Encyclopedia of the American Constitution

Editorial Board

Encyclopedia of the American Constitution

LEONARD W. LEVY, Editor-in-Chief
Claremont Graduate School, Claremont, California

KENNETH L. KARST, Associate Editor
University of California, Los Angeles

DENNIS J. MAHONEY, Assistant Editor
Claremont Graduate School, Claremont, California

MACMILLAN PUBLISHING COMPANY
A Division of Macmillan, Inc.
NEW YORK

Collier Macmillan Publishers
LONDON

Macmillan Publishing Company
A Division of Macmillan, Inc.
866 Third Avenue, New York, NY 10022

Collier Macmillan Canada, Inc.

Printed in the United States of America

printing number
1 2 3 4 5 6 7 8 9 10

Library of Congress Catalog in Publication Data

Encyclopedia of the American Constitution.

Includes index.
1. United States—Constitutional Law—Dictionaries.
I. Levy, Leonard Williams, 1923– II. Karst, Kenneth L. III. Mahoney, Dennis J.
KF4548.E53 1986 342.73'023'03 86-3038
ISBN 0-02-918610-2 347.3022303
ISBN (this edition) 0-02-918695-1

STAFF:

Charles E. Smith, *Publisher*

Elly Dickason, *Project Editor*

Morton I. Rosenberg, *Production Manager*

Joan Greenfield, *Designer*

Complete and unabridged edition 1990

J

JACKSON, ANDREW
(1767–1845)

Andrew Jackson, the seventh President of the United States, was the son of Irish immigrant parents who had settled in the South Carolina backcountry. Drifting to North Carolina after the Revolutionary war, he read enough law to gain admission to the bar. When only twenty-one he was appointed prosecuting attorney for the Western District at Nashville. There he built a flourishing practice, married, and became a leading planter-aristocrat. In 1796 he was elected a delegate to the CONSTITUTIONAL CONVENTION of Tennessee, then was chosen the new state's first representative in Congress. His service there was brief and undistinguished; it was followed by appointment to the Tennessee Superior Court, where he sat for six years, retiring in 1804. In the factional brawls of Tennessee politics Jackson won a reputation for hot-blooded courage. He killed an adversary in a celebrated duel and barely escaped with his own life in another.

Jackson rose to national fame during the War of 1812. It was mainly an Indian war on the southwest frontier. As major general of the Tennessee militia, Jackson defeated the Creeks and then imposed a humiliating treaty. In 1814 he was commissioned major general in the United States Army and was entrusted with the defense of the Gulf country from Mobile to New Orleans. He defeated the British in the Battle of New Orleans, the last and the greatest victory of the war; and although it occurred after the peace treaty was signed, the victory made Jackson a national hero. Criticized by a local citizen for refusing to lift martial law after the battle, Jackson arrested him; and when a federal judge, Dominick Hall, issued a writ of HABEAS CORPUS for the citizen, Jackson arrested the judge as well. Upon his release Judge Hall hauled the errant general into court. Jackson pleaded "the law of necessity" in his defense and got off with a thousand dollar fine. He paid, yet bristled at the alleged injustice until finally, in 1844 a Democratic Congress returned the fine with interest.

Jackson had a more serious scrape with the law in 1818. In command of an army ordered to suppress Indian disturbances along the Spanish border, he invaded Florida, executed two British subjects for stirring up the Seminoles, and captured Pensacola together with other Spanish posts. President JAMES MONROE disavowed the general's conquest, said it was unauthorized, and ordered surrender of the posts. Two cabinet officers wished to punish Jackson. Not only had he violated orders, he had violated the Constitution by making war on Spain, a power reserved to Congress. When Congress convened, a sensational month-long debate occurred in the House of Representatives on resolutions condemning Jackson for his behavior and recommending legislation to prohibit invasion of foreign territory without the consent of Congress except in direct pursuit of a defeated enemy. The resolutions failed. Jackson insisted he had acted within the broad confines of his orders. Monroe, while admitting none of this, conceded that Jackson had acted honorably on his own responsibility.

In 1822 the Tennessee legislature nominated Jackson for President. At first no one took the nomination seriously; it was obviously a stratagem of the General's political friends to avail themselves of his popularity in order to regain control of the state government. But the candidacy of "the military hero" caught fire in 1824. Jackson emerged from the election with a plurality of the popular vote; but since no candidate received a majority of the electoral vote the final choice was referred to the House, and there the influence of HENRY CLAY led to the election of JOHN QUINCY ADAMS. Jackson and his party immediately accused Adams and Clay of a "corrupt bargain." Trailing clouds of democratic rhetoric the Jacksonian politicians forged a powerful coalition that elected Old Hickory President in 1828.

The new President, though in wretched health, was a man of distinguished bearing, fascinating manners, resolute character, and still uncertain politics. In his first annual message to Congress, he called for constitutional amendments to limit the President to a single term of four or six years and, in a case like the 1824 election, to transfer the choice from the House to the people. Nothing came of this, of course. Jackson extended the old republican idea of "rotation in office" to the federal civil service, thereby laying the basis for wholesale partisan removals and appointments. He called for Indian removal. Reiterating his support for a "judicious tariff," he seemed as little inclined to back southern demands for reform as to make war on the AMERICAN SYSTEM. He pledged himself to extinguish the debt; and rather than reduce the tariff when that was accomplished, he proposed to distribute the surplus revenue to the states for works of INTERNAL IMPROVEMENTS. Finally, he pointedly raised the question of the constitutionality of the BANK OF THE UNITED STATES, whose charter would expire in 1836.

Congress responded quickly to Jackson's call for legislation to remove eastern Indian tribes west of the Mississippi. For many years he had regarded the policy of treating with the Indians "an absurdity." Now as President he sided with Georgia's policy of extending the laws of the state to Indians within its borders. When the Supreme Court in WORCESTER V. GEORGIA ruled against Georgia and upheld the Cherokee claim to federal protection, Jackson reputedly declared, "John Marshall has made his decision, now let him enforce it." The President, certainly, had no intention of coercing Georgia. By a mixture of force and persuasion he got the Cherokee and other tribes to cede their lands and migrate westward under the terms of the Removal Act. (See CHEROKEE INDIAN CASES, 1831–1832.)

Indian removal upon the pain of subjection to state authorities was the first indication of the sweeping denationalization of public policy that came to characterize the Jackson administration. Seeking to return the government to "that simple machine which the Constitution created," he struck at federal aid and planning of internal improvements by vetoing the MAYSVILLE ROAD BILL. Finding the bill unconstitutional because of its "purely local character," he nevertheless went on to express opposition to any general system of internal improvements; and after Congress adjourned he pocket-vetoed two improvement bills that could not be dismissed on local grounds. Jackson thereafter signed many improvement bills, mostly of the "pork barrel" variety, yet he repeatedly denounced the "sinister" policy matured by previous administrations and boasted of overthrowing it.

In 1832 Jackson again struck at the foundations of national authority when he vetoed the bill to recharter the Bank. The veto message adroitly combined the democratic appeals of western agrarianism with the STATES' RIGHTS prejudices of the South. On the question of constitutionality Jackson rejected the result of forty years' experience and placed his own independent judgment above that of Congress and the Supreme Court. "The opinion of the judges has no more authority over Congress than the opinion of Congress has over the judges," Jackson declared, "and on that point the president is independent of both." This was radical doctrine. In the eyes of opposition leaders, who would soon call themselves Whigs, it presaged a government of men, not of laws. (See JACKSON'S VETO OF THE BANK BILL.)

Not all of his actions were denationalizing in tendency, however. JACKSON'S PROCLAMATION TO THE PEOPLE OF SOUTH CAROLINA, condemning that state's NULLIFICATION of the protective tariff in 1832, was boldly nationalistic. Jackson ridiculed nullification as an "absurdity," defended the constitutionality of the tariff, and set forth the theory of the supremacy and indivisibility of the Union. The Constitution had created a national union, a government of "one people," to which had been committed sovereign powers heretofore belonging to the state governments; and no state could violate this union or secede from it without dissolving the whole. A month later, as South Carolina persisted in its course, Jackson called upon Congress for additional powers to enforce the revenue laws, including use of the army, navy, and militia if necessary. Congress enacted the FORCE ACT, as it was called. Use of force was averted, however, because South Carolina accepted the terms of Henry Clay's

Compromise Tariff and rescinded the ordinance of nullification.

Jackson was the first President to exercise strong, independent leadership in domestic affairs. The Bank veto, while shrinking congressional powers, expanded the President's. Overwhelmingly reelected in 1832, Jackson took his victory as a mandate to destroy the Bank. He proceeded on his own responsibility to remove the government deposits from the Bank, placing them in so-called pet banks operating under state charters. Congress had delegated authority over the government deposits to the secretary of the treasury. When that officer, William Duane, refused to remove the deposits, Jackson fired him and appointed a willing accomplice, ROGER B. TANEY, in his place. Congress convened in an uproar in December 1833. The opposition led by Clay called on the President for a paper he was known to have read to his cabinet outlining the removal policy. Jackson peremptorily refused to forward the paper on the grounds that communications to cabinet officers were privileged. (See EXECUTIVE PRIVILEGE.) Clay then introduced two resolutions censuring the President, as well as the new treasury secretary, for assuming powers "not conferred by the constitution and laws, but in derogation of both." The old issue of banking policy virtually disappeared as the opposition concentrated on the new issue of executive tyranny. The Senate, though not the House, adopted Clay's resolutions. Jackson was furious. He returned a lengthy "Protest" in which he argued that the entire executive power rested in the President, that he alone could decide how the laws should be executed, and that regardless of acts of Congress his authority to direct and remove subordinates was absolute. Congress, moreover, could not censure him; it could only impeach him. The Senate indignantly refused to enter the Protest in its journal. This bitter conflict finally came to an end in 1837, as Jackson's presidency expired, when the Senate voted to expunge the censure from the journal.

The relationship between Jackson's presidency and the Constitution was complex and confused. In the nullification crisis he placed the preservation of the Union above extravagant states' rights claims. Thirty years later, in a much deeper crisis of Union, ABRAHAM LINCOLN had no need to search for higher ground than Jackson had provided in his most famous state paper. But Jackson's presidency also gave renewed vigor to ideas of STRICT CONSTRUCTION and states' rights. It reversed the twenty-year trend toward consolidation in the general government and returned power to the states. Finally, Jackson magnified the power of the presidency at the expense of Congress. Exploiting popular democratic sentiments, he appealed to the will of the people, which he also claimed to embody, against the will of Congress. He vetoed more bills than all his predecessors combined; he was the first to employ the POCKET VETO and used it seven times. Paradoxically, his actions weakened the office. After him every President was thrown on the defensive; none would be reelected until Lincoln and none would serve two terms until ULYSSES S. GRANT. The Supreme Court, too, was challenged, for Jackson shook the ground from under the emerging consensus that the Court was the final arbiter of the Constitution. The appointment of his friend Taney as Chief Justice in 1835 terrified the Whigs, who feared that it would extend Jackson's baneful influence far into the future.

Jackson retired to his home, The Hermitage, near Nashville, and resumed the life of the planter. The patriarch of the Democratic party, he continued to influence its leaders and policies. He died at the Hermitage on June 8, 1845.

MERRILL D. PETERSON

Bibliography

BASSETT, JOHN S. and JAMESON, J. FRANKLIN, EDS. 1926–1935 *The Correspondence of Andrew Jackson,* 7 Vols. Washington: American Historical Association.

JAMES, MARQUIS 1938 *The Life of Andrew Jackson.* Indianapolis: Bobbs-Merrill.

REMINI, ROBERT 1977 *Andrew Jackson and the Course of American Empire, 1767–1821.* New York: Harper & Row.

______ 1981 *Andrew Jackson and the Course of American Freedom, 1822–1832.* New York: Harper & Row.

RICHARDSON, J. D., ED. 1896 *A Compilation of the Messages and Papers of the Presidents,* Vol. II. Washington: Government Printing Office.

JACKSON, HOWELL E. (1832–1895)

Howell Edmunds Jackson, a native of Tennessee, was appointed to the Supreme Court by BENJAMIN HARRISON in 1893. Although a Democrat, Jackson had Whig antecedents and had long been a vigorous exponent of the "New South" creed. He led the conservative opposition to repudiation of the Tennessee debt in the 1870s and represented some of the region's most prominent corporations in his law practice. GROVER CLEVELAND appointed him to a Sixth Circuit judgeship in 1886. His opinions in cases on the INTERSTATE COMMERCE ACT and the SHERMAN ANTITRUST ACT underscored his solicitude for big business.

Jackson's Supreme Court career lasted about a year and a half. Poor health precluded his participation in UNITED STATES v. E. C. KNIGHT CO. (1895) and IN RE DEBS (1895), two of the most important cases decided during his tenure. But Jackson sat with an equally divided Court at the second hearing of POLLOCK v. FARMERS LOAN & TRUST CO. (1895). His eloquent dissent, in which he insisted that the invalidation of the income tax was "the most disastrous blow ever struck at the constitutional power of Congress," remains his most famous opinion. It also sparked an enduring controversy over which, if any, of the Justices switched his vote between hearings.

CHARLES W. MCCURDY

Bibliography

SCHIFFMAN, IRVING 1970 Escaping the Shroud of Anonymity: Justice Howell Edmunds Jackson and the Income Tax Case. *Tennessee Law Review* 37:334–348.

JACKSON, ROBERT H. (1892–1954)

The orderly, middle-class world of Jamestown, New York, the economic calamity of the Great Depression, and the horrors of Nazi Germany—these were the crucial experiences that shaped the jurisprudence of Robert Houghwout Jackson, the only Supreme Court Justice to serve both as SOLICITOR GENERAL and ATTORNEY GENERAL of the United States, and the last to learn his law initially through the old-fashioned apprentice method.

Appointed to the Court by FRANKLIN D. ROOSEVELT in 1941 and facing the most important constitutional issues of the post-Depression era—the scope of federal economic management and the nationalization of the BILL OF RIGHTS—Jackson helped to accelerate the former but resisted the latter. In alliance with his close friend and colleague FELIX FRANKFURTER, he often found himself locked in combat between 1941 and 1954 with Justices HUGO L. BLACK and WILLIAM O. DOUGLAS, the ideological leaders of the Court's liberal block.

Few Justices in the Court's history articulated a more robust version of economic nationalism than Justice Jackson who, despite his small-town heritage and solicitude for independent entrepreneurship, supported consistently the expansion of federal ECONOMIC REGULATION and the growth of an integrated national marketplace, which soon became dominated by giant CORPORATIONS. Jackson wrote a sweeping validation of congressional authority under the COMMERCE CLAUSE in WICKARD v. FILBURN (1942), and he also used that provision absent federal law in *H. P. Hood & Sons v. DuMond* (1949) to strike down state regulations that insulated local economic activities from the rigors of interstate competition.

The crisis of the Great Depression convinced Jackson of the dangers of both *laissez-faire* and economic Balkanization. His later confrontation with Nazism when he served as chief American prosecutor at Nuremberg persuaded him of the dangers posed to human freedom by the growth of a monolithic police state. His firm commitment to economic nationalism never wavered, except near the end of his life in situations where the federal government began to employ the COMMERCE CLAUSE in an effort to regulate more than traditional economic activities. A year before his death, for example, Jackson narrowly construed a federal anticrime statute, voting to sustain the dismissal of INDICTMENTS for failure to register as dealers in gambling machines in *United States v. Five Gambling Devices* (1953). In the course of making their arrests in the case, FBI agents had stormed into a Tennessee country club and seized slot machines that were not shown to have been transported in interstate commerce. Jackson read into the statute a requirement of such a showing.

Jackson's fears of expanded federal police controls became so pronounced that he resisted efforts to attack RACIAL DISCRIMINATION by means of the criminal and civil provisions of the Reconstruction-era CIVIL RIGHTS ACTS, especially where these efforts threatened to undermine the autonomy of local law enforcement officials, such as SCREWS v. UNITED STATES (1945) and *Collins v. Hardyman* (1951). He also opposed federal judicial intervention under the FOURTEENTH AMENDMENT to correct local abuses in the administration of criminal justice. Although he interpreted the FOURTH AMENDMENT strictly as to federal SEARCHES AND SEIZURES, as in his dissent in BRINEGAR v. UNITED STATES (1949), he refused to extend the EXCLUSIONARY RULE to state criminal prosecutions, and he exhibited broad toleration for local police practices that shocked other members of the Court. "Local excesses or invasions of liberty," he wrote, "are more amenable to political correction," a point of view which no doubt surprised Mississippi Negroes and many state criminal suspects who endured the third degree. Even Frankfurter broke with Jackson on these issues, for example, in IRVINE v. CALIFORNIA (1954).

Jackson's small-town roots and his fear of mass-based political movements such as Nazism colored his views of other CIVIL LIBERTIES issues as well. He often defended the lone individual against the repressive machinery of the state, but he thoroughly distrusted people in groups, especially well-organized, zealous minorities who threatened to disrupt what Jackson regarded as the community's peace, stability, and proper order. The Constitution, he believed, prohibited West Virginia officials from imposing a mandatory flag salute observance on the children of Jehovah's Witnesses. (See FLAG SALUTE CASES.) The federal government, likewise, could not convict without a finding of criminal intent, condemn for TREASON without substantial proof, or hold a hapless ALIEN indefinitely on Ellis Island without charging him with a specific crime. "This man, who seems to have led a life of unrelieved insignificance," he wrote angrily, in SHAUGHNESSY V. UNITED STATES EX REL. MEZEI (1953) (dissenting opinion), "must have been astonished to find himself suddenly putting the Government of the United States in such fear that it was afraid to tell him why it was afraid of him. . . . No one can make me believe that we are that far gone."

Yet Jackson did not believe that the Constitution gave cadres of Jehovah's Witnesses the right to distribute their religious literature in defiance of local ordinances prohibiting house-to-house canvassing and ringing doorbells. "I doubt if only the slothfully ignorant wish repose in their homes," he wrote sarcastically in *Martin v. City of Struthers* (1943), responding to Justice Black's opinion upholding the Witnesses' claim, "or that the forefathers intended to open the door to such forced 'enlightenment' as we have here." A similar loathing for collective political behavior informed his attitude toward the Communist party which, like the Nazi organizations condemned at Nuremberg, he equated with a conspiracy against the social order in a concurring opinion in *Dennis v. United States* (1951).

Jackson's belief in the fragility of the political system also made him a conservative on most FREEDOM OF SPEECH issues, witness his dissenting opinion in KUNZ V. NEW YORK (1950). He objected, for instance, to the specific law upheld in the famous Illinois GROUP LIBEL case, BEAUHARNAIS V. ILLINOIS (1952), but he acknowledged the state's "commendable desire to reduce sinister abuses of our freedom of expression—abuses which I have had occasion to learn can tear society apart, brutalize its dominant elements, and persecute, even to extermination, its minorities."

Witty, combative, and gifted with an eloquent prose style, Jackson remained a person of many paradoxes: the rugged individualist who helped to fashion the New Deal's welfare state; the two-fisted prosecutor who wished to be the disinterested judge; and the economic nationalist who distrusted the growth of centralized, bureaucratic authority.

MICHAEL E. PARRISH

Bibliography

GERHART, EUGENE C. 1958 *America's Advocate: Robert H. Jackson.* Indianapolis: Bobbs-Merrill.

JAFFE, LOUIS L. 1955 Mr. Justice Jackson. *Harvard Law Review* 68:940–998.

WHITE, G. EDWARD 1976 The Dilemmas of Robert Jackson. Pages 230–250 in White, *The American Judicial Tradition: Profiles of Leading American Judges.* New York: Oxford University Press.

JACKSON v. GEORGIA

See: Capital Punishment Cases, 1972

JACKSON v. METROPOLITAN EDISON CO.
419 U.S. 345 (1974)

In the WARREN COURT years, the STATE ACTION doctrine was progressively weakened as a limitation on the FOURTEENTH AMENDMENT; more and more "private" conduct fell under the Amendment's reach. The *Jackson* decision illustrates how the BURGER COURT called a halt to this trend, limiting the substantive scope of the Amendment by giving new life to the state action limitation.

Metropolitan Edison turned off Jackson's supply of electricity, asserting that she had not paid her bill. She sued for damages and injunctive relief under federal CIVIL RIGHTS laws, claiming PROCEDURAL DUE PROCESS rights to NOTICE, hearing, and an opportunity to pay any amounts due the company. The lower courts denied relief, holding that the company's conduct did not amount to state action. The Supreme Court affirmed, 6–3, in an opinion by Justice WILLIAM H. REHNQUIST, systematically rejecting a series of arguments supporting the contention that state action was present in the case.

The fact of state regulation was held insufficient to constitute state action. As in MOOSE LODGE NO. 107 V. IRVIS (1972), there was no showing of a "close nexus" between the company's no-hearing policy and the state. The approval by the state's public utilities commission of the company's tariff, stating the right to terminate service for nonpayment, was held insufficient to demonstrate explicit state approval of the no-hearing policy. Where *Moose Lodge* had relied on the absence of a monopoly under a state liquor license, *Jackson* characterized *Moose Lodge* as a near-monopoly case and said there was no showing of a connection between the utility's monopoly status and its no-hearing policy. Finally, the Court rejected the notion that Metropolitan Edison was performing a "public function" by supplying electricity, saying there had been no delegation to the company of a power "traditionally associated with sovereignty." The latter comment looked forward to the Court's decision in FLAGG BROS., INC. v. BROOKS (1978).

Justice WILLIAM J. BRENNAN dissented without reaching the merits. Justices WILLIAM O. DOUGLAS and THURGOOD MARSHALL dissented on the merits, pointing out how the majority was departing from the teaching of the Warren Court—something that Justice Rehnquist likely did not need to have explained. *Jackson* did more than reverse currents in the various individual streams of state action DOCTRINE (public functions, monopolies, state encouragement). By taking up each of these arguments separately and rejecting them one by one, the Court also implicitly abandoned the approach of BURTON v. WILMINGTON PARKING AUTHORITY (1961), which had called for determining state action questions by looking at the totality of circumstances in a particular case.

KENNETH L. KARST

JACKSON'S PROCLAMATION TO THE PEOPLE OF SOUTH CAROLINA
(December 10, 1832)

On November 24, 1832, a state convention adopted the SOUTH CAROLINA ORDINANCE OF NULLIFICATION declaring that the federal tariff acts of 1828 and 1832 were "null, void, and no law, nor binding upon this State, its officers or citizens." Sixteen days later President ANDREW JACKSON responded with a proclamation directed at the people of South Carolina, rather than at the state government. Jackson declared the NULLIFICATION ordinance "incompatible with the existence of the Union, contradicted expressly by the letter of the Constitution, unauthorized by its spirit, inconsistent with every principle on which it was founded, and destructive of the great object for which it was formed." After a detailed and withering analysis of the legality and constitutionality of the ordinance, Jackson turned to the question of SECESSION, which South Carolina threatened if the tariffs were enforced in that state. Jackson warned the people of South Carolina that "Disunion by armed force is TREASON" and that on their heads "may fall the punishment" for that crime. Congress subsequently modified the tariffs but also passed the FORCE ACT authorizing the use of military power to enforce federal laws. South Carolina then repealed its Nullification Ordinance, but in a final flurry of defiance passed an ordinance purporting to nullify the Force Act.

PAUL FINKELMAN

Bibliography

FREEHLING, WILLIAM W. 1965 *Prelude to Civil War: The Nullification Controversy in South Carolina, 1816–1836.* New York: Harper & Row.

JACKSON'S VETO OF THE BANK OF THE UNITED STATES BILL
(July 10, 1832)

The first Bank of the United States was chartered in 1791 despite Jeffersonian opposition. In 1811 its charter expired, but in 1815 the bank was rechartered, with little opposition, as the Second Bank of the United States. The Supreme Court in MCCULLOCH v. MARYLAND (1819) upheld the constitutionality of the bank. In 1832 Congress extended the charter of the Second Bank. For a variety of reasons President ANDREW JACKSON opposed the extension. In his veto message Jackson asserted, more emphatically than previous Presidents, the necessity of exercising the presidential VETO POWER on constitutional grounds, rather than on grounds of policy or expediency. Jackson rejected *McCulloch,* arguing that "Mere PRECEDENT is a dangerous source of authority," which should not decide "questions of constitutional power except where the acquiescence of the people and the States can be considered as well settled." Furthermore, Jackson believed Supreme Court opinions "ought not to control the coordinate authorities of this Government." Rather, each branch of the government must "be guided by its own opinion of the Constitution" because a public official swears to support the Constitution "as he understands it, and not as it is understood by others." Jackson argued that the Bank was neither a necessary nor a proper subject for congressional legislation, and so he felt constitutionally obligated to veto the bill.

PAUL FINKELMAN

Bibliography

REMINI, ROBERT V. 1967 *Andrew Jackson and the Bank War: A Study in the Growth of Presidential Power.* Norton Essays in American History. New York: Norton.

JACOBELLIS v. OHIO
378 U.S. 184 (1964)

The Supreme Court reversed Jacobellis's conviction for possessing and exhibiting an obscene motion picture, finding the movie not obscene under ROTH V. UNITED STATES (1957). Justice WILLIAM J. BRENNAN's plurality opinion announced two significant constitutional developments and presaged a third. First, in any case raising the issue whether a work was obscene, the Court would determine independently whether the material was constitutionally protected. Second, in judging the material's appeal to prurient interests against "contemporary community standards," courts were to apply a national standard, not the standards of the particular local community from which the case arose. Finally, purporting to apply standards based on *Roth* and foreshadowing his opinion in MEMOIRS V. MASSACHUSETTS (1965), Brennan noted that a work could not be proscribed unless it was " 'utterly' without social importance."

Jacobellis is best known, however, for Justice POTTER J. STEWART's concurring opinion. Contending that only hard-core pornography constitutionally could be proscribed, Stewart declined to define the material that term included, stating only, "I know it when I see it."

KIM MCLANE WARDLAW

JACOBS, IN RE
98 N.Y. 98 (1885)

This exceptionally influential decision, cited hundreds of times by state and federal courts, reflected laissez-faire principles against government regulation of the economy. New York in 1884 enacted a statute to improve the public health by penalizing the manufacture of cigars on the same floor of tenement houses where people lived. Jacobs, a tenement occupant prosecuted under the statute, somehow retained WILLIAM M. EVARTS, "the Prince of the American Bar," whose powerful defense of free enterprise convinced the New York Court of Appeals to decide unanimously against the constitutionality of the regulation. Judge Robert Earl, drawing heavily on Evarts's argument, larded his opinion with polemics against state infringement on liberty and property conducted under the pretext of the POLICE POWER. The constitutional basis of the opinion is not clear because Earl stopped short of invoking the DOCTRINE of FREEDOM OF CONTRACT, but the rhetoric of SUBSTANTIVE DUE PROCESS as a limitation on LEGISLATIVE POWER to regulate the economy stands out. "Under the mere guise of police regulations," Earl said, "personal rights and private property cannot be arbitrarily invaded," and JUDICIAL REVIEW determines whether the legislative power exceeded the limits. The court found that the state plainly had not passed a health law but had trampled personal liberty.

LEONARD W. LEVY

JACOBSON v. MASSACHUSETTS
197 U.S. 11 (1905)

A Massachusetts statute required VACCINATION of a town's inhabitants when health authorities so ordered. For the Supreme Court, Justice JOHN MARSHALL HARLAN concluded the regulation was within the POLICE POWER of the commonwealth and violated no federal constitutional right.

The FIRST AMENDMENT was not then interpreted to apply to the states. Jacobson relied on the liberty guaranteed by the FOURTEENTH AMENDMENT's DUE PROCESS clause, although his objection to vaccination was religious. Harlan concluded that SUBSTANTIVE DUE PROCESS implied no absolute right to control one's body. Justices DAVID BREWER and RUFUS PECKHAM dissented.

RICHARD E. MORGAN

JAMES v. BOWMAN
190 U.S. 127 (1903)

A provision of the FORCE ACTS, passed to protect FIFTEENTH AMENDMENT guarantees, forbade bribery or intimidation to prevent the exercise of VOTING RIGHTS. Bowman, a private citizen, was indicted for preventing several blacks from voting in a Kentucky congressional election. Justice DAVID BREWER for a 6–2 Supreme Court, relying mainly on UNITED STATES V. REESE (1876), declared that the amendment applied to abridgments of the right to vote by the federal government or by a state on account of race; it did not reach private actions. A congressional measure purporting to punish "purely individual action," said Brewer, could not be sustained as an enforcement of the Fifteenth Amendment's prohibition against STATE ACTION abridging the right to vote on account of race. Further, the statute was not limited to RACIAL DISCRIMINATION denying the right to vote. Congress had not relied on its power under Article I to regulate federal elections.

DAVID GORDON

JAMES v. VALTIERRA
402 U.S. 137 (1971)

The California state constitution required voter approval in a local REFERENDUM for the building of public low-rent housing projects. The Supreme Court, 5–3, sustained this requirement against an EQUAL PROTECTION attack.

Justice HUGO L. BLACK wrote for the majority. It was not the business of the courts to analyze governmental structures to see whether they disadvantaged one group or another. In any case, advocates of low-rent housing had not been singled out for disadvantage; California required referenda for the adoption of a number of kinds of legislation. Black distinguished HUNTER V. ERICKSON (1969), which had struck down a similar referendum requirement imposed on fair housing laws. Here no RACIAL DISCRIMINATION was shown.

Justice THURGOOD MARSHALL, for the dissenters, argued that discrimination "between 'rich' and 'poor' as such" was forbidden, quoting Justice JOHN MARSHALL HARLAN's dissent in DOUGLAS V. CALIFORNIA (1963). "[S]ingling out the poor to bear a burden not placed on any other class of citizens tramples the values that the FOURTEENTH AMENDMENT was designed to protect."

KENNETH L. KARST

(SEE ALSO: *Wealth Discrimination; Indigent.*)

JAPANESE AMERICAN CASES
Hirabayashi v. United States
320 U.S. 81 (1943)
Korematsu v. United States
323 U.S. 214 (1944)
Ex parte Endo
323 U.S. 283 (1944)

For more than a month after the Japanese attack on Pearl Harbor in December 1941, no one of high authority in the armed services or elsewhere in the national government suggested seriously that persons of Japanese ancestry should be moved away from the West Coast. The Army's historian wrote that in February and March of 1942 the military estimates were that "there was no real threat of a Japanese invasion" of the area. Yet by March 1942 a program was fully underway to remove about 120,000 persons from their West Coast homes and jobs and place them in internment camps in the interior of the country. About 70,000 of these people were citizens of the United States; two out of every five people sent to the camps were under the age of fifteen or over fifty. All were imprisoned for an indefinite time without any individualized determination of grounds for suspicion of disloyalty, let alone charges of unlawful conduct, to be held in custody until their loyalty might be determined. (See PREVENTIVE DETENTION.) The basis for their imprisonment was a single common trait—their Japanese ancestry.

The military services came to discover the "military necessity" of relocating the Japanese Americans in response to pressure from the West Coast congressional delegations and from other political leaders in the region—including, to his later regret, EARL WARREN, then attorney general of California. These politicians were responding, in turn, to a clamor from certain newspapers and labor unions, along with (as U.S. Attorney General FRANCIS BIDDLE later listed them) "the American Legion, the California Joint Immigration Committee, the Native Sons and Daughters of the Golden West, the Western Growers Protective Association, the California Farm Bureau Federation [and] the Chamber of Commerce of Los Angeles." The groups' campaign was aided by newspaper accounts of American military defeats and Japanese atrocities in the early days of the war, and by false reports of sabotage at Pearl Harbor. Anti-Asian racism, long a feature of California, now had a focus. In Hawaii, which *had* been attacked, no evacuation was proposed; persons of Japanese ancestry constituted almost one third of that territory's population. On the West Coast, Japanese Americans barely exceeded one percent of the population; thus, no political force resisted the mixture of fear, racism, and greed. "The Japanese race is an enemy race," said General John DeWitt in his official report to the War Department. Once the Army urged wholesale evacuation, the opposition of Biddle and the Justice Department was unavailing. President FRANKLIN D. ROOSEVELT sided with the Army, and the evacuation began.

The program, first established by EXECUTIVE ORDER 9066 and then partly ratified by Congress, called for three measures in "military areas"—that is, the entire West Coast. First, persons of Japanese descent were placed under curfew at home from 8:00 P.M. to 6:00 A.M. Second, they would be excluded from "military areas" upon military order. Third, they would be "relocated" in internment camps until their "loyalty" could be determined. The loyalty-determining process was leisurely; as late as the spring of 1945 some 70,000 persons remained in the camps.

The three parts of the program, all of which raised serious constitutional problems, were considered separately by the Supreme Court in three cases: *Hirabayashi v. United States* (1943), *Korematsu v. United States* (1944), and *Ex Parte Endo* (1944).

The *Hirabayashi* case offered the Court a chance to rule on the validity of both the curfew and the exclusion orders. A young American citizen was charged with violating the curfew and refusing to report to a control station to be evacuated from Seattle, where he lived. He was convicted on both counts, and sentenced to three months of imprisonment. In June 1943 the Supreme Court unanimously upheld the curfew violation conviction, and said that it need not consider the validity of the exclusion order, because the two sentences were to run concurrently.

Not until December 1944 did the Court reach the other parts of the evacuation program. In *Korematsu*, the Court divided 6–3 in upholding an order excluding an American citizen from his home town, San Leandro, California. On the same day, the Court in *Endo* avoided deciding on the constitutional validity of internment. Instead, it concluded that the act of Congress ratifying the evacuation program had not authorized prolonged detention of a citizen whose loyalty was conceded. The Court assumed that some brief detention was implicitly authorized as an incident of an exclusion program aimed at preventing espionage and sabotage. Any further detention would have to rest on an assumption the Court was unwilling to make: that citizens were being detained because of their ancestry, in response to community hostility. Justice OWEN ROBERTS, concurring in the result, found congressional authority for internment in the appropriation of funds to operate the camps. Reaching the constitutional issues the majority had avoided, he concluded the Endo's detention violated "the guarantees of the BILL OF RIGHTS . . . and especially the guarantee of DUE PROCESS OF LAW."

The Japanese American cases have made two positive contributions to the development of egalitarian constitutional doctrine. The *Hirabayashi* and *Korematsu* opinions were links in a chain of precedent leading to the Supreme Court's recognition that the Fifth Amendment's due process clause contains a guarantee of equal protection as a substantive limit on the conduct of the national government. (See BOLLING V. SHARPE, 1954; EQUAL PROTECTION OF THE LAWS.) And *Korematsu* first announced the principle that legal restrictions on the civil rights of a racial group are "suspect." (See SUSPECT CLASSIFICATIONS.) Even so, these decisions deserve Eugene Rostow's epithet: "a disaster." The Supreme Court's evasion of issues, its refusal to examine the factual assumptions underlying the "military necessity" of evacuation—in short, its failures to perform as a court—are easier to forgive than to excuse. There is little comfort in the fact that the Court's *Hirabayashi* and *Korematsu* opinions were authored by Justices celebrated as civil libertarians.

Chief Justice HARLAN FISKE STONE wrote for a unanimous Court in *Hirabayashi*, approaching the validity of the curfew not so much as a question about the liberties of a citizen but as a question about congressional power. The WAR POWERS, of course, are far-reaching; they include, as Justices often repeat, "the power to wage war successfully." Thus, for Stone, the only issue before the Court was whether there was "a RATIONAL BASIS" for concluding that the curfew was necessary to protect the country against espionage and sabotage in aid of a threatened invasion. As to that necessity, the Chief Justice said: "We cannot close our eyes to the fact, demonstrated by experience, that in time of war residents having ethnic affiliations with an invading enemy may be a greater source of danger than those of a different ancestry." There was no effort to examine into the likelihood of invasion, or to specify what experience demonstrated the "fact" assumed. The one hard fact was that no sabotage or espionage had been committed by persons of Japanese ancestry at the time of the Hawaii attack or afterward. (California's Attorney General Warren had been equal to that challenge, however: ". . . that is the most ominous sign in our whole situation. It convinces me more than perhaps any other factor that the sabotage we are to get, the fifth column activities that we are to get, are timed just like Pearl Harbor was timed. . . .")

Another question remained: Why impose wholesale restrictions on persons of Japanese ancestry, when Germans and Italians were being investigated individually? Here the Court took refuge in a presumption: "We cannot say that the war-making branches of the Government did not have ground for believing that in a critical hour [disloyal] persons could not readily be isolated and separately dealt with. . . ." This is the classical language of "rational basis" review; government officials have made a factual determination, and a court "cannot say" they are mistaken. That standard of review serves well enough to test the reasonableness of a congressional conclusion that some type of activity substantially affects INTERSTATE COMMERCE. It is utterly inappropriate to test the justification for selectively imposing restrictions on a racial minority.

Justice HUGO L. BLACK began his opinion for the majority in *Korematsu* by recognizing this difference. Racial distinctions, he said, were "immediately suspect," and must be subjected to "the most rigid scrutiny." Following that pronouncement, however, all judicial scrutiny of the racial discrimination at hand was abandoned. The opinion simply quoted the "We cannot say" passage from the *Hirabayashi* opinion; stated, uncritically, the conclusions of the military authorities; observed that "war is an aggregation of hardships"; and—unkindest cut—concluded that "Citizenship has its responsibilities as well as its privileges."

Justice Roberts, dissenting, argued that Korematsu had been subjected to conflicting orders to leave the military area and to stay put, a plain due process violation. It was left to Justice FRANK MURPHY—in his finest hour—to expose the absence of imperial clothing. He demonstrated how the "military" judgment of the necessity for evacuation had departed from subjects in which Army officers were expert and had embarked on breathtaking sociological generalization: the Japanese American community were "a large, unassimilated, tightly knit racial group, bound to an enemy nation by strong ties of race, culture, custom and religion" (quoting General DeWitt).

Decades later, Peter Irons discovered in government archives irrefutable evidence that government officers had deliberately misled the Supreme Court on questions directly related to the claim of military necessity for the evacuations. In response to this evidence, in the mid-1980s federal district courts set aside the convictions of Gordon Hirabayashi, Fred Korematsu, and Minoru Yasui (whose conviction had been affirmed along with Hirabayashi's).

Justice ROBERT H. JACKSON, dissenting in *Korematsu,* said, in effect: There is nothing courts can do to provide justice in this case, or in any case in which the military and the President are determined to take action in wartime; yet we should not lend our approval to this action, lest we create a precedent for similar extraconstitutional action in the future. Of all the oft-noted ironies of the Japanese American cases, this topsy-turvy prediction may be the most ironic of all. *Korematsu* as a judicial precedent has turned out to provide a strong doctrinal foundation for the Supreme Court's vigorous defense of racial equality in the years since mid-century. The disaster of the Japanese American cases was not doctrinal. It was instead the betrayal of justice there and then for Gordon Hirabayashi, Fred Korematsu, Minoru Yasui, and some 120,000 other individuals—and thus for us all.

KENNETH L. KARST

Bibliography

GRODZINS, MORTON 1949 *Americans Betrayed: Politics and the Japanese Evacuation.* Chicago: University of Chicago Press.

IRONS, PETER 1983 *Justice at War.* New York: Oxford University Press.

ROSTOW, EUGENE V. 1949 The Japanese American Cases—A Disaster. *Yale Law Journal* 54:489–533.

JAY, JOHN
(1745–1829)

John Jay was a major figure during the Revolutionary era. Born into one of colonial New York's leading families, he was aristocratic in appearance, well educated, and a hard worker with a precise and orderly mind. He graduated from King's College in 1764, was admitted to the bar four years later, and soon had a prosperous practice. He early took an interest in the constitutional debate between England and the American colonies; although uneasy about the radical implication of some of the resistance to imperial policies in the 1770s, he nevertheless was a firm patriot. He served as a member of the New York Committee of Correspondence and in the Provincial Congress, as well as in the first and second Continental Congresses in Philadelphia. In 1776 he returned to New York to help draft a state constitution (1777) and to become New York's first chief justice. His major interests, however, lay in the field of diplomacy: he became the United States Minister to Spain in 1779 and later joined BENJAMIN FRANKLIN and JOHN ADAMS in Paris to negotiate the treaty of 1783 that recognized American independence and formally ended the fighting with Great Britain.

Returning to the United States in 1784 Jay assumed the position of secretary of foreign affairs under the ARTICLES OF CONFEDERATION. Unhappy over the weakness of the central government during the 1780s, he sympathized with the movement to create a new constitution that would strengthen the power of the federal government over the states. Jay was not a member of the CONSTITUTIONAL CONVENTION OF 1787, but he strongly advocated adoption of the Constitution in the closely contested ratification struggle in New York the following year. Joining forces with ALEXANDER HAMILTON and JAMES MADISON, Jay contributed several pieces (#2–#5 and, after a bout with illness, #64) to THE FEDERALIST. In these essays Jay warned that failure to adopt the new government would probably lead to the dissolution of the Union and the creation of separate confederacies. He also stressed that only through the creation of a strong and energetic central government could the discord and jealousies of the various states be brought under control and the territorial integrity of the United States be protected from foreign encroachment.

Shortly after becoming President, GEORGE WASHINGTON appointed Jay the first Chief Justice of the United States, a position he held from 1789 to 1795. Two main themes ran through Jay's decisions. The first stressed the supremacy of the newly created national government. CHISHOLM V. GEORGIA (1793) involved the constitutional question of whether a state could be sued in a federal court by a citizen of a different state without its permission, thus limiting its SOVEREIGNTY. The question had been raised during the debate over ratification, and the supporters of the Constitution had given assurances that such suits would not be allowed. Nevertheless, under Jay's leadership the Court handed down an affirmative decision, couched in extremely nationalistic terms. Jay stressed the role of the people of the United States in the creation of the Union, and deemphasized the powers and sovereignty of the states. A very controversial decision, *Chisholm* was vitiated when reaction to it culminated in the adoption of the ELEVENTH ADMENDMENT.

While riding circuit in 1793 Jay delivered a dissenting opinion in WARE V. HYLTON, arguing that a Virginia statute sequestering prerevolutionary debts of British creditors was invalid because it had been nullified by the Treaty of Paris (1783) which specifically indicated that such debts would be honored. The case was appealed in 1796, and the Supreme Court, from which Jay had already resigned, adopted the former Chief Justice's reasoning and reversed the lower court's decision. In another important case, *Glass v. The Sloop Betsy* (1794), the Supreme Court overturned a Maryland District Court ruling that allowed French consuls in America to function as prize courts and dispose of prizes captured by French privateers. Writing for the Court, Jay concluded that United States sovereignty required that these cases be handled by American courts.

Jay's other major concern as Chief Justice was to protect the independence of the Supreme Court by insisting on a strict SEPARATION OF POWERS. He rejected various attempts to incorporate the Court into the activities of the legislative and executive branches. For example, when Congress passed an act that required the circuit courts to review the applications of military invalids for pensions, Jay, while riding circuit in New York, declared that "neither the Legislative nor Executive branch can constitutionally assign to the Judicial any duties but such as are properly judicial and to be performed in a judicial manner." This position was upheld a short time later by the United States Circuit Court of Pennsylvania, in what has become known as HAYBURN'S CASE (1792), when the constitutionality of the law was actually challenged. Jay also rejected occasional requests from the President and Secretary of the Treasury Alexander Hamilton for ADVISORY OPINIONS on controversial matters, arguing that the Supreme Court should render opinions only in actual lawsuits brought by contending parties.

Jay was never happy serving on the Court. He thought the circuit riding duties too arduous. He also believed the Court lacked "the energy, weight and dignity which are essential to its affording due support to the national government." Hoping to return to a more active political life, he was defeated in a bid to become governor of New York in 1792. In 1794, while still holding the position of Chief Justice, he went on a special diplomatic mission to try to resolve existing controversies with Great Britain. The result was the controversial but successful JAY'S TREATY. Resigning his post on the Court, Jay became governor of New York in 1795 for two terms. Following the Jeffersonian successes in 1800 he declined reappointment as Chief Justice of the United States Supreme Court and retired from public life.

RICHARD E. ELLIS

Bibliography

MONAGHAN, FRANK 1935 *John Jay.* Indianapolis: Bobbs-Merrill.

MORRIS, RICHARD B. 1967 *John Jay, the Nation and the Court.* Boston: Boston University Press.

JAY BURNS BAKING COMPANY v. BRYAN

See: *Burns Baking Co. v. Bryan*

JAY COURT

See: Supreme Court, 1789–1801

JAY'S TREATY
8 Stat. 116 (1795)

Although obligated by the treaty that ended the Revolutionary War to evacuate its military posts in the Northwest Territory, the British government held the posts, established new ones, and, in 1793, began a policy of encouraging Indian depredations against American settlers in the territory. At the same time, the British fleet, then at war with France, began seizing American ships that called at French ports.

In April 1794, President GEORGE WASHINGTON appointed Chief Justice JOHN JAY envoy extraordinary to Britain to negotiate for neutral shipping rights and evacuation of the Northwest Territory. The treaty Jay negotiated in London and signed in November 1794 provided for both; but it also made many concessions to the British, especially at the expense of Western settlers. Several questions were left to be decided by joint commissions, which would require appropriated funds for their operation.

The congressional debate on Jay's Treaty raised constitutional issues that endure to the present day. Republicans in the House of Representatives, led by ALBERT GALLATIN, objected to a treaty with the force of supreme law that required appropriation of money but from the making of which the House was excluded. They attempted to hold the TREATY POWER hostage to the spending power.

After the treaty was ratified, during the debate on the appropriation, Gallatin induced the House to request from the President documents related to the negotiations. Washington refused to comply, invoking EXECUTIVE PRIVILEGE in order that "the boundaries fixed by the Constitution between the different departments should be preserved."

DENNIS J. MAHONEY

Bibliography

COMBS, JERALD A. 1970 *The Jay Treaty: Political Battleground of the Founding Fathers.* Berkeley: University of California Press.

JEFFERSON, THOMAS
(1743–1826)

Thomas Jefferson, statesman, philosopher, architect, champion of freedom and enlightenment, was United States minister to France when the federal CONSTITUTIONAL CONVENTION met in 1787. Long an advocate of a strengthened confederation, he applauded the convention and anxiously awaited the result of its deliberations. On seeing the roster of delegates, he exclaimed to his diplomatic colleague and friend JOHN ADAMS, "It is really an assembly of demigods." Jefferson soon made the Constitution the polestar of his politics, aligning its principles with those of aspiring American democracy, with momentous consequences for the future of the republic.

Educated for the law in his native Virginia, tutored by GEORGE WYTHE, young Jefferson was a keen student of the English constitution. Like a good Whig, he traced the venerable rights and liberties of Englishmen back to Saxon foundations. The degeneration under George III turned on the system of minsterial influence to corrupt the Parliament. This upset the balance of king, lords, and Commons upon which the freedom and order of the constitution depended; and it threatened, Jefferson came to believe, tyranny for America. He was thus led in his first published work, *A Summary View of the Rights of British America* (1774), to repudiate the political authority of the mother country over the colonies. When he penned the DECLARATION OF INDEPENDENCE two years later, he placed the American claim not in the prescriptive guarantees of the English constitution but on the Lockean ground of the NATURAL RIGHTS of man. In recoil from the treacheries of an unwritten constitution, he concluded with the mass of American patriots that a CONSTITUTION should be written; in this and other ways he sought to secure the supremacy of FUNDAMENTAL LAW over statutory law, which was the great failure of the English constitution. Finally, Jefferson entered upon the search for a new system of political balance consonant with American principles and capable of breaking the classic cycle of liberty, corruption, and tyranny, thereby ensuring the permanence of free government.

Jefferson's constitutional theory first found expression in the making of the VIRGINIA CONSTITUTION OF 1776. In June, while he was drafting the Declaration of Independence for Congress, Jefferson also drafted a plan of government for Virginia and sent it to the revolutionary convention meeting in Williamsburg. The work of framing a new government, he wrote, was "the whole object of the present controversy." In his mind, the relationship of one state paper to the other was that of theory to practice, principle to application. Endeavoring to reach all the great objects of public liberty in the constitution, he included a number of fundamental reforms in Virginia society and government. The constitution adopted at Williamsburg contained none of these reforms, however. Jefferson at once became its severest critic, not only because of its conservative character but also because it failed to meet the test of republican legitimacy. The "convention" that adopted it, as he observed, was the revolutionary successor of the House of Burgesses, elected in April to perform the ordinary business of government. It could not, therefore, frame a supreme law, a law binding on government itself. Jefferson was groping toward the conception of constituent SOVEREIGNTY, in which the government actually arises from "the consent of the governed" through the constitution-making authority of the people. Thus it was that he proposed a form of popular ratification of the constitution—a radical notion at that time. He also proposed, and included in his plan, a provision for amendment by the consent of the people in two-thirds of the counties. This proposal was unprecedented. Jefferson made the omission of any provision for constitutional change a leading count in his indictment of the Virginia frame of government.

Jefferson returned to Virginia in 1776, served his state as a legislative reformer, then as wartime governor, and reentered Congress in the fall of 1783. Turning his attention to the problems of the confederation, he followed his young friend JAMES MADISON in advocating the addition of new congressional powers to raise revenue and regulate FOREIGN COMMERCE. He persuaded Congress to try the provision of the ARTICLES OF CONFEDERATION for an interim executive in the form of a committee of the states, thereby overcoming the dilemma of a congress in perpetual session, which was one source of its debility, or virtual obliteration of the government of the United States. The plan promptly collapsed under trial. Congress seemed as incapable of exercising the powers it already had as it was of obtaining new powers from the states. Jefferson was no "strict constructionist" where the Articles were concerned. In the case of the LAND ORDINANCE OF 1784 for the government of the western territory, he prevailed upon Congress to adopt a bold nation-building measure without a stitch of constitutional authority.

Jefferson's congressional career ended in May 1784, when he was appointed minister plenipotentiary to join BENJAMIN FRANKLIN and John Adams, in Paris, on the commission to negotiate treaties of amity and commerce with European states. He had helped reformulate policy on this subject in Congress. The policy concerned trade, of course; but it also concerned the strength and character of the confederation. Although the front door to congressional commercial regulation was closed, the back door was open through the power of Congress to negotiate treaties. "The moment these treaties are concluded the JURISDICTION of Congress over the commerce of the states springs into existence, and that of particular states is suppressed," Jefferson wrote. Only in treating with foreign nations could the United States act as "one Nation," and so acting not only expand trade abroad but strengthen the bonds of union at home. Indeed, Jefferson asserted that the latter was his "primary object." His hopes were quickly disappointed, however. The European courts, with two or three exceptions, rebuffed the American overtures for freer trade; and as the various state legislatures undertook to regulate foreign trade, Jefferson's political objective was undermined. He reluctantly concluded with Madison and other nationalists that there was no alternative to the outright grant of commercial power to Congress. It was the logic of commercial policy, basically, that led Jefferson to support the federal convention.

Jefferson's position in France, where he had succeeded Franklin as minister, conditioned his response to the new constitution in opposite ways. On the one hand, he had seen the infant republic jeered, kicked, and scoffed at from London to Algiers, all respect for its government annihilated from the universal opinion of its feebleness and incompetence. He had been frustrated in commercial diplomacy even at Versailles; and he and Adams had gone begging to Dutch bankers to keep the confederation afloat. A stronger government, more national in character, with higher tone and energy, was therefore necessary to raise the country's reputation in Europe. On the other hand, Jefferson pondered the new constitution in Paris, where tyranny, not anarchy, was the problem, where the drama of the French Revolution had just begun, and where he had come to recognize the inestimable blessings of American liberty. Learning of SHAYS' REBELLION, which terrified Adams in London, Jefferson declared philosophically, "I like a little rebellion now and then. It is like a storm in the atmosphere." In this spirit, reading the convention's plan in November, he thought the delegates had overreacted to the insurrection in Massachusetts and set up "a kite to keep the hen yard in order." He was staggered, too, by the boldness of the work, a wholly new frame of government, when he had looked for reinvigorating amendments to the Articles.

But the more Jefferson studied the Constitution the more he liked it. He had two main objections. The perpetual reeligibility of the chief magistrate aroused monarchical fears in his mind. Most of the evils of European governments were traceable to their kings, he said; and an American president reeligible every fourth year would soon become a king, albeit an elective one. The fears were little felt at home, however, chiefly because of the universal confidence in GEORGE WASHINGTON, whose election to the first office was a foregone conclusion. So, increasingly, Jefferson concentrated on his second objection, the omission of a BILL OF RIGHTS. In this, of course, he was supported by the mass of anti-Federalists. At first he unwittingly played into their game of using the demand for a bill of rights to delay or defeat RATIFICATION OF THE CONSTITUTION. His suggestion in a private letter that four states withhold their assent until the demand was met contributed to the initial rejection of the Constitution in North Carolina. Actually, Jefferson always wanted speedy adoption by the necessary nine states; and when he learned of the Massachusetts plan of unconditional ratification with recommended amendments, he backed this approach. Meanwhile, in a lengthy correspondence, he converted Madison, the Federalist leader, to the cause of a bill of rights. Acknowledging the inconveniences and imperfections of all such parchment guarantees and conceding the theoretical objection to denying powers that had not been granted, he nevertheless insisted "that a bill of rights is what the people are entitled to against every government on earth, general or particular, and what no just government should refuse, or rest on inference."

Jefferson returned from France in 1789 and became secretary of state in the Washington administration. Great issues of foreign and domestic policy, which struck to the bedrock of principle, soon brought him into conflict with treasury secretary ALEXANDER HAMILTON. The conflict symbolized the rising opposition, first in the government, then in the country at large, between two nascent POLITICAL PARTIES, Republican and Federalist. The Constitution itself became an issue in February 1791, on Hamilton's plan to incorporate a national bank. After Washington received the bank bill from Congress, where Madison had pointedly questioned its constitutionality, he asked the secretaries for their opinions. Jefferson returned a brisk 2,200-word brief against the bill. No power to incorporate a bank had been delegated to Congress. None could be found among the ENUMERATED POWERS, nor could it be fairly inferred from either of the general clauses appealed to by the bank's advocates. The power of Congress to provide for the GENERAL WELFARE was only the power to lay taxes for that purpose; the NECESSARY AND PROPER CLAUSE, unless construed strictly, would "swallow up all the DELEGATED POWERS, and reduce the whole to one power." The bank bill, he concluded, would breach the limits of the Constitution, trample on the laws of the states, and open "a boundless field of power, no longer susceptible to definition." Washington, however, was persuaded by Hamilton's opinion founded on the doctrine of IMPLIED POWERS and signed the bill. The issue of congressional power was reargued a year later on Hamilton's Report on Manufactures. No legislation resulted, but Jefferson told the President that on the principles of the report Congress could tax and spend without limit on the apology of aiding the general welfare. The deeper grounds of division involved matters of morals, interests, and politics; but because policies were debated in constitutional terms, the question of who was loyal to the Constitution—whether it was best served by strict or loose construction, by STATES' RIGHTS or national consolidation, whether it ought to be viewed as a superintending rule of political action or as a point of departure for vigorous statesmanship—became a major issue between the parties.

The general doctrine of states' rights had been present from the beginning of the controversy, but only in 1798, when Jefferson was vice-president, did it become firmly associated in his mind with the preservation of the Constitution, the Union, and republican liberty. (See UNION, THEORIES OF.) All were threatened, in his opinion, by the ALIEN AND SEDITION ACTS enacted during the war crisis with France. Under the pretense of saving the country from Jacobins and incendiaries, the Federalists, he believed, aimed by these laws to cripple or destroy the Republican party. Because of the danger of criminal prosecution, the delusion of public opinion, and Federalist control of the government, including the courts, the usual means of opposition were ineffectual; so Jefferson turned to the state legislatures as the point of protest and resistance. There was nothing novel in the proceeding. As early as 1790 the Virginia assembly had protested against the allegedly unconstitutional acts of the federal government; in fact, opposition of this kind had been contemplated, and approved, in THE FEDERALIST #28. But the resolutions secretly drafted by Jefferson, and adopted by the Kentucky legislature in November, offered an authoritative theory of "state interposition" that was destined to have great influence. (See VIRGINIA AND KENTUCKY RESOLUTIONS.) The Kentucky Resolutions set forth the theory of the Constitution as a compact among the states. Acts beyond the delegated powers were unconstitutional and void; and since the contracting parties had created no ultimate arbiter, each state had "an equal right to judge for itself, as well of infractions as of the mode and measure of redress." How far Jefferson meant to go was unclear. He called for NULLIFICATION of the oppressive laws; but rather than cause overt state defiance of federal authority, his aim was to arouse opposition opinion through the legislatures to force repeal of the laws. When this political strategy failed, he got Kentucky, as well as Virginia, to renew its protest in 1799, again to no avail. Nevertheless, Jefferson always believed that the Virginia and Kentucky Resolutions were crucial to "the revolution of 1800" that elevated him to the presidency. They had saved the party and the freedom of the political process upon which victory at the polls depended. To this extent, certainly, the resolutions strengthened principles of freedom and self-government under the Constitution. But in appealing to states' rights and state resistance—interposition or nullification or SECESSION—Jefferson struck a course potentially as dangerous to the Constitution and the Union as the odious laws were to civil and political liberty.

Jefferson entered the presidency pledged to return the government to the original principles of the Constitution. These principles included, first, the protection of the state governments in all their rights as the primary jurisdictions of domestic affairs; second, a frugal and simple administration of the federal government; and third, a sharp contradiction of executive power and influence, which had threatened to "monarchize" the Constitution. Such principles were likely to prove embarrassing to the President's leadership. The story of the administration became the story of how Jefferson escaped, evaded, or overcame the restraints of his own first principles in order to provide the strong leadership the country required.

Jefferson's first test concerned the judiciary. He had always favored an independent judiciary as the guardian of individual rights against legislative and executive tyranny. But in "the crisis of '98" the courts became the destroyers rather than the guardians of the liberties of the citizen. The power of this partisan judiciary had been increased by the JUDICIARY ACT OF 1801 passed in the waning hours of the Adams administration. The Federalists, Jefferson believed, had retired to the judiciary as a stronghold from which to assail his administration; and he promptly called for repeal of the Judiciary Act. This was done, although it involved the abolition of judgeships held on GOOD BEHAVIOR tenure. The case of MARBURY v. MADISON (1803) arose at the same time. It, too, was significant primarily in its political character, as a duel between the President and the new Chief Justice, JOHN MARSHALL. Jefferson, who disliked his Virginia cousin, objected to the decision not because the Court asserted the ultimate power to interpret the Constitution, for in fact it did not go that far, but because Marshall traveled out of the case, pretending to a JURISDICTION he then disclaimed, in order to slap the chief magistrate for violating constitutional rights.

With regard to JUDICIAL REVIEW, Jefferson consistently held to the theory of "tripartite balance," under which each of the coordinate branches of government had the equal right to decide questions of constitutionality for itself. This equality of decisional power was as necessary to maintaining the constitutional SEPARATION OF POWERS, in his view, as the doctrine of states' rights was to preserving the division of authority in the federal system. Under the theory he considered the Sedition Act, which had expired, unconstitutional from the beginning and pardoned those still suffering its penalties. The idea of governmental adaptation and change through construction of the Constitution was repugnant to Jefferson. Even more repugnant was the idea of vesting the ultimate authority of interpretation in a court whose members had no accountability to the people. But Jefferson, though he held the judiciary at bay, was unwilling to push his principles to conclusion and left the foundations of judicial power undisturbed for Marshall to build upon later.

Jefferson overcame the restraints of his whiggish view of executive power by capitalizing on his personal magnetism and influence as a party leader. In FOREIGN AFFAIRS, the principal field of the general government, he had generally taken a more expansive view. Yet the foreign affairs triumph of his administration, the LOUISIANA PURCHASE, became a constitutional crisis for him. While other Republicans easily discovered legal warrant for the treaty, he could not. It was "an act beyond the Constitution," and there was nothing for the President and Congress to do but "throw themselves on the country for doing them unauthorized, what we know they would have done for themselves had they been in a situation to do it." So he drafted a constitutional amendment—"an act of indemnity"—to sanction the treaty retroactively. "I had rather ask an enlargement of power from the nation," he wrote to a Virginia senator, "than to assume it by construction which would make our powers boundless. Our peculiar security is in the possession of a written Constitution. Let us not make it a blank paper by construction." Congress was less scrupulous, however, and when it declined to follow him, he acquiesced. A revolution in the Union perforce became a revolution in the Constitution as well. He found justification for other executive actions—in foreign affairs, in the suppression of the Burr Conspiracy—above and beyond the law. "It is," he wrote, "incumbent on those only who accept of great charges, to risk themselves on great occasions, when the safety of the nation, or some of its very high interests are at stake." In Jefferson's thinking, actions of this kind, which were exceptional and uncodified, were preferable to false and frivolous constructions of the Constitution, which permanently corrupted it. Yet he took little comfort from the theory of "higher obligation" in the case of the Louisiana Purchase.

In retirement at Monticello from 1809 until his death seventeen years later, Jefferson repeatedly confronted the problem of constitutional preservation and change. He knew there could be no preservation without change, no constructive change without preservation. He knew, as he wrote in again championing reform of the Virginia constitution, "that laws and institutions must go hand in hand with the progress of the human mind." And he did not hesitate to declare again his belief, formed in 1789 in the shadow of the Bastille, that each generation, representing a new constituent majority, should make its own constitution. Change should occur, fundamentally, by CONSTITUTIONAL CONVENTION. Next to that, it should occur by regular amendment. As President he had advocated the TWELFTH AMENDMENT, approved in 1804, and several others that were stillborn. Now, from Monticello, he advocated amendments authorizing federal INTERNAL IMPROVEMENTS, the direct election of the president, and the two-term limitation on the president. Nothing happened. Finally, not long before his death, he "despair[ed] of ever seeing another amendment to the Constitution," and observed, "Another general convention can alone relieve us." Thus in the nation, as in the state, he appealed to both lawmaking and constitution-making authorities to keep the fundamental law responsive to new conditions and new demands.

Jefferson continued to the end to reject constitutional change by construction or interpretation. In the wake of the Panic of 1819, which threw his affairs into hopeless disorder, he reacted sharply against the course of consolidation in the general government, above all the bold nationalism of the Supreme Court. "The judiciary of the United States is the subtle corps of sappers and miners constantly working under ground to undermine the foundations of our confederated fabric," he wrote in 1820. "They are construing our constitution from a co-ordination of a general and special government to a general and supreme one. This will lay all things at their feet." Only by combining the revolutionary theory of "constituent sovereignty" with the rule of "strict construction" would it be possible, Jefferson believed, to maintain constitutional government on the republican foundations of "the consent of the governed."

MERRILL D. PETERSON

Bibliography

BOYD, JULIAN P., ED. 1950–1974 *The Papers of Thomas Jefferson.* 19 Vols. to date. Princeton, N.J.: Princeton University Press.

LEVY, LEONARD W. 1963 *Jefferson and Civil Liberties: The Darker Side.* Cambridge, Mass.: Harvard University Press.

LIPSCOMB, A. A. and BERGH, A. E., EDS. 1904 *The Writings of Thomas Jefferson.* 20 Vols. Washington, D.C.: Thomas Jefferson Memorial Association.

MALONE, DUMAS 1948–1982 *Jefferson and His Times.* 6 Vols. to date. Boston: Little, Brown.

PETERSON, MERRILL D. 1970 *Thomas Jefferson and the New Nation: A Biography.* New York: Oxford University Press.

JENCKS ACT
71 Stat. 595 (1957)

In *Jencks v. United States,* in June 1957, the Supreme Court, speaking through Justice WILLIAM J. BRENNAN, reversed the conviction of a labor leader, Clinton E. Jencks, charged with perjury for falsely swearing he was not a communist. The five-man majority held that reports filed by FBI-paid informants alleging Jencks's participation in Communist party activities should have been available to his counsel when requested. The majority ruled that the prosecution must either disclose to the defense statements made by government witnesses or drop the case.

Justice TOM C. CLARK wrote a near-inflammatory dissent contending that unless Congress nullified the decision, "those intelligence agencies of our government engaged in law enforcement may as well close up shop." The decision, he warned, would result in a "Roman holiday" for criminals to "rummage" through secret files. Congress seized upon Clark's dissent and a Jencks Act was quickly passed, amending the United States Code. In sharply restricting the Court's decision, the measure provided that a defendant in a criminal case could, following testimony by a government witness, request disclosure of a pretrial statement made by that witness, so long as the statement was written and signed by the witness or was a transcription of an oral statement made at the time the statement was given. Other requested material was to be screened by the trial judge for relevance, with the judge given the right to delete unrelated matters. In subsequent challenges, raised in *Rosenberg v. United States* (1959) and *Palermo v. United States* (1959), the Justices upheld the law, carefully conforming to its provisions.

PAUL L. MURPHY

Bibliography

NOTE 1958 The Jencks Legislation: Problems in Prospect. *Yale Law Journal* 67:674–699.

JENIFER, DANIEL OF ST. THOMAS (1723–1790)

Daniel of St. Thomas Jenifer signed the Constitution as a Maryland delegate to the CONSTITUTIONAL CONVENTION OF 1787. The most national-minded of Maryland's delegates, he quarreled often with LUTHER MARTIN. His late arrival on July 2 permitted approval of equal votes for the states in the Senate.

DENNIS J. MAHONEY

JENKINS v. ANDERSON 447 U.S. 231 (1980)

The Fifth Amendment allows a criminal defendant to remain silent during his trial and prevents the prosecution from commenting on his silence, in order to prevent the jury from drawing adverse inferences. In *Jenkins* the defendant surrendered to the police two weeks after killing a man and claimed that he had acted in self-defense. When he told that self-defense story at his trial, the prosecutor countered that he would have surrendered immediately had he killed in self-defense. After conviction the defendant, seeking HABEAS CORPUS relief, argued that the use of his prearrest silence violated his RIGHT AGAINST SELF-INCRIMINATION and fundamental fairness. The Supreme Court, like the federal courts below, denied relief. Justice LEWIS F. POWELL, for a 7–2 Court, ruled that the use of prearrest silence to impeach a defendant's credibility, if he testifies in his own defense, does not violate any constitutional rights. Powell's murky reasoning provoked Justices THURGOOD MARSHALL and WILLIAM J. BRENNAN, dissenting, to declare that a duty to incriminate oneself now replaced the right to remain silent. Powell had supported no such duty, but he rejected a "right to commit perjury," which no one claimed. His opinion weakened the right to remain silent.

LEONARD W. LEVY

JENSEN, MERRILL (1905–1980)

Author and editor of many books on American colonial and revolutionary history, Merrill Monroe Jensen is best known for his challenge of the traditional interpretation of the ARTICLES OF CONFEDERATION as an inadequate form of government whose weaknesses required that it be replaced by the Constitution of 1787. Jensen argued in his most influential books, *The Articles of Confederation* (1940) and *The New Nation* (1950), that the American Revolution was as much a political and social upheaval as the winning of independence from Great Britain and that the Articles of Confederation were the logical result of the democratic philosophy of the DECLARATION OF INDEPENDENCE and the state constitutions of the 1770s. Jensen also contended that the Articles' weaknesses were exaggerated both by the Federalists of 1787–1788, who actually supported the Constitution as a check on the democratic tendencies of which the Articles were the clearest expression, and by most historians.

RICHARD B. BERNSTEIN

JIM CROW LAWS

See: Segregation; Separate-but-Equal Doctrine

JOHNS, UNITED STATES v. 105 S. Ct. 881 (1985)

This case continued a trend of decisions by which the automobile exception to the FOURTH AMENDMENT's SEARCH WARRANT requirement expands without discernible limits. Warrantless AUTOMOBILE SEARCHES were first tolerated because a culprit might suddenly drive away with the evidence of his guilt before a warrant could be obtained. That possibility became the basis of holdings that if a vehicle can constitutionally be searched at the time it is found or stopped, it can be impounded and searched later; and if the vehicle can be searched, sealed containers found within may be opened and searched, too. In *Johns* the Court ruled that if officers unload the containers and store them, instead of searching them on the spot, three days later the containers may be opened without a warrant and any contraband that may be found can be introduced in EVIDENCE. Only Justices WILLIAM J. BRENNAN and THURGOOD MARSHALL dissented from the OPINION OF THE COURT by Justice SANDRA DAY O'CONNOR.

LEONARD W. LEVY

(SEE ALSO: *Chambers v. Maroney; United States v. Ross.*)

JOHNSON, ANDREW (1808–1875)

Born in 1808, Andrew Johnson became a Tennessee legislator in 1833, congressman in 1843, governor in 1853, United States senator in 1856, Tennessee's military governor in 1862, vice-president of the United States in March 1865, and, on ABRAHAM LINCOLN's death in April 1865, President. Early in his career Johnson mixed STRICT CONSTRUCTION and STATES' RIGHTS views with an unusually warm nationalism, stern loyalty to the Democratic party (until the Civil War: Johnson returned to the Democratic allegiance in late 1866), and a remarkable devotion to white supremacy. By 1860 Johnson's sponsorship of homestead legislation (see HOMESTEAD ACT) and frontier-style campaign rhetoric had won him a reputation as a latter-day Jacksonian.

In the 1860–1861 winter, Johnson, the only slave-state senator who refused to follow his state into SECESSION, openly counseled Tennesseans against seceding. For his temerity he had to flee to Washington. In the Senate, Johnson, achieving at last his homestead goal, won Republicans' appreciation also for supporting Lincoln's and Congress's policies on TEST OATHS, military arrests of civilians, confiscation, emancipation, and Reconstruction. Johnson insisted that the Constitution's WAR POWERS and TREASON clauses authorized the nation, not to coerce a state, but to punish disloyal individuals directly. This believer in a fixed, state-on-top, race-ordered FEDERALISM in 1862 accepted from Lincoln assignment as Tennessee's military governor, a position unknown to the Constitution or statutes, supportable only from the most flexible contemporary ideas on national primacy under martial law.

As military governor, Johnson employed test oaths and troops against alleged pro-Confederates, sometimes purging unfriendly government officeholders and officials of private CORPORATIONS, to rebuild local and state governments. Johnson's policies helped the Republican-War Democratic "Union" coalition win Tennessee in 1864. That party named Johnson its vice-presidential candidate in order to attract the support of other Unionists in the reconquered South and border states, who seemed to be educable on race. Then, just as the Confederacy's collapse made Reconstruction an immediate concern, Johnson became President.

Although no specific Reconstruction statute constrained him, the 1861–1862 CONFISCATION ACTS, the 1862 test oath act, and the 1865 FREEDMEN'S BUREAU law limited and defined executive actions. Johnson arrogated to himself an unprecedented right to enforce them selectively or not at all in order to further his Reconstruction policy. (For a modern parallel, see IMPOUNDMENT OF FUNDS.)

That policy (announced May 29, 1865, for North Carolina and later for other states) he based on the war powers (but Johnson later insisted that the end of hostilities cut off this source of authority) and on the GUARANTEE CLAUSE: the same authorities Lincoln and Congress employed in wartime Reconstructions (later Johnson insisted that the guarantee clause did not justify a national interest in state residents' CIVIL RIGHTS). Without authority from statute, he appointed a provisional (that is, military) governor for every defeated state, who, with Army help, initiated elections for a CONSTITUTIONAL CONVENTION among qualified voters, including ex-rebels Johnson amnestied and pardoned. The convention was to renounce secession and ratify the THIRTEENTH AMENDMENT. Johnson secretly counseled his provisional governors to appoint officials who could swear to required test oaths and even, as Lincoln had advised publicly, to grant suffrage to token Negroes. But no states obeyed their creator; several only very reluctantly ratified the Thirteenth Amendment, balking at its enforcement clause.

In "reconstructing" thirteen states, Johnson had the largest federal patronage opportunity in American history, especially with respect to postal and tax officers, traditional nuclei of political parties. He filled these influential offices with pardoned ex-Confederates who could not subscribe to the required test oaths, exempting them from the stipulation, thus returning power to recent rebels. Johnson canceled prosecutions under the confiscation laws and inhibited the work of the Freedmen's Bureau, thereby blighting blacks' prospects for a secure economic base. "Johnson" state and local officers, including judges, state attorneys, and police encouraged lawsuits against the Bureau and Army officers for alleged assaults and trespasses and for violating the BLACK CODES. Johnson did not protect his harassed military personnel under the HABEAS CORPUS ACT of 1863. In April 1866, he proclaimed that peace existed everywhere in the

South and that all federal Reconstruction authority ended.

His policies made the security of blacks, white Unionists, and federal officials woefully uncertain and seriously distorted the Constitution's CHECKS AND BALANCES. Johnson insisted that Congress should admit delegates-elect from the Southern states, though conceding that Congress had independent authority (Article I, section 5, on CONGRESSIONAL MEMBERSHIP) to judge the qualifications of its members; he reiterated that the nation had no right to intervene in those states and assigned the Army to police them. Johnson unprecedentedly enlarged the VETO POWER. His stunning vetoes of bills on CIVIL RIGHTS, the Freedmen's Bureau, and military Reconstruction, among others, antagonized even congressmen sympathetic to his views. His vetoes invoked the decision in EX PARTE MILLIGAN (1866), paid tribute to the STATE POLICE POWER, and decried the centralized military despotism he claimed to discern in these bills. But Johnson appealed also to the lowest race views of the time. And he never dealt with the question, with which congressmen at least tried to grapple, of individuals' remedies when the states failed to treat them equally in civil and criminal relationships. The President's decision to campaign in the fall 1866 elections against the party that had elected him, his opposition to the FOURTEENTH AMENDMENT (public disapprobation by a President of a proposed amendment was itself unprecedented), and his intemperate attacks against leading congressmen further alienated many persons.

Johnson rejected the idea of an adaptable Constitution and of a federal duty to seek more decent race relations. There was no halfway house between the centralization he insisted was occurring and a total abandonment of any national interest in the rights of its citizens, who were also state citizens. Johnson's rigidity reflected his heightening racism and his yearning for an independent nomination for the presidency in 1868 from Democrats and the most conservative Republicans.

Johnson himself destroyed his presidential prospects. After obeying the TENURE OF OFFICE ACT by suspending (August 1867) Secretary of War EDWIN M. STANTON, Johnson decided, upon the Senate's nonconcurrence (February 1868), to violate that law. He ousted Stanton and named ULYSSES S. GRANT as interim secretary. Republican congressmen in 1867 had shied away from IMPEACHMENT but in February 1868 the House (128–74, 15 not voting) impeached Johnson for "high crimes and misdemeanors," an offense undefined in the few earlier American impeachments, especially as to whether the "high crimes" had to be criminally indictable (Article I, section 2; Article II, sections 2, 4; Article III, section 2). Contemporary legal scholar JOHN NORTON POMEROY held that indictability was not a prerequisite for impeachability, conviction, and removal from office. The impeachment committee's charges (Articles I–X) nevertheless stressed largely indictable offenses, including Johnson's obstructions of the military Reconstruction Tenure of Office, and Army Appropriations Acts. Article XI was a catch-all to attract senators who did not hold with indictability as a minimum for impeachability. (See ARTICLES OF IMPEACHMENT, JOHNSON.)

From February through May 1868 the President's able counsel HENRY STANBERY, by insisting on indictability as the test of impeachability, confused senators who formed the court in the impeachment trial. Johnson, at last restraining his intemperateness, now enforced the military reconstruction law and other statutes he had vetoed. He replaced Grant as secretary of war with John M. Schofield, who, though conservative on race, was trusted on Capitol Hill. The Republican majority, wedded to checks and balances, hesitated to subordinate the presidency by convicting and removing Johnson. The House "managers" of the trial harassed witnesses and journalists, outraging some Republican senators. And 1868 was an election year. Johnson, his hopes for a nomination destroyed, must leave office by March 1869. These factors combined to leave Johnson unconvicted by a single Senate vote, 35–19.

Johnson was not the victim of a Radical Republican conspiracy but was the architect of his own remarkably successful effort to thwart improvements in race equality. He won because he exploited men's lowest race fears, cloaking them in glorifications of states' rights. His return to Congress in 1875 as a Tennessee senator (he died later that year), when sentiment was rising even among Republicans to dump the Negro, symbolized his triumph.

HAROLD M. HYMAN

Bibliography

BENEDICT, MICHAEL L. 1973 *The Impeachment and Trial of Andrew Johnson.* New York: Norton.

BERGER, RAOUL 1973 *Impeachment: Constitutional Problems.* Cambridge, Mass.: Harvard University Press.

SEFTON, JAMES 1980 *Andrew Johnson and the Uses of Constitutional Power.* Boston: Little, Brown.

TREFOUSSE, HANS L. 1975 *Impeachment of a President: Andrew Johnson, the Blacks, and Reconstruction.* Knoxville: University of Tennessee Press.

JOHNSON, LYNDON B.
(1908–1973)

Lyndon Baines Johnson was a strong President whose performance was tempered by an affectionate reverence for the constitutional system as a whole. He exploited the cumulative precedents for presidential leadership and authority in domestic, foreign, and military policy; protected presidential power against congressional intrusion while working with vigor to carry Congress with him; and turned the office over to his successor intact. Jointly with Congress, he extended federal power greatly in CIVIL RIGHTS, education, and welfare. He appointed the first black Supreme Court Justice, THURGOOD MARSHALL; but Johnson's attempt to assure liberal leadership beyond his term by the nomination of ABE FORTAS as Chief Justice failed when Fortas withdrew in 1968.

All this tells us little of how the American constitutional process actually operated in the turbulent, creative, and tragic days between November 22, 1963, and January 20, 1969. The agenda Lyndon Johnson confronted was unique. Aside from the urgent need to unify the nation and establish his legitimacy in the wake of JOHN F. KENNEDY's assassination, he faced simultaneous protracted crises at home and abroad: a crisis in race relations and a disintegrating position in Southeast Asia. WOODROW WILSON and FRANKLIN D. ROOSEVELT had also confronted both urgent domestic problems and war; but the course of events permitted them to be dealt with in sequence. Johnson faced them together and they stayed with him to the end.

By personality and conviction, Johnson was a man driven to grapple with problems. But he also carried into office a passionate moral vision of an American society of equal opportunity—a vision he proved capable of translating into LEGISLATION, above all in the fields of civil rights, education, and medical care. The CIVIL RIGHTS ACT OF 1964, the VOTING RIGHTS ACT OF 1965, and the Fair Housing and Federal Jury Reform Acts of 1968 were major results of his crusade for racial equality. The ELEMENTARY AND SECONDARY EDUCATION ACT and HEALTH INSURANCE FOR THE AGED ACT (MEDICARE) of 1965 were outstanding among dozens of acts passed in both fields. In carrying the religious constituencies on the Education Act, Johnson displayed skill bordering on wizardry. As proportions of gross national product, social welfare outlays of the federal government rose dramatically between 1964 and 1968 while national security outlays rose only slightly. This was possible because of an average real growth rate of 4.8 percent in the American economy.

Johnson had been a man of the Congress for some thirty years before assuming the presidency. No President ever came to responsibility with a deeper and more subtle working knowledge of the constitutional tensions between Congress and the President, and of the requirement of generating a partnership out of that tension, issue by issue. But Johnson knew from experience that, on domestic issues, a President's time for leading Congress and achieving major legislative results was short. From his first days as President, Johnson expected Congress would, in the end, mobilize to frustrate one of his initiatives and then progressively reduce or end his primacy. He was, therefore, determined to use his initial capital promptly. Although momentum slowed after mid-1965, Johnson proved capable of carrying Congress on significant domestic legislation virtually to the end of his term.

Johnson was opportunistic in the best sense. He exploited the Congress elected with him in November 1964; but he also channeled the powerful waves of popular feeling in the wake of the assassinations of John Kennedy, MARTIN LUTHER KING, JR., and ROBERT F. KENNEDY into support for his legislative program.

Johnson believed the presidency was the central repository of the nation's ideals and the energizing agent for change in the nation's policy. He understood the advantage a President enjoys relative to a fragmented Congress: the power to initiate. He brought into the White House every constructive idea he could mobilize from both private life and the bureaucracies, setting in motion some one hundred task forces, sixty within the government, forty made up of outside experts. Where possible, he also engaged members of Congress in the drafting of legislation at an early stage in the hope that their subsequent interest and support would be more energetic.

Johnson also understood that in domestic affairs there was little a President could constitutionally do on his own. His was primarily a license to persuade. He used the conventional levers of presidential influence in dealing with Congress. But his most effective instrument was his formidable power of persuasion, based on knowledge of individual members and a sensitive perception of the possibility of support from each on particular issues. He spent far more time with members of Congress than any President before or since—face to face, by telephone, or in group meetings at the White House.

Johnson judged that he had come to responsibility at a rare, transient interval of opportunity for social progress. Therefore, he used up his capital and achieved much. He left Washington with a sense of how much more he would have liked to have done; but he also realized that the nation was determined to pause and catch its breath rather than continue to plunge forward. Nevertheless, the programs initiated in Johnson's time continued to expand in the 1970s. As Ralph Ellison, the black novelist, said, Johnson will perhaps be recognized as "the greatest American President for the poor and for Negroes . . . a very great honor indeed."

But all did not go smoothly with the Great Society. In 1965, five days after the signing of the Voting Rights Act, rioting broke out in Watts, and riots in urban ghettoes continued for three years. Despite vigorous and imaginative efforts, these problems proved relatively unyielding although violence subsided in 1968 as it became increasingly clear that the costs were primarily borne by the black community. Moreover, as new welfare programs moved from law to administration, resistance gradually built up both to their cost and to intrusions on state and local authority. Although significant modifications in the Great Society programs were made in the 1970s and 1980s, it seems unlikely that the basic extensions of public policy in civil rights, education, and welfare will be withdrawn.

Although Johnson led public opinion and drove Congress in domestic affairs, he conducted the war in Southeast Asia with a reserve that did not match the nation's desire for a prompt resolution of the conflict. Johnson's relations with the Congress on the VIETNAM WAR thus differed markedly from his approach on domestic policy. HARRY S. TRUMAN had decided, with the agreement of the congressional leadership, to resist the invasion of South Korea on the basis of his powers as COMMANDER-IN-CHIEF. Johnson preferred the precedents of the Middle East and Formosa Resolutions which he, when Democratic leader in the Senate, had recommended to DWIGHT D. EISENHOWER. He followed that course in the Tonkin Gulf Resolution in 1964. Despite later controversy over the resolution, the record of the Senate debate indicates that its members understood the solemn constitutional step they were taking. Johnson consulted the bipartisan leadership and received their unanimous support on July 27, 1965, before announcing the next day that he had ordered substantial forces to Vietnam—a decision which, at the time, had overwhelming popular as well as congressional support. The possibilities of a formal DECLARATION OF WAR or new congressional mandate were examined and rejected on the ground that they might have brought into effect possible secret military agreements between North Vietnam and other communist powers.

Johnson's determination to consult with and to carry the Congress in 1964 and 1965 was real. But he knew that legislative support at the initiation of hostilities would not prevent members of Congress, disciplined by changes in public opinion, from later opposing him. In the end, he was convinced, the primary responsibility under the Constitution in matters of war and peace rested with the President; and he accepted the implications of that judgment, including the possibility that support for his decision would fade and leave him, like some of his predecessors, lonely and beleaguered.

Johnson made his decision when the entrance of North Vietnamese regular units into South Vietnam had created a crisis, compounded by the Malaysian confrontation instigated by Indonesia with Chinese support. The choice before him was to accept defeat or to fight. He chose to fight because, in his view, the Southeast Asia Treaty (SEATO) reflected authentic United States interests in Asia; a failure to honor the treaty would weaken the credibility of American commitments elsewhere; and the outcome of withdrawal would not be peace but a wider war.

The strategy Johnson adopted was gradually to reduce communist military capabilities within South Vietnam; to use air power against the lines of supply; to impose direct costs on North Vietnam by attacks on selected targets in the Hanoi area; and to support the South Vietnamese in their efforts to create a strong military establishment and to build a viable economy and a democratic political system. His objective was to convince North Vietnam that the takeover of South Vietnam was beyond its military and political grasp and that the costs of continuing the effort were excessive. From the beginning to the end of his administration, Johnson was in virtually continuous diplomatic contact with the North Vietnamese. Protracted formal negotiations began in April 1968 in the wake of the Tet offensive, during which the communist cause suffered a severe military setback but gained ground in American public opinion.

Johnson's cautious strategy in Vietnam conformed to the views of neither the hawkish majority in American public opinion and the Congress, nor the dovish minority. Johnson realized that his conduct of the war was unpopular and that public support had eroded; the nation resisted a protracted engagement with limited objectives and mounting casualties. He nevertheless held to his strategy and resisted those who advocated decisive military action on the ground outside South Vietnam. As Commander-in-Chief, Johnson was determined to conduct the war in a way that minimized the chance of a large engagement with Chinese Communist or Soviet forces. The memory of Chinese Communist entrance into the KOREAN WAR may well have played an important part in Johnson's determination; and he knew that he would be judged in history, in part, on whether his assessment of the risks of a more decisive course of action was correct. Johnson's strategy may also have been affected by two other considerations: a determination to maintain the momentum of his domestic initiatives; and fear that an all-out mobilization might regenerate an undifferentiated anticommunism, with disruptive consequences for foreign policy and McCarthyite implications at home.

The tension between impatient public opinion and Johnson's cautious strategy led to a quasi-constitutional crisis in the early months of 1968. The bipartisan unity of the American foreign policy establishment, which began in 1940, ended, for a generation at least, in 1968. Johnson's distinguished outside advisers, who had been united in November 1967 in support of Johnson's Vietnam policy, were hopelessly divided four months later.

Many complex factors contributed to the schism, but in part it was the product of conflicting images. For Johnson and others who had foreseen the Tet offensive and acted to frustrate it, the communist military failure was apparent, and Johnson's March 31 bombing reduction and proposal to negotiate were designed to exploit a position of relative strength. For those to whom the offensive was a shock and a demonstration of the futility of the American effort, Johnson's negotiation initiative seemed an admission of defeat. Johnson's simultaneous announcement of his decision not to seek reelection may have strengthened the latter image in the public mind.

Thus, Johnson left to his successor a greatly improved military, political, and economic situation in Southeast Asia, a weary and discouraged majority of Americans, and a divided foreign policy establishment in addition to an ardent minority that had been advocating withdrawal from Vietnam for several years.

The antiwar crusaders challenged Johnson's assessment on multiple grounds, among them: the importance of American interests in Southeast Asia; the legality and morality of the war itself; and the belief that Vietnamese nationalism was overwhelmingly on the side of the communists. Johnson weighed carefully the antiwar views, but he remained convinced to the end of his life that his assessment of the issues at stake was correct. He was less sure that his cautious military strategy had been correct.

There was a great deal more to Johnson's foreign policy than the war in Southeast Asia. He stabilized NATO in the wake of French withdrawal from its unified military command; saw the Dominican Republic through a crisis in 1965 to a period of economic and social progress under democracy; and encouraged regional cohesion in Latin America, Africa, and Asia.

Like all American Presidents in the nuclear age, Johnson consciously bore an extraconstitutional responsibility to the human race to minimize the risk of nuclear war. He sought to normalize relations with the Soviet Union; he carried forward efforts to tame nuclear weapons through the Non-proliferation and Outer Space treaties; and he laid the foundation for strategic arms limitation talks.

But the central fact of his administration was the convergence of war and social revolution that resulted in an accelerated inflation rate and yielded four years of antiwar demonstrations and burning ghettoes against a backdrop of prosperity and social reform. Johnson was required, at the request of the governor of Michigan, to send regular Army units to suppress riots in Detroit in July 1967; and troops had to be deployed again in Washington, D.C., in April 1968 after the assassination of Martin Luther King, Jr.

In 1967, after reading the results of a poll assessing his presidency, Johnson said: "In this job you must set a standard for making decisions. Mine is: 'What will my grandchildren think of my administration when I'm buried under the tree at the Ranch, in the family graveyard.' I believe they will be proud of two things: what I have done for the Negro and in Asia. But right now I've lost twenty points on the race issue, fifteen on Vietnam." As Lyndon Johnson's voice repeats many times each day on a tape played at the LBJ Library, ". . . it is for the people themselves and their posterity to decide."

W. W. ROSTOW

Bibliography

BURNS, JAMES MCGREGOR 1968 *To Heal and to Build: The Programs of Lyndon B. Johnson.* New York: McGraw-Hill.

JOHNSON, LYNDON B. 1971 *The Vantage Point.* New York: Holt, Rinehart & Winston.

MCPHERSON, HARRY 1972 *A Political Education.* Boston: Little, Brown.

MUELLER, JOHN E. 1973 *War, Presidents and Public Opinion.* New York: Wiley.

REDFORD, EMMETTE S. and BLISSETT, MARLAN 1981 *Organizing the Executive Branch: The Johnson Presidency.* Chicago: University of Chicago Press.
ROSTOW, W. W. 1972 *The Diffusion of Power.* New York: Macmillan.

JOHNSON, REVERDY
(1796–1876)

A leading constitutional lawyer and Maryland Unionist, Reverdy Johnson argued numerous important Supreme Court cases, including *Seymour v. McCormick* (1854), DRED SCOTT V. SANDFORD (1857), and UNITED STATES V. CRUIKSHANK (1876). At President ABRAHAM LINCOLN's request Johnson published a rebuttal to Chief Justice ROGER B. TANEY's opinion in *Ex parte Merryman* (1861), in which Johnson argued that the President had authority to suspend HABEAS CORPUS. Johnson approved the use of Negro troops and as a senator (1854–1859; 1863–1868) voted for the THIRTEENTH AMENDMENT. However, Johnson broke with Lincoln over the suppression of civilians in Maryland and war aims. Johnson believed that the Confederate states had never been legally out of the Union, and thus once the rebellion was militarily suppressed, the states should be allowed to resume their antebellum status. Johnson opposed LOYALTY OATHS and was President ANDREW JOHNSON's leading Senate supporter during the IMPEACHMENT trial.

PAUL FINKELMAN

Bibliography

STEINER, BERNARD C. 1914 *Life of Reverdy Johnson.* Baltimore: Norman, Remington Co.

JOHNSON, THOMAS
(1732–1819)

Thomas Johnson served in Maryland's colonial House of Delegates and was a member of committees to instruct delegates to the STAMP ACT CONGRESS and to draft a protest against the TOWNSHEND ACTS. He sat in the Continental Congress but was absent when the DECLARATION OF INDEPENDENCE was signed. He was a member of the convention that drafted Maryland's revolutionary constitution (1776) and served as its first governor (1777–1779). Johnson served in Congress from 1781 to 1787 and was a judge of the special federal court to settle a boundary dispute between New York and Massachusetts. He supported RATIFICATION OF THE CONSTITUTION in the state convention of 1788.

His longtime friend, President GEORGE WASHINGTON, offered Johnson a district judgeship in 1789, but Johnson accepted instead the chief judgeship of the Maryland General Court. When JOHN RUTLEDGE resigned in 1791, Washington appointed Johnson to the Supreme Court.

Serving only fourteen months on the Court, Johnson took part in no major decision. He sat for a single term (during which the JAY COURT heard only four cases) and wrote a single short opinion. In 1793, plagued by illness and fatigued by circuit duty, he resigned and was replaced by WILLIAM PATERSON.

DENNIS J. MAHONEY

JOHNSON, WILLIAM
(1771–1834)

Justice William Johnson of Charleston, South Carolina, was THOMAS JEFFERSON's first appointee to the Supreme Court. Johnson was the son of a blacksmith and revolutionary patriot. After attending Princeton and reading law with CHARLES COTESWORTH PINCKNEY, Johnson was elected to serve three terms in the state legislature as a member of the new Republican party. During his third term he became speaker of the House. In 1799, he was elected to the state's highest court, and on March 22, 1804, he was appointed to the Supreme Court, where he served until his death. Of all the fifteen Justices who sat on the MARSHALL COURT, Johnson was, at least to 1830, the most independent and vocal in advancing opinions different from those of Chief Justice JOHN MARSHALL. In treating the accountability of the members of the Court, the distribution of the national power among the three branches, the powers reserved to the states, and VESTED RIGHTS, Johnson often found himself in disagreement with the majority of the Marshall Court. At the time of his appointment, Johnson objected to Marshall's practice of rendering unaminous opinions. He felt that the judicial role required freedom of expression, and he fought to revive the practice of SERIATIM OPINIONS. "Few minds," he protested in a separate opinion in 1816, "are accustomed to the same habit of thinking. . . ." From his advent until 1822, Johnson wrote twelve of twenty-four CONCURRING OPINIONS and sixteen of thirty-two DISSENTING OPINIONS. Toward the end of his career, new Justices joined the Court who agreed with Johnson and frequently spoke out separately with him. Johnson succeeded in establishing the right to dissent, so important in later years.

Johnson also ran into conflict with other members of the Court concerning the allocation of power among the branches of the national government. Like the rest of the Marshall Court, he believed that a strong national government was vital to national unity, and he was willing to delegate broad powers to the government. However, he believed that Congress should be the chief recipient of these powers, and he was willing to construe more narrowly the powers of the judiciary and the President, as he did, for example, in *United States v. Hudson and Goodwin.* In relation to Congress, Johnson made assertions of broad power that surpassed even those of Marshall. For a unanimous Court, in *Anderson v. Dunn,* Johnson upheld Congress's LEGISLATIVE CONTEMPT POWER, and in so doing defended the legislative discretion. Every grant of congressional power draws with it "others, not expressed, but vital to its exercise; not substantive and independent, indeed, but auxiliary and subordinate." Johnson thought IMPLIED POWERS were essential to a responsive government that served the needs of the people. Securities against the abuse of discretion rested on accountability and appeals to the people. Individual liberty stood in little danger "where all power is derived from the people, and at the feet of the people, to be resumed again only at their will."

Johnson's conception of FEDERALISM was in many ways quite modern. In broadly construing powers of Congress, he looked on these less as limitations on the states than as means of strengthening national unity and improving the lot of individuals. In a separate opinion in GIBBONS V. OGDEN, Johnson wrote that where the language of the Constitution leaves room for interpretation, the judges should consult its overriding purpose: "to unite this mass of wealth and power for the protection of the humblest individual: his rights civil and political, his interests and prosperity, are the sole end; the rest are nothing but means." Chief among the means was "the independence and harmony of the states." As Justice Johnson knew from experience, some collisions between state and federal government was inevitable; the only remedy where two governments claimed power over the same individuals was a "frank and candid co-operation for the general good."

Finally, on the rights of property, Johnson showed somewhat less reverence than did the rest of the Court. Toward the end of his career, Johnson lost some of his esteem for a powerful judiciary enforcing property rights against the states, and he began to look to the states for economic and social regulation. In OGDEN V. SAUNDERS Johnson spoke for the majority. He argued that the CONTRACT CLAUSE did not prohibit "insolvent debtor laws" as applied to contracts made subsequent to the laws' enactment. In *Ogden* Johnson objected to construing that contract clause literally. He argued that contracts should receive a "relative, and not a positive interpretation: for the rights of all should be held and enjoyed to the good of the whole." Johnson seemed to foresee the notion of STATE POLICE POWERS when he insisted that the states had the power to regulate the "social exercise" of rights.

In winning tolerance for dissenting opinions and in contributing creatively and prophetically to the body of constitutional doctrine, William Johnson won a niche as an outstanding member of the early Court.

DONALD G. MORGAN

Bibliography

MORGAN, DONALD G. 1954 *Justice William Johnson: The First Dissenter.* Columbia: University of South Carolina Press.

JOHNSON, WILLIAM SAMUEL (1727–1819)

Dr. William Samuel Johnson signed the Constitution as a Connecticut delegate to the CONSTITUTIONAL CONVENTION OF 1787. A lawyer and educator, he had already served his state as a legislator and judge. Johnson, a conciliator respected by all delegates, formally proposed the Connecticut Compromise (GREAT COMPROMISE). He also proposed the words defining the extent of the JUDICIAL POWER OF THE UNITED STATES, inserting the key phrase, "all cases arising under *the Constitution and* laws of the United States," and he chaired the Committee on Style. Johnson helped keep the Convention from dissolving in the heat of factional dispute. He was later a United States senator (1789–1791).

DENNIS J. MAHONEY

JOHNSON v. AVERY 393 U.S. 483 (1969)

In a 7–2 decision, the Supreme Court, through Justice ABE FORTAS, upheld the right of state prisoners to receive the assistance of fellow convicts in the preparation of writs. The Court overturned a Tennessee prison rule aimed at abolishing the "jailhouse lawyer" practice by which a few convicts, relatively skilled at writ-writing, achieved a position of power among the inmates. Because the rule might have the effect of denying the poor and illiterate the right of HABEAS CORPUS, Tennessee was ordered either to abolish the rule or to provide alternative legal assistance for prisoners wishing to seek postconviction review of their cases.

DENNIS J. MAHONEY

JOHNSON v. LOUISIANA
406 U.S. 356 (1972)
APODACA v. OREGON
406 U.S. 404 (1972)

In DUNCAN V. LOUISIANA (1968) the Supreme Court declared that every criminal charge must be "confirmed by the unanimous suffrage of twelve jurors," and in WILLIAMS V. FLORIDA (1970) the Court found little reason to believe that a jury of six people functions differently from a jury of twelve "particularly if the requirement of unanimity is retained." Justice BYRON R. WHITE, the Court's spokesman in these cases, also wrote its opinion in *Johnson* and for a plurality of four Justices in *Apodaca;* he found nothing constitutionally defective in verdicts by a "heavy" majority vote and no constitutional mandate for verdicts by unanimous vote. The Court upheld the laws of two states that permitted verdicts of 9–3 and 10–2 respectively. These 1972 cases, according to the dissenters, diminished the BURDEN OF PROOF beyond REASONABLE DOUBT and made convictions possible by a preponderance of jurors.

For centuries the standard of proof of guilt beyond reasonable doubt was inextricably entwined with the principle of a unanimous verdict, creating a hedge against jury bias. The requirement of JURY UNANIMITY had meant that a single juror might veto all others, thwarting an overwhelming majority. Accordingly, Johnson contended that DUE PROCESS OF LAW, by embodying the standard of proof beyond a reasonable doubt, required unanimous verdicts and that three jurors who possessed such doubt in his case showed that his guilt was not proved beyond such doubt. White answered that no basis existed for believing that the majority jurors would refuse to listen to the doubts of the minority. Yet Johnson's jurors, who were "out" for less than twenty minutes, might have taken a poll before deliberating, and if nine had voted for a guilty verdict on the first ballot, they might have returned the verdict without the need of considering the minority's doubts. The dissenters saw the jury as an entity incapable of rendering a verdict by the undisputed standard of proof beyond a reasonable doubt if any juror remained unconvinced. The Court majority saw the jury as twelve individuals, nine of whom could decide the verdict if they were satisfied beyond a reasonable doubt, regardless of minority views.

If the prosecution's burden of proving guilt beyond a reasonable doubt does not change when a 9–3 verdict is permissible, verdicts returned by a nine-juror majority ought to be the same as those returned by unanimous juries of twelve. In fact, the 9–3 system yields a substantially higher conviction ratio and substantially fewer hung juries by which defendants avoid conviction, thus substantially lowering the prosecution's burden of proof.

Johnson also contended that Louisiana's complicated three-tier system of juries—unanimous verdicts of twelve in some cases, unanimous verdicts of five in others, and 9–3 verdicts in still others—denied him the EQUAL PROTECTION OF THE LAWS. In fact, the standard of proof varied with the crime, but White rejected the equal protection argument, claiming instead that Louisiana's three-tier scheme was "not invidious" because it was rational: it saved time and money. The Court hardly considered whether it diluted justice.

In *Apodaca,* the 10–2 verdict came under attack from an argument that the FOURTEENTH AMENDMENT extended to the states the same standard as prevailed in federal courts, where unanimity prevails. Four Justices, led by White, would have ruled that the SIXTH AMENDMENT does not require unanimous verdicts even in federal trials; four, led by Justice WILLIAM O. DOUGLAS, believed that because the amendment embodies the requirement of unanimous jury verdicts, no state can permit a majority verdict. LEWIS F. POWELL's opinion was decisive. He concurred with the Douglas wing to save the unanimous verdict in federal criminal trials and with the White wing to allow nonunanimous verdicts for states wanting them. In *Apodaca,* White contradictorily conceded that the reasonable doubt standard "has been rejected in *Johnson v. Louisiana.*" Douglas proved, contrary to White, that the use of the nonunanimous jury altered the way the jury functioned, stacking it against the defendant. He interpreted the majority opinions as reflecting "a 'law and order' judicial mood."

LEONARD W. LEVY

(SEE ALSO: *Jury Size.*)

Bibliography

LEVY, LEONARD W. 1974 *Against the Law: The Nixon Court and Criminal Justice.* Pages 276–298. New York: Harper & Row.

JOHNSON v. ZERBST
304 U.S. 458 (1938)

Defendants who neither sought nor were offered counsel were convicted in a federal court. The Supreme Court held that the SIXTH AMENDMENT requires counsel in all federal criminal proceedings unless the right is waived. This HOLDING is mainly of historical interest, but the case retains remarkable vitality and is often cited because of its definition of WAIVER. Starting with the proposition that there is "every reasonable presumption against 'waiver,' " the Court declared: "A waiver is ordinarily an intelligent relinquishment or abandonment of a known right or privilege."

Johnson's strong suspicion of waiver of the RIGHT TO COUNSEL is reiterated in many decisions. In *Von Moltke v. Gillies* (1948) the Supreme Court established a duty of the trial judge "to investigate [waiver of counsel] as long and as thoroughly as the circumstances of the case before him demand." The Court has also said that waiver must affirmatively appear on the record and will not be presumed from a silent record.

Although the Court's definition of waiver applies to all FUNDAMENTAL RIGHTS, and although *Johnson* is cited in FOURTH AMENDMENT and Fifth Amendment cases, the definition has been rigorously applied only in the right to counsel context that spawned it.

BARBARA ALLEN BABCOCK

JOINT ANTI-FASCIST REFUGEE COMMITTEE v. MCGRATH
341 U.S. 123 (1951)

Five members of the VINSON COURT dealt a setback to the HARRY S. TRUMAN administration's anticommunist crusade by condemning the procedures through which the ATTORNEY GENERAL of the United States listed certain organizations as "totalitarian, fascist, communist or subversive" under the President's Executive Order of 1947 creating a LOYALTY-SECURITY PROGRAM for all federal employees. Three organizations designated as "communist" by the attorney general complained that they had been stigmatized without an opportunity for a hearing at which they could rebut the government's presumption. Justice HAROLD H. BURTON concluded that the executive order did not permit the attorney general to make arbitrary, EX PARTE findings without a hearing. In separate concurring opinions, four Justices concluded that the President's order may have authorized such *ex parte* proceedings, but did so in violation of the DUE PROCESS clause. Justice HUGO L. BLACK also condemned the list as a violation of the FIRST AMENDMENT and as a BILL OF ATTAINDER. Justice STANLEY F. REED, for three dissenters, said the attorney general's actions were appropriate "to guard the Nation from espionage, subversion and SEDITION."

MICHAEL E. PARRISH

JOINT COMMITTEE ON RECONSTRUCTION

In December 1865, Congress by CONCURRENT RESOLUTION created the Joint Committee of Fifteen on Reconstruction to provide a deliberative body for consideration of Reconstruction policy, because Republicans refused to accept President ANDREW JOHNSON's "Restoration" as an accomplished fact. All legislation directly affecting Reconstruction was referred to it.

The majority report of the Joint Committee (1866), prepared by Senator WILLIAM P. FESSENDEN (Republican, Maine), rejected punitive theories of Reconstruction as "profitless abstractions" and repudiated the lenient policies of President Johnson and congressional Democrats. The Committee's Republican majority insisted that only Congress had final power to regularize the constitutional status of the seceded states. The Democratic minority report countered that the states were entitled to immediate readmission and self-government. The Joint Committee fashioned the FOURTEENTH AMENDMENT as a compendium of Republican Reconstruction objectives as of the summer of 1866: freedmen's CITIZENSHIP and voting, equality before the law and assurance of DUE PROCESS for freedmen, Confederate disfranchisement, repudiation of the Confederate war debt, denial of compensation for slaves, and confirmation of the Union debt. When the inadequacy of the Fourteenth Amendment as a comprehensive Reconstruction measure became apparent, Republican committee members drafted the first MILITARY RECONSTRUCTION ACT, which created legal machinery for beginning the process of congressional Reconstruction.

WILLIAM M. WIECEK

Bibliography

KENDRICK, BENJAMIN B. 1914 *The Journal of the Joint Committee of Fifteen on Reconstruction.* New York: Columbia University Press.

JOINT RESOLUTIONS

Joint resolutions, unlike CONCURRENT RESOLUTIONS, have the force of law and require the signature of the President to be enacted. They are therefore subject to the VETO POWER. A joint resolution may be used when a permanent statutory enactment is inappropriate. Joint resolutions may be used to issue a DECLARATION OF WAR, to end a STATE OF WAR, to annex territory, or to extend the effective life of previously enacted legislation.

As part of the AMENDING PROCESS, joint resolutions are used to propose constitutional amendments. Such resolutions require a two-thirds vote in each house, but not the President's signature.

DENNIS J. MAHONEY

JONES v. ALFRED H. MAYER CO. 392 U.S. 409 (1968)

This opinion contains important interpretations of a CIVIL RIGHTS statute and of Congress's power to prohibit private discrimination. Jones alleged that the defendants had refused to sell him a home because he was black. He brought an action under section 1982 of Title 42, United States Code, a remnant of the CIVIL RIGHTS ACT OF 1866, which states in part that all citizens shall have the same right as white citizens to purchase property.

Because Jones relied on a federal law to challenge private discrimination, and because the Supreme Court found that section 1982 encompassed Jones's claim, the case raised the question whether the Constitution grants Congress authority to outlaw private discrimination. The degree to which Congress may do so under the FOURTEENTH AMENDMENT has been a recurring unsettled question. (See UNITED STATES V. GUEST, 1966.) In *Jones,* Justice POTTER STEWART's opinion for the Court avoided that complex matter by sustaining section 1982's applicability to private behavior under Congress's THIRTEENTH AMENDMENT power to eliminate slavery. But even this HOLDING generated tension with the Court's nineteenth-century pronouncements on Congress's power to reach private discrimination.

In the CIVIL RIGHTS CASES (1883) the Court seemed to concede that the Thirteenth Amendment vests in Congress power to abolish all badges or incidents of slavery. (See BADGES OF SERVITUDE.) In that case, however, the Court viewed those badges or incidents narrowly and limited Congress's role in defining them. In striking down the CIVIL RIGHTS ACT OF 1875, a provision barring discrimination in PUBLIC ACCOMMODATIONS, the Court commented, "It would be running the slavery argument into the ground" to make it apply to every act of private discrimination in the field of public accommodations. In *Jones,* however, the Court acknowledged Congress's broad discretion not merely to eliminate the badges or incidents of slavery but also to define the practices constituting them.

Jones thus granted Congress virtually unlimited power to outlaw private RACIAL DISCRIMINATION. In later cases, *Jones* provided support for Congress's power to outlaw private racial discrimination in contractual relationships. Section 1981, another remnant of the Civil Rights Act of 1866, confers on all persons the same right "enjoyed by white citizens" to make and enforce contracts, to be parties or witnesses in lawsuits, and to be protected by law in person and property. RUNYON V. MCCRARY (1976) held section 1981 to prohibit the exclusion of blacks from private schools, and *Johnson v. Railway Express Agency, Inc.* (1974) held it to prohibit discrimination in employment.

As Justice JOHN MARSHALL HARLAN's dissent noted, *Jones*'s interpretation of section 1982 established it, more than a hundred years after its enactment, as a fair housing law discovered within months of passage of the CIVIL RIGHTS ACT OF 1968, which itself contained a detailed fair housing provision. (See OPEN HOUSING LAWS.) In finding that section 1982 reaches private discrimination not authorized by state law, *Jones* offers a questionable interpretation of the 1866 act's structure and manipulates legislative history. Whether a candid opinion could support *Jones*'s interpretation of section 1982 remains a subject of debate.

THEODORE EISENBERG

Bibliography

CASPER, GERHARD 1968 *Jones v. Mayer:* Clio, Bemused and Confused Muse. *Supreme Court Review* 1968:89–132.

FAIRMAN, CHARLES 1971 *Reconstruction and Reunion 1864–88: Part One.* Volume 6 of *The Oliver Wendell Holmes Devise History of the Supreme Court of the United States.* New York: Macmillan.

JONES v. SECURITIES & EXCHANGE COMMISSION
298 U.S. 1 (1936)

Although unimportant as a matter of constitutional law, *Jones* has significance in constitutional history. The Court's decision and the tone of Justice GEORGE SUTHERLAND's opinion for the majority helped convince President FRANKLIN D. ROOSEVELT that the Court was prejudiced against the New Deal. A Wall Street manipulator had withdrawn a securities offering on learning that the Securities and Exchange Commission was investigating his fraud. The commission had continued its investigation, raising the question whether it had exceeded its statuory authority. Sutherland called its action arbitrary, inquisitional, odious, and comparable to Star Chamber procedure. Justices BENJAMIN N. CARDOZO, LOUIS D. BRANDEIS, and HARLAN FISKE STONE answered Sutherland's charges and defended the commission. The opinion of the Court hardened Roosevelt's attitude toward it, culminating in his court-packing plan of 1937.

LEONARD W. LEVY

JONES v. VAN ZANDT

See: Fugitive Slavery

JONES v. WOLF

See: Religious Liberty

JOSEPH BURSTYN, INC. v. WILSON

See: Burstyn, Inc. v. Wilson

JUDGE PETERS, UNITED STATES v.
5 Cranch 115 (1809)

This case bears historical significance as an episode in defiance, expressed in NULLIFICATION and bordering on rebellion, by a state against the United States courts. The state was Pennsylvania, which suggests that doctrines of state sovereignty have never been merely sectional. The case was the occasion of Chief Justice JOHN MARSHALL's first nationalist opinion, but more important is the fact that Pennsylvania successfully thwarted the federal courts, exposing their helplessness in enforcing their writs, until a President of the Virginia dynasty unhesitatingly backed the judiciary, still Federalist-dominated, against the political machine of his own party in Pennsylvania.

The case originated during the Revolution as the result of a dispute between the state and Gideon Olmstead over the proceeds from the sale of a captured enemy ship. A state court denied Olmstead's claim, but a prize court established by Congress ruled in his favor; the state court refused to obey the federal order and the state treasurer retained the money. Litigation went on for years. In 1803 Judge RICHARD PETERS of the United States District court in Philadelphia decided in favor of Olmstead in his suit against the treasurer's estate, which held the money for the state. The state legislature, invoking the ELEVENTH AMENDMENT, resolved that Peters had "illegally usurped" JURISDICTION and instructed the governor to protect the rights of the state. In 1808 Olmstead, then in his eighties, obtained from the Supreme Court an order against Peters to show cause why a WRIT OF MANDAMUS should not be issued compelling him to enforce his decision of 1803. The judge stated that the state legislature had commanded the governor "to call out an armed force" to prevent the execution of a federal process. Peters asked for a resolution of the issue by the supreme tribunal of the nation, saying that he had withheld process to avoid a conflict between the state and federal governments.

In 1809, at a time when New England was disobeying the EMBARGO ACTS, Marshall, speaking for the Court, declared:

> If the legislatures of the several states may, at will, annul the judgments of the courts of the United States, and destroy the rights acquired under those judgements, the constitution itself becomes a solemn mockery, and the nation is deprived of the means of enforcing its laws by the instrumentality of its own tribunals. So fatal a result must be deprecated by all; and the people of Pennsylvania, not less than the citizens of every other state, must feel a deep interest in resisting principles so destructive of the Union, and in averting consequences so fatal to themselves.

(That passage was quoted by the Court in the 1950s and 1960s in cases involving southern defiance of federal orders commanding DESEGREGATION.) The Court awarded a "peremptory mandamus" against Peters, but neither he nor Marshall could force the state to comply.

The state governor called out the militia, and the state legislature, supporting him, announced that "*as guardians of the State rights,* we cannot permit an infringement of those rights by an unconstitutional exercise of power in the United States Courts." Those actions were not the only reply to Marshall's declaration that the Eleventh Amendment did not apply inasmuch as the suit had not been commenced against the state. Pennsylvania also denied that the Supreme Court had appellate powers over the state courts or that it was the final arbiter in a dispute between the United States and any state. When a federal marshal attempted to execute Peters's judgment, 1400 men of the state militia opposed him; he summoned a federal *posse comitatus* of 2,000 men, but to avoid bloodshed fixed the day for service in three weeks. At this juncture, while the papers in the country were still carrying news about Federalist New England's defiance of the EMBARGO ACTS, the Democratic governor of Pennsylvania turned to the Democratic national administration for support. "The issue is in fact come to this," said *The Aurora,* the administration newspaper in Philadelphia, "whether the Constitution of the United States is to remain in force or to become a dead letter. . . . The decree of the Court must be obeyed." President JAMES MADISON, mindful of the repercussions of the case, chastised the state governor. "The Executive," he replied, "is not only unauthorized to prevent the execution of a decree sanctioned by the Supreme Court of the United States, but is expressly enjoined, by statute, to carry into effect any such decree, where opposition may be made to it."

The incipient rebellion immediately collapsed. The state withdrew its militia and appropriated the money to pay Olmstead. In the aftermath of the affair, the United States arrested and tried the commanding general of the state militia and eight of his officers for having obstructed the federal marshal. A federal jury convicted them in a trial before Justice BUSHROD WASHINGTON, who sentenced the defendants to fines and imprisonment, but the President pardoned them. Eleven state legislatures adopted resolutions condemning Pennsylvania's resistance to the federal courts. Every southern state rejected Pennsylvania's doctrines of STATES' RIGHTS. That northern state had also proposed the establishment of "an impartial tribunal" to settle disputes between "the general and state governments." The legislature of Virginia replied that "a tribunal is already provided by the Constitution of the United States, *to wit:* the Supreme Court, more eminently qualified . . . to decide the disputes aforesaid . . . than any other tribunal which could be erected." In a few years, however, Virginia would be playing Pennsylvania's tune. (See MARTIN v. Hunter's Lessee, 1816.) The supremacy of the Supreme Court had by no means been established yet.

LEONARD W. LEVY

Bibliography

HIGGINBOTHAM, SANFORD W. 1952 *The Keystone in the Democratic Arch: Pennsylvania Politics 1800–1816.* Pages 177–204. Harrisburg: Pennsylvania Historical and Museum Commission.

TREACY, KENNETH W. 1957 The Olmstead Case, 1778–1809. *Western Political Quarterly* 10:675–691.

WARREN, CHARLES 1923 *The Supreme Court in American History,* 3 vols. Vol. I:375–387. Boston: Little, Brown.

JUDGMENT

The judgment of a court is its conclusion or sentence of the law applied to the facts of a case. It is the court's final determination of the rights of the parties to the case. A judgment, once entered (unless successfully appealed), is conclusive as to the rights of the parties and ordinarily may not be challenged either in a future suit by the same parties or in a collateral proceeding. The judgment is essentially equivalent to the DECISION of the court. Judgments in EQUITY and admiralty cases are called "decrees"; judgments in criminal and ecclesiastical cases are called "sentences."

DENNIS J. MAHONEY

(SEE ALSO: *Res Judicata; Habeas Corpus; Final Judgment Rule.*)

JUDICIAL ACTIVISM AND JUDICIAL RESTRAINT

"Judicial activism" and "judicial restraint" are terms used to describe the assertiveness of judicial power. In no sense unique to the Supreme Court or to cases involving some construction of the Constitution, they are editorial summations of how different courts and different judges conduct themselves.

The user of these terms ("judicial activism" and "judicial restraint") presumes to locate the relative assertiveness of particular courts or individual judges between two theoretical extremes. The extreme model of judicial activism is of a court so intrusive and ubiquitous that it virtually dominates the institutions of government. The antithesis of such a model is a court that decides virtually nothing at all: it strains to find reasons why it lacks JURISDICTION; it avows deference to the superiority of other departments or agencies in construing the law; it finds endless reasons why the constitutionality of laws cannot be examined. It is a model of government virtually without useful recourse to courts as enforcers of constitutional limits.

The uses of "judicial activism" and "judicial restraint," however, are not entirely uniform. Often the terms are employed noncommittally, that is, merely as descriptive shorthand to identify some court or judge as more activist or more restrained than some other, or more than the same court formerly appeared to be. In this sense, the usage is neither commendatory nor condemnatory. Especially with reference to the Supreme Court, however, the terms are also used polemically. The user has a personal or professional view of the "right" role of the Court and, accordingly, commends or condemns the Court for conforming to or straying from that right role. Indeed, an enduring issue of American constitutional law has centered on this lively controversy of right role; procedurally and substantively, how activist or how restrained ought the Supreme Court to be in its use of the power of constitutional JUDICIAL REVIEW?

Ought that Court to confront the constitutionality of the laws as speedily as opportunity affords, the better to furnish authoritative guidance and settle political controversy in keeping with its unique competence and function as the chief constitutional court of the nation? Or ought it, rather, to eschew any unnecessary voluntarism, recognizing that all participants in government are as bound as the Court to observe the Constitution and that the very insularity of the Supreme Court from representative government is a powerful reason to avoid the appearance of constitutional arrogance or constitutional monopoly? In brief, what degree of strict necessity should the Supreme Court require as a condition of examining the substantive constitutionality of government acts or government practices?

Substantively, the issues of "proper" activism or proper restraint are similar. When the constitutionality of governmental action is considered, what predisposition, if any, ought the Supreme Court to bring to bear? Should it take a fairly strict view of the Constitution and, accordingly, hold against the constitutionality of each duly contested governmental act unless the consistency of that act with the Constitution can be demonstrated virtually to anyone's satisfaction? Or, to the contrary, recognizing its own fallibility and the shared obligation of Congress (and the President and every member of every state legislature) fully to respect the Constitution as much as judges are bound to respect it, should the Court hold against the constitutionality of what other departments of government have enacted only when virtually no reasonable person could conclude that the act in question is consistent with the Constitution?

Disputes respecting the Supreme Court's procedural judicial activism (or restraint) and substantive judicial activism (or restraint) are thus of recurring political interest. Most emphatically is this the case with regard to judicial review of the constitutionality of legislation, as distinct from nonconstitutional judicial review. For here, unlike activism on nonconstitutional issues (such as the interpretation of statutes), the consequences of an adverse holding on the merits are typically difficult to change. An act of Congress, held inapplicable to a given transaction, need only be approved in modified form to "reverse" the Supreme Court's impression. On the other hand, a holding that the statute did cover the transaction but in presuming to do so was unconstitutional is a much more nearly permanent boundary. It may be overcome only by extraordinary processes of amending the Constitution itself (a recourse successfully taken during two centuries only four times), or by a reconsideration and overruling by the Supreme Court itself (an eventuality that has occurred about 130 times). Thus, the special force of adjudication of constitutionality, being of the greatest consequence and least reversibility, has made the proper constitutional activism (or proper restraint) of the Supreme Court itself a central question.

An appraisal of the Supreme Court in these terms involves two problems: the activism (or restraint) with which the Court rations the judicial process in developing or in avoiding occasions to decide constitutional claims; and the activism (or restraint) of its STANDARDS OF REVIEW when it does decide such claims.

The Supreme Court's own description of its proper role in interpreting the Constitution is one of strict necessity and of last resort. In brief, the Court has repeatedly held that the Constitution itself precludes the Court from considering constitutional issues unless they are incidental to an actual CASE OR CONTROVERSY that meets very stringent demands imposed by Article III. In addition, the Court holds that prudence requires the complete avoidance of constitutional issues in any case in which the rights of the litigants can be resolved without reference to such an issue.

In 1982, in VALLEY FORGE CHRISTIAN SCHOOLS V. AMERICANS UNITED, Justice WILLIAM H. REHNQUIST recapitulated the Court's conventional wisdom. Forswearing any judicial power generally to furnish advice on the Constitution, and denying that the Supreme Court may extend its jurisdiction more freely merely because constitutional issues are at stake, he declared: "The constitutional power of federal courts cannot be defined, and indeed has no substance, without reference to the necessity to 'adjudge the legal rights of litigants in actual controversies.'" Even when the stringent prerequisites of jurisdiction have been fully satisfied, moreover, "[t]he power to declare the rights of individuals and to measure the authority of governments, this Court said 90 years ago, 'is legitimate only in the last resort, and as a necessity in the determination of real, earnest, and vital controversy.'" For emphasis, he added, "The federal courts were simply not constituted as ombudsmen of the general welfare. [Such a philosophy] has no place in our constitutional scheme."

In so declaring, Justice Rehnquist was relying substantially upon a similar position adopted by Chief Justice JOHN MARSHALL in MARBURY V. MADISON (1803). Explaining that the Court's determination of constitutional questions was but an incident of its duty to pass upon legal questions raised in the due course of litigation, in no respect different from its duty when some statutory issue or COMMON LAW question might likewise be presented in a case, Marshall had insisted: "The province of the Court is, solely, to decide on the rights of individuals," and not to presume any larger role.

Accordingly, though a constitutional issue may be present, if the dispute in which it arises does not otherwise meet conventionally strict standards of STANDING, RIPENESS, genuine adverseness of parties, or sufficient factual concreteness to meet the demands of a justiciable case or controversy as required by Article III, the felt urgency or gravity of the constitutional question can make no difference. In steering a wide course around the impropriety of deciding constitutional questions except as incidental to a genuine adversary proceeding, moreover, the Court has also declared that it will not entertain COLLUSIVE SUITS. As Marshall declared in *Marbury,* "it never was the thought that, by means of a friendly suit, a party beaten in the legislature could transfer to the courts an inquiry as to the constitutionality of a legislative act." Similarly, if during the course of genuine litigation the grievance has become moot in light of subsequent events, it must then be dismissed insofar as there remains no necessity to address the original issue.

When, moreover, all requisites of conventional, genuine litigation remain such that adjudication of the parties' rights is an unavoidable judicial duty, the Court has still insisted that it should determine whether the case can be disposed of without addressing any issue requiring it to render an interpretation of the Constitution itself. Accordingly (within the conventional wisdom), even with respect to disputes properly before it, well within its jurisdiction and prominently featuring a major, well-framed, well-contested constitutional question, the Supreme Court may still refuse to address that question. In his famous concurring opinion in ASHWANDER V. TENNESSEE VALLEY AUTHORITY (1936), Justice LOUIS D. BRANDEIS insisted that constitutional questions were to be decided only as a last resort: "When the validity of an act of Congress is drawn in question, and even if a serious doubt of constitutionality is raised, it is a cardinal principle that this Court will first ascertain whether a construction of the statute is fairly possible by which the question may be avoided." Indeed, Brandeis continued, the Court will not "pass upon a constitutional question although properly presented by the record, if there is also present some other ground upon which the case may be disposed of." Moreover, though there may be no other ground, if the constitutional question arises at the instance of a public official, "the challenge by a public official interested only in the performance of his official duty will not be entertained." Even when the issue is raised by a private litigant, his challenge to the constitutionality of a statute will not be heard "at the instance of one who has availed himself of its benefits."

Self-portrayals of the Court as a wholly reluctant constitutional tribunal that is not an oracle of constitutional proclamation but a court of law that will face constitutional questions only when a failure to do so would involve it as a tribunal in an unconstitutional oppression of a litigant go even further. A litigant may have much at stake, and nothing except his reliance upon some clause in the Constitution may remain to save him from jeopardy. Still, if the clause in the Constitution is deemed not to yield objective criteria adequate to guide its application by the Court, the Court may decline to attempt to fix any meaning for the clause on the basis that it is nonjusticiable. (See POLITICAL QUESTIONS.) Similarly, if the relief requested should require the Court to consider an order against the Congress itself, an order the Court cannot be confident would be obeyed and which it is without resources otherwise to enforce, it may refuse to consider the case. Identically, if an adjudication of the constitutional question, though otherwise imperative to the litigant's case, might involve conflict with the President respecting decisions already made, communicated to, and relied upon by other governments, the case may also be regarded as nonjusticiable.

In rough outline, then, these are the principal elements of the orthodoxy of extreme judicial restraint.

Consistent with them, even when the Court does adjudicate a constitutional question, its decision is supposed to be "no broader than is required by the precise facts." Anything remotely resembling an advisory opinion or a gratuitous judicial utterance respecting the meaning of the Constitution is to be altogether avoided.

Although this combination of Article III requirements and policies has characterized a large part of the Court's history (most substantially when the constitutional questions involved acts of Congress or executive action), the Court's practice has not, in fact, been at all uniform. Collusive suits have sometimes been entertained, and the constitutional issues at once examined. Public officials sometimes have been deemed to have sufficient standing to press constitutional questions, though they have had no more than an official interest in the matter. Holdings on the Constitution occasionally have been rendered in far broader terms than essential to decide the case, often for the advisory guidance of other judges or for the benefit of state or local officials. When the constitutional issue seemed clear enough and strongly meritorious, parties placed in positions of advantage solely by force of the very condition of which they later complained on constitutional grounds have not always been estopped from securing a decision. On occasion when third parties would be unlikely or unable to raise a constitutional claim on their own behalf, moreover, other litigants deemed suitable to represent their claim have been allowed to proceed on the merits of the constitutional issues. And some utterly moot cases have been decided on the merits of their constitutional questions on the paradoxical explanation that unless the moot cases were treated as still lively, then conceivably the merits of the constitutional issues would forever elude judicial review. Indeed, the nation's most famous case, *Marbury v. Madison*, was in many respects an example of extreme procedural activism despite its disclaimer of strict necessity.

At issue in Marbury's case was the question of the Supreme Court's power to hear the case in the first instance, within its ORIGINAL JURISDICTION, rather than merely on appeal. The statute William Marbury relied upon to demonstrate his right to commence his action in the Supreme Court was altogether unclear as to whether it authorized his suit to begin in the Supreme Court. Avoidance of the necessity of examining the constitutionality of the statute was readily available merely by construing the statute as not providing for original jurisdiction: an interpretation thus making clear that Marbury had sued in the wrong court, resulting in his case's being dismissed for lack of (statutory) jurisdiction and obviating any need to say anything at all about the constitutionality of an act of Congress.

Rather than pursue that course, however, Chief Justice Marshall "actively" interpreted the act of Congress, that is, he interpreted it to draw into issue its very constitutionality and then promptly resolved that issue by holding the act unconstitutional. Beyond that, rather than be content to dismiss the case for lack of either statutory or constitutional jurisdiction, the Chief Justice also (and quite gratuitously) addressed every other question raised by the complaint, including Marbury's right to the public office he sought, the appropriateness of the remedy he asked for, the illegality of the secretary of state's refusal to give it to him, and the lack of immunity from such suits by the secretary of state. Each of these other issues was of substantial controversy. Several of them raised substantial constitutional questions. Marshall resolved all in an opinion most of which was purely advisory, that is, of no necessity in light of the ultimate holding, which was that the Court was (constitutionally) without power (jurisdiction) to address the merits of the case at all. Marshall addressed all these questions on the basis of a factual record supplied principally on affidavit of his own brother. Still, Marshall, far from recusing himself on that account or on account of his own participation as the secretary of state who failed to deliver Marbury's commission, fully participated in the case, voted, and wrote the opinion for the Court. In these many respects, the case of *Marbury v. Madison* was an extraordinary example of extreme procedural activism. Its resemblance to what the Court has otherwise said (as in the Brandeis *Ashwander* guidelines or the *Valley Forge* case) is purely ironic. Indeed, the unstable actual practices of the Court which has so often described its institutional role in constitutional adjudication as one of the utmost procedural restraint, while not uniformly adhering to that description, have contributed to the Court's great controversiality in American government.

As we have seen, procedural activism (and restraint) has consisted principally of two parts. The first part is the rigor or lack of rigor with which the Court has interpreted the limitation in Article III of the Constitution, according to which the use of the judicial power can operate solely on "cases and controversies." The second part is the extent to which the Court has also adopted a number of purely self-denying ordinances according to which it will decline to adjudicate the merits of a constitutional claim in any case in which a decision can be reached on some other ground.

In contrast, substantive activism (and restraint) has consisted principally of three parts, each reflecting the extent to which the Court has interpreted the Constitution either aggressively to invalidate actions taken by other departments of government, or diffidently to acquiesce in these actions. The first part pertains to the Court's substantive interpretations of the ENUMERATED and IMPLIED POWERS of the other departments of the national government, that is, the powers vested by Article I in Congress and the powers vested by Article II in the President. The second part pertains to the Court's interpretation of the Constitution as implicitly withdrawing from state governments a variety of powers not explicitly forbidden to them by the Constitution. And the third part pertains to the Court's interpretations of those clauses in the Constitution that impose positive restrictions on the national and the state governments, principally the provisions in Article I, sections 9 and 10, in the BILL OF RIGHTS, and in the FOURTEENTH AMENDMENT. Although there may be no a priori reason to separate the substantive activism and restraint of the Supreme Court into these three particular categories, it is nonetheless practically useful to do so: overall, the Court has responded to them quite distinctly. Indeed, in practice, despite very great differences among particular Justices, the general tendency has been to develop a constitutional jurisprudence of selective activism and selective restraint.

In respect to constitutional challenges to acts of Congress for consistency with Article I's enumeration of affirmative powers, the Court's standard of review has generally been one of extraordinary restraint. With the exception of the first three and a half decades of the twentieth century, the Court has largely deferred to Congress's own suppositions respecting the scope of its powers. During the first seventy-five years of the Constitution, for instance, only two acts of Congress were held not to square with the Constitution. During the most recent forty years (a period of intense and extremely far-reaching national legislation), again but two acts have been held to fail for want of enumerated or implied constitutional authorization. Indeed, even when the comparison is enlarged to include cases challenging acts of Congress not merely for want of enacting authority but rather because they were alleged to transgress specific prohibitions (for example, the FIRST AMENDMENT restriction that Congress shall make no law abridging the FREEDOM OF SPEECH), still the record overall is one of general diffidence and restraint. Over the entirety of the Court's history, scarcely more than 120 acts of Congress have been held invalid.

An influential rationale for such restraint toward acts of Congress was set forth in 1893, in an essay by JAMES BRADLEY THAYER that Justice FELIX FRANKFURTER subsequently identified as uniquely influential on his own thinking as a judicial conservative. Thayer admonished the judiciary to bear in mind that the executive and legislative departments of the national government were constitutionally equal to the judiciary, that they were equivalently bound by oath of office to respect the Constitution, and that each was a good deal more representative of the people than the life-tenured members of the Supreme Court. Accordingly, Thayer urged, the Court should test the acts of coordinate national departments solely according to a rule of "clear error." In brief, such acts were to be examined not to determine whether their constitutionality necessarily conformed to the particular interpretation which the judges themselves might independently have concluded was the most clearly correct interpretation of the Constitution. Rather, such acts should be sustained unless they depended on an interpretation of constitutional power that was itself manifestly unreasonable, that is, an interpretation *clearly* erroneous.

Thayer's rule provided a strong political rationale for extreme judicial deference in respect to enumerated and implied national powers. Of necessity, however, it also tended practically to the enlistment of the judiciary less as an independent guardian of the Constitution (at least in respect to the scope of enumerated and implied powers) than as an institution tending to validate claims of national authority against state perspectives on the proper boundaries of FEDERALISM. It is a thesis that has periodically attracted criticism on that account, but it does not stand as the sole explanation for the general restraint reflected in the Supreme Court's permissive construction of national legislative and executive powers. Rather, without necessarily assuming that Congress and the President possess a suitably reliable detachment to be the presumptive best judges of their respective powers, decades before the appearance of Thayer's essay the Supreme Court had already expressed a separate rationale: a judicial rule of BROAD CONSTRUCTION respecting enumerated national powers.

The most durable expression of that rule is reported in a famous OBITER DICTUM by Chief Justice John Marshall. In MCCULLOCH V. MARYLAND (1819), Marshall emphasized to his own colleagues, the federal judges: "We must never forget, that it is a *constitution* we are expounding." In full context, Marshall plainly meant that it was a Constitution for the future as well as for the present, for a nation then quite small and new but expected to become much more considerable. To meet these uncertain responsibilities, Congress would require flexibility and legislative latitude. Thus, powers granted to it by the Constitution should be read generously.

The point was expanded upon more than a century later by Justice OLIVER WENDELL HOLMES, in MISSOURI V. HOLLAND (1920), defending the judiciary's predisposition to interpret the TREATY POWER very deferentially: "When we are dealing with words that also are a constituent act, like the Constitution of the United States, we must realize that they have called into life a being the development of which could not have been foreseen completely by the most gifted of its begetters. . . . [I]t has taken a century and has cost their successors much sweat and blood to prove that they created a nation." This rule of generous construction, like Thayer's rule of "clear error," tends to support a judicial policy of substantive interpretative restraint. And while not free of criticism on its own account (as federalism critics will tend to fault it as unfaithful to their view of the extent to which substantive legislative authority was meant to be reserved to the states), it is not contingent upon doubtful assumptions respecting the capacity of the President or of the Congress fairly to assess the scope of powers they are given by the Constitution. Arguably, it is as well that this policy of judicial restraint not be made to rest on such assumptions. Although reference to the early constitutional history of the United States tends to support Thayer's thesis (early members of Congress included many persons who had participated in the shaping of the Constitution and who frequently debated proposed legislation in terms of its consistency with that Constitution), two centuries of political change have weakened its suppositions considerably. Persons serving in Congress are far removed from the original debates over enumerated powers; the business of Congress is vastly greater than it once was; the electorate is itself vastly enlarged beyond the limited numbers of persons originally eligible to vote; and such attention as may be given within Congress to issues of constitutionality is understandably likely to be principally political in its preoccupations rather than cautious and detached. Thus, the Marshall rule of generous construction in respect to national powers, rather than the Thayer proposal (of yielding to not-unreasonable interpretations by Congress), tends more strongly to anchor the general policy of judicial restraint in this area. (When the issue had been one of conflict between Congress and the President, on the other hand, the Court has tended to defer to the position of Congress as first among equals.)

In contrast, there is less evidence of a consistent policy of substantive judicial restraint in the Supreme Court's examination of state laws and state acts. Here, to the contrary, the role of the Court has emphatically been significantly more activist, procedurally as well as substantively. The Court will more readily regard the review of governmental action as within the JUDICIAL POWER OF THE UNITED STATES in the litigation of state laws. A principal example is the ease with which state TAXPAYER SUITS impugning state laws on federal constitutional grounds will be deemed reviewable in the Supreme Court, when in most instances an equivalently situated federal taxpayer is deemed to have inadequate standing in respect to an act of Congress. In addition, the Court has interpreted the Constitution to create a judicial duty to determine the constitutionality of certain kinds of state laws, though the clauses relied upon do not themselves expressly confer such a judicial duty (or power) and speak, rather, solely of some preemptive power in Congress to determine the same matter. For instance, the COMMERCE CLAUSE provides merely that Congress shall have power to regulate commerce among the several states. But in the absence of congressional regulation, the Court has actively construed the clause as directing the federal courts themselves to determine, by their own criteria, whether state statutes so unreasonably or discriminatorily burden INTERSTATE COMMERCE that they should be deemed invalid by the courts as an unconstitutional trespass upon a field of regulation reserved to Congress.

Here also the rationales have differed, and indeed not every Supreme Court Justice has embraced either rationale. (Justice HUGO L. BLACK, for instance, preferring a constitutional jurisprudence of "literal" interpretation, generally declined to find any basis in the commerce clause for judicial intervention against state statutes.) In part, the substantive activism of the Court has been explained by a "political marketplace" calculus that is the obverse of Thayer's rule for deference to Congress. According to this view, as the state legislatures are not equal departments to the Supreme Court (in the sense that Congress is an equal department), and as national interests are not necessarily as well represented in state assemblies as state interests are said to be represented in Congress (insofar as members of Congress are all chosen from state-based constituencies), there are fewer built-in political safeguards in state legislatures than in Congress. To the extent of these differences, it is said that there is correspondingly less reason for courts to assume that state legislatures will have acted with appropriate sensitivity to federal constitutional questions and, accordingly, that there is more need for closer judicial attention to their acts. The sheer nonuniformity of state legislation may be of such felt distress to overriding needs for greater uniformity in a nation with an increasingly integrated economy that a larger measure of judicial activism in adjudicating the constitutional consistency of state legislation may be warranted in light of that fact. Something of this thought may lie behind Justice Holmes's view respecting the relative importance of constitutional review itself: "I do not think the United States would come to an end if we lost our power to declare an Act of Congress void. I do think the Union would be imperiled if we could not make that declaration as to the laws of the several states." Finally, more activist substantive review of state laws has been defended on the view that, assuming Congress itself may presume to substitute a uniform rule or otherwise forbid states to legislate in respect to certain matters, the frequency with which state statutes may be adopted and the resulting interference they may impose upon matters of national importance prior to any possibility of corrective congressional action require that the federal courts exercise an interim and activist responsibility of their own. In any event, this much is clear. In respect to substantive standards of constitutional review and challenges to state laws on grounds that they usurp national authority, the overall position of the Supreme Court has been that of an activist judiciary in umpiring the boundaries of federalism.

Finally, and most prominently within the last half-century, selective judicial activism has made its strongest appearance in the judicial review of either federal or state laws that, in the Court's view, bear adversely on one or more of the following three subjects: participation in the political process, specific personal rights enumerated in the Bill of Rights, and laws adversely affecting "DISCRETE AND INSULAR MINORITIES." The scope of these respective activist exceptions (to the general rule of procedural and substantive restraint) is still not entirely settled. Indeed, each is itself somewhat unstable. Nonetheless, the indication of more aggressive, judicially assertive constitutional intervention in all three areas was strongly suggested in a footnote to UNITED STATES V. CAROLENE PRODUCTS CO. (1938). There, the Court suggested that the conventional "presumption of constitutionality" would not obtain, and that "searching judicial inquiry" would be applied to the review of laws that, on their face, appeared "to be within a specific prohibition of the Constitution," or to "restrict those political processes which can ordinarily be expected to bring about the repeal of undesirable legislation," or to bear heavily on "discrete and insular minorities" suffering from prejudice likely to lead to their neglect in the legislative process.

In respect to the first of these categories, however, it is doubtful whether the standards applied by the Supreme Court should be defined as unconventionally activist at all. To the extent that a constitutional provision explicitly forbids a given kind of statute, its mere application by the Court scarcely seems exceptional. To the contrary, it would require an extreme version of "restraint" to do otherwise.

The second category (principally concerned with limitations on voting eligibility or with varieties of unfairness in REPRESENTATION) is differently reasoned. The Court has assumed generally that deference is ordinarily due the constitutional interpretations of legislative bodies because they are themselves representatives of the people (who have the greatest stake in the Constitution). But if the law in question itself abridges the representative character of the legislatures, it tends by that fact to undermine the entire foundation of judicial restraint in respect to all other legislative acts. As it tends thereby also to reduce the efficacy of the legislative process to repeal improvident legislation, such representation-reducing statutes ought to be severely questioned.

The third category (such legislation as bears adversely on insular and discrete minorities) has emerged as by far the most controversial and unstable example of modern judicial activism. Its theory of justification is one of rationing the activism of constitutional review inversely, again in keeping with the perceived "market failure" of representative government. And, up to a point, it is quite straightforward in keeping with that theory. Thus, when the numbers of a particular class are few and their financial resources insignificant, and when the class upon whom a law falls with great force is not well-connected but, to the contrary, seems left out of account in legislative processes (by prejudices entrenched within legislatures), the resulting market place failure of political power or ordinary empathy is felt to leave a gap to be filled by exceptional judicial solicitude.

The paradigm case for such activism is that of legislation adversely affecting blacks, when challenged on grounds of inconsistency with the EQUAL PROTECTION clause of the Fourteenth Amendment. On its face, the equal protection clause provides no special standards of justification that race-related legislation must satisfy that other kinds of adverse legislative classifications need not meet. Nonetheless, on quite sound historical grounds, race-related legislation was singled out for exceptional judicial activism by the WARREN COURT. Although many of the Warren Court decisions remain of enduring controversy, it is generally conceded that the Court's STRICT SCRUTINY of such race-based laws was itself consistent with the special preoccupation of the Fourteenth Amendment with that subject. Thus, as early as 1873, in the SLAUGHTERHOUSE CASES, the Court had observed: In the light of the history of [the THIRTEENTH, Fourteenth, and FIFTEENTH] AMENDMENTS, and the pervading purpose of them, [it] is not difficult to give a meaning to [the equal protection clause]. The existence of laws in the states where the newly emancipated negroes resided, which discriminated with gross injustice and hardship against them as a class, was the evil to be remedied by this clause, and by it such laws are forbidden."

As this historical Civil War basis for that one exception was left behind, the Supreme Court plied an increasingly complicated sociology of political marketplace failure to explain an equivalent interventionism on a much broader front. Thus, gender-based laws, laws restricting ALIENS vis-à-vis citizens, and laws restricting minors vis-à-vis adults came also to be examined much more stringently under the equal protection clause than laws adversely affecting particular businesses, particular classes of property owners, certain groups of taxpayers, or others. The determination of "adequate representation" (whether direct or vicarious), the conjecture as to whether such legislative classifications were based on "stereotypes" rather than real differences, and ultimately the tentative extension of equal protection activism even to require a variety of state support for poor persons, produced unstable and largely unsustainable pluralities within the Supreme Court.

Indeed, the difficulties of selective activism in this area have been the principal object of contemporary criticism in American constitutional law. The most serious questions have been addressed to the apparent tendency of the Court to adjust its own interpretations of the Constitution not according simply to its own best understanding of that document, but rather according to its perceptions respecting the adequacy of representative government. Given the fact that far more cases compete for the opportunity to be determined by the Supreme Court than its own resources can permit it to hear, the Court might be expected to pursue a course of selective procedural activism according to which it would more readily entertain cases and more readily reach the merits of constitutional claims it should consider not to have been adequately considered elsewhere because of built-in weaknesses of representative government. On the other hand, it remains much more problematic why the Court should utilize its impressions respecting the adequacies of representative government twice over: once to determine which cases to review, and again to determine whether the Constitution has in fact been violated.

Descriptions of judicial activism and judicial restraint in constitutional adjudication are, of course, but partial truths. In two centuries of judicial review, superintended by more than one hundred Justices who have served on the Supreme Court and who have interpreted a Constitution highly ambiguous in much of its text, consistency has not been institutional but personal. Individual judges have maintained strongly diverse notions of the "proper" judicial role, and the political process of APPOINTMENT OF SUPREME COURT JUSTICES has itself had a great deal to do with the dominant perspectives of that role from time to time. Here, only the most prominent features of judicial activism and judicial restraint have been canvassed.

It is roughly accurate to summarize that in respect to interpreting the Constitution, procedurally the Supreme Court has usually exercised great restraint. Subject to some notable exceptions, it has eschewed addressing the constitutional consistency of acts of government to a dramatically greater degree of self-denial than it has exercised in confronting other kinds of legal issues seeking judicial resolution. Substantively, the Court has been predisposed to the national government in respect to the powers of that government: except for the early twentieth century, Thayer's law, requiring a showing of "clear error," has been the dominant motif. In respect to the states, on the other hand, the Court has been actively more interventionist, construing the Constitution to enforce its own notions of national interest in the absence of decisions by Congress. And, most controversially in recent decades, it has been unstably activist in deciding whether it will interpret the Constitution more as an egalitarian set of imperatives than as a document principally concerned with commerce, federalism, the SEPARATION OF POWERS, and the protection of explicitly protected liberties.

WILLIAM W. VAN ALSTYNE

Bibliography

BICKEL, ALEXANDER M. 1962 *The Least Dangerous Branch: The Supreme Court at the Bar of Politics.* Indianapolis: Bobbs-Merrill.

ELY, JOHN H. 1980 *Democracy and Distrust: A Theory of Judicial Review.* Cambridge, Mass.: Harvard University Press.

JACKSON, ROBERT H. 1941 *The Struggle for Judicial Supremacy.* New York: Knopf.

THAYER, JAMES B. 1893 "The Origin and Scope of the American Doctrine of Constitutional Law." *Harvard Law Review* 7:129.

WECHSLER, HERBERT 1959 "Toward Neutral Principles of Constitutional Law." *Harvard Law Review* 73:1.

JUDICIAL CODE

The Judicial Code of the United States is an official collection and codification of laws governing the federal judiciary and federal court procedures. Codified as Title 28 of the UNITED STATES CODE, the Judicial Code is an exercise of the Article I power of Congress to make such laws as it deems NECESSARY AND PROPER for carrying into execution the broad and ill-defined powers vested in the judiciary by Article III of the Constitution.

The present code, enacted in 1948, is the lineal descendant of the original JUDICIARY ACT OF 1789, the judiciary portions of the REVISED STATUTES of 1877, and the Judicial Code of 1911. It is an effort by judicial, legislative, and legal experts to rearrange, update, and improve the many laws dealing with the federal judicial system. Additions and improvements are periodically made by Congress, and integrated into the structural scheme of the code. The code itself is divided into six main parts, with numerous subdivisions, each relating to a particular subject matter. Among the more important subjects covered by the code are: the organization, personnel, and administration of the federal courts, including the SUPREME COURT; the JURISDICTION conferred by Congress on these various courts, including the Supreme Court; provisions for determining the proper VENUE for instituting a case in a UNITED STATES DISTRICT COURT, and provisions governing the REMOVAL to a federal court of a case instituted in a state court; and the procedures to be followed in various kinds of federal court proceedings.

The 1948 revision and recodification have been both highly praised and highly criticized. Criticism has often been focused on the provisions dealing with the jurisdiction of the federal district courts, for it is the exercise of that jurisdiction that most directly affects the delicate and controversial federal–state court relationships. Concern for these relationships led the American Law Institute to undertake a major study of the Judicial Code, culminating in a 1968 proposal to revise substantial portions of the code. Specifically, the institute suggested major modifications and limitations respecting district courts' DIVERSITY-OF-CITIZENSHIP JURISDICTION, as well as clarifications of FEDERAL QUESTION JURISDICTION and ADMIRALTY AND MARITIME JURISDICTION, and changes as to venue and removal of actions from state courts. Some of the institute's proposals bore legislative fruit and influenced judicial thinking. But the major proposals have lain fallow, and in some respects they have been outmoded by the passage of time and the birth of new tensions in the JUDICIAL SYSTEM.

Controversy about some of the Judicial Code's provisions is endless, especially those that concern the scope and exercise of the diversity jurisdiction of the federal courts. Such controversy reflects the historic and perhaps unresolvable concern that, as Chief Justice EARL WARREN once said, "we achieve a proper jurisdictional balance between the Federal and State court systems, assigning to each system those cases most appropriate in the light of the basic principles of FEDERALISM."

EUGENE GRESSMAN

Bibliography

CURRIE, DAVID P. 1968–1969 The Federal Courts and the American Law Institute. *University of Chicago Law Review* 36:1–49, 268–337.

WECHSLER, HERBERT 1948 Federal Jurisdiction and the Revision of the Judicial Code. *Law and Contemporary Problems* 13:216–243.

JUDICIAL IMMUNITY

In *Randall v. Brigham* (1869) the Supreme Court endorsed the principle of judicial immunity. Under doctrine "as old as the law," Justice STEPHEN J. FIELD wrote for the Court, judges of courts of general jurisdiction are immune from suit for judicial acts "unless perhaps where the acts, in excess of JURISDICTION, are done maliciously or corruptly." In *Bradley v. Fisher* (1872) Justice Field, again writing for the Court, extended *Randall*'s standard for protecting judges to preclude liability for all judicial acts except "acts where no jurisdiction whatever" existed and illustrated the difference between acts "in excess of jurisdiction" and acts clearly without jurisdiction. A probate judge acts clearly without jurisdiction when he tries a criminal case. A judge who improperly holds an act to be a crime or sentences a defendant to more than the statutory maximum merely acts in excess of jurisdiction. *Bradley* also disavowed the suggestion in *Randall* that a malicious or corrupt motive might affect a judge's immunity.

The Civil War Amendments, ratified at about the time *Randall* and *Bradley* were decided, led many years later to a vast growth in individual constitutional protections. This development caused both a reexamination and an eventual reaffirmation of judicial immunity. Because actions against state officials for constitutional violations are brought under SECTION 1983, TITLE 42, UNITED STATES CODE, the scope of judicial immunity from suit for constitutional violations has been defined mainly in answer to the question whether judges may be sued under section 1983.

The unequivocal language of section 1983 led some lower courts to find judges subject to suit. In TENNEY V. BRANDHOVE (1951), however, the Supreme Court held that Congress did not intend section 1983 to overturn the traditional immunity of legislators from suit. Although judicial immunity was less firmly established at COMMON LAW than was legislative immunity, *Tenney* led courts to conclude that judges, like legislators, are immune from suit under section 1983. In PIERSON V. RAY (1967), with limited discussion of the issue, the Supreme Court adopted this view in holding a judge immune from suit for convicting defendants under a statute later found to be unconstitutional.

In STUMP V. SPARKMAN (1978) the Court reaffirmed the immunity in a case that presented extreme facts. Without a hearing and without NOTICE to the victim, the defendant judge had granted a mother's petition to have her daughter sterilized. Because granting the petition was found to be a judicial act and because no state law or decision expressly denied the judge authority to grant the petition, the judge was immune.

There are, however, some limits to judicial immunity. In *Pulliam v. Allen* (1984) the Supreme Court held that state judges are not immune from section 1983 actions seeking injunctive relief or from awards of attorney's fees. In both O'SHEA V. LITTLETON (1974) and IMBLER V. PACHTMAN (1976) the Court suggested that judges are not immune from criminal prosecutions for violating constitutional rights.

A SEPARATION OF POWERS question lurks in the background of the judicial immunity DOCTRINE. Courts might well invalidate a federal statute that imposed liability on federal judges in what the courts believed to be inappropriate circumstances. Because the Court has been relatively generous in protecting its judicial colleagues from liability, and because most activity concerning judicial immunity involves actions against state judges under section 1983, the potential separation of powers issue goes largely unnoticed.

THEODORE EISENBERG

Bibliography

NOTE 1969 Liability of Judicial Officers under Section 1983. *Yale Law Journal* 79:322–337.

JUDICIAL LEGISLATION

The term "judicial legislation" appears to be something of an oxymoron, as the Constitution clearly assigns the principal task of LEGISLATION to the Congress. The Constitution does, of course, give the President a role in the legislative process through the VETO POWER and through his power to recommend legislation to Congress that "he shall judge necessary and expedient." The Framers explicitly rejected, however, a similar role for the judiciary. Several attempts to create a council of revision, composed of the executive and members of the Supreme Court, to review the constitutionality of proposed legislation, were defeated in the CONSTITUTIONAL CONVENTION. The most effective arguments against including the Court in a council of revision were derived from considerations of the SEPARATION OF POWERS. ELBRIDGE GERRY, for example, remarked that including members of the Supreme Court in a revisory council "was quite foreign from the nature of the office," because it would not only "make them judges of the policy of public measures" but would also involve them in judging measures they had a direct hand in creating. Assigning ultimate legislative responsibility to the Congress apparently reflected the Framers' belief that, in popular forms of government, primary lawmaking responsibility should be lodged with the most representative branches of the government. In JAMES MADISON's words, "the people are the only legitimate fountain of power."

Justice FELIX FRANKFURTER expressed the same view in his concurring opinion in *American Federation of Labor v. American Sash and Door Co.* (1949). "Even where the social undesirability of a law may be convincingly urged," he said, "invalidation of the law by a court debilitates popular democratic government. . . . Such an assertion of JUDICIAL POWER deflects responsibility from those on whom in a democratic society it ultimately rests—the people." Frankfurter continued his brief for judicial restraint by arguing that because the powers exercised by the Supreme Court are "inherently oligarchic" they should "be exercised with rigorous self-restraint." The

Court, Frankfurter laconically concluded, "is not saved from being oligarchic because it professes to act in the service of humane ends."

The modern Supreme Court is not so easily deterred as Frankfurter was by charges of oligarchy. Since the landmark BROWN V. BOARD OF EDUCATION decision in 1954, the Court has actively and overtly engaged in the kind of lawmaking and policymaking that in previous years was regarded as exclusively the province of the more political branches of government. William Swindler explained the Court's transition from judicial deference to judicial activisim in these terms: "If the freedom of government to act was the basic principle evolving from the Hughes-Stone decade, from 1937–1946, the next logical question—to be disposed of by the WARREN COURT—was the obligation created by the Constitution itself, to compel action in the face of inaction. This led in turn to the epochal decisions in *Brown v. Board of Education*, BAKER V. CARR, and GIDEON V. WAINWRIGHT."

Some scholars have argued that it was the identification of EQUAL PROTECTION rights as class rights and the attendant necessity of fashioning classwide remedies for class injuries that gave the real impetus to the Court's JUDICIAL ACTIVISM in the years immediately following *Brown*. The Court, in other words, effectively legislated under its new-molded EQUITY powers. (See INSTITUTIONAL LITIGATION.)

The Court's legislative role is usually justified in terms of its power of JUDICIAL REVIEW. But judicial review—even if it be regarded as a necessary inference from the fact of a written constitution—is not a part of the powers explicitly assigned to the Court by the Constitution. The Court made its boldest claim for the legitimacy of judicial legislation in COOPER V. AARON (1958). Justice WILLIAM J. BRENNAN, writing an opinion signed by all the members of the Court, outlined the basic constitutional argument for JUDICIAL SUPREMACY. Brennan recited "some basic constitutional propositions which are settled doctrine," and which were derived from Chief Justice JOHN MARSHALL's argument in MARBURY V. MADISON (1803). First is the proposition, contained in Article VI of the Constitution, that the Constitution is the supreme law of the land (see SUPREMACY CLAUSE); second is Marshall's statement that the Constitution is "the fundamental and paramount law of the nation"; third is Marshall's declaration that "[i]t is emphatically the province and duty of the judicial department to say what the law is." Justice Brennan concluded that *Marbury* therefore "declared the basic principle that the federal judiciary is supreme in the exposition of the law of the Constitution, and that principle has ever since been respected by this Court and the Country as a permanent and indispensable feature of our constitutional system. It follows that the interpretation of the FOURTEENTH AMENDMENT enunciated by this Court in the Brown Case is the supreme law of the land. . . ." The defect of Brennan's argument, of course, is that it confounds the Constitution with constitutional law.

Marshall did indeed say that the Constitution was "the fundamental and paramount law of the nation," and that any "ordinary legislative acts" "repugnant to the constitution" were necessarily void. But when Marshall wrote the famous line relied upon by Brennan that "it is emphatically the province and duty of the judicial department to say what the law is," he was referring not to the Constitution but to "ordinary legislative acts." In order to determine the law's conformity with the Constitution it is first necessary to know what the law is. And once the law is ascertained it is also necessary to determine whether the law is in conformity with the "paramount law" of the Constitution. This latter, of course, means that "in some cases" the Constitution itself "must be looked into by the judges" in order to determine the particular disposition of a case. But Marshall was clear that the ability of the Court to interpret the Constitution was incident to the necessity of deciding a law's conformity to the Constitution, and not a general warrant for CONSTITUTIONAL INTERPRETATION or judicial legislation. Marshall was emphatic in his pronouncement that "the province of the court is, solely, to decide on the rights of individuals."

"It is apparent," Marshall concluded, "that the framers of the constitution contemplated that instrument as a rule for the government of courts, as well as of the legislature." As he laconically noted in the peroration of his argument, "it is also not entirely unworthy of observation, that in declaring what shall be the supreme law of the land, the constitution itself is first mentioned; and not the laws of the United States generally, but those only which shall be made in pursuance of the constitution, have that rank." For Marshall, Brennan's assertion that the Court's decision in *Brown* was "the supreme law of the land" would indeed make "written constitutions absurd" because it would usurp the "original right" of the people to establish their government on "such principles" that must be "deemed fundamental" and "permanent." If the Supreme Court were indeed to sit as a "continuing constitutional convention," any written Constitution would certainly be superfluous since, under the circumstances there would be no "rule for the government of courts." After all, by parity of reasoning, if one were to accept Brennan's argument, it would also be necessary to hold that the Court's decision in DRED SCOTT V. SANDFORD (1857) was the supreme law of the land. But *Dred Scott* gave way because forces other than the Supreme Court decided that it was a decision not "pursuant" to the "fundamental and paramount law" of the nation. As John Agresto has cogently remarked; "If Congress can mistake the meaning of the text [of the Constitution], which is what the doctrine of judicial review asserts, so, of course, can the Court. And if it be said that it is more dangerous to have interpretive supremacy in the same body that directs the nation's public policy—that is, Congress—then (especially in this age of pervasive judicial direction of political and social life) an independent judicial interpretive power is equally fearsome for exactly the same reasons."

In SWANN V. CHARLOTTE-MECKLENBURG BOARD OF EDUCATION (1971) the Court was confronted with the question of the federal judiciary's equity powers under the equal protection clause of the Fourteenth Amendment. At issue was whether the Court could uphold SCHOOL BUSING as a "remedy for state-imposed segregation in violation of Brown I." As part of the CIVIL RIGHTS ACT OF 1964 the Congress had included in Title IV a provision that "nothing herein shall empower any official or court . . . to issue any order seeking to achieve a racial balance in any school by requiring the transportation of pupils or students from one school to another . . . or otherwise enlarge the existing power of the court to insure compliance with constitutional standards." Chief Justice WARREN E. BURGER, writing for a unanimous Court, remarked that on its face this section of Title IV is only "designed to foreclose any interpretation of the Act as expanding the *existing* powers of federal courts to enforce the Equal Protection Clause. There is no suggestion of an intention to restrict those powers or withdraw from courts their historic equitable remedial powers." According to Burger these equity powers flow directly from the Fourteenth Amendment—despite the fact that section 5 of the Amendment gives Congress explicit enforcement authority, an authority that was mistakenly restricted by the Court in the SLAUGHTERHOUSE CASES (1873) and the CIVIL RIGHTS CASES (1883).

A serious question arises, however, concerning Burger's claim that forced busing is one of the "historic" equity powers of the Court. It was never asserted as such by the Court prior to 1964, and as late as two years *after* the *Swann* decision it was still being described by Justice LEWIS F. POWELL as "a novel application of equitable power—not to mention a dubious extension of constitutional doctrine." Congress's response to *Swann*, the Equal Educational Opportunity and Transportation of Students Act of 1972, contained restrictions similar to those included in Title IV. These provisions suffered the same fate as the Title IV provisions, only now the Court was able to use *Swann* as authority for its ruling.

The *Swann* rationale derives equity powers directly from the Constitution. But the way in which the Court exercises its equity powers is indistinguishable from legislation. Thus, in effect, the Court now derives what is tantamount to legislative power from the Constitution. Because this power rests upon an interpretation of the Constitution, no act of Congress can overturn or modify the interpretation. Many scholars argue that if the Congress were to attempt to curtail the Court's power to order forced busing under the exceptions clause, the Court would be obligated, under the *Swann* reasoning, to declare such an attempt unconstitutional, because the Court's obligation to require busing as a remedy for equal protection violations is derived directly from the Constitution.

Judicial legislation incident to statutory interpretation is less controversial, for the Congress can overturn any constructions of the Court by repassing the legislation in a way that clarifies congressional intent. The interpretation of statutes necessarily involves the judiciary in legislation. In many instances the courts must engage in judicial legislation in order to say what the law is. In years past the Court's sense of judicial deference confined such judicial legislation to what Justice OLIVER WENDELL HOLMES called the "interstices" of the law. It was generally believed that the plain language of the statute should be the controlling factor in statutory construction and that extrinsic aids to construction such as legislative history should be used only where they were necessary to avoid a contradictory or absurd result.

The courts are not always the aggressive agents in the process of judicial legislation. In recent years courts have acted to fill the void created by Congress's abdication of legislative responsibility. Many statutes passed by Congress are deliberately vague and imprecise; indeed, the Congress in numerous instances charges administrative agencies and courts to supply the necessary details. This delegation of authority to administrative agencies with provisions for judicial oversight of the administrative process has contributed to the judiciary's increased participation in judicial legislation. This tendency was intensified by the

Court's decision in IMMIGRATION AND NATURALIZATION SERVICE V. CHADHA (1983), holding the LEGISLATIVE VETO unconstitutional. Congress had for years used the single-house legislative veto as a device for overseeing the activities of administrative agencies. But, as Judge Carl McGowan has noted, "the question inevitably recurs as to whether judicial review is an adequate protection against the abdication by Congress of substantive policy making in favor of broad delegation of what may essentially be the power to make laws and not merely to administer them."

The volume of litigation calling for "legislation" on the part of the courts also increases in proportion with the liberalization of the rules of STANDING. In previous years the Court's stricter requirements for standing were merely a recognition that the province of the judiciary, in the words of John Marshall quoted earlier, "was solely to decide on the rights of individuals, not to inquire how the executive, or executive officers, perform duties in which they have a discretion." Liberalized rules of standing tend to produce what Court of Appeals Judge Atonin Scalia has called "an overjudicialization of the process of self-governance." Judge Scalia reminds us of the question posed by Justice Frankfurter—whether it is wise for a self-governing people to give itself over to the rule of an oligarchic judiciary. James Bradley Thayer wrote more than eighty-five years ago that "the exercise of [judicial review], even when unavoidable, is always attended with a serious evil, namely, that the correction of legislative mistakes comes from the outside, and the people thus lose the political experience, and the moral education and stimulus that comes from fighting the question out in the ordinary way, and correcting their own errors. The tendency of a common and easy resort to this great function, now lamentably too common, is to dwarf the political capacity of the people, and to deaden its sense of moral responsibility."

If, on the other hand, the processes of democracy are unsuited for protecting democratic ends—if, that is, in the words of Jesse Choper, it is necessary for the Supreme Court generally to act "contrary to the popular will" to promote "the precepts of democracy"—then the question whether the American people can be a self-governing people is indeed a serious one. It was once thought that constitutional majorities could rule safely in the interest of the whole of society—that constitutional government could avoid the formation of majority faction. Today many scholars—and often the Supreme Court itself—simply assume that the majority will always be a factious majority seeking to promote its own interest at the expense of the interest of the minority. This requires that the judiciary intervene not only in the processes of democracy but also as the virtual representatives of the interest of those who are said to be permanently isolated from the majoritarian political process. If American politics is indeed incapable of forming nonfactious majorities—and America has never had such a monolithic majority—then the American people should give itself over honestly and openly to "government by judiciary," for if constitutional government is impossible, then so too is the possibility of self-governance.

EDWARD J. ERLER

(SEE ALSO: *Judicial Policymaking; Judicial Review and Democracy.*)

Bibliography

AGRESTO, JOHN 1984 *The Supreme Court and Constitutional Democracy.* Ithaca, N.Y.: Cornell University Press.

ERLER, EDWARD J. 1985 Sowing the Wind: Judicial Oligarchy and the Legacy of *Brown v. Board of Education. Harvard Journal of Law and Public Policy* 8:399–426.

LEVY, LEONARD W. 1967 Judicial Review, History, and Democracy. Pages 1–42 in Leonard W. Levy, ed., *Judicial Review and the Supreme Court.* New York: Harper & Row.

SWINDLER, WILLIAM 1969 *Court and Constitution in the 20th Century.* Indianapolis: Bobbs-Merrill.

JUDICIAL POLICYMAKING

Judicial policymaking and related terms—JUDICIAL ACTIVISM, judicial creativity, and JUDICIAL LEGISLATION—emphasize that judges are not mere legal automatons who simply "discover" or "find" definite, preexisting principles and rules, as the declaratory or oracular conception of the judicial function insisted, but are often their makers. As Justice OLIVER WENDELL HOLMES remarked, they often exercise "the sovereign prerogative of choice," and they "can and do legislate." Indeed, that is why the Supreme Court has often been viewed as "a continuing constitutional convention."

Policymaking is deciding what is to be done by choosing among possible actions, methods, or principles for determining and guiding present and future actions or decisions. Courts, especially high appellate courts such as the SUPREME COURT, often make such choices, establishing new rules and principles, and thus are properly called policymakers. That was emphasized by CHARLES EVANS HUGHES's famous rhetorical exaggeration, "The Constitution is what the judges say it is," and by his remark that a federal statute finally means what the Court, as ultimate interpreter of congressional LEGISLATION, says it means.

The persistent "declaratory" conception of the judicial role, a view critics derided as MECHANICAL JURISPRUDENCE, and simplistic notions of the SEPARATION OF POWERS principle long obscured the reality of judicial policymaking. Today it is widely recognized that, as C. Herman Pritchett has explained, "judges are inevitably participants in the process of public policy formulation; that they do in fact 'make law'; that in making law they are necessarily guided in part by their personal conceptions of justice and public policy; that written law requires interpretation which involves the making of choices; that the rule of STARE DECISIS is vulnerable because precedents are typically available to support both sides in a controversy."

As a system of social control, law must function largely through general propositions rather than through specific directives to particular persons. And that is especially true of the Constitution. The Framers did not minutely specify the national government's powers or the means for executing them: as Chief Justice JOHN MARSHALL said, the Constitution "is one of enumeration, rather than of definition." Many of its most important provisions are indeterminate and open-textured. They are not self-interpreting, and thus judges must read specific meanings into them and determine their applicability to particular situations, many of which their authors could not have anticipated.

Among the Constitution's many ambiguous, undefined, pregnant provisions are those concerning CRUEL AND UNUSUAL PUNISHMENT; DOUBLE JEOPARDY; DUE PROCESS OF LAW; EQUAL PROTECTION OF THE LAWS; ESTABLISHMENT OF RELIGION; excessive BAIL and fines; EX POST FACTO LAWS; FREEDOM OF SPEECH, press, assembly, and religion; life, liberty, and property; the power to regulate commerce among the several states; and unreasonable SEARCHES AND SEIZURES. Also undefined by the Constitution are such fundamental conceptions as FEDERALISM, JUDICIAL REVIEW, the RULE OF LAW, and the separation of powers. Small wonder, then, that Justice ROBERT H. JACKSON plaintively remarked that the Court must deal with materials nearly as enigmatic as the dreams of Pharaoh which Joseph had to interpret; or that Chief Justice EARL WARREN emphasized that the Constitution's words often have "an iceberg quality, containing beneath their surface simplicity submerged complexities which go to the very heart of our constitutional form of government."

Because the Constitution embodies in its ambiguous provisions both common and conflicting community ideals, the Supreme Court serves, as Edward H. Levi has said, as "a forum for the discussion of policy in the gap of ambiguity," which allows the infusion into constitutional law of new meanings and new ideas as situations and people's ideas change. That is the process which Justice FELIX FRANKFURTER described as "the evolution of social policy by way of judicial application of the Delphic provisions of the Constitution." Brief accounts of some notable Supreme Court decisions reveal their policymaking features.

Although the Constitution nowhere explicitly grants Congress the power to incorporate a national bank, the Supreme Court in MCCULLOCH V. MARYLAND (1819) held that power to be implied by the Constitution's NECESSARY AND PROPER CLAUSE. That clause empowers Congress, in executing its various enumerated powers, to make all laws for that purpose which are "necessary and proper." But those ambiguous words are not further defined by the Constitution.

In making its *McCulloch* decision, the Court chose between two historic, diametrically opposed interpretations. The narrow, STATES' RIGHTS, STRICT CONSTRUCTION, Jeffersonian interpretation of the clause was restrictive and limited Congress to legislation that was "absolutely necessary," that is, literally indispensable. The opposing interpretation, which the Court adopted, was the broad, nationalist, loose constructionist, Hamiltonian view that "necessary and proper" were equivalent to "convenient and useful" and thus were facilitative, not restrictive. The bank, declared the Court, was a convenient and useful means to legitimate ends and thus was constitutional.

Viewed broadly as the great implied powers case and the "fountainhead of national powers," *McCulloch* laid down the Hamiltonian doctrine as the authoritative rule of construction to be followed in interpreting Congress's various undefined powers. Subsequently, on that foundation, Congress erected vast superstructures of regulatory and social service legislation. The profound policy considerations underlying the Court's choices are highlighted by the contrast between Jefferson's warning that the dangerous Hamiltonian doctrine would give Congress a boundless field of undefined powers, and Chief Justice Marshall's emphasis upon the "pernicious, baneful," narrow construction which would make the national government's operations "difficult, hazardous, and expensive" and would reduce the Constitution to "a splendid bauble."

The RIGHT TO PRIVACY was recognized by the Supreme Court in GRISWOLD V. CONNECTICUT (1965). There, and in other cases, the Court variously discerned the "roots" of that right, which is not explicitly mentioned in the Constitution, in the FIRST, FOURTH, Fifth, NINTH, and FOURTEENTH AMENDMENTS and in "the penumbras of the BILL OF RIGHTS." Later, in ROE V. WADE (1973), the Court included a woman's right to an abortion in the right of privacy, and, in the detailed manner characteristic of legislation, divided the pregnancy term into three periods and prescribed specific rules governing each. Balancing a woman's interests against a state's interests during these three periods, the Court held that any decision regarding abortion during the first was solely at the discretion of the woman and her physician. But it further ruled that a state's interests in protecting maternal health, maintaining medical standards, and safeguarding potential human life—interests growing in substantiality as the pregnancy term extended—justified greater state regulation later. Thus, state regulations relating to maternal health and medical standards would be permissible in the second period, and more stringent state regulations, even extending to prohibition of abortion, would be permissible in the third period in the interest of safeguarding potential life.

The protests by dissenting Justices in the *Griswold* and *Roe* cases emphasized the judicial policymaking which those decisions revealed. The *Griswold* dissenters objected that no right of privacy could be found "in the Bill of Rights, in any other part of the Constitution, or in any case ever before decided by this Court." And dissenters in *Roe* complained that the Court's decision was "an improvident and extravagant exercise of the power of JUDICIAL REVIEW"; that the Court had fashioned "a new constitutional right for pregnant mothers"; and that the Court's "conscious weighing of competing factors" and its division of the pregnancy term into distinct periods were "far more appropriate to a legislative judgement than to a judicial one."

The Supreme Court's "REAPPORTIONMENT revolution" remedied long-standing discriminations against urban and metropolitan areas in favor of rural areas, by requiring states to reapportion their legislatures in conformity with the rule that legislative districts must be as nearly of equal population as is practicable.

That rule is not found in any constitutional provision specifically addressed to legislative apportionment, for none exists. It is a Court-created rule which clearly demonstrates the leeway for policymaking that open-ended constitutional provisions give the Court. Equal population, the Court said in WESBERRY V. SANDERS (1964), is required for congressional districts by "the command" of Article I, section 2, of the Constitution, that representatives "be chosen by the People" of the states; and is required for state legislative districts, the Court held in REYNOLDS V. SIMS (1964), by "the clear and strong command" of the FOURTEENTH AMENDMENT's equal protection clause, forbidding states to deny to any persons "the equal protection of the laws."

Courtesy may ascribe the Court's rule to CONSTITUTIONAL INTERPRETATION; but candor ascribes it to judicial policymaking. The dissenting Justices' objections in these cases made that clear. They included complaints that the Court had frozen one political theory of REPRESENTATION into the Constitution; had failed to exercise judicial self-restraint; had decided questions appropriate only for legislative judgment; had violated the separation of powers doctrine; and had excluded numerous important considerations other than population.

Supreme Court overruling decisions, in which it rejects its earlier positions for those later thought more fitting, often strikingly exemplify judicial policymaking. In MAPP V. OHIO (1961) the Court imposed upon state courts its judicially created EXCLUSIONARY RULE making illegally obtained evidence inadmissible in court. It overruled WOLF V. COLORADO (1949) which, in deference to state policies, had held an exclusionary rule not essential for due process of law.

Some overruling decisions illustrate "the victory of dissent," when earlier dissenting Justices' views in time became the law. Thus in GIDEON V. WAINWRIGHT (1963) the Court applied its rule that indigent defendants in all state felony trials must have court-appointed counsel. Overruling BETTS V. BRADY (1942), the Court adopted Justice Black's dissenting position from it, thus repudiating its *Betts* pronouncement that such appointment was "not a fundamental right, essential to a fair trial."

According to the Court in BARRON V. BALTIMORE (1833), the Bill of Rights—the first ten amendments—limits the national government but not the states. But the Court, by its INCORPORATION DOCTRINE, has read nearly all the specific guarantees of the Bill of Rights into the due process clause of the Fourteenth Amendment which provides simply that no state shall "deprive any person of life, liberty, or property, without due process of law." The incorporation has been called selective because the Court, proceeding case by case, has incorporated those guarantees which it considers "fundamental" and "of the very essence of a scheme of ORDERED LIBERTY."

Selective incorporation has involved two kinds of Supreme Court policymaking: adopting the FUNDAMENTAL RIGHTS standard for guiding incorporation, and making the separate decisions incorporating particular Bill of Rights guarantees. Thus the Court, applying its open-textured rule, has given specific meaning to "the vague contours" of the due process clause. And it has become "a perpetual censor" over state actions, invalidating those that violate fundamental rights and liberties.

Clearly the Supreme Court is more than just a legal body: the Justices are also "rulers," sharing in the quintessentially political function of authoritatively allocating values for the American polity. Representing a coordinate branch of the national government, they address their mandates variously to lawyers, litigants, federal and state legislative, executive, and judicial officials, and to broader concerned "publics." Concerning their role, no sharp line can be drawn between law and politics in the broad sense. They do not expound a prolix or rigid legal code, but rather a living Constitution "intended to be adapted to the various *crises* of human affairs," as Chief Justice Marshall said in the *McCulloch* case. And the Justices employ essentially COMMON LAW judicial techniques: they are inheritors indeed, but developers too—"weavers of the fabric of constitutional law"—as Chief Justice Hughes observed. The nature of the judicial process and the growth of the law are intertwined. The Constitution, itself the product of great policy choices, is both the abiding Great Charter of the American polity and the continual focus of clashing philosophies of law and politics among which the Supreme Court must choose: "We are very quiet there," said Justice Holmes plaintively, "but it is the quiet of a storm center, as we all know."

HOWARD E. DEAN

Bibliography

CARDOZO, BENJAMIN N. 1921 *The Nature of the Judicial Process.* New Haven, Conn.: Yale University Press.

LEVI, EDWARD H. 1948 *An Introduction to Legal Reasoning.* Chicago: University of Chicago Press.

MILLER, ARTHUR SELWYN 1978 *The Supreme Court: Myth and Reality.* Westport, Conn.: Greenwood Press.

MURPHY, WALTER F. 1964 *Elements of Judicial Strategy.* Chicago: University of Chicago Press.

PRITCHETT, C. HERMAN 1969 The Development of Judicial Research. Pages 27–42 in Joel B. Grossman and Joseph Tanenhaus, eds., *Frontiers of Judicial Research.* New York: Wiley.

JUDICIAL POWER OF THE UNITED STATES

"[T]he legislative, executive, and judicial powers, of every well constructed government," said JOHN MARSHALL in OSBORN V. BANK OF THE UNITED STATES (1824), "are co-extensive with each other; . . . [t]he executive department may constitutionally execute every law which the Legislature may constitutionally make, and the judicial department may receive from the legislature the power of construing every such law." The ARTICLES OF CONFEDERATION fell far short of this model. Not only was there no federal executive with authority to enforce congressional measures against individuals, but, apart from a cumbersome procedure for resolving interstate disputes, Congress was authorized to establish courts only for the trial of crimes committed at sea and for the determination of "appeals in all cases of captures." The remedy for these shortcomings was one of the major accomplishments of the Constitution adopted in 1789. As Article II gave the country a President with the obligation to "take care that the Laws be faithfully executed," Article III provided for a system of federal courts that more than satisfied Marshall's conditions for a "well constructed government."

Article III consists of three brief sections. The first describes the tribunals that are to exercise federal judicial power and prescribes the tenure and compensation of their judges. The second lists the types of disputes that may be entrusted to federal courts, specifies which of these matters are to be determined by the SUPREME COURT in the first instance, and guarantees TRIAL BY JURY in criminal cases. The third defines and limits the crime of TREASON.

"The judicial Power of the United States," Article III declares, "shall be vested in one Supreme Court, and in such inferior Courts as the Congress may from time to time ordain and establish." The text itself indicates that the Supreme Court was the only tribunal the Constitution required to be established, and the debates of the CONSTITUTIONAL CONVENTION demonstrate that the latter words embodied a deliberate compromise.

In fact, however, Congress created additional courts at the very beginning, in the JUDICIARY ACT OF 1789. Since 1911 the basic system has consisted of the UNITED STATES DISTRICT COURTS—at least one in every state—in which most cases are first tried; a number of regional appellate courts now called the UNITED STATES COURTS OF APPEALS; and the Supreme Court itself, which functions largely as a court of last resort. From time to time, moreover, Congress has created specialized courts with JURISDICTION to determine controversies involving relatively limited subjects. All this lies well within Congress's broad discretion under Article III to determine what lower courts to create and how to allocate judicial business among them. Specialization at the highest level, however, seems precluded; Congress can no more divide the powers of "one Supreme Court" among two or more bodies than abolish it altogether.

"The Judges, both of the supreme and inferior Courts," section 1 continues, "shall hold their Offices during GOOD BEHAVIOUR and shall, at stated Times, receive for their Services, a Compensation, which shall not be diminished during their Continuance in Office." Under the second section of Article II the judges have always been appointed by the President subject to Senate confirmation; under the fourth section of that article they may be removed from office on IMPEACHMENT and conviction of "Treason, Bribery, or other high Crimes and Misdemeanors." The central purpose of the tenure and salary provisions, as ALEXANDER HAMILTON explained in THE FEDERALIST #78, was to assure judicial independence.

The Supreme Court has repeatedly enforced the tenure and salary provisions. In EX PARTE MILLIGAN (1867), for example, the Court held even the Civil War no excuse for submitting civilians to military trials in states where the civil courts were open, and in *O'Donoghue v. United States* (1933), it held that the Great Depression did not justify reducing judicial salaries.

On a number of occasions, however, the Court has permitted matters within the judicial power to be determined by LEGISLATIVE COURTS whose judges do not possess tenure and salary guarantees. State courts may decide Article III cases, as the Framers of the Constitution clearly contemplated; the tenure and salary provisions do not apply to the TERRITORIES or to the DISTRICT OF COLUMBIA, where there is no SEPARATION OF POWERS requirement; Article III did not abolish the traditional COURT-MARTIAL for military offenses; federal magistrates may make initial decisions in Article III cases provided they are subject to unlimited reexamination by tenured judges.

Early in the twentieth century the Supreme Court appeared to give judicial blessing to the numerous quasi-judicial bodies that have grown up since the creation of the Interstate Commerce Commission in 1887, although scholars have debated heatedly whether there is any satisfactory way to distinguish them from the nontenured trial courts plainly forbidden by Article III. That these developments did not mean the effective end of the tenure and salary requirements, however, was made clear in 1982, when the Court in NORTHERN PIPE LINE CONSTRUCTION CO. V. MARATHON PIPE LINE CO. invalidated a statute empowering judges with temporary commissions to exercise virtually the entire jurisdiction of the district courts in BANKRUPTCY cases. Where to draw this line promises to be a continuing problem.

The power to be vested in federal courts is the "judicial power," and the various categories of matters that fall within this power are all described as CASES OR CONTROVERSIES—"Cases," for example, "arising under this Constitution," and "Controversies to which the United States shall be a Party." From the beginning the Supreme Court has taken this language as a limitation: federal courts may not resolve anything but "cases" and "controversies," and those terms embrace only judicial functions.

Thus, for example, when President GEORGE WASHINGTON asked the Justices for legal advice respecting the United States' neutrality during hostilities between England and France, they declined to act "extra-judicially"; and when Congress directed them to advise the war secretary concerning veterans' pensions, five Justices sitting on circuit refused, saying the authority conferred was "not of a judicial nature" (HAYBURN'S CASE, 1792). Washington's request for advice did not begin to resemble the ordinary lawsuit, but later decisions have invoked the "case" or "controversy" limitation to exclude federal court consideration of matters far less remote from the normal judicial function. The essential requirement, the Court has emphasized, is a live and actual dispute between adversary parties with a real stake in the outcome.

One dimension of this principle is the doctrine of RIPENESS or prematurity: the courts are not to give advice on the mere possibility that it might be of use in the future. Occasionally the Court has appeared to require a person to violate a law in order to test its constitutionality—causing one commentator to remark that "the only way to determine whether the subject is a mushroom or a toadstool, is to eat it." The DECLARATORY JUDGMENT ACT, passed to mitigate this hardship, has generally been applied to allow preenforcement challenges when the intentions of the parties are sufficiently firm, and it has been held consistent with the "Case" or "Controversy" requirement.

At the opposite end of the spectrum is the MOOTNESS doctrine, which ordinarily forbids litigation after death or other changed circumstances deprive the issue of any further impact on the parties. A series of debatable decisions essentially dating from *Moore v. Ogilvie* (1969), however, has relaxed the mootness DOCTRINE, especially in CLASS ACTIONS, so as to permit persons with no remaining interest to continue litigating issues deemed "capable of repetition, yet evading review."

The "case or controversy" requirement has also been held to forbid the decision of COLLUSIVE SUITS, and to preclude the courts from exercising the discretion of an administrator, as by reviewing de novo the decision to grant a broadcasting license. The most important remaining element of that requirement, however, is the constitutional dimension of the doctrine of STANDING to sue.

While standing has been aptly characterized as one of the most confused areas of federal law, its constitutional component was simply stated in *Warth v. Seldin* (1975): "[t]he Article III power exists only to redress or otherwise to protect against injury to the complaining party." Injury in this context is hardly self-defining, but it plainly requires something more than intellectual or emotional "interest in a problem." This principle puts under a serious cloud the periodic congressional attempts to authorize "any person" to obtain judicial relief against violations of environmental or other laws. On the other hand, other aspects of the standing doctrine are not of constitutional dimension and thus do not preclude Congress from conferring standing on anyone injured by governmental action.

One of the principal points of contention of the law of standing has been the right of federal taxpayers to challenge the constitutionality of federal spending programs. When a taxpayer attacked expenditures for maternal health on the ground that they exceeded the powers granted Congress by Article I, the Court in FROTHINGHAM V. MELLON (1923) found no standing: "the taxpayer's interest in the moneys of the treasury . . . is shared with millions of others, is comparatively minute and indeterminable, and the effect upon future taxation, of any payment out of the funds, so remote, fluctuating, and uncertain, that no basis is afforded for an appeal to the preventive powers of a court of EQUITY."

Although the apparent reference to equitable discretion made it uncertain that the Court was saying taxpayer suits were not "cases or controversies" within Article III, the remainder of the passage suggests that the taxpayer could not show the constitutionally required injury because it was uncertain that a victory would mean reduced taxes. Nevertheless, in FLAST V. COHEN (1968) the Court allowed a federal taxpayer to challenge expenditures for church-related education as an ESTABLISHMENT OF RELIGION in violation of the FIRST AMENDMENT. Unlike the taxpayer in *Frothingham,* who "was attempting to assert the States' interest in their legislative prerogatives," the plaintiff in *Flast* asserted "a federal taxpayer's interest in being free of taxing and spending in contravention of specific constitutional limitations," for one purpose of the establishment clause was to prevent taxation for religious ends. Whether the distinction was of constitutional scope the Court did not say; interestingly, the taxpayer opinions have tended to avoid entirely the traditional constitutional inquiry into the existence of an injury that will be redressed if the plaintiff's claim prevails.

Underlying the constitutional "case or controversy" limitation are a variety of policy concerns. The first group relates to reducing the risk of erroneous decisions. Concrete facts enable judges to understand the practical impact of their holdings; adverse parties help to assure that arguments on both sides will be considered; as argued by FELIX FRANKFURTER, "the ADVISORY OPINION deprives CONSTITUTIONAL INTERPRETATION of the judgment of the legislature upon facts." A second group of reasons focuses upon strengthening the Court's institutional position. Lawmaking by appointed judges is least difficult to reconcile with democratic principles when it is the inevitable by-product of the stock business of judging; the courts should not squander their power of moral suasion or multiply conflicts with other branches by deciding unnecessary legal questions. Third, and of considerable importance, is a concern for the separation of powers. The courts are not to exercise a general superintendence over the activities of the other branches.

The costs of the "case or controversy" limitation include the delay, uncertainty, and disruption incident to determining the constitutionality of legislation only in the course of subsequent litigation, and the danger that some legislative and executive actions may escape JUDICIAL REVIEW entirely. Whether the latter is cause for concern has much to do with one's perception of the function and importance of judicial review itself; it seems reasonable to expect that perception to influence the definition of a "case" or "controversy."

In addition to restricting federal courts to the decision of "cases" and "controversies" of a judicial nature, section 2 of Article III enumerates those categories of "cases" and "controversies" to which the "judicial Power shall extend." As the former limitation serves the interests of separating federal powers, the latter serves those of FEDERALISM. In accord with the spirit of the TENTH AMENDMENT the Supreme Court has held that Congress may not give the federal courts jurisdiction over disputes of types not listed in Article III. John Marshall set the tone in cutting down to constitutional size a statute providing for jurisdiction over cases involving ALIENS in HODGSON V. BOWERBANK in 1809: "Turn to the article of the constitution of the United States, for the statutes cannot extend the jurisdiction beyond the limits of the constitution."

Article III's provision that federal judicial power "shall extend to" certain classes of cases and controversies has generally been taken to mean that it shall embrace nothing else. From the text alone one might think it even more plain that federal courts *must* be given jurisdiction over all the matters listed, for section 1 commands that the federal judicial power "shall be vested" in federal courts. Indeed, Justice JOSEPH STORY suggested just such an interpretation in MARTIN V. HUNTER'S LESSEE in 1816. This conclusion, however, was unnecessary to the decision, contrary to the understanding of the First Congress, and inconsistent with both earlier and later decisions of the Supreme Court.

Article III, in other words, has been read to mean only that Congress may confer jurisdiction over the enumerated cases, not that it must do so. This arguably unnatural construction has been defended by reference to the limited list of controversies over which the Supreme Court has original jurisdiction, the explicit congressional power to make exceptions to the Supreme Court's appellate authority, and the compromise at the Constitutional Convention permitting Congress not to establish inferior courts at all.

This is not to say, however, that Congress has unfettered authority to deny the courts jurisdiction, for all powers of Congress are subject to limitations found elsewhere in the Constitution. A statute depriving the courts of authority to determine cases filed by members of a particular racial group, for instance, would be of highly doubtful vitality under the modern interpretation of the Fifth Amendment DUE PROCESS clause, and one part of Marshall's reasoning in MARBURY V. MADISON (1803) supports an argument that closing all federal and state courts to free-speech claims would defeat the substantive right itself. Proposals to remove entire categories of constitutional litigation from the ken of one or more federal courts often follow controversial judicial decisions. Out of respect for the tradition of CHECKS AND BALANCES, however, such bills are seldom enacted; we have so far been spared the constitutional trauma of determining the extent to which they may validly be adopted.

The cases and controversies within federal judicial power fall into two categories: those in which jurisdiction is based upon the nature of the dispute and those in which it is based upon the identity of the parties. In the first category are three kinds of disputes: those "arising under this Constitution, the Laws of the United States, and Treaties made, or which shall be made, under their Authority"; those "of ADMIRALTY AND MARITIME JURISDICTION"; and those involving competing land claims "under Grants of different States." The provision last quoted is of minor importance; the second formed the staple business of the district courts throughout their early history; the first fulfills Marshall's condition for a "well constructed government" and is by any measure the most critical ingredient of federal jurisdiction today.

The provision for jurisdiction in cases arising under the Constitution and other federal laws has two essential purposes: to promote uniformity in the interpretation of federal law, and to assure the vindication of federal rights. The First Congress sought to accomplish the second of these goals by providing, in section 25 of the 1789 Judiciary Act, for Supreme Court review of state-court decisions denying federal rights; the additional uniformity attendant upon review of state decisions *upholding* federal claims was not provided until 1914. In sustaining section 25, the opinion in *Martin v. Hunter's Lessee* demonstrated the difficulty of achieving Article III's purpose without Supreme Court review of state courts: while plaintiffs might be authorized to file federal claims directly in federal courts and defendants to remove state court actions to federal courts on the basis of federal defenses, it was not easy to see how a state court opposing removal "could . . . be compelled to relinquish the jurisdiction" without some federal court reviewing the state court decision.

Conversely, although Congress failed to give federal trial courts general jurisdiction of federal question cases until 1875, Marshall made clear as early as 1824, in *Osborn v. Bank of the United States,* that it had power to do so. Supreme Court review alone was no more an adequate protection for federal rights, Marshall argued, than was exclusive reliance on litigation beginning in federal trial courts. As the latter would leave claimants without remedy against a recalcitrant state court, the former would give a state tribunal the critical power to shape the factual record beyond assurance of federal appellate correction.

The *Osborn* opinion also settled that jurisdiction of a federal trial court over a case arising under federal law was not defeated by the presence of additional issues dependent upon state law. In a companion case, indeed, the Court upheld jurisdiction over a suit by the national bank on notes whose validity and interpretation were understood to depend in substantial part upon nonfederal law: it was enough that the plaintiff derived its existence and its right to contract from the act of Congress incorporating it. The courts have not followed this broad approach, however, in determining whether FEDERAL QUESTION JURISDICTION lies under general *statutory* provisions; when the federal ingredient of a claim is remote from the actual controversy, as in a dispute over ownership of land whose title is remotely derived from a federal land grant, the district courts lack statutory jurisdiction.

In the contract dispute discussed in *Osborn,* federal and state law were bound together in the resolution of a single claim; in such a case, as HENRY HART and Herbert Wechsler said, "a federal trial court would . . . be unable to function as a court at all" if its jurisdiction did not extend to state as well as federal matters. In the interest of "judicial economy," however, as the Supreme Court put it in *United Mine Workers v. Gibbs* (1966), jurisdiction over a case arising under federal law embraces not only a plaintiff's federal claim but also any claims under state law based on the same facts. This so-called PENDENT JURISDICTION doctrine, however, is inapplicable when the Supreme Court reviews a state court decision. With one exception, in such a case the Court may review only federal and not state questions, as the Court held in *Murdock v. Memphis* (1875); for to reverse a state court in the interpretation of its own law would be a major incursion into state prerogatives not required by the purposes for which Supreme Court review was provided.

A corollary of the *Murdock* principle is that a state court decision respecting state law often precludes the Supreme Court from reviewing even federal questions in the same case. If a state court concludes, for example, that a state law offends both federal and state constitutions, the Supreme Court cannot reverse the state law holding; thus, however it may decide the federal issue, it cannot alter the outcome of the case. This independent and ADEQUATE STATE GROUND for the state court decision means there is no longer a live case or controversy between the parties over the federal question. In light of this relation between state and federal issues, *Martin* itself announced the sole exception to the *Murdock* rule: when the state court has interpreted state law in such a way as to frustrate the federal right itself—as by holding that a contract allegedly impaired in violation of the CONTRACT CLAUSE never existed—a complete absence of power to review the state question would mean the Court's authority to protect federal rights "may be evaded at pleasure."

"The most bigoted idolizers of state authority," wrote Alexander Hamilton in *The Federalist* #80, "have not thus far shown a disposition to deny the National Judiciary the cognizance of maritime causes"; for such cases "so generally depend upon the law of nations, and so commonly affect the rights of foreigners, that they fall within the considerations which are relative to the public peace." Jurisdiction over what Article III refers to as "Cases of admiralty, and maritime Jurisdiction" has been vested by statute in the district courts since 1789. Today federal admiralty jurisdiction extends, as the Court stated in another context in *The Daniel Ball* (1871), to all waters forming part of "a continued highway over which commerce is or may be carried on with other states or foreign countries."

Not everything occurring on navigable waters, however, is a proper subject of admiralty jurisdiction; in denying jurisdiction of claims arising out of an airplane crash in Lake Erie, the Supreme Court made clear that the case must "bear a significant relationship to traditional maritime activity . . . involving navigation and commerce on navigable waters." Conversely, the relation of an activity to maritime concerns may bring it within admiralty cognizance even if it occurs on land. Marine insurance contracts, for example, are within the jurisdiction although both made and to be performed on land. Similarly, the Court has acquiesced in Congress's provision for jurisdiction over land damage caused by vessels on navigable waters.

Because an additional purpose of federal judicial power over maritime cases is understood to have been to provide a uniform law to govern the shipping industry, the Supreme Court also held in *Southern Pacific Company v. Jensen* (1917) that Article III empowers the federal courts to develop a "general maritime law" binding even on state courts, and that Congress may supplement this law with statutes under its authority to adopt laws "necessary and proper" to the powers of the courts. Indeed the Court has held that this aspect of the judicial power, like the legislative authority conferred by the commerce clause of Article I, has an implicit limiting effect upon state law. Not only does state law that contradicts federal law yield under the SUPREMACY CLAUSE, but, as the Court said in rejecting the application of a state workers' compensation law to longshoremen in the case last cited, no state law is valid if it "interferes with the proper harmony and uniformity" of the general maritime law "in its international and interstate relations."

The remaining authorization of federal court jurisdiction protects parties whose fortunes the Framers were for various reasons unwilling to leave wholly at the mercy of state courts. Many of these categories involve government litigation: "Controversies to which the United States shall be a Party; . . . between two or more States; between a State and Citizens of another State, . . . and between a State, or the Citizens thereof, and foreign States, Citizens or Subjects." A federal forum for the national government itself protects against possible state hostility; federal jurisdiction over interstate conflicts provides not only a neutral forum but also a safeguard against what Hamilton in *The Federalist* #80 called "dissentions and private wars"; that "the union will undoubtedly be answerable to foreign powers, for the conduct of its members," was an additional reason for jurisdiction over disputes involving foreign countries as well as the related jurisdiction over "Cases affecting Ambassadors, other public Ministers and Consuls."

The most interesting issue concerning these provisions has been that of SOVEREIGN IMMUNITY. In CHISHOLM V. GEORGIA (1793), ignoring the assurances of prominent Framers like James Madison and Alexander Hamilton as well as the common law tradition that the king could not be sued without his consent, the Supreme Court relied largely on the text of Article III to hold that the power over "Controversies . . . between a State and Citizens of another State" included those in which the state was an unwilling defendant. Obviously, as the Justices pointed out, this was true of the parallel authority over "Controversies . . . between two or more States," and Justice JAMES WILSON added his understanding that the English tradition was a mere formality, since consent to sue was given as a matter of course.

Whether this decision was right or wrong as an original matter, within five years it was repudiated by adoption of the ELEVENTH AMENDMENT, which provides that "[t]he Judicial power of the United States shall not be construed to extend to any suit in law or equity, commenced or prosecuted against one of the United States by Citizens or Subjects of any Foreign State." Notably, the amendment does not mention admiralty cases, suits by foreign countries, suits against a state by its own citizens under federal law, or suits against the United States. Nevertheless the Supreme Court, taking the amendment as casting doubt on the reasoning underlying *Chisholm,* has denied jurisdiction in all of these instances. The best explanation has been that, although not excepted by the amendment, they are outside the power conferred by Article III itself. One state may still sue another, however, and the United States may sue a state. The Court has found such jurisdiction "essential to the peace of the Union" and "inherent in the constitutional plan." Why this is not equally true of a suit by a state against the United States has never been satisfactorily explained.

At least since the 1824 decision in *Osborn v. Bank of the United States,* however, both the Eleventh Amendment and its related immunities have been construed to allow certain actions against state or federal officers even though the effect of the litigation is the same as if the government itself had been named defendant. The theoretical explanation that the officer cannot be acting for the state when he does what the Constitution forbids is inconsistent with the substantive conclusion, often reached in the same cases, that his action is attributable to the state for purposes of the FOURTEENTH AMENDMENT. A more principled explanation is that suits against officers are necessary if the Constitution is to be enforced at all; the response is that those who wrote the amendment could not have intended to allow it to be reduced to a hollow shell.

In any event, the *Osborn* exception has not been held to embrace all suits against government officers. At one time it was said generally that an officer could be prevented from acting but could not be ordered to take affirmative action such as paying off a government obligation, for if he was not acting for the state he had no authority to reach into its treasury. The simplicity of this distinction was shattered, however, by opinions acknowledging the availability of a WRIT OF MANDAMUS to compel an officer to perform a nondiscretionary duty. The more recent formulation in EDELMAN V. JORDAN (1974), which essentially distinguishes between prospective and retrospective relief, seems difficult to reconcile with the language of the Constitution, with its apparent purposes, or with the fiction created to support the *Osborn* rule.

Even when the government is itself a party, it may consent to be sued, and the books are filled with a confusing and incomplete array of statutes allowing suits against the United States. Some judges and scholars have argued that suits against consenting states are inconsistent with the language of the amendment, which declares them outside the judicial power; the Court's persuasive explanation has been that, like venue and personal jurisdiction, immunity is a privilege waivable by the party it protects (*Clark v. Barnard,* 1883). More debatable was the Court's decision in *Parden v. Terminal Railway* (1964) that a state had "waived" its immunity by operating a railroad after passage of a federal statute making "every" interstate railway liable for injuries to its employees; in *Edelman v. Jordan,* retreating from this conclusion, the Court emphasized that "[c]onstructive consent is not a doctrine commonly associated with the surrender of constitutional rights." Still later, however, in FITZPATRICK V. BITZER (1976) the Court held that Congress had power to override a state's immunity in legislating to enforce the Fourteenth Amendment, although it has never suggested that that amendment allowed Congress to ignore other constitutional limitations, such as the BILL OF RIGHTS.

The two remaining categories of disputes within federal judicial power are "controversies . . . between Citizens of different States" and between state citizens and "Citizens or Subjects" of "foreign States." Once again the reasons for federal jurisdiction are generally said to be the avoidance of state-court bias and of interstate or international friction. In contrast not only to the admiralty cases but also to those between states, federal jurisdiction based solely on the diverse citizenship of the parties does not carry with it authority to make substantive law. Absent a federal statute, the Court held in ERIE RAILROAD V. TOMPKINS (1938), "the law to be applied . . . is the law of the State." Later cases such as *Textile Workers Union v. Lincoln Mills* (1957) have qualified the effect though not the principle of this decision by finding in silent statutes implicit authorization to the federal courts to make law. An occasional decision has upheld FEDERAL COMMON LAW, without the pretense of statutory authority, on matters mysteriously found to be "intrinsically federal"; an example was the Court's refusal in *Banco Nacional de Cuba v. Sabbatino* (1964) to look behind official acts of foreign governments. (See ACT OF STATE DOCTRINE.)

In early decisions the Supreme Court took a narrow view of what constituted a controversy between citizens of different states for purposes of the statute implementing this provision of Article III. More recently, however, the Court has generously interpreted the power of Congress to confer DIVERSITY JURISDICTION on the federal courts. And as early as the mid-nineteenth century, recognizing that corporations can be the beneficiaries or victims of state court prejudice without regard to the citizenship of those who compose them, the Court effectively began to treat corporations as citizens by employing the transparent fiction of conclusively presuming that the individuals whose citizenship was determinative were citizens of the state of incorporation.

The best known decision involving the diversity jurisdiction was DRED SCOTT V. SANDFORD (1857), in which three Justices took the position that a black American descended from slaves could never be a state citizen for diversity purposes because he could not be a citizen of the United States. Questionable enough at the time, this conclusion was repudiated by the Fourteenth Amendment's provision that all persons born in this country are citizens of the United States "and of the state wherein they reside." Nevertheless the courts have held that only American citizens are "Citizens of . . . States" within Article III, and conversely that only foreign nationals are "Citizens or Subjects" of "foreign States."

"In all Cases involving Ambassadors, other public Ministers and Consuls, and those in which a state shall be Party," Article III, Section 2 provides, "the supreme Court shall have ORIGINAL JURISDICTION. In all the other Cases before mentioned, the supreme Court shall have APPELLATE JURISDICTION, both as to Law and Fact, with such Exceptions, and under such Regulations as the Congress shall make."

Original jurisdiction is the power to determine a dispute in the first instance; appellate jurisdiction, the power to review a decision already made. *Marbury v. Madison* (1803) held that Congress had no power to give the Supreme Court original jurisdiction of a case to which neither a diplomat nor a state was a party; a contrary result, Chief Justice Marshall argued, would make the constitutional distribution between original and appellate jurisdiction "mere surplusage." This reasoning is not especially convincing, and the converse is not true; in COHENS V. VIRGINIA in 1821 Marshall himself conceded that Congress could give the Court appellate jurisdiction over cases for which Article III provided original jurisdiction. *Cohens* also held that the Supreme Court had original authority not over all Article III cases in which a state happened to be a party but only over those "in which jurisdiction is given, because a state is a party," and thus not over a federal question case between a state and one of its own citizens. Inconsistently, however, the Court allowed the United States to sue a State in the Supreme Court in *United States v. Texas* (1892).

Marbury's implicit conclusion that the exceptions clause quoted above does not allow Congress to tamper with the original jurisdiction strongly suggests that the enumeration of original cases is a minimum as well as a maximum, and the Court has described as "extremely doubtful" the proposition that Congress may deprive it of original power over state or diplomat cases; yet the Court has concluded that it has discretion not to entertain cases within its original jurisdiction.

Unlike the original jurisdiction provision, that giving the Court appellate authority in "all the other" Article III cases contains an explicit escape valve: "with such Exceptions . . . as the Congress shall make." In *The Federalist* #81, Hamilton explained that this clause permitted Congress to limit review of facts decided by juries, but he did not say this was its sole objective. From the beginning Congress has denied the Court jurisdiction over entire classes of controversies within the constitutional reach of appellate power—such as federal criminal cases, most of which were excluded from appellate cognizance for many years even if constitutional issues were presented. The Court itself accepted this particular limitation as early as *United States v. More* (1805), without questioning its constitutionality. Moreover, when Congress repealed a statute under which a pending case attacking the Reconstruction Act had been filed, the Court in EX PARTE MCCARDLE (1869) meekly dismissed the case, observing that "the power to make exceptions to the appellate jurisdiction of this court is given by express words."

As the *McCardle* opinion noted, however, other avenues remained available for taking similar cases to the Supreme Court, and three years later the Court made clear in *United States v. Klein* (1872) that Congress could not under the guise of limiting jurisdiction effectively dictate the result of a case by directing dismissal if the Court should find for the plaintiff. Respected commentators have contended that the Supreme Court must retain appellate authority over certain constitutional questions, arguing that the exceptions clause cannot have been intended, in Henry Hart's words, to "destroy the essential role of the Supreme Court in the constitutional plan." The persuasiveness of this position depends on one's perceptions of the function of judicial review. (See JUDICIAL SYSTEM.)

In order for the Court in *Marbury v. Madison* to dismiss an action that it found Congress had authorized, it had first to conclude that it had the right to refuse to obey an unconstitutional act of Congress. Marshall's argument that this power was "essentially attached to a written constitution" is contradicted by much European experience; and his assertion that choosing between the Constitution and a statute was an inescapable aspect of deciding cases begged the question, for the Constitution might have required the courts to accept Congress's determination that a statute was valid. For the same reason one may object to his reliance on Article VI's requirement that judges swear to support the Constitution: one does not offend that oath by enforcing an unconstitutional statute if that is what the Constitution requires.

The SUPREMACY CLAUSE of Article VI is no better support; the contrasting reference to "Treaties made, or which shall be made" in the same clause strongly suggests that the phrase "laws . . . which shall be made in Pursuance of" the Constitution, also invoked by Marshall, was meant to deny supremacy to acts adopted under the Articles of Confederation, not to those that were invalid. Most promising of the provisions brought forward in *Marbury* was Article III's extension of judicial power to "Cases . . . arising under this Constitution"; as Marshall said, it could scarcely have been "the intention of those who gave this power, to say that in using it the constitution should not be looked into." Yet even here the case is not airtight. For while Article III provides for jurisdiction in constitutional cases, it is Article VI that prescribes the force to be given the Constitution; and while the latter article plainly gives the Constitution precedence over conflicting *state* laws, it appears to place *federal* statutes on a par with the Constitution itself.

Nevertheless the *Marbury* decision should be regarded as neither a surprise nor a usurpation. Though Marshall did not say so, judicial review had a substantial history before *Marbury*, and despite occasional scholarly denials it seems clear that most of the Framers expected that the courts would refuse to enforce unconstitutional acts of Congress. Moreover, there is force to Marshall's argument that a denial of this power would effectively undermine the express written limitations on congressional power; the natural reluctance to assume that the Framers meant to leave the fox in charge of the chickens lends credence to the conclusion that judicial review is implicit in the power to decide constitutional cases or in the substantive constitutional limitations themselves.

In fact the *Marbury* opinion espouses two distinct theories of judicial review that have opposite implications for a number of related issues, some of which have been discussed above. If, as Marshall at one point seemed to suggest, judicial review is only an incidental by-product of the need to resolve pending cases, it is no cause for constitutional concern if Congress eliminates the Supreme Court's jurisdiction over First Amendment cases, or if no one has standing to attack a federal spending program. If, on the other hand, as argued elsewhere in *Marbury*, judicial review is essential to a plan of constitutional checks and balances, one may take a more restrictive view of Congress's power to make exceptions to the appellate jurisdiction, and perhaps a broader view of what constitutes a case or controversy as well.

Dissenting from the assertion of judicial authority over legislative reapportionment cases in BAKER V. CARR (1962), Justice Felix Frankfurter argued for a broad exception to judicial review of both federal and state actions: even unconstitutional acts could not be set aside if they presented POLITICAL QUESTIONS. Some have attempted to trace this notion to *Marbury* itself, where the Court did say that "[q]uestions in their nature political" were beyond judicial ken. The context suggests, however, that Marshall meant only that the Court would respect actions taken by other branches of government within their legitimate authority, and Louis Henkin has shown that most later decisions using "political question" language can be so explained.

The Court itself, however, spoke in *Baker* of a general "political question" doctrine preventing decision of the merits when, among other things, there was "a lack of judicially discoverable and manageable standards for resolving" a "political" issue. A number of lower courts relied on such a doctrine in refusing to decide the legality of the VIETNAM WAR. While the doctrine as so conceived appears at cross-purposes with the checks-and-balances aspect of *Marbury*, nothing in that decision bars a finding that a particular constitutional provision either gives absolute discretion to a nonjudicial branch (such as the power to recognize foreign governments) or makes an exception to Article III's grant of the judicial power itself (as, arguably, in the case of impeachment).

In most respects, then, Article III amply satisfies Marshall's conditions for a "well constructed government." Though the governmental immunities associated with the Eleventh Amendment may seem anachronistic today, unsympathetic judicial interpretation has blunted their interference with the enforcement of federal law. Decisions since the 1950s have generally rejected Justice Frankfurter's broad conception of the political question. Thus with rare exceptions the federal judiciary, as Marshall insisted, may be given authority to construe every federal law; and the extension of judicial power to controversies between citizens of different states means that the federal courts may often be given power to apply state law as well. Though increased mobility has led to serious efforts to repeal the statutory basis for the diversity jurisdiction, it served an important function in the past and conceivably may become more important in the future. Moreover, the Framers were farsighted enough to assure federal judges the independence necessary to do their appointed job. The weakest point in the system is the arguable authority of Congress to take away all or a substantial part of the Supreme Court's appellate power in constitutional cases; for such an authority undermines other elements of the system of checks and balances that the Framers so carefully constructed.

DAVID P. CURRIE

Bibliography

BICKEL, ALEXANDER 1962 *The Least Dangerous Branch.* Pages 111–199. Indianapolis: Bobbs-Merrill.

BORCHARD, EDWIN 1928 *Hearings on H.R. 5623 before the Subcommittee of the Senate Committee on the Judiciary.* 70th Cong., 1st Sess., pp. 75–76.

FARRAND, MAX (ED.) 1911 *Records of the Federal Convention of 1787.* Vol. 1, pp. 119–129. New Haven, Conn.: Yale University Press.

HART, HENRY and WECHSLER, HERBERT 1973 *The Federal Courts and the Federal System.* Pages 309–418, 833–1103. Mineola, N.Y.: Foundation Press.

HENKIN, LOUIS 1976 Is There a "Political Question" Doctrine? *Yale Law Journal* 85:597–625.

JUDICIAL RESTRAINT

See: Judicial Activism and Restraint

JUDICIAL REVIEW

Judicial review, in its most widely accepted meaning, is the power of courts to consider the constitutionality of acts of other organs of government when the issue of constitutionality is germane to the disposition of lawsuits properly pending before the courts. This power to consider constitutionality in appropriate cases includes the courts' authority to refuse to enforce, and in effect invalidate, governmental acts they find to be unconstitutional.

Judicial review is America's most distinctive contribution to CONSTITUTIONALISM. Although courts have exercised judicial review almost from the beginning of American constitutional government, the question of the legitimacy of that JUDICIAL POWER has often provoked controversy as well as recurrent charges that American judges usurped the authority. Nearly two centuries of exercises of and popular acquiescence in the power have quieted the storms over its basic justifiability in recent decades, but vehement controversy continues regarding the proper scope and authority of judicial rulings on constitutionality. Moreover, particular exercises of judicial review continue to stir passionate political debates, as they have from the beginning.

The classic justification for judicial review was set forth by Chief Justice JOHN MARSHALL in MARBURY V. MADISON (1803). Marshall relied on general principles and constitutional text. His arguments from principle are not compelling. For example, his unchallengeable assertion that the Constitution was designed to establish a limited government does not demonstrate that *courts* should enforce those limitations. Constitutions prescribing limits on government had been adopted before 1803, as many have been since; but relatively few look to the judiciary for enforcement. Similarly, the fact that judges take an oath to support the Constitution does not imply judicial review, for the Constitution requires the oath of all federal and state officers. Far more persuasive are Marshall's references to two passages of the constitutional text. First, Article III lists cases "arising under the Constitution" as one of the subjects included within the JUDICIAL POWER OF THE UNITED STATES, suggesting that constitutional questions can give rise to judicial rulings. Second, the SUPREMACY CLAUSE of Article VI lists the Constitution first as among the legal sources that "shall be the supreme Law of the Land."

Although the inferences derivable from the constitutional text are not unchallengeable, they provide the strongest available support for Marshall's justification for judicial review. True, Article VI is specifically addressed only to state judges, for the "supreme Law of the Land" clause is followed by the statement that "Judges in every State shall be bound thereby, any Thing in the Constitution or Laws of any State to the Contrary notwithstanding." Still, the CONSTITUTIONAL CONVENTION debates and federal LEGISLATION, ever since Section 25 of the JUDICIARY ACT OF 1789, have contemplated Supreme Court review of state court rulings on constitutional questions, and it is surely plausible to argue that the Supreme Court's authority on review would be no less than that of state judges obeying the command of the supremacy clause.

Federal court review of state court judgments is an especially plausible aspect of judicial review, for it is a typical policing technique to maintain the delineations of governing authority in federal systems. That strand of judicial review is common in other federal schemes as well, as in Switzerland and Australia. Yet even federal systems are conceivable without judicial review. Thus, nationalists at the Constitutional Convention initially urged reliance on the congressional veto and on military force to curb excesses by the states. The supremacy clause, and its reliance on routine judicial power to enforce federalistic restraints, stemmed from suggestions by states' rights forces at the convention.

Judicial review in the interest of FEDERALISM has played an important role in the United States; some observers, indeed, view it as the most essential function of judicial review. As Justice OLIVER WENDELL HOLMES once put it: "I do not think the United States would come to an end if we lost our power to declare an Act of Congress void. I do think the Union would be imperiled if we could not make that declaration as to the laws of the several States." The supremacy clause goes a long way toward assuring this protection of the Union; but it provides less compelling justification for judicial review of congressional acts.

The constitutional text cited by John Marshall supports judicial review in all its aspects in a more basic sense. Article III and Article VI both reflect the premise central to judicial review—the premise that the Constitution is to be considered a species of law and accordingly cognizable in courts of law. Judicial review is essentially the judicial enforceability of constitutional norms, and viewing the Constitution as law rather than mere policy or precatory adjuration is the keystone of the more persuasive argument that the American constitutional scheme was designed to rely on judges, not merely troops or political restraints, to enforce constitutional limits.

This view of the Constitution as law—the view central to the argument for giving courts a major role in constitutional enforcement—made it relevant for Marshall to state that it was "emphatically the province and duty of the judicial department to say what the law is," and to describe judicial review as an outgrowth of the normal task of judges: to adjudicate the cases before them on the basis of all relevant rules of law, rules that include those stemming from the Constitution. And that in turn made it plausible for him to say that, where a statute and the Constitution conflict, the courts must enforce the superior Constitution and "disregard" the statute. That, to Marshall, was "of the very essence of judicial duty."

Even if Marshall's views of the Constitution as law and of the "judicial duty" were unanswerable, charges of usurpation would not be stilled. Whatever the strength of the inferences from Articles III and VI, it is undeniable that the power of judicial review is not explicitly granted by the Constitution—in contrast to the constitutions of the nations that, in modern times, have embraced systems similar to the American scheme of judicial review, such as West Germany, Italy, India, and Japan. Defenders of judicial review have accordingly sought to find added support for Marshall's conclusion in historical understandings and practices. None of the sources relied on, however, conveys overwhelming force.

For example, it is true that Marshall's argument was to a considerable extent anticipated by ALEXANDER HAMILTON in THE FEDERALIST #78; but Hamilton's essay was after all only a propagandistic defense of the Constitution during the ratification debates. Similarly, the arguments from historical practice are inconclusive at best. The much invoked statement by EDWARD COKE in BONHAM'S CASE (1610)—that "the COMMON LAW will controul Acts of Parliament, [and] adjudge them to be utterly void" when they are "against common right and reason"—was inconsistent with British practice at the time and thus is not even respectable OBITER DICTUM. More relevant was the APPELLATE JURISDICTION of the PRIVY COUNCIL over colonial courts; but invalidation of legislation through that route was rare and unpopular. And the much debated alleged PRECEDENTS in the practice of state courts during the years immediately following independence hardly establish a well-entrenched practice of judicial review in the era of the ARTICLES OF CONFEDERATION. The preconstitutional examples that withstand scrutiny are few and controversial, and in any event it is not clear that many delegates at the Constitutional Convention knew about the scattered actual or alleged instances of invalidation of state laws by state judges.

Nor do the statements in the Constitutional Convention and the state ratification debates provide ironclad proof that judicial review was intended by the Framers. While it is true that most of the statements addressing the issue supported such a judicial power, it is equally true that only a minority of speakers at the Constitution framing and ratifying conventions expressed their views. The most important statements at the Constitutional Convention came during the discussion of the council of revision proposal—a proposal that the Justices join with the President in exercising the VETO POWER. That proposal was rejected, partly on grounds supporting the legitimacy of judicial review. Thus, LUTHER MARTIN, in criticizing "the association of the Judges with the Executive" as a "dangerous innovation," argued that, "as to the Constitutionality of laws, that point will come before the Judges in their proper official character. In this character they have a negative on the laws. Join them with the Executive in the Revision and they will have a double negative."

Some scholars have argued, questionably, that judicial review was so normal a judicial function that it was taken for granted by the Framers. HENRY M. HART and Herbert Wechsler claimed to find clear support in the Convention debates: "The grant of judicial power was to include the power, where necessary in the decision of cases, to disregard state or federal statutes found to be unconstitutional. Despite the curiously persisting myth of usurpation, the Convention's understanding on this point emerges from its records with singular clarity." But with regard to original intent, EDWARD S. CORWIN's Senate testimony on the 1937 Court-packing plan still represents a fair summary of the state of the record. Corwin stated that the "people who say the framers intended [judicial review] are talking nonsense," but he added that "people who say they did not intend it are talking nonsense." As Leonard W. Levy commented after noting Corwin's assessment that there is "great uncertainty" on the issue: "A close textual and contextual examination of the evidence will not result in an improvement on these propositions."

Most important in the search for preconstitutional bases for judicial review authority is probably the late-eighteenth-century prevalence of general ideas conducive to the acceptance of the power asserted in *Marbury v. Madison.* The belief in written CONSTITUTIONS to assure LIMITED GOVERNMENT was hardly an American invention, but Americans had an unusually extensive experience with basic, HIGHER LAW documents of government, from royal charters to state constitutions and the Articles of Confederation. Yet it is possible to have constitutions without judicial review: to say that a government cannot exceed constitutional limits does not demonstrate who is to decide. It bears reiterating, then, that viewing a constitution as a species of "law" was the vital link between constitutionalism and judicial competence to decide constitutional issues. Moreover, the view that the Constitution was an act of the people rather than of the state governments helped provide an ideology congenial to Marshall's insistence that the courts could, in the name of the people, refuse to enforce the acts of the people's representatives.

Accepting the persuasiveness of Marshall's core argument is not tantamount to endorsing all of the alleged implications of judicial review that are pervasive in the late twentieth century. Marshall's stated view of the role of courts in constitutional cases was a relatively modest one; after nearly two centuries of exercise of judicial review by courts, and especially the Supreme Court, the scope and binding effect of judicial rulings are far broader. Most of Marshall's argument was largely defensive, designed to undergird judicial competence and authority to adjudicate issues of constitutionality. He insisted that the Constitution is "a rule for the government of *courts* as well as the legislature" and concluded that "*courts,* as well as other departments, are bound by that instrument." Modern perceptions, by contrast, often view the courts as playing a superior or supreme role in CONSTITUTIONAL INTERPRETATION. Claims of JUDICIAL SUPREMACY and sometimes even exclusiveness are widespread in scholarly statements and popular understandings. The extent to which such impressions are justifiable continues to give rise to sharp controversy.

Marshall's claims about judicial competence and authority were closely tied to a tripartite theory of government reflecting the SEPARATION OF POWERS. He did not deny that other branches, including the

President in the exercise of the veto power and Congress in enacting legislation, could and—under the oath to support the Constitution emphasized in *Marbury* itself—presumably must consider issues of constitutionality. Marshall's argument that courts *also* have competence to take the Constitution into account in their work was essentially a "me too" position. Modern variants on justifications for judicial review—and a number of statements from the modern Supreme Court itself—lend stronger support than anything in Marshall's reasoning to a "me superior" or even a "me only" view.

Nearly from the beginning, Presidents have taken issue with Supreme Court rulings. THOMAS JEFFERSON insisted that "nothing in the Constitution has given [the judges] a right to decide for the Executive, more than to the Executive to decide for them." And he argued that considering "the judges as the ultimate arbiters of all constitutional questions" was "a very dangerous doctrine indeed, and one which would place us under the despotism of an oligarchy." Similarly, ANDREW JACKSON insisted, in vetoing the bill to recharter the Bank of the United States in 1832, that MCCULLOCH V. MARYLAND (1819) did not preclude his action: "Mere precedent is a dangerous source of authority, and should not be regarded as deciding questions of constitutional power except where the acquiescence of the people and the States can be considered as well settled." Similar statements are found in the utterances of later Presidents, from ABRAHAM LINCOLN to FRANKLIN D. ROOSEVELT and beyond.

John Marshall was no doubt unhappy with the political statements of Jeffersonians and Jacksonians. Clearly, he would have preferred ready acceptance of his Court's glosses on the Constitution by all governmental officials and the entire nation. But nothing in the stances of the leaders of his day or since was in sharp conflict with anything in *Marbury v. Madison.* Jefferson, Jackson, and their successors did not deny the binding effect of the judges' constitutional rulings in the cases before them. But the Presidents insisted on their right to disagree with the principles underlying the Court decision. As Lincoln said in the course of his debates with STEPHEN A. DOUGLAS, he did not propose that after Dred Scott had been held to be a slave by the Court—in DRED SCOTT V. SANDFORD (1857)—"we, as a mob, will decide him to be free." But, he added, "we nevertheless do oppose that decision as a political rule which shall be binding on the voter, to vote for nobody who thinks it wrong, which shall be binding on the members of Congress or the President to favor no measure that does not actually concur with the principles of that decision. [We] propose so resisting it as to have it reversed if we can, and a new judicial rule established upon this subject."

Does it follow that, if such presidential statements are consistent with *Marbury v. Madison,* the scheme sketched by Marshall in 1803 contemplated never-ending chaos—a state of chaos in which the political branches of the national government, and the states as well, might forever disagree with the principles of Supreme Court decisions, in which the only way to implement the Court's principles would be to bring the resisting parties to court in multiple lawsuits, in which no constitutional question would ever be settled? Not necessarily, and certainly not in American experience. Judicial review has not meant that the Supreme Court's reasoning ends all constitutional debate, but neither has it meant endless litigation and dispute over every constitutional issue. Yet the reasons for the growing role of the Supreme Court in settling constitutional issues rest less on any legal principle underlying judicial review than on considerations stemming from institutional arrangements and from prudence. The only arguable basis in *Marbury* itself for viewing the courts as the ultimate arbiters of constitutional issues is Marshall's ambiguous statement that it is "emphatically the province and duty of the judicial department to say what the law is." That statement establishes judicial competence, as noted; but its ambiguity also may provide the basis for arguments for a special judicial expertise in constitutional matters and for a de facto judicial supremacy. Marshall's statement is not so strong, however, as a similar one from Hamilton, in *The Federalist* #78: "The interpretation of laws is the proper and peculiar province of the courts."

The widely observable phenomenon that a Court interpretation of the Constitution has significance beyond the parties to a particular lawsuit rests on other, stronger bases. A central one is that, to the extent a disputed constitutional issue arises in a lawsuit, and to the extent that the Supreme Court is the highest court in the judicial hierarchy, a Supreme Court interpretation is final. Technically, it is final only with respect to the parties in the case, to be sure; but the Court gives general reasons in resolving specific controversies, and the Justices normally operate under a system of PRECEDENT and STARE DECISIS. Similarly situated parties not before the Court in the particular case ordinarily recognize that, other things being equal, the Court will adhere to precedent, will apply the same rule to them if litigation ensues, and accordingly choose not to engage in needless litigation.

Basically, then, the reason that the courts generally

and the Supreme Court in particular wield such vast influence in Americans' understanding of their Constitution is that most constitutional issues can and do arise in lawsuits; and once they do, the courts, with the Supreme Court at the apex, do have the final say. As a result, most potential opponents of Court rulings follow the course implied in Lincoln's First Inaugural Address. Lincoln did not deny that Supreme Court decisions "must be binding in any case upon the parties to a suit as to the object of that suit" and "are also entitled to very high respect and consideration in all parallel cases by all other departments of the Government." He added: "And while it is obviously possible that such decision may be erroneous in any given case, still the evil effect following it, being limited to that particular case, with a chance that it may be overruled or never become a precedent for other cases, can better be borne than could the evil of a different practice." From that position, Herbert Wechsler's rhetorical question plausibly follows: When the chance that a judicial ruling "may be overruled and never become a precedent for other cases . . . has been exploited and has run its course, with reaffirmation rather than REVERSAL of decision, has not the time arrived when its acceptance is demanded, without insisting on repeated litigation? The answer here, it seems to me, must be affirmative, both as to a necessary implication of our constitutional tradition and to avoid the greater evils that will otherwise ensue." Wechsler's admonition, it should be noted, is one of prudence, not of any necessary legal mandate stemming from the *Marbury* rationale.

Beginning in the late twentieth century, however, the Supreme Court has repeatedly claimed a greater import for its exercises of judicial review than anything clearly set forth in *Marbury.* A major example came in one of the cases stemming from the school DESEGREGATION controversy, COOPER V. AARON (1958). The opinion in that case, signed by each of the Justices, provides the strongest judicial support for a view widely held by the public—that the Court is the ultimate, the supreme interpreter of the Constitution. Rejecting the premise of the actions of the legislature and of the governor of Arkansas in that case—that they were not bound by the ruling in BROWN V. BOARD OF EDUCATION (1954)—the Court purported to "recall some basic constitutional propositions which are settled doctrine." The Justices quoted Article VI and Marshall's "province and duty of the judicial department" passage in *Marbury* and added: "This decision declared the basic principle that the federal judiciary is supreme in the exposition of the law of the Constitution. [It] follows that the interpretation of the Fourteenth Amendment enunciated by this Court in the *Brown* case is the supreme law of the land, and Article VI of the Constitution makes it of binding effect on the States. [Every] state legislator and executive and judicial officer is solemnly committed by oath taken pursuant to Article VI, 3, 'to support this Constitution.' "

Similar statements have surfaced in other controversial cases in recent years, especially in BAKER V. CARR (1962) (referring to the "responsibility of this Court as ultimate interpreter of the Constitution") and POWELL V. MCCORMACK (1969) ("[It] is the responsibility of this Court to act as the ultimate interpreter of the Constitution. *Marbury v. Madison.*"). The Court in these cases was no doubt marshaling all possible rhetorical force in efforts to ward off actual or potential resistance from the states or from other branches of the federal government; but these broad modern assertions no doubt also reflect widespread popular understandings of the "ultimate" role of the Court, understandings bolstered by the nation's general acceptance of that role, despite frequent and continuing disagreements with particular decisions.

From the relatively modest assertions of the judicial review power in *Marbury v. Madison,* nearly two centuries of history have brought the Court increasingly close to the self-announced dominant role in constitutional interpretation it set forth in *Cooper v. Aaron.* That does not mean that Supreme Court interpretations are entitled to immunity from criticism, popular or academic. Nor does it signify the end of all political restraints on the Court, restraints stemming from the same Constitution that Marshall relied on in defending judicial review. Judges may be subjected to congressional IMPEACHMENT and Congress may arguably curtail the federal courts' JURISDICTION in constitutional cases. (See JUDICIAL SYSTEM.) But both weapons, though frequently brandished, have rarely been used. Moreover, the constitutional AMENDING PROCESS, albeit difficult to invoke, is available to overturn unpopular Court rulings. More significant, the composition of the Court as well as its size rest with the political branches, and the President's nominating role, together with the Senate's in confirmation, have been major safeguards against judges deviating too far from the national consensus. Despite these potential and actual checks, however, the Supreme Court's role in American government has outgrown both the view that it is the weakest branch and Marshall's own delineation of the judicial review power. What ALEXIS DE TOCQUEVILLE recognized over a century and a half ago has become ever more true since he wrote: "Scarcely any question arises in the United States which does not become, sooner or later, a subject of judicial debate."

Even though historical exercises of judicial review and popular acquiescence have largely stilled the outcries that the federal courts usurped the power to consider the constitutionality of legislation, the core arguments on behalf of the legitimacy of judicial review, summarized by Marshall in *Marbury v. Madison,* continue to generate controversial implications. Two especially important and recurrent modern debates involve arguments reaching back all the way to *Marbury.* The first issue is whether courts should strain to avoid decisions on controversial constitutional issues by invoking such devices as the POLITICAL QUESTION doctrine. The second issue concerns the proper sources of constitutional adjudication: Must courts limit themselves to "interpretation" of the Constitution, or are "noninterpretive" decisions also legitimate?

Courts confident about the legitimacy of judicial review may tend to exercise that power assertively; judges in doubt about the underpinnings of that authority may shrink from exercising the power to invalidate legislative acts and may indeed seek to escape altogether from rulings on the merits in constitutional cases. The connection between views of legitimacy and modern exercises (or nonexercises) of judicial review is illustrated by an exchange between LEARNED HAND and Herbert Wechsler. Hand insisted that there was "nothing in the United States Constitution that gave courts any authority to review the decisions of Congress" and that the text "gave no ground for inferring that the decisions of the Supreme Court [were] to be authoritative upon the Executive and the Legislature." He found the sole justification for judicial review in the practical need "to prevent the defeat of the venture at hand"—to keep constitutional government from foundering. Wechsler retorted: "I believe the power of the courts is grounded in the language of the Constitution and is not a mere interpolation."

These contending positions have contrasting implications. Thus, Hand concluded that "since this power is not a logical deduction from the structure of the Constitution but only a practical condition upon its successful operation, it need not be exercised whenever a court sees, or thinks it sees, an invasion of the Constitution. It is always a preliminary question how importunately the occasion demands an answer." Wechsler countered that there was no such broad discretion to decline constitutional adjudication in a case properly before a court: "For me, as for anyone who finds the judicial power anchored in the Constitution, there is no such escape from the judicial obligation; the duty cannot be attenuated in this way." (That "duty," he cautioned, was "not that of policing or advising legislatures or executives," but rather simply "to decide the litigated case [in] accordance with the law.")

It is true that courts do often abstain from deciding constitutional questions pressed upon them. There is no question about the legitimacy of that phenomenon to the extent that courts rely on nonconstitutional, narrower grounds of decision in disposing of a case. Nor is there any doubt that courts need not—and under the *Marbury* rationale may not—decide constitutional issues if they are not properly presented in a case because, for example, the litigation does not square with the CASE AND CONTROVERSY requirement of Article III. But twentieth-century courts have occasionally gone beyond such justifiable ABSTENTIONS to claim a more general and more questionable authority to resort to considerations of prudence in refusing to issue rulings on the merits even though a case falls within the contours of Article III and even though congressional statutes appear to confer obligatory jurisdiction on the courts.

Some commentators have defended judicial resort to the "passive virtues"; others have attacked such refusals to adjudicate as often unprincipled and illegitimate. The controversy about the political question doctrine is illustrative. To the extent that the doctrine rests on constitutional interpretation, as it does under its strand regarding what the Court in *Baker v. Carr* (1962) called "a textually demonstrable constitutional commitment of the issue to a coordinate political department," it is undoubtedly legitimate. But the courts have often gone beyond that concern to refuse adjudication on the ground of a lack of judicially "manageable standards" and on the basis of even broader, wholly prudential considerations as well. Wechsler argued that, in political question cases, "the only proper judgment that may lead to an abstention from decision is that the Constitution has committed the determination of the issues to another agency of government than the courts. [What] is involved is in itself an act of constitutional interpretation, to be made and judged by standards that should govern the interpretive process generally. That, I submit, is *toto caelo* [by all heaven] different from a broad discretion to abstain or intervene." ALEXANDER M. BICKEL strongly disagreed, insisting that "only by means of a play on words can the broad discretion that the courts have in fact exercised be turned into an act of constitutional interpretation." He saw the political question doctrine as something different from the interpretive process—"something greatly more flexible, something of prudence, not construction and not principle."

To the extent that the Supreme Court rests largely on discretionary, prudential concerns in refusing to adjudicate—as, for example, it appears to have done in holding federalistic restraints on congressional power largely nonjusticiable in GARCIA V. SAN ANTONIO METROPOLITAN TRANSIT AUTHORITY (1985)—it raises questions of legitimacy under *Marbury v. Madison.* Courts deriving their authority from a premise that the Constitution is law, as the *Marbury* argument does, are not authorized to resort to discretionary abstention devices not justified by law. As Marshall himself pointed out in COHENS V. VIRGINIA (1821): "We have no more right to decline the exercise of jurisdiction which is given, than to usurp that which is not given." But discretionary devices of self-limitation have become commonplace in judicial behavior, as a result of glosses articulated by modern judges rather than because of anything in the Constitution itself or in Marshall's reasoning. (See COMITY.)

There is a second modern issue, especially pervasive and controversial, in which the rationale of *Marbury v. Madison* affects debates about judicial review: Are the courts bound to limit themselves to "interpretations" of the Constitution in exercising judicial review? Marshall's reasoning in *Marbury* suggests that "noninterpretive" rulings are illegitimate. A justification that derives judicial review from the existence of a written constitution and from the premise that the Constitution is a species of law implies that the courts are confined by the Constitution in delineating constitutional norms. And courts indeed almost invariably purport to rest their constitutional rulings on "interpretations" of the basic document.

But modern academic commentary is sharply divided on this issue. Most scholars who insist on "interpretation" as the sole legitimate ingredient of constitutional rulings do not argue for a narrow, strict interpretation based solely on a literal reading of the constitutional text or a specific basis in the Framers' intent. But their "broad interpretivist" position does insist that constitutional rulings must rest on a clear nexus to—and plausible inference from—the Constitution's text, history, or structure. The "noninterpretivist" critics of that position emphasize the many opaque and open-ended phrases in the Constitution and the changing interpretations of these phrases over the years. They claim that the Court's behavior cannot be squared with even a broad interpretivist position and argue that the Court has always relied on extraconstitutional norms. These critics insist that "noninterpretivist" decision making is justified not only by the history of the Court's elaborations of such vague yet pervasive concepts as SUBSTANTIVE DUE PROCESS but also by the appropriate role of courts in American constitutional democracy. The noninterpretivist literature accordingly abounds with suggestions of sources courts might rely on in the search for fundamental, judicially enforceable values—sources that range from moral philosophy to contemporary political consensus and analogies to literary and scriptural analyses.

The interpretivist arguments that draw in part on Marshall's justification for judicial review have difficulty explaining the Court's performance in "reinterpreting" the Constitution in light of changing societal contexts. The noninterpretivist position has difficulty squaring its arguments with the *Marbury* view of the Constitution as a species of law. That position has difficulty as well in articulating limits on the legitimate ingredients of constitutional decision making that safeguard adequately against excessive judicial subjectivism—against the specter reflected in Learned Hand's fear of being "ruled by a bevy of Platonic Guardians." Whether constitutional decision making by judges can continue to contribute to the flexibility and durability of the Constitution without deteriorating into merely politicized and personalized rulings that risk subverting the legitimacy of constitutional government is the central and unresolved challenge confronting modern judicial review.

GERALD GUNTHER

Bibliography

BICKEL, ALEXANDER M. 1962 *The Least Dangerous Branch: The Supreme Court at the Bar of Politics.* Indianapolis: Bobbs-Merrill.

ELY, JOHN H. 1980 *Democracy and Distrust: A Theory of Judicial Review.* Cambridge, Mass.: Harvard University Press.

GREY, THOMAS 1975 Do We Have an Unwritten Constitution? *Stanford Law Review* 27:703–718.

GUNTHER, GERALD 1964 The Subtle Vices of the "Passive Virtues": A Comment on Principle and Expediency in Judicial Review. *Columbia Law Review* 64:1–25.

HAND, LEARNED 1958 *The Bill of Rights.* Cambridge, Mass.: Harvard University Press.

HART, HENRY M., JR. and WECHSLER, HERbert 1973 Pages 1–241 in Paul Bator, Paul Mishkin, David Shapiro, and Herbert Wechsler, eds., *The Federal Courts and the Federal System,* 2nd ed. Mineola, N.Y.: Foundation Press.

LEVY, LEONARD W. 1967 Judicial Review, History, and Democracy: An Introduction. Pages 1–42 in Leonard W. Levy, ed., *Judicial Review and the Supreme Court: Selected Essays.* New York: Harper & Row.

MCCLOSKEY, ROBERT G. 1960 *The American Supreme Court.* Chicago: University of Chicago Press.

McLaughlin, Andrew C. 1935 *A Constitutional History of the United States.* New York: Appleton-Century-Crofts.

Perry, Michael J. 1982 *The Constitution, the Courts, and Human Rights: An Inquiry into the Legitimacy of Constitutional Policymaking by the Judiciary.* New Haven, Conn.: Yale University Press.

Wechsler, Herbert 1961 *Principles, Politics, and Fundamental Law.* Cambridge, Mass.: Harvard University Press.

——— 1965 The Courts and the Constitution. *Columbia Law Review* 65:1001–1014.

JUDICIAL REVIEW AND DEMOCRACY

The American ideal of democracy lives in constant tension with the American ideal of JUDICIAL REVIEW in the service of individual liberties. It is a tension that sometimes erupts in crisis. THOMAS JEFFERSON planned a campaign of IMPEACHMENTS to rid the bench, and particularly the Supreme Court, of Federalist judges. The campaign collapsed when the impeachment of Associate Justice SAMUEL CHASE failed in the Senate. FRANKLIN D. ROOSEVELT, frustrated by a Court majority that repeatedly struck down New Deal economic measures, tried to "pack" the Court with additional Justices. That effort was defeated in Congress, though the attempt may have persuaded some Justices to alter their behavior. In recent years there have been movements in Congress to deprive federal courts of JURISDICTION over cases involving such matters as abortion, SCHOOL BUSING, and school prayer (see RELIGION IN PUBLIC SCHOOLS)—topics on which the Court's decisions have angered strong and articulate constituencies.

The problem is the resolution of what Robert Dahl called the Madisonian dilemma. The United States was founded as a Madisonian system, one that allows majorities to govern wide and important areas of life simply because they are majorities, but that also holds that individuals have some freedoms that must be exempt from majority control. The dilemma is that neither the majority nor the minority can be trusted to define the proper spheres of democratic authority and individual liberty.

It is not at all clear that the Founders envisaged a leading role for the judiciary in the resolution of this dilemma, for they thought of the third branch as relatively insignificant. Over time, however, Americans have come to assume that the definition of majority power and minority freedom is primarily the function of the judiciary, most particularly the function of the Supreme Court. This assumption places a great responsibility upon constitutional theory. America's basic method of policymaking is majoritarian. Thus, to justify exercise of a power to set at naught the considered decisions of elected representatives, judges must achieve, in ALEXANDER BICKEL's phrase, "a rigorous general accord between JUDICIAL SUPREMACY and democratic theory, so that the boundaries of the one could be described with some precision in terms of the other." At one time, an accord was based on the understanding that judges followed the intentions of the Framers and ratifiers of the Constitution, a legal document enacted by majorities, though subject to alteration only by supermajorities. A conflict between democracy and judicial review did not arise because the respective areas of each were specified and intended to be inviolate. Though this obedience to original intent was occasionally more pretense than reality, the accord was achieved in theory, and that theory stated an ideal to which courts were expected to conform. That is no longer so. Many judges and scholars now believe that the courts' obligations to intent are so highly generalized and remote that judges are in fact free to create the Constitution they think appropriate to today's society. The result is that the accord no longer stands even theoretically. The increasing perception that this is so raises the question of what elected officials can do to reclaim authority they regard as wrongfully taken by the judiciary.

There appear to be two possible responses to a judiciary that has overstepped the limits of its legitimate authority. One is political, the other intellectual. It seems tolerably clear that political responses are of limited usefulness, at least in the short run. Impeachment and Court-packing, having failed in the past, are unlikely to be resorted to again. Amending the Constitution to correct judicial overreaching is such a difficult and laborious process (requiring either two-thirds of both houses of Congress or an application for a convention by the legislatures of two-thirds of the states, followed, in either case, by ratification by three-fourths of the states) that it is of little practical assistance. It is sometimes proposed that Congress deal with the problem by removing federal court jurisdiction, using the exceptions clause of Article III of the Constitution in the case of the Supreme Court. The constitutionality of this approach has been much debated, but, in any case, it will often prove not feasible. Removal of all federal court jurisdiction would not return final power either to Congress or to state legislatures but to fifty state court systems. Thus, as a practical matter, this device could not be used as to any subject where national uniformity of constitutional law is necessary or highly desirable. Moreover, jurisdiction removal does not vindicate democratic governance, for it merely shifts ultimate power to different groups of judges. Democratic responses to judicial excesses probably must come through the replacement of judges who die or retire with new judges of different views. But this is a slow and uncertain process, the accidents of mortality being what they are and prediction of what new judges will do being so perilous.

The fact is that there exist few, if any, usable and effective techniques by which federal courts can be kept within constitutional bounds. A Constitution that provides numerous CHECKS AND BALANCES between President and Congress provides little to curb a judiciary that expands its powers beyond the allowable meaning of the Constitution. Perhaps one reason is that the Framers, though many of them foresaw that the Supreme Court would review laws for constitutionality, had little experience with such a function. They did not remotely foresee what the power of judicial review was capable of becoming. Nor is it clear that an institutional check—such as Senator ROBERT LA FOLLETTE's proposal to amend the Constitution so that Congress could override a Supreme Court decision by a two-thirds majority—would be desirable. Congress is less likely than the Court to be versed in the Constitution. La Follette's proposal could conceivably wreak as much or more damage to the Court's legitimate powers as it might accomplish in restraining its excesses. That must be reckoned at least a possibility with any of the institutional checks just discussed and is probably one of the reasons that they have rarely been used. In this sense, the Court's vulnerability is one of its most important protections.

If a political check on federal courts is unlikely to succeed, the only rein left is intellectual, the widespread acceptance of a theory of judicial review. After almost two centuries of constitutional adjudication, we appear to be further than ever from the possession of an adequate theory.

In the beginning, there was no controversy over theory. JOSEPH STORY, who was both an Associate Justice of the Supreme Court and the Dane Professor of Law at Harvard, could write in his *Commentaries on the Constitution of the United States,* published in 1833, that "I have not the ambition to be the author of any new plan of interpreting the theory of the Constitution, or of enlarging or narrowing its powers by ingenious subtleties and learned doubts." He thought that the job of constitutional judges was to interpret: "The first and fundamental rule in the interpretation of all instruments is, to construe them according to the sense of the terms and the intention of the parties."

The performance of the courts has not always conformed to this interpretivist ideal. In the last decade or so of the nineteenth century and the first third of the twentieth the Supreme Court assiduously protected economic liberties from federal and state regulation, often in ways that could not be reconciled with the Constitution. The case that stands as the symbol of that era of judicial adventurism is LOCHNER V. NEW YORK (1905), which struck down the state's law regulating maximum hours for bakers. That era ended when Franklin D. Roosevelt's appointments remade the Court, and *Lochner* is now generally regarded as discredited.

But, if the Court stopped defending economic liberties without constitutional justification in the mid-1930s, it began in the mid-1950s to make other decisions for which it offered little or no constitutional argument. It had been generally assumed that constitutional questions were to be answered on grounds of historical intent, but the Court began to make decisions that could hardly be, and were not, justified on that basis. Existing constitutional protections were expanded and new ones created. Sizable minorities on the Court indicated a willingness to go still further. The widespread perception that the judiciary was recreating the Constitution brought the tension between democracy and judicial review once more to a state of intellectual and political crisis.

Much of the new judicial power claimed cannot be derived from the text, structure, or history of the Constitution. Perhaps because of the increasing obviousness of this fact, legal scholars began to erect new theories of the judicial role. These constructs, which appear to be accepted by a majority of those who write about constitutional theory, go by the general name of noninterpretivism. They hold that mere interpretation of the Constitution may be impossible and is certainly inadequate. Judges are assigned not the task of defining the meanings and contours of values found in the historical Constitution but rather the function of creating new values and hence new rights for individuals against majorities. These new values are variously described as arising from "the evolving morality of our tradition," our "conventional morality" as discerned by "the method of philosophy," a "fusion of constitutional law and moral theory," or a HIGHER LAW of "unwritten NATURAL RIGHTS." One author has argued that, since "no defensible criteria" exist "to assess theories of judicial review," the judge should enforce his conception of the good. In all cases, these theories purport to empower judges to override majority will for extraconstitutional reasons.

Judges have articulated theories of their role no less removed from interpretation than those of the noninterpretivist academics. Writing for the Court in GRISWOLD V. CONNECTICUT (1965), Justice WILLIAM O. DOUGLAS created a constitutional RIGHT OF PRIVACY that invalidated the state's law against the use of contraceptives. He observed that many provisions of the BILL OF RIGHTS could be viewed as protections of aspects of personal privacy. These provisions were said to add up to a zone of constitutionally secured privacy that did not fall within any particular provision. The scope of this new right was not defined, but the Court has used the concept in a series of cases since, the most controversial being ROE V. WADE (1973). (See JUDICIAL ACTIVISM AND SELF-RESTRAINT.)

A similar strategy for the creation of new rights was outlined by Justice WILLIAM J. BRENNAN in a 1985 address. He characterized the Constitution as being pervasively concerned with human dignity. From this, Justice Brennan drew a more general judicial function of enhancing human dignity, one not confined by the clauses in question and, indeed, capable of nullifying what those clauses reveal of the Framers' intentions. Thus, the address states that continued judicial tolerance of CAPITAL PUNISHMENT causes us to "fall short of the constitutional vision of human dignity." For that reason, Justice Brennan continues to vote that capital punishment violates the Constitution. The potency of this method of generalizing from particular clauses, and then applying the generalization instead of the clauses, may be seen in the fact that it leads to a declaration of the unconstitutionality of a punishment explicitly assumed to be available three times in the Fifth Amendment to the Constitution and once again, some seventy-seven years later, in the FOURTEENTH AMENDMENT. By conventional methods of interpretation, it would be impossible to use the Constitution to prohibits that which the Constitution explicitly assumes to be lawful.

Because noninterpretive philosophies have little hard intellectual structure, it is impossible to control them or to predict from any inner logic or principle what they may require. Though it is regularly denied that a return to the judicial function as exemplified in *Lochner v. New York* is underway or, which comes to the same thing, that decisions are rooted only in the judges' moral predilections, it is difficult to see what else can be involved once the function of searching for the Framers' intent is abandoned. When constitutional adjudication proceeds in a noninterpretive manner, the Court necessarily imposes new values upon the society. They are new in the sense that they cannot be derived by interpretation of the historical Constitution. Moreover, they must rest upon the moral predilections of the judge because the values come out of the moral view that most of us, by definition (since we voted democratically for a different result), do not accept.

This mode of adjudication makes impossible any general accord between judicial supremacy and democratic theory. Instead, it brings the two into head-on conflict. The Constitution specifies certain liberties and allocates all else to democratic processes. Noninterpretivism gives the judge power to invade the province of democracy whenever majority morality conflicts with his own. That is impossible to square either with democratic theory or the concept of law. Attempts have, nonetheless, been made to reconcile, or at least to mitigate, the contradiction. One line of argument is that any society requires a mixture of principle and expediency, that courts are better than legislatures at discerning and formulating principle, and hence may intervene when principle has been inadequately served by the legislative process. Even if one assumes that courts have superior institutional capacities in this respect, which is by no means clear, the conclusion does not follow. By placing certain subjects in the legislative arena, the Constitution holds that the tradeoff between principle and expediency we are entitled to is what the legislature provides. Courts have no mandate to impose a different result merely because they would arrive at a tradeoff that weighed principle more heavily or that took an altogether different value into account.

A different reconciliation of democracy and noninterpretive judicial review begins with the proposition that the Supreme Court is not really final because popular sentiment can in the long run cause it to be overturned. As we know from history, however, it may take decades to overturn a decision, so that it will be final for many people. Even then an overruling probably cannot be forced if a substantial minority ardently supports the result.

To the degree, then, that the Constitution is not treated as law to be interpreted in conventional fashion, the clash between democracy and judicial review is real. It is also serious. When the judiciary imposes upon democracy limits not to be found in the Constitution, it deprives Americans of a right that is found there, the right to make the laws to govern themselves. Moreover, as courts intervene more frequently to set aside majoritarian outcomes, they teach the lesson that democratic processes are suspect, essentially unprincipled and untrustworthy.

The main charge against a strictly interpretive approach to the Constitution is that the Framers' intentions cannot be known because they could not foresee the changed circumstances of our time. The argument proves too much. If it were true, the judge would be left without any law to apply, and there would be no basis for judicial review.

But that is not what is involved. From the text, the structure, and the history of the Constitution we can usually learn at least the core values the Framers intended to protect. Interpreting the Constitution means discerning the principle the Framers wanted to enact and applying it to today's circumstances. As John Hart Ely put it, interpretivism holds that "the work of the political branches is to be invalidated only in accord with an inference whose starting point, whose underlying premise, is fairly discoverable in the Constitution. That the complete inference will not be found there—because the situation is not likely to have been foreseen—is generally common ground."

This, of course, requires that constitutional DOCTRINE evolve over time. Most doctrine is merely the judge-made superstructure that implements basic constitutional principles, and, because circumstances change, the evolution of doctrine is inevitable. The FOURTH AMENDMENT was framed by men who did not foresee electronic surveillance, but judges may properly apply the central value of that amendment to electronic invasions of personal privacy. The difference between this method and that endorsed by Justices Douglas and Brennan lies in the level of generality employed. Adapting the Fourth Amendment requires the judge merely to recognize a new method of governmental search of one's property. The Justices, on the other hand, create a right so general that it effectively becomes a new clause of the Constitution, one that gives courts no guidance in its application. Modifying doctrine to preserve a value already embedded in the Constitution is an enterprise wholly different in nature from creating new values.

The debate over the legitimate role of the judiciary is likely to continue for some years. Noninterpretivists have not as yet presented an adequate theoretical justification for a judiciary that creates rather than interprets the Constitution. The task of interpretation is often complex and difficult, but it remains the only model of the judicial role that achieves an accord between democracy and judicial review.

ROBERT H. BORK

Bibliography

AGRESTO, JOHN 1984 *The Supreme Court and Constitutional Democracy.* Ithaca, N.Y.: Cornell University Press.

BICKEL, ALEXANDER M. 1962 *The Least Dangerous Branch: The Supreme Court at the Bar of Politics.* Indianapolis: Bobbs-Merrill.

BORK, ROBERT H. 1985 Styles in Constitutional Theory. *South Texas Law Journal* 26:383–395.

CHOPER, JESSE 1980 *Judicial Review and the National Political Process.* Chicago: University of Chicago Press.

ELY, JOHN HART 1980 *Democracy and Distrust: A Theory of Judicial Review.* Cambridge, Mass.: Harvard University Press.

LEVY, LEONARD W., ed. 1967 *Judicial Review and the Supreme Court.* New York: Harper & Row.

JUDICIAL STRATEGY

That judges shape much public policy is a fact of political life. The significant questions are how, how often, how effectively, and how wisely they influence policy. Each of these inquiries poses normative as well as empirical problems. Here we shall be concerned only with legitimate strategies that a Justice of the United States Supreme Court can employ to maximize his or her influence. We shall focus mainly on marshalling the Court.

A Justice, like any strategist, must coordinate limited resources to achieve goals. He or she must make choices—about goals and priorities among goals and also about means to achieve those goals. Intelligent choices among means depend in part on accurate assessments of the resources the Justice controls and of the limitations that others may impose on use of those resources.

The Justices can order litigants, including government officials, to act or not act in specified ways. Less tangibly, judges also have the prestige of their office, supported by a general cultural ethos of respect for the RULE OF LAW. In particular, a Justice has a powerful weapon, an opinion—a document that will be widely distributed by the Government Printing Office and several private firms. That opinion will justify—well or poorly—a particular decision and, explicitly or implicitly, the public policy it supports.

A Justice's power is limited by the nature of judicial institutions. Judges lack self-starters. Someone has to bring a case to them. Furthermore, while they can hold acts of other public officials constitutional or unconstitutional and so allow or forbid particular policies, it is much more difficult for judges to compel government to act. The Supreme Court can rule that blacks are entitled to vote, but it cannot force Congress to pass a CIVIL RIGHTS law to make that right effective. Moreover, the Court can hear only a limited number of cases. It depends on thousands of state and federal judges to carry out its jurisprudence. And no Justice plays an *official* role in selecting, retaining, or promoting judges.

Second, a Supreme Court Justice needs the agreement of at least four colleagues. And each Justice can write a separate opinion, dissenting or concurring, in any case.

Third, and more broadly, the Court is dependent on Congress and the President for appropriations and enforcement of decisions. Each of these branches has other important checks: The House can impeach and the Senate can then remove a Justice. Congress can increase the size of the Court, remove at least part of its APPELLATE JURISDICTION, propose constitutional amendments to erase the effects of decisions or strike at judicial power itself, and use its access to mass media to challenge the Court's prestige. The President can even more effectively attack the Court's prestige, and he can persuade Congress to use any of its weapons against the Justices. He can also choose new judges who, he hopes, will change the course of CONSTITUTIONAL INTERPRETATION.

Fourth, state officials can influence public opinion to pressure Congress and the President. State officers can also drag their heels in carrying out judicial decisions and select judges who are hostile to the Court's jurisprudence.

Fifth, leaders of interest groups can pressure elected officials at all levels of government. And when judicial decisions threaten or support their values, these people seldom hesitate to apply whatever political leverage is in their self-interest.

Commentators—journalists and social scientists as well as law professors—constitute a sixth check. If judges make law, EDWARD S. CORWIN said, so do commentators. Justices who want their jurisprudence to endure must look not only to immediate reactions but also to the future. What commentators write may influence later generations of voters, lawyers, and public officials.

A Justice confronts these limitations simultaneously, and each of these groups will include a range of opinion. Any ruling will elate some and infuriate others, and the political power of various factions is likely to vary widely. In short, problems of synchronizing activities are always present and are typically complex.

The first audience a Justice must convince is composed of other Justices. The most obvious way of having one's views accepted by one's colleagues is to have colleagues who agree with one's views. Thus ability to influence the recruiting process is a difficult but fruitful means of maximizing influence. (See APPOINTMENT OF SUPREME COURT JUSTICES.) Justices who cannot choose their colleagues must consider how to persuade them.

Although treating others with courtesy may never change a vote or modify an opinion, it does make it more likely that others will listen. When others listen, intellectual capacity becomes critical. The Justice who knows "the law," speaks succintly, writes clearly, and analyzes wisely gains distinct advantages.

Practical experience can be a valuable adjunct. Logic is concerned with relations among propositions, not with their desirability or social utility. According to WILLIAM O. DOUGLAS, several Justices were converted to Chief Justice EARL WARREN's position in BROWN V. BOARD OF EDUCATION (1954) because of his vast political experience. Strength of character is also crucial. Although neither learned nor gifted as a writer, Warren led the Court and the country through a constitutional revolution. It was his "passion for justice," his massive integrity, Douglas also recalled, that made Warren such a forceful leader. "Is it right?" was his typical question, not "Do earlier decisions allow it?"

In another sense, intellect alone is unlikely to suffice. Justices are all apt to be intelligent, strong-willed people with divergent views about earlier rulings as well as public policy. They are also apt to differ about the Court's proper roles in the political system—in sum, about fundamentals of jurisprudence. At that level of dispute, it is improbable that one Justice, no matter how astute and eloquent, will convert another.

Facing disagreements that cannot be intellectually reconciled, a Justice may opt for several courses. Basically, he can negotiate with his colleagues or go it alone. Most often, it will be prudent to negotiate. Like policymaking, negotiation, even bargaining, is a fact of judicial life. Writing the opinion of the Court requires "an orchestral, not a solo performance." All Justices can utilize their votes and freedom to write separate opinions. The value of each depends upon the circumstances. If the Court divides 4–4, the ninth Justice, in effect, decides the case. On the other hand, when the Court votes 8–0, the ninth Justice's ability to negotiate will depend almost totally on his capacity to write a separate opinion that, the others fear, would undermine their position.

To be effective, negotiations must be restrained and sensitive. Justices are likely to sit together for many years. Driving a hard bargain today may damage future relations. The mores of the Court forbid trading of votes. The Justices take their oaths of office seriously; and, while reality pushes them toward accommodation, they are not hagglers in a market, peddling their views.

The most common channels of negotiating are circulation of draft opinions, comments on those drafts, and private conversations. A Justice can nudge others, especially the judge assigned the task of producing the OPINION OF THE COURT, by suggesting additions, deletions, and rephrasings. In turn, to retain a majority, the opinion writer must be willing to accede to many suggestions, even painful ones, as he tries to persuade the Court to accept the core of his reasoning. OLIVER WENDELL HOLMES once complained that "the boys generally cut one of the genitals" out of his drafts, and he made no claim to have restored their manhood.

Drafts and discussions of opinions can and do change votes, even outcomes. Sometimes those changes are not in the intended direction. After reading FELIX FRANKFURTER's dissent in BAKER V. CARR (1961), TOM C. CLARK changed his vote, remarking that if those were the reasons for dissenting he would join the majority.

Although the art of negotiation is essential, a Justice should not wish to appear so malleable as to encourage efforts to dilute his jurisprudence. He would much prefer a reputation of being reasonable but tough-minded. He thus might sometimes find it wise to stand alone rather than even attempt compromise. It is usually prudent for a Justice, when with the majority, to inject as many of his views as possible into the Court's opinion, and when with the minority to squeeze as many hostile ideas as possible out of the Court's opinion. There are, however, times when both conscience and prudence counsel standing alone, appealing to officials in other governmental processes or to future judges to vindicate his jurisprudence.

Although Justices have very limited authority to make the other branches of government act, they are not powerless. Judges can often find more in a statute than legislators believe they put there. OBITER DICTA in an opinion can also prod other officials to follow the "proper" path. The Court might even pursue a dangerous course that might push a reluctant President to carry out its decisions lest he seem either indifferent to the rule of law or unprotective of federal power against state challenges.

Lobbying with either branch is also possible. Indeed, judicial lobbying has a venerable history running back to JOHN JAY. Advice delivered through third parties may have been even more common. Over time, however, expectations of judicial conduct have risen so that even a hint of such activity triggers an outcry. Thus a judge must heavily discount the benefits of direct or indirect contacts by the probability of their being discovered.

The most obvious weapon that a Justice has against unwelcome political action is the ability to persuade his colleagues to declare that action unconstitutional or, if it comes in the shape of a federal statute or EXECUTIVE ORDER, to disarm it by interpretation. These are the Court's ultimate weapons, and their overuse or use at the wrong time might provoke massive retaliation.

A Justice must therefore consider more indirect means. Delay is the tactic that procedural rules most readily permit. The Justices can deny a WRIT OF CERTIORARI, dismiss an APPEAL, REMAND the case for clarification, order reargument, or use a dozen other tactics to delay deciding volatile disputes until the political climate changes.

Under other circumstances, it might be more prudent for a Justice to move the Court step by step. Gradual erosion of old rules and accretion of new ones may win more adherents than sudden statements of novel DOCTRINES. The Court's treatment of segregation provides an excellent illustration. If MISSOURI EX REL. GAINES V. CANADA (1938) had struck down SEPARATE BUT EQUAL, the Court could never have made the decision stick. Indeed, years later, when it excommunicated Jim Crow, enforcement created a generation of litigation that still continues.

Strategy is concerned with efficient utilization of scarce resources to achieve important objectives. Its domain is that of patience and prudence, not of wisdom in choosing among goals nor of courage in fighting for the right. The messages that a study of judicial strategy yields are: A web of checks restrains a judge's power; and If he or she wishes to maximize his or her ability to do good, a judge must learn to cope with those restrictions, to work within and around them, and to conserve available resources for the times when he or she must, as a matter of conscience, directly challenge what he or she sees as a threat to the basic values of constitutional democracy.

WALTER F. MURPHY

Bibliography

BICKEL, ALEXANDER M. 1957 *The Unpublished Opinions of Mr. Justice Brandeis.* Cambridge, Mass.: Harvard University Press.

_____ 1961 The Passive Virtues. *Harvard Law Review* 75:40–79.

DOUGLAS, WILLIAM O. 1980 *The Court Years, 1939–1975.* New York: Random House.

KLUGER, RICHARD 1976 *Simple Justice.* New York: Knopf.

MURPHY, BRUCE 1982 *The Brandeis/Frankfurter Connection.* New York: Oxford University Press.

MURPHY, WALTER F. 1964 *Elements of Judicial Strategy.* Chicago: University of Chicago Press.

O'BRIEN, DAVID M. 1986 *Storm Center: The Supreme Court in American Politics.* New York: Norton.

JUDICIAL SUPREMACY

Stripped of the partisan rhetoric that usually surrounds important decisions of the Supreme Court, debate about judicial supremacy raises a fundamental question: Who is the final, authoritative interpreter of the Constitution? The response of judicial supremacy is that courts perform that function and other officials are bound not only to respect judges' decisions in particular cases but also, in formulating future public policy, to follow the general principles judges have laid down.

JUDICIAL REVIEW does not necessarily entail or logically imply judicial supremacy. One can, as THOMAS JEFFERSON did, concede the legitimacy of courts' refusing on constitutional grounds to enforce statutes and EXECUTIVE ORDERS and still deny either that officials of a coordinate branch must obey a decision or follow its rationale in the future. This view, called "departmentalism," sees the three branches of the national government as equal in CONSTITUTIONAL INTERPRETATION: Each department has authority to interpret the Constitution for itself, but its interpretations do not bind the other two.

There are other possible answers to the basic question: Congress, the President, the states, or the people. A claim for the states presupposes the Constitution to be a compact among sovereign entities who reserved to themselves authority to construe their obligations. Such was Jefferson's assertion in the KENTUCKY RESOLUTIONS (1798), and it echoed down decades of dreary debates on NULLIFICATION and SECESSION. The Civil War settled the matter, though some southern states briefly tried to resurrect nullification to oppose BROWN V. BOARD OF EDUCATION (1954).

A claim for the President as the ultimate, authoritative interpreter smacks too much of royalty for the idea to have been seriously maintained. On the other hand, Presidents have frequently and effectively defended their independent authority to interpret the Constitution for the executive department.

A case for the people as the final, authoritative interpreter permeates the debate. American government rests on popular consent. The people can elect officials to amend the Constitution or create a new constitution and so shape basic political arrangements as well as concrete public policies. Jefferson advocated constitutional conventions as a means of popular judging between conflicting departmental interpretations.

Although even JAMES MADISON rejected Jefferson's solution, indirect appeals to the people as the ultimate interpreters are reflected in claims to the supremacy of a popularly elected legislature. On the other hand, in THE FEDERALIST #78, ALEXANDER HAMILTON rested his argument for judicial review on the authority of the people who have declared their will in the Constitution. Judicial review, he argued, does not imply that judges are superior to legislators but that "the power of the people is superior to both."

Although JOHN MARSHALL partially incorporated this line of reasoning in MARBURY V. MADISON (1803), neither he nor Hamilton ever explicitly asserted that the Supreme Court's interpretation of the Constitution was binding on other branches of the federal government. One might, however, infer that conclusion from Marshall's opinions in *Marbury* and in *McCulloch v. Maryland* (1819), where he expressly claimed supremacy as far as state governments were concerned.

We know little of the Framers' attitudes toward judicial supremacy. In *The Federalist* #51, Madison took a clear departmentalist stand, as he did in the First Congress. In 1788 Madison wrote a friend that the new Constitution made no provision for settling differences among departments' interpretations: "[A]nd as ye Courts are generally the last in making the decision, it results to them by refusing or not refusing to execute a law, to stamp it with its final character. This makes the Judiciary Dept paramount in fact to the Legislature, which was never intended and can never be proper."

In the Senate in 1802, however, GOUVERNEUR MORRIS argued that the judges derived their power to decide on the constitutionality of laws "from authority higher than this Constitution. They derive it from the constitution of man, from the nature of things, from the necessary progress of human affairs. The decision of the Supreme Court is and, of necessity, must be final."

What turns a brief for judicial review into one for judicial supremacy is, of course, the claim of finality. Partially, that claim rests on the notion that interpretation of law is a uniquely judicial function (and, by its own terms, the Constitution is "the supreme law"); partially, on the ambiguity of the Constitution about the interpretive authority of other branches; and partially on the need for a supreme arbiter to assure the supremacy and uniform interpretations of the Constitution. The claim also rests on the belief that judges, because they are protected from popular pressures, are more apt to act fairly and coherently than elected officials. "It is only from the Supreme Court," CHARLES EVANS HUGHES once asserted, "that we can obtain a sane, well-ordered interpretation of the Constitution." The Court itself has seldom explicitly claimed judicial supremacy and has never articulated a full argument for it vis-à-vis Congress or the President. Indeed, through such DOCTRINES as the presumption of constitutionality and POLITICAL QUESTIONS, the Court often defers to interpretations by other departments.

The first modern, categorical claim by the Court to supremacy came in COOPER V. AARON (1958), where the Justices said that "the federal judiciary is supreme in the exposition of the law of the Constitution," and thus that *Brown v. Board of Education* was "the supreme law of the land." But *Cooper* involved state officials as did BAKER V. CARR (1962), where the Court first referred to itself as the "ultimate interpreter of the Constitution." Still, it was not until POWELL V. MCCORMACK (1969) that the Court so designated itself in a dispute involving Congress, an assertion the Justices repeated about the President in UNITED STATES V. NIXON (1974) and about both in IMMIGRATION AND NATURALIZATION SERVICE V. CHADHA (1983). *Powell,* however, addressed only the authority of the House to exclude a duly elected member and it did not require that he be readmitted or be given back pay. *Nixon* upheld a SUBPOENA to a President whose political situation was already desperate. What would have happened to the Court's claim as "ultimate interpreter" had it faced a politically secure chief executive in *Nixon* or tried to force Congress to take action in *Powell* might well have produced examples of departmentalism, as did Jefferson's refusal to obey Marshall's subpoena in UNITED STATES V. BURR (1807). And early congressional reactions to *Chadha's* declaring the LEGISLATIVE VETO unconstitutional have been mixed. Formally as well as informally, Congress has continued the practice, though in a more guarded fashion and on a smaller scale.

Although the constitutional text does not require judicial supremacy, Congress and the President have usually gone along with the Court's constitutional interpretations. Yet the exceptions have been sufficiently frequent and important that it is difficult to demonstrate a firm tradition requiring coordinate federal branches to accept the Court's doctrines. In matters strictly judicial—whether or not courts will enforce particular statutes—judges have been supreme, though subject to checks regarding JURISDICTION and appointment of new personnel. The other branches, however, have frequently denied that they have an obligation, when setting policy, to follow the Court's constitutional interpretations.

There is a stronger argument for a duty of enforcing a judicial decision in a particular case. Certainly where the government has brought the case to the courts, an obligation to obey is obvious, as even Jefferson admitted. Where, however, the government is the defendant, the matter is much more complicated, especially when a court commands an official to perform a positive action. Jefferson and ANDREW JACKSON said they had no duty to obey such orders; ABRAHAM LINCOLN acted as if he did not; and FRANKLIN D. ROOSEVELT was prepared to ignore the GOLD CLAUSE CASES (1934) had they been decided against the government.

Typically, Congress and the President acquiesce in judicial interpretations of the Constitution because they agree with the results of judicial decisions, or fear public opinion, or recognize the difficulty of securing a congressional response. Often, too, the Justices reinforce Congress's tendency toward inertia by not pressing a claim to supremacy. Always hovering in the background of any department's assertion of supremacy is the possibility of an appeal to "the people" through the AMENDING PROCESS. Yet even such an appeal, when directed against the Court's jurisprudence, implies an admission of the tactical if not theoretical superiority of the Court as constitutional interpreter.

WALTER F. MURPHY

Bibliography

CORWIN, EDWARD S. 1914 *Marbury v. Madison* and the Doctrine of Judicial Review. *Michigan Law Review* 12:538–572.

FISHER, LOUIS 1985 Constitutional Interpretation by Members of Congress. *North Carolina Law Review* 63:701–741.

MIKVA, ABNER J. 1983 How Well Does Congress Support and Defend the Constitution? *North Carolina Law Review* 61:587–611.

MURPHY, WALTER F.; FLEMING, JAMES E.; and HARRIS, WILLIAM F., II 1986 *American Constitutional Interpretation.* Chaps. 6–7. Mineola, N.Y.: Foundation Press.

JUDICIAL SYSTEM, FEDERAL

The charter of the federal judicial system is Article III of the Constitution, authorizing the creation of federal tribunals vested with the JUDICIAL POWER OF

THE UNITED STATES, that is, the authority to adjudicate a specifically enumerated set of CASES AND CONTROVERSIES. Article III also specifies the method of appointment of federal judges and lays down rules designed to guard their independence.

The Framers, mindful of the problems that the absence of a national judiciary had caused under the ARTICLES OF CONFEDERATION, easily agreed that there must be a national Supreme Court with power to assure the uniformity and supremacy of federal law. But the Framers were divided over the question whether further provision should be made for national courts. Some favored the creation of a complete system of federal courts. Some thought that this would unnecessarily narrow the preexisting general JURISDICTION of the state courts; they argued that national interests could be sufficiently protected by providing for Supreme Court review of state court decisions involving questions of federal law. This division was settled by a compromise: Article III itself mandates that there shall be "one Supreme Court"; but beyond this the federal judicial power is simply vested in "such inferior Courts as the Congress may from time to time ordain and establish."

Article III specifies that the Supreme Court (and whatever inferior federal courts Congress may establish) are to be courts of a strictly limited jurisdiction: they may adjudicate only nine enumerated categories of cases. Some of these were included because they touch on issues of national interest: most important, cases "arising under" the Constitution and laws of the United States (the FEDERAL QUESTION JURISDICTION); cases of ADMIRALTY AND MARITIME JURISDICTION; and cases to which the United States is a party. Federal courts were also empowered to decide certain controversies implicating the nation's FOREIGN AFFAIRS (for example, disputes affecting ambassadors and other alien parties; cases arising under treaties). The remaining categories authorize the federal courts to engage in interstate umpiring in cases where it was feared that parochial interests would prevail in the state courts. Examples are controversies between states, between a state and a citizen of another state, and between citizens of different states.

Article III's specification that the judicial power consists of adjudicating "cases" or "controversies" itself embodies a fundamental political decision: the national courts were to exercise only a judicial power. Thus the CONSTITUTIONAL CONVENTION OF 1787 repeatedly and explicitly rejected a variety of proposals to allow federal courts or judges to participate as advisers or revisers in the legislative process or to render ADVISORY OPINIONS; their authority was to be limited to "cases of a judiciary nature." On the other hand, the historical evidence establishes the Framers' understanding that the grant of the judicial power was to include the authority, where necessary to the lawful decision of a case properly within a court's jurisdiction, to disregard federal or state statutes found to be unconstitutional. This power of JUDICIAL REVIEW, occasionally challenged as a usurpation because it is not explicitly mentioned in Article III, has been settled since MARBURY V. MADISON (1803).

Besides defining the outer bounds of the federal judicial power, Article III protects federal judges from political pressures by guaranteeing tenure during GOOD BEHAVIOR without reduction in compensation.

Article III is not self-executing; it needs LEGISLATION to bring it to life, most particularly because Congress must determine whether there should be "inferior" federal courts and what should be the scope of their jurisdiction. It is to this task that the First Congress turned in its twentieth enactment: the seminal JUDICIARY ACT OF 1789. Obeying the Constitution's command, the act constituted a Supreme Court, consisting of a CHIEF JUSTICE and five associates. Next, the act, establishing a tradition persisting without interruption to this day, took up the constitutional option to create a system of federal courts of ORIGINAL JURISDICTION. The structure created was curious, but survived for a century. The country was divided into districts (at least one for each state), with a district court manned by a district judge. In addition, the country was divided into circuits (originally three), each with another trial court—a CIRCUIT COURT—manned not by its own judges but by two Supreme Court Justices (sitting "on circuit") and a district judge.

Only a fraction of the constitutional potential for original federal court jurisdiction was exploited by the first Judiciary Act, attesting to the clear contemporaneous understanding of the Constitution that it is for Congress to determine which (if any) of the cases and controversies encompassed by the federal judicial power should be adjudicated in the first instance in a lower federal (rather than a state) court. (The modest original jurisdiction of the Supreme Court, limited to controversies where a state is a party and certain cases involving foreign diplomats, is thought to flow "directly" from the Constitution and thus represents a special case.) The district courts were given the jurisdiction most clearly felt to be a national one: authority to adjudicate admiralty cases. In a controversial decision, the First Congress set a precedent by opening the circuit courts to some cases involving controversies between citizens of different states and involving

ALIENS. The federal trial courts were also granted jurisdiction over most civil suits brought by the United States and over the then negligible federal criminal caseload. Notably, the act did not give the federal trial courts jurisdiction over cases "arising under" federal law, leaving these to be adjudicated in the state courts.

The appellate structure of the new court system was rudimentary. Federal criminal cases were left without direct review (and remained so for a century). The circuit courts were given a limited APPELLATE JURISDICTION over the district courts, and the Supreme Court was authorized to review civil cases decided by the circuit courts involving more than $2,000.

Finally, in its famous section 25, the act—consistent with the Framers' intention to assure the supremacy of federal law—gave the Supreme Court power to review final state court judgments rejecting claims of right or immunity under federal law. (State court judgments upholding claims of right under federal law were not made reviewable until 1914.) Supreme Court review of state judgments involving questions of federal law has been a feature of our judicial FEDERALISM ever since 1789, and has served as a profoundly significant instrument for consolidating and protecting national power.

The institutional structure created by the first Judiciary Act proved to be remarkably stable; major structural change did not come until 1891. The Supreme Court has had a continuous existence since 1789, with changes only in the number of Justices. So also have the district courts (though their number has of course undergone major change). Even the circuit courts—architecturally the weakest feature of the system—survived for more than a century.

As to the jurisdiction of the federal courts, changes were incremental in the pre-Civil War period, with the state courts acting as the primary enforcers of the still rudimentary corpus of national law. But the Civil War brought a sea change: Congress was no longer prepared to depend on the state judiciaries to enforce rights guaranteed by the new FOURTEENTH AMENDMENT and by the Reconstruction legislation. By the HABEAS CORPUS ACT of 1867 and the various CIVIL RIGHTS ACTS, Congress extended the lower federal courts' jurisdiction to include claims against state officials for invasion of federal constitutional and statutory rights. These extensions were in turn overtaken by the JUDICIARY ACT OF 1875, giving the federal courts a general jurisdiction to adjudicate civil cases arising under federal law, subject only to a minimum amount-in-controversy. These expansions, supplemented by subsequent numerous specific extensions of federal trial jurisdiction over various sorts of actions involving national law, signaled the transformation of the federal courts from narrow forums designed to resolve maritime and certain interstate disputes into catholic tribunals playing a principal role in enforcing the growing body of national rights, privileges, and immunities.

The growth of the federal judicial business in the post-Civil War era placed an ever-growing pressure on the federal judicial system. The Supreme Court was especially burdened by the duties of circuit riding and by an increasing caseload. By 1890 the Court had a backload of 1800 cases; in the same year, 54,194 cases were pending in the lower federal courts. Congress responded to the crisis in the CIRCUIT COURTS OF APPEALS ACT (Evarts Act) of 1891, which fixed the outline of the contemporary federal judicial system. The act established a system of intermediate appellate courts called Circuit Courts of Appeals (not to be confused with the old circuit courts, which were finally abolished in 1911), one for each of (the then) nine circuits and staffed with its own judges. Although a narrow category of district court decisions continued (and continue) to be reviewed directly by the Supreme Court, the Evarts Act created the standard modern practice: appeals went normally from the district courts to the new courts of appeals; the judgments of the latter were in turn reviewable by the Supreme Court.

The second major and seminal innovation of the Evarts Act related to appellate review in the Supreme Court: the act introduced the principle of review at the Court's own discretion (by writ of CERTIORARI) of judgments in the lower courts. This principle was in turn greatly expanded in the so-called Judges' Bill of 1925, which sharply reduced the availability of Supreme Court review as of right of decisions of state and federal courts and substituted for it discretionary review on certiorari—the method of review that, to this day, dominates the Court's docket.

Changes in the structure of the federal judicial system have been few and minor since 1925, although both the statutory jurisdiction and the business of the courts have undergone major transformations. In essence the system remains a three-tier system, with the district courts serving as the trial courts, the courts of appeals as the appellate tribunals of first instance, and the Supreme Court as the court of final review (having also the power to review state court decisions involving issues of federal law). The picture is completed by the existence of special federal tribunals empowered to decide particular categories of cases, and by numerous federal administrative tribunals; the decisions of all of these are typically subject to review in the regular federal courts.

The most important component of the contemporary statutory jurisdiction of the UNITED STATES DISTRICT COURTS encompasses diversity cases involving more than $10,000, criminal prosecutions and civil actions brought by the United States, a large range of actions against the United States and its agencies and officials, federal HABEAS CORPUS, and—most significant—all civil cases in which a plaintiff sues on a claim arising under the Constitution and laws of the United States. The latter, all-encompassing rubric includes not only cases brought pursuant to the hundreds of federal statutes specifying a right to sue but also the numerous cases where that right is a judge-created ("implied") right to enforce a federal statutory or—(of profound significance)—constitutional provision not itself explicitly containing a right of action. In addition, the statutes allow certain diversity and federal question cases brought in the state courts to be removed for trial to a federal district court. Finally, the district courts exercise a significant jurisdiction to review the work of many federal administrative agencies and to review and supervise the work of the system of bankruptcy courts. The jurisdiction of the district courts is occasionally specified as exclusive of the state courts (for example, admiralty, COPYRIGHT, and PATENT); most of their civil jurisdiction is, however, concurrent with that of the state courts.

The country is, in the mid-1980s, divided into ninety-seven districts (including the DISTRICT OF COLUMBIA and Puerto Rico). Each state has at least one district; districts have never encompassed more than one state. The district courts are staffed by 576 active district judges—almost three times the 1950 figure (182 new district judgeships were created between 1978 and 1984 alone). The growth in number of judges has, nevertheless, failed to keep pace with the explosive increase in the caseload that has occurred since the 1960s. In 1940 about 70,000 criminal and civil (nonbankruptcy) cases were filed in the federal courts; in 1960, about 80,000; by 1980, the figure was almost 200,000, and in 1984 it exceeded 275,000. (The compound annual rate of increase in the federal district court case load was under one percent between 1934 and 1960; it has been five percent since 1960.) The increase is due primarily and naturally to the vast growth in the total corpus of federal (constitutional, statutory, common, and administrative) law applied in turn to a growing country with an expansive and mobile economy. It has also been fed, however, in the past twenty-five years by congressional and court-initiated changes in substantive and remedial rules that have made the federal courts into powerful litigation-attracting engines for the creation and expansion of rights and the redistribution of entitlements and powers in our society. Thus open-ended constitutional and statutory formulas have been used to fuel aggressive judicial review of the validity of federal and state legislative and administrative action and to create an expansive system of remedies against federal and state government (including affirmative claims on the resources of these governments). JUSTICIABILITY requirements (such as STANDING) that previously narrowed the scope of jurisdiction over public law actions have been significantly eroded. And federal court litigation has become increasingly attractive to plaintiffs as a result of provisions for attorneys' fees, the elimination (or inflation-caused erosion) of amount-in-controversy requirements, and the increasing use of CLASS ACTIONS.

These developments are reflected in the changing content of the federal district courts' workload. There were 6,000 suits against the United States in 1960, and almost 30,000 in 1983. There were only 300 CIVIL RIGHTS cases in 1960, almost 20,000 in 1983; 2,100 prisoner postconviction cases in 1960, more than 30,000 in 1983; 500 social security law cases in 1960, more than 20,000 in 1983. In general, about thirty-five to forty percent of the mid-1980s district court civil caseload involve the United States or its officials as a plaintiff or defendant; sixty to sixty-five percent of the civil caseload is "private" (including, however, litigation against state and local governments and officials). Diversity cases have contributed about twenty percent of the caseload since the 1970s. The number of criminal prosecutions has, historically, fluctuated widely in response to special federal programs (peaking during PROHIBITION); since the mid-1970s the criminal caseload has been quite stable and in the mid-1980s contributed about fifteen to twenty percent of the total.

In response to the explosive caseload Congress has acted to allow the district courts to rely substantially on the work of so-called federal magistrates—officials appointed by district judges with wide powers (subject to review by the district judge) to issue warrants, conduct preliminary hearings, try minor criminal offenses, supervise civil discovery, rule on preliminary motions and prisoner petitions, and (with the consent of the parties) even to hear and enter judgment generally in civil cases. The conferring of additional powers on magistrates has evoked controversy as well as some (so far unsuccessful) constitutional attacks.

The UNITED STATES COURTS OF APPEALS (as they

are now called) have jurisdiction to review all final (and some interlocutory) decisions of the district courts. Pursuant to special statutory provisions they also review some cases coming directly from federal administrative agencies (this being an especially significant component of the business of the Court of Appeals for the District of Columbia Circuit). About fifteen percent of their cases are criminal cases, and another fifteen percent are federal and state prisoner postconviction and civil rights cases; only fourteen percent of their docket consists of diversity cases.

The caseload of the courts of appeals has increased dramatically in the last twenty-five years and is, in the mid-1980s, commonly described as constituting a crisis. In the forty years before 1960 that caseload hovered between 1,500 and the peak of 3,700 reached in 1960. In 1970 the figure was almost 11,500, and in 1980 it was over 21,000. From 1980 to 1983 the caseload jumped again to 29,580. From 1960 to 1983 there was an increase of almost 800 percent in the number of appeals from the district courts; the compound annual rate of increase for all cases from 1960 to 1983 was 9.4 percent (compared to 0.5 percent in the preceding twenty-five years).

To manage this workload there exist (in the mid-1980s) twelve courts of appeals assigned to geographical circuits (eleven in the states and one for the District of Columbia) and an additional one (described below) for certain special categories of subject matter. The number of judges in each circuit ranges from six (First) to twenty-eight (Ninth). There are 156 authorized circuit judgeships; in 1960 there were sixty-eight (and as recently as 1978 only ninety-seven). Cases are typically heard by panels of three judges; a few cases of special importance are in turn reheard by the court sitting EN BANC. The increase in number of judges has by no means kept pace with the expansion of the caseload since 1960. As a result, there have been substantial changes in the procedures of these courts: opportunities for oral argument (and even for briefing) have been sharply curtailed and an increasing proportion of cases is disposed of summarily, without opinion. Central staff attorneys (as well as a growing army of conventional law clerks) assist the judges.

From the beginning of our national history Congress has perceived a need to create special tribunals for the adjudication of cases falling outside the traditional areas of federal court jurisdiction. Military tribunals have, from the outset, administered a special body of law through special procedures. The administration of justice in the TERRITORIES in transition toward statehood was perceived as requiring special temporary federal tribunals that would become state courts upon statehood; the District of Columbia and the territories and dependencies of the United States also require a full panoply of special federal courts to administer local law. Beginning in 1855, with the establishment of a rudimentary Court of Claims, Congress has created a series of special tribunals to adjudicate money claims against the United States. And, particularly with the advent in this century of the modern administrative state, Congress has created numerous administrative agencies and tribunals whose business includes adjudication.

Unlike the ordinary federal courts, the institutional hallmark of most of these tribunals has been specialization. Further, the transitory nature of some of these tribunals, the perceived need to allow some of them to function inexpensively with expeditious or informal procedures, and (in the case of the administrative agencies) the equally strongly perceived need to endow them with a range of policymaking functions in addition to adjudicative functions, has typically led Congress to create them not as tribunals constituted under Article III (with lifetime judges performing an exclusively judicial function) but as special LEGISLATIVE COURTS or administrative tribunals. Their judges typically serve temporary terms and are removable for misfeasance without IMPEACHMENT. The constitutional authority for such tribunals has been much discussed and litigated; Congress's authority to constitute them has virtually always been upheld.

The most important specialized tribunals in the current federal judicial system are: the local courts of the District of Columbia, Puerto Rico, and the territories and dependencies; the system of military courts; the system of bankruptcy courts; the TAX COURT and the CLAIMS COURT, adjudicating certain tax refund claims and certain damage actions against the federal government; the Court of International Trade, adjudicating certain customs disputes; and a large and variegated array of administrative tribunals and agencies. The work of all of these tribunals is typically subject to review, through various forms of proceedings, in the regular federal courts.

In addition, in 1982 Congress created a thirteenth court of appeals, the UNITED STATES COURT OF APPEALS FOR THE FEDERAL CIRCUIT. This is a regular Article III court, whose jurisdiction is not territorial but is defined in terms of subject matter, including appeals from the Claims Court and the Court of International Trade and many patent and trademark cases.

Continuously since 1789 the Supreme Court has been the single institution with nationwide authority to supervise the inferior federal courts and to give voice to a uniform national law. The Court's size has varied from five to ten Justices; since 1869 it has consisted of a Chief Justice and eight associate Justices. The Supreme Court acts *en banc,* not in panels, though individual Justices have the conventional authority to issue stays and take emergency action. The Court acts by majority, but in this century the practice has been to grant a certiorari petition (setting the case for plenary review) if four Justices are in favor.

The caseload explosion in the lower federal courts has imposed major burdens on the Court. The Court disposed of over 4,000 cases in its 1983 term (compared to about 3,300 in 1970, 1,900 in 1960, and 1,200 in 1950). The task is possible because only a small number of cases (usually about 150) are decided on the merits by full opinion after plenary briefing and oral argument. Another 100 to 150 cases are decided on the merits by MEMORANDUM ORDER. The remaining dispositions consist of summary denials of petitions for certiorari (or other writs); there were almost 3,900 of these in 1983–1984. In 1960 there were just under 2,000 new cases docketed in the Court; in 1970, about 3,400; in 1983, about 4,200. The increase in cases docketed means more and more resources devoted to "screening" cases for decision and less to the hearing and disposition of cases on the merits. Thus the time devoted to oral argument has shrunk steadily in this century and now almost never exceeds one hour per case. The length of briefs is limited; and an ever-growing battery of law CLERKS assists in legal research and in the drafting of opinions.

The content of the Court's work reflects the scope and content of the national law. In the 1983 term the Court's decisions by full opinion included three cases within the original jurisdiction; ninety-six civil cases coming from the lower federal courts (of which forty-six involved the federal government, twenty-eight involved state and local governments, and twenty-two were private cases); sixteen federal habeas corpus cases; and thirty-two cases from the state courts (eighteen civil and fourteen criminal). Diversity cases are rarely reviewed. The Court is, increasingly, a constitutional court; about half of its cases tend to involve a constitutional question as the (or a) principal issue. The United States (as party or AMICUS CURIAE) participates in over half of the cases that the Court decides on the merits.

Although the federal judicial system has grown substantially in its 200 years, the federal courts continue to constitute only a small—though disproportionately powerful—component of the American judicial system. (Fewer than three percent of the country's judges are federal Article III judges; the biggest states have judicial systems larger than the federal system.)

The relations between state and federal courts are multifarious and exceedingly complex. Except where Congress has specified that federal court jurisdiction is exclusive, state courts of general jurisdiction exercise a normal competence to adjudicate cases involving issues of federal law (particularly in that many such issues arise by way of defense in civil and criminal cases arising under state law). Their decisions of these cases are subject to Supreme Court review, usually on certiorari; but that Court's jurisdiction in such a case is limited to the federal question in the case and may not be exercised at all if the judgment rests on a valid and dispositive state-law ground. State court judgments on issues of federal law (unless reversed by the Supreme Court) have normal RES JUDICATA effect.

The federal district courts, in turn, adjudicate many questions of state law, not only in diversity cases but also in cases arising under federal law where state law governs one or more issues. No provision for review by the state courts of the correctness of federal court decisions on issues of state law has ever existed; but in a narrow class of cases federal courts will abstain from exercising an otherwise proper federal jurisdiction in order to allow a state law issue to be determined in the state courts. (See ABSTENTION DOCTRINE.) Under the decision in ERIE RAILROAD V. TOMPKINS (1938), on issues of state law (including issues of state common law) state court precedents are accepted as authoritative by the federal courts.

Special problems are presented by the politically sensitive role of the federal courts in controlling the legality of the actions of state and local governments and their officials. Although the ELEVENTH AMENDMENT bars the federal courts from asserting jurisdiction over actions against a state as such, a wide range of remedies against state and local governments and their officials exist in the federal courts. Federal courts routinely review the constitutional validity of state criminal convictions through the writ of habeas corpus. Since the adoption of the Civil Rights Act of 1871, they have exercised jurisdiction to grant INJUNCTIONS and DAMAGES against state and local officials (and, more recently, against local governmental entities as such) for conduct under color of state law—including conduct by officials asserting official power even where the conduct is prohibited by state law—that infringes on the ever-growing corpus of federal constitutional and statutory rules governing STATE ACTION. Federal courts may enjoin state officials from enforcing unconstitutional state statutes and administrative schemes; moreover, the courts' injunctive remedial powers are frequently exercised to assume broad managerial supervision over state agencies and bureaucracies (for example, schools, mental hospitals, prisons). And the ever-burgeoning array of federal conditions and restrictions that accompany federal economic and social programs available to the states are, as a matter of routine, enforceable in the federal courts.

The political sensitivities aroused by the federal courts' jurisdiction to control the validity of state and local government action has led to some statutory and judge-made restrictions on the exercise of this jurisdiction. For over half a century federal court actions to enjoin the enforcement of state statutes on constitutional grounds had to be litigated before THREE-JUDGE COURTS and were subject to direct review by APPEAL to the Supreme Court. (The institution of the three-judge district court was virtually abolished in 1976.) During the New Deal, statutory restrictions were placed on the jurisdiction of the federal courts to interfere with state tax statutes and public utility rate orders. Statutory and judge-made rules restrict the power of the federal courts to enjoin or interfere with pending state court proceedings; and state prisoners who fail to exhaust state court remedies or fail to comply with state procedural rules do not have access to federal habeas corpus.

The federal judicial system appears to operate on one-hundred-year cycles. The structure created in 1789 became increasingly unwieldy after the Civil War and was—after some twenty years of pressure for reform—finally transformed by the Evarts Act of 1891. That act created a stable system which has, in turn, come under increasing pressure from the caseload explosion that began in the 1960s. Relief could come in the form of diminutions in the district courts' original jurisdiction (such as a long-discussed abolition of or reduction in the diversity jurisdiction); but the need for architectural revision has also become increasingly clear in the 1970s and 1980s.

Structural problems center on the appellate tiers. Further substantial increases in the number of circuit judges is an uncertain remedy. Some circuits are already unwieldy and are finding it increasingly difficult to maintain stability and uniformity in the intracircuit law. Increasing the number of circuits would increase intercircuit instability and disuniformity and place further pressure on the finite appellate capacity of our "one Supreme Court"—the latter constituting the obvious structural bottleneck in the system.

More generally, a judicial system administering an enormous and dynamic corpus of national law and adjudicating a rising caseload (approaching 300,000 cases a year) cannot operate forever on an appellate capacity that is limited to some 150–200 judicial opinions with nationwide authority. There is rising concern, too, about the quality of federal justice as the growing caseload leads to an increasing bureaucratization of the federal judicial process, with the judges reduced to an oversight capacity in managing a growing array of magistrates, central staff, and law clerks.

Since the 1970s, two methods of increasing the system's capacity to provide authoritative and uniform judicial pronouncements on issues of national law have been discussed. One consists of greater subject-matter specialization at the appellate level, with special courts of appeals having nationwide authority to deal with specified subjects of federal litigation (for instance, tax cases, administrative appeals); such courts would remove pressure from the regional courts of appeals and the Supreme Court. The alternative (or additional) possibility is to create an additional appellate "tier": a national court of appeals with power to render decisions of nationwide authority, receiving its business by assignment from the Supreme Court or by transfer from the regional courts of appeals. In addition, if the number of certiorari petitions continues to mount, the Supreme Court will eventually have to make some adjustments in its screening procedures (perhaps dealing with these petitions in panels).

Behind these structural problems lie more fundamental questions about the enormous power that the federal courts have come to exercise over the political, economic, and social policies of the nation. Throughout our history intense controversy has surrounded the question whether (and to what extent) a small corps of appointed life-tenured officials should exercise wide-ranging powers to supervise and invalidate the actions of the political branches of federal, state, and local governments. From time to time these debates have threatened to affect the independence of the federal judicial system. Thus, in the 1930s, facing wholesale invalidations of the New Deal program by a "conservative" Supreme Court, President FRANKLIN D. ROOSEVELT proposed to "pack" the Court with additional judges; his plan was widely perceived to be contrary to the spirit of the Constitution and was defeated in Congress. (Shortly thereafter a Court with a new membership and a new judicial philosophy in effect accomplished Roosevelt's purposes.)

In the second half of the twentieth century retaliatory proposals have mostly consisted of attempts to strip a "liberal" Supreme Court of appellate jurisdiction in certain categories of constitutional litigation (for example, REAPPORTIONMENT or abortion), leaving the state courts to be the final arbiters of federal law in these areas. Intense controversy surrounds the question whether Congress has constitutional power to divest the Supreme Court of appellate jurisdiction over specific categories of constitutional litigation. (The one explicit Supreme Court pronouncement on the question, the celebrated EX PARTE MCCARDLE [1869], in sweeping language upheld this power pursuant to the explicit provision of Article III providing that the Court's appellate jurisdiction is subject to "such Exceptions" and "such Regulations" as "the Congress shall make.") Even if Congress has jurisdiction-stripping power, however, its exercise—much like the exercise of the power to "pack" the Court—would be widely perceived as anticonstitutional in spirit. In fact, no such legislation has come near to achieving acceptance, attesting to the vast reservoir of ideological and political strength that the ideal of an independent federal judiciary continues to possess.

The more important and authentic debate that continues to rage as the federal court system enters its third century relates to the proper role of an independent federal judiciary in a nation that is democratic but also committed to the ideal of fidelity to law. The federal courts have come to exercise a power over the political, economic, and social life of this nation that no other independent judicial system in the history of mankind has possessed. Whether that power is wholly benign—or whether it should and can be reduced—is one of the great questions to which the twenty-first century will have to attend.

PAUL M. BATOR

Bibliography

AMERICAN LAW INSTITUTE 1969 Study of the Division of Jurisdiction Between State and Federal Courts. Washington D.C.: American Law Institute.

BATOR, PAUL M.; MISHKIN, PAUL J.; SHAPIRO, DAVID L.; and WECHSLER, HERBERT 1973 *The Federal Courts and the Federal System*, 2nd ed., with 1981 Supplement. Mineola, N.Y.: Foundation Press.

CARRINGTON, PAUL D.; MEADOR, DANIEL J.; AND ROSENBERG, MAURICE 1976 *Justice on Appeal.* St. Paul, Minn.: West Publishing Co.

DIRECTOR OF THE ADMINISTRATIVE OFFICE OF THE UNITED STATES COURTS [annually] *Annual Reports.* Washington, D.C.: United States Government Printing Office.

FRANKFURTER, FELIX and LANDIS, JAMES M. 1928 *The Business of the Supreme Court: A Study in the Federal Judicial System.* New York: Macmillan.

FRIENDLY, HENRY J. 1973 *Federal Jurisdiction: A General View.* New York: Columbia University Press.

POSNER, RICHARD A. 1985 *The Federal Courts: Crisis and Reform.* Cambridge, Mass.: Harvard University Press.

WRIGHT, CHARLES ALAN 1983 *The Law of Federal Courts.* St. Paul, Minn.: West Publishing Co.

JUDICIARY ACT OF 1789
1 Stat. 73 (1789)

Article III of the Constitution constitutes an authorizing charter for a system of national courts to exercise the JUDICIAL POWER OF THE UNITED STATES, but is not self-executing, needing legislation to bring it to life. Accordingly, the First Congress, in its twentieth enactment, turned to the creation of a JUDICIAL SYSTEM for the new nation. Its work—the First Judiciary Act, approved September 24, 1789—has ever since been celebrated as "a great law." The statute, obeying a constitutional command, constituted a SUPREME COURT. It created the office of Attorney General of the United States. It devised a judicial organization that was destined to survive for a century. And, by providing for Supreme Court review of state court judgments involving issues of federal law, it created a profoundly significant instrument for consolidating and protecting national power.

But it is the decision of the First Congress to take up the constitutional option to establish a system of federal courts "inferior" to the Supreme Court that has been characterized as the act's "transcendent achievement." The Constitution does not require the creation of inferior courts. Nevertheless, the decision to do so came swiftly, actuated by the unanimously shared view that an effective maritime commerce—trading lifeblood for the thirteen states—needed a dependable nationwide body of maritime law, and by a consensus that the most reliable method to assure its development would be to entrust it to a distinctive body of national courts. (Far more controversy surrounded the view, also finding expression in the act, that national courts were needed to assure out-of-state litigants protection against parochial prejudices.)

The act thus created a system of federal courts of original (trial) jurisdiction, establishing a tradition that has survived without interruption to this day. On the other hand, the act gave these courts the authority to adjudicate only a small fraction of the CASES AND CONTROVERSIES encompassed by the federal judicial power, attesting to the clear contemporaneous understanding of the Constitution that it is for Congress to determine which, if any, of the cases, within the federal judicial power should be adjudicated in the first instance in a federal tribunal.

The first section of the act provided for a Supreme Court, consisting of a Chief Justice and five associates. Below this, the act created a curious bifurcated system. The country was divided into districts generally coterminous with state boundaries (Massachusetts and Virginia each had two districts), each with a district court manned by a district judge. In addition, the act divided the country into three circuits, in each of which another trial court, called a CIRCUIT COURT—manned not by its own judges but by two Supreme Court Justices and a district judge—was to sit twice a year in each district within the circuit. These circuit courts, in addition, received a limited APPELLATE JURISDICTION to review district court decisions. The system of circuit courts set up in 1789, with its requirement that Supreme Court Justices sit on circuit as trial judges, persisted for more than a century; it proved to be the weakest architectural feature of the first Judiciary Act.

The act exploited only a fraction of the constitutional potential for original federal court jurisdiction. Significantly, the constitutional grant of federal judicial power over cases arising under the Constitution and laws of the United States (FEDERAL QUESTION JURISDICTION) was largely unused and remained so until 1875. (A notable exception was section 14, the All Writs Act, which, among other matters, authorized Supreme Court Justices and district judges to "grant writs of HABEAS CORPUS" to inquire into the legality of federal detentions.) The act made important use, however, of the power to locate litigation affecting out-of-staters in the new national courts. Thus, the circuit courts were given CONCURRENT JURISDICTION with the state courts over civil cases involving more than $500 "between a citizen of the State where the suit is brought, and a citizen of another State," as well as over civil cases involving more than $500 in which an ALIEN was a party.

The most important grant of jurisdiction to the new district courts gave them "exclusive original cognizance of all civil causes of ADMIRALTY AND MARITIME JURISDICTION," subject to a savings clause preserving COMMON LAW remedies.

The litigation interests of the national government were given narrow recognition in the First Judiciary Act. The circuit courts were given power to adjudicate civil cases involving more than $500 in which the United States were "plaintiffs or petitioners" (suits against the United States were not contemplated); the district courts had power to adjudicate suits at common law involving $100 brought by the United States. The act gave the district courts exclusive original cognizance over certain seizures, penalties, and forfeitures. And, finally, Congress provided for the then tiny criminal business of the national government by giving the circuit courts "exclusive cognizance of all crimes and offenses cognizable under the authority of the United States," subject to a concurrent jurisdiction in the district courts to try certain minor criminal offenses.

The circuit courts were given the authority to review final decisions of the district courts in civil and admiralty cases involving more than $50 or $300, respectively. In addition, the first Judiciary Act originated the device, in continuous use ever since, of providing for pretrial removal of certain cases from state to federal court (for example, removal in civil cases to a circuit court by alien defendants and by out-of-staters sued in the plaintiff's home-state court).

The framers of the first Judiciary Act, notwithstanding the later established DOCTRINE that the ORIGINAL JURISDICTION of the Supreme Court does not depend on legislative grant, specified in section 13 what this original jurisdiction was to be; the listing nearly (but not completely) exhausted the constitutional grant, encompassing controversies between states, between a state and a citizen of another state, and suits involving foreign diplomats. Setting another lasting precedent, the act designated only a portion of the original jurisdiction of the Supreme Court as exclusive jurisdiction. In his opinion for the Court in MARBURY V. MADISON (1803), Chief Justice JOHN MARSHALL read section B to give the Supreme Court original jurisdiction over certain cases that Article III had not expressly placed within the Court's original jurisdiction. Accordingly, the Court held this narrow provision of the 1789 act unconstitutional.

Not all lower federal court decisions were made reviewable. For instance, no provision at all was made for review of federal criminal cases (which remained, in the large, unreviewable for a century). The act authorized the Supreme Court to review final judgments in civil cases decided by the circuit courts if the matter in dispute exceeded $2,000.

In its celebrated section 25, Congress asserted the constitutional authority—sustained in MARTIN V. HUNTER'S LESSEE (1816) and COHENS V. VIRGINIA (1821)—to give the Supreme Court authority to review certain final judgments or decisions in the "highest" state court in which a decision "could be had" (language that survives to this day). Significantly, this authority did not encompass all cases involving issues of federal law: review was limited to cases where a state court had *rejected* a claim of right or immunity under federal law. (This limitation eventually proved to create an unacceptable institutional gap and was eliminated by the Judiciary Act of 1914.) A seminal feature of section 25 was its specification that Supreme Court review is limited to the question of federal law in the case.

The first Judiciary Act originated a fundamental structural feature of our legal topography in its section 34, called the Rules of Decision Act, providing (in language that still survives) that, except where federal law otherwise requires, the laws of the several states shall be regarded as "rules of decision" in trials at common law in the federal courts "in cases where they apply." Interpretations of this delphic provision—including the reversal from SWIFT V. TYSON (1842) to ERIE RAILROAD V. TOMPKINS (1938)—have had a significant impact on our judicial FEDERALISM. In addition, the act contained elaborate boilerplate with respect to many matters no longer of current interest, (for example, the exact days for court sessions, quorums, clerks, forms of oaths, bail).

The first Judiciary Act, passed by a Congress many of whose members had participated in the framing of the Constitution, has had a lasting effect, not only on the shape of the federal judicial system but on our thought about the constitutional and structural premises on which that system is based. Created by great statesmen, it set on foot an enterprise that 200 years later still bears its imprint.

PAUL M. BATOR

Bibliography

FRANKFURTER, FELIX and LANDIS, JAMES M. 1928 *The Business of the Supreme Court: A Study of the Federal Judicial System.* New York: Macmillan.

GOEBEL, JULIUS 1971 *History of the Supreme Court of the United States: Antecedents and Beginnings to 1801.* Pages 457–508. New York: Macmillan.

WARREN, CHARLES 1923 New Light on the History of the Federal Judiciary Act of 1789. *Harvard Law Review* 37:49–132.

JUDICIARY ACT OF 1801
2 Stat. 89 (1801)

This maligned congressional enactment was the final achievement of the Federalists and one of their most constructive, but the Federalists so enmeshed it in partisanship that the first important action of THOMAS JEFFERSON's administration was the repeal of the act. It created resident circuit judgeships and enormously expanded federal JURISDICTION. The JUDICIARY ACT OF 1789 had created circuit courts consisting of district court judges and Supreme Court Justices. From the outset the Justices complained about the arduous duty of riding circuit and the necessity of deciding in their appellate capacity the same cases they had decided on circuit. Congress had done nothing to separate the Justices from the circuit courts, despite presidential recommendations. The Republican victories in 1800 spurred judicial reform that was "worth an election to the [Federalist] party," said a Federalist leader. A lame-duck Congress belatedly passed a much needed bill that created six circuit courts staffed by sixteen circuit judges. More important, the bill extended the JURISDICTION OF THE FEDERAL COURTS to include virtually the entire JUDICIAL POWER OF THE UNITED STATES authorized by Article III, including a general grant of FEDERAL QUESTION JURISDICTION—something which Congress did not grant again until 1875. But the bill also reduced the size of the Supreme Court to five when the next vacancy occurred, to prevent Jefferson from making an appointment. Also, President JOHN ADAMS at the last hour appointed sixteen Federalists to the new circuit judgeships. Enraged Republicans determined to pass the JUDICIARY ACTS OF 1802.

LEONARD W. LEVY

Bibliography

TURNER, KATHRYN 1965 Federalist Policy and the Judiciary Act of 1801. *William and Mary Quarterly* 22:3–32.

JUDICIARY ACT OF 1837

See: Circuit Courts

JUDICIARY ACT OF 1869

See: Circuit Courts

JUDICIARY ACT OF 1875
18 Stat. 470 (1875)

For three-quarters of a century after the abortive JUDICIARY ACT OF 1801, federal courts lacked any general FEDERAL QUESTION JURISDICTION, that is, JURISDICTION over cases arising under federal law. The 1875 act, adopted on the same day as the CIVIL RIGHTS ACT OF 1875, was one of Congress's last pieces of nationalizing legislation during the era of Reconstruction; its primary purpose was to provide a federal judicial forum for the assertion of newly created federal rights. Using the language of Article III of the Constitution, Congress gave the CIRCUIT COURTS jurisdiction over cases "arising under the Constitution or laws of the United States" or under national treaties, provided that the matter in dispute exceeded $500. The act also authorized the REMOVAL OF CASES from state to federal courts by either plaintiffs or defendants, when those cases could have been brought originally in the federal courts.

In part, the 1875 Judiciary Act's sponsors justified this widening of federal jurisdiction as a response to a commerce that had become national in scope. In particular, they sought to relieve railroads from the need to contend with unfriendly state courts in cases involving foreclosure, receivership, taxation, and even injuries to person and property—an objective which Populists came to criticize. In the *Pacific Railroad Removal Cases* (1885) the Supreme Court read the new jurisdictional grant so expansively that in 1887 Congress increased the jurisdictional amount, eliminated removal by plaintiffs, and insulated from APPEAL federal court orders remanding removed cases to the state courts.

The chief long-term significance of the 1875 act was its establishment of a generalized federal question jurisdiction—the jurisdiction that is seen today as the federal courts' indispensable function. In FELIX FRANKFURTER's words, in 1875 the lower federal courts "ceased to be restricted tribunals of fair dealing between citizens of different states and became the primary and powerful reliances for vindicating every right given by the Constitution, the laws, and treaties of the United States."

KENNETH L. KARST

Bibliography

CHADBOURN, JAMES H. and LEVIN, LEO 1942 Original Jurisdiction of Federal Questions. *University of Pennsylvania Law Review* 90:639–674.

FRANKFURTER, FELIX and LANDIS, JAMES M. 1928 *The Business of the Supreme Court.* Pages 64–69. New York: Macmillan.

JUDICIARY ACT OF 1891

See: Circuit Courts of Appeals Act

JUDICIARY ACT OF 1911

See: Judicial Code

JUDICIARY ACT OF 1925
43 Stat. 936 (1925)

The Supreme Court's desire to reduce the burden of postwar litigation reaching its docket, combined with Chief Justice WILLIAM HOWARD TAFT's aggressive program of reform, resulted in the Judiciary Act of 1925. As litigation increased, efforts to expand the Court's discretionary control over its JURISDICTION—begun in the CIRCUIT COURTS OF APPEALS ACT of 1891—gained favor. Taft took the administrative functions of the Chief Justiceship seriously and sponsored a three-man committee of justices charged with formulating a detailed plan to regulate the Court's workload. The eventual proposal, framed mainly by Justice WILLIS VAN DEVANTER, entailed what Professor FELIX FRANKFURTER would later describe as a "drastic transfer of existing Supreme Court business to the circuit courts of appeal." This draft bill was submitted to Congress in 1922. The patchwork appearance of existing national legislation regulating the federal judiciary had prompted confusion and delay, and Taft, testifying in favor of the bill, applauded its "revision and restatement—a bringing together in a harmonious whole" of the earlier "wilderness of statutes." After three years of inaction, Congress finally passed the "Judges' Bill" in early 1925.

The new act reorganized the Court's APPELLATE JURISDICTION, allowing it to center its energies on constitutionally or nationally significant issues. Henceforth, cases would reach the Court from three avenues. Some district court decisions would go directly to the Supreme Court, but most would be shunted to the circuit courts of appeals. Among those exceptional cases that could be directly appealed because of their national importance were those arising under INTERSTATE COMMERCE or antitrust statutes, suits to enjoin enforcement of either ICC orders or state laws, and appeals by the federal government in criminal cases. Review of circuit courts of appeals' decisions was made largely discretionary; unless the Court chose to examine such a case by means of a WRIT OF CERTIORARI, most circuit decisions would be final. This provision thus superseded some of the reforms enacted in the 1891 legislation. Only two kinds of cases might be appealed directly from state courts: where a state law had been sustained against federal constitutional attack or where the state court had voided a federal law or treaty. Although the act left some problems unsolved, it successfully abated the flood of cases inundating the Court.

DAVID GORDON

Bibliography

FRANKFURTER, FELIX and LANDIS, JAMES M. 1927 *The Business of the Supreme Court.* New York: Macmillan.

JUDICIARY ACTS OF 1802
2 Stat. 132, 2 Stat. 156 (1802)

Gloating Federalists declared that the JUDICIARY ACT OF 1801 was as valuable for their party as an election victory. The appointment of only Federalists to the new circuit judgeships, the attempt by a new circuit court to get a Jeffersonian editor indicted for SEDITIOUS LIBEL, and the issuance in 1801 of the show cause order in MARBURY V. MADISON (1803) convinced President THOMAS JEFFERSON's administration that the Federalists meant to continue party warfare against them from the bench. Republicans also opposed the expanded JURISDICTION OF THE FEDERAL COURTS; they wanted litigants to remain primarily dependent on state courts and the United States as dependent as possible on the states for the execution of its laws. The upshot was the repeal of even the constructive reforms of 1801.

Federalists in Congress argued that repeal would subvert the independence of the judiciary and was unconstitutional because the circuit judges had tenure during good behavior. The Republicans answered that the Constitution empowered Congress to establish and therefore to abolish inferior federal courts. The debate on the repealer triggered a prolonged congressional discussion on national JUDICIAL REVIEW. Federalists supported the power of the Supreme Court to hold acts of Congress unconstitutional, while Republicans assaulted judicial review as an undemocratic judicial usurpation, a violation of SEPARATION OF POWERS, and a subversion of LIMITED GOVERNMENT. The only proper check on the popularity elected and politically responsible branches of the national government, Republicans argued, was the outcome of elections. Chief Justice JOHN MARSHALL's opinion in *Marbury* was the Federalist reply from the bench.

Apprehensive about the possibility that the Supreme Court might declare the repealer unconstitutional, Congress passed another judiciary act which abolished the August term of the Court. By fixing one term a year, to be held in February, Congress managed to postpone the next meeting of the Court for fourteen months, allowing a cooling-off period, during which time the Justices could resume their circuit duties. They did, and in STUART V. LAIRD (1803) they sustained the power of Congress to assign them to circuit work. The Judiciary Act of 1802 also increased the number of circuits from three to six. Until the Reconstruction period, the federal judicial system remained basically unchanged after 1802.

LEONARD W. LEVY

Bibliography

ELLIS, RICHARD E. 1971 *The Jeffersonian Crisis: Courts and Politics in the Young Republic.* Pages 4–60. New York: Oxford University Press.

JUDICIARY REFORM ACT
50 Stat. 751 (1937)

This act, a remnant of President FRANKLIN D. ROOSEVELT's court-packing proposal, provided that "whenever the constitutionality of any Act of Congress affecting the public interest is drawn in question in any court of the United States . . . the court shall permit the United States to intervene and become a party." The act further provided for direct APPEAL to the Supreme Court when a lower court held a congressional act unconstitutional in a case to which the United States or a federal officer was a party. Moreover, such appeals were to be expedited on the Court's calendar.

The act also forbade the issuance by any district court of an INJUNCTION suspending enforcement of an act of Congress upon constitutional grounds, unless approved by a specifically convened THREE-JUDGE COURT. (A single judge might grant temporary injunctive relief to prevent "irreparable loss" to a petitioner.) The three-judge court's grant or denial of an injunction was directly appealable to the Supreme Court. The remainder of the act amended the JUDICIAL CODE to provide a replacement when a district court judge was unable to perform his work. The constitutionality of the act was never challenged; although the three-judge court requirement was largely repealed in 1976, other sections are still good law.

DAVID GORDON

JUILLIARD v. GREENMAN

See: Legal Tender Cases

JULIAN, GEORGE
(1817–1899)

An Indiana abolitionist, lawyer, and congressman (1849–1851; 1861–1871), George Washington Julian was an early advocate of emancipation under the government's WAR POWERS. In 1862 he guided the HOMESTEAD ACT through Congress. Julian advocated confiscation of rebel lands and black suffrage. In 1867 he was a member of the committee of seven which drew up ARTICLES OF IMPEACHMENT against President ANDREW JOHNSON. In 1868 he introduced a constitutional amendment that would have granted women's suffrage. After 1871 Julian became a liberal Republican and then a radical Democrat. He published much, including his political memoirs (1884) and a biography of his father-in-law, Congressman Joshua R. Giddings (1892).

PAUL FINKELMAN

Bibliography

JULIAN, GEORGE W. 1884 *Political Reflections, 1840–1872.* Chicago: Jansen, McClurg & Co.

JUREK v. TEXAS

See: Capital Punishment Cases, 1976

JURISDICTION

Jurisdiction is a magical and protean term. In American law it refers to the power of legislatures, the competence of courts to deal with certain types of cases, the allocation of cases between state and federal courts, the power of both state and federal courts over defendants who have only peripheral attachments to the locale of the court, and the territory in which a unit of government exercises its power. Not surprisingly the word shifts its meanings as it moves among these quite different tasks.

The term's confusing spread of meanings has its roots in the English medieval experience. What modern observers would think of as political power accompanied the grant of property; the landlord was lord of more than land; he exercised powers of justice over the people who tilled that soil. Yet that jurisdiction also had limits: above it stood the powers of the monarch, who at least in theory had the power and responsibility to see that the lords rendered justice. Thus the word emerged from the Middle Ages carrying several meanings: the power to make law, the power to adjudicate cases, and, loosely, the territory within which that power was exercised.

We use all three senses today. We speak, for example, of legislative jurisdiction, meaning legislative power, generally allocated by state and federal constitutions. Thus the earliest opinion of the Supreme Court applying the limits of SUBSTANTIVE DUE PROCESS to state economic regulation, in ALLEGEYER V. LOUISIANA (1897), said that the state had exceeded its territorial jurisdiction. Territorial considerations aside, any decision holding a law unconstitutional can be described as a holding that the legislative body has transgressed the limits of its jurisdiction—its lawful authority. The courts have employed this rhetoric especially in defining a state's jurisdiction to tax.

We use the extended, territorial sense of the term when we write of a fugitive's having fled a jurisdiction, or when lawyers ask about which jurisdiction's law applies. Article IV, section 3, of the Constitution uses the term in this sense when it prohibits creation of a new state within the jurisdiction of an existing state without the latter's consent.

The most distinctively legal, though not exclusively constitutional, sense of the term refers to the authority of a court to decide a matter or to issue an order—its subject matter jurisdiction. Some state courts are courts of so-called general jurisdiction, competent to decide all cases within the ordinary bounds of the law. Other state courts are courts of limited jurisdiction, empowered only to decide specified types of cases or to grant only specified forms of relief. A municipal court, for example, may have jurisdiction to award damages only up to a limited dollar amount and may have no jurisdiction at all to grant an INJUNCTION.

In constitutional law jurisdiction has two special meanings, both involving civil cases. One flows from the limitation of the subject matter jurisdiction of the federal constitutional courts in Article III of the Constitution; the other grows from the due process clauses of the Fifth and FOURTEENTH AMENDMENTS.

Fundamental to the constitutional scheme is the proposition that each branch of the federal government must share powers and observe limits not only in regard to the other two branches of government but also in regard to the states. Article III and many statutes thus limit the subject matter jurisdiction of the federal courts to certain types of cases; that article, for example, ordinarily would prohibit a federal court from deciding a case between two citizens of the same state in which no question of federal or maritime law was involved. Because the limitations of Article III describe a fundamental division of authority between state and federal governments, the federal courts have been scrupulous, some would say zealous, not to overstep those subject matter boundaries. Thus even though no party to a lawsuit evinces the least concern about it, a federal court has an independent duty to investigate the basis for its subject matter jurisdiction and to dismiss the suit if jurisdiction is lacking. Such dismissals, like the jurisdictional rules that require them, protect the interests of the state court systems, to which the litigation must go if the federal courts cannot hear it.

The Constitution also limits the powers of the federal government and the states over individual citizens. State courts, for example, must observe a limitation that flows from the Fourteenth Amendment's due process clause. Since *Pennoyer v. Neff* (1878) the Supreme Court has insisted that, regardless of the kind of case involved, the defendant have some connection with the state in which the suit occurs. Over the past century the Court has remolded the basis and expanded the range of personal jurisdiction—changes that, some have suggested, have come in response to an increasingly mobile population and an economy increasingly national in scope. The Court has sometimes based the requirement of personal jurisdiction on the state's lack of power over persons not within its borders—thus harking back to the territorial sense of the term; more recently it has tended to speak less of territorial power and more of unfair inconvenience to a defendant forced to litigate in a distant forum. Whether it has grounded the requirements in FEDERALISM or in fairness to the defendant, however, the Court has insisted that such connections exist in order for a judgment of a court to be entitled to FULL FAITH AND CREDIT.

Whether similar constitutional restrictions on personal jurisdiction apply to federal courts is a more obscure matter. Because the federal government is sovereign throughout the United States, notions of geographical territoriality play no role, and only the inconvenience to the defendant would be at issue in such a case. In a number of instances involving the national economy, such as federal securities law cases, Congress has provided for nationwide personal jurisdiction in the federal courts, and such grants of power have been upheld, presumably because any harm to the defendant is outweighed by the need for a nationally available system of courts supervising the national economy. The outer limits of congressional power have not been tested, for in most cases either venue statutes (controlling the districts in which civil suits may be brought) or the FEDERAL RULES OF CIVIL PROCEDURE limit federal courts to essentially the same reach of personal jurisdiction that a state court would have.

Unlike subject matter jurisdiction, personal jurisdiction can be waived by those entitled to its protection: the Supreme Court has repeatedly held that either by prior agreement or by the simple failure to raise the issue at an early stage of litigation defendants may lose their opportunity to challenge the court's power to decide the case. COLLATERAL ATTACK on a judgment on the ground that the court lacked personal jurisdiction is available only to a defendant who did not appear in the original suit.

Article III's limits on the subject matter jurisdiction of federal courts allocate cases as between state and federal courts; the due process limitations in personal jurisdiction allocate cases between a court, either state or federal, in a particular place and courts in other places more convenient to the defendant. Though both doctrines in their more technical aspects are quintessential lawyer's law, their roots lie in the Constitution's allocations of governmental power and in a tradition of individualism. The same origins underlie the idea of jurisdiction as the limitations on the power of various branches of government. Ultimately all the uses of "jurisdiction" derive from the medieval Western tradition that distinguished between power and justice, making the ability to dispense the latter a function of allocations of the former.

STEPHEN C. YEAZELL

Bibliography

BATOR, PAUL M.; MISHKIN, PAUL J.; SHAPIRO, DAVID L.; and WECHSLER, HERBERT 1973 *Hart and Wechsler's The Federal Courts and the Federal System.* Mineoloa, N.Y.: Foundation Press.

HAZARD, GEOFFREY C. 1965 A General Theory of State-Court Jurisdiction. *Supreme Court Review* 1965:241–289.

MEHREN, ARTHUR T. VON, and TRAUTMAN, DONALD 1966 Jurisdiction to Adjudicate: A Suggested Analysis. *Harvard Law Review* 79:1121–1179.

JURISDICTION AND REMOVAL ACT

See: Judiciary Act of 1875

JURISDICTION TO TAX

Prior to the adoption of the FOURTEENTH AMENDMENT, the Supreme Court derived from principles "inhering in the very nature of constitutional government" the rule that states do not have jurisdiction to impose taxes upon persons, things, or activities outside their borders. In modern times, such limits on the legislative jurisdiction of states are derived from the DUE PROCESS clause.

The jurisdictional limitations have been applied in

a variety of settings. A state may not impose a property tax on real or tangible personal property physically located in another state, even though the owner of the property is domiciled and present in the taxing state. However, where movable instrumentalities of commerce—railroad rolling stock, ships, trucks, airplanes—are involved, a state is not limited to taxing those instrumentalities actually in the state on tax day. Instead, the state may use a formula to compute the average presence of such instrumentalities within the state. Such apportionment formulas have been upheld so long as they fairly allocate values to the taxing state.

Property taxes imposed on intangibles—such as stocks and bonds—are not subject to similar limitations. The Court initially permitted the state of domicile of the owner to tax the total value of such intangibles, reasoning that intangible property is often held secretly and might otherwise escape taxation entirely. During the 1920s and 1930s the Court attempted to derive rules that would prevent the multiple taxation of intangibles, but eventually it came to hold that any state within which some interest in an intangible exists can tax. For example, if stocks are held in a trust, the state of domicile of the trustee, the state of domicile of the beneficiary, and the state where the certificates are located may each impose a tax on the total value.

Domicile of the taxpayer is an adequate jurisdictional basis for taxing net income from property and activities outside the state. The only constitutional limitation is the COMMERCE CLAUSE. Nondomiciliary states may also tax the income arising from property and activities within their borders subject to two limitations. A 1959 federal statute (section 381, Title 18, United States Code) provides that a state may not impose a net INCOME TAX if the taxpayer does no more within the state than solicit orders to be delivered from without the state by common carrier. Formulas used to apportion income must not have the effect of reaching out and taxing values beyond the state.

The long-standing rule that states may not levy sales taxes when the seller is in another state and does no more than solicit orders in the taxing state is justified in jurisdictional terms. The buyer's state cannot impose the tax because to do so would be to project its powers beyond its boundaries. A use tax, resting on the purchaser within the state, however, is within the jurisdiction of the buyer's state. But in order to collect use taxes effectively, the buyer's state must be able to compel the seller to collect and remit the tax. The Supreme Court holds that such a duty of collection can be imposed only when there is some definite link, some minimum connection (such as ownership of property or the presence of solicitors or other employees) between the seller and the state.

Often jurisdictional and commerce problems overlap. For example, if a state seeks to tax income of an interstate business attributable to activities outside the state, the tax can be invalidated either as an assertion of jurisdiction over out-of-state activities or as disadvantaging INTERSTATE COMMERCE because more than one state taxes the same income.

EDWARD L. BARRETT, JR.

Bibliography

HELLERSTEIN, JEROME R. 1968 Recent Developments in State Tax Apportionment and the Circumscription of Unitary Business. *National Tax Journal* 21:487–503.

NOTE 1975 Developments in the Law: Federal Limitations on State Taxation of Interstate Business. *Harvard Law Review* 75:953–1036.

JURY

See: Blue Ribbon Jury; Grand Jury; Petit Jury; Trial by Jury

JURY DISCRIMINATION

Jury discrimination was first recognized as a constitutional problem shortly after the Civil War, when certain southern and border states excluded blacks from jury service. The Supreme Court had little difficulty in holding such blatant RACIAL DISCRIMINATION invalid as a denial of the EQUAL PROTECTION OF THE LAWS guaranteed by the recently adopted FOURTEENTH AMENDMENT. But, beyond such obvious improprieties, what should the principle of nondiscrimination forbid? Some kinds of "discrimination" in the selection of the jury are not bad but good: for example, those incompetent to serve ought to be excused from service, whether their incompetence arises from mental or physical defect, from demonstrably bad character, or from bias. No one has seriously argued that American jury service ought to be determined wholly by lot, as it was among the citizens of Athens. In addition, it has been the uniform policy of American jurisdictions to excuse from service some who are competent, but whose service would work a hardship on them or others: doctors, ministers, and parents who care for small children have been exempted from service on such grounds.

The history of the constitutional law regulating jury

composition has been a story of expanding and compulsory democratization. In our early national history property and voting qualifications were common, and women were systematically excluded or exempted from jury service. At COMMON LAW, indeed, special juries were sometimes employed: a jury of merchants to decide certain kinds of mercantile questions, for example, or in the trial of an ALIEN, a jury half of which spoke his language. Even in the early and middle decades of this century, the Supreme Court upheld against constitutional attack a BLUE RIBBON JURY system, by which jurors were selected supposedly for intelligence and character in a way that resulted in the vast overrepresentation of professional and business classes, in *Fay v. New York* (1947); a highly discretionary and easily abused "key man" system for selecting potential jurors by consultation with community leaders, in SWAIN V. ALABAMA (1965); and the voluntary exemption of women from jury service, in *Hoyt v. Florida* (1961). At present, however, a federal statute requires that the federal jury be drawn from a pool that represents a "fair cross section of the community," and a similar constitutional standard has been imposed by the Supreme Court on the states as well, in TAYLOR V. LOUISIANA (1975).

There are normally three stages in the selection of an American jury at which improper discrimination may occur: the establishment of the master list of all persons eligible for jury service within the JURISDICTION of a particular court (this is called the jury roll); the selection of the panel of potential jurors (called the venire) who will be asked to appear at the courthouse; and the selection from that panel of those who will actually serve on a jury in a particular case or set of cases. The question of discrimination can arise in both civil and criminal cases, but the courts have paid far more attention to the criminal jury. Two distinct provisions of the Constitution of the United States bear upon jury selection: the equal protection clause of the Fourteenth Amendment and the SIXTH AMENDMENT.

In STRAUDER V. WEST VIRGINIA (1879) and NEAL V. DELAWARE (1880) the Court held that the equal protection clause forbade a state to try a black defendant by a jury from which members of his race had been affirmatively excluded, either by statute or by administrative practice. A federal statute passed shortly after the Civil War made such discrimination a crime.

In *Hernandez v. Texas* (1954), dealing with the exclusion of Mexican-Americans, the Supreme Court extended the *Strauder* ruling to other ethnic groups. On the other hand, the Court has repeatedly said that the Constitution does not entitle a defendant to a jury that consists in whole or in part of members of his race, or of any other particular composition. The idea of the jury affirmed in these cases is not that it is a microcosm of society at large, but that it is an institution of justice for which participants may properly be required to be qualified. The equal protection clause does not guarantee a particular mix but protects only against improper exclusions.

What exclusions, beyond racial ones, are improper? In *Hernandez* the Court said that where any group in a community is systematically discriminated against it will need the protection of the Constitution, and added: "Whether such a group exists within a community is a question of fact. When the existence of a distinct class is demonstrated, and it is further shown that the laws, as written or as applied, single out that class for different treatment not based upon some reasonable classification, the guarantees of the Constitution have been violated." But what is a reasonable classification? This question is complicated by the fact that the law has traditionally imposed qualifications for jury service which may, or may not, have differential impact on racial or other protected groups. The Court has accordingly upheld, against equal protection attack, qualifications for jury service that are extremely vague and easily susceptible to abuse—"generally reputed to be honest and intelligent . . . esteemed in the community for their integrity, good character, and good judgment." The burden is on the defendant to show that such qualifications have in fact been abused. Generally speaking, racially disproportionate impact alone is not enough to invalidate a classification under the equal protection clause: actual intent to discriminate must be proved, by direct or circumstantial evidence, as the Court held in WASHINGTON V. DAVIS (1976). But in jury discrimination, proof of a substantial disproportionality in racial (or sexual) balance between the jury pool and the community at large constitutes a prima facie case of intentional discrimination which the government must rebut. (The Sixth Amendment is more protective than the equal protection clause, in those cases to which it applies, for it has no intent requirement, and the Court held in *Duren v. Missouri* (1979) that it not only prohibits discrimination but affirmatively requires that the pool from which the jury is drawn contain a "fair cross section" of the relevant community.)

Who may object to an improper exclusion? In *Peters v. Kiff* (1972), the Supreme Court held that any defendant is entitled to object to improper exclusions from the panel from which his jury is selected, whether or not he is a member of the excluded race. In addition, the Court held in *Carter v. Jury Commission of Greene County* (1976) that members of the excluded race who wish to serve on juries are entitled to bring independent proceedings to attack their exclusion, for they are deprived of equal protection with respect to an important right of CITIZENSHIP.

A separate source of constitutional restrictions on jury discrimination is the Sixth Amendment's guarantee of an "impartial jury" in criminal cases. DUNCAN V. LOUISIANA (1968) held that this provision, which originally applied only to the federal government, was "incorporated" within the Fourteenth Amendment's due process clause, and thus was applicable to the states as well. (See INCORPORATION DOCTRINE.) In *Taylor v. Louisiana* the Court held that the concept of the jury as a "fair cross section of the community" was at the core of the Sixth Amendment and thus applicable to the states. Thus exclusions will be tested not merely under the equal protection clause, which focuses on improper exclusions, but by the affirmative "cross section" principle. The latter principle conceives of the jury not as a group of citizens who are qualified for a task and chosen in a manner free from INVIDIOUS DISCRIMINATION, but as a body fairly chosen from a group that represents the community of which it is a part.

But what does "fairly chosen" mean? The federal statute requires that the jury roll reflect a fair cross section of the community, and that the venire be drawn at random from the roll; this scheme meets any standard of fairness. The courts might impose similar standards on the states. But there remains the crucial stage at which the particular jury panel is selected from the venire, and none of the rulings cited above speak to this matter. This selection is made just before trial in a process in which lawyers and the judge cooperate. Certain jurors are excused "for cause," that is, because there are good reasons why they should not sit in the particular case: admitted bias, acquaintance with one of the parties, and so on. In addition, the parties are allowed a limited number of discretionary, or "peremptory," challenges to other potential jurors. What happens if the prosecution should exercise its peremptory challenges to keep blacks or women off the jury? If that can be done with impunity, the insistence upon fairness at the other stages of jury selection becomes an empty ritual; but how can a discriminatory exercise of peremptory challenges be established? To require the prosecutor to accept any juror of a particular race or class would be unfair to the state, and upset the balance of the selection process. The Supreme Court held in *Swain v. Alabama* that the use of peremptory challenges against potential minority jurors is not always unconstitutional, but that systematic racial discrimination is impermissible under the equal protection clause. In *Batson v. Kentucky* (1986) the Court partially overruled *Swain*, holding that a prosecutor cannot constitutionally use peremptory challenges to exclude potential jurors solely on account of their race. If the circumstances raise an inference of such a use of peremptory challenges, the burden shifts to the state to provide "a neutral explanation" for the exclusions.

The effect of the antidiscrimination holdings has also been undercut by the Supreme Court's decision in APODACA V. OREGON (1972) that the states are not required to insist upon unanimous verdicts. (See JURY UNANIMITY.) Even if some members of a discriminated-against class make it to the jury, *Apodaca* means that their views can be disregarded by the majority. On the other hand, the proposition that jurors of the defendant's race or sex will be especially likely to vote for him is an assumption more easily made than proved, and arguably demeaning both to the jurors and to the class to which they belong. And even minority jurors who are outvoted will have a chance to have their views considered. The true basis of the fair cross-section requirement is assurance of the kind of diversity of view and experience that will most advance the kind of collective decision making that, as Harry Kalven and Hans Zeisel show, represents the jury at its best.

As for the distinct institution known as the GRAND JURY, which sits before trial to decide whether the evidence of a particular defendant's guilt is sufficient to justify his INDICTMENT, racial discrimination in its selection is also a violation of the equal protection clause. The indicted individual is entitled to the dismissal of his indictment, as the Court held in *Carter v. Texas* (1900), even though in some sense the defect may be thought to be cured by a properly composed trial jury. The Court has not applied the affirmative "fair cross section" requirements to the state grand jury, nor indeed, as the Court held in HURTADO V. CALIFORNIA (1884), are the states required to employ the institution of the grand jury at all. Discrimination in the selection of state grand juries remains regulated by the equal protection clause, which forbids only intentional discrimination. The federal statute does apply the "fair cross section" requirement to federal grand juries as well as trial juries.

The continued existence of both the grand jury and the trial jury appears to rest on two assumptions.

First, judicial decisions, especially in criminal cases, are assumed to be more just when they are not left to professionals but are also influenced by the views of ordinary people. Second, jury service—again, especially in the criminal process—is seen as popular participation in government. Our constitutional protections against discriminatory selection of jurors are aimed at promoting the ends of justice and the ideal of citizenship.

JAMES BOYD WHITE

Bibliography

JUDICIAL CONFERENCE OF THE UNITED STATES 1961 The Jury System in the Federal Courts. *Federal Rules Decisions* 26:411–504.

KALVEN, HARRY and ZEISEL, HANS 1966 *The American Jury.* Boston: Little, Brown.

LARUE, L. H. 1976 A Jury of One's Peers. *Washington & Lee Law Review* 33:841–876.

JURY SIZE

Traditionally, in the United States, a criminal trial jury—the PETIT JURY—has been composed of twelve persons. Early Supreme Court opinions assumed that in federal criminal cases juries of that size were required by the Constitution. In PATTON V. UNITED STATES (1930) the Court ruled that during the course of a federal trial a criminal defendant could, with the consent of the prosecutor and judge, waive the participation of one or two jurors and agree to have the verdict rendered by less than twelve.

In DUNCAN V. LOUISIANA (1968) the Supreme Court held that under the FOURTEENTH AMENDMENT a person accused of a serious crime in a state court is guaranteed the right to TRIAL BY JURY according to the same standards applied under the Sixth Amendment in the federal courts. Later, in BALDWIN V. NEW YORK (1970), the Court held that a serious, nonpetty crime for purposes of the jury trial guarantee is one where imprisonment for more than six months is authorized. In the wake of *Duncan,* the Court in WILLIAMS V. FLORIDA (1970) decided that trial of a serious crime by a jury of six persons did not violate the constitutional right to trial by jury. Eight years later, the Court in BALLEW V. GEORGIA (1978) ruled that six was the constitutional minimum—that a jury of five persons did not meet the constitutional standard. In *Colgrove v. Battin* (1973) the Court had also ruled that a six-person jury in a civil case in the federal courts did not violate the SEVENTH AMENDMENT right to jury trial.

In early England, the number of jurors on a petit jury came to be firmly fixed at twelve some time in the fourteenth century. The reasons for choosing the number twelve for the jury at common law are shrouded in obscurity; the same number was also in wide use in other countries of Europe from early times. Some writers ascribe this number to mystical and religious considerations, for example, the twelve tribes and the twelve apostles. At the time of the adoption of the Constitution and the BILL OF RIGHTS, the idea of the twelve-person jury was entrenched in the English COMMON LAW system and practice of the colonial society.

In *Williams,* the Court rejected the idea that the history of the drafting of the Sixth Amendment jury trial provision enshrined the twelve-person jury in the Constitution. Instead, the Court adopted a functional approach, relating jury size to the purposes of jury trial. The goals of the jury system were seen as interposing the common-sense judgment of laypersons, permitting community participation in the decision-making process, and making the group large enough to promote group deliberation and obtain a fair cross-section of the community. With respect to these various goals, the court majority found "little reason to think" that there is a significant difference between six and twelve, citing in support "the few experiments" and asserting that neither currently available evidence nor theory suggested contrary conclusions.

The interval between *Williams* and *Ballew* saw the publication of a significant body of SOCIAL SCIENCE RESEARCH examining the effects of changes in jury size. In *Ballew,* although the Court was unanimous on the jury size issue, only two Justices relied on these social science studies in concluding that five-person juries did not adequately fulfill the functions of jury trial outlined in *Williams.* Three Justices had "reservations as to the wisdom—as well as the necessity—of . . . heavy reliance on numerology derived from statistical studies." The same three Justices suggested that the Constitution does not require every feature of the jury to be the same in both federal and state courts, implying that a different, presumably higher, minimum size standard might be applied in the federal courts.

The studies done since *Williams,* through experiment, use of statistical analysis, and theorizing, have inquired whether the size of the jury affects: the likelihood of representation on a jury of ethnic and racial minorities and minority viewpoints that might influence results or the incidence of hung juries; the propensity of juries to reach compromise verdicts; the consistency of verdicts; the likelihood that verdicts reflect community sentiment; and the overall quality of group decision making. A few researchers have also studied the cost savings that might be achieved by reductions in jury size.

In the main, the social scientists have criticized the Court's conclusion in *Williams,* and have argued that decreasing jury size has undesirable effects. Some of these studies have been subjected to methodological criticism, such as the objections to their reliance on small group research. Definitive research on the subject remains to be done. On the issue of the jury's representative character, however, social science has already contributed fairly definitive conclusions. Although it is not possible for a single jury to be representative of the community, six-person juries are less likely than twelve-person juries to contain individuals from minority groups or those who have minority viewpoints. Richard Lempert has suggested that "there may be a positive value in minimizing the number of situations in which minority group members are judged by groups lacking minority representation. . . ."

In other constitutional contexts, judges often rely on intuition and common sense to reach judgments on functional issues, or they take into account constitutional values that transcend a functional approach. The jury size issue, however, involves specific numbers, and intuition and other constitutional values do not provide an adequate basis for drawing the required fine distinctions. One who is not persuaded by the social science studies is therefore relegated to the type of statement made by Justice Powell in *Ballew,* defending the line between five and six: "[A] line has to be drawn somewhere." Under such an approach, the constitutional line could as easily have been drawn between twelve and eleven, and with more historical justification.

Because of the Court's reluctance to overrule recent precedents and because of uncertainty whether social science research can ever demonstrate a sufficient basis for drawing a different line, it seems probable that, for a long time to come, six will remain the constitutional minimum for a criminal jury in the state courts under the Fourteenth Amendment. (Whether the Court will some day adopt Justice Powell's view and apply a different minimum size standard for juries in federal criminal trials is problematic.) Perhaps in some future century when legal historians try to deduce the reasons for choosing six as the constitutionally significant number, they, like their predecessors, may speculate about the possible mystical value of the number. In the end, they are likely to conclude that its origins, like those of the number twelve, are shrouded in obscurity.

NORMAN ABRAMS

Bibliography

LEMPERT, RICHARD 1975 Uncovering "Nondiscernible Differences: Empirical Research and the Jury Size Cases. *Michigan Law Review* 73:644–708.

JURY TRIAL

See: Trial by Jury

JURY UNANIMITY

The requirement that a jury in a criminal case reach a unanimous decision became generally established in England during the fourteenth century—about the same time that juries came to be composed of twelve persons. Unanimity began to be generally required for jury verdicts in the American colonies in the eighteenth century. The unanimity requirement as commonly applied means that all the members of the jury must agree upon the verdict—whether for conviction or acquittal. If any of the jurors fail to agree, the jury is "hung"—that is, unable to reach a verdict. Under well-established DOCTRINE, after a hung jury the defendant may be retried.

In a series of cases dating back to the end of the nineteenth century, the Supreme Court has assumed that under the Sixth Amendment the verdict of a criminal jury in the federal courts must be unanimous. This assumption has not been tested, however, for there is no provision for less than unanimous criminal verdicts in the federal courts. The decision in DUNCAN V. LOUISIANA (1968) opened the way for the Court to consider the constitutionality of efforts made by many states to change elements in the COMMON LAW jury system. *Duncan* ruled that the FOURTEENTH AMENDMENT protected the right to TRIAL BY JURY in state courts according to the same standards applied under the Sixth Amendment.

To understand the Court's subsequent decisions regarding jury unanimity, it is necessary also to consider its related decisions on JURY SIZE. The Court in WILLIAMS V. FLORIDA (1970) upheld the use of six-person juries for serious criminal cases. The question whether state criminal juries must reach unanimous verdicts was presented for the first time in 1972 in two companion cases, APODACA V. OREGON and JOHNSON V. LOUISIANA. In *Apodaca,* the constitutionality of 10–2 verdicts was sustained under the Sixth and Fourteenth Amendments. In *Johnson,* 9–3 verdicts were upheld under the Fourteenth Amendment alone. In *Apodaca,* a state case, five Justices (one concurring Justice and four dissenters) also expressed the view that the Sixth Amendment required unanimity in federal criminal trials.

In BALLEW V. GEORGIA (1978) the Court rendered its second size-of-jury decision, holding five-person juries to be unconstitutional. Thus, by the time the Court considered the issue in BURCH V. LOUISIANA (1979), it had upheld six-person juries, sustained the constitutionality of 10–2 and 9–3 majority verdicts, and held five-person juries to be unconstitutional. In *Burch,* the Court held that conviction by a 5–1 vote of a six-person jury violated the constitutional right to trial by jury.

The Court has not in modern times decided whether the SEVENTH AMENDMENT requires unanimity in federal civil trials. It can be argued that it so held in two early cases, *American Publishing Company v. Fisher* (1897) and *Springville v. Thomas* (1897), but the Court's nonunanimous verdict decisions in state criminal cases and its decision in *Colgrove v. Battin* (1973) that six-person juries are constitutional in federal civil trials, arguably have undermined those early decisions.

In addressing the unanimity issue in *Apodaca* and *Johnson,* the Court relied heavily on the analysis used in the first size-of-jury case, *Williams v. Florida,* and applied the same functional approach relating the size of the jury to the purposes of a jury trial. From a functional perspective, the unanimity issue has much in common with but is not identical to the jury size question. For example, both involve concerns that juries represent a cross-section of the community and that minority viewpoints be represented. In connection with jury size, the concern is that if the jury is too small, it will not reflect minority views. Where unanimity is departed from, the concern is that minority viewpoints represented on the jury will simply be disregarded and outvoted. A majority of the Court in *Apodaca* rejected this latter claim on the grounds that there was no reason to believe that majority jurors will fail to weigh the evidence and consider rational arguments offered by the minority. The dissenters argued that jury reliability was diminished in a nonunanimous system because there is less pressure to debate and deliberate. Professor Hans Zeisel has made a similar point: "[T]he abandonment of the unanimity rule is but another way of reducing the size of the jury. But it is reduction with a vengeance, for a majority verdict requirement is far more effective in nullifying the potency of minority viewpoints than is the outright reduction of a jury to a size equivalent to the majority that is allowed to agree on a verdict. Minority viewpoints fare better on a jury of ten that must be unanimous than on a jury of twelve where ten members must agree on a verdict" (1971, p. 722).

The less than unanimous verdict also poses a question not raised in the jury size cases. A majority of the Court in *Johnson* held that nonunanimous verdicts are not inconsistent with proof beyond a REASONABLE DOUBT and therefore do not violate DUE PROCESS. The fact that some members of the jury are not convinced of guilt does not itself establish reasonable doubt, a concept that apparently applies only to the standard of proof that each individual juror subjectively must apply, not a concept applicable to the jury as a group.

Are criminal defendants as well protected from conviction under a nonunanimous verdict system as under a unanimity requirement? The majority in *Apodoca* and *Johnson* conceded that juries would be hung somewhat less frequently under a nonunanimous system but also relied on SOCIAL SCIENCE RESEARCH for the proposition that "the probability that an acquittal minority will hang the jury is about as great as that a guilty minority will hang it." Data in the same study, however, persuaded some of the dissenters that the prosecution would gain "a substantially more favorable conviction ratio" under a nonunanimous system.

By the time *Burch* was decided in 1979, the Court, following the pattern suggested in the 1978 jury size case of *Ballew,* appears to have abandoned any attempt to rely on social science to support its conclusions regarding required jury attributes. In holding 5–1 verdicts unconstitutional, the Court concluded that "having already departed from the strict historical requirements of jury trial, it is inevitable that lines must be drawn somewhere" and relied upon "much the same reasons that led [us] in *Ballew* to decide that use of a five-member jury threatened the fairness of the proceeding. . . ."

The constitutionality of other numerical combinations—for example, 8–4 or 7–5 verdicts or the various possible majorities on juries of seven to eleven members—remains in doubt. In *Burch,* the Court expressly reserved opinion on the constitutionality of nonunanimous verdicts by juries of more than six. Only Justice HARRY A. BLACKMUN, concurring in *Apodaca,* commented that a 7–5 verdict standard would afford him "great difficulty."

The Court's decisions in the nonunanimous verdict cases have been designed to leave room for the states to experiment with different majority verdict systems. But the uncertainty produced by these decisions may discourage experimentation. If the states do introduce additional variations, the notions that "lines must be drawn somewhere" and that at some point "the fairness of the proceeding" is threatened hardly provide an adequate basis for selecting among the numerous lines that may be presented. If the Court is unwilling to rely upon social science research to back up its functional approach, it may find itself without a calculus for resolving constitutional issues in which specific numbers count.

NORMAN ABRAMS

Bibliography

ZEISEL, HANS 1971 And Then There Were None: The Diminution of the Federal Jury. *University of Chicago Law Review* 38:710–724.

JUS DARE

(Latin: "To give the law.") This is the traditional function of the legislature in a constitutional government with SEPARATION OF POWERS and is contrasted with JUS DICERE, the function of courts. A court may be said to have invaded the realm of *jus dare* when it engages in JUDICIAL POLICYMAKING.

DENNIS J. MAHONEY

JUS DICERE

(Latin: "To say [what] the law [is].") This is the traditional function of courts, and it is usually understood as a limitation upon their power (*jus dicere, et non jus dare*). "It is emphatically the province of the judicial department to say what the law is"—Chief Justice JOHN MARSHALL in MARBURY V. MADISON (1803).

DENNIS J. MAHONEY

JUST COMPENSATION

The just compensation clause of the Fifth Amendment demands that a private property owner be made whole financially when property is taken by the federal government for PUBLIC USE. The same requirement is made applicable to the states by the DUE PROCESS clause of the FOURTEENTH AMENDMENT. The requisite compensation is the monetary equivalent of the property taken, putting the owner in as good a position pecuniarily as before the taking, as the Supreme Court held in *Monongahela Navigation Co. v. United States* (1893). Compensation for losses peculiar to the owner, such as loss of investment or business profits, litigation expenses, and relocation costs, is not constitutionally required, but often is made payable by statute.

In recognition of the somewhat elusive nature of the "monetary equivalent" standard, a variety of working rules have been developed to aid the courts. The most important of these rules is the concept of fair market value. Under this concept, the owner is entitled to receive, as just compensation, the price for the property interest taken that would be agreed upon, as of the time of the taking, by a willing and informed seller and a willing and informed buyer, considering the highest and best use for which the property was available and suitable.

The market value test, however, is not an inflexible one, and other methods of estimating value have been held appropriate when reference to actual market data is impossible because there is no actual market for the property, or when the market value test would result in manifest injustice by diverging to an impermissible degree from the full indemnity principle of the Fifth Amendment.

If the property taken is only a part of a single parcel, just compensation includes payment to the owner for any diminution in value of the remainder resulting from the planned use of the part taken, but the value of benefits to the remainder may be offset against the value of the "take." These results, which ordinarily can be measured by the difference in value of the property before and after the taking, can theoretically, although seldom in fact, result in a zero award. Many states, deeming it unfair to deduct enhancements to the remainder, reject the "before and after" test and award the full value of the part taken plus any net consequential damages realized by the remainder after offsetting any special benefits thereto. That either approach is constitutionally permissible was affirmed in *Bauman v. Ross* (1897).

ARVO VAN ALSTYNE

Bibliography

ORGEL, LESTER 1953 *Valuation under the Law of Eminent Domain,* Vol. 1. Charlottesville, Va.: Michie Co.

JUSTICE DEPARTMENT

See: Attorney General and Justice Department

JUSTICIABILITY

Federal judges do not establish legal norms at will or on demand, but only when deciding cases that are justiciable, that is, appropriate for federal court decision. What makes a case justiciable is thus itself an important threshold question, because it determines whether a federal court will exercise its power to formulate and apply substantive law, rather than leaving the issues in the case to be resolved by political or other means. Hence, when the Supreme Court fashions the criteria of justiciability for itself and the lower federal courts, it effectively defines the nature and scope of the JUDICIAL POWER OF THE UNITED STATES—the power to make decisions in accordance with law.

Most justiciability issues arise when litigants who are primarily motivated to vindicate public rights seek to contest the validity of government behavior, especially on constitutional grounds. Such public interest suits are usually designed not so much to redress traditional personal grievances as to vindicate fundamental principles. Commonly the plaintiffs seek DECLARATORY JUDGMENTS or INJUNCTIONS to prevent government officials from carrying on objectionable practices that affect a wide segment of the population. These actions often test and illustrate the degree to which federal judges, particularly Supreme Court Justices, view their power of constitutional oversight as warranted only by the necessity to resolve traditional legal disputes or, instead, by a broader judicial mission to ensure government observance of the Constitution.

In demarcating the federal judicial function, the law of justiciability comprises a complex of subtle doctrines, including STANDING, RIPENESS, MOOTNESS, ADVISORY OPINIONS, and POLITICAL QUESTIONS, among others. The Supreme Court has derived that law from two sources: Article III, which limits federal judicial power to the decision of CASES AND CONTROVERSIES, and nonconstitutional "prudential" rules of the Court's own creation. Both Article III and the rules of prudence incorporate notions of the attributes or qualities of litigation that make the legal issues presented appropriate for judicial determination. The difference between the two is that if Congress wants to have the federal courts entertain public actions, it may override the Court's prudential barriers, but not the constitutional limits of "case" and "controversy."

Three primary, and often mutually reinforcing, conceptions of appropriateness shape the many manifestations of justiciability. One concerns judicial capability. It centers on making federal court adjudication competent, informed, necessary, and efficacious. In this conception, a judicial decision is proper only when adversely affected parties litigate live issues of current personal consequence in a lawsuit whose format assures adversary argument and judicial capacity to devise meaningful remedies. The second conception of appropriateness concerns fairness. It promotes judicial solicitude for parties and interests not represented in the lawsuit, whose rights might be compromised unfairly by a substantive decision rendered without their participation. The third conception concerns the proper institutional and political role in our democracy of the appointed, electorally unaccountable federal judiciary. It cautions federal courts to be sure of the need for imposing restraints, especially constitutional restraints, on other, particularly more representative, government officials.

Whether the policies underlying justiciability doctrine are (or should be) applied in a principled, consistent fashion, depending on the form and characteristics of litigation alone, as the Supreme Court professes, or whether the Court does (or should) manipulate them for pragmatic reasons, is a subject of major controversy among the Court's commentators. Inevitably, the Court has discretion to adjust the degree to which these imprecise and flexible policies must be satisfied in particular cases, given individual variations in the configuration of lawsuits and the inherently relative nature of judgments about judicial capability, litigant need, and the propriety of JUDICIAL ACTIVISM AND RESTRAINT. Assessments of the information and circumstances needed for intelligent, effective adjudication will vary with the levels of generality at which issues are posed and with judicial willingness to act under conditions of uncertainty. Appraisals frequently diverge concerning hardship to, and representation of, present and absent parties who will be affected by rendering or withholding decision. Perhaps most dramatically, Justices differ in their evaluations of the relative importance of judicial control of government behavior and the freedom of politically accountable officials to formulate policy without judicial interference.

In view of the latitude and variation in the Court's self-conscious definition of federal judicial power, it is not surprising that justiciability is a sophisticated, controversial, and difficult field, or that many decisions provoke the skepticism that justiciability DOCTRINE has been manipulated to avoid decision of some issues and advance the decision of others. The Court certainly considers (and is willing to articulate) the degree of concrete focus and clarity with which issues are presented, and how pressing is the need for judicial protection of the litigants. The Court may also consider (but almost certainly will not articulate) a number of the following factors: how substantial, difficult, and controversial the issues are; whether a decision would likely legitimate government action or hold it unconstitutional; how important the Court believes the principle it would announce is and whether the principle could be expected to command public and government acceptance; the possibility of nonjudicial resolution; whether a decision would contribute to or cut off public debate; the expected general public reaction to a decision; the Justices' own constitutional priorities; and a host of other practical considerations that may implicate the Court's capacity to establish and enforce important constitutional principles.

Such judgments appear to have influenced a number of notable justiciability rulings in diverse ways. For example, in *Poe v. Ullman* (1961) the Court held a declaratory judgment challenge to Connecticut's contraception ban nonjusticiable because the statute was not being enforced, but later held the ban unconstitutional in the context of a criminal prosecution. By contrast, in a declaratory judgment challenge to an unenforced prohibition on teaching evolution, the Court, in EPPERSON V. ARKANSAS (1968), held the case justiciable and the prohibition unconstitutional without awaiting a prosecution. Similarly, the Court twice dismissed a seemingly justiciable appeal challenging Virginia's ban on MISCEGENATION, as applied to an annulment proceeding, within a few years of declaring public school segregation unconstitutional in 1954, but in 1967, following the CIVIL RIGHTS advances of the early 1960s, held the law unconstitutional on appeal of a criminal conviction. Moreover, although the Court has deferred decision in some cases where it ultimately held state statutes unconstitutional, it also occasionally appears to have lowered justiciability barriers and rushed to uphold the constitutionality of important federal legislation (the Tennessee Valley Authority and nuclear liability limitation statutes) or to invalidate it when Congress wanted constitutional assistance with ongoing legislative reform (the FEDERAL ELECTION CAMPAIGN ACT).

Perhaps the Court is inclined to insist on a greater showing of justiciability where it expects to hold governmental action unconstitutional than where it expects to uphold the action, in part because of a substantive presumption of the constitutionality of government conduct. Yet any generalization about the relations between justiciability and the Court's substantive views is hazardous, given the many factors and subtle judgments that may be weighed in any given case. What seems certain is that decisions on questions of justiciability will always be influenced by visions of the judicial role and will be difficult to comprehend without understanding those visions.

JONATHAN D. VARAT

Bibliography

BICKEL, ALEXANDER M. 1962 *The Least Dangerous Branch: The Supreme Court at the Bar of Politics.* Chap. 4. Indianapolis: Bobbs-Merrill.

GUNTHER, GERALD 1964 The Subtle Vices of the "Passive Virtues": A Comment on Principle and Expediency in Judicial Review. *Columbia Law Review* 64:1–25.

VARAT, JONATHAN D. 1980 Variable Justiciability and the *Duke Power* Case. *Texas Law Review* 58:273–327.

WRIGHT, CHARLES A.; MILLER, ARTHUR R.; and COOPER, EDWARD H. 1984 *Federal Practice and Procedure.* Vol. 13:278–293. St. Paul, Minn.: West Publishing Co.

JUVENILE PROCEEDINGS

In a juvenile proceeding, a state court is asked to decide whether and how to intervene in the life of a child who may need supervision or protection. These proceedings often take place in a juvenile or family court and usually have two distinct phases: a "jurisdictional" stage, at which the judge must decide whether there are grounds for intervention; and a "dispositional" phase, in which the judge decides how to intervene. Juvenile court statutes typically provide for JURISDICTION in three types of cases: the delinquency case, where a young person is found to have violated a criminal law; the case where the child's conduct is not criminal, but the child is found to be beyond parental control, or in need of supervision because of improper or protocriminal conduct, such as truancy, or running away; and the dependency case, where by reason of parental neglect or abuse the child is in need of protection. Once jurisdiction is established, the court typically has broad discretionary authority in the "dispositional phase" of juvenile proceedings to intervene into the child's life through supervision, or out-of-home placement in foster care or a residential institution.

At COMMON LAW, there were neither special courts nor separate proceedings for minors accused of violating the law. "Infancy" provided a defense, somewhat akin to insanity, in a case where because of immaturity a child lacked the capacity to form the requisite criminal intent. Presumptions made it impossible to find the requisite intent in children under seven, and difficult to find it in those between seven and fourteen. Youths over fourteen were presumed capable. Except for this possible defense, a child could be arrested, indicted, tried, and convicted just like an adult. Minors were regularly charged with crimes, tried like adults, and jailed and imprisoned with adult offenders.

In the nineteenth century, reformers began questioning the appropriateness of treating youthful and adult offenders alike. A revolution began in 1899, when Illinois established the first juvenile court. Hailed as a more humane and effective way of helping children in trouble get back on the track to good citizenship, the Illinois court became a model; by 1925 nearly every state had adopted LEGISLATION providing for some sort of juvenile proceedings. For these new juvenile proceedings, the implicit model of authority was not the traditional criminal trial with adversarial procedures but the family itself, with the state as *parens patriae.*

The philosophy of the early juvenile court emphasized four tenets. The first was rehabilitation, rather than deterrence or punishment. The state's goal was to save the wayward child through appropriate treatment. The second was individualization: justice for children was to be personalized. The court's primary goal was to determine whether a child needed help, and then to prescribe on an individualized basis the appropriate treatment. The third was separation: children were to be kept away from adult criminals who might physically brutalize minors or teach them criminal habits. Finally, juvenile procedure emphasized procedural informality. Although the adversarial determination of facts might be appropriate for a criminal trial where the purpose was punishment, legalistic formalities were thought to be counterproductive in a juvenile proceeding where the purpose was rehabilitation.

Before 1967, because of the philosophy of the juvenile court and its traditions of procedural informality, juvenile proceedings typically offered none of the safeguards afforded adults in criminal trials. Juvenile court practices were virtually unaffected by the recent decisions of the Supreme Court interpreting DUE PROCESS to impose increasingly high procedural standards imposed on state criminal proceedings. Except in a few states, a young person accused of delinquency would not be assigned counsel, had no broad RIGHT AGAINST SELF-INCRIMINATION, was judged by a preponderance of the evidence standard (not proof beyond a REASONABLE DOUBT), had no right to TRIAL BY JURY, and often faced HEARSAY evidence.

The Supreme Court had hinted that due process might demand more. *Haley v. Ohio* (1948) held that a confession given by a fifteen-year-old boy and used in a criminal trial was involuntary. Justice WILLIAM O. DOUGLAS wrote that "[n]either man nor child can be allowed to stand condemned by methods that flout constitutional requirements of due process of law." More pointed doubts about the procedural informality of juvenile proceedings were expressed in *Kent v. United States* (1966). The Court's holding could be read narrowly: the District of Columbia must use fair procedures to transfer minors from juvenile to adult courts. But in Justice ABE FORTAS's opinion the landmark ruling that was to come the next year was foreshadowed in two respects: first, in the suggestion that the *parens patriae* doctrine of the juvenile court is not "an invitation to procedural arbitrariness"; and second, in the expression of the fear that notwithstanding the paternalistic philosophy of juvenile proceedings, the child may in fact receive "the worst of both worlds: that he gets neither the protections accorded to adults, nor the solicitous care and regenerative treatment postulated for children."

The constitutional watershed came in IN RE GAULT (1967), which held that due process required the states to apply various procedural safeguards to the guilt (or jurisdictional) phase of delinquency proceedings. The Court found that fifteen-year-old Gerald Gault, who had been committed for up to six years at an Arizona Industrial School for making an obscene telephone call, had been deprived of his constitutional rights to adequate written NOTICE of the charges, notice of his RIGHT TO COUNSEL, including assigned counsel, and of his right to confront and cross-examine witnesses; and advice of his privilege against self-incrimination. In a broad opinion rejecting the claim that *parens patriae* and the rehabilitative ideal justified procedural informality, Fortas declared that "unbridled discretion, however benevolently motivated, is frequently a poor substitute for principle and procedure." Although the holdings of *Gault* were expressly limited to the guilt phase of delinquency proceedings, *Gault* broadly declared a principle that children have constitutional rights of their own: "Whatever may be their precise impact, neither the FOURTEENTH AMENDMENT nor the BILL OF RIGHTS is for adults alone."

During the years following *Gault,* the Supreme Court decided several cases that expanded the constitutional rights of children in delinquency proceedings. IN RE WINSHIP (1970) held that the "beyond a reasonable doubt" standard of proof was constitutionally mandated in the adjudicatory stage of delinquency proceedings. *Breed v. Jones* (1975) held that the protections of the DOUBLE JEOPARDY clause were applicable to minors. The juvenile in *Breed* had been put in jeopardy by the original adjudicatory hearing where jurisdiction was established, and the Court found that the juvenile's subsequent criminal trial for the same offense constituted double jeopardy. But in *Swisher v. Brady* (1978) the Court held that the double jeopardy clause did not prohibit Maryland officials from taking exceptions to a SPECIAL MASTER's nondelinquency findings.

Despite the decisions in *Gault, Breed,* and *Winship,* the Court's decision in MCKEIVER V. PENNSYLVANIA (1971) reflects the Court's continued commitment to a separate system of justice for children and adults. In *McKeiver* the Court held that jury trials are not constitutionally required in delinquency proceedings. The Court reasoned that because a jury is not "a necessary component of accurate factfinding," denying a juvenile a jury trial would not violate the FUNDAMENTAL FAIRNESS component of the due process clause. In addition, the Court pointed out that "the jury trial, if required as a matter of constitutional precept, will remake the juvenile proceeding into a fully adversary process and will put an effective end to what has been the idealistic prospect of an intimate, informal protective proceeding."

Since *Gault,* juvenile proceedings involving noncriminal misbehavior, or juveniles thought to be beyond parental control, have been questioned on both procedural and substantive grounds. What does *Gault* imply about appropriate procedural safeguards? To what extent may a state restrain the liberty of a minor on the basis of acts that if committed by adults would not be criminal? The Supreme Court has not yet ruled on the due process requirements applicable to these proceedings, and most states do not provide the procedural safeguards now applicable in delinquency proceedings. In addition to voicing procedural concerns, critics have also criticized as vague and overly broad the language defining these "status offenses": running away from home, sexual promiscuity, truancy, and the like. With few exceptions, however, appellate courts have upheld the constitutional validity of these statutes against such attacks. The Supreme Court, which has written no opinion dealing with such proceedings, has sent mixed signals in summary opinions.

Today every state has juvenile proceedings that allow a court, typically a juvenile or family court, to assume jurisdiction over a neglected or abused child and remove the child from the parents' care. Although not protected by explicit language in the Constitution, the interest of parents in their children's upbringing plainly carries great constitutional weight. Beginning with MEYER V. NEBRASKA (1923), the Supreme Court has recognized the constitutional right of parents to direct the rearing of their children. The parents' claim to authority, however, is not absolute. Since the early nineteenth century, the *parens patriae* power has been held sufficient to empower courts of equity to remove a child requiring protection from parental custody and to appoint a suitable person as guardian.

Statutes authorizing state intervention have been criticized on substantive and procedural grounds. Vague substantive standards of abuse and neglect often leave judges to base their determinations on their own subjective values. As the Supreme Court noted in *Santosky v. Kramer* (1982), the Court has not precisely determined what forms of parental conduct justify state intrusion.

The Court has, however, decided several cases with respect to the procedural requirements where parental rights are terminated on grounds of abuse or neglect. In *Stanley v. Illinois* (1972) the Court relied on the doctrine of IRREBUTTABLE PRESUMPTIONS to hold that it is a denial of DUE PROCESS for unwed fathers to be disqualified from custody of their children without individualized hearings on their fitness. In *Santosky* the Court decided that the "fair preponderance of the evidence" standard, applied in New York parental rights termination proceedings, violated due process: "Before a State may sever completely and irrevocably the rights of parents in their natural child, due process requires that the State support its allegations by at least clear and convincing evidence." In LASSITER V. DEPARTMENT OF SOCIAL SERVICES (1981), however, the Court held that due process does not require assignment of counsel in every case involving the termination of parental rights. Although most jurisdictions do provide counsel for parents in such cases, few provide separate counsel for the children.

Gault has forced revolutionary changes in delinquency proceedings, but the requirements imposed in other sorts of juvenile proceedings have been modest. In the twenty years since that landmark, Supreme Court decisions have extended to young people accused of crime those procedural safeguards essential to an accurate determination of their guilt. To that extent, the Constitution no longer permits the procedural informality that characterized juvenile proceedings for over half a century. *Gault* and its progeny have substantially narrowed but not obliterated the differences between the adult criminal justice process and the juvenile justice process for delinquents. *McKeiver* underlines the conclusion that the Constitution does not require identical procedures for delinquents and adults. The Court has never held that equal protection requires the legal system to treat all those accused of crime the same, whether adults or minors.

Outside the guilt phase of delinquency proceedings, the Court has shown substantial caution, notwithstanding the potentially expansive announcement in *Gault* that children have rights, and that juvenile proceedings will be judged by their performance, not their promise. A number of factors probably underlie this caution. For one thing, the protective and rehabilitative aspirations of the juvenile court have never been rejected by the Court. As *McKeiver* suggests, the traditions of the juvenile court and the values of informality, flexibility, and protection still may carry some weight in constitutional adjudication. More fundamentally, decisions affecting children are special in two important respects that must affect constitutional analysis. First, defining constitutional rights in juvenile proceedings implicates defining parental rights, particularly in cases involving noncriminal misbehavior where the state may be reinforcing parental prerogatives, and in abuse and neglect proceedings, where the state directly challenges parental adequacy. Second, by reason of immaturity, young people may be more susceptible to coercion, and less able to make informed and responsible decisions. Whether considering the VOLUNTARINESS of a confession, the "knowing" WAIVER OF CONSTITUTIONAL RIGHTS, or the need for supervision and control, it would be foolish for the courts to conclude that age is irrelevant.

ROBERT H. MNOOKIN

(SEE ALSO: *Children's Rights; Schall v. Martin.*)

Bibliography

FLICKER, BARBARA 1982 *Standards for Juvenile Justice: A Summary and Analysis.* Juvenile Justice Standards Project. Cambridge, Mass.: Ballinger Publications.

FOX, SANFORD J. 1970 Juvenile Justice Reform: An Historical Perspective. *Stanford Law Review* 22:1187–1239.

MACK, JULIAN W. 1925 The Chancery Procedure in the Juvenile Court. Pages 310–319 in Jane Addams, ed., *The Child, the Clinic, and the Court.* New York: New Republic, Inc., and the Wieboldt Foundation.

PLATT, ANTHONY M. 1977 *The Child Savers: The Invention of Delinquency.* Chicago: University of Chicago Press.

PRESIDENT'S COMMISSION ON LAW ENFORCEMENT AND ADMINISTRATION OF JUSTICE 1967 *Task Force Report: Juvenile Delinquency and Youth Crime.* Washington, D.C.: Government Printing Office.

STAPLETON, W. VAUGHAN and TEITELBAUM, LEE E. 1972 *In Defense of Youth: A Study of the Role of Counsel in American Juvenile Courts.* New York: Russell Sage Foundation.

J. W. HAMPTON, JR. & CO. v. UNITED STATES

See: *Hampton & Co. v. United States*

K

KAHRIGER, UNITED STATES v.

See: *United States v. Marchetti*

KALVEN, HARRY, JR. (1914–1974)

Commencing the lectures that became his book, *The Negro and the First Amendment* (1965), Harry Kalven remarked that constitutional law was his hobby. He considered himself a torts teacher who had become interested in some constitutional subjects, and certainly his writings on the constitutional law of DEFAMATION and invasions of PRIVACY show deep understanding of the underlying private law. But Kalven was no constitutional amateur; his work on the jury system and on the FIRST AMENDMENT placed him in the first rank of scholars in both fields.

A long collaboration with Hans Zeisel culminated in the publication of *The American Jury* (1966), a work still hailed for its pathbreaking combination of traditional legal analysis and imaginative empirical study. His essays on defamation and OBSCENITY set patterns of thought that can be seen in scores of later scholarly works, and his article on "the PUBLIC FORUM" probably influenced the course of Supreme Court decisions more than any other single work of its era. (See also: TWO-LEVEL THEORY.)

An effervescent man, Kalven was much beloved by a generation of his students at the University of Chicago Law School, some of whom are numbered today among our leading constitutional scholars. His legacy to them, and to all of us through his scholarship, was a passion for applying careful, particularized analysis—in short, the lawyer's craft—to the ends of justice.

KENNETH L. KARST

Bibliography

In Memoriam: Harry Kalven, Jr. 1975 *The University of Chicago Law Review* 43:1–149. (Includes a complete bibliography of Kalven's writings.)

KANSAS-NEBRASKA ACT 10 Stat 277 (1854)

The Kansas-Nebraska Act declared the MISSOURI COMPROMISE of 1820 void and in its place enacted the policy of "POPULAR SOVEREIGNTY," thereby potentially opening all American territories to SLAVERY.

Democrats had extolled the finality of the COMPROMISE OF 1850 as a permanent resolution of the slavery controversy. Its constitutional elements included the stringent Fugitive Slave Act of 1850; the organization of New Mexico and Utah Territories without a prohibition of slavery; abolition of the slave trade in the DISTRICT OF COLUMBIA; and the "Clayton Compromise," which made all questions arising in the TERRITORIAL COURTS involving blacks' personal freedom or title to slaves directly appealable to the Supreme Court of the United States. The Illinois Democrat STEPHEN A. DOUGLAS, chairman of the Senate Committee on the Territories, disrupted this settlement in 1854, however, by introducing a bill to organize the remainder of the LOUISANA PURCHASE territory in order to facilitate construction of a transcontinental railroad that would have Chicago as its midcontinent terminus.

Douglas's original bill contained minor concessions to slavery, including reenactment of the Clayton Compromise provisions for Kansas Territory. But dissatisfied proslavery senators wrested further concessions. These included the declaration that the Missouri Compromise of 1820 (which prohibited slavery in the Louisiana Purchase territory north of latitude 36°30′, except Missouri) had been superseded by the Compromise of 1850 and was void. The Kansas-Nebraska Bill enacted the principle of popular sovereignty, declaring that "all questions pertaining to SLAVERY IN THE TERRITORIES . . . are to be left to the decision of the people residing therein." It included a vague suggestion that the federal Constitution might in some unspecified way inhibit the power of a territorial legislature to exclude slaves. The bill explicitly endorsed "nonintervention," a code word for an indefinite congeries of proslavery constitutional principles that hinted at an absence of power in any government to inhibit the intrusion of slavery into the territories prior to statehood.

The Kansas-Nebraska Act, together with the Compromise of 1850, surrounded the free states and the free territory of Minnesota with a cordon of territories open to slavery, thus threatening to make the Great Plains a vast proslavery chasm between the free states of the northeast and the free states and territories of the Pacific coast. The Whig party distintegrated, and its place in the North was taken by the new Republican party, which combined Whig economic objectives (free homesteads, federal aid to INTERNAL IMPROVEMENTS) with elements of the Free Soil platform of 1848. These Free Soil principles included the idea that Congress could not establish or permit slavery in a territory and that it could not constitutionally support slavery anywhere outside the extant slave states. Thus the proslavery concessions of 1854 paradoxically resulted in no immediate practical gain for slavery but rather in a widespread dissemination of antislavery constitutional beliefs.

Kansas Territory, organized by the Act, became a theater of struggle for sectional advantage between proslavery Missourians and free-state settlers. The ensuing violence disrupted the Democratic party, especially after President JAMES BUCHANAN tried to force the proslavery LECOMPTON CONSTITUTION on the free-soil majority of Kansas settlers. The Kansas-Nebraska Act thus contributed substantially to the disruption of the Union.

WILLIAM M. WIECEK

Bibliography

Russel, Robert R. 1963 The Issues in the Congressional Struggle over the Kansas-Nebraska Bill, 1854. *Journal of Southern History* 29:187–210.

KASSEL v. CONSOLIDATED FREIGHTWAYS CORPORATION

See: *Raymond Motor Transportation v. Rice*

KASTIGAR v. UNITED STATES
406 U.S. 441 (1972)

Until this case the rule was that the Fifth Amendment requires a grant of transactional immunity to displace a claim of the RIGHT AGAINST SELF-INCRIMINATION. Title II of the ORGANIZED CRIME CONTROL ACT of 1970 fixed a single comprehensive standard applicable to grants of immunity in all federal judicial, GRAND JURY, administrative, and legislative proceedings. The new law provided that when a witness is required to testify over his claim of the Fifth Amendment right, "no testimony or other information compelled under the order (or any information directly or indirectly derived from such testimony or other information) may be used against the witness in any criminal cases," except in a prosecution for perjury or failure to comply. The statute thus provided for use immunity, permitting a prosecution based on EVIDENCE not derived from the testimony forced by a grant of immunity. (See IMMUNITY GRANT.)

Kastigar was cited for contempt after he persisted in his refusal to testify concerning unnecessary dental services affecting the draft status of persons seeking to evade the draft. His refusal to testify raised the question whether the grant of use immunity was sufficient to displace the Fifth Amendment right.

A seven-member Supreme Court, voting 5–2, sustained the constitutionality of use immunity. Justice LEWIS F. POWELL declared: "We hold that such immunity from use and derivative use is coextensive with the scope of the privilege against self-incrimination, and therefore is sufficient to compel testimony over a claim of the privilege. . . . Transactional immunity, which accords full immunity from prosecution for the offense to which the compelled testimony relates, affords the witness considerably broader protection than does the Fifth Amendment privilege. The privilege has never been construed to mean that one who invokes it cannot subsequently be prosecuted." Powell dismissed COUNSELMAN V. HITCHCOCK (1892) and its progeny, which established the transactional immunity standard, as OBITER DICTA and therefore not binding. Powell reasoned that a witness who had use immunity against his compelled testimony is in substantially the same position as if he had invoked the Fifth Amendment in the absence of a grant of immunity.

But one who relies on his constitutional right to silence gives the state no possible way to use his testimony, however indirectly, against him, and he has not remotely, from the standpoint of the law, criminally implicated himself. Use immunity permits compulsion without removing the implication of criminality. On the other hand, the values of the Fifth Amendment are not infringed if the state prosecutes on evidence not related to the compelled testimony, and the state has the burden of proving that the prosecution relies on evidence from sources independent of the compelled testimony. The trouble is, as Justice THURGOOD MARSHALL pointed out in dissent, that only the prosecuting authorities know, if even they can know, the chains of information by which evidence was gathered. In any case, use immunity compels a person to be a witness against himself criminally.

LEONARD W. LEVY

Bibliography

LEVY, LEONARD W. 1974 *Against the Law: The Nixon Court and Criminal Justice.* Pages 173–187. New York: Harper & Row.

KATZ v. UNITED STATES
389 U.S. 347 (1967)

Katz ended one era of constitutional protection for FOURTH AMENDMENT rights and began another. In OLMSTEAD V. UNITED STATES (1928) the Supreme Court had virtually exempted from the Fourth Amendment's ban on UNREASONABLE SEARCHES and seizures any search that did not involve a physical intrusion on property and a seizure of tangible things. Although eroded by subsequent decisions, and superseded by a federal statute where wiretapping was required, *Olmstead*'s physical intrusion requirement inhibited constitutional control of aural and visual surveillance for forty years, until *Katz* was decided.

Federal agents, believing that Katz was using a pay telephone to transmit gambling information, attached a listening and recording device to the outside of the phone booth without trying to meet Fourth Amendment requirements. With the information obtained from the device, the police were able to convict Katz, but the Supreme Court overturned the conviction. The Court ruled that Katz was entitled to Fourth Amendment protection for his conversations and that a physical intrusion into an area occupied by Katz was not necessary to bring the amendment into play. "The Fourth Amendment protects people, not places," wrote Justice POTTER STEWART for a virtually unanimous Court (only Justice HUGO L. BLACK dissented). Justice JOHN MARSHALL HARLAN, concurring, developed a test for determining what interests are protected, which has come to be the accepted standard: "first that a person have exhibited an actual (subjective) expectation of privacy and second, that the expectation be one that society is prepared to recognize as 'reasonable.' "

The Court also set out some of the requirements for lawful ELECTRONIC EAVESDROPPING, supplementing those in BERGER V. NEW YORK (1967), many of which were incorporated in Title III of the OMNIBUS CRIME CONTROL AND SAFE STREETS ACT of 1968.

HERMAN SCHWARTZ

KATZENBACH v. MCCLUNG

See: *Heart of Atlanta Motel v. United States*

KATZENBACH v. MORGAN
384 U.S. 641 (1966)

This decision upheld the constitutionality of section 4(e) of the VOTING RIGHTS ACT OF 1965. Section 4(e) provided that no person who had successfully completed sixth grade in a school in which the language of instruction was other than English should be denied the right to vote in any election because of his inability to read or write English. In *Lassiter v. Northampton County Board of Elections* (1959) a unanimous Supreme Court had rejected a black citizen's attack on North Carolina's LITERACY TEST for voting. In *Morgan* the Court, in an opinion by Justice WILLIAM J. BRENNAN and over the dissents of Justices JOHN MARSHALL HARLAN and POTTER STEWART, rejected New York State's argument that in enforcing section 5 of the FOURTEENTH AMENDMENT Congress may prohibit enforcement of state law only if courts determine that the state law violates the FOURTEENTH AMENDMENT.

In light of *Lassiter,* it seemed unlikely that New York's literacy requirement would be judicially found to violate the Constitution. Instead, the Court found Section 4(e) appropriate legislation to enforce the Fourteenth Amendment by assuring the franchise to those who migrated to New York from PUERTO RICO after completing sixth grade, whether or not that right to vote had been unconstitutionally infringed. The *Morgan* view that the Fourteenth Amendment confers discretion upon Congress to act both remedially and prophylactically to protect Fourteenth Amendment rights makes the case a centerpiece for analysis of how far Congress may go to protect or restrict Fourteenth Amendment rights.

THEODORE EISENBERG

KEATING-OWEN CHILD LABOR ACT

39 Stat. 675 (1916)

This law marked the federal government's first attempt to regulate the use of child labor, culminating a decade-long effort by organized labor, social reformers and workers, publicists, and progressive politicians. The act prohibited the shipment in interstate or foreign commerce of any commodity produced in a mine or factory that employed children under the ages of sixteen and fourteen respectively.

Congressional debates over child labor legislation centered on the scope of national power. Opponents of the measure insisted that it involved a regulation of PRODUCTION, not commerce, and hence violated the TENTH AMENDMENT and the controlling precedent of UNITED STATES v. E. C. KNIGHT (1895). Although that decision had been distinguished in other cases involving NATIONAL POLICE POWER uses of the COMMERCE CLAUSE, such as the regulation of adulterated foods, STATES RIGHTS' oriented southern congressmen insisted that the national government could only prohibit harmful items from INTERSTATE COMMERCE. Goods made by children, they insisted, were not harmful in and of themselves. Supporters of a child labor law countered that congressional power over interstate commerce was plenary except for Fifth Amendment limitations. They also maintained that congressional action was imperative because state regulations had proven ineffective.

Supporters of the bill mobilized a broad array of interested groups, coordinated by the highly effective National Child Labor Committee. In addition, some traditionally conservative northern manufacturers lobbied for national action to counter the competitive advantage of new southern industries that operated under ineffectual state laws against child labor. A House committee report reflected this concern, noting that only national power could maintain a national marketplace and prevent unfair competition among the states. Finally, in the summer of 1916, independent progressives convinced a hitherto reluctant President WOODROW WILSON that his support was necessary to insure progressive backing in the forthcoming presidential election. Wilson decisively intervened with southern senators who had prevented passage for nearly six months, and the bill became law on September 1, 1916.

The Keating-Owen Act proved short-lived, for in less than two years the Supreme Court invalidated it in HAMMER v. DAGENHART (1918). A 5–4 majority held that the act regulated production, not interstate commerce, and violated the Tenth Amendment. The *Knight* precedent was reconfirmed, and the Court distinguished its approval of police power regulations of the flow of lottery tickets, adulterated foods, prostitutes, and liquor on the grounds that child labor products were not injurious.

Congress followed the Court's action with a new law based on the taxing power, but it, too, was voided. An effort to secure a child labor amendment to the Constitution languished in the 1920s and 1930s, but finally, in 1938, the FAIR LABOR STANDARDS ACT revived the essential elements of Keating-Owen. The Court sustained the new law in UNITED STATES v. DARBY (1941), expressly overruling *Hammer v. Dagenhart.*

STANLEY I. KUTLER

Bibliography

WOOD, STEPHEN 1968 *Constitutional Politics in the Progressive Era: Child Labor and the Law.* Chicago: University of Chicago Press.

KELLY, ALFRED H.

(1907–1976)

Alfred Hinsey Kelly taught constitutional history for many years at Wayne State University. With his colleague Winfred A. Harbison he wrote *The American Constitution: Its Origins and Development* (1948; 6th ed., with Herman Belz, 1982), now widely regarded as the best single-volume constitutional history ever written. In 1953 Kelly researched the background of the FOURTEENTH AMENDMENT for the NAACP LE-

GAL DEFENSE FUND's brief in BROWN V. BOARD OF EDUCATION (1954), concentrating on establishing the views of the framers of the amendment. He and Fund attorneys THURGOOD MARSHALL and William R. Ming prepared the final version of the historical sections of the brief submitted to the Court; in this brief and in later articles on the Amendment, Kelly distinguished "between the narrow scope of the CIVIL RIGHTS ACT OF 1866 and the much broader purposes of the Fourteenth Amendment itself" and emphasized the "broad equalitarian objectives" advocated by Representatives JOHN A. BINGHAM, THADDEUS STEVENS, and other members of Congress in the debates on the amendment. Kelly also provided inside accounts of the *Brown* litigation in his essay in *Quarrels That Shaped the Constitution* (John Garraty, ed., 1962) and in interviews with Richard Kluger for the latter's *Simple Justice* (1976).

RICHARD B. BERNSTEIN

KEMMLER, IN RE
136 U.S. 436 (1890)
MCELVAINE v. BRUSH
142 U.S. 155 (1891)
O'NEIL v. VERMONT
144 U.S. 155 (1892)

These cases dealt with the meaning of the ban on CRUEL AND UNUSUAL PUNISHMENT and with the INCORPORATION DOCTRINE of the FOURTEENTH AMENDMENT. Kemmler was sentenced to die in the electric chair, then recently invented. He argued that infliction of death by that device would violate the Fourteenth Amendment, because its PRIVILEGES AND IMMUNITIES clause or its DUE PROCESS clause meant that no state could inflict a cruel execution. The Court unanimously ruled that a cruel execution would be one involving torture or lingering death, "something inhuman and barbarous," but that the electric chair was a "humane" form of execution. The Court also held that no clause of the Fourteenth Amendment banned punishments not deemed cruel by state courts. Unlike Kemmler, McElvaine explicitly argued that the Fourteenth Amendment incorporated the Eighth Amendment's ban on cruel punishments; he also argued that solitary confinement of a convict sentenced to death was cruel. Unanimously the Court met and rejected both contentions. In O'Neil's case, however, Justices STEPHEN J. FIELD, DAVID J. BREWER, and JOHN MARSHALL HARLAN in DISSENTING OPINIONS declared that the Fourteenth Amendment applied Eighth Amendment rights and all "fundamental" rights to the states.

LEONARD W. LEVY

KENNEDY, JOHN F.
(1917–1963)

John Fitzgerald Kennedy entered the White House in 1961 as the heir to the liberal, Democratic party tradition of WOODROW WILSON, FRANKLIN D. ROOSEVELT, and HARRY S. TRUMAN. Youthful, vigorous, and blessed with extraordinary rhetorical powers, Kennedy saw himself as an activist chief executive and pledged to "get the country moving again," especially with respect to economic growth and international competition with the Soviet Union. But during his one thousand days in office, Kennedy's performance often lagged behind his promises.

His appointments to the Supreme Court were unexceptional. To the first vacancy, created by the retirement of CHARLES WHITTAKER, he named deputy attorney general BYRON R. WHITE, a former All-American football player, Rhodes Scholar, and campaign adviser. White's intellect and productivity exceeded those of his predecessor; he often aligned himself with the conservative faction on the WARREN COURT. To replace Justice FELIX FRANKFURTER and to fill the chair once occupied by OLIVER WENDELL HOLMES and BENJAMIN N. CARDOZO, Kennedy named ARTHUR GOLDBERG, a hard-working, conscientious labor lawyer, who usually voted with the liberals on the Warren Court but was blessed with neither intellectual brilliance nor a dashing prose style.

Kennedy's appointments to the lower federal courts were often dreadful, especially in the southern circuits, where "senatorial courtesy" gave great influence to segregationist Democratic senators. The result was Kennedy's appointment of a number of federal district judges who were openly segregationist and, in some instances, openly racist. On the other hand, Kennedy did place THURGOOD MARSHALL on the circuit court in New York; the Department of Justice, under the prodding of Attorney General ROBERT F. KENNEDY, began to intervene to protect CIVIL RIGHTS workers in the South; and Solicitor General Archibald Cox became a forceful and articulate spokesman for racial justice.

The struggle of black Americans to batter down the walls of segregation and win access to the voting booths of the deep South was the great domestic constitutional issue of the Kennedy years. The administration's response to this crisis blended pragmatism and expediency with idealism and occasional moral outrage. While forcing the South to accept the token integration of higher education, the administration did not push hard for similar results in the primary and secondary grades. The official violence inflicted upon civil rights activists during the Birmingham, Alabama, demonstrations led Kennedy to propose to Congress legislation which became, after his death, the landmark CIVIL RIGHTS ACT OF 1964. Many students of the Kennedy presidency regard his televised address in support of this legislation as his finest hour. On the other hand, the Kennedy brothers were not enthusiastic supporters of the 1963 March on Washington, and under pressure from FBI Director J. EDGAR HOOVER they endorsed the electronic surveillance of civil rights leader MARTIN LUTHER KING, JR.

If civil rights received growing constitutional protection from the Kennedy administration, CIVIL LIBERTIES often suffered at the hands of a regime that espoused vigorous presidential leadership and believed that the ends usually justified the means. Outraged that the nation's leading steel producers had raised prices in defiance of an informal agreement with labor and the White House, Kennedy threatened the offending corporations with tax audits, securities law investigations, and cancellation of defense contracts. Robert Kennedy's unremitting war against organized crime figures skirted the boundary of assorted illegalities, including WARRANTLESS SEARCHES and ELECTRONIC EAVESDROPPING. By waging a clandestine war against Fidel Castro's communist regime in Cuba, the Kennedy brothers also displayed a cavalier attitude about the RULE OF LAW. Operation Mongoose, directed by the attorney general, involved acts of sabotage and terrorism against the Cuban regime, most of them in violation of the neutrality laws.

Although their motives were sometimes the highest, John Kennedy and his closest advisers often fostered a disrespect for legal norms and an inflated conception of executive power that would haunt the nation during the decade after his assassination in 1963.

MICHAEL E. PARRISH

Bibliography

NAVASKY, VIÇTOR 1977 *Kennedy Justice.* New York: Atheneum.

PARMET, HERBERT S. 1983 *JFK: The Presidency of John F. Kennedy.* New York: Dial Press.

KENNEDY, ROBERT F.
(1925–1968)

After brief service in the Department of Justice, Robert F. Kennedy joined the Permanent Subcommittee on Investigations of the United States Senate (then headed by JOSEPH MCCARTHY) in 1953 as assistant counsel. When John McClellan became chairman in 1955 he appointed Kennedy chief counsel. In 1957 Kennedy became chief counsel of McClellan's Senate Rackets Committee and achieved national fame during the committee's investigations of teamsters' union leaders David Beck and James Hoffa.

Kennedy was appointed attorney general in 1961 by his brother, President JOHN F. KENNEDY. In this post he distinguished himself by vigorous enforcement of CIVIL RIGHTS—desegregating schools and interstate transportation facilities—and by finally securing the conviction of Hoffa on jury-tampering charges. (See HOFFA V. UNITED STATES, 1966.) As the President's closest adviser he exerted more influence on FOREIGN AFFAIRS than most attorneys general, heading the "executive committee" of the National Security Council during the Cuban missile crisis of 1962.

As a United States senator from New York (1965–1968), Kennedy voted for the GULF OF TONKIN RESOLUTION but later opposed President LYNDON B. JOHNSON'S conduct of the VIETNAM WAR. He was assassinated by a Palestinian nationalist while campaigning for the Democratic presidential nomination in 1968.

DENNIS J. MAHONEY

Bibliography

LASKY, VICTOR 1968 *Robert F. Kennedy: The Man and the Myth.* New York: Trident.

KENT, JAMES
(1763–1847)

James Kent, a New York jurist, influenced American constitutional jurisprudence through both his writings and his judicial opinions. Largely because of his *Commentaries on American Law,* Kent was as important a legal figure as any in nineteenth-century America. The *Commentaries* went through fourteen editions by 1900 and innumerable popular abridgments. After publication of the fifth edition, editors came and went, but they wrought their changes mostly in the notes, leaving Kent's work intact. For approximately three-quarters of a century Kent was for many lawyers, throughout the country, their primary legal authority.

Originally a two-volume set when it appeared in 1826, the *Commentaries* were quickly expanded to four. Ostensibly the book was commenced after Kent's mandatory retirement from the bench on reaching age sixty in 1823. Yet, it is possible to see the work in process through Kent's carefully crafted opinions beginning with his appointment to the New York Supreme Court in 1798, and continuing while he was the state's chancellor, 1814–1823. And it is scarcely stretching matters to consider the writing of the *Commentaries* a lifelong process.

Kent's twenty-five years of judicial opinions were imbued with the federalism of the late eighteenth century. At the heart of Kent's jurisprudence was an independent judiciary whose role was to maintain society's moral order. Because of a quirk in New York's 1777 constitution, Kent participated in the veto process as a member of the Council of Revision, which considered all bills passed by the legislature. This process meant that New York judges would have little reason to exercise JUDICIAL REVIEW when a statute's constitutionality was questioned in a case. Having approved the steamboat monopoly bill on several occasions while sitting on the council, for example, New York judges would be unlikely to declare the law contrary to the federal constitution when such a challenge was made in *Livingston v. Van Ingen* (1812) and GIBBONS V. OGDEN (1819, 1820).

The moral order that Kent and his brethren sought to maintain covered many facets of life, including freedom of expression. There was no room in Kent's order of things for BLASPHEMY—"it tends to corrupt the morals of the people, and to destroy good order," he wrote in *People v. Ruggles* (1811)—but a Federalist printer was afforded the defense of truth to the COMMON LAW charge of criminal libel against THOMAS JEFFERSON in PEOPLE V. CROSWELL (1804). The New York Supreme Court was evenly divided in *Croswell*, so that Kent's opinion, based on ALEXANDER HAMILTON's argument, did not become law in itself. A year later the legislature made truth a defense in libel suits, provided the alleged libelous matter "was published with good motives and for justifiable ends." Kent and his colleagues were careful, moreover, in their interpretation of the law, subsequently inserted in the state constitution of 1821, to protect officeholders, setting the groundwork for *Root v. King* (1829), which kept a bridle on attacks on New York public officials until NEW YORK TIMES V. SULLIVAN (1964).

Kent made another major contribution to constitutional law in *Livingston v. Van Ingen* (1812), by elaborately enunciating the doctrine of concurrent commerce powers. The Livingston-Fulton steamboat monopoly symbolized New York's encouragement of commercial enterprise. Under the statute creating the monopoly, any competitor was required to get a license in order to run a steamboat on New York waters. In his opinion for the state's court of last resort, Kent legitimized the monopoly in a decision that reversed Chancellor JOHN LANSING's refusal to grant the monopoly an INJUNCTION against unlicensed competition. Of particular constitutional moment was the argument that the monopoly violated the federal Constitution's COMMERCE CLAUSE. In rejecting this argument, Kent asserted that in the absence of actual conflict between state and national laws, states retained the powers to regulate commerce. Seven years later in *Ogden v. Gibbons* (1819), Kent found no such conflict between the monopoly and the federal coasting act of 1793. In the United States Supreme Court, however, that served as the basis for JOHN MARSHALL's invalidation of the monopoly in GIBBONS V. OGDEN (1824). Kent's doctrine of concurrent commerce powers persisted, though, largely through the efforts of his former law clerk and judicial colleague, SMITH THOMPSON, and for a time it won the support of the TANEY COURT.

Kent was also responsible for first enunciating what would become the Cherokee doctrine. Speaking for the New York court in *Goodell v. Jackson* (1823), Kent fully developed the paternalistic notion that American Indian peoples, though subject, were sovereign nations, a theme adopted by Thompson in his *Cherokee Nation v. Georgia* dissent (1831), which in turn was adopted by Marshall for the Supreme Court in *Worcester v. Georgia* (1832). (See CHEROKEE INDIAN CASES.)

Important as Kent's occasional constitutional opinions may have been, his major contribution to constitutional development remains the *Commentaries.* There is apparent irony in this accomplishment because Kent did not emphasize constitutional law; instead, he salted that subject into the great body of American law between the law of nations and the construction of wills. Kent succeeded in putting constitutional law in its proper perspective compared to other important aspects of the law. In addition, Kent admirably digested the great Marshall opinions so as, in the opinion of THOMAS REED POWELL, to make them decidedly more palatable than they were in the original. Needless to say, the *Commentaries* continued to vote Federalist.

DONALD ROPER

Bibliography

BAUER, ELIZABETH KELLEY 1952 *Commentaries on the Constitution 1790–1860.* New York: Columbia University Press.

HORTON, JOHN T. 1939 *James Kent: A Study in Conservatism 1763–1847.* New York: Appleton-Century Co.

KENT v. DULLES
357 U.S. 116 (1958)

This decision severely limited the State Department's discretionary passport policies. During the Cold War era, the department routinely denied passports to those who refused to sign a noncommunist affidavit. The Supreme Court held that the department lacked statutory authority for this policy and went on to remark in OBITER DICTUM that the RIGHT TO TRAVEL, which it traced back to MAGNA CARTA, was protected by the DUE PROCESS clause of the FIFTH AMENDMENT.

STANLEY I. KUTLER

KENTUCKY RESOLUTIONS

See: Virginia and Kentucky Resolutions

KER v. CALIFORNIA
374 U.S. 23 (1963)

In *Ker* the Supreme Court clarified the constitutional standards governing the states in SEARCH AND SEIZURE cases. MAPP V. OHIO (1961), in applying the federal EXCLUSIONARY RULE against the states, had left undetermined whether they would retain some latitude to fashion their own search rules. The Court answered this question in *Ker,* holding that the protection against state searches granted by the FOURTEENTH AMENDMENT is coextensive with that of the FOURTH AMENDMENT against federal searches. Only Justice JOHN MARSHALL HARLAN disagreed. The Court's single-standard position, he feared, might lead to dilution of federal search safeguards because the Court would be reluctant to fetter the states with standards beyond their reach.

JACOB W. LANDYNSKI

KEYES v. SCHOOL DISTRICT NO. 1
413 U.S. 189 (1973)

Keyes, the Denver school DESEGREGATION case, was the first such case to reach the Supreme Court from a district outside the South. The case gave the Court an opportunity to decide whether the fact of separation of the races in a city's schools was sufficient to justify desegregation remedies, even in the absence of any history of state law commanding SEGREGATION or any deliberate segregative action by the school board. The Court found it unnecessary to decide this question. Deliberate segregative actions of the board in one substantial part of the city, the Court said, raised a presumption of de jure segregation affecting the whole district; absent a showing that the district's parts were truly unrelated, a districtwide remedy would be approved on the basis of SWANN V. CHARLOTTE-MECKLENBURG BOARD OF EDUCATION (1971). The Court thus affirmed a busing order affecting twelve percent of the district's pupils. Justice WILLIAM J. BRENNAN wrote for a Court that was no longer unanimous.

Justice LEWIS F. POWELL, in a separate opinion that was more dissent than concurrence, argued that the time had come to scrap the DE FACTO/DE JURE distinction. In his view, *Swann* effectively required a school board to provide a remedy not only for segregation deliberately brought about by its own action or by state law but also for residential segregation—a fact of urban life throughout the country. "Segregative intent" was an illusory concept, he said. Once the fact of racial separation is shown, a board should have the duty to take appropriate steps to minimize school segregation. Massive busing, however, was not an appropriate remedy in his opinion, chiefly because of its costs to the values of the neighborhood school. Justice WILLIAM O. DOUGLAS, concurring, also thought that the de facto/de jure distinction made no sense but thought busing an appropriate remedy. Chief Justice WARREN E. BURGER concurred in the result, Justice WILLIAM H. REHNQUIST dissented, and Justice BYRON R. WHITE did not participate.

KENNETH L. KARST

(SEE ALSO: *School Busing; Columbus Board of Education v. Penick, 1979.*)

KEYISHIAN v. BOARD OF REGENTS
385 U.S. 589 (1967)

ADLER V. BOARD OF EDUCATION (1952) was one of the cases in which the Supreme Court upheld a wide range of regulations barring "subversives" from government employment. *Keyishian* overruled *Adler* and was the culmination of a series of later decisions restricting LOYALTY-SECURITY PROGRAMS, typically by invoking the VAGUENESS and OVERBREADTH doctrines. *Keyishian* struck down some parts of a complex New York law limiting employment in public teaching; the law's use of the term "seditious" was unconstitutionally vague. Other parts of the law were invalid because they prohibited *mere* knowing membership in the Communist party without the specific intent required by ELFBRANDT v. RUSSELL (1966). *Keyishian* confirmed the Court's previous decisions rejecting the doctrine that public employment is a privilege to which government may attach whatever conditions it pleases.

MARTIN SHAPIRO

KIDD v. PEARSON
128 U.S. 1 (1888)

A unanimous Court distinguished manufacturing and all forms of PRODUCTION from INTERSTATE COMMERCE, holding that a state act prohibiting the manufacture of intoxicants did not conflict with the national power to regulate interstate commerce and that the manufacture of a product for export to other states did not make it an article of interstate commerce.

LEONARD W. LEVY

KILBOURN v. THOMPSON
103 U.S. 168 (1881)

Until this case Congress believed that its power of conducting investigations was unlimited and that its judicial authority to punish contumacious witnesses for contempt was unquestionable. After this case both the investigatory and CONTEMPT POWERS of Congress were distinctly limited and subject to JUDICIAL REVIEW. Not until MCGRAIN v. DAUGHERTY (1927) did the Court firmly establish the constitutional basis for oversight and investigatory powers. The decision in *Kilbourn* was so negative in character that the legitimate area of LEGISLATIVE INVESTIGATIONS seemed murky.

Kilbourn developed out of the House's investigation, by a select committee, into the activities of a bankrupt banking firm that owed money to the United States. The committee subpoenaed Kilbourn's records, which he refused to produce, and interrogated him, but he refused to answer on the ground that the questions concerned private matters. The House cited him for contempt and jailed him. He in turn sued for false arrest, and on a writ of HABEAS CORPUS he obtained a review of his case before the Supreme Court.

Unanimously, in an opinion by Justice SAMUEL F. MILLER, the Court held that neither house of Congress can punish a witness for contumacy unless his testimony is required on a matter concerning which "the House has jurisdiction to inquire," and, Miller added, neither house has "the general power of making inquiry into the private affairs of the citizen." The subject of this inquiry, Miller said, was judicial in nature, not legislative, and a case was pending in a lower federal court. The investigation was fruitless also because "it could result in no valid legislation" on the subject of the inquiry. Thus, the courts hold final power to decide what constitutes a contempt of Congress, and Congress cannot compel a witness to testify in an investigation that cannot assist remedial legislation.

LEONARD W. LEVY

KING, MARTIN LUTHER, JR.
(1929–1968)

Martin Luther King, Jr., preeminent leader of the black freedom movement of the 1950s and 1960s, repeatedly challenged America to live up to the egalitarian principles set forth in the three Reconstruction era amendments. "If we are wrong, the Constitution of the United States is wrong," King told his Alabama colleagues in an unpublished speech on December 5, 1955, the day that Montgomery's black citizens began a year-long campaign against discriminatory seating practices on city buses. Victory in that struggle catapulted King to national prominence as an exponent of nonviolent protest against racial oppression, and throughout the twelve remaining years of his life King pursued and expanded his challenge to injustice and exploitation internationally as well as domestically.

Pointing out in his 1964 book, *Why We Can't Wait*, that the United States was "a society where the supreme law of the land, the Constitution, is rendered inoperative in vast areas of the nation" because of explicit RACIAL DISCRIMINATION, King described the CIVIL RIGHTS struggle as a resumption "of that noble journey toward the goals reflected in the PREAMBLE to the Constitution, the Constitution itself, the BILL OF RIGHTS and the THIRTEENTH, FOURTEENTH, and FIFTEENTH AMENDMENTS." Protest campaigns in segregationist strongholds such as Birmingham and Selma, Alabama, stimulated national support for landmark legislative achievements such as the CIVIL RIGHTS ACT OF 1964 and the VOTING RIGHTS ACT of 1965, and produced an all-but-complete victory over de jure segregation by the middle of that decade.

Recognizing that other evils more subtle than segregation also tangibly afflicted the daily lives of millions of black people, King broadened his attack to include all forms of poverty and economic injustice, saying that the movement had to go beyond civil rights to human rights. That progression, coupled with King's outspoken condemnations of America's militaristic foreign policy, particularly its participation in the VIETNAM WAR, led King to advocate basic changes in American society reaching far beyond his previous attacks on racial discrimination.

Identified as a prominent advocate of CIVIL DISOBEDIENCE against immoral segregation statutes even before his influential 1963 "Letter from Birmingham Jail," King defended his position by reference to the long tradition of NATURAL RIGHTS thinking. In his early years of civil rights activism King said that peaceful, willing violation of such statutes forced courts to void unconstitutional provisions, but toward the end of his life King expanded his argument, contending that the weightier moral demands of social justice sometimes required that nondiscriminatory laws also be violated. If any laws blocked the oppressed from confronting the nation with moral issues of human rights and economic justice, then such laws rightfully could be breached. Although King until 1966 had believed that depicting the brutalities of racism best attracted national support for civil rights, in his final years King repeatedly suggested that protesters might have to coerce concessions from unwilling federal officials by obstructing the orderly functioning of society until the desired policy changes were made.

King's challenge to American racism helped to close the gap between constitutional principles and discriminatory practices; his broader struggle against other forms of human injustice left a legacy that will stimulate future generations for years to come.

DAVID J. GARROW

Bibliography

GARROW, DAVID J. 1986 *Bearing the Cross: Martin Luther King, Jr., and the Southern Christian Leadership Conference, 1955–1968.* New York: William Morrow.

KING, MARTIN LUTHER, JR. 1964 *Why We Can't Wait.* New York: New American Library.

KING, RUFUS
(1755–1827)

Rufus King, a Harvard-educated lawyer who had been an officer in the Revolutionary War, represented Massachusetts in the Congress of the Confederation from 1784 to 1787. He was a principal author of the NORTHWEST ORDINANCE, and wrote its provisions prohibiting SLAVERY and protecting the OBLIGATION OF CONTRACTS against legislative impairment.

Although he originally opposed either calling a convention or radically altering the ARTICLES OF CONFEDERATION, he represented Massachusetts at the CONSTITUTIONAL CONVENTION OF 1787. King soon became a spokesman for those who favored a strong national government and for the interests of the large northern states. Very early in the debates he advocated consolidation rather than confederation: although he recognized that it was impossible to annihilate the states, he thought they should be stripped of much of their power. He argued against equal representation of the states in the Senate, and he favored popular election of the President. King proposed the CONTRACT CLAUSE, and, although it was voted down in the Committee of the Whole, he saw that it was inserted into the Constitution by the Committee on Style, of which he was a member. In opposition to GOUVERNEUR MORRIS, he supported the admission of new states on terms of equality with the old. King was also one of the first to recognize publicly that the politically important division of the country was not between large and small states, but between North and South.

Almost immediately after attending the Massachusetts ratifying convention, he moved to New York and was elected one of its original United States senators. King served in the Senate from 1789 to 1796, and was a leading spokesman for ALEXANDER HAMILTON (his political patron) and the Federalist administration.

King returned to the Senate in 1813. Although an opponent of the War of 1812, he refused to attend the HARTFORD CONVENTION, denounced New England's threat of SECESSION, and supported the government financially. Serving in the Senate until 1825, King participated in the debates over the MISSOURI COMPROMISE. Although not an abolitionist, King opposed the extension of SLAVERY, and he contended that it was within the power of Congress to make permanent abolition of slavery a condition of Missouri's admission as a state. He insisted upon constitutional guarantees of the rights of black Missourians.

In his public career, King was the Federalist candidate for vice-president (1804, 1808) and President (1816), and was twice minister to Great Britain (1796–1803, 1825–1826).

DENNIS J. MAHONEY

KINGSLEY BOOKS, INC. v. BROWN
354 U.S. 436 (1957)

Kingsley authorized broad civil remedies to control the merchandising of OBSCENITY. The Supreme Court upheld a New York statute permitting state officials to obtain INJUNCTIONS against the sale of allegedly obscene materials before a judicial determination that the materials were obscene and, after trial, to seize and destroy any material found to be obscene. Rejecting assertions that the statutory scheme was an unconstitutional PRIOR RESTRAINT, the majority concluded that the scheme in actual application did not differ from the criminal remedies sanctioned in *Alberts v. California* (1957), decided the same day. (See ROTH V. UNITED STATES, 1957.)

The dissenters argued that numerous procedural defects rendered the statute unconstitutional. The seizure and destruction of the obscene books were tantamount to "book burning," according to Chief Justice EARL WARREN, for books were judged outside the context of their use. Justices WILLIAM O. DOUGLAS and HUGO L. BLACK, jointly dissenting, argued that an injunction before trial was censorship. They also would have required a finding of obscenity for each publication of the condemned work rather than regulating speech like "diseased cattle and impure butter." Justice WILLIAM J. BRENNAN contended that the statute was vastly defective for permitting a judge, rather than a jury, to determine a work's obscenity.

KIM MCLANE WARDLAW

KINGSLEY INTERNATIONAL PICTURES CORP. v. REGENTS
360 U.S. 684 (1959)

In *Kingsley International Pictures Corp. v. Regents* the state of New York had refused to issue a license for the motion picture *Lady Chatterley's Lover* because it "alluringly portrays adultery as proper behavior." There was no claim that the film constituted an INCITEMENT TO UNLAWFUL CONDUCT. Without deciding whether all licensing schemes for motion pictures were unconstitutional the Supreme Court held that the refusal to grant this license violated the FIRST AMENDMENT. The Court reaffirmed that motion pictures were within the scope of the First Amendment and proclaimed that the amendment's "basic guarantee" is "the freedom to advocate ideas," including the idea that adultery may in some cases be justified.

STEVEN SHIFFRIN

KINSELLA v. KRUEGER

See: *Reid v. Covert*

KIRBY v. ILLINOIS
406 U.S. 682 (1972)

In an effort to eviscerate UNITED STATES V. WADE (1967) without overruling it, a plurality of the Supreme Court held that the RIGHT TO COUNSEL does not apply to pretrial identification procedures that occur before INDICTMENT or other indicia of formal criminal charges. The case involved the most suggestive confrontation imaginable: a one-to-one presentation of the person upon whom police had found a robbery victim's credit cards. Yet the Court held that because this confrontation occurred before Kirby had been formally charged, it was not a "critical stage" of the proceedings requiring counsel to preserve a future right to a FAIR TRIAL.

The distinction between pre- and postindictment identification procedures is dubious for two reasons. First, the vast majority of LINEUPS occur while cases are under investigation, and thus before indictment. Second, all the dangers of irreparable mistaken identification and the inability of counsel to reconstruct the pretrial confrontation—which had been the foundation of *Wade*—apply whether the identification occurs before or after formal charging. The plurality's startling misreading of precedent was highlighted when Justice BYRON R. WHITE, who dissented in *Wade,* dissented in *Kirby* also, saying that *Wade* compelled the opposite result.

Kirby leaves untouched the possible DUE PROCESS objections to an unfair pretrial confrontation. Proof of unfairness would require suppression of testimony about the pretrial procedure as well as the in-court identification by a witness whose perceptions were possibly tainted. A due process objection may be made whether the pretrial confrontation has occurred before or after formal charging. Of course, it is much more difficult for the accused to show that a confrontation was fundamentally unfair than to prove that it was done without counsel.

BARBARA ALLEN BABCOCK

KIRSCHBAUM v. WALLING
316 U.S. 517 (1942)

After UNITED STATES V. DARBY (1941) the Court decided many cases on the coverage of the FAIR LABOR STANDARDS ACT, which benefited employees "engaged in commerce or in the PRODUCTION of goods for commerce." Congress by no means had made the statute coextensive with the limits of its power over INTERSTATE COMMERCE, but every time the Court ruled that the statute covered certain employees, it brought their activities within the scope of the COMMERCE CLAUSE. The leading case is *Kirschbaum*, which extended statutory coverage—and thus the commerce power—to employees who were at least one step away from production. On the theory that service and maintenance employees kept a building safe and habitable, the Court held that a landlord who rented space to a firm that manufactured goods destined for interstate commerce had to pay his janitors and elevator operators the minima fixed by the statute. In *Borden Milk Co. v. Barella* (1945), the Court upheld application of the statute to service employees in a building occupied by the executive offices of a company that carried on its interstate manufacturing elsewhere. In *Martino v. Michigan Window Cleaning Co.* (1946), the employees who benefited from the statute—window cleaners employed by a company to service an industrial building—were two steps removed from production for commerce. Similarly, in *D. A. Schulte v. Gangi* (1946), the Court extended the statute and the commerce power to the maintenance people employed by a building owner who rented space to a firm that worked on intrastate goods and returned them to a contractor who subsequently shipped some of them across state lines. Employees sometimes did lose, but the Court's interpretations in these cases showed that the commerce power virtually authorized Congress to regulate any business, however remote its economic connection with interstate commerce.

LEONARD W. LEVY

KLOPFER v. NORTH CAROLINA
386 U.S. 213 (1967)

Prior to the Supreme Court's decision in *Klopfer*, only defendants in federal courts enjoyed the Sixth Amendment right to a SPEEDY TRIAL. Consequently, legislation in many states permitted prosecutors to postpone bringing pending cases to trial indefinitely. Declaring such state laws unconstitutional, the Court, in an opinion by Chief Justice EARL WARREN, held that the right to a speedy trial is a FUNDAMENTAL RIGHT incorporated by the DUE PROCESS CLAUSE of the FOURTEENTH AMENDMENT and thus fully applicable in state trials.

WENDY E. LEVY

(SEE ALSO: *Incorporation Doctrine.*)

KNIGHT COMPANY, E. C., UNITED STATES v.
156 U.S. 1 (1895)

The issue in the Supreme Court's first interpretation of the SHERMAN ANTITRUST ACT hung on the lawfulness of the Sugar Trust's acquisition of its competitors, and the decision nearly eviscerated the act. An 8–1 Court used the doctrine of DUAL FEDERALISM in dismissing a government suit to dissolve the trust.

When the American Sugar Refining Company (the Sugar Trust) acquired four Philadelphia refineries in 1892 it controlled ninety-eight percent of domestic sugar manufacturing. Attorney General RICHARD OLNEY, who inherited the case from his predecessor, believed that the Sherman Act was founded on a false economic theory; he believed that free competition had been "thoroughly discredited" and that the act should have regulated trusts as a natural development, not prohibited them. There is, however, little evidence of deliberate carelessness in Olney's preparation of the case. Although the MAJORITY OPINION commented upon a lack of EVIDENCE to demonstrate a restraint of trade, the government never believed that such a showing was necessary. Prior decisions had clearly held sales to be a part of commerce; the majority would admit as much here, and a lower court conceded that the trust had sought control of both refining and sales. Clever defense strategy successfully shifted the Court's attention from restraint of INTERSTATE COMMERCE to a consideration whether the commerce power extended to manufacturing.

Chief Justice MELVILLE W. FULLER's opinion for the Court endorsed the defendants' argument. By repeating that manufacturing was separable from commerce, the Court made a formally plausible distinction based solely on precedent. (See KIDD V. PEARSON, 1888.) Although the Sugar Trust had monopolized manufacturing, the Court found no Sherman Act violation because the acquisition of the Philadelphia refineries involved INTRASTATE COMMERCE. Although manufacturing "involves in a certain sense the control of its disposition . . . this is a secondary and not the primary sense." The trust did not lead to control of interstate commerce and so "affects it only incidentally and indirectly." This direct/indirect effects test of the reach of federal regulation had been mentioned in earlier cases (see EFFECTS ON COMMERCE) and was here employed to reach unrealistic ends: "Contracts, combinations, or conspiracies to control domestic enterprise in manufacture, agriculture, mining, PRODUCTION in all its forms, or to raise or lower prices or wages, might unquestionably tend to restrain external as well as domestic trade, but the restraint would be an indirect result, however inevitable and whatever its extent, and such result would not necessarily determine the object of the contract, combination or conspiracy."

Justice JOHN MARSHALL HARLAN, dissenting, posed the basic question: "What, in a legal sense, is a restraint of trade?" The trust was in business to sell as well as manufacture sugar, and most of its sales obviously constituted interstate commerce. Relying on GIBBONS V. OGDEN (1824), Harlan posited a broad view of the commerce power. Any obstruction of commerce among the states was an impairment of that commerce and must be treated as such. The majority's construction of the Sherman Act left the public "at the mercy of combinations." The Sugar Trust's inevitable purpose of preventing free competition doomed it as a restraint of trade. "The general government is not placed by the Constitution in such a condition of helplessness that it must fold its arms and remain inactive while capital combines . . . to destroy competition." Harlan correctly believed that the issue should not have been the contracts of acquisition but rather the trust's control over commerce in sugar.

By excluding manufacturing monopolies from the scope of the antitrust act, the decision in *Knight* cleared the way for the greatest merger and consolidation movement in American history. Chief among the industries taking advantage of the opportunities given them by the Supreme Court were manufacturing and the railroads. Such massive combines as United States Steel Corporation, American Can Company, International Harvester, and Standard Oil of New Jersey can trace their origins to this period. From 1879 to 1897 fewer than a dozen important combinations had been formed, with a total capital of around one billion dollars. Before the century ended, nearly two hundred more combinations formed, with a total capital exceeding three billion dollars. Of some 318 CORPORATIONS in business in 1904, nearly seventy-five percent had been formed after 1897.

The Court's opinion also seriously injured the concept of national supremacy; Fuller's distinction between production and commerce lasted until 1937. In the meantime, the Court had created what EDWARD S. CORWIN called a "twilight zone" in which national regulation of corporations was uncertain and haphazard. Although the Court would apply the Sherman Act to railroads within two years (see UNITED STATES V. TRANS-MISSOURI FREIGHT ASSOCIATION, 1897), not until the reinterpretation in NORTHERN SECURITIES CO. V. UNITED STATES (1904) would the Sherman Act become an effective tool against big business.

DAVID GORDON

Bibliography

EICHNER, ALFRED S. 1969 *Emergence of Oligopoly: Sugar Refining as a Case Study.* Westport, Conn.: Greenwood Press.

KNOX, PHILANDER C.
(1853–1921)

Although Philander Chase Knox, a Pittsburgh corporation lawyer, had helped create the United States Steel Corporation, he became an active antitrust prosecutor as THEODORE ROOSEVELT'S ATTORNEY GENERAL (1901–1904). Knox initiated the efficient and meticulous prosecution in NORTHERN SECURITIES CO. V. UNITED STATES (1904) and successfully argued that case before the Supreme Court. He also began victorious cases against the Salt Trust, the Coal Trust, and the Beef Trust, the latter culminating in the STREAM OF COMMERCE doctrine in SWIFT & COMPANY V. UNITED STATES (1905). Knox's actions helped revive the SHERMAN ANTITRUST ACT and insured a prominent political career after his resignation in 1904. He served as WILLIAM HOWARD TAFT'S secretary of state (1909–1913) and later, in the Senate, played a major role in railroad rate legislation. An "irreconcilable" over the League of Nations, Knox believed it imposed unconstitutional obligations under the TREATY POWER.

DAVID GORDON

KNOX v. LEE

See: Legal Tender Cases

KOLENDER v. LAWSON
461 U.S. 352 (1983)

The facts of this case, not revealed by the official report, enhanced its interest. Lawson was a law-abiding black man of unorthodox attire and grooming who suffered frequent police harassment when he walked in white neighborhoods. A 7–2 Supreme Court held VOID FOR VAGUENESS a California statute obligating persons who "wander" the streets to provide credible and reliable identification and to explain their business to the police. The majority reasoned that the statute vested excessive discretion in the police to decide whether to stop and interrogate a suspect or leave him alone in the absence of PROBABLE CAUSE to arrest him. The Court also suggested that the statute compromised the constitutional right to freedom of movement.

LEONARD W. LEVY

KONIGSBERG v. STATE BAR
353 U.S. 252 (1957)
366 U.S. 36 (1961)

In *Konigsberg* I the Supreme Court held that refusal to answer questions about political associations was constitutionally insufficient to justify a state bar association finding of failure to demonstrate good moral character, and consequent denial of bar admission. In *Konigsberg* II the Court upheld a second denial of admission based on the ground that refusal to answer obstructed full investigation of the applicant's qualifications.

MARTIN SHAPIRO

KOREAN WAR

In June 1950 North Korea attacked South Korea; within a week President HARRY S. TRUMAN committed American air, sea, and ground forces to South Korea's defense. The resulting three-year involvement lasted into the administration of DWIGHT D. EISENHOWER and became the largest undeclared war in American history prior to the Vietnam involvement.

The initial rush of events created enduring confusion about the constitutional basis for the American intervention. On June 25, the day following the attack, the United States obtained a United Nations Security Council resolution ordering North Korean withdrawal. Two days later, with fighting continuing, the Security Council requested U.N. members to assist in repelling the aggression. That day, without congressional approval, President Truman publicly ordered American air and naval support for the South Koreans, and throughout his remaining tenure in office he persistently called the conflict a United Nations POLICE ACTION. The key American decisions had actually preceded the U.N. request, however, and critics, led by Senator Robert A. Taft, convincingly demonstrated that pertinent provisions of the UNITED NATIONS CHARTER (having status as treaty law in the United States) and the United Nations Participation Act gave no constitutional authority to the American President. The necessary agreements for United States peacekeeping forces had never been concluded with the Security Council.

Careful defenders of Truman's actions, especially Secretary of State Dean Acheson, argued that Truman's authority derived from his duty as COMMANDER-IN-CHIEF to protect American interests. One such interest was the preservation of the United Nations as an instrument for peace; another was the security of American forces in the Pacific area. The defenders relied, too, on presidential control of FOREIGN AFFAIRS and on the alleged precedent of eighty-five prior instances of presidential use of military forces without a DECLARATION OF WAR. Not surprisingly, critics also found these sources insufficient, strongly disagreeing about the meaning of Congress's power "to declare war" and about the legal relevance of past episodes of unilateral presidential action. Truman nonetheless followed Acheson's advice and explicitly refused to request formal authorization from Congress.

The war had other constitutional dimensions, as well. In April 1951, after serious policy disagreements, Truman dismissed his outspoken Korean and Far Eastern commander, General of the Army Douglas MacArthur, thereby reaffirming the principle of civilian control over the military. (See CIVIL-MILITARY RELATIONS). Later, in April 1952, when a strike threatened military production for Korea, the President seized American steel mills, an action subsequently held unconstitutional in YOUNGSTOWN SHEET AND TUBE CO. V. SAWYER (1952), a decision that arguably narrowed future presidential prerogatives. The Korean engagement also intensified clashes over the FIRST AMENDMENT by contributing to the anticommunist sentiment tapped by Senator Joseph R. McCarthy. Similarly, the war provided context and impulse for the partially successful congressional effort, in the "Great Debate" of 1951, to restrict additional presidential commitment of troops to Europe. Finally, the war figured rhetorically in calls for limiting the TREATY POWER and EXECUTIVE AGREEMENTS through the BRICKER AMENDMENT.

By the time of the Korean armistice on July 27, 1953, American casualties numbered 142,000, including 33,600 deaths. The war thus stands squarely as de facto precedent for presidential war-making of substantial magnitude, and more so because American courts, in typical fashion, refrained from ruling on its constitutional base. Ironically, memories of the domestic debates over Korea helped generate later efforts, such as the Gulf of Tonkin Resolution (1964), to obtain prior congressional endorsement of foreign military ventures.

CHARLES A. LOFGREN

Bibliography

LOFGREN, CHARLES A. 1969 Mr. Truman's War: A Debate and Its Aftermath. *Review of Politics* 31:223–241.

MURPHY, PAUL L. 1972 *The Constitution in Crisis Times, 1918–1969.* New York: Harper & Row.

KOREMATSU v. UNITED STATES

See: Japanese American Cases

KOVACS v. COOPER
336 U.S. 77 (1949)

After earlier suggesting that a ban on SOUND TRUCKS would be invalid, the Supreme Court held that "loud and raucous" loudspeakers could be prohibited as a reasonable regulation of time, place, and manner of speech. The opinion by Justice STANLEY REED noted interests in residential tranquillity, and it is cited as a PRIVACY decision. Justice FELIX FRANKFURTER, concurring, delivered a major attack on the PREFERRED FREEDOM doctrine.

MARTIN SHAPIRO

KRAMER v. UNION FREE SCHOOL DISTRICT NO. 15
395 U.S. 621 (1969)

New York limited school district VOTING RIGHTS to residents who owned (or leased) real property or were parents (or guardians) of public school children. Following HARPER V. VIRGINIA BOARD OF ELECTIONS (1966), the Supreme Court held, 6–3, that this restriction denied the EQUAL PROTECTION OF THE LAWS to an adult resident living in his parents' home.

Chief Justice EARL WARREN wrote for the Court. A RATIONAL BASIS for the voting limitation was not enough; it must be justified as necessary to promote a COMPELLING STATE INTEREST. Assuming that New York could limit voting to persons especially interested in school affairs, this law's classification was insufficiently tailored to that purpose; an uninterested, non-taxpaying renter could vote, but Kramer, a taxpayer interested in school matters, could not.

The *Harper* dissenters also dissented here, speaking through Justice POTTER STEWART. The Constitution conferred no right to vote, and no racial classification was involved. Thus there was no reason to heighten judicial scrutiny, and there was a rational basis for limiting the vote to probably-interested persons.

On the same day, in *Cipriano v. Houma,* the Court unanimously invalidated a Louisiana law allowing only property taxpayers to vote on a revenue bond issue.

KENNETH L. KARST

KU KLUX KLAN ACT

See: Force Acts of 1870, 1871

KUNZ v. NEW YORK
340 U.S. 290 (1951)

In a case involving a street-corner preacher whose sermons vigorously denounced other religions, the Supreme Court struck down an ordinance requiring a permit to hold religious meetings in public places. Chief Justice FRED M. VINSON, for an 8–1 majority, wrote that "New York cannot vest restraining control over the right to speak on religious subjects in an administrative official where there are no appropriate standards to guide his action." The ordinance was "clearly invalid as a PRIOR RESTRAINT on the exercise of FIRST AMENDMENT rights."

DENNIS J. MAHONEY

L

LABOR AND THE ANTITRUST LAWS

Problems relating to the application of antitrust law to labor result from a basic incompatibility between two public policies: the first, embodied in the SHERMAN ACT of 1890, prohibits efforts by anyone to monopolize or restrain competition in the product market; the second, embodied in the NORRIS-LAGUARDIA ACT of 1932 and the WAGNER ACT of 1935, permits workers to combine into unions in order to bargain collectively with employers. COLLECTIVE BARGAINING necessarily assumes, however, the elimination of competition between employees in dealings with their employers; hence the unions' need to achieve a monopoly of the labor market. The ultimate goal of every union is to remove wages, hours, and working conditions as factors in the competition between employers.

The hotly debated question whether Congress intended to include unions within the coverage of the Sherman Act was resolved by the Supreme Court in LOEWE V. LAWLOR (1908), which held a union liable for violation of the Act. Efforts to reverse this result in the CLAYTON ACT of 1914, which declared that the "labor of a human being is not a commodity or article of commerce," and which forbade federal courts from granting INJUNCTIONS against specified kinds of peaceful conduct in labor disputes, were frustrated by extremely narrow constructions of the statutory language by the Supreme Court.

United States v. Hutcheson (1941), which held that the Sherman Act does not reach acts by a union in its own self-interest that do not involve combination with nonlabor groups, marked the beginning of a new period of virtual immunity for unions under the antitrust laws. And in *Allen Bradley v. Local 3, International Brotherhood of Electrical Workers* (1945) the Court, while holding that a conspiracy between the union and electrical parts manufacturers and contractors to monopolize the industry in New York City violated the Sherman Act, declared that if the union had achieved the same result through parallel but separate agreements with each employer, the arrangement would not have been illegal. Thus, Norris-LaGuardia's comprehensive prohibition against the issuance by federal courts of injunctions in labor disputes, the Wagner Act's authorization of the granting by the National Labor Relations Board of "official patents of monopoly" through its certification procedures, and the rise of industry-wide bargaining combined to create a doctrine of "licit monopoly" of the labor market by unions, while the Sherman Act continued to prevent similar domination of the product market by business enterprises.

By the mid-1960s, however, the pendulum had begun to swing back. In *United Mine Workers v. Pennington* (1965) a badly divided Supreme Court held that a union's conspiracy with large mine operators to drive small operators out of the market by establishing wage scales that the latter could not afford to pay violated the antitrust laws. Ten years later, in *Connell Construction Company v. Plumbers & Steamfitters Local 100* (1975), the Supreme Court distinguished union activity that eliminates competition over wages and working conditions—immune under the antitrust laws, even though it affects price competition among employers, because such restriction is the inevitable consequence of collective bargaining—from union activity restricting competition in the product market—unprotected because (in this case) its effect was to drive all nonunion employers, including the more efficient ones, out of the market, whether or not they met union standards for wages and working conditions. The Court's 5–4 decision also held that even though the union's conduct violated the secondary boycott and "hot cargo" provisions of the TAFT-HARTLEY ACT of 1947, for which express penalties are prescribed in that statute, the union was not shielded from additional liability under the Sherman Act.

The critics of the Court's decisions in *Pennington* and *Connell* point out that in both cases the issues involved were mandatory subjects of bargaining under the labor laws. They contend that the legislative history of those laws makes clear that Congress intended to provide specific and exclusive remedies for violations of their substantive provisions (e.g., illegal "secondary boycotts" and "hot cargo" clauses) and rejected the proposed revival of remedies such as injunctions at the request of private parties, as well as punitive damages, which are available under the antitrust laws.

Unquestionably, judicial application of the antitrust laws to labor not only has seriously hampered union efforts to impose uniform wages, hours, and working conditions in the labor market but also has created considerable confusion in the administration of laws governing labor–management relations. It is also true, however, that unrestricted union efforts to monopolize labor markets adversely affect product markets in respect of the cost and availability of products. The question is whether antitrust laws are the proper mechanism for striking a proper balance between the right of workers to organize and to bargain collectively and the right of employers and the general public to be free of union coercive practices that raise prices, restrict output, or otherwise control the product to the detriment of consumers.

Inasmuch as unions derive their coercive powers from industry-wide and market-wide organizations, it is often proposed that they should be precluded from organizing more than one employer in an industry, and that collusion between separate unions should be proscribed. This proposal for "fragmented bargaining" probably is not politically feasible; moreover, it would have its least effect in oligopolistic industries, where, presumably, it is needed the most, and would have its greatest impact in atomized industries, where it is needed the least. Finally, fragmented bargaining would so weaken union organizations as to undermine completely the national labor policy favoring collective bargaining.

It appears that no satisfactory way has been found to reconcile free-market competitive policies with those permitting workers to combine and to engage in peaceful concerted activities for their mutual aid and protection. The preferable way to establish the necessarily shifting equilibrium between them would seem to be through legislation dealing with specific problems rather than through the application by the judiciary of antitrust laws designed primarily for other purposes.

BENJAMIN AARON

Bibliography

HILDEBRAND, GEORGE H. 1962 *Public Policy and Collective Bargaining.* Pages 152–187. New York: Harper & Row.

MELTZER, BERNARD D. 1965 Labor Unions, Collective Bargaining, and the Antitrust Laws. *University of Chicago Law Review* 32:659–734.

ST. ANTOINE, THEODORE J. 1976 *Connell:* Antitrust Law at the Expense of Labor Law. *Virginia Law Review* 62:603–631.

LABOR AND THE CONSTITUTION

An important aspect of constitutional law has been the connection between individual rights and state or national power to regulate economic affairs. The constitutional treatment of employment is a paradigmatic example: what is the status of the relationship between employer and employee? What power does government have to change it? Of course, the answers to these questions depend on whether they are asked about the pre- or post-New Deal era.

Before the mid-1930s, labor legislation was subjected to searching JUDICIAL REVIEW by a Supreme Court committed to a laissez-faire treatment of economic issues under the DUE PROCESS clauses and a limited conception of federal authority under the COMMERCE CLAUSE. Since the New Deal, constitutional questions involving labor have been dominated by issues of expression and association, and the classification of labor activity as "economic" or "political."

The constitutional treatment of employment prior to the New Deal is best understood against the background of the COMMON LAW, a law dominated by concepts of FREEDOM OF CONTRACT and employment at will. The employer had the right to discharge an employee at any time, and the employee had supposedly equivalent right to quit at any time.

At an early stage, concerted actions by workers to affect contractual relations sometimes were treated as criminal conspiracies. Thus, in the *Philadelphia Cordwainers' Case* (1806), a strike for higher wages by a group of shoemakers was held to be illegal. "A combination of workmen to raise their wages may be considered in a twofold view: one is to benefit themselves, the other is to injure those who do not join their society. The rule of law condemns both."

Later in the nineteenth century, the courts recognized the right of workers to join together. *Commonwealth v. Hunt* (1842) is the landmark. Chief Justice LEMUEL SHAW, for the Supreme Judicial Court of Massachusetts, held that, for a combination of workers to constitute a CRIMINAL CONSPIRACY, the state must prove that the workers had specific criminal objectives or used specific criminal methods. Thereafter, the common law treatment of labor focused on the limits of legitimate labor activity—whether combinations of workers had illegal purposes or used illegal methods.

But many courts at common law continued to take a restrictive view of legal labor activity. In *Vegelahn v. Gunter* (1869), for example, the Massachusetts Court found that strikers had used "intimidation" to interfere with the contractual relationship of the employer and strikebreakers. The "coercive" methods ranged from threats of personal injury to simple "persuasion and social pressure." Similarly, in *Plant v. Woods* (1900), the same court found that a threat by strikers that the employer could "expect trouble in his business" indicated that the strike was "only the preliminary skirmish" in violent industrial warfare; the workers had given "the signal, and in doing so must be held to avail themselves of the degree of fear and dread which the knowledge of such consequences will cause in the minds of those . . . against whom the strike is directed." Thus, in measuring "illegal" objectives and methods, common law courts often assumed that even a low level of labor activity constituted a "signal" that was inherently coercive.

This common law view of the permissible limits of labor activity was read into the Constitution by the Supreme Court in the late nineteenth century, as it interpreted SUBSTANTIVE DUE PROCESS and elaborated a restrictive conception of the federal commerce power.

The Supreme Court constitutionalized the common law of employment by placing "freedom of contract" within the liberty protected by the Fifth and FOURTEENTH AMENDMENTS. Many important cases concerned legislation designed to regulate the labor market as to hours, wages, and working conditions. This type of legislation—such as the wages and hours law in the leading case of LOCHNER V. NEW YORK (1905)—was invalidated if, in the Court's view, it unreasonably interfered with the contractual freedom of employer and employee. Even when such legislation was upheld, as in MULLER V. OREGON (1908), the Court made a detailed inquiry into the substantive reasonableness of the law.

Notions of freedom of contract were also applied to the activities of labor unions. In 1898, in the aftermath of a violent Pullman strike, Congress passed the ERDMAN ACT, outlawing YELLOW DOG CONTRACTS—contracts by which employees agreed not to join labor unions. In ADAIR V. UNITED STATES (1908) the Supreme Court held that the act violated the due process clause of the Fifth Amendment: "the employer and the employee have equality of right, and any legislation that disturbs that equality is an arbitrary interference with the liberty of contract which no government can legally justify in a free land. . . ." The Court struck down a similar state statute in COPPAGE V. KANSAS (1915), and, in the 1917 case of HITCHMAN COAL V. MITCHELL, relied on the constitutional protection of yellow dog contracts in holding that federal courts could prevent unions from organizing at plants they knew to be covered by such contracts. And in TRUAX V. CORRIGAN (1921) the Court held that an Arizona statute forbidding INJUNCTIONS against PICKETING was unconstitutional, since it protected an activity (picketing) that wrongfully interfered with employers' property rights, in violation of due process.

The Supreme Court narrowly interpreted the commerce power at the beginning of the New Deal, striking down measures such as "Hot Oil" Codes, the AGRICULTURAL ADJUSTMENT ACT, and the NATIONAL INDUSTRIAL RECOVERY ACT. This development was nothing new. Although there had been swings in doctrine, the Court had generally viewed congressional power under the commerce clause with suspicion in the area of employment relations. In HAMMER V. DAGENHART (1918), for example, the Court struck down an act banning commerce in goods produced by child labor, and twenty years later, in CARTER V. CARTER COAL CO. (1936), it struck down an act regulating hours and wages in the coal industry.

The constitutional treatment of employment was changed radically by the watershed events of the New Deal. This period saw the Supreme Court reject its earlier laissez-faire interpretations of due process and its narrow vision of federal commerce power.

During the New Deal the Court abandoned its view

of freedom of contract in employment relations. In WEST COAST HOTEL V. PARRISH (1937) the Court sustained a state minimum wage law for women, holding that contractual freedom could be limited by a reasonable exercise of STATE POLICE POWERS: "Even if the wisdom of the policy be regarded as debatable and its effect uncertain, still the legislature is entitled to its judgment."

National Labor Relations Board v. Jones & Laughlin Steel Corp. (1937) upheld the WAGNER NATIONAL LABOR RELATIONS ACT (NLRA), which entitled workers to organize and required employers to bargain with their employees' chosen representatives. The Court found that the act did not invade freedom of contract: an employer was not compelled to make any agreement, but only to bargain with the employees' representatives in recognition of the "fundamental right" of workers to organize. The Court distinguished the "yellow dog" contract cases on the grounds that the NLRA did not interfere with an employer's right to discharge employees, but only prohibited coercion of employees in the guise of discharge. Despite this disclaimer, it is clear that the Court was departing radically from the rule of its prior cases: the employer was prohibited from discharging employees for union activities, and was required to bargain in good faith with its employees' unions. (See WAGNER ACT CASES.) This new treatment of labor activity was reinforced the same year in *Senn v. Tile Layers Union,* in which the Court upheld a state law permitting peaceful picketing in conjunction with a labor dispute; although the Court distinguished cases such as *Truax,* the picketing involved was neither more peaceful nor less coercive than in prior cases.

The new approach to due process was exemplified by Justice FELIX FRANKFURTER, writing for the Court in *Osborn v. Ozlin* (1940), in an opinion reminiscent of Justice OLIVER WENDELL HOLMES'S classic dissent in *Lochner:* "It is immaterial that state action may run counter to the economic wisdom either of Adam Smith or of J. Maynard Keynes, or may be ultimately mischievous even from the point of view of avowed state policy. Our inquiry must be much narrower. It is whether [the state] has taken hold of a matter within her power, or has reached beyond her borders to regulate a subject which was none of her concern. . . ."

In the 1937 *Jones & Laughlin* case, the Court upheld the NLRA under the commerce clause. The act regulated industrial strife, which had a "close and substantial relation" to commerce, and which was therefore within Congress's "plenary" power to regulate commerce.

The Court also upheld the NATIONAL POLICE POWER in the field of employment relations. UNITED STATES V. DARBY (1941) sustained the constitutionality of the FAIR LABOR STANDARDS ACT, which prohibited the interstate shipment of goods not meeting wage and hour requirements. Overruling the *Hammer* and *Carter Coal* cases, the Court confined its inquiry to the question whether the activity regulated had substantial EFFECTS ON COMMERCE. "The motive and purpose of a regulation of interstate commerce are matters for the legislative judgment upon which the Constitution places no restriction and over which the courts are given no control. . . ."

In sum, the New Deal saw the Supreme Court abandon its protection of the common law of employment in the name of the Constitution. The Court dropped its laissez-faire reading of due process and its restrictive interpretation of the commerce power. Employers are no longer apt to be successful if they claim that their constitutional rights to liberty or property are invaded by ECONOMIC REGULATION, or by state protection of union activity. They have little chance should they claim that congressional regulation of employment exceeds the commerce power.

While the Court has never explicitly revived the due process protection for freedom of contrast or similar economic rights in the context of labor relations, it has continued to see a residuum of inherent employer economic freedom that has a quasi-constitutional dimension manifested in statutory interpretation. This residuum has emerged around the issues of the right of an employer to subcontract work formerly done by its employees, or to close down all or part of its operations. Two questions have presented themselves: whether the employer may be required to bargain with its employees' union about such a decision, and whether such a decision would constitute discriminatory discharge of employees if motivated by antiunion animus.

The NLRA requires an employer to bargain over wages, hours, and working conditions; as to subjects not affecting these areas, an employer may act unilaterally. In *Fibreboard Paper Products v. NLRB* (1964) the Supreme Court held that an employer is required to bargain over a decision to subcontract work, where such subcontracting would simply replace employees with nonemployees doing the same work, and where the employer's motive is to cut costs by reducing the work force. Justice POTTER STEWART, in a concurring opinion, argued that an employer could not be compelled to bargain over managerial decisions "which lie at the core of entrepreneurial control," "those management decisions which are fundamental to the basic direction of a corporate enterprise. . . ."

The Court adopted Justice Stewart's position in *First National Maintenance v. NLRB* (1981), holding that the employer may unilaterally "shut down part of its business purely for economic reasons. . . ." The Court, as if this were a constitutional holding, read Congress's intent narrowly to avoid interference with entrepreneurial freedom: "Congress had no expectation that the elected union representative would become an equal partner in the running of the business enterprise. . . . Management must be free from the restraints of the bargaining process to the extent essential for the running of a profitable business."

The NLRA also prohibits an employer from discharging employees in retaliation for union activities. In *Textile Workers Union v. Darlington Manufacturing Co.* (1965) the Court held that it was not a discriminatory discharge for an employer to close his entire operation and discharge his entire work force, even if motivated by antiunion animus, because the employer would derive no "future benefit" from such a decision. As for a partial shutdown, this would constitute a discriminatory discharge only if it served to discourage union activity in the remainder of the employer's enterprise. Again, the Court construed congressional intent narrowly, as if it were avoiding a constitutional issue: the proposition that a single businessman cannot choose to go out of business if he wants to would represent such a startling innovation that it should not be entertained without the clearest manifestation of legislative intent or unequivocal judicial precedent so construing the Labor Relations Act. These cases were decided on statutory grounds, but they have clear constitutional emanations. The decisions are couched in terms of an inherent, absolute economic liberty untouched by regulatory statutes that look in a contrary direction.

For four decades after the New Deal, no congressional enactment was declared to have exceeded the limits of the commerce power. Congress was allowed virtually unlimited discretion. The consensus was that, as the Supreme Court stated in WICKARD V. FILBURN (1942), "effective restraints on its exercise must proceed from political rather than judicial processes"—anything Congress passed was within the commerce power.

In 1976, in NATIONAL LEAGUE OF CITIES V. USERY, however, the Court invalidated the application of the Fair Labor Standards Act to public employees, holding that the TENTH AMENDMENT prevents Congress from exercising its commerce power with respect to "functions essential to [the] separate and independent existence" of states and their subdivisions. Nevertheless, it does not seem likely in the labor field that Congress will lose much power to regulate by further restriction of the commerce power or the rebirth of economic due process. Indeed, early in 1985 in GARCIA V. SAN ANTONIO METROPOLITAN TRANSIT AUTHORITY, the Court explicitly overruled *National League of Cities.*

With the proposition established during the New Deal that government support of organized labor does not threaten the constitutional freedom of employers, the fundamental issues shifted to problems of association and expression. These problems arise in the framework of a constitutional jurisprudence which generally distinguishes sharply, for purposes of legislative authority and judicial review, between issues of economic regulation (narrow judicial review) and of the regulation of political activity (substantial review).

In this jurisprudence a key question becomes the classification of activity as "economic" or "political." With a few early exceptions, labor activity generally has been viewed, by both Congress and the Supreme Court, as economic. The "proper" role of unions has been confined to "economic" issues surrounding the collective bargaining process, with the consequence that labor's rights of expression are narrower than those attaching to organizations classified as political, and that Congress has a broader power to regulate association and expression in the labor context.

Prior to the New Deal, the right to organize a union was constitutionally unprotected. Since the New Deal, however, it has become well established (for example, in NAACP V. ALABAMA, 1958) that the protection of the FIRST AMENDMENT encompasses a right of association. But in the labor context it has not been necessary for the Supreme Court explicitly to find that the right to join a union is protected by FREEDOM OF ASSEMBLY AND ASSOCIATION. The right is protected by statute, most prominently Section 7 of the National Labor Relations Act: "Employees shall have the right to self-organization, to form, join, or assist labor organizations, to bargain collectively through representatives of their own choosing, and to engage in other concerted activities for the purpose of collective bargaining or other mutual aid or protection. . . ."

What the Supreme Court has held is that peaceful organizing activities are constitutionally protected. In HAGUE V. CONGRESS OF INDUSTRIAL ORGANIZATIONS (1939) the Court held that FREEDOM OF SPEECH and assembly attached to the dissemination of information regarding the NLRA, as well as peaceful assembly "for the discussion of the Act, and of the opportunities and advantages offered by it. . . ." And in *Thomas v. Collins* (1945) the Court held that freedom of speech and assembly were violated by a statute requiring union organizers to register prior to engaging in any organizing activities, including giving speeches to groups of workers. Although the Court characterized the union activity as economic, it rejected the proposition that "the First Amendment's safeguards are wholly inapplicable to business or economic activity." The case was therefore treated under the First Amendment's requirement that a restriction on speech or assembly be justified by clear public interest, threatened not doubtfully or remotely but by CLEAR AND PRESENT DANGER.

Most lower courts have interpreted the *Hague* and *Thomas* cases to establish a constitutional right to join a labor union. Thus, despite being clearly classified as economic activity, joining a union is protected by the First Amendment. However, the classification of labor activity as economic has consequences for the constitutional treatment of strikes and picketing.

The THIRTEENTH AMENDMENT, prohibiting involuntary servitude, probably protects the right of an individual employee to withhold his or her services. The constitutional status of strikes, however, is unclear. One reason for this is that strikes are "concerted activity" protected by the NLRA; it is therefore usually possible to decide strike questions without facing the constitutional question. However, extensive regulation and limitation of the right to strike has been permitted ever since the New Deal; it thus seems that, at most, the right has a low level of constitutional protection.

Legal limitations on strikes have been based on both their objectives and their methods. Prior to the NLRA, strikes were treated under the "illegal objectives" test of the common law; work stoppages with purposes held by courts to be illegal were prohibited. And today, strikes with certain objectives are unprotected under Section 7 of the NLRA. Thus, for example, a strike loses its protection if its purpose is to compel the employer to commit an unfair labor practice or violate other laws.

Section 7 also withholds protection from strikes that use illegal methods. For example, in *NLRB v. Fansteel Metallurgical Corp.* (1939) the Supreme Court declared unprotected a sitdown strike involving TRESPASS, destruction of property, and violation of state court injunctions. In *Mastro Plastics v. NLRB* (1956) the strike violated the NLRA's requirement of NOTICE to the employer; in *Local 174 v. Lucas Flour* (1962) the strike violated a "no-strike" clause in the union's contract with the employer.

Prior to the New Deal, labor picketing was readily enjoined, either because the ends sought were disapproved or because it was assumed to be intrinsically coercive. The Supreme Court turned this law around in the leading case of THORNHILL V. ALABAMA (1940). That case held unconstitutional a state statute banning all picketing near a business where the purpose of the picketing was to hinder the business. The Court adopted the "clear and present danger" test, treating labor activity as political activity: "The freedom of speech and of the press guaranteed by the constitution embraces at least the liberty to discuss publicly and truthfully all matters of public concern without previous restraint or fear of subsequent punishment. . . . In the circumstances of our times the dissemination of information concerning the facts of a labor dispute must be regarded as within that area of free discussion that is guaranteed by the Constitution." The Court explicitly rejected the assumption that all labor picketing is inherently coercive; it also stated that some "coercion" is permitted by the First Amendment: "Every expression of opinion on matters that are important has the potentiality of inducing action in the interests of one rather than another group in society. But the Group in power at any moment may not impose penal sanctions on peaceful and truthful discussions of matters of public interest merely on showing that others might thereby be persuaded to take action inconsistent with their interests." The Court thus treated labor picketing as full-fledged political activity.

But the Court quickly retreated from this position. Since *Thornhill,* it has become well accepted that labor picketing may be regulated, without violating freedom of speech and assembly, if the picketing is found to be illegal in method or objective.

While violence is an easy case, the Court has—to some extent—returned implicitly to the old assumption that labor picketing is an inherently coercive "signal." This means that picketing can be extensively regulated. Justice WILLIAM O. DOUGLAS, concurring in *Bakery Drivers v. Wohl* (1942), put it this way: "Picketing by an organized group is more than free speech, since it involves patrol of a particular locality and since the very presence of a picket line may induce action of one kind or another, quite irrespective of the nature of the ideas which are being disseminated."

The Court has also, as with other types of labor activity, maintained an "illegal objectives" limitation on picketing. The limitation has been most visible in two areas. The first is picketing with an objective to compel violation of state law or policy. This limitation was first articulated in *Carpenters' & Joiners Union v. Ritter's Cafe* (1942), where the Court held that the First Amendment did not protect picketing that urged an employer to act contrary to a state antitrust statute. By 1950, in *Hughes v. Superior Court,* the Court found a sufficient basis for prohibition in a purpose to violate a state "policy" announced by its courts.

The second visible category of picketing for an improper purpose is picketing for an object outlawed by the NLRA as "union unfair labor practices." For instance, the act explicitly prohibits some types of picketing designed to persuade an employer to recognize and bargain with the picketing union. But it is the secondary boycott that is the union unfair labor practice that is constitutionally most troublesome.

The act forbids a union to "threaten, coerce, or restrain" any person—usually a business—with the object of "forcing or requiring" that person to stop dealing with an employer with whom the union has a labor dispute.

The Supreme Court has recognized the potential conflict between such a prohibition and the First Amendment. In the *Tree Fruits* case, *NLRB v. Fruit & Vegetable Packers* (1964), the Court announced that it would construe the statute narrowly to avoid this constitutional difficulty: "Congress has consistently refused to prohibit peaceful picketing except where used as a means to achieve specific ends which experience has shown are undesirable." The Court therefore distinguished between picketing that attempted to persuade persons not to deal with the secondary employer (which was prohibited), and picketing attempting to persuade people not to buy products made by the primary employer (which was outside the act's prohibition). The Court thus permitted secondary picketing that was narrowly confined to the labor dispute with the primary employer. Subsequently, it limited even this narrow protection. In *Safeco NLRB v. Retail Store Employees Union* (1980), the Court held that the NLRA prohibits picketing confined to the primary employer's products, if those products constitute most of the secondary employer's business. In such a situation, boycotting the struck product is the same as boycotting the secondary employer.

Comparisons of the constitutional treatment of picketing with the treatment of other uses of the PUBLIC FORUM show that labor picketing is treated under standards different from other, similar activities. Consider two cases decided in 1982 by the Supreme Court, both decided without dissent. The cases had one thing in common: each involved a BOYCOTT and picketing by a group. The first, *Longshoremen's Association v. Allied International, Inc.,* was a suit for damages arising out of the refusal of the Longshoremen's Union to unload cargo shipped from the Soviet Union, in protest against the Russian invasion of Afghanistan. The boycott was entirely peaceful, it was totally effective, and it was unanimously held to be illegal. The boycott violated the labor statute, and that statute, as applied to this situation, did not infringe anyone's First Amendment rights.

Two months later the Court handed down its opinion in *NAACP v. Claiborne Hardware.* That case involved a suit for damages brought by white merchants in Claiborne County, Mississippi. Their businesses had been disrupted by a boycott, organized by the NAACP in protest against the failure of public officials in the county to desegregate public schools and facilities, hire black policemen, select blacks for jury duty, and end verbal abuse of blacks by law enforcement officers. The boycott, which was held by the Mississippi courts to violate state law, was executed in a less than peaceful, if considerably effective fashion. And it was—in most respects—found by the Supreme Court to be protected by the First Amendment.

Although there are a number of nice legal distinctions that might be noted between these cases and although it may be that the NAACP could not have survived if the Mississippi courts had been affirmed, one is forced to conclude that the two decisions are deeply inconsistent with one another. Of course, there is considerable inconsistency in our decisional law. The trouble here is that the inconsistency grows out of stereotypical thinking. Although labor unions ordinarily are organizations dedicated to economic activity and although economic activity is subject to substantial governmental regulation, sometimes unions engage in political action. The NAACP is often, but perhaps not always, a political action organization and political activity is rightly subject to substantial government protection.

The distinction between economic and political activity is difficult to maintain. At the margin it is difficult to designate conduct as economic and not political, or as political and not economic. But maintenance of the distinction is necessary unless we are prepared either to reduce substantially our political freedom or to reestablish substantive judicial review of economic regulation. (See COMMERCIAL SPEECH.)

Nor is the difficulty of sustaining the distinction in these cases really the problem. All legal distinctions, after all, give actors and decision makers trouble at the margin. The real problem is that even as it is wrong to stereotype individuals, so too is it wrong to stereotype the organizations through which individuals seek to achieve their economic and political goals. In deciding what is protected and what may be regulated, legislatures and courts should look at the organizations' specific conduct, not their general characteristics.

Employer speech—communications by employers with their employees during union organization campaigns—is given significantly lower protection than is the political speech often said to be at the core of the First Amendment. During the early post-New Deal period, the National Labor Relations Board viewed any antiunion speeches or literature from the employer as "interference, restraint or coercion," in violation of the NLRA. This position was rejected in *NLRB v. Virginia Electric & Power Co.* (1941). The Supreme Court held that the act could not, within the First Amendment, prohibit employer speech unless it could be demonstrated, from a total course of conduct, that the speech was coercive. This view was codified in 1947, when the NLRA was amended to provide that speech may be used as evidence of an unfair labor practice only if it contains a "threat of reprisal or force or promise of benefit." In *NLRB v. Gissel Packing* (1969), the Supreme Court made clear that employer speech is entitled to some First Amendment protection, and that the 1947 amendment to the NLRA simply "implements the First Amendment. . . ."

But the actual treatment of employer speech in union organization campaigns makes clear the low level of First Amendment protection that speech enjoys. The NLRB announced as long ago as 1948 that it would regulate union certification elections under a "laboratory conditions" standard: "it is the Board's function to provide a laboratory in which an experiment may be conducted, under conditions as nearly ideal as possible, to determine the uninhibited desires of the employees." This approach has entailed extensive restriction and regulation of employer speech, on several grounds. For example, implied threats of harm to employees for unionization have been held to be illegal except where the consequences are beyond the employer's control and are based on demonstrable probabilities. And under NLRB rulings racial appeals are prohibited unless the party making the appeal proves "that it was truthful and germane. . . ."

As with employee speech and association, this framework differs significantly from mainstream First Amendment doctrine. First, this framework suffers from a vagueness problem; the NLRB and the courts regulate, on an ad hoc basis, speech that in the political arena could be regulated, if at all, only under narrow and precise statutes. Second, with respect to employer threats, labor law turns the First Amendment on its head: an employer may not threaten to close its operation if a union wins an election despite the fact that it would be legal for the employer to close. Thus, the employer is prohibited from advocating or predicting *legal* activity.

Finally, employer speech that appeals to racial prejudice is severely restricted, even though the First Amendment protects such speech in the political arena. Indeed, Nazis may march down the streets in a predominantly Jewish community, but an employer may not state that a union advocates "race-mixing."

The rights of PUBLIC EMPLOYEES, and the relationships of such employees to their employers, raise constitutional questions different from those in private employment. Initially one might think that the major reason for treating public employees differently is that the public employer is a governmental body, and thus that STATE ACTION is involved. This distinction, however, is far less important than the differing economic and political relationships between the union and employer in the two sectors. These differences were summarized by the Supreme Court in ABOOD V. DETROIT BOARD OF EDUCATION (1977):

> A public employer, unlike his private counterpart, is not guided by the profit motive and constrained by the normal operation of the market. Municipal services are typically not priced, and where they are they tend to be regarded as in some sense "essential" and therefore are often price-inelastic. . . . The government officials making decisions as the public "employer" are less likely to act as a cohesive unit than are managers in private industry, in part because different levels of public authority . . . are involved, and in part because each official may respond to a distinctive political constituency. . . . Finally, decisionmaking by a public employer is above all a political process. The officials who represent the public employer are ultimately responsible to the electorate. . . . Through exercise of their political influence as part of the electorate, the employees have the opportunity to affect the decisions of government representatives who sit on the other side of the bargaining table. . . . [P]ermitting public employees to unionize . . . gives the employees more influence in the decision making process than is possessed by employees similarly organized in the private sector.

These differences have justified differences in the constitutional treatment of the rights of public employees to join unions and to strike.

As with private employees, the Supreme Court has never explicitly held that public employees have a constitutional right to join a labor union. The Court has, however, found that public employees do not sacrifice their freedoms of association and expression by accepting positions with government. In KEYISHIAN V. BOARD OF REGENTS (1967), for example, the Court specifically rejected the premise that "public employment . . . may be conditioned upon the surrender of constitutional rights which could not be abridged by direct government action." Based on this principle and on the implicit constitutional protection of private union membership under the right of association, the prevailing authority in the lower courts is that public employees have a constitutional right to join a labor union. This right, however, appears to be subject to greater restriction than is the similar right of private employees. Some state courts have held that certain employees, such as police officers or fire-fighters, may be prohibited from joining unions on the grounds that membership in a union would be inconsistent with the performance of their important governmental functions.

The authority is virtually unanimous that public employees do not have a constitutional right to strike. Nor does the statutory protection of strikes by private employees raise a serious question of equal protection. The test here is whether the distinction between public and private employment is rational; it plainly is.

The other side of the expression and association issue is whether employees—in the private or public sector—have the right not to associate. In other words, does the Constitution permit employees to be compelled to support a union against their wishes and beliefs? In this area the economic view of labor activity is prominent: compulsion has been permitted, but only for the economic purposes of COLLECTIVE BARGAINING.

The issue has arisen primarily with regard to agreements between unions and employers to require all employees to pay dues or "agency shop fees" to the union. Most labor statutes, including the NLRA, explicitly permit unions and employers to agree to these requirements. The Supreme Court has found such statutes to be consistent with the First Amendment. In *Railway Employees Department v. Hanson* (1956) and *Machinists v. Street* (1961) the Supreme Court upheld the relevant provision of the Railway Labor Act. In the *Abood* case, the Court upheld a similar state statute that applied to public employees. The Court reasoned that the "free rider" problem (employees who would benefit from, but not pay for, representation) was sufficient justification for Congress and states to permit these agreements.

The courts have, however, consistently emphasized the constitutional limits of this doctrine: dues collected under compulsion may be used only for collective bargaining, and not for political or ideological ends. In both *Street* and *Abood,* the Supreme Court held that, were statutes to permit political use of these funds, the statutes would violate the employees' freedom of association.

Over the years major labor issues have presented themselves as important constitutional problems. *Lochner v. New York* (1905), for example—a case involving labor legislation—is perhaps the best known substantive due process decision of the pre-New Deal period. And the downfall of that doctrine in the economic area can be observed in Court decisions upholding labor legislation; so too can the expansion of federal power under the commerce clause. Moreover, labor issues have influenced the development of the constitutional rights of speech and association.

In the future, the Supreme Court is apt to render fewer constitutional decisions involving labor. Regulation dominates the field and its constitutionality is seldom in doubt. But it can be predicted with considerable confidence that statutory interpretation of labor statutes will reflect any changes in constitutional law that may occur.

HARRY H. WELLINGTON

Bibliography

COX, ARCHIBALD; BOK, DEREK; and GORMAN, ROBERT 1981 *Labor Law: Cases and Materials,* 9th ed. Mineola, N.Y.: Foundation Press.

GETMAN, JULIUS and BLACKBURN, JOHN 1983 *Labor Relations: Law, Practice, and Policy,* 2nd ed. Mineola N.Y.: Foundation Press.

GORMAN, ROBERT 1976 *Basic Text on Labor Law: Unionization and Collective Bargaining.* St. Paul, Minn.: West Publishing Co.

GREGORY, CHARLES and KATZ, HAROLD 1979 *Labor and the Law,* 3rd ed. New York: W. W. Norton.

SUMMERS, CLYDE, WELLINGTON, HARRY, and HYDE, ALAN 1982 *Cases and Materials on Labor Law,* 2nd ed. Mineola, N.Y.: Foundation Press.

WELLINGTON, HARRY 1968 *Labor and the Legal Process.* New Haven, Conn.: Yale University Press.

WELLINGTON, HARRY and WINTER, RALPH 1971 *The Unions and the Cities.* Washington, D.C.: Brookings Institution.

LABOR BOARD CASES

See: Wagner Act Cases

LA FOLLETTE, ROBERT M. (1855–1925)

Robert Marion La Follette was one of the few giants in the history of the United States Senate, ranking with HENRY CLAY and DANIEL WEBSTER. Born in a Wisconsin log cabin, he was graduated from his state's university in Madison, began his legal practice there, and spent three undistinguished terms (1885–1891) in Congress. During the farmer-labor unrest of the 1890s, La Follette grew considerably more liberal, and in 1901 he entered the governor's mansion with a reform program later called the "Wisconsin idea." It became the basis of the Progressive movement. La Follette, always a Republican, advocated the direct PRIMARY ELECTION as a method of nominating candidates, MINIMUM WAGE AND MAXIMUM HOURS laws, trade unionism, the popular REFERENDUM, strict regulation of the rates and services of railroads and public utilities by government commissions of experts, and radical tax reforms. His success as governor led to his election in 1905 as a United States senator.

During his twenty-year career as a senator he rivaled THEODORE ROOSEVELT and WOODROW WILSON as an influence for political liberalism. The leader of the Senate's Republican insurgents, he exerted special efforts on behalf of increasing the powers of the Interstate Commerce Commission, energetic enforcement of ANTITRUST LAW, a federal income tax law, direct election of senators, and women's suffrage. After the Supreme Court decided STANDARD OIL COMPANY V. UNITED STATES (1911), La Follette denounced the RULE OF REASON and judicial usurpation of the legislative function. Unlike most Republicans he supported the appointment to the Supreme Court of LOUIS D. BRANDEIS; the two men were close friends, thought alike on most matters of political economy, and had collaborated in framing many reform measures. They differed on foreign policy. La Follette opposed American entry into World War I and the League of Nations. Although unpopular for a while during the war, because of pro-German and pacifist sympathies, La Follette emerged from the war as the undisputed leader of American liberalism.

He excoriated illiberal decisions of the Supreme Court. When the Court held unconstitutional congressional measures against child labor and construed antitrust laws to cover trade union activities, La Follette began a national campaign to curb the Court. Because he opposed JUDICIAL REVIEW over Congress, he proposed a constitutional amendment that would have authorized Congress to overcome a judicial veto in the same way as it did a presidential veto, by reenacting the statute by a two-thirds majority.

In 1924, at the peak of his career, La Follette refused to support CALVIN COOLIDGE and formed the Independent Progressive party, which nominated him and BURTON K. WHEELER, a Democrat. The party had only a presidential ticket, no local, state, or other federal candidates. It supported La Follette's Court-curbing amendment and would have restricted judicial invalidation of congressional acts to the Supreme Court only; in addition, it would have fixed a ten-year tenure for federal judges. The Progressives also denounced the Ku Klux Klan, then at the height of its popularity, and the Communist party. They also favored collective bargaining by labor through union representatives of their choice, antimonopoly measures, the restoration of competition, and extensive government ECONOMIC REGULATION. La Follette drew one vote out of every six, compared to the one in twelve received by the Populists in 1892, but carried only his own state.

When "Fighting Bob" died in 1925, his casket was placed in the rotunda of the Capitol, a rare honor, and the nation remembered him, in the words of his own epitaph, as one who "stood to the end for the ideals of American democracy."

LEONARD W. LEVY

Bibliography

LA FOLLETTE, BELLE CASE and LA FOLLETTE, FOLA 1953 *Robert M. La Follette.* 2 Vols. New York: Macmillan.

LAIRD v. TATUM 408 U.S. 1 (1972)

Protesters against American involvement in the VIETNAM WAR sued to stop Army intelligence surveillance which they claimed had a CHILLING EFFECT on the exercise of their FIRST AMENDMENT rights. Chief Justice WARREN E. BURGER's opinion for the Court, in a 5–4 decision, held that the case lacked RIPENESS because the protesters had presented no "claim of specific present objective . . . or . . . future harm" but only the fear that "the army may at some future date misuse the information in some way" that would harm them.

MARTIN SHAPIRO

LAKE COUNTRY ESTATES, INC. v. TAHOE REGIONAL PLANNING AGENCY

440 U.S. 391 (1979)

Landowners claimed that an appointed bi-state agency regulating development had, through overregulation, unconstitutionally destroyed the economic value of their property. The Supreme Court, over Justice THURGOOD MARSHALL's dissent, extended TENNEY V. BRANDHOVE (1951) to acts of unelected officials and found members of the planning agency to be absolutely immune from suit under SECTION 1983, TITLE 42, UNITED STATES CODE for their legislation-like acts. The Court also found the agency not to be protected by the ELEVENTH AMENDMENT immunity available to states.

THEODORE EISENBERG

LALLI v. LALLI

439 U.S. 259 (1978)

In *Lalli* a fragmented Supreme Court brought further confusion to the body of EQUAL PROTECTION doctrine governing classifications based on ILLEGITIMACY. A 5–4 majority upheld a New York law that allowed an illegitimate child to inherit from his or her father only if a court, during the father's lifetime and no later than two years after the child's birth, had declared the father's paternity. Justice LEWIS F. POWELL, who had written the MAJORITY OPINION in TRIMBLE V. GORDON (1977), wrote for a plurality of three Justices. Powell distinguished *Trimble* as a case in which even a judicial order declaring paternity would not have allowed inheritance; only the marriage of the child's parents would suffice. In *Lalli* the state could properly insist on the "evidentiary" requirement of a judicial order to establish paternity. The other six Justices all thought *Lalli* and *Trimble* indistinguishable: the four *Lalli* dissenters, plus two who joined the majority in upholding the law. The latter two Justices voted in accordance with their *Trimble* dissents.

The precedential force of *Trimble* may be uncertain, but at least seven Justices (the *Lalli* plurality and dissenters) all agreed that the STANDARD OF REVIEW for testing classifications based on illegitimacy was more rigorous than the RATIONAL BASIS test. Such classifications, said the plurality, would be invalid unless they were "substantially related to permissible state interests."

The state's interest in *Lalli* was the achievement of finality in the settlement of decedents' estates. The court order requirement provided sure proof of paternity. The artificiality of the requirement, however, was illustrated dramatically by the facts of *Lalli* itself, as Justice BYRON R. WHITE, for the dissenters, made clear. The decedent had often acknowledged his children openly; he had even executed a notarized document referring to one of them as "my son" and consenting to his marriage. Paternity had been proved clearly; what was missing was the formality of a court order. Such a judicial proceeding, of course, is least likely in the case in which the father and his illegitimate child are closest, and the father's acknowledgment of paternity has been most clearly established by nonjudicial means. The New York estate planners who wrote the law contrived its inertia to lean against the children of informal unions. *Lalli* is thus reminiscent of an earlier legal order designed to assure a man that his wealth and status would attach to a woman only when he chose to formalize their union and would pass only to the children of such a union.

KENNETH L. KARST

(SEE ALSO: *Freedom of Intimate Association.*)

LAMAR, JOSEPH R.

(1857–1916)

Joseph Rucker Lamar, "an old-fashioned southern gentleman," served on the Supreme Court from 1911 until his death in 1916. As a Justice, Lamar approved the received doctrines of the time such as FREEDOM OF CONTRACT and AFFECTATION WITH A PUBLIC INTEREST. Lamar had been a leading Georgia attorney and had served as a state legislator and member of the Georgia Supreme Court (1903–1905) before his appointment to the Court. He was the fourth of President WILLIAM HOWARD TAFT's appointees and replaced EDWARD D. WHITE, whom Taft had promoted from Associate to Chief Justice.

Lamar joined a Court that included Justices OLIVER WENDELL HOLMES and JOHN MARSHALL HARLAN, leaning to the progressive side. Lamar usually voted with the majority of the Court; he wrote only eight dissents in four years, and one writer counted agreement in 150 of 154 cases sustaining exercise of STATE POLICE POWER and in 71 of 74 cases striking down such legislation. Lamar's apparent conciliation should not be taken to indicate disinterested acquiescence. In UNITED STATES V. GRIMAUD (1911) Lamar substantially strengthened the force of administrative rulings. *Grimaud* placed the law squarely behind such rulings;

Lamar denied that administrative decisions constituted legislative DELEGATIONS OF POWER, and he upheld Congress's right to punish violations as criminal acts if it chose. Although he sometimes supported CIVIL RIGHTS, his most famous opinion came in a labor case: GOMPERS V. BUCK'S STOVE AND RANGE COMPANY (1911). Writing for a unanimous Court, Lamar declared that a secondary boycott constituted an illegal conspiracy in restraint of trade which could be forbidden by INJUNCTION. He rejected the union's claim of FREEDOM OF SPEECH.

Lamar served on the WHITE COURT, a Court that increasingly favored propertied interests. His lack of imagination and creativity were likely seen as virtues by his contemporaries, characteristics of a man well-fitted for the Court.

DAVID GORDON

Bibliography

DINNERSTEIN, LEONARD 1969 Joseph R. Lamar. Pages 1973–1997 in Leon Friedman and Fred L. Israel, eds., *The Justices of the United States Supreme Court, 1789–1969.* New York: Chelsea House.

LAMAR, L. Q. C.
(1825–1893)

Lucius Quintus Cincinnatus Lamar, draftsman of the Mississippi Ordinance of Secession, celebrated eulogist of CHARLES SUMNER, and "Great Pacificator" during the electoral crisis of 1877, was appointed to the Supreme Court by GROVER CLEVELAND in 1888. He was the first Democrat to be appointed in a quarter-century and the first ex-Confederate to serve on the Court. Lamar was sixty-two years old when he received his commission, the second oldest new Justice in the Court's history. But he had been the South's most prominent apostle of sectional reconciliation for more than a decade and the President was primarily interested in the nomination's symbolic dimensions.

Judging exhilarated Lamar, and he was among the Court's most productive members until debilitated by ill health in the spring of 1892. Construction of the public land laws was his specialty, reflecting his experience as Cleveland's reform-minded secretary of the interior. He was also valuable at the conference table. "His was the most suggestive mind that I ever knew," Chief Justice MELVILLE W. FULLER reported, "and not one of us but has drawn from his inexhaustible store." Lamar was equally impressed by his brethren, calling them "the smartest old fellows I ever saw." In 1893, when reminiscing about a long career of public service as Confederate diplomat, congressman, senator, and cabinet official, he described his judicial experience as "the most impressive incident in my entire intellectual and moral life."

STRICT CONSTRUCTION and traditional canons of interpretation characterized his work in constitutional law. Lamar had no sympathy for the newly fashioned concept of SUBSTANTIVE DUE PROCESS, and he concurred with Justice JOSEPH P. BRADLEY's strident dissent in CHICAGO, MILWAUKEE & ST. PAUL RY. CO. V. MINNESOTA (1890), maintaining that the REASONABLENESS of price regulations was a legislative, not a judicial, question. He also resisted extension of the SWIFT V. TYSON (1842) "general jurisprudence" doctrine to industrial accident cases. Only in the well-trodden COMMERCE CLAUSE field did Lamar consistently vote to restrict the autonomy of the states. And though he was quick to strike down tax laws and police regulations that burdened interstate transactions, Lamar remained obsessed with the necessity of setting limits to Congress's commerce power. In KIDD V. PEARSON (1888), his most influential opinion, Lamar not only formulated the mischievous distinction between commerce and manufacturing but also stated its rationale. "If it be held that the term [commerce] includes the regulation of all such manufactures as are intended to be the subject of commercial transactions in the future," he explained, "it is impossible to deny that it would also include all productive industries that contemplate the same thing. The result would be that Congress would be invested, to the exclusion of the States, with the power to regulate, not only manufacture, but also agriculture, horticulture, stock raising, domestic fisheries, mining—in short, every branch of human industry." For a former Confederate whose cherished doctrine of state SOVEREIGNTY already had been extinguished, such a state of affairs was at once imaginable and unthinkable.

CHARLES W. MCCURDY

Bibliography

MAYES, EDWARD 1896 *Lucus Q. C. Lamar, His Life, Times, and Speeches.* Nashville, Tenn.: Publishing House of the Methodist Episcopal Church South.

MURPHY, JAMS B. 1973 *L. Q. C. Lamar, Pragmatic Patriot.* Baton Rouge: Louisiana State University Press.

LAMONT v. POSTMASTER GENERAL OF THE UNITED STATES
381 U.S. 301 (1965)

A 1962 act of Congress required the postmaster general to detain all unsealed mail of foreign origin determined to be "communist political propaganda," and to notify the addressee that the mail would be delivered only if he requested it by returning an official reply card. The Supreme Court, 8–0, held the act unconstitutional as an abridgment of the addressee's FIRST AMENDMENT rights. Justice WILLIAM O. DOUGLAS, for the Court, declared that the act sought to control the flow of ideas and was at war with the wide-open discussion of ideas protected by the amendment.

LEONARD W. LEVY

(SEE ALSO: *Listeners' Rights.*)

LANDIS, JAMES M. (1899–1964)

James McCauley Landis was a gifted lawyer, professor and dean at Harvard Law School, and writer, whose outstanding contribution to American law was his theoretical analysis and practical championing of REGULATORY COMMISSIONS. He was a student of FELIX FRANKFURTER and co-authored *The Business of the Supreme Court* (1928) with him. Landis chaired both the Securities and Exchange Commission (1934–1937) and the Civil Aeronautics Board (1946–1947), served on the Federal Trade Commission (1933–1934), and wrote *The Administrative Process* (1938), a sympathetic analysis of regulatory commissions. The book discussed the limits on agencies imposed by Congress and the checks on them afforded by JUDICIAL REVIEW, and Landis downplayed the likelihood of administrative abuses of power, arguing that the true danger lay in lethargic enforcement of congressional policy. The efficiency with which these commissions could focus on economic problems by merging executive, legislative, and judicial powers impressed Landis, who saw administrative action as a practical means to achieve realistic ends.

DAVID GORDON

Bibliography

RITCHIE, DONALD A. 1980 *James M. Landis, Dean of the Regulators.* Cambridge, Mass.: Harvard University Press.

LAND ORDINANCE OF 1784

See: Ordinance of 1784

LANDRUM-GRIFFIN ACT 73 Stat. 519 (1959)

Known as the Labor Management Reporting and Disclosure Act, Landrum-Griffin brought internal administration of labor unions within the realm of federal regulation and guaranteed union members certain basic rights. Its goal was union self-regulation and voluntary democratization.

Passage of the measure resulted from a growing national concern influenced by a Senate committee's findings of union leaders' corruption and autocratic behavior. Relying on Congress's constitutional authority to insure the free flow of INTERSTATE COMMERCE, the act restricted secondary BOYCOTTS; strictly controlled union elections; required strict reporting of the unions' financial transactions; outlawed extortion PICKETING; authorized state JURISDICTION over labor disputes not handled by the National Labor Relations Board; and modified union security provisions for certain national unions. In setting forth a Bill of Rights of Members of Labor Organizations, the act reversed the courts' tendency to allow union governance by self-established rules.

The act also made it a criminal offense for a Communist party member to serve as an officer or employee of a labor union until five years after termination of party membership. In UNITED STATES v. BROWN (1965) the Supreme Court ruled this section unconstitutional as a BILL OF ATTAINDER.

PAUL L. MURPHY

Bibliography

MCLAUGHLIN, DORIS and SCHOOMAKER, ANITA 1979 *The Landrum-Griffin Act and Union Democracy.* Ann Arbor: University of Michigan Press.

LAND USE AND THE CONSTITUTION

See: Zoning

LANE v. WILSON

See: Literacy Test

LANGDON, JOHN (1741–1819)

John Langdon, a financier and businessman who risked his large personal fortune in support of the Revolution, had, by 1787, already served in the Continental Congress and as a colonel in the Revolutionary War; he had also supervised shipbuilding for the navy and had been president of New Hampshire.

As chairman of New Hampshire's delegation to the CONSTITUTIONAL CONVENTION OF 1787, Langdon personally paid the delegation's expenses. He spoke often at the Convention and served on three committees. He favored such nationalist measures as a congressional veto over state legislation and a prohibition of state taxes on exports. He advocated prohibiting Congress, as well as the states, from emitting BILLS OF CREDIT.

After signing the Constitution, Langdon returned home to become leader of the proratification forces in the state convention. He was elected to the United States Senate and became its first president *pro tempore;* and he served seven more years as governor of New Hampshire.

DENNIS J. MAHONEY

Bibliography

ROSSITER, CLINTON 1966 *1787: The Grand Convention.* New York: Macmillan.

LANSING, JOHN, JR.
(1754–1829?)

Mayor John Lansing of Albany was one of three delegates from New York to the CONSTITUTIONAL CONVENTION OF 1787. A former member of Congress and an ally of Governor George Clinton, Lansing was chosen to represent the antinationalist sentiment of the state's political leadership. Lansing was a coauthor of the PATERSON PLAN and a spokesman for the faction that opposed creating a strong national government. He and fellow New York delegate ROBERT YATES withdrew on July 10 charging that the convention was exceeding its congressional mandate to propose amendments to the ARTICLES OF CONFEDERATION.

In the New York debate over RATIFICATION OF THE CONSTITUTION Lansing was one of the anti-Federalist leaders. He was a delegate to the state ratifying convention where he urged defeat of the new Constitution and summoning of a new federal convention. After a proratification majority was assured, Lansing urged conditional ratification and then ratification reserving the right to secede. The long series of proposed amendments—including a BILL OF RIGHTS—that accompanied New York's instrument of ratification was largely Lansing's work.

After 1788 Lansing held state judicial office—serving as Chief Justice and Chancellor—but he never held any federal office except presidential elector.

DENNIS J. MAHONEY

Bibliography

ROSSITER, CLINTON 1966 *1787: The Grand Convention.* New York: Macmillan.

LANZA, UNITED STATES v.
260 U.S. 377 (1922)

There is no DOUBLE JEOPARDY when both state and federal governments outlaw an offense and each prosecutes an individual for the same act. The United States indicted Lanza for violating the VOLSTEAD ACT after the state of Washington had already prosecuted him under a state statute enforcing PROHIBITION. A unanimous Supreme Court, dismissing Lanza's double jeopardy claim, declared that the double jeopardy forbidden by the Fifth Amendment was a second trial for the same offense in the same JURISDICTION. The Court concluded: "It follows that an act denounced as a crime by both national and state sovereignties is an offense against the peace and dignity of both, and may be punished by each." *Lanza* is still good law.

DAVID GORDON

LARKIN v. GRENDEL'S DEN, INCORPORATED
459 U.S. 116 (1982)

Dissenting alone, Justice WILLIAM H. REHNQUIST observed that "silly cases" like this one, as well as great or hard cases, make bad law. Chief Justice WARREN E. BURGER for the Court aimed its "heavy FIRST AMENDMENT artillery," in Rehnquist's phrase, at a statute that banned the sale of alcoholic beverages within 500 feet of a school or church, should either object to the presence of a neighboring tavern. Originally, Massachusetts had absolutely banned such taverns but found that the objective of the STATE POLICE POWER, promoting neighborhood peace, could be fulfilled by the less drastic method of allowing schools and churches to take the initiative of registering objections. In this case a church objected to a tavern located ten feet away. Burger held that vesting the church with the state's veto power breached the prohibition against an ESTABLISHMENT OF RELIGION, on the grounds that the church's involvement vitiated the secular purposes of the statute, advanced the cause of religion, and excessively entangled state and church. Rehnquist argued that a sensible statute had not breached the wall of SEPARATION OF CHURCH AND STATE.

LEONARD W. LEVY

LARSON v. DOMESTIC AND FOREIGN COMMERCE CORPORATION
337 U.S. 682 (1949)

This is a leading decision concerning the SOVEREIGN IMMUNITY of the United States. Plaintiff sued the head of the War Assets Administration (WAA), alleging that the Administrator had sold certain surplus coal to plaintiff, had refused to deliver the coal, and had entered into a contract to sell the coal to others. Because plaintiff sought injunctive relief against WAA officials, ordering them not to sell the coal or to deliver it to anyone other than plaintiff, and because the suit concerned property of the United States, the Supreme Court found the suit to be one against the United States and, therefore, to be barred by sovereign immunity. The Court distinguished *Larson* from suits against officers for acts beyond their statutory powers and from suits seeking to enjoin allegedly unconstitutional behavior, both of which the Court stated would not constitute suits against the sovereign, even if the plaintiff alleges the officer acted unconstitutionally or beyond his statutory powers, "if the relief requested cannot be granted merely by ordering the cessation of the conduct complained of but will require affirmative action by the sovereign or the disposition of unquestionably sovereign property." In cases involving suits against state officials, part of this passage apparently was contradicted by EDELMAN V. JORDAN (1974) and MILLIKEN V. BRADLEY (1977). In each of these cases the Court found that litigation to require a state to pay the costs of future compliance with the Constitution did not constitute a suit against the sovereign. The precise holding in *Larson* became an important and debated issue in PENNHURST STATE SCHOOL AND HOSPITAL V. HALDERMAN (1984), where the Court relied in part on *Larson* to hold that actions in federal court against state officials, alleging violations of state law, are prohibited by the ELEVENTH AMENDMENT.

THEODORE EISENBERG

LARSON v. VALENTE
456 U.S. 228 (1982)

Minnesota required charitable organizations to register and make disclosure when they solicited contributions. Religious organizations were exempted if more than half their contributions came from members. Members of the Unification Church sued in federal court to challenge the law's constitutionality. The Supreme Court, 5–4, held the law invalid.

Justice WILLIAM J. BRENNAN, for the Court, said that the law effectively granted denominational preferences, favoring well-established churches and disfavoring newer churches or churches that preferred public solicitation. This discrimination took the case out of the purpose-effects-entanglement test of LEMON V. KURTZMAN (1971) for ESTABLISHMENT OF RELIGION. Instead, Brennan invoked a searching form of STRICT SCRUTINY, which the state here failed to pass. The state's purported interests in preventing abuse in solicitation were not supported in the record. In any case, Brennan said, the Minnesota law failed *Lemon*'s "entanglement" test by risking the politicizing of religion; one Minnesota legislator had remarked, "I'm not sure why we're so hot to regulate the Moonies [Unification Church] anyway."

The four dissenters thought the plaintiffs lacked STANDING to challenge the law. Two of them also dissented on the merits of the case, arguing that the law did not constitute an intentional discrimination among religions.

KENNETH L. KARST

LASKI, HAROLD J.
(1893–1950)

British political scientist and Socialist party leader Harold Joseph Laski influenced American constitutional thought both through his public writings and through his friendship with leading American jurists and political leaders. Laski studied political science at Oxford University under Ernest Barker, and from 1916 to 1920 was an instructor in government at Harvard University. While teaching at Harvard he met, and began a twenty-year correspondence with, Justice OLIVER WENDELL HOLMES, and he established an even longer-lasting friendship with Professor (later Justice) FELIX FRANKFURTER. He also numbered among his friends and correspondents President FRANKLIN D. ROOSEVELT and Justice BENJAMIN N. CARDOZO.

From 1920 until his death in 1950 Laski taught at the London School of Economics and Political Science. He continued to correspond with his American friends and frequently visited the United States. He affected American jurisprudence mainly by influencing those whose general approach to legal and constitutional problems is called LEGAL REALISM.

Although in his early books, written in America, he had embraced a pluralist doctrine of politics, Laski had by 1931 adopted the Marxist theory of history as class struggle, and thereafter he attempted to formulate a non-Soviet Marxist political theory. He never lost interest in American politics, and his last book was *The American Democracy,* a Marxist account of American history and institutions.

DENNIS J. MAHONEY

Bibliography

DEANE, HERBERT A. 1954 *The Political Ideas of Harold Laski.* Ph.D. dissertation, Columbia University.

HOWE, MARK DEWOLFE 1953 *The Holmes-Laski Correspondence.* 2 Vols. Cambridge, Mass.: Harvard University Press.

LASSITER v. DEPARTMENT OF SOCIAL SERVICES

See: Right to Counsel

LAU v. NICHOLS
414 U.S. 563 (1974)

San Francisco failed to provide non-English-speaking students of Chinese ancestry with an adequate education. The Supreme Court, without dissent, found such an effect to violate Title VI of the CIVIL RIGHTS ACT OF 1964 even absent any intent to discriminate against the students. *Lau*'s employment of an "effects" test under Title VI may not have survived REGENTS OF THE UNIVERSITY OF CALIFORNIA V. BAKKE (1978), a question that divided the Court in *Guardians Association v. Civil Service Commission* (1983). Congress later expressed approval of *Lau* in enacting legislation to assist non-English-speaking students.

THEODORE EISENBERG

LAW ENFORCEMENT AND FEDERAL–STATE RELATIONS

This country has long been committed to the notion that primary responsibility for law enforcement should reside in state and local governments. Over the past century, however, changes in the federal criminal system have affected the traditional balance among federal, state, and local responsibilities for law enforcement. We may be slowly moving in the direction of a national police force.

The Supreme Court has affirmed the constitutionality of an expanded federal legislative authority in the realm of criminal enforcement. Congress has enacted numerous statutes under this expanded federal authority. As a result, the federal criminal code has begun to look more and more like a state criminal code in its substantive content and even in its jurisdictional reach and form.

Over the long term, the balance among the several law enforcement JURISDICTIONS will be determined not only by the breadth of the law on the books but also by its implementation in practice. The type and magnitude of police resources available to the federal government and the attitudes of the electorate and decision makers in key governmental institutions are likely to determine whether a broad federal criminal authority will supplant state and local responsibilities. Here, too, some changes have begun.

The traditional allocation of law enforcement responsibilities assigns to local governments the basic policing of crimes such as homicide, theft, robbery, rape, burglary, muggings, and the like. Local police have responsibility for patrol, for immediate response to reports of crime, and for investigations. A huge number of local officers presently performs those functions nationwide, particularly in metropolitan areas. The idea of a "national police force" directed from Washington, D.C. taking over these functions seems far-reaching. But one can imagine substantial shifts in the traditional division between federal and local responsibilities that would be accompanied by growth of a significantly larger corps of federal police that might fairly be called a national police force.

The jurisdictional reach of the federal criminal code has expanded in many ways over the past century. Most federal criminal legislation not aimed at protecting direct federal interests, such as federal funds or property, has been constitutionally based in Congress's enumerated powers—for example, the POSTAL POWER, the TAXING AND SPENDING POWER, and the power to regulate commerce among the states. (See NATIONAL POLICE POWER.)

Use of the postal and taxing powers as a basis for federal criminal jurisdiction has not changed much over the years. The use of the mails was relied upon early in the mail fraud statute enacted in 1872. A comprehensive registration-tax scheme was utilized in the original major antinarcotics legislation, the HARRISON ACT of 1914. The COMMERCE CLAUSE which began its criminal law history as a fairly narrow jurisdictional base—requiring transportation or travel across a state line—in modern times has been expanded. In a number of statutes, federal jurisdiction is now based on the use of the facilities of commerce such as interstate telephone calls, telegrams, and any kind of interstate movement of persons or goods.

The EFFECT ON COMMERCE formula, originally developed in the economic regulation sphere, has also broadened the bases for federal criminal jurisdiction. The nexus with commerce required under that formula is not very substantial. And the "effect on commerce" formula itself has been extended to situations where the criminal activity merely takes place on the premises of a business whose operations affect commerce. Furthermore, in PEREZ V. UNITED STATES (1971) the Court accepted congressional findings that a type of criminal conduct was part of a class of activities affecting commerce, and held that that type of conduct could be made a federal crime without any showing of an effect upon commerce in the individual case. Although in most cases similar to *Perez* proof of an effect upon commerce probably can be shown, *Perez* represents the furthest expansion of the reach of federal criminal jurisdiction under the commerce power.

The necessity to rely upon enumerated powers led Congress to enact crimes in forms differing markedly from the usual state penal code. Often, otherwise innocuous conduct that provided the basis for federal jurisdiction became the central element of the offense. Congress made criminal the transportation in commerce of lottery tickets, or obscene literature, or women for immoral purposes; depositing a letter in the mails to execute a fraudulent scheme; or affecting commerce by robbery or extortion.

The odd form of these crimes has produced concerns peculiar to federal criminal law. The prosecution of federal crimes often overemphasizes the jurisdiction element. The Supreme Court in four decades has, in five mail fraud cases, faced the question whether mailing was done for purposes of the fraudulent scheme; during the same period, the Court has not once considered the sometimes perplexing question of what constitutes fraudulant conduct under the statute.

The jurisdictional reach of federal criminal statutes has also developed in an odd checkerboard pattern. For example, originally, federal law made it a crime to use the mails to defraud but not the telegraph or telephone. Many such inconsistencies have been eliminated, but some still remain.

The *Perez* decision may also have far-reaching effects on the form of federal crimes. The case is usually cited for its effect in expanding the jurisdictional reach of federal criminal laws. However, the more important impact of the case may be that Congress can now, if it is so minded, draft a criminal code in a form substantially identical to a state penal code. Under such a code, the federal prosecutor would not have to prove the jurisdictional element in a crime belonging to a commerce-related class of activity; the proof would resemble the evidence offered in comparable state prosecutions.

Congress has not yet fully taken up the *Perez* invitation. In addition to the consumer credit statute enacted in 1964, the most significant statutes using this drafting approach are the illegal gambling business statute and the Comprehensive Drug Abuse Prevention and Control Act, both enacted in 1970. Federal drug crimes, which were historically based on the taxing power, are now based on the commerce power and defined in traditional criminal law terms.

Many traditional crimes have long been subject to punishment under the federal criminal code where a direct federal interest is involved, when the offense occurs on federal property or in a location for which the federal government has a special responsibility, or when federal funds are involved or persons are injured. Thus murder, manslaughter, and rape are federal crimes when committed "within the special maritime and territorial jurisdiction of the United States." And where criminal conduct on federal lands is not punishable by any specific federal enactment but would be a crime under state law, federal law incorporates state law and makes the conduct punishable.

However, traditional crimes have also been made federal offenses where no direct federal interest is involved. Legislation of this type is usually justified on the ground that the crimes involved are often committed by criminal groups organized and operating in more than one state, thus calling for nationwide investigation and prosecution. Such offenses are broadly defined, however, and do not limit federal prosecution to instances where the conduct involved can conveniently only be investigated and prosecuted by federal authorities.

There is today hardly a major crime category treated in state penal codes that is not also a federal crime, even in the absence of a direct federal interest. Ignoring for the moment the jurisdictional limits, examples of such crimes include: prostitution (MANN ACT, 1910); various forms of theft involving stolen motor vehicles, other stolen property, and theft from interstate shipments (Dyer Act, 1919); bank robbery (1934); robbery (Anti-Racketeering Act, 1934); extortion (Anti-Racketeering Act, 1934); kidnaping (1932);

threats (1934); arson (Travel Act, 1961); bribery (Travel Act, 1961); rioting (1968); sexual exploitation of children (1978); and murder (Racketeer Influenced and Corrupt Organizations Act, RICO, 1970).

In several instances, state crimes have played a more direct role in the federal criminal code. In three important pieces of complex criminal legislation—the Travel Act of 1961, the gambling business statute of 1970, and the RICO statute of 1970—Congress adopted the legislative technique of making the commission of certain crimes in violation of state law a federal crime under specified circumstances. In these instances, federal law did not simply cover the same ground as the state crime; it became identical to it.

The effect of these changes in jurisdictional reach, form, and substantive coverage has been to move the federal criminal code closer to the form and content of the fifty state penal codes with which it overlaps. Certain benefits have resulted from these changes. Many anomalies and inconsistencies in federal crime coverage have been eliminated. It is now also easier for the federal government, in a limited fashion, directly to supplement state and local efforts to combat ordinary crime.

These changes also have their costs. The old emphasis on jurisdiction and the checkerboard pattern of coverage have served as a constant reminder of the limited role of the federal government in protecting local communities against ordinary crime. As these elements in the code are eliminated, it becomes easier to think in terms of an expanded federal role.

The balance of responsibility necessarily will continue to remain with the states as long as federal law enforcement resources remain small in comparison to state and local forces, and federal prosecutions remain a small percentage of the total prosecutorial caseload of the country. Overall, there are about fifty major federal criminal enforcement agencies with approximately 50,000 field personnel. Most of these have specialized duties and limited jurisdiction. Approximately 35,000 federal felony prosecutions are initiated annually by about 2,000 federal prosecutors. This federal picture should be contrasted with that at the state and local levels where approximately 19,000 police agencies employ about 500,000 sworn officers, and in excess of 700,000 prosecutions are begun each year by more than 20,000 state and local prosecutors.

A dramatic increase in the number of federal law enforcement personnel or their combination in a single agency would have to occur in order to create the conditions for a major shift of law enforcement responsibilities to the federal realm. However, such a shift could also conceivably occur through a shift of military personnel into domestic law enforcement, or by the development of federal control over state and local agencies.

The growth of existing federal law enforcement agencies has been significant although not dramatic. In the past thirty years, the Federal Bureau of Investigation, the largest federal law enforcement agency and the one with the most general criminal enforcement authority, has grown from 3,000 to 8,000 agents; the Secret Service has expanded from 300 to 1,500; and the Customs Service, from 150 to 600 agents. The Drug Enforcement Administration (DEA) has grown tenfold from 200 to 2,000 agents.

The 1970s and 1980s have seen moves toward consolidation of separate agencies. The Bureau of Narcotics, originally located in the Treasury Department, was shifted to the Department of Justice, and later became the DEA. Recently the FBI, which had never before had any significant investigative responsibility for drug matters, moved strongly into that field and began working closely with DEA. DEA personnel may eventually be absorbed into the FBI, a move that would increase the personnel of that agency by more than one-fifth.

Even if agencies continue to grow and merge, a dramatic shift of law enforcement responsibility from state and local governments to the federal government seems unlikely in the foreseeable future. The creation of a single, really large corps of federal enforcement personnel would require considerable expansion of either the rate of growth or the practice of combining agencies.

Resources for a national police operation might also conceivably become available through increased use of the military to enforce domestic law. There is a strong tradition, founded in part in the same concerns as the commitment to local responsibility for law enforcement, against the involvement of the military in law enforcement. In the context of military surveillance activities directed against civilians, Justice William O. Douglas once suggested that "turning the military loose on civilians even if sanctioned by act of Congress . . . would raise serious and profound constitutional questions." A statutory prohibition against the use of the military to enforce domestic law, the Posse Comitatus Act, was enacted in 1878. The act makes it a crime to use the military forces "to execute the laws" except as expressly authorized by Congress or the Constitution.

The Supreme Court has not yet authoritatively interpretated the Posse Comitatus Act. Existing lower court interpretations permit some limited involvement of the military in domestic law enforcement.

Several different constructions of the act were advanced in a series of decisions growing out of the occupation of Wounded Knee, South Dakota, by American Indian Movement members, for example, that the act is violated only by direct active use of federal troops in domestic law enforcement. Specific statutory exceptions also allow the domestic use of the military to enforce the laws, in cases of civil disorder, threats to federal property, and protection of federal parks, foreign dignitaries, and certain federal officials.

Increased federal efforts to combat drug smuggling have strained the Posse Comitatus Act. The desire to use navy ships and air force planes against smugglers led to enactment in 1982 of a statute that made further inroads on the act. Though limited, the new law is important because it is the first statutory modification of the Posse Comitatus Act for ordinary law enforcement purposes in the more than 100 years since its enactment. This is an area where special care should be taken; by a single stroke, Congress can effect a major change in the traditional law enforcement balance.

In the decades of the 1970s and 1980s there has been increasing federal involvement with state and local law enforcement. The Law Enforcement Assistance Administration, established in 1968 and terminated in the late 1970s, involved a massive FEDERAL GRANT-IN-AID program to state and local governments for law enforcement purposes. The potential of this technique for giving the federal government control over local law enforcement policy decisions has not been fully realized.

Formal arrangements of cooperation between federal and state and local agencies are also increasing. Fourteen federal organized crime strike forces and twelve special drug task forces involving cooperating teams of federal, state, and local law enforcement agents have been established in major cities throughout the country. Policymaking committees composed of federal, state, and local law enforcement officials also meet.

The picture presented is one of increasingly close cooperation and interdependence of law enforcement agencies at the federal, state, and local levels. The existing programs do not yet, however, add up to the establishment of a basis for federal control.

As long as there is a national consensus that the primary responsibility for law enforcement should remain at the local level there is no serious likelihood that Congress would authorize the resources to create a national police force to enforce what is becoming a true national criminal code. Any assessment of trends in the national consensus on an issue of this nature is, of course, difficult to make. One can only point to certain factors which serve as general indicators.

The focus and rhetoric of national discourse on the role of federal criminal law enforcement have changed somewhat in recent years. Crime has increasingly become a source of public concern and a standard topic of national political discussion. Correspondingly, the federal government's public pronouncements have assumed increasingly larger responsibilities for federal law enforcement. The federal emphasis in the 1950s and 1960s focused on organized crime and political corruption. In the 1970s the emphasis shifted to white-collar crime. In the 1980s the federal government has added to its emphasized responsibilities a massive attack on drugs and violence.

In the 1960s, the ATTORNEY GENERAL of the United States never spoke of the federal government's role in law enforcement without at least paying lip service to the principle that primary responsibility rests at the local level. In the 1980s the attorney general in his major addresses generally speaks of working closely with state and local law enforcement officials and the development of a national strategy.

Any serious moves toward substantial enlargement of federal law enforcement responsibilities might be opposed by state and local governments. As matters stand, these authorities typically welcome increasing federal assistance and involvement, because the crime problem is too big for local officials to handle alone. Of course, this condition augurs continued growth of the federal arm. One wonders when that growth will begin to be seen as a threat.

Congress itself continues to recite the local responsibility credo even while it expands the scope of the federal code. Although the Supreme Court has not imposed significant constitutional restraints on the reach of federal penal legislation, it has adopted a restrictive maxim of interpretation: unless Congress expresses itself unambiguously it will be presumed not to have intended to change the traditional state–federal balance in law enforcement. If the prospect of a national police force loomed on the horizon, would the Court resurrect significant constitutional limits?

Perceiving the prospect of a national police force simply in the continued expansion of the federal criminal code would be foolish. That growth, however, creates one of the conditions that would enable a national police force to function. And the very existence of an enlarged code may generate some pressure to enforce it actively. Nothing can happen, of course, unless the national consensus breaks down. There, too, some signals could mean that the "impossible" is at least possible. The development of a national police force is not imminent, but there are enough portents to suggest that we should keep in mind words uttered by Justice FELIX FRANKFURTER in YOUNGSTOWN SHEET & TUBE CO. V. SAWYER (1952), a case involving assertion of national executive power: "The accretion of dangerous power does not come in a day. It does come, however slowly, from the generative force of unchecked disregard of the restrictions that fence in even the most disinterested assertion of authority."

NORMAN ABRAMS

Bibliography

ABRAMS, NORMAN 1986 Federal Criminal Law and Its Enforcement. St. Paul, Minn.: West Publishing Co.

——— 1970 Report on Jurisdiction. Pages 33–66 in *National Commission on Reform of Federal Criminal Laws: Working Papers,* vol. 1. Washington, D.C.: The Commission.

SCHWARTZ, LOUIS B. 1948 Federal Criminal Jurisdiction and Prosecutors' Discretion. *Law and Contemporary Problems* 13:64–87.

STERN, ROBERT L. 1973 The Commerce Clause Revisited: The Federalization of Intrastate Crime. *Arizona Law Review* 15:271–285.

LAW OF THE LAND

The phrase "law of the land" has two connotations of constitutional dimension. In general usage it refers to a HIGHER LAW than that of COMMON LAW declaration or legislative enactment. As a result of the SUPREMACY CLAUSE, the Constitution is such a higher law; it is the "supreme law of the land." In the exercise of JUDICIAL REVIEW, the SUPREME COURT claims the office of ultimate interpreter of the Constitution. It has thus become commonplace to think of decisions of the Court as the law of the land.

A second connotation has a specialized meaning that reaches far back into English history and leaves its indelible mark on American constitutional law. In 1215, the barons of England forced King John to sign MAGNA CARTA, pledging his observance of obligations owed to them in return for their fealty to him. Among the provisions was one that declared (in translation from the Latin): "No freeman shall be taken or imprisoned or dispossessed or outlawed or banished, or in any way destroyed, nor will we go upon him, nor send upon him, except by the judgment of his peers, or by the law of the land." Magna Carta was necessarily a feudal document, but this provision was so worded that it retained meaning long after feudalism gave way to the modern constitutional state.

The term "law of the land" consequently continued in English usage, representing that body of FUNDAMENTAL LAW to which appeal was made against any oppression by the sovereign, whether procedural or substantive. By 1354 there had appeared an alternate formulation, "due process of law." In his *Second Institute of the Laws of England* (1642), Sir EDWARD COKE asserted that "law of the land" and "due process of law" possessed interchangeable meanings; nevertheless, the older version was not thereby supplanted. The PETITION OF RIGHT (1628) played no favorites with the two terms, demanding "that freemen be imprisoned or detained only by the law of the land, or by due process of law and not by the king's special command, without any charge."

In the politically creative period after Independence, American statesmen preferred "law of the land" to "due process," apparently because of its historic association with Magna Carta. All eight of the early state CONSTITUTIONS incorporating the guarantee in full or partial form employed the term "law of the land"; and the same was true of the NORTHWEST ORDINANCE (1787). The first appearance of "due process of law" in American organic law occurred in the Fifth Amendment to the United States Constitution (1791). But that switch of usage did not displace "law of the land." Throughout the nineteenth century state constitutions and state courts spoke in one voice or the other, or even both. As of 1903 a listing by THOMAS M. COOLEY of state constitutions incorporating the legacy from Magna Carta showed "law of the land" outrunning "due process of law." The trend subsequently has been to the latter phrase; yet a 1980 count found eleven states still expressing the guarantee as "law of the land."

The Glorious Revolution of 1688, embodying the political theory that parliamentary enactment was the practical equivalent of the "law of the land," presented a dilemma in interpretation when the versions of the guarantee were introduced into American thought and incorporated into most American constitutions. Legislative supremacy was unacceptable in the New World; the American view was that when sovereignty changed hands the English concept of limitations upon the crown now applied to the legislative as well as the executive branch. It followed that to construe the guarantee as forbidding deprivation of life, liberty, or property except by legislative enactment would be to render its protection meaningless.

The puzzlement of American judges is understandable; only in the latter part of the nineteenth century had the concept been fully disentangled from the related concepts of regularized legislative process and SEPARATION OF POWERS.

The guarantee inherited from Magna Carta is unusual among constitutional limitations. On its face it is not absolute but conditional. The government may not act against persons except by the law of the land or by due process. The thrust is arguably procedural, suggesting original intent may have been to guarantee the protection of a trial. But it can carry substantive meanings as well; those meanings emerged early and had fully developed in England by the late seventeenth century.

Although the wording and position of the state constitutional guarantees varied—some using "law of the land," others "due process of law"; some appending the guarantee to a list of procedural rights, others making it a separate provision—the variation made little difference in judicial response at the procedural level. Not so, however, with respect to substantive content. Where, as in the constitutions of the Carolinas, Illinois, Maryland, and Tennessee, the wording was close to a literal translation of Magna Carta, the guarantee was extended to VESTED RIGHTS, independently of the criminal provisions of the procedural connotation. On the other hand, Connecticut and Rhode Island courts sustained PROHIBITION laws in the 1850s, holding that the phrase "due process of law" in their state constitutions was so enmeshed with entitlements of the criminally accused as to preclude inclusion of substantive right. A third series of cases, from Massachusetts, New Hampshire, New York, and Pennsylvania, read substantive content into the guarantee despite close interrelation with procedural protections. WYNEHAMER V. NEW YORK (1856) requires special consideration. In that case the state's highest court invalidated a prohibition law, insofar as it destroyed property rights in existing liquor stocks, resting its decision on separate constitutional guarantees of both "due process" and "law of the land." Contrary to the opinion of some scholars, *Wynehamer* was not overruled by *Metropolitan Board v. Barrie* (1866); the former case applied to a law with retroactive application, the latter to one that was purely prospective.

The Fifth Amendment associates "due process" with other constitutional guarantees clearly procedural in character, and separates the guarantee of due process from the RIGHT AGAINST SELF-INCRIMINATION only by a comma. Yet in major decisions, DRED SCOTT V. SANDFORD (1857), *Hepburn v. Griswold* (1870), and ADAIR V. UNITED STATES (1908), the Supreme Court found substantive content in the clause.

In the FOURTEENTH AMENDMENT, due process is not linked to criminal procedure protections, but resembles those state constitutional provisions that had been held in state courts to have substantive content. However, the Supreme Court has disregarded the distinction between the two due process clauses in the federal Constitution. The Court has been abetted by numerous COMMENTATORS ON THE CONSTITUTION who, intent on denying the substantive element in due process, have ignored or misinterpreted the history of state constitutional guarantees of "due process" and "law of the land." The freedom from procedural connotation of Fourteenth Amendment due process made easier the path of substantive content from dissent in the SLAUGHTERHOUSE CASES (1873), to reception in CHICAGO, MILWAUKEE & ST. PAUL RAILWAY COMPANY V. MINNESOTA (1890), to full embrace in LOCHNER V. NEW YORK (1905). The Court's acceptance of the INCORPORATION DOCTRINE, with consequent reading into the Fourteenth Amendment of the various procedural protections enumerated in the BILL OF RIGHTS, largely equates the content of the two due process clauses. This development has written the final chapter in the reinterpretation of "law of the land."

FRANK R. STRONG

Bibliography

HOWARD, A. E. DICK 1968 *The Road from Runnymede: Magna Carta and Constitutionalism in America.* Charlottesville: University Press of Virginia.

REMBAR, CHARLES 1980 *The Law of the Land: The Evolution of Our Legal System.* New York: Simon and Schuster.

LEARY v. UNITED STATES
395 U.S. 6 (1969)

Timothy Leary, a celebrated 1960s connoisseur of mind-altering substances, was found in possession of marijuana and convicted of (1) failure to pay the federal marijuana tax; and (2) transportation and concealment of marijuana, knowing it had been illegally imported into the country. A unanimous Supreme Court held both convictions unconstitutional. Paying the tax would have incriminated Leary under state law; his omission to pay was justified by his RIGHT AGAINST SELF-INCRIMINATION. His other conviction had rested on a statutory presumption that a person in possession of marijuana knew it had been illegally imported. This presumption was irrational; much marijuana was grown in the United States. The presumption thus violated PROCEDURAL DUE PROCESS.

KENNETH L. KARST

LEAST RESTRICTIVE MEANS TEST

When the Supreme Court, in reviewing the constitutionality of legislation, uses the permissive RATIONAL BASIS standard, it demands only that a law be a rational means for achieving a legitimate governmental purpose. When the STANDARD OF REVIEW is more exacting, however, the Court looks more closely at the legislative choice of means, insisting on more than some minimal showing of rationality. In a SEX DISCRIMINATION case, for example, the legislation must be "substantially related" to achieving some important governmental purpose; when STRICT SCRUTINY is the appropriate standard of review, the law must be "necessary" to achieving a COMPELLING STATE INTEREST. However such a heightened standard of review may be phrased, it aims at providing as much protection for constitutional values and interests as may be consistent with the accomplishment of legislative goals. One commonly used formulation of this aim is the Court's insistence that legislation be the "least restrictive means" for attaining the ends the legislature seeks—that is, least restrictive on such constitutionally protected interests as the FREEDOM OF SPEECH, or equality, or the free flow of INTERSTATE COMMERCE.

Some commentators have urged the Supreme Court to use a similar analysis in testing the reasonableness of legislative means even under the "rational basis" standard of review, as in cases involving challenges to ECONOMIC REGULATION. Thus far, however, the Court has employed "least restrictive means" reasoning only when it has consciously used a more demanding standard of review. Thus, in DEAN MILK COMPANY V. MADISON (1951), the Court struck down an ordinance specifying that milk sold in the city as "pasteurized" be pasteurized at an approved plant within five miles of the city center. The Court emphasized that "reasonable nondiscriminatory alternatives" were available to serve the city's health interests. (See STATE REGULATION OF COMMERCE.) And in *Shelton v. Tucker* (1960) the Court invalidated a law requiring every Arkansas teacher to file an annual affidavit listing every organization to which he or she had belonged or made contributions within five years. The Court agreed that Arkansas had a strong interest in teacher fitness, but said the legislature's sweeping intrusion into associational privacy "must be viewed in the light of less drastic means for achieving the same basic purpose." A narrower inquiry, presumably, would serve that purpose.

Both decisions illustrate how the "least restrictive means" formula can help a court avoid casting aspersions on legislative motive. (See LEGISLATION; LEGISLATIVE INTENT.) Madison's ordinance might have been designed to capture the pasteurization business; Arkansas undoubtedly was seeking to expose and dismiss teachers who were members of the NAACP. In neither case did the Supreme Court openly question the legitimacy of the legislative purpose; taking the government's statement of objective at face value, it said, in effect, "There are ways you could have accomplished that without intruding on constitutionally protected ground." One excellent reason for heightening the standard of review—and thus for insisting on "least restrictive means"—is the suspicion that legislators have acted for questionable purposes. (See SUSPECT CLASSIFICATION.)

KENNETH L. KARST

Bibliography

NOTE 1969 Less Drastic Means and the First Amendment. *Yale Law Journal* 78:464–474.

LECOMPTON CONSTITUTION

In June 1857 less than thirty percent of registered voters in Kansas Territory elected a CONSTITUTIONAL CONVENTION dominated by proslavery delegates. Meeting in Lecompton, the convention drew up a constitution preparatory for statehood that guaranteed the rights of owners of slaves in the territory, excluded free blacks, and submitted to a REFERENDUM the question whether the constitution should be accepted with or without a clause prohibiting the importation of slaves into Kansas (rather than a referendum on the constitution as a whole). Viewing this as a travesty of his principle of territorial SOVEREIGNTY, Illinois Senator STEPHEN A. DOUGLAS broke with the administration of JAMES BUCHANAN, which was pressuring Congress to accept the Lecompton constitution, and led the struggle against it. In three referenda on the constitution, Kansas voted first to accept the constitution with slavery (6,226 to 569, with free-state voters abstaining), then to reject the constitution entirely (10,226 to 166 with proslavery voters abstaining), then finally to reject it entirely again (11,300 to 1,788).

The struggle over the Lecompton constitution left Kansas a territory until 1861, dissipated the influence of the Buchanan administration, drove Douglas into opposition, and destroyed the capacity of the Democratic party to serve as a unifying transsectional force.

WILLIAM M. WIECEK

Bibliography

JOHANNSEN, ROBERT W. 1973 *Stephen A. Douglas.* New York: Oxford University Press.

LEE, RICHARD HENRY (1732–1794)

Educated in England, Richard Henry Lee practiced law in his native Virginia and became a justice of the peace in 1757. The next year he was elected to the House of Burgesses where his first speech was in favor of a measure to check the spread of SLAVERY. Lee was a leader of opposition to parliamentary taxation of the colonies and wrote the protest of the House of Burgesses against the Sugar Act (1764). When the royal governor dissolved the House of Burgesses in 1774, Lee introduced a resolution, adopted by the rump of the house, calling for a continental congress. As a delegate to the FIRST CONTINENTAL CONGRESS Lee proposed formation of committees of correspondence (a plan he originated with PATRICK HENRY and THOMAS JEFFERSON) and adoption of the continental ASSOCIATION. In June 1776 Lee made the original motions in the Continental Congress for a DECLARATION OF INDEPENDENCE, confederation, and seeking of foreign alliances. He later advocated Virginia's cession of western territorial claims in order to facilitate ratification of the ARTICLES OF CONFEDERATION; and, in 1784, he was elected President of the United States in Congress Assembled.

Lee was chosen as a delegate to the CONSTITUTIONAL CONVENTION OF 1787 but declined appointment, citing conflict with his responsibilities as a member of Congress. When the new Constitution was submitted to Congress, Lee opposed it on the ground that the convention had exceeded its mandate. Seeing that he could not block the proposal, he attempted, but failed, to have Congress add a BILL OF RIGHTS (drafted by GEORGE MASON).

Lee was a leading opponent of RATIFICATION OF THE CONSTITUTION. His seventeen "Letters from the Federal Farmer," widely printed in newspapers, were among the most influential of the various anti-Federalist writings. In the letters Lee presented a wide-ranging critique of the new Constitution: it was consolidationist, not federal, and would rob the states of their SOVEREIGNTY; it was aristocratic, or even monarchical, in tendency, not republican; the coexistence of state and federal courts would lead inevitably to conflict; the JUDICIAL POWER OF THE UNITED STATES was so broadly drawn as to permit foreigners and citizens of other states to sue a state in federal court; and, most important, there was no bill of rights. Lee argued and voted against ratification in the Virginia convention of 1788.

Lee was one of Virginia's original United States senators (1789–1792). He was chairman of the committee that drafted the JUDICIARY ACT OF 1789 and floor leader in the Senate for the Bill of Rights. Later in his senatorial career he became a supporter of the Federalist party and the economic program of ALEXANDER HAMILTON. A fervent opponent of slavery, Lee himself held about three dozen slaves.

DENNIS J. MAHONEY

LEE, UNITED STATES v. 455 U.S. 252 (1982)

Members of the Amish religion object, on religious grounds, to paying taxes or receiving benefits under the SOCIAL SECURITY ACT. An Amish employer of Amish workers claimed a constitutional right to refuse to pay Social Security taxes. The Supreme Court unanimously rejected that claim. Chief Justice WARREN E. BURGER, for the Court, accepted STRICT SCRUTINY as the appropriate STANDARD OF REVIEW in cases involving RELIGIOUS LIBERTY, but concluded that the government had established that mandatory participation was necessary to achieving the "overriding governmental interest" in maintaining the Social Security system. In a concurring opinion, Justice JOHN PAUL STEVENS argued against the strict scrutiny standard, saying that claimants of special religious exemptions from laws of general applicability must demonstrate "unique" reasons for being exempted—a standard that would be nearly impossible to meet.

KENNETH L. KARST

LEGAL POSITIVISM

See: Philosophy and the Constitution

LEGAL REALISM

Legal realism was the most significant movement that emerged within American jurisprudence during the 1920s and 1930s. Numerous factors conditioned this development, including pragmatism, SOCIOLOGICAL JURISPRUDENCE, and certain ideas of Justice OLIVER WENDELL HOLMES. The legal realists were not, however, an organized or highly unified group of thinkers. Their concepts had diverse sources, their work branched out in many directions, and their responses to particular issues often varied. The substantial differences between Judge JEROME N. FRANK and Karl N. Llewellyn illustrate these tendencies. Even so, these men and the other realists shared a number of distinctive attitudes and ideas.

The term "legal realism" signifies the basic thrust of the movement, which was to uncover and to explain legal realities. This effort reflects the allegation that some of the most cherished beliefs of lawyers are myths or fictions. The major purpose of the realists' provocative criticisms of these beliefs was not, however, to undermine the American legal system. Rather, it was to facilitate development of an accurate understanding of the nature, interpretation, operation, and effects of law. The realists insisted that achievement of this goal was essential for intelligent reform of legal rules, doctrines, and practices.

This outlook contributed to the realists' intense dissatisfaction with prevailing modes of legal education and scholarship. Both were under the spell of the case method pioneered by Christopher Columbus Langdell, the influential dean of the Harvard Law School from 1870 to 1895. He conceived of legal science as a small number of fundamental principles derived from study of relatively few cases. This conception was anathema to the realists, most of whom taught at leading American law schools. Their objective was to reform and to supplement, however, rather than to discard, the case method. The changes they advocated included focus on the *behavior* of judges and other officials, on their actual *decisions* rather than broad precepts. This emphasis was essential for the understanding of "real" instead of mere "paper" rules. The realists also urged the broadening of legal education to embrace not only the law on the books but also its administration and social impact. The development of this approach required a much closer integration of law and the social sciences than was traditional.

Some of these ideas were an outgrowth of major themes of ROSCOE POUND'S sociological jurisprudence. Still, the realists tended to develop criticisms of legal orthodoxies more radical than Pound's. This tendency is apparent from both the fact-skepticism of Judge Frank and the rule-skepticism of virtually all of the realists. The first of these doctrines stresses the difficulty of predicting findings of fact by judges or jurors, while the second emphasizes the limitations of legal rules. Rule-skepticism takes various forms, one of which is the conception of law as the past or future decisions of judges or other officials. Legal rules are descriptive or predictive rather than prescriptive generalizations about their behavior. This idea stems from Justice Holmes's predictive conception of law, which is one reason for the large shadow he cast over the realist movement.

Rule-skepticism also signifies distrust of the assumption that traditional legal rules or principles are the most influential determinant of judicial decisions. Numerous considerations explain this distrust, the degree of which varied among the realists. The most important factors were: a conviction of the possibility of widely different interpretations of established legal rules and principles; a belief in the existence of competing precedents, each of which could justify conflicting decisions in most cases; an awareness of the ambiguity inherent in legal language; a perception of the rapidity of socioeconomic change; and a study of the teachings of modern psychology. This last factor also influenced the realists' critique of judicial opinions. They attacked the syllogistic reasoning of judges on the ground that it failed to explain their choice of premises, which was all-important. This failure meant that opinions were often misleading rationalizations of decisions, the real reasons for which were unstated.

Rule-skepticism is the basis of some of the most important ideas of the legal realists. Their rejection of the conventional belief that judges do or should interpret rather than make law is a significant example. That belief is untenable because judicial legislation is unavoidable. Judges frequently must choose between competing decisions or interpretations, each of which is consistent with at least some precedents, rules, or principles. Although these generalizations limit judicial freedom, judges retain a substantial amount of room to maneuver.

This analysis underlies the realists' pragmatic approach to the evaluation of law, which emphasizes its practical results or effects. Rule-skepticism also influenced their de-emphasis of legal doctrine for the purpose of explaining and predicting judicial decisions. Instead, the realists stressed the importance of such factors as the personality, attitudes, or policies of judges. A similar emphasis characterized the behavioral jurisprudence developed largely by political scientists after World War II.

Although most of the realists did not specialize in constitutional law, their ideas facilitate understanding of the decisions of the Supreme Court. The Justices frequently must choose between conflicting interpretations of the Constitution, each of which has some legal basis. Their choices depend most basically upon their values, which may vary among Justices and may change over time. These variations help to explain disagreements among the Justices as well as changes in constitutional doctrine. Realism was also a formative influence on the legal philosophy of Justice WILLIAM O. DOUGLAS.

Despite the influence of the realists on American legal thought, the reaction to their ideas has not been uniform. In fact, large numbers of lawyers expressed varying degrees of dissatisfaction with the realist movement from its inception. If some of the concepts of the realists are unsatisfactory, others are enduring contributions to the study of law and the judicial process. Legal realism therefore warrants close scrutiny by students of constitutional law and judicial behavior.

WILFRID E. RUMBLE

Bibliography

FRANK, JEROME 1949 *Law and the Modern Mind.* New York: Coward-McCann.

LLEWELLYN, KARL N. 1962 *Jurisprudence: Realism in Theory and Practice.* Chicago: University of Chicago Press.

RUMBLE, WILFRID E. 1968 *American Legal Realism: Skepticism, Reform, and the Judicial Process.* Ithaca, N.Y.: Cornell University Press.

TWINING, WILLIAM 1973 *Karl Llewellyn and the Realist Movement.* London: Weidenfeld & Nicolson.

LEGAL TENDER CASES

The Legal Tender Cases include the decisions in *Hepburn v. Griswold* (1870), invalidating Civil War legislation authorizing paper money, and *Knox v. Lee* (1871) and *Parker v. Davis* (1871), sustaining postwar legal tender legislation. The various decisions reflect important developments in the nation's economic history, as well as in the Supreme Court's history, concerning the judicial role in questions of political economy, the nature and scope of judicial power, and the relation of politics to judicial opinions.

The greenback legislation of 1862 was designed to facilitate the financing of the Civil War, authorizing payments in demand notes, redeemable not in gold or silver but in interest-bearing twenty-year bonds. The notes were made "lawful money and a legal tender in payment of all debts, public and private, within the United States." The Treasury issued over $400 million in paper money during the war. After 1865, as inflation grew and greenbacks depreciated, creditors demanded payment in specie or at least in paper money equivalent to the rising premium on specie.

Secretary of the Treasury SALMON P. CHASE presided over the government's wartime greenback program. His outward support for paper money only masked his deep-seated hostility. In March 1864, he composed an epigram reflecting his true feelings: "When public exigencies require, Coin must become paper. When public exigencies allow, Paper must become coin." Six years later, as Chief Justice, he invalidated his previous policy.

Chase's role in the first legal tender case provoked intense partisan wrangling, both on and off the bench, and raised questions of the Chief Justice's behavior as the Court's administrative leader. The legal tender controversy had become entangled in partisan politics, as Republicans defended their greenback policy and the opposition Democrats attacked it as unconstitutional and improper. The Justices lined up on the same political grounds. (Chase and the Republicans by then were mutually alienated and the Chief Justice already was courting the Democrats in hopes of winning their presidential nomination.) In numerous state cases, judges similarly voted along party lines.

Chase apparently was determined to project the Court into the political maelstrom of monetary policy. But he did so with a precarious majority. Following the arguments in *Hepburn v. Griswold* in 1869, Republican Justices DAVID DAVIS, SAMUEL F. MILLER, and NOAH SWAYNE unhesitatingly endorsed the greenback policy. Chase, joined by Democrats NATHAN CLIFFORD, STEPHEN J. FIELD, ROBERT C. GRIER, and SAMUEL NELSON voted to invalidate the 1862 law. Grier by then was so senile that his colleagues persuaded him to resign. Chase, however, included his vote in the majority.

Meanwhile, Congress had authorized increasing the number of Justices to nine, giving President ULYSSES S. GRANT two new appointments, including Grier's replacement. On February 7, 1870, he nominated WILLIAM STRONG, who as a member of the Pennsylvania Supreme Court had supported the legal tender legislation, and JOSEPH P. BRADLEY, a railroad lawyer whose clients clearly favored the paper money scheme. On that same day, Chase defiantly announced the decision holding the law unconstitutional. The resulting charge of "court packing" against Grant and the Republicans misses the point: Presidents always seek judges who will support their political goals. In this case, Chase and his allies must bear the responsibility for the Court's embarrassment when it reversed itself a year later.

Chase's opinion invoked some of JOHN MARSHALL's best aphorisms. The Court, he insisted, must declare what the law is and not enforce any law inconsistent with the Constitution. To a point, Chase followed Marshall's MCCULLOCH V. MARYLAND (1819) discussions of IMPLIED POWERS, the NECESSARY AND PROPER clause, and the validity of laws consistent with the "letter and spirit of the Constitution." But where Marshall had appealed to the "spirit" of the Constitution to justify a BROAD CONSTRUCTION of congressional powers, Chase turned the notion on its head, construed those powers narrowly, and used the spirit to discover a limitation nowhere mentioned in the Constitution.

The Constitution, Chase maintained, was designed to establish justice, and a fundamental principle of justice was that preexisting private contracts should not be impaired by governmental action. The CONTRACT CLAUSE of the Constitution, however, applied to STATE ACTION; it said nothing regarding the federal government. But, Chase argued that the Constitution's Framers "intended that the spirit" of the contract clause would apply against all legislative bodies. His reliance on the Fifth Amendment was similarly strained. He found that the prohibition of contracts requiring specie payment in effect deprived people of their property without DUE PROCESS OF LAW; indeed, he maintained that the property was "taken" for a PUBLIC USE without the required JUST COMPENSATION.

Justice Miller's dissent pleaded for judicial restraint. He rebuked Chase's "abstract and intangible" arguments about the "spirit" of the Constitution. Following Marshall's broad reading of the necessary and proper clause, Miller suggested that "the degree of that necessity is for the legislature and not for the court to determine."

Partisan reactions to the decision were predictable. But the focused concerns for the result obscured the majority's far-reaching notions of judicial authority. Chase's bold assertions of judicial superintendence provoked virtually no negative reaction. The political and public acceptance of that doctrine gave a new legitimacy to judicial power. The nation had come a great distance from the protests against judicial excesses following DRED SCOTT V. SANDFORD (1857); indeed, Chase's opinion signaled a new chapter in judicial activism.

Significantly, the newly appointed Justice Strong, and not Miller, spoke for the majority in *Knox v. Lee* (1871) when the Court reversed itself. Strong largely followed Miller's interpretation of Congress's power and the necessity of congressional control over currency policy. But he responded only indirectly to Chase's presumptions of judicial power, contending that judges must assume the constitutionality of congressional acts and rely on congressional determination of what was "necessary and proper." He failed to rebuke Chase's reliance on the "spirit" of the Constitution. Finally, anticipating criticism for the dramatic reversal, Strong chided Chase for having forced the earlier decision when the Court was so divided and on the verge of receiving new appointees. The Chief Justice, joined by Nelson, Clifford, and Field dissented, with the latter two offering additional, separate opinions. The dissenting remarks largely reiterated the majority views of *Hepburn v. Griswold.*

Thirteen years later, in *Juilliard v. Greenman,* the Court, with only Field dissenting, sustained the peacetime use of greenbacks. Justice HORACE GRAY not only used the occasion to reaffirm the constitutionality of greenbacks but flatly declared that the policy involved "a POLITICAL QUESTION, to be determined by Congress when the question of exigency arises, and not a judicial question, to be afterwards passed upon by the Court." A half century later, Chief Justice CHARLES EVANS HUGHES invoked *Juilliard* as the Court, in the GOLD CLAUSE CASES (1935), narrowly acquiesced in President FRANKLIN D. ROOSEVELT's decision to abandon the gold standard. What had begun as one of the most politically conscious and aggrandizing decisions by the Supreme Court ended in self-abnegation and deference to the political branches of the government.

STANLEY I. KUTLER

Bibliography

DAM, KENNETH W. 1982 The Legal Tender Cases. *The Supreme Court Review* 1982:367–412.

FAIRMAN, CHARLES 1971 *Reconstruction and Reunion, 1864–1888,* Vol. XVI of the Oliver Wendell Holmes Devise *History of the Supreme Court of the United States.* New York: Macmillan.

KUTLER, STANLEY I. 1968 *Judicial Power and Reconstruction Politics.* Chicago: University of Chicago Press.

LEGISLATION

In addition to the separation of powers, there are at least two intersections of the Constitution and the legislative process. One concerns the obligation and capacity of legislatures to assess the constitutionality of their proposed enactments. The other concerns the federal judiciary's role in inducing legislatures to meet their constitutional obligations. Within this context there are issues common to state and congressional lawmaking.

The American constitutional scheme obligates legislatures to assess the constitutionality of proposed enactments and to enact only legislation they deem constitutionally permissible. Although this proposition may seem obvious, it has often been contradicted by respectable lawmakers, who assert that legislatures should engage in policymaking without regard to the Constitution and leave constitutional questions exclusively to the courts. Therefore the reasons that legislatures are obligated, no less than courts, to determine the constitutionality of proposed enactments deserve explanation.

If, as Chief Justice JOHN MARSHALL asserted in MARBURY V. MADISON (1803), the Constitution is a law paramount to ordinary legislation, then to assert that legislatures need not consult the Constitution is the equivalent of asserting that individuals need not consult the law before acting. To be sure, people sometimes act in disregard of the law, subject only to the risk of sanctions if they are caught and a court holds their actions to be unlawful. But it would be perverse to conclude from this observation that we are not obligated to obey the law.

The structure and text of the Constitution certainly imply that legislatures must initially determine the legality of their enactments. For example, how would Congress know whether it had the authority to enact a bill without consulting Article I and the other provisions that delegate limited powers to the national government? Indeed, some provisions of the Constitution are explicitly addressed to legislators. Article I, section 9, provides, "No bill of attainder or ex post facto law shall be passed." The FIRST AMENDMENT says, "Congress shall make no law," and the FOURTEENTH AMENDMENT's prohibitions begin with the words, "No state shall make or enforce any law. . . ." Article VI binds legislators and officials "by Oath or Affirmation to support this Constitution. . . ." Although this command does not entail that all constitutional questions are open to all institutions at all times, it does imply that a legislator must vote only for legislation that he or she believes is authorized by the Constitution. If history matters, the obligation of legislatures to interpret the Constitution was affirmed and acted on by various of the Framers and by early legislators and Presidents—some of whom, indeed, expressed this duty or prerogative even in the face of contrary judicial interpretations.

The existence of JUDICIAL REVIEW is sometimes thought to relieve legislatures of the obligations to determine the constitutionality of their enactments. But Chief Justice Marshall's classic justifications for judicial review in *Marbury* do not necessarily imply a privileged judicial function. As Herbert Wechsler wrote: "Federal courts, including the Supreme Court, do not pass on constitutional questions because there is a special function vested in them to enforce the Constitution or police the other agencies of government. They do so rather for the reason that they must decide a litigated issue that is otherwise within their jurisdiction and in doing so they must give effect to the supreme law of the land. That is, at least, what *Marbury v. Madison* was all about." (Wechsler, 1965, p. 1006.) Other arguments for judicial review have accorded the judiciary a special role, and in COOPER V. AARON (1958) the modern Court claimed that it was "supreme in the exposition of the law of the Constitution." But the Court has never implied that JUDICIAL SUPREMACY implies judicial exclusively, or that its privileged position relieves other institutions of the responsibility for making constitutional judgments.

Indeed, some constitutional issues—so-called POLITICAL QUESTIONS—may be committed to the legislative and executive branches to the exclusion of the judiciary. For example, it is widely assumed that the Senate's judgment in an IMPEACHMENT proceeding is not reviewable by the courts even though the decision may involve controverted constitutional questions, and even though the Senate's role in cases of impeachment is more judicial than legislative. In such cases, at least, if the legislature does not consider the constitutional questions, no one will.

If legislatures are obligated to consider constitutional questions, what deference, if any, should they accord prior judicial interpretations of the Constitution? In what might be called the judicial supremacy view, a legislature is in essentially the same position as a state or lower federal court: it must treat the Supreme Court's rulings as authoritative and binding. This was the view expressed by the Court in *Cooper v. Aaron.* Quoting Marshall's assertion in *Marbury* that "[i]t is emphatically the province and the duty of the judicial department to say what the law is," the Justices continued: "This decision declared the basic principle that the federal judiciary is supreme in the exposition of the law of the Constitution, and that principle has ever since been respected by this Court and the Country as a permanent and indispensable feature of our constitutional system."

The polar view is that legislators and other officials may, or must, apply the Constitution according to their best lights. This position was asserted by THOMAS JEFFERSON, ANDREW JACKSON, and ABRAHAM LIN-

COLN, among others. In vetoing the bill to recharter the Bank of the United States in 1832, Jackson wrote:

> It is maintained by advocates of the bank that its constitutionality in all its features ought to be considered settled by the decision of the Supreme Court [in MCCULLOCH V. MARYLAND (1819)]. To this conclusion I can not assent. . . . The Congress, the Executive, and the Court must each for itself be guided by its own opinion of the Constitution. Each public officer who takes an oath to support the Constitution swears that he will support it as he understands it, and not as it is understood by others. It is as much the duty of the House of Representatives, of the Senate, and of the President to decide upon the constitutionality of any bill or resolution which may be presented to them for passage or approval as it is of the supreme judges when it may be brought before them for judicial decision. The opinion of the judges has no more authority over Congress than the opinion of Congress has over the judges, and on that point the President is independent of both. The authority of the Supreme Court must not, therefore, be permitted to control the Congress or the Executive when acting in their legislative capacities, but to have only such influence as the force of their reasoning may deserve.

The issues presented by these opposed positions are of more than theoretical or historical interest. They have surfaced in recent years in debates over Congress's authority under section 5 of the Fourteenth Amendment to interpret or apply the amendment differently from the Court, and over Congress's power to limit the JURISDICTION OF FEDERAL COURTS over particular issues. For present purposes, I will assume that Congress, as well as state legislatures, must operate within the constitutional doctrines exposited by the United States Supreme Court. What does this obligation entail?

The dimensions of legislative responsibility and some of the difficulties in meeting it are illustrated by considering a bill introduced in the 89th Congress to punish the destruction of draft cards. The bill was enacted in 1965, seemingly in response to public DRAFT CARD BURNING to protest the VIETNAM WAR. It was challenged on First Amendment grounds and upheld by the Court in UNITED STATES V. O'BRIEN (1968).

The governing constitutional standard (as the Court later recapitulated it in *O'Brien*) was that "a governmental regulation is sufficiently justified . . . if it furthers an important or substantial governmental interest; if the governmental interest is unrelated to the suppression of free expression; and if the incidental restriction on alleged First Amendment freedoms is not greater than is essential to the furtherance of that interest."

Because this area of judicial doctrine was already well developed in 1965, legislators considering the draft card destruction law did not have to engage in much independent constitutional interpretation. They were, however, required to apply existing doctrine to the situation that faced them.

First, a legislator had to determine that his or her reasons for supporting the bill were "unrelated to the suppression of free expression." This obligation meant that he could not vote for the bill if his dominant, or causative, reason for favoring it was to suppress antiwar protests (rather than, say, to facilitate the administration of the selective service). The obligation demanded only introspection, a modicum of self-awareness, and the courage or will to follow the law.

It is worth pausing for a moment to ask why the Constitution should be concerned with a legislator's motivation in voting for a measure rather than simply with the legislation itself. The answer begins with the observation that the First Amendment is designed to protect citizens' freedom to protest against government policies. The Amendment does not, however, forbid all laws that inhibit protests to any extent. For example, the Congress surely may prohibit burning anything, including draft cards, if the activity poses a fire hazard to property that Congress has the power to protect. Thus, legislators have discretion to compromise constitutional values in the pursuit of other legitimate ends of government. However, as the Court's reference to "important or substantial" interests suggests, the First Amendment demands that a legislator treat a law's inhibition of expression as a cost, indeed a cost that should not be lightly imposed. But a legislator who votes for the bill in order to suppress protest, treats the inhibition as a benefit, not a cost. He has confused the credits and debits column on the constitutional balance sheet, for he seeks to bring about the very result that the First Amendment seeks to avert.

The second factual determination—actually a mixture of law, fact, and judgment—stems from the requirement that the law further an "important or substantial governmental interest." In *O'Brien* the Court was required to speculate about the nature and importance of the interests furthered by the draft card law. As happens frequently in matters concerning the national defense, the Court gave Congress the benefit of the doubt. But, of course, the legislators know what ends they intend a law to serve. Judgments about the importance of those ends, and how well a proposed law will actually accomplish them, are among the core responsibilities of legislators—who do not owe themselves any benefit of the doubt. It would be ironic, to say the least, if the Court deferred to Congress's judgments in these matters when Congress had not actually considered the issues carefully and in good faith.

The preceding paragraphs have not distinguished between the responsibilities of "legislators" and the "legislature." How, in fact, is responsibility for constitutional decision making allocated within the lawmaking process?

The answer seems easiest with respect to motivation. Granting that not even psychoanalysis can always reveal our deepest motivations, a conscientious legislator usually knows why he or she supports or opposes a law. (A contrary position would call into doubt the very foundations of the legislative process.) The Constitution demands that legislators assure themselves that illicit motivations, such as suppressing expression or disadvantaging racial minorities, play no role in their decisions to support the legislation. A legislator who "personally" does not care to pursue an illicit end but who supports a measure to satisfy her constituents' or colleagues' desires for those ends must be taken to have incorporated their ends as her own.

However intimately legislators know their own minds, they often lack the expertise and time to assimilate the complex factual and legal information bearing on the constitutionality of a proposed law. In the ordinary run of cases, these issues must be addressed and resolved through institutional mechanisms. A number of such mechanisms exist and are actually employed.

Federal legislation is typically drafted by lawyers and other specialists—either in an executive agency or department or in a congressional committee—who are familiar with any potential constitutional issues presented by the legislation. The committee to which a bill is referred can call upon its own legal staff or on the American Law Division of the Congressional Research Service of the Library of Congress for assistance with constitutional questions. Individual legislators can also seek advice from the research service and from their own staffs, and constitutional issues may be raised in debates on the floor of the House and Senate. Before signing a bill, the President can consult with the Office of Legal Counsel or seek an opinion from the attorney general. Although most state legislators cannot avail themselves of such rich resources, all have analogous methods for assessing the constitutionality of proposed legislation.

It is sometimes said that legislators have too little time and too much political interest to take constitutional issues seriously. Surely, however, this remark cannot justify legislative inattention to questions of constitutionality—unless one believes that legislators should be held to a lower standard of law-abidingness than individuals or enterprises, who may also lack the time or inclination to follow the law. To the extent that the observation is accurate, it is a source of concern to anyone committed to constitutional democracy.

The principal deterrent against unconstitutional legislative action is the threat of judicial invalidation of a law on the ground of its substantive unconstitutionality. From time to time, courts have also engaged in what might be called "procedural review" of legislative decisions—review that focuses on the process by which the law was enacted.

Procedural review encompasses two different inquiries. One is whether the legislators acted out of unconstitutional motives; the other is whether the legislators adequately considered the factual and legal bases for the law. Chief Justice Marshall alluded to both inquiries in *McCulloch v. Maryland* (1819). With respect to unconstitutional motivation, he wrote: "Should Congress, . . . under the pretext of executing its powers, pass laws for the accomplishment of objectives not entrusted to the government, it would become the painful duty of this tribunal . . . to say that such an act was not the law of the land." And he invoked the Executive's and Congress's attention to the underlying constitutional issues as a basis for judicial deference to their decision:

> The bill for incorporating the [first] bank of the United States did not steal upon an unsuspecting legislature, and pass unobserved. Its principle was completely understood and was opposed with equal zeal and ability. After being resisted, first in the fair and open field of debate, and afterwards in the executive cabinet, with as much persevering talent as any measure has ever experienced, and being supported by arguments which convinced minds as pure and as intelligent as this country can boast, it became law. . . . It would require no ordinary share of intrepidity to assert that a measure adopted under these circumstances was a bold and plain usurpation, to which the constitution gives no countenance.

Judicial inquiry into legislative motivation has had a checkered career. The Court in HAMMER V. DAGENHART (1918) and BAILEY V. DREXEL FURNITURE COMPANY (1922) relied on Marshall's "pretext" statement to strike down federal child labor legislation, and the Court in LOCHNER V. NEW YORK (1905) expressed doubt whether the maximum hours law had been adopted for permissible motives.

Inquiries into legislative motivation declined with the judicial modesty of the late 1930s, but it reappeared with the WARREN COURT's resurgence of activism. The Court in ABINGTON SCHOOL DISTRICT

v. Schempp (1963) articulated this standard for assessing establishment of religion claims: "[W]hat are the purpose and primary effect of the enactment? If either is the advancement or inhibition of religion then the enactment exceeds the scope of legislative power as circumscribed by the Constitution." Epperson v. Arkansas (1968) applied the "purpose" aspect of this test to strike down a law forbidding the teaching of evolutionary theory. Gomillion v. Lightfoot (1960) struck down the Alabama legislature's redrawing of the boundaries of Tuskeegee on the ground that it was designed to exclude black citizens from the city limits. And Griffin v. Prince Edward County School Board (1964) held that the county could not constitutionally close its public schools with the motive of avoiding integration.

In contrast to these decisions, *United States v. O'Brien* (1968) refused to consider the defendant's contention that Congress enacted the draft-card destruction law in order to suppress antiwar protest rather than for any legitimate administrative purposes. And Palmer v. Thompson (1971) dismissed the plaintiff's claim that Jackson, Mississippi, had closed its swimming pools in order to avoid integrating them. Writing for the Court in *Palmer*, Justice Hugo L. Black emphasized that it was extremely difficult to determine an official's motivation and especially difficult "to determine the 'sole' or 'dominant' motivation behind the choices of a group of legislators." Black also remarked that "there is an element of futility in a judicial attempt to invalidate a law because of the bad motives of its supporters. If a law is struck down for this reason, rather than because of its facial contents or effect, it would presumably be valid as soon as the legislature . . . repassed it for different reasons."

More recently, the Court has repudiated the broadest implications of *O'Brien* and *Palmer*. In Arlington Heights v. Metropolitan Housing Development Corporation (1977) Justice Lewis F. Powell noted the importance of "[p]roof of racially discriminatory intent or purpose" to claims under the equal protection clause. The Court held that the complainant was entitled—indeed, required—to prove that the town's refusal to rezone an area to permit multiple-family housing was discriminatorily motivated. The relevent standard was not whether the decision was solely or even dominantly motivated by racial considerations. Rather, proof that racial motivation played any part in the decision shifts to the decision maker "the burden of establishing that the same decision would have resulted even had the impermissible purpose not been considered." In *Mt. Healthy City Board of Education v. Doyle* (1977) the Court applied a similar standard in reviewing an employee's claim that he had been discharged for exercising First Amendment rights.

The current doctrine is correct. Legislative motives are not always obscure; nor does judicial review usually require inquiring into and aggregating the motives of individual legislators. As Justice Powell noted in *Arlington Heights*, the bizarrely shaped boundaries of Tuskeegee in *Gomillion* revealed "a clear pattern, unexplainable on grounds other than race." Sometimes, as in the school- and pool-closing cases, the historical background and sequence of actions leading up to the contested event may reveal invidious purposes. Placing a substantial burden on the complainant and permitting the respondent to show that the decision was in fact overdetermined by legitimate purposes amply protect against judicial invalidation of legislative policies that were based on legitimate considerations.

Indeed, this objective might be better achieved simply by invalidating a law where unconstitutional motives played any substantial role and permitting the legislature to consider the measure anew. Justice Black's concern to the contrary, such a course is not inevitably futile. Although a legislature may disguise its motivation and reenact the law for illicit reasons, it may also choose to reenact the law for entirely legitimate reasons—or the legislature may have lost whatever interest motivated it to act in the first instance. The Alabama legislature did not attempt to gerrymander Tuskeegee again, nor did Prince Edward County try to close its schools again for a "better" reason.

Judicial inquiry into unconstitutional motivation is sometimes said to be especially intrusive because it requires the judiciary to concern itself directly with the legislative process. In an important sense, however, any form of procedural review is less intrusive than substantive review. The Court leaves to the legislature its assigned task of weighing the costs and benefits of proposed legislation, and requires only that the legislature not count a constitutionally illicit objective as a benefit.

When a law is challenged on the ground that it does not further any valid interests, or does not further them sufficiently, the Supreme Court typically does not ask what ends the legislature actually sought to achieve, but hypothesizes possible objectives and asks whether the law can be upheld in terms of them. For example, in *United States v. O'Brien*, lacking any information about what legitimate objectives Congress actually sought to achieve through the draft card destruction law, the Court upheld the law on the basis of several administrative objectives that the Justices thought the law might serve.

In a widely cited 1972 article Gerald Gunther urged that the Court should be "less willing to supply justifying rationale by exercising its imagination. . . . [It] should assess the means in terms of legislative purposes that have substantial basis in actuality, not mere conjecture." Gunther asserted that a court need not delve into "actual legislative motivation" but can rely on legislative materials such as debates and reports or on a "state court's or attorney general office's description of purpose."

The Court has sometimes taken this approach. For example, in GRISWOLD V. CONNECTICUT (1965) the Court held that the state's anticontraceptive law was not justified as a means of deterring illicit sexual intercourse—the only purpose urged by the state attorney general. The Court did not consider whether the law might be upheld on the more plausible (though constitutionally problematic) ground that the Connecticut legislature believed that contraception was immoral. Whatever the justification for this judicial strategy, it is not likely to identify the legislature's actual purposes: state courts and attorneys general have no privileged access to actual legislative purposes but must rely on the same public materials available to the Supreme Court.

In recent years some Justices, and occasionally a majority of the Court, have limited the objectives that can be considered in support of a challenged regulation to the decision maker's (supposed) actual objectives. This course is easiest for a court to follow when statutory limitations on an agency's mandate foreclose it from pursuing a broad range of objectives. For example, HAMPTON V. MOW SUN WONG (1976) invalidated a United States Civil Service regulation barring resident ALIENS from federal civil service jobs. Writing for the Court, Justice JOHN PAUL STEVENS assumed that Congress or the President might constitutionally have adopted such a requirement for reasons of foreign policy, but held that the commission's jurisdiction was limited to adopting regulations to "promote the efficiency of the federal service." Similarly, in REGENTS OF THE UNIVERSITY OF CALIFORNIA V. BAKKE (1978), Justice Powell refused to consider whether the university's preferential admissions policy was justified as a remedy for past discrimination, holding that the regents were empowered only to pursue educational objectives.

The Supreme Court has sometimes relied on legislative history to refuse to uphold legislation on the basis of objectives that were not intended. For example, in *Weinberger v. Wiesenfeld* (1975), in assessing the constitutionality of the "mother's insurance benefit" provision of the SOCIAL SECURITY ACT, Justice WILLIAM J. BRENNAN wrote for the Court that "the mere recitation of a benign, compensatory purpose is not an automatic shield which protects against an inquiry into the actual purposes underlying a statutory scheme." Although the provision might have been designed to compensate for past economic discrimination against women, the legislative history belied this purpose and the Court refused to uphold the law on a false basis.

Legislative history is often sparse or nonexistent, however. A complex legislative scheme may make a myriad of classifications; the chances are slight that legislative materials will illuminate the classification challenged in any particular case; and the absence of legislative history does not mean that the legislators did not intend to pursue a particular objective. Partly because of these complexities, judicial efforts to limit the purposes on the basis of which laws can be justified have not followed a consistent pattern. The current state of the law is captured in *Kassell v. Consolidated Freightways Corporation* (1981), which struck down a state's highway regulation prohibiting double trailers as an undue burden on INTERSTATE COMMERCE. In a concurring opinion, Justice Brennan wrote that he would give no deference to the state's arguments based on safety because the law was not actually designed to promote safety but to protect local industries. Justice WILLIAM H. REHNQUIST, dissenting, asserted that there was "no authority for the proposition that possible legislative purposes suggested by a state's lawyers should not be considered in COMMERCE CLAUSE cases." The plurality avoided the issue by rejecting the state's safety claims on the merits.

In *McCulloch* Marshall implied that the BANK OF THE UNITED STATES ACT was entitled to special deference because of the attention paid to the constitutional issues within the executive and legislative branches. Because of the difficulty of such an inquiry, however, and perhaps because of its perceived impropriety, the court has seldom conditioned deference on the extent to which the legislature actually considered the factual and legal issues bearing on the constitutional questions at stake. In *Textile Workers Union v. Lincoln Mills* (1957) the Court gave a strained interpretation to a federal statute in order to avoid a difficult constitutional question of federal jurisdiction, to which Congress had apparently paid no attention. In a separate opinion, Justice FELIX FRANKFURTER noted that "this Court cannot do what a President sometimes does in returning a bill to Congress. We cannot return this provision to Congress and respectfully request that body to assume the responsibility placed upon it by the Constitution."

In an article on the *Lincoln Mills* case, ALEXANDER M. BICKEL and Harry Wellington responded that the Court could properly perform such a "remanding function" and that it had sometimes done so, albeit surreptitiously. KENT V. DULLES (1958) is often cited as an example. Rather than decide whether the secretary of state could constitutionally refuse to issue passports to members of the Communist party, the Court held that Congress had not delegated the secretary this authority, thus in effect returning the matter to Congress. More recently, Justice Stevens, dissenting in FULLILOVE V. KLUTZNICK (1980), explicitly urged such a "remand." *Fullilove* upheld a congressional provision requiring that ten percent of the federal funds allocated to public work projects be used to procure services from minority contractors. Justice Stevens's dissent started from the premise that the Constitution disfavors all racial classifications. Noting that the challenged provision was scarcely discussed in committee or on the floor of the Congress, he wrote:

> Although it is traditional for judges to accord the same presumption of regularity to the legislative process no matter how obvious it may be that a busy Congress has acted precipitately, I see no reason why the character of their procedures may not be considered relevant to the decision whether the legislative product has [violated the Constitution]. A holding that the classification was not adequately preceded by a consideration of less drastic alternatives or adequately explained by a statement of legislative purpose would be far less intrusive than a final decision [of unconstitutionality]. . . . [T]here can be no separation-of-powers objection to a more tentative holding of unconstitutionality based on a failure to follow procedures that guarantee the kind of deliberation that a fundamental constitutional decision of this kind obviously merits.

"Procedural" judicial review, which takes account of the legislature's consideration of relevant constitutional issues, has two objectives. First, it may foster legislative attention to the Constitution in the first instance. Second, it prevents constitutional concerns from falling between two stools—which happens when a court blindly defers to a judgment that the legislature did not in fact make.

Procedural review seems appropriate where a legislature evidently has ignored issues of law or fact that bear on the constitutionality of an enactment. It is questionable whether a general practice of procedural review would prove workable, however. Among other things, a court will have difficulty in assessing the adequacy of constitutional deliberation from external indicia. Justice Powell, concurring in *Fullilove,* thus responded to the argument that the legislation was not adequately supported by factual findings or debate:

> The creation of national rules for the governance of our society simply does not entail the same concept of recordmaking that is appropriate to a judicial or administrative proceeding. Congress has no responsibility to confine its vision to the facts and evidence adduced by particular parties. One appropriate source [of facts] is the information and expertise that Congress acquires in the consideration and enactment of earlier legislation. After Congress has legislated repeatedly in an area of national concern, its Members gain experience that may reduce the need for fresh hearings or prolonged debate when Congress again considers action in that area.

In addition to the specific powers and limitations found in the Constitution, the Court has interpreted the DUE PROCESS and equal protection clauses to impose general requirements of "rationality" on the outcome of the legislative process. As stated in *F. S. Royster Guano Company v. Virginia* (1920), the equal protection STANDARD OF REVIEW requires that "the classification must be reasonable, not arbitrary, and must rest upon some ground of difference having a fair and substantial relation to the object of the legislation. . . ." The modern Court has usually articulated an even less demanding RATIONAL BASIS requirement: the law, and any classifications it makes, must plausibly promote some permissible ends to some extent.

The rationality standards may provide a minimal judicial safeguard against laws whose only purpose is constitutionally illicit, without requiring a direct inquiry into legislative motivation. But they may also impose a broader requirement on the legislative process. They may imply what Frank Michelman has described as a "public interest" rather than a "public choice" model of the legislative process.

The public interest model is premised on the possibility of shared public values or ends. "[T]he legislature is regarded as the forum for identifying or defining, and acting towards those ends. The process is one of mutual search through joint deliberation, relying on the use of reason supposed to have persuasive force" (Michelman, 1977, p. 149). The public choice model regards "all substantive values and ends . . . as strictly private. . . . There is no public or general social interest, there are only concatenations of particular interests or private preferences. There is no reason, only strategy. . . . There are no good legislators, only shrewd ones; no statesmen; only messengers" (ibid., p. 148).

The constitutional implications of the two models

can be illustrated by the city ordinance challenged in RAILWAY EXPRESS AGENCY v. NEW YORK (1949). The ordinance prohibited advertisements on the side of vehicles but exempted business delivery vehicles advertising their own business. The most obvious beneficiaries of the exemption were the city's newspapers.

If the Court had adopted a "public choice" model, it would have been pointless to subject the New York ordinance to a rationality requirement: the exemption would be permissible even if its only rationale were to "buy off" the newspapers to get the ordinance enacted or, indeed, to favor the newspapers over other advertisers. Under a "public interest" model, however, the Court would at least ask whether the exemption was related to some extrinsic purpose—and this it did. Justice WILLIAM O. DOUGLAS wrote for the Court that the "local authorities may well have concluded that those who advertise their own wares on their trucks do not present the same traffic problem in view of the nature or extent of the advertising which they use." In a concurring opinion, Justice ROBERT H. JACKSON pointed to "a real difference between doing in self-interest and doing for hire."

Thus, the Court seems nominally to adhere to a public interest model. But the weakness of the rationality standards, and the Court's generosity in imagining possible rationales for classifications (exemplified by *Railway Express Agency* itself), suggest some judicial ambivalence about the extent to which this model should be treated as a constitutional norm. There is some academic controversy about both the norm itself and its judicial enforceability.

JAMES BRADLEY THAYER asserted in his 1901 biography of John Marshall that judicial review implies a distrust of legislatures and that the legislatures "are growing accustomed to this distrust, and more and more readily incline to justify it, and to shed the consideration of constitutional restraints, . . . turning that subject over to the courts; and what is worse, they insensibly fall into a habit of assuming that whatever they can constitutionally do they may do. . . . The tendency of a common and easy resort to this great function is to dwarf the political capacity of the people, and to deaden its sense of moral responsibility." Assessing Thayer's argument is practically impossible, but it seems at least as plausible that the practice of judicial review is a necessary reminder to legislators that their actions are constrained by fundamental public law and not only by their constituents' interests or even their own moral principles.

Thayer's argument nonetheless underscores the point that the Constitution speaks directly to legislatures. In a properly functioning constitutional system, judicial review should be just that—the review of the legislature's considered judgment that the challenged act is constitutionally permissible. Whether this position is "realistic" is another matter. Surely, however, one cannot expect legislators to take their constitutional responsibilities seriously if they and the citizenry at large assume that they have none.

PAUL BREST

Bibliography

BENNETT, ROBERT 1979 "Mere" Rationality in Constitutional Law: Judicial Review and Democratic Theory. *California Law Review* 67:1049–1103.

BICKEL, ALEXANDER and WELLINGTON, HARRY 1957 Legislative Purpose and the Judicial Function: The Lincoln Mills Case. *Harvard Law Review* 71:1–39.

BREST, PAUL 1971 An Approach to the Problem of Unconstitutional Legislative Motive. *Supreme Court Review* 1971:95–146.

ELY, JOHN H. 1970 Legislative and Administrative Motivation in Constitutional Law. *Yale Law Journal* 79:1205–1341.

GUNTHER, GERALD 1982 In Search of Evolving Doctrine on a Changing Court: A Model for a Newer Equal Protection. *Harvard Law Review* 86:1–48.

LINDE, HANS 1976 Due Process of Lawmaking. *Nebraska Law Review* 55:197–255.

MICHELMAN, FRANK 1977 Political Markets and Community Self-Determination: Competing Judicial Models of Local Government Legitimacy. *Indiana Law Journal* 53:145–206.

MORGAN, DONALD G. 1966 *Congress and the Constitution: A Study in Responsibility.* Cambridge, Mass.: Belknap Press.

THAYER, JAMES BRADLEY 1901 *John Marshall.* Boston: Houghton Mifflin.

WECHSLER, HERBERT 1965 The Courts and the Constitution. *Columbia Law Review* 65:1001–1014.

LEGISLATIVE CONTEMPT POWER

Anglo-American legislative bodies have exercised the power to punish nonmembers for contempt of their dignity and proceedings since the time when the High Court of Parliament exercised undifferentiated legislative and judicial power. There is no explicit constitutional warrant for the exercise of the power by Congress, but Congress has exercised it, nonetheless, at least since 1795. There were several instances in the nineteenth century of summary judgments being rendered against nonmembers for such acts of contempt as publishing abusive language about Congress or attempting to bribe its members. In *Anderson v. Dunn* (1821) the Supreme Court held that the power to punish contempts—at least of the latter sort—was inherent in "a deliberate assembly, clothed with the majesty of the people." In KILBOURNE V. THOMPSON (1881), however, the Supreme Court held that Congress did not possess COMMON LAW power to punish as contempt Kilbourne's failure to produce documents subpoenaed by an investigatory committee for a nonlegislative purpose.

Congress defined the statutory offense of contempt of Congress in 1857; this offense was triable before the house against which the contempt was committed, and a contemnor, once convicted, might be confined in the Capitol for the duration of the congressional session. Contempt of Congress remains a statutory offense, but it is no longer prosecuted at the bar of the house. Because bribery of members of Congress is now punishable as a separate offense, the most common contemporary form of contempt of Congress is refusal to testify at or to provide evidence for LEGISLATIVE INVESTIGATIONS. The presiding officer of the offended house (ordinarily only if directed by a vote of the full house) certifies the circumstances of the contempt to the United States attorney in the district where the contempt was committed; the federal attorney may then prosecute the contemnor in federal court.

DENNIS J. MAHONEY

Bibliography

GOLDFARB, RONALD L. 1963 *The Contempt Power.* New York: Columbia University Press.

LEGISLATIVE COURT

The term "legislative court" was coined by Chief Justice JOHN MARSHALL to describe the status of courts created by Congress to serve United States TERRITORIES lying outside the boundaries of any state. Congress had not given the judges of the territorial courts the life tenure and salary guarantees that Article III of the Constitution required for judges of CONSTITUTIONAL COURTS, and Marshall needed to explain the anomaly of federal courts outside the contemplation of Article III. In AMERICAN INSURANCE CO. V. CANTER (1828) he concluded that Congress, in exercising its power to govern the territories, could establish courts that did not fit Article III's specifications. Today this concept of legislative courts embraces all courts created by Congress and staffed by judges who do not enjoy constitutional protection of their tenure and salaries. Examples include territorial courts, consular courts, the Tax Court of the United States, the Bankruptcy Court, the Court of Military Appeals, and the courts of local jurisdiction operating in the DISTRICT OF COLUMBIA and the Commonwealth of PUERTO RICO.

Just as a legislative court's judges fall outside Article III's guarantees of independence, so it is capable of handling business outside that Article's definition of "the JUDICIAL POWER OF THE UNITED STATES"—something a constitutional court cannot constitutionally do. A legislative court, for example, can be assigned JURISDICTION to give ADVISORY OPINIONS to the President or Congress. Yet, despite Marshall's OBITER DICTUM in the *Canter* opinion that a legislative court is "incapable of receiving" jurisdiction lying within the judicial power, it is clear today that such courts, like administrative agencies, can constitutionally be assigned the initial decision of a great many cases within Article III's definition of that power. (See NORTHERN PIPELINE CONSTRUCTION CO. V. MARATHON PIPE LINE CO., 1982.) Their decisions on such Article III matters are reviewable by constitutional courts, including the Supreme Court, when Congress so provides.

With some difficulty, the Supreme Court has resolved controversies over the status of several courts. The federal courts formerly serving the District of Columbia were held protected by Article III's guarantees of life tenure and salary protection. In this sense, they were constitutional courts. However, the Court also held that the same courts could constitutionally be given work falling outside Article III's specification of CASES AND CONTROVERSIES within the judicial power. In 1970, Congress replaced these "hybrid" courts with a dual court system: the constitutional courts operate under Article III's strictures and the legislative courts handle the local judicial business of the District. In *Palmore v. United States* (1973) the Supreme Court upheld the local courts' power to try local crimes (established by congressional statute), despite their judges' lack of life tenure and salary guarantees.

Similarly, in *Glidden Co. v. Zdanok* (1962), the Court staggered to the ruling—based on two inconsistent opinions, pieced together to make a majority for the result—that the old Court of Claims (see CLAIMS COURT; UNITED STATES COURT OF APPEALS FOR THE FEDERAL CIRCUIT) and the COURT OF CUSTOMS AND PATENT APPEALS were constitutional courts, not legislative courts.

In essence a legislative court is merely an administrative agency with an elegant name. While Congress surely has the power to transfer portions of the business of the federal judiciary to legislative courts, a wholesale transfer of that business would work a fundamental change in the status of our independent judiciary and would seem vulnerable to constitutional attack.

KENNETH L. KARST

Bibliography

NOTE 1962 Legislative and Constitutional Courts: What Lurks Ahead for Bifurcation. *Yale Law Journal* 71:979–1012.

LEGISLATIVE FACTS

The growth of American constitutional doctrine has been influenced, from the beginning, by the traditions of the Anglo-American COMMON LAW. Judges make constitutional law, as they make other kinds of law, partly on the basis of factual premises. Sometimes these premises are merely assumed, but sometimes they are developed with the aid of counsel. However they may be determined, the facts on which a court's lawmaking is premised are called "legislative facts." In modern usage they are sometimes contrasted with "adjudicative facts," the facts of the particular case before the court.

Not all constitutional questions concern the validity of legislation. In the 1970s and 1980s, for example, the Supreme Court went through a period of reappraisal of the EXCLUSIONARY RULE, which excludes from a criminal case some types of EVIDENCE obtained in violation of the Constitution. One factual issue repeatedly raised during this reconsideration was whether the rule actually served to deter police misconduct. In considering that question, the Court was not second-guessing the judgment of a legislature. Yet the question was properly regarded as one of legislative fact; its resolution would provide one of the premises for the Court's constitutional lawmaking.

More frequently, however, the courts consider issues of legislative fact in reviewing the constitutionality of legislation. In many cases, particularly when the laws under review are acts of Congress, the legislature itself has already given consideration to the same fact questions. Congress sometimes writes its own factual findings into the text of a law, explicitly declaring the actual basis for the legislation. In such cases the courts typically defer to the congressional versions of reality. Similar legislative findings are only infrequently written into the enactments of state and local legislative bodies, but even there the practice has recently increased. It seems unlikely, however, that judges, especially federal judges, will pay the same degree of deference to those legislative findings.

The courts' treatment of issues of legislative fact is thus seen as a function of the STANDARD OF REVIEW used to test a law's validity. When a court uses the most permissive form of the RATIONAL BASIS standard, it asks only whether the legislature could rationally conclude that the law under review was an appropriate means for achieving a legitimate legislative objective. The BRANDEIS BRIEF was invented for use in just such cases, presenting evidence to show that a legislature's factual premises were not irrational. When the standard of review is heightened—for example, when the courts invoke the rhetoric of STRICT SCRUTINY—arguments addressed to questions of legislative fact can be expected to come from both the challengers and the defenders of legislation. A court's fact-finding task in such a case is apt to be more complicated; the complication is implicit in any standard of review more demanding than the "rational basis" standard, any real interest-balancing by the courts. Arguments about the proper judicial approach to the factual premises for legislation are, in fact, arguments about the proper role of the judiciary in the governmental system. (See JUDICIAL REVIEW; JUDICIAL ACTIVISM AND JUDICIAL RESTRAINT.)

The technique of the Brandeis brief was invented for the occasion of the Supreme Court's consideration of MULLER V. OREGON (1908), upholding a law regulating women's working hours, and has been in fairly frequent use ever since. Increasingly, however, counsel have sought to present evidence on issues of legislative fact to trial courts. An early example was SOUTHERN PACIFIC CO. V. ARIZONA (1945), in which the Supreme Court struck down a law limiting the length of railroad trains. For five and a half months the trial judge heard evidence filling some 3,000 pages in the record; he made findings of legislative fact covering 148 printed pages. Justice HUGO L. BLACK, dissenting, complained that this procedure made the judiciary into a "super-legislature," but courts cannot escape from this kind of factual inquiry unless they adopt Justice Black's permissive views and abandon most constitutional limits on STATE REGULATION OF COMMERCE.

Nor are such trials of legislative fact limited to issues lying within the competence of people like safety engineers. When the California school finance case, SERRANO V. PRIEST (1972), was remanded for trial, the court took six months of expert testimony centered on a single question: Does differential spending on education produce differences in educational quality? (The court's unsurprising answer: Yes.)

As the *Serrano* and *Southern Pacific* cases show, proving legislative facts at trial is considerably more costly than filing a Brandeis brief. It permits cross-examination, however, and sharpens the focus for evidentiary offerings. Even when appellate review seems certain, the trial court's sorting and evaluation of a complex record can aid the appellate court greatly. Expert testimony, the staple of such a trial, typically rests on the sort of opinion and hearsay about which nonexperts ordinarily would not be permitted to testify. Legislative facts, of course, are tried to the judge and not to a jury; furthermore, questions of legislative fact, by definition, touch a great many "cases" not in court that will be "decided" by the precedent made in the court's constitutional ruling. Just as a constitutional case is an especially appropriate occasion for hearing the views of an AMICUS CURIAE, the widest latitude should be allowed to the parties (and to an amicus) to present evidence broadly relevant to the lawmaking issues before the court.

Ultimately there is no assurance that counsel's efforts to educate a court about the factual setting for constitutional lawmaking will improve the lawmaking itself. Yet our courts, with the Supreme Court's encouragement, continue to invite counsel to make these efforts. One of America's traditional faiths, which judges share with the rest of us, is a belief in the value of education.

KENNETH L. KARST

Bibliography

FREUND, PAUL A. 1951 *On Understanding the Supreme Court.* Boston: Little, Brown.

KARST, KENNETH L. 1960 Legislative Facts in Constitutional Litigation. *Supreme Court Review* 1960:75–112.

LEGISLATIVE IMMUNITY

The SPEECH OR DEBATE CLAUSE immunizes federal legislators from civil or criminal actions based on legislative acts. In TENNEY V. BRANDHOVE (1951) the Supreme Court, relying on the COMMON LAW immunity of legislators and the speech or debate clause, held legislators to be immune from federal civil suits based on legislative acts. This legislative immunity, however, does not preclude evidence of legislative acts in criminal prosecutions for corruption.

In what may be an expansion of common law legislative immunity, LAKE COUNTRY ESTATES, INC. V. TAHOE REGIONAL PLANNING AGENCY (1979) held that the appointed members of a bistate agency enjoyed legislative immunity from suits for constitutional violations. The Court also suggested that state legislative immunity does not depend on the existence of the speech or debate clause. *Lake Country Estates'* extension of absolute legislative immunity to un-elected officials may enable many public bodies or officials that promulgate rules of general application to rely on legislative immunity. For example, in *Supreme Court of Virginia v. Consumers Union of the United States* (1980) the Court concluded that state supreme court justices enjoyed legislative immunity from damages actions based on their promulgation of unconstitutional rules of conduct for the state bar.

THEODORE EISENBERG

Bibliography

EISENBERG, THEODORE 1982 Section 1983: Doctrinal Foundations and an Empirical Study. *Cornell Law Review* 67:492–505.

LEGISLATIVE INTENT

Legislative intent is a construct that courts use to discern the meaning of legislative action, usually in the form of LEGISLATION. The concept is employed in many fields of law—including constitutional law—in the interpretation and application of statutes. In constitutional law, courts also use the concept in determining the purposes or goals of a legislature when they are relevant to deciding the constitutionality of the legislation.

In searching for legislative intent, courts appear to assume that legislation is aimed, in an instrumentally rational fashion, at achieving certain objectives or goals. Sometimes these objectives or goals are stated in rather discrete terms. In HINES V. DAVIDOWITZ (1941), for example, the Supreme Court decided that in passing a law requiring ALIENS to register with federal authorities, Congress had the objective of barring enforcement of state laws that required aliens to register with state officials. At other times, legislative intent is cast in more general terms. Thus in RAILWAY EXPRESS AGENCY V. NEW YORK (1949), the Supreme Court decided that the legislative goal in banning advertisements from some motor vehicles was the promotion of traffic safety.

There has been controversy about reference to legislative intent as a method of giving meaning to legislation, much as there has been controversy about reference to the Framers' intent as a means of giving meaning to the provisions of the Constitution itself. Two lines of criticism have developed, one rooted in doubt about the intelligibility of the concept of legislative intent, the other grounded in skepticism about the legitimacy of the political theory that an appeal to legislative intent presupposes.

Those who question the intelligibility of attempting to ascertain the intent of a legislature argue that it is impossible to ascribe an intent to a multi-member body. First, they point out the difficulty of ascertaining the individual intents of all the legislators and, second, they argue that even if the individual intents could be ascertained, there is no theoretically sound way to combine them to produce a coherent intent of the group.

Those who question the legitimacy of an appeal to legislative intent argue that as a matter of political theory, courts should not be bound by beliefs or wishes of legislators that were not written into the text of the statute but rather only the printed words of the legislation. OLIVER WENDELL HOLMES, for example, urged that courts should ask not what the legislature intended but rather only what the statute means. Instead of looking for evidence of legislative intent, courts should, according to Holmes, consult dictionaries and evidence of contemporary usage to construct the most acceptable interpretation of the statute's meaning.

More recent scholarly criticism has also questioned the validity of the assumption about legislative behavior that legislative intent presupposes. According to these critics, legislatures are merely market arenas in which private interests trade with each other through their legislators to further their own particular advantages. A search for a legislative intent beyond the immediate effects that the statute accomplishes is, according to his view, nonsensical and perhaps politically illegitimate as well.

Legislative intent has remained an important concept in constitutional law in spite of these criticisms. First, courts have developed various methods of dealing with the practical difficulties of constructing a legislative intent. Thus the difficulties associated with discovering the intent of each legislator and of aggregating these individual intents into a group intent have been addressed through the use of presumptions and, in some cases, outright fictions. Often, particularly in the case of state legislation, there is no evidence of legislative intent beyond the words of the statute, but the courts nevertheless generally say they are seeking legislative intention when they are deciding what the legislation means.

The courts indulge in similar assumptions when additional evidence does exist. For example, courts generally credit statements in committee reports as evidence of legislative purpose, even though there may be little reason to believe that many legislators read the report or agreed with it. Similarly, the speeches of proponents during floor debates (or even in public discourse outside the legislative arena) are also treated as evidence of legislative intent, even though few legislators may have been present during the floor debate (or heard the nonlegislative remarks). Some have argued that the legislative draftsmen or proponents are the "agents" of the legislature and therefore that their intent is the relevant legislative intent. Others urge that silent legislators who vote for the enactment share the intent of those who do speak in favor of the legislation. Another view is that legislatures in effect delegate to identifiable subgroups, such as committees, the task of setting legislative goals in the areas of the subgroups' specialties. Thus the intent of the legislature with respect to a transportation law would be assumed to be the same as the intent of the legislative committee on transportation. Whatever the rationale, courts have created a concept of legislative intent that does not purport to be a true measurement of the intents of the individual legislators. In effect, courts have personified legislatures and sought to ascribe to them an intent as if the legislature were a single person, one who sometimes speaks with several, often conflicting voices about what he wants to accomplish.

The more fundamental questions of political theory which challenge the legitimacy of looking to legislative intent have not been systematically addressed, at least by the courts. Courts have, by and large, assumed that if legislative intent can be constructed, it is relevant and even controlling in the interpretation of legislative action, at least where the terms of the statute are perceived to provide leeway for interpretation.

Legislative intent may have remained important for several reasons. First, the concept is used widely outside of constitutional law for statutory interpretation. Legislatures have learned what courts will consider in searching for legislative intent, and they have adjusted their processes in some measure to provide the appropriate signals to the courts—thus encouraging continued judicial reliance on legislative intent.

Second, adherence to legislative intent may be grounded in judicial support of what the judges believe to be a political ideal. Although courts may recognize that trading among private interests does occur, they may believe that our society nevertheless aspires to a model of legislation that is an instrumentally rational pursuit of objectives that further the public interest.

Finally, courts have evolved several STANDARDS OF REVIEW in constitutional law that make the legislature's goals or objectives relevant to the constitutionality of the legislation. These standards, such as the RATIONAL BASIS test, LEAST RESTRICTIVE MEANS analysis, and the tests for federal PREEMPTION of state regulatory authority, have no doubt helped insure that the search for legislative intent remains a significant part of constitutional adjudication.

Legislative intent is thus important in several areas of constitutional adjudication. Three examples are illustrative. First, courts look to legislative intent to determine whether a legislature gave an administrative official power to take the challenged action. In KENT v. DULLES (1958), for example, the secretary of state denied a passport because the applicant failed to state whether or not he was or had been a communist. The Supreme Court held that Congress had not intended to give the secretary of state the power to deny passports on those grounds. Similarly, courts have ruled on numerous occasions—*Hines* is an example—that a state statute cannot be enforced because Congress, by enacting legislation on the same subject matter, "intended" to preempt the field from state regulation.

Second, courts often look to legislative intent because the constitutionality of the challenged legislative action depends on the legislature's purpose. Thus legislation mandating that only single-family residences may be built in a certain zone is constitutional if the purposes of the law are to reduce traffic, limit demand on municipal resources, and provide a suburban atmosphere. It will be unconstitutional, however, if the legislative purpose is to exclude minorities from the municipality, as the Supreme Court suggested in ARLINGTON HEIGHTS v. METROPOLITAN HOUSING DEVELOPMENT CORPORATION (1977).

Third, legislative intent is relevant in those areas of constitutional decision making in which courts purportedly scrutinize the "fit" between legislative means and ends. In EQUAL PROTECTION law, for example, legislative classification that disadvantages one person vis-à-vis another is said to be constitutional only if the classification is rationally related to a legitimate legislative goal. While courts tend to hypothesize rather freely about what the legislature could have intended to achieve with the classification, evidence of legislative intent is clearly relevant. More important, when circumstances call for more rigorous scrutiny—as when the classification is based on sex or race—the courts are less willing to speculate about the legislature's possible purposes, and they search for concrete evidence of legislative intent.

The meaning of legislation—what the legislature sought to accomplish—is often important in constitutional law. Even though theoretical and practical problems are attendant on the concept of legislative intent, courts use the concept in ascribing meaning to legislation in the numerous doctrinal areas in which the courts themselves have made that meaning relevant.

SCOTT H. BICE

Bibliography

DICKERSON, REED 1975 Statutory Interpretation: A Peek into the Mind and Will of a Legislature. *Indiana Law Journal* 50:206–237.

MACCALLUM, GERALD C., JR. 1966 Legislative Intent. *Yale Law Journal* 75:754–787.

RADIN, MAX 1930 Statutory Interpretation. *Harvard Law Review* 43:863–885.

LEGISLATIVE INVESTIGATION

Although congressional power to conduct investigations and punish recalcitrant witnesses is nowhere mentioned in the United States Constitution, the inherent investigative power of legislatures was well established, both in the British Parliament and in the American colonial legislatures, more than a century before the Constitution was adopted. Mention of such power in the early state constitutions was generally regarded as unnecessary, but the Massachusetts and Maryland constitutions both gave explicit authorization; the latter, adopted in 1776, empowered the House of Delegates to ". . . inquire on the oath of witnesses, into all complaints, grievances, and offenses, as the grand inquest of this state," and to ". . . call for all public or official papers and records, and send for persons, whom they may judge necessary in the course of inquiries concerning affairs relating to the public interest."

The basic theory of the power was and is that a legislative house needs it in order to obtain information, so that its law-making and other functions may be discharged on an enlightened rather than a benighted basis. Under the Constitution, the power was first exercised by the House of Representatives in 1792, when it appointed a select committee to inquire into the defeat by the Indians suffered the previous year by federal forces commanded by General Arthur St. Clair. The House empowered the committee "to call for such persons, papers and records as may be necessary to assist in their inquiries." After examining the British precedents, President GEORGE WASHINGTON and his cabinet agreed that the House "was an inquest and therefore might institute inquiries" and "call for papers generally," and that although the executive ought to refuse to release documents "the disclosure of which would endanger the public," in the matter at hand "there was not a paper which might not be properly produced," and therefore the committee's requests should be granted.

For nearly a century thereafter, investigations were conducted frequently and without encountering serious challenge, in Congress and the state legislatures alike. They covered a wide range of subjects, and their history is in large part the history of American politics. Among the most interesting state investigations were those conducted in 1855 by the Massachusetts legislature and the New York City Council, under the leadership of the "Know-Nothing" party, in which Irish Roman Catholicism was the target. Inquiries by the New York City Council into alleged Irish domination of the police force were challenged in the New York Court of Common Pleas, and Judge Charles Patrick Daly's opinion in *Briggs v. McKellar* (1855) was the first to hold that, unlike in Britain, in the United States the legislative investigative power is limited by the Constitution.

Fifteen years later, a congressional investigation was for the first time successfully challenged on constitutional grounds, in KILBOURN V. THOMPSON (1881). The House of Representatives had authorized a select committee to investigate the bankruptcy of the Jay Cooke banking firm (which was a depository of federal funds), and when the witness Kilbourn refused to answer questions, the House cited him for contempt and imprisoned him. After his release on HABEAS CORPUS, Kilbourn sued the House sergeant-at-arms for damages from false imprisonment. In an opinion by Justice SAMUEL F. MILLER, the Supreme Court sustained his claim on the grounds of constitutional SEPARATION OF POWERS, declaring that the Jay Cooke bankruptcy presented no legislative grounds for inquiry and that "the investigation . . . could only be properly and successfully made by a court of justice." The Court has never since invalidated a legislative inquiry on that particular basis, and it is probable that today, under comparable circumstances, a sufficient legislative purpose would be found. But the Court's ruling, that Congress's investigative and contempt powers are subject to JUDICIAL REVIEW and must conform to constitutional limitations, has not since been seriously questioned.

Exclusively until 1857, and commonly until 1935, Congress enforced its investigative power against recalcitrant witnesses by its own contempt proceedings: a congressional citation for contempt, and its execution through arrest and confinement of the witness by the sergeant-at-arms. (See LEGISLATIVE CONTEMPT POWER.) Judicial review of the contempt was usually obtained by habeas corpus. But the system was cumbersome, and effective only when Congress was in session. To remedy these shortcomings, Congress in 1857 enacted a statute making it a federal offense to refuse to produce documents demanded, or to answer questions put, by a duly authorized congressional investigatory committee. For some years both the contempt and the statutory criminal procedures were used, but since 1935 the contempt procedure has fallen into disuse. Challenges to congressional investigative authority are currently dealt with by INDICTMENT and trial under the criminal statute, now found in section 192, Title 2, United States Code, the constitutionality of which was upheld by the Supreme Court in *In re Chapman* (1897).

The tone of Justice Miller's opinion in the *Kilbourn* case raised doubts about the scope and even the existence of the congressional contempt power, which were repeatedly voiced during the early years of the twentieth century, when Congress conducted investigations damaging to powerful business and financial institutions. In 1912 the House Committee on Banking and Currency launched what became known as the "Money Trust Investigation," in which practically all the leading financiers of the time—J. P. Morgan the elder, George F. Baker, James J. Hill, and others—were called to answer charges of undue concentration of control of railroads and heavy industries in the hands of a few New York bankers. In 1924, Senate committees probed allegations of corruption and maladministration in the Justice, Interior, and Navy departments.

The legality and propriety of these inquiries aroused vigorous public debate. The famous jurist JOHN HENRY WIGMORE wrote of a "debauch of investigations" which raised a "stench" and caused the Senate to fall "in popular esteem to the level of professional searchers of the municipal dunghills," while then Professor FELIX FRANKFURTER accused the critics of seeking to "divert attention and shackle the future," and argued that the investigative power should be left "untrammeled." The doubters and critics were encouraged when a federal district judge, relying on the *Kilbourn* case, quashed a Senate contempt citation against Attorney General Harry M. Daugherty's brother, but the investigative and contempt powers were vindicated when the Supreme

Court reversed that decision and ruled in McGRAIN v. DAUGHERTY (1927) that the investigation was proper as an aid to legislation, and that Mally Daugherty could be required to testify on pain of imprisonment. Consequently, there were no serious or successful legal challenges to the many congressional investigations born of the Great Depression and the "New Deal" period of President FRANKLIN D. ROOSEVELT's administration. (See CONSTITUTIONAL HISTORY, 1933–1945.)

Until this time the main subjects of legislative investigations had been the civil and military operations of the executive branch, industrial and financial problems, and the operation of social forces such as the labor movement. Except for state investigations in the middle years of the nineteenth century directed at Masons and Roman Catholics, ideological matters had not been much involved.

The Russian Revolution of 1917, the spread of communist doctrine, and the Nazi seizure of dictatorial power in Germany soon emerged as major subjects of congressional concern. There were short-lived congressional investigations of communist propaganda in 1919 and 1930, and of Nazi propaganda in 1934. With the establishment of the HOUSE COMMITTEE OF UN-AMERICAN ACTIVITIES in May 1938, SUBVERSIVE ACTIVITIES emerged as the most publicized subject of congressional investigation.

During World War II, in which the United States and the Soviet Union were allies, there was a lull in these inquiries, but the "Iron Curtain" and "Cold War" revived them, and by 1947 they were again front-page news. Soon, names of prosecutors and witnesses—for example, MARTIN DIES, RICHARD M. NIXON, Alger Hiss, Whittaker Chambers, JOSEPH R. McCARTHY, and Patrick McCarran—became household words. The Senate authorized two bodies to join in the hunt for subversion: the Judiciary Committee's Subcommittee on Internal Security headed by Senator McCarran, and the Government Operations Committee's Subcommittee on Investigations under Senator McCarthy, respectively established in 1946 and 1950.

The principal activity of these agencies was summoning individuals to testify about the communist connections of themselves or others, and their proceedings contributed mightily to a period of public recrimination and bitter controversy that lasted for more than a decade. It was also a period of frequent criminal litigation involving congressional investigative power, as numerous witnesses were indicted for refusing to answer such questions. Some witnesses invoked the Fifth Amendment RIGHT AGAINST SELF-INCRIMINATION, and the Supreme Court, in three cases decided in 1955, was unanimously of the opinion that the right is available to witnesses before legislative committees, though three of the Justices thought that the witnesses had not clearly invoked it. Writing for the majority, Chief Justice EARL WARREN confirmed the congressional investigative power and stated further (*Quinn v. United States*):

> But the power to investigate, broad as it may be, is also subject to recognized limitations. It cannot be used to inquire into private affairs unrelated to a valid legislative purpose. Nor does it extend to an area in which Congress is forbidden to legislate. Similarly, the power to investigate must not be confused with any of the powers of law enforcement; these powers are assigned under our Constitution to the Executive and Judiciary. Still further limitations on the power to investigate are found in the specific individual guarantees of the BILL OF RIGHTS, such as the Fifth Amendment's privilege against self-incrimination which is in issue here.

Other witnesses, however, invoked the FIRST AMENDMENT's guarantee of FREEDOM OF SPEECH as justification for their refusal to answer, and in 1956 and 1957 two such cases, SWEEZY v. NEW HAMPSHIRE and WATKINS v. UNITED STATES, the first involving a congressional and the second a state investigation, reached the Court. With only Justice TOM C. CLARK dissenting, the Court held that, as a general proposition, First Amendment rights are enjoyed by witnesses in legislative investigations.

But did the First Amendment protect these witnesses from the obligation to answer questions about individual connections with communism? The Court did not meet that issue and based its reversal of both convictions on nonconstitutional grounds. Watkins had not been told that the questions put to him were (as the federal statute requires) "pertinent to the question under inquiry," while in Sweezy's case it was not shown that the state legislature had authorized the investigative agency to ask the questions he declined to answer.

Three years later, however, by a 5–4 vote, the Court held that the First Amendment did not bar requiring a witness to answer questions regarding his own or others' communist connections. (See BARENBLATT v. UNITED STATES; UPHAUS v. WYMAN, 1959.) In his opinion for the Court in the former case, Justice JOHN MARSHALL HARLAN undertook a "balancing . . . of the private and public interests at stake," and concluded that since the Communist party was not "an ordinary political party" and sought overthrow of the government "by force and violence," Congress had "the right to identify a witness as a member of the Communist Party." (See BALANCING TESTS.)

The authority of these two cases was somewhat tarnished in 1963 after Justice ARTHUR J. GOLDBERG had replaced Justice Frankfurter, who had been in the five-member majority. A Florida court authorized a state investigatory committee to require a local branch of the NAACP to produce its membership lists so that the committee could determine whether certain individuals suspected of communist connections were members of the NAACP. Once again the Court divided 5–4, and Justice Goldberg, writing for the majority in GIBSON v. FLORIDA LEGISLATIVE COMMITTEE, ruled that, in the absence of any prior showing of connection between the NAACP and communist activities, such required disclosure was barred by the First Amendment. Three years later, in another New Hampshire investigations case, *DeGregory v. New Hampshire Attorney General,* the Court ruled, 6–3, that the state's interest was "too remote and conjectural" to justify compelling a witness in 1964 to testify about communist activities in 1957.

Since then there have been no Supreme Court and no important state or lower federal court decisions on the constitutional aspects of legislative investigative power. The *Barenblatt* case has not been overruled, and it is perhaps noteworthy that both the *Gibson* and *DeGregory* cases involved state rather than congressional investigations. The attitudes of the Justices who have joined the Court since 1966 remain untested.

It may be surmised, for the future, that if a plausible relation between a legislative inquiry and a valid legislative purpose can be shown, and there are no procedural flaws or manifestations of gross abuse, the Court will be reluctant to deny, on constitutional grounds, the power of a legislative investigating committee to require witnesses to answer questions or produce records.

A different situation might well obtain if a congressional investigating committee should seek to enforce the production of government documents involving NATIONAL SECURITY or for some other reason inappropriate for public disclosure. Presidents have on numerous occasions exercised the right first asserted by George Washington in 1792, to withhold documents "the disclosure of which would endanger the public" or otherwise contravene the public interest. (See EXECUTIVE PRIVILEGE.) Congressional committee efforts to force the production of records of judicial conferences, or other confidential court papers, might likewise encounter constitutional objections based on the separation of powers. Up to the present time, these issues have not confronted the Supreme Court, and the political wisdom of avoiding such confrontations is manifest.

TELFORD TAYLOR

Bibliography

CARR, ROBERT K. 1952 *The House Committee on Un-American Activities.* Ithaca, N.Y.: Cornell University Press.

GOODMAN, WALTER 1968 *The Committee.* New York: Farrar, Straus & Giroux.

LANDIS, JAMES M. 1926 Constitutional Limits on the Congressional Power of Investigation. *Harvard Law Review* 40:153–226.

OGDEN, AUGUST RAYMOND 1945 *The Dies Committee.* Washington, D.C.: Catholic University of America Press.

POTTS, CHARLES S. 1926 Power of Legislative Bodies to Punish for Contempt. *University of Pennsylvania Law Review* 74:691–780.

TAYLOR, TELFORD 1955 *Grand Inquest: The Story of Congressional Investigations.* New York: Simon & Schuster.

LEGISLATIVE JURISDICTION

See: Jurisdiction

LEGISLATIVE POWER

"Legislative power" is a distinctly modern conception which presupposes a modern understanding of "law." In medieval Europe the authority of laws was variously attributed to God, nature, or custom; human authorities "found" or "declared" or enforced the law but were not thought to create it. Consequently, medieval jurists did not distinguish "legislative" from "judicial" powers. Through the end of the sixteenth century, the English Parliament (like its continental counterparts) was primarily regarded as a court, an ultimate court of APPEAL for individuals as well as communities. It was at most an incidental consideration whether Parliament was "representative" because law was not a matter of will but of knowledge.

The modern conception traces the authority of law precisely to the will of the lawmakers. It is this assumption of a pure power to make or unmake the laws that allows for our artificially clear distinction between "legislative" (that is lawmaking) and "judicial" or "executive" (law-applying) powers. In acknowledging law as the creation of particular human wills, the modern view liberates government from encrusted tradition, from folklore and superstition, above all from manipulation by legalistic conjurings. At the same time, however, this view of law opens the chilling prospect of an unlimited coercive power, since the power to create the laws seems, by its very nature, superior to the constraints of law. This sort of reasoning, powerfully advanced by theorists of SOVEREIGNTY in the seventeenth century, was treated by WILLIAM BLACKSTONE in the next century as virtually self-evident: for any court to declare invalid an act of Parliament, he observed, "were to set the judicial power above that of the legislature, which would be subversive of all government."

The Framers of the American Constitution were nonetheless intent on curbing legislative power. Historians have noted that by the standards of their European contemporaries the constitutional perspective of the American Framers was somewhat archaic, most notably in the Framers' acceptance of a HIGHER LAW limitation on legislative power and in their indifference to questions about sovereignty or ultimate authority. But in the decisive respect, the concerns and accomplishments of the Framers reflected their quite modern recognition that no laws are simply given, that the scope of legislative assertion is vast and, as THE FEDERALIST conceded, "the legislative authority necessarily predominates." Thus they set out the legislative powers in the first and longest article of the Constitution, suggesting the primacy of these powers in the governmental scheme and implicitly identifying the reach of the federal government with the reach of its legislative powers. At the same time, the language of Article I emphasizes the open-endedness of legislative power precisely by its focus on the powers rather than the duties, objectives, or obligations of the legislative branch.

Perhaps the most important checks on legislative power in the Constitution are those that seem merely procedural or institutional. In the first place, the Constitution sets up a formidable institutional gauntlet for legislative proposals, requiring that they obtain majorities in each house of Congress and then secure approval from the President (or extraordinary majorities in Congress). The Constitution also seeks to assure some independent authority for the executive branch and the judiciary by removing the selection and tenure of these officers from immediate congressional control. Ultimately, almost all executive and judicial action depends on prior statutory authority and funding from Congress. And it is impossible to say with confidence when a legislative enactment (apart from an actual BILL OF ATTAINDER—imposing criminal sanctions on particular individuals) would be so specific and peremptory as to infringe the essential law-applying authority of the executive or the judiciary. But in practice the institutional reality of the SEPARATION OF POWERS usually does preserve a protective screen of independent judgment between the legislative will and the force of law as applied.

Direct limitations on legislative power in the Constitution are perhaps the most dramatic legacy of the Framers' distrust of legislative power, but they are probably not the most efficacious or important. From the outset, Congress has been emboldened to exercise powers beyond those specifically enumerated in Article I, either by construing implied powers or appealing to the requisites of national SOVEREIGNTY. The Supreme Court sought to give some force to these limitations in the early decades of this century in order to prevent Congress from preempting the legislative authority of the states. But these efforts were repudiated by the Court after the 1930s and the repudiation of judicially enforceable limits has been explicitly reconfirmed in the current era. Even the limitations imposed by the BILL OF RIGHTS on behalf of individual liberty have very rarely been construed by the Supreme Court in ways that threatened federal legislation.

As it has expanded, however, federal legislative power has also been dispersed in striking ways. In recent decades, the federal courts, invoking vague or general constitutional clauses, have assumed the power to impose elaborate requirements on states and localities in a more or less openly legislative (law-creating) manner. Meanwhile, since the 1930s, Congress has delegated more and more legislative power to federal administrative agencies. Though Congress retains the ultimate power to block what courts and agencies do, its passivity may or may not be properly construed as acquiescence. Thus the dispersal of legislative powers seems to threaten the central promise in the modern conception of law—that there is always an identifiable human authority to hold responsible for the law.

JEREMY RABKIN

Bibliography

CORWIN, EDWARD S. 1955 *The "Higher Law" Background of American Constitutional Law.* Ithaca, N.Y.: Cornell University Press.

FISHER, LOUIS 1985 *Constitutional Conflicts between Congress and the President.* Princeton, N.J.: Princeton University Press.

LEGISLATIVE VETO

The legislative veto emerged in the 1930s as an effort to reconcile two conflicting needs. Executive officials sought greater discretionary authority, while Congress wanted to retain control over delegated authority without having to adopt new legislation for that purpose. The resulting accommodation permitted administrators to submit proposals that would become law unless Congress acted to disapprove by simple resolution (a one-house veto) or concurrent resolution (a two-house veto). Evolving forms of the legislative veto came to include requirements of congressional approval as well as opportunities for disapproval; Congress even vested some of the controls in its committees.

Although the legislative veto acquired a reputation as a congressional usurpation of executive power, initially the device favored the President. In 1932 Congress authorized President HERBERT C. HOOVER to reorganize the executive branch. His plans would become law within sixty days unless either house disapproved. The President did not have to secure the support of both houses, as would have been necessary through the regular legislative process. Instead, the burden was placed on Congress to veto his initiatives. Furthermore, to prevent presidential proposals from being buried in committee, filibustered, or changed by Congress, the law limited each opportunity for legislative veto by rules for discharging committees, restricting congressional debate, and prohibiting committee or floor amendments.

The executive branch began to view the legislative veto apprehensively when Congress attached it to statutes governing such important subjects as lend lease, IMMIGRATION, public works, energy, IMPOUNDMENT, federal salaries, foreign trade, and the WAR POWERS. As part of the congressional reassertion after the VIETNAM WAR and WATERGATE, legislative vetoes proliferated in the 1970s. By the late 1970s, Congress seemed on the verge of subjecting every federal regulation to some form of legislative veto.

The lower federal courts upheld some legislative vetoes and invalidated others, but carefully restricted their opinions to the particular statutes challenged. In 1982, however, the UNITED STATES COURT OF APPEALS for the District of Columbia Circuit struck down three laws on such broad grounds as to cast a shadow of illegality over every type of legislative veto. The Supreme Court adopted this comprehensive approach in IMMIGRATION AND NATURALIZATION SERVICE V. CHADHA (1983), invalidating the Immigration and Nationality Act's authorization for either house of Congress to set aside the attorney general's decision to suspend the DEPORTATION of an alien.

Chief Justice WARREN E. BURGER, joined by five Justices, wrote the OPINION OF THE COURT. The one-house legislative veto in *Chadha* was unconstitutional because it violated both the principle of BICAMERALISM and the presentment clause of the Constitution, which requires every bill, resolution, or vote to which the concurrence of the Senate and House is necessary (except a vote of adjournment) to be presented to the President. Whenever congressional action has the "purpose and effect of altering the legal rights, duties and relations of persons" outside the legislative branch, the Court said, Congress must act through both houses in a bill presented to the President.

Justice LEWIS F. POWELL concurred in the judgment on a narrower ground. Justice BYRON R. WHITE delivered a lengthy dissent, generally supporting the constitutionality of the legislative veto. Justice WILLIAM H. REHNQUIST also dissented, but only on the question of SEVERABILITY. He said that if the Court declared the legislative veto invalid, it should also strike down the attorney general's authority to suspend deportations.

The majority's opinion raises numerous questions. First, in holding the legislative veto severable from the attorney general's authority, the Court ignored clear evidence of a quid pro quo between Congress and the President. If severability could be discerned in this legislative history, presumably it can be found in nearly every statute establishing a legislative veto. This reasoning gives the executive branch a temporary one-sided advantage from an accommodation meant to balance executive and legislative interests.

Second, the Court asserted that the legislative veto's efficiency or convenience would not save it "if it is contrary to the Constitution. Convenience and efficiency are not the primary objectives—or the hallmarks—of democratic government. . . ." Although the legislative veto might be a "convenient shortcut" and an "appealing compromise," the Court said, it is "crystal clear from the records of the Convention, contemporaneous writings and debates, that the Framers ranked other values higher than efficiency." Here the Court played loose with history, for efficiency was indeed an important consideration for the Framers. The decade prior to the CONSTITUTIONAL CONVENTION saw an anxious and persistent search for a form of government that would perform more efficiently than the ARTICLES OF CONFEDERATION.

Third, the Court characterized the presentment

clause as a means of giving the President the power of self-defense against an encroaching Congress. The President's veto would check "oppressive, improvident, or ill-considered measures." This argument is misleading in suggesting that the legislative veto, by evading the President's veto, threatened the independence of the executive branch. In fact, the legislative veto was directed only against measures submitted by the President. Congress could not amend his proposals, but must vote yes or no. A legislative veto, if exercised, simply reestablished the status quo. For example, if either house defeated a reorganization plan the structure of government would remain as before. The President did not need his veto for purposes of "self-defense."

Fourth, the Court said that the Framers had unmistakably expressed their "determination that legislation by the national Congress be a step-by-step, deliberate and deliberative process." But both houses of Congress regularly use "shortcut" methods that pose no problems under *Chadha:* suspending the rules, asking for unanimous consent, placing legislative riders on appropriations bills, and even passing bills that have never been sent to committee.

The Court's theory of government contradicts practices developed over a period of decades by the political branches. Neither administrators nor members of Congress want the static model proffered by the Court. The conditions that spawned the legislative veto over a half-century ago have not disappeared. Executive officials still want substantial latitude in administering delegated authority; legislators still want to maintain control without having to pass new legislation. Surely the executive and legislative branches will develop substitutes to serve as the functional equivalent of the legislative veto. Forms will change; the substance will not.

Instead of a one-house veto over executive reorganization, Congress is likely to require a joint resolution of approval. This device, which satisfies the tests of bicameralism and presentment, requires the President to obtain the support of both Houses within a specified number of days. If one house withholds its support, the effect is a one-house veto.

Internal House and Senate rules offer another option. Congress can require that funds be appropriated only after an authorizing committee has passed a resolution of approval. Although this procedure amounts to a committee veto, the Justice Department may acquiesce, accepting Congress's distinction between authorization and appropriation and reasoning that Congress can control its own internal processes.

Congress can also attach a rider to an appropriations bill to prevent an agency from implementing a proposed action. Because a President will rarely veto an appropriations bill (and probably will never do so because of an objectionable rider), the practical effect of this device is that of a two-house veto. Indeed, House-Senate comity will often produce the effect of a one-house veto.

Statutes can require that selected committees be notified before agency implementation of certain programs. Notification raises no constitutional issue, for it falls within the report-and-wait category already sanctioned by court rulings. But "notification" can become a code word for prior committee approval. Only in unusual circumstances would an agency defy the wishes of its oversight committees.

After *Chadha,* Congress will continue to use informal and nonstatutory methods to control the executive branch. Congress allows agencies to shift funds within an appropriation account provided they obtain committee approval for major changes. Agencies comply because they want to retain this administrative flexibility. Because these "gentlemen's agreements" are not placed in statutes, they are unaffected by *Chadha.* They are not legal in effect. They are, however, in effect legal.

Last, Congress has continued to authorize legislative vetoes in statutes adopted after *Chadha.* Although these provisions are unconstitutional under the Court's decision, agencies are likely to abide by them rather than alienate powerful support committees on Capitol Hill. When the practical needs of executive officials and legislators coincide, they nearly always prevail over formalistic notions of SEPARATION OF POWERS.

LOUIS FISHER

Bibliography

BOLTON, JOHN R. and ABRAMS, KEVIN G. 1984 The Judicial and Congressional Response to the Invalidation of the Legislative Veto. *Journal of Law and Politics* 1:299–355.

STRAUSS, PETER L. 1983 Was There a Baby in the Bathwater? A Comment on the Supreme Court's Legislative Veto Decision. *Duke Law Journal* 1983:789–819.

SYLVESTER, KATHLEEN 1984 After Chadha, A Legal Void. *National Law Journal,* April 23, 1984, pp. 1, 8, 10.

LEHMAN v. SHAKER HEIGHTS

See: Captive Audience

LEISY v. HARDIN
135 U.S. 100 (1890)

Chief Justice MELVILLE W. FULLER, speaking for a six-member majority, ruled that because Congress possesses an EXCLUSIVE POWER under the COMMERCE CLAUSE to regulate interstate transportation, no state may enact a liquor PROHIBITION statute that bars the sale in that state of liquors imported from other states and sold in their original packages. That Congress had not exercised its commerce power was equivalent to a declaration that commerce shall be free. Any DOCTRINE to the contrary, deriving from the LICENSE CASES (1847), said Fuller, was "overthrown." Congress might, however, specifically authorize a state to ban interstate liquors; the Court sustained such an act of Congress in *In re Rahrer* (1891).

LEONARD W. LEVY

LELAND, JOHN
(1754–1841)

A native of Massachusetts and a Baptist minister, John Leland preached in Virginia from 1776 to 1791, becoming a leader in the Baptists' struggle against the Anglican church establishment there and helping to bring about its dismantlement. At first he opposed the federal Constitution on the grounds that it lacked a BILL OF RIGHTS and safeguards against tax-supported clergy; but he later switched his stand —possibly converted by JAMES MADISON personally—and swung Virginia's Baptists behind ratification.

Leland held that state attempts to foster religion only corrupted religion. A defender of both civil and RELIGIOUS LIBERTY, he supported religious rights for all, repudiating the notion of a Christian commonwealth. He opposed attempts to halt Sunday mail delivery, and by denying that government had power to pass sabbath laws, proclaim public days of prayer, or pay chaplains, he assumed a more radical stance on church and state than did most contemporary evangelicals.

THOMAS CURRY

Bibliography

BUTTERFIELD, L. H. 1952 Elder John Leland, Jeffersonian Itinerant. *American Antiquarian Society Proceedings* 62:155–242.

LEMON v. KURTZMAN
403 U.S. 602 (1971) (I)
411 U.S. 192 (1973) (II)

This case involved one of the school aid statutes produced by state legislatures in the wake of BOARD OF EDUCATION V. ALLEN (1968). *Lemon* I stands for three cases joined for decision by the Court. Lemon challenged the constitutionality of a Pennsylvania statute that authorized the Superintendent of Public Instruction to reimburse nonpublic schools for teachers' salaries, textbooks, and instructional materials in secular subjects. *Erley v. DiCenso* and *Robinson v. DiCenso* (1971) challenged a Rhode Island statute that made available direct payments to teachers in nonpublic schools in amounts of up to fifteen percent of their regular salaries.

Both statutes were unconstitutional, Chief Justice WARREN BURGER concluded, and he set forth a threefold test which continues to be invoked in ESTABLISHMENT OF RELIGION cases: any program aiding a church-related institution must have an adequate secular purpose; it must have a primary effect that neither advances nor inhibits religion; and government must not be excessively entangled with religious institutions in the administration of the program. The Pennsylvania and Rhode Island schemes provided GOVERNMENT AID TO RELIGIOUS INSTITUTIONS. Burger argued that in order to see that these dollars were not used for religious instruction, the states would have to monitor compliance in ways involving excessive entanglement.

Lemon v. Kurtzman returned to the Court (*Lemon* II) two years later on the question of whether the Pennsylvania schools could retain the monies that had been paid out in the period between the implementation of law and the decision of the Supreme Court invalidating it in *Lemon* I. In a PLURALITY OPINION for himself and Justices HARRY BLACKMUN, Lewis F. Powell, and WILLIAM H. REHNQUIST, Chief Justice Burger held that they could. An unconstitutional statute, he suggested, is not absolutely void but is a practical reality upon which people are entitled to rely until authoritatively informed otherwise. Justice BYRON R. WHITE concurred. Justice WILLIAM O. DOUGLAS, joined by Justices WILLIAM J. BRENNAN and POTTER STEWART, dissented. Douglas argued that there was "clear warning to those who proposed such subsidies" that they were treading on unconstitutional ground. "No consideration of EQUITY," Douglas suggested, should allow them "to profit from their unconstitutional venture."

RICHARD E. MORGAN

LEON, UNITED STATES v.

See: Good Faith Exception

LETTERS OF MARQUE AND REPRISAL

Letters of marque and reprisal are commissions that governments of belligerent powers grant to private shipowners (called "privateers") authorizing them to seize the vessels and property of enemy subjects on the high seas. During the Revolutionary War both the states and the Continental Congress issued letters of marque; but the Constitution grants Congress the power to issue them and denies it to the states. Although not a signatory to the Declaration of Paris (1856), which condemned privateering as contrary to the law of nations, the United States has issued no letters of marque since that time.

DENNIS J. MAHONEY

LEVER FOOD AND DRUG CONTROL ACT
40 Stat. 276 (1917)

The administration proposed this legislation to Congress, arguing that "the existence of a STATE OF WAR" made it "essential to the national security and defense" for the federal government to control the supply and pricing of food and fuel. By subjecting those industries AFFECTED WITH A PUBLIC INTEREST to federal regulation, Congress effectively delegated control of significant sectors of the economy to the President. Section 4, the heart of the act, outlawed the destruction, waste, hoarding, or price-fixing of commodities. Further sections, in an exceptionally broad DELEGATION OF POWER, authorized the President to regulate the food industry and to seize and operate "any factory, packing house, oil pipe line, mine, or other plant" engaged in commodity production.

In *United States v. L. Cohen Grocery Company* (1921), a unanimous Supreme Court struck down section 4 for failing to set adequate standards for prices. The criminal provisions unconstitutionally delegated "legislative power to courts and juries" and deprived "the citizen of the right to be informed of the nature and cause of the accusation against him," violating the Fifth and Sixth Amendments. Although the Court struck down particular provisions for VAGUENESS, it did not reach the issue of the government's authority to regulate prices under the WAR POWERS, and the Lever Act would later serve as a model for other regulatory legislation.

DAVID GORDON

LEVY v. LOUISIANA
391 U.S. 68 (1968)
GLONA v. AMERICAN GUARANTEE & LIABILITY INSURANCE CO.
391 U.S. 73 (1968)

In these decisions the Supreme Court began to subject legislative classifications based on ILLEGITIMACY of parentage to heightened judicial scrutiny. Both cases arose out of Louisiana's statute allowing an action for damages on behalf of the survivors of a decedent against a person who wrongfully caused the decedent's death. *Levy* invalidated, 6–3, a provision denying an illegitimate child the right to recover damages for the death of a parent, and *Glona* invalidated, 6–3, a corresponding provision disallowing a parent's recovery of damages for the death of an illegitimate child.

The two opinions for the Court, by Justice WILLIAM O. DOUGLAS, were very brief. Douglas purported to accept the RATIONAL BASIS STANDARD OF REVIEW. The rights asserted, however, involved "the intimate, familial relationship between a child and his own mother." And illegitimacy bore no relation to the nature of the harm inflicted in either case. The accident of a child's illegitimate birth did not justify denying his rights, and if the state sought to punish the mother of an illegitimate child for her "sin," denying her wrongful death damages was an irrational means for doing so.

It is plain that in these cases the Court was employing a standard of review considerably more demanding than its "rational basis" language suggested. Justice JOHN MARSHALL HARLAN, for the dissenters, took note of this heightened scrutiny, and opposed it. Any definition of the plaintiff class in a wrongful death statute must be artificial; a biological definition would attune the law neither to degrees of love nor to degrees of economic dependence between decedents and survivors. It was not irrational for Louisiana to "simplify" its wrongful death proceedings by using formal marriage as the key to defining the plaintiff class.

Left unspoken by both Douglas and Harlan was the time-dishonored use of the law of illegitimacy in many southern states as a covert form of RACIAL DISCRIMINATION in controlling the transmission of wealth from white fathers to their racially diverse offspring.

KENNETH L. KARST

LIBEL AND THE FIRST AMENDMENT

A central historical question about the FIRST AMENDMENT is to what extent it embodied the received eighteenth-century legal traditions of English law and governmental practice as they were reshaped and renewed in the colonial, revolutionary, and formative periods in America. Or was the amendment a break from these traditions? This issue can be stated either as a question of the intent of the Framers and ratifiers or as a matter of the normative impact of an authoritative text, elaborated in our century within an institutional matrix of JUDICIAL REVIEW radically different from that of the eighteenth century on either side of the Atlantic. However the question be stated, the historical problem is in essence whether the First Amendment is to be regarded as expressing a principle of continuity with the received legal tradition or as constituting a declaration of independence from English law, thereby projecting the American law of freedom of expression on a path of autonomous development.

The general view emphasizes continuity, both as a matter of the original understanding of the Framers of the First Amendment and as a matter of the amendment's later—much later—doctrinal elaborations. Indeed, we conventionally measure continuity or discontinuity by reference to the basic conceptual dichotomy of the English legal tradition, as formulated by WILLIAM BLACKSTONE, the oracle of the COMMON LAW for the framing generation:

> where blasphemous, immoral, treasonable, schismatical, seditious, or scandalous libels are punished by the English law . . . the liberty of the press, properly understood, is by no means infringed or violated. The *liberty of the press* is indeed essential to the nature of a free state, but this consists in laying no previous restraints upon publications, and not in freedom from censure for criminal matter when published. Every freeman has an undoubted right to lay what sentiments he pleases before the public: to forbid this is to destroy the freedom of the press: but if he publishes what is improper, mischievous, or illegal, he must take the consequences of his own temerity [*Commentaries on the Laws of England,* 1765, Bk. 4, chap. II, pp. 151–52].

The issue whether the First Amendment embraced or departed from the English legal tradition with respect to subsequent punishment tends to be fixed on the treatment of SEDITIOUS LIBEL. The historical argument for the law of seditious libel has been that government ought to have power to punish its most abusive or subversive critics because criticism of government contains the seeds of a variety of evils—disobedience to government, public disorder, even violence—and that no government can subsist if people have the right to criticize it or to call its agents corrupt or incompetent. This is seen in the work of Leonard W. Levy, ZECHARIAH CHAFEE, and others who have lately examined the First Amendment's historical foundations by looking at seditious libel as the exclusive focus for probing the question of continuity and discontinuity with respect to subsequent punishments. Having narrowed the issue to seditious libel, the scholarly tradition put the question of continuity and discontinuity in all-or-nothing terms: Does the First Amendment as a matter of original understanding, or as a matter of latter doctrinal connotation, repudiate or embrace the concept of seditious libel?

When a question about the relationship of a controversial legal tradition to a broadly phrased constitutional text is put in such terms, the answers are likely to fall out along dialectical lines. So it has been with the rejection-or-reception issue concerning seditious libel. The heated debate on the question by the Federalists and Republicans in connection with the passage of the ALIEN AND SEDITION ACTS of 1798 has been echoed through our history. In modern scholarship, the dialectic begins in 1919 when Zechariah Chafee, troubled deeply by the World War I ESPIONAGE ACT prosecutions, wrote in the *Harvard Law Review* that the Framers of the First Amendment "intended to wipe out the common law of SEDITION, and to make further prosecutions for criticism of the government, without any incitement to law-breaking, forever impossible in the United States of America." Six months later, and plainly in emulation, Justice OLIVER WENDELL HOLMES added the weight of his and LOUIS D. BRANDEIS's authority to the Chafee thesis, when he declared in his great dissent in the *Abrams* case: "I wholly disagree with the argument . . . that the first Amendment left the common law as to seditious libel in force. History seems to me against the notion." But the Chafee position never won the broad adherence that most modern scholars seem to think it had. In the World War I free speech cases before the Supreme court, John Lord O'Brien, who briefed the cases for the Justice Department, stated as the official view of the government that seditious libel prosecutions were not rendered invalid by the First Amendment, either as a matter of original intent or as correctly understood in 1919. And others, including EDWARD S. CORWIN, dissented from the Chafee position. Indeed, Chafee himself seems to have changed his tune by 1949, at least on the issue of the Framers' original intent: "The truth is, I think, that the framers had no very clear idea as to what they meant by 'the freedom of speech or the press.' " The dialectic about seditious libel and the First Amendment entered a new phase with the publication of Leonard W. Levy's seminal work, *Legacy of Suppression,* in 1960. This book argued that with respect to the general conceptions of FREEDOM OF THE PRESS prevalent at the time of the framing and ratification of the First Amendment, there was no solid evidence of a consensus to move away from a purely Blackstonian conception of freedom, that is, a conception limited to protecting only against previous restraints. In particular, Levy found considerable evidence that supported the continuing validity of seditious libel prosecutions, and no clear evidence that any lawyer, pamphleteer, philosopher, or statesman repudiated the concept of seditious libel. There was, Levy recognized, a growing sense of the necessity of the defense of truth, although far from a clear consensus even on that. And there was also a growing insistence on the independent power of the jury in a seditious libel prosecution to determine the issue of truth and the question of the seditious quality of any publication, as well as the other factual issues in the case.

Levy's account of the relationship of the First Amendment as a formal constitutional limitation on the power of Congress and his overall conception of intellectual and legal history respecting freedom of expression has from the beginning been confused by the problem of FEDERALISM. At the same time that he has insisted that the conception of freedom of the press guarded against abridgment by the First Amendment does not invalidate seditious libel, he has described the amendment as denying any power whatever by Congress to legislate with respect to the press, except to protect COPYRIGHT. Thus, he concluded that Congress had no power to pass the Sedition Act of 1798, but on federalism grounds, not because the Sedition Act violated any understandings about press freedom embodied in the First Amendment. The states and the federal courts remained empowered to try seditious libel prosecutions.

But Levy's interpretation of the "Congress shall make no law" language in the First Amendment has taken a distant backseat, in his own writing and in that of others, to his overriding emphasis that "the freedom of speech or of the press" was not understood to repudiate the concept of seditious libel. In other words, the First Amendment was understood to embody a Blackstonian conception of freedom of expression as a matter of original intent.

In NEW YORK TIMES CO. V. SULLIVAN (1964) the Supreme Court gave an authoritative modern answer to the question whether prosecution of seditious libel would survive the First Amendment. An advertisement in March 1960, placed by supporters of MARTIN LUTHER KING, JR., in the *New York Times;* recited the repressive activities of Alabama police with several minor inaccuracies and exaggerations. An Alabama jury awarded a local official $500,000 damages against the *New York Times.* The Supreme Court reacted with sweeping changes in the constitutional status of defamation law. Libel would no longer be viewed as a category of expression beneath First Amendment protection. Instead, the Court found that the political repudiation of the Sedition Act of 1798 had revealed the "central meaning" of the First Amendment: a right to criticize government and public officials. As the Court put it, "[A] rule compelling the critic of official conduct to guarantee the truth of all his factual assertions . . . leads to . . . 'self-censorship.' " The Alabama act, "because of the restraint it imposed upon criticism of government and public officials, was inconsistent with the First Amendment.

In place of actual falsity as a basis for liability, the Court imposed a new standard to govern defamation actions brought by public officials. Now, a public official could recover damages for a defamatory falsehood relating to his official conduct only upon a showing "that the statement was made with 'actual malice'—that is, with knowledge that it was false or with reckless disregard of whether it was false or not."

Sullivan effected important changes in constitutional law and practice. Defamation law previously had been left to the states, subject to gradual common law evolution in state courts not often exposed to First Amendment issues. *Sullivan* federalized this diversity of local rules into a single national body of doctrine overseen by a Court peculiarly sensitive to First Amendment problems. Furthermore, the intangibility of defamation law had left wide discretion in trial court juries; *Sullivan* imposed independent appellate court review of the facts in defamation actions as a First Amendment guarantee. And, in place of the complexity of overlapping liabilities, offsetting privileges, and jurisdictional diversity, *Sullivan* instituted a simple national rule that put a stringent burden of proof on plaintiffs.

Decisions following *Sullivan* extended the "actual malice" limitation on the law of defamation beyond the case of criticism of high public officials. The rule was expanded to apply to PUBLIC FIGURES in *Curtis Publishing Co. v. Butts* and *Associated Press v. Walker* (1967). A plurality of the Court even stretched the rule to cover private figures, if the matter was "a subject of public or general interest," in *Rosenbloom v. Metromedia, Inc.* (1971). But the Court retreated from *Rosenbloom* three years later in GERTZ V. ROBERT WELCH, INC. (1974). *Gertz* held that a private person may recover without meeting the actual malice standard. Because private figures have only limited access to the media to correct misstatements of others, and because they have not assumed the risk of injury due to defamatory falsehoods against them, the Court found the interests of private figures to weigh more heavily than those of public figures. The states were left free to establish an appropriate standard of liability, provided they do not impose liability without fault. Moreover, the states were forbidden from awarding presumed or punitive DAMAGES absent a showing of actual malice. More recently, in DUN & BRADSTREET, INC. V. GREENMOSS BUILDERS, INC. (1985), the Court retreated still further, permitting recovery of presumed and punitive damages by a private plaintiff without a showing of actual malice, because the defamatory statements did not involve a matter of public concern.

The defamation decisions beginning with *New York Times Co. v. Sullivan* have had the twofold effect of highlighting the core purpose of the First Amendment and constitutionalizing the law of defamation. By invalidating the law of seditious libel, the Court recognized that criticism of government is the type of speech most deserving of First Amendment protection. By establishing minimum standards of liability and limitations on damages for public figures and some private plaintiffs, the Court federalized the law of defamation.

BENNO C. SCHMIDT, JR.

Bibliography

KALVEN, HARRY JR. 1964 The New York Times Case: A Note on "The Central Meaning of the First Amendment." *Supreme Court Review* 1964:191.

LEVY, LEONARD W. 1984 *Emergence of a Free Press.* New York: Oxford University Press.

—— 1960 *Legacy of Suppression: Freedom of Speech and Press in Early American History.* Cambridge, Mass.: Harvard University Press.

LIBERTY OF CONTRACT

See: Freedom of Contract

LICENSE CASES
5 Howard 504 (1847)

In three related cases decided the same day, the Court sustained the constitutionality of temperance statutes of states that had restricted the sale of liquor and required all dealers to be licensed. Although the Justices unanimously concurred in the disposition of the cases, six men wrote nine opinions, and there was no opinion for the Court because a majority could not agree on the reasoning. At one extreme Justice JOHN MCLEAN took the position that the DORMANT POWERS of Congress under the COMMERCE CLAUSE utterly excluded the exercise of CONCURRENT POWERS by the states; but McLean found that the statutes were not regulations of commerce but reasonable exercises of the POLICE POWER. At the other extreme Justice PETER DANIEL supported an exaggerated view of concurrent state commerce powers.

Chief Justice ROGER B. TANEY's view was the least doctrinaire. He observed that two of the three *License Cases* dealt with the retail sale of liquor that was no longer in the original package and therefore raised no INTERSTATE COMMERCE issue. (See ORIGINAL PACKAGE DOCTRINE.) The third case, however, involved liquor imported in the original package from another state and sold in that unbroken package. Thus the business affected by the state's license law was in interstate commerce. Taney therefore confronted the question "whether the grant of power to Congress is of itself a prohibition to the States, and renders all State laws on the subject null and void." His answer to the question, unlike Chief Justice JOHN MARSHALL's, was that unless a state act came into conflict with a law of Congress, the state could constitutionally exercise a concurrent commerce power. On the other hand, he muddled his position by arguing that such a power was no more than the police power of the state, which he defined, promiscuously, as "nothing more or less than the powers of government inherent in every sovereignty to the extent of its dominions." His refusal to distinguish the police power from the commerce power and other powers left his opinion doctrinally murky, and like the opinions by the other Justices it failed to provide a usable test. At least two state judges, JAMES KENT and LEMUEL SHAW, avoided the Supreme Court's quest for a system of definitional categories by suggesting that if Congress did not brush away state legislation, it should be sustained in the absence of an actual or operational conflict with national legislation.

LEONARD W. LEVY

LIEBER, FRANCIS

See: Commentators on the Constitution

LILBURNE, JOHN
(1614–1657)

John Lilburne, whose entire career was a precedent for freedom, was the catalytic agent in the history of the RIGHT AGAINST SELF-INCRIMINATION. Primarily because of him, that right became a respected, established rule of the COMMON LAW. An agitator with an incurably inflamed sense of injustice, Lilburne was called Freeborn John, because of his incessant demands on behalf of the rights of every freeborn Englishman. No one in England could silence or outtalk him, no one was a greater pamphleteer, and no one was more principled in his devotion to political liberty, the rights of the criminally accused, and the freedoms of conscience and press. Making CIVIL DISOBEDIENCE a way of life, Lilburne successively defied king, parliament, and protectorate.

He first focused the attention of England on the injustice of forcing anyone to answer incriminating questions during his 1637 trial. After his release from prison in 1641, he joined the parliamentary cause, rose to a high military position, and became close to Oliver Cromwell; but he resigned his commission to be free to oppose the government. Four times he stood trial for his life, and he spent much of his last twenty years in jail, from which he smuggled out a torrent of tracts. He advocated a special CONSTITUTIONAL CONVENTION to write a constitution for England embodying the reforms proposed by the Levellers, the faction of constitutional democrats that he led.

When Parliament itself arrested and interrogated him, Lilburne became the first hostile witness in a LEGISLATIVE INVESTIGATION to claim a right not to answer questions against or concerning himself. He successfully made the same claim, under his view of MAGNA CARTA and the PETITION OF RIGHT, before a common law court in 1649, when tried for TREASON. He appealed to the jury above the heads of the judges and convinced the jury to decide on the injustice of the laws used to persecute political prisoners. Twice he persuaded juries to acquit him. In his trials and writings he educated England on the relation of liberty to fair play and DUE PROCESS OF LAW. At his last trial he won the unprecedented right to secure a copy of the INDICTMENT against him and to be represented by counsel in a capital case. Cromwell finally imprisoned him without trial, and Lilburne died in jail.

LEONARD W. LEVY

Bibliography

LEVY, LEONARD W. 1968 *Origins of the Fifth Amendment.* Pages 271–312. New York: Oxford University Press.

LIMITED GOVERNMENT

The idea of limited government is closely associated with political thinkers, mostly of medieval and modern periods, who placed special emphasis on preventing abuses of government. Some spoke of limitations connected with divine law and natural law; others spoke of a SOCIAL COMPACT establishing government for the sake of protecting property and other individual rights. Limited government was also a corollary of the more affirmative approach of ancient philosophers, who taught that ruling bodies could best maintain themselves by respecting social customs, moderating their policies, honoring the contributions of each social class in distributing governmental offices, and fostering self-restraint, patriotism, and other attitudes conducive to the general welfare.

In American constitutional thought limited government is often synonymous with CONSTITUTIONALISM itself. It has three more specific connotations resulting from the three principal ways in which the government can be said to be constitutionally limited: in a jurisdictional sense, limited in the objectives it may pursue; in a procedural sense, limited in the ways it may decide policy questions and adjudicate disputes involving individuals; and limited by the requirement that its policies be compatible with individual rights.

The first sense of limited government refers to the ENUMERATION OF POWERS through which the Constitution outlines the jurisdictional concerns of the national government. This method of limitation has failed. The enumeration of powers is now a dead letter as a result of the nationalizing tendencies of American economic and social life, which the Supreme Court has accommodated through its interpretations of the TENTH AMENDMENT, the COMMERCE CLAUSE, the NECESSARY AND PROPER CLAUSE, the GENERAL WELFARE CLAUSE, and the Civil War Amendments.

As for the second, or procedural, mode of limitation (structural limitations on policy formation and due process limitations on adjudication), some contemporary constitutionalists regard it as the only philosophically acceptable variety. These theorists tend to follow a value-neutral conception of constitutional democracy which is both at odds with citizen presuppositions about the goals of politics and supported by no compelling historical or philosophic argument. Respect for procedural ideas like SEPARATION OF POWERS, representative government, and DUE PROCESS is indeed central to American constitutionalism, but not because that tradition is indifferent to different ways of life and the ends of government. A traditional respect for procedure is rather an aspect of the Enlightenment commitment to liberal toleration or reasoning in human affairs, as opposed especially to precipitous decision and government in the name of divine authority. The value-neutral variety of proceduralism is inconsistent with this tradition because it denies the possibility of rationally defending the practices, conditions, and attitudes conducive to reasoning itself.

Americans typically associate limited government first and foremost with constitutional rights and JUDICIAL REVIEW. "By a limited constitution," wrote ALEXANDER HAMILTON in THE FEDERALIST #78, "I understand one which contains certain specified exceptions to the legislative authority; such, for instance, as that it shall pass no BILLS OF ATTAINDER, no EX POST FACTO laws, and the like. Limitations of this kind can be preserved in practice no other way than through the medium of courts of justice, whose duty it must be to declare all acts contrary to the manifest tenor of the Constitution void."

Yet courts are also agencies of government, and groups throughout American history have opposed judicial protection of some rights as the least majoritarian and therefore least legitimate subordination of other rights. Some theorists believe society has a way of arriving at pragmatic adjustments of conflicting views (lax enforcement of laws against CONTRACEPTION and abortion, for example) that cannot be reconciled at the level of moral principle. They regard judicial intervention in behalf of those persons who brook no compromise as divisive to the point of undermining everyone's right to live in a peaceful society. Many citizens seem profoundly bitter over their loss of freedom to live and raise their children in communities that exclude sexually suggestive entertainment, political deviants, and others, including members of other races and religions. Their criticism of the judiciary's protection of rights suggests a community oriented understanding of rights, for they themselves want the right to be members of communities that use official power to exclude some kinds of people as equals or to exclude them altogether. This community-oriented conception is highly visible in the demands of some religious groups for organized prayer in public schools despite offense to others.

But a community orientation of sorts is also implicit in demands for public recognition of the RIGHTS OF PRIVACY like those involving property, sexual freedom, and conscience. In effect, persons who demand these rights seek the right to live in communities that honor the rights demanded. Rights to property, for example, are hardly secure if the general public is unwilling to exercise the restraint and undertake the sacrifices that honoring such rights entails. It is therefore not surprising that defenders of property should treat "free enterprise" as an article of the community's gospel and special identity. For if any rights are genuine exemptions from LEGISLATIVE POWER, their enjoyment must not be left to prudential calculation. And if the government has no authority to invade them, those rights must at once be grounded in higher authority and be essential to the nation's identity in a way that it would make no sense to violate them for the sake of saving the nation. The religious right wing of American politics has a point in contending that "secular humanism" is itself something of a religious imposition on fundamentalists, who are thereby forced to live among what they regard as evil practices. Maxims of liberal toleration are no answer to these people because liberals themselves cannot tolerate being governed by thoroughly dedicated fundamentalists—those who would live every aspect of their lives as they think they should, even if that should mean employing coercive government against those who would stop them. Religiously committed folk can be excused for believing that liberalism tolerates illiberalism only by degrading it to a form of play-acting to be confined to churches, the home, or wherever one goes for respite from the serious world of education, work, and government. Defending liberalism thus requires an argument (eventually a persuasive one) that liberalism is a better way of life—that, wherever feasible, it is better for human beings to have a liberal outlook and live in secular communities that tolerate illiberal speech only, not action.

Deepening ideological divisions in American life indicate that constitutional rights can place real limits on government only where public morality favors honoring rights. Hamilton said as much in *The Federalist* #84 where he criticized naïve reliance on BILLS OF RIGHTS to protect the rights themselves. "[W]hatever fine declarations may be inserted in any constitution," he said, the security of rights "must altogether depend on public opinion, and on the general spirit of the people and of the government." It follows that governments that would honor rights effectively should work for the social and economic conditions and attitudes that are favorable to honoring rights. If rights are to remain effective limits on government, the ends of government will have to include the virtue of its citizens. Limited government in a modern sense will have to converge toward limited government in an ancient sense.

SOTIRIOS A. BARBER

(SEE ALSO: *Checks and Balances; Unwritten Constitution.*)

Bibliography

BARBER, SOTIRIOS A. 1984 *On What the Constitution Means.* Baltimore: Johns Hopkins University Press.

BERNS, WALTER 1982 Judicial Review and the Rights and Laws of Nature. *Supreme Court Review* 1982:49–83.

CORWIN, EDWARD S. 1928 The "Higher Law" Background of American Constitutional Law. *Harvard Law Review* 42:149–365.

DWORKIN, RONALD 1981 The Forum of Principle. *New York University Law Review* 56:469–518.

PURCELL, EDWARD A., JR. 1973 *The Crisis of Democratic Theory.* Lexington: University Press of Kentucky.

LINCOLN, ABRAHAM (1809–1865)

Abraham Lincoln of Illinois served as President of the United States during the nation's greatest crisis, the Civil War. He had previously represented Illinois in the House of Representatives for a single term (1847–1849), during which he introduced the SPOT RESOLUTIONS, implicitly critical of President JAMES K. POLK's administration of the Mexican War, and supported the WILMOT PROVISO, which would have banned slavery from the territory acquired in that war. Lincoln rose to national prominence opposing the policies of Senator STEPHEN A. DOUGLAS, especially Douglas's KANSAS-NEBRASKA ACT, which extended SLAVERY IN THE TERRITORIES on a local-option basis. In 1856 he joined the fledgling Republican party. Lincoln opposed Douglas's reelection to the Senate in 1858, and the two candidates toured the state together, publicly debating the issues of slavery, POPULAR SOVEREIGNTY, and CONSTITUTIONALISM. During the LINCOLN-DOUGLAS DEBATES, Lincoln severely criticized Chief Justice ROGER B. TANEY's decision in DRED SCOTT V. SANDFORD (1857) as a betrayal of the principles embodied in the DECLARATION OF INDEPENDENCE.

Lincoln's election to the presidency in 1860 triggered the long-impending SECESSION of several slaveholding southern states. Lincoln's presidency was devoted to saving the Union, which meant, in his mind, the rededication of the nation to the principles of the Declaration of Independence, and especially to the proposition that all men are created equal. This work of saving the Union, tragically cut short by an assassin's bullet, was Lincoln's great contribution to American constitutionalism.

In the Lincoln Memorial, directly behind the statue of the Great Emancipator, these words are inscribed:

In this temple
as in the hearts of the people
for whom he saved the Union
the memory of Abraham Lincoln
is enshrined forever.

Lincoln did indeed save the Union. But the Union Lincoln saved was older than the Constitution; the Constitution was intended to form a "more perfect Union." When Lincoln began the Gettysburg Address with the magisterial "Fourscore and seven years ago . . ." he intended his listeners to understand that the birth date of the nation was 1776, not 1787, and that the principles of "government of the people, by the people, for the people" were those of the Declaration of Independence. The Constitution was intended to implement those principles more perfectly than had been done by the ARTICLES OF CONFEDERATION. Lincoln at Gettysburg also intended his listeners—and the world—to know that there would be "a new birth of freedom" that would be accomplished by the EMANCIPATION PROCLAMATION, followed, as he intended that it would be, by the THIRTEENTH AMENDMENT. (We may be confident that, had he lived, Lincoln would also have given his support to the FOURTEENTH and FIFTEENTH AMENDMENTS, as part of that same "new birth.")

To understand the Constitution as Abraham Lincoln did must mean, primarily and essentially, to understand the Constitution as an expression of the principles of the Declaration. To do this is to separate the interpretation of the Constitution from all forms of legal positivism, historicism, and moral relativism, that is to say, from all those forms of interpretation that are dominant today in the law schools, universities, and courts of the nation. For, contrary to Lincoln's expectations, his words at Gettysburg have been greatly noted and long remembered: it is their meaning that has been forgotten.

Lincoln did indeed save the Union. At the time of his inauguration, March 4, 1861, seven states had already seceded and joined together to form an independent government called the Confederate States of America. JAMES BUCHANAN, the outgoing President, had been confronted with the SOUTH CAROLINA ORDINANCE OF SECESSION on December 20, 1860, six weeks after Lincoln's election, and more than ten weeks before his inauguration. Buchanan declared secession to be unconstitutional, but coupled his denunciation of secession with a much harsher denunciation of abolitionism. He denied, moreover, that he as President could take any lawful action against secession. Whatever action the federal government ought to take, he lamely concluded, must originate in laws enacted by Congress. But Buchanan had nothing to suggest to Congress, and Congress, at this juncture—the representatives of eight slave states remaining on March 4, 1861—was as divided as the nation itself. No congressional majority could have been formed then for decisive action against the rebellion. Lincoln waited until Congress had gone home, and cannily maneuvered the South Carolinians into firing those shots against Fort Sumter that electrified the North and consolidated public opinion behind his leadership. He then issued his call for 75,000 troops, and set on foot those measures that eventually resulted in the forcible subjugation of the rebellion.

Lincoln insisted that the Constitution ought not to be construed in such a way as to deny to the government any power necessary for carrying out the Constitution's commands. The Constitution required the President to take an oath "to preserve, protect, and defend the Constitution," and made it the duty of the President to "take care that the laws be faithfully executed." Lincoln held it to be absurd to suppose that it was unlawful for him to do those things that were indispensably necessary to preserve the Constitution by enforcing the execution of the laws. Even an action that might otherwise be unlawful, he said, might become lawful, by becoming thus indispensable. Lincoln never conceded that any of his wartime actions were unconstitutional. But supposing that one of them had been so, he asked, ". . . are all the laws but one to go unexecuted, and the Government itself go to pieces, lest that one be violated?"

Lincoln saved the Union. He prevented the United States from being divided into two or more separate confederacies. It was entirely likely that the North American continent would have been "Balkanized" had the initial secession succeeded. Like the Balkan states, the petty American powers would have formed alliances with greater powers, and North America would have become a cockpit of world conflict. All the evils that the more perfect Union was designed to prevent, those particularly described in the first ten numbers of THE FEDERALIST—large standing armies, heavy taxation, the restriction of individual liberties characteristic of an armed camp—would have come to pass. Civil and religious liberty, the supreme ends of republican government, would, with the failure of the American experiment, "perish from the earth." The "central idea of secession," Lincoln held, "is the essence of anarchy." A constitutional majority, checked and limited, and able to change easily with deliberate changes in public opinion and sentiment, "is the only true sovereign of a free people." To reject majority rule is to turn necessarily either to anarchy or to despotism.

The Lincoln Memorial says that Lincoln saved the Union for "the people." At the outset of the war Lincoln said, "This is essentially a people's contest." Today, when the foulest despotisms call themselves "people's republics," it requires a conscious effort to restore to our minds the intrinsic connection in Lincoln's mind between the cause of the people and fidelity to individual liberty under the rule of law in a constitutional regime. "Our adversaries," Lincoln said, at the outset of the war, "have adopted some declarations of independence, in which, unlike the good old one, penned by THOMAS JEFFERSON, they omit the words 'all men are created equal.' Why? They have adopted a temporary national constitution, in the preamble of which they omit, 'We the People,' and substitute 'We, the deputies of the sovereign and independent States.' Why? Why this deliberate pressing out of view the rights of men and the authority of the people?" Here is the core constitutional question of the Civil War. Lincoln was elected on a platform that called for the recognition of STATES' RIGHTS, "and especially the right of each State to order and control its own domestic institutions according to its own judgment exclusively." Such rights, the Republican platform asserted, and Lincoln repeated in his inaugural, were "essential to that balance of power on which the perfection and endurance of our political fabric depend." For Lincoln, however, the rights of the states were themselves the political expression of the rights of the people, which in turn were the political expression of the rights of men. The proposition that embodied the rights of men was that to which—as he said at Gettysburg—the nation was dedicated at its conception. The Civil War was a result of the fact that the idea of states' rights, and of popular sovereignty, had become divorced, in the public mind of the Confederacy, from the original doctrine of equality in the Declaration of Independence.

The question posed by the Civil War, Lincoln said, was addressed to "the whole family of man." That Lincoln conceived of mankind as in some sense a "family" was of course but another expression of his belief in human equality. Lincoln's question was essentially the same as that addressed by ALEXANDER HAMILTON in *The Federalist* #1: "whether societies of men are really capable or not of establishing good government from reflection and choice, or whether they are forever destined to depend for their political constitutions upon accident and force." The election of Abraham Lincoln was a deliberate decision of the American people, in accordance with the canons of reflection and choice embodied in the Constitution. It remained to be seen therefore whether, in Lincoln's words, "discontented individuals, too few in numbers to control administration according to organic law [can arbitrarily] break up their government, and thus practically put an end to free government upon the earth." But because the leaders of the rebellion "knew their people possessed as much of moral sense, as much devotion to law and order . . . as any other civilized and patriotic people," it was necessary for them to invent "an ingenious sophism which, if conceded, was followed by perfectly logical steps . . . to the complete destruction of the Union. The sophism itself is, that any State of the Union may, consistently with the national Constitution . . . withdraw from the Union without the consent of the Union or of any other State."

The secessionists claimed that membership in the Union resulted from the acts by which the states had ratified the Constitution and that they might therefore withdraw by the same procedure. The Constitution itself, according to this theory, had no higher authority than the will of the people of the several states, acting in their constituent capacity.

In contradiction of this position, Lincoln presented a historical argument, that the Union was older than the states, that the rights of the states were only rights within the Union, and never rights outside of it or independent of it. Although the Declaration of Independence speaks, in its next to last sentence, of all those "Acts and Things which Independent States may of right do," none of them were ever done by any of the United States independently of each other. This argument, however, is not as conclusive as that other argument, independent of history, which follows from that "abstract truth applicable to all men and all times," to which, at Gettysburg, Lincoln said the nation had been dedicated. This argument Lincoln had been developing throughout his mature life, and is the ground of his constitutionalism, as indeed it is of all his moral and political thought. According to Lincoln, the Civil War was a "people's contest" because the rights of the states, and of the United States, were the rights of the people, either severally or generally. But what are the rights of the people? They are the rights with which the Creator has equally endowed all men—all human beings. These are the unalienable rights, among which are the rights to life, to liberty, and to the pursuit of happiness. Since all men have these rights equally, no man can rule another rightfully except with that other man's consent. Nothing better illuminates the division within the American mind that brought about the Civil War than this passage from a speech in reply to Douglas in 1854: "Judge Douglas," said Lincoln, "frequently, with bitter irony and sarcasm, paraphrases our argument by saying: 'The white people of Nebraska are good enough to govern themselves, *but they are not good enough to govern a few miserable negroes!!*' Well, I doubt not that the people of Nebraska are, and will continue to be as good as the average of people elsewhere. I do not say the contrary. What I do say is, that no man is good enough to govern another man, *without that other's consent.* I say this is the leading principle—the sheet anchor of American republicanism." Slavery, Lincoln observed, is a violation of this principle, not only because "the Master . . . governs the slave without his consent; but he governs him by a set of rules altogether different from those which he prescribes for himself." Republicanism, for Lincoln, meant that those who live under the law share equally in the making of the law they live under, and that those who make the law live equally under the law that they make. Here in essence is the necessary relationship between equality, consent, majority rule, and the rule of law in Lincoln's thought. Here in essence is what unites the principles of the Declaration with the forms of the Constitution. Here is what enables us to distinguish the principles of the Constitution from the compromises of the Constitution (in particular, the compromises with slavery). Here is the essence of Lincoln's understanding of why the argument against slavery and the argument for free government are distinguishable but inseparable aspects of one and the same argument.

The people are collectively sovereign because the people individually, by their consent, have transferred the exercise of certain of their unalienable rights—but not the rights themselves—to civil society. They have done so, the better "to secure these rights." A just government will act by the majority, under a constitution devised to assure with a reasonable likelihood that the action of the majority will fulfill its purpose, which is the equal protection of the indefeasible and equal rights of all. The majority is the surrogate of the community, which is to say, of each individual. Majority rule is not merely obliged to respect minority rights; in the final analysis it has no higher purpose than to secure the rights of that indefeasible minority, the individual. The sovereignty of the people—or of the states—cannot be exerted morally or lawfully for any purpose inconsistent with the security of those original and unalienable rights. Although Lincoln denied any constitutional right to secede, he did not deny a revolutionary right, which might be exercised justly if "by the mere force of numbers, a majority should deprive a minority of any clearly written constitutional right."

In his inaugural address Lincoln repeated his oft-repeated declaration that he had no purpose, "directly or indirectly, to interfere with slavery where it exists." He had, he said, "no lawful right to do so" and he had "no inclination to do so." This, he held, was implied constitutional law, but he was willing to make it express, by an amendment to the Constitution. Lincoln would not, however, agree to any measures that might have as their consequence the extension of slavery to new lands where it did not already exist. As he wrote to his old friend ALEXANDER H. STEPHENS in 1861, "You think slavery is *right*, and ought to be extended; while we think it is *wrong* and ought to be restricted. That I suppose is the rub. It certainly is the only substantial difference between us." Many complex and elaborate explanations have been made of the causes of the Civil War. Lincoln's is at once the shortest and the most profound.

The South claimed the right to extend slavery on the ground that it was a violation of the fundamental equality of the states to allow the citizens of one state or section to emigrate into a federal TERRITORY with their property, while prohibiting the citizens of any other state or section from emigrating into that same federal territory with their property. Lincoln dealt with this argument in 1854—in his first great antislavery speech—as follows: "Equal justice to the South, it is said, requires us to consent to the extending of slavery to new countries. That is to say, inasmuch as you do not object to my taking my hog to Nebraska, therefore I must not object to you taking your slave. Now, I admit this is perfectly logical, if there is no difference between hogs and negroes."

Southerners had come to deny the essential difference between hogs and Negroes, in part because of the enormous economic stake that they had come to have in slave labor, because of the enormous burgeoning of the cotton economy. This was one cause of the change in their opinion of slavery, from a necessary evil to a positive good. Another may be seen in the following from one of Lincoln's 1859 speeches. Douglas, Lincoln said, had "declared that while in all contests between the negro and the white man, he was for the white man . . . that in all questions between the negro and the crocodile he was for the negro." Lincoln interpreted Douglas's statements as "a sort of proposition in proportion, which may be stated thus: As the negro is to the white man, so is the crocodile to the negro; and as the negro may rightfully treat the crocodile as a beast or reptile, so the white man may rightfully treat the negro as a beast or reptile." Douglas's references to "contests" between negroes and crocodiles, and between negroes and whites, reflected popular ideas of "the survival of the fittest" in the evolutionary process. Lincoln, in commenting on these remarks of Douglas, also went out of his way to deny the necessity of any such "contests." Alexander Stephens, who was inaugurated vice-president of the Confederacy in February 1861, conceded that the United States had been founded upon the proposition "that all men are created equal," and that that proposition had indeed (contrary to what Chief Justice Roger B. Taney had said in *Dred Scott v. Sandford*) included black men as well as white. But, Stephens went on, the Confederacy was "founded [and] its corner stone rests upon . . . the great truth that the negro is not the equal to the white man. That slavery—the subordination to the superior race, is his natural and normal condition." "This our new Government," Stephens added, "is the first in the history of the world, based upon this great physical and moral truth." The doctrine of racial superiority became a vital element in the conviction that slavery was a positive good. Without the conviction and the doctrine there could not have been a belief in the South of a constitutional right to extend slavery. That science, in one or another version of evolution, had established the inequality of the races, became the ground for the rejection of the doctrine that all men are created equal.

In fact, the doctrine of racial inequality involves

the denial that there is any natural right, or that there are any "laws of nature and of nature's God." And this is to deny that constitutionalism and the RULE OF LAW rest upon anything besides blind preference. Justice would then be nothing but the interest of the stronger. Abraham Lincoln's speeches, before and during the Civil War, are the supreme repository for that wisdom that teaches us that we as moral beings ought to live under the rule of law. According to this wisdom, it is also in our interest to do so, because upon our recognition of the humanity of other men depends the recognition of our own humanity. And upon the recognition of our own humanity—by ourselves and by others—depends the possibility of our own happiness as human beings. Surely Lincoln was right in saying that the source of all moral principle—no less than of all political and constitutional right—was the proposition "that all men are created equal."

It is doubtful that the history of the world records another life displaying an integrity of speech and deed equal to that of Abraham Lincoln. With an almost perfect understanding of the theoretical ground of free, constitutional government was united an unflinching courage, and a practical wisdom, in doing what had to be done, lest popular government "perish from the earth." Whether, in the third century of the Constitution, Lincoln's legacy will survive in deed depends upon whether we can recover anything of his character and intelligence. But whether or not this republic lasts, as long as the world lasts Lincoln's speeches and deeds will remain as an emblem and a beacon of humanity to all men everywhere who may be struggling out of the dark valley of despotism and aspiring to the broad, sunlit uplands of freedom.

HARRY V. JAFFA

Bibliography

BELZ, HERMAN 1969 *Reconstructing the Union.* Ithaca, N.Y.: Cornell University Press.

FEHRENBACHER, DON E. 1978 *The Dred Scott Case: Its Significance in American Law and Politics.* New York: Oxford University Press.

——— 1979 Lincoln and the Constitution. Pages 121–166 in Cullom Davis, ed., *The Public and Private Lincoln: Contemporary Perspectives.* Carbondale: Southern Illinois University Press.

JAFFA, HARRY V. (1952)1983 *Crisis of the House Divided: An Interpretation of the Lincoln–Douglas Debates.* Chicago: University of Chicago Press.

NEVINS, ALAN 1950 *The Emergence of Lincoln.* 2 Vols. New York: Scribner's.

RANDALL, JAMES G. 1951 *Constitutional Problems under Lincoln,* rev. ed. Urbana: University of Illinois Press.

LINCOLN, LEVI
(1749–1820)

Graduated from Harvard University and trained in law, Levi Lincoln fought as a Minuteman in the American Revolution and subsequently held several offices in the revolutionary government of Massachusetts. In 1780 he was a delegate to the convention that drafted the state constitution. After the Revolution he became a leader of the Massachusetts bar as well as a member of the legislature.

In 1781, Lincoln successfully argued in *Quock Walker's Case* (CALDWELL V. JENNISON) that the passage in the MASSACHUSETTS CONSTITUTION declaring that "all men are born free and equal" prohibited any legal recognition of slavery in the state. The decision effectively abolished slavery in Massachusetts.

Having early become a leader of the Republican party, Lincoln served from 1801 to 1805 as attorney general of the United States in the first administration of THOMAS JEFFERSON. In 1811 he declined, on the ground of failing eyesight, President JAMES MADISON'S offer of appointment as an associate Justice of the Supreme Court.

DENNIS J. MAHONEY

LINCOLN-DOUGLAS DEBATES
(1858)

STEPHEN A. DOUGLAS, running for reelection to the United States Senate, agreed to debate his Republican challenger, ABRAHAM LINCOLN, at seven joint appearances in rural Illinois during the summer of 1858. The resulting discourse, promptly reprinted in full in newspapers, produced a classic survey of alternatives for the future of slavery and black people in the American constitutional system.

Douglas defended the concept of territorial SOVEREIGNTY: let the people of the territories, rather than Congress, decide the future of slavery there. He stated that he "cared not whether slavery be voted up or voted down" and accused Lincoln of advocating racial equality. Lincoln emphasized the incompatibility of Douglas's position with the decision in DRED SCOTT V. SANDFORD (1857), in which Chief Justice ROGER B. TANEY had stated that a territorial legislature lacked power to exclude slavery. Douglas responded with the "FREEPORT DOCTRINE": a territorial legislature could exclude slavery simply by not enacting legislation supporting it. Lincoln hinted at a conspiracy involving Taney, Douglas, and the Pierce and BUCHANAN administrations to force slavery into the free states, an allegation Douglas indignantly denied by reasserting the power of each state to fully control its domestic policy.

WILLIAM M. WIECEK

Bibliography

JAFFA, HARRY V. 1959 *Crisis of the House Divided: An Interpretation of the Lincoln–Douglas Debates.* Garden City, N.Y.: Doubleday.

LINCOLN'S PLAN OF RECONSTRUCTION (1863)

By 1863, President ABRAHAM LINCOLN adopted policies that affected Reconstruction in some of the seceded states. He appointed military governors in Louisiana, Tennessee, and North Carolina and recognized the provisional government of Virginia. The EMANCIPATION PROCLAMATION took effect on January 1, 1863.

Lincoln issued his Proclamation of Amnesty and Reconstruction on December 8, 1863. In it, he offered AMNESTY to all participants in the rebellion, except high-ranking military and civilian officers. He announced his intention to appoint a military governor in each occupied state and to require each occupied state to accept all extant and future policy concerning slavery and emancipation. But otherwise Lincoln's policy was conservative. It assumed preservation of the states' boundaries, constitutions, and laws (except those relating to slavery) and required neither black suffrage nor confiscation. Lincoln proposed to recreate an enfranchised citizenry in each state by requiring all persons to take an oath of future loyalty and support of the laws. When ten percent of a state's 1860 voters had taken the oath, they could reorganize the state's government.

The President's authority to recreate loyal state governments derived from several provisions of Article II, including his powers as COMMANDER-IN-CHIEF, his PARDONING POWER, and his duty to see to the faithful execution of the laws. But, as with his earlier actions in calling for volunteers and suspending HABEAS CORPUS, Lincoln had to make the most of a document that had not contemplated SECESSION, civil war, or Reconstruction.

Though Arkansas and Louisiana complied with Lincoln's terms, Congress refused to seat their representatives. Lincoln and Congress clashed over the more stringent congressional plan of Reconstruction embodied in the WADE-DAVIS BILL of 1864. President ANDREW JOHNSON later pursued Reconstruction policies similar to Lincoln's.

WILLIAM M. WIECEK

Bibliography

BELZ, HERMAN 1969 *Reconstructing the Union: Theory and Policy During the Civil War.* Ithaca, N.Y.: Cornell University Press.

LINEUP

In opinions whose subtext is unease about eyewitness identification procedures and testimony, the Supreme Court ruled in 1967 that a suspect is entitled to the presence of counsel at a lineup in order to preserve a FAIR TRIAL at which the witnesses can be meaningfully cross-examined. The opinions were delivered in the cases of UNITED STATES V. WADE and *Gilbert v. California.*

If a lineup is conducted without counsel, testimony about the lineup identification is automatically excluded. The question then becomes whether the witness who attended the illegally conducted lineup should be allowed to identify the witness at trial. This question centers on whether the witness could have made the in-court identification without having attended the lineup at which counsel was not present: whether, in other words, the witness had an independent source for the identification.

The lineup cases have generated much litigation and writing, both of a practical and a scholarly sort, about the role of counsel. The Court seemed to envision the attorney as a passive observer who would use what he saw to reconstruct for the fact-finder any unfairness in the lineup procedure. But a lawyer's skills are not necessary for observing, and reconstruction on cross-examination creates the risk that through the knowledge he displays in asking questions a lawyer may become a witness in his own case. Perhaps recognizing that having counsel at lineups was an interim measure and perceiving the analytical difficulties, the Court suggested that other techniques, such as photographing or videotaping lineups, could obviate the need for counsel.

The RIGHT TO COUNSEL at lineups was greatly undercut in *Kirby v. Illinois* (1972), in which the Court held that the right begins only "at or after the initiation of adversary criminal proceedings—whether by way of formal charge, preliminary hearing, INDICT-

MENT, INFORMATION, or arraignment." Because most lineups are part of the investigative stage of a case and occur before any of the indices of a formal charge, *Kirby* necessarily implied that a lawyer or some other observer was not, in fact, generally required.

Untouched by *Kirby,* however, is the argument, made in *Stovall v. Denno* (1967), that identification procedures may be so "unnecessarily suggestive and conducive to irreparable mistaken identification" as to violate DUE PROCESS OF LAW. An example of a due process violation would be showing a crime victim only the suspect dressed in clothes like those of the perpetrator when there was time to arrange a proper lineup. Once such a due process violation is proven, the issue shifts to whether it tainted the in-court identification: whether there was "a very substantial likelihood of irreparable mistaken identification." This decision mirrors that of a court in deciding whether a victim can make an in-court identification after attending a lineup where counsel was not present.

The effect of the lineup decisions has been to focus attention on all of the procedures used in pretrial CONFRONTATION of witnesses and suspects and thus to improve the fairness of these previously unobserved, but critically important, occasions.

BARBARA ALLEN BABCOCK

Bibliography

LEVY, LEONARD W. 1974 *Against the Law.* Pages 242–258. New York: Harper & Row.

LINMARK ASSOCIATES v. WILLINGBORO
431 U.S. 85 (1977)

Without dissent, the BURGER COURT invalidated a local ordinance prohibiting real estate "For Sale" and "Sold" signs. The ordinance sought to reduce the flight by white homeowners from racially integrated neighborhoods. Although a ban upon all signs for aesthetic purposes might survive a constitutional test, wrote Justice THURGOOD MARSHALL, this ordinance violated the FIRST AMENDMENT because the township had selected a particular message for prohibitions.

MICHAEL E. PARRISH

LISTENERS' RIGHTS

The constitutional commitment to FREEDOM OF SPEECH is in part based on the simple idea that people have a right to say what they want to say without government interference. That is, freedom of speech protects the speaker. Yet the FIRST AMENDMENT themes of self-expression and speaker liberty have been recognized only sporadically in Supreme Court opinions. The more prevalent themes in First Amendment jurisprudence have been audience-oriented, albeit implicitly.

One classic justification of freedom of speech has been based on optimistic assessments about the capacity of the marketplace of ideas to distinguish between the false and the true. The emphasis of this justification is not that speakers have a right to say what they want to say, but that speakers must be free to speak so that the society can find truth, that is, so that listeners can hear and evaluate what is said. Listeners' rights are also strongly implicated by the notion that freedom of speech reflects a commitment to democratic self-government. If citizens are to decide how to respond to public issues, they must hear what others have to say. The listeners' rights emphasis of the self-government perspective is best illustrated by ALEXANDER MEIKLEJOHN's observation, approvingly cited by the Supreme Court in COLUMBIA BROADCASTING SYSTEM V. DEMOCRATIC NATIONAL COMMITTEE (1981): "What is essential is not that everyone shall speak, but that everything worth saying shall be said."

For many years, listeners' rights were protected with nary a listener before the Court. In routine cases, the aggrieved speaker invoked the rights of the listeners. In *Thomas v. Collins* (1945), for example, the Court invalidated an attempted prior restraint at the behest of the speaker, in part because of the rights of others "to hear what he had to say."

Ultimately, listeners were permitted to invoke their own rights without any speakers before the Court. In VIRGINIA STATE BOARD OF PHARMACY V. VIRGINIA CITIZENS CONSUMER COUNCIL, for example, consumers challenged a statute that prohibited pharmacists from advertising the prices of prescription drugs. No pharmacist was before the Court, only potential members of the audience for drug price advertising. The Court recognized the rights of "listener" plaintiffs to sue on their own behalf, observing that the First Amendment gives protection "to the communication, to its source and its recipients both."

LAMONT V. POSTMASTER GENERAL (1965) stands for an even broader principle. There the Court struck down a statute directing the postmaster general not to deliver certain "communist political propaganda" unless the addressee, upon notification, requested its delivery. The Court found this to be "an unconstitutional abridgment of the addressee's rights." Many of the potential senders of this "propaganda" were aliens outside the country who had no First Amendment rights of their own. The Court made this distinction explicit in *Kleindeist v. Mandel* (1972). Thus recipients of messages have a First Amendment right to hear that does not depend upon corresponding rights in the speaker. Such rights may extend to situations where the speaker is unwilling to speak; they are then usually referred to as the RIGHT TO KNOW. On the other hand, an unwilling recipient of a message may have a right not to hear, deriving from notions such as a right of privacy.

STEVEN SHIFFRIN

Bibliography

BEVIER, LILLIAN 1980 An Informed Public, an Informing Press: The Search for a Constitutional Principle. *Stanford Law Review* 68:482–517.

EMERSON, THOMAS I. 1976 Legal Foundations of the Right to Know. *Washington University Law Quarterly* 1976:1–24.

LITERACY TEST

Many states used to require voters to be literate in English. The main constitutional problems raised by this practice arose from the use of literacy tests in southern and border states as a form of RACIAL DISCRIMINATION aimed at denying black citizens their VOTING RIGHTS in violation of the FIFTEENTH AMENDMENT. A typical law conditioned voter registration on the ability to read and write a provision of the state constitution selected by the registrar, to the registrar's "satisfaction." (An Alabama registrar once wrote this explanation for rejecting a black applicant: "Error in spilling.") Some laws also required the applicant to "interpret" or "explain" the constitutional provision, offering even greater opportunities for discriminatory application.

In *Davis v. Schnell* (1949) the Supreme Court summarily affirmed a lower court decision invalidating a requirement that a voter "understand and explain" an article of the United States Constitution; the registrar's discretion was so great that the test was an obvious "device to make racial discrimination easy." However, in LASSITER V. NORTHAMPTON COUNTY BOARD OF ELECTIONS (1959) the Court unanimously upheld a bare literacy requirement, in the absence of any showing of discriminatory application. This distinction had been suggested by the Court as early as WILLIAMS V. MISSISSIPPI (1898).

Meanwhile, the Court had fought two minor voting rights skirmishes with Oklahoma. That state had required voters to pass a literacy test, but excepted any voter whose ancestors had been registered to vote in 1866. Because of this GRANDFATHER CLAUSE, only black registrants were required to take literacy tests; the Court readily invalidated this law in GUINN V. UNITED STATES (1915). After the decision, Oklahoma adopted a law requiring all new voters to register within a twelve-day period; because virtually all the new voters were black, this onerous procedure fell before the Fifteenth Amendment, which "nullifies sophisticated as well as simple-minded modes of discrimination," in *Lane v. Wilson* (1939).

The death blow to voter literacy tests was delivered not by the Court but by Congress, which approached the question gingerly. The VOTING RIGHTS ACT OF 1965 required certain states and counties to suspend their use of literacy tests for five years. This feature of the law was upheld in SOUTH CAROLINA V. KATZENBACH (1966). In the same year, KATZENBACH V. MORGAN (1966) upheld another feature of the 1965 act requiring states to confer the vote on some citizens who, having been educated in Puerto Rico, were literate in Spanish. In 1970, Congress suspended literacy tests for voting throughout the nation, a provision which the Court upheld in OREGON V. MITCHELL (1970) as a valid exercise of the power to enforce the Fifteenth Amendment. Finally, in 1975, Congress made the ban on literacy tests permanent. In practical terms, literacy tests for voters are a thing of the past, and the Supreme Court is unlikely to confront the *Lassiter* issue again.

KENNETH L. KARST

Bibliography

LEIBOWITZ, ARNOLD H. 1969 English Literacy: Legal Sanction for Discrimination. *Notre Dame Lawyer* 45:7–67.

LITIGATION STRATEGY

Litigation strategy in constitutional cases is shaped by a single animating principle—a desire to increase the likelihood that a black-robed bureaucrat called a judge will act on behalf of a politically vulnerable applicant to alter or set aside the act of a popularly accountable official. Although the degree of tension that exists between democratic political theory and constitutional litigation varies widely depending on the nature of the case and the attributes of the forum—a police brutality case litigated before an elected state judge poses no threat to democratic decision making; an EQUAL PROTECTION challenge to an act of Congress argued before an appointed, life-tenured, federal judge poses a more direct conflict—constitutional cases generally involve persons who are unable to secure redress through more conventional appeals to the political process. Litigation strategy in constitutional cases is designed to increase the potential that a judicial forum will rule in favor of such politically disfavored plaintiffs.

Sustained constitutional litigation in the United States has involved many sets of litigants, including abolitionists versus slaveholders in the period prior to the Civil War; radical reconstructionists versus southern revisionists in the period immediately following the Civil War; business CORPORATIONS versus populist reformers during the first third of the twentieth century; and civil libertarians versus majoritarians during the modern era. Although the political goals of the participants have varied widely, the strategic choices of the contestants have remained remarkably stable, involving five areas: choice of forum; selection of parties; articulation of theories of recovery; choice of tactics; and articulation of antidemocratic apologia.

Choice of forum is the most important strategic decision for a constitutional litigator. In choosing a forum, a constitutional litigator must choose between state and federal court; between a judge and jury; and sometimes between one judge and another. The outcome of many, if not most, constitutional cases turns as much on the wisdom of those strategic choices as on the intrinsic merits of the cases.

Because a constitutional plaintiff is generally seeking to trump a decision that enjoys the imprimatur of democratic decision making, the institutional capacity of the forum to render sustained anti- (or, at least, counter-) majoritarian doctrine is critical to the success of any constitutional litigation campaign. Judges who are themselves elected by the political majority or who are otherwise closely tied to the political process are least likely to enunciate sustained countermajoritarian doctrine. Judges who enjoy maximum political insulation are, on the other hand, in a position to ignore the short-term political consequences of their unpopular decisions. It would, for example, have been impossible for elected judges to have effectively enforced the fugitive slave clause in the pre-Civil War North on behalf of southern slaveholders, or the equal protection clause in the post-World War II South on behalf of black schoolchildren seeking an integrated education.

The search for an insulated judge in constitutional cases has generally led politically vulnerable plaintiffs—whether slaveholders, business corporations, or CIVIL RIGHTS activists—to seek a federal judicial forum, for federal judges are appointed and enjoy life tenure. Much of the procedural infighting that characterizes constitutional litigation revolves around attempts by plaintiffs to force claims into insulated federal forums and by defendants to deflect them to more politically accountable state courts.

The search for an insulated forum has led many constitutional litigators to view juries with suspicion. Not surprisingly, a principal litigation strategy of the abolitionist bar was to choreograph disputes about alleged fugitive slaves before free state juries in the hope that juries would decline to enforce the Fugitive Slave Act. (See FUGITIVE SLAVERY.) Modern civil rights lawyers have experienced analogous difficulty in persuading juries to return verdicts in favor of unpalatable plaintiffs whose rights may have been violated by a popularly responsible official.

Finally, the choice of forum involves a decision about the identity of the judge or, in less polite terms, judge-shopping. The identity of the judge in a constitutional case is extremely important for two reasons, one obvious and one less well understood. The obvious reason for judge-shopping involves the judge's politics. Because constitutional cases often turn on a clash of values and because the urgency with which a judge views a constitutional case may well depend on his or her view of the relative importance of the conflicting values, the same case may be decided differently by equally competent judges with differing value systems.

The less obvious reason why judge-shopping is important in constitutional cases involves the judge's technical competence. Victory for the plaintiff in constitutional cases depends upon persuading a judge that constitutional doctrine requires the overturning of a presumptively valid decision by another government official. Unless a judge is equipped to understand and evaluate complex argumentation about the meaning of ambiguous textual provisions and judicial PRECEDENT, it will be impossible to persuade the judge that doctrinal factors compel a decision for the plaintiff. Because the inertial advantage in constitutional cases almost always favors government defendants—failure to persuade the judge to act results in perpetuation of the challenged status quo—the inability of a judge to grapple with complex argumentation generally works to the disadvantage of a constitutional plaintiff.

In addition to care in selecting a forum, constitutional litigators expend a good deal of energy on the choice of a plaintiff, seeking to project the most sympathetic and appealing fact pattern. Because the judge's view of the equities may play a substantial role in the outcome of a constitutional case, the capacity of a constitutional plaintiff to evoke sympathy can be crucial. Constitutional lawyers have learned, moreover, that courts respond most favorably to fact patterns that emerge naturally from the interrelationship between a constitutional plaintiff and the government, but balk at being asked to decide artificially constructed TEST CASES.

A difficult decision constitutional litigators face in selecting a plaintiff is whether to bring the case as an individual action involving only named individuals or as a CLASS ACTION on behalf of all similarly situated persons. Militating in favor of class action status is its increased impact. A single class action can provide relief to thousands of people. Class actions, however, have drawbacks. Against the prospect of increased impact must be weighed the risk of loss, for members of a losing class are generally bound by the loss. Moreover, class actions can act as red flags to judges who would be sensitive to the claims of an individual plaintiff but who are reluctant to become involved in litigation seeking institutional change.

The selection of a defendant in a constitutional case also requires careful thought. Most important, the defendant must be capable of providing adequate relief. If injunctive relief is sought, the defendant must be sufficiently senior in the bureaucratic hierarchy to be able to promulgate and implement the changes sought by the action. At the same time, of course, the defendant must be sufficiently involved in the factual dispute giving rise to the lawsuit to justify naming him as an adverse party. If DAMAGES are sought, the defendant must have a sufficiently "deep pocket" to pay the judgment. A damage award against a judgment-proof defendant is hardly worth the effort.

One method of dealing with both the need for a high-ranking defendant and the quest for financial solvency is the naming of an entity-defendant such as the City of New York or the United States in addition to the individual defendants. The extremely complicated interplay between rules limiting the extent to which government entities can be sued in constitutional cases and plaintiffs' interest in suing government entities poses one of the serious tactical dilemmas in constitutional litigation.

A final—and less empirically verifiable—concern in selecting a defendant flows from what may be called the "Redneck-Mandarin dichotomy," which seeks to match a defendant and a judge from different educational and social backgrounds in the hope that the judge will be less constrained in exercising vigorous review powers. Although such an assumption is highly speculative, many constitutional litigators believe, for example, that they perceive a difference between many judges' willingness to exercise vigorous review of the actions of low-ranking police officers and the same judges' willingness to review the decisions of police commissioners.

Given the difficulty of overcoming the inertial advantage enjoyed by the government in constitutional cases, strategic considerations often play a role in the articulation of plaintiff's theory of recovery. It is often advisable to proceed by incremental stages and to develop alternatives to the primary constitutional theory. Thus, for example, litigation aimed at the OVERRULING of the SEPARATE BUT EQUAL DOCTRINE enunciated by PLESSY v. FERGUSON (1896) proceeded by carefully calibrated constitutional steps designed to develop sufficient momentum to make the final decision in BROWN v. BOARD OF EDUCATION (1954) possible. It is, however, extremely difficult to execute a sustained litigation campaign over time, for the factors of chance and changing tides of legal analysis are difficult to predict. On the other hand, asking for too much too soon in the absence of a carefully laid doctrinal foundation places an intolerable degree of pressure on even a sympathetic judge.

In an effort to lessen the tension between constitutional litigation and democratic political theory, litigators often seek to articulate a process-based alternative to their principal substantive theory. Thus, litigators attacking FIRST AMENDMENT violations often invite the court to seize upon a narrower, process-based claim such as VAGUENESS or OVERBREADTH as the basis for invalidating a statute, rather than confront the substantive question of the legislature's power to enact it at all. Similarly, constitutional litigators often seek to link their constitutional theories with nonconstitutional claims, such as a claim based on a statute or a COMMON LAW tort. Posing alternative theories of recovery provides a judge with a less dramatic means of protecting a constitutional value while providing effective relief to the plaintiff. Of course, many such alternative theories of recovery are subject to modification by the legislature, but the short-term result is often indistinguishable from success of the constitutional claim.

Although much litigation strategy depends on a perception of the degree to which constitutional law is shaped by value judgments, constitutional lawyers also recognize the extent to which constitutional litigation shapes community values. The process of bringing a constitutional lawsuit is educational as well as remedial. It seeks to expose the judge to a set of facts and a legal reality that would ordinarily be far from his or her consciousness. It seeks to inform the public of the existence of a social problem that, even if not ultimately amenable to constitutional resolution, requires increased public attention. Viewed as a part of the process by which the interests of the politically powerless can be protected in a democracy, constitutional litigation provides a mechanism not only for classic remedial action but for a sharpening of the underlying social issues for ultimate political resolution. Thus, for example, although under current legal standards it is difficult to establish a violation of the constitutional right of a minority community to receive equal municipal services (discriminatory purpose, not merely disparate effect, must be proven), constitutional litigation provides a forum for the dramatization of unequal treatment as a first step to a political resolution. Similarly, although only the most optimistic believed that courts would actually stop the VIETNAM WAR because it was supposedly carried on in violation of Article 1, section 8, of the Constitution, the repeated presentation of the issue both shaped public perception of the war and helped pave the way for the passage of the War Powers Resolution which attempted to deal with the legal issue of undeclared war.

Two major constraints limit the use of constitutional litigation as an educational vehicle. First is the ethical obligation to refrain from presenting frivolous or inappropriate claims to a court. Judicial attention is a scarce national resource which must be rationed, and lawyers must be prudent in presenting claims that cannot win. In the absence of a good faith belief in the legal—as opposed to the moral—soundness of a claim, it should not be presented to a court. Moreover, even if a claim is sufficiently substantial to satisfy ethical considerations, tactical considerations often argue against presenting a weak claim for adjudication. Losing a constitutional case risks the enunciation of dangerous precedent and acts to legitimate the challenged activity. Thus, although constitutional litigation plays an educational as well as a remedial role, its educational role should be a by-product of a bona fide attempt to secure a legal remedy.

A significant dilemma in planning and executing litigation strategy in constitutional cases is posed by the potential for conflict between the best interest of a plaintiff and the furtherance of the cause that precipitated the case into court. For example, a plaintiff who has gone to court to vindicate a principle and who poses a powerful TEST CASE may be confronted with a settlement offer which, while advantageous to the plaintiff, leaves the legal issue unresolved. Constitutional lawyers, while recognizing this conflict, generally resolve it in favor of the plaintiff and recommend acceptance to their clients, who then make the final decision. Despite the recognition that the interest of the client in a constitutional case should predominate over the advancement of the cause, a disturbing tendency exists on the part of both bench and bar to use a constitutional plaintiff as a convenient vehicle to trigger the enunciation of norms that may benefit society as a whole but which do little for the parties before the Court. William Marbury never did get his commission. (See MARBURY V. MADISON.)

Once a constitutional case is underway, three recurring tactical issues arise. Should immediate relief be sought, usually in the form of a preliminary INJUNCTION? Should the case be pursued as an abstract issue of law or should substantial resources be expended in developing the facts? And how broad a remedy should be sought? It is impossible to formulate even a general rule governing these three issues, except that attorneys with weak cases rarely seek preliminary injunctions and that issues of law should not be presented to a potentially hostile court in the absence of clearly established fact, given that a judge's freedom of action is greatest in determining the facts on an ambiguous record.

A parallel tactical issue defendants in a constitutional case face is whether to move to dismiss—and, thus, to assume the truth of the facts alleged in the complaint for the purposes of the motion—or to force plaintiffs to prove their facts by going to trial. Surprisingly, most defendants, in an effort to save time and resources, attempt dismissal motions, which require courts to rule on the theoretical validity of plaintiff's case without requiring plaintiff to establish the facts. Much constitutional law has been made in denying motions to dismiss and thus creating important legal precedents in cases where plaintiffs might have experienced difficulty in proving their allegations.

Finally, in presenting a constitutional case to a judge, a constitutional litigator will often seek to place it within one of three categories posing the least tension with democratic political theory in order to free the judge to exercise vigorous review. If the case involves a member of a DISCRETE AND INSULAR MINORITY, constitutional litigators will stress the inability of unpopular or disadvantaged minority groups to protect themselves within the traditional political process, thus invoking the special responsibility of courts to act as a bulwark against majoritarian overreaching. If the case involves significant political values, constitutional litigators will stress the responsibility of courts to guarantee the proper functioning of the democratic process. It is not antidemocratic, they argue, for a court to prevent the majority from refusing to permit the democratic process to function properly. If the case involves a "fundamental" value, like marriage or REPRODUCTIVE AUTONOMY, constitutional litigators will argue that the importance of such values warrants increased judicial protection. This third category involves the most controversial exercises of judicial power, because the selection of "fundamental" values appears subjective.

Ultimately, litigation strategy in constitutional cases, even at its most sophisticated, can exert only a relatively weak influence on the outcome. The adjudication of issues that impinge on deeply held values and in many other systems would be relegated solely to the political process is an inherently unpredictable phenomenon. No other area of law fits Tolstoy's vision of history so well as the claim of constitutional lawyers to be able to influence the ocean on which they most often bob like corks.

BURT NEUBORNE

Bibliography

COVER, ROBERT M. 1975 *Justice Accused: Anti-Slavery and the Judicial Process.* New Haven, Conn.: Yale University Press.

GREENBERG, JACK 1977 *Judicial Process and Social Change: Constitutional Litigation.* St. Paul, Minn.: West Publishing Co.

KLUGER, RICHARD 1975 *Simple Justice.* New York: Knopf.

NEUBORNE, BURT 1977 The Myth of Parity. *Harvard Law Review* 90:1105.

LIVINGSTON, HENRY BROCKHOLST (1757–1823)

There is a modest puzzle regarding Henry Brockholst Livingston's more than sixteen years on the Supreme Court (1806–1823): why was he comparatively silent? Livingston, a New York Jeffersonian, was among the best qualified appointees ever named to the Court. Before his appointment to the New York Supreme Court in 1802, he was at the top of the legal profession, ranked as an equal of his frequent sparring mate, ALEXANDER HAMILTON. Livingston's opinions during his five years on the New York court demonstrated legal erudition, style, and wit. Some of his opinions are still required reading for law students. The New York reports indicate that Livingston had a constant urge to express his thoughts, and he was not only an extremely active dissenter but also constantly rendered SERIATIM OPINIONS. In his four years of New York judicial tenure, Livingston dissented twenty times, concurred on fourteen occasions, and delivered twenty-four seriatim opinions. Those statistics only begin to indicate the battle on the New York court, largely between Livingston and JAMES KENT, both of whom were first-rate jurists. The business of the New York court involved many significant matters but few constitutional questions. Livingston's dissent in *Hitchcock v. Aicken* (1803) argued that the FULL FAITH AND CREDIT clause should be interpreted broadly; ultimately, the MARSHALL COURT, including Livingston, agreed with this reasoning in *Mills v. Duryee* (1813).

In contrast to his active role on the New York court, Livingston was scarcely noticeable on the Marshall Court. In fifteen TERMS he dissented but three times and delivered only five CONCURRING OPINIONS. The fact that he had not shrunk from confronting some of the ablest judges in the country when on the New York court precludes any notion that he was overwhelmed by JOHN MARSHALL and associates. The difference in Livingston's roles on the state court and the Supreme Court is important largely for what it explains about the Marshall Court's constitutional jurisprudence. By the time of Livingston's appointment, Marshall's practice of having one Justice deliver a single opinion for the Court was settled. The Justices, moreover, willingly stifled their differences, save on questions of great moment, usually constitutional. Within this practice, the Justices' common values, regardless of party affiliation, normally made compromise possible. There are indications that Livingston initially had difficulty in adjusting to the ways of the Marshall Court. In the first few cases he heard, Livingston seemed particularly active in questioning counsel, as if he might have wished to dissent, but did not. Apparently, Livingston's policy preferences blended well with the Marshall Court's general mercantile orientation. While on the New York bench Livingston had served as a precursor for nineteenth-century instrumentalist judges who shaped the law to promote commercial development. In this respect, Livingston resembled a fellow Jeffersonian on the Court, WILLIAM JOHNSON. Because of the commercial atmosphere of his home community of Charleston, South Carolina, Johnson, like Livingston, had good reason for thinking as his brethren did on commercial questions. Johnson was even more nationalistic than Marshall. Unlike Johnson, however, THOMAS JEFFERSON apparently did not attempt to goad Livingston into expressing his differences as he had done while a state judge. Another reason that Livingston did not join Johnson and make plural the "first dissenter" may have been that Livingston got along with the rest of the Court much better than Johnson did. When

Livingston died, JOSEPH STORY's rich eulogy to him indicated how fondly he was remembered. Finally, Livingston was a ready adherent to precedent, as he had demonstrated on the New York bench. When a question was settled, Livingston was unlikely to challenge its resolutions, even obliquely. In short, Livingston was a good team player, and our constitutional jurisprudence may be poorer for it. A clear example of the consequences of Livingston's proclivity for compromise is seen in STURGES V. CROWNINSHIELD (1819), in which the Court invalidated a New York insolvent law of 1811 because it had been applied retroactively. On circuit, Livingston had emphatically sustained the same law in *Adams v. Storey* (1817); yet he proceeded to compromise in *Sturges.* It seems likely that Marshall did not wish to say in his opinion that the states had CONCURRENT POWER to pass bankruptcy or insolvency laws, but he did—probably in response to Livingston's urging. Livingston's main role on the Marshall Court and in the development of constitutional jurisprudence was that of a compromiser. His opinions, with few exceptions, are forgettable.

DONALD ROPER

Bibliography

DUNNE, GERALD T. 1969 Brockholst Livingston. In Leon Friedman and Fred L. Israel, eds., *The Justices of the United States Supreme Court.* New York: Chelsea House.

HASKINS, GEORGE LEE, and JOHNSON, HERBERT A. 1981 *Foundations of Power: John Marshall, 1801–1815,* volume II of Freund, Paul A., general editor, *The Oliver Wendell Holmes Devise History of the Supreme Court of the United States.* New York: Macmillan.

LIVINGSTON, ROBERT R., JR.
(1746–1813)

The son of a New York judge, Robert R. Livingston, Jr., was a member of the committees that drafted the DECLARATION OF INDEPENDENCE (which he regarded as premature and did not sign) and the ARTICLES OF CONFEDERATION. With JOHN JAY and GOUVERNEUR MORRIS he drafted the New York constitution of 1777. From 1777 to 1801 he was chancellor of New York. In 1788 he was chairman of the New York state convention where he vigorously supported RATIFICATION OF THE CONSTITUTION. He was later minister to France (1801–1804) and, with JAMES MONROE, negotiated the LOUISIANA PURCHASE TREATY. Livingston became a partner of inventor Robert Fulton and secured a New York steamboat monopoly not broken until GIBBONS V. OGDEN (1824).

DENNIS J. MAHONEY

LIVINGSTON, WILLIAM
(1723–1790)

Governor William Livingston, poet, lawyer, and Revolutionary general, signed the Constitution as a New Jersey delegate to the CONSTITUTIONAL CONVENTION OF 1787. Unable to attend regularly, Livingston was not active in the debates; but he was influential in securing New Jersey's early and unanimous ratification. He was the father of Justice BROCKHOLST LIVINGSTON and the guardian of young ALEXANDER HAMILTON.

DENNIS J. MAHONEY

LOAN ASSOCIATION v. TOPEKA
20 Wall. (87 U.S.) 655 (1875)

The Supreme Court has frequently resorted to HIGHER LAW doctrine to buttress an opinion, but only twice in its history, in TERRETT V. TAYLOR (1815) and in this case, has it relied exclusively on the higher law as the ground for decision. An 8–1 Court, in an opinion by Justice SAMUEL F. MILLER, held unconstitutional a Kansas statute that authorized the city of Topeka to issue public bonds, payable by taxes, for the benefit of a private company that built iron bridges. In the absence of some usable clause of the Constitution, Miller relied on judicially implied limitations on government power "which grow out of the essential nature of all free governments" and protect individual rights "without which the SOCIAL COMPACT could not exist." Topeka and the state legislature had believed that attracting a bridge company promoted public prosperity as did a railroad or a public utility, but because the Court saw only an improper exercise of the tax power "to aid private enterprise and build up private fortunes," it called the statute "a robbery" of the public. Taxation, the Could held, can be exercised only for a public use or public purpose. Justice NATHAN CLIFFORD, the sole dissenter, believed that JUDICIAL REVIEW should be exercised only when the Constitution imposed a prohibition either express or necessarily implied, but not when the Court believed that a legislature had violated "natural justice" or "a general latent spirit" supposedly underlying the Constitution.

LEONARD W. LEVY

LOCHNER v. NEW YORK
198 U.S. 45 (1905)

Lochner v. New York, a landmark decision of 1905, has been discredited by the evolution of constitutional law. Justice RUFUS W. PECKHAM, writing for a 5–4 majority of the Supreme Court, invalidated a New York state statute forbidding employment in bakeries for more than sixty hours a week or ten hours a day. The rationale for the Court's opinion was that the statute interfered with the FREEDOM OF CONTRACT and thus the FOURTEENTH AMENDMENT's right to liberty afforded both the employer and the employee. The Court stated that under the statute, viewed as a labor law, the state had no reasonable ground for interfering with liberty by determining the hours of labor. Seen as a health law, the statute affected only the bakers and not the public. Accordingly, the Court concluded that the law was neither necessary nor appropriate to accomplish its health objective. Moreover, the Court was of the view that if the law were upheld for the bakers, laws designed to protect other workers would also have to be upheld. In either case, said the Court, the statute was an illegal interference with the right to contract.

Justice OLIVER WENDELL HOLMES, in an important and historic dissent, concluded that the legislature had the power to enact a law that interfered with full freedom to contract and that the personal biases of judges could not justify declaring a statute unconstitutional. Said Justice Holmes: "The constitution is not intended to embody a particular economic theory," an obvious reference to the laissez-faire view then widely accepted. Holmes's view was that a law interfered with the Fourteenth Amendment's guarantee of liberty only if "a rational and fair man necessarily would admit that the statute proposed would infringe fundamental principles of our people and our law." The dissent's view was that the statute, viewed either as a health or a labor law, did not violate these principles.

Justice JOHN MARSHALL HARLAN also dissented, arguing with Justice Holmes that the wisdom of the statute or of a particular economic theory is judicially irrelevant. Citing studies that showed the hazards of bakery work, Harlan noted that legislatures in many states had enacted legislation dealing with the number of hours in a work day. Said Justice Harlan: "[I]t is enough for the determination of this case, and it is enough for this Court, to know that the question is one about which there is room for debate and for at least honest difference of opinion." If there are "weighty substantial" reasons for enacting a law it ought "to be the end of [the] case, for the State is not amenable to the judiciary, in respect of its legislative enactments, unless such enactments are plainly, palpably, beyond all question, inconsistent with the Constitution of the United States."

The Court implicitly overruled the *Lochner* result in BUNTING V. OREGON (1917), but for three decades the decision influenced the Court as it scrutinized carefully and often struck down economic regulations as violations of SUBSTANTIVE DUE PROCESS. It was not until the mid-1930s, in the wake of the Court-packing furor and especially the Court's approval of the constitutionality of the National Labor Relations Act in *National Labor Relations Board v. Jones & Laughlin Steel Corporation* (1937), that judicial intervention in economic legislation declined. Although *Lochner* is now discredited, its focus upon substantive due process and FUNDAMENTAL RIGHTS has emerged in cases dealing with both contraception and abortion, namely GRISWOLD V. CONNECTICUT (1965) and ROE V. WADE (1973).

WILLIAM B. GOULD

LOCKE, JOHN
(1631–1704)

John Locke, the English philosopher of enlightenment, formulated the basic doctrines that influenced the American Framers of 1787. While his famous *Second Treatise,* "Of Civil Government" (1688), alludes to various traditional ways to limit governments, it sets forth an effectual new way, later called liberal CONSTITUTIONALISM. That comprised a sphere of individual liberty, fenced by a right to property, and fixed government, constituted by a majority's consent. Constitutional or civil government is to be representative, responsible, and limited, with powers separated as well as effective, and it is to be kept to its FUNDAMENTAL LAW by a perpetual threat of popular rebellion.

The first of Locke's *Two Treatises of Government* rebutted Robert Filmer's contention that monarchy exists by divine right, derived from the fatherly authority of Adam and of God. Locke thrust at paternalism, which he regarded as the natural foundation of uncivil government and of inhumane civilization in general. Mankind has inclined unthinkingly to obey fathers, who grew to be patriarchs of families and chiefs of tribes, and finally to be oppressive kings and nobles upheld by wealth, power, and the servile flatteries of traditional faiths. The *Letter concerning Toleration* (1689) espoused freedom of conscience and SEPARATION OF CHURCH AND STATE. Locke tried to remove religion from the magistrate's armory and to remake churches into voluntary associations keeping watch on government and on one another. The *Letter* counsels public toleration of religion, but as a thing merely private, and only of civil religions willing to tolerate other faiths and to obey the civil powers. In other writings Locke advocated a reasonable Christianity and a worldly and private education, and he explained human understanding prosaically, as reliably derived from sense impressions rather than from intuitions or divinations.

The first chapters of the *Second Treatise* set forth the famous doctrine of individualism: human beings are naturally free, equal, and occupied with securing themselves, not naturally subordinate to a superior or oriented to something noble or true above themselves. They are not subject to fathers or mothers so soon as they can "shift for themselves," or to husbands or wives if they no longer consent to be spouses, or to some gentleman or lord in his vineyard or estate. On the contrary, they have a natural right to acquire the means of life, to obtain the fruits of their own labor. Locke devised a private right of unlimited acquisition which implicitly indicts any leisured class, authorizes opportunity for the "industrious and rational," and provides powerful incentives for work, invention, and production. Locke was the philosophic father of capitalism, his plan whereby freedom of enterprise produces economic growth and the means of collective security. The profits of entrepreneurs, which Locke defended as incentives, occasioned the later attacks on capitalism as unjust and LIMITED GOVERNMENT as callously narrow.

The central chapters of the *Second Treatise* are Locke's prescription for public powers that will serve the people instead of exploiting them. He insisted upon powerful institutions, what THE FEDERALIST was to call effective or energetic government. A condition without government, Locke eventually maintained, is "very unsafe, very insecure," and people are "driven" to establish a LEGISLATIVE POWER to define laws, judges to apply them, and an executive to enforce them. Despite this agreement with the authoritarian Thomas Hobbes, Locke insisted that raising a state is easy compared to domesticating it. For domesticated or civil government the key is constitutionalism—government according to a man-made fundamental law agreeable to a majority. In particular, the supreme power, which Locke defines as a lawmaking power, is to be set up with a majority's consent (immediate or eventual, express or tacit). This supreme legislative power, however, is also and primarily to be shaped by Locke's enlightened prescriptions for a legislative limited, conditional, and rather democratic. Every actual legislature has by right only this legislative power, the natural CONSTITUTION behind any written constitution, and a consenting majority is to be supposed an enlightened majority. The legislature must aim to preserve individual rights, to govern by declared laws, not to impose TAXATION WITHOUT REPRESENTATION, and not to delegate its powers. Also, a legislature must be broadly representative of "populous" places filled with "wealth and inhabitants." Locke required an assembly of "deputies" of the people, while cautiously but pervasively impugning an aristocratic senate or house.

Locke provided for an executive power that is (unlike a monarch) subordinate to law and yet (like a monarch) able to act beyond law when public necessities require. The executive enforces law, unites the nation's forces for FOREIGN AFFAIRS (Locke's "federative" power), includes the judiciary, and remains, unlike the legislature, permanently on duty. For purposes of lawmaking Locke subordinated the executive to the legislature and attacked executives (such as the British king) who shared in lawmaking. Locke's argument led discreetly toward government by a responsible ministry, a dependence on a popular legislature that was rejected when the American Founders devised the Presidency, and a constitutional monarchy, which is only a "head of the republic," "a badge or emblem" representing the people. Still, executive power is extended by political necessity. In extraordinary situations, such as civil war, executive "prerogative" may extend to actions without authorization of law or even in violation of fundamental law, as when ABRAHAM LINCOLN in 1861 raised troops and monies before Congress had assembled. *Salus populi suprema lex est* is the Two Treatises' motto: the people's benefit is the supreme law. Locke repeated this maxim, which shows the limits of constitutional law, as he urged a king to reapportion an oligarchic house into a representative legislature.

The *Second Treatise* ends by insisting on an extraconstitutional RIGHT OF REVOLUTION, to secure a constitutional order against tyranny and also to help bring about popular constitutionalism. While executive prerogative may extend to reform, it is not to include a "godlike" prince with "a distinct and separate interest," a despot who violates the fiduciary "trust" of office, a conqueror, a usurper, a tyrannical king, or a clique of the rich. Such excesses make power revert to the people, who may set up anew their legislature.

Locke repeatedly called this doctrine new. Each of the last six chapters ends by holding up to governors and peoples the new right of popular rebellion. In effect, Locke justified rebellion against every regime not a constitutional republic, and justified "revolution" of traditional beliefs inimical to individualism and popular government, that is, of almost all traditional beliefs.

The American Framers accepted Locke's broad framework of NATURAL RIGHTS and civil government, while varying details of the Constitution in accord with the cautious versions of MONTESQUIEU and his followers, David Hume and Sir WILLIAM BLACKSTONE. Fearing a political zealotry that might rival the old religious wars, Montesquieu, in his *Spirit of the Laws* (1748), abstained from Locke's fiery language of natural and popular liberty. His modified Lockeanism would allow forms and structures to vary with circumstance, make the judiciary a third separate power, and allow a senate of the successful and wealthy. Montesquieu also sought to introduce humane civilization less by rebellion and more by the spread of commerce and by changes in the private law of contract and inheritance.

ROBERT K. FAULKNER

Bibliography

HARTZ, LOUIS 1955 *The Liberal Tradition in America.* New York: Harcourt, Brace.

STRAUSS, LEO 1953 *Natural Right and History.* Chicago: University of Chicago Press.

VILE, M. J. C. 1967 *Constitutionalism and the Separation of Powers.* Oxford: Clarendon Press.

LODGE, HENRY CABOT
(1850–1924)

A Harvard-trained lawyer who also earned the Ph.D. degree in history, Henry Cabot Lodge was elected three times to the House of Representatives and six times to the United States Senate from Massachusetts. He was a close friend of President THEODORE ROOSEVELT and a national leader of the Republican party.

During his second term in Congress Lodge introduced a bill that would have provided for federal supervision of elections in order to protect the VOTING RIGHTS of black citizens in southern states. But he was wary of such Progressive innovations as women's suffrage and the DIRECT ELECTION of senators. He advocated the constant expansion of the United States through the annexation of Hawaii and other island TERRITORIES, and he supported the Spanish-American War because it promised to lead to annexation of the Philippine Islands. During Roosevelt's administration Lodge was a leading congressional supporter of the Panama Canal project.

In 1918, Lodge used his position as chairman of the Senate Foreign Relations Committee to lead the fight against the Treaty of Versailles. He based his opposition to the League of Nations, a key element of the treaty, on the unconstitutionality of commiting American military forces to combat without the express consent of Congress.

Lodge was known during his lifetime as "the scholar in politics." His vision of an American constitutionalism that was both conservative and nationalistic was presented, in part, in his biographies of GEORGE WASHINGTON, ALEXANDER HAMILTON, and DANIEL WEBSTER.

DENNIS J. MAHONEY

Bibliography

GARRATY, JOHN A. 1965 *Henry Cabot Lodge: A Biography.* New York: Knopf.

LOEWE v. LAWLOR
208 U.S. 274 (1908)

This case fits a pattern of antilabor decisions that supported INJUNCTIONS against trade unions and struck down maximum hours acts, minimum wage acts, and acts prohibiting YELLOW DOG CONTRACTS. In *Loewe*, the Court, while crippling secondary boycotts, held that unions were subject to the antitrust laws and therefore were civilly liable for triple damages to compensate for injuries inflicted by their restraints on INTERSTATE COMMERCE.

Loewe originated in an attempt by the United Hatters Union, AFL, to organize a manufacturer of hats in Danbury, Connecticut. Most hat firms in the country were unionized. The few nonunion firms sweated their workers and were able to undersell unionized competitors, threatening their survival as well as the jobs of their unionized labor. Loewe's firm refused to negotiate a union contract and defeated a strike. The union retaliated with a secondary boycott, a refusal by the national membership of the AFL to buy Loewe's hats or patronize retailers who sold them. Loewe sued the union under the SHERMAN ANTITRUST ACT after the boycott resulted in a substantial loss of orders. The union demurred to the charges, admitting that it had engaged in the boycott but alleging that it had not violated the antitrust law, because that law did not cover the activities of trade unions and because the boycott in this case was not a conspiracy in restraint of commerce among the states. Invoking the DOCTRINE of the Sugar Trust Case (UNITED STATES v. E. C. KNIGHT CO., 1895) that manufacturing is a purely local activity, the union claimed that neither it nor the manufacturer engaged in interstate commerce. Although Loewe's hats, once manufactured, were shipped to purchasing retailers in twenty-one states, the union argued that it did not interfere with the actual transportation across state lines and that any restraint on interstate commerce resulting from the boycott was, according to the Sugar Trust Case, remote and indirect.

Overruling a lower federal court decision in favor of the union, the Supreme Court, in a unanimous opinion by Chief Justice MELVILLE W. FULLER, for the first time held that the Sherman Act applied to union activities; that a secondary boycott conducted across state lines is a conspiracy in restraint of interstate commerce; and that even if the restraint were remote and indirect, the Sherman Act applied because it covered "every" combination in the form of a trust "or otherwise" in restraint of interstate commerce. In 1911, however, the Court embraced the RULE OF REASON, enabling it subsequently to find that corporations, not unions, might engage in reasonable restraints; that is, the act did not prohibit all restraints except by unions. In *Loewe,* however, the Court construed the act broadly, even to the point of using the STREAM OF COMMERCE DOCTRINE to show the scope of the commerce power. There is no evidence, however, that Congress, when adopting the Sherman Act, intended to cover union activities.

The case presents the phenomenon of a labor union being held within the terms of an antitrust act and contrasting opinions of the Court. In the Sugar Trust Case the Court held a ninety-eight percent monopoly not to violate the act because manufacturing is local and any effect upon or relationship with interstate commerce is necessarily indirect; here, though, a small hatmakers' union came within the act because its boycott was interstate, despite its having done nothing to control the price or transportation of the product of a manufacturer. Moreover, the decision in this case came one week after the decision in ADAIR v. UNITED STATES (1908), where the Court declared that there is "no connection between interstate commerce and membership in a labor organization," as it struck down an act of Congress prohibiting the use of yellow-dog contracts by railroads against railroad workers engaged in interstate commerce. If *Adair* correctly invalidated the attempt by Congress to protect railroad workers under the commerce power, then a week later the Court should have decided that Congress under the same commerce power cannot, via the Sherman Act, reach an admittedly indirect relationship between a hatters' union and interstate commerce. Both the legislative history of the antitrust law and the Sugar Trust and *Adair* precedents opposed the decision in the Danbury Hatters' Case. Following the Court's decision, a triple-damages suit against the union in the lower federal court resulted in a fine of $252,000. The Danbury Hatters went unorganized, hatmakers everywhere suffered, and unionization everywhere was thwarted to an inestimable extent by the threat of Sherman Act suits. *Loewe* is one of the major cases on the subject of LABOR AND THE CONSTITUTION.

LEONARD W. LEVY

Bibliography

LIEBERMAN, ELIAS 1960 *Unions Before the Bar.* Pages 56–70. New York: Harper & Row.

LONG HAUL–SHORT HAUL DISCRIMINATION

Long haul–short haul discrimination was one of the most notorious abuses practiced by railroads in the late nineteenth and early twentieth centuries. The practice involved charging a higher rate for a short haul that was included within a longer haul over the same line. Although Congress outlawed this discriminatory practice in Section 4 of the INTERSTATE COMMERCE ACT (1887), the Supreme Court effectively nullified that section in *ICC v. Alabama Midland Railway Company* (1897). The Court rested its decision on the commission's power to grant exemptions if the long and short hauls did not occur "under substantially similar circumstances and conditions." Sufficient differences existed between hauls to justify departures from Section 4's prohibition. In 1910 Congress revived the prohibition by reenacting the long haul–short haul clause minus the "similar circumstances" clause. Carriers were now forbidden to charge higher rates for shorter (included) hauls *regardless* of different conditions, although the commission was still authorized to make exceptions. A unanimous Supreme Court sustained this provision to *United States v. Atchison, Topeka, & Santa Fe Railway Co.* (1914).

DAVID GORDON

Bibliography

SHARFMAN, ISAIAH L. 1931–1937 *The Interstate Commerce Commission.* 4 Vols. New York: Commonwealth Fund.

LONGSHOREMEN'S ASSOCIATION v. ALLIED INTERNATIONAL

See: Labor and the Constitution

LOOSE CONSTRUCTION

See: Broad Construction

LOPEZ v. UNITED STATES
373 U.S. 427 (1963)

The Supreme Court held that a government agent may surreptitiously record a conversation with a criminal suspect and use the recording to corroborate his testimony. Lopez, a tavern keeper, offered a bribe to a federal tax agent who thereupon recorded the conversation. The Court refused to exclude the recording. Because the agent was on the premises with Lopez's consent, there was no TRESPASS and therefore no violation of the FOURTH AMENDMENT. Because the agent could testify to the conversation, he could use the recording to corroborate his testimony.

HERMAN SCHWARTZ

LORETTO v. TELEPROMPTER MANHATTAN CATV CORP.
458 U.S. 419 (1982)

The Supreme Court in the modern era has used an interest balancing analysis to determine whether government regulation amounts to a TAKING OF PROPERTY for which JUST COMPENSATION must be paid. Here a New York law required landlords to allow cable television companies to install equipment on the landlords' property in order to serve tenants. The Supreme Court, 6–3, held that this governmental authorization of a "permanent physical occupation" of property was, of itself, a "taking"; in such a case no interest balancing need be done.

KENNETH L. KARST

LOTTERY CASE

See: *Champion v. Ames*

LOUISIANA PURCHASE TREATY
(1803)

The Louisiana Purchase Treaty (April 30, 1803) provided for the cession of the French province of Louisiana to the United States for approximately $11,250,000. France had reacquired Louisiana from Spain as part of Napoleon's plan to reestablish a French empire in the New World. The United States had tolerated weak Spanish control at the mouth of the Mississippi, especially since the Pinckney Treaty of 1795 gave Americans the right to navigate the river and use the port of New Orleans; but Louisiana in the hands of Napoleonic France threatened the security, commerce, and growth of the country. President THOMAS JEFFERSON sought a diplomatic resolution, hoping to obtain from France at least the continuation of Spanish guarantees and, at best, the cession of New Orleans together with the Floridas, if France possessed them. In a surprising about-face, however, Napoleon renounced the whole of Louisiana.

The acquisition of Louisiana—some 828,000 square miles, virtually doubling the land area of the United States—challenged the government in several ways. First, the boundaries were obscure. Was Texas included? Or West Florida? Jefferson made pretensions to both. Article III of the treaty said that the inhabitants should be incorporated in the Union and enjoy all the rights of citizens of the United States. Unfortunately, the Constitution Jefferson and his party were pledged to construe strictly made no provision for acquiring foreign territory, much less admitting that territory and its people into the Union. The treaty, Jefferson declared, was "an act beyond the Constitution" and ought to be sanctioned retroactively by amendment. He drafted a 375-word amendment. When congressmen objected that Louisiana might be lost because of constitutional scruples, Jefferson acquiesced in silent expansion of the TREATY POWER even as he reiterated his belief that it made the Constitution "a blank paper by construction." (The Supreme Court, in AMERICAN INSURANCE COMPANY V. CANTER, 1828, later upheld the authority to acquire and govern territory under the treaty and WAR POWERS.) The Senate ratified the treaty on October 20, 1803. Two months later the American flag was raised at New Orleans.

Government of the territory also raised constitutional difficulties. The Enabling Act, in October, vested the President and his agents with full powers, civil and military. Querulous Federalists said it made Jefferson "as despotic as the Grand Turk." The Louisiana Government Act six months later created the Orleans Territory in populous lower Louisiana, extended to it many federal laws, and vested authority in a strong governor and weak legislative council, both appointed by the President. In the view of the President and Congress the rights of self-government, for which Creole Louisianans were unprepared, should be introduced gradually as the territory became "Americanized" in its population, habits, and institutions. The Louisianans demanded immediate statehood. Although this was denied, Congress in March 1805 introduced the second stage of territorial government, including a representative assembly, more or less on the plan of the NORTHWEST ORDINANCE. Five years later the statehood commitment of the treaty was met. The American theory of an expanding union of equal self-governing states thus survived its severest test.

MERRILL D. PETERSON

(SEE ALSO: *Theories of the Union.*)

Bibliography

BROWN, EVERETT S. 1920 *The Constitutional History of the Louisiana Purchase, 1803–1812.* Berkeley: University of California Press.

LOUISVILLE JOINT STOCK LAND BANK v. RADFORD
295 U.S. 555 (1935)

During the Great Depression of the 1930s foreclosure or default on payments threatened to extinguish the small, independent farmer who owned his own property. Congress, exercising its BANKRUPTCY POWER, came to his rescue by passing the FRAZIER-LEMKE (Farm Mortgage) ACT of 1934. The act provided that bankrupt farmers might require a federal bankruptcy court to stay farm mortgage payments for a period of five years, during which time the debtor retained possession of his property and paid his creditor a reasonable rental sum fixed by the court, and at the end of the five years the debtor could buy the property at its appraised value. Because the act operated retroactively it took away rights of the mortgagee, but the CONTRACT CLAUSE limits only the states, not Congress. In the face of that clause the Court had sustained a similar state act in HOME BUILDING & LOAN ASS'N v. BLAISDELL (1934). Nevertheless Justice LOUIS D. BRANDEIS, for a unanimous Court, ruled the act of Congress void. He distinguished *Blaisdell* as less drastic: the statute there had stayed proceedings for two, not five, years. In effect Brandeis read the contract clause into the Fifth Amendment's DUE PROCESS clause, holding that the bankruptcy power of Congress must be exercised subject to SUBSTANTIVE DUE PROCESS. The statute deprived persons of property without due process by not allowing the mortgagee to retain a lien on mortgaged property. The oddest feature of this strained opinion is that it did not mention due process; Brandeis referred only to the clause that prohibited the taking of private property for a public purpose without just compensation, though the government took nothing and sought by the statute to preserve private property. The Court retreated from its position in WRIGHT v. VINTON BRANCH BANK (1937).

LEONARD W. LEVY

LOUISVILLE, NEW ORLEANS & TEXAS PACIFIC RAILWAY v. MISSISSIPPI
133 U.S. 587 (1890)

A 7–2 Supreme Court held here that a state might lawfully require railroads to provide "equal but separate accommodations" without burdening INTERSTATE COMMERCE. The majority distinguished HALL v. DECUIR (1878) because the Louisiana Supreme Court had held in that case that the state act prohibiting SEGREGATION unlawfully regulated interstate commerce. Here, the Mississippi Supreme Court had said that the Mississippi statute applied solely to INTRASTATE COMMERCE. Moreover, this case did not involve a refusal of accommodations (as in *DeCuir*), so no question of "personal rights" arose. Justice JOHN MARSHALL HARLAN, dissenting, relied on *DeCuir.*

DAVID GORDON

LOVELL v. CITY OF GRIFFIN
303 U.S. 444 (1938)

A municipal ordinance prohibited the distribution of circulars or any other literature within Griffin without a permit from the city manager. Chief Justice CHARLES EVANS HUGHES, for a unanimous Court, held the Griffin ordinance unconstitutional. The ordinance provided no standards to guide the city manager's decision. To vest an official with absolute discretion to issue or deny a permit was an unconstitutional prior restraint that violated the FIRST AMENDMENT. Because the ordinance was INVALID ON ITS FACE, Lovell was entitled to distribute her literature without seeking a permit, and to challenge the ordinance's validity when she was charged with its violation.

RICHARD E. MORGAN

LOVETT, UNITED STATES v. 328 U.S. 303 (1946)

In an opinion by Justice HUGO L. BLACK the Court declared unconstitutional a rider to an appropriation act of 1943 which provided that no salary or other compensation could be paid after November 1943 to three specified employees of the executive branch who had been branded as "subversives" by the HOUSE COMMITTEE ON UN-AMERICAN ACTIVITIES. Congress, Black wrote, had passed a BILL OF ATTAINDER, prohibited by Article I, section 9.

Justices FELIX FRANKFURTER and STANLEY F. REED rejected Black's bill of attainder analysis; but both agreed that the employees were entitled to recover money for the value of services rendered to the government, even after Congress had refused to disburse money to pay their salaries.

MICHAEL E. PARRISH

LOVING v. VIRGINIA 388 U.S. 1 (1967)

For more than a decade following its decision in BROWN V. BOARD OF EDUCATION (1954) the Supreme Court avoided direct confrontation with the constitutionality of MISCEGENATION laws. In *Loving,* the Court faced the issue squarely and held invalid a Virginia law forbidding any interracial marriage including a white partner. The decision is a major precedent in the area of RACIAL DISCRIMINATION as well as the foundation of the modern "freedom to marry." (See MARRIAGE AND THE CONSTITUTION.)

A black woman and a white man, Virginia residents, went to the DISTRICT OF COLUMBIA to be married, and returned to live in Virginia. They were convicted of violating the Racial Integrity Act and given one-year prison sentences, suspended on condition that they leave Virginia. The Virginia appellate courts modified the sentences but upheld the constitutionality of the law. The Supreme Court unanimously reversed; Chief Justice EARL WARREN wrote for the Court.

Citing the SUSPECT CLASSIFICATION language of *Korematsu v. United States* (1944) (see JAPANESE AMERICAN CASES), Warren said that a "heavy burden of justification" must be carried by a state seeking to sustain any racial classification. The fact that the law punished both the white and black partners to a marriage did not relieve the state of that burden. The law's announced goal of "racial integrity" was promoted only selectively. A white was prohibited from marrying any nonwhite except the descendants of Pocahantas; a black and an Asian, for example, could lawfully marry. The law's obvious goal was the maintenance of white supremacy; it had no legitimate purpose independent of racial discrimination and thus violated the EQUAL PROTECTION clause. PACE V. ALABAMA (1883) was assumed to be overruled.

The Court's opinion also rested on an alternative ground: the statute violated SUBSTANTIVE DUE PROCESS, by interfering with "the freedom to marry." Quoting from the STERILIZATION case, SKINNER V. OKLAHOMA (1942), Chief Justice Warren called marriage "one of the 'basic civil rights of man,' fundamental to our very existence and survival." (See ZABLOCKI V. REDHAIL, 1978; FREEDOM OF INTIMATE ASSOCIATION.)

Justice POTTER STEWART, concurring, merely repeated his earlier statement in *McLaughlin v. Florida* (1964) that a state could never make an act's criminality depend on the race of the actor.

KENNETH L. KARST

LOYALTY OATH

A mild form of loyalty oath is embedded in the Constitution itself. The President must swear (or affirm): "that I will faithfully execute the office of President of the United States, and will to the best of my ability, preserve, protect and defend the constitution of the United States." And Article VI, in conjunction with the supremacy clause, requires that members of Congress, state legislators, and "all executive and judicial officers, both of the United States and of the several states, shall be bound by oath or affirmation, to support this constitution." These are usually called affirmative oaths, in contrast to negative oaths in which oath-takers are required to abjure certain beliefs, words, or acts. In their most searching form, negative oaths probe the past as well as the future.

In Article VI, the constitutional oath of support is immediately followed by the proscription of any religious test for holding office. Loyalty oaths, called test oaths, were rife in an age of warring faiths defended by princes. They tested orthodoxy of belief and thus loyalty to the sovereign. Henry VIII launched Anglo-American constitutional practice on a sea of oaths, whose chief purpose was to root out followers of the pope of Rome. The Stuart kings exacted oaths from the first settlers, and the settlers in turn invoked them against each other. When George Calvert, the Roman Catholic first Lord Baltimore, attempted to settle in Virginia, he was confronted with an oath that he could not take. He perforce made the hard voyage back to England; his successors got their own grant to what became Maryland and promptly imposed an oath pledging fidelity to themselves.

Wary though they became of oaths with a religious content, those who made our Revolution, as well as those who resisted it, routinely exacted political loyalty oaths from military and civilians under their control. When one occupying force displaced the other, it could become a matter of life and liberty to have one's name on the wrong roster. At the same time, there was room for claims of duress and duplicity. BENJAMIN FRANKLIN expressed with his usual pithiness what was doubtless a shared cynicism when he wrote in 1776: "I have never regarded oaths otherwise than as the last recourse of liars."

One might have thought that the Framers, with revolutionary excesses fresh in their memories, meant the constitutional oaths to be exclusive of any others; but when the Civil War came, loyalty oaths again became ubiquitous. In the Confederacy, oaths were linked to the passes routinely required for any travel. Of more gravity, taking an oath was often for captives and hostile civilians the only alternative to rotting in prison or starving. The multiplicity of oaths and the pressure to yield to them resulted in their becoming unreliable indicia of loyalty. Union authorities were impelled to create a bureaucracy to interrogate oath-takers, thus anticipating modern LOYALTY-SECURITY PROGRAMS.

President ABRAHAM LINCOLN favored relatively mild oaths pledging only future loyalty. The sterner Congress fashioned the "ironclad" test oath that required denials of past conduct that secessionists could not possibly make. Those oaths barred even repentant rebels from government and the professions. The Supreme Court plausibly characterized such oaths as legislative punishment, and declared them BILLS OF ATTAINDER, in the TEST OATH CASES (1867).

Little was heard of loyalty oaths in World War I. After that war, many states singled out teachers for loyalty oaths; but they were only affirmative oaths on the constitutional model, repugnant chiefly because of the mistrust implicit in demanding them.

The waves of anticommunist sentiment that subsided only during the World War II alliance with Russia led to a new proliferation of oaths that penalized membership in subversive organizations (sometimes specifying the Communist party) and advocacy or support of violent overthrow of governments.

All this came to a boil in the tormented Cold War-McCarthy era, when oaths old and new, state and federal, were combined with loyalty-security programs to purge communist influences from public employment and licensed occupations.

When oath cases came before the Court in the 1950s, it first sustained the constitutionality of elaborate oaths, requiring only that communist affiliations must be with knowledge of illegal ends (WIEMAN V. UPDEGRAFF, 1952), and suggesting that an employee must have an opportunity for an explanatory hearing (*Nostrand v. Little,* 1960). But in the 1960s, when the tide of public opinion turned against the excesses of the 1950s, the Court turned too. In half a dozen cases, of which the climactic one was KEYISHIAN V. BOARD OF REGENTS (1967), the Court found oaths that were barely distinguishable from those it had upheld in the 1950s to be void for vagueness or overbreadth. The majority opinions paraded an alarming catalog of possible dilemmas that teachers in particular could not escape and overwhelmed the expostulations of dissenters that the Court had created a "whimsical straw man" who was "not only grim but Grimm." For good measure, the Court, in UNITED STATES V. BROWN (1965), unsheathed the bill of attainder weapon of 1867 to strike down an oath that would exclude a former communist from any office in a labor union.

Such successes against negative oaths emboldened teachers and other public servants who resented having essentially affirmative oaths directed at them. But variants of the Article VI oath to support the Constitution were uniformly upheld. The capstone case was *Cole v. Richardson* (1972). There the Court, while reaffirming in generous FIRST AMENDMENT terms the 1960s cases, found no fault in an obligation first to support and defend the constitutions of the United States and the Commonwealth of Massachusetts and, second, to oppose their violent overthrow. The second clause, Chief Justice WARREN E. BURGER wrote, "does not expand the obligation of the first; it simply makes clear the application of the first clause to a particular issue. Such repetition, whether for emphasis or cadence, seems to be the wont of authors of oaths." He added in a footnote that "The time may come when the value of oaths in routine public employment will be thought not 'worth the candle' for all the division of opinion they engender." Justice THURGOOD MARSHALL, arguing in partial dissent that the second clause should be repudiated, reflected the persisting division between willing and unwilling oath-takers when he wrote, understatedly, that "Loyalty oaths do not have a very pleasant history in this country."

The fear that hellfire would follow a false oath must have faded since the seventeenth century. Nowadays public exposure, and a perjury prosecution, are the serious sanctions. Compulsory oath-taking is welcome to some, a matter of indifference to others, an offense to conscience for a few. A notable instance of a loyalty oath that hit the wrong targets occurred at the University of California in 1949–1952. When the university regents, after prolonged and wounding controversy, insisted on their power to impose a noncommunist oath, twenty-six members of the faculty refused to take it and were ejected. They won a pyrrhic victory in the California Supreme Court, which held that the regents' oath had been supplanted by an oath required of all state employees, but that the statewide oath somehow did not contravene a state constitutional prohibition of any test oath beyond the constitutional oath of support. Some of the nonsigners in time returned; one became president of the university and so did the historian of the episode, who called it "a futile interlude."

RALPH S. BROWN

Bibliography

GARDNER, DAVID P. 1967 *The California Oath Controversy.* Berkeley and Los Angeles: University of California Press.

HYMAN, HAROLD M. 1959 *To Try Men's Souls: Loyalty Tests in American History.* Berkeley and Los Angeles: University of California Press.

SAGER, ALAN M. 1972 The Impact of Supreme Court Loyalty Oath Decisions. *American University Law Review* 22:39–78.

LOYALTY-SECURITY PROGRAMS

This hyphenated phrase refers chiefly to the measures that were taken under Presidents HARRY S. TRUMAN and DWIGHT D. EISENHOWER to exclude from public employment, and from defense industries, persons who were believed to pose risks to national security. Because the gravest threat to security was believed to flow from world communism, loyalty and security programs were designed almost entirely to counter communist influence and penetration.

In earlier periods of tension attendant upon wars, LOYALTY OATHS were the preferred device for separating the loyal from the disloyal. If oaths were taken seriously, they were self-enforcing. But when necessity or duplicity led to bales of unreliable oaths, the authorities responded by empowering officials to go behind the oaths with investigations and to make their own judgments. Such procedures, usually under military control and untrammeled by judicial control, were widespread during the Civil War and Reconstruction.

World War I was distinguished by the overzealous prying of the American Protective League and other amateurs who were given extraordinary aid and comfort by the Department of Justice. In World War II the military departments, both determined to avoid the excesses of the crusade against the Kaiser, effectively centralized loyalty screening. They emerged with a minimum of criticism. After the war, the Soviet Union abruptly came to be viewed as enemy rather than ally. The insecurities of the postwar world aroused mistrust and anxiety. President Truman, aiming to forestall harsher congressional action, launched a new kind of program with his EXECUTIVE ORDER 9835 of March 21, 1947.

The Truman loyalty program covered all civilian employees. The Department of Defense had its own program for the armed services. Defense and the Atomic Energy Commission had programs for employees of defense contractors. The Coast Guard screened maritime workers. A few states developed systematic programs of their own. Many millions thus became subject to proceedings that sought to establish whether, in the language of E.O. 9835, there were "reasonable grounds" for a belief that they were disloyal (softened in 1951 to require only a finding of "reasonable doubt" as to loyalty). In 1953 President Eisenhower's Executive Order 10450 replaced the Truman program. It required employment to be "clearly consistent with the interests of the national security." That standard remains in effect.

All of these programs worked from personal histories supplied by the employee (or applicant) backed up by investigative reports. If "derogatory information" led to a tentative adverse judgment, that was usually the end for an applicant's chances of employment. But an incumbent could have the benefit of formal charges, a hearing, and review. The trouble was that the investigations ranged widely into associations, opinions, and flimsy appraisals. The sources of none of these were accessible to the employee. He could only guess who his detractors were.

These programs were only one array in the frantic

mobilization against subversion. They were flanked by oaths and affidavits and questionnaires. To falsify any of these was a criminal offense. In order to establish what associations were forbidden, the 1947 executive order systematized the secret preparation and open use of the ATTORNEY GENERAL'S LIST of Subversive Organizations. Long before and for some years after the heyday of Senator JOSEPH R. MCCARTHY (1950–1954), congressional investigating committees took as their specialty the exposure of groups and individuals with communist ties. Their disclosures encouraged blacklists in private employment, notoriously in films and broadcasting. Senator McCarthy took the lead in stigmatizing the "Fifth-Amendment Communist"—a witness who invoked the RIGHT AGAINST SELF-INCRIMINATION. Senator Patrick A. McCarran initiated the idea that naming names was the only true badge of repentance for those who said they were no longer communists. A mass of legislation sought to expose and condemn the Communist party and its affiliates, while the Department of Justice jailed its leaders for sedition.

All of these measures raised intertwining constitutional problems, so those of loyalty-security programs are not easily isolated. However, two strands can be picked out. First, there were demands for fair process, notably to confront the source of accusations. Second, there were claims for First Amendment rights, set against the supposed necessities of national security. However, the courts often trimmed the reach of the programs without deciding such issues. They would invoke their usual preference for avoiding constitutional collisions, and simply find that executive or legislative authority was lacking.

The position that DUE PROCESS OF LAW was wanting in the rules and administration of employment tests first had to surmount the proposition that employment was not a right but only a privilege that could be summarily withheld. First Amendment claims also encountered this barrier, curtly expressed in Justice OLIVER WENDELL HOLMES'S now battered epigram: "The petitioner may have a constitutional right to talk politics, but he has no constitutional right to be a policeman." After some early hesitation, this dismissive argument was itself dismissed, notably by Justice TOM C. CLARK, who was usually a steadfast supporter of security measures. In an oath case, WIEMAN V. UPDEGRAFF (1952), he wrote for the Court: "We need not pause to consider whether an abstract right to public employment exists. It is sufficient to say that constitutional protection does extend to the public servant whose exclusion . . . is patently arbitrary or discriminatory."

What process is then due? The government perennially opposes the right of confrontation by invoking the need to protect confidential informants. The court came close to requiring a trial-type hearing, with confrontation and cross-examination, in the industrial security case of *Greene v. McElroy* (1959). But it used the avoidance technique. It said that there would have to be, at the threshold, explicit authorization from the President or Congress to conceal sources, and that it could not find such authorization. The decision had little effect. The statute authorizing security removals of government employees still requires only that charges "be stated as specifically as security considerations permit." It is doubtful that, in a time of perceived crisis, and in sensitive employment, the Constitution would be read to compel confrontation.

The Court worked its way to a firmer position on narrowing grounds for removal. It found that First Amendment rights to freedom of association were impaired by a flat proscription of employing communists in a "defense facility." In UNITED STATES V. ROBEL (1967) the employee, a shipyard worker, was an avowed Communist party member. A majority of the Court, declaring that "the statute quite literally establishes guilt by association alone," held that some less restrictive means would have to be employed to guard against disruption or sabotage. If *Robel* and like cases are followed where charges of disloyalty are brought, and where the accusation stems from political associations, the government may be unable to remove an employee except for conduct that would support a criminal prosecution.

This does not mean an end to the reliance on prying and gossiping that made loyalty-security programs disreputable. In satisfying itself of the reliability of applicants for employment, the government (or a private employer) can still probe for flaws of character, so long as standards for expulsion do not invade areas protected by the First Amendment or by ANTIDISCRIMINATION LEGISLATION. Investigators may even demand answers to questions, for example, on communist connections, that come close to protected zones, as long as the ultimate standards are correct, and the questions are helpful in seeing that the standards are satisfied. This seems to be the upshot of a tortuous line of cases involving admission to the practice of law.

From these unavoidable clashes between individual rights and security claims, a remarkable course of events has followed. Once the fevers of the 1950s had subsided, loyalty-security programs simply shrank to very modest levels. It is noteworthy that the VIETNAM WAR did not check the decline. Yet the KOREAN

WAR, which broke out in 1950, undoubtedly deepened the fears of that era.

The contraction has been helped along by the courts. Congress and the executive have perhaps done more to limit the scale at which the federal programs have been operating (the last dismissal on loyalty grounds was in 1968). The PRIVACY ACT of 1974 and similar statutes greatly restricted the flow of official information about misbehavior. President RICHARD M. NIXON abolished the Attorney General's List in the same year. Nudged by lower court decisions, the Civil Service Commission first stopped asking applicants for nonsensitive positions about subversive associations, and then in 1977 scrapped the questions for sensitive jobs too. Appropriations for investigative staff both in the Federal Bureau of Investigation and in the Defense Department have declined.

Do recent developments represent a slackening of our defenses? A revulsion against the excesses of McCarthyism? Because the prime mover in all the loyalty-security programs was hostility to communism, the programs may revive if our relations with the Soviet Union worsen. If the programs do revive, it seems unlikely that the courts will check recurrence of past excesses.

RALPH S. BROWN

Bibliography

BROWN, RALPH S. 1958 *Loyalty and Security: Employment Tests in the United States.* New Haven, Conn.: Yale University Press.

CAUTE, DAVID 1978 *The Great Fear: The Anti-Communist Purge under Truman and Eisenhower.* New York: Simon & Schuster.

DEVELOPMENTS IN THE LAW 1972 The National Security Interest and Civil Liberties. *Harvard Law Review* 85:1130–1326.

LEWY, GUENTER 1983 *The Federal Loyalty-Security Program: The Need for Reform.* Washington and London: American Enterprise Institute.

LUCAS v. 44TH GENERAL ASSEMBLY OF COLORADO

See: *Reynolds v. Sims*

LURTON, HORACE H.
(1844–1914)

President WILLIAM HOWARD TAFT's nomination of his close friend and former colleague, Horace Lurton, to replace Justice RUFUS PECKHAM in December 1909 engendered some skepticism. A Confederate veteran of the Civil War, Lurton was sixty-six and a pronounced conservative. He was, however, known as a patient and gentle man who sought compromise, and his experience clearly fitted him for the office. Lurton had sat on the Tennessee Supreme Court and the Sixth Circuit Court of Appeals (with Taft and WILLIAM R. DAY) and had also taught constitutional law and served as dean of the Law School at Vanderbilt University.

Lurton did not write many majority opinions during his tenure on the Supreme Court. He was usually among a silent majority voting in favor of government authority to sustain, for example, the NATIONAL POLICE POWER (*e.g.,* HOKE V. UNITED STATES, 1913) and the SHERMAN ANTITRUST ACT (STANDARD OIL COMPANY V. UNITED STATES, 1911); he dissented without opinion in HOUSTON, EAST & WEST TEXAS RAILWAY CO. V. UNITED STATES (1914). Most of his opinions dealt with procedural technicalities or the intricacies of employer liability laws.

One of the more frequent, though hardly regular, dissenters, Lurton was often in a minority with Justice OLIVER WENDELL HOLMES. Lurton's particular regard for precedent prompted extensive research to uncover those cases that would justify apparently inconsistent stances.

Shortly after his fourth term of court, in June 1914, Lurton died. His belief in law as the cement of society had led him to oppose JUDICIAL ACTIVISM, particularly when "a valid law, under the Constitution, is to be interpreted or modified so as to accomplish . . . [what a court] shall deem to the public advantage." Despite Lurton's prior experience, his career as a Justice provided little evidence of distinguished achievement.

DAVID GORDON

Bibliography

WATTS, JAMES F., JR. 1969 Horace H. Lurton. In Leon Friedman and Fred L. Israel, eds., *The Justices of the United States Supreme Court, 1789–1969.* New York: Chelsea House.

LUTHER v. BORDEN
7 Howard (48 U.S.) 1 (1849)

In *Luther v. Borden,* a case arising from the aftermath of the Dorr Rebellion (1842), Chief Justice ROGER B. TANEY enunciated the DOCTRINE of POLITICAL QUESTIONS and provided the first judicial exposition of the clause of the Constitution guaranteeing REPUBLI-

CAN FORMS OF GOVERNMENT (Article IV, section 4).

Though Rhode Island was in the forefront of the Industrial Revolution, its constitutional system, derived from the royal charter of 1663 (which was retained with slight modifications as the state's organic act after the Revolution), was an archaic and peculiar blend of democratic and regressive features. Malapportionment and disfranchisement grew intolerably severe as the industrial cities and mill villages filled with propertyless native and immigrant workers. (Perhaps as many as ninety percent of the adult males of Providence were voteless in 1840.) Reform efforts through the 1820s and 1830s were unsuccessful. In 1841–1842, suffragist reformers adopted more radical tactics derived from the theory of the DECLARATION OF INDEPENDENCE, asserting that the people had a right to reform or replace their government, outside the forms of law if need be. They therefore drafted a new state constitution (the "People's Constitution") and submitted it to ratification by a vote open to all adult white male citizens of the state. The regular government, meanwhile, also submitted a revised constitution (the "Freeholders' Constitution") to ratification, but only by those entitled to vote under the Charter. The people's Constitution was ratified, the Freeholders' rejected. Reform leaders then organized elections for a new state government, in which Thomas Wilson Dorr was elected governor. The two governments organized, each claiming exclusive legitimacy. The Freeholders' government declared martial law and, with the tacit support of President John Tyler, used state militia to suppress the Dorrites in an almost bloodless confrontation. It then submitted another revised constitution, ratified in late 1842, that alleviated the problems arising under the Charter.

Dorrites dissatisfied with this outcome created a TEST CASE from an incident of militia harassment and requested the Supreme Court to determine that the Freeholders' government and the subsequent 1842 constitution were illegitimate, on the grounds that the Freeholders' government was not republican and that the people of the state had a right to replace it, without legal sanction if necessary. Taney, for a unanimous Court (Justice LEVI WOODBURY dissenting in part on a martial law point), declined to issue any such ruling. After noting the insuperable practical difficulties of declaring the previous seven years of Rhode Island's government illegitimate, Taney stated that "the courts uniformly held that the inquiry proposed to be made belonged to the political power and not to the judicial." He went on to explain that Dorrite contentions "turned upon political rights and political questions, upon which the court has been urged to express an opinion. We decline doing so." Taney thus amplified a distinction, earlier suggested by Chief Justice JOHN MARSHALL, between judicial questions (which a court can resolve), and political ones, which can be resolved only by the political branches of government (executive and legislative).

Taney further held that the GUARANTEE CLAUSE committed the question of the legitimacy of a state government to Congress for resolution, and that Congress's decision was binding on the courts, a point later reiterated by Chief Justice SALMON P. CHASE in cases involving the legitimacy of congressional Reconstruction policies. Taney concluded his opinion with an empty concession to the political theory of the Dorrites: "No one, we believe, has ever doubted the proposition that, according to the institutions of this country, the SOVEREIGNTY in every State resides in the people of the State, and that they may alter and change their form of government at their pleasure. But whether they have changed it or not," Taney repeated, "is a question to be settled by the political power," not the courts.

Though the political question doctrine thereby created has never been explained by a definitive rationale, it has proved useful in enabling the courts to avoid involvement in controversies that are not justiciable, that is, not suitable for resolution by judges. (See BAKER V. CARR, 1962.)

WILLIAM M. WIECEK

LYNCH v. DONNELLY
465 U.S. 668 (1984)

The Supreme Court significantly lowered the wall of SEPARATION OF CHURCH AND STATE by sanctioning an official display of a sacred Christian symbol. Pawtucket, Rhode Island, included a crèche, or nativity scene, in its annual Christmas exhibit in the center of the city's shopping district. The case raised the question whether Pawtucket's crèche violated the Constitution's prohibition of ESTABLISHMENT OF RELIGION.

Chief Justice WARREN BURGER for a 5–4 Court ruled that despite the religious nature of the crèche, Pawtucket had a secular purpose in displaying it, as evinced by the fact that it was part of a Christmas exhibit that proclaimed "Season's Greetings" and included Santa Claus, his reindeer, a Christmas tree, and figures of carolers, a clown, an elephant, and a teddy bear. That the FIRST AMENDMENT, Burger argued, did not mandate complete separation is shown by our national motto, paid chaplains, presidential proclamations invoking God, the pledge of allegiance, and religious art in publicly supported museums.

Justice WILLIAM BRENNAN, dissenting, construed Burger's majority opinion narrowly, observing that the question was still open on the constitutionality of a public display on public property of a crèche alone or of the display of some other sacred symbol, such as a crucifixion scene. Brennan repudiated the supposed secular character of the crèche; he argued that "[f]or Christians the essential message of the nativity is that God became incarnate in the person of Christ." The majority's insensitivity toward the feelings of non-Christians disturbed Brennan.

A spokesman for the National Council of Churches complained that the Court had put Christ "on the same level as Santa Claus and Rudolph the Red-Nosed Reindeer." Clearly, the Court had a topsy-turvy understanding of what constitutes an establishment of religion, because in LARKIN V. GRENDEL'S DEN (1982) it saw a forbidden establishment in a STATE POLICE POWER measure aimed at keeping boisterous patrons of a tavern from disturbing a church, yet here saw no establishment in a state-sponsored crèche.

LEONARD W. LEVY

MACDONALD, UNITED STATES v. 456 U.S. 1 (1982)

Chief Justice WARREN E. BURGER for a 6–3 Supreme Court reaffirmed that the protection of the SPEEDY TRIAL provision of the Sixth Amendment does not extend to the period before a defendant is officially accused of the crime and ceases once charges are dismissed. Thus, the period between dismissal of military charges and indictment later in a civil court could not be considered in determining whether delay violated the right to a speedy trial. Dissenters disagreed with the majority's reasoning that the interests served by the right to a speedy trial stood in no jeopardy before accusation or after dismissal of charges.

LEONARD W. LEVY

MACON, NATHANIEL (1757–1837)

Nathaniel Macon, a North Carolina planter, opposed RATIFICATION OF THE CONSTITUTION because he thought the new government too powerful. Joining THOMAS JEFFERSON's Republican party, Macon was elected to Congress in 1791; with his party he opposed ALEXANDER HAMILTON's economic policies and the ALIEN AND SEDITION ACTS. As speaker (1801–1807), Macon, with his deputy, JOHN RANDOLPH, firmly guided the House of Representatives along administration lines. Although he briefly broke with Jefferson (1807–1809), he supported the unpopular EMBARGO ACTS. In the House (1791–1815) and later in the Senate (1815–1826), Macon was a spokesman for STATES' RIGHTS, STRICT CONSTRUCTION, and individual liberty.

DENNIS J. MAHONEY

MADDEN v. KENTUCKY 309 U.S. 83 (1940)

A Kentucky statute taxing bank deposits outside the state at a rate five times higher than the tax on intrastate deposits was assailed as breaching several clauses of section one of the FOURTEENTH AMENDMENT. By a 7–2 vote the Supreme Court, speaking through Justice STANLEY F. REED, declared that the states have broad discretion in their tax policies. Reed dismissed the arguments against the statute based on the EQUAL PROTECTION and DUE PROCESS clauses as insubstantial, but the decision in COLGATE V. HARVEY (1935) supported the argument based on the PRIVILEGES AND IMMUNITIES clause. On reconsideration the Court found that lending or depositing money is not a privilege of national CITIZENSHIP and therefore overruled *Colgate.*

LEONARD W. LEVY

MADISON, JAMES (1751–1836)

James Madison, "the father of the Constitution," matured with the American Revolution. Educated at a boarding school and at patriotic Princeton, he returned to the family plantation in Virginia at age twenty-one, two years before the infamous Coercive Acts. As Orange County mobilized behind the recommendations of the CONTINENTAL CONGRESS, he joined his father on the committee of safety, practiced with a rifle, and drilled with the local militia company. As he wrote much later, in a sketch of an autobiography, "he was under very early and strong impressions in favor of liberty both civil and religious."

Civil and religious liberty were intimately linked in Madison's career and thinking. His early revolutionary ardor is the necessary starting point for understanding his distinctive role among the Founders. The young man first involved himself in local politics, in 1774, to raise his voice against the persecution of dissenters in neighboring Virginia counties. When feeble health compelled him to abandon thoughts of active military service, the gratitude of Baptist neighbors may have helped him win election to the state convention of 1776, which framed one of the earliest, most widely imitated revolutionary constitutions. (See VIRGINIA CONSTITUTION AND DECLARATION OF RIGHTS.) It seems appropriate that Madison's first major office should have been in this convention, his first important act to prepare amendatory language that significantly broadened the definition of freedom of conscience in the Virginia Declaration of Rights. The American Revolution, as he understood it, was a grand experiment, of world-historical significance, in the creation and vindication of governments that would combine majority control with individual freedom, popular self-government with security for the private rights of all. Through more than forty years of active public service, he was at the center of the country's search for a structure and practice of government that would secure both sorts of freedom. His conviction that democracy and individual liberty are mutually dependent—and, increasingly, that neither would survive disintegration of the continental Union—guided his distinctive contributions to the writing and interpretation of the Constitution.

Defeated in his bid for reelection to the state assembly—he refused to offer the customary treats to voters—the promising young Madison was soon selected by the legislature as a member of the Council of State. Two years later, in December 1779, the legislature chose him as a delegate to Congress. Here he gradually acquired a national reputation. He was instrumental in the management of Virginia's western cession, which prepared the way for ratification of the ARTICLES OF CONFEDERATION and creation of a national domain. He introduced the compromise that resulted in the congressional recommendations of April 18, 1783, calling on the states to approve an amendment to the Articles granting Congress power to impose a five percent duty on foreign imports, to complete their western cessions, and to levy other taxes sufficient to provide for the continental debt. He learned that the confederation government's dependence on the states for revenues and for enforcement of its acts and treaties rendered it unable to perform its duties and endangered its very existence.

Reentering Virginia's legislature when his term in Congress ended, Madison became increasingly convinced that liberty in individual states depended on the Union that protected them from foreign intervention and from the wars and rivalries that had fractured Europe and condemned its peoples to oppressive taxes, swollen military forces, and the rule of executive tyrants. In 1786, as he prepared for the Annapolis Convention, Northerners and Southerners clashed bitterly in Congress over the negotiation of a commercial treaty with Spain. When Madison and other delegates decided to propose the meeting of a general convention to revise the Articles of Confederation, they acted in a context of profound, immediate concern for the survival of the Union.

By 1786, however, Madison no longer hoped that a revision of the Articles might reinvigorate the general government, nor was he worried solely by the peril of disunion. In all the states popular assemblies struggled to protect their citizens from economic troubles. Although Virginia managed to avoid the worst abuses, Madison thought continentally. Correspondents warned him of a growing disillusionment with popular misgovernment, particularly in New England, where SHAYS' REBELLION erupted in the winter of 1786. Virginia's own immunity from popular commotions or majority misrule appeared to him in doubt. He had not been able to achieve revision of the revolutionary constitution and had often suffered agonizing losses when he urged support for federal measures or important state reforms. In 1785, in his opinion, only the presence of a multitude of disagreeing sects had blocked the passage of a bill providing tax support for teachers of the Christian religion, which would have been a major blow to freedom of conscience and an egregious violation of the constitution. Personally disgusted by the changeability, injustices, and lack of foresight of even Virginia's laws, Madison feared that the revulsion with democracy, confined thus far to only a tiny (though an influential) few, could spread in time through growing numbers of the people. The crisis of confederation government, as he conceived it, was compounded by a crisis of republican convictions. Either could reverse the Revolution. Neither could be overcome by minor alterations of the Articles of Confederation. To save the Revolution, he wrote to EDMUND PENDLETON, constitutional reform must both "perpetuate the union and redeem the honor of the republican name."

No one played a more important part than Madison in bringing on the CONSTITUTIONAL CONVENTION OF 1787, turning its attention to a sweeping transformation of the federal system, or achieving national approval of its work. Returning from Annapolis, he won Virginia's quick consent to a general convention, wrote the resolutions signaling the Old Dominion's serious commitment to the project, and helped persuade GEORGE WASHINGTON to lead a delegation whose distinguished quality encouraged other states to call upon their best. Reeligible at last, he rushed from Richmond to New York, reentered the Confederation Congress, and worked successfully for measures that significantly improved the prospects for a full, successful meeting. He researched the histories and structures of other ancient and modern confederations and somehow found the time to write a formal memorandum on the "Vices of the Political System of the United States," in which he argued that the mortal ills of the confederation government and the concurrent crisis in the states alike demanded the abandonment of the Articles of Confederation and the creation of a carefully constructed national republic. In Madison's vision, the republic would rise directly from the people; would possess effective, full, and independent powers over matters of general concern; and would incorporate so many different economic interests and religious sects that majorities would seldom form "on any other principles than those of justice and the general good." Urging other members of Virginia's delegation to arrive in Philadelphia in time to frame some general propositions with which the meeting might begin, he reached the city himself the best prepared of all who gathered for the Constitutional Convention.

Madison made several distinctive contributions to the writing of the Constitution. He was primarily responsible for the VIRGINIA PLAN: the resolutions that initiated the Convention's thorough reconstruction of the federal system and served throughout the summer as the outline for reform. In the early weeks of the deliberations, he persuasively explained why no reform could prove effective if it left the general government dependent on the states. Together with JAMES WILSON, he led the delegates who insisted on proportional representation, popular ratification of the fundamental charter, and a careful balance of authority between a democratic House of Representatives and branches more resistant to ill-considered popular demands. He also urged his fellows not to limit their attention to the weaknesses of the confederation, but to come to terms as well with the vices of democratic government in the states. Constitutional reform, he argued, must also overcome the crisis of republican convictions, both by placing limitations on the states and by creating a greater republic free from the structural errors of the local constitutions. With the latter plea particularly, he opened members' minds to a complete rethinking of the problems of democracy and to the possibility that liberty and popular control might both be safest in a large republic. Although the finished Constitution differed in a number of significant respects from his original proposals, Madison was, by general agreement of historians and his colleagues, the most important of the Framers.

All of which was only part of his enormous contribution to the Constitution's great success. Before departing for Virginia, where he led the Federalists to victory in a close and capably contested state convention, Madison reassumed his seat in the Confederation Congress, helped provide some central guidance for the ratification struggle, and joined with ALEXANDER HAMILTON to write the most important explanation and defense of the completed Constitution. His numbers of THE FEDERALIST, perhaps the greatest classic in the history of American political writing, rationalized the compromises made in the Convention, rendered the document intelligible in terms of democratic theory, and thus contributed as surely to the shaping of the Constitution as the work of the preceding summer. Since early in the nineteenth century, these essays have been recognized as an essential source for understanding the intentions of the Framers, and Madison's essential theme—that the Convention's work was perfectly consistent with the principles of the Revolution, a genuinely democratic remedy for the diseases most destructive to democracy—was still but the beginning of his effort to interpret and insure the triumph of the finished plan.

The reconstructed federal government initiated operations in April 1789. Madison immediately assumed the leading role in the first Congress, which was responsible for filling in the outline of the Constitution as well as for the national legislation it had been created to permit. He drafted parts of Washington's inaugural address, prepared the House of Representatives' reply, and helped defeat proposals to address the President as "highness"—important contributions to the early effort to define the protocol between the branches and to set a democratic tone for the infant regime. He initiated the deliberations that resulted in the first federal tariff and assured a steady source of independent federal revenues. He seized the lead again in the creation of executive departments, successfully insisting that the concept of responsibility required a presidential power to remove executive officials without the consent of Congress. Finally, he took upon himself the principal responsibility for preparing the constitutional amendments that became the BILL OF RIGHTS.

Early in the contest over RATIFICATION OF THE CONSTITUTION, Madison had denied the need for such amendments. He argued that the federal government had not been granted any powers that might threaten the liberties protected in the declarations of the states, and he warned that any effort to prepare a federal bill might actually endanger rights it was intended to preserve: an inadvertent error or omission could become the basis for a claim of positive authority to act. This very train of reasoning, however, suggests why he was open to a change of mind and offers some important clues to understanding his political and constitutional position in the years after 1789.

Throughout the course of constitutional reform, Madison had insisted no less strongly on the need for an effective central government than on a governmental structure that would guarantee the continuing responsibility of rulers to the ruled, along with a considerable residual autonomy for the people in their several states. Even as he worried over the excesses of majorities, he reminded correspondents of the perils posed by rulers who escaped a due dependence on the people; and even as he warned the Constitutional Convention not to leave the general government dependent on the states, he recognized the danger of excessive concentration of authority in federal hands. His contributions to *The Federalist* describe the new regime as neither wholly national nor purely federal in nature, but as a novel, complicated mixture under which concurrent state and central governments, each possessed of only limited authority, would each perform the duties for which they were best equipped and would both resist disturbance of a federal equilibrium that offered new protection for the people. During the ratification contest, Madison was forced to promise that amendments would be added once the Constitution was approved. He realized how useful this could be in reconciling skeptics to the system. But he was also predisposed to be receptive when THOMAS JEFFERSON insisted that a bill of rights would be a valuable, additional security for the liberties and powers that the states and people had intended to reserve.

Among the most consistent themes of Madison's career was his profound respect for FUNDAMENTAL LAW. Written constitutions, in his view, were solemn compacts which created governments and granted them the only powers they legitimately possessed. Rulers guilty of transcending them, he had written in his 1785 MEMORIAL AND REMONSTRANCE against religious assessments, were "Tyrants," those who submitted "slaves." And usurpations of this sort, he added, ought to be resisted on their first appearance, as they had been early in the Revolution, before they could be strengthened by repeated exercise and "entangle the question in precedents." This scrupulous regard for fundamental charters encouraged Madison to change his mind about a bill of rights and shaped his conduct throughout the rest of his career.

Early in Washington's administration, Madison became alarmed about the sectional inequities and other consequences of Hamilton's political economy. He broke with Hamilton entirely when the secretary of the treasury proposed the creation of a national bank, protesting that the Constitution granted Congress no explicit power to charter such a corporation and that a doctrine of IMPLIED POWERS, justifying federal measures by a BROAD CONSTRUCTION of the general clauses, could completely change the character and spirit of a limited, federal system. During the 1790s, as Madison and Jefferson concluded that Hamilton and his supporters were deliberately attempting to subvert the Revolution—to concentrate all power in the general government and most of that in its executive departments—their insistence on a strict construction of the Constitution and a compact theory of its origins became an organizing theme of the Democratic-Republican opposition. Madison's Virginia Resolutions of 1798, part of a larger effort to arouse the states against the ALIEN AND SEDITION ACTS, which the Republicans regarded as a flagrant violation of the FIRST AMENDMENT, identified a Hamiltonian construction of the Constitution as a central feature of a Federalist conspiracy to sweep away all limitations on the exercise of federal power. Madison's great Report of 1800, explaining and defending the resolutions of 1798 against objections from other states, still stands as a striking landmark in the evolution of a modern, literalist interpretation of the First Amendment. In opposition to prevailing understandings that FREEDOM OF THE PRESS afforded guarantees against PRIOR RESTRAINT AND CENSORSHIP, but did not protect a publisher or author from criminal responsibility for statements tending to bring the government or its officers into disrepute, Madison insisted that the federal government was "destitute" of all authority whatever to interfere with the free development and circulation of opinion. In passages with major implications for the future, he denied that a FEDERAL COMMON LAW OF CRIMES had ever operated and suggested that the essence of elective governments was inconsistent with even STATE ACTION to restrain "that right of freely examining public characters and measures and of free communication of the people thereon, which has ever been justly deemed the only effectual guardian of every other right."

In its constitutional dimensions, the Jeffersonian "Revolution of 1800" was intended by its leaders to restore the threatened federal balance and return the general government to the role and limits originally intended by the people. As Jefferson's secretary of state, principal lieutenant, and eventual successor, Madison continued to believe that governmental actions should "conform to the constitution as understood by the Convention that produced and recommended it, and particularly by the state conventions that *adopted* it." He conceded that there were occasions that might justify or even command departures from the letter of the Constitution. He defended the LOUISIANA PURCHASE on these grounds, suggesting that a power to acquire new TERRITORIES was inherent in the concept of a sovereign nation. As President, he acted on the basis of implied executive authority in ordering the occupation of West Florida. He even came to recommend rechartering a national bank, maintaining that repeated acts of every part of government, repeatedly approved of by the nation, had overruled his earlier opinion of the institution's unconstitutionality. In his final days in office, nevertheless, he vetoed a bill providing federal support for INTERNAL IMPROVEMENTS. Although he favored federal action, he insisted on a constitutional amendment in advance. He still believed, as he had written in his "Letters of Helvidius" in 1793, that "a people who are so happy as to possess the inestimable blessing of a free and defined constitution cannot be too watchful against the introduction nor too critical in tracing the consequences of new principles and new constructions that may remove the landmarks of power."

Madison's regard for fundamental law is not to be confused with a minimalist conception of the constitutional scope of federal powers. He recommended the creation of a national university, although the Constitution delegated no explicit power to erect one. He believed that the Constitution granted Congress plenary authority over commerce, not merely ample power to impose a protective tariff but power even to require a temporary end to foreign trade as in the complete embargo or the various non-intercourse experiments preceding the War of 1812. He was as willing to defend the powers plainly granted to the federal government—over state militias, for example—as he was to guard the liberties protected by the Bill of Rights. Nevertheless, his leadership as President was characterized by deep respect for both the letter and the spirit of the federal compact. If he was diffident in leading Congress into proper preparations for a war, his serious regard for legislative independence was as much at fault as personality or circumstances. If he forbore perhaps too much in the face of flagrantly seditious opposition to the war, this forbearance was not for want of an imaginable alternative. ABRAHAM LINCOLN claimed the powers needed for a greater crisis. Madison deliberately attempted to conduct the War of 1812 at minimal expense to the republican and federal nature of the country. It was at once his weakness and his glory.

The father of the Constitution outlived all the other signers, becoming in his final years a rather troubled, though revered, authority on the creation and construction of the federal charter. The source of his discomfort was his own insistence that the Constitution was a compact among the sovereign peoples of the several states, who remained the only power competent to alter it or to deliver a definitive decision on its meaning. The great Virginian repeatedly denied that this interpretation justified the developing southern doctrine of state INTERPOSITION and NULLIFICATION. He had, in fact, warned Jefferson in 1798 against confusing the constituent authority of the peoples of the states with the powers of an individual state government. Yet neither was he willing to permit the federal courts a power of interpretation that would make the general government the final or exclusive judge in its own cause (or even to concede the courts the power to override the constitutional opinions of the executive and legislative branches). Trapped between his love of Union and his fear of grasping power, he was never able, never willing, to identify an agency or a procedure that, in case of a collision of conflicting understandings of the Constitution, could prevent a revolutionary recourse to the sovereign people. But, then, James Madison was Revolution's child. Admitting that the best constructed government could not secure a nation's liberty if it were not supported by a proper public spirit, he trusted to the end that mutual conciliation and restraint would prove sufficient to preserve the Union he had done so much to shape.

LANCE BANNING

Bibliography

BANNING, LANCE 1984 "The Hamiltonian Madison: A Reconsideration." *Virginia Magazine of History and Biography* 92:3–28.

BRANT, IRVING 1941–1961 *James Madison.* 6 Vols. Indianapolis: Bobbs-Merrill.

KETCHAM, RALPH 1971 *James Madison: A Biography.* New York: Macmillan.

MCCOY, DREW R. 1980 *The Elusive Republic: Political Economy in Jeffersonian America.* Chapel Hill: University of North Carolina Press.

WOOD, GORDON S. 1969 *The Creation of the American Republic, 1776–1789.* Chapel Hill: University of North Carolina Press.

MADISON'S "MEMORIAL AND REMONSTRANCE" (1785)

This remonstrance is the best evidence of what JAMES MADISON, the framer of the FIRST AMENDMENT, meant by an ESTABLISHMENT OF RELIGION. In 1784 the Virginia legislature had proposed a bill that benefited "Teachers of the Christian Religion" by assessing a small tax on property owners. Each taxpayer could designate the Christian church of his choice as the recipient of his tax money; the bill allowed non-church members to earmark their taxes for the support of local schools, and it upheld the "liberal principle" that all Christian sects and denominations were equal under the law, none preferred over others. The bill did not speak of the "established religion" of the state as had an aborted bill of 1779, and it purported to be based on only secular considerations, the promotion of the public peace and morality rather than Christ's kingdom on earth. Madison denounced the bill as an establishment of religion, no less dangerous to RELIGIOUS LIBERTY than the proposal of 1779 and differing "only in degree" from the Inquisition.

In an elaborate argument of fifteen parts, Madison advocated a complete SEPARATION OF CHURCH AND STATE as the only guarantee of the equal right of every citizen to the free exercise of religion, including the freedom of those "whose minds have not yet yielded to the evidence which has convinced us." He regarded the right to support religion as an "unalienable" individual right to be exercised only on a voluntary basis. Religion, he contended, must be exempt from the power of society, the legislature, and the magistrate. In his trenchant assault on establishments including the one proposed by this mild bill—"it is proper to take alarm at the first experiment on our liberties"—and in his eloquent defense of separation, Madison stressed the point that separation benefited not only personal freedom but also the free state and even religion itself. His remonstrance, which circulated throughout Virginia in the summer of 1785, actually redirected public opinion, resulting in the election of legislators who opposed the bill, which had previously passed a second reading. Madison then introduced THOMAS JEFFERSON's proposal which was enacted into law as the VIRGINIA STATUTE OF RELIGIOUS FREEDOM.

LEONARD W. LEVY

Bibliography

BRANT, IRVING 1948 *James Madison, Nationalist 1780–1787.* Pages 343–355. Indianapolis: Bobbs-Merrill.

MADISON'S *NOTES OF THE DEBATES*

In the oral arguments in OGDEN V. SAUNDERS (1824), a lawyer wondered what the intentions were of those who framed the Constitution when they included the CONTRACT CLAUSE. "Unhappily for this country and for the general interest of political science," he added, "the history of the Convention of 1787 which framed the Constitution of the United States is lost to the world." It was not lost, but no one who was not an intimate of JAMES MADISON knew that. Incredibly, JOHN MARSHALL wrote his great opinions on constitutional law and JOSEPH STORY wrote his *Commentaries on the Constitution* (1833) without knowing that Madison had in his possession his elaborate manuscript record of the CONSTITUTIONAL CONVENTION.

The Father of the Constitution not only wielded the greatest influence on its formation at the Convention, where he delivered over 200 speeches, but he also kept a record of the debates for nearly four months, a task that he later said "almost killed" him. He sat front and center in a "favorable position for hearing all that passed," and daily he composed a transcript from detailed notes kept of each session. Yet the memory that he had performed the task faded from the minds of participants.

In Madison's will of 1835, leaving his papers to his wife, he wrote that given the interest the Constitution "has inspired among friends of free Government, it was not an unreasonable inference that a report of the proceedings and discussions . . . will be particularly gratifying to the people of the United States, and to all who take an interest in the progress of political science and the course of true liberty." Why he failed to publish those records during his lifetime, indeed, why he kept them a secret, is inexplicable.

Madison worked on his manuscript intermittently for many years, revising and expanding as additional information became available. For example, he incorporated material from the official *Journal, Acts and Proceedings of the Convention* (1819) and even from ROBERT YATES's *Secret Proceedings and Debates* (1821), an Anti-Federalist work that contained useful details through July 5, 1787, including versions of Madison's own speeches. Madison's revisions of his original manuscript revealed his objective of making the record as full and accurate as possible.

After his death in 1836, Dolley Madison offered his papers to the United States. In 1837 Congress agreed on a price of $30,000, and in 1840, fifty-three years after the Convention, Madison's *Notes of the Debates* was published for the first of many times. It remains our most important source by far of what happened at the Constitutional Convention.

LEONARD W. LEVY

Bibliography

MADISON, JAMES 1977 *The Papers of James Madison,* Robert A. Rutland, ed., vol. 10. Chicago: University of Chicago Press.

WARREN, CHARLES 1928 *The Making of the Constitution.* Boston: Little, Brown.

MAGNA CARTA
(1215)

Magna Carta (Latin, great charter), one of the enduring symbols of LIMITED GOVERNMENT and of the RULE OF LAW, was forced upon an unwilling King John by rebellious barons in June of 1215. Since his accession in 1199, John had made enemies at every quarter. The barons resisted heavy taxation exacted to support the king's expensive and unsuccessful wars with the French. Lesser folk complained that royal officials requisitioned, often without payment, food, timber, horses, and carts. Justice in the courts became more sporadic. Quarreling with Pope Innocent III over the election of a new archbishop of Canterbury, John seized church properties, yielding only when the pope threatened to release the English people from their allegiance to the Crown.

By spring of 1215, the barons' discontent had ripened to the point that they formally renounced their allegiance after the king refused their demands that he confirm their liberties by a charter. Under severe pressure, John agreed to meet the barons at Runnymede. There the barons presented a list of demands, the Articles of the Barons, which were then reduced to the form of a charter—the document that later generations came to call Magna Carta.

The charter to which John agreed is an intensely practical document. Rather than being a philosophical tract redolent with lofty generalities, the charter was drafted to provide concrete remedies for specific abuses. Moreover, although the barons were rebelling against the abuse of royal power, they were not seeking to remake the fabric of feudal society. They sought instead to restore customary limits on the power of the Crown, distinguishing between rule according to law and rule by the imposition of arbitrary will.

The barons' interests were essentially selfish. They did not see themselves as disinterested advocates for the common good of the realm. Nevertheless, because the abuses of John's reign touched so many elements of English society, his opponents' demands had implications far beyond the barons' own interests. For example, the charter begins with the declaration that the liberties therein guaranteed run to "all the free men of our kingdom."

Many of Magna Carta's provisions concern feudal relationships having no counterpart in modern times. Certain of the charter's decrees, however, raise issues as vital now as then. Indeed, some of its provisions anticipate rights now embedded in American constitutional law. Among the more relevant are the following:

Chapter 39 declares, "No freed man shall be taken, imprisoned, disseised, outlawed, banished, or in any way destroyed, nor will We proceed against or prosecute him, except by the lawful judgment of his peers and by the LAW OF THE LAND." One should not read this language too broadly; for instance, "judgment of his peers" did not mean, as many have supposed, TRIAL BY JURY. But the requirement of proceedings according to the "law of the land" was significant in the development generally of the rule of law and more specifically of the concept of DUE PROCESS OF LAW. Indeed, "due process of law" and "law of the land" became interchangeable.

Chapter 40 states, "To no one will We sell, to none will We deny or delay, right or justice." Like chapter 39, this provision aimed at curbing abuses in the administration of justice. Several chapters (28, 29, 30, 31) relate to abuses in royal officials' requisitioning of private property and thus are the remote ancestor of the requirement of JUST COMPENSATION in the Fifth Amendment to the United States Constitution. Other chapters (20, 21, 22) require that fines be "according to the measure" of the offense and that fines not be so heavy as to jeopardize one's ability to make a living—reflecting the principle that the criminal law ought not to be administered in a vindictive or unduly oppressive way. Still other provisions deal with the liberties and free customs of cities and towns, with the free flow of commerce, and with church and state—all of these subjects being continuing concerns of American constitutional law.

Beginning with Henry III (who at age nine succeeded John in 1216), king after king reaffirmed Magna Carta. By the end of the fourteenth century, Magna Carta (which had been placed on the statute books in 1297) had established itself as more than a venerable statute; by then it was a FUNDAMENTAL LAW. In 1368, for example—over 400 years before MARBURY V. MADISON (1803)—a statute of Edward III commanded that Magna Carta "be holden and kept in all Points; and if there be any Statute made to the contrary, it shall be holden for none." Here one sees an early germ of the principle contained in the SUPREMACY CLAUSE of the United States Constitution.

The political turmoil of seventeenth-century England saw such parliamentarians as Sir EDWARD COKE and such pamphleteers as JOHN LILBURNE ("Freeborn John") invoking Magna Carta against the pretensions of the Stuart kings. By the end of that century, climaxed by the Glorious Revolution, three new "liberty documents" had been brought into being to stand alongside Magna Carta as assuring the liberties of the subject—the PETITION OF RIGHT (1628), the HABEAS CORPUS ACT (1679), and the BILL OF RIGHTS (1689).

Magna Carta was early carried to the New World. In 1646, some discontented freemen in the Massachusetts colony complained that the laws and liberties they were entitled to as Englishmen were not being enforced. The colony's magistrates responded by drawing up the famous "parallels" of Massachusetts—one column entitled "Magna Charta," the other "fundamentalls of the Massachusetts," the purpose being to argue that the rights assured by Magna Carta and the common law were indeed not denied to the people of Massachusetts. When WILLIAM PENN founded Pennsylvania, he drew upon Magna Carta in drafting the new colony's Frame of Government and, in 1687, was responsible for the first publication in America of Magna Carta.

In the decade between the STAMP ACT (1765) and the outbreak of hostilities with the mother country, Magna Carta became part of the fabric of colonial arguments against British policies. In the petition by the Stamp Act Congress to the king, the Congress declared that both the colonists' right to tax themselves and the right of trial by jury (a right the Crown had circumvented by giving ADMIRALTY courts JURISDICTION to try cases under the Stamp Act) were "confirmed by the Great Charter of English Liberty."

During the period leading up to revolution, the colonists' arguments, in tracts and resolutions, were essentially eclectic. Appeals to the British Constitution, including Magna Carta, were intertwined with arguments that the colonists' entitlement to such rights as taxation only with their consent were based also on the colonial charters and on natural law. As SAMUEL ADAMS put it, Magna Carta itself was a declaration of Britons' "original, inherent, indefeasible NATURAL RIGHTS."

Independence accomplished, the Americans turned to the work of building their own constitutional governments, both state and ultimately federal. The new constitutions reveal both the legacy of British institutions, including Magna Carta, and their perceived limitations. By and large, the contributions of Magna Carta and the other British "liberty" documents are most evident in American bills of rights. Virtually every state constitution has a due process clause, some using the phrase "due process," others using Magna Carta's formulation of "law of the land." For example, the debt owed Magna Carta's chapter 39 is obvious in North Carolina's Declaration of Rights, framed in 1776, "That no freeman ought to be taken, imprisoned, or disseized of his freehold, liberties, or privileges, or outlawed, or exiled, or in any manner destroyed, or deprived of his life, liberty, or property, but by the law of the land."

From the outset, however, American constitutional draftsmen understood their handiwork to go beyond Magna Carta. In North Carolina's ratifying convention (1789), JAMES IREDELL (later to serve on the Supreme Court) called Magna Carta "no constitution" but simply a legislative act, "every article of which the legislature may at any time alter." What Britain lacked, he concluded, the new American constitution supplied.

Throughout the nineteenth century, American courts, both state and federal, commonly invoked Magna Carta in shaping constitutional rights. Thus Magna Carta was relied on in cases involving (to give but a few examples) excessive court costs, open courts and certain remedies, notice and hearing, general application of the laws, and BILLS OF ATTAINDER. Gradually, as a corpus of indigenous American law developed, reliance upon Magna Carta became more and more attenuated, indeed largely rhetorical. By the twentieth century, Magna Carta had long since been irrevocably embedded into the fabric of American CONSTITUTIONALISM, both by contributing specific concepts such as due process of law and by being the ultimate symbol of constitutional government under a rule of law.

A. E. DICK HOWARD

Bibliography

HOWARD, A. E. DICK 1968 *The Road from Runnymede: Magna Carta and Constitutionalism in America.* Charlottesville: University Press of Virginia.

MAHAN v. HOWELL
410 U.S. 315 (1973)

The ideal REAPPORTIONMENT, following REYNOLDS v. SIMS (1964), would establish state legislative districts of equal populations. The question remained: How much deviation from pure mathematical equality would be tolerated? In *Mahan,* the Supreme Court approved, 6–3, a deviation of sixteen percent in the districting of Virginia's lower house, justified by the state's "policy of maintaining the integrity of district lines."

In congressional districting, no such deviation from equality is tolerated (*White v. Weiser,* 1973). However, state legislative districting may include DE MINIMIS departures from equality (up to around ten percent) without any justification (*White v. Regester,* 1973).

KENNETH L. KARST

MAHER v. ROE
432 U.S. 464 (1977)

The Supreme Court here sustained, 6–3, a Connecticut law limiting state medicaid assistance for abortions in the first trimester of pregnancy to "medically necessary" abortions (including "psychiatric necessity"), but providing such aid for childbirth. Justice LEWIS F. POWELL, for the Court, rejected both the claim that the law violated the right of PRIVACY recognized in ROE V. WADE (1973) and the claim that the state's WEALTH DISCRIMINATION violated the EQUAL PROTECTION clause.

There was to be "no retreat from *Roe,*" but Connecticut had placed "no obstacles . . . in the pregnant woman's path to an abortion." An indigent woman suffered no disadvantage from the state's funding of childbirth; she might still have an abortion if she could find the wherewithal; Connecticut had not created her indigency. Nor did the scheme deny equal protection. There was no SUSPECT CLASSIFICATION requiring STRICT SCRUTINY of the law; neither had the state invaded any FUNDAMENTAL INTEREST by discriminating against the exercise of a constitutional right. The law satisfied the RATIONAL BASIS standard, for it was rationally related to promoting the state's interest in protecting potential life—an interest recognized in *Roe* itself.

Two companion decisions, *Poelker v. Doe* and *Beal v. Doe,* upheld a city's refusal to provide hospital services for an indigent woman's nontherapeutic abortion, and read the SOCIAL SECURITY ACT not to require a state to aid nontherapeutic abortions in order to receive federal medicaid grants.

Justices WILLIAM J. BRENNAN, THURGOOD MARSHALL, and HARRY BLACKMUN all filed opinions dissenting in the three cases. They emphasized the "coercive" effect on poor women of the state's financial preference for childbirth, and the particularly harsh effect of adding unwanted children to poor households.

Even before *Roe,* wealthy women could have abortions by traveling to other states or abroad. *Roe* brought abortion within the means of middleclass women. The *Maher* majority Justices declined to extend the effective right to have an abortion beyond the boundaries of their own socioeconomic environment.

KENNETH L. KARST

(SEE ALSO: *Abortion and the Constitution; Harris v. McRae, 1980; Reproductive Autonomy.*)

MAJORITY OPINION

See: Opinion of the Court

MALLORY v. UNITED STATES

See: McNabb-Mallory Rule

MALLOY v. HOGAN
378 U.S. 1 (1964)

This is one of a series of cases in which the WARREN COURT nationalized the rights of the criminally accused by incorporating provisions of the Fourth through the Eighth Amendments into the FOURTEENTH AMENDMENT. (See INCORPORATION DOCTRINE.) In *Malloy* it was the RIGHT AGAINST SELF-IN-

CRIMINATION. Malloy, a convicted felon on probation, was ordered to testify in a judicial inquiry into gambling activities. He refused to answer any questions concerning the crime for which he had been convicted, and he was held in contempt. Connecticut's highest court, relying on TWINING V. NEW JERSEY (1908) and ADAMSON V. CALIFORNIA (1947), ruled that Malloy's invocation of the Fifth Amendment right had no constitutional basis in the state and that the Fourteenth Amendment did not extend the right to a state proceeding.

The Supreme Court reversed on the ground that the "same standards must determine whether an accused's silence in either a federal or a state proceeding is justified." Had the inquiry been a federal one, said Justice WILLIAM J. BRENNAN for a 5–4 majority, Malloy would have been entitled to refuse to answer because his disclosures might have furnished a link in a chain of evidence to connect him to a new crime for which he might be prosecuted. The Court held that "the Fifth Amendment exception from compulsory self-incrimination is also protected by the Fourteenth against abridgment by the States." *Twining* and *Adamson,* which had held to the contrary, were overruled, although the specific holding in *Adamson* relating to comments on the accused's failure to testify was not overruled until GRIFFIN V. CALIFORNIA (1965). Thus, *Malloy* stands for the DOCTRINE that the Fourteenth Amendment protects against state abridgment the same right that the Fifth protects against federal abridgment. Justices BYRON R. WHITE and POTTER STEWART did not expressly dissent from this doctrine; they contended, rather, that Malloy's reliance on his right to silence was groundless on the basis of the facts. Justices JOHN MARSHALL HARLAN and TOM C. CLARK opposed the incorporation of the Fifth Amendment right into the Fourteenth.

LEONARD W. LEVY

MANDAMUS, WRIT OF

(Latin: "We command.") A writ of mandamus is a judicial order to a lower court or to any agency or officer of any department of government, commanding the performance of a nondiscretionary act as a duty of office for the purpose of enforcing or recognizing an individual right or privilege. (See MARBURY V. MADISON, 1803.)

LEONARD W. LEVY

MANN ACT
36 Stat. 825 (1910)

Congress sought to suppress prostitution in the so-called White Slave Act under the commerce power. Anyone transporting or aiding the transportation of a woman in INTERSTATE OR FOREIGN COMMERCE "for the purpose of prostitution or debauchery, or for any other immoral purpose, or with the intent and purpose to induce, entice, or compel such woman or girl" to such immoral acts was guilty of a FELONY. Persuasion to cross state lines for these purposes "whether with or without her consent" was likewise a felony. Another section doubled the already stiff penalties (five years imprisonment or $5,000) in cases involving women under eighteen years of age. The act also authorized the Commissioner-General of Immigration to "receive and centralize information concerning the procuration of alien women and girls" for such purposes and required brothel-keepers to file statements regarding alien employees, exempting the keepers from prosecution for "truthful statements."

In HOKE V. UNITED STATES (1913) the Supreme Court sustained congressional power to enact the law under the COMMERCE CLAUSE, relying squarely on CHAMPION V. AMES (1903): "Congress, as an incident to [the commerce power] may adopt not only means necessary but convenient to its exercise, and the means may have the quality of police regulations."

DAVID GORDON

MANN-ELKINS ACT
36 Stat. 539 (1910)

The ELKINS ACT of 1903 and the HEPBURN ACT of 1906, as well as the decisions they prompted, had reinvigorated the Interstate Commerce Commission (ICC) after disastrous Supreme Court decisions such as INTERSTATE COMMERCE COMMISSION V. CINCINNATI, NEW ORLEANS & TEXAS PACIFIC RAILWAY CO. (1897). The Mann-Elkins Act granted the ICC, for the first time, the power to set original rates; it also authorized the commission to suspend applications for proposed rate increases until it had ascertained their reasonableness. Despite the statute's vesting the commission with such powers, determinations of reasonableness would still be subject to the extraordinarily flexible guidelines of the FAIR RETURN rule laid down in SMYTH V. AMES (1898). The act placed the ICC firmly in control by shifting the BURDEN OF

PROOF on the question of reasonableness from the commission to the carriers. In addition, the act revived a prohibition against LONG HAUL–SHORT HAUL DISCRIMINATION, except where specifically allowed by the commission. The act also brought telephone, telegraph, and cable lines under ICC JURISDICTION. A unanimous Supreme Court sustained many of the act's provisions in *United States v. Atchinson, Topeka & Santa Fe Railroad* (1914).

DAVID GORDON

MANSFIELD, LORD

See: Murray, William

MAPP v. OHIO
367 U.S. 643 (1961)

Mapp v. Ohio brought to a close an abrasive constitutional debate within the Supreme Court on the question whether the EXCLUSIONARY RULE, constitutionally required in federal trials since 1914, was also required in state criminal cases. *Mapp* imposed the rule on the states.

WOLF V. COLORADO (1949) had applied to the states the FOURTH AMENDMENT's prohibition against UNREASONABLE SEARCHES, but it had not required state courts to exclude from trial evidence so obtained. *Mapp*'s extension of *Wolf* was based on two considerations. First, in *Wolf* the Court had been persuaded by the rejection of the exclusionary rule by most state courts; by 1961, however, a narrow majority of the states had independently adopted the rule. Second, the *Wolf* majority was convinced that other remedies, such as suits in tort against offending officers, could serve equally in deterring unlawful searches; time, however, had shown that such remedies were useless. "Nothing can destroy a government more quickly than its failure to observe its own laws," wrote Justice TOM C. CLARK for the Court, "or worse, its disregard of the charter of its own existence."

In *Mapp v. Ohio* the Court asserted emphatically that the exclusionary rule was "an essential part" of the Fourth Amendment and hence a fit subject for imposition on the states despite "passing references" in earlier cases to its being a nonconstitutional rule of evidence. Yet, in some hazy phrasing, the opinion also suggested that the Fifth Amendment's RIGHT AGAINST SELF-INCRIMINATION was the exclusionary rule's constitutional backbone. Equally confusing was the Court's characterization of the rule as "the most important constitutional privilege" (that is, personal right) guaranteed by the Fourth Amendment while at the same time pointing to the rule's deterrent effect as justification for its imposition. More recently, the Court has settled on deterrence as the crucial consideration, and thus has refused to apply the rule in situations, such as GRAND JURY proceedings in CALANDRA V. UNITED STATES (1974), where in the Court's view the deterrent effect is minimal.

Three dissenters, in an opinion by Justice JOHN MARSHALL HARLAN, expressed "considerable doubt" that the federal exclusionary rule of WEEKS V. UNITED STATES (1914) was constitutionally based and argued that, in any event, considerations of FEDERALISM should allow the states to devise their own remedies for unlawful searches.

(Unlike the well-entrenched federal exclusionary rule, which has gone well-nigh unchallenged on the Court from the beginning, controversy concerning the rule for the states has continued unabated, both on and off the Court, since *Mapp* was decided.)

JACOB W. LANDYNSKI

MARBURY v. MADISON
1 Cranch 137 (1803)

Marbury has transcended its origins in the party battles between Federalists and Republicans, achieving mythic status as the foremost precedent for JUDICIAL REVIEW. For the first time the Court held unconstitutional an act of Congress, establishing, if only for posterity, the doctrine that the Supreme Court has the final word among the coordinate branches of the national government in determining what is law under the Constitution. By 1803 no one doubted that an unconstitutional act of government was null and void, but who was to judge? What *Marbury* settled, doctrinally if not in reality, was the Court's ultimate authority over Congress and the President. Actually, the historic reputation of the case is all out of proportion to the merits of Chief Justice JOHN MARSHALL's unanimous opinion for the Court. On the issue of judicial review, which made the case live, he said nothing new, and his claim for the power of the Court occasioned little contemporary comment. The significance of the case in its time derived from its political context and from the fact that the Court appeared successfully to interfere with the executive branch. Marshall's most remarkable accomplishment, in retrospect, was his massing of the Court behind a poorly reasoned opinion that section 13 of the JUDICIARY ACT OF 1789 was unconstitutional. Though the Court's legal craftsmanship was not evident, its judicial politics—egregious partisanship and calculated expediency—was exceptionally adroit, leaving no target for Republican retaliation beyond frustrated rhetoric.

Republican hostility to the United States courts, which were Federalist to the last man as well as Federalist in doctrine and interests, had mounted increasingly and passed the threshold of tolerance when the Justices on circuit enforced the Sedition Act. (See ALIEN AND SEDITION ACTS.) Then the lame-duck Federalist administration passed the JUDICIARY ACT OF 1801 and, a week before THOMAS JEFFERSON's inauguration, passed the companion act for the appointment of forty-two justices of the peace for the DISTRICT OF COLUMBIA, prompting the new President to believe that "the Federalists have retired into the Judiciary as a stronghold . . . and from that battery all the works of republicanism are to be beaten down and erased." The new Circuit Court for the District of Columbia sought in vain to obtain the conviction of the editor of the administration's organ in the capital for the common law crime of SEDITIOUS LIBEL. The temperate response of the new administration was remarkable. Instead of increasing the size of the courts, especially the Supreme Court, and packing them with Republican appointees, the administration simply repealed the Judiciary Act of 1801. (See JUDICIARY ACTS OF 1802.) On taking office Jefferson also ordered that the commissions for the forty-two justices of the peace for the district be withheld, though he reappointed twenty-five, all political enemies originally appointed by President JOHN ADAMS.

Marbury v. Madison arose from the refusal of the administration to deliver the commissions of four of these appointees, including one William Marbury. The Senate had confirmed the appointments and Adams had signed their commissions, which Marshall, the outgoing secretary of state, had affixed with the great seal of the United States. But in the rush of the "midnight appointments" on the evening of March 3, the last day of the outgoing administration, Marshall had neglected to deliver the commissions. Marbury and three others sought from the Supreme Court, in a case of ORIGINAL JURISDICTION, a WRIT OF MANDAMUS compelling JAMES MADISON, the new secretary of state, to issue their commissions. In December 1801 the Court issued an order commanding Madison to show cause why the writ should not be issued.

A congressman reflected the Republican viewpoint when saying that the show-cause order was "a bold stroke against the Executive," and JOHN BRECKINRIDGE, the majority leader of the Senate, thought the order "the most daring attack which the annals of Federalism have yet exhibited." When the debate began on the repeal bill, Federalists defended the show-cause order, the independence of the judiciary, and the duty of the Supreme Court to hold void any unconstitutional acts of Congress. A Republican paper declared that the "mandamus business" had first appeared to be only a contest between the judiciary and the executive but now seemed a political act by the Court to deter repeal of the 1801 legislation. In retaliation the Republicans passed the repealer and altered the terms of the Court so that it would lose its June 1802 session and not again meet until February 1803, fourteen months after the show-cause order. The Republicans hoped, as proved to be the case, that the Justices would comply with the repealer and return to circuit duty, thereby averting a showdown and a constitutional crisis, which the administration preferred to avoid.

By the time the Court met in February 1803 to hear arguments in *Marbury*, which had become a political sensation, talk of IMPEACHMENT was in the air. A few days before the Court's term, Federalists in Congress moved that the Senate should produce for Marbury's benefit records of his confirmation, provoking Senator James Jackson to declare that the Senate would not interfere in the case and become "a party to an accusation which may end in an impeachment, of which the Senate were the constitutional Judges." By no coincidence, a week before the Court met, Jefferson instructed the House to impeach a U.S. District Court judge in New Hampshire, and already Federalists knew of the plan to impeach Justice SAMUEL CHASE. Jefferson's desire to replace John Marshall with SPENCER ROANE was also public knowledge. Right before Marshall delivered the Court's opinion in *Marbury*, the Washington correspondent of a Republican paper wrote: "The attempt of the Supreme Court . . . by a mandamus, to control the Executive functions, is a new experiment. It seems to be no less than a commencement of war. . . . The Court must be defeated and retreat from the attack; or march on, till they incur an impeachment and removal from office."

Marshall and his Court appeared to confront unattractive alternatives. To have issued the writ, which was the expected judgment, would have been like the papal bull against the moon; Madison would have defied it, exposing the Court's impotence, and the

Republicans might have a pretext for retaliation based on the Court's breach of the principle of SEPARATION OF POWERS. To have withheld the writ would have violated the Federalist principle that the Republican administration was accountable under the law. ALEXANDER HAMILTON's newspaper reported the Court's opinion in a story headed "Constitution Violated by President," informing its readers that the new President by his first act had trampled on the charter of the peoples' liberties by unprincipled, even criminal, conduct against personal rights. Yet the Court did not issue the writ; the victorious party was Madison. But Marshall exhibited him and the President to the nation as if they were arbitrary Stuart tyrants, and then, affecting judicial humility, Marshall in obedience to the Constitution found that the Court could not obey an act of Congress that sought to aggrandize judicial powers in cases of original jurisdiction, contrary to Article III of the Constitution.

The Court was treading warily. The statute in question was not a Republican measure, not, for example, the repealer of the Judiciary Act of 1801. Indeed, shortly after *Marbury,* the Court sustained the repealer in STUART V. LAIRD (1803) against arguments that it was unconstitutional. In that case the Court ruled that the practice of the Justices in sitting as circuit judges derived from the Judiciary Act of 1789, and therefore derived "from a contemporary interpretation of the most forcible nature," as well as from customary acquiescence. Ironically, another provision of the same statute, section 13, was at issue in *Marbury,* not that the bench and bar realized it until Marshall delivered his opinion. The offending section, passed by a Federalist Congress after being drafted by OLIVER ELLSWORTH, one of the Constitution's Framers and Marshall's predecessor, had been the subject of previous litigation before the Court without anyone having thought it was unconstitutional. Section 13 simply authorized the Court to issue writs of *mandamus* "in cases warranted by the principles and usages of law," and that clause appeared in the context of a reference to the Court's APPELLATE JURISDICTION.

Marshall's entire argument hinged on the point that section 13 unconstitutionally extended the Court's original jurisdiction beyond the two categories of cases, specified in Article III, in which the Court was to have such jurisdiction. But for those two categories of cases, involving foreign diplomats or a state as a litigant, the Court has appellate jurisdiction. In quoting Article III, Marshall omitted the clause that directly follows as part of the same sentence: the Court has appellate jurisdiction "with such exceptions, and under such regulations as the Congress shall make." That might mean that Congress can detract from the Court's appellate jurisdiction or add to its original jurisdiction. The specification of two categories of cases in which the Court has original jurisdiction was surely intended as an irreducible minimum, but Marshall read it, by the narrowest construction, to mean a negation of congressional powers.

In any event, section 13 did not add to the Court's original jurisdiction. In effect it authorized the Court to issue writs of *mandamus* in the two categories of cases of original jurisdiction and in all appellate cases. The authority to issue such writs did not extend or add to the Court's jurisdiction; the writ of *mandamus* is merely a remedial device by which courts implement their existing jurisdiction. Marshall misinterpreted the statute and Article III, as well as the nature of the writ, in order to find that the statute conflicted with Article III. Had the Court employed the reasoning of *Stuart v. Laird* or the rule that the Court should hold a statute void only in a clear case, giving every presumption of validity in doubtful cases, Marshall could not have reached his conclusion that section 13 was unconstitutional. That conclusion allowed him to decide that the Court was powerless to issue the writ because Marbury had sued for it in a case of original jurisdiction.

Marshall could have said, simply, this is a case of original jurisdiction but it does not fall within either of the two categories of original jurisdiction specified in Article III; therefore we cannot decide: writ denied, case dismissed. Section 13 need never have entered the opinion, although, alternatively, Marshall could have declared: section 13 authorizes this Court to issue such writs only in cases warranted by the principles and usages of law; we have no jurisdiction here because we are not hearing the case in our appellate capacity and it is not one of the two categories in which we possess original jurisdiction: writ denied, case dismissed. Even if Marshall had to find that the statute augmented the Court's original jurisdiction, the ambiguity of the clause in Article III, which he neglected to quote, justified sustaining the statute.

Holding section 13 unconstitutional enabled Marshall to refuse an extension of the Court's powers and award the judgment to Madison, thus denying the administration a pretext for vengeance. Marshall also used the case to answer Republican arguments that the Court did not and should not have the power to declare an act of Congress unconstitutional, though he carefully chose an inoffensive section of a Federalist statute that pertained merely to writs of mandamus. That he gave his doctrine of judicial review the support of only abstract logic, without reference to history or precedents, was characteristic, as was the fact that his doctrine swept way beyond the statute that provoked it.

If Marshall had merely wanted a safe platform from which to espouse and exercise judicial review, he would have begun his opinion with the problems that section 13 posed for the Court; but he reached the question of constitutionality and of judicial review at the tail-end of his opinion. Although he concluded that the Court had to discharge the show-cause order, because it lacked jurisdiction, he first and most irregularly passed judgment on the merits of the case. Everything said on the merits was OBITER DICTA and should not have been said at all, given the judgment. Most of the opinion dealt with Marbury's unquestionable right to his commission and the correctness of the remedy he had sought by way of a writ of mandamus. In his elaborate discourse on those matters, Marshall assailed the President and his cabinet officer for their lawlessness. Before telling Marbury that he had initiated his case in the wrong court, Marshall engaged in what EDWARD S. CORWIN called "a deliberate partisan *coup.*" Then Marshall followed with a "judicial *coup d'état,*" in the words of ALBERT J. BEVERIDGE, on the constitutional issue that neither party had argued.

The partisan *coup* by which Marshall denounced the executive branch, not the grand declaration of the doctrine of judicial review for which the case is remembered, was the focus of contemporary excitement. Only the passages on judicial review survive. Cases on the REMOVAL POWER of the President, especially concerning inferior appointees, cast doubt on the validity of the dicta by which Marshall lectured the executive branch on its responsibilities under the law. Moreover, by statute and by judicial practice the Supreme Court exercises the authority to issue writs of mandamus in all appellate cases and in the two categories of cases of original jurisdiction. Over the passage of time *Marbury* came to stand for the monumental principle, so distinctive and dominant a feature of our constitutional system, that the Court may bind the coordinate branches of the national government to its rulings on what is the supreme LAW OF THE LAND. That principle stands out from *Marbury* like the grin on the Cheshire cat; all else, which preoccupied national attention in 1803, disappeared in our constitutional law. So too might have disappeared national judicial review if the impeachment of Chase had succeeded.

Marshall himself was prepared to submit to review of Supreme Court opinions by Congress. He was so shaken by the impeachment of Chase and by the thought that he himself might be the next victim in the event of Chase's conviction, that he wrote to Chase on January 23, 1804: "I think the modern doctrine of impeachment should yield to an appellate jurisdiction in the legislature. A reversal of those legal opinions deemed unsound by the legislature would certainly better comport with the mildness of our character than a removal of the judge who has rendered them unknowing of his fault." The acquittal of Chase meant that the Court could remain independent, that Marshall had no need to announce publicly his desperate plan for congressional review of the Court, and that *Marbury* remained as a precedent. Considering that the Court did not again hold unconstitutional an act of Congress until 1857, when it decided DRED SCOTT V. SANDFORD, sixty-eight years would have passed since 1789 without such a holding, and but for *Marbury,* after so long a period of congressional omnipotence, national judicial review might never have been established.

LEONARD W. LEVY

Bibliography

BEVERIDGE, ALBERT J. 1916–1919 *The Life of John Marshall,* 4 vols. Vol. III:50–178. Boston: Houghton Mifflin.

CORWIN, EDWARD S. 1914 *The Doctrine of Judicial Review.* Pages 1–78. Princeton, N.J.: Princeton University Press.

HAINES, CHARLES GROVE 1944 *The Role of the Supreme Court in American Government and Politics, 1789–1835.* Pages 223–258. Berkeley: University of California Press.

VAN ALSTYNE, WILLIAM W. 1969 A Critical Guide to Marbury v. Madison. *Duke Law Journal* 1969:1–47.

WARREN, CHARLES 1923 *The Supreme Court in United States History,* 3 vols. Vol. I:200–268. Boston: Little, Brown.

MARCHETTI v. UNITED STATES
390 U.S. 39 (1968)
GROSSO v. UNITED STATES
390 U.S. 62 (1968)
HAYNES v. UNITED STATES
390 U.S. 85 (1968)
UNITED STATES v. UNITED STATES COIN & CURRENCY
401 U.S. 715 (1971)

In *Marchetti* and *Grosso* the Supreme Court, in opinions by Justice JOHN MARSHALL HARLAN from which only Chief Justice EARL WARREN dissented, held that the RIGHT AGAINST SELF-INCRIMINATION constituted an ironclad defense against a criminal prosecution for failure to register as a gambler pursuant to federal gambling statutes or to pay federal occupational and EXCISE TAXES on gambling. The Court overruled *United States v. Kahriger* (1953) and *Lewis v. United States* (1955), which had held that the Fifth Amendment right could not be asserted by professional gamblers because the federal gambling laws did not compel self-incrimination. In those earlier cases the Court reasoned that the right was inapplicable to prospective acts: a gambler had the initial choice of deciding whether to continue gambling at the price of surrendering his right against self-incrimination, or cease gambling and thereby avoid the need to register and pay the taxes. In 1968 the Court found its earlier reasoning "no longer persuasive."

Justice Harlan explained how the statutes worked. A gambler had an obligation to register annually with the Internal Revenue Service as one engaged in the business of accepting wagers. He paid a $50 occupational tax plus an excise tax of ten percent on the gross amount of all bets. He had to keep daily records of all bets and reveal those records to IRS inspectors. The issue posed by such congressional requirements was not whether the United States may tax gambling, for the unlawfulness of an activity did not preclude its taxation. The issue, rather, was whether the registration, record-keeping, and tax provisions whipsawed gamblers into confessing criminal activities. Federal and state laws made gambling illegal, and the IRS made available to law enforcement agencies the identities of those who complied with the gambling statutes. Gamblers therefore confronted substantial hazards of self-incrimination. On pain of punishment for not complying, they had to provide prosecutors with evidence of their guilt.

Marchetti was convicted of failing to register and pay the occupational tax, Grosso for failing to pay that tax and the excises. Reversing their convictions, the Court distinguished their cases from those in which a criminal had failed to file income tax returns for fear of self-incrimination and another in which the government had required record keeping from persons not engaged in an inherently suspect activity. The mere filing of a tax return, required of all, or the failure to keep routine business records did not identify anyone as a suspect of a crime. In *Haynes*, the Court ruled that a person possessing a sawed-off shotgun is suspect and therefore cannot be compelled to register his weapon, under the National Firearms Act, because of the hazard of self-incrimination. In *United States Coin & Currency* a 5–4 Court applied the *Marchetti* reasoning to a forfeiture proceeding involving property used to violate federal gambling laws.

LEONARD W. LEVY

MARKETPLACE OF IDEAS

The "marketplace of ideas" argument in FIRST AMENDMENT jurisprudence was first enunciated in Justice OLIVER WENDELL HOLMES's dissenting opinion in ABRAMS V. UNITED STATES (1919):

> But when men have realized that time has upset many fighting faiths, they may come to believe even more than they believe the very foundations of their own conduct that the ultimate good desired is better reached by free trade in ideas—that the best test of truth is the power of thought to get itself accepted in the competition of the market, and that truth is the only ground upon which their wishes safely can be carried out. That at any rate is the theory of our Constitution. It is an experiment, as all life is an experiment. . . . While that experiment is part of our system I think that we should be eternally vigilant against attempts to check the expression of opinions that we loathe and believe to be fraught with death, unless they so imminently threaten immediate interference with the lawful and pressing purpose of the law that an immediate check is required to save the country.

Holmes's stirring words recall similar but distinct passages from John Milton and John Stuart Mill. Extravagant as Holmes's passage is, it is in significant respects more careful than the implications of Milton's rhetorical question: "[W]ho ever knew truth put to the worse, in a free and open encounter?" Holmes did not claim that truth always or even usually emerges in the marketplace of ideas. Holmes's claim was more confined—that the best test of truth is the competition of the marketplace.

On the other hand, Milton spoke of a free and open encounter; Holmes spoke of the competition of the marketplace. A recurrent problem in First Amendment cases is that these two notions are not the same. Those who seek access to the broadcast media, as in RED LION BROADCASTING V. FCC (1969), or to powerful newspapers, as in MIAMI HERALD PUBLISHING CO. V. TORNILLO (1974), argue that the competition of the marketplace is not free and open. They urge that truth cannot emerge in the market if the gatekeepers do not let it in. A more general criticism of the Holmes position is that the claim that the marketplace is the best test of truth cannot itself be tested without an independent test of truth, yet the argument by its terms denies any superior test of truth that is independent of the marketplace.

These criticisms aside, the question arises whether the marketplace argument overvalues truth. Holmes's view that the expression of opinion should be free until an immediate check is needed to "save the country" has never been adopted by the Supreme Court. Advocacy of illegal action, for example, may be restricted when it is directed to and likely to incite or produce imminent lawless action, whether or not the country itself is endangered. Indeed, if the marketplace argument extends to facts as well as opinions, it is clear that showings far more pedestrian than Holmes's proposed requirements are sufficient to justify repression. The expression of factual beliefs can be restricted in order to protect reputation or privacy, and, in the commercial sphere, to further any substantial government interest.

Nonetheless, the marketplace argument has been a powerful theme in First Amendment law. For example, some defamatory facts and all defamatory opinion are protected in order to guarantee the breathing space we need for robust, uninhibited, and wide-open debate. Ironically, however, the marketplace argument serves to restrict speech as well as to protect it. "Under our Constitution," said the Court in GERTZ V. ROBERT WELCH, INC. (1974), "there is no such thing as a false idea," yet obscenity is divorced from speech protection because it is thought to be unnecessary for the expression of any idea. At bottom, First Amendment methodology is grounded in a paradox. Government must be restrained from imposing its views of truth. But government itself determines when this principle has been abandoned.

STEVEN SHIFFRIN

Bibliography

SCHAUER, FREDERICK 1978 Language, Truth and the First Amendment: An Essay in Memory of Harry Canter. *Virginia Law Review* 64:263, 268–272.

MARRIAGE AND THE CONSTITUTION

Although the constitutional "right to marry" was not securely confirmed by the Supreme Court until its decision in ZABLOCKI V. REDHAIL (1978), the Court had spoken of the freedom to marry as a FOURTEENTH AMENDMENT "liberty" as early as MEYER V. NEBRASKA (1923). Two WARREN COURT decisions had also laid the foundations for SUBSTANTIVE DUE PROCESS protections of marriage. GRISWOLD V. CONNECTICUT (1965) had recognized a RIGHT OF PRIVACY for the marital relationship, and LOVING V. VIRGINIA (1967) had struck down a MISCEGENATION law not only as an unconstitutional RACIAL DISCRIMINATION but also as a due process violation. The *Loving* opinion was explicit enough in speaking of the "freedom to marry," but doubt lingered that the Court meant to carry the principle beyond the racial context of the decision.

Zablocki ended the doubt. The Court held invalid, on equal protection grounds, a law forbidding a resident to marry without a judge's approval when he or she had court-ordered child support obligations. The judge could not approve the marriage unless support payments were kept current and the children were unlikely to become public charges. Some concurring Justices thought the law defective on due process grounds. *Zablocki*'s importance turns not on this doctrinal distinction but on its explicit recognition of marriage as a FUNDAMENTAL INTEREST, requiring STRICT SCRUTINY by the courts of direct and substantial governmental interference.

Just two months earlier, however, in *Califano v. Jobst* (1977), the Court had upheld a portion of the SOCIAL SECURITY ACT terminating disability benefits for a disabled dependent child of a wage earner when the child married a person not entitled to benefits under the act, even though that person was also disabled. Much of the discussion in *Zablocki*'s several opinions was devoted to *Jobst.* The majority distinguished *Jobst* as lacking the "directness and substantiality of the interference with the freedom to marry" present in *Zablocki.* The message was clear: interferences with marriage would demand justification in proportion to their degrees of severity. In *Zablocki* as in *Jobst* a money cost was attached to marriage; in *Zablocki* that cost would be prohibitive in most cases covered by the law.

This version of judicial interest-balancing seems likely to uphold such state restrictions on marriage as blood tests, reasonable age requirements, and insistence on a mentally retarded person's ability to understand the nature of the marriage relationship, even when those restrictions are strictly scrutinized. On principle, the state's power to prohibit POLYGAMY or to deny homosexual couples marriage or some comparable status seems more vulnerable to attack. It would be unrealistic, however, to expect an extension of the constitutional right to marry to homosexuals in the near future. (See SEXUAL PREFERENCE AND THE CONSTITUTION.) And recognition of a constitutional right to multiple marriage is a poor bet even for the distant future.

The extension of constitutional protection to other intimate relationships more closely resembling traditional marriage is already at hand. *Griswold*'s "privacy" protections have been effectively extended to the unmarried in EISENSTADT V. BAIRD (1972) and CAREY V. POPULATION SERVICES INTERNATIONAL (1977). Some states continue to recognize common law marriage, and others have concluded that support obligations may attach to the partners to some informal unions, once the unions end. As the number of unmarried couples living together increases, and as the incidents of unwed union come to resemble those of traditional marriage, formal marriage itself is more clearly seen in its expressive aspects, as a statement of commitment. In these circumstances it makes good sense to think of the right to marry as, in part, a FIRST AMENDMENT right.

KENNETH L. KARST

(SEE ALSO: *Freedom of Intimate Association.*)

Bibliography

KARST, KENNETH L. 1980 The Freedom of Intimate Association. *Yale Law Journal* 89:624–692.

NOTE 1980 Developments in the Law: The Constitution and the Family. *Harvard Law Review* 93:1156–1383, 1248–1296.

MARSH v. ALABAMA 326 U.S. 501 (1946)

When a person sought to distribute religious literature on the streets of a company town, the Supreme Court, 5–3, upheld her FIRST AMENDMENT claim against the owner's private property claims. Stressing the traditional role of free speech in town shopping districts open to the general public, Justice HUGO L. BLACK for the Court noted that, aside from private ownership, this town functioned exactly as did other towns which were constitutionally forbidden to ban leafleting. *Marsh* served as the basis for the later attempt, aborted in HUDGENS V. NLRB (1976), to extend First Amendment rights to users of privately owned SHOPPING CENTERS.

MARTIN SHAPIRO

MARSH v. CHAMBERS 463 U.S. 783 (1983)

A 6–3 Supreme Court sustained the constitutionality of legislative chaplaincies as not violating the SEPARATION OF CHURCH AND STATE mandated by the FIRST AMENDMENT. Chief Justice WARREN E. BURGER for the Court abandoned the three-part test of LEMON V. KURTZMAN (1971) previously used in cases involving the establishment clause and grounded his opinion wholly upon historical custom. Prayers by tax-supported legislative chaplains, traceable to the FIRST CONTINENTAL CONGRESS and the very Congress that framed the BILL OF RIGHTS, had become "part of the fabric of our society." Justice JOHN PAUL STEVENS, dissenting, asserted that Nebraska's practice of having the same Presbyterian minister as the official chaplain for sixteen years preferred one denomination over others. Justices WILLIAM J. BRENNAN and THURGOOD MARSHALL, dissenting, attacked legislative chaplains generally as a form of religious worship sponsored by government to promote and advance religion and entangling the government with religion, contrary to the values implicit in the establishment clause—privacy in religious matters, government neutrality, freedom of conscience, autonomy of religious life, and withdrawal of religion from the political arena.

LEONARD W. LEVY

MARSHALL, JOHN (1755–1835)

John Marshall, the third CHIEF JUSTICE of the Supreme Court (1801–1835), is still popularly known as the "Great Chief Justice" and the "Expounder of the Constitution." He was raised in the simple circumstances of backwoods Virginia, but his mother was pious and well educated and his father was a leader of his county and a friend of GEORGE WASHINGTON. Even though Marshall had little formal education, his extraordinary powers of mind, coupled with equity and good humor, made him a natural leader as a young soldier of the Revolution, as a member of the Richmond bar (then outstanding in the country), and as a general of the Virginia militia. He became nationally prominent as a diplomat, having outwitted the wily Charles Talleyrand while negotiating with France's Directory (1797–1798), and as a legislator, having supported Washington's FEDERALISM first in the Virginia Assembly (1782–1791, 1795–1797) and then in the House of Representatives (1799–1800). In June 1800 President JOHN ADAMS named Marshall to replace the Hamiltonian John Pickering as secretary of state, and in January 1801, after the strife-ridden Federalists' epochal defeat, appointed him Chief Justice when JOHN JAY, the first Chief Justice, declined to preside again over "a system so defective."

From its inception Marshall had defended the Constitution. His experience in Washington's ragtag army had made him a national patriot while rousing his disgust with the palsied Confederation. At the crucial Virginia ratifying convention (June 1788) he replied in three important speeches to the fears of PATRICK HENRY and other Anti-Federalists. The proposed Constitution, he argued, was not undemocratic, but a plan for a "well-regulated democracy." It set forth in particular the great powers of taxing and warring needed by any sound government. The state governments would retain all powers not given up expressly or implicitly; they were independently derived from the people. A mix of dependence upon the people and independence and virtue in the judges would prevent federal overreaching. If a law were not "warranted by any of the powers enumerated," Marshall remarked prophetically, the judges would declare it "void" as infringing "the Constitution they are to guard." Two other nonjudicial interpretations of the Constitution are notable. In 1799 Marshall wrote a report of the Virginia Federalists defending the constitutionality of the ill-famed Sedition Act of 1798 (a law he nevertheless had opposed as divisive in the explosive political atmosphere surrounding the French Revolution). If the NECESSARY AND PROPER CLAUSE authorizes punishment of actual resistance to law, he argued, it also authorizes punishment of "calumnious" speech, which is criminal under the COMMON LAW and prepares resistance. A speech to Congress in 1800, once famous in collections of American rhetoric, defended the President's power required by JAY'S TREATY to extradite a British subject charged with murder on a British ship. Because the criminal and the location were foreign, Marshall argued, the question was not a case in law or equity for United States courts; although a treaty is a law, it is a "political law," the execution of which lies with the President, not the courts. The judiciary has no political power whatever; the President is "the sole organ of the nation in its external relations."

As Chief Justice, Marshall raised the office and the Supreme Court to stature and power previously lacking. After having two Chief Justices in eleven years, the Court had Marshall for thirty-four, the longest tenure of any Chief Justice before or since. Individual opinions SERIATIM largely ceased, and dissents were discouraged. The Court came to speak with one voice. Usually the voice was Marshall's. He delivered the OPINION OF THE COURT in every case in which he participated during the decisive first five years, three-quarters of the opinions during the next seven years, and almost all the great constitutional opinions throughout his tenure. Marshall's captivating and equable temper helped unite a diverse group of justices, many appointed by Republican Presidents bent on reversing the Court's declarations of federal power and restrictions of state power. In the face of triumphant Jeffersonian Republicans, suspicious of an unelected judiciary stocked with Federalists, Marshall was wary and astute. His Court never erred as the JAY COURT did in CHISHOLM V. GEORGIA (1793), which had provoked the ELEVENTH AMENDMENT as a corrective. Nor did he cast antidemocratic contentions in the teeth of the Jeffersonians or their Jacksonian successors, thus to provoke (as had Justice SAMUEL CHASE) IMPEACHMENT proceedings. Marshall's judicial opinions encouraged grave respect for law, treated the Constitution as sacred and its Founding Fathers as sainted men, and fashioned a protective and compelling shield of purpose, principle, and reasoning.

His crucial judicial accomplishment was MARBURY V. MADISON (1803), which laid down the essentials of the American RULE OF LAW. Judges are to oversee executive and legislature alike, keeping the political departments faithful to applicable statutes, to the written Constitution, and to "general principles" of law protecting individual rights and delimiting the functions of each department. A series of important decisions secured individual rights, especially the right to acquire property by contract, against state and general governments. UNITED STATES V. BURR (1807) expounded a narrow constitutional definition of TREASON and made prosecution difficult. STURGES V. CROWNINSHIELD (1819) set strict standards for voiding debts by bankruptcy. FLETCHER V. PECK (1810) and DARTMOUTH COLLEGE V. WOODWARD (1819) enforced as judicially protected contracts a state's sale of land and a state's grant of a corporate charter. Finally, several of Marshall's most famous opinions elaborated great powers for the national government and protected them from state encroachment. MCCULLOCH V. MARYLAND (1819) sustained Congress's authority to charter a bank and in general to employ broad discretion as to necessary and proper means for carrying out national functions. GIBBONS V. OGDEN (1824), the steamboat case, interpreted congressional power under the COMMERCE CLAUSE to protect a national market, a right of exchange free from state-supported monopoly. COHENS V. VIRGINIA (1821) eloquently defended Supreme Court review of state court decisions involving FEDERAL QUESTIONS.

The presupposition of Marshall's CONSTITUTIONAL-

ISM was that the Constitution is FUNDAMENTAL LAW, not merely a fundamental plan, written to impose limits, not just to raise powers, and designed to be permanent, not to evolve or to be fundamentally revised. Interpretation is to follow the words and purposes of the various provisions; amendment is for subordinate changes that will allow "immortality" to the Framers' primary work. Marshall called a written constitution America's "greatest improvement on political institutions." It renders permanent the institutions raised by popular consent, which is the only basis of rightful government. Besides, the American nation was fortunate in its founding: it benefited from a remarkable plan, from a fortunate ratification in the face of jealousy and suspicion in states and people, and from the extraordinary firmness of the first President. Washington had settled the new federal institutions and conciliated public opinion, despite the "infinite difficulty" of ratification and a crescendo of attacks upon his administration as monarchic, aristocratic, and anglophile. So Marshall argued in the penetrating (if somewhat wooden) *Life of George Washington,* a biography he condensed into a schoolbook to impress on his countrymen the character and political principles of "the greatest man in the world."

Marshall understood the Constitution to establish a government, not a league such as that created by the ARTICLES OF CONFEDERATION. The new government possessed sovereign powers of two sorts, legal (the judicial power) and political (legislative and executive). The special function of judges is to apply the law to individuals. It is a power extensive although not, Marshall consistently said, political or policy-oriented. Judicial JURISDICTION extends as far as does the law: common law, statute law, Constitution, treaties, and the law of nations (which Marshall influenced by several luminous opinions). In applying the law to individuals, courts are to care for individual rights, the very object of government in general. By "nature" or by "definition," courts are "those tribunals which are established for the security of property and to decide on human rights." Such rights are contained either in explicit constitutional provisions and amendments, or in "unwritten or common law," which the Constitution presupposes as the substratum of our law (and which Marshall thought was spelled out in traditional law books, such as Sir WILLIAM BLACKSTONE's *Commentaries on the Laws of England*). In short, courts are to construe all law in the light of the rights of person and property that are the object of law—as well as in the light of the constitutional authority of the other branches.

Marshall was fond of contrasting the Americans' "rational liberty," which afforded "solid safety and real security," with revolutionary France's "visionary" civic liberty, which had led to a despotism "borrowing the garb and usurping the name of freedom." While trying AARON BURR, Marshall repeatedly noted the "tenderness" of American law for the rights of the accused. His *Life of Washington* mixes praise of FREEDOM OF SPEECH and of conscience with attacks on religious persecution. Yet Marshall also said that morals and free institutions need to be "cherished" by public opinion; he would not suppose that a free MARKETPLACE OF IDEAS insures progress in public enlightenment. He did suppose that a rather free economic marketplace would lead to progress in national wealth. Marshall defended property rights in the sense of rights of contract or vested rights, rights that vest under contract and originate in a right to the fruits of one's labor and enterprise. By protecting industrious acquisitions the judiciary fosters the dynamic economy of free enterprise. Rational liberty is prudent liberty, which breeds power as well as wealth: the "legitimate greatness" of a "widespreading, rising empire," extending from "the Ste. Croix to the Gulph of Mexico, from the Atlantic to the Pacific." By directly securing the rights of property, courts indirectly secure the "vast republic."

While courts are "the mere instruments of the law, and can will nothing," or at most possess a legal discretion governed by unwritten principles of individual rights, the executive and legislature enjoy broad political discretion for the safety and interrelation of all. President and Congress are indeed subordinate to the Constitution of ENUMERATED POWERS and explicit restrictions. Marshall did not follow ALEXANDER HAMILTON, and would not have followed some later Supreme Courts, in inferring a plenary legislative power. His arguments, however, take aim at enemies on the other flank, at Jeffersonian strict constructionists who allowed only powers explicit in the Constitution or necessarily deduced from explicit powers. A constitution of government is not a "legal code," Marshall replied, and its enumerated powers are vested fully and encompass the full panoply of appropriate means. In *McCulloch,* Marshall set forth the core of the American doctrine of SOVEREIGNTY: the need for great governmental powers to confront inevitable crises. Maryland had placed a prohibitive tax on a branch of the national bank, and its counsel denied federal authority to charter a bank (a power not explicit in the Constitution). Ours is a constitution, Marshall replied, "intended to endure for ages to come, and, consequently, to be adapted to the various *crises* of human affairs." Armies must be marched and taxes raised throughout the land. "Is that construction of the Constitution to be preferred which would render these operations difficult, hazardous, and expensive?" In a similar spirit Marshall defended an executive vigorous in war and FOREIGN AFFAIRS and able to overawe faction and rebellion at home. He struck down, as violating Congress's power to regulate commerce among the states, state acts imposing import taxes or reserving monopolistic privileges. The arguments are typical. Great powers are granted for great objects. A narrow interpretation would defeat the object: the words must be otherwise construed. Thus a nation is raised. Individual enterprise, a national flow of trade, and the bonds of mutual interest breach barriers of state, section, and custom. The machinery of government is geared for great efforts of direction and coercion. The national sovereign, limited in its tasks, supreme in all means needed for their accomplishment, rises over the once independent state sovereignties. Marshall acknowledged the states' independent powers as well as the complexities of federalism: America was "for many purposes an entire nation, and for others several distinct and independent sovereignties." He tried above all to protect the federal government's superior powers from what the Framers had most feared, the encroachments of the states, more strongly entrenched in the people's affections.

Like virtually all of the Framers, Marshall was devoted to popular government. Yet SHAYS' REBELLION of western Massachusetts farmers (1786–1787) had made him wonder whether "man is incapable of governing himself." He thought the new Constitution a republican remedy for the flaws of republican government, and for some time he thought constitutional restraints might suffice to rein the people to sound government. Marshall's republicanism encompassed both representative government and balanced government. The people are to grant their sovereignty to institutions for exercise by their representatives. A more substantial, virtuous, and enlightened Senate and President would balance the more popular House of Representatives, the dangerous house in a popular republic. Marshall came to be troubled by a decline in the quality of American leaders, from the great statesmen of the Revolution and founding, notably Washington, to the "superficial showy acquirements" of "party politicians." He came to be deeply disheartened by the tumultuous growth of democratic control, inspired by THOMAS JEFFERSON and consummated by ANDREW JACKSON. A "torrent of public opinion," inflamed by the French Revolution, aroused the old debtor and STATES' RIGHTS party during Washington's administration. It led to democratic societies, set up to watch the government, and then to a legislature that conveyed popular demands without much filtering. Marshall had anticipated that Jefferson would ally himself with the House of Representatives, and become leader of the party dominating the whole legislature, thus increasing his own power while weakening the office of President and the fundamentals of balanced government. During Jackson's terms (1828–1836), with the presidency transformed from a check on the majority to the tribune of the majority, Marshall favored reduction of its power, a tenure limited to one term, and even selection of the President by lot from among the senators. He called his early republicanism "wild and enthusiastic democracy," and came to doubt that the constitutional Union could endure in the face of resurgent sectionalism and populism.

The eventual dissolution of political balances made crucial Marshall's decisive accomplishment as he and Jefferson began their terms of office: the confirmation of the judiciary as interpreter and enforcer of the fundamental law. Although Marshall's opinion in *Marbury* denied that courts can exercise political power, it gave courts power to circumscribe the forbidden sphere, to determine the powers of legislatures and executives. Marshall's argument for this unprecedented judicial authority recalled "certain principles . . . long and well established." In deciding cases judges must declare what the law is. The Constitution is the supreme law. Judges must apply the Constitution in preference to statute when the two conflict—else the Constitution is not permanent but "alterable when the legislature shall please to alter it." The argument established the Supreme Court as enforcer of the constitutional government central to America's constitutional democracy. Marshall pointed to the horrors of "legislative omnipotence," only inconspicuously bestowing on courts a ruling potency as the voice of the Constitution. Marshall's opinion, the object of intense scrutiny ever since, was faithful to the CONSTITUTIONAL CONVENTION's supposition that there will be some JUDICIAL REVIEW of statutes and to its suspicion of democratic legislatures. It did not confront certain difficulties, notably those of a Supreme Court (like the TANEY COURT in DRED SCOTT V. SANDFORD, 1857) whose decisions violate the principles of the Constitution. Marshall's judicial reasonings were his attempt to keep judges, and his country, from violating the Constitution that preserves those principles.

ROBERT K. FAULKNER

Bibliography

BEVERIDGE, ALBERT J. 1916–1919 *The Life of John Marshall.* 4 Vols. Boston: Houghton Mifflin.

CORWIN, EDWARD S. 1919 *John Marshall and the Constitution.* New Haven, Conn.: Yale University Press.

FAULKNER, ROBERT K. 1968 *The Jurisprudence of John Marshall.* Princeton, N.J.: Princeton University Press.

HOLMES, OLIVER WENDELL 1952 John Marshall. Pages 266–271 in *Collected Legal Papers.* New York: Peter Smith.

WHITE, G. EDWARD 1976 *The American Judicial Tradition.* Pages 7–34. New York: Oxford University Press.

ZIEGLER, BENJAMIN MUNN 1939 *The International Law of John Marshall.* Chapel Hill: University of North Carolina Press.

MARSHALL, THURGOOD (1908–)

Thurgood Marshall, the first black Justice of the Supreme Court, was born in Baltimore in 1908. After graduation from Lincoln University in Pennsylvania, Marshall attended Howard University Law School. Graduating first in his class in 1933, Marshall became one of CHARLES H. HOUSTON's protégés. He began practice in Baltimore, where he helped revitalize the local branch of the National Association for the Advancement of Colored People (NAACP). Houston, who had become special counsel to the NAACP in New York, was developing a program of litigation designed to attack segregated education in the South; Marshall joined the NAACP staff as Houston's assistant in 1936.

Of all the Justices who have served on the Supreme Court, Marshall has the strongest claim to having contributed as much to the development of the Constitution as a lawyer as he has done as a judge. At the start of his career, race relations law centered on the SEPARATE BUT EQUAL DOCTRINE. In his initial years at the NAACP, Marshall brought a number of lawsuits challenging unequal salaries paid to black and white teachers in the South. After Marshall succeeded Houston as special counsel in 1938, he became both a litigator and a coordinator of litigation, most of it challenging segregated education. He also successfully argued a number of cases involving RACIAL DISCRIMINATION in the administration of criminal justice before the Supreme Court. When social and political changes during World War II led to increased black militancy and support for the NAACP, Marshall was able to expand the NAACP's legal staff by hiring an extremely talented group of young, mostly black lawyers. Although he continued to conduct some litigation, Marshall gradually assumed the roles of appellate advocate and overall strategist. Relying on his staff to generate helpful legal theories, he selected the theory most likely to accomplish the NAACP's goals. This process culminated in the five lawsuits decided by the Supreme Court as BROWN V. BOARD OF EDUCATION (1954). Marshall had used his staff to develop these cases and the legal theory that segregation was unconstitutional no matter how equal were the physical facilities. After the Supreme Court held that segregation was unconstitutional and that it should be eliminated "with ALL DELIBERATE SPEED," Marshall and the NAACP staff devoted much of their attention to overcoming the impediments that southern states began to place in the way of DESEGREGATION. These impediments included school closures and investigations and harassment of the NAACP and its lawyers.

Marshall left the NAACP in 1961, having been nominated by President JOHN F. KENNEDY to a position on the UNITED STATES COURT OF APPEALS for the Second Circuit. His confirmation to that position was delayed by southern opposition for over eleven months. During Marshall's four years on the Second Circuit, he wrote an important opinion holding that the DOUBLE JEOPARDY clause applied to the states, anticipating by four years the position that the Supreme Court would adopt in BENTON V. MARYLAND (1969), a decision written by Justice Marshall. He also urged in dissent an expansive interpretation of statutes allowing persons charged with crimes in state courts to remove those cases to federal court. (See CIVIL RIGHTS REMOVAL.) Marshall was nominated as solicitor general by President LYNDON B. JOHNSON in 1965. He served as solicitor general for two years, during which he supervised the disposition of criminal cases imperiled by illegal WIRETAPPING. Johnson appointed him in 1967 to succeed Justice TOM C. CLARK on the Supreme Court.

Justice Marshall's contributions to constitutional development have been shaped by the fact that for most of his tenure his views were among the most liberal on a centrist or conservative Court. As he had at the NAACP, and as have most recent Justices, Marshall relied heavily on his staff to present his views forcefully and systematically in his opinions.

For a few years after Marshall's appointment to the Court, he was part of the liberal bloc of the WARREN COURT. Despite the tradition that newly appointed Justices are not assigned important majority opinions, Justice Marshall wrote several important free speech opinions during his first two years on the Court. In STANLEY V. GEORGIA (1969), he held that a state could not punish a person merely for possessing obscene materials in his home; the only justification for such punishment, guaranteeing a citizenry that did not think impure thoughts, was barred by the FIRST AMENDMENT. AMALGAMATED FOOD EMPLOYEES UNION v. LOGAN VALLEY PLAZA (1968) recognized the contemporary importance of privately owned SHOPPING CENTERS as places of public resort, holding that centers must be made available, over their owners' objections, to those who wish to picket or pass out leaflets on subjects of public interest. PICKERING v. BOARD OF EDUCATION (1968) established the right of public employees to complain about the way in which their superiors were discharging their responsibilities to the public.

With the appointment of four Justices by President RICHARD M. NIXON, Justice Marshall rapidly found himself in dissent on major civil liberties issues. *Stanley* was limited by *United States v. Reidel* (1971) to private possession and not extended to what might have seemed its logical corollary, acquisition of obscene material for private use. *Logan Valley Plaza* was overruled in HUDGENS v. NATIONAL LABOR RELATIONS BOARD (1976), and *Pickering* was limited by a relatively narrow definition of complaints relating to public duties in *Connick v. Myers* (1983). Marshall became part of a small liberal bloc that could prevail only by attracting more conservative members, who could be kept in the coalition by allowing them to write the majority opinions. In the series of death penalty cases, for example, Justice Marshall stated his conclusion that capital punishment was unconstitutional in all circumstances, but when a majority for a narrower position could be found to overturn the imposition of the death penalty in a particular case, he joined that majority.

Thus, after 1970, Marshall rarely wrote important opinions for the Court regarding FREEDOM OF SPEECH, CRIMINAL PROCEDURE, or EQUAL PROTECTION. Two of his opinions in cases about the PREEMPTION of state law by federal regulations, *Jones v. Rath Packing Co.* (1977) and *Douglas v. Seacoast Products* (1977), seem likely to endure as statements of general principle. More often he was assigned to write opinions in which a nearly unanimous Court adopted a "conservative" position. For example, in *Gillette v. United States* (1971), Justice Marshall's opinion for the Court rejected statutory and constitutional claims to exemption from the military draft by men whose religious beliefs led them to oppose participation in some but not all wars. Undoubtedly because of his race and because of his desire to see a majority support positions helpful to blacks, Marshall rarely wrote important opinions in cases directly implicating matters of race, although he did write two significant dissents, one defending AFFIRMATIVE ACTION in REGENTS OF THE UNIVERSITY OF CALIFORNIA v. BAKKE (1978), and another emphasizing blacks' lack of access to political power in MOBILE v. BOLDEN (1980). But Justice Marshall's major contributions have come in areas where the experience of race has historically shaped the context in which apparently nonracial issues arise.

Marshall occasionally received the assignment in important civil liberties cases. His opinion in POLICE DEPARTMENT OF CHICAGO v. MOSLEY (1972) crystallized the equality theme in the law of freedom of speech. There he emphasized the importance for free expression of the rule that governments may not regulate one type of speech because of its content, in a setting where speech with a different content would not be regulated: "[G]overnment may not grant the use of a forum to people whose views it finds acceptable, but deny use to those wishing to express less favored or more controversial views. . . . Selective exclusions . . . may not be based on content alone, and may not be justified by reference to content alone." Unless it were prohibited, discrimination based on content would allow governments, which ought to be controlled by the electorate, to determine what the electorate would hear. Although the *Mosley* principle is probably stated too broadly, because differential regulation of categories of speech such as OBSCENITY or COMMERCIAL SPEECH is allowed, still it serves as a central starting point for analysis, from which departures must be justified.

His opinion in *Memorial Hospital v. Maricopa County* (1974) synthesized a line of cases regarding the circumstances in which a state might deny benefits such as nonemergency medical care for INDIGENTS to those who had recently come to the state. If the benefit was so important that its denial could be characterized as a penalty for exercising the RIGHT TO TRAVEL, it was unconstitutional.

Because of the relatively rapid shift in the Court's composition, most of Justice Marshall's major contributions to the constitutional development have come through dissents. Several major dissenting opinions by Justice Marshall have helped shape the law of equal protection. The opinions criticize a rigid approach in which classifications based on race and a few other categories are to be given STRICT SCRUTINY while all other classifications must be "merely rational." Marshall, in dissents in DANDRIDGE v. WILLIAMS (1970) and SAN ANTONIO INDEPENDENT SCHOOL DISTRICT v. RODRIGUEZ (1973), offered a more flexible approach. He argued that the courts should examine legislation that affects different groups differently by taking into account the nature of the group—the degree to which it has been discriminated against in the past, the actual access to political power it has today—and the importance of the interests affected. Under this "sliding scale" approach, a statute differentially affecting access to WELFARE BENEFITS might be unconstitutional while one with the same effects on access to public recreational facilities might be permitted. A majority of the Court has not explicitly adopted the "sliding scale" approach, but Justice Marshall's sustained criticisms of the rigid alternative have produced a substantial, though not entirely acknowledged, acceptance of a more nuanced approach to equal protection problems.

As *Logan Valley Plaza* showed, Justice Marshall has urged, usually in dissent, an expansive definition of those actors whose decisions are subject to constitutional control. In JACKSON V. METROPOLITAN EDISON CO. (1974) the majority found that the decision of a heavily regulated utility to terminate service for nonpayment was not "state action" under any of the several strands of that DOCTRINE. Justice Marshall's dissent argued that state involvement was significant when looked at as a whole and, more important, pointed out that on the majority's analysis the utility could, without constitutional problems, terminate service to blacks. On the assumption, confirmed in later cases, that the result is incorrect, Justice Marshall's argument effectively demonstrated that the "state action" doctrine is actually a doctrine about the merits of the challenged decision: if it is a decision that the Justices believe should not be controlled by the Constitution, there is no "state action," whereas if it is a decision that the Justices believe should be controlled by the Constitution, there is state action.

Finally, after joining the seminal opinion in GOLDBERG V. KELLY (1968), which held that the Constitution defined the procedures under which public benefits, the "new property" of the welfare state, could be taken away, Justice Marshall dissented in later cases where the Court substantially narrowed the scope of *Goldberg*. His position, in cases such as BOARD OF REGENTS V. ROTH (1972), has been that everyone must be presumed to be entitled to those benefits, and that the presumption can be overcome only after constitutionality-defined procedures have been followed.

In most of the areas of law to which Justice Marshall's opinions have made significant contributions the linked strands of race and poverty appear. Discrimination by nominally private actors and suppression of speech on racial issues have played an important part in the black experience. Similarly, wealth and poverty as grounds for allocating public resources are classifications closely linked to race. Justice Marshall's desire to adopt a more flexible approach to equal protection law stems from his awareness that only such an approach would allow the courts to address difficulties that the ordinary routines of society cause for the poor. For example, his dissent in *United States v. Kras* (1973) objected to the imposition of a fifty dollar filing fee on those who sought discharges of their debts in bankruptcy. But it would be misleading to conclude that Thurgood Marshall's most important role in constitutional development was what he did as a Justice of the Supreme Court. Rather it was what he did as a lawyer for the NAACP before and after the decision in *Brown v. Board of Education.*

MARK V. TUSHNET

Bibliography

KLUGER, RICHARD 1976 *Simple Justice.* New York: Knopf.

MARSHALL v. BARLOW'S, INC. 436 U.S. 307 (1978)

In *Marshall* the Supreme Court held unconstitutional a congressional enactment authorizing Occupational Safety and Health Administration inspectors to conduct WARRANTLESS SEARCHES of employment facilities to monitor compliance with regulations. PROBABLE CAUSE for a warrant can, however, be satisfied on a lesser showing than that required in a search for criminal EVIDENCE.

JACOB W. LANDYNSKI

MARSHALL COURT (1801–1835)

In 1801 the Supreme Court existed on the fringe of American awareness. Its prestige was slight, and it was more ignored than respected. On January 20, 1801, the day President JOHN ADAMS nominated JOHN MARSHALL for the chief justiceship, the commissioners of the DISTRICT OF COLUMBIA informed Congress that the Court had no place to hold its February term. The Senate consented to the use of one of its committee rooms, and Marshall took his seat on February 4 in a small basement chamber. At the close of 1809, Benjamin Latrobe, the architect, reported that the basement had been redesigned to enlarge the courtroom and provide an office for the clerk and a library room for the Justices. In 1811, however, Latrobe reported that the Court "had been obliged to hold their sittings in a tavern," because Congress had appropriated no money for "fitting up and furnishing the Court-room. . . ." After the British burned the Capitol in 1814 Congress again neglected to provide for the Court. It held its 1815 term in a private home, and for several years after met in temporary Capitol quarters that were "little better than a dungeon." The Court moved into permanent quarters in 1819. In 1824 a New York correspondent described the Court's Capitol chamber: "In the first place, it is like going down cellar to reach it. The room is on the basement story in an obscure part of the north wing. . . . A stranger might traverse the dark avenues of the Capitol for a week, without finding the remote corner in which Justice is administered to the American Republic." He added that the courtroom was hardly large enough for a police court.

The Supreme Court, however, no longer lacked dignity or respect. It had become a force that commanded recognition. In 1819 a widely read weekly described it as so awesome that some regarded it with reverence. That year THOMAS JEFFERSON complained that the Court had made the Constitution a "thing of wax," which it shaped as it pleased, and in 1824 he declared that the danger he most feared was the Court's "consolidation of our government." Throughout the 1820s Congress debated bills to curb the Court, which, said a senator, the people blindly adored—a "self-destroying idolatry." ALEXIS DE TOCQUEVILLE, writing in 1831, said: "The peace, the prosperity, and the very existence of the Union are vested in the hands of the seven Federal judges. Without them, the Constitution would be a dead letter. . . ." Hardly a political question arose, he wrote, that did not become a judicial question.

Chief Justice Marshall was not solely responsible for the radical change in the Court's status and influence, but he made the difference. He bequeathed to the people of the United States what it was not in the political power of the Framers of the Constitution to give. Had the Framers been free agents, they would have proposed a national government that was unquestionably dominant over the states and possessed a formidable array of powers breathtaking in flexibility and scope. Marshall in more than a figurative sense was the supreme Framer, emancipated from a local constituency, boldly using his judicial position as an exalted platform from which to educate the nation to the true meaning, his meaning, of the Constitution. He wrote as if words of grandeur and power and union could make dreams come true. By the force of his convictions he tried to will a nation into being.

He reshaped the still malleable Constitution, giving clarification to its ambiguities and content to its omissions that would allow it to endure for "ages to come" and would make the government of the Union supreme in the federal system. Marshall is the only judge in our history whose distinction as a great nationalist statesman derives wholly from his judicial career. Justice OLIVER WENDELL HOLMES once remarked, "If American law were to be represented by a single figure, sceptic and worshipper alike would agree without dispute that the figure could be one alone, and that one, John Marshall." That the Court had remained so weak after a decade of men of such high caliber as JOHN JAY, OLIVER ELLSWORTH, JAMES WILSON, JAMES IREDELL, WILLIAM PATERSON, and SAMUEL CHASE demonstrates not their weakness but Marshall's achievement in making the Court an equal branch of the national government.

Until 1807 he cast but one of six votes, and after 1807, when Congress added another Justice, but one of seven. One Justice, one vote has always been the rule of the Court, and the powers of anyone who is Chief Justice depend more on the person than the office. From 1812, BUSHROD WASHINGTON and Marshall were the only surviving Federalists, surrounded by five Justices appointed by Presidents Thomas Jefferson and JAMES MADISON; yet Marshall dominated the Court in a way that no one has ever since. During Marshall's thirty-five-year tenure, the Court delivered 1,106 opinions in all fields of law, and he wrote 519; he dissented only eight times. He wrote forty of the Court's sixty-four opinions in the field of constitutional law, dissenting only once in a constitutional case. Of the twenty-four constitutional opinions for the Court that he did not write, only two were important: MARTIN v. HUNTER'S LESSEE (1816), a case in which he did not sit, and OGDEN v. SAUNDERS (1827), the case in which he dissented. He virtually monopolized the constitutional cases for himself and won the support of his associates, even though they were members of the opposing political party.

Marshall's long tenure coincided with the formative period of our constitutional law. He was in the right place at the right time, filling, as Holmes said, "a strategic place in the campaign of history." But it took the right man to make the most of the opportunity. Marshall had the character, intellect, and passion for his job that his predecessors lacked. He had a profound sense of mission comparable to a religious "calling." Convinced that he knew what the Constitution should mean and what it was meant to achieve, he determined to give its purposes enduring expression and make them prevail. The Court was, for him, a judicial pulpit and political platform from which to address the nation, to compete, if possible, with the executive and legislative in shaping public opinion.

Marshall met few of the abstract criteria for a "great" judge. A great judge should possess intellectual rectitude and brilliance. Marshall was a fierce and crafty partisan who manipulated facts and law. A great judge should have a self-conscious awareness of his biases and a determination to be as detached as human fallibility will allow. In Marshall the judicial temperament flickered weakly; unable to muzzle his deepest convictions, he sought to impose them on the nation, sure that he was right. He intoxicated himself with the belief that truth, history, and the Constitution dictated his opinions, which merely declared the law rather than made the law. A great judge should have confidence in majority rule, tempered by his commitment to personal freedom and fairness. Marshall did not think men capable of self-government and inclined to favor financial and industrial capitalism over most other interests. A great judge should have a superior technical proficiency, modified by a sense of justice and ethical behavior beyond suspicion. Marshall's judicial ethics were not unquestionable. He should have disqualified himself in MARBURY V. MADISON (1803) because of his negligent complicity. He overlooked colossal corruption in FLETCHER V. PECK (1810) to decide a land title case by a doctrine that promoted his personal interests. He wrote the opinion in MCCULLOCH V. MARYLAND (1819) before hearing the case. Marshall's "juridical learning," as Justice JOSEPH STORY, his reverent admirer and closest colleague, conceded, "was not equal to that of the great masters in the profession. . . ." He was, said Story, first, last, and always, "a Federalist of the good old school," and in the maintenance of its principles "he was ready at all times to stand forth a determined advocate and supporter." He was, in short, a Federalist activist who used the Constitution to legitimate predetermined results. A great judge should have a vision of national and moral greatness, combined with respect for the federal system. Marshall had that—and an instinct for statecraft and superb literary skills. These qualities, as well as his activism, his partisanship, and his sense of mission, contributed to his inordinate influence.

So too did his qualities of leadership and his personal traits. He was generous, gentle, warm, charming, considerate, congenial, and open. At a time when members of the Court lived together in a common boarding house during their short terms in Washington, his charismatic personality enabled him to preside over a judicial family, inspire loyalty, and convert his brethren to his views. He had a cast-iron will, an astounding capacity for hard work (witness the number of opinions he wrote for the Court), and formidable powers of persuasion. He thought audaciously in terms of broad and basic principles that he expressed axiomatically as absolutes. His arguments were masterful intellectual performances, assuming that his premises were valid. Inexorably and with developing momentum he moved from an unquestioned premise to a foregone conclusion. Jefferson once said that he never admitted anything when conversing with Marshall. "So sure as you admit any position to be good, no matter how remote from the conclusion he seeks to establish, you are gone." Marshall's sophistry, according to Jefferson, was so great, "you must never give him an affirmative answer or you will be forced to grant his conclusion. Why, if he were to ask me if it were daylight or not, I'd reply, 'Sir, I don't know. I can't tell.' " Marshall could also be imperious. He sometimes gave as the OPINION OF THE COURT a position that had not mustered a majority. According to one anecdote, Marshall is supposed to have said to Story, the greatest legal scholar in our history, "That, Story, is the law. You find the precedents."

The lengthy tenure of the members of the Marshall Court also accounts for its achievements. On the pre-Marshall Court, the Justices served briefly; five quit in a decade. The Marshall Court lasted—BROCKHOLST LIVINGSTON seventeen years, THOMAS TODD nineteen, GABRIEL DUVALL twenty-four, WILLIAM JOHNSON thirty, Bushrod Washington thirty-one, and Marshall outlasted them all. Story served twenty-four years with Marshall and ten more after his death; SMITH THOMPSON served fifteen years with Marshall and eight years after. This continuity in personnel contributed to a consistent point of view in constitutional doctrine—a view that was, substantially, Marshall's. From 1812, when the average age of the Court's members was only forty-three, through 1823—twelve successive terms—the Court had the same membership, the longest period in its history without a change, and during that period the Marshall Court decided its most important cases except for *Marbury.*

Marshall also sought to strengthen the Court by inaugurating the practice of one Justice's giving the opinion of the Court. Previously the Justices had delivered their opinions SERIATIM, each writing an opinion in each case in the style of the English courts. That practice forced each Justice to take the trouble of understanding each case, of forming his opinion on it, and showing publicly the reasons that led to his judgment. Such were Jefferson's arguments for seriatim opinions; and Marshall understood that one official opinion augmented the Court's strength by giving the appearance of unity and harmony. Marshall realized that even if each Justice reached similar conclusions, the lines of argument and explanation of doctrine might vary with style and thought of every individual, creating uncertainty and impairing confidence in the Court as an institution. He doubtless also understood that by massing his Court behind one authoritative opinion and by assigning so many opinions to himself, his own influence as well as the Court's would be enhanced. Jefferson's first appointee, Justice Johnson, sought to buck the practice for a while. He had been surprised, he later informed Jefferson, to discover the Chief Justice "delivering all the opinions in cases in which he sat, even in some instances when contrary to his own judgment and vote." When Johnson remonstrated in vain, Marshall lectured him on the "indecency" of judges' "cutting at each other," and Johnson soon learned to acquiesce "or become such a cypher in our consultations as to effect no good at all." Story, too, learned to swallow his convictions to enhance the "authority of the Court." His "usual practice," said Story, was "to submit in silence" to opinions with which he disagreed. Even Marshall himself observed in an 1827 case, by which time he was losing control of his Court, that his usual policy when differing from majority was "to acquiesce silently in its opinion."

Like other trailblazing activist judges, Marshall squeezed a case for all it was worth, intensifying its influence. For Marshall a constitutional case was a medium for explaining his philosophy of the supreme and FUNDAMENTAL LAW, an occasion for sharing his vision of national greatness, a link between capitalism and CONSTITUTIONALISM, and an opportunity for a basic treatise. Justice Johnson protested in 1818, "We are constituted to decide causes, and not to discuss themes, or digest systems." He preferred, he said, to decide no more in any case "than what the case itself necessarily requires." Ordinary Justices decide only the immediate question on narrow grounds; but Marshall, confronted by some trivial question—whether a justice of the peace had a right to his commission or whether peddlers of lottery tickets could be fined—would knife to the roots of the controversy, discover that it involved some great constitutional principle, and explain it in the broadest possible way, making the case seem as if the life of the Union or the supremacy of the Constitution were at stake. His audacity in generalizing was impressive; his strategy was to take the highest ground and make unnerving use of OBITER DICTA; and then, as a matter of tactics, almost unnoticeably decide on narrow grounds. *Marbury* is remembered for Marshall's exposition of JUDICIAL REVIEW, not for his judicial humility in declining JURISDICTION and refusing to issue the WRIT OF MANDAMUS. COHENS V. VIRGINIA (1821) is remembered for Marshall's soaring explication of the supremacy of the JUDICIAL POWER OF THE UNITED STATES, not for the decision in favor of Virginia's power to fine unlicensed lottery ticket peddlers. GIBBONS V. OGDEN (1824) is remembered for its sweeping discourse on the COMMERCE CLAUSE of the Constitution, not for the decision that the state act conflicted with an obscure act of Congress.

Marshall's first major opinion, in *Marbury,* displayed his political cunning, suppleness in interpretation, doctrinal boldness, instinct for judicial survival, and ability to maneuver a case beyond the questions on its face. Having issued the show cause order to Madison, the Court seemingly was in an impossible position once Jefferson's supporters called that order a judicial interference with the executive branch. To decide for Marbury would provoke a crisis that the Court could not survive: Madison would ignore the Court, which had no way to enforce its decision, and the Court's enemies would have a pretext for IMPEACHMENT. To decide against Marbury would appear to endorse the illegal acts of the executive branch and concede that the Court was helpless. Either course of action promised judicial humiliation and loss of independence. Marshall therefore found a way to make a tactical retreat while winning a great strategic victory for judicial power. After upbraiding the executive branch for violating Marbury's rights, Marshall concluded that the Court had no JURISDICTION in the case, because a provision of an act of Congress conflicted with Article III. He held that provision unconstitutional by, first, giving it a sweeping construction its text did not bear and, second, by comparing it to his very narrow construction of Article III. Thus he reached and decided the great question, not argued by counsel, whether the Court had the power to declare unconstitutional an act of Congress. By so doing he answered from the bench his critics in Congress who, now that they were in power, had renounced judicial review during the debate on the repeal of the JUDICIARY ACT OF 1801. Characteristically Marshall relied on no precedents, not even on the authority of THE FEDERALIST #78. Significantly, he chose a safe act of Congress to void—section 13 of the JUDICIARY ACT OF 1789, which concerned not the province of the Congress or the President but of the Supreme Court, its authority to issue writs of mandamus in cases of ORIGINAL JURISDICTION. But Marshall's exposition of judicial review was, characteristically, broader than the holding on section 13. Jefferson, having been given no stick with which to beat Marshall, privately fumed: "Nothing in the Constitution has given them a right to decide for the Executive, more than to the Executive to decide for them," he wrote in a letter. "The opinion which gives to the judges the right to decide what laws are constitutional, and what not, not only for themselves in their own sphere of action, but also for the Legislature and Executive also, in their spheres, would make the judiciary a despotic branch."

The Court did not dare to declare unconstitutional any other act of Congress which remained hostile to it throughout Marshall's tenure. STUART V. LAIRD (1803), decided shortly after *Marbury*, upheld the repeal of the Judiciary Act of 1801. (See JUDICIARY ACTS OF 1802.) A contrary decision would have been institutionally suicidal for the Court. Marshall's opinion in *Marbury* was daring enough; in effect he courageously announced the Court's independence of the other branches of the government. But he was risking retaliation. Shortly before the arguments in *Marbury*, Jefferson instructed his political allies in the House to start IMPEACHMENT proceedings against JOHN PICKERING, a federal district judge; the exquisite timing was a warning to the Supreme Court. Even earlier, Jeffersonian leaders in both houses of Congress openly spoke of impeaching the Justices. The threats were not idle. Two months after *Marbury* was decided, Justice Chase on circuit attacked the administration in a charge to a GRAND JURY, and the House prepared to impeach him. Senator WILLIAM GILES of Virginia, the majority leader, told Senator JOHN QUINCY ADAMS that not only Chase "but all the other Judges of the Supreme Court," except William Johnson, "must be impeached and removed." Giles thought that holding an act of Congress unconstitutional was ground for impeachment. "Impeachment was not a criminal prosecution," according to Giles, who was Jefferson's spokesman in the Senate. "And a removal by impeachment was nothing more than a declaration by Congress to this effect: you hold dangerous opinions, and if you are suffered to carry them into effect, you will work the destruction of the Union. We want your offices for the purposes of giving them to men who will fill them better."

Intimidated by Chase's impending impeachment, Marshall, believing himself to be next in line, wrote to Chase that "impeachment should yield to an APPELLATE JURISDICTION in the legislature. A reversal of those legal opinions deemed unsound by the legislature would certainly better comport with the mildness of our character than a removal of the Judge who has rendered them unknowing of his fault." Less than a year after his *Marbury* opinion the fear of impeachment led an anguished Marshall to repudiate his reasoning and favor Congress as the final interpreter of the Constitution. Fortunately the greatest crisis in the Court's history eased when the Senate on March 1, 1805, failed to convict Chase on any of the eight articles of impeachment. Marshall and his Court were safe from an effort, never again repeated, to politicize the Court by making it subservient to Congress through impeachment.

The Court demonstrated its independence even when impeachment hung over it. In *Little v. Barreme* (1804) Marshall for the Court held that President Adams had not been authorized by Congress to order an American naval commander to seize a ship sailing from a French port. Justice Johnson on circuit vividly showed his independence of the President who had appointed him. To enforce the EMBARGO ACTS, Jefferson had authorized port officers to refuse clearance of ships with "suspicious" cargoes. In 1808 Johnson, on circuit in Charleston, ordered the clearance of a ship and denounced the President for having exceeded the power delegated by the Embargo Acts. Jefferson could not dismiss as partisan politics Johnson's rebuke that he had acted as if he were above the law. Justice Brockholst Livingston, another Jefferson appointee, also had occasion in 1808 to show his independence of the President. Jefferson supported a federal prosecution for TREASON against individuals who had opposed the embargo with violence. Livingston, who presided at the trial, expressed "astonishment" that the government would resort to a theory of "constructive treason" in place of the Constitution's definition of treason as levying war against the United States and he warned against a "precedent so dangerous." The jury speedily acquitted. After the tongue-lashing from his own appointees, Jefferson won an unexpected victory in the federal courts in the case of the brig *William* (1808). Federal district judge John Davis in Massachusetts sustained the constitutionality of the Embargo Acts on commerce clause grounds. Davis, a lifelong Federalist, showed how simplistic was Jefferson's raving about judicial politics.

The evidence for the Court's nonpartisanship seems plentiful. For example, Justice Story, Madison's appointee, spoke for an independent Court in *Gelston v. Hoyt* (1818), a suit for damages against government officials whose defense was that they had acted under President Madison's orders. Story, finding no congressional authority for these orders, "refused an extension of prerogative" power and added, "It is certainly against the general theory of our institutions to create discretionary powers by implication. . . ."

On the other hand, the Court supported the theory of IMPLIED POWERS in *McCulloch v. Maryland* (1819), which was the occasion of Marshall's most eloquent nationalist opinion. *McCulloch* had its antecedent in *United States v. Fisher* (1804), when the Court initially used BROAD CONSTRUCTION to sustain an act of Congress that gave to the government first claim against certain insolvent debtors. Enunciating the DOCTRINE of implied powers drawn from the NECESSARY AND PROPER CLAUSE, Marshall declared that Congress could employ any useful means to carry out its ENUMERATED POWER to pay national debts. That the prior claim of the government interfered with state claims was an inevitable result, Marshall observed, of the supremacy of national laws. Although a precursor of *McCulloch, Fisher* attracted no opposition because it did not thwart any major state interests.

When the Court did confront such interests for the first time, in UNITED STATES V. JUDGE PETERS (1809), Marshall's stirring nationalist passage, aimed at states that annulled judgments of the federal courts, triggered Pennsylvania's glorification of state sovereignty and denunciation of the "unconstitutional exercise of powers in the United States Courts." The state called out its militia to prevent execution of federal judgments and recommended a constitutional amendment to establish an "impartial tribunal" to resolve conflicts between "the general and state governments." State resistance collapsed only after President Madison backed the Supreme Court. Significantly, eleven state legislatures, including Virginia's, censured Pennsylvania's doctrines and endorsed the Supreme Court as the constitutionally established tribunal to decide state disputes with the federal courts.

The *Judge Peters* episode revealed that without executive support the Court could not enforce its mandate against a hostile state, which would deny that the Court was the final arbiter under the Constitution if the state's interests were thwarted. The episode also revealed that if other states had no immediate stake in the outcome of a case, they would neither advance doctrines of state sovereignty nor repudiate the Court's supreme appellate powers. When Virginia's high court ruled that the appellate jurisdiction of the Supreme Court did not extend to court judgments and that section 25 of the Judiciary Act of 1789 was unconstitutional, the Marshall Court, dominated by Republicans, countered by sustaining the crucial statute in *Martin v. Hunter's Lessee* (1816). Pennsylvania and other states did not unite behind Virginia when it proposed the constitutional amendment initiated earlier by Pennsylvania, because *Martin* involved land titles of no interest to other states. The fact that the states were not consistently doctrinaire and became aggressive only when Court decisions adversely affected them enabled the Court to prevail in the long run. A state with a grievance typically stood alone. But for the incapacity or unwillingess of the Court's state enemies to act together in their proposals to cripple it, the great nationalist decisions of the Marshall Court would have been as impotent as the one in *Worcester v. Georgia* (1832). *Worcester* majestically upheld the supreme law against the state's despoliation of the Cherokees, but President ANDREW JACKSON supported Georgia, which flouted the Court. Even Georgia, however, condemned the SOUTH CAROLINA ORDINANCE OF NULLIFICATION, and several state legislatures resolved that the Supreme Court was the constitutional tribunal to settle controversies between the United States and the states.

The Court made many unpopular decisions that held state acts unconstitutional. *Fletcher v. Peck,* which involved the infamous Yazoo land frauds, was the first case in which the Justices voided a state act for conflict with the Constitution itself. *Martin v. Hunter's Lessee,* which involved the title to the choice Fairfax estates in Virginia, was only the first of a line of decisions that unloosed shrill attacks on the Court's jurisdiction to decide cases on a WRIT OF ERROR to state courts. In *McCulloch* the Court supported the "monster monopoly," the Bank of the United States chartered by Congress, and held unconstitutional a state tax on its Baltimore branch. In *Cohens* the Court again championed its supreme appellate powers under section 25 of the Judiciary Act of 1789 and circumvented the ELEVENTH AMENDMENT. In STURGES V. CROWNINSHIELD (1819) the Court nullified a state bankruptcy statute that aided victims of an economic panic. In GREEN V. BIDDLE (1821) the Court used the CONTRACT CLAUSE when voiding Kentucky acts that supported valuable land claims. In OSBORN V. BANK OF THE UNITED STATES (1824) it voided an Ohio act that defied *McCulloch* and raised the question whether the Constitution had provided for a tribunal capable of protecting those who executed the laws of the Union from hostile state action.

When national supremacy had not yet been established and claims of state sovereignty bottomed state statutes and state judicial decisions that the Court overthrew, state assaults on the Court were inevitable, imperiling it and the Union it defended. Virginia, the most prestigious state, led the assault which Jefferson encouraged and SPENCER ROANE directed. Kentucky's legislature at one point considered military force to prevent execution of the *Green* decision. State attacks were vitriolic and intense, but they were also sporadic and not united. Ten state legislatures adopted resolutions against the Marshall Court, seven of them denouncing section 25 of the 1789 Act, which was the jurisdictional foundation for the Court's power of judicial review over the states. In 1821, 1822, 1824, and 1831 bills were introduced in Congress to repeal section 25. The assault on the Court was sharpest in the Senate, whose members were chosen by the state legislatures. Some bills to curb the Court proposed a constitutional amendment to limit the tenure of the Justices. One bill would have required seriatim opinions. Others proposed that no case involving a state or a constitutional question could be decided except unanimously; others accepted a 5–2 vote. One bill proposed that the Senate should have appellate powers over the Court's decisions.

Throughout the 1820s the attempts to curb the Court created a continuing constitutional crisis that climaxed in 1831, when Marshall despondently predicted the repeal of section 25 and the dissolution of the Union. In 1831, however, the House, after a great debate, defeated a repeal bill by a vote of 138–51; Southerners cast forty-five of the votes against the Court. What saved the Court was the inability of its opponents to mass behind a single course of action; many who opposed section 25 favored a less drastic measure. The Court had stalwart defenders, of course, including Senators DANIEL WEBSTER and JAMES BUCHANAN. Most important, it had won popular approbation. Although the Court had enemies in local centers of power, Americans thrilled to Marshall's paeans to the Constitution and the Union and he taught them to identify the Court with the Constitution and the Union.

A perceptible shift in the decisions toward greater tolerance for state action also helped dampen the fires under the Court in Marshall's later years. The coalition that Marshall had forged began to dissolve with the appointments of Justices Smith Thompson, JOHN MCLEAN, and HENRY BALDWIN. BROWN V. MARYLAND (1827), MARTIN V. MOTT (1827), AMERICAN INSURANCE COMPANY V. CANTER (1828), WESTON V. Charleston (1829), CRAIG V. MISSOURI (1830), and the CHEROKEE INDIAN CASES (1832) continued the lines of doctrine laid down by the earlier Marshall Court. But the impact of new appointments was felt in the decisions of *Ogden v. Saunders* (1827), WILLSON V. BLACKBIRD CREEK MARSH COMPANY (1829) and PROVIDENCE BANK V. BILLINGS (1830). In Marshall's last decade on the Court, six decisions supported nationalist claims against seventeen for state claims. During the same decade there were ten decisions against claims based on VESTED RIGHTS and only one sustaining such a claim. The shift in constitutional direction may also be inferred from the inability of the Marshall Court, because of dissension and illness, to resolve CHARLES RIVER BRIDGE V. WARREN BRIDGE, MAYOR OF NEW YORK V. MILN, and BRISCOE V. BANK OF KENTUCKY, all finally decided in 1837 under Marshall's successor against the late Chief Justice's wishes. Before his last decade the only important influence on the Court resulting from the fact that Republicans had a voting majority was the repudiation of a FEDERAL COMMON LAW OF CRIMES.

What was the legacy of the Marshall Court? It established the Court as a strong institution, an equal and coordinate branch of the national government, independent of the political branches. It established itself as the authoritative interpreter of the supreme law of the land. It declared its rightful authority to hold even acts of Congress and the President unconstitutional. It maintained continuing judicial review over the states to support the supremacy of national law. In so doing, the Court sustained the constitutionality of the act of Congress chartering the Bank of the United States, laying down the definitive exposition of the doctrine of implied powers. The Court also expounded the commerce clause in *Gibbons v. Ogden* (1824), with a breadth and vigor that provided the basis for national regulation of the economy generations later. Finally, the Court made the contract clause of the Constitution into a bulwark protecting both vested rights and risk capital. *Fletcher* supported the sanctity of public land grants to private parties, encouraging capital investment and speculation in land values. NEW JERSEY V. WILSON (1812) laid down the doctrine that a state grant of tax immunity constituted a contract within the protection of the Constitution, preventing subsequent state taxation for the life of the grant. DARTMOUTH COLLEGE V. WOODWARD (1819) protected private colleges and spurred the development of state universities; it also provided the constitutional props for the expansion of the private corporation by holding that a charter of incorporation is entitled to protection of the contract clause. The Marshall Court often relied on nationalist doctrines to prevent state measures that sought to regulate or thwart corporate development. Just as national supremacy, judicial review, and the Court's appellate jurisdiction were often interlocked, so too the interests of capitalism, nationalism, and judicial review were allied. Time has hardly withered the influence and achievements of the Marshall Court.

LEONARD W. LEVY

Bibliography

BAKER, LEONARD 1974 *John Marshall.* New York: Macmillan.

BEVERIDGE, ALBERT J. 1919 *The Life of John Marshall.* Vols. 3 and 4. Boston: Houghton Mifflin.

CORWIN, EDWARD S. 1919 *John Marshall and the Constitution: A Chronicle of the Supreme Court.* New Haven: Yale University Press.

HAINES, CHARLES G. 1944 *The Role of the Supreme Court in American Government and Politics, 1789–1835.* Berkeley: University of California Press.

HASKINS, GEORGE LEE and JOHNSON, HERBERT Q. 1981 *Foundations of Power: John Marshall, 1801–1815.* Volume 2 of the *Oliver Wendell Holmes Devise History of the Supreme Court of the United States.* New York: Macmillan.

KONEFSKY, SAMUEL J. 1964 *John Marshall and Alexander Hamilton.* New York: Macmillan.

MORGAN, DONALD G. 1954 *Justice William Johnson: The First Great Dissenter.* Columbia: University of South Carolina Press.

WARREN, CHARLES 1923 *The Supreme Court in United States History,* 3 vols. Boston: Little, Brown.

MARSHALL PLAN

At the Harvard University commencement exercises on June 5, 1947, Secretary of State George C. Marshall proposed that the United States undertake a vast program of postwar economic aid to assist the countries of Europe to rebuild from World War II. Neither Secretary Marshall nor President HARRY S. TRUMAN offered any constitutional authority for such a program, although some members of Congress, led by Senator ROBERT A. TAFT of Ohio, contended that the expenditure could not be justified under either the FOREIGN AFFAIRS power or the TAXING AND SPENDING POWER. Acting on the initiative of the United States, sixteen European nations formed the Organization of European Economic Cooperation (OEEC) which in turn issued a report setting forth Europe's collective needs and resources. The Soviet Union and other East European countries were invited to participate, but declined. Thereafter, on April 3, 1948, following the Soviet-sponsored coup in Czechoslovakia, which turned the tide of congressional opinion and caused the Marshall Plan expenditures to be justified as a national defense measure, the United States Congress passed the Economic Cooperation Act, to be administered by the Economic Cooperation Administration. Within four years and after the expenditure of $12–$13 billion in American loans and grants-in-aid, Europe made tremendous strides toward economic recovery. Coupled with increased military security (evidenced primarily in the signing of the NORTH ATLANTIC TREATY in 1949 and formation of the North Atlantic Alliance), this extensive economic recovery helped quell fears of Soviet expansion into Western Europe. The Marshall Plan and the OEEC resulting from it also created a precedent for further economic integration among the participating states of Western Europe.

BURNS H. WESTON

Bibliography

PRICE, HARRY BAYARD 1955 *The Marshall Plan and Its Meaning.* Ithaca, N.Y.: Cornell University Press.

MARTIAL LAW

See: Civil–Military Relations and the Constitution

MARTIN, LUTHER (1748–1826)

Luther Martin represented Maryland in the Continental Congress and signed the DECLARATION OF INDEPENDENCE. He was attorney general of Maryland from 1778 to 1805 and one of the early leaders of the American bar. Martin also represented Maryland at the CONSTITUTIONAL CONVENTION OF 1787, where he was a leader of the small-state faction. Although he favored the Convention's purpose, he consistently advocated positions that would have prevented the establishment of a strong central government. Fearing tyranny, he endorsed a one-term presidency and opposed JAMES MADISON's plan to allow a congressional veto of state or local laws.

The question of congressional REPRESENTATION seemed to him one of the most vexing problems. He favored a unicameral legislature and spoke fervently against proportionate representation at the House of Representatives, both in the Convention and afterward. His opposition in Philadelphia helped produce the deadlock that nearly wrecked the convention, but he served on the committee that framed the GREAT COMPROMISE and supported its recommendation. Martin favored JUDICIAL REVIEW but opposed authorizing Congress to create federal courts on the ground that state courts would suffice; they were bound by federal law and their decisions could be appealed to the Supreme Court. Martin also thought that the clause prohibiting interference with the OBLIGATION OF CONTRACTS was unwise; he warned of the inevitability of "great public calamities and distress" when such intervention would become essential—an argument vindicated in HOME BUILDING & LOAN V. BLAISDELL (1934). As the summer progressed, Martin grew increasingly restive. He opposed allowing suspension of the writ of HABEAS CORPUS and he strongly favored granting Congress power to tax or completely prohibit the slave trade. An opponent of slavery, he labeled its recognition in the Constitution "absurd and disgraceful to the last degree." Martin also concluded that later changes rendered the SUPREMACY CLAUSE, which he originally had proposed, "worse than useless." For these reasons, and because the Constitution contained no BILL OF RIGHTS, he opposed its ratification. In his influential tract of 1788 against RATIFICATION OF THE CONSTITUTION, a major anti-Federalist statement, Martin presented the fullest argument of the time in favor of equal representation of the states in Congress. Despite his opposition to the Constitution, Martin later switched his party allegiance and became known as the "Federalist bulldog."

A brilliant lawyer despite his later alcoholism, Martin appeared frequently in the Supreme Court and in state trials; he defended his old friend Justice SAMUEL CHASE at the latter's IMPEACHMENT trial in 1804 and represented AARON BURR against a TREASON charge three years later, winning both cases. (See EX PARTE BOLLMAN AND SWARTWOUT, 1807.) Among dozens of Court appearances, his most famous cases were FLETCHER V. PECK (1810) and MCCULLOCH V. MARYLAND (1819). In *McCulloch,* he eloquently defended Maryland's right to tax the federally chartered Bank of the United States, arguing for the application of the Tenth Amendment. Shortly after losing *McCulloch,* Martin suffered a severe stroke. After living as a penniless derelict for some time, he was eventually taken in by Burr. He died in 1826.

DAVID GORDON

Bibliography

CLARKSON, PAUL S. and JETT, R. SAMUEL 1970 *Luther Martin of Maryland.* Baltimore: Johns Hopkins University Press.

MARTIN v. HUNTER'S LESSEE
1 Wheaton 304 (1816)

Appomattox ultimately settled the issue that bottomed this case: were the states or was the nation supreme? As a matter of law, the opinion of the Supreme Court supplied the definitive answer, but law cannot settle a conflict between competing governments unless they agree to abide by the decision of a tribunal they recognize as having JURISDICTION to decide. Whether such a tribunal existed was the very issue in this case; more precisely the question was whether the Supreme Court's APPELLATE JURISDICTION extended to the state courts. In 1810 Virginia had supported the Court against state sovereignty advocates. Pennsylvania's legislature had resolved that "no provision is made in the Constitution for determining disputes between the general and state governments by an impartial tribunal." To that Virginia replied that the Constitution provides such a tribunal, "the Supreme Court, more eminently qualified . . . to decide the disputes aforesaid in an enlightened and impartial manner, than any other tribunal which could be erected." (See UNITED STATES V. JUDGE PETERS, 1809.) The events connected with the *Martin* case persuaded Virginia to reverse its position. The highest court of the state, the Virginia Court of Appeals, defied the Supreme Court, subverted the JUDICIAL POWER OF THE UNITED STATES as defined by Article III of the Constitution, circumvented the SUPREMACY CLAUSE (Article VI), and held unconstitutional a major act of Congress—all for the purpose of repudiating JUDICIAL REVIEW, or the Supreme Court's appellate jurisdiction over state courts and power to declare state acts void.

The *Martin* case arose out of a complicated and protracted legal struggle over land titles. Lord Fairfax died in 1781, bequeathing valuable tracts of his property in Virginia's Northern Neck to his nephew, Denny Martin, a British subject residing in England. During the Revolution Virginia had confiscated Loyalist estates and by an act of 1779, which prohibited alien enemies from holding land, declared the escheat, or reversion to the state, of estates then owned by British subjects. That act of 1779 did not apply to the estates of Lord Fairfax, who had been a Virginia citizen. The Treaty of Peace with Great Britain in 1783, calling for the restitution of all confiscated estates and prohibiting further confiscations, strengthened Martin's claim under the will of his uncle. In 1785, however, Virginia had extended its escheat law of 1779 to the Northern Neck, and four years later had granted some of those lands to one David Hunter. JAY'S TREATY of 1794, which protected the American property of British subjects, also buttressed Martin's claims. By then a Virginia district court, which included Judge ST. GEORGE TUCKER, decided in Martin's favor; Hunter appealed to the state's high court. JOHN MARSHALL, who had represented Martin, and James Marshall, his brother, joined a syndicate that arranged to purchase the Northern Neck lands. In 1796 the state legislature offered a compromise, which the Marshall syndicate accepted: the Fairfax devisees relinquished claim to the undeveloped lands of the Northern Neck in return for the state's recognition of their claim to Fairfax's manor lands. The Marshall syndicate accepted the compromise, thereby seeming to secure Hunter's claim, yet thereafter completed their purchase. In 1806, Martin's heir conveyed the lands to the syndicate, and in 1808 he appealed to the Court of Appeals, which decided in favor of Hunter two years later.

The Martin-Marshall interests, relying on the Treaty of 1783 and Jay's Treaty, took the case to the Supreme Court on a WRIT OF ERROR under section 25 of the JUDICIARY ACT OF 1789. That section provided in part that the nation's highest tribunal on writ of error might reexamine and reverse or affirm the final judgment of a state court if the state court sustained a state statute against a claim that the statute was repugnant to the Constitution, treaties, or laws of the United States, or if the state court decided against any title or right claimed under the treaties or federal authority. Chief Justice Marshall took no part in the case, and two other Justices were absent. Justice JOSEPH STORY, for a three-member majority and against the dissenting vote of Justice WILLIAM JOHNSON, reversed the judgment of the Virginia Court of Appeals, holding that federal treaties confirmed Martin's title. In the course of his opinion Story sapped the Virginia statutes escheating the lands of alien enemies and ignored the "compromise" of 1796. The mandate of the Supreme Court to the state Court of Appeals concluded: "You therefore are hereby commanded that such proceedings be had in said cause, as according to right and justice, and the laws of the United States, and agreeable to said judgment and instructions of said Supreme Court . . ." (*Fairfax's Devisee v. Hunter's Lessee,* 1813).

The state court that received this mandate consisted of eminent and proud men who regarded the Supreme Court as a rival; the man who dominated the state court was SPENCER ROANE, whose opinion Story had reversed. Roane, the son-in-law of PATRICK HENRY, was not just a judge; he was a state political boss, an implacable enemy of John Marshall, and the man whom THOMAS JEFFERSON would have appointed Chief Justice, given the chance. To Roane and his brethren, Story's opinion was more than an insulting encroachment on their judicial prerogatives. It raised the specter of national consolidation, provoking the need to rally around the STATES' RIGHTS principles of the VIRGINIA AND KENTUCKY RESOLUTIONS. Roane consulted with Jefferson and JAMES MONROE, and he called before his court the leading members of the state bar, who spoke for six days. Munford, the Virginia court reporter, observed: "The question whether this mandate should be obeyed excited all that attention from the Bench and Bar which its great importance truly merited." The reporter added that the court had its opinions ready for delivery shortly after the arguments. That was in April 1814, when the Republican political organization of Virginia dared not say anything that would encourage or countenance the states' rights doctrines of Federalist New England, which opposed the War of 1812 and thwarted national policies. Not until December 1815, when the crisis had passed and secessionism in the North had dissipated, did the Virginia Court of Appeals release its opinions.

Each of four state judges wrote opinions, agreeing that the Constitution had established a federal system in which SOVEREIGNTY was divided between the national and state governments, neither of which could control the other or any of its organs. To allow the United States or any of its departments to operate directly on the states or any of their departments would subvert the independence of the states, allow the creature to judge its creators, and destroy the idea of a national government of limited powers. Although conflicts between the states and the United States were inevitable, the Constitution "has provided no umpire" and did not authorize Congress to bestow on the Supreme Court a power to pass final judgment on the extent of the powers of the United States or of its own appellate jurisdiction. Nothing in the Constitution denied the power of a state court to pass finally upon the validity of state legislation. The states could hold the United States to the terms of the compact only if the state courts had the power to determine finally the constitutionality of acts of Congress. Section 25 of the Judiciary Act was unconstitutional because it vested appellate powers in the Supreme Court in a case where the highest court of a state has authoritatively construed state acts. In sum, the position of the Court of Appeals was that the Supreme Court cannot reverse a state court on a matter of state or even federal law, but a state court can hold unconstitutional an act of the United States. Thus, Roane, with Jefferson's approval, located in the state courts the ultimate authority to judge the extent of the powers of the national government; in 1798 Jefferson had centered that ultimate authority in the state legislatures. At the conclusion of their opinions, the Virginia judges entered their judgment:

> The court is unanimously of opinion, that the appellate power of the Supreme Court of the United States does not extend to this court, under a sound construction of the constitution of the United States; that so much of the 25th section of the act of Congress to establish the judicial courts of the United States, as extends the appellate jurisdiction of the Supreme Court to this court, is not in pursuance of the constitution of the United States; that the writ of error, in this cause, was improvidently allowed, under the authority of that act; that the proceedings thereon in the Supreme Court were *Coram non judice* [before a court without jurisdiction], in relation to this court, and that obedience to its mandate be declined by the court.

When the case returned a second time to the Supreme Court on writ of error, Marshall again absented himself and Story again wrote the opinion. The *Martin* Court, consisting of five Republicans and one Federalist, was unanimous, though Johnson concurred separately. Story's forty-page opinion on behalf of federal judicial review is a masterpiece, far superior to Marshall's performance in MARBURY V. MADISON (1803) on behalf of national judicial review. In its cadenced prose, magisterial tone, nationalist doctrine, incisive logic, and driving repetitiveness, Story's opinion foreshadowed Marshall's later and magnificent efforts in MCCULLOCH V. MARYLAND (1819), COHENS V. VIRGINIA (1821), and GIBBONS V. OGDEN (1824), suggesting that they owe as much to Story as he to Marshall's undoubted influence on him. Because the Constitution, as Roane pointed out, had neither expressly empowered Congress to extend the Court's appellate jurisdiction to the state courts nor expressly vested the Court itself with such jurisdiction, Story had to justify BROAD CONSTRUCTION. The Constitution, he observed, was ordained not by the sovereign states but by the people of the United States, who could subordinate state powers to those of the nation. Not all national powers were expressly given. The Constitution "unavoidably deals in general language," Story explained, because it was intended "to endure through a long lapse of ages, the events of which were locked up in the inscrutable purpose of Providence." The framers of the Constitution, unable to foresee "what new changes and modifications of power might be indispensable" to achieve its purposes, expressed its powers in "general terms, leaving to the legislature, from time to time, to adopt its own means to effectuate legitimate objects. . . ." From such sweeping premises on the flexibility and expansiveness of national powers, Story could sustain section 25. He found authority for its enactment in Articles III and VI.

Article III, which defined the judicial power of the United States, contemplates that the Supreme Court shall be primarily an appellate court, whose appellate jurisdiction "shall" extend to specified CASES AND CONTROVERSIES. "Shall" is mandatory or imperative: the Court *must* exercise its appellate jurisdiction in *all* cases, in law and EQUITY, "arising under the Constitution, the Laws of the United States, and Treaties made. . . ." It is, therefore, the case, not the court from which it comes, that gives the Supreme Court its appellate jurisdiction, and because cases involving the Constitution, federal laws, and treaties may arise in state courts, the Supreme Court must exercise appellate jurisdiction in those cases. Contrary to Roane, that appellate jurisdiction did not exist only when the case came from a lower federal court. The Constitution required the establishment of a Supreme Court but merely authorized Congress to exercise a discretionary power in establishing lower federal courts. If Congress chose not to establish them, the Court's mandatory appellate jurisdiction could be exercised over only the state courts. The establishment of the lower federal courts meant that the appellate jurisdiction of the Supreme Court extended concurrently to both state and federal courts.

Article VI, the supremacy clause, made the Constitution itself, laws in pursuance to it, and federal treaties the supreme law of the land, binding on state courts. The decision of a state court on a matter involving the supreme law cannot be final, because the judicial power of the United States extends specifically to all such cases. To enforce the supremacy clause, the Supreme Court must have appellate jurisdiction over state court decisions involving the supreme law. That a case involving the supreme law might arise in the state courts is obvious. Story gave the example of a contract case in which a party relied on the provision in Article I, section 10, barring state impairments of the OBLIGATIONS OF A CONTRACT, and also the example of a criminal prosecution in which the defendant relied on the provision against EX POST FACTO laws. The Constitution, he pointed out, was in fact designed to operate on the states "in their corporate capacities." It is "crowded" with provisions that "restrain or annul the sovereignty of the States," making the Court's exercise of appellate power over state acts unconstitutional no more in derogation of state sovereignty than those provisions or the principle of national supremacy. Not only would the federal system survive the exercise of federal judicial review; it could not function without such review. The law must be uniform "upon all subjects within the purview of the Constitution. Judges . . . in different States, might differently interpret a statute, or a treaty of the United States, or even the Constitution itself: If there were no revising authority to control these jarring and discordant judgments, and harmonize them into uniformity, the laws, the treaties and the Constitution of the United States would be different in different states," and might never have the same interpretation and efficacy in any two states.

Story's opinion is the linchpin of the federal system and of judicial nationalism. It remains the greatest argument for federal judicial review, though it by no means concluded the controversy. Virginia's hostility was so intense that a case was contrived in 1821 to allow the Supreme Court to restate the principles of *Martin.* (See COHENS V. VIRGINIA, 1821.) As a matter of fact, though, federal judicial review and the constitutionality of section 25 remained bitterly contested topics to the eve of the Civil War.

LEONARD W. LEVY

Bibliography

BEVERIDGE, ALBERT J. 1916–1919 *The Life of John Marshall,* 4 vols. Vol. IV:145–167. Boston: Houghton Mifflin.

CROSSKEY, WILLIAM WINSLOW 1953 *Politics and the Constitution,* 2 vols. Pages 785–817. Chicago: University of Chicago Press.

HAINES, CHARLES GROVE 1944 *The Role of the Supreme Court in American Government and Politics, 1789–1835.* Pages 340–351. Berkeley: University of California Press.

MARTIN v. MOTT
12 Wheaton 19 (1827)

Mott, having avoided militia duty during the War of 1812, was fined by a court-martial. The Constitution authorized Congress to call forth the militia, and President JAMES MADISON, under congressional authority, had called upon the state militias for military service. Several states, which opposed the war, obstructed compliance, arguing that the national government had no authority to determine when the state militias could be called or to subject them to federal governance. Mott relied on such arguments. The Court unanimously held, in an opinion by Justice JOSEPH STORY, that the President, with congressional authorization, had exclusive power to decide when and under what exigencies the militia might be called to duty, and that his decision not only binds the states but places their militias under the control of officers appointed by the President.

LEONARD W. LEVY

MARYLAND TOLERATION ACT
(April 2, 1649)

This landmark in the protection of liberty of conscience was the most liberal in colonial America at the time of its passage by the Maryland Assembly under the title, "An Act Concerning Religion," and it was far more liberal than Parliament's TOLERATION ACT of forty years later. Until 1776 only the Rhode Island Charter of 1663 and Pennsylvania's "Great Law" of 1682 guaranteed fuller RELIGIOUS LIBERTY.

Maryland's statute, framed by its Roman Catholic proprietor, Lord Baltimore (Cecil Calvert), was the first public act to use the phrase "the free exercise" of religion, later embodied in the FIRST AMENDMENT. More noteworthy still, the act symbolized the extraordinary fact that for most of the seventeenth century in Maryland, Roman Catholics and various Protestant sects openly worshiped as they chose and lived in peace, though not in amity. The act applied to all those who professed belief in Jesus Christ, except antitrinitarians, and guaranteed them immunity from being troubled in any way because of their religion and "the free exercise thereof." In other provisions more characteristic of the time, the act fixed the death penalty for blasphemers against God, Christ, or the Trinity, and it imposed lesser penalties for profaning the sabbath or for reproaching the Virgin Mary or the apostles. Another clause anticipated GROUP LIBEL laws by penalizing the reproachful use of any name or term such as heretic, puritan, popish priest, anabaptist, separatist, or antinomian.

At a time when intolerance was the law in Europe and most of America, Maryland established no church and tolerated all Trinitarian Christians, until Protestants, who had managed to suspend the toleration act between 1654 and 1658, gained political control of the colony in 1689.

LEONARD W. LEVY

Bibliography

HANLEY, THOMAS O'BRIEN 1959 *Their Rights and Liberties: The Beginnings of Religious and Political Freedom in Maryland.* Westminister, Md.: Newman Press.

MASON, GEORGE
(1725–1792)

An influential Virginia leader of the Revolutionary period, George Mason served only a single term (1759–1760) in the colony's House of Burgesses. Family responsibilities and a dislike for routine legislative work kept him at his estate in Fairfax County, where he was active in local public affairs. He was a member and treasurer of the Ohio Company (1752–1773), the Virginia enterprise to explore and settle the Northwest Territory. Mason opposed parliamentary taxation of the colonies and, as justice of the peace, connived at evasion of the Stamp Act. His Fairfax Resolves of 1774 were introduced by his friend and neighbor GEORGE WASHINGTON in the House of Burgesses and prefigured the Declaration and Resolves of the FIRST CONTINENTAL CONGRESS. In 1775 Mason succeeded Washington as a member of Virginia's provisional legislature and was elected to the Committee of Safety, the de facto executive. At the Virginia convention of 1776, Mason wrote the VIRGINIA DECLARATION OF RIGHTS and a major part of the constitution. At the same convention he was appointed, along with GEORGE WYTHE, EDMUND PENDLETON, and THOMAS JEFFERSON, to a committee to revise the state's laws; and, although he resigned from the committee, many of his drafts were included in the final product. Throughout the Revolution he remained active in military and western affairs, and he was the author of an early plan for ceding the Northwest Territory to Congress and organizing its government.

Mason was at the meeting at Mount Vernon in 1785 that set in train the movement toward a constitutional convention; and he was elected to, but did not attend, the Annapolis Convention. He was a delegate to the CONSTITUTIONAL CONVENTION OF 1787 where he was one of the five most frequent speakers. He made his mark at the convention as a spokesman for republican nationalism. He favored a president elected directly by the people for a single seven-year term and assisted by a council. He opposed any mention of slavery in the Constitution as degrading to the document. He was a member of the committee that proposed the GREAT COMPROMISE but bitterly opposed the later compromise which gave twenty years' protection to the slave trade. Most decisively he desired to see a BILL OF RIGHTS included in the new constitution: "The laws of the United States are to be paramount to state bills of rights," he warned, and a constitutional guarantee of rights "would give great quiet to the people." The motion to draft a bill of rights was defeated, and Mason, who had been active in framing the new Constitution, accordingly refused to sign it. He sent his proposed bill of rights to RICHARD HENRY LEE who tried, but failed, to have Congress add it before transmitting the Constitution to the states.

Mason opposed RATIFICATION OF THE CONSTITUTION in the Virginia convention of 1788 because of its supposed antirepublican tendencies, its compromise with slavery, and its want of a bill of rights. When the convention voted to ratify the Constitution it appended a declaration of rights that closely followed Mason's declaration of 1776.

Mason thereafter retired from public life. He declined appointment as a United States senator in 1790. Shortly before his death he told Thomas Jefferson that the machinations of ALEXANDER HAMILTON in favor of urban monied interests were bearing out Mason's predictions about the Constitution.

Throughout his public career Mason adhered to principle even in apparent contradiction to his self-interest. Although he held some 300 slaves he abominated slavery as an institution and favored a plan of gradual compensated emancipation preceded by education. Although he was an active Anglican layman, he favored measures to end the ESTABLISHMENT OF RELIGION in Virginia.

DENNIS J. MAHONEY

Bibliography

ROWLAND, KATE MASON 1892 *The Life of George Mason, Including His Speeches, Public Papers, and Correspondence.* New York: Putnam's.

RUTLAND, ROBERT ALLEN 1961 *George Mason, Reluctant Statesman.* Williamsburg, Va.: Colonial Williamsburg, distributed by Holt, Rinehart & Winston, New York.

MASSACHUSETTS v. LAIRD
400 U.S. 886 (1970)

In 1969, the legislature of Massachusetts attempted to nullify the VIETNAM WAR. It passed an act declaring the war unconstitutional, exempting Massachusetts citizens from service in the war, and directing the state attorney general to seek a Supreme Court ruling on the constitutionality of the war. Accordingly, the attorney general filed suit in the state's name against the secretary of defense, Melvin Laird, requesting an order prohibiting the secretary from sending any Massachusetts citizen to Vietnam. As the suit was between a state and a citizen of another state, it would have come within the ORIGINAL JURISDICTION of the Supreme Court. The Court, however, voted 6–3 to deny leave to file the complaint. Justice WILLIAM O. DOUGLAS, who passionately desired an opportunity to rule on the constitutionality of the war, filed an unusual fourteen-page dissent from the denial memorandum.

DENNIS J. MAHONEY

MASSACHUSETTS v. MELLON

See: *Frothingham v. Mellon*

MASSACHUSETTS BAY, COLONIAL CHARTERS OF (1629, 1691)

In 1629 King Charles I granted a royal charter to Puritan leaders of the New England Company, incorporating them as the Massachusetts Bay Colony. In the same year Puritan leaders received authorization to migrate to New England and take the charter with them. As a result the Puritans controlled Massachusetts and sought to create a godly commonwealth. The charter authorized the freemen of the company to meet in a General Court or legislature, and to choose a governor, a deputy governor, and assistants, seven of whom could function as the General Court. The charter vested power in these men to govern Massachusetts Bay in every respect and guaranteed that all inhabitants "shall have and enjoy all liberties and immunities of free and natural subjects . . . as if they . . . were born within the realm of England." The Puritans, who governed themselves, enjoyed the rights of Englishmen, and put an ocean between themselves and England, became obstinately independent.

Massachusetts admitted only church members to freemanship, but the little oligarchy in control refused to allow the freemen a right to participate in governing, a violation of the charter. In 1634 the freemen, on seeing the charter for themselves, demanded full participation in government. From then on, the freemen in the towns chose two deputies from each town as members of the General Court, making it a representative body. Conflict between the freemen and the assistants led to an agreement that without a majority vote of each no law should be passed; that soon led to BICAMERALISM. In the 1640s the battle of the freemen for their charter rights led to the MASSACHUSETTS BODY OF LIBERTIES and to the MASSACHUSETTS GENERAL LAWS AND LIBERTIES, which, with the charter, became the basis of FUNDAMENTAL LAW in the colony, the functional equivalent of a written CONSTITUTION.

In the succeeding decades Massachusetts proved to be aloof from English concerns and refractory in many ways, even claiming that its charter made it independent of Parliament. Relations deteriorated after the Restoration and finally, in 1684, England vacated the charter of 1629. In 1686 James II appointed his own governor of the new Dominion of New England, which combined the New England colonies, New York, and New Jersey. The king's governor ruled without a representative legislature and sought to insinuate the Church of England into Puritan New England. News of the overthrow of James II led to a parallel Glorious Revolution in New England—and elsewhere in America. Each of the colonies that had been absorbed within the dominion resumed its prior governmental practices.

In 1691 King William III, advised by people who had experienced the independence of Massachusetts, officially restored self-government to Massachusetts on royal terms. The charter of 1691 turned Massachusetts from comparative autonomy to a royal colony. The king appointed its governor and his deputy, and the governor could veto legislation—a model for a strong executive in later American history. The General Court consisted of two houses, the lower one elected by the people of the towns who sent two deputies each to the General Court; these elected representatives chose the governor's council, which also served as the upper house. The freemanship of church members disappeared under the new charter, which replaced the religious test with a property qualification on the right to vote. The General Court was empowered to legislate, to create a judicial system, and to elect the upper house—subject to the governor's veto. The government established by the second charter recognized a clear SEPARATION OF POWERS between the three branches. The charter also embodied the principle of liberty of conscience for "all Christians (Except Papists)" and, like the first charter, also guaranteed the rights of Englishmen.

LEONARD W. LEVY

Bibliography

OSGOOD, HERBERT L. (1904)1957 *The American Colonies in the Seventeenth Century.* 3 Vols. Gloucester, Mass.: Peter Smith.

MASSACHUSETTS BOARD OF RETIREMENT v. MURGIA
427 U.S. 307 (1976)

In *Murgia* the Supreme Court, asked to subject AGE DISCRIMINATION to heightened judicial scrutiny, declined the invitation, 7–1. In a per curiam opinion the Court upheld a state law limiting membership in the uniformed state police to persons under the age of fifty, irrespective of an older person's ability to pass physical or other tests of qualification. There was not a murmur in the Court's opinion about IRREBUTTABLE PRESUMPTIONS, nor was age a SUSPECT CLASSIFICATION; although the aged were not free from discrimination, they had not experienced "purposeful unequal treatment" or disabilities imposed "on the basis of stereotyped characteristics not truly indicative of their abilities." With that breathtaking inaccuracy behind it, the Court applied the most permissive form of RATIONAL BASIS review, noted that physical ability generally declines with age, and concluded that because the mandatory retirement rule was not "wholly unrelated" to the objective of maintaining a physically fit police force, the law was valid. Justice THURGOOD MARSHALL, in lone dissent, repeated his long-standing argument that the Court should abandon its "two-tier" system of STANDARDS OF REVIEW in favor of a system that matched the level of judicial scrutiny in EQUAL PROTECTION cases to the interests at stake in each case.

KENNETH L. KARST

MASSACHUSETTS BODY OF LIBERTIES
(1641)

The Massachusetts Body of Liberties, which resulted from popular demand that the fundamental law of the colony be written, was primarily a set of constitutional safeguards protecting personal freedom and the procedures of DUE PROCESS. By 1634 the colonists were demanding publication of the colony's laws as a curb on the magistrates' discretionary powers. The magistrates opposed publication as a restraint of their lawful powers; they believed that law should develop in Massachusetts Bay as had the COMMON LAW in England, over time and by custom. More to the point, publication would invite direct comparison with English law and one provision of the charter forbade establishment of any laws repugnant to those of England.

For the remainder of the decade a number of attempts were made to formulate a document that would satisfy these demands. One plan, drawn up by the Reverend John Cotton, may have been rejected because of its biblical severity or its failure to be sufficiently comprehensive. In 1638, the Reverend Nathaniel Ward, a barrister active at Lincoln's Inn before his emigration, submitted a proposal that was eventually sent to the towns for their consideration and revision early in 1641. Despite years of inaction and obstruction by the magistrates the General Court finally adopted this draft that autumn.

The first "liberty," paraphrasing the thirty-ninth article of MAGNA CARTA, specified conformity to the traditional rights of Englishmen, as exemplified in Magna Carta and the common law, and to "the word of God." The Body of Liberties was undeniably a product of the Puritan colony: a large portion outlined ecclesiastical rights and responsibilities. One section, drawn from Cotton's code, listed twelve capital crimes and cross-referenced each one to the appropriate biblical verse.

Over forty liberties were devoted to "Juditiall Proceedings" and their adjunct rights. In addition to defining a few lesser offenses, the Body of Liberties provided extensive guarantees for each step in legal proceedings. The use of summonses was regulated and a right to BAIL was assured. Written pleadings were permitted in court and, unlike English practice, cases would not be abated for minor technical errors. Parties were granted the right to TRIAL BY JURY and to challenge any of the jurors. Other liberties protected rights now taken for granted. Among these were provisions for a SPEEDY TRIAL, a limited privilege against self-incrimination, as well as prohibitions of DOUBLE JEOPARDY and "inhumane barbarous and cruel" punishments. (See CRUEL AND UNUSUAL PUNISHMENT.) The Body of Liberties also guaranteed FREEDOM OF SPEECH in courts and public assemblies and freedom of movement. Other sections covered the "Liberties of Women," children's rights, and those of servants.

Despite these and other innovations the deputies were dissatisfied with the document. They found it overly broad and poorly defined and insisted upon specified penalties—the Body of Liberties provided them only for capital crimes—and precise limits to magisterial power. Eventually, widespread discontent resulted in the passage in 1648 of the extensively detailed MASSACHUSETTS GENERAL LAWS AND LIBERTIES.

DAVID GORDON

Bibliography

HASKINS, GEORGE L. 1960 *Law and Authority in Early Massachusetts.* New York: Macmillan.

MASSACHUSETTS CIRCULAR LETTER (February 11, 1768)

This document reveals the American conception of a CONSTITUTION as a supreme FUNDAMENTAL LAW limiting government by definite restraints upon power. SAMUEL ADAMS drafted the document, which the Massachusetts House of Representatives adopted and sent to the assemblies of other colonies to secure their assent to the contention that the TOWNSHEND ACTS of 1767 and all other taxes levied by Parliament on America were unconstitutional. The right to private property, Adams wrote, is an unalterable natural and constitutional right "engrafted into the British Constitution, as a fundamental law. . . ." Parliament had violated that right by TAXATION WITHOUT REPRESENTATION. Although Parliament was the supreme legislature in the empire, it could act lawfully only within the sphere of its legitimate powers. Echoing the Swiss jurist EMERICH DE VATTEL, who distinguished a constitution from ordinary statutory law, Adams declared that in all free states the constitution is fixed, and "as the supreme Legislative derives its Power and Authority from the Constitution, it cannot overleap the bounds of it, without destroying its own foundation. . . ." The constitution, Adams stated, "ascertains and limits" both SOVEREIGNTY and allegiance.

London censured the "Seditious Paper" of Massachusetts and declared that Massachusetts had subverted "the true principles of the constitution." To the British, as Sir WILLIAM BLACKSTONE contended in his *Commentaries,* Parliament could not act unconstitutionally; it knew no practical limits. To the Americans, an unconstitutional act was one that exceeded governmental authority. "Unconstitutional" did not mean impolitic or inexpedient, as it meant in Britain; it meant a lawless government act that need not be obeyed. The Massachusetts Circular Letter thus fortified the emergence of a new conception of constitutional law.

LEONARD W. LEVY

Bibliography

MILLER, JOHN C. 1943 *Origins of the American Revolution.* Pages 257–264. Boston: Little, Brown.

MASSACHUSETTS CONSTITUTION (October 25, 1780)

The "Constitution or Form of Government for the Commonwealth of Massachusetts" is the classic American state CONSTITUTION and the oldest surviving written constitution in the United States (or the world), distinguished in addition by the fact that it was framed by the world's first CONSTITUTIONAL CONVENTION. But for two states which merely modified their COLONIAL CHARTERS, all the original thirteen states except Massachusetts had adopted their first constitutions by 1778 and in every case the body that enacted ordinary legislation framed the constitution and promulgated it. The Massachusetts legislature also framed a constitution but resorted to the novel step of submitting it to the voters for approval, and they rejected it. Then, in accordance with a proposal first advanced in the CONCORD TOWN RESOLUTIONS of 1776, a special constitutional convention elected for the sole purpose of drawing up a document of FUNDAMENTAL LAW performed the task and sent it out for ratification, article by article. Universal manhood suffrage prevailed in the vote for delegates to the convention and for popular ratification. Massachusetts, following democratic procedures for institutionalizing the SOCIAL COMPACT THEORY of government to devise a frame of government and a supreme law, provided the model that subsequently became common throughout the United States. The Massachusetts constitution of 1780, with amendments, still continues as the constitution of that commonwealth.

JOHN ADAMS, the principal framer of the constitution, once proudly wrote, "I made a Constitution for Massachusetts, which finally made the Constitution of the United States." His exaggeration was pardonable, because no other state constitution so much influenced the framing of the national Constitution. Some earlier state constitutions had referred to the principle of SEPARATION OF POWERS but had made their legislatures dominant, even domineering. Massachusetts not only provided the fullest statement of the principle but also put it into practice. Its judges, appointed by the governor, were to hold office "during GOOD BEHAVIOR" with undiminishable salaries. Its governor was the model for the presidency of the United States. He was to be elected by the voters, rather than by the legislature as in other states, and be a strong executive. He appointed the members of his own council or cabinet and, indeed, appointed all judicial officers down to local magistrates and registers of probate as well as sheriffs, coroners, and the state attorney general. He was "commander-in-chief of the army and navy"; he had the PARDONING POWER; and he alone among the first governors of the thirteen states had a sole VETO POWER over legislation, which could be overridden only by a two-thirds vote of both houses. The state senate and house of representatives were also precursors of the national bicameral system. No original state constitution had a better system of CHECKS AND BALANCES than Massachusetts's.

Its constitution was divided into three parts: a preamble, a declaration of rights, and a frame of government. The preamble, on the general purposes of the state, explicitly embodied the social compact theory of the origin of the body politic. The declaration of rights, although containing little not found in constitutions previously framed by other states, was the most comprehensive compendium of its kind, and it phrased the rights which it guaranteed in language most influential in framing the BILL OF RIGHTS of the Constitution of the United States. The injunction against "UNREASONABLE SEARCHES and seizures" in the FOURTH AMENDMENT derives from the Massachusetts Declaration of Rights, and the injunction "shall not" instead of the pallid "ought not" ("liberty of the press ought not be restrained") was also a Massachusetts innovation. The one grave deficiency of the Massachusetts document was its creation of a multiple ESTABLISHMENT OF RELIGION that was inconsistent with its guarantee of RELIGIOUS LIBERTY.

LEONARD W. LEVY

Bibliography

ADAMS, WILLI PAUL 1980 *The First American Constitutions.* Chapel Hill: University of North Carolina Press.

PETERS, RONALD M., JR. 1978 *The Massachusetts Constitution of 1780: A Social Compact.* Amherst: University of Massachusetts Press.

MASSACHUSETTS GENERAL LAWS AND LIBERTIES

In 1646, the General Court of Massachusetts Bay appointed a committee to "correct and compose in good order all the liberties, lawes, and orders extant with us." The committee's work, publication of which was delayed until 1648, was far more comprehensive than the earlier MASSACHUSETTS BODY OF LIBERTIES. The framing of the General Laws and Liberties capped a movement for codification that had grown because the Body of Liberties had failed to curb the magistrates' discretion. Frequent legislation compounded popular confusion over the state of the law, but even so, the General Laws did not include all the laws in force.

The new code incorporated eighty-six of the one hundred items in the Body of Liberties and covered subjects from business regulations to property laws. It generally followed English practice. Plaintiffs could easily attach land, the law guaranteed a SPEEDY TRIAL, and juries could return "special" verdicts—practices foreign to English proceedings. Also unlike English practice, forms of action were relatively unimportant; substance took precedence in Massachusetts. Like contemporary English statutory abridgments and practice manuals, the General Laws were listed alphabetically to encourage reference and use. They were revised in 1660 and 1672 and served as the prototype for other colonies' legal codes.

DAVID GORDON

MASSACHUSETTS RESOLUTIONS

See: Embargo Acts

MASSES PUBLISHING COMPANY v. PATTEN

244 Fed. 535 (1917)

Judge LEARNED HAND's *Masses* opinion was one of the first federal opinions dealing with free speech. It remains influential even though Hand was reversed by the court of appeals and many years later himself abandoned his initial position. A postmaster had refused to accept the revolutionary monthly *The Masses* for mailing, citing the ESPIONAGE ACT. Hand, sitting in a federal district court, interpreted the act not to apply to the magazine. He noted that any broad criticism of a government or its policies might hinder the war effort. Nevertheless, to suppress such criticism "would contradict the normal assumption of democratic government." Hand advanced a criminal incitement test. He conceded that words can be "the triggers of action" and, if they counseled violation of law, were not constitutionally protected. If, however, the words did not criminally incite and if the words stopped short "of urging upon others that it is their duty or their interest to resist the law . . . one should not be held to have attempted to cause its violation."

Hand's concentration on the advocacy content of

the speech itself is thought by some to be more speech-protective than the CLEAR AND PRESENT DANGER rule's emphasis on the surrounding circumstances.

MARTIN SHAPIRO

MASSIAH v. UNITED STATES
377 U.S. 201 (1964)

After a defendant had been indicted and released on BAIL, a bugged co-defendant who had turned police informer, engaged him in an incriminating conversation. The Supreme Court held that the Sixth Amendment prohibits deliberate elicitation of information from an indicted person in the absence of his counsel and ruled that defendant's incriminating statements were inadmissible at trial.

BARBARA ALLEN BABCOCK

MASTER, SPECIAL

See: Special Master

MATHEWS v. ELDRIDGE
424 U.S. 319 (1976)

GOLDBERG V. KELLY (1970) established a PROCEDURAL DUE PROCESS right to an evidentiary hearing prior to the termination of state WELFARE BENEFITS. Eldridge, whose Social Security disability benefits had been terminated without a prior hearing, could be pardoned for thinking that *Goldberg* controlled his case. In the event, a 6–2 Supreme Court explained how that view was mistaken, and established its basic test for determining whether a particular procedure satisfied the demands of DUE PROCESS.

The government conceded that the disability benefit was the sort of statutory "entitlement" that constituted a "property" interest protected by the due process guarantee. The government nonetheless argued that a *prior* hearing was not required; rather, due process was satisfied by a posttermination hearing at which the beneficiary might review the evidence, submit evidence of his own, and make arguments for reconsideration. Under the existing procedures, a beneficiary who prevailed in such a posttermination hearing was entitled to full retroactive relief. A majority of the Court agreed with the government's argument.

In a passage often quoted in later opinions, the Court set out the factors relevant to determining "the specific dictates of due process," once a "liberty" or "property" interest is impaired: "First, the private interest that will be affected by the official action; second, the risk of an erroneous deprivation of such interest through the procedures used, and the probable value, if any, of additional or substitute procedural safeguards; and finally, the Government's interest, including the function involved and the fiscal and administrative burdens that the additional or substitute procedural requirement would entail." Here, eligibility for disability benefits was not based on need, the standard for welfare eligibility in *Goldberg.* The Court assumed that a delayed payment would harm the typical disability beneficiary less than the typical welfare recipient. The medical question of disability, in contrast with the "need" question in a welfare case, was more focused and less susceptible to erroneous decision. The costs of pretermination hearings would be great. In short, the Court balanced its factors on the government's side.

The *Eldridge* due process calculus implies a strong presumption of constitutionality of whatever procedures a legislative body or government agency may choose to provide persons deprived of liberty or property. This presumption grows naturally out of the Court's limited choice of factors to be balanced, emphasizing material costs and benefits and ignoring the role of procedural fairness in maintaining each individual's sense of being a respected, participating citizen.

KENNETH L. KARST

MATTHEWS, STANLEY
(1824–1889)

Stanley Matthews's political connections and his legal work for railroads led to his Supreme Court nomination in 1881; these same activities also nearly prevented him from taking a place on the bench. Like his predecessor, NOAH SWAYNE, Matthews had been an Ohio antislavery Democrat and a Democratic appointee as a United States attorney. By 1860, however, he had switched to the Republican party. After Civil War military service, he became an important leader of the Cincinnati bar. Before the Ohio Supreme Court, Matthews represented the Cincinnati Board of Education and supported its authority to abolish religious instruction in the public schools. His eloquent argument defended SEPARATION OF CHURCH AND STATE as the best way to insure RELIGIOUS LIBERTY.

Matthews served as one of RUTHERFORD B.

HAYES's lawyers during the contested electoral battle in 1877. Near the end of his administration, Hayes nominated Matthews to succeed Swayne, but because of internal Republican patronage feuds, as well as questions about Matthews's railroad connections, the Senate took no action. President JAMES A. GARFIELD, under pressure from Hayes's allies and prominent business interests, resubmitted the nomination. After a long, bitter fight, the Senate confirmed Matthews by a one-vote majority.

Matthews clearly served railroad interests when he joined the Court's decision in WABASH, ST. LOUIS & PACIFIC RAILROAD CO. V. ILLINOIS (1886), substantially weakening the state regulatory doctrine of *Munn v. Illinois* (1877). Similarly, he concurred in the nearly unanimous decision in the CIVIL RIGHTS CASES (1883), which capped a legal and political counterassault against racial equality.

The *Wabash* case, while limiting state regulation, decisively stimulated federal ECONOMIC REGULATION under the COMMERCE CLAUSE. Matthews relied on an expansive conception of national power in BOWMAN V. CHICAGO AND NORTHWESTERN RAILWAY CO. (1888), ruling invalid a state's prohibition of liquor shipments from other states. However desirable the state's regulation, Matthews said, it infringed on Congress's EXCLUSIVE POWER. In *Poindexter v. Greenhow* (1885) Matthews relied on the CONTRACT CLAUSE when he held that states could not lawfully repudiate their debts.

Matthews's most important cases involved the interpretation of the FOURTEENTH AMENDMENT. In HURTADO V. CALIFORNIA (1884) he held for the Court that even in a capital case an accusation by INFORMATION rather than INDICTMENT by a GRAND JURY did not deny DUE PROCESS OF LAW contrary to the FOURTEENTH AMENDMENT. The *Hurtado* ruling stood for nearly a half century as a barrier to any tendency toward nationalizing CIVIL RIGHTS and CIVIL LIBERTIES. Yet in YICK WO V. HOPKINS (1886) Matthews spoke for the Court on one of those rare occasions when it advanced civil rights. Holding unconstitutional the discriminatory application of a San Francisco ordinance requiring licensing of wooden laundries, used to destroy Chinese businesses, Matthews described the Fourteenth Amendment in libertarian terms that usually were reserved for corporate cases. Indeed, he cast the plight of the Chinese in language that any good entrepreneur could understand: "For, the very idea that one man may be compelled to hold his life, or the means of living, or any material right essential to the enjoyment of life, at the mere will of another, seems to be intolerable in any country where freedom prevails, as being the essence of slavery itself."

Matthews spoke for the Court in one of the Mormon antipolygamy cases, sustaining congressional action and invoking the prevailing norms of the family and marriage. He also voted to strike down the Ku Klux Klan laws in UNITED STATES V. HARRIS (1883); he agreed with the majority that AMERICAN INDIANS were not citizens in *Elk v. Wilkins* (1884); and he concurred that state MISCEGENATION laws were constitutional in PACE V. ALABAMA (1883).

Matthews epitomized the nation's retreat from the reforming zeal of Reconstruction. The controversy surrounding Matthews's appointment eventually subsided, and he carried out his duties until his death in early 1889.

STANLEY I. KUTLER

Bibliography

FILLER, LOUIS 1969 Stanley Matthews. In Leon Friedman and Fred L. Israel, eds., *The Justices of the Supreme Court,* Vol. 2:1351–1378. New York: Chelsea House.

MAGRATH, C. PETER 1963 *Morrison R. Waite: The Triumph of Character.* New York: Macmillan.

MAXIMUM HOURS AND MINIMUM WAGES LEGISLATION

Regulation of the employment relationship was an important aspect of the movement toward state intervention in economic affairs, which began in the late 1800s. The transition from small individual to large corporate employers and the development of a factory system with a numerous wage-earning class resulted in pervasive exploitation of employees. The principal method of alleviating the economic injustice was statutory regulation of employment conditions. The spectrum of protective legislation was wide, including factory safety, child labor, workers' compensation, and the hours and wages of employment. In these early days the laws were state laws.

The protracted constitutional contest over hours and wage legislation was one aspect of the larger theme of SUBSTANTIVE DUE PROCESS, a concept developed by the Supreme Court at the turn of the century. Liberty included FREEDOM OF CONTRACT, which included the employment contract, of which hours and wages were the main components. The Court held that laws regulating hours and wages violated the guarantee of DUE PROCESS OF LAW if the purpose of the law was invalid or if the means were not reasonably related to a valid purpose.

Hours legislation began in the 1870s. Reformers perceived the duration of the workday as related to the employees' health and safety, protection of which was a valid legislative purpose. In its first opinion on the subject, HOLDEN V. HARDY (1898), the Court sustained a law limiting the hours of men working in mines to eight a day. The hazardous nature of the work justified the limitation as a valid health and safety measure. In MULLER V. OREGON (1908) an hours limitation for women was sustained on the theory that the "weaker sex" required special protection.

Beyond these two exceptional situations the Court at first prohibited hours regulation. The prototype case was LOCHNER V. NEW YORK (1905). A 5–4 Court invalidated a law restricting the work of bakery employees to ten hours a day and sixty hours a week. Despite massive documentation, the Court refused to recognize that the baking industry posed any special health danger to which hours of work were reasonably related. More broadly, the Court concluded that the law was not truly a health law, but a "purely labor law" to regulate hours, an impermissible objective.

This strict view yielded to persistent pressures. In BUNTING V. OREGON (1917) hours regulation of adult males in factories was sustained as a valid health measure, a result clearly inconsistent with *Lochner,* which was not even mentioned in the opinion. Thereafter the validity of hours regulation was not seriously questioned.

Massachusetts passed the first minimum wage statute in 1912 and within ten years there were fifteen such state laws. Proponents urged that health was impaired by wages below a subsistence level. The Court was at first unpersuaded, and, in ADKINS V. CHILDREN'S HOSPITAL (1923), it invalidated a District of Columbia minimum wage law for women. Wages were the "heart of the contract" and, unlike hours, had no relation to health. Contrary to hours regulation, women were entitled to no special wage protection. The minimum wage was invalid also because it bore no relation to the value of the service rendered. But a law curing this deficiency was invalidated in MOREHEAD V. NEW YORK EX REL. TIPALDO (1936).

One principal justification for protective legislation was that the inequality of economic power between employers and employees made true freedom of contract illusory. This argument was expressly rejected by the Court, which candidly declared in COPPAGE V. KANSAS (1915) that it was "impossible to uphold freedom of contract and the right of private property without at the same time recognizing as legitimate those inequalities of fortune that are the necessary result of the exercise of those rights." Social Darwinism was thus enshrined in the Constitution.

In 1937, that year of constitutional revolution, minimum wage legislation became constitutional by a 5–4 vote. WEST COAST HOTEL CO. V. PARRISH upheld a minimum wage for women. *Adkins* was overruled. The Court purported surprise at the employer's reliance on liberty of contract. Not only was the health/subsistence rationale accepted but, more broadly, it was now accepted as a valid legislative purpose to prevent "exploitation of a class of workers who are in unequal position with respect to bargaining power."

Federal regulation of hours and wages was first exercised in limited contexts. An eight-hour day for railroad workers was upheld under the COMMERCE CLAUSE in WILSON V. NEW (1917). Congress has long regulated both wages and hours of work performed by employees of contractors with the federal government. Examples are the Davis-Bacon Act, which regulates wages for work on public buildings and other public works, and the Walsh-Healey Public Contracts Act, which regulates both wages and hours for work on supply contracts. The constitutionality of both statutes is unquestioned under the TAXING AND SPENDING POWER.

Finally, in the FAIR LABOR STANDARDS ACT of 1938, Congress legislated for private employment generally, superseding most state laws. The act required the payment of a minimum wage and overtime for all hours over forty a week to all employees engaged in commerce or the production of goods for commerce. The main purpose was not health but to bolster the economy. The FLSA was sustained under the commerce power in UNITED STATES V. DARBY (1941). A substantive due process argument was rejected without analysis. It was "no longer open to question" that neither Fifth nor FOURTEENTH AMENDMENT due process limited the fixing of minimum wages or maximum hours, and it made no difference that the regulations applied to both men and women.

That has been the view of the matter ever since. In other contexts the Court repudiated the *Lochner* substantive due process approach to protective legislation. What was once a burning issue now appears to be a closed chapter in constitutional law. The scope of the STATE POLICE POWER was underscored in striking fashion by the upholding in *Day-Brite Lighting, Inc. v. Missouri* (1952) of a law that required employers to give employees four hours off from work in order to vote—with full pay.

WILLIAM P. MURPHY

Bibliography

De Vyver, Frank T. 1939 Regulation of Wages and Hours Prior to 1938. *Law and Contemporary Problems* 6:323–332.

Dodd, E. Merrick 1943 From Maximum Wages to Minimum Wages: Six Centuries of Regulation of Employment Contracts. *Columbia Law Review* 43:643–687.

MAXWELL v. DOW
176 U.S. 581 (1900)

This case was decided at a time when the Court was subjecting the Fourteenth Amendment to an accordionlike motion, expanding substantive due process to protect the rights of property and contracting procedural due process for persons accused of crime. After Hurtado v. California (1884), when the Court held that the concept of due process did not guarantee indictment by grand jury, persons accused of crime resorted to the incorporation doctrine, claiming that the Fourteenth Amendment, through either its due process clause or its privileges and immunities clause, incorporated provisions of the Bill of Rights, thus extending to the states the same trial standards. Utah accused Maxwell by an information, rather than an indictment, and tried him by a jury of eight rather than twelve. The Fifth and Sixth Amendments would have made such procedures unconstitutional in federal courts. Maxwell argued that the Fourteenth Amendment guaranteed the federal standards in state proceedings. Justice John Marshall Harlan, dissenting, adopted Maxwell's arguments. Justice Rufus Peckham, for the remainder of the Court, held that neither the due process nor the privileges and immunities clause of the Fourteenth Amendment embodied Fifth or Sixth Amendment rights. Peckham also ruled that trial by jury "has never been affirmed to be a necessary requisite of due process of law" and that an eight-member jury was constitutional. In 1968 Duncan v. Louisiana, overruling *Maxwell,* held trial by jury to be a fundamental right of due process of law for persons accused of crime, but under today's constitutional law, the jury size need not be twelve members in a state proceeding.

Leonard W. Levy

MAYFLOWER COMPACT

See: Social Compact Theory

MAYOR OF NEW YORK v. MILN
11 Peters 102 (1837)

This was the first case decided by the Taney Court involving a commerce clause issue, and the Supreme Court finessed that issue. Justice Joseph Story, dissenting alone, said that he took consolation in knowing that the late Chief Justice (John Marshall) concurred in his view that the city of New York had unconstitutionally regulated foreign commerce, a subject exclusively belonging to Congress. The city required incoming ship captains to supply vital statistics on every immigrant they brought to harbor. The city argued that passengers were not commerce, but if they were, the voyage having ceased, no foreign commerce was involved; the requirement of the information on passengers was an exercise of the police power, a precautionary measure against paupers, vagabonds, convicts, and pestilence.

By a vote of 6–1, in an opinion by Justice Philip Barbour, the Court sustained the regulation as a valid exercise of the police power. Barbour disavowed giving any opinion on the question whether the states shared concurrent powers over foreign commerce. Justice Smith Thompson, concurring separately, agreed with Story that the facts showed a regulation of foreign commerce, but he believed that in the absence of congressional legislation, the states retained a concurrent power. The early and simplistic victory for the police power in this case solved little, because the Court did not face the question of the scope of the police powers when they affected subjects of commerce.

Leonard W. Levy

MAYSVILLE ROAD BILL
(1830)

President Andrew Jackson's veto of the Maysville Road Bill challenged the internal improvements component of Henry Clay's American System on constitutional and policy grounds and enhanced the role of the President in the legislative process.

In 1816, President James Madison vetoed the "Bonus Bill," which would have provided federal support for internal improvements such as the Cumberland Road, on the ground that the Constitution did not authorize expenditure of federal funds for anything except the powers explicitly enumerated in it. The Maysville Road Bill would have funded completion of a twenty-mile spur of the National Road entirely within the state of Kentucky. Jackson defended his veto on the ground that the Maysville Road was wholly intrastate and therefore outside the power of the federal government. Jackson also vetoed the bill in order to promote economy in the national government. He thus asserted a presidential prerogative in legislative policy, as well as a quasi-constitutional position, associated with the Democratic Party for the next thirty years, of hostility to expenditure of federal funds for internal improvements.

WILLIAM M. WIECEK

(SEE ALSO: *Veto Power.*)

MCCARDLE, EX PARTE
7 Wallace (74 U.S.) 506 (1869)

In *Ex Parte McCardle,* Chief Justice SALMON P. CHASE, for the Supreme Court, validated congressional withdrawal of the Court's jurisdiction over appeals in HABEAS CORPUS proceedings under an 1867 statute but reasserted the Court's appellate authority in all other habeas cases.

A federal circuit court remanded William McCardle, a Mississippi editor hostile to Republican Reconstruction policies, to military custody. When he appealed to the Supreme Court, Democrats predicted that the Justices would use his case as a vehicle to hold unconstitutional the trial of civilians by military commissions in southern states undergoing Reconstruction. Democrats inferred from the earlier decision of EX PARTE MILLIGAN (1866) that a majority of the Court believed that military commissions could not constitutionally try civilians accused of crimes where courts were functioning in peacetime. Alarmed congressional Republicans, seeing this essential machinery of Reconstruction threatened, enacted a narrow statute in 1868 that revoked Supreme Court appellate authority in habeas cases under the HABEAS CORPUS ACT OF 1867.

In the *McCardle* opinion, Chief Justice Chase acknowledged the validity of this repeal under the "exceptions clause" of Article III, section 2, but pointedly reminded the bar that the 1868 repealer "does not affect the JURISDICTION which was previously exercised." In *Ex Parte Yerger* (1869), the Court promptly affirmed this OBITER DICTUM, accepting a *habeas* appeal under section 14 of the JUDICIARY ACT OF 1789 and rebuking Congress for the 1868 repealer. *McCardle* is therefore historically significant as evidence not of judicial submission to political threats during Reconstruction but rather of the Court's uninterrupted determination to preserve its role in questions of CIVIL LIBERTIES.

McCardle remains important in the modern debate on congressional power to curtail the Supreme Court's APPELLATE JURISDICTION over cases raising controversial issues such as SCHOOL BUSING, school prayer, and abortion. Some constitutional scholars have argued that Congress cannot erode the substance of the JUDICIAL POWER OF THE UNITED STATES vested in the Supreme Court by Article III, section 1, through jurisdictional nibbling at the Court's appellate authority, but the extent to which Congress can affect substantive rights by jurisdictional excisions remains controverted.

WILLIAM M. WIECEK

(SEE ALSO: *Judicial System.*)

MCCARRAN ACT

See: Internal Security Act

MCCARRAN-WALTER ACT

See: Immigration

MCCARTHY, JOSEPH R.

See: McCarthyism

MCCARTHYISM

On February 9, 1950, Senator Joseph R. McCarthy of Wisconsin claimed that 205 communists were presently "working and shaping the policy of the State Department." Although McCarthy produced no documentation for this preposterous charge, he quickly emerged as the nation's dominant Cold War politician—the yardstick by which citizens measured patriotic or scurrilous behavior. McCarthy's popularity was not difficult to explain. Americans were frightened by Soviet aggression in Europe. The years since World War II had brought a series of shocks—the Hiss trial, the fall of China, the KOREAN WAR—which fueled the Red Scare and kept it alive.

President HARRY S. TRUMAN played a role as well. In trying to defuse the "Communist issue," he established a federal LOYALTY-SECURITY PROGRAM with few procedural safeguards. The program relied on nameless informants; it penalized personal beliefs and associations, not just OVERT ACTS; and it accelerated the Red hunt by conceding the possibility that a serious security problem existed inside the government and elsewhere. Before long, state and local officials were competing to see who could crack down hardest on domestic subversion. Indiana forced professional wrestlers to sign a LOYALTY OATH. Tennessee ordered the death penalty for those seeking to overthrow the *state* government. Congress, not to be outdone, passed the INTERNAL SECURITY ACT of 1950 over Truman's veto, requiring registration of "Communist action groups," whose members could then be placed in internment camps during "national emergencies."

Despite his personal commitment to CIVIL LIBERTIES, President Truman appointed four Supreme Court Justices who opposed the libertarian philosophy of WILLIAM O. DOUGLAS and HUGO L. BLACK. As a result, JUDICIAL REVIEW was all but abandoned in cases involving the rights of alleged subversives. The Court upheld loyalty oaths as a condition of public employment, limited the use of the Fifth Amendment by witnesses before congressional committees, and affirmed the dismissal of a government worker on the unsworn testimony of unnamed informants. As ROBERT G. MCCLOSKEY noted, the Court "became so tolerant of governmental restriction on freedom of expression as to suggest it [had] abdicated the field."

By the mid-1950s, the Red Scare had begun to subside. The death of Joseph Stalin, the Korean armistice, and the Senate's censure of Senator McCarthy all contributed to the easing of Cold War fears. There were many signs of this, though none was more dramatic than the Supreme Court's return to libertarian values under Chief Justice EARL WARREN. In *Slochower v. Board of Higher Education* (1956) the Court overturned the discharge of a college teacher who had invoked the Fifth Amendment before a congressional committee. In *Sweezy v. New Hampshire* (1956) it reversed the conviction of a Marxist professor who had refused, on FIRST AMENDMENT grounds, to answer questions about his political associations. In WATKINS V. UNITED STATES (1957) it held that Congress had "no general authority to expose the private affairs of individuals without justification. . . ." "No inquiry is an end in itself," wrote Warren. "It must be related to and in furtherance of a legitimate [legislative] task of Congress."

The reaction in Congress was predictable. A South Carolina representative called the WARREN COURT "a greater threat to this union than the entire confines of Soviet Russia." Bills were introduced to limit the Court's JURISDICTION in national security cases, and legislators both state and federal demanded Warren's IMPEACHMENT. Although this uproar probably caused some judicial retreat in the late 1950s, the Supreme Court played an important role in blunting the worst excesses of the McCarthy era.

DAVID M. OSHINSKY

Bibliography

OSHINSKY, DAVID M. 1983 *A Conspiracy So Immense: The World of Joe McCarthy.* New York: Free Press.

MCCLOSKEY, ROBERT G.
(1916–1969)

Robert G. McCloskey earned his Ph.D. at Harvard University, and he taught American government at Harvard from 1948 to 1969. He was by training a political scientist and by scholarly instinct a historian concerned with contemporary events; the modern Supreme Court created a challenge that filled the major portion of his intellectual life. The philosophy of judicial self-restraint in the light of the Court's limited competence and resources appealed to McCloskey at least in part because it struck a chord in his own character. He distrusted the flamboyant, preferring cautious interpretation. By nature judicious, he was suspicious of a Court that too precipitously proclaimed eternal verities. He wrote *American Conservatism in the Age of Enterprise* (1951), *The American Supreme Court* (1961), and *The Modern Supreme Court* (published posthumously in 1972), and he edited the papers of Justice JAMES WILSON.

MARTIN SHAPIRO

MCCOLLUM v. BOARD OF EDUCATION
333 U.S. 203 (1948)

During the late 1940s and 1950s "RELEASED TIME programs" were popular around the country. Public school boards and administrators cooperated with churches and synagogues to provide religious education for students according to their parents' choices. Under the arrangement in Champaign-Urbana, Illinois, students whose parents had so requested were excused from their classes to attend classes given by religious educators in the school buildings. Nonparticipating pupils were not excused from their regular classes.

McCollum, whose child Terry attended the public

schools, challenged the Illinois practice on the grounds that it violated the establishment clause of the FIRST AMENDMENT. The case was the first church-state controversy to reach the Court since EVERSON v. BOARD OF EDUCATION the year before, and Justice HUGO L. BLACK again delivered the opinion of the Court.

Referring to the theory of strict separation announced as OBITER DICTUM in his *Everson* opinion, Black held that the Illinois arrangement fell squarely within the First Amendment's ban. He stressed particularly the utilization of tax-supported facilities to aid religious teaching.

Justice FELIX FRANKFURTER concurred in an opinion in which Justices ROBERT JACKSON, WILEY B. RUTLEDGE, and HAROLD H. BURTON joined. These four had dissented from *Everson*'s approval of state aid to the transportation of children to religious schools.

Justice Jackson also concurred separately, rejecting the sweeping separationism of the Black opinion. Pointing out that there was little real cost to the taxpayers in the Illinois program, he agreed that the Court should end "formal and explicit instruction" such as that in the Champaign schools, but cautioned against inviting ceaseless petitions to the Court to purge school curricula of materials that any group might regard as religious.

Justice STANLEY F. REED, the lone dissenter, had concurred in the result in *Everson.* Here he argued that the majority was giving "establishment" too broad a meaning; unconstitutional "aid" to religion embraced only purposeful assistance directly to a church, not cooperative relationships between government and religious institutions.

McCollum seemed to represent a deepening Supreme Court commitment to the theory of strict SEPARATION OF CHURCH AND STATE, but it was significantly limited by another released-time case, ZORACH v. CLAUSEN (1952).

RICHARD E. MORGAN

MCCRAY v. UNITED STATES
195 U.S. 27 (1904)

Together with CHAMPION V. AMES (1903), the decision in *McCray* played a seminal role in the expansion of a NATIONAL POLICE POWER. Responding to lobby pressure, Congress in 1902 passed a clearly discriminatory EXCISE TAX on oleomargarine colored yellow to resemble butter. Relying on its power to regulate INTERSTATE COMMERCE, Congress sought to force yellow oleo off the market by taxing it at a rate forty times greater than naturally colored oleo. The act was attacked as an encroachment on STATE POLICE POWERS, a TAKING OF PROPERTY without DUE PROCESS, and a violation of the fundamental principles inherent in the Constitution.

Justice EDWARD D. WHITE, for a 6–3 Court, refused to inquire into Congress's intent and sustained the tax. He argued that the Court could not examine the wisdom of a particular act and, reiterating an OBITER DICTUM from *Champion,* said the remedy for "unwise or unjust" acts ". . . lies not in the abuse by the judicial authority of its functions, but in the people, upon whom . . . reliance must be placed for the correction of abuses." The Court pointedly dismissed WILLIAM GUTHRIE's argument that the validity of a tax ought to be determined by its natural and reasonable effect, regardless of pretext, though it would adopt his reasoning in BAILEY V. DREXEL (1922). The act's purpose—to suppress the sale of yellow oleo rather than to raise revenue—was immaterial. White concluded a judicial abdication of power in this case (although the Court would reassert it in *Bailey*) by stating that the Court could not help but sustain a congressional act even if that body "abused its lawful authority by levying a tax which was unwise or oppressive, or the result of the enforcement of which might be to indirectly affect subjects not within the powers delegated to Congress."

Chief Justice MELVILLE W. FULLER and Justices HENRY B. BROWN and RUFUS PECKHAM dissented without opinion.

DAVID GORDON

MCCULLOCH v. MARYLAND
4 Wheat. 316 (1819)

Speaking for a unanimous Supreme Court, Chief JUSTICE JOHN MARSHALL delivered an opinion upon which posterity has heaped lavish encomiums. JAMES BRADLEY THAYER thought "there is nothing so fine as the opinion in McCulloch v. Maryland." ALBERT BEVERIDGE placed it "among the very first of the greatest judicial utterances of all time," while William Draper Lewis described it as "perhaps the most celebrated judicial utterance in the annals of the English speaking world." Such estimates spring from the fact that Marshall's vision of nationalism in time became a reality, to some extent because of his vision. Beveridge was not quite wrong in saying that the *McCulloch* opinion "so decisively influenced the growth of the Nation that, by many, it is considered as only second in importance to the Constitution itself." On the other hand, Marshall the judicial statesman engaged in a judicial coup, as his panegyrical biographer understood. To appreciate Marshall's achievement in *McCulloch* and the intense opposition that his opinion engendered in its time, one must also bear in mind that however orthodox his assumptions and doctrines are in the twentieth century, they were in their time unorthodox. With good reason Beveridge spoke of Marshall's "sublime audacity," the "extreme radicalism" of his constitutional theories, and the fact that he "rewrote the fundamental law of the Nation," a proposition to which Beveridge added that it would be more accurate to state that he made of the written instrument "a living thing, capable of growth, capable of keeping pace with the advancement of the American people and ministering to their changing necessities."

The hysterical denunciations of the *McCulloch* opinion by the aged and crabbed THOMAS JEFFERSON, by the frenetically embittered SPENCER ROANE, and by that caustic apostle of localism, JOHN TAYLOR, may justly be discounted, but not the judgment of the cool and prudent "Father of the Constitution," JAMES MADISON. On receiving Roane's "Hampden" essays assaulting *McCulloch,* Madison ignored the threat of state nullification and the repudiation of JUDICIAL REVIEW, but he agreed with Roane that the Court's opinion tended, in Madison's words, "to convert a limited into an unlimited Government." Madison deplored Marshall's "latitude in expounding the Constitution which seems to break down the landmarks intended by a specification of the Powers of Congress, and to substitute for a definite connection between means and ends, a Legislative discretion as to the former to which no practical limit can be assigned." Few if any of the friends of the Constitution, declared Madison, anticipated "a rule of construction . . . as broad & as pliant as what has occurred," and he added that the Constitution would probably not have been ratified if the powers that Marshall claimed for the national government had been known in 1788–1789. Madison's opinion suggests how far Marshall and the Court had departed from the intentions of the Framers and makes understandable the onslaught that *McCulloch* provoked. Although much of that onslaught was a genuine concern for the prostration of STATES' RIGHTS before a consolidating nationalism, Taylor hit the nail on the head for the older generation of Jeffersonians when he wrote that *McCulloch* reared "a monied interest."

The case, after all, was decided in the midst of a depression popularly thought to have been caused by the Bank of the United States, a private corporation chartered by Congress; and *McCulloch* was a decision in favor of the hated bank and against the power of a state to tax its branch operations. The constitutionality of the power of Congress to charter a bank had been ably debated in Congress and in Washington's cabinet in 1791, when ALEXANDER HAMILTON proposed the bank bill. Constitutional debate mirrored party politics, and the Federalists had the votes. The Court never passed judgment on the constitutionality of the original BANK OF THE UNITED STATES ACT, though it had a belated opportunity. In 1809 a case came before the Court that was remarkably similar to *McCulloch:* state officials, acting under a state statute taxing the branches of the bank, forcibly carried away from its vaults money to pay the state tax. In *Bank of the United States v. Deveaux* (1809), Marshall for the Court, deftly avoiding the questions that he confronted in *McCulloch,* found that the parties lacked the DIVERSITY OF CITIZENSHIP that would authorize JURISDICTION. With the bank's twenty-year charter nearing expiration, a decision in favor of the bank's constitutionality might look like pro-Federalist politics by the Court, embroiling it in a dispute with President Madison, who was on record as opposing the bank's constitutionality, and with Congress, which supported Madison's policies.

The United States fought the War of 1812 without the bank to help manage its finances, and the results were disastrous. The war generated a new wave of nationalism and a change of opinion in Madison's party. In 1816 President Madison signed into law a bill chartering a second Bank of the United States, passed by Congress with the support of young nationalists like HENRY CLAY and JOHN C. CALHOUN and opposed by a Federalist remnant led by young DANIEL WEBSTER. The political world was turned upside down. The bank's tight credit policies contributed to a depression, provoking many states to retaliate against "the monster monopoly." Two states prohibited the bank from operating within their jurisdictions; six others taxed the operations of the bank's branches within their jurisdictions. The constitutionality of Maryland's tax was the issue in *McCulloch,* as well as the constitutionality of the act of Congress incorporating the bank.

Six of the greatest lawyers of the nation, including Webster, WILLIAM PINKNEY, and LUTHER MARTIN, argued the case over a period of nine days, and only three days later Marshall delivered his thirty-six-page opinion for a unanimous Court. He had written much of it in advance, thus prejudging the case, but in a sense his career was a preparation for the case. As

Roane conceded, Marshall was "a man of profound legal attainments" writing "upon a subject which has employed his thoughts, his tongue, and his pen, as a politican, and an historian for more than thirty years." And he had behind him all five Jeffersonian-Republican members of the Court.

Arguing that Congress had no authority to incorporate a bank, counsel for Maryland claimed that the Constitution had originated with the states, which alone were truly sovereign, and that the national government's powers must be exercised in subordination to the states. Marshall grandiloquently turned these propositions around. When Beveridge said that Marshall the solider wrote *McCulloch* and that his opinion echoed "the blast of the bugle of Valley Forge" (where Marshall served), he had a point. Figuratively, Old Glory and the bald eagle rise up from the opinion—to anyone stirred by a nationalist sentiment. The Constitution, declared Marshall, had been submitted to conventions of the people, from whom it derives its authority. The government formed by the Constitution proceeded "directly from the people" and in the words of the PREAMBLE was "ordained and established" in their name, and it binds the states. Marshall drove home that theme repeatedly. "The government of the Union . . . is, emphatically, and truly, a government of the people. In form and in substance it emanates from them. Its powers are granted by them, and are to be exercised directly on them, and for their benefit." A bit later Marshall declared that the government of the Union though limited in its powers "is supreme within its sphere of action. . . . It is the government of all; its powers are delegated by all; it represents all, and acts for all." And it necessarily restricts its subordinate members, because the Constitution and federal laws constitute the supreme law of the land. Reading this later, ABRAHAM LINCOLN transmuted it into "a government of the people, by the people, for the people."

Marshall's opinion is a state paper, like the DECLARATION OF INDEPENDENCE, the Constitution itself, or the Gettysburg Address, the sort of document that puts itself beyond analysis or criticism. But there were constitutional issues to be resolved, and Marshall had not yet touched them. Madison agreed with Roane that "the occasion did not call for the general and abstract doctrine interwoven with the decision of the particular case," but *McCulloch* has survived and moved generations of Americans precisely because Marshall saw that the "general and abstract" were embedded in the issues, and he made it seem that the life of the nation was at stake on their resolution in the grandest way.

Disposing affirmatively of the question whether Congress could charter a bank was a foregone conclusion, flowing naturally from unquestioned premises. Though the power of establishing corporations is not among the ENUMERATED POWERS, seeing the Constitution "whole," as Marshall saw it, led him to the doctrine of IMPLIED POWERS. The Constitution ought not have the "prolixity of a legal code"; rather, it marked only "great outlines," with the result that implied powers could be "deduced." Levying and collecting taxes, borrowing money, regulating commerce, supporting armies, and conducting war are among the major enumerated powers; in addition, the Constitution vests in Congress the power to pass all laws "necessary and proper" to carry into execution the powers enumerated. These powers implied the means necessary to execute them. A banking corporation was a means of effectuating designated ends. The word "necessary" did not mean indispensably necessary; it did not refer to a means without which the power granted would be nugatory, its object unattainable. "Necessary" means "useful," "needful," "conducive to," thus allowing Congress a latitude of choice in attaining its legitimate ends. The Constitution's Framers knew the difference between "necessary" and "absolutely necessary," a phrase they used in Article I, section 10, clause 2. They inserted the NECESSARY AND PROPER CLAUSE in a Constitution "intended to endure for ages to come, and, consequently, to be adapted to the various crises of human affairs." They intended Congress to have "ample means" for carrying its express powers into effect. The "narrow construction" advocated by Maryland would abridge, even "annihilate," Congress's discretion in selecting its means. Thus, the test for determining the constitutionality of an act of Congress was: "Let the end be legitimate, let it be within the scope of the Constitution, and all means which are appropriate, which are plainly adapted to that end, which are not prohibited, but consist with the letter and spirit of the Constitution, are constitutional." That formula yielded the conclusion that the act incorporating the bank was valid.

Such was the BROAD CONSTRUCTION that "deduced" implied powers, shocking even Madison. The Court, he thought, had relinquished control over Congress. He might have added, as John Taylor did, that Marshall neglected to explain how and why a private bank chartered by Congress was necessary, even in a loose sense, to execute the enumerated powers. In *Construction Construed* (1820) Taylor gave five chapters to *McCulloch,* exhibiting the consequences of Marshall's reasoning. Congress might legislate on local agriculture and manufactures, because they were necessary to war. Roads were still more necessary than banks for collecting taxes. And:

> Taverns are very necessary or convenient for the offices of the army. . . . But horses are undoubtedly more necessary for the conveyance of the mail and for war, than roads, which may be as convenient to assailants as defenders; and therefore the principle of implied power of legislation will certainly invest Congress with a legislative power over horses. In short, this mode of construction completely establishes the position, that Congress may pass any internal law whatsoever in relation to things, because there is nothing with which war, commerce and taxation may not be closely or remotely connected.

All of which supported Taylor's contention that Marshall's doctrine of implied powers would destroy the states and lead to a government of unlimited powers, because "as ends may be made to beget means, so means may be made to beget ends, until the co-habitation shall rear a progeny of unconstitutional bastards, which were not begotten by the people."

Marshall's reasoning with respect to the second question in the case incited less hostility, though not by much. Assuming Congress could charter the bank, could a state tax its branch? Marshall treated the bank as a branch or "instrument" of the United States itself, and relying on the SUPREMACY CLAUSE (Article VI), he concluded that if the states could tax one instrument to any degree, they could tax every other instrument as well—the mails, the mint, even the judicial process. The result would cripple the government, "prostrating it at the foot of the States." Again, he was deducing from general principles in order to defeat the argument that nothing in the Constitution prohibits state taxes on congressionally chartered instruments. Congress's power to create, Marshall reasoned, implied a power to preserve. A state power to tax was a power to destroy, incompatible with the national power to create and preserve. Where such repugnancy exists, the national power, which is supreme, must control. "The question is, in truth, a question of supremacy," with the result that the Court necessarily found the state act unconstitutional.

That was Marshall's *McCulloch* opinion. Roane and Taylor publicly excoriated it, and Jefferson spurred them on, telling Roane, who rejected even federal judicial review, "I go further than you do." The Virginia legislature repudiated implied powers and recommended an amendment to the Constitution "creating a tribunal for the decision of all questions, in which the powers and authorities of the general government and those of the States, where they are in conflict, shall be decided." Marshall was so upset by the public criticism that he was driven for the first and only time to reply in a series of newspaper articles. Still, Ohio allied itself with Virginia and literally defied, even nullified, the decision in *McCulloch.* (See OSBORN V. BANK OF THE UNITED STATES, 1824; COHENS V. VIRGINIA, 1821.) Pennsylvania, Indiana, Illinois, and Tennessee also conducted a guerrilla war against the Court, and Congress seriously debated measures to curb its powers. Fortunately the common enemies of the Court shared no common policies. *McCulloch* prevailed in the long run, providing, together with GIBBONS V. OGDEN (1824), the constitutional wherewithal to meet unpredictable crises even to our time. *McCulloch* had unforeseen life-giving powers. Marshall, Beveridge's "supreme conservative," laid the constitutional foundations for the New Deal and the Welfare State.

LEONARD W. LEVY

Bibliography

BEVERIDGE, ALBERT J. 1916–1919 *The Life of John Marshall,* 4 vols. Vol. IV: 283–339. Boston: Houghton Mifflin.

HAINES, CHARLES GROVE 1944 *The Role of the Supreme Court in American Government and Politics, 1789–1835 Pages 351–368. Berkeley: University of California Press.*

WARREN, CHARLES 1923 *The Supreme Court in United States History,* 3 vols. Vol. I:499–540. Boston: Little, Brown.

MCELVAINE v. BRUSH

See: *In Re Kemmler*

MCGOWAN v. MARYLAND

See: Sunday Closing Laws

MCGRAIN v. DAUGHERTY
273 U.S. 135 (1927)

In KILBOURN V. THOMPSON (1881) the Supreme Court had held that because Article I of the Constitution assigned Congress no power beyond the lawmaking power, Congress might constitutionally investigate "the private affairs of individuals" only for the purpose of gathering information to write new legislation. *McGrain* restated this requirement of legislative purpose, but rejected, 8–0, a challenge to the contempt conviction of the brother of Harry M. Daugherty who had failed to appear before a Senate committee investigating the failure of former Attorney General Daugherty to prosecute the malefactors in the Teapot Dome scandal.

In reality the investigation was not aimed at developing new legislation but at exposing malfeasance in the executive branch, a task that might have been deemed constitutionally appropriate for Congress if it were not for the simplistic *Kilbourn* theory. The gap between theory and reality was bridged by the creation of a presumption that congressional investigations had a legislative purpose, a presumption that was not to be overcome simply by showing that an investigation also had a purpose of public exposure.

The *McGrain* technique of requiring a legislative purpose for a congressional investigation, and then invoking a presumption of legislative purpose even when exposure was clearly a principal motive, had important consequences in post-World War II cases where anticommunist investigating committees were seeking to punish leftist speakers by public exposure precisely because the FIRST AMENDMENT prohibited Congress from passing legislation punishing such speech. The Court invoked the presumption of legislative purpose both to blind itself to the actual "exposure for exposure's sake" being conducted and to establish a congressional interest in lawmaking that outweighed whatever incidental infringement on speech the Court was willing to see.

MARTIN SHAPIRO

(SEE ALSO: *Legislative Investigations.*)

MCHENRY, JAMES
(1753–1816)

Irish-born physician James McHenry was a Maryland delegate to the CONSTITUTIONAL CONVENTION OF 1787 and a signer of the Constitution. Absent for most of June and July, he participated little in debate; but, when present, he took detailed notes which are a valuable record of the deliberations. He was later secretary of war (1796–1800).

DENNIS J. MAHONEY

MCILWAIN, CHARLES H.
(1871–1968)

Charles Howard McIlwain, a lawyer and political scientist, taught at Princeton and Harvard Universities. His major fields of interest were political theory and British constitutional history. His *The American Revolution: A Constitutional Interpretation* won the Pulitzer Prize in 1923. In that book he showed that the revolution was "the outcome of a collision between two mutually incompatible interpretations of the British constitution." His *Constitutionalism: Ancient and Modern* (1940, revised 1947) argued that the essence of CONSTITUTIONALISM was the balance between governmental power and the JURISDICTION of an independent judiciary and traced the roots of American constitutionalism through English history to classical Rome.

DENNIS J. MAHONEY

MCKEIVER v. PENNSYLVANIA
403 U.S. 528 (1971)

Although IN RE GAULT (1967) extended some basic procedural rights to juvenile offenders, young people continued to be tried in most states before judges who exercised great discretion, supposedly to protect juveniles. McKeiver, a juvenile defendant, faced possible incarceration for five years and requested TRIAL BY JURY, which the state denied. By a 6–3 vote, the Supreme Court decided that DUE PROCESS OF LAW does not guarantee trial by jury to juvenile offenders. Justice HARRY BLACKMUN for a plurality of four wrote an opinion based on the unrealistic premise that the juvenile system is fundamentally sound and enlightened, but he did not explain how it assured fundamental fairness. Justice JOHN MARSHALL HARLAN found Blackmun's opinion romantic but concurred nevertheless because he still opposed DUNCAN V. LOUISIANA (1968), which extended trial by jury to the states. Justice WILLIAM J. BRENNAN concurred because he thought, mistakenly, that publicity served as a check on juvenile court judges. Justices WILLIAM O. DOUGLAS, HUGO L. BLACK, and THURGOOD MARSHALL dissented. *McKeiver* short-circuited expectations that the Court would require essentially all the rights of the criminally accused for juveniles who commit adult crimes and face the prospect of serious punishment.

LEONARD W. LEVY

MCKENNA, JOSEPH
(1843–1926)

Few Justices sat longer upon the Supreme Court than Joseph McKenna, the son of an Irish immigrant baker, who served for twenty-seven years from 1898 until

1925 under three Chief Justices. During McKenna's tenure, the nation's political system grappled with the problems generated by industrialization, urbanization, and rising class conflict. The same problems followed many of the issues that came before the Court, whose decisions lacked consistency and predictability.

When President WILLIAM MCKINLEY named McKenna, his old House of Representatives colleague, to the seat vacated by Justice STEPHEN J. FIELD, he recognized not distinction at the bar or on the bench but loyal service. McKenna had been a four-term representative from California, a member of the Ninth Circuit Court of Appeals, and attorney general of the United States. In these roles McKenna had earned a justified reputation for devotion to the Republican party, the protective tariff, and the interests of his chief patron, the railroad mogul Leland Stanford. Even as a member of the circuit court, McKenna had written several opinions protecting Stanford's powerful Southern Pacific company from the unfriendly behavior of local and state officials who sought to regulate the carrier's rates and terminal facilities.

As a member of the Supreme Court during the high tide of the Progressive Era, however, McKenna supported the efforts of THEODORE ROOSEVELT's and WILLIAM HOWARD TAFT's administrations to bring the country's major railroads under a larger measure of administrative control through the Interstate Commerce Commission (ICC). Times had changed. By the turn of the century, even the railroads desired a degree of federal regulation that would protect them from conflicting state laws and the debilitating rate wars which drained away profits. McKenna wrote opinions for the Court that confirmed the new relationship between the carriers and the federal government by upholding the ICC's statutory powers with respect to fact-gathering and rate-making.

McKenna also became a robust supporter of congressional efforts to regulate other aspects of the nation's economic and social life under authority of the COMMERCE CLAUSE. He joined Justice JOHN M. HARLAN's crucial opinion in CHAMPION V. AMES (1903), which laid the foundation for a NATIONAL POLICE POWER by giving Congress the authority to exclude from the channels of INTERSTATE COMMERCE supposedly harmful goods such as lottery tickets. McKenna later applied this principle in his own opinions, which sustained the PURE FOOD AND DRUG ACT and also the Mann Act, banning the transportation of women in interstate commerce for immoral purposes.

To his great credit, McKenna was able to accept the extension of the national power doctrine to child labor in the famous case of HAMMER V. DAGENHART (1918), even while others who had endorsed the earlier decisions turned their backs upon logic and history. Nor did he join the majority in the case of ADAIR V. UNITED STATES (1908), where six Justices overturned Congress's attempt to ban YELLOW DOG CONTRACTS on the nation's railroads. McKenna's dissent placed the authority of Congress to regulate commerce above the contractual freedom of corporate management.

A stout nationalist and a moderate Republican who remained capable of accepting many progressive reforms, McKenna nonetheless displayed a checkered record with regard to state and federal efforts to assist the working class and organized labor. He refused, for example, to permit the state of Kansas to outlaw yellow dog contracts in all private industry, although he endorsed Congress's effort to do so on the interstate railroads. He cast his vote with RUFUS PECKHAM in LOCHNER V. NEW YORK (1905) and with GEORGE H. SUTHERLAND in ADKINS V. CHILDREN'S HOSPITAL (1923), when the majority struck down MAXIMUM HOURS AND MINIMUM WAGE LEGISLATION on the grounds of FREEDOM OF CONTRACT. Yet McKenna spurned that conservative shibboleth in MULLER V. OREGON (1908), WILSON V. NEW (1917), and BUNTING V. OREGON (1917). On the other hand, not many opinions could match in reactionary tone McKenna's dissent in the *Arizona Employers' Liability Cases* (1919), where he argued that liability without fault violated the DUE PROCESS clause of the FOURTEENTH AMENDMENT.

Like most of his brethren on the WHITE COURT, McKenna gave the green light to federal and state efforts to stamp out dissent during World War I. He voted to uphold the convictions of Charles Schenck and Eugene V. Debs as well as those of Jacob Abrams and Joseph Gilbert, although the latter two cases provoked sharp dissents from OLIVER WENDELL HOLMES and LOUIS D. BRANDEIS. If sometimes contractual freedom had to give way before the power of Congress, McKenna believed, so, too, did the liberty to protest against the government in time of war.

MICHAEL E. PARRISH

Bibliography

MCDEVITT, BROTHER MATTHEW 1946 *Joseph McKenna: Associate Justice of the United States.* Washington, D.C.: Catholic University Press.

SEMONCHE, JOHN E. 1978 *Charting the Future: The Supreme Court Responds to a Changing Society, 1890–1920.* Westport, Conn.: Greenwood Press.

MCKINLEY, JOHN
(1780–1852)

Like several other Jacksonian Justices on the TANEY COURT, John McKinley was a product of the Southwest. Born in Virginia, he went with his family to Kentucky where he learned law and began practice. In 1818 he moved to Huntsville, Alabama, then a frontier town, where he practiced law and pursued a diversified political career—first as a supporter of HENRY CLAY and then, when Clay's fortunes waned in Alabama, of ANDREW JACKSON. This timely shift got him a Senate seat in 1826. He served there until 1830, when he lost reelection. He then returned to the Alabama legislature, and in 1832 he went to the United States House of Representatives where he served for one term. After another term in the state legislature in 1836, he was elected by that body to the Senate but chose instead to accept an appointment to the Supreme Court from MARTIN VAN BUREN in 1837.

McKinley's legislative career lacked distinction, but the policy preferences he revealed were those that would guide his work on the Court: in addition to unswerving loyalty to Jackson and Van Buren, he was a strict states' rights man, though he never argued out his case philosophically or constitutionally. In good Jacksonian fashion he was suspicious of monopolies and hated the second Bank of the United States. He also had a strong preference for land laws that favored small settlers and a firm belief that SLAVERY was a state problem and that property in slaves was entitled to legal protection.

McKinley's fifteen years on the Supreme Court (1837–1852) were unproductive and frustrating, both for him and for those who worked with him. In general, states' rights ideas guided his judicial behavior, but he never spoke for the Court in any important cases. He took his duties seriously, as Chief Justice ROGER B. TANEY pointed out in his brief eulogy, and was decent and fairminded to the best of his ability. But during his entire tenure, which was interrupted by illness and frequent absences, he wrote only about twenty opinions for the Court, all routine.

Perhaps his most notorious opinion came in BANK OF AUGUSTA V. EARLE (1839) where, both on circuit and in a lone dissent at Washington, he held that a CORPORATION chartered in one state (a bank in the *Earle* case) could not do business within the boundaries of another state without the latter's express consent. McKinley's position was consistent with a deep concern for state SOVEREIGNTY, but it was, as Justice JOSEPH STORY observed in dismay, totally unrealistic in an age when interstate corporate business was increasingly the norm. McKinley dissented twenty-three times but none of his dissents attracted support and none pioneered new law. Many were unwritten, evidence of the Justice's increasing isolation from the ongoing operations of the Court.

McKinley was also isolated on his own circuit, although Supreme Court Justices, as senior circuit judges, ordinarily dominated the district judges with whom they sat. Not so on the Fifth Circuit where district judges Philip K. Lawrence and, to a lesser extent, Theodore H. McCaleb held the upper hand. There is evidence also that leading members of the circuit bar held the Justice in disrepute. Part of the problem was the 10,000 miles of annual travel (which left McKinley little time to study cases) and the large number of cases (2,700 at each of the two terms in 1839 by his reckoning). His circuit also included Louisiana, where the civil law received from France and the COMMON LAW formed a mixture that was well-nigh incomprehensible to all save lawyers who grew up with it. The main difficulty on circuit as on the full Court, however, was McKinley himself. His talents were simply too modest for the duties of his office. Even his eulogizers found nothing about his legal ability to praise, and all evidence points to the correctness of CARL B. SWISHER's assessment: that John McKinley, of all the Justices on the Taney Court, was the least distinguished.

R. KENT NEWMYER

Bibliography

GATELL, FRANK O. 1969 John McKinley. In Leon Friedman and Fred L. Israel (eds.), *The Justices of the United States Supreme Court 1789–1969*, Vol. 1, pages 769–792. New York: Chelsea House.

Proceedings in Relation to the Death of the Late Judge McKinley 1852 14 Howard iii–v.

MCKINLEY, WILLIAM
(1843–1901)

William McKinley, an Ohio Republican who was President of the United States from 1897 to 1901, spent most of his term in office preoccupied with foreign affairs. An imperialist, he advocated the annexation of Hawaii and, after successfully prosecuting a war against Spain, acquired the Philippines and PUERTO RICO for the United States. McKinley continued the domestic policies of his predecessor, GROVER CLEVELAND, but unlike most Chief Executives in the late nineteenth century, McKinley saw the presidency as a powerful office. He frequently relied on expert and academic commissions to offer him advice on specific problems.

McKinley's lack of interest in enforcing the SHERMAN ANTITRUST ACT paralleled BENJAMIN HARRISON's, but McKinley's failure to enforce the law vigorously is more significant because he held office during the second greatest merger movement in American history. His three attorneys general—one of whom, JOSEPH MCKENNA, would be his sole appointment to the Supreme Court—initiated only three cases under the act. The most important antitrust cases decided during McKinley's tenure, UNITED STATES V. TRANS-MISSOURI FREIGHT ASSOCIATION (1897) and *Addyston Pipe & Steel Co. v. United States* (1899), had been started under prior administrations.

DAVID GORDON

Bibliography

GOULD, LEWIS L. 1980 *The Presidency of William McKinley.* Lawrence: Regents Press of Kansas.

MCLAUGHLIN, ANDREW C. (1861–1947)

A protégé of THOMAS COOLEY at the University of Michigan, Andrew Cunningham McLaughlin took over his course in American constitutional history and later taught that subject at the University of Chicago for thirty years. In his 1914 presidential address before the American Historical Association, McLaughlin criticized CHARLES BEARD's monolithic emphasis on economic factors. McLaughlin also rejected the tone of exaltation that imbued the work of JOHN FISKE and others on the CONSTITUTIONAL CONVENTION OF 1787. In his first major book, *Confederation and Constitution* (1905), McLaughlin emphasized the constructive aspects of the ARTICLES OF CONFEDERATION and of the Confederation period. He construed the Articles as the product of a war against centralism and as the world's first written CONSTITUTION to establish a federal system, whose origins he traced to the British Empire. His other important works, distinguished for their judicious interpretations, were *Courts, Constitutions, and Parties* (1912), *Foundations of American Constitutionalism* (1932), and *Constitutional History of the United States* (1935), which won a Pulitzer Prize.

LEONARD W. LEVY

MCLAUGHLIN v. FLORIDA

See: Miscegenation

MCLAURIN v. OKLAHOMA STATES REGENTS

See: *Sweatt v. Painter*

MCLEAN, JOHN (1785–1861)

John McLean's appointment to the Supreme Court on March 6, 1829, was ANDREW JACKSON's first and the first from the old Northwest and Ohio, where McLean had grown to manhood. He studied law with Arthur St. Clair, Jr., was admitted to the bar in 1807, and maintained an active full-time practice in Lebanon, Ohio, until his 1812 election to Congress, where he served two terms. As a National Republican, he favored a protective tariff and a national bank. From 1816 to 1822 he served as judge of the Ohio Supreme Court where he gained a respect for the COMMON LAW and developed a penchant for bending it "to the diversity of our circumstances," as he put it in one case. While serving on that court, McLean assiduously cultivated political favor, first with JAMES MONROE and JOHN QUINCY ADAMS, and, when the latter began to falter, with Jackson. His efforts paid off, first in 1822 with an appointment as Commissioner of the General Land Office, then in 1823 as Postmaster General, where his brilliant administrative abilities won him a national reputation. Adams reappointed him to head the Post Office Department, and Jackson was willing to do the same but nominated him to the Supreme Court when McLean indicated an unwillingness to make political removals.

McLean served as Associate Justice from 1829 to 1861, during a period of rapid transition in American law. At the outset the new Justice inclined toward Jacksonian STATES' RIGHTS dogma, as in his dissent from CONTRACT CLAUSE orthodoxy in CRAIG V. MISSOURI (1830). More revealing yet was his practical-minded opinion for the majority in BRISCOE V. BANK OF THE COMMONWEALTH OF KENTUCKY (1837), which held that the notes of the Commonwealth Bank were not BILLS OF CREDIT prohibited by Article I, section 10, even though the state owned the bank and the notes circulated as legal tender.

Despite his result-oriented approach in such cases as *Briscoe* and MAYOR OF NEW YORK V. MILN (1837) (where he supported STATE POLICE POWER regulations against the charge that they were regulations of INTERSTATE COMMERCE), McLean was not a Jacksonian judge. Indeed, he moved steadily toward a conservative nationalism similar to that of Justice JOSEPH STORY, who became his closest friend on the Court. That McLean was solidly conservative on property rights and CORPORATION questions is clear from his majority opinion in behalf of contractual sanctity in PIQUA BRANCH BANK V. KNOOP (1854). His nationalism was apparent in the CHEROKEE INDIAN CASES (*Worcester v. Georgia*) in 1832 (where he joined JOHN MARSHALL against Georgia and Jackson), and in *Holmes v. Jennison* in 1840 (where he concurred in ROGER B. TANEY's dissent which asserted the supremacy of the federal government in the area of foreign policy). His "high-toned FEDERALISM" in COMMERCE CLAUSE cases can be seen in the LICENSE CASES (1847) and PASSENGER CASES (1849) and in his majority opinion in *Pennsylvania v. Wheeling and Belmont Bridge Company* (1852) which struck down a Virginia law authorizing a bridge that obstructed commerce over a navigable river. His dissent in COOLEY V. BOARD OF WARDENS OF PHILADELPHIA (1851) reaffirmed the theory of his friend Story that the power to regulate foreign and interstate commerce belonged exclusively to Congress.

McLean disliked slavery and his opinions often revealed his free-soil sentiments; but he regularly conceded the legality of the institution. Thus his separate opinion in PRIGG V. PENNSYLVANIA (1842) upheld the right of northern states to protect free Negroes from unlawful rendition, but it also affirmed the power of Congress to require the states to return fugitives. Equivocation was unavoidable, too, in GROVES V. SLAUGHTER (1841) where in a separate opinion McLean argued that slavery was a local institution under state control and that the power of Congress to regulate interstate commerce did not prevent a state from regulating the importation of slaves. Free states presumably could prohibit slaves from being brought into their jurisdiction and liberate slaves once they arrived, but slave states could also regulate imports and exports of slaves for sale. On circuit McLean also ruled against freedom when he thought the law obliged him to do so.

McLean's proslavery decisions, which were condemned in the free-soil press, increasingly ran counter to his presidential plans which, to the distress of some of his colleagues, he relentlessly pursued from the bench. In DRED SCOTT V. SANDFORD (1857) his political ambition, now focused on the Republican party, influenced his judicial behavior. In a separate dissent, he argued that Congress had the power to prohibit slavery in the TERRITORIES, that Negroes could be citizens, and that Dred Scott was free by virtue of his residence in a free state and a free territory. McLean has been unfairly blamed for the Court's wide-ranging, politically explosive decision—a burden we now know should fall most heavily on Taney and JAMES M. WAYNE. But there is no doubt that McLean's determination to dissent gave Taney and Wayne a good excuse to confront the whole problem of SLAVERY IN THE TERRITORIES.

McLean was not a legal scholar, he pioneered no new DOCTRINE, and he did not greatly refine the process of constitutional adjustment to new circumstances that was the hallmark of the TANEY COURT. Greatness, however, is not only rare but relative, and on a Court burdened with mediocrity McLean looked good. His opinions were generally solid and persuasive (as in the great copyright case of *Wheaton v. Peters* in 1834) and he assuredly carried more than his share of the Court's heavy work load (with nearly 250 majority opinions and numerous dissents). He was one of the few Justices of the period who went to the considerable trouble of publishing his circuit opinions (in six volumes) and whose circuit opinions were worth publishing. It is true that his political ambition contributed to the politicization of the judicial process. Still, he cherished the Court as an institution and worked diligently through it to preserve the Union under the Constitution.

R. KENT NEWMYER

Bibliography

GATELL, FRANK O. 1969 John McLean. In Leon Friedman and Fred L. Israel (eds.), *The Justices of the United States Supreme Court, 1789–1969,* Vol. 1, pages 535–567. New York: Chelsea House.

WEISENBURGER, FRANCIS P. 1937 *The Life of John McLean: A Politician on the United States Supreme Court.* Columbus: Ohio State University Press.

MCNABB v. UNITED STATES

See: McNabb-Mallory Rule

MCNABB-MALLORY RULE

Partly in response to the problem posed by the VOLUNTARINESS test, the Supreme Court made an unexpected departure from that test in *McNabb v. United States* (1943) and *Mallory v. United States* (1957). Under the "McNabb-Mallory Rule," a confession obtained by law enforcement officers during a period of unnecessary delay in bringing an arrested person before a magistrate for arraignment was inadmissible in federal prosecutions. The rule was based not on constitutional grounds but on the Court's supervisory authority over the administration of criminal justice in the federal courts. The rule created more problems than it attempted to solve, and in 1968, Congress abolished it.

In *McNabb,* five brothers were arrested for murder and held in barren detention cells for forty-eight hours. Isolated from friends and family, and without the assistance of counsel, they were repeatedly interrogated until confessions were obtained. (See POLICE INTERROGATIONS AND CONFESSIONS.) Only after they confessed were they taken before a magistrate for arraignment. The confessions were admitted into EVIDENCE at trial and the McNabbs were convicted.

The Court, with only Justice STANLEY F. REED dissenting, reversed the convictions on the ground that they were unlawfully obtained during a period of prolonged custodial delay. Federal laws in effect at the time of the Court's decision required officers to take an arrested person "immediately" before a magistrate for arraignment. At arraignment, the magistrate advises the defendant of the charges against him, of his constitutional rights, and sets a preliminary hearing date at which the government must show legal cause for the detention.

Justice FELIX FRANKFURTER devoted much of his opinion for the Court to an analysis of the policies behind the immediate arraignment laws. He concluded that they were intended to protect the rights of arrested persons and to deter the police from secret third-degree interrogation of persons not yet arraigned.

Finding that the officers who arrested the McNabbs had acted in willful disobedience of the laws requiring immediate arraignment, the Court suppressed the confessions. Suppression, Frankfurter explained, would promote the policies behind the laws and ensure the fair and effective administration of the federal criminal justice system by disallowing convictions based on unfair police procedures.

Two years after *McNabb,* Congress adopted Rule 5(a) of the FEDERAL RULES OF CRIMINAL PROCEDURE. The rule required that an arrested person be taken, "without unnecessary delay," before the nearest available commissioner or any other nearby officer empowered to commit persons charged with offenses against the laws of the United States. The rule, by failing to include remedies for its violation, left intact the *McNabb* mandate that confessions obtained during a period of unlawful detention be suppressed. Any questions regarding the continuing viability of the *McNabb* rule were put to rest by the Court's opinion in *Mallory.*

Mallory was arrested with two other suspects on rape charges. Although the police had sufficient evidence to consider Mallory the prime suspect, he was not arraigned until ten hours after his arrest, during which time he was continually interrogated and finally signed a written confession. At trial, the signed confession was introduced into evidence; Mallory was convicted and received the death sentence.

Frankfurter delivered the opinion of a unanimous Court, which held the confession inadmissible because Mallory had not been arraigned without unnecessary delay as required by Rule 5(a). The Court's interpretation of Rule 5(a) was based on the principles announced earlier in the *McNabb* decision. Delays in arraignment must be prevented in order to prevent abusive and unlawful law enforcement practices aimed at obtaining confessions of guilt from suspects in custody who have not been informed by a judicial officer of the charges against them or of their constitutional rights.

After *Mallory* the law prevailing in the federal courts, commonly referred to as the "McNabb-Mallory Rule," was that any confession made by a suspect under arrest, in violation of Rule 5(a), was inadmissible in evidence. The problem with the McNabb-Mallory Rule was that it operated arbitrarily to exclude from evidence otherwise free and voluntary confessions merely because of delay in arraignment. In other words, the United States Supreme Court had failed to consider the obvious: a delayed arraignment does not imply the involuntariness of a confession.

Criticized as illogical and unrealistic, the McNabb-Mallory Rule was abolished in 1968 when Congress enacted Title II of the OMNIBUS CRIME CONTROL AND SAFE STREETS ACT. The act provides in part that confessions shall not be inadmissible solely because of delay in arraignment, if they are voluntary and made within six hours of arrest or during a delay in arraignment that is reasonable, considering the transportation problems in getting a defendant before a magistrate. Thus, the voluntary nature of the confession is the test of its admissibility, and delay in arraignment is only one factor for the judge to consider.

WENDY E. LEVY

Bibliography

STEPHENS, OTIS H., JR. 1973 *The Supreme Court and Confessions of Guilt.* Pages 63–89. Knoxville: University of Tennessee Press.

MCREYNOLDS, JAMES C. (1862–1946)

James Clark McReynolds, a Tennessee Democrat, first came to national attention as an antitrust prosecutor during the THEODORE ROOSEVELT and WILLIAM HOWARD TAFT administrations. He was a Tennessee Gold Democrat, friendly with Colonel Edward House, WOODROW WILSON's key adviser. His antitrust reputation led to his appointment as Wilson's attorney general in 1913. Within a year, however, McReynolds found himself at odds with the administration and powerful congressmen. Wilson "kicked McReynolds upstairs" to the Supreme Court in 1914. From then until his retirement in 1941, McReynolds distinguished himself as a consistent and implacable foe of Progressive and New Deal regulatory programs.

McReynold's hostility to trusts largely derived from his ideas of individualism and freedom from arbitrary restraints. Throughout his judicial career he resolutely supported the business community and was instinctively suspicious of governmental regulation. "If real competition is to continue, the right of the individual to exercise reasonable discretion in respect of his own business methods must be preserved," McReynolds wrote in FEDERAL TRADE COMMISSION V. GRATZ (1920). In that case, the Court limited the authority of the FTC, the creation of which had been one of the Wilson administration's primary achievements; McReynolds wrote that the courts, not the commission, would decide the meaning of "unfair method of competition." In *St. Louis and O'Fallon Railroad v. United States* (1929) the Court resolved a long-standing dispute between the Interstate Commerce Commission (ICC) and railroads as to whether original or replacement costs should be considered for valuation and rate purposes. Speaking for a narrow majority, McReynolds overturned ICC policy by ruling that the commission had to base its determination of rates on replacement costs, which were higher.

McReynolds resisted the claims of organized labor. For example, he joined his colleagues in rejecting federal child labor laws and a District of Columbia minimum wage statute. When the Court in 1919 sustained an Arizona law holding employers responsible for on-the-job accidents whether or not they were negligent, McReynolds dissented, caustically arguing that such laws served "to stifle enterprise, produce discontent, strife, idleness and pauperism."

Without exception, McReynolds supported the conviction of political radicals during the "Red Scare" period following World War I. A decade later, when the Court turned against restrictive state measures on speech and press, McReynolds parted company with the majority, dissenting in STROMBERG V. CALIFORNIA (1931) and NEAR V. MINNESOTA (1931). Similarly, McReynolds's ill-concealed contempt for blacks led to dissent from decisions striking down an all-white primary law and ordering a new trial for the Scottsboro defendants. Finally, when the Court, in MISSOURI EX REL. GAINES V. CANADA (1938), began its long process of overturning segregation, McReynolds bitterly assailed the majority opinion.

Some of McReynolds's opinions defending individual rights remain relevant. In MEYER V. NEBRASKA (1923) he spoke for the Court in striking down a state statute prohibiting German language instruction in the public schools; in PIERCE V. SOCIETY OF SISTERS (1925) he ruled against an Oregon statute that had the effect of proscribing parochial school education; and in CARROLL V. UNITED STATES (1925) he vehemently protested against violations of the FOURTH AMENDMENT in enforcing PROHIBITION. In MYERS V. UNITED STATES (1926) he dissented from what he considered to be an almost unlimited approval of presidential power to remove federal officials, a view vindicated nine years later when the Court unanimously rejected President FRANKLIN D. ROOSEVELT's attempt to remove a federal trade commissioner.

The New Deal years provide the sharpest focus for McReynolds's views of constitutional law, both when he joined in majority opinions and later in the bitter dissents that represent his most familiar legacy. McReynolds combined his ideological reaction to the New Deal with a passionate, almost pathological, hatred for Franklin D. Roosevelt. The Justice was scathing in his private remarks and, at times, indiscreet in public. In his courtroom dissent in the GOLD CLAUSE CASES (1935) McReynolds emotionally proclaimed: "This is Nero at his worst. The Constitution is gone!" When the New Deal gained a few early Court victories, McReynolds dissented, as in the gold clause cases, in NEBBIA V. NEW YORK (1934), and in ASHWANDER V. TENNESSEE VALLEY AUTHORITY (1936). As one of the "Four Horsemen," he participated in striking down thirteen New Deal measures between 1934 and 1936. When the Court made its famous shift, beginning in 1937 with WEST COAST HOTEL COMPANY V. PARRISH and the WAGNER ACT CASES, McReynolds joined his fellow conservatives in outraged dissent. As their spokesman in *National Labor Relations Board v. Friedman-Marks Clothing* (1937), he argued that the WAGNER ACT regulated production, not commerce, and thus exceeded the boundaries of congressional power as set in long-standing precedents. Similarly, he considered the SOCIAL SECURITY ACT unconstitutional; he registered a lone dissent against the approval of the securities registration provisions of the PUBLIC UTILITIES HOLDING COMPANY ACT; and, finally, he provided the sole dissent to the Court's recognition in 1940 that labor PICKETING was entitled to protection as an exercise of FREEDOM OF SPEECH.

Few Supreme Court Justices have been more outspoken or more doctrinaire than McReynolds; and few have been so incompatible with colleagues. McReynolds refused to speak to fellow Wilson appointee John H. Clarke, who was too liberal, and to LOUIS D. BRANDEIS and BENJAMIN N. CARDOZO, who were both liberal and Jewish. Even Chief Justice Taft found him "selfish and prejudiced" and difficult to like. He was committed to laissez-faire individualism and racial segregation, and he was unyielding and hostile to any political beliefs he regarded as deviant.

STANLEY I. KUTLER

Bibliography

MASON, ALPHEUS THOMAS 1956 *Harlan Fiske Stone: Pillar of the Law.* New York: Viking.

PASCHAL, JOEL F. 1951 *Mr. Justice Sutherland: A Man Against the State.* Princeton, N.J.: Princeton University Press.

MECHANICAL JURISPRUDENCE

This pejorative epithet was introduced in 1908 by the American jurist ROSCOE POUND. It and similar rubrics—"the jurisprudence of conceptions," "slot machine, phonograph, T-square theories of law"—were widely used to caricature patterns of juristic thought and judicial action that deduced conclusions from unexamined, predetermined conceptions by purely mechanical logical processes, disregarded socioeconomic realities and practical consequences, and understated the degree of judicial lawmaking by attributing a machinelike automatism to the judicial process.

The "sociological jurisprudence" and "legal realism" of Justices OLIVER WENDELL HOLMES, HARLAN FISKE STONE, and BENJAMIN N. CARDOZO were often hailed as correctives for mechanical jurisprudence because they viewed law and logic instrumentally as means to social ends, and they acknowledged judicial lawmaking.

A perennial juristic allurement, mechanical jurisprudence was exemplified by many Supreme Court "economic DUE PROCESS" and COMMERCE CLAUSE decisions between 1895 and 1937. In due process cases such as LOCHNER V. NEW YORK (1905) and ADKINS V. CHILDREN'S HOSPITAL (1923), the Court invoked the laissez-faire doctrine, FREEDOM OF CONTRACT, which regarded workers and employers as bargaining equals, in holding state and federal legislation unconstitutional. In commerce clause cases such as UNITED STATES V. E. C. KNIGHT CO. (1895) and CARTER V. CARTER COAL CO. (1936), the Court used economically unrealistic distinctions between "commerce" and PRODUCTION, and "direct" and "indirect" EFFECTS ON COMMERCE in invalidating federal legislation. A classic expression of mechanical jurisprudence is the passage of Justice Owen Roberts's opinion in UNITED STATES V. BUTLER (1936) where he said the Court had only to compare the statute with the appropriate constitutional clause to see if they squared.

Such decisions led finally to President FRANKLIN D. ROOSEVELT's 1937 "Court reform" bill, designed, he said, "to save the Constitution from the Court and the Court from itself." But the Court swiftly reversed and reformed itself, abandoning these mechanical constitutional interpretations. Later, in WICKARD V. FILBURN (1942), it reemphasized that its recognition of economic realities had made "the mechanical application of legal formulas no longer feasible."

HOWARD E. DEAN

Bibliography

POUND, ROSCOE 1908 Mechanical Jurisprudence. *Columbia Law Review* 8:605–623.

STERN, ROBERT L. 1951 The Problems of Yesteryear—Commerce and Due Process. *Vanderbilt Law Review* 4:446–468.

MEIKLEJOHN, ALEXANDER (1872–1964)

Alexander Meiklejohn was a philosopher, president of Amherst College, and director of an experimental college at the University of Wisconsin. After his long academic career he became a CIVIL LIBERTIES publicist. His *Free Speech and Its Relation to Self-Government* (1948) presented the FIRST AMENDMENT as the foundation of political democracy. He advocated that citizens should have the same unlimited FREEDOM OF SPEECH as their representatives. Regarding the CLEAR AND PRESENT DANGER TEST and BALANCING TESTS as annulments of the First Amendment, he criticized OLIVER WENDELL HOLMES and ZECHARIAH CHAFEE as proponents of a stunted interpretation of free speech. In the McCarthy period he defended the right of communists to teach. His essay, "The First Amendment Is An Absolute," written when he was almost ninety, summarized his position, which was not really absolutist. Distinguishing "the freedom of speech" from "speech," he believed that private defamation, OBSCENITY, perjury, false advertising, and solicitation of crime were not constitutionally protected. His ABSOLUTISM seems to have extended to speech concerning all matters of public policy, education, philosophy, arts, literature, and science, but he believed that even protected speech was subject to reasonable regulations of time and place. Meiklejohn was closer to Holmes and Chafee than he admitted.

LEONARD W. LEVY

MEMOIRS v. MASSACHUSETTS
383 U.S. 413 (1966)

Nine years after ROTH V. UNITED STATES, still unable to agree upon a constitutional definition of OBSCENITY, the Supreme Court reversed a state court determination that John Cleland's *Memoirs of a Woman of Pleasure,* commonly known as *Fanny Hill,* was obscene. The three-Justice PLURALITY OPINION, written by Justice WILLIAM J. BRENNAN, held that the constitutional test for obscenity was: "(a) the dominant theme of the material taken as a whole appeals to a prurient interest in sex; (b) the material is patently offensive because it affronts contemporary community standards relating to the description or representation of sexual matters; and (c) the material is utterly without redeeming social value."

Despite an OBITER DICTUM in JACOBELLIS V. OHIO (1964), it was believed—and the Massachusetts courts had held—that *Roth* did not require unqualified worthlessness before a book might be deemed obscene. Justice Brennan twisted the *Roth* reasoning (that obscenity was unprotected because it was utterly worthless) into a constitutional test that was virtually impossible to meet under criminal standards of proof. Thus a finding of obscenity would become rare, even where the requisite prurient interest appeal and offensiveness could be demonstrated.

The Massachusetts courts had tried the book in the abstract; a host of literary experts testified to its social value. The circumstances of the book's production, sale, and publicity were not admitted. Justice Brennan noted that evidence that distributors commercially exploited *Fanny Hill* solely for its prurient appeal could have justified a finding, based on the purveyor's own evaluation, that *Fanny Hill* was utterly without redeeming social importance.

Justices HUGO L. BLACK, WILLIAM O. DOUGLAS, and POTTER J. STEWART concurred in the result, Black and Douglas adhering to their view that obscenity is protected expression. Stewart reiterated his view that the First Amendment protected all but "hard-core pornography."

Justice TOM C. CLARK, dissenting, rejected the importation of the "utterly without redeeming social value" standard into the obscenity test, which he believed would give the "smut artist free rein." Reacting against the continuous flow of pornographic materials to the Supreme Court, he reasserted that the Court should apply a "sufficient evidence" standard of review of lower courts' obscenity decisions.

Justice JOHN MARSHALL HARLAN, dissenting, argued that although the federal government could constitutionally proscribe only hard-core pornography, the states could prohibit material under any criteria rationally related to accepted notions of obscenity.

Justice BYRON R. WHITE, also dissenting, argued that *Roth* counseled examination of the predominant theme of the material, not resort to minor themes of passages of literary worth to redeem obscene works from condemnation.

KIM MCLANE WARDLAW

MEMORANDUM ORDER

Most orders of any court are not accompanied by opinions, but are simply stated in memorandum form. The Supreme Court issues thousands of such memorandum orders each year, granting or denying such requests as applications for review, applications for permission to appear IN FORMA PAUPERIS, applications for permission to file briefs AMICI CURIAE, or PETITIONS FOR REHEARING.

Some memorandum orders effectively decide cases; the denial of a petition for CERTIORARI is one example, and another is the dismissal of an APPEAL "for want of a substantial federal question." Occasionally the Court summarily affirms the decision of a lower court, issuing no opinion but only a memorandum order. The denial of certiorari generally has little force as a PRECEDENT; however, both lower courts and commentators do draw conclusions concerning the Court's view when they see a consistent pattern of refusal to review lower court decisions reaching the same conclusion. The summary affirmance of a decision in a memorandum order does establish a precedent, but the precedent is limited to the points necessarily decided by the lower court, and does not extend to the reasoning in that court's opinion. The practice of deciding major issues through memorandum orders is often criticized on the ground that decisions will not be understood as principled if they are not explained.

KENNETH L. KARST

Bibliography

BROWN, ERNEST J. 1958 The Supreme Court, 1957 Term—Foreword: Process of Law. *Harvard Law Review* 72:77–95.

MEMPHIS v. GREENE
451 U.S. 100 (1981)

Because the City of Memphis blocked a street at the point where a white neighborhood bordered a black neighborhood, residents of the black neighborhood had to drive around the white neighborhood in order to get to and from the city center. Black residents brought a CLASS ACTION against the city, seeking an INJUNCTION to keep the street open. They failed in the federal district court, but the court of appeals held that the closing violated their right to hold and enjoy property, guaranteed by the CIVIL RIGHTS ACT OF 1866.

The Supreme Court, with Justice JOHN PAUL STEVENS writing for a 6–3 majority, rejected the statutory claim, saying the street closing had caused only minor inconvenience, and had not damaged the plaintiff's property values. The question remained whether the THIRTEENTH AMENDMENT, of its own force, forbade anything but slavery itself. The Court did not reach this broad question, saying only that the street closing here was not a BADGE OF SERVITUDE. Justice THURGOOD MARSHALL, for the dissenters, scored the majority for ignoring "the plain and powerful symbolic message of the 'inconvenience' ": to fence out "undesirables."

KENNETH L. KARST

MENTAL ILLNESS AND THE CONSTITUTION

Mental illness has played two apparently different roles in American law generally: as a limitation on state authority to impose ordinary legal standards on individuals and as a basis for increasing state authority over individuals. The paradigmatic limiting use of mental illness is the defense of insanity for conduct that would otherwise be subject to criminal liability. Its paradigmatic use to increase state authority is in civil commitment of people who, apart from their mental illness, would not be subject to state confinement or control. In both guises, however, the same underlying justification is advanced—that a mentally ill person deserves specially beneficial treatment from the state, either to excuse him from ordinary standards of criminal liability or to protect and treat him under civil commitment laws.

Until the 1960s, constitutional doctrine paid scant attention to any of the legal usages for mental illness. Beginning in that decade, lower federal courts began to scrutinize these uses and to invoke constitutional norms in the service of that scrutiny. The central problem was that the promise of special beneficence for mental illness proved false on close examination. Although insanity was denoted a defense to criminal liability, in practice defendants thus found "not guilty" were automatically confined to state maximum security institutions indistinguishable from prisons (and often with harsher custodial conditions), were provided with virtually no psychiatric treatment, and were typically held for longer terms than if they had been convicted of the offenses charged. Similarly, individuals who were civilly committed, ostensibly for protection and treatment, in fact were regularly confined in brutal state institutions, provided no semblance of psychiatric treatment, subjected to degrading impositions such as numbing, physically harmful drug dosages, strait-jacketed isolation, and confined for long terms.

Confronted with these facts, federal courts found various violations of constitutional rights, all derived essentially from the proposition that DUE PROCESS required the state to justify any deprivation of liberty and, where that justification was based on a promise of beneficent treatment, to fulfill that promise. Thus the District of Columbia Circuit Court held in *Rouse v. Cameron* (1966) that those found not guilty by reason of insanity had a "right to treatment" and not simply custodial confinement, and in *Bolton v. Harris* (1968) that these defendants could not be automatically confined after an insanity acquittal but only if found "mentally ill" and "in need of treatment" according to civil commitment standards. For civilly committed people generally, that court found in *Lake v. Cameron* (1966) a liberty-based presumption against automatic commitment to a secure institution and a consequent right to treatment in the "least restrictive alternative" setting. Other federal courts concluded that civilly committed people generally had a constitutional right to treatment and that civil commitment must rest on proof of "danger to self or others," not simply mental illness as such, and proof moreover that would satisfy the criminal law "beyond REASONABLE DOUBT."

For more than a decade after these rulings, the Supreme Court held back from any definitive holding either to endorse or to reject these doctrinal innovations. During the 1960s, the Court did demonstrate concern for the problem of unfulfilled and even hypocritical state promises of therapeutic benefits as a justification for increased social controls. The most significant context for this Supreme Court concern was not mental illness but rather the juvenile court system, where states sought to justify the absence of criminal law procedural protections by invoking the promise of therapy. In IN RE GAULT (1967) the Court found these promises insufficiently convincing and required extensive recasting of juvenile court procedures.

In 1972 the Supreme Court first addressed the systemic implications of this same problem for state authority generally premised on mental illness. In *Jackson v. Indiana* the Court overturned common state practice regarding criminal defendants found mentally incompetent to stand trial. Traditional doctrine purported to excuse such disabled defendants from standing trial, ostensibly to benefit them; but the practical consequence was that these defendants were treated in the same way and as badly as those found not guilty by insanity. The defendants were given long-term, even lifetime, confinement in harsh facilities without semblance of psychiatric care, even if the offense charged were a petty MISDEMEANOR. The Court ruled in *Jackson* that this disposition violated due process; the conditions of this confinement must provide treatment with reasonable prospect that the defendant will be made competent to stand trial. The practical result of this ruling has been substantially to increase the treatment resources provided to defendants found incompetent for trial. To justify the confinement of defendants who, after a substantial period of confinement, remain disabled for trial purposes, a state must invoke its civil commitment laws.

With this one exception, however, the Supreme Court was hesitant during the 1970s to address the constitutional law issues raised by state invocations of mental illness. The dominant motif of the Court's work during this time can be seen in its resolution in 1979 of the question of the requisite BURDEN OF PROOF in civil commitment proceedings. The Court acknowledged that substantial due process liberty interests were at stake, but nonetheless concluded that the state's beneficent purpose toward the allegedly mentally ill person justified a less stringent burden than the criminal standard of proof; hence in *Addington v. Texas* (1979) the Court required an intermediate standard of "clear and convincing evidence."

This impulse to find some seeming middle ground between fundamentally opposed premises is also apparent in the Court's equivocal approach to the question of a constitutional right to treatment for persons confined to state mental institutions. In O'CONNOR v. DONALDSON (1975) the Court ruled that a state could not commit a person on grounds of mental illness alone but only with an added finding of danger to self or others. The Court refused, however, to decide whether a state was obliged to provide treatment to such a person rather than impose merely custodial confinement. The same issue returned to the Court in *Youngberg v. Romeo* (1982), this time regarding an institutionalized person who was retarded rather than mentally ill. Again the Court avoided a definitive resolution, ruling that the plaintiff was constitutionally entitled to "minimal treatment" that reasonably promised to reduce his aggressive outbursts—as opposed to the harsh behavior controls, such as prolonged shackling, that the state had used. The Court did not, however, reach the broader issue whether the state was obliged to provide treatment with any promise of greater benefits such as ultimate freedom from confinement.

In 1983 the Court departed from its previous pattern of equivocation in these matters. In a 5–4 decision the Court held in *Jones v. United States* that a criminal defendant found not guilty by insanity could be confined to a mental institution without regard to the maximum term for which he might have been sentenced for the offense charged. The Court ruled, moreover, that the insanity acquittal itself justified the defendant's confinement without any necessary invocation of civil commitment standards, thus effectively disapproving the 1968 court of appeals decision in *Bolton.* The Court in effect treated the "criminally insane" as different from either "criminals" or the "insane." This differential treatment can work a marked disadvantage, as the defendant in the *Jones* case found. But, the Court appeared to conclude, the defendant chooses to plead criminal insanity and thus knowingly embraces the risk of his ultimate disadvantage. Indeed, in AKE v. OKLAHOMA (1985) the Court made it easier to invoke the insanity defense by ruling that an indigent defendant is entitled to a court-appointed psychiatrist. The specific context of that case was a capital offense, where the risk of indefinite confinement following an insanity acquittal might seem invariably worthwhile; but the Court did not limit its holding to capital cases.

It is not clear whether the Court's definitive rulings in the context of criminal insanity will be followed by similar resolutions in other aspects of state authority regarding mentally ill people. The Court may have felt a special need to address criminal insanity as such because of the extraordinary public attention resulting from John Hinckley's acquittal for insanity in 1982 on the charge of attempting to assassinate President RONALD REAGAN. Whatever the future directions of judicial rulings, however, the underlying questions regarding the justifications for and scope of state authority in these matters remain difficult.

The dominant theme of the constitutional principle set out by lower courts in the 1960s and 1970s has been that mental illness is relevant to the exercise of state power only where the state promises therapeutic benefit, and that the Constitution requires that this promise be kept. Keeping the promise, however, is easier said than done. Both diagnosis and treatment of mental illness is uncertain. Furthermore, adequate therapy, either in state institutions or in community treatment facilities, will require supervision of complex bureaucracies and large expenditures of funds. Supervision of this process will severely strain both the courts' enforcement capacities and traditional conceptions of judicial authority. Some observers thus conclude that the lower courts were correct in seeing the failure and even hypocrisy of states regarding their therapeutic promises, but these courts merely compounded this error by invoking the Constitution to add new promises that similarly cannot be fulfilled.

If courts cannot and should not attempt to enforce the promise of therapy, what response is proper in the face of egregious state abuses? Some have argued that states should simply be barred from giving mental illness special legal relevance in any circumstances, as a justification either for increasing or withholding state power over individuals. In this view, states could confine people for "dangerousness" only by applying ordinary criminal law standards, and those standards should make no special dispensation for the mentally ill. A few states have essentially abolished the insanity defense and sharply limited the availability of civil commitment. Similarly, some judicial decisions such as *Rogers v. Okin* (1980) have found a constitutional right to *refuse* treatment, notwithstanding that a person has been civilly committed as mentally ill and dangerous. The premise of these decisions is not that the state might fail to keep its therapeutic promise; it is rather that the promise may be kept with excessive rigor, and that the state may thereby transgress valued boundaries of individual integrity and dignity. Though these lower court decisions do not directly embrace the view that would abolish all state mental illness powers, they share the underlying suspicion of therapeutically justified state impositions, and they apparently prefer modes of social control that do not directly purport to invade mental processes, such as imprisonment for criminal convictions.

This underlying premise is a temptingly plausible response to the sorry history of state abuse of the mentally ill. But the premise fails both as social policy and as constitutional doctrine. The consequences were disastrous for large numbers of people who were removed from state institutions in the 1960s and 1970s, in part as a response to court decisions, and were "dumped" into communities with no facilities to receive them or willingness to respond to their special needs. As constitutional doctrine, the abolitionist doctrine relies on a conception of due process "liberty" that takes insufficient account of the psychological conditions of individual autonomy that lie beneath this prized constitutional right. This conception ignores the ways in which mental illness can distort an individual's capacity to acknowledge his need for help, including state-administered assistance. It may be that state power can never be trusted to provide this help, that this is the lesson of the history of state abuse of mentally ill people in the criminal and civil law context. But this lesson has not yet been clearly written into constitutional doctrine.

ROBERT A. BURT

Bibliography

BROOKS, ALEXANDER D. 1974 *Law, Psychiatry and the Mental Health System,* and 1980 *Supplement.* Boston: Little, Brown.

BURT, ROBERT A. 1979 *Taking Care of Strangers: The Rule of Law in Doctor–Patient Relations.* New York: Free Press.

SCULL, ANDREW 1977 *Decarceration: Community Treatment and the Deviant: A Radical View.* Englewood Cliffs, N.J.: Prentice-Hall.

MENTAL RETARDATION AND THE CONSTITUTION

The Supreme Court first addressed the constitutional status of mentally retarded people in BUCK V. BELL (1927). In an opinion by Justice OLIVER WENDELL

HOLMES, the Court upheld a state statute authorizing compulsory STERILIZATION of "mental defectives." In dismissing the claim that this imposition wrongly discriminated against retarded people and thereby denied them EQUAL PROTECTION under the FOURTEENTH AMENDMENT, Holmes appeared to invoke "minimal scrutiny" (as it was later termed), holding that the legislature might reasonably find retardation both inheritable and socially harmful. It was not until the 1970s that courts took a different, more protective stance toward retarded people. In so doing, they challenged the social attitudes of fear and aversion that lay beneath not only sterilization laws but also the general state policy, dating from the late nineteenth century, of excluding retarded people from community facilities (such as public schools) and consigning them to large, geographically isolated residential institutions.

The modern decisions involved two constitutional approaches. The first approach was to recognize a constitutional "right to treatment" for residents of state institutions. This right was initially formulated in 1971 when a federal district court held that brutal custodial conditions in an Alabama institution must be remedied by intensive educational and treatment programs conducted by new cadres of professionally qualified staff. In *Youngberg v. Romeo* (1982) the Supreme Court effectively endorsed this constitutional holding, deriving as a proposition of SUBSTANTIVE DUE PROCESS that, although the state was not required to offer any services to retarded people, if the state chose to provide residential facilities, then those facilities must meet certain minimal standards.

The second constitutional approach was initially formulated in 1972, when a federal district court overturned a state statute excluding retarded children from public schools on the ground that they were "ineducable." The court appeared to conclude that all retarded people were educable to some degree. This holding was quickly adopted by other federal courts to overturn similar state statutes and, moreover, was endorsed by Congress in the EDUCATION OF ALL HANDICAPPED CHILDREN ACT (1975) requiring education of all children, no matter how severely impaired, as a condition on federal funding of public schools.

These two constitutional approaches of substantive due process and equal protection analysis were blended by a 1977 district court ruling that a state institution for the retarded must be wholly closed and its residents moved to small-scale community homes on the grounds that the "right to treatment" could not be effectively protected in any large, isolated institutional setting and that, like racial SEGREGATION, separation of retarded people from contact with mentally normal people was INVIDIOUS DISCRIMINATION. A congressional act of 1975 also indicated preference for community over institutional retardation facilities; but the Supreme Court, in PENNHURST STATE SCHOOL V. HALDERMAN (1981) without addressing the initial constitutional ruling, held that Congress had spoken only with "hortatory" rather than mandatory intention.

In 1985 the Supreme Court finally did address the question whether mentally retarded people warranted specially protected constitutional status, but its answer was ambiguous. The specific issue in *Cleburne v. Cleburne Living Center* (1985) was the validity of a local ZONING ordinance that specifically excluded group residences for "feeble-minded" people, even though fraternity and sorority houses, dormitories, and nursing homes for "convalescents or aged" people were explicitly permitted. The Fifth Circuit overturned the ordinance, citing the immutability of retardation, its stigmatized social history (as evidenced by sterilization laws based on spurious scientific findings and by brutalizing, isolated institutional residences), and the political vulnerability of retarded people. Because retardation could be relevant to some state classifications such as school programming or employment eligibility, however, the court found that it was more like gender than like race, a "quasi-suspect" rather than a SUSPECT CLASSIFICATION. Applying intermediate scrutiny, the court found insufficient justification for the zoning exclusion.

The Supreme Court declined to follow this analysis. It concluded that retardation classifications warranted no special judicial scrutiny for several reasons: the legitimate relevance of retardation for some classificatory purposes, the nonjudicial expertise seemingly required to evaluate such purposes, and the political strength of retardation advocates as evidenced by the 1975 congressional acts (notwithstanding that Congress had also acted against race and gender discrimination in recent decades). The Court nonetheless invalidated the zoning ordinance on the ground that it was based merely on "vague, undifferentiated fears" about retarded people. This rationale does not readily fit the conventional conception of "minimal scrutiny" equal protection analysis, given that fears regarding the irrationality and uncontrollability of retarded people have some plausible claim to factuality, even though this claim is unreliably documented and inapplicable to most retarded people.

The Court's invalidation of the zoning ordinance in *Cleburne* must thus rest on an unacknowledged premise, either that minimal scrutiny equal protection analysis (as applied to all state classifications) now requires more clearly demonstrated reasonableness than has heretofore been demanded or that retarded people do warrant some degree of special judicial protection to ensure that differential classifications of them have factual bases beyond "vague, undifferentiated fears."

ROBERT A. BURT

Bibliography

BURT, ROBERT A. 1985 Pennhurst: A Parable. Pages 265–364 in Robert Mnookin, ed., *In the Interest of Children.* New York: W. H. Freeman.

MERE EVIDENCE RULE

A SEARCH WARRANT must identify the place to be searched and the items to be seized. Such items may include fruits or instrumentalities of crime (such as stolen money or burglar's tools) or contraband (such as illegal drugs). In *Gouled v. United States* (1921) the Supreme Court held that search warrants could not issue to seize mere EVIDENCE of crime.

In WARDEN V. HAYDEN (1967), however, the Court held that warrants could issue for mere evidence so long as there was a "nexus" between the evidence and the criminal behavior. ZURCHER V. STANFORD DAILY (1978) illustrates the effect of the rule's abandonment. The Stanford University student newspaper published photographs of a campus disturbance between the police and demonstrators. Because the police observed only two of their assailants, a warrant was obtained for a search of the newspaper's offices. The warrant affidavit did not allege any involvement in the unlawful acts by newspaper staff members. During the search, police examined the paper's photographic labs, files, desks, and waste paper baskets. Since no new evidence was discovered, no items were taken.

One commentator has summarized the "mere evidence rule" after *Zurcher* as follows: *Zurcher* represents a case in which none of the items searched for by the police was a fruit or instrumentality of a crime, or contraband. Under the pre-*Hayden* rule, the warrant used in *Zurcher* could not have been issued. Yet the present broad rule is so well established that the Supreme Court's majority opinion did not even discuss the issue.

CHARLES H. WHITEBREAD

Bibliography

WHITEBREAD, CHARLES H. 1980 *Criminal Procedure.* Mineola, N.Y.: Foundation Press.

METROPOLITAN LIFE INSURANCE CO. v. WARD
470 U.S. (1985)

This decision departed from a long series of Supreme Court decisions upholding the constitutionality of state taxes against attack under the EQUAL PROTECTION clause. Alabama taxed the gross premiums of insurance companies by imposing a one percent tax on companies organized in Alabama, and a tax of three percent or four percent on companies organized in other states. In an opinion by Justice LEWIS F. POWELL, the Supreme Court held, 5–4, that this discrimination failed even the RATIONAL BASIS test, because its only articulated purpose—to create a tax advantage for domestic economic interests over out-of-state interests—was illegitimate. Congress, in its 1945 act permitting the states to discriminate in favor of local insurance companies, had insulated such laws from attack under the COMMERCE CLAUSE, but had not purported to speak to any issue of equal protection.

In an unusual division of the Court, Justice SANDRA DAY O'CONNOR dissented, joined by Justices WILLIAM J. BRENNAN, THURGOOD MARSHALL, and WILLIAM H. REHNQUIST. Justice O'Connor pointed to previous decisions recognizing the legitimacy of state efforts to promote domestic industry, and made the unanswerable point that Alabama's tax scheme was rationally related to such a purpose. Furthermore, she said, Congress in 1945 understood that it was authorizing laws of this very kind. She also accused the majority of reviving active judicial scrutiny of state ECONOMIC REGULATION. Although the latter prediction seems unlikely to come true, the fear that it expresses is not dispelled by the majority's opinion.

KENNETH L. KARST

Bibliography

COHEN, WILLIAM 1985 Federalism in Equality Clothing: A Comment on Metropolitan Life Insurance Company v. Ward. *Stanford Law Review* 38:1–27.

MEYER v. NEBRASKA
262 U.S. 390 (1923)

Meyer represented an early use of SUBSTANTIVE DUE PROCESS doctrine to defend personal liberties, as distinguished from economic ones. Nebraska, along with other states, had prohibited the teaching of modern foreign languages to grade school children. Meyer, who taught German in a Lutheran school, was convicted under this law. The Supreme Court, 7–2, held the law unconstitutional. Justice JAMES C. MCREYNOLDS wrote for the Court in *Meyer* and in four companion cases from Iowa, Ohio, and Nebraska. Justice OLIVER WENDELL HOLMES, joined by Justice GEORGE SUTHERLAND, dissented in all but the Ohio cases.

McReynolds began with a broad reading of the "liberty" protected by the FOURTEENTH AMENDMENT: "it denotes not merely freedom from bodily restraint, but also the right of the individual to contract, to engage in any of the common occupations of life, to acquire useful knowledge, to marry, establish a home and bring up children, to worship God according to the dictates of his own conscience, and, generally, to enjoy those privileges long recognized at common law as essential to the orderly pursuit of happiness by free men." State regulation of this liberty must be reasonably related to a proper state objective; the legislature's view of reasonableness was "subject to supervision by the courts." The legislative purpose to promote assimilation and "civic development" was readily appreciated, given the hostility toward our adversaries in World War I. However, "no adequate reason" justified interfering with Meyer's liberty to teach or the liberty of parents to employ him during a "time of peace and domestic tranquillity."

Holmes concurred in the Ohio cases, because Ohio had singled out the German language for suppression. But he could not say it was unreasonable for a state to forbid teaching foreign languages to young children as a means of assuring that all citizens might "speak a common tongue." Because "men might reasonably differ" on the question, the laws were not unconstitutional.

Meyer was thus a child of LOCHNER V. NEW YORK (1905), taking *Lochner*'s broad view of the judicial role in protecting liberty. Yet, although substantive due process has lost its former vitality in the field of ECONOMIC REGULATION, *Meyer*'s precedent remains vigorous in the defense of personal liberty. *Meyer* was reaffirmed in GRISWOLD V. CONNECTICUT (1965), LOVING V. VIRGINIA (1967), and ZABLOCKI V. REDHAIL (1978), three modern decisions protecting the FREEDOM OF INTIMATE ASSOCIATION.

KENNETH L. KARST

MIAMI HERALD PUBLISHING COMPANY v. TORNILLO
418 U.S. 241 (1974)

It may be argued that FREEDOM OF SPEECH is meaningless unless it includes access to the mass media so that the speech will be heard. Here the Supreme Court unanimously struck down a Florida statute requiring a newspaper to provide a political candidate free space to reply to its attacks on his personal character. Noting that the statute infringed upon "editorial control and judgment," the Court held that "any [governmental] compulsion to publish that which 'reason' tells . . . [the editors] . . . should not be published is unconstitutional."

Tornillo was a major blow to proponents of a right of access. When compared to RED LION BROADCASTING COMPANY V. FEDERAL COMMUNICATIONS COMMISSION (1969), it raises the question whether the FIRST AMENDMENT provides greater protection for the press than for the electronic media. In light of the large number of one-newspaper towns, the scarcity rationale for allowing government to compel access to broadcast channels would seem to apply even more strongly to the print media. Ultimately the distinction may be between the public ownership of the channels and the private ownership of the print media. If so, the Court has not explained or defended this linking of speech rights to property rights.

MARTIN SHAPIRO

MICHAEL M. v. SUPERIOR COURT
450 U.S. 464 (1981)

A boy of 17½ was convicted of rape under a California statute making it a crime for a male to have intercourse with a female under 18; the girl's age was 16½. A fragmented Supreme Court voted 5–4 to uphold the conviction against the contention that the statute's SEX DISCRIMINATION—the same act was criminal for a male but not for a female—denied the EQUAL PROTECTION OF THE LAWS.

There was no opinion for the Court. The majority Justices, however, agreed in accepting the California Supreme Court's justification for the law: prevention of illegitimate teen-age pregnancies. The risk of pregnancy itself, said Justice WILLIAM H. REHNQUIST, served to deter young females from sexual encounters; criminal sanctions on young males only would roughly "equalize" deterrents.

The dissenters argued that California had not demonstrated its law to be a deterrent; thirty-seven states had adopted gender-neutral statutory rape laws, no doubt on the theory that such laws would provide even more deterrent, by doubling the number of persons subject to arrest. When both parties to an act are equally guilty, argued Justice JOHN PAUL STEVENS, to make the male guilty of a FELONY while allowing the female to go free is supported by little more than "traditional attitudes toward male–female relations."

KENNETH L. KARST

MICHELIN TIRE COMPANY v. ADMINISTRATOR OF WAGES
423 U.S. 276 (1976)

Opening the way for increased local revenue, a unanimous Court overruled *Low v. Austin* (1872) and sustained a state property tax on imported goods even though they retained their character as imports. The Court held that the IMPORT-EXPORT CLAUSE did not prohibit such a tax if it were imposed without discrimination on all goods in the state.

DAVID GORDON

(SEE ALSO: *Original Package Doctrine.*)

MICHIGAN v. LONG

See: Adequate State Grounds; Stop and Frisk

MICHIGAN v. SUMMERS
452 U.S. 692 (1981)

A 6–3 Supreme Court held that if the police had a valid warrant to search a home for illegal drugs, they had authority to detain the occupants of the premises during the search. They could therefore lawfully require a suspect to remain in the house, arrest him after finding the contraband, and search his person incident to the arrest. The dissenters argued that the FOURTH AMENDMENT prevented the police from seizing a person without PROBABLE CAUSE in order to make him available for arrest should probable cause be revealed by the search.

LEONARD W. LEVY

MIDDENDORF v. HENRY
425 U.S. 25 (1976)

A 5–3 Supreme Court ruled that servicemen have no RIGHT TO COUNSEL in summary courts-martial. Justice WILLIAM H. REHNQUIST's majority opinion concluded that such proceedings did not constitute criminal prosecutions within the Sixth Amendment's guarantee, and he also disposed of a Fifth Amendment DUE PROCESS claim as without merit.

DAVID GORDON

MIFFLIN, THOMAS
(1744–1800)

General Thomas Mifflin, a wealthy Philadelphia Quaker, was a member of the Pennsylvania Assembly and of the First and Second Continental Congresses before serving as quartermaster general of the Army (1775–1778). He was elected to Congress in 1782, and in 1783 became President of the United States in Congress Assembled. Mifflin was speaker of the Pennsylvania Assembly in 1787, when he was chosen as chairman of his state's delegation to the CONSTITUTIONAL CONVENTION OF 1787. The records of the convention do not indicate that Mifflin ever spoke in the debates, although he did sign the Constitution. In 1790 he presided over the state CONSTITUTIONAL CONVENTION. He served as governor of Pennsylvania from 1790 to 1799, a period that included the WHISKEY REBELLION.

DENNIS J. MAHONEY

Bibliography

ROSSITER, CLINTON 1966 *1787: The Grand Convention.* New York: Macmillan.

MILITARY JUSTICE

The Constitution, in language taken from the ARTICLES OF CONFEDERATION, empowers Congress to "make Rules for the Government and Regulation of the land and naval Forces." Congress has enacted Articles of War and Articles for the Government of the Navy since 1775, but in 1950 the two systems were fused in the Uniform Code of Military Justice (UCMJ).

Criminal justice under the UCMJ resembles that in civilian courts more than it differs. As in most states, the type of trial court depends on the gravity of the offense. Petty offenses are dealt with by nonjudicial punishment or summary court-martial; more serious offenses may be tried before a special or general court-martial. The types of court-martial differ in number of members and in the maximum punishment they may impose. The rules of EVIDENCE are about the same as in the federal courts; and a defendant tried by a special or general court-martial enjoys the RIGHT TO COUNSEL at government expense. The Supreme Court held in *Middendorf v. Henry* (1976) that the right to free counsel does not apply in summary courts-martial, which more closely resemble administrative hearings than criminal trials.

The major difference between military and civilian criminal justice is the absence of a jury. The members of the court are appointed by the convening authority, who can, theoretically, "pack the court." However, the accused can avoid the possibility of command influence by electing trial by a military judge sitting alone, who is responsible only to the Judge Advocate General of his service. When the military judge sits with members of a court-martial his role is like that of a civilian judge, except that the members determine the sentence if the accused is convicted. There is an elaborate system of review but, except in a limited class of cases, APPEAL to the Court of Military Appeals (three civilian judges appointed by the President) is not by right.

The UCMJ does not provide for review by any civilian court: findings and sentences of courts-martial, as affirmed under the code, are "final and conclusive" and "binding upon all . . . courts . . . of the United States." The Supreme Court has always held that, absent provision by Congress, there can be no direct appeal from the decisions of military tribunals. The federal courts have, however, developed several techniques of collateral review—notably HABEAS CORPUS, MANDAMUS, and suits for back pay in the COURT OF CLAIMS—which effectively ensure that military courts are subject to constitutional supervision.

The federal courts had long collaterally reviewed court-martial convictions to ensure that there was JURISDICTION over person, offense, and sentence. The Supreme Court after World War II imposed new limits on court-martial jurisdiction over person and offense. In the UCMJ, courts-martial were granted jurisdiction over many categories of civilians, including honorably discharged servicemen and civilians accompanying the armed forces outside the United States. In a series of decisions, including UNITED STATES EX REL. TOTH V. QUARLES (1955) and REID V. COVERT (1956), the Supreme Court held that a court-martial could not constitutionally try any civilian in peacetime. There are still some gray areas, such as jurisdiction over retired regulars and certain reservists.

Thereafter the Court held that a court-martial could not constitutionally try a member of the armed forces for an offense that had no "service connection"; the leading case, *O'Callahan v. Parker* (1969), involved the attempted rape of a civilian by a soldier off-post, on leave, and out of uniform. Despite a subsequent decision in which the Court suggested a dozen factors to be considered in determining whether a crime was "service-connected," there are still many doubtful cases, particularly those involving off-post use or possession of drugs. The Court of Military Appeals and the inferior federal courts have made two exceptions to the requirement of service connection. Considering that *O'Callahan* was based on the loss of TRIAL BY JURY, they have permitted courts-martial to try offenses regardless of service connection committed outside the jurisdiction of American civilian courts or punishable by not more than six months' confinement, so that the accused would not in any case be constitutionally entitled to a jury.

Until after World War II the BILL OF RIGHTS had no application to courts-martial: if jurisdiction existed over person, offense, and sentence, federal courts would not consider allegations of even the grossest unfairness. Chief Justice SALMON P. CHASE, concurring in EX PARTE MILLIGAN (1866), declared that "the power of Congress, in the government of the land and naval forces, is not affected by the fifth or any other amendment." Historical evidence concerning the framers of the Bill of Rights justifies Chase's dictum: President JAMES MADISON, for example, approved the conviction of General William Hull in 1814, although the court-martial had denied Hull's request for the assistance of counsel.

The Supreme Court has never set aside a court-martial conviction for denial of constitutional DUE PROCESS, but it would almost certainly do so if confronted with a clear case of such denial. No such case has yet reached the Court because the protections of the Bill of Rights (except trial by jury and the right to BAIL) are embodied in the UCMJ. A coerced confession, for example, would violate not only the Fifth Amendment but also the UCMJ and thus constitute a denial of "military due process." In addition the Court of Military Appeals has consistently construed the UCMJ in such a way as to avoid conflict with the Supreme Court's construction of the Constitution. Military exigency may, however, justify some relaxation of civilian standards. Military rulings on constitutional issues must conform to Supreme Court standards, absent a showing that special military conditions require a different rule. Thus PARKER v. LEVY (1974) held that the "general articles" which prohibit "conduct unbecoming an officer and a gentleman" and "disorders and neglects to the prejudice of good order and discipline" are not unconstitutionally vague or overbroad.

JOSEPH W. BISHOP, JR.

Bibliography

BISHOP, JOSEPH W., JR. 1974 *Justice under Fire: A Study of Military Law.* Chaps. 2, 3, 4. New York: Charterhouse.

WIENER, FREDERICK BERNAYS 1958 Courts-Martial and the Bill of Rights: The Original Practice. *Harvard Law Review* 72:1–49, 266–304.

MILITARY RECONSTRUCTION ACTS

14 Stat. 428 (1867)
15 Stat. 2 (1867)
15 Stat. 14 (1867)

The first Military Reconstruction Act established procedures for the resumption of self-government and normalized constitutional status for ten states of the former Confederacy. Though it preserved extant governments intact for the time being, it authorized military peacekeeping and required adoption of new state constitutions. It also mandated black suffrage.

By February 1867, congressional Republicans realized that the FOURTEENTH AMENDMENT, even if ratified, constituted an insufficient program of Reconstruction. They were unwilling to accept the forfeited-rights theory of southern state status propounded by Rep. THADDEUS STEVENS, or to sanction indefinite military governance. However, the intransigence of President ANDREW JOHNSON and the Machiavellian politics of congressional Democrats, who both demanded immediate and unconditional restoration of white rule in the South, convinced the Republicans that federal supervision of the process of recreating state governments was essential if the freedmen and Republican war objectives were not to be abandoned.

The first Military Reconstruction Act divided the ex-Confederate states (Tennessee excepted) into five military districts each under the command of a regular brigadier general, who was charged with peacekeeping responsibilities. He was empowered to use either ordinary civilian officials or military commissions to accomplish this objective. Though the commissions were authorized to overrule civilian authorities if necessary, the act did not replace the state governments previously created under presidential authority. Rather, under the first and subsequent Military Reconstruction Acts (1867–1868), the commanding general was required to call for the election of delegates to CONSTITUTIONAL CONVENTIONS. In these elections, blacks were entitled to vote, and whites disfranchised by the Fourteenth Amendment were excluded. The new state constitution had to enfranchise blacks. When it was ratified by a majority of eligible voters, elections were to be held under it for new state governmental officials. Only then would the existing governments cede authority. The new legislature had to ratify the Fourteenth Amendment and present its state constitution to Congress. Congress would then complete the process by admitting the state's congressional delegation to their seats.

President Johnson vetoed the first measure, asserting several grounds for its unconstitutionality. First, it imposed an "absolute domination of military rulers" whose "mere will is to take the place of all law," subjecting the southern people to "abject slavery." Second, Congress lacked power to impose governments on the southern states, particularly because those states remained part of the Union. Third, the act would deny individual liberties, including the requirements of TRIAL BY JURY, warrants, DUE PROCESS, and HABEAS CORPUS. Johnson also opposed the measure because the requirements of black suffrage would "Africanize the southern part of our territory," and, finally, because the anomalous status of the ten states which had been denied representation in Congress since 1865 cast a cloud over legislation affecting them. Congress immediately overrode the veto.

Under the procedure specified by the Military Reconstruction Acts, all southern states were reorganized and readmitted between 1868 and 1870. The military presence remained for nearly another decade, however, because of turbulence caused by anti-black and anti-Unionist terrorism. The Republican governments established under congressional Reconstruction were overthrown by "Conservative" or "Redeemer" white-supremacist Democratic regimes by 1877, when the process of Reconstruction was effectively terminated.

WILLIAM M. WIECEK

(SEE ALSO: *Constitutional History, 1865–1877.*)

MILLER, SAMUEL F. (1816–1890)

Samuel Freeman Miller was a towering figure on the Supreme Court from his appointment by ABRAHAM LINCOLN in 1862 until his death in 1890. He sat with four Chief Justices, participated in more than 5,000 decisions of the Court, and was its spokesman in ninety-five cases involving construction of the Constitution. No previous member of the Court had written as many constitutional opinions. Miller's contemporaries regarded him as one of the half-dozen great Justices in American history, a remarkable achievement for a self-educated lawyer who had never held public office, either in his native Kentucky or in adopted Iowa, prior to his appointment to the Court. Justice HORACE GRAY claimed that if his legal training had been less "unsystematic and deficient," Miller would have been "second only to [JOHN] MARSHALL."

Miller looked and acted the part of a great magistrate. He was tall and massive; he had a warm, unaffected disposition and was said to be "as ready to talk to a hod-carrier as to a cardinal." His instinct for what he often called "the main points, the controlling questions," his impatience with antique learning and philosophical abstraction, and his unrivaled reputation for industry, integrity, and independence all enhanced his stature. Candor and intellectual self-reliance pervaded his opinions, and he often stated quite bluntly his assumption that law and practical good sense were of one piece: "This is the honest and fair view of the subject, and we think it conflicts with no rule of law" (*Pettigrew v. United States,* 1878); "if this is not DUE PROCESS OF LAW it ought to be" (*Davidson v. New Orleans,* 1878); "this is just and sound policy" (*Iron Silver Mining Co. v. Campbell,* 1890).

Statecraft rather than formal jurisprudence was Miller's forte, and he emerged as the Court's balance-wheel soon after coming to the bench. His career ultimately spanned three tumultuous decades in which the Justices constantly quarreled, often rancorously, about the scope of federal and state powers and the Court's role in protecting private rights against the alleged usurpations of both. Scores of cases involved highly charged political issues. Yet Miller always remained detached. He never permitted differences of opinion to affect personal relations with his brethren; he met counsels of heat and passion with chilly distaste. Miller's capacity for detachment was, in part, a matter of personality. But it was also a function of his modest view of the Court's role in the American system of government. He resisted doctrinal formulations that curtailed the discretion of other lawmakers, spoke self-consciously about "my conservative habit of deciding no more than is necessary in any case," and often succeeded in accommodating warring factions of more doctrinaire colleagues by narrowing the issue before the Court. As early as 1870, Chief Justice SALMON P. CHASE said he was "beyond question, the dominant personality upon the bench."

The first principles of Miller's constitutional understanding were derived from HENRY CLAY and the Whig party. Although he abandoned the Whigs for the Republican party in 1854, Miller never ceased to regard Clay as the quintessential American statesman or to reaffirm the Kentucky sage's belief in a BROAD CONSTRUCTION of national powers, the primacy of the legislative department in shaping public policy, and the duty of government at all levels to encourage material growth. Miller's adherence to the first two principles was especially apparent in his work on the CHASE COURT. In EX PARTE MILLIGAN (1866), he joined the minority of four, concurring, who suggested that Congress might constitutionally have established martial rule in Indiana. And in *Tyler v. Defrees* (1870), a confiscation case, Miller flatly rejected the doctrine "long inculcated, that the Federal Government, however strong in a conflict with a foreign foe, lies manacled by the Constitution and helpless at the feet of a domestic enemy." Early in 1868, when the movement to impeach President ANDREW JOHNSON gathered momentum and the Court initially established jurisdiction in EX PARTE MCCARDLE, Miller conceded privately that "in the threatened collision between the Legislative branch of the government and the Executive and judicial branches I see consequences from which the cause of free government may never recover in my day." He added, however, that "the worst feature I now see is the passion which governs the hour in all parties and persons who have a controlling influence." In contrast, Miller not only counseled caution and delay while Congress proceeded to divest the Court of jurisdiction over *McCardle* but also dissented in TEXAS V. WHITE (1869). He regarded the status of states still undergoing military reconstruction as a POLITICAL QUESTION which only Congress could decide. *Hepburn v. Griswold* (1870), the first of the LEGAL TENDER CASES, evoked his most celebrated defense of congressional authority. There Miller sharply criticized the majority's reliance on the "spirit" of the Constitution, which, he insisted, "substitutes . . . an undefined code of ethics for the Constitution, and a court of justice for the National Legislature. . . . Where there is a choice of means, the selection is for Congress, not the Court."

Miller was not always such a positivist in rejecting considerations arising from the spirit of the Constitution. In the SLAUGHTERHOUSE CASES (1873), which came up during fierce public debate over the Enforcement and Klu Klux Klan Acts, Miller intervened decisively to preserve "the main features" of the federal system. Although the powers of Congress were not directly at issue, his opinion for the Court undercut every FOURTEENTH AMENDMENT theory that had been advanced in other cases to justify federal jurisdiction over perpetrators of racially motivated private violence. The Fourteenth Amendment's PRIVILEGES AND IMMUNITIES clause, Miller explained for a majority of five, protected only the handful of rights that necessarily grew out of "the relationship between the citizen and the national government." The really fundamental privileges and immunities of CITIZENSHIP, including the rights to protection by the government, to own property, and to contract, still remained what they had been since 1789—rights of state citizenship. To bring all CIVIL RIGHTS under the umbrella of national citizenship, Miller concluded, would be "so great a departure from the structure and spirit of our institutions" and would so "fetter and degrade the State governments by subjecting them to the control of Congress" that it should not be permitted "in the absence of language which expresses such purpose too clearly to admit of doubt."

Over the succeeding seventeen years, Miller's voting record in civil rights cases remained consistent with the views he expounded in 1873. He joined the majority in UNITED STATES V. CRUIKSHANK (1876) and the CIVIL RIGHTS CASES (1883), both of which severely reduced the range of "appropriate legislation" Congress was authorized to enact; he voted to invalidate the Ku Klux Klan Act altogether in UNITED STATES V. HARRIS (1883). In EX PARTE YARBROUGH (1884), an important Enforcement Act case, Miller consolidated his formal approach to protecting civil rights in a federal system. Speaking for a unanimous Court, he sustained federal jurisdiction over persons who violently interfered with the exercise of VOTING RIGHTS in a federal election. Congress's authority to reach private action in *Yarbrough,* he explained, flowed not from the FIFTEENTH AMENDMENT but from both its power to regulate the time, place, and manner of federal elections and its duty "to provide, in an election held under its authority, for security of life and limbs to the voter." By emphasizing the national ramifications of private action in *Yarbrough,* Miller managed to distinguish *Cruikshank* in much the same way that he had distinguished between rights of national citizenship and rights of state citizenship in the *Slaughterhouse Cases.* Both formulations were designed to set principled limits to the exercise of Congress's affirmative powers to protect civil rights.

The impulse to preserve "the main features" of the federal system also shaped Miller's work in cases involving governmental interventions in economic life. He was certainly not immune to the laissez-faire ethos of the late nineteenth century, and his opinion for the Court in LOAN ASSOCIATION V. TOPEKA (1875) has long been regarded as one of the most significant expressions of natural law constitutionalism in American history and as an important building block in the growth of SUBSTANTIVE DUE PROCESS. There he held that a contract for $100,000 in municipal bonds, issued to lure a manufacturing firm to Topeka, was unenforceable. The people's tax dollars, he proclaimed, could not "be used for purposes of private interest instead of public use." Yet Miller resisted the urge, spearheaded by Justice STEPHEN J. FIELD, to link the "public use" principle with the Fourteenth Amendment and the concept of "general jurisprudence" in order to limit the exercise of all the states' inherent powers—police, taxation, and eminent domain.

The sweeping doctrines advanced by Field and other doctrinaire advocates of laissez-faire conflicted with three working principles of Miller's constitutional understanding, each of which militated against dramatic enlargement of federal judicial power at the expense of the states. The first was his Whiggish predisposition to allow state governments ample room to channel economic activity and develop resources for the general good. A broad construction of the Fourteenth Amendment, he asserted in the *Slaughterhouse Cases,* "would constitute this Court a perpetual censor upon all legislation of the States" and generate state inaction, even in the face of clear public interests, for fear of endless litigation. Miller also believed that it was not the function of federal courts to sit in judgment on state courts expounding state law. He repeatedly invoked this second working principle in the long line of cases that began with GELPCKE V. DUBUQUE (1864). There the Court insisted that municipal bonds issued to subsidize railroad construction were unquestionably for a "public use" despite recent state court decisions to the contrary. The *Gelpcke* majority defended federal judicial intervention on the ground that municipal bonds were a species of commercial paper and therefore the question of bondholder rights "belong[ed] to the domain of general jurisprudence." Miller dissented. In his view, extension of the principle of SWIFT V. TYSON (1842) to the construction of state statute law was an unconscionable act of federal usurpation, and he accurately predicted that it would spawn a generation of conflict between federal courts and recalcitrant state and local officials.

The apparent inconsistency between Miller's opinion in *Loan Association v. Topeka* and his stance in the *Slaughterhouse Cases* and in the *Gelpcke* line of municipal-bond cases is readily explained. All of them did raise similar conceptual issues; each hinged, in part, on the application of the "public use" principle to governmental aid of private enterprise in the form of either monopoly grants or cash subsidies. But for Miller, if not for his colleagues, the controlling factor in *Loan Association v. Topeka* was that it had been tried under the DIVERSITY JURISDICTION of a federal court, and pertinent state law had not yet been framed on the subject. As a result, Miller later explained in *Davidson v. New Orleans* (1878), the Court had been free to invoke "principles of general constitutional law" which the Kansas court was equally free to adopt or reject in subsequent cases involving similar circumstances. The concepts of substantive due process and "general jurisprudence," on the other hand, failed to maintain the ample autonomy for state governments which Miller regarded as an indispensable component of the American polity.

Miller ultimately failed to stave off the luxuriation of substantive due process, just as he had failed to curb the majority's impulse to invoke *Swift* in the municipal-bond cases. "It is in vain to contend with judges who have been at the bar the advocates for forty years of rail road companies, and all the forms of associated capital," he told his brother-in-law late in 1875. "I am losing interest in these matters. I will do my duty but will fight no more." Yet Miller's views did make a difference, particularly in the conference room. What remained influential was Miller's third working principle of constitutional interpretation. He recommended resistance to Field's syllogistic reasoning and quest for immutable principles; he suggested, instead, that once the Court had determined to protect private rights against state interference, it was best to decide cases on the narrowest possible grounds, to employ open-ended doctrinal formulas amenable to subsequent alteration, and to elaborate the meaning of due process through what he called a "gradual process of inclusion and exclusion." Thus Miller described local aid of manufactures as "robbery" in *Loan Association v. Topeka,* but he added that "it may not be easy to draw the line in all cases so as to decide what is a public use in this sense and what is not." He also endorsed the notoriously vague doctrine of "business AFFECTED WITH A PUBLIC INTEREST" in *Munn v. Illinois* (1877). And in CHICAGO, MILWAUKEE & ST. PAUL RY. V. MINNESOTA (1890), when the Court finally invalidated a state law on due process grounds, Miller concurred "with some hesitation" but filed an opinion cautioning his colleagues against the adoption of a rigid formula, such as "fair value," to determine whether rate-making authorities had acted "arbitrarily and without regard to justice and right."

Miller's immediate successors disregarded the advice, but during the 1930s interest revived in his conception of the judicial function, particularly among FELIX FRANKFURTER's circle at the Harvard Law School. Frankfurter, who called Miller "the most powerful member of his Court," insisted in 1938 that judging was not at all like architecture. Rather than framing doctrinal structures with clean lines and the appearance of permanence, Frankfurter explained, "the Justices are cartographers who give temporary location but do not ultimately define the evershifting boundaries between state and national power, between freedom and authority." Miller could not have described his own views with greater clarity or force.

CHARLES W. MCCURDY

Bibliography

FAIRMAN, CHARLES 1938 *Mr. Justice Miller and the Supreme Court, 1862–1890.* Cambridge, Mass.: Harvard University Press.

FRANKFURTER, FELIX (1938)1961 *Mr. Justice Holmes and the Supreme Court.* Cambridge, Mass.: Harvard University Press.

GILLETTE, WILLIAM 1969 Samuel Miller. Pages 1011–1024 in Leon Friedman and Fred Israel, eds., *The Justices of the Supreme Court, 1789–1965.* New York: Chelsea House.

MILLER v. CALIFORNIA
413 U.S. 15 (1973)
PARIS ADULT THEATRE I v. SLATON
413 U.S. 49 (1973)

For the first time since ROTH V. UNITED STATES (1957), a Supreme Court majority agreed on a definition of OBSCENITY. The Court had adopted the practice of summarily reversing obscenity convictions when at least five Justices, even if not agreeing on the appropriate test, found the material protected. The states were without real guidelines; and the requirements of JACOBELLIS V. OHIO (1964) that each

Justice review the material at issue had transformed the Court into an ultimate board of censorship review.

To escape from this "intractable" problem, the *Miller Court* reexamined obscenity standards. Chief Justice WARREN E. BURGER's majority opinion, reaffirming *Roth*, articulated specific safeguards to ensure that state obscenity regulations did not encroach upon protected speech. The Court announced that a work could constitutionally be held to be obscene when an affirmative answer was appropriate for each of three questions:

(a) whether "the average person applying contemporary community standards" would find that the work, taken as a whole, appeals to the prurient interest . . .;
(b) whether the work depicts or describes, in a patently offensive way, sexual conduct specifically defined by the applicable state law; and
(c) whether the work, taken as a whole, lacks serious literary, artistic, political or scientific value.

Three aspects of the *Miller* formula are noteworthy. First, the work need not be measured against a single national standard, but may be judged by state community standards. Second, state obscenity regulations must be confined to works that depict or describe sexual conduct. Moreover, the states must specifically define the nature of that sexual conduct to provide due NOTICE to potential offenders. Third, the Court rejected the "utterly without redeeming social value" standard of MEMOIRS V. MASSACHUSETTS (1966). To merit FIRST AMENDMENT protection, the work, viewed as a whole, must have serious social value. A token political or social comment will not redeem an otherwise obscene work; nor will a brief erotic passage condemn a serious work.

In a COMPANION CASE, *Paris Adult Theater I*, the Court held that regulations concerning the public exhibition of obscenity, even in "adult" theaters excluding minors, were permissible if the *Miller* standards were met. The prohibition on privacy grounds against prosecuting possession of obscene material in one's home, recognized in STANLEY V. GEORGIA (1969), does not limit the state's power to regulate commerce in obscenity, even among consenting adults.

Justice WILLIAM J. BRENNAN, joined by Justices POTTER J. STEWART and THURGOOD MARSHALL, dissented in both cases. Abandoning the views he expressed in *Roth* and *Memoirs*, Brennan concluded that the impossibility of definition rendered the outright suppression of obscenity irreconcilable with the First Amendment and the FOURTEENTH AMENDMENT. The Court's inability to distinguish protected speech from unprotected speech created intolerable fair notice problems and chilled protected speech. Furthermore, "institutional stress" had resulted from the necessary case-by-case Supreme Court review. Instead of attempting to define obscenity, Brennan would balance the state regulatory interest against the law's potential danger to free expression. He recognized the protection of juveniles or unconsenting adults as a state interest justifying the suppression of obscenity. Justice WILLIAM O. DOUGLAS, separately dissenting, also denounced the vague guidelines that sent persons to jail for violating standards they could not understand, construe, or apply.

The Court's attempt to articulate specific obscenity standards was successful to the extent it reduced the number of cases on the Supreme Court docket. Nevertheless, as Justice Brennan noted, and the history of obscenity decisions confirms, any obscenity definition is inherently vague. The Court thus remains the ultimate board of censorship review.

KIM MCLANE WARDLAW

Bibliography

LOCKHARD, WILLIAM B. 1975 Escape from the Chill of Uncertainty: Explicit Sex and the First Amendment. *Georgia Law Review* 9:533–587.

MILLETT v. PEOPLE OF ILLINOIS
117 Illinois 294 (1886)

This was the first case in which a court held a regulatory statute unconstitutional on the ground that it violated the doctrine of FREEDOM OF CONTRACT. Illinois required coalmine owners to install scales for the weighing of coal in order to determine the wages of miners. Millett, an owner, contracted with his miners, in violation of the statute, to pay by the boxload rather than by weight. The state supreme court, overturning his conviction, unanimously declared that the statute deprived him of DUE PROCESS substantively construed. Miners, the court said, could contract as they pleased in regard to the value of their labor, and owners had the same freedom of contract. The court summarily dismissed the contention that the regulation was a valid exercise of the POLICE POWER on the ground that the legislature had not protected the miners' safety or the property of others. A few months later the Pennsylvania high court, in *Godcharles v. Wigeman* (1886), held unconstitutional a state act that prohibited owners of mines or factories from paying workers in kind rather than in money wages. Such cases were forerunners of LOCHNER v. NEW YORK (1905) and its progeny.

LEONARD W. LEVY

MILLIGAN, EX PARTE
4 Wallace 2 (1866)

In 1861, Chief Justice ROGER B. TANEY contrived a possibility of executive–judicial, civil–military clashes (*Ex parte Merryman*); in 1863 the Supreme Court averted similar confrontations (EX PARTE VALLANDIGHAM; PRIZE CASES). But in 1866–1867, the CHASE COURT, in the TEST OATH and *Ex parte Milligan* decisions, overcame its restraint.

In 1864, an Army court sentenced Lambden (spelling various) Milligan, a militantly antiwar, Negrophobe Indianan, to death for overtly disloyal activities. President ANDREW JOHNSON commuted the sentence to life imprisonment. Milligan's lawyer, employing the 1863 HABEAS CORPUS ACT, in 1865 appealed to the federal circuit court in Indiana for release. The judges, including Justice DAVID DAVIS, divided on whether a civil court had JURISDICTION over a military tribunal and on the legitimacy of military trials of civilians. This division let the petition go to the Supreme Court. There, in 1866, Attorney General HENRY STANBERY denied that any civil court had jurisdiction; special counsel BENJAMIN F. BUTLER insisted on the nation's right to use military justice in critical areas.

Milligan's lawyers included JAMES A. GARFIELD, JEREMIAH BLACK, and DAVID DUDLEY FIELD. Milligan, they argued, if indictable, was triable in civil courts for TREASON. Alternatively, they insisted that the Army court had failed to obey the 1863 Habeas Corpus Act's requirement to report on civilian prisoners. Further, they asserted that the Constitution's barriers against the use of military power in a state not in rebellion were fixed and unmodifiable, though Congress, they admitted, had authority to use military justice in the South.

All the Justices concurred about the military court's dereliction in not reporting Milligan's arrest. For the Court's bare majority, Justice Davis held that neither President nor Congress could establish military courts to try civilians in noninvaded areas, and, implicitly, that the final decision as to what areas were critical was the Court's. Martial law must never exist where civil courts operated, he stressed, although both had co-existed since the war started. SALMON P. CHASE, speaking also for Justices SAMUEL MILLER, NOAH SWAYNE, and JAMES WAYNE, disagreed. Congress could extend military authority in Indiana under the WAR POWERS without lessening BILL OF RIGHTS protections, Chase asserted. The option was Congress's, not the Court's.

The majority view in *Milligan* was at once seized upon by supporters of President Johnson, the white South, and the Democratic party, though even Justice Davis stressed that he referred not at all to the South. Until military reconstruction clarified matters, the duties of the Army, acting under President Johnson's orders and the FREEDMEN'S BUREAU statute, were complicated greatly by misuses of the *Milligan* decision in the southern state courts, complications increased by the Test Oath decisions. Taken together, the *Milligan* and the Test Oath decisions greatly limited the capacity of both the nation and the states to provide more decent, color-blind justice in either civil or military courts (including those of the Freedmen's Bureau), and to exclude from leadership in politics and the professions persons who had sparked SECESSION and war.

In subsequent decades, legal writers THOMAS COOLEY and ZECHARIAH CHAFEE reconstructed *Milligan* into a basic defense of individual liberty and of civilian primacy over the military. Both men were flaying dragons perceived by Victorian Social Darwinists and by critics of World War I witch-hunts. Milligan was never a merely theoretical threat. Neither the civil police and courts of Indiana nor the federal government, except for the Army, evidenced capacity to deal with him. In light of existing alternatives, the Army's decision to try Milligan (not its failure to report its decision and verdict) is defensible.

Republican criticism of the *Milligan* decision never threatened the Court. Instead, from 1863 through 1875, the Congress increased the Court's habeas corpus jurisdiction as well as that in admiralty, bankruptcy, and claims. The *Milligan* decision, paradoxically, became a major step in the Court's successful effort to regain the prestige that it had squandered in DRED SCOTT v. SANDFORD (1857), and that Taney had risked dissipating altogether in *Merryman.*

HAROLD M. HYMAN

Bibliography

GAMBIONE, JOSEPH G. 1970 *Ex Parte Milligan:* The Restoration of Judicial Prestige? *Civil War History* 16:246–259.

KUTLER, STANLEY I. 1968 *Judicial Power and Reconstruction Politics.* Chaps. 6–8. Chicago: University of Chicago Press.

MILLIKEN v. BRADLEY
418 U.S. 717 (1974)
433 U.S. 267 (1977)

The DESEGREGATION of public schools in many large cities poses a problem: the cities are running out of white pupils, as white families move to the suburbs. In the early 1970s, some federal district judges began to insist on desegregation plans embracing not only city districts but also surrounding suburban districts. In the first such case to reach the Supreme Court, the Justices divided 4–4, thus affirming without opinion the DECISION of the court of appeals, which had reversed the district court's order for metropolitan relief. The case had come from Richmond, Virginia; Justice LEWIS F. POWELL, the former president of the Richmond school board, had disqualified himself.

Milliken, the Detroit school desegregation case, came to the Court the next year. Justice Powell participated, and a 5–4 Court held that interdistrict remedies were inappropriate absent some showing of a constitutional violation by the suburban district as well as the city district. Chief Justice WARREN E. BURGER wrote for the majority, joined by the other three appointees of President RICHARD M. NIXON and by Justice POTTER STEWART. Justices THURGOOD MARSHALL, BYRON R. WHITE, and WILLIAM O. DOUGLAS all wrote dissenting opinions, and Justice WILLIAM J. BRENNAN also dissented.

This decision was the first major setback for school desegregation plaintiffs, but it did not entirely foreclose metropolitan relief. Justice Stewart, who joined the majority opinion, concurred separately as well, saying he would be prepared to accept metropolitan relief not only where a suburban district had committed a constitutional violation, but also where state officials had engaged in racially discriminatory conduct such as racial gerrymandering of district lines or discriminatory application of housing or ZONING laws.

When the Detroit case returned to the Court three years later, it added a weapon to the arsenal of desegregation remedies. As part of a desegregation decree, the district court ordered the establishment of remedial education programs; the Supreme Court unanimously affirmed, with the Chief Justice again writing for the Court. The remedy must not exceed the constitutional violation, he wrote, but here, unlike the situation in *Milliken I,* the remedy was "tailored to cure the condition that offend[ed] the Constitution."

KENNETH L. KARST

MINERSVILLE SCHOOL DISTRICT v. GOBITIS

See: Flag Salute Cases

MINIMUM WAGES

See: Maximum Hours and Minimum Wages Legislation

MINISTERIAL ACT

A ministerial act is one an official performs as a matter of legal duty, without any personal discretion and without judging the merits. For example, in MARBURY V. MADISON (1803), Chief Justice JOHN MARSHALL described delivery of an appointee's commission as a ministerial act of the secretary of state.

DENNIS J. MAHONEY

MINNESOTA v. BARBER
136 U.S. 313 (1890)

The Supreme Court unanimously held unconstitutional as a violation of the COMMERCE CLAUSE a Minnesota statute that prohibited the sale for human consumption of meat slaughtered in another state and not inspected in Minnesota. The statute, the Court declared, forced citizens to buy only Minnesota meat, denying them the benefits of competition in INTERSTATE COMMERCE.

LEONARD W. LEVY

MINNESOTA RATE CASES
230 U.S. 352 (1913)

In these cases a unanimous Supreme Court reaffirmed state power to regulate INTRASTATE COMMERCE even if it should indirectly affect INTERSTATE COMMERCE. Justice CHARLES EVANS HUGHES stressed the supremacy of federal authority but, reaching back to COOLEY V. BOARD OF WARDENS OF PHILADELPHIA (1852), held that states could regulate interstate commerce when Congress had not yet chosen to act.

The cases before the Court represented extensive litigation throughout the country. The Railroad & Warehouse Commission of Minnesota and the state legislature had issued orders fixing maximum rail rates within the state. Although the rates they set were purely intrastate, both sides agreed that interstate rates would be affected. The cases arose as STOCKHOLDERS' SUITS to prevent the application of the prescribed rates to interstate operators. (See EX PARTE YOUNG, 1908.) On the principal question whether the orders fixed rates that interfered with interstate commerce, Hughes agreed that if the rates imposed a direct burden on commerce, they must fall. He then began a lengthy exposition of the nature of commercial regulation in the federal system, concluding that "it is competent for a state to govern its internal commerce . . . although interstate commerce may incidentally or indirectly be involved." Unless and until Congress acted, state action might well be legal even if touching interstate commerce. Only Congress could judge the necessity for action and, having decided to, it could intervene "at its discretion for the complete and effective government" of even local conduct affecting interstate commerce. The Minnesota actions were, therefore, within the state's power but would be superseded if Congress acted. The Court thus broadly upheld state ratemaking authority; it also implicitly affirmed federal power over intrastate railroad activity affecting interstate commerce, a significant step it would take explicitly the following year in HOUSTON, EAST & WEST TEXAS RAILWAY COMPANY v. UNITED STATES (1914).

DAVID GORDON

MINOR v. HAPPERSETT
21 Wallace 162 (1875)

MORRISON R. WAITE delivered the unanimous opinion of the Supreme Court holding that a woman, though a citizen of the United States and of the state in which she resides, had no right to vote as a privilege of national CITIZENSHIP protected by the PRIVILEGES AND IMMUNITIES clause of the FOURTEENTH AMENDMENT. The laws of her state allowed only men to vote, and the amendment did not change that by making any new voters.

LEONARD W. LEVY

MINTON, SHERMAN
(1890–1965)

Born in Indiana in 1890, Sherman Minton attended Indiana University and Yale Law School. After military service during World War I, several years in private practice, and brief service as attorney for an Indiana state agency, Minton was elected to the United States Senate in 1934. A fervent advocate of President FRANKLIN D. ROOSEVELT's "New Deal," Minton supported measures expanding the federal government's role in ECONOMIC REGULATION powers despite his concern that the Supreme Court might declare such measures unconstitutional. As the Court repeatedly struck down New Deal legislation, Minton proposed that the votes of at least seven Justices be necessary to invalidate an act of Congress; in 1937, Minton worked vigorously for the enactment of Roosevelt's Court reorganization plan. After Minton was defeated for reelection in 1940, he served briefly as one of Roosevelt's special assistants. In the spring of 1941 Roosevelt appointed Minton to the Seventh Circuit Court of Appeals. In 1949 President HARRY S. TRUMAN appointed Minton to the Supreme Court to fill the vacancy created by the death of Justice WILEY B. RUTLEDGE; this appointment was as much a product of Truman's close friendship with Minton as of Truman's desire to appoint Justices with prior judicial experience. Ill health forced Minton's retirement in 1956.

Minton believed that the Supreme Court could not impose libertarian standards upon a government and a people that did not favor them. Minton's commitment to judicial restraint and his resistance to what he perceived as JUDICIAL POLICYMAKING followed directly from his frustration as a senator with the Court's opposition to New Deal legislation and his participation in efforts to curb the Court's powers.

Minton disappointed liberals who had hoped that he would work as vigorously for judicial protection of individual liberties as for the legitimation of governmental economic regulation. He consistently voted to uphold statutes and other governmental programs intended to protect the national security, rejecting challenges asserting violation of individual liberties. In CRIMINAL PROCEDURE cases, Minton tended to uphold convictions. For example, in UNITED STATES v. RABINOWITZ (1950) Minton held for the Court that the FOURTH AMENDMENT permits WARRANTLESS SEARCHES and seizures, so long as they are reasonable. Where litigants sought review of state criminal decisions, Minton was reluctant to disturb state procedures or court decisions absent a showing of significant unfairness affecting the verdict. Minton was ready to invalidate STATE ACTION discriminating against minorities, but he was disinclined to find state action. He emphasized the literal meaning of congressional statutes, rarely resorting to external aids or evidence of legislative intent; in the absence of express statutory language, federal regulation did not preempt concurrent state regulation.

Minton stressed the importance of the Court's collegial atmosphere. He disliked personal disputes among the Justices and did his best to reduce their intensity or to dissipate them altogether. Minton viewed the task of writing opinions for the Court as the preparation of functional instruments of collective policy. He rarely wrote concurrences or dissents, for he believed that separate opinions tended to vitiate the authority of majority opinions and to sow discord among the Justices. After his retirement in 1956, Minton minimized the significance of his tenure on the Court; he believed that his most important judicial act was his vote in BROWN V. BOARD OF EDUCATION (1954) to strike down SEGREGATION of public schools.

RICHARD B. BERNSTEIN

Bibliography

WALLACE, HARRY L. 1959–1960 Mr. Justice Minton: Hoosier Justice on the Supreme Court. *Indiana Law Journal* 34:145–205, 383–424.

MIRANDA v. ARIZONA 384 U.S. 436 (1966)

Miranda is the best known as well as the most controversial and maligned self-incrimination decision in the history of the Supreme Court. Some of the harshest criticism came from the dissenters in that case. Justice BYRON R. WHITE, for example, declared that the rule of the case, which required elaborate warnings and offer of counsel before the RIGHT AGAINST SELF-INCRIMINATION could be effectively waived, would return killers, rapists, and other criminals to the streets and have a corrosive effect on the prevention of crime. The facts of *Miranda,* one of four cases decided together, explain the alarm of the four dissenters and of the many critics of the WARREN COURT. The majority of five, led by Chief Justice EARL WARREN, reversed the kidnap-and-rape conviction of Ernesto Miranda, who had been picked out of a LINEUP by his victim, had been interrogated without mistreatment for a couple of hours, and had signed a confession that purported to have been voluntarily made with full knowledge of his rights, although no one had advised him that he did not need to answer incriminating questions or that he could have counsel present. The Court reversed because his confession had been procured in violation of his rights, yet had been admitted in EVIDENCE. Warren conceded that the Court could not know what had happened in the interrogation room and "might not find the . . . statements to have been involuntary in traditional terms." Justice JOHN MARSHALL HARLAN, dissenting, professed to be "astonished" at the decision. Yet the Court did little more than require that the states follow what was already substantially FBI procedure with respect to the rights of a suspect during a custodial interrogation.

The doctrinal significance of the case is that the Fifth Amendment's self-incrimination clause became the basis for evaluating the admissibility of confessions. The Court thus abandoned the traditional DUE PROCESS analysis that it had used in state cases since BROWN V. MISSISSIPPI (1936) to determine whether a confession was voluntary under all the circumstances. (See POLICE INTERROGATIONS AND CONFESSIONS.) Moreover, the Court shifted to the Fifth Amendment from the Sixth Amendment analysis of ESCOBEDO V. ILLINOIS (1964), when discussing the RIGHT TO COUNSEL as a means of protecting against involuntary confessions. *Miranda* stands for the proposition that the Fifth Amendment vests a right in the individual to remain silent unless he chooses to speak in the "unfettered exercise of his own will." The opinion of the Court lays down a code of procedures that must be respected by law enforcement officers to secure that right to silence whenever they take a person into custody or deprive him of his freedom in any significant way.

In each of the four *Miranda* cases, the suspect was not effectively notified of his constitutional rights and was questioned incommunicado in a "police-dominated" atmosphere; each suspect confessed, and his confession was introduced in evidence against him at his trial. The Court majority demonstrated a deep distrust for police procedures employed in stationhouse interrogation, aimed at producing confessions. The *Miranda* cases showed, according to Warren, a secret "interrogation environment," created to subject the suspect to the will of his examiners. Intimidation, even if only psychological, could undermine the will and dignity of the suspect, compelling him to incriminate himself. Therefore, the inherently compulsive character of in-custody interrogation had to be offset by procedural safeguards to insure obedience to the right of silence. Until legislatures produced other procedures at least as effective, the Court would require that at the outset of interrogation a person be clearly informed that he has the right to remain silent, that any statement he makes may be used as evidence against him, that he has the right to the presence of an attorney, and that if he cannot afford an attorney, one will be appointed to represent him.

These rules respecting mandatory warnings, Warren declared, are "an absolute prerequisite to interrogation." The presence of a lawyer, he reasoned, would reduce coercion, effectually preserve the right of silence for one unwilling to incriminate himself, and produce an accurate statement if the suspect chooses to speak. Should he indicate at any time before or during interrogation that he wishes to remain silent or have an attorney present, the interrogation must cease. Government assumes a heavy burden, Warren added, to demonstrate in court that a defendant knowingly and intelligently waived his right to silence or to a lawyer. "The warnings required and the waiver necessary in accordance with our opinion today are prerequisites," he emphasized, "to the admissibility of any statement made by a defendant."

Warren insisted that the new rules would not deter effective law enforcement. The experience of the FBI attested to that, and its practices, which accorded with the Court's rules, could be "readily emulated by state and local law enforcement agencies." The Constitution, Warren admitted, "does not require any specific code of procedures" for safeguarding the Fifth Amendment right; the Court would accept any equivalent set of safeguards.

Justice TOM C. CLARK, dissenting, observed that the FBI had not been warning suspects that counsel may be present during custodial interrogation, though FBI practice immediately altered to conform to Warren's opinion. Clark, like Harlan, whose dissent was joined by Justices POTTER STEWART and Byron White, would have preferred "the more pliable dictates" of the conventional due process analysis that took all the circumstances of a case into account. Harlan also believed that the right against self-incrimination should not be extended to the police station and should not be the basis for determining whether a confession is involuntary. White wrote a separate dissent, which Harlan and Stewart joined, flaying the majority for an opinion that had no historical, precedential, or textual basis. White also heatedly condemned the majority for weakening law enforcement and for prescribing rules that were rigid, but still left many questions unanswered. (See MIRANDA RULES.)

LEONARD W. LEVY

Bibliography

KAMISAR, YALE 1980 *Police Interrogations and Confessions.* Pages 41–76. Ann Arbor: University of Michigan Press.

WHITEBREAD, CHARLES H. 1980 *Criminal Procedure.* Pages 292–310. Mineola, N.Y.: Foundation Press.

MIRANDA RULES

In MIRANDA V. ARIZONA (1966) the Supreme Court held that a person subject to custodial POLICE INTERROGATION must be warned that any statement he makes can be used against him, that he has a right to remain silent, and that he has a right to the presence of an attorney and that one will be appointed for him if he is indigent. A defendant may waive these rights. A WAIVER must be voluntary and intelligent. In the absence of a fully effective alternative, these warnings must be given and a valid waiver taken as the constitutional prerequisite to the admissibility of any product of custodial police interrogation.

The *Miranda* opinion left unresolved numerous issues. For example: When is a person in custody? What constitutes interrogation? What are the standards for measuring the validity of a purported waiver of the *Miranda* rights? May voluntary statements that are inadmissible for failure to comply with *Miranda* be introduced to impeach the credibility of a defendant's trial testimony? How is the burden of proving VOLUNTARINESS and compliance with the *Miranda* requirements allocated?

Post-*Miranda* cases have lessened considerably the constraints the decision had imposed upon law enforcement officials. For example, the police are required to give a suspect the *Miranda* warnings only if the suspect is in custody at the time of interrogation. In OROZCO V. TEXAS (1969) the Court held that a person is in custody any time that he is not free to leave whether in his own home, a hospital, a police car, or the stationhouse. ESTELLE V. SMITH (1981) held that when an indicted defendant, who has not put his mental state in issue, is compelled to undergo a court-ordered psychiatric examination, he is in custody and is entitled to the *Miranda* warnings prior to the evaluation by a mental health professional. However, most courts have held that a suspect is not in custody when in an open, natural environment. Examples include STOP AND FRISK situations, traffic arrests, accident investigations, or searches at international borders.

The second prerequisite to requiring the *Miranda* warnings is that the suspect be the subject of interrogation. The *Miranda* opinion defined interrogation as "questioning initiated by law enforcement officers." In RHODE ISLAND V. INNES (1980), the Court elaborated, stating that "interrogation" meant "express questioning or its functional equivalent" including "any words or actions on the part of the police . . . reasonably likely to elicit an incriminating response from the subject." By contrast, a statement freely and voluntarily made without any interrogation is admissible as a "threshold confession" or "spontaneous statement." If, for example, a person walks into a police station and states that he has killed someone, the police are not required to stop the person wishing to speak and give that person the warnings.

If both custody and interrogation are present, the police must give the warnings or take a valid waiver before proceeding. The police may not presume that a suspect knows of the *Miranda* rights. The form of the warnings may vary, however, so long as the words used give a clear, understandable warning of all the rights, taking into account the circumstances and the characteristics of the suspect.

In OREGON V. ELSTAD (1985) the Supreme Court held that an invalid confession obtained without the suspect being informed of his *Miranda* rights would not invalidate a later confession made after the suspect was informed of his rights, so long as the confession was obtained without coercion. However, in NEW YORK V. QUARLES (1984) the Court established a "public safety" exception, stating that if reasonable concern for public safety is present, a police officer need not recite the *Miranda* warnings before questioning a suspect in custody.

The accused, after receiving the warnings, may voluntarily waive any of his *Miranda* rights. The government must demonstrate voluntariness under all the circumstances. A signed waiver form is strong, but not conclusive, evidence of voluntariness. An effective waiver need not be written, however, and it may be implied from the accused's conduct.

Once the suspect terminates the interrogation or requests counsel, he may not be reinterviewed without being provided access to the requested attorney even if the suspect is given a second set of *Miranda* warnings. In EDWARDS V. ARIZONA (1981) the Court held that once an accused requests counsel, questioning must cease until counsel is present or until the accused "initiates further communication, exchanges or conversation with the police." In *Smith v. Illinois* (1984), the Court followed this precedent by holding that, once the accused has requested an attorney, no further questions or responses may be used to cast doubt on the request.

By contrast, in *Fare v. Michael C.* (1979) the Court held that a juvenile's request for a probation officer during questioning does not have the same constitutional effect as a request for a lawyer. The Court based its distinction on the fact that a lawyer's principal responsibility is to defend his client, while a probation officer has a duty to report and prosecute misconduct by a juvenile. In addition, probation officers are not necessarily qualified to provide legal assistance. Consequently, a juvenile's request for his probation officer is not a per se invocation of the *Miranda* RIGHT TO COUNSEL.

The issue of voluntariness arises in nonwaiver contexts as well. The Court has held that voluntary confessions obtained in violation of the *Miranda* rules, though not admissible in the State's case-in-chief as evidence of guilt, may be admitted to impeach a testifying defendant's credibility. In the leading case, HARRIS V. NEW YORK (1971), the defendant denied in court that he had sold heroin to an undercover agent. During cross-examination, Harris was asked whether he had made certain statements following his arrest that were inconsistent with his in-court testimony. Even though the prosecution conceded that the statements were obtained in violation of *Miranda,* the Supreme Court upheld the trial judge's ruling that the statements could be considered by the jury in evaluating the defendant's credibility.

When the defendant's statements are truly involuntary, they may not be admitted into evidence for any purpose. *Mincey v. Arizona* (1978) is illustrative, holding that the defendant's statements were inadmissible because they were obtained while the defendant was hospitalized and barely able to speak.

Whether the issue arises in the waiver or in the impeachment context, the burden of proving voluntariness under all the circumstances rests on the government. *Miranda* described it as a "heavy burden," a term which a number of courts have interpreted as requiring proof beyond a REASONABLE DOUBT. The Supreme Court, however, stopped this trend by holding, in *Lego v. Twomey* (1972), that proof by a preponderance of the evidence will suffice in federal court, though the states may impose a higher burden in state proceedings.

CHARLES H. WHITEBREAD

Bibliography

WHITEBREAD, CHARLES H. 1980 *Criminal Procedure.* Mineola, N.Y.: Foundation Press.

MISCEGENATION

The fear of racial mixture migrated to the New World with the earliest colonists. In 1609, planters headed for Virginia were reminded by a preacher of the injunction that "Abrams posteritie keepe to themselves." Of course, they did no such thing. From the beginning, there was a shortage of women; white men freely interbred with both Indian and black women, even before the great waves of slave importation. During the era of slavery, interracial sex cut across all strata of the white male population, from the poorest indentured servants to the wealthiest planters. THOMAS JEFFERSON was merely the most celebrated of the latter. Mulattoes were, in fact, deliberately bred for the slave market. Miscegenation laws, forbidding an interracial couple to marry or live together, were not designed to prevent interracial sex but to prevent the transmission of wealth and status from white fathers to their interracial offspring. Laws governing ILLEGITIMACY served a similar purpose, particularly in southern states. To this day, a majority of "blacks" in the United States are of interracial descent.

The adoption of the FOURTEENTH AMENDMENT offered an obvious opportunity for the Supreme Court to hold miscegenation laws unconstitutional on EQUAL PROTECTION grounds. When the occasion arose in PACE V. ALABAMA (1883), however, the Court unanimously upheld such a law, saying that it applied equally to punish both white and black partners to an intimate relationship. The constitutional validity of miscegenation laws went largely unquestioned until the great mid-twentieth-century rediscovery of racial equality as the Fourteenth Amendment's central meaning. Following BROWN V. BOARD OF EDUCATION (1954), it was only a matter of time before the miscegenation issue would reach the Supreme Court. As it happened, the period of time was short. In *Naim v. Naim* (1955–1956) the Court fudged, dismissing an appeal in a jurisdictional evasion that Herbert Wechsler properly scored as "wholly without basis in the law." Unquestionably, the Court adopted this avoidance technique because of the political storm that had greeted the *Brown* decision. Playing on the white South's fear of race mixture was a standard scare tactic of politicians favoring SEGREGATION. Recognizing this fear, the NAACP, in planning its assault on segregated higher education, had deliberately chosen as its plaintiff in MCLAURIN V. OKLAHOMA STATE REGENTS (1950) a sixty-eight-year-old graduate student. The *Brown* opinion itself had been carefully limited to the context of education, and the *Naim* evasion was cut from the same political cloth.

For a decade, the Court was spared the inevitable confrontation. In *Mclaughlin v. Florida* (1964), it invalidated a law forbidding unmarried cohabitation by an interracial couple. Assuming for argument the validity of the state's law forbidding interracial marriage, the Court nonetheless held that the cohabitation law denied equal protection. The reasoning of *Pace v. Alabama,* the Court said, had not withstood analysis in more recent decisions. Finally, in LOVING V. VIRGINIA (1967), the Court put an end to the whole ugly pretense about "racial purity," holding invalid a law forbidding interracial marriage. Equal protection and SUBSTANTIVE DUE PROCESS grounds served as alternative basis for the decision. *Loving* thus stands not only for a principle of racial equality but also for a broad "freedom to marry." (See FREEDOM OF INTIMATE ASSOCIATION.) The principle of equality is often liberty's cutting edge.

KENNETH L. KARST

Bibliography

FRAZIER, E. FRANKLIN 1939 (rev. ed. 1966). *The Negro Family in the United States.* Chap. IV. Chicago: University of Chicago Press.

MYRDAL, GUNNAR 1944 *An American Dilemma: The Negro Problem and Modern Democracy.* Chap. 5. New York: Harper & Brothers.

MISDEMEANOR

A misdemeanor is one of a class of offenses considered less heinous, and punished less severely, than FELONIES. Generally, misdemeanors are punishable by fine or by incarceration in facilities other than penitentiaries for terms of up to one year. Federal law and most state statutes classify all crimes other than felonies as misdemeanors. Two standards have traditionally been used to distinguish felonies from misdemeanors: the place of imprisonment (a penitentiary as opposed to a jail); and the length of imprisonment (more than one year for felonies, a lesser term for misdemeanors).

The Supreme Court has held that criminal defendants charged with misdemeanors are entitled to certain guarantees of the BILL OF RIGHTS. In ARGERSINGER V. HAMLIN (1972), an indigent defendant was convicted of carrying a concealed weapon, a misdemeanor offense, and sentenced to ninety days in jail. An attorney was not appointed to represent the defendant even though he did not waive this right. The Supreme Court ruled that the RIGHT TO COUNSEL was applicable to misdemeanors where the defendant received a jail term. In *Scott v. Illinois* (1979), however, the Supreme Court declined to find a right to counsel at trial where loss of liberty is merely a possibility and does not, in fact, occur.

The Supreme Court also held, in BALDWIN V. NEW YORK (1970), that the Sixth Amendment requires that defendants accused of serious crimes be afforded the right to TRIAL BY JURY. This right applies to misdemeanors where imprisonment for more than six months is authorized. (See INFORMATION.)

CHARLES H. WHITEBREAD

Bibliography

LAFAVE, W. and SCOTT, A. 1972 *Criminal Law.* St. Paul, Minn.: West Publishing Co.

MISHKIN v. NEW YORK

See: *Memoirs v. Massachusetts*

MISSISSIPPI v. JOHNSON
4 Wallace (71 U.S.) 475 (1867)
GEORGIA v. STANTON
6 Wallace (73 U.S.) 50 (1868)

In these cases, the Supreme Court refused to enjoin President ANDREW JOHNSON and Secretary of War EDWIN M. STANTON from enforcing the MILITARY RECONSTRUCTION ACTS. The Justices unanimously refused to act in the Mississippi case, holding that legislatively mandated executive duties were not enjoinable. Georgia subsequently argued that the military laws threatened its corporate sovereignty, but Justice SAMUEL NELSON found this a POLITICAL QUESTION unfit for judicial scrutiny. Nelson hinted, however, that the Court might favorably consider an action based on property rights. Shortly afterward, in an unreported case (*Mississippi v. Stanton,* 1868), the Justices evenly divided on that question. Consequently, the judiciary never ruled on the constitutionality of military reconstruction; yet these decisions involved an important recognition of SEPARATION OF POWERS and the limits of JUDICIAL POWER.

STANLEY I. KUTLER

MISSISSIPPI UNIVERSITY FOR WOMEN v. HOGAN
458 U.S. 718 (1982)

Joe Hogan, a male registered nurse, was rejected by a state university's all-female school of nursing. A 5–4 Supreme Court held that Hogan's exclusion violated his right to EQUAL PROTECTION OF THE LAWS. For the majority, Justice SANDRA DAY O'CONNOR rejected the argument that, by excluding males, the university was compensating for discrimination against women. Rather, the all-female policy "tends to perpetuate the stereotyped view of nursing as an exclusively woman's job." The university thus failed the test set by CRAIG V. BOREN (1976) for SEX DISCRIMINATION cases. The dissenters, making a case for diversity of types of higher education, emphasized that Hogan could attend a coeducational state nursing school elsewhere in Mississippi.

KENNETH L. KARST

MISSOURI v. HOLLAND
252 U.S. 416 (1920)

MISSOURI V. HOLLAND confirmed the status of treaties as supreme law. Although becoming "perhaps the most famous and most discussed case in the constitutional law of foreign relations" it arose from a narrower Progressive Era desire to prevent indiscriminate killing of migratory birds, which key states had proved unable or unwilling to end by themselves. Congress first legislated hunting restrictions in March 1913, but lower federal courts invalidated them on TENTH AMENDMENT grounds as exceeding the federal government's commerce power, intruding on STATE POLICE POWERS, and usurping the states' well-established position in American law as trustees for their citizens of wild animals. The federal government feared the outcome of a final test of the 1913 act sufficiently to delay Supreme Court action. Instead, responding to suggestions from Elihu Root and others, the Wilson administration concluded the Migratory Bird Treaty of 1916 with Great Britain (acting on behalf of Canada). This committed both nations to restrict hunting of the birds, and in the United States President WOODROW WILSON signed implementing legislation in July 1918.

Several lower courts, including one that had ruled against the 1913 legislation, quickly upheld the 1918 act. In one of these cases the state of Missouri had sought to enjoin federal game warden Ray P. Holland from enforcing the new law. Appealing to the Supreme Court, Missouri argued that because, in the absence of a treaty, the legislation would be clearly invalid on Tenth Amendment grounds, it must fall even with a treaty base, for otherwise constitutional limitations would become a nullity. The Supreme Court upheld the 1918 legislation in a 7–2 vote (but with no written dissent filed).

Echoing the government's defense of the challenged act, the core of Justice OLIVER WENDELL HOLMES's opinion for the Court was a standard federal supremacy argument. Whether or not the 1913 legislation had been invalid, the 1918 act implemented a treaty; because the Constitution explicitly delegated the TREATY POWER to the federal government and gave status as supreme law to treaties made "under the authority of the United States," Tenth Amendment objections had no force.

Less restrained, even cryptic, was Holmes's language, which provided a basis for years of controversy. After questioning whether the requirement that treaties be made under the authority of the United States meant more than observance of the Constitution's prescribed forms for treaty-making, Holmes defended an organic, expansive conception of the Constitution. Its words had "called into life a being the development of which could not have been foreseen completely by the most gifted of its begetters." The Migratory Bird Case needed consideration "in light of our whole experience." The question finally became whether the treaty was "forbidden by some invisible radiation from the general terms of the 10th Amendment." Holmes thereby camouflaged his admissions that treaties must involve matters of national interest and must not contravene specific constitutional prohibitions.

In the 1920s and early 1930s, when the Court often adhered to the doctrine of DUAL FEDERALISM, MISSOURI V. HOLLAND arguably offered constitutional grounds for otherwise suspect federal legislation if appropriate treaties were concluded. (Proponents of child labor regulation toyed with the approach.) Fears about its potential in this respect lingered into the 1950s, when the case was a frequent target for backers of the BRICKER AMENDMENT. Yet after 1937 the Supreme Court routinely accepted broader interpretations of TAXING AND SPENDING POWERS, the COMMERCE CLAUSE, and the FOURTEENTH AMENDMENT, so in practice the case's importance diminished.

CHARLES A. LOFGREN

Bibliography

HENKIN, LOUIS 1972 *Foreign Affairs and the Constitution.* Mineola, N.Y.: Foundation Press.

LOFGREN, CHARLES A. 1975 *Missouri v. Holland* in Historical Perspective. *Supreme Court Review* 1975:77–122.

MISSOURI COMPROMISE (1820)

The Missouri Compromise provided a simple constitutional and geographical expedient for resolving a crisis of the Union growing out of slavery's expansion into the western TERRITORIES. Because the compromise formed the basis of a balance of the free and slave states in the Union for a generation, its abrogation in the 1850s destabilized the constitutional system and intensified the disruption of the Union.

In 1819, Representative James Tallmadge of New York offered an amendment to the Missouri statehood enabling bill that would prohibit the further introduction of slavery into Missouri and would free all children born to slaves after the state's admission, but hold them in servitude until age 25. Free-state congressmen supported congressional power thus to restrict the admission of Missouri by arguments derived from four constitutional sources: the new states clause of Article IV, section 3, giving Congress discretionary authority to admit new states into the Union; the territories clause of the same article and section, empowering Congress to make "Regulations respecting the Territory" of the nation; the slave trade clause of Article I, section 9, permitting congress to control the "Migration" of persons; and the GUARANTEE CLAUSE of Article IV, section 4, which required all states to have a REPUBLICAN FORM OF GOVERNMENT. Supporters of the Tallmadge amendment, citing the DECLARATION OF INDEPENDENCE, argued that slavery was incompatible with republican government.

Opponents of the Tallmadge amendment rejected all these arguments, insisting particularly that the logical implications of the republicanism argument would subvert slavery in the states where it already existed. The first Missouri crisis was resolved by a package of statutes that admitted Missouri without the Tallmadge restriction, admitted Maine as a free state, and prohibited the introduction of slavery into the remainder of the Louisiana Purchase territory north of Missouri's southern boundary. This compromise was subsequently supplemented by an informal process of admitting paired free and slave states, thus preserving a balance between the sections in the Senate.

On the eve of its statehood Missouri precipitated the second crisis by adopting provisions in its new constitution that would have prohibited the abolition of slavery without the consent of slaveholders and that required the state legislature to prohibit the ingress of free blacks. Constitutional arguments over the second controversy turned on the PRIVILEGES AND IMMUNITIES clause of Article IV, section 2, which introduced the question of the constitutional status of free black people. This issue went unresolved because the compromise that settled the second crisis simply provided that nothing Missouri might do in legislative compliance with the constitutional mandate should be construed to deny any citizen a privilege or immunity to which he was entitled, a toothless provision that Missouri flouted in 1847 by excluding free blacks.

THOMAS JEFFERSON warned at the time that "a geographical line, coinciding with a marked principle, moral and political, once conceived and held up to the angry passions of men, will never be obliterated." His somber prediction was fulfilled in the 1850s. The WILMOT PROVISO of 1846, which would have prohibited the introduction of slavery into territories acquired as a result of the Mexican War, inaugurated a period of controversy that terminated in the destruction of the Union in 1860. Democrats and southern political leaders in 1848 began to insist that the first Missouri restriction was unconstitutional and to demand its repeal. Repeal was accomplished by the KANSAS-NEBRASKA ACT of 1854; and Chief Justice ROGER B. TANEY gratuitously held that the Missouri Compromise had been unconstitutional all along in his opinion in DRED SCOTT V. SANDFORD (1857). Yet during Secession Winter, Senator JOHN J. CRITTENDEN resurrected the Missouri Compromise as the centerpiece of his compromise proposals, which recommended extrapolating the Missouri line all the way to the Pacific. But by 1860 sectional developments had made the constitutional settlement of 1820 obsolete.

WILLIAM M. WIECEK

Bibliography

MOORE, GLOVER 1953 *The Missouri Controversy, 1819–1821.* Lexington: University of Kentucky Press.

MISSOURI ex rel. GAINES v. CANADA
305 U.S. 337 (1938)

This was the first decision establishing minimum content for equality within the SEPARATE BUT EQUAL DOCTRINE. Missouri law excluded blacks from the state university; Gaines, a black applicant, was thus rejected by the university's law school. Missouri's separate university for blacks had no law school, and so the state offered to pay his tuition at a law school in a neighboring state. Represented by NAACP lawyers, Gaines sought a WRIT OF MANDAMUS to compel his admission to the state university law school. The state courts denied relief, and the Supreme Court reversed, 6–2.

Chief Justice CHARLES EVANS HUGHES, for the majority, said, "The admissibility of laws separating the races in the enjoyment of privileges afforded by the State rests wholly upon the equality of the privileges which the laws give to the separated groups within the State." The case was thus a doctrinal milestone on the road to BROWN V. BOARD OF EDUCATION (1954). Henceforth the Court would demand real equality in a segregated system of education. Because the education of blacks in the southern and border states had emphasized separateness and deemphasized equality—even equality of physical facilities and school spending—it would have been enormously expensive for the states to satisfy the test of *Gaines* by providing parallel educational systems. *Brown*'s question—whether segregation itself imposed an unconstitutional inequality—was a natural extension of the inquiry launched in *Gaines.*

KENNETH L. KARST

MISSOURI PACIFIC RAILROAD v. HUMES
115 U.S. 512 (1885)

A CORPORATION, invoking the FOURTEENTH AMENDMENT, employed SUBSTANTIVE DUE PROCESS against a state statute, but the Supreme Court, led by Justice STEPHEN J. FIELD, unanimously construed due process in an exclusively procedural sense. A statute might seriously depreciate the value of property, Field declared, but "if no rule of justice is violated in the provisions for the enforcement of such a statute," it could not be said to deprive a person of property without due process. The case was a replay of *Davidson v. New Orleans* (1878), which Field quoted. In 1886, the Court began to abandon the *Davidson-Humes* view of due process. (See STONE V. FARMERS' LOAN & TRUST CO.)

LEONARD W. LEVY

MITCHUM v. FOSTER
407 U.S. 225 (1972)

The federal anti-INJUNCTION statute prohibits a federal court from granting an injunction to stay state court proceedings "except as expressly authorized by Act of Congress, or where necessary in aid of its JURISDICTION, or to protect or effectuate its judgments." In *Mitchum,* relying on the "basic alteration" in our federal system wrought by the Reconstruction-era legislation, the Supreme Court decided that SECTION 1983, TITLE 42, UNITED STATES CODE (originally part of the Civil Rights Act of 1871), constituted an exception to the prohibition despite the absence of an express reference in section 1983 to the anti-injunction statute. Recent scholarship, which implicitly supports *Mitchum,* suggests that the original 1793 version of the anti-injunction statute sought merely to prohibit individual Supreme Court Justices from enjoining state proceedings and was not intended to be a comprehensive ban on federal injunctions against state proceedings. The Court's prior decision in YOUNGER v. HARRIS (1971) limits *Mitchum*'s practical importance. *Younger,* which relied on nonstatutory grounds, severely restricted federal courts' discretion to enjoin pending state proceedings.

THEODORE EISENBERG

MOBILE v. BOLDEN
446 U.S. 55 (1980)

A fragmented Supreme Court majority upheld, 6–3, Mobile's at-large system for electing city commissioners, although the system diluted the voting strength of black voters by submerging them in a white majority. The plurality found that purposeful RACIAL DISCRIMINATION had not been demonstrated. (See WASHINGTON V. DAVIS, 1976; ROGERS V. LODGE, 1982.) In 1982 Congress amended the VOTING RIGHTS ACT OF 1965 to permit reliance on racially discriminatory "results" to show a violation of the act's prohibitions.

KENNETH L. KARST

MONELL v. DEPARTMENT OF SOCIAL SERVICES
436 U.S. 658 (1978)

In 1961, MONROE V. PAPE had held municipalities effectively immune from suit under SECTION 1983, TITLE 42, UNITED STATES CODE. *Monell* reinterpreted the legislative history relied upon in *Monroe* to conclude that municipalities may be sued under section 1983 but are liable only for acts constituting official policy. Not every violation of federal rights by municipal employees gives rise to an action against the municipality.

THEODORE EISENBERG

MONETARY POWER

The monetary power of Congress flows from one express constitutional grant and a melange of others, cemented by the NECESSARY AND PROPER CLAUSE. The enumerated power deals with coin and has never been significant in American constitutional law. Congress's more important powers over the money supply—to charter banks and endow them with the right to issue circulating notes, to emit BILLS OF CREDIT, and to make government paper a legal tender—are only implied. From the administration of GEORGE WASHINGTON to the age of FRANKLIN D. ROOSEVELT, few questions were debated with more intensity than the nature and scope of Congress's IMPLIED POWERS over the currency. At no point, however, did the Supreme Court offer sustained resistance to the extension of Congress's authority. In MCCULLOCH V. MARYLAND (1819), the lodestar case on the monetary power, the MARSHALL COURT upheld incorporation of a bank as an appropriate means for executing "the great powers, to lay and collect taxes; to borrow money; to regulate commerce; to declare and conduct a war; and to raise and support armies and navies." The HUGHES COURT invoked the same undifferentiated list of enumerated powers, reinforced by the necessary and proper clause, in the GOLD CLAUSE CASES (1935), where the last potential limitation on Congress's monetary power was swept away.

Two factors account for the Court's acquiescence. The ambiguous legacy of the CONSTITUTIONAL CONVENTION OF 1787 was especially important. Monetary questions loomed large in the political history of the Confederation era, and some of the Founders, perhaps a majority, wanted to constitutionalize a settlement. They acted decisively to curtail state power. Article I, section 10, provides that "no state shall . . . coin money; emit bills of credit; [or] make anything but gold and silver coin a tender in payment of debts." But the Founders were more circumspect when dealing with the scope of national power. JAMES MADISON's motion to vest Congress with a general power "to grant charters of incorporation" was not adopted because, as RUFUS KING explained, the bank question might divide the states "into parties" and impede ratification. JAMES WILSON suggested that the power to incorporate a bank was implied anyway; but GEORGE MASON, the only other delegate to speak on the matter, disagreed.

Conflicting conceptions of implied powers also materialized without being resolved in the much longer debate on Congress's authority to augment the money supply with government paper. The original draft of the Constitution, as reported to the convention by the Committee of Detail, empowered Congress "to borrow money and emit bills on the credit of the United States." When this section was reached in debate, GOUVERNEUR MORRIS moved to strike out the emission clause; the motion was ultimately carried by a vote of nine states to two. Yet there was no meeting of minds on the implications of Morris's motion before the roll call. Wilson, Mason, and virtually everyone else who spoke assumed that striking out the emission power was equivalent to prohibiting congressional exercise of such a power. Morris said that "the monied interest will oppose the plan of government if paper emissions be not prohibited." But NATHANIEL GORHAM remarked that he was for "striking out, without inserting any prohibition." And that was precisely what happened. Gorham neither mentioned the concept of implied powers nor flatly stated that eliminating the power to emit was by no means equivalent to prohibiting it. His remarks nonetheless suggest that at least some of the Founders assumed, despite Morris's protestations to the contrary, that to vote for his motion was to leave the paper money question to be settled as problems arose.

The sequence of federal legislation on banking and the currency was the second factor that shaped the growth of Congress's monetary power in constitutional law. Once the Constitution had been ratified, Congress was required to assert implied powers either to incorporate a bank or to issue paper money. Sanctioned exercise of one power could be expected to provide at least a modicum of constitutional authority for assertion of the other. Yet the Founders' distrust of government paper was so intense that it was possible for a skillful statesman to obscure the close constitutional relationship between the powers to incorporate banks and emit paper money by treating the former as a conservative policy alternative to the latter. ALEXANDER HAMILTON was such a statesman.

In his Report on the National Bank (1790) Hamilton stressed the "material differences between a paper currency, issued by the mere authority of Government, and one issued by a Bank, Payable in coin." The proposed national bank, he said, would serve as a financial arm of the government and a ready lender to the Treasury; its capital stock, consisting primarily of public securities, would be monetized in the form of bank notes redeemable in specie, thereby multiplying the nation's active capital and stimulating trade. Paper money, in contrast, was just too "seducing and dangerous an expedient," for "there is almost a moral certainty of its becoming mischievous." Much of the constitutional theory he mustered later to justify Congress's power to incorporate a bank was equally applicable to its power to issue paper money. But it is unlikely that the congressmen who approved the BANK OF THE UNITED STATES ACT or President Washington, who signed the bill despite forceful constitutional arguments against it by THOMAS JEFFERSON and others, would have sanctioned Hamilton's BROAD CONSTRUCTION of the government's implied powers in order to facilitate emissions of paper money. In view of JOHN MARSHALL's language regarding the sanctity of contracts in OGDEN V. SAUNDERS (1827), it is equally significant the *McCulloch* involved national bank notes rather than depreciated government paper.

Between 1812 and 1815 there occurred another series of events with implications almost as great as *McCulloch* for the development of Congress's monetary power. The First Bank's charter expired in 1811; its successor was not created until 1816. When the War of 1812 began, then, the government had to finance its operations without the aid of a national banking system. On four separate occasions Congress followed President Madison's recommendation and authorized the emission of Treasury notes, fundable into government bonds and receivable for all duties and taxes owed to the government. Every piece of paper issued in 1812, 1813, and 1814 had a large denomination, carried a fixed term, and bore interest. But the 1815 issue was of bearer notes without interest, in denominations from three, five, and ten dollars upward, receivable in payments to the United States without time limit. Debate in Congress suggests that the notes were fully expected to circulate as currency. Nobody objected to them on constitutional grounds and all were retired soon after the war. Nevertheless, the 1815 Treasury notes provided what John Jay Knox later called "a fatal precedent."

Knox's was a shrewd observation. The Madison administration's Treasury notes were indistinguishable from the bills of credit which Gouverneur Morris and others thought they had prohibited at the Constitutional Convention. In defense of his motion to strike the emission clause, Morris had emphasized that "a responsible minister" could meet emergencies without resort to bills of credit. The remaining power "to borrow money," he had explained, would enable the Treasury to issue "notes"—a term which he understood to mean interest-bearing, fixed-term paper in contradistinction to "bills" which he defined as interest-free paper issued by the government in payment of its obligations. The Treasury notes emitted by the Madison administration were clearly of the latter variety. Moreover, the receivability of those notes for all public debts undermined Madison's own constitutional understanding of 1787. He had suggested that the Convention ought to retain the emission power while expressly prohibiting the power to make government paper a legal tender.

As he noted in his journal, however, Madison had "acquiesce[d]" in the Convention's decision once he "became satisfied that striking out the words would not disable the Government from the use of public notes as far as they could be safe and proper; and would only cut off the pretext for a paper currency and particularly for making the bills a tender either for public or private debts." At Philadelphia, moreover, only Madison had emphasized the legal tender question. And as the bullionists on the Court learned during the post-Civil War LEGAL TENDER CASES, it was extremely difficult to deny Congress the legal tender power once its power to emit bills of credit had been conceded and *McCulloch* had established its discretion in the choice of appropriate means.

Yet the distrust of money-supply decisions made by legislation retained such great vitality during the nineteenth century that an attempt was made to proscribe irredeemable government paper on constitutional grounds. It came in *Hepburn v. Griswold* (1870). Speaking for a 4–3 majority, Chief Justice SALMON P. CHASE declared that the legal tender legislation he had recommended during his tenure as ABRAHAM LINCOLN's secretary of the treasury was invalid insofar as it impaired the value of preexisting private debts. Chase began by reiterating Marshall's *McCulloch* commentary on implied powers and "the painful duty of this tribunal" with regard to laws inconsistent with the "letter and spirit" of the Constitution. He admitted that Congress had an "undisputed power" to emit bills of credit; in VEAZIE BANK V. FENNO (1869) he had said that Congress might even levy prohibitive taxes on the notes of state-chartered banks in order "to provide a currency for the whole country." But the legal tender power was distinguishable. It was not necessary, though perhaps convenient, for Congress to impart legal tender qualities to its paper in order to guarantee circulation. And legislation that impaired contracts was not only contrary to the "spirit" of the Constitution as Marshall and others had understood it but also deprived creditors of property without DUE PROCESS or JUST COMPENSATION.

The narrow construction of Congress's authority expounded in *Hepburn* did not endure. SAMUEL MILLER, dissenting along with NOAH SWAYNE and DAVID DAVIS, had claimed that the majority's reliance on the "spirit" of the Constitution substituted "an undefined code of ethics for the Constitution." In their view, *McCulloch* had established that "where there is a choice of means, the selection is for Congress, not the Court." WILLIAM STRONG and JOSEPH BRADLEY, whom ULYSSES S. GRANT nominated to the Court on the very day *Hepburn* was decided, agreed with the *Hepburn* dissenters and voted to overrule Chase's previous majority in *Knox v. Lee* (1871). Bradley stated in a concurring opinion that once the power to emit bills of credit had been conceded, "the incidental power of giving such bills the quality of legal tender follows almost as a matter of course." Strong's opinion for the Court responded forcefully to the "TAKING" claims advanced in *Hepburn.* An 1834 act passed pursuant to Congress's power "to coin money and regulate the value thereof," he pointed out, had established a new regulation of the weight and value of gold coins. Creditors had sustained consequential injuries as a result, for antecedent debts had become "solvable with six per cent less gold than was required to pay them before." But it had never been imagined that Congress had taken property without due process of law. Congress's implied monetary powers, Strong concluded, were as plenary as its enumerated monetary power: "Contracts must be understood as made in reference to the possible exercise of the rightful authority of the government, and no obligation of contract can extend to the defeat of legitimate governmental authority."

Two other Chase Court decisions, *Bronson v. Rodes* (1869) and *Trebilock v. Wilson* (1872), reflected the law's continuing favor for freedom in private contract despite Strong's sweeping language regarding the plenary nature of Congress's monetary power. There the Court held that agreements specifically requiring payment in gold and silver coin could not be satisfied by tenders of irredeemable government paper. Coin was still a legal tender under federal law, the Court explained; because the Legal Tender Acts did not expressly prohibit parties from drafting contracts requiring payment in specie, it remained "the appropriate function of courts . . . to enforce contracts according to the lawful intent and understanding of the parties." Creditors found *Bronson* and *Trebilock* particularly reassuring in the Populist era. Although the Civil War greenbacks became redeemable at par in 1879, apprehensions of currency devaluation by "free coinage" of silver prompted virtually all draftsmen of long-term debt obligations to specify repayment in gold coin of a given weight and fineness. But the monetary crisis of 1933 led not only to another, apparently final abandonment of the gold standard and a substantial depreciation of the currency but also to a joint resolution of Congress that proclaimed gold clauses in private contracts to be "against public policy" and void. Eight years later, EDWARD S. CORWIN remarked that "no such drastic legislation from the point of view of property rights had ever before been enacted by the Congress."

The Court nonetheless sustained the resolution by a 5–4 margin in the GOLD CLAUSE CASES (1935). In *Bronson* and *Trebilock*, Chief Justice CHARLES EVANS HUGHES explained for the majority, the Court had mandated the enforcement of contracts containing gold clauses at a time when Congress had not prohibited such agreements. Now Congress had acted; "parties cannot remove theirs transactions from the reach of dominant constitutional power by making contracts about them." JAMES MCREYNOLDS filed a discursive dissent in which he claimed, among other things, that the Constitution "is gone." In one respect his argument had some merit. Many of the Founders, perhaps a majority, had assumed that adoption of Gouverneur Morris's motion to strike the power to emit bills of credit precluded all government paper designed to circulate as money. Yet contracts were enforceable in government paper and only government paper after 1933. From another perspective, however, McReynolds's claim was simply perverse. The constitutional text does not forbid Congress to issue paper money, and American constitutional law not only sets limitations on what government does but also legitimizes government's authority to act affirmatively in the face of changing public interests. It was no accident that when Marshall emphasized the importance of remembering that "it is a *constitution* we are expounding," he did so in the leading case involving Congress's monetary power.

CHARLES W. MCCURDY

Bibliography

CORWIN, EDWARD S. 1941 *Constitutional Revolution, Ltd.* Claremont, Calif.: Claremont Colleges.

DAM, KENNETH W. 1982 The Legal Tender Cases. *Supreme Court Review* 1981:367–412.

HURST, JAMES WILLARD 1973 *A Legal History of Money in the United States, 1774–1970.* Lincoln: University of Nebraska Press.

KNOX, JOHN JAY 1882 *United States Notes: A History of the Various Uses of Paper Money by the Government of the United States.* New York: Scribner's.

MONROE, JAMES
(1758–1831)

James Monroe was the last veteran of the American Revolution to serve as President of the United States. He had abandoned his studies at the College of William and Mary to join the army, and he rose to the rank of lieutenant colonel. He later read law under THOMAS JEFFERSON and, in 1782, was elected to the legislature of his native Virginia. From 1783 to 1786 he represented Virginia in Congress, where one of his chief concerns was the unsuccessful attempt to amend the ARTICLES OF CONFEDERATION to provide for a stronger central government. A committee chaired by Monroe drafted an amendment that would have given Congress the power to regulate commerce, but no action was taken on the amendment.

Notwithstanding his views on the Confederation, Monroe opposed RATIFICATION OF THE CONSTITUTION, primarily because it created too strong a central government and vested too much power in the President. He publicly professed to see in the proposed system a tendency toward monarchy and aristocracy, and he privately complained that the South would be outvoted on sectional issues.

From 1790 to 1794, Monroe represented Virginia in the United States Senate. There he was a leader of the Republican party and an opponent of the programs of ALEXANDER HAMILTON and especially of the BANK OF THE UNITED STATES ACT. He left the Senate in 1794 to become ambassador to France. He served as governor of Virginia (1799–1802), then held diplomatic posts abroad for the Jefferson administration, including an assignment as one of the negotiators of the LOUISIANA PURCHASE TREATY. He was again elected governor in 1811 but resigned to become secretary of state under President JAMES MADISON. During the War of 1812 he also acted as secretary of war.

Monroe's presidency (1817–1825) was notable for the rhetoric of constitutional literalism and STRICT CONSTRUCTION. He opposed congressional schemes for federally funded INTERNAL IMPROVEMENTS (such as highways and canals) on the grounds that there was no constitutional authority for them; but he suggested a constitutional amendment to confer such authority. In 1820, despite reservations about the constitutionality of its conditions on admission of a state, Monroe approved the MISSOURI COMPROMISE limiting expansion of SLAVERY IN THE TERRITORIES. And in 1823, on the advice of Secretary of State JOHN QUINCY ADAMS, he asserted presidential control over FOREIGN AFFAIRS by proclaiming the MONROE DOCTRINE. During his administration, the opportunity for peaceful westward development was assured by the negotiation of treaties fixing the borders of the United States with Canada and with the Spanish and Russian possessions in North America.

The most pressing constitutional question of his time was the place of slavery in the American republic. Himself a slaveholder, Monroe favored gradual, compensated emancipation followed by settlement of ex-slaves in Africa. To that end he was a founding member of the American Colonization Society; and the capital of Liberia, the African state settled through the society's efforts, was named in his honor.

Monroe's last active role in public affairs was as president of the Virginia CONSTITUTIONAL CONVENTION of 1829.

DENNIS J. MAHONEY

Bibliography

AMMON, HARRY 1971 *James Monroe: The Quest for National Identity.* New York: McGraw-Hill.

MONROE *v.* PAPE
365 U.S. 167 (1961)

This case, a fountainhead of modern CIVIL RIGHTS doctrine, arose out of an unconstitutional search conducted by Chicago police officers. The victim sought damages in an action brought under SECTION 1983, TITLE 42, UNITED STATES CODE, which authorizes suits for deprivations, under COLOR OF LAW, of rights, privileges, or immunities secured by the Constitution and laws of the United States. *Monroe* settled that section 1983 protects all FOURTEENTH AMENDMENT rights and not merely those narrowly defined rights that the SLAUGHTERHOUSE CASES (1873) found to be protected by the Fourteenth Amendment's PRIVILEGES AND IMMUNITIES clause. Early litigation under section 1983 had suggested possible links between the scope of the privileges and immunities clause and the rights protected by section 1983. *Monroe* also confirmed earlier holdings in federal civil rights cases that the phrase "under color of" law in section 1983 includes official acts not authorized by state law. *Monroe*'s third holding, that cities could not be made defendants in section 1983 cases, was overruled in MONELL V. DEPARTMENT OF SOCIAL SERVICES (1978).

THEODORE EISENBERG

MONROE DOCTRINE
2 Richardson, *Messages and Papers of the Presidents* 207 (1823)

The United States, the first true revolutionary nation, became, in 1823, the guardian of the emerging revolutionary states of the New World. The American constitutional ideal of republican, LIMITED GOVERNMENT, founded on NATURAL RIGHTS and SOCIAL COMPACT, stood in opposition to the constitutional system of Europe, based on hereditary privilege. The countries of the Western Hemisphere, becoming independent in the early nineteenth century, would, in rejecting the European system, seem naturally to embrace the American ideal.

JOHN QUINCY ADAMS, secretary of state to President JAMES MONROE, perceived the threat to the Americas from the reactionary Concert of Europe and the Holy Alliance. Adams formulated, and Monroe announced, a policy of resistance to any attempt to restore European hegemony in the Americas. Although Adams counseled use of diplomatic channels, Monroe, on the advice of Secretary of War JOHN C. CALHOUN, announced the doctrine in his 1823 State of the Union Message.

The proclamation of the Monroe Doctrine was a significant assertion of executive power in FOREIGN AFFAIRS. Although Monroe's address repeatedly stressed America's neutrality in European wars and in the colonial revolutions against Spain, his declaration that "we should consider any attempt on their part to extend their system to any portion of this hemisphere as dangerous to our peace and safety" was a clear warning that American interests would be vindicated by force, if necessary. The President, therefore, committed the country to potential military action outside its borders and announced the fact to Congress rather than asking for congressional authorization.

The Constitution, of course, makes no provision for so sweeping an assertion of executive authority over foreign affairs or so general a commitment of American power abroad. Yet the Monroe Doctrine swiftly became part of the UNWRITTEN CONSTITUTION, the accretion of customs and precedents that fill the constitutional lacunae.

DENNIS J. MAHONEY

Bibliography

PERKINS, DEXTER 1955 *A History of the Monroe Doctrine.* Boston: Little, Brown.

MONTESQUIEU
(1689–1755)

The political philosophy of Charles de Secondat, Baron de la Brede et de Montesquieu, was an important influence on American constitutional thought. The leading republican theorist of the generation immediately preceding the American Revolution, he was referred to more frequently by the delegates to the CONSTITUTIONAL CONVENTION OF 1787 than any other theoretical writer. JAMES MADISON (in THE

FEDERALIST #43) called him "the oracle . . . who is always consulted and cited." In the debates on the RATIFICATION OF THE CONSTITUTION the authority of Montesquieu was invoked by partisans ranging from LUTHER MARTIN to ALEXANDER HAMILTON.

Montesquieu's most important work was *The Spirit of the Laws* (1748). The book seems obscure and difficult to most readers, at least partly because the author tried to combine a philosophic inquiry, intended for a few readers only, with practical political advice meant for a much wider audience. In Montesquieu's practical teaching, based on observation, philosophic reflection, and first-hand experience, the American founders found the apparent resolution of two key problems of American politics: how to reconcile popular government with a vast extent of territory and how to reconcile energetic government with the security of liberty.

Montesquieu was the first political philosopher to treat FEDERALISM at any length. He believed, with the classical theorists, that republican government was possible only in small societies, for there alone could be found the virtue and public-spiritedness necessary if people are to govern themselves. But small republics are in constant danger from larger, despotic neighbors. The solution was the federal republic: "a convention by which several bodies politic consent to become citizens of a larger state . . . a society of societies who form a new one, which can enlarge itself through new associates who join."

But a large republic, even a federal republic, is liable to destruction through internal strife. Sectional and religious differences divide the people and make republican virtue impossible. For this, too, Montesquieu had an answer: "Commerce cures destructive prejudices; and it is almost a general rule that wherever there is commerce there are gentle ways of life." Commerce tends to make people peaceful and tolerant, and it makes them aware of their interdependence for security and comfort.

Montesquieu's greatest influence on American CONSTITUTIONALISM is seen in the twin doctrines of SEPARATION OF POWERS and CHECKS AND BALANCES. Montesquieu adopted the idea of separation of powers from JOHN LOCKE, but he fundamentally modified it by defining the three branches of government as legislative, executive, and judicial. Although Montesquieu introduced separation of powers in a famous chapter "On the Constitution of England," that chapter actually comprises not a description of the English government but rather a presentation of the conditions necessary for liberty and safety. Checks and balances, according to Montesquieu, are modifications of separation of powers necessary to keep any one branch of government from becoming despotic and to promote harmony of action.

DENNIS J. MAHONEY

Bibliography

ALLEN, WILLIAM BARCLAY 1972 Montesquieu: The Federalist-Anti-Federalist Debate. Unpublished Ph.D. dissertation, Claremont Graduate School.

PANGLE, THOMAS L. 1973 *Montesquieu's Philosophy of Liberalism.* Chicago: University of Chicago Press.

MOODY, WILLIAM H.
(1853–1917)

After studying law in the offices of novelist-lawyer Richard Henry Dana, William Henry Moody of Massachusetts first came to national attention as a special prosecutor in the Fall River ax-murder case of Lizzie Borden (1892). In 1895 he went to Congress where he served as a Republican until President THEODORE ROOSEVELT appointed him secretary of the navy in 1902. When PHILANDER C. KNOX left the administration for the Senate in 1904, Moody replaced him as attorney general. Philosophically comfortable with the President, Moody spent much of his tenure directing the prosecution of the Beef Trust. Although Knox had begun the case, Moody successfully argued SWIFT & COMPANY V. UNITED STATES (1905) before the Supreme Court, helping to lay the basis for the STREAM OF COMMERCE doctrine. As attorney general, Moody directed active participation by the Department of Justice in many facets of national ECONOMIC REGULATION, from antitrust proceedings to railroad regulation under the ELKINS ACT.

Roosevelt rewarded Moody's service and his commitment to a strong national government by appointing him to succeed Justice HENRY B. BROWN on the Supreme Court in 1906. Although Moody's service on the Court formally lasted until 1910, he was rarely present the last two years. Moody took part in relatively few cases during his tenure, but his opinions fulfilled Roosevelt's expectations and reflected Moody's moderate Progressivism. As a Justice, Moody continued his support of regulatory legislation, often voting with the Court to extend or strengthen federal authority. Moody joined the majority in LOEWE V. LAWLOR (1908), holding that the SHERMAN ANTITRUST ACT covered labor boycotts, and he wrote for the dissenters in the first EMPLOYERS' LIABILITY CASES (1908), asserting that Congress had power to regulate employer–employee relations in INTERSTATE COMMERCE issues. Although that dissent typified Moody's willingness to expand the reach of federal powers, he also supported exercises of STATE POLICE POWER when they worked no interference with federal powers. An adherent of judicial self-restraint, Moody opposed judicial legislation and he silently concurred in MULLER V. OREGON (1908), in which the BRANDEIS BRIEF offered convincing EVIDENCE to the Court of the benefits of maximum hours legislation. In TWINING V. NEW JERSEY (1908), perhaps his best-known opinion, Moody, for the Court, declared that the RIGHT AGAINST SELF-INCRIMINATION was not an "essential element" of DUE PROCESS OF LAW incorporated in the FOURTEENTH AMENDMENT and applicable to the states. If the people of the state were dissatisfied with the law, he declared, recourse "is in their own hands."

Stricken with acute rheumatism, Moody retired in 1910 and died, a semi-invalid, seven years later.

DAVID GORDON

MOORE, ALFRED
(1755–1810)

A staunch Federalist in an Anti-Federalist state, Alfred Moore served as North Carolina's attorney general from 1782 to 1791 and was prominent in securing RATIFICATION OF THE CONSTITUTION there. He defended the state Confiscation Act in BAYARD V. SINGLETON (1787), opposing JUDICIAL REVIEW. President JOHN ADAMS appointed him to the Supreme Court in 1799 but he resigned in 1804 because of ill health. During his tenure Moore wrote only one opinion, in *Bas v. Tingy* (1800), a prize case. Moore's unexceptional opinion, together with those of the other Justices, lent support to congressional legislation dealing with the quasi-war with France.

DAVID GORDON

MOORE v. CITY OF EAST CLEVELAND
431 U.S. 494 (1977)

Although it produced no OPINION OF THE COURT, *Moore* is a major modern Supreme Court precedent confirming the Constitution's protection of the family. A 5–4 Court held invalid a city ordinance limiting occupancy of certain residences to single families and defining "family" in a way that excluded a family composed of Inez Moore, her son, and two grandsons who were not brothers but cousins. Justice LEWIS F. POWELL, for a plurality of four Justices, concluded that "such an intrusive regulation of the family" required careful scrutiny of the regulation's justification. The city's asserted justifications—avoiding overcrowding, traffic and parking problems, and burdens on its schools—were served only marginally by the ordinance. The plurality thus concluded that the ordinance denied Mrs. Moore liberty without DUE PROCESS OF LAW.

Justice JOHN PAUL STEVENS, concurring, characterized the ordinance as a TAKING OF PROPERTY without due process or compensation. Chief Justice WARREN E. BURGER, dissenting, would have required Moore to exhaust her state administrative remedies before suing in federal court. Three other Justices dissented on the merits, rejecting both due process and EQUAL PROTECTION attacks on the ordinance and more generally opposing heightened judicial scrutiny of legislation merely on the basis of its effect on a family like the Moores.

The plurality opinion has become a standard citation for the reemergence of SUBSTANTIVE DUE PROCESS, and more specifically for a constitutional right of an extended—but traditional—family to choose its own living arrangements. In a wider perspective the decision can be seen as part of the growth of a FREEDOM OF INTIMATE ASSOCIATION. The decision was not, however, a blow against covert RACIAL DISCRIMINATION. East Cleveland was a predominantly black city, with a black commission and city manager. The ordinance, like ordinances in many white communities, was designed to maintain middle-class nuclear family arrangements. In this perspective, the plurality opinion is seen to collide with *Village of Belle Terre v. Boraas* (1974), which had upheld an ordinance excluding "unrelated" groups from single-family residences. Justice Powell's distinction of *Belle Terre* amounted to this: families are different. But he offered no definition of "family" apart from a generalized bow to "a larger conception of the family," including an extended family of blood relatives, for which he found support in "the accumulated wisdom of civilization." Of such stuff is substantive due process made.

KENNETH L. KARST

Bibliography

BURT, ROBERT A. 1979 The Constitution of the Family. *Supreme Court Review* 1979:329, 388–391.

MOORE v. DEMPSEY
261 U.S. 86 (1923)

Moore was a landmark for two of the twentieth century's most important constitutional developments: the emergence of the DUE PROCESS clause of the FOURTEENTH AMENDMENT as a limitation on state CRIMINAL PROCEDURE, and the assumption by the federal judiciary of a major responsibility for supervising the fairness of state criminal processes, through HABEAS CORPUS proceedings.

For all its importance, the case began as a squalid episode of racist ferocity. Returning from World War I, a black Army veteran sought to organize black tenant farmers of Phillips County, Arkansas, into a farmers' union. In October 1919—a year disfigured by racial violence in both North and South—these farmers held a meeting in a rural church to plan efforts to obtain fair accountings from their white landlords. At this remove in time it requires effort to understand that such a meeting, in such a place, for such a purpose, was seen as revolutionary. A sheriff's deputy fired at the church; blacks who were armed fired back, killing the deputy and wounding his companion. Hundreds of new deputies were sworn; they and hundreds of troops arrested most of the county's black farmers, killing resisters. Responsible estimates of the black dead ranged from twenty-five to 200.

About 120 blacks were indicted for various crimes, including the murder of the deputy. The trial juries, like the grand jury that had issued the INDICTMENTS, were all white. Twelve men were convicted of murder and sentenced to death; dozens of others were sentenced to long prison terms. The twelve sentenced to death filed APPEALS in two groups of six each. One group, after multiple appeals, was released in 1923 by order of the Arkansas Supreme Court, for excessive delay in their retrial. The convictions of the remaining six, however, were affirmed by the state supreme court, and the U.S. Supreme Court denied certiorari. They unsuccessfully sought habeas corpus in the state courts, and again the Supreme Court declined to review the case.

By now the NAACP had mounted a national fund-raising drive to support the six petitioners. Their execution, set for September 1921, was postponed by the filing of a habeas corpus petition in the federal district court. That court dismissed the writ. On direct appeal, the Supreme Court reversed, 7–2, with an opinion by Justice OLIVER WENDELL HOLMES. (The opinion refers, apparently erroneously, only to the five petitioners who were tried together; the petition of the sixth was consolidated for hearing and decision.)

On REMAND to the district court, counsel for the six petitioners struck a deal; the habeas corpus petition would be dismissed and the sentence commuted to twelve years' imprisonment, making the men eligible for immediate parole. In 1925 the governor of Arkansas granted an "indefinite furlough," releasing them along with the others convicted following the Phillips County "insurrection."

The federal habeas corpus petition in *Moore* alleged that counsel appointed to represent the five defendants tried together did not consult with his clients before the trial; requested neither delay nor change of VENUE nor separate trials; challenged not a single juryman; and called no defense witnesses. The trial took forty-five minutes, and the jury "deliberated" less than five minutes. A lynch mob had been dissuaded from carrying out its purpose by a local committee, appointed by the governor to combat the "insurrection," who assured the mob that justice would be done swiftly. Two black witnesses swore they had been whipped and tortured into testifying as the prosecution wished. Holmes summarized the petition: "no juryman could have voted for an acquittal and continued to live in Phillips county, and if any prisoner, by any chance, had been acquitted by a jury, he could not have escaped the mob."

The Supreme Court held that these facts, if proved, justified two conclusions: the state had violated PROCEDURAL DUE PROCESS, and the federal district court should grant the writ of habeas corpus. Today both conclusions seem obvious. In 1923, however, the Supreme Court had not yet begun to impose significant federal constitutional limitations on the fairness of state criminal proceedings. *Moore* lighted the path that would lead, in less than half a century, to an expansion of the liberty protected by the due process clause, applying virtually the entire BILL OF RIGHTS to the states. (See INCORPORATION DOCTRINE.)

Moore's other conclusion, concerning the reach of federal habeas corpus, also broke new ground. In FRANK V. MANGUM (1915), a case involving strikingly similar facts, the Court had rejected a claim to federal habeas corpus relief on the ground that the state courts had provided a full "corrective process" for litigating the accused's federal constitutional claims. Only in the absence of such a corrective process, the Court had held, could a federal habeas corpus court intervene. *Moore* did not explicitly overrule *Frank*, but it did look in a different direction. Justice Holmes, in his characteristically laconic way, said only that if "the whole proceeding is a mask," with all participants in the state trial swept to their conclusion by a mob, and if the state courts fail to correct the wrong, "perfection in the [state's] machinery for correction" could not prevent the federal court from securing the accused's constitutional rights. The right claimed in *Moore,* of course, goes to the essence of due process of law; when the basic fairness of a state criminal trial is challenged, the fact that the state courts have already had a chance to look into the matter seems a weak justification for barring federal habeas corpus.

From *Moore* through FAY V. NOIA (1963), the Supreme Court steadily widened access to federal habeas corpus for persons challenging constitutionality of state convictions. STONE V. POWELL (1976) and WAINWRIGHT V. SYKES (1977) marked the BURGER COURT's reversal of the direction of doctrinal change. Indeed, *Stone* revived the doctrine of *Frank v. Mangum* in cases involving claims based on the FOURTH AMENDMENT's guarantee against UNREASONABLE SEARCHES and seizures. Yet, despite these limitations, *Moore*'s legacy, even in the field of federal habeas corpus, remains vital to a system of national constitutional standards of fairness for persons accused of crime.

KENNETH L. KARST

Bibliography

BATOR, PAUL M. 1963 Finality in Criminal Law and Federal Habeas Corpus for State Prisoners. *Harvard Law Review* 76:441, 483–493.

WATERMAN, J. S. and OVERTON, E. E. 1933 The Aftermath of Moore v. Dempsey. *St. Louis Law Review* (now *Washington University Law Review*) 18:117–126.

MOOSE LODGE #107 v. IRVIS
407 U.S. 163 (1972)

Irvis, a black, was refused service at a Harrisburg, Pennsylvania, branch of the Moose Lodge, a fraternal organization whose fraternity knew bounds. Irvis sued under federal CIVIL RIGHTS laws for an INJUNCTION requiring the Pennsylvania liquor board to revoke the lodge's license so long as it continued to discriminate on the basis of race. The Supreme Court held, 6–3, in an opinion by Justice WILLIAM H. REHNQUIST, that Irvis was not entitled to the relief he sought. The state's licensing was not, of itself, sufficient to satisfy the STATE ACTION limitation of the FOURTEENTH AMENDMENT, and the Constitution offered no protection against RACIAL DISCRIMINATION by a private club.

In the majority's view, nothing in the case approached the "symbiotic relationship" between the state and private racial discrimination shown in BURTON V. WILMINGTON PARKING AUTHORITY (1961). Although Pennsylvania liquor licensees were subjected to a number of state regulations, that supervision did not "encourage" racial discrimination. Furthermore, because many liquor licenses had been issued in the area, the lodge's license fell short of creating a state-supported monopoly. Thus the state had not implicated itself in the lodge's discriminatory policies.

Justices WILLIAM O. DOUGLAS and WILLIAM J. BRENNAN wrote separate DISSENTING OPINIONS, each joined by Justice THURGOOD MARSHALL. The dissenters emphasized the degree of monopoly power of clubs licensed to sell liquor and the state's detailed regulation of licensees.

KENNETH L. KARST

MOOTNESS

Article III's CASE OR CONTROVERSY restriction precludes federal courts from declaring law except in the context of litigation by parties with a personal stake in a live dispute that judicial decision can affect. They may not resolve moot questions—questions whose resolution can no longer affect the litigants' dispute because events after the commencement of litigation have obviated the need for judicial intervention. However live the issues once were, however much the parties (and the public) may desire a declaration of law, and however far the litigation may have progressed when the mooting events occur, Article III requires dismissal of the lawsuit. Common examples include a criminal defendant's death during appeal of a jail sentence, enactment of a new statute superseding one whose enforcement the plaintiff seeks to enjoin, or full satisfaction of a party's litigation demands.

Other cases exhibit less certainty that the substantive issues raised no longer need judicial action to forestall anticipated harm. In these cases, mootness questions are more troublesome. They inevitably introduce discretion to exercise or withhold judgment, discretion potentially influenced by the substantive issues' public importance. Thus, in DEFUNIS V. ODEGAARD (1974) a divided Supreme Court refused to decide the constitutionality of a race-conscious AFFIRMATIVE ACTION program for law school admissions when it appeared fairly certain that the challenger, who had only become a student through lower court victories, would be graduated irrespective of the lawsuit's outcome.

Several DOCTRINES reveal mootness to be a matter of degree. First, when changed circumstances moot the main dispute, but adjudication could produce collateral consequences, the issue is not moot, as when a prisoner's sentence expires before his appeal is decided, but the conviction might subject him to other civil or criminal penalties. Second, cases where defendants voluntarily agree to refrain from challenged behavior are not moot absent proof that they are unlikely to resume the behavior. This rule protects plaintiffs by preventing defendants from manipulating the mootness doctrine to avoid adverse decisions. Third, issues are not moot, despite passage of the immediate problem, when they are "capable of repetition, yet evading review," that is, when they arise sporadically, do not persist long enough to be reviewed before ceasing each time, and are reasonably likely to threaten the challengers again. Suits challenging ELECTION rules, where the immediate election passes before judicial resolution but the rules probably would affect the challengers in subsequent elections, or litigation challenging an abortion restriction that necessarily can apply to a woman only during the term of pregnancy are important instances where an unbending application of the mootness doctrine might deny judicial protection to persons periodically subject to harm. Finally, the Court generously allows a CLASS ACTION to continue, despite developments eliminating any need to protect the party bringing the lawsuit on behalf of the class, if the case is not moot as to other members of the class.

These refinements give federal courts some flexibility either to reach issues of their choice without pressing necessity to protect the parties or to decline to rule by insisting on a higher degree of probability that the threat of harm continues. Like other JUSTICIABILITY doctrines, mootness is not only a constitutional doctrine itself but a somewhat pliable tool of constitutional governance.

JONATHAN D. VARAT

Bibliography

NOTE 1974 The Mootness Doctrine in the Supreme Court. *Harvard Law Review* 88:373.

MOREHEAD v. NEW YORK ex rel. TIPALDO

298 U.S. 587 (1936)

In June 1936 the Supreme Court ended its term with an opinion so startling that even the Republican party repudiated it at the party's national convention. The Republican plank read: "We support the adoption of State laws to abolish sweatshops and child labor and to protect women and children with respect to MAXIMUM HOURS, MINIMUM WAGES and working conditions. We believe that this can be done within the Constitution as it now stands." "This" was precisely what the Court had ruled could not be done. It had defended STATES' RIGHTS as it struck down national legislation, and in NEBBIA V. NEW YORK (1934) it had declared, "So far as the requirement of DUE PROCESS of law is concerned, a state is free to adopt whatever economic policy may reasonably be deemed to promote public welfare. . . ." Just two weeks before the *Tipaldo* decision, the Court had announced, in CARTER V. CARTER COAL COMPANY (1936), as it had in the SCHECHTER POULTRY CORP. V. UNITED STATES (1935), that the regulation of labor was a local matter reserved by the TENTH AMENDMENT to the states, and specifically the Court had referred to the fixing of wages as a state function. Thus the resolution of *Tipaldo* came as a surprise. The Court used the FREEDOM OF CONTRACT doctrine, derived from SUBSTANTIVE DUE PROCESS, to hold that the states lack power to enact minimum wage laws. The precedent that controlled the case, the Court ruled, was ADKINS V. CHILDREN'S HOSPITAL (1923).

Although *Adkins* had seemed to block minimum wage legislation, the Court grounded that decision on the statute's failure to stipulate that prescribed wages should not exceed the value of labor services. New York had carefully framed a minimum wage law for women and children that embodied the Court's *Adkins* standard: the state labor commission was empowered to fix wages "fairly and reasonably commensurate with the value of the service or class of service rendered." By a 5–4 vote the Court held the state act unconstitutional. Justice PIERCE BUTLER, speaking for the majority, declared, "Forcing the payment of wages at a reasonable value does not make applicable the principle and ruling of the Adkins Case." The right to make contracts for wages in return for work "is part of the liberty protected by the due process clause," Butler said, and the state was powerless to interfere with such contracts. Women were entitled to no special consideration. Any measure that deprived employers and women employees the freedom to agree on wages, "leaving employers and men employees free to do so, is necessarily arbitrary."

Chief Justice CHARLES EVANS HUGHES dissented on ground that the statute was a reasonable exercise of the POLICE POWER, and he distinguished this case from *Adkins* because the *Tipaldo* statute laid down an appropriate standard for fixing wages. Justices HARLAN FISKE STONE, LOUIS D. BRANDEIS, and BENJAMIN N. CARDOZO concurred in Hughes's opinion but in a separate dissent by Stone they went much further. Stone accused the majority of having decided on the basis of their "personal economic predilections." He repudiated the freedom of contract DOCTRINE, adding: "There is grim irony in speaking of the freedom of contract of those who, because of their economic necessities, give their services for less than is needful to keep body and soul together." Following the reasoning of Justice OLIVER WENDELL HOLMES, dissenting in *Adkins,* Stone declared that it made no difference what wage standard the statute fixed, because employers were not compelled to hire anyone and could fire employees who did not earn their wages. Stone would have followed the principle of *Nebbia,* which the majority ignored, and he would have overruled *Adkins.* A year later, after President FRANKLIN D. ROOSEVELT proposed packing the Court, it overruled *Adkins* and *Tipaldo* in WEST COAST HOTEL V. PARRISH (1937).

LEONARD W. LEVY

Bibliography

LEONARD, CHARLES A. 1971 *A Search for a Judicial Philosophy: Mr. Justice Roberts and the Constitutional Revolution of 1937.* Pages 88–93. Port Washington, N.Y.: Kennikat Press.

MORGAN v. VIRGINIA
328 U.S. 373 (1946)

This was the first transportation SEGREGATION case brought to the Supreme Court by the NAACP; counsel for the appellant were THURGOOD MARSHALL and WILLIAM H. HASTIE. A Virginia law required racial segregation of passengers on buses. A black woman, riding from Virginia to Maryland, refused to move to a rear seat; she was convicted of a MISDEMEANOR and fined $10. Eighteen states forbade such segregation of passengers, and ten states required it. In 1878 the Supreme Court had invalidated a state law forbidding racial segregation on an interstate carrier as an undue burden on INTERSTATE COMMERCE in HALL V. DECUIR. The NAACP lawyers rested on the *Hall* precedent, and did not argue that the Virginia law violated the FOURTEENTH AMENDMENT.

In an opinion by Justice STANLEY F. REED, the Supreme Court held, 7–1, that the law unduly burdened interstate commerce. Although the usual analysis of a STATE REGULATION OF COMMERCE involves a balance of burdens on commerce against competing state interests such as health or safety, the Court avoided any discussion of a state interest in segregation, saying only that a uniform national rule of passenger seating was required for interstate carriers, if any rule was to be adopted. Justice HAROLD BURTON dissented.

KENNETH L. KARST

MORMON CHURCH v. UNITED STATES

See: *Church of Jesus Christ of Latter-Day Saints v. United States*

MORRILL ACT
12 Stat. 503 (1862)

The Morrill Land Grant College Act provided a basis for state support of public universities and thereby profoundly influenced the course of American higher education.

Under the Land Ordinance of 1785, section 16 of every township was sold and the proceeds used to create a "school fund." In the late 1850s, Vermont Republican Justin Morrill promoted the "Illinois Idea," which would have authorized further land grants to create an "industrial college" in each state. But southern Democrats objected on constitutional grounds, seeing in Morrill's bill a threat to STATES' RIGHTS. In 1862, with these opponents withdrawn from Congress, the Land Grant College Act was passed. It provided that 30,000 acres of public lands be assigned to each state for each of its senators and representatives (or land scrip in an equivalent amount issued to states lacking available public lands). The proceeds of the land sales were to be invested to support a college "to teach such branches of learning as are related to agriculture and the mechanic arts," as well as "military tactics," "in order to promote the liberal and practical education of the industrial classes." The American land-grant colleges are the result of this policy.

WILLIAM M. WIECEK

MORRIS, GOUVERNEUR
(1752–1816)

A lawyer and businessman descended from a wealthy, landed family, Gouverneur Morris was elected to New York's first provincial congress in 1775. The next year, he was a member of the committee that drafted the state's first CONSTITUTION and wrote the message to New York's delegates to the Continental Congress instructing them to vote for the DECLARATION OF INDEPENDENCE. He was himself sent to the Continental Congress in 1778 and was a signer of the ARTICLES OF CONFEDERATION. In 1780 he moved to Philadelphia and served as assistant superintendent of finance under ROBERT MORRIS. In this last capacity, he drafted a report to Congress that contained the first official proposal for a national currency: a decimal coinage based on the Spanish dollar.

Gouverneur Morris was elected to Pennsylvania's delegation to the CONSTITUTIONAL CONVENTION OF 1787. In the debates of the Convention he spoke more frequently than any other delegate. He was an advocate of strong national government, but also of aristocratic privilege. His view of humankind was extraordinarily cynical, and, distrusting any higher motives, he desired to institutionalize private interests as a guarantee of liberty. Although, like Robert Morris, he proposed a senate chosen for life from men of great wealth, the proposal arose partly out of fear that otherwise the rich would corrupt the democratic elements of the regime. He favored a provision to allow Congress to veto state laws and wanted to unite the executive and judiciary in a council of revision to veto national legislation. He favored direct election of the President and congressional representation proportional to taxation; he opposed any constitutional protection of slavery or the slave trade. He was against giving Congress the power to admit new states on terms of equality, and throughout his life he advocated governing the western territories as provinces while retaining power in the East.

Morris was elected to the Committee on Style, along with WILLIAM SAMUEL JOHNSON (its chairman), JAMES MADISON, JAMES WILSON, and RUFUS KING. The committee entrusted Morris with the duty of preparing its report, and so Morris became the principal author of the actual words of the Constitution. He also devised the formula for signing the document—the signatures bearing witness to the unanimous consent of the states—and drafted the letter by which the Convention transmitted its work to Congress.

ALEXANDER HAMILTON asked Morris to collaborate in writing THE FEDERALIST, but Morris declined. He served as a senator from New York from 1800 to 1803, supporting the JUDICIARY ACT OF 1801 and advocating the annexation—by force if necessary—of Louisiana. His public career also included a brief term as minister to France and the founding chairmanship of the Erie Canal Commission.

Morris opposed the War of 1812 as sectional and ill-conceived. The former champion of strong national government became an advocate of STATES' RIGHTS; he even counseled SECESSION of New York and New England from the Union. Morris was disappointed when the HARTFORD CONVENTION resolutions failed to embody that step.

DENNIS J. MAHONEY

Bibliography

MINTZ, MAX M. 1970 *Gouverneur Morris and the American Revolution.* Norman: University of Oklahoma Press.

ROOSEVELT, THEODORE 1888 *Gouverneur Morris.* (American Statesman Series.) Boston: Houghton Mifflin.

MORRIS, ROBERT
(1734–1806)

The English-born merchant and patriot Robert Morris was an early supporter of colonial rights, opposing the Stamp Act and signing the Non-Importation Agreement in 1765. As a member of the Second Continental Congress (1776–1788), Morris voted against the DECLARATION OF INDEPENDENCE because it was premature; but he later signed the Declaration as well as the ARTICLES OF CONFEDERATION. He earned the nickname "Financier of the Revolution" because of his role in raising money to support the Army. In 1781, Congress chose him to be superintendent of finance. While serving in that capacity he organized the Bank of North America, chartered by Congress as a device for borrowing money to pay the costs of the new government. In 1783, he resigned the "insupportable situation" of superintendent of finance, giving as his reason that "to increase our debts while the prospect of paying them diminishes does not consist with my ideas of integrity."

He was a member of the Pennsylvania delegation to the CONSTITUTIONAL CONVENTION OF 1787. There he nominated GEORGE WASHINGTON to be presiding officer, but otherwise, despite his reputation in Pennsylvania politics as a speaker who "bears down all before him," he remained silent throughout the debates. He was a strong nationalist, and desired a Senate comprising men of great and established property appointed for life. Morris signed the Constitution, and, in a letter, recommended it as "the subject of infinite investigation, disputation, and declamation," but still the work not of angels or devils but of "plain, honest men."

Morris and his friends supported the Constitution not least because it promised economic stability, security of contracts, and relief from the harassment of the Bank of North America by the state governments. But Morris's support for ratification seems only to have increased the fervor of some anti-Federalists.

Morris would have been a leading candidate to become the first secretary of the treasury, but he did not want the post. Instead, in 1789, he was elected to the United States Senate, where he became a leader of the Federalist faction and a key ally of ALEXANDER

HAMILTON in the matter of the assumption of state debts.

Morris retired from public life in 1795, and devoted his time to the management of his financial affairs, including his speculation in western lands. That speculation brought him, in 1797, to financial ruin and to three and one-half years in debtors' prison.

DENNIS J. MAHONEY

MORROW, WILLIAM W. (1843–1929)

William W. Morrow served nearly thirty-two years on the federal bench. President BENJAMIN HARRISON in 1892 appointed him to the Northern District of California; President WILLIAM MCKINLEY in 1897 elevated him to the Ninth Circuit Court of Appeals, where he served until retirement in 1923.

His most influential opinion came in *In Re Wong Kim Ark* (1897). Morrow relied on history and precedent in the Ninth Circuit to define a COMMON LAW basis for CITIZENSHIP. He held that under the first section of the FOURTEENTH AMENDMENT a child whose parents were subjects of the emperor of China but domiciled in the United States at the time of the child's birth derived his citizenship from the place of birth rather than the father's citizenship. Morrow's opinion, which the Supreme Court affirmed in UNITED STATES V. WONG KIM ARK (1898), confirmed the claims of thousands of Chinese to American citizenship.

Morrow's opinion in *United States v. Wheeler et al.* (1912) revealed his profound suspicion of federal authority. Arizona officials had refused to prosecute the perpetrators of the Bisbee deportations, in which private citizens had forcibly removed over 200 members of the Industrial Workers of the World from Arizona to New Mexico. The United States sought to prosecute the leaders of the deportation under the conspiracy section of the FORCE ACT OF 1870. Morrow, however, rejected federal intervention. He held that the Fourteenth Amendment applied only to those rights explicitly provided for by Congress and which had not been historically entrusted to the states. Morrow reasoned that the acts of private individuals did not constitute STATE ACTION under the amendment, that the 1870 act applied only to the rights of freedmen, and that Congress had not passed any statute making kidnapping a federal crime. Morrow refused to allow the federal government to intervene, no matter how just the cause, in an area traditionally left to the STATE POLICE POWER.

Morrow's conservative jurisprudence paralleled his Republican politics. Through three decades of service on the Ninth Circuit he provided leadership to a court committed, like himself, to precedent and DUAL FEDERALISM.

KERMIT L. HALL

Bibliography

JURY, JOHN G. 1921 William W. Morrow. *California Law Review* 10:1–7.

MUELLER v. ALLEN 463 U.S. 388 (1983)

In this major case on the SEPARATION OF CHURCH AND STATE, the Supreme Court altered constitutional law on the issue of state aid to parents of parochial school children. The precedents had established that a state may not aid parochial schools by direct grants or indirectly by financial aids to the parents of the children; whether those aids took the form of tax credits or reimbursements of tuition expenses did not matter. In this case the state act allowed taxpayers to deduct expenses for tuition, books, and transportation of their children to school, no matter what school, public or private, secular or sectarian.

Justice WILLIAM H. REHNQUIST for a 5–4 Court ruled that the plan satisfied all three parts of the purpose, effect, and no-entanglement test of LEMON V. KURTZMAN (1971). That all taxpaying parents benefited from the act made the difference between this case and the precedents, even though parents of public school children could not take advantage of the major tax deduction. Rehnquist declared that the state had not aided religion generally or any particular denomination and had not excessively entangled the state with religion even though government officials had to disallow tax deductions for instructional materials and books that were used to teach religion. According to the dissenters, however, the statute had not restricted the parochial schools to books approved for public school use, with the result that the state necessarily became enmeshed in religious matters when administering the tax deductions. The dissenters also rejected the majority point that the availability of the tax deduction to all parents distinguished this case from the precedents. The parents of public school children simply were unable to claim the large deduction for tuition. Consequently the program had the effect of advancing the religious mission of the private sectarian schools.

LEONARD W. LEVY

MUGLER v. KANSAS
123 U.S. 623 (1887)

In *Mugler* the Supreme Court took a significant step toward the acceptance of SUBSTANTIVE DUE PROCESS, announcing it would henceforth examine the reasonableness involved in an exercise of STATE POLICE POWER. A Kansas statute prohibited the manufacture or sale of intoxicating liquor; the state arrested Mugler for making and selling malt liquor and also closed a brewery for being a public nuisance.

Justice JOHN MARSHALL HARLAN addressed the issue: did the Kansas statute violate the FOURTEENTH AMENDMENT guarantee of DUE PROCESS OF LAW? He declared that such a prohibition "does not necessarily infringe" any of those rights. Although an individual might have an abstract right to make liquor for his own purposes, as Mugler contended, that right could be conditioned on its effect on others' rights. The question became who would determine the effects of personal use on the community? Harlan found that power lodged squarely in the legislature which, to protect the public health and morals, might exercise its police power. But, bowing to JOSEPH CHOATE'S argument, he admitted that such power was limited. Harlan asserted that the courts would not be bound "by mere forms [or] . . . pretenses." They had a "solemn duty—to look at the substance of things"; absent a "real or substantial relation" of the act to its objects, the legislation must fall as a "palpable invasion of rights secured by the FUNDAMENTAL LAW." The Kansas statute easily passed this test, however, and Harlan denied any interference or impairment of property rights. Harlan likewise dismissed the contention that the closing of a brewery amounted to a TAKING OF PROPERTY without JUST COMPENSATION, thereby depriving its owners of due process. Justice STEPHEN J. FIELD dissented in part, urging the Court to adopt substantive due process.

DAVID GORDON

(SEE ALSO: *Allgeyer v. Louisiana, 1897.*)

MULLER v. OREGON
208 U.S. 412 (1908)

Despite the Supreme Court's previous rejection of a maximum hour law for bakers in LOCHNER V. NEW YORK (1905), here the Justices unanimously sustained an Oregon statute limiting women to ten hours' labor in "any mechanical establishment, or factory, or laundry." The sole issue was the law's constitutionality as it affected female labor in a laundry. Lawyers for Muller contended that the law violated FREEDOM OF CONTRACT, that it was class legislation, and that it had no reasonable connection with the public health, safety, or welfare. The state countered with LOUIS D. BRANDEIS's famous brief elaborately detailing similar state and foreign laws, as well as foreign and domestic experts' reports on the harmful physical, economic, and social effects of long working hours for women.

Justice DAVID BREWER, speaking for the Court, based his opinion on the proposition that physical and social differences between the sexes justified a different rule respecting labor contracts, thereby allowing him to distinguish *Lochner.* Although the Constitution imposed unchanging limitations on legislative action, Brewer acknowledged that the FOURTEENTH AMENDMENT's liberty of contract doctrine was not absolute. He invoked HOLDEN V. HARDY (1898), sustaining an eight-hour day for Utah miners, and portions of *Lochner* that similarly approved some exceptional regulations. Brewer declared that although the legislation and opinions cited in the BRANDEIS BRIEF were not "authorities," the Court would "take judicial cognizance of all matters of general knowledge."

The accepted wisdom that women were unequal and inferior to men animated Brewer's opinion. Women's physical structure and their maternal functions, he said, put them at a disadvantage. Long hours of labor, furthermore, threatened women's potential for producing "vigorous" children; as such their physical well-being was a proper object of interest "in order to preserve the strength and vigor of the race." Beyond Brewer's concerns for the "future well-being of the race," he contended that the long historical record of women's dependence upon men demonstrated a persistent reality that women lacked "the self-reliance which enables one to assert full rights." Legislation such as the Oregon maximum hour law, Brewer concluded, was necessary to protect women from the "greed" and "passion" of men and therefore validly and properly could "compensate for some of the burdens" imposed upon women.

Taken out of context, Brewer's remarks obviously reflected paternalistic and sexist notions. Yet they also reflected prevailing sentiments, which he invoked to justify an exception to his normally restrictive views of legislative power. The same arguments were advanced by those who sought an opening wedge for ameliorating some of the excesses of modern industrialism.

Although the *Muller* decision did not overrule *Lochner*, it reinforced a growing line of precedents to counter *Lochner*. *Muller* eventually led to BUNTING V. OREGON (1917), approving maximum hour laws for both sexes, a decision that Chief Justice WILLIAM HOWARD TAFT believed in 1923 had tacitly overruled *Lochner*—mistakenly, as it turned out, for the Court invoked *Lochner* to strike down a minimum wage law in ADKINS V. CHILDREN'S HOSPITAL (1923).

STANLEY I. KUTLER

(SEE ALSO: *Sex Discrimination.*)

Bibliography

MASON, ALPHEUS T. 1946 *Brandeis: A Free Man's Life.* New York: Viking Press.

MULTIMEMBER DISTRICT

A multimember district (MMD) is a political district with more than one representative. European countries with proportional REPRESENTATION divide multiple representatives proportionally by party vote, normally producing many small, doctrinaire parties and volatile, schismatic governments. In United States MMDs, at-large, winner-take-all elections have been the rule, notably with ELECTORAL COLLEGE delegations. Winner-take-all puts more than proportional value on shiftable votes. Scholars believe that it has helped produce the American pattern of stable, center-seeking, two-party coalitions attentive to minorities who can form part of a winning coalition.

A ten-member, winner-take-all MMD offers less demographic variety—and less direct claim on any particular representative—than ten single-member districts; so MMDs have often been attacked for depersonalizing representation and submerging minorities. On the other hand, voters in MMDs have a mathematical advantage over voters in single-member districts (SMDs) because a 1/10 vote for ten representatives has more chance of affecting the overall election outcome than a full vote for one representative. Moreover, MMD representatives, who answer to one large constituency rather than to ten small ones, are thought more likely to vote as a bloc than SMD representatives. Hence, an MMD voter may have less access to his representative than does an SMD voter, but he also may have more power over electoral and legislative outcomes.

MMDs share with GERRYMANDERS the "standards problem": the incommensurability of the various ways in which dilution or concentration of a group can enhance or diminish the group's power for different purposes. Short of ordering proportional representation, there is no way to equalize a group's (or a group member's) effective power. Accordingly, the Supreme Court has been cautious in intervening against MMDs, as it has against gerrymanders. In *Delaware v. New York* (1966) it was unmoved by Delaware's argument that New York voters, with sixty-four delegates to the Electoral College, has 2.3 times as much chance to affect the election outcome as Delaware voters, with only three delegates.

Likewise, with the exceptions of judicially created MMDs and legislatively created ones drawn with the proven intent of submerging minorities, the Court has been tolerant of MMDs, even where their effect has been to submerge minorities. In *Whitcomb v. Chavis* (1971) and MOBILE V. BOLDEN (1980) the Court held that submerging a minority is not per se a violation of the FOURTEENTH or FIFTEENTH AMENDMENT. Purposeful discrimination must also be shown, as in *White v. Regester* (1973) and ROGERS V. LODGE (1982), where the plaintiffs demonstrated intentional discrimination against minority groups. Congressional critics (of the *Mobile* case) in 1982 succeeded in amending the VOTING RIGHTS ACT of 1965 to make racially disproportionate election results one "circumstance" relevant to the determination of a violation of the act. The amendment added a proviso that racially proportional representation is not required, but it left to the courts the task of giving meaning to its calculatedly uncertain operative language.

WARD E. Y. ELLIOTT

Bibliography

BANZHAF, JOHN E. 1966 Multi-Member Electoral Districts—Do They Violate the "One Man, One Vote" Principle? *Yale Law Journal* 75:1309–1338.

ELLIOTT, WARD E. Y. 1975 *The Rise of Guardian Democracy: The Supreme Court's Role in Voting Rights Disputes, 1845–1969.* Cambridge, Mass.: Harvard University Press.

MUNDT-NIXON BILL (1948–1949)

Karl Mundt of South Dakota and RICHARD M. NIXON of California, members of the HOUSE COMMITTEE ON UN-AMERICAN ACTIVITIES, sponsored the first anticommunist bill of the Cold War era. They contended that a house-cleaning of the executive department and a full exposure of past derelictions regarding communists would come only from a body in no way corrupted by ties to the administration. The measure (HR 5852) contained antisedition provisions but also reflected the view that the constitutional way to fight communists was by forcing them out into the open. The bill thus would have required the Communist party and "front" organizations to register with the Department of Justice and supply names of officers and members. It would also require that publications of these organizations, when sent through the mails, be labeled "published in compliance with the laws of the United States, governing the activities of agents of foreign principals."

The measure passed the House by a large margin but failed in the Senate after becoming a controversial factor in the presidential campaign of 1948. The bill was denounced by the Republican candidate, Thomas E. Dewey, and numerous respected national publications as a form of unwarranted thought control.

PAUL L. MURPHY

(SEE ALSO: *Subversive Activities and the Constitution.*)

Bibliography

COHEN, MURRAY and FUCHS, ROBERT F. 1948 Communism's Challenge and the Constitution. *Cornell Law Quarterly* 34:182–219, 352–375.

MUNICIPAL BANKRUPTCY ACT
48 Stat. 798 (1934)

This legislation, amending the Bankruptcy Act of 1898, declared "a national emergency caused by increasing financial difficulties of many local governmental units." Hearings on the bill disclosed that over 2,000 municipalities in all forty-eight states were in default—including such cities as Detroit and Miami—to an estimated total of nearly three billion dollars. The act conferred ORIGINAL JURISDICTION on federal bankruptcy courts in proceedings for the relief of "any municipality or other political subdivision of any State." Such taxing districts were thus enabled to file petitions asserting their inability to meet their debts. The act required submission of a "plan of readjustment" to accommodate a municipality's debts. The courts could enforce a plan that was "fair [and] equitable" and was approved by either two-thirds or three-quarters of the creditors, depending on the nature of the district. Section 80(k) stated that "nothing contained in this chapter shall be construed to limit or impair the power of any State to control . . . any political subdivision" and required state approval of these bankruptcy petitions.

A 5–4 Supreme Court invalidated this act in ASHTON V. CAMERON COUNTY WATER DISTRICT (1936), but the Court sustained a substantially similar act in *United States v. Bekins* (1938).

DAVID GORDON

Bibliography

JACKSON, ROBERT H. 1941 *The Struggle for Judicial Supremacy.* New York: Knopf.

MUNICIPAL IMMUNITY

Although precise practice varied among the states, two distinctions shaped municipalities' COMMON LAW liability. First, cities were immune from harms resulting from the exercise of governmental functions, such as fire protection, but they were not immune for harms attending proprietary functions, such as running a business. This sovereignlike immunity drew upon cities' legal connection to sovereign states, but it was independent of the ELEVENTH AMENDMENT immunity which states enjoy from suit in federal court. Since *Lincoln County v. Luning* (1890), cities and counties have not been viewed as part of the state for Eleventh Amendment purposes. Second, courts distinguished between discretionary functions, for which cities were immune, and ministerial activities, for which cities were not immune. As long as municipal liability was largely a branch of common law liability, courts articulated no significant distinctions between the treatment of federal claims against cities and claims brought under state law.

MONROE V. PAPE (1961), which reinvigorated SECTION 1983, TITLE 42, UNITED STATES CODE, and transformed the liability of state and local officials for violations of federal law into a question of federal statutory interpretation, laid the groundwork for greater municipal liability for violations of federal rights. But *Monroe* also retarded this development by interpreting section 1983 not to authorize suits against municipalities for violations of federal law. Indeed, the Court suggested that Congress doubted its constitutional authority to do so.

Between 1961 and 1978 litigants employed, with mixed success, various techniques to exploit *Monroe*'s federalization of official liability law, while at the same time avoiding *Monroe*'s holding that section 1983 did not authorize suits against cities. While these techniques were still developing, MONELL V. DEPARTMENT OF SOCIAL SERVICES (1978) drastically changed the law of municipal liability. *Monell* reinterpreted the legislative history relied on in *Monroe,* concluded that Congress had meant to subject cities to suit for violations of federal law, and overruled *Monroe*'s limitation on suits against cities. But *Monell* also held that Congress had not intended cities to be liable merely because they had employed an individual wrongdoer. Under *Monell*, cities are liable for violation of federal law only if the violation is "by its lawmakers or by those whose edicts or acts may fairly be said to represent official policy."

The question whether an alleged violation of federal law may be characterized as official policy became even more critical when, in OWEN V. CITY OF INDEPENDENCE (1980), the Court held that cities may not rely on the good faith defense available to individual officials as part of the law of EXECUTIVE IMMUNITY. *Owen* also severed the final links between municipalities' common law immunities and their modern amenability to suit under federal law. The Court rejected reliance by cities on sovereign-based immunities; a higher sovereign, the United States, had in section 1983 commanded municipal liability. The immunity for discretionary acts fell because "a municipality has no 'discretion' to violate the Federal Constitution." Cities achieved a modest victory when, in *City of Newport v. Fact Concerts, Inc.* (1981), the Court reaffirmed their traditional immunity from punitive damages claims.

THEODORE EISENBERG

Bibliography

SCHNAPPER, ERIC 1979 Civil Rights Litigation After *Monell. Columbia Law Review* 79:213–266.

MUNN v. ILLINOIS

See: Granger Cases

MURDOCK v. PENNSYLVANIA
319 U.S. 105 (1943)

A city ordinance required anyone offering goods for sale or engaged in solicitation (as opposed to sale from fixed premises) to obtain a license and pay a fee. Jehovah's Witnesses charged with violating the ordinance challenged it as a violation of the free exercise clause of the FIRST AMENDMENT.

Justice WILLIAM O. DOUGLAS, delivering the OPINION OF THE COURT, held that although the Witnesses offered literature for sale, their activity was "as evangelical as the revival meeting," occupying the same high estate under the First Amendment as worship in churches and preaching from pulpits. On the same day the Court vacated the judgment in *Jones v. Opelika* (1942), where the Court had previously upheld such an ordinance against a similar challenge.

Justice STANLEY F. REED dissented, arguing that JONES V. OPELIKA had been correctly decided. Justices OWEN ROBERTS, FELIX FRANKFURTER, and ROBERT H. JACKSON joined Reed's dissent. Justice Frankfurter also dissented separately, arguing that persons are not constitutionally "exempt from taxation merely because they may be engaged in religious activities or because such activities may constitute the exercise of a constitutional right."

Murdock represented a step away from the traditional doctrine of REYNOLDS V. UNITED STATES (1879) which had held that otherwise valid secular regulations could be enforced against nonconforming behavior even if that behavior were religiously motivated. (See RELIGIOUS LIBERTY.)

RICHARD E. MORGAN

MURPHY, FRANK
(1890–1949)

President FRANKLIN D. ROOSEVELT appointed Frank Murphy to the Supreme Court in 1940. Murphy, who had been mayor of Detroit and governor of Michigan, was ATTORNEY GENERAL at the time of his appointment as a Justice. As attorney general he created the Civil Rights Section (now division) of the Department of Justice and supported a vigorous antitrust program. As spokesman for the Supreme Court in constitutional matters, Murphy made modest but significant contributions. But as author of CONCURRING and DISSENTING OPINIONS in constitutional areas of individual freedom, Murphy voiced some of the more eloquent and impassioned defenses of human liberty in the Court's history.

Murphy's tenure on the Court spanned the decade of the 1940s. That period witnessed the consolidation of the federal and state power to deal with pressing economic and social problems. Murphy eagerly joined in this judicial retreat from the philosophy of LOCHNER V. NEW YORK (1905). Murphy's contribution to the de-Lochnerization of constitutional law was highlighted by his opinions for the Court in *North American Co. v. Securities & Exchange Commission* (1946) and *American Power & Light Co. v. Securities & Exchange Commission* (1946). Those decisions validated the "death sentence" clauses of the PUBLIC UTILITY HOLDING COMPANY ACT of 1935, the last major piece of New Deal legislation to be challenged. In language reminiscent of JOHN MARSHALL's language in GIBBONS V. OGDEN (1824), Murphy declared that the COMMERCE CLAUSE is "an affirmative power commensurate with the national needs." It gives Congress authority "to undertake to solve national problems directly and realistically, giving due recognition to the scope of state power," as well as to other constitutional provisions.

His first assignment to write a Court opinion produced a historic chapter in the development of FREEDOM OF SPEECH. In THORNHILL V. ALABAMA (1940) the Court held an Alabama antipicketing statute unconstitutional on its face. Murphy wrote that information concerning labor disputes is "within the area of free discussion . . . guaranteed by the Constitution." Such speech can be abridged only if there is a CLEAR AND PRESENT DANGER that substantive evils may arise before the merits of the discussion can be tested in the market of public opinion. The Court, though later permitting certain "time, place, and manner" restrictions on picketing, has never repudiated the *Thornhill* doctrine.

Another landmark free speech opinion written by Murphy was CHAPLINSKY V. NEW HAMPSHIRE (1942). Although controversial, the decision proved to be an influential forerunner of the Court's doctrinal notion that certain kinds of speech are of such slight social value as not to deserve full FIRST AMENDMENT protection. Such speech, said Murphy, includes "the lewd and obscene, the profane, the libelous, and the insulting or 'FIGHTING' WORDS—those which by their very utterance inflict injury or tend to incite an immediate BREACH OF THE PEACE."

Murphy also made a provocative contribution to the once raging judicial battle over whether the FOURTEENTH AMENDMENT totally or only selectively incorporates the BILL OF RIGHTS. While agreeing with Justice HUGO L. BLACK's total INCORPORATION DOCTRINE, Murphy in a dissent in ADAMSON V. CALIFORNIA (1947) proposed an "incorporation-plus" approach. A state proceeding, he wrote, may be so wanting in DUE PROCESS as to warrant constitutional condemnation "despite the absence of a specific provision in the Bill of Rights." Murphy's suggestion has proved functionally similar to the Court's final choice of the "selective incorporation approach."

Murphy was seldom assigned to write majority opinions in other constitutional areas. Among the few that he did write were the short-lived Fourth Amendment opinion in TRUPIANO V. UNITED STATES (1948) and the influential FULL FAITH AND CREDIT opinion in *Industrial Commission v. McCartin* (1947). Thus most of his deeply held views on the constitutional rights of individuals had to find expression in concurring and dissenting opinions. Through these he developed his judicial philosophy and expressed his ardent opposition to restricting the constitutional rights of racial and religious minorities, the economically disadvantaged, and those accused of crime.

The most durable and the most highly praised of all these individualized opinions is his dissent from what Murphy called "this legalization of racism" in KOREMATSU V. UNITED STATES (1944). The Court there upheld the wartime relocation of all persons of Japanese ancestry residing on the West Coast. Murphy dissected the military report upon which the relocation was based, and found the report filled with discredited and questionable racial and sociological factors beyond the realm of expert military judgment. To Murphy, the relocation was nothing more than racial discrimination that was "utterly revolting among a free people who have embraced the principles set forth in the Constitution of the United States." This dissent has been described by commentators as a classic in Supreme Court literature, and as one that "should be engraved in stone."

In *Falbo v. United States* (1944), Justice Murphy wrote that the law "knows no finer hour than when it cuts through formal concepts and transitory emotions to protect unpopular citizens against discrimination and persecution." His instinctive empathy for the constitutional rights of the oppressed and the unpopular constitutes Murphy's lasting contribution to the development of constitutional law.

EUGENE GRESSMAN

Bibliography

FINE, SIDNEY 1984 *Frank Murphy: The Washington Years.* Ann Arbor: University of Michigan Press.

HOWARD, J. WOODFORD 1968 *Mr. Justice Murphy.* Princeton, N.J.: Princeton University Press.

MURPHY v. FLORIDA
421 U.S. 794 (1975)

Jack "Murph the Surf" Murphy appealed a Florida robbery conviction. He claimed that he was denied a FAIR TRIAL because the jurors learned about his previous robbery and murder convictions, and about the circumstances of the instant case, from newspaper reports. The Supreme Court, 8–1, sustained his conviction.

Speaking through Justice THURGOOD MARSHALL, the Court held that juror exposure to information concerning the accused does not presumptively deny DUE PROCESS OF LAW. Since the VOIR DIRE did not discover juror hostility and there was no inflamed community sentiment, the totality of circumstances did not show inherent or actual prejudice.

DENNIS J. MAHONEY

(SEE ALSO: *Free Press/Fair Trial.*)

MURPHY v. FORD
390 F. Supp. 1372 (1975)

On September 8, 1974, President GERALD R. FORD granted to his predecessor, RICHARD M. NIXON, a "full, free and absolute pardon . . . for all offenses" that he might have committed while President. A Michigan lawyer brought suit in federal District Court for a DECLARATORY JUDGMENT invalidating the pardon. The District Court judge dismissed the suit, holding that the PARDONING POWER is unlimited, except in cases of IMPEACHMENT, and may as properly be exercised before criminal proceedings begin as after conviction. Citing THE FEDERALIST, the judge argued that the intention of the Framers in establishing the pardoning power was to provide for just such instances.

DENNIS J. MAHONEY

(SEE ALSO: *Articles of Impeachment [Nixon]; Watergate and the Constitution.*)

MURPHY v. WATERFRONT COMMISSION OF N.Y. HARBOR

See: Two Sovereignties Rule

MURRAY, WILLIAM
(Lord Mansfield)
(1705–1793)

The leading Tory constitutionalist of the eighteenth century, William Murray was appointed a judge after a career as a barrister and parliamentarian and service as attorney general. As Baron (later Earl) Mansfield, he was Lord Chief Justice of the Court of King's Bench from 1756 until 1788. He was active in the debates of the House of Lords and served for fifteen years in the cabinet. He opposed repeal of the Stamp Act in 1766, arguing that since the colonists were virtually represented in Parliament their complaints of TAXATION WITHOUT REPRESENTATION were without merit. Mansfield was a firm advocate of coercion in dealing with America, and he was the author of the Quebec Act of 1775.

In the WILKES CASES of 1763–1770 he held GENERAL WARRANTS illegal. He was tolerant of religious deviance and disapproved of prosecution of either Roman Catholic recusants or Protestant dissenters. In SOMERSET'S CASE (1772) he freed an escaped slave who had been recaptured in England, ruling that slavery was too odious to be supported by COMMON LAW. In SEDITIOUS LIBEL cases he allowed the jury to decide only the fact of publication, reserving the question of law—whether the published words were libelous—to be decided by the judge.

DENNIS J. MAHONEY

MURRAY'S LESSEE v. HOBOKEN LAND & IMPROVEMENT COMPANY
18 Howard 272 (1856)

This case raised the question whether an act of Congress provided DUE PROCESS OF LAW in the proceedings it laid down for exacting payments due to the treasury by collectors of the customs. For the first time the Supreme Court expounded the meaning of due process of law, which limited all branches of government. The Court interpreted due process exclusively in terms of PROCEDURAL DUE PROCESS. The settled usages and modes of proceedings in English law, "before the emigration of our ancestors," that were not unsuited to the civil and political conditions of America constituted due process.

LEONARD W. LEVY

MUSKRAT v. UNITED STATES
219 U.S. 346 (1911)

In one of a series of TEST CASES, the Court here refused to hear the suits involved because the parties failed to meet the constitutional requirement of CASES OR CONTROVERSIES (Article III, section 2). Congress had authorized certain INDIANS to sue the United States in the COURT OF CLAIMS and directed the ATTORNEY GENERAL to defend. The object was to determine the validity of certain congressional acts regarding Indian lands. The Court dismissed the suits, denying that Congress had the authority to create a case and designate parties to it.

DAVID GORDON

(SEE ALSO: *Ashwander v. Tennessee Valley Authority, 1936; Collusive Suit.*)

MYERS v. UNITED STATES
272 U.S. 52 (1926)

An 1876 statute authorized presidential appointment and removal of postmasters with the ADVICE AND CONSENT of the Senate. (See APPOINTING AND REMOVAL POWER.) President WOODROW WILSON appointed Myers with Senate consent but later removed him without consulting that body. Myers filed suit in the COURT OF CLAIMS and appealed that court's adverse decision to the Supreme Court.

Chief Justice, and former President, WILLIAM HOWARD TAFT, in a broad construction of Article II, found the statute unconstitutional. For a 6–3 majority he insisted upon the necessity for the nation's chief executive officer to be able to remove subordinates freely: "To hold otherwise would make it impossible for the President . . . to take care that the laws be faithfully executed."

Justices OLIVER WENDELL HOLMES, JAMES C. MCREYNOLDS, and LOUIS D. BRANDEIS dissented. Brandeis declared that implying an unrestricted power of removal from the power of appointment "involved an unnecessary and indefensible limitation upon the constitutional power of Congress." History and present state practice demonstrated "a decided tendency to limit" the executive's removal power, and he also cited the DOCTRINES of CHECKS AND BALANCES and the SEPARATION OF POWERS.

The Court limited the doctrinal reach of *Myers* in HUMPHREY'S EXECUTOR V. UNITED STATES (1935).

DAVID GORDON

NAACP v. ALABAMA
357 U.S. 449 (1958)

In this decision the Supreme Court first recognized a FREEDOM OF ASSOCIATION guaranteed by the FIRST AMENDMENT. Alabama, charging that the NAACP had failed to qualify as an out-of-state CORPORATION, had sought an INJUNCTION preventing the association from doing business in the state. In that proceeding, the state obtained an order that the NAACP produce a large number of its records. The association substantially complied, but refused to produce its membership lists. The trial court ruled the NAACP in contempt and fined it $100,000. The state supreme court denied review, and the U.S. Supreme Court unanimously reversed.

Justice JOHN MARSHALL HARLAN wrote for the Court. First, the NAACP had STANDING to assert its members' claims; to rule otherwise would be to require an individual member to forfeit his or her political privacy in the act of claiming it. On the constitutional merits, Harlan wrote: "Effective advocacy . . . is undeniably enhanced by group association"; thus "state action which may have the effect of curtailing the freedom to associate is subject to the closest scrutiny." The privacy of association may be a necessary protection for the freedom to associate "where a group espouses dissident beliefs." Here, disclosure of NAACP membership in Alabama during a time of vigorous civil rights activity had been shown to result in members' being fired from their jobs, physically threatened, and otherwise harassed. Only a COMPELLING STATE INTEREST could justify this invasion of political privacy. That compelling interest was not shown here. The names of the NAACP's rank-and-file members had no substantial bearing on the state's interest in assuring compliance with its corporation law.

This same technique—solemnly accepting the state's account of its purposes, ignoring possible improper motives, and concluding that those state interests were not "compelling"—was employed in other cases involving efforts by southern states to force disclosures of NAACP membership such as *Bates v. Little Rock* (1960) and *Shelton v. Tucker* (1960).

KENNETH L. KARST

(SEE ALSO: *Gibson v. Florida Legislative Investigation Commission, 1963.*)

NAACP v. BUTTON
371 U.S. 415 (1962)

The Supreme Court held that Virginia statutes forbidding one person to advise another that his legal rights had been violated and to refer him to a particular attorney were unconstitutional as applied to activities of the NAACP and its legal defense fund. The furtherance of litigation designed to challenge the constitutionality of RACIAL DISCRIMINATION was a mode of expression and association protected by the FIRST and FOURTEENTH AMENDMENTS. The Court acknowledged that INTEREST GROUP LITIGATION, aimed at changing constitutional law through TEST CASES, was not only professional legal activity subject to state regulation but also constitutionally protected political activity.

MARTIN SHAPIRO

(SEE ALSO: *NAACP Legal Defense & Educational Fund.*)

NAACP v. CLAIBORNE HARDWARE COMPANY

See: Labor and the Constitution

NAACP LEGAL DEFENSE & EDUCATIONAL FUND

The NAACP Legal Defense & Educational Fund, Inc., was founded in 1939 by board members of the National Association for the Advancement of Colored People to conduct the legal program of the association through a corporation qualified to receive tax deductible contributions. The association was not tax exempt, because it lobbied. Board members of the association served on the board of the Fund; the Fund's director and some of its lawyers also were employees of the association.

In 1957 the Internal Revenue Service (IRS) objected to the interlocking staff and board because it enabled an organization not tax exempt to influence one entitled to tax exemption. The IRS required termination of the interlocking arrangement. Thereafter the Fund and the association were no longer formally linked, and the Fund functioned entirely independently with its own board, staff, budget, and policies. The Fund has since represented individuals and organizations with no relationship to the association at all as well as members and branches of the association.

In 1984 the Fund's staff consisted of twenty-four lawyers, with offices in New York and Washington, D.C., and several hundred cooperating lawyers across the United States. Its budget was $6.7 million. It has served as a model for the public interest law movement generally, including other legal defense funds, such as those dealing with discrimination against Hispanics, Asians, women, the handicapped, homosexuals, and the aged, as well as public interest firms representing environmental, consumer, migrant worker, and other groups.

The Fund's director-counsel was THURGOOD MARSHALL, who served until 1961 and was succeeded by Jack Greenberg, who directed the organization until 1984, when he was succeeded by Julius L. Chambers. The Fund has been involved in most of the leading cases dealing with racial discrimination in the United States, including BROWN V. BOARD OF EDUCATION (1954), which held unconstitutional racial SEGREGATION in public education, the principle of which was ultimately extended to all other governmental activities. *Brown* was the culmination of a planned litigation effort which built upon earlier Fund cases involving RACIAL DISCRIMINATION in graduate and professional schools. In the 1960s, the Fund provided representation in most of the cases generated by the CIVIL RIGHTS movement, including representation of MARTIN LUTHER KING, JR. Thereafter, following passage of the Civil Rights Acts of the mid-1960s, the Fund brought most of the leading cases enforcing those laws. The Fund has represented civil rights claimants in more than 2,000 cases dealing with education, employment, VOTING RIGHTS, housing, PRISONERS' RIGHTS, CAPITAL PUNISHMENT, health care, and other areas of the law.

JACK GREENBERG

Bibliography

RABIN, ROBERT L. 1976 Lawyers for Social Change: Perspectives on Public Interest Law. *Stanford Law Journal* 28:207–261.

NARCOTICS REGULATION

See: Drug Regulation

NARDONE v. UNITED STATES
302 U.S. 379 (1937)

After the Supreme Court largely exempted ELECTRONIC EAVESDROPPING from constitutional control in OLMSTEAD V. UNITED STATES (1928), protection against WIRETAPPING was sought legislatively. In 1934, Congress passed the COMMUNICATIONS ACT, section 605 of which provided that "no person" could intercept and divulge radio and wire communications. In *Nardone v. United States* the Supreme Court ruled that section 605 extended to federal agents; later the Court applied it also to state officers in *Benanti v. United States* (1957). The Justice Department construed section 605 very narrowly, however, and it was rarely invoked. It has been largely superseded by Title III of the OMNIBUS CRIME CONTROL AND SAFE STREETS ACT (1968).

HERMAN SCHWARTZ

NASHVILLE CONVENTION RESOLUTIONS
(1850)

Fearing that Congress might enact the WILMOT PROVISO, abolish the slave trade in the DISTRICT OF COLUMBIA, or adopt other antislavery measures, southern separatists called for a convention of slave states to meet at Nashville in June 1850. The convention adopted resolutions asserting that: the TERRITORIES were the joint property of the people of all the states; Congress could not discriminate among owners of different kinds of property in the territories, and hence could not exclude slaves; and the federal government must protect all forms of property, including slaves, in the territories. However, the moderates who dominated the convention added that if the free states refused to recognize these principles, the slave states would accept a division of the territories by extending the MISSOURI COMPROMISE line to the Pacific, an extraordinary concession on the central constitutional issue that disgusted the radicals. A poorly attended adjourned session of the convention, dominated by radicals, met in November 1850, denounced the COMPROMISE OF 1850, advocated SECESSION, but proposed no immediate program. The resolutions of the Nashville Convention are thus significant principally as an indication of the slave states' inability to unite on a secessionist platform.

WILLIAM M. WIECEK

(SEE ALSO: *Slavery and the Constitution.*)

Bibliography

POTTER, DAVID M. 1976 *The Impending Crisis, 1848–1861.* New York: Harper & Row.

NATIONAL ASSOCIATION FOR THE ADVANCEMENT OF COLORED PEOPLE

See: NAACP Legal Defense & Educational Fund

NATIONAL EMERGENCIES ACT

See: Emergency Powers

NATIONAL ENVIRONMENTAL POLICY ACT

See: Environmental Regulation

NATIONAL INDUSTRIAL RECOVERY ACT
48 Stat. 195 (1933)

The National Industrial Recovery Act (NIRA) was the best-known and, perhaps, in President FRANKLIN D. ROOSEVELT's words, "the most important and far-reaching legislation ever enacted" by the New Deal Congress. The act was designed to curb unemployment, stimulate business recovery, and end the competitive wars of the Great Depression. By May 1935, over 750 codes covering some twenty-three million people had been created under the NIRA's authority. Even before Roosevelt's inauguration, his "brain trust" had begun to plan a recovery bill. Introduced May 17, 1933, the bill raised questions of constitutionality. Congress passed it, however, and Roosevelt signed it into law on June 16.

The act declared a national emergency and justified congressional action under the COMMERCE CLAUSE and the GENERAL WELFARE CLAUSE. Section 2 established the National Recovery Administration (NRA) to supervise the NIRA, limiting its operation to two years. The heart of the act, section 3, provided for the framing of "codes of fair competition" by private businessmen and trade associations. After meeting certain requirements and obtaining presidential approval, these codes became "standards of fair competition" with the full force of federal law, regulating industrywide prices, wages, and practices. Such an extraordinary DELEGATION OF POWER was unprecedented: it allowed private citizens to draft codes to rule industry and provided, at best, minimal policy guidelines and standards. Violations of the codes "in any transaction in or affecting INTERSTATE OR FOREIGN COMMERCE [were] deemed an unfair method of competition in commerce within the meaning of the FEDERAL TRADE COMMISSION ACT." Upon complaint or failure of an industry to formulate a code, the President could establish a compulsory code. Section 7 prescribed three mandatory provisions for every code: availability of COLLECTIVE BARGAINING, employee freedom from coercion to join or refrain from joining a union, and compliance with regulated MAXIMUM HOURS AND MINIMUM WAGES. The various clauses of this section constituted the broadest regulation of wages and hours in American history to that date. The NRA also incorporated in its "blanket code" a provision outlawing child labor in industries without specific codes. Although the NIRA prohibited monopolies and monopolistic practices, it exempted code-covered industries from the antitrust laws. Title II of the NIRA established a Public Works Administration to stimulate construction and, by spending its $3.3 billion budget, to increase purchasing power.

Serious questions of the act's constitutionality eventually reached the Supreme Court, however, and in SCHECHTER POULTRY CORP. v. UNITED STATES (1935) a unanimous Court voided the NIRA for unconstitutionally delegating power to the President and exceeding the limits of the commerce power. Despite this decision and PANAMA REFINING COMPANY v. RYAN (1935), invalidating other provisions, Congress gradually replaced the act with new and more effective legislation. Although historians debate whether the NRA impeded or encouraged recovery and reform, the lessons of this experiment in economic planning provided valuable experience for drafting later legislation such as the WAGNER (NATIONAL LABOR RELATIONS) and FAIR LABOR STANDARDS ACTS.

DAVID GORDON

Bibliography

LYON, LEVERETT S. ET AL. 1935 *The National Recovery Administration: An Analysis and Appraisal.* Washington, D.C.: Brookings Institution.

ROOS, CHARLES F. 1937 *NRA Economic Planning.* Bloomington: Indiana University Press.

NATIONAL LABOR RELATIONS ACTS

See: Taft-Hartley Act; Wagner Act

NATIONAL LEAGUE OF CITIES v. USERY
426 U.S. 833 (1976)

This case proved that obituaries for DUAL FEDERALISM were premature. It arose after Congress amended the FAIR LABOR STANDARDS ACT (FLSA), in 1974, to extend wages-and-hours coverage to nearly all public employees. Several states, cities, and intergovernmental organizations sought to enjoin enforcement of the new provisions. Admitting that the employees in question would come within the federal commerce power if they worked in the private sector, the plaintiffs argued that congressional regulation of employment conditions for state and municipal workers violated "the established constitutional DOCTRINE of INTERGOVERNMENTAL IMMUNITY." A three-judge district court disagreed, ruling that under MARYLAND v. WIRTZ (1968), which had upheld the application of WAGES AND HOURS REGULATIONS to public schools and hospitals, an employee's public status was irrelevant to the scope of congressional authority. On APPEAL, the Supreme Court reversed the lower court, 5–4, holding that the FLSA amendments could not constitutionally be applied to public employees performing "traditional governmental functions."

Writing for the Court, Justice WILLIAM H. REHNQUIST initially confronted the sweep of the COMMERCE CLAUSE recognized in GIBBONS v. OGDEN (1824). The grant of congressional power was plenary, he conceded, but did not override "affirmative limitations" on Congress. The TENTH AMENDMENT provided the most explicit source for such a limitation, for in FRY v. UNITED STATES (1975) the Court had offered the dictum that the amendment "expressly declared the constitutional policy that Congress may not exercise power in a fashion that impairs the States' integrity or their ability to function effectively in a federal system." Yet Rehnquist emphasized a less explicit limitation—the overall federal structure. Within it, states perform essential governmental functions, and state decisions about these functions, which include fire protection and law enforcement, must be free from federal interference. Wages and hours legislation constituted a forbidden infringement, because it "operate[s] directly to displace the States' freedom to structure integral operations in areas of traditional governmental functions. . . ." Indeed, he expressly held the Court had wrongly decided *Wirtz.*

But the meaning of *National League of Cities* as precedent is not clear. Justice HARRY A. BLACKMUN qualified his crucial fifth vote with a concurrence that interpreted the Court as "adopt[ing] a balancing approach." For him, the decision did not preclude regulation of states in areas, such as environmental protection, where the federal interest was demonstrably greater. And the Court itself expressly left open the power of Congress to regulate even traditional state functions by employing the TAXING AND SPENDING POWER or by enforcing the FOURTEENTH AMENDMENT. (See FITZPATRICK v. BITZER, 1976.)

In dissent, Justice WILLIAM J. BRENNAN charged that the decision contained "an ominous portent of destruction of our constitutional structure" and delivered a "catastrophic body blow" to the commerce power. In his view, Rehnquist had misread earlier case law and had abandoned the plain meanings of the commerce and SUPREMACY CLAUSES. Moreover, Rehnquist's "essential function test" was "conceptually unworkable," for it failed to clarify the distinction between essential and other state activities.

The Court's opinion did lack a reasoned test for

determining the essential functions of states "*qua* states." It also ran counter to forty years of judicial acceptance of broad congressional power under the commerce clause. Accordingly, *National League of Cities* led to further litigation over state immunity from federal regulation and injected the Supreme Court into issues long dormant. In GARCIA V. SAN ANTONIO METROPOLITAN TRANSIT AUTHORITY (1985) a different 5–4 majority flatly overruled *National League of Cities,* but the dissenters promised that disinterment of the 1976 decision awaited only one more vote.

CHARLES A. LOFGREN

Bibliography

BARBER, SOTIRIOS A. 1976 *National League of Cities v. Usery:* New Meaning for the Tenth Amendment? *Supreme Court Review* 1976:161–182.

LOFGREN, CHARLES A. 1980 The Origins of the Tenth Amendment: History, Sovereignty, and the Problem of Constitutional Intention. Pages 331–357 in Ronald K. L. Collins (ed.), *Constitutional Government in America.* Durham, N.C.: Carolina Academic Press.

NAGEL, ROBERT F. 1981 Federalism as a Fundamental Value: *National League of Cities* in Perspective. *Supreme Court Review* 1981:81–109.

NATIONAL POLICE POWER

The "national police power" is not, strictly speaking, a constitutional power of Congress. Rather, it is a phrase describing the power of Congress, acting under the enumerated powers, to enact "police legislation." The term "police legislation" includes criminal law as well as health, morals, safety, antidiscrimination, and environmental statutes.

Under our federal system, national police power regulation has always been controversial. Police matters are historically state or local concerns, and yet some problems seem to call for a national solution. The recurring issues, therefore, are whether Congress should address a problem that has historically been attacked at the state or local level and whether the courts can articulate any principled limits on congressional power to do so.

The Constitution provides a number of sources of power for national police legislation. The most important are the congressional powers to regulate commerce, to tax, and to spend. However, several other powers should not be overlooked. The postal power makes possible laws to protect consumers from fraudulent or obscene materials transmitted through the mails, subject to significant First Amendment limitations. The enabling clauses of the THIRTEENTH and FOURTEENTH AMENDMENTS open the way for a variety of antidiscrimination laws. (See JONES V. ALFRED H. MAYER CO. [1968], racial discrimination in housing; UNITED STATES V. GUEST [1966], violence against minorities in the use of public facilities.)

Because such local activities as manufacturing or gambling are not themselves interstate commerce, they are not, without more, subject to federal commerce clause regulation. However, constitutional developments during the twentieth century have marked out two techniques which, alone or in combination, permit virtually unlimited regulation of local activity under the aegis of the COMMERCE CLAUSE: prohibition of INTERSTATE COMMERCE and linking a local activity to an "effect" on interstate commerce.

A few early statutes prohibited particular forms of interstate commerce (such as transportation of diseased cattle or use of unsafe locomotives) because they physically endangered the stream of commerce. In 1895, however, Congress took a further critical step by prohibiting the interstate transportation of lottery tickets. Transportation of the tickets harmed nobody; Congress was obviously concerned that the use of the tickets in the receiving state was harmful to public morals. Thus the prohibition on transportation really was a technique to assist the states in stamping out national (or international) lotteries. Under traditional assumptions, of course, the regulation of gambling or of consumer fraud was a state responsibility, but individual state regulation of lotteries had proved ineffectual.

In CHAMPION V. AMES (1903), often referred to as "The Lottery Case," the Supreme Court upheld the federal statute by a 5–4 vote. The majority believed that the shipment of articles in interstate commerce that were harmful to the public safety or morals was a "misuse" of commerce, the prohibition of which lay well within the commerce power. This rationale paved the way for many later statutes which treated various goods or persons as "outlaws" of commerce and thus prohibited their shipment. For example, the courts upheld regulation or prohibition of interstate transportation of adulterated food, prostitutes, obscene literature, and stolen cars upon the authority of *Champion.* In addition, the Court upheld statutes banning the interstate shipment of items (such as liquor or goods produced by convict labor) that violated the laws of the receiving state.

In addition to permitting regulation of interstate transportation of goods, *Champion* provided authority for regulation of the use of the goods after they arrived. Finally, although most of the commerce-prohibition cases involved regulation of purely commercial activity, the Court in *Caminetti v. United States* (1917) found no constitutional objection to punishing a man for transporting a woman to whom he was not married across the state lines for immoral, but wholly noncommercial, purposes. (See HOKE V. UNITED STATES, 1913.)

The usefulness of the commerce-prohibiting technique suffered a temporary but sharp reverse after Congress decided to use it for the purpose of abolishing child labor. In HAMMER V. DAGENHART (1918) the Supreme Court held that Congress could not prohibit the transportation in interstate commerce of goods made by children, because the goods were lawfully produced in the state of origin and harmless both to interstate commerce and to users in the receiving state. The government tried to show that the law was necessary to achieve fair interstate competition, because states allowing child labor had an unfair advantage over those prohibiting it. The Court said that Congress had no power to equalize comparative advantages or disadvantages among the states.

Justices OLIVER WENDELL HOLMES'S dissent in *Hammer* seemingly demolished the majority opinion and ultimately became the law when UNITED STATES V. DARBY overruled *Hammer* in 1941. *Darby* made clear that Congress could prohibit the interstate shipment of harmless goods manufactured by workers whose wages or working hours violated the FAIR LABOR STANDARDS ACT. The Court in *Darby* accepted the theory, rejected by the *Hammer* majority, that Congress could use the commerce-prohibiting technique to improve labor conditions in the state of origin and to achieve fair competition among states. After *Darby*, therefore, there was no longer any obstacle to the achievement of police goals by the prohibition of interstate commerce in people or goods, absent the violation of some other constitutional norm.

In the landmark commerce clause case of GIBBONS V. OGDEN (1824) Chief Justice JOHN MARSHALL seemingly established that a local activity could be regulated by Congress under the commerce clause if the activity "affected" other states. Nevertheless there arose a confusing body of case law on the extent to which local affairs could be regulated because of their effect on interstate commerce. On the one hand, for example, the Shreveport case, HOUSTON, EAST AND WEST TEXAS RAILWAY V. UNITED STATES (1914), allowed the Interstate Commerce Commission to regulate intrastate railroad rates because low rates for intrastate hauls and high rates for interstate hauls unfairly discriminated against interstate commerce. On the other hand, early antitrust cases, including UNITED STATES V. E. C. KNIGHT CO. (1895), cast doubt on Congress's power to regulate monopolies in manufacturing because manufacturing was considered local; the Court evidently assumed that granting regulatory power to the national government would prevent the states from regulating the activity.

In several cases during the 1930s, narrow majorities of the Supreme Court invalidated New Deal legislation that sought to regulate local activity affecting interstate commerce (such as labor relations in coal mining in CARTER V. CARTER COAL CO., 1936). By the late 1930s, however, these cases had been disapproved. By the time of WICKARD V. FILBURN (1942) there was no longer any doubt that Congress had power to regulate purely local and individually trivial activities which (when cumulated) substantially affected interstate commerce. In that case the Court ruled that Congress could regulate home consumption of wheat because of its aggregate effect on an interstate market.

Thus the "affecting commerce" rationale was available when Congress turned to national police legislation. The Fair Labor Standards Act not only prohibited interstate transportation of goods manufactured by persons whose wages or hours violated the act; it also directly prohibited the production of such goods for interstate commerce. *United States v. Darby* upheld the manufacturing prohibition on two distinct theories. The Court held that manufacturing could be prohibited (even if transportation had not been prohibited) because production of goods under substandard labor conditions was a form of unfair competition that substantially affected interstate commerce. In addition, the Court upheld the manufacturing ban as a necessary and proper incident of Congress's power to prohibit interstate transportation of the goods. This latter theory opened the way for Congress to ban virtually any local activity if it also bans interstate transportation of the persons who conduct the activity or the goods produced by it.

Congress has frequently resorted to the "affecting commerce" rationale when it pursues fundamentally noneconomic objectives. The Court has generously upheld federal statutes upon determining that Congress has "rationally" concluded that a local activity substantially affected commerce. For example, the Court upheld in KATZENBACH V. MCCLUNG (1964) a federal prohibition on racial discrimination, as applied to a restaurant that had purchased food from a local seller who had purchased it in interstate commerce. The Court's tenuous theory was that Congress could rationally conclude that discrimination in such restaurants decreased interstate sales of food.

(See HEART OF ATLANTA V. UNITED STATES, 1964.)

The "affecting commerce" rationale has opened the way for a vast expansion of federal criminal law. In PEREZ V. UNITED STATES (1971) the Court upheld a conviction under the federal loan-sharking statute, even though the defendant had no apparent contact with interstate commerce. In previous cases, such as *Katzenbach v. McClung,* the characteristic used to identify the regulated party had a connection to interstate commerce, but in *Perez,* the characteristic ("loan-sharking") had no such connection. However, the Court deferred to congressional findings that loan-sharking is used by multistate organized crime rings to raise or launder money to take over legitimate businesses. It then held that because loansharks as a "class" substantially affect interstate commerce, any member of the class can be reached by a federal criminal statute, regardless of the individual's actual interstate connections. Of course, this approach is drastically overinclusive, but it is justifiable because it is difficult to ascertain in a given case whether a particular loan-shark has connections to organized crime and thus to interstate commerce. The *Perez* theory that Congress can criminalize an entire class, when some members of that class substantially affect interstate commerce, undergirds several other federal racketeering, gambling, and drug abuse statutes. (See LAW ENFORCEMENT AND FEDERAL–STATE RELATIONS.)

The "prohibiting commerce" and the "affecting commerce" techniques, used separately or together, thus provide the authority for virtually limitless expansion of national police power. Given only slight ingenuity in statute-drafting, a local activity which Congress wishes to regulate or prohibit can be linked somehow to interstate commerce.

Nevertheless, the Court has employed a number of low-visibility judicial techniques to slow the federalization of police power. It has frequently construed narrowly statutes that make unexpected intrusions into local domains, reasoning that Congress should clearly state its intention to expand national police power. Moreover, in construing federal criminal statutes, the Court takes into account its view of an appropriate balance between state and federal law enforcement. These constructional techniques require Congress at least to face and consider the implications of a drastic extension of federal power. Similarly, the Court may hold that an ambiguous criminal statute fails to give fair warning to those affected by it if a broad construction would punish essentially local activity.

In considering congressional police power under the commerce clause, the most important open question is whether a majority of the Supreme Court will hold that a "trivial" effect on interstate commerce is an insufficient foundation. A number of Justices have written that questions of degree are important to them and that the cumulative effect on commerce of the class of regulated activities must be "substantial." In several cases involving federal stripmining legislation, for example, including HODEL V. VIRGINIA SURFACE MINING AND RECLAMATION ASSOCIATION and *Hodel v. Indiana* (1981), the court unanimously upheld statutes which regulated stripmining on steep slopes and on farmland against claims that land use control is a uniquely local function. The Court found that Congress had acted rationally in identifying the environmental effects of stripmining as substantial burdens on interstate commerce and that the means chosen by Congress were rational. Two Justices wrote separately to emphasize that their concurrence was based on the substantiality of the effect. In the past, other Justices have expressed similar reservations. If a majority of the Supreme Court were actually to assess the substantiality of the effect on commerce of the class of regulated activities before upholding a statute, it would be much less clear than it seems today that the Constitution imposes no effective limit on the national police power under the commerce clause.

By using its power to tax an activity, Congress can discourage, regulate, or prohibit the activity. Consequently, a power intended to furnish Congress with the means for raising revenue can be effectively employed for police purposes. Occasional taxpayers have contended that a so-called tax is really regulatory in purpose and effect, and consequently not a tax at all. In early cases, such as UNITED STATES V. DOREMUS (1919), the Court upheld tax statutes with patently obvious regulatory goals, taking the tax label at face value. The court turned a blind eye to the fact that the tax would destroy the taxed business, that it produced little or no revenue, or that its administrative provisions were inappropriate for tax collection.

However, when Congress sought to prohibit child labor by taxing income from the sale of products made by children, the Court rebelled. In BAILEY V. DREXEL FURNITURE CO. (1922) it concluded that the tax was actually a regulatory measure, for it provided for a tax of ten percent on annual net income if the taxpayer knowingly used child labor on even a single occasion. Thus, said the Court, Congress had used the taxing power as a pretext for an attempt to regulate manufacturing—something it had previously held beyond Congress's power.

Ultimately, the court abandoned any effort to distinguish taxation from regulation. In upholding the federal gambling tax, which obviously was intended to stamp out illegal gambling rather than to raise revenue, the Court noted that a federal tax is valid even though it may destroy the taxed activity, raises little revenue, and contains enforcement provisions more appropriate to a criminal statute than a tax provision. In *United States v. Kahriger* (1953), decided over a strong dissent by Justice FELIX FRANKFURTER, the Court held that unless the tax law contains penalty or administrative provisions "extraneous to any tax need," it is valid.

The Court later limited its *Kahriger* precedent. MARCHETTI V. UNITED STATES (1968) held that the registration requirement for gamblers entailed coerced self-incrimination, in violation of the Fifth Amendment. Nevertheless, unless a tax runs afoul of a specific provision of the Bill of Rights, it seems unlikely that the Court will ever again seek to patrol the troubled border between taxation and regulation. There is little need for the distinction, now that virtually any activity it seeks to regulate through taxation could be easily reached through the commerce power.

Through its power to spend for the general welfare, Congress can enlist state or private cooperation in achieving an endless list of regulatory goals. All it needs to do is place conditions on offers of federal money. If the offer is sufficiently generous, the recipients are virtually certain to accept the conditions.

In the 1930s the Supreme Court made a doomed attempt to limit the traditional practice of regulation through conditional grants. It held that a federal program of payments to farmers, upon condition that they contractually agree to limit their acreage, was an invalid attempt to regulate agriculture and thus an incursion into a matter left to the states. In UNITED STATES V. BUTLER (1936) it declared that Congress could not purchase submission to a regulation that it could not impose directly.

The *Butler* prohibition on conditional spending lasted only a year. The SOCIAL SECURITY ACT contained a joint federal-state taxing and spending program to pay unemployment compensation. To induce the states to participate, Congress imposed a payroll tax on employers. However, a taxpayer received a credit of ninety percent of the federal tax if its state levied a payroll tax and adopted a system for distributing benefits that complied with the federal statute. As a practical matter, this credit, which had the effect of a federal expenditure, required states to participate in the program. Nevertheless, the court upheld that statute in STEWARD MACHINE COMPANY V. DAVIS (1937), approving the concept of "cooperative federalism" and declaring that no state was coerced into adopting an unemployment compensation system. However, the Court indicated that it might have some doubts if the federal law imposed conditions that were unreasonable or unrelated in subject matter to legitimate national objectives or entailed surrender by states of quasi-sovereign powers.

Since *Steward Machine,* the Court has consistently upheld conditional spending programs in the few cases that have raised the issue. For example, in *Oklahoma v. Civil Service Commission* (1947) it sustained a system of conditional highway construction grants to states. A recipient state had to consent to a provision in the HATCH ACT precluding administration by any person involved in political campaigns. Because the state was free to reject federal funding, no coercion was involved.

Conditional federal grants have been used to achieve a wide variety of federal police objectives, particularly in the areas of environmental protection, affirmative action, education, and health services. However, in PENNHURST STATE SCHOOL V. HALDERMAN (1981) the Court sounded a warning. If a state is to be bound by a condition on its receipt of federal funds, the condition must be unambiguously stated in the statute. Otherwise, a state's acceptance might not have been knowing and voluntary. Like the requirement that Congress make a clear statement that it intends a criminal statute to reach an essentially local activity, the clear statement rule of *Pennhurst* requires Congress to focus on the issue of federalism when it adopts a conditional spending program.

Congress has ample power to achieve national police power objectives. The commerce clause, the postal, taxing, and spending power, and the enabling clauses of the Thirteenth and Fourteenth Amendments furnish authority for almost any conceivable expansion of national regulatory jurisdiction. However, the Court has suggested (sometimes in OBITER DICTUM) potential limitations on these powers which might someday be invoked to constrain an extension of federal authority.

Much more important than any judicially imposed limits are the political constraints on the national police power. Various structural elements of the national government assure sympathetic treatment for arguments based on federalism; for example, states opposing federal intrusion are protected by the fact that each state has two senators (regardless of population). Among other factors, state legislative control over House districting and the state-oriented organization of national political parties also assure respectful treatment for state or local contentions that extension of federal regulation is unnecessary. Similarly, the selection of the President by the Electoral College emphasizes the importance of states. The powerful representation of states at the national level, the tradition that police regulation is performed at the state level, and the inertia of Congress all work together to assure that intrusions by the national government into matters of state concern are likely to occur only when a broad national consensus emerges that centralization is necessary.

MICHAEL ASIMOW

Bibliography

CUSHMAN, ROBERT E. 1919 National Police Power under the Commerce Clause of the Constitution. *Minnesota Law Review* 3:289–319, 381–412, 452–483.

——— 1920 National Police Power under the Postal Power of the Constitution. *Minnesota Law Review* 4:402–440.

KADEN, LEWIS B. 1979 Politics, Money and State Sovereignty: The Judicial Role. *Columbia Law Review* 79:847–897.

STERN, ROBERT L. 1973 The Commerce Clause Revisited: Federalization of Intrastate Crime. *Arizona Law Review* 15:271–285.

WECHSLER, HERBERT 1954 The Political Safeguards of Federalism: The Role of the States in the Composition and Selection of the National Government. *Columbia Law Review* 54:543–560.

NATIONAL PROHIBITION CASES

See: Amending Process; Eighteenth Amendment

NATIONAL SECURITY ACT
69 Stat. 495 (1947)

This act embodies the most comprehensive reorganization ever undertaken of the means by which the WAR POWERS are to be exercised. The act unified the command of the armed forces, officially organized the Joint Chiefs of Staff, created the Air Force department, and established the office of secretary of defense. The separate army and navy establishments recognized in the Constitution, together with the air force, became a single, permanent "National Military Establishment."

Furthermore, the act erected, within the executive branch, the National Security Council. The original intention of Congress seems to have been to constrict the President's freedom of action in defense and FOREIGN AFFAIRS by prescribing the persons to be consulted and the manner of consultation in national security decision making. In fact, however, strong and politically skillful Presidents have used the council to strengthen their own positions, as, for example, President JOHN F. KENNEDY did during the Cuban missile crisis of 1962.

Under the National Security Council the act created the Central Intelligence Agency (CIA), with a broad charter to conduct foreign intelligence-gathering activities, as well as to process and disseminate intelligence gathered by other agencies. The act specifically prohibited domestic intelligence activities on the part of the CIA.

DENNIS J. MAHONEY

NATIONAL SECURITY AND THE FOURTH AMENDMENT

The right to individual privacy and the preservation of national security have jarred against each other for centuries. "National security cases . . . often reflect a convergence of First and FOURTH AMENDMENT values not present in cases of 'ordinary' crime," wrote Justice LEWIS F. POWELL for a unanimous Supreme Court in UNITED STATES V. UNITED STATES DISTRICT COURT (1972). The early English cases, such as the WILKES CASES (1763–1770), establishing the right to keep the government out of a home unless it has PROBABLE CAUSE and a judicially approved warrant to enter, arose from successful challenges by political dissidents to searches by royal officers hunting for seditious writings. Preventing such infringements on both personal security and free expression was the main purpose of the Fourth Amendment. Today, Presidents claim inherent executive power to break into homes, to make physical SEARCHES AND SEIZURES, to open mail, and to video-tape, WIRETAP, and bug—again in order to protect national security.

Where the surveillance is directed against national security threats by *domestic* groups or individuals, the Supreme Court has held that the President has no inherent executive power, and a warrant must first be obtained. The government's needs will not be presumed to outweigh the threats such a power poses for the rights of free speech and personal security; rather, a search against domestic threats must be approved in advance by a neutral magistrate. The Court did suggest that Congress could authorize less stringent procedures for domestic intelligence gathering than for crime detection, but so far Congress has not done so.

Foreign national security issues have been treated very differently. Courts have generally accepted the claim of inherent presidential power to use electronic surveillance, video-tapes, and physical entries against both foreigners and Americans in order to obtain foreign intelligence, without obtaining prior judicial approval. The power is justified on several grounds: the need for stealth, speed, and secrecy to counter foreign threats; the executive's superior experience and knowledge of FOREIGN AFFAIRS and the judiciary's relative lack of competence in such matters; and the executive's primacy in foreign affairs in the constitutional scheme. This power is limited to intelligence gathering, so that when the investigation becomes a criminal investigation and the warrantless interception is made for the purpose of gathering evidence for a prosecution, the requirements of Title III of the OMNIBUS CRIME CONTROL AND SAFE STREETS ACT must be satisfied. This inherent intelligence gathering power, moreover, can be exercised only by the President or the attorney general; a lower-level official cannot authorize intelligence-gathering break-ins or wiretaps on his own, without judicial approval.

In 1976, a Senate committee issued a massive documentation of the many abuses of Fourth Amendment rights perpetrated by executive officers and the intelligence agencies from the 1930s through the 1970s. The Central Intelligence Agency, for example, admitted wiretapping people it considered "left-wingers" both in this country and abroad in a project it called "Operation Chaos," even though the agency had no authority to operate domestically. It was trying to find links between antiwar groups and foreign powers, which were never found. The military eavesdropped on radio messages in the late 1960s and early 1970s in connection with civil disorders, with full knowledge that such eavesdropping was illegal. In 1969, President RICHARD M. NIXON authorized taps on four journalists and thirteen government employees, allegedly to discover who was leaking foreign affairs information; these taps were kept in operation for over two years even though it quickly became clear that nothing pertinent to the leaks was being learned.

In reaction to these revelations and to the Watergate abuses, Congress in 1978 banned electronic surveillance for foreign national security purposes within the United States, without prior judicial approval. Under the Foreign Intelligence Surveillance Act (FISA) the executive branch no longer has inherent power to tap and bug for foreign intelligence-gathering purposes. With the approval of the attorney general, a federal official may apply to a specially selected court (composed of regular federal judges) which sits in secret. The court must issue a warrant if it finds probable cause to believe, first, that the target is a foreign power or agent, and, second, that certain procedures to minimize the interception have been set up; an American who, on behalf of a foreign power, engages in clandestine intelligence gathering that may involve criminal activity, may be considered a foreign agent, though not for activities protected by the FIRST AMENDMENT. Other control procedures are also established, though they are less stringent than those for electronic surveillance for crime detection under Title III. The FISA applies to foreign intelligence gathering by any type of electronic, mechanical, or other surveillance device, but not to physical break-ins, mail openings, and the like—these remain subject to the more traditional claims of inherent presidential power.

Although the FISA was held constitutional by a federal district court, there is still no definitive Supreme Court ruling on the existence of inherent executive power to break into homes for foreign national security purposes or to eavesdrop on Americans without a warrant.

HERMAN SCHWARTZ

Bibliography

CARR, JAMES G. 1977 (1981 supp.) *The Law of Electronic Surveillance.* New York: Clark Boardman.

SCHWARTZ, HERMAN 1977 *Taps, Bugs, and Fooling the People.* New York: Field Foundation.

UNITED STATES, CONGRESS, SENATE SELECT COMMITTEE TO STUDY GOVERNMENTAL OPERATIONS WITH RESPECT TO INTELLIGENCE ACTIVITIES 1976 *III Final Report.* 94th Congress, 2d session.

NATURAL GAS REGULATION

See: Economic Regulation

NATURALIZATION

Naturalization was defined by the Supreme Court in BOYD V. NEBRASKA EX REL. THAYER (1892) as "the act of adopting a foreigner, and clothing him with the privileges of a native citizen." Congress, under Article I, section 8, of the Constitution, has complete discretion to determine what classes of ALIENS are eligible for naturalization; an individual may claim naturalization as a right only upon compliance with the terms that Congress imposes. Exercising this discretion in the Immigration and Nationality Act of 1952, Congress denied eligibility to those persons who advocate the violent overthrow of the government and limited it to those who have resided in the United States for at least five years, are of "good moral character," and take an oath in open court to support and defend the Constitution, to bear true faith and allegiance to the same, and to bear arms or perform noncombative service in behalf of the United States.

Any naturalized citizen who is proved to have taken the oath of citizenship with mental reservations or to have concealed acts or affiliations that, under the law, would disqualify him for naturalization, is subject, upon these facts being conclusively shown in a proper proceeding, to cancellation of his certificate of naturalization. While this action remedies a fraud on the naturalization court that the United States would otherwise be powerless to correct, it subjects a naturalized citizen to possible loss of CITIZENSHIP from which native-born citizens are spared and thus arguably calls into question Justice WILLIAM O. DOUGLAS's announcement in *Schneider v. Rusk* (1964) that "the rights of citizenship of the native-born and of the naturalized person are of the same dignity and are co-extensive."

Although naturalization normally is accomplished through individual application and official response on the basis of general congressional rules, naturalization can also be extended to members of a group, without consideration of their individual fitness. Such collective naturalization can be authorized by Congress, as in cases of naturalization of all residents of an annexed TERRITORY or of a territory made a state, or by a treaty.

RALPH A. ROSSUM

Bibliography

GORDON, CHARLES and ROSENFIELD, HARRY N. 1984 *Immigration Law and Procedure,* Vol. 3, chaps. 14–18. New York: Matthew Bender.

HERTZ, MICHAEL T. 1976 Limits to the Naturalization Power. *Georgetown Law Journal* 64:1007–1045.

NATURAL LAW

See: Higher Law; Natural Rights

NATURAL RIGHTS AND THE CONSTITUTION

The Constitution as it came from the Philadelphia convention contained no bill of rights. Indeed, the word right (or rights) appears only once in it, and there only in the context of Congress's power to promote the progress of science and useful arts "by securing for limited Times to Authors and Inventors the exclusive Right to their respective Writings and Discoveries" (Article 1, section 8). In the view of the Anti-Federalists, the Constitution should have begun with a statement of general principles, or of "admirable maxims," as PATRICK HENRY said in the Virginia ratifying debates, such as the statement in the VIRGINIA DECLARATION OF RIGHTS of 1776: "That all men are by nature equally free and independent, and have certain inherent rights, of which, when they enter a state of society, they cannot by any compact deprive or divest their posterity; namely, the enjoyment of life and liberty, with the means of acquiring and possessing property, and pursuing and obtaining happiness and safety." In short, a bill of rights ought to be affixed to the Constitution containing a statement of natural rights.

The Federalists disagreed. They conceded that the Constitution might properly contain a statement of *civil* rights, and they were instrumental in the adoption of the first ten amendments which we know as the BILL OF RIGHTS, but they were opposed to a general statement of first principles in the text of the Constitution. However true, such a statement, by reminding citizens of the right to abolish government, might serve to undermine government, even a government established on those principles. And, as Publius insisted, the Constitution was based on those principles: "the Constitution is itself, in every rational sense, and to every useful purpose, A BILL OF RIGHTS" (THE FEDERALIST #84). It is a bill of natural rights, not because it contains a compendium of those rights but because it is an expression of the natural right of everyone to govern himself and to specify the terms according to which he agrees to give up his natural freedom by submitting to the rules of civil government. The Constitution emanates from us, "THE PEOPLE of the United States," and here in its first sentence, said Publius, "is a better recognition of popular rights than volumes of those aphorisms which make the principal figure in several of our State bills of rights and which would sound much better in a treatise of ethics than in a constitution of government." Natural rights point or lead to government, a government with the power to secure rights, and only secondarily to limitations on governmental power.

This is not to deny the revolutionary character of natural rights, or perhaps more precisely, of the natural rights teaching. The United States began in a revolution accompanied by an appeal to the natural and unalienable rights of life, liberty, and the pursuit of happiness. But these words of the DECLARATION OF INDEPENDENCE are followed immediately by the statement that "to secure these rights, Governments are instituted among Men." Natural rights point or lead to government in the same way that the Declaration of Independence points or leads to the Constitution: the rights, which are possessed by all men equally by nature (or in the state of nature), require a well-governed civil society for their security.

The link between the state of nature and civil society, or between natural rights and government, is supplied by the laws of nature. The laws of nature in this (modern) sense must be distinguished from the natural law as understood in the Christian tradition, for example. According to Christian teaching, the natural law consists of commands and prohibitions derived from the inclinations (or the natural ordering of the passions and desires), and is enforced, ultimately, by the sanction of divine punishment. According to Hobbes and Locke, however—the principal authors in the school of natural rights—the laws of nature are merely deductions from the rights of nature and ultimately from the right of self-preservation. Because everyone has a natural right to do whatever is necessary to preserve his own life, the state of nature comes to be indistinguishable from the state of war where, in Hobbes's familiar phrase, life is solitary, poor, nasty, brutish, and short; even in Locke's more benign version, and for the same reason, the state of nature is characterized by many unendurable "inconveniences." In short, in the natural condition of man the enjoyment of natural rights is uncertain and human life itself becomes insufferable. What is required for self-preservation is peace, and, as rational beings, men can come to understand "the fundamental law of nature" which is, as Hobbes formulates it, "to seek peace, and follow it." From this is derived the second law of nature, that men enter in a contract with one another according to which they surrender their natural rights to an absolute sovereign who is instituted by the contract and who, from that time forward, represents their rights. More briefly stated, each person must consent to be governed, which he does by laying down his natural right to govern himself. In Locke's version, political society is formed when everyone "has quitted his natural power"—a power he holds as of natural right—and "resigned it up into the hands of the community." In the same way, Americans of 1776 were guided by "the Laws of Nature and of Nature's God" when they declared their independence and constituted themselves as a new political community. Commanding nothing—for these are not laws in the proper sense of commands that must be obeyed—the laws of nature point to government as the way to secure rights, a government that derives its "just powers from the consent of the governed." (See SOCIAL COMPACT THEORY.)

It is important to understand that in the natural rights teaching neither civil society nor government exists by nature. By nature everyone is sovereign with respect to himself. Civil society is an artificial person to which this real person, acting in concert with others, surrenders his natural and sovereign powers, and upon this agreement civil society becomes the sovereign with respect to those who consented to the surrender. It is civil society, in the exercise of this sovereign power, that institutes and empowers government. So it was that "we [became] the People of the United States" in 1776 and, in 1787–1788, that we ordained and established "this CONSTITUTION for the United States of America." The Constitution is the product of the "will" of the sovereign people of the United States (*The Federalist* #78).

The power exercised by this people is almost unlimited. Acting through its majority, the people is free to determine the form of government (for, as the Declaration of Independence indicates, any one of several forms of government—democratic, republican, or even monarchical—may serve to secure rights) as well as the organization of that government and the powers given and withheld from it. It will make these decisions in the light of its purpose, which is to secure the rights of the persons authorizing it. This is why the doctrine of natural rights, if only secondarily, leads or points to limitations on government; and this is why the people of the United States decided to withhold some powers and, guided by the new "science of politics" (*The Federalist* #9), sought to limit power by means of a number of institutional arrangements.

Among the powers withheld was the power to coerce religious opinion. Government can have authority over natural rights, said THOMAS JEFFERSON, "only as we have submitted [that authority] to them, [and] the rights of conscience we never submitted, we could not submit."

Among the institutional arrangements was the SEPARATION OF POWERS, and the scheme of representation made possible by extending "the sphere of society so as to take in a greater variety of parties and interests thus making it less probable that a majority of the whole will have a common motive to invade the rights of other citizens" (*The Federalist* #10). First among these rights, according to Locke, is the property right, for, differing somewhat from Hobbes in this respect, Locke understood the natural right of self-preservation primarily as the right to acquire property. Publius had this in mind when he said that "the first object of government . . . [is] the protection of different and unequal faculties of acquiring property" (*The Federalist* #10). The large (commercial) republic is a means of securing this natural right as well as the natural right of conscience, for, within its spacious boundaries, there will be room for a "multiplicity of [religious] sects" as well as a "multiplicity of [economic] interests" (*The Federalist* #51).

Just as a "respect to the opinions of mankind" required Americans to announce the formation of a people that was assuming its "separate and equal station . . . among the powers of the earth," so a jealous concern for their natural rights required this people to *write* a Constitution in which they not only empowered government but, in various complex ways, limited it.

WALTER BERNS

Bibliography

JAFFA, HARRY V. 1975 *The Conditions of Freedom: Essays in Political Philosophy.* Pages 149–160. Baltimore: Johns Hopkins University Press.

STORING, HERBERT J. 1978 The Constitution and the Bill of Rights. Pages 32–48 in M. Judd Harmon, ed., *Essays on the Constitution of the United States.* Port Washington, N.Y.: Kennikat.

STRAUSS, LEO 1953 *Natural Right and History.* Introduction and chap. 5. Chicago: University of Chicago Press.

NAVIGABLE WATERS

See: Subjects of Commerce

NEAGLE, IN RE

See: Sawyer, Lorenzo

NEAL v. DELAWARE
103 U.S. 370 (1881)

Justice JOHN MARSHALL HARLAN, for a majority of 7–2, laid down an important principle in JURY DISCRIMINATION cases: the fact that no black person had ever been summoned as a juror in the courts of a state presents "a *prima facie* case of denial, by the officers charged with the selection of grand and petit jurors, of that equality of protection" secured by the FOURTEENTH AMENDMENT. *Neal* differed from VIRGINIA V. RIVES (1880), here reaffirmed, because the prisoner in *Rives* had merely alleged the exclusion of blacks, which the state denied, while here the state conceded the exclusion. The state chief justice explained that "the great body of black men residing in this State are utterly unqualified by want of intelligence, experience or moral integrity, to sit on juries." Harlan called that a "violent presumption." *Neal* did nothing to prevent the elimination of blacks from juries in the South, because in the absence of a state confession of constitutional error, blacks had the burden of proving deliberate and systematic exclusion of their race. (See NORRIS V. ALABAMA, 1935.)

LEONARD W. LEVY

NEAR v. MINNESOTA
283 U.S. 697 (1931)

Although GITLOW V. NEW YORK (1925) had accepted for the sake of argument that the FIRST AMENDMENT'S FREEDOM OF SPEECH guarantees were applicable to the states through the DUE PROCESS clause of the FOURTEENTH AMENDMENT, *Near* was the first decision firmly adopting the INCORPORATION DOCTRINE and striking down a state law in its totality on free speech grounds. Together with STROMBERG V. CALIFORNIA (1931), decided in the same year and also with a 5–4 majority opinion by Chief Justice CHARLES EVANS HUGHES, *Near* announced a new level of Supreme Court concern for freedom of speech.

A Minnesota statute authorizing injunctions against a "malicious, scandalous and defamatory newspaper, magazine or other periodical" had been applied against a paper that had accused public officials of neglect of duty, illicit relations with gangsters, and graft. Arguing that hostility to PRIOR RESTRAINT AND CENSORSHIP are the very core of the First Amendment, the Court struck down the statute. Yet *Near*, the classic precedent against prior restraints, is also the doctrinal starting point for most defenses of prior restraint. The Court commented in OBITER DICTUM that "the protection even as to previous restraint is not absolutely unlimited," and listed as exceptions wartime obstruction of recruitment and publication of military secrets, OBSCENITY, INCITEMENTS to riot or forcible overthrow of the government, and words that "may have all the effect of force."

In emphasizing the special First Amendment solicitude for criticisms of public officials, whether true or false, *Near* was an important way station between

Gitlow's implicit acceptance of the constitutional survival in the United States of the English COMMON LAW concept of SEDITIOUS LIBEL and the rejection of that concept in NEW YORK TIMES V. SULLIVAN (1964).

MARTIN SHAPIRO

NEBBIA v. NEW YORK
291 U.S. 502 (1934)

Both the desperate economic conditions in the American dairy industry and the legal responses to the dairy crisis, during the depression years 1929–1933, exemplified the dilemmas that the Great Depression posed for American law. Vast, unmarketable surpluses of fluid milk and other dairy products, widespread mortgage foreclosures in dairy centers of rural America, and wild swings in dairy prices and consumption, all spelled extreme distress for the industry and its marketing institutions.

Among the states that responded with new legislation was New York, whose dairy industry constituted about half the value of its farm income and served the great urban concentration of population in the city of New York and its metropolitan area. In framing a program to deal with the crisis, New York's lawmakers knew they were forced to walk through a constitutional minefield. Despite provisions of the 1933 federal AGRICULTURAL ADJUSTMENT ACT intended to give the states some latitude in control of dairy commerce involving interstate milksheds, federal district courts around the country had struck down state laws seeking to control interstate movements of fluid milk or the terms on which it could be marketed. In addition, even laws seeking to regulate only in-state production and distribution were challenged as invalid under the AFFECTED WITH A PUBLIC INTEREST rule; indeed, in numerous previous decisions the Supreme Court had in obiter dicta listed dairies among the enterprises that clearly were "ordinary" or "purely private" businesses, not affected with a public interest and therefore not subject to price regulation. In NEW STATE ICE CO. V. LIEBMANN (1932), for example, the Court had denied the legislature of Oklahoma authority to regulate ice manufacturing and selling on the ground that it was "a business as essentially private in its nature as the business of the grocer, the dairyman, the butcher, the baker, the shoemaker, or the tailor."

Mindful of this background, the New York legislature conducted a lengthy investigation of the fluid milk industry and its travails. In addition to making a record, thereby, as to the condition of the farmers and distribution system, the price collapse and its consequences, and the extensive effects of the crisis on the state's economy, when the legislature drafted a new Milk Control Law in March 1933, it explicitly denominated it as emergency legislation and provided for its termination one year following. By this maneuver, the legislators hoped to slip the knot of "affected with a public interest" and give the Milk Control Law safe harbor in the EMERGENCY POWERS and POLICE POWER area in the event that courts proved unimpressed with the statute's assertion that the milk industry was "a business affecting the public health and interest."

Like similar legislation enacted in New Jersey, Illinois, and other dairy states, the New York law included power to fix prices in the virtually plenary grant of authority to the milk control agency that was established. The board was also empowered to license producers, establish maximum retail prices and the spread between prices paid producers and charged consumers, and regulate interstate fluid milk entrants to the New York market.

The price-fixing provision came before the bench in an appeal from the conviction of a storekeeper for selling milk at retail below the price established by the new milk control agency. When the New York Court of Appeals affirmed the conviction, the case was carried to the Supreme Court. Counsel contended that price control violated the "affected with a public interest" standard, subjecting Nebbia to improper regulation in violation of his FOURTEENTH AMENDMENT right to DUE PROCESS.

By a 5–4 vote, the Court upheld the New York law. Justice OWEN J. ROBERTS's opinion did not rest on the narrow grounds that the milk control program was of an emergency nature; instead, it addressed in broadest possible terms the nature of the police power and the constitutional limitations upon which states might exercise it. The long history of the "affected with a public interest" doctrine came to an end with *Nebbia,* the majority opinion going back to Chief Justice MORRISON R. WAITE's language in *Munn v. Illinois* (1877). (See GRANGER CASES.) Waite had used the phrase "affected with a public interest" as the equivalent of "subject to the exercise of the police power," the Court now declared: "It is clear that there is no closed class or category of businesses affected with a public interest, and the function of courts in the application of the Fifth and Fourteenth Amendments is to determine in each case whether circumstances vindicate the challenged regulation as a reasonable exertion of governmental authority or condemn it as arbitrary or discriminatory." By repudiating the doctrine of affection with a public interest, which was based on SUBSTANTIVE DUE PROCESS OF LAW, the Court weakened the due process clause as a bastion of property rights. The due process clause, Roberts observed, made no mention of sales, prices, business, contracts, or other incidents of property. Nothing, he added, was sacred about the prices one might charge. The state, Roberts declared, "may regulate a business in any of its aspects, including the prices to be charged for the products or commodities it sells." The crux of this opinion, which prefigured a transformation in constitutional law, was this statement: "So far as the requirement of due process is concerned . . . a state is free to adopt whatever economic policy may reasonably be deemed to promote public welfare, and to enforce that policy by legislation adapted to its purpose. The courts are without authority either to declare such policy, or, when it is declared by the legislature, to override it."

Handed down not long after HOME BUILDING & LOAN ASSOCIATION V. BLAISDELL (1934), a decision that did extensive damage to once sacrosanct CONTRACT CLAUSE doctrine, the *Nebbia* decision was anathema to property-minded conservatives who saw the juridical scaffolding for VESTED RIGHTS as collapsing in the early New Deal years, even before the Court fight and the wholesale reversal of doctrine that came after 1935. Indeed, *Nebbia* may be read as present-day constitutional law.

HARRY N. SCHEIBER

Bibliography

GOLDSMITH, IRVING B. and WINKS, GORDON W. 1938 Price Fixing: From *Nebbia* to *Guffey*. Pages 531–553 in Douglas B. Maggs, ed., *Selected Essays on Constitutional Law.* Chicago: Association of American Law Schools.

NEBRASKA PRESS ASSOCIATION v. STUART

427 U.S. 539 (1976)

In *Nebraska Press Association v. Stuart* the Court addressed for the first time the constitutionality of a prior restraint on pretrial publicity about a criminal case. Noting the historic conflict between the FIRST and Sixth AMENDMENTS, the Court refused to give either priority, recognizing that the accused's right to an unbiased jury must be balanced with the interests in a free press. At issue was a narrowly tailored GAG ORDER in a sensational murder case restraining the press from publishing or broadcasting accounts of the accused's confessions or admissions or "strongly implicative" facts until the jury was impaneled.

Applying the standard of DENNIS V. UNITED STATES (1951) and inquiring whether "the gravity of the 'evil,' discounted by its improbability justified such invasion of free speech as is necessary to avoid the danger," the Court struck down the gag order. To determine whether the record supported the extraordinary measure of a prior restraint on publication, the Court considered the nature and extent of pretrial news coverage, the likelihood that other measures would mitigate the effects of unrestrained pretrial publicity, and the effectiveness of a restraining order to prevent the threatened danger, and, further, analyzed the order's terms and the problems of managing and enforcing it. The gag order was critically flawed because it prohibited publication of information gained from other clearly protected sources.

Justice WILLIAM J. BRENNAN, joined by Justices POTTER J. STEWART and THURGOOD MARSHALL, concurring, argued that a prior restraint on the press is an unconstitutionally impermissible method for enforcing the Sixth Amendment. Refusing to view the First and Sixth Amendments as in irreconcilable conflict, he noted that there were numerous less restrictive means by which a fair trial could be ensured. Justice BYRON R. WHITE doubted whether prior restraints were ever justifiable, but did not believe it wise so to announce in the first case raising that question. Justice LEWIS F. POWELL emphasized the heavy burden resting on a party seeking to justify a prior restraint.

KIM MCLANE WARDLAW

(SEE ALSO: *Free Press/Fair Trial; Prior Restraint and Censorship.*)

NECESSARY AND PROPER CLAUSE

The enumeration of powers in Article I, section 8, gives Congress the power to do such specific things as "regulate commerce . . . among the several States" and "raise and support Armies." At the end of the list is the power "to make all Laws which shall be necessary and proper for carrying into execution the foregoing Powers, and all other Powers vested by this Constitution in the Government of the United States, or in any Department or Officer thereof." The Anti-Federalists called this the "elastic clause" or the "sweeping power." They predicted it would centralize all governmental power in the national government. JAMES MADISON denied this charge in THE FEDERALIST #23. He observed that the clause spoke of power to execute only those powers that were specified elsewhere in the document, and that the power vested by the clause would have been implicit in the grant of other powers even without the clause. (See IMPLIED POWERS.) The clause, therefore, did not conflict with the principle of enumerated national powers, Madison argued. Events have vindicated Anti-Federalist fears.

THOMAS JEFFERSON and ALEXANDER HAMILTON took opposing positions on the meaning of the word "necessary" in the clause during their debate in 1791 on the constitutionality of the first BANK OF THE UNITED STATES ACT. Hamilton argued that the nation needed a BROAD CONSTRUCTION of congressional powers so that the government could employ a wide variety of means useful to the discharge of its responsibilities. Jefferson countered that a broad construction would enable Congress to encroach upon the reserved powers of the states whenever its measures might serve as means to ends within its enumerated powers. To safeguard STATES' RIGHTS, such encroachments should be permitted only when "absolutely necessary," said Jefferson—only, that is, when failure to encroach would nullify the grant of federal power. Hamilton's view prevailed first with President GEORGE WASHINGTON in 1791 and later in the Supreme Court, when JOHN MARSHALL's opinion in MCCULLOCH V. MARYLAND upheld the second national bank in 1819.

Marshall construed national powers in terms of a few authorized national ends. Most important, he understood the COMMERCE POWER and related powers as authorizing the pursuit of national prosperity and the various military and diplomatic powers as authorizing the pursuit of national security. This ends-oriented conception of national powers was the view of *The Federalist* #41, which also gave greatest emphasis to the goals of national prosperity and security. When Marshall held in *McCulloch* that Congress could pursue its authorized ends without regard for the reserved powers of the states, he was saying, in effect, that Congress could do what it wanted to relative to state powers so long as it gave the right reasons. Marshall suggested a hierarchy of constitutional values, with state powers subordinated to Congress's version of national prosperity and security. The opinion thus brought virtually all state powers within Congress's potential control, because, with changing conditions, Congress might consider any social practice (education, for example) as an instrument of the nation's prosperity and security.

But to suggest that Congress can act for the right reasons is not to say that Congress can disregard states' rights at will. Marshall's theory of the necessary and proper clause was still consistent with the idea of enumerated powers because it presupposed a limited number of nationally authorized ends. Marshall thus stated that the judiciary would be prepared to invalidate pretextual uses of national power to reach ends reserved to the states. In the twentieth century, the Supreme Court refused to give effect to Marshall's commitment to invalidate pretextual uses of congressional power, thus fulfilling the Anti-Federalist prediction of what the clause eventually would be.

The Court first upheld pretextual uses of power as means to eliminating state bank notes in VEAZIE BANK V. FENNO (1869) and margarine colored to resemble butter in MCRAY V. UNITED STATES (1904). These acts were aimed at what Congress considered the nation's economic health. They were therefore valid under Marshall's theory of the commerce power. But, in the meanwhile, the Court had moved away from Marshall's conception to a limited view of the nation's commerce as those things that crossed state lines. Pretexts were necessary unless the Court chose to abandon this artificial view; instead of correcting the mistake which necessitated pretexts, the Court established precedents for them. Later the Court upheld enactments that obviously were not aimed at the national goals implicit in Congress's enumerated powers. The Court thus upheld the TAXING POWER as a weapon against drug abuse in UNITED STATES V. DOREMUS (1919) and the commerce power as a means of combating gambling, illicit sex, and other practices usually said to be reserved to the STATE POLICE POWER, as in HOKE V. UNITED STATES (1913). These decisions turned Marshall's theory of the necessary and proper clause on its head. Where Marshall had upheld incursions into state powers as means to nationally authorized ends, the Court was now upholding national powers as means to state ends. As a result the NATIONAL POLICE POWER can today be used to reach an indefinite variety of purposes, and the necessary and proper clause authorizes almost anything that might be useful for addressing what Congress views as a national problem.

Limits on national power do remain in the BILL OF RIGHTS, in other sources of individual rights such as the Civil War amendments, and in principles derived from the Constitution's institutional arrangements. Because the states do constitute a part of those arrangements, the Court still says it will protect various state rights to participate in federal government action, such as the right to equal representation in the Senate. But such states' rights limitations on national power are of little contemporary significance. For the most part, the necessary and proper clause has been construed in a way that has destroyed the notion that the enumeration of powers limits the national government.

SOTIRIOS A. BARBER

Bibliography

BERNS, WALTER 1961 The Meaning of the Tenth Amendment. Pages 126–148 in Robert A. Goldwin, ed., *A Nation of States.* Chicago: Rand McNally.

GUNTHER, GERALD, ED. 1969 *John Marshall's Defense of McCulloch v. Maryland.* Stanford, Calif.: Stanford University Press.

NELSON, SAMUEL (1792–1873)

On March 5, 1845, Samuel Nelson became a Justice of the Supreme Court and judge of the Second Circuit. President JOHN TYLER nominated the New York Democrat in the belief that his record of moderation compiled over twenty-one years in the New York courts, including thirteen as associate and then chief justice of the state supreme court, would resolve eighteen months of wrangling between the chief executive and the Senate over the high court vacancy. Unanimous Senate confirmation made Nelson the Court's thirty-first justice.

Nelson's most significant contribution to constitutional development involved the admiralty clause in Article III, section 2, of the Constitution. That clause specified that the federal courts should exclusively exercise the ADMIRALTY AND MARITIME JURISDICTION. He interpreted the clause to extend federal JURISDICTION while retaining for the states an area of constitutional responsibility. Nelson first suggested the position, later adopted by the full Court in PROPELLER GENESEE CHIEF V. FITZHUGH (1851), that where INTERSTATE COMMERCE was involved the admiralty clause extended federal jurisdiction to inland rivers and lakes (*New Jersey Steam Navigation Co. v. Merchant's Bank,* 1848). He carefully rooted this expansion in an 1845 act that established admiralty jurisdiction in "certain cases, upon the lakes and navigable waters connecting with" the oceans. Nelson left to state courts responsibility for vessels that operated on lakes and rivers exclusively within the same state. This interpretation rested on two constitutional themes that pervaded his other opinions: congressional domination of matters of law as opposed to constitutional principles, and belief in a scheme of dual SOVEREIGNTY.

Even in this single instance of doctrinal leadership Nelson lost the initiative. New members of the Court and the quickening tempo of commercial life in the western United States rendered his emphasis on dual sovereignty obsolete. Almost always eager for accommodation, he acquiesced. In 1869 he spoke for the Court in holding that from the time of *Genesee Chief* federal admiralty jurisdiction on the lakes and rivers stemmed from the JUDICIARY ACT OF 1789 rather than from the act of 1845 (*The Eagle v. Frazer,* 1869). Through this about-face, Nelson acknowledged that litigants could use federal district courts in admiralty cases arising in INTRASTATE COMMERCE.

The concept of dual sovereignty also informed his attitude toward the COMMERCE CLAUSE. In the LICENSE CASES (1847) and PASSENGER CASES (1849) he concurred with Chief Justice ROGER B. TANEY's opinions sustaining STATE POLICE POWER, and in the 1849 cases he was the only Justice not to write a separate opinion. When Congress acted under the commerce clause, Nelson supported national power. Speaking for the Court in *Pennsylvania v. Wheeling and Belmont Bridge Co.* (1856), his most important commerce clause opinion, he confirmed Congress's power to deal with navigation and interstate commerce on inland rivers.

Nelson's constitutional jurisprudence also stressed JUDICIAL SELF-RESTRAINT and SEPARATION OF POWERS. He voted only once with a majority to strike down a federal law in *Hepburn v. Griswold* (1870). He deferred to presidential management of FOREIGN AFFAIRS, but dissented in the PRIZE CASES (1863) because he thought President ABRAHAM LINCOLN had infringed on Congress's war-making powers.

Nelson believed that federal JUDICIAL POWER should protect slaveholders, but that the Court should exercise it benignly. Acting on this belief, he persuaded the Court in 1856 to rehear DRED SCOTT V. SANDFORD (1857). In his draft opinion for the Court, he argued that the laws of Missouri made Scott a slave and that the Court could ignore the questions of the legal status of slaves and the constitutionality of the MISSOURI COMPROMISE. This position raised the hackles of Justices JOHN MCLEAN and BENJAMIN R. CURTIS, and Chief Justice Taney took from Nelson responsibility for preparing the Court's opinion. Nelson, believing that the Chief Justice's decision to reach major issues was unwise, submitted his draft opinion for the Court as his own, even retaining the pronoun "we" in the printed version.

Nelson continued in the post-Civil War era as a

hardworking jurist and able legal technician. He agreed in February 1871 to serve on the *Alabama* Claims Commission. His appointment by a Republican president underscored as much his reputation as an impartial jurist as it did his knowledge of admiralty, maritime, and prize law.

Nelson resigned from the Court on November 28, 1872. Often described as a doughface (a Northerner who took a southern view on slavery), Nelson is better understood as a political moderate concerned about the fate of the Union, disposed to antislavery rather than proslavery views, and committed to the position that the judicial role should emphasize discretion, restraint, and deference to legislative leadership. In view of his twenty-six years on the Court, he contributed surprisingly little to constitutional jurisprudence.

KERMIT L. HALL

Bibliography

GATELL, FRANK OTTO 1969 Samuel Nelson. Pages 817–839 in Leon Friedman and Fred L. Israel, eds., *The Justices of the United States Supreme Court 1789–1969: Their Lives and Major Opinions.* New York: Chelsea House.

NEW HAMPSHIRE SUPREME COURT v. PIPER
470 U.S. (1985)

In *Piper* the Supreme Court followed *United Building and Construction Trades Council v. Camden* (1984) and applied a two-step analysis for applying the PRIVILEGES AND IMMUNITIES clause of Article IV. The Court held, 8–1, that New Hampshire's rule limiting the practice of law to New Hampshire citizens violated the clause. First, the clause was properly invoked; doing business in the state is a privilege that is "fundamental" to the preservation of interstate harmony. Second, the state had not sufficiently justified its exclusion of Piper, who lived in Vermont, 400 yards from the New Hampshire border, and intended to maintain a law office in New Hampshire.

KENNETH L. KARST

NEW JERSEY v. T.L.O.
469 U.S. (1985)

In *New Jersey v. T.L.O.* a unanimous Supreme Court held that the FOURTH AMENDMENT's prohibition against unreasonable SEARCHES AND SEIZURES applies to searches of students conducted by public school officials. A majority of the Court (6–3) also held that school officials need not obtain a SEARCH WARRANT before searching a student under their authority and that their searches can be justified by a lower standard than probable cause to believe that the subject of the search has violated or is violating the law. Instead, the legality of the search depends on the reasonableness of the search under all the circumstances.

According to Justice BYRON R. WHITE's majority opinion, determining reasonableness requires a twofold inquiry: first, whether the search was justified at its inception, and, second, whether the search as actually conducted was reasonably related in its scope to the circumstances that initially justified it. Ordinarily, the search is justified at its inception if there are reasonable grounds for suspecting that the search will produce EVIDENCE that the student has violated or is violating either the law or the school rules. The search is permissible in scope if the measures adopted are reasonably related to the objectives of the search and are not excessively intrusive in light of the age and sex of the student and the nature of the infraction.

PATRICK DUTTON

Bibliography

DUTTON, PATRICK 1985 School Searches: Recent Applications of the United States and California Constitutions. *Journal of Juvenile Law* 9:106–128.

NEW JERSEY v. WILSON
7 Cranch 164 (1812)

This case was the vehicle by which the Supreme Court made a breathtaking expansion of the CONTRACT CLAUSE. In the colonial period New Jersey had granted certain lands to an Indian tribe in exchange for a waiver by the Indians of their claim to any other lands. The grant provided that the new lands would be exempt from taxation in perpetuity. In 1801, over forty years later, the Indians left the state after selling their lands with state permission. The legislation repealed the tax exemption statute and assessed the new owners, who challenged the constitutionality of the repeal act.

A unanimous Supreme Court, overruling the state court, held that the grant of a tax immunity was a contract protected by the contract clause. By some species of metaphysics the Court reasoned that the tax immunity attached to the land, not to the Indians, and therefore the new holders of the land were tax exempt. Chief Justice JOHN MARSHALL's opinion, voiding the state tax, gave a retroactive operation to the contract clause; the grant of tax immunity predated the clause by many years. More important, Marshall ignored the implications of his DOCTRINE that such a grant was a contract. According to this decision, a state, by an act of its legislature, may contract away its sovereign power of taxation and prevent a successive legislature from asserting that power. The doctrine of VESTED RIGHTS, here converted into a doctrine of tax immunity, handicapped the revenue capabilities of the states, raising grave questions about the policy of the opinion. As a matter of political or constitutional theory, the Court's assumption that an attribute of SOVEREIGNTY can be surrendered by a legislative grant to private parties or to their property was, at the least, dubious. Although Marshall restricted the states, he allowed them to cede tax powers by contract rather than thwart the exercise of those powers on rights vested by contract.

The growth of CORPORATIONS revealed the significance of the new doctrine of tax immunity. States and municipalities, eager to promote the establishment of banks, factories, turnpikes, railroads, and utilities, often granted corporations tax immunity or other tax advantages as an inducement to engage in such enterprises, and the corporations often secured their special privileges by corrupt methods. This case permitted the granting of tax preferences and constitutionally sanctioned political corruption and the reckless development of economic resources. But permission is not compulsion; the legislatures, not the judiciary, granted the contracts. The Court simply extended the contract clause beyond the intentions of its framers to protect vested rights and promote business needs.

LEONARD W. LEVY

NEW JERSEY COLONIAL CHARTERS

New Jersey received its first charter from its proprietors, John Berkeley and George Carteret, in 1664. The charter established representative institutions of government, contained a clause on RELIGIOUS LIBERTY similar to that in the RHODE ISLAND CHARTER of 1663, and guaranteed that only the general assembly could impose taxes. In 1676 Berkeley sold his share of New Jersey to Quakers, leaving Carteret proprietor of East New Jersey. In 1677 the Quaker proprietors issued a "Charter or Fundamental Laws, of West New Jersey," the work, probably, of WILLIAM PENN. The charter included clauses on liberty of conscience, TRIAL BY JURY, and several protections for the criminally accused; the charter is memorable, however, because it functioned as a written CONSTITUTION of FUNDAMENTAL LAW. It began with the provision that the "COMMON LAW or fundamental rights" of the colony should be "the foundation of the government, which is not to be altered by the Legislative authority . . . constituted according to these fundamentals. . . ." The legislature was enjoined to maintain the fundamentals and to make no laws contradicting or varying from them.

In 1682 a Quaker group headed by Penn gained control of East New Jersey and in the following year issued "The Fundamental Constitutions" for that province. The charter of 1683, which was modeled on the Pennsylvania Frame of Government of 1682 (see PENNSYLVANIA COLONIAL CHARTERS), recognized CONSCIENTIOUS OBJECTION, banned any ESTABLISHMENT OF RELIGION, paraphrased chapter 39 of MAGNA CARTA, and included a variety of provisions that resembled a bill of rights, far more numerous than in the English BILL OF RIGHTS of 1689. Although New Jersey became a royal colony in 1702, the seventeenth-century Quaker charters are significant evidence of the grip which CONSTITUTIONALISM had upon influential colonial thinkers.

LEONARD W. LEVY

Bibliography

ANDREWS, CHARLES MCLEAN 1936 *The Colonial Period of American History.* Vol. 3:138–180. New Haven, Conn.: Yale University Press.

NEW JERSEY PLAN

The adoption of the VIRGINIA PLAN by the CONSTITUTIONAL CONVENTION OF 1787 frightened state sovereignty supporters and nationalists from small states. A bicameral Congress apportioned on the basis of population would have enabled the great states to dominate the new government. On June 15, 1787, WILLIAM PATERSON of New Jersey introduced a substitute plan that retained the "purely federal" (confederated) character of the ARTICLES OF CONFEDERATION. Under the Article a unicameral Congress in which each state had one vote preserved the principle of state equality.

As CHARLES PINCKNEY observed, if New Jersey had an equal vote, she would "dismiss her scruples, and concur in the national system." The New Jersey plan, though merely amending the Articles, was a small states' nationalist plan, not a state sovereignty plan. It recommended a Congress with powers to regulate commerce and to raise revenue from import and stamp duties, and it would have authorized requisitions from the states enforceable by a national executive empowered to use the military against states defying national laws and treaties. The plan recommended a national judiciary with broad JURISDICTION, extending to cases arising out of the regulation of commerce and the collection of the revenue. The nucleus of the SUPREMACY CLAUSE, making national law the supreme law of the states, was also part of the plan. It was a warning to large-state nationalists that they would have to compromise on the issue of REPRESENTATION. The Committee of the Whole defeated the plan 7–3, with one state divided. The Convention was thereafter stymied until the GREAT COMPROMISE was adopted. (See CONSTITUTIONAL HISTORY, 1776–1789.)

LEONARD W. LEVY

Bibliography

BRANT, IRVING 1950 *James Madison: Father of the Constitution, 1787–1800.* Pages 46–54. Indianapolis: Bobbs-Merrill.

NEW ORLEANS v. DUKES
427 U.S. 297 (1976)

Only once since 1937 has the Supreme Court struck down a state ECONOMIC REGULATION as a denial of the EQUAL PROTECTION OF THE LAWS. That case was *Morey v. Doud* (1957). In *Dukes,* the Court unanimously overruled *Morey;* a per curiam opinion reaffirmed the appropriateness of the RATIONAL BASIS standard of review in testing economic regulations against the demands of both equal protection and SUBSTANTIVE DUE PROCESS.

Dukes involved a New Orleans ordinance prohibiting the sale of food from pushcarts in the French Quarter, but exempting vendors who had been selling from pushcarts for eight years. This GRANDFATHER CLAUSE, said the Court, was rationally related to the city's legitimate interest in preserving the area's distinctive character while accommodating substantial reliance interests of long-term businesses.

KENNETH L. KARST

NEWSMAN'S PRIVILEGE

See: Reporter's Privilege

NEW STATE ICE COMPANY v. LIEBMANN
285 U.S. 262 (1932)

An Oklahoma law required ice dealers to obtain a license before entering the market because their business was AFFECTED WITH A PUBLIC INTEREST. A 6–2 majority could find no exceptional circumstances such as monopoly or emergency—that is, no public interest in regulation—justifying the restriction and so struck down the law as a violation of DUE PROCESS. Echoing Justice OLIVER WENDELL HOLMES's dissent in TYSON & BROTHER V. BANTON (1927), Justice LOUIS D. BRANDEIS, with Justice HARLAN FISKE STONE concurring, insisted that the assessment of local conditions and requirements was a legislative concern. Seeking to justify a state's right to experiment with social and economic legislation, Brandeis wrote: ". . . we must be ever on our guard, lest we erect our prejudices into legal principles."

DAVID GORDON

(SEE ALSO: *Ribnik v. McBride, 1928; Nebbia v. New York, 1934.*)

NEW YORK v. BELTON

See: Automobile Searches

NEW YORK v. FERBER
458 U.S. 747 (1982)

This decision demonstrated the BURGER COURT's willingness to add to the list of categories of speech excluded from the FIRST AMENDMENT's protection. New York, like the federal government and most of the states, prohibits the distribution of material depicting sexual performances by children under age 16, whether or not the material constitutes OBSCENITY. After a New York City bookseller sold two such films to an undercover police officer, he was convicted under this law. The Supreme Court unanimously affirmed his conviction.

Justice BYRON R. WHITE, for the Court, denied that state power in this regulatory area was confined to the suppression of obscene material. The state's interest in protecting children against abuse was compelling; to prevent the production of such materials, it was necessary to forbid their distribution. Child PORNOGRAPHY—the visual depiction of sexual conduct by children below a specified age—was "a category of material outside the protection of the First Amendment."

The Court also rejected the argument that the law was overbroad, thus abandoning a distinction announced in BROADRICK V. OKLAHOMA (1973) to govern OVERBREADTH challenges. Henceforth the overbreadth doctrine would apply only in cases of "substantial overbreadth," whether or not the state sought to regulate the content of speech.

KENNETH L. KARST

NEW YORK v. MILN

See: *Mayor of New York v. Miln*

NEW YORK v. QUARLES

467 U.S. 649 (1984)

Justice WILLIAM REHNQUIST, for a 5–4 Supreme Court, announced a public safety exception to the MIRANDA RULES. In a situation where concern for the public safety must supersede adherence to MIRANDA V. ARIZONA (1966), the prosecution may use in EVIDENCE incriminating statements made during a custodial interrogation before the suspect receives notice of his constitutional rights. Here, the Court reinstated a conviction based on the evidence of a gun and information concerning its whereabouts. Dissenters disagreed on whether the case showed a threat to the public safety, but produced no principled argument against the exception to *Miranda.*

LEONARD W. LEVY

NEW YORK v. UNITED STATES

See: *Graves v. New York*

NEW YORK CENTRAL RAILROAD COMPANY v. WHITE

243 U.S. 188 (1917)

The New York Workmen's Compensation Act of 1914 made employers liable to compensate injured workers in certain cases without regard to fault. The statute thereby departed from time-honored COMMON LAW rules of liability, particularly the fellow-servant doctrine and contributory negligence. The act established a graduated scale of compensation based on the loss of earning power, prior wages, and the character and duration of the disability suffered. Death benefits would be paid according to the survivors' needs.

Here, a night watchman was injured while guarding tools and materials used in the construction of a new station and tracks designed for INTERSTATE COMMERCE. A 9–0 Supreme Court held that the watchman was not in interstate commerce within the meaning of the first EMPLOYERS' LIABILITY ACT. Justice MAHLON PITNEY, for the Court, declared that his work "bore no direct relation to interstate transportation." Pitney rejected claims that the New York act violated the FOURTEENTH AMENDMENT's prohibition against a TAKING OF PROPERTY without DUE PROCESS OF LAW and deprived both parties of the FREEDOM OF CONTRACT. "It needs no argument to show that such a rule [fellow-servant] is subject to modification or abrogation by a state upon proper occasion." Because "the public has a direct interest in this as affecting the common welfare," the Court sustained the act as a reasonable exercise of the STATE POLICE POWER. Pitney also rejected the argument that the exclusion of certain workers from the statute's coverage was an arbitrary classification in violation of the EQUAL PROTECTION clause of the Fourteenth Amendment. He concluded that the classification was reasonable in view of the "inherent risks" associated with the various occupations.

DAVID GORDON

NEW YORK CHARTER OF LIBERTIES AND PRIVILEGES

(October 30, 1683)

The first enactment of the first general assembly in New York was a statute but had the characteristics of a charter or CONSTITUTION of FUNDAMENTAL LAW. Its purpose was to establish a government "that Justice and Right may be Equally done to all persons . . . ," an early forerunner of the principle of EQUAL PROTECTION OF THE LAWS. After describing the organs of government and empowering every freeholder to vote for representatives, the statute paraphrased chapter 39 of MAGNA CARTA and provided that no taxes should be imposed but by the general assembly. Then followed protections of the rights of the criminally accused, including a right to INDICTMENT by GRAND JURY in criminal cases. Another provision of the document, after protecting RELIGIOUS LIBERTY, created a multiple ESTABLISHMENT OF RELIGION. It allowed the towns on Long Island to elect Christian ministers of their choice, to be supported by town rates, and declared that "all" the other Christian churches in the province were "priviledged Churches . . . Established" by law. Elsewhere in Christendom, an established church meant a church of a single denomination preferred over all others.

The Privy Council disallowed the statute in 1686. In 1691, after James II was overthrown, the general assembly substantially reenacted it but again it was disallowed, probably because it curbed the royal prerogative. Although the statute never became law, it is early evidence of the high regard that colonists had for Magna Carta, written guarantees of their liberties, and the principle that there should be no TAXATION WITHOUT REPRESENTATION.

LEONARD W. LEVY

Bibliography

ANDREWS, CHARLES MCLEAN 1936 *The Colonial Period of American History.* Vol. 3:114–121. New Haven, Conn.: Yale University Press.

NEW YORK TIMES CO. v. SULLIVAN 376 U.S. 254 (1964)

MARTIN LUTHER KING, JR., was arrested in Alabama in 1960 on a perjury charge. In New York a group of entertainers and civil rights activists formed a committee to help finance King's defense. They placed a full-page advertisement in the *New York Times* appealing for contributions. The ad charged that King's arrest was part of a campaign to destroy King's leadership of the movement to integrate public facilities and encourage blacks in the South to vote. It asserted that "Southern violators" in Montgomery had expelled King's student followers from college, ringed the campus with armed police, padlocked the dining hall to starve them into submission, bombed King's home, assaulted his person, and arrested him seven times for speeding, loitering, and other dubious offenses.

L. B. Sullivan, a city commissioner of Montgomery, filed a libel action in state court against the *Times* and four black Alabama ministers whose names had appeared as endorsers of the ad. He claimed that because his duties included supervision of the Montgomery police, the allegations against the police defamed him personally.

Under the common law as it existed in Alabama and most other states, the *Times* had little chance of winning. Whether the statements referred to Sullivan was a fact issue; if the jury found that readers would identify him, it was immaterial that the ad did not name him. Because the statements reflected adversely on Sullivan's professional reputation they were "libelous per se"; that meant he need not prove that he actually had been harmed. The defense of truth was not available because the ad contained factual errors (for example, police had not "ringed the campus," though they had been deployed nearby; King had been arrested four times, not seven). A few states recognized a privilege for good faith errors in criticism of public officials, but Alabama was among the majority that did not.

The jury awarded Sullivan $500,000. In the Alabama Supreme Court, the *Times* argued such a judgment was inconsistent with FREEDOM OF THE PRESS, but that court merely repeated what the United States Supreme Court had often said: "The First Amendment of the United States Constitution does not protect libelous publications."

When the case reached the Supreme Court in 1964, it was one of eleven libel claims, totaling $5,600,000, pending against the *Times* in Alabama. It was obvious that libel suits were being used to discourage the press from supporting the CIVIL RIGHTS movement in the South. The *Times* urged the Court to equate these uses of libel law with the discredited doctrine of SEDITIOUS LIBEL and to hold that criticism of public officials could never be actionable.

Only three Justices were willing to go that far. The majority adopted a more limited rule, holding that public officials could recover for defamatory falsehoods about their official conduct or fitness for office only if they could prove that the defendant had published with "actual malice." This was defined as "knowledge that [the statement] was false or with reckless disregard of whether it was false or not." The Court further held that this element had to be established by "clear and convincing proof," and that, unlike most factual issues, it was subject to independent review by appellate courts. The Court then reviewed Sullivan's evidence and determined that it did not meet the new standard.

The decision was an important breakthrough, not only for the press and the civil rights movement but also in FIRST AMENDMENT theory. Until then, vast areas of expression, including libel and commercial speech, had been categorically excluded from First Amendment protection. Also, the decision finally repudiated the darkest blot on freedom of expression in the history of the United States, the Sedition Act of 1798.

Over the next few years, the Court went out of its way to make the new rule effective. It defined "reckless disregard" narrowly (*St. Amant v. Thompson,* 1967). It extended the *Sullivan* rule to lesser public officials (*Rosenblatt v. Baer,* 1966), to candidates for public office (*Monitor Patriot Co. v. Roy,* 1971), to PUBLIC FIGURES (*Associated Press v. Walker,* 1967), and to criminal libel (*Garrison v. Louisiana,* 1964). After 1971 the Court retreated somewhat, declining to extend the *Sullivan* rule to private plaintiffs and permitting a de facto narrowing of the public figure category.

From its birth the rule has been criticized, by public officials and celebrities who believe it makes recovery too difficult, and by the news media, which argue that the rule still exposes them to long and expensive litigation, even though ultimately they usually win. The Court, however, has shown no inclination to revise the rule. In *Bose Corp. v. Consumers Union* (1984), the Court was invited to dilute it by abandoning independent appellate review of findings of "actual malice." The Court refused, holding such review essential "to preserve the precious liberties established and ordained by the Constitution."

DAVID A. ANDERSON

Bibliography

KALVEN, HARRY, JR. 1964 The New York Times Case: A Note on "The Central Meaning of the First Amendment." *Supreme Court Review* 1964:191–221.

PIERCE, SAMUEL R., JR. 1965 The Anatomy of an Historic Decision: *New York Times Co. v. Sullivan. North Carolina Law Review* 43:315–363.

NEW YORK TIMES CO. v. UNITED STATES

403 U.S. 713 (1971)

New York Times Co. v. United States, more commonly known as the Pentagon Papers case, is one of the landmarks of contemporary prior restraint doctrine. Only NEAR V. MINNESOTA (1931) rivals it as a case of central importance in establishing the FIRST AMENDMENT's particular and extreme aversion to any form of official restriction applied prior to the act of speaking or the act of publication.

The dramatic facts of the case served to keep it before the public eye even as it was being litigated and decided. On June 12, 1971, the *New York Times* commenced publication of selected portions of a 1968 forty-seven-volume classified Defense Department study entitled "History of United States Decision Making Process on Vietnam Policy" and a 1965 classified Defense Department study entitled "The Command and Control Study of the Tonkin Gulf Incident Done by the Defense Department's Weapons Systems Evaluation Group in 1965." Collectively these documents came to be known as the Pentagon Papers. Within a few days other major newspapers, including the *Washington Post,* the *Los Angeles Times,* the *Detroit Free Press,* the *Philadelphia Inquirer,* and the *Miami Herald* also commenced publication of the Pentagon Papers. The papers had been provided to the *New York Times* by Daniel Ellsberg, a former Defense Department official and former government consultant. Ellsberg had no official authority to take the Pentagon Papers; his turning over the papers to the *New York Times* was similarly unauthorized.

When the newspapers commenced publication, the United States was still engaged in fighting the VIETNAM WAR. Claiming that the publication of the Pentagon Papers jeopardized national security, the government sought an INJUNCTION against any further publication of the papers, including publication of scheduled installments yet to appear. In the United States District Court for the Southern District of New York, Judge Murray Gurfein issued a temporary restraining order against the *New York Times,* but then denied the government's request for a preliminary injunction against publication, finding that, in light of the extremely high hurdle necessary to justify a prior restraint against a newspaper, "the publication of these historical documents would [not] seriously breach the national security." (See PRIOR RESTRAINT AND CENSORSHIP.) The United States immediately appealed, and the Court of Appeals for the Second Circuit, on June 23, 1971, remanded the case for further consideration in light of documents filed by the United States indicating that publication might pose "grave and immediate danger to the security of the United States." The Second Circuit continued to enforce the stay it had previously issued, in effect keeping the *Times* under the restraint of the temporary restraining order. On the same day, however, the United States Court of Appeals for the District of Columbia Circuit, in a case involving the *Washington Post's* publication of the Pentagon Papers, affirmed a decision of the district court refusing to enjoin further publication. On June 24, the *New York Times* filed a petition for a WRIT OF CERTIORARI and motion for expedited consideration in the Supreme Court, and on the same day the United States asked that Court for a stay of the District of Columbia circuit's ruling in the *Washington Post* case. The two cases were consolidated and accelerated, with briefs filed on June

26, oral argument the same day, and a decision of the Supreme Court on June 30, only seventeen days after the first publication of the papers in the *New York Times.*

In a brief PER CURIAM opinion, the Supreme Court affirmed the District of Columbia Circuit, reversed the Second Circuit, and vacated the restraints. Noting the "heavy presumption" against prior restraints, and the consequent "heavy burden of . . . justification" necessary to support a prior restraint, the Court found that the United States had not met that especially heavy burden.

The Court's per curiam opinion was accompanied by a number of important separate opinions by individual Justices. Justices HUGO L. BLACK and WILLIAM O. DOUGLAS made it clear that in their view prior restraints were never permissible. Justice WILLIAM J. BRENNAN would not go this far, but found it noteworthy that "never before has the United States sought to enjoin a newspaper from publishing information in its possession." For him "only governmental allegation and proof that publication must inevitably, directly, and immediately cause the occurrence of an evil kindred to imperiling the safety of a transport already at sea [citing *Near v. Minnesota*] can support even the issuance of an interim restraining order." In agreeing that the restraint was improper, Justice THURGOOD MARSHALL emphasized the absence of statutory authorization for governmental action to enjoin a newspaper. And Justice JOHN MARSHALL HARLAN, joined by Chief Justice WARREN E. BURGER and Justice HARRY A. BLACKMUN, dissented. The dissenters were disturbed by the alacrity of the proceedings, and in addition thought that the executive's "constitutional primacy in the field of FOREIGN AFFAIRS" justified a restraint at least long enough to allow the executive to present its complete case for the necessity of restriction. The most doctrinally illuminating opinions, however, were those of Justices POTTER J. STEWART and BYRON R. WHITE. For them only the specific nature of the restriction rendered it constitutionally impermissible. Had the case involved criminal or civil sanctions imposed after publication—subsequent punishment rather than prior restraint—they indicated that the First Amendment would not have stood in the way.

As highlighted by the opinions of Justices Stewart and White, therefore, the *Pentagon Papers* case presents the problem of prior restraint in purest form. The judges had the disputed materials in front of them, and thus there was no question of a restraint on materials not before a court, or not yet published. And the evaluation of the likely effect of the materials was made by the judiciary, rather than by a censorship board, other administrative agency, or police officer. Under these circumstances, why might a prior restraint be unconstitutional when a subsequent punishment for publishing the same materials would be upheld? What justifies a constitutional standard higher for injunctions than for criminal sanctions? It cannot be that prior restraints in fact "prevent" more things from being published, for the deterrent effect of a criminal sanction is likely to inhibit publication at least as much as an injunction. Someone who is willing knowingly to violate the criminal law, in order to publish out of conscience, may also be willing to violate an injunction. Is the special aversion against prior restraint, visible in the Pentagon Papers case, based on principle, or is it little more than an anachronism inherited from John Milton and WILLIAM BLACKSTONE, and transferred from a milieu in which prior restraint was synonymous with unreviewable determinations of an administrative censorship board?

The result in the Pentagon Papers case was not inconsistent with prior cases. The case did, however, present more clearly the puzzling nature of the virtually absolute prohibition against prior restraints under circumstances in which subsequent punishment of the very same material would have been permissible. Yet the case is also significant for reasons that transcend the doctrine of prior restraint. When confronted with a constitutional objection to a governmental policy, a court typically must evaluate the justification for the policy, and assess the likelihood of some consequences that the policy is designed to prevent. When that consequence and the governmental attempt to forestall it relates to war, national security, or national defense, judicial deference to governmental assertions of likely consequences has traditionally been greatest, even if the putative restriction implicates activities otherwise protected by the Constitution. When national security has been invoked, constitutional protection has often been more illusory than real. At every level in the Pentagon Papers case the courts conducted their own independent assessments of the likely dangers to national security and to troops overseas. The Supreme Court's decision was at least partly a function of the Justices' unwillingness to accept governmental incantation of the phrase "national security" as dispositive. Certainly executive determinations concerning the effect of publications on national security still receive greater deference than do other executive predictions about the effect of publications. But the Pentagon Papers case stands for the proposition that even when national security is claimed the courts will scrutinize for themselves the necessity of restriction. The decision, therefore, speaks not only to prior restraint but also, and more pervasively, to the courts' willingness to protect constitutional rights even against wartime governmental restrictions imposed in the name of national security.

FREDERICK SCHAUER

Bibliography

HENKIN, LOUIS 1971 The Right to Know and the Duty to Withhold: The Case of the Pentagon Papers. *University of Pennsylvania Law Review* 120:271–280.

JUNGER, PETER 1971 Down Memory Lane: The Case of the Pentagon Papers. *Case Western Reserve Law Review* 23:3–75.

KALVEN, HARRY, JR. 1971 Foreword: Even When a Nation Is at War. *Harvard Law Review* 85:3–36.

NIEMOTKO v. MARYLAND 340 U.S. 268 (1951)

The VINSON COURT here unanimously reversed the convictions of two Jehovah's Witnesses who had been charged with disorderly conduct for attempting to hold religious services in a city park without a permit. Local officials had refused to issue the permit, citing ordinances or administrative standards that governed the procedure, but such permits had been routinely approved for other religious and patriotic groups. The city's refusal to issue a permit to the Jehovah's Witnesses under these circumstances, the Court held, was both an unconstitutional prior restraint on speech and a denial of EQUAL PROTECTION.

MICHAEL E. PARRISH

NINETEENTH AMENDMENT

Ratification of the women's suffrage amendment in 1920 marked the culmination of a struggle spanning three quarters of a century. Under the leadership of organizations including the National Woman's Suffrage Association and the National Women's Party, over 2 million women participated in some 900 campaigns before state and federal legislators, party officials, and referendum voters. By the time the amendment was adopted, a majority of the states had already given some recognition to women's VOTING RIGHTS.

Political agitation for enfranchisement began in 1848, at the first women's rights convention in Seneca Falls, New York. In its Declaration of Sentiments, the convention included suffrage as one of the "inalienable rights" to which women were entitled. As the century progressed, the vote assumed increasing importance, both as a symbolic affirmation of women's equality and as a means to address a vast array of sex-based discrimination in employment, education, domestic law, and related areas. Once the Supreme Court ruled in MINOR V. HAPPERSETT (1875) that suffrage was not one of the PRIVILEGES AND IMMUNITIES guaranteed by the FOURTEENTH AMENDMENT to women as citizens, the necessity for a state or federal constitutional amendment became apparent.

The struggle for women's rights was a response to various forces. Urbanization, industrialization, declining birth rates, and expanding educational and employment opportunities tended to diminish women's role in the private domestic sphere while encouraging their participation in the public sphere. So too, women's involvement, first with abolitionism and later with other progressive causes, generated political commitments and experiences that fueled demands for equal rights.

Those demands provoked opposition from various quarters. The liquor industry feared that enfranchisement would pave the way for PROHIBITION, while conservative political and religious leaders, as well as women homemakers, painted suffrage as an invitation to socialism, anarchism, free love, and domestic discord. Partly in response to those claims, many leading suffragists became increasingly conservative in their arguments and increasingly unwilling to address other causes and consequences of women's inequality. That strategy met with partial success. As they narrowed their social agenda, women's rights organizations expanded their political appeal. The growing strength of the suffrage movement, together with women's efforts in World War I, finally helped prompt the United States to join the slowly increasing number of Western nations that had granted enfranchisement.

Yet to many leading women's rights activists, the American victory proved scarcely less demoralizing than defeat. The focus on enfranchisement had to some extent deflected attention from other issues of critical importance for women, such as poverty, working conditions, birth control, health care, and domestic relations. Without a unifying social agenda beyond the ballot, the postsuffrage feminist movement foundered, splintered, and for the next half century, largely dissolved. During that period, women did not vote as a block on women's issues, support women candidates, or, with few exceptions, agitate for women's rights. Despite their numerical strength and access to the ballot, women remained subject to a vast range of discrimination in employment, education, WELFARE BENEFITS, credit standards, family law, and related areas. Although the Nineteenth Amendment itself was urged as a ground for qualifying women to serve on juries, most courts rejected this argument except where jury service was tied to voter status.

Yet however limited its immediate affects, the Nineteenth Amendment marked a significant advance toward equal rights. Enfranchisement was a necessary if not sufficient condition for women to exercise significant political leverage. Moreover, the skills, experience, and self-esteem that women gained during the suffrage campaign helped lay the foundation for a more egalitarian social order.

DEBORAH L. RHODE

Bibliography

CATT, CARRIE CHAPMAN and SHULER, NETTIE ROGERS 1970 *Woman Suffrage and Politics.* New York: Americana Library Edition.

STANTON, ELIZABETH CADY; ANTHONY, SUSAN B., GAGE, MATILDA JOSLYN; and HARPER, IDA H., eds. 1881–1922 *History of Woman Suffrage.* New York: Fowler & Wells.

NINTH AMENDMENT

Largely ignored throughout most of our history, the Ninth Amendment has emerged in the past twenty years as a possible source for the protection of individual rights not specifically enumerated in the Constitution's text. Although no Supreme Court decision has yet been based squarely on an interpretation of the Ninth Amendment, it has been mentioned in several leading cases in which the Court enlarged the scope of individual rights. Lawyers, scholars, and judges are understandably intrigued by a provision that, on the basis of language, seems ideally suited to provide a constitutional home for newly found rights: "The enumeration of certain rights in the Constitution shall not be construed to deny or disparage others retained by the people."

The historical origins of the Ninth Amendment lay in JAMES MADISON's concern that the inclusion of specified rights in the BILL OF RIGHTS might leave other rights unprotected. He recognized, moreover, that the inherent limitations of language could thwart the intent of the authors of the Bill of Rights to provide a permanent charter of personal freedom. These concerns, which led Madison originally to question the wisdom of a Bill of Rights, caused him to propose, in the First Congress, a resolution incorporating the present language of the Ninth Amendment. It was adopted with little debate.

It is not surprising that the Ninth Amendment lay dormant throughout most of our history. The holding in BARRON V. BALTIMORE (1833) that the Fifth Amendment was not applicable to the states limited the scope of the Ninth Amendment also: all provisions of the Bill of Rights restricted the United States only. Moreover, the federal government, being one of limited powers, did not move into those areas of activity that would trigger claims of infringement of rights not specified in the Constitution. Challenges to federal actions were more likely to take the form that the President or Congress lacked power under the Constitution rather than that the actions abridged an individual right. Even the specific guarantees of the Bill of Rights spawned only a trickle of litigation until well into the twentieth century.

The states, of course, had broad POLICE POWERS to legislate in the areas of welfare, health, education, morality, and business. Until the latter part of the nineteenth century, however, the Supreme Court's review of state legislation served primarily to assure that states did not unduly burden or tax interstate businesses. Court decisions in these areas were not based on individual rights but rather on a judicially created doctrine that Congress's power to regulate INTERSTATE COMMERCE carried with it a prohibition against state laws that were viewed by the Court as unreasonably burdensome or discriminatory as applied to interstate businesses. The post-Civil War Amendments provided the textual basis for challenges to state law as violating individual rights.

The Supreme Court, however, moved quickly to limit the scope of the THIRTEENTH AMENDMENT and FOURTEENTH AMENDMENT. In the famous SLAUGHTERHOUSE CASES (1873) the Court virtually eliminated the PRIVILEGES AND IMMUNITIES clause of the Fourteenth Amendment as a protection for individual rights by limiting the clause to such rights as interstate travel, petitioning the federal government for redress of grievances, protection while abroad, or the privilege of HABEAS CORPUS. The EQUAL PROTECTION and DUE PROCESS clauses were also narrowly interpreted so as to preclude broad challenges to state regulatory statutes, as was the Thirteenth Amendment in *Slaughterhouse* and the CIVIL RIGHTS CASES (1883).

Despite the *Slaughterhouse Cases,* those seeking constitutional support for the protection of property rights against ECONOMIC REGULATION looked elsewhere in the Fourteenth Amendment, and ultimately found a home in the due process clause. Toward the end of the nineteenth century the Court expanded the meaning of "liberty" and "property" to include the right to enter into business relationships. Hundreds of state laws were invalidated under this expanded concept of SUBSTANTIVE DUE PROCESS. This view of the Fourteenth Amendment, together with narrow interpretations of Congress's power under the COMMERCE CLAUSE and the TAXING AND SPENDING POWER, led to the New Deal constitutional crisis of the 1930s. In the spring of 1937 a narrow Court majority shifted ground, broadening Congress's enumerated powers and limiting the due process clause to its present scope, namely, that state regulatory laws should bear a reasonable relationship to a valid legislative purpose. Throughout this long constitutional journey the Ninth Amendment was an unused instrument, because those who challenged state laws relied primarily on the Fourteenth Amendment's due process clause whose scope had been so broadened that there was no need to develop a theory of unenumerated rights.

As the Court in the 1930s and 1940s finally rejected the claim that the Constitution contained rights that protected business against government regulation, the enumerated rights in the Bill of Rights were gradually being incorporated into the meaning of the words "liberty" and "property" of the Fourteenth Amendment's due process clause. By the end of the 1960s, substantive rights guaranteed by the FIRST AMENDMENT, and most of the procedural rights of the Fourth, Fifth, Sixth, and Eighth Amendments were made binding on the states. In this legal development the Ninth Amendment was inconsequential, because the Court employed the judicial technique of incorporating into the due process clause rights enumerated in the Bill of Rights. There was little need to develop the concept of "unenumerated" rights, so long as the due process clause of the Fourteenth Amendment provided the vehicle for making the Bill of Rights binding on the states.

Thus, during the early 1960s, as the process of incorporating the Bill of Rights into the Fourteenth Amendment was moving forward, the Supreme Court maintained a consensus developed as early as UNITED STATES V. CAROLENE PRODUCTS CO. (1938). On matters of economic and social legislation (the type of law that gave rise to the substantive due process controversies of the pre-New Deal era) the Supreme Court would have a limited role to play. Legislation (either state or federal) would be assumed to be valid unless arbitrary or unreasonable, or unless shown to violate a specific provision of the Constitution. Laws reflecting prejudice against certain minorities, or laws infringing personal liberties of the kind enumerated in the Bill of Rights, or other specific provisions of the Constitution, would be subject to a more demanding form of judicial scrutiny.

The Court remained divided on the meaning of specific constitutional guarantees, but these divisions resulted from differences over the meaning of enumerated rights, rather than from differences over whether newly identified, unenumerated, rights should be read into the Constitution. In this constitutional world, an amendment that spoke of unenumerated rights had little to offer as a defense of personal rights. However, a Connecticut law that prohibited the use of contraceptives jolted this consensus and led to the emergence of the Ninth Amendment as a possible vehicle for the protection of rights not specifically guaranteed in other provisions of the Constitution. After two decades of not enforcing its statute, and after thwarting attempts to overturn it in the Supreme Court, Connecticut prosecuted a doctor who was giving contraceptive advice to a married couple in a BIRTH CONTROL clinic. He was charged with "aiding and abetting" a violation of the law prohibiting the use of contraceptives.

The case, GRISWOLD V. CONNECTICUT (1965), presented a difficult problem for a Court majority wedded to the notion that only arbitrary, or capricious, or invidiously discriminatory laws, or those that violated a specific constitutional right, could be invalidated. All of the Justices agreed that the Connecticut statute was foolish, but the Court was obviously troubled as to why it was unconstitutional for a state to decide that it wished to discourage extramarital sexual relations and that the ready availability of contraceptives, including contraceptives for married persons, increased the likelihood of extramarital sex by eliminating the fear of pregnancy. Connecticut claimed that in order to achieve the objective of deterring sex outside of marriage the state could prohibit the use of all contraceptives, thus making them less available. If no specific constitutional right had been violated, why could not Connecticut make its own mistakes, leaving it to the people, through their elected representatives, to correct them?

The Supreme Court's answer, in an opinion by Justice WILLIAM O. DOUGLAS, was to create a right of marital privacy which was found in "penumbras, formed by emanations" from other guarantees found in enumerated rights, specifically those in the First, Third, Fourth, and Fifth Amendments. The Ninth Amendment was also mentioned, but the constitutional approach of the majority was to expand existing rights in order to create a new right of marital privacy which the Connecticut law was held to contravene.

Three Justices (Chief Justice EARL WARREN and Justices ARTHUR GOLDBERG and WILLIAM J. BRENNAN), in an opinion by Goldberg, relied specifically on the Ninth Amendment as an additional basis for striking down the law. Justice Goldberg's standard for defining rights "retained by the people" seemed to strike a widely criticized note of open-ended substantive due process. He referred to FUNDAMENTAL RIGHTS and to the "traditions" and "conscience of our people" in order to determine whether a right was to be regarded as "fundamental." It is not surprising that this language prompted a vigorous dissent from Justice HUGO L. BLACK, who regarded the majority and concurring Justices as having engaged in the same unprincipled personal jurisprudence as the conservative Justices who had written the concept of FREEDOM OF CONTRACT into the Constitution in the early part of the twentieth century.

Viewed in isolation, the *Griswold* case might have been regarded merely as involving a slight broadening of enumerated rights to encompass the basic right to decide whether or not to conceive a child. Whether the Court reached this result by finding the new right lurking in "penumbras" formed by "emanations" from existing rights, or by discovering new "unenumerated" rights, was probably of no great concern, because the Connecticut statute was so unreasonable, even in the context of the state's asserted objective of promoting moral behavior, that the law should have been declared invalid under a REASONABLENESS standard. But strong movements were developing in the country during the 1960s and 1970s. Women were moving rapidly toward equality of opportunity to participate in American life. Attitudes about private sexual behavior, marriage, cohabitation, and family relationships were all changing toward an increased respect for individual choice.

In the 1970s the Court responded by recognizing some of these new attitudes and enshrining them in constitutionally protected rights. In EISENSTADT V. BAIRD (1972), for example, the principles of *Griswold* were extended to include the right of an unmarried person to the acquisition and use of contraceptives. The culmination of this trend was ROE V. WADE (1973), where the Court recognized constitutional protection of a woman's right to procure an abortion, particularly during the first twenty-six weeks of pregnancy. *Roe v. Wade,* in turn, generated renewed debate among constitutional scholars over the proper role of the Court in intervening to overturn the legislative decisions of democratically elected legislatures. In this debate the Ninth Amendment started to assume new significance because it provided a possible textual basis for an expanded jurisprudence of individual liberty.

The Ninth Amendment was mentioned in *Roe v. Wade,* but only as one of a number of constitutional provisions to support the Court's conclusion that "liberty" encompassed a woman's child-bearing decision. Justice Douglas, who had written the majority opinion in *Griswold,* based his concurrence in *Roe v. Wade* primarily on the Ninth Amendment and suggested a broad range of personal autonomy rights such as "control over development and expression of one's intellect, interest, tastes, and personality," "freedom of choice in the basic decisions of one's life respecting marriage, divorce, procreation, contraception, and the education and upbringing of children," "freedom to care for one's health and person, freedom from bodily restraint or compulsion, freedom to walk, stroll, or loaf."

After *Roe v. Wade* (perhaps relying on Justice Douglas's expansive concurrence) some litigants sought to use the Ninth Amendment as a basis for expanding personal autonomy rights beyond the scope of sexual privacy. Many lower courts appeared receptive to such claims as the right, under the Ninth Amendment, to control one's personal grooming and appearance and the right to be protected from disclosing personal information. However, in *Kelley v. Johnson* (1976) the Supreme Court upheld a regulation limiting the length of a police officer's hair. Personal autonomy issues continue to be litigated, but the Ninth Amendment is rarely involved as a basis for decision.

Because interest in the Ninth Amendment started with cases involving sexual privacy, it is not surprising that the amendment continues to be used to attack state antisodomy laws. Apart from a summary affirmance in 1976 of a district court opinion, the Court has not specifically addressed the issue of the rights of homosexuals. In 1985 the Court of Appeals for the Fourth Circuit upheld a Ninth Amendment claim that right of private consensual sexual behavior was beyond the reach of state regulation. But even if the Supreme Court should sustain the decision of the Circuit Court the Supreme Court's preferred rationale is likely to be substantive due process, that is, enlarging the definition of "sexual privacy" as part of the "liberty" protected by the Fourteenth Amendment.

One could well conclude that the Ninth Amendment should be allowed to return to the oblivion it experienced prior to the *Griswold* case. Persistent references to the Ninth Amendment by lower court judges, however, and even by Supreme Court Justices (for example, Chief Justice WARREN E. BURGER in RICHMOND NEWSPAPERS, INC. V. VIRGINIA, 1980) suggest that the amendment could serve as an analytical tool for the appraisal of new claims of constitutional rights. If it is to serve as something more than a superfluous additional citation, the Ninth Amendment must offer the promise of the development of a more coherent body of law than has thus far emerged as the Court has recognized new claims of unenumerated constitutional rights.

At present the Court deals with such rights primarily through the technique employed in *Griswold* and its progeny. The Court usually tries to base its decisions on one or more specific constitutional provisions, and then expands those provisions to include new rights. Typical was the *Richmond Newspaper* case, where the Court held that the public had a right of access to criminal trials. Chief Justice Burger's plurality opinion was based on principles said to derive from the First Amendment, even though the amendment itself specifically guarantees, for these purposes, only the rights of speech, press, and assembly. The Chief Justice made specific reference to rights that were not "enumerated" in the Constitution and pointed out that James Madison's concern with the danger of protecting only enumerated rights led to the adoption of the Ninth Amendment.

Despite his reference to the Ninth Amendment, the Chief Justice's approach in *Richmond Newspapers* would appear to be similar to earlier cases, including *Griswold,* where new rights were recognized because they were analogous to existing rights. Freedom of association is a judicially recognized derivation of the First Amendment protection for freedom of expression, and the requirement of proof beyond a REASONABLE DOUBT is derived from the enumerated guarantee of due process. Recognizing the right of marital privacy or the right to terminate a pregnancy may involve a greater leap from the enumerated rights in the First, Fourth, and Fifth Amendments, but the technique of deriving the rights from enumerated rights did not start with *Griswold* or *Roe v. Wade.* Once the leap is made, the further development of the right becomes merely a matter of interpretation of the newly perceived rights.

An alternate approach to the development of unenumerated rights would look instead to the open-ended clauses of the Constitution such as the PRIVILEGES AND IMMUNITIES clauses in Article IV and the Fourteenth Amendment, or the due process clause—or even no clause at all. Some Justices have viewed the developments since *Griswold* as a revival of open-ended substantive due process. This view has characterized the approach of Justices FELIX FRANKFURTER and JOHN MARSHALL HARLAN to the incorporation of procedural rights into the Fourteenth Amendment. They would have relied on the meaning of "liberty" rather than on the lifting of a "right" from the Bill of Rights and transferring the right to the Fourteenth Amendment (the approach of Justice Brennan and ultimately a majority of the Court).

If the Ninth Amendment is to serve as a meaningful vehicle for the protection of unenumerated rights, it should, at the least, have something more to offer than the expansion of enumerated rights exemplified by *Roe v. Wade* and *Richmond Newspapers* or the open-ended substantive due process approach of Justices Frankfurter, Harlan, and Stewart. The Ninth Amendment offers two potential contributions: historical justification and constitutional standard. The historical justification, articulated by Justice Goldberg in *Griswold* and by Chief Justice Burger in *Richmond Newspapers,* provides a powerful support for the argument that "unenumerated rights" have a place in the Constitution.

The same history also suggests a constitutional standard: a range of rights protected by the entire text of the Constitution. To leave the Ninth Amendment open-ended, with no obligation on the part of judges to link unenumerated rights to enumerated rights, would render the amendment indistinguishable from the nontextually based substantive due process. Moreover, confining "retained" rights to those analogous to enumerated rights would be consistent with Madison's conception of the Ninth Amendment. He was not seeking to create new rights. He was concerned that the enumeration of the rights in the Bill of Rights could not possibly take into account similar but undefined rights that could not be fully delineated in a constitutional text. The Ninth Amendment was the original "safety net" to compensate for the imperfection of language and the inability to provide for changing circumstances. Such an approach leaves room for a gradual expansion of rights, but requires some grounding for each newly recognized right in the constitutional text. A text-based standard is one that requires far less justification, in terms of democratic political theory, than a frankly noninterpretivist standard.

Does the Ninth Amendment, as so limited, add an additional dimension to the technique employed in

Griswold or *Richmond Newspapers?* If rights "retained" under the Ninth Amendment are those analogous to rights found elsewhere in the Constitution, how does this approach differ from the approach of Justice Douglas in *Griswold,* which found rights in the "penumbras" formed by "emanations" from existing rights?

One obvious response is that the Ninth Amendment is itself a textual, historically valid justification for this approach to the enforcement of enumerated rights. It thus has a "leg-up" in the quest for legitimacy of judicial intervention. Moreover, Ninth Amendment analysis should derive from the entire text of the Constitution and not merely from other rights. Thus, as Justice Brennan noted in *Zobel v. Williams* (1982), the RIGHT TO TRAVEL can be discerned as a necessary consequence of nationhood as embodied in several constitutional provisions. Similarly, protection of VOTING RIGHTS can be derived from constitutional provisions that contemplate broad voter participation. The Ninth Amendment has never defined absolute rights. Rather, jurisprudence based on the Ninth Amendment will require placing on the balancing scales those individual unenumerated rights that might otherwise be ignored but that are sufficiently analogous to enumerated rights, or to our governmental structure, as to require constitutional protection.

NORMAN REDLICH

Bibliography

BLACK, CHARLES 1981 *Decision According to Law.* New York: Norton.

DUNBAR, L. 1956 James Madison and the Ninth Amendment. *Virginia Law Review* 42:627–643.

ELY, J. H. 1980 *Democracy and Distrust: A Theory of Judicial Review.* Cambridge, Mass.: Harvard University Press.

LAYCOCK, DOUGLAS 1981 Taking Constitutions Seriously: A Theory of Judicial Review by John Hart Ely. *Texas Law Review* 59:343–394.

PATTERSON, B. 1955 *The Forgotten Ninth Amendment* 27; *The Constitution of the United States of America: Analysis and Interpretations,* S. Doc. No. 92–82, 92d Cong.

REDLICH, N. 1961 Are There Certain Rights . . . Retained by the People? *NYU Law Review* 37:787, 802–808.

RHOADES, LYMAN AND PATULA, RODNEY R. 1973 The Ninth Amendment: A Survey of Theory and Practice in the Federal Courts Since *Griswold v. Connecticut. Denver Law Journal* 50:153–176.

VAN ALSTYNE, WILLIAM 1981 Slouching Toward Bethlehem with the Ninth Amendment. *Yale Law Journal* 91:207–216.

NIX v. WILLIAMS
104 S. Ct. 2501 (1984)

A 7–2 Supreme Court held that although an accused's incriminating statements could not be admitted as EVIDENCE because police had interrogated him in violation of his RIGHT TO COUNSEL, physical evidence discovered on the basis of his incriminating statements could be introduced against him if the prosecution, by a preponderance of proof, could show that such evidence would inevitably have been discovered even in the absence of accused's statements. The case produced an "inevitable discovery" exception to the EXCLUSIONARY RULE: any FRUIT OF THE POISONOUS TREE may be used as evidence if it would have been inevitably or ultimately discovered, just as if it had been discovered on the basis of independent or uncontaminated leads. (See BREWER V. WILLIAMS, 1977.)

LEONARD W. LEVY

NIXON, RICHARD M.
(1913–)

Richard Milhous Nixon, the thirty-seventh President of the United States, was born in Yorba Linda, California. An alumnus of Whittier College and Duke University Law School, he practiced law in Whittier, California, from 1937 to 1942. After a brief stint in the enforcement of wartime price controls, he entered the Navy and served with it in the South Pacific. Upon his release from duty he was elected to the House of Representatives from the Twelfth District of California. Shortly he gained national prominence as a member of the HOUSE COMMITTEE ON UN-AMERICAN ACTIVITIES, and he played a decisive role in generating the perjury case against Alger Hiss. Nixon was elected to the Senate from his home state in 1950, gaining new notoriety in denouncing the Democrats for having "lost" China to communism. In 1952 he was elected vice-president as the running mate of DWIGHT D. EISENHOWER. Nixon had riveted national attention—once again—with an impassioned defense on radio and television of his acceptance of money from a political "slush" fund. As vice-president he drew international notice through his "kitchen debate" with Soviet Premier Nikita Khrushchev. Nixon was nominated for President by his party in 1960, but lost to the Democrats' JOHN F. KENNEDY in a close election. Two years later Nixon ran for governor of California and lost. He reentered the private practice of law, this time in New York City. Maintaining and broadening his political contacts, he was again nominated for the presidency by the Republicans in 1968. His campaign theme was a pledge to heal the divisions in the nation that the Vietnam War had created and to bring the hostilities to an honorable conclusion. He won a plurality of the popular vote over the Democrats' HUBERT H. HUMPHREY and George C. Wallace, candidate of the American Independence Party.

As President, Nixon took advantage of the dramatic expansion of the office that had been taking place since the time of FRANKLIN D. ROOSEVELT, recognizing that the public had grown accustomed to regarding the Chief Executive as the undisputed architect of national policies. But Nixon stretched his authority with less restraint than his predecessors, undertaking steps violative of the law and of the Constitution itself. A full explanation for his actions may never be forthcoming. Possibly he felt keenly that his party's inability to capture or control Congress would continue to frustrate his desire to dismantle many New Deal and Great Society programs. He may also have been guided by inner compulsions of ambition and feelings of inadequacy he never articulated. Nixon, at any rate, interpreted by his own lights the constitutional prerogatives of his office, including an assumed right to ignore or modify the letter and intent of laws.

Nixon, for example, did not consider himself obligated to respect the law of 1972 requiring that EXECUTIVE AGREEMENTS arrived at with foreign governments be reported to Congress within sixty days, cavalierly submitting them late. Moreover, he sometimes negotiated them at a lower diplomatic level and labeled them "arrangements." Under Nixon's stewardship, executive agreements were entered into on major matters and formal treaties almost invariably on minor matters—a reversal of the traditional relationship between the two forms of diplomatic undertakings.

Although a few Presidents had sometimes impounded funds appropriated by Congress, the step was generally taken in conformity with congressional intent or under the President's authority as COMMANDER-IN-CHIEF. Nixon broke fresh ground in his assertion of a constitutional power to decline to spend appropriated funds. For him IMPOUNDMENT was a legitimate tool of the President to alter policy set by Congress—and he employed it on a scale hitherto unknown. While some of the funds he refused to release came out of military, space, and public works appropriations, vast amounts also came out of social and environmental programs. By 1973 Nixon's impoundments totaled about $18 billion, between seventeen and twenty percent of the funds he could claim to control. Nixon and his aides maintained that he was following patterns established by previous Presidents. The evidence is, however, that his predecessors did not aim to contravene the will of Congress, but merely postpone immediate expenditure. Nixon, on the other hand, used impoundment to terminate or curtail programs. He defended his actions on the ground that the executive power of the President included a constitutional right to be the people's defender against Congress's inability to hold down nondefense spending.

Nixon's boldness had the effect of giving the executive an item veto of appropriation bills—a remedy long sought by Presidents, and provided for in the CONFEDERATE CONSTITUTION, but consistently withheld from Presidents since first requested by President ULYSSES S. GRANT in 1873. Whatever the merit of the device, Nixon's insistence on exercising it in defiance of Congress was a usurpation of power.

Although WIRETAPPING without formal authorization had long been employed occasionally by Presidents, Nixon was the first Chief Executive who systematically resorted to its use. His practice of it grew out of a determination to keep under wraps the "secret" B-52 raids over Cambodia in 1969. Nixon was apparently fashioning a new conception of his office, metamorphosing it into a "plebiscitary presidency"—one in which the Chief Executive would assume widened power under the Constitution, relying on a reshaped Supreme Court to validate his actions. Nixon's expressed concern was that leaks of information about the "secret war" were putting national security in jeopardy. He ordered the tapping of telephones of members of the National Security Council staff and of several newspaper reporters. The taps were conducted without court order and in patent violation of Title III of the OMNIBUS CRIME CONTROL AND SAFE STREETS ACT of 1968. By countenancing not only illegal wiretapping but, shortly, burglary (in the case of Daniel Ellsberg, who revealed the so-called Pentagon Papers), the hiring of *agents provacateurs* (to conduct "dirty tricks" in election campaigns), and the subverting of the Internal Revenue Service (to punish "enemies"), Nixon was substituting his personal sanction for established law.

In assuming this prerogative, Nixon believed he was exercising what he regarded as INHERENT POWER to maintain national and domestic security. This claim of "inherent power," sometimes also set forth by previous Presidents, has never been recognized as valid by the courts. In UNITED STATES V. UNITED STATES DISTRICT COURT (1972) the Supreme Court by an 8–0 vote ruled unconstitutional the Nixon administration's practice of engaging in domestic electronic surveillance without a judicial warrant.

Nixon's assertion of an EXECUTIVE PRIVILEGE to reject a SUBPOENA became the issue in the case of UNITED STATES V. NIXON (1974). The suit revolved around Nixon's refusal to surrender tapes containing information relevant to the prosecution of some of his close aides for offenses that included obstruction of justice by "covering up" the administration's involvement in the Watergate break-in. In its unanimous decision requiring the President to turn over the tapes, the Supreme Court recognized that a President is entitled to confidentiality of communication—needful for "protection of the public interest in candid, objective, and even blunt or harsh opinion in presidential decisionmaking." But, the Court concluded, "when the ground for asserting privilege as to subpoenaed material sought for use in a criminal trial is based only on the generalized interest in confidentiality, it cannot prevail over the fundamental demands of DUE PROCESS OF LAW in the fair administration of criminal justice. The generalized assertion of privilege must yield to the demonstrated, specific need for EVIDENCE in a pending criminal trial."

Nixon toyed with the idea of disobeying the decision, but decided to comply, surrendering the tapes covered in the decision. Indeed, he published their contents, thus providing the House Judiciary Committee with the "smoking gun"—the now famous words in which the President counseled inducing the Central Intelligence Agency to limit the FBI's investigation of the Watergate burglary.

Nixon's use of the POCKET VETO was also remarkable. As intended by the Framers of the Constitution it may be used at the end of a session of Congress when a President who does not sign a bill cannot return it to Congress because it stands adjourned. Nixon unhesitatingly used pocket vetoes when Congress was merely in brief recess. In *Kennedy v. Simpson* (1973) a district court overturned as misused Nixon's pocket veto of the Family Practice of Medicine Bill, which had been opposed by only three members of Congress.

Nixon's transgressions of the law and the Constitution contributed to the passage of two major pieces of legislation. One was the CONGRESSIONAL BUDGET AND IMPOUNDMENT CONTROL ACT of 1974, which detailed the arrangements under which Congress may monitor the deferral by a President of appropriated funds. The second law, responding to the deployment of troops in Asia, first by President LYNDON B. JOHNSON and then by Nixon, was the War Powers Resolution of 1973, severely restricting the ability of a President to use military force outside the United States without congressional authorization. Nixon and all succeeding Presidents have denounced this law as an unconstitutional abridgment of the power of the President to direct the armed forces.

Nixon made two nominations to the Supreme Court that failed of confirmation. In 1969 he submitted the name of Judge Clement F. Haynsworth of South Carolina, a designation that met implacable opposition from CIVIL RIGHTS groups and labor unions. Early the following year Nixon sent forward the name of Judge G. Harrold Carswell of the Fifth Circuit Court of Appeals in Florida. Denounced as a racist in many quarters, although he had renounced his older views on race, Carswell was also opposed as lacking the superior qualifications required for a seat on the highest court.

In addition to placing HARRY A. BLACKMUN of Minnesota, LEWIS F. POWELL, Jr., of Virginia, and WILLIAM H. REHNQUIST of Arizona on the Supreme Court, Nixon also appointed the fourteenth Chief Justice, Judge WARREN E. BURGER of the District of Columbia Court of Appeals, whose conservative speeches and advocacy of judicial restraint appealed to the President. Nixon had been especially impressed by an address that Burger delivered in 1967 on the subject of "law and order," from which Nixon had borrowed during the 1968 campaign for the Presidency. He was mindful, too, of the support Burger had given him during his critical time in the 1952 campaign.

Nixon was the first Chief Executive to resign the Presidency—a consequence of the Watergate affair that convulsed the nation from 1972 to 1974. The reasons for the burglary—carried out by Nixon's political aides at the headquarters of the Democratic party—have never been adduced. From the start of the investigation the administration tried to cover up its connection to the crime. In the long drawnout effort to get at the truth, the focus of the quest became the President himself: what did he know and when did he know it? The evidence lay in the recordings of conversations in his office that Nixon was revealed to have been making for years. The President turned over the critical tapes just as the House of Representatives seemed on the verge of voting to impeach him. He surrendered his office on August 9, 1974. The following month, his successor, GERALD R. FORD, issued the former President a "full, free, and absolute" pardon for any crimes he may have committed.

HENRY F. GRAFF

Bibliography

KURLAND, PHILIP B. 1978 *Watergate and the Constitution.* Chicago: University of Chicago Press.

NATHAN, RICHARD P. 1973 *The Plot That Failed: Nixon and the Administrative Presidency.* New York: Wiley.

NIXON, RICHARD M. 1978 *R.N.: The Memoirs of Richard Nixon.* New York: Grosset & Dunlap.

SCHLESINGER, ARTHUR M., JR. 1973 *The Imperial Presidency.* Boston: Little, Brown.

WHITE, THEODORE H. 1975 *Breach of Faith: The Fall of Richard Nixon.* New York: Atheneum.

NIXON, UNITED STATES v.
418 U.S. 683 (1974)

This litigation unfolded contemporaneously with congressional investigation of the Watergate affair and with proceedings in the House of Representatives for the IMPEACHMENT of President RICHARD M. NIXON. (See WATERGATE AND THE CONSTITUTION.) A federal GRAND JURY had indicted seven defendants, including Nixon's former attorney general and closest White House aides, charging several offenses, including conspiracy to obstruct justice by "covering up" the circumstances of a burglary of Democratic party offices in Washington. The grand jury named Nixon as an unindicted co-conspirator. A special prosecutor had been appointed to handle this prosecution. To obtain evidence, the special prosecutor asked Judge John Sirica to issue a SUBPOENA ordering Nixon to produce electronic tapes and papers relating to sixty-four White House conversations among persons named as conspirators, including Nixon himself.

Judge Sirica issued the subpoena in mid-April 1974; on May 1, Nixon's counsel moved to quash the subpoena and to expunge the grand jury's naming of the President as a co-conspirator. Sirica denied both motions and ordered Nixon to produce the subpoenaed items. When Nixon appealed, the special prosecutor asked the Supreme Court to hear the case, bypassing the court of appeals. The Court granted that motion and advanced argument to July 8. On July 24 the Court upheld the subpoena, 8–0, including the votes of three Nixon appointees. Justice WILLIAM H. REHNQUIST, formerly a Justice Department official under the indicted ex-attorney general, had disqualified himself. A week following the decision, before Nixon had complied with it, the House Judiciary Committee recommended his impeachment. When Nixon turned over the tapes on August 5, they included a conversation that even his strongest supporters called a "smoking gun." On August 9 the President resigned.

A year earlier a White House press officer had said Nixon would obey a "definitive" decision of the Supreme Court about the tapes. At ORAL ARGUMENT in the Supreme Court, however, Nixon's counsel, pressed to say that the President had "submitted himself" to the Court's decision, evaded any forthright promise of compliance. Even after the Court's decision, the press reported, Nixon and his aides debated for some hours whether he should comply with the subpoena. Some have reported that the Court's unanimity was an important factor influencing that decision.

The Court itself seems to have been impressed with the need for unanimity; its bland opinion, formally attributed to Chief Justice WARREN E. BURGER, bore the external marks of a document hurriedly negotiated—as investigative reporters have said it was. The Court brushed aside objections to its JURISDICTION, such as the FINAL JUDGMENT RULE. Nixon also argued that the courts had no jurisdiction over an "intrabranch" dispute between the President and his subordinate, the special prosecutor. Responding, the Court emphasized the "uniqueness" of the conflict, but apart from that comment its argument bordered on incoherence. After gratuitously remarking that the executive branch had exclusive discretionary control over federal criminal prosecutions, the Court reversed field, discovering a guarantee of independence for the special prosecutor in the regulation that appointed him and promised not to remove him absent a consensus among certain congressional leaders. Both the Court's propositions were dubious. (See APPOINTING AND REMOVAL POWER.) Yet the Court marched on to some heroic constitutional issues concerning relations between the executive and judicial branches.

Both sides had appealed to the abstraction of SEPARATION OF POWERS. Nixon argued first that the judiciary lacked power "to compel the President in the exercise of his discretion," and second that the President enjoyed an EXECUTIVE PRIVILEGE to keep confidential his conversations with his advisers. The first argument blurred two separate issues: the President's immunity from judicial process and the POLITICAL QUESTION issue of his discretion to control disclosure of his conversations. This latter claim of absolute executive privilege overlapped his second main argument.

That argument began with an absolute privilege claim, but if that claim failed the President sought to persuade the Court to recognize a wide scope for a qualified privilege.

The special prosecutor, opposing both presidential immunity and the claim of absolute privilege, assumed the existence of a qualified privilege. That privilege was lost, he argued, when there was substantial reason to believe that the participants in a presidential conversation had been planning a crime.

The Court's opinion, like Nixon's argument, blurred the boundaries of separate issues in the case. The decision to uphold the subpoena, however, implicitly rejected the claim of presidential immunity, and the Court expressly rejected the claim of absolute privilege. A qualified privilege did exist, the Court said—by way of assumption, not demonstration—but the privilege was defeated when the specific confidential information sought was shown to be relevant, admissible evidence for a pending federal prosecution. The Court thus disposed of the case without mentioning Nixon's own possible complicity in crime; it dismissed the question whether the President could constitutionally be named as a co-conspirator.

Today some form of a qualified executive privilege is assumed to exist, but the scope of the privilege remains largely undefined. *Nixon*'s most important contribution to our constitutional law, however, lay elsewhere: in its reaffirmation that even the highest officer of government is not beyond the reach of the law and the courts. Nixon's brief had included this remark, designed to reassure: "it must be stressed we do not suggest the President has the attributes of a king. *Inter alia,* a king rules by inheritance and for life." The *Nixon* decision reminded us that there are also other differences.

KENNETH L. KARST

Bibliography

SYMPOSIUM 1974 United States v. Nixon. *UCLA Law Review* 22:1–140.

WOODWARD, BOB and ARMSTRONG, SCOTT 1979 *The Brethren: Inside the Supreme Court.* Pages 285–347. New York: Simon & Schuster.

NIXON v. ADMINISTRATOR OF GENERAL SERVICES
433 U.S. 425 (1977)

Ex-president RICHARD M. NIXON sued to prevent implementation of the Presidential Recordings and Materials Preservation Act. In upholding the constitutionality of the act, the Supreme Court rejected Nixon's contentions that it violated SEPARATION OF POWERS and EXECUTIVE PRIVILEGE, abridged Nixon's RIGHT OF PRIVACY and FREEDOM OF ASSOCIATION, and constituted a BILL OF ATTAINDER.

DENNIS J. MAHONEY

NIXON v. CONDON
286 U.S. 73 (1932)

After the decision in NIXON V. HERNDON (1927), Texas amended its statute, giving a political party's state executive committee the power to set voting qualifications for the party's PRIMARY ELECTIONS. The Democratic party's committee limited primary voting to whites. Nixon, a black, again was denied a primary ballot and again sued election officials for DAMAGES. The Supreme Court reversed a dismissal of the action, holding, 5–4, that the committee's conduct was STATE ACTION in violation of the FOURTEENTH AMENDMENT. The line of "Texas primary cases" continued with GROVEY V. TOWNSEND (1935).

KENNETH L. KARST

NIXON v. FITZGERALD
457 U.S. 731 (1982)
HARLOW v. FITZGERALD
457 U.S. 800 (1982)

In these cases the Supreme Court significantly expanded the scope of EXECUTIVE IMMUNITY in actions for DAMAGES brought by persons injured by official action. Fitzgerald sued former President RICHARD M. NIXON and two of his aides, alleging that he had been dismissed from an Air Force job in retaliation for revealing to a congressional committee a two billion dollar cost overrun for a transport aircraft.

In *Nixon* the Court held, 5–4, that the President is absolutely immune from civil damages—not merely for the performance of particular functions but for all acts within the "outer perimeter" of his official duties. Justice LEWIS F. POWELL, for the majority, rested his decision not on the text of the Constitution but on "the constitutional tradition of the SEPARATION OF POWERS." Unlike other executive officers, who have only a qualified immunity from damages actions, the President occupies a unique place in the government. He must be able to act without fear of intrusive inquiries into his motives. The dissenters agreed that some of the President's functions should be clothed in absolute immunity, but argued that a qualified immunity from suit was sufficient in most cases to protect presidential independence.

In *Harlow* the Court, 8–1, rejected the aides' claim of absolute immunity, but broadened the scope of qualified executive immunity. Under previous decisions, this immunity was lost when the official negligently violated "clearly established" rights or acted with malicious intention to deprive constitutional rights or to cause harm. The Court here eliminated the "malicious intention" test for losing the immunity. A great many actions for damages against executive officials are based on claims of right that are not "clearly established." *Harlow* forbids damages in such a case even though the official acts with malice.

KENNETH L. KARST

NIXON v. HERNDON
273 U.S. 536 (1927)

This decision was the first in a series of "Texas primary cases." Texas law disqualified blacks from voting in Democratic party PRIMARY ELECTIONS. Nixon, refused a ballot under this law, sued election officers for damages under the federal CIVIL RIGHTS laws, asserting a denial of EQUAL PROTECTION OF THE LAWS under the FOURTEENTH AMENDMENT and a denial of the right to vote on account of race, in violation of the FIFTEENTH AMENDMENT. (See VOTING RIGHTS.) The Supreme Court reversed a dismissal of the action, holding for Nixon on his equal protection claim and not discussing the Fifteenth Amendment. The next case in the series was NIXON V. CONDON (1932).

KENNETH L. KARST

NLRB v. FRIEDMAN-HARRY MARKS CLOTHING CO.

See: Wagner Act Cases

NLRB v. FRUEHAUF TRAILER COMPANY

See: Wagner Act Cases

NLRB v. JONES & LAUGHLIN STEEL CORP.

See: Wagner Act Cases

NO-KNOCK ENTRY

Police are not allowed to enter a house to search or make an ARREST unless they have procured a warrant based on PROBABLE CAUSE, according to PAYTON V. NEW YORK (1980) and *Vale v. Louisiana* (1970). If police cannot get a warrant because of EXIGENT CIRCUMSTANCES, they may act on probable cause alone. In either case, the Supreme Court has not articulated specific rules for no-knock entries. At COMMON LAW, police could not make a forcible entry unless admittance was refused after they announced their authority and purpose, and the FEDERAL CODE OF CRIMINAL PROCEDURE prescribes the same requirements. But the Court has not made this rule into a formal FOURTH AMENDMENT requirement. Rather, the Court emphasizes that entries must always be reasonable, and forcible entries must be based on exigent circumstances. A few states authorize by statute the issuance of no-knock warrants, but any blanket sanctioning of such entries probably would be held to violate the Fourth Amendment.

CATHERINE HANCOCK

Bibliography

LAFAVE, WAYNE R. 1978 *Search and Seizure: A Treatise on the Fourth Amendment.* Vol. 2:122–140. St. Paul, Minn.: West Publishing Co.

NOLO CONTENDERE

(Latin: "I do not choose to contest [it].") This statement, variously defined as plea and not a plea, indicates that the defendant will not fight a charge against him. Of the same immediate effect as a guilty plea, it admits the facts charged but cannot be used as a confession of guilt in any other proceeding. Acceptance by a court is discretionary.

DAVID GORDON

NONINTERPRETIVISM

See: Constitutional Interpretation

NONTESTIMONIAL COMPULSION

See: Testimonial Compulsion

NORMAN v. BALTIMORE & OHIO RAILROAD COMPANY

See: Gold Clause Cases

NORRIS, GEORGE W.
(1861–1944)

George William Norris, a progressive Republican from Nebraska, served in the House of Representatives from 1903 to 1913. He led the revolt against Speaker Joseph Cannon that, in 1910, broke the power of the speaker to control virtually all legislation in the house. As a United States senator (1913–1943) Norris was the author of the TWENTIETH AMENDMENT, which ended the "lame duck" sessions of Congress, and co-author of the NORRIS-LAGUARDIA ACT (1932), which outlawed YELLOW DOG CONTRACTS and restricted use of federal court INJUNCTIONS against labor strikes, and of the TENNESSEE VALLEY AUTHORITY ACT (1933). Norris supported most of President FRANKLIN D. ROOSEVELT's "New Deal" and criticized Supreme Court decisions that held such legislation unconstitutional. Although he favored a constitutional amendment to restrict national JUDICIAL REVIEW, he opposed Roosevelt's plan to pack the Court with pro-administration justices.

DENNIS J. MAHONEY

Bibliography

LOWITT, RICHARD 1963–1978 *George W. Norris.* 3 Vols. Syracuse, N.Y.: Syracuse University Press; Urbana, Ill.: University of Illinois Press.

NORRIS v. ALABAMA
294 U.S. 587 (1935)

Clarence Norris, one of the Scottsboro boys (see POWELL V. ALABAMA, 1932), on retrial moved to quash the INDICTMENT and trial venire (pool of potential jurors) on the ground that qualified black citizens were systematically excluded from jury service solely on the basis of race. On denial of his motion by the trial judge, Norris was retried and again found guilty. The state supreme court affirmed the JUDGMENT of the trial court that no JURY DISCRIMINATION existed. The Supreme Court, voting 8–0, reversed the judgment after reviewing the evidence for itself for the first time in such a case. The evidence showed that for a generation or more no black person had been called for jury service in the county and that a substantial number of black persons qualified under state law. In an opinion by Chief Justice CHARLES EVANS HUGHES, the Court ruled that the evidence of black exclusion made a *prima facie* case of denial of the EQUAL PROTECTION guaranteed by the FOURTEENTH AMENDMENT. *Norris* began a line of cases that led to the virtual extinction of RACIAL DISCRIMINATION in the composition of juries.

LEONARD W. LEVY

NORRIS-LAGUARDIA ACT
47 Stat. 70 (1932)

Reeling from a string of adverse court decisions, labor saw the Norris-LaGuardia Act of 1932 as Congress's long overdue remedy for Supreme Court antipathy. A panel of experts, including Professor FELIX FRANKFURTER, helped to draft a bill to end the abuse of labor INJUNCTIONS, and, as eventually passed by large majorities in Congress, the act greatly diminished the use of federal injunctions in labor disputes. The act recognized the need for COLLECTIVE BARGAINING and encouraged union formation, ending years of misinterpretation of the spirit, if not the letter, of the CLAYTON ACT. One of the key provisions of the new act (section 4) outlawed the issuance of federal injunctions against those who "whether acting singly or in concert" might strike, aid, or publicize strikes, join unions, or assemble peacefully. YELLOW DOG CONTRACTS, sustained in HITCHMAN COAL & COKE COMPANY V. MITCHELL (1917), were also rendered unenforceable (section 3). In DUPLEX PRINTING PRESS COMPANY V. DEERING (1921) the Court had unjustifiably declared that the Clayton Act provision covering labor disputes applied only to related parties, employer and employee, not to those engaged in a secondary boycott. Section 13 rewrote that practice by redefining "labor dispute" so that the parties need no longer be in "proximate relation" to each other. Although the act divested federal courts of injunctive power, it provided exceptions where illegal acts or injury were likely. Moreover, the employers had to make "every reasonable effort" to negotiate a settlement before seeking an injunction (section 8).

The act's explicitly stated purpose was to foster labor's right to organize and act without federal judicial interference. The act created no new substantive rights but enlarged the area in which labor could operate. The act's procedures would be upheld in *Lauf v. E. G. Shinner & Company* (1938) and its substance upheld in *New Negro Alliance v. Sanitary Grocery Company* (1938).

DAVID GORDON

NORTH ATLANTIC TREATY
63 Stat. 2241 (1949)

Following World War II, the Soviet Union rapidly expanded its influence in Eastern and Central Europe. Fearing a further "Communist offensive," the West, led initially by Belgium, Canada, France, Luxembourg, the Netherlands, the United Kingdom, and the United States, negotiated the North Atlantic Treaty which, it was hoped, would deter Soviet expansionism. The treaty was signed by twelve countries on April 4, 1949, and presently lists a total of sixteen countries among its signatories. The primary objectives of the treaty are as stated in its preamble: "to promote stability and well-being in the North Atlantic area" and "to unite . . . for collective defense and for the preservation of peace and security." The treaty stipulates that "an armed attack against one or more of the [State] Parties in Europe or North America shall be considered an attack against them all" and that, in the event of such an attack, each State Party shall take "such action as it deems necessary, including the use of armed force, to restore and maintain the security of the North Atlantic area." Some commentators have suggested that this language may effect an unconstitutional delegation of United States authority to declare war. The argument is of minimal concern, however, inasmuch as Article 11 of the treaty provides that all of the treaty's provisions shall be "carried out by the Parties in accordance with their respective constitutional processes." The discretionary language of Article 5 ("such action as it deems necessary") reinforces this conclusion.

BURNS H. WESTON

(SEE ALSO: *Status of Forces Agreements; Treaty Power.*)

Bibliography

FOX, WILLIAM T. and SCHILLING, WARNER R., EDS. 1973 *European Security and the Atlantic System.* New York: Columbia University Press.

SAULLE, MARIA RITA 1979 *NATO and Its Activities.* Dobbs Ferry, N.Y.: Oceana Publications.

NORTHERN PIPELINE CONSTRUCTION COMPANY v. MARATHON PIPE LINE COMPANY
458 U.S. 50 (1982)

If Congress were to make a wholesale transfer of JURISDICTION over matters within the JUDICIAL POWER OF THE UNITED STATES to administrative agencies or LEGISLATIVE COURTS, the result would be a serious risk of undermining the independence of the judiciary. Then, under what circumstances can Congress make any such transfer? The question blurs constitutional doctrine with practical statecraft. In *Marathon* the Supreme Court had an opportunity to illuminate this subject, which has long seemed impervious to light.

In the BANKRUPTCY ACT (1978) Congress created a category of bankruptcy judges, who would hold office not during good behavior (as do judges of CONSTITUTIONAL COURTS) but for fourteen-year terms. The act authorized the bankruptcy judges to decide not only matters peculiar to bankruptcy, such as the marshaling and distribution of assets and the discharge of bankrupts from certain liabilities, but also "related" matters, including actions on behalf of bankrupts against other persons, based on state law. The Supreme Court, 6–3, held that the grant of jurisdiction over the "related" matters exceeded the limits of Article III.

Four Justices concluded that federal jurisdiction over matters not involving "public rights"—dealings between the national government and others, or subject to that government's regulation—must be vested in constitutional courts, with certain limited exceptions. Three Justices espoused balancing Article III's concerns for judicial independence against other practical needs of administering the governmental system. Neither view commanded a majority of the Court, and the doctrinal murk deepened.

KENNETH L. KARST

(SEE ALSO: *Thomas v. Union Carbide Agricultural Products Company, 1985.*)

NORTHERN SECURITIES CO. v. UNITED STATES
193 U.S. 197 (1904)

A bare majority of the Supreme Court, in a broad construction of congressional power under the COMMERCE CLAUSE, upheld the constitutionality of the SHERMAN ANTITRUST ACT as applied to holding companies. The Court thus extended the scope of the Sherman Act to companies not directly engaged in such commerce which nevertheless controlled INTERSTATE COMMERCE.

The formation in 1901 of the Northern Securities Company, a holding company comprising both the Hill-Morgan and the Harriman interests, united parallel competing lines. In March 1902, the government filed an EQUITY suit to dissolve the company. The question was clear: was a holding company, whose subsidiaries' operations were its only connection with interstate commerce, exempt from the Sherman Act? The Court split 5–4 but without a majority opinion.

Justice JOHN MARSHALL HARLAN, for the plurality, followed UNITED STATES v. TRANS-MISSOURI FREIGHT ASSOCIATION (1897) and other cases, arguing that the Sherman Act established competition as a test for interstate commerce. Harlan declared that a combination need not be directly in commerce to restrain it: intent to restrain or potential for restraint was all that was needed, and here potential restraint could be found in the reduction of competition resulting from the holding company's formation. Harlan refused to interpret the statute using the RULE OF REASON. He also broadly construed the commerce clause, curtly dismissing defense allegations that the INJUNCTION violated state sovereignty and the TENTH AMENDMENT. Justice DAVID J. BREWER concurred only in Harlan's result. Abandoning his earlier opinions, Brewer now embraced the rule of reason but concluded that even under that rule the Northern Securities Company clearly constituted an unlawful restraint of trade.

Justices EDWARD D. WHITE and OLIVER WENDELL HOLMES each wrote dissents. The former followed the definition of interstate commerce in UNITED STATES v. E. C. KNIGHT COMPANY (1895), stressing that stock ownership did not place the defendants within the scope of the Sherman Act. Holmes's first written dissent on the Supreme Court emphasized a COMMON LAW reading of the statute. He believed that the holding company device was neither a combination nor a contract in restraint of trade. Holmes asserted that this case so nearly resembled *Knight* as to require no deviation from that opinion.

Counted by THEODORE ROOSEVELT "one of the greatest achievements of my administration because it emphasized the fact that the most powerful men in this country were held to accountability before the law," this decision's importance lay both in Harlan's insistence on the supremacy of federal law and in the reinvigoration of a law that business had hoped the Court rendered ineffectual in *Knight.*

DAVID GORDON

Bibliography

APPEL, R. W., JR. 1975 The Case of the Monopolistic Railroadman. In John A. Garraty, ed., *Quarrels That Have Shaped the Constitution.* New York: Harper & Row.

NORTHWESTERN FERTILIZER CO. v. HYDE PARK
97 U.S. 659 (1878)

In 1867 the Illinois legislature chartered the company for a term of fifty years to manufacture fertilizer, from dead animals, outside the city limits of Chicago. The nearby village of Hyde Park regarded the company's factory as an unendurable nuisance, injurious to the public health. Immediately before the legislature chartered the company it empowered the village to abate public nuisances excepting the company. The village passed an ordinance prohibiting the existence of any company engaged in any offensive or unwholesome business within a distance of one mile. The ordinance put the fertilizer company out of business. It invoked its chartered rights against the ordinance, which it claimed violated the CONTRACT CLAUSE.

On the basis of past decisions the Court should have accepted the company's argument, holding that the village had no authority to abate its factory. By a vote of 7–1, however, the Supreme Court ruled that the village had validly exercised its police power to protect the public health. Justice NOAH SWAYNE for the Court declared that the company's charter must be construed narrowly and held that it provided no exemption from liability or nuisances. Swayne quoted from the decision earlier that term in BOSTON BEER CO. v. MASSACHUSETTS in which the Court announced the DOCTRINE of INALIENABLE POLICE POWER. Both cases had the result of weakening the contract clause's traditional protection of chartered rights.

LEONARD W. LEVY

NORTHWEST ORDINANCE
(1787)

This congressional enactment, which applied to the territory northwest of the Ohio River, was the most significant accomplishment of the United States under the ARTICLES OF CONFEDERATION. In effect the ordinance provided for self-government under constitutional law in the TERRITORIES, thus "solving" a colonial problem by avoiding it. The pattern for government, which subsequently was extended to other western territories, allowed for growth from a system of congressional government to statehood and admission to the Union "on an equal footing with the original States, in all respects whatever. . . ." As soon as a district reached a population of 5,000 males of voting age, each one possessing a fifty-acre freehold was entitled to vote for representatives to a general assembly. The assembly had authority to elect a delegate to Congress with the right to debate but not to vote. When the population reached 60,000, the territory could apply for admission as a state, on condition that it had a REPUBLICAN FORM OF GOVERNMENT and a state constitution. Ohio, Illinois, Indiana, Michigan, and Wisconsin were formed out of the Northwest Territory; this ordinance established a model for territorial governance and the admission of other states in the American West.

The ordinance was the first federal document to contain a bill of rights. To extend "the fundamental principles of civil and RELIGIOUS LIBERTY," Congress provided articles that were to have constitutional status, remaining "forever . . . unalterable" except by common consent. These articles guaranteed that the inhabitants of a territory should always be entitled to the writ of HABEAS CORPUS, TRIAL BY JURY, representative government, and judicial proceedings "according to the course of the COMMON LAW" (in effect, a provision for DUE PROCESS OF LAW.) As an extra safeguard the articles encapsulated a provision from MAGNA CARTA by insuring that no person should be deprived of liberty or property "but by the judgment of his peers, or the LAW OF THE LAND." In addition, the articles protected the right to BAIL except in capital cases, enjoined that all fines should be "moderate," and prohibited CRUEL OR UNUSUAL PUNISHMENT. Another article that provided a federal precedent for a similar provision in the BILL OF RIGHTS of the Constitution of the United States dealt with EMINENT DOMAIN: no person's property could be taken except in a public exigency, when he must be fully compensated for its value. The CONTRACT CLAUSE of the Constitution also originated in this ordinance: one article declared that no law should ever be made or have force that in any manner interfered with or affected existing private contracts made in good faith and without fraud. Other articles encouraged "schools and the means of education" and protected Indian lands and liberties. One provision of the ordinance had the effect of reducing sex discrimination in land ownership and preventing the introduction of the law of primogeniture; it ordained that the property of anyone dying intestate (without a will) should be distributed in equal parts to all children or next of kin. The ordinance also protected the religious sentiments and modes of worship of all orderly persons, without exception, and in a precedent-making clause declared, "There shall be neither slavery nor involuntary servitude" in the Northwest Territory or states formed from it. The ordinance, which was probably drafted in the main by RUFUS KING and NATHAN DANE, remains one of the most constructive and influential legislative acts in American history.

LEONARD W. LEVY

Bibliography

PHILBRICK, FRANCIS S. 1965 *The Rise of the New West, 1754–1830.* Pages 120–133. New York: Harper & Row.

NORTZ v. UNITED STATES

See: Gold Clause Cases

NOTICE

When unsure what is right, American society often falls back on a process in which people on all sides of a disputed question have their say before a decision is rendered. Moreover, even if one cannot participate in a governmental decision, our notions of the state require that one know in advance the standards by which officials will judge us. To have one's say or to conform one's behavior to a standard one must know of the proceeding or the standard. Because such knowledge is so essential to this scheme of things, the Constitution at numerous points requires that those affected by governmental actions receive notice.

Clauses as diverse and specific as the requirement that Congress publish a journal and the prohibitions against EX POST FACTO laws and BILLS OF ATTAINDER, as well as the more general requirements of the DUE PROCESS clauses require notice in various circumstances. Because of its generality the due process clause has generated most of the litigation about constitutionally required notice. In PROCEDURAL DUE PROCESS cases courts have struggled to distinguish two situations: those in which persons need have only the *opportunity* of finding out about contemplated government actions, and situations in which they must receive more individualized attention. The maxim that ignorance of the law is no excuse expresses the proposition that the legislature need not tell each of us that it has passed some law. We rely instead on the hope that our legislators represent us and on the opportunity we have to adjust our behavior after the law takes effect. The Supreme Court has, however, required that laws defining criminal acts be sufficiently specific to enable persons who *do* look at them to tell what acts are prohibited.

As the focus of government attention narrows from all citizens (the subject of statutes) to more specific contexts, the Constitution requires more elaborate and specific forms of notice, notice that is often linked with a subsequent hearing. Thus the Court has not required the Colorado legislature to notify all the citizens of Denver before altering their property assessments, but it has required notice (and a hearing) for individual property owners on a block to be assessed on the basis of frontage feet. Similarly with administrative or judicial adjudication: persons whose property or liberty stands in jeopardy must receive notice of the threatened governmental action.

Even in such individual adjudication, however, due process requires only that parties who will be bound by official decisions receive the best notice practicable given the circumstances. For example, in a suit to approve the trustee's stewardship of a common trust fund with more than a hundred beneficiaries, the Court required individual notice only to those beneficiaries who could easily be located; members of the group thus notified shared an interest with the unnotified and would represent them, the Court said in *Mullane v. Central Hanover Bank & Trust* (1950).

Once it has notified them with appropriate specificity, government requires much of its citizens; until such notice, however, it can require little.

STEPHEN C. YEAZELL

Bibliography

TRIBE, LAURENCE H. 1978 *American Constitutional Law.* Chap. 10. Mineola, N.Y.: Foundation Press.

NOXIOUS PRODUCTS DOCTRINE

The first step in development of a NATIONAL POLICE POWER was the "noxious products doctrine," which Justice JOHN MARSHALL HARLAN propounded in CHAMPION V. AMES (1903). According to this doctrine, Congress has the power to prohibit INTERSTATE COMMERCE in any item that is so injurious to the public—in this case, lottery tickets—as to pollute the commerce of which it is a part. In HAMMER V. DAGENHART (1918), the doctrine became a limitation on the commerce power: because the products of child labor were not inherently more harmful than those of adult labor, Congress lacked power to forbid their interstate transportation. The doctrine was abandoned after UNITED STATES V. DARBY LUMBER (1941).

DENNIS J. MAHONEY

NULLIFICATION

THOMAS JEFFERSON first suggested the doctrine of nullification in the second Kentucky Resolutions (1799), where he asserted that the sovereign states are the only proper judges of whether the federal government has violated the Constitution and "that a nullification . . . [by] those sovereignties, of all unauthorized acts . . . is the rightful remedy." (See VIRGINIA AND KENTUCKY RESOLUTIONS.) In the 1820s, South Carolinians Robert J. Turnbull and Whitemarsh Seabrook laid the doctrinal foundations of an expanded nullification argument by denouncing the expansion of federal authority. In *Consolidation* (1824), THOMAS COOPER argued that the states remained independent sovereigns, having given only limited and express powers to Congress.

JOHN C. CALHOUN systematized and refined the Carolinians' constitutional arguments. He maintained that the people of the separate states never relinquished their SOVEREIGNTY, and that sovereignty was indivisible. In ratifying the Constitution, the states created a government of limited, specified, and delegated authority. Calhoun used the legal doctrine of agency to explain the federal relationship: "The States . . . formed the compact, acting as sovereign and independent communities. The General Government is but [their] creature . . . a government emanating from a compact between sovereigns . . . of the character of a joint commission . . . having, beyond its proper sphere, no more power than if it did not exist." ("Address on the Relation of the States and the Federal Government," 1831.) When the federal government (the agent) exceeded its authority, the states (the principals), in the exercise of their sovereign power, could "interpose" their authority by nullifying the federal statute or action, which would be void in the nullifying states. If three-fourths of the other states adopted a constitutional amendment empowering the federal government to perform the nullified act, the state then had the choice of acquiescing or of withdrawing from the compact (the federal Constitution) by SECESSION. But Calhoun emphasized that nullification was a peaceable alternative, not a preliminary step, to secession.

Calhoun's theory found application in a dispute, ostensibly over protective tariffs, that produced the Nullification Crisis of 1832. For a decade, Carolinians had declared that their objections to specific federal programs such as INTERNAL IMPROVEMENTS or the national bank were merely specific parts of a larger objection to federal intrusion into the states' internal autonomy. The antitariff struggle was, in James Henry

Hammond's metaphor, a "battle at the outposts" to prevent an assault on the real "citadel," slavery. When the Tariff of 1832 failed to meet Carolinian demands for an abrogation of the 1828 Tariff of Abominations, a South Carolina convention adopted an ordinance nullifying it and prohibiting its enforcement in the state.

President ANDREW JACKSON reacted forcefully. In his "Proclamation to the People of South Carolina" (1832), he denounced the theory of secession, insisting that the federal government was a true government to which the states had surrendered a part of their sovereignty. (See JACKSON'S PROCLAMATION.) "Disunion by armed force is treason," he warned. Congress enacted the FORCE ACT (1833), which provided for alternative means of collecting the tariff in South Carolina and enhanced the president's power to use militia and regular forces to suppress resistance to federal authority. Congress also began a downward revision of the tariff. With the crisis over the tariff assuaged, the South Carolina legislature denounced Jackson's "Proclamation" and a subsequent convention made the empty gesture of nullifying the Force Act.

In 1837, Calhoun offered six congressional resolutions that would have opened all federal TERRITORIES to slavery. Congress adopted four of these, including one declaring that the federal government was only a "common agent" of the states and possessed only "delegated" powers. But antislavery agitation in the North increased, and many Northerners endorsed the WILMOT PROVISO (1846), which would have excluded slavery from the territories acquired as a result of the Mexican War. To meet this threat, other southern radicals, including Robert Barnwell Rhett, Edmund Ruffin, and William Lowndes Yancey, turned to secession, which subsumed nullification.

Though the Union victory in the Civil War left the doctrines of state sovereignty, INTERPOSITION, nullification, and secession all defunct, southern political leaders briefly and ineffectually exhumed interposition theories during efforts in the late 1950s to thwart desegregation in southern universities and schools.

WILLIAM M. WIECEK

Bibliography

CURRENT, RICHARD W. N. 1963 *John C. Calhoun.* New York: Washington Square Press.

FREEHLING, WILLIAM W. 1965 *Prelude to Civil War: The Nullification Controversy in South Carolina, 1816–1836.* New York: Harper & Row.

NULLIFICATION CONTROVERSY

See: Constitutional History, 1829–1848

O

OBITER DICTUM

(Latin: "Said in passing.") In an opinion, a judge may make observations or incidental remarks. Because these comments are unnecessary to the DECISION, they are not a part of the HOLDING and thus do not bind the court in later cases. Such statements are often referred to by the plural, dicta.

DAVID GORDON

OBLIGATION OF CONTRACTS

The CONSTITUTIONAL CONVENTION OF 1787, engaged as it was in producing a frame of national government, provided in the Constitution for only a very few restrictions on the LEGISLATIVE POWER of the STATES. Among these was the proscription of any state law impairing the obligation of contracts; that the delegates omitted to include a similar prohibition as to Congress is attributable entirely to the fact that they did not contemplate the existence of national contract law. The phrase "obligation of contracts" did not exist as a term of art, but originated in the Constitution; its meaning is not as obvious as it may seem.

The moral obligation of contracts derives from the voluntary agreement of parties who promise to perform certain duties in exchange for some valuable consideration. In the NATURAL RIGHTS political philosophy of the Framers of the Constitution, the obligation to obey the law itself derives from a SOCIAL COMPACT, in which the individual obliges himself to obey in exchange for the state's guarantee of security for his life, liberty, and property. The moral obligation of contracts, of course, cannot be impaired by state law.

But contracts are also legally binding under the COMMON LAW (as modified from time to time by statute). One of the things that induces men to enter into contracts is the knowledge that the state, by its courts and officers, stands ready to enforce the contractual duties undertaken by the parties. This knowledge is especially important when, as in contracts for lending money, one party will have already performed his side of the bargain while the promise of the other party remains "executory," that is, to be performed in the future. The CONTRACT CLAUSE of the Constitution was intended to prevent state law from undermining the enforceability at law of obligations voluntarily entered into.

The Framers of the Constitution well knew the temptation to repudiate obligations improvidently undertaken. SHAYS' REBELLION, which had just been suppressed in Massachusetts, had been directed against judicial enforcement of farm mortgage loans. The CONTINENTAL CONGRESS, sitting at the same time as the Convention, recognized the same danger and wrote into the NORTHWEST ORDINANCE a provision that "no law ought ever to be made or have force in the said territory, that shall, in any manner whatever, interfere with or affect private contracts, or engagements, *bona fide,* and without fraud previously formed."

The history of the constitutional guarantee against impairment of contracts has been the story of slow, but steady, erosion. Much of the erosion has been effected by limiting the extent of the legal obligation or by discovering remedies that purport to leave the obligation intact while depriving the obligee of the benefit of his bargain. In STURGES V. CROWNINSHIELD (1819) Chief Justice JOHN MARSHALL defined the obligation of a contract as "the law which binds the parties to perform their agreement." Subsequently, in OGDEN V. SAUNDERS (1827), over Marshall's vigorous dissent, the majority held that the "law" in Marshall's definition was the municipal law of contracts in force where and when the contract was entered into, which local law became part of the contract regardless of any contrary intent of the parties to it. The legislature (or courts) may alter the law of contracts so long as the alteration is prospective in effect. Even after *Ogden v. Saunders,* however, the Supreme Court continued to read the contract clause as proscribing retroactive state legislation affecting contracts.

In times of economic distress, when the number of debtors exceeds the number of creditors, the majority tends to use the political process to shield itself from the consequences of improvident engagements. When the economic hardship is prolonged, even constitutional barriers may be unable to withstand the pressure for relief. Under such pressure, courts have held debtors' relief legislation constitutional by distinguishing the obligation of the contract from the remedies available when the contract is breached. Thus, for example, in HOME BUILDING AND LOAN COMPANY V. BLAISDELL (1933) the HUGHES COURT held that a state law extending the contractual time for repayment of mortgage loans and precluding creditors from exercising their contractual right to sell the mortgaged property to satisfy the debt did not impair the obligation of the loan contract (because the debtor still owed the money) but merely altered the remedy. This sophistical holding permitted the form of the constitutional guarantee to endure even as its substance drained away.

In recent years the Court has partially repudiated the rationale of *Blaisdell* and has revived the contract clause as a check on state ECONOMIC REGULATION. In UNITED STATES TRUST CO. V. NEW JERSEY (1977) as regards public contracts, and in ALLIED STRUCTURAL STEEL CO. V. SPANNAUS (1978) as regards private contracts, the Court subjected statutes that apparently impaired the obligation of contracts to a higher STANDARD OF REVIEW than is commonly applied to economic legislation.

DENNIS J. MAHONEY

Bibliography

FRIED, CHARLES 1981 *Contract as Promise: A Theory of Contractual Obligation.* Cambridge, Mass.: Harvard University Press.

O'BRIEN, UNITED STATES v. 391 U.S. 367 (1968)

The *O'Brien* opinion is today widely cited in briefs and judicial opinions defending governmental action against claims of violation of the FREEDOM OF SPEECH. In 1965 Congress amended the SELECTIVE SERVICE ACT to make it a crime to destroy or mutilate a draft registration card. The amendment's legislative history made clear that it was aimed at antiwar protest, but the Supreme Court nonetheless upheld, 8–1, the conviction of a protester for DRAFT CARD BURNING, rejecting his FIRST AMENDMENT claims.

Writing for the Court, Chief Justice EARL WARREN assumed that SYMBOLIC SPEECH of this kind was entitled to First Amendment protection. However, he announced a doctrinal formula now dear to the hearts of government attorneys, a formula that seemed to apply generally to all First Amendment cases: "[W]e think it clear that a government regulation is sufficiently justified if it is within the constitutional power of the Government; if it furthers an important or substantial governmental interest; if the governmental interest is unrelated to the suppression of free expression; and if the incidental restriction on alleged First Amendment freedoms is no greater than is essential to the furtherance of that interest."

This very case seemed appropriate for application of the formula to overturn the protesters' conviction, but it was not to be. Here, Warren said, the power of the federal government to "conscript manpower" was clear; further, he placed great importance on the government's interests in keeping draft cards intact. As for the purpose to suppress expression, the Chief Justice took away what he had just given to First Amendment challengers: the Court should not inquire, he said, into possible improper congressional motivations for an otherwise valid law. (See LEGISLATION.) Finally, he said, the government's interests could not be served by any less restrictive means.

It is hard to avoid the conclusion that the Justices, embattled on political fronts ranging from SEGREGATION to school prayers, thought it prudent not to add to the Court's difficulties a confrontation with Congress and the President over the VIETNAM WAR. Justice WILLIAM O. DOUGLAS, however, dissented alone on the ground that the Court should consider the constitutionality of military CONSCRIPTION in the absence of a DECLARATION OF WAR by Congress.

KENNETH L. KARST

Bibliography

ELY, JOHN HART 1975 Flag Desecration: A Case Study in the Roles of Categorization and Balancing in First Amendment Analysis. *Harvard Law Review* 88:1482–1508.

NIMMER, MELVILLE B. 1973 The Meaning of Symbolic Speech under the First Amendment. *UCLA Law Review* 21:29–62.

O'BRIEN v. BROWN
409 U.S. 1 (1972)

This decision involved challenges to the unseating of delegates to the Democratic National Convention. The Supreme Court refused to decide the case and stayed the lower court's decision, since the full convention had not met on the question and little time was available to decide delicate, "essentially political" issues. Three Justices dissented.

WARD E. Y. ELLIOTT

OBSCENITY

Obscenity laws embarrass ALEXIS DE TOCQUEVILLE's claim that there is "hardly a political question in the United States which does not sooner or later turn into a judicial one." It is not merely that the obscenity question became a serious judicial issue rather much later than sooner. It is that the richness of the questions involved have been lost in their translation to the judicial forum.

Obscenity laws implicate great questions of political theory including the characteristics of human nature, the relationship between law and morals, and the appropriate role of the state in a democratic society. But these questions were barely addressed when the Court first seriously considered a constitutional challenge to obscenity laws in the 1957 cases of ROTH v. UNITED STATES and *Alberts v. California.*

The briefs presented the Court with profoundly different visions of FIRST AMENDMENT law. Roth argued that no speech including obscenity could be prohibited without meeting the CLEAR AND PRESENT DANGER test, that a danger of lustful thoughts was not the type of evil with which a legislature could be legitimately concerned, and that no danger of antisocial conduct had been shown. On the other hand, the government urged the Court to adopt a balancing test that prominently featured a consideration of the value of the speech involved. The government tendered an illustrative hierarchy of nineteen speech categories with political, religious, economic, and scientific speech at the top; entertainment, music, and humor in the middle; and libel, obscenity, profanity, and commercial PORNOGRAPHY at the bottom. The government's position was that the strength of public interest needed to justify speech regulation diminished as one moved down the hierarchy and increased as one moved up.

In response to these opposing contentions, the Court took a middle course. Relying on cases like BEAUHARNAIS V. ILLINOIS (1952), the Court seemed to embrace what HARRY KALVEN, JR., later called the TWO-LEVEL THEORY of the First Amendment. Under this theory, some speech is beneath the protection of the First Amendment; only that speech within the amendment's protection is measured by the clear and present danger test. Thus some speech is at the bottom of a two-level hierarchy, and the *Roth* Court sought to explain why obscenity deserved basement-level nonprotection.

History, tradition, and consensus were the staple of the Court's argument. Justice WILLIAM J. BRENNAN explained that all "ideas having even the slightest redeeming social importance" deserve full First Amendment protection. But, he said, "implicit in the history of the First Amendment is the rejection of obscenity as utterly without redeeming social importance." Then he pointed to the consensus of fifty nations, forty-eight states, and twenty obscenity laws passed by the Congress from 1842 to 1956. Finally, relying on an OBITER DICTUM from CHAPLINSKY V. NEW HAMPSHIRE (1942), the Court explained that obscene utterances "are of such slight social value as a step to truth that any benefit that may be derived from them is clearly outweighed by the social interest in order and morality."

From the perspective of liberal, conservative, or feminist values, the Court's reliance on the *Chaplinsky* quotation amounts to a cryptic resolution of fundamental political questions. Liberals would advance several objections. Some would suggest that the Court underestimates the contribution to truth made by sexually oriented material. David Richards, for example, has suggested that

> pornography can be seen as the unique medium of a vision of sexuality . . . a view of sensual delight in the erotic celebration of the body, a concept of easy freedom without consequences, a fantasy of timelessly repetitive indulgence. In opposition to the Victorian view that narrowly defines

proper sexual function in a rigid way that is analogous to ideas of excremental regularity and moderation, pornography builds a model of plastic variety and joyful excess in sexuality. In opposition to the sorrowing Catholic dismissal of sexuality as an unfortunate and spiritually superficial concomitant of propagation, pornography affords the alternative idea of the independent status of sexuality as a profound and shattering ecstasy [1974, p. 81].

Even some liberals might find these characterizations overwrought as applied to Samuel Roth's publications, such as *Wild Passion* and *Wanton by Night.* Nonetheless, many of them would argue that even if such publications have no merit in the MARKETPLACE OF IDEAS, individuals should be able to decide for themselves what they want to read. Many would argue along with John Stuart Mill that "[T]he only purpose for which power can be rightfully exercised over any member of a civilized community, against his will, is to prevent harm to others." Such a principle is thought to advance the moral nature of humanity, for what distinguishes human beings from animals is the capacity to make autonomous moral judgments. From this perspective, the *Roth* opinion misunderstands the necessity for individual moral judgments and diminishes liberty in the name of order without a proper showing of harm.

Conservatives typically agree that humans are distinguished from animals by their capacity to make rational moral judgments. They believe, however, that liberals overestimate human rational capacity and underestimate the importance of the state in promoting a virtuous citizenry. Moreover, they insist that liberals do not sufficiently appreciate the morally corrosive effects of obscenity. From their perspective, obscenity emphasizes the base animality of our nature, reduces the spirituality of humanity to mere bodily functions, and debases civilization by transforming the private into the public. As Irving Kristol put it, "When sex is a public spectacle, a human relationship has been debased into a mere animal connection."

Feminists typically make no objection to erotic material and make no sharp separation between reason and passion. Their principal objection is to the kind of sexually oriented material that encourages male sexual excitement in the domination of women. From their perspective, a multibillion dollar industry promotes antifemale propaganda encouraging males to get, as Susan Brownmiller put it, a "sense of power from viewing females as anonymous, panting playthings, adult toys, dehumanized objects to be used, abused, broken and discarded." From the feminist perspective, the *Roth* opinion's reference to the interests in order and morality obscures the interest in equality for women. From the conservative perspective, the opinion is underdeveloped. From the liberal perspective, it is wrong-headed.

Liberals gained some post-*Roth* hope from the Court's treatment of the obscenity question in STANLEY V. GEORGIA (1969). In *Stanley* the Court held that the possession of obscenity in the home could not be made a criminal offense without violating the First Amendment. More interesting than the holding, which has since been confined to its facts, was the Court's rationale. The Court insisted that "our whole constitutional heritage rebels at the thought of giving government the power to control men's minds." It denied the state any power "to control the moral content of a person's thoughts." It suggested that the only interests justifying obscenity laws were that obscene material might fall into the hands of children or that it might "intrude upon the sensibilities or privacy of the general public."

Many commentators thought that *Stanley* would be extended to protect obscene material where precautions had been taken to avoid exposure to children or nonconsenting adults. Indeed such precautions were taken by many theaters, but the Supreme Court (the composition of which had changed significantly since *Stanley*) reaffirmed *Roth* and expanded on its rationale in *Paris Adult Theatre I v. Slaton* (1973).

The Court professed to "hold that there are legislative interests at stake in stemming the tide of commercialized obscenity, even assuming it is feasible to enforce effective safeguards against exposure to the juvenile and the passerby. These include the interest of the public in the quality of life and the total community environment, the tone of commerce in the great city centers, and, possibly, the public safety itself." The Court did not suggest that the link between obscenity and sex crimes was anything other than arguable. It did insist that the "States have the power to make a morally neutral judgment that public exhibition of obscene material, or commerce in such material, has a tendency to injure the community as a whole . . . or to jeopardize, in Chief Justice Earl Warren's words, the State's 'right . . . to maintain a decent society.' "

Several puzzles remain after the Court's explanation is dissected. First, "arguable" connections to crime do not ordinarily suffice to justify restrictions of First Amendment liberties. A merely arguable connection to crime supports restriction only if the speech involved is for some other reason outside First

Amendment protection. Second, as the Court was later to recognize in YOUNG V. AMERICAN MINI THEATRES, INC. (1976), the reference to quality of life, the tone of commerce in the central cities, and the environment have force with respect to all sexually oriented bookstores and theaters whether or not they display obscene films or sell obscene books. The Court in MILLER V. CALIFORNIA (1973) limited the definition of obscenity to that material which the "average person, applying contemporary community standards" would find that "taken as a whole appeals to the prurient interest" and "depicts and describes, in a patently offensive way, sexual conduct specifically defined by the applicable state law"; and which, "taken as a whole, lacks serious literary, artistic, political, or scientific value." No one has suggested that these restrictions on the definition bear any relationship to the tone of commerce in the cities.

Moreover, if the intrusive character of public display were the issue, mail order sales of obscene material should pass muster under the First Amendment; yet there is no indication that the Court is prepared to protect such traffic. As interpreted in the *Paris Adult Theatre* opinion, *Stanley v. Georgia* appears to protect only those obscene books and films created and enjoyed in the home; the right to use in the home amounts to no more than that. There is no right to receive obscene material—even in plain brown wrappers.

Perhaps least convincing is the Court's attempt to harmonize its *Paris Adult Theatre* holding with liberal thought. It claims to have no quarrel with the court's insistence in *Stanley* that the state is without power "to control the moral content of a person's thoughts." Because obscene material by the Court's definition lacks any serious literary, artistic, political, or scientific value, control of it is said to be "distinct from a control of reason and the intellect." But this is doubletalk. The power to decide what has serious artistic value is the power to make moral decisions. To decide that material addressing "reason" or the "intellect" is all that is important to human beings is ultimately to make a moral decision about human beings. Implicit in the latter idea, of course, is the belief that the enjoyment of erotic material for its own sake is unworthy of protection. But the view is much more general. The Court supposes that human beings have a rational side and an emotional side, that the emotional side needs to be subordinated and controlled, and that such suppression or control is vital to the moral life. That is why the Court believes that the contribution of obscenity to truth is outweighed by the state's interest in morality. The Court's insistence on the right to maintain a decent society is in fact an insistence on the state's interest in the control of the "moral content of a person's thoughts."

Finally, it is simply dazzling for the Court to suggest that the states are engaged in a "morally neutral" judgment when they decide that obscene material jeopardizes the right to maintain a decent society. When states decide that "a sensitive key relationship of human existence, central to family life, community welfare, and the development of human personality can be debased and distorted by commercial exploitation of sex," they operate as moral guardians, not as moral neutrals. Nonetheless, the Courts' bows to liberal theory in *Paris Adult Theatre* are revealing, and so are the guarded compromises of the obscenity test adopted in *Miller v. California.* The bows and compromises reflect, as do the opinions of the four dissenting Justices in *Paris Adult Theatre,* that America is profoundly divided on the relationship of law to morality and on the meaning of free speech. Since *Paris Adult Theatre* and *Miller,* and despite those decisions, the quantity of erotic material has continued to grow. At the same time, feminist opposition to pornography has ripened into a powerful political movement. The Supreme Court's decisions have neither stemmed the tide of commercial pornography nor resolved the divisions of American society on the issue. These political questions will continue to be judicial questions.

STEVEN SHIFFRIN

Bibliography

CLOR, HARRY M. 1969 *Obscenity and Public Morality.* Chicago: University of Chicago Press.

KALVEN, HARRY, JR. 1960 The Metaphysics of the Law of Obscenity. *Supreme Court Review* 1960:1–45.

LEDERER, LAURA, ed. 1980 *Take Back the Night: Women on Pornography.* New York: Bantam Books.

RICHARDS, DAVID A. J. 1974 Free Speech and Obscenity Law: Toward a Moral Theory of the First Amendment. *University of Pennsylvania Law Review* 123:45–99.

O'CONNOR, SANDRA DAY
(1930–)

Sandra Day O'Connor, the first woman Justice to serve on the Supreme Court, was appointed by President RONALD REAGAN in 1981. She had served previously as the nation's first woman senate majority leader in her home state of Arizona and as a member of the Arizona Court of Appeals. In announcing her nomination the President extolled her as someone who would be a rigid adherent of constitutional principles, taking an exacting view of the SEPARATION OF POWERS as a limitation on JUDICIAL ACTIVISM, and respecting the role of FEDERALISM in the constitutional scheme. Although there is little doubt that one motivation in appointing O'Connor was to deprive the Democrats of the opportunity of appointing the first woman Justice, the President's expectations have, by and large, not been disappointed.

For O'Connor constitutional jurisprudence means, above all, an adherence to enduring constitutional principles, recognizing that, while the application of these principles may change, the principles themselves are rooted in the constitutional text and in the precepts that animate the Constitution. In her dissent in *Akron v. Akron Center for Reproductive Health* (1983), O'Connor complained that the majority's decision rested "neither [on] sound constitutional theory nor [on] our need to decide cases based on the application of neutral principles." It is not entirely clear yet whether the Justice mistakenly identifies constitutional principles with "neutral principles." Her opinions generally indicate an awareness that the Constitution is not neutral with respect to its ends and purposes. She has refused to accept the prevailing view that the Constitution is merely a procedural instrument that is informed by no purposes or principles beyond the procedures themselves.

In CRIMINAL PROCEDURE cases O'Connor has adhered to the principle she enunciated in KOLENDER V. LAWSON (1983): "Our Constitution is designed to maximize individual freedoms within a framework of ORDERED LIBERTY. Statutory limitations on those freedoms are examined for substantive authority and content as well as for definiteness or certainty of expression." The Justice has used this rationale to resist unwarranted attempts to expand criminal DUE PROCESS rights beyond those clearly prescribed or fairly implied by the Constitution. For example, in OREGON V. ELSTAD (1985) O'Connor refused to extend the FRUIT OF THE POISONOUS TREE doctrine either to uncoerced inculpatory statements made after police violation of the MIRANDA RULES, or as in NEW YORK V. QUARLES (1984), to nontestimentary EVIDENCE produced as a result of a *Miranda* violation. In the latter case O'Connor concluded that Justice WILLIAM H. REHNQUIST's majority opinion had created "a finespun new DOCTRINE on public safety exigencies incident to custodial interrogation, complete with the hair-splitting distinctions that currently plague our FOURTH AMENDMENT jurisprudence." Moreover, dissenting in *Taylor v. Alabama* (1982), O'Connor would not have allowed an illegal ARREST to taint a confession that followed appropriate *Miranda* warnings; nor in *South Dakota v. Neville* (1983) would she allow the claim that the refusal to take a blood-alcohol test is protected by the RIGHT AGAINST SELF-INCRIMINATION.

O'Connor has been no less resolute in her efforts to protect the constitutional role of the states in the federal system. In her dissent in GARCIA V. SAN ANTONIO METROPOLITAN TRANSIT AUTHORITY (1985) she remarked that the principle of "state autonomy . . . requires the Court to enforce affirmative limits on federal regulation of the states." The majority opinion, she continued, created the "real risk that Congress will gradually erase the diffusion of power between state and nation on which the Framers based their faith in the efficiency and vitality of our Republic." O'Connor has also staunchly supported the "exhaustion" doctrine of federal HABEAS CORPUS review as a means "to protect the state courts' role in the enforcement of federal law and prevent disruption of state judicial proceedings." The rule that all federal claims must first be exhausted in state court proceedings is, as she wrote in *Engle v. Isaac* (1982), a recognition that "the State possesses primary authority for defining and enforcing the criminal law." She continued that "[f]ederal intrusions into State criminal trials frustrate both the States' sovereign power to punish offenders and their good-faith attempts to honor constitutional rights." And in HAWAII HOUSING AUTHORITY V. MIDKIFF (1984) O'Connor made clear that the Court would accord the utmost deference to state legislatures in matters of "social legislation."

O'Connor was less deferential, however, in the instance where a state maintained a women-only nursing school. Writing for the majority in MISSISSIPPI UNIVERSITY FOR WOMEN V. HOGAN (1982), O'Connor stated that in "limited circumstances a gender-based classification favoring one sex can be justified if it intentionally and directly assists members of the sex that is disproportionately burdened." Here, the SEX DISCRIMINATION actually harmed the intended beneficiaries by perpetuating "stereotyped" and "archaic" notions about the role of women in society.

O'Connor has urged the Court to reexamine some important issues connected with the ESTABLISHMENT OF RELIGION clause of the FIRST AMENDMENT. Concurring in WALLACE V. JAFFREE (1985), O'Connor agreed that an Alabama law providing for a moment of silence was unconstitutional because it sought to sanction and promote prayer in public schools. She dissented, however, from the Court's decision in AGUILAR V. FELTON (1985) striking down the use of federal funds to provide remedial education by public school teachers for parochial school students. While agreeing in LYNCH v. DONNELLY (1983) that every governmental policy touching upon religion must have a secular purpose, O'Connor suggested that the entanglement test propounded in LEMON v. KURTZMAN (1971) should be reexamined.

In the area of EQUAL PROTECTION rights, O'Connor has taken the firm stance that rights belong to individuals. In *Ford Motor Company v. Equal Employment Opportunity Commission* (1982), and in her concurring opinion in FIREFIGHTERS LOCAL #1784 v. STOTTS (1984), O'Connor argued that remedies must be limited to those who can demonstrate actual injury and must be fashioned in a way that protects the settled expectations of innocent parties. She thus adheres to the original intention of the framers of the FOURTEENTH AMENDMENT and of the CIVIL RIGHTS ACT OF 1964, reaffirming the principle that lies at the heart of constitutional jurisprudence—that rights belong to individuals and not to the racial or gender group of which they are members. Employing narrowly construed and analytical opinions, O'Connor has begun to build a solid base for the Court's return to a jurisprudence that looks to the articulation of the Constitution's enduring principles.

EDWARD J. ERLER

Bibliography

CORDRAY, RICHARD A. and VRADLIS, JAMES T. 1985 The Emerging Jurisprudence of Justice O'Connor. *University of Chicago Law Review* 52:389–459.

O'CONNOR, SANDRA DAY 1981 Trends in the Relationships between the Federal and State Courts from the Perspective of a State Court Judge. *William and Mary Law Review* 22:801–815.

O'CONNOR v. DONALDSON
422 U.S. 563 (1975)

Donaldson was initially billed as the case that would decide whether a mental patient held in custody had a constitutional "right to treatment." Ultimately the Court did not decide that issue, but it did make some important pronouncements on the relation between MENTAL ILLNESS AND THE CONSTITUTION.

Kenneth Donaldson was committed to a state hospital at the request of his father; the committing judge found that he suffered from "paranoid schizophrenia." Although the commitment order specified "care, maintenance, and treatment," for almost fifteen years Donaldson received nothing but "milieu therapy"—the hospital superintendent's imaginative name for involuntary confinement. Donaldson finally sued the superintendent and others for damages under SECTION 1983, TITLE 42, UNITED STATES CODE, claiming they had intentionally denied his constitutional rights. The federal district judge instructed the jury that Donaldson's rights had been denied if the defendants had confined him against his will, knowing that he was neither dangerous nor receiving treatment. The jury awarded damages, and the court of appeals affirmed, specifically endorsing the district court's theory of a mental patient's constitutional right to treatment.

The Supreme Court unanimously held that Donaldson had stated a valid claim, but remanded the case for reconsideration of the hospital superintendent's assertion of EXECUTIVE IMMUNITY. Justice POTTER STEWART, for the Court, said that a finding of mental illness alone could not justify a state's confining a person indefinitely "in simple custodial confinement." The Court did not reach the larger question of a "right to treatment"; it disclaimed any need to decide whether persons dangerous to themselves or others had a right to be treated during their involuntary confinement by the state, or whether a nondangerous person could be confined for purposes of treatment. But when the state lacked any of the usual grounds for confinement of the mentally ill—the safety of the person confined or others, or treatment for illness—involuntary confinement was a denial of liberty without DUE PROCESS OF LAW. Confinement was not justified, for example, in order to provide the mentally ill with superior living standards, or to shield the public from unpleasantness. To support the latter point, the Court cited FIRST AMENDMENT decisions including COHEN v. CALIFORNIA (1971). Chief Justice WARREN E. BURGER concurred in the Court's opinion, but wrote separately to express his opposition to any constitutional "right to treatment."

KENNETH L. KARST

OFFICE OF MANAGEMENT AND BUDGET

The rapid growth of the federal government in the twentieth century has created the need for an institution to coordinate both fiscal and substantive policy. In 1921, Congress empowered the President to prepare and submit a BUDGET for the government. Previously, the government had had no central budgeting function: the various agencies had made funding requests directly to the appropriations committees in Congress. The President exercises the budgeting function through the Office of Management and Budget (OMB). Although OMB controls the requests that Congress receives, Congress is free to appropriate any amount that it considers appropriate.

The budgeting function accords the President an important opportunity to set the agenda for congressional deliberations over appropriations. Notwithstanding the modern presence of a budget process within Congress itself, Congress finds itself responding initially to the President's views of the best resource allocation for the government. And, of course, Congress is aware that its departure from the President's recommended budget may result in the presidential veto of an appropriations bill. In consequence, through OMB the President exercises great influence on actual appropriations. Moreover, appropriations usually confer discretion concerning the amounts to be spent and the precise uses to be made of the funds. The President supervises the agencies' actual spending through OMB.

OMB also exercises limited control over the substantive policies that the agencies follow. The Supreme Court, in MYERS V. UNITED STATES (1926), recognized presidential power to "supervise and guide" the executive agencies in their exercise of power that Congress has delegated to them. This does not extend to the independent regulatory commissions because, in HUMPHREY'S EXECUTOR V. UNITED STATES (1935), the Supreme Court declared those commissions to be independent of the President except for the constitutional power to appoint their members, and except for powers over them that Congress explicitly grants the President, such as budget review.

Policy supervision therefore concentrates on the executive agencies. In part because of doubts about the extent of the President's power to dictate policy even when it is formed in the executive agencies, OMB has usually limited its supervision to requiring agencies to comply with procedural directives imposed by Presidential EXECUTIVE ORDERS. These directives are thought to be less intrusive than outright commands setting substantive policy. Several Presidents have directed the agencies to prepare analyses of the costs and benefits of their regulations, and to submit them to OMB for review and comment. In view of the size of the executive establishment and the complexity of the issues it considers, this kind of procedural supervision and occasional ad hoc consultation on major policy decisions is the most that the relatively small bureaucracy that serves the President in OMB can hope to accomplish.

HAROLD H. BRUFF

Bibliography

MILLS, GREGORY B. and PALMER, JOHN L., eds. 1984 *Federal Budget Policy in the 1980s.* Washington D.C.: The Urban Institute Press.

OFFICIAL IMMUNITY

See: Executive Immunity; Judicial Immunity; Legislative Immunity; Municipal Immunity; Sovereign Immunity

OGDEN v. SAUNDERS
12 Wheaton 213 (1827)

Ogden established the doctrine that a state bankruptcy act operating on contracts made after the passage of the act does not violate the OBLIGATION OF A CONTRACT. The majority reasoned that the obligation of a contract, deriving from positive law, is the creature of state laws applicable to contracts. A contract made after the enactment of a bankruptcy statute is, therefore, subject to its provisions; in effect the statute enters into and becomes part of all contracts subsequently made, limiting their obligation but not impairing it.

For a minority of three, Chief Justice JOHN MARSHALL dissented, losing control of his Court in a constitutional case for the first and only time during his long tenure. He would have voided all state bankruptcy acts that affected the obligation of contracts even prospectively. Grounding his position in the immutable HIGHER LAW principles of morality and natural justice, he maintained that the right of contract is an inalienable right not subject to positive law. The parties to a contract, not society or government, create its obligation. Marshall believed that the majority's interpretation of the CONTRACT CLAUSE would render its constitutional prohibition on the states "inanimate, inoperative, and unmeaning." Had his opinion prevailed, contractual rights of property vested by contract would have been placed beyond government regulation, making the contract clause the instrument of protecting property that the Court later fashioned out of the DUE PROCESS clause substantively construed. Until then, despite Marshall's fears, the contract clause remained the principal bastion for the

DOCTRINE of VESTED RIGHTS. This case, however, ended the Court's doctrinal expansion of that clause. *Ogden* prevented constitutional law from confronting the nation with a choice between unregulated capitalism and socialism.

LEONARD W. LEVY

OHIO LIFE INSURANCE AND TRUST CO. v. DE BOLT

See: *Piqua Branch Bank v. Knoop*

OKANOGAN INDIANS v. UNITED STATES

See: Pocket Veto Case

OLIVER, IN RE
333 U.S. 257 (1948)

Since 1917 Michigan had maintained a unique GRAND JURY system, allowing a single judge to be a grand jury with all its inquisitorial powers as well as retain his judicial power to punish for contempt any witness whose testimony he believed to be false or evasive. In the course of a secret grand jury proceeding, a judge summarily sentenced Oliver for contempt. The Supreme Court held the Michigan procedure a violation of SIXTH AMENDMENT rights—denial of PUBLIC TRIAL and of an opportunity to defend himself—without DUE PROCESS OF LAW, contrary to the FOURTEENTH AMENDMENT. Justice HUGO L. BLACK spoke for a 7–2 majority.

LEONARD W. LEVY

OLIVER v. UNITED STATES
466 U.S. 170 (1984)

A 6–3 Supreme Court, speaking through Justice LEWIS F. POWELL, reinvigorated the sixty-year-old "open fields" DOCTRINE, according to which the FOURTH AMENDMENT, whose language protects "persons, houses, papers, and effects," does not extend to open fields. No one doubts that the police, or public, may view land from a plane. The question in *Oliver* was whether the police could ignore "No Trespassing" signs and make a warrantless investigation of fenced-in backlands used to grow marijuana, seize EVIDENCE, and introduce it in court despite a TRESPASS on private property. Powell declared that no one could reasonably have a constitutionally protected expectation of privacy in an open field, well away from the curtilage or land immediately surrounding a house (and therefore part of the area to which the Fourth Amendment's protection extends). The dissenters objected that the language of the amendment does not expressly include many areas which the Court has ruled to be within its protection, such as telephone booths, offices, curtilages, and other places which one may reasonably expect to be secure against warrantless police intrusion.

LEONARD W. LEVY

OLMSTEAD v. UNITED STATES
277 U.S. 438 (1928)

Federal agents installed WIRETAPS in the basement of a building where Roy Olmstead, a suspected bootlegger, had his office and in streets near his home. None of Olmstead's property was trespassed upon. A sharply divided Supreme Court admitted the wiretap EVIDENCE in an opinion that virtually exempted ELECTRONIC EAVESDROPPING from constitutional controls for forty years. The dissents by Justices OLIVER WENDELL HOLMES and LOUIS D. BRANDEIS are classic statements of the government's obligation to obey the law.

Olmstead argued that because the prosecution's evidence came entirely from the wiretaps, it could not be used against him; wiretapping, he claimed, was a SEARCH AND SEIZURE under the FOURTH AMENDMENT, and because the amendment's warrant and other requirements had not been met, the wiretap evidence was illegally obtained. He also claimed that use of the wiretap evidence violated his RIGHT AGAINST SELF-INCRIMINATION under the Fifth Amendment; further, that because the agents had violated a state statute prohibiting wiretapping, the evidence was inadmissible, apart from the Fourth and Fifth Amendments.

Chief Justice WILLIAM HOWARD TAFT, writing for a five-Justice majority, rejected all Olmstead's contentions. The self-incrimination claim was dismissed first: the defendants had not been compelled to talk over the telephone but had done so voluntarily. This aspect of *Olmstead* has survived to be applied in cases such as HOFFA V. UNITED STATES (1966). As to the Fourth

Amendment claims: first, the Court ruled that the amendment was violated only if officials trespassed onto the property of the person overheard, and no such trespass had taken place—the agents had tapped Olmstead's telephones without going onto his property. Second, the Court limited Fourth Amendment protection to "material things," not intangibles like conversations. Third, the Court seemed to deny any protection for the voice if projected outside the house. As to the claim that the agents' violation of the state statute required excluding the evidence, the Chief Justice found no authority for such exclusion.

Justice Holmes wrote a short dissent, condemning the agents' conduct as "dirty business." Justice Brandeis wrote the main dissent in which he disagreed with the majority's reading of the precedents, its very narrow view of the Fourth Amendment, and its willingness to countenance criminal activity by the government. For him, the Fourth Amendment was designed to protect individual privacy, and he warned that the "progress of science in furnishing the Government with means of espionage" called for a flexible reading of the amendment to "protect the right of personal security." He stressed that because a tap reaches all who use the telephone, including all those who either call the target or are called, "WRITS OF ASSISTANCE or GENERAL WARRANTS are but puny instruments of tyranny and oppression when compared with wiretapping." Responding to the argument that law enforcement justified both a narrow reading of the amendment and indifference to the agents' violation of state law, he wrote: "Experience should teach us to be most on our guard to protect liberty when the Government's purposes are beneficent. . . . The greatest dangers to liberty lurk in insidious encroachment by men of zeal, well-meaning but without understanding. . . . Our Government is the potent, the omnipresent teacher. For good or for ill, it teaches the whole people by its example."

Although the decision was harshly criticized, it endured. In *Goldman v. United States* (1942), *Olmstead* was read to allow police to place a microphone against the outside of a wall, because no trespass onto the property was involved. Wiretapping itself remained outside constitutional controls, though section 605 of the COMMUNICATIONS ACT of 1934 was construed by the Supreme Court in NARDONE V. UNITED STATES (1937) to bar unauthorized interception and divulgence of telephone messages.

In 1954, however, *Olmstead* began to be undermined. In IRVINE V. CALIFORNIA (1954), the Court indicated that intangible conversations were protected by the Fourth Amendment. The Court found a trespass when the physical penetration was only a few inches into a party wall as in SILVERMAN V. UNITED STATES (1961) or by a thumbtack as in *Clinton v. Virginia* (1964). Finally, in KATZ V. UNITED STATES (1967), the Supreme Court overruled *Olmstead*, holding that a trespass was unnecessary for a violation of the Fourth Amendment and that the amendment protects intangibles, including conversations.

HERMAN SCHWARTZ

Bibliography

MURPHY, WALTER F. 1966 *Wiretapping on Trial: A Case Study in the Judicial Process.* New York: Random House.

OLNEY, RICHARD
(1835–1917)

In 1893 President GROVER CLEVELAND offered the post of ATTORNEY GENERAL to Richard Olney. A Massachusetts Democrat and highly successful railroad lawyer, Olney sought the advice of his major clients. All agreed he should accept the office and one even continued him on the payroll after he took the post, a conflict of interest that reflected the biases Olney allowed to influence his actions in office.

Olney was one of a few lawyers in the country who had litigated the recently passed SHERMAN ANTITRUST ACT; he had successfully defended the Whiskey Trust, and he believed that section 2 of the act was "void because of vagueness, indefiniteness, and ambiguity." While Olney served as attorney general, the Department of Justice initiated no new antitrust suits against business combinations.

Olney is most often remembered for his weak presentation of the government case in UNITED STATES V. E. C. KNIGHT & COMPANY (1895). Although the prosecution had been begun under President BENJAMIN HARRISON, Olney was responsible for choosing *Knight* to test the Sherman Act's constitutionality. Even as attorney general he specifically rejected the belief that "the aim and effect of this statute are to prohibit and prevent" trusts, and he contended that "literal interpretation" of the act was "out of the question" because of the act's overbroad terms. His ineffective prosecution contributed to a government loss, crippling enforcement of the Sherman Act for nearly a decade. Olney saw *Knight* as a vindication of his personal views and as an excuse to ignore the law; although he ought to have chosen a stronger case, the federal judges who so narrowly construed the act must share responsibility for the outcome.

Olney's antipathy to the Sherman Act ran deep.

He was determined to break the Pullman strike in 1894, and although he had to rely on the Sherman Act to secure lower court INJUNCTIONS, he abandoned that successful tack in the Supreme Court. He convinced a unanimous Court in IN RE DEBS (1895) to rely instead upon the inherent power of the executive branch to protect the national interest in the flow of INTERSTATE COMMERCE.

Olney also argued POLLOCK V. FARMERS' LOAN & TRUST COMPANY (1895) before the Supreme Court, although his actions resulted in insufficient time for government preparation and may have cost the government its case. The Court struck down the tax, a decision Olney considered "a great blow to the power of the Federal government . . . a national misfortune."

DAVID GORDON

Bibliography

EGGERT, GERALD 1974 *Richard Olney: Evolution of a Statesman.* University Park: Pennsylvania State University Press.

OLSEN v. NEBRASKA EX REL. REFERENCE & BOND ASSOCIATION

313 U.S. 236 (1941)

Sustaining a Nebraska statute regulating fees charged by private employment agencies, the Supreme Court specifically reversed RIBNIK V. MCBRIDE (1928). Justice WILLIAM O. DOUGLAS reiterated earlier dissents of Justices OLIVER WENDELL HOLMES (see TYSON & BROTHER V. BANTON, 1927) and LOUIS D. BRANDEIS (see NEW STATE ICE COMPANY V. LIEBMANN, 1932), declaring that the need and appropriateness of legislation concerning the public interest ought to be left to state legislatures.

DAVID GORDON

OMNIBUS ACT

15 Stat. 73 (1868)

The Omnibus Act readmitted six of the Confederate states to full congressional representation and terminated military governance in them.

After the process of restoration mandated by the MILITARY RECONSTRUCTION ACTS was largely completed, Congress readmitted Arkansas in June 1868 and, three days later, by the Omnibus Act readmitted Alabama, Florida, Georgia, Louisiana, North Carolina, and South Carolina. The Omnibus Act declared that each of the six states had complied with the conditions specified in the Military Reconstruction Acts, required each to ratify the FOURTEENTH AMENDMENT, and imposed the "fundamental condition" that the state constitutional provisions for black suffrage be inviolate. All the congressmen and senators of these states were seated by late July 1868.

Georgia's full readmission was delayed for two years, however, because the state legislature excluded all black members and admitted several whites disfranchised by the Fourteenth Amendment or the Military Reconstruction Acts. Congress by special legislation forced a rescission of these actions, and Georgia once again underwent military supervision until its readmission. Virginia, Mississippi, and Texas were also readmitted in 1870, thus bringing the formal process of Reconstruction to a close.

WILLIAM M. WIECEK

OMNIBUS CRIME CONTROL AND SAFE STREETS ACT

92 Stat. 3795 (1968)

The most extensive anticrime legislation in the nation's history, this measure reflected the public's fear of rising crime and its demand for federal protection. Congress enacted a massive and restrictive piece of legislation, called by its critics an invasion of basic CIVIL LIBERTIES. Particularly distasteful to President LYNDON B. JOHNSON, who signed it with reluctance, were titles permitting broad use of WIRETAPPING in federal and state cases, and a section seeking to overturn controversial Supreme Court rulings on the rights of defendants.

The act authorized law enforcement grants to aid local police departments in planning, training, and research and a block grant procedure whereby funds were given to the states to be allocated to their communities under a statewide plan. It channeled funds to improve techniques for combating organized crime and for preventing and controlling riots. The most controversial provision of the act purported to overturn Supreme Court decisions in *Mallory v. United States* (1957), MIRANDA V. ARIZONA (1966), and UNITED STATES V. WADE (1967), authorizing greater freedom in POLICE INTERROGATION of suspects accused of crimes against the United States, and in the use of LINEUPS to identify criminals.

The measure specified permissive new conditions

under which confessions could be introduced in federal courts. The trial judge was to determine the issue of voluntariness, out of the hearing of the jury, basing that determination on such criteria as time lapse between arrest and arraignment, whether the defendant knew the nature of the charged offense, when the defendant was advised of or knew of the right to remain silent and the RIGHT TO COUNSEL, and whether the defendant was without assistance of counsel when questioned and giving the confession.

The act's provisions on ELECTRONIC EAVESDROPPING permitted warrant-approved wiretapping and bugging in investigations of a wide variety of specified crimes, and authorized police to intercept communications for forty-eight hours without a warrant in an "emergency" where organized crime or NATIONAL SECURITY was involved. Further, it authorized any law officer or any other person obtaining information in conformity with such a process to disclose or use it as appropriate. The law forbade the interstate shipment to individuals of pistols and revolvers, and over-the-counter purchase of handguns by individuals who did not live in the dealer's state. But it specifically exempted rifles and shotguns from these controls.

Passed overwhelmingly a few hours after the assassination of ROBERT F. KENNEDY, the act still drew the opposition of liberals troubled by its criminal law sections and concerned that its permissive wiretap section did not contain proper constitutional safeguards. Constitutional issues aside, the act failed to achieve its objectives.

PAUL L. MURPHY

Bibliography

NATIONAL COMMISSION ON THE CAUSES AND PREVENTION OF VIOLENCE 1970 *Law and Order Reconsidered.* Washington, D.C.: Government Printing Office.

O'NEIL v. VERMONT

See: *In Re Kemmler*

ONE PERSON, ONE VOTE

The National Municipal League popularized the slogan "one man, one vote" from the 1920s to the 1960s to promote REAPPORTIONMENT to equalize political districts. Reapportionment had lagged far behind urban growth, leaving the largest urban districts by 1960 with only half the legislative representatives per capita of the smallest rural ones.

Urban spokesmen claimed that "malapportionment" produced stagnant "barnyard governments" indifferent to urban concerns and needs. They demanded one person, one vote to stop urban blight and revitalize state governments. These conjectural claims did not win reapportionment from legislators reluctant to tamper with their own districts, nor from voters, who repeatedly defeated reapportionment INITIATIVES. But they did persuade political and legal writers and study commissions, who called for courts or commissions to order reapportionment where legislators and voters would not.

The Supreme Court declined this invitation in COLEGROVE V. GREEN (1946) but accepted one person, one vote in REYNOLDS V. SIMS (1964) as the "fundamental principle" of the Constitution. Political scientists, black rights groups, the *New York Times,* and the DWIGHT D. EISENHOWER and JOHN F. KENNEDY administrations had endorsed that principle.

Some critics thought that the Court had confused individual suffrage with group REPRESENTATION, misconstrued the FOURTEENTH AMENDMENT, and ignored the "standards problem" of equalizing group representation, because gerrymandering could still deny equal weight to votes. Others saw little evidence of revitalization or greater equality in substance to match the greater equality in form, and they believed that by overriding legislative and popular majorities, the Court seemed to have devalued the very representative institutions to which it granted equal access in form.

The WARREN COURT's adoption of one person, one vote was a remarkable political success, affecting more people than school DESEGREGATION or criminal justice cases, with less help from Congress and less damaging backlash. But its practical contributions to equal representation and vital government remain a matter of dispute.

WARD E. Y. ELLIOTT

Bibliography

ELLIOTT, WARD E. Y. 1975 *The Rise of Guardian Democracy: The Supreme Court's Role in Voting Rights Disputes, 1845–1969.* Cambridge, Mass.: Harvard University Press.

ON LEE v. UNITED STATES
343 U.S. 737 (1952)

The Supreme Court held, 5–4, that government informers who deceptively interrogated criminal suspects and simultaneously transmitted the conversations to other government agents via electrical transmitters had not violated the FOURTH AMENDMENT or the antiwiretap provisions of section 605 of the COMMUNICATIONS ACT; the agents who listened might testify to the overheard conversations. Because entry had been consented to—although the consent was obtained deceptively—it was not a TRESPASS, and under OLMSTEAD V. UNITED STATES (1927) the intrusion did not violate the Fourth Amendment. It was also not WIRETAPPING, nor did it become illegal because it might be immoral. The Court reaffirmed *On Lee* in UNITED STATES V. WHITE (1971).

HERMAN SCHWARTZ

OPEN HOUSING LAWS

Many believe housing, the last major area covered by Congress's 1960s CIVIL RIGHTS program, to be the key to at least short-term progress in INTEGRATION. Despite numerous ANTIDISCRIMINATION LAWS, segregated housing patterns threaten much of the civil rights agenda, including integrated public education. Yet until the 1960s the federal government promoted segregated housing. Federal housing agencies, such as the Federal Housing Administration, required racially RESTRICTIVE COVENANTS in federally assisted projects. In Executive Order 11063 (1962), President JOHN F. KENNEDY prohibited housing discrimination in federal public housing and in housing covered by mortgages directly guaranteed by the federal government. Title VI of the CIVIL RIGHTS ACT OF 1964, which outlawed discrimination in programs receiving federal financial assistance, extended the ban to nearly all federally assisted housing.

Title VIII of the CIVIL RIGHTS ACT OF 1968 was the first comprehensive federal open housing law. Title VIII bans discrimination on the basis of race, color, religion, or national origin in the sale, lease, and financing of housing, and in the furnishing of real estate brokerage services. A 1974 amendment extends the ban to discrimination on the basis of sex. Title VIII exempts single-family houses sold or rented by owners and small, owner-occupied boarding houses. Congress's consideration of Title VIII was affected by the assassination of Martin Luther King, Jr. House opponents of the measure had tried to delay its consideration in the hope that intervening national events would sway Congress against it. But during the delay, Dr. King was assassinated and passage of the act followed swiftly.

Courts have construed Title VIII to cover activities other than the direct purchase, sale, or lease of a dwelling. For example, Title VIII prohibits discriminatory refusals to rezone for low-income housing. Most courts find that practices with greater adverse impact on minorities, even if undertaken without discriminatory purposes, impose some burden of justification. This view links Title VIII litigation to a similar line of EMPLOYMENT DISCRIMINATION cases decided under Title VII of the Civil Rights Act of 1964.

To enforce its provisions, Title VIII authorizes the secretary of housing and urban development to seek to conciliate disputes, but the Department of Housing and Urban Development (HUD) initially must defer to state or local housing agencies where state law provides relief substantially equivalent to Title VIII. In *Gladstone, Realtors v. Village of Bellwood* (1979) the Supreme Court held that Title VIII also authorized direct civil actions in federal court without prior resort to HUD or to state authorities. An ATTORNEY GENERAL finding a pattern or practice of housing discrimination is authorized to seek relief in federal court.

Two months after Title VIII's enactment the Supreme Court found Section 1982, Title 42, United States Code, a remnant of section 1 of the CIVIL RIGHTS ACT OF 1866, to be another federal open housing law. Section 1982 grants all citizens the same right "as is enjoyed by white citizens" to purchase and lease real property. In JONES V. ALFRED H. MAYER CO. (1968) the Court construed section 1982 to prohibit a racially motivated refusal to sell a home to a prospective black purchaser. In *Sullivan v. Little Hunting Park, Inc.* (1969) the Court found that violations of section 1982 may be remedied by damages awards or by injunctive relief. There are, therefore, two federal open housing laws, which, in the area of RACIAL DISCRIMINATION, overlap. But section 1982 contains none of Title VIII's exemptions, provides for none of its administrative machinery, and contains no express list of remedies.

THEODORE EISENBERG

Bibliography

BELL, DERRICK A., JR. 1980 *Race, Racism and American Law,* 2nd ed. Boston: Little, Brown.

DORSEN, NORMAN; BENDER, PAUL; NEUBORNE, BURT; and LAW, SYLVIA Emerson, Haber and Dorsen's *Political and Civil Rights in the United States,* 4th ed. II:1063–1149. Boston: Little, Brown.

OPINION OF THE COURT

An appellate court would give little guidance to inferior courts, the legal community, or the general public concerning the law if it merely rendered a DECISION and did not explain the RATIO DECIDENDI, or the grounds for its decision. It is the court's reading of the law and the application of legal principles to the facts that gives a reported case value as PRECEDENT and permits the judicial system to follow the doctrine of STARE DECISIS. By ancient custom, Anglo-American judges, at least at the appellate level, publish opinions along with their decisions.

The general practice of English courts at the time of the American Revolution, and the general practice today in most of the British Commonwealth, is for the members of multijudge courts to deliver their opinions SERIATIM, that is, severally and in sequence. This practice was followed by the United States SUPREME COURT during its early years. However, when JOHN MARSHALL became CHIEF JUSTICE in 1801 he instituted the practice of delivering a single "opinion of the court." The effect of this change was to put the weight of the whole Court behind a particular line of reasoning (usually Marshall's), and so to make that line of reasoning more authoritative. At the time, Marshall's innovation was criticized by many, including President THOMAS JEFFERSON, either because it permitted lazy Justices to evade the responsibility of thinking through the cases on their own or because it fortified the Federalist majority in its conflicts with Republican legislators and state governments.

The opinion of the court is not necessarily unanimous. A majority of the Justices customarily endorses a single opinion, however, and that majority opinion is issued as the opinion of the court, with the Chief Justice—or the senior Justice, if the Chief Justice is not in the majority—assigning responsibility for writing the opinion. A Justice who disagrees with the decision of the case may file a DISSENTING OPINION; a Justice who agrees with the result, but disagrees with the rationale, or desires to supplement the majority opinion, may file a CONCURRING OPINION. When there is no majority opinion, the opinion signed by the largest number of Justices in support of the decisions is called the PLURALITY OPINION, and no opinion of the court is issued. In some important cases in the past, and increasingly during the BURGER COURT years, the number of separate opinions has presented an appearance resembling a return to seriatim opinions.

DENNIS J. MAHONEY

ORAL ARGUMENT

Lawyers argue points of law orally before courts at all levels. The Supreme Court regulates oral argument by court rule. Some cases are decided summarily, without full briefing and argument, on the papers filed by the parties seeking and opposing Supreme Court review. About 150 cases per TERM are decided with briefs and oral argument. The arguments begin in October, early in the term, and (absent extraordinary circumstances) end in the following April, so that all opinions can be finished by the end of the term.

In the Court's early years oral argument was a leisurely affair; argument in MCCULLOCH V. MARYLAND (1819) lasted nine days. Today, given the increase in the Court's business and increasing doubt that illumination is proportional to talk, argument is normally limited to one-half hour for each side. More time may be allocated to a case that is unusually complicated or important. Permission to argue is only rarely granted to an AMICUS CURIAE, except for the SOLICITOR GENERAL, who is often allowed to argue orally for the United States as amicus curiae.

The Justices have already read the briefs when they hear counsel. Accordingly, oral argument is no longer a place for oratory. Justices interrupt with their questions and even conduct debates with each other through rhetorical questions to counsel. Time limits on argument are strictly enforced; the red light flashes on the lectern, and counsel stops.

Normally within a few days after oral argument the Justices meet in CONFERENCE to discuss groups of cases and vote tentatively on their disposition. The Justices regularly say that oral argument, fresh in their minds, influences their thinking in "close" cases. Whether a case is close, however, is a characterization very likely formed before a Justice hears what counsel have to say.

KENNETH L. KARST

Bibliography

STERN, ROBERT L. and GRESSMAN, EUGENE 1978 *Supreme Court Practice,* 5th ed. Chap. 14. Washington, D.C.: Bureau of National Affairs.

ORDERED LIBERTY

A loosely used term, diversely applied in scholarly literature and judicial opinions, "ordered liberty" suggests that fundamental constitutional rights are not absolute but are determined by a balancing of the public (societal) welfare against individual (personal) rights. In this dialectical perspective, the thesis is "order," its antithesis "liberty"; the synthesis, "ordered liberty," describes a polity that has reconciled the conflicting demands of public order and personal freedom.

Justice BENJAMIN N. CARDOZO's majority opinion for the Court in PALKO V. CONNECTICUT (1937) provided what was probably the first judicial recognition of "ordered liberty." Acknowledging the difficulty of achieving "proper order and coherence," Cardozo identified some constitutionally enumerated rights that were *not* of the essence of a scheme of "ordered liberty," and thus not incorporated in the FOURTEENTH AMENDMENT and applied to the states: "to abolish [these rights] is not to violate a principle of justice so rooted in the traditions and conscience of our people as to be ranked fundamental." On the other hand, rights such as "freedom of thought and speech" were "of the very essence of a scheme of ordered liberty" because they constituted "the matrix, the indispensable condition, of nearly every other form of freedom."

HENRY J. ABRAHAM

Bibliography

ABRAHAM, HENRY J. 1987 *Freedom and the Court: Civil Rights and Liberties in the United States,* 5th ed. New York: Oxford University Press.

ORDINANCE OF 1784

One of the most important constitutional questions of the founding era was that of the status of the western TERRITORIES. In 1783, as a concession to secure ratification of the ARTICLES OF CONFEDERATION, states with claims to western lands ceded them to Congress. In April 1784 Congress adopted an ordinance of government for the ceded territory drafted by THOMAS JEFFERSON. That ordinance, although it never went into effect, embodied the principle that the territories were not to be mere colonies but would become states within the Union. The principle was fulfilled under the NORTHWEST ORDINANCE and the Constitution.

The Ordinance of 1784 created eight "states" in the West and prescribed for them three stages of evolution culminating in full equality with the original thirteen states. But, unlike the Northwest Ordinance, which provided for gradual advance toward self-government by the settlers, the Ordinance of 1784 conferred self-government immediately. Jefferson's proposal to ban SLAVERY from the territories was defeated in Congress by a vote of seven states to six.

Rather than allow squatters to benefit, Congress made the Ordinance effective only when the western lands were officially offered for sale, and that did not happen until after the Ordinance was superseded.

DENNIS J. MAHONEY

OREGON v. BRADSHAW

See: *Edwards v. Arizona*

OREGON v. ELSTAD
470 U.S. (1985)

The Supreme Court reaffirmed MIRANDA V. ARIZONA (1966) yet made another exception to it. For a 6–3 majority, Justice SANDRA DAY O'CONNOR held that initial failure to comply with the MIRANDA RULES does not taint a second confession made after a suspect has received the required warnings and has waived his rights. In this case the suspect had not blurted out an incriminating statement before police questioned him. They arrested him, with a warrant, at his home and began an interrogation without advising him of his rights. He confessed. They took him to the station and gave him the warnings, but they did not inform him that his prior confession could not be used against him as proof of his guilt. O'Connor, commenting that a contrary decision might "disable the police," ruled that the second confession need not be suppressed because of the illegality of the first. She treated the illegal confession as if it had been voluntarily made. Her focus on the voluntariness of that initial confession suggested that if coercion had then been present, it would have tainted a second confession made after the *Miranda* warnings. The Court, therefore, reaffirmed *Miranda.* Nevertheless, the case taught that the police may ignore *Miranda,* secure a confession, and then give the warnings in the hope of getting an admissible confession once the suspect thinks "the cat is out of the bag." Justice WILLIAM J. BRENNAN savaged the Court's opinion in a dissent that O'Connor claimed had an "apocalyptic tone" and distorted much of what she had said. She denied Brennan's accusation that the majority's opinion had a "crippling" effect on *Miranda.*

LEONARD W. LEVY

OREGON v. HASS

See: Police Interrogation and Confessions

OREGON v. MITCHELL
400 U.S. 112 (1970)

This decision suggested some short-lived constitutional limits on Congress's power to regulate voting. The 1970 amendments to the VOTING RIGHTS ACT

OF 1965 lowered from twenty-one to eighteen the minimum voting age for federal, state, and local elections, suspended LITERACY TESTS throughout the nation, prohibited states from imposing RESIDENCE REQUIREMENTS in presidential elections, and provided for uniform national rules for absentee registration and voting in presidential elections. (See VOTING RIGHTS AMENDMENTS.) The Supreme Court unanimously upheld the suspension of literacy tests and, over Justice JOHN MARSHALL HARLAN's dissent, found the residency and absentee voting provisions valid. Four Justices found the age limit reduction constitutional for all elections and four Justices found it unconstitutional for all elections. Because Justice HUGO L. BLACK found the age limit reduction constitutional only for federal elections, the case's formal HOLDING, though reflecting only Justice Black's view, was to sustain the age reduction only in federal elections. The many separate opinions in *Mitchell* also reviewed the question, first addressed in KATZENBACH V. MORGAN (1966), of Congress's power to interpret and alter the scope of the FOURTEENTH AMENDMENT. In 1971, in response to *Mitchell,* the TWENTY-SIXTH AMENDMENT lowered the voting age to eighteen in all elections.

THEODORE EISENBERG

ORGANIZED CRIME CONTROL ACT

84 Stat. 922 (1970)

Heralded as the most comprehensive federal law ever enacted to combat organized crime, this act was not limited to that use alone. Its provisions applied to a wide range of offenses, on the theory that the involvement of organized crime in a particular criminal act is not always clear. The detection of such involvement was one purpose of the law.

The legislation contained thirteen titles, a number of which aroused sharp criticism on constitutional grounds. One controversial title reinforced and expanded the investigatory power of GRAND JURIES by authorizing special grand juries to return INDICTMENTS and to report to UNITED STATES DISTRICT COURTS concerning criminal misconduct by appointive public officials involving organized criminal activity or concerning organized crime conditions in their areas. An individual named in such a report was entitled to a grand jury hearing, with the right to call witnesses and to file a rebuttal to the report. Another title replaced all previous laws governing witness IMMUNITY GRANTS; the title authorized federal legislative, administrative, and judicial bodies to grant witnesses immunity from prosecution using their testimony. The new section thus substituted "use immunity" for the "transaction immunity" that had previously protected such witnesses from prosecution for any events mentioned in or related to their testimony regardless of independent evidence against them.

Other provisions authorized detention of recalcitrant witnesses for CONTEMPT until they complied with court orders to testify, but for no longer than eighteen months, authorized convictions for perjury based on obviously contradictory statements made under oath (no longer requiring proof of the crime by any particular number of witnesses or by any particular type of EVIDENCE), and the use of depositions in criminal cases subject to constitutional guarantees and certification by the ATTORNEY GENERAL that the case involved organized crime. Still other sections limited to five years the period in which government action to obtain evidence could be challenged as illegal and limited the disclosure of government records previously required by ALDERMAN V. UNITED STATES (1969). Finally, the act authorized increased sentences up to twenty-five years for persons convicted of felonies, provided they were found to be dangerous and to be "habitual" offenders, "professional" criminals, or "organized crime figures."

Although the whole measure was denounced by the New York City Bar Association as containing "the seeds of official repression," only the narrowed witness immunity provisions were challenged. In KASTIGAR V. UNITED STATES (1972) the Supreme Court ruled that they did not violate the Fifth Amendment RIGHT AGAINST SELF-INCRIMINATION.

PAUL L. MURPHY

Bibliography

CONGRESSIONAL QUARTERLY 1973 *Congress and the Nation,* vol. 3. Washington, D.C.: Congressional Quarterly.

ORIGINAL JURISDICTION

The original jurisdiction of a court (as distinguished from APPELLATE JURISDICTION) is its power to hear and decide a case from the beginning. In the federal court system, the district courts originally hear the overwhelming majority of cases. Most discussion and litigation concerning the JURISDICTION OF FEDERAL COURTS centers on the district courts' original JURISDICTION. Yet the term "original jurisdiction" is heard most frequently in discussion and litigation concerning the jurisdiction of the Supreme Court.

The Constitution itself establishes the Supreme Court's original jurisdiction. After setting out the types of cases subject to the JUDICIAL POWER OF THE UNITED STATES, Article III distributes the Supreme Court's jurisdiction over them: "In all cases affecting ambassadors, other public ministers and consuls, and those in which a state shall be a party, the Supreme Court shall have original jurisdiction. In all other cases mentioned, the Supreme Court shall have appellate jurisdiction. . . ."

From the beginning, Congress has given the district courts CONCURRENT JURISDICTION over some of the cases within the Supreme Court's original jurisdiction, offering plaintiffs the option of commencing suit in either court. The Supreme Court has given this practice its stamp of constitutional approval. Furthermore, because the Court is hard-pressed by a crowded docket, it has sought ways of shunting cases to other courts. Thus, even when a case does fall within the Court's original jurisdiction, the court has conferred on itself the discretion to deny the plaintiff leave to file an original action. Typically the Court decides only three or four original jurisdiction cases each year, conserving its institutional energies for its main task: guiding the development of federal law by exercising its appellate jurisdiction.

Congress, however, cannot constitutionally diminish the Court's original jurisdiction. Nor can Congress expand that jurisdiction; the dubious reading of Article III in MARBURY V. MADISON (1803) remains firmly entrenched. However, the Supreme Court does entertain some actions that have an "original" look to them, even though Article III does not list them as original jurisdiction cases: HABEAS CORPUS is an example; so are the common law WRITS OF MANDAMUS and PROHIBITION. The Court hears such cases only when they can be characterized as "appellate," calling for Supreme Court supervision of actions by lower courts.

Of the two types of original jurisdiction cases specified in Article III, the state-as-party case has produced all but a tiny handful of the cases originally decided by the Supreme Court. Officers of foreign governments enjoy a broad diplomatic immunity from suit in our courts, and, for motives no doubt similarly diplomatic, they have not brought suits in the Supreme Court. (The "ambassadors" and others mentioned in Article III, of course, are those of foreign governments, not our own.)

The state-as-party cases present obvious problems of SOVEREIGN IMMUNITY. The ELEVENTH AMENDMENT applies to original actions in the Supreme Court; indeed, the amendment was adopted in response to just such a case, CHISHOLM V. GEORGIA (1793). Thus a state can no more be sued by the citizen of another state in the Supreme Court than in a district court. However, when one state sues another, or when the United States or a foreign government sues a state, there is no bar to the Court's jurisdiction.

The spectacle of nine Justices of the Supreme Court jointly presiding over a trial has a certain Hollywood allure, but the Court consistently avoids such proceedings. The SEVENTH AMENDMENT commands TRIAL BY JURY in any common law action, and at first the Supreme Court did hold a few jury trials. The last one, however, took place in the 1790s. Since that time the Court has always managed to identify some feature of an original case that makes it a suit in EQUITY; thus jury trial is inappropriate, and findings of fact can be turned over to a SPECIAL MASTER, whose report is reviewed by the Court only as to questions of law.

The source of the substantive law applied in original actions between states is FEDERAL COMMON LAW, an amalgam of the ANGLO-AMERICAN COMMON LAW, policies derived from congressional statutes, and international law principles. Thus far no state has defied the Supreme Court sufficiently to test the Court's means of enforcing its decrees, but some states have dragged out their compliance for enough years to test the patience of the most saintly Justice.

KENNETH L. KARST

Bibliography

NOTE 1959 The Original Jurisdiction of the United States Supreme Court. *Stanford Law Review* 11:665–719.

ORIGINAL PACKAGE DOCTRINE

In BROWN V. MARYLAND (1827) the Supreme Court had before it a challenge to a state statute requiring all importers of goods from foreign countries to take out a $50 license. Instead of simply holding that such a license tax imposed only on importers from foreign countries violated the constitutional clause prohibiting states from laying "any IMPOSTS or duties on imports or exports," Chief Justice JOHN MARSHALL used the occasion to decide just when goods imported from abroad ceased being imports exempted from taxation by the states. He concluded that no tax could be imposed on the goods or their importer so long as the goods had not been sold and were held in the original packages in which they were imported. He also said the principles laid down "apply equally to importations from a sister state."

The original package DOCTRINE had a long career

as applied to goods imported from abroad. In *Low v. Austin* (1872) the Court held that a state could not collect its uniform property tax on cases of wine which the importer held in their original package on tax day. Much later, in *Hooven & Allison Co. v. Evatt* (1945), the Court applied the doctrine to immunize bales of hemp from state property taxation, so long as the importer held them in their original package—the bales. Along the way, not surprisingly, the Court struggled in many cases with such problems as what constitutes the original package, and when it is broken.

Finally, in MICHELIN TIRE CORP. V. WAGES (1976) the Court upheld the imposition of a nondiscriminatory property tax upon tires imported from abroad and held in their original packages. It discussed at length the decision in *Low v. Austin*, overruled it, and appeared to be saying that only taxes discriminating against FOREIGN COMMERCE will be held invalid. Hence, it appears that the rules governing taxation of imports will now be similar to those applied to taxing such goods from other states, with the original package doctrine playing no part in the decisions.

Marshall's suggestion in *Brown v. Maryland* that the original package doctrine applied to state *taxation* of goods imported from other states was early rejected. In WOODRUFF V. PARHAM (1869) the Court upheld a state sales tax applied to an auctioneer who brought goods from other states and sold them in the taxing state in the original and unbroken packages. The IMPORT-EXPORT CLAUSE was determined to apply only to traffic with foreign nations, not to interstate traffic. The Court indicated its feeling that it would be grossly unfair if a resident of a state could escape from state taxes on all merchandise that he was able to import from another state and keep in its original package.

In 1890, however, the Court held that the original package doctrine applied to invalidate state *regulations* of goods imported from other states until the goods were sold or the package broken. The decision, LEISY V. HARDIN (1890), invalidated a state prohibition law as applied to sales within the state by the importer of kegs and cases of beer. Federal statutes were then enacted permitting states to exclude alcohol even in original packages. But the original package doctrine persisted with reference to other state regulations for nearly half a century. The Court found reasons in many cases to avoid applying the doctrine but did not effectively repudiate it until 1935. In *Baldwin v. G. A. F. Seelig* (1935) the Court, after reviewing the cases applying the original package doctrine said:

"In brief, the test of the original package is not an ultimate principle. . . . It makes a convenient boundary and one sufficiently precise save in exceptional conditions. What is ultimate is the principle that one state in its dealing with another may not place itself in a position of economic isolation. Formulas and catchwords are subordinate to this overmastering requirement."

Today the original package doctrine is of interest only to historians.

EDWARD L. BARRETT, JR.

(SEE ALSO: *State Regulation of Commerce; State Taxation of Commerce.*)

Bibliography

NOWAK, JOHN E.; ROTUNDA, RONALD D.; and YOUNG, NELSON J. 1979 *Handbook on Constitutional Law.* Pages 285–290. St. Paul, Minn.: West Publishing Co.

POWELL, THOMAS R. 1945 State Taxation of Imports: When Does an Import Cease to Be an Import? *Harvard Law Review* 58:858–876.

RIBBLE, F. D. G. *State and National Power over Commerce.* Pages 196–199. New York: Columbia University Press.

OROZCO v. TEXAS
394 U.S. 324 (1969)

In an opinion by Justice HUGO L. BLACK, the Supreme Court held that a conviction based on incriminating admissions obtained by police in the absence of notification of the MIRANDA RULES, even though the prisoner was at home, away from the coercive surroundings of a stationhouse, violated the RIGHT AGAINST SELF-INCRIMINATION.

LEONARD W. LEVY

OSBORN v. BANK OF THE UNITED STATES
9 Wheaton 738 (1824)

On its constitutional merits, *Osborn* was a replay of MCCULLOCH V. MARYLAND (1819). Ohio had sought to drive out the congressionally chartered bank by taxing its branches $50,000 each and by seizing money from its vaults. The bank sued the state auditor in a federal court for recovery of the money. The state argued that the ELEVENTH AMENDMENT barred the court from taking JURISDICTION, but, on APPEAL to the Supreme Court, Chief Justice JOHN MARSHALL concluded that the amendment applied only when the state was named as a party defendant—a position abandoned by the Court in later decisions. (See EX PARTE YOUNG, 1908.) On the principles of *McCulloch*, the auditor was liable for his TRESPASS.

Osborn's lasting doctrinal contribution was its sweeping definition of congressional power under Article III to confer FEDERAL QUESTION JURISDICTION on the federal courts. Marshall's view, which remains good law, was that cases "arising under" the Constitution, or federal laws, or treaties included—for purposes of defining congressional power to confer jurisdiction—any case in which federal law might *potentially* be dispositive. It made no difference that federal law was not implicated in the bank's complaint for trespass; the arguable invalidity of the bank's charter might possibly be raised as a defense to such an action. Although similar words ("arises under") are used in the statutes defining federal question jurisdiction, they have been interpreted more narrowly. *Osborn* thus defines congressional power, not its exercise.

The *Osborn* decision heightened the vehemence of state denunciations of the Court's judicial nationalism and even of its appellate jurisdiction. President ANDREW JACKSON's veto of the bank bill of 1832 probably reflected the prevailing belief—despite *McCulloch* and *Osborn*—that Congress had no constitutional authority to charter a corporation.

LEONARD W. LEVY
KENNETH L. KARST

O'SHEA v. LITTLETON
414 U.S. 488 (1974)

Protesters against RACIAL DISCRIMINATION in Cairo, Illinois, obtained a federal court INJUNCTION against a state judge and magistrate, forbidding continuation of various discriminatory BAIL, sentencing, and jury-fee practices in criminal cases. The Supreme Court reversed, 6–3, on RIPENESS grounds. Although some plaintiffs had previously suffered such discrimination, none were now threatened with prosecution. Thus there was no live CASE OR CONTROVERSY.

Once a prosecution was commenced, YOUNGER V. HARRIS (1971) would forbid a federal injunction. (See ABSTENTION DOCTRINE.) Thus potential plaintiffs in such cases must file their complaints within a narrow time period.

KENNETH L. KARST

OTIS, JAMES, JR.
(1725–1783)

Massachusetts lawyer, Harvard graduate (1743), and ideologue of the American Revolution, James Otis, Jr., became constitutionally significant with PAXTON'S CASE (1761), which concerned the issuance of WRITS OF ASSISTANCE by the Superior Court of Massachusetts. Confronted with the reality that the writs, which empowered customs officers to search all suspected houses, typified many kinds of general SEARCH WARRANTS within British law, Otis resorted to the HIGHER LAW. Using sources from MAGNA CARTA to BONHAM'S CASE (1610), Otis argued not only that incompatibility with natural and COMMON LAW rendered general searches void but also that the court should proclaim that invalidity. Although he did not advocate outright JUDICIAL REVIEW of an act of Parliament by a colonial court, the interpretation of the writs that Otis urged on the court would have had that result.

Although Otis's present fame derives heavily from *Paxton's Case,* he gained little contemporary notice from his performance in it, for his brief was not published until 1773. Rather, the principal constitutional services of the case were that it resulted in Otis's election to the Massachusetts General Court (legislative), thereby giving him a forum for his views and enabling him to assemble and rehearse the constitutional arguments that he later applied to those issues that directly generated the American Revolution.

Limiting the power of Parliament was central to Otis's thought: "To say the Parliament is absolute and arbitrary is a contradiction. The parliament cannot make 2 and 2, 5; Omnipotency cannot do it; the supreme power in a state is JUS DICERE [to announce the law] only;—JUS DARE [to construct the law] strictly speaking belongs only to God. . . . Should an act of Parliament be against any of his natural laws, which are immutably true, their declaration would be contrary to eternal truth, equity and justice, and consequently void." Otis's constitutional significance, however, does not emanate from this belief, which most contemporaries shared, but from the corollaries he extracted from it. Otis first transformed the British constitution into a fixed rather than a flexible barrier to Parliament, which he redefined as a subordinate creature of the constitution rather than one of its components. Of even greater import, Otis characterized the courts as umpires of Parliament's power. "The judges of England," he wrote, "have declared in favor of these sentiments when they expressly declare; that acts of Parliament against natural equity are void. That acts against the fundamental principles of the British Constitution are void." To assert that all earthly power, even that of Parliament, had limits was a ubiquitous platitude; to imply that agencies outside Parliament could calibrate and enforce these limits challenged the axiom of parliamentary supremacy that, for most Englishmen, lay at the foundation of their constitution.

A disembodied and didactic use of sources, ranging from Magna Carta to Hugo Grotius, provided Otis's intellectual ammunition. In *Bonham's Case,* for example, the *Reports* of Sir EDWARD COKE mentioned courts' controlling acts of Parliament and adjudging them void. Coke's meaning, however, was constructive rather than constitutional and involved no judicial effort to subjugate Parliament. The case pitted not the legislature against the courts but two clashing private parties and raised questions of which conflicting laws applied. Coke reasoned that the common law courts, acting with, rather than against, another court in the form of Parliament, should give the laws a reasonable construction that was jointly desired. Otis bloated the case, however, into precedent for constitutional regulation of Parliament under judicial aegis.

Otis repeatedly denied the revolutionary implications of his ideology, stressing that Parliament was the British Empire's supreme but not absolute legislature and could alone rescind its statutes. Despite these denials, however, Otis's assumptions intrinsically approached the threshold of the right to revolution against unconstitutional parliamentary acts.

Having asserted limits to Parliament's authority, Otis enumerated the colonial rights that lay beyond them. As a delegate to the STAMP ACT CONGRESS (1765) and in his *Rights of the British Colonies* (1764), written against the Sugar Act, Otis condemned taxation of the colonists by a Parliament to which they had directly elected no representatives. (See TAXATION WITHOUT REPRESENTATION.) As moderator of the Boston town meetings, he also opposed juryless trials under the TOWNSHEND ACTS of 1767.

Widely regarded as the premier theorist of the radical cause in the 1760s, Otis had great influence on the constitutional ideology of the developing revolution. He edited many of the *Farmer's Letters* (1767) by JOHN DICKINSON, while JOHN ADAMS adapted much of Otis's reasoning in *Paxton's Case* against juryless ADMIRALTY trials in *Sewall v. Hancock* (1768–1769).

WILLIAM CUDDIHY

Bibliography

WATERS, JOHN 1968 *The Otis Family.* Chapel Hill: University of North Carolina Press.

OVERBREADTH

Judges frequently encounter the claim that a law, as drafted or interpreted, should be invalidated as overbroad because its regulatory scope addresses not only behavior that constitutionally may be punished but also constitutionally protected behavior. The normal judicial response is confined to ruling on the law's constitutionality as applied to the litigant's behavior, leaving the validity of its application to other people and situations to subsequent adjudication. Since THORNHILL V. ALABAMA (1940), however, the Supreme Court has made an exception, most frequently in FIRST AMENDMENT cases but applicable to other precious freedoms, when it is convinced that the very existence of an overbroad law may cause knowledgeable people to refrain from freely exercising constitutional liberties because they fear punishment and are unwilling to litigate their rights. In such cases, the aggregate inhibition of guaranteed freedom in the regulated community is thought to justify both holding the overbroad law INVALID ON ITS FACE and allowing one to whom a narrower law could be applied constitutionally to assert the overbreadth claim. Unlike the alternative of narrowing the unconstitutional portions of an overbroad statute case by case, facial invalidation prevents delay in curing the improper deterrence. Moreover, courts most effectively can address the inhibition of those who neither act nor sue by allowing those who do to raise the overbreadth challenge.

Like a VAGUENESS challenge, an overbreadth challenge implicates judicial governance in two controversial ways. First, if successful, the challenge completely prohibits the law's enforcement, even its constitutional applications, until it is narrowed through reenactment or authoritative interpretation. Second, the challenge requires a court to gauge the law's applications to unidentified people in circumstances that must be imagined, often ignoring the facts of the situation before them—a practice of hypothesizing that is at odds with the court's usual application of law to the facts of concrete CASES OR CONTROVERSIES.

Overbreadth differs from vagueness in that the constitutional defect is a law's excessive reach, not its lack of clarity; yet the defects are related. A law that punished "all speech that is not constitutionally protected" would, by definition, not be overbroad, but it would be unduly vague because people would have to speculate about what it outlawed. A law that prohibited "all speaking" would be unconstitutionally overbroad, but it also might be vague. Although clear enough if taken literally, it might be understood that the legislature did not intend the full reach of its broadly drafted law, and the public would have to speculate about what the contours of the intended lesser reach might be. A law that banned "all harmful speech" would be both overbroad and vague on its face. The key connection, however, is the improper inhibiting effect of the broad or vague law.

As with vagueness, the federal courts approach overbreadth challenges to state and federal laws differently. A federal court must interpret a federal law before judging its constitutionality. In doing so, the court may reduce the law's scope, if it can do so consistently with Congress's intent, a course that may minimize constitutional problems of overbreadth. Only state courts may authoritatively determine the reach of state laws, however. Consequently, when the Supreme Court reviews an overbreadth challenge to a state law on appeal from a state court—which review usually occurs because the challenger raised the claim in defense of state court proceedings against him—the Court must accept the state court's determination of the law's scope and apply its own constitutional judgment to the law as so construed. By contrast, if parties threatened with enforcement of a state statute sue in federal court to have the law declared unconstitutionally overbroad before they are prosecuted or sued in state court, the federal court faces the additional complication of determining the overbreadth question without the guidance of any state court interpretation of the law in this case. If past interpretations of the law's terms make its breadth clear, there is no more difficulty than in Supreme Court review of a state court case. But if there is some question whether a state court might have narrowed the state law, especially in light of constitutional doubts about it, the federal court faces the possibility of making its own incorrect interpretation and basing an overbreadth judgment on that unstable premise.

With other constitutional claims involving uncertain state laws, a federal court normally will abstain from deciding the constitutional question until clarification is sought in state court. However, because the prolongation of CHILLING EFFECTS on constitutionally protected conduct is the basis of the vagueness of overbreadth doctrines, the Supreme Court indicated in DOMBROWSKI V. PFISTER (1965) and *Baggett v. Bullitt* (1964) that abstention is generally inappropriate if the problem would take multiple instances of adjudication to cure. *Babbitt v. United Farm Workers* (1979) followed the implicit corollary, requiring abstention where a single state proceeding might have obviated the need to reach difficult constitutional issues. But BROCKETT V. SPOKANE ARCADES, INC. (1985) shunned abstention in a case where state court clarification was feasible in an expeditious single proceeding, but where the litigants objecting to overbreadth were not people to whom the law could be validly applied but people who desired to engage in constitutionally protected speech. In that circumstance, at least where the unconstitutional portion of the statute was readily identifiable and severable from the remainder, the Court chose to strike that portion rather than abstain to see if the state court would remove it by interpretation.

Brockett also expressed a preference for partial over facial invalidation whenever challengers assert that application of a statute to them would be unconstitutional. The Court's ultimate objective is to invalidate only a statute's overbroad features, not the parts that legitimately penalize undesirable behavior. It permits those who are properly subject to regulation to mount facial overbreadth attacks only to provide an opportunity for courts to eliminate the illegitimate deterrent impact on others. Partial invalidation would do such people no good, and those who are illegitimately deterred from speaking may never sue. In order to throw out the tainted bathwater, the baby temporarily must go too, until the statute is reenacted or reinterpreted with its flaws omitted. Where, as in *Brockett,* one asserts his own right to pursue protected activity, however, no special incentive to litigate is needed. The Court can limit a statute's improper reach through partial invalidation and still benefit the challenger. *Brockett*'s assumption that the tainted part of the statute does not spoil the whole also undercuts Henry Monaghan's important argument that allowing the unprotected to argue overbreadth does not depart from normal STANDING rules because they always assert their own right not to be judged under an invalid statute. The part applied to them is valid, and they are granted standing to attack the whole only to protect others from the invalid part. Finally, the claim that a law is invalid in all applications because based on an illegitimate premise has elements of both partial and facial invalidation. As the invalid premise affects the challenger as well as everyone else, there is no need to provide a special incentive to litigate, but because the whole law is defective, total invalidation is appropriate.

The seriousness of striking the whole of a partially invalid law at the urging of one to whom it validly applies, together with doubts about standing and the reliability of constitutional adjudication in the context of imagined applications, renders overbreadth an exceptional and controversial DOCTRINE. The determination of what circumstances are sufficiently compelling to warrant the doctrine's use has varied from time to time and among judges. The WARREN COURT focused mainly on the scope of the laws' coverage, the chilling effect on protected expression, and the ability of the legislature to draw legitimate regulatory boundaries more narrowly. The Court seemed convinced that overbroad laws inhibited freedom substantially, and thus made that inhibition the basis of invalidation, especially when the laws were aimed at dissidents and the risk of deliberate deterrence was high, as in APTHEKER V. SECRETARY OF STATE (1964), *United States v. Robel* (1967), and *Dombrowski v. Pfister* (1965). The BURGER COURT has continued to employ the overbreadth doctrine when deterrence of valued expression seems likely, as in *Lewis v. New Orleans* (1974), which struck down a law penalizing abusive language directed at police, and in SCHAD V. MT. EPHRAIM (1981), which struck down an extremely broad law banning live entertainment.

Justice BYRON R. WHITE has led that Court, however, in curtailing overbreadth adjudication. As all laws occasionally may be applied unconstitutionally, there is always a quantitative dimension of overbreadth. White's majority opinion in BROADRICK V. OKLAHOMA (1973) held that the overbroad portion of a law must be "real and substantial" before it will be invalidated. That standard highlights the magnitude of deterrent impact, which depends as much on the motivations of those regulated as on the reach of the law. *Broadrick* also emphasized the need to compare and offset the ranges of a statute's valid and invalid applications, rather than simply assess the dimensions of the invalid range. This substituted a judgment balancing a statute's legitimate regulation against its illegitimate deterrence of protected conduct for a judgment focused predominantly on the improper inhibition.

Broadrick initially limited the "substantial overbreadth" approach to laws seemingly addressed to conduct, leaving laws explicitly regulating expression, especially those directed at particular viewpoints, to the more generous approach. In *Ferber v. New York* (1982) and *Brockett,* however, substantial overbreadth was extended to pure speech cases as well. That these cases involved laws regulating OBSCENITY might suggest that some Justices find the overbreadth doctrine an improper means to counter deterrence of marginally valued expression. More likely, however, the Court generally is abandoning its focus on the subject of a law's facial coverage in favor of a comparative judgment of the qualitative and quantitative dimensions of a law's legitimate and illegitimate scope, whatever speech or conduct be regulated.

Still, the reality of deterrence and the value of the liberty deterred probably remain major factors in overbreadth judgments, even if more must be considered. For example, the Court's pronouncement in BATES V. STATE BAR OF ARIZONA (1977) that overbreadth analysis generally is inappropriate for profit-motivated advertising rested explicitly on a judgment that advertising is not easily inhibited and implicitly on the historic perception of COMMERCIAL SPEECH as less worthy of protection.

Overbreadth controversies nearly always reflect different sensitivities to the worth of lost expression and of lost regulation of unprotected behavior, or different perceptions of the legitimacy and reliability of judicial nullification of laws that are only partially unconstitutional, or different assessments of how much inhibition is really likely, how easy it would be to redraft a law to avoid overbreadth, and how important broad regulation is to the effective control of harmful behavior. Despite controversy and variations in zeal for application of the overbreadth doctrine, however, its utility in checking repression that too sweepingly inhibits guaranteed liberty should assure its preservation in some form.

JONATHAN D. VARAT

Bibliography

ALEXANDER, LAWRENCE A. 1985 Is There an Overbreadth Doctrine? *San Diego Law Review* 22:541–554.

MONAGHAN, HENRY P. 1981 Overbreadth. *Supreme Court Review* 1981:1–39.

NOTE 1970 The First Amendment Overbreadth Doctrine. *Harvard Law Review* 83:844–927.

OVERRULING

The authority of the Supreme Court to reconsider and overrule its previous decisions is a necessary and accepted part of the Court's power to decide cases. By one estimate, the Supreme Court overruled itself on constitutional issues 159 times through 1976 and in each case departed from the doctrine of STARE DECISIS.

The basic tenet of *stare decisis,* as set forth by WILLIAM BLACKSTONE, is that PRECEDENTS must generally be followed unless they are "flatly absurd" or "unjust." The doctrine promotes certainty in the law, judicial efficiency (by obviating the constant reexamination of previously settled questions), and uniformity in the treatment of litigants. The roots of the doctrine, which is fundamental in Anglo-American jurisprudence, have been traced to Roman civil law and the Code of Justinian.

Justices and commentators have disagreed about the proper application of *stare decisis* to constitutional decision making. Justice (later Chief Justice) EDWARD D. WHITE, in his dissenting opinion in POLLOCK V. FARMERS LOAN & TRUST CO. (1895), observed:

> The fundamental conception of a judicial body is that of one hedged about by precedents which are binding on the court without regard to the personality of its members. Break down this belief in judicial continuity, and let it be felt that on great constitutional questions this court is to depart from the settled conclusions of its precedessors, and to determine them all according to the mere opinion of those who temporarily fill its bench, and our Constitution will, in my judgment, be bereft of value and become a most dangerous instrument to the rights and liberties of people.

Under this view, *stare decisis* should be applied with full force to constitutional issues.

The more commonly accepted view is that *stare decisis* has a more limited application in CONSTITUTIONAL INTERPRETATION than it does in the interpretation of statutes or in ordinary common law decision making. Although Congress, by a simple majority, can override the Supreme Court's erroneous interpretation of a congressional statute, errors in the interpretation of the Constitution are not easily corrected. The AMENDING PROCESS is by design difficult. In many instances only the Court can correct an erroneous constitutional decision.

Moreover, the Court will on occasion make decisions that later appear to be erroneous. As Chief Justice JOHN MARSHALL remarked in MCCULLOCH V. MARYLAND (1819), the Constitution requires deductions from its "great outlines" when a court decides specific cases. Because the modern Supreme Court generally accepts for review only cases in which principles of broad national importance are in competition, its decisions necessarily involve difficult questions of judgment. In view of the difficulties inherent in amending the Constitution, any errors made by the Court in the interpretation of constitutional principles must be subject to correction by the Court in later decisions.

The classic statement of this view was expressed by Justice LOUIS D. BRANDEIS in his dissenting opinion in *Burnet v. Coronado Oil & Gas Co.* (1932): "[I]n cases involving the Federal Constitution, where correction through legislative action is practically impossible, this Court has often overruled its earlier decisions. The Court bows to the lessons of experience and the force of better reasoning, recognizing that the process of trial and error, so fruitful in the physical sciences, is appropriate also in the judicial function." The Court has relied on Brandeis's reasoning in later decisions, such as EDELMAN V. JORDAN (1974), overruling previous constitutional precedents.

An additional reason for applying *stare decisis* less rigidly to constitutional decisions is that the judge's primary obligation is to the Constitution itself. In the words of Justice FELIX FRANKFURTER, concurring in *Graves v. New York* (1939), "the ultimate touchstone of constitutionality is the Constitution itself and not what we have said about it."

Some critics of *stare decisis* suggest that it has no place whatsoever in constitutional cases. For example, Chief Justice ROGER B. TANEY reasoned in the PASSENGER CASES (1849) that a constitutional question "is always open to discussion" because the judicial authority of the Court should "depend altogether on the force of the reasoning by which it is supported." The more generally accepted view, however, was stated by the Court in *Arizona v. Rumsey* (1984): "Although adherence to precedent is not rigidly required in constitutional cases, any departure from the doctrine of *stare decisis* requires special justification." Consistent with this view, the Supreme Court generally seeks to provide objective justification for the overruling of past precedents, apart from the fact that the Court's personnel may have changed.

One of the most commonly expressed reasons for overruling a previous decision is that it cannot be reconciled with other rulings. This rationale is in a sense consistent with *stare decisis* in that the justification for the overruling decision rests on competing but previously established judicial principles. In GIDEON V. WAINWRIGHT (1963), for example, which overruled BETTS V. BRADY (1942), the Court asserted not only that the rationale of *Betts* was erroneous but also that *Betts* had abruptly departed from well-established prior decisions. *Betts* had held that the DUE PROCESS clause of the FOURTEENTH AMENDMENT does not impose on the states, as the Sixth Amendment imposes on the federal government, the obligation to provide counsel in state criminal proceedings. *Gideon* expressly rejected this holding, thereby ruling that indigent defendants have the right to appointed counsel in such cases. Similarly, in WEST COAST HOTEL CO. v. PARRISH (1937) the Court concluded that it had no choice but to overrule its earlier decision in ADKINS v. CHILDREN'S HOSPITAL (1923), which had held a minimum wage statute for women unconstitutional under the due process clause. The Court reasoned that *Adkins* was irreconcilable with other decisions permitting the regulation of maximum hours and other working conditions for women.

The Court frequently argues, too, that the lessons of experience require the overruling of a previous decision. In ERIE RAILROAD CO. v. TOMPKINS (1938), for example, the Court reasoned that in nearly one hundred years the doctrine of SWIFT v. TYSON (1842) "had revealed its defects, political and social." And in MAPP v. OHIO (1961) the Court held the EXCLUSIONARY RULE applicable to the states, saying that the experience of various states had made clear that remedies other than the exclusionary rule could not effectively deter unreasonable searches and seizures. The Court therefore overruled WOLF v. COLORADO (1949), which only two decades earlier had ruled that states were free to devise their own remedies for enforcing SEARCH AND SEIZURE requirements applicable to the states through the due process clause of the Fourteenth Amendment.

The Court also justifies overruling decisions on the basis of changed or unforeseen circumstances. In BROWN v. BOARD OF EDUCATION (1954), for example, the Court referred to the change in status of the public schools in rejecting the application of the SEPARATE BUT EQUAL DOCTRINE of PLESSY v. FERGUSON (1896). And in PROPELLER GENESEE CHIEF v. FITZHUGH (1851), one of the earliest overruling decisions, the Court stressed that when it had erroneously held in *The Thomas Jefferson* (1825) that the ADMIRALTY AND MARITIME JURISDICTION of the federal government was limited "to the ebb and flow of the tide," commerce on the rivers of the West and on the Great Lakes had been in its infancy and "the great national importance of the question . . . could not be foreseen."

Other considerations may also suggest a decision's susceptibility to being overruled. Thus a decision on an issue not fully briefed and argued may be entitled to less precedential weight than one in which the issue received full and deliberate consideration. Or, the fact that an issue was decided by a closely divided Court may suggest a higher probability of error and make later reconsideration more likely. By contrast, as the Court recognized in *Akron v. Akron Center for Reproductive Health* (1983), a carefully considered decision, repeatedly and consistently followed, may be entitled to more respect than other constitutional holdings under principles of *stare decisis.*

As the Court develops constitutional doctrine, it may limit or distinguish a previous decision, gradually eroding its authority without expressly overruling it. Such a doctrinal evolution may both portend an overruling decision and establish the groundwork for it.

The Court's willingness to reconsider its prior constitutional decisions and in some instances to overrule itself is implicit in the general understanding of the Constitution as a document of broad outlines intended to endure the ages. Yet it has been suggested that the Court risks a loss of confidence as a disinterested interpreter of the Constitution whenever it overrules itself. Because of its antimajoritarian character, the Court must be sensitive to the need for restraint in exercising its power of JUDICIAL REVIEW. If it overrules itself too frequently and without adequate justification, its reputation may suffer. The Constitution's general language, however, leaves wide room for honest differences as to its interpretation and application. An objective and detached overruling opinion, which faithfully seeks to apply constitutional principles on the basis of the constitutional text and history, is on occasion to be expected and need not jeopardize public confidence in the Court.

JAMES R. ASPERGER

Bibliography

BERNHARDT, CHARLOTTE C. 1948 Supreme Court Reversals on Constitutional Issues. *Cornell Law Quarterly* 34:55–70.

BLAUSTEIN, ALBERT P. and FIELD, ANDREW H. 1958 "Overruling" Opinions in the Supreme Court. *Michigan Law Review* 57:151–194.

ISRAEL, JEROLD H. 1963 Gideon v. Wainwright: The "Art" of Overruling. *Supreme Court Review* 1963:211–272.

NOLAND, JON D. 1969 Stare Decisis and the Overruling of Constitutional Decisions in the Warren Years. *Valparaiso University Law Review* 4:101–135.

REED, STANLEY 1938 Stare Decisis and Constitutional Law. *Pennsylvania Bar Association Quarterly* 1938:131–150.

OVERT ACTS TEST

The overt acts test originated in the seventeenth century in suggestive remarks by ROGER WILLIAMS, William Walwyn, and Baruch Spinoza, primarily to promote the cause of RELIGIOUS LIBERTY. To the same end, PHILLIP FURNEAUX, in the next century, developed the test and THOMAS JEFFERSON adopted it.

Such libertarians advocated the test as an alternative to the prevailing BAD TENDENCY TEST, according to which the expression of an opinion was punishable if it tended to stir animosity to the established religion of a state or to the government or its officers or measures. Thus, the preamble to Jefferson's VIRGINIA STATUTE OF RELIGIOUS FREEDOM declared that allowing the civil magistrate to restrain the profession of opinions "on the supposition of their ill tendency . . . at once destroys all religious liberty." The government's rightful purposes, Jefferson continued, were served if its officers did not interfere until "principles break out into overt acts against peace and good order." The overt acts test, therefore, sharply distinguished words from deeds, and, in Furneaux's words, was based on the proposition that the "penal laws should be directed against overt acts only."

When the Sedition Act of 1798 incorporated the principles of ZENGER'S CASE (1735), libertarians who had advocated those principles finally abandoned them as inadequate protections of the FREEDOM OF THE PRESS and embraced the overt acts test. Only a radical minority ever advocated the test in cases of political expression, yet it survived down to the twentieth century. Justices HUGO L. BLACK and WILLIAM O. DOUGLAS found the test admirably suited to their ABSOLUTISM. Dissenting in YATES V. UNITED STATES (1957), Black said, "I believe that the FIRST AMENDMENT forbids Congress to punish people for talking about public affairs, whether or not such discussion incites to action, legal or illegal."

The overt acts test would provide the utmost protection for words and make the principle of FREEDOM OF SPEECH immunize every kind of verbal crime. The test ignores the fact that in some instances words themselves can be crimes (contempt of court, perjury, OBSCENITY, the verbal agreement in a CRIMINAL CONSPIRACY) or can violate laws validly governing the time and place of assemblies, parades, PICKETING, and SOUNDTRUCKS AND AMPLIFIERS. Words can also cause severe injury, constitute INCITEMENT TO UNLAWFUL CONDUCT, or otherwise solicit crime. The overt acts test draws a bright but fake constitutional line between speech and action; an indistinct zone would be more appropriate. Nevertheless, the Supreme Court in BRANDENBURG V. OHIO (1969), a leading free speech case, almost flirted with the overt acts test when it held that a state may not constitutionally "forbid or proscribe advocacy of the use of force or of law violation except where such advocacy is directed to inciting or producing imminent lawless action and is likely to incite or produce such action."

The Constitution contains a different overt acts test in the TREASON clause (Article 3, section 3), which specifies that unless a person accused of treason confesses in open court, two witnesses to the same overt act must prove his guilt. The clause also defines the required overt act as making war against the United States or "adhering to their Enemies, giving them aid and comfort." The treason clause, therefore, prevents the punishment of "constructive" treason, which consists of any words or acts construed by the government or a court to be tantamount to treason. Thus, the overt acts provision of the treason clause helps guarantee CIVIL LIBERTY by preventing the crime of treason from being used expansively to silence opponents of the government.

LEONARD W. LEVY

Bibliography

GREENAWALT, KENT 1980 Speech and Crime. *American Bar Foundation Research Journal* 1980:647–785.

OWEN v. CITY OF INDEPENDENCE
445 U.S. 622 (1980)

In MONELL V. DEPARTMENT OF SOCIAL SERVICES (1978) the Supreme Court held that municipalities may be liable under SECTION 1983, TITLE 42, UNITED STATES CODE, for deprivations of constitutional rights if the deprivation results from official policy. In *Owen,* the Court held that municipalities may not avail themselves of the good-faith defense or qualified immunity enjoyed by individual defendants in section 1983 cases. Thus, a municipality may be liable for unconstitutional acts even if its officials reasonably believe in good faith that their acts are constitutional.

THEODORE EISENBERG

OYAMA v. CALIFORNIA
332 U.S. 633 (1948)

In *Terrace v. Thompson* (1923) the Supreme Court had upheld the power of a state to limit land ownership to U.S. citizens. *Oyama,* together with TAKAHASHI V. FISH AND GAME COMMISSION (1948), both undermined *Terrace* and signaled a changing judicial attitude toward RACIAL DISCRIMINATION.

California's Alien Land Law forbade land ownership by ALIENS ineligible for CITIZENSHIP; under existing federal law, that category was largely limited to persons of Asian ancestry. Invoking its law, California sought to take over title to land held in the name of a young U.S. citizen, on the ground that it was really owned by his father, an alien ineligible for citizenship. The father had paid for the land, and so under the law was presumed its owner. A similar presumption would not apply to ownership of land by citizens of other races. Without purporting to rule on the general validity of the Alien Land Law, the Supreme Court held, 7–2, that the presumption denied the EQUAL PROTECTION OF THE LAWS.

KENNETH L. KARST

PACE v. ALABAMA
106 U.S. 583 (1883)

To white supremacists, the miscegenation issue was crucially important. The often unexpressed fear of interracial sex involving white women underlay all sorts of RACIAL DISCRIMINATION. The states punished adultery and fornication much more severely when the parties were of different races than when both were of the same race. *Pace* challenged the constitutionality of Alabama's statute, but the Supreme Court unanimously held that the unequal punishment did not violate the EQUAL PROTECTION clause of the FOURTEENTH AMENDMENT because both the interracial fornicators were subject to the same punishment.

LEONARD W. LEVY

(SEE ALSO: *Loving v. Virginia, 1967.*)

PACIFISTS

See: Conscientious Objection

PACKERS & STOCKYARDS ACT
42 Stat. 159 (1921)

After a Federal Trade Commission investigation damaging to the meat-packing industry in 1919–1920, popular sentiment demanded decisive action. Congress responded with this statute regulating both the packers and the stockyards. As one of its sponsors declared, the statute merely reenacted old principles in order to restore and maintain competition. Indeed, the clause banning "unfair" competition restated section 5 of the FEDERAL TRADE COMMISSION ACT. Other provisions forbade giving "undue or unreasonable advantage" (repeating section 3 of the INTERSTATE COMMERCE ACT) or apportioning items by geographic area (I.C.A., section 5; SHERMAN ANTITRUST ACT, section 1). Violators might be brought before the secretary of agriculture, who could issue CEASE-AND-DESIST ORDERS; APPEALS lay to federal CIRCUIT COURTS. Stockyards subject to the act were required to register and provide "reasonable" services and charges. The secretary could determine new rates and order compliance, although the act provided no standards for his guidance. Perhaps because of a CONSENT DECREE negotiated with the industry in 1920, the Department of Justice was reluctant to prosecute the packers. Their disinclination, and the packers' efforts to avoid the consent decree, materially contributed to the act's passage. In enacting this statute, Congress emphasized public concern over and commitment to strict accountability to the nation's antitrust laws. (See STAFFORD V. WALLACE, 1922.)

DAVID GORDON

Bibliography

GORDON, DAVID 1983 The Beef Trust: Antitrust Law and the Meat Packing Industry, 1902–1922. Ph.D. diss., Claremont Graduate School.

PAINE, THOMAS
(1737–1809)

Thomas Paine, the son of an English Quaker tradesman, became the great propagandist of the American and French revolutions. Before sailing to Philadelphia in 1774, with a letter of recommendation from BENJAMIN FRANKLIN, Paine had been a corsetmaker, a privateer, a tax assessor, a songwriter, and a tobacconist. In Philadelphia, he became editor of the *Pennsylvania Magazine,* crusading for abolition of slavery, proscription of dueling, greater rights for women, and easier availability of divorce.

Paine became the spokesman for the American Revolution when, in January 1776, he published a pamphlet called *Common Sense.* The pamphlet sharply attacked "the constitutional errors of the English form of government," including monarchy and CHECKS AND BALANCES. Paine declared that "the constitution of England is so complex, that the nation may suffer for years together without being able to discover in which part the fault lies." He argued for minimal government: "Society is in every state a blessing, but government even in its best state is but a necessary evil." Paine concluded *Common Sense* with a proposal for a "Continental Charter" of government based on large and equal REPRESENTATION and featuring a presidency rotated among the provincial delegations.

Between 1776 and 1783, Paine published a series of thirteen essays called *The Crisis,* chronicling "the times that try men's souls." Although in *Common Sense* he had denounced the English constitution, by the time he wrote *The Crisis* #7 in 1778, Paine had come to wonder "whether there is any such thing as the English constitution?" *The Crisis* #13, published in 1783, presented an argument for a strong and permanent national union, because "we have no other national SOVEREIGNTY than as the United States."

As the CONSTITUTIONAL CONVENTION OF 1787 met, however, Paine was en route to Europe to promote a scheme for building iron bridges. The outbreak of the French Revolution in 1789 found him in Paris. He became a French citizen and a member of the revolutionary Convention; he was the principal author of the Declaration of the Rights of Man and Citizen. When Edmund Burke denounced the French Revolution, Paine responded with *The Rights of Man,* the nearest thing he ever wrote to a systematic treatise on politics. Not an originator of ideas but a popularizer, Paine grounded his case for the revolution in the concepts of NATURAL RIGHTS and SOCIAL COMPACT. "Every civil right," he wrote, "has for its foundation some natural right pre-existing in the individual, but to the enjoyment of which his individual power is not, in all cases, sufficiently competent."

In 1792 the French revolutionary government fell into the hands of a radical faction; Paine was imprisoned and only narrowly escaped the guillotine. During his year in prison he wrote *The Age of Reason,* an apology for deism and religious rationalism with an anti-Christian tenor.

Paine's release from prison was arranged by the American ambassador, JAMES MONROE. For nearly a decade Paine remained in France as a journalist and political commentator. In 1802 he returned to America where he wrote polemical articles for the newspapers in support of THOMAS JEFFERSON's Republican party until his death in 1809.

DENNIS J. MAHONEY

Bibliography

CANAVAN, FRANCIS 1972 Thomas Paine. Pages 652–658 in Leo Strauss and Joseph Cropsey, eds., *History of Political Philosophy.* Chicago: Rand McNally.

HAWKE, DAVID FREEMAN 1974 *Paine.* New York: Harper & Row.

PALKO v. CONNECTICUT
302 U.S. 319 (1937)

Palko, decided in the sesquicentennial year of the Constitution, highlights the difference between the constitutional law of criminal justice then and now. The *Palko* Court, which was unanimous, included five of the greatest judges in our history—CHARLES EVANS HUGHES, LOUIS D. BRANDEIS, HARLAN FISKE STONE, HUGO L. BLACK, and the Court's spokesman, BENJAMIN N. CARDOZO. In one respect Cardozo's opinion is a historical relic, like HURTADO V. CALIFORNIA (1884), MAXWELL V. DOW (1900), and TWINING V. NEW JERSEY (1908), which he cited as governing precedents. In another respect, *Palko* rationalized the Court's INCORPORATION DOCTRINE of the FOURTEENTH AMENDMENT by which it selected FUNDAMENTAL RIGHTS to be safeguarded against state violation.

Palko was sentenced to life imprisonment after a jury found him guilty of murder in the second degree. The state sought and won a new trial on the ground that its case had been prejudiced by errors of the trial court. Palko objected that a new trial on the same INDICTMENT exposed him to DOUBLE JEOPARDY, but he was overruled. At the second trial the jury's verdict of murder in the first degree resulted in a sentence of death. Had the case been tried in a federal court, the double jeopardy claim would have been good. The question raised by Palko's case was whether a double standard prevailed—one for state courts and the other for federal—or whether the Fifth Amendment's guarantee against double jeopardy applied to the state through the DUE PROCESS clause of the Fourteenth Amendment.

Cardozo declared that Palko's contention was even broader: "Whatever would be a violation of the original BILL OF RIGHTS (Amendments 1 to 8) if done by the federal government is now equally unlawful by force of the Fourteenth Amendment if done by a state." The Court answered, "There is no such general rule," thus rejecting the theory of total incorporation. Nevertheless, said Cardozo, by a "process of absorption"—now referred to as selective incorporation—the Court had extended the due process clause of the Fourteenth Amendment to include FIRST AMENDMENT freedoms and the RIGHT TO COUNSEL in certain cases, yet it had rejected the rights of the criminally accused, excepting representation by counsel for ignorant INDIGENTS in capital prosecutions. The rationalizing principle that gave coherence to the absorption process, Cardozo alleged, depended on a distinction among the various rights. Some were "fundamental" or "of the very essence of a scheme of ORDERED LIBERTY," like FREEDOM OF SPEECH or religion. By contrast, TRIAL BY JURY, indictment by GRAND JURY, and the RIGHT AGAINST SELF-INCRIMINATION were not: justice might be done without them. The right against double jeopardy, the Court ruled summarily, did not rank as fundamental and therefore received no protection against the states from the due process clause of the Fourteenth Amendment. BENTON V. MARYLAND (1969) overruled *Palko,* showing that even "fundamental" value judgments change with time. All that remains of *Palko* is the abstract principle of selective incorporation.

LEONARD W. LEVY

Bibliography

ABRAHAM, HENRY J. 1977 *Freedom and the Court,* 3rd ed. Pages 64–70. New York: Oxford University Press.

PALMER, ALEXANDER M.
(1872–1936)

Appointed attorney general in 1919, Alexander Mitchell Palmer soon faced violence stirred up by the extreme left. After a series of bombings, Palmer campaigned against CIVIL LIBERTIES and unsuccessfully urged adoption of a new SEDITION law. His overreaction to alleged domestic radicals, particularly his "Red Raids" into private homes, mass arrests, and deportations of aliens, earned him widespread censure. Palmer also used the emergency WAR POWERS to attempt an end to the coal strike in 1919, exciting further criticism. These circumstances all contributed to his losing the 1920 Democratic presidential nomination for which he had been a leading contender. He nevertheless remained a party regular and helped write the 1932 party platform.

DAVID GORDON

Bibliography

COBEN, STANLEY (1963) 1972 *A. Mitchell Palmer: Politician.* New York: Da Capo Press.

PALMER v. THOMPSON
402 U.S. 217 (1971)

Under a federal court order to integrate its public recreational facilities, Jackson, Mississippi, closed four of its five public swimming pools and surrendered the city's lease on the fifth pool. In a 5–4 decision, the Supreme Court sustained the closings, stating that a legislative act does not "violate EQUAL PROTECTION solely because of the motivations of the men who voted for it." *Palmer*'s statement that legislative motive is irrelevant was undermined in WASHINGTON V. DAVIS (1976) and ARLINGTON HEIGHTS V. METROPOLITAN HOUSING DEVELOPMENT CORPORATION (1977).

THEODORE EISENBERG

PALMER RAIDS
(1919–1920)

In the aftermath of World War I and the Russian Revolution, waves of European immigration aggravated domestic inflation and unemployment. Labor strikes, often violent, were rampant, and the Communist party was organized.

Under pressure from the press and the public, WOODROW WILSON's attorney general, A. MITCHELL PALMER, conducted a series of raids between autumn 1919 and spring 1920 against the homes and offices of suspected ALIENS and radical leaders. The raids were conducted without ARREST WARRANTS or SEARCH WARRANTS, and those detained were denied the right to HABEAS CORPUS. Several thousand persons were detained, and over 500 alien radicals were deported.

DENNIS J. MAHONEY

PALMORE v. SIDOTI
466 U.S. 429 (1984)

When Linda Palmore was divorced from Anthony Sidoti, a Florida court awarded custody of their daughter to Palmore. Later, Sidoti sought custody on the ground that Palmore, a white woman, had been cohabiting with a black man, whom she shortly married. The state court changed the custody on the sole ground that the mother had "chosen for herself and her child, a life-style unacceptable to her father and to society." The child would, if she remained with her mother, be "more vulnerable to peer pressures" and would suffer from "social stigmatization." The Supreme Court unanimously reversed.

For the Court, Chief Justice WARREN E. BURGER reaffirmed the need for STRICT SCRUTINY of governmental action based on race. Racial prejudice indeed existed, but the potential injury from such private biases was not a constitutionally acceptable basis for the custody change. The decision has symbolic importance, but seems unlikely to make much difference in actual awards of child custody, which can be rested on a variety of grounds in the name of the "best interests of the child" without any explicit consideration of race.

KENNETH L. KARST

PANAMA CANAL TREATIES
33 Stat. 2234 (1903)
TIAS 10030 (1977)

At the turn of the twentieth century the United States emerged as a major power in world politics. Central to that major-power status were America's merchant shipping and the navy that protected it. The disadvantage of being a continental power with shores on two oceans became obvious during the Spanish-American War when redeployment of warships from the Pacific to the Atlantic Ocean, by way of Cape Horn, took two months to complete. The United States government determined to construct a canal across Central America through the Isthmus of Panama. The United States negotiated a treaty with Colombia, in which the isthmus was located, but that treaty was rejected by the Colombian Senate in August 1903.

In November 1903, with American encouragement, Panama declared its independence from Colombia; two weeks later Panama signed a treaty (sometimes called the Hay-Bunau Treaty) permitting the United States to build the Panama Canal. The United States Senate gave its ADVICE AND CONSENT to ratification of the treaty the following February.

In the treaty the United States undertook to defend both the canal and the Republic of Panama and to make nominal annual payments to Panama from the revenue of the canal. The treaty gave the United States permanent control "as if it were sovereign" over the Panama Canal Zone, a strip of land ten miles wide dividing the republic—which retained nominal sovereignty over the zone—in two. For nearly three-quarters of a century the Canal Zone was governed as an American TERRITORY. When President LYNDON B. JOHNSON made (mostly symbolic) concessions to Panama following civil unrest there in the 1960s, members of Congress accused him of usurping Congress's exclusive power over the territories.

Negotiations between four successive administrations and the Panamanian government, conducted over more than thirteen years, resulted in two pacts signed in 1977, the Panama Canal Treaty and the Panama Canal Neutrality Treaty. Together, these agreements abolished the Canal Zone, returned the zone and the canal to Panamanian SOVEREIGNTY, and provided for the future operation of the waterway under joint, and ultimately under Panamanian, control. The campaign to win the advice and consent of the Senate to the treaties proved to be a major test of the constitutional roles of the executive and the Senate in the exercise of the TREATY POWER. The original Panama Canal Treaty had been approved after an unprecedentedly short debate; the length of the debate over the new treaties was exceeded in the twentieth century only by that over the TREATY OF VERSAILLES.

Ratification of the treaties in 1978, with numerous amendments and "conditions," proved to be only the beginning of a new struggle. The treaties were not self-executing but required implementing legislation; that gave members of the House of Representatives, some of whom objected to the President and the Senate giving away "American territory" without their participation, a chance to affect the terms of the transfer. Over the objections of both President JIMMY CARTER and the Panamanian government, Congress wrote into the implementing legislation provisions authorizing the President to intervene militarily to protect American interests in the former Canal Zone. The episode serves to illustrate the extent of congressional power, under the Constitution, to influence the conduct of FOREIGN AFFAIRS, over which the President is often assumed to have exclusive control.

DENNIS J. MAHONEY

Bibliography

CRABB, CECIL V. and HOLT, PAT M. 1980 The Panama Canal Treaties. *Invitation to Struggle: Congress, the President and Foreign Policy.* Chap. 3. Washington, D.C.: Congressional Quarterly.

PANAMA REFINING CO. v. RYAN
293 U.S. 388 (1935)

In 1933 the price of wholesale gasoline had fallen to two and a half cents a gallon, that of crude oil to ten cents a barrel. The states, unable to cut production and push up prices, clamored for national controls. Congress responded with section 9(c) of the NATIONAL INDUSTRIAL RECOVERY ACT, authorizing the President to prohibit the shipment in INTERSTATE COMMERCE of petroleum produced in excess of quotas set by the states. By a vote of 8–1 the Supreme Court, in an opinion by Chief Justice CHARLES EVANS HUGHES, for the first time in history held an act of Congress unconstitutional because it improperly delegated legislative powers to the President without specifying adequate standards to guide his discretion. Moreover, the act did not require him to explain his orders. Vesting the President with "an uncontrolled legislative power," Hughes said, exceeded the limits of delegation; he did not explain how much delegation is valid and by what standards.

Justice BENJAMIN N. CARDOZO disagreed. He found adequate standards in section 1 of the statute: the elimination of unfair competitive practices and conservation of natural resources. These objectives guided the President's discretion, Cardozo explained. The principle of SEPARATION OF POWERS, which the majority used to underpin its opinion, should not be applied with doctrinaire rigor. Moreover, the statute, Cardozo observed, "was framed in the shadow of a national disaster" which raised unforeseen contingencies that only the President could face from day to day. The standards for his discretion had to be broad, and he need never give reasons for EXECUTIVE ORDERS. Cardozo's opinion notwithstanding, the Court in effect removed the oil industry from effective controls, to its detriment and that of the national economy. This case marked the New Deal's debut before the Court.

LEONARD W. LEVY

(SEE ALSO: *Delegation of Power.*)

PAPACHRISTOU v. JACKSONVILLE

See: Vagrancy Laws

PARDEE, DON ALBERT
(1837–1919)

President JAMES A. GARFIELD on May 3, 1881, appointed Don Albert Pardee judge of the Fifth Circuit Court. From 1891 to his death Pardee presided as senior judge of the Fifth Circuit Court of Appeals.

Pardee's most significant constitutional opinions involved the STATE POLICE POWER and VESTED RIGHTS. In *New Orleans Water-Works Co. v. St. Tammany Water-Works Co.* (1882) the judge held that the Louisiana legislature had exceeded its powers by incorporating a new company to compete with an enterprise that had enjoyed a monopoly over the distribution of the water supply to the city of New Orleans. "Arguments in cases like the one under consideration," Pardee observed, "are generally based on the assumption that the sovereign . . . is absolutely unfettered with regard to . . . all the rights of property. I am not prepared to take this advanced ground." He enjoined the new company from further construction and held that the legislature could not invoke its police power "without compensation of the vested rights of the New Orleans Water-Works Company."

Pardee did accept broader legislative discretion under the police power when moral objectives were involved. In *United States ex rel. Hoover v. Ronan, Sheriff* (1887) he rejected an argument that a Georgia statute violated the DUE PROCESS and EQUAL PROTECTION provisions of the FOURTEENTH AMENDMENT by requiring would-be saloonkeepers in unincorporated towns and cities to obtain signatures from residents in order to secure a retail license. In *Ex Parte Kinnerbrew* (1888), he found on moral benefit grounds that the Georgia local option liquor law was compatible with the federal COMMERCE CLAUSE.

Pardee insisted on the power of the federal judiciary to frame a constitutional jurisprudence that separated the state police power into public and private sector concerns. As a result, reverence for vested property rights and public morality gilded his judicial conservatism.

KERMIT L. HALL

Bibliography

BRYAN, PAUL E. 1964 Don Albert Pardee. *Dictionary of American Biography,* Vol. 14:201–202. New York: Scribner's.

PARDONING POWER

The power of pardon—the power to relieve a person of the legal sanctions imposed for illegal conduct—was reluctantly put in the hands of the President by the CONSTITUTIONAL CONVENTION OF 1787. The reluctance derived from the fact that it was too much akin to the royal prerogative to afford dispensation to favorites from obedience to the law, a prerogative supposedly eliminated by the English BILL OF RIGHTS in 1689. The Framers were concerned lest the power should be used to shelter the treasonous activities of a President and his henchmen. The most persuasive argument on behalf of a presidential pardoning power was its potential use to reconcile warring factions. Because it would, for this purpose, be an effective tool only if it were readily available to strike a deal at any time, and because Congress was not expected to be in session all, or even most, of the time, it properly devolved on the executive.

The power of pardoning for criminal activities is all but plenary. There is the constitutional limitation that pardon may not be used to relieve from impeachment or its sanctions. Otherwise, a pardon can be granted before conviction, indeed before indictment, and it can be conferred absolutely or conditionally, provided that the conditions themselves are not unconstitutional. However, whether a pardon can be conferred over the objection of the grantee is not clear, for acceptance of a pardon is generally thought to be an acknowledgment of commission of a crime.

On the whole, the pardon power has not been used for political ends as was anticipated. The partisan strife of the Old World did not, with rare exceptions, see its counterpart on the American scene. The political nature of the power can be seen in the pardons to the WHISKEY REBELS, to those convicted under the ALIEN AND SEDITION ACTS, and in the AMNESTY—granted by Congress—to the rebels of the Civil War. President GERALD R. FORD's pardon of ex-President RICHARD M. NIXON after the Watergate affair was, perhaps, the most blatant partisan use of the power.

The Supreme Court, in SCHICK V. REED (1974), has legitimated the almost unlimited power of executive pardon. Although the history of the origins as recounted in *Schick* is somewhat suspect, *Schick* remains the definitive statement, unless and until the Court revises it through later opinions.

PHILIP B. KURLAND

Bibliography

CORWIN, EDWARD S. 1957 *The President: Office and Powers 1787–1957,* 4th ed. New York: New York University Press.

PARHAM v. HUGHES

See: Illegitimacy

PARHAM v. J. R.
442 U.S. 584 (1979)

The notion of "voluntary" civil commitment of mental patients takes on a special meaning when the patients are children: under a typical state's law they can be committed by the joint decision of their parents and mental hospital authorities. This case, a CLASS ACTION on behalf of all children detained in Georgia mental hospitals, was brought in order to establish a child's PROCEDURAL DUE PROCESS right to an adversary hearing before being so committed. Although the lower federal court agreed with the plaintiff's theory, the Supreme Court reversed in an opinion by Chief Justice WARREN E. BURGER.

The Court was unanimous in rejecting the broadest due process claim in behalf of the children. There were constitutionally protected "liberty" interests at stake in a commitment, both the freedom from bodily restraint and the freedom from being falsely labeled as mentally ill. However, applying the interest-balancing calculus suggested in MATHEWS V. ELDRIDGE (1976), the Court concluded that a child's due process rights did not extend to an adversary precommitment hearing. The majority concluded that due process required no more than informal "medical" inquiries, once near the time of commitment and periodically thereafter, by a "neutral fact-finder" who would determine whether the standards for commitment were satisfied. There need be no adversary proceeding, but this neutral decision maker should interview the child.

The Court's opinion emphasized the importance of maintaining parents' traditional role in decision making for their children. (See CHILDREN'S RIGHTS.)

Although some parents might abuse their authority, the law had historically "recognized that natural bonds of affection lead parents to act in the best interests of their children." On the surface, *J. R.* is a "family autonomy" decision. Yet, as Robert Burt has shown, the Court's solicitude for parental authority was expressed in the context of parental decisions validated by state officials. Other decisions suggest that the Court's primary deference runs not to parents but to "state-employed behavioral professionals."

Justice WILLIAM J. BRENNAN, for three partially dissenting Justices, agreed that pre-confinement hearings were not constitutionally required in all cases where parents sought to have their children committed, but he argued that due process did require at least one postadmission hearing. The informal inquiries approved by the Court did not meet this standard.

KENNETH L. KARST

(SEE ALSO: *Mental Illness and the Constitution.*)

Bibliography

BURT, ROBERT A. 1979 The Constitution of the Family. *Supreme Court Review* 1979:329–395.

PARIS ADULT THEATRE I v. SLATON

See: *Miller v. California*

PARKER v. BROWN
317 U.S. 341 (1943)

A California statute compelled raisin growers to comply with the orders of a state-sponsored marketing monopoly. Farmers could sell thirty percent of their crop on the open market; the remainder went to the state commission, which controlled the interstate supply and price. This law survived challenge when a unanimous bench followed reasoning laid out earlier by Justice HARLAN FISKE STONE in DISANTO V. PENNSYLVANIA (1927). Here Stone dismissed statutory objections: the SHERMAN ANTITRUST ACT applied only to individual, not state, action; neither did the COMMERCE CLAUSE forbid this state regulation. Most important, Congress, in the AGRICULTURAL MARKETING AGREEMENT ACT, did not preempt this state legislation but reflected a congressional policy to encourage it.

DAVID GORDON

(SEE ALSO: *State Regulation of Commerce.*)

PARKER v. DAVIS

See: Legal Tender Cases

PARKER v. LEVY
417 U.S. 733 (1974)

In a celebrated trial of the VIETNAM WAR era, Captain Howard Levy, an Army physician, was convicted by COURT MARTIAL for violating provisions of the UNIFORM CODE OF MILITARY JUSTICE that penalized willful disobedience of the lawful command of a superior officer, "conduct unbecoming an officer and a gentleman," and conduct "to the prejudice of good order and discipline in the armed forces." The Third Circuit Court of Appeals had held that these provisions were unconstitutionally vague in violation of the DUE PROCESS clause of the Fifth Amendment and overbroad in violation of the FIRST AMENDMENT.

Justice WILLIAM H. REHNQUIST, for the Supreme Court, reversed and upheld Levy's conviction. Rehnquist's opinion rejected the contention that the provisions of the Uniform Code of Military Justice were too vague and overbroad. "The fundamental necessity for obedience, and the consequent necessity for imposition of discipline, may render permissible within the military that which would be constitutionally impermissible outside it," he wrote. Justices WILLIAM O. DOUGLAS, WILLIAM J. BRENNAN, THURGOOD MARSHALL, and POTTER STEWART dissented. The last wrote, "I cannot believe that such meaningless statutes as these can be used to send men to prison under a Constitution that guarantees due process of law."

MICHAEL E. PARRISH

PARLIAMENTARY PRIVILEGE

Parliamentary privilege, a term originating in England, refers to a bundle of rights that Parliament and every American legislature claimed and exercised. Article I of the Constitution safeguards several of these rights, including the right of the House of Representatives to choose its speaker, the right of each house to judge the elections and qualifications of members, the right of the houses to determine their own rules of procedure, and the rights of members to be free from arrest while performing their duties and to enjoy FREEDOM OF SPEECH in carrying out their duties. (See SPEECH OR DEBATE CLAUSE.) In addition, parliamentary privilege included the right, which derived from the judicial authority of Parliament, to punish for contempt.

The power to punish for contempt in both England and America proved to be incompatible with freedom of speech for critics of government, especially of the legislature. In colonial America the most suppressive body was the popularly elected assembly, which in effect enforced the law of SEDITIOUS LIBEL by punishing contempts or breaches of parliamentary privilege. An assembly, needing no GRAND JURY to indict and no PETIT JURY to convict, could summon, interrogate, and fix criminal penalties against anyone who had written, spoken, or printed words tending to impeach the assembly's conduct, question its authority, derogate from its honor, affront its dignity, or defame its members.

The practice of punishing seditious scandals or contempts against the government began in America with the first assembly that met in Virginia and continued well after the adoption of the Constitution. In 1796, for example, the New York Assembly jailed a lawyer for his offensive publications, and in 1800 the United States Senate found a Jeffersonian editor guilty of a "high breach of privileges" because of his seditious libels. As late as 1874 the Texas legislature, having expelled a hostile journalist, ordered his imprisonment for violating its order. The Supreme Court has held that the House of Representatives has the implied power to punish for contempt. Theoretically Congress still retains that power; in practice Congress refers its charges to a federal prosecutor who seeks a grand jury INDICTMENT. (See LEGISLATIVE CONTEMPT POWER.)

LEONARD W. LEVY

Bibliography

CLARKE, MARY PATTERSON (1943)1971 *Parliamentary Privilege in the American Colonies.* New York: Da Capo Press.

WITTKE, CARL (1921)1970 *The History of English Parliamentary Privilege.* New York: Da Capo Press.

PAROCHIAL SCHOOLS

See: Government Aid to Religious Institutions

PARTIES, POLITICAL

See: Political Parties and the Constitution; Political Parties in Constitutional Law

PASSENGER CASES
7 Howard 283 (1849)

Two states imposed a tax on the masters of vessels for each alien passenger they landed in the country. By a 5–4 vote, the Supreme Court held the state acts unconstitutional. Each of the Justices in the majority wrote an opinion, and none spoke for the Court. Three of the four dissenters wrote opinions. The report of the cases takes 290 pages and reflects chaos in judicial interpretation. The Justices squabbled about DORMANT POWERS, EXCLUSIVE POWERS, CONCURRENT POWERS, and the COMMERCE CLAUSE in relation to the POLICE POWER, but they settled nothing doctrinally.

LEONARD W. LEVY

PATENT

Article I grants to Congress the power to "promote the Progress of Science and useful Arts, by securing for limited times to Authors and Inventors the exclusive Right to their respective Writings and Discoveries." This clause confers on the federal government authority to provide for both patents and COPYRIGHTS.

United States patent law derives from the English experience. During Tudor times, English monarchs granted various monopolies (such as ones over salt) to royal favorites. The populace arose against the high prices charged by such monopolies. In 1623, Parliament enacted the germinal Statute of Monopolies. The statute declared monopolies void but as an exception allowed letters patent for fourteen years to the "true and first inventors" of "new manufactures."

In America, some states prior to adoption of the Constitution granted patents to inventors. But in listing the limited and specific powers of the federal legislature, the drafters of the Constitution agreed that patents and copyrights should be among those powers. As JAMES MADISON argued in THE FEDERALIST #43, "the States cannot separately make effectual provision for either." The drafters perceived that the interests of both a unified national economy and a strong system of incentives for invention required that a patent power lie in the federal government.

The constitutional power specifies both the *end* of the patent system (progress of the useful arts) and the *means* for achieving it (secure for a limited time to inventors the exclusive right to their discoveries). The power is only an enablement and does not of its own force create any patent rights. Nevertheless, the first Congress in 1790 enacted a patent statute. An 1836 statute revised the patent laws and created the Patent Office. A 1952 statute restated the patent laws in their current form. An inventor of a new and useful product or process may obtain from the Patent Office a patent granting for a number of years (currently seventeen) the right to exclude others from making, selling, or using the invention defined by the claims in the patent.

Although most questions concerning patentability are defined by statute, the Constitution limits Congress's power to authorize patent monopolies. In *Graham v. John Deere Co. of Kansas City* (1966), the Supreme Court stressed that Congress may not authorize patents that "remove existent knowledge from the public domain." Rejecting a NATURAL RIGHTS theory of patents for inventions, the Court emphasized the utilitarian function of patents: they stimulate innovation and the disclosure of new knowledge. Patents may issue only for inventions that advance the state of technology. This constitutional standard of innovation finds expression in the patent law DOCTRINE of "nonobviousness," which bars a patent for any discovery that would have been obvious at the time of invention to a person with ordinary skill in the pertinent art who had knowledge of all the prior art.

A patent may issue for virtually any type of useful product or process. In *Diamond v. Chakrabarty* (1980), the Supreme Court upheld the potential patentability of a live, genetically altered strain of microorganism.

DONALD S. CHISUM

Bibliography

CHISUM, DONALD S. 1978 *Patents: A Treatise on the Law of Patentability, Validity and Infringement.* New York: Matthew Bender.

MACHLUP, FRITZ 1958 An Economic Review of the Patent System. Study No. 15, Subcommittee on Patents, Trademarks & Copyrights, Judiciary Committee, 85th Congress, 2d Session.

PATERSON, WILLIAM (1745–1806)

William Paterson played a major role in the framing of the United States Constitution. His stubborn advocacy of state equality influenced the kind of government that was formed. He also was an active member of the United States Supreme Court who served as an important link between the Framers of the Constitution and the Supreme Court of JOHN MARSHALL.

Born in Ireland, Paterson moved to New Jersey at an early age, graduated from the College of New Jersey (Princeton), studied law, and was admitted to the bar in 1768. Supporting the movement for independence, he soon became a prominent member of New Jersey's revolutionary generation and served in its provincial legislature. Paterson drafted the state's first constitution and became its first attorney general. During the 1780s he built up his legal practice by defending the interests of wealthy landowners and creditors. In the political battles of that decade he advocated the supremacy of the peace treaty of 1783 over state laws, opposed the emission of paper money, and supported the movement to create a strong central government.

In 1787 New Jersey selected Paterson as one of its delegates to the CONSTITUTIONAL CONVENTION. Although he favored increasing the power of the national government, Paterson vigorously opposed the proposal of the VIRGINIA PLAN, as drafted by JAMES MADISON and presented by EDMUND RANDOLPH, that REPRESENTATION in both houses of the national legislature be apportioned according to population. Paterson feared this provision would give too much power to the larger states and place smaller states like New Jersey, Connecticut, and Delaware at a disadvantage. As an alternative he proposed the NEW JERSEY PLAN of government. Its principal feature was the continuance of the unicameral legislature of the ARTICLES OF CONFEDERATION in which each state had only one vote. The plan also would have: provided the federal government with the power to levy imposts and regulate trade and collect funds from states that did not comply with federal requisitions; created a Supreme Court with broad powers; and made the laws and treaties of the United States the supreme law of the land, with the state judiciaries bound to obey them despite any contrary state laws. Should a state or individuals within a state refuse to obey the laws of Congress or its treaties, the federal government would have had the right to use force to compel obedience. In other words, the central issue separating the proponents of the New Jersey Plan from those who favored the Virginia Plan was representation, not nationalism. Although the convention rejected Paterson's proposal, the delegates from the small states remained strongly opposed to proportional representation in Congress. In fact, the convention almost foundered on this issue, but it finally resolved the matter by adopting the so-called GREAT COMPROMISE that provided for representation by population in the lower house of a bicameral Congress and equal representation of each state in the upper house. With this matter settled, Paterson threw his complete support behind the new Constitution.

In 1789 the New Jersey legislature elected Paterson to the first United States Senate where, along with OLIVER ELLSWORTH, he helped to write the JUDICIARY ACT OF 1789. This law created a system of lower federal courts, broadly defined their JURISDICTION, created the office of attorney general, and gave the Supreme Court APPELLATE JURISDICTION over the final decisions of state courts in all matters relating to the Constitution and federal laws and treaties. As a senator, Paterson also enthusiastically supported ALEXANDER HAMILTON's proposals to fund the national debt at face value with full interest, and for the federal government to assume all state debts. In November 1790 Paterson resigned his seat in the Senate to become governor of New Jersey. In this capacity he undertook the task of codifying the state's laws, which were published in 1800. He also worked closely with Hamilton in 1791 to form the generally unsuccessful "Society for Establishing Useful Manufactures"; the society created a small industrial city on the banks of the Passaic River, which became known as Paterson.

Early in 1793 President GEORGE WASHINGTON appointed Paterson to the United States Supreme Court. For the next decade he had an active career on the bench participating in almost all the important decisions rendered by the high court. These decisions reveal Paterson to have been, above all else, a firm advocate of the supremacy of the federal over the state governments. In *Penhallow v. Doane's Administrators* (1795) he expounded an extremely nationalist interpretation of the origins and nature of the Union, arguing that even during the 1780s the Continental Congress represented the "supreme will" of the American people. In the important and controversial case of WARE V. HYLTON (1796) Paterson held that the treaty of peace with Great Britain (1783), which guaranteed that no legal obstacles would be placed in the way of the recovery of debts owed by Americans to British creditors, was part of the "supreme law of the land," rendering invalid a Virginia statute (1777) that allowed the sequestration of debts owed to British subjects before the Revolution.

Paterson also believed in a strong and independent judiciary. In 1795 while on circuit in Pennsylvania he delivered an opinion in VAN HORNE'S LESSEE V. DORRANCE that espoused the doctrine of VESTED RIGHTS and the right of the courts to void a statute repugnant to the Constitution. Although the case involved a state law that contradicted a state constitution, Paterson's argument had broader theoretical implications, and his remarks on the subject of JUDICIAL REVIEW are the fullest and most important statements by a Justice of the United States Supreme Court before John Marshall's opinion in MARBURY V. MADISON (1803). In HYLTON V. UNITED STATES (1796) Paterson agreed with the other Justices in upholding the constitutionality of a federal tax on carriages enacted in 1794. Because the key issue was whether the carriage tax was a DIRECT TAX or an excise tax, Paterson's opinion contained a long discussion of the intention of the Framers of the Constitution as to what kinds of taxes required apportionment among the states according to population. Paterson also expounded on the intention of the Framers in *Calder v. Bull* (1798) when he concurred with the rest of the Court in interpreting the provision of Article I, section 10, prohibiting state legislatures from enacting EX POST FACTO laws as extending only to criminal, not civil laws.

Like so many Federalists, Paterson refused to recognize the legitimacy of the Republican opposition during the 1790s. When Congress passed the ALIEN AND SEDITION ACTS, in 1798, he vigorously enforced them. While riding circuit in Vermont he urged a federal grand jury to indict Democratic-Republican Congressman Matthew Lyon for bringing the President and the federal government into disrepute with his various criticisms. "No government," Paterson observed, "can long subsist when offenders of this kind are suffered to spread their poison with impunity." In the trial that followed Paterson continued to pursue Lyon, emphasizing that the tendency of the Congressman's words be made the test of his intent. Paterson also made clear his belief that the Supreme Court alone had the final authority to determine the constitutionality of laws of Congress, a position the Republican defense had denied. After the jury convicted Lyon, Paterson imposed a harsh sentence of four months in jail and a $1,000 fine. In 1800 Paterson also presided over the trial of Anthony Haswell, a Bennington, Vermont, newspaperman who had rallied to Lyon's defense, and following Haswell's conviction sentenced him to two months in prison and fined him $200. Paterson's actions during the crisis of 1798, along with those of SAMUEL CHASE, are among the clearest examples of the partisan nature of the Federalist judiciary during the late 1790s. Many Jeffersonians were incensed by the proceedings, and had the attempt to remove Chase from the Supreme Court proven successful in 1805, they probably would have gone after Paterson next.

When Oliver Ellsworth resigned as Chief Justice

in 1800, most Federalists in the Senate felt the post should go to Paterson. But by then President JOHN ADAMS had openly broken with the Hamiltonian wing of the party, and he appointed John Marshall instead. Paterson accepted this development graciously; in fact, he described the new Chief Justice as "a man of genius" whose "talents have at once the lustre and solidity of gold." When the Jeffersonians took political power in 1801, Paterson backed away from his earlier extremism and supported Marshall's strategy of avoiding direct political confrontations with the Republican majority in Congress. When the JUDICIARY ACT OF 1801 was repealed, some of the more belligerent Federalists, including Justice Chase, wanted the Supreme Court to declare the repeal act unconstitutional. Riding circuit in Virginia, Marshall opposed this strategy, and declared the law constitutional in STUART V. LAIRD. The decision was immediately appealed to the Supreme Court where Marshall would not be allowed to participate in the case because he had already ruled on it in the lower court. In early 1803 Paterson delivered the Supreme Court's decision on the question. Not only did he side with Marshall, he delivered a warning to the more combative Federalists that "the question is at rest and ought not now to be disturbed." Among other things, the decision clearly indicated that the Federalist-dominated Supreme Court was willing to acquiesce in the "Revolution of 1800." It also went a long way toward reducing concerns, at least among moderates in THOMAS JEFFERSON's administration, about the high court's tendency to engage in partisan politics.

In the fall of 1803, Paterson was injured in a carriage accident. He missed the February 1804 term of the Supreme Court; and although he rode circuit the following year, he never fully recovered. He died in 1806.

RICHARD E. ELLIS

Bibliography

GOEBEL, JULIUS, JR. 1971 *History of the Supreme Court of the United States, Vol. I: Antecedents and Beginnings to 1801.* New York: Macmillan.

O'CONNOR, JOHN E. 1979 *William Paterson: Lawyer and Statesman, 1745–1806.* New Brunswick, N.J.: Rutgers University Press.

PATERSON PLAN

See: New Jersey Plan

PATTON v. UNITED STATES
281 U.S. 276 (1930)

In this case a unanimous Supreme Court, speaking through Justice GEORGE SUTHERLAND, held that the constitutional right to a jury in a federal court included exactly twelve members who were to render a unanimous verdict. (See JURY SIZE; JURY UNANIMITY.) Sutherland also declared that a defendant might waive his right to a jury or consent to a jury of less than twelve. Forty years later, in WILLIAMS V. FLORIDA (1970), a case involving a state court, the Court held that fixing the number of required jurors at twelve was a "historical accident" and "cannot be regarded as an indispensable component of the Sixth Amendment."

DAVID GORDON

(SEE ALSO: *Waiver of Constitutional Rights.*)

PAUL v. DAVIS
424 U.S. 693 (1976)

Even before GOLDBERG V. KELLY (1970) the Supreme Court assumed that the guarantee of PROCEDURAL DUE PROCESS attached to state impairments of "liberty" or "property" interests—concepts that bore their own constitutional meanings as well as their traditional COMMON LAW meanings. *Goldberg* and its successors added to those meanings a new category of protected "entitlements" established by statute or other state action. BISHOP V. WOOD (1976) and *Paul v. Davis* turned this development upside down, using the idea of "entitlements" under state law to *confine* the reach of due process.

In *Paul,* police officers circulated a flyer containing the names and photographs of persons described as "active shoplifters." Davis, one of those listed, had been arrested and charged with shoplifting, but the case had not been prosecuted and the charge had been dismissed. He sued a police officer in a federal district court, claiming damages for a violation of his federal constitutional rights. The Supreme Court held, 5–3, that the alleged harm to Davis's reputation did not, of itself, amount to impairment of a "liberty" interest protected by the due process guarantee. For the majority, Justice WILLIAM H. REHNQUIST manhandled precedents that had established reputation as a "core" constitutionally protected interest, asserting that the Court had previously offered protection to reputation only when it was harmed along with some other interest established by state law, such as a right to employment. Justice WILLIAM J. BRENNAN, for the dissenters, showed how disingenuous was this characterization of the precedents.

Probably the majority's main concern was to keep the federal CIVIL RIGHTS laws from becoming a generalized law of torts committed by state officers, with the federal courts as the primary forum. Yet the majority opinion cannot be taken at face value. Unquestionably the notion of "liberty" interests protected by due process still includes a great many interests not defined by state law, such as FIRST AMENDMENT liberties.

KENNETH L. KARST

PAUL v. VIRGINIA
8 Wallace 168 (1869)

In 1866, Virginia prohibited out-of-state insurance companies from doing business without a substantial deposit; domestic companies were not so required. Convicted of violating the 1866 act, Paul filed a WRIT OF ERROR and BENJAMIN R. CURTIS argued his case. Justice STEPHEN J. FIELD, for a unanimous Supreme Court, rejected Paul's Article IV PRIVILEGES AND IMMUNITIES argument, declaring that CITIZENSHIP could apply only to natural persons. Field further asserted that insurance contracts were not articles of commerce and that the issuance of a policy was not a transaction in INTERSTATE COMMERCE. *Paul* was often cited as a limitation on congressional power on the incorrect assumption that congressional and state regulatory power were mutually exclusive. *Paul* remained law until virtually overturned in UNITED STATES V. SOUTH-EASTERN UNDERWRITERS ASSOCIATION (1944), involving congressional power, after which Congress authorized state regulation.

DAVID GORDON

PAXTON'S CASE
Gray, *Mass. Repts.*, 51 469 (1761)

In *Paxton's Case,* the Massachusetts Superior Court considered whether to continue issuing WRITS OF ASSISTANCE, which, by a British statute of 1662, empowered customs officers to search all houses for contraband. Massachusetts opposed these writs; its legislation had repudiated the general SEARCH WARRANTS they resembled in favor of uniformly specific warrants. Other stimulants to the case were frequent searches under the writs, tense relations with local British customs officers, the belief that customs regulations had been enforced against local merchants with discriminatory rigor, and the thwarted ambitions of the powerful Otis family for appointment to the Superior Court.

The death of King George II terminated existing writs after six months, and local merchants asked the court not to replace them. In the initial hearing Josiah Gridley argued the positions of the customs establishment that the act of 1662 defined writs of assistance as general search warrants and that a local statute had empowered the court to issue them by giving it the same jurisdiction as the one that issued them in England. Oxenbridge Thacher and JAMES OTIS, JR., representing the merchants, inaccurately replied that the local court had not recently exercised the powers of the English tribunal, the Court of Exchequer.

Otis, son of the candidate for a seat on the Superior Court, cited a magazine article to prove that the writs did not currently operate as GENERAL WARRANTS in Britain and had not been so intended by the statute of 1662. Legions of British laws authorized general searches, however, and Otis relied primarily on the HIGHER LAW. Since general searches allegedly violated natural and COMMON LAW, Otis reasoned that writs of assistance were intrinsically void if worded as the statute prescribed and should be judicially construed as specific search warrants.

Otis's use of sources was heavily didactic. He cited Sir EDWARD COKE, whose *Institutes* exaggerated MAGNA CARTA into a prohibition of general search warrants, and he wrongly read into Coke a further requirement that all search warrants be specific. Otis also stretched BONHAM'S CASE (1610) to hold that common law courts could "control" unreasonable Parliamentary legislation and render it void. Only private interests had actually clashed in *Bonham's Case,* not levels of law or government as Otis implied. Although Otis had not advised the court explicitly to disallow a Parliamentary statute, he misused *Bonham's Case* to advocate a judicial construction of the act that would have had the effect of disallowance.

Persuaded by Otis's eloquence, the court delayed its decision, found that the writs used in England were general, and approved their local issuance over Otis's continued objections. The Massachusetts legislature responded by reducing the salaries of the judges and passing a bill, vetoed by the governor, to define the writs as specific warrants. THOMAS HUTCHINSON, whose appointment as Chief Justice had blocked the judicial aspirations of the Otises, later traced his political demise to his courtroom support of writs of assistance. *Paxton's Case* is one of the leading precedents for the FOURTH AMENDMENT and probably inspired the rejection by later Massachusetts courts (1763–1766) of customary search warrants against felons in *Bassett v. Mayhew* and other cases.

WILLIAM CUDDIHY

Bibliography

SMITH, M. H. 1978 *The Writs of Assistance Case.* Berkeley: University of California Press.

PAYTON v. NEW YORK
445 U.S. 573 (1980)

The FOURTH AMENDMENT, which the FOURTEENTH makes applicable to the states, says that the "right of people to be secure in their . . . houses . . . shall not be violated." *Payton* was the first case in which the Supreme Court confronted the issue whether police may enter a private home, without an ARREST WARRANT or consent, to make a FELONY arrest. New York, sustained by its courts, authorized warrantless ARRESTS, by forcible entry if necessary, in any premises, if the police had PROBABLE CAUSE to believe a person had committed a felony. In Payton's case the police seized EVIDENCE in PLAIN VIEW at the time of arrest and used it to convict him.

A 6–3 Supreme Court, in an opinion by Justice JOHN PAUL STEVENS, reversed and held the state statute unconstitutional. Absent EXIGENT CIRCUMSTANCES, "a man's house is his castle" and unlike a public place may not be invaded without a warrant. Stevens found slight guidance in history for his position on the special privacy of the home in the case of a felony arrest, but he insisted that the Fourth Amendment required a magistrate's warrant. Justice BYRON R. WHITE for the dissenters declared that the decision distorted history and severely hampered law enforcement; the amendment required only that a warrantless felony arrest be made on probable cause in daytime. (See STEAGALD V. UNITED STATES, 1981.)

LEONARD W. LEVY

PECKHAM, RUFUS W.
(1838–1909)

Rufus Wheeler Peckham, the last of President GROVER CLEVELAND's four appointees to the Supreme Court, was commissioned in 1896 following eight years of service on the New York Court of Appeals. His name is linked most often with one of the half dozen most fulsomely denounced Supreme Court decisions in American history. Speaking for a majority of five in LOCHNER V. NEW YORK (1905), Peckham invoked the SUBSTANTIVE DUE PROCESS doctrine of "liberty of contract," which he had established in an incipient form in ALLGEYER V. LOUISIANA (1897), and invalidated a statute regulating the hours worked by bakeshop employees. (See FREEDOM OF CONTRACT.) Peckham's opinion infuriated progressive reformers, evoked one of Justice OLIVER WENDELL HOLMES's most famous dissents, and ultimately contributed a new term to the lexicon of constitutional discourse in America. More than four generations later, "Lochnerism" is habitually used by commentators to describe the horrible consequences of interventionist JUDICIAL REVIEW in defense of doctrinally abstract constitutional rights.

Holmes once remarked that the "major premise" of Peckham's jurisprudence was "God damn it." It was an apt observation. Peckham was outraged by the increasing propensity of state legislatures and the Congress to transcend "the proper functions of government," and he not only conceptualized the judicial function in essentially negative terms but also regarded the Court as an appropriate forum for battling the ominous evils of centralization and socialism. For Peckham, the Court's role in constitutional adjudication was to police the boundaries separating the rights of the individual, the powers of the states, and the authority of the general government in such a way as to keep each within its proper sphere. Otherwise, he warned while still on the New York bench, "in addition to the ordinary competition that exists throughout all industries, a new competition will be introduced, that of competition for the possession of the government."

Peckham had boundless confidence in his capacity to draw objective lines between these mutually limiting spheres. He dissented in CHAMPION V. AMES (1903) on the ground that a federal statute prohibiting interstate distribution of lottery tickets was not a regulation of commerce at all but rather an attempt by Congress to usurp the reserved power of the states to regulate public morals. And in *Lochner* Peckham conceded that state governments might prevent individuals from making certain kinds of contracts, only to conclude that there was no "direct relation" between the hours worked by bakeshop employees and either the public health or the health, safety, and morals of the workers. Peckham, in short, knew a police regulation or an exercise of the commerce power when he saw one. Holmes may have been astonished when Peckham claimed that legitimate governmental interventions were readily distinguishable from those with only a "pretense" of legitimacy. But most Americans were accustomed to the claim. The spate of veto messages issued by President Cleveland were strikingly similar to Peckham's judicial opinions in both substance and style.

Peckham's voting record in cases involving race relations reflected another principal goal of the Cleveland Democracy—"home rule" for the South. The great spokesman for liberty of contract joined the majority in HODGES V. UNITED STATES (1906), which denied federal JURISDICTION over conspiracies to prevent blacks from making or carrying out labor contracts. He also concurred in BEREA COLLEGE V. KENTUCKY (1908), where the Court upheld a statute prohibiting even voluntary interracial education. If Peckham perceived a principled difference between the right of employers and employees to contract in *Lochner* and the right of individuals freely to associate in *Berea College,* he never described it. Yet it appears that Peckham rarely worried about such overarching conceptual problems. He not only managed to keep race relations and employment contract issues in separate analytical compartments but also voted to impose more stringent PUBLIC USE requirements on state governments when they regulated prices under the POLICE POWER than when they exercised the EMINENT DOMAIN power. Peckham stridently criticized the DOCTRINE of *Munn v. Illinois* (1877) throughout his career, arguing that storage rates charged by grain elevator firms were not subject to regulation because the owners had not devoted their property "to any public use, within the meaning of the law." (See GRANGER CASES.) In *Clark v. Nash* (1905), however, he sustained a law that permitted individuals to condemn rights-of-way across their neighbors' land for irrigation and mining purposes. "What is a public use," Peckham declared, "may frequently and largely depend upon the facts surrounding the subject, and . . . the people of a State . . . must in the nature of things be more familiar with such facts" than the federal judiciary.

Peckham wrote 448 opinions during his fourteen years on the Court, more than thirty percent of which were dissents. Very few of his majority opinions have stood the test of time. Modern commentators almost unanimously regard most of the results he reached to be insupportable and his mode of reasoning unfathomable. But it was Peckham himself who best summed up both the implications of his work for American public life and the internal contradictions that hastened its demise. "At times there seems to be a legal result which takes no account of the obviously practical result," he wrote in *Sauer v. City of New York* (1907). "At times there seems to come an antithesis between legal science and common sense."

CHARLES W. MCCURDY

Bibliography

SKOLNIK, RICHARD 1969 Rufus Peckham. Pages 1685–1703 in Leon Friedman and Fred L. Israel, eds., *The Justices of the United States Supreme Court, 1789–1967.* New York: Chelsea House.

PEIK v. CHICAGO & NORTHWESTERN RAILWAY COMPANY

See: Granger Cases

PELL v. PROCUNIER
417 U.S. 817 (1974)

In a case that helped delineate the boundaries between the traditional FIRST AMENDMENT freedoms and the expanding area of PRISONERS' RIGHTS, several prisoners and professional journalists challenged the constitutionality of a California prison regulation that forbade press interviews with particular inmates. The argument for the prisoners' rights was that this regulation abridged their FREEDOM OF SPEECH; the journalists claimed the rule inhibited their newsgathering capabilities, thus violating the FREEDOM OF PRESS. The Justices voted 6–3 against the inmates and 5–4 against the journalists. Because the prisoners had alternative means of communication (friends or family, for example) the California regulation did not violate their rights. The majority based its rejection of the journalists' position on the purpose of the regulation—to prevent particular individuals from gaining excessive influence through special attention—and the reporters' otherwise free access to prisoners. Furthermore, the regulation did not prohibit the press from publishing what it chose.

DAVID GORDON

PENDENT JURISDICTION

When a federal court has JURISDICTION over a case presenting a FEDERAL QUESTION, the court may also take jurisdiction over closely related claims based on state law. According to *Gibbs v. United Mine Workers of America* (1966), pendent jurisdiction over a state law claim is appropriate when the state and federal claims share "a common nucleus of operative fact." If the federal claim is itself insubstantial, or is dismissed before the case is tried, it will not serve as a basis for getting a state claim heard by the federal court; such a case should be dismissed. The federal court has discretion to decline pendent jurisdiction over a state claim when the state issues are apt to predominate in the case (making it more appropriate for hearing in a state court), or when the combination of federal and state claims is apt to produce jury confusion. (See ANCILLARY JURISDICTION.)

In PENNHURST STATE SCHOOL & HOSPITAL V. HALDERMAN (1984) the Supreme Court drastically curtailed use of pendent jurisdiction in CIVIL RIGHTS cases. The Court held that the ELEVENTH AMENDMENT bars a federal court from entertaining an action—whether for DAMAGES or for INJUNCTION—against a state officer, when the action is based on an alleged violation of state law.

KENNETH L. KARST

Bibliography

WRIGHT, CHARLES ALAN 1983 *The Law of Federal Courts,* 4th ed. Pages 103–109. St. Paul, Minn.: West Publishing Co.

PENDLETON, EDMUND
(1721–1803)

Admitted to the bar in 1745, Edmund Pendleton became a justice of the peace in 1751 and a member of the Virginia House of Burgesses in 1752. He was a leader of the conservative patriot faction in Virginia and opposed PATRICK HENRY on many issues, including colonial reaction to the Stamp Act of 1765. Pendleton opposed the act and, as a justice of the peace, declared it unconstitutional, but he did not approve of Henry's famous resolutions against it. He became a member of the committee of correspondence in 1773 and a delegate to the FIRST CONTINENTAL CONGRESS in 1774. Between 1774 and 1776 he was president of both the Virginia convention (the provisional legislature) and the Committee of Safety (the de facto executive). He presided over the Virginia convention of 1776 which passed the resolution Pendleton had drafted instructing Virginia's delegates to the Continental Congress to seek a DECLARATION OF INDEPENDENCE, adopted the VIRGINIA DECLARATION OF RIGHTS AND CONSTITUTION, and appointed a committee, including Pendleton, GEORGE WYTHE, and THOMAS JEFFERSON, to revise the state's laws. He was elected speaker of the first House of Delegates under the new constitution (1776–1777) and then appointed first presiding judge of the court of chancery (1777–1779). In 1779 he became presiding judge of the court of appeals, the state's highest court, a position he held until his death. In COMMONWEALTH V. CATON (1782), he stated that laws repugnant to the state constitution were void, but he reserved the question of whether his court could so declare them.

Pendleton was unanimously chosen president of the Virginia convention of 1788 at which he argued and voted for the RATIFICATION OF THE CONSTITUTION. He declined President GEORGE WASHINGTON'S offer of a federal district judgeship in order to remain on the state court. As an indication of his virtues as a judge, it is said that only one of his judicial decisions was ever reversed, and in that case he reversed himself.

DENNIS J. MAHONEY

PENDLETON ACT
22 Stat. 403 (1883)

A fundamental change in the operation of American government began with the adoption of the Civil Service Act of 1883—known as the Pendleton Act, for its sponsor, Senator George H. Pendleton (Democrat of Ohio). The act created a merit system for selection of non-policymaking employees of the United States government to replace the "spoils" system which rewarded political supporters. Although the immediate stimulus for adoption of the act was the assassination of President JAMES GARFIELD by a disappointed office seeker, a politically independent civil service had been a major goal of reformers for many years.

The act based eligibility for affected federal employment on performance in competitive examinations, and it created a Civil Service Commission to supervise the examinations and handle personnel administration. Initially extending to less than ten percent of federal employees, the competitive civil service now includes over ninety percent. Much of this growth was a result of the Ramspeck Act (Civil Service Act of 1940) which authorized the President to place virtually all federal employment under the system by EXECUTIVE ORDER. The Civil Service Reform Act (1978) abolished the Civil Service Commission but retained the principle of political neutrality established by the Pendleton Act.

DENNIS J. MAHONEY

Bibliography

ROSENBLOOM, DAVID H. 1971 *Federal Service and the Constitution.* Ithaca, N.Y.: Cornell University Press.

PENN, WILLIAM
(1644–1718)

The scion of a wealthy English family, William Penn attended Oxford University, studied law, and managed the family's estates before becoming a Quaker in the mid-1660s. Throughout the rest of his life Penn engaged in Quaker preaching and propaganda. He was imprisoned on at least three occasions for publishing pamphlets about his religious beliefs. His acquittal in 1670 on a charge of unlawful preaching led to BUSHELL'S CASE, which ended the punishment of jurors who decided contrary to a judge's instructions. In the political campaigns of the late 1670s, Penn agitated for RELIGIOUS LIBERTY and frequent parliamentary elections.

Penn's involvement with America began in 1682, when he became a trustee of the colony of West Jersey, which he and eleven others had purchased for settlement by Quakers, and helped to frame its charter. King Charles II granted the proprietary colony of Pennsylvania to Penn in 1681 as settlement of a large debt that the king owed Penn's father; the following year Penn leased the area now known as Delaware and added it to the colony. Penn described his intentions for the colony as a "holy experiment" in religious and political liberty. In 1682, during a two-year sojourn in America, he wrote a Frame of Government (constitution) for the colony, granting the settlers freedom of religion, procedural guarantees in criminal cases, and limited self-government.

In 1697 Penn drafted, and submitted to the Board of Trade, the first proposal for a federal union of the English colonies in North America. His plan would have created a "congress," comprising two representatives from each colony, competent to legislate on any matter related to "the public tranquility and safety."

During a visit to Pennsylvania in 1701 Penn granted the residents a new charter, the Charter of Privileges, creating a unicameral legislature, greatly expanding the scope of colonial self-government, and providing for Delaware's establishment as a separate entity. Shortly thereafter, he returned to England, where he died.

DENNIS J. MAHONEY

(SEE ALSO: *Pennsylvania Colonial Charters.*)

Bibliography

WILDES, HARRY E. 1974 *William Penn.* New York: Macmillan.

PENN CENTRAL TRANSPORTATION CO. v. NEW YORK CITY
438 U.S. 104 (1978)

Some governmental regulations of the use of property are severe enough to be called TAKINGS OF PROPERTY, for which JUST COMPENSATION must be made under the explicit terms of the Fifth Amendment (governing federal government action) or interpretations of the FOURTEENTH AMENDMENT'S DUE PROCESS clause (governing state action). This decision illustrates how difficult it is to persuade the Supreme Court that a regulation constitutes a "taking."

A New York City ordinance required city approval before a designated landmark's exterior could be altered. The owner of Grand Central Terminal sought to build a tall office building on top of the terminal, and was refused permission on aesthetic grounds. The Supreme Court held, 6–3, that this regulation did not constitute a "taking."

Justice WILLIAM J. BRENNAN, for the majority, conceded that the taking/regulation distinction had defied clear formulation, producing a series of "ad hoc factual inquiries." This regulation, however, was analogous to ZONING under a comprehensive plan; over 400 landmarks had been designated. Further, the owner's loss was reduced by transferring its air-space development rights to other property in the city.

For the dissenters, Justice WILLIAM H. REHNQUIST argued that the law's severely destructive impact on property values was not justified by either of the usual "exceptions": the banning of "noxious uses," or the imposition of widely shared burdens to secure "an average reciprocity of advantage" (as in the case of zoning). Penn Central had suffered a huge loss of value, not offset by benefits under the landmark law.

KENNETH L. KARST

PENNHURST STATE SCHOOL & HOSPITAL v. HALDERMAN
451 U.S. 1 (1981)
457 U.S. 1131 (1984)

Pennhurst worked major changes in the interpretation of the ELEVENTH AMENDMENT and in the PENDENT JURISDICTION of federal courts over claims based on state law. These changes remove one important weapon from the arsenal of CIVIL RIGHTS plaintiffs.

Terri Lee Halderman, a resident of Pennhurst, a state institution for the mentally retarded, commenced a CLASS ACTION in federal district court against Pennhurst and a number of state and local officials. She alleged that squalor, abuse of residents, and other conditions at Pennhurst violated the federal DEVELOPMENTALLY DISABLED ASSISTANCE AND BILL OF RIGHTS ACT of 1975, the DUE PROCESS clause of the FOURTEENTH AMENDMENT, and Pennsylvania's statute governing mental retardation. After a long trial, the district court agreed with her on all counts, and held that mentally retarded people in the state's care had a due process right to live in "the least restrictive setting" that would serve their needs. The court's INJUNCTION ordered the defendants to close Pennhurst and place its residents in "suitable living arrangements." The court of appeals affirmed, but rested decision only on the federal statute. The Supreme Court reversed, instructing the lower courts to consider whether the district court's order was justified on the basis of the Constitution or state law. On REMAND, the court of appeals avoided the constitutional issue, holding that state law required reaffirmance of the "least restrictive setting" ruling. When the case returned to the Supreme Court, the Court held, 5–4, that the Eleventh Amendment barred the district court's injunction. (The case was then settled, with the state agreeing to close Pennhurst and to move its residents to their home communities, or to other institutions if they were aged or ill.)

Justice LEWIS F. POWELL's OPINION OF THE COURT announced that the doctrine of SOVEREIGN IMMUNITY is a constitutional principle, based on the Eleventh Amendment, which gives a state immunity from suit in a federal court by an individual plaintiff. In Powell's novel reading, EX PARTE YOUNG (1908) stands for a narrow exception to this immunity, allowing a suit in federal court for an injunction against a state officer only when the plaintiff's claim is based on a violation of the federal Constitution. (Perhaps violations of federal statutes will fit within this category, because of the operation of the SUPREMACY CLAUSE.) Suits in federal court against state officers—even suits for injunctive relief—are thus barred by the Eleventh Amendment when they are based on claimed violations of state law.

Prior to *Pennhurst* an action in federal court founded on FEDERAL QUESTION JURISDICTION could include a claim for relief on state law grounds, when both the federal and state claims arose out of the same facts. However, Powell said, this doctrine of pendent jurisdiction rests only on concerns for efficiency and convenience, concerns that must give way to the force of the Eleventh Amendment.

For the dissenters, Justice JOHN PAUL STEVENS decried the Court's overruling of some two dozen precedents, and defended the long-established understanding of *Ex parte Young:* that when a state officer's conduct is illegal (under either federal or state law), the officer is "stripped" of the cloak of the sovereign's immunity. Here it was perverse to clothe Pennsylvania's officers with the state's Eleventh Amendment immunity when they were acting in violation of their sovereign's commands as embodied in state law. Justice WILLIAM J. BRENNAN, dissenting separately, argued that the amendment does not bar a suit by a citizen against the citizen's own state.

The *Pennhurst* majority opinion is vulnerable to criticism for its historical analysis of the Eleventh Amendment, for its casual dismissal of the importance of the federal courts' pendent jurisdiction, and for its choice to confer immunity on wrongdoing officials in the name of the sovereignty of the very state that had made the officials' conduct illegal. These criticisms seem minor, however, in the light of another one that is far more grave. The majority, in denying private citizens a vital judicial remedy against official lawlessness, weakened the rule of law.

KENNETH L. KARST

Bibliography

SHAPIRO, DAVID L. 1984 Wrong Turns: The Eleventh Amendment and the Pennhurst Case. *Harvard Law Review* 98:61–85.

PENNSYLVANIA v. NELSON
350 U.S. 497 (1956)

The Supreme Court banned outright state prosecutions for SEDITION against the United States by ruling, in *Pennsylvania v. Nelson,* that Congress had already preempted that field of SOVEREIGNTY. The decision had the effect of limiting the states to punishing sedition against state or local, but not federal, government.

Steve Nelson, an avowed communist, had been convicted for violating Pennsylvania's stringent sedition law by his words and actions concerning the federal government; he was sentenced to serve twenty years in prison and pay large fines. The state supreme court reversed, holding the state law had been superseded by the Smith Act. The Supreme Court upheld and extended this ruling. Chief Justice EARL WARREN used three criteria or a three-part criterion in ruling that there was no longer room for state action in this field. The scheme of federal regulation, he maintained, which included the Smith Act, the INTERNAL SECURITY ACT of 1950, and the COMMUNIST CONTROL ACT of 1954, was "so pervasive" as to leave no room for state regulation. Further, these federal statutes demonstrated a federal interest "so dominant" as to preclude state action on the same subject; and for the state to enforce its federal law presented a "serious danger of conflict" with the administration of the federal program. Three Justices dissented, arguing that Congress had not intended to preempt the internal security field.

Following the decision all pending proceedings under the state sedition laws were dismissed or abandoned. Congress considered a measure to set aside the decision but failed to enact it.

PAUL L. MURPHY

PENNSYLVANIA COLONIAL CHARTERS
(April 25, 1682; October 28, 1701)

WILLIAM PENN, the proprietor of Pennsylvania, was a Quaker, a humanitarian, a champion of RELIGIOUS LIBERTY, and a stalwart advocate of CIVIL LIBERTIES. His two charters for his colony gave it representative institutions of government and bills of rights far in advance of the times. The 1682 Frame of Government called itself a "charter of liberties" that had the character of FUNDAMENTAL LAW. Any act of government that "infringed" on the designated liberties, said the Frame, "shall be held of no force or effect." Inhabitants possessing one hundred acres of land "at one penny an acre" were declared "freemen" capable of electing or being elected representatives, including members of the upper house—an innovation. The Frame separated church and state and guaranteed religious liberty by its provision that all persons professing God should be free to worship as they pleased and not be compelled to frequent or maintain any worship or ministry. FAIR TRIAL, which Penn and the Quakers had been denied in England, was here protected. At a time when defendants could not testify on their own behalf, the Frame allowed all persons to plead their own cases. Trial by a twelve-member jury of the VICINAGE, whose judgment was to be "final" (see BUSHELL'S CASE, 1670) and INDICTMENT by GRAND JURY in capital cases were guaranteed. The RIGHT TO BAIL was recognized and excessive fines were banned.

The 1701 Charter of Privileges, which replaced the Frame and remained the basis of government in Pennsylvania until 1776, also had the character of a CONSTITUTION to which ordinary legislation must conform or be of no effect. Its provisions for the "Enjoyment of Civil Liberties" and for religious liberty, and its ban against an ESTABLISHMENT OF RELIGION extended to all inhabitants "for ever." Among their innovations was a guarantee that "all criminals shall have the same Privileges of Witnesses and Council [sic] as their Prosecutors," the source of the comparable clauses in the SIXTH AMENDMENT. England did not allow counsel to all defendants until 1836. Pennsylvania's colonial charters had a marked influence on the development of the concept of a bill of rights in America.

LEONARD W. LEVY

Bibliography

PERRY, RICHARD L., ed. 1959 *Sources of Our Liberties.* Pages 204–221, 251–260. New York: American Bar Foundation.

PENNSYLVANIA CONSTITUTION OF 1776
(August 16, 1776)

Pennsylvania's short-lived first CONSTITUTION, superseded in 1790, is notable because it was the most unorthodox and democratic of the constitutions of the original states. Although the extralegal "convention" that framed the document exercised full powers of government and remained in session as the legislature, the constitution was FUNDAMENTAL LAW. Its preamble, stressing NATURAL RIGHTS theory, declared that it was "for ever" unalterable; its declaration of rights was made part of the constitution and inviolable; and its frame of government created a legislature without the power "to add to, alter, abolish, or infringe" any part of the constitution.

The declaration of rights was superior to the more famous VIRGINIA DECLARATION OF RIGHTS, Pennsylvania's model. Pennsylvania omitted the right to BAIL and the ban against excessive fines and CRUEL AND UNUSUAL PUNISHMENTS but added FREEDOM OF SPEECH, assembly, and petition; separated church and state; recognized the right of CONSCIENTIOUS OBJECTION; protected the RIGHT TO COUNSEL in all criminal cases; and provided for the right to bear arms and the RIGHT TO TRAVEL or emigrate—all constitutional "firsts" in the United States. To create a political democracy controlled by the people, the frame of government established a powerful unicameral legislature, with no upper house to check the lower and no governor to veto its legislation. The legislature's proceedings had to be made public and its doors were to be open to the public. In effect all males of voting age could vote, because the constitution enfranchised all taxpayers (all men had to pay a POLL TAX) and their sons, and anyone who could vote was eligible to hold office. Proportional representation, based on the number of taxable inhabitants, governed the apportionment of the legislature.

In place of a governor the constitution established a council, elected by the people, representing each county, with a president or chairman. The council had weak executive powers but for the power to make appointments, including all judges. The constitution instituted few checks and did recognize SEPARATION OF POWERS. Its strangest institution was the council of censors, a popularly elected body that met for one year in every seven and was charged with the responsibility of seeing that the constitution was preserved inviolate; it could review the performance of all public officers, order IMPEACHMENTS, recommend repeal of legislation, and call a convention to revise the constitution. That council met only once and was so politically divided that it did nothing. But the VERMONT CONSTITUTION OF 1777, based on Pennsylvania's, copied the council of censors and kept it until 1869. The Pennsylvania Constitution of 1790 followed the MASSACHUSETTS CONSTITUTION OF 1780.

LEONARD W. LEVY

Bibliography

SELSON, J. PAUL (1936)1971 *The Pennsylvania Constitution of 1776.* New York: Da Capo Press.

PENSACOLA TELEGRAPH CO. v. WESTERN UNION TELEGRAPH CO.
96 U.S. 1 (1878)

This case is significant because the Supreme Court, following GIBBONS V. OGDEN (1824), declared that the congressional power to regulate INTERSTATE COMMERCE extends to newly invented instrumentalities of commerce, here the telegraph. In 1866 Congress had prohibited the states from granting telegraph monopolies. Florida, seeking to control telegraphic transmission within its JURISDICTION, conferred exclusive rights on the Pensacola company. A 7–2 Court, speaking through Chief Justice MORRISON R. WAITE, held the state act unconstitutional for conflict with the act of Congress. Accordingly, the company had no valid chartered right to exclude competitors.

LEONARD W. LEVY

PENUMBRA THEORY

Writing for the Supreme Court in GRISWOLD V. CONNECTICUT (1965), Justice WILLIAM O. DOUGLAS commented that "specific guarantees in the BILL OF RIGHTS have penumbras, formed by emanations from those guarantees that help give them life and substance." The occasion for this shadowy suggestion was the Court's decision holding unconstitutional the application to a BIRTH CONTROL clinic of a state law forbidding the use of contraceptive devices, even by the married couples whom the clinic had aided. Although nothing in the Constitution specifically forbade such a law, Justice Douglas rested decision on a RIGHT OF PRIVACY founded in this "penumbra" theory. A number of constitutional guarantees created "zones of privacy." One such zone included the "right of association contained in the FIRST AMENDMENT." Other protections of privacy were afforded by the THIRD AMENDMENT'S limitations on the quartering of troops, the FOURTH AMENDMENT'S protections against unreasonable SEARCHES AND SEIZURES, and the Fifth Amendment's RIGHT AGAINST SELF-INCRIMINATION. "The present case, then, concerns a relationship lying within the zone of privacy created by several fundamental constitutional guarantees."

This "penumbra" theory, which has had no generative power of its own, is best understood as a last-ditch effort by Justice Douglas to avoid a confrontation with Justice HUGO L. BLACK over a doctrinal issue dear to Black's heart. In his famous dissent in ADAMSON V. CALIFORNIA (1947), Black had derided "the natural-law–due-process formula" that allowed judges, with no warrant in the constitutional text, "to trespass, all too freely, on the legislative domain of the States as well as the Federal Government." Douglas had joined Black's *Adamson* dissent, and perhaps hoped that his *Griswold* opinion, by maintaining a formal tie to the specifics of the Bill of Rights, might persuade Black to come along. Black, of course, would have none of it: "I get nowhere in this case by talk about a constitutional 'right of privacy' as an emanation from one or more constitutional provisions. I like my privacy as well as the next one, but I am nevertheless compelled to admit that government has a right to invade it unless prohibited by some specific constitutional provision."

The Court subsequently relocated its new right of privacy in the liberty protected by the DUE PROCESS clause of the FOURTEENTH AMENDMENT, and no further "penumbras" have been seen in the land. Nonetheless, the *Griswold* decision has been an unusually influential precedent, not only for the Supreme Court's abortion decisions but also for the development of a generalized FREEDOM OF INTIMATE ASSOCIATION. Not every penumbra darkens the road ahead.

KENNETH L. KARST

Bibliography

KAUPER, PAUL G. 1965 Penumbras, Peripheries, Emanations, Things Fundamental and Things Forgotten: The Griswold Case. *Michigan Law Review* 64:235–282.

PEONAGE

Peonage is a system of debt bondage, in which a laborer is bound to personal service in order to work off an obligation to pay money. The system originated in the newly independent countries of Spanish America early in the nineteenth century, and in Hawaii and the Philippines later, as a substitute for various institutions used in the colonial era to marshal a labor force. In some of these countries the system continues to exist. In its classic form, peonage involves a trivial advance of money to a worker, in exchange for a contractual obligation to work for a term, or until the debt is repaid. From then on, the laborer is bound by law to serve the employer, and efforts to quit are met with the force of the state: arrest, imprisonment, return to the employer's service.

Peonage was also part of a larger system of involuntary servitude that emerged in the American South after the Civil War. As such, though whites have sometimes been its victims, peonage has served as a substitute for black slavery. After the slave states were forced by emancipation to shift from a labor regime based on status and force to one of free labor based on contract and choice, peonage emerged as a system that hid the wolf of involuntary servitude in the sheep's clothing of contract.

Peonage as a customary system for coerced black labor had its origin in the contract-enforcement sections of the BLACK CODES (1865–1875) and other labor-related statutes of the era. These provided both civil and criminal penalties for breach of labor contracts, punished VAGRANCY, prohibited enticement of laborers from their jobs, and hampered or penalized agents inducing the emigration of laborers. Southern states also permitted the leasing of convict labor and adopted a criminal-surety system, whereby a person convicted of a MISDEMEANOR would have his fine and costs paid by a prospective employer and then be obliged to work for the surety. Though the Black Codes were soon repealed, the FREEDMEN'S BUREAU at the same time emphasized labor contracts as the nexus of the employer–employee relationship for former slaves, and this later encouraged the use of contracts as a device for forcing black labor.

In 1867, when Congress enacted the Peonage Act to abolish peonage in New Mexico Territory, it also made it applicable to "any other Territory or State of the United States." The act made it a FELONY to hold a person in a condition of peonage, or to arrest a person for that purpose. It voided statutes and "usages" enforcing the "voluntary or involuntary service or labor of any persons as peons in liquidation of a debt or obligation, or otherwise."

United States District Judge Thomas G. Jones began the legal struggle against peonage in a vigorous GRAND JURY charge, reported as *The Peonage Cases* (1903), defining peonage broadly as "the exercise of dominion over their persons and liberties by the master, or employer, or creditors, to compel the discharge of the obligation, by service or labor, against the will of the person performing the service." In *Clyatt v. United States* (1905), the Supreme Court upheld the use of the Peonage Act for the prosecution of a peonmaster. Brushing aside both STATE ACTION and DUAL SOVEREIGNTY arguments, Justice DAVID J. BREWER found authorization for direct federal power over peonage in the enforcement clause (section 2) of the THIRTEENTH AMENDMENT. But he also held that debt was the "basal fact" of peonage, thus limiting federal action to cases where an actual debt could be shown.

After publication of the "Report on Peonage" (1908) by the United States Department of Justice, prompted by discovery of occasional instances of white peonage (usually of immigrants), the Supreme Court, in BAILEY V. ALABAMA (1911), used the Peonage Act to strike down Alabama contract-enforcement statutes that permitted quitting to be *prima facie* evidence of an intent to defraud the employer. The Court held that the Peonage Act voids "all legislation which seeks to compel the service or labor by making it a crime to refuse or fail to perform it." In *United States v. Reynolds* (1914), the Court invalidated Alabama criminal-surety statutes, describing the plight of a black peon caught in them as being "chained to an everturning wheel of servitude." But peonage has proved to be a remarkably tenacious form of servitude for blacks in the rural South, highlighted by the 1921 massacre of eleven black peons by their Georgia master, and by the establishment of peonage under federal and state auspices in refugee camps after the 1927 Mississippi River flood.

While physical force or threat of prosecution plainly constitute peonage, other forms of compulsion present interpretive problems. Thus subterfuges as well as outright violations of the Peonage Act persist into the present, despite the invalidation or repeal of the state labor-contract statutes that provided the original basis of peonage. The threat of deportation has proved an effective means of keeping alien migrant workers in a condition of involuntary or underpaid labor, and lower federal courts have divided as to whether this constitutes peonage.

WILLIAM M. WIECEK

Bibliography

COHEN, WILLIAM 1976 Negro Involuntary Servitude in the South, 1865–1940: A Preliminary Analysis. *Journal of Southern History* 42:31–60.

DANIEL, PETE 1972 *The Shadow of Slavery: Peonage in the South, 1901–1969.* Urbana: University of Illinois Press.

NOVAK, DANIEL A. 1978 *The Wheel of Servitude: Black Forced Labor After Slavery.* Lexington: University Press of Kentucky.

PEOPLE v. CROSWELL
3 Johnson's Cases (N.Y.) 336 (1804)

The state of New York, run by Jeffersonians, indicted Harry Croswell, a Federalist editor, for the crime of SEDITIOUS LIBEL, because he wrote that President THOMAS JEFFERSON had paid a scurrilous journalist to defame GEORGE WASHINGTON. Croswell was convicted at a trial presided over by the Jeffersonian chief justice of the state, Morgan Lewis, who embraced the position of the prosecution in ZENGER'S CASE (1735). Lewis ruled that truth was not a defense against a charge of seditious libel and that the jury's sole task was to decide whether the defendant had published the statements charged, leaving the court to decide their criminality as a matter of law.

ALEXANDER HAMILTON, representing Croswell on his appeal to the state's highest court, advocated the protections of the Sedition Act of 1798: truth as a defense and determination by the jury of the criminality of the publication. FREEDOM OF THE PRESS, declared Hamilton, was "the right to publish, with impunity, truth, with good motives for justifiable ends, though reflecting on government, the magistracy, or individuals." Spenser Ambrose, the Jeffersonian prosecutor, defended the remote BAD TENDENCY TEST. By the time the court decided the case, Ambrose had become a member of it. Had he been eligible to vote, the court would have supported the suppressive views of Lewis and Ambrose. As it was, the court split 2–2. Judge BROCKHOLST LIVINGSTON joined Lewis, while Judge SMITH THOMPSON joined the opinion of JAMES KENT, a Federalist who adopted Hamilton's argument.

In 1805 the state legislature enacted a bill allowing the jury to decide the criminality of a publication and permitted truth as a defense if published "with good motives for justifiable ends." On the whole that was the standard that prevailed in the United States until NEW YORK TIMES V. SULLIVAN (1964).

LEONARD W. LEVY

PER CURIAM

(Latin: "By the court.") A *per curiam* opinion represents the views of the court and summarily disposes of the issue before the court by applying settled law. (See RES JUDICATA). Generally the opinion is short and it is always unsigned, although dissents will occasionally be filed.

DAVID GORDON

PEREZ v. BROWNELL

See: *Trop v. Dulles*

PEREZ v. UNITED STATES
402 U.S. 146 (1971)

In sustaining a conviction for the federal crime of "loan-sharking," the Supreme Court upheld Title II of the CONSUMER CREDIT PROTECTION ACT as valid under the COMMERCE CLAUSE. For an 8–1 Court, Justice WILLIAM O. DOUGLAS rehearsed a congressional committee's finding that extortionate credit practices were linked to organized, interstate crime and vitally affected INTERSTATE COMMERCE. He rejected petitioner's contention that the crime of loan-sharking was necessarily local in nature. Justice POTTER STEWART, in dissent, argued that there had been no showing of interstate movement or effect in Perez's case, and worried that Congress might preempt the whole field of criminal law.

DENNIS J. MAHONEY

PERRY v. UNITED STATES

See: Gold Clause Cases

PERRY EDUCATION ASSOCIATION v. PERRY LOCAL EDUCATORS' ASSOCIATION
460 U.S. 37 (1983)

Perry provided the leading modern opinion setting guidelines governing FIRST AMENDMENT claims of access to the PUBLIC FORUM. A school district's collective bargaining agreement with a union (PEA) provided that PEA, but no other union, would have access to the interschool mails and to teacher mailboxes. A rival union (PLEA) sued in federal district court, challenging the constitutionality of its exclusion from the school mails. The district court denied relief, but the court of appeals held that the exclusion violated the EQUAL PROTECTION clause and the First Amendment. The Supreme Court reversed, 5–4, rejecting both claims.

Justice BYRON R. WHITE wrote for the Court, setting out a three-category analysis that set the pattern for later "public forum" cases such as CORNELIUS V. NAACP LEGAL DEFENSE AND EDUCATIONAL FUND, INC. (1985). First, the streets and parks are "traditional" public forums, in which government cannot constitutionally forbid all communicative activity. Any exclusion of a speaker from such a traditional public forum based on the content of the speaker's message must be necessary to serve a COMPELLING STATE INTEREST. Content-neutral regulations of the "time, place, and manner" of expression in such places may be enforced when they are narrowly tailored to serve significant state interests and they leave open "ample alternative channels" of communication.

Second, the state may open up other kinds of public property for use by the public for expressive activity. The state may close such a "designated" public forum, but so long as it remains open it must be made available to all speakers, under the same constitutional guidelines that govern traditional public forums.

Third, communicative uses of public property that is neither a traditional nor a designated public forum may be restricted to those forms of communication that serve the governmental operation to which the property is devoted. The only constitutional limits on such restrictions on speech are that they be reasonable, and that they not be imposed in order to suppress a particular point of view. The *Perry* case, said Justice White, fit this third category: the school mail system was neither a traditional public forum nor designated for public communicative use; rather it could be limited to school-related communications, including those from PEA, the teachers' elected bargaining agent. Such a limitation did not exclude PLEA because of its point of view.

Justice WILLIAM J. BRENNAN, for the four dissenters, argued that the exclusion of PLEA was "viewpoint discrimination," and thus that the case did not turn on the characterization of the school mails as a public forum.

The *Perry* formula capped a process of doctrinal development focused on what HARRY KALVEN, JR., named "the concept of the public forum." In its origin, the concept expanded the First Amendment's protections of speech. *Perry* marks the success of a campaign, highlighted by Justice WILLIAM H. REHNQUIST's opinion in *United States Postal Service v. Greenburgh Civic Association* (1981), to convert the public forum concept into a preliminary hurdle for would-be speakers to clear before they can establish their claims to the FREEDOM OF SPEECH on government property or in government-managed systems of communication.

KENNETH L. KARST

PERSON

The Constitution contains dozens of references to "persons" but nowhere defines the term. When the Framers of the original document identified persons who might hold federal office or be counted in determining a state's representation in Congress or the ELECTORAL COLLEGE, they used "persons" in its everyday sense—even when they provided that slaves should be counted as "three fifths of all other Persons." Focusing on the allocation of governmental powers, they had little occasion to ponder the philosopher's question: what does it mean to be a person? It was the addition to the Constitution of a body of constitutional rights against the government—first in the BILL OF RIGHTS and later in the FOURTEENTH AMENDMENT—that gave the philosopher's question constitutional significance.

In court, that question is never raised in wholesale terms but always in the context of particular issues. The Fourteenth Amendment's DUE PROCESS and EQUAL PROTECTION clauses, for example, offer their protections to "any person." Should those protections extend to a corporation? To a fetus? A philosopher, asked to say whether a corporation or a fetus more closely resembles some ideal model of a person, might be forgiven for failing to predict the Supreme Court's conclusions in *Santa Clara County v. Southern Pacific Railroad* (1886) and ROE V. WADE (1973) that corporations were included but fetuses were not. The Court, like many another human institution, defines its terms with substantive purposes in mind.

The notion that a corporation might be a "person" for some constitutional purposes had been suggested early in the nineteenth century. The point was not explicitly argued to the Supreme Court, however, until *San Mateo County v. Southern Pacific Railroad* (1882). In that case former Senator ROSCOE CONKLING, representing the railroad, made use of the journal of the joint congressional committee that had drafted the Fourteenth Amendment, a committee on which he had served. Conkling strongly intimated that the committee had used the word "person" for the specific purpose of including corporations. The case was dismissed for MOOTNESS, but in the *Santa Clara* case Chief Justice MORRISON R. WAITE interrupted ORAL ARGUMENT to say that the Court had concluded that the equal protection clause, in referring to a "person," extended its benefit to a corporation—a ruling that has since been followed consistently in both equal protection and due process decisions. Much of the later development of SUBSTANTIVE DUE PROCESS as a guarantee of FREEDOM OF CONTRACT and a protection against ECONOMIC REGULATION thus rested on a proposition of law whose basis was never articulated in an opinion of the Supreme Court.

To be a person, for constitutional purposes, is to be capable of holding constitutional rights. Our system of rights is premised on the idea that a right either "belongs" to someone—some person—or does not exist. The DOCTRINES of STANDING and mootness, as they govern our federal courts, reflect this assumption. We are accustomed to speak of "individual rights." Yet any claim to any right is an appeal to principle—and a principle is an abstraction that governs a great many "cases" not in court. Every claim of "individual" right, in other words, is a claim on behalf of a group composed of all those who fit the claim's underlying principle. Only a person can claim a constitutional right, but every such claim is made by a person as an occupant of a role: a homeowner whose house has been searched by the police, a would-be soapbox orator, a natural father disqualified from having custody of his child.

Although corporations—or even whole states—are capable of asserting constitutional claims, and although every "individual" constitutional right is capable of being generalized to extend to a group, nonetheless there remains an important sense in which we hold constitutional rights as persons. Today's constitutional law recognizes a body of substantive rights founded on the essentials of being a person. Here the philosopher's question must be asked; some model of what it means to be a person is implicit in such developments as the emergence of a RIGHT OF PRIVACY or a FREEDOM OF INTIMATE ASSOCIATION.

These rights of "personhood" (to use the Supreme Court's expression in *Roe v. Wade*) attach to natural persons. They rest on the assumption, usually not articulated, that although each human being is unique, we all share certain elements of our common humanity. The assumption is that each of us is conscious of a continuing identity; has some conception of his or her own good; is capable of forming and changing purposes; has a sense of justice—is, in short a "moral person" and not just a biological organism. Of course, the biological person has received its own constitutional protections: the FOURTH AMENDMENT'S guarantee against unreasonable searches and seizures runs in part to our "persons"; a woman's right to have an abortion is based on her right to control the use of her body. It is the moral person, however, who is the focus of the newer rights of "personhood."

The principal doctrinal foundation for these rights has been a renascent SUBSTANTIVE DUE PROCESS. Yet similar values form the substantive core of the Fourteenth Amendment's guarantee of the equal protection of the laws. That guarantee originated as part of the nation's response to slavery and to efforts in the postabolition South to create a system of serfdom to substitute for slavery. In law, of course, a slave was not a person; an item of property could claim no rights. Yet the original Constitution's two provisions recognizing slavery referred not to "slaves" but to "persons"—as if the draftsmen, resigned to the necessity of their unholy bargain with the southern states, nonetheless could not bring themselves to deny their common humanity with the men and women held as slaves. Seventy years later, in DRED SCOTT V. SANDFORD (1857), Chief Justice ROGER B. TANEY expressed quite another view of the Framers' understanding. At the nation's founding, Taney said, blacks had been considered "an inferior class of beings," incapable of CITIZENSHIP. The modern revival of the Fourteenth Amendment's principle of equal citizenship serves, above all, to protect the claim of each of us to be treated by the society as a person—one who has rights as a respected, responsible, participating member of our community.

KENNETH L. KARST

Bibliography

GRAHAM, HOWARD JAY 1938 The "Conspiracy Theory" of the Fourteenth Amendment. *Yale Law Journal* 47:371–403; 48:171–194.

HORWITZ, MORTON J. 1985–1986 *Santa Clara* Revisited: The Development of Corporate Theory. *West Virginia Law Review* 88:173–224.

NOONAN, JOHN T., JR. 1976 *Persons and Masks of the Law: Cardozo, Holmes, Jefferson, and Wythe as Makers of the Masks.* New York: Farrar, Straus & Giroux.

TRIBE, LAURENCE H. 1978 *American Constitutional Law.* Chap. 15. Mineola, N.Y.: Foundation Press.

VINING, JOSEPH 1978 *Legal Identity: The Coming of Age of Public Law.* New Haven, Conn.: Yale University Press.

PERSONAL LIBERTY LAWS

Between 1826 and 1858, all the free states east of Illinois enacted "personal liberty laws" providing one or more procedural remedies to persons seized as fugitive slaves. These included the writs of HABEAS CORPUS and personal replevin. Some personal liberty laws also provided jury trial to alleged fugitives; prohibited kidnaping or enticement of black persons out of state; imposed more stringent state procedures for recaptions; or provided the services of state's attorneys to alleged fugitives. The Vermont Freedom Act of 1858 declared every slave who came into the state free.

In PRIGG V. PENNSYLVANIA (1842), Justice JOSEPH STORY held that state statutes interfering with recaptures under the 1793 Fugitive Slave Act were unconstitutional. But in an OBITER DICTUM unique to him, Story stated that state officials need not participate in a recapture under federal authority. This spurred enactment of statutes prohibiting state officials such as judges and sheriffs from participating in fugitive recaptures and prohibiting the use of state facilities such as jails to slave-catchers trying to hold runaways. Proslavery spokesmen tirelessly denounced the personal liberty laws. In his last annual message, President JAMES BUCHANAN blamed the crisis of 1860 on them. South Carolina cited the laws as justification for its SECESSION.

WILLIAM M. WIECEK

Bibliography

MORRIS, THOMAS D. 1974 *Free Men All: The Personal Liberty Laws of the North, 1780–1861.* Baltimore: Johns Hopkins University Press.

PERSONNEL ADMINISTRATOR OF MASSACHUSETTS v. FEENEY
442 U.S. 256 (1979)

In selecting applicants for state civil service positions, Massachusetts preferred all qualifying veterans of the armed forces over any qualifying nonveterans. Because fewer than two percent of Massachusetts veterans were women, the preference severely restricted women's public employment opportunities. A nonveteran woman applicant challenged the preference as a denial of the EQUAL PROTECTION OF THE LAWS; the Supreme Court, 7–2, upheld the preference's constitutionality.

The Court, speaking through Justice POTTER STEWART, followed WASHINGTON V. DAVIS (1976) and held that SEX DISCRIMINATION, like RACIAL DISCRIMINATION, is to be found only in purposeful official conduct. A discriminatory impact, of itself, is thus insufficient to establish the sex discrimination that demands the judicial scrutiny set out in CRAIG V. BOREN (1976). Here the veterans preference disadvantaged nonveteran men as well as women; there was no basis for assuming that the preference was "a pretext for preferring men over women." Rather it was aimed at rewarding the sacrifices of military service and easing the transition from military to civilian life.

Justice THURGOOD MARSHALL dissented, joined by Justice WILLIAM J. BRENNAN: legislators act for a variety of reasons; the question is whether an improper purpose was one motivating factor in the governmental action. Here the discriminatory impact of the law was not merely foreseeable but inevitable. The result was to relegate female civil servants to jobs traditionally filled by women. Other less discriminatory means were available for rewarding veterans (bonuses, for example); the state's choice of this preference strongly suggested intentional gender discrimination. A similar "foreseeability" argument was persuasive to a majority of the Court four weeks later, in the context of school segregation. (See COLUMBUS BOARD OF EDUCATION V. PENICK, 1979.)

KENNETH L. KARST

PETERS, RICHARD
(1744–1828)

President GEORGE WASHINGTON on April 11, 1792, commissioned Richard Peters judge of the United States District Court for Pennsylvania, a position he filled until his death. His duties included presiding with a Supreme Court Justice over the federal CIRCUIT COURT in the state.

Peters contributed significantly to the development of a distinctly American ADMIRALTY AND MARITIME LAW, including features borrowed from civil and COMMON LAW precedents. In cases like *Warder v. La-Belle Creole* (1792), he was among the first American judges to advance a risk-reward calculus intended to facilitate the expansion of commerce.

His constitutional opinions touched the civil and criminal JURISDICTIONS of the lower federal courts and the law of TREASON. Peters in 1792 joined his fellow circuit court judges in HAYBURN'S CASE in refusing to determine the qualifications of Revolutionary War pensioners under a congressional act. This task, the judges concluded, fell outside the JUDICIAL POWER OF THE UNITED STATES. Peters, however, had a broad view of federal judicial power. In *United States v. Worrall* (1798) he urged recognition of a FEDERAL COMMON LAW OF CRIMES, a position subsequently rejected by the Supreme Court.

Peters's nationalism also shaped his views of treason and the supremacy of the federal courts. In *United States v. John Fries* (1800) he charged the jury that "levying war against the United States" included armed opposition to the collection of taxes. (See FRIES' REBELLION.) During the famous *Olmstead* controversy in Pennsylvania, Peters ordered the governor and the General Assembly to pay a judgment outstanding against the state in the federal court. Peters withheld issuing compulsory process for fear of an armed clash, but Chief Justice JOHN MARSHALL in UNITED STATES V. JUDGE PETERS (1809) vindicated the judge's nationalism.

Peters's Federalist political principles flowed into his jurisprudence. He was a "Republican Schoolmaster," who exploited the lower federal bench to promote commercial development, federal judicial independence, and national authority.

KERMIT L. HALL

Bibliography

PRESSER, STEPHEN B. 1978 A Tale of Two Judges: Richard Peters, Samuel Chase, and the Broken Promise of Federalist Jurisprudence. *Northwestern University Law Review* 73:26–111.

PETITION FOR REDRESS OF GRIEVANCES

See: Freedom of Petition

PETITION OF RIGHT
(June 7, 1628)

This statute is among the foremost documents in Anglo-American constitutional history. The Petition of Right protected the liberty of the subject and contributed to the development of the RULE OF LAW and the concept of FUNDAMENTAL LAW. The Framers of the Constitution regarded the act of 1628 as part of their COMMON LAW inheritance establishing rights against government. In its time, however, the statute limited only the royal prerogative or executive authority.

In 1626 Charles I, exercising his prerogative, had exacted a "forced loan" from his subjects. The poor paid it by having to quarter soldiers in their homes and having to serve in the army or face trial by a military tribunal. Five knights refused to make a contribution of money to the crown on the grounds that it was an unconstitutional tax; they were imprisoned by order of the king's council. When they sought a writ of HABEAS CORPUS, the Court of King's Bench, in *Darnel's Case* (1627), ruled that because the return to the writ showed the prisoners to be held on executive authority, no specific cause of imprisonment had to be stated.

The forced loan and the resolution of *Darnel's Case* caused a furor. After the House of Commons adopted resolutions against arbitrary taxation and arbitrary imprisonment, Sir EDWARD COKE introduced a bill to bind the king. The House of Lords sought to "save" the SOVEREIGNTY of the king by allowing a denial of habeas corpus for reasons of state. Coke, opposing such an amendment to the bill, argued that it would weaken MAGNA CARTA, and he warned: "Take heed what we yield unto: Magna Charta [sic] is such a fellow that he will have no 'sovereign.' " The Lords finally agreed and the king assented.

The Petition of Right reconfirmed Magna Carta's provision that no freeman could be imprisoned but by lawful judgment of his peers or "by the LAW OF THE LAND." The Petition also reconfirmed a 1354 reenactment of the great charter which first used the phrase "by DUE PROCESS OF LAW" instead of "by the law of the land." By condemning the military trial of civilians, the Petition invigorated due process and limited martial law. One section of the Petition provided that no one should be compelled to make any loan to the crown or pay any tax "without common consent by act of parliament." Americans later relied on this provision in their argument against TAXATION WITHOUT REPRESENTATION. Other sections of the act of 1628 provided that no one should be imprisoned or be forced to incriminate himself by having to answer for refusing an exaction not authorized by Parliament. Condemnation of imprisonment without cause or merely on executive authority strengthened the writ of habeas corpus. (See HABEAS CORPUS ACT OF 1679; BILL OF RIGHTS [ENGLISH].) The THIRD AMENDMENT of the Constitution derives in part from the Petition of Right.

LEONARD W. LEVY

Bibliography

RELF, FRANCIS H. 1917 *The Petition of Right.* Minneapolis: University of Minnesota Press.

PETIT JURY

The petit jury is the trial jury, as distinguished from the GRAND JURY. The petit jury decides questions of fact in cases at law, and renders the verdict, formally declaring its findings. Traditionally, in Anglo-American law, the jury decided by unanimous vote of twelve members, but this is not constitutionally required.

DENNIS J. MAHONEY

(SEE ALSO: *Jury Discrimination; Jury Size; Jury Unanimity; Trial by Jury.*)

PHELPS, EDWARD J.
(1822–1900)

Edward John Phelps was a Vermont Democrat who, in frequent appearances before the Supreme Court, championed the rights of private property. An outstanding orator—he was frequently likened to DANIEL WEBSTER or WILLIAM EVARTS—Phelps served as president of the American Bar Association (1880–1881) and as Kent Professor of Law at Yale (1881–1900). He declared that America's problems stemmed from "a vicious and altogether unnecessary enlargement of the electorate"; this attitude explained his belief that the Constitution was too hallowed to be "hawked about the country, debated in the newspapers . . . [and] elucidated by pot-house politicians, and dung-hill editors."

DAVID GORDON

PHILADELPHIA v. NEW JERSEY
437 U.S. 617 (1978)

In a 7–2 decision, the Supreme Court invalidated a New Jersey environmental protection law that prohibited the importation of solid waste originating or collected out of state. Justice POTTER STEWART, writing for the majority, concluded that the law unduly burdened INTERSTATE COMMERCE. The worthlessness of the regulated commodity did not exclude it from the operation of the COMMERCE CLAUSE; nor was the law permissible because its goals were environmental rather than economic. New Jersey could not require other states to bear the whole burden of conservation of its landfill sites. (See ENVIRONMENTAL REGULATION AND THE CONSTITUTION.)

DENNIS J. MAHONEY

PHILADELPHIA & READING RAILROAD CO. v. PENNSYLVANIA
(State Freight Tax Case)
15 Wallace 232 (1873)

Pennsylvania imposed a tonnage tax on all freight transported within the state, including freight shipped out of and into the state. The transportation of freight for exchange or sale, said Justice WILLIAM STRONG for a 7–2 Supreme Court, is commerce, and a clear tax on such commerce among states is an unconstitutional burden on INTERSTATE COMMERCE that might injure commercial intercourse in the country. Strong added that the transportation of persons or merchandise through a state or from one to another is a subject of national importance requiring, under the rule of COOLEY V. BOARD OF WARDENS (1852), uniform and exclusive regulation by Congress. This still is an important case on STATE TAXATION OF COMMERCE.

LEONARD W. LEVY

PHILOSOPHY AND THE CONSTITUTION

The Constitution is one of the great achievements of political philosophy; and it may be the only political achievement of philosophy in our society. The Framers of the Constitution and the leading participants in the debates on RATIFICATION shared a culture more thoroughly than did any later American political elite. They shared a knowledge (often distorted, but shared nevertheless) of ancient philosophy and history, of English COMMON LAW, of recent English political theory, and of the European Enlightenment. They were the American branch of the Enlightenment, and salient among their membership credentials was their belief that reasoned thought about politics could guide them to ideal political institutions for a free people. They argued passionately about the nature of SOVEREIGNTY, of political REPRESENTATION, of republicanism, of CONSTITUTIONALISM; and major decisions in the ferment of institution-building that culminated in 1787 were influenced, if never wholly determined, by such arguments. The final form of the new federal Constitution embodied radically new views about the location of sovereignty—now located "in the people" in a stronger sense than any philosopher except Jean-Jacques Rousseau would have recognized—and about the function of the SEPARATION OF POWERS and BICAMERALISM.

Philosophy has never again played the role it played at the founding of the Republic, except perhaps in inspiring some ABOLITIONIST CONSTITUTIONAL THEORY. To be sure, "philosophy" in a loose sense has always influenced politicians and judges, who are part of society. The Supreme Court in the late nineteenth and early twentieth centuries expressed in its decisions a laissez-faire "philosophy" compounded of Darwinism, a version of NATURAL RIGHTS theory, and conservative economic beliefs. When the Court abandoned that "philosophy," they adopted another, more progressivist and pragmatic, and more attuned to, though at most only loosely connected with, the renascent empiricism among academic philosophers. Occasionally, the Court has adverted to specific philosophical doctrines, from JOHN MARSHALL in FLETCHER V. PECK (1810) to GEORGE H. SUTHERLAND in UNITED STATES V. CURTISS-WRIGHT EXPORT CORP. (1936) (on the necessary existence of sovereign power). Individual Justices like OLIVER WENDELL HOLMES may have been influenced by philosophical reading and by contact with professional philosophers. But, on the whole, while "philosophy" has had an influence, philosophy has had little—except to the extent that the "philosophy" of the present is always shaped in part by the philosophy of the past. (The decreased influence of philosophy has not lessened the relevance of philosophical issues.)

There are a number of reasons for the decreased influence of philosophy. In the open society the Framers helped to create, their style of argument, dependent on a relatively homogeneous and classically educated elite, could not maintain its political importance. Also, political philosophy itself became less unified. Widely divergent views were united under the umbrella of the Enlightenment by common opposition to entrenched privilege and hieratic religion. Once common enemies were vanquished, philosophical comrades parted company.

Another reason for the decreased influence of philosophy is that philosophy admits of no binding authorities, while law does, and does essentially. The Framers were creating a new political system. No one since then, except to some extent the Reconstruction Congresses, has had that luxury. Later contributors to our constitutional development have always had to interpret, and to attempt to maintain at least the appearance of continuity with, what has gone before.

Curiously, while recent philosophical thinking has had little discernible influence on constitutional law, the reverse is not true. The decisions of the WARREN COURT and the public discussion they generated certainly contributed, probably significantly, to the revival of interest among American philosophers in social and political questions, a revival that became apparent in the CIVIL RIGHTS era of the 1950s and 1960s and that is still in full flower.

Whatever the influence or lack of it of philosophy on constitutional law, philosophical discussion among academic constitutional lawyers may have reached greater intensity in the 1980s than at any time since the 1780s. Constitutional law, like law in general, raises deep and perplexing philosophical questions. The questions that arise most immediately are questions of political philosophy, and of these the one that has generated most discussion is what is known as the "antimajoritarian difficulty": how can it be appropriate for the enormously consequential power of JUDICIAL REVIEW to be vested ultimately in nine individuals who are not chosen by the people and who are not politically accountable to anyone at all? The problem is especially vexing when the Court, in the space of three decades, has outlawed SEGREGATION, forbidden religious activity in the public schools, required REAPPORTIONMENT of the state legislatures and local government, created a constitutional code of CRIMINAL PROCEDURE, established a right to abortion, and found in the EQUAL PROTECTION clause a command that government shall not engage in SEX DISCRIMINATION.

There are three principal types of answer to the question how a democratic society can countenance such judicial power. The first answer, and the natural answer for any lawyer, is the claim that the Supreme Court has this power because the Constitution says it does. But the Constitution does not say that, at least not explicitly. The power of judicial review is nowhere explicitly granted. Now, in a sense, the lawyer's answer is still right. The Constitution as it has been interpreted from 1803 to the present does create the power of judicial review. The propriety of some form of judicial review is disputed by no one. Even so, it is noteworthy that at the very foundation of American constitutional law we encounter the problem of CONSTITUTIONAL INTERPRETATION.

Given a document, and given agreement that its commands are to be put into practice by legal institutions, how do we decide what it commands? How do we decide what it means? Neither the words alone nor anything we know about the writers' intentions is likely to answer straightforwardly all the questions time will bring forth. For that matter, is it the document we are primarily concerned to interpret, or the political and doctrinal tradition proceeding from the document that we are concerned to interpret and to continue? And how are interpretation and continuation related?

It is important to distinguish between the document and the tradition and to ask how our commitments to each are interrelated. For example, we are firmly committed, by our allegiance to the tradition, to certain DOCTRINES, such as the effective application of the BILL OF RIGHTS to the states and of the equal protection clause to the federal government, which can be deduced from the document only by extremely generous canons of interpretation. Some argue that if we are committed to these doctrines, then we must accept and continue to apply those generous canons. But that conclusion does not follow at all. Law, like any tradition, can sanctify mistakes.

The problem of interpretation does not arise only at the stage of justifying judicial review. It arises also at every application of judicial review. What is the Court to do with this power? The lawyerly answer, and again clearly the right answer in some sense, is that the Court should enforce the Constitution. But once more, how do we decide what the Constitution means?

The lawyerly exponent of judicial review also invites, by appealing to the Constitution, the most fundamental question: why do we care about the document or the tradition at all? It may be that to ask this question is to go beyond the domain of the lawyer as lawyer; but lawyers and judges are people, and every person who bears allegiance to the document or the tradition must face this question. Note, however: even though all lawyers and judges must face this question of political philosophy in deciding whether to carry out their roles, it does not follow that they must also appeal to substantive political philosophy in the course of carrying out their roles. Whether they must do that, and whether they could avoid doing that if they tried, are further issues.

The difficulties with the lawyerly justification and exposition of judicial review have prompted two other main theories of judicial review. In one theory, judicial review is justified by the need to protect individual rights against infringement by majoritarian government. Exponents of this theory have drawn heavily on a neo-Kantian strain of contemporary American political philosophy in attempting to elucidate individual rights and the limits of the majority's legitimate power. In the other theory, judicial review does not purport to limit but merely to purify the democratic process. Judicial intervention is necessary to protect political speech and participation and to prevent distortion of the process by majority prejudice, but all in the name of more perfect majoritarianism.

Opposed as they are on the significance of individual rights, these two theories share an ambivalent relationship to the Constitution and the interpretive tradition. Whence comes the notion that individual autonomy should be protected, or that majoritarian democracy should be purified but not otherwise limited? Is it just that the Constitution says so? The Constitution says neither of these things explicitly; and it says both too much and too little to make either of these views a completely satisfactory reading of the document as a whole.

On the other hand, if someone claims to read the Constitution as protecting individuality (or purified majoritarianism) because of the independent moral weight of those values, why does the historical document come into it at all? Is not every appeal to the Constitution by a proponent of independently grounded values of autonomy or purified majoritarianism in some sense mere manipulation of other people's allegiance to the Constitution for itself?

We see that the questions raised by the lawyerly approach to judicial review are not so easily avoided. Still, the competing approaches we have noted alert us to dimensions of the problem not previously apparent. First, if the justification for judicial review is to promote general values such as autonomy or purified majoritarianism, that may help us decide how specific bits of the Constitution should be interpreted. Second, the tradition may refer to certain goals—justice, autonomy, democracy—which the tradition itself views as having a value and grounding outside and independent of the tradition. If the tradition commands allegiance both to its own specific content and to external values, it contains within itself the seeds of possible contradiction. What does faithfulness to the tradition then require?

As of the 1980s, the newest philosophical interest of academic constitutional lawyers is in hermeneutics. Whether there are answers here, and whether any such answers will influence the course of constitutional law, remains to be seen. Hermeneutics may bring new insight into the various meanings of the idea of operating in a tradition. Barring some remarkable feat of philosophical bootstrapping, hermeneutics will not answer the most fundamental philosophical question about constitutional law: why care about the tradition at all? And there is a final irony. Because the political community is made up of individuals who must confront this fundamental question, the community must confront it also, even though from another perspective it is by shared allegiance to the tradition that the community is defined.

DONALD H. REGAN

Bibliography

DWORKIN, RONALD (1977)1978 *Taking Rights Seriously.* Cambridge, Mass.: Harvard University Press.

ELY, JOHN H. 1980 *Democracy and Distrust: A Theory of Judicial Review.* Cambridge, Mass.: Harvard University Press.

LAYCOCK, DOUGLAS 1981 Taking Constitutions Seriously: A Theory of Judicial Review. *Texas Law Review* 59:343–394.

TRIBE, LAURENCE H. 1978 *American Constitutional Law.* Mineola, N.Y.: Foundation Press.

WOOD, GORDON S. 1969 *The Creation of the American Republic, 1776–1787.* Chapel Hill: University of North Carolina Press for the Institute of Early American History and Culture at Williamsburg, Va.

PICKERING, JOHN
(1738?–1805)

In March 1803 the House of Representatives impeached John Pickering, federal district judge for New Hampshire, of habitual drunkenness, uttering blasphemy and profanity from the bench, and making decisions contrary to law. During his Senate trial Pickering introduced a defense of insanity; but the Senate, in a partisan vote, found him "guilty as charged" and removed him from office. The vote was a warning to other Federalist judges that Congress did not need to convict them of a specific crime in order to remove them. (See IMPEACHMENT.)

DENNIS J. MAHONEY

PICKETING

Picketing typically consists of one or more persons patrolling or stationed at a particular site, carrying or wearing large signs with a clearly visible message addressed to individuals or groups approaching the site. Some form of confrontation between the pickets and their intended addressees appears an essential ingredient of picketing. Congress and the National Labor Relations Board have distinguished between picketing and handbilling, however, and merely passing out leaflets without carrying a placard does not usually constitute picketing. What stamps picketing as different from more conventional forms of communication, for constitutional and other legal purposes, ordinarily seems to be the combination of a sign big enough to be seen easily and a confrontation between picketer and viewer.

Constitutional determinations concerning picketing have usually involved LABOR unions that are advertising a dispute with employers and appealing to the public or fellow employees for support. The assistance sought might be a refusal by customers to patronize the picketed business or a refusal by workers to perform services or make deliveries there. In addition, picketing has often been a weapon of CIVIL RIGHTS demonstrators, political and religious activists, environmentalists, and other interest groups.

The leading Supreme Court decision upholding picketing as an exercise of FREEDOM OF SPEECH protected by the FIRST AMENDMENT is THORNHILL V. ALABAMA (1940). In striking down a state antipicketing statute, Justice FRANK MURPHY declared that an abridgment of the right to publicize through picketing or similar activity "can be justified only where the clear danger of substantive evils arises under circumstances affording no opportunity to test the merits of ideas by competition for acceptance in the market of public opinion." Despite this sweeping language, the actual holding in *Thornhill* was narrow. The Alabama courts were prepared to apply a criminal statute to prohibit a single individual from patrolling peacefully in front of an employer's establishment carrying a sign stating truthfully that the employer did not employ union labor.

Following *Thornhill* two principal themes have dominated the Supreme Court's analysis of the constitutional status of picketing. One is the "unlawful objectives" test and the other is the concept of picketing as "speech plus." Under the first approach, as illustrated by GIBONEY V. EMPIRE STORAGE & ICE CO. (1949), even peaceful picketing may be proscribed if its "sole, unlawful immediate objective" is the violation of a valid public policy or statutory mandate. Picketing is treated like any other type of communication, oral or written, which may also be forbidden if it produces a CLEAR AND PRESENT DANGER of, or a direct INCITEMENT to, substantive evils that government is entitled to prevent. A message delivered by pickets, however, might constitute a clearer and more present danger than the same message in a newspaper advertisement, for picketing physically confronts the addressee at the very moment of decision.

A conceptual weakness of the "unlawful objectives" test is that it can sustain almost any restriction on picketing by too loose a characterization of the pickets' purpose as illegal. In *Teamsters Local 695 v. Vogt, Inc.* (1957), a 5–3 Supreme Court upheld a state court INJUNCTION against peaceful organizational picketing on the ground that its purpose was to coerce the employer to force its employees to join the union. Even so, in *Amalgamated Food Employees Union v. Logan Valley Plaza* (1968) Justice THURGOOD MARSHALL could sum up the prior DOCTRINE by declaring that the cases in which picketing bans had been approved "involved picketing that was found either to have been directed at an illegal end . . . or to have been directed to coercing a decision by an employer which, although in itself legal, could validly be required by the State to be left to the employer's free choice."

Picketing as "speech plus" refers to two elements that arguably distinguish it from pure speech. First, it involves physical activity, usually the patrolling of a particular location. It is therefore subject to TRESPASS laws, and to other laws governing the time, place, and manner of expression, such as laws limiting sound levels, regulating parades, or forbidding the obstruction of public ways. Furthermore, picketing enmeshed with violence or threats of violence may be enjoined or prosecuted as assault and battery. Second, picketing may serve as a "signal" for action, especially by organized groups like labor unions, without regard to the ideas being disseminated. Some scholars have challenged the "pure speech/speech plus" dichotomy, contending that all speech, oral or written, has certain physical attributes, and can evoke stock responses from a preconditioned audience.

A further strand of Supreme Court free speech analysis is the notion that government may not engage in "content control." Thus, in POLICE DEPARTMENT OF CHICAGO V. MOSLEY (1972) the Court invalidated a city ordinance that forbade all picketing next to any school while it was in session, but exempted "peaceful picketing of any school involved in a labor dispute." That constituted "an impermissible distinction between labor and other peaceful picketing." The "no content control" doctrine obviously must be qualified by the "unlawful objectives" test.

In 1980 the Supreme Court extended the "unlawful objectives" test so far as to strip it of any practical limitations. A 6–3 majority held in *NLRB v. Retail Employees Local 1001* (*Safeco*) that picketing asking customers not to buy a nonunion product being distributed by a second party was an unlawful BOYCOTT of the distributor. Six Justices considered the prohibition justified constitutionally by Congress's purpose of blocking the "coercing" or "embroiling" of neutrals in another party's labor dispute. In *Safeco,* for the first time ever, the Supreme Court clearly sustained a ban on peaceful and orderly picketing addressed to, and calling for seemingly lawful responses by, individual consumers acting on their own.

Safeco might be explained on the basis that labor picketing is only "economic speech," like commercial advertising, and thus subject to lesser constitutional safeguards than political or ideological speech. Although such a distinction would contradict both established precedent and the traditional recognition of picketing as the working person's standard means of communication, at least it would preserve full-fledged free speech protections for picketing to promote political and ideological causes.

THEODORE J. ST. ANTOINE

Bibliography

COX, ARCHIBALD 1951 Strikes, Picketing and the Constitution. *Vanderbilt Law Review* 4:574–602.

GREGORY, CHARLES O., and KATZ, HAROLD A. (1946) 1979 *Labor and the Law.* New York: Norton.

JONES, EDGAR A., JR. 1956 Free Speech: Pickets on the Grass, Alas!—Amidst Confusion, a Consistent Principle. *Southern California Law Review* 29:137–181.

PIERCE, FRANKLIN
(1804–1869)

A New Hampshire attorney and politician, Pierce was nominated as a compromise presidential candidate by the Democrats in 1852. Pierce was a supporter of the COMPROMISE OF 1850 and a long-time opponent of abolitionists and antislavery Democrats. In 1854 he supported the KANSAS-NEBRASKA ACT, which led to a mini-civil war in "bleeding Kansas." Pierce's role in the passage of this act and his generally pro-southern positions undermined most of his other legislative proposals and his popularity in the North. During the Civil War Pierce's shrill attacks on ABRAHAM LINCOLN's administration made Pierce appear to be a full-fledged Copperhead.

PAUL FINKELMAN

Bibliography

NICHOLS, ROY F. 1931 *Franklin Pierce: Young Hickory of the Granite State.* Philadelphia: University of Pennsylvania Press.

PIERCE, WILLIAM
(1740?–1789)

William Pierce, a veteran of the Revolutionary War and a member of Congress, was a delegate from Georgia to the CONSTITUTIONAL CONVENTION OF 1787. He spoke only infrequently, and he left the Convention on July 1, under pressure of private business difficulties. Pierce did not sign the Constitution but wrote to ST. GEORGE TUCKER: "I approve of its principles and would have signed it with all my heart, had I been present."

Pierce kept fairly detailed notes of the debates while he was present. The notes were published in 1828 and include brief character sketches of each of the delegates.

DENNIS J. MAHONEY

PIERCE v. SOCIETY OF SISTERS
268 U.S. 510 (1925)

Pierce provided a doctrinal link between the SUBSTANTIVE DUE PROCESS of the era of LOCHNER V. NEW YORK (1905) and that of our own time. The Supreme Court unanimously invalidated an Oregon law requiring children to attend public schools. A church school and a military school, threatened with closure, sued to enjoin the law's enforcement. Although the law threatened injury to the schools, their challenge to it was based not on their own constitutional rights but on the rights of their pupils and the children's parents. By allowing the schools to make this challenge, the Court made a major exception to the usual rule denying a litigant's STANDING to assert the constitutional rights of others. Here there was a close relationship between the schools and their patrons, and failure to allow the schools to assert the patrons' rights might cause injury to the schools that no one would contest in court. Parents, fearing prosecution and unwilling to bear the expense of suit, might simply send their children to public schools.

In an opinion by Justice JAMES C. MCREYNOLDS, the Court held that the law unconstitutionally invaded the parents' liberty, guaranteed by the FOURTEENTH AMENDMENT's due process clause, to direct their children's education and upbringing. The decision rested squarely on the notion that important personal liberties could be seriously restricted by the state only upon a showing of great public need. Although *Pierce* thus traced its lineage to earlier decisions protecting economic liberty, it provided support for a later generation of decisions protecting marriage and family relationships against state intrusion. (See FREEDOM OF INTIMATE ASSOCIATION.)

Pierce is also cited regularly as a RELIGIOUS LIBERTY precedent, defending the right of parents to choose religious education for their children. (See WISCONSIN V. YODER, 1971.)

KENNETH L. KARST

PIERSON v. RAY
386 U.S. 547 (1967)

Pierson is an important case involving individual immunities from suits under SECTION 1983, TITLE 42, UNITED STATES CODE. Clergymen who violated an unlawful "whites only" waiting room policy in a Jackson, Mississippi, bus terminal were arrested and convicted. They brought an action under section 1983 against the arresting police officers and a state judge for depriving the clergymen of their constitutional rights. The Supreme Court both reaffirmed what it asserted to be the absolute immunity of judges from suit at COMMON LAW and refused to interpret section 1983 to abolish that traditional immunity. Although the police officer defendants were not granted absolute immunity, the Court did grant them a defense if the otherwise unconstitutional arrests were made in good faith and with PROBABLE CAUSE.

THEODORE EISENBERG

PINCKNEY, CHARLES
(1757–1824)

Charles Pinckney, a wealthy and ambitious young lawyer from South Carolina, was one of the most active members of the CONSTITUTIONAL CONVENTION OF 1787. A supporter of strong national government, Pinckney had already proposed in Congress several amendments to strengthen the government under the ARTICLES OF CONFEDERATION. He had unsuccessfully urged Congress to call a convention to amend the Articles.

Selected as a delegate to the Federal Convention, Pinckney drafted a comprehensive plan for revising the articles which he introduced immediately after EDMUND RANDOLPH proposed the VIRGINIA PLAN. The PINCKNEY PLAN was never debated in the Convention or the Committee of the Whole, although the Committee of Detail may have drawn some ideas or phrases from it.

Pinckney was one of the most frequent speakers in the debates, but the Constitution, as written, reflected his influence only in minor points and details. In a speech before signing, Pinckney announced that he would support the Constitution despite "the contemptible weakness and dependence of the Executive."

In his later career, Pinckney was a delegate to the South Carolina ratifying convention and to the state CONSTITUTIONAL CONVENTION of 1790, three times governor, a member of the legislature and of both houses of Congress, and minister of the United States to Spain.

DENNIS J. MAHONEY

PINCKNEY, CHARLES COTESWORTH
(1746–1825)

A British-educated, slaveholding lawyer, General Charles Cotesworth Pinckney represented South Carolina at the CONSTITUTIONAL CONVENTION OF 1787 and signed the Constitution. In the convention he worked for a strong national government and for protection of the slaveholding interests. As a leading spokesman for RATIFICATION in South Carolina, he defended the compromises on SLAVERY and argued that a BILL OF RIGHTS was unnecessary.

In 1791, Pinckney declined President GEORGE WASHINGTON's offer of a seat on the Supreme Court. The chief leader of the southern Federalists, Pinckney was nominated for vice-president in 1800, and for President in both 1804 and 1808.

DENNIS J. MAHONEY

Bibliography

ZAHNISER, MARVIN R. 1967 *Charles Cotesworth Pinckney, Founding Father.* Chapel Hill: University of North Carolina Press.

PINCKNEY PLAN
(1787)

The brash young South Carolinian CHARLES PINCKNEY arrived at the CONSTITUTIONAL CONVENTION OF 1787 bearing his own comprehensive draft of a new CONSTITUTION based on proposals he had made to amend the ARTICLES OF CONFEDERATION during his three years in Congress. He presented it to the convention immediately after EDMUND RANDOLPH presented the VIRGINIA PLAN. The Pinckney Plan was never debated, but it was referred to the Committee on Detail which may have drawn some ideas or phrases from it.

There was no copy of the Pinckney Plan among the papers of the convention. Pinckney himself later published what he claimed was his plan, but this was actually a fabrication closely resembling the finished Constitution. On the basis of this (fraudulent) published version and Pinckney's own extravagant claims about his influence, many historians and popular writers have attributed more significance to the Pinckney Plan and its author than either actually had.

In the twentieth century, historians J. Franklin Jameson and ANDREW C. MCLAUGHLIN reconstructed the details of the original Pinckney Plan. The proposal was certainly quite nationalistic, with no state role in the election of either house of Congress, an unconditional congressional veto over state laws, and a very powerful national executive.

DENNIS J. MAHONEY

Bibliography

MCLAUGHLIN, ANDREW C. 1904 The Pinckney Plan. *American Historical Review* 9:135–147.

PINK, UNITED STATES v.
315 U.S. 203 (1942)

In *Pink,* the Supreme Court reaffirmed a DOCTRINE articulated five years earlier in UNITED STATES V. BELMONT (1937): that the President has exclusive constitutional authority to recognize foreign governments and to take all steps necessary to effect such recognition. In *Belmont,* the Court recognized the federal government's STANDING to sue to enforce an EXECUTIVE AGREEMENT known as the "Litvinov Agreement." As part of the process of recognition of the Soviet Union by the United States in 1933, this agreement assigned to the United States nationalized Russian assets located within the United States.

In *Pink,* the Court was again confronted with the controversial Litvinov Assignment. In this case, while recognizing the federal government's rights under the Litvinov Assignment as required by *Belmont,* the New York courts rejected the government's claims of ownership of the assets in question, contending that to enforce the assignment would violate New York public policy against the confiscation of private property. The Supreme Court reversed, 5–2, emphasizing that an executive agreement, like a TREATY, is part of the "supreme law of the land" that no state may frustrate without interfering unconstitutionally with the federal government's exclusive competence in respect of FOREIGN AFFAIRS. In so doing, the Court reasserted the supremacy of an executive agreement over all inconsistent state law or policy.

BURNS H. WESTON

Bibliography

CARDOZO, MICHAEL H. 1962 The Authority in Internal Law of International Treaties: The Pink Case. *Syracuse Law Review* 13:544–553.

FORKOSCH, MORRIS D. 1975 The Constitution and International Relations. *California Western International Law Journal* 5:219, 246–249.

HENKIN, LOUIS 1972 *Foreign Affairs and the Constitution.* Mineola, N.Y.: Foundation Press.

LEARY, M. A. 1979 International Executive Agreements: A Guide to the Legal Issues and Research Sources. *Law Library Journal* 72:1–11.

PINKNEY, WILLIAM
(1764–1822)

William Pinkney studied law under SAMUEL CHASE and subsequently practiced in Baltimore. Although he opposed the RATIFICATION OF THE CONSTITUTION in the Maryland convention of 1788, he later became one of the nation's foremost constitutional lawyers. He held public office continuously from 1788 until his death, serving in the state legislature, in both houses of Congress, as a diplomat in important foreign capitals, and as ATTORNEY GENERAL of the United States under President JAMES MADISON. Although as a young man he favored gradual compensated emancipation in Maryland, Pinkney was a vigorous spokesman for the slave states in the Senate debates over the MISSOURI COMPROMISE (1820).

Between political and diplomatic assignments Pinkney conducted what was probably the most lucrative legal practice in the United States, arguing seventy-two cases before the Supreme Court. He was counsel for the New Hampshire state appointed board of trustees in DARTMOUTH COLLEGE V. WOODWARD (1819), unsuccessfully arguing that the college was a public CORPORATION whose charter could be altered by the state. In MCCULLOCH V. MARYLAND (1819), however, he won the day, contending for the constitutionality of a congressionally chartered bank and against the power of the state to tax it. And in COHENS V. VIRGINIA (1821) he successfully argued for the Supreme Court APPELLATE JURISDICTION over state criminal cases.

As an advocate, Pinkney won the praise of both judges and opposing counsel. Chief Justice JOHN MARSHALL called him "the greatest man I ever saw in a court of justice" and Marshall's successor, ROGER B. TANEY, said that in thirty years, "I have seen none to equal Pinkney." His enduring significance in American constitutional history derives from his incisive and original arguments in cases of first impression.

PAUL FINKELMAN

Bibliography

PINKNEY, REV. WILLIAM 1853 *The Life of William Pinkney.* New York: D. Appleton & Co.

PIQUA BRANCH OF THE STATE BANK OF OHIO v. KNOOP
16 Howard 369 (1854)

In NEW JERSEY V. WILSON (1812) the Supreme Court had held that a state grant of a tax immunity was a contract within the protection of the CONTRACT CLAUSE. In this case Ohio chartered a bank with the proviso that six percent of its net profits would be taxed in lieu of other taxation. The states competed with each other to entice private business to settle within their borders on the supposition that the more banks, railroads, and factories a state had, the greater would be its prosperity. Special privileges to CORPORATIONS were common, and they often wrote their own charters. Ohio, gripped by an anticorporate movement, reneged by passing an act to tax banks at the same rate as other properties. The bank refused to pay the new tax on the ground that its charter was a contract the obligation of which had been impaired by the tax. (See OBLIGATION OF CONTRACTS.) By a vote of 6–3 the Supreme Court invalidated the tax. To the contention that the power to tax was an inalienable attribute of SOVEREIGNTY, which could not be contracted away, the Court replied that the making of a public contract is an exercise of sovereignty. To the argument that one legislature, by granting a charter of tax immunity, could not bind its successors, the Court replied that the contract clause made the charter binding. In effect the Court cautioned the states to govern wisely, because the Court would not shield them from their imprudence if it took the form of contracts. Corporations throughout the country profited enormously.

LEONARD W. LEVY

PITNEY, MAHLON
(1858–1924)

Mahlon Pitney was the last of President WILLIAM HOWARD TAFT's appointments to the Supreme Court. Organized labor and some progressives vigorously protested the nomination because of Pitney's antilabor opinions as a New Jersey state judge, but his views paralleled Taft's. During Pitney's decade on the bench (1912–1922), he made prophets of his critics, as his opinions reflected a consistent hostility to the claims of organized labor. Nevertheless, Taft, as Chief Justice, derided Pitney as a "weak" member of his Court.

In COPPAGE V. KANSAS (1915) Pitney concluded that a Kansas statute prohibiting YELLOW DOG CONTRACTS violated FREEDOM OF CONTRACT. The opinion largely followed doctrine laid down in LOCHNER V. NEW YORK (1905), and reinforced in ADAIR V. UNITED STATES (1908), when the Court nullified an 1898 congressional law prohibiting railroads from imposing yellow dog contracts. In *Coppage,* Pitney attacked the state law as a restraint on a worker's right to contract, a right he saw as essential to the laborer as to the capitalist, "for the vast majority of persons who have no other honest way to begin to acquire property, save by working for money." Rejecting the statute's avowed intent of enabling workers to organize and bargain collectively, Pitney held that its primary effect was to interfere with "the normal and essentially innocent exercise of personal liberty or of property rights."

Two years later, Pitney wrote the Supreme Court's opinion favoring labor INJUNCTION and again sustained the validity of yellow dog contracts. In HITCHMAN COAL AND COKE CO. V. MITCHELL (1917) he upheld an injunction forbidding the United Mine Workers from seeking to organize workers who had previously agreed not to join a union. Every miner who had affiliated with the union "was guilty of a breach of contract," he said; furthermore, Pitney found that the union knowingly had violated the employer's "legal and constitutional right to run its mine 'non-union.' " Pitney's implacable defense of yellow dog contracts and injunctions galvanized labor's growing antagonism to the federal judiciary and its demands for congressional relief. Eventually, in 1932, the NORRIS-LAGUARDIA ACT forbade federal courts to enforce yellow dog contracts or issue labor injunctions, thus severely limiting the effects of Pitney's COPPAGE and HITCHMAN opinions.

In DUPLEX PRINTING CO. V. DEERING (1921) Pitney reinforced the judicial ban on secondary BOYCOTTS, thus frustrating organized labor's understanding that the CLAYTON ACT (1914) had legalized such practices. Pitney followed an earlier decision against secondary boycotts (LOEWE V. LAWLOR, 1908) and argued that a sympathetic strike supporting a secondary boycott could not be deemed "peaceful and lawful persuasion as allowed in the Clayton Act." Although Pitney regularly invoked judicial doctrines that inhibited labor's right to organize, he occasionally defied prediction. In *Mountain Timber Co. v. Washington* (1917) Pitney led a 5–4 majority that sustained a state WORKERS' COMPENSATION law requiring all employers to contribute to a general state fund, regardless of whether their employees had been injured. He found that the statute did not deprive employers of their property without DUE PROCESS OF LAW, and furthermore, it had a reasonable relationship to the GENERAL WELFARE. Four years later, in TRUAX V. CORRIGAN (1921), he joined OLIVER WENDELL HOLMES, LOUIS D. BRANDEIS, and JOHN H. CLARKE in dissent against Chief Justice Taft's opinion invalidating an Arizona law modeled on the labor provisions of the Clayton Act. In another rare deviation from his norm, Pitney joined the dissenters who favored the dissolution of the United States Steel Corporation.

Typically, judges such as Pitney would presume that regulatory laws such as Kansas's prohibition of yellow dog contracts and the labor provisions of the Clayton Act violated liberty of contract or property rights. Yet Pitney made no such assumption when an individual confronted the criminal process. In the notorious case of FRANK V. MANGUM (1915), for example, Pitney maintained that the state of Georgia had "fairly and justly" done its duty. Pitney also vigorously supported the national government's prosecution of dissenters and radicals following World War I. In *Pierce v. United States* (1920) he sustained the conviction of socialists who "knowingly" and "recklessly" distributed "highly colored and sensational" and "grossly false" statements about the government's conduct of the war. The *Pierce* decision solidified the Court's shift from Holmes's CLEAR AND PRESENT DANGER interpretation of the FIRST AMENDMENT to the less speech-protective BAD TENDENCY TEST.

Pitney approved the Court's invalidation of the child labor laws; he dissented from the majority's approval of widening the authority of the Interstate Commerce Commission; and he dissented from Justice CHARLES EVANS HUGHES's expansive reading of the COMMERCE CLAUSE in the "Shreveport Case," HOUSTON, EAST AND WEST TEXAS RAILWAY COMPANY V. UNITED STATES (1914). In short, Pitney's judicial career faithfully reflected the conservative reaction to much of the political and legal thrust of the Progressive movement.

STANLEY I. KUTLER

Bibliography

LEVITAN, DAVID M. 1954 Mahlon Pitney—Labor Judge. *Virginia Law Review* 40:733–770.

PITT, WILLIAM (Lord Chatham) (1708–1778)

William Pitt the elder was one of Britain's greatest statesmen and one of freedom's staunchest friends. He led Britain from near defeat in the Seven Years War to victory and worldwide empire.

In the WILKES CASES debates (1763–1770) Pitt denounced GENERAL WARRANTS as illegal and subversive of liberty and opposed any surrender of PARLIAMENTARY PRIVILEGE. During the 1766 debate over repeal of the Stamp Act, Pitt insisted that "the distinction between legislation and taxation is essentially necessary to liberty," and that while Britain was "sovereign and supreme, in every circumstance of government and legislation whatsoever," Parliament had no right to tax those not represented therein. "There is," he declared, "a plain distinction between taxes levied for purposes of raising a revenue, and duties imposed for the regulation of trade." Later that year, as earl of Chatham, Pitt was again called to head the government. During his administration (but while he was incapacitated by illness) his chancellor of the exchequer procured passage of the TOWNSHEND ACTS.

In the 1770s Chatham urged conciliation with the American colonies, but he opposed any measure tending toward dissolution of the empire. His final speech, delivered in 1778, was against a motion to withdraw British troops and recognize American independence.

DENNIS J. MAHONEY

PLAIN VIEW DOCTRINE

The FOURTH AMENDMENT protects persons and their effects against unreasonable SEARCHES AND SEIZURES. However, articles exposed to the plain view of others are subject to a warrantless seizure on PROBABLE CAUSE, for no search is involved and hence no invasion of privacy results. (Plain view differs from abandonment. Exposure of an article to plain view may result from carelessness; abandonment signifies a deliberate relinquishment of the right of ownership. In either case, there is no constitutionally protected interest in the privacy of the article.)

Three conditions must be met for a plain view seizure to be constitutional, according to the decision in COOLIDGE V. NEW HAMPSHIRE (1971). First, the officer who sees the article must have a legal right to be where he is. Second, discovery of the article by the police must be "inadvertent," not a result of prior information that would have enabled the police to obtain a warrant beforehand. (This requirement is relaxed in a SEARCH INCIDENT TO ARREST, where a seizure made within the limited scope of the authorized search is lawful even if the finding of the evidence was anticipated.) Finally, the incriminating nature of the evidence must be "immediately apparent," so that no additional intrusion on privacy is necessary in order to establish that fact. (The term "immediately apparent" was modified in *Brown v. Texas* (1983) to mean probable cause; certainty is not required.)

An emergency "hot pursuit" of a suspect into private premises, as in WARDEN V. HAYDEN (1967), provides the widest latitude for a plain view seizure; the search for the suspect and his weapons is permitted to extend throughout the entire place until he is apprehended. Barring emergencies, however, a plain view of the interior of a house, obtained through a window or open door, does not permit a warrantless entry of premises any more than does testimony of the senses (say, the odor of marijuana) that criminal activity is afoot. In searches of buildings, therefore, the plain view serves to authorize a seizure only when a lawful search is already in progress when the view is obtained. A different standard applies to automobiles: a plain view of evidence in an automobile on the road not only permits seizure of the evidence but also may provide probable cause for a WARRANTLESS SEARCH of the entire vehicle. Since *Brown,* even a closed container may be seized under the plain view doctrine if the contents can be reliably inferred from its outside appearance—for example, a tied balloon of a type commonly used to carry narcotics.

JACOB W. LANDYNSKI

Bibliography

LAFAVE, WAYNE R. 1978 *Search and Seizure: A Treatise on the Fourth Amendment.* Vol. 2:589–595, 601–605. St. Paul, Minn.: West Publishing Co.

PLANNED PARENTHOOD v. ASHCROFT

See: Reproductive Autonomy

PLANNED PARENTHOOD OF CENTRAL MISSOURI v. DANFORTH
428 U.S. 52 (1976)

Following ROE V. WADE (1973), Missouri adopted a comprehensive law regulating abortion. Planned Parenthood, which operated an abortion clinic, and two eminent physicians sued in federal district court challenging the constitutionality of most of the law's provisions. On appeal, the Supreme Court unanimously upheld three of the state's requirements and by divided vote invalidated four others. Justice HARRY A. BLACKMUN wrote for the Court.

The Court sustained the law's definition of "viability" of a fetus: "when the life of the unborn child may be continued indefinitely outside the womb by natural or artificial life-supportive systems." The state's failure to set a specific time period survived a challenge for VAGUENESS; the Court assumed that the physician retained the power to determine viability. The Court also upheld a requirement of written certification by a woman of her "informed" consent to an abortion, and certain record-keeping requirements.

The Court invalidated, 6–3, a requirement of consent to an abortion by the husband of the pregnant woman, and invalidated, 5–4, a parental consent requirement for unmarried women under age eighteen. Recognizing the husband's strong interest in the abortion decision, the Court concluded that when spouses disagreed, only one of them could prevail; that one must be the woman. As for parental consent, the opinion offered no broad charter of CHILDREN'S RIGHTS but concluded that a "mature" minor's right to have an abortion must prevail over a parent's contrary decision (*H. L. v. Matheson,* 1981). The state had little hope of restoring a family structure already "fractured" by such a conflict.

The Court invalidated, 6–3, a prohibition on saline amniocentesis as an abortion technique. The procedure was used in more than two-thirds of all abortions following the first trimester of pregnancy; its prohibition would undermine *Roe.* Finally, the state had required a physician performing an abortion to use professional skill and care to preserve the life and health of a fetus. The requirement was held invalid, 6–3, because it was not limited to the time following the stage of fetal viability.

The question of the doctor's role in determining viability and preserving fetal life returned to the Court in *Colautti v. Franklin* (1979). There the Court invalidated, 6–3, on vagueness grounds, a Pennsylvania law requiring a doctor to exercise care to protect a fetus when there was "sufficient reason to believe that the fetus may be viable." As in *Roe* and *Danforth,* the Court paid considerable deference to physicians, leaving undefined their control over their patients' constitutional rights.

KENNETH L. KARST

(SEE ALSO: *Abortion and the Constitution; Reproductive Autonomy.*)

Bibliography

COHEN, LESLIE ANN 1980 Fetal Viability and Individual Autonomy: Resolving Medical and Legal Standards for Abortion. *UCLA Law Review* 27:1340–1364.

PLEA BARGAINING

The overwhelming majority of convictions in American criminal courts occur when the accused pleads guilty to a charge; few defendants receive a full judicial trial. "Plea bargaining" describes a variety of incentives and pressures that produce this result and that are commonly encountered in American criminal courts. Some plea bargaining is explicit: defendants are led by the prosecutor or the judge to plead guilty in return for the promise of some concession or in fear of harsh treatment meted out to those who insist on a trial. The reward for defendants may be release on bail before trial, the dropping or reduction of charges, or the lightening of punishment imposed after conviction. Some defendants may plead guilty out of a sense of contrition, but more probably acquiesce in conviction because they expect more lenient treatment if they do not insist on their right to trial.

Overt negotiation to induce a defendant to plead guilty is often not necessary. The incentive structure is built into the culture of the courthouse and into the substantive criminal code itself. Those accused of crime learn the culture from cellmates, friends, and lawyers. Under most modern American penal codes, the same criminal conduct typically permits the defendant to be charged with one or more of several distinct offenses, each carrying different levels of potential punishment. Some of the potential sentences are severe: not just CAPITAL PUNISHMENT but punishment for common offenses by prison terms that may exceed the length of a person's vigorous adulthood. It would be practically impossible and morally unthinkable to apply such severe sanctions in a substantial portion of the cases.

The system is thus dominated at every level by official discretion; police, prosecutors, judges, and correctional officials are expected to extend leniency to most offenders lest the system become brutal and the courthouses overloaded. The guilty plea thus provides incentives for the state as well as the defendant. The courts are prepared to try only about ten percent of the cases potentially before them, and prosecutors value convictions obtained without the effort and expense of trial.

The relationship of this system of official discretion, including plea bargaining, with constitutional norms is strained, to say the least. Enforcement of criminal laws in America is predominantly the responsibility of over 3,000 distinct and varying local systems for the administration of criminal justice. The system generally gives a central role to professional police and prosecutorial organizations rather than to the active supervising magistracy that the Fourth, Fifth, and Sixth Amendments apparently contemplated for federal prosecutions.

The dominance of plea bargaining and the discretionary power to bring and dismiss charges tend to reduce the likelihood of direct confrontation between constitutional doctrine and everyday law enforcement practice. Officials are motivated to settle cases in which the lawfulness of their behavior appears likely to be challenged. Moreover, the dominance of discretion permits some rationalization of enforcement policies, better managerial control of scarce resources, and reduction of the uncertainties of trial for both officials and defendants. The system also permits the public at large to avoid facing the contradictions inherent in the penal policies embodied in the criminal codes of most states.

The guilty plea system potentially conflicts with constitutional norms in three principal ways. First, the system is in some tension with DUE PROCESS standards. In America the guilty plea wholly substitutes for a judicial trial. In Europe, the judge typically must conduct an independent investigation of guilt, whether or not the accused confesses. Even before the modern constitutional revolution in criminal justice, the Supreme Court recognized the dangers inherent in convictions based solely upon guilty pleas, insisting in such cases that convictions be based on knowing and voluntary WAIVER OF RIGHTS. In a series of decisions between 1960 and 1970 the Court spelled out this requirement in specific terms: an admission of guilt in open court by an accused who is adequately counseled and informed by a neutral judge of his rights and of the possible consequences of waiving them by pleading guilty. This formula requires only a rather formalistic colloquy between defendant and judge in open court to ascertain the accused's knowledge and VOLUNTARINESS of the plea. It also precludes active participation by the judge in the negotiations that induce the plea, through promises of leniency or threats of severity. It is also understood that bargains, once struck, must be observed by the government. Beyond these requirements due process is satisfied so long as the bargaining is fair according to the standards of commercial bargaining. Thus a defendant may be held to his plea despite his insistence that he is innocent. Troubling issues arise when an accused pleads guilty, despite his belief in his own innocence, because he recognizes the long odds against acquittal and the high risk of a more severe penalty after conviction at trial. Although the Court has held such pleas to be voluntary and to satisfy due process standards, doubts continue regarding the voluntariness of many such pleas.

A second cluster of constitutional concerns about the guilty plea system centers on the question of equal treatment for all similarly situated defendants. The guarantees of due process and EQUAL PROTECTION somewhat limit the arbitrary and disparate imposition of punishment. Yet the plea bargaining system grants to some defendants concessions that are unlikely to be extended to all. Indeed, if the concessions were equally available, they would lose much of their force in persuading defendants to plead guilty. Moreover, the process of negotiation operates outside the formal protections of the criminal process, within an area of official discretion that is seldom subjected to independent scrutiny. Opportunities abound for arbitrary discrimination.

The third and most pressing set of constitutional concerns about plea bargaining has received the least satisfactory treatment by the Supreme Court. When a defendant pleads guilty, he waives a host of constitutionally protected rights, including TRIAL BY JURY or by a judge, the RIGHT AGAINST SELF-INCRIMINATION, the right to CONFRONTATION and cross-examination of witnesses, and the right to challenge evidence against him. Government officials encourage the waiver of these rights by promising reduced punishment, and by threatening greater punishment for those who insist on their constitutionally guaranteed rights. This process appears to be an UNCONSTITUTIONAL CONDITION on the exercise of rights.

Despite these constitutional concerns, and despite widespread public dissatisfaction, plea bargaining seems to be a permanent feature of the American system of criminal justice. If the Supreme Court has thus far acquiesced in the system's constitutionality, perhaps the Court is not yet persuaded that a satisfactory alternative has been demonstrated.

ARTHUR ROSETT

Bibliography

ROSETT, ARTHUR I. and CRESSY, DONALD 1976 *Justice by Consent: Plea Bargains in the American Courthouse.* Philadelphia: Lippincott.

SCHULHOFER, STEPHEN J. 1984 Is Plea Bargaining Inevitable? *Harvard Law Review* 97:1037–1107.

PLESSY v. FERGUSON
163 U.S. 537 (1896)

Until BROWN V. BOARD OF EDUCATION (1954), *Plessy* was the constitutional linchpin for the entire structure of Jim Crow in America. Borrowed from LEMUEL SHAW in ROBERTS V. BOSTON (1851), the *Plessy* Court established the SEPARATE BUT EQUAL DOCTRINE: black persons were not denied the EQUAL PROTECTION OF THE LAWS safeguarded by the FOURTEENTH AMENDMENT when they were provided with facilities substantially equal to those available to white persons.

Florida enacted the first Jim Crow transportation law in 1887, and by the end of the century the other states of the old Confederacy had followed suit. Louisiana's act, which was challenged in *Plessy,* required railroad companies carrying passengers in the state to have "equal but separate accommodations" for white and colored persons by designating coaches racially or partitioning them. Black citizens, who denounced the innovation of Jim Crow in Louisiana as "unconstitutional, unamerican, unjust, dangerous and against sound public policy," complained that prejudiced whites would have a "license" to maltreat and humiliate inoffensive blacks. Plessy was a TEST CASE. Homer A. Plessy, an octoroon (one-eighth black), boarded the East Louisiana Railroad in New Orleans bound for Covington in the same state and sat in the white car; he was arrested when he refused to move to the black car. Convicted by the state he appealed on constitutional grounds, invoking the THIRTEENTH and Fourteenth AMENDMENTS. The Court had already decided in LOUISVILLE, NEW ORLEANS & TEXAS PACIFIC RY. V. MISSISSIPPI (1890) that Jim Crow cars in INTRASTATE COMMERCE did not violate the COMMERCE CLAUSE.

Justice JOHN MARSHALL HARLAN was the only dissenter from the opinion by Justice HENRY B. BROWN. That the state act did not infringe the Thirteenth Amendment, declared Brown, "is too clear for argument." The act implied "merely a legal distinction" between the two races and therefore had "no tendency to destroy the legal equality of the two races, or reestablish a state of involuntary servitude." Harlan, believing that STATE ACTION could have no regard to the race of citizens when their CIVIL RIGHTS were involved, would have ruled that compulsory racial SEGREGATION violated the Thirteenth Amendment by imposing a BADGE OF SERVITUDE.

The chief issue was whether the state act abridged the Fourteenth Amendment's equal protection clause. One reads Brown's opinion with an enormous sense of the feebleness of words as conveyors of thought, because he conceded that the object of the amendment "was undoubtedly to enforce the absolute equality of the two races before the law," yet he continued the same sentence by adding, "but in the nature of things it could not have been intended to abolish distinctions based on color. . . ." As a matter of historical fact the intention of the amendment was, generally, to abolish legal distinctions based on color. The Court pretended to rest on history without looking at the historical record; it did not claim the necessity of adapting the Constitution to changed conditions, making untenable the defense often heard in more recent years, that the decision fit the times. *Plessy* makes sense only if one understands that the Court believed that segregation was not discriminatory, indeed that it would violate the equal protection clause if it were discriminatory. Brown conceded that a statute implying a legal inferiority in civil society, lessening "the security of the right of the colored race," would be discriminatory, but he insisted that state-imposed segregation did not "necessarily imply the inferiority of either race to the other. . . ." There was abundant evidence to the contrary, none of it understandable to a Court that found fallacious the contention that "the enforced separation of the two races stamps the colored race with a badge of inferiority. If this be so, it is not by reason of anything found in the act, but solely because the colored race chooses to put that construction on it." That segregation stamped blacks with a badge of inferiority was not fallacious. The fallacy was that only they imputed inferiority to segregation. Jim Crow laws were central to white supremacist thought. That blacks were inherently inferior was a conviction being stridently trumpeted by white supremacists from the press, the pulpit, and the platform, as well as from the legislative halls, of the South. The label, "For Colored Only," was a public expression of disparagement amounting to officially sanctioned civil inequality. By the Court's own reasoning, state acts compelling racial segregation were unconstitutional if inferiority was implied or discrimination intended.

The separate but equal doctrine was fatally vulnerable for still other reasons given, ironically, by the

Court in *Plessy.* It sustained the act as a valid exercise of the POLICE POWER yet stated that every exercise of that power "must be reasonable, and extend only to such laws as are enacted in good faith for the promotion of the public good, and not for the annoyance or oppression of a particular class." Jim Crow laws were not only annoying and oppressive to blacks; they were not reasonable or for the public good. The Court asserted that the question of reasonableness must be determined with reference "to the established usages, customs and traditions" of the people of the state. The proper standard of reasonableness ought to have been the equal protection clause of the Constitution, not new customs of the white supremacists of an ex-slave state. Even if the custom of segregation had been old, and it was not, the Court was making strange doctrine when implying that discrimination becomes vested with constitutionality if carried on long enough to become customary. Classifying people by race for the purpose of transportation was unreasonable because the classification was irrelevant to any legitimate purpose.

The only conceivable justification for the reasonableness of the racial classification was that it promoted the public good, which Brown alleged. The effects of segregation were inimical to the public good, because, as Harlan pointed out, it "permits the seeds of race hate to be planted under the sanction of law." It created and perpetuated interracial tensions. Oddly the Court made the public-good argument in the belief that the commingling of the races would threaten the public peace by triggering disorders. In line with that assumption Brown declared that legislation is powerless to eradicate prejudice based on hostile "racial instincts" and that equal rights cannot be gained by "enforced commingling." These contentions seem cynical when announced in an opinion sanctioning inequality by sustaining a statute compelling racial segregation. The argument that prejudice cannot be legislated away overlooked the extent to which prejudice had been legislated into existence and continued by Jim Crow statutes.

Harlan's imperishable dissent repeated the important Thirteenth Amendment argument that he had made in the CIVIL RIGHTS CASES (1883) on badges of servitude. That amendment, he declared, "decreed universal civil freedom in the country." Harlan reminded the Court that in STRAUDER V. WEST VIRGINIA (1880), it had construed the Fourteenth Amendment to mean that "the law in the States shall be the same for the black as for the white" and that the amendment contained "a necessary implication of a positive immunity, or right . . . the right to exemption from unfriendly legislation against them distinctively as colored—exemption from legal discriminations, implying inferiority in civil society, lessening the security of their enjoyment of rights which others enjoy. . . ." To Harlan, segregation was discriminatory per se. The state act was unreasonable because segregation was not germane to a legitimate legislative end. He meant that the Fourteenth Amendment rendered the state powerless to make legal distinctions based on color in respect to public transportation. A railroad, he reminded the Court, was a public highway exercising public functions available on the same basis to all citizens. "Our Constitution," said Harlan, "is color-blind, and neither knows nor tolerates classes among citizens." He thought the majority's decision would prove in time to be as pernicious as DRED SCOTT V. SANDFORD (1857). As for the separate but equal doctrine, he remarked that the "thin disguise" of equality would mislead no one "nor atone for the wrong this day done."

Plessy cleared the constitutional way for legislation that forced the separation of the races in all places of public accommodation. Most of that legislation came after *Plessy.* In the CIVIL RIGHTS CASES, the Court had prevented Congress from abolishing segregation, and in *Plessy* the Court supported the states in compelling it. Not history and not the Fourteenth Amendment dictated the decision; it reflected its time, and its time was racist. As Justice Brown pointed out, even Congress in governing the DISTRICT OF COLUMBIA had required separate schools for the two races. The Court did not invent Jim Crow but adapted the Constitution to it.

LEONARD W. LEVY

Bibliography

KLUGER, RICHARD 1973 *Simple Justice: The History of Brown v. Board of Education and Black America's Struggle for Equality.* Pages 71–83. New York: Knopf.

OBERST, PAUL 1973 The Strange Career of *Plessy v. Ferguson. Arizona Law Review* 15:389–418.

OLSON, OTTO, ed. 1967 *The Thin Disguise: Turning Point in Negro History: Plessy v. Ferguson.* New York: Humanities Press.

WOODWARD, C. VANN 1971 The National Decision Against Equality. Pages 212–233 in Woodward, *American Counterpoint: Slavery and Racism in the North–South Dialogue.* Boston: Little, Brown.

PLURALITY OPINION

In some cases the majority of Justices of the Supreme Court, although agreeing on the DECISION, do not agree on the reasoning behind the decision. In such cases, there is no OPINION OF THE COURT; instead there are two or more opinions purporting to explain the decision. If one opinion is signed by more Justices than any other, it is called the "plurality opinion." A plurality opinion may be cited as precedent in later cases, but, unlike a majority opinion, it is not an authoritative statement of the Court's position on the legal or constitutional issues involved.

DENNIS J. MAHONEY

PLYLER v. DOE
457 U.S. 202 (1982)

Experimenting with ignorance, the Texas legislature authorized local school boards to exclude the children of undocumented ALIENS from the public schools, and cut off state funds to subsidize those children's schooling. The Supreme Court, 5–4, held that this scheme denied the alien children the EQUAL PROTECTION OF THE LAWS. The OPINION OF THE COURT, by Justice WILLIAM J. BRENNAN, contains the potential for important future influence on equal protection DOCTRINE.

The Court was unanimous on one point: the FOURTEENTH AMENDMENT's guarantee of equal protection for all PERSONS extends not only to aliens lawfully admitted for residence but also to undocumented aliens. The question that divided the Court was what that guarantee demanded—an issue that the Court's recent opinions had typically discussed in language about the appropriate STANDARD OF REVIEW. In SAN ANTONIO INDEPENDENT SCHOOL DISTRICT V. RODRIGUEZ (1973) the Court had rejected the claim that EDUCATION was a FUNDAMENTAL INTEREST, and had subjected a state system for financing schools to a deferential RATIONAL BASIS standard. A significant OBITER DICTUM, however, had suggested that a total denial of education to a certain group of children would have to pass the test of STRICT SCRUTINY. (See GRIFFIN V. COUNTY SCHOOL BOARD OF PRINCE EDWARD COUNTY, 1964.) Furthermore, although alienage was, for some purposes, a SUSPECT CLASSIFICATION, the Court had not extended that characterization to laws discriminating against aliens who were not lawfully admitted to the country.

Justice Brennan's analysis blurred the already indistinct lines dividing levels of judicial scrutiny in equal protection cases. He suggested that some form of "intermediate scrutiny" was appropriate, and even hinted at a preference for strict scrutiny. Eventually, though, he came to rest on rhetorical ground that could hold together a five-Justice majority. Because the Texas law imposed a severe penalty on children for their parents' misconduct, it was irrational unless the state could show that it furthered "some substantial goal of the State," and no such showing had been made. In a concurring opinion, Justice LEWIS F. POWELL remarked that heightened scrutiny was proper, on analogy to the Court's decisions about classifications based on ILLEGITIMACY. Justice THURGOOD MARSHALL, also concurring, repeated his argument for recognition of a "sliding scale" of standards of review, and accurately noted that this very decision illustrated that the Court was already employing such a system. No one should be surprised when the Court holds invalid a supremely stupid law that imposes great hardship on a group of innocent people.

Chief Justice WARREN E. BURGER, writing for the four dissenters, agreed that the Texas policy was "senseless." He argued nonetheless that the Court, by undertaking a "policymaking role," was "trespass[ing] on the assigned function of the political branches." In allocating scarce state resources, Texas could rationally choose to prefer citizens and lawfully admitted aliens over aliens who had entered the country without permission; for the dissenters, that was enough to validate the law.

The *Plyler* opinion was narrow, leaving open the question whether a similar burden of substantial justification would be imposed on a discrimination against undocumented aliens who were adults, or even against innocent children when the discrimination was something less than a total denial of education. Justice Brennan did suggest that judicial scrutiny might properly be heightened in cases of discrimination against aliens—even undocumented aliens—who had established "a permanent attachment to the nation." Although it is unlikely that this view could command a majority of the Court today, the remark may bear fruit in the future.

KENNETH L. KARST

(SEE ALSO: *Immigration*.)

POCKET VETO

If Congress adjourns within ten days after passing a bill, the President can prevent the bill's enactment by merely withholding his signature (Article I, section 7, clause 3, of the Constitution). By means of this extension of the VETO POWER, the President can kill legislation without giving any reason and without the possibility of being overridden.

DENNIS J. MAHONEY

POCKET VETO CASE

Okanogan Indians v. United States 279 U.S. 655 (1929)

A unanimous Supreme Court, speaking through Justice EDWARD SANFORD, held that a bill passed by Congress, but not signed by the President, had died when the 69th Congress adjourned between its first and second sessions. The POCKET VETO may therefore be used during the adjournment between sessions, and not merely at the final adjournment, of a particular Congress.

In *Wright v. United States* (1938) and *Kennedy v. Sampson* (1965) federal courts established that the pocket veto could not be used during intrasession adjournments.

DENNIS J. MAHONEY

POELKER v. DOE

See: *Maher v. Roe*

POINTER v. TEXAS

380 U.S. 400 (1965)

A state court had allowed the introduction in EVIDENCE of the transcript of an absent witness's testimony given at a preliminary hearing when the defendant, unrepresented by counsel, could not effectively cross-examine. The Supreme Court, disallowing an exception to the HEARSAY RULE, held that "the SIXTH AMENDMENT's right of an accused to confront the witnesses against him is a fundamental right and is made obligatory on the State by the FOURTEENTH AMENDMENT." The Court also held that the RIGHT OF CONFRONTATION is governed by the same standards in state and federal courts.

LEONARD W. LEVY

POLICE ACTION

The phrase "police action" is not a term of art, or one having any precise legal significance, but simply an expression or euphemism occasionally employed to describe the use of the armed forces of the United States and other nations to resist what is perceived as a violation of international law, a notable example being American use of the armed forces against the North Korean invasion of South Korea in 1950. (See KOREAN WAR AND THE CONSTITUTION.) President HARRY S. TRUMAN based his decision to use American forces to defend South Korea on the fact that the North Korean aggression constituted a violation of the UNITED NATIONS CHARTER, as declared in a resolution of the Security Council. (The Soviet Union, which of course treated the North Korean invasion as "self-defense," chose to absent itself from that meeting of the Council and thereby lost the opportunity to veto the resolution.) Subsequently, in 1957, Senator John Bricker and other conservative congressmen who were opposed to American intervention in Korea (not because they had any sympathy for communist imperialism but because they were isolationists) attempted to remove such justifications of presidential use of troops by unsuccessfully proposing that the Constitution be amended to require affirmative action by Congress before a treaty obligation could be implemented. (See STATE OF WAR; BRICKER AMENDMENT.)

The phrase has occasionally been employed, although not officially, in other situations in which the United States has used its armed forces without a DECLARATION OF WAR or other explicit sanction by Congress, such as President JOHN F. KENNEDY's 1962 blockade of Cuba. A pejorative variation of it was sometimes employed by opponents of American intervention in VIETNAM, who contended that the United States should not act as an "international policeman" or "international gendarme." Although it would have been appropriate, it seems to have been used by no one to describe President Jimmy Carter's unsuccessful attempt, in April 1980, to mount a military raid to free American hostages in Iran.

The characterization has never been officially or generally applied to a declared war.

JOSEPH W. BISHOP, JR.

Bibliography

SEARS, KENNETH C. 1956 Bricker-Dirksen Amendment. *Hastings Law Journal* 8:1–17.

POLICE DEPARTMENT OF CHICAGO v. MOSLEY

408 U.S. 92 (1972)

Mosley is the leading modern decision linking EQUAL PROTECTION doctrine with the FIRST AMENDMENT. Chicago adopted an ordinance prohibiting PICKETING within 150 feet of a school during school hours, but excepting peaceful labor picketing. Earl Mosley had been picketing on the public sidewalk adjoining a high school, carrying a sign protesting "black discrimination," and after the ordinance was adopted he sought declaratory and injunctive relief, arguing that the ordinance was unconstitutional. The Supreme Court unanimously agreed with him.

Justice THURGOOD MARSHALL, for the Court, concluded that the exemption of labor picketing violated the equal protection clause of the FOURTEENTH AMENDMENT. This conclusion followed the lead of Justice HUGO L. BLACK, concurring in COX V. LOUISIANA (1965). Yet Justice Marshall's opinion speaks chiefly to First Amendment values and primarily cites First Amendment decisions. "[A]bove all else, the First Amendment means that government has no power to restrict expression because of its message, its ideas, its subject matter, or its content." As Chief Justice WARREN E. BURGER noted in a brief concurrence, so broad a statement is not literally true; the Court has upheld regulations of speech content in areas ranging from DEFAMATION to OBSCENITY. Yet *Mosley* properly stakes out a presumption in favor of "equality of status in the field of ideas"—a phrase borrowed from ALEXANDER MEIKLEJOHN.

The *Mosley* opinion makes two main points. First, regulations of message content are presumptively unconstitutional, requiring justification by reference to state interests of compelling importance. Second, "time, place, and manner" regulations that selectively exclude speakers from a PUBLIC FORUM must survive careful judicial scrutiny to ensure that the exclusion is the minimum necessary to further a significant government interest. Together, these statements declare a principle of major importance: the principle of equal liberty of expression.

KENNETH L. KARST

Bibliography

KARST, KENNETH L. 1976 Equality as a Central Principle of the First Amendment. *University of Chicago Law Review* 43:20–68.

POLICE INTERROGATION AND CONFESSIONS

In the police interrogation room, where, until the second third of the century, police practices were unscrutinized and virtually unregulated, constitutional ideals collide with the grim realities of law enforcement. It is not easy to talk about the defendant's right to silence and his RIGHT TO COUNSEL when the defendant has confessed to a heinous crime—for example, the rape and murder of a small child as in BREWER V. WILLIAMS (1977) or the kidnapping, robbery, and murder of a cab driver, by a shotgun blast to the back of the head, as in RHODE ISLAND V. INNIS (1980)—and the confession seems quite credible. Thus, for many years few matters have split the Supreme Court, troubled the legal profession, and agitated the public as much as the confession cases.

Not surprisingly, the most famous confession case of all, MIRANDA V. ARIZONA (1966), is regarded as the high-water mark of the WARREN COURT'S "DUE PROCESS revolution." Nor is it surprising that the decision became the prime target of those who attributed an increase of crime to the softness of judges. *Miranda*, which finally applied the RIGHT AGAINST SELF-INCRIMINATION to the informal proceedings in the interrogation room, emerged only after a long struggle, and increasing dissatisfaction, with the test for admitting confessions that preceded it—the "voluntariness" test based on the "totality of circumstances." *Miranda* can be understood only in light of the Court's prior efforts to deal with the intractable confession problem.

Until well into the eighteenth century, doctrines concerning confessions did not affect the admissibility of extrajudicial narrative statements of guilt offered as EVIDENCE, but dealt only with the conditions under which immediate conviction followed a confession as a plea of guilty. It was not until *The King v. Warickshall* (1783) that an English court clearly expressed the notion that confessions might be unworthy of credit because of the circumstances under which they were obtained. In that case the judges declared: "A free and voluntary confession is deserving of the highest credit, because it is presumed to flow from the strongest sense of guilt, and therefore it is admitted as proof of the crime to which it refers; but a confession forced from the mind by the flattery of hope, or by the torture of fear, comes in so questionable a shape when it is to be considered as the evidence of guilt, that no credit ought to be given to it; and therefore it is rejected."

Because a separate rule against coerced confessions emerged in eighteenth-century English cases nearly a century after the right against self-incrimination had become established, JOHN H. WIGMORE, the great master of the law of evidence, concluded that the two rules had no connection. But Leonard W. Levy, the leading student of the origins of the right against self-incrimination, strongly disagrees. He maintains that "[t]he relationship between torture, *compulsory* self-incrimination, and *coerced* confessions was an historical fact as well as a physical and psychological one" and that "in the 16th and 17th centuries, the argument against the three, resulting in the rules that Wigmore said had no connection, overlapped" (Levy 1968, pp. 265, 288–289 n.102).

Levy points out that Baron Geoffrey Gilbert, in his *Law of Evidence,* "written before 1726 though not published until thirty years later, stated that though the best evidence of guilt was a confession, 'this confession must be voluntary and without compulsion; for our Law in this differs from the Civil Law, that it will not force any Man to accuse himself; and in this we do certainly follow the Law of Nature, which commands every Man to endeavor his own Preservation . . .' " (Levy 1968, p. 327). Baron Gilbert's phrasing, "our Law . . . will not force any Man to accuse himself," Levy says, "expressed the traditional English formulation of the right against self-incrimination, or rather against *compulsory* self-incrimination. The element of compulsion or involuntariness was always an essential ingredient of the right and, before the right existed, of protests against incriminating interrogations" (ibid., pp. 327–328).

Although Levy insists that this was a historical blunder, both in the United States and in England the confession rules and the right against self-incrimination were divorced and, with the one notable exception of *Bram v. United States* (1897), went their separate ways—until the two rules were intertwined in MALLOY V. HOGAN (1964) and fused in the famous *Miranda* case (1966). Moreover, for most of its life the voluntariness test was essentially an alternative statement of the rule that a confession was entitled to credit so long as it was free of influence that made it untrustworthy or "probably untrue." Wigmore reflected the law prevailing at the time when in 1940 he pointed out that a confession was not inadmissible because of "any *breach of confidence*" or "any *illegality* in the method of obtaining it," or "because of any connection with the *privilege against self-incrimination.*"

In *Bram v. United States* (1897) the Supreme Court did rely explicitly on the self-incrimination clause of the Fifth Amendment in holding a confession inadmissible. But the Court soon abandoned the *Bram* approach, perhaps stung by the criticism of Wigmore and others that it had misread history, and until the mid-1960s *Bram* amounted only to an early excursion from the prevailing due process–voluntariness test.

The right against self-incrimination was not deemed applicable to the states until 1964, and by that time the Supreme Court had decided more than thirty state confession cases. Moreover, even if the Fifth Amendment right against self-incrimination had been deemed applicable to the states much earlier, the law pertaining to "coerced" or "involuntary" confessions still would have developed without it. For until *Miranda* (1966), the prevailing view was that the suspect in the police interrogation room was not being compelled to be a witness against himself within the meaning of the privilege; he was threatened neither with perjury for testifying falsely nor contempt for refusing to testify at all. Because the police have no legal authority to compel statements, there is no legal obligation to answer, ran the argument, to which a privilege can apply.

So long as police interrogators were not required to advise suspects of their rights nor to permit them to consult with lawyers who would do so, there could be little doubt that many a suspect would assume that the police had a legal right to an answer. Still worse, there could be little doubt that many a suspect would assume, or be led to believe, that there were *extralegal* sanctions for refusing to cooperate. Small wonder that commentators decried the legal reasoning that excluded the privilege against self-incrimination from the stationhouse for so many years as "casuistic," "a quibble," and a triumph of logic over life.

Wigmore long condemned the statement of the confession rule in terms of voluntariness for the reason that "the fundamental question for confessions is whether there is any danger that they may be untrue . . . and that there is nothing in the mere circumstance of compulsion to speak in general . . . which creates any risk of untruth." But only two years after the Supreme Court handed down its first FOURTEENTH AMENDMENT due process cases, BROWN V. MISSISSIPPI (1936), Charles McCormick defended the voluntariness terminology on the ground that it might reflect a recognition that the confession rule not only protects against the danger of untrustworthiness but also protects an interest closely akin to that protected by the right against compulsory self-incrimination. Three decades later, the *Miranda* Court would agree. McCormick also suggested that the entire course of decisions in the confessions field could best be understood as "an application to confessions both of a privilege against evidence illegally obtained . . . and of an overlapping rule of incompetency which excludes the confessions when untrustworthy" (1954, p. 157). In the advanced stages of the voluntariness test, the Court would again make plain its agreement with McCormick.

Thus, in *Spano v. New York* (1959) the Court, speaking through Chief Justice EARL WARREN, pointed out that the ban against involuntary confessions turns not only on their unreliability but also on the notion that "the police must obey the law while enforcing the law; that in the end life and liberty can be as much endangered from illegal methods used to convict those thought to be criminals as from the actual criminals themselves." And the following year, in *Blackburn v. Alabama* (1960), the Court, again speaking through Chief Justice Warren, recognized that "a complex of values underlies the stricture against use by the state of confessions which, by way of convenient shorthand, this Court terms involuntary."

The "untrustworthiness" rationale, the view that the rules governing the admissibility of confessions were merely a system of safeguards against false confessions, could explain the exclusion of the confession in *Brown v. Mississippi* (1936), where the deputy sheriff who had presided over the beatings of the defendants conceded that one had been whipped, "but not too much for a Negro." And the untrustworthiness rationale was also adequate to explain the exclusion of confessions in the cases that immediately followed the *Brown* case such as CHAMBERS V. FLORIDA (1940), *Canty v. Alabama* (1940), *White v. Texas* (1940), and *Ward v. Texas* (1942), for they, too, involved actual or threatened physical violence.

As the crude practices of the early cases became outmoded and cases involving more subtle pressures began to appear, however, it became more difficult to assume that the resulting confessions were untrustworthy. In *Ashcraft v. Tennessee* (1944), for example, although the confession was obtained after some thirty-six hours of almost continuous interrogation, there was good reason to think that the defendant had indeed been involved in the murder. The man whom the defendant named as his wife's killer readily admitted his involvement and accused the defendant of hiring him to do the job. Moreover, after the interrogation had ceased and the defendant had been examined by his family physician, he made what the doctor described as an "entirely voluntary" confession, in the course of which he explained why he wanted his wife killed. Nevertheless, calling the extended questioning "inherently coercive," a 6–3 majority, speaking through Justice HUGO L. BLACK, held that Ashcraft's confession should not have been allowed into evidence. Under the circumstances, the *Ashcraft* case seemed to reflect less concern with the reliability of the confession than disapproval of police methods which appeared to the Court to be dangerous and subject to serious abuse.

Although he dissented in *Ashcraft*, Justice FELIX FRANKFURTER soon became the leading exponent of the "police misconduct" or "police methods" rationale for barring the use of confessions. According to this rationale, in order to condemn and deter abusive, offensive, or otherwise objectionable police interrogation methods, it was necessary to exclude confessions produced by such methods regardless of how relevant and credible they might be, a point underscored in ROGERS V. RICHMOND (1961). After more conventional methods had failed to produce any incriminating statements, a police chief pretended to order petitioner's ailing wife brought down to headquarters for questioning. Petitioner promptly confessed to the murder for which he was later convicted. The trial judge found that the police chief's pretense had "no tendency to produce a confession that was not in accord with the truth" and in his charge to the jury he indicated that the admissibility of the confession should turn on its probable reliability. But the Court, speaking through Justice Frankfurter, held that convictions based on involuntary confessions must fall

> not because such confessions are unlikely to be true but because the methods used to extract them offend an underlying principle in the enforcement of our criminal law; that ours is an accusatorial and not an inquisitorial system. . . . Indeed, in many of the cases in which the command of the Due Process Clause has compelled us to reverse state convictions involving the use of confessions obtained by impermissible methods, independent corroborating evidence left little doubt of the truth of what the defendant had confessed. Despite such verification, confessions were found to be the product of constitutionally impermissible methods in their inducement. . . . The attention of the trial judge should have been focused, for purpose of the Federal Constitution, on the question whether the [police behavior] was such as to overbear petitioner's will to resist and bring about confessions not freely self-determined—a question to be answered with complete disregard of whether or not petitioner in fact spoke the truth.

The "voluntariness" test seemed to be at once too wide and too narrow. In the sense of wanting to confess, or doing so in a completely spontaneous manner, as one might confess to rid one's soul of guilt, no confession reviewed by the Court under the "voluntariness" test had been voluntary. On the other hand, in the sense that the situation always presented a choice between two alternatives, all confessions examined by the Court had been voluntary.

As the voluntariness test evolved, it became increasingly clear that terms such as "voluntariness" and "coercion" were not being used as tools of analysis, but as mere conclusions. When a court concluded that the police had resorted to unacceptable interrogation techniques, it called the resulting confession "involuntary" and talked of "overbearing the will." When, on the other hand, a court concluded that the methods the police had employed were permissible, it called the resulting confession "voluntary" and talked of "self-determination." Moreover, such terms as "voluntariness," "coercion," and "overbearing the will" focused directly on neither of the two underlying reasons that led the courts to bar the use of confessions—the offensiveness of police interrogation methods or the risk that these methods had produced an untrue confession.

Another problem with the due process "totality of the circumstances"-voluntariness test was that it was amorphous, elusive, and largely unmanageable. Almost everything was relevant—for example, whether the suspect was advised of his rights; whether he was held incommunicado; the suspect's age, intelligence, education, and prior criminal record; the conditions and duration of his detention—but almost nothing was decisive. Except for direct physical coercion no single factor or combination of them guaranteed exclusion of a confession as involuntary. Because there were so many variables in the voluntariness equation that one determination seldom served as a useful precedent for another, the test offered police interrogators and trial courts little guidance. Trial courts were encouraged to indulge their subjective preferences, and appellate courts were discouraged from active review.

In the thirty years between *Brown* (1936) and *Miranda* (1966) the Court had reviewed about one state confession case per year and two-thirds of these had been death penalty cases. Indeed, the Court's workload had been so great that it had even denied a hearing in most death penalty cases. Not surprisingly, Justice Black remarked in the course of the oral argument in *Miranda:* "If you are going to determine [the admissibility of the confession] each time on the circumstances, [if] this Court will take them one by one, [it] is more than we are capable of doing."

The Supreme Court's dissatisfaction with the elusive "voluntariness" test and its quest for a more concrete and manageable standard led to the decisions in MASSIAH V. UNITED STATES (1964) and ESCOBEDO V. ILLINOIS (1964) and culminated in the 1966 *Miranda* decision.

Massiah grew out of the following facts: After he had been indicted for various federal narcotics violations and retained a lawyer, and while he was out on bail, Massiah was invited by his codefendant, Colson, to discuss the pending case in Colson's car. Massiah assumed that he was talking to a partner in crime, but Colson had become a secret government agent. A radio transmitter had been concealed in Colson's car to enable a nearby federal agent to overhear the Massiah-Colson conversation. As expected, Massiah made incriminating statements.

Despite the fact that Massiah was neither in "custody" nor subjected to "police interrogation," as that term is normally used, the Supreme Court held that his damaging admissions should have been excluded from evidence. The decisive feature of the case was that after adversary criminal proceedings had been initiated against him—and Massiah's RIGHT TO COUNSEL had "attached"—government agents had deliberately elicited statements from him in the absence of counsel.

Massiah was soon overshadowed by *Escobedo,* decided a short five weeks later. When Danny Escobedo had been arrested for murder he had repeatedly but unsuccessfully asked to speak to his lawyer. Instead, the police induced Escobedo to implicate himself in the murder. Although Escobedo had incriminated himself before he had been indicted or adversary criminal proceedings had otherwise commenced against him, a 5–4 majority held that under the circumstances "it would exalt form over substance to make the right to counsel . . . depend on whether at the time of the interrogation, the authorities had secured a formal indictment." At the time the police had questioned him, Escobedo "had become the accused and the purpose of the investigation was to 'get him' to confess his guilt despite his constitutional right not to do so."

Until *Miranda* moved the case off center-stage two years later, the meaning and scope of *Escobedo* was a matter of widespread disagreement. In large part this was due to the accordion-like quality of Justice ARTHUR J. GOLDBERG's majority opinion. At some places the opinion suggested that a suspect's right to counsel was triggered once the investigation ceased to be a general inquiry into an unsolved crime and began to "focus" on him, regardless of whether he was in "custody" or asked for a lawyer. Elsewhere, however, the opinion seemed to limit the holding to its special facts (Escobedo had specifically requested and been denied an opportunity to seek his lawyer's advice, the police had failed to warn him of his right to remain silent, and he was in police custody).

The *Escobedo* dissenters read the majority opinion broadly: "The right to counsel now not only entitles the accused the counsel's advice and aid in preparing for trial but stands as an impenetrable barrier to any interrogation once the accused has become suspect. From that very moment apparently his right to counsel attaches." The dissenters expressed a preference for a self-incrimination approach, rather than a right to counsel approach. The right against self-incrimination, after all, proscribed only compelled statements. "It is incongruous to assume," they argued, "that the provision for counsel in the Sixth Amendment was meant to amend or supersede the self-incrimination provision of the Fifth Amendment, which is now applicable to the States." Two years later, in *Miranda,* the Court would focus on the Fifth Amendment, but it would define "compulsion" within the meaning of the privilege in a way that displeased the four *Escobedo* dissenters (all of whom also dissented in *Miranda*).

Dissenting in *Ashcraft* in 1944, Justice ROBERT H. JACKSON agreed that custody and questioning of a suspect for thirty-six hours is "inherently coercive," but quickly added: "And so is custody and examination for one hour. Arrest itself is inherently coercive and so is detention. . . . But does the Constitution prohibit use of all confessions made after arrest because questioning, while one is deprived of freedom, is 'inherently coercive'?" Both Jackson and Justice Black, who wrote the majority opinion in *Ashcraft,* knew that in 1944 the Court was not ready for an affirmative answer to Jackson's question. But by 1966 the Court had grown ready.

Ernesto Miranda had been arrested for rape and kidnapping, taken to a police station, and placed in an "interrogation room," where he was questioned about the crimes. Two hours later the police emerged from the room with a signed confession. In the 1940s or 1950s Miranda's confession unquestionably would have been admissible under the voluntariness test; his questioning had been mild compared to the objectionable police methods that had rendered a resulting confession involuntary in past cases.

The Supreme Court, however, had become increasingly dissatisfied with the voluntariness test. Miranda's interrogators admitted that neither before nor during the questioning had they advised him of his right to remain silent or his right to consult with an attorney before answering questions or his right to have an attorney present during the interrogation. These failures were to prove fatal for the prosecution.

In *Miranda* a 5–4 majority, speaking through Chief Justice Warren, concluded at last that "all the principles embodied in the privilege [against self-incrimination] apply to informal compulsion exerted by law-enforcement officers during in-custody questioning." Observed the Court:

> An individual swept from familiar surroundings into police custody, surrounded by antagonistic forces, and subjected to the persuasions [described in various interrogation manuals, from which the Court quoted at length] cannot be otherwise than under compulsion to speak. As a practical matter, the compulsion to speak in the isolated setting of the police station may well be greater than in courts or other official investigations, where there are often impartial observers to guard against intimidation or trickery. . . . Unless adequate protective devices are employed to dispel the compulsion inherent in custodial surroundings, no statement obtained from the defendant can truly be the product of his free choice.

The adequate protective devices necessary to neutralize the compulsion inherent in the interrogation environment are the now familiar "*Miranda* warnings." Although *Miranda* is grounded primarily in the right against self-incrimination, it also has a right to counsel component designed to protect and to reinforce the right to remain silent. Thus, prior to any questioning a person taken into custody or otherwise deprived of his freedom of action in any significant way must not only be warned that he has a right to remain silent and that "anything said can and will be used against [him]," but must also be told of his right to counsel, either retained or appointed. "[T]he need for counsel to protect the Fifth Amendment privilege," stated the Court, "comprehends not merely a right to consult with counsel prior to any questioning but also to have counsel present during any questioning if the defendant so desires."

A suspect, of course, may waive his rights, provided he does so voluntarily, knowingly, and intelligently. But no valid WAIVER OF CONSTITUTIONAL RIGHTS can be recognized unless specifically made after the warnings have been given. Moreover, "[t]he mere fact that [a person] may have answered some questions or volunteered some statements . . . does not deprive him of the right to refrain from answering any further inquiries until he had consulted with an attorney and thereafter consents to be questioned."

Although a great hue and cry greeted the case, *Miranda* may fairly be viewed as a compromise between the old voluntariness test (a standard so elusive and unmanageable that its safeguards were largely illusory) and extreme proposals (based on an expansive reading of *Escobedo*) that threatened to "kill" confessions.

Miranda allows the police to conduct general on-the-scene questioning even though the person arrested is both uninformed and unaware of his rights. It allows the police to question a person in his home or office, provided they do not restrict the person's freedom to terminate the meeting. (Indeed, the opinion seems to recommend that the police question a suspect in his home or place of business.) Moreover, "custody" alone does not call for the *Miranda* warnings. The Court might have held that the inherent pressures and anxieties produced by arrest and detention are substantial enough to require neutralizing warnings. But it did not. Thus, so long as the police do not question one who has been brought to the station house, *Miranda* leaves them free to hear and act upon volunteered statements, even though the volunteer neither knows nor is advised of his rights. (This point was recognized by dissenting Justice BYRON R. WHITE in *Miranda.*)

Surprisingly, *Miranda* does not strip police interrogation of its characteristic secrecy. To the extent that any lawyer worth his salt will tell a suspect to remain silent it is no less clear that any officer worth his salt will be sorely tempted to get the suspect to do just the opposite. But no stenographic transcript (let alone an electronic recording) of the waiver transaction, or the questioning that follows a waiver, need be made; no disinterested observer (let alone a judicial officer) need be present. There is language in *Miranda* suggesting that the police must make an objective record of the waiver transaction but this language has been largely overlooked or disregarded by the lower courts. And nowhere in the *Miranda* opinion does the court explicitly require the police to make either tape or verbatim stenographic recordings of the crucial events.

On the eve of *Miranda*, there were doubts that law enforcement could survive if the Court were to project defense counsel into the police station. But the *Miranda* Court did so only in a quite limited way. It never took the final step (and, as a practical matter, the most significant one) of requiring that the suspect first consult with a lawyer, or actually have a lawyer present, in order for his waiver of constitutional rights to be considered valid.

Whether suspects are continuing to confess because they do not fully grasp the meaning of the *Miranda* warnings or because the police are mumbling, hedging, or undermining the warnings, or whether the promptings of conscience and the desire "to get it over with" are indeed overriding the impact of the warnings, or whether admissions of guilt are quid pro quos for reduced charges or lighter sentences, it is plain that in-custody suspects are continuing to confess with great frequency. This result would hardly have ensued if *Miranda* had fully projected counsel into the interrogation process, requiring the advice or presence of counsel before a suspect could waive his rights.

Because *Miranda* was the centerpiece of the Warren Court's revolution in CRIMINAL PROCEDURE, and one of the leading issues of the 1968 presidential campaign, almost everyone expected the BURGER COURT to treat *Miranda* unkindly. And it did, but only for a decade.

The first blow was struck in HARRIS V. NEW YORK (1971), which held that statements preceded by defective *Miranda* warnings, and thus inadmissible to establish the prosecution's initial case, could nevertheless be used to impeach the defendant's credibility if he took the stand. The Court noted, but seemed untroubled, that some comments in the landmark opinion seemed to bar the use of statements obtained in violation of *Miranda* for any purpose.

A second impeachment case, *Oregon v. Hass* (1975), seemed to inflict a deeper wound. In *Hass,* the police advised the suspect of his rights and he asserted them. Nevertheless, the police refused to honor the suspect's request for a lawyer and continued to question him. That such a flagrant violation of *Miranda* should produce evidence that may be used for impeachment purposes is especially troublesome; under these circumstances, unlike those in *Harris,* it is fair to assume that no hope of obtaining evidence usable for the government's case-in-chief operates to induce the police to comply with *Miranda. Hass,* then, was a more harmful blow to *Miranda* that was *Harris.*

Even more disturbing than the impeachment cases is their recent extension to permit the use of a defendant's prior silence to impeach his credibility if he chooses to testify at his trial. In JENKINS V. ANDERSON (1980) the Court held that a murder defendant's testimony that he had acted in self-defense could be impeached by showing that he did not go to the authorities and report his involvement in the stabbing. In *Fletcher v. Weir* (1982) the Court held that even a defendant's post-arrest silence—so long as he was not given and need not have been given the *Miranda* warnings—could be used to impeach him if he decided to testify at trial.

Still other blows were struck by *Michigan v. Mosley* (1975) and *Oregon v. Mathiason* (1977). Although language in *Miranda* can be read as establishing a per se rule against any further questioning of one who had asserted his right to silence, *Mosley* held that under certain circumstances, which the case left unclear, if the police cease questioning on the spot, they may try again and succeed at a later interrogation session. *Mathiason,* a formalistic, crabbed reading of *Miranda,* demonstrates that even police station interrogation is not necessarily "custodial." (The suspect had agreed to meet a police officer in the state patrol office and had come to the office alone.)

For supporters of *Miranda,* the most ominous note of all was struck by Justice WILLIAM H. REHNQUIST, speaking for the Court in *Michigan v. Tucker* (1974). The *Tucker* Court viewed the *Miranda* warnings as "not themselves rights protected by the Constitution" but only "prophylactic standards" designed to "safeguard" or to "provide practical reinforcement" for the right against self-incrimination. And it seemed to equate "compulsion" within the meaning of that right with "coercion" or "involuntariness" under the pre-*Miranda* due process test. It seemed to miss the point that much greater pressures were necessary to render a confession "involuntary" under the old test than are needed to make a statement "compelled" under the new. That was one of the principal reasons the old test was abandoned in favor of *Miranda.*

A lumping together of self-incrimination "compulsion" and pre-*Miranda* "involuntariness," which appears to be what the Court did in *Tucker,* seemed to approach a rejection of the central premises of *Miranda.* Moreover, the Supreme Court has no supervisory power over state criminal justice. By stripping *Miranda* of its most apparent constitutional basis without explaining what other bases for it there might be, the Court in the *Tucker* opinion seemed to be preparing the way for the eventual overruling of *Miranda.*

A decade later, in NEW YORK V. QUARLES (1984) and in OREGON V. ELSTAD (1985), a majority of the Court, relying heavily on language in the *Tucker* opinion, again drew a distinction between statements that are actually "coerced" or "compelled" and those that are obtained merely in violation of *Miranda*'s "procedural safeguards" or "prophylactic rules." *Quarles* admitted a statement a handcuffed rape suspect had made when questioned by police about the whereabouts of a gun he had earlier been reported to be carrying. The Court, speaking through Justice Rehnquist, "conclude[d] that the need for answers to questions in a situation posing a threat to the public safety outweighs the need for the prophylactic rule protecting [the] privilege against self-incrimination." *Elstad* held that the failure to give *Miranda* warnings to a suspect who made an incriminating statement when subjected to custodial interrogation in his own home did not bar the use of a subsequent station house confession by the suspect when the second confession was immediately preceded by *Miranda* warnings. The court, speaking through Justice SANDRA DAY O'CONNOR, rejected the argument that a *Miranda* violation "necessarily breeds the same consequences as police infringement of a constitutional right, so that evidence uncovered following an unwarned statement must be suppressed as 'fruit of the poisonous tree.' " Although *Quarles* and *Elstad* can be read very narrowly, and *Tucker,* too, can be limited to its special facts, the Court's language in these cases—language that "deconstitutionalizes" *Miranda*—may prove to be far more significant than the cases' specific holdings.

In light of the *Tucker* majority's undermining of the basis for *Miranda* and against the background of such cases as *Harris, Hass,* and *Mathiason,* a 1980 confession case, *Rhode Island v. Innis,* posed grave dangers for *Miranda.* The defendant had been convicted of heinous crimes: kidnapping, robbery, and murder. He had made incriminating statements while being driven to a nearby police station, only a few minutes after being placed in the police vehicle. Any interrogation that might have occurred in the vehicle was brief and mild—much more so than the direct, persistent police station interrogation in *Miranda* and its companion cases. Two police officers conversing with one another in the front of the car, but in Innis's presence, had expressed concern that because the murder occurred in the vicinity of a school for handicapped children, one of the children might find the missing shotgun and injure himself. At this point, Innis had interrupted the officers and offered to lead them where the shotgun was hidden.

The Court might have taken an approach suggested by earlier dissents and limited *Miranda* to custodial station house interrogation or its equivalent (for example, a five-hour trip in a police vehicle). It did not do so. The Court might have taken a mechanical approach to interrogation and limited it, as some lower courts had, to situations where the police directly address a suspect. Again, it did not do so. It might have limited interrogation to situations where the record establishes (as it did not in *Innis*) that the police intended to elicit an incriminating response, an obviously difficult test to administer. It did not do this either.

Instead, the Court, speaking through Justice POTTER STEWART (one of the *Miranda* dissenters), held that "*Miranda* safeguards come into play whenever a person in custody is subjected to either express questioning or its functional equivalent." The term "interrogation" includes "any words or actions on the part of the police (other than those normally attendant to arrest and custody) that the police should know are reasonably likely to elicit as incriminating response from the suspect." Although the *Innis* case involved police "speech," the Court's definition embraces police tactics that do not. Thus, the Court seems to have repudiated the position taken by a number of lower courts that confronting a suspect with physical evidence or with an accomplice who has already confessed is not interrogation because it does entail verbal conduct on the part of the police.

One may quarrel, as the three dissenters did, with the Court's application of its definition of "interrogation" to the *Innis* facts (the Court concluded that the defendant had not been interrogated). But *Innis* ia a harder case than most because there was "a basis for concluding that the officer's remarks were for some purpose *other* than that of obtaining evidence from the suspect. An objective listener could plausibly conclude that the policeman's remarks . . . were made solely to express their genuine concern about the danger posed by the hidden shotgun" and thus not view their conversation "as a demand for information" (White 1980, pp. 1234–1235).

In any event, considering the various ways in which the *Innis* Court might have given *Miranda* a grudging interpretation, its generous definition of "interrogation" seems much more significant than its questionable application of the definition to the particular facts of the case. In *Innis* the process of qualifying, limiting, and shrinking *Miranda* came to a halt. Indeed, it seems fair to say that in *Miranda*'s hour of peril the *Innis* Court rose to its defense.

If *Innis* encouraged *Miranda*'s defenders, EDWARDS V. ARIZONA (1981) gladdened them even more. For *Edwards* was the first clear-cut victory for *Miranda* in the Burger Court. Sharply distinguishing the *Mosley* case, which had dealt with a suspect's assertion of his right to remain silent, the *Edwards* Court, speaking through Justice White (another of the *Miranda* dissenters), held that when a suspect invokes his right to counsel the police cannot try again. Under these circumstances, a valid waiver of the right to counsel cannot be established by showing "only that [the suspect] responded further to police-initiated custodial interrogation," even though he was again advised of his rights at a second interrogation session. He cannot be questioned anew "until counsel has been made available to him, unless [he] himself initiates further communication, exchanges or conversation with the police." Thus, *Edwards* reinvigorates *Miranda* in an important respect. (But a more recent case, *Oregon v. Bradshaw* (1983), interprets "initiation of further communication" so broadly that it seems to sap *Edwards* of much of its vitality.)

Although *Miranda* maintained the momentum generated by *Escobedo,* it represented a significantly different approach to the confession problem. Although the *Miranda* Court understandably tried to preserve some continuity with the loose, groping *Escobedo* opinion, it has become increasingly clear that, by shifting from a right to counsel base to a self-incrimination base, *Miranda* actually marked a fresh start in describing the circumstances under which Fifth and Sixth Amendment protections attach. *Escobedo* assigned primary significance to the amount of guilt available to the police at the time of questioning; the opinion therefore contains much talk about "focal point" and the "accusatory stage." But *Miranda* attaches primary significance to the conditions surrounding or inherent in the interrogation setting; thus the opinion contains much discussion of the "interrogation environment" or the "police-dominated" atmosphere that "carries its own badge of intimidation."

If the requisite inherent pressures exist, *Miranda* applies whether or not the individual being questioned is a "prime suspect" or has become "the accused." On the other hand, if these pressures are not operating, an individual is not entitled to the *Miranda* warnings—no matter how sharply the police have focused on him or how much they consider him the "prime suspect" or "the accused." In short, *Miranda* did not enlarge *Escobedo* so much as displace it.

The same, however, cannot be said for *Massiah.* Although *Miranda* has dominated the confessions scene ever since it was handed down, *Massiah* has emerged as the other major Warren Court confession doctrine. As strengthened by two Burger Court decisions, *Brewer v. William* (1977) (often called "the Christian burial speech" case) and *United States v. Henry* (1980), the *Massiah* doctrine holds that once "adversary" or "judicial" proceedings have commenced against an individual (by way of INDICTMENT, INFORMATION, or initial appearance before a magistrate), deliberate government efforts to elicit incriminating statements from him, whether done openly by uniformed police officers (as in *Williams*) or surreptitiously by secret government agents (as in *Massiah* and *Henry*) violate the individual's right to counsel.

Williams revivified *Massiah.* Indeed, one might even say that *Williams* disinterred it. For until the decision in *Williams* there was good reason to think that *Massiah* had only been a steppingstone to *Escobedo* and that both cases had been largely displaced by *Miranda.*

But *Massiah* is alive and well. And the policies underlying the *Massiah* doctrine are quite distinct from those underlying *Miranda.* The *Massiah* doctrine represents a pure right to counsel approach. It comes into play regardless of whether a person is in custody or is being subjected to interrogation in the *Miranda* sense. There need not be any compelling influences at work, inherent, informal, or otherwise.

The most recent *Massiah* case, *United States v. Henry* (1980), applied *Massiah* to a situation where the Federal Bureau of Investigation (FBI) had instructed its secret agent, ostensibly a fellow prisoner, not to question the defendant about the crime and there was no showing that he had. Nevertheless, the defendant's incriminating statements were held inadmissible. It sufficed that the government had "intentionally create[d] a situation likely to induce [the defendant] to make incriminating statements without the assistance of counsel." The FBI created such a situation when it instructed its secret agent to be alert to any statements made by the defendant, who was housed in the same cellblock. Even if the agent's claim were accepted that he did not intend to take affirmative steps to obtain incriminating statements, the agent "must have known that such propinquity likely would lead to that result." *Henry* not only reaffirmed the *Massiah* doctrine but significantly expanded it. Thus, the *Massiah* doctrine has emerged as a much more potent force than it ever had been during the Warren Court era.

The Burger Court's generous reading of *Miranda* in *Innis* and *Edwards* and its even more generous reading of *Massiah* in the *Henry* case have reaffirmed the Court's commitment to control police efforts to obtain confessions by constitutional rules that transcend "untrustworthiness' and "voluntariness."

Regardless of its shortcomings and the hopes it never fulfilled (or the fears about the case that proved unfounded), *Miranda* was an understandable and long-overdue effort—and the Court's most ambitious effort ever—to solve the police interrogation–confession problem. At the very least it formally recognized an interrogated suspect's self-incrimination privilege, and a right to counsel for rich and poor alike designed to protect and effectuate that privilege; generated a much greater general awareness of procedural rights; and emphatically reminded the police that they neither create the rules of interrogation nor act free of JUDICIAL REVIEW.

Miranda was an attempt to do in the confessions area what the Warren Court had done elsewhere—take the nation's ideals down from the walls, where they had been kept framed to be pointed at with pride on ceremonial occasions, and live up to them. The degree to which *Miranda* actually succeeded is debatable, but the symbolic quality of the decision extends far beyond its actual impact upon police interrogation methods.

YALE KAMISAR

Bibliography

BAKER, LIVA 1983 *Miranda: Crime, Law and Politics.* New York: Atheneum.

BERGER, MARK 1980 *Taking the Fifth: The Supreme Court and the Privilege against Self-Incrimination.* Lexington, Mass.: Lexington Books.

GRAHAM, FRED 1970 *The Self-Inflicted Wound.* New York: Macmillan.

KAMISAR, YALE 1980 *Police Interrogation and Confessions: Essays in Law and Policy.* Ann Arbor: University of Michigan Press.

LEVY, LEONARD W. 1968 *Origins of the Fifth Amendment.* New York: Oxford University Press.

MCCORMICK, CHARLES T. 1954 *Evidence.* St. Paul, Minn. West Publishing Co.

STEPHENS, OTIS 1973 *The Supreme Court and Confessions of Guilt.* Knoxville: University of Tennessee Press.

WHITE, WELSH S. 1981 Interrogation without Questions. *Michigan Law Review* 78:1209–1251.

WIGMORE, JOHN HENRY 1940 *Evidence,* 3rd ed. Boston: Little, Brown.

POLICE POWER

The police power is the general power of a government to legislate for the comfort, safety, health, morals, or welfare of the citizenry or the prosperity and good order of the community.

DENNIS J. MAHONEY

(SEE ALSO: *Inalienable Police Power; National Police Power; Reserved Police Power; State Police Power.*)

POLITICAL PARTIES AND THE CONSTITUTION

The United States Constitution is virtually silent on politics. It touches upon elections, but even here the subject is treated in a most gingerly fashion by delegating the power to set the "Times, Places and Manner of holding Elections for Senators and Representatives" to the legislature of each state. Even the qualification for voting in national elections was left to the states, by the provision that whoever was qualified to vote for members of the "most numerous branch of the State Legislature" could also vote for members of the House of Representatives.

The Founders saw peril in politics. The Constitution was an effort to provide a solution to politics. To JAMES MADISON in THE FEDERALIST #10, one of the greatest virtues of the Constitution was that it provided an antidote to the "mischiefs of faction." Because attempting to prevent the emergence of faction would be a cure worse than the disease, the only alternative was to provide a system of FEDERALISM on a continental scale so that no faction or conspiracy among factions could reach majority size, thereby becoming a party. Representative government centered in a legislature became the superior form of government because the "temporary or partial considerations" of factions would be regulated by "passing them through the medium of a chosen body of citizens, whose wisdom . . . will be more consonant to the public good than if pronounced by the people themselves. . . ." GEORGE WASHINGTON in his Farewell Address (the drafting of which was shared by Madison and ALEXANDER HAMILTON) warned of "the danger of parties in the State [founded on] geographical discriminations [and] against the baneful effects of the spirit of party generally."

The Constitution was designed also to solve the political problems inherent in the presidency. In effect, Article II provided for a two-tiered presidential selection: *nomination* by the electors and *election* by the House of Representatives. Under the original Article II the process began with selection of electors in a manner provided by each state legislature. In the first election under the Constitution, in 1788–1789, the electors were chosen by legislature in seven states and by voters in six. Next, electors were to meet in their state capitals, never nationally. There is no ELECTORAL COLLEGE; that term is nowhere to be found in the Constitution or in *The Federalist.* At the prescribed meeting at the state capital each elector had the right and obligation to cast ballots for *two persons*—not two votes, but separate votes for two different people, one not from the same state as the elector. If a candidate received an absolute majority of all electoral votes, he was declared the President; the candidate with the second largest vote became vice-president. If no candidate received an absolute majority, the House of Representatives would choose from the top five names, with each state having one vote, regardless of the population of the state. If two candidates received an absolute majority in a tie vote (as happened between THOMAS JEFFERSON and AARON BURR in 1800), the House would choose between the top two.

This system was virtually designed to produce a *parliamentary* government—a strong executive elected by the lower house of the legislature. During the first two decades of the Republic, the primary functions of the national government were to implement the scheme of government contemplated by the Constitution, and that required one-time-only policies, such as the establishment of the major departments, the establishment of the judiciary, and the exercise of SOVEREIGNTY as a nation-state among nation-states, manifest in various kinds of treaties. Policies had to be adopted to assume all the debts previously incurred by the CONTINENTAL CONGRESS and the national government under the ARTICLES OF CONFEDERATION; laws were also adopted to assume all the debts incurred during the war by the thirteen states. All these policies and many others emanated from the executive branch. Congress looked to President Washington for leadership and accepted Secretary of the Treasury Alexander Hamilton as Washington's representative. Although consensus around Washington was replaced with polarization, even before JOHN ADAMS became President, the Federalists carried the necessary majorities through legislative meetings (caucuses) led mainly by Hamilton. But at the same time, all the power to enact the policies—all the power "expressly delegated" to the national government by Article I, section 8—was lodged in Congress. Inevitably, politics came out as a modified parliamentarism, with a strong executive elected by the lower house.

These arrangements seem to have been intentional on the part of the Framers of the Constitution. Without a national meeting, and with each elector having to cast ballots for two separate persons, it was to be expected that several candidates for President would be identified. The concept of the "favorite son" actually goes back to George Washington himself, and the expectation that there would be a large number of favorite sons is strongly implied by the provision that in the event of no absolute majority the top five names would be submitted to the House. Surely this means that more than five meaningful candidates would normally be produced and that final election in the House would be the norm also. With this modified parliamentary system, the Constitution and politics became synonymous. The politics of the two to three decades of the founding period followed the lines prescribed by the Constitution—or, to put it another way, flowed fairly strictly within channels established by the Constitution.

This original system was transformed within a generation following the founding. At some point during the Jefferson administration, the regime of the founding was replaced by a regime of ordinary government. One-time-only policies were replaced by routine and repeatable policies, such as INTERNAL IMPROVEMENTS, land grants, personal claims, tariffs, PATENTS, surveys, and other services. This type of national government is precisely what was intended by Article I, section 8. The TENTH AMENDMENT (1791) merely made more explicit what was already unmistakably clear in Article I, that the important powers of governing were to be reserved to the states. What was not intended, however, was that the political solution prevailing during the first generation would come unstuck. Political parties had already emerged despite Washington's warnings, and the discipline of their members virtually destroyed the so-called Electoral College by requiring that each elector be pledged to a presidential candidate "nominated" prior to their selection as electors. Political parties captured the *nominating* phase of presidential selection. For twenty years thereafter the method of nomination was by legislative caucus—derisively called King Caucus. As the two major parties spread their influence to districts where they had voters but no members of Congress, the party leaders had to work out a method of nomination more representative than King Caucus. That solution, the presidential nominating convention, was adopted in 1832 and remained the institution of party government until 1952.

The national party system was by this time no longer working within prescribed constitutional channels but had created some new channels for itself. *More significantly, the party system in the 1820s and 1830s created a realm of politics independent of the Constitution.*

In another sense, however, the Constitution was having the last word. First, Congress had become the central power of the national government. There was no longer any development toward parliamentary government but clearly toward congressional government, as WOODROW WILSON put it in his important text later in the nineteenth century. Second, the nominating convention, in providing the President with a popular base independent of Congress, produced the SEPARATION OF POWERS that many feel the Constitution had intended—a system of coequal branches each with its own separate constituency.

Third, and most important, the functions of the national government had come more into proportion with the intent of Article I, section 8. That is to say, a politics independent of the Constitution came only at the expense of the kinds of functions the national government had been required to perform during the founding decades. In fact, the relationship ought to be put the other way around. The change of functions from the one-time-only policies of the founding to the ordinary policies of the rest of the nineteenth century had been responsible for the political changes, thus confirming a fundamental and well-nigh universal pattern: *every regime tends to create a politics consonant with itself.* Thus, when the regime (the Constitution and its government) of the founding shifted to a regime of policies arising literally under the provisions of Article I, section 8, politics changed accordingly. For more than a century after 1832 the national government was congressional government; the national politics during that epoch was a function of party government; and together, government and politics were consistent with, and reinforced, a strictly *federal* Constitution in which the national government had a highly limited and specialized role in the life of the country.

A third regime emerged out of the New Deal, not from the increased size of the national government but from the addition to that government of significant new functions. The significant departure from tradition arose out of the enactment of a large number of policies that can be understood only as regulatory and redistributive policies. In effect, the national government acquired its own POLICE POWERS and added its own regulatory and redistributive policies to those of the states. These additions—which were validated by the Supreme Court—brought on a third regime.

Congress did more than enact the new policies that gave the national government its new functions and its directly coercive relationship to citizens. Congress also literally created a new form of government by delegating powers to the executive branch. Each of the new regulatory policies adopted by Congress identified broadly the contours of a problem and then delegated to the executive virtually all the discretion necessary to formulate the actual rules to be imposed on citizens. Technically, this is called the DELEGATION OF POWER, and the rationalization was that Congress had indeed passed the law and left to administrative agencies the power only to "fill in the details." But in fact the executive branch filled in more than details. Just as Woodrow Wilson called the national government of the nineteenth century congressional government, we can with no greater distortion entitle the regime following the New Deal as presidential government.

National politics began to change accordingly. Signs of the weakening of party democracy were already fairly clear during the New Deal. President FRANKLIN

D. ROOSEVELT had tried to rebuild the Democratic party into a programmatic kind of presidential party. The most dramatic moment in that effort was the "purge of 1938," an unprecedented effort by a President to defeat or demote the opposition within his own party in order to make it into a modern instrument of program development and enactment. History records that Roosevelt failed, but the meaning of that failure was not lost on the Democrats or Republicans: the President can no longer depend on locally organized opportunistic parties and must develop his own, independent base of popular support. If this support could no longer be found through political parties, the President would have to do it directly, through the media of mass communication. The President's constituency became the public *en masse.*

The presidential conventions of 1952 were the last of the traditional conventions, where parties still controlled the nominations through the control that state party leaders had over the delegates. And if ANDREW JACKSON can be considered the revolutionary who gave birth to the national conventions, DWIGHT D. EISENHOWER was a revolutionary who turned them into vestigial organs. As the 1952 Republican Convention approached, the Eisenhower forces had to confront the fact that ROBERT A. TAFT was ahead. Their only available strategy was to question the credentials of several state delegations whose members, pledged to Taft, had been selected by the traditional method of virtual appointment by state leaders and were pledged to vote slavishly for the candidate designated by the state leadership. Failing to convince the credentials committee, the Eisenhower leaders took their objections to the convention floor in the form of a "fair play" motion. The debate took place over national television—despite Taft's objections—and the Eisenhower motion swayed enough neutral delegations to gain the majority vote and the momentum sufficient to win the nomination. More important than the immediate victory was the long-range result, which was to weaken the foundations of the traditional party system itself. Progressively from that time, delegates came to be treated as factors in their own right, as individuals to be courted rather than as pawns within a state delegation controlled by state party leaders.

Once the delegates became meaningful individuals, the process of selection had to be democratized. Just as the nominating convention once was a means of democratizing the legislative caucus, the primaries became the means of democratizing conventions. But the primaries are as much a reflection as a cause of the decline of party government, including the decline of party control of the presidential selection process. Party government was already seriously undermined before the spread of selection of pledged delegates by primary elections. The transformed convention was, then, a reflection of the broader process of the decline of state and national political parties. The presidential nomination was becoming an open process by which presidential candidates amassed individual delegates, who had little in common with each other or with the candidate to whom they were pledged. The popular base of the presidency became a mass base. It was no longer the outcome of a process by which state party leaders and their delegations formed coalitions around the candidate most likely to win the nomination and election for President.

Serious students of American political parties have been arguing for more than a decade over the political reforms of the 1960s and 1970s associated with the loosening of the national parties and the virtual displacement of the national conventions. Some argue that the decline of political parties and of the convention as the institution of party government was unintentionally caused by the reforms. Others argue that parties had already declined and that the decline of conventions as the real decision-making body was already happening; therefore, the reforms were more a reflection of the decline than a cause of it. Most significant, however, is the emergence of the new regime: a new form of politics consonant with the regime of regulation and redistribution, with its presidential government.

Many of the current disagreements continue because we are still in the midst of the transformation and the ultimate form has not yet fully emerged. Two distinct scenarios or models can be drawn from the prevailing political analyses. One is "dealignment," tending toward mass democracy—that is, a direct relationship between the President and the masses of people unmediated by any representative institution at all, whether party or legislature. The second scenario is an alignment or realignment model anticipating the restoration of the two major parties. Such a development could require the abolition of some reforms instituted in the 1960s and 1970s that radically unhinged certain features of the traditional party system, and adoption of new measures aimed at restoring the power of party bosses in the presidential nominating process.

The resolution is likely to be a fusion of the two models. The entire functioning of the national government has come to rest upon the President; the expectations of all Americans focus there, and the relationship between the President and the people will continue to be direct. This is the essence of mass politics. At the same time, however, there is strong evidence of a resurgence in the headquarters of the national political parties. Yet there is no place for these parties in the direct line of communication between the President and his mass base. Thus, if these parties are to survive and prosper at the national level they will have to find functions other than the traditional ones of intervening between the masses and the President by controlling the nominating process and political campaigns. The creation of such new functions would require the national leadership to organize from the bottom up, district by district, but in fact the national headquarters are organizing from the top down. They are developing their base in the electorate by collecting data for the computerized analysis of categories of voters. These techniques permit efficient mass mailings to solicit voters and, more important, sponsors who will make millions of donations in units of less than $50 apiece. These are not electoral parties in the traditional sense. Nor are they European-style "mass parties" or social democratic parties. They are what, for lack of an established word, can be called "taxation parties," whose main function is to defray the tremendous cost of the capital necessary to maintain the computers, collect the data, analyze the data, write the letters and stuff the envelopes, and design and communicate the spot announcements and other commercial messages on extremely expensive network television.

American national politics has been in a state of transition for a long time. Professional students of elections, polling, and political parties have all been expecting some kind of "realignment" at least since 1964. Major reforms of the parties and of elections have followed each presidential election since that time; their main result has been to prevent forever the outcome of the previous convention and election. Although the Democrats have been the major reformers, mainly because they have been the major losers in national elections, the Republicans have followed them in these reforms almost immediately. The national political process has not yet adjusted effectively to the regime of regulation and redistribution. In other words, although politics ultimately takes some form consonant with the regime, there is no guaranteeing that the adjustments will be successful and stable.

This fact points to the most important contrast between the present regime and the two previous ones: National politics is flowing through channels increasingly independent of the Constitution; that is, efforts to restore party government have been oblivious to the historic relationship between the Constitution and politics.

This is not to suggest that politics is operating unconstitutionally or outside the spirit of Supreme Court decisions. It means only that efforts to restore the parties, and to reform nominations and elections accordingly, have concentrated on the flow itself rather than on the constitutional structure that ultimately determines the flow. Having recognized the many problems with American politics since the New Deal, reformers have attempted to change the politics. They have persisted in this approach even while recognizing two grievous perils in it. First, because some interests inevitably gain or lose from any political reform, there is always a suspicion that these gains were known and sought in advance. The legitimacy of the system can be badly hurt by the more generalized suspicion that the established electoral process is being manipulated. Second, some reform efforts have come close to violating the FIRST AMENDMENT, and in fact the Supreme Court declared such a violation in BUCKLEY V. VALEO (1976), striking down a law attempting to set limits on the amounts individuals could spend in campaigns. That case is definitely not the end of litigation involving First Amendment rights involved in political reforms. (See POLITICAL PARTIES AND THE SUPREME COURT.)

Politics can be understood as the never-ending process of adjusting to a given structure of government, or regime, by seeking sufficient power and consensus to change the structure or influence its direction. If a change in the conduct of politics is sought, the appropriate route is the exercise of the historic right to change the Constitution and the structure of government. The forms of politics would change accordingly. We have constitutional rights to change our government. As Madison argued in *The Federalist* #10, the attempt to regulate politics is a cure worse than the disease. If there are problems with American national politics—and there appears to be wide agreement on this proposition throughout the political spectrum—then the time may have come to reexamine the structure of government, including the Constitution itself. An extensive revision of the Constitution is neither necessary nor appropriate. The last major constitutional change was triggered by the New Deal, without a single constitutional amendment. Once we recognize that politics is most stable and most respected when it is consonant with constitutional forms, reformers might be convinced to focus at least some of their energies away from political reform and toward constitutional reform.

THEODORE J. LOWI

Bibliography

AGAR, HERBERT 1966 *The Price of Union.* Boston: Houghton Mifflin.

BINCKLEY, WILFRED 1947 *President and Congress.* New York: Knopf.

BURNHAM, WALTER DEAN 1970 *Critical Elections and the Mainsprings of American Politics.* New York: Norton.

CHARLES, JOSEPH 1961 *The Origins of the American Party System.* New York: Harper & Row.

GINSBERG, BENJAMIN 1982 *The Consequences of Consent.* Reading, Mass.: Addison-Wesley.

LOWI, THEODORE J. (1967)1975 Party, Policy and Constitution in America. In William N. Chambers and Walter Dean Burnham, eds., *The American Party System—Stages of Political Development.* New York: Oxford University Press.

POLSBY, NELSON 1983 *Consequences of Party Reform.* New York: Oxford University Press.

SHEFTER, MARTIN 1978 Party Bureaucracy and Political Change. In Louis Maisel and Joseph Cooper, eds., *Political Parties: Development and Decay.* Beverly Hills, Calif.: Sage Publications.

POLITICAL PARTIES IN CONSTITUTIONAL LAW

"No America without democracy, no democracy without politics, no politics without parties. . . ." So begins Clinton Rossiter's commentary on American political parties. Nonetheless, the Supreme Court has said in *Elrod v. Burns* (1976) that "partisan politics bears the imprimatur only of tradition, not the Constitution." Despite the absence of constitutional reference to political parties, the Constitution has had substantial influence in shaping the two-party system and in defining the contested boundary between governmental authority and political party autonomy.

Frank Sorauf has observed that "[t]he major American political parties are in truth three-headed political giants, tripartite systems of interactions. . . . As a political structure they include a party organization, a party in office, and a party in the electorate. . . ." All three branches of political parties are defined, limited, and authorized, at least in part, by constitutional DOCTRINE. All three are shaped in part by specific constitutional arrangements.

Two-party politics, which has persisted throughout the nation's history, began in the struggle between Federalists and Anti-Federalists over the RATIFICATION OF THE CONSTITUTION. Provisions of the Constitution have reinforced the two-party system, especially Article II, section 1, empowering each state to select presidential electors, and the TWELFTH AMENDMENT, requiring an absolute majority of the ELECTORAL COLLEGE or, failing that, of state delegations in the House of Representatives for election of the President. The majority rule tends to compel the coalition of disparate factions into two parties, because only the establishment of broad coalitions offers any prospect of securing the majority necessary for election of the President.

Although no constitutional rule requires that members of the House of Representatives be elected by plurality vote or from single-member districts, these understandings soon took root after ratification of the Constitution. The popular election of the United States senators mandated by the SEVENTEENTH AMENDMENT has the effect of creating single-member districts for the selection of members of that house. These constitutional practices strengthen the two-party system, requiring broad coalitions to secure a majority, the only guarantee of electoral victory under these rules.

The Constitution's provision for a federal structure of government also shapes the party system. Unlike the majority rule's incentive for factions to consolidate into two parties, the federal structure encourages wide dispersion of influence within the party ranks. Because offices and powers at the state and local levels are more accessible and often more important than those in the national government, party organizations in each state and locale grow independent of one another and are largely free from sanctions imposed by any national party organization. This dispersion of party organization is heightened by the mandate of Article I, section 1, and the Twelfth Amendment for state-by-state selection of the electors who choose the President.

States began to regulate political parties in the late eighteenth century, and these regulations became commonplace during the Progressive era. The STATE POLICE POWER was regarded as a sufficient basis for the imposition of governmental authority upon the parties. The state-prescribed Australian ballot, antifusion legislation, and state-operated primaries were introduced at the same time as laws regulating the structure and activities of political parties. All of these were intended to curb political "bosses" and "machines."

By the beginning of World War II, the constitutions of seventeen states and the statutes in virtually all states referred to political parties—conferring rights on them, regulating their activities, or both. State regulatory schemes went beyond prescribing the methods by which parties would select nominees for office and the qualifications of parties for places on the ballot. Many states also regulated the selection and composition of district, county, and state political party committees, the authority and duties of those committees, and the rules for their operation.

Whether the national government has similar authority to regulate political parties has seldom been tested, for Congress has not chosen to enact legislation recognizing party associations or regulating their structure and activities. Any such federal power could, however, be thought to derive from several constitutional sources.

Article IV, section 1, of the Constitution grants Congress a broad power to regulate the time, place, and manner of electing senators and representatives. In UNITED STATES V. CLASSIC (1941) the Supreme Court construed this provision to allow Congress to regulate individual conduct and also to modify those state regulations of federal elections that the Constitution authorizes. The Court has also cited the NECESSARY AND PROPER CLAUSE as an additional source of congressional authority over federal elections, and in EX PARTE YARBROUGH (1884) it declared that Congress has the power, as an attribute of republican government, to pass laws governing federal elections, especially to protect them against fraud, violence, and other practices that undermine their integrity. And, although no constitutional provision explicitly extends the authority of Congress to regulate presidential elections, the Court affirmed this power in *Burroughs v. United States* (1934), OREGON V. MITCHELL (1970), and BUCKLEY V. VALEO (1976).

Congressional power to regulate elections does not necessarily imply power to regulate political parties. But the Supreme Court has taken a major step in that direction by bringing federal PRIMARY ELECTIONS, which are principally a party process for selecting candidates, within the ambit of Article I. In *United States v. Classic* the Justices held that: "Where state law has made the primary an integral part of the procedure of choice, or where in fact the primary effectively controls the choice, the right of the elector to have his ballot counted at the primary is . . . included in the right [to vote in congressional elections] protected by Article I, sec. 2." This right to vote in congressional elections may be protected by Congress under Article I, section 4. Subsequently, the Court has treated *Classic* as recognizing a general congressional power to regulate primary elections for federal offices.

A wholly distinct doctrinal technique for imposing judicial limits upon party affairs, which may extend congressional legislative authority to party activities, grew out of the White Primary Cases. In NIXON V. HERNDON (1927) the Supreme Court held that because the sponsorship of a primary election by a state was STATE ACTION subject to the FOURTEENTH AMENDMENT, the exclusion of black voters from such a primary was unconstitutional. Even when the state authorized the party executive committee to determine party membership, NIXON V. CONDON (1932) held the ensuing primary to constitute state action. State authorization of a ballot position for candidates selected in party-sponsored primaries, without any state-prescribed primary rules or state operation of the primary, was held in SMITH V. ALLWRIGHT (1944) to be state action in violation of the FIFTEENTH AMENDMENT.

Many commentators and judges regard TERRY V. ADAMS (1953)—the last of the White Primary Cases—as extending constitutional limitation to party activities beyond primary elections. In *Terry* the Supreme Court held that the Fifteenth Amendment prohibited a local group, the Jaybird Democratic Association, from excluding blacks from a preprimary straw vote, paid for and operated exclusively by the association, to endorse candidates to run in the statutorily recognized Democratic party primary. The four-member plurality of the *Terry* Court concluded that the Jaybirds were part of the Democratic party. Only three Justices said that the Jaybird straw vote was limited by the Fifteenth Amendment because it was "an integral part, indeed the only effective part, of the electoral process."

Nonetheless, most judicial decisions now treat party organizations as state-affiliated agencies. State laws often closely prescribe the structure, organization, and duties of local, district, and state party units. Hence, the lower federal court cases have held that the EQUAL PROTECTION CLAUSE governs the selection and apportionment of members of local, district, and state party committees and conventions. Several decisions of the Court of Appeals for the District of Columbia have also applied the Fourteenth Amendment to national party conventions, because those conventions are integral parts of the process of selecting the President. But in at least one case that court suggested that the developing law of "state action," as defined by the Supreme Court, had excluded party conventions from the scope of the Fourteenth Amendment.

In defining the scope of the Fourteenth and Fifteenth Amendments, and thus the scope of congressional power to enforce those amendments, several appellate courts have distinguished between parties' candidate selection activities and their management of "internal affairs." Ronald Rotunda has suggested "a functional standard" in which "all integral steps in an election for public office are public functions and therefore state action subject to some judicial scrutiny." The functional distinction, though plausible and attractive, is difficult to apply in practice. Party activists often seek to influence the selection of party candidates, presumably to assure that party nominees reflect the policies of the party organization. Working through party organizations, they endorse candidates in the primary, expend money on their behalf, and mobilize primary voters for them. These activities could easily be construed as part of the selection of candidates; yet it seems unlikely that they fall within the reach of the prohibitions of the Fourteenth and Fifteenth Amendments—and thus the reach of Congress's power to enforce those amendments.

One further source of governmental authority to regulate political parties is the power to attach restrictions to special statuses or benefits accorded to candidates and parties under federal and state laws. Generally, the Supreme Court has rejected legislation that requires the surrender of constitutional rights as a condition for attaining a governmental benefit. (See UNCONSTITUTIONAL CONDITIONS.) Although it recognized in *Buckley v. Valeo* (1976) that political expenditures constitute protected speech under the FIRST AMENDMENT, the Supreme Court nonetheless upheld the PRESIDENTIAL ELECTION CAMPAIGN FUND ACT's limits on political party expenditures for nomination conventions and on candidate spending in presidential nomination and general election campaigns subsidized by federal money. This decision has broad implications for state regulatory authority in the thirteen states that provide public grants to candidates and political parties.

In virtually all states political parties receive automatic access to the ballot if they obtain a certain percentage of votes cast in a prior election. And in every state the ballot carries the party label to identify the candidates nominated by qualified political parties. These state benefits to political parties may justify state regulation of the structure, organization, and operation of political parties. Moreover, these benefits may strengthen claims that party activities constitute state action, thus bringing them within the ambit of both judicial and congressional authority under the Civil War amendments.

Although the Constitution has been interpreted to allow government to extend special recognition to political parties, especially major parties, governmental assistance to parties is circumscribed by constitutional limits. In *Buckley v. Valeo* the Supreme Court not only held that financial subventions were within congressional authority under the GENERAL WELFARE CLAUSE; it also sustained definitions of eligibility that tended to reinforce the position of the major parties. Full public financing is available only to a party whose presidential candidate in the previous election received at least 25 percent of the popular vote. Some minor parties and candidates are eligible for lesser funding; others are not.

The party, seen as part of the electorate, is recognized by state eligibility requirements for voter participation in primary elections. Connecticut's closed party primary survived the challenge that it abridged independent voters' right to vote and freedom of association. A lower federal court held that the state law validly served "to protect party members from 'intrusion by those with adverse political principles,' and to preserve the integrity of the electoral process," and the Supreme Court affirmed in *Nader v. Schaffer* (1976). The courts have not decided whether political parties' freedom of association protects them from intrusion into the nominating process by persons who are not party members.

State authority to protect the integrity of party membership rolls is limited by the Fourteenth Amendment. A voter's freedom to associate with a party is apparently abridged if state-mandated enrollment rules unduly delay participation in a party primary. In *Kusper v. Pontikes* (1973) the Supreme Court invalidated a law requiring party enrollment twenty-three months in advance of a primary in which the voter wished to participate.

States also have power to protect the integrity of party nominating procedures by limiting independent or third-party candidacies by those who have been affiliated with another party. Hence, in *Storer v. Brown* (1974) the Supreme Court sustained a state law requiring an independent or new-party candidate to disaffiliate from his prior party at least a year in advance of his new party's primary. And in *American Party of Texas v. White* (1974) the Justices upheld a state law prohibiting persons who had voted in a party's most recent primary from signing petitions to qualify another party's candidate or an independent candidate for the ballot. The Court has also intimated that it would sustain "sore loser" statutes which prohibit a candidate who has participated in a party's nominating contest from subsequently qualifying as an independent candidate or opposition party aspirant in the same election. But in the same case, *Anderson v. Celebrezze* (1983), the Court held that states may not protect established parties by setting early filing deadlines that bar independent candidates arising from opposition to the platforms or candidates of major parties, when those become known.

The Constitution has been interpreted to allow preferred ballot access to established parties. Hence, in *Jennes v. Fortson* (1971) the Court sustained a statute giving automatic ballot access to parties that had obtained twenty percent or more of the vote in the prior election, while requiring others to gain ballot placement by obtaining petition signatures equivalent to five percent of those eligible to vote in the prior election. Nonetheless, in *Williams v. Rhodes* (1968) the Court rejected statutory schemes so complex or burdensome as to make it virtually impossible for any but the Democratic and Republican parties to obtain ballot access.

Promotion of political parties through minimal restrictions on the First Amendment right to associate and on the right to vote are justified by a wide array of governmental interests. The Supreme Court has said that states may protect political parties in order to assure "stability of the political system," to avoid confusion or deception, to "avoid frivolous or fraudulent candidacies prompted by short-range political goals, pique, or personal quarrel." Congress, in providing public financing of parties and candidates, can seek to avoid funding hopeless candidacies with large sums of public money or fostering proliferation of splinter parties. In the aggregate these justifications represent a constitutional hospitality toward political parties, at least when legislators grant them special statuses.

Several developments in constitutional doctrine suggest that long-established governmental regulation of political parties may now stand on treacherous ground. The 1950s saw the emergence of an independent First Amendment freedom of association, principally in cases involving dissident or oppressed groups, especially the Communist party. As early as 1952, in *Ray v. Blair,* the Supreme Court sustained a Democratic party requirement that candidates for presidential elector swear to vote for the presidential and vice-presidential candidates selected by the national Democratic party. Such an oath "protects a party from intrusion by those with adverse political principles." But until the 1970s there was little other judicial recognition that the freedom of association might secure rights of major political parties against governmental regulation.

In *Cousins v. Wigoda* (1975) and *Democratic Party v. LaFollette* (1981) the Supreme Court specifically announced that the First Amendment protected national party conventions in their establishment of rules for the selection of delegates, even in the face of contrary state laws or local party practices. In both cases, the Supreme Court announced that "the National Democratic party and its adherents enjoy a constitutionally protected right of political association." Both cases also applied the traditional standard in First Amendment cases; only a COMPELLING STATE INTEREST warranted abridgment of the "rights of association" of the national Democratic party.

In *LaFollette* the Court concluded that Article II, section 1, of the Constitution, which empowers each state to "appoint" presidential electors in the manner directed by the legislature, bears such a "remote and tenuous" connection to "the means by which political party members in a State associate to elect delegates to party nominating conventions . . . as to be wholly without constitutional significance." This conclusion sets aside one possible constitutional basis for state power to regulate party activities in selecting presidential nominees. Together, *Cousins* and *LaFollette* signal judicial reluctance to sweep every stage in the candidate selection process, especially those conducted by the parties themselves, within the scope of governmental regulation.

Indeed, in *Cousins* the Supreme Court specifically declined to "decide" or to "intimate" decisions on several critical issues of governmental authority to regulate parties, thus suggesting that large areas of the law remain open despite the assumption of past practices and of lower court decisions that party affairs are subject to extensive regulation. First, the Court did not decide "whether the decisions of a National Political Party in the area of selection constitute state or governmental action" limited by the Fourteenth and Fifteenth Amendments, and thus subject to congressional regulation. Second, the Justices left open the question "whether national political parties are subject to the principles of the REAPPORTIONMENT decisions, or other constitutional restraints, in their methods of delegate selection or allocation." Third, the Court did not decide "whether or to what extent national political parties and their nominating conventions are regulable by, or only by, Congress."

Although the sweeping associational rights of political parties recognized in *Cousins* and *LaFollette* have sometimes been regarded as limited by the Supreme Court's reference to the special "national interest" in presidential nominating conventions, the Court has relied on those decisions to protect party autonomy below the national level. In *Rivera-Rodriguez v. Popular Democratic Party* (1982) the Court cited *Cousins* and *LaFollette* in holding that a territorial political party, empowered by law to select a replacement for a deceased territorial legislator originally elected on the party ticket, was "entitled to adopt its own procedures to select . . . [a] replacement" and "was not required to include nonmembers in what can be analogized to a party primary election."

These developments suggest that the emerging First Amendment rights of parties may give them broad autonomy to order their affairs. At a minimum, party organizations can make a strong claim to order the selection, structure, and operation of party committees and conventions free from state regulation, even if those committees and conventions participate actively in candidate selection primaries. The federal courts have held that a state law prohibiting party committees from endorsing candidates in primaries violated First Amendment speech and associational rights; they avoided deciding, however, whether party campaign activities such as contributing money were similarly protected in those primary contests. If party assemblies actually select candidates, they may claim autonomy under *Cousins* and *LaFollette*, which held that party rules overrode contrary state laws in prescribing the selection of delegates to national party nominating conventions.

At the farthest reaches, the First Amendment might be construed to allow parties a substantial role in prescribing party membership and qualifying candidates for participation in party primaries established by the states. A state has a legitimate interest in an orderly election process that encourages qualified persons to participate in elections free of fraud, intimidation, and corruption; but its interests do not warrant limitations on the First Amendment associational rights of political parties. Parties may therefore establish voter enrollment and candidate eligibility rules to prevent the intrusion into party primaries of candidates and voters who do not share the party's goals. These party rules would, of course, be subject to the limits that the Supreme Court has already imposed to protect the constitutional rights to vote and associate. Such a theory of party autonomy is consistent with the modern understanding of the First Amendment and with contemporary Supreme Court declarations of party associational rights. It is a theory awaiting full explication and recognition.

DAVID ADAMANY

Bibliography

GEYH, CHARLES 1983 "It's My Party and I'll Cry If I Want To": State Intrusions upon the Associational Freedoms of Political Parties. *Wisconsin Law Review* 1983:211–240.

GOTTLIEB, STEPHEN E. 1982 Rebuilding the Right of Association: The Right to Hold a Convention as a Test Case. *Hofstra Law Review* 11:191–247.

KESTER, JOHN G. 1974 Constitutional Restrictions on Political Parties. *Virginia Law Review* 60:735–784.

NOTE 1978 Equal Representation of Party Members on Political Party Central Committees. *Yale Law Journal* 88:167–185.

ROSSITER, CLINTON L. 1960 *Parties and Politics in America.* Ithaca, N.Y.: Cornell University Press.

ROTUNDA, RONALD D. 1975 Constitutional and Statutory Restrictions on Political Parties in the Wake of *Cousins v. Wigoda. Texas Law Review* 53:935–963.

SORAUF, FRANK J. 1980 *Party Politics in America.* Boston: Little, Brown.

POLITICAL PHILOSOPHY OF THE CONSTITUTION

It is a commonplace that the Constitution provides for a LIMITED GOVERNMENT, one that depends upon a system of CHECKS AND BALANCES. And this in turn is said to reflect a realistic opinion both about the nature of man and about the purposes and risks of government. The general government is limited in that much is left to the states to do, to the extent and in the ways the states choose to act. The very existence of the states and many of the things they do are taken for granted; they do not depend upon the Constitution. Even the states formed pursuant to the Constitution automatically assumed, upon admission to the Union, virtually all of the prerogatives (or STATES' RIGHTS) of the original thirteen, including the status of being largely independent of the other states and in many respects independent of the general government.

The states play vital parts in the periodic choices of United States senators, representatives, and presidential electors. Otherwise, the Constitution, once ratified, depends upon the states for relatively few things in order to permit the general government to function within its appointed sphere. Various restrictions are placed upon the states, primarily with a view to preventing interferences by them with the proper activities of the general government. In addition, the states are obliged by the Constitution to respect various legal determinations in other states. But, by and large, the states are left fairly autonomous, however republican they are required and helped to be under the Constitution. (Although the Civil War and its Reconstruction amendments had effects upon the original constitutional dispensation, these amendments are consistent with, if not the natural culmination of, the initial dedication of the Constitution to liberty and equality.)

The general government is limited in still another critical respect by the SEPARATION OF POWERS, which makes the Constitution seem far less simple than it really is. Virtually everything that may be done by any branch of that government must take account, if it does not require the immediate cooperation, of the other two branches. Thus, Congress can enact laws alone, but it is easier to do so in collaboration with the President; how the judges will understand and how the President will execute these laws must be anticipated. The President alone commands the armed forces, but what those forces consist of and how they are equipped depends on congressional provisions, as does the very declaration of the wars in which such forces may be used. The judges interpret and apply laws, but, apart from the Supreme Court, all courts of the general government depend for their JURISDICTION and for their very existence upon the Congress, and for the execution of their decrees upon the President. Many other such interdependencies are evident.

We can even see in the references to divinity in the DECLARATION OF INDEPENDENCE an oblique anticipation of the qualified separation of powers found in the Constitution itself. There are four references of this kind in the Declaration. The first reference to God, and perhaps the second as well, regarded God as legislator; it is He that orders things, ordaining what is to be. That is, He first comes to sight as lawgiver or lawmaker. Next, God is seen as judge. Finally, He is revealed as executive, as One Who extends protection, enforcing the laws that have been laid down (with a suggestion as well of the dispensing power of the executive). Thus, the authors of the Declaration portrayed even the government of the world in the light of their political principles.

The constitutional dispersal of powers (between state and general governments, among branches of the general government, and between congressional houses with quite different constituencies) testifies to the recognition that those who wield power have to be watched, and perhaps shackled or at least hobbled. This understanding may be seen also in the ways the people discipline themselves, agreeing to proceed in accordance with constitutional forms. Such precautions make sense, however, only if there is indeed a considerable power to be exercised.

Preeminent among the powers of the general government are those that must be exercised countrywide if they are to be used effectively. These include the plenary (but not necessarily exclusive) powers of the general government with respect to commerce "among the several States," taxes, "the common defense," and international relations, all of which are reinforced by the NECESSARY AND PROPER CLAUSE. And so there has been no need for a "living" Constitution to "grow," except perhaps to grow out of the artificial limitations imposed by those periodic misinterpretations of the Constitution that have failed to appreciate the full extent of the powers intended to be vested in the general government.

Here and there the Constitution restricts the exercise of the plenary powers conferred upon the general government—but those restraints tend to be "procedural." "Substantive" restraints upon such powers would be unreasonable should they have to be employed in unpredictable but grave circumstances. The Constitution assumes the prudence of those who wield power. Thus, for example, no matter how the tax power is hedged in, Congress can still so use its discretion here as to ruin the country.

The prudence relied upon is to be directed to the advancement of the goals enumerated in the PREAMBLE. There are elsewhere in the Constitution further indications of what is taken for granted as legitimate ends of government, such as in references to "the Progress of Science and useful Arts," to "public safety," to the control of "disorderly Behaviour," to a "Republican Form of Government," and to "the Law of Nations." And, of course, the Declaration of Independence states in an authoritative manner the enduring ends of American government rooted in the inalienable rights of men.

That the Declaration of Independence is taken for granted is evident even in the way the Constitution is dated: "in the Year of our Lord one thousand seven hundred and Eighty seven and of the Independence of the United States of America the Twelfth." It seems to be taken for granted as well that the prudence relied upon both in the Declaration and in the Constitution is generally to be promoted by free discussion of public issues, however salutary a temporary secrecy may be on occasion. Such discussion is presupposed by the relations of the various branches of government to one another and by what they say to each other. Thus, judges deliberate and set forth their conclusions in published opinions; the President, in exercising his VETO POWER, is to give "his Objections," which objections are to be considered by Congress; the members of Congress are protected in their exercise of freedom of speech as legislators. A continental FREEDOM OF SPEECH and FREEDOM OF THE PRESS were presupposed as well, even before the ratification of the FIRST AMENDMENT, by the repeated indications in the Constitution of 1787 that it is an ultimately sovereign people who establish and continually assess the government.

The SOVEREIGNTY of the people is central to the constitutional system, moderated though the people's control may be by the use of representatives and by indirect selections of various officers of government. Each of the seven articles of the original Constitution, including the judiciary article, testifies to the understanding that the people are ultimately to have their way, however carefully they have disciplined themselves in restricting the manner in which they insist upon having their way. The people are sovereign, and for good reasons: it is a government designed for their happiness; they themselves have ordained it and are to support it. Besides, no one else is obviously better qualified to decide what is in the best interests of the country.

An essential equality among people is indicated in various ways, including in the equal status of the states and in the freedom of citizens to move among the states. Majority rule is taken for granted again and again. No male–female or rich–poor distinction is recognized. The Constitution does not even recognize an intrinsic difference among the races, however much grudging accommodation there may have had to be to existing slavery institutions. And, of course, no government in the United States may grant TITLES OF NOBILITY.

To defer to the genuine sovereignty of the people is to submit, in effect, to that rule of law contemplated by MAGNA CARTA. It is only through law that a people, in their political capacity, can truly speak or be spoken to. Dependence upon the RULE OF LAW points to LEGISLATIVE SUPREMACY, which is indicated again and again in the Constitution, not least in its IMPEACHMENT provisions. It is peculiar, then, that we rely as much as we now do on JUDICIAL REVIEW—that is, on the duty of courts to assess congressional enactments for their constitutionality. Of course, this duty, too, can be put in terms of respect for the rule of law. But it is difficult to find in the text of the Constitution any provision for judicial review or even any indication that it was ever anticipated by the Framers. In fact, the care with which the President's veto (the executive counterpart to judicial review) is established argues against the opinion that judges are intended by the Constitution to examine formally sufficient acts of Congress for their constitutionality, except perhaps whenever the prerogatives of the courts themselves are immediately threatened. What does seem to be anticipated by the Constitution is an even more considerable power for judges than judicial review seems to offer, but one which the appellate courts of the general government have largely surrendered. This is their indirect but nevertheless critical power of supervising the COMMON LAW (and hence the moral sensibilities) of the country, subject to whatever regulations legislatures may choose to provide. In any event, these courts are entitled, perhaps even obliged, to interpret acts of Congress in accordance with the Constitution, proceeding in each case before them on the reasonable assumption (until Congress clearly indicates otherwise) that nothing unconstitutional or unjust is intended.

In the American constitutional system, both the rule of law and an ultimate dependence upon the sovereignty of the people mean that property is to be respected. (And this respect probably implies, considering the evident commercial presuppositions of the Constitution, that economic interests are to be advanced.) Respect for property is the private counterpart to that political deference to the public seen in genuine republican government. The protections of property in the THIRD, FOURTH, Fifth, SEVENTH, and Eighth Amendments draw upon a principle that is already evident in the original Constitution.

Deference to the public, and to republicanism, also takes the form of a concern for "the Blessings of Liberty." That a considerable liberty is taken for granted by the Constitution may be seen in its assurances with respect to HABEAS CORPUS, to BILLS OF ATTAINDER, to the crime of TREASON, to RELIGIOUS TESTS, and to "INDICTMENT, Trial, Judgment and Punishment, according to Law." It may be seen as well in the spirit of liberty which pervades the governmental system, making much of a people's freely choosing what they will have done for them, by whom, and upon what terms.

But however much liberty, property, and equality are to be respected, there is no question under the Constitution but that there should be effective governance, and governance with respect to the most important matters facing the country as a whole. However "limited" the exercise of power may be, primarily because of the different parts played by the three branches of the general government and by the states, great powers do exist for the general government to exercise. In any extended contest, the Constitution assumes that a determined Congress can have its way both with the President and with the courts. The Constitution was itself fashioned by a deliberative body which resembles much more the Congress than it does either the presidency or the judiciary. In the very nature of things, lawmaking (whether entrusted to one hand or to many) is at the heart of sovereignty, providing the necessary mandates for those who either interpret or execute the laws.

Lawmaking may be seen as well in what the people at large in their sovereign capacity have done in "ordain[ing] and establish[ing] this Constitution." Thus, the preeminence of lawmaking may be seen not only in what the CONSTITUTIONAL CONVENTION did in drafting the Constitution but even more in what the people did in the RATIFICATION OF THE CONSTITUTION. The provision of a workable AMENDING PROCESS also presupposes that the people retain their ultimate authority—and that standards exist by which they may examine and modify constitutional arrangements from time to time.

The Framers of the Constitution applied those standards, set forth in the Declaration of Independence, to the needs and opportunities of their day. Such standards were understood to be rooted in nature. The American people considered themselves sanctified by Providence, or at least peculiarly fitted because of their experiences and circumstances, to discern and to follow the guidance of nature. Americans looked to political philosophers and other students of law and government for help in their recourse to nature—and they invoked with confidence writers from Plato and Aristotle to John Locke and Adam Smith. But none of these writers was authoritative; all of them could be exploited, along with the considerable historical record (sacred and profane, ancient and modern) repeatedly drawn upon in debate. The diversity of the many sources casually, if not cavalierly, put to use by the Framers suggests that the astute political thought of eighteenth-century Americans was, in certain respects, distinctive to them. They were eminently practical and yet high-minded constitutionalists who seemed willing to leave many private concerns, and vital personal virtues, to the ministrations of local government and of common-law judges (as well as to church and family), while they entrusted the government of the United States both with the GENERAL WELFARE (including the economy of the country) and with external affairs (including the common defense).

However extensive and even awesome those governmental powers may be, the powers retained by the people to revise whatever is done by government in their name remain even greater. The ultimate sovereignty of the people may be seen not only in the constitutional provision for amendments but also in that natural RIGHT OF REVOLUTION vigorously relied upon in the Declaration of Independence.

Intrinsic to the political philosophy of the Constitution is the recognition that a bad law may still be constitutional, and hence that the political must be distinguished from the legal (or judicial). This understanding means that in order for the constitutional government empowered by the people (as well as for the all-powerful people themselves) to contribute to the common good in a regular and enduring manner, there must be constant and informed recourse by Americans (citizens and public servants alike) to the instructive dictates of prudence.

GEORGE ANASTAPLO

Bibliography

ALVAREZ, LEO PAUL DE, ED. 1976 *Abraham Lincoln, the Gettysburg Address and American Constitutionalism.* Irving, Texas: University of Dallas Press.

ANASTAPLO, GEORGE 1971 *The Constitutionalist: Notes on the First Amendment.* Dallas, Texas: Southern Methodist University Press.

______ 1965 The Declaration of Independence. *St. Louis University Law Journal* 9:390–415.

______ 1984 Mr. Crosskey, the American Constitution, and the Natures of Things. *Loyola University of Chicago Law Journal* 15:181–260.

______ 1987 *The Constitution of 1787: A Commentary.* Athens, Ohio: Swallow Press/Ohio University Press. (Reprinted from *Loyola University of Chicago Law Journal* [1986] 18:1.)

CROSSKEY, WILLIAM W. 1953 *Politics and the Constitution in the History of the United States.* Chicago: University of Chicago Press.

EIDELBERG, PAUL 1968 *The Philosophy of the American Constitution: A Reinterpretation of the Intentions of the Founding Fathers.* New York: Free Press.

SHARP, MALCOLM P. 1973 Crosskey, Anastaplo and Meiklejohn on the United States Constitution. *University of Chicago Law School Record* 20:3–18.

STORY, JOSEPH 1833 *Commentaries on the Constitution of the United States.* Boston: Hilliard, Gray & Co.

POLITICAL QUESTION

As early as MARBURY V. MADISON (1803) the Supreme Court recognized that decisions on some governmental questions lie entirely within the discretion of the "political" branches of the national government—the President and Congress—and thus outside the proper scope of JUDICIAL REVIEW. Today such questions are called "political questions."

Among the clauses of the federal Constitution held

to involve political questions, the one most frequently cited has been Article IV, section 4, under which the federal government "shall guarantee to every State in this Union a REPUBLICAN FORM OF GOVERNMENT." Federal courts, and particularly the Supreme Court, have argued that as the definition of "republican" is at the heart of the American political system, only the "political branches," which are accountable to the sovereign people, can make that definition. The electorate can ratify or reject the definition by reelecting or defeating their representatives at the next election. The choice of definition, Justice FELIX FRANKFURTER said, dissenting in BAKER V. CARR (1962), entails choosing "among competing theories of political philosophy," which is not a proper judicial function.

Thus the Supreme Court has refused to review political decisions in cases involving two governments, each claiming to be the legitimate one of a state (LUTHER V. BORDEN, 1849); the question whether the post-Civil War Reconstruction governments in southern states were republican (*Georgia v. Stanton* and MISSISSIPPI V. JOHNSON, 1867); the "republican" nature of the INITIATIVE and REFERENDUM (*Pacific Telephone & Telegraph Co. v. Oregon*, 1912; *Hawke v. Smith*, 1920); lack of REAPPORTIONMENT by state legislatures (COLEGROVE V. GREEN, 1946); contested elections (*Taylor & Marshall v. Beckham*, 1900); certain presidential actions (*Mississippi v. Johnson*, 1867); certain cases arising in Indian territory (CHEROKEE INDIAN CASES, 1831–1832); and FOREIGN AFFAIRS (*Foster v. Neilson*, 1829; *Charlton v. Kelly*, 1913).

The Supreme Court has never successfully differentiated those questions proper for judicial interpretation from those that are reserved to the "political" branches. A plurality of the Justices having held in *Colegrove v. Green* (1946) that a state legislature's failure to reapportion itself after the decennial federal census was a political question, for example, the Court in *Baker v. Carr* decided that such inaction raised a question under the equal protection clause of the FOURTEENTH AMENDMENT rather than the guarantee clause, and therefore raised an issue proper for judicial decision. After having handed down a line of cases holding that contested elections were matters in which the final decision could come only from the relevant legislative body, the Court overturned the refusal by the House of Representatives (POWELL V. MCCORMACK, 1969) to seat a member who, in the Court's view, had been excluded unconstitutionally.

The Court has been relatively consistent in holding various foreign relations issues to constitute political questions, because of the necessity for the country to speak with one voice, the inability of courts to develop a body of principles to govern such issues, and what Justice Frankfurter described in *Perez v. Brownell* (1958) as the "constitutional allocation of governmental function" concerning foreign affairs to the President and Congress. Matters such as the existence of a state of war, the relevance of a treaty, the boundaries of the nation, and the credentials of foreign diplomats have been left to congressional and presidential diplomats. But the Court stated in REID V. COVERT (1957) that even the provisions of a treaty or EXECUTIVE AGREEMENT are reviewable if citizens assert violations of their rights. And, in the face of government claims that the travel of Americans abroad raises diplomatic issues fit only for executive discretion, the Court has enunciated the RIGHT TO TRAVEL abroad and has made substantive rulings for and against claims of that right (KENT V. DULLES, 1958; APTHEKER V. SECRETARY OF STATE, 1964; ZEMEL V. RUSK, 1965).

The Supreme Court's variable commitment to the political question doctrine may be explained by reasons that are nondoctrinal. The Court appears to resort to the doctrine when only two substantive judgments are possible, the first being unacceptable to the Court because it would likely go unenforced and the second being equally unacceptable because it would violate a major tenet of American political ideology. In *Colegrove v. Green*, for example, the plurality suggested that the Illinois legislation might ignore a HOLDING that the legislature's refusal to redesign badly malapportioned congressional districts was unconstitutional—and the House of Representatives might take no action. Yet upholding such a malapportionment, which gave some citizens a vote of far greater weight than that of others, would have run contrary to the American belief that all citizens are equal in the electoral process. Similarly, the Court in *Mississippi v. Johnson* had the choice of deciding that the Reconstruction state governments were illegitimate, a ruling that the President and Congress surely would have ignored; or that the governments, which had been imposed by the federal government on citizens denied the right to participate in the election process, were legitimate—which would have offended the basic American idea of SOVEREIGNTY of the people. In both cases the Court invoked the political question doctrine and left decision in the hands of the "political branches."

The very notion of "political branches," however, is untenable. Article III of the Constitution makes the federal judiciary indirectly accountable insofar as it may enable the people's representatives in Congress to strip the courts of JURISDICTION over matters the people believe the courts to have mishandled. Federal judges, too, are liable to IMPEACHMENT—although this resource has never been taken for purely political purposes since the earliest days of the nineteenth century.

Court decisions necessarily affect power. The decision in PLESSY V. FERGUSON (1896) legitimizing SEPARATE BUT EQUAL railroad cars for black and white passengers encouraged southern states to establish racially segregated schools; the holding of BROWN V. BOARD OF EDUCATION (1954) that "separate but equal" schools violated the equal protection clause stripped the states of that power, transferring the power to define SEGREGATION and integration to the federal courts, the Congress, and, in some cases, to the President. The Court's upholding of ECONOMIC REGULATION affecting wages, hours, unionization, social security, job safety, and competition shifted power from employers to state and federal legislatures, executives, and REGULATORY AGENCIES, as well as to unions, and enabled the United States to consolidate a system of welfare capitalism under which privately owned property is systematically regulated by governmental bodies.

The Court nonetheless insists that the judicial branch is apolitical, because its own institutional power depends on the electorate's belief that the Court is above politics. As JAMES MADISON pointed out in THE FEDERALIST #51, the Court possesses neither the power of the purse nor that of the sword. It is entirely dependent for the enforcement of its decisions on the willingness of the population and public officials to carry them out. Were the Court's decisions to be ignored, the Court's prestige would suffer; in a circular fashion, the loss of prestige would increase the possibility that subsequent decisions would go unheeded.

The Court's decisions find ready compliance when the decisions reflect a societal consensus. The difference between the Court's 1946 *Colegrove* decision that malapportionment was a political question and its contrary 1962 *Baker* decision can be linked to the large-scale movement of population to urban areas underrepresented in the legislatures. By 1962 a majority of the nation's population could be expected to concur in a decision that enhanced its political power. Promise of additional support from the President was implicit in the appearance of Attorney General ROBERT F. KENNEDY before the Court to argue as AMICUS CURIAE for reapportionment, for Kennedy was, of course, the brother of President JOHN F. KENNEDY, who owed his office to urban votes.

The political question device derives its legitimacy from the necessity to preserve an independent judiciary in the American political system. The device is justifiable because it enables the judiciary to maintain its independence by withdrawing from no-win situations. In addition, it prevents the courts from usurping the role of the ballot box. The Supreme Court, declaring the presence of a political question, tacitly admits that it cannot find and therefore cannot ratify a social consensus that does not violate basic American beliefs. The Court has no moral right to impose rules upon a country not yet ready for them. The political question doctrine, which permits the Court to restrain itself from precipitating impossible situations that might tear the social fabric, gives the electorate and its representatives time to work out their own rules, which can ultimately be translated into constitutional doctrine through judicial decision. The doctrine of political questions is more than a self-saving mechanism for the Court; it is also an affirmation of a governmental system based on popular sovereignty.

PHILIPPA STRUM

Bibliography

BICKEL, ALEXANDER M. 1962 *The Least Dangerous Branch.* Indianapolis: Bobbs-Merrill.

SCHARPF, FRITZ W. 1966 Judicial Review and the Political Question: A Functional Analysis. *Yale Law Journal* 75:517–546.

STRUM, PHILIPPA 1974 *The Supreme Court and "Political Questions."* University: University of Alabama Press.

POLK, JAMES KNOX
(1795–1849)

The eleventh President's constitutional beliefs blended STRICT CONSTRUCTION, expediency, and continental vision. He returned to a central theme of Jacksonian constitutionalism to harmonize these divergent interests: the President was the tribune of the people, the only nationally elected federal official.

Polk stressed the SEPARATION OF POWERS in order to legitimate the popularly based presidential power he exercised. He recognized that congressional committees had legitimate claims to information held by the executive branch, but he spurned congressional requests that intruded upon areas of constitutional responsibility he believed assigned to the President, most notably FOREIGN AFFAIRS. He rebuffed, in 1848, Senate advice to negotiate a treaty of extradition with Prussia and to secure the purchase rights of the Hudson's Bay Company on the Columbia River. Yet Polk acknowledged that Congress commanded a broad sphere of constitutional responsibility; he vetoed only three legislative acts.

Polk contributed significantly to the constitutional development of the COMMANDER-IN-CHIEF clause. Unlike ABRAHAM LINCOLN, he believed that the clause granted only military leadership to the President. Yet Polk made use of this power to implement his policy of continentalism. He ordered General ZACHARY TAYLOR into disputed territory between the United States and Mexico knowing that such actions were likely to precipitate hostilities. When the Mexicans responded with force, Congress was left to ratify a war rather than to fulfill its constitutional mandate to declare it. Throughout the ensuing conflict Polk established the precedent that a vigorous conception of the commander-in-chief clause meant control over military affairs.

Tough and efficient, Polk was a transitional figure in the constitutional evolution toward the modern presidency. Unlike his twentieth-century counterparts, Polk, with his strict constructionist beliefs, did not think that the right of self-defense or the inherent authority of the commander-in-chief bestowed on him the power to wage war against another country without congressional authorization.

KERMIT L. HALL

Bibliography

MCCOY, CHARLES A. 1960 *Polk and the Presidency.* Austin: University of Texas Press.

POLLAK, WALTER H.
(1887–1940)

Walter H. Pollak, an active supporter of CIVIL LIBERTIES, argued a number of important cases before the Supreme Court. He represented the defendant in GITLOW V. NEW YORK (1925) and, although he lost that case, succeeded in convincing the Court that the FOURTEENTH AMENDMENT incorporates the FIRST AMENDMENT guarantees of FREEDOM OF THE PRESS and FREEDOM OF SPEECH against the states. With ZECHARIAH CHAFEE, Pollak served on the Wickersham Committee and investigated "lawlessness in law enforcement." He also took part in WHITNEY V. CALIFORNIA (1927) and successfully defended the "Scottsboro boys" in POWELL V. ALABAMA (1932) and NORRIS V. ALABAMA (1935).

DAVID GORDON

POLLOCK v. FARMERS' LOAN & TRUST CO.
157 U.S. 429 and 158 U.S. 601 (1895)

CHARLES EVANS HUGHES called these decisions a "self-inflicted wound" comparable to the decision in DRED SCOTT V. SANDFORD (1857). Here the Supreme Court held unconstitutional an 1894 act of Congress that fixed a flat tax of two percent on all annual incomes over $4,000. Pollock filed a STOCKHOLDER'S SUIT against the trust company to prevent it from complying with the statute which, he claimed, imposed a DIRECT TAX without apportioning it among the states on the basis of population. The trust company, the party of record on the side of the tax, avoided the appearance of collusion by hiring the president of the American Bar Association, JAMES COOLIDGE CARTER; RICHARD OLNEY, attorney general of the United States, was on the same side as AMICUS CURIAE. Theirs was the easy task because history and all the precedents proved that the clause of Article 1, section 9, referring to direct taxes, meant only taxes on people or on land. The Court had so declared in HYLTON V. UNITED STATES (1796) and in several other cases, especially SPRINGER V. UNITED STATES (1881), a direct precedent; the Court there had unanimously sustained an earlier income tax as imposing an indirect tax and therefore not subject to the requirement of apportionment.

Counsel for Pollock, led by JOSEPH H. CHOATE, buttressed a weak case with an impassioned argument intended to provoke judicial fear and reflecting the panic felt by many conservatives. Choate warned that the Court had to choose between "the beginning of socialism and communism" and the preservation of private property, civilization, and the Constitution. He appealed to the Court to substitute its discretion for that of Congress.

Justice HOWELL E. JACKSON not having participated, an eight-member Court decided the case. All agreed that the federal tax on municipal bonds was unconstitutional, because government instrumentalities were exempt from taxation (see INTERGOVERNMENTAL IMMUNITIES). On the question of the validity of the tax on income from personal property, the

Court divided evenly. But on the question of the validity of the tax on income from real estate, the Court voted 6–2 that it was a direct tax unconstitutionally assessed. Nothing favorable can be said about Chief Justice MELVILLE W. FULLER's opinion for the majority. He took for granted the very proposition he should have proved, asserting that a tax on the income from land was indistinguishable from a tax on the land itself. Clearly, however, the income that may derive from rents, timber, oil, minerals, or agriculture is distinguishable from a tax on acreage or on the assessed value of the land itself. Fuller distinguished away the precedents: *Hylton* had decided only that a tax on carriages was not a direct tax, and *Springer* had decided only the narrow point that a tax on a lawyer's fees was not a direct one. Neither case, Fuller declared, dealt with a tax on the income from land, and he made much of the point that such a tax is unique because of the undisputed fact that a tax on the land itself is undoubtedly a direct tax. Justices EDWARD D. WHITE and JOHN MARSHALL HARLAN, dissenting, concluded that history and STARE DECISIS demanded a different ruling, and they warned that when the Court virtually annulled its previous decisions on the basis of the policy preferences of a majority that happened to dominate the bench, the Constitution was in jeopardy.

The tie vote of the Court on all other issues meant that the decision of the CIRCUIT COURT prevailed, leaving in force the taxes on corporate income, wages and salaries, and returns from investments. Accordingly, Choate moved for a rehearing, which was granted, and Justice Jackson attended. The trust company, which was supposed to defend the income tax act, did not retain Carter or replace him, thus leaving Olney to defend it. He took half the time permitted by the Court for his presentation.

The arguments the second time focused on the validity of the tax on the income from personal property, mainly interest and dividends. Fuller, speaking for a bare majority, again read the Court's opinion. Six weeks earlier he had based his position on the uniqueness of a tax on the income from land; now he took the opposite view, reasoning that if a tax on the income from land is a direct tax, so is a tax on the income from personal property. Having found the statute void in significant respects, he reasoned next that the invalidity of some sections contaminated the rest: since the sections were inseparable, all were void because some were.

When Fuller finished his opinion, Harlan began to read his dissent; it sizzled in its language and delivery. He ended a systematic refutation by pounding his desk, shaking his finger in the face of the Chief Justice, and shouting, "On my conscience I regard this decision as a disaster!" (*The Nation* magazine described Harlan as an "agitator" who expounded "the Marx gospel from the bench.") He accused the majority of an unprecedented use of judicial power on behalf of private wealth by striking down a statute whose policy they disliked and by doing it against all law and history. He also pointed out, as did the other dissenters, Justices White, Jackson, and HENRY B. BROWN, that the parts of the statute that were not unconstitutional per se, and might be reenacted if Congress chose, taxed the income of people who earned their money from wages and salaries but who derived no income from land or invested personal property. The decision, said Brown, is "nothing less than a surrender of the taxing power to the moneyed class" making for "a sordid despotism of wealth." It "takes invested wealth," said White, and "reads it into the Constitution as a favored and protected class of property. . . ." It was, said Jackson, "the most disastrous blow ever struck at the constitutional power of congress" and made the tax burden fall "most heavily and oppressively upon those having the least ability" to pay.

Public opinion was opposed to the Court, though it had vigorous supporters especially among the Republican newspapers in the East. The *New York Sun* exclaimed in delight, "Five to Four, the Court Stands Like a Rock." The *New York Herald Tribune* hailed the Court for halting a "communist revolution." The Democratic party, however, recommended an amendment to the Constitution vesting Congress with the power denied by the Court. The SIXTEENTH AMENDMENT was not ratified, though, until 1913, by which time the nation's maldistribution of wealth had intensified. For eighteen years, as EDWARD S. CORWIN wrote, "the veto of the Court held the sun and moon at pause," while the great fortunes went untaxed. The government during that time raised almost all of its revenues from EXCISE TAXES and tariffs, whose burden fell mainly on consumers. In 1913 the average annual income in the United States was $375 per capita.

LEONARD W. LEVY

Bibliography

CORWIN, EDWARD S. 1932 *Court over Constitution.* Pages 177–209. Princeton, N.J.: Princeton University Press.

KING, WILLARD L. 1950 *Melville Weston Fuller.* Pages 193–221. New York: Macmillan.

PAUL, ARNOLD M. 1960 *Conservative Crisis and the Rule of Law: Attitudes of Bar and Bench, 1887–1895.* Pages 159–220. Ithaca, N.Y.: Cornell University Press.

SHIRAS, GEORGE, 3RD and SHIRAS, WINFIELD 1953 *Justice George Shiras Jr. of Pittsburgh.* Pages 160–183. Pittsburgh: University of Pittsburgh Press.

POLLOCK v. WILLIAMS
322 U.S. 4 (1944)

A Florida statute made the failure to perform services according to an agreement (for which an advance had been made) *prima facie* evidence of an intent to defraud. The Supreme Court, in an opinion by Justice ROBERT H. JACKSON, voided the statute, 7–2, as a violation of the THIRTEENTH AMENDMENT and of the Anti-Peonage Act of 1867. At issue before the Court was a HABEAS CORPUS petition for "an illiterate Negro laborer in the toils of law for the want of $5." His failure to perform agreed-upon labor for that advance resulted in a $100 fine, in default of which he was sentenced to sixty days' imprisonment. Jackson held that the Thirteenth Amendment and the Anti-Peonage Act "raised both a shield and a sword against forced labor because of debt."

DAVID GORDON

POLL TAX

A poll tax (CAPITATION TAX, head tax) is typically levied on every adult (or adult male) within the taxing JURISDICTION. An old technique for raising revenue, the tax in its compulsory form raises no important constitutional questions. (Under Article I, section 9, Congress can levy a poll tax only by apportionment to the national census. Congress has not in fact raised revenue this way.)

Serious constitutional issues have been raised in this century by poll taxes whose payment is "voluntary," enforced only by conditioning voter registration on their payment. Early in the nation's history, payment of such taxes came to replace property ownership as a qualification for voting. By the Civil War, however, widespread acceptance of universal suffrage had virtually eliminated the poll tax as a condition on voting.

In a number of southern states, the poll tax returned in the 1890s along with SEGREGATION as a means of maintaining white supremacy. In theory and in early practice, poor whites as well as blacks were kept from voting by this means. Later, however, some registrars learned to use the device mainly for purposes of RACIAL DISCRIMINATION, requiring only black would-be voters to produce their receipts for poll tax payments—in some states for payments going back to the voter's twenty-first year. The poll tax gradually fell from favor as a means of keeping blacks from voting; "good character" requirements and LITERACY TESTS, for example, were more readily adapted to this purpose. By 1940 only seven states retained the poll tax as a voting condition.

In BREEDLOVE V. SUTTLES (1937), a case involving a white applicant for registration, the Supreme Court upheld Georgia's use of the poll tax as a condition on voting. The poll tax remained a CIVIL RIGHTS issue, kept alive in Congress by the regular introduction of bills to abolish its use. Southern committee chairmanships and senatorial filibusters succeeded in sidetracking this legislation. When the TWENTY-FOURTH AMENDMENT was finally submitted to the states in 1962, it forbade the use of poll taxes as a condition on voting only in federal, not state, elections. The Amendment was ratified in 1964.

Two years later, the Supreme Court held, in HARPER V. VIRGINIA BOARD OF ELECTIONS (1966), that conditioning voting in state elections on poll tax payments denied the EQUAL PROTECTION OF THE LAWS. Only four states still retained the device, but its elimination eloquently symbolized the relation between VOTING RIGHTS and the equal CITIZENSHIP of all Americans.

KENNETH L. KARST

Bibliography

MYRDAL, GUNNAR 1944 *An American Dilemma: The Negro Problem and Modern Democracy.* Chaps. 22–23. New York: Harper & Brothers.

POLYGAMY

Because polygamy was one of the early tenets of the Mormon Church, the movement to eradicate plural marriage became bound up with religious persecution. The Supreme Court has consistently held that the FIRST AMENDMENT'S protections of RELIGIOUS LIBERTY do not protect the practice of plural marriage. Thus REYNOLDS V. UNITED STATES (1879) upheld a criminal conviction for polygamy in the Territory of Utah, and DAVIS V. BEASON (1880) upheld a conviction for voting in the Territory of Idaho in violation of an oath required of all registrants forswearing belief in polygamy. The corporate charter of the Mormon Church in the Territory of Utah was revoked, and its property forfeited to the government, in CHURCH OF JESUS CHRIST OF LATTER-DAY SAINTS V. UNITED STATES (1890). The church's First Amendment claim was waved away with the statement that belief in polygamy was not a religious tenet but a "pretense" that was "contrary to the spirit of Christianity."

It would be comforting if this judicial record were confined to the nineteenth century, but it was not. In *Cleveland v. United States* (1946), the Court upheld a conviction of Mormons under the MANN ACT for transporting women across state lines for the purpose of "debauchery" that took the form of living with them in polygamous marriage. The Court's opinion, citing the nineteenth-century cases and even quoting the "spirit of Christianity" language with approval, was written by none other than Justice WILLIAM O. DOUGLAS.

More recently, the Court has recognized a constitutional right to marry, and in a number of contexts has afforded protection for a FREEDOM OF INTIMATE ASSOCIATION. (See MARRIAGE AND THE CONSTITUTION.) With or without the ingredient of religious freedom, SUBSTANTIVE DUE PROCESS doctrine seems amply to justify an extension of these rights to plural marriage among competent consenting adults. Yet the force of conventional morality in constitutional adjudication should not be underestimated; the Supreme Court is not just the architect of principle but an institution of government. Polygamy is not on the verge of becoming a constitutional right.

KENNETH L. KARST

Bibliography

LARSON, GUSTAVE O. 1971 *The "Americanization" of Utah for Statehood.* San Marino, Calif.: Huntington Library.

POMEROY, JOHN NORTON

See: Commentators on the Constitution

POPULAR SOVEREIGNTY

"Popular sovereignty" was a solution proposed by some northern Democrats to the problem of slavery's access to the TERRITORIES. As an alternative to the WILMOT PROVISO, Michigan Senator Lewis Cass proposed in 1847 that slavery be left "to the people inhabiting [the territories] to regulate their internal concerns their own way." He later concluded that congressional prohibition of SLAVERY IN THE TERRITORIES was unconstitutional. Popular sovereignty was a radical innovation: never before had residents of the territories been thought to be invested with SOVEREIGNTY, let alone a territorial sovereignty implying that the federal government lacked substantive regulatory power over the territories.

Illinois Senator STEPHEN A. DOUGLAS took up popular sovereignty in 1854, recommending that the MISSOURI COMPROMISE be jettisoned in order to get the slavery question out of Congress and leave it to the settlers of the territories. Though adopted in the KANSAS-NEBRASKA ACT, popular sovereignty soon fell into disfavor in both the North and the South. Douglas and other northern Democrats rejected the travesty made of it by President JAMES BUCHANAN in his attempt to force slavery into Kansas, while southern leaders abandoned it in favor of a constitutional program that would have forced slavery into all the territories.

WILLIAM M. WIECEK

Bibliography

JOHANNSEN, ROBERT W. 1973 *Stephen A. Douglas.* New York: Oxford University Press.

POPULAR SOVEREIGNTY (in Democratic Political Theory)

The Constitution's first words bespeak its derivation from popular authority: "We the people of the United States . . . do ordain and establish this Constitution." The DECLARATION OF INDEPENDENCE expresses the principle of this act: "to secure these rights, governments are instituted among men, deriving their just powers from the consent of the governed." The specific doctrine of popular sovereignty behind these familiar phrases still needs to be clarified and distinguished from related but distinct doctrines.

This doctrine of popular SOVEREIGNTY relates primarily not to the Constitution's operation but to its source of authority and supremacy, ratification, amendment, and possible abolition. When JAMES MADISON wrote in THE FEDERALIST #49 that "the people are the only legitimate fountain of power," he referred to what he had called in *The Federalist* #40 (paraphrasing the Declaration) "the transcendent and precious right of the people to 'abolish or alter their governments.' " Legitimate power derives primarily from the people's original consent to their form of government, not from their continuing role in it. Because popular consent is the "pure, original fountain of all legitimate authority," ALEXANDER HAMILTON, in *The Federalist* #22, presents the RATIFICATION OF THE CONSTITUTION by conventions specially elected by the people, a mode recently pioneered by the states, as crucial to its legitimacy. *The Federalist* both opens and closes remarking that for a whole people so to choose their constitution by voluntary consent, far from being typical, is an unprecedented prodigy.

This American mode of popular consent to the institution of government formalized the notion in JOHN LOCKE's *Second Treatise* of "the Constitution of the Legislative being the original and supreme act of the Society, antecedent to all positive Laws in it, and depending wholly on the People." It provides a peaceful, certain, and solemn alternative to violent and irregular acts but remains ultimately an expression of the right to revolution; Madison almost admits in *The Federalist* #40 that adoption of the Constitution was authorized not under the ARTICLES OF CONFEDERATION but only by popular consent as an exercise of revolutionary right. Such popular sovereignty could always be exercised again not only by regular amendment but by revolution.

For the Founders, legitimate government not only had to derive its powers originally from the consent of the people but also had to gain the consent of their regularly elected representatives to legislate for them and tax them. The revolutionary controversy was fundamentally waged, first, over the American invocation of Locke's position that government "must *not raise Taxes* on the Property of the People, *without the Consent of the People,* given by themselves, or their Deputies," and then over its extension to no legislation without REPRESENTATION.

Such popular sovereignty still is not identical with popular government. The Founders generally regarded the British constitution, for example, with its hereditary king and lords, as a legitimate and even free government because the British (unlike the American) people were represented (albeit imperfectly) in the House of Commons. Republican government, although the form of government best exhibiting the capacity of mankind for self-government, was not the only form compatible with popular consent as the basis of legitimate power. Because Madison correctly believed that the character of the American people makes them unlikely to exercise their sovereign right to replace their republican government with one of another form, this point is relevant less to our domestic than to our foreign policy, which in principle should recognize the right of other sovereign peoples to consent to other forms of government.

Republican government itself differs for the Founders from the populism some later doctrines equate with popular sovereignty. *The Federalist* treats republican government as a species of popular government in that it is administered by officials appointed directly or indirectly by the people and holding office for limited periods or during GOOD BEHAVIOR. It differs from the other species, which they called "democracy" and by which they meant direct democracy, by its reliance on representation. *The Federalist* regards this difference not as an evil necessitated by size (as some Anti-Federalists did) but as a superiority making possible both size, with all its advantages, and government by "men who possess most wisdom to discern, and most virtue to pursue, the common good of the society." (THOMAS JEFFERSON in a letter to JOHN ADAMS called such republican officials "the natural aristocracy.") Republican representatives should refine and enlarge the public views because the reason, not the passion, the cool and deliberate sense, not the temporary errors and delusions, of the public should prevail. The Founders regarded the American republic as embodying the sovereignty of the public reason because it was so constructed as to encourage representatives, especially the Senate, President, and courts, to withstand popular error and passion until popular good sense could respond to argument and events. Their opinion that such an outcome would generally emerge in the few years allowed by the Constitution reveals confidence in both representatives and constituents as well as distrust.

The supremacy of the Constitution and JUDICIAL REVIEW, distinctive features of American CONSTITUTIONALISM, are paradoxical results of this doctrine of popular sovereignty. Hamilton in *The Federalist* #78, like JOHN MARSHALL in MARBURY V. MADISON (1803), based them on the Constitution's being the special act of the sovereign people: "the Constitution ought to be preferred to the statute, the intention of the people to the intention of their agents." The equation of popular sovereignty with the supremacy of the Constitution, let alone with judicial review, may become problematic once the people who ordained and established the Constitution are long dead. Jefferson suggested in a letter to an unpersuaded Madison that all constitutions naturally expire every generation. Madison in reply adduced the danger of faction and the need of even the most rational government for the prejudice that results from stability, but Jefferson continued to believe in the right of each generation to choose its own form of government. The jural argument for constitutional supremacy was stated by Hamilton in *Phocion* #2 (and echoed in *The Federalist* #78): "The constitution is the compact made between the society at large and each individual. The society therefore, cannot without breach of faith and injustice, refuse to any individual, a single advantage which he derives under that compact . . . until the compact is dissolved with the same solemnity and certainty with which it was made." Ultimately the identity of popular sovereignty with constitutional supremacy depends on an enlightened public opinion animated by the spirit of the Constitution.

That the Founders tended not to call the doctrine expounded here "popular sovereignty" reflects their being republicans and constitutionalists rather than populists. Not the people simply but their reason especially as solemnly embodied in their Constitution is sovereign. More fundamentally, since governments are instituted by consent "to secure these rights," their legitimacy depends not only on consent but on the security of individual rights. Debates such as that over "popular sovereignty" between ABRAHAM LINCOLN and STEPHEN DOUGLAS reveal the potential tension between popular consent and equal rights.

NATHAN TARCOV

Bibliography

EPSTEIN, DAVID F. 1984 *The Political Theory of the Federalist.* Chicago: University of Chicago Press.

JAFFA, HARRY V. (1959)1982 *Crisis of the House Divided: An Interpretation of the Issues in the Lincoln-Douglas Debates.* Chicago: University of Chicago Press.

TARCOV, NATHAN 1985 American Constitutionalism and Individual Rights. Pages 101–125 in Robert Goldwin and William Schambra, eds., *How Does the Constitution Secure Rights?* Washington, D.C.: American Enterprise Institute.

PORNOGRAPHY

The Supreme Court's OBSCENITY decisions define the forms of pornography that are protected from censorship by the FIRST AMENDMENT. As a practical matter, this protection is quite broad. Most pornography is also a unique kind of speech: about women, for men. In an era when sexual equality is a social ideal, the constitutional protection of pornography is a vexing political issue. Should pornographic imagery of male dominance and female subordination be repudiated through censorship, or will censorship inevitably destroy our commitment to free speech?

In ROTH V. UNITED STATES (1957) the Court found obscene speech to be unworthy of First Amendment protection because it forms "no essential part of any exposition of ideas." Yet precisely because of pornography's ideational content, some of it was deemed harmful and made criminal. The Court could avoid examining the specific nature of this harm, once it had located obscenity conveniently outside the constitutional pale. But it could not avoid defining obscenity, and thereby identifying the justification for its censorship.

The essential characteristic of "obscene" pornography is its appeal to one's "prurient interest," which is a genteel reference to its capacity to stimulate physical arousal and carnal desire. But such pornography must also be "offensive," and so, to be censored, sex-stimulant speech must be both arousing and disgusting. The meaning of offensiveness depends upon the subjective judgment of the observer, and is best captured by Justice POTTER STEWART's famous aphorism in JACOBELLIS V. OHIO (1964): "I know it when I see it."

Given the limitations of the criminal process, obscenity laws did not make offensive pornography unavailable in the marketplace. As HARRY KALVEN, JR. pointed out, few judges took the evils of obscenity very seriously, although constitutional rhetoric made the law appear to be "solemnly concerned with the sexual fantasies of the adult population." The Court's chief goal was the protection of admired works of art and literature, not the elimination of pornographic magazines at the corner drug store. Sporadic obscenity prosecutions may occur in jurisdictions where the "contemporary community standard" of offensiveness allows convictions under MILLER V. CALIFORNIA (1973). But the constitutional validity of a legal taboo on "hard-core" pornography became largely irrelevant to its suppliers and consumers, even as that material became sexually explicit and more violent in its imagery during the 1970s.

That same decade saw a legal revolution in equality between the sexes, embodied in judicial decisions based on the guarantees of EQUAL PROTECTION and DUE PROCESS. Women won legal rights to control and define their own sexuality, through litigation establishing rights to contraception and abortion, and through legislative reforms easing restrictions on prosecutions for sexual assault. Pornography also became a women's issue, as feminists such as Catharine MacKinnon attacked it as "a form of forced sex, a practice of sexual politics, an institution of gender inequality." Women marched and demonstrated against films and magazines portraying them as beaten, chained, or mutilated objects of sexual pleasure for men. In 1984, their protests took a legal form when MacKinnon and Andrea Dworkin drafted an ordinance adopted by the Indianapolis City Council, outlawing some types of pornography as acts of SEX DISCRIMINATION.

By using the concept of equal protection as a basis to attack pornographic speech, the council set up a dramatic assault upon First Amendment doctrine, making embarrassed enemies out of old constitutional friends. As a strategic matter, however, the council needed a COMPELLING STATE INTEREST to justify censorship of speech that did not fall into the obscenity category. The ordinance defined offensive pornography more broadly than *Miller*'s standards allow, because it went beyond a ban on displays of specific human body parts or sexual acts. Instead, it prohibited the "graphic sexually explicit subordination of women" through their portrayals as, for example, "sexual objects who enjoy pain or humiliation," or "sexual objects for domination, conquest, violation, exploitation, possession or use."

As a philosophical matter, sex discrimination is a good constitutional metaphor for the harms attributed to pornography, namely, the loss of equal CITIZENSHIP status for women through the "bigotry and contempt" promoted by the imagery of subordination. But as a matter of DOCTRINE, the causal link between the social presence of pornography and the harms of discrimination is fatally remote. Free speech gospel dictates that "offensive speech" may be censored only upon proof of imminent, tangible harm to individuals, such as violent insurrection (BRANDENBURG V. OHIO, 1969), a physical assault (COHEN V. CALIFORNIA, 1971), or reckless tortious injury to reputation (NEW YORK TIMES V. SULLIVAN, 1964). The closest historical analogue to the creation of a cause of action for classwide harm from speech is the criminal GROUP LIBEL statute upheld by a 5–4 Supreme Court in BEAUHARNAIS V. ILLINOIS (1952). But this remedy has been implicitly discredited by *New York Times* and *Brandenburg*, given its CHILLING EFFECT upon uninhibited criticism of political policies and officials.

It came as no surprise when early court decisions struck down Indianapolis-type ordinances as void for vagueness, as an unlawful PRIOR RESTRAINT on speech, and as an unjustified restriction of protected speech as defined by the earlier obscenity decisions. The courts could accept neither the equal protection rationale nor the breadth of the ordinances' scope, as both would permit too great an encroachment upon the freedoms of expression and consumption of art, literature, and political messages. Ironically, it is the potentially endemic quality of the imagery of women's subordination that defeats any attempt to place a broad taboo upon it.

Eva Feder Kittay has posed the question, "How is it that within our society, men can derive a sexual charge out of seeing a woman brutalized?" Her answer to that loaded question is that our conceptions of sexuality are permeated with conceptions of domination, because we have eroticized the relations of power: men eroticize sexual conquering, and women eroticize being possessed. Pornography becomes more than a harmless outlet for erotic fantasies when it makes violence appear to be intrinsically erotic, rather than something that is eroticized. The social harm of such pornography is that it brutalizes our moral imagination, "the source of that imaginative possibility by which we can identify with others and hence form maxims having a universal validity."

The constitutional source for an analysis of brutalizing pornography lies in the richly generative symbols of First Amendment law itself. That law already contains the tolerance for insistence "on observance of the civic culture's norms of social equality," in the words of Kenneth L. Karst. Any acceptable future taboo would be likely to take the form of a ban on public display of a narrowly defined class of pictorial imagery, simply because that would be a traditional, readily enforceable compromise between free speech and equality. Any taboo would be mostly symbolic, but it would matter. Only by limiting the taboo can we avoid descending into the Orwellian hell where censorship is billed as freedom.

CATHERINE HANCOCK

Bibliography

BRYDEN, DAVID 1985 Between Two Constitutions: Feminism and Pornography. *Constitutional Commentary* 2:147–189.

KALVEN, HARRY, JR. 1960 The Metaphysics of Obscenity. *Supreme Court Review* 1960:1–45.

KITTAY, EVA FEDER 1983 Pornography and the Erotics of Domination. Pages 145–174 in Carol C. Gould, ed., *Beyond Domination: New Perspectives on Women and Philosophy.* Totowa, N.J.: Rowman & Allanheld.

MACKINNON, CATHARINE A. 1984 Not a Moral Issue. *Yale Law & Policy Review* 2:321–345.

NOTE 1984 Anti-Pornography Laws and First Amendment Values. *Harvard Law Review* 98:460–481.

POSSE COMITATUS ACT
20 Stat. 145 (1878)

Representative James P. Knott (Democrat of Kentucky) introduced this act as an amendment to the Army Appropriation Act of 1878. It provides that "it shall not be lawful to employ any part of the Army of the United States, as a posse comitatus, or otherwise, for the purpose of executing the laws" except as specifically authorized by Congress. The act has applied to the Air Force since 1947; it has been extended to the Navy and Marine Corps by administrative regulations. Originally enacted as a step in the dismantling of Reconstruction, this provision banned the practice implicitly authorized by the JUDICIARY ACT OF 1789, and used before the Civil War to enforce the FUGITIVE SLAVE ACT, of including military forces in the federal marshal's posse. The act remains on the books (section 1835, Title 18, United States Code) as an expression of the fundamental division between the military and civilian realms: the armed forces are not a LAW ENFORCEMENT agency.

Congress has authorized the use of the armed forces to suppress insurrection, domestic violence, unlawful combination, or conspiracy that obstructs the execution of federal law or impedes the course of justice, or that deprives any class of people of constitutional rights that the state authorities cannot or will not protect. That provision of the FORCE ACT OF 1871 (now section 333, Title 10, United States Code) was invoked by President DWIGHT D. EISENHOWER in 1958 when he used Army units to disperse the mob in Little Rock, Arkansas, that resisted a federal court's school DESEGREGATION order (see COOPER V. AARON), and by President RICHARD M. NIXON, in 1970, when he ordered federal troops to assist in quelling a riot in Detroit, Michigan.

DENNIS J. MAHONEY

POSTAL POWER

Seven words of Article I, section 8, of the Constitution grant the postal power to Congress. Under the power "To Establish Post Offices and Post Roads" liberally construed, Congress has built offices and constructed roads for handling the mails and maintained an extensive nationwide delivery service. Congress has vested in the Postal Service, now in corporate form, monopoly powers over the delivery of letters and extensive, though often untested, POLICE POWERS over the mails.

The postal system in the United States traces its roots to a 1692 crown patent to Thomas Neale by William and Mary, granting a monopoly of the colonial posts, including all profits therefrom. The Post Office was established on July 26, 1775, by the CONTINENTAL CONGRESS to assure effective communications and to eliminate what was viewed as a tax by the British Post Office. The ARTICLES OF CONFEDERATION granted exclusive postal power to Congress, and the Constitution carried forward the congressional power over the mails.

At the time of the CONSTITUTIONAL CONVENTION the activities of the Post Office were widely accepted, and there was little sentiment for change or elaboration. Indeed, the postal power was virtually undebated, and only one reference to it is to be found in THE FEDERALIST. The breadth of the congressional interpretation of the postal power, therefore, finds neither support nor contradiction in the Constitution or the debates concerning its adoption.

The postal monopoly, contained in the so-called private express statutes, generally makes it unlawful for private carriers to carry letters and packets, unless postage has been paid thereon and canceled. This provision is, in effect, a 100 percent tax on the carrying of letters outside the Postal Service. The monopoly dates from colonial days, and it was and is justified on the economic grounds that it is necessary to retain monopoly power over profitable routes and services so that the Postal Service can provide uniform and inexpensive service nationwide, even along uneconomic and remote routes. The Articles of Confederation specifically granted the monopoly, giving the Congress "sole and exclusive power." The absence of these words in Article I, section 8, leaves the constitutionality of the monopoly unclear, but the few courts that have considered the question have held in its favor. Historically, monopoly had been an integral feature of the British and colonial postal systems, as well as those of many other Western nations.

The extent of the postal power has been the subject of debate in the Congress and of occasional litigation. The earliest questions concerned post roads: did Congress have authority to construct new roads, or only to designate existing state roads as postal routes? The issue had not been discussed by the Framers or, with one exception (New York), at the state conventions. Congress determined that it had power to appropriate funds to construct post roads, but not to construct them directly. The Supreme Court had never decided the question, although Chief Justice JOHN MARSHALL in OBITER DICTUM in MCCULLOCH V. MARYLAND (1819) suggested that the power included construction. In the construction of the first of these roads, the Cumberland Road, Congress and the President adopted a working compromise by seeking the consent of the affected states prior to approval of the bill. Many other post roads were constructed following similar procedures. The Supreme Court ultimately put the question of construction authority to rest in *Kohl v. United States* (1876) by holding that the federal government may condemn land, by analogy to EMINENT DOMAIN, for a post office site.

Postal statutes and regulations grant police powers to the Postal Service, imposing rules designed to protect the public welfare and limiting mailability. Safety regulations (for example, mailability of poisons and explosives) and mechanical rules (size and packaging standard), have not been the subject of serious challenge. The statute imposing fines and imprisonment for mail fraud was held constitutional in *Public Clearing House v. Coyne* (1904) and several later cases. Other statutory determinations of nonmailability have similarly been upheld. *Ex parte Jackson* (1878) upheld a criminal conviction under a federal statute prohibiting mailing of newspapers containing advertisements for lotteries. In the late eighteenth and early nineteenth centuries, relying on *Jackson* and other holdings, Congress greatly expanded the exclusionary power to cover libelous matter, OBSCENITY, and the like, and these provisions remain a part of present law. The Supreme Court has repeatedly upheld the constitutionality of the congressional power to exclude obscene materials from the mails.

From 1872 until 1970, the Post Office was an executive department and the postmaster general had CABINET status. Prompted by heavy economic losses from Post Office operations, problems with postal deliveries, and charges of political inefficiency, Congress in 1970 created the United States Postal Service to take over the functions of the Post Office Department. Removing the operations of the Post Office (including appointment of the postmaster general) from direct political influence and granting to the Post Office a substantial degree of fiscal autonomy were among the major objects of the reorganization. The new Postal System is organized as a public CORPORATION, owned entirely by the federal government, under the management of a board of governors. The board appoints the postmaster general, who is the chief executive officer of the Postal Service, but is no longer a cabinet member. The board and the officers have wide discretion with respect to management, services, and expenditures, subject to congressional oversight. Postal rates, formerly established directly by Congress, are now determined by a presidentially appointed Postal Rate Commission on the basis of recommendations made by the board of governors.

STANLEY SIEGEL

Bibliography

JOHNSTON, JOSEPH F., JR. 1968 The United States Postal Monopoly. *Business Lawyer* 23:379–405.

PAUL, JAMES C. and SCHWARTZ, MURRAY L. 1961 *Federal Censorship: Obscenity in the Mail.* New York: Free Press.

PROJECT: POST OFFICE 1968 *Southern California Law Review* 41:643–727.

ROGERS, LINDSAY 1916 *The Postal Power of Congress.* Baltimore: Johns Hopkins University Press.

POUND, ROSCOE
(1870–1964)

Roscoe Pound was a prominent legal educator, a distinguished philosopher of law, and a prolific writer. His major contribution to American law was his formative role in the development of SOCIOLOGICAL JURISPRUDENCE. He elaborated this instrumentalist approach during the Progressive era, the spirit of which pervaded his writings. His thought had a conservative side to it, however, which became more influential in the latter stages of his life. He expressed this conservatism not only in his eulogies of the COMMON LAW but also in his criticism of the New Deal and the "service state," his indictment of administrative tribunals, and his fulminations against LEGAL REALISM.

Although Pound did not specialize in constitutional law, he promoted better understanding of the realities of the judicial process in this field through his critique of MECHANICAL JURISPRUDENCE, his explanation of the broad scope of judicial discretion and JUDICIAL POLICYMAKING, and his contrast between the "law in the books and the law in action." He was also a trenchant critic of the extreme individualism underlying numerous decisions of the Supreme Court well into the twentieth century.

The quality of Pound's voluminous writings, which spanned almost the entire *corpus juris,* varied substantially. His best scholarship consisted, in the main, of his influential articles on legal thought and reform published from 1905 to 1916. These works included "Liberty of Contract" (1909), which was one of his few publications to focus on constitutional questions. *The Spirit of the Common Law* (1921), *The Formative Era of American Law* (1938), and *The Development of Constitutional Guarantees of Liberty* (1957) are today his most useful books for students of constitutional law and history. His *Jurisprudence* (1959) was the most comprehensive statement of his legal philosophy.

WILFRID E. RUMBLE

Bibliography

WIGDOR, DAVID 1974 *Roscoe Pound.* Westport, Conn.: Greenwood Press.

POVERTY

See: Indigent; Wealth Discrimination

POWELL, LEWIS F.
(1907–)

Lewis Franklin Powell, Jr., has always eluded conventional portraiture. In broad brush, Powell appears the archetypal conservative: a successful corporate lawyer, a director of eleven major companies, a pillar of Richmond, Virginia's civic and social life. The roll call of legal honors—president of the American Bar Association, the American College of Trial Lawyers, and the American Bar Foundation—does little to dispel the impression.

The portrait, however, needs serious refinement. During Virginia's "massive resistance," when the Byrd organization chose to close public schools rather than accept racial integration, Powell, as chairman of the Richmond Public School Board, fought successfully to keep Richmond's open. As vice-president of the National Legal Aid and Defender Society, he helped persuade the organized bar to support publicly financed legal services for the poor. Jean Camper Cahn, a black leader with whom he worked in that endeavor, found Powell "so curiously shy, so deeply sensitive to the hurt or embarrassment of another, so self-effacing that it is difficult to reconcile the public and private man—the honors and the acclaim with the gentle, courteous, sensitive spirit that one senses in every conversation, no matter how casual. . . ."

The portrait of the private practitioner parallels that of the Supreme Court Justice. The broad picture is again one of orthodox adherence to the canons of restraint. Powell labored diligently to limit the powers of the federal courts. He sought to narrow the STANDING of litigants invoking federal JURISDICTION to instances of actual injury in WARTH V. SELDIN (1975). He dissented when the Court in *Cannon v. University of Chicago* (1979) inferred from federal statutes a private cause of action. He greatly restricted the power of federal judges to review claims of unlawful SEARCH AND SEIZURE raised by state defendants in STONE V. POWELL (1976). And he urged the sharp curtailment of federal equitable remedies such as student BUSING for racial balance, in cases like KEYES V. DENVER SCHOOL DISTRICT #1 (1973).

While working to limit federal judicial power, Powell championed the power of others to operate free of constitutional strictures. Thus prosecutors should enjoy discretion in initiating prosecution, police and GRAND JURIES in pursuing EVIDENCE, trial judges in questioning jurors, welfare workers in terminating assistance, and military officers in conducting training. The "hands-off" view applied especially to public education. Powell, a former member of the Virginia Board of Education, wrote the Court opinion preserving the rights of states to devise their own systems of public school finance in SAN ANTONIO SCHOOL DISTRICT V. RODRIGUEZ (1973). And the former chairman of the Richmond School Board spoke for the broad discretion of school authorities to administer student suspensions and corporal punishment, dissenting in GOSS V. LOPEZ (1975) and writing for the Court in INGRAHAM V. WRIGHT (1977).

Even so, a corner of the jurist's nature has been reserved for personal circumstances of particular poignancy. An early opinion afforded a black construction worker in Mississippi, father of nine, the opportunity to confront his accusers and establish his innocence in *Chambers v. Mississippi* (1973). Another Powell opinion, in MOORE V. EAST CLEVELAND (1977), voided a municipal housing ordinance that prevented an elderly woman from living with her adult sons and grandchildren. Another, SOLEM V. HELM (1983), held unconstitutional a life sentence without parole imposed by state courts on the perpetrator of seven nonviolent felonies. Even in the sacrosanct area of education, the Justice concurred in PLYLER V. DOE (1982) rather than leave children of illegal aliens "on the streets uneducated."

The cases of compassion are remarkable in one respect. Vindication of the individual claims meant overriding the most cherished of Powell's conservative tenets: the protection of state criminal judgments from meddlesome review on petition for federal writs of HABEAS CORPUS, and the recognition of only those rights tied closely to the constitutional text. Powell, plainly nervous about damaging these principles, narrowed the rulings almost to their actual facts. The cases thus testify both to a strength and a weakness in the jurist, the strength being that of an open mind and heart, the weakness being that of cautious case-by-case adjudication that leaves law bereft of general guidance and sure content.

The dichotomy between the cases of compassion and the towering doctrinal efforts of the school finance case (*Rodriguez*) and the search and seizure case (*Stone*) illustrates the different dimensions of the man himself. Powell, for example, privately deplored the arrogance of the national communications media and the maleficence of the criminal element. But he was, by nature, reserved, considerate, as eager to listen as to talk. Thus, even on subjects of strong feeling, the tempered judgment often triumphed. This quality marked his opinions dealing with the press. In a concurrence more libertarian than the Court opinion he joined in BRANZBURG V. HAYES (1972), Powell urged that "a proper balance" be struck on a "case-by-case basis" between the claims of newsmen to protect the confidentiality of sources and the need of grand juries for information relevant to criminal conduct. In GERTZ V. ROBERT WELSH INC. (1974), perhaps his most important opinion on the FIRST AMENDMENT, Powell balanced a plaintiff's interest in his good reputation against press freedoms, permitting private citizens to recover in libel on a standard less than "knowing or reckless falsehood" but greater than liability without fault. Balancing of individual and societal claims characterized Powell's opinions involving the rights of radical campus organizations, the unconventional use of national symbols, and even many criminal cases, where fact-specific rulings on the admissibility of suspect LINEUPS, for example, began to replace the per se EXCLUSIONARY RULES of the WARREN COURT.

Balancing does not permit confident forecasting of appellate outcomes. Case-by-case weighing of facts and circumstances can constitute a dangerous delegation of the Supreme Court's own authority on constitutional matters to trial judges, police and prosecutors, and potential litigants, all of whom capitalize on the uncertainty of law to work their own wills. But balancing suited Powell's preference for a devolution of authority and, in cases like GERTZ, achieved a thoughtful accommodation of competing interests.

In his most famous opinion, UNIVERSITY OF CALIFORNIA REGENTS V. BAKKE (1978), Powell, the balancer, struck a middle course on the flammable question of benign preferences based on race. The immediate question in *Bakke* was whether the medical school of the University of California at Davis could set aside sixteen of one hundred places in its entering class for preferred minorities. Eight Justices took polar positions. Four argued that Title VI of the CIVIL RIGHTS ACT OF 1964 prohibited any preference based on race. Four others contended that both the act and the constitution permitted the Davis program. Powell, the ninth and deciding Justice, alone sought to accommodate both the American belief in the primacy of the individual and the need to heal a history of oppression based on race.

It has become common to note that the Supreme Court under WARREN E. BURGER did not, as some feared, dismantle the activist legacy of the Warren Court. Many of the influential Justices, Powell, POTTER STEWART, and BYRON R. WHITE among them, were more pragmatic than ideological. Thus the Court trimmed here, expanded there, and approached complex questions cautiously. Powell's opinions exhibit, as much as those of any Justice, this Court's composite frame of mind. Like him, the Court he served has eluded conventional description.

J. HARVIE WILKINSON III

Bibliography

GUNTHER, GERALD 1972 In Search of Judicial Quality in a Changing Court: The Case of Justice Powell. *Stanford Law Review* 24:1001–1035.

HOWARD, A. E. DICK 1972 Mr. Justice Powell and the Emerging Nixon Majority. *Michigan Law Review* 70:445–468.

SYMPOSIUM 1977 [Justice Lewis F. Powell] *University of Richmond Law Review* 11:259–445.

SYMPOSIUM 1982 [Justice Lewis F. Powell] *Virginia Law Review* 68:161–458.

POWELL, THOMAS REED
(1880–1955)

Constitutional lawyer and political scientist Thomas Reed Powell taught for twenty-five years at Harvard Law School. He was a prolific writer of articles on constitutional law and especially on the issues of STATE TAXATION OF COMMERCE and INTERGOVERNMENTAL IMMUNITIES from taxation. His published analyses of constitutional DOCTRINES and Supreme Court decisions frequently influenced the future course of constitutional law, as, for example, in reducing the protection from taxation afforded by the ORIGINAL PACKAGE DOCTRINE. He was also a commentator on the activities of the Supreme Court: he was critical of its anti-New Deal decisions in the 1930s, of the proliferation of separate opinions in the 1940s, and of the prevalence of rhetorical excess over rigorous logic at all times. His last public lectures were published in 1956 as *Vagaries and Varieties in Constitutional Law.*

DENNIS J. MAHONEY

POWELL v. ALABAMA
287 U.S. 45 (1932)

Powell was the famous "Scottsboro boys" case in which "young, ignorant, illiterate blacks were convicted and sentenced to death without the effective appointment of counsel to aid them. The trials were in a hostile community, far from the defendants' homes; the accusation was rape of two white women, a crime "regarded with especial horror in the community."

In an early major use of the DUE PROCESS clause to regulate the administration of criminal justice by the states, the Supreme Court held that the trials were fundamentally unfair. The facts of the case made this portentous holding an easy one: the defendants were tried in one day, the defense was entirely pro forma, and the death sentence was immediately imposed on all seven defendants without regard to individual culpability or circumstance. *Powell* was not a Sixth Amendment RIGHT TO COUNSEL case; three decades would pass before that guarantee was imported into due process in GIDEON V. WAINWRIGHT (1963). But the language of the Court in expounding the importance of counsel to a fair trial was repeatedly quoted as the Sixth Amendment right developed: "[the layman] lacks both the skill and knowledge adequately to prepare his defense, even though he has a perfect one. He requires the guiding hand of counsel at every step in the proceedings against him. Without it, though he be not guilty, he faces the danger of conviction because he does not know how to establish his innocence."

Although *Powell* is usually cited as a case in which defendants had no counsel at all, there was actually a lawyer at their side, but he came late into the case and was unfamiliar with Alabama law. In discussing the failure of due process, the Court referred to the lack of investigation and consultation by this last-minute volunteer. Thus, *Powell* has implications for the developing doctrine of ineffective assistance of counsel.

BARBARA ALLEN BABCOCK

POWELL v. MCCORMACK
395 U.S. 486 (1969)

Adam Clayton Powell, Jr., a flamboyant clergyman of indifferent ethics, for many years represented a New York City district in Congress. In 1967, after Powell won reelection despite a conviction for criminal contempt of court and a record of misappropriation of public funds, the House of Representatives denied him a seat. In a special election, he received eighty-six percent of the votes and again appeared to take his seat. The House then passed a resolution "excluding" Powell.

Powell and thirteen of his constituents then sued Speaker John McCormack and several other officers of the House of Representatives. Powell lost in both the District Court and the Court of Appeals, and his case was not heard by the Supreme Court until after the Ninetieth Congress had adjourned. Powell had, in the meanwhile, been reelected, and was seated as a member of the Ninety-First Congress.

The Supreme Court, in an 8–1 decision, declined to hold the case moot, finding that Powell's claim for back pay was sufficient for a justiciable controversy. In an opinion by Chief Justice EARL WARREN, the Court proceeded to overturn some long-standing assumptions about the constitutional status of CONGRESSIONAL MEMBERSHIP.

The Court held that the houses of Congress, although they are the judges of the qualifications provided in the Constitution itself (Article I, section 5) may not add to the qualifications provided in the Constitution (Article I, section 2). If a person elected to the House is qualified by age, CITIZENSHIP, and residence, he may not be excluded. Of course, once a member has been seated, he may be expelled by a two-thirds vote for any offense the House believes is "inconsistent with the trust and duty of a member" (*In re Chapman,* 1897). But, in Powell's case the Court held that exclusion was not equivalent to expulsion. (See POLITICAL QUESTIONS.)

DENNIS J. MAHONEY

POWELL v. PENNSYLVANIA

See: Waite Court

PRATT, CHARLES
(Lord Camden)
(1714–1794)

The leading Whig constitutionalist of eighteenth-century England, Charles Pratt was appointed a judge after a career as a barrister and parliamentarian and service as attorney general. Arguing SEDITIOUS LIBEL cases, he had maintained that the jury was competent to decide the questions both of law and of fact. He was Chief Justice of the Court of Common Pleas from 1762 until 1766. In the WILKES CASES he declared GENERAL WARRANTS contrary to the principles of the constitution and held their issuance by secretaries of state illegal. He also discouraged prosecution of Roman Catholic recusants. As Baron (later Earl) Camden, he made his first speech in the House of Lords in 1765 supporting the American position on the Stamp Act. In the debates on the Declaratory Act he called TAXATION WITHOUT REPRESENTATION "sheer robbery" and denounced the fiction of virtual representation. He became Lord Chancellor in 1766 but resigned in 1770 after disagreeing with the cabinet about several matters, including policy toward America. He continued to support the American position in the House of Lords and, with Lord Chatham, favored reconciliation with the colonies. He returned to the cabinet in 1782 and was Lord President of the Council from 1784 until his death.

DENNIS J. MAHONEY

PRAYER, SCHOOL

See: Religion in Public Schools

PREAMBLE

The part of the Constitution that we read first is the part of the original Constitution that was written last. The Preamble, which sets forth the noble purposes for which the Constitution is "ordained and established," was composed by the CONSTITUTIONAL CONVENTION's Committee of Style. The committee sat between September 8 and September 11, 1787, after the Convention had debated and voted on all of the substantive provisions of the Constitution; its mandate was to arrange and harmonize the wording of the resolutions adopted by the delegates during the preceding four months. The task of actually drafting the document fell to GOUVERNEUR MORRIS of New York, and so the authorship of the Preamble must be ascribed to him.

Morris made two major changes in the Preamble as it was reported by the Committee of Detail and referred to the Committee of Style. The earlier version had begun, "We, the people of the states of . . ." and then had listed the thirteen states in order, from north to south; Morris changed this to the now familiar "We, the people of the United States. . . ." And the earlier version had merely stated that the people ordained and established the Constitution; Morris added the list of purposes for which they did so. Each of these changes has been the occasion of some controversy.

The reference to the "people of the United States" was a source of irritation to the Anti-Federalists. PATRICK HENRY, for example, in the Virginia ratifying convention, denounced the use of the phrase as a harbinger of a national despotism. The Convention, he said, should have written instead, "We, the States. . . ." In ANTI-FEDERALIST CONSTITUTIONAL THOUGHT, only the states, as the existing political units, to which the people had already delegated all the powers of government, could constitute a federal union and redelegate some of their powers to the national government. Reference to the constituent authority of "the people of the United States" seemed to imply consolidation, not confederation.

It is unlikely that Morris, the Committee of Style, or the Convention had any such implication in mind. The Convention had approved a preamble that referred to the people of all thirteen states. The committee had to "harmonize" that with the provision that the Constitution would become effective when it was ratified by any nine states. There would likely be a time, therefore, when there would be nine states in the Union and four outside of it; but no one could predict which would be the nine and which the four. So long as the Constitution would become effective with less than thirteen states in the Union, listing the thirteen states in the Preamble would be misleading and inaccurate. Whichever states did ratify the Constitution would be the "United States," and it would be the people of those "United States" that had ordained the Constitution. Moreover, the Constitution provided for the future admission of additional states, and the people of those states, too, would ordain and establish the Constitution.

But Henry's objection was ill-founded for another reason. The DECLARATION OF INDEPENDENCE had pronounced the Americans "one people" and had given to their political Union the name of the "United States of America." The states and the Union had been born together on July 4, 1776, when a new nation was brought forth upon this continent. The one people certainly possessed the right to alter or abolish their former government and to establish a new government more conducive to their future safety and happiness. "We, the people of the United States," are identical to the "one people" that in the Declaration of Independence dissolved the political bonds that formerly connected us to Great Britain.

The list of purposes for ordaining and establishing the Constitution is perhaps more perplexing. The Convention had never debated or voted on such a list; and yet each delegate must have had some such purposes in mind throughout the deliberations. How else could he have gauged or judged the propriety of the measures upon which he did debate and vote? Morris and the Committee of Style must have thought it fitting to provide this terse apologia for their summer's deliberations; and the delegates apparently agreed, for there is no record of any objection to the Preamble as it was reported by the committee.

The Preamble lists the purposes for which the Constitution was created: to form a more perfect Union, to establish justice, to insure domestic tranquillity, to provide for the common defense, to promote the general welfare, and to secure the blessings of liberty, not only for the founding generation but also for "posterity." It, in effect, declares to a candid world the causes for which the people have chosen to replace the ARTICLES OF CONFEDERATION with a new Constitution. The purposes listed in the Preamble are consistent with what the Declaration of Independence asserts to be the end of all governments instituted among men, namely to secure the equal and inalienable natural rights of all to life, liberty, and the pursuit of happiness.

The Preamble does not purport to create any offices or to confer any powers; as JOSEPH STORY later wrote, "Its true office is to expound the nature and extent and application of the powers actually conferred by the Constitution, and not substantially to create them." Although COMMENTATORS ON THE CONSTITUTION have, over the years, purported to find in the Preamble justification for the exercise of INHERENT POWERS of government, no court has ever held that the Preamble independently grants power to the government or to any of its officers or agencies. In fact, in *Jacobson v. Massachusetts* (1905), the Supreme Court specifically rejected that interpretation.

The Preamble concludes by proclaiming that the people "do ordain and establish this Constitution." EDWARD S. CORWIN correctly pointed to the active voice and present tense of this phrase. The act of constituting a government occurs at a particular moment in time; but the authority of the Constitution depends on the continuous consent of the governed. The people, as Corwin wrote, " 'do ordain and establish,' *not* did ordain and establish." Thus does the Preamble play its role in the preservation of constitutional government. An afterthought of the Constitutional Convention, a rhetorical flourish by the Committee of Style, the Preamble has been memorized by schoolchildren and declaimed by orators and statesmen on public occasions for two centuries. And every time it is recited it calls to mind the purposes of our federal Union and unites the people more firmly to the cause of republican liberty.

DENNIS J. MAHONEY

Bibliography

CORWIN, EDWARD S. 1920 *The Constitution and What It Means Today.* Princeton, N.J.: Princeton University Press.

EIDELBERG, PAUL 1968 *The Political Philosophy of the Constitution.* New York: Free Press.

ROSSITER, CLINTON 1966 *1787: The Grand Convention.* New York: Macmillan.

PRECEDENT

In MARBURY V. MADISON (1803) Chief Justice JOHN MARSHALL rested the legitimacy of JUDICIAL REVIEW of the constitutionality of legislation on the necessity for courts to "state what the law is" in particular cases. The implicit assumption is that the Constitution is law, and that the content of constitutional law is determinate—that it can be known and applied by judges. From the time of the nation's founding, lawyers and judges trained in the processes of the COMMON LAW have assumed that the law of the Constitution is to be found not only in the text of the document and the expectations of the Framers but also in judicial precedent: the opinions of judges on "what the law is," written in the course of deciding earlier cases. (See STARE DECISIS.)

Inevitably, issues that burned brightly for the Framers of the Constitution and of its various amendments have receded from politics into history. The broad language of much of the Constitution's text leaves open a wide range of choices concerning interpretation. As the body of judicial precedent has grown, it has taken on a life of its own; the very term "constitutional law," for most lawyers today, primarily calls to mind the interpretations of the Constitution contained in the Supreme Court's opinions. For a lawyer writing a brief, or a judge writing an opinion, the natural style of argumentation is the common law style, with appeals to one or another "authority" among the competing analogies offered by a large and still growing body of precedent.

The same considerations that support reliance on precedent in common law decisions apply in constitutional adjudications: the need for stability in the law and for evenhanded treatment of litigants. Yet adherence to precedent has also been called the control of the living by the dead. Earlier interpretations of the Constitution, when they seem to have little relevance to the conditions of society and government here and now, do give way. As Chief Justice EARL WARREN wrote in BROWN V. BOARD OF EDUCATION (1954), "In approaching [the problem of school SEGREGATION], we cannot turn the clock back to 1868 when the [FOURTEENTH] AMENDMENT was adopted, or even to 1896 when PLESSY [V. FERGUSON] was written. We must consider public education in the light of its full development and its present place in American life. . . ." Justice OLIVER WENDELL HOLMES put the matter more pungently: "It is revolting to have no better reason for a rule of law than that so it was laid down in the time of Henry IV."

Although the Supreme Court decides only those issues that come to it in the ordinary course of litigation, the Court has a large measure of control over its own doctrinal agenda. The selection of about 150 cases for review each year (out of more than 4,000 cases brought to the Court) is influenced most of all by the Justices' views of the importance of the issues presented. (See CERTIORARI, WRIT OF.) And when the Court does break new doctrinal ground, it invites further litigation to explore the area thus opened. For example, scores of lawsuits were filed all over the country once the Court had established the precedent, in BAKER V. CARR (1962), that the problem of legislative REAPPORTIONMENT was one that the courts could properly address. The Justices see themselves, and are seen by the Court's commentators, as being in the business of developing constitutional DOCTRINE through the system of precedent. The decision of particular litigants' cases today appears to be important mainly as an instrument to those lawmaking ends. The theory of *Marbury v. Madison*, in other words, has been turned upside down.

Lower court judges pay meticulous attention to Supreme Court opinions as their main source of guidance for decision in constitutional cases. Supreme Court Justices themselves, however, give precedent a force that is weaker in constitutional cases than in other areas of the law. In a famous expression of this view, Justice LOUIS D. BRANDEIS, dissenting in *Burnet v. Coronado Oil & Gas Co.* (1932), said, "in cases involving the Federal Constitution, where correction through legislative action is practically impossible, this court has often overruled its earlier decisions. The court bows to the lessons of experience and the force of better reasoning, recognizing that the process of trial and error, so fruitful in the physical sciences, is appropriate also in the judicial function."

Although this sentiment is widely shared, Justices often are prepared to defer to their reading of precedent even when they disagree with the conclusions that produced the earlier decisions. Justice JOHN MARSHALL HARLAN, for example, regularly accepted the authoritative force of WARREN COURT opinions from which he had dissented vigorously. The Court as an institution occasionally takes the same course, making clear that it is following the specific dictates of an earlier decision because of the interest in stability of the law, even though that decision may be out of line with more recent doctrinal developments.

The Supreme Court is regularly criticized, both from within the Court and from the outside, for failing to follow precedent. But a thoroughgoing consistency of decision cannot be expected, given the combination of three characteristics of the Court's decisional process. First, the Court is a collegiate body, with the nine Justices exercising individual judgment on each case. Second, the body of precedent is now enormous, with the result that in most cases decided by the Court there are arguable precedents for several alternative doctrinal approaches, and even for reaching opposing results. Indeed, the system for selecting cases for review guarantees that the court will regularly face hard cases—cases that are difficult because they can plausibly be decided in more than one way. Finally, deference to precedent itself may mean that issues will be decided differently, depending on the order in which they come before the Court. The Court's decision in *In re Griffiths* (1973), that a state cannot constitutionally limit the practice of law to United States citizens, is still a good precedent; yet, if the case had come up in 1983, almost certainly it would have been decided differently. (See ALIENS.)

The result of this process is an increasingly fragmented Supreme Court, with more PLURALITY OPINIONS and more statements by individual Justices of their own separate views in CONCURRING OPINIONS and dissents—thus presenting an even greater range of materials on which Justices can draw in deciding the next case. In these circumstances, it is not surprising that some plurality opinions, such as that in MOORE V. CITY OF EAST CLEVELAND (1977), are regularly cited as if they had a precedent value equal to that of OPINIONS OF THE COURT.

The range of decisional choice offered to a Supreme Court Justice by this process is so wide as to call into the question the idea of principled decision on which the legitimacy of judicial review is commonly assumed to rest. Yet the hard cases that fill the Supreme Court's docket—the very cases that make constitutional law and thus fill the casebooks that law students study—do not typify the functioning of constitutional law. A great many controversies of constitutional dimension never get to court, because the law seems clear, on the basis of precedent; similarly, many cases that do get to court are easily decided in the lower courts. Although we celebrate the memory of our creative Justices—Justices who are remembered for setting precedent, not following it—the body of constitutional law remains remarkably stable. In a stable society it could not be otherwise. As Holmes himself said in another context, "historic continuity with the past is not a duty, it is only a necessity."

KENNETH L. KARST

Bibliography

EASTERBROOK, FRANK H. 1982 Ways of Criticizing the Court. *Harvard Law Review* 95:802–832.

LEVI, EDWARD H. 1949 *An Introduction to Legal Reasoning.* Chicago: University of Chicago Press.

LLEWELLYN, KARL N. 1960 *The Common Law Tradition.* Boston: Little, Brown.

MONAGHAN, HENRY P. 1979 Taking Supreme Court Opinions Seriously. *Maryland Law Review* 39:1–26.

PREEMPTION

The SUPREMACY CLAUSE of the Constitution (Article VI, clause 2) requires that inconsistent state laws yield to valid federal laws. Preemption is the term applied to describe invalidation of state laws by superior federal law.

Strictly speaking, the issue of preemption is not one of constitutional law. The issue is not what Congress has the power to do, but what Congress has done. Where Congress has made an articulate decision whether particular state laws should survive a new scheme of federal regulation, the issue is settled. For example, in enacting minimum federal standards for automobile pollution control equipment in 1967, Congress prohibited states from enforcing more restrictive standards but made an exception for the State of California. There has been no need for litigation to mark the contours of preemption in that context. Insofar as there is a "doctrine" of preemption, it concerns the treatment of preemption by federal laws where Congress has ignored the issue.

Since preemption cases theoretically turn on construction of federal statutes to determine whether Congress intended to preempt state laws, there are limits to generalizations that can be drawn from the decisions. Each case construes a federal statute with a distinct regulatory structure and legislative history. It is particularly difficult to classify the simplest form of preemption cases—those where the claim is made that the terms of federal and state law are flatly inconsistent. Federal law may, for example, give express permission to engage in conduct prohibited by state law. An early famous case of this type was GIBBONS v. OGDEN (1824).

The most complex issues of preemption arise where it is concededly possible to comply with mandates of both state and federal law. The question then arises whether Congress intended to "occupy the field," or whether the challenged state law's enforcement would interfere inordinately with the policies of the federal law. State law may provide additional sanctions for conduct prohibited by federal law. (In *California v. Zook,* 1949, the Court sustained a state law that punished interstate motor transport operating without a federal permit.) State law may impose more stringent regulations than federal law. (In *Napier v. Atlantic Coast Line R.R.,* 1926, the Court held that a state law requiring railroad safety equipment was preempted by a federal law that required less equipment.) Finally, it may be argued that state law is, in some general way, inconsistent with the purposes of federal law. (In *New York Telephone Co. v. New York State Department of Labor,* 1979, the Court sustained state payment of unemployment compensation benefits to strikers as not inconsistent with the policy of free COLLECTIVE BARGAINING under federal labor law.)

The Court has announced general tests for determining whether Congress has "occupied the field." An often-quoted summary of the standards for finding congressional intent to preempt state law is contained in *Rice v. Santa Fe Elevator Corp.* (1947). "The scheme of federal regulation may be so pervasive as to make reasonable the inference that Congress left no room for the States to supplement it. . . . Or the Act of Congress may touch a field in which the federal interest is so dominant that the federal system will be assumed to preclude enforcement of state laws on the same subject. . . . Or the state policy may produce a result inconsistent with the objective of the federal statute." These standards are peculiarly devoid of content, as the Court admitted in the sentence following those just quoted: "It is often a perplexing question whether Congress has precluded state action or by the choice of selective regulatory measures has left the POLICE POWER of the States undisturbed except as the state and federal regulations collide."

The lack of any pattern to the preemption cases can be explained in that each case seeks to ascertain congressional intent in a unique context. Since, however, contentious preemption questions arise precisely because Congress has ignored the existence of related state laws, the "intent of Congress" is a fiction that fails to describe the Court's decision process. The controlling factors in judicial decision are similar to those that would have confronted the intelligent legislator who had grappled with them. The judges' social values, views as to the legislative wisdom of the federal and state laws, and general views of the federal system may be as decisive as technical consideration of how well the federal and state schemes would mesh.

In many cases, there are potential issues of constitutional validity of the challenged state law in addition to the preemption question. Some preemption decisions can be explained as a part of the Court's general practice of avoiding unnecessary constitutional questions. Often, the preemption question is decided, articulately or *sub silentio,* by the same criteria that would have governed the avoided constitutional question. The preemption doctrine may be preferred by the Court because the judicial decision striking down a state law is tentative, and congressional attention is invited to the issue. If Congress does nothing, the issue is avoided. If Congress makes an articulate choice to withdraw the preemption barrier, the inescapable constitutional question benefits from the additional data supplied by congressional decision. A final attraction of the preemption rationale, beyond the tentativeness of a preemption decision, may be that each decision can be truly ad hoc, resting on a fictional finding of congressional intent to preempt that governs only the particular federal statutory scheme before the Court.

WILLIAM COHEN

Bibliography

COHEN, WILLIAM 1982 Congressional Power to Define State Power to Regulate Commerce: Consent and Preemption. Pages 523–547 in Terrance Sandalow and Eric Stein, eds., *Courts and Free Markets: Perspectives from the United States and Europe.* Oxford: Clarendon Press.

CRAMTOM, ROGER 1956 Pennsylvania v. Nelson: A Case Study in Federal Preemption. *University of Chicago Law Review* 26:85–108.

PREFERRED FREEDOMS

Because FIRST AMENDMENT freedoms rank at the top of the hierarchy of constitutional values, any legislation that explicitly limits those freedoms must be denied the usual presumption of constitutionality and be subjected to STRICT SCRUTINY by the judiciary. So went the earliest version of the preferred freedoms doctrine, sometimes called the preferred position or preferred status doctrine. It probably originated in the opinions of Justice OLIVER WENDELL HOLMES, at least implicitly. He believed that a presumption of constitutionality attached to ECONOMIC REGULATION, which needed to meet merely a RATIONAL BASIS test, as he explained dissenting in LOCHNER V. NEW YORK (1905). By contrast, in ABRAMS V. UNITED STATES (1919) he adopted the CLEAR AND PRESENT DANGER test as a constitutional yardstick for legislation such as the ESPIONAGE ACT OF 1917 or state CRIMINAL SYNDICALISM statutes, which limited FREEDOM OF SPEECH.

Justice BENJAMIN N. CARDOZO first suggested a more general hierarchy of constitutional rights in PALKO V. CONNECTICUT (1937), in a major opinion on the INCORPORATION DOCTRINE. He ranked at the top those "fundamental principles of liberty and justice which lie at the base of all our civil and political institutions." He tried to distinguish rights that might be lost without risking the essentials of liberty and justice from rights which he called "the matrix, the indispensable condition, of nearly every other form of freedom." These FUNDAMENTAL RIGHTS came to be regarded as the preferred freedoms. A year later Justice HARLAN F. STONE, in footnote four of his opinion in UNITED STATES V. CAROLENE PRODUCTS (1938), observed that "legislation which restricts the political processes" might "be subjected to more exacting judicial scrutiny" than other legislation. He suggested, too, that the judiciary might accord particularly searching examination of statutes reflecting "prejudice against DISCRETE AND INSULAR MINORITIES."

The First Amendment freedoms initially enjoyed a primacy above all others. Justice WILLIAM O. DOUGLAS for the Court in MURDOCK V. PENNSYLVANIA (1943) expressly stated: "FREEDOM OF THE PRESS, freedom of speech, FREEDOM OF RELIGION are in a preferred position." In the 1940s, despite bitter divisions on the Court over the question whether constitutional rights should be ranked, as well as the question whether the Court should ever deny the presumption of constitutionality, a majority of Justices continued to endorse the doctrine. Justice WILEY B. RUTLEDGE for the Court gave it its fullest exposition in *Thomas v. Collins* (1945). Justice FELIX FRANKFURTER, who led the opposition to the doctrine, called it "mischievous" in KOVACS V. COOPER (1949); he especially disliked the implication that "any law touching communication" might be "infected with presumptive invalidity." Yet even Frankfurter, in his *Kovacs* opinion, acknowledged that "those liberties . . . which history has established as the indispensable conditions of an open as against a closed society come to the Court with a momentum for respect lacking when appeal is made to liberties which derive merely from shifting economic arrangements."

The deaths of Murphy and Rutledge in 1949 and their replacement by TOM C. CLARK and SHERMAN MINTON shifted the balance of judicial power to the Frankfurter viewpoint. Thereafter little was heard about the doctrine. The WARREN COURT vigorously defended not only CIVIL LIBERTIES but CIVIL RIGHTS and the rights of the criminally accused. The expansion of the incorporation doctrine and of the concept of EQUAL PROTECTION OF THE LAWS in the 1960s produced a new spectrum of FUNDAMENTAL INTERESTS demanding special judicial protection. Free speech, press, and religion continued, nevertheless, to be ranked, at least implicitly, as very special in character and possessing a symbolic "firstness," to use EDMOND CAHN's apt term. Although the Court rarely speaks of a preferred freedoms doctrine today, the substance of the doctrine has been absorbed in the concepts of strict scrutiny, fundamental rights, and selective incorporation.

LEONARD W. LEVY

Bibliography

MCKAY, ROBERT B. 1959 The Preference for Freedom. *New York University Law Review* 34:1184–1227.

PRESENTMENT

A presentment is a written accusation of criminal offense prepared, signed, and presented to the prosecutor by the members of a GRAND JURY, acting on their own initiative rather than in response to a bill of INDICTMENT brought before them by the government. By returning a presentment, the grand jury forces the prosecutor to indict. The presentment procedure permits the grand jury to circumvent prosecutorial inertia or recalcitrance to initiate criminal proceedings. The grand jury's presentment power originated long before there were government prosecutors. The presentment is a descendant of the grand jury's original function: to initiate criminal proceedings by accusing those whom the grand jurors knew to have reputedly committed offenses.

CHARLES H. WHITEBREAD

Bibliography

TESLIK, W. RANDOLPH 1975 *Prosecutorial Discretion: The Decision to Charge.* Washington, D.C.: National Criminal Justice Reference Service.

PRESIDENTIAL ELECTION CAMPAIGN FUND ACT

See: Federal Election Campaign Acts

PRESIDENTIAL ORDINANCE-MAKING POWER

As a means of carrying out constitutional and statutory duties, Presidents issue regulations, proclamations, and EXECUTIVE ORDERS. Although this exercise of legislative power by the President appears to contradict the doctrine of SEPARATION OF POWERS, the scope of administrative legislation has remained broad. Rules and regulations, as the Supreme Court noted in *United States v. Eliason* (1842), "must be received as the acts of the executive, and as such, be binding upon all within the sphere of his legal and constitutional authority."

It is established DOCTRINE that "the authority to prescribe rules and regulations is not the power to make laws, for no such power can be delegated by the Congress," as a federal court of appeals declared in *Lincoln Electric Co. v. Commissioner of Internal Revenue* (1951). Nevertheless, vague grants of delegated authority by Congress give administrators substantial discretion to make federal policy. Over a twelve-month period from 1933 to 1934 the National Recovery Administration issued 2,998 orders. This flood of rule-making activity was not collected and published in one place, leaving even executive officials in doubt about applicable regulations.

Legislation in 1935 provided for the custody of federal documents and their publication in a "Federal Register." The Administrative Procedure Act of 1946 established uniform standards for rule-making, including notice to the parties concerned and an opportunity for public participation. Recent Presidents, especially GERALD FORD, JIMMY CARTER, and RONALD REAGAN, have attempted to monitor and control the impact of agency regulations on the private sector.

Proclamations are a second instrument of administrative legislation. Sometimes they are hortatory in character, without legislative effect, such as proclamations for Law Day. Other proclamations have substantive effects, especially when used to regulate international trade on the basis of broad grants of statutory authority. Still other proclamations have been issued solely on the President's constitutional authority, as with pardons and AMNESTIES and ABRAHAM LINCOLN's proclamations in April 1861. When a statute prescribes a specific procedure in an area reserved to Congress and the President follows a different course, proclamations are illegal and void.

From ancient times a proclamation was literally a public notice, whether by trumpet, voice, print, or posting. Yet in 1873 the Supreme Court in *Lapeyre v. United States* declared that a proclamation by the President became a valid instrument of federal law from the moment it was signed and deposited in the office of the secretary of state, even though not published. These early proclamations eventually found their way into the *Statutes at Large,* but not until the Federal Register Act of 1935 did Congress require the prompt publication of all proclamations and executive orders that have general applicability and legal effect.

Executive orders are a third source of ordinance-making power. They draw upon the constitutional power of the President or powers expressly delegated by Congress. Especially bold were the orders of President FRANKLIN D. ROOSEVELT from 1941 to 1943; without any statutory authority he seized plants, mines, and companies. Actions that exceed legal bounds have been struck down by the courts, a major example being the Steel Seizure Case (YOUNGSTOWN SHEET AND TUBE CO. V. SAWYER, 1952). Executive orders cannot supersede a statute or override contradictory congressional expressions.

Congress has used its power of the purse to circumscribe executive orders. After President RICHARD M. NIXON issued executive order 11605 in 1971, rejuvenating the SUBVERSIVE ACTIVITIES CONTROL BOARD, Congress reduced the agency's budget and expressly prohibited it from using any of the funds to implement the President's order. Congress has also prevented the President from using appropriated funds to finance agencies created solely by executive order.

LOUIS FISHER

Bibliography

FLEISHMAN, JOEL L. and AUFSES, ARTHUR H. 1976 Law and Orders: The Problem of Presidential Legislation. *Law and Contemporary Problems* 40:1–45.

HART, JAMES 1925 *The Ordinance Making Powers of the President of the United States.* Baltimore: Johns Hopkins University Press. [Reprinted in 1970 by Da Capo Press.]

PRESIDENTIAL POWERS

The powers of the American presidency are amorphous and enormous. Perhaps they can be defined only by saying that they are made adequate to the problems to which the power is addressed. Although these powers purportedly derive from the specifications of the Constitution itself, in fact their definition is to be found in the behavior of the American Presidents since 1789. During this time the executive branch, largely with the acquiescence of Congress and the encouragement of the Supreme Court, has come to resemble the monolithic authority to be found in governments that have succeeded to the authority of czars and emperors. LIMITED GOVERNMENT is now constitutionally limited only by the first eight Amendments and Article I, section 9, and even then only at the discretion of the Supreme Court.

The reason for the accumulation of power in the presidency is not hard to find. Power goes to the official who can use it. It is easy for the President to be that official because, as Justice ROBERT H. JACKSON wrote in YOUNGSTOWN SHEET & TUBE CO. V. SAWYER (1952):

> Executive power has the advantage of concentration in a single head in whose choice the whole Nation has a part, making him the focus of public hopes and expectations. In drama, magnitude and finality his decisions so far overshadow any others that almost alone he fills the public eye and ear. No other personality in public life can begin to compete with him in access to the public mind through modern methods of communications. By his prestige as head of state and his influence upon public opinion he exerts a leverage upon those who are supposed to check and balance his power which often cancels their effectiveness.

The doctrine of SEPARATION OF POWERS, not to be found in terms in the Constitution, has receded to the vanishing point so far as the presidency is concerned. And the principle of CHECKS AND BALANCES, intrinsic in the Constitution as a whole, has also been diminished when it comes to putting restraints on the President.

Essentially there are two conflicting theses on the powers of American Presidents, depending in large part on whether it is believed that the opening words of the Second Article: "The Executive power shall be vested in a President of the United States," is itself a grant of power or, as was the case with Articles I and III, is simply a designation of the office with the powers of that official to be found in the provisions that followed. In sum, the question is whether everything that comes after the first sentence in Article II is a redundancy so far as presidential powers are concerned. A reading of the origins of the article would clearly deflate the concept of a presidency replete with the royal prerogatives that the nation had so roundly condemned in the DECLARATION OF INDEPENDENCE itself.

Even the view taken by THEODORE ROOSEVELT, however, is not so broad as to leave no need for separation of powers. Roosevelt asserted "that the executive power was limited only by specific restrictions and prohibitions appearing in the Constitution or imposed by Congress under its Constitutional powers." Roosevelt's immediate successor in office, WILLIAM HOWARD TAFT, had espoused a different reading: "The true view of the executive function is . . . that the President can exercise no power which cannot be fairly and reasonably traced to some specific grant of power or justly implied and included within such grant as proper and necessary." Taft's was the better reading of the origins of the constitutional provisions, although even he later turned to the Roosevelt reading when he was on the Supreme Court. But Roosevelt's was the better reading of the history of the presidency and a better prediction of what the presidency was to become.

The last important Supreme Court opinion on presidential powers, perhaps because it was one of the few outside the area of CIVIL LIBERTIES that rejected a presidential reach for power beyond his grasp, came in 1952 in the Steel Seizure Case. There the Court was thoroughly divided. The dissenters, led by Chief Justice FRED M. VINSON, read the INHERENT POWERS of the presidency as all but limitless, in keeping with the construction given by most political scientists. Justice HUGO L. BLACK went to the other extreme in his opinion for the Court. For him the chief magistrate had only those powers specifically provided by the terms of the Constitution and those powers properly conferred upon him by Congress. But of all the opinions in *Youngstown,* the one most often looked to by constitutional lawyers, including those sitting on the Court, has been that of Justice Robert H. Jackson, for whom there was no plain rule but rather a sliding scale:

> 1. When the President acts pursuant to an express or implied authorization of Congress, his authority is at its maximum, for it includes all that he possesses in his own right plus all that Congress can delegate. . . .
>
> 2. When the President acts in absence of either a congressional grant or denial of authority, he can only rely upon his own independent powers, but there is a zone of twilight in which he and Congress may have concurrent authority, or in which its distribution is uncertain. Therefore, congressional inertia, indifference or quiescence may sometimes, at least as a practical matter, enable, if not invite, measures of independent presidential responsibility. In this area, any test of power is likely to depend on the imperative of events and contemporary imponderables rather than on abstract theories of law.
>
> 3. When the President takes measures incompatible with the express or implied will of Congress, his power is at its lowest ebb, for then he can rely only upon its constitutional powers minus any constitutional powers of Congress over the matter. . . . Presidential claim to a power at once so conclusive and preclusive must be scrutinized with caution, for what is at stake is the equilibrium established by our constitutional system.

Jackson concluded his opinion, saying: "With all its defects, delays and inconveniences, men have discovered no technique for long preserving free government except that the Executive be under the law, and that the law be made by parliamentary deliberations. Such institutions may be destined to pass away. But it is the duty of the Court to be the last, not first, to give them up."

The concept of the RULE OF LAW continues to diminish as the nation embraces first the description in CLINTON ROSSITER's *Constitutional Dictatorship,* and then that of Arthur Schlesinger in his *Imperial Presidency.* We continue, however, to parse the sentences of the Constitution in order to justify or oppose presidential authority. But there is less reality in this exercise as each day succeeds the next.

The catalogue of presidential powers specifically stated in the Constitution is neither long nor extensive. He is given a conditional power of veto of all legislation, subject to being overridden by a two-thirds vote of each house. The remainder of his powers are specified in Article II, section 7: he is to be COMMANDER-IN-CHIEF of the armed forces, including the militia when in the service of the United States; he may require opinions from his principal cabinet officers; he may grant pardons and reprieves for offenders against the national laws; he may enter into TREATIES with foreign nations with the ADVICE AND CONSENT of two-thirds of the Senate; he is to nominate ambassadors, ministers, and consuls, members of the Supreme Court, and such other officers as are not otherwise provided for by the Constitution, plus such other officers as Congress shall provide; he may fill vacancies while the Senate is not in session; he shall address Congress on the state of the union and recommend the passage of measures he deems necessary and expedient; he may convene Congress and adjourn it when the two houses do not agree on adjournment; he shall receive ambassadors and other public ministers from foreign countries; "he shall take Care that the Laws be faithfully executed"; and he shall commission all officers of the United States. In fact, however, these bare bones of presidential authority have had much meat placed on them by presidential practices, by legislative delegation, and by judicial approval. It can hardly be gainsaid that the authors of the constitutional language would be much surprised were they to return to the scene to see what it is said that they have wrought.

The slivers of presidential power specifically authorized by the Constitution have been bundled like fasces to create huge authority in the President under the banners of FOREIGN AFFAIRS powers; WAR POWERS; fiscal powers; legislative powers and administrative powers. None of these rests exclusively on any specific authority granted by the Constitution but rather on combinations and permutations of them combined with "intrinsic" or "necessary and proper" powers, although the NECESSARY AND PROPER

CLAUSE itself was a grant only to the legislative branch.

Probably the most extensive, and perhaps the most important, of the modern President's powers is to be found in his hegemony over the nation's foreign relations. As Archibald Cox has written: "The United States' assumption of a leading role in world affairs built up the presidency by focussing world attention upon the president. The constitution, combined with necessity, gives the president greater personal authority in foreign affairs than domestic matters. A succession of presidents pushed these powers to, and sometimes beyond, their limits. The personal manner in which they conducted international relations doubtless influenced their style in dealing with domestic matters." But it has been "necessity," not the Constitution, that vested this great personal power in the President. There are only two plausible grounds in the Constitution for great presidential authority in the area of foreign relations. It is he who names and receives ambassadors, which was early construed to mean that he was the sole spokesman of the nation with regard to foreign nations. It is he who is charged with the negotiation of treaties. But both in the appointment of ambassadors and in the making of treaties, the Founders required the collaboration of the Senate: a majority vote of acquiescence in the case of ambassadors and a two-thirds vote of the Senate to validate a treaty.

What the Constitution did not give the President by way of powers in this area, he has been given by Congress or he has taken for himself, and what he has taken for himself has generally been legitimated by Supreme Court decision. Much of relations with foreign nations that was committed to Congress—for example, the power over FOREIGN COMMERCE, the war-making authority—has become irrelevant to the modern Constitution. For the Supreme Court has declared that the powers over foreign affairs that are the President's do not derive from the Constitution but rather are a direct inheritance from the Crown of England. In UNITED STATES v. CURTISS-WRIGHT EXPORT CORP. (1936) the Court said: "As a result of the separation from Great Britain by the colonies acting as a unit, the powers of external SOVEREIGNTY passed from the Crown not to the colonies severally, but to the colonies in their collective and corporate capacity as the United States. . . . Sovereignty is never held in suspense. When, therefore, the external sovereignty of Great Britain in respect to the colonies ceased, it immediately passed to the Union." Not only did this power inhere in the Union; it belonged directly to the President, although where it was before there was a President is not made clear. But, said the Court, it did not come through the Constitution or the Congress. It is a "very delicate, plenary and exclusive power of the President as the sole organ of the federal government in the field of international relations—a power which does not require as a basis for its exercise an act of Congress." It is somewhat strange, if the foreign relations power never belonged to the states, that the Founders thought it necessary to take it from them in the specific words of Article I, section 10: "No state shall enter into any treaty, alliance, or confederation; grant LETTERS OF MARQUE AND REPRISAL; . . . No state shall, without the consent of Congress . . . keep troops, or ships of war in time of peace, enter into any agreement or compact with another state, or with a foreign power, or engage in war, unless actually invaded. . . ." It is strange, too, that Congress can consent to the exercise of foreign affairs powers by the states, if that power properly belongs exclusively to the President.

The coalescence of this power over foreign relations solely in the President has also had the effect of eliminating specific checks on him by the Senate. The Constitution clearly gives the power to negotiate treaties to the President, but it requires the consent of two-thirds of the Senate to validate a treaty. The requirement of Senate approval has often proved a stumbling block, as it was when the Senate refused to consent to the United States' entry into the League of Nations and when the Senate imposed qualifications on the treaty ceding the Panama Canal Zone back to Panama. But the President and the Supreme Court have found a way out of some of these restraints. An agreement with a foreign nation may be called an EXECUTIVE AGREEMENT rather than a "treaty," and an "executive agreement" does not require Senate approval, according to the decisions in UNITED STATES v. BELMONT (1937) and UNITED STATES v. PINK (1942). There is no guide, however, to say what the province of a treaty may be to distinguish it from that of an executive agreement. The justification for evading presidential responsibility to the Senate is, however, often founded on the ground that effectuation of such agreements usually requires congressional legislation, and a majority of both houses is said to be as good as or better than two-thirds of the Senate in ratifying the presidential action and easier to secure.

It has been argued, but not very cogently, that the foreign affairs powers of the President somehow derive from the Commander-in-Chief Clause of Article II. ALEXANDER HAMILTON's explanation of that provision in THE FEDERALIST #69 as to the limited authority of the commander-in-chief still seems to be the better understanding of it: "It would amount to nothing more than the supreme command and direction of the military and naval forces, as first General and Admiral of the Confederacy."

The foreign affairs powers of the President are as broad as they have become not because of constitutional delegation but because of the exigencies that have caused the Presidents to seize the power to meet the problems. Neither the public nor the Congress has shown much aversion to this presidential usurpation.

Presidential war powers, like presidential foreign affairs powers, rest on practice and precedent rather than on constitutional authorization. Thus, despite the provision of Article 1, section 8, giving Congress the power to declare war, wars have tended to be a consequence of executive action, sometimes confirmed by a congressional DECLARATION OF WAR and sometimes carried on without one. Five times in American history, Congress has declared war: the War of 1812, the Mexican War of 1848, the Spanish American War of 1898, and World Wars I (1917) and II (1941). Each time American military and naval forces had been committed to action before the actual declaration took place. In most instances when military forces have been engaged against foreign powers there has been no declaration of war even when the conflict reached such vast scales as the country's commitments to the KOREAN WAR and VIETNAM WAR. It has been argued that there were de facto declarations in such instances as Korea and Vietnam by congressional silence or appropriations for the military, but that was not what the Founders had in mind. For them war was thought too serious a matter to be left to generals and Presidents.

Congress has come up with a statute attempting to resolve the problem of presidential usurpation of the war power. The WAR POWERS RESOLUTION of 1973 provides that a President can order military action without a declaration of war by Congress, but he must inform Congress within forty-eight hours of doing so. Troops cannot be committed for more than sixty days except when Congress so authorizes, and Congress is empowered to order an immediate withdrawal of American forces by CONCURRENT RESOLUTION not subject to presidential veto. The statute is of dubious constitutional validity, giving presidential powers to Congress and congressional powers to the President. It is not likely to be the subject of a successful court test, for courts cannot act expeditiously enough nor can they effectuate a decree against the will of either of the other branches.

The essential fact is that the Constitution gives to Congress the power to declare war, to raise and support the armed forces, to make rules for the governance of the armed forces, to call up the militia, and to regulate it. It gives to the President the powers of commander-in-chief, which is only an authority to act in command of the military services so that no mere military officer shall be without civilian oversight.

The greater problem with presidential war powers is whether they enhance his authority over domestic civilian affairs. The Court has tended to sustain extraordinarily broad powers for the executive during the course of a war, as in the JAPANESE AMERICAN CASES (1943–1944), allowing relocation of native and foreign-born Japanese from the West Coast into concentration camps. When war has ended, the Court tends to look more dubiously on executive war powers, holding in DUNCAN V. KAHANOMOKU (1946), for example, that it was an abuse of authority to declare martial law in Hawaii on the day after the Japanese bombed Pearl Harbor. So far as civilian activities are concerned, it is said that war does not give the executive any new powers but simply justifies the use of granted powers reserved for emergencies. The fact is that, in contemporary times, Congress has provided the President with more EMERGENCY POWERS than he ever has occasion to use, generally leaving to him the discretion to determine whether an emergency warrants calling such powers into play. The concept of emergency powers, itself nowhere to be found in the Constitution, has long since expanded beyond the realms of war powers to justify presidential action in the economic and social realm as well as in the areas of military combat and foreign affairs. The confiscation of Iranian assets in the United States to ransom American captives from the Iranians in 1980 affords an example of the extension of presidential authority far beyond what the Constitution provided; but in DAMES & MOORE V. REGAN (1981) the flimsiest statutory delegation was held sufficient to justify the President's actions.

The Constitution gave the President no powers over the national fisc. It was very clear at the CONSTITUTIONAL CONVENTION OF 1787 that the authority over national finance—what went into the national purse and what came out of it—belonged to Congress and Congress alone, subject, of course, to the presidential power of veto. Article 1, section 7, commands that the House of Representatives alone shall originate revenue measures. Article 1, section 8, gives to the Congress the "power to lay and collect taxes," "to pay the debts," "to borrow money," "to coin money," and to punish counterfeiting. And Article 1, section 9, clause 7, provides that "no money shall be drawn from the Treasury, but in consequence of appropriations made by law." If any principle of responsible government can be said to have been derived from the Glorious Revolution of 1688 in England and the American Revolution, it is that a popularly elected legislature is the only safe place in which to place the power of the purse.

This is not to deny that at all times in our history the executive branch has played a more or less important role in the creation and effectuation of fiscal policy, from the roles of Secretaries of the Treasury Hamilton and ALBERT GALLATIN and ANDREW JACKSON's war on the BANK OF THE UNITED STATES to contemporary times when it would appear that the executive is dominant and Congress subordinate with regard to all the fiscal powers that the Constitution gave to the Congress. But the role of the executive branch has essentially been defined by the Congress. If the executive power is now so great in fiscal matters, the reason is not that the Constitution has conferred the power on the President but that Congress has done so. Thus, one frustrating restraint on presidential fiscal policy derives from the autonomy over the money supply granted by Congress to the Federal Reserve Board, an agency independent of the President.

The nation has evolved from one in which the national government's principal role was that of the protector of the lives and property of the citizenry against encroachment by foreign governments and other citizens to one in which the government manages the economy, for better or worse, in a state where the government has assumed responsibility for the social welfare as well as the physical protection of the citizenry. And as the progression has gone on, so too has Congress relinquished more and more authority to the President. But the President can be said to have these powers only at the will of Congress and to exercise them only in order to enforce the laws faithfully. Indeed, the DELEGATION OF POWER has gone so far as for Congress to have provided by law that the President may refuse to enforce its legislation by IMPOUNDMENT of appropriated funds, provided notice is given to Congress and Congress acquiesces.

Although Congress now has its own budget-making procedures, the dominant BUDGET, derived from the President's Office of Management and Budget, is submitted to Congress more by way of command than suggestion. The concept of an executive budget derives from the 1920s when Congress first enacted a demand that the President supply one. Since then, however, the Office of Management and Budget has grown from a simple accounting agency into a fiscal ombudsman for the entire government. It is a force second only to that of the President himself within the executive branch and it has not been bashful about exercising its powers. But if the beast is a presidential pet, it is nonetheless a creature of a Congress dedicated to transferring to the President the powers that the Constitution gave to Congress.

In constitutional terms, the President's role in the legislative process was originally to be very small. Most important, of course, was the power to veto the acts passed by Congress. And even here, unlike the power of the Crown to forestall parliamentary will as expressed in legislation, the President was given only a conditional veto, subject to being overridden by two-thirds of each house of Congress. The VETO POWER is, however, fully effective only for a President who prefers a limited role for government. Obviously, his veto cannot create legislation but only prevent it. A forceful President seeking to impose his will by way of persuading Congress to action rather than inaction can, however, use the veto as a bargaining-tool, a threat to cancel what Congress wants unless it gives the President what he wants. Stalemate is a frequent consequence of a profligate use of the veto power.

The President also has the power by constitutional provision to adjourn Congress, when the two houses are unable to agree on adjournment, and to convene Congress. The power to prorogue Parliament was a sore point with the colonists and they had no intention of conferring such authority on any executive of their own.

There was an imitation of the royal prerogative that was to come into existence even though it was not planned by the Founders. The Constitution provides that the President "shall from time to time give the Congress information of the state of the union, and recommend to their consideration such measures as he shall judge necessary and expedient." Like the Queen's message to the opening of Parliament, this device has been used by the executive administration to offer a legislative program to Congress. Indeed, most legislation of importance that comes to enactment in Congress tends to be that which the President has recommended to it or which the President supports by lobbying in Congress. Legislation that does not bear the imprimatur of the President seldom makes its way to enactment, although presidential recommendations are frequently amended in the process of legislative consideration and sometimes are unrecognizable by the time they emerge from both houses. But the influence of the President, utilizing the Office of Management and Budget for details, on the making of the laws is extraordinarily strong. And while there is no provision for presidential budget making in the Constitution, the fact is that the budget that he submits is the foundation on which the congressional budget-making process depends.

In fact, the President indulges in a great deal of lawmaking himself. With the demise of the ban on the delegation of legislative power, which occurred when the Supreme Court was reconstituted by FRANKLIN D. ROOSEVELT, most of the rules governing American society are made by the executive branch. Legislation has tended to take the form of generalized programs whose details are to be filled by agencies of the executive branch. Indeed, some legislation is created by the President even in the absence of authorization for it by the Congress. This takes the form of so-called EXECUTIVE ORDERS theoretically directed to the enforcement of the laws by persons in the executive branch, but usually with the same effect as rules directed to the governed rather than the governors. Very rare indeed is the instance, like the steel seizure case, when the Court has throttled an executive order. Thus, most of the rules governing the lives of Americans are to be sought not in the statutes-at-large but rather in the Federal Register where are to be found the results of the exercise of delegated legislative authority as well as executive orders that do not rest on any actual delegation.

It would seem that the originators of the departments of government thought of them as semiautonomous, with their functions defined by Congress and their secretaries responsible to either the President or the Congress, or both, as prescribed by the legislation creating those offices. The provision for a power in the President to call on the principal officers of government for their opinions would have been redundant if in fact it had been anticipated that all executive officials were directly subordinate to the President. It was probably GEORGE WASHINGTON's organization of his department chiefs into a cabinet rather than the words of the Constitution that made for the hierarchical system headed by the President that has been taken for granted since early in the nineteenth century. The cabinet is not a constitutional body and has no constitutional powers. The powers of the department heads are dependent on legislative rather than constitutional provision, except for their duties to give opinions to the President on demand. Thus by custom and by legislation, and perhaps through the charge of the Constitution to the President faithfully to execute the laws, it has come to be accepted that the executive branch, for all its multitude of offices, is an entity for which the President is responsible both to Congress through the legislature's oversight function, and to the voting public. Surely this notion of the unitary nature of the executive branch and the exceptions thereto—independent administrative agencies—underlies the judgment of the Supreme Court in MYERS V. UNITED STATES (1926) establishing the right of the President to remove officials at his will. This accepted principle is not contradicted by the obligation of the President or other executive officials to abide by their own regulations, which are created by him or them and which are subject to change by him or them. (See APPOINTMENT AND REMOVAL POWER.)

The whole of the executive branch acts subordinately to the command of the President in the administration of federal laws, so long as they act within the terms of those laws. Their offices confer no right to violate the laws, whether they take the form of constitution, statute, or treaty.

The United States does have in the presidency a "constitutional dictatorship" or a "plebiscitary President." The "benevolent monarch" of contemporary times, however, is still subject to the force of public opinion, sometimes expressed through representatives, sometimes expressed through the print and electronic media, sometimes expressed in the streets, and every four years expressed through the ballot boxes. One-term Presidents may become the rule. Despite all the centralization of authority, however, the greatest power of the presidency in this democracy is not the power of command. It is the power to lead a nation by moral suasion. It takes a great President to do that well, and that is why history records so few great Presidents.

PHILIP B. KURLAND

Bibliography

CORWIN, EDWARD S. 1957 *The President: Office and Powers 1787–1957.* 4th rev. ed. New York: New York University Press.

COX, ARCHIBALD 1976 Watergate and the Constitution of the United States. *University of Toronto Law Journal* 26:125–139.

KOENIG, LOUIS W. 1975 *The Chief Executive.* 3d ed. New York: Harcourt, Brace, Jovanovich.

KURLAND, PHILIP B. 1978 *Watergate and the Constitution.* Chicago: University of Chicago Press.

NEUSTADT, RICHARD E. 1960 *Presidential Power.* New York: John Wiley & Sons.

PIOUS, RICHARD M. 1979 *The American Presidency.* New York: Basic Books.

ROSSITER, CLINTON 1948 *Constitutional Dictatorship.* Princeton, N.J.: Princeton University Press.

SCHLESINGER, ARTHUR M., JR. 1973 *The Imperial Presidency.* Boston: Houghton Mifflin Co.

PRESIDENTIAL SPENDING POWER

The Constitution assigns to Congress the exclusive power to authorize spending. Article I, section 9, prohibits money being drawn from the Treasury "but in Consequence of Appropriations made by law." Nevertheless, the power of the purse is shared with the President because Congress has found it necessary to delegate substantial discretion over the expenditure and allocation of funds.

In his first message to Congress, President THOMAS JEFFERSON recommended that Congress appropriate "specific sums to every specific purpose susceptible of definition." He quickly recognized the impracticability of this principle, later admitting that "too minute a specification has its evil as well as a too general one." Lump-sum appropriations are routinely passed by Congress, especially during emergency periods. The magnitude of these lump sums, frequently in the billions of dollars, overstates the amount of flexibility available to administrators. Their scope of discretion is narrowed by general statutory controls, nonstatutory controls embedded in committee reports and other parts of the legislative history, and agreements and understandings entered into by Congress and the agencies.

The conflicting needs of administrative flexibility and congressional control are often reconciled by "reprogramming" agreements. An agency is given some latitude to shift funds *within* an appropriation account, moving them from one program to another. Legislative controls have gradually tightened. Initially the appropriation committees required regular reporting by the agencies, but reprogrammings over a designated dollar threshold must now be approved by appropriations subcommittees and, in some cases, by authorizing committees that have JURISDICTION over the program. Although these reprogramming procedures are largely nonstatutory and therefore fall short of legally binding requirements, they have become highly formalized and structured. They are incorporated not only in congressional documents but also in agency directives, instructions, and financial management manuals.

Another form of executive spending discretion results from transfer authority. A transfer involves the shifting of funds from one appropriation account to another (in contrast to reprogramming, where funds remain within an account). Moreover, the authority to transfer funds must be explicitly granted by statute. Transfer authority is usually accompanied by limitations, such as allowing a five percent leeway, that help preserve the general budgetary priorities of Congress. When agencies use transfer or reprogramming authority to spend funds on programs that had been previously rejected by Congress, or to enter into long-term financial commitments, Congress responds by adopting additional statutory and nonstatutory restrictions.

Agencies have access to billions of dollars that are hidden from public and congressional view. Confidential and secret funding collides with the requirement of Article I, section 9, of the Constitution: "A regular Statement and Account of the Receipts and Expenditures of all public Money shall be published from time to time." Confidential funds appeared as early as 1790, when Congress appropriated $40,000 to the President to pay for special diplomatic agents. Congress let the President decide the degree to which these expenditures would be made public. Since that time confidential (unvouchered) funds have been made available to many agencies that have domestic as well as foreign responsibilities.

Confidential funding is overt at least in the sense that the amounts are identified in appropriation or authorization bills. Secret funding is covert at every stage, from appropriation straight through to expenditure and auditing. Appropriations, ostensibly for the Defense Department or other agencies, are later siphoned off and allocated to the Central Intelligence Agency and other parts of the intelligence community. Absent congressional authorization, a federal taxpayer lacks STANDING to challenge the constitutionality of confidential or secret funding. The establishment of intelligence committees in the 1970s restored some semblance of congressional control. Legislation for the White House and the General Accounting Office has also tightened legislative control over unvouchered funds. With each increase in the scope of executive spending discretion, Congress participates ever more closely in administrative matters.

LOUIS FISHER

(SEE ALSO: *Impoundment.*)

Bibliography

FISHER, LOUIS 1975 *Presidential Spending Power.* Princeton, N.J.: Princeton University Press.

WILMERDING, LUCIUS, JR. 1943 *The Spending Power: A History of the Efforts of Congress to Control Expenditures.* New Haven, Conn.: Yale University Press.

PRESIDENTIAL SUCCESSION

The framework for electing a President and vice-president every four years is spelled out in the Constitution. As originally adopted, the Constitution was not clear about certain aspects of succession to the Presidency in the event something happened to the elected President. The Framers were content to establish the office of vice-president and to add the general provisions of Article II, section 1, clause 6: "In Case of the Removal of the President from Office, or of his Death, Resignation, or Inability to discharge the Powers and Duties of the said Office, the same shall devolve on the vice-president and the Congress may by Law provide for the Case of Removal, Death, Resignation or Inability, both of the President and Vice-President, declaring what Officer shall then act as President, and such officer shall act accordingly, until the Disability be removed, or a President shall be elected."

The Framers left unanswered questions concerning the status of a vice-president in cases of removal, death, resignation, and inability, the meaning of the term "inability," and the means by which the beginning and ending of an inability should be determined. Because no event occurred to trigger the succession provision, these ambiguities were of no consequence during the first half century of our nation's existence. Although three vice-presidents died in office and another resigned, the presidency and vice-presidency never became vacant at the same time. If that eventuality had come to pass, the president pro tempore of the Senate would have served as President under the provisions of a 1792 statute on presidential succession.

The ambiguities inherent in the succession provision surfaced in 1841 when President William Henry Harrison died in office. Despite protests that he had become only the "acting president," Vice-President JOHN TYLER assumed the office and title of President for the balance of Harrison's term. Tyler's claiming of the presidency, said JOHN QUINCY ADAMS, was "a construction in direct violation both of the grammar and context of the Constitution. . . ."

The precedent established by Tyler was followed twice within the next twenty-five years when Vice-Presidents MILLARD FILLMORE and ANDREW JOHNSON became President upon the deaths in office of Presidents ZACHARY TAYLOR and ABRAHAM LINCOLN. In 1881 the precedent became an obstacle to Vice-President CHESTER A. ARTHUR's acting as President during the eighty days that President JAMES A. GARFIELD hovered between life and death after being shot by an assassin. The view was strongly expressed at the time that if Arthur were to succeed to the presidency, then according to the Tyler precedent he would be President for the remainder of the presidential term regardless of whether Garfield recovered. Arthur made clear that he would not assume presidential responsibility lest he be labeled a usurper.

In the twentieth century the Tyler precedent was followed on the four occasions when Presidents died in office (WILLIAM MCKINLEY, WARREN G. HARDING, FRANKLIN D. ROOSEVELT, and JOHN F. KENNEDY). Once again, however, it became an obstacle to a vice-president's acting as President during the lengthy period WOODROW WILSON lay ill, unable to discharge the powers and duties of office. For the most part, presidential responsibility was assumed by the President's wife, doctor, and secretary.

Between 1955 and 1957 the lack of clarity in the succession provision was highlighted when President DWIGHT D. EISENHOWER sustained a heart attack, an attack of ileitis, and a stroke. Efforts to have Congress address the question were unsuccessful, but important groundwork for reform was established. President Kennedy's assassination in 1963 became the catalyst for implementing that reform. Congress proposed and the states ratified the TWENTY-FIFTH AMENDMENT to the Constitution to resolve the major issues surrounding the subject of presidential succession. The amendment confirmed that the vice-president becomes President for the remainder of the term in the case of death, removal, or resignation. In the case of an inability, the amendment provided that the vice-president serves as acting President only for the duration of the inability. The amendment provided for two methods of establishing the existence of an inability. The President was authorized to declare his own inability and, in such event, its termination. For the case where the President does not or cannot declare his own inability, it empowered the vice-president and a majority of the Cabinet to make the decision. If the President should dispute their determination, Congress decides the issue.

The amendment also established a mechanism for filling a vice-presidential vacancy: presidential nomination and confirmation by a majority of both houses of Congress. The Twenty-Fifth Amendment is supplemented by a statute on presidential succession adopted in 1947 which provided for the Speaker of the House of Representatives to serve as President in the event of a double vacancy in the offices of President and vice-president.

The Twenty-Fifth Amendment served the nation well in the 1970s when both a President and vice-president resigned from office during the same presidential term. Twice vice-presidents were nominated by the President and confirmed by Congress. The first of those vice-presidents, GERALD R. FORD, became President of the United States upon the resignation of RICHARD M. NIXON on August 9, 1974. Ford's succession, as did the eight preceding successions of vice-presidents, took place in a manner that demonstrated the stability and continuity of government in the United States.

JOHN D. FEERICK

Bibliography

BAYH, BIRCH 1968 *One Heartbeat Away.* Indianapolis: Bobbs-Merrill.

FEERICK, JOHN D. 1965 *From Failing Hands.* New York: Fordham University Press.

——— 1976 *The Twenty-Fifth Amendment.* New York: Fordham University Press.

SILVA, RUTH 1951 *Presidential Succession.* Ann Arbor: University of Michigan Press.

PRESUMPTION OF CONSTITUTIONALITY

See: Rational Basis; Standard of Review

PRETRIAL DISCLOSURE

The rules and practices governing pretrial disclosure to the opposing party differ dramatically in criminal and civil litigation. In civil disputes, each side has access to virtually all relevant information possessed by the other. In criminal cases, however, there has been a continuing debate which has focused on how much disclosure the prosecutor, with his superior investigative resources, should be required to make. The argument against wide-ranging disclosure is that it will result in witness intimidation and perjury. The arguments for disclosure are that a criminal trial should not be a "sporting event" in which one side tries to surprise the other, and that disclosure of the prosecution's EVIDENCE would aid the effective assistance of counsel to the accused guaranteed by the Sixth Amendment. (See RIGHT TO COUNSEL.)

Proponents of greater disclosure in criminal cases have made some gains in recent years through the expansion of DISCOVERY statutes. Rule 16 of the FEDERAL RULES OF CRIMINAL PROCEDURE is typical. The rule currently provides that, absent special circumstances, the government must disclose upon request: the defendant's own statements; his record of prior convictions; and documents, tangible evidence, or reports of examinations of the defendant or scientific tests the government intends to introduce at trial. The most striking difference between this rule and civil practice is that the criminal rule does not give the defense the power either to discover the identity of government witnesses or to compel them to testify under oath prior to trial. Several states provide for disclosure of prosecution witness lists, but Congress in 1974 rejected such a provision in the federal rules on the usual argument that disclosure of the identity of witnesses would possibly subject them to intimidation.

In addition to the slow but steady statutory expansion of pretrial disclosure by the government to the defense, there has been a reciprocal movement to entitle the prosecution to learn more about the defense case before trial. The argument that the policies underlying the Fifth Amendment RIGHT AGAINST SELF-INCRIMINATION shield the defense from any disclosure has largely been unsuccessful. Under the federal and many state rules, the defense can be requested to disclose any tangible evidence or results of physical or mental examinations it intends to introduce at trial, and to give notice of an alibi or insanity defense. The Supreme Court has upheld the constitutionality of compelling defense disclosure, provided that discovery is a two-way street; if the defendant is required to disclose alibi witnesses, for example, the government must also disclose any evidence that refutes the alibi.

Against the background of limited formal discovery rules, prosecutors frequently open files to the defense in an attempt to induce guilty pleas. Sometimes, also, judges exert informal pressure toward open discovery in order to avoid trial delays that might be caused by surprise evidence.

The Supreme Court has repeatedly held that a defendant has no general constitutional right to discovery, but it has required that the prosecution sometimes reveal "favorable" evidence. In *Brady v. Maryland* (1963) the government failed to disclose to a murder defendant that his companion had once admitted to a government agent that he had done the actual killing. The Court held that such a failure to disclose violates DUE PROCESS where the evidence is "material to guilt or punishment," irrespective of the good faith of the prosecution.

The lower courts generally gave an expansive reading to the *Brady* decision, but the Supreme Court curbed this development in *United States v. Agurs* (1976). The *Agurs* Court held that if the defense has not requested favorable evidence, or has made only a general request, a failure to disclose gives the defendant no constitutional right to a new trial unless there is a strong probability that the result of the first trial would not have been different had the favorable evidence been disclosed. Moreover, an appellate court should not grant a new trial so long as the trial judge remains reasonably convinced of the defendant's guilt. The *Agurs* Court also said that the failure to disclose evidence that reveals that the prosecution's case includes perjured testimony or the failure to disclose favorable evidence after it has been specifically requested by the defense, is "rarely excusable." In these two situations, the Constitution requires that the defendant be given a new trial if there is any reasonable possibility that the verdict would have been different had the undisclosed evidence been admitted.

Thus, *Agurs* provided some ammunition to both sides of the debate over criminal discovery: it limited the general due process right but also created a category for all but automatic reversal when the prosecution fails to respond to a defense request for specific information or when the prosecution case includes the knowing use of perjury.

BARBARA ALLEN BABCOCK

Bibliography

BABCOCK, BARBARA 1982 Fair Play: Evidence Favorable to an Accused and Effective Assistance of Counsel. *Stanford Law Review* 34:1133–1182.

PREVENTIVE DETENTION

Preventive detention is the jailing of an accused not to prevent bail-skipping but to protect public safety pending trial. Although pretrial incarceration of criminal defendants has long been condoned when necessary to assure their appearance in court, the constitutional status of preventive detention is far less certain. The Supreme Court has never directly addressed the issue, in part because until quite recently it was rendered largely academic by a federal statutory right to BAIL in noncapital cases and by similar rights granted in most state constitutions. Since 1970, however, District of Columbia courts have been authorized to deny pretrial release in certain cases to suspects charged with "dangerous" crimes, and several states have recently amended their constitutions to allow detention under similar circumstances. Following this activity, Congress in 1984 passed a nationwide program of preventive detention, substantially curtailing the federal statutory right to bail for the first time since the right was enacted in 1789.

The constitutionality of these programs is not altogether free from doubt. To begin with, the Eighth Amendment bars the federal government from requiring "excessive bail." Commentators have waged a spirited debate over whether that prohibition implies that some bail must be set. Many constitutional scholars have argued that the Framers intended to provide an affirmative right to bail to all defendants who do not pose an unacceptable risk of flight, and that without such a right the "excessive bail" clause would be a senseless bar against the government's doing indirectly what it remained free to do directly. Others have contended that the clause is aimed at the courts, not at Congress, and that a restriction on judicial discretion in setting bail is fully consistent with legislative authority to determine the circumstances under which bail should be granted at all.

The Supreme Court's decisions and opinions on the issue have been inconclusive. In *Stack v. Boyle* (1951) the Court held that bail was "excessive" when set higher than necessary to assure the accused's presence at trial. Strictly speaking, the ruling concerned only the level at which bail may be set if it is set, but the Court also hinted that the right to bail in the first place, long accorded by federal statute, might have a constitutional dimension: "Unless this right to bail before trial is preserved, the presumption of innocence, secured only after centuries of struggle, would lose its meaning."

The rule of *Stack v. Boyle* regarding bail amounts has remained undisturbed, despite general recognition that in practice bail is frequently set with a covert eye to whether the defendant seems likely to commit crimes before trial. The Supreme Court quickly backed away, however, from its strong if cryptic endorsement of the "right to bail." In *Carlson v. Landon* (1952) the Court approved the denial of bail, for reasons of public safety, to alien communists held pending deportation hearings. The Eighth Amendment, the Court explained, does not grant "a right to bail in all cases," but only provides "that bail shall not be excessive in those cases where it is proper to grant bail." The Court noted in particular that the amendment "has not prevented Congress from determining the classes of cases in which bail should be allowed."

Despite these seemingly categorical remarks, the effect of *Carlson* on the legacy of *Stack v. Boyle* remains unclear. The *Carlson* decision seems to have been based primarily on the differences between a criminal prosecution against a citizen and a deportation proceeding against an alien; the Court concluded only that "the Eighth Amendment does not require that bail be allowed under the circumstances of these cases."

Whether or not the Eighth Amendment provides a right to bail, preventive detention may raise questions of constitutionality under the DUE PROCESS clauses of the Fifth and FOURTEENTH AMENDMENTS. In *Bell v. Wolfish* (1979) the Supreme Court rejected a related argument, suggested in part by its own opinion in *Stack v. Boyle,* that the "presumption of innocence" limits what the government may do to a criminal defendant before conviction. The Court explained in *Wolfish* that the presumption of innocence is nothing but an evidentiary rule to be applied at trial; "it has no application to a determination of the rights of a pretrial detainee." The due process clauses, however, do apply before the commencement of trial, and *Wolfish* and later decisions have made clear that those clauses, in addition to constraining the permissible forms of detention and setting minimum procedural safeguards, also bar absolutely the "punishment" of an accused before conviction.

In testing for punishment in this context, the Supreme Court has considered, among other things, the government's reasons for imposing a given measure. The highest local court in the District of Columbia concluded in 1981 that incarceration for preventive purposes is nonpunitive and hence may be imposed before trial. The Supreme Court reasoned differently in BROWN V. UNITED STATES (1965), concluding that a preventive rationale should not stop confinement from being punishment for purposes of the BILL OF ATTAINDER clauses, but it has made no similar determination under the due process clauses.

The question whether the Constitution permits pretrial detention for purposes other than assuring a defendant's appearance in court thus remains open. A small part of the question was answered in SCHALL V. MARTIN (1984), where the Court upheld a state program of preventive detention for accused juvenile delinquents, but *Schall* relied heavily on the special prerogatives which the Constitution allows the state with respect to juveniles. Whether unconvicted adults may be jailed to keep them from committing future crimes remains a question to be decided.

The difficulty of the question reflects the strain placed on constitutional norms by the exigencies of the pretrial period. Preventive detention is difficult to reconcile with the ideal of due process, but many people are understandably made uneasy by the thought of defendants "walking the streets" while awaiting trial for serious crimes. A partial solution to the dilemma may be found in the Sixth Amendment's guarantee of a speedy trial: greater fidelity to that provision would alleviate to some extent both the risks associated with pretrial release and the inherent tension between due process and any restraint on the liberty of unconvicted defendants.

ABNER J. MIKVA

Bibliography

VERRILLI, DONALD B., JR. 1982 The Eighth Amendment and the Right to Bail: Historical Perspectives. *Columbia Law Review* 82:328–362.

PRICE, UNITED STATES v.
383 U.S. 787 (1966)

Eighteen defendants implicated in the murder of three CIVIL RIGHTS workers in Mississippi challenged the INDICTMENTS against them under the federal CIVIL RIGHTS ACT OF 1866 and that of 1870. One act applied only to persons conspiring to violate any federally protected right, the other only to persons acting "under COLOR OF LAW" who willfully violated such rights. Previous decisions of the Supreme Court had limited the two statutes. "Under color of law" covered only officers and in effect meant STATE ACTION, thus excluding private persons from prosecution. The language of the conspiracy statute notwithstanding, the Court had previously applied it to protect only the narrow class of rights that Congress could, apart from the FOURTEENTH AMENDMENT, protect against private individuals' interference, thus excluding the bulk of civil rights. Justice ABE FORTAS for a unanimous Court ruled that when private persons act in concert with state officials they all act under color of law, because they willfully participate in the prohibited activity (deprivation of life without DUE PROCESS OF LAW) with the state or its agents. Fortas also ruled that the 1870 act meant what it said: it safeguarded *all* federally protected rights secured by the supreme law of the land. By remanding the cases for trial, the Court made possible the first conviction in a federal prosecution for a civil rights murder in the South since Reconstruction.

LEONARD W. LEVY

PRICE-FIXING

See: Antitrust Law and the Constitution; Economic Regulation

PRIGG v. PENNSYLVANIA
16 Peters 539 (1842)

In 1839 Edward Prigg was convicted of kidnapping for removing an alleged fugitive slave from Pennsylvania without obtaining a warrant from a state judge as required by a Pennsylvania act of 1826. Prigg eventually appealed to the United States Supreme Court. Justice JOSEPH STORY, speaking for the Court, overturned his conviction. Story determined: (1) The federal Fugitive Slave Law of 1793 was constitutional. This was the first Supreme Court decision on that issue. (2) All state laws interfering with the rendition of fugitive slaves were unconstitutional. (3) The Fugitive Slave clause of the United States Constitution (Article IV, section 2, clause 3) was in part self-executing, and a slaveowner or his agent could capture and return a runaway slave under a right of self-help, without relying on any statute or judicial procedure, as long as the capture did not breach the peace. (4) State jurists and officials ought to help enforce the federal act of 1793, but Congress could not compel them to do so. Chief Justice ROGER B. TANEY concurred in Story's decision, but not his reasoning. Taney distorted Story's opinion by erroneously asserting that Story had declared it was illegal for state officials to aid in the rendition of fugitive slaves. In fact, Story encouraged the states to aid in the rendition process, but he believed Congress could not compel state assistance. After the decision many free states enacted PERSONAL LIBERTY LAWS which removed state support for the federal act of 1793. With few federal officials to help masters, the law went unenforced in much of the North. This situation helped lead to the passage of a new and harsher fugitive slave law in 1850.

PAUL FINKELMAN

Bibliography

FINKELMAN, PAUL 1979 *Prigg v. Pennsylvania* and Northern State Courts: Antislavery Use of a Proslavery Decision. *Civil War History* 25:5–35.

PRIMARY ELECTION

The primary election for selecting candidates is a uniquely American innovation. First adopted in Wisconsin in 1905, it has since spread to every other state. Generally it is the required method for selecting major POLITICAL PARTIES' nominees, whose names are automatically placed on the general election ballot, and for narrowing the field in nonpartisan elections.

The Supreme Court has not heard a modern constitutional challenge to state authority to compel political parties to select their candidates at primaries or to define party membership for these purposes. In *Cousins v. Wigoda* (1975), however, the Supreme Court held that Illinois could not require the Democratic National Convention to seat delegates selected in the state's primary; and in *Democratic Party v. La-Follette* (1981) the Court held that Wisconsin's delegates could not be bound by state law to follow candidate preferences expressed by voters in the state's presidential primary. In both cases, the Justices declared that the "party and its adherents enjoy a constitutionally protected right of political association." And in *Democratic Party* the Court said that "the freedom to associate . . . necessarily presupposes the freedom to identify the people who constitute the association, and to limit association to those people only." The Justices recognized state interests in the conduct of primary elections, however, and their decisions specifically addressed attempts to regulate the conduct of national party conventions and delegates. States might be able to limit the privilege of automatic access to the ballot to those parties conforming with state primary laws.

The Supreme Court has upheld state primary laws that protect the interests of political parties. In 1976 it affirmed a lower court judgment upholding a state's closed primary against a challenge that it abridged the right to vote and violated the RIGHT OF PRIVACY in political affiliation and belief. Similarly, the Court upheld, in *Rosario v. Rockefeller* (1973), an extended waiting period for voters wishing to change party registration, thus protecting party primaries from invasion by opposition party adherents and from casual participation by independent voters. But in *Kusper v. Pontikes* (1973), the Court acknowledged a competing interest in voter participation by rejecting a waiting period so long that the voter wishing to change party affiliation was excluded entirely from at least one primary election.

The Supreme Court has concluded that Congress has authority to regulate primary elections to nominate candidates for federal office, including prohibition of fraud, bribery, and other practices that deprive voters of rights, in UNITED STATES v. CLASSIC (1941) and *Burroughs v. United States* (1934), and regulation of political finance practices, in BUCKLEY v. VALEO (1976). Additional authority to regulate primaries is encompassed within the enforcement clauses of the FOURTEENTH and FIFTEENTH AMENDMENTS.

The principal clauses of these amendments also have independent application to primary elections, apart from any regulatory legislation Congress may enact. Once a state has established the primary for nominating candidates, the ONE PERSON-ONE VOTE principle of the apportionment cases applies. RACIAL DISCRIMINATION in primaries has been held unconstitutional, whether these barriers are established by the state, as in NIXON V. HERNDON (1927), or by political parties pursuant to state authorization to define party membership, as in NIXON V. CONDON (1932) and SMITH V. ALLWRIGHT (1944). Racial discrimination has also been held unconstitutional in a primary operated exclusively by a political party following the state's repeal of its primary election system. The most far-reaching application of the Fifteenth Amendment, in TERRY V. ADAMS (1953), prohibited racial discrimination in a "pre-primary" straw vote conducted by an all-white political club, when such "pre-primaries" had regularly proved determinative of elections.

In *Cousins v. Wigoda* the Supreme Court held that state primary laws do not supersede the authority of national party conventions over the selection and seating of delegates, but it did not choose to make a broad decision between competing claims of FREEDOM OF ASSOCIATION of political parties and governmental authority to regulate nomination activities. On one side of this continuing constitutional controversy lie assertions of FIRST AMENDMENT rights of parties to define their own membership, to control the composition and operation of party bodies, and to nominate candidates. On the other side lie assertions of state and congressional authority to regulate elections, of congressional power specifically granted in the enforcement clauses of the Fourteenth and Fifteenth Amendments, and of the independent operation of the principal clauses of those amendments. Notwithstanding the Supreme Court's reluctance to decide this question broadly, the Court's decisions have increasingly recognized the freedom of association of political parties.

DAVID ADAMANY

PRINCE v. MASSACHUSETTS
321 U.S. 158 (1944)

Massachusetts law provided that no boy under twelve or girl under eighteen could engage in street sale of any merchandise. Prince was the guardian of a nine-year-old girl. Both were Jehovah's Witnesses and sold Witness literature. The question was whether the statute impermissibly infringed on the free exercise of religion.

Writing for the Court, Justice WILEY B. RUTLEDGE balanced the broad powers of the state to protect the health and welfare of minors against the FIRST AMENDMENT claims and held that the state's power prevailed. Justices FRANK MURPHY and ROBERT H. JACKSON dissented.

Prince follows the "secular regulation" approach to RELIGIOUS LIBERTY introduced by UNITED STATES V. REYNOLDS (1879).

RICHARD E. MORGAN

PRIOR INCONSISTENT TESTIMONY

See: Confrontation

PRIOR RESTRAINT AND CENSORSHIP

History has rooted in our constitutional tradition of freedom of expression the strongest aversion to official censorship. We have learned from the English rejection of press licensing and from our own experiences that the psychology of censors tends to drive them to excess, that censors have a stake in finding things to suppress, and that—in systems of wholesale review before publication—doubt tends to produce suppression. American law tolerated motion picture censorship for a time, but only because movies were not thought to be "the press" in FIRST AMENDMENT terms. Censorship of the movies is now virtually dead, smothered by stringent procedural requirements imposed by unsympathetic courts, by the voluntary rating system, and, most of all, by public distaste for the absurdities of censorship in operation.

American law has tolerated requirements of prior official approval of expression in several important areas, however. No one may broadcast without a license, and the government issues licenses without charge to those it believes will serve the "public interest." Licensing is also grudgingly tolerated—because of the desirability of giving notice and of avoiding conflicts or other disruptions of the normal functions of public places—in the regulation of parades, demonstrations, leafleting, and other expressive activities in public places. But the courts have taken pains to eliminate administrative discretion that would allow officials to censor PUBLIC FORUM expression because they do not approve its message.

Notwithstanding these areas where censorship has been permitted, the clearest principle of First Amendment law is that the least tolerable form of official regulation of expression is a requirement of prior official approval for publication. It is easy to see the suffocating tendency of prior restraints where all expression—whether or not ultimately deemed protected by the First Amendment for publication—must be submitted for clearance before it may be disseminated. The harder question of First Amendment theory has been whether advance prohibitions on expression in specific cases should be discredited by our historical aversion to censorship. The question has arisen most frequently in the context of judicial INJUNCTIONS against publication. Even though injunctions do not involve many of the worst vices of wholesale licensing and censorship, the Supreme court has tarred them with the brush of "prior restraint."

The seminal case was NEAR V. MINNESOTA (1931), handed down by a closely divided Court but never questioned since. A state statute provided for injunctions against any "malicious, scandalous, and defamatory newspaper," and a state judge had enjoined a scandal sheet from publishing anything scandalous in the future. The Minnesota scheme did not require advance approval of all publications, but came into play only after a publication had been found scandalous, and then only to prevent further similar publications. Nevertheless, the majority of the Justices concluded that to enjoin future editions under such vague standards in effect put the newspaper under judicial censorship. Chief Justice CHARLES EVANS HUGHES's historic opinion made clear, however, that the First Amendment's bar against prior restraint was not absolute. Various exceptional instances would justify prior restraints, including this pregnant one: "No one would question but that a government might prevent actual obstruction to its recruiting service or the publication of the sailing dates of transports or the number and location of troops."

It was forty years before the scope of the troop ship exception was tested. The *Pentagon Papers* decision of 1971, NEW YORK TIMES CO. V. UNITED STATES, reaffirmed that judicial injunctions are considered prior restraints and are tolerated only in the most compelling circumstances. This principle barred an injunction against publication of a classified history of the government's decisions in the Vietnam war, although—unlike *Near*—the government had sought to enjoin only readily identifiable material, not unidentified similar publications in the future. Ten different opinions discussed the problem of injunctions in national security cases, and the only proposition commanding a majority was the unexplained conclusion that the government had not justified injunctive relief.

The central theme sounded in the opinions of the six majority Justices was reluctance to act in such difficult circumstances without guidance from Congress. Accepting the premise that there was no statutory authority for an injunction, several considerations support the Court's refusal to forge new rules concerning the disclosure of national secrets. First, the Court's tools are inadequate for the task; ad hoc evaluations of executive claims of risk are not easily balanced against the First Amendment's language and judicial interpretation. Second, dissemination of secret information often arises in the context of heated disagreements about the proper direction of national policy. One's assessment of the disclosure's impact on security will depend on one's reaction to the policy. Third, it would be particularly unsatisfactory to build a judge-made system of rules in an area where much litigation must be done *in camera.* Thus, general rules about specific categories of defense-related information cannot be fashioned by courts. The best hope in a nuclear age for accommodating the needs of secrecy and the public's RIGHT TO KNOW lies in the legislative process where, removed from pressures of adjudicting particular cases, general rules can be fashioned. The courts' proper role in this area is to review legislation, not try to devise rules of secrecy case by case.

Chilling this victory for freedom of the press were admonitions, loosely endorsed by four Justices, that the espionage statutes might support criminal sanctions against the *New York Times* and its reporters. No journalists were indicted, but the prosecutions of Daniel Ellsberg and Anthony Russo rested on a view of several statutes that would reach the press by punishing news-gathering activities necessarily incident to publication. Since the dismissal of these cases for reasons irrelevant to these issues, the extent of possible criminal liability for publishing national security secrets remains unclear.

The *Pentagon Papers* case underlines how little the United States has relied on law to control press coverage of national defense and foreign policy matters. For most of our history the press has rarely tested the limits of its rights to publish. Secrets were kept because people in and out of government with access to military and diplomatic secrets shared basic assumptions about national aims. The Vietnam war changed all that. The *Pentagon Papers* dispute marked the passing of an era in which journalists could be counted on to work within understood limits of discretion in handling secret information.

The third major decision striking down a judicial order not to publish involved neither national security nor scandal but the right of a criminal defendant to a fair trial. A state court enjoined publication of an accused's confession and some other incriminating material on the ground that if prospective jurors learned about it they might be incapable of impartiality. In NEBRASKA PRESS ASSOCIATION V. STUART (1976) the Supreme Court decided that the potential prejudice was speculative, and it rejected enjoining publication on speculation. The majority opinion examined the evidence to determine the nature and extent of pretrial publicity, the effectiveness of other measures in mitigating prejudice, and the effectiveness of a prior restraint in reducing the dangers. This opinion determined that the impact of pretrial publicity was necessarily speculative, that alternative measures short of prior restraint had not been considered by the lower courts, and that prior restraint would not significantly reduce the dangers presented.

On one issue of considerable importance, the Court seemed to be in full agreement. The opinions endorsed controls on parties, lawyers, witnesses, and law enforcement personnel as sources of information for journalists. These GAG ORDERS have been controversial among many journalists and publishers who think the First Amendment should guarantee the right to gather news. Although freeing the press from direct control by limiting prior restraint, the Court approved an indirect method of reaching the same result, guaranteeing that the press print no prejudicial publicity, by approving direct controls on sources of prejudicial information. The Court has subsequently held that pretrial motions may be closed to the public and the press with the consent of the prosecutor and the accused but over the objection of the press, in GANNETT CO. V. DEPASQUALE (1979). This case involved access to judicial proceedings, not prior restraints on the press, and was decided largely on Sixth Amendment grounds. The Court reached the opposite result with respect to trials in RICHMOND NEWSPAPERS V. VIRGINIA (1980), but acknowledged that the right of access to trials is not absolute.

These decisions and others have firmly established that the First Amendment tolerates virtually no prior restraints. This DOCTRINE is one of the central principles of our law of FREEDOM OF THE PRESS. On the surface, the doctrine concerns only the form of controls on expression. It bars controls prior to publication, even if imposition of criminal or civil liability following publication would be constitutional. But, as with most limitations of form, the prior restraint doctrine has important substantive consequences. Perhaps the most important of these consequences is that the doctrine is presumably an absolute bar to any wholesale system of administrative licensing or censorship of the press, which is the most repellent form of government suppression of expression. Second, the prior restraint doctrine removes most of the opportunities for official control of those types of expression for which general rules of control are difficult to formulate. The message of the prior restraint doctrine is that if you cannot control expression pursuant to general legislative standards, you cannot control it at all—or nearly at all, as the *Pentagon Papers* decision suggests, by suggesting an exception allowing an injunction in a truly compelling case of national security. A third effect of the doctrine is that by transferring questions of control over expression from the judiciary to the legislatures, it provides an enormously beneficial protection for the politically powerful mass media, if not for other elements of society with strong First Amendment interests but weaker influence in the legislative process.

Although the Supreme Court has exceeded its historical warrant in subjecting judicial injunctions to the full burden of our law's traditional aversion to prior restraints, there are sound reasons for viewing all prior controls—not only wholesale licensing and censorship—as dangerous to free expression. Generally it is administratively easier to prevent expression in advance than to punish it after the fact. The inertia of public officials in responding to a *fait accompli*, the chance to look at whether expression has actually caused harm rather than speculate about the matter, public support for the speaker, and the interposition of juries and other procedural safeguards of the usual criminal or civil process all tend to reinforce tolerance when expression can only be dealt with by subsequent punishment. Moreover, all prior restraint systems, including injunctions, tend to divert attention from the central question of whether expression is protected to the subsidiary problem of promoting the effectiveness of the prior restraint system. Once a prior restraint is issued, the authority and prestige of the restraining agent are at stake. If it is disobeyed, the legality of the expression takes a back seat to the enforcement of obedience to the prior restraint process. Moreover, the time it takes a prior restraint process to decide produces a systematic delay of expression. On the other hand, where law must wait to move against expression after it has been published, time is on the side of freedom. All in all, even such prior restraints as judicial injunctions—which are more discriminating than wholesale censorship—tend toward irresponsible administration and an exaggerated assessment of the dangers of free expression.

BENNO C. SCHMIDT, JR.

Bibliography

BLASI, VINCENT 1981 Toward a Theory of Prior Restraint: The Central Linkage. *Minnesota Law Review* 66:11.

EMERSON, THOMAS 1955 The Doctrine of Prior Restraint *Law and Contemporary Problems* 20:648.

SCHMIDT, BENNO C., JR. 1977 Nebraska Press Association: An Expansion of Freedom and Contraction of Theory. *Stanford Law Review* 29:431.

PRISONERS' RIGHTS

Some might think that the very term "prisoners' rights" is an oxymoron, because the essence of being imprisoned is the reduction or elimination of rights. Prisoners have traditionally been deprived of VOTING RIGHTS and, obviously, of the right to travel outside the prison confines, often of the right to communicate freely with the outside world and of the right of conjugal relationships, and, at times, of the right of ACCESS TO COURTS to complain about even those rights that they retain.

There is a tension in constitutional doctrine between the need to enforce discipline in the difficult circumstances of the prison and the necessity of recognizing that in a society of law, even prisoners ought to have remedies for violation of whatever constitutional rights they possess and also to have the right to be immune from arbitrary and capricious actions of the prison hierarchy. This tension has expressed itself in judicial opinions in two major ways: first, the enunciation of a "hands-off doctrine" that precludes JURISDICTION to review complaints of inmates; and second, the determination, either broadly or narrowly, of the nature of the rights that a prisoner might have. In times when the cluster of rights is extremely narrow, the distinction between the first mode of analysis and the second is not great.

As late as 1963 a commentator could write that there is a "conviction held with virtual unanimity by the courts that it is beyond their power to review the internal management of the prison system." Much of this changed, however, when the Supreme Court held in *Wolff v. McDonnell* (1974), as part of its expansion of PROCEDURAL DUE PROCESS to the decision making of many institutions, that "a prisoner is not wholly stripped of constitutional protections when he is imprisoned for crime. There is no iron curtain drawn between the Constitution and the prisons of this country."

Still, the definition of rights for prisoners is almost always husbanded with conditions and recognition of concerns for the difficulties the warden faces. Where the FIRST AMENDMENT is concerned, RELIGIOUS LIBERTY is guaranteed but only to the extent that the opportunities to exercise that freedom must be "reasonable." Similarly, when the right to speak and communicate is concerned, the Court limited it in PELL V. PROCUNIER (1974) to the kind of expression that is "not inconsistent with [their] status as . . . prisoner[s] or with the legitimate penological objectives of the corrections system." In *Lee v. Washington* (1968) the Court implied that even racial SEGREGATION may be tolerated when it is essential to "prison security and discipline." And the Court held in *Hudson v. Palmer* (1984), a departure from previous expansion of privacy rights, that "the FOURTH AMENDMENT had no applicability to a prison cell."

With the wonderful perversity that makes legal development fascinating, the Supreme Court, in the late 1970s, expanded prisoners' rights of access to courts, while almost simultaneously narrowing the grounds for constitutional challenge.

Litigation concerning prisoners' rights is an indicator of concern about individual rights generally. As the Court changes its views of the breadth and definition of such rights, the treatment of alleged institutional wrongs in a correctional setting is like the canary a miner takes along down the shaft. Constitutional litigation during the 1960s and 1970s created massive exposure of the internal workings of correctional institutions and pressure for change. In many instances, wholesale reforms were imposed upon these institutions as a consequence of the litigation. But the canary is weakening. (See INSTITUTIONAL LITIGATION.)

MONROE E. PRICE

Bibliography

NOTE 1963 Beyond the Ken of the Courts: A Critique of Judicial Refusal to Review the Complaints of Convicts. *Yale Law Journal* 72:506.

PRIVACY

See: Right of Privacy

PRIVACY ACT
88 Stat. 1896 (1974)

The Privacy Act was passed in response to public concern about "data banks" maintained by United States government agencies. Often, a person did not know what agencies held files on him or what such files contained. In addition, information provided to one government agency—often under a promise of confidentiality—was passed on to a second agency to be used for a different purpose, and that without the knowledge or consent of the individual concerned.

The act was passed by Congress and signed by President GERALD R. FORD in December 1974. According to its provisions: an individual is to have access to any files concerning him maintained by a government agency (except law-enforcement and national security files); an individual who believes that information about him in a government file is inaccurate or incomplete may seek injunctive relief to correct the file; no agency is to use information provided by an individual for other than the original purpose, or to provide the information to another agency, without the individual's consent; no agency may deny benefits to individuals who refuse to disclose their social security numbers; and no agency may maintain records describing the exercise of rights protected by the FIRST AMENDMENT.

DENNIS J. MAHONEY

Bibliography

O'BRIEN, DAVID M. *1979 Privacy, Law, and Public Policy.* New York: Praeger.

PRIVACY AND THE FIRST AMENDMENT

William L. Prosser has listed four categories of invasion of privacy: intrusion upon the plaintiff's seclusion or solitude, or into his private affairs; public disclosure of embarrassing private facts about the plaintiff; publicity which places the plaintiff in a false light in the public eye; and appropriation, for the defendant's advantage, of the plaintiff's name or likeness. Absent the communication of information disclosed by the intrusion, the first category of invasion raises no FIRST AMENDMENT issue.

The second category, the public disclosure of embarrassing private facts, clearly does raise a First Amendment issue. When does the FREEDOM OF THE PRESS to report "news" outbalance the individual's RIGHT TO PRIVACY, even if the disclosure is of embarrassing private facts? Thus far, the Supreme Court has only partially answered that question. In COX BROADCASTING CORPORATION V. COHN (1975) the Court held that the state could not impose liability for invasion of privacy by reason of the defendant's television news disclosure of the name of a rape victim. The Court held that the First Amendment immunized the press from such liability where the information disclosed was truthful and had already been publicly disclosed in court records. Subsequent decisions have indicated that such a First Amendment privilege applies as well to the publication of material in at least some official records designated confidential—for example, information about a criminal proceeding involving a juvenile, even though it was obtained from sources other than the public record. But what of intimate private fact disclosures that do not involve criminal proceedings, or other official action? Or suppose the disclosure of private facts is embarrassing to the subject, but does not injure reputation. Which prevails, the plaintiff's right of privacy or the defendant's FREEDOM OF SPEECH? The Supreme Court thus far has been silent on these issues, and the lower courts have offered no satisfactory answers.

The third category, known as "false light" privacy, was the subject of the Supreme Court's decision in *Time, Inc. v. Hill* (1967). Defendant's report in *Life* magazine of plaintiffs' encounter with gangsters was in part false, though not reputation injuring. The Supreme Court held that the defendant was entitled to a First Amendment defense in a false-light privacy action unless the defendant knew the matter reported was false or published with reckless disregard of the truth. The Court acknowledged that this standard was borrowed from the First Amendment defense to DEFAMATION which it had fashioned in NEW YORK TIMES V. SULLIVAN (1964). Where *Sullivan* had involved statements about a public official, *Hill* seemingly extended the First Amendment privilege to statements about "a matter of public interest." The First Amendment defamation defense was later expanded in GERTZ V. ROBERT WELCH, INC. (1974) to apply to reports involving "public figures" as well as "public officials," and to require at least a negligence standard of liability as regards defamation of nonpublic figures. The Supreme Court has not had occasion to reconsider the impact of the First Amendment upon "false light" privacy cases since its decision in *Gertz.*

The fourth category is more generally referred to as the "right of publicity." It differs fundamentally from the other categories in that the injury does not consist of embarrassment and humiliation. It is based rather upon the wrongful appropriation of a person's (usually a celebrity's) name or likeness for commercial purposes. The measure of recovery is based upon the value of the use, not the injury suffered from mental distress. The only Supreme Court decision to consider the impact of the First Amendment upon the right of publicity has been *Zacchini v. Scripps-Howard Broadcasting Co.* (1977). The plaintiff performed a "human cannonball" act at a county fair. The defendant photographed his entire act and broadcast it in a local television news program. Plaintiff sued for infringement of his right of publicity. The Supreme Court held that the defendant was not entitled to a First Amendment defense. The Court regarded this as "the strongest case" for the right of publicity because it involved "the appropriation of the very activity by which the entertainer acquired his reputation in the first place." Even in the usual case, where a celebrity's name or likeness is used in order to sell a product, the lower courts have not found the First Amendment to constitute a defense, and it seems unlikely that the Supreme Court would take a contrary view. On the other hand, where the name or likeness is used as a part of an informational work, such as a biography or a biographical motion picture, in most cases the First Amendment would appear to constitute a valid defense.

MELVILLE B. NIMMER

Bibliography

NIMMER, MELVILLE B. 1968 The Right to Speak from *Times* to *Time:* First Amendment Theory Applied to Libel and Misapplied to Privacy. *California Law Review* 56:935–967.

PROSSER, WILLIAM L. 1971 *Torts,* 4th ed. St. Paul, Minn.: West Publishing Co.

PRIVILEGE, EVIDENTIARY

See: Evidentiary Privileges

PRIVILEGE AGAINST SELF-INCRIMINATION

See: Right Against Self-Incrimination

PRIVILEGED COMMENT

See: Libel and the First Amendment

PRIVILEGE FROM ARREST

That legislators should be free from the threat of arrest except for notorious crimes while attending legislative sessions or en route to or from them has been recognized in English law for at least 1300 years. After the American Revolution that privilege was inserted into several state constitutions and the ARTICLES OF CONFEDERATION.

Because the privilege does not extend to "TREASON, FELONY, or BREACH OF THE PEACE," it amounts in practice to immunity from arrest in civil matters, such as nonpayment of debts. The privilege is less a guarantee of legislative independence from executive abuse than a protection of public business from interference growing out of private disputes.

DENNIS J. MAHONEY

PRIVILEGES AND IMMUNITIES

The Constitution's two privileges and immunities clauses were born of different historical circumstances and inspired by different purposes. Yet they are bound together by more than their textual similarity. Both clauses look to the formation of "a more perfect Union," both sound the theme of equality, and both have raised questions about the role of the federal judiciary in protecting NATURAL RIGHTS.

The original Constitution's Article IV set out several principles to govern relations among the states. The FULL FAITH AND CREDIT CLAUSE established one such principle, and so did the clauses providing for interstate rendition of fugitive felons and fugitive slaves. (See SLAVERY AND THE CONSTITUTION; FUGITIVE SLAVERY; FUGITIVE FROM JUSTICE.) Along with these "interstate comity" provisions was included this guarantee: "The citizens of each state shall be entitled to all privileges and immunities of citizens in the several states." Called "the basis of the Union" by ALEXANDER HAMILTON in THE FEDERALIST #80, the first privileges and immunities clause aimed at preventing a state from subjecting another state's citizens to discriminatory treatment of the kind customarily given to ALIENS. The framers saw the clause as embodying the principles of a much longer provision in the ARTICLES OF CONFEDERATION, which had begun with this statement of objective: "The better to secure and perpetuate mutual friendship and intercourse among the people of the different states in this union. . . ."

From the beginning everyone understood that Article IV's privileges and immunities clause could not mean exactly what it said. A Virginian who came to Boston surely had a right to engage in trade, but just as surely could not expect to be a candidate for governor of Massachusetts. What principle distinguished these two activities? Early in the nineteenth century, Justice BUSHROD WASHINGTON, sitting on circuit in CORFIELD V. CORYELL (1823), read the clause to guarantee equality for out-of-state citizens only as to "those privileges and immunities which are, in their nature, fundamental; which belong, of right, to the citizens of all free governments; and which have, at all times, been enjoyed by the citizens of the several states which comprise this Union. . . ." Washington went on to list "some" of those "fundamental" privileges, in language broadly inclusive of nearly every sort of right imaginable. Not only did a citizen of one state have a right "to pass through, or to reside in any other state for purposes of trade, agriculture, professional pursuits, or otherwise"; he also had the right, said Washington, to "enjoyment of life and liberty, with the right to acquire and possess property of every kind, and to pursue and obtain happiness and safety; subject nevertheless to such restraints as the government may justly prescribe for the general good of the whole." Other rights were listed, such as a right of access to a state's courts and a right to nondiscriminatory taxation. Portentously, the passage ended by mentioning "the elective franchise" as a fundamental right.

No one, not even Washington, thought a state had a constitutional duty to let out-of-staters vote in state elections. The inference arises that in offering his list of "fundamental" privileges and immunities Washington had in mind something beyond a catalogue of rights of interstate equality. That broader objective may have been to make Article IV's privileges and immunities clause into a generalized federal constitutional guarantee of liberty, available to local citizens and out-of-staters alike—with identification and enforcement of "fundamental" liberties in the hands of the federal judiciary.

This "natural rights" vision of the privileges and immunities clause of Article IV has never found favor in the Supreme Court. The Court has not interpreted the clause as a source of substantive rights, apart from the right to some measure of equality in a state's treatment of citizens of other states. The term "citizens" has been consistently limited, in this context, to natural persons who are citizens of the United States, thus excluding both corporations and aliens from the clause's protection. The substantive reach of the clause, too, was narrow in the Court's early interpretations: the right to pursue a common calling, the right to own and deal with property, the right of access to state courts.

Even in this restrictive interpretation, the interstate equality demanded by the clause overlaps with the antidiscrimination principle that restricts STATE REGULATIONS OF COMMERCE. The same law, in other words, might violate both the implied limitations of the COMMERCE CLAUSE and the privileges and immunities clause of Article IV. Yet the commerce clause has been a more significant guarantee against interstate discrimination. The commerce clause presumptively forbids a state to discriminate against INTERSTATE (or FOREIGN) COMMERCE, even when the persons engaging in that commerce are the state's own citizens. And the commerce clause, unlike the privileges and immunities clause, protects both corporations and aliens from discrimination against their activities in commerce.

A major shift in judicial attitude toward the privileges and immunities clause was signaled by TOOMER V. WITSELL (1948). South Carolina licensed shrimp boats in coastal waters, demanding license fees of $25 per boat from residents and $2,500 from nonresidents. (Since the adoption of the FOURTEENTH AMENDMENT, state residence and state citizenship have been treated as virtually equivalent.) The Supreme Court held this discrimination a violation of both the commerce clause and the privileges and immunities clause, and in its opinion reformulated the latter clause's governing doctrine. Henceforth any state discrimination against citizens of other states would be held invalid unless the state demonstrated a "substantial reason for the discrimination" apart from their out-of-state citizenship. In *Doe v. Bolton* (1973), a companion case to ROE V. WADE (1973), the Court applied the *Toomer* formula to strike down a Georgia law allowing only state residents to obtain abortions in Georgia.

Toomer seemed to have dispatched the "fundamental" privileges limitation in favor of a straightforward requirement of substantial justification for discrimination against out-of-staters. But here as elsewhere in constitutional law the idea of FUNDAMENTAL INTERESTS has had remarkable recuperative power. BALDWIN V. FISH & GAME COMMISSION (1978) revived the doctrine to uphold a Montana law that charged a state resident $9 for an elk hunting license and a nonresident $225. (The nonresident might also use the license to kill one bear and one deer, to shoot game birds, and to fish. The same package of sanguinary privileges would cost a resident $30.) Elk hunting, said the Court, was a sport, not a means to livelihood; equal access for out-of-staters to Montana elk was "not basic to the maintenance of well-being of the Union," and thus not a "fundamental" privilege protected by Article IV against interstate discrimination. Only four weeks later, in HICKLIN V. ORBECK (1978), the Court returned to the *Toomer* approach to invalidate an Alaska law giving preference to state residents in employment in jobs related to construction of the Alaska pipeline. The state had not offered substantial justification for the discrimination, the Court said, and therefore it was invalid. *Baldwin* was not cited.

The cleanest way to resolve the tension between these two decisions would have been to abandon *Baldwin* as a doctrinal sport. Instead, the Supreme Court combined both lines of decision in a new formula. In *United Building & Construction Trades Council v. Mayor and Council of Camden* (1984) and SUPREME COURT OF NEW HAMPSHIRE V. PIPER (1985) the Court established a two-part test for determining the validity of a state law challenged under Article IV's privileges and immunities clause. The first inquiry follows *Baldwin:* the law is limited by the clause only when its discrimination against out-of-staters touches a privilege that is "fundamental" to interstate harmony. The Court made clear in *Piper* that access to a means of livelihood is such a privilege. The second inquiry follows *Toomer* and *Hicklin:* if the privilege in question is "fundamental," the discrimination is invalid unless there is a "substantial" reason for treating out-of-staters differently, and the law's discrimination bears a "substantial relationship" to that objective. The second requirement states an intermediate STANDARD OF REVIEW for judicial scrutiny of both the state's purposes and its discriminatory means.

Special problems have plagued the Supreme Court's efforts to apply the privileges and immunities clause of Article IV to cases in which the discriminating states have acted as purchasers of goods and services, or owners of property, or proprietors of enterprises. In the *Camden* case, the Court refused to recognize a general exemption of such activities from the strictures of the clause; if the activities affected a "fundamental" interest, the clause would be implicated. In the same breath, however, the Court suggested that the state's interests as a market participant might be relevant to the second part of the new two-part inquiry: the question of justification for discriminating against out-of-staters. Justification for some state preferences for local citizens may be found in the citizens' obligations to support local government. *Toomer*'s teaching is that the justification must be substantial.

Thus far the privileges and immunities clause of Article IV has been applied only to state laws discriminating against out-of-staters. Concurring in *Zobel v. Williams* (1982), Justice SANDRA DAY O'CONNOR argued for a broader application of the clause that would place constitutional limits on any state law—even a law discriminating between different groups of the state's own citizens—when the law disadvantages persons who have only recently arrived in the state. Justice O'Connor would have found a violation of the clause in Alaska's law distributing the state's oil revenues to Alaska citizens in proportion to the length of their residence; she argued that the law imposed "disabilities of alienage"—a result the clause was designed to forbid. The majority, holding the law invalid on equal protection grounds, rejected this novel interpretation in favor of the conventional view: the privileges and immunities clause of Article IV is inapplicable to such a case, for the clause speaks only to discrimination against citizens of other states.

A second privileges and immunities clause was added to the Constitution in 1868 as part of the Fourteenth Amendment: "No state shall make or enforce any law which shall abridge the privileges or immunities of citizens of the United States." Justice ROBERT H. JACKSON, concurring in EDWARDS V. CALIFORNIA (1941), said expansively that "[t]his clause was adopted to make United States citizenship the dominant and paramount allegiance among us." The fact is that the amendment's framers did not sharply differentiate the functions of the various clauses of the amendment's first section and did not speak with one voice concerning the purposes of the privileges and immunities clause. Undoubtedly, however, the clause was meant to have some effect as a limitation on the states. The amendment's opening sentence "overruled" DRED SCOTT V. SANDFORD (1857) by conferring United States citizenship and state citizenship on "all persons born or naturalized in the United States and subject to the jurisdiction thereof." The privileges and immunities clause, following immediately in the amendment's text, surely was intended to give some substantive content to the rights of citizenship, and particularly to the equal citizenship of blacks. (See EQUAL PROTECTION OF THE LAWS.) Yet the Supreme Court, in its first encounter with the clause, read it, as Justice STEPHEN J. FIELD aptly said in dissent, to be "a vain and idle enactment, which accomplished nothing." In the SLAUGHTERHOUSE CASES (1873) a 5–4 majority, distinguishing the privileges and immunities of national citizenship from those of state citizenship, confined the former to rights established elsewhere in the Constitution and federal laws and to rights that were already fairly inferable from the relation of a citizen to the national government. (Examples of the latter would be the right to United States protection in other countries, the right to enter public lands, or the right to inform federal authorities of violations of federal law.) The majority described *Corfield*'s list of "fundamental" rights as privileges of state citizenship, subject to Article IV's guarantee of interstate equality but untouched by the new privileges and immunities clause of the Fourteenth Amendment.

The Court feared that a contrary reading of the privileges and immunities clause, coupled with the power of Congress to enforce the Fourteenth Amendment, would not only "constitute this court a perpetual censor upon all legislation of the states" but also "bring within the power of Congress the entire domain of civil rights heretofore belonging exclusively to the states." Such a result, the Court accurately said, would radically restructure the federal union, centralizing power in the national government. No doubt some congressional proponents of the Fourteenth Amendment had hoped for precisely that result. The *Slaughterhouse Cases* dissenters viewed the prospect with equanimity and even sought to revive the natural rights philosophy of *Corfield* in the name of the Fourteenth Amendment. In doctrinal terms, however, they lost the battle decisively. The Court has never given the Fourteenth Amendment's privileges and immunities clause any significant content that is distinctively its own.

Occasional flurries of activity have suggested impending revitalization of the clause. Justice HUGO L. BLACK made the clause a centerpiece in his effort to persuade the Court to recognize the total incorporation of the Bill of Rights into the Fourteenth Amendment. (See INCORPORATION DOCTRINE.) And for a season the clause came to life as a limitation on state taxing power, until MADDEN v. KENTUCKY (1940) overruled COLGATE v. HARVEY (1935). Individual Justices have promoted the clause in concurring opinions, such as that of Justice Jackson in *Edwards v. California* (1941) (right to move freely from state to state) and that of Justice OWEN ROBERTS in HAGUE v. COMMITTEE FOR INDUSTRIAL ORGANIZATION (1939) (right to assemble to discuss national legislation), but these ventures have been largely superseded by the development of other constitutional limitations on the states.

In the modern era, Justice Jackson's *Edwards* argument has borne fruit in the development of a constitutional RIGHT TO TRAVEL. The right is now well established as a limitation on state power, but the right's source in the Constitution remains unspecified. The commerce clause is one obvious candidate, and not just one but both privileges and immunities clauses have also been nominated. (Congressional interferences with the freedom of foreign travel have been tested against the Fifth Amendment's DUE PROCESS clause.) Plainly, the Supreme Court has no need to rely on either privileges and immunities clause as an independent source for the right to travel.

Although the natural rights approach to constitutional adjudication failed to make headway in the name of either of the privileges and immunities clauses, in the field of ECONOMIC REGULATION the views of the *Slaughterhouse Cases* dissenters came to prevail for almost half a century under the banner of SUBSTANTIVE DUE PROCESS. (See FREEDOM OF CONTRACT.) That experiment in JUDICIAL ACTIVISM was closed in the 1930s, but a similar philosophy has informed the revival of substantive due process as a protection of personal freedoms. Some commentators have suggested that the Fourteenth Amendment's privileges and immunities clause may be an apt vessel for these newer constitutional liberties, or even for yet-to-be-discovered affirmative constitutional obligations of government. After a century and more on the constitutional shelf, all the vessel needs is a little polishing.

KENNETH L. KARST

Bibliography

ELY, JOHN HART 1980 *Democracy and Distrust: A Theory of Judicial Review.* Pages 22–30. Cambridge, Mass.: Harvard University Press.

FAIRMAN, CHARLES 1971 *Reconstruction and Reunion, 1864–88, Part One.* Chap. 20. (Volume VI, History of the Supreme Court of the United States.) New York: Macmillan.

KURLAND, PHILIP B. 1972 The Privileges and Immunities Clause: "Its Hour Come Round at Last?" *Washington University Law Quarterly* 1972:405–420.

SIMSON, GARY J. 1979 Discrimination against Nonresidents and the Privileges and Immunities Clause of Article IV. *University of Pennsylvania Law Review* 128:379–401.

VARAT, JONATHAN D. 1981 State "Citizenship" and Interstate Equality. *University of Chicago Law Review* 48:487–572.

PRIVY COUNCIL

The Privy Council together with the monarch constitutes "the Crown," which is, in theory, the executive branch of the British government. Association of the council in the exercise of executive power was a check against the abuse of that power. The council is appointed for life and comprises members of the royal family, ministers and former ministers of state, judges, and distinguished subjects. In practice, the cabinet has become, through an evolutionary process, the executive committee of the Privy Council.

In the seventeenth and eighteenth centuries the Privy Council exercised the royal prerogative of disallowing acts of the colonial legislatures. At the same time the council was the highest court of appeal from the colonial courts (a function now exercised by the judicial committee of the Privy Council). The role of the Privy Council in the political order of the British Empire was thus suggestive of both the VETO POWER and JUDICIAL REVIEW.

Some of the early state constitutions provided for a council to share the executive power or to review acts of the legislature. At the CONSTITUTIONAL CONVENTION OF 1787 various unsuccessful proposals for a plural executive reflected the British notion of the Privy Council as a check against royal tyranny.

DENNIS J. MAHONEY

PRIZE CASES
2 Black (67 U.S.) 635 (1863)

In the *Prize Cases,* a 5–4 majority of the Supreme Court sustained the validity of President ABRAHAM LINCOLN's blockade proclamations of April 1861, refusing to declare unconstitutional his unilateral actions in meeting the Confederacy's military initiatives.

Lincoln proclaimed a blockade of southern ports on April 19 and 27, 1861. Congress authorized him to declare a state of insurrection by the Act of July 13, 1861, thereby, at least in the view of the dissenters, giving formal legislative recognition to the existence of civil war. By the Act of August 6, 1861, Congress retroactively ratified all Lincoln's military actions. The *Prize Cases* involved seizures of vessels bound for Confederate ports prior to July 13, 1861.

For the majority, Justice ROBERT C. GRIER held that a state of civil war existed de facto after the firing on Fort Sumter (April 12, 1861) and that the Supreme Court would take judicial notice of its existence. Though neither Congress nor President can declare war against a state of the Union, Grier conceded, when states waged war against the United States government, the President was "bound to meet it in the shape it presented itself, without waiting for Congress to baptize it with a name." Whether the insurgents were to be accorded belligerent status, and hence be subject to blockade, was a POLITICAL QUESTION to be decided by the President, whose decision was conclusive on the courts. Grier reproved the dissenters by reminding them that the court should not "cripple the arm of the government and paralyze its power by subtle definitions and ingenious sophisms."

Justice SAMUEL NELSON for the dissenters (Chief Justice ROGER B. TANEY, and Justices JOHN CATRON and NATHAN CLIFFORD) argued that only Congress can declare a war and that consequently the President can neither declare nor recognize it. A civil war's "existence in a material sense . . . has no relevancy or weight when the question is what constitutes war in a legal sense." Lincoln's acts before 13 July 1861 constituted merely his "personal war against those in rebellion." Therefore seizures under the blockade proclamations were illegal.

The *Prize Cases* permitted the federal government the convenient ambiguity of treating the Confederacy as an organized insurgency and as a conventional belligerent. The opinions also had an implicit relevance to other disputed exercises of presidential authority. Defenders of a broad executive power could argue that the majority opinion's reasoning supported the constitutionality of Lincoln's call for volunteers, of his suspension of the writ of HABEAS CORPUS, and perhaps also of the EMANCIPATION PROCLAMATION.

WILLIAM M. WIECEK

PROBABLE CAUSE

The FOURTH AMENDMENT guarantees in part that "The right of the people to be secure in their persons, houses, papers and effects, against UNREASONABLE SEARCHES and seizures shall not be violated, and no warrants shall issue but upon probable cause. . . ." The determination of probable cause necessarily turns on specific facts and often requires the courts and the police to make most difficult decisions. The need for probable cause in American CRIMINAL PROCEDURE arises in three instances: probable cause to ARREST or detain, probable cause to search, and probable cause to prosecute. The first two derive constitutional status directly from the Fourth Amendment and govern the conduct of the police. An inquiry by a judge or GRAND JURY into probable cause for prosecution is not constitutionally required in state cases; however, this check on the exercise of prosecutorial discretion is prescribed by statute or state constitutional mandate in most states and is constitutionally required by the Fifth Amendment in federal cases.

As to arrest and search, the language of the Fourth Amendment does not distinguish between SEARCHES AND SEIZURES of objects, and arrests—"seizures" of the person. While one might assume that the term would have equivalent meanings in both the search and arrest contexts, the differences between arrests of suspects and searches for evidence or contraband require the probable cause standard to be applied to different types of data for the two procedures. Probable cause for a search does not automatically support an arrest, nor does a valid ARREST WARRANT necessarily support a search.

Probable cause in the arrest context was defined by the United States Supreme Court in *Beck v. Ohio* (1964) as turning on "whether at that moment [of arrest] the facts and circumstances within [the officers'] knowledge and of which they [have] reasonably trustworthy information [are] sufficient to warrant a prudent man in believing that the [suspect] had committed or was committing an offense. There are two potential sources of information—personal knowledge and "trustworthy" secondary data. The Supreme Court has clearly established that secondary data—information not within the officer's personal knowledge—can supply sufficient grounds for an arrest. Thus, the police may rely on reports from other cities or states to support valid arrests, as in *Whitely v. Warden* (1971). Credible information supplied by an informant may also be used.

The officer's specific knowledge derived from direct contact with the arrestee is usually the primary support for a finding of probable cause. It is clear such information must be specific. Mere knowledge that, for example, a suspect has been convicted in the past coupled with an unidentified INFORMANT'S TIP alleging current criminal activity has been held to be insufficient.

Even specific EVIDENCE linking an individual to a crime will not justify an arrest if the evidence has been discovered unconstitutionally. An arrest cannot be justified by evidence seized pursuant to the arrest; as the Court said in *Sibron v. New York* (1968): "An incident search may not precede an arrest and serve as part of its justification."

Evidence discovered in an on-street investigative encounter that has not yet reached the level of an arrest may be properly used to create probable cause. For example, if as a result of a STOP-AND-FRISK encounter on the street, authorized by TERRY V. OHIO (1968), an officer feels a weapon, he has probable cause to arrest for carrying a concealed weapon. Similarly, if in the course of a temporary detention the suspect fails adequately to account for his suspicious actions or if he affirmatively discloses incriminating evidence, probable cause to arrest may be established. The same is true if the suspect runs away. While flight alone does not create probable cause to arrest, it is a significant factor to be considered in the overall assessment.

By contrast, however, as the Court held in *Brown v. Texas* (1979), the mere failure of a suspect to identify himself, without more, does not supply probable cause. Nor may a valid arrest rely on an individual's failure to protect his innocence when found with suspects for whom probable cause exists, as in *United States v. Di Re* (1948).

Di Re also stands for the proposition that mere presence of an individual in the company of others who are properly suspected of criminal activity does not constitute probable cause. Subsequent cases, however, have made clear that there are limits to this principle. The difficulties here have largely come with possessory offenses. On the one hand, the Court in *Johnson v. United States* (1947) held that a tip that opium was being smoked coupled with the smell of opium outside a hotel room did not give rise to probable cause to arrest everyone in the room. Although there was probable cause to believe a crime was being committed, there was insufficient information to determine who was committing it. Yet in KER V. CALIFORNIA (1963) the Court upheld the arrest of a married couple found in their kitchen with a brick of marijuana, even though the tip leading them there had linked only the husband to the contraband. The Court reasoned that the combination of the wife's presence in a small kitchen with obvious contraband, coupled with information that the husband had been using the apartment as a base for his drug activities, gave sufficient grounds for a reasonable belief that they were both in possession of marijuana.

This requirement of linking probable cause specifically to the arrestee was again mentioned by the Court in YBARRA V. ILLINOIS (1979). There the police procured a valid warrant to search a tavern believed to be the center of drug activity. In executing the warrant, the police searched about a dozen of the tavern's patrons, including Ybarra. While the case thus actually dealt with the legitimacy of the search rather than an arrest, the Court stated: "[W]here the standard is probable cause, a search or *seizure of a person* must be supported by probable cause particularized with respect to that person. This requirement cannot be undercut or avoided by simply pointing to the fact that coincidentally there exists probable cause to search or seize another or to search the premises where the person may happen to be." (Emphasis added.) *Ybarra* thus reinforces the requirement that probable cause be particularized to the person arrested; mere presence at a place connected with criminal activity, or in the company of suspected criminals, without more, is inadequate.

Finally, the Court held in *Gerstein v. Pugh* (1975) that whenever a suspect has been arrested without a warrant and with no prior INDICTMENT, he is entitled to a quick judicial check on the police conclusion that there is probable cause to detain him if he will undergo a "significant pretrial restraint on liberty"—more than the mere condition that he return for trial. This hearing, while constitutionally required if these conditions are met, need not be adversary and does not give rise to a RIGHT TO COUNSEL. As with the hearing to obtain an arrest warrant, this proceeding does not even require the accused's presence. The standard of proof is simply whether there is probable cause to believe the suspect has committed a crime.

The search context is the second major area in which the issue of probable cause arises. Most courts hold that probable cause for a search exists when the facts and circumstances in a given situation are sufficient to warrant a man of reasonable caution to believe that seizable objects are located at the place to be searched. (See BRINEGAR V. UNITED STATES, 1949; CARROLL V. UNITED STATES, 1925.)

The probable cause determination is generally based on the information supplied to the magistrate in the application for a search warrant. An application must be sworn to and must allege the place to be searched, the property to be seized, the person having the property if it is to be taken from his control, and the underlying crime. There is no requirement that everything must be set out in the application itself; affidavits may be attached or sworn statements taken before the magistrate. Because applications are usually submitted by police officers who do not have legal training, the language of the application is to be construed in a nontechnical way. Nevertheless, if the application is all that is submitted, and it is expressed in "conclusory" terms only, it will be insufficient to establish probable cause. Sufficient data must be contained in either the application itself or the supporting affidavits to justify the magistrate in issuing the warrant.

Although no blanket assertion can explain all cases involving probable cause for the issuance of search warrants, one useful rule of thumb is that if the affidavit and supporting documents allege facts that can explain to the magistrate the basis for the probable cause determination, a warrant based on such an affidavit is likely to be good. On the other hand, when an affidavit asserts a mere conclusion such as "we have it on good information and do believe there are drugs at the suspect's home," there is no independent basis for the magistrate's determination. A warrant based on such a showing is likely to be invalid.

The hardest issue arises when the affiant police officer is not the source of the information but is relying on an informant. Most of the Supreme Court's decisions concerning the required credibility of informants have arisen in cases involving SEARCH WARRANTS rather than arrest warrants, but the standards for use of informants in both contexts are the same.

The Supreme Court first enunciated the requirements for a valid informant-based warrant in AGUILAR V. TEXAS (1964). According to this test, the affidavit must: (a) set forth sufficient underlying circumstances to demonstrate to a neutral and detached magistrate how the informant reached his/her conclusion; *and* (b) establish the reliability or credibility of the informant. In the subsequent case, SPINELLI V. UNITED STATES (1969), the Supreme Court explained that the absence of a statement detailing the manner in which the informant's data were gathered renders it especially important that "the tip describe the accused's criminal activity in sufficient detail that the magistrate may know that he is relying on something more substantial than a casual rumor . . . or an accusation based merely on an individual's general reputation."

The *Aguilar/Spinelli* test has, however, been rejected by ILLINOIS V. GATES (1983). The Court in *Gates* introduced a totality-of-the-circumstances test, stating that it was not necessary to establish the credibility of the informant as a separate element to a valid search warrant. Instead, reliability and credibility of the informer and his basis of knowledge are considered as intertwining considerations that may illuminate the probable cause issue. In *Gates* the police received an anonymous informant's letter containing details of the defendants' involvement in drug trafficking which were corroborated by police investigations. The Court held that this provided a sufficient basis for a finding of probable cause.

Finally, according to *Henry v. United States* (1959), if the police had probable cause to arrest or search, the fact that the information on which they relied turns out to be false does not invalidate the arrest or search. Sufficient probability is the touchstone of Fourth Amendment reasonableness. (See PRELIMINARY HEARING.)

CHARLES H. WHITEBREAD

Bibliography

LAFAVE, WAYNE R. 1978 *Search and Seizure: A Treatise on the Fourth Amendment.* St. Paul, Minn.: West Publishing Co.

PROCEDURAL DUE PROCESS OF LAW, CIVIL

The Fifth Amendment forbids the United States to "deprive" any person of "life, liberty, or property without DUE PROCESS OF LAW." The FOURTEENTH AMENDMENT imposes an identical prohibition on the states.

Due process is the ancient core of CONSTITUTIONALISM. It is a traditional legal expression of concern for the fate of persons in the presence of organized social power. The question of according due process arises when governments assert themselves adversely to the interests of individuals.

In modern usage "due process" connotes a certain normative ideal for decisions about the exercise of power. Very broadly, it has come to mean decisions that are not arbitrary, but are aligned with publicly accepted aims and values; are not dictatorial, but allow affected persons a suitable part in their making; and are not oppressive, but treat those affected with the respect owed political associates and fellow human beings. It is from the liberal individualist tradition that these abstract due process standards—of reason, voice, and dignity—have drawn their more concrete content. That content includes the definition of proper aims for state activity, the canons of legitimating participation and consent, and the conceptions of human personality that set the threshold of respectful treatment.

The law distinguishes between "substantive" and "procedural" due process. An arbitrary or groundless decision may violate substantive due process regardless of how it came to be made. O'CONNOR V. DONALDSON (1975), for example, held that no antecedent procedure will justify incarceration of a harmless eccentric. Conversely, a peremptory decision may violate procedural due process regardless of purposive justification. Guilt in fact will not justify sudden, final dismissal of a faithless government employee without a hearing, as the Supreme Court stated in ARNETT V. KENNEDY (1974). The due process claim is "procedural" rather than "substantive" when it questions not the state's authority to impose the harm in question by an adequate decision process, but rather the adequacy of the process actually used.

Of course, procedural demands gain much of their power from their perceived contribution to substantive accuracy and enlightenment. Justice FELIX FRANKFURTER stated in JOINT ANTI-FASCIST COMMITTEE V. MCGRATH (1951): "No better instrument has been devised for arriving at truth than to give a person in jeopardy of serious loss notice of the case against him and an opportunity to meet it. Nor has a better way been found for generating the feeling, so important to a popular government, that justice has been done."

The focal concern of procedural due process is the set of procedures, epitomized by the judicial trial, whereby governing rules and standards are brought to bear on individuals in specific cases. The doctrine also has some further extension to the formation of the governing rules and standards. Due process can support a claim for direct voice in the formation process, for example, by industry members regarding regulatory standards under consideration by an administrative agency. It can also be the ground of an objection to the nonrepresentative character of the political process in which a standard originates, for example, a restriction on professional entry adopted by a board composed of self-interested professionals. There may also be a due process failure in the way a legal standard is formulated. The standard may be too vague and ill-defined to ensure even-handed application or allow for effective submission of proofs and arguments by someone contesting its application; or, conversely, it may be so narrowly drawn as to represent an arbitrary or vindictive discrimination against a disfavored few. Lawmaking defects of these various kinds are chiefly the concern of doctrines of SEPARATION OF POWERS, unconstitutional delegation, VAGUENESS, and prohibition of BILLS OF ATTAINDER, but they cannot in practice be held entirely separate from procedural due process claims.

In *Joint Anti-Fascist Refugee Committee v. McGrath* Justice Frankfurter invoked a history in which the adversary judicial trial has dominated our law's vision of procedural due process, as the model of a procedure designed to assure reason, voice, and dignity to individuals threatened with harm by the state. Criminal due process shows the fullest development of the adversarial model, just as criminal proceedings tend to maximize the conditions bespeaking the need for adversarial safeguards: charges specifically directed against the accused individual, by highly visible officers acting in the state's name, threatening not only tangible deprivation of liberty or wealth but also public degradation. Some state-initiated proceedings against individuals, such as those brought to establish paternity or terminate parental status, while nominally civil in character, resemble criminal prosecutions in their accusatory and stigmatic implications or in the gravity of their threatened sanctions, leaving little doubt about the need to grant respondents something approaching the full set of due process safeguards. Such safeguards were required by the Court in LASSITER V. DEPARTMENT OF SOCIAL SERVICES (1981). As cases of impending state-imposed harm depart further from the criminal prosecution paradigm, however, they reveal that puzzling issues of political and legal principle are latent in the general ideal of due process. Such cases pose two distinct questions for due process doctrine. First, does the occasion demand any kind of proceeding at all? Assuming an affirmative answer, the second question is, what process is due?

Events that from certain perspectives are describable as deprivations of life, liberty, or property in which the state is implicated—for example, a creditor acting under a legal privilege to repossess consumer goods from an assertedly defaulting debtor—may occur with no provision in the law for any process at all. The most theoretically telling of recent judicial encounters with due process doctrine has been concerned with defining the occasions when some trial-type process is constitutionally required.

Due process further stands for a constitutionally mandated procedural code for the fair conduct of whatever trial-type proceedings are to occur. In this second aspect, due process doctrine is a compendium of answers to such varied questions as: May the hearing be postponed until after the onset of the deprivation (such as a summary suspension of a student from school) or must there be a predeprivation hearing? May the state depart from COMMON LAW rules regarding HEARSAY evidence, allow its judges to interrogate witnesses, use publication rather than personal contact as a means of notifying concerned parties of pending proceedings, or deny parties the assistance of counsel in small claims tribunals?

The answers found in due process doctrine to such questions will bind a government just insofar as it chooses, or is required by the first aspect of the doctrine, to use judicial-type forums or trial-type proceedings to carry out their pursuits. The chief problems posed by such questions are the recurrent ones of JUDICIAL REVIEW and CONSTITUTIONAL INTERPRETATION: from what sources, by what modes of reasoning, shall the answers be drawn, given the breadth and imprecision of constitutional text? Historically, the main methodological alternatives and debates have arisen in the context of criminal prosecutions and been thence carried over to the civil side.

Constitutional claims to trial-type proceedings are most obviously compelling when individuals stand to be harmed by actions of officials performing state functions or wielding state powers. Yet even in such cases the individual interests at stake may be found insufficient to call due process rights into play. On a textual level, the question plainly is whether the affected interest is identifiable as "life, liberty, or property." History, however, discloses contrasting approaches to that question. It was once commonly supposed that any serious imposition on an individual—any "grievous loss"—could qualify as a constitutionally significant deprivation. A chief feature of contemporary due process doctrine is that the potency of a harm as a due process trigger turns not on such an ordinary assessment of its weight or practical severity but rather on a technical, categorical judgment about its legal "nature." In adjudicating what categories of interests legally qualify as "life," "liberty," or "property" for due process analysis, the Court has drawn eclectically on sources both naturalistic and positivistic—on both a HIGHER LAW tradition and on currently enacted law.

This eclecticism, and indeed the entire complex practice of categorically excluding some concededly weighty interests from due process protection, has apparently evolved out of the Court's encounters with modern welfare state activism. Consider the case of a government worker unceremoniously fired, or of a disability pensioner whose monthly payments are cut off. In such cases the underlying due process values of reason, voice, and dignity may seem to call as strongly for a chance to be heard as in cases of revocation of a professional license or dispossession of land or goods. Yet neither a government job nor a disability benefit is "property" in the common speech of our own culture or that of the constitutional Framers; and although their loss might be called a loss of liberty, to speak so broadly would bring within the sweep of procedural due process many cases that evidently do not belong there, for example, denial of admission to a state university.

The Court's response, in cases like GOLDBERG V. KELLY (1970) and BISHOP V. WOOD (1976), has been to say that "property" may, indeed, include all manner of beneficial relations with the state or others, but only insofar as those relations are legal entitlements in the sense that explicit (or positive) law protects against their impairment. Thus a probationary employee lacking contractual term or statutory tenure may be peremptorily dismissed and the mere applicant peremptorily rejected; but the tenured employee has a right to be heard on the question of cause for dismissal, and the disability claimant under a statute containing definite eligibility rules may not be delisted—or even denied initial admission to benefits—without some opportunity to be heard on the issue of eligibility.

The method of equating due process protected "property" with positive legal entitlement—that is, by reference to clearly ordained, subconstitutional law—has several attractive features. It flows easily from the observation in BOARD OF REGENTS V. ROTH (1972) that a chief purpose of "the ancient institution of property" has been to "protect . . . expectations upon which people must rely in their daily lives" against being "arbitrarily undermined." Moreover, the positive-entitlement conception makes a neat fit with the idea that a fair hearing is the nub of due process. Entitlement makes directly clear what the hearing shall be about, for any law framing an entitlement must specify issues available for contest by anyone complaining of deprivation. Finally, entitlement analysis may seem to keep the judiciary clear of imposing on popularly accountable branches of government any political values or ends not accepted by those branches themselves. A judge enforcing due process rights appears to do little more than take seriously the decision of the lawmakers to create the entitlement in the first place.

The Court on some occasions has gone so far as to say that no interest qualifies as due process protected property except insofar as a legal rule safeguards its continued enjoyment. It seems clear that such statements cannot be taken literally. For example, the Court consistently refuses to approve procedures involving state officers in the repossession of goods bought on credit, without affording a prompt hearing to the buyer, no matter how clearly the applicable state law states that the buyer's entitlement to continued possession is to lapse upon the creditor's filing of notice of default (as distinguished from a judicial finding of default). Here it must be the brute reality of the buyer's established possession of the goods that comprises the constitutionally protected property, regardless of the explicit legal rules concerning its protection or duration.

The possession cases illustrate the naturalistic or higher law side of the Court's eclectic method of interest characterization. Protection of established possession against disorderly or unjustified incursion is an ancient fixture in both the rhetoric and the practice of Anglo-American common law and liberty. There are other common liberties similarly, if not all quite so anciently, esteemed: personal mobility and bodily security; liberties of conscience, intellect, and expression; domestic sanctuary, marital intimacy, and family solidarity; occupational freedom and professional autonomy. Although some of these interests find mention in the Bill of Rights, they mostly lack specific constitutional recognition.

The Court has used the "liberty" branch of the due process guarantee as a warrant for procedural protection for such interests, quite apart from their status as entitlements under positive law—and without overprecious worry about their status at ancestral common law. Regardless of whether the state's law purports, or ever did purport, to make into legal rights a schoolchild's security against corporal punishment (INGRAHAM V. WRIGHT, 1977), a parent's retention of child custody (*Santosky v. Kramer,* 1982), or a parolee's preference for remaining at liberty (*Morrissey v. Brewer,* 1972), those interests have been held protected, by the due process clause itself, against peremptory impairment by STATE ACTION. They are treated as constitutional entitlements regardless of whether they are statutory ones. It is easy to imagine why naturalist as well as positivist elements thus enter into the Court's characterizations. Welfare state activism positively invites forms of reliance and dependence which, however historically novel, evoke the essential purposes of due process; but the activist state is also prone to tread insensitively on old but still vital concerns that courts recognize as traditional freedoms.

The conclusion that an interest jeopardized by government action does qualify as someone's "life, liberty, or property" does not end the due process inquiry, for the question then remains of how much "process" is "due." It has been said that due process entails, at a minimum, "some kind of hearing" for the exposed individual. Precisely what kind depends on a judicial assessment: one which, according to the formulation in MATHEWS V. ELDRIDGE (1976), is supposed to take account of the gravity of the individual interest at stake, the utility of the requested procedures in avoiding factually misinformed or legally erroneous decisions, and the cost of those procedures to the pursuit of legitimate state objectives. The results of such a calculus can range from the heavy procedural armor available to criminal defendants in capital cases to the simple "opportunity to present his side of the story" that, under GOSS V. LOPEZ (1975), is due a student facing a short disciplinary suspension from school.

An important and oft-contested feature of the constitutionally guaranteed process is its timing relative to the deprivation. The Court long stood by the general proposition that (apart from "emergency" situations, such as seizure of contraband) due process meant predeprivation process. The Court continues to insist on some opportunity for in-person hearing prior to "core" deprivations such as dispossession of tangible property. In several cases, such as *Arnett v. Kennedy* and *Mathews v. Eldridge,* involving government jobs and other "benefits," the Court has accepted postponement of a live hearing until after the fall of the axe, when there has been predeprivation notice and opportunity for written protest, as long as there is adequate assurance for reparation in case the deprivation is eventually found unjustified.

Under pressure of the "mass justice" conditions imposed by modern governmental benefit programs involving very large numbers of eligibility decisions, there has been indication in recent cases and commentaries of tolerance for an alternative due process model, one less concerned than the traditional trial-type model with participation values. In this alternative managerial model, the measure of due process is not the quality of the opportunity given affected individuals for a say in the resolution of their own cases but quality control in the production of decisions. The aim is not voice for the individual but accuracy in the aggregate of the resolutions reached over a period of program administration. As advocates of this alternative model recognize, two factors are required to justify the model's use in any given setting: first, the relative dominance of individuals' interests in receiving their entitlements over their dignitary interests in participation; and, second, the value of such a systems management approach in maximizing the receipt of entitlements.

When judges find constitutional protection, under the broad cover of "liberty," for selected interests not specified as rights by constitutional text or other clearly uttered law, and when they determine just what form and quantum of process is "due" in respect of particular kinds of deprivations, they have obviously entered on the work of ranking substantive ends and values. Yet courts doing this kind of due process adjudication have not evinced great worry about usurpation of the lawmaking function. One reason may be that by merely requiring the state to provide some kind of hearing when it acts adversely to some individual's interests, a court does not consider itself ultimately to be preventing lawmakers from reaching whatever substantive results they choose.

However, the judicial act of fashioning procedural requirements, and attaching these to a select set of liberties, is not without substantive force. Procedural requirements can place serious practical obstacles in the way of legislative pursuits. They may be expensive. They may cause a formalization or distancing of some relations that lawmakers could reasonably prefer to leave more informal, close, or open, such as the relations among teachers and students in a school. They may deter valued candor—as from evaluators of candidates for jobs, promotions, university admissions, professional licenses—insofar as due process entitles the subjects of adverse reports to disclosure or CONFRONTATION. Procedural requirements may thus force lawmakers to weigh some programmatic objectives against others that would be jeopardized by pursuing the former within the procedural rules laid down by courts.

Due process protection for interests that are not entitlements established by positive law may have a subtler substantive import. If the jeopardized interest enjoys no specific protection under any law aside from the due process clause itself, there is no obvious focus for the required process. A hearing on the issue of whether the contested deprivation is "without due process" may seem pointless, lacking some legal restriction on the conditions in which the deprivation is authorized. This problem has arisen in a number of cases involving dispossession of public housing tenants, when neither the laws governing the housing programs not the leases issued to tenants purported to restrict in any way the power of administrators to evict tenants at any time, for any reason or no reason.

Courts in this situation may supply the missing substantive entitlement on their own, by finding in the due process guarantee a protection against deprivations not rationally related to the purposes of the governmental activity in question. Thus a court may bar a public housing administrator from evicting a tenant who has been cohabiting with a nonspouse, if the court concludes that excluding the cohabitation is not rationally related to the court's understanding of the purposes of public housing. In such a case, the crossover from procedural to substantive concerns is glaringly evident.

A similar crossover is less evident, but still detectible, when a court responds to the lack of a positive law entitlement by requiring the state itself to enunciate some restrictions of purpose or circumstance on lawful impairment of the protected interest, which can provide a basis for due process hearings when official deprivations impend. For the court must then stand ready to decide whether the state's restrictions measure up to constitutional standards of protectiveness. A statute solemnly declaring that tenants may not be evicted "except as the Administrator shall decide is required for the general good" could not satisfy a court determined to afford procedural due process protection to the tenant's possessory interest viewed as an entitlement.

The alternative possibility, of requiring procedural protection even in the absence of legal restrictions on official discretion, rarely seems to have caught the Supreme Court's attention. Responsible officials, even when legally free to act at will, can always try to explain their decisions to persons adversely affected, and give the latter a chance to respond. Such an interchange will sometimes make a practical difference, by changing the officials' perceptions of the relevant facts or values. But even when it does not it may well serve any or all of the elemental purposes of due process: ensuring a voice in decisions for affected individuals, securing their recognition as persons deserving respect, and promoting consistency of official actions with goals and values that responsible officials are prepared to state and defend publicly.

Why has such a view of procedural due process, as serving process values apart from the aim of ensuring that persons receive the treatment legally due them, failed to gain judicial support? Most obviously, such an approach would cast very widely the due process net. If we see due process as broadly concerned with the quality of interaction between official and citizen, rather than more narrowly with vindication of the citizen's legal rights, then any state-inflicted "grievous loss" will seem to bring into play the constitutional standards of decisional procedure—a perhaps daunting result in light of the ubiquity of the welfare state.

The Court's limited extension of procedural protection beyond positive legal entitlements to possessory interests and a select set of liberties seems to represent its aversion to three unpalatable alternatives: first, deformation of the constitutional due process mandate by restricting its reach to entitlements specifically found in subconstitutional positive law; second, intrusive overextension of the mandate to all cases of palpably harmful state action; and third, free-form judicial choice among substantive values and policy goals. The Court apparently cannot avoid all three dangers fully and simultaneously. It has needed supplementary techniques to make good the avoidance of both trivialization and globalization of the range of the due process mandate, and these techniques have put heavy pressure on both doctrinal shapeliness and judicial self-discipline.

For example, the danger of trivialization constantly lurks in a crucial indeterminacy in the concept of legally defined entitlement as the equivalent of due process protected property. The problem is that of distributing components of a positive legal regime between the categories of substance and procedure. Suppose, as in *Bishop v. Wood,* that police officers are dismissable whenever, but only when, a designated superior has given the employee a written notice of dismissal for malfeasance in the performance of duty. Straightforwardly read, the law means to make the legal condition of dismissability not actual malfeasance but delivered written notice of dismissal. An entitlement-based due process doctrine then would logically require a hearing but only on the bootless issue of delivery of the notice. A judge can logically avoid that result by reading the law to condition dismissability on actual malfeasance, although that reading will make the law unconstitutional if the law includes no adequate provision for hearing on the malfeasance question. Whether such a reading seems unacceptably self-destructive will depend on the primacy of due process values in the reader's constitutional understanding.

Similar puzzles affect questions about whose entitlement is established by a plain statutory restriction on official discretion. A striking example is *O'Bannon v. Town Court Nursing Center* (1980), where a statute provided for financial assistance to needy elderly persons in meeting their costs of residence in officially approved nursing homes, and also set conditions of approval for the homes. Thus it was apparently unlawful for officials either to deny certification to homes meeting the conditions or to deny benefits to eligible residents of certified homes. When officials proposed to decertify a certain home, its residents claimed a due process right to be heard on the issued of the home's certifiability. The Supreme Court concluded that the residents had no constitutional right to such a hearing because their entitlement was just to benefits while residing in a certified home; the entitlement to certification belonged strictly to the nursing home operators.

Given the close practical resemblance of the residents' interests to the strongly protected interests of tenants in uninterrupted possession, a court could reasonably have concluded that they, too, were entitled to certification of their home if in fact it met the legal standards, and therefore they had due process rights to be heard on that issue. The Court's contrary conclusion was obviously influenced by concerns about overextended application of the constitutional due process mandate.

Claims to due process are not confined to situations in which the claimant's legal posture is defensive or the adversaries are government officials. They may arise also where individuals are exposed to the state's judicial power by their involvement in private legal controversies; and even where (the due process claim aside) there impends no legal proceeding at all but just some harm at a fellow citizen's hands.

The defendant in a private civil lawsuit faces possible deprivation, by officers wielding state powers, of wealth through a money judgment or of personal liberty through an injunctive decree. The occasion is obviously one to activate due process concerns, and civil defendants are held entitled to such procedural due process essentials as a fair and orderly hearing before an unbiased judge.

For reasons not quite so obvious, so are civil plaintiffs. A tempting explanation is that having allowed its courts to take charge of a private dispute, the state is obliged to have them do so in a way that satisfies the due process demand for reason, voice, and dignity. Yet this explanation seems incomplete. Some assistance is better than none. The state does not injure or oppress claimants to whom it offers procedurally flawed assistance against violators of the kinds of interests typically at stake in civil cases, unless the state is affirmatively obligated to secure those interests against violations by private as well as governmental agents. Suppose, for example (as the Supreme Court apparently did in TRUAX V. CORRIGAN, 1921) that the state is constitutionally obligated to protect landowners against disturbance by PICKETING. On such a view, a disturbed landowner can cite a refusal of protection as a deprivation of property and demand a hearing on the question of the state's justification for refusal. In other words, the landowner can demand a hearing on whether the picketing is for some special reason legally privileged. The state can meet this demand by letting the landowner sue the picketers for injunctive relief, but only if the procedural conditions of the suit satisfy due process standards of fairness from the plaintiff's point of view.

Thus denial of fair procedure to a civil plaintiff comes within the traditional due process concern about injurious treatment of individuals by the state, just insofar as we see the state's failure to protect the plaintiff's interests against the defendant's encroachments as itself a form of injury. Such is the SOCIAL COMPACT view according to which persons entering political association surrender to the state the use of force, for the safer protection of their several "lives, liberties, and estates." The state's regime of law and order then overrides the natural liberty of self-help, but only by replacing it with the state's obligation to protect.

Some such account seems necessary to complete the explanation of the conceded due process rights of civil plaintiffs. Yet other current law ostensibly rejects this account. *United States v. Kras* (1973) and *Logan v. Zimmerman Brush Co.* (1982) together indicate that the state may usually condition a would-be civil plaintiff's ACCESS TO THE COURTS on payment of filing fees, thus effectively excluding whoever cannot pay. Such a doctrine is hard to square with the idea of a state's affirmative duty to protect the litigable interests of its citizens, arising out of the latter's relinquishment of self-help by private force.

When a government sues a citizen in an otherwise ordinary civil dispute, involving property or contract rights or tort claims, the citizen sued will of course have the due process rights normally enjoyed by privately sued civil defendants. The reverse case, of a civil dispute in which the citizen is the one seeking relief for a TRESPASS, breach of contract, or other civil wrong by a governmental defendant, is complicated by the doctrine of SOVEREIGN IMMUNITY. In general, that doctrine means that the governments of the states and the Union may not be sued without the consent of their respective legislatures. If the courts find that such consent has not been given, the citizen alleging deprivation by governmental action will lack recourse in the ordinary courts, a situation presenting an obvious and a serious due process concern. In many such cases, the constitutionally guaranteed right of due process must prevail over sovereign immunity and entitle the victimized citizen to relief in constitutional litigation. That would surely be the result, for example, if government officials sought to imprison someone, or seize privately held land or goods, without ever giving the victim a fair chance to contest the legal and factual basis for such action. The citizen would be able to gain preventive relief or compensation in a CIVIL RIGHTS action based on the due process clause of the Fifth or Fourteenth Amendment.

The question of due process rights is most puzzling when seizures of possessions, or other violations of core interests generally given legal protection, are carried out by private agents with no apparent state complicity—a finance company sending its own forces to repossess an automobile securing an overdue debt, or a repair shop collecting an unpaid bill by retaining and eventually selling the repaired article. People do not usually take such "self-help" actions, or think them prudent, unless the actions are in some sense authorized, if not positively enabled, by state law. Thus lawmakers may authorize and enable a creditor's private repossession of chattel security by exempting such activity from liability for crime (theft) or civil wrong (conversion of goods). Indeed, the law usually goes farther, making it wrongful for the debtor to resist the seizure by force. The law doubtless otherwise contributes to the ability of creditors to make their seizures effective, as by securing the wealth used to pay for the requisite services. The utility of the repair shop's liquidation-by-sale depends on law allowing extinction of the debtor's legal claim to the goods in favor of the person who buys them from the repair shop. In short, self-help creditor remedies are evidently deliberate creations of state law, particular components of the state's total scheme of legally recognized and sanctioned rights and liabilities. In that sense, at least, the self-helping creditor inflicts significant deprivations under cover of the state's power, while affording no opportunity for the deprivee to be heard on the matter.

Even so, the Supreme Court concluded in FLAGG BROTHERS V. BROOKS (1978) that laws authorizing creditor self-help do not in general violate due process. In defense of this result, it might have been urged that the due process requirement is satisfied by the debtor's opportunity to sue later for restorative or compensatory relief in case the creditor's seizure was in fact unjustified. Such a rationale would accord with the holding in *Ingraham v. Wright* that paddling a student without a hearing comports with due process so long as compensatory relief for an unjustified paddling can be obtained later in a lawsuit. Yet courts have not usually explained in this way their tolerance for unilateral, peremptory creditor self-help, apparently seeing the difficulty of reconciling such an account with prevailing due process doctrine for cases of seizure by state officers, which strictly requires the state to provide some kind of judicial supervision, and a hearing for the deprivee as promptly as the case permits.

Courts instead have seen the issue presented by private self-help activities as one of state action, and, as in the *Flagg Brothers* case, have concluded that the due process guarantee has no application to such activities however much they may practically depend on the support of law. The reason for this judicial diffidence, as important as it is simple, is the difficulty of distinguishing in principle between the due process claim raised by the case of the self-helping creditor and that raised by many, if not all, other cases of intentional or foreseeable infliction, by private agents, of civilly actionable harm, that is, of torts, breaches of contract, breaches of trust, and so forth. Often, if not always, it will be possible to show compellingly how the law has contributed directly to the occasion or motive for committing the injurious act or to the injurer's practical power to inflict it, or to the practical defenselessness of the victim. But the idea of a constitutional right to a predeprivation hearing, or even an accelerated postdeprivation hearing, in all cases of ordinary private legal wrongs stretches due process too far. Every ordinary contract dispute cannot be a constitutional case.

Thus courts have been led to conclude that the deprivations of property wrought by private creditor self-help are not violations of due process for the reason that they are not attributable to the state. The position is that due process generally is not concerned with exercises of power by persons not identified with the state or perceived as acting on its behalf, in forms not conventionally understood as distinctive to the state. This position is unfortunately at odds with the premise which apparently underlies recognition of the due process rights of civil plaintiffs—the premise, that is, of an affirmative state duty to protect the persons and possessions of inhabitants against gross violation by private as well as public agents.

The difficulty is of a kind that logically must appear somewhere within any body of constitutional doctrine in which a first aim is that of securing spheres of individual liberty against social coercion, and a first institutional device is that of legal rights, themselves an obvious form of collective force. In the constitutionalist vision there is indissoluble tension between law's aim, personal liberty, and its instrument, state power. In this field of contradictory forces are situated all legal rights, including due process rights. Thus it happens that the same due process claims which from one viewpoint represent the state's liberating engagement to protect each person against incursion by others or by the social aggregate, from another perspective represent the state's oppressive oversight of affairs perhaps better and more properly left to the concerned individuals.

In no setting is the dilemma more evident than in that of the family, which in our culture has most strongly represented the value of social solidarity as opposed to that of individuals severally free to treat at arm's length in civil society. PARHAM V. J. R. (1979), a case in which due process claims were asserted on behalf of a minor child being committed by parents to a mental institution, illustrates the difficulty. The Court there assumed "that a [minor] child has a protectable interest . . . in not being . . . erroneously" committed; said that parents must be generally supposed to act in their children's best interests; said that "the risk of error inherent in the parental decision . . . [is] sufficiently great" that parental discretion cannot be "absolute and unreviewable"; and concluded, not resoundingly, that "some kind of inquiry should be made by a 'neutral fact finder' to determine whether . . . [the child] satisf[ies] the medical standards for admission."

Of the largest questions of current meaning and future role for due process in our civic culture, the Supreme Court's irresolute posture in the *Parham* case is emblematic. If due process is an epitome of libertarian law, it is also—by the same token, Max Weber would advise—an epitome of bureaucratic law. Due process as we know it is a hallmark of a formally rational law designed to liberate as it organizes and orders: to liberate energy and will by the promise of regularity, calculability, and impartiality, and by insistent strong demarcation of the private from the public sphere.

But our due process is a hallmark, too, of hierarchical formal ordering; that is, of ordering by preordained rules emanating from specialized governing authorities (representative or accountable as those authorities may be, of or to the governed). There are always spheres of life in which due process is problematic because those spheres want ordering that is more contextual and less abstract, more responsive and less prefigured, more empathic and less impersonal, more interactive and less distanced, more participatory and less authoritative, than what "due process" has traditionally signified. Conversely, "due process" invokes sensibilities resistant to a general movement toward a more thoroughly democratized polity, in which the personal and the political aspects of life would be much less sharply separated than we have tended to keep them. In any such movement due process would necessarily be transformed—transformed but not discarded, since we are unlikely to forsake the ideals of reason, voice, and dignity, or the conviction that individuals are not just parts of social wholes.

FRANK I. MICHELMAN

Bibliography

BREST, PAUL 1982 State Action and Liberal Theory: A Casenote on *Flagg Brothers v. Brooks. University of Pennsylvania Law Review* 130:1296–1330.

FRIENDLY, HENRY J. 1975 Some Kind of Hearing. *University of Pennsylvania Law Review* 123:1267–1317.

KADISH, SANFORD 1957 Methodology and Criteria in Due Process Adjudication—A Survey and Criticism. *Yale Law Journal* 66:319–363.

MASHAW, JERRY L. 1983 *Bureaucratic Justice: Managing Social Security Disability Claims.* New Haven, Conn.: Yale University Press.

MICHELMAN, FRANK 1977 Formal and Associational Aims in Procedural Due Process. Pages 126–171 in J. Roland Pennock and John Chapman, eds., *Nomos XVIII: Due Process* New York: New York University Press.

MINOW, MARTHA 1985 Beyond State Intervention in the Family: For Baby Jane Doe. *Michigan Journal of Law Reform* 18:933–1014.

MONAGHAN, HENRY 1977 Of "Liberty" and "Property." *Cornell Law Review* 62:405–444.

REICH, CHARLES 1964 The New Property. *Yale Law Journal* 73:733–787.

VAN ALSTYNE, WILLIAM 1977 Cracks in "The New Property": Adjudicative Due Process in the Administrative State. *Cornell Law Review* 62:445–493.

PROCEDURAL DUE PROCESS OF LAW, CRIMINAL

The Barons at Runnymede did better than they knew. When they induced King John in 1215 to announce in MAGNA CARTA that no man should be imprisoned or dispossessed "except by the lawful judgment of his peers and by the LAW OF THE LAND," they laid the basis for a text that was to have greater significance in the development of American constitutional law than any other. In time "judgment of his peers" and "law of the land" came to be rendered alternatively as DUE PROCESS OF LAW and in that form were adopted in the Fifth Amendment to the United States Constitution as a restriction upon the federal government: "No person shall . . . be deprived of life, liberty or property, without due process of law." In 1868, substantially the same language was employed in the FOURTEENTH AMENDMENT as a restriction upon the states. Thus was embedded in the Constitution a phrase whose exegesis was to generate hundreds of decisions, libraries of commentary, and unending controversy, to this day. The Supreme Court has, over the years, used the due process clause to develop a variety of substantive restraints upon the power of government. This article, however, will deal only with the sense of due process closest to its original conception, namely, as the source of restrictions on the procedures through which governmental authority may be exercised over the individual in criminal cases.

In determining the procedures the Constitution requires of the federal government in criminal cases, the due process clause of the Fifth Amendment has been of limited significance. The BILL OF RIGHTS contains a variety of provisions explicitly directed to CRIMINAL PROCEDURE, and these rather than the due process clause have served as the principal vehicles for the development of a constitutional law of criminal procedure. So, for example, the Supreme Court has developed the constitutional law of permissible SEARCH AND SEIZURE through interpretations of the

FOURTH AMENDMENT; the constitutional law with respect to DOUBLE JEOPARDY and the RIGHT AGAINST SELF-INCRIMINATION through interpretations of the Fifth Amendment; the constitutional law with respect to SPEEDY and PUBLIC TRIAL, TRIAL BY JURY, NOTICE, CONFRONTATION of opposing witnesses, and the RIGHT TO COUNSEL through interpretations of the Sixth Amendment; and the constitutional law barring excessive BAIL, fines, and CRUEL AND UNUSUAL PUNISHMENT through interpretations of the Eighth Amendment. On the other hand, in determining the procedures the Constitution requires of state governments the due process clause of the Fourteenth Amendment has played the significant and decisive role.

What due process of law required and by what principles its meaning was to be ascertained were questions that were to preoccupy the Court for generations. They were raised early in MURRAY'S LESSEE V. HOBOKEN LAND & IMPROVEMENT CO. (1856), a civil case involving the meaning of the Fifth Amendment's due process clause: "The Constitution contains no description of those procedures which it was intended to allow or forbid. It does not even declare what principles are to be applied to ascertain whether it be due process. It is manifest that it was not left to the legislative power to enact any process that might be devised. The article is a restraint on the legislative as well as on the executive and judicial powers of government, and cannot be so construed as to leave Congress free to make any process 'due process of law' by its mere will." Nor, as the Court might have added, could the article be so construed as to leave the Court free to determine what is and what is not due process by *its* mere will. The effort of the Court to come to terms with this challenge is the central feature of the constitutional history of due process.

An early effort to state a principle for interpreting due process was the test of whether a procedure was in accord with settled practices in England before the Revolution and not rejected here after settlement. A practice that met this test accorded due process; a practice that did not failed to accord due process. The test served its purpose in some cases, but it soon proved insufficient, for whatever value it had as a fixed determinant of meaning was overbalanced by its inability to reflect changing times and needs and evolving perceptions of what fairness requires. For example, the settled English practice of initiating a prosecution, customarily continued in this country, was INDICTMENT by a GRAND JURY. Did this mean that due process fastened that procedure upon the states? This was the question at issue in HURTADO V. CALIFORNIA (1884), where the Court faced a California innovation permitting a prosecutor to initiate a prosecution by filing an INFORMATION on his own, after a preliminary hearing before a magistrate on whether there was sufficient cause. The Court upheld the procedure despite its deviance from settled practice because it could find in the new procedure no significant prejudice to the rights of the accused. More decisive than the state of English practice was whether the challenged procedure comported with "those fundamental principles of liberty and justice which lie at the base of all our civil and political institutions." To regard established usage as "essential to due process of law would be to deny every quality of the law but its age, and to render it incapable of progress or improvement." Thus, the Court limited the traditional test: a practice sanctioned by immemorial usage necessarily accorded due process, but one not so sanctioned was not necessarily inconsistent with due process. In time, however, the Court rejected the remaining limb of the test as well. It had been well settled in England that a FELONY defendant had no right to be represented by counsel, and although that had been rejected in the United States Constitution and in the states, the change had not gone so far as to require appointment of counsel for INDIGENT defendants. In POWELL V. ALABAMA (1932) the Court held nevertheless that the failure to appoint counsel for uneducated and indigent defendants in a capital case in circumstances in which they had no real opportunity to present a defense denied due process of law. Of more significance to the Court was its judgment of the "fundamental nature" of the right to be represented by counsel, which in these circumstances was essential to the right to be heard at all.

The test, then, that came to prevail in judging the constitutionality of procedures in state criminal prosecutions was that of fundamental fairness in the circumstances of the particular case. Over the years a variety of formulations were used in an effort to give greater content to the test. Concerning each procedural safeguard that was being asserted, the Court would ask whether it was "of the very essence of a scheme of ORDERED LIBERTY," or whether a "fair and enlightened system of justice would be impossible without it," or whether "liberty and justice" would exist if it were sacrificed, or whether it was among those "immutable principles of justice, acknowledged . . . wherever the good life is a subject of concern." Concerning the procedure applied in the contested prosecution, the Court asked whether it violated a "principle of justice so rooted in the traditions and conscience of our people as to be ranked as fundamental," or whether its use subjected a person to "a hardship so acute and shocking that our polity would not endure it," or whether it offended "those canons of decency and fairness which express the notions of justice of English-speaking peoples even toward those charged with the most heinous offenses," for due process "embodies a system of rights based on moral principles so deeply imbedded in the traditions and feelings of our people as to be deemed fundamental to a civilized society as conceived by our whole history."

Whether any or all of these phrases succeeded in accomplishing anything more than to remit the issue to the intuitive sense of fairness of each Justice; whether, as Justice HUGO L. BLACK asked in ROCHIN V. CALIFORNIA (1952), there could possibly be "avenues of investigation . . . open to discover 'canons' of conduct so universally favored that this Court should write them into the Constitution" were issues that troubled the Justices and commentators alike. These doubts led to the development of an alternative test to determine the meaning of due process; namely, that due process should be taken to mean no more and no less than the specific guarantees of the Bill of Rights. In short, the due process clause of the Fourteenth Amendment "incorporated" as restrictions upon the states the provisions of the first eight amendments originally written as restrictions upon the federal government. The first Justice JOHN MARSHALL HARLAN was the first to advance the argument in several of his dissenting opinions, including *Hurtado* and *O'Neil v. Vermont* (1892). The issue was revived in modern times when Justice Black took up the cudgels in ADAMSON V. CALIFORNIA (1947).

The *Adamson* case involved the constitutionality of California law allowing adverse comment to the jury on a defendant's failure to explain or deny evidence against him. In a federal prosecution this practice would have violated the Fifth Amendment's right against self-incrimination. But, of course, under the settled doctrine this was not determinative. The Court had to find that this particular aspect of the self-incrimination privilege—that which disallowed comment on its exercise—was essential to fundamental fairness to the defendant, and this the majority declined to do. The majority could find nothing in the California practice that denied the defendant a FAIR TRIAL. He was not compelled to testify. True, if he did testify he would open the record to evidence of his prior convictions, but, "When evidence is before a jury that threatens conviction, it does not seem unfair to require him to choose between leaving the adverse evidence unexplained and subjecting himself to impeachment through disclosure of former crimes." Justice Black dissented, arguing that a violation of the Fifth Amendment right against self-incrimination was necessarily a denial of due process under the Fourteenth Amendment.

Justice Black's arguments in favor of the INCORPORATION DOCTRINE, as first announced in *Adamson* and developed in later opinions, notably in his concurrence in DUNCAN V. LOUISIANA (1968), were grounded in a study of the history of the adoption of the Fourteenth Amendment, which convinced him that it was the intent of the amendment's framers that it should incorporate the Bill of Rights as a restraint upon the states. For Black, the Constitution did not endow the Court with power to expand and contract the meaning of due process to accord with the Court's assessment of what fundamental fairness required at any particular time. The fundamental fairness test was a resort to "natural law," depending "entirely on the particular judge's idea of ethics and morals instead of requiring him to depend on the boundaries fixed by the written words of the Constitution." Such a test was inconsistent with "the great design of a written Constitution." The specific language of the Bill of Rights would confine the power of the Court to read its own predilections into the Constitution.

Moreover, Black believed that the Bill of Rights, more reliably than the fundamental fairness test, would guide the Court to outcomes consistent with the values of a democratic society. In Black's view the judgment of the Framers of the Constitution would serve better than each Justice's personal judgment in determining what fairness required in criminal prosecutions. Indeed, the record of the Court's administration of its fundamental fairness test was for Black the clearest demonstration of his argument. He was speaking hyperbolically when he said in *Rochin* that the traditional test had been used "to nullify the Bill of Rights," but the fact was that in most instances the Court, as in *Adamson,* had used the fairness standard to uphold state convictions that would have been reversible had the specific provisions of the Bill of Rights been applicable.

Black's primary antagonist on this use, as on many others, was Justice FELIX FRANKFURTER, in later years joined by the second Justice JOHN MARSHALL HARLAN. They rejected Black's interpretation of the history of the Fourteenth Amendment's adoption, finding no plausible evidence that it was intended to incorporate the Bill of Rights as a restraint upon the states. But, beyond that, they advanced a very different approach to CONSTITUTIONAL INTERPRETA-

TION. According to Frankfurter and Harlan, the provisions of the first eight amendments were not equally fundamental. Some, like the guarantees of FREEDOM OF SPEECH and religion, stated enduring values and were, therefore, binding on the states through the "independent potency" of the Fourteenth Amendment. Others, such as those protecting the right against self-incrimination and jury trials, "express the restricted views of Eighteenth-Century England regarding the best methods for the ascertainment of facts." Not every procedure that was historically protected by these provisions was necessary for fundamental fairness, though some might be of this character. Still others, such as the requirement of a grand jury indictment and the right to a jury in civil cases where the amount in controversy exceeded twenty dollars, were largely historical relics. The terms of the Bill of Rights, all of them and only them, were, therefore, an unsuitable text for carrying out the commands of fundamental justice embodied in the requirement of due process of law. Changing circumstances would create new and unforeseen problems, casting new light on the question whether a given procedural guarantee was "fundamental." Only an evolving and flexible due process could assure preservation of the procedural requirements of a free society without binding the criminal process unnecessarily to the forms of the past.

Justices Frankfurter and Harlan conceded that the Court had sustained state procedures whose use would have been forbidden under the Bill of Rights. What mattered, however, was that it had done so only after satisfying itself in each case that the defendant had not been denied fundamental fairness. For example, the Fifth Amendment might forbid a federal prosecutor to APPEAL a conviction of a lesser offense than that charged and to prosecute under the original indictment if the appeal succeeds, but, as the Court held in *Palko v. Connecticut* (1937), the requirements of civilized justice would not be compromised by permitting a state to continue a similar prosecution until it achieved a trial free of substantial error. A jury of twelve persons might be required of federal prosecutions by the Sixth Amendment, but, as the Court held in *Maxwell v. Dow* (1900), it did not follow that a person could not receive a fundamentally fair trial in a state court before a jury of fewer members. Where, on the other hand, state practices fatally infected the justice of the convictions—as in *Powell v. Alabama* (1932) where the accused was deprived of a fair opportunity to present a defense, or in BROWN V. MISSISSIPPI (1936), where torture was used to extract a confession, or in MOORE V. DEMPSEY (1923) where the trial itself was a sham and a pretense—the Court did not hesitate to employ the fundamental fairness standard of due process to strike down the convictions.

In addition, Justices Frankfurter and Harlan emphasized the importance of the Court's avoiding excessive intrusions into the autonomy of the states. The Framers had deliberately chosen to create a federal rather than a wholly centralized system, partly to assure the limitation of power through its dispersal but also to obtain the benefits of autonomy and diversity in state government. Total incorporation of the Bill of Rights into the Fourteenth Amendment would impose a constitutional straitjacket on the states, stifling experimentation by the states in the administration of justice in the name of an unneeded uniformity.

As for the peril of judges' confusing their purely personal preferences with the requirements of the Constitution, Frankfurter and Harlan argued that this risk was inherent in JUDICIAL REVIEW—no less under the incorporation doctrine than under the fundamental fairness test. Giving meaning to particular provisions of the Bill of Rights, whose major provisions were written in open and general terms, would require judicial inquiry equally broad and open. The peril of judgment on the basis of personal preferences, they argued, must be met by judicial deference to the judgment of state governments and by a rigorous search for the fundamentals of fairness required by the nature and commitments of our society.

Though Justice Black lost the debate in *Adamson*, he continued to advance the cause of total incorporation to his final days on the Court. He never succeeded in persuading a majority, but although he lost some battles he won the war. When the dust cleared two decades after *Adamson*, the fundamental fairness standard (though significantly modified) still reigned as the accepted test of due process, but every provision of the Bill of Rights bearing on criminal procedure, with the single exception of the requirement of grand jury indictments, had been held applicable to the states.

This development occurred through the increased use of the strategy of SELECTIVE INCORPORATION, under which selected clauses of the Bill of Rights were held to be binding on the states as such in the view that they were required by fundamental fairness. Consistency with prior decisions was grounded in the view that what the Court had repeatedly rejected was the theory of total incorporation, not the view that some provisions of the Bill of Rights could be binding on the states through the due process clause. As Justice BENJAMIN N. CARDOZO, an early opponent of the total incorporation doctrine, had observed in PALKO V. CONNECTICUT (1937): "In [certain] situations immunities that are valid as against the federal government by force of the specific pledges of particular amendments have been found to be implicit in the concept of ordered liberty and thus, through the Fourteenth Amendment, become valid as against the states." Yet it is important to note that this justification for the new doctrine blurred an important distinction in the traditional view, which was that some *rights* protected by the provisions of the Bill of Rights might prove so central to ordered liberty that they were also binding on the states through the due process clause. This was not to say, however, that certain *provisions* of the Bill of Rights, in their entirety with all their interpretations, were incorporated by the due process clause.

In the decade following *Adamson* the Court was apparently not yet ready to take this leap from the traditional view to the new doctrine of selective incorporation. Instead, the Court developed a number of significant expansions in its conception of what fundamental fairness required that prepared the ground for the flowering of the selective incorporation theory a decade later. An early important instance was WOLF V. COLORADO (1949), in which the Court held, in an opinion by Justice Frankfurter, that "the security of one's privacy against arbitrary intrusion by the police—which is at the core of the Fourth Amendment— . . . is implicit in 'the concept of ordered liberty'" and hence enforceable against the states through the due process clause. Still, the opinion was careful not to say that the Fourth Amendment as such was applicable to the states, and the Court declined to apply the remedy it had developed for enforcing the Fourth Amendment in federal prosecutions—excluding the unlawfully seized evidence. Other cases carried the movement forward. The Court in *Rochin* found that pumping an accused's stomach to obtain incriminating evidence was so "shocking to the conscience" that due process required the conviction to be reversed. Increasingly the Court found the failure to appoint counsel for indigent defendants to violate due process under the "totality of circumstances" rule of BETTS V. BRADY (1942), which required specific prejudice to be identified in the record. The circumstances in which the Court held confessions involuntary and, therefore, barred by due process were extended in *Spano v. New York* (1959) beyond physical coercion to include situations in which the defendant's will had been overborne by more subtle means of influence, such as persistent interrogation and trickery.

In the 1960s, however, the traditional test of fundamental fairness yielded to selective incorporation as the Court's dominant approach in reviewing the constitutionality of state prosecutions. A change of mood had taken place. For a variety of reasons—change in the composition of the Court, the CIVIL RIGHTS movement, the "War against Poverty"—the consensus on the Supreme Court moved toward greater intervention on behalf of criminal defendants, the great majority of whom were poor and members of minority groups. The continued enlargement case by case of the requirements of "fundamental fairness" was one possible alternative. But if, as the Justices apparently increasingly believed, excesses in the states' administration of criminal justice required extensive judicial correction, then something more was needed than the power to intervene in occasional cases of gross injustice. As a consequence the 1960s saw one of the remarkable accomplishments of the Warren Court—the federalization of state criminal procedure through the selective incorporation of the Bill of Rights.

Mapp v. Ohio (1961) marked the beginning. Effective control of state law enforcement required a constitutional remedy for law enforcement excesses. The EXCLUSIONARY RULE, which barred admission of unconstitutionally obtained evidence, had been developed decades earlier as a remedy in federal prosecutions. In *Wolf v. Colorado* the Court had declined to apply the exclusionary rule to the states, saying that a conviction based on reliable physical evidence was not fundamentally unfair just because the police had obtained the evidence by unconstitutional means. In *Mapp* the Court overruled that holding. The Court had, after all, already held in *Wolf* that the Fourth Amendment's RIGHT OF PRIVACY was enforceable against the states. It seemed natural to take the further step of holding that the remedy used to enforce Fourth Amendment privacy rights against federal violations was no less required to enforce "due process" privacy rights against state violations. If Fourth Amendment rights were basic to liberty, so must be the only practical means for their enforcement.

The next major case, GIDEON V. WAINWRIGHT (1963), also had features that made it a relatively easy case for extending selective incorporation. The Court had earlier held in *Betts* that appointment of counsel for indigents, though required by the Sixth Amendment for federal prosecutions, was not necessarily a fundamental right protected by due process. In the special circumstances of some particular prosecution, failure to appoint counsel might constitute a lack of fundamental fairness, but absence of counsel would not necessarily create this level of prejudice in every case. However, the "special circumstances" doctrine was gradually undermined in successive cases as the Court increasingly was able to find those circumstances in cases that were typical. As Justice Harlan observed, "The Court had come to realize . . . that the mere existence of a serious criminal charge constituted in itself special circumstances requiring the services of counsel at trial." Against this background there was little resistance to overruling *Betts* and, in the process, holding that the Sixth Amendment's guarantee of counsel was one of those clauses which fundamental fairness required to be imposed upon the states by the Fourteenth Amendment.

From then on scarcely a TERM of Court in the 1960s went by without the Court's OVERRULING some prior case to hold that an additional provision of the Bill of Rights was necessary to fundamental fairness and was, therefore, incorporated in due process. In 1965, in *Griffin v. California,* the Court overruled *Adamson* and held that the Fifth Amendment right against self-incrimination was protected by due process. The Sixth Amendment right to confrontation of witnesses was held to be incorporated in *Pointer v. Texas* (1965), and the rights to a speedy and public trial and to compulsory process for obtaining witnesses were also held to be incorporated in KLOPFER V. NORTH CAROLINA and *Washington v. Texas* (1967). In DUNCAN V. LOUISIANA (1968), the Court overruled earlier decisions and held that the Sixth Amendment's right to a jury trial was incorporated in due process. In BENTON V. MARYLAND (1969), *Palko* was overruled and the double jeopardy provision was held applicable to the states. The job was done. To all intents and purposes, the contours of due process of law required of the states by the Fourteenth Amendment had come to be defined by the specific guarantees of the Bill of Rights limiting the federal government.

One may fairly ask of this constitutional tour de force how well it was defended in doctrinal analysis. The position favoring total incorporation had a forceful logic: once the initial premise was accepted, it followed that every provision of the Bill of Rights and every interpretation of those provisions developed for federal prosecutions should apply equally to state prosecutions. But how was the theory of selective incorporation to be justified? Did the Court seriously mean that all the rights the Court had previously found in selected provisions of the Bill of Rights—such as the jury trial provision of the Sixth Amendment, the Fifth Amendment's protection against self-incrimination, the Fourth Amendment restraints upon search and seizure (including the right to have even reliable evidence excluded if it were unlawfully obtained)—all were so fundamental that "a fair and enlightened system of justice would be impossible" without them? This conclusion could scarcely stand scrutiny. As the Court had noted in earlier cases holding these guarantees unprotected by due process, a large portion of the democratic world, with claims to a civilized and enlightened system of justice no less strong than ours, offers no such guarantees.

Very little effort was made to address this challenge until Justice BYRON R. WHITE (in a footnote, ironically) did so in his opinion for the Court in *Duncan v. Louisiana* (1968), holding the jury trial guarantee of the Sixth Amendment incorporated by the due process clause. He ascribed the rejection of the earlier holdings to a new interpretation of what fundamental fairness meant. The Court had previously understood it to require those guarantees that a system of justice anywhere at any time would have to accord to be called civilized. In the newer cases, however, the Court proceeded on the view that fairness required those guarantees that are necessary to an "Anglo-American regime of ordered liberty." It is not required, White noted, that a procedural guarantee be "necessarily fundamental to fairness in every criminal system that might be imagined," but that it be fundamental "in the context of the criminal processes maintained by the American states."

Whether this revision of the fundamental fairness test suffices as a basis for selecting particular provisions of the Bill of Rights for incorporation is problematic. If the new test refers to practices that have so long been accorded in American systems of justice that they have come to be regarded as among the distinguishing characteristics of American justice, then "fundamental" becomes equivalent to "traditional," all the provisions of the Bill of Rights are fundamental, and the accepted test of selective incorporation becomes in fact the rejected test of total incorporation. It would appear, however, that something more was meant. Criminal justice systems, like other social institutions, are complex and comprise a variety of elements that function in a delicate ecological relationship. Given the particular functioning of some procedural protection in the American system, it may be that the protection is fundamental to fairness in that system, although it would not be in a system with a different assortment of procedural elements with differing functional relationships. So, in the *Duncan* case, Justice White noted that although it was easy to imagine a fair system that used no juries, in which alternative guarantees and protections would serve the purposes the jury serves in English and American systems, no American jurisdiction had undertaken to construct such a system.

If this latter interpretation of fundamental fairness were taken seriously, the Court would be obliged to undertake in each case a factual examination of the complex functioning of the state's criminal justice system, with particular attention to how the functioning of the system as a whole colors the significance of the practice at issue. But no such inquiry was made in the *Duncan* case. The opinion drew attention to the long-standing concern about overzealous prosecutors and biased judges. But it made no effort to examine such questions as whether the routine availability of appellate review in the state courts and COLLATERAL ATTACK in the federal courts rendered a jury trial less indispensable as a protection against such abuses; or why, if the use of a jury for this purpose made it a requirement of fundamental fairness in the American system, it was not required in all civilized systems; or whether a jury of randomly chosen citizens in fact served as a check against bias rather than as a source of bias. The Court also pointed generally to the traditional acceptance in America of a jury power of nullification in the application of the law. But the Court failed to consider why this power is significant, and why, in other systems, a comparable power of nullification is not seen to be required by fundamental fairness.

The point is not that the Court could not have made a case for the conclusion that fundamental fairness required the jury in the American system of justice, but that it did not try. Nor did the Court do better in the other cases applying the doctrine of selective incorporation. In the end, therefore, there is force in the conclusion that the Court's attempt to shore up the doctrinal case for selective incorporation was an illusory post hoc rationalization.

An additional consideration, strongly pressed by Justice Harlan in his dissenting opinions, lends further support to that conclusion. Even if it be granted that a guarantee to be found in a provision of the Bill of Rights is required by fundamental fairness in an American system of justice, it does not follow that each and every interpretation of that provision developed in federal prosecutions is equally required for fundamental fairness. For example, the Fifth Amendment's privilege against self-incrimination has been held in federal prosecutions to preclude judicial or prosecutorial comment on the failure of the defendant to respond to the evidence against him. The Fifth Amendment's protection against double jeopardy has been interpreted to attach at the time the jury is first sworn. The Sixth Amendment's guarantee of a jury trial in criminal cases had once been held to require a unanimous verdict of the jury. But even if the core concept of the privilege against self-incrimination, the double jeopardy protection, and the jury trial guarantee were found to be necessary for fundamental fairness, it would scarcely follow that each and every one of these interpretations of the federal guarantees is also necessary. Yet, in sharp contrast to the requirements of the avowed theory of selective incorporation, this is what the Court had held in every instance: a conclusion that a clause of the Bill of Rights is applicable to the states necessarily entails that each and every interpretation of that clause developed in federal prosecutions, regardless of its rationale or significance, becomes fully applicable as well, as Harlan said, "jot-for-jot and case-for-case" and "freighted with [its] entire accompanying body of federal doctrine" (*Duncan v. Louisiana,* 1968; *Malloy v. Hogan,* 1964). This conclusion constitutes further evidence that the Court was not taking seriously the only theory it had advanced to support its doctrine of selective incorporation.

Putting aside the doctrinal warrant of the approach to procedural due process that has come to prevail, what has been its impact on the administration of criminal justice in the states and what is its likely bearing on the future of due process? It is clear that the values of federalism have been heavily overrun. Given the expansive, pervasive, and often highly detailed regulations the Court has imposed on the processes of criminal justice under warrant of the Bill of Rights, one has to conclude that the autonomy of state government has been drastically curtailed.

At the same time, it is almost certainly true that the procedural rights accorded the accused in state courts have been greatly expanded over what they would have been had this federalization not taken place. The expansion of constraints upon the administration of justice during the era of the Warren Court in the 1960s has been one of the notable characteristics of that Court. Few state courts and no state legislatures could have been expected on their own to have achieved anything like a comparable expansion. People will differ over whether the balance between effective law enforcement and the rights of the accused thereby achieved resulted in a preferable system of criminal justice than would have been obtained under the earlier doctrine. Most would agree, however, that the coalescing of the minimum constitutional rights of the accused in both state and federal prosecutions has tended to produce a constitutional jurisprudence more understandable to the citizen who does not typically distinguish between state and federal government in considering the rights of the accused.

On the other hand, the presumed advantage in

using the Bill of Rights to measure what due process requires of the states—that it eliminates the uncertainty and the need for personal, subjective decision-making by judges imposed by the traditional view—has hardly been evident. In deciding what searches are "reasonable" within the Fourth Amendment, how far that Amendment protects a right of privacy against new forms of ELECTRONIC EAVESDROPPING, when noncoercive POLICE INTERROGATION becomes violative of the Fifth Amendment's right against self-incrimination, what punishment, including CAPITAL PUNISHMENT, is "cruel and unusual" within the Eighth Amendment (which the Court in TROP V. DULLES (1958) conceded had to be determined by "the dignity of man" and "evolving standards of decency"), it was readily apparent that the text of the Bill of Rights scarcely spoke for itself and in fact invited no less an assessment and choice among competing values on the basis of the Justice's sense of what justice and fairness required. Fixed meanings have not triumphed over flexible ones, and judicial subjectivity has not been contained. More seriously, insofar as the Court has proceeded on the false assumption that the need for judicial value choosing has been overcome, it has handicapped itself in the task of developing a well-considered method of decision-making that would discipline and make more rational the inevitable process of choosing among competing values.

This concern is particularly pressing because the Court has recognized that due process is still open-ended, that although due process includes the incorporated clauses of the Bill of Rights, those clauses do not exhaust the content of due process. The 1952 decision in *Rochin*, that a state denied due process by using evidence pumped from the accused's stomach against his will, was reaffirmed in SCHMERBER V. CALIFORNIA (1966) under the principle that due process precludes action against an accused that "shocks the conscience" and violates one's "sense of justice," notwithstanding the inapplicability of any other provision of the Bill of Rights. Similar evidence of the vitality of the older tests of due process where the Bill of Rights does not reach are the Court's decisions in IN RE WINSHIP (1970), holding that an essential requirement of due process in criminal cases is proof of guilt beyond a REASONABLE DOUBT, and in the CAPITAL PUNISHMENT CASES OF 1976, finding in due process a requirement of articulated criteria to guide the judge or jury in determining whether to impose capital punishment.

One may conclude that despite the victory of selective incorporation the task of developing a defensible method and set of criteria to govern the determination of those criminal procedures that are constitutionally permissible is very much before the Court. How it could best be met is uncertain. One proposed approach would entail a consideration of a number of issues. In this view the Court would begin by drawing out the implications of the basic values animating constitutional restraints on the criminal process: fairness to the accused, protection of personal dignity, and the reliability of the processes for determining guilt. Next, the Court would determine how gravely the controverted procedure impugned those values and how seriously certain restraints would prejudice the due administration of criminal justice. Finally, the Court would seek ways of rooting the inevitable final choices in ground more secure than the personal judgment of the majority of the Justices on the optimum operation of the system of criminal justice. Another approach, less oriented to consequentialist considerations, would have the Court determine the fundamental legal rights of persons, including the constitutional rights of the accused, in terms of the requirements of a general political theory that best account for the moral principles embedded in the Constitution, laws, and culture of our society. Whatever the answer, the task is a formidable one. Indeed, the effort may ultimately be futile, as those believe who view the Court as indistinguishable from any other political body in the exercise of its power. But to the extent that the Court accepts the claim that its exercise of political power is based on reason and disinterestedness—that is, on law—it can scarcely abandon the goal of writing opinions that give credence to the claim. However one may approve its results, the doctrine of selective incorporation, with its oversimplifications and misperceptions, and its dubious doctrinal underpinnings, has not served that goal well.

SANFORD H. KADISH

Bibliography

ALLEN, FRANCIS A. 1953 Due Process and State Criminal Procedures: Another Look. *Northwestern University Law Review* 48:16–35.

DWORKIN, RONALD M. 1975 Hard Cases. *Harvard Law Review* 88:1057–1109.

FAIRMAN, CHARLES 1949 Does the Fourth Amendment Incorporate the Bill of Rights? The Original Understanding. *Stanford Law Review* 2:5–173.

FRIENDLY, HENRY 1965 The Bill of Rights as a Code of Criminal Procedure. *California Law Review* 53:929–956.

HENKIN, LOUIS 1963 "Selective Incorporation" in the Fourteenth Amendment. *Yale Law Journal* 73:74–88.

KADISH, SANFORD H. 1957 Methodology and Criteria in

Due Process Adjudication—A Survey and Criticism. *Yale Law Journal* 66:319–363.

NOTE 1949 The Adamson Case: A Study in Constitutional Technique. *Yale Law Journal* 58:268–287.

NOWAK, JOHN E. 1979 Foreword: Due Process Methodology in a Post-Incorporation World. *Journal of Criminal Law and Criminology* 70:397–423.

PROCLAMATION OF NEUTRALITY (1793)

The Proclamation of Neutrality (April 22, 1793) was issued by President GEORGE WASHINGTON upon notification that France and Britain were at war. It pledged the United States to "pursue a course friendly and impartial" toward the belligerents and enjoined observance on all citizens upon pain of prosecution. Neutrality was bound to be difficult because of intense partisan feelings about the war, the privileges and obligations of the French alliance, and British rejection of American claims of neutral rights on the seas.

The importance of the proclamation for the Constitution was twofold. First, as a unilateral declaration by the President it seemed to preempt the power of Congress to decide questions of war and peace. Secretary of State THOMAS JEFFERSON, although he acquiesced in the proclamation, had made this objection in the cabinet, and it was taken up by the Republicans. In a notable series of articles under the signature Pacificus, Secretary of the Treasury ALEXANDER HAMILTON defended the proclamation. His claim of independent executive authority in FOREIGN AFFAIRS was opposed by JAMES MADISON as Helvidius, who compared it to the royal prerogative of the English constitution. (Hamilton's argument prevailed in history, though Madison's antipathy to overriding executive power has not lacked supporters.) Second, as the conduct of neutrality was executive altogether, it afforded the first instance of government by administrative lawmaking. Decisions were made in the cabinet, without statutory authority, with the guidance only of the customary law of nations. Divided and uncomfortable in this work, the cabinet officers submitted twenty-nine questions to the ruling of the Supreme Court. The court declined to rule, however, and thus established the precedent against ADVISORY OPINIONS. Meanwhile, the government's attempt to prosecute violators of the proclamation was defeated by unsympathetic juries. Not until June 1794 did Congress enact a neutrality law, which codified the rules developed in the cabinet during the preceding year.

MERRILL D. PETERSON

Bibliography

THOMAS, CHARLES M. 1931 *American Neutrality in 1793: A Study in Cabinet Government.* New York: Columbia University Press.

PROCUNIER v. MARTINEZ 416 U.S. 396 (1974)

Speaking through Justice LEWIS F. POWELL, the Supreme Court invalidated California prison regulations censoring inmates' correspondence and prohibiting attorney–client interviews conducted by law students and legal paraprofessionals. The censorship provisions had permitted prison officials to ban correspondence in which inmates "unduly complain," "magnify grievances," or expressed "inflammatory political, racial, religious or other views or beliefs." These vague standards, the Court held, violated the FIRST AMENDMENT rights of prisoners and those with whom they corresponded. The prohibition on the use of law students and paralegals was held to be an unjustified restriction on prisoners' ACCESS TO THE COURTS.

MICHAEL E. PARRISH

PRODUCTION

Until the transformation of the constitutional law of ECONOMIC REGULATION, beginning in 1937, "production" described economic activities that the Supreme Court regarded as local or intrastate in character and therefore beyond Congress's power to regulate under the COMMERCE CLAUSE. In 1895 the Court ruled in UNITED STATES v. E. C. KNIGHT CO. that every form of production and matters related to it were stages of economic activity that preceded the buying, selling, and transportation of goods among the states. Manufacturing, mining, agriculture, domestic fisheries, stock raising, and labor had only an "indirect" effect upon commerce, by judicial definition. Because commerce came after production the United States had no constitutional authority to extend the SHERMAN ANTITRUST ACT to monopolies in production, nor could it control the trade practices of poultry dealers, or regulate agricultural production, or fix the MAXIMUM HOURS AND MINIMUM WAGES of miners. In UNITED STATES v. DARBY (1941) the Court sustained the constitutionality of the FAIR LABOR STANDARDS

ACT, which applied to workers engaged in production of goods for sale in INTERSTATE COMMERCE; in the next year the Court in WICKARD v. FILBURN (1942) ended any remaining vestiges of the doctrine that Congress could not regulate production. The Court ruled that, although certain economic activities are local or intrastate, the commerce clause extends Congress's power to them if they affect commerce, making their regulation an appropriate way of governing commerce among the states.

LEONARD W. LEVY

PROFFITT v. FLORIDA

See: Capital Punishment Cases, 1976

PROGRESSIVE CONSTITUTIONAL THOUGHT

During the Progressive era, roughly from 1900 to 1920, the Constitution and the SUPREME COURT came in for considerable criticism on the part of historians, political theorists, statesmen, intellectuals, and journalists. The criticisms involved five issues: the origins of the Constitution's authority; claims that the Constitution, and the system of government it supported, were antiquated and needed to be modified in light of developments in modern science; protests that the Supreme Court functioned as an instrument of business interests; demands that the Constitution be reinterpreted to allow for federal regulation of industry; and similar demands that it become the agency of social reform.

Prior to the Progressive era the Constitution's authority rested on the assumption that it was a neutral document capable of rendering objective judgments based on either transcendent religious principles or secular doctrines like natural law. The first challenge to that assumption came from J. ALLEN SMITH's *The Spirit of American Government* (1907), in which the Constitution was alleged to be a "reactionary" document designed to thwart the democratic principles of the DECLARATION OF INDEPENDENCE by means of CHECKS AND BALANCES and JUDICIAL REVIEW of legislative actions of popular majorities. But the most thorough critique of the Constitution's presumed disinterested authority fell like a blockbuster with the publication of CHARLES A. BEARD's *An Economic Interpretation of the Constitution* (1913). Here readers discovered that the movement toward RATIFICATION OF THE CONSTITUTION in 1787–1789 was led by merchants, manufacturers, creditors, and land speculators whose primary concern was to protect their own interests from what JAMES MADISON called "overbearing factions." THE FEDERALIST's authors, Beard was aware, hardly concealed the fact that they regarded protection of property as the essence of liberty. But Beard's exposure of the economic motives of the Framers did much to demystify the moral character of the Constitution by disclosing the "interests" behind it.

While the historian Beard tried to unmask the sacred image of the Constitution, political theorists tried to reestablish it on a more scientific foundation. In *The Process of Government* (1908) Arthur Bentley suggested that the scholar must penetrate beyond the formal structure of the Constitution to appreciate the forces and pressures that act upon it through interest group demands. But the dynamic of amoral interest politics was precisely what troubled WOODROW WILSON and other Progressive idealists. First in *Congressional Government* (1884), then in *Constitutional Government in the United States* (1908), and finally in a series of campaign speeches published as *The New Freedom* (1912), Wilson indicted the Constitution for weakening the executive branch of government, allowing interests and power to prevail in the legislature's standing committees, accepting as inevitable factional antagonisms detrimental to the public good, and upholding the letter of the law rather than the life of the state. Criticizing *The Federalist* for bequeathing a static, mechanist concept of government, Wilson wanted a Constitution "accountable to Darwin, not to Newton," a Constitution as "a living organism" capable of growth and adaption, one that would coordinate the branches of government so that liberty could be preserved not on the basis of diversity—Madison's premise—but of unity forged by presidential leadership.

Critical of the Constitution, Progressives also became disillusioned with a Supreme Court as an obstacle in the path of social reform. THEODORE ROOSEVELT exploded in anger when the Court invalidated state LEGISLATION involving child labor, tenement house reform, and other goals of Progressivism. Yet, curiously, Progressives disagreed whether the Court had a right to do so. In *The Supreme Court and the Constitution* (1912), Beard argued that the right of judicial review was the clear intent of *The Federalist.* In *Our Judicial Oligarchy* (1912) Gilbert E. Roe expounded the opposing case, arguing that the courts had usurped authority in reviewing legislative acts. While both authors scorned judges disposed to preserving property rights at the cost of social justice, they continued to differ as to whether the Supreme Court could hold unconstitutional laws void or whether it should defer to the legislative process and exercise what the followers of OLIVER WENDELL HOLMES called "judicial restraint."

Progressives were far more unified in advocating regulation. All the writers associated with the liberal *New Republic*—HERBERT CROLY, Walter Weyl, Walter Lippmann, John Dewey, and LOUIS D. BRANDEIS—wanted to see corporate enterprise subordinated to the public good by means of industrial commissions, surveillance of trusts and monopolies, banking and railroad legislation, and the like. All also agreed that standing in the way of federal regulatory policies was a debilitating Jeffersonian heritage that made private rights anterior to public responsibilities, a destructive individualism that frustrated the ideals of political authority and civic duty. "Only by violating the spirit of the Constitution," Lippmann boldly declared, "have we been able to preserve the letter of it." Many of the Progressives were Hamiltonian nationalists convinced that both the Constitution and the Republic could be preserved from the corruptions of business interests only by augmenting the authority of an efficient and enlightened state. Many were also pragmatists who believed that the Constitution should be interpreted not from within but from without, not in terms of its inherent logic or precedent but in light of its consequences as society experiences the Court's rulings.

Progressives succeeded in realizing a number of reforms through the AMENDING PROCESS, specifically the income tax, women's suffrage, and the DIRECT ELECTION of senators. As with the INITIATIVE, RECALL, and REFERENDUM in state governments, and direct PRIMARY ELECTIONS in national politics, the constitutional amendments aimed to allow people to participate more directly in the decisions affecting their lives. Whereas *The Federalist*'s authors believed that liberty could best be preserved by distancing the people from the immediate operations of government, the Progressives saw no conflict between republican liberty and participatory democracy.

JOHN PATRICK DIGGINS

Bibliography

COMMAGER, HENRY STEELE 1950 *The American Mind: An Interpretation of American Thought and Character Since the 1890s.* New Haven, Conn.: Yale University Press.

ROSTOW, EUGENE V. 1970 The Realist Tradition in Law. Pages 203–218 in Arthur M. Schlesinger, Jr., and Morton White, eds., *Paths of American Thought.* Boston: Beacon Press.

PROHIBITION

A recurring theme in American constitutional history is the attempt of a majority to impose its moral standards on society by legislation. The nineteenth-century temperance movement, along with its close ally, the ABOLITIONIST movement, constituted such a moral majority. That movement sought the legal prohibition of alcoholic beverages.

State and local prohibition statutes were accepted by the Supreme Court in MUGLER V. KANSAS (1887) as valid applications of the STATE POLICE POWER. That such laws deprived citizens of their liberty and property without DUE PROCESS OF LAW had been asserted, before the Civil War, only in the state court case of WYNEHAMER V. NEW YORK (1856).

In the early twentieth century the prohibition movement acquired a new ally in the Progressive movement, and, after nineteen states adopted prohibition laws, agitation shifted to the national level. In 1917 Congress enacted prohibition as a wartime austerity measure. The same year Congress proposed the EIGHTEENTH AMENDMENT, which, when ratified in 1919, raised prohibition to constitutional status. Repeal came fourteen years later with adoption of the TWENTY-FIRST AMENDMENT.

The failure of the "noble experiment" of national prohibition is frequently cited by opponents of other types of majoritarian legislation on moral issues, such as laws against SEGREGATION, handguns, abortion, and drugs.

DENNIS J. MAHONEY

PROHIBITION, WRIT OF

To lawyers as well as others, the term PROHIBITION calls to mind a law forbidding the making, distribution, or possession of intoxicating liquors. In law, however, the term has an ancient COMMON LAW meaning that retains vitality today. The writ of prohibition is an order from a higher court commanding a lower court to stop hearing a matter outside the lower court's JURISDICTION. From the beginning prohibition has been considered an extraordinary writ, one that the higher court may or may not grant, in its discretion. It is not normally to be used as a substitute for an APPEAL or a petition for a WRIT OF CERTIORARI.

A statute dating from the JUDICIARY ACT OF 1789 is interpreted to empower the UNITED STATES COURTS OF APPEALS and the Supreme Court to issue writs of prohibition to lower federal courts. Under this law, the Supreme Court can also issue writs of prohibition to state courts.

KENNETH L. KARST

PROHIBITION OF SLAVE TRADE ACT
2 Stat. 426 (1807)

Colonial legislatures had often tried to restrict the importation of slaves for economic reasons, and THOMAS JEFFERSON's famous deleted passage in the DECLARATION OF INDEPENDENCE denounced the royal disallowance of these bills. After Independence, all the states (except Georgia until 1798) prohibited the importation of slaves from abroad. The CONSTITUTIONAL CONVENTION OF 1787 permitted Congress to legislate against the international trade but at the insistence of the South Carolina delegates prohibited it from exercising that power for twenty years (Article I, section 9). After 1790, the Pennsylvania Abolition Society and the American Convention of Abolition Societies demanded interim legislation against the trade. Their lobbying produced the Act of March 22, 1794, prohibiting Americans from fitting out in American ports for the international trade. But South Carolina shocked the nation's conscience by reopening the trade in 1803.

President Jefferson urged Congress to ban the international trade at the earliest possible moment, and Congress responded with the Act of March 2, 1807, which prohibited the importation of slaves from foreign nations and dependencies, penalized persons engaging in the trade and purchasers from them, and provided for forfeiture of slaving vessels. The Act of May 15, 1820, declared slaving to be piracy, punishable by death. But enforcement of the ban was deliberately half-hearted, and the illegal trade brought in approximately a thousand blacks a year from Africa and the Caribbean. Though some southern spokesman in the late 1850s demanded a reopening of the trade, the CONFEDERATE CONSTITUTION also prohibited it.

WILLIAM M. WIECEK

Bibliography

WIECEK, WILLIAM M. 1977 *The Sources of Antislavery Constitutionalism in America, 1760–1848.* Ithaca, N.Y.: Cornell University Press.

PROPELLER GENESEE CHIEF v. FITZHUGH
12 Howard 443 (1851)

An act of Congress extended the ADMIRALTY AND MARITIME JURISDICTION of the United States Courts in matters of contract and tort arising upon the Great Lakes and connecting navigable rivers. In the case of *The Thomas Jefferson* (1825), the Court had confined federal admiralty and maritime jurisdiction to tide waters. Here, the Supreme Court, by a vote of 8–1, sustained the constitutionality of the act of Congress by ruling that JURISDICTION should not depend on the ebb and flow of the tide as in England but on the fact that the United States has "thousands of miles" of public navigable waters in which there is no tide. The TANEY COURT thus considerably expanded federal jurisdiction.

LEONARD W. LEVY

PROVIDENCE BANK v. BILLINGS
4 Peters 514 (1830)

This case anticipated the DOCTRINE of the CHARLES RIVER BRIDGE CO. V. WARREN BRIDGE CO. (1837) case and limited the doctrine of tax immunity established by NEW JERSEY V. WILSON (1812). The Court here, through Chief Justice JOHN MARSHALL, established the principle that a corporate charter should not be construed to vest more rights than are found in its express provisions. A state taxed a bank for the first time long after chartering it. The bank contended that its charter implied a tax immunity, because a state power to tax the bank could destroy it, contrary to its charter. The Court sustained the tax against the CONTRACT CLAUSE argument, reasoning that the state had made no express contract to relinquish its power to tax and that the relinquishment of that power "is never to be assumed." Chartered privileges "must be expressed . . . or they do not exist."

LEONARD W. LEVY

PRUDENTIAL INSURANCE COMPANY v. BENJAMIN
328 U.S. 408 (1946)

The dissenters in UNITED STATES V. SOUTH-EASTERN UNDERWRITERS (1944) feared that declaring insurance to be INTERSTATE COMMERCE, subject to congressional regulation, would create chaos by rendering state regulation of that industry void. An act of Congress, however, left most such regulation standing and Justice WILEY RUTLEDGE headed a unanimous Court sustaining a state tax that discriminated against interstate commerce. Assuming that such a tax would be invalid in the absence of congressional action, here Congress had decided that uniformity of regulation and taxation was necessary and had authorized even discriminatory state regulation and taxation of the insurance business.

DAVID GORDON

(SEE ALSO: *State Regulation of Commerce.*)

PRUNEYARD SHOPPING CENTER v. ROBINS
447 U.S. 74 (1980)

HUDGENS V. N.L.R.B. (1976) had held that the FIRST AMENDMENT did not compel private owners of SHOPPING CENTERS to permit their property to be used for expressive activity. In *PruneYard,* California's supreme court held that the state constitution required a shopping center owner to permit the collection of signatures on a petition. The Supreme Court unanimously affirmed. Justice WILLIAM H. REHNQUIST, for the Court, concluded that the state law did not work an uncompensated TAKING OF PROPERTY. Nor did it violate the owner's First Amendment rights by compelling it to convey a message. Justice LEWIS F. POWELL, concurring, argued that under other circumstances an owner might have such a First Amendment right.

KENNETH L. KARST

PUBLIC ACCOMMODATIONS

The refusal of hotels, restaurants, theaters, and other public accommodations to serve blacks was not exclusively a southern phenomenon. In the South, however, the practice was an essential part of a system of racial dominance and dependency, long after the THIRTEENTH AMENDMENT abolished slavery and the FOURTEENTH AMENDMENT recognized the CITIZENSHIP of the freed slaves. Aware of the role played by this form of RACIAL DISCRIMINATION in the system of white supremacy, Congress adopted the CIVIL RIGHTS ACT OF 1875, the last major CIVIL RIGHTS act of the Reconstruction era. The law prohibited public accommodations, including railroads along with the types already mentioned, from denying access to any person on account of race. The Supreme Court held this law unconstitutional, saying that when Congress enforced the Fourteenth Amendment it had no power to reach private action. (See CIVIL RIGHTS CASES, 1883; STATE ACTION.)

Later came the Jim Crow laws—state laws requiring racial SEGREGATION in all manner of public places, including public accommodations. This practice received the Court's blessing in PLESSY V. FERGUSON (1896), a case involving the segregation of seating in railroad cars. (See SEPARATE BUT EQUAL DOCTRINE.) By the end of the nineteenth century, the denial of access for blacks to public accommodations in the South was firmly rooted in both law and custom.

Soon after the Supreme Court decided BROWN V. BOARD OF EDUCATION (1954), the modern civil rights movement turned to the problem of access to public accommodations. The reason for direct action such as freedom rides and SIT-INS was not that seats in the front of the bus arrive at a destination before back seats do, or that black college students yearn to perch on lunch counter stools. Public accommodations became a target for civil rights demonstrators for exactly the same reason that they had been made the vehicles for racial discrimination in the first place: segregation and the refusal of service to blacks were powerful symbols of racial inferiority, highly visible denials of the entitlement of blacks to be treated as persons and citizens. Employment discrimination and housing discrimination might touch material interests of great importance, but no interest is more important than self-respect. The primary target of the civil rights movement was the stigma of caste.

Within a few years after the *Brown* decision, the Supreme Court had held unconstitutional nearly the whole range of Jim Crow laws. Racial segregation practiced by state institutions, or commanded or authorized by state laws, failed the test of the Fourteenth Amendment even before Congress reentered the public accommodations field. In most of the states of the North and West, civil rights laws commanded equal access not only to public accommodations—such laws merely reinforced the common law duties of innkeepers and common carriers—but also to other businesses. In the South, however, private discrimination continued in most hotels, restaurants, and barber shops. The Supreme Court was repeatedly invited to decide whether the Fourteenth Amendment established a right of access to such places, free of racial bias, but the Court repeatedly declined the invitation. (See BELL V. MARYLAND, 1964.)

As part of the CIVIL RIGHTS ACT OF 1964, Congress adopted a comprehensive public accommodations law, forbidding discrimination in the same types of places that had been covered by the 1875 act. (Railroads were forbidden to discriminate by modern interpretations of the INTERSTATE COMMERCE ACT of 1887.) Before the year was out, the Supreme Court had upheld the public accommodations portion of the 1964 act, on the basis of the power of Congress to regulate interstate commerce. (See HEART OF ATLANTA MOTEL V. UNITED STATES, 1964.)

The 1964 act is limited in its coverage, reaching an establishment only if it "affects commerce" or if its discrimination is "supported by STATE ACTION." The act exempts both private clubs and small rooming houses lived in by their proprietors. Now that the Supreme Court has interpreted the CIVIL RIGHTS ACT OF 1866 as a broad guarantee against private racial discrimination in the sale of property and other contracting, and validated the law as a congressional enforcement of the Thirteenth Amendment, at least some of the limitations of the 1964 act have been made irrelevant. For example, a barber shop is covered by the 1964 act if it is located in a covered hotel, but not if it is independent. Under recent interpretations of the 1866 act, any barber shop would violate the law by refusing service on the basis of the customer's race. (See JONES V. ALFRED H. MAYER CO., 1968; RUNYON V. MCCRARY, 1976.)

The substantive core of the Fourteenth Amendment is a principle of equal citizenship. (See EQUAL PROTECTION OF THE LAWS.) Even in the absence of civil rights legislation, that principle demands that the organized community treat each of us, irrespective of race, as a respected, participating member. Racially based denial of access or segregation in places of public accommodations—even those privately owned—is a deliberate denial of the status of equal citizenship, as the sit-in demonstrators knew and helped the rest of us to understand.

KENNETH L. KARST

Bibliography

LEWIS, THOMAS P. 1963 The Sit-in Cases: Great Expectations. *Supreme Court Review* 1963:101–151.

POLLITT, DANIEL H. 1960 Dime Store Demonstrations: Events and Legal Problems of the First Sixty Days. *Duke Law Journal* 1960:315–365.

WOODWARD, C. VANN 1966 *The Strange Career of Jim Crow*, 2d (rev.) ed. New York: Oxford University Press.

PUBLIC EMPLOYEES

The government may regulate public employees more extensively than citizens at large because legitimate employer interests in controlling job-related behavior supplement the government's general constitutional power to control the behavior of private citizens. Government employers constitutionally are less free than private employers to control their employees, however, for the simple reason that the Constitution primarily limits government, not private, power. Eligibility criteria, work rules, and myriad personnel decisions take on constitutional dimensions in public sector employment that are absent from the private sector.

The competing analogies of government as citizen-regulator and government as private employer raise related questions. How much more power may the government exercise over its employees than over citizens at large? What constitutional limits bind public employers that do not bind private employers? The two questions tend to converge because, inevitably, the government affects its employees as regulator and employer simultaneously.

The constitutional issues comprise both substance and process. What substantive freedoms may the government require its employees to forgo as a condition of employment and what are the permissible and impermissible bases for disadvantaging public employees? Procedurally, when, how, and with what opportunity to respond, must government employers inform their employees of the reasons for adverse personnel actions?

The constitutional values at stake clash and mesh in complex ways. Government workers have individual rights to exercise substantive freedoms without improper penalty and to be treated fairly by the government. These often vie with government interests in effective, honest, efficient, and democratic management of the public's business. The government also has interests in employee loyalty and in the confidential execution of public policy. These may war with the value of freedom for dissident employees to bring important information to public attention and to check abuse of government power by other officials. Inevitably, public employees have greater opportunities than ordinary citizens both to impede legitimate government action and to prevent government abuse.

Public employees' own rights and the implication of their activities for public governance make the constitutional balance important and intricate, especially given this century's extensive increase in public employment. The existence of 3 million federal employees and 13 million more state and local government workers makes sacrifices of their constitutional freedoms of considerable consequence, both personal and societal. Yet their numbers create a potent political force able to secure statutory job protection and to fend off arbitrary treatment as a group, diminishing the need for constitutional protection. In addition, the size of the public work force increases legitimate government claims to constitutional flexibility in employee management.

Speaking in broad historical terms, Supreme Court decisions on the constitutional status of public employees reflect varying sensitivity to one or a combination of these competing considerations at different periods. Three major themes are discernible, however. The earliest, simplest, and perhaps most powerful is broad deference to government employment prerogatives. This deference rests on the common understanding that the Constitution creates no constitutional right to government employment. The frequently invoked corollary is that those who want the privilege of government work may be compelled to forgo exercising constitutional rights that the government cannot deny private citizens. Justice OLIVER WENDELL HOLMES, then still a state court judge, succinctly expressed this RIGHT–PRIVILEGE DISTINCTION theme in *McAuliffe v. Mayor of New Bedford* (1892). Holmes rejected a policeman's claim that his discharge for political activity violated his right of free expression, commenting that the officer "may have a constitutional right to talk politics, but he has no constitutional right to be a policeman."

The Supreme Court invoked this theme before and after *McAuliffe.* At very different stages of constitutional development over the past century, the Court has consistently upheld government power to foster a nonpartisan civil service by requiring vast numbers of public employees to refrain from active participation in politics, a cherished right of the citizenry at large. The Court has also upheld government requirements that public employees vow to uphold and defend the federal and state constitutions and not attempt their unlawful overthrow, that they live in the employing JURISDICTION, and that national security employees not publish writings about their work until the intended publication is screened to cull out classified information. In the early 1950s, moreover, the Court tolerated government efforts to disqualify from public jobs people who had advocated the forceful overthrow of the government, or who belonged to groups that did, or who refused to reveal their association with such groups, even in circumstances in which private citizens could not be punished for saying or doing the same things.

The right–privilege distinction remains a powerful influence, but Cold War hysteria and McCarthy-era purges of government employees suspected of subversive beliefs provoked the realization that adverse personnel decisions may involve more than legitimate government interests in employee relations, worker loyalty, bureaucratic neutrality, and government efficiency. The Court began to impose constitutional limits narrowly designed to protect public employees from invidiously selective maltreatment. This second theme protects against improper government motivation, but not against broad impact. Restrictions on the political freedom of numerous public employees are tolerated for the legitimate advantages of having a nonpartisan bureaucracy, but government may not penalize even a few for constitutionally unacceptable reasons, such as dislike of their beliefs. In UNITED STATES V. LOVETT (1946), for example, the Court struck down as a BILL OF ATTAINDER a provision of an appropriations law prohibiting payment of the salaries of three named government employees declared guilty of SUBVERSIVE ACTIVITY not by a court but by a House of Representatives subcommittee. Similarly, WIEMANN V. UPDEGRAFF (1952) took a stand against GUILT BY ASSOCIATION and held that government employment could not be denied for membership in a group advocating unlawful overthrow of the government if the member lacked knowledge of the group's unlawful aim.

With the advent of the WARREN COURT, constitutional protection for public employees expanded with the gradual adoption of a third, more complex approach that perceived several values at risk in government treatment of public employees. Increased solicitude for the employees' personal freedom, heightened awareness that jobs often carry some sense of entitlement, and growing appreciation of the part that government workers play in citizen self-government, intensified objections to blatant instances of ideologically discriminatory treatment. Reports of the death of the right–privilege distinction may have been exaggerated, but its hold weakened considerably. Various methods used to weed out allegedly subversive public employees, especially LOYALTY OATHS and compelled disclosure of an individual's associations, were invalidated on VAGUENESS and OVERBREADTH grounds, because the Court thought those methods of employment disqualification would excessively inhibit freedom of expression and association. Those developments paralleled the Warren Court's general expansion of citizen immunity from regulation affecting individual liberty and culminated in a series of decisions between 1966 and 1968, including ELFBRANDT V. RUSSELL (1966) and KEYISHIAN V. BOARD OF REGENTS (1967), that forbade public employers from requiring their employees as a condition of employment to relinquish the expanded constitutional freedoms they enjoyed as citizens. *Pickering v. Board of Education* (1968) appeared to complete the rejection of Holmes's view in *McAuliffe* by holding that a teacher could not be dismissed for speaking on issues of public concern involving her employer.

After the Warren Court era ended, the broadest implications of the demise of the right–privilege distinction were curtailed when the Court reaffirmed the constitutionality of government efforts to keep the civil service broadly—and neutrally—apolitical. The opposition to narrower but selective disadvantaging based on ideological viewpoint remained, however. The Court has disallowed the firing of public employees for belonging to the wrong political party, except where party affiliation is a legitimate qualification for the particular job. The political patronage practice may distort the political beliefs of public employees, but because it represents discrimination against ideologically disfavored viewpoints, it also elicits the narrower concern for preventing selective arbitrariness. In 1983 the Court drew an uncertain line between a worker grievance and a citizen complaint, allowing dismissal of public employees without constitutional restraint for employee speech on matters of personal interest, but retaining *Pickering*'s FIRST AMENDMENT protection against dismissal for speech as a citizen on matters of public concern. It endorsed neither government's right to impose any conditions on public employment it chooses, nor the employees' personal rights of self-expression. Rather, the Court stressed the government's need for flexibility in employee discipline and the public, not personal, value of employee freedoms.

Protection against employment sanctions imposed for constitutionally unacceptable reasons also underlies the Court's public employees PROCEDURAL DUE PROCESS decisions. Significantly, these protections developed after, not before, the Court established substantive limits on the reasons the government legitimately could invoke to disadvantage its employees. The possibility of intentional government arbitrariness, rather than government indifference to valuable employment opportunities, seems to have prompted the development of procedural protections surrounding the loss of government employment benefits.

The development was part of the procedural due process revolution of the Warren Court. Government benefits that did not have to be granted at all, including employment, could not be taken away once awarded without providing certain constitutionally imposed minimum procedures. Rejecting both extremes, the Court never recognized a right to government work but also denied the government the unrestricted freedom to withhold it. Nor has the Court required that reasons and a fair process always be provided before an individual loses an employment opportunity. Instead, the Court has let the government decide whether to hold out a job as offering some job protection or security of employment. If the government bestows no entitlement by statute or practice, several rules apply. No reason is needed to discharge or refuse to hire. If defamatory reasons nonetheless are given for an adverse personnel action, the employee must have an opportunity to defend against the charge. In any event, constitutionally illegitimate reasons may not form the public basis of the adverse action. If the government does hold out a job as offering employment security of any sort, moreover, the Court disallows deprivation of the secured position until constitutionally adequate notice, reasons, and other procedures are followed. The government worker may not be deprived of employment prospects either for illegitimate reasons or for legitimate reasons that do not apply to his circumstances.

The constitutional law of public employee regulation inevitably affects the efficiency of government operations, the personal freedoms of the workers, and the public interest in checking government abuse and being apprised of how public policy is being enforced. Accommodating these interests is, and will remain, an important and complex constitutional problem.

JONATHAN D. VARAT

Bibliography

NOTE 1984 Developments in the Law—Public Employment. *Harvard Law Review* 97:1611, 1738–1800.

VAN ALSTYNE, WILLIAM W. 1969 The Constitutional Rights of Public Employees. *UCLA Law Review* 16:751–772.

PUBLIC FIGURE

The concept of a public figure features prominently in modern FIRST AMENDMENT law involving libel suits. NEW YORK TIMES V. SULLIVAN (1964) prevented public officials (officeholders and candidates for office) from recovering damages for defamation without proof of actual malice, that is, proof that the statement was made with the knowledge that it was false or with reckless disregard whether it was or not. In *Curtis Publishing Company v. Butts* (1967) the Supreme Court extended the actual malice rule to public figures, described by the Court as private persons in positions of considerable influence or able to attract attention because they had thrust themselves into public controversies. A public figure commands public interest and therefore has sufficient access to the mass media to be able, like an officeholder, to publicize his response to falsehoods about him. He invites comment and his remarks make news. The Justices unanimously agreed that for the sake of a robust FREEDOM OF THE PRESS, the actual malice rule applies to public figures, but they disagreed in specific cases on the question whether a particular person, such as the former wife of the scion of a famous family is a public figure, the question before the court in *Time Incorporated v. Firestone* (1976). The Court has tended to deny the press's claim that the party suing for damages is a public figure.

LEONARD W. LEVY

PUBLIC FORUM

Laws that regulate the time, place, and manner of speech are not considered inherently problematic under the FIRST AMENDMENT, in contrast to laws that regulate the content of speech. As a general matter, would-be speakers can be denied the use of a particular public space for their expressive activities if other proper uses of that space would be unduly disturbed and if different speakers with different messages also would be denied use of the space.

The "public forum" DOCTRINE represents an important gloss on the general doctrine that accords government fairly wide authority to regulate speech in public places. For spaces that are designated public forums—streets, parks, and sidewalks, for example—the regulatory authority of government is subject to careful scrutiny under the First Amendment. Public forums, unlike other public spaces, cannot be devoted entirely to nonexpressive uses; some accommodation of the claims of would-be speakers must be made. In addition, when the content of the speech is taken into account in governing the use of a public forum, as when political criticism or commercial advertising but not expression of a labor grievance is disallowed on a public sidewalk, an especially strong presumption of invalidity stalks the regulation. Even content-neutral regulations regarding the time and manner of speech in a public forum pass muster under the First Amendment only if they are "narrowly tailored to serve a significant government interest, and leave open ample alternative channels of communication."

The historical derivation of the public forum doctrine can be traced to an oft-quoted OBITER DICTUM by Justice OWEN J. ROBERTS in HAGUE V. CIO (1939):

> Wherever the title of streets and parks may rest, they have immemorially been held in trust for the use of the public and, time out of mind, have been used for purposes of assembly, communicating thoughts between citizens, and discussing public questions. The privilege of a citizen of the United States to use the streets and parks for communication of views on national questions may be regulated in the interest of all; it is not absolute, but relative, and must be exercised in subordination to the general comfort and convenience, and in consonance with peace and good order; but it must not, in the guise of regulation, be abridged or denied.

The dictum repudiated the doctrine, endorsed by the Supreme Court forty years earlier, that government's ownership of the land on which streets and parks are situated gave officials the nearly plenary authority of a private landlord to regulate access to those spaces. The phrase "public forum" was first employed as a legal term of art by HARRY KALVEN, JR., in an influential article on the topic of speech in public places. The Supreme Court's most comprehensive discussion of the public forum doctrine is in PERRY EDUCATION ASSOCIATION V. PERRY LOCAL EDUCATORS' ASSOCIATION (1983).

Public streets, parks, state capitol grounds, and sidewalks have been held by the Court to be "quintessential" public forums. Public auditoriums and meeting rooms, state fair grounds, and public school classrooms have also been held to be public forums, although the tenor of judicial opinions suggests that officials may have somewhat more regulatory authority to preserve the special character of such places than may be exercised over open spaces such as streets and parks. The Court has denied public forum status to a jailyard, a military base portions of which were open to the public, residential mailboxes, and an internal communications system used for delivering messages and posting notices within a school district. The most important criterion for deciding whether a space constitutes a public forum is the traditional use of that type of space, not necessarily in the particular locale but rather as a general practice nationwide. Some Justices have contended that the dominant consideration should be whether the use of the space for expressive purposes is basically incompatible with other legitimate uses, but that position has not won acceptance by a majority of the Court.

The public forum doctrine has been criticized, primarily on two counts. First, it is claimed that the analytical device of categorizing public places on the basis of their general characteristics fails to give sufficient weight to considerations peculiar to each particular dispute over the use of public property for expressive purposes. Case-by-case variations in the degree to which expressive and regulatory values are implicated tend, so this criticism goes, to be overshadowed by the characterization of a place in gross as either a public forum or not. Particularly as applied to places that do not qualify as public forums, the categorization approach of the public forum doctrine permits government to regulate speech that may be highly appropriate in the particular circumstances and that may not impose serious burdens on other uses of the public space.

Second, and somewhat in tension with the first criticism, it is sometimes maintained that the public forum doctrine is misleading in that the designation of a place as a public forum or not has little resolving power in actual cases. Thus, the regulation of speech based on its content is highly disfavored, even as applied to places that are not public forums. It is not clear what the public forum doctrine adds to the presumption against regulation based on content. In addition, because a COMPELLING STATE INTEREST can justify the regulation of speech in a public forum and because places that are not public forums typically are devoted to activities that conflict somewhat with the use of such places for expressive purposes, it is not obvious that the public forum designation alters dramatically the balancing of conflicting uses that must take place in all disputes over access to public land.

Probably the most important aspect of the public forum doctrine is the principle that public forums cannot be closed off entirely to marches, DEMONSTRATIONS, rallies, and individual acts of expression. In contrast, uniformly enforced blanket prohibitions on expressive activities in places that are not public forums are permissible as a general matter under the First Amendment. Apart from this issue of blanket prohibitions, the significance of the public forum doctrine lies mainly in the tendency of courts to weigh competing particularistic considerations more favorably to speakers when the situs in dispute is a public forum.

VINCENT BLASI

(SEE ALSO: *City of Los Angeles v. Taxpayers for Vincent, 1984.*)

Bibliography

KALVEN, HARRY, JR. 1965 The Concept of the Public Forum. *Supreme Court Review* 1965:1–32.

STONE, GEOFFREY 1974 Fora Americana: Speech in Public Places. *The Supreme Court Review* 1974:233–280.

PUBLIC PURPOSE DOCTRINE

The DOCTRINE of public purpose has been used, in the course of American constitutional history, as a standard by which courts have determined the legitimacy of state EMINENT DOMAIN and taxation legislation. In different periods the doctrine has been mobilized to advance divergent ideological causes and varying constitutional interpretations.

The first distinct phase in the doctrine's history ran from the early nineteenth century to the 1870s, when it was prominent as a justification for new and often far-reaching uses of eminent domain and taxation. During that period the doctrine was a bulwark of positive government. From the 1870s to the World War I period, the doctrine became something quite different in the hands of conservatives who sought to enshrine laissez-faire policy as constitutional law. Arguments treating the public purpose doctrine as a limitation on government action were often prominent, in the new constitutional view of VESTED RIGHTS, as arguments based on FREEDOM OF CONTRACT. A third phase began in the 1930s, when state and federal courts were confronted with challenges to urban slum clearances and redevelopment projects that involved new uses of both eminent domain and taxation powers. Again the doctrine of public purpose found a prominent place in constitutional law, with legal opinion and judicial rulings seriously divided for a time as to what view of public purpose ought to prevail.

Formulation of a "public purpose" standard as a canon for testing the legitimacy of governmental action first became prominent in American decisions when states began to expand the reach of their transportation policies in the early nineteenth century. Projects such as the great Erie Canal enterprise in New York, and similar public works in other states, required powers of eminent domain for the agencies responsible for construction. When legislatures devolved the eminent domain power upon private chartered corporations that built bridges, roads, canals, and railroads, there was widespread agreement that some constitutional limitation should be formulated to prevent indiscriminate delegation of such high sovereign powers. Legal commentators and judges often invoked the Fifth Amendment's reference to PUBLIC USE as a limitation upon eminent domain TAKINGS OF PROPERTY by state authority; many state constitutions used the same phrase in their takings clauses, and even when no express constitutional limitation referred to public use the state courts read it into their law as a fundamental principle of justice. Was a privately owned turnpike corporation engaged in a "public" activity, however? How was the distinction between "public" activities and those merely "private" to be drawn?

Gradually the phrase "public purpose" assumed

nearly the same standing, as a measure of legitimacy, as "public use." One of the early decisions on turnpikes, for example, acknowledged the uniquely "public" character of such roads. They were, a New York judge declared in 1823, "the most public roads or highways that are known to exist, and in point of law, they are made entirely for public use, and the community has a deep interest in their construction and preservation." A few years later, New York's chancery court upheld the exercise of eminent domain powers by a privately owned railroad corporation. It was legitimate for the state to devolve the power to expropriate, on payment of compensation, the court declared, "not only where the safety but also where the interest or even the expediency of the state is concerned." In WEST RIVER BRIDGE V. DIX (1848), the earliest Supreme Court case during the first sixty years of the Republic's history where the eminent domain power was ruled upon directly, it was a direct taking by a state—not devolution of the power on a corporation—that was challenged; but the opinions in the case left no doubt that states enjoyed wide discretion in deciding what activities should qualify as "public" in use or purpose, hence were eligible to exercise the eminent domain power if vested in them by the legislatures.

A parallel development in legal doctrine reinforced the impact of the foregoing line of decisions. This other development was in riparian law and its relationship, which changed over time, to public law in the states. As the state legislatures enacted a growing body of law regulating interests in streams—fisheries, navigation, shoreline development, damming of waters for millpower—the courts were called upon to rule on the legitimate reach of the regulatory power. The courts derived from English COMMON LAW distinctions between streams owned by the sovereign; streams "private in ownership but public in use" and so subject to broad regulatory control; and streams strictly private in ownership and in use, whose private character immunized owners against loss from regulation or taking without compensation. Repeatedly, lawyers and judges drew the analogy between waterways in public use and the chartered railroad, canal, bridge, and road companies that were private in ownership, yet "public" in purpose and use. The analogy lent additional legitimacy to "public purpose" as a doctrine which supported state action that forced private rights to yield to communal needs. Private companies were given special privileges in promotion of drainage, wharf facilities, supply of water to urban centers, and transportation facilities, as the Ohio Supreme Court declared in 1836, "because the public has an interest in them." Hence it was consistent to force private owners to yield to takings, for purposes of such enterprises, under eminent domain.

Although the doctrine had been used initially to support a large view of eminent domain power, it was soon employed also in support of tax-financed subsidies to private business firms. As enthusiasm for railroad construction swept the country in the middle decades of the nineteenth century, voters in hundreds of local communities and many state legislatures proved willing to extend cash subsidies—money raised through taxation—to private railroads, to guarantee railroad bonds, or to purchase stock in such railroads. Again, "public purpose" proved to be the vehicle for legitimation of such use of public funds. The Michigan high court, for example, in 1852 turned back a challenge to the constitutionality of such tax-supported aid on the ground that railroad corporations were "created for public benefit" and so were distinguishable from "strictly private corporations . . . [in which] private advantage is the ultimate as well as the immediate object of their creation." The landmark state case, widely followed, was *Sharpless v. Philadelphia*, decided by the Pennsylvania court in 1853. Termed in the court's decision "beyond all comparison, the most important cause that has ever been in this Court," the case was decided in favor of the constitutionality of state subsidies. Taxation must be for a public purpose, the court emphasized, and despite private ownership the railroad companies receiving aid represented such a purpose.

The spreading practice of extending public aid to corporations alarmed many jurists, however; and by the late 1860s, opposition to such a broad reading of "public purpose" and "public use" concepts had grown strong. Emblematic of the issue was the policy of Wisconsin, where the legislature by 1874 had authorized public, tax-supported aid to telegraph, steamship, hotel, waterworks, gas, construction, bridge, canal, river improvement, and dry-dock corporations. The constitutions of the newly admitted western states commonly designated as "public purpose" enterprises firms engaged in logging, road building, irrigation and reclamation, railroads, river improvement, and drainage for mining or agriculture. Such enterprises were routinely granted eminent domain power, and many of them received subsidies. In the East and Midwest, several states allowed manufacturing corporations of all kinds to condemn and flood lands for power sites. Such laws were defended as aid to companies with an important public purpose, comparable to the grants of similar eminent domain powers to gristmills in colonial Massachusetts. In a few states—

among them Georgia, New York, Alabama, and Vermont—the courts invalidated such grants of power. In most state tribunals, however, the broad view of "public purpose" continued to prevail.

Indicative of the emerging conservative jurisprudence on the issue were decisions of Judge THOMAS M. COOLEY's Michigan court in 1870 against public aid to railroads and in 1877 against a milldam flooding act. In Cooley's view, set forth more systematically in his treatise, *Constitutional Limitations* (1868), "Everything that may be done under the name of taxation is not necessarily a tax; and it may happen that an oppressive burden imposed by the government, when it comes to be carefully scrutinized, will prove, instead of a tax, to be an unlawful confiscation of property, unwarranted by any principle of constitutional government." Further distinguished authority for the same view came from the Iowa Supreme Court. Chief Justice JOHN F. DILLON—like Cooley, a treatise writer who pressed his concern for vested rights on the legal profession and the courts in the late nineteenth century—wrote an opinion for the Iowa court in 1862 that struck down railroad bond aid as a confiscation of citizens' property without compensation and a violation of DUE PROCESS.

The conservative assault led by Dillon and Cooley soon enlisted the aid of the Supreme Court. In LOAN ASSOCIATION V. TOPEKA (1874) the Court declared unconstitutional a Kansas municipal bond issue in aid of a bridge-manufacturing company. Justice SAMUEL F. MILLER's opinion for the majority denounced the use of tax funds for a "private interest instead of a public use"; and he termed it robbery to exercise the taxing power in this way. It was a sudden and surprising use of the public purpose doctrine to limit state legislative power—in contrast with its earlier use to enlarge state power and legitimate new activities.

The conservative version of public purpose did not carry the day altogether, even as the jurisprudence of vested rights was gaining ascendancy. Thus the Supreme Court repeatedly turned back assaults on state aid to railroads, with a solid majority maintaining that transportation had always been considered a "public purpose" activity and so eligible for eminent domain power and aid with tax funds. *Olcott v. The Supervisors* (1873) upheld the validity of local bonds issued to aid railroads in a Wisconsin municipality, in the face of efforts to repudiate them. In language squarely in the line of doctrine that had come down from JAMES KENT's views on turnpikes half a century earlier, the Court asserted that railroads had a "public highway character. . . . Though the ownership is private, the use is public." Use of tax funds to subsidize manufacturing companies suffered a different fate, however, in light of the *Loan Association* decision. Thus Clyde Jacobs calculated that from 1870 to 1910 some forty public purpose cases challenging tax aid to businesses came before the federal courts and state high courts. In thirty-nine of the forty, public aid was found invalid on the ground that it was not for a public purpose. Moreover, numerous state courts interpreted the "public purpose" provisions in state constitutions to forbid subsidies or relief payments to the blind, for example, or to farmers who had suffered from weather or crop failure.

In the Supreme Court, however, a manifest softening of the commitment to public purpose as a limiting doctrine became evident in decisions on the constitutionality of grants of taxing and eminent domain power to special-purpose irrigation districts. The Court ruled in *Fallbrook Irrigation District v. Bradley* (1896) that local geographical and climatic conditions required a considerable legislative discretion as to what constituted public purpose. In other cases that tested the constitutionality of using tax revenues to finance state enterprises such as public utilities and even grain warehouses, the Court moved still further toward allowing legislatures to do so. By the early 1920s public purpose as a national constitutional doctrine was no longer a major support for vested property rights or limitation upon governmental power, even though the Court, beginning with *Fallbrook*, explicitly treated public purpose as a FOURTEENTH AMENDMENT issue.

The Supreme Court also abandoned in 1916 a residual doctrine that had enjoyed considerable judicial respect in many jurisdictions since the 1850s, the doctrine that "public use" (justifying takings by the state) should be interpreted as "use by the public" and not in broad "public purpose" terms. In *Mt. Vernon-Woodberry Company v. Alabama Power Company* (1916), Justice OLIVER WENDELL HOLMES, writing for the Court, declared flatly that "the inadequacy of the use by the general public as a universal test is established."

The deep economic crisis in the 1930s and the social dislocations it generated led to the third distinct phase of the public purpose doctrine's history. The application, throughout the nation, of federal aid to urban slum clearance and housing development produced challenges in both federal and state courts to the constitutionality of using eminent domain and taxation powers for such purposes. Especially where private real-estate and financial interests were given a key role in housing, the public purpose of takings and public expenditures for such programs was questioned. By 1940 such objections had been rejected, and the public programs upheld, in the courts of twenty-eight states. Many of these opinions concluded that where "public welfare" was served the public purpose test was met—a broad concept of legitimacy for eminent domain (and taxation) that found expression also in *United States ex rel. Tennessee Valley Authority v. Welch* (1946), a leading Supreme Court decision validating takings by a federal agency for purposes of regional development. It was for Congress to decide what was a public use, the Court declared; no "departure . . . [from] judicial restraint," with deference to the legislative branch, was warranted.

The language of the *Welch* decision was imported into state and federal courts' review of another wave of urban slum clearance programs in the 1940s and 1950s, following World War II. In this later period, more than mere slum clearance was at issue; the urban programs often embraced comprehensive "urban redevelopment" objectives, typically employed private financial and entrepreneurial interests in the projects, and often involved sweeping condemnation programs that took land and buildings that did not fit the "slum" classification. Rejecting a public purpose challenge to comprehensive redevelopment, in which some of the property taken ended up in the hands of private developers, not government itself, a federal district court in a landmark 1953 ruling, *Schneider v. District of Columbia,* declared: "the term 'public use' has progressed as economic facts have progressed, and so projects such as railroads, public power plants, the operation of mines under some conditions, and, more recently, low-cost housing have been held to be public uses for which private property may be seized. Moreover, . . . the variation in the term from '[public] use' to '[public] purpose' indicates a progression in thought." So long as the taking is necessary to the public purpose that the legislature has determined and defined, the court concluded, eminent domain powers necessary to accomplishment of that purpose must be deemed legitimate.

The valedictory came in *Berman v. Parker* (1954), when the Supreme Court affirmed that public purpose was a concept coterminous with "public welfare," hence embraced objectives across a broad spectrum that included "public safety, public health, morality, peace and quiet, law and order," to list only "some of the more conspicuous examples." Once pursuit of public purpose in these terms was accepted, then eminent domain, taxation, or the STATE POLICE POWER might be used to accomplish the goals set forth. Judicial review under the Fifth and Fourteenth Amendments was not out of the question, at least in some jurists' views. Justice FELIX FRANKFURTER, for example, in a concurring opinion in *Welch,* wrote: "But the fact that the nature of the subject matter gives the legislative determination nearly immunity from judicial review does not mean that the power to review is wanting." In the subsequent history of taking, however, it was the eminent domain/police power distinction, and not the public purpose doctrine, on which constitutional challenges to regulation would turn. The purposes for which eminent domain or taxation could be used did seem "nearly immune," in light of modern constitutional interpretation of the GENERAL WELFARE CLAUSE.

HARRY N. SCHEIBER

Bibliography

JACOBS, CLYDE E. 1954 *Law Writers and the Courts: The Influence of Thomas M. Cooley, Christopher G. Tiedman, and John F. Dillon upon American Constitutional Law.* Berkeley and Los Angeles: University of California Press.

NICHOLS, PHILIP, JR. 1940 The Meaning of Public Use in the Law of Eminent Domain. *Boston University Law Review* 20:615–624.

SCHEIBER, HARRY N. 1971 The Road to *Munn:* Eminent Domain and the Concept of the Public Purpose in the State Courts. *Perspectives in American History* 5:327–402.

WOODBURY, COLEMAN, ED. 1953 *Urban Redevelopment: Problems and Practices.* Chicago: University of Chicago Press.

PUBLIC TRIAL

"In all criminal prosecutions, the accused shall enjoy the right to a speedy and public trial. . . ." The language of the Sixth Amendment appears to assure that criminal courtrooms in the United States will be open—that there will be no secret trials. But the issue of openness in the process of criminal justice has only recently reached a point of consensus in the Supreme Court after nearly forty years of experimentation with successive constitutional tests.

Conflicting values underlay the debate. One was that of the open society, with the public free to observe and criticize the activities of government, including the courts. The other was fairness to someone accused of a crime: his or her right to a trial uninfluenced by public passion or prejudice. The two values do not usually conflict, but it hardly needs to be said that they may clash in a country that has known mob-dominated courtrooms and lynchings.

The constitutional conflict first surfaced in a series of cases starting with BRIDGES V. CALIFORNIA (1941).

The issue was whether American, like British, judges could punish as a contempt of court any comment on a pending criminal case that had a tendency to interfere with the administration of justice. In *Bridges* two persons had been held in contempt: a labor leader for a telegram criticizing a judicial decision against his union, and a newspaper editor for an editorial admonishing a judge not to grant probation to two convicted union members. By a 5–4 vote the Supreme Court reversed both contempt convictions. The Court's opinion, by Justice HUGO L. BLACK, said the FIRST AMENDMENT barred punishment for such comments unless they presented a CLEAR AND PRESENT DANGER—the test framed by Justice OLIVER WENDELL HOLMES in the early sedition cases such as ABRAMS V. UNITED STATES (1919)—of causing "disorderly and unfair administration of justice." Later decisions made plain that it would be extremely difficult for authorities to meet that test. Justice WILLIAM O. DOUGLAS said in *Craig v. Harney* (1947): "A trial is a public event. What transpires in the courtroom is public property. . . . There is no special perquisite of the judiciary which enables it, as distinguished from other institutions of democratic government, to suppress, edit, or censor events which transpire in proceedings before it."

Nevertheless, concern remained about the possible effect of outside comment on the criminal justice process, especially on the impartiality of jurors. Justice FELIX FRANKFURTER felt so strongly about the matter that he wrote an impassioned opinion in *Maryland v. Baltimore Radio Show* (1950), when the Supreme Court refused to review a state appellate court decision reversing on First Amendment grounds the contempt conviction of a radio broadcaster who had broadcast, before a murder trial, the record of the defendant and alleged evidence of his guilt.

The Supreme Court dealt with the problem of prejudicial press comment on criminal cases another way: by reversing convictions when there was reason to think the jury might have been improperly influenced by the outside comment. The Court first found that prejudicial comment had violated a defendant's constitutional right to fair trial in IRVIN V. DOWD (1961). Justice Frankfurter, still preferring to proceed against the press itself, wrote bitterly in a concurring opinion: "The Court has not yet decided that, while convictions must be reversed and miscarriages of justice result because the minds of jurors or potential jurors were poisoned, the poisoner is constitutionally protected in plying his trade." But the device of contempt to prevent prejudicial comment never found favor with a majority. In *Sheppard v. Maxwell* (1966) the Court outlined other measures to prevent the prejudicing of juries in notorious cases: delaying or moving the trial, for example, or sequestering the jury once it had been selected.

Then a new prophylactic device was taken up by some trial courts around the country: INJUNCTIONS against press institutions and representatives forbidding reports, before trial, of evidence and other material that might prejudice potential jurors. These gag orders, as the press angrily called them, followed the approach adopted by Britain in the Criminal Justice Act of 1967. That act allowed the press to attend pretrial committal proceedings, thereby assuring scrutiny of the process, but forebade reporting on them until after the trial itself was completed—unless the defendant waived the restriction. But in 1976 the Supreme Court held that the First Amendment stood in the way of this approach, too. In NEBRASKA PRESS ASSOCIATION V. STUART the press had been enjoined from reporting, before trial, the alleged confession and other especially prejudicial matters about the defendant in a gruesome multiple murder case in a small Nebraska town. The Court's opinion, by Chief Justice WARREN E. BURGER, declined to adopt an absolute rule against such restraints. But the decision against them, on the extreme facts of that case, made it most unlikely that gag orders would ever be permissible; and trial courts stopped issuing them.

A last round of the constitutional debate about fair trial and free speech tested still another prophylactic device: closing the courtroom to the public and the press during sensitive phases of pretrial or trial proceedings. In GANNETT V. DEPASQUALE (1979) counsel for the defendants moved to close a pretrial hearing on motions to suppress confessions and other EVIDENCE, arguing that reports of the hearing would prejudice future jurors if the evidence were in fact suppressed. The prosecutor did not object, and the trial judge closed the courtroom. A newspaper then challenged the order. The Supreme Court decided that the "public trial" clause of the Sixth Amendment was for the benefit of the defendant alone, who could waive it, and that outsiders had no STANDING to insist on an open courtroom. The majority put aside First Amendment considerations.

A year later the Court did consider the First Amendment and decided that it limited the closing of courtrooms. In RICHMOND NEWSPAPERS V. VIRGINIA a 7–1 majority found unconstitutional the exclusion of the public (and with it the press) from a criminal trial. There was no opinion of the Court, but various Justices shared the view expressed by Chief Justice Burger that the First Amendment assures the public a "right of access" to criminal trials that can be denied only for strong and articulated reasons. Indications are that the right extends also to civil cases, and to pretrial proceedings as well as trials.

The decision was an extraordinary doctrinal conclusion to the long cycle of constitutional litigation. For the Supreme Court had for the first time said that the First Amendment was not only a shield protecting the right to speak or publish but also a sword helping the public to gain access to information about government institutions. How far that new doctrine would be taken was uncertain. But in American courtrooms, at least, a constitutional presumption favors openness.

ANTHONY LEWIS

Bibliography

LEWIS, ANTHONY 1980 A Public Right to Know about Public Institutions: The First Amendment as Sword. *The Supreme Court Review* 1980:1–25.

SCHMIDT, BENNO C. 1977 Nebraska Press Association: An Expansion of Freedom and Contraction of Theory. *Stanford Law Review* 29:431–476.

PUBLIC USE

The "taking" clause of the Fifth Amendment limits the power of EMINENT DOMAIN by demanding that governmental taking of private property be for a public use. The Supreme Court held in CHICAGO, BURLINGTON & QUINCY RAILROAD CO. V. CHICAGO (1897) that the same requirement applies to the states through the FOURTEENTH AMENDMENT.

Although some early decisions defined the public use standard to include a right of "use by the public," that approach was repudiated by the Court. As early as 1905 in *Clark v. Nash,* the Court held that a state could authorize a private person to condemn an easement for irrigation across a neighbor's land. "What is a public use," said the Court, "may frequently and largely depend upon the facts surrounding the subject." In the arid environment of Utah, the taking of a private irrigation easement could properly be deemed a public use, because it was "absolutely necessary" to agricultural development. On similar grounds, the Court's decision in *Strickley v. Highland Boy Gold Mining Co.* (1906) sustained the statutory authority of a mining company to condemn a private easement for transporting ore to a railroad loading site. These decisions were followed by many others intimating that any use conducive to the public benefit was a public use for which eminent domain could be invoked, including reclamation of swamp lands, establishment of water and electrical power systems, development of transportation facilities, and creation of public parks.

The broad public benefit test has, in recent years, been assimilated with the RATIONAL BASIS approach invoked by the Supreme Court in reviewing regulations of economic interests under the DUE PROCESS clause. In the leading case, *Berman v. Parker* (1954), the court sustained the use of eminent domain to acquire various separate parcels of private property in blighted areas in furtherance of a community redevelopment project. The fact that the property to be condemned would be resold or leased to private persons for redevelopment purposes did not transgress the public use limitation, for "when the legislature has spoken, the public interest has been declared in terms well-nigh conclusive. In such cases the legislature, not the judiciary, is the main guardian of the public needs to be served. . . . The concept of the public welfare is broad and inclusive."

Under this expansive and deferential approach, eminent domain may be exercised as a means for achieving practically any use or objective within the power of the legislative body.

ARVO VAN ALSTYNE

Bibliography

NICHOLS, PERRY 1983 *The Law of Eminent Domain,* Vol. 2A. New York: Matthew Bender & Co.

PUBLIC UTILITIES REGULATION

See: Economic Regulation

PUBLIC UTILITY HOLDING COMPANY ACT
49 Stat. 803 (1935)

This measure was an important part of the legislative program of President FRANKLIN D. ROOSEVELT. Two leading supporters of the bill were Senators GEORGE NORRIS and HUGO L. BLACK. The act's objective was to disperse ownership and control of the nation's gas and electric utilities, then highly concentrated in pyramids of corporations with holding companies at the top. The act required holding companies to register with the Securities and Exchange Commission and authorized the SEC to limit a company's operations to a single region. A "death sentence" provision authorized dissolution of a company that did not show, within five years, that it was serving an efficient local function.

The great holding companies sought to challenge the constitutionality of the entire act in an early TEST CASE, but government lawyers managed to persuade the Supreme Court to defer the omnibus attack and consider the act's registration requirement separately. The Court upheld that requirement in *Electric Bond & Share Co. v. SEC* (1938). The other provisions of the law came before the Court after Roosevelt had appointed seven Justices. Those provisions were sustained, with broad readings of Congress's power under the COMMERCE CLAUSE, in *North American Co. v. SEC* (1946) and *American Power & Light Co. v. SEC* (1946). By 1952, more than 750 holding companies had been dissolved.

KENNETH L. KARST

Bibliography

FREUND, PAUL A. 1951 *On Understanding the Supreme Court.* Pages 99–110. Boston: Little, Brown.

PUERTO RICO, CONSTITUTIONAL STATUS OF

No clear definition exists of how and to what extent the Commonwealth of Puerto Rico fits within the federal constitutional system. Undoubtedly, the *Puerto Rican Federal Relations Act,* enacted by Congress in 1950 "in the nature of a compact" between Congress and the people of Puerto Rico, and the adoption by Puerto Ricans of their own constitution in 1952 were intended to work a significant change in the previous colonial relationship between the island and the United States. The nature and scope of this change, however, have not been conclusively ascertained by federal courts ruling on the matter.

Puerto Rico, which had become a self-governing overseas province of the Kingdom of Spain under the Royal Decree of 1897, was ceded to the United States in 1898 under the Treaty of Paris which ended the Spanish-American War. It became an unincorporated TERRITORY of the United States, subject to the plenary command of Congress. Under various Supreme Court decisions it is clear that, until 1952, Puerto Rico was a domestic possession of the United States, neither a foreign country nor an integral part of the nation, merely belonging to it. Congressional authority over the island and its people encompassed the entire domain of SOVEREIGNTY, both national and local, and was completely unconstrained by the federal Constitution, except as regards those basic prohibitions which go "to the very root of the power of Congress to act at all" and "which the Constitution has established in favor of human liberty and are applicable to every condition or status." (See INSULAR CASES.) Wielding its plenary powers, the United States established a military government in Puerto Rico from 1898 to 1900, when a civil regime was installed under the Foraker Act, providing a meager participation of Puerto Ricans in the island's government. In 1917 Congress enacted a second Organic Act (Jones Act) providing a measure of self-government and granting United States CITIZENSHIP collectively to the people of Puerto Rico, while retaining all major elements of sovereignty.

In 1950 a bill to provide for the organization of a constitutional government by the people of Puerto Rico was introduced in Congress. Its provisions were not to be effective until accepted in a REFERENDUM by Puerto Rican voters. After a favorable vote on the new federal act by the island electorate, a CONSTITUTIONAL CONVENTION was held in Puerto Rico and the fundamental law drafted there was adopted by the majority of the islanders in 1952. In transmitting the newly adopted Puerto Rican Constitution to Congress, President HARRY S. TRUMAN recognized that with such approval "full authority and responsibility for local self-government [would] be vested in the people of Puerto Rico." In 1953 the United Nations recognized that Puerto Ricans, exercising the right of self-determination, had achieved a new constitutional status, and had "been invested with attributes of political sovereignty which clearly identify the status of self-government attained by the Puerto Rican people as that of an autonomous political entity."

It is generally accepted by federal courts that after 1952 "Puerto Rico's status changed from that of a mere territory to the unique status of COMMONWEALTH." The Supreme Court itself stated in *Examining Board v. Flores* (1976) that "the purpose of Congress in its 1950 and 1952 legislation was to accord to Puerto Rico the degree of autonomy and independence normally associated with a State of the Union." However, the precise extent of the referred "autonomy" and the constitutional basis for statelike status are very much in doubt. Thus, while the Supreme Court has now accepted that "Puerto Rico is to be deemed sovereign over matters not ruled by the federal Constitution" and that Puerto Rican legislation and court decisions deserve the same regard in federal courts as those of a state, it has also ruled in *Harris v. Rosario* (1980) that Congress under the territorial clause may still "treat Puerto Rico differently from States so long as there is a rational basis for its actions."

Likewise, the Court, after acknowledging that Puerto Rico is subject to federal constitutional requirements regarding FREEDOM OF SPEECH, DUE PROCESS, EQUAL PROTECTION, and reasonable SEARCH AND SEIZURE, has indicated that such guarantees are binding either directly under the BILL OF RIGHTS or indirectly by operation of the FOURTEENTH AMENDMENT, expressly refusing to fix one or the other as the source or basis of their applicability. The Court has yet to write on a clean slate in dealing with the new constitutional status of Puerto Rico.

JAIME B. FUSTER

Bibliography

FUSTER, JAIME B. 1974 Origin of the Doctrine of Territorial Incorporation and Its Implications for the Power of the Commonwealth of Puerto Rico. *University of Puerto Rico Law Review* 43:259–294.

PURE FOOD AND DRUG ACT
34 Stat. 768 (1906)

Typical of the progressive legislation passed after the turn of the century, this act extended the NATIONAL POLICE POWER to regulate the quality of food and drugs in INTERSTATE COMMERCE. A personal crusade by the chief chemist of the Department of Agriculture together with the muckrakers' stomach-churning exposés fanned public opinion. President THEODORE ROOSEVELT's backstage maneuvering also helped secure passage of this federal inspection act on June 30, 1906.

The act outlawed the manufacture of "adulterated or misbranded" food or drugs and prohibited their introduction into interstate or FOREIGN COMMERCE. Congress gave the secretaries of agriculture, treasury, and commerce and labor authority to issue regulations enforcing the act and specifically provided PROCEDURAL DUE PROCESS for violators. The act forbade: misbranding of food; the use of imitations, substitutes, harmful additives, rotten ingredients; and concealment of "damage or inferiority." Drugs were required to meet federal standards of quality, purity, and strength or clearly label their departures from the standards.

The Supreme Court sustained this act in HIPOLITE EGG COMPANY V. UNITED STATES (1911) as a legitimate exercise of congressional power over commerce. Congress substantially tightened and extended it in the FOOD, DRUG, AND COSMETIC ACT of 1938.

DAVID GORDON

Q

QUERN v. JORDAN
440 U.S. 332 (1979)

This case held that SECTION 1983, TITLE 42, UNITED STATES CODE, does not abrogate the states' ELEVENTH AMENDMENT immunity from suit in federal court. The amendment therefore precludes retroactive damage awards against states. States, however, may be forced to bear the costs of future compliance with the Constitution and state officials may be enjoined to comply with the Constitution.

THEODORE EISENBERG

QUIRIN, EX PARTE
317 U.S. 1 (1942)

In 1942 President FRANKLIN D. ROOSEVELT issued a proclamation subjecting enemies entering the United States through the coastal defense zones to trial by military tribunal and denying them access to the civil courts. Seven German saboteurs, who had been set ashore in the United States from submarines and who had subsequently been captured, were tried under the terms of the proclamation. The saboteurs petitioned for a writ of HABEAS CORPUS, arguing that, so long as the regular courts were open and operating, they were entitled to TRIAL BY JURY, and citing as PRECEDENT the Civil War case EX PARTE MILLIGAN.

The Supreme Court, then in summer recess, met in extraordinary session to hear the petition. An 8–0 Court, speaking through Chief Justice HARLAN F. STONE, upheld the constitutionality of military trial for offenses against the law of war. But the Court also insisted upon the right of the civil courts to review the constitutionality or applicability of Roosevelt's proclamation in individual cases.

DENNIS J. MAHONEY

(SEE ALSO: *Cramer v. United States; Haupt v. United States.*)

Bibliography

BELKNAP, MICHAL R. 1980 The Supreme Court Goes to War: The Meaning and Implications of the Nazi Saboteur Case. *Military Law Review* 89:59–95.

QUOCK WALKER CASES

See: *Commonwealth v. Jennison*

QUOTAS, RACIAL

See: Racial Quotas

RABINOWITZ, UNITED STATES v.

See: Search Incident to Arrest

RACIAL BALANCE

The idea of racial balance is a product of the DESEGREGATION of public schools in the years since BROWN V. BOARD OF EDUCATION (1954–1955). The term refers to the racial distribution of students in particular schools in relation to the racial distribution of school children in an entire district. If a district's children are seventy percent white and thirty percent black, then a hypothetically perfect balance would produce these same percentages in each school. By extension, the notion of racial balance may be used in discussing other institutions: a housing project, a factory's work force, a state university's medical school. (See RACIAL QUOTAS; AFFIRMATIVE ACTION.)

In the school cases, the Supreme Court has held that racial balance is an appropriate "starting point" for a lower court to use in fashioning a remedy for de jure SEGREGATION. (See DE FACTO/DE JURE; SWANN V. CHARLOTTE-MECKLENBURG BOARD OF EDUCATION, 1971.) However, even where segregation has been deliberately caused by school board actions, there is no constitutional requirement of racial balance throughout the district's schools. Although one-race schools are presumptively to be eliminated, the school board will be allowed to prove that the racial distribution in those schools results from something other than the board's deliberate policy. SCHOOL BUSING over very long distances, for example, would not be required under this approach; distance alone would be a racially neutral explanation for the board's failure to remedy racial imbalance.

In the absence of previous legislation commanding or authorizing school segregation, or school board actions with segregative intent, the fact of racial imbalance in a district's schools, standing alone, does not amount to a constitutional violation. However, intentional acts of segregation by the board in the remote past, coupled with current racial imbalance, will place on the board an almost impossible burden of proving that it has dismantled its "dual" (segregated) system. (See COLUMBUS BOARD OF EDUCATION V. PENICK, 1979.)

The term racial balance is sometimes used in a different sense. Some discussions of school segregation use the term to describe a school that includes a "critical mass" of students from each race. Social scientists disagree over the educational value to minority students of having a significant number of white students in the classroom. The suggestion that minority students learn better in the company of whites has roots in the Supreme Court's pre-*Brown* decisions on graduate education. (See SWEATT V. PAINTER, 1950.) And where segregation is imposed by official action, *Brown* itself takes the view that the resulting stigma impairs minority students' ability to learn. But the abstract proposition that minority students cannot learn effectively outside the presence of whites is more than a little patronizing. And the notion of racial balance in this sense is immensely complicated in a multiethnic community: is a school integrated if it contains significant numbers of both white and minority students, or should the category of minority students be broken down into its black, Hispanic, and other components? Merely to ask this question is to understand why the Supreme Court has avoided speaking of racial balance in this latter sense and has used the idea in its mechanical racial-percentages sense only as a "starting point."

KENNETH L. KARST

Bibliography

FISS, OWEN M. 1975 The Jurisprudence of Busing. *Law and Contemporary Problems* 1975:194–216.

RACIAL CLASSIFICATION

See: Benign Racial Classification; Invidious Discrimination; Racial Discrimination; Suspect Classification

RACIAL DISCRIMINATION

The nation was founded with the enslavement of blacks as an established and ongoing institution, and though we were not particularly proud of the institution, we were prepared to live with it. The Constitution did not mention the word "slave," and contemplated the eventual closing of the slave trade (referred to simply as the "importation of persons"), but, through similar circumlocutions, also created obligations to return fugitive slaves, and included a proportion of the slaves within the population base to be used for the apportionment of representatives and taxes. In DRED SCOTT V. SANDFORD (1857) the Supreme Court viewed slaves as property and declared that the right of slaveholders to take their slaves to the territories was protected by the DUE PROCESS CLAUSE of the Fifth Amendment.

The Civil War brought slavery to an end and reversed the basic commitment of the Constitution toward blacks. The law sought equality rather than enslavement, and it was through the elaboration of this egalitarian commitment that the concept of racial discrimination emerged. Prohibiting racial discrimination became the principal strategy of the American legal system for achieving equality for blacks. The laws against racial discrimination typically protect all racial minorities, not just blacks, and yet, for purely historical reasons, the development of those laws would be unimaginable apart from the struggle of blacks for equality in America. That struggle has been the source both of the achievements of antidiscrimination law and of its recurrent dilemmas.

The three amendments adopted following the Civil War constitute the groundwork of this branch of the law, although only one—the FIFTEENTH AMENDMENT—actually speaks of racial discrimination. It provides that "the right . . . to vote shall not be denied or abridged . . . on account of race, color, or previous condition of servitude." The other Civil War amendments are not cast in terms of racial discrimination. The THIRTEENTH AMENDMENT prohibits slavery and involuntary servitude, and the FOURTEENTH AMENDMENT, in relevant aspect, prohibits states from denying "the EQUAL PROTECTION OF THE LAWS." But the Supreme Court has interpreted both these amendments to prohibit racial discrimination. With respect to the Thirteenth Amendment, the Court reasoned in JONES V. ALFRED H. MAYER CO. (1968) that racial discrimination is a badge or incident of slavery. (See BADGES OF SERVITUDE.) Similarly, in interpreting the Fourteenth Amendment, the Court, as early as STRAUDER V. WEST VIRGINIA (1880), declared racial discrimination to be the kind of unequal treatment that constitutes a denial of equal protection of the laws. Indeed, over the years, racial discrimination came to be seen as the paradigmatic denial of equal protection, and supplied the standard against which all other equal protection claims came to be measured, even when pressed by nonracial groups such as the poor or women. They too had to show that they were discriminated against on the basis of some impermissible criterion such as their wealth or sex. The promise of equal protection was thus transformed into a promise not to discriminate.

It was, moreover, through the enforcement of the Fourteenth Amendment that the prohibition against racial discrimination achieved its greatest prominence. Antidiscrimination was the instrument that finally put to an end the system of white supremacy that emerged in the late nineteenth and early twentieth centuries and that worked by separating whites and blacks—Jim Crow. The discrimination appeared on the very face of Jim Crow laws and a principle that condemned racial discrimination easily brought those laws within the sweep of the Fourteenth Amendment. All that was needed was an understanding of how the separatism of Jim Crow worked to the disadvantage of blacks; that was the burden of BROWN V. BOARD OF EDUCATION (1954) and the cases that followed. As the principle controlling the interpretation of the Fourteenth Amendment, antidiscrimination was a limitation only upon the actions of states, but once the step entailed in *Brown* was taken, the federal government was, in BOLLING V. SHARPE (1954), made subject to an identical prohibition by a construction of the due process clause of the Fifth Amendment. Racial discrimination was deemed as inconsistent with the constitutional guarantee of liberty as it was with equal protection.

Statutes, too, have been concerned with racial equality. In the years immediately following the Civil War, Congress passed a comprehensive program to protect the newly freed slaves, and defined the conduct it sought to prohibit in a variety of ways. In the CIVIL RIGHTS ACT OF 1866 Congress promised that blacks would enjoy the same rights as whites; in the FORCE ACTS (1870, 1871) it guaranteed all citizens the rights and privileges arising from the Constitution or laws of the United States. In the decades following *Brown v. Board of Education,* however, when the antidiscrimination principle of the Fourteenth Amendment received its most strenuous affirmation and the nation embarked on its Second Reconstruction, Congress cast the substantive standard in terms of a single idiom—do not discriminate. (See CIVIL RIGHTS ACT OF 1964; VOTING RIGHTS ACT OF 1965; CIVIL RIGHTS ACT OF 1968.)

During this period, Congress introduced new mechanisms to enforce the equal protection clause; for example, it authorized the attorney general to bring injunctive school desegregation suits, required federal administrative agencies to terminate financial assistance to segregated school systems, and provided for criminal prosecutions against those who forcibly interfered with desegregation. Congress also broadened the reach of federal antidiscrimination law beyond the scope of the Fourteenth Amendment by regulating, in the name of racial equality, activities of private agencies (for example, restaurants, employers, or landlords), which otherwise would not have been covered by that amendment because of its "state action" requirement. In each of these measures, Congress used the language of antidiscrimination. So did the President in promulgating EXECUTIVE ORDER 11246 (1965), which regulates government contractors. Many state legislatures also intervened on behalf of racial equality during the Second Reconstruction, and these enactments were also couched in terms of prohibiting discrimination.

Sometimes Congress and the state legislatures exempted certain discriminatory practices from the laws they enacted. One instance is the federal open housing law, which exempts discrimination by small residences ("Mrs. Murphy's roominghouse"); another is the federal fair employment statute, which exempts from its coverage small businesses (at first businesses with fewer than twenty-five employees, later reduced to fifteen). Apparently Congress viewed the interest in associational liberty present in these settings as sufficiently strong to justify limited exemptions to the ban on racial discrimination. Yet, putting these exemptions and a handful of others to one side, it is fair to say that today, primarily as a result of the Second Reconstruction, the prohibition against racial discrimination is all-encompassing. It has both constitutional and statutory bases and is the subject of an executive order. It is a pervasive feature of both federal and state law and calls forth a broad array of civil and criminal remedies. It almost has the status of a moral imperative, like the norm against theft or killing. The issue that divides Americans today is thus not whether the law should prohibit racial discrimination but what, precisely, doing so entails.

The antidiscrimination norm, as already noted, was largely fashioned at a time when the nation was swept by the SEPARATE-BUT-EQUAL DOCTRINE of Jim Crow and when blacks were disadvantaged in a rather open and crude manner. In such a context, the principle of antidiscrimination invites a color blindness: When allocating a scarce opportunity, such as a job or a place in a professional school, the decision maker should not prefer a white candidate over a black one on the basis of the individual's color or race. Here antidiscrimination requires that individuals be judged independently of race. This much is settled. Interpretive problems arise, however, when the social context changes—when we have moved beyond Jim Crow and blacks have come to be disadvantaged primarily in ways that are hidden and systematically entrenched. Then we confront two issues. One arises from the exclusion of blacks on the basis of a seemingly innocent criterion such as performance on a standardized test; the other from the preference given to blacks to correct for long-standing unequal distributional patterns.

To clarify the first issue, it should be understood that the appearance of innocence might be misleading. Although a black scores higher than a white on a test, the employer might manipulate or falsify the scores so that the white is given the job. In this case, the apparent use of an innocent criterion is simply a mask for racial discrimination. The decision is still directly based on race and would be deemed unlawful. The most straightforward remedy would be to set aside the decision and allow an honest application of the test.

There are, moreover, situations when a test is honestly administered and yet the very decision to use the test in the first place is based on an illegitimate concern, namely, a desire to exclude blacks. A highly sophisticated verbal aptitude test might be used, for example, to select employees for manual work because the employer, wanting to maintain a predominantly white work force, assumes that fewer whites than blacks will be screened out by the test. Here again, the "real" criterion of selection is race; a court would disallow the use of the irrelevant test, and require the employer to choose a criterion that serves a legitimate end. In both of these cases—the dishonest application of legitimate criteria and the honest application of illegitimate criteria—the appearance of color blindness is a sham and a court could use the simple, colorblind form of the antidiscrimination norm to void the results.

The more troublesome variant of the first issue arises when (1) the facially innocent criterion is adopted in order to serve a legitimate interest; (2) the criterion in fact furthers that interest; and (3) the application of the criterion disadvantages the racial minority in much the same way as would the use of race as the criterion of selection. The job may in fact require sophisticated verbal skills and the test that measures these skills may screen out more blacks than whites. The test is job-related but has a disparate adverse impact on blacks. The question then is whether an employment decision based on the test violates the antidiscrimination prohibition. This is a question of considerable difficulty because while the law, strictly speaking, prohibits distinctions based on race, this particular decision is based on a criterion other than race.

One school of thought answers this question in the negative. This view stresses process, and interprets antidiscrimination in terms of the integrity of the selection process: A selection process based on race is corrupt and cannot be allowed. A selection process free of racial influence might redound to the benefit of the racial minority, since it would allow them to compete on equal footing with other groups and thus give them a chance to alter the distributional inequalities that occurred under a regime such as Jim Crow, where they were penalized because of their race. Any actual effect on their material status as a group, however, would represent just an agreeable by-product, or a background assumption, not the purpose of antidiscrimination law. According to this school, the aims of antidiscrimination law are fulfilled when the process of selection is purified of all racial criteria or motivations.

Another viewpoint stresses results or effects, not process; it would find the use of the innocent criterion unlawful even if it serves legitimate ends. What is decisive, according to this school of thought, is the actual disadvantaging of blacks, not the way the disadvantage comes about. If the application of a criterion has a disproportionately adverse impact on the racial minority, in the sense that it excludes substantially more blacks than whites, the criterion should be treated as the functional equivalent of race.

At the heart of this interpretation of antidiscrimination is a concern for the social status of blacks. It is motivated by a desire to end all practices that would tend to perpetuate or aggravate their subordinate position. Admittedly, the costs of this program are real, for it is stipulated that the contested criterion serves some legitimate end; the test is job-related. But these costs are seen as a necessary price of justice. Only when the costs become extraordinarily large or achieve a special level of urgency, as when the criterion serves some "compelling" (and not just a "legitimate") interest, will the use of the criterion be allowed.

The theorist who so emphasizes effects rests his argument principally on the Fourteenth Amendment and ascribes to it the grandest and noblest of purposes—the elimination of caste structure. He insists that antidiscrimination, as the principle that controls the application of that amendment, be construed with this broad purpose in mind and if need be, that a new principle—the group-disadvantaging principle—be articulated in order to make this purpose even more explicit. He also insists that the various statutes that prohibit discrimination—the principal argumentative props of the process school—should be construed derivatively. These statutes, unlike the Fourteenth Amendment, may contain in so many words a specific ban on "discrimination based on race," but, so the effects theorist argues, these statutes should be seen as a legislative adoption of the prevailing constitutional principle. When that principle is interpreted to forbid the use of criteria that effectively disadvantage blacks, the statutes should be interpreted in a similar fashion.

The process school emphasizes not only the precise language in which the statutory norm is cast but also the traditional rule that conditions judicial intervention on a finding that the defendant is at fault. This fault exists when a white is given a job over a black even though the black scored higher on a test; the employer is said to be acting wrongfully because race is unrelated to any legitimate purpose and is a factor over which individuals have no control. But the requisite fault is said to be lacking when the selection is made on the basis of the individual's performance under some nonracial standard, such as a job-related test. On the other hand, those who subscribe to an effects test emphasize the prospective nature of the remedy typically sought in these cases (an injunction to forbid the use of the criterion in the future) and deny the need for a finding of fault. Such a finding may be necessary to justify damages or the criminal sanction, because these remedies require the defendant to pay for what he did in the past, and presumably such a burden can be placed only on someone who acted wrongfully. But an injunction simply directs that the defendant do what is just and does not presuppose that the defendant has acted wrongfully. Alternatively, the effects theorist might contend that if fault is necessary, it can be found in the defendant's willingness to persist in the use of the contested criterion with full knowledge of its consequences for the racial minority. Such persistence connotes a certain moral indifference.

The disadvantaging that the effects test seeks to avoid is usually defined in terms of the status of a group (for example, the criterion has a greater adverse impact on blacks than on whites and thus tends to perpetuate their subordinate position). Some see this group orientation as alien to our jurisprudence, and thus find a further reason for turning away from an effects test. Borrowing the Court's language in SHELLEY V. KRAEMER (1948), they insist that "[t]he rights created by the first section of the Fourteenth Amendment are, by its terms, guaranteed to the individual" and that "[t]he rights established are personal rights." But those who subscribe to the effects test see the well-being of individuals and of groups as inextricably linked: They believe that the status of an individual is determined in large part by the status of the group with which he is identified. Slavery itself was a group phenomenon, and any corrective strategy must be structured in group terms. Effects theorists also point to practices outside the racial context that display a concern for the welfare of groups such as religious minorities, women, the handicapped, labor, and consumers, and for that reason insist that a group orientation is thoroughly compatible with American legal principles.

In the late 1960s and early 1970s, the Supreme Court responded to these arguments and moved toward adopting an effects test in cases such as *Gaston County v. United States* (1969), GRIGGS V. DUKE POWER CO. (1971), and SWANN V. CHARLOTTE-MECKLENBURG BOARD OF EDUCATION (1971). There was, however, an element of ambiguity or hesitation in the Court's response. The Court prohibited the use of seemingly innocent criteria that disadvantaged blacks, even when their use served some legitimate interests, but the Court did not justify its decisions solely in terms of the adverse effects of the criteria. In addition, the Court characterized the adverse effect as a vestige of an earlier use of race. For example, a literacy test was disallowed as a qualification for voting not simply because it disqualified more blacks than whites but also because it perpetuated the disadvantages previously imposed on blacks in segregated schools. This insistence on analyzing the disadvantage as a vestige of past discrimination may have reflected a commitment to the process test insofar as the Court treated the earlier procedural imperfection (the assignment to schools on the basis of race) as the legally cognizable wrong and the present practice (the literacy test) as merely a device that perpetuates that wrong. But at the same time, the concern with past discrimination surely reflected some commitment to the effects test, for it resulted in the invalidation of facially innocent criteria that in fact served legitimate ends. Disallowing today's literacy test would avoid perpetuating yesterday's discrimination in the educational system, but only by compromising an interest the Court had previously deemed legitimate, namely, that of having a literate electorate. In fact, an interpretation of antidiscrimination law to forbid practices that perpetuate past discrimination could become functionally coextensive with an interpretation that makes effects decisive if some global practice such as slavery is taken as the relevant past discrimination, if the victims of past discrimination are identified in group terms, and if the remedial burden is placed on parties who had no direct role in the earlier discrimination. All disparate effects can be seen as a vestige of the special and unfortunate history of blacks in America.

By the mid-1970s, however, it became clear that the Court was not inclined to broaden its concern with past discrimination so as to make it the functional equivalent of the effects test. In fact, the Court turned in the opposite direction—away from effects and toward process. As Justice POTTER STEWART announced, "Reconstruction is over." The Court did not flatly repudiate its earlier decisions, but instead tried to limit them by confining the effects test to those antidiscrimination norms that were embodied in statutes. For constitutional claims of discrimination, the Court in cases such as WASHINGTON V. DAVIS (1976) and MOBILE V. BOLDEN (1980) required a showing that the process was flawed, or more precisely, that the defendant "intended to discriminate." The plaintiff had to show that the defendant's decision was based on race, or that he chose the seemingly innocent criterion not to further legitimate ends but to exclude or disadvantage blacks. The Court continued to honor claims of past discrimination, but by and large insisted that those claims be advanced by individually identifiable victims of the earlier discrimination, that past acts of discrimination be defined with a great deal of specificity, and that the causal links of those acts to the present racially disparate effects be manifest. No global claims of past discrimination have been allowed.

There is a certain irony in this distinction between statutory and constitutional claims, and in the Supreme Court's decision to confine the effects test to the statutory domain, for the statutes are couched in terms less congenial to such a test. The statutes speak specifically in terms of decisions based on race, while the Fourteenth Amendment speaks of equal protection. (Antidiscrimination is but the judicially constructed principle that is to guide the application of that provision.) Arguably, the distinction between statute and Constitution might reflect the Court's desire to find some way of limiting the practical impact of the effects test, for under the Fourteenth Amendment an effects test would have the widest scope and present the greatest possibilities of judicial intervention. The Fourteenth Amendment extends to all state practices and, because of its universality (it protects every "person"), could be used to protect even those groups that are not defined in racial terms. Indeed, in *Washington v. Davis* the Court expressed the fear that under the effects test the Fourteenth Amendment might even invalidate a sales tax because of its disproportionately adverse impact on the poor (never for a moment pausing to consider whether suitable limiting principles could be developed for avoiding such a result). The Court's distinction between statutory and constitutional claims might also stem from a desire to devise a means for sharing with other political institutions responsibility for the sacrifice of legitimate interests entailed in the application of an effects test. When attached to the statute, the effects test and its disruptive impact become the responsibility of both Court and Congress, since Congress remains free to repeal the statute or otherwise disavow the test.

In the mid-1970s, at the very moment the Court was struggling to identify the circumstances in which the use of a seemingly innocent criterion could be deemed a form of racial discrimination and was moving away from an effects test, it also had to confront the other major interpretive issue posed by antidiscrimination law, the issue of AFFIRMATIVE ACTION. The Court had to decide whether the norm against racial discrimination prohibits giving preference to blacks.

For much of our history, it was assumed that race-based action would be hostile to blacks and that therefore colorblindness would work to the advantage of blacks or at least shield them from hostile action. During the Second Reconstruction, however, as the drive for racial equality grew stronger, an assertedly "benign" use of race became more common. Many believed that even the honest application of legitimate criteria would not significantly alter the unequal distributional patterns that were produced among the races first under slavery and then under Jim Crow, and that it would be necessary, at least for the immediate or foreseeable future, to give blacks a preference in order to improve their status relative to other groups.

These affirmative action programs typically included other minorities, such as Hispanics, as beneficiaries, but were primarily seen as addressed to blacks and did not extend to all disadvantaged groups, such as the poor or white ethnic minorities. They had a distinctive racial cast and were sometimes described as a form of "reverse discrimination." These programs were also typically structured so as to require the decision maker to achieve a certain number of blacks or other minorities within the institution, say, as employees or students. Often that number equaled the percentage of blacks or other minorities in the general population, and was variously described as a goal or quota, depending on which side of the issue one was on. A "goal" was said to establish the minimum rather than the maximum and to be more flexible than a "quota." But more significantly, the term "goal" did not have the odious connotations of the term "quota," which had been used in the past to describe numerical limits on the admission of minorities, limits that were designed to preserve rather than eradicate the caste structure.

For the most part, these affirmative action programs were not treated as a constitutional or statutory requirement. Some of those who subscribed to an effects test argued that the failure to institute preferential programs would constitute a practice that perpetuated the subordinate position of blacks and thus would be itself a form of racial discrimination. But this argument equated inaction with action, and either for that reason or because the effects test was having difficulties of its own, this argument never established a toehold in the law. Equally unsuccessful were the arguments that emphasized those antidiscrimination laws, such as the federal fair employment statute or the executive order governing government contractors, that not only prohibited discrimination but also commanded in so many terms "affirmative action"; the inclusion of these two words were deemed insufficient to alter or add to the basic obligations of the law. The issue posed by affirmative action programs was therefore one of permissibility, rather than obligation: Were these programs consistent with the prohibition against racial discrimination?

Sometimes the purported beneficiaries of the programs (or people speaking on their behalf) objected to them on the theory that the use of race was not wholly benign. Affirmative action was premised on the view that the racial minorities would not fare well under a colorblind policy, thus implying that these minorities are not as well equipped as whites to compete under traditional meritocratic criteria. They are being told, as they were under Jim Crow, that they are inferior—nothing "reverse" about this distinction. This complaint forced those who ran affirmative action programs to be secretive or discreet about what they were doing, but it did not bring those programs to an end or even present an especially formidable obstacle. The proponents of affirmative action explained that the race-based preference was premised on an assessment of the group's history in America, on the wrongs it suffered, not on a belief about innate ability, and as such could not justifiably be seen as giving rise to a slight. The use of race is benign, they insisted, because it improves the status of blacks and other racial minorities by giving them positions, jobs, or other concrete material advantages that they otherwise would not enjoy, at least not in the foreseeable future.

Affirmative action programs have also been attacked by whites, especially when there are discernible differences in the applicants under standard nonracial criteria and when scarce goods, such as highly desired jobs or places in professional schools, are being allocated. In such circumstances favoring a black because of his race necessarily means disfavoring a white because of his race; a job given to one is necessarily denied another. The rejected white applicant cannot truly claim that he is stigmatized even in these circumstances; no one is suggesting he is inferior. His exclusion comes as the by-product or consequence of a program founded on other principles—not to hurt him or the members of his group, but to help the disadvantaged. On the other hand, the rejected white applicant does not rest his complaint solely on the fortuity of the general, racially unspecific language of the antidiscrimination norm, the fact that discrimination based on *any* race is prohibited. The white applicant can also claim that he is being treated unfairly, since he is being judged on the basis of a criterion over which he has no control and which is unrelated to any conception of merit. The rejected white applicant might not be stigmatized, but he can insist that he is being treated unfairly.

This claim of individual unfairness finds support in the process theory of antidiscrimination: If the purpose of antidiscrimination law is to preserve the integrity of a process, to insure that individuals are treated fairly and to prevent them from being judged on the basis of irrelevant criteria, then it would not seem to matter whether the color used in the process were white or black. In either instance, the selection process would be unfair. The program may be well-intentioned, but the intention is of little solace to the rejected white applicants who, as Justice LEWIS F. POWELL put it, are being forced "to bear the burdens of redressing grievances not of their making."

Some of the proponents of affirmative action deny that there is any unfairness to the rejected white applicant. They argue that the claim of unfairness presupposes a special moral status for certain nonracial or meritocratic standards of evaluation, such as grades or performance on a standardized test, and that the requisite moral status is in fact lacking. The white has no "right" to be judged on the meritocratic standard. The more widely shared view among the proponents of affirmative action, however, acknowledges the unfairness caused to individual whites by the preference for blacks but treats it as a necessary, yet regrettable cost of eliminating caste structure. As Justice HARRY A. BLACKMUN put it, "In order to get beyond race, we must first take account of race. There is no other way." Those who take this position, like those who support an effects test, argue that the purpose of antidiscrimination law is to guard against those practices that would perpetuate or aggravate the subordinate position of blacks and other racial minorities and that it would be a perversion of history now to use that law to stop programs designed to improve the status of these groups.

The Supreme Court confronted the issue of affirmative action and weighed these arguments in two different settings. In one, affirmative action was undertaken at the behest of a court order. The theory underlying such orders is not that affirmative action is directly required by an antidiscrimination statute or by the Constitution but rather that it is needed to remedy a pattern or practice of discrimination. Affirmative action is part of the court's corrective plan. A court might, for example, require a company to grant a preference in the seniority system to blacks who were previously excluded from the company and thus unable to earn seniority rights equal to those of whites. The Supreme Court has accepted such remedial uses of race, although it has insisted that this kind of preference be limited to identifiable victims of past discrimination and that some regard be given to the interests of the innocent whites who might be adversely affected by the preferences. For example, blacks might be preferred for vacancies, but will not necessarily be allowed to force the layoff of whites.

The second setting consists of the so-called voluntary affirmative action programs, which are adopted not under orders from a court but out of a sense of moral duty or a belief that the eradication of caste structure is a desirable social policy. These voluntary affirmative action programs have proved more troublesome than the remedial ones, in part because they are not limited to individually identifiable victims of past discriminations (they are truly group oriented), but also because they are not preceded by a judicial finding that the institution has previously discriminated and they are not carried out under the close supervision of a court. The Supreme Court approved these affirmative action programs, but its approval has not been a blanket one. By the mid-1980s, it was established that under certain circumstances color consciousness is permissible, but the Court has been divided in its effort to define or limit these circumstances.

These divisions have been especially pronounced when the voluntary programs were used in higher education. In the first case, DEFUNIS V. ODEGAARD (1974), involving admissions to a state law school, the Court heard arguments and then dismissed the case on grounds of MOOTNESS because the rejected white applicant had graduated by the time the Court came to decide the case—a disposition that underscored the difficulty of the issue and the internal divisions on the Court. A few years later, the Court took up the issue again, in REGENTS OF UNIVERSITY OF CALIFORNIA V. BAKKE (1978), this time at the insistence of a rejected white applicant to a state medical school. In this case the Court reached the merits, but the divisions were even more apparent. No single opinion commanded a majority.

Four Justices thought the preferential program in *Bakke* unlawful. They stressed an antidiscrimination statute, which prohibited, in so many terms, discrimination based on race. These Justices reasoned that a preference for blacks is as much a discrimination based on race as one for whites. No discrimination means no discrimination. Another Justice thought preferential programs could be justified as a means of diversifying the student body, but he objected to the manner in which the particular program before the Court had been implemented. He would allow race to be considered in the admissions process, but would not permit separate tracks for applicants according to race. The remaining four Justices joined in an opinion that would sustain the program as it was in fact implemented, but two of these Justices also wrote separate opinions.

These deep-seated divisions did not resolve themselves substantially in the years following *Bakke.* One voluntary program received a slightly more resolute acceptance by the Court, however, in FULLILOVE V. KLUTZNICK (1980). This program was established by Congress and required a preference for minority-owned businesses in awarding contracts for federally funded public works projects. Although, once again, no single opinion commanded a majority of the Court, the vote of the Justices shifted from 1–4–4 to 6–3, and Chief Justice WARREN E. BURGER, who had objected (without qualification) to the preferential program in *Bakke,* voted to uphold this one. He also wrote one of three opinions that supported the constitutionality of the program. The Chief Justice studiously avoided choosing among "the formulas of analysis" articulated in *Bakke;* that is, he refused to say whether the affirmative action program had to meet the "compelling" interest standard or whether it was sufficient if the corrective ends of the program were deemed "important" or just "legitimate" and the means substantially related to those ends. He simply said, whatever the standard, this program meets it. He did, however, specifically and repeatedly mention one factor that might be the key to the change in his position and the Court's attitude in general: "Here we pass, not on a choice made by a single judge or a school board, but on a considered decision of the Congress and the President."

With this emphasis on the role played by the coordinate branches of government in the affirmative action program, the Chief Justice returned to an idea that emerged in the analysis of the Court's treatment of facially innocent criteria, and that might well explain the Court's determination to confine the effects test to statutes: The Court is more prepared to accept the costs and dislocations that are entailed in the eradication of caste structure when it can share the responsibility for this project with the other branches of government. The Court does not want to go it alone. This suggests that the fate of equality will depend not only on the substantive commitments of the

Justices, on their determination to bring the subordination of blacks and other racial minorities to an end, but also on their views about the role of the Court. The content of antidiscrimination law will in good measure depend on the willingness of the Justices to use their power to lead the nation, or if that impulse is lacking, on the willingness of the other branches of government to participate aggressively in the reconstruction of a society disfigured by one century of slavery and another of Jim Crow.

OWEN M. FISS

Bibliography

BELL, DERRICK 1980 *Race, Racism and American Law.* Boston: Little, Brown.

BREST, PAUL 1976 In Defense of the Antidiscrimination Principle. *Harvard Law Review* 90:1–54.

COHEN, MARSHALL; NAGEL, THOMAS; and SCANLON, THOMAS 1977 *Equality and Preferential Treatment.* Princeton, N.J.: Princeton University Press.

EISENBERG, THEODORE 1981 *Civil Rights Legislation.* Charlottesville, Va.: Michie Co.

FISHKIN, JAMES 1983 *Justice, Equal Opportunity and the Family.* New Haven, Conn.: Yale University Press.

FISS, OWEN 1971 A Theory of Fair Employment Laws. *University of Chicago Law Review* 38:235–314.

——— 1976 Groups and the Equal Protection Clause. *Philosophy and Public Affairs* 5:107–177.

FREEMAN, ALAN 1978 Legitimizing Racial Discrimination through Antidiscrimination Law: A Critical Review of Supreme Court Doctrine. *Minnesota Law Review* 62:1049–1119.

GARET, RONALD 1983 Communality and Existence: The Rights of Groups. *Southern California Law Review* 56:1001–1075.

GUNTHER, GERALD 1972 In Search of Evolving Doctrine on a Changing Court: A Model for Newer Equal Protection. *Harvard Law Review* 86:1–48.

KARST, KENNETH and HOROWITZ, HAROLD 1974 Affirmative Action and Equal Protection. *Virginia Law Review* 60:955–974.

RAE, DOUGLAS 1981 *Equalities.* Cambridge, Mass.: Harvard University Press.

TUSSMAN, JOSEPH and TEN BROEK, JACOBUS 1949 The Equal Protection of the Laws. *California Law Review* 37:341–381.

RACIAL QUOTAS

Programs of AFFIRMATIVE ACTION, aimed at increasing opportunities for women and members of racial and ethnic minorities in employment and higher education, have sometimes taken the form of numerical quotas. In REGENTS OF UNIVERSITY OF CALIFORNIA V. BAKKE (1978) sixteen places in a state university medical school's entering class were reserved for minority applicants; in FULLILOVE V. KLUTZNICK (1980) ten percent of funds in a federal public works program were reserved for minority-owned businesses. Such quotas have been challenged as denials of the EQUAL PROTECTION OF THE LAWS, with mixed doctrinal results.

Opponents of racial quotas maintain that it is offensive to penalize or reward people on the basis of race—in short, that the Constitution is, or ought to be, colorblind. Opponents discern in quotas a subtle but pervasive racism, in the patronizing assumption that persons of particular colors or ethnic backgrounds cannot be expected to meet the standards that apply to others. This assumption, the opponents argue, is, in its own way, a BADGE OF SERVITUDE, stigmatizing the quotas' supposed beneficiaries. Some opponents see quotas as part of a general trend toward dehumanization, robbing individuals of both personal identity and human dignity, lumping them together in a collectivity based on other people's assumptions about racially defined traits.

Unfortunately for today's America, race has never been a neutral fact in this country. Those who defend affirmative action generally admit to some uneasiness about the potential abuse of racial distinctions. They argue, however, that there is no real neutrality in a system that first imposes on a racial group harsh disadvantages, readily transmitted through the generations, and then tells today's inheritors of disadvantages that from now on the rules prohibit playing favorites. If either compensation for past RACIAL DISCRIMINATION or the integration of American institutions is a legitimate social objective, the proponents argue, a government in pursuit of those objectives can hardly avoid taking race into account.

The recent attack on racial quotas draws fuel from an emotional reservoir filled two generations ago by universities that limited admission of racial and religious minorities—most notably Jews—to specified small quotas. This ugly form of discrimination was part of a systematic stigmatization and subordination of minority groups by the dominant majority. The recent quotas are designed to remedy the effects of past discrimination, and—when they serve the objective of compensation or integration—are not stigmatizing. They do, however, use race or ethnic status as a means of classifying persons, and thus come under fire for emphasizing group membership rather than "individual merit."

The right to equal protection is, indeed, an individual right. Yet the term "individual merit" misleads in two ways. The word "individual" misleads by obscuring the fact that every claim to equality is a claim made on behalf of the group of persons identified by some set of characteristics: race, for example, or high college grades and test scores. To argue against a racial preference is not to support individual merit as against a group claim, but to argue that some other group, defined by other attributes, is entitled to preference.

"Merit" misleads by conveying the idea of something wholly intrinsic to an individual, apart from some definition of community needs or purposes. When we reward achievement, we are not merely rewarding effort, but are also giving out prizes for native talents and environmental advantages. Mainly, we reward achievement because society wants the goods produced by the combination of talents, environment, and effort. But it is also reasonable to look to past harms and potential contributions to society in defining the characteristics that deserve reward. We admit college achievers to law schools not to reward winners but to serve society with good lawyers. If it be legitimate to seek to end a system of racial caste by integrating American society, nothing in the idea of individual merit stands in the way of treating race as one aspect of "merit."

Race-conscious remedies for past governmental discrimination were approved in decisions as early as SWANN v. CHARLOTTE-MECKLENBURG BOARD OF EDUCATION (1971). Affirmative action quotas pose another question: can government itself employ race-conscious remedies for the effects of past societal discrimination? In *Fullilove,* six Justices agreed on an affirmative answer to that question, at least when Congress prescribes the remedy. *Bakke* was complicated by a statutory claim; its result—and its practical effect in professional school admissions—was a distinction between racial or ethnic quotas, which are unlawful, and the use of racial or ethnic status as "one factor" in admission, which is lawful.

The distinction was a political success; it drew the fangs from a controversy that had turned venomous. But the distinction between a quota and a racial factor is more symbol than substance. If race is a factor, it will decide some cases. How many cases? The weight assigned to race surely will be determined by reference to the approximate number of minority admittees necessary to achieve the admitting university's goals of educational "diversity." The difference between saying "sixteen out of a hundred" and "around sixteen percent" is an exercise in constitutional cosmetics—but it seems to have saved affirmative action during a critical season.

KENNETH L. KARST

Bibliography

KARST, KENNETH L. and HOROWITZ, HAROLD W. 1974 Affirmative Action and Equal Protection. *Virginia Law Review* 60:955–974.

VAN ALSTYNE, WILLIAM W. 1979 Rites of Passage: Race, the Supreme Court, and the Constitution. *University of Chicago Law Review* 46:775–810.

RAILROAD COMMISSION OF TEXAS v. PULLMAN COMPANY

See: Abstention Doctrines

RAILROAD CONTROL ACT
40 Stat. 451 (1918)

Railroad service virtually ceased during the severe winter of 1917–1918. The extraordinary wartime volume of traffic and the railroads' fiscal and physical inability to meet its demands prompted President WOODROW WILSON to take control of all railway transport in the country on December 26, 1917. Congress ratified his proclamation in March 1918, by "emergency legislation enacted to meet conditions growing out of war."

The substance of the act concerned reimbursement of the owners for the use of their property while under government management. Congress set JUST COMPENSATION for this TAKING OF PROPERTY at the average operating income for the prior three years and also insured "adequate and appropriate [monies] for the maintenance, repair, renewals and depreciation of property." This legislation temporarily superseded much of the regulatory power of the Interstate Commerce Commission (ICC). It authorized the President to initiate "reasonable and just" rates which became effective without the ordinarily required wait and without ICC approval. That body could review the reasonableness of the rates but must give "due consideration" to the "unified and coordinated national control" and the stipulation that the roads "are not in competition." The constitutionality of the act as a whole was never challenged but separate sections were sustained under the WAR POWERS in a series of cases.

DAVID GORDON

RAILROAD REGULATION

See: Economic Regulation

RAILROAD RETIREMENT ACT
48 Stat. 1283 (1934)

This act established a retirement and pension plan for railroad employees engaged in INTERSTATE COMMERCE. Congress specified "promoting efficiency and safety in interstate transportation" among the purposes of the act. Each employee, whose participation was mandatory, would be required to retire after thirty years service or at sixty-five, receiving thereafter an annuity based upon his length of service. Contributions from both employee and the carrier would finance these payments. A Railroad Retirement Board would adjust the contributions, initially set at two percent of a worker's salary and doubled by the carrier, and would administer the act. Congress further authorized the board to make actuarial surveys and keep pertinent records and data. The act vested district courts with JURISDICTION to enforce board orders and to review administrative questions.

A 5–4 Supreme Court voided the law in RAILROAD RETIREMENT BOARD V. ALTON (1935) as a violation of DUE PROCESS OF LAW and outside the commerce power, a decision effectively nullified in STEWARD MACHINE CO. V. DAVIS (1937).

DAVID GORDON

RAILROAD RETIREMENT BOARD v. ALTON RAILWAY COMPANY
295 U.S. 330 (1935)

In the spring of 1935, as the FRANKLIN D. ROOSEVELT administration made plans for a general SOCIAL SECURITY ACT, the Supreme Court held unconstitutional the RAILROAD RETIREMENT ACT of 1934, which established a program of compulsory retirement and old age pensions for railroad workers engaged in INTERSTATE COMMERCE. Justice OWEN ROBERTS, for a five-member majority, found the act violative of DUE PROCESS OF LAW and unauthorized by the COMMERCE CLAUSE. By exacting a percentage of payrolls for a pension fund, the act, Roberts said, was a "naked appropriation of private property" for the benefit of workers. The act was also "bad" because no reasonable connection existed between the welfare of railroad workers and the efficiency or safety of interstate transportation.

Chief Justice CHARLES EVANS HUGHES, joined by Justice LOUIS D. BRANDEIS, BENJAMIN N. CARDOZO, and HARLAN FISKE STONE, dissented. The MAJORITY OPINION shocked Hughes because it went beyond the invalidation of this particular pension plan; the majority's "unwarranted limitation" on the commerce clause denied wholly and forever the power of Congress to enact any social welfare scheme. Relying on GIBBONS V. OGDEN (1824) for the scope of the commerce power, Hughes observed that its exercise had the widest range in dealing with interstate railroads. He accepted Congress's judgment that the plan enhanced efficiency and safety. Moreover, the precedents supported the constitutionality of the act, he argued; the act did not differ in principle from workmen's compensation acts for railroad employees, which the Court had sustained. It had also upheld a congressional enactment that empowered the Interstate Commerce Commission to take excess profits from some railroads for the benefit of others. (See DAYTON GOOSE CREEK RAILROAD CO. V. UNITED STATES, 1924.) The Court's opinion helped provoke the constitutional crisis of 1937.

LEONARD W. LEVY

RAILWAY EXPRESS AGENCY v. NEW YORK
336 U.S. 106 (1949)

Railway Express is a leading modern example of the Supreme Court's deference to legislative judgments in the field of ECONOMIC REGULATION. The Court unanimously upheld a New York City "traffic safety" ordinance forbidding advertisements on vehicles but exempting delivery vehicles advertising their owners' businesses. No one mentioned the FIRST AMENDMENT. (See COMMERCIAL SPEECH.) Justice WILLIAM O. DOUGLAS, for the Court, first waved away a DUE PROCESS attack on the ordinance. Turning to the companion EQUAL PROTECTION attack, Douglas said that the city "may well have concluded" that advertising vehicles presented a greater traffic hazard than did trucks carrying their owners' messages. "We cannot say that that judgment is not an allowable one." The opinion typifies the Court's use of the most deferential RATIONAL BASIS review of economic regulation.

Justice ROBERT H. JACKSON expressed some doubt as to the Court's reasoning but concurred, referring to the law's historic distinctions between "doing in self-interest and doing for hire." Along the way he uttered the decision's most memorable words: "there is no more effective practical guarantee against arbitrary and unreasonable government than to require that the principles of law which officials would impose on a minority must be imposed generally."

KENNETH L. KARST

RANDOLPH, EDMUND
(1753–1813)

In 1776 Edmund Jenings Randolph, lawyer, mayor of Williamsburg, and aide to General GEORGE WASHINGTON, was the youngest delegate to the convention that adopted the VIRGINIA DECLARATION OF RIGHTS AND CONSTITUTION. He became the state's first attorney general under the new constitution and was later a delegate to Congress, where he favored amending the ARTICLES OF CONFEDERATION to give Congress the power to levy import duties. He was a member of the Annapolis Convention of 1786 and later the same year defeated RICHARD HENRY LEE to become governor of Virginia.

Randolph led Virginia's delegation to the CONSTITUTIONAL CONVENTION OF 1787, where he introduced the VIRGINIA PLAN. He did not, however, sign the finished Constitution, which, he believed, gave too much power to the President and so tended toward monarchy. Nevertheless, in 1788 he argued and voted in the state convention for RATIFICATION OF THE CONSTITUTION. He argued that there was no alternative except disunion and that a second convention could be called to perfect the document.

President Washington appointed Randolph the first attorney general of the United States, making him a colleague of and mediator between THOMAS JEFFERSON and ALEXANDER HAMILTON. When Jefferson resigned in 1794, Randolph succeeded him as secretary of state, but he was himself forced to resign the next year when British publication of captured French dispatches led to charges of TREASON and bribery against Randolph. This disgrace ended his political career, but he remained an eminent lawyer. In 1807 he was chief defense counsel when AARON BURR was tried for and acquitted of treason.

DENNIS J. MAHONEY

RANDOLPH, JOHN
(1773–1833)

John Randolph of Roanoke, Virginia, congressman and sometime senator, advocated the constitutional doctrines of STATES' RIGHTS and STRICT CONSTRUCTION that became identified with southern opposition to the federal government and that eventuated in SECESSION. Excepting his support for the LOUISIANA PURCHASE, Randolph consistently preferred the claim of state to federal SOVEREIGNTY. A bitter critic of the Federalist federal judiciary, he managed or mismanaged the IMPEACHMENT of Justice SAMUEL CHASE in 1804.

Breaking with THOMAS JEFFERSON in 1806, Randolph commenced a career of opposition to almost every sitting President and to most national policies. His principles were straightforward. He believed that the Constitution was a compact among sovereign states. Sovereignty did not inhere in the federal government, and the admission of new states was a device to weaken the original, compacting states. He espoused the southern view that regarded every attempt to expand federal power as an attack on SLAVERY, and he regarded democracy and nationalism as leveling and centralizing invasions of ancient state privileges and mores. He viewed with especial bitterness the rulings of the MARSHALL COURT.

ROBERT DAWIDOFF

Bibliography

DAWIDOFF, ROBERT 1979 *The Education of John Randolph.* New York: Norton.

RASMUSSEN v. UNITED STATES

See: Insular Cases

RATE REGULATION

See: Economic Regulation

RATIFICATION OF CONSTITUTIONAL AMENDMENTS

The delegates to the CONSTITUTIONAL CONVENTION OF 1789 decided upon the outlines of the AMENDING PROCESS after only a few hours of debate. The requirement that any proposed amendment be ratified by three-fourths of the states was adopted unanimously, but was, like so much of the Constitution, the result of a compromise. Initially the convention seems to have assumed that amendments to the federal charter would require ratification by all the states; but five state delegations were willing to set the requirement as low as two-thirds of the states. No form of ratification other than by the states as entities was proposed or discussed in the convention.

JAMES MADISON, writing in THE FEDERALIST # 39, described the method of ratifying amendments to the new Constitution as "partly federal, partly national." The method is [con]federal in that ratification is accomplished by the states as states, and not by a referendum of the people or a national majority. At the same time, the method is national in that it does not require the assent of all the constituent states to alter the terms of the federal union. A pure theory of FEDERALISM, as it was understood by the founding generation, would not have sanctioned imposition of an amended compact upon unconsenting parties.

Our first constitution, the ARTICLES OF CONFEDERATION, had required the unanimous consent of the states to any amendment. For that reason, during the "critical period" between 1781 and 1789 no amendments were adopted, even when decisive weaknesses in the confederal system were apparent. The requirement for unanimous ratification of amendments made the Constitutional Convention and the new Constitution necessary.

Article V in fact provides for state ratification of constitutional amendments in one or the other of two distinct modes, leaving the choice of mode to Congress. The first mode is ratification by state legislatures, the second is ratification by conventions. In two centuries of government under the Constitution Congress has proposed thirty-three constitutional amendments and in thirty-two cases has prescribed state legislatures as the agents of ratification. The single exception was ratification of the TWENTY-FIRST AMENDMENT, repealing PROHIBITION.

The constitutional provision relating to ratification is little more than an outline. The details have been filled in as the need has arisen. Although the state legislatures derive their authority to ratify amendments from the federal Constitution, the size of the majority required to effect ratification is determined by the constitution, statutes, or legislative rules of each state. Many, perhaps most, prescribe an extraordinary majority for that purpose.

An amendment automatically becomes part of the Constitution when it is ratified by the requisite number of states, but someone must be designated to receive the certificates of ratification, to count them, and to announce publicly that ratification is complete. Originally Congress delegated this task to the secretary of state, but it is now performed by a relatively minor official, the director of general services. Congress itself proclaimed the ratification of the FOURTEENTH AMENDMENT.

Article V sets no time limit within which the states must act on proposed amendments. The Framers supposed that the ratification process would occur at roughly the same time throughout the country. RATIFICATION OF THE CONSTITUTION itself took nine months; the BILL OF RIGHTS was ratified in just over two years. The convention provided no definite time period after which a proposal for amendment would lapse. Therefore, a recurring question has been how long the states have to ratify proposed amendments.

The principles of democracy and CONSTITUTIONALISM would be ill-served if ratification of constitutional amendments by the several states did not have to be accomplished roughly contemporaneously. This goal has been met in the case of every successful amendment. Although seven years has become the standard period for the states to consider ratification, no amendment has, in fact, required as long as four years for ratification. The TWENTY-SECOND AMENDMENT required the longest time, forty-seven and one-half months; the TWENTY-SIXTH AMENDMENT required the shortest period, four months. The average time for ratification of a constitutional amendment has been eighteen months.

As a legal matter, ratification must be accomplished within a "reasonable" time, but no statute or court decision has defined just how long a period that is. The CHILD LABOR AMENDMENT, proposed in 1924, was ratified by three state legislatures as late as 1937, and the Supreme Court declined to hold that those ratifications were ineffective. The Supreme Court, in *Dillon v. Gloss* (1920), upheld the power of Congress to set a seven-year limit on the ratification period; but in *Coleman v. Miller* (1939) the Court refused to set such a limit on its own account where Congress failed to exercise the power.

The EIGHTEENTH, TWENTIETH, Twenty-First, and Twenty-Second AMENDMENTS comprise the ratification time limit within their texts. In several other cases, Congress has prescribed the time limit (invariably seven years) in the JOINT RESOLUTION proposing the amendment. Only once did Congress attempt to extend the prescribed time limit: when the seven years allotted for ratification of the so-called EQUAL RIGHTS AMENDMENT (ERA) expired in 1979, Congress—by less than the two-thirds majority required for the original proposal—voted to extend the ratification period for an extra three and one-half years. The failure of the proposed amendment's supporters to garner sufficient ratifications even in the extended time period averted a constitutional crisis over the issue of time limits.

A matter frequently debated but never definitively resolved is whether the states, during the period for consideration of a proposed amendment, may alter a decision once one is taken. The question arose with regard to the Fourteenth Amendment and was revived during the controversy over the ERA. Indeed, there seems to be no doubt that a state, having declined to ratify a proposed amendment, may, within the allotted time, alter that decision and ratify the amendment. It is less certain whether a state that has voted to ratify a proposed amendment may subsequently rescind such a ratification. In 1868 Congress and Secretary of State WILLIAM H. SEWARD declared the Fourteenth Amendment ratified, apparently counting the ratifications of two states (New Jersey and Ohio) that had voted to rescind their ratifications. On the date of the declaration a sufficient number of states had ratified to render the disputed votes irrelevant. Expiration in 1983 of the extended time limit for ratification of the ERA made the question of rescinded ratifications of that proposal moot.

The requirement of state ratification presupposes that the state legislatures are free to choose whether or not to ratify a proposed amendment. But this is not always true. Ratification of the Fourteenth Amendment was secured, in part, because Congress made such ratification a condition for readmission of the states of the former Confederacy. Clearly Congress, amidst the crisis of Civil War and Reconstruction, stretched the limits of its authority by imposing that condition.

Controversies concerning the ratification of constitutional amendments are almost prototypically POLITICAL QUESTIONS. Only rarely has the Supreme Court decided such controversies. In *Hawke v. Smith* (1920) and *Leser v. Garnett* (1922) the Court rejected attempts to submit the question of ratification to a popular vote or to condition ratification on approval in a REFERENDUM. In *United States v. Sprague* (1931) the Court refused to impose any limit on Congress's freedom to choose between the two constitutional modes of ratification. The effect of the few cases the Court has decided has been, as in *Dillon* and *Coleman*, to reserve the power of final determination to Congress.

DENNIS J. MAHONEY

Bibliography

FREEDMAN, SAMUEL S. and NAUGHTON, PAMELA J. 1978 *ERA: May a State Change Its Vote?* Detroit, Mich.: Wayne State University Press.

ORFIELD, LESTER 1942 *The Amending of the Federal Constitution.* Ann Arbor: University of Michigan Press.

RATIFICATION OF THE CONSTITUTION

Plans for a convention to revise the ARTICLES OF CONFEDERATION were in fact a subterfuge, because the delegates in Philadelphia convened in May 1787 with no serious thought whatever of an attempt to keep that instrument in force. But a legal problem had to be resolved, for the Articles were a fact and their revision was to be made only by unanimous agreement of the Continental Congress which "the legislatures of every state" would later confirm. Delegates to the CONSTITUTIONAL CONVENTION OF 1787, including several lawyers who later became Supreme Court Justices, wasted little time in disposing of such restrictions, but they were wary of the manner in which the Constitution could be made acceptable to the people. The solution hit upon by JAMES MADISON in his VIRGINIA PLAN was to circumvent the state legislatures and ask Congress to send whatever plan they adopted in Philadelphia to "assemblies of Representatives . . . expressly chosen by the people, to consider & decide thereon." Frankly fearful of local officeholders who would see the new Constitution as a threat to "the importance they now hold," the Virginia delegates were united on this point. "Nine States had been required in all great cases under the Confederation & that number was on that account preferable," GEORGE MASON suggested, and his logic prevailed.

After some maneuvering, the expiring Continental Congress by unanimous resolution forwarded the Constitution to the states for their approbation, thus placing an implicit seal of congressional approval on Article VII. The principle of a two-thirds majority rather than unanimity was crucial. Ominously, Rhode Island had sent no delegate to the convention. To avoid embarrassing obstructions, prudence dictated a fair trial for the Constitution, provided key state conventions ratified the document. Rarely in American history has such a sweeping change moved so rapidly through the cumbersome machinery of disparate state governments, and the phenomenon can be explained only in the adroit handling of GEORGE WASHINGTON's implied endorsement along with the urgency which supporters of the Constitution preached in pamphlets and newspapers or wherever influential citizens congregated.

Much of the credit for the Federalists' strategy must go to James Madison. As a central figure at the convention and in the Continental Congress he carefully brought forward the accompanying documents which gave an impression of unanimity by the framers and the forwarders. Using his franking privilege (as a congressman), Madison maintained a correspondence with colleagues in the principal state capitals and coordinated plans to hold conventions at the proper tactical time. Ratification by the conventions in Pennsylvania, Massachusetts, and Virginia was essential, for these three states contained most of the nation's people and much of its wealth. In New York a surly band controlled the state government and was in no hurry to surrender its profitable customs collecting to a national government, but these men could not withstand pressure from the commercial community if all the other large states ratified. Rhode Island was doubtful, and New Jersey and Georgia were unnecessary, owing to the smallness of their populations and their geographic positions.

The Federalists had powerful allies in the newspapers, some ninety-eight in number, most of which printed the Constitution *in toto* shortly after September 17. In Philadelphia, Boston, and New York the leading journals soon printed essays favoring the Constitution and denouncing the opposition Anti-Federalists as obstinate "placemen" (state officeholders) fearful of losing their jobs or "wrongheaded" on other grounds. Pennsylvania Federalists moved swiftly but could not outrace their friends in Delaware, who hurriedly called a three-county convention and became the first ratifying state on December 7 (30–0). In Philadelphia, the first stirrings of Anti-Federalist activity included publication of attacks on the Constitution's lack of a BILL OF RIGHTS, but as that argument was picked up elsewhere the high-handed legislature called a convention that was heavily weighted with delegates from eastern counties favorable to the Federalist cause. Before farming communities in western counties could organize, the Pennsylvania convention ratified on December 12 (46–23). New Jersey fell in line on December 18 (38–0). Then word came that Georgia had also unanimously ratified on January 2, 1788 (26–0). After perfunctory debate, Connecticut ratified on January 9 (128–40).

Before they could enjoy these triumphs, the Federalists learned that the failure to include a bill of rights, the fears of an overbearing (and tax-hungry) "consolidated" government, and a variety of local circumstances would slow ratification and might jeopardize the whole process. Massachusetts became the focal point of Federalist efforts, for rumblings from town meetings indicated that opposition was greater than anticipated. A phalanx of Harvard-trained lawyers, supported by commercial and shipping interests, accepted a set of recommendatory amendments to weaken the major Anti-Federalist positions, and on February 6 the Federalists won, 187–168.

New York Anti-Federalists began to counterattack. They urged friends in New Hampshire to reject the Constitution, and there is some murky evidence that a quick vote would have gone against ratification. Both sides finally settled on a postponement until June. Madison helped ALEXANDER HAMILTON write the essays of "Publius" (these became a classic treatise titled THE FEDERALIST) for the New York newspapers and continued to send his morale-building, organizing letters to friends in the South. An unexpected stumbling block to ratification came from Baptist ministers and congregations, who voiced concern that freedom of conscience was not safeguarded by the Constitution.

Meanwhile, Maryland Federalists lost patience with their long-winded opponents in the Annapolis convention and ratified on April 28 (63–11). The recommended amendments from Massachusetts Anti-Federalists were used as a talking point, but when the argument came to whether amendments could be part of a conditional ratification, the Federalists lost their tempers. Madison hurried back to Virginia, aware that PATRICK HENRY and Mason would form the most powerful Anti-Federal combination possible. New York seemed safely Anti-Federalist, for Governor George Clinton and his friends talked and printed venomous attacks on the Constitution and its Federalist drafters. Hamilton counted heads and asked Madison if a conditional ratification would suffice. No, Madison replied, a ratification with any strings attached would leave New York out of the Union. After slight Anti-Federal resistance, South Carolina ratified on May 23 (149–73). In Rhode Island, the people rejected ratification directly, 237 yeas to 2,708 nays.

Ratification by Virginia on June 25 was uncertain until a crucial ballot was won by Federalists, who captured the eight doubtful votes from western areas. Madison, JOHN MARSHALL, and EDMUND RANDOLPH led the charge against Henry and Mason, but they agreed to recommend amendments adding a bill of rights to preserve some good will on the final roll call (89–79). The ninth state, New Hampshire, had already ratified on June 21, 1788 (57–46). The news from Virginia, however, sent a thrill through the North. Diarist JOHN QUINCY ADAMS noted that jubilant Federalists fired muskets far into the night when the tidings from Richmond reached Boston. With ten states now committed, the Constitution was sure of a trial. Even so, a powerful, entrenched Anti-Federal faction prevented action by the North Carolina convention, which adjourned to await future developments and a possible second convention that diehard Anti-Federalists thought might patch up another version of the Constitution (with a bill of rights among the additions). A test vote on ratification lost, 184–84, but New York fooled everybody by ratifying on July 26 (30–27).

Within four months, all the states except North Carolina and Rhode Island had set in motion machinery to elect the new federal Congress and a President. The knowledge that Washington supported the Constitution and would be the first President tipped the balance in crucial situations. Washington's stature, the concession by Madison and others that amendments adding a bill of rights would be proposed forthwith, and the overwhelming support of the press were the chief reasons that ratification proceeded with relative speed. The new government was operating, and Madison had introduced a bill of rights by the time North Carolina ratified on November 21, 1789 (197–99). Rhode Island narrowly ratified on May 29, 1790 (34–32), to become a fully participating member of the Union. Few scars remained. The hastily drawn lines of the ratification battle soon faded, and the divergent political philosophies that emerged in the next decade had little to do with the intense struggle of 1787–1788.

ROBERT A. RUTLAND

Bibliography

FARRAND, MAX, ed. (1911)1966 *The Records of the Federal Convention of 1787,* 4 vols. New Haven, Conn.: Yale University Press.

MAIN, JACKSON TURNER 1961 *The Antifederalists: Critics of the Constitution, 1781–1788.* Chapel Hill: University of North Carolina Press.

RUTLAND, ROBERT A. 1966 *The Ordeal of the Constitution: The Antifederalists and the Ratification Struggle of 1787–1788.* Norman: University of Oklahoma Press.

WOOD, GORDON S. 1969 *The Creation of the American Republic, 1776–1787.* Pages 306–344. Chapel Hill: University of North Carolina Press.

RATIO DECIDENDI

(Latin: "Reason for being decided.") A statement made in an OPINION OF THE COURT is either *ratio decidendi* or OBITER DICTUM. *Ratio decidendi* refers to a statement that is a necessary part of the chain of reasoning leading to the DECISION of the case, while obiter dictum ("said by the way") refers to any other statement in the opinion. The distinction is clear in theory but, in practice, may be difficult to apply to any given case.

No federal court may properly pass on a legal or constitutional question that is not brought before it in a CASE OR CONTROVERSY, and a court properly resolves only those questions necessary to decide a case before it. The resolution of a particular question is the court's HOLDING on that question, and the reasoning necessary to the resolution of a question properly before the court is *ratio decidendi.* The *ratio decidendi* is thereafter binding as a rule of law when the case is cited as precedent. Although a judge may have a clear idea of what arguments were necessary to reach the decision in a case and may attempt to convey that idea in his opinion, it is the courts that apply the case as precedent in future decisions that finally establish which statements were obiter dicta and which *ratio decidendi.*

DENNIS J. MAHONEY

RATIONAL BASIS

The "rational basis" STANDARD OF REVIEW emerged in the late 1930s, as the Supreme Court retreated from its earlier activism in the defense of economic liberties. We owe the phrase to Justice HARLAN FISKE STONE, who used it in two 1938 opinions to signal a new judicial deference to legislative judgments. In UNITED STATES V. CAROLENE PRODUCTS CO. (1938), Stone said that an ECONOMIC REGULATION, challenged as a violation of SUBSTANTIVE DUE PROCESS or of EQUAL PROTECTION, would be upheld unless demonstrated facts should "preclude the assumption that it rests upon some rational basis within the knowledge and experience of the legislators." In *South Carolina State Highway Department v. Barnwell Brothers, Inc.* (1938), Stone proposed "rational basis" as the standard for reviewing STATE REGULATIONS OF COMMERCE. (Later, Stone would accept the necessity for more exacting judicial scrutiny of such laws.) To complete the process, the Court adopted the same deferential posture toward congressional judgments that local activities substantially affected INTERSTATE COMMERCE and thus might be regulated by Congress under the COMMERCE POWER. In all its uses, "rational basis" represents a strong presumption of the constitutionality of legislation.

Yet even so minimal a standard of JUDICIAL REVIEW does, in theory, call for some judicial scrutiny of the rationality of the relationship between legislative means and ends. And that scrutiny of means makes sense only if we assume that the ends themselves are constitutionally required to serve general, public aims; otherwise, every law would be self-justifying, as precisely apt for achieving the advantages and disadvantages it achieves. Although the Court has sometimes suggested in economic regulation cases that even a search for legislative rationality lies beyond the scope of the judicial function, some such judicial scrutiny is required if our courts are to give effect to generalized constitutional guarantees of liberty and equality. Today's assumption, therefore, is that a law depriving a person of liberty or of equal treatment is invalid unless, at a minimum, it is a rational means for achieving a legitimate legislative purpose.

Even so relaxed a standard of review appears to call for a judicial inquiry always beset by uncertainties and often dominated by fictitious assumptions. Hans Linde has demonstrated the unreality attendant on judicial efforts to identify the "purposes" served by a law adopted by legislators with diverse objectives, or objectives only tenuously connected to the public good. Lacking sure guidance as to those "purposes"—which may have changed in the years since the law was adopted—a court must rely on counsel's assertions and its own assumptions. But in its inception the rational basis standard was not so much a mode of inquiry as a formula for validating legislation. Thus, in McGOWAN v. MARYLAND (1961), the Supreme Court said, "A statutory discrimination will not be set aside if any state of facts reasonably may be conceived to justify it." Part of the reason why the rational basis standard survives in federal constitutional law is that it is normally taken seriously only in its permissive feature (*United States Railroad Retirement Board v. Fritz,* 1980). A number of state courts, interpreting STATE CONSTITUTIONAL LAW, do take the rational basis standard to require a serious judicial examination of the reasonableness of legislation. And the Supreme Court itself, in its late-1960s forays into the reaches of equal protection doctrine lying beyond racial equality, sometimes labeled legislative classifications as "irrational" even as it insisted that state-imposed inequalities be justified against more exacting standards of review. (See HARPER v. VIRGINIA STATE BOARD OF ELECTIONS, 1966; LEVY v. LOUISIANA, 1968; SHAPIRO v. THOMPSON, 1969.) Since that time, the explicit recognition of different levels of judicial scrutiny of legislation has allowed the Court to reserve the rhetoric of rational basis for occasions thought appropriate for judicial modesty, in particular its review of "economic and social regulation." Some substantive interests call for heightened judicial scrutiny of legislative incursions into them; absent such considerations, the starting point for constitutional analysis remains the rational basis standard.

KENNETH L. KARST

Bibliography

LINDE, HANS A. 1976 Due Process of Lawmaking. *Nebraska Law Review* 55:197–255.

RAWLE, WILLIAM
(1759–1836)

A Philadelphia lawyer and Federalist, Rawle declined GEORGE WASHINGTON's offer to become the first attorney general of the United States. As United States attorney for Pennsylvania, he was the government prosecutor in the cases arising from the WHISKEY REBELLION (1794) and FRIES' REBELLION (1798). Rawle also advocated the existence of a FEDERAL COMMON LAW OF CRIMES. He is best remembered as one of the earliest COMMENTATORS ON THE CONSTITUTION. His *New View of the Constitution* (1825) was widely used as a textbook. Although he was a nationalist, he was the first to advocate the right of state SECESSION.

LEONARD W. LEVY

RAYMOND MOTOR TRANSPORTATION COMPANY v. RICE
434 U.S. 429 (1978)

Continuing a line of decisions begun in SOUTHERN PACIFIC COMPANY v. ARIZONA (1945), an 8–0 Supreme Court struck down a state highway regulation as an unconstitutional burden on INTERSTATE COMMERCE. A Wisconsin statute barred trucks over fifty-five feet in length from state highways as a safety measure. Two trucking companies challenged the law under the COMMERCE CLAUSE. A strong demonstration that the law made, at best, a negligible contribution to highway safety combined with the state's failure to provide an adequate defense of the measure led the Court to override the strong presumption usually given such laws.

In *Kassel v. Consolidated Freightways Corp. of Delaware* (1981), Iowa made a "more serious effort to support the safety rationale of its [fifty-five foot limit] than did Wisconsin in *Raymond,*" but a 6–3 Court, relying on *Raymond,* struck down the Iowa statute on the same grounds.

DAVID GORDON

READ, GEORGE
(1733–1798)

George Read of Delaware was a signer of both the DECLARATION OF INDEPENDENCE and the Constitution. A frequent speaker at the CONSTITUTIONAL

CONVENTION OF 1787, he favored a consolidated national government and proposed abolition of state boundaries. He was a leader of the ratification movement in Delaware, and later he served as state chief justice and as a United States senator.

DENNIS J. MAHONEY

REAGAN, RONALD
(1911–)

Born in Tampico, Illinois, brought up in Dixon, Illinois, a graduate of Eureka College, Illinois, Ronald Reagan came from the American Midwest, while his adult life was largely spent in California, leading to a classic California combination of midwestern seriousness of purpose and California casualness of style. Coming to maturity in 1932, he was first a convinced follower of FRANKLIN D. ROOSEVELT, changing his political beliefs in response to his perceptions of communist infiltration in the late 1940s, and formally becoming a Republican only in 1962. A radio announcer as a young man, then an actor (playing in more than fifty motion pictures), then for three years an Army captain, then for five years president of the Screen Actors Guild, he became a spokesman for the General Electric Company, traveling nationally to speak to company employees and civic groups on domestic and patriotic themes. In 1966 he defeated five other candidates to win the Republican nomination for governor of California and was then elected over the incumbent Edmund Brown by a historic margin of nearly one million votes. He was easily reelected in 1970. His two terms as governor of the most populous state in the Union were marked by a dramatic reduction in the number of welfare recipients, a small increase in the number of state employees, and a large increase in the funding of higher education.

In 1976 he fell sixty votes short of defeating President GERALD R. FORD for the Republican nomination for the presidency. In 1980 he defeated five other candidates to capture the nomination, and he won the presidential election by a landslide of 489 electoral votes. In 1984 he was reelected, this time taking the votes of forty-nine of the fifty states and emerging in a position to put his stamp on the judiciary of the nation.

Three themes characterize President Reagan's approach to the Constitution. They are the necessity of moral virtue if American democracy is to work; the importance of FEDERALISM; and the guiding force of American practices approved by the Founding Fathers. These themes run through Reagan's public pronouncements on a variety of specific topics bearing on constitutional law. For example, he has seen the solution to the problem of curbing crime in America as first restoring a sense of moral seriousness to the criminal trial, so that it is not seen as a bureaucratized bargaining process. At the same time, he has criticized courts for taking on tasks for which they are unfitted and so slighting their essential role of determining guilt or innocence; and he has proposed legislation limiting the use of HABEAS CORPUS review of state courts by federal judges.

Traditional functions for the courts, less federal supervision, an infusion of moral purpose—these are remedies that Reagan sees as congruent with the Constitution even as interpreted by the Supreme Court. For another example, he has opposed the imposition of RACIAL QUOTAS in EDUCATION, hiring, or housing, even when the quotas are disguised as AFFIRMATIVE ACTION. Belief in equality under the law does not in his view require reverse discrimination. Nothing in a Constitution he sees as colorblind supports a contrary conclusion. In other areas his views require constitutional amendment.

Religion is the foundation of morality, and morality is inseparable from government—this note in American politics is as old as WASHINGTON'S FAREWELL ADDRESS, which Reagan has frequently invoked. In Reagan's own words, "We poison our society when we remove its theological underpinnings," and again, "Without God there is no virtue because there is no prompting of conscience."

From this perspective, the Court-compelled exclusion of religious exercises from the public schools is disastrous and is unwarranted by the Constitution, which, Reagan has repeatedly remarked, says nothing about public education or prayer. In Reagan's words, the FIRST AMENDMENT "was not meant to exclude religion from our schools." Reagan has affirmed his belief in a "wall of separation" between church and state. In an American tradition as old as ROGER WILLIAMS, he sees the primary function of that wall as protecting religion from governmental intrusion. The Supreme Court, in his view, has been guilty of such intrusion.

Federalism influences this approach. The Supreme Court, interpreting the Constitution, often conceives of itself as though it were a superior, benign, and neutral agency that is not part of the national government. Reagan has cut through this position and identified the Court as the champion of a particular ideology, imposing uniform requirements in disregard of local custom. Justified where there was a national mandate to eliminate RACIAL DISCRIMINATION, the Court has acted in this way even, he believes, where it has discovered no national mandate. Reagan's criticism of the Court on RELIGION IN THE PUBLIC SCHOOLS not only affirms earlier American traditions; it also reflects attachment to the local autonomy that federalism fosters.

The religion Reagan refers to is biblical religion, described by him as "our Judaeo-Christian heritage." He quotes both Old and New Testaments in his public addresses. The Ten Commandments, he has observed, have not been improved upon by the millions of laws enacted since their promulgation. He issued a proclamation of National Bible Week and rejoiced that twenty-five states followed suit. He sees no constitutional barrier to a believer, as President, acknowledging the God of the Bible, speaking of the moral values he derives from his belief in God, and taking seriously such slogans as "one nation under God" and "in God we trust."

Public testimony to moral values based on religion has been conjoined with insistent rejection of religious intolerance. Reagan has consistently denounced bigotry, but he contends that those who have excluded biblical religion from the schools are themselves "intolerant of religion." They have denied a freedom to exercise religion as old as the practice of prayers in legislatures, the employment of chaplains by the military, and the invocation of God before opening any court. Such American traditions are his guide to the meaning of the Constitution in an area crucial for him in the formation of morality.

Critical of the Supreme Court's individual decisions in a manner sanctioned by the example of THOMAS JEFFERSON, ABRAHAM LINCOLN, and FRANKLIN D. ROOSEVELT, Reagan has not denied the Court's authority. He has favored correction of the prayer decision by the adoption of a constitutional amendment permitting voluntary group prayer in the schools. The government in his view should tolerate and accommodate the religious beliefs, speech, and conduct of the people; it should not direct their religious beliefs, speech, or conduct. For that reason, Reagan's school prayer amendment expressly prohibits any governmental role in composing the words of prayers to be said in the public schools.

The constitutional right to abortion, announced by the Supreme Court in ROE V. WADE (1973), has been the object of repeated criticism by Reagan. He has taken the extraordinary step, for a sitting President, of publishing a book, *Abortion and the Conscience of a Nation* (1984), in which he declares that "there is no cause more important than affirming the transcendent right to life of all human beings, the right without which no other rights have any meaning." On January 22, 1985, the twelfth anniversary of *Roe v. Wade,* he addressed the prolife march in Washington as the marchers prepared once again to ask the Supreme Court to change its position, and told them that he was "proud to stand with you in the long march to protect life." No other constitutional decision of the Supreme Court has been so vigorously, persistently, and personally condemned by an American President.

Reagan has consciously used the presidency as "a bully pulpit" to proclaim that there is no proof that the child in the womb is *not* human; that the child in midterm and later abortion feels pain; and that over 4,000 such children are killed every day in America, 15,000,000 in the first decade since ROE V. WADE. Such facts alone, he believes, will make most people reconsider and seek reversal of *Roe.*

How the reversal is accomplished has not been a matter of great concern to Reagan. He endorsed reversal by amendment of the Constitution. He attempted to persuade the Senate to end a FILIBUSTER that killed the Helms Bill that would have used Congress's power under section 5 of the FOURTEENTH AMENDMENT to define life as including the unborn. Passage of the bill (itself without sanctions) would undoubtedly have led to state legislation on abortion that would have given the Supreme Court the opportunity of looking at abortion in the light of the congressional definition. It has been speculated that Reagan believes the most practical way of effecting the result he desires is by his appointments to the Supreme Court.

In the cases of abortion and of prayer, Reagan has sought amendments reversing Supreme Court decisions that upset traditional balances. In the case of the balanced BUDGET, he has asked for something new, a constitutional restraint that would prevent federal expenditures exceeding federal revenues. The desirability of such an amendment had, however, been voiced as early as 1798 by Thomas Jefferson. In Reagan's view, a balanced budget amendment could be a powerful tool for reducing the federal establishment and restoring economic power to the states. Federalism would be enhanced by its enactment. The traditional role of the states would very likely be increased. Reagan also perceives a moral element: habitual deficit spending by the federal government is an easy evasion of responsibility. In his second Inaugural Address, on January 21, 1985, Reagan called for passage of the Balanced Budget Amendment.

Citizens and Presidents must interpret the Constitution as well as lawyers and judges. President Reagan's approach to the Constitution is not dependent on the reasoning advanced by recent Justices of the Supreme Court to justify or rationalize their decisions. He has employed older and broader criteria. For him the Constitution does not mean the gloss put upon it by opinions of the Court but the original document illumined by tangible traditions and by reflection on its foundation in moral realities. He has evidenced a strong commitment to the essentials that the Constitution presupposes and at the same time preserves.

JOHN T. NOONAN, JR.

Bibliography

REAGAN, RONALD 1984 *Abortion and the Conscience of a Nation.* New York: Thomas Nelson.

REAGAN, RONALD 1981–1985 *Presidential Papers.* Washington, D.C.: Government Printing Office.

SMITH, HEDRICK; CLYMER, ADAM; SILK, LEONARD; LINDSEY, ROBERT; AND BURT, RICHARD 1980 *Reagan the Man, the President.* New York: Macmillan.

WHITE, F. CLIFTON 1980 *Why Reagan Won: A Narrative History of the Conservative Movement.* Chicago: Regnery Gateway.

REAGAN v. FARMERS' LOAN & TRUST CO.

154 U.S. 362 (1894)

In a grotesque opinion the Supreme Court unanimously held unconstitutional a rate schedule fixed by a state railroad commission. Justice DAVID BREWER for the Court had no doubt that the economic validity of rates was subject to JUDICIAL REVIEW, and he found that these rates were "unjust and unreasonable," meaning too low in the estimate of the Court. They resulted, he said with exaggeration, in "a practical destruction to rights of property." Four years later, in SMYTH V. AMES (1898), the Court finally adopted SUBSTANTIVE DUE PROCESS as the basis for such a ruling, but in this case the Court seemed unready to embrace such an extravagant position, despite previous flirtations with it. Here the Court cast about for something more familiar and found it in the concepts of EQUAL PROTECTION and JUST COMPENSATION, which it united. The difficulty was that the just compensation clause of the Fifth Amendment bound only the national government, not the states, and it applied only in cases of EMINENT DOMAIN, when private property was taken for a PUBLIC PURPOSE. Nothing of that sort had happened here. Brewer, however, declared that the commission's rates denied "equal protection which is the constitutional right of all owners of other property," and then he ruled that the equal protection clause "forbids legislation . . . by which the property of one individual is, without compensation, wrested from him for the benefit of another, or of the public." Thus the Court incorporated the substance of the just compensation clause of the Fifth Amendment into the Fourteenth for the benefit of railroads, though the Court refused in other cases of this period to incorporate into the FOURTEENTH AMENDMENT the rights that protected accused persons or victims of RACIAL DISCRIMINATION. (See INCORPORATION DOCTRINE.) Moreover, this was not a case of eminent domain and the property of the railroad was not "wrested" without compensation. More rationally, Brewer sought to devise an economic test for determining the reasonableness of a rate schedule: whether the rate was equivalent to the market value of the use of the property. That economists found such a test to be unsound was not so significant as the Court's arrogating to itself the power to determine reasonableness by economic criteria that thrust it into judgments better suited to legislative and administrative agencies. (See ECONOMIC REGULATION AND THE CONSTITUTION.)

LEONARD W. LEVY

REAL EVIDENCE

Real evidence is supplied by a thing that is inspected by the jury, or other trier of fact. (Statements by witnesses are called testimonial evidence.) The acquisition and use of real evidence in the criminal process intersects with constitutional doctrine in various ways. For example, the EXCLUSIONARY RULE may forbid the offering of evidence—such as a gun or a bag containing marijuana—that has been obtained in an unconstitutional SEARCH AND SEIZURE. Correspondingly, the probability that such real evidence will be found in a particular place may, under the doctrine of PROBABLE CAUSE, justify the issuance of a SEARCH WARRANT.

KENNETH L. KARST

REAPPORTIONMENT

Direct democracy is not possible in a nation as populous as the United States is now, or even as it was in 1787 when the Constitution of the United States was drafted. Accordingly, the objective was then, and is now, to devise and implement as fair and effective a plan of democratic REPRESENTATION as possible.

The idea of fair and effective representation at each level of government was not new in 1787. The search for such a formula lies at the center of Anglo-American political thought. In 1690 JOHN LOCKE sought to abolish England's rotten boroughs by urging that, "it being the interest as well as the intention of the people, to have a fair and equal representation, whoever brings it nearest to that is an undoubted friend to and establisher of the government, and cannot miss the consent and approbation of the community."

Although Britain did not put an end to its rotten boroughs until near the middle of the twentieth century, the issue of how best to structure a truly representative government was very much alive at the time the various proposals for the American Constitution were being debated. At last a compromise was struck in the CONSTITUTIONAL CONVENTION OF 1787, giving equal representation to each state in the Senate and representation based on population in the House of Representatives. Article I, section 2, of the Constitution provides that "Representatives . . . shall be apportioned among the several states . . . according to their respective numbers . . . ," with recomputation of the apportionment every ten years, and each state to have at least one representative regardless of population. But the task of fixing the formula for the apportioning process was left to Congress, and no directions at all were established to guide the states in the parallel function of allocating seats in the state legislature or in local governmental bodies. We are not, however, left entirely in doubt about what Congress thought appropriate for apportionment in the states. The NORTHWEST ORDINANCE of 1787 provided that representation in the territorial legislatures to be created in that area should be based on population. In general, the states accepted the principle of reasonably equal population among legislative districts, but the principle was often modified by assurances of at least one representative from each county or township or municipality. Departures from population equality may not have been egregious in this time of mostly rural dispersal; but by the late nineteenth and early twentieth centuries what had once been minor deviations became major divergences.

JOHN QUINCY ADAMS observed in 1839 that the division of sovereign powers between the states and the nation, as set out in the Constitution, gave us "the most complicated government on the face of the globe." The twentieth century has proved how right he was. The interaction between increasingly potent national and state governments, frequently aggravated by friction arising out of competition for power, has produced a delicately balanced division of power and a complexity of relationships probably unsurpassed in the history of governmental institutions.

Yet it is the proud boast of FEDERALISM in the United States that the governments of the fifty states and that of the nation can work together in common purpose rather than in a relationship of competition and mistrust. Moreover, it is a basic premise of representative democracy in the United States that the people are entitled to representation somewhat in proportion to their numbers, at every level of government. The tradition of majority rule cannot otherwise be attained. Neither the division of sovereign powers prescribed in the federal system nor the fairness of legislative representation formulas can long be left unattended. Vigilant superintendence by an informed electorate is essential.

Even the wisest political scientists have difficulty in defining the precise meaning of representative democracy. There is, however, general agreement that representative democracy in the United States includes something of liberty, equality, and majority rule. Even though these qualities are scarcely less abstract, it can surely be said that representative democracy relates to the processes by which citizens exert control over their leaders. From the time of the Constitutional Convention debate has centered on the extent to which, and the ways in which, majority control over leaders should be exercised. Congress has wrestled with the issue, with inconclusive results. In 1842, for example, Congress required each state to establish compact, contiguous, single-member congressional districts as nearly equal in population as possible. These criteria, however, lapsed in 1911. In any event, no enforcement method had been established, and the courts considered the issue none of their business.

Not until more than a hundred years after the RATIFICATION OF THE CONSTITUTION in 1789 did such states as California, Illinois, Michigan, New York, Ohio, and Pennsylvania, responding to new pressures, abandon the equal-population principle in one or both houses. So widespread had been the original acceptance of the equality concept that no fewer than thirty-six of the original state constitutions provided that representation in both houses of the state legislature would be based completely, or predominantly, on population. Between 1790 and 1889 no state was admitted to the Union in which its original constitution did not provide for representation principally based on population in both houses of the state legislature.

To speak of the equal-population principle as the basis for apportionment of those nineteenth-century legislatures is not to say that there was mathematically precise equality among the districts at that time. The western states, for example, commonly relied on county lines in drawing their apportionment formulas. The distortions that resulted from assuring each county at least one representative, for example, or from grouping whole counties to form election districts, were much less pronounced in agricultural and rural America than in present-day industrial and urban America. The population of the United States, outside the few great commercial centers in the East, was spread thinly across the face of the country.

The drift from relative equality to substantial inequality would have moved at about the same pace as the shift in population from rural to urban America; and that would have been bad enough. But some states accelerated the trend away from the equality principle by other devices as well. As state legislatures were enlarged, additional seats were granted to the areas of new growth without diminishing representation of the declining population areas. As the population of rural areas declined, state legislatures abandoned even the formal acceptance of equal population as a controlling principle, typically guaranteeing each county (or township) one representative. Some states, unable or unwilling to change the constitutional requirement for equality among districts, simply ignored the mandate for decennial change. (Tennessee is a good example; the state constitutional requirement of reapportionment every ten years was ignored between 1901 and 1961, giving rise in 1962 to BAKER V. CARR.)

The consequence of these factors, singly or in combination, was by the middle of the twentieth century a remarkable skewing of voter impact, ordinarily giving the less populated areas of a state a disproportionate influence in legislative representation. The impact was most marked at the state and local legislative levels, but not without considerable influence on congressional districting as well.

By the middle of the twentieth century the disparities in legislative representation were marked. Thus, in the then ninety-nine state legislative chambers (forty-nine bicameral legislatures plus the Nebraska unicameral legislature), thirty-two relied in large part on population; eight used population, but with weighted ratios; forty-five combined population and area considerations; eight granted representation to each unit; five had fixed constitutional apportionments; and one (the New Hampshire Senate) was based on state tax payments. These conclusions somewhat understate the actual disregard of population as the basis of representation because this summary is drawn exclusively from the state constitutional requirements, without adjustment for violation of those provisions.

The time has come to ask: what is (re)apportionment and what is (re)districting? The question is well put, for the terms are sometimes (confusingly) used interchangeably. But there is a difference. Apportionment is ordinarily described as the allocation of legislative seats by a legislative body to a subordinate unit of government, and districting as the process of drawing the final lines by which each legislative district is bounded. Thus, Congress apportions the number of congressional districts to which each state is entitled, based on population figures disclosed at each decennial census. Each state legislature then draws lines that divide the state into as many congressional districts as have been allocated to it by Congress.

State legislatures, on the other hand, both apportion the distribution of state legislative seats *and* draw the district lines that determine which voters will make each selection. Therein lies the problem, clearly rooted in the political ambition of each political group to overcome its opposition, before the voting begins, on the basis of the dispersion of voters eligible to vote for one candidate rather than another.

By the early 1960s the act and the impact of malapportionment were everywhere apparent, typically to the apparent disadvantage of individual voters in heavily populated districts and to the apparent advantage of voters in sparsely populated districts. Despite the fact that many state constitutions required reapportionment every ten years and included formulas requiring approximate population equality, no legislative chamber came closer to that goal than two to one, and the disparity between most populous to least populous district was in many states more than ten to one and in several more than one hundred to one. To put the matter another way, in twelve states fewer than twenty percent of the voters lived in districts that elected a majority of the state senators, and in seven states fewer than thirty percent of the voters lived in districts that elected a majority of the members of the lower house.

State courts occasionally acted to deal with the most egregious abuses, but the federal courts, until 1962, adamantly refused to intervene. Although the Supreme Court had long recognized the right of citizens to vote free of arbitrary impairment by STATE ACTION when such impairment resulted from dilution by false tally or by stuffing of the ballot box, the Court had declined to deal with apportionment and districting abuses on the grounds that the issue was not justiciable, that is, not appropriate for federal judicial intervention. As Justice FELIX FRANKFURTER said in COLEGROVE V. GREEN (1946), "Courts ought not to enter this political thicket."

Finally, the case of interference with the exercise of the franchise was made so clearly that a majority of the Court was persuaded that only federal judicial intervention could put an end to this denial of equality. The case that triggered this change in attitude provided a dramatic illustration of flagrant abuse of voter rights by a state legislature that had openly flouted its own state constitution for more than half a century.

The Tennessee Constitution had required, since 1870, that the number of senators and representatives in the general assembly "be apportioned among the several counties or districts, according to the number of qualified electors in each. . . ." Moreover, the state constitution required reapportionment in accordance with the equal-population standard every ten years. Between 1901 and 1961, however, the legislature had not acted on the matter. As a result, thirty-seven percent of the Tennessee voters lived in districts that elected twenty of the thirty-three senators, and forty percent of the voters lived in districts that elected sixty-three of the ninety-nine members of the lower house. The federal court challenge was brought by voters in urban areas of the state, who invoked the Constitution of the United States and claimed that they had been denied the EQUAL PROTECTION OF THE LAWS, "by virtue of the debasement of their votes."

The resulting Supreme Court decision, *Baker v. Carr,* did not rule on the substance of the equality claim, but did hold that the issue was properly within the JURISDICTION OF THE FEDERAL COURTS and was justiciable. Only Justices Frankfurter and JOHN MARSHALL HARLAN dissented.

Within two years the Supreme Court signaled how it would decide the equality issue. GRAY V. SANDERS (1963), while not strictly an apportionment case, involved the closely related issue of voter discrimination. The election practice there challenged was the Georgia "county-unit" system, as it applied to statewide primaries: a candidate for nomination who received the highest number of popular votes in a county was considered to have carried the county and to be entitled to two votes for each representative to which the county was entitled in the lower house of the general assembly. The majority of the county unit vote was required to nominate a candidate for United States senator or state governor, while a plurality was sufficient for nomination of candidates for other offices. Because the most populous county (Fulton, with a 1960 population of 556,326) had only six unit votes, while the least populous county (Echols, with a 1960 population of 1,876) had two unit votes, "one resident in Echols County had an influence in the nomination of candidates equivalent to 99 residents of Fulton County."

Georgia argued that, because the ELECTORAL COLLEGE permitted substantial inequalities in voter representation in a "winner-take-all" system, parallel systems should be permitted to the states. Moreover, the state argued that because United States senators represent widely divergent numbers of voters, the same should be permitted in one house of a state legislature. But the Supreme Court rejected all such analogies as inapposite: "The inclusion of the electoral college in the Constitution, as the result of specific historical concerns, validated the collegiate principle despite its inherent numerical inequality, but implied nothing about the use of an analogous system by a State in a statewide election. No such specific accommodation of the latter was ever undertaken, and therefore no validation of its numerical equality ensued."

While conceding that states "can within limits specify the qualifications of voters both in state and federal elections," the Court denied that a state is entitled to weight the votes "once the geographical unit for which a representative is to be chosen is designated. . . ." Accordingly, the Court concluded: "The conception of political equality from the DECLARATION OF INDEPENDENCE, to Lincoln's Gettysburg Address to the FIFTEENTH, SEVENTEENTH and NINETEENTH AMENDMENTS can mean only one thing—ONE PERSON, ONE VOTE." The fatal defect in the Georgia plan was that the votes were weighted on the basis of geography as an expression of legislative preference for rural over urban voters.

The next franchise case decided by the Supreme Court with full opinion, WESBERRY V. SANDERS (1964), was also not a state legislative apportionment case; it was a congressional districting case not very dissimilar from *Colegrove v. Green*—except in result. Plaintiffs were qualified voters of Fulton County, Georgia, entitled to vote in the state's fifth congressional district, which had a 1960 population of 823,680, as compared with the 272,154 residents of the ninth district.

After the decision in *Baker v. Carr,* the Court had little difficulty deciding that such issues were justiciable in federal courts. The substantive ruling, however, came as something of a surprise. Plaintiffs had argued principally that the gross population disparities violated the equal protection clause of the FOURTEENTH AMENDMENT. The Supreme Court, however, adopted what had been a subordinate contention, that the Georgia arrangement violated Article I, section 2, of the Constitution, which prescribed that representatives be chosen "by the People of the several States." Justice HUGO L. BLACK, writing for the majority of six, stated that this provision, when construed in its historical context, means "that as nearly as practicable one man's vote in a congressional election is to be worth as much as another's. . . . To say that a vote is worth more in one district than in another would not only run counter to our fundamental ideas of democratic government, it would cast aside the principle of a House of Representatives elected 'by the People,' a principle tenaciously fought for and established at the Constitutional Convention." That result, at first surprising in view of the nonspecific constitutional text, was well supported in the Court's review of the relevant history. For example, at the Constitutional Convention JAMES WILSON of Pennsylvania had said that "equal numbers of people ought to have an equal number of representatives," and representatives "of different districts ought clearly to hold the same proportion to each other, as their respective constituents hold to each other."

Reliance on section 2 of Article I rather than on the equal protection clause has had significant consequences. From that date forward the Court has been less tolerant of population variations among congressional districts than of those in state legislative districts, as to which the population-equality principle has, since REYNOLDS V. SIMS (1964), been based on the equal protection clause of the Fourteenth Amendment.

Reynolds v. Sims and its five companion cases completed the original round of apportionment and districting cases and constituted the foundation on which all subsequent litigation has built. On June 15, 1964, the Court invalidated the state legislative apportionment and districting structure in Alabama (the *Reynolds* case), Colorado, Delaware, Maryland, New York, and Virginia. One week later the Court struck down the formulas in nine additional states, foretelling a complete reapportionment revolution.

Reynolds v. Sims was illustrative. The complaint in that case alleged that the last legislative reapportionment in the state had been based on the 1900 federal census despite a state constitutional requirement for decennial reapportionment. Accordingly, because the population growth had been uneven, urban counties were severely disadvantaged by the state legislature's failure to reapportion every ten years and by the state constitution's provision requiring each of the sixty-seven counties to have at least one representative in the lower house with a membership of 106. The Supreme Court of the United States ruled unequivocally in favor of the equal-population principle: "We hold that, as a basic constitutional standard, the Equal Protection Clause requires that the seats in both houses of a bicameral state legislature must be apportioned on a population basis. Simply stated, an individual's right to vote for state legislators is unconstitutionally impaired when its weight is in a substantial fashion diluted when compared with votes of citizens living in other parts of the state."

The decisions in *Wesberry* and *Reynolds* required adjustment of congressional districting practices in all states (except the few states with only one representative each) and of all state legislative districting practices. Despite considerable adverse reaction in the beginning and substantial litigation to determine the full significance of the decisions, by and large compliance was secured; and further adjustments were made after the results of the 1970 and 1980 censuses were determined.

Two principal types of questions remained to be worked out after the first decisions were announced: how equal is "equal" in congressional districting and in state legislative apportionment and districting? and to what extent does the equal-population principle apply to the thousands of local governmental units and the even larger number of special districts that serve multitudinous quasi-governmental purposes?

Despite criticism of the *Reynolds* decision based on an assumption that the Court had demanded mathematical exactness among election districts, the Court explicitly acknowledged the permissibility of some variation: "We realize that it is a practical impossibility to arrange legislative districts so that each one has an identical number of residents, or citizens, or voters. Mathematical exactness or precision is hardly a workable constitutional requirement." The important obligation is for each state to "make an honest and good faith effort to construct districts, in both houses of its legislature, as nearly of equal population as is practicable."

From the beginning the *Reynolds* Court acknowledged that states could continue to place some reliance on political subdivision lines, at least in drawing the lines for state legislative bodies. "Since almost invariably there is a significantly larger number of seats in state legislative bodies to be distributed within a state than congressional seats, it may be feasible to use political subdivision lines to a greater extent in establishing state legislative districts than in congressional districting while still affording adequate representation to all parts of the State." A further reason for at least limited adherence to local political subdivision lines is the highly pragmatic proposition that, to do otherwise, "[i]ndiscriminate districting, without any regard for political subdivisions, may be little more than an invitation to partisan gerrymandering."

Acknowledging the principle that population deviations are permissible in state districting implementation of rational state policy, the Supreme Court has recognized that de minimis numerical deviations are unavoidable. Maximum deviations in Connecticut of 7.83 percent among house districts and 1.81 percent among senate districts were upheld in *Gaffney v. Cummings* (1973). Texas deviations of 9.9 and 1.82 percent respectively among house and senate districts were similarly approved in *White v. Regester* (1973). In MAHAN V. HOWELL (1973) the Court upheld a Virginia plan despite a maximum deviation of 16.4 percent, on the grounds that the plan could "reasonably be said to advance the rational state policy of respecting the boundaries of political subdivisions," but cautioned that "this percentage may well approach tolerable limits."

The requirement of population equality is far more exacting in the drawing of congressional district lines. In *Kirkpatrick v. Preisler* (1969) the Court struck down Missouri's 1967 Redistricting Act despite the fact that the most populous district was 3.13 percent larger and the least populous 2.84 percent smaller than the average district. In explanation the Court stated, "Since 'equal representation for equal numbers of people [is] the fundamental goal for the House of Representatives,' the 'as nearly as practicable' standard requires that the State make a good faith effort to achieve precise mathematical equality. Unless population variances among congressional districts are shown to have resulted despite such effort, the State must justify each variance, no matter how small." In *Karcher v. Daggett* (1983) the Supreme Court invalidated a deviation of less than one percent among New Jersey congressional districts because the state had failed to make "a good-faith effort to achieve precise mathematical equality" in population among its congressional districts. In sum, because local units of government are less important as factors in the representation of relatively large numbers of persons in the Congress than for smaller numbers of persons in the state legislature, population deviations among congressional districts are strictly scrutinized, while a more tolerant review is accorded state districting. But even in state districting the excesses of the past are no longer tolerable; above the *de minimis* level deviations must be held within narrow limits and must be justified in terms of preservation of political subdivisions, compactness and contiguity of districts, and respect for natural or historical boundaries.

No matter how close the judicial superintendence of population equality, one problem remains. In congressional and state legislative districting alike, even the most exact adherence to the equal-population principle does not assure protection against legislative line-drawers who seek partisan advantage out of the process. "Gerrymander" is the term used to describe such efforts to preserve partisan power or to extend such power through manipulative use of the process. The term originated in 1812 in Massachusetts, where political maneuvering had produced a salamander-shaped district which was named after ELBRIDGE GERRY, then governor. From that time forward the gerrymander has been an altogether too-common fact of American political life. Nevertheless, despite repeated attempts to persuade the Supreme Court to enter this new "political thicket," the Court has denied that there is any constitutional ground for superintending the apportionment and districting process other than the equal-population principle. Accordingly, the states remain free, so far as the United States Constitution is concerned, to construct congressional and state legislative districts that resemble salamanders or other equally peculiar creatures. And many state legislatures have done just that, particularly where one party is in secure control of the state legislative process. Where party control of the two houses of a bicameral legislature is divided, or where the governor is of a different party, the drawing of congressional and state legislative district lines is likely to be worked out by political compromise or, that failing, by the courts.

More seemly alternatives are possible, but they are not often adopted in the absence of JUDICIAL REVIEW over the process except as to population equality among districts. Congress has the authority to set standards of compactness and contiguity that would avoid the worst abuses and could be enforced in the courts. State legislatures could adopt similar standards to control the process within their own states, but few political leaders are willing to relinquish the prospect of present or future partisan advantage to be secured out of the districting process.

Like state legislative districting, the districting of counties, municipalities, or other local governmental units is constitutionally permitted to deviate to some extent from full equality if it can be demonstrated that the governmental unit has made "an honest and good faith effort" to construct districts "as nearly of equal population as practicable." Local governments may use MULTIMEMBER DISTRICTS if there is a history of such representation and if such plans are not part of a deliberate attempt to dilute or cancel the voting strength of racial or political elements in the governmental unit. Despite that limitation, local governments, like states, may use ethnic or minority population data in constructing districts designed to elect representatives of that minority or ethnic group. (See UNITED JEWISH ORGANIZATION V. CAREY, 1977.)

Supreme Court intervention in the apportionment and districting process has unquestionably restructured congressional and state legislative representation. Gross population disparities among election districts have been evened out so that the democratic promise of fair representation has been made possible of realization. But no court, even so powerful a body as the Supreme Court of the United States, can assure democratic representation. The ultimate test of the democratic process will depend upon the level of concern of the voters and their willingness to insist that their legislative representatives take whatever action is necessary to prevent excesses.

There are two principal types of gerrymandering, both of which should be controlled. The bipartisan or "incumbent survival" plan is designed to assure as far as possible the reelection of incumbents, sometimes regardless of party affiliation; the technique is to distribute party registration or proven party supporters to the legislators who will benefit most. The partisan plan is designed to maintain or increase the number of seats held by the majority party; the technique is to "waste" votes of the opposition party either by concentrating the voters loyal to that party in as few districts as possible, or by dispersing the opposition voting strength among a number of districts in which it cannot command majorities. Control of these abuses is not likely to come from party leadership. Voters concerned with the integrity of the process must demand an end to such practices, calling for state constitutional amendments or statutes requiring that districts be compact and contiguous.

Redistricting should be a matter of special concern for ethnic and racial minorities, many of whom are concentrated in urban centers. Typically, minority spokesmen claim that fair representation requires districts that will elect members of their own groups. When legislatures act to meet such demands, other groups are likely to feel disadvantaged. That issue was litigated to the Supreme Court in *United Jewish Organization v. Carey.* In that case a New York redistricting plan had been modified to bring it into compliance with the VOTING RIGHTS ACT OF 1965. In the process the act divided a community of Hasidic Jews in order to establish several substantially nonwhite districts. The Court upheld the plan, ruling that such a use of racial criteria was justified in fulfillment of congressional legislative policy in the Voting Rights Act.

Somewhat related to the issue just discussed is the question whether municipalities and other local legislative bodies should be permitted to require at-large elections for all the seats in the legislative unit. Such a practice may make it impossible for a minority group in the community to secure representation, even though one or more members of that minority might be elected if single-member districts were used. The Supreme Court held, in MOBILE V. BOLDEN (1980), that multimember district elections would be tolerated, even where the impact on minority groups was demonstrated, unless it could be shown that the plan was adopted with racially discriminatory intent. However, the Voting Rights Act of 1982 overturned that ruling; under the act, invidious intent need not be shown if impact disadvantageous to identifiable minorities can be established.

In the era before the application of computer technology to politics, it was common for politicians and their staffs to spread out maps on office floors, using adding machines for their arithmetic, slowly building new districts from census tracts and precinct figures. Because most redistricting decisions must be made sequentially—one boundary change requires another, which requires yet another—the computer is perfectly designed to speed the process and allow for more sophisticated analysis. The computer not only makes available numerical population counts, voter history, and party registration, but also permits a graphic display of the areas represented.

These technical advances have resulted in what may be styled the second reapportionment revolution. They place in the hands of those responsible for redistricting a vast array of information for use in drawing district lines. It follows, for better or for worse, that the computer's twin features of speed and accuracy can advance the goal of "fair and effective representation" as well as engineer the nearly perfect gerrymander.

At the time of the reapportionment decisions of the early 1960s, commentators speculated about the decisions' likely impact on the representational process. The most common prediction was that the urban areas would dominate state legislatures, with a general tendency toward liberal legislative policies. It is by no means clear that this prediction has come true. Enlarged influence of the suburbs, often with a conservative representation and not infrequently allied with rural representatives, has been the more typical reality. The one thing that can be said with confidence is that adoption of the equal-population principle has ended the worst abuses and assured basic fairness in the most important features of the democratic process.

ROBERT B. MCKAY

Bibliography

ADAMS, BRUCE 1977 A Model State Reapportionment Process: The Continuing Quest for "Fair and Effective Representation." *Harvard Journal on Legislation* 14:825–904.

COMMON CAUSE 1977 *Reapportionment: A Better Way.* Washington, D.C.: Common Cause.

DIXON, ROBERT G. 1968 *Democratic Representation: Reapportionment in Law and Politics.* New York: Oxford University Press.

GROFMAN, BERNARD; LIJPHART, AREND; MCKAY, ROBERT B.; and SCARROW, HOWARD (EDS.) 1981 *Representation and Redistricting Issues.* Lexington, Mass.: D. C. Heath.

MCKAY, ROBERT B. 1965 *Reapportionment: The Law and Politics of Equal Representation.* New York: Twentieth Century Fund.

POLSBY, NELSON, ED. 1971 *Reapportionment in the 1970s.* Berkeley: University of California Press.

REASONABLE DOUBT

Proof beyond a reasonable doubt is the highest level of proof demanded in American courts. It is the usual standard for criminal cases, and in criminal litigation it has constitutional grounding in decisions of the United States Supreme Court. Although the reasonable doubt standard is not often used in noncriminal settings, there are exceptional situations, usually where liberty is placed in jeopardy, when a JURISDICTION will borrow the criminal standard of proof for a civil case.

Any standard of proof chosen by an American court recognizes that in all litigation there is the chance of a mistake. If opposing litigants agree on the various matters that constitute their case, usually the case is settled. There is little for a judge or a jury to do. Once a dispute arises, however, adversaries offer conflicting EVIDENCE and conflicting interpretations of evidence to decision makers. Rarely, if ever, is there a dispute in which every witness and every aspect of physical and scientific evidence presented by opposing parties point with perfect certainty to one specific conclusion. Witnesses may suffer from ordinary human frailties—they have memory problems; they sometimes confuse facts; they see events differently from each other; they have biases and prejudices that call into question their judgment; and they may be frightened and have trouble communicating on the witness stand. Physical evidence might be damaged or destroyed and thus of minimal or no use at trial. Or, it might be difficult to connect physical evidence with the parties before the court. Even scientific tests often provide little more than probabilities concerning the relationship of evidence to the issues in a case.

Were judges and juries required to decide cases on the basis of absolute certainty about what occurred, it is doubtful that they ever would find the standard satisfied. Whoever was required to prove the case would always lose. Recognizing that absolute certainty is not reasonably possible, American courts have chosen to demand less. How much less determines the extent to which they are willing to accept the risk of error in the course of litigation.

In criminal cases the typical requirement is that the government must prove the essential elements of any offense it chooses to charge beyond a reasonable doubt. This means that, although the decision maker need not be certain that a defendant is guilty before convicting, any reasonable doubt requires that it find the defendant not guilty. Such a standard allocates most of the risk of error in criminal cases to the state. It cannot assure that no innocent person will ever be convicted, but the standard is demanding enough to make it most unlikely that someone who is actually innocent will be found guilty. It is more likely that truly guilty persons may go free, but that is the price American criminal justice pays to avoid mistakes that harm the innocent.

It is uncertain when this standard of proof was first used in criminal cases. In early England, whether or not a person would be convicted depended on his ability to produce compurgators or to avoid misfortune in an ordeal. Subsequently, success turned on whether or not a suspect could succeed in trial by combat. As trial by jury replaced other forms of proof, the jurors originally decided cases on the basis of their own knowledge, and even if they relied on informants, the jurors themselves were responsible for the accuracy of the facts. Not until the notion of an independent fact finder, typically a jury, developed was a standard of proof very meaningful. With the development of the independent and neutral fact finder, the "beyond a reasonable doubt" concept took on importance.

Although there is no mention of the proof beyond a reasonable doubt concept in the United States Constitution, trial by jury is in all but petty cases guaranteed by the Sixth Amendment, and with the Supreme Court's decision in DUNCAN V. LOUISIANA (1968), this right is now binding on the states. By the time the Sixth Amendment was adopted, proof beyond a reasonable doubt was closely associated with the right to an impartial jury guaranteed by the Constitution in criminal cases.

Thus, it is not surprising that the Supreme Court has found the proof beyond a reasonable doubt standard to be constitutionally required in criminal cases with respect to all essential elements of offenses charged, whether the criminal case is litigated in state or federal court (IN RE WINSHIP, 1970). The Court associated the high proof standard with the strong presumption of innocence in criminal cases and observed that before a defendant may be stigmatized by criminal conviction and punished for criminal wrongdoing, DUE PROCESS requires the state to prove guilt beyond a reasonable doubt. (See JACKSON V. VIRGINIA, 1979).

There is little agreement on exactly what a reasonable doubt is. No single definition of reasonable doubt has ever gained acceptance in American courts. There does seem to be some consensus that a decision maker should understand that a reasonable doubt is one based in reason as applied to the proof offered in a case. This elaboration of the standard is consistent with the oath that judges administer to jurors who are called upon to decide a case. Beyond this, it is difficult to define the term. Any language that is used is likely to be challenged as being either too demanding or not demanding enough.

Judges and juries have come to know that the proof beyond a reasonable doubt standard represents American regard for liberty and the dignity of the individual who stands against the state and who seeks to preserve his freedom and independence. A reasonable doubt will protect him.

STEPHEN A. SALTZBURG

(SEE ALSO: *Burden of Proof.*)

Bibliography

KALVEN, HARRY, JR. and ZEISEL, HANS 1966 *The American Jury.* Boston: Little, Brown.

TRIBE, LAURENCE H. 1971 Trial by Mathematics: Precision and Ritual in the Legal Process. *Harvard Law Review* 84:1329–1393.

REASONABLE SEARCH

See: Unreasonable Search

RECALL

Among the reforms introduced during the Progressive era was the recall, a device by which the people, at an election, can remove an official from office before his term expires. Unlike IMPEACHMENT, recall does not involve an accusation of criminality or misconduct, and it is commonly used when the official decides or acts contrary to the opinion of a significant segment of his constituency.

Although recall is widely used at the state and local levels, there is no provision for recall of national officials. Moreover, because senators and representatives hold office under the United States Constitution, they are not subject to recall under state law.

DENNIS J. MAHONEY

RECIPROCAL TAX IMMUNITIES

See: Intergovernmental Immunities

RECONSTRUCTION AMENDMENTS

See: Fifteenth Amendment; Fourteenth Amendment; Thirteenth Amendment

RED LION BROADCASTING CO. v. FEDERAL COMMUNICATIONS COMMISSION 395 U.S. 367 (1969)

The Federal Communications Commission promulgated fairness rules requiring balanced BROADCASTING on public issues. The Court answered FIRST AMENDMENT challenges by arguing that different media required different constitutional standards, and that the scarcity of frequencies both necessitated government allocation and justified requirements that allocatees insure balanced programming. Comparing *Red Lion* to MIAMI HERALD PUBLISHING CO. V. TORNILLO (1974) indicates that electronic media enjoy less editorial freedom than do the print media. As technological developments undercut the scarcity rationale, the Court shifted toward an intrusiveness-into-the-home rationale for greater regulation of broadcasters.

MARTIN SHAPIRO

(SEE ALSO: *Fairness Doctrine.*)

REED, STANLEY F.
(1884–1980)

Stanley Forman Reed, a descendant of Kentucky gentry, was educated at Kentucky Wesleyan College, Yale, Columbia, the University of Virginia, and the Sorbonne. He then returned to Maysville, Kentucky, where he entered private law practice and Democratic party politics. After serving two terms in the Kentucky General Assembly, he was called to Washington as counsel to the Federal Farm Board during HERBERT C. HOOVER's administration. His competence as a legal technician led to his promotion to general counsel to the Reconstruction Finance Corporation (RFC) and his retention at that post when FRANKLIN D. ROOSEVELT came to power. During the early years of the New Deal, Reed played an important role in the attempts at economic revival through the RFC and in the framing of new legislation by the Brain Trust. He defended New Deal measures before an unreconstructed Supreme Court, first as special counsel arguing the GOLD CLAUSE CASES and then as solicitor general from 1935 to 1938. Reed was Roosevelt's second appointee to the Supreme Court, taking office January 15, 1938, and replacing Justice GEORGE H. SUTHERLAND.

Reed was a moderate man in both personal style and constitutional views. He occupied a position of influence between the Court's liberal and conservative wings, between activists and advocates of judicial self-restraint. He was most comfortable with the majority and was willing to modify his views as the Court majority shifted. In a Court marked by strong personalities, Reed was able to maintain cordial relations with colleagues of different ideological persuasions.

Reed's opinions are not noted for ringing phrases or rigid insistence on principled positions. The discussion places great weight on the specifics of factual circumstances and often takes on a dialectic quality, a paragraph-by-paragraph dialogue between the Justice and a holder of divergent views whom Reed is trying to accommodate and coopt. The other voice may be internal; perhaps, if it is not that of the Justice himself it may belong to a defeated law clerk, echoing the heated in-chambers arguments Reed relished.

A central theme that runs through Reed's views on many constitutional issues is his willingness to uphold the exercise of governmental power by both the federal government and the states. He had faith in the good intentions of government officials, and was rarely willing to infer impermissible motives behind their actions. These attitudes are consistent with Reed's experience as the architect and legal manager of New Deal programs and as the advocate who defended these laws before a hostile Supreme Court. Justice Reed was a key part of the new majority of the Court that upheld federal regulation in the face of challenges under the DUE PROCESS clause. In dissent with Chief Justice FRED M. VINSON he was a staunch defender of presidential power in YOUNGSTOWN SHEET & TUBE COMPANY V. SAWYER (1952). Similarly, he was notably willing to defer to administrative fact-finding and interpretation of statutes.

These same attitudes can be seen in Reed's approach to CRIMINAL PROCEDURE, particularly in cases presenting claims of abusive police behavior. His deference to what he saw as another administrative agency was reinforced by the attitudes of a Mason County, Kentucky, landowner, whose experience led him to think of the police as a benevolent small-town constabulary. Beginning with his lone dissent in *United States v. McNabb* (1943), Reed deferred to the police and to state procedural rules in ways that led him to accept behavior that a majority of his colleagues found unacceptable. "I am opposed to broadening the possibilities of defendants escaping punishment by these more rigorous technical requirements on the administration of justice," he wrote in *McNabb.*

Reed occupied a pivotal position on the Court in CIVIL RIGHTS cases. He joined with and frequently wrote for the majority in vindication of the rights of blacks, including MORGAN V. VIRGINIA (1945), SMITH V. ALLWRIGHT (1943), and BROWN V. BOARD OF EDUCATION (1954). However, like a majority of his colleagues, he saw the treatment of Japanese Americans during World War II in a different light. (See JAPANESE AMERICAN CASES.)

Reed was slow to join the emerging majority during the 1940s that protected Jehovah's Witnesses in the exercise of their religion; his view on RELEASED TIME for religious instruction of public school pupils, expressed originally in his sole dissent in MCCOLLUM V. BOARD OF EDUCATION (1948), became substantially the majority position in ZORACH V. CLAUSEN (1952). He was relatively permissive of local time, place, and manner regulations of SOUNDTRUCKS in KOVACS V. COOPER (1948), but often voted with the absolutist position of Justices HUGO L. BLACK and WILLIAM O. DOUGLAS regarding other public speech issues, as he did in BEAUHARNAIS V. ILLINOIS (1952) and TERMINIELLO V. CHICAGO (1947). Nonetheless, Reed sided with the finding of necessity of police action against a public speaker in FEINER V. NEW YORK (1951).

A more consistent theme in Reed's positions was his opposition to what he saw as political radicalism. He upheld federal and state statutes as well as legislative and grand jury investigative powers and deportation aimed at the removal of "security risks." Writing for the Court majority, he also upheld the power of the federal government to limit the political activities of its employees in *United Public Workers v. Mitchell* (1947).

Justice Reed retired from active service on the Supreme Court in 1957, but continued to sit on the Court of Claims and Court of Appeals for the District of Columbia, as special master for the Supreme Court in original jurisdiction cases, and briefly as chairman of the CIVIL RIGHTS COMMISSION. He died in 1980 at the age of ninety-five, having lived longer than any other Justice in history.

ARTHUR ROSETT

Bibliography

PRITCHETT, C. HERMAN 1969 Stanley Reed. In Leon Friedman and Fred L. Israel, eds., *The Justices of the United States Supreme Court: 1789–1969,* Vol. 3:2373–2389. New York: Chelsea House.

REESE v. UNITED STATES
92 U.S. 214 (1876)

Reese was the first VOTING RIGHTS case under the FIFTEENTH AMENDMENT and, among the early decisions, the most consequential. The Supreme Court crippled the attempt of the federal government to protect the right to vote and made constitutionally possible the circumvention of the Fifteenth Amendment by formally nonracial state qualifications on the right to vote. Congress had made election officials subject to federal prosecution for refusing to qualify eligible voters or not allowing them to vote. Part of the statute specified denial on account of race, part did not. One section, for example, provided for the punishment of any person who prevented any citizen from voting or qualifying to vote. A black citizen offered to pay his POLL TAX to vote in a municipal election, but the election officials refused to receive his tax or to let him vote. The United States prosecuted the officials.

The Court, by an 8–1 vote, in an opinion by Chief Justice MORRISON R. WAITE, held the act of Congress unconstitutional because it swept too broadly: two sections did not "confine their operation to unlawful discriminations on account of race, etc." The Fifteenth Amendment provided that the right to vote should not be denied because of race, but Congress had overreached its powers by seeking to punish the denial on any ground. The Court voided the whole act because its sections were inseparable, yet refused to construe the broadly stated sections in terms of those sections that did refer to race. By its pinched interpretation of the amendment, the Court made it constitutionally possible for the states to deny the right to vote on any ground except race, thus allowing the use of poll taxes, LITERACY TESTS, good character tests, understanding clauses, and other devices to achieve black disfranchisement.

LEONARD W. LEVY

REFERENDUM

Among the political reforms introduced during the Progressive Era was the referendum, by which acts of the legislature are referred to the people for their approval or rejection at an election. Referenda may be initiated by the legislature itself or by petition of the people. The referendum is a check on such abuses as corrupt legislation or blatantly partisan gerrymandering of legislative districts (see GERRYMANDER); but it also provides a way for politicians to avoid responsibility for controversial measures.

Reformers have frequently advocated a national referendum procedure. However, legislation authorizing a national referendum would probably be unconstitutional, and an amendment authorizing it would almost certainly fail to receive congressional approval.

DENNIS J. MAHONEY

REGAN v. WALD
468 U.S. 222 (1984)

A 1982 Treasury Department regulation prohibited travel-related business transactions with Cuba. Persons who wished to travel to Cuba, but were inhibited from doing so by the regulation, sued to enjoin its enforcement. The Supreme Court, 5–4, followed ZEMEL V. RUSK (1965) and HAIG V. AGEE (1981) in rejecting claims based on the RIGHT TO TRAVEL protected by the Fifth Amendment's DUE PROCESS clause. The dissenters argued that Congress had not authorized the regulation.

KENNETH L. KARST

REGENTS OF UNIVERSITY OF CALIFORNIA v. BAKKE
438 U.S. 265 (1978)

Perhaps the Supreme Court's majority in DEFUNIS V. ODEGAARD (1974) thought a delay in deciding on the constitutionality of racial preferences in state university admissions would give time for development of a political consensus on the issue. The result was just the opposite; by the time *Bakke* was decided, the question of RACIAL QUOTAS and preferences had become bitterly divisive. Bakke, a nonminority applicant, had been denied admission to the university's medical school at Davis. His state court suit had challenged the school's program setting aside for minority applicants sixteen places in an entering class of 100. Bakke's test scores and grades exceeded those of most minority admittees. The California Supreme Court held that the racial preference denied Bakke the EQUAL PROTECTION OF THE LAWS guaranteed by the FOURTEENTH AMENDMENT.

A fragmented United States Supreme Court agreed, 5–4, that Bakke was entitled to admission, but concluded, in a different 5–4 alignment, that race could be taken into account in a state university's admissions. Four Justices thought the Davis quota violated Title VI of the CIVIL RIGHTS ACT OF 1964, which forbids the exclusion of anyone on account of race from any program aided by federal funds. This position was rejected, 5–4. Four other Justices argued that the Davis quota was constitutionally valid as a reasonable, nonstigmatizing remedy for past societal discrimination against racial and ethnic minorities. This view was rejected by Justice LEWIS F. POWELL, who concluded that the Davis quota was a denial of equal protection. His vote, along with the votes of the four Justices who found a Title VI violation, placed Bakke in Davis's 1978 entering class.

Justice Powell's opinion on the constitutional question began by rejecting the notion of a "BENIGN" RACIAL CLASSIFICATION. He concluded that the burden of remedying past societal discrimination could not constitutionally be placed on individuals who had no part in that discrimination—absent the sort of constitutional violation that had been found in school DESEGREGATION cases such as SWANN V. CHARLOTTE-MECKLENBURG BOARD OF EDUCATION (1971), where color-conscious remedies had been approved. While rejecting quotas, Justice Powell approved the use of race as one factor in a state university's admissions policy for the purpose of promoting diversity in its student body.

Race is relevant to "diversity," of course, mainly because past societal discrimination has made race relevant to a student's attitudes and experiences. And if one's membership in a racial group may be a factor in the admissions process, it may be the decisive factor in a particular case. The Powell opinion thus anticipates a preference for minority applicants; how much of a preference will depend, as he says, on "some attention to numbers"—that is, the number of minority students already admitted. The difference between such a system and a racial quota is mostly symbolic.

The press hailed Justice Powell's opinion as a judgment of Solomon. As a contribution to principled argument about equal protection doctrine, it failed. As a political solution, however, it was a triumph. The borders of preference became blurred, so that no future applicant could blame her rejection on the preference. At the same time, a university following a "diversity" approach to admissions was made safe from constitutional attack. AFFIRMATIVE ACTION was thus saved, even as Bakke was ushered into medical school and racial quotas ringingly denounced. Almost miraculously, the issue of racial preferences in higher education virtually disappeared from the political scene, and legislative proposals to abolish affirmative action were shelved. Solomon, it will be recalled, succeeded in saving the baby.

KENNETH L. KARST

Bibliography

BLASI, VINCENT 1979 Bakke as Precedent: Does Mr. Justice Powell Have a Theory? *California Law Review* 67:21–68.

KARST, KENNETH L. and HOROWITZ, HAROLD W. 1979 The Bakke Opinions and Equal Protection Doctrine. *Harvard Civil Rights–Civil Liberties Law Review* 14:7–29.

WILKINSON, J. HARVIE, III 1979 *From Brown to Bakke.* New York: Oxford University Press.

REGULATORY AGENCIES

Regulatory agencies are governmental bodies created by legislatures to carry out specified state or national policies. Such an agency is typically responsible for regulating one particular area of social or economic life; it is staffed by specialists who develop the knowledge and experience necessary to enforce complex regulatory laws. Regulatory agencies normally combine the powers to make rules, to adjudicate controversies, and to provide ordinary administrative services, functions corresponding to the legislative, judicial, and executive powers of the separate branches of government. They fill in the gaps of general policy by bringing order, method, and uniformity to the process of modern government.

Although administrative agencies are as old as the federal government, the national regulatory process as we know it today began with the creation of the Interstate Commerce Commission in 1887. Granted extensive authority over the booming railroad industry, the commission received broad rule-making and adjudicatory powers, broader than those of any previous agency. It set the trend, and the goal, for future agencies by being the first governmental unit "whose single concern was the well-being," as James Landis said, "in a broad public sense, of a vital and national industry."

Since the New Deal, regulatory agencies have become the most visible tool for the achievement of national policy. They provide a form of centralized supervision which in earlier periods of American history was deemed neither necessary nor desirable. Their proliferation paralleled the development of national industries and the emergence of Congress as a policymaking body unable to supervise the details of administration. At the same time, a growing welfare state has recognized new interests such as welfare entitlements and equal employment opportunity. New regulatory agencies have been created to provide sympathetic administration of the new national policy goals, and to resolve conflicts by procedures less formalized and adversarial—and far less costly—than those prevailing in courts of law.

The character and origin of a regulatory agency depend on the nature of its tasks. Generally, such agencies fall into three main categories: independent regulatory commissions; executive agencies; and government corporations. The independent commissions, so called because of their relative freedom from executive control, are the most important, and include such agencies as the Interstate Commerce Commission (ICC), Securities and Exchange Commission (SEC), Federal Trade Commission (FTC), National Labor Relations Board (NLRB), and Nuclear Regulatory Commission (NRC). Each independent commission is headed by a multimember board appointed by the President with the ADVICE AND CONSENT of the Senate. Congress has sought to guarantee the commissions' independence by establishing their governing boards on a bipartisan basis, providing fixed terms of office for board members, and authorizing the President to remove them only for reasons specified by statute.

The executive agency, an example of which is the Environmental Protection Agency, is one whose administrator and top assistants are appointed by the President, to whom they report directly and who may remove them freely. The executive agency lies squarely within the executive branch; its position within the constitutional framework of SEPARATION OF POWERS is thus more clearly defined than that of the independent regulatory agencies. The government corporation, an example of which is the Tennessee Valley Authority, is created by statute for a stated purpose and is wholly owned by the government. This model has been used when a project, because of its duration or its required investment, cannot easily be achieved through private development.

Regulatory agencies differ significantly in the range of their powers and their modes of operation. For example, the work of the NLRB is almost exclusively judicial in character. Although it has broad authority under the WAGNER ACT and TAFT-HARTLEY ACT, the NLRB has chosen to exercise only adjudicatory powers. The Equal Employment Opportunity Commission, on the other hand, has no formal power to adjudicate claims or impose administrative sanctions. The sensitive and highly controversial character of its mission—to carry out the antidiscrimination provisions of Title VII of the CIVIL RIGHTS ACT OF 1964—prompted Congress to limit EEOC's authority to "informal methods of conference, conciliation, and persuasion." If these methods fail the alleged victim of discrimination may sue in federal court. Even though EEOC itself may not issue final orders, its guidelines for dealing with patterns of discrimination in employment, together with its field investigations in particular cases, often induce compliance. The result is a significant regulatory effect.

An immense body of administrative law, found in the voluminous *Code of Federal Regulations* and in a multitude of specialized publications, has been created by these and other administrative agencies.

The development and structure of regulatory agencies have strained the constitutional theory of separation of powers, for the agencies typically blend functions of all three branches of government. Yet the Supreme Court has sought to accommodate the constitutional theory with the needs of effective government, and thus to preserve the constitutional balance underscored by the principle of separation of powers. The constitutional basis for Congress's power to create regulatory agencies is derived from Article I. Section 1 grants "[a]ll legislative powers" to Congress; section 8 enumerates these powers and vests Congress with the additional power to make laws NECESSARY AND PROPER for carrying them into effect. Regulatory agencies have always been regarded as necessary and proper means of achieving the ends of national policy.

Implicit in the theory of separation of powers is the doctrine that delegated authority cannot be redelegated. Under this principle Congress cannot constitutionally invest the executive (or, for that matter, the judiciary) with the power of legislation. How then is it possible to justify the rule-making power conferred on agencies? The Supreme Court's answer is that such authority is permissible if the authorizing statute embodies a policy and provides guidelines to channel administrative action. Of course, within these guidelines agencies exercise considerable discretion. In theory, however, they are not legislating in a constitutional sense when exercising their discretion; they are simply carrying out legislative policies established by Congress.

Reality, however, had not easily converged with theory. Despite its reiteration of the doctrine forbidding delegation, the Supreme Court has consistently allowed "directionless" delegations of legislative authority. Not until the 1930s did the Court actually invalidate congressional statutes for excessive delegation of legislative power. But these precedents soon fell from favor as the Court proceeded to uphold subsequent legislative mandates as vague as those previously nullified. Some delegations have been disturbingly broad. For example, the Federal Communications Commission is to use its licensing power in the "public convenience, interest, or necessity." The Court upheld this "supple instrument" of delegation as being "as concrete as the complicated factors for judgement in such a field" permit. Nevertheless, the doctrine forbidding delegation still lives in theory. As recently as 1974, in *National Cable Television v. United States,* the Supreme Court construed a federal statute narrowly so as to avoid the implication from a literal reading of the statute that taxing power—clearly a legislative function—had been conferred on the Federal Communications Commission.

The doctrine forbidding legislative delegation has had its corollary in challenges to the constitutionality of regulatory agencies' exercise of judicial functions. The contention is that these functions are inconsistent with Article III's grant of the JUDICIAL POWER to courts. Yet the Supreme Court has upheld the delegation of adjudicatory functions to regulatory agencies, so long as the courts retain power to determine whether the agencies have acted within their legislative mandates.

The obverse of the delegation issue concerns strategies by which Congress may take back authority it has granted. Despite congressional efforts to ensure their independence, regulatory agencies came under criticism of liberals who complained that, instead of regulating in the public interest, the agencies had become the clients of the special interest they were supposed to regulate. More recently, conservatives have attacked regulatory agencies for pervasive bureaucratization, for growing unaccountability, and for disregard of their legislative mandates. The congressional response to these criticisms has taken a number of forms, including attempts to deregulate certain industries and the effort to reserve a power of LEGISLATIVE VETO of agency actions.

The legislative veto, adopted by Congress with increasing frequency in the 1970s, when public criticism of regulatory agencies was at its zenith, poses serious constitutional issues. Congress required various executive agencies to report to it in advance of specified kinds of proposed action. Then, if Congress (or, in some cases, one house of Congress) should adopt a resolution of disapproval within a certain time, the proposed action was effectively "vetoed." The Supreme Court held this mechanism unconstitutional in IMMIGRATION AND NATURALIZATION SERVICE V. CHADHA (1983), as applied to the one-house veto of a deportation order. First, the Court held, the congressional veto was a legislative act requiring passage by both houses of Congress. Second, and more serious, the congressional veto offended Article II, which requires any legislative act to be presented to the President for his approval before it takes effect.

The President as chief executive is commanded by Article II of the Constitution to "take care that the Laws be faithfully executed." From an early time, Presidents claimed an inherent constitutional power to remove any executive official whom they or their predecessors had appointed. This claim was vindicated in MYERS V. UNITED STATES (1926). But in HUMPHREY'S EXECUTOR V. UNITED STATES (1935) the Supreme Court refused to apply this theory of inherent power to the removal of a member of an independent agency exercising quasi-legislative and quasi-judicial powers. Distinguishing between a "purely executive" officer and an officer of an independent agency, the Court sustained Congress's authority, when creating regulatory agencies, to fix the terms of commissioners and specify the exclusive grounds for their removal. In *Weiner v. United States* (1958) this principle was applied to the removal of a member of the War Claims Commission, whose organizing statute specified no grounds for removal. The Court noted the adjudicatory nature of the agency's work, and thus concluded that Congress had not made it part of the executive establishment under the political control of the President. The Supreme Court has recognized that independent agencies cannot exercise their statutory duties fairly or impartially, as Congress intended, unless they are free from executive control.

The combination of investigatory, prosecutorial, and adjudicatory functions within the same regulatory agency has also been the subject of constitutional litigation. In *Winthrop v. Larkin* (1975), however, the Supreme Court reaffirmed its long-standing view that the mixture of these functions within a single agency or person does not violate DUE PROCESS unless the presumption of honesty and integrity of officers exercising these functions is overcome by evidence of actual bias or prejudgment in a particular case. Even though the separation of these functions within the regulatory context is not constitutionally commanded, legislators have often concluded that the best mix of efficiency and impartiality is maintained when prosecutorial and judicial functions are performed by different officers within an agency.

All regulatory agencies are subject to the constitutional requirement of PROCEDURAL DUE PROCESS. The right to a hearing must be granted when an agency takes action directly affecting rights and obligations: those affected must be given NOTICE and an opportunity to present their case in a FAIR HEARING. The process due in any particular case depends on the nature of the liberty or property interest involved. If these interests are constitutionally recognized then notice and even a prior hearing may be required before agency action can be taken. Whether the RIGHT TO COUNSEL, cross-examination, and other trial-type procedures will be required depends on the importance of the private interest at stake when balanced against the government's interest and the risk of erroneous deprivation under an agency's normal operating procedures.

The extent to which agency determinations are subject to judicial review is governed by the Administrative Procedure Act. Generally, administrative action is unreviewable if committed by statute to agency discretion. Courts may, however, set aside even discretionary action when it is "arbitrary, capricious, an abuse of discretion, or otherwise not in accordance with law." Under the act, the courts are to sustain agency findings of fact if they are supported by substantial evidence. Although the definition of "substantial" may differ from court to court, the Supreme Court retains the final say on whether the rule has been properly applied in a given case.

DONALD P. KOMMERS

Bibliography

DAVIS, KENNETH C. 1969 *Discretionary Justice.* Baton Rouge: Louisiana State University Press.

FREEDMAN, JAMES O. 1978 *Crisis and Legitimacy.* Cambridge: At the University Press.

KOHLMEIER, LOUIS M. 1969 *The Regulators.* New York: Harper & Row.

LANDIS, JAMES 1938 *The Administrative Process.* New Haven, Conn.: Yale University Press.

REDORD, EMMETT S. 1969 *The Regulatory Process.* Austin: University of Texas Press.

REHABILITATION ACT
87 Stat. 355 (1973)

In addition to providing funding and research incentives for various programs to aid the handicapped, Congress incorporated antidiscrimination provisions into the Rehabilitation Act. In federally assisted programs, the act prohibits discrimination solely by reason of handicap against an "otherwise qualified handicapped individual." In addition, the act requires federal executive agencies to take AFFIRMATIVE ACTION to employ handicapped individuals. In *Southeastern Community College v. Davis* (1979) the Supreme Court held that the Rehabilitation Act does not forbid a nursing school from imposing relevant physical qualifications upon participants in its training programs.

THEODORE EISENBERG

Bibliography

BURGDORF, ROBERT L., JR. 1980 *The Legal Rights of Handicapped Persons.* Baltimore: Paul H. Brookes Publishing Co.

REHEARING

A party who is dissatisfied with the court's decision or opinion in a case may request the court to reconsider. The term "rehearing" refers to such a reconsideration, usually by an appellate court.

By statute, the Supreme Court's APPELLATE JURISDICTION over cases coming from the state courts is limited to questions of federal law that have been properly drawn in question in the lower courts. This requirement normally is not satisfied by a litigant who raises a federal question for the first time in a petition for rehearing after a state supreme court has decided the case. However, if the state court entertains the petition and actually considers the federal question, the question can be brought to the Supreme Court.

The Supreme Court itself receives between 100 and 200 petitions for rehearing each year, seeking reconsideration of its own decisions or opinions. Fewer than one percent of these petitions are granted. By rule, the Court has provided that a petition for rehearing will be granted only by the vote of a majority of the Justices, including at least one Justice who concurred in the decision. By custom, a Justice who did not participate in that decision does not vote on the petition for rehearing.

One occasion for granting a petition for rehearing is the case in which the Supreme Court has affirmed the lower court's decision by a 4–4 vote. If the missing Justice was ill and has recovered, or if a ninth Justice has been appointed to fill a vacancy, it may seem likely that a majority will be mustered once the Court returns to full strength. Absent such a circumstance, the typical petition for rehearing achieves little but delay and the chance for a parting shot.

KENNETH L. KARST

Bibliography

STERN, ROBERT L. and GRESSMAN, EUGENE 1978 *Supreme Court Practice,* 5th ed. Chap. 15. Washington, D.C.: Bureau of National Affairs.

REHNQUIST, WILLIAM H. (1924–)

William Rehnquist joined the Supreme Court in 1971 at age forty-seven. He had been a clerk to Justice ROBERT H. JACKSON and a practitioner in Arizona. At the time of his appointment, he was the assistant attorney general for legal counsel—as President RICHARD M. NIXON described the post on appointing him, "the President's lawyer's lawyer."

Brilliant, charming, and deeply conservative, he has become the intellectual leader of the court—a fact that is not obvious from the statistics. Many terms he has dissented more than any other Justice, often alone. Rehnquist's influence lies in setting the terms of the debate. His dissents mark the path for future developments. His MAJORITY OPINIONS have been unusually influential, in part because Chief Justice WARREN E. BURGER regularly assigns him the most difficult and interesting cases, and in part because the opinions articulate approaches that have substantial general importance.

Rehnquist follows a structural approach in which the original understanding and the text of the Constitution assume great importance. The states play a substantial role in this structure, and a vision of an allocation of functions between state and federal governments lies at the center of Rehnquist's thought. He takes seriously the proposition that the federal government has limited powers and that the states hold sway over substantial fields. The Justice also has a view of the allocation of powers within the federal government in which judges play only a limited role. Judges may enforce some explicit guarantees, such as the right to FREEDOM OF SPEECH, but Rehnquist sees their more important function as enforcing the decisions of the political branches rather than questioning them. Judges must patrol the allocation of powers among other contending claimants, but once a political branch acts within its capacity, the decision, no matter how unwise, binds the courts.

This highly deferential approach follows from a belief that the Framers of the Constitution settled little but governmental structure, leaving the rest to future generations. Judges have no authority to restrict the powers of the political branches. They cannot invoke a decision by the Framers or political branches allocating power to the courts, and they cannot point to any other source of authority. Rehnquist is a moral skeptic and so rejects arguments that the Constitution authorizes judges to insist that other branches keep up with evolving notions of decent conduct; he believes that only the political process can define decency.

Justice Rehnquist outlined his approach in a solitary dissent to TRIMBLE v. GORDON (1977). The majority held that a statute discriminating against illegitimate children violated the EQUAL PROTECTION clause of the FOURTEENTH AMENDMENT. Calling that clause a "classic paradox" that "makes sense only in the context of a recently fought Civil War," Rehnquist continued:

> In the case of equality and equal protection, the constitutional principle—the thing to be protected to a greater or lesser degree—is not even identifiable from within the four corners of the Constitution. For equal protection does not mean that all persons must be treated alike. Rather, its general principle is that persons similarly situated should be treated similarly. But that statement of the rule does little to determine whether or not a question of equality is even involved in a given case. For the crux of the problem is *whether persons are similarly situated* for purposes of the STATE ACTION in issue.

Rehnquist therefore finds the constitutional guarantee of equality empty and thus vulnerable to being made a mere vessel for the beliefs of modern judges about what things *should* count as the pertinent similarities and differences. In his view, however, the Constitution does not resolve that question, which is at root political, to be resolved by political processes. The equal protection clause is limited to the Civil War concern, race. Within that field the prohibition is absolute, and race is a forbidden classification. Rehnquist has opposed governmental racial distinctions of all sorts, preferential "set-asides" for construction work, which the majority approved in FULLILOVE V. KLUTZNICK (1980), and preferences for private employment, which were sustained in UNITED STEELWORKERS V. WEBER (1979), as well as those stigmatizing blacks.

He applies the same approach to almost every other aspect of the Constitution. The FIRST AMENDMENT disables government from stopping speech—the subject debated by the Framers—but does not require government to facilitate speech, for example, by creating rights of access to information. Judicial expansion of the amendment's core meaning is unauthorized. A judge may not properly pursue the principles or values that underlie the document, because every principle has its limit, and the Constitution left adjustments to the political branches. As Rehnquist wrote in an article published in 1976: "Even in the face of a conceded social evil, a reasonably competent and reasonably representative legislature may decide to do nothing. It may decide that the evil is not of sufficient magnitude to warrant any governmental intervention. It may decide that the financial cost of eliminating the evil is not worth the benefit which would result from its elimination. It may decide that the evils which might ensue from the proposed solution are worse than the evils which the solution would eliminate." The judge must accept the political answers to these problems.

This limitation does not imply judicial passivity. The judge must rigorously enforce any actual constitutional decisions to remove issues from the political process. The BILL OF RIGHTS contains some of these decisions, but the most important are those concerning the structure of government. Rehnquist is perhaps best known for his enforcement of principles of FEDERALISM that cannot be found in the constitutional text. Writing for a bare majority in NATIONAL LEAGUE OF CITIES V. USERY (1976), he concluded that the structure of the Constitution withheld from Congress any power to regulate the operation of "states as states." As a result, the Court held, Congress could not require state and local governments to pay the minimum wages applicable to private parties. The Justice also has read into many statutes limits founded on a perceived need to maintain the role of states as coordinate centers of power.

But decisions based on the structure of the Constitution do not always favor the states. Often Rehnquist has joined holdings under the COMMERCE CLAUSE restricting the powers of states to levy discriminatory taxes or otherwise hinder INTERSTATE COMMERCE, even though neither legislation not any clear textual command prohibits this discrimination. He wrote the court's opinion in FITZPATRICK V. BITZER (1976), holding that in the exercise of its power under the Fourteenth Amendment, Congress may authorize suits against the states, even though the ELEVENTH AMENDMENT appears to deprive federal courts of JURISDICTION to entertain such suits.

The allocation of powers within the federal government also has been a theme of Rehnquist's work. He has attempted to revive the "antidelegation" doctrine, arguing that Congress may not grant uncertain decision-making powers to the executive branch. He joined the Court's opinion in BUCKLEY V. VALEO (1976), invalidating Congress's effort to appoint officers to administer the election laws, characterizing that effort as an intrusion on the executive power. And he supplied the theory and vote necessary to strike down in NORTHERN PIPELINE CONSTRUCTION CORP. V. MARATHON PIPE LINE CO. (1982) a grant of judicial power to BANKRUPTCY judges who lacked life tenure of office.

Part of Rehnquist's influence among the Justices comes from his distinctive style. Most judicial opinions come in shades of gray, following a dull formula notable only for turgid prose and abundant footnotes. Justice Rehnquist's opinions come closer to lavender than gray. They are relatively short and lively. One began with a limerick. Rehnquist often uses colorful (if strained) metaphors. The opinions are less copiously documented than those of his colleagues, but not because he does not know the references—they appear in the appropriate quantities in his articles. The Justice has simply chosen to write in an entertaining style. His opinions are read, and being read is the first step in being influential.

Some critics, including David L. Shapiro, have accused Rehnquist of intellectual dishonesty, because he is willing to distinguish a case on a marginally relevant basis, or to purport to honor PRECEDENT while disavowing the earlier case's rationale. Timid or weak Justices routinely treat precedents so, but Rehnquist is neither timid nor weak. That is why his nimble treatment of precedent is troubling. No one can attribute his conduct to inadvertence or to the work of a law clerk.

Justice Rehnquist is not always cavalier in distinguishing or narrowing unpleasant precedents. He will attack earlier cases openly in separate or DISSENTING OPINIONS, only to distinguish them in opinions for the Court. His opinion in *National League of Cities* purported to preserve some cases he had attacked, in solitary dissent, a year before, in *Fry v. United States* (1975). Part of his approach to precedent arises from his understanding that the author of a majority opinion speaks not for himself but for the Court as institution. He therefore tries to preserve precedents with which he does not agree, by flimsy distinctions if necessary. The result may seem contrived, but it is often essential to the functioning of the Court.

The ultimate test of honesty is whether a Justice faithfully distinguishes his constitutional views from his personal ones. Most Justices see little difference, leading to the conclusion that the Constitution follows the personal view rather than the reverse. Yet Rehnquist, who generally opposes governmental control of economic affairs, believes that the Constitution allows the political branches to establish and maintain a welfare state with extensive ECONOMIC REGULATION. He follows his jurisprudence to its logical conclusions. Though he supports property rights, he wrote an opinion in PRUNEYARD SHOPPING CENTER v. ROBINS (1980) sustaining the authority of a state to restrict those rights in the interest of fostering political speech with which the property owner disagreed.

In 1986 President RONALD REAGAN nominated Rehnquist to succeed Warren Burger as Chief Justice of the United States. One may expect Chief Justice Rehnquist to retain the same coherent picture of a government in which judges police structure rather than substance.

FRANK H. EASTERBROOK

Bibliography

POWELL, JEFF 1982 The Compleat Jeffersonian: Justice Rehnquist and Federalism. *Yale Law Journal* 91:1317–1370.

REHNQUIST, WILLIAM H. 1976 The Notion of a Living Constitution. *Texas Law Review* 54:693–706.

SHAPIRO, DAVID L. 1976 Mr. Justice Rehnquist: A Preliminary View. *Harvard Law Review* 90:293–357.

REID v. COVERT
KINSELLA v. KRUEGER
354 U.S. 1 (1957)

In a 6–2 decision, the Supreme Court invalidated a provision making the Uniform Code of Military Justice applicable to civilians accompanying the armed forces abroad, and reversed the COURT-MARTIAL convictions of two women who had murdered their servicemen husbands on military bases overseas.

Justice HUGO L. BLACK, for a plurality, held that neither the power to make rules for governing the armed forces nor any international agreement could free the government from the procedural requirements of Article III, Section 2, and the Fifth and Sixth Amendments.

DENNIS J. MAHONEY

REITMAN v. MULKEY
387 U.S. 369 (1967)

By an overwhelming majority, California's voters adopted an INITIATIVE measure ("Proposition 14") adding to the state constitution a provision repealing existing OPEN HOUSING LAWS and forbidding the enactment of new ones. Following the lead of the state supreme court, the Supreme Court held, 5–4, that the circumstances of Proposition 14's adoption demonstrated state encouragement of private RACIAL DISCRIMINATION in the sale and rental of housing. Justice BYRON R. WHITE, for the majority, said this encouragement amounted to STATE ACTION in violation of the FOURTEENTH AMENDMENT. Justice JOHN MARSHALL HARLAN, for the dissenters, argued that Proposition 14 merely withdrew the state from regulation of private conduct; the state court determinations of "encouragement" were not fact findings, but mistaken readings of the Supreme Court's own precedents.

Taken seriously, the *Reitman* decision implies an affirmative state obligation to protect against private racial discrimination in housing. The Supreme Court, far from reading the decision in this manner, has consistently rejected litigants' efforts even to invoke the "encouragement" doctrine there announced. *Reitman* thus lies in isolation, awaiting resurrection. But the trumpet call announcing the end of the world of state action doctrine, seemingly so close in the final years of the WARREN COURT, now seems far away.

KENNETH L. KARST

RELEASED TIME

Twice, in MCCOLLUM V. BOARD OF EDUCATION (1948) and again in ZORACH V. CLAUSEN (1952), the Supreme Court considered FIRST AMENDMENT challenges to the practice of releasing public school pupils from their regular studies so that they might participate in programs for religious instruction.

The first such program, in Gary, Indiana, in 1914, provided that, with parental consent and cooperation of church authorities, children could be released for one or more periods each week to go to churches of their own faith and there participate in religious instruction, returning to the public school at the end of the period, or if the period was the last of the day, going home.

The idea spread to other communities, but, for a variety of reasons, quite slowly. In rural and small urban communities, such as Champaign, Illinois, it was found more effective to have the religious instruction take place within the public schools rather than in the church schools.

In Champaign in 1940, an interfaith council with Protestant, Roman Catholic, and Jewish representatives was formed to offer religious instruction within the public schools during regular school hours. Instructors of religion were to be hired and paid by or through the interfaith council, subject to the approval and supervision of the public school superintendent. Each term the public school teachers distributed to the children cards on which parents could indicate their consent to the enrollment of their children in the religion classes. Children who obtained such consent were released by the school authorities from the secular work for a period of thirty minutes weekly in the elementary schools and forty-five minutes in the junior high school. Only Protestant instruction was conducted within the regular classroom; children released for Roman Catholic or Jewish instruction left their classroom for other parts of the building. Nonparticipants were also relocated, sometimes accompanied by their regular teachers and sometimes not. At the end of each session, children who had participated in any religious instruction returned to the regular classroom, and regular class work was resumed.

McCollum v. Board of Education (1948) was a suit, brought in a state court by the mother of a fifth grader, challenging the constitutionality of Champaign's program. In the Supreme Court, counsel for the school authorities argued that the establishment clause did not apply to the states, and that the contrary HOLDING in EVERSON V. BOARD OF EDUCATION (1947) should be overruled. This the Court refused to do, reasserting *Everson*'s conclusion about the scope of the establishment clause.

No more successful was the argument that historically the establishment clause had been intended to forbid only preferential treatment of one faith over others, whereas the Champaign program was open equally to Protestants, Roman Catholics, and Jews. Here, too, the Court found no reason to reconsider its statement in *Everson* that the clause barred aid not only to one religion but equally to all religions.

Where, the Court said, pupils compelled by law to go to school for secular education are released in part from their legal duty if they attend religious classes, the tax-supported public school system's use to aid religious groups to spread their faiths falls squarely under the ban of the First Amendment. Not only are the public school buildings used for the dissemination of religious doctrines, but the state also affords sectarian groups an invaluable aid, helping to provide pupils for their religious classes through the use of the state's compulsory public school machinery. This, the Court concluded, was not SEPARATION OF CHURCH AND STATE.

Although the Court's language appeared to encompass in its determination of unconstitutionality released time plans providing for off-school religious instruction (and Justice HUGO L. BLACK who wrote the opinion so interpreted it), the majority reached a contrary conclusion in *Zorach v. Clausen* (1952).

Zorach involved New York City's program, which restricted public school participation to releasing children whose parents had signed consent cards and specifically forbade comment by any principal or teacher on the attendance or nonattendance of any pupil upon religious instruction. This situation, said the Court speaking through Justice WILLIAM O. DOUGLAS, differed from that presented in the *McCollum* case. There, the classrooms had been used for religious instruction and the influence of the public school used to promote that instruction. Here, the public schools did no more than accommodate their schedules to allow children, who so wished, to go elsewhere for religious instruction completely independent of public school operations. The situation, Douglas said, was not different from that presented when a Roman Catholic student asks his teacher to be excused to attend a mass on a Holy Day of Obligation or a Jewish student to attend synagogue on Yom Kippur.

Government, Justice Douglas said further, may not finance religious groups nor undertake religious instruction nor blend secular and sectarian education nor use secular institutions to force one or some religion on any person. Government, however, must be neutral in respect to religion, not hostile. "We are," he said, "a religious people whose institutions presuppose a Supreme Being. When the state encourages religious instruction or cooperates with religious authorities, it follows the best of our traditions. For it then respects the religious nature of our people and accommodates the public service to their spiritual needs."

On the basis of *McCollum* and *Zorach*, the present law is that released time programs are constitutional so long as the religious instruction is given off the public school premises and the public school teachers and authorities are involved in it only by releasing uncoerced children who choose to participate in it.

LEO PFEFFER

Bibliography

PFEFFER, LEO (1953)1967 *Church, State and Freedom.* Boston: Beacon Press.

Released Time for Religious Education in New York City Schools. 1949 Public Education Association.

STOKES, A. P. and PFEFFER, LEO 1964 *Church and State in the United States.* New York: Harper & Row.

RELIGION AND FRAUD

Few responsibilities are more sensitive and difficult to meet than drawing a line between punishable obtaining of property under false pretenses and constitutionally protected free exercise of religion. In the one major case to reach the Supreme Court, *United States v. Ballard* (1944), the Court split three ways in its decision.

Ballard involved the conviction of organizers of the "I Am" movement, indicted for using the mails to defraud because they falsely represented that they had supernatural powers to heal the incurably ill, and that as "Divine messengers" they had cured hundreds of afflicted persons through communication with Saint Germain, Jesus, and others. The trial court had instructed the jury that they should not decide whether these statements were literally true, but only whether the defendants honestly believed them to be true.

On appeal the majority of the Supreme Court agreed with the trial judge. Under the principles of SEPARATION OF CHURCH AND STATE and RELIGIOUS LIBERTY, it held, neither a jury nor any other organ of government had the competence to pass on whether certain religious experiences actually occurred. A jury could no more constitutionally decide that defendants had not shaken hands with Jesus, as they claimed, than they could determine that Jesus had not walked on the sea, as the Bible related. The limit of the jury's power was a determination whether defendants actually believed that what they recounted was true.

Chief Justice HARLAN FISKE STONE dissented on the ground that the prosecution should be allowed to prove that none of the alleged cures had been effected. On the other extreme Justice ROBERT H. JACKSON urged that the prosecution should not have been instituted in the first place, for few juries would find that the defendants honestly believed in something that was unbelievable. Nevertheless the majority decision remains the law, and is not likely to be OVERRULED after a half-century of acceptance.

LEO PFEFFER

Bibliography

PFEFFER, LEO (1953)1967 *Church, State and Freedom.* Boston: Beacon Press.

RELIGION IN PUBLIC SCHOOLS

For centuries in the Western world, organized education was church education; colonial schools established on the American shores therefore naturally reflected a religious orientation. Prior to the early nineteenth-century migration of Irish to this country, the orientation of these schools was Protestant—a fact that contributed to the establishment and growth of the Roman Catholic parochial school system. Nevertheless, when the RELEASED TIME plan for religious instruction was initiated in 1914, the majority of Roman Catholic children still attended public schools. The plan thus provided for separate religious instruction classes for Protestants, Roman Catholics, and Jews. Roman Catholic Church spokesmen condemned the Supreme Court's decision in MCCOLLUM V. BOARD OF EDUCATION (1948) invalidating the program. Previously, however, Roman Catholics had protested against public school religious instruction with a Protestant orientation, and had instituted lawsuits challenging such programs' constitutionality. Public school authorities in New York chose to formulate their own "non-sectarian" prayer, which was submitted to and received the approval of prominent religious spokesmen of the three major faiths. The twenty-two-word prayer read: "Almighty God, we acknowledge our dependence upon Thee, and beg Thy blessings upon us, our parents, our teachers and our country."

The denominational neutrality of the prayer, the Supreme Court held in ENGEL V. VITALE (1962), was immaterial. Nor was it relevant that observance on the part of students was voluntary (nonparticipating students were not even required to be in the classroom or assembly hall while the prayer was recited). Under the establishment clause, the Court said, aid to all religions was as impermissible as aid to one religion, even if the aid was noncoercive. The constitutional prohibition against laws respecting an ESTABLISHMENT OF RELIGION means at least that it is "no part of the business of government to compose official prayers for any group of the American people to recite as part of a religious program carried on by government."

One year after *Engel,* the Court, in ABINGTON SCHOOL DISTRICT V. SCHEMPP, was called upon to rule on the constitutionality of two practices in the public schools common throughout the nation, prayer recitation and devotional Bible reading. In respect to the former it ruled immaterial the fact that, unlike *Engel,* the recited prayer had not been formulated by public school authorities, but was the Lord's Prayer taken from the Bible. The fatal flaw in the *Engel* regulation lay not in the authorship of the prayer but in the fact that its purpose and primary effect were the advancement of religion. This fact mandated invalidation of both Lord's Prayer recitation and devotional Bible reading. The Court rejected the claim that the purposes of the challenged program were the secular ones of promoting moral values, contradicting the materialistic trends of our time, perpetuating our institutions, and teaching literature. None of these factors, the Court said, justified use of the Bible as an instrument of religion or resort to a ceremony of pervasive religious character. Nothing in its decision, it concluded, was intended to cast doubt on the study of comparative religion or the study of the Bible for its literary and historic qualities, so long as these were presented as part of a secular program of education.

McCollum, Engel, and *Schempp* involved efforts to introduce religious teachings or practices into the public schools. EPPERSON V. ARKANSAS (1968) presented the converse, that is, religiously motivated exclusion of secular instruction from the public school curriculum. A statute forbade teaching "the theory or doctrine that mankind ascended or descended from a lower order of animals." The Court held that the statute violated the establishment clause, because its purpose was to protect religious orthodoxy from inconsistent secular teaching of evolution.

In *Stone v. Graham* (1980) the Court struck down a Kentucky statute requiring the posting of copies of the Ten Commandments (purchased with private contributions) on the walls of all the public school classrooms in the state. The statute, it held, had no secular purpose; unlike the second part of the Commandments, the first (worshiping God, avoiding idolatry, not taking the Lord's name in vain, and observing the Sabbath) concerned religious rather than secular duties.

WIDMAR V. VINCENT (1981) manifests a more tolerant approach in respect to colleges than to elementary and secondary schools. With but one dissent, the Court held that where state university facilities were open to groups and speakers of all kinds, they must also be open for use by an organization of evangelical Christian students for prayer, hymns, Bible commentary, and discussion of religious views and experience. As construed by the Court, the establishment clause did not mandate such exclusion; on the contrary, the state's interest in enforcing its own constitution's church–state separation clause was not sufficiently "compelling" to justify content-barred discrimination forbidden by the FREEDOM OF SPEECH clause.

However, in *Jaffree v. Board of School Commissioners* (1984) the Court affirmed without opinion a Court of Appeals decision ruling unconstitutional an Alabama law authorizing voluntary participation in a prayer formulated by the legislators; and a year later, in WALLACE V. JAFFREE (1985) it invalidated another section of the statute that required a one-minute period of silence for "meditation or voluntary prayer." The provision, the Court said, did not have a valid secular purpose, but rather one that sought to return prayer to the public schools.

LEO PFEFFER

Bibliography

PFEFFER, LEO (1953)1967 *Church, State and Freedom.* Boston: Beacon Press.

STOKES, A. P. and PFEFFER, LEO 1964 *Church and State in the United States.* New York: Harper & Row.

TRIBE, LAURENCE H. 1984 *American Constitutional Law.* Chap. 14. Mineola, N.Y.: Foundation Press.

RELIGIOUS LIBERTY

Although the FIRST AMENDMENT's mandate that "Congress shall make no law respecting an ESTABLISHMENT OF RELIGION, or prohibiting the free exercise thereof" is expressed in unconditional language, religious liberty, insofar as it extends beyond belief, is not an absolute right. The First Amendment, the Supreme Court said in CANTWELL V. CONNECTICUT (1940), "embraces two concepts—freedom to believe and freedom to act. The first is absolute but, in the nature of things, the second cannot be. Conduct remains subject to regulation of society."

Although the Court has repeated this dualism many times, it does not explain what the free exercise clause means. There is no need for a constitutional guarantee protecting freedom to believe, for, as the COMMON LAW had it, "the devil himself knows not the thoughts of man." Even if freedom to believe encompasses freedom to express what one believes, the clause adds nothing, since FREEDOM OF SPEECH and FREEDOM OF THE PRESS are specifically guaranteed in the amendment. Indeed, before *Cantwell* was decided, the Court applied the free speech rather than free exercise guarantee to challenges against state laws allegedly impinging upon religious liberty. Moreover, the word "exercise" connotes action or conduct, thus indicating that the framers had in mind something beyond the mere expression of a belief even if uttered in missionary activities.

In America the roots of religious liberty can be traced to ROGER WILLIAMS, whose pamphlet, "The Bloudy Tenent of Persecution for cause of Conscience, discussed in a Conference between Truth and Peace," asserted that it was God's command that "a permission of the most Paganish, Jewish, Turkish, or Antichristian consciences and worships, be granted to all men in all Nations and Countries." Another source was THOMAS JEFFERSON's VIRGINIA STATUTE OF RELIGIOUS LIBERTY, adopted in 1786, which declared that no person should be compelled to frequent or support any religious worship nor suffer on account of religious opinions and beliefs.

By the time the First Amendment became part of the Constitution in 1791, practically every state in the Union, to a greater or lesser degree, had enacted constitutional or statutory provisions securing the free exercise of religion. Indeed, it was the absence of a BILL OF RIGHTS whose proponents invariably called for a guarantee of religious freedom, that was the most frequently asserted objection to the Constitution presented to the states for approval. The necessary approval was obtained only because the Constitution's advocates promised that such a bill would be added by amendment after the Constitution was adopted.

Although the First Amendment was framed as a limitation of congressional powers, Supreme Court decisions have made it clear that executive and judicial action were likewise restricted by the amendment. Thus in *Anderson v. Laird* (1971) the Supreme Court refused to review a decision that the secretary of defense violated the First Amendment in requiring cadets in governmental military academies to attend chapel. As to the judiciary, unquestionably a federal court could not constitutionally disqualify a person from testifying as a witness because he was an atheist. (See TORCASO V. WATKINS, 1961.)

Since the Court's decision in *Cantwell* the states are subject to the restrictions of the free exercise clause no less than the federal government. Because our federal system leaves to the states what is generally called the POLICE POWER, there were few occasions, prior to *Cantwell,* when the Supreme Court was called upon to define the meaning of the clause. The few that did arise involved actions in the TERRITORIES, which were subject to federal laws and thus to the First Amendment. Most significant of these was REYNOLDS V. UNITED STATES (1879), wherein the Supreme Court upheld the constitutionality of an act of Congress criminalizing POLYGAMY in any American territory. In rejecting the defense that polygamy was mandated by doctrines of the Holy Church of Latter-Day Saints (Mormons) and thus was protected by the free exercise clause, the Court stated what was later echoed in *Cantwell,* that although laws "cannot interfere with mere religious belief, they may with practice." It could hardly be contended, the Court continued, that the free exercise clause barred prosecution of persons who engaged in human sacrifice as a necessary part of their religious worship.

Since Reynolds was charged with practicing polygamy, the Court's decision did not pass upon the question whether teaching it as a God-mandated duty was "mere religious belief" and therefore beyond governmental interference. In DAVIS V. BEASON (1890) the Court decided that such teaching was "practice," and therefore constitutionally subject to governmental restrictions.

Teaching or preaching, even if deemed action, is however not beyond all First Amendment protection, which encompasses freedom of speech as well as religion. In GITLOW V. NEW YORK (1925) the Supreme Court declared for the first time that the free speech guarantee of the First Amendment was incorporated into the FOURTEENTH AMENDMENT by virtue of the DUE PROCESS clause in the latter and thus was applicable to the states. Accordingly, the Jehovah's Witnesses cases that first came to the Court in the 1930s were initially decided under the speech rather than the religion clause (LOVELL V. GRIFFIN, 1938; *Schneider v. Irvington,* 1939). It was, therefore, natural for the Court to decide the cases under the CLEAR AND PRESENT DANGER test that had first been announced in SCHENCK V. UNITED STATES (1919), a case involving prosecution for speaking against United States involvement in World War I.

In another sense, this too was quite natural since, like Schenck, the Witnesses were pacifists, at least in respect to wars in this world. (In *Sicurella v. United States,* the Court in 1955 ruled that a member of the sect was not disqualified from conscientious objector exemption because the sect's doctrines encompassed participation by believers in serving as soldiers in the Army of Christ Jesus at Armageddon.) Nevertheless, unlike Schenck and other opponents to American entry in World War I, the Witnesses (like the Friends) did not vocally oppose American entry into the war but limited themselves to claiming CONSCIENTIOUS OBJECTION status.

The Court did not apply the clear and present danger test in a case involving a member of the Jehovah's Witnesses whose child was expelled from public school for refusing to participate in the patriotic program of flag salute. In that case, *Minersville School District v. Gobitis* (1940), the Court, in an opinion by Justice FELIX FRANKFURTER, rejected the assertion as a defense of religious freedom. (See FLAG SALUTE CASES.) The antipolygamy law, he stated, was upheld in *Reynolds* not because it concerned action rather than belief, but because it was a valid general law, regulating the secular practice of marriage.

The majority of the Court, however, soon concluded that *Gobitis* had been incorrectly decided, and three years later the Court overruled it in *West Virginia State Board of Education v. Barnette* (1943). There the Court treated the Witnesses' refusal to salute the flag as a form of speech and therefore subject to the clear and present danger test. In later decisions, the Court returned to *Cantwell* and treated religious freedom cases under the free exercise rather than free speech clause, although it continued to apply the clear and present danger test.

Unsatisfied with that test, Justice Frankfurter prevailed upon his colleagues to accept a differently worded rule, that of BALANCING competing interests, also taken from Court decisions relating to other freedoms secured in the Bill of Rights. When a person complains that his constitutional rights have been infringed by some law or action of the state, it is the responsibility of the courts to weigh the importance of the particular right in issue as against the state's interest upon which its law or action is based. For example, the right of an objector not to violate his religious conscience by engaging in war must be weighed against the nation's interest in defending itself against foreign enemies, and, in such weighing, the latter interest may be adjudged the weightier.

The majority of the Court accepted this rule, but in recent years it has added an element that has almost turned it around. Justice Frankfurter believed that a citizen who challenged the constitutionality of state action had the burden of convincing the court that his interest was more important than the state's and should therefore be adjudged paramount. Establishing an individual's right superior to the state's interest was a particularly heavy burden to carry, but it was made even heavier by Justice Frankfurter's insistence that any doubt as to relative weights must be resolved in favor of the state, which would prevail unless its action were patently unreasonable. Recently, however, the Court has taken a more libertarian approach, requiring the state to persuade the courts that the values it seeks to protect are weightier. In the language of the decisions, the state must establish that there is a COMPELLING STATE INTEREST that justifies infringement of the citizen's right to the free exercise of his religion. If it fails to do so, its law or action will be adjudged unconstitutional. (See THOMAS V. REVIEW BOARD OF INDIANA, 1981; UNITED STATES V. LEE, 1982.)

In accord with this rule, the Court, in the 1972 case of WISCONSIN V. YODER, expressly rejected the belief–action test, holding that Amish parents could not be prosecuted for refusing to send their children to school after they had reached the age of fourteen. "Only those interests of the highest order," the Court said, "and those not otherwise served can overbalance the legitimate claim to the free exercise of religion."

Religious liberty is protected not only by the free exercise clause but also by the clause against ESTABLISHMENTS OF RELIGION. In EVERSON V. BOARD OF EDUCATION (1947) and later cases, the Court has stated that under the establishment clause, government cannot force a person to go to church or profess a belief in any religion. In later decisions, the Court has applied a three-pronged purpose–effect–entanglement test as a standard of constitutionality under the establishment clause. The Court has held, in *Committee for Public Education and Religious Liberty v. Nyquist* (1973), for example, that a challenged statute must have a primary effect that neither advances nor inhibits religion, and must avoid government entanglement with religion. (See SEPARATION OF CHURCH AND STATE.)

The Supreme Court's decisions in the arena of conflict between governmental concerns and individuals' claims to religious liberty can be considered in relation to the four categories suggested by the PREAMBLE to the Constitution: national defense, domestic tranquillity, the establishment of justice, and GENERAL WELFARE. In resolving the issues before it in these decisions the Court has spoken in terms of clear and present danger, balancing of competing interests, or determination of compelling governmental interests, depending upon the date of the decision rendered.

Probably no interest of the government is deemed more important than defense against a foreign enemy. Individual liberties secured by the Constitution must yield when the nation's safety is in peril. As the Court ruled in the SELECTIVE DRAFT LAW CASES (1918), the prohibition by the THIRTEENTH AMENDMENT of involuntary servitude was not intended to override the nation's power to conscript an army of—if necessary—unwilling soldiers, without which even the most just and defensive war cannot be waged.

By the same token, exemption of Quakers and others whose religious conscience forbids them to engage in military service cannot be deemed a constitutional right but only a privilege accorded by Congress and thus subject to revocation at any time Congress deems that to be necessary for national defense. However, even in such a case, Congress must exercise its power within the limitations prescribed by the First Amendment's mandate of neutrality among religions and by the EQUAL PROTECTION component of the Fifth Amendment's due process clause. Hence, in exercising its discretion, Congress could not constitutionally prefer some long-standing pacifist religions over others more recently established.

Exemption of specific classes—the newly betrothed, the newly married, the fainthearted, and others—goes back as far as Mosaic times (Deuteronomy 20:1–8). Since all biblical wars were theocratic, there was no such thing as religious exemption. In England, Oliver Cromwell believed that those whose religious doctrine forbade participation in armed conflict should constitute an exempt class. So too did the legislatures in some of the American colonies, the Continental Congress, and a number of the members of the Congress established under the Constitution. Madison's original draft of what became the SECOND AMENDMENT included a provision exempting religious objectors from compulsory militia duty; but that provision was deleted before Congress proposed the amendment to the states. The first national measure exempting conscientious objectors was adopted by Congress during the Civil War; like its colonial and state precedents, it was limited to members of well-recognized religious denominations whose articles of faith forbade the bearing of arms.

The SELECTIVE SERVICE ACT of 1917 exempted members of recognized denominations or sects, such as the Friends, Mennonites, and Seventh-Day Adventists, whose doctrine and discipline declared military service sinful. The 1940 act liberalized the requirements for exemption to encompass anyone who by "reason of religious training and belief" possessed conscientious scruples against "participation in war in any form." In 1948, however, the 1940 act was further amended, first, to exclude those whose objection to war was based on "essentially political, sociological or philosophical views or a mere personal code," and second, to define religion as a belief in a "Supreme Being."

In view of the Court's holding in *Torcaso v. Watkins* (1961) that the Constitution did not sanction preferential treatment of theistic religions over other faiths, limitation of exemption to persons who believe in a "Supreme Being" raised establishment clause issues. In UNITED STATES V. SEEGER (1965) the Court avoided these issues by interpreting the statute to encompass a person who possessed a sincere belief occupying a place in the life of its possessor parallel to that filled by the orthodox belief in God of one who clearly qualified for the exemption. Applying this definition to the three cases before it, the Court held that Selective Service boards had erroneously denied exemption: to one who expressed a "belief in and devotion to goodness and virtues for their own sakes, and a religious faith in a purely ethical creed"; to another who rejected a relationship "vertically towards Godness directly," but was committed to relationship "horizontally towards Godness through Mankind and the World"; and to a third who defined religion as "the supreme expression of human nature," encompassing "man thinking his highest, feeling his deepest, and living his best."

Because exemption of conscientious exemption is of legislative rather than constitutional origin, Congress may condition exemption on possession of belief forbidding participation in all wars, excluding those whose objection is selective and forbids participation only in what they personally deem unjust wars, such as that in Vietnam. The Court sustained such an act of Congress in *Gillette v. United States* (1971). However, independent of any statutory exemption, the Court held in *Thomas* that, at least in peacetime, disqualification of a person from unemployment insurance benefits for conscientious refusal to accept an offered job in a plant that manufactured arms violated the free exercise clause.

Closely related to military service as an aspect of national defense is national unity, cultural as well as political. The relevant constitutional issues reached the Supreme Court in 1923 in three cases involving Lutheran and Reformed schools, and, two years later, in two cases involving a Roman Catholic parochial and a nonsectarian private school. The former cases, reflecting post-World War I hostility to German-speaking Americans, were decided by the Court in MEYER V. NEBRASKA (1923) and two companion cases. These involved the conviction of teachers of German who violated statutes forbidding the teaching of a foreign language to pupils before they had completed eight grades of elementary schooling. The Court, in reversing the convictions, relied not only on the constitutional right of German teachers to pursue a gainful occupation not inherently evil or dangerous to the welfare of the community, but also the right of parents to have their children taught "Martin Luther's language" so that they might better understand "Martin Luther's dogma." The cases were decided long before the Court held that the free exercise clause was incorporated in the Fourteenth Amendment's due process clause and therefore were technically based upon the teachers' due process right to earn a livelihood and the parents' due process right to govern the upbringing of their children.

In PIERCE V. SOCIETY OF SISTERS and its companion case, *Pierce v. Hill Military Academy* (1925), the Court invalidated a compulsory education act that required all children, with limited exceptions, to attend only public schools. A single opinion, governing both cases, relied upon *Meyer v. Nebraska* and based the decision invalidating the law on the due process clause as it related to the school owners' contractual rights and the parents' right to control their children's education, rather than to the free exercise rights of teachers, parents, or pupils. Nevertheless, since the Court's ruling in *Cantwell* that the free exercise clause was applicable to the states, *Pierce* has often been cited by lawyers, scholars, and courts as a free exercise case, and particularly one establishing the constitutional rights of churches to operate parochial schools. Had *Pierce* been decided after *Cantwell* it is probable that free exercise would have been invoked as an additional ground in respect to the Society of Sisters' claim; the opinion as written did note that the child was not the mere creature of the state and that those who nurtured him and directed his destiny had the right, coupled with the high duty, to recognize and prepare him for additional obligations.

Reference has already been made to the Supreme Court's decision in *West Virginia State Board of Education v. Barnette* upholding the First Amendment right of Jehovah's Witnesses public school pupils to refrain from participating in flag salute exercises, although there the Court predicated its decision on the free speech rather than the free exercise mandate of the Amendment.

Jehovah's Witnesses' creed and conduct affected not only national defense through pacifism and alleged failure to pay respect to the flag but also governmental concern with domestic tranquillity. What aggravated hostility to the sect beyond its supposed lack of patriotism were its militant proselytizing methods, encompassing verbal attacks on organized religion in general and Roman Catholicism in particular. In their 1931 convention the Witnesses declared their mission to be "to inform the rulers and the people of and concerning Satan's cruel and oppressive organization, and particularly with reference to Christiandom, which is the most visible part of that visible organization." God's purpose was to destroy Satan's organization and bring quickly "to the obedient peoples of the earth peace and prosperity, liberty and health, happiness and life."

This is hardly new or surprising. Practically every new religion, from Judaism through Christianity and Islam to the present, has been predicated upon attacks against existing faiths; indeed, this is implied in the very term "Protestant." Clearly, those who wrote the First Amendment intended it to encompass attacks upon existing religions. (In BURSTYN V. WILSON, 1952, the Court invalidated a statute banning "sacrilegious" films.) Attacks on existing religions are almost invariably met with counterattacks, physical as well as verbal, by defenders of the accepted faiths.

The assaults upon the Jehovah's Witnesses were particularly widespread and intense for a number of reasons. Their conduct enraged many who felt that their refusal to salute the flag was unpatriotic, if not treasonous. Their attacks upon the Christian religion infuriated many others. The evidence in *Taylor v. Mississippi* (1943), for example, included a pamphlet suggesting that the Roman Catholic Church was responsible for flag saluting. The book *Religion*, by the Witnesses' first leader, Charles T. Russell, described their operations: "God's faithful servants go from house to house to bring the message of the kingdom to those who reside there, omitting none, not even the houses of the Roman Catholic hierarchy, and there they give witness to the kingdom because they are commanded by the Most High to do so. . . . They do not loot nor break into the houses, but they set up their phonographs before the doors and windows and send the message of the kingdom right into the ears of those who might wish to hear; and while those desiring to hear are hearing, some of the 'sourpusses' are compelled to hear."

The predictably resulting resort to violence and to law for the suppression of the Witnesses' activities gave rise to a host of Supreme Court decisions defining for the first time both the breadth and the limitations of the free exercise clause (and also, to some extent, the free speech clause). Most of the Jehovah's Witnesses cases were argued before the Supreme Court by Hayden Covington; his perseverance, as well as that of his client, was manifested by the fact that before *Minersville School District v. Gobitis* was decided, the Court had rejected his appeals in flag salute cases four times. The Court had accepted JURISDICTION in *Gobitis,* as well as its successor, *Barnette,* because, notwithstanding these previous rejections, the lower courts had decided both cases in the Witnesses' favor.

The Witnesses were not the only persons whose aggressive missionary endeavors and verbal attacks upon other faiths led to governmental actions that were challenged as a violation of the free exercise clause and were defended as necessary to secure domestic tranquillity. In KUNZ V. NEW YORK (1951), the Court held that a Baptist preacher could not be denied renewal of a permit for evangelical street meetings because his preachings, scurrilously attacking Roman Catholicism and Judaism, had led to disorder in the streets. The Court said that appropriate public remedies existed to protect the peace and order of the communities if the sermons should result in violence, but it held that these remedies did not include prior restraint under an ordinance that provided no standards for the licensing official.

Jehovah's Witnesses were the major claimants to religious liberty in the two decades between 1935 and 1955. During that period they brought to the Supreme Court a large number of cases challenging the application to them of a variety of laws forbidding disturbing the peace, peddling, the use of SOUNDTRUCKS, as well as traffic regulations, child labor laws, and revenue laws.

In *Cantwell v. Connecticut* (1940) the Court held that the First Amendment guaranteed the right to teach and preach religion in the public streets and parks and to solicit contributions or purchases of religious materials. Although a prior municipal permit might be required, its grant or denial might not be based upon the substance of what is taught, preached, or distributed but only upon the need to regulate, in the interests of traffic control, the time, place, and manner of public meetings. In COX V. NEW HAMPSHIRE (1940) the Court ruled that religious liberty encompassed the right to engage in religious processions, although a fee might be imposed to cover the expenses of administration and maintenance of public order. The Constitution, however, does not immunize from prosecution persons who in their missionary efforts use expressions that are lewd, obscene, libelous, insulting, or that contain "fighting" words which by their very utterance, the Court declared in CHAPLINSKY V. NEW HAMPSHIRE (1942), inflict injury or tend to incite an immediate breach of the peace. The Constitution also secures the right to distribute religious handbills in streets and at publicly owned railroad or bus terminals, according to the decision in *Jamison v. Texas* (1943), and, according to *Martin v. City of Struthers* (1943), to ring doorbells in order to offer house occupants religious literature although, of course, not to force oneself into the house for that purpose.

Related to the domestic tranquillity aspects of Jehovah's Witnesses claims to use public streets and parks are the claims of other feared or unpopular minority religious groups (often referred to as "sects" or, more recently, "CULTS") to free exercise in publicly owned areas. In HEFFRON V. INTERNATIONAL SOCIETY FOR KRISHNA CONSCIOUSNESS (ISKCON) (1981) the Court held that a state rule limiting to specific booths the sale or distribution of merchandise, including printed material, on public fair grounds did not violate the free exercise clause when applied to members of ISKCON whose ritual required its members to go into all public places to distribute or sell its religious literature and to solicit donations.

Discriminatory treatment, however, is not constitutionally permissible. Thus, in *Cruz v. Beto* (1972) the Supreme Court upheld the claim of a Buddhist prisoner in Texas that his constitutional rights were violated by denying him use of the prison chapel, punishing him for sharing his Buddhist religious materials with other prisoners, and denying him other privileges, such as receiving points for attendance at religious services, which enhanced a prisoner's eligibility for early parole consideration. While a prisoner obviously cannot enjoy the free exercise of religion to the same extent as nonprisoners, the Court said, he is protected by the free exercise clause subject only to the necessities of prison security and discipline, and he may not be discriminated against simply because his religious belief is unorthodox. This does not mean that every sect within a prison, no matter how few in number, must have identical facilities or personnel; but reasonable opportunities must be afforded to all persons to exercise their religion without penalty.

One of the most difficult problems facing a court arises when it is called upon to decide between free exercise and the state's interest in preventing fraud. The leading case on the subject is *United States v. Ballard* (1944), which involved a prosecution for mail fraud. The INDICTMENT charged that the defendants, organizers of the "I Am" cult, had mulcted money from elderly and ill people by falsely representing that they had supernatural powers to heal and that they themselves had communicated personally with Heaven and with Jesus Christ.

The Court held that the free exercise clause would be violated if the state were allowed to seek to prove to a jury that the defendants' representations were false. Neither a jury nor any other organ of government had power to decide whether asserted religious experiences actually occurred. Courts, however, could constitutionally determine whether the defendant himself believed that what he recounted was true, and if a jury determined that he did not, they could convict him of obtaining money under false pretenses. The difficulty with this test, as Justice ROBERT H. JACKSON noted in his dissenting opinion, is that prosecutions in cases such as *Ballard* could easily degenerate into religious persecution; juries would find it difficult to accept as believed that which, by reason of their own religious upbringing, they deemed unbelievable.

In providing for "affirmation" as an alternative to "oath" in Article II, section 1, and Article VI, section 3, the framers of the Constitution, recognizing that religious convictions might forbid some persons (specifically Quakers) to take oaths, manifested their intention that no person in the judicial system—judge, lawyer, court official, or juryman—should be disqualified from governmental service on the ground of religion. In *Torcaso v. Watkins* (1961) the Court reached the same conclusion under the First Amendment as to state officials (for example, notaries public), and in *In re Jenison* (1963), the Court refused to uphold a conviction for contempt of court of a woman who would not serve on a jury because of the biblical command "Judge not that ye not be judged."

Resort to secular courts for resolution of intrachurch disputes (generally involving ownership and control of church assets) raises free exercise as well as establishment problems. As early as 1872 the Court held in *Watson v. Jones* that judicial intervention in such controversies was narrowly limited: a court could do no more than determine and enforce the decision of that body within the church that was the highest judicatory body according to appropriate church law. If a religious group (such as Baptist and Jewish) were congregational in structure, that body would be the majority of the congregation; if it were hierarchical (such as Roman Catholic or Russian Orthodox), the authority would generally be the diocesan bishop.

That principle was applied by the Supreme Court consistently until *Jones v. Wolf* (1979). There the court held that "neutral principles of law developed for use in all property disputes" could constitutionally be applied in church schism litigation. This means that unless the corporate charter or deeds of title provide that the faction loyal to the hierarchical church will retain ownership of the property, such a controversy must be adjudicated in accordance with the laws applicable to corporations generally, so that if recorded title is in the name of the local church, the majority of that body is entitled to control its use and disposition. The Court rejected the assertion in the dissenting opinion that a rule of compulsory deference to the highest ecclesiastical tribunal is necessary in order to protect the free exercise of those who formed the association and submitted themselves to its authority.

Where a conflict exists between the health of the community and the religious conscience of an individual or group, there is little doubt that the free exercise clause does not mandate risk to the community. Thus, as the Court held in JACOBSON V. MASSACHUSETTS (1905), compulsory VACCINATION against communicable diseases is enforceable notwithstanding religious objections to the procedure. So, too, fluoridation of municipal water supplies to prevent tooth cavities cannot be enjoined because of objection by some that drinking fluoridated water is sinful.

Where the life, health, or safety of individuals, rather than communities at large, is involved the constitutional principles are also fairly clear. When the individuals are children, a court may authorize blood transfusions to save their lives notwithstanding objection by parents (such as Jehovah's Witnesses) who believe that the procedure violates the biblical command against the drinking of blood. The underlying principle was stated by the Court in PRINCE V. MASSACHUSETTS (1944) upholding the conviction of a Jehovah's Witness for violating the state's child labor law in allowing her nine-year-old niece to accompany and help her while she sold the sect's religious literature on the city's streets. "Parents," the Court said, "may be free to become martyrs themselves. But it does not follow that they are free, in identical circumstances, to make martyrs of their children before they have reached the age of full and legal discretion when they can make that choice for themselves." It follows from this that unless mental incompetence is proved, a court may not authorize a blood transfusion upon an unconsenting adult.

The Court also balances competing interests in determining the constitutionality of enforcing compulsory Sunday laws against those whom religious conscience forbids labor or trade on the seventh rather than the first day of the week. In MCGOWAN V. MARY-

and and *Two Guys from Harrison-Allentown v. McGinley* (1961) the Court upheld the general validity of such laws against an establishment clause attack. Although their origin may have been religious, the Court said, the laws' present purpose was secular: to assure a weekly day for rest, relaxation, and family companionship.

Two other cases, *Gallagher v. Crown Kosher Super Market* (1961) and *Braunfeld v. Brown* (1961), decided at the same time, involved Orthodox Jews who observed Saturday as their day of rest and refrained from business on that day. In these cases the Court rejected the argument that requiring a Sabbatarian either to abstain from engaging in his trade or business two days weekly or to sacrifice his religious conscience, while requiring his Sunday-observing competitors to abstain only one day, imposed upon the Sabbatarian a competitive disadvantage, thereby penalizing him for his religious beliefs in violation of the free exercise clause. Exempting Sabbatarians, the Court held, might be administratively difficult, might benefit non-Sabbatarians motivated only by a desire for a competitive advantage over merchants closing on Sundays, and might frustrate the legitimate legislative goal of assuring a uniform day of rest. Although state legislatures could constitutionally elect to grant an exemption to Sabbatarians, the free exercise clause does not require them to do so.

In SHERBERT V. VERNER (1963), however, the Court reached a conclusion difficult to reconcile with that in *Gallagher* and *Braunfeld.* Denial of unemployment insurance benefits to a Seventh-Day Adventist who refused to accept tendered employment that required working on Saturday, the Court held, imposed an impermissible burden on the free exercise of religion. The First Amendment, it said, forbids forcing an applicant to choose between following religious precepts and forfeiting government benefits on the one hand, or, on the other, abandoning the precepts by accepting Sabbath work. Governmental imposition of such a choice, the Court said, puts the same kind of burden upon the free exercise of religion as would a fine imposed for Saturday worship.

The Court upheld statutory tax exemptions for church-owned real estate used exclusively for religious purposes in WALZ V. TAX COMMISSION (1970), rejecting an establishment clause attack. In *Murdock v. Pennsylvania* (1943) and *Follett v. Town of McCormack* (1944), however, the Court ruled that under the free exercise clause a revenue-raising tax on the privilege of canvassing or soliciting orders for articles could not be applied to Jehovah's Witnesses who sold their religious literature from door to door; in the same cases, the Court stated that an income tax statute could constitutionally be applied to clergymen's salaries for performing their clerical duties.

In *United States v. Lee* (1982) the Court upheld the exaction of social security and unemployment insurance contributions from Amish employers. The employers argued that their free exercise rights had been violated, citing 1 Timothy 5:8: "But if any provide not . . . for those of his own house, he hath denied the faith, and is worse than an infidel." Compulsory contribution, the Court said, was nonetheless justified; it was essential to accomplish the overriding governmental interest in the effective operation of the social security system.

To sum up, the Supreme Court's decisions in the arena of religious liberty manifest a number of approaches toward defining its meaning, specifically clear and present danger, the balancing of competing interests, and the establishment of a compelling state interest justifying intrusion on free exercise. On the whole, the Court has been loyal to the original intent of the generation that wrote the First Amendment to accord the greatest degree of liberty feasible in our society.

LEO PFEFFER

(SEE ALSO: *Widmar v. Vincent, 1981.*)

Bibliography

GIANELLA, DONALD 1968 Religious Liberty: Non-Establishment and Doctrinal Development: Part I, The Religious Liberty Guarantee. *Harvard Law Review* 80:1381–1431.

HOWE, MARK DEWOLFE 1965 *The Garden and the Wilderness: Religion and Government in American Constitutional History.* Chicago: University of Chicago Press.

KAUPER, PAUL G. 1964 *Religion and the Constitution.* Baton Rouge: Louisiana State University Press.

MANWARING, DAVID R. 1962 *Render unto Caesar: The Flag Salute Controversy.* Chicago: University of Chicago Press.

PFEFFER, LEO (1953) 1967 *Church, State and Freedom.* Boston: Beacon Press.

STOKES, ANSON P. 1950 *Church and State in the United States.* New York: Harper & Brothers.

______ and PFEFFER, LEO 1965 *Church and State in the United States.* New York: Harper & Row.

TRIBE, LAWRENCE H. 1978 *American Constitutional Law.* Mineola, N.Y.: Foundation Press.

RELIGIOUS SCHOOLS

See: Government Aid to Religious Institutions

RELIGIOUS TEST FOR PUBLIC OFFICE

As early as the seventeenth century ROGER WILLIAMS expressed his dissent from the common practice, inherited from England, of imposing a religious test for public office. However, by the beginning of the eighteenth century even Rhode Island had adopted the pattern prevailing among the other colonies and had enacted a law that limited CITIZENSHIP and eligibility for public office to Protestants.

Most liberal of these was Pennsylvania's law, which required a belief that God was "the rewarder of the good and punisher of the wicked." At the other extreme was that of North Carolina, which disqualified from office any one who denied "the being of God or the truth of the Protestant religion, or the divine authority of either the Old or New Testament."

After the Revolutionary War, however, the states began the process of disestablishment, including the elimination of religious tests. The 1786 VIRGINIA STATUTE OF RELIGIOUS LIBERTY, for example, asserted that "our CIVIL RIGHTS have no dependence on our religious opinions," and "the proscribing of any citizen as unworthy of being called to office of trust and emolument, unless he profess or renounce this or that religious opinion, is depriving him injuriously of those privileges and advantages to which in common with his fellow citizens he has a NATURAL RIGHT." The CONSTITUTIONAL CONVENTION OF 1787 unanimously adopted the clause of Article VI providing that "no religious Test shall ever be required as a qualification to any Office or public Trust under the United States."

The prohibition applies only to federal offices, and some states having religious tests in their constitutions or laws did not repeal them but contented themselves with limiting them to belief in the existence of God. One of these was Maryland, where an otherwise fully qualified appointee to the office of notary public was denied his commission for the office for refusing to sign the oath.

In TORCASO V. WATKINS (1961) the Supreme Court ruled the denial unconstitutional, relying upon both the no-establishment and the free exercise clauses of the FIRST AMENDMENT. As to the former, it asserted that the clause does not bar merely preferential treatment of one religion over others (although even such limited interpretation would require invalidation since the oath preferred theistic over nontheistic faiths such as "Buddhism, Taoism, Ethical Culture and Secular Humanism and others") but also preferential treatment of religion as against nonreligion. The opin ion also invoked the free exercise clause in concludin that the provision invades "freedom of religion an belief."

The converse of religious tests for public office, re flecting a prevalent anticlericalism, was the disqualifi cation of clergymen from serving in public office. majority of the states had such provisions when th Constitution was written, but in *McDaniel v. Pat* (1978) the Supreme Court held such laws violativ of the First Amendment's free exercise clause.

LEO PFEFFE

Bibliography

PFEFFER, LEO (1953)1967 *Church, State and Freedon* Boston: Beacon Press.

——— 1975 *God, Caesar and the Constitution.* Bostor Beacon Press.

RELIGIOUS USE OF STATE PROPERTY

In WIDMAR V. VINCENT (1981) the Supreme Cour ruled that a state university's exclusionary policy i respect to students' use for prayer or religious instruc tion of premises generally available to students fo nonreligious use violated the FIRST AMENDMENT' guarantee of FREEDOM OF SPEECH.

Earlier, relevant decisions, mostly involving Jeho vah's Witnesses, were handed down before the Cour ruled in CANTWELL V. CONNECTICUT (1940) that th free exercise of religion clause, like the free speec clause, was applicable to the states no less than t the federal government. Quite naturally, therefore it applied to religious meetings and conversionary ef forts the CLEAR AND PRESENT DANGER (later COMPEL LING STATE INTEREST) test formulated in SCHENC V. UNITED STATES (1919) in respect to political speec and meetings and continued to do so after *Cantwel*

In *Jamison v. Texas* (1943) the Court rejected contention that a city's power over streets and park is not limited to making reasonable regulations fo the control of traffic and maintenance of order, bu encompasses power absolutely to prohibit use for com munication of ideas, including religious ones. N doubt, it ruled in NIEMOTKO V. MARYLAND (1951 a municipality may require a permit to hold religiou meetings or, as in *Cox v. New Hampshire* (1941), pub lic parades or processions, in streets and parks, bu only to regulate time and place, and it may not refus a permit by reason of the meeting's content, even i it includes verbal attacks upon some religions. Th s so, the Court ruled in KUNZ V. NEW YORK (1941), even where prior missionary meetings had resulted in disorder because of the minister's scurrilous attacks on Roman Catholicism and Judaism, because the added cost of providing police to prevent possible violence does not justify infringement upon First Amendment rights.

Nor, as the Court held in *Schneider v. Irvington* (1939), may a municipality prohibit distribution of leaflets, including religious ones, on public streets and parks in order to prevent littering; the constitutional way to avoid littering is by arresting litterers, rather than restricting rights secured by the amendment. For the same reason, it reversed the conviction of a Jehovah's Witness who rang door bells to distribute religious handbills, in violation of an ordinance (enacted in part to prevent criminal entry) prohibiting ringing of doorbells or knocking on doors to distribute handbills.

The Court, in *Widmar,* did not hold that a state university must provide premises for student prayer and religious instruction, but only that it may not exclude such use if premises are provided for other noncurricular purposes. It is hardly likely that it intended thereby to overrule MCCOLLUM V. BOARD OF EDUCATION (1948), wherein it outlawed religious instruction in public schools even where limited to pupils whose parents consent thereto. The distinction between the two situations lies in the fact that *McCollum* involved students of elementary and secondary school ages, whereas *Widmar* concerned students of college age who are generally less likely to be unduly influenced by on-premises prayer meetings.

In LYNCH V. DONNELLY (1984) the Court upheld the use of municipal funds to finance the cost of erecting and illuminating a life-size nativity scene in Pawtucket, Rhode Island, as part of an annual Christmas display. (Although the display was on private property, the Court made it clear that the result would have been the same had it been on town-owned property.) The Court based its decision on the recognition that Christmas had become a national secular holiday in American culture.

LEO PFEFFER

Bibliography

PFEFFER, LEO 1985 *Religion, State and the Burger Court.* Buffalo, N.Y.: Prometheus.

REMAND

A remand is an appellate court's act in returning a case to a lower court, usually unnecessary when the appellate court affirms the lower court's judgment. When the Supreme Court reverses or vacates a state court judgment, it customarily remands for "proceedings not inconsistent" with the Court's decision.

KENNETH L. KARST

REMEDIES

See: Constitutional Remedies; Exhaustion of Remedies

REMOVAL OF CASES

When a civil or criminal case within CONCURRENT federal and state JURISDICTION is filed in state court, Congress may choose to offer the parties the right to remove it from state to federal court. Indeed, removal is the only way to provide for ORIGINAL federal JURISDICTION in some cases, such as those in which a FEDERAL QUESTION appears for the first time in the defendant's answer to the complaint. Because federal removal jurisdiction is treated as derivative from state jurisdiction, a suit improperly filed in state court may not be removed.

Congress has employed removal ever since the JUDICIARY ACT OF 1789. The device serves two principal purposes. First, removal can equalize the position of plaintiffs and defendants with respect to choice of forum. For example, federal statutes allow defendants to remove most DIVERSITY JURISDICTION and federal question cases that the plaintiff could have brought initially in federal court. Second, removal can provide access to a more sympathetic federal forum for defendants who are asserting federal rights as defenses. For example, statutes permit federal officers and others acting under federal authority to remove suits brought against them for conduct within the scope of that authority. Another statute authorizes removal of suits by individuals whose rights under federal equal rights laws cannot be enforced in state court. (See CIVIL RIGHTS REMOVAL.)

Federal statutory law provides that if a removable claim is joined in the same suit with a nonremovable claim, the entire suit may be removed if the two claims are "separate and independent." If the nonremovable claim is sufficiently separate to satisfy the statutory requirement, however, it may not be within the federal court's PENDENT OR ANCILLARY JURISDICTION. In such cases, the statute resolves the constitutional problem by granting the federal court discretion to remand the nonremovable claim to state court.

CAROLE E. GOLDBERG-AMBROSE

Bibliography

COHEN, W. 1961 Problems in the Removal of a "Separate and Independent Claim or Cause of Action." *Minnesota Law Review* 46:1–41.

REMOVAL POWER (PRESIDENTIAL)

See: Appointing and Removal Power, Presidential

RENDELL-BAKER v. KOHN

See: *Blum v. Yaretsky*

RENDITION

See: Fugitive from Justice; Fugitive Slavery

REPEAL ACT (1894)

See: Civil Rights Repeal Act

REPORTER'S PRIVILEGE

The reporter's privilege issue posed in BRANZBURG V. HAYES (1972) is a microcosm of the difficulties of both journalism and law in accommodating traditional procedures and principles to the development of widespread disenchantment and disobedience in American society. For knowledge about dissident groups we must depend on the efforts of journalists, efforts that will be impeded if the subjects believe that reporters' information will become available to law enforcement agencies. Yet the legal system has important interests in prompt detection and prosecution of crimes. Anglo-American judges have long boasted that no person is too high to escape the obligation of testifying to a GRAND JURY. This obligation is an important guarantee of equality in the operation of criminal law. Thus, courts have historically been unsympathetic to claims that certain kinds of information should be privileged from disclosure before the grand jury. Only the RIGHT AGAINST SELF-INCRIMINATION and the attorney–client privilege have achieved general recognition from American courts.

In *Branzburg,* three cases joined for decision, three reporters had declined to provide requested information to a grand jury. The reporters argued for a special privilege, arguing that compulsory testimony would significantly diminish the flow of information from news sources.

The opinions of a closely divided Supreme Court spanned the spectrum of possible FIRST AMENDMENT responses. Justice BYRON R. WHITE's majority opinion rejected the notion of a journalist's claim of privilege, calling the journalists' fear speculative. Even assuming some constriction in the flow of news, White argued the public interest in investigating and prosecuting crimes reported to the press outweighs that in the dissemination of news about those activities when the dissemination rests upon confidentiality.

After seemingly rejecting both the theoretical and the empirical arguments for a journalist's privilege, the majority opinion concluded with an enigmatic suggestion that the door to the privilege might not be completely closed. "Newsgathering," the majority noted obliquely, "is not without its First Amendment protection": "[G]rand jury investigations if instituted or conducted other than in good faith, would pose wholly different issues for resolution under the First Amendment. Official harassment of the press undertaken not for purposes of law enforcement but to disrupt a reporter's relationship with his news sources would have no justification."

Moreover, the majority opinion made clear that the subject of reporter's privilege is an appropriate one for legislative or executive consideration. It noted that several states already had passed SHIELD LAWS embodying a journalist's privilege of the kind sought.

In a brief but important concurring opinion, Justice LEWIS F. POWELL emphasized that "we do not hold that . . . state and federal authorities are free to 'annex' the news media as an investigative arm of government." No "harassment" of newsmen will be tolerated, Powell continued, if a reporter can show that the grand jury investigation is "not being conducted in good faith" or if he is called upon for information "bearing only a remote and tenuous relationship to the subject of the investigation." Lower courts have generally followed the Powell approach to claims of reporter's privilege.

Four Justices dissented. For Justice WILLIAM O. DOUGLAS, the First Amendment offered immunity from appearing or testifying before a grand jury unless the reporter were implicated in a crime. Justice POTTER J. STEWART, for himself and Justices WILLIAM J. BRENNAN and THURGOOD MARSHALL, wrote a careful but impassioned dissent. From the right to publish Stewart deduced corollary right to gather news. This right, in turn, required protection of confidentia ources. Stewart recognized that the interest of the government in investigating crime could properly outweigh the journalist's privilege if the government could show that the information sought were "clearly relevant to a precisely defined subject of governmental inquiry"; that the reporter probably had the relevant information; and that there were no other available source for the information.

Later decisions have uniformly rejected claims of special privilege for reporters in other factual settings. In ZURCHER V. STANFORD DAILY (1978) the Supreme Court denied that the First Amendment gave any special protection to newsrooms against police searches and seizures. And in HERBERT V. LANDO (1979) the Court rejected a claim that journalists should be privileged not to respond to questions about the editorial processes or their subjective state of mind concerning stories involved in libel actions. Thus the Court has left the question of reporter's privilege to legislative treatment through shield laws and to prosecutorial discretion.

BENNO C. SCHMIDT, JR.

Bibliography

BLASI, VINCENT 1971 The Newsman's Privilege: An Empirical Study. *Michigan Law Review* 70:229.

REPORT OF THE CONFERENCE OF CHIEF JUSTICES ON FEDERAL–STATE RELATIONSHIPS (August 23, 1958)

By the late 1950s resentment grew among many state officials over the Supreme Court's increasing monitoring of state policies and activities. The Conference of State Chief Justices, with Southerners among the prime movers, issued a long critique of the Supreme Court's rulings, condemning the body's activism, "policy making," and departures from STARE DECISIS. The report chiefly criticized the Court for: increasing national power at the expense of the states through the use of the GENERAL WELFARE CLAUSE, FEDERAL GRANTS-IN-AID, and the doctrine of PREEMPTION; and curtailing state authority in state LEGISLATIVE INVESTIGATIONS, public employment, admission to the bar, and administration of the criminal law. The report called for rebuilding a strong FEDERALISM; the Court's curtailment of its own policymaking; and restoration of the "great principle of distribution of powers among the various branches of government and between levels of government—the crucial base of our democracy." Court defenders responded by pointing to the need for uniform national constitutional standards, particularly in THE CIVIL RIGHTS area, maintaining the "democracy" of JUDICIAL REVIEW.

PAUL L. MURPHY

Bibliography

PRITCHETT, C. HERMAN 1961 *Congress versus the Supreme Court, 1957–1961.* Minneapolis: University of Minnesota Press.

REPRESENTATION

Representation is standing or acting in the place of another, normally because a group is too large, dispersed, or uninformed for its members to act on their own. It is not necessarily democratic; nor is it necessarily connected to the idea of government by consent. Democratic representation, based on the concept that governmental legitimacy rests on the reasoned assent of individual citizens, dates from the seventeenth century.

This concept has long been taken seriously in the United States. Colonial assemblies won as much domestic legislative power in the fifty years before the American Revolution as Parliament had won in 500, with broader voting constituencies than Parliament's and more conviction that the representatives should speak for their local constituencies rather than for the nation at large. Both this "inner revolution" and the outward break with England asserted a NATURAL RIGHT to government by consent of the governed and treated consent as more than a legal fiction. "NO TAXATION WITHOUT REPRESENTATION" was the slogan asserting this right. A guarded commitment to majority rule has helped put the right into practice. As THOMAS JEFFERSON declared in his first inaugural address, "though the will of the majority is in all cases to prevail, that will to be rightful must be reasonable."

The Constitution put certain restraints on majority rule: it banned some acts outright; it divided its majorities by SEPARATION OF POWERS and FEDERALISM; and it permitted an electorate that was restricted mostly to white male landowners. Yet the Constitution was democratic for its day; it has since expanded both the number of elective offices and the franchise; and its very barriers to majority whim, requiring the creation of broad, stable coalitions to rule, have brought about a majority rule stronger and more reasonable than might have evolved from a less fettered regime. JAMES MADISON, explaining and defending the Constitution in THE FEDERALIST, extolled the principle of representation as the device that made majority rule compatible with good government. Representation made possible the extended republic, embracing a large enough territory and population to be safe from foreign aggression and a great enough diversity of economic and other interests to minimize the danger of majority faction. Indirect self-government through a limited number of representatives required coalition-building, with diverse factions compromising their antagonistic goals. Representation also facilitated deliberation: direct democracy (exemplified by the Athenian Assembly) smacked too much of mob rule.

But the Constitution left many questions of representation unsettled. Whom, exactly, do the representatives represent? Does the representative speak for his district, state, or nation? Does he speak only for his supporters and his party, or for opponents, nonvoters, and the unfranchised as well? Does he speak for the whole people or for a coalition of interests? Answers depend on what representation is expected to accomplish and how it is structured.

There has been little agreement in American history about the goals of representation. Some, such as Jefferson and ABRAHAM LINCOLN, have argued that the purpose of the regime is to protect individual rights of liberty and equality. Others, such as JOHN C. CALHOUN, with his doctrine of concurrent majorities, have argued that protection of STATES' RIGHTS or property rights is the basic goal. Still others, such as ALEXANDER HAMILTON and STEPHEN A. DOUGLAS, have emphasized institutional stability and regularity.

Structural variation can drastically affect the quality of representation. A representative can be a symbol, a sample, an agent, or a trustee, elected directly or through intermediaries, individually or jointly accountable to a territorial or an ideological constituency. The American system, with two-party competition for single-member districts, bicameral legislatures, and separate executive branch, has had accessible representatives who speak for their local constituencies (though they are more than agents and are not bound by detailed constituent "instruction") but may be hard to unite on national issues. The British system, combining legislative and executive powers, and with disciplined national parties, has produced representatives who speak for the nation and coalesce easily on national issues but are much less accessible and attentive to district interests than American representatives. Proportional representation, used by several European governments since World War I, usually has MULTIMEMBER DISTRICTS, with seats divided by proportion of vote for each party. Proportional representation reflects public ideological variety, often with a small party for every view. By focusing on ideological issues, it tends to discourage compromise and produce weak, volatile coalitions, such as those of Weimar Germany and the Fourth French Republic.

American reformers have greatly extended the franchise without greatly changing the structure or working of government. In the Progressive Era, 1880–1920, they also sought to cleanse elections of control by party and financial bosses with "good government" reforms: Australian ballot; PRIMARY ELECTIONS, INITIATIVE, REFERENDUM, and RECALL; nonpartisan civil service; nonpartisan local elections, corrupt practices acts, and weakening of the speaker's control over the House of Representatives. These reforms reduced corruption but also undermined party discipline and lowered voter turnout.

Academic reformers responded to these changes in three different ways. Some called for less separation of powers and more disciplined national parties on the British model. Others wanted to make every office elective, including party, cabinet, and corporate leaders, and to make elections more "representative" with public funding, REAPPORTIONMENT, proportional representation, or quotas. Yet others called for councils of experts to take over problems that elected representatives had failed to solve.

These prescriptions have been partially fulfilled in the adoption of structural change but less so in the delivery of promised results. National power has been enlarged over state, public over private, expert over amateur, and judicial over legislative. Blacks have the right to political equality; legislative districts are equalized; public funding of presidential campaigns has been increased; presidential nomination has been made almost plebiscitary. But these reforms did not still complaints that the system was producing unrepresentative leadership. Reformers deplored most of the candidates in the reformed presidential elections of the 1970s and public turnout sank to new lows. The winning candidate in 1980 and 1984 argued that private consumer sovereignty was the truest form of democracy.

Over the years the Supreme Court, though once reluctant to take sides on POLITICAL QUESTIONS, has become an important player in the game of reform. Chief Justice JOHN MARSHALL first laid down the political question doctrine in OBITER DICTUM in MARBURY V. MADISON (1803), forbearing to "intermeddle with the prerogatives of the executive." "Questions, in their nature political," he wrote, "can never be made in this court." Chief Justice ROGER B. TANEY, in LUTHER V. BORDEN (1849), declared that the republican or representative character of state domestic government was "political in its nature" and reserved by judicial prudence—and perhaps also by constitutional mandate under the GUARANTEE CLAUSE—for resolution by the "political branches, not the judiciary." The Dorr controversy in *Luther* involved many of the same issues as BAKER V. CARR (1962), but the Court lacked the political strength, the appearance of constitutional authority, and the enforcement technique to intervene effectively.

Against the disfranchisement of blacks, prohibited on paper after 1870 by the FIFTEENTH AMENDMENT, the Court provided no lasting protection until 1944, when it ended the white primary—although it had intervened against some administrative abuses and would later intervene aggressively against franchise restrictions under both the Fourteenth and Fifteenth Amendments. Almost all other state representation questions—validity of delegations of authority, of legislative enactments, of party nomination decisions, and of initiatives and referenda—the Court found nonjusticiable.

The Court's list of nonjusticiable political questions appeared to include unequal or "malapportioned" electoral districts, especially after COLEGROVE V. GREEN (1946). But in *Baker v. Carr,* over objections from Justices FELIX FRANKFURTER and JOHN MARSHALL HARLAN that the Court was entering a "quagmire" of insoluble questions, the majority held that apportionment was not a political question and was "within the reach of judicial protection under the FOURTEENTH AMENDMENT." In REYNOLDS V. SIMS (1964), the Court proclaimed that "ONE PERSON, ONE VOTE" is the "fundamental principle" of the Constitution, applicable to both houses of state legislatures and to local and special-purpose elections—even if most of the voters involved opposed it. The principle does not, however, apply to the United States Senate, the ELECTORAL COLLEGE, or most aspects of party organization. Nor does it seem to apply to the manipulation of effective votes through gerrymandering (see GERRYMANDER) and multimember districting unless these are surgically exclusive of a protectable minority, as in GOMILLION V. LIGHTFOOT (1960). *Gomillion* invalidated a law excluding from the city limits of Tuskegee, Alabama, all but four or five black voters while keeping every white voter. In a series of cases beginning with *Wright v. Rockefeller* (1965) and highlighted by UNITED JEWISH ORGANIZATIONS V. CAREY (1977) and MOBILE V. BOLDEN (1980), the Court has repeatedly refused to interfere with nonsurgical districting to the obvious disadvantage of racial or religious minorities who as individuals would have been eminently protectable against franchise discrimination. The difference between districting discrimination against groups and franchise discrimination against individuals is that franchise discrimination is easy to remedy, but districting discrimination is not. Courts have equalized nominal votes by equal apportionment but not effective votes—votes that actually elect the voter's candidate—because there is no way short of proportional representation to equalize every group's effective vote.

Besides holding apportionment justiciable, the reapportionment cases did something more radical: they treated districting discrimination and franchise discrimination as if they were virtually interchangeable, and they invoked the EQUAL PROTECTION clause of the Fourteenth Amendment to protect a "right to vote" against "dilution" by unequal districts. But the framers of the Fourteenth Amendment had insisted that it left suffrage "exclusively under the control of the states"; construing it to grant a federal right to vote would seem to render at least five subsequent voting rights amendments, including section 2 of the Fourteenth Amendment, superfluous. This "parthenogenesis of a VOTING RIGHT," combined with an aggressive application of STRICT SCRUTINY, led to the judicial abolition of POLL TAX, property, and taxpayer qualifications on voting, and all but the shortest RESIDENCY REQUIREMENTS. It also cleared the way for the passage of the VOTING RIGHTS ACT of 1965 and, paradoxically, gave a boost to the TWENTY-SIXTH AMENDMENT (eighteen-year-old vote)—and, possibly, to the proposed DISTRICT OF COLUMBIA REPRESENTATION AMENDMENT.

These voting rights decisions substantially aided the "inclusion process" in a formal sense. Some critics feel that this aid was a desirable end in itself; others argue that, by overriding the choices of elected representatives and creating constitutional authority *ex nihilo,* the Court has debased the vote in substance more than it has enlarged it in form. As the nation enters its third century under the Constitution, the inclusion process has been judicialized but hardly completed—and the same may be said of the ancient debate over political representation.

WARD E. Y. ELLIOTT

Bibliography

ELLIOTT, WARD E. Y. 1975 *The Rise of Guardian Democracy: The Supreme Court's Role in Voting Rights Disputes, 1845–1969.* Cambridge, Mass.: Harvard University Press.

REPRODUCTIVE AUTONOMY

Commencing in 1942 in SKINNER V. OKLAHOMA, and most intrepidly in 1973 in ROE V. WADE, the Supreme Court has secured against unwarranted governmental intrusion a decision fundamental to the course of an individual's life—the decision whether to beget or bear a child. Government action in this area bears significantly on the ability of women, particularly, to plan and control their lives. Official policy on reproductive choice may effectively facilitate or retard women's opportunities to participate in full partnership with men in the nation's social, political, and economic life. Supreme Court decisions concerning BIRTH CONTROL, however, have not yet adverted to evolving sex equality-equal protection doctrine. Instead, high court opinions rest dominantly on SUBSTANTIVE DUE PROCESS analysis; they invoke basic liberty-autonomy values difficult to tie directly to the Constitution's text, history, or structure.

Skinner marked the first occasion on which the Court referred to an individual's procreative choice as "a basic liberty." The Court invalidated a state statute providing for compulsory STERILIZATION of habitual offenders. The statute applied after a third conviction for a FELONY "involving moral turpitude," defined to include grand larceny but exclude embezzlement. The decision ultimately rested on an EQUAL PROTECTION ground: "Sterilization of those who have thrice committed grand larceny, with immunity for those who are embezzlers, is a clear, pointed, unmistakable discrimination." Justice WILLIAM O. DOUGLAS's opinion for the Court, however, is infused with substantive due process tones: "We are dealing here with legislation which involves one of the basic CIVIL RIGHTS of man. Marriage and procreation are fundamental to the very existence and survival of the race." Gerald Gunther has noted that, in a period marked by a judicial hands-off approach to economic and social legislation, *Skinner* stood virtually alone in applying a stringent review standard favoring a "basic liberty" unconnected to a particular constitutional guarantee.

Over two decades later, in GRISWOLD V. CONNECTICUT (1965), the Court grappled with a state law banning the use of contraceptives. The Court condemned the statute's application to married persons. Justice Douglas's opinion for the Court located protected "zones of privacy" in the penumbras of several specific BILL OF RIGHTS guarantees. The law in question impermissibly intruded on the marriage relationship, a privacy zone "older than the Bill of Rights" and "intimate to the degree of being sacred."

In EISENSTADT V. BAIRD (1972) the Court confronted a Massachusetts law prohibiting the distribution of contraceptives, except by a registered pharmacist on a doctor's prescription to a married person. The Court avoided explicitly extending the right announced in *Griswold* beyond use to distribution. Writing for the majority, Justice WILLIAM J. BRENNAN rested the decision on an equal protection ground: "whatever the rights of the individual to access to contraceptives may be," the Court said, "the rights must be the same for the unmarried and the married alike." *Eisenstadt* thus carried constitutional doctrine a considerable distance from "the sacred precincts of marital bedrooms" featured in *Griswold.*

The Court's reasoning in *Eisenstadt* did not imply that laws prohibiting fornication, because they treat married and unmarried persons dissimilarly, were in immediate jeopardy. Rather, Justice Brennan declined to attribute to Massachusetts the base purpose of "prescrib[ing] pregnancy and the birth of an unwanted child as punishment for fornication."

In 1977, in CAREY V. POPULATION SERVICES INTERNATIONAL, the Court invalidated a New York law prohibiting the sale of contraceptives to minors under age sixteen and forbidding commercial distribution of even nonprescription contraceptives by anyone other than a licensed pharmacist. Justice Brennan reinterpreted the pathmarking precedent. *Griswold,* he noted, addressed a "particularly 'repulsive' " intrusion, but "subsequent decisions have made clear that the constitutional protection of individual autonomy in matters of childbearing is not dependent on [the marital privacy] element." Accordingly, "*Griswold* may no longer be read as holding only that a State may not prohibit a married couple's use of contraceptives. Read in light of [*Eisenstadt* and *Roe v. Wade*] the teaching of *Griswold* is that the Constitution protects individual decisions in matters of childbearing from unjustified intrusion by the State."

Roe v. Wade declared that a woman, guided by the medical judgment of her physician, has a FUNDAMENTAL RIGHT to abort her pregnancy, a right subject to state interference only upon demonstration of a COMPELLING STATE INTEREST. The right so recognized, Justice HARRY L. BLACKMUN wrote for the Court, falls within the sphere of personal privacy recognized or suggested in prior decisions relating to marriage, procreation, contraception, family relationships, child-rearing and education. The "privacy" or individual autonomy right advanced in *Roe v. Wade* is not explicit in our fundamental instrument of government, Justice Blackmun acknowledged; however, the Court viewed it as "founded in the FOURTEENTH AMENDMENT's [and presumably the FIFTH AMEND-

MENT's] concept of personal liberty and restrictions upon state action." Justice Blackmun mentioned, too, the district court's view, derived from Justice ARTHUR J. GOLDBERG's concurring opinion in *Griswold,* that the liberty at stake could be located in the NINTH AMENDMENT's reservation of rights to the people.

The Texas criminal abortion law at issue in ROE v. WADE was severely restrictive; it excepted from criminality "only a *lifesaving* procedure on behalf of the mother, without regard to pregnancy stage and without recognition of the other interests involved." In the several years immediately preceding the *Roe v. Wade* decision, the Court noted, the trend in the states had been "toward liberalization of abortion statutes." Nonetheless, the Court's rulings in *Roe v. Wade* and in a companion case decided the same day, *Doe v. Bolton* (1973), called into question the validity of the criminal abortion statutes of every state, even those with the least restrictive provisions.

The sweeping impact of the 1973 rulings on state laws resulted from the precision with which Justice Blackmun defined the state interests that the Court would recognize as compelling. In the first two trimesters of a pregnancy, the state's interest was confined to protecting the woman's health: during the first trimester, "the abortion decision and its effectuation must be left to the medical judgment of the pregnant woman's attending physician"; in the next three-month stage, the state may, if it chooses, require other measures protective of the woman's health. During 'the stage subsequent to viability" (roughly, the third trimester), the state may protect the "potentiality of human life"; at that stage, the state "may, if it chooses, regulate, and even proscribe, abortion except where it is necessary, in appropriate medical judgment, for the preservation of the life or health of the mother."

Sylvia Law has commented that no Supreme Court decision has meant more to women. Wendy Williams has noted that a society intent on holding women in their traditional role would attempt to deny them reproductive autonomy. Justice Blackmun's opinion indicates sensitivity to the severe burdens, mental and physical, immediately carried by a woman unable to terminate an unwanted pregnancy, and the distressful life she and others in her household may suffer when she lacks the physical or psychological ability or financial resources necessary for child-rearing. But *Roe v. Wade* bypassed the equal protection argument presented for the female plaintiffs. Instead, the Court anchored stringent review to the personal autonomy concept found in *Griswold.* Moreover, *Roe v. Wade* did not declare an individual right; in the Court's words, the decision stated a joint right of "the woman and her responsible physician . . . in consultation."

The 1973 abortion rulings have been called aberrational, extraordinarily activist interventions by a Court reputedly deferential to STATES' RIGHTS and legislative judgments. John Hart Ely criticized *Roe v. Wade* as a decision the Court had no business making because freedom to have an abortion "lacks connection with any value the Constitution marks as special."

Archibald Cox described his own view of *Roe v. Wade* as "less rigid" then Ely's. He said in a 1975 lecture: "The Court's persistent resort to notions of substantive due process for almost a century attests the strength of our natural law inheritance in constitutional adjudication." Cox considered it "unwise as well as hopeless to resist" that strong tradition. *Roe v. Wade* nevertheless foundered, in his judgment, because the Court did not (and, he believed, could not) articulate an acceptable "precept of sufficient abstractness." The critical parts of the opinion, he commented, "read like a set of hospital rules and regulations."

Paul Freund expressed a similar concern in 1982. He thought *Roe v. Wade* epitomized a tendency of the modern Supreme Court (under Chief Justice WARREN E. BURGER as well as Chief Justice EARL WARREN) "to specify by a kind of legislative code the one alternative pattern which will satisfy the Constitution, foreclosing further experimentation by Congress or the states." In his view, "a law which absolutely made criminal all kinds and forms of abortion could not stand up; it is not a reasonable accommodation of interests." But the Court "adopted what could be called the medical point of view—making distinctions that turn on trimesters." The Court might have drawn other lines, Freund suggested; it might have adopted an ethical rather than a medical approach, for example, by immunizing abortions, in a manner resembling the American Law Institute proposal, "where the pregnancy was the result of rape or incest, where the fetus was severely abnormal, or where the mother's health, physical or mental, would be seriously impaired by bringing the fetus to term." (The Georgia statutes struck down in *Doe v. Bolton,* companion case to *Roe v. Wade,* were patterned on the American Law Institute's model.) If the Court had proceeded that way, Freund commented, perhaps "some of the bitter debate on the issue might . . . have been averted; at any rate the animus against the Court might have been diverted to the legislative halls."

Animus there has been, in the form of anti-abortion constitutional amendments introduced in Congress in 1973 and each session thereafter; proposals for "human life" legislation, in which Congress, upon the vote of a simple majority, would declare that the Fourteenth Amendment protects the life of "persons" from the moment of conception; and bills to strip the Supreme Court of JURISDICTION to decide abortion cases. State legislatures reacted as well, adopting measures aimed at minimizing the impact of the 1973 ruling, including notice and consent requirements, prescriptions for the protection of fetal life, and bans on public expenditures or access to public facilities for abortion.

Some speculated that the 7–2 judgments in the 1973 cases (Justices BYRON R. WHITE and WILLIAM H. REHNQUIST dissented) were motivated in part by population concerns and the specter of unwanted children born to women living in grinding poverty. But in 1977, the Court voted 6–3 against pleas to extend the 1973 rulings to require public assistance for an indigent woman's elective (not medically necessary) abortion. First, in *Beal v. Doe,* the Court held that the federally established Medicaid program did not require Pennsylvania, as a condition of participation, to fund elective abortions. Second, in MAHER V. ROE the Court ruled that the equal protection clause did not command Connecticut, which furnished Medicaid funds for childbirth, to pay as well for elective abortions. Finally, *Poelker v. Doe* held that the city of St. Louis did not violate the equal protection clause by providing publicly financed hospital services for childbirth but not for elective abortions.

The impoverished Connecticut women who sought Medicaid assistance in *Maher* maintained that, so long as their state subsidized childbirth, it could not withhold subsidy for abortion, a far less expensive and, at least in the first trimester, less risky procedure. Stringent equal protection review was required, they urged, because the state had intruded on the "fundamental right" declared in *Roe v. Wade.* Justice LEWIS F. POWELL, writing for the Court, responded that the right recognized in *Roe* did not require government neutrality as to the abortion decision; it was not a right to make a choice unchecked by substantive government control. Rather, it was a right restraining government from obstructing a woman's access to private sources to effectuate her decision. Because the right *Roe v. Wade* secured, as explained in *Maher,* was not impinged upon (and because disadvantageous treatment of needy persons does not alone identify SUSPECT CLASSIFICATION requiring close scrutiny), Connecticut's funding refusal could be sustained if it related "rationally" to a "constitutionally permissible" purpose. The policies to encourage childbirth in preference to abortion and to protect potential life supported the *Maher* regulation. There was, in the Court's view, no issue here, as there had been in *Roe v. Wade,* of an attempt "to impose [the state's] will by force of law."

Although criticized as irrational in the reproductive choice context, the distinction Justice Powell drew between government carrot and government stick had been made previously in other settings. But in *Maher,* unlike other cases in which the carrot/stick distinction had figured, the state could not justify its funding bar as an attempt to conserve public funds. In comparison to the medical costs of childbirth and the subsequent costs of child-rearing borne by public welfare programs, the costs of elective abortions are insubstantial.

The *Maher* logic was carried further in HARRIS V. MCRAE (1980). The federal law at issue, known as the HYDE AMENDMENT, excluded even therapeutic (medically needed) abortions from the Medicaid program. In holding, 5–4, that the Hyde Amendment survived constitutional review, the Court reiterated the distinction drawn in *Maher.* Justice JOHN PAUL STEVENS, who had joined the majority in *Maher,* switched sides in *McRae* because he discerned a critical difference between elective and therapeutic abortions in the context of the Medicaid program. Congress had established two neutral criteria for Medicaid benefits—financial need and medical need. The pregnant women who challenged the Hyde Amendment met both criteria. By creating an exception to the medical need criterion for the sole purpose of deterring exercise of the right declared "fundamental" in *Roe v. Wade,* Justice Stevens reasoned, the sovereign had violated its "duty to govern impartially."

Following the bold step in the 1973 abortion rulings, the public funding rulings appear incongruous. The direct, practical effect of the funding rulings will not endure, however, if the legislative trend again turns in the direction discernible at the time of the *Roe v. Wade* decision. National and state legislators may come to question the wisdom of a childbirth-encouragement policy trained on Medicaid-eligible women, and to comprehend more completely the centrality of reproductive autonomy to a woman's control of her life's course.

May the state require spousal consent to the abortion decision of a woman and her physician when the state itself may not override that decision? In PLANNED PARENTHOOD V. DANFORTH (1976) the Court held unconstitutional Missouri's requirement of spousal consent to a first-trimester abortion. Justice Blackmun, for the six-member majority, declared that the state may not delegate authority to any person, even a spouse, to veto abortions which the state may not proscribe or regulate. A husband, of course, has a vital interest in his wife's pregnancy, Justice Blackmun acknowledged. But the woman's stake is more compelling; therefore the final decision must rest with her.

Although government may not remove the abortion decision from the woman and her physician unless its action demonstrably serves a compelling interest in the woman's health or in potential life, a state may act to ensure the quality of the decision. In *Danforth* the Court unanimously upheld Missouri's requirement that, prior to a first-trimester abortion, a woman certify that she has given her informed, uncoerced consent. The abortion decision is stressful, the Court observed; it should be made with "full knowledge of its nature and consequences." A state's authority in this regard, however, is limited. Regulations must be genuinely necessary to secure enlightened consent; they must be designed to inform rather than persuade; and they must not interfere with the physician's counseling discretion.

In *Akron v. Akron Center for Reproductive Health* (1983) the Court, 6–3, speaking through Justice Powell, struck down a series of regulations that exceeded these limits. One regulation required the physician to tell any woman contemplating an abortion that the unborn child is a human life from conception; to tell her the details of the anatomical characteristics of the fetus; and to enumerate the physical and psychological risks of abortion. The Court held this regulation invalid because it was designed to persuade women to forgo abortions, and because it encroached upon the physician's discretion to decide how best to advise the patient. The Court also invalidated as unnecessary to secure informed, uncoerced consent a twenty-four-hour waiting period between consent and abortion and a requirement that the physician personally convey information to the woman.

The Court has not yet had occasion to pass upon a regulation designed to render the birth-control-through-contraception decision an informed one. In *Bolger v. Youngs Drug Product Corporation* (1983), however, a majority held that government may not block dissemination of information relevant to that decision. At issue was a federal statute (the Comstock Act) prohibiting the mailing of contraceptive advertisements. All eight participating Justices held the statute unconstitutional as applied to the promotional and informational literature in question because the legislation impermissibly regulated COMMERCIAL SPEECH. (Earlier, in *Carey,* the Court had invalidated an analogous state regulation on the same ground.) Five Justices joined in a further ruling that the federal statute violated the right to reproductive autonomy because it denied adults truthful information relevant to informed contraception decisions.

The trimester scheme established in *Roe v. Wade* has guided the Court's ruling on state regulation of abortion procedures. Under that scheme, the state may not interfere with a physician's medical judgment concerning the place and manner of first-trimester abortions because abortions performed at that stage are less risky than childbirth. Thus in *Doe v. Bolton* (1973), the companion case to *Roe v. Wade,* the Court invalidated a Georgia requirement that even first-trimester abortions be performed in a full-service hospital. In *Connecticut v. Menillo* (1975), however, the Court, per curiam, explicitly relied upon one of the underpinnings of *Roe v. Wade,* the need for a physician's medical judgment, to uphold a state's conviction of a nonphysician for performing an abortion.

The ban on state regulation of a physician's performance of first-trimester abortions is not absolute; it does not exclude regulation serving an important state health interest without significantly affecting the abortion decision. A unanimous bench in *Danforth* so indicated in upholding a Missouri regulation requiring maintenance of records of all abortions, for disclosure only to public health officials, for seven years.

Roe v. Wade declared that after the first trimester, because an abortion entails greater risks, the state's interest in women's health could justify "place and manner" regulations even if the abortion decision itself might be affected. However, the Court has attentively scrutinized procedural regulations applicable after the first trimester to determine whether, in fact, they are reasonably related to the protection of the patient's health in light of current medical knowledge. Several regulations have failed to survive the court's scrutiny. In *Doe v. Bolton,* for example, the Court struck down Georgia's requirement that a hospital committee and two doctors, in addition to the woman's physician, concur in the abortion decision. And in *Danforth,* the Court struck down a Missouri ban on use, after the first trimester, of saline amniocentesis, then the most widely used second-trimester abortion procedure. Justice Blackmun, for the majority, observed that although safer procedures existed, they were not generally available. Consequently, the regulation in practice would either require the use of more dangerous techniques or compel women to forgo abortions.

The Court had three 1983 encounters with regulations alleged to connect sufficiently with a women's health: *Akron, Planned Parenthood Association v. Ashcroft,* and *Simopoulos v. Virginia.* In *Akron* and *Ashcroft,* the Court invalidated regulations requiring that abortions, after the first trimester, be performed in licensed acute-care hospitals. Justice Powell, for the majority, said that although current medical knowledge justified this requirement during much of the relevant period, it was unnecessary during the first four weeks of the second trimester; medical advances had rendered abortions safe at that stage even when performed in less elaborate facilities. The hospital requirement significantly burdened a woman's access to an abortion by raising costs substantially; therefore it must be tied more precisely to the period in which it was necessary. In *Simopoulos,* on the other hand, the Court upheld the limitation of second-trimester abortions to licensed facilities (including nonacute care facilities licensed to perform abortions during the first four to six weeks of the second trimester).

These three decisions indicate the Court's readiness to test specific second-trimester regulations that increase the cost of abortions against advances in medical technology. However, the majority in *Akron,* although aware that medical advances had rendered early second-trimester abortions safer than childbirth, explicitly refused to extend beyond the first trimester an across-the-board proscription of burdensome "place and manner" regulations.

Only in the last stage of pregnancy, after viability, does the state's interest in potential life become sufficiently compelling to allow the state to forbid all abortions except those necessary to preserve the woman's health. The point at which viability occurs is a medical judgment, the Court said in *Roe v. Wade, Danforth,* and *Colautti v. Franklin* (1979); the state may not establish a fixed measure of that point after which nontherapeutic abortions are illegal.

When postviability abortions occur, may the state impose manner requirements in the interest of preserving a viable fetus? The answer appears to be yes, if the regulations are not overbroad. In *Danforth* the Court invalidated a regulation requiring the physician to exercise due care to preserve the fetus; the regulation was not limited to postviability abortions. In *Ashcroft,* however, a 5–4 majority sustained a law requiring a second physician to attend a postviability abortion and attempt to preserve the life of the fetus. Even the dissenters agreed that such a regulation could stand if trimmed; they objected to Missouri's regulation because it required a second physician even at abortions using techniques that eliminated any possibility of fetal survival.

Dissenting in *Akron,* Justice SANDRA DAY O'CONNOR, joined by Justices White and Rehnquist, strongly criticized the Court's trimester approach to the regulation of abortion procedures. *Roe v. Wade's* medical model, she maintained, had been revealed as unworkable in subsequent cases. Advances in medical technology would continue to move forward the point during pregnancy when regulation could be justified as protective of a woman's health, and to move backward the point of viability, when the state could forbid abortions unless they were necessary to preserve the patient's life or health. The *Roe v. Wade* framework thus impelled legislatures to adjust their laws to changing medical practices, and called upon courts to examine legislative judgments, not as jurists applying "neutral principles" but as "science review boards."

More fundamentally, Justice O'Connor disapproved the interest balancing exhibited by the Court in the 1973 decisions. Throughout pregnancy, she said, the state has "compelling interests in the protection of potential human life and in maternal health." (In *Beal* the Court had said that the state does have an interest in potential life throughout a pregnancy, but that the interest becomes *compelling* only in the postviability stage.) Justice O'Connor's analysis, it appears, would permit from the beginning of pregnancy the regulation *Roe v. Wade* permits only in the final trimester: state proscription of abortion except to preserve a woman's health.

Vagueness doctrine has occasionally figured in the Court's review of state regulation of abortion procedures. In *Colautti,* the Court invalidated as too vague to supply adequate notice a statute attaching a criminal sanction to a physician's failure to exercise due care to preserve a fetus when there is "sufficient reason to believe that the fetus may be viable." And in *Akron,* a vagueness handle was employed to strike down a provision mandating the sanitary and "humane" disposal of aborted fetuses.

Minors have constitutional rights, but state authority over CHILDREN'S RIGHTS is greater than over adults'; the state may protect minors because of their immaturity and "peculiar vulnerability," and in recognition of "the importance of the parental role in child rearing." Justice Powell so observed in his plurality opinion in *Bellotti v. Baird* (1979), and no Justice has disagreed with these general statements. In concrete cases concerning the reproductive autonomy of minors, however, the Court has been splintered.

In *Danforth,* the Court invalidated, 5–4, a law requiring a parent's consent for most abortions performed on unmarried women under the age of eighteen. The majority did not foreclose a parental consent requirement for minors unable to make the abortion decision in an informed, mature manner.

The Court "continue[d] the inquiry" in *Bellotti.* Massachusetts required unmarried minors to obtain the consent of both parents or, failing that, the authorization of a state judge "for good cause shown." The Court voted 8–1 to invalidate the law, but split 4–4 on the rationale. Justice Stevens, writing for four Justices, thought the case governed by *Danforth.* Justice Powell, writing for four other Justices, attempted to provide guidance for state legislators. The abortion decision is unique among decisions facing a minor, he observed; it cannot be postponed until attainment of majority, and if the fetus is carried to term, the new mother will immediately face adult responsibilities. A blanket requirement of parental consent, using age as a proxy for maturity, was too sweeping. Yet the state's interest in ensuring the quality of a minor's abortion decision and in encouraging family participation in that decision would justify a law requiring either parental consent or the determination of an independent decision maker that abortion is in the minor's best interest, or that she is mature enough to decide for herself.

Justice Powell's *Bellotti* framework, although by 1983 only a two-member view, became, in *Akron* and *Ashcroft,* the de facto standard governing consent statutes. In *Ashcroft,* the Court upheld, 5–4, a statute conditioning a minor's abortion on either parental consent or a juvenile court order. Justice Powell and Chief Justice Burger voted to uphold the provision because, as indicated in *Bellotti,* the juvenile court must authorize an abortion upon finding that the abortion is in the minor's best interest or that the minor is mature enough to make her own decision. Three other Justices viewed the consent requirement as imposing "no undue burden on any right that a minor [arguably] may have to undergo an abortion." Four Justices dissented because the statute permitted an absolute veto, by parent or judge, "over the decision of the physician and his patient."

In *Akron,* however, the Court struck down, 6–3, an ordinance requiring all minors under age fifteen to have either parental or judicial consent. Because *Akron* failed to provide explicitly for a judicial determination of the minor's maturity, Justice Powell and the Chief Justice joined the four *Ashcroft* dissenters in condemning the consent provision.

With respect to contraception, no clear statement has emerged from the Court on the extent of state and parental authority over minors. In *Carey* the Court, 7–2, struck down a ban on the distribution of contraceptives to persons under age sixteen. The state sought to justify the measure as a means of deterring sexual activity by minors. There was no majority decision, but six Justices recognized that banning birth control would not in fact deter sexual activity.

May the state require parental consent to the minor's use of contraceptives? At least five Justices, it appears from the *Carey* decision, would state unequivocally that minors have no right to engage in sexual activity in face of disapproval of the state and of their parents. But it is hardly apparent that any minor-protective interest supports stopping the young from effectuating a decision to use nonhazardous contraceptives when, despite the views or commands of the state and their parents, they do engage in sexual activity.

Arguably, such a provision would serve to preserve parental authority over a decision many people consider a moral one. *Danforth* indicated that this end is insufficient to justify requiring parental consent for an abortion. Yet, as Justice Powell's *Bellotti* opinion illustrates, at least some Justices consider the abortion decision unique. Perhaps the issue will remain undecided. For practical reasons, lawmakers may be deterred from conditioning a minor's access to contraceptives on parental consent or notification. Many minors whose parents would wish them to use birth control if they engaged in sexual activity would nevertheless fail to seek parental consent for fear of disclosing their sexual activities. As five Justices indicated in *Carey,* deliberate state policy exposing minors to the risk of unwanted pregnancies is of questionable rationality.

In *Akron,* which came to the Court a decade after *Roe v. Wade,* Justice Powell acknowledged the continuing argument that the Court "erred in interpreting the Constitution." Nevertheless, *Akron* commenced with a reaffirmation of the 1973 precedent. As *Akron* itself illustrates, the Court typically has applied *Roe v. Wade* to restrict state efforts to impede privately financed access to contraceptives and abortions.

It appears safe to predict continued "adher[ence] to STARE DECISIS in applying the principles of *Roe v. Wade.*" But other issues remain beyond the zone of secure prediction. Current opinions do not indicate whether the Court eventually will relate its reproductive autonomy decisions to evolving law on the equal status of men and women. Nor can one forecast reliably how science and population will influence the next decades' legislative and judicial decisions in this area.

The development of a safe, efficient, inexpensive

morning-after pill, for example, may alter the reproductive autonomy debate by further blurring distinctions between contraceptives and abortifacients, and by sharply reducing occasions for resort to clinical procedures. A development of this order may diminish in incidence and detail both legislative activity and constitutional review of the kind sparked in the decade following *Roe v. Wade.* Moreover, it is at least possible that a different question will confront the Court by the turn of the century: If population size becomes a larger governmental concern, legislators may change course, and measures designed to limit childbirth may become the focus of constitutional controversy.

RUTH BADER GINSBURG

Bibliography

BREST, PAUL 1981 The Fundamental Rights Controversy: The Essential Contradictions of Normative Constitutional Scholarship. *Yale Law Journal* 90:1063–1112.

BYRN, ROBERT 1973 An American Tragedy: The Supreme Court on Abortion. *Fordham Law Review* 41:807–862.

COX, ARCHIBALD 1976 *The Role of the Supreme Court in American Government.* New York: Oxford University Press.

DEMBITZ, NANETTE 1980 The Supreme Court and a Minor's Abortion Decision. *Columbia Law Review* 80:1251–1263.

DESTRO, ROBERT 1975 Abortion and the Constitution: The Need for a Life Protective Amendment. *California Law Review* 63:1250–1351.

ELY, JOHN HART 1973 The Wages of Crying Wolf: A Comment on *Roe v. Wade. Yale Law Journal* 82:920–949.

ESTREICHER, SAMUEL 1982 Congressional Power and Constitutional Rights: Reflections on Proposed "Human Life" Legislation. *Virginia Law Review* 68:333–458.

FREUND, PAUL 1983 Storms over the Supreme Court. *American Bar Association Journal* 69:1474–1480.

HEYMANN, PHILIP and BARZELAY, DOUGLAS 1973 The Forest and the Trees: *Roe v. Wade* and its Critics. *Boston University Law Review* 53:765–784.

LAW, SYLVIA 1984 Rethinking Sex and the Constitution. *University of Pennsylvania Law Review* 132:955–1040.

PERRY, MICHAEL 1976 Abortion, the Public Morals, and the Police Power: The Ethical Function of Substantive Due Process. *UCLA Law Review* 23:689–736.

——— 1978 The Abortion Funding Cases: A Comment on the Supreme Court's Role in American Government. *Georgetown Law Journal* 66:1191–1245.

REGAN, DONALD 1979 Rewriting *Roe v. Wade. Michigan Law Review* 77:1569–1646.

TRIBE, LAURENCE H. 1978 *American Constitutional Law* Pages 921–934. Mineola, N.Y.: Foundation Press.

REPUBLICAN FORM OF GOVERNMENT

The Constitution requires that "The United States shall guarantee to every State in this Union a Republican Form of Government" (Article IV, section 4). The ideal of republican government antedated the Constitution and supplied some substantive criteria for the guarantee. The concept of republican government has changed and expanded over time, but it has influenced constitutional development only indirectly.

THOMAS JEFFERSON's 1776 draft constitution for Virginia, various Revolutionary-era state constitutions, and the NORTHWEST ORDINANCE (1787) mandated republican government in the states or TERRITORIES. When the GUARANTEE CLAUSE was adopted at the CONSTITUTIONAL CONVENTION OF 1787, the concept of republican government had identifiable connotations to the Revolutionary generation. In a negative sense, it excluded monarchical government and the creation of nobility. Because the Framers believed that internal disorder threatened republican institutions, they fused the guarantee clause with the clause in Article IV authorizing the federal government to suppress domestic violence. But in its positive connotations, republican government implied popular SOVEREIGNTY, a balance and SEPARATION OF POWERS, and LIMITED GOVERNMENT.

The contributions of ALEXANDER HAMILTON and JAMES MADISON in THE FEDERALIST reflected these negative and positive emphases. In numbers 6, 21, 22, 25, 34, and 84, Hamilton stressed the nonmonarchical character of republican governments and the need for a central authority powerful enough to suppress insurrections so as to forestall republican degeneration into absolutism. Madison, however, in numbers 10, 14, 39, and 43, emphasized the representative and majoritarian nature of republican government, contrasting it with direct democracies. SHAYS' REBELLION in central Massachusetts (1786–1787), rumors of monarchical plots and overtures late in the Confederation period, and federal response to the WHISKEY REBELLION (western Pennsylvania, 1794) lent weight to the emphasis that Hamilton reflected.

Conservative judges in the antebellum period insisted that statutes must conform to "certain vital principles in our free republican governments," in the words of Justice SAMUEL CHASE in CALDER V. BULL (1798) (SERIATIM OPINION). He claimed that "the genius, the nature, and the spirit of our state governments" voided unconstitutional legislation even without specific constraints in the state constitutions. Thus the concept of republican government became a fecund source of authority for judges seeking to restrain legislative innovation that affected property in such matters as liquor PROHIBITION and the Married Women's Property Acts.

In Rhode Island's Dorr Rebellion (1842), frustrated suffrage reformers abandoned hope that the state's conservative political leadership (called the "Freeholders' Government") would rectify the severe malapportionment and disfranchisement that existed under the royal charter of 1662, which still served as the state's constitution. They therefore applied the DECLARATION OF INDEPENDENCE literally to write a new constitution at a convention elected by the votes of all adult males, including those not entitled by existing law to vote. They then elected a government under the new constitution, including the "People's Governor," Thomas Wilson Dorr. The Freeholders, relying on Hamilton's nonmonarchic conception of republican government, insisted that a government was republican if it enjoyed the support of the enfranchised voters. By imposing martial law, the Freeholders crushed the Dorrite government. They then instituted suffrage reforms under a new state constitution.

The Dorr Rebellion was the matrix for LUTHER v. BORDEN (1849), where Chief Justice ROGER B. TANEY provided the first significant judicial hints about the meaning of republican government. Though Taney rebuffed Dorrite efforts to have the Court declare the Freeholder and subsequent regimes illegitimate, he conceded that "according to the institutions of this country, the sovereignty in every State resides in the people of the State, and . . . they may alter and change their form of government at their own pleasure." But he nullified this concession by applying the POLITICAL QUESTION doctrine: whether the people have altered their government is a question to be decided by the political branches of the national government (Congress and the President), whose determination is binding on the courts.

The constitutional controversy over slavery turned partly on the nature of republican forms of government. In the debates over the admission of Missouri in 1819–1821, antislavery congressmen asserted that slavery was inconsistent with republican government. ABOLITIONISTS later maintained that slavery violated natural law by depriving slaves of the right to their liberty, their persons, and their labor. Southern spokesmen after 1835 developed the position that slavery was not only compatible with republicanism, but actually conducive to it, creating a leisured master class freed for the disinterested pursuit of civic responsibilities.

The slavery controversy echoed in debates on Reconstruction between 1862 and 1875. Many Republicans supported policies that would have given blacks the vote, assured equal rights for all, and excluded southern states from representation in Congress until they had eradicated the vestiges of slavery and secessionist sentiment. They demanded that Congress force these improvements on the southern state governments. Democrats and other conservatives, on the other hand, identified the essence of republicanism with self-government—for whites only. Though adoption of the MILITARY RECONSTRUCTION ACTS (1867–1868) evidenced a Republican willingness to exact certain minima from the southern states, such as the program reflected in sections 1 through 4 of the FOURTEENTH AMENDMENT, the party soon fell back to a more compromising position. Senator JACOB HOWARD of Michigan reflected a Republican consensus late in Reconstruction when he defined a republican form of government as one "in which the laws of the community are made by their representatives, freely chosen by the people. . . . [I]t is popular government; it is the voice of the people expressed through their representatives." He was echoed by Chief Justice MELVILLE W. FULLER in *In re Duncan* (1891): the "distinguishing feature of [the republican] form is the right of the people to choose their own officers for governmental administration, and pass their own laws in virtue of the legislative power reposed in representative bodies."

However, the Supreme Court has otherwise consistently declined to specify substantive characteristics of a republican form of government, sometimes using the political-question doctrine to avoid doing so. Chief Justice MORRISON R. WAITE observed in MINOR v. HAPPERSETT (1875) that "no particular government is designated as republican, neither is the exact form to be guaranteed, in any manner especially designated." In *Pacific States Telephone and Telegraph Co. v. Oregon* (1912) Chief Justice EDWARD D. WHITE refused to declare that direct-democracy innovations such as the REFERENDUM or the INITIATIVE fell afoul of the constitutional guarantee. In the previous year, though, President WILLIAM HOWARD TAFT vetoed the Arizona/New Mexico admissions bill because it provided for judicial RECALL. Taft condemned the "possible tyranny of a popular majority." In BAKER v. CARR (1962) Justice WILLIAM J. BRENNAN refused to use the guarantee clause as a basis for requiring REAPPORTIONMENT, relying instead on the EQUAL PROTECTION clause. But he trimmed back the breadth of the political question DOCTRINE, leaving open the remote possibility that the Supreme Court might someday take on a more active role in delineating the substantive content of republican forms of government.

Unless it does so, however, the nature of republican government will be determined largely outside judicial forums, and the constitutional guarantee of republican government in the states will be enforced, as it has been consistently since before the Civil War, by Congress and, derivatively, the President.

WILLIAM M. WIECEK

Bibliography

BONFIELD, ARTHUR 1962 Baker v. Carr: New Light on the Constitutional Guarantee of Republican Government. *California Law Review* 1962:245–263.

——— 1962 The Guarantee Clause of Article IV Section 4: A Study in Constitutional Desuetude. *Minnesota Law Review* 46:513–572.

WIECEK, WILLIAM M. 1972 *The Guarantee Clause of the U.S. Constitution.* Ithaca, N.Y.: Cornell University Press.

WOOD, GORDON S. 1969 *The Creation of the American Republic, 1776–1787.* Chapel Hill: University of North Carolina Press.

RESERVED POLICE POWER

If a state reserves a power to alter, amend, or repeal a charter of incorporation before or when granting that charter, the CONTRACT CLAUSE is not necessarily a bar to the exercise of the state police power. In HOME BUILDING AND LOAN ASSOCIATION V. BLAISDELL (1934), the Court ruled that a state may modify or abrogate contracts because existing laws, by becoming part of the contracts, limit their obligations and because "the reservation of essential attributes of sovereign power is also read into contracts." That principle had originated in the concurring opinion of Justice JOSEPH STORY in DARTMOUTH COLLEGE V. WOODWARD (1819), when he declared that a corporate charter could not be changed unless a power for that purpose were reserved in the charter itself. Thereafter the states began to reserve such a power not only in charters, but in general acts of incorporation and in state constitutions, which applied to all charters subsequently granted. In 1877, when the court sustained a rate-fixing statute enacted under the reserved police power, it declared that the power must be reasonably exercised, consistent with the objects of the charter, and must not violate VESTED RIGHTS. In a 1936 case in which the Court repeated that formulation, as it had many times before, it stated that the reserved power prevented reliance on the contract clause. Never has the Court clarified its standards to explain why it has struck down some regulations under the reserved power yet has sustained others.

The reserved power nevertheless weakened the contract clause's service as a bastion of inviolable corporate charters. In 1884, for example, the Court held that because a private water works company was a public utility, its rates could be fixed by government authority under a reservation clause enacted after the state granted a charter giving the company an equal voice in the fixing of rates. The rise of the DOCTRINE of the reserved police power and the related doctrine of the INALIENABLE POLICE POWER forced the defenders of property rights to seek a more secure constitutional base than the contract clause, thus contributing to the emergence of SUBSTANTIVE DUE PROCESS OF LAW in the 1890s. Dozens of cases involved the application of the reserved police power even after the FOURTEENTH AMENDMENT replaced the contract clause as the main basis for invalidating state regulations. These cases did not, however, produce consistent principles that fixed ascertainable limits on the reserved power. The Court reserved to itself the final power to decide when it will enforce constitutional limitations on the reserved police power. Today the Court speaks of "the reserved powers doctrine" without making the "formalistic distinction" between powers that are reserved and those that are inalienable. *Home Building and Loan Association v. Blaisdell* (1934) obliterated a distinction between the reserved police power and the inalienable police power.

LEONARD W. LEVY

Bibliography

WRIGHT, BENJAMIN F. 1938 *The Contract Clause of the Constitution.* Pages 195–213. Cambridge, Mass.: Harvard University Press.

RESERVED POWERS (OF STATES AND PEOPLE)

See: Tenth Amendment

RESIDENCE REQUIREMENTS

Most states limit some benefits, such as welfare payments or free medical care for indigents, to state residents; all states limit voting to residents. Legislative classifications based on nonresidence or out-of-state CITIZENSHIP are not subjected to heightened judicial scrutiny under the EQUAL PROTECTION clause, and these residence requirements consistently pass the relaxed RATIONAL BASIS test.

Because state citizenship and residence are "essentially interchangeable" for purposes of the PRIVILEGES AND IMMUNITIES clause of Article IV, however, discriminations against nonresidents are scrutinized more carefully under that provision. The state must justify such discriminations by showing that they are substantially related to dealing with some special problem or condition caused by nonresidents. A state might constitutionally charge out-of-staters more than residents for a license to cut timber, if the increased charge bore some fair relation to increased costs of enforcing conservation laws against nonresidents. Similarly, nonresidents might constitutionally be denied WELFARE BENEFITS or charged higher tuition for attending a state university, because residents have supported the welfare system and the university out of general tax revenues. The notion of a "political community" justifies limiting the vote to residents.

Discriminations not so justified, however, violate Article IV's privileges and immunities clause when they touch privileges that are deemed "fundamental" to interstate harmony. (See TOOMER V. WITSELL, 1948, commercial shrimping; HICKLIN V. ORBECK, 1978, employment; DOE V. BOLTON, 1973, abortion; NEW HAMPSHIRE SUPREME COURT V. PIPER, 1985, practice of law.)

Requirements of residence for a specified period raise an additional constitutional problem. The Court has invalidated a number of these durational residence requirements on EQUAL PROTECTION grounds, also invoking the RIGHT TO TRAVEL or migrate interstate. (See SHAPIRO V. THOMPSON, 1969, welfare benefits; DUNN V. BLUMSTEIN, 1972, one-year requirement for voting invalid; later decisions allow fifty-day residence qualification; *Memorial Hospital v. Maricopa County,* 1974, nonemergency medical care for indigents; *Zobel v. Williams,* 1982, payment of bonuses apportioned to length of residence in the state. But see SOSNA V. IOWA, 1975, one year's residence a valid requirement for access to divorce court.) William Cohen has argued persuasively that these decisions are consistent with a theory that validates a state's durational residence requirement only when the requirement is a reasonable test of a newcomer's intent to remain a resident of the state. The Supreme Court has not yet embraced this theory—or, indeed, any coherent theory explaining its decisions concerning durational residence requirements.

KENNETH L. KARST

Bibliography

COHEN, WILLIAM 1984 Equal Treatment for Newcomers: The Core Meaning of National and State Citizenship. *Constitutional Commentary* 1:9–19.

VARAT, JONATHAN D. 1984 "Citizenship" and Interstate Equality. *University of Chicago Law Review* 48:487–572.

RES JUDICATA

(Latin: "The thing has been adjudicated.") The term is used broadly to refer to two kinds of effect given to a court's judgment: extinguishing claims and thus barring future litigation ("claim preclusion"), or conclusively determining certain issues that might arise in future litigation ("issue preclusion").

KENNETH L. KARST

(SEE ALSO: *Collateral Attack; Full Faith and Credit; Habeas Corpus.*)

RESOLUTIONS OF STAMP ACT CONGRESS

See: Stamp Act Congress

RESTRAINT OF TRADE

See: Antitrust Law and the Constitution

RESTRICTIVE COVENANT

Until the Supreme Court ruled their judicial enforcement unconstitutional in SHELLEY V. KRAEMER (1948), restrictive covenants were widely employed to achieve the racial SEGREGATION of urban neighborhoods in America. A restrictive covenant is a contract among owners of land, mutually limiting the uses of land covered by the covenant. Many such covenants have benign purposes: all the owners on a residential block, for example, might agree that houses will be set back thirty feet from the street. Racial covenants, however, limited the occupancy of homes on the basis of the occupants' race. They rested on an ugly premise: excluding blacks or Asians would, as one Louisiana court put it, make a neighborhood "more attractive to white people."

Such covenants were commonly adopted by landowners, or written into deeds of newly developed land, beginning in the late nineteenth century. Under existing property law, they were enforceable not only against their signers, but against the signers' heirs, assignees, and purchasers—at least so long as "conditions" had not changed. The use of the covenants accelerated after the Supreme Court decided, in BUCHANAN V. WARLEY (1917), that municipal ZONING ordinances specifying where persons of one race or another might live were unconstitutional. The typical covenant ran for twenty-five years, but some ran for fifty years or even in perpetuity.

Restrictive covenants cannot be said to be the sole cause, or even the primary cause, of residential segregation before 1948. The poverty of most blacks was itself a severe restriction on the purchase of homes; and middle-class blacks who could afford to buy were steered to "colored sections" by real estate brokers and lenders. (The latter practices became violations of federal law only in 1968.) Yet the covenants surely played their part in the segregative process, a part they could play only because they were enforceable in court.

If an owner started to build a house too close to the street, in violation of a restrictive covenant, the neighbors would be entitled to an INJUNCTION ordering the owner to stop. They might also be entitled to damages, if they could demonstrate some loss. But, subject to the covenant's limitations, the owner would be entitled to occupy the property, or sell it to any purchaser. The owner of property subject to a racial covenant, however, could not—so long as the covenant was enforceable—sell it to blacks for their use as a residence. The racial covenants, then, not only restricted black would-be buyers but also restricted the owners' free alienation of property—an interest recognized in the COMMON LAW since the thirteenth century. Yet the state courts regularly enforced the covenants.

The Supreme Court lent its approval in 1926, in CORRIGAN V. BUCKLEY, holding that judicial enforcement of a racial covenant did not even raise a substantial federal question; any discrimination was private action, not STATE ACTION. (The case arose not in a state, covered by the FOURTEENTH AMENDMENT, but in the DISTRICT OF COLUMBIA. The Court correctly sensed, however, that a similar problem would arise if an EQUAL PROTECTION guarantee were found applicable to governmental action in the District.)

Over the next two decades, the NAACP searched for opportunities to bring to the Court new challenges to the judicial enforcement of racially restrictive covenants. They finally succeeded in *Shelley,* where the Court did find state action in a state court's injunctive relief to enforce a covenant against black buyers of a home. On the same day, in *Hurd v. Hodge* (1948), the Court reached a comparable result in an attack on judicial enforcement of a covenant in the District of Columbia. No constitutional issue was decided in *Hurd;* the Court based its decision on "the public policy of the United States."

Five years later, the Court took away the last remaining weapon of persons who would seek to use racial covenants as a way of keeping their neighborhoods white. In BARROWS V. JACKSON (1953) the Court held that a state court violated the Fourteenth Amendment by using a covenant as a basis for awarding damages against persons who sold their house to black buyers.

One of the worst features of the racial covenants was their contribution to the symbolism of black inferiority. The removal of that symbolism, wherever it may be found, is necessary if the Fourteenth Amendment's promise of equal CITIZENSHIP is to be fulfilled. But ending the judicial enforcement of racial covenants did not end residential segregation, a phenomenon that has declined only slightly since 1940.

KENNETH L. KARST

Bibliography

HENKIN, LOUIS 1962 Shelley v. Kraemer: Notes for a Revised Opinion. *University of Pennsylvania Law Review* 110:473–505.

VOSE, CLEMENT E. 1959 *Caucasians Only.* Berkeley: University of California Press.

RETROACTIVITY OF JUDICIAL DECISIONS

LEGISLATION ordinarily does not apply retroactively to conduct occurring prior to its adoption but only to actions taking place after enactment. Indeed, the potential unfairness of some retroactive legislation is so great that certain forms of legislative retroactivity are specifically prohibited by the Constitution. The EX POST FACTO clauses of the Constitution prohibit retroactive criminal penalties, and the CONTRACT CLAUSE limits state legislation that would impair the obligation of pre-existing contracts. In addition, certain other fundamentally unfair forms of legislative retroactivity may violate constitutional due process guarantees.

Judicial decisions, on the other hand, ordinarily *are* retroactive in application. To some extent, such retroactivity is a consequence of the nature and function of the judicial decision-making process. Traditional lawsuits and criminal prosecutions concern the legal consequences of acts that have already taken place. If judicial decisions in such cases are to adjudicate the issues between the parties, those decisions necessarily must apply to prior events. The retroactive effect of judicial decisions, however, commonly extends beyond application to the particular parties involved in a case. To the extent that a judicial decision constitutes a new legal precedent, it will ordinarily be applied to all undecided cases that are subsequently litigated, regardless of whether the relevant events occurred before or after the new precedent was announced.

Although traditional judicial decisions are, in theory, completely retrospective in nature, two sets of legal doctrines place important practical limits on the actual breadth of decisional retroactivity. Statutes of limitations, which require suits to be brought within some specified period of time after the relevant events occur, limit the retrospective application of new precedents to the length of the prescribed limitations period; and the doctrines of RES JUDICATA and collateral estoppel prevent the relitigation of cases and issues that have been finally decided before the new precedent is announced. In addition, as in the case of retroactive legislation, there are some circumstances of fundamental unfairness in which constitutional principles may prevent the retroactive use of judicial decisions. By analogy to the constitutional prohibition of ex post facto laws, for example, the Supreme Court in *Bowie v. City of Columbia* (1964) held it unconstitutional to apply a new expansive judicial interpretation of a criminal statute to prior conduct.

The principal theoretical basis supporting the broad traditional retroactivity of judicial decisions is the abstract idea that courts (unlike legislatures) do not make, but merely find, the law. This theory in effect denies the existence of retroactivity; under the theory the events in question were always subject to the newly announced rule, although that rule had not been authoritatively articulated.

The theory that judicial decisions do not make law does not always reflect reality. Perhaps the clearest example of apparent judicial lawmaking is a court's overruling of an earlier judicial decision regarding the meaning of the COMMON LAW, a statute, or a constitutional provision. Even when no earlier decision is overruled, judicial decisions or interpretations may announce genuinely new principles. When judicial decisions thus create new law, it is plausible to argue that the new principles should not be given the retroactive effect normally accorded to judicial decisions, but should instead be treated more like new legislation and given prospective effect only. These arguments are strongest when individuals or governments have relied (perhaps irrevocably) upon earlier decisions in shaping their conduct. In such circumstances, retroactive application may cause unanticipated and harmful results.

In response to these and similar considerations, some courts have used the practice of PROSPECTIVE OVERRULING of prior decisions. Such a court, in overruling a precedent upon which substantial reliance may have been placed, may announce in OBITER DICTUM its intention to reject the old doctrine for the future, but nevertheless apply the old rule to the case at hand and to other conduct prior to the new decision. Alternatively, the court may apply the new rule to the parties before it, thus making the announcement of the new rule HOLDING rather than "dictum," but may otherwise reserve the rule for future application. In *Great Northern Railway Company v. Sunburst Oil and Refining Company* (1932) the Supreme Court held that the Constitution permits either of these forms of prospective overruling. The *Sunburst* decision gave constitutional approval to prospective judicial overruling of common law precedents and of decisions interpreting statutes. Such prospective overruling has primarily been used in two kinds of cases: new interpretations of statutes relating to property and contract rights, and the overruling of doctrines of municipal and charitable immunity from tort liability.

The most prominent and controversial recent issue concerning prospective overruling, however, has involved the retroactivity of new Supreme Court decisions enlarging the constitutional rights of defendents in criminal proceedings. During the 1950s and 1960s, the Court significantly broadened the rights of criminal defendants with respect to unconstitutional SEARCHES AND SEIZURES, POLICE INTERROGATION AND CONFESSIONS, the scope of the RIGHT AGAINST SELF-INCRIMINATION, and the inadmissibility of unconstitutionally obtained evidence. The Court has ruled that some of these new constitutional interpretations should not be given general retrospective application.

The extent of the possible retroactive application of new doctrines affecting the constitutionality of criminal convictions is greater than in most other areas of law because of the potential availability of postconviction relief to prisoners whose convictions might be effectively challenged if the newly announced rules were applicable to prior convictions. Petitions for HABEAS CORPUS are not subject to statutes of limitations or to the ordinary operation of the doctrine of *res judicata.* Thus, in 1961, when the Supreme Court decided in MAPP V. OHIO that the Constitution prohibits states from basing criminal convictions upon EVIDENCE obtained in violation of the FOURTH and FOURTEENTH AMENDMENTS, full retroactivity of that decision would have permitted a great many prisoners to challenge their convictions, no matter when their trials had occurred. Because the *Mapp* decision was based upon the interpretation of constitutional provisions dating from 1791 and 1868, the theoretical arguments for full retroactivity were strong. However, *Mapp* overruled the opinion of the Court in WOLF V. COLORADO (1949), which had held, directly contrary to *Mapp*, that the states were free to use unconstitutionally obtained evidence in most circumstances. Although police could hardly have legitimately relied upon *Wolf* in engaging in unconstitutional searches, state prosecutors and courts might have relied upon *Wolf* in using unconstitutionally obtained evidence. The primary reason given by the Court for the *Mapp* decision, moreover, was to deter police misconduct; the *Mapp* EXCLUSIONARY RULE is not a safeguard against conviction of the innocent. Retroactive application of *Mapp* to nullify pre-existing convictions would thus arguably contribute little to the main purpose of the *Mapp* rule while permitting guilty defendants to escape their just punishment. Similar issues have surrounded the potential retroactivity of other new Supreme Court decisions enlarging the constitutional rights of criminal defendants.

The Supreme Court has resolved these retroactivity issues by employing a test focusing on three main criteria: whether the purpose of the new rule would be furthered by its retroactive application; the extent of the reliance by law enforcement authorities and courts on prior decisions and understandings; and the likely effect of retroactive application on the administration of justice. Using this approach the Court held, in *Linkletter v. Walker (1965)*, that the *Mapp* decision would be applied to trials and direct APPEALS pending at the time of the *Mapp* decision, but not to state court convictions where the appeal process had been completed prior to announcement of the *Mapp* opinion. The same rule of general nonretroactivity has been applied to new constitutional interpretations prohibiting comment on a defendant's failure to take the witness stand at trial; establishing the MIRANDA RULES for police warnings to persons interrogated; prohibiting WIRETAPPING without judicial SEARCH WARRANTS; and limiting the permissible scope of SEARCHES INCIDENT TO ARRESTS. On the other hand, full retroactivity has been accorded to new decisions requiring provision of free counsel for INDIGENTS in criminal trials; requiring proof beyond a REASONABLE DOUBT in state criminal proceedings; and broadening the definition of constitutionally prohibited DOUBLE JEOPARDY. In general, rules designed to protect innocent persons from conviction have been given full retroactive application, while rules primarily intended to correct police and prosecutorial abuses that do not implicate guilt have been given limited retroactivity. The practical significance of these retroactivity decisions has been diminished in recent years by Supreme Court decisions that limit the availability of post-conviction relief to incarcerated persons (for example, STONE V. POWELL, 1976) and by the current Supreme Court's general opposition to continued expansion of defendants' constitutional rights in criminal proceedings.

PAUL BENDER

Bibliography

FIELD, OLIVER P. 1935 *The Effect of an Unconstitutional Statute.* Minneapolis: University of Minnesota Press.

RETROACTIVITY OF LEGISLATION

A characteristic of arbitrary government is that the state can alter retroactively the legal status of acts already done. Therefore, proposals to prohibit various types of retroactive LEGISLATION encountered the opposition of those delegates to the CONSTITUTIONAL CONVENTION OF 1787 who believed such laws were "void of themselves" and that a formal prohibition would "proclaim that we are ignorant of the first principles of legislation." There are, nevertheless, three such prohibitions in the Constitution: Congress may not pass EX POST FACTO laws and the states may not pass ex post facto laws or laws impairing the OBLIGATION OF CONTRACTS.

There are sound historical reasons for supposing that the Framers meant to proscribe both criminal and civil legislation with retrospective application. But JOHN DICKINSON had warned the convention that WILLIAM BLACKSTONE'S commentaries treated "ex post facto" as a technical term applying only to criminal law. In CALDER V. BULL (1798), the Supreme Court relied on Blackstone's authority to confine the constitutional prohibition to criminal laws.

The CONTRACT CLAUSE ultimately proved a mere parchment barrier to retroactive legislation. It does not apply to the federal government and the courts have so interpreted it as to make it a weak defense against retroactive state laws.

DENNIS J. MAHONEY

REVENUE SHARING

One consequence of the massive increase in the size and power of the federal government that began in the 1930s was the preemption by the federal government of the sources of revenue that had previously supported the state and local governments. The inability of such governments to find adequate stable sources of income seemed to pose grave problems for American FEDERALISM.

Funds appropriated by the federal government already flowed to state and local governments in the form of FEDERAL GRANTS-IN-AID, often with the effect of coopting those governments as administrators of federally mandated programs. The federal grants brought with them various restrictions as well as burdensome paperwork requirements.

One solution was to return to the state and local governments a share of the tax revenues collected by the federal government, not in support of particular federal programs but as general revenue to be spent for local purposes, with a minimum of restrictions. In the late 1960s, the idea of general revenue sharing was adopted by the Republican party as part of its proposal for a "new federalism." In 1972, Congress, at the urging of President RICHARD M. NIXON, enacted the State and Local Fiscal Assistance Act. The act authorized the distribution of $30 billion to state and local governments over a five-year period. Of that sum, one-third was allocated to the states and two-thirds to counties, cities, and other local governments to be distributed according to a flexible formula taking into account population, locally generated revenues, and other factors. The major restriction was a ban on RACIAL DISCRIMINATION in funded activities.

The program was extended in 1976; in 1980, a revised version was enacted that eliminated the states from the distribution scheme. Any revitalization of federalism as a result of revenue sharing has been less than apparent.

DENNIS J. MAHONEY

Bibliography

SCHEFFER, WALTER F., ed. 1976 *General Revenue Sharing and Decentralization.* Norman: University of Oklahoma Press.

REVISED STATUTES OF THE UNITED STATES

18 Stat. 1 (1875)

In 1866, Congress authorized the President to appoint a commission "to revise, simplify, arrange, and consolidate all statutes of the United States." The revision, completed in 1874 and modified in 1878, constituted the first official codification of the general and permanent laws of the United States. The revision supersedes the original public laws it consolidated. Except for those portions of the revision that have been repealed, amended, or superseded by subsequent compilations of federal statutes, the revision remains the authoritative statement of federal statutes enacted prior to 1874.

The revision was not supposed to work substantive changes in the code. But some relatively straightforward statutes became hopelessly confused as a result of the revision. Its most drastic effects may have been upon CIVIL RIGHTS statutes designed to enhance and protect constitutional rights. The revision's treatment of the JURISDICTION of the federal courts to hear civil rights cases brought under SECTION 1983, TITLE 42, UNITED STATES CODE, generated a century of confusion that was furthered by Justice HARLAN FISKE STONE's opinion in HAGUE V. CIO (1939) and that culminated in *Lynch v. Household Finance Corporation* (1972), *Chapman v. Houston Welfare Rights Organization* (1979), and a 1980 amendment providing for jurisdiction in all such cases. The revision's scattering of the CIVIL RIGHTS ACT OF 1866 throughout the Code contributed to that provision's century of near dormancy, to the Court's questionable reading of the 1866 act's intended scope in JONES V. ALFRED H. MAYER CO. (1968) and RUNYON V. MCCRARY (1976), to a confusing of CIVIL RIGHTS REMOVAL statutes that the Court only slightly illuminated in *Georgia v. Rachel* (1966) and *City of Greenwood v. Peacock* (1966), and to a misunderstanding, manifested in *Robertson v. Wegmann* (1978) and *Board of Regents v. Tomanio* (1980), of Congress's intent with respect to the role of state law in federal civil rights cases.

THEODORE EISENBERG

Bibliography

SUNSTEIN, CASS 1982 Section 1983 and the Private Enforcement of Federal Law. *University of Chicago Law Review* 49:401–409.

REYNOLDS v. SIMS

377 U.S. 533 (1964)

Once the Supreme Court declared in BAKER V. CARR (1962) that legislative districting presented a justiciable controversy, lawsuits were filed in more than thirty states challenging existing legislative apportionments. Six of these cases were decided by the Court on the same day, and the Court held all six states' apportionments unconstitutional. The main opinion was written in *Reynolds v. Sims,* the Alabama case; all six opinions of the Court were by Chief Justice

EARL WARREN, who believed until his death that *Reynolds* was the most important decision rendered by the Court during his tenure. The vote in four of the cases was 8–1, and in the other two, 6–3. Justice JOHN MARSHALL HARLAN dissented in all six cases, joined in two of them by Justices POTTER STEWART and TOM C. CLARK.

Baker v. Carr had been a response to decades of stalemate in the political process. Population shifts from rural areas to cities in the twentieth century had not been accompanied by changes in the electoral maps of most states. As a result, vast disparities in district populations permitted control of both houses of the typical state legislature to be dictated by rural voters. In Alabama, for example, Mobile County, with a population over 300,000, had three seats in the lower house, while Bullock County's two representatives served a population under 14,000. If JUDICIAL REVIEW normally defers to majoritarian democracy, here the premise for that deference was lacking; legislators favored by these apportionment inequalities were not apt to remedy them.

Baker had rested decision not on the GUARANTEE CLAUSE but on the EQUAL PROTECTION clause of the FOURTEENTH AMENDMENT. In the early 1960s, the Court had heightened the STANDARD OF REVIEW in equal protection cases only when RACIAL DISCRIMINATION was present; for other cases, the relaxed RATIONAL BASIS standard prevailed. Some Justices in the *Baker* majority had based their concurrence on the total arbitrariness of the Tennessee apportionment scheme there challenged. Justice WILLIAM O. DOUGLAS, concurring, had even said, "Universal equality is not the test; there is room for weighting." The *Baker* dissenters and academic critics had argued that the apportionment problem was unsuitable for judicial determination because courts would be unable to devise principled standards to test the reasonableness of the "weighting" Justice Douglas had anticipated; the problem belonged, they had said, in the category of POLITICAL QUESTIONS. The *Baker* majority had replied blandly: "Judicial standards under the Equal Protection Clause are well developed and familiar," and courts could determine that malapportionment represented "*no* policy, but simply arbitrary and capricious action." The suggestion was plain: departures from district population equality would be valid if they rested on legitimate policies.

Reynolds belied this suggestion. In a sweeping opinion that Archibald Cox called a *coup de main,* the Court discarded almost all possible justifications for departing from a strict principle of equal district populations and established for state legislative districts the ONE PERSON, ONE VOTE formula it had recently used in other electoral contexts. (See GRAY V. SANDERS 1963; WESBERRY V. SANDERS, 1964.) The Court thus solved *Baker*'s problem of judicially manageable standards by resort to a mechanical test that left no "room for weighting"—and, not incidentally, no room for legislative evasion. The companion cases to *Reynolds* demonstrated the strength of the majority's conviction. *Maryland Committee for Fair Representation v. Tawes* (1964) rejected the "federal analogy" and imposed the population equality principle on both houses of a bicameral legislature, and LUCAS V. FORTY-FOURTH GENERAL ASSEMBLY OF STATE OF COLORADO (1964) insisted on the principle in the face of a popular REFERENDUM approving an apportionment that departed from it. In *Reynolds* itself the Court made clear that the states must keep their legislative apportionments abreast of population shifts as reported in the nation's decennial census.

In short, numbers were in, and a political theory of interest representation was out: "Citizens, not history or economic interests, cast votes." Justice Stewart, dissenting in two of the cases, took another view: "Representative government is a process of accommodating group interests through democratic institutional arrangements." Fairness in apportionment thus requires effective representation of the various interests in a state, a concern that the principle of district population equality either ignored or defeated. But Justice Stewart's premise—that equal protection required only an apportionment scheme that was rationally based and did not systematically frustrate majority rule—was rejected by the Court. Because voting "is a fundamental matter in a free society," the Chief Justice said, the dilution of the strength of a citizen's vote "must be carefully and meticulously scrutinized." *Reynolds* was the crucial decision in the line of equal protection cases developing the doctrine that voting is a FUNDAMENTAL INTEREST, whose impairment calls for STRICT SCRUTINY. (See HARPER V. VIRGINIA BOARD OF ELECTIONS, 1966; KRAMER V. UNION FREE SCHOOL DISTRICT NO. 15, 1969.)

The Court's disposition of the six REAPPORTIONMENT cases, and its memorandum orders in other cases in succeeding months, left little doubt that the Justices had learned a lesson from their experience in BROWN V. BOARD OF EDUCATION (1954–1955). Here there would be no ALL DELIBERATE SPEED formula to extend the time for compliance with the decision. Lower courts were expected to move quickly—and did move quickly—to implement the doctrine announced in *Reynolds.* Even so, politicians had some time to mount a counterattack. Thirty-two state legislatures requested the calling of a CONSTITUTIONAL CONVENTION to overturn *Reynolds.* Senator Everett Dirksen gained substantial support when he introduced a proposed constitutional amendment to the same end. Bills were offered in both houses of Congress to withdraw the federal courts' JURISDICTION over reapportionment cases. But all these efforts came to nothing. The jurisdictional bills failed; the Dirksen proposal did not pass either house; the constitutional convention proposal, which had been carried forward with little publicity, withered in the remaining state legislatures when it was exposed to political sunlight.

The reason for the politicians' protest was obvious to all: many of them anticipated losing their own seats, and many others foresaw reduced influence for certain interests that rural representatives had favored. The public, however, overwhelmingly approved the principle of "one person, one vote" when the issue was tested in opinion polls; the politicians' counterattack failed because the people sided with the Court.

Academic criticism of the WARREN COURT has prominently featured *Reynolds* as a horrible example. The Court, the critics say, failed to write an opinion that reasoned from generally accepted premise to logically compelled conclusion. That is a telling criticism if, as HENRY HART was fond of saying, "reason is the life of the law." But reason is not the *life* of the law, or of anything else. It is a mental instrument to be used by judges and other humans along with their capacities for other ways of knowing: recognizing textures, patterns, analogies, relations that are not demonstrated by "if . . . then" syllogisms but grasped intuitively and at once. Perhaps the public was more ready to accept "one person, one vote" than were the Warren Court's critics because people who are not lawyers understand that the Supreme Court's most important product is justice. Surely they understood that the *Reynolds* formula, for all its inflexibility, more truly reflected our national sense of political justice than did the "cancer of malapportionment"—the term is Professor Cox's—that preceded it.

It is, by definition, hard to justify innovation by reference to the conventional wisdom. The beginnings of judicial DOCTRINE, like other beginnings, may be more easily felt than syllogized. Ultimately, if constitutional intuitions are to be translated into constitutional law, coherent explanation must come to replace the vague sense of doing the right thing; consolidation is an essential part of the Supreme Court's task. Yet to deny the legitimacy of a decision whose underlying value premises are clear, on the ground that the decision does not follow deductively from what has gone before, is to deny the legitimacy of judicial creativity—and it is our creative judges whom we honor most.

Reynolds v. Sims did not remake the political world; it mostly transferred power from rural areas to the conservative suburbs of large cities. But the decision touched a deep vein of American political egalitarianism and gave impetus to a doctrinal development as important as any in our time: recognition of the values of equal citizenship as the substantive core of the Fourteenth Amendment.

KENNETH L. KARST

Bibliography

CASPER, GERHARD 1973 Apportionment and the Right to Vote: Standards of Judicial Scrutiny. *Supreme Court Review* 1973:1–32.

DIXON, ROBERT G., JR. 1968 *Democratic Representation: Reapportionment in Law and Politics.* New York: Oxford University Press.

MCKAY, ROBERT B. 1965 *Reapportionment: The Law and Politics of Equal Representation.* New York: Twentieth Century Fund.

REYNOLDS v. UNITED STATES
98 U.S. 145 (1879)

This case established the principle that under the guarantee of RELIGIOUS LIBERTY, government may not punish religious beliefs but may punish religiously motivated practices that injure the public interest. Reynolds violated a congressional prohibition on bigamy in the territories and appealed his conviction in Utah on FIRST AMENDMENT grounds, alleging that as a Mormon he had a religious duty to practice POLYGAMY. Chief Justice MORRISON R. WAITE for a unanimous Supreme Court ruled that although government might not reach opinions, it could constitutionally punish criminal activity. The question, Waite declared, was whether religious belief could be accepted as justification of an overt act made criminal by the law of the land. Every government, he answered, had the power to decide whether polygamy or monogamy should be the basis of social life. Those who made polygamy part of their religion could no more be exempt from the law than those who believe that human sacrifice was a necessary part of religious worship. Unless the law were superior to religious belief, Waite reasoned, every citizen might become a law unto himself and government would exist in name only. He did not explain why polygamy and human sacrifice were analogous, nor did he, in his simplified exposition, confront the problem whether an uncontrollable freedom of belief had much substance if the state could punish the dictates of conscience: belief without practice is an empty right. Moreover, Waite did not consider whether belief should be as absolutely free as he suggested; if polygamy was a crime, its advocacy had limits.

LEONARD W. LEVY

RHODE ISLAND v. INNES
446 U.S. 291 (1980)

Innes explained the meaning of "interrogation" under MIRANDA V. ARIZONA (1966). *Miranda* declared, "If the individual states that he wants an attorney, the interrogation must cease until an attorney is present." Everyone agreed that the suspect in *Innes* had received his *Miranda* warnings and invoked his RIGHT TO COUNSEL, and that he was in custody. The question was whether he had been interrogated.

Police arrested a man suspected of a shotgun murder. Repeatedly they advised him of his *Miranda* rights, and a captain instructed officers about to transport him to the stationhouse not to question him in any way. During a brief automobile ride, one officer said to another, within the suspect's hearing, that they ought to try to find the shotgun because a child might discover it and kill herself. The suspect promptly volunteered to take the police to the shotgun. Again the police gave the *Miranda* warnings. The suspect replied that he understood his rights but wanted the gun removed from the reach of children. His statements and the gun were introduced in EVIDENCE at his trial, over his objection. The state supreme court reversed his conviction, finding a violation of *Miranda.*

A 6–3 Supreme Court decided that the police had not interrogated the suspect. Justice POTTER STEWART for the majority construed *Miranda* broadly to mean that interrogation includes questioning or a "functional equivalent"—any words or actions by the police reasonably likely to elicit any response from their suspect. Here there was no interrogation, only a spontaneous admission. The dissenters believed that an officer deliberately referred to the missing gun as a danger to innocent children in the hope of eliciting from the suspect an incriminating statement; whether that happened cannot be known. If the Court majority had believed that the officer making the remark had understood the suspect's psychological makeup and that an appeal to his conscience might have worked, that majority would have decided that the suspect had been interrogated. Contrary to the view of Justice JOHN PAUL STEVENS, dissenting, *Miranda* was not narrowed.

LEONARD W. LEVY

(SEE ALSO: *Police Interrogations and Confessions.*)

RHODE ISLAND AND PROVIDENCE PLANTATIONS, CHARTER OF
(July 8, 1663)

ROGER WILLIAMS founded Providence in 1636 as a shelter for anyone "distressed in conscience." His covenant was the first anywhere to exclude the civil government from religious matters. From the beginning the towns that became Rhode Island practiced RELIGIOUS LIBERTY, welcoming Quakers and Jews, and enjoyed SEPARATION OF CHURCH AND STATE. John Clarke, a Baptist minister who was Williams's friend and co-worker, was influential in the framing of the code of laws of 1647 establishing a "democratical" government. The restoration of the Stuarts in 1660 forced Rhode Island to secure a charter; Clarke was Williams's emissary to Charles II, who granted the first American charter guaranteeing religious liberty. The MARYLAND ACT OF TOLERATION (1649) was a statute; the charter of Rhode Island, which remained its constitution until 1842, made the guarantee a part of FUNDAMENTAL LAW. The language of the charter on this key provision was Clarke's. It referred to the colony's "livlie experiment" to show that a civil state could best be maintained if the inhabitants were secured "in the free exercise and enjoyment of all theire civill and religious rights." All peaceable persons might "freelye and fullye hav and enjoye his and theire owne judgments."

LEONARD W. LEVY

Bibliography

PERRY, RICHARD L., ed. 1959 *Sources of Our Liberties.* Pages 162–179. New York: American Bar Foundation.

RIBNIK v. MCBRIDE
277 U.S. 350 (1928)

Guided by TYSON AND BROTHER V. BANTON (1927), the Supreme Court voided a New Jersey statute regulating fees charged by employment agencies. The majority held that although widespread evils existed which were subject to regulation, the establishment of prices for a private business was outside legislative power. Justice HARLAN FISKE STONE'S dissent, joined by Justices OLIVER WENDELL HOLMES and LOUIS D. BRANDEIS, denied any distinction between illegal price controls and other, acceptable regulations. (See OLSEN V. NEBRASKA EX REL. REFERENCE & BOND ASSOCIATION, 1941; ADAMS V. TANNER, 1917.)

DAVID GORDON

RICHMOND NEWSPAPERS, INC. v. VIRGINIA
448 U.S. 555 (1980)

Richmond Newspapers recognized a constitutional right of access to criminal trials. It marked the first time a majority embraced any such FIRST AMENDMENT claim. Yet division and bitterness obviously remained from the splintered decision a year earlier in GANNETT V. DEPASQUALE, which had held that the Sixth Amendment did not preclude closing a pretrial suppression hearing to the press and public.

In *Richmond Newspapers*, a 7–1 majority distinguished *Gannett* and held that the press and public share a right of access to actual criminal trials, though the press may enjoy some preference. In the PLURALITY OPINION, Chief Justice WARREN E. BURGER found a right to attend criminal trials within "unarticulated rights" implicit in the First Amendment rights of speech, press, and assembly, as well as within other constitutional language and the uninterrupted Anglo-American tradition of open trials. This right to an open trial prevailed over efforts by Virginia courts to close a murder trial, premised on the defendant's request to do so. The trial judge had made no particularized finding that a FAIR TRIAL could not be guaranteed by means less drastic than total closure.

Justice WILLIAM H. REHNQUIST was alone in dissent, but only Justices BYRON R. WHITE and JOHN PAUL STEVENS concurred in Burger's opinion. Justice LEWIS F. POWELL took no part in the decision. Four Justices concurred separately in the JUDGMENT. They differed about whether *Gannett* actually was distinguishable, what weight to give history, and what particular constitutional basis mandated the result.

Richmond Newspapers decided only the UNCONSTITUTIONALITY of a total ban on public access to actual criminal trials when there is no demonstration that alternative means could not guarantee a fair trial. Yet the decision is significant for its recognition of a First Amendment right to gather newsworthy information; moreover, some Justices identified a broad right to receive information about government, including the activities of the judicial branch.

AVIAM SOIFER

RIGHT . . .

See also: Freedom of . . .

RIGHT AGAINST SELF-INCRIMINATION

The Fifth Amendment is virtually synonymous with the right against self-incrimination. One who "pleads the Fifth" is not insisting on grand jury INDICTMENT, freedom from DOUBLE JEOPARDY, or JUST COMPENSATION for property taken by the government—all safeguarded in the same amendment. He is saying that he will not reply to an official query because his truthful answer might expose him to criminal jeopardy. He seems to be saying that he has something to hide, making the Fifth appear to be a protection of the guilty; it is, but probably no more so than other rights of the criminally accused. The right against self-incrimination is the most misunderstood, unrespected, and controversial of all constitutional rights.

Its very name is a problem. It is customarily referred to as "the privilege" against self-incrimination, following the usage of lawyers in discussing evidentiary privileges (for example, the husband–wife privilege, the attorney–client privilege). Popular usage, however, contrasts "privilege" with "rights," and the Fifth Amendment's clause on self-incrimination creates a constitutional right with the same status as other rights. Its "name" is unknown to the Constitution, whose words cover more than merely a right or privilege against self-incrimination: "no person . . . shall be compelled in any criminal case to be a witness against himself." What does the text mean?

The protection of the clause extends only to natural persons, not organizations like corporations or unions. A member of an organization cannot claim its benefits if the inquiry would incriminate the organization but not him personally. He can claim its benefits only for himself, not for others. The text also suggests that a prime purpose of the clause is to protect against government coercion; one may voluntarily answer any incriminating question or confess to any crime—subject to the requirements for WAIVER OF CONSTITUTIONAL RIGHTS. In some respects the text is broad, because a person can be a witness against himself in ways that do not incriminate him. He can, in a criminal case, injure his civil interests or disgrace himself in the public mind. Thus the Fifth can be construed on its face to protect against disclosures that expose one to either civil liability or INFAMY. The Fifth can also be construed to apply to an ordinary witness as well as the criminal defendant himself. In Virginia, where the right against self-incrimination first received constitutional status, it appeared in a paragraph relating to the accused only. The Fifth Amendment is not similarly restrictive, unlike the Sixth Amendment which explicitly refers to the accused, protecting him alone. The location of the clause in the Fifth, rather than in the Sixth, and its reference to "no person" makes it applicable to witnesses as well as to the accused.

On the other hand, the clause has a distinctively limiting factor: it is restricted on its face to criminal cases. The phrase "criminal case" seems to exclude civil cases. Some judges have argued that no criminal case exists until a formal charge has been made against the accused. Under such an interpretation the right would have no existence until the accused is put on trial; before that, when he is taken into custody, interrogated by the police, or examined by a GRAND JURY, he would not have the benefit of the right. Nor would he have its benefit in a nonjudicial proceeding such as a LEGISLATIVE INVESTIGATION or an administrative hearing. The Supreme Court has given the impression that the clause, if taken literally, would be so restricted; but the Court refuses to take the clause literally. Thus, in COUNSELMAN V. HITCHCOCK (1892), the Court held that the Fifth does protect ordinary witnesses, even in federal grand jury proceedings. Unanimously the Court declared, "It is impossible that the meaning of the constitutional provision can only be that a person shall not be compelled to be a witness against himself in a criminal prosecution against himself." Although the Court did not explain why it was "impossible," the Court was right. Had the framers of the Fifth intended the literal, restrictive meaning, their constitutional provision would have been a meaningless gesture. There was no need to protect the accused at his trial; he was not permitted to give testimony, whether for or against himself, at the time of the framing of the Fifth. Making the criminal defendant competent to be a witness in his own case was a reform of the later nineteenth century, beginning in the state courts with Maine in 1864, in the federal courts by an act of Congress in 1878.

Illumination from the face of a text that does not mean what it says is necessarily faint. Occasionally the Court will display its wretched knowledge of history in an effort to explain the right against self-incrimination. Justice FELIX FRANKFURTER for the Court, in ULLMANN V. UNITED STATES (1956), drew lessons from the "name" of "the privilege against self-incrimination," but conceded that it is a provision of the Constitution "of which it is peculiarly true that 'a page of history is worth a volume of logic.' " TWINING V. NEW JERSEY (1908), the most historically minded opinion ever delivered for the Court on the right, was misleading and shallow when it was not inaccurate on the question whether the right was "a fundamental principle of liberty and justice which inheres in the very idea of free government."

The American origins of the right derive largely from the inherited English COMMON LAW system of criminal justice. But the English origins, so much more complex, spill over legal boundaries and reflect the many-sided religious, political, and constitutional issues that racked England during the sixteenth and seventeenth centuries: the struggles between Anglicanism and Puritanism, between Parliament and king, between limited government and arbitrary rule, and between freedom of conscience and suppression of heresy and SEDITION. Even within the more immediate confines of law, the history of the right against self-incrimination is enmeshed in broad issues: the contests for supremacy between the accusatory and the inquisitional systems of procedure, the common law and the royal prerogative, and the common law and its canon and civil law rivals. Against this broad background the origins of the concept that "no man is bound to accuse himself" (*nemo tenetur seipsum accusare*) must be understood and the concept's legal development traced.

The right against self-incrimination originated as an indirect product of the common law's accusatory system and of its opposition to rival systems which employed inquisitorial procedures. Toward the close of the sixteenth century, just before the concept first appeared in England on a sustained basis, all courts of criminal jurisdiction habitually sought to exact self-incriminatory admissions from persons suspected of or charged with crime. Although defendants in crown cases suffered from this and many other harsh procedures, even in common law courts, the accusatory system afforded a degree of fair play not available under the inquisitional system. Moreover, torture was never sanctioned by the common law, although it was employed as an instrument of royal prerogative until 1641.

By contrast, torture for the purpose of detecting crime and inducing confession was regularly authorized by the Roman codes of the canon and civil law. "Abandon all hope, ye who enter here" well describes the chances of an accused person under inquisitorial procedures characterized by PRESENTMENT based on mere rumor or suspicion, indefiniteness of accusation, the oath *ex officio,* secrecy, lack of CONFRONTATION, coerced confessions, and magistrates acting as accusers and prosecutors as well as "judges." This system of procedure, by which heresy was most efficiently combated, was introduced into England by ecclesiastical courts.

The use of the oath *ex officio* by prerogative courts, particularly by the ecclesiastical Court of High Commission, which Elizabeth I reconstituted, resulted in the defensive claim that "no man is bound to accuse himself." The High Commission, an instrument of the Crown for maintaining religious uniformity under the Anglican establishment, used the canon law inquisitorial process, but made the oath *ex officio,* rather than torture, the crux of its procedure. Men suspected of "heretical opinions," "seditious books," or "conspiracies" were summoned before the High Commission without being informed of the accusation against them or the identity of their accusers. Denied DUE PROCESS OF LAW by common law standards, suspects were required to take an oath to answer truthfully to interrogatories which sought to establish guilt for crimes neither charged nor disclosed.

A nonconformist victim of the High Commission found himself thrust between hammer and anvil: refusal to take the oath or, having taken it, refusal to answer the interrogatories meant a sentence for contempt and invited Star Chamber proceedings; to take the oath and respond truthfully to questioning often meant to convict oneself of religious or political crimes and, moreover, to supply evidence against nonconformist accomplices; to take the oath and then lie meant to sin against the Scriptures and risk conviction for perjury. Common lawyers of the Puritan party developed the daring argument that the oath, although sanctioned by the Crown, was unconstitutional because it violated MAGNA CARTA, which limited even the royal prerogative.

The argument had myth-making qualities, for it was one of the earliest to exalt Magna Carta as the symbol and source of English constitutional liberty. As yet there was no contention that one need not answer incriminating questions after accusation by due process according to common law. But a later generation would use substantially the same argument—"that by the Statutes of Magna Charta . . . for a man to accuse himself was and is utterlie inhibited"—on behalf of the contention that one need not involuntarily answer questions even after one had been properly accused.

Under Chief Justice EDWARD COKE the common law courts, with the sympathy of Commons, vindicated the Puritan tactic of litigious opposition to the High Commission. The deep hostility between the canon and common law systems expressed itself in a series of writs of prohibition issued by Coke and his colleagues, staying the Commission's proceedings. Coke, adept at creating legal fictions which he clothed with the authority of resurrected "precedents" and inferences from Magna Carta, grounded twenty of these prohibitions on the allegedly ancient common law rule that no man is bound to accuse himself criminally.

In the 1630s the High Commission and the Star Chamber, which employed similar procedures, reached the zenith of their powers. But in 1637 a flinty Puritan agitator, JOHN LILBURNE, refused the oath. His well-publicized opposition to incriminatory questioning focused England's attention upon the injustice and illegality of such practices. In 1641 the Long Parliament, dominated by the Puritan party and common lawyers, condemned the sentences against Lilburne and others, abolished the Star Chamber and the High Commission, and prohibited ecclesiastical authorities from administering any oath obliging one "to confess or to accuse himself or herself of any crime."

Common law courts, however, continued to ask incriminating questions and to bully witnesses into answering them. The rudimentary idea of a right against self-incrimination was nevertheless lodged in the imperishable opinions of Coke, publicized by Lilburne and the Levellers, and firmly associated with Magna Carta. The idea was beginning to take hold of men's minds. Lilburne was again the catalytic agent. At his various trials for his life, in his testimony before investigating committees of Parliament, and in his ceaseless tracts, he dramatically popularized the demand that a right against self-incrimination be accorded general legal recognition. His career illustrates how the right against self-incrimination developed not only in conjunction with a whole gamut of fair procedures associated with "due process of law" but also with demands for freedom of conscience and expression. After Lilburne's time the right became entrenched in English jurisprudence, even under the judicial tyrants of the Restoration. As the state became more secure and as fairer treatment of the criminally accused became possible, the old practice of bullying the prisoner for answers gradually died out. By the early eighteenth century the accused was no longer put on the stand at all; he could not give evidence in his own behalf even if he wished to, although he was permitted to tell his story, unsworn. The prisoner was regarded as incompetent to be a witness for himself.

After the first quarter of the eighteenth century, the English history of the right centered primarily upon the preliminary examination of the suspect and the legality of placing in evidence various types of involuntary confessions. Incriminating statements made by suspects at the preliminary examination could be used against them at their trials; a confession, even though not made under oath, sufficed to convict. Yet suspects could not be interrogated under oath. One might be ensnared into a confession by the sharp and intimidating tactics of the examining magistrate; but there was no legal obligation to answer an incriminating question—nor, until 1848, to notify the suspect or prisoner of his right to refuse answer. One's answers, given in ignorance of his right, might be used against him. However, the courts excluded confessions that had been made under duress. Only involuntary confessions were seen as a violation of the right. Lord Chief Baron Geoffrey Gilbert in his *Law of Evidence* (1756) declared that although a confession was the best evidence of guilt, "this Confession must be voluntary and without compulsion; for our Law . . . will not force any Man to accuse himself; and in this we do certainly follow that Law of Nature" that commands self-preservation.

Thus, opposition to the oath *ex officio* ended in the common law right to refuse to furnish incriminating evidence against oneself even when all formalities of common law accusation had first been fulfilled. The prisoner demanded that the state prove its case against him, and he confronted the witnesses who testified against him. The Levellers, led by Lilburne, even claimed a right not to answer any questions concerning themselves, if life, liberty, or property might be jeopardized, regardless of the tribunal or government agency directing the examination, be it judicial, legislative, or executive. The Leveller claim to a right against self-incrimination raised the generic problem of the nature of SOVEREIGNTY in England and spurred the transmutation of Magna Carta from a feudal relic of baronial reaction into a modern bulwark of the RULE OF LAW and regularized restraints upon government power.

The claim to this right also emerged in the context of a cluster of criminal procedures whose object was to ensure fair play for the criminally accused. It harmonized with the principles that the accused was innocent until proved guilty and that the BURDEN OF PROOF was on the prosecution. It was related to the idea that a man's home should not be promiscuously broken into and rifled for evidence of his reading and writing. It was intimately connected to the belief that torture or any cruelty in forcing a man to expose his guilt was unfair and illegal. It was indirectly associated with the RIGHT TO COUNSEL and the right to have witnesses on behalf of the defendant, so that his lips could remain sealed against the government's questions or accusations. It was at first a privilege of the guilty, given the nature of the substantive law of religious and political crimes. But the right became neither a privilege of the guilty nor a protection of the innocent. It became merely one of the ways of fairly determining guilt or innocence, like TRIAL BY JURY itself; it became part of due process of the law, a fundamental principle of the accusatorial system. It reflected the view that society benefited by seeking the defendant's conviction without the aid of his involuntary admissions. Forcing self-incrimination was thought to brutalize the system of criminal justice and to produce untrustworthy evidence.

Above all, the right was closely linked to FREEDOM OF SPEECH and RELIGIOUS LIBERTY. It was, in its origins, unquestionably the invention of those who were guilty of religious crimes such as heresy, schism, and nonconformity, and later, of political crimes such as TREASON, SEDITIOUS LIBEL, and breach of PARLIAMENTARY PRIVILEGE. More often than not, the offense was merely criticism of the government, its policies, or its officers. The right was associated, then, with guilt for crimes of conscience, of belief, and of association. In the broadest sense it was not so much a protection of the guilty, or even the innocent, but a protection of freedom of expression, of political liberty, and of the right to worship as one pleased. The symbolic importance and practical function of the right certainly settled matters, taken for granted, in the eighteenth century. And it was part of the heritage of liberty that the common law bequeathed to the English settlers in America.

Yet, the right had to be won in every colony, invariably under conditions similar to those that generated it in England. The first glimmer of the right in America was evident in the heresy case of John Wheelwright, tried in 1637 in Massachusetts. In colony after colony, people exposed to the inquisitorial tactics of the prerogative court of the governor and council refused to answer to incriminating interrogatories in cases heavy with political implications. By the end of the seventeenth century the right was unevenly recognized in the colonies. As the English common law increasingly became American law and the legal profession grew in size, competence, and influence,

Americans developed a greater familiarity with the right. English law books and English criminal procedure provided a model. From Edmond Wingate's *Maxims of Reason* (1658), which included the earliest discussion of the maxim, *"Nemo tenetur accusare seipsum,"* to Gilbert's *Evidence,* law books praised the right. It grew so in popularity that in 1735 BENJAMIN FRANKLIN, hearing that a church wanted to examine the sermons of an unorthodox minister, could declare: "It was contrary to the common Rights of Mankind, no Man being obliged to furnish Matter of Accusation against himself." In 1754 a witness parried a Massachusetts legislative investigation into seditious libel by quoting the well-known Latin maxim, which he freely translated as "A Right of Silence as the Priviledge of every Englishman." In 1770 the attorney general of Pennsylvania ruled that an admiralty court could not oblige people to answer interrogatories "which may have a tendency to criminate themselves, or subject them to a penalty, it being contrary to any principle of Reason and the Laws of England." When, in 1770, New York's legislature jailed Alexander McDougall, a popular patriot leader who refused answer to incriminating queries about a seditious broadside, the public associated the right with the patriot cause, and the press printed the toast, "No Answer to Interrogatories, when tending to accuse the Person interrogated." Thereafter the New York legislature granted absolute immunity to recalcitrant malefactors whose testimony was required in trials or investigations.

In 1776 the VIRGINIA CONSTITUTION AND DECLARATION OF RIGHTS provided that in criminal prosecutions the accused party cannot "be compelled to give evidence against himself." Every state (eight including Vermont) that prefaced its constitution with a bill of rights imitated Virginia's phrasing, although two, by placing the clause in a section apart from the rights of the accused, extended the right to third parties or witnesses. Whether the right was constitutionally secured or was protected by common law made little difference, because the early decisions, even in states that constitutionally secured the right, followed the common law rather than the narrower phrasing of their constitutions. For example, the PENNSYLVANIA CONSTITUTION of 1776 had a self-incrimination clause that referred to "no man," which the 1790 constitution narrowed to "the accused." Nevertheless, in the first case on this clause the state supreme court applied it to the production of papers in civil cases and to questions involving exposure to "shame or reproach."

During the controversy over the RATIFICATION OF THE CONSTITUTION of 1787, only four states recommended that a comprehensive bill of rights should be added to the new document, but those four demanded a self-incrimination clause modeled on the conventional phrasing that no person should be compelled to give evidence against himself. JAMES MADISON, in framing what became the Fifth Amendment, urged in sweeping language that no person should be "compelled to be a witness against himself." That phrasing was amended to apply only to criminal cases, thereby permitting courts to compel a civil defendant to produce documents against himself, injuring his civil interest without infringing his traditional rights not to produce them if they could harm him criminally. Whether the framers of the clause in the Fifth meant it to be fully coextensive with the still expanding common law principle is unknown. The language of the clause and its framers' understanding may not have been synonymous, especially because a criminal defendant could not testify under oath even in the absence of the self-incrimination clause. It was intended as a ban on torture, but it also represented the opinion of the framers that the right against self-incrimination was a legitimate defense possessed by every individual against government. The framers were tough-minded revolutionaries who risked everything in support of their belief that legitimate government exercises its powers in subordination to personal rights. The framers were not soft, naive, or disregardful of the claims of law and order. They were mindful that the enduring interests of the community required justice to be done as fairly as possible: that no one should have to be a witness against himself in a criminal case was a central feature of the accusatory system of criminal justice, which the framers identified with fairness. Deeply committed to a system of criminal justice that minimized the possibilities of convicting the innocent, they were not less concerned about the humanity that the law should show even to the offender. The Fifth Amendment reflected their judgment that in a society based on respect for the individual, the government shouldered the entire burden of proving guilt and the accused need make no unwilling contribution to his conviction.

What is the present scope of the right and how have the Supreme Court's interpretations compared with the history of the right? Generally the Court has construed the clause of the Fifth as if the letter killeth. Seeking the spirit and policies of the clause, the Court has tended to give it an ever widening meaning, on the principle that "it is as broad as the mischief against which it seeks to guard," as the Court said in *Counselman.* In effect the Court has taken the position that the Fifth embodied the still evolving common law of the matter rather than a rule of fixed meaning. Often the Court has had history on its side without knowing it, with the result that many apparent innovations could have rested on old practices and precedents.

History supported the decision in BOYD V. UNITED STATES (1886) connecting the Fifth and FOURTH AMENDMENTS and holding that the seizure of one's records for use as evidence against him compels him to be a witness against himself. Beginning in the early eighteenth century the English courts had widened the right against self-incrimination to include protection against the compulsory production of books and papers that might incriminate the accused. In a 1744 case a rule emerged that to compel a defendant to turn over the records of his corporation would be forcing him to "furnish evidence against himself." In the 1760s in WILKES'S CASES, the English courts extended the right to prevent the use of GENERAL WARRANTS to seize private papers in seditious libel cases. Thus the right against self-incrimination and FREEDOM OF THE PRESS, closely allied in their origins, were linked to freedom from unreasonable SEARCHES AND SEIZURES. In *Entick v. Carrington* (1765), Lord Camden (CHARLES PRATT) declared that the law obliged no one to give evidence against himself "because the necessary means of compelling self-accusation, falling upon the innocent as well as the guilty, would be both cruel and unjust; and it should seem that search for evidence is disallowed upon the same principle." American colonists made similar arguments against WRITS OF ASSISTANCE, linking the right against UNREASONABLE SEARCH to the right against self-incrimination. UNITED STATES V. WHITE (1944), which required the production of an organization's records even if they incriminated the witness who held them as custodian, was a departure from history.

That the right extends to witnesses as well as the accused is the command of the text of the Fifth. Protection of witnesses, which can be traced to English cases of the mid-seventeenth century, was invariably accepted in American manuals of practice as well as in leading English treatises throughout the eighteenth century. The Supreme Court's decision in *McCarthy v. Arndstein* (1924), extending the right to witnesses even in civil cases if a truthful answer might result in a forfeiture, penalty, or criminal prosecution, rested on dozens of English decisions going back to 1658 and to American precedents beginning in 1767. In a little known aspect of MARBURY V. MADISON (1803), Chief Justice JOHN MARSHALL asked Attorney General LEVI LINCOLN what he had done with Marbury's missing commission. Lincoln, who probably had burned the commission, refused to incriminate himself by answering, and Marshall conceded that he need not reply, though he was a witness in a civil suit.

Many early state decisions held that neither witnesses nor parties were required to answer against themselves if to do so would expose them to public disgrace or infamy. The origins of so broad a right of silence can be traced as far back as sixteenth-century claims by Protestant reformers such as William Tyndale and Thomas Cartwright in connection with their argument that no one should be compelled to accuse himself. The idea passed to the common lawyers and Coke, was completely accepted in English case law, and found expression in WILLIAM BLACKSTONE'S *Commentaries* as well as American manuals of practice. Yet the Supreme Court in BROWN V. WALKER (1896) restricted the scope of the historical right when ruling that the Fifth did not protect against compulsory self-infamy. Its decision was oblivious to history as was its reaffirmation of that decision in *Ullmann v. United States* (1956).

From the standpoint of history that 1896 holding and its 1956 reaffirmation correctly decided the main question whether a grant of full immunity supersedes the witness's right to refuse answer on Fifth Amendment grounds. Colonial precedents support absolute or transactional immunity, as did the IMMUNITY GRANT decisions in 1896 and 1956. The Court departed from its own precedents and history when ruling in KASTIGAR V. UNITED STATES (1972) that limiting the right to use and derived-use immunity does not violate the right not to be a witness against oneself.

History supports the decisions made by the Court for the first time in *Quinn v. United States* (1955) and WATKINS V. UNITED STATES (1957) that the right extends to legislative investigations. As early as 1645 John Lilburne, relying on his own reading of Magna Carta and the PETITION OF RIGHT, claimed the right, unsuccessfully, before a parliamentary committee. In 1688 the Pennsylvania legislature recognized an uncooperative witness's right against self-incrimination. Other colonial assemblies followed suit though New York's did not do so until forced by public opinion after McDougall's case. That Parliament also altered its practice is clear from the debates in 1742 following the refusal of a witness to answer incriminatory questions before an investigating committee. The Commons immunized his testimony against prosecution, but the bill failed in the Lords in part because it violated one of the "first principles of English law," that no person is obliged to accuse himself or answer any questions that tend to reveal what the nature of his defense requires to be concealed. In 1778 the Continental Congress investigated the corrupt schemes of Silas Deane, who invoked his right against self-incrimination, and Congress, it seems, voted that it was lawful for him to do so.

History belies the TWO-SOVEREIGNTIES RULE, a stunting restriction upon the Fifth introduced by the Court in 1931 but abandoned in MURPHY V. WATERFRONT COMMISSION (1964). The rule was that a person could not refuse to testify on the grounds that his disclosures would expose him to prosecution in another jurisdiction. The Court mistakenly claimed that the rule had the support of historical precedents; history clearly contradicted that rule as the Court belatedly confessed in 1964.

History supports the rule of *Bram v. United States* (1897) that in criminal cases in the federal courts—this was extended by MALLOY V. HOGAN (1964) to the state courts, too—whenever a question arises whether a confession is incompetent because it is involuntary or coerced, the issue is controlled by the self-incrimination clause of the Fifth. Partly because of JOHN H. WIGMORE's intimidating influence and partly because of the rule of *Twining* denying that the FOURTEENTH AMENDMENT extended the Fifth to the states, the Court until 1964 held that the coercion of a confession by state or local authorities violated due process of law rather than the right against self-incrimination. Wigmore, the master of evidence, claimed that the rule against coerced confessions and the right against self-incrimination had "no connection," the two being different in history, time or origin, principle, and practice.

Wigmore was wrong. From the fact that a separate rule against coerced confessions emerged in English decisions of the eighteenth century, nearly a century after the right against self-incrimination had become established, he concluded that the two rules had *no* connection. That the two operated differently in some respects and had differing rationales in other respects led him to the same conclusion. But he focused on their differences only and so exaggerated those differences that he fell into numerous errors and inconsistencies of statement. The relationship of the two rules is apparent from the fact that the shadow of the rack was part of the background from which each rule emerged. The disappearance of torture and the recognition of the right against compulsory self-incrimination were victories in the same political struggle. The connections among torture, *compulsory* self-incrimination, and *coerced* confessions was a historical fact as well as a physical and psychological one. In the sixteenth and seventeenth centuries, the argument against the three, resulting in the rules that Wigmore said had no connection, overlapped. Compulsory self-incrimination was always regarded by its opponents as a species of torture. An act of 1696 regulating treason trials required that confessions be made willingly, without violence, and in open court. The quotation above from Geoffrey Gilbert disproves Wigmore's position. When the separate rule against coerced confessions emerged, its rationale was that a coerced confession is untrustworthy evidence. There remained, however, an indissoluble and crucial nexus with the right against self-incrimination because both rules involved coercion or the involuntary acknowledgment of guilt. Significantly the few references to the right against self-incrimination, in the debates on the ratification of the Constitution, identified the right with a protection against torture and inquisition, that is, against coerced confessions. Wigmore fell into error by assuming that the right against self-incrimination had a single rationale and a static meaning. In fact it always had several rationales, was an expanding principle of law, and spun off into different directions. One spin-off was the development of a separate rule against coerced confessions. If there was "an historical blunder," it was made by the English courts of the eighteenth century when they divorced the confessions rule from the self-incrimination rule.

History is not clear on the Court's distinction between TESTIMONIAL COMPULSION, which the Fifth prohibits, and nontestimonial compulsion, which it does not prohibit. Blood samples, photographs, fingerprints, voice exemplars, and most other forms of nontestimonial compulsion are of modern origin. The fact that the Fifth refers to the right not to be a witness against oneself seems to imply the giving of testimony rather than keeping records or revealing body characteristics for identification purposes. The distinction made by the Court in SCHMERBER V. CALIFORNIA (1966) was reasonable. Yet, limiting the Fifth to prohibit only testimonial compulsion poses problems. The accused originally could not testify at all, and the history of the right does not suggest the *Schmerber* limitations. The common law decisions and the wording of the first state bills of rights explicitly protected against compelling anyone to give or furnish "evidence" against himself, not just testimony.

The fact that history does not support some of the modern decisions limiting the scope of the right hardly means that history always substantiates decisions expanding it. Decisions like *Slochower v. Board of Education* (1956) and GARRITY V. NEW JERSEY (1967), which protect against penalizing the invocation of the right or chilling its use, draw no clear support from the past. Indeed, the decision in GRIFFIN V. CALIFORNIA (1965) which prohibited comment on the failure of a criminal defendant to testify on ground that such comment "is a remnant of the inquisitorial system" is historically farfetched.

Finally, history is ambiguous on the controversial issue whether the right against self-incrimination extends to the police station. When justices of the peace performed police functions and conducted the preliminary examination of suspects, their interrogation was inquisitorial in character (as it is in the interrogation rooms of modern police stations) and it usually had as its object the incrimination of the suspect. Yet he could not be examined under oath, and he did have a right to withhold the answer to incriminating questions. On the other hand, he had no right to be told that he need not answer or be cautioned that his answers could be used against him. However, the right against self-incrimination grew out of a protest against incriminating interrogation *prior to* formal accusation. That is, the maxim *nemo tenetur seipsum prodere* originally meant that no one was obligated to supply the evidence that could be used to indict him. Thus, from the very inception of the right, a suspect could invoke it at the earliest stages of his interrogation.

In MIRANDA V. ARIZONA (1966) the Supreme Court expanded the right beyond all precedent, yet not beyond its historical spirit. *Miranda's* purpose was to eliminate the inherently coercive and inquisitional atmosphere of the interrogation room and to guarantee that any incriminating admissions are made voluntarily. That purpose was, historically, the heart of the Fifth, the basis of its policy. Even the guarantee of counsel to effectuate that purpose has precedent in a historical analogy: the development of the right to counsel originally safeguarded the right against self-incrimination at the trial stage of prosecution. When the defendant lacked counsel, he had to conduct his own case, and although he was not put on the stand and did not have to answer incriminating questions, his failure to rebut accusations and insinuations by the prosecution prejudiced the jury, vitiating the right to silence. The right to counsel permitted the defendant's lips to remain sealed; his "mouthpiece" spoke for him. In *Miranda* the Court extended the protection of counsel to the earliest stage of a criminal action, when the need is the greatest because the suspect is most vulnerable.

Nevertheless, the *Miranda* warnings were an invention of the Court, devoid of historical support. Excepting rare occasions when judges intervened to protect a witness against incriminatory interrogatories, the right had to be claimed or invoked by the person seeking its protection. Historically it was a fighting right; unless invoked it offered no protection. It did not bar interrogation or taint an uncoerced confession as improper evidence. Incriminating statements made by a suspect could always be used at his trial. That a person might unwittingly incriminate himself when questioned in no way impaired his legal right to refuse answer. He lacked the right to be warned that he need not answer; he lacked the right to have a lawyer present at his interrogation; and he lacked the protection of the strict waiver requirements that now accompany the MIRANDA RULES. From a historical view, the decision in BREWER V. WILLIAMS (1977) and the limits on interrogation imposed by RHODE ISLAND V. INNES (1980) extraordinarily inflate the right. What was once a fighting right has become a pampered one. Law should encourage, not thwart, voluntary confessions. The Fifth should be liberally construed to serve as a check on modern versions of the "third degree" and the spirit of McCarthyism, but the Court should distinguish rapists and murderers from John Lilburne and realize that law enforcement agencies today are light years away from the behavior revealed in BROWN V. MISSISSIPPI (1936) and CHAMBERS V. FLORIDA (1940).

The Court said in PALKO V. CONNECTICUT (1937) that the right against compulsory self-incrimination was not a fundamental right; it might be lost, and justice might still be done if the accused "were subject to a duty to respond to orderly inquiry." Few would endorse that judgment today, but it is a yardstick for measuring how radically different the constitutional law of the Fifth became in half a century.

History surely exalts the right if precedence be our guide. It won acceptance earlier than did the freedoms of speech, press, and religion. It preceded a cluster of procedural rights such as benefit of counsel. It is older, too, than immunities against BILLS OF ATTAINDER, EX POST FACTO laws, and unreasonable searches and seizures. History also exalts the origins of the right against self-incrimination, for they are related to the development of the accusatorial system of criminal justice and the concept of FAIR TRIAL; to the principle that FUNDAMENTAL LAW limits government—the very foundation of CONSTITUTIONAL-

ISM; and to the heroic struggles for the freedoms of the FIRST AMENDMENT. History does not, however, exalt the right against the claims of justice.

LEONARD W. LEVY

Bibliography

FRIENDLY, HENRY J. 1968 The Fifth Amendment Tomorrow: The Case for Constitutional Change. *University of Cincinnati Law Review* 37:671–726.

GRISWOLD, ERWIN 1955 *The 5th Amendment Today.* Cambridge, Mass.: Harvard University Press.

HOOK, SIDNEY 1957 *Common Sense and the Fifth Amendment.* New York: Criterion.

KAMISAR, YALE 1980 *Police Interrogation and Confessions: Essays in Law and Policy.* Ann Arbor: University of Michigan Press.

LEVY, LEONARD W. 1968 *Origins of the Fifth Amendment: The Right against Self-Incrimination.* New York: Oxford University Press.

MAYERS, LEWIS 1959 *Shall We Amend the Fifth Amendment?* New York: Harper & Row.

MORGAN, EDMUND M. 1949 The Privilege against Self-Incrimination. *Minnesota Law Review* 34:1–37.

WIGMORE, JOHN HENRY 1961 *Evidence in Trials at Common Law,* vol. 8, rev. by John T. McNaughton. Boston: Little, Brown.

RIGHT OF PRIVACY

Long before anyone spoke of privacy as a constitutional right, American law had developed a "right of privacy," invasion of which was a tort, justifying the award of money damages. One such invasion would be a newspaper's embarrassing publication of intimate facts about a person, or a statement placing someone in a "false light," when the story was not newsworthy. Other invasions of this right were found in various forms of physical intrusion, or surveillance, or interception of private communications. The Constitution, too, protected some interests in privacy: the FOURTH AMENDMENT forbade unreasonable SEARCHES AND SEIZURES; the Fifth Amendment offered a RIGHT AGAINST SELF-INCRIMINATION; the THIRD AMENDMENT, a relic of the Revolutionary War, forbade the government to quarter troops in a private house in peacetime without the owner's consent. Even so, despite Justice LOUIS D. BRANDEIS's famous statement in the WIRETAPPING case of OLMSTEAD V. UNITED STATES (1928), there was no general constitutional "right to be let alone." Nor does any such sweeping constitutional right exist today. Beginning with GRISWOLD V. CONNECTICUT (1965), the Supreme Court has recognized a constitutional right of privacy, but the potentially broad scope of that right remains constricted by the Court's current interpretations of it.

Griswold held invalid a Connecticut law forbidding the use of contraceptives, in application to the operators of a BIRTH CONTROL clinic who were aiding married couples to violate the law, offering them advice and contraceptive devices. Justice WILLIAM O. DOUGLAS, writing for the Court, disavowed any reliance on SUBSTANTIVE DUE PROCESS to support the decision. Although the statute did not violate the terms of any specific guarantee of the BILL OF RIGHTS, said Douglas, the Court's decisions had recognized that "specific guarantees in the Bill of Rights have penumbras, formed by emanations from those guarantees that help give them life and substance." The FREEDOM OF ASSOCIATION, although not mentioned in the FIRST AMENDMENT, had been protected against intrusions on the privacy of political association. The Third, Fourth, and Fifth Amendments also created "zones of privacy." The *Griswold* case concerned "a relationship lying within the zone of privacy created by several fundamental constitutional guarantees." Furthermore, the idea of allowing police to enforce a ban on contraceptives by searching the marital bedroom was "repulsive to the notions of privacy surrounding the marriage relationship."

Connecticut had not been enforcing its law even against drugstore sales of contraceptives; the governmental prying conjured up in the *Griswold* opinion was not really threatened. What *Griswold* was protecting was not so much the privacy of the marital bedroom as a married couple's control over the intimacies of their relationship. This point emerged clearly in EISENSTADT V. BAIRD (1972), which extended the right to practice contraception to unmarried persons, and in CAREY V. POPULATION SERVICES INTERNATIONAL (1977), which struck down three laws restricting the sale and advertisement of contraceptives.

In *Eisenstadt* the Court characterized the right of privacy as the right of an individual "to be free from unwarranted intrusion into matters so fundamentally affecting a person as the decision whether to bear or beget a child." The prophecy in those words came true the following year when the Court, in ROE V. WADE (1973), held that the constitutional right of privacy recognized in *Griswold* was "broad enough to encompass a woman's decision whether or not to terminate her pregnancy." This right to decide whether to have an abortion was qualified only in the later stages of pregnancy; during the first trimester of pregnancy it was absolute. Abandoning *Griswold*'s PENUMBRA THEORY, the Court placed the right of privacy within the liberty protected by the DUE PROCESS clause of the FOURTEENTH AMENDMENT. (See ABORTION AND THE CONSTITUTION.)

As the *Roe* dissenters pointed out, an abortion operation "is not 'private' in the ordinary usage of that word." Liberty, not privacy, was the chief constitutional value at stake in *Roe.* In later years various Justices have echoed the words of Justice POTTER STEWART, concurring in *Roe,* that "freedom of personal choice in matters of marriage and family life" is a due process liberty. Indeed, Justice Stewart's formulation was too narrow; the Court's decisions have gone well beyond formal marriage and the traditional family to protect a much broader FREEDOM OF INTIMATE ASSOCIATION. Yet that freedom is often defended in the name of the constitutional right of privacy.

From the time of the *Griswold* decision forward, privacy became the subject of a body of legal and philosophical literature notable for both analytical quality and rapid growth. The term "privacy" cried out for definition—not merely as a feature of constitutional law, where the Supreme Court had offered no more than doctrinal impressionism, but more fundamentally as a category of thought. Is privacy a situation, or a value, or a claim of right? Is privacy itself the subject of our moral and legal claims, or is it a code word that always stands for some other interest? However these initial questions be answered, what are the functions of privacy in our society? These are not merely philosophers' inquiries; in deciding "right of privacy" cases judges also answer them, even if the answers are buried in assumptions never articulated.

Not until 1977 did the Supreme Court begin to map out the territory occupied by the constitutional right of privacy. In WHALEN V. ROE the Court upheld a state law requiring the maintenance of computerized records of persons who obtained various drugs by medical prescription. "The cases sometimes characterized as protecting 'privacy,'" said the Court, "have in fact involved at least two different kinds of interests. One is the individual interest in avoiding disclosure of personal matters, and another is the interest in independence in making certain kinds of important decisions." This passage is noteworthy in two respects: first, its opening words suggest a new awareness that "privacy" may not be the most informative label for an interest in freedom of choice whether to marry, or procreate, or have an abortion, or send one's child to a private school. Second, the passage strongly hints that some interests in informational privacy—freedom from disclosure—are constitutionally protected not only by the First, Fourth, and Fifth Amendments but also by a more general right of privacy.

The *Whalen* opinion was written by Justice JOHN PAUL STEVENS, who has consistently urged an expansive reading of the "liberty" protected by the due process clauses. As if to emphasize that the right of privacy is merely one aspect of a broadly defined right of substantive due process, Justice Stevens cited, to support his reference to the interest in independence in making important decisions, ALLGEYER V. LOUISIANA (1897), which established the FREEDOM OF CONTRACT as a due process right. If the "important decisions" part of the right of privacy is to be absorbed back into the body of substantive due process, and if informational privacy is to become part of a redefined constitutional right of privacy, the contours of this new right will for the first time approach the meanings of "privacy" in common speech. Before *Whalen,* it was possible to say that the one interest most conspicuously left unprotected by the constitutional right of privacy was privacy itself. In any event, even after *Whalen*'s suggestive analysis, the Supreme Court has continued to speak of "the" constitutional right of privacy.

There is a sense in which personal decisions about sex and marriage and procreation are private decisions. Indeed, the word "private" serves better than "privacy" to indicate the interests in personal autonomy at stake in such cases. Both words can refer to such forms of privacy as seclusion and secrecy; to do something in private is to do it free from public or general observance, and private information consists of facts not publicly or generally known. But "private" has another meaning that lacks any similar analogue in the idea of privacy. Private property, for example, is property that is one's own, subject to one's control, from which one has the right to exclude others if one chooses to do so. It makes perfect sense to speak of a power of decision as private in this sense. From this perspective the line of "privacy" opinions from *Griswold* to *Roe* and beyond can be seen as seeking to identify the circumstances in which the decision "to bear or beget a child" is one that "belongs" to the individual, one from which the public—even the state—can be excluded. Calling such an interest "privacy," however, is a play on words; any freedom from governmental regulation might just as easily be called "privacy." Perhaps Justice Stevens was making this point in his *Whalen* opinion when he cited *Allgeyer,* a case in which the liberty at stake was freedom to buy insurance from an out-of-state company.

Much of what government does in the way of regulating behavior intrudes on privacy in its commonly understood senses of solitude and nondisclosure. Yet even when these forms of privacy are assimilated to the constitutional right of privacy, the result is not wholesale invalidation of governmental action. The *Whalen* decision itself is illustrative. Recognizing that the drug records law threatened some impairment of both the interest in nondisclosure and the interest in making personal decisions, the Court nonetheless concluded that the law's informational security safeguards minimized the chances of serious harm to those interests and that the law was a reasonable means of minimizing drug abuse. More serious threats of disclosure of accumulated personal information, the Court said, might exceed constitutional limitations. The clear implication is that future claims to a constitutional right of privacy in the form of nondisclosure will be evaluated through a process of judicial interest balancing.

Even a judge who regards privacy as a constitutional value in itself, something more than a label for other interests, will be pressed to consider why privacy is important, in order to place the proper weights in a given case's decisional balance. The commentary on privacy regularly identifies several overlapping values. If governmental "brainwashing" would be unconstitutional, as all observers assume, the reason surely lies in the widely shared sense that the essentials of due process "liberty" include a healthy measure of control over the development of one's own individuality. That control undoubtedly requires some amount of privacy in the form of nondisclosure and seclusion. To have the sense of being a person, an individual needs some degree of control over the roles she may play in various social settings; control over the disclosure of personal information contributes to this process. Similarly, both learning and creative activity require a measure of relaxation and refuge from the world's intrusions.

A closely related function of informational privacy is its value as a foundation for friendship and intimacy. Although a cynic might say that the most effective way for an individual to preserve the privacy of his thoughts and feelings would be never to disclose them, that course would sacrifice the sort of sharing that constitutes a central value of intimate association—which, in turn, is crucial to the development of individuality. It is here that we can see clearly the overlap between privacy as selective nondisclosure and "privacy" as autonomy in intimate personal decisions. Justice Douglas's *Griswold* opinion spoke to both concerns: he sought to defend the privacy of the marital bedroom against hypothetical government snooping and to defend a married couple's autonomy over the intimacies of their relationship. The special constitutional status of the home, recognized in decisions ranging from search and seizure doctrines to the "private" possession of OBSCENITY protected in STANLEY V. ILLINOIS (1969), draws not only on the notion of the home as a sanctuary and place of repose but also on the home's status as the main locus of intimate associations.

Finally, privacy in the sense of seclusion or nondisclosure serves to encourage freedom, both in the sense of political liberty and in the sense of moral autonomy. The political privacy cases from NAACP V. ALABAMA (1958) to GIBSON V. FLORIDA LEGISLATIVE INVESTIGATION COMMITTEE (1963) and beyond rest on the premise that disclosure of political associations is especially harmful to members of political groups that are unpopular or unorthodox. When the Army engaged in the domestic political surveillance that produced the Supreme Court's 5–4 nondecision in LAIRD V. TATUM (1972), its files were filled with the names of those who "were thought to have at least some potential for civil disorder," not with the names of Rotarians and Job's Daughters. A similar threat is posed by disclosure of one's homosexual associations or other intimate associations outside the mainstream of conventional morality. Such a case, like *Griswold*, implicates both privacy as nondisclosure or seclusion and "privacy" as associational autonomy.

On the other side of the constitutional balance, opposed to the interest in informational privacy, may be ranged any of the interests commonly advanced to support the free exchange of information. To further many of those interests, the common law of defamation erected an elaborate structure of "privileges," designed to protect from liability persons who made defamatory statements in the course of exchanging information for legitimate purposes: a former employer might give a servant a bad reference; a newspaper might criticize the town mayor. As these examples show, informational privacy is by no means the only constitutional interest that may be raised in such cases. Not only has the law of defamation been hedged in with First Amendment limitations; liability for the tort of invasion of privacy must also pass judicial scrutiny aimed at avoiding violations of the FREEDOM OF THE PRESS. Although the Supreme Court has not ruled on the matter, undoubtedly the First Amendment will be read to include a "newsworthiness" defense to an action for damages for invasion of privacy by publication of intimate facts. Even where the First Amendment is not involved directly as a constitutional limit on the award of damages or the imposition of punishment under state law, that amendment's values must be taken into account in evaluating any claim that a state has violated an individual's constitutional right of informational privacy. (See GOVERNMENT SPEECH.) Perhaps for this reason, most lower federal courts have been reluctant to find in Justice Stevens's *Whalen* opinion a general invitation to expand the constitutional right of privacy's protections against disclosure of information.

Nor has the Supreme Court been ready, in the years since ROE V. WADE, to extend either branch of the constitutional right of privacy. The Court's best-known opportunities for widening the scope of the right have come in "important decisions" cases involving nonmarital intimate relationships (including homosexual ones; see SEXUAL PREFERENCE AND THE CONSTITUTION) and the asserted right to control one's own personal appearance (including dress and hair length). In some of these cases the Court has avoided deciding cases on their constitutional merits; in no case has the Court validated the claim of a right of privacy. On principle, the intimate association cases seem clearly enough to be governed by *Griswold* and its successor decisions. Yet the Court has temporized, displaying what ALEXANDER BICKEL once called "the passive virtues," evidently awaiting the formation of a sufficient political consensus before extending constitutional protection to unconventional intimate associations.

One factual context in which the Court seems likely to continue its hospitality to "privacy" claims touching intimate personal decisions is that of governmental intrusions into the body. The abortion decisions, of course, are the modern starting point. Compulsory smallpox VACCINATION, once upheld as a health measure, stands on shakier constitutional ground now that smallpox has been virtually eradicated. Compulsory STERILIZATION, too, is unconstitutional in the absence of justification by some COMPELLING STATE INTEREST. The Supreme Court has explicitly redescribed SKINNER V. OKLAHOMA (1942) as a "privacy" case. By analogy, the right of a competent adult to refuse medical treatment seems secure, even when that choice will probably lead to death. (See EUTHANASIA.)

If the Supreme Court comes to accept Justice Stevens's broad reading of due process "liberty," it makes little difference whether the bodily intrusion cases be seen as raising "privacy" issues. There are occasions, however, when governmental invasions of the body implicate not only the interest in autonomy over one's own body but also privacy in its true sense of nondisclosure and seclusion. An appalling case in point is *Bell v. Wolfish* (1979). Inmates of a federal detention center, held in custody before being tried on criminal charges, sued to challenge the constitutionality of various conditions of their confinement. One challenged practice was the systematic subjection of every inmate to visual inspection of his or her body cavities after every "contact visit" with a person from outside the center, whether or not anyone had any suspicion that contraband was being smuggled into the center. A 5–4 Supreme Court held that the searches were not unreasonable and thus presented no Fourth Amendment problem; the majority did not separately consider any constitutional right of privacy founded on due process. The two main dissenting opinions, emphasizing substantive due process, insisted that the government must offer substantial justification for such a degrading invasion of privacy. (See ROCHIN V. CALIFORNIA, 1952.) Justification was lacking: the lower court had found that the searches were ineffective in detecting smuggled goods, and the government's argument that the searches deterred smuggling was an obvious makeweight.

There was no significant physical invasion of the body in the *Wolfish* case. Yet the privacy interests of the individuals searched were not far removed from those involved in the abortion and sterilization cases. The detainees sought vindication of their right to be afforded the dignity of respect, not just for their bodies but for their persons. The very pointlessness of the searches in cases where suspicion was lacking heightened the humiliation, to the point that many inmates had given up visits by family members. The case illustrates perfectly the convergence of the interests in personal autonomy and informational privacy in an individual's control over his own personality. When government seriously invades that sphere, due process demands important justification.

Several states guarantee a right of privacy in their state constitutions. The various state supreme courts have relied on these provisions to hold unconstitutional not only invasions of informational privacy, such as police surveillance, but also invasions of personal autonomy, such as laws limiting the occupancy of a house to members of a family, or forbidding the possession of marijuana for personal use. If the Supreme Court were to follow the doctrinal leadership of these courts, it would not be the first time. (See INCORPORATION DOCTRINE.)

Both types of interests protected by the federal constitutional right of privacy are susceptible to either broad or narrow interpretation. A generalized "privacy" right to make important decisions, like a generalized right of informational privacy, resists clear-cut definition. Every extension of a constitutional right of personal autonomy detracts from the power of government to regulate behavior in the public interest (as government defines that interest); and every extension of a constitutional right of informational privacy detracts from the free flow of communication. The problem for the courts, here as in EQUAL PROTECTION and other areas of constitutional growth, is the stopping-place problem. It is no accident that most discussions of the newer constitutional right of privacy turn to questions about the proper role of the judiciary—a theme that has dominated discussion of substantive due process since it appeared on the constitutional scene a century ago. The problem of defining a constitutional right and the problem of establishing the courts' proper constitutional role are two faces of the same inquiry. A constitutional right that defies description not only fails to protect its intended beneficiaries but also undermines the position of the courts in the governmental system.

Justice Stevens's opinion in WHALEN V. ROE begins to point the way toward the resolution of the uncertainties that have surrounded the constitutional right of privacy ever since the *Griswold* decision. It does aid constitutional analysis to separate the right into the two strands of personal autonomy and informational privacy. Yet it remains useful to recognize, as Justice Stevens has continued to remind us, that both strands remain part of a single substantive due process principle: significant governmental invasions of individual liberty require justification, scaled in importance according to the severity of the invasions. The right of privacy, then, is no more susceptible to precise definition than are such rights as due process or equal protection. What can be identified are the substantive values that inform the right of privacy. These values, as the Supreme Court's decisions show, are centered in the respect owed by the organized society to each individual as a person and as a member of a community. When governmental officers invade a person's control over her own body, or development of individual identity, or intimate associations—either by restricting decisional autonomy or by intruding on privacy in the sense of nondisclosure or solitude—then the Constitution demands that they be called to account and made to justify their actions.

For the future, the fate of the right of privacy, like that of all constitutional rights, will depend on the courts only secondarily. In the long run, the crucial questions will be how much privacy and what kinds of privacy we value. Total privacy—that is, isolation from others—is not merely unattainable; hardly anyone could stand it for long. In some societies people neither have nor want much of what we call privacy. Yet even among Australian aborigines who eke out their precarious living in a desert that often fails to provide walls, there are rules of restraint and social distance, and, when all else fails, the magic of secret names. Our own constitutional right of privacy will grow or wither as our own society's rules of restraint and social distance form and dissolve.

KENNETH L. KARST

(SEE ALSO: *Privacy and the First Amendment.*)

Bibliography

BOSTWICK, GARY L. 1976 A Taxonomy of Privacy: Repose, Sanctuary, and Intimate Decision. *California Law Review* 64:1447–83.

GAVISON, RUTH 1980 Privacy and the Limits of Law. *Yale Law Journal* 89:421–71.

GERETY, TOM 1977 Redefining Privacy. *Harvard Civil Rights–Civil Liberties Law Review* 12:233–96.

GREENAWALT, KENT 1974 Privacy and Its Legal Protections. *Hastings Center Studies* 2:45–68.

HENKIN, LOUIS 1974 Privacy and Autonomy. *Columbia Law Review* 74:1410–33.

PENNOCK, J. ROLAND and CHAPMAN, JOHN W., eds. 1971 *Privacy.* NOMOS XIII. New York: Atherton Press.

Symposium on Privacy 1966 *Law and Contemporary Problems* 31:251–435.

TRIBE, LAURENCE H. 1978 *American Constitutional Law.* Chap. 15. Mineola, N.Y.: The Foundation Press.

WESTIN, ALAN F. 1967 *Privacy and Freedom.* New York: Atheneum.

RIGHT OF REVOLUTION

The right of revolution is not a right that is defined and protected by the Constitution but a NATURAL RIGHT. It would be absurd for a constitution to authorize revolutionary challenges to its authority. However, it would not have been absurd for the preamble to the Constitution to have acknowledged the right of revolution, as, for example, the preamble to the PENNSYLVANIA CONSTITUTION of 1776 had done. It was unnecessary to include such an acknowledgment in the Constitution of 1787, for the Constitution did not supplant the DECLARATION OF INDEPENDENCE of 1776, which remained the first organic law of the United States. The "people" who "ordain and establish this Constitution" are the same "people" who in 1776 "assume among the powers of the earth, the separate and equal station to which the Laws of Nature and of Nature's God entitle them." The Declaration, borrowing the reasoning of JOHN LOCKE, succinctly states the American doctrine of the right of revolution:

> We hold these truths to be self-evident, that all men are created equal, that they are endowed by their Creator with certain unalienable Rights, that among these are Life, Liberty and the pursuit of Happiness. That to secure these rights, Governments are instituted among Men, deriving their just powers from the consent of the governed, That whenever any Form of Government becomes destructive of these ends, it is the Right of the People to alter or abolish it, and to institute new Government, laying its foundation on such principles and organizing its powers in such form, as to them shall seem most likely to effect their Safety and Happiness. Prudence, indeed, will dictate that Governments long established should not be changed for light and transient causes; and accordingly all experience hath shown, that mankind are more disposed to suffer, while evils are sufferable, than to right themselves by abolishing the forms to which they are accustomed. But when a long train of abuses and usurpations, pursuing invariably the same Object evinces a design to reduce them under absolute Despotism, it is their right, it is their duty, to throw off such Government, and to provide new Guards for their future security.

Recognition of the right of revolution is, in this view, implicit in the recognition of human equality. A people who recognize that they are equal members of the same species—that no human being is the natural ruler of another—accept that the inequalities necessarily involved in government are not natural but must be "instituted" and operated by "consent"; and that the primary end of government is not the promotion of the interests of one allegedly superior class of human beings but the security of all citizens' equal rights to "life, liberty, and the pursuit of happiness." It follows that it is the right and the duty of such a people to change their government when it persistently fails to effect this end. This right and duty, the Declaration says, belongs not to all peoples but only to those enlightened peoples who recognize human equality and natural rights, and who will therefore exercise their revolutionary right to establish right-securing government by consent.

Not only the revolutionaries of 1776 but also the Framers of the Constitution of 1787 justified their actions on this basis. In THE FEDERALIST #40 and #43 JAMES MADISON cites the Declaration's right of revolution to explain and to support the revolutionary proposals of the CONSTITUTIONAL CONVENTION. Madison argues that political leadership (by patriots like those assembled in Philadelphia) is needed in a revolution because "it is impossible for the people spontaneously and universally to move in concert towards their object." Thus, while the right of revolution is justly exercised when an enlightened people feel and judge that their government threatens to lead them back into an anarchical state of nature by failing to fulfill the duties they have entrusted to it, a revolution need neither wait for nor involve an anarchical disruption of society. However, exercise of the right of revolution (in contrast to mere CIVIL DISOBEDIENCE) can well necessitate and justify war. Those who exercise the right of revolution must prudently measure their forces.

ALEXANDER HAMILTON, in *The Federalist* #16, acknowledged that no constitution can guarantee that a widespread revolutionary opposition to the government will never occur; such opposition might well proceed "from weighty causes of discontent given by the government" itself. In contrast to Marxist doctrines of revolution, the American doctrine does not anticipate a future in which the right of revolution can safely disappear. It is therefore a cause for concern that today the right of revolution is obscured not only because it is a natural rather than a constitutional right but also because natural rights are no longer generally recognized by political theorists and jurists.

JOHN ZVESPER

Bibliography

MANSFIELD, HARVEY C., JR. 1978 *The Spirit of Liberalism.* Cambridge, Mass.: Harvard University Press.

STOURZH, GERALD 1970 *Alexander Hamilton and the Idea of Republican Government.* Stanford, Calif.: Stanford University Press.

RIGHT–PRIVILEGE DISTINCTION

There are at least two ways of distinguishing between "privileges" and "rights" in the context of American constitutional law and history, and careful analysis does not confound the two. The text of the Constitution refers to both privileges and rights, and uses "privileges" as a term of art denoting a class of rights that may be invoked defensively, to excuse one from a legal restraint or obligation. In another usage, privileges have both an inferior status to and a less permanent existence than rights, being subject to revocation by the government or to the imposition of conditions on their exercise. There is no foundation in the Constitution for the latter distinction.

In the Constitution, a privilege is one kind of right. The word privilege appears four times. The first appearance is in the PRIVILEGE FROM ARREST in civil cases enjoyed by members of Congress during congressional sessions. The second appearance is the guarantee of the "privilege of the writ of HABEAS CORPUS," yet that "privilege" has at least as great a degree of status and permanence as any right in the Constitution. The other appearances are in the PRIVILEGES AND IMMUNITIES clauses of Article IV and of the FOURTEENTH AMENDMENT: the citizens of each state are entitled to the privileges and immunities of citizens in the several states; and no state may abridge the privileges or immunities of citizens of the United States.

Privileges are associated with, but are distinct from, immunities. A privilege is an exemption from a legal restraint or duty (such as the duty to testify in court), while an immunity is an exemption from liability (usually civil liability). Thus members of Congress are privileged from arrest and immune from having to answer in another place for their SPEECH OR DEBATE. The way in which the word is used in the Constitution suggests that a privilege is a kind of right distinguished not by revocability or conditionability but by the fact that it cannot be asserted until some authority has taken action against one. One can exercise the right of RELIGIOUS LIBERTY or the right of peaceable assembly on one's own initiative; but one cannot demand that the state show cause for holding one in jail until one is actually held, and one cannot refuse to answer questions until questions are asked. A constitutional privilege is defensive, but it may be asserted as of right. Thus there is not necessarily a diminution of the RIGHT AGAINST SELF-INCRIMINATION when that right is called a privilege.

The word "right," standing alone, along with the word "freedom" and the phrase "right of the people," is used in the Constitution to designate a right that one may assert affirmatively and which the government is precluded from invading. Among these are NATURAL RIGHTS, which antedate the Constitution, such as the FREEDOM OF SPEECH, the right of the people to keep and bear arms, and the right of the people to be secure in their persons, houses, papers, and effects. Another category of constitutional rights comprises procedural rights, both civil and criminal.

Precise usage of constitutional terms is hampered by an unfortunate rhetorical use of the terms "right" and "privilege." Even JAMES MADISON seems, on occasion, to have used "privilege" to mean a special boon conferred by authority and subject to revocation at the pleasure of the grantor. Subsequently, because the power to revoke a right includes the power to impose conditions upon its exercise, "privilege" came, in certain rhetorical circumstances, to stand for rights that were conditionable.

This rhetorical use of "right" and "privilege" was introduced into American public law by OLIVER WENDELL HOLMES. Writing as a justice of the Massachusetts Supreme Judicial Court, Holmes commented in 1892 on the freedom of speech of PUBLIC EMPLOYEES: "The petitioner may have the constitutional right to talk politics, but he has no constitutional right to be a policeman." Public employment was, for Holmes, not a right but a privilege. In GOLDBERG V. KELLY (1970) the Supreme Court stated that it had abandoned the right–privilege distinction. WELFARE BENEFITS might be a privilege, in the sense that the state could constitutionally abolish a welfare program, but a particular beneficiary's benefits could not be terminated except by procedures that satisfied the requirements of PROCEDURAL DUE PROCESS.

Similarly, the federal courts today interpret the FIRST AMENDMENT to protect public employees against at least some restrictions on their constitutional freedoms. Government, the Court has said, "may not deny a benefit to a person because he exercises a Constitutional right." Yet rights—even First Amendment rights—are defined more narrowly for public employees than they are for others, as the validation of the HATCH ACT demonstrated. (See UNCONSTITUTIONAL CONDITIONS.)

In recent years the Court has erected new barriers to the invocation of the right to procedural due process, requiring that a claimant establish deprivation of a liberty or property interest before due process even becomes an issue and paying considerable deference to state law in defining both types of interest. In refusing to characterize some important interests as liberty or property, the Court has relegated those interests to an inferior status. Thus the Holmesian right–privilege distinction, once abandoned, has been welcomed home in new clothes.

DENNIS J. MAHONEY
KENNETH L. KARST

Bibliography

HOHFELD, WESLEY N. 1923 *Fundamental Legal Conceptions.* New Haven, Conn.: Yale University Press.

MONAGHAN, HENRY P. 1977 Of "Liberty" and "Property." *Cornell Law Review* 62:401–444.

VAN ALSTYNE, WILLIAM W. 1968 The Demise of the Right–Privilege Distinction in Constitutional Law. *Harvard Law Review* 81:1439–1464.

_____ 1977 Cracks in "The New Property": Adjudicative Due Process in the Administrative State. *Cornell Law Review* 62:445–493.

RIGHT TO BAIL

See: Bail

RIGHT TO BEAR ARMS

See: Second Amendment

RIGHT TO BE INFORMED OF ACCUSATION

The Sixth Amendment provides that "[i]n all criminal prosecutions, the accused shall enjoy the right . . . to be informed of the nature and cause of the accusation. . . ." The right was recognized in English law prior to adoption of the Constitution and exists today in every state, under state law and through judicial interpretation of the DUE PROCESS clause of the FOURTEENTH AMENDMENT. The notice of accusation contemplated by the Sixth Amendment is the formal charge of crime to which the accused must respond by pleading guilty or not guilty; it does not include the notice issues that may arise in the investigative phase of a criminal proceeding.

The "notice clause" makes no reference to the institution that must produce the charge, the instrument through which notice must be given, or the precise function of the notice. But these details are supplied by other provisions of the Constitution, by history, and by judicial opinions. Where the accused is charged with an infamous federal crime, usually a FELONY, the Fifth Amendment requires that the accusation must be made by the INDICTMENT of a GRAND JURY. For lesser federal crimes, an INFORMATION drafted by a prosecutor or even a complaint will suffice. In the states, any of these processes may be used because indictment by grand jury is not required by the Fourteenth Amendment.

Over the years, the charging instrument has been assigned several roles by the courts. It provides the notice required by the Sixth Amendment, and it assists in enforcing the provisions of the Fifth Amendment dealing with the grand jury, DOUBLE JEOPARDY, and due process. For example, indictments and informations must demonstrate that the offense charged is not the same as one for which the accused has already been placed in jeopardy. And indictments must reflect the decisions of the grand juries that returned them.

The unique function of the Sixth Amendment's notice clause—as distinct from the facilitative role it plays for the Fifth Amendment—is to require advice to the accused of the charge against him so that he may decide whether to concede his guilt or, if he does not, so that he may prepare to defend himself at trial. The notice must also contain enough detail to enable the court to determine whether the charge is sufficient in law to support a conviction. To perform these functions, the notice must state the basic facts regarding each element of the offense with "reasonable particularity of time, place and circumstances." Such notice is especially important in an adversary system that contemplates a trial as a climactic event. Without notice, defendants would find it difficult to proceed expeditiously, and frequent continuances might be necessary; trial judges would have no manageable criterion for determining the relevance of EVIDENCE or the instructions to be given to juries; and appellate courts would have inadequate standards for review.

Few cases have tested the limits of the notice clause, for both the federal government and the states now have statutes or rules of court that define what must appear in the charging instrument and these requirements usually reflect the constitutional standard. For example, Rule 7 of the FEDERAL RULES OF CRIMINAL PROCEDURE requires a "plain, concise and definite written statement of the essential facts constituting the offense charged." There are state decisions, however, that suggest how little might now be constitutionally required of the initial charge in a criminal case. In these cases, state laws authorized indictments that informed defendants only of the names or citations of the statutes they were accused of violating. In *People v. Bogdanoff* (1930) New York's high court upheld the constitutionality of such a "short form indictment." Although the New York statute involved in that case has not survived, the opinion called attention in dramatic fashion to changes that may have made the law of "notice" partially obsolete. The routine maintenance of trial records was said to provide a basis for determining whether a prior proceeding involved the same offense as the one charged in the indictment. And the availability of grand jury minutes made it possible to determine whether the offense charged at trial was the same as the one contemplated by the grand jury. The only interest of the accused remaining to be protected by the charging instrument itself, said the court, was an adequate opportunity to prepare for trial; that interest could be served by a bill of particulars, continuances, and other measures. In sum, the notice clause—stripped of its relation to the jeopardy and grand jury provisions—may be satisfied not only by a single charging document but also by a process of notice that enables the defendant to understand the charge and defend against it.

The logic of a flexible conception of notice, rooted less in form than in concern for the defendant's need to prepare for trial, led inevitably to the position that many defects in the indictment or information—which might have led to dismissal in an earlier, more formalistic period—were now regarded as merely technical. For example, the doctrine of "fatal variance" had prohibited any departure in the course of trial from the offense charged. Such variances are now held to be HARMLESS ERROR so long as the defendant has not been materially prejudiced in making his defense and, if an indictment is involved, the trial falls fairly within the scope of the grand jury's charge.

As the specificity demanded of indictments and informations declined, defendants lost one of the principal means for learning about the prosecution's case in advance of trial. Pleadings in criminal cases had been assimilated to an increasingly liberal law of civil procedure, but those changes had not been accompanied in CRIMINAL PROCEDURE by the pretrial DISCOVERY which had emerged to compensate for looser pleadings in civil cases. Beginning in the 1960s, however, pretrial disclosure of the prosecution's case has become more available to the defendant, some of it mandated by the due process clause. This expansion of the process of notice before and during trial has minimized the problems of law and policy which relatively spare charges might otherwise have presented under the notice clause of the Sixth Amendment.

ABRAHAM S. GOLDSTEIN

Bibliography

GOLDSTEIN, ABRAHAM S. 1960 The State and the Accused: Balance of Advantage in Criminal Procedure. *Yale Law Journal* 69:1149, 1172–1180.

SCOTT, AUSTIN, JR. 1982 Fairness in Accusation of Crime. *Minnesota Law Review* 41:509–546.

WRIGHT, CHARLES ALAN 1982 *Federal Practice and Procedure, Criminal,* 2nd ed. Vol. 1, Sections 125–126. St. Paul, Minn.: West Publishing Co.

RIGHT TO CONFRONT WITNESSES

See: Confrontation, Right of

RIGHT TO COUNSEL

The constitutional right to counsel in American law encompasses two broad categories of rights: first, rights of persons to retain and employ counsel in official proceedings and, second, rights of persons who because of financial incapacity or other reasons are unable to procure the assistance of lawyers, to have counsel appointed in their behalf.

The modern rights to counsel are the product of a historical evolution extending over a half-millennium. English criminal procedure in the early modern era diverged sharply from today's institutions of adversary criminal justice. In the Tudor and Stuart regimes, legal proceedings in which the crown's interests were strongly implicated were heavily tilted in favor of the state and against the accused. Thus it was only in the least serious cases, those involving MISDEMEANORS, that the privilege of the accused to present his defense by counsel was recognized. Not until the end of the seventeenth century was a similar right granted defendants in TREASON trials (along with the right to have counsel appointed by the court when requested). Over 140 years were to elapse before Parliament recognized the right of the accused to retain and employ counsel in FELONY trials. The earlier recognition of the right to counsel in treason cases reflects the fact that members of Parliament were themselves frequent targets of treason prosecutions launched by the crown. Throughout the eighteenth century the incongruity of a system that recognized counsel rights in misdemeanor and treason cases but withheld them in felony cases at a time when as many as 150 felonies were punishable by death was widely perceived and sometimes protested.

In the American colonies there was great variation in practices and statutory provisions relating to rights of counsel in criminal cases. By 1776, however, the right of attorneys retained by the accused to perform defense functions in courts appears to have been widely conceded, and in several of the colonies practices were considerably in advance of those then prevailing in England. In Pennsylvania, for example, the appointment of counsel for impoverished defendants in capital cases was mandated by statute; and in Connecticut even more liberal practices of appointment were established in the quarter-century before the American revolution.

Rights to counsel entered American constitutional law through provisions included in the early state constitutions and with the ratification of the Sixth Amendment to the federal Constitution in 1791. Seven of the original states and Vermont adopted constitutional provisions relating to the rights to counsel, and the right so protected was that to retain and employ lawyers in criminal trials. By the beginning of the nineteenth century only two states, Connecticut and

New Jersey, appear clearly to have recognized a right in the accused to request appointment of counsel in all serious cases; and in neither was the privilege created by a constitutional provision.

Included in the Sixth Amendment, upon which most of the modern law of counsel rights depends, is the following clause: "In all criminal prosecutions, the accused shall enjoy the right . . . to have the Assistance of Counsel for his defense." There is no direct evidence of the framers' intentions in drafting the language or of the understanding of those who ratified the amendment. Yet the general assumption until well into the present century was that the right constitutionally protected was one to employ counsel, not to have counsel assigned.

One of the most remarkable features of Sixth Amendment history is the paucity of judicial authority on the counsel clause for nearly a century and a half after the amendment's ratification. There was no comprehensive exegesis in the Supreme Court, and only a scattering of holdings in the lower federal courts. The relative absence of authoritative interpretation may be explained in part by the long delay in establishing a system of federal criminal APPEALS and the strict limitations applied to the HABEAS CORPUS remedy in the federal courts. The landmark decision in JOHNSON V. ZERBST was not handed down until 1938, six years after the Court had begun its delineation of the rights to counsel protected by the DUE PROCESS clause of the FOURTEENTH AMENDMENT in state criminal prosecutions. (See POWELL V. ALABAMA, 1932.) *Johnson* was comprehensive and far-reaching. The Court, through Justice HUGO L. BLACK, without pausing to canvass the historical understanding of the counsel clause, held that a federal trial court lacked power "to deprive an accused of his life and liberty unless he has or waives the assistance of counsel." Second, the assistance of counsel "is an essential jurisdictional prerequisite" to a federal court's power to try and sentence a criminal defendant. Hence the habeas corpus remedy may be invoked by a prisoner to set aside his conviction if the Sixth Amendment right to counsel was withheld at his trial. Third, although the right to have counsel assigned may be waived, allegations of waiver will be closely scrutinized. WAIVER OF CONSTITUTIONAL RIGHTS involves "an intentional relinquishment of a known right or privilege." The trial judge has a "protecting duty" to see that the accused understands his rights to legal assistance, and if the judge determines that the defendant has waived his rights, the record of the trial should clearly reveal the judge's determination and the basis for it.

In holding that the counsel clause not only creates a right to make use of a retained lawyer in federal criminal proceedings but also mandates the assignment of counsel for an accused otherwise unable to procure legal assistance, *Johnson v. Zerbst* upset the long-prevailing understanding to the contrary. Yet the decision did not immediately produce a major alteration in the actual practices of federal criminal justice. Many federal district courts before 1938, with the active encouragement of the Department of Justice, had been assigning counsel to indigent defendants in felony cases. The lawyers so appointed typically received no compensation for their services and were hampered in having no resources for pretrial investigations of their cases or for many other incidents of trial. *Johnson v. Zerbst* did little to improve this situation. It was not until a quarter-century later that Congress enacted the Criminal Justice Act of 1964 and for the first time provided, however inadequately, a system of compensated legal assistance in the federal courts.

In the celebrated case of *Powell v. Alabama*, decided in 1932, the Supreme Court made its first significant contribution to the constitutional law of counsel rights in Fourteenth Amendment cases. *Powell*, in addition, was one of the great seminal decisions in the Court's history and strongly influenced the development of the entire modern constitutional law of CRIMINAL PROCEDURE. The decision arose out of one of the most famous of twentieth-century criminal prosecutions, that of the Scottsboro defendants. Seven illiterate young blacks were arrested on the charge of raping two white women. After INDICTMENT the accused were divided into groups and tried in three separate trials. No lawyer having come forward to represent the defendants, the trial judge appointed "all the members of the bar" to assist in the arraignment, an act later described by the Supreme Court as merely "an expansive gesture." At the trial no lawyer was designated to assume personal responsibility for protecting the defendants' interests. Each trial was completed in a single day, and in each the jury convicted the accused and sentenced them to death. The convictions were affirmed in the Alabama Supreme Court, the chief justice vigorously dissenting.

At the time of the *Powell* decision, the Supreme Court had rarely employed the federal judicial power to upset state criminal prosecutions. (See MOORE V. DEMPSEY, 1923.) The determination of the Court that the procedures in the Alabama trial had violated the accused's rights to due process of law protected by the Fourteenth Amendment was, therefore, an event of portentous significance. The Court held that both the right of the defendants to retain counsel and the right to have counsel assigned in their behalf had been nullified. The speed with which the Scottsboro defendants had been rushed to trial and conviction deprived them of an opportunity to secure legal assistance, and the arrival of lawyers eager to provide representation for the defendants shortly thereafter indicated that the haste was seriously prejudicial. Beyond this, the Court found that the failure to make an effective appointment of counsel in behalf of the accused, given the circumstances of the case, constituted a denial of due process.

The constitutional theory of Justice GEORGE SUTHERLAND's opinion for the court is important, for it dominated thought about the rights of counsel for the next three decades. Whatever else the protean phrase "due process of law" contemplates, argued the Court, it encompasses the requirement of NOTICE and hearing in criminal cases. A FAIR HEARING, in turn, encompasses the right to counsel. In one of the Court's best-known OBITER DICTA, Justice Sutherland wrote: "The right to be heard would be, in many cases, of little avail if it did not comprehend the right to be heard by counsel. [Even the intelligent and educated layman] requires the guiding hand of counsel at every step of the proceedings against him. Without it, though he be not guilty, he faces the danger of conviction because he does not know how to establish his innocence."

Although the *Powell* decision was placed on a broad constitutional base, one susceptible of future doctrinal development, the actual HOLDING of the case was narrowly drawn. Thus the right of the accused to receive an assignment of counsel in *Powell* was made to rest on such considerations as that the charge was a capital offense, that the defendants were young, inexperienced, illiterate, and the like. The question that immediately became pressing was how far the *Powell* precedent would be extended when one or more of the circumstances in that case were absent. It was widely assumed that the Fourteenth Amendment might require the state to appoint counsel for an INDIGENT defendant in any capital case, even though a considerable interval elapsed before the proposition was authoritatively stated in *Bute v. Illinois* (1948). The more important question, however, was whether a "flat requirement" of counsel similar to the Sixth Amendment rule imposed on the federal courts in *Johnson v. Zerbst* would also be found applicable to state prosecutions by reason of the Fourteenth Amendment. A definitive negative answer came in BETTS V. BRADY (1942).

In *Betts* the defendant was convicted of robbery, a noncapital felony. At his trial in the state court, the accused, an unemployed farm hand said by the Supreme Court to be "of ordinary intelligence," requested the appointment of counsel to assist in his defense. The request was denied by the trial judge, and the accused participated in the defense by examining his own witnesses and cross-examining those of the prosecution. When, after conviction, defendant was denied *habeas corpus* relief in the state courts, he took his case to the Supreme Court alleging that the denial of counsel at his trial violated due process of law. Justice OWEN ROBERTS for the Court denied that due process required the assignment of counsel for indigent defendants in every state felony case. There was, in the view of the Court's majority, nothing in historical or contemporary practice to validate the claim. Rather, the question in each case was whether in the totality of circumstances presented, appointment of counsel was required to insure the accused a fair hearing. In the present case, the Court said, there was no such necessity. The issue upon which the defense rested, that of alibi, was simple and straightforward. There were no special circumstances of mental incapacity or inexperience that placed defendant at a serious disadvantage in maintaining his defense.

Criticism of the *Betts* decision began with Justice Black's vigorous dissent in that case and was promptly amplified in the press and the writings of legal commentators. Two principal reasons for the reluctance of the Court's majority to impose the obligation of assigning counsel in all state felony prosecutions can be identified. First, the prevailing opinion in *Betts* reflected the Court's deference to state autonomy, a deference widely believed at the time to be mandated by the nature of American FEDERALISM. The administration of criminal justice was an area in which state powers of self-determination were thought to be particularly broad. Second, there was the related concern that the states were poorly prepared suddenly to assume the obligation of providing legal aid for unrepresented defendants in all state felony cases. The problem was not only that lawyers and resources would have to be supplied in pending and future cases, but also that hundreds of state prisoners had been convicted in trials in which no assistance of counsel was received. The concern was freely articulated by Justice FELIX FRANKFURTER when in *Foster v. Illinois* (1947) he wrote: "Such an abrupt innovation . . . would furnish opportunities hitherto uncontemplated for opening wide the prison doors of the land."

Nevertheless, with the passage of time opinion increasingly supported the overturning of *Betts* and recognition of a "flat requirement" of counsel in state as well as federal prosecutions. The *Betts* rule, far from strengthening federalism, exacerbated the relations of state and federal courts. Because under *Betts* the requirement of appointing counsel depended on the unique circumstances of the particular case, the resulting decision often provided little guidance to state judges dealing with cases in which the facts were significantly different. Many state judges came to favor the broader rule of *Johnson v. Zerbst* because of its greater certainty. It became apparent to many state officials that ultimately *Betts v. Brady* would be overruled, and in anticipation of the event they created systems of legal aid on their own initiative, supplying counsel for unrepresented defendants in all serious state cases. Meanwhile it had become increasingly difficult for the states to protect convictions in the Supreme Court when defendants argued that "special circumstances" had required appointment of counsel at the trial. In the thirteen years before *Betts* was overruled in GIDEON V. WAINWRIGHT (1963), no state conviction was upheld by the Court against a claim of special circumstances. It is significant also that when the *Gideon* case was pending before the Court, the attorneys general of twenty-two states filed AMICUS CURIAE briefs asking that *Betts* be overruled and the broader rule of appointment recognized.

Although the opinion of Justice Black for the court is unprepossessing, *Gideon v. Wainwright* marked a new era in the constitutional law of counsel rights. Portions of the opinion appear to pay deference to the older theories of fair hearing, and others seem to suggest that counsel must be assigned to unrepresented defendants on grounds of equality. Ultimately, however, *Gideon's* constitutional basis is the Sixth Amendment: the Sixth Amendment is "subsumed" in the provisions of the Fourteenth Amendment, and hence the same obligations relating to assignment of counsel for the indigent accused in federal courts are also owed in state prosecutions. Since the *Gideon* case there has been a flowering of constitutional doctrine relating to counsel rights in many important areas of the criminal process.

Although the prevailing opinion in the *Gideon* case did not specifically limit its holding to felony trials, most observers believed that the right to counsel for indigent defendants would not apply in all misdemeanor cases. Following *Gideon,* state and lower federal courts devised various formulas for dealing with counsel rights in small-crime prosecutions. The state of Florida, borrowing from cases involving the constitutional right to jury trial, provided that counsel rights should not attach in prosecutions for "petty offenses," *i.e.,* crimes punishable by not more than six months' imprisonment. (Cf. BALDWIN V. NEW YORK, 1970.) In ARGERSINGER V. HAMLIN (1972), nine years after *Gideon,* the Supreme Court rejected Florida's use of the petty-offense concept. In effect, the Court ruled that any deprivation of liberty, even for a few days, is a sanction of significant gravity. Accordingly, no unrepresented defendant may be jailed for any term unless he has waived counsel at the trial. The *Argersinger* holding dramatically expanded the legal aid obligations of state systems of criminal justice. Adequate practical implementation of counsel rights in small-crimes courts is yet to be fully attained in many jurisdictions.

The right recognized in *Argersinger* was defined further in *Scott v. Illinois* (1979). In the latter case an unrepresented defendant was sentenced for an offense which under state law was punishable by both fines and imprisonment. The sentence actually imposed, however, was a monetary fine. The Court, through Justice WILLIAM H. REHNQUIST, ruled that because the unrepresented accused was not actually sentenced to jail, his constitutional rights had not been denied. Ironically, Scott's rights were given less protection than he would have received if the Court had adopted the petty-offense formula in *Argersinger;* that formula would have looked to the penalties authorized by a statute, not solely to those actually imposed.

Because of the comparative modernity of criminal appeals in Anglo-American legal history, the Supreme Court's consideration of constitutional rights of representation in appellate proceedings was not preceded by extensive COMMON LAW experience. The first substantial discussion of constitutional rights to counsel on appeal occurred in DOUGLAS V. CALIFORNIA (1963) decided on the same day as the *Gideon* case. A California rule of court authorized the state intermediate appellate court to scrutinize the record in a pauper's appeal "to determine whether it would be of advantage to the defendant or helpful to the appellate court to have counsel appointed." Pursuant to this authority the court denied counsel to defendant, adjudicated his appeal, and affirmed his criminal conviction. In the Supreme Court the defendant successfully asserted that the California procedures violated his Fourteenth Amendment rights.

In reaching its result the Court relied primarily on an obligation in the state to accord equal treatment to rich and poor appellants and revived an earlier dictum of Justice Black in GRIFFIN V. ILLINOIS (1956): "There can be no equal justice where the kind of trial a man gets depends on the amount of money he has." Here the obligation of equal treatment was not met. Had defendant been able to retain his own lawyer, his appeal, regardless of its merits, would have been presented by counsel. Because of his poverty and the decision of the appellate court not to assign a lawyer to him, he was unrepresented on appeal. Whatever the implications of the Court's theory, the obligation of the state to provide "equal treatment" to the poor does not necessarily mean that the treatment must be identical to that meted out to appellants able to hire their own lawyers. Thus, the opinion asserts, "absolute equality is not required." In illustrating this possibility, the Court strongly implied that the constitutional obligation to assign counsel involved in *Douglas* may apply only to the first appeal. If an indigent represented by an assigned counsel is unsuccessful in the intermediate appellate court and decides to seek further review in the state's highest court, he may submit to the latter the brief prepared by counsel in the intermediate court, but the highest court may not be under obligation to assign a lawyer to conduct the second appeal. A decade later the Court made explicit what had been suggested in the *Douglas* case. In ROSS V. MOFFITT (1974) the Court sustained the validity of North Carolina procedures that provided the indigent with counsel in the first appeal but denied his requests for representation when he sought a discretionary review in the state supreme court and later, when seeking a WRIT OF CERTIORARI in the United States Supreme Court.

The limitations recognized by the Court, however, do not appear to have seriously inhibited the availability of appellate remedies to indigent defendants. Arguably, this may be true in part because the Court was essentially correct in concluding that the decencies of fair hearing and reasonable equality of treatment can be accorded such appellants without offering counsel in all stages of the appellate procedure. Also, many jurisdictions have gone beyond the constitutional minima and supply counsel throughout the review process. Perhaps of equal importance is a series of cases that have overcome many of the difficulties that earlier confronted impoverished criminal litigants in the appellate courts. As early as 1956, the Court in *Griffin v. Illinois* held that a convicted defendant may not be denied access to an appellate remedy because of his poverty. Under state law the appellant could perfect his appeal only by use of a stenographic transcript of the trial proceedings, the latter being unavailable to him because he had no funds to purchase it. Under these circumstances, the Court ruled, the state must furnish the prisoner with a transcript. In the years following, the *Griffin* principle was broadly applied. (For example, *Burns v. Ohio,* 1950; see WEALTH DISCRIMINATION.)

Recognition of counsel rights and the removal of obstacles to review for indigent prisoners have greatly widened opportunities for appellate regulation of the trial process. They have, at the same time, created substantial problems for the administration of justice in the appellate courts. Economic constraints may operate on appellants "paying their own way" so as to deter the filing of frivolous appeals. No such constraints influence the indigent prisoner. The resulting problems go beyond the swelling of the dockets of appellate courts and also include certain difficulties for lawyers assigned by the courts to represent indigent appellants. Many such attorneys believe, often rightly, that the appeals of their clients cannot be supported on any substantial legal grounds. Yet efforts by the lawyers to withdraw from representation may, on occasion, prejudice the interests of their clients and, in some instances, may be motivated by the lawyers' design to escape onerous and unprofitable obligations. Efforts to balance such considerations have not as yet resulted in a satisfactory resolution. The rule announced by the Supreme Court requires the appointed lawyer seeking to be relieved of the case to allege that it is "wholly frivolous." The motion must be accompanied by a brief referring to anything in the record that might arguably support the appeal. How matters may be both "arguable" and "wholly frivolous" is not explained, and the effect of the rule must be to induce the lawyer to remain in the case regardless of his professional judgment of frivolity. The Massachusetts Supreme Judicial Court, in *Commonwealth v. Moffett* (1981) recognizing this effect, simply refused to permit counsel to withdraw solely on grounds of absence of merit in the appeal.

Other questions relating to counsel rights have arisen in the postconviction criminal process. As early as *Mempa v. Ray* (1967) a unanimous Court held that an indigent defendant, who had been placed on probation after conviction and given a deferred sentence, was entitled to be represented by counsel when his probation was revoked and he was sentenced to imprisonment. In *Gagnon v. Scarpelli* (1973), however, the Court ruled that although due process requires a hearing whenever a probation or parole is revoked, counsel need not be appointed unless special circumstances dictate the need for legal representation. This dubious resurrection of the *Betts v. Brady* doctrine, long since rejected at the criminal trial, was justified in part by the need to preserve "flexibility" in procedures leading to revocation. The American Bar Association in its *Standards of Criminal Justice* repudiated the *Gagnon* rule and called for appointment of counsel in such cases.

One of the most striking characteristics of the WARREN COURT was its allegiance to the adversarial system of criminal justice. This dedication inevitably resulted in the expansion of constitutional rights to counsel. Thus, the adversary system was strengthened in areas where it already existed, such as the criminal trial, and also extended to other areas where it had had little or no operation, such as pretrial police interrogations. Clearly the Court's attitudes toward a rejuvenated adversarial process reflected some of its deepest convictions about the proper containment of state power in the administration of criminal justice. Introducing lawyers into the interrogation rooms of police stations, for example, was intended to achieve values going beyond those ordinarily associated with counsel rights. In addition to advising his client, the lawyer could serve as a witness to police interrogatory activity and a deterrent to police abuse. His presence might often be indispensable to the preservation of the suspect's RIGHT AGAINST SELF-INCRIMINATION and other constitutional rights.

Concern with proper representation of defendants' interests in the pretrial phases of the criminal process was expressed by the Supreme Court in its earliest cases involving rights to counsel. Even in *Powell v. Alabama* (1932) the Court had referred to the pretrial preparation of the defense as "the most critical" period in the criminal proceedings. Before the decision of *Gideon v. Wainwright* (1963) the Court had begun mandating the appointment of counsel for unrepresented accused persons at various "critical stages of the proceedings." Thus in *Hamilton v. Alabama* (1961) the murder conviction of the indigent accused was reversed because of the absence of defense counsel at the pretrial arraignment.

The more difficult problems, however, were those of the accused's rights after ARREST but before formal commencement of the judicial proceedings by bringing the accused into court for preliminary hearing or arraignment. The issues were squarely drawn in the companion cases of *Crooker v. California* and *Cicenia v. La Gay* (1958). In the former, petitioner, who was under sentence of death, complained that the confession introduced against him at his trial had been obtained in a period of incommunicado questioning during which time he was denied the opportunity to confer with his own attorney. A narrowly divided Court affirmed the conviction, Justice TOM C. CLARK emphasizing the "devastating effect" of the presence of counsel in the interrogation room on criminal law enforcement.

Crooker and *Cicenia* were overruled in ESCOBEDO V. ILLINOIS (1964) which represented the high-water mark of judicial protection of Sixth Amendment counsel rights in the pretrial interrogatory process. In a 5–4 decision the Court ruled that at the point in questioning when suspicions of the police have "focused" on the party being interrogated, even if this occurs before defendant is indicted for a criminal offense, the right of the party to consult with an attorney cannot constitutionally be denied. Two years later the Court decided the famous case of MIRANDA V. ARIZONA (1966), holding that whenever a suspect has been taken into custody he may not be interrogated until he has been given the "fourfold" warning: the arrested party must be advised that he has a right to remain silent, that he is entitled to consult with a lawyer, that the lawyer may be present at the interrogation, and that if he is unable to hire an attorney, counsel will be supplied. (See MIRANDA RULES.)

Although the prevailing opinion in *Miranda* reaffirmed the holding of the *Escobedo* case, the impact of the latter was considerably modified. Thus, use of the "focus" concept, while not expressly rejected, was for practical purposes abandoned. Again, although the *Miranda* opinion reaffirmed the existence of Sixth Amendment counsel rights in pretrial interrogation, the emphasis of the opinion is significantly different. The dominant view regarded the right to counsel in the interrogation situation as an incident to and a necessary means for protection of the Fifth Amendment's right against self-incrimination. The emphasis on that right is so dominant that the rights to representation recognized in *Miranda* have sometimes been referred to as Fifth Amendment rights to counsel.

The *Miranda* case did not bring lawyers into interrogation rooms so frequently as was hoped or feared at the time the decision was handed down. One principal weakness of the prevailing opinion was its failure to insist that a suspect's decision to waive the presence of counsel must itself be made only with the advice of a lawyer. In consequence, rights to counsel are frequently waived by persons in police custody. One study published shortly after the *Miranda* ruling revealed as few as seven percent of the suspects requesting stationhouse counsel. The tendency toward widespread waiver of *Miranda* rights appears to have continued in the intervening years.

Even before *Escobedo,* the Court had contributed another important strand to counsel doctrine in MASSIAH V. UNITED STATES (1964). After the defendant in that case had been indicted for a narcotics offense, government agents induced an accomplice of Massiah to draw him into conversation in an electronically "bugged" automobile. Incriminating admissions made by the defendant were overheard by the agents and introduced against him at the trial. In reversing Massiah's conviction, the Court ruled that the ELECTRONIC EAVESDROPPING violated defendant's rights to counsel, which rights had "attached" when the INDICTMENT against him was returned. Contemporary reaction to the *Massiah* decision was generally critical. Many commentators believed that if a wrong had been done to Massiah it consisted not of a denial of counsel rights, but rather an invasion of his Fourth Amendment RIGHT TO PRIVACY, or perhaps of the introduction of an "involuntary" confession against him. Again, to conceive of the rights to counsel attaching only at the return of the indictment leaves open to police officials an opportunity of frustrating the rule by simply delaying the indictment or INFORMATION.

After the decision of *Escobedo* it was widely assumed that the *Massiah* precedent had been drained of vitality. Yet in the widely noted case of BREWER V. WILLIAMS (1977) *Massiah* was invested with renewed significance. Although *Brewer* might readily have been decided by an application of the *Miranda* rule, the Court chose instead to reverse the conviction on the grounds of denial of counsel, reliance being placed on the *Massiah* precedent. Later decisions, building on *Massiah,* appear to assert a right in the defendant not to be approached by the government for evidence of his own guilt in the absence of counsel, once judicial proceedings are initiated by return of an indictment or other in-court proceedings (*United States v. Henry,* 1980). In New York the state courts have transcended the *Massiah* precedent by interpreting state law to mean that whenever a lawyer enters a case in behalf of the defendant, even when this occurs before indictment, the accused in custody may not waive his right to counsel in the absence of his lawyer (*People v. Hobson,* 1976). Although the New York rule alleviates the restrictions imposed by the Supreme Court on the *Massiah* doctrine, it is of limited value to indigent defendants, who ordinarily do not acquire counsel before the commencement of judicial proceedings.

A final area of pretrial counsel rights involves LINEUPS. Misidentification of the accused by prosecution witnesses constitutes perhaps the most prolific source of erroneous convictions; police lineups and other identification procedures often spawn such errors. In UNITED STATES V. WADE (1967) the Court responded to these problems by designating the pretrial identification confrontation between witnesses and the accused as a "critical stage" of the proceedings and hence one requiring the presence of the accused's attorney. An identification made at a lineup in which the suspect's right to counsel was not honored may not be introduced at the criminal trial. An in-court identification is not summarily barred, but before it can be employed as evidence, the prosecution must establish by "clear and convincing evidence" that it was based on observations other than those made at the flawed lineup. After this promising beginning the Court backed away, and the view appears established that unless the identification evidence was obtained by methods so defective as to deny due process of law, an identification obtained in the absence of counsel may be introduced in court if the lineup occurred before return of an indictment. (See KIRBY V. ILLINOIS, 1972.) Limiting rights of counsel to the postindictment period is especially devastating in these areas because identification efforts are typically undertaken before formal charges are made. In UNITED STATES V. ASH (1973) the Court has also refused to supervise other identification procedures, such as those involving the use of photographic files. The problems of convicting the innocent through misidentification persist, and the Court has relegated their solutions largely to administrative and legislative action.

Basic to the rights of counsel is the quality of the legal representation supplied the criminal accused. Yet growth of the law in this area is inhibited by the fear that close judicial scrutiny of the competency of such representation will provide numerous and unwarranted opportunities for disappointed criminal litigants to attack their convictions. Such administrative concerns resulted in the once widely recognized rule that convictions were not to be reversed on incompetency grounds unless the performance of defense counsel constituted a "mockery of justice." The formula employed in the Supreme Court today is considerably more demanding: counsel's advice must not fall "outside the range of competence demanded of attorneys in criminal cases" (*Tollet v. Henderson,* 1953). The application of the "ordinary competence" test, however, results in the reversal of comparatively few criminal convictions. Thus in *United States v. Decoster* (1979) the District of Columbia Court of Appeals refused to upset a conviction in which a court-appointed lawyer failed to interview his client's codefendants or any other witnesses before trial. Failures to achieve the objective of adequate defense in criminal cases are often not the product of the professional incompetence of lawyers. In many cases the court-appointed lawyer is on the staff of an inadequately funded legal aid agency that must impose wholly unrealistic case loads on its attorneys. Similar problems also often affect the privately retained lawyer who because of the economics of criminal law practice may be under pressure to accept more cases than he can adequately handle. The courts alone cannot be expected to solve problems of this sort, but it is doubtful that instances of inadequate defense will be significantly abated until the courts articulate and apply specific minimum standards of counsel performance.

The right of an indigent litigant to demand appointment of counsel from the state in noncriminal proceedings has received comparatively little judicial consideration or development. In the famous case of IN RE GAULT (1967) the Court recognized a right to counsel in a state juvenile court delinquency proceeding. Some courts have held that, where necessary to a fair hearing, a similar right is possessed by an indigent petitioner in an habeas corpus action. Since juvenile court and habeas corpus proceedings, although "civil" in form, are analogous or intimately related to the criminal process, the precedents in neither category represent a significant expansion of counsel rights into noncriminal areas.

In *Lassiter v. Department of Social Services* (1981) the question was whether counsel must be appointed to represent an indigent mother in a proceeding brought by the state to terminate her parental rights. In such a proceeding the defendant faces a sanction often considered more severe than a sentence of imprisonment, and, given the nature of the issues, the defendant's need for professional assistance is at least as great as that of the accused in many criminal cases. Although recognizing these considerations, the Court's majority limited the right to counsel to the situation in which all the circumstances in a particular case make legal representation necessary for a fair hearing, and it concluded that such considerations were not shown to be present in the *Lassiter* case. This latter-day revival of the *Betts v. Brady* precedent is regrettable in view of the needs for counsel in these proceedings and the comparatively small social costs involved in making counsel available routinely in all such cases. Like *Betts,* however, the *Lassiter* holding may represent a step toward a more satisfactory ultimate result.

In the development of the modern constitutional law of criminal procedure, questions of the rights of counsel have held a central position. This centrality is not surprising; counsel rights are integral to an adversarial system of justice, and the expansion and refurbishing of that system have been a dominant objective of constitutional procedural law from the decision of *Powell v. Alabama* in 1932 to the present. In the intervening years, issues of counsel rights have continued to emerge in a variety of contexts. It may be anticipated that this course of constitutional events will continue so long as the Supreme Court places significant reliance on the adversarial system as the principal mechanism to control and order the applications of state power in the criminal process.

FRANCIS A. ALLEN

(SEE ALSO: *Nix v. Williams, 1986.*)

Bibliography

ALLEN, FRANCIS A. 1975 The Judicial Quest for Penal Justice: The Warren Court and the Criminal Cases. *Illinois Law Forum* 1975:518–542.

ATTORNEY GENERAL'S COMMITTEE 1963 *Poverty and the Administration of Federal Criminal Justice.* Washington: Government Printing Office.

BEANEY, WILLIAM A. 1955 *The Right to Counsel in American Courts.* Ann Arbor: University of Michigan Press.

HOLTZOFF, A. 1944 Right to Counsel under the Sixth Amendment. *New York University Law Review* 20:1–22.

KAMISAR, YALE 1962 Betts v. Brady Twenty Years Later. *Michigan Law Review* 61:219–282.

——— 1978 Brewer v. Williams, Massiah and Miranda: What Is Interrogation? When Does It Matter? *Georgetown Law Journal* 67:1–101.

LEVINE, F. and TAPP, J. 1973 The Psychology of Criminal Identification: The Gap from Wade to Korley. *University of Pennsylvania Law Review* 121:1079–1131.

RIGHT TO JURY TRIAL

See: Trial by Jury

RIGHT TO KNOW

The phrase "right to know" does not appear in the text of the FIRST AMENDMENT, nor has it been used as an organizing category in Supreme Court opinions. Nonetheless, the phrase captures several major themes in First Amendment law, and its frequent appearance in editorials concerning FREEDOM OF THE PRESS attests to its rhetorical appeal. The phrase conjures up the citizen critic responsible for democratic decision making and a vigilant press acting as public trustee in gathering and disseminating vital information. It recalls the companion ideas of LISTENERS' RIGHTS and the MARKETPLACE OF IDEAS.

The "right to know" is a slogan, but it is not empty and its content is not exhausted by conceptions of self-government, the marketplace of ideas, or listeners' rights. To be sure, such conceptions provide rationales for a right to know. Most court decisions preventing government from interfering with speakers' liberty have the effect of protecting the right to know. Some decisions are explicitly founded upon theories of listeners' rights, and, indeed, listeners have occasionally been the plaintiffs challenging the offending government action. Not every decision protecting a speaker's liberty, however, is appropriately characterized as protecting a right to know. For example, opinions in which the court has used the OVERBREADTH DOCTRINE to invalidate convictions for using fighting words find little support in any claim of a right to know. A police officer may learn something by being exposed to insulting language, but protection of speech in such decisions rests on a defense of speaker liberty for its own sake, wholly apart from anything the audience may learn.

If decisions protecting speaker's liberty are not always premised upon a right to know, neither are claims of the right to know limited to assertions of speaker's liberty. Indeed, the most intriguing question begged by the expression "right to know" is the scope of such a right. Does the public have a constitutional right to know anything that speakers themselves are unwilling to provide? To date, there is no judicial authority for the proposition that the public or the press has any First Amendment right to information voluntarily withheld by private actors. Indeed, even though the press is sometimes said to act as trustee for the public in getting information, the public has no constitutional right to compel the press to disclose any information it may choose to withhold.

The fighting issue is the extent to which the public or press has a constitutional right to know information that government officials wish to withhold. For a long time it appeared there was no such right. By 1978, no Supreme Court holding contradicted Chief Justice WARREN E. BURGER'S contention in *Houchins v. KOED* that "neither the First not Fourteenth Amendment mandates a right of access to government information or sources of information within the government's control." Or, as Justice POTTER STEWART put it in an often-quoted statement, "[T]he First Amendment is neither a Freedom of Information Act nor an Official Secrets Act."

RICHMOND NEWSPAPERS, INC. V. VIRGINIA (1980) constituted the Court's first break with its past denials of constitutional rights of access to information within government control. The Court held that in the absence of some overriding consideration requiring closure, the public possessed a First Amendment right to be present at a criminal trial. Some of the Justices in *Richmond Newspapers* would have opted for a general right of access to governmental information subject to a degree of restraint dictated by the nature of the information and the strength of the government's interests in nondisclosure. Other Justices would have confined the right of access to places traditionally open to the public. What *Richmond Newspapers* makes clear, however, is that the First Amendment is a sword as well as a shield and that the right to know promises to be a developing area of First Amendment law.

STEVEN SHIFFRIN

Bibliography

BEVIER, LILLIAN 1980 An Informed Public, an Informing Press: The Search for a Constitutional Principle. *Stanford Law Review* 68:482–517.

EMERSON, THOMAS I. 1976 Legal Foundations of the Right to Know. *Washington University Law Quarterly* 1976:1–24.

RIGHT TO TRAVEL

The right to travel is a doctrinal orphan grown to vigorous adulthood. As the ARTICLES OF CONFEDERATION (1781) recognized expressly, the freedom of interstate movement follows logically from the recognition of our nationhood. The Constitution contains no similarly explicit guarantee, but the logic of nationhood remains, reinforced by two centuries of nationlizing experience. The modern right to travel may still be searching for its doctrinal sources, but its historical base is secure.

Personal mobility is a value Americans have always prized. FRANKLIN D. ROOSEVELT brushed the edges of this idea when he greeted the Daughters of the American Revolution as fellow "immigrants." The nineteenth century, the formative era for our constitutional law, was also the century of the frontier. The twentieth century brought the automobile—and the moving van; each year nearly one family in five changes residence.

The power of Congress to protect the freedom of interstate movement is a theme both old and new. The great decision in GIBBONS V. OGDEN (1824) recognized that the COMMERCE CLAUSE authorized congressional regulation of the interstate transportation of persons as well as goods. The modern reach of congressional power is illustrated by the holding in GRIF-

FIN V. BRECKINRIDGE (1971) that Congress can protect CIVIL RIGHTS by prohibiting private interferences with the right of black persons or civil rights workers to travel interstate.

The commerce power of Congress has long been held to imply limits on STATE REGULATION OF COMMERCE. When a state interferes with the interstate movement of persons, it must provide weighty justification for so burdening commerce. EDWARDS V. CALIFORNIA (1941) shows how difficult it is for a state to justify this sort of regulation.

The *Edwards* majority, resting decision on the commerce clause, said nothing about the right to travel. Four Justices, while not disputing the commerce ground, preferred to base decision on the PRIVILEGES AND IMMUNITIES clause of Article IV. This clause, which superseded the Articles of Confederation provision guaranteeing "free ingress and egress" from one state to another, had been interpreted early in the nineteenth century (in CORFIELD V. CORYELL, 1823) to include the "fundamental" right of a citizen of one state to travel through or migrate to another.

The Constitution's other privileges and immunities clause—that of the Fourteenth Amendment—is yet another potential source for a right of interstate travel. The concurring Justices in *Edwards* echoed the words of Chief Justice ROGER B. TANEY, dissenting in the PASSENGER CASES (1849), when they said that the freedom of interstate travel was one of the privileges of national citizenship. (See CRANDALL V. NEVADA, 1868; SLAUGHTERHOUSE CASES, 1873.)

This doctrinal untidiness has the blessing of the Supreme Court. Speaking for the Court in UNITED STATES V. GUEST (1966), Justice POTTER STEWART, who yielded to no one in expressing his affection for the right to travel, said: "The constitutional right to travel from one State to another . . . occupies a position so fundamental to the concept of our Federal Union. It is a right that has been firmly established and repeatedly recognized. . . . Although there have been recurring differences in emphasis within the Court as to the source of the constitutional right to travel, there is no need to canvas those differences further. All have agreed that the right exists. . . . We reaffirm it now."

Guest involved the power of Congress to protect interstate travel, a power easily inferable from the commerce clause. When the WARREN COURT expanded the reach of the right to travel as a limit on the states, the Court selected still another constitutional weapon: the EQUAL PROTECTION clause. SHAPIRO V. THOMPSON (1969) established the modern pattern. The Court invalidated state laws limiting WELFARE BENEFITS to persons who had been residents for a year. Such a durational RESIDENCE REQUIREMENT impaired the right to travel, which was a FUNDAMENTAL INTEREST; accordingly, the states must justify the impairment by showing its necessity as a means for achieving a COMPELLING STATE INTEREST. The justifications offered in *Shapiro* failed this STRICT SCRUTINY standard of review.

In two decisions following *Shapiro,* the Court refined its analytical style for cases implicating the right to travel interstate. Both opinions were written by Justice THURGOOD MARSHALL. DUNN V. BLUMSTEIN (1972) held unconstitutional a state law limiting voting to persons with one year of residence in the state and three months in the county. Justice Marshall elaborated on *Shapiro:* That opinion had emphasized the illegitimacy of a state's purpose to deter interstate migration, but had not insisted on a showing that any welfare applicants had, in fact, been deterred from migrating. Strict judicial scrutiny was required, irrespective of any such showing, whenever a state law penalized interstate migration, and here the durational residence qualifications for voting amounted to a penalty. Failing the test of strict scrutiny, they must be invalidated. A year later, in MARSTON V. LEWIS (1973) and BURNS V. FORTSON (1973), the Court upheld fifty-day residence qualifications for voting, remarking that "the 50-day registration period approaches the outer constitutional limits in this area."

The "penalty" analysis was fully developed in MEMORIAL HOSPITAL V. MARICOPA COUNTY (1974), when the Court struck down a one-year county residence qualification for an indigent to receive free nonemergency hospital or health care. Denial to new residents of "a basic necessity of life" amounted to a "penalty" on interstate migration and medical care was as much a necessity as welfare subsistence. This analysis allowed Justice Marshall to distinguish STARNS V. MALKERSON (1971), in which the Court had summarily affirmed a lower court's decision upholding a one-year durational requirement for receiving state higher education at reduced tuition rates.

Beyond elucidating the sort of penalty on interstate travel that would require strict judicial scrutiny, the *Dunn* and *Memorial Hospital* opinions also emphasized the right to migrate to another state for the purpose of settling there, as differentiated from the right merely to travel. Commentators have made much of this distinction, but little turns on it in practice, and any serious effort to reduce the right to travel to a right of migration would turn away from the right's historical sources in national citizenship.

By 1975, the right to travel's doctrinal state was cluttered with furniture. The stage direction for the next event might read: "Enter Justice WILLIAM H. REHNQUIST, bearing an axe." SOSNA V. IOWA (1975) confronted the Court with a one-year residence qualification for access to the state's divorce court. Writing for the majority, Justice Rehnquist (the only dissenter in *Memorial Hospital*) not only concluded that the limitation was valid; he reached that conclusion without discussing "penalties" or even the equal protection clause. Indeed, the only doctrinal reference in his whole treatment of the merits of the case was a summary rejection of a marginal argument addressed to the short-lived doctrine of IRREBUTTABLE PRESUMPTIONS.

Doctrinal demolition seems to have been Justice Rehnquist's aim; throughout his opinion he referred abstractly to "the constitutional issue," without saying what the issue was, and he concluded by saying that the one-year qualification was "consistent with the provisions of the United States Constitution." Distinguishing *Shapiro* and the other recent precedents, he remarked that the states' interests in those cases had touched nothing more than budgetary or recordkeeping considerations. In *Sosna,* the state was concerned to protect the interests of defendant spouses and possible minor children, and also to make its divorce decrees safe from COLLATERAL ATTACK. Thus the state might "quite reasonably" choose not to be a divorce mill. Predictably, the *Sosna* dissenters were led by Justice Marshall, who expressed his dismay over the dismantling of the only theory yet constructed to explain the modern right to travel decisions. What had happened to strict scrutiny, to the notion of penalties on interstate travel, to the link between the right to travel and the equal protection clause? The majority's silence on all these questions persisted for seven years.

In ZOBEL V. WILLIAMS (1982) an 8–1 Supreme Court struck down an Alaska law that would have distributed much of the state's vast oil revenues to its adult residents, apportioning distributions on the basis of length of residence in the state. For the Court, Chief Justice WARREN E. BURGER rested decision on the equal protection clause, remarking that "right to travel analysis" was "little more than a particular application of equal protection analysis." The state's purpose to reward citizens for past contributions was ruled out by SHAPIRO V. THOMPSON; to uphold Alaska's law would invite apportionment of all manner of taxes and benefits according to length of residence, a result that was "clearly impermissible." Concurring, Justice SANDRA DAY O'CONNOR rejected the equal protection ground, but argued that requiring nonresidents settling in the state "to accept a status inferior to that of old-timers" would impose one of the "disabilities of alienage" prohibited by the privileges and immunities clause of Article IV. In a separate concurrence, Justice WILLIAM J. BRENNAN returned to the origins of the right to travel; even if no specific provision of the Constitution were available, he found that right's "unmistakable essence in that document that transformed a loose confederation of States into one Nation."

William Cohen has suggested a sensible rule of thumb for the durational residence decisions: Equality of treatment for newcomers is required, but durational residence requirements are permitted as tests for residents' intention to remain in the state, that is, tests for state citizenship. Until the Court accepts this view, constitutional doctrine concerning the right to interstate travel remains where it was in the mid-1960s: "All are agreed that the right exists," but it has itself become a rootless wanderer.

The right to international travel is quite another matter. Its doctrinal location is clear: the Fifth Amendment's due process clause. Congressional power to regulate this liberty is wide-ranging. ZEMEL V. RUSK (1966) sustained the government's refusal to issue a passport valid for travel to Cuba, and CALIFANO V. AZNAVORIAN (1978) upheld the withholding of social security benefits during months when beneficiaries are out of the country. In the latter case, the Court remarked that "indirect" congressional burdens on the right of international travel should not be tested by the strictness attending penalties on interstate travel, but were valid unless they were "wholly irrational." Direct restrictions on travel, such as the denial of a passport, are undoubtedly to be tested against a somewhat higher—but as yet unspecified—level of judicial scrutiny. And when Congress regulates foreign travel in a way that discriminates against the exercise of FIRST AMENDMENT freedoms, strict scrutiny is called for. Thus APTHEKER V. SECRETARY OF STATE (1964) held unconstitutional the denial of passports to members of the Communist party.

The decisions recognizing a right to travel abroad have been concerned with travel itself, and not with a more limited right to migrate. The reasoning of those decisions is readily extended to congressional regulation of interstate travel. The commerce clause unquestionably empowers Congress to control the interstate movement of persons, but, like all the powers of Congress, that clause is subject to the provisions of the BILL OF RIGHTS. Congress obviously could not constitutionally forbid members of the Communist party to travel interstate. First Amendment considerations aside, the liberty protected by the Fifth Amendment's due process clause bars Congress from any arbitrary restrictions on interstate travel. The point has practical importance, for the broad sweep of the commerce power has made the prohibition of interstate movement one of the favorite regulatory techniques of Congress. Almost certainly the extremely permissive standard of the *Aznavorian* decision (upholding restrictions unless they are "wholly irrational") would apply to "indirect" congressional regulations of interstate travel. A direct prohibition, however, very likely would encounter a judiciary ready to insist on a more substantial justification.

The notion that the freedom to travel is a liberty protected by the guarantee of due process need not be limited to congressional restrictions on travel. The Fourteenth Amendment's due process clause surely is equally capable of absorbing the right to travel as a limitation on the states. The main barrier to recognizing the right to travel as an aspect of SUBSTANTIVE DUE PROCESS, no doubt, is the Supreme Court's reluctance to contribute further to the development of substantive due process as a vehicle for active judicial intervention in legislative policymaking.

For a season, then, the right of interstate travel is left without certain doctrinal underpinnings. Its capacity to survive on its own, cut off from the usual doctrinal supports, indicates that it draws nourishment from something else. The something else is our strong sense that we are not only a collection of states but a nation.

KENNETH L. KARST

Bibliography

BAKER, STEWART A. 1975 A Strict Scrutiny of the Right to Travel. *UCLA Law Review* 22:1129–1160.

BARRETT, EDWARD L., JR. 1976 Judicial Supervision of Legislative Classification—A More Modest Role for Equal Protection? *Brigham Young University Law Review* 1976:89–130.

BLACK, CHARLES L., JR. 1969 *Structure and Relationship in Constitutional Law.* Pages 27–30. Baton Rouge: Louisiana State University Press.

COHEN, WILLIAM 1984 Equal Treatment for Newcomers: The Core Meaning of National and State Citizenship. *Constitutional Commentary* 1:9–19.

RIGHT TO VOTE

See: Voting Rights

RIGHT-TO-WORK LAWS

Union security provisions in labor contracts have required membership in, or financial support of, the signatory union by employees, as a condition of employment by the signatory employer. Concern that such provisions could be used to restrict employment unduly, to penalize dissent, and to infringe on employees' associational interests, stimulated the enactment of state right-to-work laws. Such laws, now operative in approximately twenty states, prohibit conditioning of employment on union membership or, generally, on financial support of a union.

The TAFT-HARTLEY ACT (1947) amended the National Labor Relations Act (NLRA) (1935) and imposed new restrictions on union security provisions, barring requirements of full-fledged union membership before or after employment and limiting compulsory membership to payment of uniform dues and initiation fees. Congress's approach appeared responsive to the argument that unions should be permitted, through collective bargaining, to secure financial support from all members of a bargaining unit, including those not members of the union, because the union's duty of fair representation encompasses all of them. Nonetheless, section 14(b), enacted by the Taft-Hartley Act, permitted states to prohibit union security provisions otherwise legal under the NLRA. This extraordinary deference to state labor law contrasts sharply with the preemption of more restrictive state laws by the 1951 Railway Labor Act amendments (now applicable to both airline and railway employees).

The Supreme Court, in *Lincoln Federal Labor Union v. Northwestern Iron & Metal Co.* (1949) and a companion case, *American Federation of Labor v. American Sash Co.*, upheld state right-to-work laws against challenges based on the CONTRACT CLAUSE and constitutional guarantees of FREEDOM OF SPEECH, FREEDOM OF PETITION and assembly, EQUAL PROTECTION, and DUE PROCESS OF LAW. The Court, moreover, negated any equal protection requirement that state remedies for discrimination against union members and nonmembers, respectively, be coextensive. The Court wryly observed that the unions' due process contentions were a reversion to the doctrines of LOCHNER V. NEW YORK (1905), ADAIR V. UNITED STATES (1908), and COPPAGE V. KANSAS (1915), which the Court had discarded—after having used them to invalidate prohibitions of YELLOW DOG CONTRACTS and other measures designed to protect workers' associational interests.

In *Retail Clerks v. Schermerhorn* (1963) the Supreme Court upheld state power "to enforce their laws restricting the execution and enforcement of union-security agreements." The Court, however, significantly limited state authority, stating that "[it] begins only with the actual negotiation and execution of the type of agreement described by §14(b)." Consequently, under section 14(b), a state could not properly enjoin PICKETING for an agreement proscribed by state law. The Court did not explain the reasoning behind the apparent anomaly of permitting a state to prohibit a completed agreement but not economic pressure to secure it. The Court may, however, have feared that state authority over such antecedent pressures would too often be used to restrict activity protected by the NLRA, such as peaceful picketing that publicizes substandard working conditions.

Otherwise valid union security agreements raise questions under the FIRST AMENDMENT when dissidents object to the use of compulsory financial exactions for political and other purposes not central to collective bargaining.

BERNARD D. MELTZER

Bibliography

HAGGARD, T. 1977 *Compulsory Unionism, the NLRB and the Courts: A Legal Analysis of Union Security Agreements.* Philadelphia: Industrial Research Unit, Wharton School, University of Pennsylvania.

RIPENESS

People who anticipate harm occasionally attack a law's constitutionality before it is applied to them, or even before the law takes effect. A federal court may decline to decide such a case for lack of ripeness if it is unclear that adjudication is needed to protect the challengers, or if information sufficient to permit intelligent resolution is not yet available. A matter of timing and degree, ripeness is grounded both in Article III's CASE OR CONTROVERSY requirement and the federal courts' reluctance to issue constitutional decisions needlessly or prematurely. Delaying decision may cause interim hardship and allow unconstitutional harm to occur, but further developments may narrow the issues, or produce important information, or even establish that no decision is needed.

The Supreme Court's ripeness decisions display varying sensitivity to these sometimes conflicting factors. Normally, a court is more likely to defer resolution of fact-dependent issues, like those based on a particular application of a law, than it is to defer adjudication of strictly legal issues. A single case may present some issues ripe for adjudication, but others not ripe. Ripeness decisions mainly respond, however, to the degree of contingency or uncertainty of the law's expected effect on the challenger.

Where leeway exists, the court may be influenced by determining whose interests a quicker decision would serve. Thus, when federal civil servants fearing dismissal for violation of the HATCH ACT asked that the political activities they were contemplating be declared constitutionally protected in *United Public Workers v. Mitchell* (1947), the Court found the case unripe absent enforcement of the act against some particular employee behavior. Similarly, a challenge to IMMIGRATION policy was held unripe in *International Longshoremen's Union v. Boyd* (1954) despite a strong indication that, without a ruling, resident ALIENS risked jeopardizing their right to return to the United States. With little doubt that the laws would be applied, the challengers nonetheless were forced to act at their peril. By contrast, when a delay in decision has threatened to frustrate government policy, the Court has resolved anticipatory challenges to laws whose future application appeared inevitable, including legislation restructuring some of the nation's railroads in the *Regional Rail Reorganization Act Cases* (1974) and the FEDERAL ELECTION CAMPAIGN ACTS in BUCKLEY V. VALEO (1976).

Sensitivity to the government's interest in quick resolution even led the Court to uphold a federal statute limiting aggregate operator liability for nuclear power plant explosions in *Duke Power Co. v. Carolina Environmental Study Group, Inc.* (1978), despite evidence that explosions are unlikely and serious doubt that this statute would ever be applied. Because injury to the asserted right of unlimited recovery for nuclear disaster was unlikely to occur soon, if at all, the constitutional issues did not seem ripe; yet the Court concluded that the case was ripe, because the normal operation of nearby nuclear plants (whose development the statute had facilitated) threatened imminent pollution—even though the suit had not questioned the pollution's legality.

As the *Duke Power* case illustrates, the inherent policy choice in ripeness decisions—between finding constitutional adjudication premature and finding prevention of harm or validation of government policy timely—embodies important perceptions of judicial role in a regime characterized by the SEPARATION OF POWERS.

JONATHAN D. VARAT

Bibliography

WRIGHT, CHARLES A.; MILLER, ARTHUR R.; and COOPER, EDWARD H. 1984 *Federal Practice and Procedure.* Vol. 13A:112–214. St. Paul, Minn.: West Publishing Co.

RIZZO v. GOODE
423 U.S. 362 (1978)

Rizzo exemplifies the BURGER COURT's inhospitability to INSTITUTIONAL LITIGATION aimed at broad structural reform. Philadelphia citizens sued the mayor and other officials in federal court, alleging condonation of a pattern of police mistreatment of minority residents and others. The district court held long hearings, validated the plaintiffs' charges, and ordered the defendants to submit a comprehensive plan to improve complaint procedures and police discipline.

The Supreme Court, 5–3, held this order improper. The Court implied that the controversy lacked RIPENESS, and suggested that YOUNGER V. HARRIS (1971) might protect the action of state executives as well as state courts. The decision, however, rested on the ground that police supervisors had been insufficiently involved in the proved misconduct to justify the court's systemwide order.

KENNETH L. KARST

ROANE, SPENCER
(1762–1822)

Spencer Roane, a Virginian, was the foremost judicial exponent of STATES' RIGHTS in the era of the MARSHALL COURT, and President THOMAS JEFFERSON would have made him Chief Justice of the United States had the opportunity arisen. Roane served for twenty-eight years (1794–1822) on Virginia's highest court. Before then he was a state legislator. He opposed RATIFICATION OF THE CONSTITUTION and never abandoned his belief that the national government possessed powers dangerous to the states.

Roane supported the authority of his court to hold unconstitutional a state act and even a congressional act, but he denied the authority of the Supreme Court to hold a state act unconstitutional. As leader of the nation's most influential state court he regarded the Supreme Court as a rival, and his words carried extrajudicial influence. He founded the Richmond *Enquirer* and ran Virginia politics. By the close of his life he headed an organization that controlled Virginia's press, its banks, its congressional delegation, and all three branches of its state government. He was JOHN MARSHALL's most formidable foe and outspoken opponent.

In the controversy leading to MARTIN V. HUNTER'S LESSEE (1816), Roane's court held unconstitutional section 25 of the JUDICIARY ACT OF 1789. In 1815 he described the United States as "a confederation of distinct sovereignties." His constitutional decisions differed from the Marshall Court's even on matters not involving the nature of the Union. He sustained the act later held void in TERRETT V. TAYLOR (1815) and supported the state in a case similar to DARTMOUTH COLLEGE V. WOODWARD (1819).

His vehement opposition to the nationalist doctrines of MCCULLOCH V. MARYLAND (1819) and COHENS V. VIRGINIA (1821) led him to denounce the Marshall Court in a series of essays in the Richmond *Enquirer,* which Jefferson warmly acclaimed and even JAMES MADISON tentatively endorsed. Roane's views on the Union were probably closer to those of 1787 than Marshall's. Doubtlessly Roane loved the "federal union" as he understood it, although Marshall called him "the champion of dismemberment." Roane was an able, orthodox judge who died a sectional advocate.

LEONARD W. LEVY

Bibliography

MAYS, DAVID J. 1928 Judge Spencer Roane. *Proceedings of the Thirty-Ninth Annual Meeting of The Virginia State Bar Association* 39:446–464.

ROBBINS v. CALIFORNIA

See: *Ross, United States v.*

ROBEL v. UNITED STATES
389 U.S. 258 (1967)

Over two dissents, the WARREN COURT struck down on FIRST AMENDMENT grounds a section of the SUBVERSIVE ACTIVITIES CONTROL ACT of 1950 that prohibited the employment of members of the Communist party in "defense facilities" designated by the secretary of defense. Because the statute failed to distinguish between those who supported the unlawful goals of the party and those who did not, wrote Chief Justice EARL WARREN, its OVERBREADTH violated the right of association protected by the FIRST AMENDMENT. Warren rejected government arguments seeking to justify the provision by the WAR POWER and national security interests. "It would indeed be ironic if, in the name of national defense, we would sanction the subversion of one of those liberties—the freedom of association—which makes the defense of the Nation worthwhile." Justices BYRON R. WHITE and JOHN MARSHALL HARLAN dissented, observing that the majority "arrogates to itself an independent judgement of the requirements of national security."

MICHAEL E. PARRISH

ROBERTS, OWEN J. (1875–1955)

Best known as an Associate Justice of the United States Supreme Court, Owen Josephus Roberts had a varied preliminary career—law practice and teaching, administration, and public service. In 1930, after the Senate Judiciary Committee rejected the nomination of Circuit Judge John J. Parker, President HERBERT C. HOOVER appointed Roberts, a Philadelphia Republican, who was approved without a dissenting vote. That same year, CHARLES EVANS HUGHES returned to the Court as Chief Justice of the United States.

Roberts and Hughes came to the Court in a period of sharp disagreement concerning not only the role of government in economic and social affairs but also the nature and scope of the judicial function itself. Both men were destined to play significant roles. Examples abound, and Hughes and Roberts were often joined. They agreed, for example, in sustaining Minnesota's moratorium on mortgage foreclosures in HOME BUILDING AND LOAN ASSOCIATION V. BLAISDELL (1934).

In NEBBIA V. NEW YORK (1934) Roberts, without using the word "emergency," upheld a New York statute regulating the price of milk. In WOLFF PACKING COMPANY V. COURT OF INDUSTRIAL RELATIONS (1923) Chief Justice WILLIAM HOWARD TAFT had invoked the concept of business AFFECTED WITH A PUBLIC INTEREST as a test of legitimate government power. Rejecting this test, Roberts observed: "The phrase can mean no more than that an industry for adequate reason is subject to control for the public good." Roberts also opposed the judicial notion that prices and wages were constitutionally immune from regulation. Thus the constitutional barriers Justice GEORGE H. SUTHERLAND had erected in ADKINS V. CHILDREN'S HOSPITAL (1923) against the District of Columbia minimum wage for women as the "heart of a contract" were weakened. Citing *Munn v. Illinois* (1877), Roberts recalled: "The DUE PROCESS clause makes no mention of sales or prices. . . . The thought seems, nevertheless, to have persisted that there is something peculiarly sacrosanct about prices and wages."

Roberts's *Nebbia* opinion also disavowed a broad scope of judicial power. Here, as in UNITED STATES V. BUTLER (1936), the judicial function involved "only one duty, to lay the article of the Constitution which is involved beside the statute which is challenged and to decide whether the latter squares with the former." The *Nebbia* opinion was thus hailed as indicating fair weather for FRANKLIN D. ROOSEVELT's New Deal legislation. Without specifying any particular level of government, Roberts declared: "This Court from the early days affirmed that the power to promote the general welfare is inherent in government." Yet, speaking for the Court in RAILROAD RETIREMENT BOARD V. ALTON RAILWAY COMPANY (1935), Roberts argued that Congress lacked power under the COMMERCE CLAUSE to pass any compulsory pension act for railroad workers. Hughes, LOUIS D. BRANDEIS, BENJAMIN N. CARDOZO, and HARLAN F. STONE dissented, the last rating this decision "the worst performance of the Court in my time."

UNITED STATES V. BUTLER apparently put the New Deal's legislative program beyond the scope of the TAXING AND SPENDING POWER. Roberts, invoking the TENTH AMENDMENT, argued that judicial endorsement of the AGRICULTURAL ADJUSTMENT ACT would "sanction legislative power without restriction or limitation" and convert Congress into a "parliament of the whole people, subject to no restrictions save such as are self-imposed." Roberts also voted with the conservatives in CARTER V. CARTER COAL COMPANY (1936), which set aside the Coal Conservation Act. Again the stumbling block was the Tenth Amendment. Coal mining, like agriculture, was local and therefore beyond the reach of national authority.

Meanwhile, overwhelming popular approval of the New Deal in the 1936 presidential election and the continuing high level of unemployment made it apparent that reliance on the states to cope with the economic emergency was misplaced. Blocking national action were four Supreme Court Justices, sometimes joined by Hughes and Roberts.

Roberts's judicial record appears inconsistent. Although the cases involved different issues, the shift between *Nebbia* on the one hand and *Alton* and *Butler* on the other is a clear instance of change. Some observers charged that Roberts, alarmed by Roosevelt's court-packing proposal of February 1937, shifted from a vote against the minimum wage in MOREHEAD V. NEW YORK EX REL. TIPALDO (1936) to one in favor of it in WEST COAST HOTEL COMPANY V. PARRISH (1937). Thus Roberts became famous as "a man of many minds."

In the personal rights area Roberts was, on occasion, conspicuously on the liberal side. Joined by Brandeis, Sutherland, and Butler, he dissented in *Snyder v.*

Massachusetts (1934), insisting that when a jury visits the scene of a crime, the defendant and counsel must be present. In *Schneider v. Irvington* (1939) he voted to set aside a city ordinance restricting FREEDOM OF THE PRESS and distribution of nonadvertising circulars and pamphlets.

In HERNDON V. LOWRY (1937) Roberts wrote for the Court, which reversed the conviction of Angelo Herndon, a black organizer for the Communist party, who had been found guilty of inciting insurrection by trying to enlist other blacks in that organization. The Georgia courts sentenced Herndon to eighteen years in prison. Said Roberts of the state act that penalized any attempt to incite an insurrection against the state: "The statute, as construed and applied, amounts merely to a dragnet which may enmesh anyone who agitates for a change of government if a jury can be persuaded that he ought to have foreseen his words would have some effect in the future conduct of others. No reasonably ascertainable standard of guilt is prescribed. So vague and indeterminate are the boundaries thus set to the FREEDOM OF SPEECH and assembly that the law necessarily violates the guarantees of liberty embodied in the FOURTEENTH AMENDMENT." In BETTS V. BRADY (1942), however, Roberts for the Court held that the right to be represented by counsel in a noncapital felony case was not essential to due process of law (overruled in GIDEON V. WAINRIGHT, 1961).

During World War II, when the Court, speaking through Justice HUGO L. BLACK in *Korematsu v. United States* (1944), upheld the compulsory transfer of Japanese American citizens to relocation centers, Roberts wrote an eloquent dissent. Joined by FRANK MURPHY and ROBERT H. JACKSON, he challenged Black's majority opinion, then the prevailing public view. He wrote: "[This] is the case of convicting a citizen as a punishment for not submitting to imprisonment in a concentration camp, based on his ancestry, and solely because of his ancestry, without evidence or inquiry concerning his loyalty and good disposition towards the United States. . . . I need hardly labor the conclusion that constitutional rights have been violated."

Roberts and all his colleagues, including Stone, had held in GROVEY V. TOWNSEND (1935) that voting in PRIMARY ELECTIONS was not a constitutional prerogative but a privilege of party membership. In the famous case of UNITED STATES V. CLASSIC (1941) the Court, again speaking through Stone, without mentioning *Grovey,* ruled that participation in primaries was a right secured by the Constitution. Thus, with the adherence of Roberts, but without discussing *Grovey,* Stone brought traditional southern election customs to the brink of destruction. More alert than Roberts, commentators knew that another precedent had been broken. In 1944, when the Court overruled *Grovey,* Roberts exploded. "Not a fact differentiates that case (*Grovey*) from this, except the names of the parties. . . . If this Court's opinion in the *Classic* case discloses its method of overruling earlier decisions, I can protest that in 'fairness,' it should rather have adopted the open and frank way of saying what it was doing. . . ." "The instant decision," Roberts fumed in SMITH V. ALLWRIGHT (1944), "tends to bring the adjudication of this tribunal into the same class as a restricted railroad ticket, good for this day and train only."

New trends and new judicial personnel in a rapidly changing world disturbed Roberts. He asserted that law had become not a chart to govern but a game of chance. By 1941 the cordial relations he had previously enjoyed with his colleagues became strained. When Roberts retired in 1945, Chief Justice Stone drafted the customary letter to a departing colleague commenting: "You have made fidelity to principle your guide to decision." Black and WILLIAM O. DOUGLAS strongly objected, contending that this was precisely the quality Roberts lacked. Consequently no farewell letter was sent.

Roberts was a modest man, sensitive to his shortcomings. On leaving the bench he commented: "I have no illusion about my judicial career. . . . Who am I to revile the good God that did not make me a Marshall, a Taney, a Bradley, a Holmes, a Brandeis, or a Cardozo?"

ALPHEUS THOMAS MASON

Bibliography

LEONARD, CHARLES A. 1971 *A Search for Judicial Philosophy: Mr. Justice Roberts.* Port Washington, N.Y.: Kennikat Press.

MASON, ALPHEUS T. 1956 *Harlan Fiske Stone: Pillar of the Law.* New York: Viking.

NOTE 1955 Owen J. Roberts—In Memoriam. *University of Pennsylvania Law Review* 104:311–317.

ROBERTS v. CITY OF BOSTON
5 Cush. (Mass.) 198 (1850)

In BROWN V. BOARD OF EDUCATION (1954) the Court observed that the SEPARATE BUT EQUAL DOCTRINE "apparently originated in *Roberts* v. *City of Boston*." Chief Justice LEMUEL SHAW's opinion in that case had an extraordinary influence. The courts of at least ten states relied on it as a precedent for upholding segregated education. In HALL v. DECUIR (1878) the Supreme Court cited it as an authority for the rule that "equality does not mean identity." In PLESSY v. FERGUSON (1896) the Court relied on it as the leading precedent for the validity of state legislation requiring racial SEGREGATION in places where whites and blacks "are liable to be brought in to contact," and in GONG LUM v. RICE (1927) the Court explained *Roberts* as having sustained "the separation of colored and white schools under a state constitutional injunction of EQUAL PROTECTION, the same as the FOURTEENTH AMENDMENT. . . ."

Roberts arose as a TEST CASE to determine the validity of Boston's requirement that black children attend segregated schools. CHARLES SUMNER, attacking that requirement, denied that a racially separate school could be equal, because it imposed a stigma of caste and fostered prejudice.

Shaw, for a unanimous Supreme Judicial Court, agreed that the case presented the question whether the separate schools for blacks violated their constitutional right to equality. But he reasoned that all rights must depend on laws adapted to the "respective relations and conditions" of individuals. He believed that the school committee had exercised "a discriminating and honest judgment" in deciding that the good of both races was best promoted by the separate education of their children. The law, Shaw said in reply to Sumner, did not create prejudice, probably could not change it, and might only foster it by "compelling" both races to attend "the same schools." Thus, by a singular absence of considered judgment, the court found no constitutional violation of equal protection in compulsory racial segregation as long as blacks had an equal right to attend public schools.

LEONARD W. LEVY

ROBERTS v. LOUISIANA

See: Capital Punishment Cases, 1976

ROBINSON, UNITED STATES v.
414 U.S. 218 (1973)

The Supreme Court here resolved the question whether the FOURTH AMENDMENT permits a full search of the person INCIDENT TO ARREST for a minor offense. This question is particularly acute in cases of traffic offenses, where police commonly make arrests in order to search drivers and their automobiles.

In *Robinson* the police stopped an automobile and arrested its driver for operating the vehicle without a license. A search of his clothing uncovered heroin. Because searches incident to arrest are allowed for the purpose of discovering concealed weapons and evidence, Robinson's counsel argued that such searches are unjustified in connection with routine traffic arrests: they will seldom yield evidence related to the traffic offense itself, and the chances of the driver's being armed are usually minimal.

The Supreme Court ruled, however, that a search incident to a custodial arrest requires no justification beyond the arrest; it is not an exception to the warrant requirement, but rather is itself a reasonable search. It was "speculative" to believe that those arrested for driving without a license "are less likely to be armed than those arrested for other crimes." Any lawful arrest justifies "a full search of the person."

JACOB W. LANDYNSKI

ROBINSON-PATMAN ACT
49 Stat. 1526 (1936)

The rapid growth of chain stores during the Depression effectively bypassed the price discrimination prohibitions of the CLAYTON ACT by altering the basic lines of competition which that act addressed. Shortly after the Supreme Court invalidated the NATIONAL INDUSTRIAL RECOVERY ACT's codes of fair competition (beginning in SCHECHTER POULTRY CORPORATION v. UNITED STATES, 1935), Representative Wright Patman introduced a corrective bill into the House designed to regulate chain stores' use of economies of scale. As finally passed, the act amended section 2 of the Clayton Act. Although one section of the new act allowed price discrimination made "in good faith" to match a competitor's price, the act generally outlawed discrimination that "substantially lessened" competition or tended to create a monopoly. Other provisions prohibited the taking or making of allowances or commissions to buyers if not made proportionally. Buyers were also forbidden from "knowingly receiving" or inducing any discrimination. Although the act provided for suits by the Department of Justice and private individuals, the burden of enforcement fell on the FEDERAL TRADE COMMISSION. By tightening and narrowing section 2 of the Clayton Act, this legislation protected smaller firms by reducing the competitive advantages of large chains.

DAVID GORDON

Bibliography

HANSEN, HUGH C. 1983 Robinson Patman Law: A Review and Analysis. *Fordham Law Review* 51:1113.

ROCHIN v. CALIFORNIA
342 U.S. 165 (1952)

To dispose of evidence, Rochin swallowed drug capsules. Officers pummeled his stomach and jumped on him in an effort to make him throw up the evidence. That failing, they rushed him to a hospital where a doctor, on police instructions, pumped an emetic solution through a tube into Rochin's stomach, forcing him to vomit the capsules. With that evidence the state convicted Rochin as a drug pusher. The Supreme Court unanimously reversed his conviction. Justice FELIX FRANKFURTER, for the Court, held that the state had violated Rochin's right to DUE PROCESS OF LAW. Due process, said Frankfurter, however "indefinite and vague," outlawed "conduct that shocks the conscience." State prosecutions must not, at the risk of violating due process, offend the "sense of justice" or of "fair play." Due process enjoined a respect for the "decencies of civilized conduct."

Justices HUGO L. BLACK and WILLIAM O. DOUGLAS, concurring separately, repudiated Frankfurter's reasoning as excessively subjective. His "nebulous" standard of due process, they believed, allowed the Court to draw upon undefinable notions of justice or decency or fairness. They would have ruled that the state violated Rochin's Fifth Amendment RIGHT AGAINST SELF-INCRIMINATION, which the FOURTEENTH AMENDMENT incorporated.

LEONARD W. LEVY

ROCK ROYAL CO-OPERATIVE, UNITED STATES v.

See: *Wrightwood Dairy, United States v.*

RODNEY, CAESAR A.
(1772–1824)

Elected to the House of Representatives in 1802, Jeffersonian Congressman Caesar Augustus Rodney became one of the managers of the IMPEACHMENT of Justice SAMUEL CHASE. In that capacity he argued that any deviation from GOOD BEHAVIOR on the part of a judge constituted a MISDEMEANOR in the constitutional sense and was, therefore, an impeachable offense even if not an indictable crime.

As attorney general of the United States (1807–1811), Rodney asserted President THOMAS JEFFERSON's right to overrule a federal court decision on enforcement of the EMBARGO ACTS and defended, in EX PARTE BOLLMAN AND SWARTWOUT (1807), prosecutions for constructive TREASON.

DENNIS J. MAHONEY

ROE v. WADE
410 U.S. 113 (1973)
DOE v. BOLTON
410 U.S. 179 (1973)

In these cases the Supreme Court confronted the emotionally charged issue of abortion. The decisions invalidated two states' abortion laws—and, by inference, similar laws in a majority of states. As a result, the Court was plunged into prolonged and intense controversy, ranging from questions about the bearing of morality on constitutional law to questions about the proper role of the judiciary in the American system of government. The Court held unconstitutional a Texas law forbidding abortion except to save the pregnant woman's life and also invalidated several features of a Georgia law regulating abortion procedures and limiting abortion to Georgia residents.

The two women whose fictitious names grace the cases' titles were pregnant when they filed their actions in 1970, but not at the time of the Supreme Court's decision. The Court nonetheless held that their cases were not moot; rigid application of the MOOTNESS doctrine would prevent appellate review of an important issue that was capable of repetition. Nine doctors were also held to have STANDING to challenge the Georgia law; the intervention of a doctor under prosecution in Texas was held improper under the equitable ABSTENTION principle of YOUNGER V. HARRIS (1971); and a Texas married couple was denied standing because the woman had not been pregnant. The Court thus proceeded to the constitutional merits.

The *Roe* opinion, by Justice HARRY A. BLACKMUN, reviewed the history of abortion laws and the recent positions on abortion taken by medical groups and the American Bar Association, but the Court grounded its decision on neither history nor current professional opinion. Instead, the Court relied on a constitutional right of PRIVACY previously recognized in GRISWOLD V. CONNECTICUT (1965) and now relocated in the "liberty" protected by the DUE PROCESS clause of the FOURTEENTH AMENDMENT. This right included "a woman's decision whether or not to terminate her pregnancy," which decision was a FUNDAMENTAL INTEREST that could be restricted only on a showing of a COMPELLING STATE INTEREST.

The Court identified two state interests that would qualify as "compelling" at different stages in pregnancy: protection of maternal health and protection of potential life. Before discussing these interests, however, the Court dealt with a preliminary question: whether a fetus was a PERSON within the meaning of the Fourteenth Amendment. In an abortion, of course, it is not the state that denies life to a fetus; presumably the point of the Court's question was that if a fetus were a "person," the amendment should not be read to bar a state from protecting it against being aborted. The Court concluded, however, that a fetus was not a "person" in the amendment's contemplation. In reaching this conclusion, Justice Blackmun said: "We need not resolve the difficult question of when life begins." Absent a consensus among doctors, philosophers, or theologians on the issue, "the judiciary, at this point in the development of man's knowledge, is not in a position to speculate as to the answer." In any event, the law had never recognized the unborn "as persons in the whole sense." That conclusion alone, however, could not dispose of the question of the state's power. A state can constitutionally protect beings (or even things) that are not persons—including fetuses, which surely can be protected by law against certain kinds of experimentation or disposal, even though the law may be motivated by a feeling that fetuses share our common humanity.

The Court did recognize the state's interests in protecting maternal health and potential life; each would become "compelling" at successive stages of pregnancy. During the first trimester of pregnancy, neither interest is compelling; the abortion decision and its implementation must be left to the woman and her doctor. During the second trimester, the interest in maternal health becomes sufficiently compelling to justify some state regulations of the abortion procedure. When the fetus becomes "viable"—capable of life outside the womb, around the beginning of the third trimester of pregnancy—the state's interest in potential life becomes sufficiently compelling to justify prohibiting abortion except to preserve the "life or health" of the mother.

This scheme of constitutional rights has the look of a statute and evidently was influenced by New York's liberal law and the American Bar Association's model abortion law. Investigative reporters tell us that the three-part scheme resulted from negotiation among the Justices, and it is hard to see it as anything but a compromise between banning abortion altogether and turning over the entire abortion decision to the pregnant woman.

Justice BYRON R. WHITE, dissenting, complained that the Court had permitted abortion to satisfy "the convenience, whim or caprice of the putative mother." Chief Justice WARREN E. BURGER, concurring, responded that the Court had rejected "any claim that the Constitution requires abortion on demand" in favor of a scheme relying on doctors' "medical judgments relating to life and health." The Court's opinion deals ambiguously with the doctor's decisional role. At one point it states that the abortion decision "must be left to the medical judgment of the pregnant woman's attending physician." Yet the Court's decision rests on the constitutional right to privacy, which includes "a woman's decision whether or not to terminate her pregnancy." Very likely Justice Blackmun, a former general counsel of the Mayo Clinic, was influenced by the medical authorities he cited. Indeed, the Blackmun and Burger opinions both convey an inclination to convert abortion issues into medical questions. Linking the state's power to forbid abortions with "viability" is one example—although it is unclear how the Court will respond when medical technology permits the preservation of very young fetuses outside the womb. Similarly, a supposed lack of medical consensus made the Court reluctant to decide when life begins.

The issues in *Roe,* however, were not medical issues. First, there is no medically correct decision concerning an abortion when the pregnant woman's health is not endangered. Second, there is no lack of medical consensus about what happens in the normal process of reproduction from insemination to birth. In some sense "life" begins at conception; to say otherwise is not to make a medical judgment but to decide a question of law or morality. The problem before the Court in *Roe* was to determine whether (or when) a state could constitutionally protect a fetus. The state's interest in potential life surely begins at the time of conception, and arguably before. Yet if *Griswold* and EISENSTADT V. BAIRD (1972) remained good law, the state could not constitutionally protect that interest by forbidding contraception. Most people do not equate the use of "morning after" pills or intrauterine devices with murder, although these forms of "contraception" are really ways of effecting abortion after conception. In 1973 no state was enforcing its abortion laws against such practices. Yet the argument that "life" begins at conception, for purposes of defining legal or moral rights, embraced the claims of both the newest embryo and the eight-month fetus. There was evident artificiality in the Court's selection of "viability" as the time when the state's concerns for potential life became "compelling," but there would have been artificiality in any resolution of the issue of state power other than an all-or-nothing decision.

In *Roe*'s companion case, *Doe v. Bolton*, the Court held invalid four provisions of Georgia law, requiring that abortions be: (1) performed in hospitals accredited by the Joint Commission on Accreditation of Hospitals; (2) approved by hospital staff committees; (3) approved in each case by two physicians other than the pregnant woman's doctor; and (4) limited to Georgia residents. The latter requirement was an obvious violation of Article IV's PRIVILEGES AND IMMUNITIES clause, and the other three were held to impose unreasonable restrictions on the constitutional right recognized in *Roe.*

The *Roe* opinion has found few defenders; even the decision's supporters are inclined to offer substitute justifications. *Roe*'s critics divide roughly into two groups: those who regard abortion as murder, and those who think the Supreme Court exceeded its proper institutional bounds, failing to ground its decision in the Constitution and merely substituting its own policy judgment for that of the people's elected representatives.

The latter criticism touched off an impressive succession of essays on JUDICIAL REVIEW. It was the former group of critics, however, who dominated the politics of abortion. The "right to life" movement was, for a time, one of the nation's most effective "single issue" groups, achieving enough respect from legislators to permit the adoption of laws withdrawing governmental financial aid to poor women who seek abortions. (See MAHER V. ROE, 1977); HARRIS V. MCRAE, 1980.) Various constitutional amendments to overturn *Roe* were proposed in Congress, but none was submitted to the states for ratification. In the early 1980s Congress considered, but did not adopt, a bill declaring that "human life begins from the moment of conception." Congress also heard proposals to withdraw federal court jurisdiction over abortion cases. (See JUDICIAL SYSTEM.) Yet the *Roe* decision has weathered all these political storms.

Roe's stability as a precedent is founded on the same social and political base that initially supported the decision. It was no accident that *Roe* was decided in the 1970s, when the movement against SEX DISCRIMINATION was winning its most important constitutional and political victories. The abortion question was not merely an issue between pregnant women and their unwanted fetuses; it was also a feminist issue, going to women's position in society in relation to men. Even today American society imposes a greater stigma on unmarried women who become pregnant than on the men who father their children, and society still expects women to take the major responsibility for contraception and child care. The implications of an unwanted pregnancy or parenthood for a woman's opportunities in education, employment, and personal association—indeed, for the woman's definition of self—are enormous. Justice White's dissenting remark, that abortion regulation is an issue about which "reasonable men may easily and heatedly differ," perhaps said more than he intended to say.

KENNETH L. KARST

(SEE ALSO: *Abortion and the Constitution; Reproductive Autonomy.*)

Bibliography

ELY, JOHN HART 1973 The Wages of Crying Wolf: A Comment on *Roe v. Wade. Yale Law Journal* 82:920–949.

HENKIN, LOUIS 1974 Privacy and Autonomy. *Columbia Law Review* 74:1410–1433.

Symposium on the Law and Politics of Abortion. 1979 *Michigan Law Review* 77:1569–1646.

TRIBE, LAURENCE H. 1978 *American Constitutional Law.* Pages 923–934. Mineola, N.Y.: Foundation Press.

WOODWARD, BOB and ARMSTRONG, SCOTT 1979 *The Brethren: Inside the Supreme Court.* Pages 165–189, 229–240. New York: Simon & Schuster.

ROGERS v. LODGE
458 U.S. 613 (1982)

Rogers v. Lodge involved a successful challenge to an at-large electoral scheme for county commissioners in Burke County, Georgia. The Supreme Court noted that at-large systems are not unconstitutional per se and that a challenge could succeed only upon a showing that the system was established or maintained for a discriminatory purpose. All sides conceded that blacks in Burke County had free access to registration, voting, and candidacy for office. The issue was not, therefore, equal participation in the electoral process but "effective" participation. The Court held that where there was evidence of the lingering effects of past RACIAL DISCRIMINATION that had limited "the ability of blacks to participate effectively in the political process," the district court was justified in finding that an electoral scheme that did not hold at least the potential of electing minority members to office in proportion to their numbers was maintained for discriminatory purposes in violation of the EQUAL PROTECTION clause. Thus the Court, while not requiring proportional representation, nevertheless permitted it to be used as the test in determining whether an electoral system worked to "diminish or dilute the political efficacy" of minorities.

EDWARD J. ERLER

ROGERS v. RICHMOND 365 U.S. 534 (1961)

This is one of numerous cases prior to MALLOY V. HOGAN (1964) dealing with the question whether a confession was voluntary under a DUE PROCESS standard or coercive in violation of that standard. *Rogers* is significant because it was the first case in which the Court repudiated the test of trustworthiness as an element of the due process standard. Justice FELIX FRANKFURTER, for a 7–2 Court, declared that even if a confession were true or reliable, it should be excluded from admission in evidence if involuntary. Our system is accusatorial, not inquisitorial, Frankfurter said, and therefore the state must establish guilt by evidence not coerced from the accused.

LEONARD W. LEVY

ROOSEVELT, FRANKLIN D. (1882–1945)

Franklin Delano Roosevelt, four-time President of the United States, received his formal instruction in the constitutional system at Harvard College (1900–1904) and Columbia Law School (1904–1907). The mood of the Progressive period, however, was more potent than academic doctrine in shaping his understanding of the constitutional process.

His kinsman Theodore Roosevelt, for whom he cast his first presidential vote in 1904, saw the Constitution "not as a straitjacket . . . but as an instrument designed for the life and healthy growth of the Nation." T. R. further saw the courts as "agents of reaction" and the President as the "steward of the people." If necessary, the President must be prepared to act as the savior of the Constitution against the courts, a role in which T. R. cast himself when he proposed the recall of judicial decisions in 1912. Service under WOODROW WILSON confirmed the young Franklin Roosevelt's belief in a spacious reading of executive authority, and experience as assistant secretary of the navy in wartime Washington showed him how emergency expanded presidential initiative.

After the Wilson administration, Roosevelt's return to legal practice was interrupted when he was crippled in 1921 by poliomyelitis. Elected governor of New York in 1928, he soon confronted the consequences of the Wall Street crash of 1929. He foresaw no constitutional objections to his state programs of unemployment relief, public power development, and land planning. "The United States Constitution," he said in a 1930 speech, "has proved itself the most marvelously elastic compilation of rules of government ever written." Though Roosevelt's purpose in that speech was to vindicate STATES' RIGHTS, he proved marvelously elastic himself when elected President in 1932. Favoring the concentration of power at whatever level of government he happened to be serving, he became thereafter a resolute champion of federal authority.

"Our Constitution," he said in his first inaugural address, "is so simple and practical that it is possible always to meet extraordinary needs by changes in emphasis and arrangement without loss of essential form." He hoped, he continued, to preserve the normal balance between executive and legislative authority. However, if the national emergency remained critical, "I shall ask the Congress for the one remaining instrument to meet the crisis—broad Executive power to wage a war against the emergency." He thus combined optimism about the essential elasticity of the Constitution with an understanding that extraordinary executive initiative must rest, not on inherent presidential power, but on the delegation to the President of powers possessed by Congress. To this he added a certain pessimism about the federal courts, assuming, as he had said during the 1932 campaign, that the Republican party had been in "complete control of all branches of the Federal Government . . . the Supreme Court as well."

For this last reason he was in no hurry to send New Deal legislation through the gantlet of the Supreme Court. The first major test came in February 1935 over the constitutionality of the congressional JOINT RESOLUTION of June 1933 abrogating the so-called gold clause in public and private contracts. If the Court invalidated the resolution, the result would increase the country's total debt by nearly $70 billion. Roosevelt prepared a radio speech attacking an adverse decision and planned to invoke EMERGENCY POWERS to mitigate the effects. But while the Court, in PERRY V. UNITED STATES (1935), held the repudiation of the gold clause unconstitutional with regard to government bonds (though not to private obligations), it also held that, because the plaintiff had suffered no losses, he was not entitled to compensation. The administration's monetary policy remained precariously intact. (See GOLD CLAUSE CASES.)

But three months later in a 5–4 decision the Court nullified the Railroad Retirement Act as an invalid use of the commerce power. Then on May 27, in SCHECHTER POULTRY CORP. v. UNITED STATES it struck down the NATIONAL INDUSTRIAL RECOVERY ACT on two grounds: that the act involved excessive DELEGATION OF POWER by Congress, and that it exceeded the reach of congressional power under the COMMERCE CLAUSE. The vote against the National Recovery Administration was unanimous, as were two other decisions the same day—"Black Monday" in the eyes of New Dealers—one holding the FRAZIER-LEMKE FARM BANKRUPTCY ACT unconstitutional, the other denying the President the power to remove a member of a regulatory commission without congressional consent. If the Court was warning Roosevelt not to go to extremes, Roosevelt responded by warning the Court not to go to extremes either. Calling the SCHECHTER decision "more important probably than any decision since [DRED SCOTT v. SANFORD (1857)]," he said that it carried the Constitution back to "the horse-and-buggy definition of INTERSTATE COMMERCE."

Undeterred, the Court majority prosecuted its attack. In January 1936 six Justices in UNITED STATES v. BUTLER pronounced agriculture a "local" subject, beyond Congress's power, and set aside the AGRICULTURAL ADJUSTMENT ACT. Justice HARLAN F. STONE protested a "tortured construction of the Constitution" in an eloquent dissent. The Court majority, however, proceeded to strike down the Guffey Bituminous Coal Conservation Act, the Municipal Bankruptcy Act, and, finally, in MOREHEAD v. NEW YORK EX REL. TIPALDO (1936), a New York minimum wage law. The Court, Roosevelt now said, had thereby created a " 'no-man's-land' where no Government—State or Federal—can function." Between 1789 and 1865 the Court had declared only two acts of Congress unconstitutional; now, between 1934 and 1936, it invalidated thirteen. Doctrines propounded by the Court majority held out small hope for the SOCIAL SECURITY ACT, the WAGNER NATIONAL LABOR RELATIONS ACT, and other New Deal laws awaiting the judicial test. Roosevelt concluded that "[JOHN] MARSHALL's conception of our Constitution as a flexible instrument—adequate for all times, and, therefore, able to adjust itself as the new needs of new generations arose—had been repudiated."

By 1936 apprehension was spreading about the destruction of the New Deal by the unelected "Nine Old Men." Congress and the law schools were astir with proposals to rein in the Court. Roosevelt outlined three possibilities to his cabinet: limiting the power of the Court to invalidate congressional legislation; making an explicit grant to Congress of powers now in dispute; or ("a distasteful idea") packing the Court by appointing new judges. The first two courses required constitutional amendments. Roosevelt soon decided that an amendment would be difficult to frame, even more difficult to ratify, and in any event subject to judicial interpretation. The problem lay not in the Constitution but in the Court. In early 1936 he instructed Attorney General HOMER CUMMINGS to prepare in utmost secrecy a plan, short of amendment, that would overcome the Court's resistance.

Roosevelt did not make the Court an issue in the 1936 campaign. But his smashing victory in November convinced him that the moment had arrived. Cummings proposed legislation providing for the appointment of new Justices when sitting Justices failed to retire at the age of seventy. Roosevelt sprang the plan in a message to Congress on February 5, 1937. Claiming overcrowded dockets and overworked and overage judges, Roosevelt requested legislation that would enable him to appoint as many as six new Justices.

Postelection euphoria had evidently marred Roosevelt's usually astute political judgment. Wider consultation might at least have persuaded him to make his case as an honest confrontation of power. The pretense that he was seeking merely to ease the burdens of the Court relied on arguments that Chief Justice CHARLES EVANS HUGHES soon demolished in a letter to the Senate Judiciary Committee. By the time Roosevelt began to present the true issue—"We must take action to save the Constitution from the Court and the Court from itself"—his initial trickiness had lost the court plan valuable momentum.

The Chief Justice had further resources. On March 29, in WEST COAST HOTEL v. PARRISH, a 5–4 Court upheld a Washington minimum wage law, thereby in effect overruling the *Tipaldo* decision taken the preceding term. The "switch in time" that "saved nine" was provided by Justice OWEN J. ROBERTS; because *Parrish* had been argued in December, Roberts's second thoughts, if affected by external circumstances, responded to the election, not to the Court plan. In March, the Court also upheld a slightly modified version of the Farm Bankruptcy Act rejected two years earlier. In April, in *National Labor Relations Board v. Jones & Laughlin Steel Corporation,* the

Court approved the National Labor Relations Act in a 5–4 decision in which, as Roberts later conceded, both he and Hughes reversed the position they had taken in condemning the Guffey Act the year before. In May the Court upheld the Social Security Act.

In two months, the Court, under the pressure of the election and the Roosevelt plan, wrought a constitutional revolution, recognizing in both federal and state governments powers it had solemnly denied them in the two previous years as contrary to the Constitution. It greatly enlarged the federal commerce power and the TAXING AND SPENDING POWER, gave new force to the GENERAL WELFARE CLAUSE, altered the application of the DUE PROCESS clause to the states, and abandoned the doctrine of excessive delegation as a means of invalidating federal legislation.

The Court's revisionism, by lessening the felt need for reform, strengthened opposition, already vehement, to the President's plan for the Court. Democrats joined Republicans in denouncing "court-packing." In May the decision of Justice WILLIS VAN DEVANTER to resign, opening the way for Roosevelt's first Supreme Court appointment, further weakened pressure for the plan. In the interests of Senate passage, Roosevelt promised the vacancy to the majority leader Senator Joseph T. Robinson. As Robinson was both old and conservative, he was an anomalous reform choice. By summer Roosevelt was belatedly ready to entertain compromise. But Robinson's death in July brought the bitter struggle to an end.

The insouciance with which Roosevelt presented the Court plan exacted heavy costs in the future of his domestic program, the unity of his party, the confidence of the electorate, and his own self-confidence. Still, the plan attained its objective. As ROBERT H. JACKSON summed it up, "The President's enemies defeated the court reform bill—the President achieved court reform." The plan forced the Court to abandon rigid and restrictive constitutional views; at the same time, the plan's rejection eliminated Court packing as a precedent for the future. History may well conclude both that Roosevelt was right to propose the plan and that the opposition was right to beat it.

In the next half dozen years Roosevelt made the Court his own, appointing HUGO L. BLACK (1937), STANLEY F. REED (1938), FELIX FRANKFURTER (1939), WILLIAM O. DOUGLAS (1939), FRANK MURPHY (1940), JAMES F. BYRNES (1941), Robert H. Jackson (1941), and WILEY B. RUTLEDGE (1943) as Associate Justices and Harlan F. Stone as Chief Justice (1941). In time the Roosevelt Court itself split between the apostles of judicial restraint, who had objected to the methods of the "Nine Old Men," and the activists, who had objected only to their results. But the new Court was united in affirming the reach of the national government's constitutional power to meet the social and economic problems created by the Great Depression.

With the status of New Deal legislation thus assured, Roosevelt's next tangle with constitutional issues took place in FOREIGN AFFAIRS. The Court in UNITED STATES V. CURTISS-WRIGHT EXPORT CORPORATION (1936) had unanimously endorsed the propositions that "the powers of external SOVEREIGNTY did not depend upon the affirmative grants of the Constitution" and that the President had in foreign affairs "a degree of discretion and freedom from statutory restriction which would not be admissible were domestic affairs alone involved." But Congress still had statutory control over vital areas of foreign policy. Neutrality, for example, had been a congressional prerogative since 1794. While Roosevelt requested discretionary neutrality legislation, he saw no practical choice but to accept mandatory laws passed by a stubbornly isolationist Congress. These laws placed the administration in a foreign policy straitjacket from which it sought to wriggle free to the very eve of Pearl Harbor.

Congress, too, retained the constitutional power to declare war. As Roosevelt reminded the French prime minister during the fall of France in 1940, assurance of aid did not imply military commitments; "only the Congress can make such commitments." And legislative power extended to a variety of defense questions. When Winston S. Churchill asked for the loan of old American destroyers, Roosevelt initially responded that "a step of that kind could not be taken except with the specific authorization of the Congress." Later Roosevelt was persuaded that he could make the transfer through executive action. Attorney General Robert H. Jackson's official opinion to this effect rested not on claims of inherent power as President or COMMANDER-IN-CHIEF but on the construction of laws passed by Congress. Critics found the argument strained, but public opinion supported the action.

The decisive step marking the end of American neutrality was the Lend-Lease Act, passed after full and vigorous debate in March 1941. Once Congress had authorized the lending and leasing of goods to keep Britain in the war, did this authority not imply an effort to make sure that the goods arrived? So Roosevelt evidently assumed, trusting that a murky proclamation of "unlimited national emergency" in May 1941 and the impact of Nazi aggression on public opinion would justify his policy. When Grenville Clark urged a joint resolution by which Congress would explicitly approve measures necessary to assure the delivery of supplies, Roosevelt replied in July that the time was not "quite right." The renewal of the draft the next month by a single-vote majority in the House of Representatives showed the fragility of congressional support. By autumn the navy, on presidential orders and without congressional authorization (until Neutrality Act revision in November), was fighting an undeclared war against Germany to protect convoys in the North Atlantic.

Roosevelt's actions in the latter part of 1941, like ABRAHAM LINCOLN'S after the fall of Fort Sumter, were arguably unconstitutional, though not without historical precedent. He did not seek to justify the commitment of American forces to combat by pleas of inherent power as President or as Commander in Chief, and thereby proposed no constitutional novelties. If pressed, he perhaps would have associated himself with JOHN LOCKE, THOMAS JEFFERSON, and Abraham Lincoln in asserting not continuing presidential power but emergency prerogative to be exercised only when the life of the nation was at stake.

Entry into war, as always, increased unilateral presidential authority. When under the New Deal Roosevelt had acted most of the time on the basis of specific statutes, as a war President he acted very often on the basis of general powers claimed as "Commander in Chief in wartime" and on emergency powers activated by proclamation and conferred on an all-purpose agency, the Office of Emergency Management. Of the agencies established in 1940–1943 to control the war economy, only one, the Office of Price Administration, rested on a specific statute.

This statute ironically provoked Roosevelt's most notorious assertion of unilateral authority. The Price Control Act contained a farm parity provision deemed threatening to the anti-inflation program. Roosevelt told Congress in September 1942 that, if it did not repeal the provision within three weeks, he would refuse to execute it. "The President has the powers, under the Constitution and under Congressional Acts," he declared, "to take measures necessary to avert a disaster which would interfere with the winning of the war." He added, "When the war is won, the powers under which I act automatically revert to the people—to whom they belong."

The international threat, as always, increased pressure on CIVIL LIBERTIES. In 1940, while protesting his sympathy with OLIVER WENDELL HOLMES's condemnation of wiretapping in OLMSTEAD V. UNITED STATES (1928), Roosevelt granted his attorney general qualified permission to wiretap "persons suspected of SUBVERSIVE ACTIVITIES against the United States." Given the conviction Roosevelt shared with most Americans that a Nazi victory in Europe would have endangered the United States, he would have been delinquent in his duty had he not taken precautionary measures. Though we know now that the internal menace was exaggerated, no one could be sure of that at the time.

Roosevelt, however, extended his concern to include Americans honestly opposed to intervention, directing the Federal Bureau of Investigation to investigate isolationists and their organizations. There was so little government follow-up of Roosevelt's prodding, however, that the prods were evidently taken by his subordinates as expressions of passing irritation rather than constant purpose. In 1941 Roosevelt appointed FRANCIS BIDDLE, a distinguished civil libertarian, as attorney general and kept him on the job throughout the war despite Biddle's repeated resistance to presidential requests that threatened the BILL OF RIGHTS.

Roosevelt's preoccupation with pro-Nazi agitation increased after Pearl Harbor. "He was not much interested in the theory of SEDITION," Biddle later recalled, "or in the constitutional right to criticize the government in wartime. He wanted this anti-war talk stopped." In time, his prods forced a reluctant Biddle to approve the indictment of twenty-six pro-Fascist Americans under a dubious application of the law of CRIMINAL CONSPIRACY. A chaotic trial ended with the death of the judge, and the case was dropped.

Biddle also resisted the most shameful abuse of power within the United States during the war—the relocation of Americans of Japanese descent. Here Roosevelt responded both to local pressure, including that of Attorney General EARL WARREN of California, and to the War Department, where such respected lawyers as Henry L. Stimson and John J. McCloy demanded action. Congress ratified Roosevelt's EXECUTIVE ORDER before it was put into effect, so the relocation did not represent a unilateral exercise of presidential power. The Supreme Court upheld the program in the JAPANESE AMERICAN CASES (1943–1944).

Still, despite Roosevelt's moments of impatience and exasperation, his administration's civil liberties record during World War II was conspicuously better than that of the Lincoln administration during the Civil War or of the Wilson administration during World War I. In 1944 the AMERICAN CIVIL LIBERTIES UNION saluted "the extraordinary and unexpected record . . . in freedom of debate and dissent on all public issues and in the comparatively slight resort to war-time measures of control or repression of opinion."

Roosevelt's presidency vindicated his conviction that social reform and military victory could be achieved without breaching the Constitution. A believer in a strong presidency, he was himself a strong President within, on the whole, constitutional bounds. His deviations from strict constitutional propriety were mostly under impressions, sometimes mistaken, of clear and present international danger. Those of his successors who claimed inherent presidential WAR POWERS went further than he ever did.

Roosevelt was a political leader, not a constitutional lawyer, and he correctly saw that in its major phase constitutional law is often a question of political and economic philosophy. No doubt his understanding of the practical necessity of consent was more important than technical appreciation of constitutional limitations in keeping his actions within the frame of the basic charter. But his presidency justified his inaugural assertion that the Constitution could meet extraordinary needs by changes in emphasis and arrangement without loss of essential form. His legacy was a revivified faith in the adequacy of the Constitution as a progressive document, equal to domestic and foreign emergency and "capable of meeting evolution and change."

ARTHUR M. SCHLESINGER, JR.

Bibliography

ALSOP, JOSEPH and CATLEDGE, TURNER 1938 *The 168 Days.* Garden City, N.Y.: Doubleday.

BIDDLE, FRANCIS 1962 *In Brief Authority.* Garden City, N.Y.: Doubleday.

FREEDMAN, MAX, ed. 1967 *Roosevelt and Frankfurter: Their Correspondence, 1928–1945.* Boston: Little, Brown.

JACKSON, ROBERT H. 1941 *The Struggle for Judicial Supremacy: A Study of a Crisis in American Power Politics.* New York: Knopf.

MASON, A. T. 1956 *Harlan Fiske Stone: Pillar of the Law.* New York: Viking.

SCHLESINGER, ARTHUR M., JR. 1957–1960 *The Age of Roosevelt,* vols. I–III. Boston: Houghton Mifflin.

ROOSEVELT, THEODORE
(1858–1919)

The son of a New York City merchant and philanthropist and a descendant of the original Dutch settlers of New Amsterdam, Theodore Roosevelt was graduated magna cum laude from Harvard College in 1879. He studied law for one year at Columbia University, but never completed law school or practiced law. When he was twenty-three years old he published his first book (the influential *Naval War of 1812*) and was elected to the New York state legislature on the Republican ticket. In his second term, having successfully campaigned for a LEGISLATIVE INVESTIGATION of statewide corruption, he was chosen minority leader of the state Assembly, and from that position he engineered passage of the state civil service reform measures proposed by Democratic Governor GROVER CLEVELAND.

In 1886, after two years of ranching in the Dakota badlands, Roosevelt returned to New York City and attempted to resume his political career, but he was defeated in his race for mayor. He held no political office until 1889, when President BENJAMIN HARRISON appointed him to the United States Civil Service Commission, a post in which he was retained when Cleveland returned to the presidency. In 1895, Roosevelt became president of the New York City Police Commission; for more than two years he did public battle with police corruption and demon rum.

When William McKinley was elected President, Roosevelt went back to Washington as the vigorous assistant secretary of the Navy. At the beginning of the Spanish-American War in 1898, Roosevelt resigned his office in the Navy Department and raised a regiment of volunteer cavalry, which he subsequently led in combat in Cuba. Riding the crest of fame from his wartime exploits, Roosevelt was elected governor of New York in 1898 and vice-president of the United States in 1900.

Roosevelt succeeded to the presidency when McKinley was assassinated in September 1901. He immediately pledged that his aim was "to continue, absolutely unbroken, the policy of President McKinley." But neither his love of fame nor his reformist impulses would permit him to redeem that pledge. Having reached the highest office in the land at a younger age than anyone before or since, he displayed a degree of vigor and impatience far greater than his predecessors had done. He also had a more expansive view of the powers and duties of the President than any of his predecessors since ABRAHAM LINCOLN. Not only did he think of the presidency as a "bully pulpit" from which one might lead, rather than follow, public opinion, but he also conceived of the office as having a roving commission to do anything the public weal might require so long as the Constitution did not by its terms prohibit the proposed course of action.

In FOREIGN AFFAIRS, Roosevelt acted with particular energy. On his own initiative he imposed a form of government in the Philippines (a commission headed by WILLIAM HOWARD TAFT) that Congress subsequently confirmed in the Philippine Organic Act (1902). He arranged by treaty for America to take over the British interest in construction of a canal across the Isthmus of Panama and subsequently fomented a revolt of Panamanians against the government of Colombia so that a favorable PANAMA CANAL TREATY could be negotiated (1903) and work on the canal begun. When the Latin American countries of Venezuela and Santo Domingo (now the Dominican Republic) defaulted on loans from European banks, Roosevelt put those countries under American occupation and receivership rather than risk military intervention by Europeans in the Western Hemisphere. This policy he called his "corollary" to the MONROE DOCTRINE. When an American citizen was kidnapped in 1904 by a band of Moroccan brigands, Roosevelt ordered a force of sailors and marines to invade a neutral and sovereign state to secure the citizen's release. Roosevelt also personally mediated the settlement of the Russo-Japanese War in 1905 (thereby earning the Nobel Peace Prize), and his administration was instrumental in achieving agreements to guarantee the independence of Morocco (1906) and to settle disputes among the Central American republics (1907). When Congress refused to appropriate funds so that the United States fleet could make a round-the-world show-the-flag cruise, Roosevelt used his power as COMMANDER-IN-CHIEF to order the ships to go as far as they could, confident that Congress would appropriate the funds to bring them home.

In domestic policy, Roosevelt's administration was both nationalist and interventionist. Roosevelt resumed prosecutions under the SHERMAN ANTITRUST ACT (albeit not so vigorously as his later critics would have liked) and proposed what became the HEPBURN ACT (1906), giving the Interstate Commerce Commission authority to set railroad rates nationwide. He put the federal government into the business of conserving America's wild places and natural resources, creating the Inland Waterways Commission (1907) and the National Conservation Commission (1908).

Roosevelt was generally critical of the constitutional jurisprudence of his day, and especially of the Supreme Court's protection of SUBSTANTIVE DUE PROCESS OF LAW in cases relating to ECONOMIC REGULATION. He emphatically rejected the contention that criticism of the judiciary weakens respect for law and undermines the independence of the judiciary. In his sixth state-of-the-Union message, he said: "The judge has a power over which no review can be exercised; he himself sits in review upon the acts of both the executive and legislative branches of the government; save in the most extraordinary cases he is amenable only at the bar of public opinion; and it is unwise to maintain that public opinion in reference to a man with such power shall neither be exprest nor led." Influenced by some of the more radical strains of PROGRESSIVE CONSTITUTIONAL THOUGHT, he favored a right of popular "recall" of state judicial decisions, that is, of allowing decisions to be overturned by a vote of the people. His first appointee to the Supreme Court, OLIVER WENDELL HOLMES of Massachusetts, initially so disappointed Roosevelt that the President remarked that he could "carve a judge with more backbone from a banana." Roosevelt's two other appointees, WILLIAM R. DAY and WILLIAM MOODY, both generally provided judicial support for state and federal regulation of business enterprise.

In 1908, Roosevelt did not seek reelection, but hand-picked as his successor William Howard Taft. He then retired from politics to a life of writing and adventuring. But Roosevelt disapproved of the conservative tone assumed by the Taft administration and attempted to wrest the 1912 Republican nomination for himself. When Taft was renominated, Roosevelt formed his own party, the Progressive party, and ran for President anyway. Roosevelt's candidacy split the Republican vote and permitted the election of WOODROW WILSON.

Roosevelt was later reconciled to the Republican party and in 1916 campaigned for the Republican presidential candidate, CHARLES EVANS HUGHES. When the United States entered World War I, Roosevelt asked President Wilson to authorize him to raise and command a volunteer division to serve in the expeditionary force; Wilson refused. After the war, Roosevelt opposed Wilson's plan for a League of Nations, preferring that the postwar world be dominated by an Anglo-American alliance. When he died, in 1919, Roosevelt was beginning to plan for yet another attempt at reelection to the presidency.

DENNIS J. MAHONEY

Bibliography

BLUM, JOHN MORTON 1954 *The Republican Roosevelt.* Cambridge, Mass.: Harvard University Press.

MORRIS, EDMUND 1979 *The Rise of Theodore Roosevelt.* New York: Coward, McCann & Geohegan.

MOWRY, GEORGE E. 1958 *The Era of Theodore Roosevelt: 1900–1912.* New York: Harper & Brothers.

ROSENBERG v. UNITED STATES
346 U.S. 273 (1953)

Over the vehement protests of three of its members (HUGO BLACK, FELIX FRANKFURTER, and WILLIAM O. DOUGLAS), the VINSON COURT vacated a STAY OF EXECUTION issued by Douglas that had halted the scheduled electrocution of Julius and Ethel Rosenberg. The Rosenbergs had been convicted and sentenced to death in 1951 for allegedly violating the 1917 ESPIONAGE ACT by passing secret information about the atomic bomb to the Soviet Union. Douglas had refused to join Black, Frankfurter, and HAROLD BURTON in earlier efforts to review the case by means of CERTIORARI and HABEAS CORPUS, but on June 17, 1953, after the Court had recessed for the term, he stayed the Rosenbergs' execution on the ground that their lawyers had raised a new argument deserving judicial scrutiny—the couple should have been tried under the Atomic Energy Act of 1946 rather than the earlier statute.

Responding to intense pressure from the Eisenhower administration, Chief Justice FRED VINSON recalled the Justices to Washington for special session. On June 19, a 6–3 majority overturned the stay and rejected Douglas's interpretation of the Atomic Energy Act. The Rosenbergs were executed that same evening. Frankfurter, who, with Black, had urged a full review of the case since the earliest appeals, later wrote that this last act of the Vinson Court was "the most disturbing single experience I have had during my term of service on the Court."

MICHAEL E. PARRISH

Bibliography

RADOSH, RONALD and MILTON, JOYCE 1983 *The Rosenberg File: A Search for the Truth.* New York: Holt, Rinehart & Winston.

ROSS, UNITED STATES v.
456 U.S. 798 (1982)

Ross altered the constitutional law of AUTOMOBILE SEARCHES. A UNITED STATES COURT OF APPEALS, following Supreme Court precedents, had held that although police had PROBABLE CAUSE to stop an automobile and make a WARRANTLESS SEARCH of its interior, including its closed areas, they should have had a SEARCH WARRANT before opening closed containers that they had searched for evidence. And in *Robbins v. California* (1981) the Court had declared that unless a closed container, by its shape or transparency, revealed contraband, it might not be opened without a warrant. The rationale of requiring a warrant for such a search turned on the reasonable expectation of privacy protected by the FOURTH AMENDMENT. *Ross,* however, substantially expanded the automobile exception to the warrant requirement.

Justice JOHN PAUL STEVENS for a 6–3 Court declared that the question for decision was whether the police, making a warrantless search with probable cause, had a right to open containers found in a vehicle. A lawful search of any premises extended to the whole area where the object of the search might be found. Thus a warrant to search a vehicle authorizes the search of all closed areas within it, including containers. "The scope of a warrantless search based on probable cause," Stevens said, "is no narrower—and no broader—than the scope of a search authorized by a warrant supported by probable cause." Accordingly, the scope of the search depended on the EVIDENCE sought for, not on the objects containing that evidence. Having so reasoned, the Court necessarily overruled the *Robbins* holding.

Justices THURGOOD MARSHALL, WILLIAM J. BRENNAN, and BYRON R. WHITE, dissenting, lamented that "the majority today not only repeals all realistic limits on warrantless automobile searches, it repeals the Fourth Amendment warrant requirement itself"—patently an exaggeration. *Ross* did make a shambles of the reasoning in earlier cases on searching closed containers in automobiles, but the Court finally delivered an unambiguous opinion for the guidance of law enforcement officers. Whether or not the Court based the new rule on expediency for the purpose of assisting prosecutorial forces, it will likely have serious implications for the privacy of Americans using their vehicles.

LEONARD W. LEVY

ROSS v. MOFFITT
417 U.S. 600 (1974)

Ross sharply limited the requirement of DOUGLAS V. CALIFORNIA (1963) that counsel be provided, free of charge, to INDIGENTS seeking to appeal from state convictions. The *Douglas* opinion had referred only to the "first appeal as of right," and here the Supreme Court's 6–3 majority drew the line defining the state's constitutional responsibility at precisely that point. There was no obligation to furnish counsel to pursue discretionary appeals or applications for Supreme Court review. Justice WILLIAM H. REHNQUIST's majority opinion did distinguish *Douglas,* but its reasoning drew heavily on the *Douglas* dissent of Justice JOHN MARSHALL HARLAN.

KENNETH L. KARST

ROSSITER, CLINTON
(1917–1970)

Clinton Lawrence Rossiter III was a political scientist, constitutional scholar, and historian. His fascination with the response of constitutional government to the exigencies of crisis and war led to his first two books, *Constitutional Dictatorship* (1948) and *The Supreme Court and the Commander in Chief* (1951). His most widely read work, *The American Presidency* (1956, rev. ed. 1960), a deft and approving account of the Presidency's growth in power, influence, and responsibility, was perhaps the most influential study of that institution before Watergate. *Seedtime of the Republic,* a monumental intellectual history of the American Revolution, traced the roots of the Revolutionary generation's political ideas to seventeenth-century English republican thought. Rossiter's other works include *Parties and Politics in America* (1960), *Conservatism in America* (1955, rev. ed. 1962), *Alexander Hamilton and the Constitution* (1964), *1787: The Grand Convention* (1966), and the posthumously published *The American Quest, 1790–1860* (1971).

RICHARD B. BERNSTEIN

ROSTKER v. GOLDBERG
453 U.S. 57 (1981)

Men subject to registration for possible military CONSCRIPTION challenged the exclusion of women from the registration requirement as a denial of EQUAL PROTECTION. The Supreme Court, 6–3, rejected this claim. Justice WILLIAM H. REHNQUIST, for the majority, paid great deference to Congress's authority over military affairs; with the most minimal judicial second-guessing of the congressional judgment, he concluded that men and women were "not similarly situated," because any draft would be designed to produce combat troops, and women were ineligible for combat. SEX DISCRIMINATION, in other words, was its own justification.

As the dissenters demonstrated, the exclusion of women from draft registration had resulted from no military judgment at all; the President and the Joint Chiefs of Staff had urged that women be registered. Rather, Congress had heard the voice of public opinion. It is not impossible that the Court itself heard that voice. Thus do sex-role stereotypes perpetuate themselves.

KENNETH L. KARST

ROTH v. UNITED STATES
354 U.S. 476 (1957)
ALBERTS v. CALIFORNIA
354 U.S. 476 (1957)

Until *Roth* and *Alberts,* argued and decided on the same days, the Supreme Court had assumed that the FIRST AMENDMENT did not protect OBSCENITY. Squarely confronted with the issue by appeals from convictions under the federal obscenity statute (in *Roth*) and a California law outlawing the sale and advertising of obscene books (in *Alberts*), the Court held that obscenity was not constitutionally protected speech.

Justice WILLIAM J. BRENNAN, for the majority, relied on historical evidence that the Framers of the First Amendment had not intended to protect all speech, but only speech with some redeeming social value. Thus, the First Amendment protected even hateful ideas that contributed toward the unfettered exchange of information that might result in desired political and social change. Obscenity, however, was utterly without redeeming social importance, and was not constitutionally protected.

Neither statute before the Court defined obscenity; nor did the Court examine the materials to determine whether they were obscene. The Court nevertheless rejected the appellants' due process objections on the grounds that the statutes had given sufficient warning as to the proscribed conduct and the trial courts had applied the proper standard for judging obscenity.

The Court rejected the widely used test based on *Queen v. Hicklin* (1868) which judged a work's obscenity by the effect of an isolated excerpt upon particularly susceptible persons. The proper standard was "whether to the average person, applying contemporary community standards, the dominant theme taken as a whole appeals to prurient interest," that is, has a tendency to excite lustful thoughts. Because the obscenity of the materials involved in *Roth* was not at issue, the Court escaped the task of applying its definition. Ironically, the definition of obscenity was to preoccupy the Court for the next sixteen years. The Court, having designated a category of speech that could be criminally proscribed, now confronted the critical task of delineating that category.

Chief Justice EARL WARREN and Justice JOHN MARSHALL HARLAN, separately concurring, sought to limit the scope of the majority opinion. Warren, concurring in the result, agreed that the defendants' conduct in commercially exploiting material for its appeal to prurient interest was constitutionally punishable. Harlan, concurring in *Alberts* and dissenting in *Roth,* believed the Court was required to examine each work individually to determine its obscene character, and argued that the Constitution restricted the federal government in this field more severely than it restricted the states. Justices WILLIAM O. DOUGLAS and HUGO L. BLACK, dissenting in both cases, enunciated the positions they were to take in the wave of obscenity cases soon to overwhelm the Court: obscenity, like every other form of speech, is absolutely protected by the First Amendment.

KIM MCLANE WARDLAW

RULE OF FOUR

Even before Congress expanded the Supreme Court's discretionary CERTIORARI jurisdiction in 1925, the Court had adopted the practice of granting certiorari whenever four of the nine Justices agreed that a case should be heard. This "rule of four" was first made public in testimony concerning the bill that became the 1925 act. Some commentators have seen the adoption of that act as a congressional ratification of the practice; in any case, the rule is well established. In *Rogers v. Missouri Pacific R.R.* (1957) a majority agreed that the rule required the Court to hear a petition granted on the vote of four Justices, even though the other five might still think the case unworthy of review, unless new considerations had come to light in the meanwhile. As *New York v. Uplinger* (1984) makes clear, however, the vote of four Justices to *hear* a case does not require the Court to *decide* it if the other five Judges think a decision inappropriate.

The Court follows a similar practice in APPEAL cases coming from the state courts. The Court has even dismissed such an appeal "for want of a substantial FEDERAL QUESTION" over the expressed dissent of three Justices. When three members of the Court argue that a question is a substantial one, it probably is. The dismissal of an appeal under these circumstances reinforces the view that appeal, despite its theoretically obligatory nature as defined by Congress, has taken on much of the discretionary quality of the Court's certiorari policy.

KENNETH L. KARST

Bibliography

LEIMAN, JOAN MEISEL 1957 The Rule of Four. *Columbia Law Review* 57:975–992.

RULE OF LAW

The rule of law is the general principle that government and the governed alike are subject to law, as regularly adopted and applied. The principle is nowhere express in the United States Constitution, but it is a concept of basic importance in Anglo-American constitutional law. In that context, it is not merely a positivist doctrine of legality, requiring obedience to any duly adopted doctrine, but a means to assure that the actions of all branches of government are measured against the fundamental values enshrined in the COMMON LAW and the Constitution.

The rule of law has its roots in classical antiquity, in the *Politics* of Aristotle and the works of Cicero. As an Anglo-American legal principle, the concept may be traced to MAGNA CARTA (1215). In the thirty-ninth clause of that instrument, King John promised the barons that "No free man shall be taken, imprisoned, disseized, outlawed, or banished, or in any way destroyed, nor will we proceed against or prosecute him, except by the lawful judgment of his peers and the LAW OF THE LAND." Four centuries later, with the principle well entrenched in the theory and practice of the English common law, EDWARD COKE challenged James I's assertion of the right to exercise an independent judicial power with the words of Henry Bracton: "Quod Rex non debet esse sub homine, sed sub Deo et lege" [The King ought not to be under man, but under God and the law.] After the chaos of revolution, commonwealth, and restoration, the Glorious Revolution of 1688 established the permanent subjection of the king to the law, both of the common law courts and of Parliament.

Coke's *Reports* and *Institutes,* JOHN LOCKE's *Second Treatise of Government* (1691), and the flood of English radical political writing that accompanied the events of the seventeenth and eighteenth centuries carried these ideas to the American colonies. They became a key element in the ideology of the American Revolution. THOMAS PAINE's *Common Sense* (1776) proclaimed, "that in America, *the law is king.* For as in absolute governments, the king is law, so in free countries the law ought to be king; and there ought to be no other." As the unprecedented era of constitution making that succeeded the American Revolution provoked more sophisticated analysis of the structure of government, it became clear that not only the executive but also the legislature must be subject to law. Thus, JOHN ADAMS more temperately but more tellingly expressed the principle of the rule of law in drafting the MASSACHUSETTS CONSTITUTION of 1780. The Declaration of Rights in that instrument called for the SEPARATION OF POWERS, "to the end it may be a government of laws and not of men." Chief Justice JOHN MARSHALL gave practical effect to Adams's words in the actual application of the new federal Constitution, using them in MARBURY V. MADISON (1803) to bolster his argument that William Marbury had a judicial remedy for the withholding of his commission by the secretary of state.

The principle was elaborated and definitively labeled "the Rule of Law" by the leading nineteenth-century English constitutional theorist Albert Venn Dicey (1835–1922). In his influential work, *Introduction to the Study of Law of the Constitution* (1885), Dicey ranked the rule of law with parliamentary SOVEREIGNTY and constitutional conventions as one of the three fundamental elements of the unwritten British constitution. He gave the term "rule of law" three meanings: a requirement that government act against the citizen only in accordance with "regular law" enforced in the "ordinary courts" and not arbitrarily or in the exercise of "wide discretionary authority"; a requirement that the government and all citizens be equal before the law and equally subject to the ordinary courts; and a formulation reflecting the fact that constitutional rights were grounded not in abstract principles but in "the ordinary law of the land" as enforced in the courts.

Dicey's views of the rule of law have been rigorously elaborated by later political theorists, notably Friedrich Hayek in his *Constitution of Liberty* (1960) and other works. The fundamental nature of the rule of law as the basis of a moral and just social order has been recognized in more general terms in works such as Lon Fuller's *The Morality of Law* (1964) and John Rawls's *A Theory of Justice* (1971). It is also seen in the efforts of internationalists in the 1960s to establish international doctrines of world peace and human rights through a "world rule of law." More recently, critics have challenged the legitimacy of the rule of law, characterizing it as simply a cover for the maintenance of power by privileged social classes. Roberto Unger, in *Law and Modern Society* (1976), questioned the viability of the rule of law in the modern welfare/corporate state as the liberal premises upon which it is based decline.

Dicey's elaboration of the rule of law has also been forcefully criticized in England and the United States because its prohibition of discretionary action is inconsistent with the widespread use of the administrative process that has become characteristic of modern democratic government. Kenneth Culp Davis, a leading American critic, attributed the virtual nonuse of the phrase in American judicial opinions to the unreality of Dicey's "extravagant version" of the doctrine. Its occasional appearance to highlight a discussion of fairness or legality reflects, according to Davis, only the tendency of some judges "to add the touch of poetry" to their work.

Nevertheless, the concept of the rule of law remains fundamental to Anglo-American constitutional jurisprudence. In Britain, it remains a device for calling upon the protections of the common law against legislative and executive intrusion. In the United States, at the most general level, the rule of law is invoked by judges as they seek to assure compliance by the federal and state governments with the guarantees of the BILL OF RIGHTS. Those guarantees, as interpreted by the courts, are binding upon the governments and individuals to whom they are addressed. The Supreme Court made this point clear in COOPER V. AARON (1958), rejecting the position of defiance toward a federal court's school desegregation order taken by the governor and legislature of Arkansas.

More specifically, the concept of the rule of law embodies what Laurence H. Tribe has characterized as "the Model of Governmental Regularity." This model describes requirements of generality and prospectivity of legislation and procedural regularity in administration and adjudication that are articulated in and enforced through the EX POST FACTO and BILL OF ATTAINDER clauses of the Constitution and the DUE PROCESS clauses of the Fifth and FOURTEENTH AMENDMENTS. Finally, the element of equality in Dicey's rule of law has received fundamental expression in the development of the EQUAL PROTECTION clause of the Fourteenth Amendment. That clause, as interpreted and applied by the Supreme Court in the second half of the twentieth century, has provided constitutional support for the most profound changes that our society has seen, short of revolution or civil war.

L. KINVIN WROTH

Bibliography

ALLAN, T. R. S. 1985 Legislative Supremacy and the Rule of Law. *Cambridge Law Journal* 44:111–143.

DICEY, ALBERT VENN 1885 *Introduction to the Study of the Law of the Constitution.* London: Macmillan.

TRIBE, LAURENCE H. 1978 *American Constitutional Law.* Mineola, N.Y.: Foundation Press.

RULE OF REASON

The rule of reason was a statutory construction of the SHERMAN ANTITRUST ACT by the Supreme Court. Nothing better illustrated JUDICIAL POLICYMAKING than the rule of reason, which held that the Sherman Act excepted from its scope "good trusts" or "reasonable restraints of trade." The statute expressly declared illegal "every" contract, combination, and conspiracy in restraint of trade, and as a result the Court in several early cases rejected the argument that "every" did not mean what it said. The Court also denied that the statute should be construed in the light of the COMMON LAW, which had recognized the legality of certain ancillary restraints of trade on the ground that they were reasonable. For example, in UNITED STATES V. TRANS-MISSOURI FREIGHT ASSOCIATION (1897) the Court rejected the proposition that "Congress, notwithstanding the language of the [Sherman] act, could not have intended to embrace all contracts, but only such contracts as were in unreasonable restraint of trade." Said Justice RUFUS PECKHAM for the Court: "[w]e are, therefore, asked to hold that the act of Congress excepts contracts which are not in unreasonable restraint of trade." To read that rule of reason into the statute, Peckham answered, would be an exercise of JUDICIAL LEGISLATION.

That remained the Court's view until 1911, when it ignored its PRECEDENTS, the text of the statute, and the views of the Senate and the President. In 1909 the Senate had rejected a bill that proposed to amend the Sherman Act by incorporating the rule of reason. "To amend the antitrust act, as suggested by this bill," declared a subcommittee of the Senate Judiciary Committee, "would be to entirely emasculate it, and for all practical purposes render it nugatory as a remedial statute." In 1910 President WILLIAM HOWARD TAFT in a message to Congress had argued that no need existed to amend the scope of the Sherman Act. Yet in 1911, in two major antitrust cases, UNITED STATES V. STANDARD OIL COMPANY OF NEW JERSEY and *United States v. American Tobacco Co.*, Chief Justice EDWARD D. WHITE, who had dissented from earlier opinions repudiating the rule of reason, explicitly adopted it for an 8–1 Court. The sole dissenter, Justice JOHN MARSHALL HARLAN, echoing the *Trans-Missouri Freight* case, assaulted "judicial legislation"—the usurpation by the Court of a congressional function. The Sherman Act, Harlan insisted, included "every" restraint of trade, even a reasonable one. But Congress, in its 1914 antitrust legislation of the CLAYTON ACT and the FEDERAL TRADE COMMISSION ACT, by failing to attack the rule of reason acquiesced in it.

As a result of its rule of reason, the Supreme Court prevented effective use of the Sherman Act to prevent industrial consolidations of a monopolistic character. Thus, in *United States v. United Shoe Machinery Company* (1918), the Court held that the antitrust act did not apply to the company even though its dominating position in the industry approached that of an absolute monopoly which had restrained trade by its use of exclusive PATENT rights. In UNITED STATES V. UNITED STATES STEEL CORPORATION (1920) the Court held that the nation's largest industrial enterprise had reasonably restrained trade despite its "attempt to monopolize" in violation of the act. Similarly, in *United States v. International Harvester Company* (1927) the rule of reason defeated the government's case once again even though the company controlled a big proportion of the market and used exclusive dealer contracts to eliminate competition. Although the Court ruled that trade union activities came within the scope of the antitrust act, no union ever benefited from a Court finding that its restraint of trade was reasonable. The rule of reason, in short, proved to be of considerable importance in the history of JUDICIAL REVIEW, of the economy, and of government efforts to regulate monopolistic practices.

LEONARD W. LEVY

(SEE ALSO: *Antitrust Law and the Constitution.*)

Bibliography

NEALE, A. D. 1970 *The Antitrust Laws of the United States of America.* Cambridge: At the University Press.

RUMMEL v. ESTELLE
445 U.S. 263 (1980)

OLIVER WENDELL HOLMES once said that the Supreme Court sits to expound law, not do justice. This case is proof. On the premise that the length of a sentence is "purely a matter of legislative judgment," Justice WILLIAM H. REHNQUIST for a 5–4 Court found no CRUEL AND UNUSUAL PUNISHMENT in Rummel's mandatory life sentence after his third felony conviction for obtaining $120.75 by false pretenses. Rummel argued that his sentence was disproportionate to his crime. Rehnquist replied that the possibility of a parole in twelve years and the right of a state legislature to fix penalties against recidivists overcame Rummel's argument. Rehnquist declared that the state legislature was acting within its competence in prescribing punishment and that the state has a legitimate interest in requiring extended incarceration of habitual criminals. The Court would not substitute its judgment for the legislature's and overturn a sentence which was neither inherently barbarous nor grossly disproportionate to the offense.

Justice LEWIS F. POWELL for the dissenters believed that Rummel's life sentence "would be viewed as grossly unjust by virtually every layman and lawyer." The cruel and unusual punishment clause of the Eighth Amendment, extended by the FOURTEENTH AMENDMENT to the states, Powell argued, prohibited grossly disproportionate punishments as well as barbarous ones. Rummel's three felonies netted him about $230 in frauds. He never used violence, threatened anyone, or endangered the peace of society. Texas treated his crimes as no different from those of a three-time murderer. The Court's decision weakened the use of the cruel and unusual punishment clause in noncapital cases.

LEONARD W. LEVY

RUNYON v. MCCRARY
427 U.S. 160 (1976)

The CIVIL RIGHTS ACT OF 1866 gives all persons "the same right . . . to make and enforce contracts . . . as is enjoyed by white persons." In the *Runyon* case the Supreme Court, following its 1968 decision in JONES V. ALFRED H. MAYER CO., relied on the THIRTEENTH AMENDMENT as a source of congressional power and upheld the application of this provision to two private schools' exclusion of qualified black applicants.

Justice POTTER STEWART, writing for the Court, made clear that several issues concerning the act's coverage were being left open. The Court was not deciding whether the act forbade a private social organization to impose a racial limitation on its membership; nor was it deciding whether a private school might limit its students to boys or girls, or to members of some religious faith. *Runyon* itself involved "private, commercially operated, non-sectarian schools."

Although Congress is empowered to enforce the Thirteenth Amendment, the provisions of the BILL OF RIGHTS limit congressional power here as elsewhere. The school operators argued unsuccessfully that the application of the 1866 act to their admissions practices violated rights of association, parental rights, and the RIGHT OF PRIVACY.

In responding to the associational freedom claim, Justice Stewart came close to saying that the freedom to practice racial discrimination in the choice of one's associates is not entitled to constitutional protection—a view that surely would not survive in the context of marriage or other intimate association. Concurring specially, Justice LEWIS F. POWELL remarked on the strength of the associational freedoms that would be involved if the 1866 Act were applied to a racially discriminatory selection of a home tutor or babysitter.

The Court dismissed the parental rights claim with the comment that parents and school operators retained the right to use the schools to inculcate the values of their choice. The privacy claim was similarly rejected; parents had a right to send their children to private schools, but the schools remained subject to reasonable government regulation.

Justices BYRON R. WHITE and WILLIAM H. REHNQUIST dissented, arguing that *Jones* was wrongly decided and that the 1866 act had not been intended to forbid a private, racially motivated refusal to contract. Justice JOHN PAUL STEVENS, in a special concurrence, agreed with the dissenters' view of the 1866 act's purposes. However, he concluded, "for the Court now to overrule *Jones* would be a significant step backwards" in the process of eliminating RACIAL DISCRIMINATION; thus he joined the Court's opinion. It was ever so; today's history almost always prevails in a contest with yesterday's.

KENNETH L. KARST

RUTGERS v. WADDINGTON
(New York Mayor's Court, 1784)

Decided in 1784 by the Mayor's Court of New York City, this was an early state precedent for JUDICIAL REVIEW and the first reported case in which the constitutionality of a state act was attacked on the ground that it violated a treaty of the United States. The state's Trespass Act allowed Rutgers, who had fled New York when the British occupied the city, to sue for the value of rents lost while her property was held by British merchants under military authority. The statute barred defendants from pleading that military authority justified the "trespass" under acts of war and the law of nations. The Treaty of Peace, however, canceled claims for injuries to property during the war. ALEXANDER HAMILTON, representing the defendants, expressly argued that the court should hold the Trespass Act unconstitutional.

Chief Judge JAMES DUANE, for the court, declared that the state constitution embodied the COMMON

LAW and that the common law recognized the law of nations. Duane also declared that the union of the states under the ARTICLES OF CONFEDERATION constituted "a FUNDAMENTAL LAW," according to which Congress had exclusive powers of making war and peace: "no state in this union can alter or abridge, in a single point, the federal articles or the treaty." His logic having led him to the brink of holding the Trespass Act void, Duane abruptly endorsed the prevailing Blackstonian theory of legislative supremacy. When the legislature enacted a law, "there is no power which can controul them . . . the Judges are not at liberty, altho' it appear to them to be unreasonable, to reject it: for this were to set the judicial above the legislative, which would be subversive of all government." Duane then declared that the legislature had not intended to revoke the law of nations and that the court had to expound the statute to give the legislature's intention its effect, whereupon the court emasculated the statute. The judgment was that for the time the property was held under military order, acts done according to the law of nations and "buried in oblivion" by the treaty could not be redressed by the statute; Rutgers could not recover for trespass.

Technically the court had construed the act to conform to the treaty and the law of nations, but the legislature angrily resolved that the adjudication was "subversive of all law and good order" and that if a court could "dispense with" state law, "Legislatures become useless." Although a motion to remove the judges failed, a public protest meeting adopted "An Address to the People," angrily accusing the court of having "assumed and exercised a power to set aside an Act of the State." The "Address," severely condemning judicial review, was widely circulated, as was the pamphlet report of the case.

LEONARD W. LEVY

RUTLEDGE, JOHN
(1739–1800)

John Rutledge, a wealthy lawyer, represented South Carolina in the STAMP ACT Congress (1765) and chaired that state's delegations to the First and Second Continental Congresses. He was a member of the committee that drafted the South Carolina Constitution (1776) and was elected the state's first president (1776–1778) and second governor (1779). He led his state's delegation to the CONSTITUTIONAL CONVENTION OF 1787, where he used his oratorical skill to advance a moderate STATES' RIGHTS position and to defend the interests of the southern slaveholding aristocracy. He opposed creation of a separate federal judiciary, but favored a provision making the federal Constitution and laws binding on state courts. After signing the Constitution, he served as a member of the South Carolina ratifying convention.

In 1789, President GEORGE WASHINGTON appointed Rutledge one of the original associate justices of the Supreme Court, but he resigned in 1791—having done only circuit duty—to become Chief Justice of South Carolina. In 1795, Washington appointed him Chief Justice of the United States, and he presided over the August 1795 term of the Court; but an intemperate speech against JAY'S TREATY alienated the Federalists, and the Senate refused to confirm his nomination. (See SUPREME COURT, 1789–1801.)

DENNIS J. MAHONEY

RUTLEDGE, WILEY B.
(1894–1949)

When Wiley B. Rutledge joined the Supreme Court in January 1943, succeeding JAMES F. BYRNES, he helped to forge a liberal coalition that substantially redirected constitutional developments for the next six years. His sudden death in the summer of 1949, two months after the passing of Justice FRANK MURPHY, ended a brief era of liberal activism and ushered in the bleakest period for CIVIL LIBERTIES in the Court's history. President FRANKLIN D. ROOSEVELT's eighth and last appointment to the high bench, Rutledge remained, with the exception of Murphy, the most consistently liberal member of the STONE and VINSON COURTS.

When dean of the law school of the University of Iowa, Rutledge's support for FDR's New Deal, including the "court-packing" proposal, earned him an appointment to the Circuit Court of Appeals for the District of Columbia in 1939. There he consistently endorsed the social and economic reforms of the Roosevelt administration and also compiled a strong record on civil liberties. In one opinion Rutledge dissented on FIRST AMENDMENT grounds when the judges upheld a local license tax levied against itinerant religious preachers.

A year later, as the newest member of the Stone Court, Rutledge provided the fifth and crucial vote in a coalition including HUGO L. BLACK, WILLIAM O. DOUGLAS, Murphy, and Chief Justice HARLAN FISKE STONE that overturned the Supreme Court's own ruling in a similar case decided six months earlier

(*Jones v. Opelika,* 1943; MURDOCK V. PENNSYLVANIA, 1943). He also joined Justice ROBERT H. JACKSON's opinion in *West Virginia State Board of Education v. Barnette* (1943). (See FLAG SALUTE CASES.)

Rutledge's jurisprudence blended economic nationalism with compassion for the economically disadvantaged and extreme sensitivity to individual rights. He endorsed, for example, interpretation of the WAGNER ACT to cover local newspaper carriers and believed that the minimum wage provisions of the FAIR LABOR STANDARDS ACT benefited all employees "throughout the farthest reaches of the channels of INTERSTATE COMMERCE."

To protect workers from exploitation, Rutledge believed, the federal government could prohibit entirely homework in the embroidery industry. To protect consumers from abuses, the federal government could prosecute insurance companies under the SHERMAN ANTITRUST ACT, despite more than a half century of precedent to the contrary. (See UNITED STATES V. SOUTH-EASTERN UNDERWRITERS ASSOCIATION, 1944.) He consistently supported the constitutional and statutory rights of working-class Americans, even when the legislative history of the particular law under discussion appeared in doubt (UNITED STATES V. UNITED MINE WORKERS, 1947).

At the same time, Rutledge's concern for individual rights extended even to corporations and capitalists, two groups which often lay beyond the constitutional protection offered by other New Deal liberals on the Court. Unlike Justice FELIX FRANKFURTER, for example, he did not believe that Congress had intended in the pure FOOD AND DRUG LAWS to impose criminal liability upon corporate executives without a finding of personal culpability or negligence. Nor did he believe that Congress could punish violators of wartime price regulations without jury trials and without opportunity to contest the regulations' legality in enforcement proceedings. (See YAKUS V. UNITED STATES, 1944; JUDICIAL SYSTEM.)

Rutledge endorsed without hesitation the concept of PREFERRED FREEDOMS articulated by Justice Stone in UNITED STATES V. CAROLENE PRODUCTS CO. (1938). FREEDOM OF SPEECH and PRESS, RELIGIOUS LIBERTY, the right to vote, and judicial protection for "discrete and insular minorities" served as the cornerstones of his philosophy. Like Stone, he, too, failed to implement these ideals in the infamous JAPANESE AMERICAN CASES, but, those apart, his civil liberties record remained impeccable. His most memorable CIVIL LIBERTIES opinions came in *Thomas v. Collins* (1944), where he wrote for a five-man majority that reversed the conviction of a labor organizer who had been convicted of contempt for speaking at a union rally without a permit; in EVERSON V. BOARD OF EDUCATION (1947), where he dissented against an opinion that sustained the constitutionality of state aid to the parents of children in parochial schools for bus transportation; and IN RE YAMASHITA (1946), where he and Murphy alone dissented against the drumhead trial of a vanquished Japanese general before an American military commission. With eloquence, heat, and sarcasm, Rutledge denounced the proceedings as "the most flagrant . . . departure . . . from the whole British-American tradition of the COMMON LAW and the Constitution."

He subscribed as well to Justice Black's notion that the DUE PROCESS clause of the FOURTEENTH AMENDMENT "incorporated" the specific protections of the BILL OF RIGHTS, but in the case of ADAMSON V. CALIFORNIA (1947), Rutledge and Murphy were also prepared to go far beyond Black's reasoning to hold that "occasions may arise where a proceeding falls so far short of conforming to fundamental standards of procedure as to warrant constitutional condemnation in terms of a lack of due process despite the absence of a specific provision in the Bill of Rights." (See INCORPORATION DOCTRINE.)

Had Rutledge and Murphy lived, the course of constitutional development in the McCarthy era of the early 1950s might have been healthier for both the Court and the country.

MICHAEL E. PARRISH

Bibliography

HARPER, FOWLER 1965 *Justice Rutledge and the Bright Constellation.* Indianapolis: Bobbs-Merrill.

MANN, W. HOWARD 1950 Rutledge and Civil Liberties. *Indiana Law Journal* 25:532–558.

RUTLEDGE COURT

See: Supreme Court, 1789–1801

Encyclopedia of the American Constitution

Editorial Board

Encyclopedia of the American Constitution

LEONARD W. LEVY, Editor-in-Chief
Claremont Graduate School, Claremont, California

KENNETH L. KARST, Associate Editor
University of California, Los Angeles

DENNIS J. MAHONEY, Assistant Editor
Claremont Graduate School, Claremont, California

MACMILLAN PUBLISHING COMPANY
A Division of Macmillan, Inc.
NEW YORK

Collier Macmillan Publishers
LONDON

Macmillan Publishing Company
A Division of Macmillan, Inc.
866 Third Avenue, New York, NY 10022

Collier Macmillan Canada, Inc.

Printed in the United States of America

printing number
1 2 3 4 5 6 7 8 9 10

Library of Congress Catalog in Publication Data

Encyclopedia of the American Constitution.

Includes index.
1. United States—Constitutional Law—Dictionaries.
I. Levy, Leonard Williams, 1923– II. Karst, Kenneth L. III. Mahoney, Dennis J.
KF4548.E53 1986 342.73'023'03 86–3038
ISBN 0–02–918610–2 347.3022303
ISBN (this edition) 0-02-918695-1

STAFF:

Charles E. Smith, *Publisher*
Elly Dickason, *Project Editor*
Morton I. Rosenberg, *Production Manager*
Joan Greenfield, *Designer*

Complete and unabridged edition 1990

SACCO AND VANZETTI CASE

See: *Commonwealth v. Sacco and Vanzetti*

SAN ANTONIO INDEPENDENT SCHOOL DISTRICT v. RODRIGUEZ
411 U.S. 1 (1973)

Rodriguez was the BURGER COURT's definitive statement on the subject of EQUAL PROTECTION guarantees against WEALTH DISCRIMINATION—and the statement was that the Court wanted the subject to go away.

Under Texas law, the financing of local school districts relies heavily on local property taxes. Thus a district rich in taxable property can levy taxes at low rates and still spend almost twice as much per pupil as a poor district can spend, even when the poor district taxes its property at high rates. A federal district court, relying on WARREN COURT precedents, concluded that wealth was a SUSPECT CLASSIFICATION, that education was a FUNDAMENTAL INTEREST, and thus that strict judicial scrutiny of the state-imposed inequalities was required. The trial court also concluded that, even if the permissive RATIONAL BASIS standard of review were appropriate, the Texas school finance system lacked any reasonable basis. The Supreme Court reversed, 5–4, in an opinion by Justice LEWIS F. POWELL that was plainly designed as a comprehensive pronouncement about equal protection doctrine.

The opinion was definitive, as a coffin is definitive. Despite what the Court had said in BROWN V. BOARD OF EDUCATION (1954) about education as the key to effective citizenship, here it said that education was not a fundamental interest in the sense that triggered STRICT SCRUTINY—at least not when some minimal level of education was being provided. Indeed, said the majority, the courts lacked power to create new substantive rights by defining interests as "fundamental," unless those interests were already guaranteed elsewhere in the Constitution. Here was formal recognition of the Burger Court's zero-population-growth policy for fundamental interests.

Nor was wealth a suspect classification. Decisions such as GRIFFIN V. ILLINOIS (1956) and DOUGLAS V. CALIFORNIA (1963) had involved INDIGENTS "completely unable to pay" for the benefits at stake, who "sustained an absolute deprivation" of the benefits. Here, the deprivation was only relative; pupils in poor districts were receiving some education. Furthermore, although the trial court had found a significant correlation between district wealth and family wealth, the Supreme Court held the proof of that correlation insufficient; poor children, after all, might live in the shadows of a rich district's factories. In any case, Justice Powell concluded, the evidence was mixed on the question whether school spending affected the quality of education.

Because there was no occasion for strict scrutiny, the Court employed the rational basis standard of review. Contrary to the district court's conclusion, the Texas financing scheme was rationally designed to maintain local control over school spending and educational policy. Justice BYRON R. WHITE, dissenting, attacked this asserted rationality. If "local control" flowed from control over the spending of money, then Texas, by relying heavily on the property tax and by drawing its district lines, had parceled out that choice in an irrationally selective way, to rich districts and not to poor ones.

Justice THURGOOD MARSHALL's dissent was the most powerful equal protection opinion of the Burger Court era. He elaborated on his DANDRIDGE V. WILLIAMS (1970) dissent, rejecting a two-tier system of standards of review in favor of a "sliding-scale" approach tying the level of judicial scrutiny to the importance of the interests at stake and the degree to which the state's classification bore on the powerless. Here, on both counts, judicial scrutiny should be heightened well above the level of requiring only minimal rationality. In any case, the Court had not, in the *Griffin/Douglas* line of cases, insisted on a showing of absolute deprivation as a condition of strict scrutiny of wealth discrimination; the problem in those cases was the *adequacy* of an appeal, as affected by a discrimination between rich and poor. The Texas scheme could not survive any heightened judicial scrutiny—as the majority itself had virtually conceded.

Justice Powell, a former school board president, surely feared judicial intrusion into the decisions of local school officials. Beyond that narrow concern, the majority undoubtedly worried about judicial intrusion into the allocation of state resources. These are legitimate concerns. The question was, and remains, what kinds of economic inequality, *imposed by the state itself,* can be tolerated in the face of a constitutional guarantee of the equal protection of the laws.

KENNETH L. KARST

(SEE ALSO: *Education and the Constitution; Plyler v. Doe, 1982.*)

Bibliography

MICHELMAN, FRANK I. 1969 The Supreme Court, 1968 Term—Foreword: On Protecting the Poor Through the Fourteenth Amendment. *Harvard Law Review* 83:7–59.

SANFORD, EDWARD T.
(1865–1930)

Edward Terry Sanford was the last of WARREN HARDING's four Supreme Court appointments. He had served fifteen years as a federal judge in Tennessee and, as with many of Harding's judicial appointments, he was chosen in large part because of Chief Justice WILLIAM HOWARD TAFT's lobbying activities.

For nearly seven years, Sanford loyally followed and served Taft. He began his tenure by joining a rare Taft dissent when the Court invalidated the DISTRICT OF COLUMBIA MINIMUM WAGE LAW in ADKINS V. CHILDREN'S HOSPITAL (1923). He was a regular member of the Chief Justice's Sunday afternoon extracurricular conferences, which excluded the Court's more liberal members such as OLIVER WENDELL HOLMES, LOUIS D. BRANDEIS, and HARLAN F. STONE. In a final coincidence, Sanford died on March 8, 1930, the same day as Taft.

Sanford's most important contribution to constitutional law during his brief tenure came in the area of CIVIL LIBERTIES. In GITLOW V. NEW YORK (1925) he led the Court in sustaining New York's criminal anarchy statute. Sanford's opinion largely reiterated the Court's BAD TENDENCY TEST regarding FREEDOM OF SPEECH, arguing that the state had a right to protect itself against speech that called for the overthrow of government. The state could not, he said, "reasonably be required to measure the danger from every such utterance in the nice balance of a jeweler's scale." But Sanford also acknowledged that the FOURTEENTH AMENDMENT incorporated the FIRST AMENDMENT's guarantees of free speech and FREEDOM OF THE PRESS against STATE ACTION. That INCORPORATION DOCTRINE had momentous consequences for the Court's later views of CIVIL RIGHTS and LIBERTIES.

In WHITNEY V. CALIFORNIA (1927) Sanford again sustained a criminal anarchy conviction. But the same day, in *Fiske v. Kansas,* he spoke for the Court when for the first time the Justices overturned a state conviction on the ground that a criminal anarchy statute had been applied to deny the defendant his freedom of speech, as guaranteed by the First and Fourteenth Amendments. Sanford found that the state had failed to provide evidence of the organization's criminal or violent purposes. Shortly after Sanford's death, the Court nullified a state criminal anarchy statute and a state law sanctioning the suppression of certain newspapers, with both decisions (STROMBERG V. CALIFORNIA, 1931; NEAR V. MINNESOTA, 1931) implementing Sanford's *Gitlow* incorporation doctrine.

Sanford generally concurred with the Court's decisions involving national and state ECONOMIC REGULATION. For example, he joined in approving ZONING laws in EUCLID V. AMBLER REALTY CO. (1926), and he agreed that a Pennsylvania statute requiring drugstore owners to be registered pharmacists was unconstitutional in *Lambert v. Yellowley* (1926). But in *Ma-*

ple Floor Association v. United States (1925) Sanford joined Taft's dissent protesting the Court's holding that trade associations did not violate the SHERMAN ANTITRUST ACT. In *Tyson v. Banton* (1927) Sanford, dissenting from a ruling that invalidated regulations of theater ticket brokers, invoked the STATE POLICE POWER doctrine of the GRANGER CASES (1877); he argued that because the brokers' business was AFFECTED WITH A PUBLIC INTEREST, the legislature could protect "the public from extortion and exorbitant rates."

Sanford's Supreme Court tenure was, on the whole, unremarkable. There is irony in that his *Gitlow* opinion, despite its antilibertarian result, laid the foundation for the mid-twentieth-century libertarian revolution and the nationalization of American CIVIL RIGHTS and CIVIL LIBERTIES.

STANLEY I. KUTLER

Bibliography

RAGAN, ALLEN E. 1943 Mr. Justice Sanford. *East Tennessee Historical Society Publications* 15:74–88.

SAN MATEO COUNTY v. SOUTHERN PACIFIC RAILROAD

See: Person

SANTA CLARA COUNTY v. SOUTHERN PACIFIC RAILROAD

See: Person

SAWYER, LORENZO (1820–1891)

In 1870 ULYSSES S. GRANT commissioned Lorenzo Sawyer of California judge of the Ninth Circuit Court, a position he filled until his death. Throughout these years, Sawyer shared circuit court duties with Supreme Court Justice STEPHEN J. FIELD.

Sawyer formulated a narrow interpretation of the PUBLIC PURPOSE DOCTRINE and STATE POLICE POWERS. He declared that a state could not, consistently with the FOURTEENTH AMENDMENT, define the public purpose to permit mining companies to cause flooding of private lands. Sawyer also resisted local efforts to discriminate against the Chinese under the guise of the POLICE POWER. In 1890 he struck down a San Francisco ordinance, which required Chinese to live and work in a designated area of the city, as an "arbitrary confiscation of property without DUE PROCESS or any process of law." Sawyer also invalidated other suspect uses of the police power that sought to harass the Chinese by outlawing the operation of laundries and opium parlors. Such measures, he ruled, placed "an unlawful inhibition upon the inalienable rights and liberties of [all] citizens. . . ."

Sawyer subscribed to the doctrine of DUAL FEDERALISM, but in *In Re Neagle* he forcefully recited the supremacy of the federal government. David Neagle, a United States marshal and bodyguard for Justice Field, had killed a man to protect Field. Sawyer issued a writ of HABEAS CORPUS releasing Neagle from custody by California officials on charges of murder. He held that the marshal had acted in pursuance of the laws of the United States and that "a state law, which contravenes a valid law of the United States, is, in the nature of things, necessarily void—a nullity."

Justice Field cast a large shadow over jurisprudence of the Ninth Circuit, but Sawyer also significantly shaped American constitutional law. His opinions were a major source of authority on the police powers of the states, the public purpose doctrine, and the Fourteenth Amendment.

KERMIT L. HALL

Bibliography

SWISHER, CARL BRENT 1930 *Stephen J. Field, Craftsman of the Law.* Pages 325–326, 332, 337, 342, 352, 353, 355, 358–359. Washington, D.C.: Brookings Institution.

SCALES v. UNITED STATES 367 U.S. 203 (1961)

The Supreme Court, always careful to avoid declaring the Smith Act unconstitutional, instead employed statutory interpretation to emasculate its provisions. Here the Court held that the act's clause banning "membership" in certain organizations applied only to members active in the organization's affairs, knowing that its purpose was to bring about the overthrow of the government by force and violence as speedily as circumstances would permit, and with the specific purpose to bring about that overthrow. In the *Scales* case itself, the Court affirmed a conviction under the membership clause. Since that time, however, the act's forbidding BURDEN OF PROOF has discouraged further prosecutions.

MARTIN SHAPIRO

SCHAD v. MOUNT EPHRAIM
452 U.S. 61 (1981)

The Supreme Court, 7–2, reversed the conviction of the operators of an "adult" bookstore for violating a ZONING ordinance of a residential town by presenting live entertainment in the form of nude dancing. The state courts had construed the ordinance to forbid all live entertainment; so read, it fell afoul of the FIRST AMENDMENT doctrine of OVERBREADTH. The Court concluded that the state's asserted justifications (limiting commerce to residents' "immediate needs," and avoiding problems with parking, trash, and the like) were unsupported by the record, which showed that live entertainment was offered in three other establishments. The dissenters argued that, although banning other entertainment might present First Amendment problems, banning nude dancing did not.

KENNETH L. KARST

SCHALL v. MARTIN
467 U.S. 253 (1984)

This is one of several cases showing that legal fictions infect JUVENILE PROCEEDINGS involving criminal conduct. *Schall* reflected the fictions that juveniles, unlike adults, "are always in some form of custody" and that PREVENTIVE DETENTION is not punitive and is designed to protect the youthful offender as well as society from the consequences of his uncommitted crimes. New York, without distinguishing first offenders from recidivists and without distinguishing trivial offenses from major crimes of violence, allowed juveniles, aged seven to sixteen, to be jailed for up to seventeen days pending adjudication of guilt. Justice WILLIAM H. REHNQUIST, for a 6–3 Supreme Court, ruled that preventive detention in the case of juveniles is compatible with the FUNDAMENTAL FAIRNESS required by the FOURTEENTH AMENDMENT's guarantee of DUE PROCESS OF LAW. Rehnquist found adequate procedural safeguards in the New York statute, noted that every state permitted preventive detention of juveniles accused of crime, and declared that the juveniles' best interests were served because preventive detention disabled them from committing other crimes prior to the date of court appearance. Justices THURGOOD MARSHALL, WILLIAM J. BRENNAN, and JOHN PAUL STEVENS, dissenting, insisted that the majority's factual argument did not survive critical scrutiny any more than did the statute provide due process.

LEONARD W. LEVY

SCHECHTER POULTRY CORP. v. UNITED STATES
295 U.S. 495 (1935)

After the decision in this case, striking down the NATIONAL INDUSTRIAL RECOVERY ACT, a conservative gave thanks that the Constitution still stood, while a liberal wondered whether it stood still. The Supreme Court's "horse and buggy" interpretation, as President FRANKLIN D. ROOSEVELT called it, imperiled the power of the United States to control any part of the economy that the Court regarded as subject to the exclusive control of the states. Chief Justice CHARLES EVANS HUGHES, for the Court, first held the statute void because it improperly delegated legislative powers. Private business groups might frame codes governing their industries as long as NRA officials approved and the president promulgated them. Hughes said the president's discretion was "unfettered," and even Justice BENJAMIN N. CARDOZO, who had dissented in PANAMA REFINING CO. V. RYAN (1935), separately concurred and spoke of "delegation running riot." Improper DELEGATION [of power] could have been rectified by new legislation, but the Court also held the act unauthorized by the COMMERCE CLAUSE, leaving the impression that labor matters and trade practices were beyond the scope of congressional power unless in INTERSTATE COMMERCE or directly affecting it.

The government argued that although Schechter sold only in the local market, its business was in the STREAM OF COMMERCE. Ninety-six percent of the poultry sold in New York City came from out of state. Hughes rejected that argument by ruling that the flow of interstate commerce had ceased, because the poultry had come to a permanent rest in the city: it was sold locally and did not again leave the state. The government also invoked the SHREVEPORT DOCTRINE, arguing that even if the commerce here were local, it had so close and substantial a relationship to interstate commerce that its federal regulation was necessary to protect interstate commerce. Schechter's preferential trade practices, low wages, and long hours, in violation of the poultry code, enabled it to undersell competitors, diverting the interstate flow of poultry to its own market, injuring interstate competitors, and triggering a cycle of wage and price cutting that threatened to extend beyond the confines of the local market. This entire line of reasoning, Hughes said, proved too much. It laid the basis for national regulation of the entire economy, overriding state authority. It also ignored the fundamental distinction between direct and indirect effects upon interstate commerce. What that distinction was Hughes did not explain, but he asserted that Schechter's violations of the code only indirectly affected interstate commerce and therefore stood beyond national reach. Even Cardozo, joined by Justice HARLAN FISKE STONE, declared that "to find immediacy or directness here is to find it almost everywhere."

Schechter temporarily ended national regulation of industry and allowed Roosevelt to blame the Court, even though the NRA's code programs were cumbersome, unpopular, and scheduled for political extinction. The Court's views of the commerce clause made no substitute constitutionally feasible.

LEONARD W. LEVY

SCHENCK v. UNITED STATES
249 U.S. 47 (1919)

The FREEDOM OF SPEECH provisions of the FIRST AMENDMENT played a singularly retiring role in American constitutional law until the time of World War I or, more precisely, until the Russian Revolution and the Red Scare that it generated in the United States. The Sedition Act of 1798 (see ALIEN AND SEDITION ACTS) obviously posed serious First Amendment questions but was not tested in the Supreme Court and was soon repealed. A scattering of free speech claims and oblique pronouncements by the federal courts occurred after 1900, but speech issues, even when they did arise, typically appeared in state courts in the contexts of OBSCENITY prosecutions and labor disputes. The Court did not declare the First Amendment applicable to the states through the due process clause of the FOURTEENTH AMENDMENT (see INCORPORATION DOCTRINE) until GITLOW V. NEW YORK (1925). Furthermore, in its most direct pronouncement on the freedom of speech provision of the First Amendment, *Patterson v. Colorado* (1907), the Court, speaking through Justice OLIVER WENDELL HOLMES, had suggested that the provision barred only prior restraints, a position that Holmes abandoned in *Schenck*.

In 1917 Congress passed an ESPIONAGE ACT making it a crime to cause or attempt to cause insubordination in the armed forces, obstruct recruitment or enlistment, and otherwise urge, incite, or advocate obstruction or resistance to the war effort. Although there had been much bitter debate about U. S. entry into World War I, the speakers whose prosecutions raised First Amendment issues that ultimately reached the Supreme Court were not German sympathizers. They were left-wing sympathizers with the Russian Revolution who were provoked by the dispatch of Allied expeditionary forces to Russia. If the American war machine was to be turned on the Revolution, it must be stopped.

Prosecutions of such revolutionary sympathizers triggered three important federal court decisions that initiated the jurisprudence of the First Amendment: MASSES PUBLISHING COMPANY V. PATTEN (1917), *Schenck v. United States*, and ABRAMS V. UNITED STATES (1919). *Schenck* was the first major Supreme Court pronouncement on freedom of speech.

Schenck was general secretary of the Socialist Party which distributed to prospective draftees a leaflet denouncing CONSCRIPTION and urging recipients to assert their opposition to it. He was convicted of conspiracy to violate the Espionage Act by attempting to obstruct recruiting. Following his own earlier writing on attempts, Holmes, writing for a unanimous Court, said: It seems to be admitted that if an actual obstruction of the recruiting service were proved, liability for words that produced that effect might be enforced. The statute of 1917 . . . punishes conspiracies to obstruct as well as actual obstruction. If the act (speaking, or circulating a paper), its tendency and the intent with which it is done are the same, we perceive no ground for saying that success alone warrants making the act a crime. In response to Schenck's First Amendment claims, Holmes said:

> We admit that in many places and in ordinary times the defendants in saying all that was said in the circular would have been within their constitutional rights. But the character of every act depends upon the circumstances in which it is done. The most stringent protection of free speech would not protect a man in falsely shouting fire in a theatre and causing a panic. . . . The question in every case is whether the words used are used in such circumstances and are of such a nature as to create a CLEAR AND PRESENT DANGER that they will bring about the substantive evils that Congress has a right to prevent. It is a question of proximity and degree.

That the clear and present danger test was first announced in a context in which speech was treated as an attempt to commit an illegal act rather than in a situation in which the statute declared certain speech itself criminal was important for several reasons. First, the attempts context necessarily drew the judicial focus to the nexus between speech and criminal action and thus to the circumstances in which the speech was uttered rather than to the content of the speech itself. Questions of intent and circumstances, crucial to the law of attempts, thus became crucial to the danger test. Second, if the link between speech and illegal act was necessarily a question of degree, then much discretion was necessarily left to the judge. The clear and present danger test has often been criticized for leaving speakers at the mercy of judicial discretion. Having invoked the danger test, the Court affirmed Schenck's conviction. Third, supporters of judicial self-restraint subsequently sought to narrow the scope of the danger test by insisting that it was to be employed only in situations where the government sought to prosecute speech under a statute proscribing only action. In this view, the test was inapplicable when the legislature itself had proscribed speech, having made its own independent, prior judgment that a certain class of speech created a danger warranting suppression.

Although Holmes wrote in Schenck for a unanimous court, he and Justice LOUIS D. BRANDEIS were the danger test's sole supporters in the other leading cases of the 1920s: *Abrams, Gitlow,* and WHITNEY V. CALIFORNIA (1927). A comparison of these cases indicates that Holmes's "tough guy" pose was deeply implicated in his clear and present danger decisions. In the later cases, Holmes seemed to be saying that a self-confident democracy ought not to descend to the prosecution of fringe-group rantings about socialist revolution. In *Schenck,* however, where the speech was concretely pointed at obstructing war time recruitment, Holmes said: "When a nation is at war, many things that might be said in time of peace are such a hindrance to its effort that their utterance will not be endured so long as men fight and that no Court could regard them as protected by any constitutional right."

MARTIN SHAPIRO

Bibliography

CHAFEE, ZECHARIAH 1941 *Free Speech in the United States.* Cambridge, Mass.: Harvard University Press.

SCHEUER v. RHODES
416 U.S. 236 (1974)

This decision established that high state officers are not absolutely immune from suit for constitutional violations. Ohio National Guard troops shot and killed four students demonstrating against the VIETNAM WAR. The deceased students' representatives sued Governor James Rhodes and other state officials, alleging reckless deployment of the Guard and unlawful orders to the Guard which led to the shootings. The Supreme Court held Rhodes not to be absolutely immune from suit. The Court did indicate that officials with substantial discretionary responsibilities are to be given greater deference than officials with more limited tasks. *Rhodes* connects the first SECTION 1983 case on EXECUTIVE IMMUNITY, PIERSON V. RAY (1967), with later decisions such as WOOD V. STRICKLAND (1975) and *Procunier v. Navarette* (1978).

THEODORE EISENBERG

SCHICK v. REED
419 U.S. 256 (1974)

In a 5–4 decision, the Supreme Court upheld the President's right to grant conditional clemency. Maurice Schick, convicted of murder in 1954 by a court-martial, was sentenced to death. In 1960, under Article II, section 2, clause 1, of the Constitution, President DWIGHT D. EISENHOWER commuted the sentence to life imprisonment without parole. Citing FURMAN V. GEORGIA (1972), Schick asked the Court to hold the no-parole condition unconstitutional. But the court held that the PARDONING POWER flows from the Constitution alone and may not be limited except by the Constitution itself.

DENNIS J. MAHONEY

SCHMERBER v. CALIFORNIA
384 U.S. 757 (1966)

Justice WILLIAM J. BRENNAN, for a 6–3 majority of the Supreme Court, ruled that the taking of a blood sample from the petitioner over his objections, to prove his guilt for driving under the influence of alcohol, did not constitute TESTIMONINAL COMPULSION and therefore did not violate the RIGHT AGAINST SELF-INCRIMINATION, nor did it constitute an invalid WARRANTLESS SEARCH under the EXIGENT CIRCUMSTANCES.

LEONARD W. LEVY

SCHNECKLOTH v. BUSTAMONTE
412 U.S. 218 (1973)

The police may conduct a search without a warrant when consent is freely given. Before *Schneckloth,* some lower courts had taken the position that consent was not voluntary unless the prosecution could demonstrate that the person was aware of his right to refuse consent. Others held that knowledge of the right to refuse was merely one element to be considered, and that consent was established by the totality of the circumstances. In *Schneckloth* the Supreme Court adopted the latter position.

The Court distinguished the FOURTH AMENDMENT from other constitutional guarantees (for example, the RIGHT TO COUNSEL) for which the Court had required an intentional relinquishment of the right. The other guarantees intend to promote the ascertainment of truth in a trial; the Fourth Amendment, on the other hand, does not promote pursuit of truth but secures PRIVACY. The requirement of MIRANDA RULE warnings prior to POLICE INTERROGATION was also an inapposite analogy, for the coercion inherent in a custodial environment is unlikely to be duplicated "on a person's own familiar territory."

Justice LEWIS POWELL, concurring, set forth views later adopted by the Court in STONE v. POWELL (1976), proposing radical restrictions on the use of HABEAS CORPUS to review Fourth Amendment violations by state officers. Three dissenting Justices took the position that mere absence of coercion is not the equivalent of a meaningful choice; that "a decision made without actual knowledge of available alternatives" is not "a choice at all."

JACOB W. LANDYNSKI

SCHNELL v. DAVIS
336 U.S. 933 (1949)

In a PER CURIAM opinion, the Supreme Court affirmed a district court JUDGMENT. Davis had brought a CLASS ACTION, arguing that enforcement of Alabama's "Boswell Amendment" violated the VOTING RIGHTS of blacks. The amendment, adopted in 1946 to circumvent the decision in SMITH v. ALLWRIGHT (1944), made the ability to "understand and explain" the Constitution a requirement for voter registration. The record showed that this "understanding clause" was used exclusively to deny registration to blacks. The Court held that the requirement violated the FIFTEENTH AMENDMENT because it was used to deny the right to vote on account of race or color.

DENNIS J. MAHONEY

SCHOOL BUSING

Before BROWN v. BOARD OF EDUCATION (1954–1955) was decided, many a southern child rode the bus to school, passing on the way a bus headed in the other direction, loaded with children of another race. The busing of children was "one tool" used to maintain a system of school SEGREGATION. As late as 1970, before the Supreme Court had approved a single busing order, about forty percent of the nation's children rode buses to school. The school bus had permitted the replacement of rural one-room schoolhouses with consolidated schools; in the city, riding the bus had been thought safer than walking. School busing did not become the object of majoritarian anger until the 1970s, when the Supreme Court described it as "one tool" for dismantling a segregated system and affirmed its use not only in the South but also in the cities of the North and West.

In a rural southern county, the simplest form of DESEGREGATION might drastically reduce school busing; racial living patterns would permit integration of the schools through the discontinuation of racial assignments and assignment of children to the schools nearest their homes. In the cities, however, residential segregation had been so thorough that the abandonment of racial assignments and the substitution of a neighborhood school policy would not end the separation of school children by race. The question was asked: Would the Supreme Court insist on more than the end of racial assignments—on the actual mixing of black and white children in the schools—by way of dismantling segregation produced by deliberate official policy? In SWANN v. CHARLOTTE-MECKLENBURG BOARD OF EDUCATION (1971), the Court answered that question affirmatively. Then, in KEYES v. SCHOOL DISTRICT NO. 1 (1973) and COLUMBUS BOARD OF EDUCATION v. PENICK (1979), the Court extended *Swann*'s commands to the North and West, in ways that blurred the DE FACTO/DE JURE distinction. Once a constitutional violation is found, even in remote acts of deliberate segregation by a school board, then as a practical matter the district court's remedial goal becomes "the greatest possible degree of actual desegregation"—and that, in a large city, means the busing of massive numbers of children for the purpose of achieving the maximum practicable RACIAL BALANCE.

Apart from the busing ordered by courts, some busing for integration purposes has resulted from voluntary programs, mostly involving the busing of minority children to schools formerly populated by non-Hispanic whites. Political resistance has been directed not to those programs but to busing ordered by a court over the opposition of the school board and of large numbers of parents and children. The most outspoken protest has come from white parents. The responses of school board majorities have varied, from political warfare in Boston and Los Angeles to the "let's-make-it-work" attitude in Columbus.

President RICHARD M. NIXON, whose first electoral campaign adopted a "Southern strategy" and whose campaign for reelection included an attack on school busing, proposed congressional legislation to restrict busing. In 1974 Congress purported to forbid a federal court to order a student's transportation to a school "other than the school closest or next closest to his place of residence." This statute's constitutionality would have been dubious but for a proviso that canceled its effect: the law was not to diminish the authority of federal courts to enforce the Constitution.

The school busing issue has forced a reevaluation of the goals of desegregation. In *Brown* the chief harm of school segregation imposed by law was said to be the stigma of inferiority, which impaired black children's motivation to learn. The fact of separation of the races in urban schools may or may not have the same stigmatic effect—even though deliberately segregative governmental actions have contributed to residential segregation in cities throughout the nation. Stigma aside, it is far from clear that racial isolation alone impairs minority children's learning. In communities with substantial Hispanic or Asian-American populations, concerns about the maintenance of cultural identity are apt to be expressed in opposition to taking children out of neighborhood schools and away from bilingual education programs. The call for "community control" of schools is heard less frequently in black communities today than it was around 1970, but some prominent black CIVIL RIGHTS leaders have placed increasing emphasis on improvement of the schools and decreasing emphasis on the busing of children.

Part of the reason for this shift in emphasis surely is a sense of despair over the prospects of busing as an effective means of achieving integration. Social scientists disagree on the amount of "white flight" that has resulted from court-ordered busing. Some demographic changes are merely extensions of a long-established pattern of middle-class migration to the suburbs. The Supreme Court in MILLIKEN V. BRADLEY (1974) made clear that metropolitan relief, combining city and suburban districts for purposes of school integration, was allowable only in rare circumstances. "White flight" can also take the form of withdrawal of children from public schools; recent estimates suggest that about one-fifth of the students in the nation's private schools have fled from desegregation orders. In this perspective, the neighborhood school is seen not only as a focus for community but also, less appetizingly, as a means for controlling children's associations and passing social advantage from one generation to the next. Either strategy of "white flight" costs money. It is no accident that the hottest opposition to court-ordered school busing has come from working-class neighborhoods, where people feel that they have been singled out to bear a burden in order to validate an ideal they have come to doubt.

School busing for integration purposes has come under strong political attack. Neither Congress nor a state can constitutionally prohibit busing designed to remedy *de jure* segregation. However, state measures limiting busing designed to remedy *de facto* segregation may or may not be upheld, depending on the legislation's purposes and effects. (See WASHINGTON V. SEATTLE SCHOOL DISTRICT NO. 1, 1982; CRAWFORD V. LOS ANGELES BOARD OF EDUCATION, 1982.)

Sadly, it is realistic to assume the continuation of urban residential segregation, which has diminished only slightly since 1940, despite nearly half a century of civil rights litigation and legislation. (Even the migration of increasing numbers of middle-class black families to the suburbs has not significantly diminished residential segregation.) Given that assumption, the nation must choose between accepting racially separate schools and using school busing to achieve integration. The first choice will seem to many citizens a betrayal of the promise of *Brown.* The second choice faces opposition strong enough to threaten not only the nation's historic commitment to public education but also its commitment to obedience to law. The resolution of this dilemma is a challenge not only to courts but also to school board members and citizens, demanding imagination, patience, and good will in quantities far beyond their recent supply.

KENNETH L. KARST

Bibliography

BELL, DERRICK A., JR. 1976 Serving Two Masters: Integration Ideals and Client Interests in School Desegregation Litigation. *Yale Law Journal* 85:470–516.

DIMOND, PAUL R. 1985 *Beyond Busing: Inside the Challenge to Urban Segregation.* Ann Arbor: University of Michigan Press.

FISS, OWEN M. 1975 The Jurisprudence of Busing. *Law and Contemporary Problems* 39:194–216.

WILKINSON, J. HARVIE, III 1979 *From Brown to Bakke.* New York: Oxford University Press.

SCHOOL DESEGRATION

See: Desegregation

SCHOOL PRAYER

See: Religion in Public Schools

SCHOULER, JAMES
(1839–1920)

Massachusetts-born James Schouler, while a Union officer in the Civil War, contracted a fever that left him nearly deaf. He nevertheless rose to national prominence as an attorney and historian. Although his law practice was successful—his first Supreme Court victory was *Hosmer v. United States,* 1872)—he gave it up (because of his disability) in favor of teaching. His main historical work was the nationalistic *History of the United States under the Constitution* (7 volumes, 1880–1913), which he conceived as the first comprehensive account of American political and legal history. He also wrote *Constitutional Studies: State and Federal* (1897) and biographies of THOMAS JEFFERSON and ALEXANDER HAMILTON.

DENNIS J. MAHONEY

SCHROEDER, THEODORE
(1864–1953)

Before World War I, Theodore Schroeder, as FELIX FRANKFURTER said, was the foremost authority in the field of FIRST AMENDMENT rights. A prosperous lawyer, he could afford to be a full-time publicist in the cause of opposing all censorship and prosecutions for seditious, blasphemous, and obscene libels. In 1902 he founded the Free Speech League, the mainstay of CIVIL LIBERTIES until the founding of the AMERICAN CIVIL LIBERTIES UNION. ROGER BALDWIN, one of the many civil libertarians whom Schroeder influenced, declared that Schroeder "was the Free Speech League." Schroeder was an uncompromising First Amendment absolutist who defended anarchists, freethinkers, and pornographers. He also advocated equal rights for women and defended Emma Goldman and Margaret Sanger. His major works include *"Obscene" Literature and Constitutional Law* (1911), *Free Speech for Radicals* (1916), *Constitutional Free Speech Defined and Defended* (1919), and *Free Speech Bibliography* (1922).

LEONARD W. LEVY

Bibliography

AUERBACH, JEROLD 1972 (1911) Introduction to Schroeder, Theodore, *"Obscene" Literature and Constitutional Law.* New York: Da Capo Press.

SCHWARE v. NEW MEXICO BOARD OF BAR EXAMINERS
353 U.S. 232 (1957)

Schware was one of the early cases in which state bar examiners refused bar admission to persons suspected of communism. The Court overturned the refusal on DUE PROCESS grounds, holding that a finding that the applicant was a Communist party member before 1940 was constitutionally insufficient to overcome evidence of his later good moral character.

MARTIN SHAPIRO

SCHWIMMER, UNITED STATES v.
279 U.S. 644 (1929)

When Rosiki Schwimmer applied for NATURALIZATION, officials questioned whether she could take the oath to "uphold and defend the Constitution against all enemies" without reservation. She opposed war in all forms.

The question before the Supreme Court was whether Congress had intended to require willingness to perform combatant military service as a condition of naturalization. Justice PIERCE BUTLER spoke for the Court and held that Congress had. Justice OLIVER WENDELL HOLMES dissented, joined by Justice LOUIS D. BRANDEIS. Holmes noted that Schwimmer, a woman of almost sixty years, would never actually be called upon to serve. Furthermore, taking a position against resort to armed forces was simply a reform objective no different from favoring a unicameral legislature. Justice EDWARD T. SANFORD also dissented.

Schwimmer was overruled by GIROUARD V. UNITED STATES (1946).

RICHARD E. MORGAN

SCOPES v. STATE OF TENNESSEE

See: *State of Tennessee v. Scopes*

SCOTT v. ILLINOIS

See: Right to Counsel

SCOTTSBORO CASES

See: *Norris v. Alabama; Powell v. Alabama*

SCREWS v. UNITED STATES
325 U.S. 91 (1945)

Southern law enforcement officers were prosecuted under section 242 of Title 18, United States Code, a federal CIVIL RIGHTS statute, for beating to death a black arrestee. Because section 242 proscribes only action "under COLOR OF LAW," and because congressional power to enforce the FOURTEENTH AMENDMENT was assumed to be limited to reaching STATE ACTION, the question arose whether behavior not authorized by state law could be either state action or action under color of law. The Court's affirmative answer, which relied in part on UNITED STATES V. CLASSIC (1941), both established section 242 as a weapon against police misconduct and nourished the post-1960 expansion of noncriminal civil rights litigation. MONROE V. PAPE (1961), relying on *Screws* and *Classic,* similarly interpreted the "under color of" law requirement for noncriminal civil rights actions brought under SECTION 1983, TITLE 42, UNITED STATES CODE. Exclusive reliance on state law to remedy police misconduct, a position advocated in dissent in *Screws* by Justices OWEN ROBERTS, FELIX FRANKFURTER, and ROBERT H. JACKSON, would never again be the rule.

Screws also raised the question whether federal criminal civil rights statutes are unconstitutionally vague. Section 242 outlaws willful deprivations of rights secured by the Constitution. Because constitutional standards change constantly, there was doubt that section 242 provided potential defendants with adequate warning of proscribed behavior. In *Screws,* the Court sought to avoid this difficulty by holding that the word "willfully" in section 242 connotes "a purpose to deprive a person of a specific constitutional right." The Court's remand of the case to reinstruct the jury on the meaning of "willful" prompted Justice FRANK MURPHY to dissent, pointing out that the officers had contrived to beat their victim for fifteen minutes after he lost consciousness and arguing that the right to "life" protected by the Fourteenth Amendment surely included a right not to be murdered by state officials. The specific intent requirement has generated confusion in subsequent interpretations of the criminal civil rights statutes.

THEODORE EISENBERG

SEARCH, UNREASONABLE

See: Unreasonable Search

SEARCH AND SEIZURE

The FOURTH AMENDMENT has the virtue of brevity and the vice of ambiguity. It does not define the PROBABLE CAUSE required for warrants or indicate whether a WARRANTLESS SEARCH or seizure is inevitably "unreasonable" if made without probable cause, so that the factual basis required for a constitutional search or seizure is unclear. The amendment does not define the relationship of the word "unreasonable" to the clause setting forth the conditions under which warrants may issue; it is thus unclear when a judicial officer's approval must be obtained before an ARREST or search is made. There is also uncertainty as to what official conduct is subject to the amendment's restraints, that is, just what actions amount to "searches and seizures" and threaten the "right of the people to be secure." Finally, there is ambiguity concerning how that right is to be enforced; unlike the Fifth Amendment RIGHT AGAINST SELF-INCRIMINATION, no mention is made of barring from EVIDENCE the fruits of a violation of the amendment. The Supreme Court has had to respond to each of these four fundamental questions. (See RIGHT–PRIVILEGE DISTINCTION.)

The warrant clause of the Fourth Amendment makes it apparent that a valid ARREST WARRANT or SEARCH WARRANT may issue only upon a showing of probable cause to the issuing authority. This requirement is intended to prohibit resort to GENERAL WARRANTS and arrest and search on suspicion. As the Court noted in BRINEGAR V. UNITED STATES (1949), it is also intended "to give fair leeway for enforcing the law in the community's protection," and thus is best perceived as "a practical, nontechnical conception affording the best compromise that has been found for accommodating these often opposing interests" of individual privacy and collective security.

Though a literal reading of the Fourth Amendment does not compel this result, the prohibition upon "UNREASONABLE" SEARCHES and seizures has been construed to mean that even searches and seizures conducted without a warrant require probable cause. As explained in WONG SUN V. UNITED STATES (1963), "the requirements of reliability and particularity of the information on which an officer may act . . . surely cannot be less stringent [when an arrest is made without a warrant] than where an arrest warrant is obtained. Otherwise, a principal incentive now existing for the procurement of arrest warrants would be destroyed." But the amount of probable cause required for with-warrant and without-warrant searches is not exactly the same; the Court stated in *United States v. Ventresca* (1965) that because of the preference accorded to warrants, "in a doubtful or marginal case a search under a warrant may be sustainable where without one it would fail."

The same quantum of evidence is required whether one is concerned with probable cause to arrest or to search. Thus in SPINELLI V. UNITED STATES (1969), concerning probable cause for a search warrant, the Court found its earlier decision in DRAPER V. UNITED STATES (1959), concerning probable cause to arrest, to be a "suitable benchmark." But the arrest and search situations differ in important respects. For arrest, it must be sufficiently probable that an offense has been committed and that the particular individual to be arrested has committed it; for a search, it must be sufficiently probable that specified items are evidence of criminal activity and are to be found in the specified place. On a given set of facts one type of probable cause may be present but not the other.

The probable cause test is an objective rather than a subjective one. "If subjective good faith alone were the test," the Supreme Court said in *Beck v. Ohio* (1964), "the protections of the Fourth Amendment would evaporate, and the people would be 'secure in their houses, papers, and effects,' only in the discretion of the police." The question, therefore, is not what the arresting or searching officer thought but rather what a reasonable person with the experience and expertise of the officer would have thought. That assessment is to be made on all available information regardless of its admissibility in a criminal trial because, as the Court said in *Brinegar,* the probable cause test is "not technical" and involves "the factual and practical considerations of everyday life on which reasonable and prudent men, not legal technicians, act." Thus credible HEARSAY may be considered, but a person's reputation, at least when stated in terms of unsubstantiated conclusions, cannot.

Although *Brinegar* declares that probable cause requires "less than evidence which would justify . . . conviction" but yet "more than bare suspicion" and also that the question is one of "probabilities," it gives no indication as to what degree of probability is required. Some of the Court's decisions—for example, *Johnson v. United States* (1948), holding that the smell of burning opium from within a hotel room did not amount to probable cause to arrest a particular occupant because until the subsequent entry she was not known to be the sole occupant of the room—suggest a more-probable-than-not standard. But the Supreme Court has never explicitly held that the Fourth Amendment requires this standard, and the lower courts have understandably found such an interpretation too stringent in at least some circumstances. Thus, it is not uncommon to find an appellate decision holding that an arrest near a crime scene was lawful even though the victim's description was not exact or detailed enough to single the arrested person out from all other persons in the vicinity, or that a search of a number of different places under a suspect's control is permissible even though no one of them is the more-probable-than-not location of the evidence sought.

Most of the Supreme Court's probable cause cases involve information from police informants, denizens of the criminal milieu who provide information in exchange for money or informal immunity regarding their own criminal conduct. In AGUILAR V. TEXAS (1964), where the search warrant affidavit merely recited that the affiants had "received reliable information from a credible person" that "narcotics and narcotics paraphernalia are being kept at the above described premises," the Court adopted a two-pronged test. This affidavit was held insufficient because, first, it did not disclose how the informant knew what he claimed to know concerning what was in the house; and second, it did not disclose how the affiants concluded that their informer was reliable. The first prong of this test has usually been met with details about how the informant acquired his knowledge (for instance, that he had just been inside the house and saw there a cache of narcotics from which the occupant made a sale), though it can be indirectly satisfied by self-verifying detail. As explained in *Spinelli,* if the informant gives a great many details about the criminal scheme (the precise amount of narcotics in the house, how it is wrapped, exactly where it is stored), then it may be inferred "that the informant had gained his information in a reliable way."

The second or "veracity" prong of *Aguilar* has typically been met on the basis of past performance, that is, by a recitation that this same informant previously has given information that turned out to be correct. Alternatively, it has sufficed to show, as in UNITED STATES V. HARRIS (1971), that the informant's statement included an admission against penal interest ("I bought some narcotics while I was in that house"), as people "do not lightly admit a crime and place critical evidence in the hands of the police in the form of their own admissions." The Supreme Court sometimes stressed that the informer's tale was partly corroborated, but there was considerable uncertainty as to just what deficiencies under the *Aguilar* two-pronged test this corroboration overcomes. (Because the use of informants raises special concerns not present in other situations, no comparable showing of veracity is needed when the information has been obtained from a police officer or a cooperative citizen.)

The *Aguilar* test was abandoned in ILLINOIS V. GATES (1983) in favor of a more general "totality of the circumstances" approach. The *Aguilar* factors of veracity and basis of knowledge remain as "relevant considerations," but are no longer two independent requirements; "a deficiency in one may be compensated for . . . by a strong showing as to the other." This is an unfortunate development, for the *Aguilar* rule provided a necessary structure and more precise guidance to police and judges. Moreover, the *Gates* approach is unsound, for surely—as the Court has often held—a conclusory allegation ("there are narcotics in that house") is insufficient even when it comes from a source of unquestioned reliability. *Gates* will doubtless make it easier to establish probable cause than it has been previously; the Court deemed it sufficient that the police had received an anonymous letter with a conclusory assertion of drug trafficking and then had corroborated the letter with certain predicted behavior that was not otherwise suspicious.

One extremely important question regarding the Fourth Amendment probable cause test is whether it is fixed or variable, that is, whether it always requires the same quantum of evidence or whether this compromise between privacy and law enforcement interests may be struck differently on a case-by-case basis. For example, may it be concluded that the solution of an unsolved murder is of greater public concern than the solution of an unsolved shoplifting, so that an arrest or search concerning the former would require less evidence than one respecting the latter offense? When confronted with that question in *Dunaway v. New York* (1979), the Court answered in the negative, saying such a variable standard would be impracticable: "A single, familiar standard is essential to guide police officers, who have only limited time and expertise to reflect on and balance the social and individual interests involved in the specific circumstances they confront."

Another supposed variable in *Dunaway* was that the police action at issue was a brief detention of the suspect at the police station, not recorded as an arrest. Though the Court there found the detention "indistinguishable from a traditional arrest" and thus subject to the usual probable cause requirement, on other occasions the Supreme Court has used a BALANCING TEST: when the police action is significantly less intrusive than the usual arrest or search, there is a corresponding reduction in the required factual basis justifying that action. The leading decision is the STOP AND FRISK case, TERRY V. OHIO (1968), which with later decisions may be taken to mean, first, that a brief on-the-street detention of a suspect, a distinct police practice significantly less intrusive than a full-fledged arrest, is lawful upon a reasonable suspicion of criminality falling short of that needed to arrest; and second, that a frisk of that suspect for purposes of self-protection, a distinct police practice significantly less intrusive than a complete search of the person, is lawful upon a reasonable suspicion that the suspect is armed falling short of the probable cause required for a full search.

Although this balancing in *Terry* upheld a limited seizure and search on a watered-down version of probable cause, in other situations the Supreme Court has permitted very limited routine seizures or searches even absent any case-by-case showing of suspicion. Thus CAMARA V. MUNICIPAL COURT (1967) allowed a safety inspection of a dwelling, without any showing of the likelihood of code violations in that particular dwelling, where the inspection followed "reasonable legislative or administrative standards," such as those authorizing periodic inspection. And in *Delaware v. Prouse* (1979) the Court indicated its approval of stopping a vehicle for a driver's license and vehicle registration check, even absent suspicion that the driver was unlicensed or the car unregistered, as part of a roadblock conducted under standardized procedures.

Still another line of cases requires no factual basis for a particular seizure or search provided it is conducted in connection with some other search or seizure for which there is a sufficient basis. Where such relationships exist, the law would be very complex and difficult to apply if multiple factual bases were required, and thus sophistication has been rejected in favor of certain "bright lines" clearly marking the boundaries of permissible police conduct. Illustrative is UNITED STATES V. ROBINSON (1973), holding that a search of a person is permissible whenever that individual has just been subjected to a lawful custodial arrest. Though the Court in *Robinson* understood that search of the arrestee's person serves only to ensure that he does not have a weapon by which to make an escape or evidence of the crime which he might try to destroy or dispose of, it was not thought realistic to require separate police determinations whether there were grounds for arrest and whether the arrestee might be armed or in possession of evidence. Rather, the right to search was "piggybacked" onto the authority to arrest. By like reasoning, the Court held in *New York v. Belton* (1981) that the search of an automobile's passenger compartment can be piggybacked onto the contemporaneous arrest of an occupant, and in MICHIGAN V. SUMMERS (1981) that the brief detention of an occupant of a house can be piggybacked onto the contemporaneous execution of a search warrant for contraband there.

The Supreme Court has often expressed a preference for searches and seizures made pursuant to a warrant, reasoning that the warrant process protects Fourth Amendment rights by ensuring that critical decisions are made by "a neutral and detached magistrate." Thus the warrant-issuing authority may not be given to a prosecutor (COOLIDGE V. NEW HAMPSHIRE, 1971), or to a justice of the peace who receives a fee for warrants issued (*Connally v. Georgia,* 1977), but at least as to minor offenses may be granted to a clerk of the court acting under the supervision of a judge (*Shadwick v. City of Tampa,* 1972). The magistrate's responsibility is to make the critical probable cause decision which otherwise would be left to the police, and to ensure, as the Fourth Amendment requires, that the warrant describes the place to be searched and the person or things to be seized with such specificity that an officer can, as the Court put it in *Steele v. United States* (1925), "with reasonable effort ascertain and identify" the place, person, or thing intended.

Despite this preference for warrants, in many circumstances a search or seizure may constitutionally be made without a warrant. For one thing, no warrant need be obtained when EXIGENT CIRCUMSTANCES make a detour to a magistrate impracticable. Illustrative is the seminal AUTOMOBILE SEARCH case of CARROLL V. UNITED STATES (1925), where it was stressed that "it is not practicable to secure a warrant because the vehicle can be quickly moved out of the locality or jurisdiction in which the warrant must be sought." However, the Court has not always dealt with the exigent circumstances issue in a consistent fashion. In CHAMBERS V. MARONEY (1970) the Court extended the *Carroll* rule to a vehicle that was in police custody and inaccessible to anyone else. On the other hand, in *Vale v. Louisiana* (1970) the Court chastised the police for not having obtained a search warrant a day earlier, though the probable cause needed for its issuance had unexpectedly come to the attention of the officer for the first time just minutes before the warrantless search of the arrestee's dwelling.

These different attitudes suggest that considerations other than "exigent circumstances" are at play. For example, the Court is less willing to recognize exceptions to the warrant requirement for dwelling searches than for vehicle searches. Apparently perceiving that its expanded vehicle search rule could not be explained in terms of exigent circumstances, the Court in *United States v. Chadwick* (1977) offered another explanation: vehicles have a "diminished expectation of privacy" which makes them unworthy of the usual Fourth Amendment warrant requirement. Yet in *Arkansas v. Sanders* (1979) the Court found no such diminished expectation in a suitcase, even when placed in a vehicle. It is not immediately apparent why placing one's personal items in the trunk of a car manifests less of a privacy expectation than placing those same items in some other type of container. Perhaps that is why the Court responded in *United States v. Ross* (1982) with this curious rule for the container-in-a-car cases: the *Chambers* no-warrant rule applies if there is probable cause to search the entire vehicle, but the *Sanders* warrant rule applies if there is probable cause to search only the container in the vehicle.

Some decisions reflect the Court's belief that certain police intrusions are more serious than others and that the warrant process is necessary only for the more serious ones. Intrusions upon a possessory interest are generally viewed as less serious than intrusions into a privacy interest; the former alone do not require warrants. *Coolidge v. New Hampshire* teaches that if the police are lawfully present in a place executing a search warrant and find items they believe are subject to seizure but which are not named in the warrant, they usually may make a warrantless seizure of them and need not return to the magistrate for another warrant. By contrast, when the police come into lawful possession of a closed container, for example, one which was turned over to them because misdelivered, as in *Walter v. United States* (1980), further intrusion into the privacy of the container ordinarily requires a warrant.

Similar analysis partly explains the rule of UNITED STATES V. WATSON (1976) that an arrest in a public place may be made without a warrant even if there was ample opportunity to obtain one. The Court did not consider such a seizure as great a threat to Fourth Amendment values as, say, the search of a dwelling. Thus the situation changes if the arrest can be made only by entering private premises; the Court held in PAYTON V. NEW YORK (1980) that a warrant is then required absent true exigent circumstances. The situation also changes if the seizure of the person becomes more intrusive. As the Court explained in *Gerstein v. Pugh* (1975), no warrant is needed merely for "a brief period of detention to take the administrative steps incident to arrest," but if the arrestee is not promptly released then "the Fourth Amendment requires a judicial determination of probable cause as a prerequisite to extended restraint on liberty following arrest."

Yet another theme runs through the Court's decisions: no warrant is necessary when there is little for the magistrate to decide. The most obvious illustration is the rule that no search warrant is required for an inventory of an impounded vehicle because there are no special facts for the magistrate to evaluate. The point is also illustrated by comparing *Payton* with STEAGALD V. UNITED STATES (1981). Together the two cases stand for the proposition that an arrest warrant alone justifies entry into the intended arrestee's home to arrest him but not entry into a third party's home, which usually requires a search warrant. In the former situation, unlike the latter, there is no substantial need for a magistrate to determine on a case-by-case basis whether the suspect will probably be found in his own home. Sometimes, as in *Camara v. Municipal Court,* requiring warrants for housing inspections but permitting their issuance without a case-by-case probable cause showing, the Court has been sharply divided on the question of whether resort to the warrant process would be meaningful.

Still another consideration in the warrant cases of the Court is the need for "bright lines," the notion that case-by-case assessments simply are not feasible as to certain matters, so that a general rule applicable to all cases of a certain type is necessary. An example is *United States v. Watson,* holding that no warrant is required to arrest in a public place; a contrary holding, the Court said, would "encumber criminal prosecutions with endless litigation with respect to the existence of exigent circumstances, whether it was practicable to get a warrant, whether the suspect was about to flee, and the like." But in CHIMEL V. CALIFORNIA (1969) the Court overruled cases permitting a warrantless search of premises contemporaneous with a lawful arrest therein, rejecting the dissenters' claim that the earlier "bright line" rule was necessary because there often is "a strong possibility that confederates of the arrested man will in the meanwhile remove the items for which the police have probable cause to search."

The probable cause and warrant requirements of the Fourth Amendment limit the government only. They have no application to private illegal searches and seizures, as where a private person breaks into premises, seizes evidence of crime found therein, and turns that evidence over to the authorities. But if a government official should instigate or participate in such an activity, that involvement would make the private person an agent of the government. Though most Fourth Amendment cases involve the actions of police officers, the amendment unquestionably applies to other government officials as well.

The limitations of the Fourth Amendment extend only to "searches" and "seizures." The term "seizure" is considerably broader than "arrest"; thus the fact that a particular detention is not called an arrest or is less intrusive than an arrest does not mean the amendment is inapplicable. As the Court put it in *Terry v. Ohio,* "whenever a police officer accosts an individual and restrains his freedom to walk away, he has 'seized' that person." That formulation leaves unresolved an issue of perspective: is the question whether the officer intended to restrain, or whether the suspect believed he was restrained? Either of these subjective states of mind would be difficult to prove apart from the self-serving statements of the officer and suspect, respectively, and thus an objective test is preferable. The courts, including the Supreme Court, have given insufficient attention to this matter. In *Florida v. Royer* (1983) a majority of the Court expressed the view "that a person has been 'seized' within the meaning of the Fourth Amendment only if, in view of all of the circumstances surrounding the incident, a reasonable person would have believed that he was not free to leave." But few people feel free to walk away during a police–citizen encounter, and thus a workable test may require consideration whether the officer added to the inherent pressures by engaging in menacing conduct significantly beyond that accepted in social intercourse. Some governmental pressure causing a person to be in a certain place at a certain time, such as the GRAND JURY subpoena upheld in UNITED STATES V. DIONISIO (1973), does not amount to a Fourth Amendment seizure.

More difficult is the definition of a "search" within the meaning of the Fourth Amendment. The view requiring a physical intrusion into "a constitutionally protected area" was finally abandoned in KATZ V. UNITED STATES (1967), which involved ELECTRONIC EAVESDROPPING upon one end of a telephone conversation with a device attached to the outside of a public telephone booth. The Court held that this conduct was a search because the government "violated the privacy upon which [Katz] justifiably relied while using the telephone booth." Justice JOHN MARSHALL HARLAN, concurring in *Katz* in an opinion often relied upon by lower courts, enunciated "a twofold requirement, first that a person have exhibited an actual (subjective) expectation of privacy and, second, that the expectation be one that society is prepared to recognize as 'reasonable.' "

The first of these two requirements clearly deserves no place in a theory of what the Fourth Amendment protects. Were it otherwise, as Anthony Amsterdam aptly put it, "the government could diminish each person's subjective expectation of privacy merely by announcing half-hourly on television . . . that we were all forthwith being placed under comprehensive electronic surveillance." Justice Harlan later came around to this position, counseling in his dissenting opinion in UNITED STATES V. WHITE (1971) that analysis under *Katz* must "transcend the search for subjective expectations," because our expectations "are in large part reflections of laws that translate into rules the customs and values of the past and present." A majority of the Court continues to use the "actual (subjective) expectation of privacy" formulation, but cautioned in *Smith v. Maryland* (1979) that in some situations it "would provide an inadequate index of Fourth Amendment protection."

The Court has sometimes referred to the second *Katz* requirement simply as the "reasonable 'expectation of privacy' " test. From this, it might be assumed that investigative activity constitutes a search whenever it uncovers incriminating actions or objects which the law's hypothetical reasonable man would have expected to remain private, that is, those which as a matter of statistical probability were not likely to be discovered. But such an approach is unsound. Rather, as Justice Harlan later explained in his *United States v. White* dissent, the question here must "be answered by assessing the nature of a particular practice and the likely extent of its impact on the individual's sense of security balanced against the utility of the conduct as a technique of law enforcement." In Amsterdam's words, at the heart of the matter is "a value judgment": "whether, if the particular form of surveillance practiced by the police is permitted to go unregulated by constitutional restraints, the amount of privacy and freedom remaining to citizens would be diminished to a compass inconsistent with the aims of a free and open society."

Although *Katz,* so viewed, offers a useful approach to the question of what the Fourth Amendment protects, the Court's application of the test has been neither consistent nor cautious, as can be seen by comparing MARSHALL V. BARLOW'S INC. (1978) with *Smith v. Maryland* (1979). In *Marshall,* holding unconstitutional the warrantless inspection of business premises, the Court expressly rejected the government's claim that a businessman lacked any privacy expectation vis-à-vis the government when there was no such expectation as to others (in this instance, his employees). Rather, the Court reached the sensible conclusion that an unconsented entry would be a Fourth Amendment search even though the area entered was regularly used by the company's employees. But a year later, in *Smith,* rejecting the claim that there was a "legitimate expectation of privacy" in the numbers one dials on his telephone, the Court, though asserting that "our lodestar is *Katz,*" concluded there was no such privacy expectation vis-à-vis the government because the telephone company's switching equipment had the capacity to record that information for certain limited business purposes. This unfortunate all-or-nothing view of privacy, as Justice THURGOOD MARSHALL noted in dissent, means that "unless a person is prepared to forego use of what for many has become a personal or professional necessity, he cannot help but accept the risk of surveillance."

In still another situation the Fourth Amendment's probable cause and warrant requirements are not applicable. This situation is most commonly called a CONSENT SEARCH, although when the facilitating party is active rather than passive it may be characterized as involving no search at all. At one time the consent doctrine was assumed to be grounded on the concept of waiver, but in SCHNECKLOTH V. BUSTAMONTE (1973) the Court, saying such an approach "would be thoroughly inconsistent with our decisions," held that the underlying issue was whether the person's consent was "voluntary." One reason the concept of waiver is inappropriate here is because it has long been recognized that sometimes one party may give a consent that will be effective against another. As the Court put it in *United States v. Matlock* (1974), where two or more persons have joint access to or control of premises "it is reasonable to recognize that any of the coinhabitants has the right to permit the inspection in his own right and that the others have assumed the risk that one of their number might permit the common area to be searched." The Court in *Matlock* found it unnecessary to pass upon the correctness of a position taken by several lower courts, namely, that the Fourth Amendment's reasonableness requirement is met if the police reasonably but mistakenly conclude that the consenting person has such authority.

The Fourth Amendment was a largely unexplored territory until BOYD V. UNITED STATES (1886), where the Supreme Court, weaving together the Fourth and Fifth Amendments, concluded that "the seizure of a man's private books and papers to be used in evidence against him" was not "substantially different from compelling him to be a witness against himself" and thus held that physical evidence the defendant was required to produce was inadmissible. *Boyd* was later confined by *Adams v. New York* (1904) to the situation in which a positive act was required of the defendant, but in WEEKS V. UNITED STATES (1914) the Court ruled that the "effect of the 4th Amendment" is to forbid federal courts to admit into evidence the fruits of Fourth Amendment violations. The same could not be said of the state courts, the Supreme Court decided in WOLF V. COLORADO (1949); whether exclusion of evidence was the best way to enforce the Fourth Amendment was "an issue as to which men with complete devotion to the protection of the RIGHT OF PRIVACY might give different answers." *Wolf* was overruled in MAPP V. OHIO (1961), where the majority concluded that other remedies for Fourth Amendment violations had proven worthless. Without an EXCLUSIONARY RULE operative at both the state and the federal level, the Constitution's assurance against unreasonable searches and seizures "would be 'a form of words,' valueless and undeserving of mention in a perpetual charter of inestimable human liberties."

Over the years the Court has given various explanations of the rationale for this exclusionary rule. In ELKINS V. UNITED STATES (1960) the Court emphasized "the imperative of judicial integrity"—that the courts not become "accomplices in the willful disobedience of a Constitution they are sworn to uphold." A second purpose, articulated by Justice WILLIAM J. BRENNAN, dissenting in UNITED STATES V. CALANDRA (1974), is that "of assuring the people—all potential victims of unlawful government conduct—that the government would not profit from its lawless behavior, thus minimizing the risk of seriously undermining popular trust in government." This second purpose is reflected in opinions as early as *Weeks.* Yet a third purpose, not explicitly mentioned in the earlier cases, is that of deterring unreasonable searches and seizures. Thus, in *Elkins* the Court emphasized: "The rule is calculated to prevent, not to repair. Its purpose is to deter—to compel respect for the constitutional guaranty in the only effectively available way—by removing the incentive to disregard it." In recent years the Court has relied almost exclusively upon this deterrence rationale.

Over the years the deterrence issue has occasioned intense debate; some claim the exclusionary rule does not deter and should be abandoned, and others claim that it does and should be retained. Hard evidence supporting either claim is unavailable, but some argue that a deterrent effect may be assumed because of such post-exclusionary-rule phenomena as the dramatic increase in the use of warrants and stepped-up efforts to educate the police on the law of search and seizure. The debate has recently centered on a proposed "good faith" exception to the Fourth Amendment exclusionary rule, allowing admission of illegally obtained evidence if the searching or seizing officer acted in a reasonable belief that his conduct was constitutionally permissible. A limited version of the exception was adopted by the Court in UNITED STATES V. LEON (1984), where the exclusionary rule was "modified so as not to bar the use in the prosecution's case-in-chief of evidence obtained by officers acting in reasonable reliance on a search warrant issued by a detached and neutral magistrate but ultimately found to be unsupported by probable cause." The majority reasoned that exclusion for purposes of deterrence was unnecessary in such circumstances, as exclusion would have no significant deterrent effect on the magistrate who issued the warrant, and there is no need to deter the policeman who justifiably relied upon the prior judgment of the magistrate. Whether *Leon* will be a stepping-stone to adoption of a broader (and, it would seem, less justifiable and more difficult to apply) "good faith" exception, applicable also in without-warrant cases, remains to be seen.

The current dimensions of the Fourth Amendment exclusionary rule are mostly tailored to the deterrence rationale. The rule is not used in certain settings on the assumption that the incremental gain in deterrence is not worth the cost. Illustrative are *United States v. Calandra,* refusing to compel exclusion at the behest of a grand jury witness because it "would achieve a speculative and undoubtedly minimal advance in the deterrence of police misconduct at the expense of substantially impending the role of the grand jury"; and *United States v. Janis* (1976), declining to require exclusion in federal tax litigation of evidence uncovered in a state criminal investigation of gambling because "common sense dictates that the deterrent effect of the exclusion of relevant evidence is highly attenuated when the 'punishment' imposed upon the offending criminal enforcement officer is the removal of that evidence from a civil suit by or against a different sovereign." Even in the context of a criminal trial the deterrent objective of the exclusionary rule is sometimes perceived as outweighed by competing considerations. This explains the rule in *Walder v. United States* (1954) that the government may use illegally obtained evidence to impeach the defendant's testimony, so that the defendant cannot "turn the illegal method by which evidence in the Government's possession was obtained to his own advantage, and provide himself with a shield against contradiction of his untruths."

Who may invoke the exclusionary rule? The rule of STANDING generally is that a constitutional challenge may be raised only by those who have an interest in the outcome of the controversy, and who are objecting to a violation of their own rights. A defendant in a criminal case against whom illegally obtained evidence is being offered certainly meets the first requirement, but he does not necessarily meet the second. As to the latter, the fundamental question is whether the challenged conduct intruded upon his freedom or expectation of privacy or only that of someone else, as *Rakas v. Illinois* (1978) illustrates. The Court held that passengers in a car did not have standing to object to a search under the seats and in the glove compartment of that vehicle. Essential to the holding were the conclusions that these passengers were not claiming that the car had been illegally stopped, that they "asserted neither a property nor a possessory interest in the automobile, nor an interest in the property seized," and that the areas searched were ones "in which a passenger *qua* passenger simply would not have a legitimate expectation of privacy." The Supreme Court refused in ALDERMAN V. UNITED STATES (1969) to adopt a rule of "target standing" allowing a defendant to object to any Fourth Amendment violation committed for the purpose of acquiring evidence for use against him. This refusal limits to some extent the deterrent effect of the exclusionary rule, for police sometimes deliberately direct an illegal search at one person because they are seeking evidence to use against another person they know will not be able to question their conduct.

What evidence is subject to challenge under the exclusionary rule? Under the FRUIT OF THE POISONOUS TREE doctrine, the exclusionary rule applies not only to the immediate and direct fruits of a Fourth Amendment violation (the physical evidence found in a search), but also to secondary or derivative evidence (a confession acquired by confronting a person with that physical evidence). Of course, in a criminal investigation the discovery of one fact often plays some part in the discovery of many others, and they in turn contribute to the uncovering of still others, and so on, but the fruits doctrine is not pushed this far. Even the fact first discovered by an illegal act does not become forever "inaccessible" for court use: it may still be proved "if knowledge of [the fact] is [also] gained from an independent source," as in SILVERTHORNE LUMBER CO. V. UNITED STATES (1920). The "inevitable discovery" doctrine accepted in *Nix v. Williams* (1984), whereunder illegally obtained evidence is admissible if "the prosecution can establish by a preponderance of the evidence that the information ultimately or inevitably would have been discovered by lawful means," likewise serves to put the police in no worse position than they would have been if their misconduct had not occurred. Another limitation is provided by the test in *Wong Sun v. United States*: "whether, granting establishment of the primary illegality, the evidence to which instant objection is made has been come at by exploitation of that illegality or instead by means sufficiently distinguishable to be purged of the primary taint." In that case the taint of one defendant's illegal arrest was deemed dissipated by his release on his own recognizance, so that the taint did not reach a subsequently given confession. Considerations close to the deterrent function of the exclusionary rule also come into play here. Thus, suppression of derivative evidence is much more likely if it appears that the primary illegality was a clearly unconstitutional act or that it was undertaken for the purpose of acquiring that derivative evidence. For example, a confession will be deemed the fruit of an obviously illegal arrest made in the hope of acquiring a confession.

It cannot be denied that there is ample room for reasonable disagreement regarding the rationales and results of a number of the Supreme Court's Fourth Amendment decisions. In the main, however, the Court's response to the four fundamental questions just discussed has been indisputably appropriate and sound. The decisions on the requisite factual basis for a seizure or search have generally struck a fair balance between privacy and law enforcement interests. The Court's rulings regarding the warrant requirement have prevented the warrant process from becoming so overburdened as to become a mechanical and meaningless routine, yet have provided added protection to those Fourth Amendment interests that are valued most. The decisions defining the activities to which the amendment applies—especially *Katz* and its justified expectation of privacy test—provide an approach that should enable the Court to protect against new threats to the individual's right to be free of intrusive government surveillance. Finally, it is the Court's insistence upon an exclusionary rule as an enforcement mechanism that has kept the Fourth Amendment from being reduced to "a form of words."

WAYNE R. LAFAVE

Bibliography

AMSTERDAM, ANTHONY G. 1974 Perspectives on the Fourth Amendment. *Minnesota Law Review* 58:349–477.

GRANO, JOSEPH D. 1978 Perplexing Questions about Three Basic Fourth Amendment Issues: Fourth Amendment Activity, Probable Cause, and the Warrant Requirement. *Journal of Criminal Law and Criminology* 69:425–463.

KAMISAR, YALE 1983 Does (Did) (Should) the Exclusionary Rule Rest on a "Principled Basis" Rather Than an "Empirical Proposition"? *Creighton Law Review* 16:565–667.

LAFAVE, WAYNE R. 1978 *Search and Seizure: A Treatise on the Fourth Amendment,* 3 vols. St. Paul, Minn.: West Publishing Co.

LANDYNSKI, JACOB W. 1966 *Search and Seizure and the Supreme Court.* Baltimore, Md.: Johns Hopkins University Press.

OAKS, DALLIN H. 1970 Studying the Exclusionary Rule. *University of Chicago Law Review* 37:665–757.

UNITED STATES, CONGRESS, SENATE COMMITTEE ON THE JUDICIARY, SUBCOMMITTEE ON CRIMINAL LAW 1982 *The Exclusionary Rule Bills,* 97th Cong., 1st & 2d sess.

SEARCH INCIDENT TO ARREST

WEEKS V. UNITED STATES (1914) recognized, as an exception to the FOURTH AMENDMENT's requirement of a SEARCH WARRANT, the authority of police to search a person incident to his arrest in order to discover concealed weapons or evidence. This principle has remained essentially unchallenged, although its application to a person arrested for a minor offense, such as a traffic violation, involving small likelihood of danger to the officer, was severly criticized by some Justices in UNITED STATES V. ROBINSON (1973). Extension of the allowable search from the person of the arrestee to include the area "in his control," in AGNELLO V. UNITED STATES (1925), planted the seed of conflict between those Justices who would allow a complete search of the premises and those who would limit the search to the area from which the arrestee could conceivably reach for weapons to wield or evidence to destroy.

Marron v. United States (1927) allowed the search to cover "all parts of the premises," but in *Go Bart v. United States* (1931) and *United States v. Lefkowitz* (1932) the Court condemned wholesale "rummaging of the place." Again, *Harris v. United States* (1947) upheld the search of an entire apartment, but *Trupiano v. United States* (1948) forebade even the seizure of contraband in PLAIN VIEW of the arresting officers. The pendulum again swung in *United States v. Rabinowitz* (1950), which authorized search of the whole place. By now the field was "a quagmire," as Justice TOM C. CLARK exclaimed, dissenting in CHAPMAN V. UNITED STATES (1961). One group of Justices took the position, essentially, that once officers are legitimately on premises to make an arrest, the accompanying search, no matter how extensive, is only a minor additional invasion of privacy and therefore reasonable. They conceded that the arrest must not serve as a pretext for the search, and that the search must be limited to objects for which the arrest was made, but these limitations are easily evaded. Justice FELIX FRANKFURTER provided intellectual leadership for the opposing view, arguing that when a search incident to arrest is allowed to extend beyond the need that gave rise to it, the exception swallows up the rule that a warrant must be obtained save in EXIGENT CIRCUMSTANCES. Moreover, because a warrant often will strictly limit the area to be searched, to authorize search of the entire premises has the novel effect of allowing searches incident to arrest a broader scope than searches under warrant.

So the matter stood until CHIMEL V. CALIFORNIA (1969). There the Court restored the balance between theory and practice by overruling *Harris* and *Rabinowitz* and limiting the scope of incident searches to the person of the arrestee and his immediate environs. Still, the *Chimel* limitation may not always apply. Where the police have strong reason to believe that confederates of the arrestee are hidden on the premises, they are presumably entitled, under the "hot pursuit" doctrine of WARDEN V. HAYDEN (1967), to make a "sweep" of the place in order to minimize the danger. The reverse would also seem to follow: once the arrestee has been subdued (assuming there is no reason to suspect the presence of confederates), the police no longer have authority to search even a limited area.

An important legal difference between search of the person's clothing and search of property within the area of his reach should be noted. Property under the arrestee's control, which might have been searched without a warrant immediately following the arrest, may not be searched later; to be lawful under *United States v. Chadwick* (1977) the search must be substantially contemporaneous with the arrest. However, in a radical departure from the spirit, if not the letter, of the *Chimel* rule, the Court held in *United States v. Edwards* (1974) that authority to search the arrestee's clothing is not lost by the passage of time and may be exercised hours later, following his incarceration. The rationale for this difference appears to be that the arrestee's expectation of privacy in property not associated with his person remains undiminished. Absent a warrant, the property search must therefore be carried out promptly, as an exigency measure, or not at all.

Under ILLINOIS V. LAFAYETTE (1983), an arrestee's

possessions may be inventoried in the police station prior to his incarceration so as to safeguard them against theft and protect the officers against spurious claims. Because it is considered a reasonable administrative procedure, "the inventory search constitutes a well-defined exception to the warrant requirement."

JACOB W. LANDYNSKI

Bibliography

LAFAVE, WAYNE R. 1978 *Search and Seizure: A Treatise on the Fourth Amendment.* Vol. 2:406–466. St. Paul, Minn.: West Publishing Co.

LANDYNSKI, JACOB W. 1966 *Search and Seizure and the Supreme Court.* Pages 87, 98–117. Baltimore: Johns Hopkins University Press.

_____ 1971 The Supreme Court's Search for Fourth Amendment Standards. *Connecticut Bar Journal* 45:2–30.

SEARCH WARRANT

The FOURTH AMENDMENT to the Constitution prohibits unreasonable SEARCHES AND SEIZURES and provides that "No Warrants shall issue, but upon PROBABLE CAUSE, supported by Oath or Affirmation, and particularly describing the place to be searched, and the persons or things to be seized." The Framers adopted the warrant clause in response to the use by British customs officers of GENERAL WARRANTS, known as WRITS OF ASSISTANCE, to enforce British trade laws.

A writ of assistance conveyed virtually unbridled discretion to search under the authority of the Crown. The writ was not required to be based on any facts giving reason to believe that a crime had been committed. Nor did it contain an inventory of things to be taken, the names of alleged offenders, or any limitation on the places to be searched. Once issued, a writ remained valid during the lifetime of the reigning sovereign.

Judicial interpretations of the warrant clause have expressed a strong preference for the use of a neutral and detached magistrate over the "hurried action" of a police officer engaged in the often competitive enterprise of ferreting out crime. Since COOLIDGE V. NEW HAMPSHIRE (1971) searches conducted outside the judicial process have been considered by the Supreme Court to be unreasonable per se unless they fall within one of the exceptions to the warrant requirement.

A magistrate who issues a search warrant may not occupy a dual role, both reviewing the facts presented to justify the warrant and actively participating in the criminal investigation or prosecution. Such a dual role creates a conflict of interest that is inimical to the objectives of the warrant clause. As the Supreme Court observed in UNITED STATES V. UNITED STATES DISTRICT COURT (1972), the Fourth Amendment protections cannot be properly guaranteed if searches "may be conducted solely within the discretion of the Executive Branch."

An important part of the Fourth Amendment's proscription against general warrants is that a warrant may be issued only upon probable cause. This requirement necessarily limits each warrant to a particular set of circumstances relating to a suspected criminal offense. The alleged facts must establish a reasonable basis to believe that the offense was committed and that contraband or EVIDENCE of the offense is located at the place to be searched. Although a finding of probable cause may rest upon HEARSAY or other evidence that would not be admissible at trial, the issuing magistrate must nonetheless carefully consider the reliability of such evidence. According to ILLINOIS V. GATES (1983), in assessing probable cause, a magistrate must make a "practical, commonsense" decision in view of all the circumstances set forth in the affidavit, including the "veracity" and "basis of knowledge" of the persons supplying the information.

The information that forms the basis for the search warrant must be sworn to by "oath and affirmation" at the time the warrant is issued. To ensure an independent review by the magistrate, the oath must attest to facts and circumstances, not merely to the affiant's conclusion that he believes he has probable cause for the search. Moreover, an insufficient affidavit cannot be rehabilitated later by testimony concerning facts known by the affiant or otherwise available, but not disclosed to the magistrate at the time of issuance of the warrant. A contrary rule, of course, would render the warrant requirement meaningless.

An important issue that remained unresolved until *Franks v. Delaware* (1978) was whether the accuracy of the information relied on to justify a search warrant may be challenged. In *Franks* the Supreme Court held that if it can be shown that the affiant intentionally or recklessly gave false or misleading information to the magistrate, a reviewing court may invalidate the warrant if the magistrate's finding of probable cause was based on the misinformation.

The warrant clause also precludes the issuance of general search warrants, for it commands that the warrant describe with particularity the place to be searched and the objects to be seized. In *Gouled v. United States* (1921) the Supreme Court held that law enforcement officers could not seize property, even though particularly described in a search warrant, when the property was merely of evidentiary value in a criminal proceeding. This MERE EVIDENCE RULE, which attempted to distinguish between mere evidence and contraband or other property that was a fruit or instrumentality of a crime, was both unsound and lacking in reason and historical support. The Court abandoned the rule in WARDEN V. HAYDEN (1967).

The purpose of the particularity requirement is to limit implicitly the scope of what the officer executing the warrant may do. As the Court stated in *Marron v. United States* (1927): "The requirement that warrants shall particularly describe the things to be seized makes general searches under them impossible and prevents the seizure of one thing under a warrant describing another. As to what is to be taken, nothing is left to the discretion of the officer executing the warrant." With respect to the place to be searched, the description must be such that the officer executing the warrant can, with reasonable effort, ascertain and identify the place intended.

As a practical matter, of course, law enforcement officers may not be completely divested of all discretion in executing search warrants. Moreover, notwithstanding the language in *Marron,* the Court has held that incriminating evidence not listed in a search warrant may be seized when observed in plain view by officers executing the warrant, provided that the officers inadvertently come upon the evidence. The particularity requirement, however, greatly circumscribes the officer's discretion and therefore plays an important role in minimizing the likelihood of police abuse.

JAMES R. ASPERGER

Bibliography

LAFAVE, WAYNE R. 1978 *Search and Seizure: A Treatise on the Fourth Amendment.* Vol. 2:1–213. St. Paul, Minn.: West Publishing Co.

LASSON, NELSON B. 1937 *The History and Development of the Fourth Amendment to the United States Constitution.* Baltimore: Johns Hopkins University Press.

SECESSION

Secession, the withdrawal of a state from the American Union, first appeared as an impulse rather than an articulated constitutional doctrine. Inchoate secessionist movements agitated the southwestern frontier after the signing of JAY'S TREATY (1794). AARON BURR's alleged conspiracy was linked to them. Massachusetts Federalists who were disgruntled about the rising political power of the South and the western territories between 1803 and 1814 contemplated secession in correspondence among themselves. Before the Civil War, Garrisonian abolitionists developed doctrines of disunion, calling for both individual disallegiance and the withdrawal of the free states from a union with the slave states. Southern political leaders, uneasy about the spread of abolitionist and Free Soil sentiment in the north, occasionally voiced threats of secession.

JOHN C. CALHOUN developed the theoretical framework for secession, though ironically, he did so in order to avoid secession through the alternatives of INTERPOSITION and NULLIFICATION. Drawing on the thought of earlier STATES' RIGHTS ideologues such as JOHN TAYLOR of Caroline, JOHN RANDOLPH, and THOMAS COOPER, as well as the concepts of state sovereignty and the Union broached in the VIRGINIA AND KENTUCKY RESOLUTIONS of 1798–1799, Calhoun insisted that SOVEREIGNTY in America resided not in the nation but severally in the people of each of the states. The states created the national government, giving it only limited, specific, and delegated powers. The national government was thus the agent or the trustee for the people of the states, and the federal Constitution was merely a "compact" among sovereign states. If the national government abused its delegated powers by unconstitutional legislation or executive acts, the states could interpose their authority between the federal government and their people and could nullify federal legislation within their territory. But if enough other states ratified an amendment to the federal Constitution that authorized the nullified act, then the states had only the option of submitting to or withdrawing from the Union.

After the election of ABRAHAM LINCOLN in 1860, South Carolina radicals induced the legislature to call a convention to consider secession. The convention voted unanimously for secession, and in the "Declaration of the Immediate Causes [of] Secession" (1860) they asserted that the free states had violated the constitutional compact by failing to enforce the Fugitive Slave Acts vigorously and by enacting PERSONAL LIBERTY LAWS that impeded the recapture of fugitive slaves. The free states also had denied slaveholders' right of transit through their territory with their slaves, agitated against slavery, tolerated abolitionist societies, and permitted dissemination of abolitionist propaganda. They had permitted blacks to vote and had elected a sectional presidential candidate determined to effect the eventual abolition of slavery. Thus South Carolina, in order to protect its people and its peculiar institution, severed the union binding it to the other states and reassumed its status as "a separate and independent state."

Though all slave states were deeply divided over the wisdom and constitutionality of secession, Mississippi, Florida, Alabama, Georgia, Louisiana, and Texas also seceded by February 1, 1861. These seven states formed the Confederate States of America in February. After the firing on Fort Sumter, Virginia, North Carolina, Tennessee, and Arkansas seceded. A proslavery rump session of the Missouri legislature and a convention of Kentucky Confederate soldiers declared their states seceded, but both states, as well as the other border slave states, remained in the Union. After the defeat of southern forces in 1865, most of the Confederate states repudiated secession, but diehards in South Carolina merely repealed their secession ordinance instead of nullifying it. Nonetheless, secession as a constitutional remedy was dead, and the United States was thenceforth "one nation, indivisible."

WILLIAM M. WIECEK

SECOND AMENDMENT

However controversial the meaning of the Second Amendment is today, it was clear enough to the generation of 1789. The amendment assured to the people "their private arms," said an article which received JAMES MADISON's approval and was the only analysis available to Congress when it voted. Subsequent contemporaneous analysis is epitomized by the first American commentary on the writings of WILLIAM BLACKSTONE. Where Blackstone described arms for personal defense as among the "absolute rights of individuals" at COMMON LAW, his eighteenth-century American editor commented that this right had been constitutionalized by the Second Amendment. Early constitutional commentators, including JOSEPH STORY, William Rawle, and THOMAS M. COOLEY, described the amendment in terms of a republican philosophical tradition stemming from Aristotle's observation that basic to tyrants is a "mistrust of the people; hence they deprive them of arms." Political theorists from Cicero to JOHN LOCKE and Jean-Jacques Rousseau also held arms possession to be symbolic of personal freedom and vital to the virtuous, self-reliant citizenry (defending itself from encroachment by outlaws, tyrants, and foreign invaders alike) that they deemed indispensable to popular government.

These assumptions informed both sides of the debate over RATIFICATION OF THE CONSTITUTION. While Madison, in THE FEDERALIST #46 assured Americans that they need never fear the federal government because of "the advantage of being armed, which you possess over the people of almost every other nation," opponents of ratification such as PATRICK HENRY declaimed: "The great principle is that every man be armed. Everyone who is able may have a gun." SAMUEL ADAMS proposed that "the Constitution never be construed . . . to prevent the people of the United States who are peaceable citizens from keeping their own arms." As much of this debate used the word "militia," it is necessary to remember that in the eighteenth century the militia was coextensive with the adult male citizenry. By colonial law every household was required to possess arms and every male of military age was required to muster during military emergencies, bearing his own arms. The amendment, in guaranteeing the arms of each citizen, simultaneously guaranteed arms for the militia.

In contrast to the original interpretation of the amendment as a personal right to arms is the twentieth-century view that it protects only the states' right to arm their own military forces, including their national guard units. This view stresses the Anti-Federalists' bitter opposition to the provisions of Article I, section 8, authorizing a standing army and granting the federal government various powers over state militias. Both textual and historical difficulties preclude acceptance of this exclusively STATES' RIGHTS view. For instance, Madison's proposed organization for the provisions of the BILL OF RIGHTS was not to append them, but to interpolate each amendment into the Constitution following the provision to which it pertained. Had he viewed the amendment as modifying the military-militia clauses of the Constitution (which he strongly defended against Anti-Federalist criticism), he would have appended it to those clauses in section 8. Instead, he planned to place what are now the First and Second Amendments in Article I, section 9, along with the original Constitution's guarantees against BILLS OF ATTAINDER and EX POST FACTO LAWS and against suspension of HABEAS CORPUS.

The states' rights interpretation simply cannot be squared with the amendment's words: "right of the people." It is impossible to believe that the First Congress used "right of the people" in the FIRST AMENDMENT to describe an individual right (FREEDOM OF ASSEMBLY), but sixteen words later in the Second Amendment to describe a right vested exclusively in the states. Moreover, "right of the people" is used again to refer to personal rights in the FOURTH AMENDMENT and the NINTH AMENDMENT, and the TENTH AMENDMENT expressly distinguishes "the people" from "the states."

Interpreting the Second Amendment as a guarantee of an individual right does not foreclose all gun controls. The ownership of firearms by minors, felons, and the mentally impaired—and the carrying of them outside the home by anyone—may be limited or banned. Moreover, the government may limit the types of arms that may be kept; there is no right, for example, to own artillery or automatic weapons, or the weapons of the footpad and gangster, such as sawed-off shotguns and blackjacks. Gun controls in the form of registration and licensing requirements are also permissible so long as the ordinary citizen's right to possess arms for home protection is respected.

DON B. KATES, JR.

Bibliography

HALBROOK, STEVEN 1984 *That Every Man Be Armed: The Evolution of a Constitutional Right.* Albuquerque: University of New Mexico Press.

KATES, DON B., JR. 1983 Handgun Prohibition and the Original Meaning of the Second Amendment. *Michigan Law Review* 82:204–273.

MALCOLM, JOYCE 1983 The Right of the People to Keep and Bear Arms: The Common Law Tradition. *Hastings Constitutional Law Quarterly* 10:285–314.

SHALHOPE, ROBERT E. 1982 The Ideological Origins of the Second Amendment. *Journal of American History* 69:599–614.

SECONDARY BOYCOTT

See: Boycotts and the Constitution

SECOND EMPLOYERS' LIABILITY CASES

See: Employers' Liability Cases

SECTION 1983, TITLE 42, UNITED STATES CODE
(Judicial Interpretation)

Few statutes have fluctuated in importance as wildly as section 1983. From near total disuse—twenty-one reported cases from 1871 to 1920—it became one of the most litigated provisions of federal law. This drastic change is attributable both to developments in constitutional law and to developments peculiar to section 1983.

Section 1983's ascension matches the twentieth-century expansion of constitutional rights. As originally enacted in the Civil Rights Act of 1871, section 1983 at most provided a cause of action for deprivations, under color of state law, of constitutional rights. Until relatively recently, citizens had few constitutional rights enforceable against the states. In section 1983's early years, the modern expansions of the EQUAL PROTECTION and DUE PROCESS clauses had not occurred, the STATE ACTION doctrine immunized a broad range of activity from constitutional scrutiny, and the FOURTH AMENDMENT was in the infancy of its constitutional development.

An ill-considered dichotomy between classes of constitutional rights also hindered section 1983's growth. In an influential separate opinion in HAGUE V. CIO (1939), Justice HARLAN FISKE STONE argued that section 1983's jurisdictional counterpart, section 1343(3), should be interpreted to authorize federal courts to hear cases involving personal rights but not to hear cases involving mere property rights. This view influenced many courts' interpretations of section 1983 itself, again with limiting effect. In *Lynch v. Household Finance Corporation* (1972) the Court rejected the personal rights/property rights distinction. Paradoxically, a similar dichotomy between personal interests and economic interests continues to shape, indeed govern, interpretation of the equal protection clause.

Section 1983's text generated interpretive problems that might have hindered its widespread use even if the Constitution had enjoyed a broader scope. As enacted, section 1983 protected "rights, privileges or immunities" secured by the Constitution. Its scope therefore depended upon what were viewed as rights, privileges, or immunities secured by the Constitution. Until the SLAUGHTERHOUSE CASES (1873), one might have thought the rights, privileges, or immunities so secured simply to be all constitutional rights. But the *Slaughterhouse Cases* narrowly interpreted the FOURTEENTH AMENDMENT's privileges or immunities clause to protect only a small subclass of constitutional rights. Some courts adopted a similar interpretation of section 1983. In addition, section 1983 reaches only deprivations "under color of" state law. Not until well into the twentieth century was it clearly recognized that behavior not authorized by state law might constitute action under COLOR OF LAW. A narrowly construed Constitution, the shadow cast by the *Slaughter-*

house Cases, the state action doctrine, and section 1983's text combined to minimize section 1983's importance.

In the 1920s, section 1983 provided actions for some deprivations of VOTING RIGHTS. Perhaps the Court relied on the section when, in NIXON V. HERNDON (1927), it allowed a damage action to go forward against state officials. In *Lane v. Wilson* (1939), another voting rights case, the Court expressly referred to section 1983 in approving a damage action. But these cases did not erode the important limitations on section 1983.

The erosion process commenced with early twentieth-century cases that construed state action to include some actions taken in violation of state law, and with EX PARTE YOUNG (1908), which held that the ELEVENTH AMENDMENT does not bar injunctive actions against state officials. In the 1940s, criminal CIVIL RIGHTS decisions also interpreted the phrase "under color of" law to include some unauthorized action. MONROE V. PAPE (1961) capped the process by interpreting section 1983 to protect at least all constitutional rights embodied in the Fourteenth Amendment and by holding the color of law requirement in section 1983 to be satisfied by the unauthorized action of police officers. *Monroe,* together with the wide expansion of constitutional rights of the 1950s and 1960s, assured section 1983's importance.

But section 1983's growth triggered a reaction, one that began with *Monroe* itself. If every constitutional violation generated a cause of action for damages there must be limits as to when defendants actually would be held liable. In *Monroe,* the Court, giving a questionable reading to section 1983's history, held that the section was not meant to render cities liable for constitutional violations. This limitation survived until MONELL V. DEPARTMENT OF SOCIAL SERVICES (1978), when the Court held that cities may be liable under section 1983 but that, in yet another questionable reading of the section's history, Congress did not intend cities to be liable for acts of city officials unless the acts constituted "official policy," a phrase destined to be the subject of much litigation. The reaction also includes some sentiment to impose an EXHAUSTION OF REMEDIES requirement in one or more classes of section 1983 cases.

With respect to individual defendants, the Court in a series of cases read into section 1983 an array of LEGISLATIVE, JUDICIAL, prosecutorial and EXECUTIVE IMMUNITIES. And in QUERN V. JORDAN (1979) the Court held that section 1983 was not meant to abrogate the Eleventh Amendment immunity of states. In OWEN V. CITY OF INDEPENDENCE (1980), however, the Court declined to extend to municipalities the good faith defense available to executive officials. The reaction to section 1983's expansion may also encompass a series of cases, including *Parratt v. Taylor* (1981), PAUL V. DAVIS (1976), INGRAHAM V. WRIGHT (1977), and *Estelle v. Gamble* (1976), narrowly interpreting constitutional rights. If a private cause of action accompanies every constitutional right, the Court may be hesitant to "constitutionalize" many rights. Finally, the Court held in *Carey v. Piphus* (1978) that a violation of PROCEDURAL DUE PROCESS, standing alone, will not support a substantial recovery of damages; to recover more than nominal damages a plaintiff in such a case must show actual harm. The Court left open the question whether this rule would apply to other types of constitutional violation.

For many years, courts disagreed over whether section 1983 provided a cause of action for violations of federal statutes by state officials. The REVISED STATUTES of 1874, which were not supposed to make substantive changes in the law, expanded section 1983's wording to include "laws." Over a century later, in *Maine v. Thiboutot* (1980), the Court interpreted section 1983 to provide a cause of action for at least some federal statutory claims.

THEODORE EISENBERG

Bibliography

EISENBERG, THEODORE 1982 Section 1983: Doctrinal Foundations and an Empirical Study. *Cornell Law Review* 67:482–556.

——— 1981 *Civil Rights Legislation.* Charlottesville, Va.: Michie Co.

FRIENDLY, HENRY J. 1973 *Federal Jurisdiction: A General View* Pp. 87–107. New York: Columbia University Press.

NAHMOD, SHELDON H. 1979 *Civil Rights & Civil Liberties Litigation.* Colorado Springs, Colo.: Shepard's.

NOTE 1977 Developments in the Law: Section 1983 and Federalism. *Harvard Law Review* 90:1133–1361.

SECURITIES LAW AND THE CONSTITUTION

Following the 1929 stockmarket crash and the ensuing economic depression, Congress enacted the Securities Act of 1933 and the Securities Exchange Act of 1934 to restore investor confidence and provide for more efficient securities markets. Although both disclosure and regulatory provisions of the two statutes were challenged during the 1930s on constitutional grounds, the lower federal courts consistently held that both statutes were within Congress's power to regulate INTERSTATE COMMERCE and did not violate any other constitutional guarantees. In *Electric Bond & Share Co. v. Securities and Exchange Commission* (1937) the Supreme Court rejected constitutional attacks on certain provisions of the PUBLIC UTILITY HOLDING COMPANY ACT similar to the disclosure and registration requirements of the 1933 and 1934 acts, although the Court did not discuss the general validity of federal securities regulation.

Because both the states and the federal government regulate the securities markets, the Supreme Court has periodically undertaken to define the relationship between federal and state regulatory schemes by interpreting federal securities statutes. The first such case to raise constitutional questions of FEDERALISM grew out of the dramatic increase in hostile corporate takeover attempts in the late 1960s. In 1968 and 1970 Congress amended the 1934 act by adding certain provisions, known as the Williams Act, to regulate tender offers. A number of states immediately adopted takeover statutes of their own, presumably in order to protect local businesses from hostile takeovers. Because the state statutes gave more protection to target companies than did the Williams Act, tender offerors immediately challenged the state statutes as either invalid under the COMMERCE CLAUSE or preempted by the Williams Act.

In *Edgar v. Mite Corporation* (1982) the Supreme Court held that the Illinois takeover statute impermissibly burdened interstate commerce because the statute's nationwide reach significantly interfered with the economic benefits of tender offers while providing few benefits to Illinois. The Court's opinion was limited to the commerce clause holding, although three Justices also argued that the Williams Act preempted the Illinois regulatory scheme. A number of similar state takeover laws have subsequently been invalidated by lower federal courts on either commerce clause or PREEMPTION grounds.

Recent constitutional developments have suggested the possibility of FIRST AMENDMENT restraints on the disclosure aspects of securities regulation. Both the 1933 and 1934 acts regulate extensively the speech of corporate issuers and securities professionals by mandating some disclosures, prohibiting others, and by policing the content of various disclosure documents, all in the interest of preventing securities fraud, facilitating corporate suffrage, and providing investors with full and accurate information about securities and the securities markets. In VIRGINIA STATE BOARD OF PHARMACY V. VIRGINIA CITIZENS CONSUMER COUNCIL (1976) the Court extended First Amendment protection to COMMERCIAL SPEECH, and in FIRST NATIONAL BANK OF BOSTON V. BELLOTTI (1978) the Court confirmed that corporate speakers could claim the benefits of the First Amendment. In CENTRAL HUDSON GAS & ELECTRIC CORP. V. PUBLIC SERVICE COMMISSION (1980) the Court indicated that while misleading commercial speech may be regulated, remedies must be "no broader than reasonably necessary to prevent the deception."

In 1985, the Supreme Court confronted the question of First Amendment constraints on federal securities regulation. In *Lowe v. Securities and Exchange Commission* the petitioner argued that First Amendment notions of prior restraint barred the SEC from enjoining publication of petitioner's securities newsletter under the Investment Advisers Act of 1940 after petitioner's investment adviser registration was revoked because of his illegal conduct. The Court avoided the First Amendment issue by holding that the petitioner was the publisher of a "bona fide newspaper" and thus statutorily exempt from regulation under the 1940 act. Justices BYRON R. WHITE and WILLIAM H. REHNQUIST and Chief Justice WARREN E. BURGER concurred in the result but argued that the First Amendment question should have been reached and decided. They indicated that the total bar on publication required by the 1940 act was too drastic a remedy for possibly deceptive speech, whether that speech was fully protected or merely commercial speech.

Although many of the disclosure provisions of the 1933 and 1934 acts presumably satisfy the *Central Hudson* tests, those aspects of both statutes requiring prepublication clearance of disclosure by the SEC or limiting informational activities by securities professionals may be regarded as sweeping too broadly to meet First Amendment requirements. In some areas, moreover, as in the application of the proxy rules to corporate and shareholder speech concerning issues of social and political significance, corporate speech may be entitled to full First Amendment protection. All these issues remain to be raised in the courts.

ALISON GREY ANDERSON

SEDITION

Sedition is a comprehensive term for offenses against the authority of the government not amounting to TREASON. Such offenses might include the spreading of disaffection or disloyalty, conspiracy to commit insurrection, or any SUBVERSIVE ACTIVITY. Sedition tends toward treason, but does not reach the constitutionally defined offense of "levying war against the

United States or adhering to their enemies, giving them aid and comfort."

Historically, the broad category of "sedition" has comprised several kinds of activity, although there has not always been consistency about which constituted criminal offenses. SEDITIOUS LIBEL, the uttering of words bringing the government or its officers into ridicule or disrepute, was an offense at COMMON LAW and under the ALIEN AND SEDITION ACTS of 1798. Seditious membership, that is, active, knowing, and purposeful membership in an organization committed to the overthrow of the government by unlawful means, is an offense under the Smith Act. Seditious advocacy, the public promotion of insurrection or rebellion, and seditious conspiracy, combining with others to subvert the government, violate several statutory provisions; but those offenses must be very carefully defined lest the statutes exert a CHILLING EFFECT on legitimate criticism of government.

The possibility of sedition poses a particular problem for constitutional democracy. Democratic governments, no less than any other kind, need to protect themselves against seditious activity. But measures taken in self-defense must not be so broad in their scope as themselves to become a threat to individual liberty. In the United States, the FIRST AMENDMENT to the Constitution protects FREEDOM OF SPEECH, FREEDOM OF THE PRESS, and FREEDOM OF ASSEMBLY AND ASSOCIATION; these specific constitutional guarantees limit the power of Congress and of the states to legislate against sedition.

For most of American history, the national and state governments exercised a CONCURRENT POWER to define and punish sedition. The power of Congress to legislate against sedition does not derive from any of the specific ENUMERATED POWERS, but is NECESSARY AND PROPER for the carrying out of several of them. In PENNSYLVANIA V. NELSON (1956) the Supreme Court held that Congress, by enacting a pervasive scheme of regulation, had preempted the field of legislation concerning sedition against the United States.

DENNIS J. MAHONEY

(SEE ALSO: *Sedition Act of 1918.*)

SEDITION ACT
40 Stat. 553 (1918)

As World War I progressed, enthusiastic war supporters argued more and more that the ESPIONAGE ACT OF 1917 did not adequately restrict domestic critics of the war effort. Advocates of additional restriction argued that weakness of the existing loyalty legislation forced citizens to take the law into their own hands. If firmer federal policies could be established, such distasteful forms of repression might be averted. Thus a more restrictive amendment to the Espionage Act was proposed and, despite strong congressional protest that the measure virtually terminated freedom of expression, was signed into law on May 16, 1918. The amendment, called the Sedition Act, defined eight offenses punishable by $10,000 fine or more than twenty years in prison, or both. The new offenses included: uttering, printing, writing, or publishing any disloyal, profane, scurrilous, or abusive language intended to cause contempt, scorn, contumely or disrepute as regards the form of government of the United States, or the Constitution, or the flag, or the uniform or the Army or Navy, or any language intended to incite resistance to the United States or to promote the cause of its enemies; urging any curtailment of production or anything necessary to the prosecution of the war with intent to hinder its prosecution; advocating, teaching, defending, or suggesting the doing of any of these acts; and words or acts supporting or favoring the cause of any country at war with the United States, or opposing the cause of the United States therein.

The 1918 act also enlarged the censorship functions of the postmaster general, empowering him to refuse to deliver mail to any individual or business employing the mails in violation of the statute. He was to order a letter that he deemed undeliverable to be returned to the sender with the phrase "Mail to this address undeliverable under the Espionage Act" stamped on the envelope. Thus the postmaster general was empowered to damage or destroy the business or reputation of any American citizen.

Enforced extensively in the period from May to November 1918, the measure virtually terminated wartime criticism until the Armistice. While efforts were made to reenact its provisions in a peace-time sedition statute during the A. MITCHELL PALMER "red scare" period, Congress balked and ultimately took the act off the books in March 1921.

The extremely broad language of the act would today make it vulnerable to attack on the grounds of OVERBREADTH. In 1919, however, the Supreme Court upheld the conviction of five anarchists for circulating a leaflet urging curtailment of war production and encouraging resistance to the participation of U.S. forces in opposition to the Russian revolution. Justice OLIVER WENDELL HOLMES wrote a famous dissent, joined by Justice LOUIS D. BRANDEIS, in ABRAMS V.

UNITED STATES (1919). (See CLEAR AND PRESENT DANGER.)

PAUL L. MURPHY

Bibliography

MURPHY, PAUL L. 1979 *World War I and the Origin of Civil Liberties in the United States.* New York: Norton.

SEDITIOUS LIBEL

Though its scope has varied greatly with time and place, the heart of the doctrine of seditious libel is the proposition that government may punish its critics for words it perceives as a threat to its survival. The offending words may be criticism of the government itself, or, more often, of its leaders. What constitutes seditious libel tends to be whatever the government fears most at the time. In fifteenth-century England, where reverence for the crown was considered essential to the safety of the realm, it was a crime to call the king a fool or to predict his death. In colonial America the most frequent offense was criticizing local representatives of the crown. In 1798, the Federalist party feared that Jeffersonian attacks would so undermine public confidence that the fledgling Republic would fall—or at least that the Federalists would lose the election of 1800. They therefore made it a crime to publish any false, scandalous, and malicious writing about either house of Congress or the President of the United States.

In England, seditious libels were once prosecuted as treason, punishable by death. Thus in 1663 William Twyn, who printed a book endorsing the right of revolution, was hanged, emasculated, disemboweled, quartered, and beheaded. Not until the eighteenth century did the law clearly distinguish seditious libel from treason; the latter then was confined to cases in which the seditious words were accompanied by some overt act. Seditious libel became a misdemeanor, punishable by fines, imprisonment, and the pillory. Prosecutions were common in England until the mid-nineteenth century.

Seditious libel was part of the received law in the American colonies, but it was received unenthusiastically. There probably were no more than a dozen seditious libel prosecutions in the entire colonial period, and few were successful. Although no one seems to have doubted that government should have some power to protect itself from verbal attacks, many complained that the doctrine as it had evolved in England allowed legitimate criticism to be swept within the ambit of the seditious libel proscription. The law allowed no defense of truth; the objective was to preserve respect for government, to which truthful criticism was an even greater threat than falsehood. And because the interests to be protected were the government's, it would hardly do to let a jury decide whether the words were actionable. The judges therefore kept for themselves the power to determine whether the speaker's intent was seditious; the jury was only allowed to decide whether he had uttered the words charged.

As ideas of POPULAR SOVEREIGNTY grew, critics on both sides of the Atlantic attacked these rules. In America the issue jelled in the 1735 trial of John Peter Zenger, a New York printer who had criticized the royal governor. Zenger's lawyer, Andrew Hamilton, argued that he should be allowed to defend Zenger by proving the truth of the publication, and that the jury should be allowed to decide whether the words were libelous. The judge rejected both arguments, but the jury acquitted Zenger anyway, even though he had admitted publishing the words. (See ZENGER'S CASE.)

The case made popular heroes of Zenger and Hamilton and destroyed the effectiveness of seditious libel law as a tool for English control of American dissent. There were few, if any, successful common law prosecutions in the colonies after *Zenger.* Colonial legislatures sometimes punished their critics for breaches of "parliamentary privilege," but public resentment eventually made this device ineffective, too.

The intended effect of the FIRST AMENDMENT on the law of seditious libel is still in dispute. It is clear that seditious libel was still the law in 1789, and that the Framers expressed no intent to preclude prosecutions for seditious libel. They certainly did not intend to prevent the states from prosecuting seditious libels; all agreed that the First Amendment was a limitation on federal power only. And within a decade, Congress passed the Sedition Act of 1798, under which the Federalists prosecuted a number of prominent Republican editors. Several Justices of the Supreme Court, sitting as circuit judges, enforced the act. This evidence has persuaded some modern scholars that the Framers had no intention of abolishing seditious libel.

Others have argued that the Framers had at least a nascent understanding that some freedom to criticize government was a prerequisite to self-government, and that England's rigorous concept of seditious libel was inconsistent with that need. Their failure explicitly to condemn it might be explained by the fact that seditious libel prosecutions had not been a serious threat in their lifetimes. The Sedition Act may have been an unprincipled effort by desperate Federalist partisans to keep control of the government, rather than a considered affirmation of the constitutionality of seditious libel.

The Supreme Court has never squarely held that the First Amendment forbids punishment of seditious libels. From World War I through the McCarthy era, state and federal governments prosecuted numerous anarchists, socialists, and communists for advocating draft resistance, mass strikes, or overthrow of the government. Although the statutes authorizing these prosecutions were not called seditious libel acts, they had much the same effect. The Court generally upheld these convictions (usually over the dissents of the more libertarian Justices) until the 1960s, when in BRANDENBURG V. OHIO (1969) it adopted the view that punishment of mere advocacy is unconstitutional unless it is intended to produce imminent lawless action and is likely to do so.

Garrison v. Louisiana (1964) closely resembled a traditional seditious libel prosecution. A district attorney had been convicted of criminal libel for accusing local judges of laziness and corruption. The Court reversed his conviction, but implied that the prosecution might have been permissible if the state had proved that the defendant spoke with reckless disregard of the truth or falsity of his statements.

Nevertheless, the judgment of history is that seditious libel laws are inconsistent with FREEDOM OF SPEECH and FREEDOM OF THE PRESS. JAMES MADISON and THOMAS JEFFERSON argued in 1799 that the Sedition Act was unconstitutional. Justice OLIVER WENDELL HOLMES, dissenting in ABRAMS V. UNITED STATES (1919), wrote, "I wholly disagree with the argument of the Government that the First Amendment left the common law as to seditious libel in force. . . . I had conceived that the United States through many years had shown its repentance for the Sedition Act . . . by repaying the fines that it imposed." And in NEW YORK TIMES V. SULLIVAN (1964) the Court said, "Although the Sedition Act was never tested in this Court, the attack upon its validity has carried the day in the court of history."

DAVID A. ANDERSON

(SEE ALSO: *Alien and Sedition Acts.*)

Bibliography

ANDERSON, DAVID A. 1983 The Origins of the Press Clause. *University of California at Los Angeles Law Review* 30:455–537.

LEVY, LEONARD W. 1984 *Emergence of a Free Press.* New York: Oxford University Press.

NELSON, HAROLD L. 1959 Seditious Libel in Colonial America. *American Journal of Legal History* 3:160–172.

SEEGER, UNITED STATES v. 380 U.S. 163 (1965)

At issue in the *Seeger* case was Section 6(j) of the Universal Military Training and Service Act. Originally enacted in 1940, the act exempted those who, as a matter of "religious training and belief," were opposed to participation in a war. In 1948, Congress amended this provision and defined religious belief as "an individual's belief in a relation to a supreme being involving duties superior to those arising from any human relation, but [not including] essentially political, sociological, or philosophical views. . . ."

Despite the textual evidence of a congressional intent to condition exemption on the theistic belief, Justice TOM C. CLARK, for the Supreme Court, interpreted the provision as requiring only a sincere and meaningful belief occupying in the life of its possessor a place parallel to that filled by the belief in God of those admittedly qualified for the exemption. Seeger had argued that if section 6(j) granted exemptions only on the basis of conventional theistic belief, it amounted to an ESTABLISHMENT OF RELIGION. Facing the unattractive alternatives of finding section 6(j) unconstitutional or reading it in a sufficiently broad fashion so as to secularize the exemption, the majority chose the latter.

RICHARD E. MORGAN

(SEE ALSO: *Conscientious Objection.*)

SEGREGATION

From the beginning, RACIAL DISCRIMINATION in America has been a national phenomenon. Jim Crow was a southern name for the segregation of the races as part of a system of caste. But segregation antedated Jim Crow, and it began in the North and the West. The leading judicial decision upholding school segregation before the Civil War bears a name Northerners prefer to forget: ROBERTS V. BOSTON (1850). Blacks were either excluded entirely from PUBLIC ACCOMMODATIONS such as hotels, railroads, and theaters, or given separate accommodations. They were segregated in prisons and in churches. Several northern and western states even sought to bar the immigration of blacks; such a legal provision was adopted by Oregon voters by an eight-to-one margin.

Nor has this country's segregation been limited to blacks. As late as 1947, a federal court of appeals held that the segregation of Chicano children in a school district in California was invalid. The decision's ground was itself depressing: the state's statute authorized only the segregation of children whose ancestry was Indian, Chinese, Japanese, and Mongolian.

Still, it was the postabolition South that carried the segregation of the races to its fullest development, and blacks were the chief victims of the practice. Before slavery was abolished, of course, the dominance of whites was assured without any call for segregation. After abolition, the southern states adopted severe legal restrictions on blacks, which served to maintain white supremacy. (See BLACK CODES.) When the CIVIL RIGHTS ACT OF 1866 and the FOURTEENTH AMENDMENT not only ended these legal restrictions but also positively declared the CITIZENSHIP of the freed slaves, segregation was the southern response. By 1870, Tennessee had forbidden interracial marriages (see MISCEGENATION), and later came the "Jim Crow car" laws segregating railroad passenger seating.

Segregation was not, however, merely a creature of state legislation. It also resulted from private action: a hotel would refuse to take black guests; homeowners in a neighborhood would agree not to sell to black buyers. In such cases law played a role that was less obvious on the surface of events but was vital nonetheless. A black who sought the aid of the state courts in overcoming private discrimination would simply be turned away; state laws would deny any remedy.

Late in the nineteenth century, the Supreme Court gave its support to this system of interlocking discriminations. In the CIVIL RIGHTS CASES (1883), the Court held invalid a congressional statute forbidding racial discrimination by railroads, hotels, theaters, and restaurants. (See STATE ACTION.) And in PLESSY V. FERGUSON (1896) the Court upheld a Jim Crow car law against an EQUAL PROTECTION attack. (See SEPARATE BUT EQUAL DOCTRINE.) By the early twentieth century, the South was racially segregated to extremes that were at once tragic and ludicrous: separate telephone booths for blacks in Oklahoma; separate storage for textbooks used by black children in North Carolina and Florida schools; separate elevators for blacks in Atlanta; separate Bibles for swearing black witnesses in Georgia courts. The point of all this was nothing less than the denial to blacks of membership in a white-dominated society—the denial of citizenship itself, in defiance of the Fourteenth Amendment.

Some of the harms caused by racial segregation are harms to material interests: a black is denied accommodation at a hotel, or admission to a state university medical school (and thus to the medical profession), or the chance to live in a particular neighborhood or be a factory foreman. These material harms are serious, but the worst harms of segregation are psychic harms. The primary reason for segregating railroad passengers, of course, is to symbolize a caste system. The stigma of inferiority is a denial of a person's humanity, and the result is anguish and humiliation. The more the races are separated, the more natural it is for members of the dominant white race to see each black person not as an individual but simply as a black. Ralph Ellison, in his novel *Invisible Man* (1952), makes the point: "I am invisible, understand, simply because people refuse to see me. . . . When they approach me they see only my surroundings, themselves, or figments of their imagination—indeed, everything and anything except me. . . . You ache with the need to convince yourself that you do exist in the real world." To be a citizen, on the other hand, is to be respected as a person and recognized as a participating member in the society.

Jim Crow was a complex living system, and its dismantling would be no simple task. The field of segregation in housing exemplifies the difficulties. The NAACP's first major victory against segregation came in BUCHANAN V. WARLEY (1917), when the Supreme Court struck down a local ZONING ordinance aimed at maintaining segregated residential neighborhoods. But the decision by no means ended housing segregation, which continued as a result of private conduct. When the private discrimination was sufficiently connected with state action, as in the case of racially RESTRICTIVE COVENANTS enforced by state courts, the Fourteenth Amendment was an effective weapon against residential segregation. (See SHELLEY V. KRAEMER, 1948.) But in the absence of such state support, a landowner might simply refuse to rent or sell to blacks, and the would-be buyers would be without remedy. Two events in 1968 altered this portion of the doctrinal landscape. In JONES V. ALFRED H. MAYER CO. the Supreme Court concluded that the Civil Rights Act of 1866 forbade private discrimination in the sale of property. In the same year, Congress adopted a comprehensive fair housing law as part of the CIVIL RIGHTS ACT OF 1968. The new law forbade various forms of racial discrimination by lenders and brokers as well as private landlords and sellers. The combination of constitutional litigation and legislation aimed at ending housing segregation had achieved a radical restructuring of the law.

The restructuring of racial patterns in the neighborhoods where people live, however, has proved to be quite another matter. Middle-class blacks have largely left the core cities to live in suburbs, but the degree of racial segregation in residences has changed only slightly since 1940. The term "white flight," coined in the context of school desegregation, seems even more clearly applicable to residential patterns. It is hard to find stable interracial neighborhoods in any large city in the country, at any income level. (For discussion of related questions concerning the public schools—where continued patterns of segregation are related directly to residential segregation—see DESEGREGATION.)

In contrast, racial segregation in transportation and other public accommodations has come to an end. (See SIT-IN; CIVIL RIGHTS ACT OF 1964.) And laws forbidding interracial marriage collapsed under the double weight of equal protection and DUE PROCESS in LOVING V. VIRGINIA (1967). (See FREEDOM OF INTIMATE ASSOCIATION.) EMPLOYMENT DISCRIMINATION, too, is in retreat—including the segregation of job categories by race—as a result of enforcement of the fair employment portions of the 1964 Act.

The segregation that remains in American society, then, is chiefly residential segregation—with its concomitant, a substantial extent of separation of the races in the public schools. There is irony here: the decision in the school segregation case, BROWN V. BOARD OF EDUCATION (1954), was the critical event in the demise of Jim Crow, but our big city schools are the one set of public institutions in which the races remain largely separated. Yet *Brown*'s impact on American life was important. The decision began more than a doctrinal movement; its implicit affirmation of the equal citizenship of all our people accelerated forces that have markedly changed not only race relations but also a wide range of other relationships formerly characterized by dominance and dependency.

It is easy now to see the social and economic changes in the country that permitted the success of the movement to end officially sponsored segregation. World War II was the great watershed. By the time the war began, there was a critical mass of educated blacks, enough to provide a national movement not only with its great chiefs but with local leadership as well—and with a trained cadre of lawyers. The war produced waves of migration of blacks out of the rural South and into the cities of the North and West, where they very soon found a political voice. In part, too, the war had been billed as a war against Nazi racism—whatever we might be doing on the home front. (See JAPANESE AMERICAN CASES, 1943–1944.) The expected postwar depression failed to appear, and the 1950s and 1960s were a time of economic expansion, conducive to a sympathetic reception for egalitarian claims. All this is familiar learning. Yet in the early 1950s there was no sense of inevitability surrounding the assault on segregation. If the sudden collapse of Jim Crow now seems inevitable, that in itself is a measure of the distance we have come. And if the end of segregation did not end a system of racial caste, that is a measure of the distance we have yet to travel.

KENNETH L. KARST

Bibliography

BELL, DERRICK 1980 Brown v. Board of Education and the Interest-Convergence Dilemma. *Harvard Law Review* 93:518–533.

LEVY, LEONARD W. and JONES, DOUGLAS 1972 Jim Crow Education: Origins of the "Separate but Equal" Doctrine. In Levy, Leonard W., *Judgments: Essays on American Constitutional History*. Chicago: Quadrangle Books.

LITWACK, LEON F. 1961 *North of Slavery*. Chicago: University of Chicago Press.

MYRDAL, GUNNAR 1944 *An American Dilemma*. New York: Harper & Brothers.

WOODWARD, C. VANN 1966 *The Strange Career of Jim Crow*, 2nd rev. ed. New York: Oxford University Press.

SELDEN, JOHN
(1584–1654)

A jurist, antiquary, and occasional member of Parliament, John Selden wrote extensively on the history of English law. With Sir EDWARD COKE he championed individual liberties and helped frame the PETITION OF RIGHT. He contended that Parliament's rights were secured by COMMON LAW and not enjoyed at the Crown's discretion.

DAVID GORDON

SELECTIVE CONSCIENTIOUS OBJECTION

See: Conscientious Objection

SELECTIVE DRAFT LAW CASES
Arver v. United States
245 U.S. 366 (1918)

In 1917, Congress authorized CONSCRIPTION as a means of rapidly increasing the strength of the armed forces. All males between twenty-one and thirty were to register for the draft, and up to one million were selectively to be called up. The six petitioners were all convicted of failure to register.

A unanimous Supreme Court, speaking through Chief Justice EDWARD D. WHITE, rejected each of several constitutional arguments against the draft law. Since the power to raise armies is specifically granted, the Court held that Congress might adopt any means necessary to call the required number of men into service. Compulsion might be used since "a governmental power which has no sanction to it . . . is in no substantial sense a power." A number of ingenious arguments based on the historic nature and uses of the militia were rejected because the power to raise armies is distinct from the militia clause.

For the argument that conscription violated the THIRTEENTH AMENDMENT, White had only eloquent scorn: "We are unable to conceive upon what theory the exaction by the government from the citizen of his supreme and noble duty of contributing to the defense of the rights and honor of the nation . . . can be said to be the imposition of involuntary servitude."

DENNIS J. MAHONEY

SELECTIVE EXCLUSIVENESS

Selective exclusiveness, or the *Cooley* doctrine, derives from the opinion of Justice BENJAMIN R. CURTIS for the Supreme Court in COOLEY V. BOARD OF PORT WARDENS (1852). Before that case, conflict and confusion characterized the Court's decisions in COMMERCE CLAUSE cases. Some Justices believed that Congress's power to regulate interstate and FOREIGN COMMERCE was an EXCLUSIVE POWER and others that the states shared CONCURRENT POWER over commerce. Some believed that a distinction existed between the national power over commerce and the STATE POLICE POWER.

Cooley provided a compromise doctrine that transformed judicial thinking. The Court recognized that commerce embraces a vast field of diverse subjects, some demanding a single uniform rule that only Congress might make, and others best served by state regulations based on local needs and differences. Thus the doctrine treated congressional power as exclusive on a selective basis—in only those cases requiring uniform legislation; and the states shared a concurrent power in other cases. In cases of conflict, of course, congressional action would prevail.

The *Cooley* formulation necessarily failed to provide a means by which the Court could discern which subjects were national and which local. Accordingly the Justices were able to manipulate the doctrine to sustain or invalidate state legislation as they wished. In time, judicial analysis focused on the purposes of the legislation and the degree to which it adversely affected the flow of commerce, rather than on the nature of the subject regulated. No formulation could diminish the free play of judicial discretion.

LEONARD W. LEVY

Bibliography

FRANKFURTER, FELIX 1937 *The Commerce Clause under Marshall, Taney, and Waite.* Chapel Hill: University of North Carolina Press.

SELECTIVE INCORPORATION

See: Incorporation Doctrine

SELECTIVE SERVICE ACT
40 Stat. 76 (1917)

In the National Defense Act of 1916, the General Staff prepared a blueprint for increasing the military, but it failed to recruit adequate personnel through a voluntary system. With war declared, President WOODROW WILSON in April 1917 sent to Congress a bill to "Authorize the President to Increase Temporarily the Military Establishment." After a six-week debate, the Selective Service Act of 1917 was enacted. The measure vested the President with the power to raise an army by CONSCRIPTION. Enrollment and selection were to be carried out by 4,000 local civilian boards, appointed by the President and organized under federally appointed state directors. Although these boards operated under uniform federal regulations, they were given considerable discretion in meeting quotas and handling deferment applications. The manpower requirements for the war period were developed by the army General Staff and apportioned to the states. The order of induction was determined by lottery. Over twenty-four million American males were registered under the law. Nearly three million were selected and inducted.

The constitutionality of the law was early challenged by its opponents on the grounds of illegal DELEGATION OF POWER and a violation of the THIRTEENTH, Fifth, TENTH, and FIRST AMENDMENTS. The Supreme Court brushed aside such challenges in the SELECTIVE DRAFT LAW CASES (1918), determining that the powers of the central government to make war and support armies encompass the authority to impose compulsory military service.

PAUL L. MURPHY

Bibliography

DUGGAN, JOSEPH S. 1946 *Legislative and Statutory Development of the Federal Concept of Conscription for Military Service.* Washington: Catholic University Press.

SELECTIVE SERVICE ACTS

Conscription Act
12 Stat. 731 (1863)

Burke-Wadsworth Selective Training and Service Act
54 Stat. 885 (1940)

Universal Military Training and Service Act
62 Stat. 604 (1948)

The Constitution gives Congress the power to "raise and support armies" and to "provide and maintain a navy." The traditions of the American people have dictated that throughout most of our history peacetime military service has been voluntary and emergencies have been met, in the first instance, by activating the organized state militias. CONSCRIPTION, drafting men for compulsory military duty, is available for the gravest emergencies. During the War of 1812, Congress considered, but did not adopt, a Draft Bill.

The first federal military draft in American history was authorized by the Conscription Act of 1863. That act required registration of all able-bodied male citizens eighteen to forty-five years old, and provided that whenever a congressional district failed to provide its quota of volunteers the deficiency should be made up by drawing from the pool of registrants. The act further provided that the draftee could avoid service by providing a substitute or by paying $300. The first draft under the act, in July 1863, was the occasion of a week-long riot in New York City, in which over one thousand people were killed and over one-and-a-half million dollars worth of property was destroyed.

The first peacetime selective service law was the Burke-Wadsworth Act of 1940, requiring registration in anticipation of American entry into World War II. The act, also known as the Selective Training and Service Act, was patterned after the SELECTIVE SERVICE ACT OF 1917: universal registration and classification administered by local boards. The 1940 act expired in 1947 and was replaced by the Universal Military Training and Service Act of 1948, which continued the basic scheme of the 1917 and 1940 statutes. The first draft under this act was in 1950, and conscription for the KOREAN WAR and VIETNAM WAR was done under provisions of that act. Registration under the act (renamed the Military Selective Service Act in 1967) ceased in 1975.

President Jimmy Carter in 1980 sought and received congressional authorization to reimplement peacetime draft registration, but the 1980 measure provided for registration only, not for classification or conscription. (See ROSTKER V. GOLDBERG, 1981.)

DENNIS J. MAHONEY

SELF-INCRIMINATION

See: Right against Self-Incrimination

SEPARATE BUT EQUAL DOCTRINE

The first type of racial SEGREGATION law to spread over the South was the "Jim Crow car" law, requiring blacks and whites to be seated separately in railroad passenger cars. When the Supreme Court held such a law valid in PLESSY V. FERGUSON (1896), the majority concluded that, so long as the facilities for each race were equal, the enforced separation of the races did not itself impose any inequality on black persons. In support of this separate but equal DOCTRINE, the Court drew on a pre-Civil War decision in Massachusetts, upholding racial segregation in the public schools. (See ROBERTS V. BOSTON, 1850.)

Although the doctrine originated in the context of state regulation of private conduct, it was soon extended to validate segregation in state-operated facilities. The races were separated by the law's command in courtrooms; in the public schools (see GONG LUM V. RICE, 1927); in state offices; in public parks, beaches, swimming pools, and golf courses; in prisons and jails. Some state institutions, such as universities, simply excluded blacks altogether; in most southern states there were separate state colleges for blacks. Throughout this system of segregation, the formal assumption was that facilities for blacks and whites might be separate, but they were equal.

Given the undoubted fact that segregation was imposed for the purpose of maintaining blacks in a condition of inferiority, the very term separate but equal is internally inconsistent. But the *Plessy* opinion had rejected the claim that racial separation itself imposed on blacks an inequality in the form of inferiority. (See BADGES OF SERVITUDE.) Yet *Plessy* set the terms of judicial inquiry in a way that ultimately undermined the separate but equal principle. The question of *justifications* for inequality was largely neglected; the Court focused on the question whether inequality *existed*.

In railroad cars, it was easy to achieve a rough equality of physical facilities. Similarly, a public swimming pool might be reserved for whites three days a week, reserved for blacks three days, and closed the other day. In education, however, inequalities of enormous proportion persisted up to the decision in BROWN V. BOARD OF EDUCATION (1954) and beyond. Black colleges lacked professional schools; black high schools emphasized vocational training and minimized preparation for college. In physical plants, teachers' salaries, levels of teacher training, counseling services, curricula—in every measurable aspect—the separate education offered blacks was anything but the equal of the education offered whites.

One strategy devised by the NAACP for ending school segregation was thus the filing of lawsuits aimed at forcing school boards to equalize spending for black education—at crushing expense. At the same time, a direct assault was made on segregation in higher education, and especially graduate education, where it was easiest to prove the inequality of facilities. (See MISSOURI EX REL. GAINES V. CANADA, 1938; SWEATT V. PAINTER, 1950.) These decisions, following *Plessy*'s lead, focused on the bare question of inequality. Inevitably, these cases came to touch the question whether segregation itself implied unequal education. The *Brown* opinion pursued that inquiry, found educational inequality in the fact of enforced separation, and—without discussing any purported justifications for segregation—held school segregation unconstitutional.

Separate but equal thus ended its doctrinal sway in the field of education. Within a few years the Supreme Court, in a series of PER CURIAM opinions consisting entirely of citations to *Brown*, had invalidated all state-sponsored segregation. The separate but equal doctrine was laid to rest.

KENNETH L. KARST

Bibliography

LEVY, LEONARD W. and JONES, DOUGLAS 1972 Jim Crow Education: Origins of the "Separate but Equal" Doctrine. In Levy, Leonard W., *Judgments: Essays on American Constitutional History*. Chicago: Quadrangle Books.

OBERST, PAUL 1973 The Strange Career of *Plessy v. Ferguson*. *Arizona Law Review* 15:389–418.

WOODWARD, C. VANN 1966 *The Strange Career of Jim Crow*, 2nd rev. ed. New York: Oxford University Press.

SEPARATION OF CHURCH AND STATE

The first provision of the BILL OF RIGHTS—known as the establishment clause—states that "Congress shall make no law respecting an ESTABLISHMENT OF RELIGION. . . ." This constitutional mandate seeks to assure the separation of church and state in a nation characterized by religious pluralism.

Justice WILEY B. RUTLEDGE observed in EVERSON V. BOARD OF EDUCATION (1947) that "no provision of the Constitution is more closely tied to or given content by its generating history than the religious clause of the FIRST AMENDMENT." Justice HUGO L. BLACK recounted in *Everson* that in the old world, "with the power of government supporting them, at various times and places, Catholics had persecuted Protestants, Protestants had persecuted Baptists, Protestant sects had persecuted other Protestant sects, Catholics of one shade of belief had persecuted Catholics of another shade of belief, and all of these had from time to time persecuted Jews." And, he added, "these practices of the old world were transplanted to and began to thrive in the soil of the new America." For example, in Massachusetts, Quakers, Baptists, and other religious minorities suffered harshly and were taxed for the established Congregational Church. In 1776, the Maryland "Declaration of Rights" stated that "only persons professing the Christian religion" were entitled to religious freedom, and not until 1826 were Jews permitted to hold public office. The South Carolina Constitution of 1778 stated that "the Christian Protestant religion shall be deemed . . . the established religion of this state."

The specific historical record, rather than disclosing a coherent "intent of the Framers," suggests that those who influenced the framing of the First Amendment were animated by several distinct and sometimes conflicting goals. Thus, THOMAS JEFFERSON believed that the integrity of government could be preserved only by erecting "a wall of separation" between church and state. A sharp division of authority was essential, in his view, to insulate the democratic process from ecclesiastical depradations and excursions. JAMES MADISON shared this view, but also perceived church–state separation as benefiting religious institutions. Even more strongly, ROGER WILLIAMS, one of the earliest colonial proponents of religious freedom, posited an evangelical theory of separation, believing it vital to protect the sanctity of the church's "garden" from the "wilderness" of the state. Finally, there is evidence that one purpose of the establishment clause was to protect the existing state-established churches from the newly ordained national government. (Indeed, although disestablishment was then well under way, the epoch of state-sponsored churches did not close until 1833 when Massachusetts separated church and state.)

Even if the Framers' intent were unanimous and unambiguous, it still could not provide ready answers for many contemporary problems. First, a number of present-day church–state issues were not foreseen by the founders. For example, public education was virtually unknown in the eighteenth century; the Framers could have no position on the matter of RELIGION IN PUBLIC SCHOOLS—one of the most frequently adjudicated modern establishment clause questions. Second, implementing the Framers' precise thinking, even if discernible, might jeopardize values now considered secured by the establishment clause. As Justice WILLIAM J. BRENNAN speculated in ABINGTON TOWNSHIP SCHOOL DISTRICT V. SCHEMPP (1963), perhaps because the nation has become more religiously heterogeneous, "practices which may have been objectionable to no one in the time of Jefferson and Madison may today be highly offensive to . . . the deeply devout and the non-believers alike."

The varied ideologies that prompted the founders do, however, disclose a dominant theme: according constitutional status to RELIGIOUS LIBERTY and the integrity of individual conscience. Moreover, one of the main practices seen by many Framers as anathema to religious freedom was forcing the people to support religion through compulsory taxation. Jefferson viewed this as "sinful and tyrannical," and Madison found it abhorrent to compel "a citizen to contribute three pence only of his property" to a religious cause. The founders recognized that although government subsidy of religion may not directly influence people's beliefs, it coerces citizens either to contribute to their own religions or, worse, to support sectarian doctrines antithetical to their convictions.

By its terms, the establishment clause applies only to the federal government ("*Congress* shall make no law . . ."), but in *Everson* (1947) the Court ruled that the FOURTEENTH AMENDMENT made the clause applicable to the states. Before then, only two Supreme Court decisions had produced any significant consideration of the establishment clause. *Bradfield v. Roberts* (1899) had upheld federal appropriations to a Roman Catholic hospital for care of indigent patients. *Quick Bear v. Leupp* (1908) had sustained federal disbursement of funds, held in trust for the Sioux Indians, to Roman Catholic schools designated by the Sioux for payment of tuition. Neither opinion, however, attempted any comprehensive definition of the nonestablishment precept, an effort first undertaken in *Everson* where the Court stated:

> The "establishment of religion" clause of the First Amendment means at least this: Neither a state nor the Federal government can set up a church. Neither can pass laws which aid one religion, aid all religions, or prefer one religion over another. Neither can force nor influence a person to go to or to remain away from church against his will or force him to profess a belief or disbelief in any religion. No person can be punished for entertaining or professing religious beliefs or disbeliefs, for church attendance or nonattendance. No tax in any amount, large or small, can be levied to support any religious activities or institutions, whatever they may be called, or whatever form they may adopt to teach or practice religion. Neither a state nor the Federal Government can, openly or secretly, participate in the affairs of any religious organization or groups and *vice versa.* In the words of Jefferson, the clause against establishment of religion by law was intended to erect "a wall of separation between church and state."

Since then, there has been little agreement among the Justices, lower courts, and scholars as to what constitutes impermissible "aid" to, or "support" of, religion.

Beginning in the early 1960s and culminating in LEMON V. KURTZMAN (1971), the Court developed a three-part test for reviewing establishment clause challenges: "First, the statute must have a secular legislative purpose; second, its principal or primary effect must be one that neither advances nor inhibits religion . . . ; finally, the statute must not foster 'an excessive government entanglement with religion.' " The *Lemon* test, despite its consistent invocation by the Court, has not been a model of coherence. Indeed, in an unusually candid OBITER DICTUM in COMMITTEE FOR PUBLIC EDUCATION V. REGAN (1980) the Court conceded that its approach "sacrifices clarity and predictability for flexibility," a state of affairs that "promises to be the case until the continuing interaction between the courts and the states . . . produces a single, more encompassing construction of the Establishment Clause." A better approach would read the establishment clause to forbid government action when its purpose is religious *and* it is likely to impair religious freedom by coercing, compromising, or influencing religious beliefs.

One of the nation's most politically divisive issues has been the proper place of religion in public schools. Decisions in the early 1960s, holding that prayer and Bible reading violate the establishment clause, precipitated serious efforts to reverse the Court by constitutional amendment. Later legislative proposals have sought to strip the federal courts of JURISDICTION over cases challenging voluntary school prayer.

The first cases concerning religion in public schools involved RELEASED TIME. In MCCOLLUM V. BOARD OF EDUCATION (1948) the Court invalidated an Illinois program of voluntary religious instruction in public school classrooms during school hours by privately employed teachers. Students whose parents signed "request cards" attended weekly classes in religion; others pursued secular studies elsewhere in the school during this period. The Court's opinion emphasized use of "the state's tax-supported public school buildings" and "the state's compulsory public school machinery." Four years later, in ZORACH V. CLAUSEN (1952), the Court upheld a New York City "off-premises" released time program. Released students attended classes at their respective religious centers; neither public funds nor public classrooms directly supported religion. In a much quoted and controversial passage, the Court observed: "We are a religious people whose institutions presuppose a Supreme Being. We guarantee the freedom to worship as one chooses. We make room for as wide a variety of beliefs and creeds as the spiritual needs of man deem necessary. . . . When the state encourages religious instruction or cooperates with religious authorities by adjusting the schedule of public events to sectarian needs, it follows the best of our traditions."

Neither *McCollum* nor *Zorach* propounded any specific STANDARD OF REVIEW. A decade later, in ENGEL V. VITALE (1962), the Court invalidated a New York law providing for recitation of a state-composed prayer at the beginning of each public school day. Although the prayer was denominationally "neutral," and students could remain silent or leave the room, the Court declared that this "breaches the constitutional wall of separation between Church and State," because "it is no part of the business of government to compose official prayers."

The Court's approach soon underwent a dramatic revision. In *Abington Township v. Schempp* the Court held it unconstitutional for public schools to conduct daily exercises of reading student-selected passages from either the Old or New Testaments (without teacher comment) and recitation of the Lord's Prayer. Drawing on its rationale in the SUNDAY CLOSING CASES (1961), the Court articulated a "test" for government action challenged under the establishment clause: "[W]hat are the purpose and the primary effect of the enactment? If either is the advancement or inhibition of religion then the enactment exceeds the scope of legislative power as circumscribed by the Constitution. That is to say that to withstand the strictures of the Establishment Clause there must be a secular legislative purpose and a primary effect that neither advances nor inhibits religion." The Court ruled that the "opening exercise is a religious ceremony," emphasizing, however, that "objective" study of the Bible (presumably for its literary and historical value) was constitutionally permissible.

There are two difficulties with the Court's declared willingness—reaffirmed regularly since *Schempp*—to invalidate government action solely on the basis of a nonsecular "purpose." First, although *Schempp* emphasized the establishment clause's requirement of a "wholesome neutrality" by the state toward religion, the Court has also made clear that the Constitution does not mandate an "untutored devotion" to this precept. Indeed, it has sometimes held that the free exercise clause *obliges* government to act with a nonsecular purpose—actually, to give a preference to religion—when the action is necessary to permit the unburdened exercise of religion.

Second, despite the *Schempp* test's condemnation of laws whose purpose is to "advance religion," the Court in *Zorach* had previously conceded that the released time program upheld had a nonsecular purpose: facilitation of religious instruction. *Zorach* has been specifically reaffirmed since *Schempp* was decided. Thus, the Court itself is not fully committed to its articulated doctrine that a religious purpose alone is sufficient to invalidate government action.

Although both *Engel* and *Schempp* declared that religious coercion was irrelevant under the establishment clause, the Court has nevertheless often carefully analyzed the elements of coercion and influence in programs it has considered. For example, in *Engel* the Court remarked on "the indirect coercive pressure upon religious minorities to conform to the prevailing officially approved religion." In *Zorach*, the Court emphasized its questionable conclusion that there was no "coercion to get public school students into religious classrooms." And in WIDMAR V. VINCENT (1981), in requiring a state university to provide student religious groups equal access to its facilities, the Court noted: "University students are . . . less impressionable than younger students and should be able to appreciate that the university's policy is one of neutrality towards religion."

The Court's sensitivity to religious coercion and influence in establishment clause challenges, its doctrinal pronouncements to the contrary notwithstanding, comports with an approach that recognizes that in accommodating the values underlying both the establishment and free exercise clauses, a nonsecular purpose cannot always be avoided, and that the primary offense to the establishment clause is some meaningful intrusion upon religious liberty.

Nearly two decades elapsed between *Schempp* and the BURGER COURT's first major decision on religion in public schools. In *Stone v. Graham* (1980) a Kentucky statute required posting a copy of the Ten Commandments (purchased with private funds) in all public school classrooms, with the notation: "The secular application of the Ten Commandments is clearly seen in its adoption as the fundamental legal code of Western Civilization and the COMMON LAW of the United States." Although the state court found that the legislature's purpose was not religious and sustained the law, the Supreme Court reversed.

The *Stone* opinion is significant for several reasons. First, it sheds further light on how the Court decides whether a legislative purpose is secular or religious. In *Schempp,* when the school board contended that the Bible reading program was not instituted for religious reasons (but rather to promote moral values, teach literature, and inspire student discipline), the Court brusquely replied that "surely, the place of the Bible as an instrument of religion cannot be gainsaid." In *Stone,* the Court stated that the Ten Commandments were not confined to "arguably secular matters" such as prohibition of murder and adultery but also prescribed religious duties such as observing the Sabbath and avoiding idolatry—adding that the law did not integrate the Bible or the commandments into an ethics, history, or comparative religion course. It quite peremptorily concluded that the program "serves no . . . educational function" and that "the Ten Commandments is undeniably a sacred text in the Jewish and Christian faiths, and no legislative recitation of a supposed secular purpose can blind us to that fact." *Stone* also reaffirms that a nonsecular purpose is itself enough to condemn a law under the establishment clause. Although the Court briefly considered the state program's potential for coercing or influencing children—observing that "if the posted copies of the Ten Commandments are to have any effect at all, it will be to induce the school children to read, meditate upon, perhaps to venerate and obey, the Commandments"—it nevertheless held that the law lacked a secular purpose and was invalid on that basis alone. This doctrine was vigorously reinforced in WALLACE V. JAFFREE (1985), which invalidated an Alabama statute authorizing a period of silence in public schools "for meditation or voluntary prayer," because the law was "entirely motivated by a purpose to advance religion." (The Justices plainly indicated that only a slightly different statutory formulation "protecting every student's right to engage in voluntary prayer during an appropriate moment of silence during the school day" would pass constitutional muster.)

Although regulatory laws allegedly enacted to aid religion have generated only a few Supreme Court decisions, they have significantly affected establishment clause jurisprudence. In MCGOWAN V. MARYLAND (1961) the Court upheld prohibition of the sale of most merchandise on Sundays. The Court conceded that the original purpose of Sunday closing laws was to encourage observance of the Christian Sabbath. But it found that, as presently written and administered, most such laws "are of a secular rather than of a religious character," seeking "to set one day apart from all others as a day of rest, repose, recreation and tranquility." The choice of Sunday, "a day of particular significance for the dominant Christian sects," did not "bar the state from achieving its secular goals."

McGowan emphasized that a Sunday closing law might violate the establishment clause if its purpose were "to use the State's coercive power to aid religion." This warning was fulfilled in EPPERSON V. ARKANSAS (1968), when the Court invalidated a law that excised the theory of human biological evolution from public school curricula. Reviewing the circumstances of its adoption in 1928, the Court found that "fundamentalist sectarian conviction was and still is the law's reason for existence."

Although Arkansas probably exceeded what the free exercise clause required for "accommodation" of fundamentalist religious doctrine, there was no indication that its anti-evolution statute coerced, compromised, or influenced school children to embrace fundamentalist doctrine. The Arkansas statute thus satisfied religious needs with no meaningful threat to religious liberty—the chief danger the establishment clause was intended to avoid. Yet, as in the Ten Commandments and moment-of-silence cases, a religious purpose alone proved fatal.

The Court first gave plenary consideration to the problem of public aid to church-related schools in *Everson v. Board of Education* (1947). A New Jersey township reimbursed parents for the cost of sending their children on public buses to and from schools, including Roman Catholic parochial schools. Although the Court asserted that "no tax . . . can be levied to support any religious activity or institution," it upheld the New Jersey program by a 5–4 vote. The majority conceded that without the program's subsidy some children might not be sent to church schools. But it reasoned that funding bus transportation for all pupils in both public and sectarian schools accomplished the "public purpose" of aiding parents in getting their children "safely and expeditiously to and from accredited schools." In this respect, New Jersey's aid program was similar to providing all schools with basic municipal services, such as fire and police protection. Furthermore, the state could not constitutionally exclude persons from its aid "because of their faith, or lack of it." (The *Everson* majority indicated that bus transportation might be the limit of permissible assistance.) The dissenters protested that the program aided children "in a substantial way to get the very thing which they are sent to [parochial schools] to secure, namely, religious training and teaching."

The Court did not again confront the issue of aid to church-related schools until BOARD OF EDUCATION v. ALLEN (1968). During the intervening two decades, the Court had developed the "secular purpose-secular effect" standard. *Allen* held that New York's lending secular textbooks, approved by local school boards, to all secondary school students, including those in church-related schools, had the secular purpose of furthering education and a primary effect that benefited students and parents, not religious schools.

The "excessive entanglement" prong of the Court's establishment clause test emerged two years later. WALZ v. TAX COMMISSION (1970) rejected the claim that New York's tax exemption for "real or personal property used exclusively for religious, educational or charitable purposes" supported religion in violation of the establishment clause. After finding that the exemption had the nonreligious purpose of avoiding inhibition on the activities of charities and other community institutions, the Court continued: "We must also be sure that the end result—the effect—is not an excessive government entanglement with religion. The test is inescapably one of degree. Either course, taxation of churches or exemptions, occasions some degree of involvement with religion. . . . [The question is] whether it is a continuing one calling for official and continuing surveillance leading to an impermissible degree of entanglement." The Court conceded that tax exemption accorded an indirect economic benefit to religion, but concluded that it gave rise to less government involvement than nonexemption. Taxing the churches would occasion "tax valuation of church property, tax liens, tax foreclosures, and the direct confrontations and conflicts that follow in the train of those legal processes."

In LEMON v. KURTZMAN (1971) the Court returned to the problem of church-related schools. Rhode Island subsidized public and private school teachers of secular subjects (not to exceed fifteen percent of their salaries); parochial school teachers agreed not to teach religion during the subsidy. The legislature had found that "the quality of education available in nonpublic elementary schools has been jeopardized [by] rapidly rising salaries." Pennsylvania reimbursed nonpublic schools for the salaries of teachers of "secular" subjects such as mathematics, physical science, physical education, and foreign languages. Church-related schools maintained accounts, subject to state audit, that segregated the costs of "secular educational service." Reimbursement for religiously oriented courses was prohibited.

The Court held that both programs violated the establishment clause. It acknowledged a secular purpose, but reasoned that the states' efforts to avoid a primary effect that advanced religion produced "excessive entanglement between government and religion." In the Court's view, church-related elementary and secondary schools had as their mission the inculcation of religious doctrine, especially among "impressionable" primary school pupils. Continuing state evaluation of school records "to establish the cost of secular as distinguished from religious instruction," and the state "surveillance necessary to ensure that teachers play a strictly nonideological role" were "pregnant with dangers of excessive government direction of Church schools and hence of Churches." Although this "administrative" entanglement was fatal, both laws risked another sort of entanglement: their "divisive political potential" along religious lines, given the likely demand for continuing and ever increasing annual appropriations.

The excessive entanglement criterion has been prominent in establishment clause adjudication since 1970; but it does not represent a value that either can or should be judicially secured by the establishment clause. The major fear of administrative entanglement between government and religion is that state regulation impairs the ability of religious groups to pursue their mission. This concern, however, is unfounded both doctrinally and empirically. At least since PIERCE v. SOCIETY OF SISTERS (1925) it has been understood that the Constitution permits the state to regulate church-related institutions whether or not it provides them financial assistance. Parochial school curricula, for example, have long been regulated without significant evidence of infringement of religious values. And if there were, the regulation would be invalid whether or not tied to monetary aid.

Another form of administrative entanglement regularly occurs when the state seeks to distinguish religion from nonreligion in order to grant an exemption from civil regulations. Although government scrutiny of religious beliefs is a sensitive task, the need for that scrutiny springs from the Constitution's explicit definition of religion as a subject for special treatment.

Similar objections can be raised to using "avoidance of political strife along religious lines" as a criterion for establishment clause adjudication. Indeed, if government were to ban religious conflict in the legislative process, serious questions of First Amendment political liberty would arise. But practical considerations, more than doctrinal ones, demonstrate the futility of making "political divisiveness" a constitutional determinant. Legislation does not violate the establishment clause simply because religious organizations support or oppose it. Religious groups have frequently differed on secular political issues—gambling, OBSCENITY, drug and gun control, CONSCRIPTION, PROHIBITION, abolition of slavery, racial integration, prostitution, sterilization, abortion, BIRTH CONTROL, divorce, the VIETNAM WAR, the EQUAL RIGHTS Amendment, and CAPITAL PUNISHMENT, to name but a few. Churches and other religious groups have markedly influenced resolution of some of these matters. In the early 1980s, they actively debated the question of the nation's nuclear arms policy. Although a law may in fact promote a religious purpose, if the law serves genuinely secular ends—and impairs no one's religious liberty by coercing, compromising, or influencing religious beliefs—it should not be unconstitutional simply because its proponents and antagonists were divided along religious lines.

Moreover, even if government could or should eliminate religious fragmentation in the political arena, the establishment clause is an ineffective tool for the task. For example, forbidding aid to parochial schools does not effect a truce, but only moves the battleground; if children in parochial schools are excluded from school aid, their parents will tend to oppose increased funding of public schools.

The Court has viewed aid to church-related higher education more favorably than it has viewed aid to elementary and secondary schools. *Tilton v. Richardson* (1971), a companion case to *Lemon,* upheld federal construction grants to colleges for buildings and facilities that applicants agreed not to use for religious instruction. The government enforced this promise by on-site inspections. The Court easily found a secular purpose in the expansion of higher education opportunities. In reasoning that the subsidy's primary effect did not advance religion, it stated that, unlike elementary and secondary schools, church-related colleges were not "permeated" by religion. Their dominant motive is secular education; they normally afford a high degree of ACADEMIC FREEDOM for faculty and students; and their students are less susceptible to religious indoctrination than are school children. In sharp contrast to its generalized appraisal of parochial schools, the Court rejected a "composite profile" of a "typical sectarian" college. Instead, the Court found, on the record before it, that courses at the four recipient Roman Catholic institutions were taught according to professional academic standards. Moreover, the aid took the form of a one-time, single-purpose construction grant. Thus no appreciable governmental surveillance was required. Finally, the Court found the potential for "religious fragmentation in the political arena" lessened by the religious colleges' geographically diverse student bodies and the absence of religious affiliation of a majority of recipient colleges.

Decisions since *Tilton* have continued to sustain aid to religiously affiliated colleges. In *Hunt v. McNair* (1973) the Court upheld the use of South Carolina tax-exempt bonds to finance facilities for all colleges, so long as the facilities were limited to nonsectarian purposes. The Court placed the burden on those challenging the aid to establish that recipient colleges are "permeated" with religion. And in *Roemer v. Board of Public Works* (1976) the Court upheld Maryland grants of fifteen percent of the student cost in the state college system to all private colleges, if they certified that they used the funds for nonreligious purposes.

Subsequent decisions on aid to elementary and secondary schools have generally, but not unexceptionally, followed the path of *Lemon. Meek v. Pittenger* (1975) involved a program under which Pennsylvania lent instructional materials (such as maps, films, projectors, and laboratory equipment) to private schools, seventy-five percent of which were church-related. The Court agreed that the aid was ideologically neutral, but held that "when it flows to an institution in which religion is so pervasive that a substantial portion of its functions are subsumed in the religious mission," it has the primary effect of advancing religion. The Court also invalidated "auxiliary services" (such as standardized testing, speech therapy, and psychological counseling) by public employees for private school children on their schools' premises: "To be certain that auxiliary teachers remain religiously neutral . . . the State would have to impose limitations . . . and then engage in some form of continuing surveillance to ensure that those restrictions were being followed." In addition to this "administrative entanglement," the Court observed that the program promised to generate "political entanglement" in the form of "continuing political strife." (The Court reaffirmed this holding as to auxiliary services in 1985 in the COMPANION CASES of *Grand Rapids School District v. Ball* and AGUILAR V. FELTON.)

Two years after *Meek, Wolman v. Walter* (1977) illustrated how constitutionality may turn on slight changes in form. The Court upheld Ohio's provision of (1) speech, hearing, and psychological diagnostic services by public employees on private school premises; (2) therapeutic and remedial services by public employees at a "neutral site off the premises" of the private school (even if in an adjacent mobile unit); and (3) payment for standardized tests used in private schools (the dispositive factor being that the tests were drafted and scored by public employees). The Court distinguished *Meek* on paperthin grounds relating to the closeness of the connection between the services provided and the religious school's educational mission and to the likelihood that public employees would "transmit ideological views" to children.

Wolman invalidated state payment for field trips of private school pupils, distinguishing *Everson* on the basis of the school's control over the expenditure of the funds and the close relation of the expenditure to the school's curriculum. The Court also invalidated a program for lending instructional materials to students, but, as in *Meek,* reaffirmed *Allen* and upheld lending students secular textbooks.

COMMITTEE FOR PUBLIC EDUCATION V. REGAN (1980) upheld New York's reimbursing private schools for performing testing and reporting services mandated by state law. The tests were prepared by the state, but, unlike those in *Wolman,* some were administered and scored by private school personnel. Nevertheless, because the tests were mostly objective, the Court concluded that there was little risk of their religious use. The Court distinguished *Levitt v. Committee for Public Education* (1973), which had invalidated a similar New York statute because it did not provide for state audits to ensure that the public funds did not exceed the nonpublic school's actual cost. In *Regan,* the occasional audits were found adequate to prevent a religious effect but not so intrusive as to produce excessive entanglement.

As of the mid-1980s, the most effective way for government to assist elementary and secondary parochial schools is through the tax system. In COMMITTEE FOR PUBLIC EDUCATION V. NYQUIST (1973) the Court invalidated a New York program, which the Court agreed had a "secular purpose," that gave tuition grants to low-income parents and tax relief to middle-income parents of children in private schools. The Court held that this had the effect of aiding the religious functions of sectarian schools. The Court distinguished *Walz* on several grounds. First, unlike the *Nyquist* programs, tax exemptions for church property had ample historical precedent, being "widespread during colonial days" and currently "in force in all 50 states." Second, although property tax exemption tended to lessen involvement between church and state, the programs in *Nyquist* tended to increase it. Finally, the tax exemption in *Walz* went to a broad class of charitable, religious, and educational institutions, but the record in *Nyquist* showed that eighty-five percent of the children benefited attended sectarian schools, practically all run by the Roman Catholic Church.

A decade later, in MUELLER V. ALLEN (1983), the Court upheld a Minnesota program granting a state income tax deduction for parents with children in *any* nonprofit school, public or private. This deduction could be used for expenditures for tuition and transportation, as well as for textbooks and instructional materials and equipment (so long as they were not used to teach religion). The Court conceded that the "economic consequences" of the Minnesota program were "difficult to distinguish" from the New York program in *Nyquist.* But that it was difficult did not make it impossible. One difference the Court found was that *Mueller* involved "a genuine tax deduction," whereas the *Nyquist* tax credit was more like a direct grant than a tax benefit. The Court found most significant that the *Mueller* plan was available to all parents, not just those with children in private schools. Thus, the plan was "facially neutral" and its "primary effect" did not advance religion. The Court reached this conclusion even though ninety-six percent of the Minnesota deductions were taken by parents who sent their children to parochial schools—mainly Roman Catholic and Lutheran. As for the other four percent, there were only seventy-nine public school students who deducted tuition, which they paid because they attended public schools outside their districts for special reasons. Of course, children who attended public schools in their districts did get some deductions—for the cost of pencils, notebooks, and other incidentals not customarily provided.

The lesson to be drawn from all the elementary and secondary school decisions is that states wishing to provide significant financial assistance may do so simply by adopting the proper form. For example, New York could successfully revive its program invalidated in *Nyquist* by providing a tax benefit to all parents, including those whose children attend public schools, knowing that this would not appreciably increase the cost of the plan. But New York might be required to use the form of a tax deduction (rather than a tax credit or direct grant as in *Nyquist*), a difference of vital importance to parents with low incomes, who would obtain little benefit from a tax deduction.

Application of the Court's three-part test to the problem of GOVERNMENT AID TO RELIGIOUS INSTITUTIONS has generated ad hoc judgments incapable of being reconciled on a principled basis. The Court has assumed that the entire program of parochial schools is "permeated" with religion. But there is much dispute as to the facts. Some "secular" subjects in some parochial schools are unquestionably courses of religious indoctrination; other courses are truly secular; many probably fall between these polar characterizations. Thus, public aid incidentally benefits religion. But virtually all government services to church-related facilities—whether bus transportation, police and fire protection, sewage connections, sidewalks, tuition grants, or textbooks—incidentally benefit their sectarian functions by releasing church funds for religious purposes.

The critical inquiry should be whether direct or indirect government assistance to parochial schools exceeds the value of the secular educational service the schools render. If it does not, there is no use of tax-raised funds to aid religion, and thus no danger to religious liberty. This inquiry differs from the Court's approach, which has often invalidated laws with secular purposes because of their effects in advancing religion. A state program with both a secular purpose and a secular effect does not threaten values underlying the establishment clause. Furthermore, when the Court invalidates such a law simply because it incidentally furthers religious interests, the Justices assert the power to assess the multiple impacts of legislation, to separate religious from secular effects, and then to determine which are paramount. Ultimately the Justices must then rely on their own subjective notions of predominance.

In the mid-1980s, the Court was twice confronted with the problem of government practices that specifically acknowledge religion. MARSH V. CHAMBERS (1983) upheld Nebraska's paying a chaplain to open each legislative session with a prayer. Proceeding unusually, the Court did not apply its three-part test. Rather, it relied first on history and tradition—pointing out that paid legislative chaplains and opening prayers existed in the Continental Congress, the First Congress, and every Congress thereafter, as well as in most states today and in colonies such as Virginia and Rhode Island, both of which were bastions of religious liberty. Second, the Court rested on the intent of the Framers, noting that just three days after the First Congress had authorized paid chaplains it approved the Bill of Rights; this made it difficult to believe that the Framers could conceive of the establishment clause as prohibiting legislative chaplains. Thus, the practice survived challenge even though Nebraska's purpose was unquestionably religious and the Court's doctrine is that such purpose alone produces an establishment clause violation.

A year later, in LYNCH V. DONNELLY (1984), the Court sustained Pawtucket, Rhode Island's inclusion of a nativity scene in the city's annual Christmas season display. The cost was nominal, unlike the $320 expended monthly for Nebraska's chaplain in *Marsh*. The Court reasoned that the purpose and effect were not exclusively religious but, rather, that "the creche in the display depicts the historical origins of this traditional event long recognized as a National Holiday." The opinion also emphasized that our history was replete with government recognition of religion's role in American life and with government expressions of religious belief. As examples, it pointed to presidential proclamations of national days of prayer and of Thanksgiving and Christmas as national holidays, public funding of a chapel in the Capitol and of chaplains in the legislature and in the military, "In God We Trust" as our statutorily prescribed national motto, the language "One Nation under God" as part of the Pledge of Allegiance, and the plethora of religious paintings in publicly supported galleries and in public buildings. Stating that "this history may help explain why the Court consistently has declined to take a rigid, absolutist view of the Establishment Clause," the Court strongly suggested that all these deeply ingrained practices were constitutional.

The final important church–state separation issue concerns the tension between the First Amendment's two religion clauses, one forbidding government to promote or "establish" religion, the other forbidding government to abridge the "free exercise" of religion. As observed in *Walz*, both "are cast in absolute terms, and either . . . if expanded to a logical extreme, would tend to clash with the other." Charting a course that offends neither provision presents a continual challenge for the Court; yet its few direct confrontations with the problem have been unsatisfying.

The two most celebrated free exercise clause decisions illustrate the inherent conflict. In SHERBERT V. VERNER (1962) a Seventh-Day Adventist was discharged by her employer because she would not work on Saturday, her Sabbath. South Carolina denied her unemployment compensation for refusing "suitable work," that is, a job requiring Saturday labor. The

Court held that this denial violated the free exercise clause by conditioning benefits on a violation of her religious faith. Although the Court's decision implements the free exercise clause, the purpose of its ruling—like the purpose of the released time program in *McCollum*—is clearly to facilitate religious practice. Thus, the exemption required by the Court in the name of the free exercise clause appears to violate the Court's establishment clause doctrine, which renders invalid any government action with a nonsecular purpose. The Court's conclusory response was that "plainly we are not fostering the 'establishment' of the Seventh-day Adventist religion" but rather governmental "neutrality in the face of religious differences."

In WISCONSIN V. YODER (1971) the Court held that application of school attendance requirements to the Old Order Amish violated the free exercise clause. In characterizing this as an "accommodation" for the Amish, the Court rejected the contention that this religious exemption violated the establishment clause: "The purpose and effect of such an exemption are not to support, favor, advance or assist the Amish, but to allow their centuries-old religious society . . . to survive free from the heavy impediment compliance with the Wisconsin compulsory-education law would impose."

In THORNTON V. CALDOR, INC. (1985), however, the Court ruled that a state had gone too far in "accommodating" religion. It held that a Connecticut law that required employers to give a day off to employees on their Sabbath, "no matter what burden or inconvenience this imposes on the employer or fellow workers," had the "primary effect" of advancing "a particular religious practice" and thus violated the establishment clause. The Court emphasized the "absolute and unqualified right not to work" afforded the employees, although this appeared to be little different from the exemption that the Court itself had ordered in *Sherbert.*

Although there is considerable overlap in the purposes of the establishment and free exercise clauses—their central function being to secure religious liberty—the decisions disclose that each has an identifiable emphasis. In the main, the free exercise clause protects adherents of religious faiths from secularly motivated laws whose effect burdens them because of their particular beliefs. When the Court finds a violation of the free exercise clause, the law is normally held invalid as applied; all that is required is an exemption for the claimant from the law's otherwise proper operation. In contrast, the principal thrust of the establishment clause concerns religiously motivated laws that pose the danger to believers and nonbelievers of being required to support their own religious observance or that of others. When the Court finds a violation of the establishment clause, ordinarily the offensive provision is entirely invalid and may not be enforced at all.

A better approach would reconcile the conflict between the clauses by interpreting the establishment clause to forbid only those laws whose purpose is to favor religion, and then only if such laws tend to coerce, compromise, or influence religious beliefs. Under this standard, the religious exemption that the Court required in *Sherbert* would itself be unconstitutional because it impairs religious liberty by supporting religion with funds raised by taxation. Although the core value of religious liberty may forbid government to interfere with Sherbert's practice of Seventh-Day Adventism, it similarly forbids forcing other citizens to subsidize a religious practice. On the other hand, the proposed alternative approach probably would not change the result in *Yoder;* it is doubtful that exempting the Amish from the compulsory education law (or giving employees a day off on their Sabbath, as in *Thornton*) would tend to coerce, compromise, or influence religious choice. Finally, the alternative approach would distinguish *Yoder* from those decisions—such as *McCollum, Engel,* and *Schempp*—that have invalidated religious practices in public schools. Neither these programs nor the exemption in *Yoder* had a "secular" purpose. But, unlike *Yoder* and *Thornton,* the public school programs threatened religious liberty and were thus properly held to abridge the constitutional separation of church and state.

JESSE H. CHOPER

Bibliography

ANTIEAU, CHESTER J.; DOWNEY, ARTHUR T.; and ROBERTS, EDWARD C. 1964 *Freedom from Federal Establishment.* Milwaukee, Wisc.: Bruce Publishing Co.

CHOPER, JESSE H. 1963 Religion in the Public Schools: A Proposed Constitutional Standard. *University of Minnesota Law Review* 47:329–416.

——— 1968 The Establishment Clause and Aid to Parochial Schools. *California Law Review* 56:260–341.

——— 1980 The Religion Clauses of the First Amendment: Reconciling the Conflict. *University of Pittsburgh Law Review* 41:673–701.

CURRY, THOMAS 1986 *The First Freedoms.* New York: Oxford University Press.

HOWE, MARK D. 1965 *The Garden and the Wilderness.* Chicago: University of Chicago Press.

KURLAND, PHILIP B. 1962 *Religion and the Law.* Chicago: Aldine Publishing Co.

LEVY, LEONARD W. 1986 *An Establishment of Religion.* New York: Macmillan.

MURRAY, JOHN C. 1960 *We Hold These Truths.* Chap. 2. New York: Sheed & Ward.

NOWAK, JOHN E.; ROTUNDA, RONALD D.; and YOUNG, J. NELSON 1983 *Handbook on Constitutional Law,* 2nd ed. Pages 1229–1281. St. Paul, Minn.: West Publishing Co.

PFEFFER, LEO 1984 *Religion, State, and the Burger Court.* Buffalo, N.Y.: Prometheus Books.

SCHWARTZ, ALAN 1968 No Imposition of Religion: The Establishment Clause Value. *Yale Law Journal* 77:692–737.

STOKES, ANSON PHELPS 1950 *Church & State in the United States.* 3 Vols. New York: Harper.

TRIBE, LAURENCE H. 1978 *American Constitutional Law.* Chap. 14. Mineola, N.Y.: Foundation Press.

SEPARATION OF POWERS

Any system of constitutional government must have as one of its central principles some degree of separation of powers. A system of government in which all legal power and authority is exercised by one person or group of people must depend entirely upon their self-restraint in the exercise of that power. The history of government does not suggest that such self-restraint is likely this side of heaven or utopia, and efforts to prevent the abuse of the powers of government have therefore focused on constitutional arrangements that divide and limit the powers of government.

The doctrine of the separation of powers consists of a number of elements: the idea of three separate branches of government, the legislature, the executive, and the judiciary; the belief that there are unique functions appropriate to each branch; and the assertion that the personnel of the branches of government should be kept distinct, no one person being able to be a member of more than one branch of government at the same time. The more pure or extreme the form of the doctrine, the greater the extent to which all three of these elements are insisted upon without reservation or modification. In past centuries political writers have proposed such extreme solutions in France, Britain, and America, and attempts have been made, unsuccessfully, to approximate as closely as possible to this extreme in practice. The spirit of the doctrine was expressed clearly in the Constitution of Virginia in 1776: "The legislature, executive and judiciary departments shall be separate and distinct, so that neither exercise the powers properly belonging to the other: nor shall any person exercise the powers of more than one of them at the same time. . . ."

A further aspect of the doctrine is the concern with the method by which the members of the executive and judicial branches are selected, for this will have implications for the extent to which the members of one branch may be able to influence the behavior of members of another. The more extreme versions of the doctrine therefore demand the direct election of members of all three branches of government in order that they should be responsible directly to the people, and not dependent upon each other. In the words of Samuel Williams, historian of Vermont, in 1794, "the security of the people is derived not from the nice ideal application of checks, balances, and mechanical powers, among the different parts of the government, but from the responsibility, and dependence of each part of the government, on the people."

The doctrine of the separation of powers, standing alone, however, has never been able to provide the kind of safeguards against the abuse of governmental power which it claims to provide. In practice we find that CHECKS AND BALANCES are required to prevent one or another branch of government from becoming too dominant. The idea of internal checks, exercised by one branch of government over the others, is drawn from the ancient theory of mixed government, and from the eighteenth-century "mixed and balanced constitution" of Great Britain. Thus JAMES MADISON, in THE FEDERALIST #48, undertook to show that unless the branches of government "be so far connected and blended as to give each a constitutional control over the others, the degree of separation which the maxim requires, as essential to a free government, can never in practice be duly maintained." All constitutional systems of government are therefore an amalgam of the separation of powers and checks and balances. The exact composition of this mixture was a central problem for the Framers of the federal Constitution, and their solution distinguished presidential-congressional government from parliamentary systems.

The emergence of a full-blown doctrine of the separation of powers was the result of a long process of development, involving the refinement of a set of concepts, including the idea of law itself, which today we largely take for granted. In early times the idea of law was very different from the modern concept of legislation or statute law. The latter view of law, consciously drafted and adopted by human rather than divine will, did not emerge clearly until the battle between king and parliament in seventeenth-century England sharpened the perception of law, lawyers, and politicians. The more radical opponents of royal power conceived of a parliament that was representative of the people, making laws which the king, or some other executive power, should put into effect. In the turmoil of civil war, this doctrine of the separation of powers was fashioned by a number of writers until it reached a recognizably modern form.

As the British constitutional crisis deepened, the doctrine was refined by those who, like John Milton, pointed to the arbitrary character of the Long Parliament, Henry Ireton in the Whitehall debates of 1649, and JOHN LILBURNE in *The Picture of the Councel of State* asserting that "the House itself was never (neither now, nor in any age before) betrusted with a Law executing power, but only with a Law making power." John Sadler in his *The Rights of the Kingdom* of 1649 asserted the basis of the separation of powers very clearly. The three powers of government, legislative, judicial, and executive, "should be in Distinct Subjects; by the Law of Nature, for if Lawmakers be judges, of those that break their Laws; they seem to be judges in their own cause: which our Law, and Nature itself, so much avoideth and abhorreth, so it seemeth also to forbid, both the Lawmaker, and the Judge to Execute."

The execution of Charles I and the establishment of republican government stripped away the remaining vestiges of mixed government and left the separation of powers as the sole constitutional principle for the organization of the government of Great Britain. The Commonwealth produced the first written constitution of modern times, the Instrument of Government of 1653, and the doctrine of the separation of powers clearly inspired its authors. This document vested the supreme legislative authority in the lord protector and the people assembled in Parliament, but in effect the role of the protector in legislation was to be limited to a suspensive veto of twenty days. The Instrument also provided that "the exercise of the Chief Magistracy and the administration of the Government . . . shall be in the Lord Protector, assisted with a Council." Although the Instrument of Government was never an effective basis for government, from that time on the theory of the separation of powers emerged and reemerged whenever demands were made to limit the power of governments. The official defense of the Instrument, *A True State of the Case of the Commonwealth,* published in 1654, and probably written by Marchamont Nedham, expressed the theory behind the constitution when it criticized earlier institutional arrangements "which placing the legislative and executive powers in the same persons is a marvellous in-let of corruption and tyranny." At this point the idea of a judicial power distinct from the executive was still relatively undeveloped, to emerge more fully at the end of the seventeenth century, and then to blossom in the work of MONTESQUIEU and WILLIAM BLACKSTONE, and to be embodied in the Constitution of the United States.

With the restoration of Charles II in 1660 the basis of a new theory of the constitution was required. The principle of the separation of powers must be reasserted, as it was by JOHN LOCKE, but in the context of a "mixed and balanced" constitution, incorporating a role for the monarch and for the House of Lords. This amalgam of the separation of powers and checks and balances, the constitution of the Augustan Age of British politics, was lauded as the model of "a constitution of liberty." Montesquieu is popularly credited with a major role in the development of the separation of powers, but the theory was developed a hundred years before the publication of *The Spirit of the Laws* (1748). Indeed it is the influence of his work, particularly in the American colonies, rather than any intellectual contribution to the separation of powers, that gives such significance to the work of Montesquieu. Montesquieu's contribution to the separation of powers was essentially his modern emphasis upon the three powers of government and the clear recognition of the importance of the power to judge, a point driven home by Blackstone in his *Commentaries on the Laws of England* (1765–1769). Blackstone, whose work was known to every lawyer in the American colonies, took Montesquieu's rather feeble notion of the judicial power and clothed it with the majesty of the English judges.

From the time of the first English settlements in America there was a continual interplay between ideas and events in the home country and the developing politics of the colonies. Mixed government and the separation of powers were common subjects of discussion in Massachusetts in the seventeenth century, and the constitutional debates over the role of king and parliament in England had their repercussions in America. In 1644, the elders of the church described the government of Massachusetts Bay as not a "pure aristocracy, but mixt of an aristocracy and democracy" and defended the "negative voice" which the governor and assistants exercised over decisions of the legislature. In 1679 the elders affirmed that the government of Massachusetts consisted in the "distribution of differing interest of power and privilege between the magistrates and freemen, and the distinct exercise of legislative and executive power." This statement preceded by eleven years the publication of Locke's *Second Treatise.* In the eighteenth century American thought fell into the same mold as that of other eulogists of the English constitution, adapting the terminology where necessary to fit the circumstances of colonial governments, until the increasing conflict between the English Parliament and the colonists brought to the foreground those aspects of the English system that were attracting criticism both at home and abroad, the cabinet system and the corrupt and unrepresentative House of Commons. In the colonies, Americans saw the mixing of legislative, executive, and judicial functions in the governors' councils and in the abuse of power by royal governors. With the upsurge of revolutionary fervor the doctrine of the separation of powers lay ready to hand, both as a stick with which to beat the British and as the basis for a truly American system of government.

The American achievement was to transform the theory of the mixed constitution, in which the powers of government were distributed among monarchy, aristocracy, and democracy, into a functionally divided system in which king and peers had no part, turning a class-based structure into one in which all the different branches of government drew their authority from the people. The first step in this process was taken when the revolutionary state constitutions were established in 1776 and succeeding years. These constitutions contained broad affirmations of the separation of powers, but the checks and balances of the British model were out of favor. Consequently, popularly elected legislatures became the dominant branch of government.

The state legislatures soon began to act in ways that raised fears that the separation of powers, if not buttressed in some other way, meant that in practice, in THOMAS JEFFERSON's words, "All the powers of government, legislative, executive, and judiciary, result to the legislative body." The need for positive checks to the exercise of power was increasingly apparent. The *Essex Result* of 1778, recommending the form which the new constitution for Massachusetts should take, noted that "Each branch is to be independent, and further, to be so balanced, and able to exert such checks upon the others, as will preserve it from dependance on, or a union with them." Madison summed up the situation in *The Federalist* #48: "The conclusion that I am warranted in drawing from these observations is, that a mere demarcation on parchment of the constitutional limits of the several departments is not a sufficient guard against those encroachments which lead to a tyrannical concentration of all the powers of government in the same hands."

It was necessary therefore that the departments of government should "be so far connected and blended as to give to each a constitutional control over the others": the President to have a qualified VETO POWER and the PARDONING POWER, the Senate to play a part in appointments and in the ratification of treaties, and the Supreme Court, by implication at least, to have the power to declare legislative acts to be unconstitutional. As Madison observed in *The Federalist* #48, the three branches of government, although separate, must be "connected and blended" to ensure that each has some "constitutional control over the others."

Thus the separation of powers was not destroyed but rather reinforced by the adoption in the Constitution of a number of checks and balances. Although in some degree this represented a reversion to the pattern of the English Constitution, there was one vital respect in which no one wished to see the English model adopted. The popular denigration of George III as a tyrant in the revolutionary situation was understandable, but the members of the CONSTITUTIONAL CONVENTION had a much deeper understanding of the British political system. They understood the nature of the "*Cabinet Council* composed entirely of the principal officers of the great departments," they understood the role of the king's ministers in the legislature, and they knew well the system of crown influence and the role of unqualified members of the House of Commons. Their rejection of the whole basis of linking the executive and legislative branches of government in this way was complete, and Article I, section 6, of the Constitution, which provided that "no Person holding any Office under the United States, shall be a Member of either House during his Continuence in Office," was adopted without hesitation.

What then have been the practical effects of the separation of powers on the legal and political system of the United States? These effects can be seen in two broad, related areas: the decisions of the Supreme Court relating to "the powers of government," and the political articulation of the American system.

The Supreme Court has faced a number of difficulties which arise from the confusions inherent in the way the "separation of powers" evolved. The term "separation of powers" is sometimes used, as here, to refer to the doctrine that the major branches of government should be kept separate and limited to their own functions, but quite often the term is also used to include the checks and balances in the Constitution, which derive their rationale from a different source. Second, the word "power" is used ambiguously to mean both "branch" and "function." Finally, most of the Court's problems arise from the need to define the functions of government when it is argued that a particular branch has engaged in an activity outside its "proper" function. When the Constitution itself makes what the Court in BAKER V. CARR (1962) called "a textually demonstrable commitment" of an issue to a coordinate branch of government, then the Court has only to determine that to be the case, but what does the text demonstrate when it refers to "the legislative power" or "the executive power"? Such terms are vague indeed. The nub of the problem is that the functions of government can be defined only in the broadest conceptual terms—making rules, carrying rules into effect, and settling disputes arising out of the application of rules—but few activities of government fall unambiguously into such categories. The difficulty is particularly acute in any effort to categorize the exercise of the discretionary powers of government which the traditional doctrine of the separation of powers did not encompass. Indeed, the doctrine had been developed largely to render ineffective the exercise of such discretion in the form of the prerogatives of the Crown in England, or in the exercise of the powers of the governors in the American colonies.

As a consequence of these difficulties the Court has generally followed a pragmatic course in its decisions on the separation of powers. In practice the Court has generally accepted that no precise "watertight definition of government powers is possible." The first major issue facing the Supreme Court was to define its own role in the system of separation of powers and checks and balances. The Anti-Federalist and Jeffersonian interpretations of the Constitution looked back to the strict view that each branch of government not only should be separate from the others but also should not be dependent upon them, and therefore not subject to their control. Such an interpretation would rule out JUDICIAL REVIEW as it has come to be exercised in the United States, and faint echoes of this attempt to escape the JURISDICTION of the Court have been heard as recently as President RICHARD M. NIXON's claim to an absolute EXECUTIVE PRIVILEGE for tape recordings of his conversations with his aides. However, in MARBURY V. MADISON (1803) Chief Justice JOHN MARSHALL emphatically asserted that it was "the province and duty of the judicial department to say what the law is"—and, in the course of doing so, to rule upon the extent of the power and functions of the other branches of government. Respect is due to the interpretations put on the Constitution by other branches, but in the end, as the Court said in UNITED STATES V. NIXON (1974), "the 'JUDICIAL POWER OF THE UNITED STATES' vested in the federal courts by Art. III Sec. 1, of the Constitution can no more be shared with the Executive Branch than the Chief Executive, for example, can share with the Judiciary the power to override a Presidential veto. Any other conclusion would be contrary to the basic concept of separation of powers and checks and balances that flow from the scheme of a tripartite government." The Court has, of course, accepted that interference in the activities of the other branches of government, in particular the Congress, is a delicate and sensitive matter. The POLITICAL QUESTIONS doctrine protects the Court against becoming embroiled in matters that could drag it down into the morass of day-to-day politics, but the Court itself retains the right to determine what is, and what is not, a political question.

The Supreme Court has set limits to the exercise of the legislative powers of Congress either to interfere directly in litigation, to interpret earlier legislation, or to set aside decisions of courts already made. It has also ruled that, as in HAYBURN'S CASE (1792) and *United States v. Ferreira* (1853), Congress cannot impose upon the courts duties not considered to be judicial in character. In two major decisions the Supreme Court announced that the houses of Congress could not properly appropriate to themselves a judicial function. In KILBOURN V. THOMPSON (1881) the Court concluded that in committing a witness to prison for refusing to testify before a committee the House of Representatives had "not only exceeded the limit of its own authority, but assumed power which could only be properly exercised by another branch of the government, because the power was in its nature clearly judicial." And OBITER DICTUM in WATKINS V. UNITED STATES (1957), the Court said, "Nor is the Congress a law enforcement or trial agency. These are functions of the executive and judicial departments of government."

The Supreme Court has also prevented Congress from trenching upon the powers of the executive branch. In MYERS V. UNITED STATES (1926) the Court held that Congress could not limit by statute the President's power to remove executive officers, although in HUMPHREY'S EXECUTOR V. UNITED STATES (1935) it upheld congressional restrictions on the President's power to dismiss officers of independent regulatory agencies; and in BUCKLEY V. VALEO (1976) the Court invalidated the attempt by Congress itself to make appointments to the Federal Elections Commission. The Court quoted with approval the decision in *Springer v. Philippine Islands* (1928): "Legislative power, as distinguished from executive power, is the authority to make laws, but not to enforce them or appoint the agents charged with the duty of such enforcement. The latter are executive functions."

In general the Supreme Court has been generous in its interpretation of the powers of the President. However, in two important instances the Court has checked presidential power. In YOUNGSTOWN SHEET AND TUBE COMPANY V. SAWYER (1951) the Court held unconstitutional President Harry S. Truman's attempt to take over steel mills by EXECUTIVE ORDER, on the ground that "the President's power to see that the laws are faithfully executed refutes the idea that he is to be a lawmaker. The Constitution limits his functions in the lawmaking process to the recommending of laws he thinks wise and the vetoing of laws he thinks bad." And in *United States v. Nixon* (1974) the Court rejected the President's claim of executive privilege against a court order to produce tapes and documents relating to the Watergate investigations.

The area in which the Supreme Court has been subjected to the greatest degree of criticism for failing to maintain the spirit and practice of the separation of powers has been the way in which it has handled the question of the DELEGATION OF POWER by Congress to the executive branch and to independent regulatory commissions. In the modern administrative state, complex regulatory activities on the part of government necessitate agencies that will make rules (subordinate to statute law), apply those rules, and decide disputes arising out of their actions. The United States Congress, in establishing a large number of such agencies, has created a "headless fourth branch" of government. These agencies, in the words of Justice ROBERT H. JACKSON in *Federal Trade Commission v. Ruberoid Company* (1952), "have been called quasi-legislative, quasi-executive or quasi-judicial, as the occasion required, in order to validate their function within the separation of powers scheme of the Constitution. The mere retreat to the qualifying 'quasi' is implicit with confession that all recognized classifications have broken down, and 'quasi' is a smooth cover which we draw over our confusion as we might use a counterpane to conceal a disordered bed." Although the Court has said "that the legislative power of Congress cannot be delegated," in practice it has allowed very broad and ill-defined delegations of power to administrative agencies. In two instances such delegation of power has been disallowed: PANAMA REFINING CO. V. RYAN (1935) and SCHECHTER POULTRY CORP. V. UNITED STATES (1935). In the latter case the Court asserted that the proper delegation of power required Congress to establish "standards of legal obligation, thus performing its essential legislative function." Failure to enact such standards for the administrative agency to follow would be an attempt to transfer the legislative function of Congress to others. However, in numerous cases the Court has allowed delegation with little in the way of effective standards set by Congress, and giving to the administrative agency, as in the *Permian Basin Area Rate Cases* (1968), a wide and uncontrolled discretion. In the field of FOREIGN AFFAIRS the delegation of legislative power to the President and his ability to negotiate with foreign powers and make EXECUTIVE AGREEMENTS with them, are very wide indeed, as the Court recognized in UNITED STATES V. CURTISS-WRIGHT EXPORT CORP. (1936).

In all these areas of tension between the branches of government, therefore, the Supreme Court, despite the broad generalizations which appear from time to time in its opinions, has followed a pragmatic approach to the separation of power. However, in IMMIGRATION AND NATURALIZATION SERVICE V. CHADHA (1983) the Court, in the opinion of some, adopted a more theoretical and formal line of argument. In *Chadha* the Court invalidated the use of the LEGISLATIVE VETO, the device by which Congress reserved to itself the right to review administrative regulations and decisions taken under some 200 different statutes. The opinion, written by Chief Justice WARREN E. BURGER, concentrated on the narrow constitutional issues of "presentment" of legislation and BICAMERALISM, but referred to the theory of the separation of powers in the Constitution as dividing the powers of government into "three defined categories, legislative, executive and judicial" which are "functionally identifiable." An alternative approach was put by Justice LEWIS F. POWELL in a CONCURRING OPINION. His objection to the use of the legislative veto in this particular instance was that the House of Representatives had improperly exercised a judicial power by ruling on the case of a particular individual rather than making a general rule. In taking this position Justice Powell was appealing to an element of the separation of powers of long standing and of great importance: the generality of law, restricting the legislative power to the general rather than the particular.

Some critics of the Supreme Court argue with Philip Kurland that as a consequence of its decisions "the ancient concept of the separation of powers and checks and balances has been reduced to a slogan, to be trotted out by the Supreme Court from time to time as a substitute for reasoned judgment." Whether or not this assessment of the judicial history of the separation should be considered too harsh, the impact of the concept upon the day-to-day working of the American political system has undoubtedly been enormous in terms of the relationship between the administration and the Congress. The prohibition on simultaneous membership of the legislative and executive branches in Article I, section 6, of the Constitution distinguishes the American system from the vast majority of genuinely democratic regimes in the world, most of which follow the parliamentary model. The fact that the President and his administration must operate from outside the legislature, rather than from within it, makes a vast difference to the techniques that must be employed to gain the acquiescence of the legislature to policies proposed by the executive. Much more important than the distinction between legislative and executive functions is the fact of two distinct branches of government with no overlapping of personnel (the VICE-PRESIDENT of the United States excepted). This strict separation of the personnel of government is certainly not the only reason why American political parties are so decentralized, diffuse, and undisciplined, but it is certainly a very important factor. The consequences for the way in which government policies are formulated, evolved, enacted, and implemented are immeasurable.

M. J. C. VILE

Bibliography

BARBER, SOTIRIOS A. 1975 *The Constitution and the Delegation of Congressional Power.* Chicago: University of Chicago Press.

ELLIOTT, E. DONALD 1984 INS v. Chadha: The Administrative Constitution, the Constitution, and the Legislative Veto. *Supreme Court Review* 1983:125–176.

GWYN, W. B. 1965 *The Meaning of the Separation of Powers.* New Orleans: Tulane University Press.

KURLAND, PHILIP B. 1978 *Watergate and the Constitution.* Chicago: University of Chicago Press.

SCHWARTZ, BERNARD 1963 *A Commentary on the Constitution of the United States.* New York: Macmillan.

VILE, M. J. C. 1967 *Constitutionalism and the Separation of Powers.* Oxford: Oxford University Press.

SERIATIM

(Latin: "Severally" or "in series.") Members of multijudge courts sometimes deliver individual opinions seriatim rather than joining in a single "OPINION OF THE COURT." Before JOHN MARSHALL became Chief Justice, the Supreme Court followed this practice, requiring each Justice to explain his DECISION. Opinions delivered seriatim are necessarily less authoritative than those that carry the weight of the full Court or a majority of the Justices. For that reason Marshall abandoned the established practice in favor of giving an opinion of the court. THOMAS JEFFERSON, both in 1787 and later as President, favored a constitutional requirement that Supreme Court opinions be rendered seriatim.

DENNIS J. MAHONEY

SERRANO v. PRIEST
5 Cal. 3d 584, 487 P.2d 1241, 96 Cal. Rptr 601 (1971)

This decision of the California Supreme Court produced a flurry of hope that the disgraceful inequalities in the financing of public schools might fall to an EQUAL PROTECTION attack. Two years after the *Serrano* decision, the Supreme Court of the United States dashed that hope in SAN ANTONIO INDEPENDENT SCHOOL DISTRICT V. RODRIGUEZ (1973).

Public schools throughout the nation are financed in major part through reliance on the local property tax. School districts that are property-wealthy thus can levy relatively low taxes and support their schools at high levels of spending per pupil. Poor districts, however, must levy taxes at much higher rates in order to spend at much lower levels per pupil. The California court in *Serrano* held this system unconstitutional, 6–1, both under the equal protection clause of the FOURTEENTH AMENDMENT and under parallel provisions of the state constitution. Because the decision merely reversed a trial court's determination that the complaint had not stated a valid constitutional claim, and remanded the case for trial, it was not a FINAL JUDGMENT and was not reviewable by the United States Supreme Court. Similarly, the ruling on state constitutional law was an ADEQUATE STATE GROUND, insulating the case from Supreme Court review.

The California court's opinion was devoted mainly to a discussion of the equal protection clause. Two grounds were found for subjecting the school finance scheme to STRICT SCRUTINY: the interest in education was held to be a FUNDAMENTAL INTEREST, and WEALTH DISCRIMINATION was held to be a SUSPECT CLASSIFICATION. Absent a showing of a COMPELLING STATE INTEREST justifying the inequalities in the state's statutory scheme, that scheme must fall.

The Supreme Court's *Rodriguez* decision, rejecting both the California court's bases for strict scrutiny, ended *Serrano*'s brief influence on the course of federal constitutional DOCTRINE. But other state courts reached similar results on the basis of their own state constitutions, and in California itself *Serrano* produced significant efforts to restructure public school finance.

KENNETH L. KARST

SEVENTEENTH AMENDMENT

Proposed by Congress on May 16, 1912, the Seventeenth Amendment went into effect on May 31, 1913. The amendment provided for DIRECT ELECTION of United States senators by the people of the states. Previously, under the first clause of Article I, section 3, senators had been chosen by the state legislatures.

Selection of United States senators by state legislatures had been an object of criticism for many years. Direct election of senators was first proposed in 1826; and after 1893 a constitutional amendment to establish direct election was proposed in Congress every year. Even without a constitutional amendment, popular choice of senators was becoming the rule. By 1912, twenty-nine of the forty-eight states had provided either for nomination by party primaries, with the individual legislators bound to vote for their party's nominee, or for a statewide general election, the result of which was binding on the legislature.

The objectives of direct election included reducing corruption in selection of senators, elimination of national-party domination of state legislatures, and immediate representation of the people in the Senate. But there was actually little change in the characteristics of persons elected to the Senate or in the proceedings and activities either of the Senate or of the state legislatures as a result of the Seventeenth Amendment.

The amendment has not occasioned much litigation. In 1915, the Supreme Court held that the right to vote for United States senators was a privilege of United States CITIZENSHIP, protected by the PRIVILEGES AND IMMUNITIES clause; and in 1946 it held that that right could not be denied on account of race. The Court has also held that the Seventeenth Amendment does not require that a candidate receive a majority of the votes cast in order to be elected.

DENNIS J. MAHONEY

SEVENTH AMENDMENT

An unexpectedly controversial provision of the document that emerged from the CONSTITUTIONAL CONVENTION OF 1787 was that giving the Supreme Court APPELLATE JURISDICTION "both as to law and fact." Anti-Federalists argued that the provision worked to abridge or deny the COMMON LAW right of TRIAL BY JURY in civil cases. Some, including PATRICK HENRY, went so far as to contend that it introduced the continental European civil law into the American court system. Although the convention had considered a clause protecting the right to a jury trial in civil cases, the clause was omitted; because the jury system varied somewhat from state to state, the meaning of the clause would not be certain. In the course of the RATIFICATION OF THE CONSTITUTION, five state conventions recommended an amendment to give the right explicit constitutional status.

The Seventh Amendment was proposed by Congress in 1789 and was ratified in 1791, as part of the BILL OF RIGHTS. As originally introduced by JAMES MADISON, the restriction on review of a jury's findings would have been inserted in Article III immediately after the definition of the Supreme Court's appellate jurisdiction. When the Bill of Rights was reorganized into a series of new articles, the restriction was joined to the general guarantee of a jury trial in federal civil cases.

The purpose of the amendment was not to extend the right to a jury trial but to preserve it as it then existed. The phrase "common law" did not purport to exclude cases arising under federal statutes but rather those cognizable in EQUITY or under ADMIRALTY AND MARITIME JURISDICTION. The word "jury" originally meant the common law jury of twelve men; but the Supreme Court held in *Colegrove v. Battin* (1973) that a jury of six members satisfied the general intent of the amendment. The Seventh Amendment is one of the very few provisions of the Bill of Rights not made applicable to the states under the INCORPORATION DOCTRINE. State courts would thus be free, under federal constitutional law, to dispense with juries altogether in civil cases.

Since the FEDERAL RULES OF CIVIL PROCEDURE in 1934 united the formerly discrete procedures of law and equity, new questions have emerged under the Seventh Amendment. In BEACON THEATRES INC. V. WESTOVER (1959) and DAIRY QUEEN INC. V. WOOD (1962) the Supreme Court held that the right to jury trial attached to all issues of law of the type formerly triable to a jury at common law, even when those issues were "incidental" to equitable issues. In *Ross v. Bernhard* (1970) this principle was extended to STOCKHOLDER'S SUITS, which previously had been heard only under the rules of equity.

DENNIS J. MAHONEY

SEVERABILITY

A court determines whether a statute is severable (or separable) in order to decide one of two different questions: When part of the law is unconstitutional, should the court hold the entire statute invalid, or merely the offending part? When the law can be applied validly to the litigant in court, should the court nonetheless hold the law invalid because it is capable of being applied unconstitutionally to others?

The first question was presented in CARTER V. CARTER COAL CO. (1936). Congress had regulated coal prices and the wages and hours of coal miners. After holding the wage and hour regulations invalid, the Supreme Court posed the severability issue in the usual way, as a question of LEGISLATIVE INTENT: if Congress had known the wage and hour provisions would be held invalid, would it still have regulated prices? Congress had stated plainly that if any part of the coal act were held invalid, the rest of the law remained effective. Nonetheless, the Court said, the price controls were so closely related to the labor provisions that Congress would not have enacted them alone. The price controls were thus invalid, whether or not they would have been valid if considered by themselves. The issue of severability calls into play the same kind of judgment employed in JUDICIAL REVIEW of the constitutionality of LEGISLATION.

Carter involved a federal statute. When a state law presents a similar question of severability, the Supreme Court ordinarily leaves that question to the state courts. However, a state statute may present the Court with the second type of severability issue. When a state law is INVALID ON ITS FACE—for example, under the FIRST AMENDMENT doctrine of OVERBREADTH—the Court refuses to enforce the law because of its potential unconstitutional application to persons not in court. This practice moderates the effect of the rule denying a litigant STANDING to raise other persons' legal rights.

KENNETH L. KARST

Bibliography

MONAGHAN, HENRY P. 1982 Overbreadth. *Supreme Court Review* 1982:1–39.

NOTE 1984 Severability of Legislative Veto Provisions: A Policy Analysis. *Harvard Law Review* 97:1182–1197.

STERN, ROBERT L. 1937 Separability and Separability Clauses in the Supreme Court. *Harvard Law Review* 51:76–128.

SEWARD, WILLIAM H. (1801–1872)

William Henry Seward was a New York lawyer, governor (1838–1842), United States senator (1849–1861), and secretary of state (1861–1869). As governor he prevented the extradition to Virginia of three men accused of helping a slave escape, and thus set off a minor interstate squabble. In *Jones v. Van Zandt* (1847) Seward, as cocounsel with SALMON P. CHASE, unsuccessfully appealed the conviction of an Ohio Quaker accused of aiding fugitive slaves. In the Senate, Seward opposed the COMPROMISE OF 1850, asserting that on the issue of slavery there was "HIGHER LAW than the Constitution." He supported the admission of Kansas as a free state, attacked the Supreme Court's decision in DRED SCOTT V. SANDFORD (1857), and in 1858 declared that slavery had created "an irrepressible conflict" for the Union. During the SECESSION crisis Seward served on the Committee of Thirteen, and proposed that Congress guarantee to protect slavery wherever it existed. Seward thought secession was illegal, but he urged Lincoln to evacuate Fort Sumter and negotiate with Confederate officials. Seward initially opposed the EMANCIPATION PROCLAMATION and successfully urged Lincoln to delay it until after a Union military victory. In FOREIGN AFFAIRS he deftly negotiated to keep Britain and France out of the war, and avoided a conflict with Britain over the *Trent* affair. He also laid out the legal argument that led to a successful damage claim against Britain over the *Alabama.* During Reconstruction, Seward supported ANDREW JOHNSON's policies, and drafted many of his veto messages. He also negotiated the acquisition of Alaska (1867) from Russia.

PAUL FINKELMAN

Bibliography

VAN DEUSEN, GLYNDON G. 1967 *William Henry Seward.* New York: Oxford University Press.

SEX DISCRIMINATION

The application of constitutional principle to government action that distinguishes on the basis of sex is a late-twentieth-century development. From the 1860s until 1971, the record remained unbroken: the Supreme Court rejected every effort to overturn sex lines in the law. Equalizing the rights, responsibilities, and opportunities of men and women was not considered a judicial task; without offense to the Constitution, women could be kept off juries and barred from occupations ranging from law to bartending. Women could also be "protected" from long hours, night work, and hazardous jobs, as in MULLER V. OREGON (1908), but protection of this order limited women's opportunities and relied upon the notion that a woman "looks to her brother and depends upon him."

The Court explained its position in *Fay v. New York* (1947). The NINETEENTH AMENDMENT's ratification in 1920 gave women the vote, but only that; in other respects, the Constitution remained an empty cupboard for sex equality claims. Nearly a decade and a half later, in *Hoyt v. Florida* (1961), a unanimous bench reaffirmed the traditional view. The Court held that a volunteers-only system for females serving on juries encountered no constitutional shoal; it was rational to spare women from the obligation to serve in recognition of their place at the "center of home and family life."

Pervasive social changes following World War II undermined the *Hoyt* assumptions. That period saw unprecedented growth in women's employment outside the home, a revived feminist movement, changing marriage patterns, and a decline in necessary home-centered activity. Expansion of the economy's service sector opened places for women in traditional as well as new occupations. Curtailed population goals, facilitated by more effective means of controlling reproduction, and extended lifespans counted as well among important ingredients in this social dynamic. These last two developments created a setting in which the typical woman, for the first time, was experiencing most of her adult years in a household not dominated by child care requirements. Columbia economics professor Eli Ginzberg appraised the sum of these changes as "the single most outstanding phenomenon of our century." The BURGER COURT, not noted for its activism in other areas, responded.

Through the 1960s, the Supreme Court had explained its EQUAL PROTECTION rulings in terms of a two-tier model. Generally, challenged legislation was ranked at the lower tier and survived judicial inspection if rationally related to a permissible government objective. Exceptional cases, ranged on the upper tier, involved FUNDAMENTAL RIGHTS (voting is a prime example) or SUSPECT CLASSIFICATIONS (race is a paradigm). Review in these exceptional cases was rigorous. To survive inspection, the legislative objective had to be compelling, and the classification, necessary to its accomplishment. (See STRICT SCRUTINY; COMPELLING STATE INTEREST.)

Equal protection adjudication in gender discrimination cases prompted "in between" standards. As the 1970s wore on, the STANDARD OF REVIEW for sex-based classification inched up toward the higher tier. The process commenced with *Reed v. Reed* (1971). A unanimous Court held that an Idaho estate administration statute, giving men preference over similarly situated women, denied would-be administrator Sally Reed the equal protection of the laws. *Reed* attracted headlines; it marked the first solid break from the Supreme Court's consistent affirmation of government authority to classify by sex. The terse *Reed* opinion acknowledged no departure from precedent, but Court-watchers recognized something new was in the wind.

Less than a year and a half after the laconic *Reed* decision, the Court came within one vote of declaring sex a "suspect" category. In FRONTIERO V. RICHARDSON (1973) the Justices held 8–1 that married women in the uniformed services were entitled to the same fringe benefits as married men. Under the laws declared unconstitutional, men received a housing allowance and health care for their civilian wives automatically; women received these family benefits only if they supplied over three-fourths of the couple's support.

Four of the Justices ranked sex a suspect classification. Justice LEWIS F. POWELL, concurring, articulated a prime reservation of the remaining five Justices: our eighteenth- and nineteenth-century Constitution-makers had evidenced no concern at all about the equality of men and women before the law. The Court must tread lightly, Justice Powell cautioned, when it enters the gray zone between CONSTITUTIONAL INTERPRETATION, a proper judicial task, and constitutional amendment, a job for the people's elected representatives.

No fifth vote has emerged for explicit placement of sex at the top tier of equal protection analysis, although the Court has repeatedly acknowledged that it applies a standard considerably more exacting than the lower tier RATIONAL BASIS test. If a classification based upon gender is to withstand constitutional challenge, the defender of the sex criterion must establish what the Court in *Kirchberg v. Feenstra* (1981) called "exceedingly persuasive justification"; the sex-based distinction will be condemned unless it "substantially furthers an important government interest." In MISSISSIPPI UNIVERSITY FOR WOMEN V. HOGAN (1982) the Court noted that it was unnecessary to "decide whether classifications based upon gender are inherently suspect," for the classification challenged there could not survive even intermediate tier scrutiny. If the Court continues to review categorization by gender with the rigor displayed in many of its 1973–1982 decisions, however, the "suspect" seal may eventually be placed on accumulated precedent.

Despite the absence of a majority opinion, the 8–1 *Frontiero* JUDGMENT was a notable way-paver for challenges to statutes that openly disadvantage or denigrate women. First, the Court did not invalidate the flawed legislation; it repaired it. Congress provided benefits for the military man's family; the Court, in effect, extended the same benefits to families in which the service member was female. Second, in contrast to the statute that figured in *Reed*—a nineteenth-century hangover repealed prospectively months before the Court heard Sally Reed's appeal—post–World War II legislation was at issue in *Frontiero.* Most significantly, *Frontiero* invalidated the type of gender line found most frequently in federal and state legislation. Wives were deemed dependent regardless of their own economic circumstances. Husbands were ranked independent unless they contributed less than one-fourth of the couple's support. In disallowing resort to this particular stereotype the Court set the stage for its subsequent disallowance of similar stereotypes in other settings.

Since *Frontiero,* with few exceptions, the Court has regularly overturned legislation explicitly invoking a male/female criterion and perceived by the Justices as denigrating women. A Utah statute that required a parent to support a son until age twenty-one but a daughter only until eighteen was struck down in *Stanton v. Stanton* (1975). Using DUE PROCESS analysis, the Court invalidated laws excluding all women from jury duty save those who volunteered (TAYLOR V. LOUISIANA, 1975) or chose not to opt out (*Duren v. Missouri,* 1979). In *Kirchberg v. Feenstra* (1981) a unanimous bench condemned Louisiana's "head and master" law, which gave the husband alone a unilateral right to dispose of property jointly owned with his wife.

Even a noncontributory welfare program—the type of governmental largess generally left untouched by the judiciary—has been revised by Court decree to eliminate the law's discrimination against women. Congress had provided for public assistance benefits to families where dependent children had been deprived of parental support because of the father's unemployment; no benefits were allowed when mother, rather than father, qualified as the unemployed parent. "Congress may not legislate 'one step at a time' when that step is drawn along the line of gender, and the consequence is to exclude one group of families [those in which the female spouse is a wage earner] altogether from badly needed subsistence benefits," Justice HARRY BLACKMUN concluded for a Court unanimous on the constitutional issue in CALIFANO V. WESTCOTT (1979). Although the Justices divided 5–4 on the appropriate remedy (the majority extending the benefit to families of unemployed mothers, the dissenters preferring to invalidate the entire program), all subscribed solidly to the equal protection ruling.

In 1837 Sarah Grimke made this plea: "I ask no favors for my sex, I surrender not our claim to equality. All I ask of our brethren, is that they . . . take their feet . . . off our necks. . . ." Does the equal protection principle operate with the same bite when men rather than women are the victims of explicit gender-based discrimination? Constitutional doctrine after *Reed* has evolved, with some insecurity, through three stages. In the first, statutes ostensibly favoring women were upheld if they were seen as "compensatory," even if that rationalization was entirely post hoc. Then the Court recognized more consistently that gender-based classifications rooted in "romantic paternalism" reinforce stereotypes and perpetuate anachronistic social assumptions that confine women's opportunities. In the third stage, the Court attempted a reconciliation of these two strands of doctrine: a classification that favors women can survive an equal protection attack, but only if it reflects a conscious legislative choice to compensate for past, gender-based inequities.

In two first-stage decisions the Court upheld laws that appeared to favor women. *Kahn v. Shevin* (1974) involved a $15-per-year state property tax saving for widows (along with the blind and the totally disabled) but not widowers. The classification, as the Court appraised it, was genuinely "benign"—it helped some women and harmed none. Following on the heels of *Kahn,* the Court ruled, in *Schlesinger v. Ballard* (1975), that it was not a denial of equal protection to hold a male naval officer to a strict "up or out" (promotion or discharge) system, while guaranteeing a female officer thirteen years of duty before mandatory discharge for lack of promotion.

Kahn and *Ballard* were greeted by some in a Panglossian manner. The decisions could be viewed as offering women the best of both worlds—a High Court ready to strike down classifications that discriminate against females, yet vigilant to preserve laws that prefer or favor them. But this analysis was uncritically optimistic. The classification attacked in *Kahn* was barely distinguishable from other products of paternalistic legislators who had regarded the husband more as his wife's guardian than as her peer. And in *Ballard,* neither contender challenged the anterior discrimination that accounted, in large measure, for the navy's promoting men more rapidly than women—the drastically curtailed opportunities and assignments available to navy women.

Sex as a proxy for need, or as an indicator of past discrimination in the marital unit, is a criterion too gross to survive vigorous equal protection scrutiny. The Court eventually demonstrated its appreciation that discrimination by gender generally cuts with two edges, and is seldom, if ever, a pure favor to women. A young widower whose wage-earning wife had died giving birth to the couple's son brought suit in *Weinberger v. Wiesenfeld* (1975). The unanimous Court declared unconstitutional the SOCIAL SECURITY ACT's provision of a mother's benefit for the caretaker of a deceased wage-earner's child. As in *Frontiero,* the remedy was extension of the benefit in question to the entire class of similarly situated individuals, males as well as females. In effect, the *Wiesenfeld* judgment substitutes functional description (sole surviving parent) for the gender classification (widowed mother) employed in the statute.

The government had urged that the sex differential in *Wiesenfeld* operated "to offset the adverse economic situation of women." But the Court read the legislative history closely and rejected "the mere recitation of a benign, compensatory purpose" as a hindsight apology for laws in fact based on twin assumptions: that man's primary place is at work, woman's at home; and that a gainfully employed woman is a secondary breadwinner whose employment is less crucial to her family than her husband's.

Wiesenfeld's focus on actual legislative purpose set a penetrating standard for sex classifications defended as "benign" or "compensatory." Gender classifications superficially favoring women and affecting interests ranging from the purchase of beer to attendance at a nursing school have accordingly been struck down.

CRAIG V. BOREN (1976) held unconstitutional an Oklahoma law allowing young women to purchase 3.2 percent beer at age eighteen, but requiring young men to wait until age twenty-one. *Orr v. Orr* (1979) declared violative of equal protection a statute that required husbands, but never wives, to pay alimony. CALIFANO V. GOLDFARB (1977) rejected social security classifications qualifying a widow for survivor's benefits automatically, a widower only upon proof that his wife supplied three-fourths of the couple's support.

The 4–1–4 judgment in *Goldfarb,* in contrast to the *Wiesenfeld* decision on which *Goldfarb* built, was a cliffhanger. The PLURALITY OPINION concentrated on discrimination against women as breadwinners. Justice JOHN PAUL STEVENS, who cast the swing vote in favor of widower Goldfarb, focused on the discrimination against the surviving male spouse. Why this discrimination against a class of men? Like the plurality, Justice Stevens refused to accept the government's hindsight compensatory justification for the scheme. Congress, the record suggested, had ordered different treatment for widows and widowers out of longstanding "habit"; the discrimination encountered by widower Goldfarb was "merely the accidental byproduct of [the legislators'] traditional way of thinking about females." Four members of the Court, in dissent, repeated a long rehearsed argument: the sex-based classification accurately reflects the station in life of most women, it operates benignly in women's favor, and it is administratively convenient. In 1980, however, the Court adhered to *Goldfarb* with a clearer (8–1) majority, in WENGLER V. DRUGGISTS MUTUAL INSURANCE CO.

The most emphatic reaffirmation of *Wiesenfeld's* skeptical view of benign gender-based classification came in 1982, one day after expiration of the extended deadline for ratification of the proposed EQUAL RIGHTS AMENDMENT. The Court decided, 5–4, in *Mississippi University for Women v. Hogan,* that Mississippi's single-sex admissions policy for a nursing school failed to meet the heightened standard of review. Justice SANDRA DAY O'CONNOR, who, a century earlier under BRADWELL V. ILLINOIS (1873), could have been barred from practicing law without offense to the Constitution, wrote the majority opinion.

Challengers in most of the cases just surveyed contended against gross assumptions that females are (and should be) concerned primarily with "the home and the rearing of the family," males with "the marketplace and the world of ideas" (*Stanton v. Stanton,* 1975). The complainants did not assail the accuracy of these assumptions as generalizations. Rather, they questioned each law's erroneous treatment of men and women who did not fit the stereotype, and the fairness of gender pigeonholing in lieu of neutral, functional description. The traditional legislative slotting, they argued, amounted to self-fulfilling prophecy. A Court that in 1948, in GOESAERT V. CLEARY, had declared "beyond question" the constitutionality of legislation "drawing a sharp line between the sexes," was receptive in the 1970s to argument to which it would not "give ear" a generation earlier.

The Court has left a narrow passage open, however, for compensatory legislation that does not rest on traditional role-typing. In *Califano v. Webster* (1977) the Court distinguished from habitual categorization by sex a law designed, at least in part, to ameliorate disadvantages women experienced. A social security benefit calculation, effective from 1956 to 1972, established a more favorable formula for retired female workers than for retired male workers. The legislative history indicated that this scheme, unlike those in *Wiesenfeld* and *Goldfarb,* had been conceived in light of the discrimination commonly encountered by gainfully employed women, specifically, depressed wages for "women's work" and the early retirement that employers routinely forced on women but not on men. While tilting toward a general rule of equal treatment, the *Webster* PER CURIAM opinion approves genuinely compensatory classifications that are adopted for remedial reasons rather than out of prejudice about "the way women are," and are trimly tailored in scope and time to match the remedial end.

Neutrally phrased laws that disproportionately affect one sex have not attracted the heightened scrutiny generally accorded explicit gender-based classifications that serve as a proxy for a characteristic or condition susceptible of individual testing. Citing RACIAL DISCRIMINATION precedent, the Court has held that facially neutral classifications that disproportionately affect members of one sex are not necessarily sex-based. The Court has not yet considered in a constitutional setting whether official lines may be drawn based on actuarial differences, but statutory precedent indicates the answer will be "no."

"[G]ood intent or absence of discriminatory intent" does not immunize an employment practice from the equal opportunity requirement of Title VII of the CIVIL RIGHTS ACT OF 1964, which now covers both public and private employment. GRIGGS V. DUKE POWER CO., a notable 1971 Title VII race discrimination decision, so held. But in WASHINGTON V. DAVIS (1976) the Court held the *Griggs* principle inapplicable to race discrimination claims invoking the Constitution rather than Title VII. PERSONNEL ADMINISTRATOR OF MASSACHUSETTS V. FEENEY (1979) expanded the *Washington v. Davis* reasoning. *Feeney* involved an assault on exorbitant veterans' preferences in civil service as impermissibly gender-biased. Helen Feeney challenged the nation's most extreme veterans' preference—an absolute lifetime preference Massachusetts accorded veterans in a range of civil service positions. The preference had "a devastating impact upon the employment opportunities of women"; it operated to reserve top jobs for a class almost exclusively male. The purpose? Purely to aid veterans, surely not to harm women, Massachusetts (and the United States, AMICUS CURIAE) maintained. Of course, to become a veteran one must be allowed to serve her country, and the military had maintained highly restrictive quotas and more exacting qualification standards for females. When litigation in *Feeney* commenced, over ninety-eight percent of Massachusetts veterans were male.

Feeney sought accommodation of the conflicting interests—aiding veterans and opening to women civil service employment beyond the "pink-collar" ghetto. The typical "points-added" preference, she said, was not at issue, only the extreme arrangement Massachusetts had legislated, which placed a veteran with a minimum passing grade ahead of a woman with a perfect score, and did so for each promotion as well as for initial hiring. A preference so large, she argued, took too much from Pauline to pay Paul.

The Court rejected the proffered distinction between moderate and exorbitant preferences. The "discriminatory purpose" hurdle could not be surmounted absent proof that the Massachusetts preference "was originally devised or subsequently re-enacted because it would accomplish the collateral goal of keeping women in a stereotypic and predefined place in the Massachusetts Civil Service." The lawmaker must *want,* not merely anticipate, the consequences. Alone, disparate impact on one sex, however "devastating" and "inevitable," does not violate equal protection.

The discriminatory purpose requirement, as elaborated in *Feeney,* leaves a slack rein for legislative choices with foreseeable but undesigned adverse effects on one of the sexes. Suppose, for example, that the social security payments at issue in *Wiesenfeld* or *Goldfarb* had turned not on sex but on the deceased wage-earner's status as the family's principal breadwinner. In most families, husbands would fit that neutrally phrased description, wives would not. May Congress, without violating equal protection, resort to a "principal breadwinner" standard in social welfare legislation in the interest of fiscal economy? Would use of a "principal breadwinner" criterion survive constitutional review as a measure enacted "in spite of," rather than "because of" its practical effect—its reduction of the value to the family of the wife's earnings? The only, uncertain, guide is an obiter dictum from *Feeney,* in which the Court accepted that "covert" sex classifications, ostensibly neutral but in fact a pretext for sex-based discrimination, are vulnerable to equal protection attack.

Can actuarial differences, for example, in life expectancies, health records, or accident experiences, provide constitutionally valid grounds in any context for gender-based categorizations? Sex averaging has not fared well in post-1970 constitutional litigation. Thus, *Reed v. Reed* and *Frontiero v. Richardson* rejected as a basis for government action the generalization that "men [are] as a rule more conversant with business affairs than women"; *Craig v. Boren,* the fact that more 18–20-year-old males than females drink and drive; *Orr v. Orr* (1979), the reality that wives far more often than husbands "need" alimony. Legislation resting on characteristics, attributes, habits, or proclivities of the "typical man" or "typical woman" have been rejected for two reasons: they reinforce traditional restrictive conceptions of the social roles of men and women; and they burden members of one sex by employing gender as a proxy for a characteristic susceptible to individual testing or at least capable of sex-neutral description. But actuarial tables, their defenders point out, are used in situations in which individual testing is not feasible. The Court has not yet explicitly confronted actuarial tables in a constitutional context, but a Title VII decision may indicate the position the Court will take in an equal protection challenge to government action.

Los Angeles Department of Water and Power v. Manhart (1978) raised the question whether women could be required to pay more currently in order to receive monthly benefits on retirement equal to those received by men. The majority held the two-tier charges inconsistent with Title VII's prohibition of sex-based classification. All recognized in *Manhart* that the statement, "on the average, women live longer than men," is accurate, and that an individual's lifespan generally cannot be forecast with precision. But the majority refused to countenance a break from the general Title VII rule against sex averaging. Unquestionably, for pension purposes, women destined to die young are burdened by placement in an all-female class, and men destined to live long are benefited by placement in an all-male class. Moreover, Justice Stevens suggested for the majority, the group insurance context may not be an ideal setting for urging a distinction other than age: "To insure the flabby and the fit as though they were equivalent risks may be more common than treating men and women alike; but nothing more than habit makes one 'subsidy' seem less fair than the other." The Court adhered to *Manhart,* when invited to reconsider, or contain the holding, in *Arizona Governing Committee v. Norris* (1983).

Are women to have the opportunity to participate in full partnership with men in the nation's social, political, and economic life? Kenneth L. Karst has identified this overarching question, in its constitutional dimension, as one ripe for synthesis in the final quarter of the twentieth century. The synthesis envisioned would place within an encompassing sex equality framework cases involving explicit male/female classification as well as cases on REPRODUCTIVE AUTONOMY and pregnancy-linked regulation. That synthesis, however, may well depend on the clarity of directions from the political arena. The Court has treated reproductive choice cases under a "personal autonomy," not a "sex equality" rubric, and it has resisted argument that separate classification of pregnant women is sex-based.

In a bold 1973 ruling, ROE V. WADE, the Court struck down an anti-abortion law as unwarranted state intrusion into the decision of a woman and her doctor to terminate a pregnancy. *Roe v. Wade* has been typed aberrational—an extraordinarily activist decision issued from a bench reputedly deferential to legislative judgments. It bears emphasis, however, that the Court bypassed an equal protection argument presented for the female plaintiffs. Rather, the Court anchored stringent review to a concept of personal autonomy derived from the due process guarantee. Two decisions, particularly, had paved the way: GRISWOLD V. CONNECTICUT (1965), which held inconsistent with due process Connecticut's ban on use of contraceptives even by married couples, and EISENSTADT V. BAIRD (1972), which extended *Griswold* to strike down Massachusetts' prohibition on sales of contraceptives except to married persons by prescription.

Some speculated that *Roe v. Wade* and a companion 1973 decision, *Doe v. Bolton,* were motivated, at least in part, by concerns about unwanted children born into impoverished families. But in MAHER V. ROE (1977) the Court indicated that such speculations had been mistaken. The Court declined to extend the 1973 rulings to require state support for an indigent woman's elective abortion.

The impoverished women, on whose behalf constitutional claims to public assistance for abortion were pursued, relied primarily on the equal protection principle. They maintained that, so long as government subsidized childbirth, it could not withhold subsidy for abortion, a far less expensive, and, at least in the first trimester, less risky procedure. If government pays for childbirth but not abortion, then, the *Maher* plaintiffs argued, government intrudes upon a choice *Roe v. Wade* said the state must leave to doctor and patient. The Court, however, distinguished government prohibition from government support. Though the state could not bar access to a woman able to pay for an abortion, it was not required to buy an admission ticket for the poor woman. Rather, government could pursue a policy of encouraging childbirth (even if that policy would affect only the poor) by refusing Medicaid reimbursement for nontherapeutic abortions and by banning such abortions in public hospitals. Though widely criticized in the reproductive-choice context, the distinction between government stick and government carrot had been made in other settings to which the Court referred in its 1977 ruling.

The *Maher* logic was carried further in HARRIS

v. McRae (1980). The federal law at issue excluded even medically needed abortions from a medical benefits program. In holding, 5–4, that this exclusion violated neither the due process nor the equal protection clause, the Court reiterated the distinction drawn in *Maher:* though the government may not proscribe abortion, it need not act affirmatively to assure a poor woman's access to the procedure.

Following after the intrepid 1973 abortion decisions, the later public-funding-of-abortion rulings appear incongruous. The *Roe v. Wade* decision was not easy to reach or explain. Social and economic conditions that seem irreversible, however, suggest that the ruling made by the Court in 1973 will remain with us in the long run, while the later dispositions may eventually succumb to a different legislative view of state and national policy, and of the centrality of choice with respect to childbearing to a woman's control of her life's course.

When does disadvantageous treatment of pregnant workers operate to discriminate on the basis of sex? High Court decisions on that question display less than perfect logic and consistency.

School teachers may not be dismissed or placed on forced leave arbitrarily at a fixed stage in pregnancy well in advance of term. Such a rule conflicts with due process, the Court ruled in Cleveland Board of Education v. LaFleur (1974). Similarly invoking due process, the Court held in *Turner v. Department of Employment Security* (1975) that pregnant women willing and able to work may not be denied unemployment compensation when jobs are closed to them. It is unlawful under Title VII, as interpreted by the Court in *Nashville Gas Co. v. Satty* (1977), for an employer to deprive women disabled by pregnancy of accumulated job-bidding seniority when they return to work.

But *Geduldig v. Aiello* (1974) held that a state-operated disability income protection plan could exclude pregnancy without offense to the equal protection principle. And in an analogous Title VII case, *General Electric Company v. Gilbert* (1976), the Court held that a private employer's exclusion of pregnant women from disability coverage did not discriminate on the basis of sex because all "nonpregnant persons," women along with men, were treated alike.

Lawyers may attempt to square the apparently contradictory constitutional decisions by referring to the different principles employed in the Court's analyses—equal protection in *Aiello,* due process in both *LaFleur* and *Turner.* But the particular due process theory of irrebuttable presumptions the Court pressed into service in *LaFleur* has lost favor with the Justices in other contexts. A factor not fully acknowledged in the written opinions, and based more on the Justices' experience than on legal analysis, may account for the divergent responses. Perhaps the able pregnant woman seeking only to do a day's work for a day's pay, or the woman seeking to return to her job relatively soon after childbirth, is a credible figure to the Court, while the woman who asserts she is disabled by pregnancy is viewed with suspicion. Is she really incapacitated physically or is she malingering so that she may stay "where she belongs"—at home tending baby?

With respect to Title VII, Congress in 1978 simplified the judicial task by prospectively overruling *General Electric.* It amended the statute to say explicitly that classification on the basis of sex includes classification on the basis of pregnancy. The Court gave the amended statute a cordial reception in *Newport News Shipbuilding of Drydock Co. v. EEOC* (1983). The congressional definition placed in Title VII is not controlling in constitutional adjudication, but the Court may be stimulated by the legislature's action to revise its view, expressed in *Aiello* and *General Electric,* that singling out "pregnant persons" is not a sex-based action. Coming full circle, there will be pressure on the Court not simply to check regulation disadvantageous to pregnant women but to uphold new-style protective legislation—for example, laws requiring employers to grant to pregnant women a voluntary leave period not accorded others with temporarily disabling physical conditions.

In what areas does the Constitution allow explicit male/female classification? A few idiosyncratic problems survive.

According to current doctrine, the Constitution affords some leeway for discrimination with respect to parental rights and relationships, at least when children are born out of wedlock. A unanimous Court held in *Quilloin v. Walcott* (1978) that an unwed father who "has never exercised actual or legal custody over his child" has no constitutional right to block adoption approved by the mother. (In contrast, the Court held in *Caban v. Mohammed* [1979] that a state statute discriminated on the basis of sex in violation of equal protection when it permitted adoption of a child born out of wedlock solely on the mother's consent, even when the father's parental relationship with the child was substantial.) And according to *Parham v. Hughes* (1979) a state may condition an unwed father's (but not an unwed mother's) right to recover for wrongful death upon his legitimation of his child by court order. The main theme of the *Parham* opinion had been sounded earlier: women and men were not similarly situated for the purpose at hand—maternity is rarely in doubt, but proof of paternity is often difficult. Hence, as the Court held in LALLI v. LALLI (1978), the state may erect safeguards against spurious filiation claims. Those safeguards may be applied even when, as in *Parham,* father and child had a close and constant relationship.

MICHAEL M. v. SUPERIOR COURT (1981) upheld, 5–4, California's "statutory rape" law, under which a male who engages in sexual intercourse with an underage female commits a crime; a female who engages in sexual intercourse with an underage male does not. Both participants in the act that precipitated the prosecution in *Michael M.* were underage.

There was no majority opinion in *Michael M.* Justice WILLIAM H. REHNQUIST wrote for the Court's plurality. He postulated as the statute's purpose, as California had argued, the prevention of teenage pregnancy, and reasoned that males and females were not similarly situated in this setting. Nature inhibited the female, for she would suffer the consequences. The law could legitimately take into account this fact of life by punishing the male, who lacked a biological deterrent. Moreover, the plurality found persuasive California's further contention that sparing the female from criminal liability might encourage her to report the unlawful activity.

Given the ancient roots of the California law, Justice WILLIAM J. BRENNAN pointed out in dissent, it was plain that the sex classification "was initially designed to further . . . outmoded sexual stereotypes" (young women are not capable of consenting to an act of sexual intercourse, young men can make such decisions for themselves). For Justice Stevens, who dissented separately, the critical question in *Michael M.* was whether "the sovereign . . . govern[s] impartially" under a statute that authorizes punishment of the male, but not the female, even "when they are equally responsible" for the disfavored conduct, indeed even "when the female is the more responsible of the two." The answer, it seemed to Justice Stevens, was clearly "no."

Although by 1980 many states had amended all of their sex crime laws to render them equally applicable to males and females, *Michael M.* touched a sensitive nerve. In view of the 4–1–4 division, the decision may well remain an isolated instance.

ROSTKER v. GOLDBERG (1981) presented the politically loaded question whether Congress could confine draft registration to males. Congress had thought about the matter and decided it in 1980. It considered, on the administration's recommendation, authorizing the President to require registration by both sexes. But it decided on registration for males only. The Court's 6–3 decision upheld the sex classification. The opinion, written by Justice Rehnquist, underlined the special deference due congressional judgments in the areas of national defense and military affairs.

The *Rostker* opinion asserted that men and women were not similarly situated for the purpose at hand because women were excluded from combat service, an exclusion "Congress specifically recognized and endorsed . . . in exempting women from registration." Reminiscent of *Schlesinger v. Ballard,* where no party challenged the dissimilar promotion opportunities for male and female naval officers, no party challenged the combat exclusion in *Rostker.* Even so, the executive branch had estimated that in the event of a major mobilization there would be a substantial number of noncombat positions in the armed services that conscripted women could fill. Against this backdrop *Rostker* may be explained as a WAR POWERS case, unlikely to have a significant influence in future sex discrimination cases.

Constitutional doctrine relating to gender discrimination, although still evolving, and variously interpreted, is nonetheless a remarkable judicial development. In contrast to race discrimination, an area in which constitutional interpretation is tied to amendments drawn with a view to the eradication of the legacy of black slavery, gender discrimination was not a concern to which the Reconstruction Congress (or the Founding Fathers) adverted. Nonetheless, the Court, since 1970, has creatively interpreted clauses of the Constitution (equal protection and, less securely, due process) to accommodate a modern vision of sexual equality in employment, in access to social benefits, in most civic duties, in reproductive autonomy. Such interpretation has limits, but sensibly approached, it is consistent with the grand design of the Constitution-makers to write a charter that would endure as the nation's fundamental instrument of government.

RUTH BADER GINSBURG

Bibliography

BABCOCK, BARBARA A.; FREEDMAN, ANN E.; NORTON, ELEANOR H.; and ROSS, SUSAN C. 1974 *Sex Discrimination: Causes and Remedies* (Wendy Williams, Supplement 1978). Boston: Little, Brown.

GINSBURG, RUTH BADER 1978 Sex Equality and the Constitution. *Tulane Law Review* 52:451–475.

______ 1979 Sexual Equality under the Fourteenth and the Equal Rights Amendments. *Washington University Law Quarterly* 1979:161–178.

______ 1983 The Burger Court's Grapplings with Sex Discrimination. In V. Blasi, ed. *The Burger Court: The*

Counter-Revolution That Wasn't. Pages 132–156. New Haven, Conn.: Yale University Press.

GUNTHER, GERALD 1972 Foreword: In Search of Evolving Doctrine on a Changing Court: A Model for a Newer Equal Protection. *Harvard Law Review* 86:1–48.

KANOWITZ, LEO 1981 *Equal Rights: The Male Stake.* Albuquerque: University of New Mexico Press.

——— 1969 *Women and the Law.* Albuquerque: University of New Mexico Press.

KARST, KENNETH L. 1976 Book Review. *Harvard Law Review* 89:1028–1036.

——— 1977 Foreword, Equal Citizenship under the Fourteenth Amendment. *Harvard Law Review* 91:1–68.

——— 1984 Woman's Constitution. *Duke Law Journal* 1984:447–508.

KAY, HERMA H. (1974)1981 *Sex-Based Discrimination,* 2nd ed. St. Paul: West Publishing Co.

——— 1985 Models of Equality. *University of Illinois Law Review* 1985:39–88.

LAW, SYLVIA 1984 Rethinking Sex and the Constitution. *University of Pennsylvania Law Review* 132:955–1040.

TRIBE, LAURENCE H. 1978 *American Constitutional Law.* Pages 1060–1077. Mineola, N.Y.: Foundation Press.

WASSERSTROM, RICHARD A. 1977 Racism, Sexism, and Preferential Treatment: An Approach to the Topics. *UCLA Law Review* 24:581–622.

SEXUAL PREFERENCE AND THE CONSTITUTION

Since the 1960s both legislation and judicial decisions have moved toward decriminalization of homosexual conduct and toward increased acceptance of homosexuals as parents, professionals, and public employees. A number of legal restrictions remain, however, mostly concerning employment and other material benefits. The Supreme Court has not fully considered the constitutional issues raised by these restrictions. In DOE V. COMMONWEALTH'S ATTORNEY (1976) the Court summarily affirmed, 6–3 and without opinion, a federal district court's dismissal of a constitutional challenge to Virginia's sodomy law, brought by two adult males who lived in a stable homosexual relationship. The absence of any serious threat of prosecution suggests that the Court's decision may have rested on a RIPENESS ground. In any case, *Doe* surely is not the Court's last word on the subject—although it provides an object lesson for anyone who would ignore the influence of conventional morality on the development of coherent constitutional principle.

Doe had been argued on the theory of a RIGHT OF PRIVACY, by analogy to the Court's decisions on BIRTH CONTROL and abortion. But "privacy," in its ordinary usage, fails to capture the essence of the constitutional claim. A middle-class homosexual couple need fear no prosecution if they keep their relationship private. It is precisely the public expression of homosexuality that produces sanctions; the interest at stake is in some sense the opposite of privacy, more akin to a FIRST AMENDMENT freedom of expression. Similarly, the issue of homosexual marriage, which has been addressed by some commentators as an issue of SEX DISCRIMINATION, seems better approached as a problem in symbolic expression of a homosexual couple's identity.

Recognition of homosexual relationships within a FREEDOM OF INTIMATE ASSOCIATION would place on government the burden of justifying its interference with those relationships. If a state had to prove that homosexuality alone disqualified a person from child custody or employment as a school teacher, its efforts to do so would demonstrate that the operative factor in the law's disqualifications was not risk of harm but stigma. Commentators have suggested that homosexuality be added to the list of SUSPECT CLASSIFICATIONS calling for STRICT SCRUTINY under the EQUAL PROTECTION clause, and there is force to the argument. Whether the problem be seen as one of equality or as an aspect of SUBSTANTIVE DUE PROCESS, most laws regulating homosexual conduct seem unlikely to survive serious constitutional scrutiny. What remains in question is the willingness of a majority of Justices for the Supreme Court to engage in that scrutiny.

KENNETH L. KARST

Bibliography

PROJECT 1966 The Consenting Adult Homosexual and the Law: Empirical Study of Enforcement and Administration in Los Angeles County. *UCLA Law Review* 13:643–832.

RIVERA, RHONDA R. 1979 Our Straight-Laced Judges: The Legal Position of Homosexual Persons in the United States. *Hastings Law Journal* 30:799–955.

SYMPOSIUM 1985 The Legal System and Homosexuality—Approbation, Accommodation, or Reprobation? *University of Dayton Law Review* 10:445–813.

SHAPIRO v. THOMPSON
394 U.S. 618 (1969)

Two states and the DISTRICT OF COLUMBIA denied WELFARE BENEFITS to new residents during a one-year waiting period. The Supreme Court, 6–3, held that the state schemes denied the EQUAL PROTECTION OF THE LAWS and that the District's law violated the

Fifth Amendment's equal protection component, as recognized in BOLLING v. SHARPE (1954).

Justice WILLIAM J. BRENNAN wrote for the Court. The RIGHT TO TRAVEL from one state to settle in another was a FUNDAMENTAL INTEREST, whose impairment was justified only on a showing of a COMPELLING STATE INTEREST. These statutes served to deter the entry of INDIGENTS and to discourage interstate travel for the purpose of obtaining increased welfare benefits, but those objectives were constitutionally illegitimate efforts to restrict the RIGHT TO TRAVEL. Equal protection considerations forbade a state to apportion its benefits and services on the basis of past tax contributions. The saving of welfare costs similarly could not "justify an otherwise invidious classification." Various arguments addressed to administrative convenience were also insufficiently compelling.

The Court also hinted that WEALTH DISCRIMINATION against the indigent might constitute a SUSPECT CLASSIFICATION, or, alternatively, that minimum subsistence might be a fundamental interest. Both these suggestions were sidetracked in later decisions such as SAN ANTONIO INDEPENDENT SCHOOL DISTRICT v. RODRIGUEZ (1973).

Chief Justice EARL WARREN dissented, joined by Justice HUGO L. BLACK. Warren argued that Congress had approved the one-year waiting periods in the SOCIAL SECURITY ACT. The majority rejected this statutory interpretation but added that in any event "Congress may not authorize the States to violate the Equal Protection Clause."

Justice JOHN MARSHALL HARLAN, in a long dissent, mounted a frontal attack on the WARREN COURT'S expansion of the judicial role in equal protection cases through its heightening of the STANDARDS OF REVIEW in cases involving fundamental interests and suspect classifications. Here, as in other decisions of the same period, the Harlan dissent illuminates the Court's doctrinal path more effectively than does the majority opinion. It has always been possible for a Justice to combine clarity of vision with the wrong conclusion.

KENNETH L. KARST

(SEE ALSO: *Invidious Discrimination.*)

SHAUGHNESSY v. UNITED STATES ex rel. MEZEI
345 U.S. 206 (1953)

Over the dissent of four Justices, the VINSON COURT upheld the authority of the ATTORNEY GENERAL to exclude and detain indefinitely an ALIEN without a hearing at Ellis Island solely on the basis of confidential information, "the disclosure of which would be prejudicial to the public interest." Justice ROBERT H. JACKSON, dissenting, wrote that he could not imagine how a hearing "would menace the security of this country."

MICHAEL E. PARRISH

SHAW, LEMUEL
(1781–1861)

Lemuel Shaw was chief justice of Massachusetts from 1830 to 1860, during which time he wrote a record number of opinions, over 2,200, only one in dissent. He dominated his court as no other judge has. His opinions were often comprehensive, ponderous, analytical treatises. He often explained guiding principles in terms of policy or social advantage, placing his decisions on the broadest grounds. Justice OLIVER WENDELL HOLMES, attributing Shaw's influence to his "accurate appreciation of the requirements of the community," declared that "few have lived who were his equals in their understanding of the grounds of public policy to which all laws must be ultimately referred. It was this which made him . . . the greatest magistrate which this country has produced."

Before his appointment to the Supreme Judicial Court, Shaw had been a Federalist lawyer, a member of both branches of the state legislature, and a bank director. Shaw did not, however, fit the stereotype of the conservative Whig judge seeking DOCTRINES of VESTED RIGHTS to ward off legislative controls over business enterprise. He was the foremost champion of the power of government to promote and regulate the economy in the public interest. To call the POLICE POWER Shaw's invention would be an exaggeration, but not a great one. Unlike JOHN MARSHALL and ROGER B. TANEY, who viewed the police power as the residual powers of the state, Shaw defined it as the power of government "to trench somewhat largely on the profitable use of individual property" for the public good, and he distinguished the police power from other state powers. Shaw laid the foundations for the legal character of power companies, railroads, and water suppliers as public utilities, privately owned but subject to regulation for the public benefit. He would even have included manufacturers and banks. He was the first to hold that the power of EMINENT DOMAIN cannot be restrained by or contracted away under the CONTRACT CLAUSE. At a time when that clause had become a bulwark of vested rights, making it a link between capitalism and constitutionalism, Shaw voided legislative alterations of chartered rights in only three cases, and in each the essential regulatory powers of the state were undiminished. Shaw was profoundly committed to JUDICIAL RESTRAINT. He held statutes unconstitutional in only nine reported cases, most often to protect the rights of the criminally accused. In as many cases Shaw repudiated the doctrine of SUBSTANTIVE DUE PROCESS drawn from WYNEHAMER V. NEW YORK (1856). Community rights rather than vested ones were Shaw's foremost concern.

In his COMMERCE CLAUSE opinions, too, Shaw sustained state powers. The Supreme Court agreed with him in the LICENSE CASES (1847) but reversed him in the PASSENGER CASES (1849), despite the sagacity of his empirical test to determine whether state and federal laws actually conflicted in their operation. In the absence of a federal law, Shaw would have sustained state legislation. He handed down the leading opinion on the constitutionality of the Fugitive Slave Act of 1850 in SIMS' CASE (1851), though he freed every sojourner slave (not a runaway) who reached Massachusetts. (See COMMONWEALTH V. AVES, 1836.) He originated the SEPARATE BUT EQUAL DOCTRINE that became the legal linchpin of racial SEGREGATION, and he upheld a conviction for BLASPHEMY in an opinion that abridged RELIGIOUS LIBERTY. In such cases he carried his doctrine of judicial restraint too far, but he towered over class and party, and his name became a synonym for judicial integrity and impartiality.

LEONARD W. LEVY

Bibliography

ADLOW, ELIJAH 1962 *The Genius of Lemuel Shaw.* Boston: Court Square Press.

LEVY, LEONARD W. 1957 *The Law of the Commonwealth and Chief Justice Shaw.* Cambridge, Mass.: Harvard University Press.

SHAYS' REBELLION
(1786–1787)

The economic depression following the Revolutionary War fell especially harshly upon small farmers who relied on borrowed money to finance their crops. Falling prices led to default and foreclosure. Seven states resorted to deliberate inflation (through large issues of unsecured paper currency), stay laws, and other forms of DEBTOR'S RELIEF LEGISLATION.

The Massachusetts legislature, however, defeated all such proposals. Beginning in August 1786, mobs of impoverished farmers in central and western Massachusetts prevented the courts from functioning and ordering foreclosures. In September an armed force assembled at Springfield under Daniel Shays, a farmer and one-time Revolutionary army captain. On January 25, 1787, Shays attempted to seize the federal arsenal at Springfield, but his men were repulsed by artillery. On February 4, the rebels were routed and the leaders captured by the state militia.

Meanwhile, Massachusetts had applied to Congress for assistance. Although Congress authorized raising a small force to protect the arsenal, no aid was actually sent.

The effect of the rebellion was to raise the specter of disintegration of civil government and so to hasten the process of constitutional reform. Less than three weeks after the collapse of Shays Rebellion, Congress passed a resolution giving official sanction to the Annapolis Convention's call for the CONSTITUTIONAL CONVENTION OF 1787.

DENNIS J. MAHONEY

Bibliography

SZATMARY, DAVID P. 1980 *Shays' Rebellion: The Making of an Agrarian Insurrection.* Amherst: University of Massachusetts Press.

SHELLEY v. KRAEMER
334 U.S. 1 (1948)
HURD v. HODGE
334 U.S. 24 (1948)

In 1926, in CORRIGAN V. BUCKLEY, the Supreme Court rejected a constitutional attack on judicial enforcement of racially RESTRICTIVE COVENANTS—contractual agreements between neighboring residential landowners limiting the occupancy of their houses to white persons. From that time forward, the NAACP sought to persuade the Court to reconsider and find the covenants' enforcement to constitute STATE ACTION in violation of the FOURTEENTH AMENDMENT. Finally, in *Shelley,* the Court granted review in two such cases, one from Missouri and one from Michigan. In both, white neighbors obtained INJUNCTIONS forbidding black buyers to occupy houses subject to racial covenants. The decision was widely anticipated to be important, both doctrinally and practically. Eighteen AMICUS CURIAE briefs supported the NAACP's position, and on the other side three white "protective associations" filed briefs, as did the National Association of Real Estate Boards. Counsel for the NAACP included CHARLES HOUSTON and THURGOOD MARSHALL.

The time was ripe for an overruling of *Corrigan's* casual acceptance of racially restrictive covenants as a "private" means of imposing residential segregation. The armed forces had integrated at the end of the World War II; in 1947 the President's Committee on Civil Rights had published a report calling attention to the importance of judicial enforcement to the effectiveness of the covenants; and President HARRY S. TRUMAN, a strong CIVIL RIGHTS advocate, had placed the weight of the executive branch on the NAACP's side by authorizing the SOLICITOR GENERAL to file an AMICUS CURIAE brief. The Supreme Court held, 6–0, that state courts could not constitutionally enjoin the sale to black buyers of property covered by restrictive covenants.

Shelley's result seems inescapable. Yet hardly anyone has a kind word for the *Shelley* opinion, written by Chief Justice FRED VINSON. *Corrigan* was not overruled but was characterized as a case involving only the validity of restrictive covenants and not their enforcement in courts. Standing alone, said Vinson, the racial covenants violated no rights; their enforcement by state court injunctions, however, constituted state action in violation of the Fourteenth Amendment. Taken for all it is worth, this reasoning would spell the end of the state action limitation—a loss many could cheerfully bear. But it is plain the Court had no such heroics in mind. The Justices were not ready to find state action in any private conduct the state might fail to prohibit. Yet the opinion never quite explained why, given the *Shelley* result, those larger doctrinal consequences do not follow. The opinion's elusive quality led Philip Kurland to call it "constitutional law's *Finnegans Wake.*"

Two decades later, in EVANS V. ABNEY (1970), the Court picked up the first shoe. *Shelley* was limited severely, and the power of a private owner to call on the courts to enforce his or her control over property was largely freed from constitutional limitations.

A companion case to *Shelley, Hurd v. Hodge* (1948), involved a racial covenant covering land in the DISTRICT OF COLUMBIA. Without reaching the question whether the Fifth Amendment guaranteed EQUAL PROTECTION (see BOLLING V. SHARPE, 1954), the Court held the judicial enforcement of the covenant to violate "the public policy of the United States."

KENNETH L. KARST

Bibliography

HENKIN, LOUIS 1962 Shelley v. Kraemer: Notes for a Revised Opinion. *University of Pennsylvania Law Review* 110:473–505.

HOROWITZ, HAROLD W. 1957 The Misleading Search for "State Action." *Southern California Law Review* 30:208–221.

SHELTON v. TUCKER

See: Least Restrictive Means Test

SHEPPARD-TOWNER MATERNITY ACT

42 Stat. 224 (1921)

FEDERAL GRANTS-IN-AID to the states began in the mid-nineteenth century. As the federal government, in its new capacity as a welfare state, funded important social services, some congressmen and senators considered this form of federal spending socialistic and questioned its constitutionality.

In 1921, Congress passed the Maternity Act, a measure recommended by President WARREN G. HARDING, allocating funds to the states for health service for mothers and children, particularly in rural communities. This welfare measure sought to reduce maternal and infant mortality. Critics argued that federal funds could lawfully be spent only in connection with the ENUMERATED POWERS of Congress, and they asserted that the grant-in-aid was a subtle method of extending federal power and usurping functions properly belonging to the states. Further, since the formal acceptance of such grants by state legislatures brought federal supervision and approval of the funded state activities, the measure placed too much potentially coercive power in the hands of federal bureaucracies.

The Supreme Court was asked to rule on the act's constitutionality in separate suits brought by a taxpayer and the Commonwealth of Massachusetts. The Court did not rule on the merits in either case, holding that the state presented no justiciable controversy and that the taxpayer lacked STANDING to sue. (See TAXPAYERS' SUITS; FROTHINGHAM V. MELLON, 1923.) Still, many states refused to avail themselves of the provisions of the act, and Congress failed to renew it in 1929. Nonetheless, the projects of this period were a political precedent for much of the modern system of federally dispensed welfare.

PAUL L. MURPHY

Bibliography

LEMONS, J. STANLEY 1960 The Sheppard-Towner Act: Progressivism in the 1920's. *Journal of American History* 55:776–786.

SHERBERT v. VERNER
374 U.S. 398 (1963)

Sherbert, a Seventh-Day Adventist, lost her job after the mill at which she had been working went on a six-day work week and she refused Saturday work. She filed for unemployment compensation, was referred to a job, but declined it because it would have required Saturday work. By declining proffered employment she was no longer "available for work" under South Carolina's rules and hence no longer eligible for unemployment benefits.

Justice WILLIAM J. BRENNAN, speaking for the Supreme Court, concluded that the disqualification imposed a burden on Mrs. Sherbert's free exercise of religion. The FIRST AMENDMENT, he declared, protected not only belief but observance. Even an incidental burdening of religion could be justified only if the state could show a COMPELLING STATE INTEREST in not granting an exemption.

This decision was a significant departure from the secular regulation approach to free exercise claims which had been affirmed by the Court as recently as *Braunfeld v. Brown* (1961). Brennan made little attempt to distinguish *Sherbert* from *Braunfeld.* Justice WILLIAM O. DOUGLAS, concurring, rejected the secular regulation approach.

Justice POTTER STEWART concurred in the result, disassociating himself from Brennan's reasoning. Stewart saw tension developing between the Court's interpretation of the free exercise and establishment clauses. To grant free exercise exemptions from otherwise valid secular regulations preferred religious over nonreligious people. In establishment clause cases, however, any governmental action that had the effect of advancing religion was forbidden. Stewart would have relieved the tension by relaxing the establishment clause rule.

Justice JOHN MARSHALL HARLAN, joined by Justice BYRON R. WHITE, dissented. For Harlan, the notion of a constitutional compulsion to "carve out an exception" based on religious conviction was a singularly dangerous one.

RICHARD E. MORGAN

SHERMAN, ROGER
(1721–1793)

Roger Sherman was one of the leading members of the founding generation. For more than two decades he was simultaneously mayor of New Haven, Connecticut, a member of the state legislature, and a judge of the Superior Court. He was a delegate to the Continental Congress almost continuously from 1774 to 1784. He signed the DECLARATION OF INDEPENDENCE, the ARTICLES OF CONFEDERATION, and the Constitution, the only person to sign all these founding documents.

At the CONSTITUTIONAL CONVENTION OF 1787, Sherman was a respected elder statesman. He distrusted a large and ill-informed populace and wanted all elections to national office mediated by the state legislatures. He formally introduced the GREAT COMPROMISE and argued strongly for its passage. He wrote the contingency provision prescribing election of the President by the House of Representatives if there was no majority in the ELECTORAL COLLEGE. He opposed giving the President an absolute VETO POWER and erecting a system of federal courts inferior to the Supreme Court. He originally favored, but later gave up, a unicameral national legislature chosen by the state legislatures. He strongly supported the prohibitions on export duties and BILLS OF CREDIT

After the Convention, Sherman worked hard for RATIFICATION OF THE CONSTITUTION, writing newspaper articles (as "A Countryman") and attending the state ratifying convention. He was a member of the first House of Representatives (1789–1791) and of the United States Senate (1791–1793). In Congress, as in the Convention, Sherman opposed as unnecessary and unwise the enactment of a federal BILL OF RIGHTS.

DENNIS J. MAHONEY

Bibliography

BOARDMAN, ROGER SHERMAN 1938(1971) *Roger Sherman: Signer and Statesman.* Philadelphia: University of Pennsylvania Press. (Reprint, New York: Da Capo).

SHERMAN ANTITRUST ACT
26 Stat. 209 (1890)

This concisely worded law represented the first congressional attempt at antitrust legislation. Neither the reasons for its approval nor its framers' intent are clear, but several circumstances ordained its passage.

Individual state attempts to regulate monopoly were often unsuccessful; a federal statute would satisfy the need for uniform national policy as well as consistent practice. In addition, a heritage of antimonopoly sentiment and an economic depression combined to inflame public opinion against the industrial giants. Consequently, the platforms of both major parties contained antimonopoly planks in 1888, and, following his election, President BENJAMIN HARRISON asked Congress to redeem this pledge. Of sixteen bills introduced into the next Congress, one, sponsored by Senator John Sherman (Republican, Ohio), was briefly debated and then referred to the Judiciary Committee. Six days later the committee reported out a completely rewritten bill which received only cursory debate and passed 52–1 in the Senate and 242–0 in the House. The lack of debate, particularly over such a potentially controversial bill, has never been satisfactorily explained. Often-cited possibilities include fierce interparty competition for support from the vigorously antimonopoly West and an underestimation of the act's importance. Contemporaries paid it little attention—the trusts and their congressional allies did not even bother to oppose the bill. Its proponents conceded that the act was an experimental entry into a new field of ECONOMIC REGULATION. In fact, it contained nothing new.

Although Senator Sherman was the moving force behind the bill, Senator George Edmunds (Republican, Vermont), chairman of the Senate Judiciary Committee, wrote most of it. Despite Edmunds's claim that it was "clear in its terms . . . [and] definite in its definitions," the act failed to define the two most important concepts in it: monopoly and restraint of trade. Although there is a debate over the (Anglo-American) COMMON LAW underpinnings of the act, most scholars agree that the common law forbade agreements in restraint of trade and CRIMINAL CONSPIRACY to monopolize. The controversy arises over these doctrines' application in America and the extent of their incorporation into the Sherman Act. The final bill also omitted any specific exemption for labor or farm organizations. Congress either meant to leave the issue to the courts (see LOEWE V. LAWLOR, 1908) or, more likely, believed an exemption was self-evident from the text.

The first section of the act outlawed "every contract, combination . . . or conspiracy, in restraint of trade" or INTERSTATE COMMERCE and was directed against joint action. Section 2—equally applicable to individuals—outlawed any means of achieving monopoly. Broader than section 1, this clause declared void any attempt, combination, or conspiracy to monopolize. It did not outlaw monopoly per se. Among the remaining provisions were those granting JURISDICTION to the CIRCUIT COURTS, providing for EQUITY proceedings, and authorizing treble damage suits.

Even with public support, the Sherman Act proved ineffective initially. The economic depression of the 1890s adversely affected business, and the general terms of the act required interpretation which could only come with time. The Court hamstrung the act in UNITED STATES V. E. C. KNIGHT (1895), holding that it did not apply to manufacturing. Even though a bare majority of the Court resuscitated the act against pooling arrangements in UNITED STATES V. TRANS-MISSOURI FREIGHT ASSOCIATION (1897), the government would not achieve any notable success until PHILANDER C. KNOX became ATTORNEY GENERAL under THEODORE ROOSEVELT. Then, in quick succession, the government won major victories in NORTHERN SECURITIES CO. V. UNITED STATES (1904) and SWIFT & CO. V. UNITED STATES (1905). The next decade saw a limitation on antitrust policy as the Court formulated the RULE OF REASON and additional implementation by Congress which passed the CLAYTON and FEDERAL TRADE COMMISSION ACTS.

DAVID GORDON

Bibliography

NEALE, A. D. and GOYDER, D. G. 1980 *The Antitrust Laws of the United States of America,* 3rd ed. Cambridge: At the University Press.

THORELLI, HANS B. 1955 *The Federal Antitrust Policy.* Baltimore: Johns Hopkins University Press.

SHIELD LAWS

In BRANZBURG V. HAYES (1972) and later decisions relating to an asserted REPORTER'S PRIVILEGE, the Supreme Court rejected the claim that the FIRST AMENDMENT should privilege reporters from having to respond to proper inquiries incident to legal proceedings. However, before and after *Branzburg,* more than half the states have passed legislation, called shield laws, that give reporters such a privilege. These laws vary considerably, as has their reception in the state courts. Some laws privilege reporters as to all information gathered in the course of their journalistic activities. Others privilege reporters only as to information gathered from confidential informants. Some laws make an exception to the privilege if a reporter has witnessed the commission of a crime.

A number of state courts have found state constitutional grounds for cutting back on shield laws. Thus one California decision held that a shield law could not immunize a reporter from having to answer a judge's questions about who had violated a judicial GAG ORDER against informing the press about evidence in a notorious criminal trial. And New Jersey's supreme court held that the state's law could not shield a reporter from inquiries by a defendant in a criminal case concerning information relevant to his defense.

BENNO C. SCHMIDT, JR.

SHIRAS, GEORGE, JR.
(1832–1924)

George Shiras, Jr., was appointed to the Supreme Court by BENJAMIN HARRISON in 1892 and served for slightly more than a decade. A native of Pittsburgh and a Yale graduate, Shiras had maintained an independent, yet prosperous and varied law practice for nearly forty years before his appointment. He came to the Court without previous experience in public life and charted an independent course. His voting record suggests that he remained aloof from the era's policy debates yet maintained a fundamental distrust of institutional change. His unadorned and cool style and his emphasis on precedent and conventional rules of interpretation reflected his personality as well as his conception of the judicial function.

The 1890s were a transitional period in American public life, and the questions that crowded the Court's docket indicated the increasing scope and intensity of governmental interventions in economy and society. Three major classes of constitutional issues came up during Shiras's tenure. The first involved petitioners who sought enlarged judicial protection under the FOURTEENTH AMENDMENT for FREEDOM OF CONTRACT in the face of state laws regulating labor relations and the price of essential services. They got no encouragement from Shiras. In *Brass v. North Dakota* (1894), a grain elevator case, he refused to restrict the range of "businesses AFFECTED WITH A PUBLIC INTEREST" to those with a "virtual monopoly" at a particular location; he also spoke for the Court in *Knoxville v. Harbison* (1901), sustaining a Tennessee statute that required employers to pay their workers in cash or company-store scrip redeemable in cash. Justices DAVID J. BREWER and RUFUS PECKHAM, the FULLER COURT's leading apostles of laissez-faire, dissented in each instance. Yet Shiras was consistently aligned with Brewer and Peckham in the second class of cases, including UNITED STATES V. E. C. KNIGHT CO. (1895) and CHAMPION V. AMES (1903), involving federal authority under the COMMERCE CLAUSE in policy domains traditionally reserved to the states. Congressional regulation of manufacturing CORPORATIONS and public morals, like federal JUDICIAL REVIEW of STATE POLICE POWER regulations under the Fourteenth Amendment, necessitated new and, in Shiras's view, illegitimate departures in the organization of constitutional power.

Shiras wrote his most powerful opinions in the third class of cases, involving petitioners whose liberty or property was jeopardized by intensified federal activity in areas of acknowledged federal competence. He complained repeatedly about the majority's penchant for narrow construction of the Fifth Amendment's JUST COMPENSATION clause when riparian land was damaged by federal construction of dams and other river improvements. He also dissented sharply in BROWN V. WALKER (1896), contending that a federal immunity statute for persons required to testify before the Interstate Commerce Commission was an inadequate substitute for the Fifth Amendment RIGHT AGAINST SELF-INCRIMINATION. And in *Wong Wing v. United States* (1896) Shiras spoke for a unanimous Court that finally curbed Congress's draconian anti-Chinese program at the point where immigration officials were authorized to sentence illegal aliens to as much as one year of hard labor prior to deportation. The sentence of hard labor was an "infamous" one, Shiras explained. Consequently it could be invoked only after the Fifth and Sixth Amendment requirements of due process and TRIAL BY JURY had been met.

Shiras had determined at the time of his appointment to retire at seventy to avoid burdening his brethren because of age. He underscored his habitual divergence from conventional norms by carrying through his resolve. His retirement in 1903 attracted little notice, and his death more than twenty years later even less. Shiras's constitutional jurisprudence was simply too idiosyncratic to generate a significant following at the bar, in the law schools, or among the general public.

CHARLES W. MCCURDY

Bibliography

PAUL, ARNOLD 1969 George Shiras, Jr. Pages 1577–1591 in Leon Friedman and Fred L. Israel, eds., *The Justices of the United States Supreme Court, 1789–1969: Their Lives and Major Opinions.* New York: Chelsea House.

SHIRAS, WINFIELD 1953 *Justice George Shiras, Jr. of Pittsburgh.* Pittsburgh: University of Pittsburgh Press.

SHOPPING CENTERS

By the 1960s, shopping centers accounted for more than one-third of the nation's retail sales. Crowds of shoppers made the centers attractive places for the exercise of FIRST AMENDMENT rights such as PICKETING, leafleting, and the circulation of petitions. Two decades earlier, in MARSH V. ALABAMA (1946), the Supreme Court had assimilated the "company town" to the First Amendment DOCTRINE governing the use of an ordinary city street as a PUBLIC FORUM. When shopping center owners sought to prevent the use of their property for communications they had not approved, the question arose whether the centers, too, would be assimilated to the public forum doctrine.

The problem first came to the Supreme Court near the zenith of WARREN COURT activism in the defense of CIVIL LIBERTIES. In *Amalgamated Food Employees Union v. Logan Valley Plaza, Inc.* (1968), a bare majority held that union picketing of a store in a shopping center was protected by the First Amendment. Justice THURGOOD MARSHALL, for the Court, described the shopping center as the functional equivalent of the business district of the company town in *Marsh.* The author of the *Marsh* opinion, Justice HUGO L. BLACK, led the four dissenters.

When the issue returned to the Court, President RICHARD M. NIXON's four appointees were sitting. A new 5–4 majority now held, in *Lloyd Corp v. Tanner* (1972), that the distribution of leaflets opposing the VIETNAM WAR could be forbidden by a shopping center's private owner. Justice LEWIS F. POWELL, for the majority, distinguished *Logan Valley:* the leafleting here had no relation to the center's activities, and here alternative means of communication were reasonably available on nearby streets. Justice Marshall led the dissenters.

The circle closed four years later, when a 7–2 majority, speaking through Justice POTTER STEWART (a *Lloyd Corp.* dissenter), said that *Lloyd Corp.* really had overruled *Logan Valley.* HUDGENS V. N.L.R.B. (1976), like *Logan Valley,* was a union picketing case. Justice Stewart pointed out that *Lloyd Corp.* had drawn an untenable distinction based on the content of messages being conveyed; because that distinction failed, it was necessary to make a yes-or-no decision on the assimilation of shopping centers to the doctrine governing company towns—and the majority's answer was "no."

Some passages in the *Lloyd Corp.* opinion had suggested that a shopping center owner had a constitutionally protected property right to exclude leafleters. That argument was flatly rejected by the Court in PRUNEYARD SHOPPING CENTER V. ROBBINS (1980). California's supreme court had ruled that the state constitution protected the right to collect signatures for a petition in a shopping center. The U.S. Supreme Court unanimously held that this principle of state constitutional law did not violate any federal constitutional rights.

KENNETH L. KARST

Bibliography

TRIBE, LAURENCE H. 1978 *American Constitutional Law.* Pages 693–696, 1163–1167. Mineola, N.Y.: Foundation Press.

SHREVEPORT DOCTRINE

In the early twentieth century, the Supreme Court employed several DOCTRINES to sustain federal regulation of INTRASTATE COMMERCE. Among these, the Shreveport doctrine enjoyed a long tenure in the service of the COMMERCE CLAUSE. Since its elaboration, the Court has approved its use as a means of reaching a variety of activities, including professional football, minimum wages, crop control, and RACIAL DISCRIMINATION.

First announced in HOUSTON, EAST & WEST TEXAS RAILWAY V. UNITED STATES—the Shreveport Rate Case—(1914), the doctrine permitted congressional regulation of purely local freight rates when, unmodified, they would have impeded INTERSTATE COMMERCE. The doctrine drew sustenance from the Court's distinction between direct and indirect EFFECTS ON COMMERCE in UNITED STATES V. E. C. KNIGHT COMPANY (1895) but reflected a new economic pragmatism. The Court recognized the integrated nature of the railroad system before it in the Shreveport Rate Case. It asserted that the commerce power "necessarily embraces the right to control . . . [intrastate] operations in all matters having such a close and substantial relation to interstate traffic that the control is essential or appropriate" to maintain a free flow of interstate commerce. The Court applied the doctrine throughout the 1920s in railroad cases such as DAYTON-GOOSE CREEK RAILWAY V. UNITED STATES (1924).

The judicial "revolution" of 1937 enhanced the use of the Shreveport doctrine. Earlier, the Court had struck down federal regulation in CARTER V. CARTER COAL COMPANY (1936) as an attempt to control activities only indirectly affecting interstate commerce, but it soon held that the WAGNER (NATIONAL LABOR RELATIONS) ACT legitimately regulated PRODUCTION (heretofore considered local), reiterating the "close and substantial relation" test of the Shreveport doctrine. (See N.L.R.B. V. JONES & LAUGHLIN STEEL CORP., 1937.)

The doctrine continued to grow in the 1940s. After several predictable decisions allowing federal regulation of intrastate milk prices (UNITED STATES V. WRIGHTWOOD DAIRY, 1942), the Court greatly expanded the doctrine in WICKARD V. FILBURN (1942) by subjecting to federal control a local wheat crop "where no part of the product is intended for interstate commerce or intermingled with the subjects thereof." The Court declared that even local activity that "may not be regarded as commerce . . . may still . . . be reached by Congress if it exerts a substantial economic effect on interstate commerce . . . irrespective of whether such effect is what might at some earlier time have been defined as 'direct' or 'indirect'." This interpretation invited increasing use of the doctrine in antitrust cases, particularly under the SHERMAN ANTITRUST ACT, where, along with the STREAM OF COMMERCE DOCTRINE, it became a test of the law's applicability.

Congress and the Supreme Court continued this expansion in the 1960s. The CIVIL RIGHTS ACT OF 1964, based on the commerce clause, prohibits racial discrimination in PUBLIC ACCOMMODATIONS. The Court sustained application of the act to a local restaurant because "the absence of direct evidence connecting discriminatory restaurant service with the flow of interstate food . . . is not . . . a crucial matter." (See KATZENBACH V. MCCLUNG, 1964; *Daniel v. Paul*, 1969.) Criminal activity, too, fell within the doctrine's scope when the Court found ties between local loansharking and interstate commerce in PEREZ V. UNITED STATES (1971). The Court also included firearms in the doctrine's reach, sustaining a conviction under the OMNIBUS CRIME CONTROL AND SAFE STREETS ACT for illegal possession, despite a minimal demonstration of the requisite connection with commerce (*Scarborough v. United States*, 1977).

The Shreveport doctrine helped bring about the demise of DUAL FEDERALISM. Because of the Justices' willingness to accede to congressional determinations, the Court's application of the doctrine has consistently followed its statement in *Board of Trade v. Olsen* (1923) that "this court will certainly not substitute its judgment for that of Congress in such a matter unless the relation of the subject to interstate commerce, and its effect upon it, are clearly nonexistent."

DAVID GORDON

SIBRON v. NEW YORK

See: *Terry v. Ohio*

SIERRA CLUB v. MORTON
405 U.S. 727 (1972)

Acting as a public defender of the environment, the Sierra Club sued the secretary of the interior to enjoin approval of a ski resort development at Mineral King Valley in Sequoia National Forest. The Supreme Court, 4–3, denied the Club's right to JUDICIAL REVIEW of claimed statutory violations, for failure to allege harm to its members in their personal use of Mineral King. Significantly, however, the Court declared aesthetic and environmental interests, though widely shared, to be as deserving of judicial protection as economic interests. Thus, persons whose individual enjoyment of the environment is impaired by government action have STANDING to contest the action's legality.

JONATHAN D. VARAT

SILVERMAN v. UNITED STATES
365 U.S. 505 (1961)

To investigate gambling, DISTRICT OF COLUMBIA police officers inserted a microphone into a wall. The device touched a heating duct, enabling the police to overhear conversations throughout the house.

In *Goldman v. United States* (1942) the Court had afforded no constitutional protection against a microphone placed *against* a wall. By 1961 the Court, concerned about new methods of electronic surveillance, ruled that because there was a physical penetration, albeit only a few inches, the overhearing was subject to the FOURTH AMENDMENT with no need to reconsider *Goldman* or earlier cases; that reconsideration occurred in KATZ V. UNITED STATES (1967).

HERMAN SCHWARTZ

(SEE ALSO: *Electronic Eavesdropping.*)

SILVER PLATTER DOCTRINE

WEEKS V. UNITED STATES (1914), which formulated the EXCLUSIONARY RULE for federal prosecutions, made an exception for EVIDENCE seized by state officers in searches that did not meet FOURTH AMENDMENT standards. The evidence was usable in a federal trial when it was handed by the state to federal officers on "a silver platter" (Justice FELIX FRANKFURTER's phrase in *Lustig v. United States,* 1949). Participation by federal officers in the state search, no matter how minor, rendered the evidence inadmissible in federal cases under *Byars v. United States* (1927), as did even a search conducted by state officers alone if its purpose was the gathering of evidence for the federal government under *Gambino v. United States* (1927).

A combination of several factors led to the overruling of the silver platter doctrine in ELKINS V. UNITED STATES (1960). First, in WOLF V. COLORADO (1949), the Supreme Court had applied "the core" of the Fourth Amendment's standard (which did not, however, include the exclusionary rule) to the states. It therefore became incongruous to admit in federal court evidence which state officials had seized in violation of the Constitution. In addition, about half the states had adopted an exclusionary rule for unlawfully seized evidence; to allow federal authorities to use evidence which would have been excluded in the state courts served to frustrate the exclusionary policies of those states and to undermine the principle of FEDERALISM on which the silver platter doctrine was itself premised. The expansion of federal criminal law also undermined the vitality of the doctrine: a growing catalogue of crimes punishable by both federal and state governments evidently alerted the Court to the attendant possibilities of abuse by cooperative law enforcement.

Thus far the *Elkins* principle applies only to evidence in criminal cases. In *Janis v. United States* (1976), the Court held that evidence unlawfully seized by state officers can be used by the federal government (and vice versa) in civil proceedings (for instance, in a tax assessment case). The Court reasoned that the main purpose of the exclusionary rule is to deter unlawful searches, and that application of the rule should be tailored to this end. When the officer is prevented from using the seized evidence to further a criminal prosecution, the principle of deterrence is amply served; exclusion of the evidence in a civil case would provide no significant reinforcement for Fourth Amendment values.

JACOB W. LANDYNSKI

(SEE ALSO: *Two Sovereignties Rule.*)

Bibliography

LANDYNSKI, JACOB W. 1966 *Search and Seizure and the Supreme Court.* Pages 70–73, 149–158. Baltimore: Johns Hopkins University Press.

SILVERTHORNE LUMBER CO. v. UNITED STATES
251 U.S. 385 (1920)

Silverthorne was the first case to test the scope of the EXCLUSIONARY RULE, formulated in WEEKS V. UNITED STATES (1914), requiring exclusion from a federal trial of EVIDENCE obtained in an unconstitutional search.

Federal officers searched the Silverthorne Company's office; "without a shadow of authority," in Justice OLIVER WENDELL HOLMES's words, they "made a clean sweep of all the books, papers, and documents found there." Compounding the "outrage," the records were copied and photographed, and an INDICTMENT was framed on the basis of the information uncovered. The district court ordered the return of the originals but allowed the copies to be retained by the government, which then subpoenaed the originals. The Supreme Court reversed.

Holmes asserted that to allow the government to use the derivatively acquired evidence would mean that "only two steps are required [to render the evidence admissible] instead of one. In our opinion such is not the law. It reduces the 4th Amendment to form of words." Holmes added: "The essence of a provision forbidding the acquisition of evidence in a certain way is that not merely evidence so acquired shall not be used, but that it shall not be used at all." On this principle, an admission made by a suspect while he is under illegal arrest, as in WONG SUN V. UNITED STATES (1963), like a lead furnished by an illegally placed wiretap, as in NARDONE V. UNITED STATES (1939), may not be introduced into evidence because it is directly derived from an unlawful act. In *Nardone,* Justice FELIX FRANKFURTER dubbed the doctrine of the *Silverthorne* case as the FRUIT OF THE POISONOUS TREE.

JACOB W. LANDYNSKI

SIMON v. EASTERN KENTUCKY WELFARE RIGHTS ORGANIZATION
426 U.S. 26 (1976)

In 1969 the Internal Revenue Service (IRS) amended its regulations governing nonprofit hospitals' obligations to provide care for INDIGENTS. A number of individuals and service organizations sued to set aside the modifications, claiming they would cause the denial of services to indigents. Following WARTH V. SELdin (1975), the Supreme Court held that the plaintiffs lacked standing. Justice LEWIS F. POWELL, for the Court, declared that it was "purely speculative" whether any denials of hospital service to the plaintiffs could be traced to the IRS changes, or whether judicial relief against the IRS would increase the availability of such services to them. The plaintiffs thus could not meet Article III's requirement of CASES OR CONTROVERSIES. Justice WILLIAM J. BRENNAN, joined by Justice THURGOOD MARSHALL, argued that the plaintiffs had alleged a cognizable injury, but concurred in the result on grounds of RIPENESS.

DAVID GORDON

SIMOPOULOS v. VIRGINIA

See: Reproductive Autonomy

SIMS' CASE
7 Cushing (Mass.) 285 (1851)

Chief Justice LEMUEL SHAW of Massachusetts, denying a writ of HABEAS CORPUS for a fugitive slave, delivered the first and most influential opinion sustaining the constitutionality of the Fugitive Slave Act of 1850. The case, which riveted national attention, had political and moral as well as constitutional significance; it reproduced hateful scenes of slavery in the North. The capture and rendition of a black man provoked denunciations of the COMPROMISE OF 1850. Without military force to execute the rendition, Shaw's decision would have been a dead letter in Massachusetts.

LEONARD W. LEVY

(SEE ALSO: *Fugitive Slavery.*)

SINKING FUND CASES
Union Pacific Railroad Co. v. United States
99 U.S. 700 (1879)
Central Pacific Railroad Co. v. Gallatin
99 U.S. 727 (1879)

Congress authorized the construction of transcontinental railroads and made massive grants and loans to them. Following the exposure of enormous corruption in the management of the roads, Congress enacted a statute requiring that twenty-five percent of the annual net earnings of the CORPORATIONS be paid into a sinking fund to guarantee payment of the debts owed to the federal treasury. The Supreme Court sustained the second statute on ground that Congress had reserved the power to alter or amend its original grant. However, Chief Justice MORRISON R. WAITE, for a 6–3 Court, said in an OBITER DICTUM that the United States binds itself by its contracts and that, although the CONTRACT CLAUSE applied only to the states, the Fifth Amendment's DUE PROCESS clause effectuated the binding by preventing the deprivation of property. Three Justices, WILLIAM STRONG, JOSEPH P. BRADLEY, and STEPHEN J. FIELD, wrote dissenting opinions based on Waite's dictum; they believed that the sinking-fund statute violated the Fifth Amendment. The decision is significant, therefore, because of the strong boost it gave to the emerging concept of SUBSTANTIVE DUE PROCESS. In effect, too, the Court incorporated contract clause reasoning into the due process clause as a means of protecting property when Congress "improperly interferes with VESTED RIGHTS." This strange doctrine operated, though infrequently, as late as 1936. (See LOUISVILLE JOINT STOCK LAND BANK V. RADFORD.)

LEONARD W. LEVY

SIPUEL v. OKLAHOMA STATE BOARD OF REGENTS
332 U.S. 631 (1948)

PER CURIAM, reaffirming MISSOURI EX REL. GAINES V. CANADA (1938), the Supreme Court ordered Oklahoma to provide a black applicant with legal education in a state law school. Rather than admit her to the state university, the state roped off part of the state capitol, called it a law school for blacks, and provided three instructors. The Supreme Court avoided ruling on this mockery, saying the case had not presented the issue whether separate law schools satisfied the Constitution.

KENNETH L. KARST

(SEE ALSO: *Sweatt v. Painter, 1950.*)

SIT-IN

The CIVIL RIGHTS movement of the 1960s embraced more than lawsuits aimed at ending racial SEGREGATION in southern public institutions. It also included several forms of direct action, such as "freedom rides," in which blacks would ride on buses and trains, refusing to confine themselves to places set aside for black passengers. The quintessential form of direct action was the sit-in demonstration. The practice began in Greensboro, North Carolina, in 1960. Four black college freshmen went to a dime store lunch counter and ordered coffee. When they were told they would not be served, they sat at the counter, waiting, in silent protest against the indignity of RACIAL DISCRIMINATION. The next week they returned, joined by increasing numbers of students, white and black. Soon the sit-in technique spread to lunch counters throughout the South.

The impact of the sit-ins was enormous. Many stores and restaurants abandoned their discriminatory policies within a matter of weeks. Most, however, held out, and called the police. Sit-in demonstrators by the hundreds were arrested and charged with criminal TRESPASS. From 1960 to 1964, the problem of the sit-ins came to the Supreme Court over and over again.

When the segregating restaurant was a state operation (for example, a lunch counter in a courthouse), the Court could reverse the conviction by analogy to BROWN V. BOARD OF EDUCATION (1954). Even when the lunch counter was privately owned, the Court would reverse the conviction if it could find some public policy in the background, requiring or encouraging segregation. During the early 1960s the Court was pressed to abandon, or drastically alter, the STATE ACTION limitation, so as to create an equivalent FOURTEENTH AMENDMENT right to be free from racial discrimination in all privately owned PUBLIC ACCOMMODATIONS, irrespective of any state participation. The issue reached a climax—but not a resolution—in BELL V. MARYLAND (1964), when the Court again struck down a conviction on a narrow ground, without deciding the larger constitutional issue.

The Court was relieved of the need to face that issue when Congress adopted the CIVIL RIGHTS ACT OF 1964, which included a broad prohibition against racial discrimination in public accommodations. The Supreme Court quickly upheld the law's constitutionality in HEART OF ATLANTA MOTEL V. UNITED STATES (1964). Further, the Court held that the 1964 act applied with retroactive force, invalidating trespass convictions for sit-ins at public accommodations before the law's effective date (*Hamm v. City of Rock Hill*, 1964).

KENNETH L. KARST

Bibliography

LEWIS, THOMAS P. 1963 The Sit-In Cases: Great Expectations. *Supreme Court Review* 1963:101–151.

PAULSEN, MONRAD G. 1964 The Sit-In Cases of 1964: But Answer Came There None. *Supreme Court Review* 1964:137–170.

SIXTEENTH AMENDMENT

The Sixteenth Amendment was designed to circumvent POLLOCK V. FARMERS' LOAN AND TRUST CO. (1895), in which the Supreme Court had held that a federal tax on income from property was a DIRECT TAX on that property and therefore invalid for want of apportionment among the states on the basis of population (Article I, sections 2 and 9). Following *Pollock*, powerful political forces continued to press for an income tax to replace the regressive consumption taxes then employed to finance the federal government. Indeed, an amendment might have been unnecessary, given the Supreme Court's philosophical shift in *Flint v. Stone Tracy Co.* (1911), upholding a corporate income tax as an excise on doing business in corporate form, not a tax on property.

Although there was sentiment for challenging *Pollock* by reenacting a personal income tax, President WILLIAM HOWARD TAFT urged a constitutional amendment. The Sixteenth Amendment was speedily passed and ratified in 1913. It provides: "The Congress shall have power to lay and collect taxes on incomes, from whatever source derived, without apportionment among the several States, and without regard to any census or enumeration."

Since the enactment of a new income tax statute in 1913, only a single Supreme Court decision has held an income tax provision unconstitutional. EISNER V. MACOMBER (1920) ruled that a stock dividend of common stock on common stock was not "income" because the element of "realization" was lacking. *Macomber* has been greatly undermined by subsequent cases, such as *Helvering v. Bruun* (1940) which treated the return of a lessor's property to him at the termination of a lease as a realization of income. Indeed, the current Court would probably dispense entirely with any constitutional requirement of a realization (or alternatively view a stock dividend as a realization). In *Helvering v. Griffiths* (1943) three dissenters would have overruled *Macomber* but the majority held that the constitutional issue had not been presented by the statute.

Eisner v. Macomber also purported to define "income" for constitutional purposes as "the gain derived from capital, from labor, or from both combined." This definition proved far too narrow; in *Commissioner v. Glenshaw Glass Co.* (1955), the Court rejected all considerations of source, holding a windfall constitutionally taxable as income.

Unlike *Macomber,* modern decisions go to considerable lengths to uphold the constitutionality of income tax provisions. For example, the lower courts upheld an income tax provision that taxed mutual insurance companies on their gross receipts in *Penn Mutual Indemnity Co. v. Commissioner* (1976). Because no deductions were allowed, the tax might have been levied even though the taxpayer had no gain. Similarly, lower courts have upheld a Code section that values property received for services by ignoring value-depressing restrictions on the property (*Sakol v. Commissioner,* 1978). Although the Supreme Court has not had occasion to confirm these broad holdings, the modern approach to claims of constitutional invalidity of tax statutes is to uphold them as indirect taxes or alternatively to define "income" with sufficient breadth to accommodate the provision in issue within the Sixteenth Amendment.

MICHAEL ASIMOW

Bibliography

PAUL, RANDOLPH 1954 *Taxation in the United States.* Boston: Little, Brown.

SIXTH AMENDMENT

See: Confrontation, Right of; Counsel, Right to; Criminal Procedure; Fair Trial; Speedy Trial

SKINNER v. OKLAHOMA 315 U.S. 535 (1942)

In *Skinner* the Supreme Court laid a doctrinal foundation for two of the most important constitutional developments of the twentieth century: the expansion of the reach of the EQUAL PROTECTION clause and the reemergence of SUBSTANTIVE DUE PROCESS as a guarantee of personal freedoms. The case arose out of an Oklahoma law authorizing STERILIZATION of a person convicted three times of "felonies involving moral turpitude." Skinner, convicted first of chicken stealing and then twice of armed robbery, was ordered sterilized by the state courts. The Supreme Court unanimously reversed, holding the sterilization law unconstitutional. Surely the decision seemed easy; no doubt the only serious question was the appropriate ground for decision.

The opinion of the Court, by Justice WILLIAM O. DOUGLAS, rested on equal protection grounds. The sterilization law contained an exception for violations of "prohibitory [liquor] laws, revenue acts, embezzlement, or political offenses." Although the state might constitutionally impose different penalties on embezzlement and other forms of stealing, it could not use so artificial a distinction as the basis for depriving someone of the right of procreation, "one of the basic civil rights of man." Because sterilization permanently deprived a person of a "basic liberty," said Justice Douglas, the judiciary must subject it to "STRICT SCRUTINY." Here the state had offered no justification for the belief that inheritability of criminal traits followed the line between embezzlement and chicken stealing.

Surely the Court also recognized that the sterilization law's exceptions were white collar crimes. Justice Douglas said, "In evil or reckless hands" sterilization could "cause races or types which [were] inimical to the dominant group to wither and disappear." (The year was 1942; the Nazi theory of a "master race" was a major ideological target in World War II.) Sterilization of some but not all who commit "intrinsically the same quality of offense" was "INVIDIOUS" DISCRIMINATION in the same way that RACIAL DISCRIMINATION was.

Chief Justice HARLAN FISKE STONE, concurring, found the Court's equal protection rationale unpersuasive, but found a denial of PROCEDURAL DUE PROCESS in the sterilization law's failure to give a three-time felon like Skinner an opportunity to show that his criminal tendencies were not inheritable. Given the prevailing scientific opinion that criminal traits were not generally inheritable, an individual should have a chance to contest the law's assumption. (This style of reasoning was in vogue briefly during the 1970s under the name of IRREBUTTABLE PRESUMPTIONS.) Justice ROBERT H. JACKSON agreed with both the Douglas and the Stone approaches.

Close to the surface of both the Douglas and the Stone opinions was a strong skepticism that any criminal traits were inheritable. Such an objection would seem fatal to Oklahoma's law on substantive due process grounds. But the Court had very recently abandoned substantive due process as a limit on ECONOMIC REGULATION, and in doing so had used language suggesting the complete demise of substantive due process. Both Douglas and Stone seemed to be avoiding the obvious ground that the law arbitrarily deprived Skinner of liberty. But *Skinner* can be seen today as not only a forerunner of a later Court's strict scrutiny analysis of equal protection cases involving FUNDAMENTAL INTERESTS and SUSPECT CLASSIFICATIONS but also a major early precedent for the development of a constitutional RIGHT OF PRIVACY as a branch of substantive due process.

KENNETH L. KARST

(SEE ALSO: *Reproductive Autonomy: Freedom of Intimate Association.*)

Bibliography

KARST, KENNETH L. 1969 Invidious Discrimination: Justice Douglas and the Return of the "Natural-Law-Due-Process Formula." *UCLA Law Review* 16:716–750.

SLANDER

See: Libel and the First Amendment

SLAUGHTERHOUSE CASES
16 Wallace 36 (1873)

Most histories of the Constitution begin consideration of the judicial interpretation of the THIRTEENTH and FOURTEENTH AMENDMENTS with the *Slaughterhouse* decision of 1873. The decision is, to be sure, of vast significance. Justices JOSEPH P. BRADLEY and STEPHEN J. FIELD, dissenting, expressed embryonic DOCTRINES of FREEDOM OF CONTRACT and SUBSTANTIVE DUE PROCESS that were to dominate American jurisprudence for two generations.

In 1869, Louisiana, ostensibly as a public health measure, incorporated the Crescent City Stock Landing and Slaughterhouse Company and granted it a monopoly of licensed butchering in New Orleans. Butchers not parties to the lucrative arrangement, after failing to crack the monopoly in the state courts, employed as counsel, in an appeal to the federal courts, former Supreme Court Justice JOHN A. CAMPBELL, who more recently had been a Confederate assistant secretary of war. Campbell argued before the Supreme Court that the excluded butchers had been deprived of their livelihoods by the state's deliberate discrimination, although Louisiana had disguised the corrupt monopoly as a health measure. Therefore the disputed statute violated the Thirteenth Amendment's ban on involuntary servitude, the 1866 CIVIL RIGHTS ACT's enforcements of that ban, and the Fourteenth Amendment's guarantees of PRIVILEGES AND IMMUNITIES, EQUAL PROTECTION OF THE LAWS, and due process.

Among prominent counsel for the state, Senator MATTHEW HALE CARPENTER responded to Campbell's innovative brief. Carpenter easily assembled case law that sustained state restrictions on private economic relationships. He insisted that the STATE POLICE POWER amply undergirded the Louisiana statute. No federal constitutional question existed, Carpenter asserted. Both the Thirteenth and the Fourteenth Amendments were irrelevant to the litigants' rights and remedies. And, he prophesied, the federal system would be virtually revolutionized if the Court accepted Campbell's notions and legitimized a federal interest in individuals' claims to be exempt from state regulation.

Speaking through Justice SAMUEL F. MILLER, a majority of the Court was unready to accept Campbell's view that federal guarantees to individuals extended to trades (although, in the TEST OATH CASES, 1867, the Court had extended other federal guarantees to lawyers, ministers, and teachers). Instead, having accepted Carpenter's arguments, Miller reviewed the tradition of judicial support for state determination of ways to meet POLICE POWER responsibilities. Miller denied that exclusion from butchering deprived the appellants of federally protected rights to freedom, privileges and immunities, equal protection, or due process; the "one pervading purpose" of the postwar amendments, he said, was to liberate black slaves, not to enlarge whites' rights. The monopoly created by the state law could not be perceived as imposing servitude; the Thirteenth Amendment was irrelevant as a protection for livelihoods.

Turning to the Fourteenth Amendment, Miller separated federal from state privileges and immunities. He assigned to the states the definition of ordinary marketplace relationships essential to the vast majority of people. More important, he assigned to state privileges and immunities all basic CIVIL LIBERTIES and rights, excluding them from federal protection. Miller's sweeping interpretation relegated everyone, including Negroes, who had assumed that the Fourteenth Amendment had assigned the federal government the role of "guardian democracy" over state-defined CIVIL RIGHTS, to the state governments for effective protection. The national government could protect only the few privileges and immunities of national citizenship: the RIGHT TO TRAVEL, access to Washington, D.C., FREEDOM OF ASSEMBLY and PETITION, and HABEAS CORPUS. Miller and the majority ignored contemporary evidence that many of the framers of both amendments and of the 1866 Civil Rights Act did perceive federally protectable privileges and immunities in broad terms; did assign to federal courts the duty to protect those rights; did envision national civil rights as the essential bridge connecting individuals and states to the nation in a more perfect union. And the majority overlooked earlier contrary case law that spoke directly to the point of the amendments as requirements for federal protection against both state and private discriminations: *In re Turner* (1867) and *Blyew v. U.S.* (1872).

Ignoring also prewar uses of due process in DRED SCOTT V. SANDFORD (1857) and in LAW OF THE LAND clauses in state constitutions, and shrugging off the equal protection argument Campbell had advanced for the appellants, Miller reiterated his position that the postwar amendments protected only blacks against STATE ACTION. The federal protection the Court allowed was minimal and virtually irrelevant to the needs of freedmen, and, for all Americans, left the protection of rights fundamentally unchanged from the prewar condition.

Dissenting, Justices Joseph P. Bradley and Stephen J. Field dredged up Justice SAMUEL CHASE's 1798 opinion in CALDER V. BULL and that of Justice BUSHROD WASHINGTON in his much-quoted 1823 circuit opinion in CORFIELD V. CORYELL, plus the augmented emphases on judicial discretion in a long line of decisions. Bradley emphasized the Fourteenth Amendment's due process clause. Advancing beyond the views of Chief Justice ROGER B. TANEY in *Dred Scott,* he justified judicial intervention to defend substantive due process rights and insisted that a right to choose a calling is a property, a FUNDAMENTAL RIGHT that no state might demean casually. That right was the base for all liberty. The federal courts must repel any state attack on that right, even though the attack might be disguised as a health measure under police powers.

Field argued that the butchering monopoly created servitudes forbidden by the Thirteenth Amendment, but he concentrated on the Fourteenth's privileges and immunities clause. It embraced all the fundamental rights belonging to free men. The national Constitution and laws affirmed those rights. Arbitrary state inhibitions on access to a trade or professions demeaned national rights. Field conceded that states were free to exercise their police powers, even to regulate occupations. But state regulations must apply equally to all citizens who met the standards of the state regulations.

Later, jurists less respectful than Field of state-based FEDERALISM were to cut his *Slaughterhouse* dissent free of its privileges and immunities moorings. Combining his views with Bradley's emphases on the broad effect of the Fourteenth Amendment, later jurists and legal commentators were to transform them into doctrines of freedom of contract and substantive due process. Those doctrines, which were to reign until the twentieth century was well advanced, constrained needful state actions in numerous areas of life and labor.

HAROLD M. HYMAN

Bibliography

BETH, LOREN P. 1963 The Slaughter-House Cases—Revisited, *Louisiana Law Review* 23:487–505.

FAIRMAN, CHARLES 1971 Reconstruction and Reunion, 1864–1868. Chap. 21 in Vol. VI, part 1, of the *Oliver Wendell Holmes Devise History of the Supreme Court of the United States.* New York: Macmillan.

HAMILTON, WALTON H. 1938 The Path of Due Process of Law. Pages 167–179 in Conyers Read, ed., *The Constitution Reconsidered.* New York: Columbia University Press.

HYMAN, HAROLD M. and WIECEK, WILLIAM M. 1982 *Equal Justice under Law: Constitutional Development 1835–1875.* Pages 472–483. New York: Harper & Row.

SLAVERY AND THE CONSTITUTION

Long before the CONSTITUTIONAL CONVENTION OF 1787 the question of slavery had become the prime concern of many Americans. In the first and second Continental Congresses, the matter arose when several groups of slaves petitioned for their manumission. Nothing came of their pleas, of course. In THOMAS JEFFERSON's draft of the DECLARATION OF INDEPENDENCE, he accused the king of waging cruel war against human nature itself, "violating its most sacred rights of life and liberty in the persons of a distant people . . . captivating and carrying them into slavery in another hemisphere. . . ." Although slavery existed throughout the English colonies in 1776, the southern slaveholders in Congress forced rejection of this indictment of the king. If they won their independence on the basis of such an argument, they feared that there would no longer be any justification for slavery.

In some colonies the sentiment against slavery grew during the war for Independence; and the eventual use of slaves as soldiers in the war contributed to the feeling that they should be free. As the states gained their independence some prohibited the slave trade. Some went beyond that enacting legislation looking to the abolition of slavery altogether. Pennsylvania and Massachusetts passed such laws in 1780, followed by Connecticut and Rhode Island in 1784, New York in 1785, and New Jersey in 1786. While no states south of Pennsylvania abolished slavery during this period, several enacted laws facilitating manumission by slaveholders.

Meanwhile, the Continental Congress began to look at the question of slavery as it undertook to develop a national land policy. When Thomas Jefferson framed the ORDINANCE OF 1784 for the organization of government in the western territory, he included a provision that after the year 1800 there should be no slavery or involuntary servitude in any of the states to be organized. That provision was rejected. The idea persisted, however, that slavery should not be extended indefinitely. In the NORTHWEST ORDINANCE of 1787 Jefferson's language of 1784 was adopted with the caveat that fugitive slaves escaping into the Northwest Territory from one of the original states "may be lawfully reclaimed and conveyed to the person claiming his or her labor or service. . . ." The Ordinance did not apply south of the Ohio River, where slaveholders were more likely to settle than in the Northwest Territory.

It was inevitable that slavery should have been an important consideration at the Constitutional Convention. At a time when slavery was waning in the North, the southern states saw in slavery an increasing source of wealth both in the market value of slaves and in what slaves could produce. An economic interest so important could not be ignored by a convention one of whose major concerns was to protect property and to advance the economic interests of those who were to live within the new frame of government. Although there were numerous points at which the emerging document affected the institution of slavery, four were of prime significance to the future of slavery and, indeed, the fate of the Constitution.

One point had to do with the TAXING POWER of Congress. Southern delegates generally feared that in levying taxes, especially POLL TAXES, the federal government might discriminate against the South in the way it counted slaves. Closely connected with this was the perception that in apportioning representation, the South would suffer from any arrangement that did not recognize and count slaves as people. After considerable debate, some of it acrimonious, a compromise was reached. Direct taxes were to be apportioned among the several states according to population, thus making it impossible to raise a major portion of federal revenue by taxing property that existed only in one section of the country. In determining the basis of taxation *and* representation, five slaves were to be counted as equal to three free persons. The cryptic language in Article I, Section 2, reads: "Representatives and direct Taxes shall be apportioned among the several States which may be included within this Union, according to their respective Numbers, which shall be determined by adding to the whole Number of free Persons, including those bound to Service for a Term of Years, and excluding Indians not taxed, three fifths of all other persons."

The other two points regarding slavery were handled with some dispatch, not because they were unimportant but because they did not come up until late in the session, when the weary delegates were eager to return to their homes. On the slave trade, several southern delegates were uncompromising. While those from Virginia and Maryland appeared to favor a prohibition of the trade, those from South Carolina and Georgia were unalterably opposed to the prohibition. To avoid a rupture between the delegates of the upper South and the North, who favored prohibition, and those of the lower South, the compromise was reached that the slave trade could not be ended before twenty years had elapsed. This language was added in Article II, Section 9: "The Migration or Importation of such Persons as any of the States now shall think proper to admit, shall not be prohibited by the Congress prior to the Year one thousand eight hundred and eight, but a Tax or duty may be imposed on such Importation, not exceeding ten dollars for each Person."

Significantly, there was almost no opposition to the proposal that fugitive slaves be returned to their masters. The public obligation to return slaves, which had already been provided for in several Indian treaties between 1781 and 1786, was established in the Northwest Territory in 1787 along with the prohibition of slavery in that region. When the provision came before the Convention in late August, the delegates were in no mood for a protracted debate. The slaveholders had already won such sweeping constitutional recognition of slavery, moreover, that the question of fugitive slaves was something of an anticlimax. Without serious challenge, the provision was inserted in Article IV, Section 2: "No person, held to Service or Labour in one State, under the Laws thereof, escaping into another, shall, in Consequence of any Law or Regulation therein, be discharged from such Service or Labour, but shall be delivered up on Claim of the party to whom such Service or Labour may be due."

In dealing with slavery the delegates to the Convention made certain, as if out of a sense of guilt or shame, never to use the word "slave" or any of its variations in the Constitution itself. "Three fifths of all other persons," "Persons held to Service or Labour," and "Migration or Importation of Such Persons," were all mere euphemisms. Everyone knew what they meant. They were meant to shield the consciences of the delegates just as the clauses themselves were meant to protect the institution of slavery. In none of the deliberations did the delegates give serious consideration to abolishing slavery, even though slavery made a mockery of freedom, equality, and the rights of man. It did not make a mockery, however, of the rights of property. American independence and the new Constitution had the effect of giving slavery a longer life than it was to have in the British Empire.

It was the business of the Congress to enact legislation to carry out the objectives set forth in the Constitution. As far as slaves were concerned, this meant the enactment of legislation to facilitate the recovery of runaway slaves by their masters. The impetus for legislation came, however, not from concerns about fugitive slaves but in the call for a statute to facilitate the surrender of FUGITIVES FROM JUSTICE. When the governor of Pennsylvania was unable to persuade the governor of Virginia to give up three white men accused of kidnapping a Pennsylvania free Negro, he presented the facts in the case to President GEORGE WASHINGTON. When the President transmitted the matter to Congress, it responded by passing the Fugitive Slave Act of 1793. After dealing with the matter of the surrender of fugitives from justice in the first two sections, the law turned to the rendition of fugitive slaves.

Under the law a slaveholder could apply to a federal district or circuit judge for a certificate authorizing him to return his slave to the state from which he had fled. This certificate was to be granted after the master had captured his slave, and there were few federal judges at the time; therefore, the master was compelled to go to considerable expense and travel before enjoying the protection of the federal courts. The law did not authorize judges to issue warrants for the arrest of slaves and it did not compel federal authorities to aid in the pursuit of fugitive slaves. The lack of such provisions generated criticism by slaveholders for years to come.

Although under the law of 1793 many fugitives were recaptured and returned to the places from which they had fled, masters continued to complain about the difficulties of reclaiming their human property. Meanwhile, as antislavery sentiment gained momentum in the first decade of the century, opponents of slavery placed additional obstacles in the way of slaveholders seeking the return of their runaways. They began actively to aid fugitives, to urge federal judges not to issue certificates for the return of runaways, and to persuade local officers not to cooperate in their rendition. Slavemasters soon called for a more effective law, and in 1818, a stronger bill was introduced in the House of Representatives. As it made its way through Congress, it was burdened with amendments introduced by antislavery legislators requiring proof of ownership before a court of record and making masters criminally liable for false claims. Although a version of the proposed law passed both houses, it was tabled when the conference committee was unable to resolve the problem of amendments.

As the new century began, many Americans turned their thoughts to the provision of the Constitution prohibiting Congress from closing the slave trade before 1808. The slave trade was flourishing, and the slave interests faced a curious dilemma. If the trade continued they risked increasing the chances of violence as unruly blacks from Africa or revolutionary and resourceful blacks from the Caribbean were imported. On the other hand, they required a larger number of slaves to tend their burgeoning plantations. Hoping that the national and state governments would provide safeguards against uprisings and insurrections, they were tempted to favor the continued importation of slaves. At least, they wished to keep their options open.

Ending the slave trade under the provision set forth in the Constitution was not a foregone conclusion, and the antislavery forces knew it. All through the decade they pressed for stringent federal legislation to end the trade. In January 1800, a group of free Negroes in Philadelphia called on Congress to revise its laws on the slave trade and on fugitives. When South Carolina reopened its ports to the trade in 1803, antislavery groups began to press Congress to act. Several resolutions were introduced in Congress condemning the slave trade, but that body took no conclusive steps. The question was brought dramatically before the country in December 1805, when Senator Stephen R. Bradley of Vermont introduced a bill to prohibit the slave trade after January 1, 1808, but the bill was indefinitely tabled. This measure set the stage for President Jefferson to address the issue in his annual message to Congress in December 1806. He called attention to the approaching date when Congress could constitutionally prohibit "all further participation in those violations of human rights which have been so long continued on the unoffending inhabitants of Africa, and which the morality, the reputation, and the best interests of our country have long been eager to proscribe."

Pursuant to the President's eloquent call, which was reminiscent of his draft of the Declaration of Independence, Congress proceeded to consider legislation outlawing the trade. Every provision of the proposed law was debated vigorously. Slaveholders, fearing that Africans smuggled into the United States would not be under the control of the law, wanted them seized and sold into slavery. The antislavery members of

Congress strongly objected. The PROHIBITION OF THE SLAVE TRADE ACT (1807) was a compromise. It directed federal officers to be "governed by the provisions of the laws, now existing, of the several states prohibiting the admission or importation . . . of any Negro, mulatto, or other person of color."

In 1818 in the first supplementary act to the law of 1807, Congress sought to make the trade less attractive by increasing the penalty for anyone engaged in it. For example, a fine of $20,000 was replaced by a lowered fine and imprisonment for three to seven years. There were stiffer penalties for persons who knowingly purchased illegally imported Negroes; one-half of all forfeitures and fines were to go to informers. In 1819 Congress directed the President to use armed cruisers on the coasts of the United States and Africa to suppress the trade. Half the proceeds of a condemned ship would go to the captor as bounty, and the captured slaver was to be returned to the port from which it sailed. In the following year Congress provided that direct participation in the slave trade was an act of piracy, punishable by death.

The slave trade was profitable, and it continued despite federal legislation. State laws on the disposition of illegally imported Africans varied. North Carolina directed that such Africans "be sold and disposed of for the state." Georgia directed that the Africans either be sold or given to the Colonization Society for transportation to Africa, with the Society bearing all expenses. Despite these laws, most imported slaves seem to have escaped capture. There were so few captures and the federal officials did so little to enforce the statute of 1807 that it was nearly a dead letter. Slavers introduced their cargo into the United States from Galveston, then a part of Mexico, from Amelia Island in Florida, until 1819 a part of the Spanish Empire, and at various ports on the eastern and southern coasts of the United States. Secretary of the Treasury William H. Crawford confessed that the United States had failed to enforce the law.

Estimates regarding the numbers involved in the illicit slave trade varied. In the decades following passage of the supplementary acts, slavers easily evaded federal authorities, and enforcement received no more than lip service in Washington. In 1839 President MARTIN VAN BUREN called for revision of the laws covering the slave trade in order that "the integrity and honor of our flag may be carefully preserved." A decade later President Zachary Taylor invited the attention of Congress "to an amendment of our existing laws relating to the African slave trade, with a view to the effectual suppression of that barbarous traffic." Nothing happened, and the trade continued down through the Civil War. Because of its clandestine nature, precise figures are impossible; a recent student of the trade estimates that some 51,000 slaves were illegally imported by 1860.

Shortly after the United States purchased Louisiana in 1803, inhabitants from the older states began to settle in the newly acquired territory. When Louisiana entered the Union in 1812 as a slave state, eastern and northern interests began to appreciate the political and economic consequences of slave states entering the Union. They believed that under the Constitution the federal government could prevent the creation of slave states in the territories. They were determined, therefore, to prevent slave states from entering the Union, or, failing that, to limit the number of new slave states. When Missouri sought admission in 1818, northern members of Congress said that they would agree only on condition that the Missouri constitution forbid slavery. Southerners claimed that the restriction was discriminatory; some threatened disunion. After bitter debate, the impasse was resolved when Maine sought admission. Congress admitted Maine as a free state and Missouri as a slave state and declared that in the Louisiana territory slavery should not exist north of the southern boundary of Missouri.

The MISSOURI COMPROMISE stimulated the rivalry between the slave and free states, with each side searching for ways to enhance its advantage. While southern spokesmen insisted that the problems of slavery were local, they relied on the federal Constitution and laws to protect slavery in defiance of the FIRST AMENDMENT; they demanded that antislavery petitions to Congress be laid on the table without receiving notice. At the same time they demanded that Congress act to facilitate the return of fugitive slaves. As antislavery sentiment in the North increased and abolitionists became more active in obstructing the return of fugitives, the Southerners' demands for protection became more shrill. There were numerous dramatic moments between 1830 and 1860, when abolitionists seized fugitive slaves from their captors or interrupted court proceedings to give accused fugitives the opportunity to flee.

In some northern states residents feared that the Fugitive Slave Law of 1793 would operate to the disadvantage of kidnapped whites and free Negroes accused of being runaway slaves. Consequently, state legislatures empowered state courts to rule in matters arising out of the 1793 law. The Pennsylvania statute of 1826 required the master to present to a magistrate proof of his claim to the alleged fugitive. If the magistrate was convinced the claim was well founded, he was to issue a certificate authorizing the removal of the runaway from the state. If, on the other hand, anyone had seized a person suspected of being a runaway and wrongfully removed him, he would, upon conviction, be deemed guilty of a felony and suffer fine and imprisonment. In due course and by amicable arrangement the Supreme Court ruled on the constitutionality of the Pennsylvania statute in PRIGG V. PENNSYLVANIA (1842), thereby significantly affecting the slavery question for the next two decades.

Edward Prigg, a slave catcher, seized a Negro woman and her children in Pennsylvania with the intention of returning them to their alleged owner in Maryland. When Prigg sought a certificate authorizing their removal, the magistrate, dissatisfied with the proof of ownership, declined to issue the certificate. Prigg took them anyway and was subsequently convicted for violating the 1826 law. The Supreme Court reversed the state court in a decision that had far greater significance than merely exonerating Prigg. Speaking for the Court, Associate Justice JOSEPH STORY declared the Pennsylvania PERSONAL LIBERTY LAW unconstitutional, because it invaded a field placed within the exclusive domain of the federal government by the Fugitive Slave Act of 1793 and by the Constitution itself. "Under the Constitution," said Story, the right to seize a runaway and the duty to deliver him pervaded "the whole Union with an equal and supreme force, uncontrolled and uncontrollable by State SOVEREIGNTY or State legislation." States could enforce the law of 1793, if they wished; but they could not be required to do so, Story added. Further, if an owner recaptured his fugitive slave he did not need a state magistrate's permission to return him to his place of abode.

By placing the fugitive slave question within the exclusive JURISDICTION of the federal government, Justice Story implicitly encouraged northern states that did not wish to cooperate in the enforcement of federal legislation on the subject. The decision promoted the belief, moreover, that antislavery forces could work through sympathetic state and local officials to prevent the recovery of fugitive slaves. Accordingly ten free states enacted personal liberty laws.

When slaveholders felt the impact of *Prigg* in relieving states of responsibility in enforcing the Fugitive Slave Law, they agitated for a more stringent federal law that neither abolitionists nor hostile state laws could nullify. Because the annual pecuniary loss in fugitive slaves was in the hundreds of thousands of dollars, slaveholders increased their pressure on Congress to act. Despite its validation in *Prigg*, the Act of 1793 was inadequate. State courts seemed to vie with abolitionists in their disregard for federal authority. What was needed was a new act of Congress providing effective federal machinery for its successful enforcement. Early in 1850, Senator James Mason of Virginia introduced a bill to that end. Thus began the long and tortuous route by which a new fugitive slave law made its way through Congress.

The debate on the bill was extensive and, at times, acrimonious, connected as it was with other matters that were to constitute the COMPROMISE OF 1850. In the Senate, WILLIAM H. SEWARD of New York wanted to guarantee to every alleged fugitive slave the right to TRIAL BY JURY. HENRY CLAY of Kentucky, on the other hand, wished to emphasize the right of the aggrieved master to recover his property from any place, including a free state, where the slave had fled. DANIEL WEBSTER of Massachusetts, to the surprise of many Northerners and Southerners, agreed with Clay and declared that "in regard to the return of persons bound to service, who have escaped into the free States . . . it is my judgment that the South is right, and the North is wrong." After the bill passed both houses, President Millard Filmore signed it on September 18, 1850.

The new fugitive slave law undertook to establish adequate federal machinery for its enforcement. Circuit courts were to appoint commissioners who, concurrently with circuit and district judges, had authority to grant certificates for the return of fugitive slaves. United States marshals were to execute warrants issued under the act, and a failure of diligent execution was punishable by a $1,000 fine. If a fugitive should escape from a marshal's custody, the marshal was liable for the slave's full value. When the marshal or claimant brought the slave before the court to request a certificate for his return, the alleged fugitive was not permitted to testify in his own behalf. Court disturbances, aiding or abetting fugitives, and harboring or concealing fugitives were punishable by a $1,000 fine and six months imprisonment.

Abolitionists and others attacked the Fugitive Slave Law as unconstitutional. Horace Mann said that it made war on the fundamental principles of human liberty. CHARLES SUMNER called it a "flagrant violation of the Constitution, and of the most cherished rights—shocking to Christian sentiments, insulting to humanity, and impudent in all its pretensions." Others argued that the fugitive slave clause of the Constitution did not confer on Congress any power to enact laws for the recovery of fugitive slaves. They questioned the power of Congress, moreover, to give commissioners authority to render judgments that only United States judges could properly render under the

Constitution. The denial to fugitives by the law of 1850 of the right to trial by jury and to CONFRONT and cross-examine witnesses was itself an unconstitutional denial of DUE PROCESS, its opponents argued. The fact that commissioners received fees instead of fixed salaries meant that they were themselves interested parties in fugitive slave cases. If the commissioner turned over the fugitive to his claimant, he received a ten dollar fee. If he freed the fugitive, the commissioner received only five dollars. What commissioner could be trusted to render impartial justice when his income depended on the kind of decision that he rendered?

The flight into Canada from northern cities of numerous free Negroes and fugitive slaves dramatized for many Northerners the new role of the federal government in obstructing the efforts of those who sought freedom. Many Northerners vowed to prevent enforcement of the new fugitive slave law. Fugitive slave cases increased, but so did rescues, accompanied by denunciations of federal officials. Friends of fugitives resorted to desperate measures such as kidnapping slave hunters and poisoning their bloodhounds. They organized vigilance committees not only to engage in action but also to express their moral revulsion to every effort to enforce the new law. In 1852 the Boston committee unsuccessfully attempted to prevent the rendition of Thomas Sims, an alleged fugitive from Georgia. Composed of such men as Theodore Parker, Wendell Phillips, Horace Mann, and Charles Sumner, the committee, on April 13 at 3 A.M., watched as the United States marshal walked Sims down State Street, past the spot where Crispus Attucks fell and to the wharf where the ship was waiting to take him back to Savannah. Six days later Sims was publicly whipped in Savannah, the first slave Massachusetts had returned.

Opponents of the Fugitive Slave Law of 1850 challenged it in the same way that opponents had challenged its predecessor. The Supreme Court ruling in STRADER V. GRAHAM (1851) could well have controlled the problem for years to come. After Jacob Strader, a citizen of Kentucky, helped several Negroes leave Kentucky, their alleged master sued Strader for damages. Strader claimed that the blacks were not slaves and that they made regular visits to Ohio where they worked as entertainers. These visits, Strader claimed, had caused them to become free even if they had previously been slaves because the Ordinance of 1787 forbade slavery in the Northwest Territory of which Ohio had been a part. When the case reached the Supreme Court, Chief Justice ROGER B. TANEY, speaking for the entire bench, declared that whatever the status of the blacks while outside Kentucky, they were subject to Kentucky laws upon their return. Nothing in the Constitution, he insisted, could control the law of Kentucky on this subject.

Meanwhile, opposing forces in Kansas were attempting to settle the issue in their own way. The bill to organize Kansas and Nebraska as territories had repealed the Missouri Compromise and left to the inhabitants of the respective territories the decision whether the states-to-be would be slave or free. Abolitionists, believing there should be no more slave states under any circumstances, were determined to make Kansas as well as Nebraska free states. To that end, they undertook first to settle Kansas with persons who would vote for a free constitution and thus to discourage slaveholders from settling in Nebraska, which they were certain would become a free state. Proslavery forces were determined at least to make Kansas a slave state. Both sides were certain they had the Constitution on their side. After bitter arguments and bloody battles, Kansas voted for a free constitution. The South felt that its ambitions had been frustrated and its rights under the Constitution violated as well.

The antislavery forces would not let the decision in *Strader* stand without challenge. They hoped it might be modified, or even overruled, in another decision offering some protection to slaves who had been in free states. Soon another case, DRED SCOTT V. SANDFORD (1857), presented an ideal opportunity, they thought, to secure an unequivocal statement on the status of slaves in the free states and in the territories. Dred Scott, a Missouri slave, traveled with his master to the free state of Illinois, where they lived for a time, then to Minnesota, a free territory under the provisions of the Missouri Compromise. Upon their return to Missouri, his master sold Scott to a New York resident in a vain attempt to establish federal DIVERSITY JURISDICTION when Scott subsequently sued for his freedom. When the Supreme Court announced its decision on March 6, 1857, Chief Justice Taney was again the spokesman.

Taney declared that because Negroes had been viewed as belonging to an inferior order at the time that the Constitution was ratified, they were not citizens within the meaning of the Constitution's provision defining the permissible JURISDICTION of federal courts in cases between citizens of different states. Moreover Scott had not become free by virtue of the Missouri Compromise, because the Compromise was unconstitutional; Congress had no authority to prohibit slavery in the territories. In any case, Taney concluded, once Scott returned to Missouri his status was determined by Missouri law. In Missouri he was still a slave, and thus not a citizen of any state. The case was dismissed for want of jurisdiction.

The decision gave the proslavery forces more support than they could possibly have expected. Slavery's opponents called the decision wicked, atrocious, and abominable. Others hoped the decision would settle once and for all the grievous sectional issues that were about to destroy the Union. But the decision remained controversial. Its impact on events of the next few years is unclear. Perhaps it did not contribute significantly to the critical disputes and eventual divisions in the Democratic party. Perhaps the decision did not greatly stimulate the growth of the Republican party. Yet, as Don E. Fehrenbacher, the leading historian of the decision, has said, "it was a conspicuous and perhaps an integral part of a configuration of events and conditions that did produce enough changes of allegiance to make a political revolution and enough intensity of feeling to make that revolution violent."

The abolitionists, although embittered by the decision, did not relent in their effort to secure judicial support for their position. In a Wisconsin case, which came to the Supreme Court as ABLEMAN V. BOOTH (1859), they attempted once again to have the Fugitive Slave Law of 1850 declared unconstitutional. Sherman M. Booth, an abolitionist editor in Milwaukee, had been arrested for helping a Negro escape from a United States deputy marshal. The state courts pronounced the law unconstitutional and ordered Booth released. When the case reached the Supreme Court in 1859, Chief Justice Taney reversed the state courts, censured them for presuming to pass judgment on federal laws, and held that the Fugitive Slave Law was fully authorized by the Constitution.

Booth was the last opportunity the abolitionists would have to take their cause to the Supreme Court. They would win local victories, such as the denial of the right of transit by slaves through a free state, but the Fugitive Slave Law remained intact until the Civil War. It would take much more than court challenges or even local disturbances to dislodge the institution of slavery. The fact remained that slavery was so deeply imbedded in the Constitution itself and so firmly protected by it that both violent action and a constitutional amendment would be required to effect far-reaching and lasting change.

The violent action was not long in coming, but the outbreak of the Civil War did not put an end to slavery. President ABRAHAM LINCOLN insisted that the Confederate states were still in the Union and continued to enjoy the constitutional protection of slave property. Once the war began in earnest, however, there was no enforcement of the fugitive slave laws, and as slaves escaped to the Union lines, their emancipation became increasingly a part of the war's objectives. Congress early took steps to free certain slaves. The CONFISCATION ACT of August 6, 1861, declared that owners forfeited slaves engaged in hostile military service. In July 1862 Congress took additional steps in the Second Confiscation Act by granting freedom to slaves of traitors. Furthermore, the slaves of all persons supporting the rebellion were "forever free of their servitude. . . ." Although Lincoln had serious doubts about the constitutionality of the act, he signed it.

Meanwhile, Congress was moving speedily to emancipate the slaves whom it constitutionally could. It could not pass a universal emancipation bill, but it could and did abolish slavery in the DISTRICT OF COLUMBIA and the TERRITORIES. The emancipation bill for the District of Columbia precipitated a lengthy debate, during which President Lincoln persuaded the lawmakers to include an appropriation of $1,000,000 for compensation to owners not exceeding $300 for each slave and for the removal and colonization of the freedmen. Even so, Lincoln was reluctant to sign the bill. He signed it after Senator CHARLES SUMNER of Massachusetts and Bishop Daniel A. Payne of the African Methodist Episcopal Church pleaded with him to approve it. On June 19, 1862, Congress passed and sent to the President a bill abolishing slavery in the territories, with no provision for the compensation of owners, and Lincoln signed it.

The President continued to argue that the federal government could not emancipate the slaves unless it also compensated the owners and colonized the freedmen. Unfortunately for him, his arguments convinced neither the representatives of the border slave states nor the Negro delegations that visited him. Consequently, he was compelled to face the mounting pressures to free the slaves without any apparent constitutional means of doing so. Even as he moved toward an emancipation policy, Lincoln kept his own counsel. He listened patiently to the constant stream of delegations, some urging him to free the slaves, others insisting that he do nothing. The only thing he revealed was that the matter was on his mind, day and night, "more than any other."

In the late spring of 1862 Lincoln decided that he would emancipate the slaves by proclamation. The bleak military outlook pressed the decision on Lincoln. In July he read to the Cabinet a recently completed draft and solicited suggestions regarding language and timing. The members confined their remarks to possible political and military consequences. Lincoln agreed that a propitious moment to issue it would be in the wake of a Union victory, lest some view it as an act of desperation.

Although the battle of Antietam, September 17, 1862, was not the clear-cut victory for which Lincoln had been waiting, he decided to act anyway. On September 22, 1862, he issued the Preliminary EMANCIPATION PROCLAMATION, to take effect on January 1, 1863. Abandoning the notion of colonization, the President, in the final Proclamation, declared free those slaves in states or parts of states under Confederate control. He further declared that the freedmen would be received into the armed service of the United States "to garrison forts, positions, stations, and other places, and to man vessels in said service." Even without a comprehensive emancipation policy, Lincoln is reported to have said as he signed the document, "I never, in my life, felt more certain that I was doing right than I do in signing this paper."

Lincoln realized, of course, that his proclamation, primarily a war measure, did not actually free the slaves. Although military action set many of them free, either state or federal action or both were needed to achieve real and permanent freedom in law and practice. By early 1865, Tennessee, West Virginia, Maryland, and Missouri had taken steps to free their slaves. Delaware and Kentucky, like the Confederate states, had taken no such action by the end of the war.

It early became clear that only national action, preferably through a constitutional amendment, could provide a uniform emancipation policy. Yet some doubted the wisdom or even the prudence of using the Constitution to reform a domestic institution such as slavery. Others questioned the legality of amending the Constitution while eleven states remained outside the Union. The latter circumstance was a major reason why the proposed amendment to forbid slavery throughout the nation initially failed to get the necessary two-thirds approval of the House after it had passed the Senate in the spring of 1864. After the election of 1864 and with the war winding down, the House finally approved the amendment on January 31, 1865. The following day, Lincoln was pleased to sign the resolution submitting the amendment to the states for ratification.

By December 18, 1865, twenty-seven states, including eight former Confederate states, had ratified the THIRTEENTH AMENDMENT, and it became part of the Constitution. One of the ironies was that the amendment could not have been ratified without the concurrence of the slave states whose governments Congress did not recognize in 1865. This seemed an appropriate way to end slavery, which was itself the most remarkable anomaly in the history of the country.

JOHN HOPE FRANKLIN

Bibliography

BECKER, CARL (1942)1953 *The Declaration of Independence: A Study in the History of Political Ideas.* New York: Knopf.

BOWEN, CATHERINE DRINKER 1966 *Miracle at Philadelphia: The Story of the Constitutional Convention May to September 1787.* Boston: Little, Brown.

CURTIN, PHILIP 1969 *The Atlantic Slave Trade: A Census.* Madison: University of Wisconsin Press.

DUBOIS, W. E. BURGHARDT (1896)1954 *The Suppression of the African Slave Trade to the United States of America.* New York: Social Science Press.

FEHRENBACHER, DON E. 1978 *The Dred Scott Case: Its Significance in American Law and Politics.* New York: Oxford University Press.

FINKELMAN, PAUL 1981 *An Imperfect Union: Slavery, Federalism, and Comity.* Chapel Hill: University of North Carolina Press.

FRANKLIN, JOHN HOPE 1963 *The Emancipation Proclamation.* Garden City, N.Y.: Doubleday.

LEVY, LEONARD W. 1950 Sims' Case: The Fugitive Slave Law in Boston in 1851. *Journal of Negro History* 35:39–74.

ZILBERSMIT, ARTHUR 1967 *The First Emancipation: The Abolition of Slavery in the North.* Chicago: University of Chicago Press.

SLAVERY IN THE TERRITORIES

Slavery was confirmed by statute or royal decree in all the English, Spanish, and French colonies of North America. After American Independence, slavery therefore enjoyed a legal existence in all the states. In the NORTHWEST ORDINANCE of 1787, the Confederation Congress prohibited slavery in the Northwest Territory, although it also provided for the recapture of slaves escaping there. The First Congress reenacted this ban, but in legislation for the area southwest of the Ohio River it omitted the exclusion of slavery, so that slavery was free to penetrate into the TERRITORIES ceded by Virginia, New York, North Carolina, South Carolina, and Georgia. Slavery also existed in the French settlements that were to become Louisiana, Missouri, Illinois, and Indiana. The treaty of cession with France (1803), by which the United States acquired the LOUISIANA PURCHASE, guaranteed extant property rights, thus assuring slavery's perpetuation in those territories.

Despite the ban of the Northwest Ordinance, settlers in Ohio (particularly in the Virginia Military Reserve in the southwest quadrant of the territory), Indiana, and Illinois tried to introduce slavery, with the connivance of Indiana territorial governor William Henry Harrison in the case of Ohio, and at least the tacit consent of President THOMAS JEFFERSON. They failed in Ohio and Indiana, but in Illinois slavery continued in subterfuge forms in the lead mines of Galena and the salt mines of Shawneetown, and only a vigorous abolitionist effort prevented its legalization throughout the state in 1822.

The Constitution contained no direct allusion to slavery in the territories; the new states and territories clauses did not refer to it, although the fugitive slave clause permitted recapture of fugitives only from the states, not the territories. Consequently, when Missouri sought admission as a slave state in 1819, Congress had no textual guidance, and for the first time it had to extrapolate from what it could determine of the Framers' intent concerning the territories. The result was a long and bitter debate in which restrictionists argued that slavery was hostile to the spirit of republican government and should not be extended to the new lands, while slavery's supporters insisted that Congress lacked power to exclude slavery from any territory. Jefferson at the time joined the antirestrictionists, arguing that as slavery spread it would diffuse to the point where the black population, relative to the white, would dwindle in both the old states and the new territories. The Missouri controversy was settled by admitting Missouri as a slave state and Maine as a free state, while prohibiting slavery in all the Louisiana Purchase territory north of Missouri's southern boundary (36°30′). (See MISSOURI COMPROMISE.) Jefferson likened the Missouri debates to a "firebell in the night," the "knell of the union."

As the confrontation over slavery intensified in the 1830s, abolitionists and defenders of slavery amplified their constitutional and policy arguments about slavery's future in the territories. Abolitionists found two sources of congressional power to exclude slavery. They saw the territories clause (Article IV, section 3) as a plenary grant of power to the national government to regulate all matters of property and personal status in the territories. Further, the new states clause (Article IV, section 3) implicitly permitted restriction because it gave Congress power to prohibit a state's admission if it recognized slavery. Abolitionists also maintained that slavery was contrary to the principles of a republican form of government, which the United States must guarantee to each of the states.

Alarmed by such doctrines, JOHN C. CALHOUN in the period 1837–1847 elaborated doctrines that denied any exclusionary power to Congress. He insisted that the territories were the common property of all the states, and that it would be unjust to the slave states to exclude one form of property and its owners (slaves) when all other forms of property were not similarly restricted. Calhoun regarded Congress as the agent of the states (they being the principals) or as their trustee (they being the beneficiaries). By either legal metaphor, Congress lacked power to exclude slavery because that would discriminate against one group of states. He maintained that slavery was not only a positive good but also an essential element in the domestic and political structure of the slave states. Efforts to impede its spread were therefore not only insulting but threatening to the security of the states themselves.

This debate remained academic until 1845. Arkansas had been admitted as a slave state in 1836, the unorganized Indian Territory (modern Oklahoma) was not then targeted for white settlement, and many still considered the remainder of the Louisiana Purchase uninhabitable. But Texas's independence, followed by its request for admission, thrust the territorial debates to center stage, and for over a decade after the outbreak of the Mexican War the territorial issue eclipsed all other topics of the slavery controversy except the problem of fugitive slaves. Texas, a slaveholding Republic that had struck for Independence partly because the Mexican constitution had abolished slavery, presented the potential for more than one slave state; the JOINT RESOLUTION admitting it to statehood recognized its potential subdivision into five states.

When war with Mexico broke out in 1846, the future of the territories to be acquired from that country became a more urgent issue. A few persons suggested that the United States acquire no new territories, but that idea was lost in the tide of Manifest Destiny flooding the country in the 1840s. In 1846, Representative David Wilmot, a Pennsylvania Democrat, offered a proviso to an appropriations bill that used the language of the Northwest Ordinance to exclude slavery from all territories acquired as a result of the Mexican War. Democrats and other defenders of slavery were alarmed by the WILMOT PROVISO's popularity in the North (nearly all free state legislatures endorsed it), and especially by the Proviso's appeal to Northern Democrats, who resented Southern dictation of party policy on slavery-related subjects and wanted to preserve the new territories for free white settlement.

The Proviso's opponents introduced four alternative proposals. Many Southerners at first found the idea of extending the Missouri Compromise line attractive. The Polk administration, Justice JOHN CATRON of Tennessee, the NASHVILLE CONVENTION of 1850, and Senator JOHN J. CRITTENDEN of Kentucky in 1860 all suggested extrapolating the 36°30′ line as a simple and arbitrary solution to the Gordian knot of slavery in the territories. Despite its simplicity, the idea repeatedly failed. One of the reasons for its failure was that other Southern leaders, more determined to protect the South than to compromise the territorial issue, revised their 1820 position and insisted that any exclusion of slavery from the territories was unconstitutional. Their theories for a time were subsumed under the shorthand term "non-intervention," a name for a cluster of doctrines that adopted Calhoun's premises and went on to demand that the federal government protect slavery in all the territories and even establish it there by a federal territorial slave code if necessary.

Northern Democrats rejected this position, but they did not want to split the party by endorsing the Wilmot Proviso. Under the leadership of Lewis Cass of Michigan and STEPHEN A. DOUGLAS of Illinois, they proposed a third alternative: the doctrine of territorial sovereignty, more often but less accurately referred to as POPULAR SOVEREIGNTY or squatter sovereignty. Cass and Douglas insisted that the future of slavery in the territories be decided by the settlers of the territories themselves, not by Congress. After 1850, they also began to adopt the Southern position that slavery's exclusion was not only unnecessary and gratuitously offensive to the South but also unconstitutional. Territorial sovereignty contained a central ambiguity: when were the settlers to decide? If, as Southern spokesmen demanded, territorial settlers could not exercise this prerogative until the eve of statehood, then slavery would establish a foothold, as it had in Missouri, and be impossible to dislodge. Northern proponents of territorial sovereignty, on the other hand, insisted that the settlers had a right to exclude slavery at any point after the organization of the territory. This view, in turn, forced Southerners to another doctrinal redoubt, when they claimed that just as Congress could not exclude slavery, neither could its creature, the territorial legislature. In this view, slavery could establish itself anywhere in American territories.

The Free Soil coalition of 1848, made up of New York Democrats, antislavery Whigs, and former political abolitionists, adopted the Wilmot Proviso as a principal plank in their program. But the COMPROMISE OF 1850 decisively rejected the Wilmot Proviso. In admitting California as a free state and organizing New Mexico and Utah Territories without restrictions as to slavery, Congress also rejected the Missouri Compromise line. But it also adopted the fourth alternative to the Wilmot Proviso, the "Clayton Compromise." Senator John Clayton of Delaware had proposed that all questions arising in TERRITORIAL COURTS concerning title to slaves or a black's claim to freedom be appealable directly to the United States Supreme Court, in effect inviting the Justices of the high court to try their hand at resolving the seemingly insoluble territorial issue. By adopting the Clayton Compromise, Congress admitted its inability to deal with the most exigent political issue of the day. Its desperate grasp at nonpolitical solutions not only confessed its impotence but also assumed the finality of an unpredictable resolution of a question that was ultimately metajudicial.

The KANSAS-NEBRASKA ACT of 1854 adopted the principle of territorial sovereignty, along with some vague and ambiguous allusions to nonintervention. It declared the Missouri Compromise defunct and implied that it was unconstitutional, thus representing a victory for both northern Democrats and Southerners. But this accommodation did not last long, as Kansas filled with authentic settlers and Missouri sojourners. Because most of the former hoped to see Kansas free and because all the latter were determined to make it a slave state, political controversy erupted into guerrilla warfare in the period known as "Bleeding Kansas." President JAMES BUCHANAN tried to force the proslavery LECOMPTON CONSTITUTION on the territory, over the wishes of a large majority of bona fide settlers, and thereby split the Democratic party into Southern-dominated and Douglas wings.

Meanwhile, Chief Justice ROGER B. TANEY and his colleagues took up the invitation tendered by Congress in DRED SCOTT V. SANDFORD (1857). Taney held, in the latter part of his opinion, that the Missouri Compromise was unconstitutional, and that Congress could not exclude slavery from a territory. He adopted three Calhounite positions in OBITER DICTA: the federal government had to protect slavery in the territories; territorial legislatures could not exclude slavery at any time before statehood; and the federal government was the trustee of the states or the territories. In passing, Taney suggested that congressional exclusion would deprive a slaveowner of rights to property protected by the DUE PROCESS clause of the Fifth Amendment. This adumbration of SUBSTANTIVE DUE PROCESS was merely a passing allusion, however, the emphasis of Taney's opinion lying instead in his interpretation of the new states clause.

In the LINCOLN–DOUGLAS DEBATES of 1858, ABRA-

HAM LINCOLN challenged Douglas to explain what was left of territorial sovereignty after *Dred Scott.* Douglas suggested the FREEPORT DOCTRINE: that Congress could for all practical purposes exclude slavery from a territory simply by not enacting a territorial slave code or extending any other protection for it there. Under one interpretation of SOMERSET V. STEWART (1772), there being no positive law to keep a person enslaved, slavery effectively could not establish itself. This led Mississippi Senator JEFFERSON DAVIS to demand that the federal courts protect slavery in the territories somehow, and, if this proved unavailing, that Congress enact a territorial slave code.

The Constitution of the Confederate States of America extended full federal protection to slavery in any territories the Confederacy might acquire. The Congress of the United States abolished slavery in all federal territories in 1862 (Act of June 19, 1862).

WILLIAM M. WIECEK

(SEE ALSO: *Constitutional History, 1829–1848.*)

Bibliography

BESTOR, ARTHUR 1961 State Sovereignty and Slavery: A Reinterpretation of Proslavery Constitutional Doctrine, 1846–1860. *Journal of the Illinois State Historical Society* 54:117–180.

QUAIFE, MILO M. 1910 *The Doctrine of Non-Intervention with Slavery in the Territories.* Chicago: Chamberlin.

RUSSEL, ROBERT R. 1966 Constitutional Doctrines with Regard to Slavery in the Territories. *Journal of Southern History* 32:466–486.

SLOAN v. LEMON

See: Committee v. Nyquist

SMITH, J. ALLEN
(1860–1924)

Lawyer, economist, and political scientist James Allen Smith was an influential spokesman for PROGRESSIVE CONSTITUTIONAL THOUGHT. His most important book was *The Spirit of American Government* (1901), subtitled "A Study of the Constitution: Its Origins, Influence and Relation to Democracy." Smith contended that the Constitution represented a reactionary and undemocratic retreat from the revolutionary principles of the DECLARATION OF INDEPENDENCE. He proposed to make the Constitution more democratic by eliminating CHECKS AND BALANCES, curbing the SUPREME COURT, and introducing DIRECT ELECTIONS for the President and Senate along with INITIATIVE, REFERENDUM, and RECALL.

DENNIS J. MAHONEY

SMITH v. ALLWRIGHT
321 U.S. 649 (1944)

In 1935 the Supreme Court had held in GROVEY V. TOWNSEND that the Texas Democratic party convention's rule excluding black voters from PRIMARY ELECTIONS was not STATE ACTION and thus violated no constitutional rights. *Allwright* involved the same question, raised in the same manner; Smith alleged that he was excluded from the Texas Democratic primary because of his race and sought damages from election officials under federal CIVIL RIGHTS laws. The case had become a plausible candidate for Supreme Court review because in UNITED STATES V. CLASSIC (1941) the Court had reconsidered the nature of a primary election by way of upholding Congress's power to forbid fraud in primary elections of nominees for federal offices. In *Classic,* the Court had concluded that Louisiana primary elections were, by law, an integral part of the machinery for electing officers.

Applying the *Classic* reasoning in *Allwright,* the Court overruled *Grovey v. Townsend* and held that the state's provision of machinery for primary elections was sufficiently connected with the party's conduct of those elections to satisfy the state action limitation of the FIFTEENTH AMENDMENT. Because that amendment forbade a state to deny or abridge the right to vote on account of race, Smith was entitled to damages if he could prove his allegations. Justice STANLEY F. REED wrote for the Court.

Justice OWEN ROBERTS, who had written for a unanimous Court in *Grovey,* dissented, complaining that the OVERRULING of a DECISION after only nine years tended "to bring adjudications of this tribunal into the same class as a restricted railroad ticket, good on this day and train only." The obvious question was: why had Roberts joined in the *Classic* decision? Contemporary accounts suggest that at least some of the other Justices thought Roberts had been "duped" into concurring in *Classic,* and that Roberts knew they thought so. In the years between *Grovey* and *Allwright,* President FRANKLIN D. ROOSEVELT had made seven appointments to the Court. Justice Roberts's lone companion from the earlier days was Chief Justice HARLAN FISKE STONE, who had written the *Classic* opinion.

KENNETH L. KARST

SMITH ACT

See: Alien Registration Act

SMYTH v. AMES
169 U.S. 466 (1898)

A unanimous Supreme Court, in this arrogation of power, proclaimed its acceptance of SUBSTANTIVE DUE PROCESS in rate regulation. The Court refused to "shrink from the duty" of exercising its judgment in a highly technical area of ECONOMIC REGULATION best left to experts. For the next forty years, the Court would review the rate schedules of REGULATORY COMMISSIONS seeking to accommodate shifting and illusory judicial standards of fairness.

In 1893 a Nebraska statute prescribed maximum rail rates for intrastate transportation. William Jennings Bryan defended the state legislature's power to fix reasonable rates for INTRASTATE COMMERCE; JAMES COOLIDGE CARTER urged that the Court limit the power when unreasonable rates effectively divested a railroad of its property. The question presented by the three cases consolidated here was whether those rates amounted to a TAKING OF PROPERTY without JUST COMPENSATION, thereby depriving the railroads of their property without DUE PROCESS OF LAW. Justice DAVID J. BREWER, sitting as a circuit judge in one of the cases, invented a "FAIR RETURN ON FAIR VALUE" test. He struck down the rates because they failed to provide a fair return on a fair valuation of the railroad property and thereby they effectively destroyed property.

Accepting Brewer's opinion, Justice JOHN MARSHALL HARLAN, for the Court, asserted that REAGAN V. FARMERS' LOAN & TRUST COMPANY (1894) demonstrated the appropriateness of a judicial determination of the question. Courts, he said, must be free to inquire into the sufficiency of the rates set by the state legislature, even though the Nebraska constitution only granted the legislature the power to prescribe " 'reasonable' maximum rates." Admitting that the question could be "more easily determined by a commission" of experts, Harlan pursued the "considerations" which, "given such weight as may be just and right in each case," would allow a determination of reasonable rate. He declared that the "basis of all calculations . . . must be the fair value of the property being used." Then he listed a number of various aids to determine fair value: original construction costs, replacement or reproduction costs, stock values, the cost of permanent improvements, earning power under the prescribed rate structure, operating expenses, and other unspecified matters. The company, he concluded, was justified in asking a "fair return upon the value of that which it employs for the public convenience." The Nebraska statute had failed to provide that fair return and so deprived the railroad of its property without just compensation, thereby depriving it of due process of law under the FOURTEENTH AMENDMENT.

In *Smyth* the Court readily substituted its judgment on a question of policy for other branches of government. Regulatory commissions of all sorts would spend four decades attempting to second-guess the courts' efforts to determine what constituted a "fair return" on "fair value." Over those decades, the Court manipulated the fair value standards to the benefit of corporations. The Court relied primarily on two of Harlan's factors in assessing fair value. Until about 1918, high original costs governed the Court's determination of fair value. When the war ended and both costs and prices rose, the Court turned to replacement costs as a means of deciding fair value, again keeping rates high. The Court consistently avoided using earnings—perhaps the best economic measure—as a guide. Justices LOUIS D. BRANDEIS and OLIVER WENDELL HOLMES denounced the fair return rule throughout the 1920s and 1930s; their views gained adherents by the early 1940s. In *Federal Power Commission v. Natural Gas Company* (1942) the Court asserted that property value was not an essential factor in calculating a fair return, and the Supreme Court finally disavowed a judicial control of the question in FEDERAL POWER COMMISSION V. HOPE NATURAL GAS COMPANY (1944).

DAVID GORDON

Bibliography

HALE, ROBERT LEE 1952 *Freedom through Law: Public Control of Private Governing Power.* Pages 461–500. New York: Columbia University Press.

SNEPP v. UNITED STATES
444 U.S. 507 (1980)

A former Central Intelligence Agency (CIA) employee, Frank W. Snepp III, published a book containing unclassified information about CIA activities in South Vietnam. Snepp did not submit the book to the CIA for prepublication review, in breach of his express employment agreement not to publish any information without the agency's prior approval or to disclose any *classified* information. In a decision remarkable for its procedural setting and for its failure to meet head-on the FIRST AMENDMENT issues implicated by the prior restraint, the Supreme Court, PER CURIAM, sanctioned the imposition of a constructive trust on all proceeds from the book's sales.

The Court recognized, as the government conceded, that Snepp had a First Amendment right to publish unclassified information. The Court found, however, that by virtue of his employment as a CIA agent, Snepp had entered a fiduciary relationship with the agency. Snepp breached the special trust reposed in him by failing to submit *all* material, whether classified or not, for prepublication review. That breach posed irreparable harm to the CIA's relationships with foreign governments and its ability to perform its statutory duties. The constructive trust remedy was thereby warranted.

Justice JOHN PAUL STEVENS, joined by Justices WILLIAM J. BRENNAN and THURGOOD MARSHALL, dissented, arguing that the remedy was unsupported by statute, the contract, or case law. He urged that the contract be treated as an ordinary employment covenant. On this theory, its enforcement would be governed by a rule of reason that would require a balancing of interests, including Snepp's First Amendment rights, and might justify an equity court's refusal to enforce the prepublication review covenant. Further, the alleged harm suffered by the government did not warrant the Court's "draconian" remedy, especially because the government had never shown that other remedies were inadequate. Stevens noted that the Court seemed unaware that it had fashioned a drastic new remedy to enforce a species of prior restraint on a citizen's right to criticize the government.

KIM MCLANE WARDLAW

(SEE ALSO: *Prior Restraint and Censorship.*)

SOCIAL COMPACT THEORY

An invention of political philosophers, the social contract or social compact theory was not meant as a historical account of the origin of government, but the theory was taken literally in America where governments were actually founded upon contract. The words "compact" and "contract" are synonymous and signify a voluntary agreement of the people to unite as a political community and to establish a government. The theory purports to explain why individuals should obey the law: each person, in a government that exists with the consent of the governed, freely and, in effect, continuously gives consent to the constitution of his community.

The theory hypothesizes a prepolitical state of nature in which people were governed only by the law of nature, free of human restraints. From the premise that man was born free, the deduction followed that he came into the world with God-given or NATURAL RIGHTS. Born without the restraint of human laws, he had a right to possess liberty and to work for his own property. Born naked and stationless, he had a right to equality. Born with certain instincts and needs, he had a right to satisfy them—a right to the pursuit of happiness. These natural rights, as JOHN DICKINSON declared in 1766, "are created in us by the decrees of Providence, which establish the laws of our nature. They are born with us; exist with us; and cannot be taken from us by any human power without taking our lives."

When people left the state of nature and compacted for government, the need to make their rights secure motivated them. ALEXANDER HAMILTON observed that "Civil liberty is only natural liberty modified and secured by the sanctions of civil society. . . . The origin of all civil government, justly established, must be a voluntary compact between the rulers and the ruled, and must be liable to such limitations as are necessary for the security of the absolute rights of the latter." The most detailed exposition of this theory was by JOHN LOCKE, the most brief and eloquent by THOMAS JEFFERSON in the preamble of the DECLARATION OF INDEPENDENCE. One of the self-evident truths in the latter is "That to secure these rights, Governments are instituted among Men, deriving their just powers from the consent of the governed. . . ."

The compact theory of government colored the thought and action of Americans during the colonial period and through the period of constitution making. The new world actually seemed like a state of nature, and Americans did in fact compact with each other; the theory seemed to fit the circumstances under which American political and constitutional institutions grew. Our system developed as a self-conscious working out of some of the implications of the compact theory.

The related but distinct idea, so important in Puritan thought, that people covenant with each other to make a church for their ecclesiastical polity, was extended to their secular polity. Even before the founding of Virginia a Separatist leader asked, "What agreement must there be of men? For church governors there must be an agreement of the people or commonwealth." A half century before Locke's *Second Treatise,* THOMAS HOOKER, a founder of Connecticut, explained that in any relationship that involved authority there must be free agreement or consent. "This," he said, "appears in all covenants betwixt Prince and People, Husband and Wife, Master and Servant, and most palpable is the expression of this in all confederations and corporations . . . They should first freely engage themselves in such covenants. . . ." The first concrete application of the covenant theory to civil government was the Mayflower Compact (1620). The Pilgrims, putting theory into practice, solemnly did "covenant and combine . . . into a civil body politick," an experience multiplied over and again with the founding of numerous settlements in New England. (See FUNDAMENTAL ORDERS OF CONNECTICUT.)

The colonists also regarded their charters as compacts. As Hamilton said later, George III was "King of America, by virtue of a compact between us and the Kings of Great Britain." These colonies, Hamilton explained, were settled under charters granted by kings who "entered into covenants with us. . . ." Over a period of a century and a half, Americans became accustomed to the idea that government existed by consent of the governed, that the people created government, that they did it by written compact, and that the compact constituted their FUNDAMENTAL LAW. From practical experience as well as from revolutionary propaganda, Americans believed in the compact theory and they acted it out.

It was a useful tool, immediately at hand and lending historical and philosophical credibility, for destroying the old order and creating a new one. William Drayton, the chief justice of South Carolina, echoed a commonplace idea when he said that George III had "unkinged" himself by subverting the "constitution of this country, by breaking the original contract. . . ." The compact theory legitimated the right of revolution, as the Declaration of Independence made clear. Even before that declaration, colonial radicals contended that the Coercive Acts (see FIRST CONTINENTAL CONGRESS) "have thrown us into a state of nature," and justified contracting for a new government. After Independence a town orator in Boston declared that the people had reclaimed the rights "attendant upon the original state of nature, with the opportunity of establishing a government for ourselves. . . ." The colonies became states by a practice that mirrored the theory; they drew up written constitutions, often phrased as compacts, and purposefully put formal statements of the compact theory into those documents. The MASSACHUSETTS CONSTITUTION OF 1780 (still operative) declares: "The body politic is formed by a voluntary association of individuals; it is a social compact by which the whole people covenants with each citizen and each citizen with the whole people. . . ." A minister, Jonas Clark, said in a sermon that just government is founded in compact "and in compact alone." The new state constitution, he declared, was "a most sacred covenant or contract. . . ." The state CONSTITUTIONAL CONVENTION that framed that constitution was devised to institutionalize the compact theory.

Although the ARTICLES OF CONFEDERATION do not formally state that theory, letters of the members of the Continental Congress that framed the Articles show that they regarded themselves as making a compact for the union of states, and THE FEDERALIST #21 refers to "the social compact between the States. . . ." Similarly, at the Philadelphia CONSTITUTIONAL CONVENTION OF 1787, JAMES MADISON declared that the delegates had assembled to frame "a compact by which an authority was created paramount to the parties, and making laws for the government of them." GEORGE WASHINGTON, on behalf of the "Federal Convention," when sending the new Constitution to the Congress of the Confederation for submission to the states, drew an analogy from compact theory: individuals left a state of nature by yielding up some liberty to preserve the rest, and the states surrendered some of their SOVEREIGNTY to consolidate the union. Some of the states, when formally ratifying the new Constitution, considered themselves to be "entering into an explicit and solemn compact," as New Hampshire declared. Chief Justice JOHN JAY observed, in CHISHOLM V. GEORGIA (1793), that every state constitution "is a compact . . . and the Constitution of the United States is likewise a compact made by the people of the United States to govern themselves."

The compact theory answers one of the most profound questions of political philosophy: why do people submit to the compulsions of government? The answer is that when they established government they consented to its exercise of power and agreed to obey it if it secured their rights. The compact theory has been remarkably fecund. From government by consent it led to political democracy. It also led to CONSTITUTIONALISM as LIMITED GOVERNMENT, to a concept of a constitution as fundamental law, to constitutions as written documents, to the constitutional convention as a way of writing the document, to the right of revolution when the government is destructive of the ends of the compact, and to concepts of civil liberty and written BILLS OF RIGHTS.

LEONARD W. LEVY

Bibliography

MCLAUGHLIN, ANDREW C. 1932 *The Foundations of American Constitutionalism.* New York: New York University Press.

ROSSITER, CLINTON 1953 *Seedtime of the Republic: The Origin of the American Tradition of Political Liberty.* New York: Harcourt, Brace.

TATE, THAD W. 1965 The Social Contract in America, 1774–1787: Revolutionary Theory as a Conservative Instrument. *William and Mary Quarterly* 22:375–391.

WOOD, GORDON S. 1969 *The Creation of the American Republic, 1776–1787.* Chapel Hill: University of North Carolina Press.

SOCIAL SCIENCE IN CONSTITUTIONAL LITIGATION

All litigation, including constitutional litigation, resolves issues of law and fact. Social science research can help to clarify the facts on which a case may turn; and it can help the resolution of legal issues by laying before the courts data and analyses that bear on the choice of an appropriate legal rule.

Legal lore has it that the rise of social science in the law began with the BRANDEIS BRIEF, in which LOUIS D. BRANDEIS, special counsel for the state of Oregon, successfully bolstered the state's claim in MULLER V. OREGON (1908) that its statute limiting the working hours for women was constitutional. Although in theory the state merely had to show that such a regulation was not unreasonable, previous decisions had struck down laws regulating working hours of other employees as unreasonable invasions of the liberty of contract. The brief supported the reasonableness of the law in part by showing that a great many American states and even more countries abroad had similar statutes. It was an effective if modest social science effort.

More sophisticated techniques are to be found in contemporary constitutional litigation. Sampling, the most powerful tool of social science research, is now firmly established as an appropriate means of gathering EVIDENCE. If the survey was conducted without bias and if the technical requirements are met, a sample may be accepted as a reasonably accurate representation of the sampled universe. For instance, in support of a motion for change of VENUE in a criminal case, a sample survey measures the extent and depth of pretrial prejudice in the community. If a voluminous body of communications is at issue, sampling may be combined with a technique called content analysis. Thus, when the constitutionality of the work of the House Committee on Un-American Activities was litigated, a sample of the committee's public hearings was examined. This approach yielded a numerical statement of the frequency with which the committee asked its witnesses questions that transcended its constitutional authority. Similar content analysis has sometimes been used in support of a motion for change of venue, documenting the charge that a substantial part of the pretrial publicity originated in the prosecutor's office.

Proof of racial or other discrimination in jury selection, employment, and other contexts frequently employs sampling and subsequent statistical analysis. Such proof involves an analysis of the differences between the actual outcome of the selection process and the outcome that would have been expected if discrimination had no role in the process.

In *United States v. Hazelwood School District* (1977), for instance, the Supreme Court made its own probability computations to determine whether excluding the metropolitan area from the labor market in which a suburban school district hired its teachers would substantially weaken the government's statistical proof that the district had engaged in discrimination. Although the Court's statistical performance in *Hazelwood* was flawed in certain respects, similar methods in proving discrimination have become accepted in both federal and state courts.

Of particular interest are the cases in which the judicial system itself is charged with discrimination. The two main targets here are the administration of the death penalty and the selection of jurors. Evidence has been mounting, and finally has drawn the attention of the Supreme Court, that the death penalty is administered with bias, discriminating against black offenders who killed white victims. The major technical problem in distilling this evidence is to assure comparability of the homicides under analysis.

In the jury selection area, the statistical analysis of discrimination has had more impact. Despite substantial efforts in this direction, the lower courts have rejected these efforts. In *Castandeda v. Partida* (1977), for instance, the Court used a standard statistical formula to compute the probability that the disparity between the proportion of Mexican-Americans serving on GRAND JURIES and their proportion in the county population could have arisen if grand jurors had been selected at random. The majority found the probability to be so minute (about one in a number with 140 zeros) that the discrepancy was sufficient to establish discrimination even though there were problems with the data used to estimate these proportions and even though the majority of jury commissioners were themselves Mexican-Americans.

In the trial of Dr. Benjamin Spock and others accused of conspiring to obstruct the draft, the alleged discrimination involved female jurors. The allegation of bias in that case was directed not against the system but against the particular judge who consistently selected juries with significantly fewer women than those of his colleagues, although all drew from the same pool of potential jurors.

At times experimental social science research is offered to aid a court in assessing the consequences of its legal options or in ascertaining facts relevant to the choice of these options. When the Supreme Court in BROWN V. BOARD OF EDUCATION (1954) held that segregated education was inherently unequal, the Court quoted with approval a lower court's finding that school segregation with the sanction of law produced feelings of inferiority among black children, affecting their motivation to learn. The Court remarked that its conclusion was "amply supported by modern authority." That authority, cited in a footnote, consisted of seven items. Five, such as Gunnar Myrdal's *American Dilemma,* dealt generally with problems of black education. Two bore more directly on the issue: a statement by thirty-two leading social scientists and an experiment conducted by the psychologist Kenneth Clark. Clark had given sixteen black children in a South Carolina elementary school a sheet of paper on which two dolls were drawn, identical in every respect except that the one was black, the other white. The children were asked, "Which doll would you like to play with?" "Which is the nice and which the bad doll?" "Which doll looks like you yourself?" Ten of the children liked the white doll best; eleven called the black doll the "bad" one; seven of the black children, when asked which doll was like themselves, picked the white one. From these answers and earlier research, Clark concluded "that these children . . . like other human beings who are subjected to an obviously inferior status in the society in which they live, have been definitely harmed in the development of their personalities. . . ."

Later, scholars disputed both the evidentiary power of that study and the weight the Justices had attached to it. The study, obviously limited in size and structure, today would hardly survive cross-examination. Most likely its major function was to buttress a position the Justices had reached on their own.

Social science research has provided more solid evidence in litigation over the constitutionality of juries with fewer than twelve members. In the two decisions that affirmed the legality of such juries, the Court cited a number of empirical studies purporting to show that these modifications did not affect the quality of the verdicts rendered by the smaller juries. Subsequently these studies were severely criticized, and five years later BALLEW V. GEORGIA held five-member criminal juries unconstitutional. Justice HARRY A. BLACKMUN's opinion repeatedly cited these critical views.

Most social science operations suffer from some imperfection, partly because their subject matter is so complex, and partly because of methodological flaws. Even if such imperfections are minor, courts may hesitate to accept social science findings that threaten to dislodge established rules. One type of effort to compensate for imperfection is "triangulation"—the confluence of evidence from independent studies that approach the same problem from different angles. An example is the series of studies of "death qualified" juries.

At one time, a New York statute allowed New York City to try murder and other crimes of public notoriety before specially selected BLUE RIBBON JURIES, whose members, among other qualifications, were required to have no objection to the death penalty. When the Court was asked to declare these juries unconstitutional because of alleged bias in favor of the prosecution, it declined by a bare majority on the ground that there was no proof of such bias. Speculation as to how such proof might be established led to the first study which found that jurors who were in favor of the death penalty were indeed more likely to convict, not only in capital trials, but generally. Six other studies followed, with different approaches; each replicated the result.

Witherspoon v. Illinois (1968), decided halfway through these studies, did not reach the issue. Although the Court agreed that merely having scruples about the death penalty was not sufficient cause for eliminating jurors, it dismissed the first few research findings, indicating that the exclusion of jurors with scruples against the death penalty would bias the jury in favor of conviction, as "too tentative and fragmentary." Subsequent efforts to convince other courts that the post-*Witherspoon* juries, too, were biased in favor of convicting defendants failed until 1983 and 1984 when two federal district courts in HABEAS CORPUS proceedings accepted the evidence provided in these studies and invalidated the convictions. Although the federal Courts of Appeals have divided on this issue and the Supreme Court has agreed to review one of these cases, these two decisions mark a preliminary acceptance of proof by triangulation.

The role of social science research in litigation is bound to grow in spite of deep-seated hesitancy on the part of the courts to look at statistical evidence. It is difficult to predict how fast and where the use of social science techniques will increase in constitutional litigation. Much will depend on the resourcefulness of social scientists in developing new research and the initiative of attorneys in presenting evidence that can sharpen the perception of litigated facts and aid courts in judging the consequences of their legal options.

HANS ZEISEL
DAVID KAYE

Bibliography

BALDUS, D. and COLE, J. 1980 *Statistical Proof of Discrimination.* Colorado Springs, Colo.: Shepard's.

CAHN, EDMOND 1962 A Dangerous Myth in the School Segregation Cases. In Kenneth Clark, ed., *Confronting Injustice.* Pages 329–345. Boston: Little, Brown.

KAYE, DAVID 1980 And Then There Were Twelve: Statistical Reasoning, the Supreme Court, and the Size of the Jury. *California Law Review* 68:1004–1043.

—— 1982 Statistical Evidence of Discrimination. *Journal of the American Statistical Association* 77:773–783.

LEMPERT, RICHARD O. 1975 Uncovering "Nondiscernible" Differences: Empirical Research and the Jury-Size Cases. *Michigan Law Review* 73:643–708.

LOH, WALLACE D. 1984 *Social Research in the Judicial Process: Cases, Readings and Text.* New York: Russell Sage Foundation.

SAKS, MICHAEL J. 1974 Ignorance of Science Is No Excuse. *Trial* 10:18–20.

WALBERT, DAVID 1971 The Effect of Jury Size on the Probability of Conviction: An Evaluation of *Williams v. Florida. Case Western Law Review* 22:529–554.

ZEISEL, HANS 1971 And Then There Were None: The Diminution of the Federal Jury. *University of Chicago Law Review* 38:710–724.

—— 1980 Reflections on Experimental Techniques in the Law. *Journal of Legal Studies* 2:107–124.

—— 1968 *Some Data on Juror Attitudes Towards Capital Punishment.* Chicago: University of Chicago Center for Studies in Criminal Justice.

—— 1985 *Say It with Figures,* 6th ed. Chap. 14. New York: Harper & Row.

—— and DIAMOND, SHARI 1974 "Convincing Empirical Evidence" on the Six-Member Jury. *University of Chicago Law Review* 41:281–295.

SOCIAL SECURITY ACT
49 Stat. 620 (1935)

The Social Security Act of 1935, as subsequently amended, is the primary source of federal and federal–state cooperative social welfare programs. In addition to the program popularly denominated "social security," which now includes old age, survivors, and disability insurance, and the fiscally related medical assistance program for the aged (Medicare), the current Social Security Act also provides grants to states for many federally regulated programs, such as unemployment compensation, services to poor families with children (Aid to Families with Dependent Children), services to the aged, blind, and disabled (Supplementary Security Income), health care for the poor (Medicaid), and maternal and child welfare services.

The act has been a fertile source of constitutional litigation. The cooperative federal-state unemployment compensation scheme was narrowly sustained as a legitimate congressional exercise of the power "to lay and collect taxes . . . to . . . provide . . . for the GENERAL WELFARE of the United States" in STEWARD MACHINE CO. V. DAVIS (1937). In a companion case, HELVERING V. DAVIS (1937), seven Justices agreed that the federal social security old age retirement benefits program was well within the purview of Congress's TAXING AND SPENDING POWER.

The act has generated a number of important PROCEDURAL DUE PROCESS cases. GOLDBERG V. KELLY (1970) held that due process requires an evidentiary hearing *prior* to the termination of WELFARE BENEFITS. Justice WILLIAM J. BRENNAN, writing for a majority of six, reasoned that a subsequent hearing would be inadequate to protect the interests of the eligible recipient deprived of basic subsistence while she awaited her opportunity to challenge termination of benefits. *Goldberg v. Kelly* was narrowly construed in MATHEWS V. ELDRIDGE (1976), which held that due process does not require a prior evidentiary hearing when social security disability benefits are terminated after a Social Security Administration determination that the worker is no longer disabled. The Court distinguished *Goldberg* on two grounds: *Goldberg* involved public assistance for the INDIGENT while social security disability benefits are not based on financial need; and the opportunity for a prior hearing is less valuable to the recipient when the administrative conclusion is based on expert medical testimony, as in a disability termination case, rather than on a wide variety of facts and witness credibility, as in a public assistance case.

The social security program embodied a number of gender-based assumptions about economic dependence that were challenged as violative of the EQUAL PROTECTION guarantee in *Weinberger v. Wiesenfeld* (1975) and CALIFANO V. GOLDFARB (1977). In *Wiesenfeld,* the Court required that "mother's benefits," payable to an insured worker's widow who cares for the worker's child, be extended equally to similarly situated widowers. In *Goldfarb,* the Court held invalid a requirement that widowers but not widows prove actual dependency on the deceased insured worker.

In another group of cases prospective social welfare beneficiaries have constitutionally challenged the substantive conditions of individual grants. In *Flemming v. Nestor* (1960), *Weinberger v. Salfi* (1975), and *Mathews v. DeCastro* (1976), the Supreme Court rejected such challenges.

GRACE GANZ BLUMBERG

Bibliography

ALTMEYER, ARTHUR 1968 *The Formative Years of Social Security.* Madison: University of Wisconsin Press.

DEPARTMENT OF HEALTH, EDUCATION AND WELFARE 1960 *Basic Readings in Social Security: The 25th Anniversary of the Social Security Act.* Washington, D.C.: Government Printing Office.

WITTE, EDWIN 1962 *The Development of the Social Security Act.* Madison: University of Wisconsin Press.

SOCIOLOGICAL JURISPRUDENCE

Sociological jurisprudence is one of the most important schools of legal thought in the twentieth century. Its major proponent in the United States was ROSCOE POUND (1870–1964), a prolific writer who was dean of the Harvard Law School from 1916 to 1936. A number of other legal educators and judges also contributed in varying degrees to the theory or practice of sociological jurisprudence. They included five former members of the Supreme Court—OLIVER WENDELL HOLMES, LOUIS D. BRANDEIS, HARLAN FISKE STONE, BENJAMIN N. CARDOZO, and FELIX FRANKFURTER. Even though the doctrines of these jurists were anything but uniform, they shared a number of important attitudes and ideas.

The movement for a sociological jurisprudence emerged during the Progressive Era. Pound interpreted it as the "movement for pragmatism as a philosophy of law," the purpose of which was to facilitate legal reform and social progress. Although legal change should take place under the leadership of lawyers, the agenda of sociological jurisprudence did not focus on changes in legal institutions. Rather, it stressed reform of prevailing conceptions of the study, interpretation, and application of law.

This emphasis reflected a particular diagnosis of the ills of the American legal system at the outset of the twentieth century. These problems included judicial hostility to laws designed to protect workers, which courts often construed narrowly or held unconstitutional. Decisions of the Supreme Court applying the doctrine of SUBSTANTIVE DUE PROCESS are a classic example of the tendency. The advocates of sociological jurisprudence assailed this judicial response to social legislation, which they attributed to several factors. One was the isolation of the study of law from the social sciences. This condition allegedly fostered an ignorance of social realities and needs that contributed to unjust decisions. "Unless we know the facts on which legislators may have acted," Justice Brandeis pointed out in BURNS BAKING CO. V. BRYAN (1924), "we cannot properly decide whether they were . . . unreasonable, arbitrary, or capricious. Knowledge is essential to understanding; and understanding should precede judging."

Pound maintained that another factor contributing to judicial decisions that obstructed social progress was MECHANICAL JURISPRUDENCE, or the rigid deduction of decisions from established principles without regard to their practical effects. He argued that this kind of syllogistic reasoning not only obscured judges' wide range of choice in selecting premises but also contributed to their intolerance of laws limiting FREEDOM OF CONTRACT. The very different attitude of Justice Holmes was one reason why advocates of sociological jurisprudence held him in such high esteem.

These criticisms were the basis of the characteristic reform objectives of sociological jurisprudence. A fundamental goal was the development of a better factual understanding of the practical effects of legal precepts and institutions. Cardozo proposed a Ministry of Justice which would study and observe the "law in action." In "The Living Law" Brandeis recommended "broader education . . . continued by lawyer and judge throughout life: study of economics and sociology and politics which embody the facts and present the problems of today." This idea strongly conditioned the unorthodox BRANDEIS BRIEF in MULLER V. OREGON (1908), an approach that Brandeis and other lawyers such as Felix Frankfurter used in a number of subsequent cases. Only two of the 113 pages of this brief presented the traditional kind of legal argument, while the rest consisted largely of factual evidence of the bad effects on women of excessive hours of work. Brandeis argued that these data showed that the Oregon law, which limited women's working hours to ten per day, was a reasonable limitation of freedom of contract. His argument favorably impressed the Justices, who unanimously upheld the law.

The prescription for abandoning "mechanical jurisprudence" was a more pragmatic approach to judicial decision making. No one expressed this idea better than Cardozo, who insisted that law is a means to the end of "social welfare" or "social justice." He argued that judges should interpret general constitutional limitations to serve this end. The changing meaning of the word "liberty" in the due process clauses of the Fifth and FOURTEENTH AMENDMENTS is an example. (See INCORPORATION DOCTRINE.) Similar beliefs conditioned Frankfurter's suggestion that constitutional law "in its relation to social legislation, is . . . but applied politics, using the word in its noble sense."

These ideas reflected a justifiable dissatisfaction with the content of American constitutional law earlier in this century. The adequacy of the sociological jurists' diagnosis of and reforms for these evils is another matter. To begin with, they tended to exaggerate the causal significance of "mechanical jurisprudence" and judicial ignorance of social needs. Neither of these factors ordinarily influence the actual decisions of the Justices or their choice of premises as much as their policy preferences or attitudes. Furthermore, conservative Justices might (and did) use Cardozo's "method of sociology" for their own purposes. "Social welfare" and "social justice" are subject, after all, to a multitude of interpretations. In some cases a majority of the Justices invalidated laws defended by a "Brandeis brief." The extent to which that technique influenced them to uphold other laws is uncertain, but its impact may have been corroborative rather than decisive. The use of social science evidence in BROWN V. BOARD OF EDUCATION (1954) illustrates this tendency. Finally, social scientists often disagree about the interpretation of the facts or their implications for public policy.

To say this is not to imply that the value of sociological jurisprudence was negligible. Its greatest contribution to constitutional law was that it served as a positive force for upholding social legislation. If its efficacy in this regard was limited, at least it provided support for judges inclined to hold such legislation constitutional. Moreover, knowledge of the actual effects of legal precepts and institutions is essential for informed evaluations of them. The call of sociological jurisprudence for studies of these effects was, thus, a step in the right direction.

WILFRID E. RUMBLE

Bibliography

BRANDEIS, LOUIS D. 1916 The Living Law. Address before the Chicago Bar Association, January 3, 1916.

CAHILL, FRED V. 1952 *Judicial Legislation.* New York: Ronald Press.

ROSEN, PAUL L. 1972 *The Supreme Court and Social Science.* Urbana: University of Illinois Press.

RUMBLE, WILFRID E. 1968 *American Legal Realism.* Ithaca, N.Y.: Cornell University Press.

WHITE, G. EDWARD 1978 *Patterns of American Legal Thought.* Indianapolis: Bobbs-Merrill.

SOLEM v. HELM
463 U.S. 277 (1983)

Expanding the coverage of the Eighth Amendment's CRUEL AND UNUSUAL PUNISHMENT clause, the Supreme Court held that in addition to barbaric sentences it prohibits criminal sentences that are disproportionate to the crime for which a defendant is convicted. Jerry Helm, a habitual offender, passed a bad check and received the most severe punishment—life imprisonment without possibility of parole—that South Dakota could impose for any crime. A 5–4 Court decided that because Helm's six prior FELONY convictions were for relatively minor nonviolent crimes against property and because he was treated more severely than other criminals who had committed more serious crimes, his sentence was significantly disproportionate to his crime. The dissenting Justices saw "judicial usurpation" of state sentencing discretion, especially in cases of incorrigible recidivists.

LEONARD W. LEVY

SOLICITOR GENERAL

The solicitor general is a senior officer of the United States Department of Justice with special responsibilities in the representation of the United States and its officers and agencies before the Supreme Court, and in the administration of justice in the federal appellate courts.

The title—solicitor general—like that of ATTORNEY GENERAL is derived from English usage, but the functions of the offices are quite different in the United States. In England, both offices are political in the sense that they are filled by members of Parliament. In the United States, neither the attorney general nor the solicitor general is a member of Congress. The attorney general is a member of the Cabinet. He advises the President, works with members of Congress on legislative matters and judicial appointments, holds press conferences and is otherwise responsible for governmental and public relations. He is also charged with administering a large department which includes the Federal Bureau of Investigation, the Bureau of Prisons, the Immigration and Naturalization Service, and other important agencies. Though he has policy and administrative responsibilities of great importance, he has virtually no time to be a lawyer in the traditional sense.

Until 1870, the attorney general functioned alone with only a small staff, and in association with the United States attorneys in the various states, over whom he had little authority. In 1870, apparently as an economy device (to eliminate the cost of retaining private lawyers in the increasing number of cases), Congress established the Department of Justice, with the attorney general as its head. The statute provided that there should be in the Department "an officer learned in the law, to assist the Attorney-General in the performance of his duties, to be called the solicitor-general." Under the statute the solicitor general was authorized in the attorney general's discretion to argue "any case in which the government is interested" before the Supreme Court, or in any federal or state court." These statutory provisions remain to the present day, essentially unchanged.

In the years since 1870, the duties of the Department of Justice have greatly increased. Until 1953 the solicitor general was the second officer in the Department of Justice and served as acting attorney general in the attorney general's absence. The responsibilities of the attorney general have made it necessary to add a deputy attorney general and an associate attorney general, so that the solicitor general is now the fourth ranking officer in the department. But the solicitor general's responsibilities have remained essentially unchanged in substance—though greatly increased in volume—over the past sixty years. He remains the leading officer in the department functioning primarily as a lawyer.

As the pattern has developed, the solicitor general is not a politician, and he has only a minimum of political responsibility. His function is to be the government's top lawyer in the courts, particularly the Supreme Court, and by well-established tradition he is allowed considerable independence in carrying out this role. Bent and Schloss, describing the office as "the bridge between the Executive and the Judiciary," have said that "[t]he Solicitor General must often choose between incongruous roles and differing loyalties. He is still the government's lawyer, and he most frequently acts as an advocate. On the other hand, he also functions as a reviewer of government policies, an officer of the Court, and . . . a protector of the public interest."

In more specific terms, the organization of the Department of Justice assigns to the solicitor general four areas of responsibility. Two of these are of primary importance. First, the solicitor general is responsible for the representation of the United States and its officers and agencies in all cases before the Supreme Court of the United States. The BRIEFs which are filed on behalf of the government in the Supreme Court are prepared by him or under his direction. He argues the most important cases himself, and assigns the argument in other cases to members of his staff, to other lawyers in the Department of Justice or to lawyers for the agencies which may be involved in the cases before the Court. Second, the Solicitor General decides whether the United States will APPEAL in any case which it loses in any court, state or federal, or indeed in foreign courts. This function is not widely known, even in the legal profession. It is, however, a very important means of coordinating and controlling the government's litigation, so that cases of little importance are not taken to the appellate courts. It also serves to minimize the taking of inconsistent positions before the various appellate courts.

This function includes determining whether any case will be taken by the government to the Supreme Court. This is probably the most important responsibility assigned to the solicitor general. With few exceptions, no case can now be taken to the Supreme Court except on application for review—called a petition for a WRIT OF CERTIORARI. In recent years, some four thousand such applications are made to the Court by all parties each year. Yet the Court can hear on the merits only about a hundred and fifty cases a year. This means that it is of great importance for the solicitor general to select with care the relatively small number of cases in which the government will file petitions. A high proportion of the solicitor general's petitions are in fact granted by the Court, which means that he has, as part of his responsibility, carried out an important part of the selection process necessarily confronting the Court.

In addition to the two functions just outlined, the solicitor general has two other responsibilities. These assist him in carrying out his role as overall controller of Government APPELLATE JURISDICTION. First his authorization must be obtained before the United States or one of its officers or agencies files a brief as friend of the court—AMICUS CURIAE—in any appellate court. Second his authorization must be obtained before a petition for REHEARING *en banc*—before the whole court—is filed in any UNITED STATES COURT OF APPEALS. The courts of appeals are overburdened, and hearings EN BANC present serious logistical problems. Requiring authority from the solicitor general means that such petitions are rarely filed, and only in the most important cases.

The solicitor general's office is a relatively small one, though it has grown slowly in recent years. At the present time it numbers about twenty lawyers in addition to the solicitor general himself; and, including secretaries and aides, the total number of personnel in the office is about fifty. Thus it can operate in much the same way as a moderate-sized law firm. There is considerable pressure in the office as the cases keep coming in, from all parts of the country, and almost all of them are subject to relatively short deadlines.

In the nature of things, the solicitor general cannot be a specialist. The cases coming to his desk involve every field of law—constitutional law, ADMINISTRATIVE LAW, criminal law, tax law, antitrust law, labor law, international law, ENVIRONMENTAL PROTECTION, energy, and every other field with which the government is concerned. Inevitably, the staff in the office specialize to some extent, and there are four deputy solicitors general, each of whom has special responsibilities for particular areas. But there are no rigid lines, and all lawyers in the office are available to handle the various types of cases as they come in.

The solicitor general's role in the Supreme Court is limited to the representation of the United States, its officers, and its agencies. Other cases which may be of great importance involve private parties, or states or their subsidiaries. Thus, the cases involving BIRTH CONTROL (GRISWOLD V. CONNECTICUT, 1965) and abortion (ROE V. WADE, 1973) were not handled by the solicitor general. But more than half of the cases before the Supreme Court (particularly those heard by the Court on the merits) are "government cases," that is, cases in which the United States, or its officers or agents, are parties. It is important to the Court to have these cases handled in competent fashion, and the research and ideas, and policy decisions, lying behind the solicitor general's advocacy before the Supreme Court can influence the decisions reached by the Court.

Much of the government's litigation before the Supreme Court, though important, does not attract wide public attention. From time to time, though, cases coming before the Court are rather spectacular in terms of public interest. Reference may be made, for example, to YOUNGSTOWN SHEET & TUBE CO. V. SAWYER (1952), where the Court invalidated the action of President HARRY S. TRUMAN in seizing the steel industry during the KOREAN WAR, the Pentagon Papers case (NEW YORK TIMES CO. V. UNITED STATES, 1971), and UNITED STATES V. NIXON (1974), where the Court held that the White House tapes made under the direction of President RICHARD M. NIXON must be turned over in response to a SUBPOENA from a GRAND JURY. For the most part, though, the work of the solicitor general and his staff is rather straightforward professional work.

It is important to recognize that in all cases the solicitor general is an advocate and not a judge. However, he is a very special sort of advocate. There are some positions which he will not support because he thinks the government's position is clearly wrong in law. On rare occasions, in such cases, he "confesses error" before the Court. The Court is not bound by such a confession, but it usually accepts the solicitor general's conclusion. There are other cases where the solicitor general will not himself defend the government's position, but he thinks a "respectable" defense can be made, and he assigns another government lawyer who is willing to do so to present that defense. Illustration of this may be found in *Peters v. Hobby* (1955), involving the LOYALTY-SECURITY PROGRAM during the 1950s, and in *Gutknecht v. United States* (1970), involving "delinquency reclassification" under the SELECTIVE SERVICE ACT. But the solicitor general will frequently advocate a position which he believes to be worthy of presentation to the Court even though he might not decide in favor of that position if he were a judge. Laymen sometimes have difficulty in accepting this, but, within limits, it is inherent in the role of a lawyer, and it is inherent in the position of the solicitor general. For he is the government's chief advocate. The function of deciding cases is assigned to others.

In this situation, the solicitor general's role is sometimes a difficult one. Whenever he decides not to take a case before the Supreme Court, he is in effect depriving the Court of the opportunity to decide it. This is, indeed, an important part of his function, in view of the fact that many more applications come to the Court than it can possibly accept. The solicitor general's judgment that the chances of success in a particular case are slim is obviously a relevant consideration. Yet there are cases of such importance that he should take the case to the Court, in order to obtain a definitive decision, even though he has little faith in the government's position.

An illustration is found in UNITED STATES V.

UNITED STATES DISTRICT COURT (1972). This involved the validity of so-called national security WIRETAPS, made on executive authority (the President or the attorney general) alone, without a judicial warrant. As the cases before the Supreme Court developed, it seemed unlikely that the Court would uphold such wiretaps, at least in cases of domestic security. Yet the attorney general needed to know. If he had such authority, cases might develop where he would need to use it. If he did not have the authority, he should have the definitive decision of the Supreme Court, by which he would, of course, abide. A petition was filed with the Court in order that the question might be definitively settled, and the Court granted the petition. In due course, the Court held that domestic "national security" wiretaps are illegal under the FOURTH AMENDMENT, when made without a court warrant. Thus the solicitor general, though himself dubious about the government's case, played his appropriate role in obtaining a definitive decision on an important public question.

In the daily routine of his office the solicitor general has many decisions to make. In making these decisions, he may be subject to various pressures. These pressures may be wholly legitimate professional pressures from other lawyers in the government seeking to persuade him to accept their view. He frequently gives hearings, too, to opposing lawyers. There may also be various forms of political pressure—rarely presented as such—from Capitol Hill, or from other officers of the government. The solicitor general should be able to receive such representations and come to his own conclusions. Attorneys general have usually been firm in their support of the solicitor general. And, indeed, the fact that the decision is assigned to the solicitor general may serve to protect the attorney general from such pressures. But the attorney general and the President are the solicitor general's superiors, and if he receives an order from above he must decide whether the matter is one of principle for him; if it is, he must resign. As far as is known, no solicitor general has ever resigned for such a reason. But this is what happened to Attorney General Elliott Richardson and Deputy Attorney General William Ruckelshaus, when they refused to comply with President Nixon's order to discharge Archibald Cox as Special Prosecutor in 1973.

Special problems arise when officers or agencies differ from the position of the solicitor general, and especially when two or more agencies have different interests or points of view which they present vigorously to the solicitor general or his staff. A situation of this sort arose in the case of *Fortnightly Corp. v. United Artists Television, Inc.* (1968), involving cable television. The Copyright Office in the Library of Congress had one view about the case. The Federal Communications Commission had another. And the Antitrust Division in the Department of Justice had still a third. All views were strongly advocated. The solicitor general negotiated separately with the lawyers for each office concerned. None would yield. Then he held a meeting at which all interested lawyers were present, hoping that some sort of a consensus would emerge. Unfortunately, none did, and the solicitor general concluded that he had no alternative but to formulate his own view, which he submitted to the Court.

This case exemplifies one of the important roles of the solicitor general, in resolving differences within the government, so that a single position may be presented to the Court. When these differences arise within the Justice Department, or between the several executive departments, the solicitor general seeks to persuade but eventually may have to make his own decision. The situation is somewhat more difficult when the difference is with one of the "independent agencies," such as the Federal Trade Commission or the Securities and Exchange Commission.

For historical reasons, it has long been settled that the Interstate Commerce Commission and the Maritime Commission can appear before the Supreme Court through their own lawyers. With respect to the other agencies, however, the statutory provisions are not explicit. Though there is occasionally some tension, the solicitor general has been able to maintain effective control over agency cases in the Supreme Court. In this process, various devices are used. He sometimes advises the Court that the agency has a different view. He sometimes authorizes the agency to file a brief stating its view. By and large, the agencies believe that the solicitor general's support is important and helpful, and this belief is reinforced by the standing of the solicitor general before the Court. Cases of this sort are carefully considered in the solicitor general's office, and full hearings are given to the lawyers from the agencies involved. In this way problems of real difficulty have been resolved with substantial satisfaction on the part of all concerned.

There is a final role of the solicitor general which, though long an important one, has been of increasing significance in recent years. This is the preparation and filing of briefs in the Supreme Court as a friend of the Court—amicus curiae. Under the Rules of the Supreme Court, the solicitor general is authorized to file such a brief without consent of the parties or special leave of the Court. Frequently a case between private parties, or a state criminal prosecution, may raise a question of great interest to the federal government, though the latter is not a party. An example is TERRY V. OHIO (1968), involving the validity of a STOP AND FRISK by local police. The solicitor general filed an amicus brief in that case because of the great interest of the federal government in law enforcement. Through such briefs, the solicitor general protects the interests of the federal government, aids the Court by furnishing information and relevant legal materials, facilitates the handling of difficult questions with the "independent agencies" of the government, and, on occasion, presents his own views on novel constitutional questions.

In this way, the solicitor general has participated in cases involving SCHOOL DESEGREGATION, legislative REAPPORTIONMENT, CAPITAL PUNISHMENT, CIVIL RIGHTS, and many other important questions of developing constitutional and statutory law. Within wide limits, the solicitor general has freedom to develop his own position in such briefs. The solicitor general and his staff have great experience in Supreme Court cases, and well-considered and carefully prepared briefs can be of considerable assistance to the Court through impartial and informed analysis of novel questions.

Indeed, a high proportion of briefs amicus filed by the solicitor general are prepared because of direct invitation from the Court. Such invitations are always treated as commands, and great care is taken in determining the position to be taken and in developing the materials to be included in the brief. In many ways, such briefs are the purest expression of the relation of trust and confidence which has long been established between the solicitor general and the Court.

It is this trust and confidence on which the position of the solicitor general before the Court, and his effective representation of the United States, in the long run depend.

ERWIN N. GRISWOLD

Bibliography

NOTE 1969 Government Litigation in the Supreme Court: The Roles of the Solicitor General. *Yale Law Journal* 78:1442–1481.

SOMERSET'S CASE
98 Eng. Rep. 499 (K.B., 1772)

The case of *Somerset v. Stewart,* decided by King's Bench (the highest COMMON LAW court in England) in 1772, profoundly affected the constitutional status of slavery in England and in the United States after independence (because the precedent had become part of American common law). In a brief opinion, Lord Mansfield, Chief Justice, held that slavery "must be recognized by the law of the country where it is used." He further declared that "the state of slavery is of such a nature, that it is incapable of being introduced on any reasons, moral or political; but only [by] positive law." *Somerset's Case* did not abolish slavery in England or America, but until the 1850s it was interpreted to mean that slavery did not exist where it was not established by positive law (which, according to Chief Justice JOHN MARSHALL in *The Antelope* [1825], might include custom as well as statutory law). Abolitionists construed Mansfield's words to mean either that slavery was universally illegitimate or that it had a legal existence only where affirmatively established by a slave code. They denied that the federal government had power to establish slavery in any territory or district, or to protect it anywhere. (See ABOLITIONIST CONSTITUTIONAL THEORY.) This argument became the basis of the Republican "Freedom national, slavery local" slogan of the 1850s and was reflected in STEPHEN A. DOUGLAS's FREEPORT DOCTRINE of 1858. *Somerset's Case* also complicated interstate relations in the matter of fugitive and sojourning slaves; some free states in the 1850s refused to recognize the continuation of an individual's slave status in a free JURISDICTION. (See FUGITIVE SLAVERY.) Southern jurists responded by repudiating the liberating potential of the *Somerset* doctrine after 1851, dismissing Mansfield's words as OBITER DICTA or error.

WILLIAM M. WIECEK

SONZINSKY v. UNITED STATES
300 U.S. 506 (1937)

The unanimous opinion in this case indicated that the spirit animating the decision in BAILEY V. DREXEL FURNITURE CO. (1922) was dead: the Supreme Court would no longer inquire into Congress's motives in enacting a tax measure. The National Firearms Act of 1934 imposed an annual EXCISE TAX on manufacturers and dealers of firearms, excepting handguns. The Court refused to consider that the tax was not imposed to raise a revenue and was a penalty to suppress traffic in a commodity normally subject only to state regulation. Compulsory registration provisions of such statutes, however, were later held unconstitutional in MARCHETTI V. UNITED STATES (1968).

LEONARD W. LEVY

SOSNA v. IOWA
419 U.S. 393 (1975)

Iowa limited access to its divorce court to persons who had resided in the state for one year. Sosna, denied a divorce under this law, brought suit in a federal court challenging the one-year limitation's constitutionality. By the time her case reached the Supreme Court, the year had passed. Because the case had been properly certified as a CLASS ACTION, however, the Court rejected the state's invitation to dismiss the action for MOOTNESS. On the merits, a six-Justice majority, speaking through Justice WILLIAM H. REHNQUIST, upheld the statute.

Justice Rehnquist breathed no word concerning "penalties" on the exercise of the RIGHT TO TRAVEL interstate. Instead, he merely noted that previous decisions had struck down durational RESIDENCE REQUIREMENTS only when they were justified entirely on the basis of budgetary or record-keeping considerations. Here, he said, the state had an interest in protecting the rights of defendant spouses and of any minor children. Further, the state might wish to avoid "officious intermeddling" in another state's primary concerns and to protect its own divorce decrees against COLLATERAL ATTACK. "A state such as Iowa may quite reasonably decide that it does not wish to become a divorce mill." In any event, an Iowa plaintiff was merely delayed in getting a divorce, not denied one altogether.

Justice BYRON R. WHITE dissented, arguing that the case was moot. Justice THURGOOD MARSHALL dissented on the merits, joined by Justice WILLIAM J. BRENNAN: The Court's analysis did not subject this penalty on exercise of the right to travel to the STRICT SCRUTINY it deserved but improperly employed a functional equivalent of the RATIONAL BASIS standard of review. Iowa's most important interest, protecting the integrity of its decrees, could be achieved by the less restrictive means of merely requiring a divorce plaintiff to be domiciled in the state. And the delay/denial distinction was false; a plaintiff would be denied marital freedom (and the freedom to remarry) during an entire year.

KENNETH L. KARST

SOUNDTRUCKS AND AMPLIFIERS

When the Framers of the FIRST AMENDMENT wrote a ban on laws "abridging" FREEDOM OF SPEECH into the Constitution, the range of the human voice was relatively limited. The invention of electronic sound amplification equipment in the twentieth century potentially extended that range even into distant buildings and behind locked doors. Loudspeakers and bullhorns, whether stationary or mobile, present a particular problem of speech regulation: to what extent does the right to speak override the expectation of peace and privacy enjoyed by members of the public? Especially troubling are soundtrucks, amplifier-equipped motor vehicles that blare political slogans or advertising messages while roving the streets of residential neighborhoods.

The problem of soundtrucks and amplifiers was addressed by the Supreme Court in two famous cases. In *Saia v. New York* (1948) a 5–4 Court struck down a city ordinance requiring permission of the chief of police before a soundtruck could be used within the city limits. The ordinance provided no standard for the police chief to apply in granting or withholding permission. Eight months later, in KOVACS V. COOPER (1949), a five-Justice majority (including the *Saia* dissenters) upheld an ordinance prohibiting the operation within a city of soundtrucks that emitted "loud or raucous noises." The plurality thought the "loud and raucous" test an adequate standard of regulation, while two concurring Justices understood the ordinance as a ban on all soundtrucks.

The danger of public regulation of amplified speech is that restrictions ostensibly directed to the time, place, and manner of speaking will be used as a pretext for controlling the content of speech. But, as technology makes the outside world ever more intrusive into the realm of individual privacy, the right of the people to provide themselves freedom from loud and raucous utterance, whatever its content, can only become more valuable.

DENNIS J. MAHONEY

SOUTH CAROLINA v. KATZENBACH
383 U.S. 301 (1966)

This decision upheld the constitutionality of portions of the VOTING RIGHTS ACT OF 1965. Southern states attacked, as an intrusion upon state SOVEREIGNTY and on other grounds, portions of the act suspending tests or devices used to measure voter qualifications, barring new voter qualifications pending approval by federal authorities, providing for the appointment of federal voting examiners to register voters, and determining which states and political subdivisions were subject to the act's coverage. In sustaining the legislation under the FIFTEENTH AMENDMENT, the Supreme Court, in an opinion by Chief Justice EARL WARREN, rejected the argument that Congress could do no more than forbid violations of the Fifteenth Amendment and must leave the fashioning of remedies for violations to the courts. Congressional findings that case-by-case litigation was inadequate to vindicate VOTING RIGHTS justified the decision "to shift the advantage of time and inertia from the perpetrators of the evil to its victims."

THEODORE EISENBERG

SOUTH CAROLINA EXPOSITION AND PROTEST

See: Exposition and Protest

SOUTH CAROLINA ORDINANCE OF NULLIFICATION (1832)

South Carolinians' objections to the expansion of federal authority focused on protective tariffs enacted in 1828 and 1832. They were most concerned, however, about potential external threats to the security of slavery, including threats from the federal government. Inspired by constitutional theories of JOHN C. CALHOUN, the South Carolina legislature called a convention to nullify the tariff.

On November 24, 1832, the convention adopted the Ordinance of Nullification, which declared that Congress lacked power to adopt a protective tariff. The tariff measures were therefore "null, void, and no law, nor binding upon this State, its officers or citizens." The ordinance voided all contracts and judicial proceedings designed to collect the tariff, prohibited state officials from enforcing it, required the state legislature to enact legislation that would "prevent the enforcement and arrest the operation" of the tariffs, prohibited appeals of tariff-related cases to the Supreme Court, required all public officials and jurors to take an oath to support the ordinance and supportive legislation, and warned that any coercive federal act would trigger the state's SECESSION. South Carolina also subsequently nullified the federal FORCE ACT that empowered President ANDREW JACKSON to collect the tariff. Though the Nullification Ordinance produced a major constitutional crisis in 1832, it was a short-term failure. President Jackson and all the Southern states denounced it, and South Carolina never found occasion to put its requirements to the test. But the Ordinance was a major step in implementing the theory of NULLIFICATION and, as such, pointed to secession.

WILLIAM M. WIECEK

Bibliography

CURRENT, RICHARD N. 1963 *John C. Calhoun.* New York: Washington Square Press.

SOUTH CAROLINA ORDINANCE OF SECESSION (1860)

JOHN C. CALHOUN, the foremost theorist of SECESSION, had argued that the United States Constitution was a compact among sovereign states. When one of the parties to the compact (federal government or other state) had violated its terms by enacting or condoning unconstitutional acts, and other remedies such as INTERPOSITION and NULLIFICATION proved futile, an aggrieved party could withdraw from the compact and resume the independent status it enjoyed previously.

In response to ABRAHAM LINCOLN's election, the South Carolina legislature called a convention to consider secession. On December 20, 1860, the convention, meeting at Charleston, unanimously adopted the Ordinance of Secession, a brief statement declaring that "the union now subsisting . . . is hereby dissolved." Four days later, the Convention approved the "Declaration of the Causes of Secession," a brief exposition of secessionist and compact theory. In it, the Carolinians accused the free states of violation or half-hearted enforcement of the Fugitive Slave Acts, tolerating abolitionist agitation, and electing a presidential candidate pledged to the eventual abolition of slavery. Therefore South Carolina declared itself an "independent state, with full power to levy war, conclude peace, contract alliances, establish commerce, and to do all other acts and things which independent States may of right do."

WILLIAM M. WIECEK

Bibliography

POTTER, DAVID M. 1976 *The Impending Crisis,* 1848–1861. New York: Harper & Row.

SOUTH DAKOTA v. NEVILLE
459 U.S. 553 (1983)

In this case the Supreme Court answered a question left unresolved by earlier decisions: can a state use as evidence the fact that a person arrested for drunk driving refused to take a blood-alcohol test? GRIFFIN V. CALIFORNIA (1965) had held that adverse comment on a defendant's refusal to testify impermissibly burdened the RIGHT AGAINST SELF-INCRIMINATION, and SCHMERBER V. CALIFORNIA (1966) had held that a state could compel the taking of a blood-alcohol test without violating that right, which protected against testimonial compulsion only, not compulsion of physical evidence drawn from the body. In *Neville* the Court ruled that a state that authorized a driver to refuse a blood-alcohol test could introduce that refusal as evidence against him. The Court relied not on the earlier distinction between TESTIMONIAL AND NONTESTIMONIAL COMPULSION but on the fact that the element of compulsion was altogether absent here because the state did not require the test.

LEONARD W. LEVY

SOUTH-EASTERN UNDERWRITERS ASSOCIATION v. UNITED STATES
322 U.S. 533 (1944)

The statement in PAUL V. VIRGINIA (1869) that insurance did not constitute INTERSTATE COMMERCE underlay seventy-five years of acquiescence and spawned an intricate network of state regulation. The question of federal regulation did not come before the Court until this indictment of an underwriters' association for violating the SHERMAN ANTITRUST ACT. A 4–3 Court, led by Justice HUGO L. BLACK, declared that insurance was commerce subject to federal regulation. Moreover, the Sherman Act applied, and the underwriters could properly be convicted for its violation. Justice ROBERT H. JACKSON, dissenting in part, conceded the fact of interstate commerce but felt obliged to follow the well-established legal fiction to the contrary until Congress acted to regulate. Chief Justice HARLAN FISKE STONE dissented, predicting chaos when state regulation was discontinued because federal controls did not exist. Justice FELIX FRANKFURTER joined Stone, admitting the reach of federal power but denying that the Sherman Act was intended to extend to insurance.

DAVID GORDON

(SEE ALSO: *Prudential Insurance Company v. Benjamin, 1946.*)

SOUTHERN MANIFESTO
(March 11, 1956)

Southern politicians generally opposed the Supreme Court's ruling in BROWN V. BOARD OF EDUCATION (1954). Virginia and other states resurrected the doctrine of INTERPOSITION, and Georgia threatened NULLIFICATION. The most considered statement of segregationist constitutional theory was the declaration against INTEGRATION made by ninety-six southern congressmen and senators, in March 1956, led by Senator Harry F. Byrd of Virginia. The manifesto argued: *Brown* represented a clear abuse of judicial power; the FOURTEENTH AMENDMENT, which did not mention education, was not intended to affect state educational systems; PLESSY V. FERGUSON (1896) was still good law; DESEGREGATION would cause chaos and confusion in the states affected. The manifesto called upon the people of the states to "resist forced integration by any lawful means" and concluded with a pledge "to use all lawful means to bring about a reversal of this decision which is contrary to the Constitution, and to prevent the use of force in its implementation." Federal response to such abstract defiance was notably lacking, although a group of distinguished leaders of the American bar denounced attacks on the Supreme Court as "reckless in their abuse, . . . heedless of the value of JUDICIAL REVIEW and . . . dangerous in fomenting disrespect for our highest law."

PAUL L. MURPHY

Bibliography

MUSE, BENJAMIN 1964 *Ten Years of Prelude: The Story of Integration Since the Supreme Court's 1954 Decision.* New York: Viking.

SOUTHERN PACIFIC CO. v. ARIZONA
325 U.S. 761 (1945)

Arizona prohibited operation of a railroad train more than fourteen passenger cars or seventy freight cars long. The Supreme Court, 7–2, held the law an unconstitutional burden on INTERSTATE COMMERCE. Chief Justice HARLAN FISKE STONE, for the Court, emphasized the magnitude of that burden; the law forced the railroad to operate thirty percent more trains in the state, and to break up and remake trains; its total yearly cost to both railroads operating in the state was a million dollars. Stone also noted that requiring more trains would produce more accidents; the state's safety argument was weak. This interest-balancing analysis was far more demanding than the "RATIONAL BASIS" STANDARD OF REVIEW Stone had employed in *South Carolina State Highway Department v. Barnwell Bros., Inc.* (1938), upholding limits on truck widths and weights. *Southern Pacific* set the standard for future challenges to STATE REGULATIONS OF COMMERCE in the transportation field.

KENNETH L. KARST

SOVEREIGN IMMUNITY

At COMMON LAW the sovereign, although subject to the law, was immune from the JURISDICTION of its own courts. The English doctrine of sovereign immunity was established at an early time, probably in the thirteenth century; but long before the American Revolution the jurisdictional exemption of the sovereign, though remaining theoretically absolute, was riddled with exceptions. Judicial process against the sovereign was available through petition of right and other procedures resting upon waiver of immunity, and subordinate officers could be sued for damages attributable to official acts and were subject to process by prerogative writ.

Because sovereign immunity was part of the common law heritage existing when the Constitution was adopted, the courts later embraced the doctrine as an implicit limitation upon their jurisdiction. Hence, some provisions of Article III of the Constitution were interpreted as subject to this qualification. The immunity of the United States, first acknowledged by the Supreme Court in *United States v. McLemore* (1846), became a complete exemption, protecting the federal government and its agencies from unconsented suit in any court by any plaintiff. State immunity was initially rejected by the Court in CHISHOLM V. GEORGIA (1793), but that unpopular HOLDING was quickly reversed by the ELEVENTH AMENDMENT. The amendment, in juxtaposition with Article III, was subsequently construed to immunize the states from unconsented suits by private plaintiffs and by foreign governments in federal court.

The states, however, are not immune from suit by either the United States or other states. As a matter of state law, states commonly have claimed immunity from suit by private plaintiffs in state court. The power of Congress to lift the states' common law immunity seems restricted only by the limitations of the JUDICIAL POWER OF THE UNITED STATES as defined in Article III, the general limitations of congressional power, and—arguably—some core notion of state sovereignty. (See NATIONAL LEAGUE OF CITIES V. Usery, 1976.)

The immunity doctrine is in tension with the RULE OF LAW, and pragmatic justifications for its perpetuation are unpersuasive. By means of statutes waiving immunity and through judicial interpretation, the ambit of the exemption has been drastically reduced. Congressional legislation creating the COURT OF CLAIMS in 1855 and later enactments, such as the Tucker Act (1887) and the FEDERAL TORT CLAIMS ACT (1946), subject the United States to suit on many kinds of claims. The states, by state constitutional provision or statute, have abolished completely or restricted their own immunity—often in state judicial proceedings only, less commonly in federal court actions. Moreover, as a practical matter, the impact of the doctrine is significantly restricted by differentiating suits against public officers for official acts done or threatened pursuant to unconstitutional or legally deficient authorization from suits against the government itself. Although the courts permit state and federal officers to assert sovereign immunity where the suit against them is adjudged to be substantially against the government itself, such cases are generally limited to suits seeking damages or restitution for past acts where judgment will expend itself upon the public treasury, those seeking to dispossess the government of property, and some suits seeking specific performance. As a consequence of these developments, sovereign immunity has become a narrow and ill-defined jurisdictional bar, whose contemporary legitimacy and utility are doubtful.

CLYDE E. JACOBS

Bibliography

DAVIS, KENNETH C. 1970 Supp. *Administrative Law Treatise.* Pages 895–940. St. Paul, Minn.: West Publishing Co.

HOLDSWORTH, SIR WILLIAM S. 1944 *A History of English Law.* Vol. 9 of 15. London: Methuen.

SOVEREIGNTY

The single term "sovereignty" is used to denote two distinct (although related) concepts of constitutional significance. It refers both to the autonomy of a state with respect to its legislative JURISDICTION and to the supreme authority within the state. There are historical reasons why the same term is used for both, but to confound them is a serious and all-too-common error. The term itself comes from the Latin *superans* (meaning "rising above" or "overcoming") through the French *souverain.*

Sovereignty, in the first sense, is a concept derived from international law. A state is sovereign if it is independent of other states and possesses the authority to determine its relationship to other states and to regulate its own internal affairs. Sovereignty, in this sense, is the essential condition required for membership in the family of nations. Sovereign states do not ordinarily make treaties or wage formal war except with other states recognized as sovereign. International law also recognizes some communities as semisovereign, that is, as possessing certain, but not all, of the attributes of sovereignty. The member states of a federal union are in this category.

Internally the several states of the United States are legally sovereign in this sense insofar as they possess jurisdiction, the legitimate authority to declare the law within their territory. But this sovereignty is not unlimited. As the Supreme Court said in PARKER V. BROWN (1943), "The governments of the states are sovereign within their territory save only as they are subject to the prohibitions of the Constitution or as their action in some measure conflicts with powers delegated to the National Government, or with Congressional legislation enacted in the exercise of those powers." The jurisdiction of the states is constitutionally limited by subject as well as by territory, but within their sphere the state governments are as supreme as the national government is within its sphere. This is the meaning of what JAMES MADISON in THE FEDERALIST #39 called the "compound republic."

The states enjoy some other attributes of sovereignty: they may not without their consent be sued in their own courts or in the courts of the United States (see SOVEREIGN IMMUNITY; ELEVENTH AMENDMENT) and they possess independent and plenary authority to lay and collect taxes on persons, things, or transactions within their jurisdiction. Among themselves, also, the states are sovereign. The jurisdiction of a state is exclusive of the other states. Disputes between or among states in cases not governed by the Constitution, an INTERSTATE COMPACT, or a federal statute are resolved according to the principles of international law. But the sovereignty of the states does not limit or diminish the sovereignty of the Union. In all international affairs and in domestic affairs properly subject to it, the government of the United States is sovereign. Without its consent, the United States may not be sued in the courts either of the United States or of the several states.

In political theory sovereignty is generally held to be indivisible; careful writers thus distinguish between the indivisible sovereignty of the people and the powers or attributes of sovereignty that are divided between the national and state governments. Hence ALEXANDER HAMILTON, in *The Federalist* #32, wrote of "the division of the sovereign power." But not all political actors are so careful; it is not uncommon for politicians, judges, or commentators to refer to a "division of sovereignty" in the federal system.

The second meaning of sovereignty as the single, supreme authority within a state, above the law and uncontrollable except by its own will, was introduced into political theory by Jean Bodin in his *Six Bookes of the Commonwealth* (1576). Its most extreme expression was given by Thomas Hobbes who, in *Leviathan* (1651), asserted that opposition to tyranny was identical with opposition to sovereignty, or, in other words, that there is no standard except its own will against which the actions of the sovereign can be judged. A democratic, but no less radical, form was given to this concept of sovereignty by Jean-Jacques Rousseau in *The Social Contract* (1762).

Originally an analytical or explanatory formulation, the notion of a single, indivisible power in the state became a prescriptive article of the Tory political creed. WILLIAM BLACKSTONE identified the King-in-Parliament as the sovereign in England. Governor THOMAS HUTCHINSON, in his famous dispute with the Massachusetts Assembly in 1773, ascribed that same status to Parliament within the British Empire—denying that the provincial legislatures of America had any power or authority except by Parliament's grace. To the Whigs of America the Hobbesian idea of sovereignty, as it was stated by Hutchinson, represented a threat to the liberty they had inherited and the self-government they had established. As an empirical assertion the indivisibility of sovereignty seemed to be disproved by the federal systems of Germany, Switzerland, and the Netherlands, as well as by the British imperial system as it existed in the mid-eighteenth century; and as a prescriptive formula it was all too clearly intended to subvert American home rule.

The social contract theory expressed in the DECLARATION OF INDEPENDENCE and the first state constitutions was a rejection of the Tory doctrine of sovereignty. Neither the government nor any branch or officer of the government justly exercises any power except by the consent of the governed. The doctrine of equality of rights means that no person or body of persons is above the law. The claim of the Declaration, our most fundamental constitutional document, is that there can be no sovereign but the people. This doctrine of POPULAR SOVEREIGNTY was identified by ALEXIS DE TOCQUEVILLE as the defining characteristic of American constitutionalism. Both the national and state governments derive their powers from the people through the Constitution. Each exercises jurisdiction, but neither possesses sovereignty in the absolute, Hobbesian sense.

The Hobbesian notion of sovereignty was translated from a political to a legal concept in the nineteenth century by the British jurist John Austin, who argued that there was no HIGHER LAW against which the decrees of the state could be measured, and so the power of the legislature was absolute. In this revived form it was brought to America as part of the intellectual baggage of legal positivism.

Throughout American history a favorite rhetorical device has been to identify one level of government—usually the state—as sovereign. The success of this device depends upon the ambiguity of the term. That a political body exercises jurisdiction, is supreme within its sphere, and is autonomous in its internal affairs does not mean that it, its government, or its legislature is immune to the sanctions of the law or is free of the constraints of higher law. To speak of the "sovereign states" is not entirely inaccurate if the speaker refers to their autonomy within their own sphere, but it derives its force by evoking the notion of indivisibility and illimitability drawn from the other sense of the term. The rhetoric seemingly denies that the sovereign states are comprised within a sovereign Union.

Within the American regime the ultimate power and authority to alter or abolish the constitutions of government of state and Union resides only and inalienably with the people. If it be necessary or useful to use the term "sovereignty" in the sense of ultimate political power, then there is no sovereign in America but the people.

DENNIS J. MAHONEY

Bibliography

DIAMOND, MARTIN (1970)1981 *The Founding of the Democratic Republic.* Itasca, Ill.: F. E. Peacock.

JAFFA, HARRY V. 1965 *Equality and Liberty: Theory and Practice in American Politics.* New York: Oxford University Press.

LASKI, HAROLD J. 1921 The Foundations of Sovereignty. Pages 1–29 in *The Foundations of Sovereignty and Other Essays.* New Haven, Conn.: Yale University Press.

SPAIGHT, RICHARD DOBBS (1758–1802)

Richard Dobbs Spaight represented North Carolina at the CONSTITUTIONAL CONVENTION OF 1787 and signed the Constitution. An infrequent speaker, Spaight favored strong national government. He was a leader of the RATIFICATION movement in North Carolina and was later elected governor and congressman. In a controversy with JAMES IREDELL over BAYARD V. SINGLETON (1787), he denounced JUDICIAL REVIEW as undemocratic.

DENNIS J. MAHONEY

SPECIAL MASTER

A special master is an officer appointed by a court to assist it in a particular proceeding. When the Supreme Court exercises its ORIGINAL JURISDICTION, normally it appoints a special master to take EVIDENCE, make findings of fact, and submit a draft decree. The master's recommendations are advisory; decision rests with the Court. Many of the Supreme Court's special masters are former federal judges.

KENNETH L. KARST

SPEECH OR DEBATE CLAUSE

The Constitution's speech or debate clause provides that "for any Speech or Debate in either House, [members of Congress] shall not be questioned in any other Place." Despite its narrow phrasing, the clause was read in GRAVEL V. UNITED STATES (1972) and other cases as protecting all integral parts "of the deliberative and communicative process by which Members participate in committee and House proceedings with respect to the consideration and passage or rejection of proposed legislation." The clause also protects members' aides in performing tasks that would be protected if performed by members. An act protected by the clause may not be the basis of a civil or criminal judgment against a member of Congress. Under *Doe v. McMillan* (1973), actions by private citizens are barred even though the English PARLIAMENTARY PRIVILEGE from which the clause derives was concerned with executive encroachments on legislative prerogatives.

There are three inroads upon the speech or debate clause's protection. First, criminal prosecutions for corrupt behavior, such as accepting a bribe to influence legislation, may go forward, as in BREWSTER V. UNITED STATES (1972), on the theory that even if legislative acts were performed in exchange for payment, accepting a bribe is not a legislative act. But this area is not without difficulty, as was evidenced by the Court's refusal in *United States v. Johnson* (1966) and *United States v. Helstoski* (1979) to allow the use of legislative acts as evidence in corruption cases.

Second, in *Gravel v. United States* and HUTCHINSON V. PROXMIRE (1979), the Court implicitly held that communications with a member's constituents are not legislative functions and expressly held that members of Congress could be made to answer for words, written or spoken, or deeds done, outside formal congressional communications channels. Thus Senator Mike Gravel (or his aide) could be interrogated about republishing the Pentagon Papers with a private publisher, even though he could not be asked about reading the papers into the record of a committee hearing (see NEW YORK TIMES CO. V. UNITED STATES, 1971). And Senator William Proxmire could be held liable for defamatory communications.

Third, a citizen aggrieved by a subpoena to appear before, or furnish documentary evidence to, a congressional committee may challenge the subpoena by refusing to comply and defending any resulting contempt citation on the ground that the subpoena was unconstitutional or otherwise defective.

The speech or debate clause also plays a central but somewhat confusing role in delineating state legislators' immunity from suit under SECTION 1983, TITLE 42, UNITED STATES CODE. (See LEGISLATIVE IMMUNITY.) In TENNEY V. BRANDHOVE (1951) the Court relied in part on the speech or debate clause, which by its terms applies only to members of Congress, to find state legislators absolutely immune from damages actions under section 1983. In *United States v. Gillock* (1980), however, the Court held that in a federal criminal prosecution of a state legislator, the speech or debate privilege does not bar using legislative acts as evidence.

THEODORE EISENBERG

Bibliography

REINSTEIN, ROBERT J. and SILVERGATE, HARVEY A. 1973 Legislative Privilege and the Separation of Powers. *Harvard Law Review* 86:1113–1182.

YANKWICH, LEON R. 1951 The Immunity of Congressional Speech—Its Origin, Meaning and Scope. *University of Pennsylvania Law Review* 99:960–977.

SPEEDY TRIAL

The Sixth Amendment provides that "in all criminal prosecutions, the accused shall enjoy the right to a speedy . . . trial." The Supreme Court in KLOPFER V. NORTH CAROLINA (1967) held that the guarantee is applicable to the states through the DUE PROCESS clause of the Fourteenth Amendment. The origin of the right can be traced back at least to MAGNA CARTA (1215) and perhaps to the Assize of Clarendon (1166). On different occasions the Supreme Court has described it as "fundamental," "slippery," and "amorphous."

Denial of a speedy trial may result in prolonged incarceration prior to trial and exacerbation of the anxiety and concern that normally accompany public accusations of crime. Prolonged incarceration before trial inevitably involves a disruption of normal life and imposition of a substantial sanction at a time when innocence is still presumed. It causes loss of productive labor, normally without opportunity for training or rehabilitation, and frequently interferes with preparation of a defense.

Pretrial release can ameliorate these conditions, but a defendant who achieves pretrial release may be subject to significant restraints on his freedom of action, his job may be threatened, his resources may be dissipated, and he and his family may suffer from understandable concern about his future while his reputation in the community is impaired. For these reasons courts have enforced the right in a variety of contexts. Charges were dismissed in *Smith v. Hooly* (1969) when a state failed to bring a defendant to trial on state charges while he was serving a federal sentence despite demands for trial by the accused, and in *Klopfer* when a state suspended prosecution indefinitely although the defendant was not in custody.

Not all defendants want a speedy trial; many want no trial at all. Delay is a common defense tactic and in some cases an accused may benefit from prolonged delay, particularly when pretrial release has been achieved. In such cases, although only the defendant has a right to demand a speedy trial, the state may desire a speedy trial. Prolonged delay contributes to court backlog and places pressure on prosecutors to make concessions in PLEA BARGAINING. Defendants released pending trial may commit additional crimes. Witnesses may die. Memories fade. The risk of escape or bail-jumping cannot be ignored.

Not infrequently, delay may serve the interests of both an accused and a prosecutor for different reasons. Even if public interest would be better served by a prompt trial, there may be no effective way of expediting trial. Nor is the public interest served by dismissing charges if a trial is not held promptly.

One answer to the problem would be a requirement that trial take place within a specified time. The variety of factual situations confronting prosecutors and defense counsel has prevented agreement on an appropriate time interval between charge and trial that should govern all cases. The absence of such a litmus test has deterred the Court from proclaiming any single period of delay as the maximum permitted by the constitutional imperative.

There are good reasons for requiring a defendant to make an appropriate demand before he can complain of a denial of his right to speedy trial, but the Court has also declined to place such an obligation upon a defendant as an absolute requirement. Instead, in BARKER V. WINGO (1972), it chose to consider the facts of each case, examining the length of the delay, the prejudice it might cause, the presence or absence of a demand for trial by the defendant, and the justification asserted by the state for its failure to try the accused earlier.

Courts have been remarkably receptive to government justification for significant delays. For example, in *Barker* a delay of five and one half years and sixteen state-requested continuances was permitted because of the need to convict a co-defendant before proceeding against the accused, illness of the chief investigating officer, and acquiescence by the defendant during most of the period. The willingness of a court to accept government assertions of good cause may be influenced by recognition that a dismissal of pending charges is required by the Supreme Court holding in *Strunk v. United States* (1973) if it decides a speedy trial has been denied. Unlike the EXCLUSIONARY RULE or other sanctions for violation of rights, dismissal resulting from a finding of a deprivation of the right to speedy trial may fully immunize a defendant from prosecution.

According to the Court's holding in *United States v. Marion* (1971) only "an accused" may assert a right to speedy trial and a prosecution must have been initiated by arrest and filing of charges before the right attaches. The period between the charge and trial is crucial. Delay between commission of the crime and formal charge is not significant to a claim of a Sixth Amendment violation, although the identity of the accused was or might have been known and PROBABLE CAUSE for arrest or INDICTMENT may have existed. In UNITED STATES V. MACDONALD (1982) the Supreme Court held that prosecutorial delay between dismissal of initial charges by military authority and reassertion of the charges in a civilian forum at a later time was beyond the purview of the Sixth Amendment.

Many of the disadvantages caused an accused by unreasonable delay between charge and trial also ensue when there is an unreasonable delay before charges are brought against him. In *United States v. Lovasco* (1977) the Supreme Court indicated that, in unusual cases, an accused may be able to establish a violation of the due process clause as a result of oppressive pretrial delay where actual prejudice can be demonstrated and inadequate justification exists. Government "bad faith," as when a charge is delayed, or dismissed and subsequently asserted at a later time in order to "forum shop," stockpile charges, or achieve some other tactical advantage, might also constitute a denial of due process. But the degree of protection afforded to an accused against unreasonable delay between commission of an offense and formal charges will depend on the applicable statute of limitations in most cases.

Statutory provisions implement the constitutional provision in many states and in federal prosecution. Encouraged by the *American Bar Association Standards for Criminal Justice, Speedy Trial* (1968), many jurisdictions have set specific legislative time limits within which a defendant must be brought to trial. Perhaps the most important of these statutes is the federal Speedy Trial Act of 1974, defining in detail permissible time periods in different types of cases and setting forth grounds for dismissal of charges with and without prejudice. Assertion of rights under these statutes is more likely to provide effective protection to an accused than reliance on the Constitution except in extraordinary cases.

A. KENNETH PYE

Bibliography

AMSTERDAM, ANTHONY G. 1975 Speedy Criminal Trial: Rights and Remedies. *Stanford Law Review* 27:525–543.

GODBOLD, JOHN C. 1972 Speedy Trial—Major Surgery for a National Ill. *Alabama Law Review* 24:265–294.

LAFAVE, WAYNE R. and ISRAEL, JEDD H. 1985 *Criminal Procedure.* St. Paul, Minn.: West Publishing Co.

WHITEBREAD, CHARLES H. 1980 *Criminal Procedure.* Mineola, N.Y.: Foundation Press.

SPEISER v. RANDALL
357 U.S. 513 (1958)

The Supreme Court invalidated on DUE PROCESS grounds a noncommunist oath required for a California property tax exemption. *Speiser* is a leading early case in the series breaking down the RIGHT–PRIVILEGE DISTINCTION and establishing that due process must be strictly observed where FUNDAMENTAL RIGHTS are infringed.

MARTIN SHAPIRO

SPENDING POWER

See: Taxing and Spending Power

SPINELLI v. UNITED STATES
393 U.S. 410 (1969)

In *Spinelli* the Supreme Court explicated and expanded the PROBABLE CAUSE standards for SEARCH WARRANTS set forth in AGUILAR V. TEXAS (1964).

Spinelli was convicted under federal law of crossing state lines to conduct gambling operations. A detailed FBI affidavit, on which the search warrant was based, stated in part that Spinelli was "known" to law enforcement officers as a bookmaker, and that a confidential informant had established that Spinelli was operating as a bookmaker.

The Court ruled that the INFORMANT's testimony could not count toward the establishment of probable cause, because the affidavit failed to establish the informant's reliability or to clarify his relationship to Spinelli. The Court rejected the government's claim that the tip gave "suspicious color" to Spinelli's activities, and that, conversely, the surveillance helped corroborate the informant's tip (he had, for example, provided the correct numbers of two telephones listed in someone else's name in an apartment frequented by Spinelli). Such a "totality of the circumstances" approach, said the Court, painted "with too broad a brush." The *Spinelli* approach was abandoned in ILLINOIS V. GATES (1983).

JACOB W. LANDYNSKI

SPOT RESOLUTIONS
(1847)

Congressman ABRAHAM LINCOLN (Whig, Illinois) introduced a series of eight resolutions in the House of Representatives on December 22, 1847. Intended to show the illegality of the Mexican War, the resolutions were in the form of interrogatories, challenging President JAMES K. POLK to name the exact spot upon which American blood was first shed in the war and to concede that that spot was on soil rightfully claimed by Mexico. The contention of the northern Whigs, including Lincoln, was that Polk had used his power as COMMANDER-IN-CHIEF of the Army to provoke the Mexicans into war in order to seize new territory into which SLAVERY could be extended.

In a brilliant speech in January 1848 Lincoln explained that accurate answers to his interrogatories would demonstrate that "the War with Mexico was unnecessarily and unconstitutionally commenced by the President." He claimed that the President had usurped Congress's constitutional power to declare war and disputed Polk's claim that Congress, by appropriating money for the conduct of the war, had sanctioned its commencement.

The Spot Resolutions, like the WILMOT PROVISO, were meant to embarrass the administration by linking the Mexican War with the slave power in the public mind. The House tabled Lincoln's resolutions but passed another resolution condemning Polk's conduct.

DENNIS J. MAHONEY

Bibliography

JOSEPHY, ALVIN M., JR. 1975 *History of the Congress of the United States.* Pages 188–193. New York: American Heritage Publishing Co.

SPRINGER v. UNITED STATES
102 U.S. 586 (1881)

Springer contested the constitutionality of a federal income tax statute on ground that it was a DIRECT TAX not apportioned on the basis of state population. The Supreme Court unanimously upheld the tax on ground that the only direct taxes are taxes on land and CAPITATION TAXES.

LEONARD W. LEVY

(SEE ALSO: *Pollock v. Farmers' Loan and Trust Co.*)

STAFFORD v. WALLACE
358 U.S. 495 (1922)

Seventeen years after SWIFT & COMPANY V. UNITED STATES (1905), the Supreme Court again approved the extension of federal authority to local activities. A nationalistic exposition of the COMMERCE CLAUSE ran through the opinion in which the Court not only reaffirmed but also extended the STREAM OF COMMERCE DOCTRINE. Commission men, who sold animals on consignment, sued to enjoin enforcement of the PACKERS & STOCKYARDS ACT. They asserted that because they provided only "personal services" and were not engaged in INTERSTATE COMMERCE, they were not subject to the act. For a 7–1 Court, Chief Justice WILLIAM HOWARD TAFT followed Justice OLIVER WENDELL HOLMES's opinion in *Swift* and sustained the act. Congress had acted reasonably in securing an "unburdened flow" of interstate commerce. Moreover, the stockyards were "not a place of rest or final destination . . . but a throat through which the current [of commerce] flows." Because the commission men were essential to maintaining this flow, their activities were properly part of interstate commerce and subject to the act. Justice JAMES C. MCREYNOLDS dissented without opinion. By reviving and reapplying the stream of commerce doctrine, the Court built a foundation on which the New Deal would later support its ECONOMIC REGULATIONS.

DAVID GORDON

STAMP ACT CONGRESS, RESOLUTIONS OF (October 19, 1765)

These resolutions, adopted by the delegates of nine American colonies meeting in an intercolonial congress, expressed the basis of the American constitutional position in the quarrel with Great Britain leading to the American Revolution. The mother country, financially exhausted by a great war from which the American colonies stood to gain the most, decided to retain an army in America and to require the colonists to pay a small fraction of the cost of their defense. Parliamentary legislation aimed at raising a revenue in America was, however, unprecedented before the Sugar Act of 1764. That act provoked the first constitutional protests from the colonies. In form the 1764 legislation had regulated their ocean trade, thus imposing an "external" tax. The Stamp Act of 1765 imposed "internal" taxes on every sort of legal document and most business documents; on college diplomas, liquor licences, and appointments to offices; and on playing cards, newspapers, advertisements, almanacs, books, and pamphlets. Admiralty courts, which operated without juries and used inquisitional procedures, had JURISDICTION over offenses against the act. American opposition was so vehement and widespread that the act proved to be unenforceable.

The Stamp Act Congress addressed itself to two constitutional issues raised by the act of Parliament. After asserting that the colonists were entitled to all the rights and liberties of Englishmen, the congress resolved that Parliament, a body in which the colonists were not represented and which could not represent them, had no constitutional authority to tax them. Several resolutions condemned TAXATION WITHOUT REPRESENTATION and endorsed the principle that only their own assemblies could constitutionally tax the American colonists. The congress also endorsed the right to TRIAL BY JURY and condemned the unprecedented extension of admiralty court jurisdiction as subversive of colonial liberties.

The Stamp Act was in force for only four months before Parliament repealed it, not because of the American constitutional protests but because of the protests of British merchants who suffered from a boycott of their goods by American importers. To save face, Parliament accompanied its repealer with the Declaratory Act of 1766, which insisted that Great Britain had full power to make laws for America "in all cases whatsoever." The American position, that "no taxes . . . can be constitutionally imposed . . . but by their respective legislatures," was founded on a different view of the British constitution, even a different understanding of the meaning of a CONSTITUTION and of the word "unconstitutional." A local court in Virginia gratuitously condemned the Stamp Act as unconstitutional and therefore not binding.

LEONARD W. LEVY

Bibliography

MORGAN, EDMUND S. and HELEN M. 1953 *The Stamp Act Congress.* Chapel Hill: University of North Carolina Press.

STANBERY, HENRY S. (1803–1881)

An Ohio lawyer and United States attorney general (1866–1868), Henry Stanbery opposed congressional reconstruction and prepared many of President ANDREW JOHNSON's veto messages. Nevertheless, in MISSISSIPPI V. JOHNSON (1867) Stanbery successfully defended executive enforcement of congressional statutes by arguing that the SEPARATION OF POWERS barred the Supreme Court from issuing an INJUNCTION against the President. Similarly, in *Georgia v. Stanton* (1868) he successfully argued that the case involved POLITICAL QUESTIONS beyond the Court's JURISDICTION. In 1868 Stanbery resigned his office to defend Johnson at his IMPEACHMENT trial. Stanbery's insistence on DUE PROCESS slowed the trial and helped achieve Johnson's acquittal.

PAUL FINKELMAN

Bibliography

MENEELY, A. HOWARD 1935 Henry Stanbery. In *Dictionary of American Biography,* Vol. 27:498–499. New York: Scribner's.

STANDARD OF REVIEW

Some constitutional limitations on government are readily susceptible to "interpretation," in the sense of definition and categorization. Once a court categorizes a law as a BILL OF ATTAINDER, for example, it holds the law invalid. Other limitations, however, are expressed in terms that make this sort of interpretation awkward: the FREEDOM OF SPEECH, the EQUAL PROTECTION OF THE LAWS, DUE PROCESS OF LAW. The judicial task in enforcing these open-ended limitations implies an inquiry into the justifications asserted by government for restricting liberty or denying equal treatment. The term "standards of review," in common use since the late 1960s, denotes various degrees of judicial deference to legislative judgments concerning these justifications.

The idea that there might be more than one standard of review was explicitly suggested in Justice HARLAN FISKE STONE's opinion for the Supreme Court in UNITED STATES v. CAROLENE PRODUCTS CO. (1938). Confirming a retreat from the JUDICIAL ACTIVISM that had invalidated a significant number of ECONOMIC REGULATIONS over the preceding four decades, Stone concluded that such a law would be valid if the legislature's purpose were legitimate and if the law could rationally be seen as related to that purpose. Stone added, however, that this permissive RATIONAL BASIS standard might not be appropriate for reviewing laws challenged under certain specific prohibitions of the BILL OF RIGHTS, or laws restricting the political process, or laws directed at DISCRETE AND INSULAR MINORITIES. Such cases, Stone suggested, might call for a diminished presumption of constitutionality, a "more exacting judicial scrutiny."

The WARREN COURT embraced this double standard in several doctrinal areas, most notably in equal protection cases. The permissive rational basis standard continued to govern review of economic regulations, but STRICT SCRUTINY was given to laws discriminating against the exercise of FUNDAMENTAL INTERESTS such as voting or marriage and to laws employing SUSPECT CLASSIFICATIONS such as race. The strict scrutiny standard amounts to an inversion of the presumption of constitutionality: the state must justify its imposition of a racial inequality, for example, by showing that the law is necessary to achieve a COMPELLING STATE INTEREST. Today active judicial review of both the importance of legislative purposes and the necessity of legislative means is employed not only in some types of equal protection cases but also in fields such as the freedom of speech and RELIGIOUS LIBERTY. It has even attended the rebirth of SUBSTANTIVE DUE PROCESS.

Inevitably, however, cracks appeared in this two-tier system of standards of review. The Court used the language of "rational basis" to strike down some laws, and in cases involving SEX DISCRIMINATION it explicitly adopted an intermediate standard for reviewing both legislative ends and means: discrimination based on sex is invalid unless it serves an "important" governmental purpose and is "substantially related" to that purpose. A similar intermediate standard is now part of the required analysis of governmental regulations of COMMERCIAL SPEECH. In practical effect, the Court has created a "sliding scale" of review, varying the intensity of judicial scrutiny of legislation in proportion to the importance of the interests invaded and the likelihood of legislative prejudice against the persons disadvantaged. The process, in other words, is interest-balancing, pure and simple. Justice WILLIAM H. REHNQUIST, writing for the Court in ROSTKER v. GOLDBERG (1981), remarked accurately that the Court's various levels of scrutiny "may all too readily become facile abstractions used to justify a result"—a proposition well illustrated by the *Rostker* opinion itself.

KENNETH L. KARST

Bibliography

GUNTHER, GERALD 1972 The Supreme Court, 1971 Term—Foreword: In Search of Evolving Doctrine on a Changing Court: A Model for a Newer Equal Protection. *Harvard Law Review* 86:1–48.

STANDARD OIL COMPANY v. UNITED STATES

221 U.S. 1 (1911)

UNITED STATES v. AMERICAN TOBACCO COMPANY

211 U.S. 106 (1911)

John D. Rockefeller, owner of the nation's first, largest, and richest trust and controller of the nation's oil business, scorned his competitors and contemned the law. His disregard for the SHERMAN ANTITRUST ACT helped earn him, in 1909, a dissolution order which the trust appealed to the Supreme Court. Rockefeller thereby provided Chief Justice EDWARD D. WHITE with the occasion to celebrate the conversion of a majority of the Court to his viewpoint, enabling him to write the RULE OF REASON into antitrust law. After nearly fifteen years of effort, White had managed to enlarge judicial discretion in antitrust cases, even though the oil trust did not urge the doctrine upon the Court; indeed, it was unnecessary to the case's disposition.

Chief Justice White, leading an 8–1 Court, ruled that only an "unreasonable" contract or combination in restraint of trade would violate the law. White had effectively amended the law to insert his test: section 1 of the Sherman Act would henceforth be interpreted as if it said, "Every unreasonable contract, combination . . . or conspiracy in restraint of trade . . . is hereby declared to be illegal."

Standard Oil, however, lost the case. The record, said White, showed clearly and convincingly that this trust was unreasonable. Systematic attempts to exclude or crush rivals and the trust's astounding success demonstrated the violation beyond any doubt.

Justice JOHN MARSHALL HARLAN concurred in the result but dissented from the Court's announcement of the rule of reason. Harlan observed that Congress had refused to amend the act to incorporate the rule of reason, and he lashed out at the majority's "judicial legislation," predicting that the new policy would produce chaos. His call echoed in Congress where Democratic pressure grew to write the rule of reason out of the Sherman Act. That pressure would eventually find partial release in supplementary antitrust legislation, passage of the CLAYTON ACT in 1914. The rule of reason prevailed, however, although the Court applied a double standard. When massive business combinations such as United States Steel Corporation, United Shoe Machinery Company, and International Harvester came before the Court, they were found to have acted reasonably, restraints of trade notwithstanding. In antitrust action against labor unions, however, the Court ignored that rule.

In the companion *American Tobacco* case, Chief Justice White attempted to mitigate a too vigorous federal antitrust policy by ordering reorganization, not dissolution, of the Tobacco Trust. He thereby heartened business interests by showing solicitousness for property rights and a stable economy.

DAVID GORDON

Bibliography

BRINGHURST, BRUCE 1979 *Antitrust and the Oil Monopoly: The Standard Oil Cases, 1890–1914.* Westport, Conn.: Greenwood Press.

STANDING

In the United States, unelected, life-tenured federal judges may decide legal issues only when they are asked to do so by appropriate litigants. Such litigants are said to have standing to raise certain legal claims, including constitutional claims, in the federal courts.

A litigant's standing depends on two sets of criteria, one constitutionally required and one not, each ostensibly having three parts. The constitutional criteria derive from Article III's job description for federal judges, which permits them to declare law only when such a declaration is necessary to decide CASES AND CONTROVERSIES. These criteria center on the notion of an injured person's asking a court for a remedy against the responsible party, and each criterion corresponds to one of the three participants—to the plaintiff, the defendant, and the court, respectively. The plaintiff must assert that he suffered a cognizable personal injury; that the defendant's conduct caused the injury; and that the court's judgment is substantially likely to relieve it. The three nonconstitutional criteria for standing are "prudential" rules, self-imposed by the courts for their own governance, rules which Congress can eliminate if it chooses. These criteria, too, serve to diminish the frequency of substantive pronouncements by federal judges, but they focus on the legal basis of the suit, not on the plaintiff's actual injury. The first nonconstitutional criterion concerns representation: to secure judicial relief, injured litigants normally must assert that the injurious conduct violated their own legal rights, not the rights of third parties. The second assumes that government violations of everyone's undifferentiated legal rights are best left to political, not judicial, response: no one has standing if his or her legal position asserts "only the generalized interest of all citizens in constitutional governance." The third "prudential" criterion for standing seeks assurance that the law invoked plausibly protects the legal interest allegedly invaded: whatever interest is asserted must be "arguably within the zone of interests to be protected or regulated by the statute or constitutional guarantee in question."

Standing issues rarely surface in traditional suits, but federal courts applying these guidelines frequently deny standing to "public interest" plaintiffs anxious to challenge the legality of government behavior. The aim is not only to prevent federal judges from proclaiming law unless such declarations are needed to resolve concrete disputes, but also to promote proper conditions for intelligent adjudication (including adversary presentation of the facts and legal arguments) and to foster adequate representation of affected interests. When litigants ask federal courts to restrict the constitutional authority of politically accountable public officials, moreover, apprehension about unwise or excessive judicial intervention heightens, and the standing limitations may be applied with particular force.

Collectively, the Supreme Court's standing criteria often overlap; they are applied flexibly—sometimes inconsistently—to give the Supreme Court considerable discretion to exercise or withhold its power to declare law. The way that discretion is exercised reflects any particular Court's ideology of JUDICIAL ACTIVISM AND RESTRAINT and the substantive, constitutional rights it is either eager or reluctant to enforce.

The refinements of standing doctrine illustrate this flexibility and discretion. The core requirement of cognizable personal injury, for example, demands that the plaintiff have suffered injury to an interest deemed deserving of judicial protection. Over time, the Court has expanded the category of judicially acknowledged injuries beyond economic harm to include reputational, environmental, aesthetic, associational, informational, organizational, and voter harms, among others. Because of its vision of constrained judicial power in a representative democracy, however, the Court steadfastly forbids TAXPAYERS' SUITS and citizens' suits asserting purely ideological harm, particularly the harms of frustration, distress, or apprehension born of unlawful government conduct. Resting on lack of cognizable injury, the ban on citizen standing thus appears constitutionally compelled, although it effectively duplicates the nonconstitutional barrier to asserting generalized grievances, which appears to rest on the absence of a cognizable legal interest. Less diffuse, but in ALLEN v. WRIGHT (1984) nonetheless held an insufficiently personal injury, is the feeling of stigma arising from discrimination directed, not personally, but against other members of the plaintiff's race. If the type of injury is judicially approved and the plaintiff personally suffered it, however, the fact that many others have suffered it will not negate standing. For example, in UNITED STATES v. SCRAP (1973) a student activist group was deemed to have standing based on widespread environmental injury.

Flexibility also characterizes the Court's degree of insistence on the remaining constitutional criteria. The closeness of the causal link between defendant's conduct and plaintiff's injury has varied from *United States v. SCRAP,* which accepted a loose connection between the Interstate Commerce Commission's approval of freight rate increases for scrap materials and increased trash problems in national parks, to *Allen v. Wright* (1984), which found too attenuated a seemingly closer link between the Internal Revenue Service's allegedly inadequate enforcement of the law requiring denial of tax exemptions to racially discriminatory private schools and "white flight" in public school districts undergoing DESEGREGATION. Similarly, insistence that judicial relief be substantially likely to redress plaintiff's injury has varied from *Linda R. S. v. Richard D.* (1973), where mothers of illegitimate children seeking to force prosecution of the fathers for nonsupport were denied standing because a court order supposedly would result only in jailing the fathers, not in increased support, to *Duke Power Co. v. Carolina Environmental Study Group* (1978), where neighbors of nuclear power plants, seeking relief from present injury caused by normal plant operation, were granted standing to contest (unsuccessfully) the constitutional validity of a federal statute limiting recovery of DAMAGES for potential nuclear disasters, despite considerable uncertainty that a legal victory for the plaintiffs would stop the plants' normal operations.

Of the nonconstitutional criteria, only the usual prohibition against representing third-party rights needs elaboration, primarily because of its different forms and its significant exceptions. When a personally injured plaintiff seeks to argue that the injurious conduct violated the legal rights of others, the prohibition, beyond serving the usual objectives of standing, serves also to protect nonlitigants who may not wish to assert their own rights or would do so differently (and perhaps more effectively) if they became litigants. Major exceptions to that prohibition respond to this policy by allowing representation, even of constitutional rights, when the Court concludes that the absent third parties would benefit rather than suffer from a substantive decision. One important example of this exception is the case in which third parties would have difficulty asserting their own rights, as in NAACP v. ALABAMA (1958), where the CIVIL RIGHTS group was permitted to assert its members' right to remain anonymous. Another example is the case in which the disputed conduct affects special plaintiff–third party relationships in ways suggesting that the plaintiff and third-party interests coincide. Under this exception doctors can represent patient rights to abortion, private schools can represent parent rights to choose private education, and sellers can represent the rights of young consumers to buy beer or contraceptives.

The Court generally denies standing when persons constitutionally subject to regulation urge that the regulation would be unconstitutional in application to others. This rule preserves legislative policy in cases where the law is applied constitutionally. Again, however, there is an exception, invoked most often in FIRST AMENDMENT challenges of VAGUENESS and OVERBREADTH, when the law's very existence would significantly inhibit others from exercising important constitutional rights and thus deter them from mounting their own challenge.

A final example is the case in which uninjured representatives seek to champion the legal rights of injured persons they represent outside of litigation. Thus, associations, not injured themselves, may sue on behalf of their members' injuries, provided that the members would have standing, the associations seek to protect interests germane to their purposes, and the claims and requested relief do not require individual member participation. And a state, which normally lacks standing as *parens patriae* to represent the claims of individual citizens, or even of all its citizens in opposition to the federal government, may represent its citizens when the injury alleged substantially affects the state's general population, especially if suit by individual citizens seems unlikely.

Like other JUSTICIABILITY doctrines, standing rules often thwart attempts to induce federal courts to make or reform constitutional or other law. How often the rules have that result will depend not only on the articulated criteria of standing but also on the Supreme Court's receptivity to the substance of the underlying claims and its judgment of the desirability and likelihood of political solutions.

JONATHAN D. VARAT

Bibliography

NICHOL, GENE R., JR. 1984 Rethinking Standing. *California Law Review* 72:68–102.

SCOTT, KENNETH E. 1973 Standing in the Supreme Court: A Functional Analysis. *Harvard Law Review* 86:645–692.

VINING, JOSEPH 1978 *Legal Identity: The Coming of Age of Public Law.* New Haven, Conn.: Yale University Press.

STANLEY v. GEORGIA
394 U.S. 557 (1969)

Authorized by a SEARCH WARRANT, federal and state agents entered and searched Stanley's home for evidence of bookmaking activities. Instead they found film, which was used to convict him for possession of obscene material. The Supreme Court reversed, holding that mere possession of obscenity in one's home cannot constitutionally be made a crime.

Prior OBSCENITY decisions had recognized a legitimate state interest in regulating public dissemination of obscene materials. In *Stanley,* however, the Court recognized two fundamental constitutional rights that outweighed the state interest in regulating obscenity in a citizen's home: the FIRST AMENDMENT right to receive information and ideas, regardless of their social worth, and the constitutional right to be free from unwanted government intrusion into one's privacy.

As justification for interfering with these important individual rights, the state asserted the right to protect individuals from obscenity's effects. The Court rejected that argument, viewing such "protection" as an attempt to "control . . . a person's thoughts," a goal "wholly inconsistent with the philosophy of the First Amendment."

Justices POTTER J. STEWART, WILLIAM J. BRENNAN, and BYRON R. WHITE concurred in the result, on the ground that the SEARCH AND SEIZURE were outside the lawful scope of the officers' warrant, and thus violated Stanley's FOURTH AMENDMENT rights.

KIM MCLANE WARDLAW

STANTON, EDWIN M.
(1814–1869)

A prominent antebellum attorney, Edwin McMasters Stanton was an active member of the Supreme Court bar and was the chief government investigator and counsel in the California land claims cases. In 1859 he successfully defended Congressman Daniel Sickles in a murder trial with the then novel defense of temporary insanity.

In 1860 Stanton became JAMES BUCHANAN's lame duck ATTORNEY GENERAL. An ardent Unionist, Stanton urged support for the garrison at Fort Sumter and the arrest for TREASON of the South Carolina commissioners. During the interregnum Stanton secretly met with Republican senators informing them of the administration's complicity with secessionists. He also worked secretly with General Winfield Scott to move troops to protect Washington while preventing the shipment of arms to the South.

As secretary of war (1862–1868) Stanton vastly reduced corruption and political influence on promotions, while building a highly efficient military. Stanton was an early advocate of emancipation and the use of black troops. Zealous in supporting the Union, Stanton used the War Department to arrest civilians suspected of treason, disloyalty, or disrupting recruitment and rigorously enforced internal security. During the 1863 and 1864 elections Stanton furloughed troops so they could return home to vote, used the army to intimidate opponents, and allowed officers to campaign.

After ABRAHAM LINCOLN's assassination Stanton was ruthless in finding and prosecuting anyone connected with John Wilkes Booth's plot. Despite President ANDREW JOHNSON's opposition, Stanton supported the CIVIL RIGHTS ACT OF 1866 and the FREEDMAN'S BUREAU, while working closely with Congress to support MILITARY RECONSTRUCTION. Stanton's backing of generals sympathetic to congressional goals prevented Johnson from implementing his reconstruction program. Fear that Johnson would fire Stanton led to the TENURE OF OFFICE ACT and then to IMPEACHMENT proceedings when Johnson tried to replace Stanton. Stanton aided the impeachment managers by giving them war department documents and information, lobbying wavering senators, and writing "anonymous" editorials denouncing Johnson. After Johnson's acquittal Stanton resigned. In 1869 President ULYSSES S. GRANT nominated Stanton to the Supreme Court, but he died before confirmation.

PAUL FINKELMAN

Bibliography

THOMAS, BENJAMIN P. and HYMAN, HAROLD M. 1962 *Stanton: The Life and Times of Lincoln's Secretary of War.* New York: Knopf.

STARE DECISIS

(Latin: "to stand by decided [cases].") The DOCTRINE of *stare decisis,* one of the key elements of Anglo-American COMMON LAW, embodies the principle that PRECEDENTS are to be followed in the adjudication of cases. The substance of the law is revealed through the decisions of courts in cases between individuals or between an individual and the government, and adherence to precedent transforms the decisions in those cases into a settled body of public law. Once an issue of law has been resolved in a case by a court of competent JURISDICTION, the HOLDING in the case is determinative of the issue for that court and subordinate courts; and it offers guidance, as well, to courts of coordinate jurisdiction. Courts proceed, as a general rule, by following and applying precedents or else by distinguishing them (that is, by showing how the facts of the instant case render the precedent inapposite). Most frequently a court faces the question of which of two or more lines of precedent to follow. The doctrine of *stare decisis* lends stability and predictability to the legal order, but it is not absolute: courts may dispose of precedents that are outdated, or that have undesirable consequences, by OVERRULING them. The federal courts, and especially the Supreme Court, have tended in recent years to diminish the force of *stare decisis* in constitutional cases.

DENNIS J. MAHONEY

STATE

The DECLARATION OF INDEPENDENCE declares that the "united colonies" are, as they ought to be, "free and independent states." The term "states" was chosen to indicate their status as autonomous political communities. The state was the result of the SOCIAL COMPACT, binding man to man and subjecting all to rule by some part of the community. The term also carried a connotation, already obsolescent in England, of a republican form of government; the seventeenth-century British political writers with whose works the Americans were familiar had generally contrasted "state" with "monarchy" or "principality."

But the Declaration of Independence was, after all, the unanimous declaration of the *united* states. Although the Declaration proclaims that the states are "free and independent," they were not thereby made independent of one another. By the Declaration, the one American people assumes among the powers of the earth the separate and equal station to which it is entitled by natural and divine law. Thus is the American people declared to possess SOVEREIGNTY, and not the several states, although in the common usage, of the eighteenth as well as of the twentieth century, the term "state" refers to a sovereign entity.

The central paradox of American politics has always been, from the time of the Declaration and of the Constitution, the existence of ineradicable states within an indissoluble Union. The sovereignty of the people, from whom both the national and the state governments derive their just powers, is the basis for the distinctively American form of FEDERALISM. Neither is the central government the creature of the states nor do the states exist at the mercy of the central government, but both exercise those limited and delegate powers that are assigned them by the sovereign people.

Each of the original thirteen states had been founded and administered as a British colony prior to 1776. They had, therefore, established forms of government under their COLONIAL CHARTERS. During the Revolution, most of them adopted CONSTITUTIONS providing for government of the same persons and territory as the colonies had comprised. The fourteenth and fifteenth states, Vermont and Kentucky, had experienced provisional self-government before they were admitted to the Union. Before the ANNEXATION OF TEXAS, that state had revolted against Mexico and governed itself as an independent republic. California's brief existence as the "Bear Flag Republic" (1846) scarcely qualifies as independence or self-government; but, when the controversy over slavery prevented Congress from organizing the lands won in the Mexican War, California proceeded to adopt a constitution (1849) and to govern its own affairs until its admission to the Union (1850). Hawaii was an independent kingdom for centuries before American immigrants revolted against the native monarchy and engineered the annexation of those islands by the United States.

All of the rest of the states—thirty-two to date—have been formed out of the national dominion of the United States and have been admitted to the Union as states following a probationary period as TERRITORIES. The process by which the national dominion was to be settled and transformed into states was devised by THOMAS JEFFERSON and adopted by the CONTINENTAL CONGRESS as the ORDINANCE OF 1784, although that ordinance was never actually enforced. Essentially the same scheme was enacted in the NORTHWEST ORDINANCE (1787), which was the model for all subsequent treatment of the territories of the United States. At the CONSTITUTIONAL CONVENTION OF 1787 the delegates rejected GOUVERNEUR MORRIS's proposal that states formed from the western territories should have a status inferior to the original states, and they provided instead that new states should be admitted to the Union on terms of full equality with the existing states.

Under the ARTICLES OF CONFEDERATION the national government was entirely the creature of the state governments. The confederation derived its formal existence from a compact among the states, and the members of Congress were chosen by the state legislatures. Most of the delegates to the Constitutional Convention were convinced of the necessity of creating a national government directly responsible to the people of the nation. JAMES MADISON, for one, arrived in Philadelphia prepared to argue for a pure separation of state from national government, according to which the two tiers of government would be separately elected and separately responsible to the people in their respective spheres. But the Convention chose instead to give the institutions of the states a share in the government of the nation, and to provide, in the national constitution, for certain guarantees to the people of the states, including guarantees against their state governments.

In the Constitution, representatives in Congress are allocated to the states on the basis of population, and the state governments are left free to apportion them among districts and to provide for their election. Each state is allotted two senators, and until adoption of the SEVENTEENTH AMENDMENT (1913) the senators were chosen by the state legislatures. The President and vice-president are chosen by an ELECTORAL COLLEGE whose members are apportioned to, chosen by, and convened in the several states. The Constitution became effective only upon ratification by conventions in the several states, and amendment of the Constitution is impossible without the concurrence of the legislatures of (or conventions in) three-fourths of the states. And the TENTH AMENDMENT, adopted in 1791 as part of the BILL OF RIGHTS, reserves all governmental power not delegated to the national government by the Constitution to the states or the people.

On the other hand, Article I, section 10, prohibits the states from entering into treaties or alliances or granting LETTERS OF MARQUE AND REPRISAL; coining money, issuing BILLS OF CREDIT to circulate as currency, or making anything but gold or silver legal tender for payment of obligations; enacting EX POST FACTO laws or BILLS OF ATTAINDER, legislating to impair the OBLIGATION OF CONTRACTS, or conferring TITLES OF NOBILITY. The exercise of certain other powers by the states is made contingent upon the consent of Congress: taxation of imports or exports, maintenance of armies or navies, entering into INTERSTATE COMPACTS, and making war (unless actually invaded or imminently threatened by a foreign power). Moreover, the SUPREMACY CLAUSE subordinates the enactments of the states to the Constitution and to laws and treaties of the national government, and all state officers and judges are bound by oath to follow these, as the supreme law, whenever there is a conflict with state enactments or decisions.

But a proposal that the national Congress should have the power to review and "negative" state legislation failed to win a majority at the Constitutional Convention; and more drastic proposals that the states be abolished, or realigned, or reduced to the status of provinces or administrative districts were rejected almost without discussion. The Convention did not adopt the VIRGINIA PLAN's wording, granting the national Congress the power to legislate in any field wherein the states were "incompetent," which would effectively have made Congress the only judge of the limits of its own power, and instead listed the fields in which national legislation was, or might be, required.

The sphere of state authority that the Constitution left untouched was vast, and included almost every governmental function with which most citizens were likely to come into direct contact. The laws of property, of inheritance, of marriage, of contract, of debt, of liability for civil wrongs, of employer–employee (or master–servant) relations, of commercial transactions, of banking, of business incorporation, and of common police were left to the states. The law of crimes and punishments, except for crimes against the national government, on the high seas, or in the armed forces, was left to the states. The nineteenth-century French political scientist ALEXIS DE TOCQUEVILLE referred to these as functions of "administration," distinguishing them from such high political functions as national defense, foreign affairs, and acquisition and settlement of territory. But, precisely because the administrative functions of government are those with which the people are in daily contact, Tocqueville concluded that the affections and loyalties of the people would always be directed first to the states in preference to the national government.

The primary loyalty to the state, rather than to the Union, was one of the chief problems of American politics at least until the end of the Civil War. When regional interests, particularly regional economic interests, ran contrary to the course of national legislation, politicians at the state level frequently attempted to rally the people to the cause of disunion. There were many delegates to the HARTFORD CONVENTION (1814) who advocated the SECESSION of the New England states to protest the War of 1812, and the TARIFF ACT OF 1828 led to South Carolina's attempt at NULLIFICATION. Politicians attempted to justify such acts by resort to THEORIES OF THE UNION that regarded the national government as the product of a compact among the states, the breach of which freed the offended states from their obligations.

The great tragedy of American constitutional history was the coincidence of state loyalties with attachment to the peculiar institution of human slavery. In 1861 eleven states attempted to secede from the federal union and to form a confederacy in which the existence of both slavery and state sovereignty would be permanently guaranteed. Some adherents of ABOLITIONIST CONSTITUTIONAL THOUGHT were content to permit the secession on the ground that the Union was better off without the slave states. Some national politicians, including President JAMES BUCHANAN, were willing to tolerate the secession on the ground that the national government lacked constitutional authority to coerce the states.

President ABRAHAM LINCOLN rejected Buchanan's position, arguing that the federal Union was the permanent creation of the whole American people and dating the creation of the Union from the Declaration of Independence. In this way, Lincoln tied the preservation of the Union to the antislavery cause, making the Civil War not a mere war between the states but a struggle to complete the constitution of the Republic upon the foundation of natural rights and the consent of all the governed, in accordance with the principles of the Declaration. The completion of the Constitution required the addition of the THIRTEENTH AMENDMENT (abolishing slavery), the FOURTEENTH AMENDMENT (guaranteeing individual rights against state interference), and the FIFTEENTH AMENDMENT (prohibiting RACIAL DISCRIMINATION as a limitation on VOTING RIGHTS). The settlement of the crisis that had caused the Civil War necessitated these additional constitutional guarantees to the people against abuses by the state governments.

However, neither the Civil War nor the constitutional amendments adopted in its aftermath transferred significant additional power to the national government. Although there were new constitutional restrictions on the states, and although the national Congress was given power to enforce those restrictions, the distribution of substantive powers within the federal system remained essentially unaltered. What did change was the attitude of the people toward the two levels of government: CITIZENSHIP of the United States became, in most of the country, the primary source of political allegiance, and state citizenship became secondary. Constitutional expression of this change was embodied in the SIXTEENTH AMENDMENT (authorizing an income tax as an independent source of revenue for the national government) and the SEVENTEENTH AMENDMENT (providing for DIRECT ELECTION of United States senators).

In PROGRESSIVE CONSTITUTIONAL THOUGHT it was fashionable to speak of the states as the "laboratories" of the federal system, where experiments in political reform could be carried out. Like the abolition of slavery, all of the important reform measures of the Progressive era began at the state level and were enacted at the national level, if at all, only after successful adoption in the states. Such measures included women's suffrage, direct elections, and the PROHIBITION of alcoholic beverages.

In the twentieth century the states suffered a radical change of relative status. That change had two aspects: the expansion of national power into fields previously regarded as belonging to the states, and the subordination of the states in the administration of national programs. The change of relative status was probably an inevitable consequence of the shift of loyalties as well as of the increased mobility, communication, and interaction attendant upon industrialization.

World War I and the Great Depression of the 1930s were great national emergencies, and the national government strained the limits of its power to effect national measures in response. Ultimately, the COMMERCE CLAUSE became the source of constitutional authority for comprehensive national regulation of the economy, and ECONOMIC REGULATION based on that authority received the approbation of the Supreme Court beginning with the WAGNER ACT CASES (1937). The last vestiges of limitation inherent in the concept of INTERSTATE COMMERCE were swept away in WICKARD V. FILBURN (1941). By the middle of the twentieth century it was no longer true that state law alone governed most ordinary economic relationships. In the 1960s the commerce power became the basis for national CIVIL RIGHTS legislation and had already become the basis for a NATIONAL POLICE POWER generally.

If there is any type of activity that could with certainty be distinguished from "commerce," that would be the activity of governing. Whether on the basis of that distinction, or on some more general basis in the idea of federalism, the state and local governments were long excluded from national regulation under the commerce clause. NATIONAL LEAGUE OF CITIES V. USERY (1976) made that exclusion a matter of constitutional law, at least insofar as the activity that the national government sought to regulate was traditionally or inherently a governmental function and not just a publicly operated business. However, over vigorous dissent, a narrow majority overruled *Usery* in GARCIA V. SAN ANTONIO METROPOLITAN TRANSIT AUTHORITY (1984), and the exclusion was thereby judicially abolished.

The TAXING AND SPENDING POWER and the GENERAL WELFARE CLAUSE form the constitutional basis for coopting the states as administrators of national programs. The Constitution gives Congress the power to lay and collect taxes for the purpose of providing for the general welfare of the United States. Under this authority, Congress may appropriate public monies, raised through taxation, for programs beyond the scope of the ordinary legislative power and may make the appropriation conditional on compliance with nationally established guidelines. Beginning with the SHEPPARD-TOWNER ACT (1921), Congress has appropriated money to the states to support programs conforming to national standards. Such appropriations, and the standards upon which they are conditioned, are virtually immune to constitutional challenge because of judicial rules of STANDING. Thus in cases like FROTHINGHAM V. MELLON (1923) and HELVERING V. DAVIS (1937) neither states nor taxpayers could state a case permitting review of FEDERAL GRANTS-IN-AID or the regulations accompanying them. One result of this is that by the mid-1980s federal grants made up a significant share of the revenues of the state governments and federal regulations dictated the operation of state programs in highway construction, traffic control, driver licensing health care, public relief, education, and most other areas.

Twentieth-century court decisions have also served to change the status of the states. The Fourteenth Amendment's guarantee that the states could not deprive persons of life, liberty, or property without due process of law has formed the basis for federal court intervention in many substantive areas. At the beginning of the century, state economic regulation was often held unconstitutional when it was found to conflict with the due process clause. Later in the century, through the INCORPORATION DOCTRINE, the Supreme Court extended SUBSTANTIVE DUE PROCESS protection to most of the rights that the first ten amendments protect against national government intrusion. In the 1950s and 1960s the Supreme Court used the concept of PROCEDURAL DUE PROCESS effectively to rewrite the state codes of criminal procedure, and in the 1970s and 1980s it expanded SUBSTANTIVE DUE PROCESS to preclude state interference with such RIGHTS OF PRIVACY as abortion and REPRODUCTIVE AUTONOMY.

Nevertheless, the twentieth century did not herald a radical reduction of state power and influence. Government power and government expenditure have grown continuously at all levels; but the states have been largely displaced or coopted in the exercise of some functions as they have expanded their reach into other areas previously left to private activity and enterprise. Although both President RICHARD M. NIXON and President RONALD REAGAN publicly advocated a "new federalism" in which the states and their governments would enjoy greater freedom of action, the tendency toward centralization has continued, and state governments have attempted to maintain their importance not by recovering autonomy in old areas but by expanding their activity into new areas.

DENNIS J. MAHONEY

Bibliography

ELAZAR, DANIEL J. 1972 *American Federalism: A View from the States,* 2nd ed. New York: Thomas Y. Crowell Co.

GOLDWIN, ROBERT, ED. 1962 *A Nation of States.* Chicago: Rand-McNally.

GRODZINS, MORTON 1966 *The American System: A New View of Government in the United States,* ed. Daniel J. Elazar. Chicago: Rand-McNally.

HAWKINS, ROBERT B., ED. 1982 *American Federalism: A New Partnership for the Republic.* San Francisco: Institute for Contemporary Studies.

MORLEY, FELIX 1959 *Freedom and Federalism.* Chicago: Henry Regnery Co.

SANFORD, TERRY 1967 *Storm over the States.* New York: McGraw-Hill.

VILE, M. J. C. 1961 *The Structure of American Federalism.* Oxford: Oxford University Press.

STATE ACTION

The phrase "state action," a term of art in our constitutional law, symbolizes the rule—or supposed rule—that constitutional guarantees of human rights are effective only against *governmental* action impairing those rights. (The word "state," in the phrase, denotes any unit or element of government, and not simply one of the American states, though the "state action" concept has been at its most active, and most problematic, with respect to these.) The problems have been many and complex; the "state action" doctrine has not reached anything near a satisfactory condition of rationality.

A best first step toward exploring the problems hidden in the "state action" phrase may be a look at its development in constitutional history. The development has revolved around the first section of the FOURTEENTH AMENDMENT, wherein the problem is in effect put forward by the words here italicized:

> All persons born or naturalized in the United States, and subject to the jurisdiction thereof, are citizens of the United States and of the State wherein they reside. *No State* shall make or enforce any law which shall abridge the privileges or immunities of citizens of the United States; *nor shall any State* deprive any person of life, liberty, or property, without due process of law; nor deny to any person within its jurisdiction the equal protection of the laws.

An early "state action" case under this section, *Ex parte Virginia* (1880), raised an audacious claim as to the limiting effect of the words emphasized above. A Virginia judge had been charged under a federal statute forbidding racial exclusion from juries. He was not directed by a state statute to perform this racial exclusion. The judge argued that the action was not that of the state of Virginia, but rather the act of an official, proceeding wrongfully on his own. On this theory, a "state" had not denied EQUAL PROTECTION. The Fourteenth Amendment, the judge contended, did not therefore forbid the conduct charged, or authorize Congress to make it criminal. The Supreme Court, however, declined to take such high ground.

"The constitutional provision," it said, ". . . must mean that no agency of the state, or of the officers or agents by whom its powers are exerted, shall deny . . . equal protection of the laws." But probably the only fully principled and maximally clear rule as to "state action" would have been that the "state," as a state, does not "act" except by its official enactments—and so does not "act" when one of its officers merely abuses his power. "Fully principled and maximally clear"—but, like so many such "rules," aridly formalistic, making practical nonsense of any constitutional rule it limits. There were gropings, around the year of this case, toward a "state action" requirement with bite, but the modern history of the concept starts with the CIVIL RIGHTS CASES of 1883, wherein many modern problems were foreshadowed. In the CIVIL RIGHTS ACT OF 1875, Congress had enacted "[t]hat all persons . . . shall be entitled to the full and equal enjoyment of the accommodations, advantages, facilities, and privileges of inns, public conveyances on land or water, theatres, and other places of public amusement . . . [regardless of race]."

Persons were indicted for excluding blacks from hotels, theaters, and railroads. The Court considered that the only possible source of congressional power to make such a law was section 5 of the Fourteenth Amendment: "The Congress shall have power to enforce, by appropriate legislation, the provisions of this article." This section the Court saw as authorizing only those laws which *directly* enforced the guarantees of the amendment's section 1 (quoted above), which in turn referred only to a *state.* The amendment therefore did not warrant, the Court held, any congressional dealing with racially discriminatory actions of individuals or CORPORATIONS.

Few judicial opinions seem to rest on such solid ground; at the end of Justice JOSEPH BRADLEY's performance, the reader is likely to feel, "Q.E.D." But this feeling of apparent demonstration is attained, as often it is, by the passing over in silence of disturbing facts and thoughts. Many of these were brought out in the powerful dissent of Justice JOHN MARSHALL HARLAN.

One of the cases involved racial discrimination by a railroad. The American railroads, while they were building, were generally given the power of EMINENT DOMAIN. Eminent domain is a sovereign power, enjoyed par excellence by the state, and given by the state to "private" persons for public purposes looked on as important to the state; the Fifth Amendment's language illustrates the firmness of the background assumption that "private property" shall be taken, even with JUST COMPENSATION, only for PUBLIC USE. The American railroads were, moreover, very heavily assisted by public subsidy from governmental units at all levels. Both these steps—the clothing of railroad corporations with eminent-domain power, and their subsidization out of public funds—were justified, both rhetorically and as a matter of law, on the grounds that the railroads were *public instrumentalities,* fulfilling the classic state function of furnishing a transportation system. Regulation of railroads was undertaken under the same theory.

Railroads and hotel-keepers, moreover, followed the so-called common callings, traditionally entailing an obligation to take and carry, or to accommodate, all well-behaved persons able to pay. The *withdrawal* of protection of such a right to equal treatment might be looked on as "state action," and Congress might well decide, as a practical matter, either that the right had been wholly withdrawn as to blacks (which was in many places the fact of the matter) or that the state action supporting these rights of access was insufficient and required supplementation; only the most purposefully narrow construction could deny to such supplementation the name of "enforcement."

Indeed, this line of thought, whether as to the *Civil Rights Cases* or as to all other "equal protection" cases, is fraught with trouble for the whole "state action" doctrine, in nature as in name. "Action" is an exceedingly inapt word for the "denial" of "protection." Protection against lynching was, for example, usually "denied" by "inaction." Inaction by the state is indeed the classic form of "denial of protection." The Civil Rights Cases majority did not read far enough, even for the relentless literalist; it read as far as "nor shall any State . . ." but then hastily closed the book before reading what follows: ". . . *deny* to any person . . . the equal *protection* of the laws." Contrary to the majority's reading, the state's affirmative obligation of protection should have extended to the protection of the traditional rights of resort to public transport and common inns; it was notorious that the very people (blacks) whose "equal protection" was central to the Fourteenth Amendment were commonly the only victims of nominally "private" denial of these rights.

Justice Harlan pointed out that in its first sentence, conferring CITIZENSHIP on the newly emancipated slaves, the first section of the Fourteenth Amendment did not use any language in any way suggesting a "state action" requirement, so that there was not even the verbal support for the "state action" requirement that the Court had found in the other phrases of that section. The question then became, in Harlan's view, what the legal consequences of "citizenship" were; for purposes of the particular case at hand, he said:

> But what was secured to colored citizens of the United States—as between them and their respective States—by the national grant to them of State citizenship? With what rights, privileges, or immunities did this grant invest them? There is one, if there be no other—exemption from race discrimination in respect of any civil right belonging to citizens of the white race in the same State. . . . Citizenship in this country necessarily imports at least equality of civil rights among citizens of every race in the same State. It is fundamental in American citizenship that, in respect of such rights, there shall be no discrimination by the State, or its officers, or by individuals or corporations exercising public functions or authority, against any citizen because of his race or previous condition of servitude. . . .

There is a third, most interesting aspect to Harlan's dissent. The majority had summarily rejected the argument that under the THIRTEENTH AMENDMENT—forbidding SLAVERY and involuntary servitude and giving Congress enforcement power—racial exclusion from public places was one of the "badges and incidents" of slavery. Harlan argued that forced segregation in public accommodations was a BADGE OF SERVITUDE, and he pointed out that no "state action" requirement could be found in the words of the Thirteenth Amendment. This argument was plowed under and was heard from no more for many decades, but it is of great interest because it was revived and made the basis of decision in a leading case in the 1960s, JONES V. ALFRED H. MAYER CO. (1968).

The *Civil Rights Cases,* in the majority opinion, brushed past contentions that were in no way frivolous. Very many discriminatory actions of public scope are taken by persons or corporations enjoying special favor from government and heavily regulated by government; one cannot easily see their actions as isolated from public power. "Denial of equal protection," the central constitutional wrong in racial cases, seems to refer at least as naturally to inaction as it does to action. If any positive rights at all inhere in citizenship—and if there are no such rights, the citizenship clause is a mere matter of nomenclature—these rights are set up by the Fourteenth Amendment without limitation as to the source of their impairment. Nevertheless, the holdings and doctrine of the *Civil Rights Cases* fell on a thirstily receptive society. The "state action" doctrine became one of the principal reliances of a racist nation, North as well as South.

In a society where so much of access to goods and values is managed by nominally "private" persons and corporations—railroads, restaurants, streetcars, cinemas, even food and clothing—a protection that runs only against the government, strictly defined, can work out to very little effective protection. If the official justice system is hampered by inconvenient constitutional safeguards, the sheriff can play cards while the lynch mob forms, and there is "no state action." A nightclub may refuse to serve a black celebrity, and there is "no state action." The "state action" doctrine protected from constitutional scrutiny an enormous network of racial exclusion and humiliation, characterizing both North and South.

Paradoxically, the "state action" requirement may

for a long time have been more important to the maintenance of northern racism than to that of the cruder racism of the South. The South developed SEGREGATION by law, in all phases of public life, and this regime was broadly validated by the notorious 1896 decision in PLESSY V. FERGUSON. For complex political reasons—and perhaps because of a faintly lingering adherence to scraps of Civil War idealism—segregation by official law was not widely imposed in the North. But the practices of real-estate agents, mortgage lenders, restaurant keepers, and a myriad of other "private" people and corporations added up to a pervasive custom of racial segregation in many phases of life, a custom less perfectly kept than the official legal dictates of the southern regime, but effectively barring most blacks from much of the common life of the communities they lived in.

A striking case in point was *Dorsey v. Stuyvesant Town Corporation* (1949–1950). The Metropolitan Life Insurance Company, having much money to invest, struck a complicated deal with the State and the City of New York. The contemplated end-result was the conversion of a large section of New York City—from 14th to 23rd Streets, and from Avenue A to the East River—into a vast complex of apartments, to be owned and run by a Metropolitan subsidiary. By formal statute and ordinance, the State and City acquiesced in this scheme, agreeing to use (and later using) the sovereign "eminent domain" power to acquire title to all the needed land, which was, as prearranged, later transferred to Metropolitan. Again by formal arrangement, a quarter-century tax exemption was granted on "improvements"—that is to say, on the immensely valuable apartment buildings. The public easement on certain streets was extinguished, and control over them turned over to Stuyvesant Town Corporation, a Metropolitan subsidiary; various water, sewage, and fire-protection arrangements were altered to suit the needs of the project. And all this was done, visibly and pridefully, as a joint effort of public and "private" enterprise; politicians as well as insurance men took bows. Then, when the whole thing was built, with "title" safely vested in "private" hands, Stuyvesant Town Corporation announced that no blacks need apply for apartments. The suit of a black applicant reached the highest court of New York, and that court held, 4–3, that there was not enough "state action" in all this to make applicable the Fourteenth Amendment prohibition of racial discrimination. The Supreme Court of the United States denied CERTIORARI.

The *Stuyvesant Town* case illustrates very well what could be done with the "state action" formula. With the fullest cooperation from government at all levels, as much of any city as might be desired (strictly public buildings alone excepted) could be turned into a "whites only" preserve. With the necessary cooperation, the process could be extended to a whole county, or a whole state. If they were prudent, the political partners in such deals would not put anything in writing about the racial exclusion contemplated.

But the essentiality of the "state action" formula to the success of northern racism must not obscure its considerable strategic importance even in the South. Segregation by law had in the main been validated, and this was the South's main reliance, but there were gaps, and the "state action" formula filled them in.

First, there was the role of nominally "private" violence against blacks, as the ultimate weapon of the racist regime—with lynching at the top of the arsenal's inventory. At this point the disregard of the Fourteenth Amendment's words, "nor shall any State *deny* . . . equal *protection* of the laws," is most surprising. But for a long time a whole lot of seemingly serious people saw no "denial of protection" in the de facto denial of protection to blacks against a great deal of "private" violence.

Second, outright racial residential zoning by law—just one form of segregation—had been struck down by the Supreme Court, in the 1917 case of BUCHANAN V. WARLEY. The opinion in that case does not adequately distinguish *Plessy v. Ferguson,* but it was the law, and nominally "private" methods of racial zoning had often to be resorted to in the South—just as they were, pervasively, in the North. Real-estate agents and mortgage banks played their accustomed part; until astonishingly recent times, the actually published codes of "ethics" of "realtors" forbade (under some transparent euphemism) actions tending toward spoiling the racial homogeneity of any neighborhood. But more was needed, and that more was found—South and North—in the "racially RESTRICTIVE COVENANT." These "covenants" were neither necessarily nor commonly mere casual contractual arrangements between parties dickering at random. Very commonly, when an "addition" was "subdivided," all the first deeds restricted ownership or occupancy, or both, to whites only—or to white Gentiles only, or to white Gentiles of northern European extraction. These covenants, recorded at the courthouse in a registry furnished by the State for this purpose, were ordained by many states' laws to "run with the land"—that is, they had to be put in all subsequent deeds forever, and usually were binding whether so inserted or not, since any buyer, examining title, could find them in the title-chain. These "covenants"—often functionally equivalent to racial zoning by law, enforced by court orders, and kept on file at the courthouse—were for a long time looked on as "merely private" action, in no way traceable to the state, and so not amenable to constitutional command.

A third and even more important use of the "state action" doctrine (or a doctrine closely akin) was peculiar to the South, and was the rotting-out base of southern politics for generations. The FIFTEENTH AMENDMENT forbade racial exclusions from voting—but, like the Fourteenth, it directed its prohibition at governments: "The right of citizens of the United States to vote shall not be denied or abridged by the United States or by any State on account of race, color, or previous condition of servitude."

The general response in the South to this politically inconvenient constitutional mandate was the all-white Democratic PRIMARY ELECTION. This primary was colloquially known as "the election"; its nominees virtually always won in the November balloting, when all the whites who had voted in the Democratic primary were expected to vote for its nominee, and enough did so to wipe out any scattered Republican votes, including the votes of those blacks who could surmount the other barriers to their voting—LITERACY TESTS, difficult registration procedures, and even more violent discouragements. This plain fraud on the Constitution did not rest wholly on the concept that the action of the Democratic party was not "state action," but the even bolder idea behind it—the idea, namely, that the practical substitution of a "party" election for the regular election could altogether escape the Fifteenth Amendment mandate, even when the State commanded the all-whiteness of the Party—was related in more than spirit to the "state action" doctrine as illustrated in the Stuyvesant Town case. Its basis was the thought that racial voting requirements were not "official" if a nominally "private" organization was put in as a buffer between the wrong done and state power. And the all-white primary in the end had to rely (vainly, as at last it turned out) on the "state action" requirement.

The "state action" doctrine is not a mere interesting footnote in constitutional law. It has served as an absolutely essential and broadly employed component in the means by which black equality, theoretically guaranteed by the post-Civil War amendments, was made to mean next to nothing. It could do this because of the fact that, in our society, vast powers over all of life are given to formally private organizations—the Democratic party, the realtors' association, the mortgage bank, the telephone company, and so on—and because, further and indispensably, the courts were (as is illustrated by a line of decisions from the *Civil Rights Cases* to the Stuyvesant Town case) willing in case after case to gloss over the fact that large organized enterprises can rarely if ever be successfully conducted without very considerable help from the government. Intermixed in these racial cases was, moreover, the disregard of the Fourteenth Amendment's textual condemnation of governmental *inaction,* where that inaction amounted to *denial of equal protection,* as inaction obviously may. And constitutional guarantees that were implicit rather than explicit as limits on government were mostly ignored. A doctrine that went to the length of seeming to make of lynching a thing untouched by the Constitution and (as in UNITED STATES V. CRUIKSHANK, 1875) untouchable by Congress was and could be again a powerful tool indeed for bringing national human rights, nationally enjoyed, to nothing, on the plane of life as lived.

The "state action" requirement thus served the major strategic goal of a nation to which racism, in practice, was utterly essential. But even outside the field of race, its incidence, though spotty, was wide-ranging. As late as 1951, in *Collins v. Hardyman,* the Supreme Court, obviously under the influence of the doctrine though not directly relying on it, forcibly construed a federal statute, in plain contradiction to the law's clear terms, as not to reach the "private" and violent breaking up of a political meeting of citizens.

But a strong countercurrent developed in the 1940s. Without entire consistency, the Supreme Court uttered a striking series of decisions that promised to clip the claws of the "state action" requirement. The Court declared the all-white Democratic primary unlawful in SMITH V. ALLWRIGHT (1944) and extended this ruling in TERRY V. ADAMS (1953) to a local primary serving the same function under another name and form. MARSH V. ALABAMA (1946) held that the FIRST AMENDMENT, as incorporated into the Fourteenth, forbade the barring of Jehovah's Witnesses from distributing leaflets in a company-owned town. And SHELLEY V. KRAEMER (1948) held that judicial enforcement of restrictive covenants was unlawful.

In the "white primary" cases the Court was doing no more than refusing to persevere in self-induced blindness to an obvious fraud on the Fifteenth Amendment. But *Marsh v. Alabama* suggested that the formality of "ownership" could not immunize from constitutional scrutiny the performance of a governmental function—an idea big with possibility. And the

Shelley case even more profoundly stirred the foundations. Of course it was difficult to say that judicial enforcement of a racial-restrictive covenant, recorded at the courthouse, with the attendant implication that such covenants are not (as some others are) "against public policy," did not amount to "state action of some kind"—the requirement as worded in the fountainhead *Civil Rights Cases* of 1883. The difficulty in assimilation of *Shelley* arose from the fact that "state action of some kind" underpins and in one way or another enforces every nominally "private" action; the states had facilitated and lent their aid, indeed, to the very acts of discrimination considered in the 1883 cases. *Shelley,* therefore, forced a more searching analysis of the theory of "state action"; academic commentators became exceedingly eager and thorough, and in later decisions the Court became more willing to find "state action" and to move toward a fundamental doctrinal revision.

This process was accelerated by the civil rights movement that gained strength in the late 1950s, and grew to major force in the 1960s. In 1954, the famous case of BROWN V. BOARD OF EDUCATION had outlawed racial segregation in the public schools; a number of other decisions had extended this rule to all forms of segregation imposed by law or by uncontestable official action. Though enforcement of these decisions was to be difficult, the first of two principal jural supports of American racism—legal prohibition of participation by blacks in the common society—had crumbled. Naturally attention turned—whether with the aim of continuing racism or of completing its demolition—to the second of the pillars of American racism, the "state action" requirement.

Segregation and state action were now clearly seen to have a close functional similarity. Before the decisions following *Brown,* the blacks in a typical southern town could not eat in the good restaurants because state law commanded their exclusion. After these decisions, the proprietors of the restaurants, by and large, went on excluding blacks. (In this they were simply following a practice widely followed in the North already). There was a difference in legal theory, but no difference to the black people. The city-owned bus system could not make black people sit in the back—but most bus companies were "private" in form; seating in the back was "privately" commanded.

The resistance to this widespread public segregation under "private" form was led (actively in part and symbolically throughout) by Dr. Martin Luther King, Jr. Thousands of black people—most, but not all, young—defied the system by "sitting-in"—insisting upon service at "private" establishments open to the general public. They were in great numbers convicted of "crimes" selected with careful attention to the appearance of neutrality, such as "trespass after warning" or BREACH OF THE PEACE, and their cases reached the Supreme Court in some number.

The net result up to about 1965 was a considerable practical loosening up of the "state action" requirement, but no satisfactory theoretical reworking of that doctrine. A very few examples must be selected from the abundant case law.

The 1961 case of BURTON V. WILMINGTON PARKING AUTHORITY is an interesting example. The parking authority, a state agency, leased space in its parking building to a restaurateur, who forthwith refused to serve blacks. One might have thought it all but frivolous to contend that "state action of some kind" was absent here. The state had gone with open eyes into a transaction that empowered the restaurateur to insult and inconvenience citizens, in a public building owned by itself, and its police stood ready to make his rule stick. The state had done this—in effect certainly, if not in intent—for rent money. It had had the easy recourse of inserting in the lease a provision against racial discrimination; one has to wonder how the omission of that provision, obviously available under "the laws," can be anything but a "denial" of "equal protection of the laws," on the part of government. Yet the Court majority, though striking down the discrimination in the very case, roamed back and forth amongst the minutiae of facts—gas, service for the boiler-room, responsibility for structural repairs—and carefully confined its ruling to a lease of public property "in the manner and for the purpose shown to have been the case here. . . ." Still, the Wilmington case might have contributed toward some generality of constitutional theory.

As the "sit-in" issue heated up, however, the Court became even more evasive of the central issues. As cases reached the Court in great numbers, no "sit-in" conviction was ever affirmed. But neither the whole Court nor any majority ever reached and decided the central issue—whether *Shelley v. Kraemer* fairly implied that the knowing state use of state power to enforce discrimination, in publicly open facilities, constituted such action of the state as "denied equal protection of the laws." Instead the cases were decided on collateral grounds peculiar to each of them.

The culminating case was BELL V. MARYLAND (1964). Trespass convictions of Maryland civil-rights "sitters-in" were reversed, on the grounds (available by chance) that a newly enacted Maryland antidiscrimination statute might be held, in the state courts, to "abate" prosecution for prior attempts to get the service now guaranteed; nothing was actually decided on the more fundamental issues. Six Justices reached the "state action" issue, but of those six, three would have found it and three would not.

At this dramatic moment, with indefinite postponement of a major doctrinal decision seemingly impossible, Congress stepped in and solved the immediate problem, by passing the CIVIL RIGHTS ACT OF 1964, Title 2 of which made unlawful nearly all the discriminatory exclusions that had generated the sit-in prosecutions, making future prosecutions of sit-ins impossible. Then, in 1964, in *Hamm v. City of Rock Hill,* the Court held that the act compelled dismissal of all such prosecutions begun before its passage. Thus vanished the immediate problem of the sit-ins, and of many other claims to nondiscrimination previously based purely on the Constitution. It is noteworthy that Congress chose to base this Title 2, dealing with PUBLIC ACCOMMODATIONS, mainly on the COMMERCE CLAUSE rather than on the Fourteenth Amendment. This legislative decision reflected uncertainty as to whether the Court could be persuaded to overrule the 1883 *Civil Rights Cases,* which had severely limited congressional power to enforce the Fourteenth Amendment. In HEART OF ATLANTA MOTEL V. UNITED STATES (1964) and KATZENBACH V. MCCLUNG (1964) the Court construed the 1964 provisions broadly, and upheld them under the commerce clause theory that Congress had emphasized. The public accommodations crisis was over, and with it the really agonizing social crisis as to "state action."

Nevertheless, important problems continued to present themselves after 1964. It seemed for a time that, though no longer under the intense pressure of the public accommodations issue, the Court might be moving along the road toward relaxation of the state action requirement—a road along which travel had begun at least as early as the cases of *Smith v. Allwright* (1944—knocking out the all-white Democratic primary), *Marsh v. Alabama* (1946—the "company-town" case), and *Shelley v. Kraemer* (1948—the case of the racial-restriction covenants). (Indeed, no case actually denying relief on the "no-state-action" ground was decided by the Supreme Court from 1906 to 1970, except the 1935 case upholding the white primary, overruled nine years later).

In 1966 the Court held, in *Evans v. Newton,* that a huge public park in the center of Macon, Georgia, could no longer be operated as a park "for whites only," pursuant to the directions in the 1911 will of the man who had given it to the city, even though the city, for the purpose of seeing this all-white status maintained, had resigned as trustee, and had acquiesced in the appointment of a set of "private" trustees. In *Amalgamated Food Employees v. Logan Valley Plaza* (1968) the Court applied *Marsh v. Alabama* to hold a large SHOPPING CENTER subject to the First Amendment, and REITMAN V. MULKEY (1967) struck down under the Fourteenth Amendment a California constitutional amendment that would have forbidden state or local "fair" (i.e., anti-racist) housing ordinances until such time as the state constitution might be amended again—a process substantially more difficult than the enactment of ordinary legislation. This opinion, by Justice BYRON R. WHITE, encouraged much hope, because it explicitly undertook to judge this state constitutional amendment "in terms of its 'immediate objective,' its 'ultimate effect,' and its 'historical context and the conditions existing prior to its enactment.' " This attitude, if adhered to, would in every case bring the "state action" question down to the earth of reality. The Court would recognize the impact of formal state "neutrality" on the actual patterns of American racism, and would ask in each case whether such seeming "neutrality" operated as a *denial of equal protection* to the group principally marked for protection. This hope was further encouraged in 1969 in *Hunter v. Erickson* wherein the Court struck down an Akron, Ohio, requirement that fair-housing ordinances run an especially difficult gauntlet before they became effective; it was especially striking that Justices JOHN MARSHALL HARLAN and POTTER STEWART, who had dissented in *Reitman,* found the Akron provision too much, because on its face it discriminated against anti-racist laws.

But the current of doctrine changed after President RICHARD M. NIXON made the most of his chance to put his stamp on the Court. The change was signaled by the 1970 decision in EVANS V. ABNEY, a follow-up to the first Macon park case, *Evans v. Newton,* above. After the Newton decision, the heirs of the donor of the park applied for a reverter to them. The Court held this time that the state court's decision in their favor, in effect imposing a penalty on the citizens of Macon for their being unable under the Fourteenth Amendment to keep the park all-white, did not constitute "such state action" as to implicate the equal protection clause.

In 1971, in PALMER V. THOMPSON, the Court upheld the City of Jackson in its closing the city swimming pools and leasing one of them to the "private" YMCA, rather than having blacks swim in them. Here the Court found no state encouragement of discrimination, although the pools had been closed in response to a desegregation order. This was a total turn-about, in just four years, from the *Reitman v. Mulky* resolution to tie the operation of state-action law to the facts of life, and Justice White, the author of the *Reitman* opinion, dissented, with three other pre-Nixon Justices.

In 1974 the Court decided JACKSON V. METROPOLITAN EDISON COMPANY. A heavily regulated "private" electric company, enjoying a monopoly and a state-issued certificate of public convenience, terminated service to a customer without offering her any chance to be heard. This practice was allowed by a "tariff" on file with and at the least acquiesced in by the Public Utilities Commission. Justice WILLIAM H. REHNQUIST's opinion for the Court found insufficient "state action" in any of this to implicate the DUE PROCESS clause. This opinion and judgment, if adhered to in all their implications, would put us at least as far back as the 1883 Civil Rights Cases. Then, in 1976, HUDGENS V. NATIONAL LABOR RELATION BOARD explicitly overruled the *Logan Valley Shopping Center* case and made authoritative for the time being a very narrow view of *Marsh v. Alabama.*

Meanwhile, however, a new doctrinal thread had become visible. In the 1883 *Civil Rights Cases* the first Justice Harlan had argued that the Thirteenth Amendment, which contains no language to support a state-action requirement, proscribes all "badges and incidents" of slavery—which, historically, would mean a great many if not all racially discriminatory and degrading actions. This argument was a long time in coming into its own, but in 1968, in *Jones v. Alfred H. Mayer Co.,* the Court made it the ground of a decision upholding an old act of Congress which the Court interpreted to command nondiscrimination in the sale of housing. And in 1976, GRIFFIN V. BRECKENRIDGE, overruling *Collins v. Hardyman,* based decision solidly on the Thirteenth Amendment, holding that the amendment authorizes Congress to secure its beneficiaries against "racially discriminatory private action aimed at depriving them of . . . basic rights. . . ." Under the very formula of the 1883 *Civil Rights Cases* themselves—Congress may "enforce" only that which is substantively there—this should imply a large substantive content in the Thirteenth Amendment, far beyond literal "slavery." In RUNYON V. MCCRARY (1976) the Court extended much the same rationale to the condemnation of racial exclusion from a "private, commercially operated, nonsectarian" school.

"State action" doctrine has remained intractable to being made rational. What is wanted is attention to these points:

1. In almost any impingement by one person or more on another person or more, there is some contribution by the state: empowerment, support, or threatened support. Thus the presence or absence of "state action" is not a "test" at all; this has led to the spinning out of enormous series of subtests, hard to express and even harder to comprehend, none of which has much if any warrant in law.

2. Concomitantly, "state action" may not legitimately be confined—as the Supreme Court's recent opinions have confined it—to one or more neatly defined categories such as "command," "encouragement," or "public function." One may identify ten ways in which so infinitely complicated and subtle a being as the "state" may act—and the "state" may then act in an eleventh and then in a twelfth way—*all* "state action."

3. There is no warrant whatever in law for the assumption that "state action," to be significant, must be at a *high level* of involvement, or that a *very close* "nexus" must be found between "state action" and the wrong complained of.

4. Many constitutional guarantees do not explicitly require "state action" as a component. The modern "state action" requirement purported to draw its life from the words of the Fourteenth Amendment. Many rights and relationships set up by the Constitution and enforceable by Congress do not refer to the state at all, for example, the prohibition of slavery (and, as now held, its badges and incidents), the right to vote for congressmen and senators, the RIGHT TO TRAVEL. It is only custom-thought, which usually means half-thought, that would think it obvious that an impediment to INTERSTATE COMMERCE would be unconstitutional only if it were state-created.

5. A citizen of the United States should be regarded as having *relational* rights—rights of membership in the organized community—which nobody, state or private person, may interfere with. This principle has some life in the cases; in *Bewer v. Hoxie School District* (8th Cir. 1956), for example, an INJUNCTION was upheld that restrained private persons from interfering with state officials' attempts to comply with the national Constitution. But the principle deserves a greater generality. Anybody who tries forcibly to keep another person from getting his mail is interfering with a legitimate relation between citizen and government, even though the wrongdoer's own actions may not be "state action" at all. (See also UNITED STATES V. GUEST, 1966.)

6. There is broad scope in the natural meaning of the Fourteenth Amendment's words: "deny to any person within its jurisdiction the equal protection of

the laws." These words, even as a matter of "narrow verbal criticism," do not require "action."

7. Above all, while much of the defense of the "state action" requirement is conducted in the name of the private, personal lives of people whose conduct, it is said, ought not to be constitutionalized, it is very, very rare that any real "state action" case involves these values at all. The conduct of public transportation and restaurants, the operation of carnivals and parks, dealings with city swimming pools, the way the light company collects its bills, the character of a whole section of town—these are the usual stuff of "state action" problems in real life. If anybody ever files a lawsuit praying a mandatory injunction that he be included on somebody else's dinner list, that will be time enough to begin devising a well-founded "rule of reason" fencing constitutional prohibition out of the genuinely private life. This "genuinely private" life may be hard to define, but surely no harder to define than the "state action requirement" has turned out to be, and continues to be. And at least one would be trying to define the right thing.

CHARLES L. BLACK, JR.

Bibliography

BLACK, CHARLES L., JR. 1962 The Constitution and Public Power. *Yale Review* 52:54–66.

BLACK, CHARLES L., JR. 1967 "State Action," Equal Protection, and California's Proposition 14. *Harvard Law Review* 81:69–109.

HALE, ROBERT L. 1952 *Freedom through Law.* Chap. 11. New York: Columbia University Press.

HOROWITZ, HAROLD W. 1957 The Misleading Search for "State Action" under the Fourteenth Amendment. *Southern California Law Review* 30:208–221.

VAN ALSTYNE, WILLIAM W. 1965 Mr. Justice Black, Constitutional Review, and the Talisman of State Action. *Duke Law Journal* 1965:219–247.

STATE ACTION—BEYOND RACE

For most of its century-long existence, the STATE ACTION limitation of the reach of the FOURTEENTH Amendment and FIFTEENTH AMENDMENT has had its chief importance in cases involving RACIAL DISCRIMINATION. From the CIVIL RIGHTS CASES (1883) until the 1940s, the state action barrier impeded both judicial and congressional protection of CIVIL RIGHTS. As the civil rights movement gathered force in the years following World War II, relaxation of the state action limitation was essential to the vindication of the rights of blacks and others who were making claims to constitutional equality. The WARREN COURT accelerated the erosion of the state action barrier, bringing more and more private conduct within the reach of the Fourteenth Amendment. ALEXANDER M. BICKEL accurately described the effects of the Court's decisions as "egalitarian, legalitarian, and centralizing." By the late 1960s some commentators were predicting the state action doctrine's early demise.

Those predictions missed the mark; today the state action limitation remains very much alive. Yet the doctrine's revival has not signaled a return to a restricted role for the national government in protecting rights of racial equality. By the time the BURGER COURT set about rebuilding the state action barrier, the Court had provided Congress with a firm basis for federal civil rights legislation in the THIRTEENTH AMENDMENT, which has never been interpreted to contain a state action limitation. Furthermore, the Court had generously interpreted various federal civil rights laws to forbid most types of private racial discrimination that had flourished behind the state action barrier in the prewar years.

Although the revival of the state action doctrine has offered little new support for private racial discrimination, that revival has diminished the "legalitarian" and "centralizing" effects of the Warren Court's decisions. Indeed, recent Supreme Court majorities have explicitly extolled the Court's use of the state action doctrine to promote the values of individual autonomy and FEDERALISM. The Warren Court had blurred the distinction between state and society, between what is "public" and what is "private." In so doing, the Court assumed that the force of law underlay all private dealings. It is only a short step from this assumption to the judicial creation of a great many constitutional rights of private individuals against other private individuals. Justice JOHN MARSHALL HARLAN, deploring the trend, argued in UNITED STATES V. GUEST (1966) that "[the] CONSTITUTIONAL CONVENTION was called to establish a nation, not to reform the COMMON LAW."

The Burger Court has viewed its revival of the state action barrier in precisely these terms, as a contraction of the reach of the Constitution—and especially the reach of the federal judiciary—with a corresponding expansion of both individual autonomy and state SOVEREIGNTY. The Court's recent majorities have drawn a sharp distinction between society's "public" and "private" spheres, and two implications have followed. First, the Constitution limits governmental, but not private, conduct. Second, if private conduct is to be regulated by government, the preferred regulator is the state government, and not Congress or the federal courts. The result has been a marked reduction in the Fourteenth Amendment's potential applications to private conduct, even when that conduct is carried on with what the Warren Court used to call "significant state involvement."

Indeed, the very search for "significant state involvement" has been replaced by a new analytical approach. Where the Warren Court determined the existence of state action by considering the totality of interconnections between government and private conduct, today's majority separately examines various arguments for finding state action underpinning private conduct—and typically, as in JACKSON V. METROPOLITAN EDISON COMPANY (1974) and BLUM V. YARETSKY (1982), rejects those arguments one by one.

In doctrinal terms, the current majority of the Supreme Court has narrowed both of the principal avenues for finding state action in private conduct. First, the "public function" theory that informed the "white primary" cases from NIXON V. HERNDON (1927) to TERRY V. ADAMS (1953) and the "company town" decision in MARSH V. ALABAMA (1946) has been confined to cases in which the state has delegated to a private party a function traditionally performed exclusively by the state. In FLAGG BROTHERS, INC. V. BROOKS (1978) the Court even tightened its rhetoric for such cases, referring to "the sovereign function doctrine."

Second, the various types of state support that previously contributed to findings of "significant state involvement" in private conduct, having been disaggregated in the Court's analysis, have been strictly limited in their separate meanings. Thus: heavy state financial aid to a private school was insufficient to establish state action in RENDELL-BAKER V. KOHN (1982); the theory of REITMAN V. MULKEY (1967) that the state had "encouraged" private racial discrimination has yet to be employed to find state action in another case; the state's licensing and comprehensive regulation of a public utility was insufficient to establish state action in *Jackson v. Metropolitan Edison Company;* the precedent of BURTON V. WILMINGTON PARKING AUTHORITY (1961) has been restricted to cases in which government and private actors are so intimately interconnected that their relationship can be called one of "symbiosis"—or, as in LUGAR V. EDMONDSON OIL COMPANY (1982), "joint participation"; and the RESTRICTIVE COVENANT precedent of SHELLEY V. KRAEMER (1948) has become a one-case category. Even a public defender, employed by the state to represent indigent defendants in criminal cases, was held in *Polk County v. Dodson* (1981) not to be acting under COLOR OF LAW as required by SECTION 1983, TITLE 42, OF THE U.S. CODE, statutory words that are interpreted to track the state action limitation.

The insight that law—and thus the coercive power of the state—provides the foundation for claims of right in human society is not new. Indeed, the proposition teeters on the edge of tautology. To say that a person owns land, for example, is mainly a shorthand statement about the readiness of state officials to employ force to protect that person's exercise of certain rights to control the use of that land. To speak of law itself is to speak of a power relationship. In a large and complex society the point may sometimes become diffused, but the potential application of coercive power, wielded by governmental officials, is one of the chief features differentiating interactions in nearly all human societies from those in a jungle. The public/private distinction may have its uses, but candid description is not one of them.

Nonetheless, Justice WILLIAM H. REHNQUIST, writing for the Supreme Court in the *Flagg Brothers* case, reaffirmed "the 'essential dichotomy' between public and private acts" as a feature of American constitutional law. State action, for purposes of interpreting the Fourteenth Amendment, could not be found on the potential enforcement of law by state officials, but only on its actual enforcement. To rule otherwise, Rehnquist said, would "intolerably broaden" the notion of state action. Unquestionably, the public/private distinction is secure in American constitutional law.

The appeal of the public/private distinction for the judges and commentators who create constitutional DOCTRINE is readily identified. If any one value lies at the core of American CONSTITUTIONALISM, it is the protection of individual freedom against arbitrary exercises of governmental power. A central assumption in this value scheme is that a "neutral" body of law is no more than the playing field on which individuals autonomously pursue their own goals. The same assumption is also reassuring about autonomy itself—not just that autonomy is valuable, but that autonomy exists. It is hard to see how American constitutionalism could get along without some form of the public/private distinction, absent a fundamental transformation of the idea of constitutionalism.

Plainly, the public/private distinction would be compatible with a definition of state action much broader than the current one. The present restrictive interpretation of the state action limitation, in other words, serves purposes beyond the maintenance of a zone of individual freedom against arbitrary governmental interference. Those purposes are not far below the surface of the Supreme Court's recent state action opinions. The Supreme Court's current restrictive readings of the state action limitation are congenial to Justices who want to preserve state power against the intrusion of the federal government, and who want to restrict the role of the judiciary in second-guessing the political process. One's attitude toward the state action issue, as toward a great many constitutional issues in the last generation, will reflect one's general views about JUDICIAL ACTIVISM AND RESTRAINT. The consequences of these choices are not merely institutional; they affect substantive rights of liberty and equality. Every decision reinforcing the Fourteenth Amendment's state action barrier is a decision not to vindicate a claim of Fourteenth Amendment rights.

KENNETH L. KARST

Bibliography

NOTE 1974 State Action: Theories for Applying Constitutional Restrictions to Private Activity. *Columbia Law Review* 74:656–705.

SYMPOSIUM 1982 The Public/Private Distinction. *University of Pennsylvania Law Review* 130:1289–1608.

TRIBE, LAURENCE H. 1985 *Constitutional Choices.* Pages 246–268. Cambridge, Mass.: Harvard University Press.

STATE AID TO PAROCHIAL SCHOOLS

See: Government Aid to Religious Institutions

STATE AND LOCAL FISCAL ASSISTANCE ACT

See: Revenue Sharing

STATE CONSTITUTIONAL LAW

American constitutionalism is more than the United States Constitution as interpreted by the United States Supreme Court. Each of the fifty states has its own constitution, which is the chief charter of government and of limitations on government in that state. State constitutions offer contrasts to common assumptions, based only on the United States Constitution, concerning both government and constitutional law.

State constitutions preceded the Constitution of the United States. State governments had to be formed when colonial governments were displaced in the move to American independence. The CONTINENTAL CONGRESS called upon each colony to establish its own government, but the Congress decided not to propose a single model for all. Eleven of the original thirteen states adopted written constitutions between 1776 and 1780; Connecticut and Rhode Island established their governing institutions without adopting constitutions until well into the nineteenth century. The generation that drafted the United States Constitution and the BILL OF RIGHTS first applied many of its political theories to forming the state constitutions.

One tradition dating from the early state constitutions is to place the declaration of rights at the beginning of the document. The rights so declared differed among the states, but together they covered virtually all of the guarantees later added to the United States Constitution. As to the structure of government, all states except Pennsylvania adopted bicameral legislatures (today only Nebraska's is unicameral), but they diverged on how and by whom representatives were elected. The theory of a separation of legislative, executive, and judicial powers was widely approved and expressly incorporated in Virginia's and other constitutional texts, but the legislatures were dominant in most states, electing governors, other executive officers, and judges.

By 1800 most of the original state constitutions had been replaced by revised documents. Nineteenth-century constitutions reflected the changing political concerns of old and new states as the nation expanded westward. Jeffersonian and Jacksonian views of democracy and equality broadened political participation and extended popular election from legislative to virtually all executive, administrative, and judicial offices. By mid-century, legislative profligacy with public credit in pursuit of economic development led to constitutional restraints on taxing and borrowing, on "lending the state's credit" or granting special PRIVILEGES OR IMMUNITIES to private persons, and on individual incorporation acts or other special or local laws. New governmental programs such as public education and regulation of banks, railroads, and public utilities were not left to ordinary legislation but were added to state constitutions, often to be administered by separately elected officials. State constitutions address such social problems as alcoholic beverages, gambling, and lotteries. The movement toward populist government reached its climax at the beginning of the twentieth century when many states provided for referenda on legislation and constitutional amendments upon petition by the requisite numbers of voters. Eventually many states had constitutions resembling haphazard legal codes.

After World War II a number of states adopted substantially new or modernized constitutions, including Missouri (1945), New Jersey (1947), Hawaii and Alaska (1959), Michigan (1960), Connecticut (1965), Florida and Pennsylvania (1968), Illinois and Virginia (1970), Montana (1972), Louisiana (1974), California (1976), and Georgia (1982). Others retain their original constitutions as revised by individual amendments. Altogether the fifty states have had a total of nearly 150 constitutions, with corresponding diversity among the states.

Although guarantees of individual rights dominate judicial and public attention, the primary function of constitutions is the organization and allocation of governmental authority. When this is done in a written constitution, the legitimacy of actions even by the highest elected officials depends upon compliance with the constitution and can be challenged for failure to comply. A comparison shows that in a number of respects the constitutional law of state government is more complex than that of the United States, although in one respect it is not.

The authority of states as such is not derived from their constitutions, as the early examples of Connecticut and Rhode Island show; unless limited, state authority is as plenary as that of the British Parliament. State constitutions therefore have no need for lists of legislative "powers" like those granted Congress in the United States Constitution. The great residue of the COMMON LAW concerning private transactions and property is state law. Although elected officials of local governments exercise lawmaking, taxing, and executive powers, their relation to the state is the reverse of that between the state and the federal government insofar as local governments have only the powers defined in state law. The "home rule" provisions found in many state constitutions, however, introduce one complexity comparable to the constitutional problems of FEDERALISM.

There are other contrasts. Federal executive officers are appointed by the President and must trace their actions to some act of Congress except for those powers given the President directly by the Constitution. Although the typical state constitution refers to an executive department of government, many executive officials, such as state treasurers, attorneys general, superintendents of public instruction and prosecutors, are separately elected to carry out functions described in the constitution. In fiscal matters many state constitutions, unlike the United States Constitution, require a balanced budget and allow the governor an item veto. Constitutional issues arise from provisions governing uniformity and limits on taxes and procedures for issuing bonds. Others arise in the administration of the election laws, especially the popular initiative and referendum. They result in a body of constitutional law that has no federal parallel.

When parallels do exist, experience under state constitutional law often provides a test for conceptions assumed at the national level or accepted by the United States Supreme Court, for instance, in questions of executive power and privileges. The Alaska court in *State v. A.L.I.V.E.* (1980) invalidated the LEGISLATIVE VETO device before the United States Supreme Court did so in IMMIGRATION AND NATURALIZATION SERVICE V. CHADHA (1983).

The role of state judges in reviewing acts of government developed early and was generally accepted. New York's first constitution included judges in a Council of Revision that exercised the power to veto legislation. Under seven state constitutions the judges of the highest courts may be called upon to render ADVISORY OPINIONS.

Constitutional entrenchment of individual rights began with the earliest state constitutions in 1776 and is universal throughout the states, though the statements of rights differ. The common tradition includes procedural guarantees such as speedy and public trial by jury upon known charges, the right to call and to confront witnesses, freedom from warrantless and unreasonable searches and seizures and from compelled self-incrimination, as well as guarantees of property rights and freedom of expression, assembly, and petition. Many constitutions prescribed the law governing libel actions. The equality posited in the DECLARATION OF INDEPENDENCE was not translated into general state constitutional doctrine, being denied to slaves, women, and unpropertied citizens. But hereditary inequality was proscribed, as were, in the words of the Virginia Bill of Rights (1776), "exclusive or separate emoluments or privileges from the community, but in consideration of public services."

Differences among state provisions were not accidental. The status of religion varied among the early states, some favoring Protestant denominations or Christianity generally. Different views of punishment resulted in different provisions on that subject. Some states limited the right to bear arms to public defense; others extended it to self-defense. Conventions debated such issues as the role of GRAND JURIES. New states adopting constitutions throughout the nineteenth century drew their models not from the United States Constitution but from earlier states.

In the catalogue of guaranteed rights, too, many state provisions have no federal parallel. They may command open court proceedings, a result that the United States Supreme Court has strained to develop indirectly from FREEDOM OF THE PRESS. Many guarantee legal remedies for private injuries, a subject not generally within the powers granted to Congress. Some prescribe humane treatment of prisoners. In modern times some states have added guarantees of workers' rights, environmental values, rights of privacy, and equal rights of men and women. Constitutional rights, in the sense of rights guaranteed by constitutions rather than other law, are by no means identical throughout the United States.

State constitutions have provided almost the only guarantees against the states' laws through most of the nation's history. The United States Constitution denied the states authority to enact BILLS OF ATTAINDER, EX POST FACTO LAWS, and laws impairing the obligation of contracts, but the first ten amendments that are commonly called the Bill of Rights were addressed only to the federal government. When a Maryland property owner in 1833 sought to invoke the just compensation clause of the Fifth Amendment against the City of Baltimore, Chief Justice JOHN MARSHALL wrote in BARRON V. BALTIMORE (1833) that adoption of these amendments "could never have occurred to any human being, as a mode of doing that which might be effected by the state itself"; Congress would not engage in "the extraordinary occupation of improving the constitutions of the several states, by affording the people additional protection from the exercise of power by their own governments, in matters which concerned themselves alone."

After the Civil War, Congress began a process of constitutional amendments that did afford new protections to people who were excluded from political power in their own states. The THIRTEENTH AMENDMENT ended slavery, and the FOURTEENTH AMENDMENT defined CITIZENSHIP and restrained states from denying their own residents as well as other persons national privileges and immunities, DUE PROCESS, or the EQUAL PROTECTION OF THE LAWS. Thereafter, the FIFTEENTH, NINETEENTH, TWENTY-FOURTH, and TWENTY-SIXTH AMENDMENTS, respectively, forbade all states to deny voting rights to any citizen by reason of race or color, or sex, or failure to pay a tax, or to eighteen-year-old citizens. Except for this progressive expansion of the franchise, the Thirteenth and Fourteenth Amendments are the only federal constitutional provisions since 1789 to guarantee individual rights against the states.

With the turn of the twentieth century, the United States Supreme Court began to construe the Fourteenth Amendment's guarantee of "due process" so as to strike down substantive state regulations, first of property and economic activities, and later of activities involving speech, press, assembly, and religion that the FIRST AMENDMENT would protect against federal infringement. Theoretically, each state's bill of rights remained the primary and independent guarantee against oppressive action by that state, but state courts had provided little protection in interpreting and enforcing these guarantees. In the thirty years after 1935, claims to rights equivalent to those under the First Amendment and federal restraints on the criminal law process were increasingly pressed upon and accepted by the United States Supreme Court under the Fourteenth Amendment, until practically all provisions of the federal Bill of Rights were incorporated into "due process" under that amendment. (See INCORPORATION DOCTRINE.)

Because most state constitutions are easily amended, they often reflect the shifting popular concerns of an era as the United States Constitution does not. Although a federal EQUAL RIGHTS AMENDMENT proposed in 1972 failed to win ratification, similar texts were adopted by twelve states. Eight states incorporated guarantees of "privacy" into their bills of rights, creating new conundrums about the intended meaning and scope of that term. Some states sought to halt or reverse the ending of racial SEGREGATION by constitutional amendments, futile in the face of the Fourteenth Amendment, to forbid the operation of integrated public schools or the enactment of OPEN HOUSING LAWS. Some sought to stem the costs of social programs by new limits on taxes and spending.

State constitutions also were amended in reaction to judicial decisions under state bills of rights. The record of state constitutional amendments must be considered in any theory that would locate changing social values in the changeless terms of the Fourteenth Amendment.

State courts have a mixed record in enforcing their states' guarantees of liberty, equality, and fair procedures. Defendants' procedural rights in principle were well protected at trial, but not in police investigations and prearraignment procedures. About half the states followed the federal rule to exclude illegally seized evidence before the United States Supreme Court mandated exclusion under the Fourteenth Amendment. State courts gave some force to constitutional clauses concerning the SEPARATION OF CHURCH AND STATE but practically none to FREEDOM OF SPEECH or of the press, the latter often being threatened as much by orders of the courts themselves as by legislation. Much of the United States Supreme Court's case law after 1930 responded to state court failures to protect individual rights. With the growth of this case law, lawyers began to argue only under the developing federal jurisprudence, and state courts gave no independent application to their states' own guarantees, with one exception: They continued to strike down state regulations of business and property under notions of SUBSTANTIVE DUE PROCESS long after the Supreme Court disavowed this practice under the Fourteenth Amendment.

Since the 1970s, however, there has been a dramatic revival of state court decisions under state constitutions. Some of these were independent of any decision of the United States Supreme Court; many others turned to state constitutions in reaction to Supreme Court holdings or doctrines denying claims under the United States Constitution. The revival was encouraged in a 1977 speech by Justice WILLIAM J. BRENNAN, himself a former member of the New Jersey Supreme Court. The theme was taken up by other Justices and state judges.

The result is a rapidly growing diversity of constitutional decisions among state and federal courts. The California court in SERRANO V. PRIEST (1977) and the New Jersey court in *Robinson v. Cahill* (1973) held that equal rights under their states' constitutions required equalization of financial support to public schools after the Supreme Court denied this claim under the Fourteenth Amendment in SAN ANTONIO SCHOOL DISTRICT V. RODRIGUEZ (1972). Similar holdings followed when the Supreme Court allowed the exclusion of abortion from state-paid medical services. After the United States Supreme Court limited rights of access to shopping centers in *Lloyd Corp., Ltd. v. Tanner* (1972), several state courts found such rights in their state constitutions, some on the far-reaching premise that their state's speech guarantees did not run only against government. State decisions have invalidated services to parochial school students that pass muster under the First Amendment. The Oregon Supreme Court in *Wheeler v. Green* (1979) forbade punitive damages for defamation, though the United States Supreme Court has indicated that they are permissible.

The most numerous and most controversial constitutional guarantees apply to criminal law. Their protection is not so generally valued by twentieth-century citizens as it was by those who gave them constitutional stature. State supreme courts have struck down the death penalty as cruel or unusual punishment and have departed from federal holdings on such issues as DOUBLE JEOPARDY, right to jury trial and to counsel for petty offenses, and SEARCHES INCIDENT TO ARREST. The response has included constitutional amendments by INITIATIVES to reinstate CAPITAL PUNISHMENT and to tie state provisions relating to police seizures to FOURTH AMENDMENT holdings of the United States Supreme Court.

Before the United States Supreme Court bound the states to most federal constitutional rights through the Fourteenth Amendment, courts had to decide only whether and how to apply each state's bill of rights. After the Supreme Court's incorporation doctrine decisions, most courts again applied only a single body of law, the federal case law. The revival of state constitutional guarantees raised problems inherent in the dual legal system of federalism that had long been forgotten. Some of these are procedural problems; others concern the substance of constitutional interpretation.

When state law, including state constitutional law, protects whatever right a person claims, it cannot logically be said that the state violates any federal guarantee that the person otherwise might invoke. Logical procedure, therefore, requires that the state's ordinary law and thereafter its constitutional law be determined before reaching any claim that the state falls short of federally mandated standards. This principle has been recognized by some state courts, for example Oregon's in *Sterling v. Cupp* (1981), Maine's in *State v. Cadman* (1984), and New Hampshire's in *State v. Ball* (1983). Other courts, however, apply their own state constitutions selectively when they perceive a reason to differ from federal doctrine or to insulate a decision from review by the United States Supreme Court, or they cite both federal and state constitutions for the same holding. These hybrid practices have been criticized as unprincipled because state constitutions are invoked only when necessary to diverge from less protective decisions of the United States Supreme Court, or because citation of both constitutions simultaneously prevents further review by the United States Supreme Court and discourages amendment of the state constitution. In 1983 the United States Supreme Court and some state courts called for "clear statements" whether the claimed right was grounded in the state or the federal constitution.

Many lawyers and judges routinely use contemporary Supreme Court pronouncements on federal constitutional law as benchmarks also for interpretation of state constitutions, particularly when similar texts are involved. But state courts need not regard these pronouncements as authoritative in state constitutional interpretation, whether or not the texts are the same. The fact that state and federal texts were adopted with the same intent or purpose does not make the federal interpretation presumptively correct; a difference in texts only makes this point easier to see. The principle is true both for results and for methodology; many state decisions do not follow the mid-century Supreme Court's formulas for analyzing and resolving constitutional issues, while others do so.

Responsible interpretation of state constitutions often presents problems unique to the state. Historical records are not readily available to lawyers; sometimes none were preserved. When old texts are repeated in successive constitutions, it is debatable which generation's understanding should matter. The uneven quality of opinions requires reliance on precedents to be selective yet not capricious. The ever present temptation held out to courts is to act as pragmatic policymakers in the guise of constitutional interpreters, without excessive scruple whether anyone placed the supposed principle of decision into the constitution, or whether the principle as stated can be given consistent application.

For many reasons constitutional law has long been equated with the decisions of the Supreme Court of the United States. The Court as an institution is the subject of extensive and continuing writings by social scientists and journalists as well as by legal scholars. Only its decisions apply throughout the nation. The Court's nationalization of individual rights in mid-twentieth century, coinciding with the development of dominant national news media and with the emphasis of professional education on national materials, obscures the fact that the federal system makes the states responsible for large and important areas of law over which the Supreme Court has no jurisdiction unless a state administers this responsibility in a manner contrary to the United States Constitution or laws.

The late-twentieth-century revival of state constitutions has served to remind the general public as well as legal professionals of the essentials of the federal system. Its importance is not measured by the instances in which state courts have enforced individual rights beyond decisions of the United States Supreme Court. Many important functions, problems, and innovations of state constitutions do not concern individual rights. Moreover, citizens sometimes were quick to repeal constitutional guarantees of rights when these were enforced by their courts. State constitutions provide no security for dispensing with the national guarantees of the Fourteenth Amendment.

Even debates over repealing guaranteed rights, however, brought citizen responsibility for these rights close to home as no United States Supreme Court decision could do. Although citizens in some states amended their constitutions to revive capital punishment and relinquish protections against police abuses, similar proposals were defeated in other states.

Experience in the states, in the conduct of state government as well as in state court decisions of constitutional issues, continues to offer alternative models and concepts by which to test, and sometimes to gain, ideas for the nation. After two centuries, independent constitutional thought and action in the states remains an essential strength of federalism as well as a guarantee of individual freedom.

HANS A. LINDE

Bibliography

ABRAHAMSON, SHIRLEY S. 1982 Reincarnation of State Courts. *Southwestern Law Journal* 36:951–974.

BRENNAN, WILLIAM J. 1977 State Constitutions and the Protection of Individual Rights. *Harvard Law Review* 90:459–504.

DOUGLAS, CHARLES G. 1978 State Judicial Activism—The New Role for State Bills of Rights. *Suffolk University Law Review* 12:1123–1150.

ELAZAR, DANIEL J. and SCHECHTER, STEPHEN L., eds. 1982 State Constitutional Design in Federal Systems. *Publius* 12:1–185.

LINDE, HANS A. 1984 E Pluribus—Constitutional Theory and State Courts. *Georgia Law Review* 18:165–200.

MCGRAW, BRADLEY D. 1984 *Developments in State Constitutional Law.* St. Paul, Minn.: West Publishing Co.

POLLOCK, STEWARD G. 1983 State Constitutions as Separate Sources of Fundamental Rights. *Rutgers Law Review* 35:705–722.

PORTER, MARY C. and TARR, G. ALAN, eds. 1982 *State Supreme Courts.* Westport, Conn.: Greenwood Press.

UTTER, ROBERT F. 1984 Freedom and Diversity in a Federal System. *University of Puget Sound Law Review* 7:491–525.

STATE FREIGHT TAX CASE

See: *Philadelphia & Reading Railroad Co. v. Pennsylvania*

STATE OF . . .

See entry under name of state

STATE OF EMERGENCY

See: Emergency Powers

STATE OF TENNESSEE v. SCOPES 289 SW 363 (1925)

In 1925 Dayton, Tennessee, authorities arrested a local high school teacher, John T. Scopes, for violating the state's Butler Act, which prohibited public school instructors from teaching "any theory that denies the story of the Divine Creation of man as taught in the Bible, and to teach instead that man has descended from a lower order of animals." Scopes admitted to teaching about evolution from George Hunter's *Civic Biology,* a book approved by Tennessee's textbook commission. The Scopes trial, soon known throughout the nation as "the monkey trial," came in the middle of a decade punctuated by the Red Scare, increased urban–rural tensions, and the resurgence of the Ku Klux Klan. The Dayton courtroom soon became an arena of cultural and political conflict between fundamentalist Christians and civil libertarians.

The former, led by William Jennings Bryan, a three-time presidential candidate and ardent prohibitionist who joined the prosecution staff, argued that the Butler Act was a traditional exercise of STATE POLICE POWER with respect to public education, little different from mandating other curricula and fixing the qualifications of teachers. They also saw the statute as a defense of traditional folk values against the moral relativism of modern science and other contemporary religious beliefs. Scopes's defenders, including the AMERICAN CIVIL LIBERTIES UNION (ACLU) and the celebrated criminal lawyer Clarence Darrow, saw in the Butler Act a palpable threat to several constitutional guarantees, including SEPARATION OF CHURCH AND STATE and FREEDOM OF SPEECH.

The trial judge, John T. Raulston, rejected all constitutional attacks against the statute; he also declined to permit testimony by scientific and religious experts, many of whom hoped to argue the compatibility between evolution and traditional religious values, including the belief in a supreme being. The only issue for the jury, Raulston noted, was the narrow one of whether or not John Scopes had taught his class that man had descended from a lower form of animals. Because Scopes has already admitted doing so, the jury's verdict was never in doubt. Darrow and the defense gained a public relations triumph by putting Bryan on the stand to testify as an expert about the Bible. The Great Commoner, who collapsed and died several days after the trial ended, affirmed his faith in biblical literalism, including the story of Jonah and the whale. The jury, however, found Scopes guilty and Raulston fined him the statutory minimum of $100.

Darrow and the ACLU encountered only frustration when they attempted to APPEAL the conviction. The state supreme court, with one judge dissenting, upheld the constitutionality of the Butler Act. However, they reversed Scopes's conviction on a technicality, holding that the Tennessee constitution prohibited trial judges from imposing fines in excess of $50 without a jury recommendation. The state supreme court also urged Tennessee officials to cease further prosecution of John Scopes—advice which the attorney general followed. The Butler Act remained on the Tennessee statute books but was not enforced against other educational heretics.

MICHAEL E. PARRISH

Bibliography

GINGER, RAY 1958 *Six Days or Forever? Tennessee v. John Thomas Scopes.* New York: Oxford University Press.

STATE OF WAR

The existence of a "state of war" for various purposes of domestic and international law is not generally controlled by the existence or absence of a congressional DECLARATION OF WAR. The federal courts, including the Supreme Court, have often held that hostilities, not accompanied by any formal declaration of war (as has been the case in all but five of the approximately 160 occasions in which American armed forces have been committed to combat), were "war" and, conversely, that "peace" existed despite the fact that war had been declared and not terminated by a peace treaty or legislative action. Sometimes the same hostilities have been treated as "war" for one purpose and "peace" for another. Examples can describe the judicial approach better than generalities.

The undeclared naval combat with France in 1798–1799 was treated as war for the purpose of a statute rewarding those who recaptured American vessels "from the enemy" (*Bas v. Tingy,* 1800) but (many years later) as peace under the Franco-American treaty of 1778 (*Gray v. United States,* 1884). The Civil War, though of course never declared by Congress, created a state of war under international law, so that neutral vessels running the Union blockade of Confederate ports could lawfully be captured and sold as prizes. (See PRIZE CASES, 1863). American forces sent to China to help suppress the Boxer Uprising of 1900 were engaged in war under Article of War 58, which permitted courts-martial to try charges of murder only "in time of war" (*Hamilton v. McClaughry*, 1905). But although on June 10, 1949, a declared war still existed between the United States and Germany and Japan, the Supreme Court held that, since there were no hostilities, that date was "time of peace" under a similar Article of War (*Lee v. Madigan*, 1959; the decision effectively overruled *Kahn v. Anderson*, 1921). The COURT OF MILITARY APPEALS and at least one civilian court held that the Korean and Vietnam conflicts, though not declared wars, were nonetheless "war" under provisions of the Uniform Code of Military Justice, which suspended the statute of limitations and increased penalties for certain military offenses in wartime (*Broussard v. Patton*, 1972; *United States v. Bancroft*, 1953; *United States v. Anderson*, 1968). But the Court of Military Appeals and the COURT OF CLAIMS also held that only a declared war could trigger a provision of the Code which gives courts-martial JURISDICTION "in time of war [over] persons serving with or accompanying an armed force in the field." The principle that emerges from examination of these and many similar cases is that the existence of a "state of war" depends principally on the amount of violence, unless a holding that "war" existed would raise serious constitutional questions, as by giving courts-martial jurisdiction over civilians.

The question can, of course, be of profound importance, for war is chief among the great emergencies that may be held to justify actions of the executive and the legislature which would in normal times be plainly unconstitutional. The most extreme example is the Supreme Court's refusal to strike down the 1942 exclusion of American citizens of Japanese descent from the West Coast and their confinement in "relocation centers," under an EXECUTIVE ORDER of President FRANKLIN D. ROOSEVELT, which had been ratified by an act of Congress. (See EXECUTIVE ORDER 9066; JAPANESE AMERICAN CASES.) As a general proposition it may be said that the Supreme Court's unwillingness to hold unconstitutional the actions of the President and Congress in such emergencies varies in inverse ratio to the size of the emergency and the decision's chronological closeness to it. It has been the practice of the Court to scrutinize emergency measures much more closely and to give the executive and legislature much less leeway if the case reaches the Court after the war is over. (See EX PARTE MILLIGAN, 1866; DUNCAN V. KAHANAMOKU, 1946.)

JOSEPH W. BISHOP, JR.

Bibliography

BISHOP, JOSEPH W., JR. 1974 *Justice under Fire: A Study of Military Law.* Pages 178–180, 192–201. New York: Charterhouse.

RATNER, LEONARD G. 1971 The Coordinated Warmaking Power—Legislative, Executive and Judicial Roles. *Southern California Law Review* 44:461–489.

STATE POLICE POWER

The POLICE POWER of the states is one of the most important concepts in American constitutional history; yet, like PRIVACY or FREEDOM OF CONTRACT, its historic significance derives from usage and application, not from the language of the Constitution itself. Nowhere in the Constitution does the term appear.

In his *Commentaries on the Laws of England* (1769) WILLIAM BLACKSTONE provided a definition of public police as "the due regulation and domestic order of the kingdom, whereby the inhabitants of the State, like members of a well-governed family, are bound to conform their general behavior to the rules of propriety, good neighborhood, and good manners, and to be decent, industrious, and inoffensive in their respective stations." Some of the early American treatises quoted this definition, but in fact it serves badly as a guide to constitutional doctrine and governmental realities in the United States in the 1790s or the early nineteenth century. Nor was the Supreme Court much more effective in providing guidance as to the substance and limits of the police power. Chief Justice JOHN MARSHALL verged perilously near outright tautology in GIBBONS V. ODGEN (1824), when he referred to the police power of the states as "that immense mass of legislation, which embraces every thing within the territory of a State, not surrendered to the general [national] government," and as the "acknowledged power of a State to regulate its police, its domestic trade, and to govern its own citizens." Left entirely open, of course, was the matter of what indeed had not been "surrendered" in the way of state powers as well as the matter of what was "acknowledged" as a legitimate part of residual state SOVEREIGNTY in light of the Constitution. The Court itself, clearly, would acknowledge positive powers and define the terms of "surrender." As late as 1847, in his opinion in the LICENSE CASES, Chief Justice ROGER B. TANEY was referring to the state police power in terms that hardly improved upon Marshall's, so far as specificity was concerned, but that at least had a more positive (if not to say sweeping) rhetorical thrust: that power was, Taney declared, "nothing more or less than the powers of government inherent in every sovereignty to the extent of its dominions." Not until the post-Civil War years, when FOURTEENTH AMENDMENT litigation paraded state regulatory laws before the Supreme Court for review, did the Court begin to grapple more tellingly with the problem of definition. Even in contemporary times, however, fitting the police power into the constellation of constitutional ideas has remained one of the Court's most perplexing concerns. There was as much critical acumen as despair in Justice WILLIAM O. DOUGLAS's plaint, in *Berman v. Parker* (1954), that "an attempt to define its reach or trace its outer limits is fruitless, for each case must turn on its own facts." In the last analysis, Douglas contended, "the definition is essentially the product of legislative determinations. . . ."

The Marshall and Taney approach to definition of the police power was sufficient, in a sense, because it sought only to place some sort of label on the powers that remained with the states once the Court had determined the legitimate reach of the CONTRACT CLAUSE and of the COMMERCE CLAUSE; the police power was what the states had left when such determinations had been made. From the standpoint of state lawmakers, however, the approach of the two great Chief Justices was not at all sufficient. First, it did not make even the most basic conceptual distinctions among the fundamental types of governmental power; and so defining the police power as coextensive with sovereignty meant that police subsumed the powers of taxation and EMINENT DOMAIN. Second, the Marshall-Taney approach did not come to grips with power and its legitimate reach in a positive sense. What were the sources of state authority in its exercise of sovereign power? On what basis could a state court, for example, weigh the legitimacy of a regulatory law (even if clearly not beyond the bounds set by federal contract clause and commerce clause rules) against state constitutional limitations such as those prohibiting TAKINGS without JUST COMPENSATION?

It fell to one of the nation's greatest state judges, Chief Justice LEMUEL SHAW of Massachusetts, to produce a doctrinal exposition on the police power that would establish the framework for subsequent adjudication and debate. Shaw's formulation was set forth in *Commonwealth v. Alger* (1851), in which the Massachusetts high court upheld as a proper exercise of "the police power" (so explicitly called) a statute that forbade construction of any wharf in specified areas of Boston harbor. Shaw's great achievement was twofold. He broke out of the *cul de sac* to which Marshall and Taney had driven, addressing the legitimacy of the police power in terms liberated from boundaries set by commerce and contract clause doctrine; and he offered a jurisprudential foundation for positive governmental action.

Shaw conceded at the outset that the police power challenged head-on any efforts to tame it and bring it within bounds. Yet, while it was "not easy to mark its boundaries, or prescribe limits to its exercise," the police power must be acknowledged as superior in some reasoned way to private rights and claims. It was so, Shaw contended, as "a settled principle, growing out of the nature of well-ordered civil society." And so he turned to the task of giving substance to what the Supreme Court had lately termed "the police power belonging to the states, in virtue of their general sovereignty" (Justice JOSEPH STORY in PRIGG V. PENNSYLVANIA, 1842). One of the foundations of that power was the COMMON LAW rule *sic utere tuo ut alienum non laedas* (use your own property in such manner as not to injure that of another). Historically, the rule had been invoked to justify private nuisance and PUBLIC NUISANCE actions alike; in either way, however, it had been used in essentially defensive modes. Shaw linked the *sic utere* concept with a positive obligation of government to impose a system of reasonable restraints on private property uses. "Rights of property," he contended, are properly subject "to such reasonable restraints and regulations established by law, as the legislature, under the governing and controlling power vested in them by the Constitution, may think necessary and expedient." As Leonard W. Levy, the biographer of Shaw, has shown, Shaw thus advanced doctrine well beyond the old common law framework; although Shaw held out the possibility of judicial overturning of laws that were not "reasonable" and violated private VESTED RIGHTS, he stressed the propriety of the legislature's acting when necessary and expedient to impose restraints for the public good.

But Shaw also undertook to define a related, yet in some measure conceptually distinct, foundation for the police power: the concept of "rights of the public." Thus Shaw insisted on the "expediency and necessity of defining and securing the rights of the public," and elsewhere on "the acknowledged public right." Even acts not necessarily punishable by common law might properly be declared illegal by regulatory legislation, Shaw wrote, "for the sake of having a definitive, known and authoritative rule which all can understand and obey." Thus, from the Shaw court in 1851, American police power doctrine emerged in its essentials. As in an earlier decision in 1837 (*Commonwealth v. Blackington*), Shaw asserted the legislature's power to act for the public good to be "the general rule," whereas restraint of the legislature should be the "specific exception."

The next step in elaboration of police power doctrine was the specification of positive purposes, more detailed than the public good or "rights of the public" broadly stated, for which the power would justify regulatory legislation. Early efforts at specification along these lines, before Shaw reformulated the whole issue, had tended simply to codify the common law categories of behavior and property uses constituting nuisance. (Such, for example, is what one finds in Chancellor JAMES KENT's *Commentaries.*) Here again, the arsenal of the common law held an instrument potentially powerful—the principle *salus populi suprema lex* (the welfare of the people is the supreme law), which in the seventeenth and eighteenth centuries in England had often been invoked to assert the plenary powers of Parliament restricted only by accumulated constitutional liberties. In an influential Vermont decision, handed down three years after Shaw's great effort, Chief Justice Isaac Redfield declared that "the general comfort, health, and prosperity of the State" warranted state regulatory powers on the same basis of power as "resides in the British parliament, except where they are restrained by written constitutions" (*Thorpe v. Rutland Railroad,* 1855).

In some other state courts, judges proved reluctant to endorse wholly such broad definitions of legitimate intervention; yet even these more conservative jurists, while looking for principles on which to support JUDICIAL REVIEW, contributed to specification of the bases of positive authority. Thus one of the Michigan judges in *People v. Jackson & Co.* (1861) contended that powers "which can only be justified on [the] specific ground" of the police power or general legislative power must be "clearly necessary to the safety, comfort and well being of society." This line of reasoning was reflected in the 1877 decision of the Supreme Court in BOSTON BEER CO. V. MASSACHUSETTS, in which Justice JOSEPH P. BRADLEY stated for the Court that a PROHIBITION statute against sale of alcoholic beverages did not violate the rights of a brewery company, for clearly such legislation was warranted under the police power: "However difficult it may be to render a satisfactory definition of it," Bradley wrote, "there seems to be no doubt that it does extend to the protection of the lives, health, and property of the citizens, and to the preservation of good order and the public morals."

Two other doctrinal arguments found their way into antebellum state jurisprudence on the police power. The first, which was rooted in the notion that the power was part of the residuary sovereignty and of legislative authority comparable to that of Parliament, was that the police power was inalienable. That is, states could not bargain away their power—and obligation—to look after the public interest. (See INALIENABLE POLICE POWER.) The second, a pragmatic strain that would doubtless frighten those who believed that vested rights in property deserved more rigid protection, was the view that the police power needed to be consonant with the changing character and needs of the society. This latter, expansive view of the police power found vivid expression in decisions of the 1850s upholding new regulations which permitted railroads to use the public streets to gain access to urban centers. How the imperatives of material progress inspired this expansive doctrine was illustrated in the language of an Illinois decision in 1859 (*Moses v. Railroad*) declaring that to deny a railroad the use of public streets, "no matter how much the general good may require it, simply because streets were not so used in the days of Blackstone, would hardly comport with the advancement and enlightenment of the present age."

Although the antebellum state courts had provided them with a doctrinal foundation for expanded regulatory initiatives, the state legislatures in fact were slow to extend the range or increase the intensity of regulation. Still, grist for judicial mills was provided by laws that were challenged in the long-established areas of state intervention—that is, in such matters as the regulation of streams to protect navigation and fisheries, marketing regulations and standards, laws requiring the fencing-in of livestock, rudimentary safety legislation (especially against fire dangers), and the control of operations on public works such as bridges, highways, and canals. In the late 1840s and the 1850s, police-power measures proliferated as both the regulation of railroad operations and prohibition of alcoholic beverages became common. Astute lawyers were quick to resist expansive claims for the police power, especially when they limited the freedom that powerful economic interests enjoyed in the use of their property. Prior to 1833, challenges to the police power were often based on the Fifth Amendment as well as on comparable provisions of the state constitutions; but the decision of BARRON V. BALTIMORE cut off that line of defense for propertied interests. Still, lawyers continued to rely on the DUE PROCESS provisions of state constitutions; and they contended regularly that regulations took away the value of private property without just compensation—in other words, that the regulations effectively were "takings" and amounted to INVERSE CONDEMNATION. Despite the doctrinal contribution of Chief Justice Shaw and others in the 1850s, moreover, lawyers resorted commonly to the view that only uses of property that were actionable under the common law (as noxious uses, nuisances, or trespasses) could be reached by state regulations. In few cases did courts respond favorably to such arguments. Still, the intellectual and to some degree political groundwork was thereby laid for future attacks on the police power.

Adoption of the Fourteenth Amendment gave new impetus and hope to defenders of private property, who presented arguments in the courts that the PRIVILEGES AND IMMUNITIES clause and the due process clause alike afforded new protections against interventions under the police power. Simultaneously with adoption of the amendment, in 1868, came publication of THOMAS M. COOLEY's treatise, *Constitutional Limitations,* in its first edition. Of basic importance to Cooley's view of the limitations that ought to confine the power of state legislatures was his premise that the "due bounds of legislative power" were not set alone by "express constitutional provisions." The implied limitations that he believed ought to apply all hinged on a generalized "due process" concept. Due process, he contended, forbade enactment of what he termed "class legislation" (laws imposing burdens or granting privileges to specific groups or interests that were arbitrarily singled out instead of being "reasonably" classified). Moreover, his generous definition of due process would forbid laws that were "arbitrary and unusual [in] nature," and as such "unknown to the law of the land." The champions of laissez-faire, if given reason for optimism by the Fourteenth Amendment and the views in Cooley's treatise, were provided with a source of unbounded joy by publication in 1886 of CHRISTOPHER G. TIEDEMAN's *Limitations of the Police Power in the United States.* Tiedeman's great contribution was his attempt to turn the clock back altogether, to negate the principal contribution the Shaw Court had made in *Alger,* by resurrecting wholesale the doctrine that the old common law limits also constituted the proper limits of the positive police power. In effect, Tiedeman attempted to fuse the concept of due process, in the Constitution, with the traditional common law limits of *sic utere.* By the late 1870s, the Supreme Court itself had become divided on the crucial question: how far could state regulation go in limiting the actions of private persons and corporations in the marketplace?

The subsequent battle was not confined to the courts; it extended to the legislatures and the political hustings. Indeed, the question of regulatory power was at the very vortex of the storm in both national and state politics for three-quarters of a century. Three issues were involved in the debates. The first was whether specific types of regulatory actions by government abridged, unconstitutionally, what came to be called FREEDOM OF CONTRACT. The second was whether the courts or, instead, the legislatures were supreme in determining whether specific regulations were constitutionally permissible. Finally, there was the issue of what standards the courts should apply generally—if indeed the judicial branch had the power to review specific regulatory measures—to distinguish constitutional measures from those that were unconstitutional. All these issues centered on the rights of property.

Supreme Court doctrine continued to echo pre-Civil War formulations, even expanding them (rhetorically, at least) at the height of conservative, property-minded influence on the Court. Thus in *Barbier v. Connolly* (1884) Justice STEPHEN J. FIELD declared that neither the Fourteenth Amendment nor any other "was designed to interfere with the power of the State, sometimes termed its police power, to prescribe regulations to promote the health, peace, morals, education, and good order of the people, and to legislate so as to increase the industries of the State, develop its resources, and to add to its wealth and prosperity." Going as far, but in terms perhaps even more open-ended and expansive, Justice JOHN MARSHALL HARLAN asserted in *Chicago, Burlington & Quincy Railway v. Commissioners* (1906) that the legitimate police power of the state "embraces regulations designed to promote the public convenience or the general prosperity, as well as regulations designed to promote the public health, the public morals or the public safety." Despite such assertions of legitimacy for regulatory power, virtually every new or proposed regulation threatening to impose costs or restraints on private interests met with resistance in the state legislatures and the courts. Regulation varied in scope and effectiveness, from one state to another. The latitude and potential for diversity within the legal system offered by FEDERALISM was never more apparent. Nonetheless, the emergent industrial order, the rapid growth of population and absorption of millions of immigrants, urbanization, and the social dislocations that attended the acceleration of technological change and the growth of large-scale firms with enormous leverage over their employees and markets all served to focus political and legislative attention on expansion of the states' regulatory activities. Soon the courts were crowded with cases challenging regulative innovations.

The threshold question, of course, was whether legislative discretion should be permitted or whether the courts should impose constitutional standards that went to questions of substance such as "reasonableness." Before the Civil War, "due process" had been understood as referring to procedural requirements (right to a FAIR HEARING, specification of procedural steps and forms, NOTICE, and the like). In the 1870s, counsel in both the SLAUGHTERHOUSE CASES of 1873 and *Munn v. Illinois* and the other GRANGER CASES of 1877 argued that state regulatory legislation should be overturned on grounds of "due process" deprivation now defined as deprivation of substantive rights in violation of the Fourteenth Amendment. However, the right to regulate private interests, the Court declared in *Munn*, is one "which may be abused," to be sure; but "for protection against abuses by legislatures the people must resort to the polls, not to the courts."

Within a short time, though, the Court reversed itself and began to review state legislation under the police power with a view toward deciding whether "abuse" had occurred. Expansion of the concepts of SUBSTANTIVE DUE PROCESS and freedom of contract, in the hands of a Court whose personnel and social philosophy had changed radically by the 1890s, brought the Court into the business of acting regularly as censor of legislation on substantive grounds. Despite the continued ascendancy in national politics of Republican and conservative-Democratic regimes that resisted pressures for sweeping social-reform legislation, still a flood of new state legislation came forth in such areas as municipal public health, franchise law affecting public utilities, factory and mining safety, maximum hours, child labor, building codes, and railroad safety and operating practices. Neither the state courts nor the Supreme Court lacked for opportunities to play the role of censor and apply the new substantive due process reading of the Fourteenth Amendment.

Thus the courts turned to the last of the great questions regarding constitutional definition of the police power and its limits in the post-Civil War era: the question of standards or formulae for determining constitutionality. One of those standards emerged early in the period—ironically, in *Munn v. Illinois*, in which the new Fourteenth Amendment claims were decisively rejected by the Court. In deciding the case, however, the Court set forth the new principle of AFFECTATION WITH A PUBLIC INTEREST, asserting that warehouses and railroad companies were subject to regulation because they were virtual monopolies. They were comparable to bridges and ferries, long held by the common law to be a special category of business dedicated to service to the public, standing athwart essential lines of commerce and travel. Citizens were compelled, in effect, to resort to them; hence they were classified by the Court as being in the regulable category. The "affectation" doctrine was a Trojan horse. If there was a line to be drawn between businesses regulable because of their essential character—that is, because the public was compelled to use them for vital activities—then on the other side of that line were types of business immune from regulation. Such was the logic of *Munn*. In later years, the Court struck down a great variety of state regulatory laws on the grounds they were aimed at businesses not affected with a public interest. Indeed, not until 1934 in NEBBIA V. NEW YORK did the Court finally abandon the affectation distinction, ruling that a state could properly regulate any economic interest. "It is clear," the Court declared, "that there is no closed class or category of businesses affected with a public interest."

"Freedom of contract" similarly served as a standard for the Court to strike down regulatory legislation. Thus in LOCHNER V. NEW YORK (1905) and ADKINS V. CHILDREN'S HOSPITAL (1923), as well as in other decisions, the Court invalidated various state laws that regulated the terms of industrial employment. Like the "affectation" standard, however, the freedom of contract formulation as a restriction on the police power was destined to be discarded in the course of the New Deal period of the Court's history.

Other limitations on state exercise of the police power proved to be more enduring. They are, in part, the limitations rooted in the older, antebellum concept of due process as a procedural concept, reinforced by the terms of the EQUAL PROTECTION clause of the Fourteenth Amendment. Not only the Supreme Court but also the state courts—both in periods when many courts were inclined to invalidate social-reform legislation on the grounds of freedom of contract and in periods when they were more inclined to be deferential to legislatures—have contributed to the formulation of continuing restraints on the police power. Thoroughly accepted in American constitutional law, in recent decades, is Justice OLIVER WENDELL HOLMES's warning, in *Noble State Bank v. Haskell* (1911), that regulatory legislation by its definition will "more or less limit the liberty of the individual or . . . diminish property to a certain extent"—but government would be paralyzed if such limitations should regularly fall afoul of constitutional objections. Yet Holmes himself conceded in his opinion in the controversial case of *Pennsylvania Coal Company v. Mahon* (1922) when the Court invalidated a Pennsylvania law curbing mining companies' property rights in an effort to save urban structures from collapsing, that there must be some definable "limits" to the police power: "While property may be regulated to a certain extent, if regulation goes too far it will be recognized as a taking." Thus a line must be drawn between the police power, which permits diminution of property or liberty, and the power of eminent domain, which authorizes a taking only for a public purpose and on payment of adequate compensation.

To this specific consideration of when regulation encroaches on the realm of eminent domain taking, the Supreme Court and state courts have welded the more traditional procedural concerns. Exemplary of the latter was the doctrine of the Tennessee high court in *Vanzant v. Waddel* (1829) to the effect that to be valid a regulation must be "a general public law, equally binding upon every member of the community . . . under similar circumstances." Chief Justice Shaw of Massachusetts elaborated the theme in decisions upholding forfeiture of property deemed unwholesome or a PUBLIC NUISANCE, but requiring TRIAL BY JURY and judicial process. So long as the legislature established a precise statutory rule, applied it evenhandedly, and provided traditional procedural safeguards, the Shaw court would uphold police power regulation. Later, from the Supreme Court opinion in MUGLER V. KANSAS (1887), came the formulation that to be valid a police power regulation must have a "real or substantial relation" to public health, morals, safety, and welfare; and in 1936 (*Treigle v. Homestead Association*) the Court also declared that a regulation must be enacted "for an end which is in fact public and the means adopted must be reasonably adapted to the accomplishment of that end." These considerations of due process, too, have survived even though the restraining concepts to which they were once wedded—the "affectation" idea, and substantive due process concepts such as judicial determination of reasonableness—have largely been stripped from them.

In recent times, and particularly since the expansion of the positive state in the New Deal era, constitutional challenges to the police power have come to a focus on the question of how much administrative discretion ought to be allowed to state regulatory agencies. Agricultural marketing commissions, fish and game control agencies, mining-safety authorities, factory inspection boards, fire- and building-code enforcement agencies, air and water pollution control boards, and other regulatory agencies of government have been held to standards of administrative due process. Their substantive powers of regulation, however, have been generally upheld broadly by state and federal courts.

Emblematic of modern police power issues in the law is the history of land-use ZONING. Even prior to the decision in 1926 of EUCLID V. AMBLER REALTY, in which the Supreme Court upheld zoning that excluded industrial use, several of the states' appellate courts had validated such legislation. In each instance, they rejected claims that property owners had suffered from an effective "taking," hence ought to be compensated. As the Supreme Court itself noted in *Euclid,* such regulations a half century earlier "probably would have been rejected as arbitrary and oppressive"; now they were found necessary and valid because they were consonant with the magnitude of emergent industrial and urban problems. As the California Supreme Court declared in *Miller v. Board of Public Works* (1925), widely cited in other cases involving expansion of administrative discretion: "The police power, as such, is not confined within the narrow circumspection of precedents, resting upon past conditions which do not cover and control present-day conditions. . . . [It] is elastic and, in keeping with the growth of knowledge and the belief in the popular mind in the need for its application, capable of expansion. . . ."

The presumption of constitutionality against claims based on due process was explicitly stated in opinions of the Supreme Court again in the 1930s, echoing the majority's views in *Munn.* In *Nebbia,* for example, the Court not only laid to rest "affectation with a public interest" as a limitation on the police power; it also held that a regulation should be accorded "every possible presumption . . . in favor of its validity . . . unless palpably in excess of legislative power." When the Court upheld a statute regulating prices charged by employment agencies, in OLSEN V. NEBRASKA (1941), it couched its holding in terms that made its new posture unmistakable: "We are not concerned," wrote Justice William O. Douglas, "with the wisdom, need, or appropriateness of the legislation. . . . There is no necessity for the state to demonstrate before us that evils persist." In FERGUSON V. SKRUPA (1963) the Court refused to strike down a state law that prohibited anyone from engaging in the business of debt-adjusting except as incidental to the practice of law.

Justice HUGO L. BLACK, writing for the Court, acknowledged that good arguments doubtless could be made for the social utility of the activity thus restricted. But he concluded that though the regulation might be "wise or unwise," this substantive issue was not the Court's concern; it belonged to the state legislature. In *Agins v. Tiburon* (1980) a municipal zoning ordinance severely limited development of open-space lands; the Court again upheld a sweeping use of the police power and turned away due process arguments against the ordinance. So long as even a greatly reduced use of the land was permitted, the Court ruled, claims that "justice and fairness" had been denied would not be upheld. Although the Court still imposed commerce power limitations on the states' regulatory activities, by the 1980s it seemed that the presumption of constitutionality against due process, contract clause, and inverse condemnation claims was firmly entrenched.

A decision ostensibly on a narrow technical point yet vitally important for expansion of discretionary power's real-life effectiveness was *Morrissette v. United States* (1951). In this decision the Court reaffirmed state court rulings dating back to pre-Civil War years that when criminal penalties are used to enforce police power regulations regarding "public health, safety and welfare," the state is not constitutionally required to prove criminal intent, as in ordinary criminal cases.

In response to the emergence of the modern state police power, there has been abundant scholarly debate and legal controversy regarding its impact on private economic rights. Some have welcomed the enlarged regulatory power and administrative discretion, declaring them to be indispensable in the complex world of modern economic and social change. These same features of the modern police power have been condemned heatedly by others, however, as unfair in their application. That eminent domain takings, which do require compensation, and actions under the police power, which do not, are on a continuous spectrum of state power has long been recognized. Numerous scholarly formulations have been offered to distinguish the two powers. The classic distinction was given in ERNST FREUND's great treatise, *The Police Power: Public Policy and Constitutional Rights*, published in 1904. Freund contended that "the state takes property by eminent domain because it is useful to the public, and under the police power because it is harmful." Modern critics of the expanded police power and the positive state deplore restrictions upon uses of property that impose costs upon a private owner in order to benefit the public, rather than to prevent harm to the public; thus, the person prevented from building on his or her land where it stands in the flight path of an airport's runway is said by these critics to be harmed unfairly, forced in effect to bear alone the cost of a public benefit.

There are some, indeed, who take a hard-line position on the police power by arguing that virtually all restraints—but certainly those that deprive private property owners of what previously had been "reasonable expectations" of use and profit from regulated property—ought to be accompanied by reasonable compensation. Only the narrowest sort of regulation, based on common law nuisance and *sic utere* doctrine, would be exempt as these property-minded conservatives formulate their theory. The possibility that paralysis of the regulatory process might be caused by the sheer volume of government compensation payments required by this theory is a source of satisfaction rather than dismay to the most doctrinaire proponents of this view. Posed against it, and in favor of a definition of police power broad in its terms and consonant with recent decisions, is a theory that when government undertakes the role of "enterpriser" (creating parks, building highways, sponsoring urban renewal projects) it ought to compensate owners whose property is taken or damaged; but in its role as "arbiter" of contending social interests, as Joseph Sax has written, its actions for regulation of private uses of property should require no compensation. Other commentators, taking a middle position, urge that courts should give fresh recognition to considerations of "fairness" in these matters—for example, guarding against the possibility of a property owner's becoming the victim of more or less systematic deprivation, and also distinguishing degrees of harm and damage to the private owners affected by a STATE ACTION. These commentators also urge that administrators and legislators should be aware of "demoralization costs" when no effort is made to ameliorate the suffering of those hit hardest by regulatory activities.

The conflict between claims of the public under the police power and the claims of private property thus constitutes one major area of constitutional adjudication and current debate. Another area, no less turbulent and controversial, is the conflict between the police power and personal freedoms. Virtually all confrontations between persons and the state on matters of FREEDOM OF SPEECH, FREEDOM OF THE PRESS, FREEDOM OF ASSEMBLY, SEPARATION OF CHURCH AND STATE, or discrimination based on sex or religion or race are confrontations involving the police power. The whole corpus of constitutional doctrine based on the BILL OF RIGHTS and on the Fourteenth Amendment, in this area, together with such federal statutes as the various CIVIL RIGHTS acts, serve as a comprehensive set of limitations upon exercise of the state police power. The states remain free, however, to impose a higher standard in regard to constitutional liberties than is required by prevailing Supreme Court doctrine based on the federal Constitution.

As the uses of the federal regulatory powers have expanded, especially since 1933, there has been increasing need for the courts to examine the question of PREEMPTION—that is, the supersession of state laws when federal regulation has occupied a given policy area. In cases such as PARKER V. BROWN in 1943, and *Florida Avocado Growers v. Paul* twenty years later, the Supreme Court has upheld state marketing regulations affecting agricultural products even though both federal antitrust regulation and federal farm policies presented serious preemption questions. In the fields of labor law and transportation regulation, however, the Court has been more inclined to curb the scope of state activity in fields regulated by federal statutes and administrative regulations. Since the mid-1960s, a wave of consumer-oriented, industrial safety, and environmental legislation enacted by Congress has brought national power into regulatory areas previously occupied largely by state law. These initiatives have occasioned considerable litigation centering on preemption and congressional intent. In a few instances, the new federal statutes specifically authorize imposition of higher regulatory standards by individual states; other statutes have provided for federal preemption after a specified period, in states that do not meet certain minimum standards of regulation and enforcement.

The complexities of the preemption issue in modern constitutional law concerning the state police power are emblematic of the differences between government intervention in the present day and intervention on the modest scale of the eighteenth and nineteenth centuries. In 1836 Justice Joseph Story summarized the limited functions of the state in his day: to protect the persons and property of citizens from harm, to guard personal rights; to establish courts of justice and enforce laws against crimes, to enforce contracts, and to encourage moral behavior. These functions, together with state promotion of economic development, were justified because they were "conducive to the strength and the happiness of the people." What Story could not anticipate—and what is at the core of the modern constitutional history of the state police power—is the enormous expansion of regulatory activity and the accompanying shift toward enlarged administrative discretion in the modern state. Recent decisions and treatises are no longer much concerned with issues concerning the legitimacy of the police power as such issues were defined in Field's and Cooley's day, or even in the early years of the New Deal. Nonetheless, changing values as to equality, fairness, and rights of the public—and, to an increasing degree in the 1980s, a revival of issues concerning efficiency criteria and the wisdom of regulatory policies—continue to be expressed both in policy debates and in scholarly dialogue on the place of the state police power in the constitutional system.

HARRY N. SCHEIBER

Bibliography

FREUND, ERNST 1904 *The Police Power: Public Policy and Constitutional Rights.* Chicago: Callaghan.

HASTINGS, W. A. 1900 The Development of the Law as Illustrated by the Decisions Relating to the Police Power of the State. *Proceedings of the American Philosophical Society* 39:359–554.

LEVY, LEONARD W. 1957 *The Law of the Commonwealth and Chief Justice Shaw.* Cambridge, Mass.: Harvard University Press.

REZNICK, SCOTT M. 1978 Empiricism and the Principle of Conditions in the Evolution of the Police Power: A Model for Definitional Scrutiny. *Washington University Law Quarterly* 1978:1–92.

SCHEIBER, HARRY N. 1982 Law and the Imperatives of Progress: Private Rights and Public Values in American Legal History, *Nomos: Yearbook of the American Society for Political and Legal Philosophy* 24:303–320.

SCHWARTZ, BERNARD 1965 *A Commentary on the Constitution of the United States, Part II: The Rights of Property.* New York and London: Macmillan.

STOEBUCK, WILLIAM V. 1980 Police Power, Takings, and Due Process. *Washington and Lee Law Review* 37:1057–1099.

STATE REGULATION OF COMMERCE

When the Framers of the Constitution granted Congress the power "to regulate Commerce with foreign Nations, and among the several States, and with the Indian Tribes," they did not specify what regulatory powers were to be left to the states. Did they intend simply to grant a power to Congress which left the states free to regulate until such time as Congress acted? Were states restrained only from enacting statutes inconsistent with federal statutes? Or was the grant of power to Congress intended to be exclusive, forbidding the states to regulate commerce among the states even though Congress had not acted?

These questions troubled the Court several times

during JOHN MARSHALL's tenure as Chief Justice. As a strong nationalist, he was attracted by the argument presented by DANIEL WEBSTER in GIBBONS v. OGDEN (1824) that the word "regulate" implied full power over the thing to be regulated and necessarily excluded the power of the states to regulate the same thing. But Congress could not be expected to regulate all commerce among the states. Most transportation was by water. Inland transportation was slow and difficult. It could take a week or ten days to travel from Boston to New York, and in practical effect Georgia was more remote from New York than from the ports of Europe.

Marshall's solution was to suggest that Congress had full power to regulate INTERSTATE COMMERCE but that in the absence of conflicting federal regulations, the states had power to enact local police laws—inspection laws, quarantine laws, health laws, laws respecting turnpike roads and ferries—even though such laws might affect commerce. After Marshall's death the Justices were sharply divided between those advocating the position that exclusive power to regulate interstate commerce was vested in Congress and those, led by the new Chief Justice, ROGER B. TANEY, advocating the position that states had full power to regulate interstate commerce so long as Congress had not acted.

In 1851, in COOLEY v. BOARD OF WARDENS OF PHILADELPHIA, the Court arrived at a compromise of the conflicting views. In upholding a state law requiring vessels in interstate and FOREIGN COMMERCE to accept local pilots, the Court said that when the subjects being regulated "are in their nature national, or admit only of one uniform system, or plan of regulation" they "require exclusive legislation by Congress." On the other hand, when the subjects were local, as in the case of pilotage regulations attuned to individual conditions of the various ports, the states could regulate until Congress might intervene.

During the next half century the Court struggled to limit the negative implications of its notion of broad federal powers to regulate during a time when the federal government regulated little outside of water transportation. Some theory was needed to support the necessary state regulation of commerce. One way to do this was to narrow the definition of interstate commerce. In PAUL v. VIRGINIA (1868) the Court held that the insurance business was not commerce among the states and so could be regulated by the states. In KIDD v. PEARSON (1888) it upheld an Iowa statute forbidding the manufacture of intoxicating beverages as applied to a manufacturer who sold all his output in other states. The Court said that manufacturing was not commerce. If it were commerce, the Court assumed, "Congress would be invested, to the exclusion of the States, with the power to regulate not only the manufacturers, but also agriculture, horticulture, stock raising, domestic fisheries, mining—in short, every branch of human industry." In other cases the Court decided when an interstate journey began (when the goods had been actually shipped, or delivered aboard a common carrier for shipment, across state borders) and when it ended (when it came to rest at the end of its journey available for final disposition or use).

Toward the end of the century the Court devised another method for enabling states to regulate in areas Congress had not chosen to regulate. In *Cooley* the Court had said that a federal statute consenting to all present and future state pilotage regulations was invalid insofar as it incorporated future regulations because the division of power between state and nation was fixed in the Constitution and Congress could not change it. In LEISY v. HARDIN (1890) the Court held that one state could not forbid the sale of liquor brought in from another state while still in its ORIGINAL PACKAGE, but added that "so long as Congress does not pass any law to regulate it, or allowing the States so to do, it thereby indicates its will that such commerce shall be free and untrammelled." Congress took the hint and enacted a law permitting states to regulate such traffic in liquor, and the Court upheld the law in *In re Rahrer* (1891). Since then it has been settled that Congress may, if it wishes, permit states to regulate in areas otherwise reserved for Congress.

But even these rules did not result in agreement on the principles to be used in deciding individual cases. Despite the fact that *Cooley* appeared to have established that the states sometimes could regulate, the Court continued to refer from time to time to the "exclusive" power of Congress to regulate interstate commerce. In other cases the Court suggested that the test of validity of a state regulation of interstate commerce was whether it imposed a forbidden "direct" burden on commerce or a permitted "indirect" burden. By the beginning of the twentieth century there was clear agreement on only one principle: state regulations that clearly discriminated against interstate commerce by imposing burdens on such commerce beyond those imposed on comparable INTRASTATE COMMERCE were invalid.

During the first third of this century the Court dealt with a large mass of state regulations of transportation. A fair characterization of the cases would be one of doctrinal confusion. While the Court affirmed that states could not ban interstate transportation or discriminate against it for economic reasons, it had great difficulty in deciding when formally nondiscriminatory state regulations might be invalid because of the burdens they cast on commerce.

Today the Court does not get transportation cases involving state discrimination against interstate commerce. Instead, it is asked to determine that even nondiscriminatory regulations may be invalid if they impose substantial burdens on commerce without compensatory state advantages. *South Carolina State Highway Department v. Barnwell Bros.* (1938) involved a state statute prohibiting the use on state highways of any trucks wider than ninety inches. Although nondiscriminatory, the statute had a major impact on interstate commerce; all other states permitted a width of ninety-six inches, and thus most trucks engaged in interstate commerce would not be able to enter South Carolina. The Court said that few matters of state regulation were "so peculiarly of local concern" as was the use of state highways. The problem was one of determining whether local conditions demanded the regulation in the interests of safety. That determination was "a legislative, not a judicial choice," and the state's conclusion that the regulation was necessary was presumed correct unless "upon the whole record . . . it [was] without a RATIONAL BASIS."

But seven years later, in SOUTHERN PACIFIC V. ARIZONA EX REL. SULLIVAN (1945), the Court indicated that the courts rather than the state legislatures would have the final say in such commerce cases. A state statute limited the length of all trains in Arizona to fourteen passenger cars or seventy freight cars. The Court declared that Congress could "permit the states to regulate the commerce in a manner which would otherwise not be permissible . . . or exclude state regulations even of matters of peculiarly local concern which nevertheless affect interstate commerce." But when Congress had not acted, the final determination was for the courts. The question was whether the state interest in preventing injuries to railroad employees due to the slack action of cars on longer trains was outweighed by the burden the statute would have upon interstate commerce. The Court concluded that the state justification was weak and the burden heavy and so invalidated the statute. *Barnwell* was said to be different because it had dealt with the peculiarly local nature of state highways.

In recent years the Court has struggled with the question whether the *Barnwell* or the *Southern Pacific* approach should be used to judge state regulations of highways. In BIBB V. NAVAJO FREIGHT LINES, INC. (1959) the Court held invalid an Illinois statute requiring trucks to use contour mudguards when all other states permitted, and Arkansas required, straight mudflaps. The Court reaffirmed *Barnwell*, saying that courts should not engage in rebalancing the interests which the state legislature had, but added that this was "one of those cases—few in number—where local safety measures that are nondiscriminatory place an unconstitutional burden on interstate commerce." The Court has also dealt with state laws forbidding the use of trucks pulling double trailers as applied to interstate carriers. In RAYMOND MOTOR TRANSPORTATION, INC. V. RICE (1978) the Court unanimously invalidated a Wisconsin statute, noting that extensive evidence showed the law's heavy burden on interstate commerce and that the state had made no effort to demonstrate any safety interest. In *Kassel v. Consolidated Freightways Corp.* (1981) the Court invalidated a similar Iowa statute but was unable to agree upon an opinion or upon the way in which such regulations should be judged. Only four Justices clearly applied the *Southern Pacific* approach in highway regulation cases; the others were willing to leave the matter to the states when the safety interests at stake were substantial.

Cases involving regulation of production and trade also give the Court difficulty in arriving at consistent standards. Some governing rules are fairly straightforward. A state cannot ban the importation of goods, except in the rare case when goods must be excluded to avoid substantial damage to persons or property. So the Court in GREAT ATLANTIC & PACIFIC TEA CO. V. COTTRELL (1976) held that Mississippi could not forbid the importation of milk from Louisiana which had refused to sign a reciprocity agreement with Mississippi. In PHILADELPHIA V. NEW JERSEY (1978) the Court held invalid a state law banning importation of garbage destined for private landfills. The Court said: "[W]here simple economic protectionism is effected by state legislation, a virtually *per se* rule of invalidity has been erected. . . . The clearest example of such legislation is a law that overtly blocks the flow of interstate commerce at a State's borders."

Nor can a state ban the exportation of goods, even for the purpose of conserving scarce goods for use by citizens of the state. Thus in HOOD & SONS V. DU MOND (1949) the Court held that New York could not deny a milk dealer the right to purchase milk and ship it out of state, even though milk was short for a nearby city. In *Hughes v. Oklahoma* (1979) the Court said the commerce clause forbade the state from preventing the transportation or sale outside the state of minnows procured within the state. And an attempt by New Hampshire to make sure that electricity generated by water power served first the needs of local citizens, by forbidding the export of such power without permission of the state, was invalidated in *New England Power Co. v. New Hampshire* (1982). The Court said that the regulation was "precisely the sort of protectionist regulation that the COMMERCE CLAUSE declares off-limits to the States." However, *Sporhase v. Nebraska* (1982) suggests that a state restriction on the exportation of ground water may be upheld when done "to conserve and preserve for its own citizens this vital resource in times of severe shortage."

Regulations which discriminate against interstate commerce or otherwise operate to protect local commerce against competition are also invalidated. In *Baldwin v. G. A. F. Seelig, Inc.* (1935) the Court held unconstitutional a New York statute that made it unlawful to sell milk purchased from out-of-state producers at prices less than those paid local producers. The Court said: "If New York, in order to promote the economic welfare of her farmers, may guard them against competition with the cheaper prices of Vermont, the door has been opened to rivalries and reprisals that were meant to be averted by subjecting commerce between the states to the power of the nation." A Louisiana statute forbidding the export of shrimp unless the heads and hulls had been removed was held invalid in *Foster-Fountain Packing Co. v. Haydel* (1928) because the effect was to favor the canning of meat and the manufacture of bran in Louisiana.

Much more difficult for the Court have been cases that do not overtly discriminate against interstate commerce. In DEAN MILK CO. V. MADISON (1951) the Court invalidated a city ordinance forbidding the sale of milk as pasteurized unless it had been processed and bottled at an approved plant located within five miles of the center of Madison. Although the criterion excluded in-state as well as out-of-state milk, the Court said it discriminated against interstate commerce. The Court recognized that Madison had a legitimate interest in the purity of milk, but held it could not give an economic preference to local businesses if there were reasonable nondiscriminatory alternatives, such as inspection outside the state.

In *Pike v. Bruce Church, Inc.* (1970) the Court held unconstitutional, as applied to a grower with a substantial packing plant in California, an Arizona statute forbidding shipment of fruit out of the state unless it was packed in containers bearing the name of Arizona. The court set out a series of tests which have been frequently referred to in later cases: "Where the statute regulates even-handedly to effectuate a legitimate local public interest, and its effects on interstate commerce are only incidental, it will be upheld unless the burden imposed on such commerce is clearly excessive in relation to the putative local benefits. . . . If a legitimate local purpose is found, then the question becomes one of degree. And the extent of the burden that will be tolerated will of course depend on the nature of the local interest involved, and on whether it could be promoted as well with a lesser impact on interstate activities."

The Court has difficulty in applying the *Pike* formula. The major problem comes in deciding whether a case presents a nondiscriminatory statute with an incidental EFFECT ON COMMERCE or one which can be characterized as discriminatory, hence requiring the higher STANDARD OF REVIEW. In *Hunt v. Washington State Apple Advertising Commission* (1977) a North Carolina statute requiring all closed containers of apples sold in the state to bear no grade other than the applicable U.S. grade or standard was challenged by Washington, which marketed under its own grades which were equivalent or superior to the U.S. grades. Even though the statute applied equally to local and out-of-state shippers of apples, the Justices found that the statute discriminated against the Washington apples and held it invalid. The principal difficulty appeared to be that the statute took from Washington the market advantages it had earned through its own grading system.

The next year, in *Exxon Corp. v. Maryland* (1978), however, the Court upheld a state law forbidding a producer or refiner of petroleum products to operate any retail service station within the states. Maryland had no in-state oil production or refining. The Court said that the act did not affect the interstate transportation of gasoline—presumably the same volume would come in after the statute as before—but merely the structure of retailing. Further, since owners of multi-state chains of retail stations who did not produce gas could continue to compete, there was not even a preference for locally owned stations. The Court said that *Hunt* was different because there the statute favored in-state operators over out-of-state ones.

More recently, in MINNESOTA V. CLOVER LEAF CREAMERY CO. (1981), the Court upheld a Minnesota statute banning the retail sale of milk in plastic nonreturnable, nonrefillable containers while permitting such sale in other nonreturnable, nonrefillable containers such as paperboard milk cartons. The Court noted that the statute did not discriminate. The burden imposed on commerce was very slight since most dairies packaged their milk in various kinds of containers, and the shifts in the business would not be distributed on in-state, out-of-state lines.

Finally, the Court has held that when the state itself is in the market producing or selling goods, the commerce clause does not restrict the state. Thus in *Reeves, Inc. v. Stake* (1980) the Court upheld, 5–4, a decision by South Dakota to cease selling cement which the state manufactured to out-of-state customers in order to supply the needs of South Dakota customers. The Court said that the state, as a market participant, was free to prefer its own citizens, even though it could not order private businesses to do the same. The Court distinguished the manufacture of cement from regulating private use of natural resources such as coal, timber, wild game, or minerals. The cement was the end product of a complex process in which a physical plant and human labor of the state had acted on raw materials. The dissenters said the policy upheld was "precisely the kind of economic protectionism that the Commerce Clause was intended to prevent."

Today, as in 1824, the Court has great difficulty in defining its place with reference to state regulation of interstate commerce. States can regulate commerce in the absence of conflicting federal regulation so long as they do not go too far. The Court will strike down clear discriminations or economic preferences for local economic interests. But, when confronted with a nondiscriminatory regulation that imposes an incidental burden on commerce, the Court will sometimes let the regulation stand until Congress acts and in other cases will intervene to protect commerce. This uncertainty is likely to persist.

EDWARD L. BARRETT, JR.

Bibliography

DOWLING, NOEL T. 1940 Interstate Commerce and State Power—Revised Version. *Virginia Law Review* 27:1–28.

NOWAK, JOHN E.; ROTUNDA, RONALD D.; and YOUNG, NELSON J. 1978 *Handbook on Constitutional Law.* Pages 243–266. St. Paul, Minn.: West Publishing Co.

RIBBLE, F. D. G. 1937 *State and National Power over Commerce.* New York: Columbia University Press.

TRIBE, LAURENCE H. 1978 *American Constitutional Law.* Pages 319–344. Mineola, N.Y.: Foundation Press.

VARAT, JONATHAN D. 1981 State "Citizenship" and Interstate Equality. *University of Chicago Law Review* 48:487–572.

STATES' RIGHTS

"States' rights" is better understood not as a term of art denoting a constitutional principle but as a slogan with tactical value in political controversy. The slogan of states' rights has been raised at one time or another by advocates from every region of the country and by partisans of every political persuasion. The phrase emphasizes one element of FEDERALISM, but it is a serious error to equate federalism with states' rights.

Although the states' rights are often asserted in terms of state SOVEREIGNTY, the claim of states' rights is really a claim on behalf of the sovereignty of the people. No government, national or state, properly exercises any power that has not been delegated to it by the people. The assertion of states' rights is most often made by those who oppose a policy of the national government and who claim that the people have not delegated to the national government the power to implement the policy. Less often the assertion is made by those who believe that the states, or at least their own states, are more likely than the federal government to implement a desired policy.

The idea of states' rights is as old as the Republic. The jealousy with which the colonial legislatures guarded their limited local powers against the British Parliament and the royal government was carried over into ANTI-FEDERALIST CONSTITUTIONAL THOUGHT. To the extent that the argument for states' rights is one of principle, it is based on the classical notion that public virtue flourishes only in relatively small political communities. The French political philosopher MONTESQUIEU, whom JAMES MADISON called the "oracle" for American constitutionalists of the Founding Era, restated the classical view in modern terms and maintained that the best practical regime was a small republic confederated for military and commercial purposes with similar small republics. Many Anti-Federalists opposed the Constitution from a genuine fear of consolidation into a continental empire that only a despot could govern effectively.

But there was also a practical factor in the Anti-Federalist opposition. In the years between 1776 and 1789, the state governments had assumed responsibility for their internal affairs to a far greater degree than the colonial governments had ever done. Individual leaders, parties, cliques, and factions had arisen and assumed their places in state politics; creation of a national political environment was bound to reduce the power of most of them. Familiar ways of dealing with problems would be replaced with strange ones.

After the RATIFICATION OF THE CONSTITUTION, the erstwhile opponents of the new frame of government, along with some of its defenders, sought to interpret it in Anti-Federalist, or Montesquian, terms. The Constitution, according to this interpretation, was a compact between the people of each state and the people of the other states. When the Federalist-dominated national government adopted the ALIEN AND SEDITION ACTS (1798), "states' rights" became the battle cry of the Republican party, whose leaders, JAMES MADISON and THOMAS JEFFERSON, gave the slogan substantive expression in the VIRGINIA AND KENTUCKY RESOLUTIONS (1799).

In the nineteenth century the growing sectional rivalry between the commercial, and increasingly industrial, North and the agrarian South was reflected in competing THEORIES OF THE UNION. The states' rights position came to be identified in public discourse with the interest of the slave power. It found its champion in JOHN C. CALHOUN, who, in the South Carolina EXPOSITION AND PROTEST (1828–1829), announced the doctrine of NULLIFICATION as a logical consequence of the state compact theory. Nullification, of course, was an empty threat unless it was backed up by the possibility of SECESSION.

One attempt was made to implement Calhoun's doctrine, the SOUTH CAROLINA ORDINANCE OF NULLIFICATION directed against the TARIFF ACT OF 1828, and that was a failure. In 1861, when the election of ABRAHAM LINCOLN as President clearly signaled that slavery had been belatedly set upon its course of ultimate extinction, eleven southern states withdrew from the Union. Lincoln denied not only the legitimacy but also the very possibility of secession, and the victory of the Union in the Civil War vindicated his position for all practical purposes. Whatever rights the states have they have as members of the Union.

The FOURTEENTH AMENDMENT, adopted after the Civil War, proved an obstacle to state regulation of economic activity begun under the influence of the Populist and Progressive movements. Because the BILL OF RIGHTS applied only to the federal government, individuals whose rights were infringed by actions of the state governments (unless they were the victims of BILLS OF ATTAINDER, EX POST FACTO LAWS, or laws impairing the OBLIGATION OF CONTRACTS) previously had been able to rely only on the state constitution, political system, or courts for redress. In the late nineteenth and early twentieth centuries, however, the Supreme Court held the substantive guarantees (life, liberty, and property) of the Fourteenth Amendment's due process clause to be effective limitations on state legislative power. In the rhetoric of the reformers, the federal government (or at least its judicial branch) had infringed on the states' right to regulate their internal affairs.

In the 1920s the cry of "states' rights" was raised both by those who opposed federal intrusions into areas of state legislative concern and by those states that were frustrated in the attempt to expand state regulatory power. It is instructive that states' rights claims were raised in both MASSACHUSETTS V. MELLON (1923) and PIERCE V. SOCIETY OF SISTERS (1925), the first in the interest of less and the second in the interest of more governmental regulation.

Between the late 1940s and the late 1960s, the cause of states' rights became virtually identified with the cause of southern opposition to CIVIL RIGHTS legislation. The national commitment to abolishing racial SEGREGATION, first in publicly owned facilities and then in private establishments dealing with the public, aroused fierce opposition among those who were destined to lose their privileged position. Despite its long history of service to every shade of political opinion, the slogan of "states' rights" may have been permanently tarnished by its association with state-sponsored RACIAL DISCRIMINATION.

If the states, as states, have a valid claim of right to any particular field of legislation, that field would seem to be legislation concerning the internal workings of the governmental apparatus of the state. In the twentieth century the federal government undertook to regulate the compensation and working conditions of state employees, incidentally to its regulation of compensation and working conditions of private employees under the COMMERCE CLAUSE. In NATIONAL LEAGUE OF CITIES V. USERY (1976) the Supreme Court struck down such regulation insofar as the employees concerned were involved in the essential governmental operations of the states. The distinction was undermined in EQUAL EMPLOYMENT OPPORTUNITY COMMISSION V. WYOMING (1983), and discarded as unworkable in GARCIA V. SAN ANTONIO METROPOLITAN TRANSIT AUTHORITY (1985). In *Garcia* a 5–4 Supreme Court explicitly overruled *Usery,* and—unless the dissenters were accurate in predicting that the *Usery* doctrine would one day be revived—effectively put an end to the last vestige of states' rights in constitutional law.

DENNIS J. MAHONEY

(SEE ALSO: *Tenth Amendment.*)

Bibliography

ELAZAR, DANIEL J. 1972 *American Federalism: A View from the States,* 2nd ed. New York: Thomas Y. Crowell Co.

GRODZINS, MORTON 1966 *The American System: A New View of Government in the United States,* ed. Daniel J. Elazar. Chicago: Rand-McNally.

SANFORD, TERRY 1967 *Storm over the States.* New York: McGraw-Hill.

VILE, M. J. C. 1961 *The Structure of American Federalism.* Oxford: Oxford University Press.

STATES' RIGHTS AMENDMENTS (1963–1967)

The decisions of the WARREN COURT radically altered the constitutional balance of power to the disadvantage of the several states. In 1963, the Council of State Governments recommended three constitutional amendments that would, respectively, have established a third variation of the AMENDING PROCESS by which the states could alter the Constitution without the participation of Congress; denied the Supreme Court JURISDICTION over apportionment of state legislatures; and created a Court of the Union, comprising all the state chief justices, with power to overrule the Supreme Court on questions of federal–state relations.

The amendments were introduced in Congress by Senator J. Strom Thurmond of South Carolina but were buried in committee. Supporters hoped to have two-thirds of the state legislatures petition Congress and thereby oblige Congress to call an amending convention. The first and third proposals encountered widespread opposition—including public denunciation by Chief Justice EARL WARREN. But the 1964 REAPPORTIONMENT decisions, REYNOLDS V. SIMS and *Lucas v. Forty-Fourth General Assembly,* spurred the legislatures to act on the remaining proposal. By the time the agitation ceased in 1967, thirty-three states (only one less than necessary) had petitioned for an amending convention on the apportionment issue.

DENNIS J. MAHONEY

STATE SUICIDE THEORY

Massachusetts Senator CHARLES SUMNER, like most abolitionists and all Republicans before the Civil War, believed that the federal government lacked constitutional power to abolish slavery in the states. By early 1862, however, he and some other Republicans sought a theoretical basis for the exercise of congressional authority to govern occupied areas of the Confederacy and to eliminate slavery there. While other Republicans flirted with theories of territorialization or the CONQUERED PROVINCES concept of Representative THADDEUS STEVENS, Sumner developed his own unique amalgam of constitutional ideas for Reconstruction, which came to be known as the state suicide theory.

Sumner believed that the Confederate states, by seceding, had committed a sort of constitutional suicide, dissolving their "peculiar local institutions" (that is, slavery) and leaving their territory and inhabitants to be governed by Congress. This conception derived from three constitutional sources. The idea that the seceded states had reverted to the condition of TERRITORIES was widely discussed among Republicans after the outbreak of war. The belief that slavery, because it required positive law for its existence, would expire when that law expired, was derived from implications of the doctrine of SOMERSET'S CASE (1772) and had appeared in abolitionists' constitutional arguments before the war. Abolitionists also found a basis of congressional power to govern the states (including the power to abolish slavery there) in the clause of Article IV, section 4, that requires the United States to guarantee a REPUBLICAN FORM OF GOVERNMENT to each of the states. (See ABOLITIONIST CONSTITUTIONAL THEORY.)

Democrats, conservatives, and even moderate Republicans deplored the state suicide theory, regarding it as unconstitutional because it recognized the validity, or at least effectiveness, of SECESSION. Sumner abandoned his insistence on the constitutional death of the states but continued to maintain that Congress had plenary governmental power in the occupied states.

WILLIAM M. WIECEK

Bibliography

DONALD, DAVID 1970 *Charles Sumner and the Rights of Man.* New York: Knopf.

STATE TAXATION OF COMMERCE

Since BROWN V. MARYLAND in 1827 the Supreme Court has decided hundreds of cases determining the extent to which the COMMERCE CLAUSE immunizes from state taxation property moving in INTERSTATE COMMERCE or businesses engaged in such commerce. From the outset, agreement has existed on one principle—state taxes that discriminate against interstate commerce are invalid. In WELTON V. MISSOURI (1876) the Court held invalid a state tax on local sales because it applied only to goods produced outside the state. Recently, in *Boston Stock Exchange v. State Tax Commission* (1977), the Court stated that the "fundamental principle" that no state may impose a tax that discriminates against interstate commerce "follows inexorably from the basic purpose of the [Commerce] Clause. Permitting individual states to enact laws that favor local enterprises at the expense of out-of-state businesses 'would invite a multiplication of preferential trade areas destructive' of the free trade which the Clause protects."

The Supreme Court recognized early, however, that even formally nondiscriminatory taxes might put interstate commerce at a competitive disadvantage. In PHILADELPHIA & READING RAILROAD V. PENNSYLVANIA (1873) a tax on transportation companies measured by cents per ton of freight carried within the state (but not apportioned to distance) was held invalid as applied to goods in interstate commerce even though local commerce paid the same tax. The Court noted that if one state could impose this tax all states could and commercial intercourse between states remote from each other might be destroyed. Interstate commerce could bear the imposition of a single tax but "it would be crushed under the load of many." To avoid such burdens the Court formulated broad prophylactic rules. States were not permitted to tax interstate commerce by laying taxes on property in transit in interstate commerce, the business which constituted such commerce, the privilege of engaging in it, or the receipts derived from it.

The Supreme Court did not go so far, however, as to hold that states could never secure revenue from interstate businesses. An immunity that broad would have placed the states in the position of being required to provide governmental services to interstate property and businesses within their borders without being able to secure from them any contribution to the costs of such governmental services. Hence the Court came to recognize a variety of avenues through which states could derive revenue from interstate commerce.

The principal state revenue producer in the last century was the *ad valorem* property tax. Although property taxes on goods actually moving in interstate commerce were forbidden (because of the risk that they would be applied by more states than one), states were permitted to impose property taxes upon railroad cars and barges if they were apportioned (usually by mileage) so as to apply, in effect, only to the average number of cars present in the state on any one day. The Supreme Court even went so far as to permit states to levy property taxes on the intangible values of interstate transportation companies by permitting the imposition of taxes upon the proportion of the total going-concern value of the companies that track mileage within the state bore to total track mileage.

In other cases activities were characterized as intrastate in order to permit state taxation. Manufacturing, mining, and PRODUCTION were held to be INTRASTATE COMMERCE and taxes upon such activities were permitted even though substantially all of the goods produced were shipped in interstate commerce. Sales involving the transfer of goods from seller to buyer within the state were regarded as intrastate while sales involving no more than solicitation of orders within the state followed by delivery from without were interstate sales. Hence, states could impose nondiscriminatory license taxes on peddlers who carried with them the goods they sold but not on drummers who merely took orders. Later, when modern sales taxes came into existence, the Court applied the same principles. A sales tax could not be imposed when the seller outside the state shipped goods to the purchaser inside the state, but it could be imposed upon the local retailer who brought the goods from outside and then sold and delivered them to customers. In order to protect local merchants from competition by out-of-state sellers, states imposed on purchasers a tax on the "first use" within the state of goods purchased, with an exemption for goods on which the sales tax had been paid. The Supreme Court sustained such taxes on the theory that they were imposed on a local transaction—the use—rather than upon the interstate sale.

Another major boost to the power of states to secure revenues from interstate commerce came in *United States Glue Co. v. Town of Oak Creek* (1918). The Supreme Court upheld the power of a state to impose taxes measured by net income derived within the state, including net income from interstate activities. The Court distinguished earlier decisions forbidding the imposition of taxes on gross income from commerce by saying that such taxes burdened commerce directly while net income taxes, applied only to the taxpayers' net profits, bore only indirectly upon commerce. The power of the states to impose net INCOME TAXES was initially limited only by two principles. First, a net income tax could not be collected if the taxpayer did only interstate commerce within the state, because it would constitute an imposition on the privilege of engaging in interstate commerce—a privilege that the state did not grant. Second, the tax could be imposed only upon that portion of the net income fairly attributable to activities within the taxing state. A rational apportionment formula was required.

In *Western Livestock v. Bureau of Revenue* (1938), Justice HARLAN FISKE STONE sought to derive from the cases a general principle that would abrogate the general rule that interstate commerce itself could not be taxed. He said that it was not the purpose of the commerce clause "to relieve those engaged in interstate commerce from their just share of state tax burden even though it increases the cost of doing business." He noted that gross receipts taxes had often been held invalid. "The vice characteristic of those which have been held invalid is that they have placed on commerce burdens of such a nature as to be capable in point of substance, of being imposed . . . or added to . . . with equal right by every state which the commerce touches, merely because interstate commerce is being done, so that without the protection of the commerce clause it would bear cumulative burdens not imposed on local commerce."

The decision in *Western Livestock* did not mark an end to the older idea that interstate commerce itself could not be directly taxed. As recently as 1946 in *Freeman v. Hewit,* Justice FELIX FRANKFURTER speaking for the Court said:

> Nor is there any warrant in the constitutional principles heretofore applied by this Court to support the notion that a State may be allowed one single-tax-worth of direct interference with the free flow of commerce. An exaction by a State from interstate commerce falls not because of a proven increase in the cost of the product. What makes the tax invalid is the fact that there is interference by a State with the freedom of interstate commerce. . . . Trade being a sensitive plant, a direct tax upon it to some extent at least deters trade even if its effect is not precisely calculable.

For nearly three decades after *Western Livestock* the cases continued to reflect first one and then the other of these conflicting approaches.

Recently, however, the Supreme Court has cleared out most of the underbrush of the cases from the past and has established some relatively simple guidelines for the future. In *Complete Auto Transit, Inc. v. Brady* (1977) the Court said that it considers not the "formal language" of the tax statute but its "practical effect" and sustains "a tax against commerce clause challenge when the tax is applied to an activity with a substantial nexus with the taxing state, is fairly apportioned, does not discriminate against interstate commerce, and is fairly related to the services provided by the State."

With respect to *ad valorem* property taxation, the Court continues to forbid such taxes on goods moving in interstate commerce while reaffirming the rule that properly apportioned taxes may be imposed upon the instrumentalities of commerce such as railroad cars and airplanes. In *Japan Line, Ltd. v. County of Los Angeles* (1979), however, the Court limited this rule as applied to foreign-owned instrumentalities. It held that a country could not impose even an apportioned tax on the value of shipping containers owned by a Japanese shipping company because Japan was taxing the entire value of the containers. The Court said that its rule permitting apportioned property taxation was based on its ability to force apportionment on all potential taxing jurisdictions. Since Japan could not be required to apportion, the county could not tax at all even though it provided governmental services to the containers when they were in the state.

The distinction between taxes measured by gross income and those by net income has been abolished, along with the rule that states may not tax the privilege of engaging in interstate commerce. In the *Brady* case and in *Department of Revenue of Washington v. Association of Washington Stevedoring Companies* (1978) the Court upheld privilege taxes measured by gross receipts derived from exclusively interstate commerce within the taxing state. The Court indicated that the key is apportionment, which avoids multiple burdens. In *Washington Stevedoring,* for example, it upheld a tax on the gross receipts of a stevedoring company which had as its entire activity loading and unloading in Washington ships engaged in interstate and FOREIGN COMMERCE. It said that the state had "a significant interest in exacting from interstate commerce its fair share of the cost of state government. . . . The Commerce Clause balance tips against the tax only when it unfairly burdens commerce by exacting more than a just share from interstate activity."

A 1959 federal statute (section 381, Title 18, United States Code) provides that a state may not impose a net income tax if the taxpayer does no more within the state than solicit orders. Beyond that limit the major, current problems relate to the apportionment of an interstate business's income among the states having JURISDICTION TO TAX it. Nearly half of the states are adherents to the Multistate Tax Compact which calls for net income to be apportioned by a three-factor formula based on property, payroll, and sales. Most states, whether or not adherents to the Compact, utilize similar three-factor formulas. Iowa, however, applies a formula under which it taxes that proportion of net income that gross sales within the state bear to total gross sales. In *Moorman Manufacturing Co. v. Blair* (1978) a challenge to this formula was rejected. The taxpayer argued that to permit Iowa to use a single-factor formula when other states in which it did business used a three-factor formula would result in the taxation by Iowa of income that had been taxed in other states. The Supreme Court would go no further than to examine the particular formula to see that it is reasonable and does not allocate disproportionate amounts of income to the taxing state, leaving to Congress the question whether a uniform formula should be imposed on all states. The

Court has also recently rejected challenges to the application of apportionment formulas to the entire net income of integrated companies engaged in production, refining, and distribution of petroleum products. In *Exxon Corporation v. Wisconsin Department of Revenue* (1980) the Court held that so long as the taxpayer is engaged in a "unitary business" any state in which it does business may apply its apportionment formula to the entire net income of the business without regard to how the taxpayer's own accounting system allocates profits and losses.

With respect to taxes on the sales transaction, existing doctrines permit the state in which goods are sold to tax through either a sales or a use tax. However, collection of the use tax is often impossible if the state cannot compel the seller to collect the tax from the purchaser and remit it to the state. Recent concern has been with the DUE PROCESS jurisdictional problem. The state must show some definite link, some minimum connection, between the seller and the state, before it can impose the duty of collection.

A century and a half after *Brown v. Maryland* the Supreme Court's approach to state taxation of interstate commerce is relatively simple: so long as the state taxes do not discriminate against such commerce or create a risk of multiplication of similar levies on the same property or activity, they will be upheld. States will be given wide latitude in devising formulas for apportioning income and allocating values. If more protection for commerce is desired, it will have to come from Congress.

EDWARD L. BARRETT, JR.

(SEE ALSO: *Excise Taxes; Import-Export Clause; Imposts; Original Package Doctrine; State Regulation of Commerce.*)

Bibliography

BARRETT, EDWARD L., JR. 1953 "Substance" vs. "Form" in the Application of the Commerce Clause to State Taxation. *University of Pennsylvania Law Review* 101:740–791.

HARTMAN, PAUL J. 1953 *State Taxation of Interstate Commerce.* Buffalo, N.Y.: Dennis Co.

NOTE 1975 Developments in the Law: Federal Limitations on State Taxation of Interstate Business. *Harvard Law Review* 75:956–1036.

STATUS OF FORCES AGREEMENT

Following World War II, as a consequence of entering into a series of mutual defense pacts, the United States established a continuing military presence in a number of foreign countries. To deal with the legal questions that inevitably arose because of this presence, the United States entered into a number of agreements—known as "status of forces agreements"—with the receiving (that is, host) countries involved.

Typically, status of forces agreements exempt visiting forces from the receiving state's passport and immigration regulations, and from its customs duties and taxes on personal property also. Further, the sending state is permitted to issue driving permits and licenses to members of its forces, to purchase goods locally for local consumption, and to employ indigenous civilian labor. In addition, provision usually is made for the settlement of claims for property damage allegedly caused by the visiting forces.

The heart of a status of forces agreement, however, is its allocation of JURISDICTION in respect of criminal offenses putatively committed by the members and accompanying civilians of the visiting forces. In general, the sending state and the receiving state retain exclusive jurisdiction over offenses not punishable by the laws of the other. Where an offense is punishable by the laws of both states, concurrent jurisdiction prevails, with either the sending state or the receiving state retaining the primary right to exercise criminal jurisdiction, depending on the nature of the offense and the circumstances of its occurrence. Where the receiving state exercises jurisdiction, it ordinarily guarantees a prompt and speedy trial, timely notice of charges, the right to confront hostile witnesses, satisfactory legal representation, and a competent interpreter. The accused is usually guaranteed the right to communicate with her or his governmental representatives and to have them present at trial, if possible.

BURNS H. WESTON

(SEE ALSO: *North Atlantic Treaty; Treaty Power.*)

Bibliography

LAZAREFF, S. 1971 *Status of Military Forces under Current International Law.* Leyden, Netherlands: A. W. Sijthoff.

SNEE, J. and PYE, A. K. 1957 *Status of Forces Agreements and Criminal Jurisdiction.* Dobbs Ferry, N.Y.: Oceana Publications.

STATUTORY CONSTRUCTION

See: Legislation

STAY OF EXECUTION

A stay of execution is an order commanding that the enforcement (execution) of a lower court JUDGMENT be suspended (stayed) pending further proceedings before that court or an appeal of the judgment to a higher court. The entry of such an order is essentially a matter of judicial discretion, tempered by various principles developed in court rules and judicial precedents. In a civil case, a stay order may be conditioned on the posting of a bond to protect the interests of the prevailing party; in a criminal case a stay of a prison sentence raises the question of the defendant's entitlement to release or continued freedom, often conditioned on posting a bail bond.

In the federal court system, stays can be sought in district courts, courts of appeals, and ultimately in the Supreme Court. Generally speaking, a litigant must exhaust all possibilities of securing a stay from a lower court or courts before applying to a higher court. Stays are of two categories: a stay of a district court judgment pending an appeal to a court of appeals, and a stay of a court of appeals judgment or mandate pending application to the Supreme Court to review the judgment of the court of appeals. The Supreme Court or an individual Justice has statutory authority to grant both types of stays, provided that all efforts to secure a stay from the lower courts have failed.

Most stay applications in the Supreme Court are addressed to and resolved by individual Justices, acting in their capacity as circuit Justices "in chambers," although application can be made to the entire Court for reconsideration of an individual Justice's denial of a stay. Generally, a stay will be granted when there is a "reasonable probability" that four Justices, the minimum needed to grant review, will vote to review the case; that there is "a fair prospect" that the decision below will be reversed; that irreparable harm to the applicant will likely result if a stay is denied; and that the balance of equities, to the parties and to the public, favors a stay.

EUGENE GRESSMAN

Bibliography

STERN, ROBERT L.; GRESSMAN, EUGENE; and SHAPIRO, STEPHEN M. 1986 *Supreme Court Practice,* 6th ed. Chap. 17. Washington, D.C.: Bureau of National Affairs.

STEAGALD v. UNITED STATES
451 U.S. 204 (1981)

A 7–2 Supreme Court extended to third parties the rule of PAYTON V. NEW YORK (1980) that, absent consent or exigent circumstances, law enforcement officers may not enter a home to make an arrest without a SEARCH WARRANT. Here the officers sought to execute an ARREST WARRANT for one person by entering the home of another and found EVIDENCE that served to convict that other party. The Court supported his contention that the FOURTH AMENDMENT required a warrant for the search of his home, reasoning that privacy, especially in one's home, outweighed the inconvenience to the officers of having to obtain a search warrant.

LEONARD W. LEVY

STEEL SEIZURE CONTROVERSY

In the latter part of 1951, a dispute arose between the nation's steel companies and their employees over terms and conditions of employment. On December 18, the steelworkers union gave notice of intention to strike when existing agreements expired on December 31. On December 22, President HARRY S. TRUMAN referred the dispute to the federal Wage Stabilization Board and the strike was canceled. The Board's subsequent report produced no settlement. Early in April 1952, the United Steel Workers of America called a nationwide strike to begin April 9.

President Truman and his advisers feared that the interruption of production would jeopardize national defense, particularly in Korea. The President thus issued EXECUTIVE ORDER 10340 to Secretary of Commerce Charles Sawyer, instructing him to take possession and operate the steel mills in the name of the United States government. Truman's authority to take such action was not granted specifically by the statute, and he cited none, although the Selective Service Act of 1948 and the Defense Production Act of 1950 authorized the seizure of industrial plants failing to give priority to defense orders. Although the TAFT-HARTLEY ACT of 1947 had a procedure for injunctive relief in a strike situation affecting an entire industry, or imperiling the national health and safety, it did not contain seizure provisions. Truman preferred to act on the basis of what Department of Justice attorneys assured him was the INHERENT POWER in the office of the President, stemming from his authority as COMMANDER-IN-CHIEF and "in accordance with the Constitution and the laws of the United States."

The steel companies obeyed Secretary Sawyer's order under protest but brought suit to enjoin the seizure in the District Court for the District of Columbia. There Judge David Pine granted a preliminary injunction restraining the secretary from continuing the seizure. Pine's ruling on the merits and the stay of the injunction by the United States Court of Appeals compelled the Supreme Court to face the constitutional issue also, on final appeal. (See YOUNGSTOWN STEEL AND TUBE V. SAWYER, 1952.)

PAUL L. MURPHY

Bibliography

MARCUS, MAEVA 1977 *Truman and the Steel Seizure Case: The Limits of Presidential Power.* New York: Columbia University Press.

STEPHENS, ALEXANDER H. (1812–1883)

A successful self-taught Georgia lawyer, Alexander Hamilton Stephens was a congressman (1843–1859, 1873–1882), vice-president of the Confederacy (1861–1865), and a lifelong defender of STATES' RIGHTS. As a southern Whig, Stephens sought to protect state SOVEREIGNTY and preserve the Union. These objectives led to apparent inconsistencies. Thus, he opposed JOHN C. CALHOUN and NULLIFICATION while arguing for the abstract right of SECESSION. Similarly, Stephens was a slaveowner who declared that "I am no defender of slavery in the abstract." He supported ANNEXATION OF TEXAS to preserve the balance of free and slave states, but he did not support slave extension generally. He opposed the Mexican War because of his unrelenting hatred of President JAMES K. POLK, his honest belief that the war was unjust, and his fear that it would reopen the divisive issue of SLAVERY IN THE TERRITORIES. But once the war was over he advocated opening the Mexican Cession to slavery. Ironically, he successfully moved to table the Clayton Compromise (1848), even though he supported its purpose, because he believed the Supreme Court would declare that existing Mexican law prohibited slavery in the new territories.

Stephens opposed the COMPROMISE OF 1850, warning: "Whenever this Government is brought in hostile array against me and mine, I am for disunion—openly, boldly and fearlessly for *revolution.*" Nevertheless, once the compromise passed, Stephens supported it in Georgia, and at the state's secession convention of 1850 he helped write the Georgia Platform which denounced disunion. Stephens then joined ROBERT TOOMBS and Howell Cobb in organizing a Union Party in Georgia.

In 1854 Stephens became a Democrat. He was the floor manager for the KANSAS-NEBRASKA ACT (1854) and worked closely with STEPHEN A. DOUGLAS. As chairman of the House Committee on the Territories Stephens supported the LECOMPTON CONSTITUTION, unlike his Senate counterpart (Douglas). Despite Douglas's apostacy on this issue, Stephens supported his presidential nomination in 1860 and futilely campaigned for Douglas in Georgia.

In November 1860 Stephens opposed secession in Georgia, arguing that Southerners and northern Democrats could block any bill that threatened slavery or the South. His pro-Union speech, reprinted throughout the North, led to a brief correspondence with President-elect ABRAHAM LINCOLN. As a delegate to the Georgia secession convention (January 1861), Stephens supported the creation of a southern nation, provided that it adopted a CONSTITUTION similar to that of the United States. In the provisional Confederate Congress Stephens helped draft the CONFEDERATE CONSTITUTION, which owing in part to his influence resembled the Constitution of 1787. Stephens was then chosen vice-president of the Confederacy. As a moderate who had long opposed secession, Stephens gave the new government legitimacy. On slavery, Stephens was by this time quite "sound." As early as 1855 he had defended slavery on biological and biblical grounds, as well as its role in creating southern society, which Stephens believed was the greatest in history. By 1860 he owned more than thirty slaves. In March 1861 he told the South and the world, in his most famous speech, that slavery was the "cornerstone of the Confederacy."

Throughout the Civil War Stephens's relationship with JEFFERSON DAVIS was stormy. Stephens opposed CONSCRIPTION, martial law, and the suspension of the writ of HABEAS CORPUS. He accused Davis of becoming a dictator and advocated that Georgia seceded from the confederacy to seek peace and sovereignty on its own. Stephens urged that the Confederacy support George McClellan's presidential bid and then seek peace with the United States. He made numerous peace overtures, and in early 1865 met with Lincoln in an unrealistic attempt to negotiate a peace that would preserve a separate southern nation.

Arrested for TREASON in May 1865, Stephens was incarcerated at Fort Warren (Boston) until President ANDREW JOHNSON pardoned him in October. He then returned to Georgia where an unreconstructed state legislature elected him to the United States Senate. The Senate responded to this affront by denying Stephens his seat.

In a ponderous and tedious book, *A Constitutional View of the Late War Between the States* (2 vols., 1868, 1870), Stephens presented an elaborate and unconvincing defense of secession. He responded to his many hostile critics with an even duller book, *The Reviewers Reviewed* (1872). Reelected to Congress in 1873, Stephens remained for nearly a decade as an ineffectual and somewhat scorned relic of the past. He continued to defend slavery and states' rights, while opposing reconstruction and black rights.

PAUL FINKELMAN

Bibliography

VON ABELE, RUDOLPH 1946 *Alexander H. Stephens: A Biography.* New York: Knopf.

STERILIZATION

Late in the nineteenth century, when simple and safe medical procedures for sterilization became available, the eugenics movement began to promote compulsory sterilization laws. A few laws were enacted specifying sterilization as punishment for sex crimes, but they were rarely enforced. In 1907 Indiana adopted a law authorizing sterilization of persons deemed "feebleminded," or, as one leading proponent put it, "socially defective." Other states soon followed. The Supreme Court lent both practical and moral support in its 1927 decision in BUCK V. BELL, upholding the constitutionality of Virginia's law. By 1935 more than thirty states had adopted forced sterilization laws, and 20,000 "eugenic" sterilizations had been performed. The victims of such laws tended to be poor; indeed, in the view of eugenics proponents, poverty and other forms of dependence were the marks of the "socially inadequate classes" that needed eradication.

Times have changed, and constitutional law has changed. Concurring in GRISWOLD V. CONNECTICUT (1965), Justice ARTHUR GOLDBERG said, "Surely the Government, absent a showing of a COMPELLING subordinating STATE INTEREST, could not decree that all husbands and wives must be sterilized after two children have been born to them." After SKINNER V. OKLAHOMA (1942) the point seems incontestable. Yet some state courts, following *Buck,* still uphold laws authorizing the involuntary sterilization of institutionalized mental patients. Although only fifteen years separated the *Buck* and *Skinner* decisions, their doctrinal foundations were worlds apart. *Skinner,* calling procreation "one of the basic civil rights of man," insisted on STRICT SCRUTINY by the Court of the justifications supporting a compulsory sterilization law. *Buck,* on the other hand, had employed a deferential form of RATIONAL BASIS review, analogizing forced sterilization to forced VACCINATION.

Skinner's crucial recognition was that sterilization was more than an invasion of the body; it was an irrevocable deprivation of the right to define one's life and one's identity as a biological parent. Vaccination implies no such consequences for one's self-identification and social role. The constitutional issues presented by sterilization thus bear a strong analogy to the issues raised by laws restricting other forms of BIRTH CONTROL and abortion. (See FREEDOM OF INTIMATE ASSOCIATION.) The Supreme Court has characterized all these forms of state interference with REPRODUCTIVE AUTONOMY as invasions of FUNDAMENTAL INTERESTS, and has subjected them to close scrutiny in the name of both EQUAL PROTECTION, as in *Skinner,* and that form of SUBSTANTIVE DUE PROCESS that goes by the alias of a RIGHT OF PRIVACY, as in *Griswold* and ROE V. WADE (1973).

The issue of *Buck* seems certain to return to the Supreme Court one day, to be decided on the basis of a much heightened STANDARD OF REVIEW. Similarly, a state law requiring consent of a spouse before a person could be sterilized would surely be held invalid, on analogy to PLANNED PARENTHOOD OF MISSOURI V. DANFORTH (1976). If a law calling for involuntary sterilization must pass the test of strict scrutiny, and if a competent adult has a corresponding right to choose to be sterilized, then the critical ingredient is choice. An "informed consent" requirement thus seems defensible against constitutional attack, provided that the required "informing" procedure does not unreasonably burden the decision to be sterilized. (An informed consent requirement for abortion was upheld by the Supreme Court in *Danforth.*)

As Justice WILLIAM O. DOUGLAS noted in his *Skinner* opinion, sterilization in "evil or reckless hands" can be an instrument of genocide. Even the most devoted partisan of reproductive choice cannot be entirely comfortable knowing that the percentage of sterilized nonwhite women in the United States is almost triple that for white women, or that among public assistance recipients blacks are twice as likely to "choose" sterilization as are whites. Under current interpretations the Constitution has nothing to say about the bare fact of this disparity; yet it reflects a condition of constitutional dimension that deserves to be addressed, at least in the domain of PROCEDURAL DUE PROCESS. And if nonwhite women are led by government officers to believe that sterilization is voluntary in theory but somehow compulsory in fact, that form of "engineering of consent" appears reachable in actions for damages under SECTION 1983, TITLE 42, UNITED STATES CODE, based on the deprivation of substantive due process.

KENNETH L. KARST

Bibliography

KELLY, MARY E. 1979 Sterilization Abuse: A Proposed Regulatory Scheme. *DePaul Law Review* 28:731–768.

KEVLES, DANIEL J. 1985 *In the Name of Eugenics: Genetics and the Uses of Human Heredity.* New York: Knopf.

PILPEL, HARRIET F. 1969 Voluntary Sterilization: A Human Right. *Columbia Human Rights Law Review* 7:105–119.

STETTLER v. O'HARA
243 U.S. 629 (1917)

An Oregon Supreme Court decision sustained that state's minimum wage law for women on the basis of the STATE POLICE POWER argument approved in MULLER V. OREGON (1908). A 4–4 Supreme Court affirmed that ruling in *Stettler.* Several state courts drew the inference that a properly drawn law regulating women's wages would be upheld and sustained such laws in reliance on *Stettler.* The DISTRICT OF COLUMBIA MINIMUM WAGE ACT nonetheless fell, 5–3, in ADKINS V. CHILDREN'S HOSPITAL (1923).

DAVID GORDON

STEVENS, JOHN PAUL
(1920–)

When President GERALD R. FORD named him to the Supreme Court in 1975, John Paul Stevens had all the conventional qualifications for the job. He had served for five years on the UNITED STATES COURT OF APPEALS for the Seventh Circuit, had been a distinguished antitrust law practitioner, a law school teacher, and a law clerk to Justice WILEY B. RUTLEDGE. But those who expected this conventional background to yield a conventional Justice soon learned better. Most new Justices write first for a unanimous Court; Justice Stevens's maiden effort, HAMPTON V. MOW SUN WONG (1976), included a combination of EQUAL PROTECTION and DELEGATION OF POWERS doctrine so novel that only four other Justices joined in it—and two of those added their own concurrence. In the terms that followed, Justice Stevens found it necessary to write separately far more often than any of his colleagues.

Many of his concurrences and dissents were sparked by disagreement with the substance of the BURGER COURT's decisions. He is the only Justice appointed since 1968 who does not regularly vote against criminal defendants, and his strong defense of PRISONERS' RIGHTS clearly runs counter to the majority's thinking. So too does his STRICT CONSTRUCTION of the ESTABLISHMENT OF RELIGION clause; and he is among the least receptive of the Justices when states assert local interests against the workings of a national economy, let alone the voice of Congress.

Overall, however, his moderate pragmatism puts him close to the center of the Court on most issues. What divides him from his colleagues is not so much substance as his fundamental dissatisfaction with the Court's judicial style. That style was summed up in UNITED STATES V. NIXON (1974), the year before Stevens's appointment. It is "emphatically the province and duty" of the judiciary, the Court quoted from MARBURY V. MADISON (1803), "to say what the law is." Left, right, and center, the Court he joined was nearly unanimous in wanting to say as much as possible about what the law is.

Stevens came from a different school. His first constitutional law professor, Nathaniel Nathanson, taught him that abstract talk about constitutional issues is usually misleading. In Nathanson's words, "we are the sworn enemies of the glittering half-truths, the over-simplified explanations. We are constantly at war with . . . the black-letter law, the restatements, the horn books." Another teacher soon reinforced the lesson; years after his clerkship, Stevens remembered: "Justice Rutledge exhibited great respect for experience and practical considerations. He was critical of broadly phrased rules which deceptively suggested that they would simplify the decision of difficult questions."

To a degree, this focus on the practical, the concrete, makes Stevens a spokesman for judicial restraint and narrow opinions. He can be relied upon, for example, to protest when the Court reaches out to decide constitutional issues on an insufficient record, as in *Globe Newspaper Co. v. Superior Court* (1982); when it leaps to interpret the Constitution despite a statute that would do the job, as in REGENTS OF THE UNIVERSITY OF CALIFORNIA V. BAKKE (1978); when it insists on reviewing for federal error a state court decision that will likely be restored on ADEQUATE STATE GROUNDS, as in *Michigan v. Long* (1983); or when it invokes the OVERBREADTH DOCTRINE to discuss facts not before the Court, as in *Metromedia, Inc. v. San Diego* (1981). And despite his reputation for unorthodox and strongly held views, some of Stevens's best work has been done in painstaking opinions such as *NAACP v. Claiborne Hardware Co.* (1982), where he held together a diverse group of Justices by saying no more than was necessary to resolve the case.

But Stevens's rejection of glittering half-truths and over-simplified explanations is no mere passive virtue. It has a radical side. In YOUNG V. AMERICAN MINI THEATRES, INC. (1976), for example, where Stevens defended the constitutionality of special ZONING for theaters showing sexually explicit movies, he did so by launching a frontal attack on that most glittering of half-truths—the assertion that government must ignore the content of the speech that it regulates. Only three other Justices joined him in *Mini Theatres*, but he persisted, pointing out in case after case that the principle of "content neutrality" was plainly too sweeping, that content-based distinctions had been employed for years in OBSCENITY, libel, and COMMERCIAL SPEECH cases. Ultimately he prevailed. In *New York v. Ferber* (1982) the Court explicitly endorsed Stevens's *Mini Theatres* analysis in the course of making child PORNOGRAPHY a new class of unprotected speech. Perhaps characteristically, Stevens refused to join the Court's opinion; in his view, the *Ferber* Court had fallen victim to an equally egregious half-truth—the notion that some kinds of speech are wholly beyond the scope of the FIRST AMENDMENT's protection.

By stripping away the slogans that obscured the First Amendment, Justice Stevens left himself free to follow what he had so admired in Rutledge: he could seek "a practical solution to a practical problem," exercising "the faculty of judgment and not merely the logical application of unbending principles." Recognizing that even obscene speech is still speech, he looked at the practical effect of criminal obscenity prosecutions. In an analysis strikingly parallel to his CAPITAL PUNISHMENT opinions, he concluded that the Court's obscenity decisions had produced laws so vague that they supplied juries with little or no guidance. The result was that, for most pornography, criminal penalities were applied too arbitrarily to withstand scrutiny.

At the same time, it was plain to him that the reasons for restricting sexually offensive speech do not die at the indistinct boundary between the obscene and the merely indecent. Although speech bordering on obscenity cannot be wholly suppressed, Stevens concluded, the practical—and so the constitutionally permissible—solution was to confine such speech to contexts that minimize or even eliminate its offensiveness. Thus, in SCHAD V. VILLAGE OF MT. EPHRAIM (1981) he would have allowed the town to bar nude dancing from quiet shopping centers and neighborhoods—but apparently not from "a local replica of Place Pigalle." In FEDERAL COMMUNICATIONS COMMISSION V. PACIFICA FOUNDATION (1978) he would have let the government keep four-letter words off afternoon radio—but not out of the United States Reports.

This insistence that constitutional issues be examined context by context marks all of Stevens's campaigns against the artificiality of black-letter constitutional law. When he joined the Court, for example, EQUAL PROTECTION analysis had split into two tiers, each with its own set of incantations; the prevailing doctrinal dispute was whether and where to add yet a third, "intermediate" tier between STRICT SCRUTINY and RATIONAL BASIS review. Again Justice Stevens's solution was a striking doctrinal departure: not more tiers but fewer. "There is only one Equal Protection Clause," he wrote in CRAIG V. BOREN (1976), and so only one basic STANDARD OF REVIEW. By demanding that legislative classifications be genuinely relevant to a legitimate purpose, Justice Stevens produces results not unlike those that emerge from the clanking operation of two- or even three-tiered review. The difference is that Stevens candidly exercises judgment, taking account of the context, the offensiveness of the classification, and the credibility of the legislative purpose.

Though his approach pays dividends in candor and flexibility, it has its costs. Among the first casualties, ironically, are some of the pieties of judicial restraint. Stevens's equal protection analysis, for example, does not allow him to pretend that laws are invalidated by some brooding three-tiered omnipresence in the sky. Instead, it demands a far more skeptical and probing look at legislative politics than is usual for advocates of restraint. His First Amendment analysis, for example, would replace the discredited "content neutrality" standard with a narrower requirement that government not display bias against a particular viewpoint. This practical and pointed inquiry would save some laws that do not survive the Court's more abstract standard. But the price of this restraint is high. To uphold some lawmakers' actions, as in *FCC v. League of Women Voters* (1984), he must bluntly accuse others of actions "obviously directed at spokesmen for a particular point of view."

Perhaps it is a recognition of these costs that makes Stevens adroit at using such techniques as "legislative remand," particularly when federal policies are at stake. His opinion in *Hampton v. Mow Sun Wong* (1976), for example, struck down a civil service rule barring ALIENS from federal employment—not because the asserted federal purposes were insufficient but because they were none of the Civil Service Commission's business. If the President or Congress adopted the same rule, he suggested, it might well withstand review. Similarly, in FULLILOVE V. KLUTZNICK (1980) he would have invalidated a federal law reserving ten percent of certain construction grants for minority-owned businesses—not because such a set-aside was necessarily unconstitutional but because it raised profound constitutional questions that Congress had failed even to consider in its "slapdash" rush to enactment.

What does this unique mix of radicalism and restraint mean for Stevens's role on the Court? It seems clear, first, that his candor will always make him something of an outsider; it shows a glint of cheerful mischief too often for him to be a classic majority-building centrist. It may be true, as Stevens said in *Lakeside v. Oregon* (1978), that "most people formally charged with crime are guilty" or that "most people who remain silent in the face of serious accusations have something to hide and therefore are probably guilty." It may also be true, as Stevens wrote in *Fullilove,* that so-called benign racial preferences make it easier for "representatives of minority groups to disseminate patronage to their political backers." But as bracing as these unwelcome truths can be in the opinions of a single Justice, they will not, and probably should not, find their way soon into opinions of the Court.

More important over the long run is Stevens's campaign to win back broad fields of constitutional judgment from the logicians and their half-truths. Here he has had occasional victories, but he is battling uphill. Justices write opinions that leave much unsaid only when they have faith in the wisdom of those who will finally fill the gaps—the lower courts, their colleagues, future Justices. So long as most members of the Court lack that faith, Stevens's campaign for institutional humility will face long odds. Even when the Court adopts his practical, contextual approach, as it essentially has in equal protection cases, its opinions are likely to cling to the words and forms of a more MECHANICAL JURISPRUDENCE.

Of course no Justice can expect to impose the full range of his or her views on the Supreme Court. It is when one looks at individual doctrines that the impact of Stevens's iconoclastic creativity becomes clear. At times the power of his attack has swept away entrenched dogma and cleared the way for new thinking, as it did in *Ferber.* More important still is his ability to come fresh to new constitutional problems and to tailor new solutions for them. This talent showed even on the Seventh Circuit, where, for example, he preceded the Court in declaring that the First Amendment is a safeguard against patronage dismissals and that state tort remedies are a way of providing due process to a prisoner deprived of his property. On the Court, by joining with other Justices in the center, Stevens has set new terms of constitutional debate in areas as diverse as the death penalty, SEARCH AND SEIZURE, and gerrymandering. As new Justices and new issues come to the Court, as the shock of his challenge to the old bromides fades, it is this practical creativity that will ultimately make his mark upon the law.

STEWART ABERCROMBIE BAKER

Bibliography

STEVENS, J. P. 1956 Mr. Justice Rutledge. Pages 176–202 in Allison Dunham and Philip B. Kurland, eds., *Mr. Justice.* Chicago: University of Chicago Press.

——— 1985 Judicial Restraint. *San Diego Law Review* 22:437–452.

STEVENS, THADDEUS
(1792–1868)

A Pennsylvania lawyer, state legislator (1833–1841), and congressman (1849–1853, 1859–1868), Thaddeus Stevens was the most powerful Republican congressman throughout the Civil War and beginning of Reconstruction. During this period Stevens was the earliest and most consistent congressional supporter of black rights and opponent of slavery. Stevens initiated, sponsored, or helped pass all key Reconstruction acts from 1865 to 1868. More than any other individual, Stevens was responsible for making the ex-slaves citizens.

After reading law, Stevens began practicing in 1816. In 1817 his unsuccessful defense of an accused murderer with the then novel plea of insanity brought Stevens fame and clients. After an initial case in which he represented a master in regaining fugitive slaves, Stevens never again defended slavery. Throughout the rest of his career Stevens took numerous cases on behalf of fugitive slaves, free blacks, and abolitionists. As one congressman said after his death, Stevens "was an abolitionist before there was such a party name." By 1831 he was one of Pennsylvania's most successful lawyers and a national leader of the Anti-Masonic movement. In 1835 Stevens single-handedly convinced the legislature to create a system of free public education for Pennsylvania. His passionate defense of public education stemmed from his own poverty-stricken background.

In 1848 Stevens was elected to Congress as a Whig, campaigning against slavery in lands ceded by Mexico. In Congress he was an acerbic, sarcastic, unrelenting opponent of slavery. Opposing the COMPROMISE OF 1850, he predicted it would be "the fruitful mother of future rebellion, disunion, and civil war." One of the first bloody fruits of the Compromise was the Christiana Riot, in Stevens's own county; a slaveowner was killed attempting to seize his fugitive slaves. Stevens helped organize the successful defense of Caster Hanway who was indicted for TREASON for refusing to help the master. A backlash against the riot and abolition cost Stevens his congressional seat the following year. After a short time in the Know-Nothing Party, he became a Republican in early 1855. In 1858 he was again elected to Congress, as a staunch opponent of his fellow Pennsylvanian, President JAMES BUCHANAN.

At the beginning of the Civil War Stevens became a leader of congressional Republicans. As chairman of the House Ways and Means Committee he influenced all legislation requiring appropriation of funds. Stevens was largely responsible for the Internal Revenue Act of 1862 and the Legal Tender Acts which were necessary to finance the war. As a member of the Joint Committee on the Conduct of the War Stevens helped insure that civilian, and not military, authority would be pre-eminent during the war. Stevens used this position, as well as his Ways and Means chairmanship, to press ABRAHAM LINCOLN's administration to stop the military from returning fugitive slaves and to allow blacks to enlist.

In 1861 Stevens was one of the few men in Washington who publicly recognized that slavery was the root cause of SECESSION and that the war required its destruction. In July 1861 he was one of two House members to oppose the Crittenden resolution, which declared that the North had no interest in interfering with slavery. In December 1861 Stevens helped defeat a reaffirmation of that resolution. From the outbreak of hostilities Stevens argued that the seceding states should be dealt with according to the "laws of war." He asserted that constitutional obligations and protections—such as those involving fugitive slaves, the protection of private property, or the writ of HABEAS CORPUS—should not be "binding on one party while they are repudiated by the other." Thus, he supported the creation of the new state of West Virginia on the theory that Virginia had ceased to exist as a state when it left the Union, so that it was unnecessary for Virginia to agree to the division of the state. Stevens's theory of STATE SUICIDE was never fully adopted by the Congress or the courts, but it was influential in persuading many congressmen to support his legislation during both the war and Reconstruction.

As early as August 1861 Stevens urged the abolition of slavery as a war measure. In 1862 he tried to secure legislation that would lead to the confiscation of plantations in the rebel states. He believed that such land could be constitutionally seized, not because it was owned by men who could be convicted of treason, but because it was the fruit of war. He subsequently introduced legislation to end slavery in the DISTRICT OF COLUMBIA, prevent the Army from returning fugitive slaves, and provide equal pay for black soldiers. He was a leader in securing other legislation that protected blacks and allowed them to serve in the military, even if they were owned by loyal masters.

During Reconstruction Stevens was the House Republican whip, a member of the Joint Committee on Reconstruction, and probably the most powerful politician in Washington. In early 1866 Stevens introduced legislation for the continuation of the FREEDMEN'S BUREAU, the adoption of the FOURTEENTH AMENDMENT to protect the freedmen, and the enfranchisement of blacks in Washington, D.C. President ANDREW JOHNSON's unexpected veto of the Freedmen's Bureau Bill, his subsequent attempts to prevent ratification of the Fourteenth Amendment, and his vehement opposition to voting by blacks led to congressional Reconstruction. Stevens sponsored legislation that prevented the former Confederate states from sending representatives to Congress without congressional approval. The legislation was specifically aimed at Johnson's home state of Tennessee, but applied to all the Confederate states.

During the election of 1866 Stevens openly argued for complete racial equality while campaigning for Republicans and against Andrew Johnson's administration. Johnson, meanwhile, publicly accused Stevens, CHARLES SUMNER, and the abolitionist Wendell Phillips of treason and suggested they ought to be hanged. The election gave the Republicans more than a two-thirds majority in both houses. Although ill through much of the Fortieth Congress, Stevens nevertheless sponsored the TENURE OF OFFICE ACT, which set the stage for Johnson's IMPEACHMENT, and the MILITARY RECONSTRUCTION ACT of 1867, which placed all former Confederate states, except Tennessee, under military rule. Stevens successfully backed many CIVIL RIGHTS measures introduced by others. He was the prime mover in requiring the former Confederate states to ratify the Fourteenth Amendment and enfranchise blacks. He supported legislation authorizing the army to protect the freedmen from white vigilantes. Virtually all this legislation was enacted over Johnson's veto, with Stevens, as majority whip, guiding it through Congress. Stevens failed, however, to persuade Congress to confiscate Southern plantations and provide land for the freedmen.

In 1866 and 1867 Stevens unsuccessfully supported Congressman James Ashley's motions for impeachment. In early 1868 Stevens himself sought Johnson's impeachment, but could not get committee support for it. However, after Johnson fired Secretary of War EDWIN M. STANTON, in violation of the Tenure of Office Act, an impeachment committee was quickly formed. Stevens, as a member of that committee, helped draft the ARTICLES OF IMPEACHMENT and later was a manager of the prosecution. However, he was quite ill by then and took little part in the trial. Ten weeks after the trial Stevens died.

PAUL FINKELMAN

Bibliography

BRODIE, FAWN M. 1959 *Thaddeus Stevens: Scourge of the South.* New York: Norton.

KORNGOLD, RALPH 1955 *Thaddeus Stevens.* New York: Harcourt Brace & World.

STEWARD MACHINE COMPANY v. DAVIS
301 U.S. 548 (1937)

Plaintiff, an employer, challenged the 1935 SOCIAL SECURITY ACT unemployment compensation provisions, which imposed a payroll tax on employers and directed that the tax receipts be paid to the general revenue. To offset part of this tax, the act granted employers a credit for taxes paid to a state unemployment fund conforming to federal benefit and solvency requirements. One such requirement was that state funds be held for safekeeping by the secretary of the treasury and invested in federal government securities. Plaintiff invoked UNITED STATES V. BUTLER (1936), which had invalidated AGRICULTURAL ADJUSTMENT ACT price support provisions that enabled the secretary of agriculture to contract with farmers to reduce agricultural production in exchange for payments funded by a federal tax levied on agricultural commodity processing. *Butler* had generally addressed the scope of Congress's power "to lay and collect taxes . . . to . . . provide . . . for the GENERAL WELFARE of the United States." While ostensibly rejecting the narrowest reading of the clause, originally proposed by JAMES MADISON, that the taxation power could be exercised only to carry out specifically ENUMERATED POWERS, and purporting to adopt a broader, though undefined, interpretation of the TAXING AND SPENDING POWER, *Butler* nevertheless had treated the TENTH AMENDMENT as a limitation on the federal taxation power. In *Steward Machine Co.*, plaintiff argued that the unemployment taxation scheme, like the agricultural price support provisions, exceeded congressional powers because it infringed the Tenth Amendment's reservation to the states of power not delegated by the Constitution to the United States.

The unemployment compensation scheme was sustained, 5–4. Justice BENJAMIN N. CARDOZO, writing for the majority, distinguished *United States v. Butler* on two grounds: the unemployment tax proceeds were to be used for the "general welfare" because they were not earmarked for any special group; and the unemployment compensation plan did not infringe state prerogatives because state participation in this cooperative federal-state program was entirely voluntary. The Court described unemployment as a "problem . . . national in area and dimensions." Many states wished to develop unemployment compensation programs but feared economic competition from those states without such plans. Hence a federal tax was necessary to enable states to accomplish their general welfare goals.

In its permissive, though vague, interpretation of the term "general welfare," *Steward Machine Co.* and its companion case, HELVERING V. DAVIS (1937), seem to repudiate the *United States v. Butler* view that Congress, in exercising its power to tax for the general welfare, is required by the Tenth Amendment to eschew regulation of matters historically controlled by the states. *Steward Machine Co.* is also noteworthy for its sympathetic appraisal of joint federal-state welfare ventures. Justice Cardozo amply demonstrated that the competitive pressures of a national economy make it increasingly difficult for the states to perform traditional welfare functions without the national uniformity made possible by federal assistance and regulation.

GRACE GANZ BLUMBERG

STEWART, POTTER J.
(1915–1985)

When DWIGHT D. EISENHOWER nominated Potter Stewart to the United States Supreme Court, the President was recognizing the perfect embodiment of Midwest Republican civic virtues. Born in Cincinnati, Stewart was the son of a popular reformist and Republican mayor who was later appointed to the Ohio Supreme Court. Stewart went from Cincinnati to Yale College where he was a class leader, then to Harvard for graduate study, and then back to Yale Law School. He returned to Cincinnati, after service in the Navy and on Wall Street to practice law and engage in civic affairs. In 1954, at the age of thirty-nine, he was named to the Court of Appeals for the Sixth Circuit. In October 1958, as a recess appointment, Stewart became an Associate Justice of the Supreme Court.

Stewart's tenure on the Court—more than twenty-three years—was atypically long. Only eighteen Justices have served a longer term. Yet Stewart did not seek to place a sharp imprint on the work of the Court, an imprint of the sort Justice HUGO L. BLACK or Justice FELIX FRANKFURTER had brought to their work. Nor did he seek to build a constituency within the Court or outside it. During two periods, at the outset of his tenure and shortly after the transition to the BURGER COURT, Stewart's vote was of great significance in determining the outcome of the Court's work. Because he was not a member of a dominant and consistent majority, it would not be the case, under the customs of the Court, that the most significant cases of the quarter-century were his to write.

Stewart was guided in his decisions and his actions as a judge by a sense of decency and proportion. He believed in a nation in which order, partially derived from privately inculcated values, offered the opportunity for advancement, creativity, and freedom. His sense of propriety led him to decline the possibility of becoming Chief Justice, according to then-President RICHARD M. NIXON, because Stewart thought it inappropriate for a sitting Justice to aspire to a presidential elevation. Even his resignation was characteristic. Stewart resigned not out of illness, nor out of ambition, nor for alternative appointment, but merely because he felt that limited service was correct.

These themes of propriety, of respect for structure and rules, permeate the jurisprudence of Justice Stewart. He was a firm adherent to the principles of STARE DECISIS, even when its application led to a result varying from his own previously expressed view. In a 1974 DISSENTING OPINION he wrote: "A basic change in the law upon a ground no firmer than a change in our membership invites the popular misconception that this institution is little different from the two political branches of the Government. No misconception could do more lasting injury to this Court and to the system of law which it is our abiding mission to serve."

An elegant and careful treatment of the facts was often at the core of a Stewart opinion because an understanding of the facts was central to the way he approached the issues in a case. Regularly, he would indulge his belief that a decision should be of appropriately narrow scope by stating what the case was not about. For him, a deep understanding of context was a prophylactic against undue haste in constitutional decision making. Dissenting in ESTES v. TEXAS (1965), for example, Stewart sought to demonstrate that the use of television cameras in the courtroom in that criminal case did not provide the factual predicate for the sweeping pronouncements in the Court's opinion concerning rights of defendants. Context yielded DOCTRINE, and not the reverse. If the result of an understanding of the facts was increased doctrinal complexity, then that could not be helped. "The time is long past when men believed that development of the law must always proceed by the smooth incorporation of new situations into a single coherent analytical framework," he wrote in COOLIDGE v. NEW HAMPSHIRE (1971). He thought it wrong that doctrine, sometime encapsulated in a "sterile metaphor" should seem to substitute for careful analysis, a point he made in his dissenting opinion in ABINGTON SCHOOL DISTRICT v. SCHEMPP (1963).

Much of Stewart's most significant work dealt with defining those rules, especially the FIRST AMENDMENT and the FOURTH AMENDMENT, which constrain the activities of government. There was a sharp tinge of the radical in Stewart's protection of the individual from government intervention. He celebrated the Fourth Amendment's warrant clause as a carefully conceived limitation on precipitate government searches and persistently opposed a reading that cheapened the clause. According to his colleague Justice LEWIS F. POWELL, Stewart's opinion in KATZ v. UNITED STATES (1967) "revitalized the fourth amendment" by rejecting the notion first espoused in OLMSTEAD v. UNITED STATES (1928) that the amendment applied only to physical trespass by police officers. In *Katz,* the court held that private conversations even outside the home must be secure from unwarranted police interception. "The Fourth Amendment," Stewart declared in characteristically pithy style, "protects people not places." Thus a Federal Bureau of Investigation microphone placed against the wall of a telephone booth was held to be an invasion of the RIGHT OF PRIVACY. Similarly, Stewart led the Court in a series of opinions that valued the doctrinal purity of a judicially sanctioned warrant requirement for a valid police search. Stewart sought to place the doctrine and its numerous exceptions in proper balance. At the same time, Stewart strongly recognized that in the field of ECONOMIC REGULATION legislatures should not be subject to similar constraints. He especially admired Justice ROBERT H. JACKSON and was fond of quoting Jackson's aphorism that "[t]he view of JUDICIAL SUPREMACY . . . has been its progressive closing of the avenues to peaceful and democratic conciliation of our social and economic conflicts."

Stewart's opinions gave important strength to the First Amendment guarantee of FREEDOM OF SPEECH and FREEDOM OF THE PRESS. He set as a task for himself a clearer and longer-lasting basis for the protection of the press so that it could monitor the government and inform the populace. In NEW YORK TIMES CO. V. UNITED STATES (1971) he wrote that only material that would cause "direct, immediate, and irreparable harm to the nation or its people" could be subject to prior restraint through court-ordered publication restrictions. In an early opinion for the Court, *Shelton v. Tucker* (1960), Stewart proclaimed that government cannot pursue even a legitimate end "by means that broadly stifle fundamental personal liberties when the end can be more narrowly achieved."

Stewart could be bold as well as forceful. It was his influence that led the Court to revitalize the THIRTEENTH AMENDMENT, validating Congress's power to establish a sweeping ban on RACIAL DISCRIMINATION in private housing. In JONES V. ALFRED H. MAYER CO. (1967) a land developer refused to sell a house to Joseph Lee Jones because Jones was black. By invoking the Thirteenth Amendment, Stewart's far-reaching opinion bypassed the limited and often confusing STATE ACTION requirement of the FOURTEENTH AMENDMENT and held that discrimination in private housing violated a previously dormant Reconstruction-era CIVIL RIGHTS statute, the CIVIL RIGHTS ACT OF 1866. In general, his civil rights opinions had a refreshing simplicity and directness that avoided temporizing and recognized statutory and constitutional imperatives.

Stewart was influential in other areas as well. For a time, his was one of the most original and radical views on the freakishness of the imposition of CAPITAL PUNISHMENT. It was his reconception of the criminal law in *Robinson v. California* (1962) that established new categories of thinking about sanctions and stigma. In *Carrington v. Rash* (1965) he broke new ground in his constitutional measure of state-imposed vote eligibility restrictions based on occupation, residency, and similar grounds.

Earlier than many of his colleagues Stewart brought to his analyses of the antitrust laws a keen sense of the economic impact of various approaches to the CLAYTON ACT and the SHERMAN ACT: his perceptions about the inappropriateness of a "per se" approach in vertical integration cases, stated in dissent in *United States v. Arnold, Schwinn & Co.* (1967), became the view of the Court in *Continental T.V. Inc. v. GTE Sylvania Inc.* (1977); his scorn for mechanical reliance on market shares as a test for invalidating mergers, articulated in dissent in *United States v. Von's Grocery Co.* (1966), became the text of his majority opinion in *United States v. General Dynamics Corp.* (1973).

Stewart was a bridge, a point of continuity from the Court of the late 1950s to the Court of the 1980s. Throughout, he prized what he viewed as the qualities of being a judge. In HARRIS V. MCRAE (1980) he wrote—upholding the constitutionality of a law restricting federal funding for abortions—that it was not the mission of the Court to decide whether "the balance of competing interests" in that legislation, or any other, "is wise social policy." Citing one of his favorite cases, WILLIAMSON V. LEE OPTICAL, INC. (1955), Stewart concluded that "we cannot, in the name of the Constitution, overturn duly enacted statutes simply 'because they may be unwise, inprovident, or out of harmony with a particular school of thought.' " Stewart's philosophy of law, his jurisprudence of appropriateness, his respect for the role of the Court, transcend categories as his devoted service on the Court transcended categorization.

MONROE E. PRICE

Bibliography

FRIEDMAN, LEON 1978 Potter Stewart. In Leon Friedman and Fred L. Israel, eds., *The Justices of the United States Supreme Court: Their Lives and Major Opinions*, 2nd ed. New York: Chelsea House.

MERESMAN, BARNETT, MERESMAN GOLDMAN & MORRIS 1982 A Lawyer's Lawyer, A Judge's Judge: Justice Potter Stewart and the Fourth Amendment. *University of Chicago Law Review* 51:509–544.

STEWART, POTTER 1975 Or of the Press. *Hastings Law Journal* 26:631–637.

STOCKHOLDER'S SUIT

Stockholders suing their CORPORATIONS rarely raise constitutional questions, although the Supreme Court accepted jurisdiction of a case involving such a suit as early as 1856. (See DODGE V. WOOLSEY.) Yet several celebrated constitutional decisions in review of acts of Congress have come in stockholder actions brought to prevent corporate compliance with tax or regulatory programs the stockholders deemed unconstitutional. Having failed to convince management to challenge the programs' constitutionality, dissenting stockholders have used the device of a stockholder's action to accomplish the same result. In most nonconstitutional cases, dissenting stockholders are not permitted to bypass the business judgment of corporate managers and sue on the corporation's behalf, but—ironically, and controversially—this rule has not always prevailed in constitutional cases. The device has not been used effectively since the New Deal era, but when it was used, the Supreme Court seemed eager to render major constitutional decisions, an orientation perennially opposed to the Court's professed practice.

Three celebrated examples tell the story. In POLLOCK V. FARMERS' LOAN & TRUST CO. (1895) the Supreme Court held a federal income tax law unconstitutional. The corporate taxpayer had planned to accept the tax obligation, and a federal statute prevented an INJUNCTION suit by the corporation, but the dissenting stockholders were permitted to seek an injunction preventing compliance. No one objected to the stockholders' right to sue; the plaintiff asserted that the suit was not a COLLUSIVE SUIT between the stockholder and the company; and the Court rendered its controversial decision on the merits—a decision subsequently overturned by the SIXTEENTH AMENDMENT (1913). In ASHWANDER V. TENNESSEE VALLEY AUTHORITY (1936) preferred stockholders of the Alabama Power Company sued to prevent their corporation from performing a contract with the TVA, claiming that Congress lacked constitutional power to authorize the TVA to develop and contract for the sale of electricity. The Supreme Court, over Justice LOUIS D. BRANDEIS's famous objection that the stockholders lacked STANDING to sue and that the Court generally should seek to avoid constitutional questions, permitted the suit. The Court held the TVA's action constitutional, thereby ending a major legal threat to an important New Deal program. A few months later, however, in CARTER V. CARTER COAL CO. (1936), another stockholder suit, the Court invalidated the Guffey Act of 1935, an important anti-Depression measure. The president of Carter Coal, whose parents were majority stockholders and who had set company policy in compliance with the act, initiated the suit as a dissenting stockholder the day after the law was enacted.

These stockholder actions raise several questions of JUSTICIABILITY. One is similar to that raised in taxpayers' and citizens' suits: are they suits to prevent individual injury, suits that incidentally necessitate constitutional interpretation, or are they public actions to assure constitutional governance for the whole citizenry? The allegation that corporate compliance with the questioned law will injure the corporation's (and therefore the stockholders') financial interests, may distinguish stockholder from taxpayer or citizen standing, despite a similar element of remoteness. A second question is raised by the possibility of a collusive suit, with both the dissenting stockholder and the corporate management desiring the same result. The possibility is real, but the drawbacks of collusive suits have not been a serious problem in stockholder suits. Despite the trumped-up appearance of *Carter v. Carter Coal Co.*, for example, the federal government vigorously opposed Carter. There was strongly adversary presentation, and, in a COMPANION CASE, another company directly challenged the government's enforcement of the new act. The most significant danger may be that the stockholder suit is really a request for a premature advisory opinion, because stockholder, corporation, and government all want a constitutional ruling when the corporation plans to comply with the law and no present controversy exists. The Court was eager to rule in *Pollock*, *Carter*, and *Ashwander*. The first two produced substantial interferences with congressional power, both subsequently overturned, and the last consciously legitimated government policy. Plainly, the stockholder suit has been used as an instrument of the Supreme Court's judicial activism in the exercise of JUDICIAL REVIEW.

JONATHAN D. VARAT

STONE, HARLAN F.
(1872–1946)

After finishing Amherst College and Columbia Law School (where in 1906 he became dean), Harlan F. Stone divided his time between teaching and practice in New York City. In 1923, President CALVIN COOLIDGE, a former college mate from Amherst, appointed him attorney general of the United States. Less than a year later he became Associate Justice of the United States Supreme Court. In 1941 President FRANKLIN D. ROOSEVELT, ignoring party labels, appointed him Chief Justice.

Experience gained as a teacher at the Columbia Law School had contributed directly to his preparation for the supreme bench. At the university, where he had time and opportunity for study and reflection, he developed ideas about the nature of law and the function of courts. Before donning judicial robes, Stone had argued only one case, *Ownbey v. Morgan* (1921), before the Supreme Court, adumbrating what was to become the major theme of his constitutional jurisprudence—judicial self-restraint. The correction of outmoded processes, he argued, ought to be left to legislatures rather than assumed by courts.

It seems ironical that Stone, a solid, peace-loving man, should have been in the crossfire of controversy throughout his judicial career. On the TAFT COURT, and also during a good part of Chief Justice CHARLES EVANS HUGHES's regime, he differed from colleagues on the right who interposed their economic and social predilections under the guise of interpreting the Constitution. During his own chief justiceship Stone was sometimes at odds with colleagues on the left who were equally intent on using their judicial offices to further particular preferences.

Stone's moderate approach is revealed in his consideration of INTERGOVERNMENTAL IMMUNITIES from taxation—a vexing problem throughout the chief justiceships of Taft and Hughes. Rejecting the facile reciprocal immunities doctrine established in MCCULLOCH V. MARYLAND and COLLECTOR V. DAY, respectively, he held that the federal system does not establish a total want of power in one government to tax the instrumentalities of the other. For him, the extent and locus of the tax burden were the important considerations. No formula, no facile "black and white" distinctions sufficed to determine the line between governmental functions that were immune from taxation and those that were not. Stone elaborated these views in *Helvering v. Gerhardt* (1938) and GRAVES V. NEW YORK EX REL O'KEEFE (1939). Similarly, in cases concerning state regulations of economic affairs and STATE TAXATION OF COMMERCE, Stone rejected question-begging formulas such as "business AFFECTED WITH A PUBLIC INTEREST" or "direct and indirect effects."

Though habitually a Republican, Stone believed that increased use of governmental power was a necessary concomitant of twentieth-century conditions. "Law," he said, "functions best only when it is fitted into the life of a people." He made this point specific in his law lectures. This conviction sometimes aligned him with OLIVER WENDELL HOLMES and LOUIS D. BRANDEIS. Uniting the triumvirate was their view that a Justice's personal predilections must not thwart the realization of legislative objectives not clearly violative of the Constitution.

Stone's constitutional jurisprudence crystallized during 1936, the heyday of the Court's resistance to President Roosevelt's program of government control and regulation. In the leading case of UNITED STATES V. BUTLER (1936) the Court voted 6–3 to invalidate the AGRICULTURAL ADJUSTMENT ACT (AAA). Justice OWEN J. ROBERTS and dissenting Justice Stone were about equally skeptical of the wisdom of the AAA. Their differences concerned the scope of national power and the Court's role in the American system of government. Stone thought that the majority had come to believe that any legislation it considered "undesirable" was necessarily unconstitutional. The Court had come to think of itself, as Stone said, as "the only agency of government that must be assumed to have capacity to govern."

The majority was haunted by the possibility that Congress might become "a parliament of the whole people, subject to no restrictions save such as are self-imposed." But, Stone countered, "consider the status of our own power." The President and Congress are restrained by the "ballot box and the processes of democratic government," and "subject to judicial restraint. The only check on our own exercise of power is our own sense of self-restraint."

Butler was neither the first nor the last time a dissenter expressly accused the court of "torturing" the Constitution under the guise of interpreting it. But no other Justice had previously used such strong language in condemning the practice.

In ADKINS V. CHILDREN'S HOSPITAL (1923) the Court had declared unconstitutional the minimum wage for women. Justice GEORGE H. SUTHERLAND was the spokesman. Holmes dissented as did Chief Justice Taft. *Adkins* was still in good standing in MOREHEAD V. NEW YORK EX REL. TIPALDO (1936) when Stone repeated his indictment: "It is not for the Court to resolve doubts whether the remedy by regulation is as efficacious as many believe, or better than some other, or is better even than blind operation of uncontrolled economic forces. The legislature must be free to choose unless government is rendered impotent. The Fourteenth Amendment has no more imbedded in the Constitution our preference for some particular set of economic beliefs, than it has adopted in the name of liberty the system of theology which we happen to approve."

In his war on the recalcitrant four (PIERCE BUTLER, JAMES C. MCREYNOLDS, Sutherland, and WILLIS VAN DEVANTER) Stone was sometimes allied with Holmes and Brandeis. Chief among points of agreement was their recognition of the need for a living law. As Holmes put it: "A slumber when prolonged means death." The essence of their creed was judicial self-restraint, recognized as a desirable rather than a realizable role.

The bond uniting them strengthened as the majority's doctrinaire approach became increasingly reactionary. Differences were exposed when Holmes, Brandeis, and Stone sometimes filed separate opinions in support of the same decision. In dissent Holmes, a gifted essayist addicted to generalization, often avoided the tough issues and "failed to meet the majority on its own ground." "This is a pretty good opinion," Stone remarked on one occasion, "but the old man leaves out all the troublesome facts and ignores all the tough points that worried the lower courts." "I wish," he once observed in grudging admiration, "I could make my cases sound as easy as Holmes makes his."

Stone's divergence from Brandeis was likewise most vividly portrayed in dissent. When the Court struck down legislation Brandeis favored in terms of policy, the erstwhile "People's Attorney" did not hesitate to use the Court as a forum to persuade others of its wisdom. "I told him [Brandeis] long ago," Holmes commented in 1930, "that he really was an advocate rather than a judge. He is affected by his interest in a cause, and if he feels it, he is not detached." Stone took specific exception to Brandeis's JUDICIAL ACTIVISM. In reply to a note in which Brandeis invited Stone to join his dissent in *Liggett Co. v. Lee* (1931), Stone said: "Your opinion is a very interesting and powerful document. But it goes further than I am inclined to go, because I do not think it necessary to go that far in order to deal with this case. . . . I think you are too much an advocate of this particular legislation. I have little enthusiasm for it, although I think it constitutional. In any case, I think our dissents are more effective if we take the attitude that we are concerned with power and not with the merit of its exercises. . . ."

Without minimizing the great contributions of Holmes and Brandeis, it seems fair to conclude that in a logical as well as a chronological sense Stone was the one who, in both the old and the new Court, carried their tradition to fulfillment. Perforce it fell to him, as his former law clerk, Herbert Wechsler, said, "to carry through to victory and consolidate the gain."

Chief Justice Taft paid high tribute to Stone's pioneering, even as he warned of the danger in the former law teacher's method. Said Taft: "He is a learned lawyer in many ways, but his judgement I do not altogether consider safe and the ease with which he expresses himself, and his interest in the whole branch of the law in which he is called upon to give an opinion on a single principle makes the rest of the Court impatient and doubtful. . . . Without impeaching at all his good faith in matters of that sort, we find we have to watch closely the language he uses."

Viewing Stone's dissent in *United States v. Butler* as a "lodestar for due regard between legislative and judicial power," some commentators interpreted the 1937 judicial about-face as signifying well-nigh complete withdrawal of the Court from the governing process.

After 1937, when the Court's Maginot Line crumbled, Justice Stone feared that the guarantees of CIVIL LIBERTIES might be wanting in effective safeguards. At first glance it does seem paradoxical that the leader of the campaign for judicial self-restraint in cases involving governmental ECONOMIC REGULATION should have articulated the PREFERRED FREEDOMS doctrine. In an otherwise obscure case, Stone suggested in the body of the opinion that he would not go so far as to say that no economic legislation would ever violate constitutional restraints, but he did indicate that in this area the Court's role would be strictly confined. Attached to this opinion is a famous footnote suggesting special judicial responsibility in the orbit of individual liberties. (See UNITED STATES V. CAROLENE PRODUCTS COMPANY, 1938.)

Two years later, in *Minersville School District v. Gobitis* (1940), the Court voted 8–1 to uphold Pennsylvania's compulsory flag salute as applied to Jehovah's Witnesses schoolchildren against their parents' religious beliefs. Justice FELIX FRANKFURTER, who spoke for the majority, wrote privately to Stone: "We are not the primary resolver of the clash. What weighs strongly on me in this case is my anxiety that while we lean in the direction of the libertarian aspect, we do not exercise our judicial power unduly, and as though we ourselves were legislators by holding too tight a rein on organs of popular government." (See FLAG SALUTE CASES.)

When Frankfurter learned that Stone was the lone dissenter, he was deeply disturbed. He pleaded: "That you should entertain doubts has naturally stirred me to an anxious re-examination of my own view. . . . I can assure you that nothing has weighed as much on my conscience since I came on this Court as has this case.. . . I'm aware of the important distinction which you so skillfully adumbrated in your footnote 4 in the *Carolene Products Co.* Case. I agree with that distinction: I regard it as basic. I have taken over that distinction in its central aspect."

Adolph Hitler had already unleashed his diabolical forces in Europe, and a widening conflict seemed inevitable. Frankfurter continued: "For time and circumstances are surely not irrelevant in resolving the conflict that we have to resolve in this particular case. . . . But certainly it is relevant to make the adjustment that we have to make within the framework of present circumstances and those that are clearly ahead of us."

Reflecting his New England heritage of RELIGIOUS LIBERTY, Stone was not convinced. He replied: "I am truly sorry not to go along with you. The case is peculiarly one of the relative weight of imponderables and I cannot overcome the feeling that the Constitution tips the scales in favor of religion."

Stone won this battle in a second case involving

the compulsory flag salute, *West Virginia State School Board of Education v. Barnette* (1943). By 1943 three other justices, HUGO L. BLACK, WILLIAM O. DOUGLAS, and FRANK MURPHY, who had joined Frankfurter in upholding the compulsory flag salute in *Gobitis,* changed their minds. Two new appointees, ROBERT H. JACKSON and WILEY B. RUTLEDGE, agreed with Stone's dissent in the earlier case, thus transforming a vote of 8–1 to uphold the compulsory salute to a vote of 6–3 striking it down. Speaking through Justice Jackson, the Court declared: "If there is any fixed star in our constitutional constellation, it is that no official, high or petty, can prescribe what shall be orthodox in politics, nationalism, religion, or other matters of opinion, or force citizens to confess by word or act their faith therein. If there are any circumstances which permit an exception, they do not occur to us."

Stone had initially expressed the "preferred freedoms" doctrine tentatively, merely raising the question whether in the case of legislation touching rights protected by the FIRST AMENDMENT there may be "narrower scope for the operation of the presumption of constitutionality" and whether such legislation might not be "subjected to more exacting judicial scrutiny." He first used the expression "preferred freedoms" in JONES V. OPELIKA (1942).

After Stone's death in 1946, the passing of Justices Murphy and Rutledge in 1949, and the intensification of the Cold War, the "preferred freedoms" doctrine fell into a constitutional limbo. Justice Frankfurter, still smarting from the second flag salute case, attacked the doctrine fiercely in KOVACS V. COOPER (1949) where, referring to "preferred freedoms," he wrote: "This is a phrase which has crept into some recent decisions of the Court. I deem it a mischievous phrase if it carries the thought, which it may subtly imply, that any law touching communication is infected with invalidity. . . . I say that the phrase is mischievous because it radiates a constitutional doctrine without avowing it."

DENNIS V. UNITED STATES (1951), a case involving the last stage of the 1949 trial of eleven leaders of the Communist party of the United States for violation of the Smith Act of 1940, dealt the doctrine a serious blow. Yet even after *Dennis* some substance of the doctrine remained. In dissent Justice Black expressed the hope "that in calmer times, when present pressure, passions, and fear subside, this or some later Court will restore the First Amendment liberties to the high preferred place where they belong in a free society."

Stone's guiding rule was judicial self-restraint, not self-abnegation. Before 1937 he criticized right-wing colleagues who equated what they considered economically undesirable legislation with unconstitutionality. After Roosevelt had reconstructed the Court, he was at loggerheads with judges on the left, equally intent, he thought, on reading their preferences into the constitution.

Repeated conflicts with Black and Douglas, who, he felt, were prone to resolve all doubt in labor's favor, alienated him. Stone's creativity was confined by the boundaries of the known. Any marked departure from existing principles left him "a little hurt, a little bewildered and sometimes even a little angry." When in 1945 he found himself pitted against judicial activists on the left, he dolefully reminisced: "My more conservative brethren in the old days enacted their own economic prejudices into law. What they did placed in jeopardy a great and useful institution of government. The pendulum has now swung to the other extreme, and history is repeating itself. The Court is now in as much danger of becoming a legislative Constitution making body, enacting into law its own predilections, as it was then. The only difference is that now the interpretation of statutes, whether 'over-conservative' or 'over-liberal' can be corrected by Congress."

Stone's conception of judicial conduct was almost monastic. He strove against almost insuperable odds to keep the Court within what he considered appropriate bounds. A judge should limit himself precisely to the issue at hand. Contradictory precedents should usually be specifically overruled. The Court ought "to correct its own errors, even if I help in making them." Stone's judicial technique recognized complexity. "The sober second thought of the community," he urged, "is the firm base on which all law must ultimately rest."

Stone advocated restraint, not because he believed a judge's preference should not enter law, but precisely because it inevitably did. The sharp barbs of his thought were intended for the flesh of judges, both right and left, who, without weighing social values, prematurely enforced private convictions as law. He strove not to eliminate subjectivity but to tame it.

As Chief Justice he was less impressive. In 1929, when it was rumored that President HERBERT C. HOOVER might elevate Stone as Taft's successor, the Chief Justice had opposed it, saying that the Associate Justice was "not a great leader and would have a great deal of trouble in massing the Court." Years later, Taft's assessment proved true. The bench Stone headed was the most frequently divided, the most quarrelsome in history. If success be measured by the

Chief's ability to maintain harmony, he was a failure. Solid convictions handicapped him. Nor would he resort to the high-pressure tactics of Chief Justices Taft and Hughes. Believing profoundly in freedom of expression for others, no less than himself, he was slow to cut off debate.

Stone had an abiding faith in free government and in JUDICIAL REVIEW as an essential adjunct to its operation. He believed that radical change was neither necessary not generally desirable. Drastic change could be avoided "if fear of legislative action, which Courts distrust or think unwise, is not overemphasized in interpreting the document." A free society needed continuity, "not of rules but of aims and ideals which will enable government in all the various crises of human affairs, to continue to function and to perform its appointed task within the bounds of reasonableness."

ALPHEUS THOMAS MASON

Bibliography

DOUGLAS, WILLIAM O. 1946 Chief Justice Stone. *Columbia Law Review* 46:693–695.

DOWLING, NOEL T. 1941 The Methods of Mr. Justice Stone in Constitutional Cases. *Columbia Law Review* 41:1160–1181.

DOWLING, NOEL T.; CHEATHAM, E. E.; and HALE, R. L. 1936 Mr. Justice Stone and the Constitution. *Columbia Law Review* 36:351–381.

FRANK, JOHN P. 1957 Harlan Fiske Stone: An Estimate. *Stanford Law Review* 9:621–632.

HAND, LEARNED 1946 Chief Justice Stone's Conception of the Judicial Function. *Columbia Law Review* 46:696–699.

KONEFSKY, S. J. 1946 *Chief Justice Stone and the Supreme Court.* New York: Macmillan.

MASON, ALPHEUS THOMAS 1956 *Harlan Fiske Stone: Pillar of the Law.* New York: Viking.

WECHSLER, HERBERT 1946 Stone and the Constitution. *Columbia Law Review* 46:764–800.

STONE v. FARMERS' LOAN & TRUST CO.
116 U.S. 307 (1886)

This case marks a transition in our constitutional law from the Supreme Court's use of the CONTRACT CLAUSE as a bastion of VESTED RIGHTS protected by corporate charter to its use of SUBSTANTIVE DUE PROCESS as a check on state regulation of business. Here, however, the Court sustained the regulation before it even as it laid the basis for the new DOCTRINE. The facts seemingly constituted an open-and-shut case for a victory of the contract clause. A railroad company's charter explicitly authorized the railroad to set rates for carrying passengers and freight. Thirty-eight years after granting the charter, the state of Mississippi empowered a railroad commission to revise rates. The trust company, a stockholder of the railroad, sued to enjoin Stone and other members of the commission from enforcing the state rate regulations. In past rate cases, whenever the contract clause argument had lost, the RESERVED POLICE POWER doctrine had prevailed; in this case the state had reserved no power to alter the company's charter. The INALIENABLE POLICE POWER doctrine had defeated the contract clause argument only in cases involving the public health, safety, or morals. Yet the Court, by a vote of 7–2, held that the state had not violated the company's charter.

Chief Justice MORRISON R. WAITE, in his opinion for the Court, reasoned that the explicit grant of rate-making powers to the railroad did not imply either a grant of exclusive powers or that the state had surrendered a power to revise rates set by the railroad. The state's power to regulate rates, Waite declared, cannot be "bargained away" except by a positive grant. Never before had the Court construed a contract so broadly in favor of the public and so strictly against a corporation.

Waite added, however, that the regulatory power was not unlimited: under pretense of regulating rates, the state could not require the railroad to carry persons or property free, and "neither can it do that which in law amounts to a taking of private property . . . without DUE PROCESS OF LAW. What would have this effect we need not now say, because no tariff has yet been fixed by the commission." Waite also declared that state rate-making does "not necessarily" deny due process. In effect he undercut his own proposition, asserted in *Munn v. Illinois* (1877), that the question of the reasonableness of rates is purely legislative in nature. (See GRANGER CASES.) In *Stone* the implied principle was that reasonableness was subject to JUDICIAL REVIEW. Moreover, the references to due process of law in effect reflected substantive due process, because a rate regulation could not violate due process except in a substantive sense. *Stone* heralded a new era in constitutional law, which the Court entered during the next decade.

LEONARD W. LEVY

STONE v. GRAHAM

See: Religious Liberty

STONE v. MISSISSIPPI
101 U.S. 814 (1880)

Chief Justice MORRISON R. WAITE for a unanimous Supreme Court held that the state might revoke the chartered right of a lottery company to do business in the state, without violating the CONTRACT CLAUSE. Because the company was not subject to the state's reserved POLICE POWER to alter or repeal the contract, the Court relied on the doctrine of INALIENABLE POLICE POWER, here the power to protect the public morals by outlawing gambling.

LEONARD W. LEVY

STONE v. POWELL
428 U.S. 465 (1976)

By act of Congress, a state prisoner may petition a federal court for a writ of HABEAS CORPUS on a claim that he was imprisoned in violation of his constitutional rights. In *Stone,* however, the Supreme Court ruled that federal courts should not entertain habeas corpus claims by prisoners who charge that they were convicted on unconstitutionally seized EVIDENCE, when the prisoner has had an opportunity for a full and fair hearing on the issue in the state courts.

The Court differentiated, for habeas corpus purposes, between the guarantees of the Fifth and Sixth Amendments, which are vital to the trustworthiness of the fact-finding process, and the FOURTH AMENDMENT, which is not. Exclusion of evidence is not a personal right of the defendant but a judicial remedy designed to deter the police from unlawful searches. Thus the EXCLUSIONARY RULE is not an "absolute" but must be balanced against competing policies. Indiscriminate application of the rule, far from fostering respect for constitutional values, might generate disrespect for the judicial system. On the other hand, denying the right to raise SEARCH AND SEIZURE claims in habeas corpus proceedings would not seriously diminish the educational effect of the rule; it was scarcely likely that police would be deterred by the possibility that the legality of the search would be challenged in habeas corpus proceedings after the state courts had upheld it.

Dissenting Justices WILLIAM J. BRENNAN and THURGOOD MARSHALL averred that the exclusionary rule is a right of the defendant and not a "mere utilitarian tool" which turns on its deterrent value.

JACOB W. LANDYNSKI

STONE COURT
(1941–1946)

When Associate Justice HARLAN FISKE STONE moved over to the central seat of the Chief Justice in October 1941, he presided over a bench seven of whose nine members had been appointed to the Court by President FRANKLIN D. ROOSEVELT. All seven, who were sympathetic to the mass of new regulatory laws and welfare measures sponsored by the President, could be expected to develop approvingly the constitutional revolution of 1937. Surely they would sustain vast congressional expansion of federal power under the COMMERCE CLAUSE and drastically curtail the scope of JUDICIAL REVIEW. Stone himself had been appointed Associate Justice by President CALVIN COOLIDGE, but he had long advocated newly dominant constitutional principles in dissenting opinions. OWEN J. ROBERTS, now the senior Associate Justice, was a Republican appointed by President HERBERT C. HOOVER, but it was the shift of his vote, along with Chief Justice CHARLES EVANS HUGHES's, that had tipped the scales for change. Outside observers expected "a new unity in Supreme Court DOCTRINE, based upon a clearer philosophy of government than has yet been expressed in the swift succession of decisions rendered by a Court standing in the shadow of political changes."

But there was no unity. The new Chief Justice soon came to view his brethren as "a team of wild horses." DISSENTING OPINIONS and CONCURRING OPINIONS proliferated in numbers previously inconceivable. The controversies ranged from major jurisprudential differences to unworthy personal squabbles over such matters as the phrasing of the Court's letter to Justice Roberts upon his retirement.

The sources of disunity were both philosophical and temperamental. All but one or two of the Justices were highly individualistic, each was accustomed to speak his mind. All, with the possible exception of Justice Roberts, accepted the new regulatory and welfare state; but there were sharp differences over the proper pace and extent of change. The Chief Justice and Justices Roberts, STANLEY F. REED, JAMES F. BYRNES, and to a lesser degree Justices FELIX FRANKFURTER and ROBERT H. JACKSON, were more conservative in disposition than Justices HUGO L. BLACK, WILLIAM O. DOUGLAS, FRANK MURPHY, and Justice Byrnes's successor, WILEY B. RUTLEDGE. The temperamental differences were sometimes matched by differences in legal philosophy. The Chief Justice, Justice Frankfurter, and to a lesser degree Justice Jackson, were craftsmen of the law deeply influenced by a strong sense of the importance of the judge's loyalty to a growing, changing, but still coherent set of legal principles. For them, such institutional concerns were often more important than immediate, practical consequences. Justices Black, Douglas, and Murphy gave far more emphasis to the redistribution of social and economic power and to progressive reform. In conflicts between the individual and his government outside the economic area, the conservatives' instinct for order would often clash with the progressive liberals' enthusiasm for CIVIL LIBERTIES and CIVIL RIGHTS. The marked dissension indicates the difficulty any President of the United States faces in stamping one pattern upon the work of the Court.

Viewed in the sweep of constitutional history, the Stone years, 1941–1946, were the first part of a period of transition also encompassing the VINSON COURT, 1946–1953. By 1940 the main lines of CONSTITUTIONAL INTERPRETATION under the commerce clause and GENERAL WELFARE CLAUSE had been adapted to centralized ECONOMIC REGULATION and the welfare state. After 1953, when EARL WARREN became Chief Justice of the United States, the driving force would be a new spirit of libertarianism, egalitarianism, and emancipation. It remained for the Stone Court to complete the reinterpretation of the commerce clause and to pursue the philosophy of judicial deference to legislative determinations, whether state or federal. But harbingers of the new age of reform by constitutional adjudication also began to appear. The first explicit challenges to an across-the-board philosophy of judicial self-restraint were raised in the Stone Court. From the seeds thus scattered would grow the doctrinal principles supporting the subsequent vast expansion of constitutionally protected civil liberties and civil rights.

In interpreting the commerce clause, the Stone Court, whenever faced with a clear assertion of congressional intent to exercise such wide authority, did not shrink from pressing to its logical extreme the doctrine that Congress may regulate any local activities that in fact affect INTERSTATE COMMERCE. For example, in WICKARD V. FILBURN (1942) the Court sustained the imposition of a federal penalty upon the owner of a small family farm for sowing 11.9 acres of wheat in excess of his 11.1 acre federal allotment, upon the ground that Congress could rationally conclude that small individual additions to the total supply, even for home consumption, would cumulatively affect the price of wheat in interstate markets. The reluctance of the more conservative Justices to sanction unlimited expansion of federal regulation into once local affairs took hold when federal legislation was couched in terms sufficiently ambiguous to permit limitation. Decisions putting marginal limits upon the coverage of the federal wage and hour law are the best examples. Only a bare majority of four of the seven Justices participating could be mustered in UNITED STATES V. SOUTHEASTERN UNDERWRITERS ASSOCIATION (1944) for holding the insurance industry subject to the SHERMAN ANTITRUST ACT. In PAUL V. VIRGINIA (1879) the Court had first ruled that writing an insurance policy on property in another state was not interstate commerce. Later decisions and an elaborate structure of regulation in every state were built upon that precedent. Congress had essayed no regulation of insurance. The executive branch had not previously sought to apply the Sherman Act. Justices Black, Douglas, Murphy, and Rutledge seemed not to hesitate in sustaining the Department of Justice's novel assertion of federal power, a position supportable by the literal words of the statute and the logic of the expansive view of the commerce power. Respect for precedent and a strong sense of the importance of institutional continuity led the Chief Justice and Justices Frankfurter and Jackson to protest so sharp a departure from the status quo in the absence of a specific congressional directive: "it is the part of wisdom and self-restraint and good government to leave the initiative to Congress. . . . To force the hand of Congress is no more the proper function of the judiciary than to tie the hands of Congress." Congress responded to the majority by limiting the application of the Sherman Act to the insurance business, and by confirming the states' powers of regulation and taxation.

New constitutional issues that would lead to the next major phase in the history of constitutional adjudication began to emerge as wartime restrictions and the multiplication of government activities stirred fears for personal liberties. The war against Nazi Germany reinvigorated ideals of human dignity, equality, and democracy. As more civil liberties and civil rights litigation came upon the docket, a number of Justices began to have second thoughts about the philosophy of judicial deference to legislative determinations. That philosophy had well fitted the prevailing desire for progressive social and economic reform so long as the states and the executive and legislative branches of the federal government were engaged in the redistribution of power and the protection of the disadvantaged and distressed. The recollection of past judicial mistakes and the need for consistency of institutional theory cautioned against activist judicial ventures even in so deserving an area as civil liberty. On the other hand, continued self-restraint would leave much civil liberty at the mercy of executive or legislative oppression. The libertarian judicial activist could achieve a measure of logical consistency by elevating civil liberties to a PREFERRED POSITION justifying stricter standards of judicial review than those used in judging economic measures. The older dissenting opinions by Justices OLIVER WENDELL HOLMES and LOUIS D. BRANDEIS pleading for greater constitutional protection for FREEDOM OF SPEECH pointed the way even though they had failed to rationalize a double standard.

Stone himself, as an Associate Justice, had suggested one rationale in a now famous footnote in UNITED STATES V. CAROLENE PRODUCTS CO. (1938). Holding that the Court should indulge a strong presumption of constitutionality whenever the political processes of representative government were open, he nonetheless suggested that stricter judicial review might be appropriate when the challenge was to a statute that interfered with the political process—for example, a law restricting freedom of speech—or that was a result of prejudice against a DISCRETE AND INSULAR MINORITY—for example, a law discriminating against black people.

The issue was first drawn sharply under the FIRST and FOURTEENTH AMENDMENTS in the FLAG SALUTE CASES (1940, 1943). The substantive question was whether the constitutional guarantees of the freedom of speech and free exercise of religion permitted a state to expel from school and treat as truants the children of Jehovah's Witnesses, who refused to salute the United States flag. In the first case, the expulsions were sustained. Speaking for the Court, Justice Frankfurter invoked the then conventional rationale of judicial self-restraint. National unity and respect for national tradition, he reasoned, were permissible legislative goals. The compulsory flag salute could not be said to be an irrational means of seeking to secure those goals, even though the Court might be convinced that deeper patriotism would be engendered by refraining from coercing a symbolic gesture. To reject the legislative conclusion "would amount to no less than the pronouncement of pedagogical and psychological dogma in a field where courts possess no marked and certainly no controlling competence." The lone dissent came from Stone, who was still an Associate Justice.

Three years later the Court reversed itself. Justice Jackson, for the Court, summarized the core philosophy of the First Amendment: "If there is any fixed star in our constitutional constellation, it is that no official, high or petty, can prescribe what shall be orthodox in politics, nationalism, religion, or other matters of opinion or force citizens to confess by word or act their faith therein." First Amendment freedoms, the Court reasoned, rejecting Justice Frankfurter's plea for consistent application of the principle of judicial self-restraint, might not be curtailed for "such slender reasons" as would constitutionally justify restrictions upon economic liberty. Freedom of speech, of assembly, and of religion were susceptible of restriction "only to prevent grave and immediate danger to interests that the State may lawfully protect. We cannot because of modest estimates of our competence in such specialities as public education, withhold the judgment that history authenticates as the function of this Court when liberty is infringed."

Even in the 1980s, the deep and pervasive cleavage between the advocates of judicial self-restraint and the proponents of active judicial review in some categories of cases still divides both the Justices and constitutional scholars. It is now pretty clear, however, that judicial review will be stricter and there will be little deference to legislative judgments when restrictions upon freedom of expression, religion, or political association are at stake. (See JUDICIAL ACTIVISM AND RESTRAINT.)

In later years the Court would come also to scrutinize strictly, without deference to the political process, not only some laws challenged as denials of the EQUAL PROTECTION OF THE LAWS guaranteed by the Fourteenth Amendment but even statutes claimed to infringe FUNDAMENTAL RIGHTS in violation of the DUE PROCESS clauses of the Fifth and Fourteenth Amendments. The Stone Court broke the ground for STRICT SCRUTINY of statutory classifications prejudicing an "insular minority" in a opinion in one of the JAPANESE AMERICAN CASES declaring that "all legal restrictions which curtail the civil rights of a single racial group are immediately suspect . . . the courts must subject them to the most rigid scrutiny." In later years the constitutional standard thus declared became the basis for many decisions invalidating hostile RACIAL DISCRIMINATION at the hands of government, segregation laws, and other "invidious" statutory classifications.

Earlier the Stone Court opened the door to strict review in a second and still highly controversial class of cases under the equal protection clause. An Oklahoma statute mandated the STERILIZATION of persons thrice convicted of specified crimes, including grand larceny, but not of persons convicted of other crimes of much the same order and magnitude, such as embezzlement. The somewhat obscure opinion by Justice Douglas in SKINNER V. OKLAHOMA (1942), holding the differential treatment to violate the equal protection clause, emphasized the need for "strict scrutiny" of classifications made in a sterilization law, and referred to procreation as "a basic liberty." Later reforms by constitutional adjudication in the area of VOTING RIGHTS and legislative REPRESENTATION would be based upon the proposition that a legislative classification is subject to strict scrutiny not only when it is invidious but also when it differentiates among individuals in their access to a basic liberty. The precedent would also be invoked to support still later controversial decisions upholding claims of individual liberty in matters of sexual activity, childbirth, and abortion.

The Stone Court also sharpened the weapons for challenging crucial discrimination in the processes of representative government. In most of the states of the Old South, nomination as the candidate of the Democratic party still assured election to office. A political party was regarded as a private organization not subject to the equal protection clause of the Fourteenth Amendment or to the FIFTEENTH AMENDMENT's prohibition against denial or abridgment of VOTING RIGHTS by reason of race or color. Even after PRIMARY ELECTIONS regulated by state law became the standard method for nominating party candidates, "white primaries" remained an accepted method of excluding black citizens from participation in self-government.

The first step in upsetting this neat device was taken in an opinion by Justice Stone just before he became Chief Justice. Interference with the right to cast an effective ballot in a primary held to nominate a party's candidate for election as senator or representative was held in UNITED STATES V. CLASSIC (1938) to interfere with the election itself and thus to be punishable under legislation enacted by Congress pursuant to its power to regulate the time, place, and manner of holding elections under Article I, section 4. Next, in SMITH V. ALLWRIGHT (1944) the Stone Court ruled that if black citizens are excluded because of race or color from a party primary prescribed and extensively regulated by state law, their "right . . . to vote" has been denied or abridged by the state in violation of the Fifteenth Amendment. Opening the polls to effective participation by racial minorities throughout the South, in accordance with the promise of the Fifteenth Amendment, would have to await the civil rights revolution and the enactment of the VOTING RIGHTS ACT OF 1965, but these decisions eliminating "white primaries" were the first major steps in that direction.

While marking its contributions to the mainstream of constitutional history, one should not forget that the Stone Court was a wartime court subject to wartime pressures as it faced dramatic cases posing the underlying and unanswerable question, "How much liberty and judicial protection for liberty may be sacrificed to ensure survival of the Nation?" Economic measures were uniformly upheld, even a scheme for concentrating the review of the legality of administrative price regulations in a special EMERGENCY COURT OF APPEALS, thus denying a defendant charged in an ordinary court with a criminal violation the right to assert the illegality of the regulation as a defense. Extraordinary deference to military commanders under wartime pressures alone can account for the Court's shameful decision sustaining the constitutionality of a military order excluding every person of Japanese descent, even American-born United States citizens, from most of the area along the Pacific Coast.

More often, the majority resisted the pressures when individual liberty was at stake. In DUNCAN V. KAHANAMOKU (1946), an opinion with constitutional overtones, the substitution of military tribunals for civilian courts in Hawaii was held beyond the statutory authority of Army commanders. Prosecution of a naturalized citizen of German descent who had befriended a German saboteur landed by German submarine and who took his funds for safekeeping was held in CRAMER V. UNITED STATES (1945) not to satisfy the constitutional definition of TREASON because the only overt acts proved by the testimony of two witnesses—meetings with the enemy saboteur in public places—were not shown to give aid and comfort to the enemy. In *Schneiderman v. United States* (1943) the Court held that proof that a naturalized citizen was an avowed Marxist and long-time active member, organizer, and officer of the Communist Party of the United States, both before and after his NATURALIZATION, was insufficient to warrant stripping him of CITIZENSHIP on the ground that, when naturalized, he had not been "attached to the principles of the Constitution . . . and well disposed to the good order and happiness of the United States."

The delicate balance that the Stone Court maintained between the effective prosecution of the war and the constitutional safeguards of liberty is perhaps best illustrated by the dramatic proceedings in EX PARTE QUIRIN (1942). In June 1942 eight trained Nazi saboteurs were put ashore in the United States by submarine, four on Long Island and four in Florida. They were quickly apprehended. President Roosevelt immediately appointed a military commission to try the saboteurs. The President was determined upon swift military justice. The proclamation declared the courts of the United States closed to subjects of any nation at war with the United States who might enter the United States and be charged with sabotage or attempt to commit sabotage. The trial was prosecuted with extraordinary speed and secrecy. Before the trial was complete, counsel for the saboteurs sought relief by petition for HABEAS CORPUS. By extraordinary procedure the case was rushed before the Supreme Court. The Justices broke their summer recess to hear oral argument. An order was promptly entered denying the petitions and promising a subsequent opinion. Within a few days the military tribunal passed sentence and six of the saboteurs were executed.

In the post-execution opinion the Court explained that the offense was triable by military commission; that the military commission was lawfully constituted; and that the proceedings were conducted without violation of any applicable provision of the Articles of War. The Justices were greatly troubled upon the last question. Some realized that in truth the swift and secret procedure ordained by the President left them with little ability to give meaningful protection to the saboteurs' legal rights in the military proceedings. Yet, even while recognizing that wartime pressures bent traditional legal safeguards in this as in other instances before the Stone Court, one should not conclude "inter arma silent leges." The hard core of the Court's decision was that judicial review of the saboteurs' constitutional contentions could not be barred even by the President as COMMANDER-IN-CHIEF. One may therefore hope that, if similar circumstances again arise, the Stone Court's basic defense of CONSTITUTIONALISM in time of war will prove more significant than its occasional yielding to the pressures of emergency.

ARCHIBALD COX

Bibliography

MASON, ALPHEUS 1956 *Harlan Fiske Stone, Pillar of the Laws.* Chaps. 34–42. New York: Viking Press.

ROSTOW, EUGENE 1945 The Japanese American Cases: A Disaster. *Yale Law Journal* 54:489–533.

SWINDLER, WILLIAM F. 1970 *Court and Constitution in the Twentieth Century,* Vol. 2, chaps. 6–10. Indianapolis: Bobbs-Merrill.

WOODWARD, J. 1968 *Mr. Justice Murphy.* Chaps. 11–13. Princeton, N.J.: Princeton University Press.

STOP AND FRISK

Most courts recognize that a police officer has the authority to detain a person briefly for questioning even without PROBABLE CAUSE to believe that the person is guilty of a crime. The Supreme Court first addressed the "stop and frisk" issue in TERRY V. OHIO (1968). In *Terry,* an experienced police officer observed three unknown men conducting themselves in a manner that suggested the planning of an imminent robbery. With his suspicion aroused—but clearly without probable cause to make an ARREST—the officer stopped and patted the men down, finding weapons on two of them. The holders of the two guns were arrested and convicted of possession of a concealed weapon. The Supreme Court ruled that the officer's actions in stopping the suspects were constitutional.

Terry, therefore, authorized law enforcement officials, on the grounds of reasonable suspicion, to stop briefly a suspicious person in order to determine his identity or to maintain the status quo while obtaining more information. Such a "stop" is proper when: the police observe unusual conduct; the conduct raises reasonable suspicion that criminal activity may be afoot; and the police can point to specific and articulable facts that warrant that suspicion. A "frisk" is proper when the following prerequisites are met: a "frisk" cannot be justified on "inchoate and unparticularized suspicion or 'hunch'," but must be grounded on facts which, in light of the officer's experience, support "specific reasonable inferences" that justify the intrusion; a "frisk" is proper only after "reasonable inquiries" have been made, although such inquiries need not be extensive; and a "frisk" is authorized where an officer reaches a reasonable conclusion that the person stopped for questioning may be armed and presently dangerous.

Further clarifying the test permitting a valid "stop and frisk," the Supreme Court has stated that the totality of the circumstances must be taken into account. Looking at the whole picture, the detaining officers must have a particularized and objective basis for suspecting the particular person stopped of criminal activity. The Court has emphasized that the process of assessing all the circumstances often will not involve hard certainties but rather probabilities; the evidence to justify the stop must be weighed in accordance with the understanding and experience of law enforcement personnel.

Applying that standard in UNITED STATES V. CORTEZ (1981), the Court upheld the propriety of stopping a defendant whose camper van was observed late at night near a suspected pick-up point for illegal ALIENS. The size of the vehicle, the lateness of the hour, and the remoteness of the spot all combined to make the stop reasonable.

Moreover, in *Adams v. Williams* (1972) the Supreme Court extended the *Terry* DOCTRINE in the following ways: (1) a "stop and frisk" is authorized for such offenses as possession of illegal drugs or a concealed weapon; (2) an informant's tip may provide reasonable cause for a "stop and frisk" even where no unusual conduct has been observed by an officer; and (3) the "identification" and "reasonable inquiries" requirements of the *Terry* decision are no longer absolute prerequisites. The *Terry* doctrine was again extended in *Michigan v. Long* (1983) where a "frisk" for weapons was not restricted to the person but was extended to any area that might contain a weapon posing danger to the police. A search of the passenger compartment of a car was held reasonable due to the observance of a hunting knife, the intoxicated state of the defendant, and the fact that the encounter took place at night in an isolated rural area.

In *Pennsylvania v. Mimms* (1977) the Court held that, whenever a vehicle is lawfully detained for a traffic violation, the police officer may order the driver out of the vehicle for questioning without violating the proscriptions of the FOURTH AMENDMENT.

In SIBRON V. NEW YORK (1968) a patrolman observed Sibron with a group of known drug addicts. The officer approached Sibron in a restaurant and ordered him outside. During a brief conversation with the officer, Sibron reached into his pocket. The patrolman promptly thrust his hand into the same pocket and found several glassine envelopes containing heroin.

The Supreme Court found the search to be unlawful on several grounds, including the fact that the "mere act of talking with a number of known addicts" was not enough to produce a reasonable inference that a person was armed and dangerous. The officer's motive, which was clearly to search for drugs, not for a weapon, invalidated the search as well. The *Sibron* decision is important because it made clear that *Terry* established only a narrow power to search on less than probable cause to arrest, and that the right to frisk is not an automatic concomitant to a lawful stop. *Sibron* also established proper motive as a prerequisite to a proper frisk.

In *Peters v. New York* (1968), *Sibron*'s companion case, an off-duty policeman saw through the peephole of his apartment door two strangers tiptoeing down the hallway. After calling the police station, dressing, and arming himself, the officer pursued the men and questioned Peters. Peters said he was visiting a married girlfriend but would not identify her. The officer then patted down Peters and felt in his pocket a hard, knife-like object. He removed the object, which turned out to be a plastic envelope containing burglar's tools. Peters was charged with unlawful possession of burglar's tools. The search was held proper as incident to a lawful arrest because the circumstantial EVIDENCE available to the officer reached the level of probable cause to arrest Peters for attempted burglary.

After *Sibron* and *Peters,* the issue arises as to the legal consequences when a police officer pats down a suspect, reaches into the suspect's pocket, and pulls out evidence of a crime but not a weapon. The questions are whether the officer could reasonably have believed the item was a weapon, and whether the item was visible even without removing it. Using *Sibron* and *Peters* as models, a box of burglar's tools would satisfy the test (*Peters*), while a soft bag of heroin would not be admissible (*Sibron*).

The lower courts have expanded the scope of a constitutionally permissible frisk beyond a limited patdown of a suspect's outer clothing. Courts have included within the scope of a permissible frisk the area under a suspect's car seat, after the suspect appeared to hide something there, and a glove compartment within the reach of a suspect. In addition, the lower courts have relaxed their supervision over police judgments concerning objects that seem to be weapons when suspects are frisked, allowing officers to search after they have touched objects such as razor blades, cigarette lighters, and even lipstick containers.

The Supreme Court has declined to impose a rigid time limit for stop and frisk situations. In *United States v. Sharpe* (1985), where a pickup truck involved in drug trafficking was detained for twenty minutes, the Court determined that the length of the stop was reasonable by considering the purpose of the stop, the reasonableness of the time in effectuating the purpose, and the reasonableness of the means of investigation. In *United States v. Hensley* (1985) the Court widened the application of permissible investigative stops to include investigations of completed crimes. The Court also articulated that a police officer's reliance on a "wanted flyer" issued by another police department provided reasonable basis to conduct a stop if the flyer was based on "specific and articulable facts."

Finally, courts have handled the special case of airport "stop and frisk" situations in three ways. The first treats the problem through a straightforward application of the *Terry* test. The second method involves courts lowering the *Terry* level of "reasonable suspicion" to a less stringent standard. The third approach overtly abandons the *Terry* formula, opting for an ADMINISTRATIVE SEARCH consent rationale which does not even require reasonable suspicion. Today, the use of electronic scanning devices at most airports has diminished this area of "stop and frisk" concern.

CHARLES H. WHITEBREAD

Bibliography

WHITEBREAD, CHARLES H. 1980 *Criminal Procedure.* Mineola, N.Y.: Foundation Press.

STORING, HERBERT J. (1928–1977)

Herbert Storing established the American Founding as a special field of study, both in his teaching at the University of Chicago and in his scholarship. Storing's monumental work, *The Complete Anti-Federalist,* contains introductions to and annotated, accurate texts of all substantial Anti-Federalist writings, along with the essay, "What the Anti-Federalists were *For.*" This material plus his essay on "The 'Other' Federalist Papers," facilitates a full study of the dialogue over RATIFICATION OF THE CONSTITUTION in 1787–1788. It also explains why the Constitution's opponents "must be seen as playing an indispensable, if subordinate, part in the founding process." Storing argued that the Anti-Federalists lost the debate, ultimately, because they could not reconcile the contradiction of supporting union while opposing adequate powers for the federal government, but he regarded as well taken their criticism of the Constitution as not providing for, and even undermining, republican virtue.

Elsewhere, in essays on slavery, CIVIL DISOBEDIENCE, the political thought of black Americans, and statesmanship, and in congressional testimony concerning the ELECTORAL COLLEGE, Storing demonstrated the continuing relevance of the founding dialogue for American politics.

MURRAY DRY

Bibliography

STORING, HERBERT J. 1981 *The Complete Anti-Federalist.* 7 Vols. Chicago: University of Chicago Press. (Volume 1 was also published separately under the title, *What the Anti-Federalists were* For.)

——— 1976 "The 'Other' Federalist Papers." *Political Science Reviewer* 6:215–247.

STORY, JOSEPH (1779–1845)

Joseph Story's contributions to American nationalism were as great as those of any other figure in American judicial history. The record of his career—his thirty-four years as an associate Justice of the Supreme Court, his hundreds of opinions delivered from the First Circuit Court (of Appeals), his many influential *Commentaries,* his contributions to the creation of admiralty and commercial law and EQUITY jurisprudence, his re-creation of the Harvard Law School—is more abundant, more distinguished, and more fertile than that of any jurist of his generation. Imbued with a deep pride in the American nation, Story believed that nationalism should proclaim itself in the might of the government and the majesty of the law, and in the expression of this philosophy he was articulate beyond any of his fellow jurists. Ceaselessly—in Congress, on the bench, from the professor's podium and the speaker's platform, in his study, and through his voluminous correspondence—he admonished the American people to exalt the nation and to preserve the Constitution and adapt it to the exigencies of history.

Born in Marblehead, Massachusetts, in 1779, Story graduated from Harvard College in 1798, read law, and began legal practice in Salem in 1801. In 1807 New England land speculators retained him to protect their interests in the notorious Yazoo lands controversy; his argument before the Supreme Court in their behalf was accepted by Chief Justice JOHN MARSHALL for the Court in FLETCHER V. PECK (1810).

A conservative Republican in a predominantly Federalist state, Story served for three years (1805–1808) in the Massachusetts legislature and then briefly (1808–1809) in the national House of Representatives. Though nominally a Republican, Story early displayed his independence by openly challenging President THOMAS JEFFERSON'S policies on naval preparedness and on the Embargo; Jefferson blamed the "pseudo-Republican," Story, for the repeal of that Embargo, which he had hoped would be a substitute for war. On returning to Massachusetts, Story reentered the state legislature and in 1811 was elected its speaker. When Justice WILLIAM CUSHING of Massachusetts died in 1810, Story was one of four candidates proposed to President JAMES MADISON as Cushing's successor. Not having forgiven Story's opposition to the Embargo, Jefferson protested to Madison that Story was "unquestionably a tory . . . and too young." Only after three other prospective nominees—LEVI LINCOLN, Alexander Wolcott, and JOHN QUINCY ADAMS—had declined the nomination or were rejected by the Senate did Madison turn to Story. At thirty-two, he was—and remains—the youngest appointee in the history of the Court.

When Story took his seat on the Bench in 1812, he was already an ardent nationalist. From the beginning he endorsed that BROAD CONSTRUCTION of the Constitution that we associate with Marshall, and throughout Marshall's life he was not so much a disciple of as a collaborator with the Chief Justice. For the next quarter century, these two magisterial jurists presented a united front on most major constitutional issues; only on the issue of PRESIDENTIAL POWERS in wartime, raised in *Brown v. United States* (1814), and a few issues of admiralty, international, and prize law did they ever disagree. Yet throughout his judicial career, Story's was an independent and original mind different in style if not in philosophy from Marshall's. Story respected and even venerated the Chief Justice, and the respect was mutual. If Story looked to Marshall for authoritative exposition of the Constitution, Marshall looked to Story for the substantiation of his logic and for help in other areas of law—notably in admiralty, conflict of laws, and equity. And when Story spoke on constitutional issues, it was in no mere imitative tones; frequently he pointed the way that Marshall later followed, as when his great opinion in MARTIN V. HUNTER'S LESSEE (1816) anticipated Marshall's opinion in COHENS V. VIRGINIA (1821). Although in some areas—such as the interpretation of the COMMERCE, NECESSARY AND PROPER, and CONTRACT CLAUSES of the Constitution—Marshall blazed the way, in others—notably those concerning the proper realms of executive and judicial power, issues of concurrent state and national power, and the creation of a uniform national commercial law—Story's was the greater overall achievement.

What emerges most strikingly from a study of Story's constitutional opinions is his passionate commitment to the authority of the national government in the federal system. He was quick to counter any attack or limitation upon its powers; he was alert to the potentialities of the concept of IMPLIED POWERS; he was ambitious to extend federal JURISDICTION by judicial opinion, legislation, or doctrinal writing. His ambitions were chiefly for the judiciary, for whose authority he was acquisitive and even belligerent, but he made bold claims for the national executive and legislative powers as well.

Story's solicitude for national executive authority was early asserted in *Brown v. United States* (1814), one of the few constitutional cases where he and Marshall disagreed. The issue presented was the validity of the confiscation of enemy property during the War of 1812 by the local United States district attorney without express legislative authority. Marshall, speaking for the Court, held such seizures illegal absent express authority granted by Congress. Story claimed that under the WAR POWER, the executive had full authority to direct such seizures, for in the absence of legislation he was bound only by international law, which countenanced such action. Not content to vindicate the executive power merely under the rules of international law, Story rested his case upon the doctrine of implied powers in the Constitution, here anticipating Marshall's statement of that doctrine in MCCULLOCH V. MARYLAND (1819). Story later seized the opportunity to restate and expand on his views on the implied powers of the executive in national emergencies in MARTIN V. MOTT (1827), which established the constitutional authority of the President to use his discretion as to the exigency that justified calling out the militia.

Though Story was not as jealous for legislative as for executive authority, in cases where the distribution of powers in the federal system was at issue he ranged himself strongly on the nationalist side. Thus, in PRIGG V. PENNSYLVANIA (1842), which presented the grave question whether authority to enforce the FUGITIVE SLAVE ACT of 1793 was vested exclusively in the national government or concurrently in the national and state governments, the Court held unconstitutional a Pennsylvania statute setting up parallel state enforcement machinery and imposing heavy penalties on any person who should seize or remove from the state anyone who had not been adjudged a fugitive from service. Story held for the Court that Congress had preempted the field by passing the 1793 act. This general argument was nothing new, being derived from Marshall's statement of the PREEMPTION doctrine in GIBBONS V. OGDEN (1824), but Story went further, arguing in dictum that the Constitution's fugitive slave clause did not impose upon the states any obligation to carry it into effect. Congressional authority was exclusive, so that the states not only could not cooperate with it through parallel legislation but might even prohibit their officials from acting under it. This was nationalism with a vengeance—as well as an escape hatch for northern states' PERSONAL LIBERTY LAWS. Only Justice JAMES M. WAYNE accepted Story's reasoning entirely; Chief Justice ROGER B. TANEY and Justices PETER V. DANIEL and HENRY BALDWIN agreed that the state statute was unconstitutional but denied that a state could release its officers from the obligation to enforce a federal law, while Justice JOHN MCLEAN dissented *in toto,* upholding the state statute's constitutionality.

Story's ambiguous views on slavery, exemplified by his opinion in *Prigg,* merit special discussion. Story detested slavery and denounced it in charges to federal GRAND JURIES, and it was the source of his sole extrajudicial public statement on political issues—his condemnation of the MISSOURI COMPROMISE. Yet he generally yielded to the countervailing pull of his belief in the necessity to support and sustain the authority of the legal system. Thus, his opinion in *The Amistad* (1841), while upholding the claims for freedom of Africans who had liberated themselves from captivity and seized control of the slave ship carrying them to Latin America, rested solidly upon principles of international law, not on the noble rhetoric of John Quincy Adams's argument in the Africans' behalf. And while his OBITER DICTUM in *Prigg* might be read as flowing from hostility to slavery, his appeals in his lectures at the Harvard Law School that all citizens faithfully obey the Fugitive Slave Act indicate that it was his zeal for the RULE OF LAW and for exclusive national authority rather than sympathy for the fugitive slave that dictated the ingenious reasoning in *Prigg*.

Story's support for exclusive congressional authority extended to other areas as well. In *Houston v. Moore* (1820) he argued (in dissent) that by providing for the trial and punishment of offenses against the federal militia act, Congress had preempted the field, thereby precluding the states from making similar provisions; it followed that the criminal jurisdiction of the United States in this area could not be delegated in whole or in part to state tribunals. In his dissent in MAYOR OF NEW YORK V. MILN (1837) Story asserted that congressional authority to regulate commerce was supreme and exclusive and that a state law requiring the master of a foreign vessel to supply elaborate information about his passengers was an unconstitutional regulation of commerce rather than a constitutional exercise of the STATE POLICE POWER. Similarly, in *United States v. Coombs* (1838), he expanded the reach of federal power under the commerce clause, holding for the Court that a federal statute prohibiting as a crime against the United States the theft of goods from wrecked or stranded ships was a constitutional regulation of commerce, even though it might not fall within federal admiralty jurisdiction.

Ready as Story was to vindicate national executive and legislative powers, it was the judicial prerogative that was closest to his heart. In his eyes the judiciary was the bulwark of the Constitution, and the courts' role in maintaining the balance of the departments and the federal system was of supreme importance.

Key to this balance was Section 25 of the JUDICIARY ACT OF 1789, which provided for APPEALS from state to federal courts, guaranteeing the harmonious interpretation of the Constitution throughout the United States. In *Martin v. Hunter's Lessee* (1816), Story upheld the constitutionality of Section 25. In one form or another, this case had dragged its tortuous way through the courts for almost a quarter of a century. While the legal issues were complicated, the constitutional question was comparatively simple: was the authoritative interpretation of the Constitution lodged finally in the Supreme Court or did it share this prerogative with the highest state courts? The Court had already decided the legal issues in *Fairfax v. Hunter's Lessee* (1813), but the Virginia courts refused to be bound by that decision. Marshall disqualified himself from the case for reasons of judicial propriety, so Story spoke for the Court in his first great opinion. To him the case presented the simple question of national versus state supremacy, and his answer was equally simple, in contrast to his opinion's verbosity: the national government was supreme. Appeals from state to national courts did not involve any infringement upon the SOVEREIGNTY of the state, for the people of the state, acting in their sovereign capacity, had already provided for such appeals through their ratification of the Constitution. Building on *Martin*, Marshall later seized his chance to vindicate Section 25 anew in *Cohens v. Virginia*.

Story's other efforts to expand federal judicial power were to prove no less significant than *Martin*. While early in his judicial career he had unsuccessfully advocated common-law jurisdiction for the federal courts, Story achieved that goal indirectly in SWIFT V. TYSON (1842). In *Swift*, Story held that Section 34 of the Judiciary Act of 1789, which provided that "the laws of the several States, except where the Constitution, treaties, or statutes of the United States shall otherwise require or provide, shall be regarded as rules of decision in trials at common law in the courts of the United States," did not always bind federal courts to follow the decisions of state courts. He contended rather that Section 34 required federal courts to follow state court decisions only in strictly state matters, and that federal courts were free in cases posing "questions of general commercial law" to follow "the general principles and doctrines of commercial jurisprudence."

Swift was the entering wedge for the gradual creation of a FEDERAL COMMON LAW, but the decision had a troubled history until, after repeated challenge and criticism, the Court overruled it in ERIE RAILROAD CO. V. TOMPKINS (1938). Despite *Erie*, the need for uniformity of interpretation in contracts, sales, commercial paper, secured transactions, and other branches of commercial law resulted in the gradual though somewhat disorderly creation of a common commercial law. Through federal legislation, uniform state laws (such as the Uniform Commercial Code), the American Law Institute's promulgation of Restatements of the various branches of the law, and the publication of authoritative treatises and reports of decisions, Story's dream of a national commercial law has been substantially vindicated.

Story helped to establish uniformity in many areas of commercial law. Almost single-handed, he shaped American admiralty law in his opinions on the First Circuit Court and the Supreme Court. More important, however, were his many authoritative *Commentaries,* which he composed as part of his responsibilities as Dane Professor of Law at Harvard, a position which he held from 1829 until his death. Story was "driven to accept" this post by his old friend Nathan Dane, who conditioned his gift to the near moribund Harvard Law School on Story's acceptance of the chair. His lectures gave rise to commentaries on *Bailments* (1832), the *Constitution* (3 vols., 1833), *Conflict of Laws* (1834), *Equity Jurisprudence* (1836), *Equity Pleading* (1838), *Agency* (1839), *Partnership* (1841), *Bill of Exchange* (1843), and *Promissory Notes* (1845), which together comprise the most impressive body of scholarship on commercial law ever to come from the pen of one scholar. These commentaries, together with his authority and prestige, made the Harvard Law School the largest and most distinguished in the nation.

To three fields particularly Story's contributions were of outstanding importance. His *Commentaries on the Constitution* molded constitutional law and history for half a century; in light of their influence on DANIEL WEBSTER and ABRAHAM LINCOLN, it might be said that it was Story who triumphed in the Civil War and the FOURTEENTH AMENDMENT. His works on equity established its popularity in the American legal system by giving equity (in the words of an English commentator) "a philosophical character with which it never had been invested by any preceding author." His *Conflict of Laws,* the most original and learned of all his books, opened up a relatively new subject and revealed the possibilities of Continental to American and—even more remarkable—of American to English and Continental law, as well as winning for Story a distinguished international reputation.

Equally characteristic of Story's zeal for national authority and uniformity was his legal and judicial conservatism. His belief in natural law—that laws are discovered rather than made—was part and parcel of the thinking of his generation, as of that earlier generation which had fought the American Revolution and framed state and national constitutions. Of the talismanic trio of life, liberty, and property, Story emphasized property—an emphasis peculiarly congenial to his temperament. The society in which Story lived was acquisitive and speculative—more fully so than the society that produced Marshall and Taney—and Story, along with JAMES KENT, came to be its most persuasive legal representative.

TERRETT V. TAYLOR (1816) gave Story his first opportunity to uphold property rights from the bench; writing for the Court, he struck down Virginia's attempt to revoke grants of glebe lands to the Episcopal Church, on the HIGHER LAW ground that legislative grants of land could not constitutionally be revoked by a subsequent legislative act. Similarly, Story's learned concurring opinion in DARTMOUTH COLLEGE V. WOODWARD (1819) supported Marshall's conclusion that the Constitution's contract clause forbade the revision or revocation by a state legislature of a college's charter. In the hands of Marshall and Story, the contract clause proved a powerful weapon for the maintenance of the status quo and the frustration of legislative experiments.

Marshall's death in 1835 and his replacement by Taney created a situation in which Story was increasingly uncomfortable. In three cases in the 1837 Term—*Mayor of New York v. Miln* (discussed above), CHARLES RIVER BRIDGE CO. V. WARREN BRIDGE, and BRISCOE V. BANK OF KENTUCKY—Story found himself in lonely and eloquent dissent, mourning the passing of the "old law." In *Charles River Bridge,* Story's most famous dissent, he bitterly countered the Court's decision upholding the Massachusetts legislature's grant of a permit to a new bridge company to build a bridge across the Charles River in competition with an existing bridge authorized by an earlier charter. Story's opinion ransacked the history of the COMMON LAW to establish that public grants were to be construed in the same manner as private grants—against the grantor; thus, the earlier grant of permission to build the first bridge should be read as granting an irrevocable monopoly. In *Briscoe,* Story dissented from a decision upholding Kentucky's creation of a state bank authorized to issue bank notes. Invoking the departed Marshall, Story argued that because a state could not do through an agent what it was barred from doing directly, Kentucky had violated the constitutional prohibition against the issuing by a state of BILLS OF CREDIT. These three cases dramatized the contrast between the Story-Marshall interpretation of the Constitution and that advanced by Taney and his colleagues; they illustrate the TANEY COURT's modification of the MARSHALL COURT's earlier positions to favor the states' police powers and a greater exercise of judicial continence.

Although Story died suddenly in 1845, leaving unwritten his projected works on admiralty and insurance and his memoirs, he had in large part succeeded in his determination to create a rounded system of law not only through judicial opinions but also through systematic treatises and teaching. His judicial opinions helped to formulate our constitutional, equity, PATENT, COPYRIGHT, admiralty, insurance, and commercial law. His *Commentaries* did more than those of any other expositor until our own day to mold popular ideas about the American constitutional system and to influence professional ideas about law, while they all but created the fields of commercial law and conflict of laws. And from the great law school which was so largely of his making and the extension of his shadow, he sent forth lawyers, judges, and teachers imbued with his nationalist philosophy of law and politics. Nor, indeed, did his influence end here; through such disciples as CHARLES SUMNER, TIMOTHY WALKER, and FRANCIS LIEBER, he handed on a vital and persistent tradition.

HENRY STEELE COMMAGER
RICHARD B. BERNSTEIN

Bibliography

COMMAGER, HENRY STEELE 1953 Joseph Story. In *Gaspar G. Bacon Lectures on the Constitution of the United States, 1940–1950.* Boston: Boston University Press.

DUNNE, GERALD T. 1970 *Justice Joseph Story and the Rise of the Supreme Court.* New York: Simon & Schuster.

MCCLELLAN, JAMES 1971 *Joseph Story and the American Constitution: A Study in Political and Legal Thought.* Norman: University of Oklahoma Press.

NEWMYER, R. KENT 1985 *Supreme Court Justice Joseph Story: Statesman of the Old Republic.* Chapel Hill: University of North Carolina Press.

STORY, WILLIAM W. 1851 *Life and Letters of Joseph Story,* 2 vols. Boston: Little, Brown.

STRADER v. GRAHAM
10 Howard (51 U.S.) 83 (1851)

In a suit under a Kentucky statute making an abettor of fugitive slaves liable to the master for their value, defendant attempted to evade liability by arguing that the slaves, who had previously been permitted by their master, the plaintiff, to sojourn in free states, became free there and retained that status upon their return to their slave-state domicile. Defendant sought a reversal of the Kentucky Court of Appeals' determination that their slave status reattached.

On the central question, Chief Justice ROGER B. TANEY held that a state court's determination of the status of blacks was conclusive on federal courts. But he went on to assert in dictum that every state had the right to determine the status of persons within its territory "except in so far as the powers of the states in this respect are restrained, or duties and obligations imposed on them" by the federal Constitution, thus suggesting that the Constitution might somehow invalidate northern abolition statutes or statutes regulating the permissible stay of sojourning slaves. He also insisted that the NORTHWEST ORDINANCE was defunct, its famous sixth article no longer a basis for the exclusion of slavery from the five states of the former Northwest Territory, thus suggesting that Congress might not be able to impose an enforceable antislavery condition on a territory's admission as a state.

Had the United States Supreme Court in 1857 wished to evade the controversial question raised in DRED SCOTT V. SANDFORD of the constitutionality of congressional prohibition of SLAVERY IN THE TERRITORIES, it might have used *Strader* to hold that the determination of Scott's status by the Missouri Supreme Court was binding on federal courts. Justice SAMUEL NELSON's concurrence in *Dred Scott,* originally intended to be the opinion for the Court, did in fact adopt this approach.

WILLIAM M. WIECEK

STRAUDER v. WEST VIRGINIA
100 U.S. 303 (1880)
VIRGINIA v. RIVES
100 U.S. 313 (1880)
EX PARTE VIRGINIA AND J. D. COLES
100 U.S. 339 (1880)

On a day in 1880 the Supreme Court handed down three opinions that fixed the constitutional law of JURY DISCRIMINATION for over half a century. The effect of the three, taken collectively, barred overt state denial of the rights of blacks to serve on juries and effectively barred blacks from jury service in the South. Anything so crude as an announced and deliberate effort to exclude persons on ground of race was unconstitutional; but if official policy did not refer to race and yet blacks were systematically excluded by covert practices, the Constitution's integrity remained unimpaired. No estimate can be made of the miscarriages of justice that occurred in the South and border states where only whites sat in judgment in civil cases involving the property of blacks or in criminal cases involving their life and liberty over a period of at least fifty-five years.

Strauder was a case in which official state policy was overtly discriminatory on racial grounds. West Virginia by statute declared that only whites might serve on juries. Justice WILLIAM STRONG, for the Court, holding the act to be a violation of the EQUAL PROTECTION clause of the FOURTEENTH AMENDMENT, declared that denying citizens the right to participate in the administration of justice solely for racial reasons "is practically a brand upon them, affixed by law; an assertion of their inferiority, and a stimulant to that race prejudice which is an impediment to securing to individuals of the race that equal justice which the law aims to secure to all others." The Court also sustained the constitutionality of a section of the CIVIL RIGHTS ACT OF 1866 by which Congress authorized the removal of a case from a state court to a federal court in order to prevent the denial of CIVIL RIGHTS by the state court. Justice STEPHEN J. FIELD and NATHAN CLIFFORD dissented without opinion.

In *Ex Parte Virginia and J. D. Coles,* the Court sustained the constitutionality of an act of Congress which provided that no qualified person should be disqualified because of race for service as a grand or petit juror in any court, state or federal. Coles, a county court judge of Virginia charged with selecting jurors, excluded from jury lists all black persons. He was indicted by the United States and was liable to be fined $5,000. On petition for a writ of HABEAS CORPUS, he alleged that the federal court had no JURISDICTION over him and that the act of Congress was unconstitutional. Strong declared that under the Fourteenth Amendment, Congress could reach any act of a state that violated the right of black citizens to serve on juries or their right to be tried by juries impartially selected without regard to race. The act of Judge Coles was the act of the state of Virginia, for a state acts through its officers and agents, none of whom may deny the equal protection of the laws. By so ruling, the Court prepared the ground for the doctrine of STATE ACTION. Field and Clifford, again dissenting, thought the act of Congress regulated purely local matters and destroyed state autonomy.

The effects of *Strauder* and *Ex Parte Virginia* were vitiated by the *Rives* decision. Two black men, indicted for the murder of a white man, sought to have their cases removed from a state court to a federal court on the ground that the GRAND JURY that indicted them and the PETIT JURY summoned to try them were composed entirely of whites. The prisoners claimed that the jury lists should include one third blacks, in proportion to the population, and, most important, that no blacks had ever been allowed to serve on juries in the county where they were to be tried. In this case the record did not show, as it did in the other two, overt and direct exclusion of blacks. Strong, for the Court, this time supported by Field and Clifford concurring separately, simply stated, without further ado, that the "assertions" that no blacks ever served on juries in the county "fall short" of showing the denial of a civil right or the existence of racial discrimination. The defendants might still be tried impartially. Similarly, they had no right to a jury composed in part of members of their race. A mixed jury, said the Court, is not essential to the equal protection of the laws. There was no "unfriendly legislation" in this case. In effect the Court placed upon black prisoners the burden of proving deliberate and systematic exclusion on ground of race. As a result, blacks quickly disappeared from jury service in the South.

LEONARD W. LEVY

(SEE ALSO: *Neal v. Delaware,* 1881; *Norris v. Alabama,* 1935.)

Bibliography

SCHMIDT, BENNO C. 1983 Juries, Jurisdiction, and Race Discrimination: The Lost Promise of *Strauder v. West Virginia. Texas Law Review* 61:1401–1499.

STREAM OF COMMERCE DOCTRINE

The Supreme Court introduced the "stream" or "current" metaphor in SWIFT & CO. v. UNITED STATES (1905) to represent the movement of goods in INTERSTATE COMMERCE. The DOCTRINE is significant because it marks the Court's first recognition that commercial markets ignored state lines; the Justices departed from decades of CONSTITUTIONAL INTERPRETATION in which economic reality had yielded to formal legal discrimination. The doctrine itself may be stated as follows: what appears, when out of context, to be INTRASTATE COMMERCE comes within the reach of the interstate commerce power if that commerce is but an incident related to an interstate continuum. Thus Congress can regulate the local aspects of commerce that are inseparably related to the current of interstate commerce, even though the flow has been temporarily interrupted by a kind of whirlpool or eddy while the product goes through some stage in the transformation of the raw material into the finished goods before being shipped again in the interstate stream to reach its final destination.

In *Swift* the government charged the nation's largest meat packers with conspiring to monopolize interstate commerce in violation of the SHERMAN ANTITRUST ACT. The packers asserted that their activities took place at the stockyards—solely within the boundaries of a single state—and thus involved only local or intrastate commerce. Justice OLIVER WENDELL HOLMES, for a unanimous Court, rejected the packers' contentions.

> [C]ommerce among the states is not a technical legal conception, but a practical one drawn from the course of business. When cattle are sent for sale from a place in one state, with the expectation that they will end their transit, after purchase, in another, and when in effect they do so, with only the interruption necessary to find a purchaser at the stock yards, and when this is a typical, constantly recurring course, the current thus existing is a current of commerce among the states, and the purchase of cattle is a part and incident of such commerce.

The opinion struck hard at the rigid separation between PRODUCTION and commerce approved in UNITED STATES v. E. C. KNIGHT & CO. (1895). In recognizing that the United States no longer comprised a group of small, discrete markets, the Court began to confront the legal implications of the transportation and communications revolutions.

Although Holmes did not create the pithy metaphor, it stuck. In STAFFORD v. WALLACE (1922) Chief Justice WILLIAM HOWARD TAFT declared that the stockyards were "a throat through which the current flows, and the transactions which occur therein are only incident to this current." The doctrine marked the "inevitable recognition of the great central fact" that such streams of commerce are interstate "in their very essence."

By the 1930s, as the circumstances that had given rise to the doctrine disappeared, the doctrine's pragmatism became increasingly well-accepted. Though the stream of commerce terminology made frequent appearances, the Court began to ignore the doctrine itself. In SCHECHTER POULTRY CORP. v. UNITED STATES (1935) and CARTER v. CARTER COAL CO. (1936) the Court refused to apply it. When a 5–4 Court sustained government regulation of interstate commerce in NLRB v. Jones & Laughlin Steel Corp. (1937), the Justices still chose not to base their opinion merely on the stream of commerce doctrine. Drawing upon both *Stafford* and HOUSTON, EAST & WEST TEXAS RAILWAY CO. v. UNITED STATES (1914), Chief Justice CHARLES EVANS HUGHES declared that only those intrastate activities that had "such a close and substantial relation" to interstate commerce would be subject to congressional control.

The Supreme Court continued to use Holmes's language into the 1940s, but the doctrine almost disappeared. Indeed, although the phrase "stream of commerce" has enjoyed renewed use in the 1970s and 1980s, the Court almost never invokes the doctrine. Instead, the Justices have echoed Holmes's rejection of technical legal inquiries.

DAVID GORDON

Bibliography

GORDON, DAVID 1984 Swift & Company v. United States: The Beef Trust and the Stream of Commerce Doctrine. *American Journal of Legal History* 28:244–279.

STRICT CONSTRUCTION

This phrase purports to describe a method of CONSTITUTIONAL INTERPRETATION. Those using it, however, often are not referring to the same interpretive method. Classically, a strict construction is one that narrowly construes Congress's power under Article I, section 8. But some use strict construction to mean interpretations that limit the situations to which a constitutional provision applies, without regard to the interpretations' effect on the scope of federal power. Despite the existence of these and other definitions, one theme unites many uses of the phrase. Most users employ strict construction to support political positions by portraying them as the result of what at least sounds like a value-neutral interpretive technique. The phrase's political use now outweighs any technical legal significance it may have.

The term's greatest historical importance stems from its use to describe restrictive interpretations of the federal government's constitutional powers. Modern constitutional interpretations render strict construction of federal power a remnant of the past. In the nation's early years, however, the question of strict versus BROAD CONSTRUCTION of federal power was as critical as any question facing the country. The dispute over whether to establish a BANK OF THE UNITED STATES provided the setting for the first debate over the construction to be afforded Congress's powers. THOMAS JEFFERSON and JAMES MADISON, who both opposed the Bank, "strictly construed" the federal government's powers and concluded that Congress lacked power to create the Bank. ALEXANDER HAMILTON, who favored the Bank, advocated a more flexible view of federal power. In disputes over federal power, the phrase would continue to characterize these early Jeffersonian positions opposed by Federalists.

Chief Justice JOHN MARSHALL's reputation as a non-strict-constructionist owes much to his opinion for the Court sustaining the validity of the act creating the second Bank of the United States. In MCCULLOCH V. MARYLAND (1819) Marshall endorsed Hamilton's view of Congress's powers in an opinion that included the oft-quoted passage, "Let the end be legitimate, let it be within the scope of the constitution, and all means which are appropriate, which are plainly adapted to that end, which are not prohibited, but consist with the letter and spirit of the constitution, are constitutional." In GIBBONS V. OGDEN (1824), again speaking through Marshall, the Court expressly rejected strict construction of federal power as a proper method of interpretation. It found not "[o]ne sentence in the Constitution . . . that prescribes this rule."

Strict construction becomes a much more complex concept when offered, as it has been, as a method of interpreting the entire Constitution. Strict construction then means interpretations that restrict the situations in which constitutional grants of power, or limitations on them, are deemed applicable. A strict construction simply limits the cases in which the Constitution applies. In this sense, a strict construction need not correspond to a constitutional interpretation that limits federal power. This difference results from the variable structure of constitutional provisions.

Some constitutional provisions are phrased positively in the sense that they confer powers upon Congress, the President, or the courts. Other provisions, such as the FIRST AMENDMENT, are phrased negatively. A strict construction—in the sense of limiting the Constitution's applicability—of the positive powers limits federal authority, as Marshall did in MARBURY V. MADISON (1803), when he construed Article III not to authorize the Supreme Court to issue original writs of MANDAMUS. But strict (that is, narrow) construction of a negative provision such as the First Amendment expands governmental authority. Even if strict construction had become the accepted technique for interpreting grants of power to Congress, it is questionable whether, in a government of limited powers, strict construction would be an appropriate technique for interpreting express constitutional limitations on Congress's power.

When used to interpret the entire Constitution, strict construction fails as a guiding principle in the large class of cases in which one constitutional provision can be interpreted narrowly only by broadly interpreting another provision. DRED SCOTT V. SANDFORD (1857) highlights this problem. *Dred Scott,* which restricted Congress's power to regulate slavery in the territories and assured Chief Justice ROGER B. TANEY's reputation as a strict constructionist, is the Court's most famous strict construction of federal power. Yet, while Taney construed strictly Congress's power, he simultaneously construed broadly constitutional limitations on Congress's authority and the constitutional rights of slaveholders.

A similar problem undermines efforts to embrace strict construction as a politically conservative technique for judicial decision making. The conservative Supreme Court of the late nineteenth and early twentieth centuries did limit Congress's powers by, among other things, invalidating federal statutes as exceeding Congress's power under the commerce clause and by finding, in UNITED STATES V. BUTLER (1936), short-lived limitations on Congress's TAXING AND SPENDING POWER. But in relying on the due process clauses to invalidate many federal and state enactments, the same Court offered broad interpretations of those limitations on government power.

The ambiguity attending strict construction has not deterred many from trying to exploit the concept for political advantage. Even in the early disputes between Federalists and Jeffersonians, when strict construction may have had its clearest meaning, there is a hint of hypocrisy in the reliance placed on strict construction. It is unlikely that insufficient strictness is what really troubled early critics of Marshall's and other Federalists' loose constructions. When it suited their goals, Marshall's critics supported loose construction. For example, to justify an administrative and legislative program imposing an embargo on France and England, President Jefferson interpreted broadly presidential and congressional authority to terminate and influence commerce. And Marshall did not always generously interpret the federal government's powers. At AARON BURR's treason trial, Marshall strictly, that is to say, narrowly, construed Article III, section 3, the constitutional provision on treason.

Although many have tried to rely on strict constructionism to political advantage, this trend reached its modern peak under President RICHARD M. NIXON. He referred to strict construction as a characteristic he sought in a Supreme Court appointee. Nixon probably did not primarily mean one who narrowly construed the federal government's powers. He was most dissatisfied with the Supreme Court's CRIMINAL PROCEDURE decisions. In his 1968 campaign, Nixon announced his preference for Supreme Court appointees who would aid the society's peace forces in combating criminals. In this context strict construction was a double negative: limiting the situations in which the Constitution restricted states' criminal procedures. Only coincidentally would such constructions reduce the federal government's role.

Like previous users of the term, Nixon employed strict construction for political advantage, not to facilitate discussion of theories of CONSTITUTIONAL INTERPRETATION. He never articulated his understanding of the phrase, and Justice HARRY BLACKMUN, one of his Supreme Court appointees, disclaimed an understanding of it. Nixon once described Justice FELIX FRANKFURTER as exemplifying what he sought in a Justice, yet Frankfurter delivered nonstrict criminal procedure opinions. In ROCHIN V. CALIFORNIA (1952) he wrote that forcing an emetic into a suspect's stomach to gather recently swallowed evidence shocked the conscience and, therefore, violated the DUE PROCESS CLAUSE of the FOURTEENTH AMENDMENT. And Frankfurter dissented from the Court's decision upholding the admissibility of conversations overheard by means of ELECTRONIC EAVESDROPPING. In addition, in assessing a president's constitutional powers, Nixon was anything but a strict constructionist. The impoundment of funds appropriated by Congress, the invasion of Cambodia, the assertion of EXECUTIVE PRIVILEGE, and many of Nixon's domestic security measures all suggest an expansive, nonstrict view of a president's constitutional authority.

Finally, "strict construction" may have other sensible meanings that do not refer to narrow interpretations. Justice HUGO BLACK may have thought himself to be construing the Constitution strictly when he applied it literally, as in First Amendment cases. Another plausible meaning is strict adherence to the letter and spirit of the Constitution. Under this view, everyone can claim to be a strict constructionist, adhering to what he or she ascertains to be the principles embodied in the Constitution. Strict construction also may characterize a passive judiciary. For example, many believe legislative apportionment to be a POLITICAL QUESTION, a matter of concern only for the legislative and executive branches. A judge who invades the area is deemed active and, therefore, not a strict constructionist. Judge LEARNED HAND may have used strict construction in this sense when he stated that the Supreme Court's failure to define political questions is "a stench in the nostrils of strict constructionists."

THEODORE EISENBERG

Bibliography

BLACK, CHARLES L., JR. 1960 *The People and the Court.* New York: Macmillan.

KELLY, ALFRED H.; HARBISON, WINFRED A., and BELZ, HERMAN 1983 *The American Constitution,* 6th ed. New York: Norton.

KOHLMEIER, LOUIS M., JR. 1972 *God Save This Honorable Court.* New York: Scribner's.

MURPHY, WILLIAM P. 1967 *The Triumph of Nationalism.* Chicago: Quadrangle Books.

STRICT SCRUTINY

In its modern use, "strict scrutiny" denotes JUDICIAL REVIEW that is active and intense. Although the "constitutional revolution" of the late 1930s aimed at replacing JUDICIAL ACTIVISM with a more restrained review using the RATIONAL BASIS formula, even that revolution's strongest partisans recognized that "a more exacting judicial scrutiny" might be appropriate in some cases. Specific prohibitions of the BILL OF RIGHTS, for example, might call for active judicial defense, and legislation might be entitled to a diminished presumption of validity when it interfered with the political process itself or was directed against DISCRETE AND INSULAR MINORITIES. (See UNITED STATES V. CAROLENE PRODUCTS CO., 1938.) The term "strict scrutiny" appears to have been used first by Justice WILLIAM O. DOUGLAS in his opinion for the Supreme Court in SKINNER V. OKLAHOMA (1942), in a context suggesting special judicial solicitude both for certain rights that were "basic" and for certain persons who seemed the likely victims of legislative prejudice.

Both these concerns informed the WARREN COURT's expansion of the reach of the EQUAL PROTECTION clause. "Strict scrutiny" was required for legislation that discriminated against the exercise of FUNDAMENTAL INTERESTS or employed SUSPECT CLASSIFICATIONS. In practice, as Gerald Gunther put it, the Court's heightened scrutiny was " 'strict' in theory and fatal in fact." The Court took a hard look at both the purposes of the legislature and the means used for achieving them. To pass the test of strict scrutiny, a legislative classification must be "necessary to achieve a COMPELLING STATE INTEREST." Thus the state's objectives must be not merely legitimate but of compelling importance, and the means used must be not merely rationally related to those purposes but necessary to their attainment.

The same demanding standard of review has emerged in other areas of constitutional law. Thus even some "indirect" regulations of the FREEDOM OF SPEECH—that is, regulations that do not purport to regulate message content—must be strictly scrutinized. Similarly, strict scrutiny is appropriate for general legislation whose application is attacked as a violation of the right of free exercise of religion. (See RELIGIOUS LIBERTY.) And in those places where SUBSTANTIVE DUE PROCESS has made a comeback—notably in defense of liberties having to do with marriage and family relations, abortion and contraception, and more generally the FREEDOM OF INTIMATE ASSOCIATION—the same strict judicial scrutiny is the order of the day.

The Court has developed intermediate STANDARDS OF REVIEW falling between the rational basis and strict scrutiny standards. Not every heightening of the intensity of judicial review, in other words, implies strict scrutiny. Most critics of the Supreme Court's modern activism reject not only its employment of the strict scrutiny standard but also its use of any heightened standard of review. For these critics, there is little room in the Constitution for any judicial inquiry into the importance of governmental goals or the utility of governmental means. Some action by the state is forbidden by the Constitution, more or less explicitly. Beyond these prohibitions, say these critics, lie no principled guides to judicial behavior.

Yet strict judicial scrutiny of legislation is almost as old as the Constitution itself. From one season to another, the special objects of the judiciary's protection have varied, but from JOHN MARSHALL's day to our own the courts have always found *some* occasions for "a more exacting judicial scrutiny" of the political branches' handiwork. It is hard to imagine what our country would be like if they had not done so.

KENNETH L. KARST

Bibliography

GUNTHER, GERALD 1972 The Supreme Court, 1971 Term—Foreword: In Search of Evolving Doctrine on a Changing Court: A Model for a Newer Equal Protection. *Harvard Law Review* 86:1–48.

STROMBERG v. CALIFORNIA 283 U.S. 359 (1931)

A California law made it a crime to display a red flag or banner "as a sign, symbol or emblem of opposition to organized government or as an invitation or stimulus to anarchistic action or as an aid to propaganda that is of a seditious character. . . ." A member of the Young Communist League who ran a summer camp where the daily ritual included the raising of "the workers' red flag" was convicted for violating the statute, although a state appellate court noted that the prohibition contained in the first clause—"opposition to organized government"—was so vague as to be constitutionally questionable. That court nonetheless upheld the conviction on the grounds that the defendant had been found guilty of violating the entire statute and that the other two clauses relating to "anarchistic action" and "seditious character" were sufficiently definite.

Chief Justice CHARLES EVANS HUGHES and six other members of the Supreme Court reversed the conviction. In his opinion, Hughes pointed out that, the jury having rendered a general verdict, it was impossible to know under which clause or clauses the defendant had been convicted. If any of the three clauses were invalid, the conviction could not stand. The Court found the first clause "so vague and indefinite" that it violated the DUE PROCESS clause of the FOURTEENTH AMENDMENT because it prohibited not only violent, illegal opposition to organized government but also "peaceful and orderly opposition to government by legal means. . . ." Justices JAMES C. MCREYNOLDS and PIERCE BUTLER dissented.

MICHAEL E. PARRISH

STRONG, WILLIAM (1808–1895)

Strong was a learned, able, hard-working Supreme Court Justice who competently handled the tedious routine of COMMON LAW, admiralty, PATENT, and revenue law cases. Except for sustaining legal tenders and invalidating state-authorized exclusion of blacks from jury service, he rarely spoke for the Court in constitutional matters during his ten-year career. Strong's appointment in 1870 was viewed as part of an alleged court-packing scheme to reverse a recent decision invalidating legal tender legislation. But President ULYSSES S. GRANT had decided to nominate Strong and JOSEPH P. BRADLEY in January 1870, a month before an eight-man court, including a Justice who already had resigned, narrowly decided *Hepburn v. Griswold.* Grant, meanwhile, was well aware that Strong had written an opinion for the Pennsylvania Supreme Court sustaining the laws.

Strong did not disappoint Grant. In May 1871, he

wrote the majority opinion in *Knox v. Lee* and *Parker v. Davis,* reversing *Hepburn.* He largely based his argument on the NECESSARY AND PROPER clause, finding the legal tender legislation a necessary concomitant to the WAR POWER. He also refuted the *Hepburn* argument that the laws violated the "spirit of the Constitution" because they impaired the OBLIGATION OF CONTRACTS. All contracts, Strong contended, had to anticipate the rightful exercise of congressional power.

Strong generally defended vested contractual and property rights, the LEGAL TENDER CASES notwithstanding. He joined Justice STEPHEN J. FIELD's dissent in *Munn v. Illinois* (1877). In his own dissent in the SINKING FUND CASES (1879), he maintained that the government could not require railroads to divert part of their earnings into a special fund for payment of their federal debts. The original railroad grant contained no such provision, but Congress had reserved the right to alter, amend, or repeal the act. Strong nevertheless insisted that the new requirement was "plainly transgressive of legislative power" for it violated an implied contractual promise not to call for debt payment before 1897. Strong's dissent, along with those by JOSEPH BRADLEY and Field, heralded the procorporation, antistatist tendencies that dominated the Court for several decades.

The Court's concern with state economic regulation inevitably provoked operations of national authority. In the *State Freight Tax Case* (1873) (see PHILADELPHIA AND READING R.R. CO. V. PENNSYLVANIA) Strong offered a significant commentary on the scope of the COMMERCE CLAUSE when it conflicted with traditional state power. Pennsylvania had imposed a tonnage tax on railroad freight carried within and out of the state, but Strong held that the transportation of goods was a "constituent of commerce" and the tax's "effect" unduly burdened INTERSTATE COMMERCE. In a comparison case, Strong held valid a tax on corporate gross receipts irrespective of whether they came from interstate or intrastate businesses (*State Tax on Railway Gross Receipts,* 1873). In effect, the commerce clause was not a shield for private enterprise against STATE TAXATION.

Strong's record on CIVIL RIGHTS was mixed. He joined the Court's majority in the SLAUGHTERHOUSE CASES (1873) to restrict the scope of the FOURTEENTH AMENDMENT. Similarly, he voted to limit federal guarantees for voting and civil rights. In *Blyew v. United States* (1872), he wrote the Court's first opinion restricting the CIVIL RIGHTS ACT OF 1866. The act authorized federal trials for crimes "affecting persons" denied rights secured by law. Strong held, however, that federal courts lacked JURISDICTION over a defendant accused of murdering three blacks on the ground that the dead persons could not be affected by any prosecution. Although Strong favored upholding a state statute requiring equal access in public transportation, he silently acquiesced when the Court held that the law unduly burdened interstate commerce (HALL V. DECUIR, 1878). But he spoke for the Court in a series of cases that marked some exceptional, however limited, victories for blacks.

In STRAUDER V. WEST VIRGINIA (1880) the Court invalidated a state statute excluding blacks from juries. Strong conceded that blacks were not entitled to have other blacks sit on their juries, but he held that they had a right to have juries selected impartially. The protection of one's life and liberty against racial prejudice was, Strong contended, a "legal right" under the Fourteenth Amendment and therefore the state's exclusion law constituted a denial of EQUAL PROTECTION OF THE LAWS. In a companion case, *Ex parte Virginia* (1880), Strong upheld a section of the 1875 CIVIL RIGHTS ACT which prohibited RACIAL DISCRIMINATION in jury selection. Although state law forbade such discrimination, a state judge had refused to call blacks as jurors. Strong brushed aside arguments that the judge's refusal was not the same as STATE ACTION, which Congress concededly could prohibit. The judge, he insisted, held state office and acted for the state; as such he was obligated to obey the federal constitution and law. But in a third case decided that day, *Virginia v. Rives* (1880), Strong denied a plea for removal of a cause to a federal court on the ground of JURY DISCRIMINATION. Here blacks had been excluded as a result of discretionary action by jury commissioners, not as a result of state law as in *Strauder.* The decision in effect condoned the practical exclusion of blacks from southern juries for the next seventy-five years. Nevertheless, Strong's opinion in *Ex Parte Virginia* preserved a vestige of federal power that was revived in the CIVIL RIGHTS ACT OF 1957, the first such legislation since Reconstruction.

Strong did not have the domineering intellectual force of a Bradley, Field, or Miller, but he performed capably during his career. He was admired and respected by his diverse colleagues, and he managed to avoid the intense personal and ideological conflicts that characterized the period. He abruptly resigned in 1880. Strong was in good health, but he supposedly stepped down as an example to NATHAN CLIFFORD, WARD HUNT, and NOAH SWAYNE who were ill and frequently absent from the bench. Within two years, the three resigned. In retirement, Strong publicized the Court's burdensome workload, and his efforts contributed to the creation of new courts of appeal in 1891. (See CIRCUIT COURTS OF APPEALS ACT.)

STANLEY I. KUTLER

Bibliography

KUTLER, STANLEY I. 1969 William Strong. In Friedman, Leon, and Israel, Fred L., eds., *The Justices of the United States Supreme Court, 1789–1969: Their Lives and Major Opinions,* pages 1153–1178. New York: Chelsea House.

STUART v. LAIRD
1 Cranch 299 (1803)

The JUDICIARY ACT OF 1802, having repealed the JUDICIARY ACT OF 1801 before it could go into operation, abolished the new CIRCUIT COURTS and returned the Justices of the Supreme Court to circuit duty under the JUDICIARY ACT OF 1789. The *Stuart* case raised the constitutionality of the repeal act of 1802. Although Chief Justice JOHN MARSHALL despised the repeal act and believed it to be unconstitutional, on circuit duty he sidestepped the constitutional issue. When the case came before the Court on a WRIT OF ERROR, Justice WILLIAM PATERSON for the Court, with Marshall abstaining, ruled that the practice of riding circuit had begun under the act of 1789 and that long acquiescence "has fixed the construction. It is a contemporary interpretation of the most forcible nature." Thus the Court avoided holding unconstitutional an act of THOMAS JEFFERSON's administration.

LEONARD W. LEVY

(SEE ALSO: *Marbury v. Madison.*)

STUDENTS CHALLENGING REGULATORY AGENCY PROCEDURES (SCRAP), UNITED STATES v.
412 U.S. 669 (1973)

Environmentalists sued to force the Interstate Commerce Commission to suspend a freight rate surcharge announced by the nation's railroads. Plaintiffs claimed the surcharge would raise the cost of transporting recyclable materials and thus injure their recreational and aesthetic use of areas around Washington, D.C., by increasing pollution from waste disposal and causing greater consumption of natural resources.

In one of its most generous rulings on STANDING, the Court held that environmental advocates could raise a statutory claim that, according to three dissenters, was based on injuries that were too remote, speculative, and insubstantial to confer standing. Justice POTTER J. STEWART followed the implications of SIERRA CLUB V. MORTON (1972): environmental harm, however widespread, satisfies the "injury in fact" requirement of standing, and the case will be heard if those who complain allege harm to themselves. The harm need not be "substantial." Nor did it matter that the line of causation between the challenged government act and the asserted environmental harm was "attenuated." Several subsequent decisions, such as *Warth v. Seldin* (1975) and SIMON V. EASTERN KENTUCKY WELFARE RIGHTS ORGANIZATION (1976), differ from *SCRAP,* insisting that the causal link between act and harm be more clearly shown. *SCRAP*'s relaxed view of causal nexus in standing may reflect a special judicial receptivity to environmental litigation.

JONATHAN D. VARAT

STUMP v. SPARKMAN
435 U.S. 349 (1978)

This decision confirmed judges' absolute immunity from damage suits for alleged constitutional violations. At the request of a mother who was displeased with her "somewhat retarded" fifteen-year-old daughter's behavior, and in EX PARTE proceeding in which the child was not represented, Judge Stump ordered the child to be sterilized. The girl was told she was having an appendectomy, and she discovered some years later she had been sterilized. In an action brought by the sterilization victim and her husband, the Supreme Court held, 5–3, that the judge was immune from liability. Because signing the sterilization order was a judicial act, and because there was no express statement in state law that judges lacked JURISDICTION to entertain sterilization requests, the judge's behavior was covered by the doctrine of JUDICIAL IMMUNITY. In the name of judicial independence, the majority immunized conduct that the three dissenters aptly called "lawless," "beyond the pale of anything that could sensibly be called a judicial act."

THEODORE EISENBERG

STURGES v. CROWNINSHIELD
4 Wheaton 122 (1819)

This was the first of the very rare CONTRACT CLAUSE cases decided by the Supreme Court involving private executory contracts. The case arose during a depression, when many states had enacted bankruptcy or insolvency statutes. Chief Justice JOHN MARSHALL, for a unanimous Court, agreed that the states possessed a concurrent power to enact such statutes in the absence of the exercise by Congress of its power to establish uniform bankruptcy laws but held that New York's act violated the contract clause. Crowninshield had declared his bankruptcy under that state's act to protect himself from paying a debt contracted before its passing. The doctrine of the case is that a state act cannot operate retroactively on previously existing contracts; a statute that relieves the debtor from imprisonment is valid but not one that cancels the obligation of his contract. The case left uncertain the constitutionality of bankruptcy acts that operate prospectively on contracts formed after their enactment. (See OGDEN V. SAUNDERS, 1827.)

LEONARD W. LEVY

SUBJECTS OF COMMERCE

A chief purpose of the COMMERCE CLAUSE of the federal Constitution is to assure the free movement of the subjects of commerce among the several states. What are these subjects? Essentially, the term refers to things sold or transported in INTERSTATE COMMERCE. But they need not be articles of trade or even of value. Nor are they confined to objects as such. They may include PERSONS. All are included as subjects or articles of commerce when they begin to move from one state to another. They remain articles of commerce until they fall into the possession of the ultimate buyer or reach their final stage of repose within a given state. Thus, at any point between the beginning and the end of their journey among the states, they are legitimate candidates for congressional regulation. With respect to these subjects, as with interstate commerce generally, Congress may, in the words of GIBBONS V. OGDEN (1824), "prescribe the rule by which commerce is to be governed."

Congress ordinarily exerts its power over the subjects of commerce in order to protect their free movement across state borders. But this power has also been construed to permit Congress to divest some subjects of their interstate character. Divestment occurs when Congress prohibits the interstate transportation of certain goods or persons. Examples of such subjects are stolen automobiles, intoxicating beverages, forged checks, convict-made goods, explosives, prostitutes, firearms, lottery tickets, and kidnaped children. Federal laws prohibiting commerce in such subjects are usually designed to assist the states in fighting crime or protecting their citizens against social, moral, or economic harm. (See NATIONAL POLICE POWER.) But Congress has also banned the interstate shipment of ordinary objects of trade, like lumber, in opposition to state policy. Any such federal law must of course bear a reasonable relationship to interstate commerce. Thus, according to UNITED STATES V. DARBY (1941), Congress may validly bar the interstate shipment of goods produced in violation of a federal MAXIMUM HOUR AND MINIMUM WAGE law so that "interstate commerce [does not become] the instrument of competition in the distribution of goods produced under substandard labor conditions."

The commerce clause, however, is not merely an authorization to Congress to enact laws for the protection of the subjects of commerce. It serves also by its own force to prevent the states from erecting trade barriers or passing any legislation that would obstruct the movement of goods from state to state. As a practical matter the states, not Congress, regulate most subjects (and aspects) of commerce. They may do so out of a legitimate concern for the health, welfare, and safety of their own citizens. Yet, the exercise of this valid STATE POLICE POWER is often in tension with the value of free and open borders that informs the commerce clause. (See STATE REGULATION OF COMMERCE; STATE TAXATION OF COMMERCE.)

A central development in modern commerce clause jurisprudence is the Supreme Court's identification as legitimate articles of commerce many subjects historically regarded as the exclusive preserve of the states. Such subjects include insurance contracts, natural resources, fish and wild game, and even valueless material such as solid and liquid wastes. Prevailing DOCTRINE holds that the shipment in and out of the states of these subjects of commerce is protected by the commerce clause unless Congress ordains otherwise. Most recently, in *Sporkase v. Nebraska* (1982), the Supreme Court added ground water to its list of legitimate subjects of commerce. As the Court noted in PHILADELPHIA V. NEW JERSEY (1978), no object of interstate trade is excluded by definition from this list.

Still the tension between state power and the commerce clause remains. In the watershed case of COOLEY V. BOARD OF WARDENS (1851) the Court tried to resolve this tension by declaring that states may not regulate a subject of commerce the *nature* of which requires a single (national) uniform plan of regulation, even in the absence of any federal law. The *Cooley* rule has not yielded a long list of particular subjects requiring exclusive national regulation. It has been applied mainly to identify subjects whose number and diversity might require, when regulated, local knowledge and experience. State or local regulation of such subjects, whether justified to facilitate trade or to protect the public, is valid unless it conflicts with a law of Congress. *Cooley* itself upheld state regulation of harbor traffic, over commerce clause objections, because of the local peculiarities of port facilities.

Today, however, the Court rarely finds the *Cooley* rule applicable. The modern approach to commerce clause analysis applies a "balancing" test that weighs the interest served by a local regulation of a subject of commerce against the regulation's burden upon interstate commerce. If the burden substantially outweighs the local benefit, even if the legislation is nondiscriminatory, the regulation is unlikely to survive constitutional analysis. (If the *Cooley* rule forbids state regulation there is of course no balancing.) Generally, an article of commerce, although it may be taxed or regulated by the state, may not be so burdened as to prevent or seriously to obstruct its transportation in interstate commerce.

Yet the states do bar some "subjects of commerce" from entering their borders. Local inspection laws, for example, may exclude goods such as diseased cattle, adulterated food, and infectious plants. Such articles do not fall within the Court's classification of *legitimate* subjects of commerce. Correspondingly, the states may validly prevent some goods from leaving their borders. Certain natural resources, like rare birds and fish, may be withheld from commercial exploitation altogether. Such resources assume the character of subjects of commerce, however, when they are permitted legally to be sold or are reduced to personal possession. At that point, even though the private acquisition of such resources may be regulated by law in the interest of their preservation, the states are generally forbidden to restrict their use or sale to their own citizens.

DONALD P. KOMMERS

Bibliography

BENSON, PAUL R., JR. 1970 *The Supreme Court and the Commerce Clause, 1937–1970.* Cambridge, Mass.: Dunnellen.

CORWIN, EDWARD S. 1936 *The Commerce Power Versus States Rights.* Princeton, N.J.: Princeton University Press.

SCHWARTZ, BERNARD 1979 Commerce, the States, and the Burger Court. *Northwestern University Law Review* 74:409–439.

SUBPOENA

A subpoena is a court order that compels a person to appear for the purpose of giving testimony at a trial or a pretrial proceeding, such as a preliminary examination or pretrial deposition. A court also can issue a subpoena for documents or other items of tangible EVIDENCE. Parties to civil suits, and the prosecution in criminal cases, had a COMMON LAW right to compel testimony before the creation of the Constitution. The Sixth Amendment provides defendants in criminal cases a basis for fairly presenting their defense by giving them the power to subpoena witnesses. The government in some circumstances may have an affirmative duty to help a defendant find a witness, such as a government informer, or to refrain from restricting the defendant's ability to locate a witness essential to the presentation of a defense.

The Sixth Amendment, in part, provides that accused persons have the right of witnesses and the right "to have compulsory process" for obtaining witnesses in their behalf. The confrontation and compulsory process clauses permit the defendant to use the power of the courts to obtain witnesses and they limit governmental interference with the defendant's ability to examine witnesses at trial. These clauses have been incorporated into the FOURTEENTH AMENDMENT by the Supreme Court; thus they govern both federal and state prosecutions.

A defendant may compel a person to testify in a court proceeding by applying to the court for a subpoena ordering the person to appear in court or at a pretrial hearing. However, the defendant's ability to use the court's subpoena power is not unlimited. A court can require a defendant to provide it with information that justifies the production of the witness.

When a defendant has a court issue a subpoena to a witness, the witness normally is entitled to a statutory fee to offset his expenses for attendance at the judicial proceeding. An INDIGENT defendant may use the court's subpoena power to compel witnesses to testify in his behalf even though he cannot pay the witness fee. In these circumstances, however, a court may require the indigent defendant to show that the persons whom he subpoenas are likely to give testimony relevant to the charge.

An indigent defendant may try to use the subpoena power to compel an expert (such as a psychiatrist or a ballistics expert) to attend court to testify on the defendant's behalf. Whether the government must pay the cost for providing the defendant with an expert witness is primarily a DUE PROCESS, rather than a subpoena power, issue. However the issue be phrased, courts must determine whether, under the circumstances of the case, a fair trial depends on government provision of the expert witness.

The Sixth Amendment's confrontation clause, together with the compulsory process clause, restricts the government's ability to limit the testimony of potential defense witnesses and the cross-examination of prosecution witnesses. If a person who has received a subpoena to give testimony believes that his testimony would not be relevant to the trial, or that his testimony is subject to an EVIDENTIARY PRIVILEGE, he may move to quash the subpoena. A witness may assert a constitutionally based privilege, such as the RIGHT AGAINST SELF-INCRIMINATION, or a common law or statutory privilege, such as a doctor–patient privilege. One who has no such privilege may not refuse to respond to the subpoena or refuse to give testimony.

JOHN E. NOWAK

Bibliography

LAFAVE, WAYNE R. and ISRAEL, JEDD H. 1984 *Criminal Procedure.* Section 23.3. St. Paul, Minn.: West Publishing Co.

WRIGHT, CHARLES ALAN and GRAHAM, K. 1980 *Federal Practice and Procedure: Evidence.* Section 5436. St. Paul, Minn.: West Publishing Co.

SUBSTANTIVE DUE PROCESS OF LAW

To say that governmental action violates "substantive due process" is to say that the action, while adhering to the forms of law, unjustifiably abridges the Constitution's fundamental constraints upon the content of what government may do to people in the name of "law." As the Supreme Court put the matter most succinctly in HURTADO V. CALIFORNIA (1884), "Law is something more than mere will exerted as an act of power. . . . [It] exclud[es], as not due process of law, acts of attainder, bills of pains and penalties, acts of confiscation . . . and other similar special, partial and arbitrary exertions of power under the forms of legislation. Arbitrary power, enforcing its edicts to the injury of the persons and property of its subjects, is not law, whether manifested as the decree of a personal monarch or of an impersonal multitude."

Substantive due process thus restricts government power, requiring coercive actions of the state to have public as opposed to merely private ends, defining certain means that government may not employ absent the most compelling necessity, and identifying certain aspects of behavior which it may not regulate without a clear showing that no less intrusive means could achieve government's legitimate public aims.

The phrase DUE PROCESS OF LAW derives from King John's promise in MAGNA CARTA to abide "by the law of the land," as translated four centuries later by Sir EDWARD COKE. But the belief that even the sovereign must follow a HIGHER LAW can be traced further back still. Even before the Middle Ages, kings symbolically acknowledged their limitations when they accepted their crowns; royal coronations were religious rites in which the rulers supposedly received power directly from God. The medieval notion of a divine law that even the sovereign might not transgress lay at the heart of English COMMON LAW and of the barons' demands at Runnymede. By the eighteenth century, the idea was phrased in terms of a natural law philosophy of SOCIAL COMPACT between sovereign and citizen. Although individuals were thought to surrender certain freedoms to the state, other rights were considered so much a part of personhood that they lay outside the scope of the social compact. Indeed, protection of such rights had to be the aim of any valid government; a state would abrogate its essential function were it to deny its citizens these fundamental freedoms.

The most famous articulation of that social compact philosophy in American history is the statement in the DECLARATION OF INDEPENDENCE that "all men . . . are endowed by their Creator with certain unalienable Rights . . . among these are Life, Liberty and the Pursuit of Happiness . . . to secure these Rights, Governments are instituted among Men, deriving their just Powers from the Consent of the Governed." Although the Declaration of Independence does not, of course, use the words "due process," the notion that substantive limits may be implied from the character of our society and from our reasons for ceding coercive authority to the state underlies both that document and the system of law and politics structured by our Constitution. The Fifth and FOURTEENTH AMENDMENTS to the Constitution provide, respectively, that neither the federal government nor the states may deprive persons "of life, liberty, or property, without due process of law." The Supreme Court has long recognized that STATE ACTION that follows fair procedures and thus satisfies PROCEDURAL DUE PROCESS may nonetheless violate substantive due process by exceeding the limits of the proper sphere of government. In the name of substantive due process, the Supreme Court has accordingly struck down hundreds of statutes governing matters ranging from wages and hours to sexual conduct.

Some commentators have called "substantive due process" a contradiction in terms. But a dismissal on semantic grounds of the very notion of substantive due process is unwarranted. First, the very idea of "process" has often been taken to include concerns as to the nature of the body taking an action, and legislatures have at times been understood as structurally improper sources of particular kinds of public actions. Second, the Constitution guarantees "due process *of law*," and, as the passage quoted above from *Hurtado* suggests, the term "law" can itself be taken to imply various normative requirements. Third, even the purest "procedural" norms inevitably embody substantive choices. Finally, the choice of the constitutional phrase on which substantive review has been pinned is to a large degree accidental; the Fourteenth Amendment's "privileges or immunities" clause might have been a happier selection—but the real question is whether and how individual rights not explicitly guaranteed by the Constitution should be protected under that document taken as a whole, not whether courts have picked a felicitous phrase to describe that protective task.

The Constitution, however, does not specify the essential rights of personhood; the BILL OF RIGHTS lists only certain rights that particularly warranted articulation in 1791, and the NINTH AMENDMENT makes clear that the list is not to be taken as exhaustive. It is on a largely open landscape that courts, including the Supreme Court, have had to mark out our fundamental freedoms. The process has necessarily been one of continual redefinition, responding to the changing—one hopes evolving—values and concerns of the Justices and the nation. Due process, as FELIX FRANKFURTER noted, has a "blessed versatility."

Not until the adoption of the Fourteenth Amendment in 1868 did the Constitution explicitly require state deprivations of liberty or property to comply with "due process of law"; BARRON V. BALTIMORE (1833) had interpreted the parallel Fifth Amendment bar to limit only the federal government. Well before 1868, however, both the Supreme Court and various state courts had begun to articulate inherent, judicially enforceable bounds on governmental interference with individual autonomy. Insofar as these limits were announced and enforced by federal judges, such holdings occurred in cases not involving specific provisions of the United States Constitution but falling within the DIVERSITY JURISDICTION of federal courts because the opposing parties were citizens of different states. The liberties the courts protected were almost exclusively economic: the ability to contract as one wished and to do as one pleased with one's own property.

Thus, as early as 1798, Justice SAMUEL CHASE wrote in CALDER V. BULL that any law that "takes property from A. and gives it to B." is invalid as contrary to "general principles of law and reason," even if it is not "expressly restrained" by the Constitution. Justice Chase reasoned that such a law would usurp judicial authority if intended to correct an injustice A had done to B, and, if intended simply to improve matters, would not be "law" at all but would instead transgress limitations implied by the very notion of representative government: "the nature, and ends of legislative power will limit the exercise of it."

From time to time throughout the nineteenth century, the Supreme Court struck down state statutes it judged to exceed these inherent limits on legislative power. Typically, however, the Court left unclear whether the limits derived from the purpose and character of legislatures, as Justice Chase had argued; or from an ahistorical body of natural law; or from specific, if unnamed, provisions of the Constitution. In FLETCHER V. PECK (1810), for example, the Supreme Court invalidated a Georgia statute that attempted to revoke state land grants. Writing for the Court, Chief Justice JOHN MARSHALL explained only that the statute was rendered invalid "either by general principles which are common to our free institutions, or by the particular provisions of the Constitution." Similarly, when the Supreme Court in TERRETT V. TAYLOR (1815) struck down Virginia's attempt to divest the Episcopal Church of its property, it rested its holding on "principles of natural justice" and "fundamental laws of every free government," as well as on the "spirit and letter" of the Constitution.

Within a decade or so after the Civil War, however, the Supreme Court more clearly embraced a theory of implied limitations. When, in LOAN ASSOCIATION V. TOPEKA (1875), the Court invalidated a tax designed to finance a bonus for local industry, it did not mention the Constitution at all; exercising the common law power of a federal court sitting in a diversity case, the Court simply found the tax "purely in aid of private or personal objects" and hence "beyond the legislative power and . . . an unauthorized invasion of private right." Echoing *Calder v. Bull*, the *Loan Association* Court declared that there are "rights in every free government beyond the control of the state" and that limitations on sovereign power "grow out of the essential nature of free governments."

Ironically, it was a notion of intrinsic limits on proper government action, including judicial action—a notion similar to that underlying the Court's invalidation of state and local laws in *Fletcher v. Peck, Terrett v. Taylor,* and *Loan Association v. Topeka*—that initially constrained substantive review of state legislation under the Fourteenth Amendment. By prohibiting state laws that "abridge the PRIVILEGES OR IMMUNITIES of citizens of the United States," the amendment's framers may have intended to provide federal protection against state encroachment of fundamental rights, but the Supreme Court in the SLAUGHTERHOUSE CASES (1873) construed the clause narrowly to safeguard only rights peculiarly associated with national CITIZENSHIP, such as the right to vote in national elections. In the Court's view, the clause did not protect the essential freedoms traditionally protected by the states themselves in intrastate disputes and protected by federal courts under Article IV, section 2, only from state laws unjustly discriminating against out-of-staters. Upholding the constitutionality of a state-granted monopoly on slaughterhouses around New Orleans, the *Slaughterhouse* Court held that the right to pursue one's trade was a right of state not national citizenship.

Writing for the Court in *Slaughterhouse,* Justice SAMUEL F. MILLER—who two years later penned the majority opinion in *Loan Association v. Topeka*—made clear that the main motivation for the *Slaughterhouse* decision lay in the Court's fear that a more expansive interpretation of the Fourteenth Amendment would allow the federal government to exceed the proper bounds of its authority and to intrude on the regulatory domain of the states. Construing the amendment's privileges or immunities clause or its due process clause to protect all fundamental rights, Miller explained, "would constitute this Court a perpetual censor upon all legislation of the states" and, by virtue of the affirmative enforcement power granted Congress in section 5 of the Fourteenth Amendment, would allow Congress to "pass laws in advance, limiting and restricting the exercise of legislative power by the states in their most ordinary and useful functions." In contrast, the largely nonconstitutional review carried out in *Fletcher, Terrett,* and *Loan* was seen by the Court as guided and constrained by well-developed common law notions of the inherent limits of legitimate state action, gave no affirmative power to Congress, and fell within one of the federal government's clearly proper roles: adjudicating cases in which diversity of citizenship cast doubt on the impartiality of state tribunals.

But the doctrinal distinction between constitutional and common law review of the substantive legitimacy of state legislation was internally unstable: if natural law limitations on government could guide and constrain the Court in diversity-of-citizenship cases, they could do the same in cases brought pursuant to the Fourteenth Amendment. Moreover, the Court could apply common law principles to invalidate any congressional attempt under the guise of the Fourteenth Amendment to prohibit perfectly legitimate state activity.

Partly because of this doctrinal instability, and partly because of strong pressure from the organized bar for a more expansive review of state ECONOMIC REGULATION, the Court moved rapidly in the years following *Loan Association* and *Slaughterhouse* toward substantive review of state legislation under the Fourteenth Amendment's due process clause. Throughout the last quarter of the nineteenth century, the Court often warned in OBITER DICTA that the due process clause prohibited states from transgressing common law limitations on legitimate governmental action. In particular, the Court gave notice that unreasonable state deprivations of property or of the FREEDOM OF CONTRACT would be struck down as unconstitutional. In ALLGEYER V. LOUISIANA (1897) this line of dicta finally ripened into a landmark HOLDING: the Court there invalidated a Louisiana restriction on insurance contracts as substantively incompatible with due process of law. By barring companies not licensed by the state from insuring Louisiana property, the Court held, Louisiana had exceeded its STATE POLICE POWER and had unconstitutionally impaired the freedom of contract.

In the four decades following *Allgeyer,* the Supreme Court scrutinized socioeconomic legislation more aggressively and persistently than ever before or since, striking down scores of federal and state statutes as violative of substantive due process. The period from 1897 to 1937 has come to be known as "the *Lochner* era," after its most infamous product, LOCHNER V. NEW YORK (1905). *Lochner* invalidated a New York law limiting the work week of bakery employees to sixty hours; the Court found the statute an unreasonable infringement of the freedom of contract. In dissent, Justice OLIVER WENDELL HOLMES protested that "[t]he fourteenth amendment does not enact Mr. Herbert Spencer's *Social Statics.*"

Throughout the *Lochner* era, the Court closely examined both the means and the ends of socioeconomic legislation. The Court required that the relationship between a statute and its legitimate objectives be "real and substantial," and it repeatedly invalidated laws that it deemed to burden individual economic liberty more than strictly necessary to accomplish the goals of such laws. Thus, the majority in *Lochner* reasoned that regulation of bakery work hours exceeded the proper bounds of the police power in part because the state could protect the health of bakery employees without infringing so fundamentally on contractual freedom. Similarly, ADKINS V. CHILDREN'S HOSPITAL (1923) struck down minimum wage laws for women partly because the Court deemed narrower wage regulations sufficient to achieve the legislature's legitimate ends, and *Liggett Co. v. Baldridge* (1928), which invalidated Pennsylvania restrictions on corporate ownership of pharmacies, noted less objectionable regulatory means the state could employ to protect the same interests in public health.

In addition to demanding a tight fit between ends and means, the *Lochner* Court required that the statutory ends themselves fit its sense of the proper aims of lawmaking. Informed by earlier doctrines of implied limitations, as well as by the popular notions of social Darwinism and the writings of conservative legal COMMENTATORS ON THE CONSTITUTION such as THOMAS M. COOLEY and CHRISTOPHER G. TIEDEMAN, the Court viewed protection of individual common law rights and advancement of the general health, safety, and moral welfare to be the only valid objectives of government regulation. Laws aimed at redistributing economic and social power—giving A's property to B—by their very nature fell outside the realm of legitimate legislative action. Thus, for example, in ADAIR V. UNITED STATES (1908) and COPPAGE V. KANSAS (1915), the Court invalidated prohibitions against YELLOW DOG CONTRACTS that conditioned employment on workers' promises not to join unions. Writing for the majority in *Coppage,* Justice MAHLON PITNEY rejected the argument that inequality of bargaining power could justify infringing contractual liberty: it is "impossible to uphold freedom of contract and the right of private property without at the same time recognizing as legitimate those inequalities of fortune that are the necessary result of the exercise of those rights."

Although the Court in the *Lochner* era struck down close to 200 statutes under the due process clauses, it upheld even more. Many of the laws sustained were distinguished from invalidated statutes only by subtle factual differences supporting findings that they served the Court's narrow vision of the general welfare. After repeatedly striking down price controls, for example, the Court in NEBBIA V. NEW YORK (1934) upheld regulation of milk prices, concluding that the regulation was plausibly connected to public health on the theory that price competition encouraged suppliers to cut corners on sanitation. Other statutes, however, were sustained for a more specific reason: the Court exempted from its general liberty-of-contract approach statutes designed to protect especially disadvantaged or vulnerable groups. Thus, in HOLDEN V. HARDY (1897), the Court upheld restrictions on the hours worked by coal miners; the Court stressed the ultrahazardous nature of coal mining and the ability of coal companies in company-run towns virtually to dictate the terms of employment. Similarly, the Court in MULLER V. OREGON (1908), moved in part by the supposed physical vulnerability of women and by sexist notions of their maternal mission, permitted Oregon to limit women's hours of work outside the home.

Just as prior doctrinal instabilities had helped to usher in the *Lochner* era, so these exceptions to the regime of laissez-faire presaged the era's close. By acknowledging that a state could protect at least some groups at the expense of others, *Holden* and *Muller* made available in every substantive due process case the argument that the legislature might reasonably have determined that the class protected by the challenged statute was unable to, or should not be forced to, fend for itself. Indeed, *Lochner v. New York* was itself drastically limited *sub silentio* in 1917, when the Court in BUNTING V. OREGON (1917) relied on *Muller* in upholding a state law limiting to ten hours the work day of manufacturing employees.

With the onset of the Depression, moreover, it became progressively more difficult to view the relative wealth of A and B as a matter of purely private concern, outside the domain of proper governmental authority. Increasingly, economic transactions were seen as interrelated, and the general welfare was understood as intimately linked to the welfare of disadvantaged groups. The Supreme Court's persistent invalidation of redistributive legislation was sharply criticized by labor unions, the liberal press, and New Deal politicians, all of whom argued that extensive economic regulation, both state and federal, was necessary to alleviate the Depression. The perceived legitimacy of such regulation was further bolstered by the work of "realist" legal scholars such as MORRIS R. COHEN and Robert Hale, who portrayed distributions of private wealth and power as the results of public choices expressed, for example, in the law of property and contract.

After much outcry, the Supreme Court parted dramatically with *Lochner* in WEST COAST HOTEL V. PARRISH (1937), which abandoned earlier precedent and upheld a statutory minimum wage for women as reasonable in light of women's vulnerability to economic exploitation and the public interest in minimizing the number of workers requiring government relief. In the years that followed, the Court confirmed its abandonment of *Lochner* by repeatedly rejecting challenges to expansive New Deal regulation of private economic arrangements, and in 1949 the Court unanimously and explicitly rejected the *"Allgeyer-Lochner-Adair-Coppage* constitutional doctrine."

Never, however, did the Supreme Court explicitly abandon *Lochner*'s substantive theory of what constitutes legitimate legislation; it remains the official dogma to this day that regulatory power may not be exercised solely to transfer property from one private party to another. Instead, the Court relaxed the STANDARD OF REVIEW it applied to socioeconomic regulation: the close scrutiny of the *Lochner* era was replaced with extreme deference to legislative determinations. Thus, in UNITED STATES V. CAROLENE PRODUCTS CO. (1938) the Court promised to uphold socioeconomic legislation if any known or reasonably inferable state of facts supported the legislature's judgment.

In the intervening decades, this extreme deference has become virtually complete judicial abdication. Although substantive scrutiny has occasionally been smuggled in through the privileges or immunities clause of Article IV or the CONTRACT CLAUSE, in due process review the Court has required of economic regulation only "minimum rationality" and has shown itself willing to uphold laws on the basis of purely hypothetical facts or objectives, or on blind trust in legislative rationality. Justice WILLIAM H. REHNQUIST carried the Court's approach to its logical extreme in his opinion for the majority in *Railroad Retirement Board v. Fritz* (1980). Rejecting a due process challenge to legislation that phased out the eligibility of long-retired railroad employees to receive both social security and railroad retirement benefits, but preserved the similar eligibility of more recently retired employees of equally long (or longer) tenure, the majority reasoned that the statute was clearly a rational way to accomplish its precise result: cutting off the dual benefits of the very employees adversely affected by the law. "The plain language" of the statute, Justice Rehnquist wrote, "marks the beginning and end of our inquiry."

The Supreme Court has not been entirely without textual guidance in its post-1937 effort to define the fundamental freedoms protected by the Fourteenth Amendment's due process clause. Although the Bill of Rights formally applies only to the federal government, the Court has relied heavily on the first eight amendments in determining which rights—both procedural and substantive—are so essential that governmental action abrogating them violates due process of law. Most of the guarantees in the Bill of Rights have now been "selectively incorporated" into the Fourteenth Amendment, although the Court has decisively repudiated the view, espoused by Justice HUGO L. BLACK, that the Fourteenth Amendment applies the Bill of Rights to the states *in toto*.

At the close of the *Lochner* era, the Justices laid down a fairly restrictive rule for determining which provisions of the Bill of Rights were "incorporated." Writing for the Court in PALKO V. CONNECTICUT (1937), Justice BENJAMIN N. CARDOZO limited incorporation to those rights "implicit in the concept of ORDERED LIBERTY." Eventually recognizing the irrelevance of an inquiry into whether "a civilized system could be imagined that would not accord the particular protection," the Court in the late 1960s adopted a more contextual approach, asking whether a particular right was essential to the American political order. Thus, in DUNCAN V. LOUISIANA (1968) the Court held that criminal trial safeguards provided by the Bill of Rights are absorbed by the Fourteenth Amendment if they are "fundamental in the context of the criminal processes maintained by the American states." Over time, *Duncan* has come to stand for the more general proposition that guarantees in the Bill of Rights should be incorporated—and guarantees not expressly mentioned should be added—if they are necessary to protect values basic to our society. (See INCORPORATION DOCTRINE.)

Although substantive due process protection of implied rights to contractual liberty virtually vanished with the close of the *Lochner* era, judicial solicitude has grown in the ensuing years for a different set of liberties not expressly protected by the Constitution—a diverse group of claims to personal autonomy that have been collectively labeled the RIGHT OF PRIVACY. In contrast to the narrow contractual liberty to which the *Lochner* Court devoted the bulk of its concern, the right of privacy has come to embrace a wide array of freedoms, including rights of association and reproduction as well as of seclusion and intellectual independence. Some of these freedoms have been derived by extrapolation (or, perhaps, excavation) from the Bill of Rights or other clauses of the Fifth and Fourteenth Amendments. Yet the stirring rhetoric that has typically accompanied the elaboration of these personal freedoms testifies to a judicial perception that they are in some way more fundamental than the textual provisions to which they are pegged.

The Supreme Court made clear the essential nature of these "privacy" or "personhood" rights when it gave them their earliest articulation during the *Lochner* era itself. Striking down a state law that forbade the teaching of foreign languages before the eighth grade, the Court in MEYER V. NEBRASKA (1923) stressed the importance of allowing teachers to pursue their calling and parents to raise their children as they saw fit. Justice JAMES C. MCREYNOLDS's majority opinion gave broad scope to the liberty protected by the due process clauses: "Without doubt, [it] denotes not merely freedom from bodily restraint but also the right of the individual to contract, to engage in any of the common occupations of life, to acquire useful knowledge, to marry, establish a home and bring up children, to worship God according to the dictates of his own conscience, and generally to enjoy those privileges long recognized at common law as essential to the orderly pursuit of happiness by free men." Two years later, in PIERCE V. SOCIETY OF SISTERS (1925), the Court marshaled similar rhetoric in invalidating a state requirement that all students attend public schools. Still more sweeping—and perhaps of more lasting influence—was Justice LOUIS D. BRANDEIS's formulation in his dissent in OLMSTEAD V. UNITED STATES (1928): "The makers of our Constitution . . . sought to protect Americans in their beliefs, their thoughts, their emotions, and their sensations. They conferred, as against the government, the right to be let alone—the most comprehensive of rights and the right most valued by civilized men."

Despite the broad language of these early opinions, *Meyer* and *Pierce* evinced special judicial solicitude primarily for family autonomy—freedom from government intrusion into the traditionally intimate realms of marriage, reproduction, and child-rearing. That emphasis, along with recognition of personal autonomy rights as fundamental, was furthered by the watershed case of SKINNER V. OKLAHOMA (1942), the Supreme Court's first important privacy decision following the demise of *Lochner.* Invalidating a state statute providing for the STERILIZATION of persons convicted two or more times of "felonies involving moral turpitude," the Court termed the right to reproduce "one of the basic civil rights of man." Part of the Court's concern stemmed from fear of the invidious and possibly genocidal ways in which government control over reproduction might be exercised: the Court observed that the "power to sterilize, . . . [i]n evil or reckless hands . . . can cause races or types which are inimical to the dominant group to wither and disappear."

The right to REPRODUCTIVE AUTONOMY recognized in *Skinner* has since been elaborated and considerably expanded. As recently as 1978, the Court in ZABLOCKI V. REDHAIL "reaffirm[ed] the fundamental character of the right to marry," holding that a state may not forbid marriage of parents unable to meet their child support obligations. More controversial has been the extension of *Skinner* to BIRTH CONTROL practices. In GRISWOLD V. CONNECTICUT (1965) the Supreme Court ruled that a married couple's decision to purchase and use contraceptives is a private matter beyond the proper reach of government authority. Perhaps not surprisingly, Justice WILLIAM O. DOUGLAS's majority opinion focused on the intimacy of marital choices, invoking "a right of privacy older than the Bill of Rights" and defending the "sacred precincts of marital bedrooms." The freedom to practice contraception was not freed of its familial trappings until 1972, when Justice WILLIAM J. BRENNAN wrote for the Court in EISENSTADT V. BAIRD that, if "the right of privacy means anything, it is the right of the *individual,* married or unmarried, to be free from unwarranted governmental intrusions into matters so fundamentally affecting a person as the decision whether to bear or beget a child." That *Baird* singled out as decisive in *Griswold* the element of reproductive autonomy was made clear by CAREY V. POPULATION SERVICES INTERNATIONAL (1977), which invalidated a state statute allowing contraceptives to be sold only by licensed pharmacists and only to persons over sixteen.

When the Court assessed the constitutionality of ABORTION laws in ROE V. WADE (1973), its commitment to reproductive autonomy collided with an equally basic concern for the sanctity of human life. Writing for the majority, Justice HARRY L. BLACKMUN reasoned that the liberty protected by the due process clauses includes a woman's fundamental right to decide, with her physician, whether to end or to continue a pregnancy, but that certain state interests are sufficiently compelling to override that right. During the final trimester of pregnancy, the state's interest in preserving the fetus, by then viable, justifies a ban on abortions; before the third trimester, however, abortions may not be prohibited and may be regulated only as necessary to protect the woman's health; and, before the second trimester, the state may require only that abortions be performed by licensed physicians.

As an element of substantive due process, the right to privacy has received its doctrinally purest exposition in reproductive autonomy cases. Equally important rights to personal autonomy, however, have been found in the "penumbras" of constitutional provisions less abstract than the requirement of "due process of law," most notably the FIRST AMENDMENT. In *West Virginia State Board of Education v. Barnette* (1943) the Court construed the First Amendment, along with the Fifth and the Fourteenth, to establish for each individual a sphere of intellectual and spiritual independence. Striking down a compulsory flag salute in public schools, Justice ROBERT H. JACKSON wrote for the Court that, "[i]f there is any fixed star in our constitutional constellation, it is that no official, high or petty, can prescribe what shall be orthodox in politics, nationalism, religion, or other matters of opinion or force citizens to confess by word or act their faith therein." The Court appealed to the same notion when it held, in *Wooley v. Maynard* (1977), that New Hampshire could not punish a person for obscuring the words "Live Free or Die" on his license plate because he found it religiously or philosophically repugnant to display the state's slogan on his car. The Court reasoned that the state had impermissibly invaded the private "sphere of intellect and spirit" by requiring individuals "to use their private property as a 'mobile billboard' for the State's ideological message."

In NAACP V. ALABAMA (1958) and *Talley v. California* (1960) the Court found in the First Amendment guarantees of associational and expressive freedom correlative rights to anonymity. And in MOORE V. CITY OF EAST CLEVELAND (1977) the Court protected a special right to familial association by invalidating a single-family zoning ordinance that prevented a woman from living with her son and two grandsons. Renewing its special commitment to traditional visions of family autonomy, the Court distinguished the zoning law upheld in *Village of Belle Terre v. Boraas* (1974) on the basis that "the ordinance there affected only *unrelated* individuals," whereas East Cleveland had "chosen to regulate the occupancy of its housing by slicing deeply into the family itself."

Other penumbral rights to personal autonomy have been found in the intersection of several textual provisions, or in the constitutional system taken as a whole. In SHAPIRO V. THOMPSON (1969), for example, the Court alluded to the COMMERCE CLAUSE, the privileges or immunities clause of the Fourteenth Amendment, and the similar language in Article IV, section 2, as well as to the Fifth Amendment's due process clause and "the nature of our Federal Union" in finding that "our constitutional concepts of personal liberty" imposed a general requirement that "all citizens be free to travel throughout the length and breadth of our land uninhibited by statutes, rules, or regulations which unreasonably burden or restrict this movement." The newly vitalized RIGHT TO TRAVEL had earlier been recognized in the context of international mobility, at least when other First Amendment rights were also at stake: the Court in APTHEKER V. SECRETARY OF STATE (1964) had struck down a congressional denial of passports to members of the Communist party. In HAIG V. AGEE (1981) the Court sustained revocation of the passport of a former intelligence agent who was engaged in exposing undercover agents stationed abroad. In *Haig* the Court distinguished sharply between the "right" of inter*state* travel and the "freedom" of inter*national* travel, refusing to extend to congressional regulation of the latter the close scrutiny it had given state regulation of the former.

The Supreme Court attempted to unify some of these disparate doctrinal threads in WHALEN V. ROE (1976), its most comprehensive treatment thus far of the right of privacy. Writing for a unanimous Court, Justice JOHN PAUL STEVENS upheld a carefully crafted state scheme for maintaining computerized records of prescriptions for certain dangerous drugs, but only after examining the statute's implications for what he described as the two components of the right to privacy: an interest in confidentiality—"avoiding disclosure of personal matters"—and an interest in free choice—"independence in making certain kinds of important decisions."

Despite this seemingly broad formulation, the Court has resisted the creation of a generic right to choose how one lives. In *Kelley v. Johnson* (1976), for example, the Court upheld police department rules regulating officers' hair styles and prohibiting them from having beards. Writing for the majority, Justice Rehnquist argued that the rules did not violate the right of privacy recognized in *Roe, Baird,* and *Griswold;* he distinguished those cases as involving "substantial claims of infringement on the individual's freedom of choice with respect to certain basic matters of procreation, marriage, and family life." Nor is the Court apparently prepared to protect even all intimate decisions central to one's self-definition; the Justices have, for example, passed up several opportunities to review statutes punishing or burdening private homosexual activity between consenting adults. (See FREEDOM OF INTIMATE ASSOCIATION.)

Some lower courts have been more willing to expand the protected sphere of personal autonomy, recognizing broad rights of lifestyle choice as well as, in some cases, freedom to decide how and when one will die. The Supreme Court, however, appears unlikely to follow very quickly. Not only are some Justices concerned about the open-ended and potentially radical nature of such decisions, but the Court has repeatedly dropped unsubtle hints that there are fairly sharp limits to its tolerance. The "blessed versatility" of substantive due process is limited by the Justices' awareness that the Supreme Court is an institution of government.

LAURENCE H. TRIBE

Bibliography

BLACK, CHARLES L. 1969 *Structure and Relationship in Constitutional Law.* Baton Rouge: Louisiana State University Press.

BREST, PAUL and LEVINSON, SANFORD 1983 *Processes of Constitutional Decisionmaking: Cases and Materials.* Boston: Little, Brown.

CHOPER, JESSE H. 1980 *Judicial Review and the National Political Process: A Functional Reconsideration of the Role of the Supreme Court.* Chicago: University of Chicago Press.

ELY, JOHN HART 1980 *Democracy and Distrust: A Theory of Judicial Review.* Cambridge, Mass.: Harvard University Press.

GUNTHER, GERALD 1975 *Cases and Materials on Constitutional Law.* Mineola, N.Y.: Foundation Press.

KENNEDY, DUNCAN 1980 Toward an Historical Understanding of Legal Consciousness: The Case of Classical Legal Thought in America 1850–1940. *Research in Law & Sociology* 3:3–57.

LOCKHART, WILLIAM B., KAMISAR, YALE, and CHOPER, JESSE H. (1964)1980 *Constitutional Law: Cases—Comments—Questions.* St. Paul, Minn.: West Publishing Co.

PENNOCK, ROLAND J. and CHAPMAN, JOHN W., eds. 1977 *Due Process.* New York: New York University Press.

TRIBE, LAURENCE H. 1978 *American Constitutional Law.* Mineola, N.Y.: Foundation Press.

——— 1985 *Constitutional Choices.* Cambridge, Mass.: Harvard University Press.

SUBVERSIVE ACTIVITIES CONTROL BOARD

The INTERNAL SECURITY ACT of 1950 created the Subversive Activities Control Board (SACB). This agency was to determine, on request of the ATTORNEY GENERAL, whether a particular organization was a communist-action, communist-front, or communist-infiltrated organization. After SACB had issued an order so designating an organization and after the order had been sustained by the courts, various disabilities and sanctions could be imposed on the group and its members. These included being barred from federal jobs, being denied employment in defense-related industries, and being prohibited from using United States passports.

Eleven years after SACB's creation, the Supreme Court sustained its findings that the Communist party was a communist-action organization as defined by the act and upheld an order requiring the party to register. (See COMMUNIST PARTY V. SACB, 1961.) The Court subsequently declared unconstitutional attempts to implement the sanctions of the act, and in 1965 (ALBERTSON V. SACB) it ruled that the forced registration of individual members of the party would violate the RIGHT AGAINST SELF-INCRIMINATION. By the late 1960s, SACB was moribund. Congress, attempting salvage, gave it authority to register with the attorney general the names of persons it had determined were members of communist organizations, and SACB eventually declared seven persons to be in this category. Such limited action, as well as a 1967 decision holding unconstitutional provisions barring members of registered organizations from jobs in defense-related industries, further limited SACB's utility. In 1974, the RICHARD M. NIXON administration, bowing to SACB's critics, requested no further funding, effectively ending its life.

PAUL L. MURPHY

Bibliography

MURPHY, PAUL L. 1972 *The Constitution in Crisis Times, 1918–1969.* New York: Harper & Row.

SUBVERSIVE ACTIVITY

Activity is "subversive" if it is directed toward the overthrow of the existing form of government by force or other unlawful means. Subversive activity comprises TREASON, SEDITION, insurrection, and sabotage, as well as other unlawful acts committed with the requisite intent. Although individuals may engage in subversive activity, concerted or organized subversion is more common and excites more public concern. Active, purposive membership in subversive organizations—such as the Communist party, the American Nazi party, or the Ku Klux Klan—is a federal crime, and between 1950 and 1974 the ATTORNEY GENERAL'S LIST was maintained as an official catalog of such groups.

In twentieth-century America, the suppression of subversion has been controversial where the "activity" has seemed to consist primarily of SUBVERSIVE

ADVOCACY. But the controversy should not obscure the fact that there is such a thing as subversive activity and that the survival of constitutional government requires that such activity be controlled.

The critical distinction is not between words and deeds, speech and action. Even the staunchest defenders of CIVIL LIBERTIES agree that INCITEMENT TO UNLAWFUL CONDUCT may be punished by law, at least when the speaker has the intention and capability of inducing his hearers to engage in insurrection, riot, or disobedience of law. Some forms of subversive activity—for example, the attack on the House of Representatives by Puerto Rican nationalists in 1954—are extreme forms of SYMBOLIC SPEECH, known in revolutionary jargon as "propaganda of the deed." The political goal toward which it is aimed is precisely what distinguishes subversive activity.

Because the government of the United States is one of limited and ENUMERATED POWERS, its authority to define and punish subversive activities as crimes is not entirely clear. Treason is defined in Article III, section 2, of the Constitution, and as the same section limits the range of punishment for treason, it implies the power of Congress to prescribe punishment within the permitted range. The Constitution does not define any lesser degree of subversive activity, nor does it expressly grant to Congress the power to define and punish such crimes. Instead, the power must be an IMPLIED POWER incidental to the power to punish treason or else NECESSARY AND PROPER for the carrying out of one or more of the enumerated powers.

In the absence of statutes against insurrection or rebellion, the perpetrators of FRIES' REBELLION and the WHISKEY REBELLION were tried for treason. The prosecutors argued that an armed rising to prevent the execution of federal law—the normal definition of insurrection—was at least a constructive treason as the COMMON LAW had understood the term. Similarly, when AARON BURR assembled an armed force in the Western territories, for purposes that are still not entirely clear, the only federal offense for which he could be tried was treason. But a charge of treason seems manifestly to have been inappropriate in each of these cases.

On the other hand, the ALIEN AND SEDITION ACTS, enacted when the country was on the brink of war with France, generously defined offenses against the United States. Although section 2, defining SEDITIOUS LIBEL, is more famous, section 1 of the Sedition Act proscribed certain subversive activities: combination or conspiracy to impede the operation of law or to intimidate government officials, procuring or counseling riot or insurrection—whether or not the activity was successful. The ESPIONAGE ACT OF 1917, enacted while the country was fighting World War I, treated as criminal any attempt to procure draft evasion or to interfere with military recruitment while the Sedition Act of 1918 proscribed all advocacy of revolution, however remote the prospect of success.

In the latter half of the twentieth century, the phenomenon of political terrorism raised new problems. Frequently directed from outside the United States, terrorist activity, like the extreme forms of subversive activity, employs politically motivated violence. Although the aim of terrorism may not be the overthrow of the American government, terrorism shares with the more extreme forms of subversive activity the substitution of violence for public deliberation and constitutional government.

DENNIS J. MAHONEY

Bibliography

GRODZINS, MORTON 1956 *The Loyal and the Disloyal: Social Boundaries of Patriotism and Treason.* Chicago: University of Chicago Press.

HURST, JAMES WILLARD 1971 *The Law of Treason in the United States.* Westport, Conn.: Greenwood Press.

SUBVERSIVE ADVOCACY

The quest for NATIONAL SECURITY has placed strains on the FIRST AMENDMENT when the country has been at war, or threatened by war, or torn by fear of an external enemy or domestic social unrest. Federal and state governments have sought to silence those regarded as "subversives" and internal enemies because they supported a foreign cause or advocated revolutionary change in American institutions.

The ALIEN AND SEDITION ACTS, passed only seven years after ratification of the First Amendment, were the most extreme of these measures in our history. President JOHN ADAMS and the Federalist Congress used them to stifle the opposition Republicans who were accused of being "servile minions" of France, with which war seemed imminent in early 1798. Seventeen prosecutions were instituted against Republican newspaper editors, officeholders, and adherents, with only one acquittal.

The constitutionality of the Sedition Act was never tested in the Supreme Court, which then had no JURISDICTION to review federal criminal convictions. But the act was sustained by the lower federal courts, including three Supreme Court Justices sitting as trial judges. The modern Supreme Court, in NEW YORK

TIMES CO. v. SULLIVAN (1964), has stated that the First Amendment bars prosecution for SEDITIOUS LIBEL. Opposition to the government in power, accompanied by criticism of official policy and conduct, cannot constitutionally be proscribed as "seditious" or "subversive."

During the nineteenth century there was no federal legislation limiting FREEDOM OF SPEECH or FREEDOM OF THE PRESS. No official efforts were made to silence the Federalist denunciation of the War of 1812. Abolitionist sentiment did not fare so well in the succeeding decades of bitter controversy over slavery. Southern states passed laws limiting the freedom to criticize slavery. During the Civil War no sedition act was passed to suppress the widespread opposition to the war in the North. But President ABRAHAM LINCOLN suspended the writ of HABEAS CORPUS, controlled the mails, telegraph, and passports, and approved military detention of thousands of persons accused of disloyalty.

The rapid industrialization and urbanization of the country after the Civil War was accompanied by social unrest. The Haymarket Square bombing in Chicago in 1886, the violent Homestead and Pullman strikes in the 1890s, the assassination of President WILLIAM MCKINLEY in 1901 by a presumed "anarchist," and the militant tactics of the Industrial Workers of the World led to the passage of the first state Criminal Anarchy Law in New York in 1902. By 1921, thirty-three states had enacted similar laws making it a crime to advocate the overthrow of existing government by force or violence. Unlike the Sedition Act of 1798, these laws forbade only the advocacy of illegal means to effect political change.

Together with the federal ESPIONAGE ACT of 1917, these state laws were used to suppress opposition to World War I voiced by pacifists, sympathizers with Germany, and international socialists. The 1917 act made it criminal to obstruct recruiting, cause insubordination in the armed forces, or interfere with military operations. Amendments to the Espionage Act (the SEDITION ACT of 1918) made it an offense, among other things, to say or do anything that would favor any country at war with the United States, oppose the cause of the United States in the war, or incite contempt for the American form of government or the uniform of the Army or Navy. Under the Espionage Act 877 people were convicted, almost all for expressing opinions about the merits and conduct of the war. The Supreme Court sustained these convictions, rejecting the contention that they violated the First Amendment.

SCHENCK v. UNITED STATES (1919) was the first of the Espionage Act cases to reach the Supreme Court. Justice OLIVER WENDELL HOLMES wrote the Court opinion affirming the conviction and, for the first time, enunciated the CLEAR AND PRESENT DANGER test to determine when advocacy of unlawful conduct is protected by the First Amendment. Holmes also wrote the opinions of the Court in FROHWERK v. UNITED STATES (1919) and DEBS v. UNITED STATES (1919), sustaining the convictions of a newspaper editor for questioning the constitutionality of the draft and charging that Wall Street had dragged the country into the war, and of Eugene V. Debs, the railroad union and Socialist party leader, for denouncing the war as a capitalist plot. Just what the "clear and present danger" was in these cases was doubtful, and Holmes and Brandeis soon began to dissent from the way the majority used the test.

Their first great dissent came in ABRAMS v. UNITED STATES (1919). In his dissenting opinion, which Brandeis joined, Holmes gave new content to the clear and present danger test by emphasizing the immediacy of the danger that must exist. Although Holmes would have softened this requirement, permitting punishment of speech with the specific intent to bring about the danger even if the danger itself was not "immediate," he did not think the necessary intent had been shown in *Abrams.*

The Red Scare of 1919 and 1920 was induced not only by fear of the Bolshevik revolution and the Communist International but also by the economic and social insecurity that accompanied demobilization after World War I. The PALMER RAIDS expressed the federal government's fears and antiradical sentiments. The states resorted to their criminal anarchy laws and the Supreme Court sustained convictions under these laws in GITLOW v. NEW YORK (1925) and WHITNEY v. CALIFORNIA (1927).

In *Gitlow* the Court assumed that freedom of speech and press, protected by the First Amendment from abridgment by Congress, was a "liberty" protected by the DUE PROCESS clause of the FOURTEENTH AMENDMENT against state impairment. In both *Gitlow* and *Whitney* the Court refused to apply the clear and present danger test because the state legislatures had prohibited a particular class of speech—the advocacy of the doctrine that the government should be overthrown by violence. Gitlow's advocacy of violent revolution violated the law even if there were no clear and present danger of revolution. The legislature might reasonably seek "to extinguish the spark without waiting until it has enkindled the flame or blazed into the conflagration."

Dissenting in *Gitlow,* Holmes argued for application of the clear and present danger test, but did not confront the majority's position. But Brandeis, concurring in *Whitney,* insisted that courts and juries must be free to decide whether, under the circumstances of each case, "the evil apprehended is [relatively serious and its incidence] so imminent that it may befall before there is opportunity for full discussion. . . . Only an emergency can justify repression."

From the end of the Red Scare to the outbreak of World War II, federal action against alleged subversives was limited to deportation of alien communists. State prosecutions under criminal anarchy laws were infrequent after the middle 1920s. The Sedition Act of 1918 was repealed in 1921 and has never been revived.

The Smith Act of 1940 was modeled on the New York Criminal Anarchy law. During World War II, twenty-eight pro-Nazi individuals were prosecuted under it for conspiring to cause insubordination in the armed forces, but the judge died and the prosecution was dropped. Eighteen members of the Trotskyist Socialist Workers party, which opposed the war, were convicted of conspiracy to cause insubordination in the armed forces and to advocate violent overthrow of the government.

On the whole, the country supported World War II. After the Nazi invasion of the Soviet Union, in June 1941, communists became the staunchest supporters of the war. But as soon as the war was won, the activities of the international communist movement resumed. In 1949 eleven leaders of the Communist party were convicted under the Smith Act for conspiring to advocate violent overthrow of the United States government and establishment of a dictatorship of the proletariat, and to organize the Communist party to advocate these goals. The Supreme Court affirmed the convictions, 6–2, in DENNIS V. UNITED STATES (1951).

In 1948 the Soviet Union had blockaded Berlin and engineered the communist coup that overthrew the parliamentary regime in Czechoslovakia. By the time the Supreme Court decided *Dennis,* several Soviet spy rings in the West had been exposed, the communists had taken control in China, and Americans were dying in the KOREAN WAR. The domestic and foreign policies of the American Communist party were consistent with Soviet policies and directives. In light of these events, a plurality of four Justices, speaking through Chief Justice FRED M. VINSON, reformulated the clear and present danger test into a BALANCING TEST that weighed the seriousness of the danger, discounted by its improbability, against the degree of invasion of freedom of speech.

Justice FELIX FRANKFURTER concurred, deferring to Congress's judgment regarding the extent of the danger posed by the Communist party and the world communist movement. With the experience of the Nuremberg war crimes trials still fresh in his memory, Justice ROBERT H. JACKSON also concurred, joining Frankfurter in rejecting the appropriateness of the clear and present danger test to the communist conspiracy.

Though not purporting to overrule *Dennis,* the Supreme Court, in YATES V. UNITED STATES (1957), reversed convictions of the officers of the Communist party in California. Justice JOHN MARSHALL HARLAN's plurality opinion read the Smith Act as requiring proof that the defendants had advocated "unlawful action" and not merely "abstract doctrine" that the United States government should be overthrown. *Yates* did not represent a return to the Holmes-Brandeis version of the clear and present danger test. It emphasized the content of the advocacy, not its consequences. On this view, advocacy of unlawful action was punishable, irrespective of the immediacy of the danger.

After *Yates* was decided, the government concluded that it could not satisfy the requirements of proof demanded by the Supreme Court and abandoned all prosecutions under the Smith Act. Altogether twenty-nine communists were convicted under that act, including the leaders involved in *Dennis* and the only person convicted under the provision proscribing membership in the Communist party. His conviction was upheld in SCALES V. UNITED STATES (1961) because he was an "active member" who knew of the Party's unlawful goals and had a "specific intent" to achieve them.

In 1950, shortly after the outbreak of the Korean War, Congress enacted the SUBVERSIVE ACTIVITIES CONTROL ACT, which required communist organizations to register with the ATTORNEY GENERAL. When the Communist party failed to register, the attorney general asked the Subversive Activities Control Board to order it to register and list its members. In COMMUNIST PARTY V. SUBVERSIVE ACTIVITIES CONTROL BOARD (1961) the Court upheld the board's finding that the party was a communist-action organization and its order requiring the party to register. Only Justice HUGO L. BLACK dissented from the majority view that the First Amendment did not prohibit Congress from removing the party's "mask of anonymity."

The Supreme Court in 1961 did not pass upon the contention that compulsory registration would violate the RIGHT AGAINST SELF-INCRIMINATION afforded by the Fifth Amendment because it would subject party members to prosecution under the Smith Act and the

1954 COMMUNIST CONTROL ACT. This contention was eventually sustained in ALBERTSON V. SUBVERSIVE ACTIVITIES CONTROL BOARD (1965). As a result, neither the Communist party nor any of its members ever registered under the act, and no organization ever registered as a communist front. In 1968, Congress removed the registration obligation. Instead, the Subversive Activities Control Board was authorized to keep records, open to public inspection, of the names and addresses of communist organizations and their members. But in 1969 and 1970 the courts held that mere membership in the party was protected by the First Amendment, and the board was disbanded in 1973.

The Communist Control Act of 1954 purported to deprive the Communist party of the "rights, privileges, and immunities attendant upon legal bodies." It was not clear whether Congress intended this provision to dissolve the party as a legal organization or only to bar it from the ballot and benefits such as mailing privileges. Though the Supreme Court has not passed upon its constitutionality, the act has become a dead letter.

Although the Espionage Act and the Smith Act remained in force during the VIETNAM WAR, no prosecutions were brought under either measure. In *Bond v. Floyd* (1966) the Supreme Court assumed that opposition to the war and the draft was protected by the First Amendment.

In 1967 a Ku Klux Klan leader was convicted of violating the Ohio CRIMINAL SYNDICALISM LAW by making a speech at a Klan rally to which only television newsmen had been invited. The speech was derogatory of blacks and Jews and proclaimed that if the white race continued to be threatened, "it's possible that there might have to be some revengence [sic] taken." In a PER CURIAM opinion in BRANDENBURG V. OHIO (1969) the Supreme Court reversed the conviction and held the Ohio statute unconstitutional. In so doing, it overruled *Whitney v. California* and again reformulated the clear and present danger doctrine: "constitutional guarantees of free speech and free press do not permit a State to forbid or proscribe advocacy of the use of force or of law violation except where such advocacy is directed to inciting or producing such action." Although the Court purported to follow *Dennis*, commentators generally conclude that *Brandenburg* overruled *Dennis*. In *Communist Party of Indiana v. Whitcomb* (1974) the Supreme Court held that it was unconstitutional for Indiana to refuse a place on the ballot to the Communist party of Indiana because its officers had refused to submit an oath that the party "does not advocate the overthrow of local, state or national government by force or violence."

The *Brandenburg* formula, the most speech-protective standard yet evolved by the Supreme Court, has been criticized from opposing sides. Concurring in *Brandenburg*, Justices WILLIAM O. DOUGLAS and Black would have abandoned the clear and present danger test in favor of a distinction between ideas and overt acts. Some critics reject even this concession on the ground that an incitement-of-overt-acts test can be manipulated by the courts to cut off speech just when it comes close to being effective.

Others argue that advocacy of the forcible overthrow of the government, or of any unlawful act, is not protected by the First Amendment. Such advocacy is not political speech because it is a call to revoke the results that political speech has produced; violent overthrow destroys the premises of our system. An organization that seeks power through illegal means refuses to abide by the legitimate conditions of party competition in a democracy.

Furthermore, in suppressing totalitarian movements, even if they purport to reject illegal means, a democratic society is not acting to protect the status quo but the very same interest which freedom of speech itself seeks to secure—the possibility of peaceful progress under freedom. In this view, the *Brandenburg* formula would deny our democracy the constitutional right to act until it might be too late to prevent a totalitarian victory.

Although one may disagree with the view that the problem of a totalitarian party's competing for political power in a democracy is solely one of "freedom of expression," the reasons for toleration—to keep even the freedom of expression open to challenge lest it become a "dead dogma," and to allow extremist groups to advocate revolution because they may represent real grievances that deserve to be heard—must be seriously considered by legislators in determining whether suppression is a wise policy. But if wisdom may sometimes dictate toleration, that conclusion does not imply that the Constitution gives the enemies of freedom the right to organize to crush it.

CARL A. AUERBACH

Bibliography

GUNTHER GERALD 1975 Learned Hand and the Origins of Modern First Amendment Doctrine: Some Fragments of History. *Stanford Law Review* 27:719–773.

LEVY, LEONARD W. 1985 *Emergence of a Free Press.* New York: Oxford University Press.

LINDE, HANS A. 1970 "Clear and Present Danger" Reexamined: Dissonants in the Brandenburg Concerto. *Stanford Law Review* 22:1163–1186.

NATHANSON, NATHANIEL L. 1950 The Communist Trial and the Clear-and-Present-Danger Test. *Harvard Law Review* 63:1167–1175.

SUGARMAN v. DOUGALL
413 U.S. 634 (1973)
GRIFFITHS, IN RE
413 U.S. 717 (1973)

In *Sugarman,* the Supreme Court held, 8–1, that New York's law making ALIENS ineligible for civil service employment was unconstitutional. In *Griffiths,* the Court held, 7–2, that Connecticut could not constitutionally bar resident aliens from the practice of law. Both decisions rested on EQUAL PROTECTION grounds. Justice LEWIS F. POWELL, writing for the Court in *Griffiths,* concluded that the state had not shown that excluding aliens from law practice was necessary to serve an interest sufficiently substantial to justify the rule. In *Sugarman,* Justice HARRY A. BLACKMUN wrote for the Court, repeating what he had said in GRAHAM V. RICHARDSON (1971), that discrimination against aliens must survive STRICT SCRUTINY by the courts. Here the bar to aliens was not necessary to achieve any substantial interest. Justice Blackmun added that some discrimination against aliens would be justified in the name of "political community": the right to vote or to hold high public office, for example, might be limited to citizens. These OBITER DICTA assumed importance in the later cases of FOLEY V. CONNELIE (1978) and AMBACH V. NORWICK (1979).

KENNETH L. KARST

SUGAR TRUST CASE

See: *Knight Co., E. C., United States v.*

SULLIVAN, UNITED STATES v.
332 U.S. 689 (1948)

In no other case has the Supreme Court more sweepingly construed the COMMERCE CLAUSE. To protect consumers the Federal Food, Drug, and Cosmetic Act of 1938, passed under the NATIONAL POLICE POWER, prohibited the misbranding of drugs "held for sale after interstate shipment." Nine months after a bottle of sulfathiazole tablets had been shipped from Chicago to Atlanta, a retail druggist in Columbus, Georgia, who had purchased the bottle, properly labeled with a warning that the drug could be toxic, sold twelve tablets in a box without the mandatory warning. The local druggist thereby committed a federal crime. A federal court of appeals reversed his conviction on the ground that the words "held for sale after interstate shipment" extended only to the first intrastate sale and could not apply to all subsequent local sales after any lapse of time.

The Supreme Court, in an opinion by Justice HUGO L. BLACK for a bare majority, reversed and sustained the constitutionality of the statute. Black declared that it prohibited misbranding no matter when the drug was sold and without regard to how many local sales intervened; the statute remained in force "to the moment of . . . delivery to the ultimate consumer" in an intrastate transaction. Sullivan, the druggist, had contended that the statute so construed exceeded the commerce power and invaded powers reserved to the states under the TENTH AMENDMENT. Black replied merely that a 1913 precedent, *McDermott v. Wisconsin,* which had sustained the misbranding provision of the PURE FOOD AND DRUG ACT of 1906, controlled the case. He thought that the "variants" between the two cases were "not sufficient" to distinguish *McDermott,* although he conceded that the retailer in *McDermott* had been the direct consignee of an interstate shipment. That fact should have made the precedent inapplicable. Black did not take notice that in *McDermott* the Court had reversed the state conviction of a grocer who misbranded under state law but complied with federal law. Black did not consider that under the ORIGINAL PACKAGE DOCTRINE the druggist sold local merchandise. Justice WILEY RUTLEGE concurred without reaching the constitutional issue and like the three dissenters wrote only on the construction of the statute.

After *Sullivan* the commerce power seemed to have no statable limits, though the rationale of the decision is unclear. The transaction involved in *Sullivan* was neither INTRASTATE COMMERCE that affected INTERSTATE COMMERCE, nor the PRODUCTION of goods for interstate commerce. The reach of the national police power, which began with CHAMPION V. AMES (1903), seems to have no end.

LEONARD W. LEVY

SUMNER, CHARLES
(1811–1874)

In 1833 Charles Sumner, a protégé of JOSEPH STORY, graduated from Harvard Law School. Until 1851 he practiced law, taught at Harvard Law School, annotated Vesey's Chancery Reports, and became a well-known lecturer advocating, among other reforms, world peace and abolition of slavery. In 1848 Sumner was an unsuccessful Free Soil candidate for Congress, campaigning against the "lords of the lash and the lords of the loom." In ROBERTS V. BOSTON (1849) Sumner unsuccessfully challenged government compulsion of SEGREGATION in Boston schools, arguing that racially separate schools denied equality. In upholding segregation, Massachusetts Chief Justice LEMUEL SHAW enunciated, for the first time, the doctrine of SEPARATE BUT EQUAL.

In 1851 Sumner won the Senate seat once held by DANIEL WEBSTER. In his first speech, "Freedom National, Slavery Sectional," Sumner attacked the fugitive slave law and congressional support of slavery for nearly four hours. In an 1856 speech, "The Crime Against Kansas," Sumner vilified senators who had supported the KANSAS-NEBRASKA ACT. He described STEPHEN A. DOUGLAS as "the squire of slavery, its very Sancho Panza, ready to do all its humiliating offices." South Carolina's Andrew Butler was, in Sumner's view, the Don Quixote of slavery who had "chosen a mistress to whom he has made his vows, and who, though ugly to others . . . is chaste in his sight; I mean the harlot slavery." Two days later Congressman Preston Brooks, a relative of Butler, repaid Sumner for these remarks by beating him insensible with a cane. Many Northerners viewed this incident as a symbol of a violent slavocracy which threatened the Constitution and the nation. After a three-and-a-half-year convalescence Sumner returned to the Senate in 1860, renewing his crusade against bondage with a four-hour oration, "The Barbarism of Slavery." This speech became a Republican campaign document in 1860.

From the beginning of the Civil War Sumner urged the abolition of slavery. He argued that secession was STATE SUICIDE, that the Confederate States had reverted to territorial status, and that, despite the decision in DRED SCOTT V. SANDFORD, Congress had the power to end slavery in these TERRITORIES. On a less theoretical level Sumner successfully sponsored legislation to repeal the fugitive slave laws and to allow black witnesses to testify in federal courts. Sumner was unsuccessful, however, in his attempts to gain congressional support for the integration of Washington's street railroads and other facilities. As chairman of the Senate Foreign Relations Committee, Sumner was constantly at odds with Secretary of State WILLIAM SEWARD, and often served as President ABRAHAM LINCOLN's unofficial adviser on foreign policy. Sumner exploited that position to gain diplomatic recognition for Haiti and Liberia and to secure a passport for a black constituent. As chairman of the Select Committee on Slavery and Freedmen, Sumner laid the groundwork for the FREEDMEN'S BUREAU.

During Reconstruction, Sumner was the Senate's most vociferous advocate of black rights and an early opponent of ANDREW JOHNSON. Sumner's increasingly moralistic and uncompromising posture undermined his legislative effectiveness during Reconstruction. Sumner initially opposed the THIRTEENTH and FOURTEENTH AMENDMENTS because they failed to give blacks enough rights. He gave little support to the FIFTEENTH AMENDMENT because he believed the Constitution embodied the highest moral principles and thus enabled Congress under existing constitutional powers to enfranchise blacks. After 1870 Sumner devoted himself to a comprehensive CIVIL RIGHTS bill, which would give the freedmen complete equality. Its passage, in a somewhat truncated form, as the CIVIL RIGHTS ACT OF 1875 was a posthumous tribute to Sumner's integrity and his passionate devotion to racial equality.

PAUL FINKELMAN

Bibliography

DONALD, DAVID HERBERT 1960 *Charles Sumner and the Coming of the Civil War.* New York: Knopf.

——— 1970 *Charles Sumner and the Rights of Man.* New York: Knopf.

SUNDAY CLOSING LAWS

The first compulsory Sunday observance law in what is now the United States was promulgated in Virginia in 1610. It made absence from church services punishable by death for the third offense. Although there is no record of any person suffering the death penalty, lesser penalties, including whipping, were in effect in all the colonies and were continued after independence. Implicit constitutional recognition of Sunday observance is found in Article I, section 7, which excepts Sundays from the ten days wherein the President is required to exercise his veto of bills adopted by Congress.

Before the Supreme Court ruled that the FIRST AMENDMENT was applicable to the states, it held, in *Hennington v. Georgia* (1896), that Georgia had not unconstitutionally burdened INTERSTATE COMMERCE by regulating the movement of freight trains on Sundays. Four years later, it held, in *Petit v. Minnesota* (1900), that the state had not denied DUE PROCESS in refusing to classify barbering as an act of necessity or charity that could legally be performed on Sundays.

In 1961, after the Court had ruled the First Amendment applicable to the states, it considered the constitutionality of three state Sunday closing laws under that Amendment in four cases, known collectively as the Sunday Closing Law Cases. Two, *McGowan v. Maryland* and *Two Guys from Harrison-Allentown, Inc. v. McGinley,* concerned owners of highway discount stores that were open for business seven days a week. The other two, *Gallagher v. Crown Kosher Super Market* and *Braunfeld v. Brown,* involved stores owned by Orthodox Jews, who, by reason of religious convictions, abstained from all business activities on Saturdays.

In these cases the statutes were challenged on three principal grounds: that the laws violated the ban on the ESTABLISHMENT OF RELIGION; that the statutes' crazy-quilt pattern of exemptions was arbitrary, constituting a denial of due process and the EQUAL PROTECTION OF THE LAWS (for example, in one of the states it was legal to sell fish and food stuffs wholesale, but not at retail; in another, merchandise customarily sold at beaches and amusement parks might be sold there, but not elsewhere); that, at least in respect to Jews, Seventh-Day Adventists, and others whose religions required rest on Saturday, the laws violated the constitutional protection of RELIGIOUS LIBERTY by making it economically difficult if not impossible for them to observe their own Sabbath when their competitors operated six days each week.

In all four cases the Court upheld the constitutionality of the challenged laws, with all the prevailing opinions written by Chief Justice EARL WARREN. He recognized that the laws challenged in these cases had been enacted in colonial times with the purpose of ensuring observance of the majoritarian Christian Sabbath as a religious obligation. However, he said, the religious origin of these statutes did not require their invalidation if their present purpose was secular.

Warren said that the modern purpose of the challenged statutes was to set aside a day for "rest, repose, relaxation, tranquillity"; the purpose was therefore secular rather than religious. The Maryland statutes, for example, permitted such Sunday activities as the operation of bathing beaches, amusement parks, and even pinball and slot machines, as well as the sale of alcoholic beverages and the performance of professional sports. That such exemptions are directly contrary to the religiosity of the Sabbath indicated clearly that the Sunday laws' present purpose was not religious.

Viewed as welfare legislation, the Sunday laws presented little constitutional difficulty. The Chief Justice noted in *McGowan* that numerous federal and state laws affecting public health, safety, conditions of labor, week-end diversion at parks and beaches, and cultural activities of various kinds, had long been upheld. To forbid a state from prescribing Sunday as a day of rest solely because centuries ago such laws had their genesis in religion would be a CONSTITUTIONAL INTERPRETATION based on hostility to the public welfare rather than the SEPARATION OF CHURCH AND STATE.

The Court had more difficulty in sustaining laws applied against persons observing a day other than Sunday as their divinely ordained day of rest. Six Justices agreed that state legislatures, if they so elected, could constitutionally exempt Sabbatarians from complying with Sunday law restrictions, but the free exercise clause did not mandate that they do so. However, a majority of the Court could not agree upon one opinion to that effect. The Chief Justice, speaking for a plurality of four, noted that while the clause secured freedom to hold any belief, it did not forbid regulation of secular practices merely because some persons might suffer economically if they obeyed the dictates of their religion. Income tax laws, for example, did not violate the clause even though they limited the amount of deductions for religious contributions. If a state regulated conduct by a general law, the purpose and effect of which were to advance secular goals, its action was valid despite its indirect burden on the exercise of religion unless the purpose could practicably be otherwise accomplished. A sabbatarian exemption would be hard to enforce, and would interfere with the goal of providing a uniform day of rest that as far as possible eliminated the atmosphere of commercial activity. The laws thus did not violate the free exercise clause.

In THORNTON V. CALDOR, INC. (1985) the Court went even further. It ruled unconstitutional, under the effect aspect of the purpose-effect-entanglement test of constitutionality under the establishment clause, a Connecticut law that accorded employees an absolute right not to work on their chosen Sabbath.

LEO PFEFFER

Bibliography

PFEFFER, LEO (1953)1967 *Church, State and Freedom.* Boston: Beacon Press.

——— 1975 *God, Caesar, and the Constitution.* Boston: Beacon Press.

STOKES, ANSON PHELPS 1950 *Church and State in the United States.* New York: Harper & Brothers.

SUPREMACY CLAUSE

The supremacy clause of Article VI, clause 2, declares: "This Constitution and the Laws of the United States which shall be made in Pursuance thereof; and all

Treaties made, or which shall be made, under the authority of the United States, shall be the supreme law of the Land." This principle of national supremacy was a radical departure from the constitutional order that prevailed under the ARTICLES OF CONFEDERATION. Whereas the Articles created a short-lived confederation of states—according to its terms a mere "league of friendship" founded on the good faith of sovereign states—the Constitution established a federal union designed to last in perpetuity. The distinguishing feature of the "more perfect union" created by the Constitution was a strong national government capable of dealing with the problems and complexities of a growing nation and strong state governments acting within their sphere of authority. The Constitution does not establish the supremacy of the national government in all things. National supremacy is limited to laws made PURSUANT TO THE CONSTITUTION. What is not granted to the national government under its ENUMERATED POWERS is, as a general rule, reserved to the people or to the states under the TENTH AMENDMENT.

The supremacy clause may truly be regarded as the linchpin of American FEDERALISM. It holds the republic together by providing a principle for the resolution of conflicts between the states and the nation. Valid national law is clearly paramount in the face of conflicting state law. But whether a state law conflicts with federal law or a federal constitutional provision is not always clear. When doubts exist over the compatibility of federal and state law, and a real controversy arises from these doubts, the judiciary is usually called upon to work out the implications of the supremacy clause through interpretation. The outcome of such cases often depends on inferences drawn by the courts from the structure of the federal system and the values it represents.

The problems of interpretation generated by the supremacy clause have taken two forms epitomized by the celebrated cases of MCCULLOCH V. MARYLAND (1819) and GIBBONS V. OGDEN (1824). In the first Maryland taxed a national bank doing business within its borders; in the second New York granted a monopoly over steamboat navigation on its internal waterways. The supremacy clause operated to invalidate both measures. *McCulloch* stands for the principle that even a power reserved to the states—here the ordinary and indispensable power of taxation—may not be exercised in such a way as to impede or unduly burden a federal agency or activity; *Gibbons* stands for the principle that the state's regulation of a subject matter within its territory, and normally under its control, must give way before a conflicting, and valid, federal statute. "It is of the very essence of [national] supremacy," wrote Chief Justice JOHN MARSHALL, "to remove all obstacles to its action within its own sphere, and to so modify every power vested in subordinate governments as to exempt its own operation from . . . their influence." In both cases, Marshall underscored the plenary nature of the enumerated powers of Congress; they admit of no limitations save those prescribed in the Constitution. When combined with *McCulloch*'s doctrine of IMPLIED POWERS, fortified by the NECESSARY AND PROPER CLAUSE, the reach of federal power cuts a potentially deep furrow into the field of state SOVEREIGNTY.

This expansive view of federal power was for almost a century strongly contested by the doctrine of DUAL FEDERALISM. It held that nation and states were essentially equal in their respective spheres of influence. The doctrine did not hold that the states could decide for themselves the extent of their sovereign powers. Once again this was a judicial task, for dual federalism was an axiom of CONSTITUTIONAL INTERPRETATION. Beginning roughly in 1835, shortly after ROGER B. TANEY replaced Marshall as Chief Justice, the Supreme Court deployed and developed the concept of STATE POLICE POWER—broadly characterized as the power of a state to provide for the general welfare of its people—to limit the reach of national law. This movement attained its apogee in the first third of the twentieth century when the Supreme Court used the Tenth Amendment to invalidate numerous federal laws, all of them regulating various aspects of the economy. Most of these decisions supported the ideology of individualism and capitalism. The national statutes struck down by the Court were deemed to interfere with state police power yet arguably enacted pursuant to the delegated powers of Congress and clearly not expressly forbidden by the Constitution.

The year 1937 marks the collapse of the doctrine that state sovereignty constitutes a limitation on the exercise of power delegated by the Constitution to Congress. Since then the Supreme Court has returned and held steadfastly to the spirit of *McCulloch* and *Gibbons.* Even activities sponsored or operated by the state are subject to federal regulation when imposed pursuant to a delegated power. NATIONAL LEAGUE OF CITIES V. USERY (1976) is the only exception to this principle: in striking down a federal wage and hour provision as applied to state and local public employees, a closely divided Supreme Court ruled that such power—in this instance the federal commerce power—may not be exercised to interfere with "functions essential to the separate and independent existence" of the "states as states." The ghost of dual federalism lurks in *Usery*. In 1985, however, a closely divided Court overruled *Usery* in GARCIA V. SAN ANTONIO METROPOLITAN TRANSIT AUTHORITY.

In interpreting the supremacy clause today, the Supreme Court has given up the search for bright lines separating federal and state authority. The two levels of government are no longer perceived as antagonistic rivals, whatever the tensions between them. The supremacy clause once operated to immunize persons closely related to the federal government from most forms of state taxation. The pre-1937 doctrine of federal tax immunity, based on the generalized notion of federal supremacy rooted in *McCulloch*, was construed to invalidate such levies as state or local taxes on the income of federal employees, on interest income from federal bonds, on income derived from property leased by the federal government, and on sales to the United States. Since 1937, however, the Supreme Court with the help of Congress has wiped out most of this RECIPROCAL TAX IMMUNITY. The prevailing doctrine today, particularly after *United States v. New Mexico* (1982), is that a nondiscriminatory state tax even upon private contractors with close and intricate relationships with the federal government will not violate the supremacy clause unless the tax is imposed *directly* upon the United States.

In the field of regulation, too, sharp lines between federal and state authority are often difficult to find. Modern government is complex, involving the entanglement of federal and state policy in fields once regarded as exclusively state concerns. Education, conservation, aid to the poor and the handicapped, and environmental protection are prominent examples of such fields. The relationship between levels of government in all these areas today is one of cooperation and reciprocity. By means of FEDERAL GRANTS-IN-AID and other funding programs the national government, pursuant to its power of taxing and spending for the GENERAL WELFARE, has actually encouraged the states to pass laws and adopt policies in response to local needs. This new context of COOPERATIVE FEDERALISM does not mean, however, that the supremacy clause has lost its bite. Indeed, it has operated to establish the primacy of the national government even in some of the aforementioned fields. An example is *Blum v. Bacon* (1982), where the Supreme Court invalidated a New York law excluding recipients of a federal program aiding poor families with dependent children from receiving aid under the state's federally funded emergency welfare program. (*Blum* involved a state statutory policy that conflicted with a federal administrative regulation.)

As the preceding suggests, contemporary supremacy clause analysis is largely a matter of statutory interpretation. The supremacy clause has not been interpreted to prevent federal and state governments from regulating the same subject, partly out of the judiciary's recognition of the reality of cooperative federalism. The nature of some subjects (e.g., IMMIGRATION and NATURALIZATION, bankruptcy, PATENTS, and some articles of commerce) may require national uniform legislation. But most problems of American national life are valid topics of both national and state legislation (e.g., air and water pollution, motor carrier transportation, labor relations, consumer protection, and CIVIL RIGHTS). States and nation may legislate on these topics for similar or different reasons. The key to the validity of such concurrent or parallel legislation is whether both federal and state regulations can be enforced without impairing federal superintendence of the field. Even apparently conflicting state legislation may survive supremacy clause analysis if the state law deals with a field traditionally occupied by the state and the state's interest is substantial enough to offset any presumption that Congress may have intended to occupy the field all by itself. A principle of comity has thus replaced the earlier antagonism between nation and states characteristic of dual federalism. Today, as a general rule, unless Congress statutorily declares its intent to occupy a field, federal regulation preempts state law only where the latter seriously impedes the former.

Jones v. Roth Packing Company (1977) is a leading example of a case in which federal policy displaced state law notwithstanding the absence of explicit preemptive language in the congressional statute. Here the federal Fair Packaging and Labeling Act, enacted under the COMMERCE CLAUSE, was construed to conflict with a state consumer protection law dealing with the weight of certain goods packaged for sale. The Supreme Court read into the federal statute a congressional intent to supersede state law. Supersession was inferred from the supremacy clause because the enforcement of the state law was an obstacle to the full accomplishment and execution of the congressional purpose. In other cases federal PREEMPTION has been inferred because "[t]he scheme of federal regulation may be so pervasive as to make reasonable the inference that Congress left no room for the states to supplement it" or because "the Act of Congress may touch a field in which the federal interest is so dominant that the federal system will be assumed to preclude enforcement of state laws on the same subject." The supremacy clause thus remains a vital operative principle of American constitutional law even though the Supreme Court tends to presume the validity of concurrent state legislation, barring proof of its interference with federal policy.

DONALD P. KOMMERS

Bibliography

CORWIN, EDWIN S. 1913 *National Supremacy: Treaty Power versus State Power.* New York: Holt.

SCHMIDHAUSER, JOHN R. 1958 *The Supreme Court as Final Arbiter of Federal–State Relations.* Chapel Hill: University of North Carolina Press.

SUPREME COURT
(History)

The only court whose existence is mandated by the Constitution is the Supreme Court. Article III states: "The judicial power of the United States shall be vested in one supreme court, and in such inferior courts as the Congress may from time to time ordain and establish." Besides its existence, a few attributes are constitutionally entrenched by Article III. The tenure of the judges is to be "during GOOD BEHAVIOR," and their compensation "shall not be diminished during their continuance in office." These provisions, modeled on English law and made applicable to all federal judges, were obviously intended to assure the independence of a judiciary appointed, pursuant to Article II, by the President with the ADVICE AND CONSENT of the Senate.

Other features having a bearing on the character and independence of the Court were not addressed, presumably to be left at large or determined from time to time by Congress. Qualifications for membership on the Court were not specified; nor were the size of the Court, the period of its TERMS, or the level of the judges' compensation. The Court was to have both ORIGINAL JURISDICTION and APPELLATE JURISDICTION, but the latter was subject to "such exceptions, and under such regulations, as the Congress shall make." Nothing was said concerning the relation of the Supreme Court to the courts of the STATES.

Thus from the outset the Court was only partially sheltered from the politics of republican government. The status of the Court was one of those creative ambiguities that have marked the Constitution as no less an organism than a mechanism, Darwinian as well as Newtonian. The position of the Court may have been in the mind of an eminent modern foreign-born mathematician who, contemplating American CITIZENSHIP, regretted that he could not swear allegiance to the Constitution because "it is full of inconsistencies." In a self-governing nation, to be sure, the Court is detached but not disengaged, distant but not remote. Therein lay its potential either for popular neglect and scorn or for power and prestige.

The need for a federal judiciary, and so for an ultimate tribunal, was felt by the Framers as part of the transition from a confederation to a federal union. The ARTICLES OF CONFEDERATION supplied no such institution, except a supreme tribunal for prize and admiralty cases. A system of federal courts, parallel to those of the states, was one of the innovative conceptions of 1787. Their function was to serve as impartial tribunals, free of local bias, in suits between states, or controversies involving citizens of different states or a foreign country; to establish a uniform interpretation of federal laws; and to maintain the supremacy of federal law in cases where a state law conflicted with the Constitution, federal statutes, or treaties of the United States. In sum, the JURISDICTION OF THE FEDERAL COURTS could rest on the nature of the parties or of the question presented. Only in cases where a state, or a foreign country or its diplomatic representative, was a party was the Supreme Court given original (nonappellate) jurisdiction.

These skeletal provisions of Article III were fleshed out by Congress in the JUDICIARY ACT OF 1789. That act set the number of Supreme Court Justices at five associate Justices and one CHIEF JUSTICE, with salaries of $3,500 and $4,000, respectively. (The monetary differential remained at $500 until 1969, when it was increased to $2,500.) Three provisions of the act led to developments that proved to be of seminal importance for the prestige and power of the Supreme Court: a requirement that the Justices serve on regional CIRCUIT COURTS ("circuit riding"); a provision in section 13 that seemed to grant original jurisdiction to the Court to issue WRITS OF MANDAMUS; and a grant of power in section 25 to review the decisions of state supreme courts in cases turning on the Constitution, laws, or treaties of the United States. Each of these merits attention.

The circuit duties meant sitting with a federal district judge to form a circuit court, which heard appeals from district courts and had original jurisdiction in diversity of citizenship cases. In the early years circuit riding consumed the greater part of a Justice's time and surely his energy; travel by carriage or horseback over rough roads and stopovers at uncomfortable inns resulted in a weariness of flesh and spirit, against which the Justices complained bitterly, but which they forbore to resist. Yet these excursions into the local courthouses brought them into touch with lawyers, journalists, and townspeople, and gave a reality to the Supreme Court that its functioning in the capital city could not match. Moreover, the assignment of each Justice to a particular circuit affected significantly the appointments to the Court, for a vacancy on the Court would normally be filled by an appointment from the same circuit, and so at any time the practical range of nominees was limited and the influence of a small group of senators was proportionately great. Not until 1891, with the passage of the CIRCUIT COURTS OF APPEALS ACT, were the Justices fully relieved of circuit-riding duties. Thereafter geography played a decreasing role in appointments. A striking instance was the widely acclaimed appointment by President HERBERT C. HOOVER in 1932 of Judge BENJAMIN N. CARDOZO of New York to succeed Justice OLIVER WENDELL HOLMES of Massachusetts, although two New Yorkers, Chief Justice CHARLES EVANS HUGHES and Justice HARLAN FISKE STONE, were already on the Court. A comparable instance was the appointment by President Reagan in 1981 of Judge SANDRA DAY O'CONNOR of Arizona to succeed Justice POTTER STEWART of Ohio even though another Arizonan, Justice WILLIAM H. REHNQUIST, was already serving.

As circuit riding was a cardinal factor in gaining popular recognition of the Court (at considerable cost to the Justices) and in determining appointments, so did the practice furnish an early opportunity for the Court to judge the validity of an act of Congress. In the waning days of the Federalist administration, Congress passed the JUDICIARY ACT OF 1801, compounded of partisanship and principle, which created new judgeships and abolished circuit riding. When the Jeffersonians took office, however, they countered with the JUDICIARY ACT OF 1802, which abolished the judgeships and restored circuit riding. Chief Justice JOHN MARSHALL, sensing a political crisis for the Court, solicited the opinions of his brethren on the question of complying with the law or treating it as beyond the authority of Congress. The Justices had serious doubts about the law's validity, and a strong distaste for the resumption of the burden it imposed, yet a majority counseled compliance, in accord with Marshall's own inclination. But a private litigant, defeated in a circuit court in Virginia at which Marshall himself presided, appealed to the Supreme Court, arguing the unconstitutionality of the 1802 act. The Congress, fearing a judgment voiding the act, had abolished the 1802 term of the Supreme Court. When the case, STUART V. LAIRD, was decided, in February of 1803, the Court, with Marshall not participating, surprised and gratified the Jeffersonians by upholding the act, in a brief opinion which simply declared that acquiescence by the Court in circuit duty for twelve years under the Judiciary Act of 1789 had given a practical construction of the Constitution that would not now be disturbed. That the Court would at least consider the validity of an act of Congress had been resolved just six days earlier in the landmark case of MARBURY V. MADISON (1803).

That case, establishing the power of JUDICAL REVIEW of acts of Congress, marked the second of the three germinal developments from the Judiciary Act of 1789. Section 13, which gave the Court power to issue mandamus and other writs, might have been read simply as conferring the power where the jurisdiction of the Court rested on one of the grounds specified in Article III. But the Court was not of a mind for so narrow a reading. When William Marbury of Maryland invoked the original jurisdiction of the Court to enforce a right to an office of justice of the peace pursuant to an appointment by President JOHN ADAMS, and sought a mandamus to compel Secretary of State JAMES MADISON to deliver his commission, the Court regarded section 13 as conferring jurisdiction, and as so construed beyond the ambit of original jurisdiction defined in Article III. The suit for mandamus was therefore dismissed, again to the gratification of the Jeffersonians, but in the process the Court had declared the far more significant principle that in the decision of a case where a federal law was arguably incompatible with the Constitution, the Court, in deciding what "the law" was, must, if necessary, vindicate the HIGHER LAW and treat the legislative act as ineffectual.

Despite some provocative language in Marshall's opinion (the executive branch cannot "sport away" the rights of others), the Jeffersonians focused on the immediate result and regarded it as a victory at the hands of a still-Federalist Court. Indeed, judicial review was not then the divisive party issue; the Jeffersonians would have welcomed a Supreme Court decision holding the Sedition Act of 1798 unconstitutional. Whether Marshall's doctrine of judicial review was a usurpation later became a subject of heated debate, scholarly and unscholarly. Although the Constitution contains no specific mention of the power, and although Marshall's opinion, resting on the logic of the decisional process, can be said to beg the question of who is to decide, the debates in the CONSTITUTIONAL CONVENTION do indicate obliquely an acceptance of the power, in explaining the rejection of attempts to involve judges in an extrajudicial power of veto of legislation. But the debates were not cited in *Marbury;* MADISON'S NOTES, the most authoritative source, pursuant to the policy of secrecy, were not published until fifty years after the Convention.

The third of the salient projections from the Judiciary Act of 1789, involving section 25, produced more immediate partisan repercussions. Section 25 empowered the Court to review decisions of state courts that denied rights claimed under the federal Constitution, statutes, or treaties. Again, no constitutional provision explicitly conferred such power on the Supreme Court, although Article VI does declare the supremacy of federal law: "the judges in every state shall be bound thereby." By their silence, the Framers may have sought to avoid confrontations in the ratifying process, as in forbearing to be explicit about a national power to issue paper money or to establish a national bank.

The storm over the Court's power to review state court decisions was precipitated by its decision in MARTIN v. HUNTER'S LESSEE (1816) sustaining the validity of section 25. The case was a contest over title to the extensive Fairfax estate in the northern neck of Virginia, turning on the intricate interrelations of Virginia land law and treaties of the United States with Great Britain concerning ownership of land by British nationals. Holding that the Virginia court had misapplied both Virginia and federal law, the Supreme Court in 1813, through Justice JOSEPH STORY, reversed the state court's judgment and remanded the case to that court. A number of factors weakened the force of the decision. Story's opinion controverted the state court's even on points of the interpretation of state law, although section 25 itself limited review to federal questions. At a time when seven Justices constituted the Court, only four participated in the decision; the vote was 3–1, and the mandate to the Virginia court was unfortunately in the traditional form addressed to an inferior court, "you are hereby commanded, etc." The Virginia court was outraged and refused to obey the mandate. On a new WRIT OF ERROR to the Supreme Court, Story elaborated the justification of Supreme Court review in terms of the need for uniformity and supremacy of national law. The nature of the cause, not the court, was determinative of the Supreme Court's power to review (though critics wondered, no doubt unfairly, if the Supreme Court could then be given authority to review certain decisions of the House of Lords). John Marshall could not have uttered a pronouncement more nationalistic than that of the New England Republican appointed by President JAMES MADISON. (Marshall had excused himself because of his family's ownership of part of the land. Story, appointed in 1811 at the age of thirty-two, one of the most learned and powerful of Justices and a firm ally of Marshall, had been Madison's fourth choice to succeed WILLIAM CUSHING of Massachusetts: LEVI LINCOLN declined the nomination, Alexander Wolcott was rejected by the Senate, and JOHN QUINCY ADAMS also declined. Thus are the inevitabilities of history determined.)

In a sequel to the decision, the Court took the further step of sustaining its power to review even criminal judgments of state courts where a federal question, such as the interpretation of a federal law, was implicated. The opinion by Chief Justice Marshall in COHENS v. VIRGINIA (1821) was the climactic realization of the Court's vision of a uniform federal law and a Constitution that was supreme in reality as well as in principle.

Reaction to the *Cohens* decision by Jeffersonians, particularly in Virginia, was intense. Judge SPENCER ROANE, who instead of Marshall would probably have become Chief Justice if OLIVER ELLSWORTH had not resigned before Jefferson took office, published a series of bitter letters under pseudonyms, paying his respects to "A most monstrous and unexampled decision. It can only be accounted for from that love of power which all history informs us infects and corrupts all who possess it, and from which even the upright and eminent Judges are not exempt." The Court's "extravagant pretension" reached "the zenith of despotic power." In the following years a series of bills were introduced in Congress to repeal, in whole or in part, the appellate jurisdiction of the Supreme Court. Under these genial auspices was thus established a particularly sensitive and probably the most crucial power of the highest court in our federal union: the review of decisions of state courts in the interest of vindicating rights secured by the Constitution.

Conflicts between the Supreme Court, on the one hand, and the executive or legislative branches, or both, on the other, have occurred continually. The other branches have utilized the full spectrum of measures made available by the constitution. The most drastic of these, IMPEACHMENT, was the first to be tried; indeed it was designed as a trial run by Jefferson to prepare the way for a similar attack on Chief Justice Marshall. The immediate target was Justice SAMUEL CHASE, ardent Federalist, whose partisan outbursts in charges to the grand jury in Maryland furnished the occasion. The attempt misfired, however; Chase was narrowly acquitted in the Senate, owing probably to comparable overreaching by the fiery JOHN RANDOLPH, who managed the case for the Jeffersonians.

A milder form of resistance to the Court was the doctrine of departmental independence, whereby the

President was as free to act on his view of constitutional authority as the Court was to act on its own. Despite the prospect of endless oscillation that this theory implied, it was espoused in some form by Jefferson, ANDREW JACKSON, and ABRAHAM LINCOLN. President JACKSON'S VETO OF THE BANK BILL (1832) was based partly on grounds of unconstitutionality, although the earlier law creating the bank had been sustained by the Supreme Court. In his message justifying the veto, Jackson had the advice and aid of his attorney general, ROGER B. TANEY. By an irony of history, when President Lincoln in his first inaugural address dealt with Taney's opinion in DRED SCOTT v. SANDFORD (1857), he adopted something of the Jackson-Taney philosophy, maintaining that although he offered no resistance to the decision as a settlement of the lawsuit he could not regard it as binding on the political branches for the future.

The indeterminate size of the Court became a weapon in the contest between President ANDREW JOHNSON and Congress over Reconstruction. By successive statutory changes, following the admission of new states and the creation of new circuits, the authorized membership of the Court had been increased to ten. A radical Congress, distrustful of Johnson and wishing to deprive him of the power to make new appointments to the Court, reduced the number of seats prospectively to seven. (Contributing to the move was a plan of Chief Justice SALMON P. CHASE to induce a reluctant Congress to increase the Justices' salaries in return for a decrease in the number to be compensated. That plan failed, but Chase did succeed in having the title of his office changed from Chief Justice of the Supreme Court to Chief Justice of the United States.) The actual number of Justices did not fall below eight, and in 1869 the number was fixed at nine.

More famous is the action of the same Congress in withdrawing the appellate jurisdiction of the Supreme Court in cases under a HABEAS CORPUS act, giving rise to the decision in EX PARTE MCCARDLE in 1869. While the immediate issue in the case was whether a military commission in Mississippi could try a newspaper editor for inflammatory writings urging citizens not to cooperate with the military government, Congress was fearful that a politically minded majority on the Court would hold the entire plan of Reconstruction unconstitutional. The Court, which had already heard argument in the case, bowed to the withdrawal of jurisdiction, but carefully pointed out that another appellate route remained unaffected by the repealing statute. Consequently the value of *McCardle* as a PRECEDENT, which is the centerpiece of constitutional argument on the extent of congressional power to limit the Court's jurisdiction, is at best doubtful.

The post-Reconstruction Court alienated labor and progressives by decisions taking a narrow view of state power to regulate and tax business; the COMMERCE CLAUSE and FREEDOM OF CONTRACT protected by SUBSTANTIVE DUE PROCESS served as shields for industry. The Progressive party platform in 1912, under the aegis of THEODORE ROOSEVELT, advocated the RECALL of judges and judicial decisions by popular vote. Although this thrust was aimed at state courts rather than the Supreme Court, the latter had set a tone for judicial review in a triad of decisions in 1895. UNITED STATES v. E. C. KNIGHT CO. held that a combination of sugar refiners controlling ninety percent of sugar production in the nation was not subject to the SHERMAN ANTITRUST ACT because processing is not commerce. IN RE DEBS held that a labor leader could be imprisoned for violating a federal court's INJUNCTION in a railroad labor strike, without judicial reliance on any statutorily defined offense. POLLOCK v. FARMERS LOAN AND TRUST CO. held the federal income tax law unconstitutional as applied to income from real property, stocks, and bonds, though valid as applied to wages, because an income tax is tantamount to a tax on its source, and where the source is property in some form the tax is a DIRECT TAX which under the constitution is forbidden to Congress unless apportioned according to population.

The most serious conflict with the Court, certainly since Marshall's time, culminated in President FRANKLIN D. ROOSEVELT's Court reorganization plan in early 1937. The Court had held unconstitutional a series of major New Deal measures designed for economic recovery and reform: the NATIONAL INDUSTRIAL RECOVERY ACT; AGRICULTURAL ADJUSTMENT ACT; Railway Pension Act; Farm Mortgage Act; Guffey-Snyder Bituminous Coal Act; Municipal Bankruptcy Act; and a state minimum wage law for women. Still to be decided was the validity of the WAGNER NATIONAL LABOR RELATIONS ACT, the SOCIAL SECURITY ACT, the PUBLIC UTILITY HOLDING COMPANY ACT, and the TENNESSEE VALLEY AUTHORITY ACT in its full scope. The administration was persuaded that the barrier did not inhere in the Constitution but was the handiwork of Justices who were out of sympathy both with the New Deal and with the best traditions of constitutional decision. Apparently accepting the validity of this analysis, Chief Justice Hughes, appointed by President Hoover, though he greatly disliked 5–4 decisions, nevertheless joined Justices LOUIS D. BRANDEIS, Stone, and Cardozo as dissenters in the last five of the cases listed above as holding measures invalid. During his first term President Roosevelt had no opportunity to make an appointment to the Court.

The reorganization plan, which was formulated by Attorney General HOMER S. CUMMINGS, called for the appointment of an additional member of the Court for each Justice who did not retire at the age of seventy, up to a maximum membership of fifteen. Despite the President's sweeping electoral victory in 1936, and intensive political efforts by the administration for four months, the plan failed to pass the Senate. A number of factors contributed to the result. The argument based on age and inefficiency, stressed by proponents at the outset, was transparently disingenuous. A letter from Chief Justice Hughes, joined by Justices WILLIS VAN DEVANTER and Brandeis, to Senator Burton K. Wheeler, at the latter's request, effectively refuted the charge that the Court needed additional members to keep abreast of its docket. The Court itself, while the bill was pending, sustained a state minimum wage law, the National Labor Relations Act, an amended Farm Bankruptcy Act, and the Social Security Act. As one senator remarked, "Why keep on running for the bus after you've caught it?" Moreover, Congress enacted a new retirement act for Supreme Court Justices, which made retirement more acceptable. Since 1869 a full pension had been provided for, but as retirement was equivalent to resignation under the statute, the pension was subject to the will of Congress and in 1932, as an economy measure, it had been reduced by half and was later restored. The act of 1937, by enabling retired Justices to serve on the lower federal courts, placed their retirement compensation under constitutional protection against diminution. Justice Van Devanter availed himself of this new law, giving the President his first opportunity to make an appointment and lessening further the need for enactment of his plan. But perhaps the most powerful factor leading to its defeat was a pervasive feeling, even among groups holding grievances against particular decisions, that the independence of the judiciary was too important a principle to be sacrificed, even under the extreme provocation furnished by a majority of the Court itself.

The appellate jurisdiction of the Court became a target of attack in 1958, as it had been in the early nineteenth century. Senator William E. Jenner of Indiana, reacting against decisions curtailing governmental actions in the field of loyalty investigations, introduced a series of bills withdrawing Supreme Court jurisdiction in this and related classes of cases. Passage was narrowly averted by the efforts of the then majority leader, Senator LYNDON B. JOHNSON. Comparable bills were introduced in 1982 to preclude review of decisions concerning abortion and school prayers. Such efforts, if successful, would produce chaotic results. In the name of the federal Constitution, varying decisions, for and against local laws, would stand unreconciled; the Supreme Court would have no opportunity to reconsider or modify its precedents; state and federal judges would be left to take different positions on the binding effect of prior Supreme Court decisions.

It is apparent that in the recurrent clashes of party, section, and class that have marked American history, the Court, whose role, in principle, is that of an arbiter, has not escaped the role of participant. In these judicial involvements, extraordinary force on one side has induced similar force on the other. A dramatic example is the contest over the production of the White House tapes for use as evidence in the prosecutions growing out of the Watergate break-in. President RICHARD M. NIXON refused to comply with a subpoena issued by the district court, on the ground of EXECUTIVE PRIVILEGE. The tension between the rule of law and presidential immunity from suit had been resolved in part by bringing suit against a subordinate who was carrying out presidential orders, as in the steel seizure case, YOUNGSTOWN SHEET AND TUBE CO. V. SAWYER (1952), where the named defendant was the secretary of commerce. President Nixon, however, forced the issue by taking sole custody of the tapes. On appeal, the Supreme Court responded with the countervailing measure of holding the President amenable to the process of a court where the need of EVIDENCE in a criminal trial outweighs a generalized claim of privilege. The unanimity of the decision (with one abstention) was doubtless a factor impelling the President to yield, thus avoiding an ultimate confrontation.

That the supreme judicial tribunal, without the power of purse or sword, should have survived crises and vicissitudes and maintained its prestige can be ascribed partly to its own resourcefulness and partly to the recognition by a mature people of the Court's necessary functions in the American constitutional democracy. The Court's resourcefulness owes much to the central paradox of its work: it decides issues of great political moment, yet it does so in the context of a controversy between ordinary litigants in a conventional lawsuit. That setting provides a test of concreteness in the formulation of DOCTRINE, allows flexibility of development, and enables the Court to adapt and refine doctrine as new factual and procedural settings may suggest.

The Supreme Court's essential functions, performed within the framework of conventional lawsuits, are fourfold: to resolve controversies between states; to assure the uniform application of national law; to maintain a common market in a continental union; and to enforce the guarantees of liberty and equality embodied in the BILL OF RIGHTS, the post-Civil War Amendments, and other provisions of the Constitution.

Although the Court's jurisdiction over suits between states is statistically insignificant, the function is of practical and symbolic importance, serving as a substitute for diplomacy and war in disputes over boundaries, allotment of waters, and the like. Because these cases originate in the Supreme Court, factual disputes are referred to a SPECIAL MASTER for hearings, findings, and recommendations, which are then presented to the Court for argument and decision.

The uniform interpretation and application of national law has become increasingly important with the proliferation of federal regulatory statutes and administrative rules. For almost a century, until 1938, the Supreme Court essayed a broader concept of uniformity in the COMMON LAW itself, in fields such as commercial law and torts, under the doctrine of SWIFT V. TYSON (1842), which empowered the federal courts to pronounce a FEDERAL COMMON LAW without regard to the common law of particular states. Sweeping as it was, the doctrine was truncated, for the federal common law could have no binding authority in state courts, and thus a bifurcated system of common law developed, along with a practice of forum shopping by lawyers as between federal and state courts. The doctrine was repudiated by the Court in ERIE RAILWAY V. TOMPKINS (1938) in an opinion by Justice Brandeis that branded as unconstitutional the course theretofore pursued by the federal courts. With the demise of *Swift v. Tyson* the rationale for retaining DIVERSITY OF CITIZENSHIP JURISDICTION in the federal courts, for the decision of matters of state law, was materially weakened.

The maintenance of a common market is a modern description of a historic function of the Court, exercised since Marshall and his colleagues decided in GIBBONS V. OGDEN (1824) that the constitutional power of Congress over commerce among the states implied a negative on state power, even when Congress has not acted, and that the Supreme Court would enforce that implied prohibition. For a generation these commerce clause cases elicited a series of decisions upholding or setting aside state regulations—of quarantine, pilotage, intoxicating liquors, entry fees—by classifying them as either regulations of commerce, and so invalid, or regulations of local health or safety, and so valid as POLICE POWER measures. This effort at classification obscured the process of judgment by treating a conclusory label as if it were a premise for reasoning. A pivotal change in methodology occurred in COOLEY V. BOARD OF WARDENS (1852), a pilotage case where the opinion by Justice BENJAMIN CURTIS recognized that commercial regulation and police power were not mutually exclusive categories, and that decision should turn on an empirical judgment, weighing the necessity of the local law, the seriousness of the impact on commerce, the need for uniformity of treatment, and the possible discriminatory impact on out-of-state enterprise. This kind of scrutiny, and comparable analysis of local taxation when challenged by multistate business, have been staples of Supreme Court adjudication and exemplars for other economic federations struggling to accommodate local interests and those of a union.

The most intensive, acclaimed, and in some quarters questioned, aspects of the Court's work has been the elaboration of fundamental human rights. While in England the great expressions of these rights are found in the writings of philosophers and poets—the secular trinity of John Milton, JOHN LOCKE, and John Stuart Mill—in America the pronouncements are embodied—Jefferson apart—in the judicial opinions of Holmes, Brandeis, Hughes, Stone, ROBERT H. JACKSON, HUGO L. BLACK, and other Justices. The development of a body of CIVIL LIBERTIES guarantees, mainly under the Bill of Rights and the FOURTEENTH AMENDMENT, reached its fullest flowering during the Chief Justiceship of EARL WARREN (1953–1969), though the seeds were planted in the HUGHES COURT.

During the 1930s, while public attention was focused on the Court's struggle with national power over the economy, path-breaking advances were made in a series of decisions applying federal constitutional guarantees against the states. It is more than coincidence that this development occurred at a time of rising totalitarianism abroad. FREEDOM OF THE PRESS and FREEDOM OF ASSOCIATION AND ASSEMBLY were unmistakably put under the protection of the liberty secured by the Fourteenth Amendment in NEAR V. MINNESOTA (1931) and DEJONGE V. OREGON (1937), respectively. The principle that a conviction in a state court following the use of a coerced confession is a violation of DUE PROCESS OF LAW was announced for the first time BROWN V. MISSISSIPPI (1936). A state's duty to afford racial equality in education was sharpened in MISSOURI EX REL. GAINES V. CANADA (1938): it could not be satisfied by resort to a neighboring state. Mayors and governors were subjected to the reach of federal judicial process in HAGUE V. CIO (1939) and *Sterling v. Constantin* (1932), an accountability that came to be important in later contests over desegregation.

If the drama of these seminal developments was largely overlooked, the same cannot be said of the great expansion of civil liberties and CIVIL RIGHTS by the WARREN COURT. The leading decisions have become familiar landmarks. BAKER V. CARR (1962), requiring substantial equality of population in electoral districts within a state, asserted judicial power over what had previously been deemed a POLITICAL QUESTION; Chief Justice Warren regarded it as the most important decision of his tenure, because of its potential for redistributing basic political power. BROWN V. BOARD OF EDUCATION (1954, 1955) was both the culmination and the beginning in the long drive against RACIAL DISCRIMINATION: doctrinally a climax, practically a starting point in the devising of remedies. MIRANDA V. ARIZONA (1966), limiting POLICE INTERROGATION of suspects in custody and giving suspects the RIGHT TO COUNSEL during interrogation, has become a symbol of the Court's intense concern for standards of CRIMINAL PROCEDURE, a concern that has sometimes been viewed as an index to a society's civilization. The EQUAL PROTECTION guarantee, which Justice Holmes in 1927 could call the last refuge of a constitutional lawyer, was revitalized in the service not only of racial minorities but of other stereotyped groups: ALIENS, illegitimates, and women. Freedom of the press was extended well beyond freedom from restraint on publication: In actions for LIBEL brought by PUBLIC FIGURES following NEW YORK TIMES V. SULLIVAN (1964), the defendant publisher would be liable only if he acted with legal malice, that is, with knowledge of the publication's falsity or with reckless disregard for its truth or falsity.

A constitutional RIGHT OF PRIVACY, of uncertain scope, extending beyond the explicit SEARCH AND SEIZURE guarantee to encompass at least certain conjugal intimacies, was established in GRISWOLD V. CONNECTICUT (1965). The religion clauses of the FIRST AMENDMENT were given new vitality in decisions rejecting organized prayer in the public schools, such as ENGEL V. VITALE (1962).

On any measure, it is an impressive performance. The momentum was somewhat slackened during the first decade and a half of Chief Justice WARREN E. BURGER's tenure, particularly in the areas of criminal procedure and nonestablishment of religion; yet during this period the Court reached the high-water mark of constitutionally protected autonomy in ROE V. WADE (1973), upholding freedom of choice respecting abortion in the first two trimesters of pregnancy.

Criticism of the modern Court has taken diverse directions. Some critics have complained that the Court has been unfaithful to the historic meaning of constitutional provisions. But the argument begs the question of "meaning." If the term signifies denotative meaning, the particular instances that the Framers envisioned as comprehended in the text, the original meaning has indeed been departed from. If, however, the purposive meaning is accepted, and the application does not contradict the language of the text, there is no infidelity. Such an analysis will not disapprove, for example, the "meaning" ascribed to the freedom of the press in the First Amendment.

Another criticism charges defenders of the Court with a double standard: the modern Court is a mirror image of the pre-1937 Court, the judicial vetoes coming now from the left instead of the right. The asserted parallel, however, is inexact. The problem is to identify the appropriate role for judicial review in a representative democracy. The older Court set aside such products of the political process as minimum wage, price control, and tax legislation. The modern Court, by and large, has given its intensive scrutiny to two areas of law that are of peculiarly legitimate concern to the judiciary. One is the field of procedure, in a large sense, civil and criminal. The other is the set of issues concerning representation of interests in the formation of public opinion and lawmaking. This category would include FREEDOM OF SPEECH and press and association, VOTING RIGHTS, education, and the interests of groups underrepresented in the formulation of public policy. This approach gives a certain coherence to constitutional theory: as the commerce clause protects out-of-state enterprise against hostility, open or covert, the Bill of Rights and the Civil War amendments especially protect the political, social, or ethnic "outsider" against official neglect or ostracism.

A more qualified criticism is addressed to two tendencies of the modern Court. One is a perceived disposition to carry a constitutional safeguard to excessive lengths, as in BUCKLEY V. VALEO (1976), which held invalid, in the name of freedom of expression, statutory limits on expenditures by or on behalf of candidates for federal offices. The other, illustrated by the abortion and police interrogation cases, is an inclination, when holding a state law or practice invalid, to prescribe only a single form of corrective that will not offend constitutional standards.

A problem faced by the Court throughout much of its history, one that has again become acute, is the burden of an expanding caseload. In the last hundred years two statutory jurisdictional revisions brought temporary relief. The Circuit Courts of Appeals Act of 1891, by establishing a system of regional appellate courts, assured litigants of one opportunity for review without resort to the Supreme Court. The JUDICIARY ACT OF 1925, sponsored by the Justices themselves and promoted by Chief Justice WILLIAM HOWARD TAFT, made discretionary review by WRIT OF CERTIORARI, instead of APPEAL as of right, the normal mode of access to the Supreme Court.

Each solution, however, has in time become part of the problem. With thirteen courts of appeals, and the burgeoning of federal statutory law, there is a growing incidence of conflicting decisions calling for review. Moreover, the disposition of petitions for certiorari has occupied an increasing amount of the Justices' time, with more than 4,000 filed each term. Of these, approximately 175 are granted and the cases decided with full opinion after oral argument.

A study group appointed under the auspices of the Federal Judicial Center reported in 1972 that the caseload was reaching the saturation point. Certain ameliorative measures had already been taken. The normal time allowed for oral argument had been reduced from an hour to a half hour for each side. The number of law CLERKS had been increased in stages from one to four for each Justice. The study group expressed disquiet at what it viewed as a bureaucratic movement, and recommended the creation of a national court of appeals to review decisions that warranted review but not necessarily by the Supreme Court. Others proposed variations on this plan, notably one or more courts of appeals having specialized jurisdiction, in tax or criminal or regulatory cases. Sixty years after the 1925 act, the problem has not been resolved. And yet without adequate time for reflection, collegial discussion, critical scrutiny, mutual accommodation, and persuasive exposition, the Court cannot function at its best.

At its best, the Court can recall the legal profession and the people to an appreciation of their constitutional heritage, by translating the ideals and practices embodied in an eighteenth-century charter of the Enlightenment into the realities of a modern industrial democracy.

PAUL A. FREUND

Bibliography

BICKEL, ALEXANDER M. 1962 *The Least Dangerous Branch.* Indianapolis: Bobbs-Merrill.

CONGRESSIONAL QUARTERLY 1981 *The Supreme Court and Its Work.* Washington, D.C.: Congressional Quarterly.

FREUND, PAUL A. 1961 *The Supreme Court of the United States.* Cleveland and New York: Meridian Books.

FREUND, PAUL A. and KATZ, STANLEY N. 1971– The Oliver Wendell Holmes Devise History of the Supreme Court of the United States. 11 Vols. New York: Macmillan. The following volumes have been published: vol. I, GOEBEL, JULIUS, JR. 1971 *Antecedents and Beginnings to 1801;* vol. II, HASKINS, GEORGE L. AND JOHNSON, HERBERT A. 1981 *Foundations of Power: John Marshall, 1801–1815;* vol. V, SWISHER, CARL B. 1974 *The Taney Period, 1836–1864;* vols. VI and VII, FAIRMAN, CHARLES 1971 *Reconstruction and Reunion, 1864–1888, Part One;* 1986 *Part Two;* vol. IX, BICKEL, ALEXANDER M. and SCHMIDT, BENNO C., JR. 1984 *The Judiciary and Responsible Government, 1910–1921.*

FRIEDMAN, LEON and ISRAEL, FRED L., eds. 1969–1978 *The Justices of the United States Supreme Court, 1789–1969.* 5 Vols. New York: Chelsea House.

LEWIS, ANTHONY 1964 *Gideon's Trumpet.* New York: Random House.

POLLAK, LOUIS H., ed. 1966 *The Constitution and the Supreme Court: A Documentary History.* 2 Vols. Cleveland: World Publishing Co.

SWINDLER, WILLIAM F. 1970 *Court and Constitution in the Twentieth Century: The New Legality, 1932–1968.* Indianapolis: Bobbs-Merrill.

WARREN, CHARLES 1926 *The Supreme Court in United States History.* 2 Vols. Boston: Little, Brown.

WESTIN, ALAN, ed. 1961 *The Supreme Court: Views from Inside.* New York: Norton.

SUPREME COURT
(Role in American Government)

The Supreme Court is the only court in the United States whose existence is mandated by the Constitution, yet the Constitution designates no number of judges for the Supreme Court and sets no qualifications for judicial service. So far as the Constitution is concerned, the Supreme Court could as readily consist of two or of twenty-two judges, rather than of nine as has been the case since 1870. And so undemanding is the Constitution in setting qualifications for appointment to the Supreme Court that its members could consist entirely of persons not qualified to serve in either House of Congress, for which at least a few minimum standards of eligibility (of age and of CITIZENSHIP) are constitutionally prescribed. The Constitution speaks simply to the vesting of the JUDICIAL POWER OF THE UNITED STATES in "one supreme court, and in such inferior Courts as the Congress may from time to time ordain and establish," but it leaves much else to discretion and a great deal to chance.

The role of the Supreme Court in American government is much like this overall. Some impressions of what the Court's role was meant to be can be gained from what the Constitution says and from the immediate history of 1789, as well as from the categories of JURISDICTION assigned to the Court by Article III. But much of that role is also the product of custom and of practice about which the Constitution itself is silent.

The constitutional text itself suggests several ways of describing the Supreme Court's role, in conformity with Article III's prescriptions of the Court's jurisdiction. The useful jurisdictional distinctions are of four principal kinds, each providing some insight into what the Court was originally expected to do.

First mentioned is the Supreme Court's jurisdiction as a trial court, an ORIGINAL JURISDICTION invocable by certain parties in particular (states and representatives of foreign states) but by no one else. Second is that branch of its appellate jurisdiction applicable also solely because of who the parties are, irrespective of the nature of the dispute between them. Third is the Court's appellate jurisdiction that attaches solely because the case involves a federal statute or treaty of the United States, or arises under ADMIRALTY AND MARITIME LAW, without regard to who the parties may be and whether or not any constitutional question may be involved. Finally, the Court may exercise an appellate jurisdiction over "all cases arising under [the] Constitution," a phrase construed broadly to include any case in which the outcome may be affected by a question of constitutional law. It is the application of this phrase, of course, that tends to fix the Supreme Court's most important role, but as can be seen from the foregoing larger enumeration, it is not by any means the sole business to which the Court was expected to attend.

The role of the Supreme Court as a court of original jurisdiction has been useful but minor. Ordinarily, the Court's small complement of original jurisdiction has merely expedited its speedy examination of certain legal issues raised by states against other states (typically involving boundary or interstate river claims) or against the national government, as in OREGON V. MITCHELL—a 1970 decision holding unconstitutional one portion of an act of Congress that sought to override state voting age restrictions. Because Congress can provide for expedited Supreme Court review of cases originating in other courts, however, it is doubtful whether this feature of Article III has been terribly vital. Its one theoretical importance may be that the original jurisdiction it provides to the states is guaranteed against elimination by Congress—for unlike the Court's appellate jurisdiction, its original jurisdiction is not subject to the "exceptions" clause of Article III.

Dwarfing the Court's role as a court of original jurisdiction is its much larger and more familiar role as the ultimate appellate court in the United States for a vastly greater number and variety of disputes, although the Court is not obliged to review all such cases and in fact hears but a small fraction of those eligible for review. The cases eligible for review, some on APPEAL and a larger number on petition for a WRIT OF CERTIORARI, are divisible into two principal categories: those in which the character of the contesting parties makes the case reviewable, and those in which the nature of the legal issue raised by the case makes the case reviewable.

In the first category of cases within the Court's appellate jurisdiction there are many that raise no constitutional questions and indeed need not raise any kind of federal question. As these cases are within the Court's power of review solely because of the parties, regardless of the subject in dispute between them, they may involve very ordinary legal issues (for example, of contract, tort, or property law) as to which there is no special expertise in the Supreme Court and no obvious reason why they need be considered there. And in practice, they are not reviewed.

Part of the original interest in providing the Supreme Court as the ultimate appellate tribunal in the United States reflected the Framers' desire to provide an appellate court for litigants likely to be sued in hostile jurisdictions—cases, for instance, arising in state courts which nonresident defendants might fear would be inclined to favor local parties as against outsiders. Since the furnishing of lower federal courts (to hear such cases) was left entirely optional with Congress to provide or not provide as it liked, the Supreme Court's appellate jurisdiction even from state court diversity cases was directly provided for in Article III. Nonetheless, in the course of 200 years the felt need for such cases to be heard in the Supreme Court has never materialized—although such cases remain a staple of lower federal court jurisdiction. (Efforts in Congress to repeal this entire category of lower federal court jurisdiction are more than a half-century old, but they have been only partly successful, largely in restricting such cases to those involving sums in excess of $10,000.) In the meantime, however, the Supreme Court does not review such cases and, by act of Congress, it is under no obligation to take them. This particular anticipated role of the Supreme Court, as an active court in hearing appeals in ordinary diversity cases presenting no federal question and implicating no general interest of the United States, has never been significant in fact.

In contrast, the second branch of the Supreme Court's appellate jurisdiction—identified not by the parties but by the nature of the legal questions—remains intensely active. Indeed, the principal role the Court plays today as an appellate court undoubtedly arises almost entirely from this subject matter assignment of appellate jurisdiction of cases involving disputes of national law. In these cases the Court interprets acts of Congress and treaties of the United States as well as the Constitution as the ultimate source of governing law in the United States.

Specifically, these cases may raise any of the following four kinds of basic conflicts: conflicts between claims relying upon mutually exclusive interpretations of concededly valid acts of Congress or treaties of the United States; between constitutional claims of state power and claims of federal power (FEDERALISM conflicts); between constitutional claims by Congress and claims by the President or claims by the judiciary (SEPARATION OF POWERS conflicts); or between constitutional claims of personal right and claims of either state or of national power (personal rights conflicts). A principal function of Article III was to establish the Supreme Court as the ultimate national court of appeals to provide finality and consistency of result in the interpretation and application of all federal and constitutional law in the United States, within the full range of these four fundamental and enduring concerns.

For nearly the first hundred years (1789–1875), almost all appeals to the Supreme Court on such federal questions as these came from state courts rather than from lower federal courts. Not until 1875, in the aftermath of the Civil War, were lower federal courts given any significant original (trial) jurisdiction over private civil cases arising under acts of Congress or treaties of the United States. Since 1875, moreover, many federal question cases still proceed from state courts to the Supreme Court, because reliance on some federal law or on the Constitution often arises only in answer to some claim filed in a state court and thus emerges only by way of defense rather than as the basis of complaint.

The fact that this arrangement of the Court's appellate jurisdiction places the Supreme Court in appellate command over all other courts in the United States in all federal question cases is exactly what makes the Supreme Court supreme. In constitutional matters, for instance, this fact is the basis of Justice ROBERT H. JACKSON's observation, in speaking of the Court, that "[w]e are not final because we are infallible, but we are infallible only because we are final," that is, superior in constitutional authority to review the determinations of other courts and in turn unreviewable by any other court. It likewise animates the 1907 observation by CHARLES EVANS HUGHES (later Chief Justice of the United States). "We are under a Constitution," Hughes acknowledged, "but the Constitution is what the judges say it is," since it is their view and, most important, the Supreme Court's view, that ultimately controls in each case. And even when no constitutional issue is present, but the issue is how an act of Congress shall be interpreted and applied, the finality of the Supreme Court's appellate jurisdiction is equally pivotal; it is the Americanized version of Bishop Hoadley's observation in 1717, in reference to the power of the English courts in interpreting acts of Parliament. "Whoever hath an absolute authority to interpret any written or spoken laws," Hoadley observed, "it is he who is truly the lawgiver, to all intents and purposes, and not the person who first spoke or wrote them." From an early time Americans seem to have believed in the wisdom of reposing in the courts—and ultimately in the Supreme Court—the responsibility of substantive constitutional review, and it seems clear (despite some scholars' qualified doubts) that the Supreme Court was indeed meant to exercise that responsibility. (See JUDICIAL REVIEW.) It is unquestionably this role of substantive constitutional review that marks the special position of the Supreme Court.

The Supreme Court's decisions in constitutional cases may be roughly divided into three kinds, according to which its role in American government is occasionally assessed or described. The three kinds of decisions are these: legitimizing, braking, and catalytic.

A decision is said to be legitimizing whenever the Court examines any act of government on constitutional grounds and finds it not wanting. In holding that the act as applied is in fact authorized by the

Constitution and not offensive to any of its provisions (for example, the BILL OF RIGHTS or the FOURTEENTH AMENDMENT), the Court thus vouches for its constitutional legitimacy. A decision may be called a braking decision whenever its immediate effect is necessarily to arrest the further application of an act of Congress because the Court holds the act either inapplicable or unconstitutional, or whenever OBITER DICTA accompanying the decision serve notice of constitutional barriers in the way of similar legislation. Finally, a decision may be called catalytic when its immediate practical effect is to compel highly significant action of a sort not previously forthcoming from national or state government.

A significant and controversial example of the legitimizing sort is PLESSY V. FERGUSON (1896), the case sustaining certain state racial SEGREGATION laws as not inconsistent with the Fourteenth Amendment, despite intense argument to the contrary. A modern example of the same sort may be FULLILOVE V. KLUTZNICK (1980), a case sustaining a limited form of RACIAL DISCRIMINATION in favor of certain minority contractors as not inconsistent with the Fifth Amendment, despite intense argument as well. In each case, the Court considered a previously untested kind of race-related law. In each, the Supreme Court's decision could be said effectively to have impressed the operative law with a judicial imprimatur of constitutional legitimacy, given that in each case the challenged statute was sustained.

Examples of the braking sort may be found in the Court's early New Deal decisions holding Congress unauthorized by the COMMERCE CLAUSE to supplant state laws with its own much more sweeping and detailed ECONOMIC REGULATIONS. In this instance, the critical decisions of the Court forced a momentary pause in the onrush of legislation, compelling more deliberate attention to what the nation had been and what it meant to become. As it happened, the braking effect of these cases was eventually overcome, but it is nonetheless true that in the meantime the position taken by the Court played a sobering role. In a few other instances, the braking effect of equivalent cases was overcome by formal amendment of the Constitution itself: the SIXTEENTH AMENDMENT, for instance, was adopted principally to overcome the effect of the Court's decision in POLLOCK V. FARMERS' LOAN & TRUST (1895); the Thirteenth Amendment and Fourteenth Amendment displaced the Court's decision in DRED SCOTT V. SANDFORD (1857); and the TWENTY-SIXTH AMENDMENT displaced the decision in *Oregon v. Mitchell.* These reactions are by themselves not an indication that the Court has erred, of course, since the Constitution itself separates the role of the Court from the formal processes of constitutional modification. (See AMENDING PROCESS.) Any decision in the Supreme Court holding a statute unconstitutional may provide occasion to activate the AMENDING PROCESS provided for in Article V. Amendments by themselves are not proof that the decisions they effectively overrule were necessarily poorly conceived. They may, rather, but mark new Cambrian rings in what is meant to be a living constitution.

An example of a catalytic decision would be one holding certain prison conditions to be so inadequate as to constitute a form of CRUEL AND UNUSUAL PUNISHMENT, such that either the prisoners must be released (which public authorities are loath to do), or large sums must be raised and less congested prisons must be built. The change-forcing nature of the Court's catalytic decision is but descriptive of its practical implications. By itself it thus carries no suggestion that the Court acted from impulse rather than from obligation, in ruling as it did. The same observation may apply equally to the other two categories of decisions.

Thus, in the "legitimizing" decision there is no necessary insinuation that the measure that has been sustained is on that account also necessarily desirable or well-taken legislation; such questions are ordinarily regarded as no proper part of the judicial business. Adjudicated constitutionality properly vouches solely for an act's consistency with the Constitution, which consistency may still leave much to be desired, depending upon one's own point of view and one's feeling of constitutional adequacy. Similarly, it does not follow that an act's adjudicated unconstitutionality necessarily implies its undesirability or, indeed, that there would be anything terribly wrong were the Constitution amended so that similar legislation might subsequently be reenacted and sustained. It means merely that the act does not pass muster under the Constitution as it is and as the judges are oath-bound to apply it until it is altered.

So also with catalytic decisions: such forced change as a particular decision may produce is required simply to bring the conduct of government back within constitutional lines as they are, and not as they need be. As conscientiously applied by the Court, the Constitution thus speaks to such constitutional boundaries as were put in place sometime in the past, from a considered political judgment of the time that such boundaries would be important. The judgment is wholly an inherited one, however, and contemplates the possibility of amendment to cast off such restraints as subsequent extraordinary majorities may find unendurable. Viewed in this way, the Constitution is a device by means of which past generations signal to subsequent generations their cumulative assessment of what sorts of restraints simple majoritarianism needs most. The Supreme Court is the ultimate judicial means by which the integrity of those restraints is secured against the common tendency to think them ill-conceived or obsolete, sustaining them when pressed by proper litigants with suitable standing, until instructed by amendment to acknowledge the change. It is a signal responsibility and an unusual power—one which few other national supreme courts have been given.

On the other hand, the phrases "legitimizing," "braking," and "catalytic" are not always used so descriptively, however well they capture the by-products of the Court's work. Rather, they are sometimes used prescriptively, and thus in an entirely different sense. In this different usage they presume to provide a more jurisprudential blueprint for the role of the Supreme Court: that it is appropriate for the Court actively to serve these three functions politically as it were, and to involve the Constitution only instrumentally in their service. Employed in this different locution, they are phrases used to express faith in a specific kind of judicial activism, according to which the right role of the Court is to identify the needs of efficient and humane government and to adjust its own adjudications accordingly.

In this view, it is in fact the proper role of the Supreme Court to legitimate (by holding constitutional) such laws as circumstances persuade it ought not be disapproved, to brake (by adverse construction or by holding unconstitutional) such developments as it determines to have been precipitously taken or otherwise to have been ill-advised, and to catalyze (by artful action) such changes it deems highly desirable but unlikely to be forthcoming from government unless the Court so requires. The persuasive justification for the Supreme Court lies in what it can do best as a distinct institution, in this view, and only secondarily in adhering to the Constitution. And what the Supreme Court can do better than others is to compensate for such gaps as it finds in the Constitution or in the political process, and to take such measured steps as it can to repair them. Accordingly, the more appropriate role of the Supreme Court is to conduct itself institutionally as best it can to contribute actively to a better political quality of life in the United States: in deciding which cases to hear, when to hear them, on what grounds to decide them, and how to make them come out in ways most in keeping with these three vital functions of granting legitimacy to the good, putting brakes on the bad, and compelling such changes as are overdue.

As an original jurisprudence of proposed judicial role, this perspective on the Supreme Court has had considerable occasional support. In the concrete, moreover, there is good reason to believe that certain Justices—probably a nontrivial number—have embraced it in selected aspects of their own work. At the least, there are a large number of constitutional decisions that appear to reflect its view of what judges should seek to do, as indeed some Justices have virtually absorbed it as an articulate feature of proper judicial review; their decisions seem sometimes to be based on little else.

Still, and for obvious reasons, it remains deeply problematic, for at bottom it would have the judges struggle against the obligation of their oaths. Insofar as cases such as *Plessy* or *Fullilove* were to any extent self-conscious efforts by a Supreme Court majority simply to legitimate race-based arrangements it thought desirable, and not decisions reporting a difficult judicial conclusion respecting the lack of constitutional restrictions on the legislative acts at issue, for instance, it is doubtful whether the "legitimacy" thus established was appropriate or, indeed, constitutionally authorized. Likewise, insofar as the early New Deal cases were to any extent simply a deliberate institutional attempt by the majority Justices to arrest what they thought to be ill-advised varieties of market intervention, and not decisions reflecting an attentive interpretation respecting the limits of Congress's commerce power, it is debatable whether the "braking" thus applied was appropriate or authorized. So, too, with such decisions as may be catalytic, but which may be driven more by a judicial desire to see changes made than by a mere firm resolve that the Constitution shall be obeyed.

Without doubt, however, the tendency to urge the Supreme Court to compose its interpretations of the Constitution in subordination to allegedly significant social tasks remains widespread. Moreover, the malleability of many constitutional clauses invites it, and the political staffing mechanism (provided by Article III) for selecting the judges may appear obliquely to legitimate it. The tendency to rationalize its propriety is deeply entrenched.

Even so, the conscious treatment of constitutional clauses as but textual or pretextual occasions for judicial legitimation, braking, or social catalysis, does tend to pit the Court against itself in its disjunction of fundamentally incompatible roles. The resulting tension has split the Court virtually from the beginning. It divides it even now: between these two visions of the Court, as a professional court first of all or as a political court first of all, lie two centuries of unsteady swings of actual judicial review. The history of the Supreme Court in this respect but reiterates a classic antinomy in American constitutional law. It doubtless reflects the conflicts Americans tend to sense within themselves—as to what role they genuinely wish this Court to fulfill.

With certain highly notable exceptions (including West Germany, Japan, Australia, and most recently Canada), the written CONSTITUTIONS of most modern nation-states serve merely as each nation's explanation of itself as a government. Such a constitution typically presents a full plan of government, a statement of its purposes and powers, and an ample declaration of rights. Yet, unlike the Constitution of the United States, such a constitution cannot be invoked by litigants and does not require or even permit courts of law to use it as against which all other laws may be examined. It is, rather, a nonjusticiable document. It is intended to be taken seriously (at least this is the case generally), but only in the political sense that legislative and executive authorities are meant to reconcile their actions with the constitution at the risk of possible popular disaffection should they stray too far from what the constitution provides. Whether the authorities have thus strayed, however, and what consequences shall follow if they have, is not deemed to be the appropriate business of courts of law.

The enormous distinction of American constitutional law has thus rested in the very different and exceptional role of the judiciary, from the most unprepossessing county courts through the hierarchy of the entire federal court system. The unique role of the Supreme Court has been its own role as the ultimate appellate court in reference to that judiciary, most critically in all constitutional cases. The arrangement thus established does not lessen the original obligation of other government officials separately to take care that their own actions are consistent with the Constitution, but it is meant to provide—as effectively as human institutions can arrange—an additional and positive check. When official action is not consistent with the Constitution, as ultimately determined under the Supreme Court's authority, the courts are given both the power and the obligation to intercede: to interpose such authority as they have and to provide such redress as appears to be due. Judged even by international standards, this is an ample role. It is not this role that now appears fairly open to question, moreover, but rather the definition of role that would assume something more or accept something less.

WILLIAM VAN ALSTYNE

Bibliography

ABRAHAM, HENRY J. 1986 *The Judicial Process.* 5th ed. New York: Oxford University Press.

AGRESTO, JOHN 1984 *The Supreme Court and Constitutional Democracy.* Ithaca, N.Y.: Cornell University Press.

BICKEL, ALEXANDER M. 1962 *The Least Dangerous Branch: The Supreme Court at the Bar of Politics.* Indianapolis, Ind.: Bobbs-Merrill.

COX, ARCHIBALD 1976 *The Role of the Supreme Court in American Government.* New York: Oxford University Press.

ELY, JOHN HART 1980 *Democracy and Distrust: A Theory of Judicial Review.* Cambridge, Mass.: Harvard University Press.

FREUND, PAUL 1961 *The Supreme Court of the United States.* Cleveland, Ohio: World Publishing Company.

HOROWITZ, DONALD L. 1977 *The Courts and Social Policy.* Washington, D.C.: The Brookings Institution.

JACKSON, ROBERT H. 1955 *The Supreme Court in the American System of Government.* New York: Harper & Row.

MASON, ALPHEUS THOMAS 1979 *The Supreme Court from Taft to Burger.* 3d ed. Baton Rouge: Louisiana State University Press.

MCCLOSKEY, ROBERT G. 1960 *The American Supreme Court.* Chicago: University of Chicago Press.

WOLFE, CHRISTOPHER 1986 *The Rise of Modern Judicial Review.* New York: Basic Books.

SUPREME COURT, 1789–1801

On January 8, 1801, twelve days before President JOHN ADAMS appointed JOHN MARSHALL as Chief Justice, a Jeffersonian newspaper reported: "JOHN JAY, after having thru' decay of age become incompetent to discharge the duties of Governor, has been appointed to the sinecure of Chief Justice of the United States. That the Chief Justiceship is a sinecure needs no other evidence than that in one case the duties were discharged by one person who resided at the same time in England, and by another during a year's residence in France." The one in France was OLIVER ELLSWORTH, sent there by President Adams as a special ambassador to negotiate peace. Ellsworth had recently resigned, and Jay, whose appointment as Ellsworth's successor had been confirmed by the Senate, had himself been the first Chief Justice, whom President GEORGE WASHINGTON had sent to England to negotiate a treaty that bore Jay's name. The chief justiceship was no sinecure: although the Supreme Court then met for only two short terms a year, the Justices also served as circuit court judges, and riding circuit was extremely arduous. When Jay was offered the position again, he declined it because of the circuit responsibilities and because the Court had neither "the energy, weight and dignity" necessary for it to support the national government nor "the public confidence and respect."

Jay's judgment was harsh although the Court did have problems, some of its own making. All the Justices were Federalists; their decisions EN BANC or on circuit seemed partisan—pro-Administration, pro-English, or procreditor—and they presided at trials under the infamous Sedition Act, whose constitutionality they affirmed. But the Court was not responsible for most of its difficulties. It had no official reporter (ALEXANDER J. DALLAS'S unofficial reports first appeared in 1798) and the press publicized only a few of the Court's decisions. The public knew little about the Court, and even members of its own bar were unfamiliar with its decisions. Nothing better symbolizes the nation's neglect of the Court than the fact that when the United States government moved to Washington, D.C., in late 1800, the Court had been forgotten. Not only did it lack a building; it had no courtroom. Congress hastily provided a small committee room in the basement of the Senate wing of the Capitol for the Court to meet.

The Court's beginnings were hardly more auspicious, however distinguished its membership. At its first term in February 1790 it had nothing to do except admit attorneys to its bar, and it shortly adjourned. It began as a court without a reporter, litigants, a docket, appeals, or decisions to make. It was chiefly an appellate court whose APPELLATE JURISDICTION scarcely matched the breadth of the JUDICIAL POWER OF THE UNITED STATES stated in Article III. Congress in the JUDICIARY ACT OF 1789 had authorized the Court to review state court decisions that denied claims based on federal law, including the Constitution. Review was not authorized when the state court upheld a claim of federal right. The system of appellate jurisdiction thus permitted the Supreme Court to maintain federal law's supremacy but not its uniform interpretation. The Court's review of civil decisions of the lower federal courts was limited to cases involving more than $2,000 in controversy, and it could not review criminal cases from those courts. Congress had stingily authorized the Court to hear cases in its appellate capacity in order to keep it weak, to prevent centralization of judicial powers, to preserve the relative importance of state courts, and to insulate the Court from many matters that concerned ordinary citizens. For its first two years it heard no cases, and it made no substantive decisions until 1793. Its docket never got crowded. Dallas reported less than seventy cases for the pre-Marshall Court, and fewer than ten percent of them involved constitutional law. The Court was then first a COMMON LAW court, second a court of ADMIRALTY AND MARITIME JURISDICTION.

Although its members were able, the pre-Marshall Court had difficulty attracting and keeping them. When Marshall became Chief Justice, only WILLIAM CUSHING of the original six Justices appointed by Washington remained. Robert H. Harrison, one of the original six, was confirmed but declined appointment, preferring instead the chancellorship of Maryland. JAMES IREDELL accepted Harrison's place, so that the first Court consisted of Chief Justice Jay and Justices Cushing, JOHN BLAIR, JOHN RUTLEDGE, JAMES WILSON, and Iredell. Rutledge performed his circuit duties but had never attended a session of the Court when he resigned after two years to become chief justice of South Carolina. CHARLES C. PINCKNEY and Edward Rutledge declined appointment to John Rutledge's seat, preferring to serve in their state legislature. THOMAS JOHNSON accepted that seat but resigned it in less than two years because circuit riding was too strenuous. WILLIAM PATERSON succeeded him. The February 1794 term was Jay's last. That he reentered New York politics after negotiating JAY'S TREATY says something about the Court's prestige at the time. So too does the fact that ALEXANDER HAMILTON preferred private practice to the chief justiceship. At that point, John Rutledge, who had quit the Court, applied for the post vacated by Jay. Washington appointed Rutledge, who attended the August 1795 term of the Court when it decided only two cases. The Senate, having reconvened, rejected him because of his opposition to Jay's Treaty. Washington offered the chief justiceship to PATRICK HENRY who declined it. The President then named Justice Cushing, whom the Senate confirmed; but he too declined, preferring to remain Associate Justice. In 1796, Oliver Ellsworth became Chief Justice but quit after four years. John Blair retired early in 1796 and Washington again had to fill a vacancy on the Court. After EDMUND RANDOLPH refused the position, SAMUEL CHASE accepted. In 1798, Wilson became the first Justice to die in office. RICHARD PETERS refused to be considered for the position, and John Marshall also declined. Adams then appointed BUSHROD WASHINGTON, and after Iredell died in 1798, he appointed ALFRED MOORE, who resigned within five years. When Ellsworth resigned and Jay declined reappointment, even though the Senate confirmed him, Adams turned to Marshall. The rapid turnover in personnel during the Court's first decade did not ease its work or enhance its reputation.

Jeffersonians grumbled about the Court's Federalist constitutional theories, but Jay kept his Court out of politics and established its independence from the other branches of the government. That achievement and the Court's identification of its task as safeguarding the supreme law of the land kept the Court a viable institution, despite its many problems during the first decade, and laid the groundwork for the achievements of the MARSHALL COURT.

Late in 1790, Virginia's legislature denounced as unconstitutional the bill for national assumption of state debts. Washington allowed Hamilton to send a copy of the Virginia resolves to Jay and to inquire whether the various branches of the government should employ their "collective weight . . . in exploding [Virginia's STRICT CONSTRUCTION] principles." Hamilton warned that Virginia had shown "the first symptom of a spirit which must either be killed or it will kill the Constitution of the United States." However, Jay, who privately advised Washington and drafted his PROCLAMATION OF NEUTRALITY, recognized the difference between a judicial pronouncement and an extrajudicial one. The Court, strongly believing in the principle of SEPARATION OF POWERS, would not express ex officio opinions except in judicial cases before it. Jay calmly declined the executive's invitation.

Similar principles motivated the Justices when confronted by Congress's Invalid Pensioners' Act of 1792 which required the circuit courts to pass on the pension applications of disabled veterans, subject to review by the secretary of war and Congress. Justices Wilson and Blair together with Judge Peters on circuit in the district of Pennsylvania, having refused to pass on an application from one Hayburn, explained their conduct in a letter to the President. They could not proceed because first, the business directed by the statute was not judicial in nature, there being no constitutional authority for it, and second, because the possible revision of the Court's judgment by the other branches of government would be "radically inconsistent with the independence" of the judiciary. In their circuits, Jay, Cushing, and Iredell similarly explained that a judicial decision must be a final decision. HAYBURN'S CASE (1792), which was not really a "case" and in which nothing was judicially decided, was important because the Court, in Wilson's words, affirmed "a principle important to freedom," that the judicial branch must be independent of the other branches.

Similarly, Jay established another principle vital to the Court's independent, judicial, and nonpolitical character when he declined Washington's request for an ADVISORY OPINION. That request arose out of apparent conflicts between American treaty obligations to France and the Proclamation of Neutrality. The French commissioned privateers in American ports and established prize courts to condemn vessels captured by those privateers. Washington sought the Court's opinion on twenty-nine questions involving international law and treaty interpretation, in connection with the French practices. Jay, relying again on the principle of separation of powers, observed that the Court should not "extra-judicially" decide questions that might come before it in litigation. Thus, by preserving its purely judicial character, the Court was free to decide some of those questions when real cases posed them. From the beginning, the Court staked its power and prestige on its special relationship to the supreme law of the land, which it safeguarded, expounded, and symbolized.

The pre-Marshall Court also exercised the power of JUDICIAL REVIEW. The Justices on circuit quickly held state acts unconstitutional for violating the supreme law of the land. Jay and Cushing on circuit in the district of Connecticut held that that state, by adversely affecting debts owed to British creditors, had violated the treaty of peace with Britain; Iredell in Georgia and Paterson in South Carolina made similar decisions. The Justices held that United States treaties were superior to state laws. The Supreme Court confronted the issue in WARE V. HYLTON (1796). With Iredell alone dissenting, the Court rejected the arguments of John Marshall, making his only appearance before the Justices, as counsel for the debtor interests of Virginia. He opposed "those who wish to impair the sovereignty of Virginia" and contended first that the Constitution had not authorized the Court to question the validity of state statutes and, second, that a treaty could not annul them. SERIATIM opinions by Chase, Paterson, Wilson, and Cushing held otherwise.

In *Clarke* v. *Harwood* (1797) the Court ruled that *Ware* "settled" the question before it. *Clarke* was the Court's first decision against the validity of a state act in a case arising on a WRIT OF ERROR to a state court under section 25 of the Judiciary Act of 1789. Section 25 authorized the Court to reverse or affirm state decisions that denied rights claimed under United States treaties. Maryland's high court, relying on a state statute sequestering debts owed to British creditors, had barred a claim based on the treaty of peace with Britain. By reversing the Maryland court, the Supreme Court in effect voided the state act. However, the Court rarely heard cases on a writ of error to a state court. Indeed, it had not decided its first such case until shortly before *Clarke.* In *Olney v. Arnold* (1796) the Court had reversed a Rhode Island decision that misconstrued a revenue act of Congress. The Court's power of reviewing state decisions under Section 25 did not become controversial until 1814. (See MARTIN v. HUNTER'S LESSEE, 1816.) During the Court's first decade, judicial review of state legislation was uncontested, and it was exercised.

On circuit the Justices also struck down state acts as violating the CONTRACT CLAUSE of the Constitution. The first such decision occurred in 1792 in CHAMPION AND DICKASON v. CASEY, which voided a Rhode Island state law. Given the hullaballoo in that state when its own judiciary was suspected of having voided a state act in TREVETT v. WEEDEN (1787), the meek acceptance of the 1792 decision showed the legitimacy of judicial review over the states.

In HYLTON v. UNITED STATES (1796) the Court for the first time determined the constitutionality of an act of Congress, ruling that an EXCISE on carriages, not being a DIRECT TAX, was valid even if not apportioned among the states. Those hoping for the Court to hold the federal excise unconstitutional were Jeffersonians; they did not then or at any time during the Court's first decade challenge the legitimacy of the Court's power to refuse to enforce an unconstitutional statute. Until the debate on the repeal of the JUDICIARY ACT OF 1801 (see JUDICIARY ACTS OF 1802), scarcely anyone opposed judicial review, whether over state or over congressional legislation. *Hayburn's Case* in 1792 was misunderstood throughout the nation. Not only did Attorney General Randolph believe that the Court had annulled an act of Congress; so did Congress. The House established an investigating committee, "this being the first instance in which a Court of Justice had declared a law of Congress unconstitutional." Jeffersonians gleefully praised the Justices and hoped the Court would extend the precedent by holding unconstitutional other congressional legislation that promoted Hamilton's economic programs. Later, Jeffersonians in Sedition Act trials sought to persuade the Justices on circuit that they should declare the statute void. Repeatedly during the first decade, bills arose in Congress that provoked members in both houses to state that the Court should and would hold them unconstitutional. The way to the doctrine of judicial review announced in MARBURY v. MADISON (1803) was well paved, and the opposition to the Court's opinion did not derive from its assumption of a power to void an act of Congress.

Another major theme in the work of the Court during its first decade was nationalism. Once again, the Marshall Court built on what the Jay and Ellsworth Courts had first shaped. The early Courts helped vindicate the national character of the United States government, maintain the supremacy of the nation over the states, and keep the states from undermining the new constitutional system. On circuit duty the Justices frequently lectured federal GRAND JURIES, inculcating doctrines from THE FEDERALIST, and these grand jury charges were well publicized in the newspapers. In one of his charges, Jay, in 1790, having declared, "We had become a Nation," explained why national tribunals became necessary for the interpretation and execution of national law, especially in a nation accustomed only to state courts and state policies. Circuit court opinions striking down state laws in violation of the contract clause or federal treaties preached nationalism and national supremacy. Many of the criminal prosecutions before the federal circuit courts during the first decade were connected with national suppression of the WHISKEY REBELLION and the FRIES REBELLION. Similarly, prosecutions under the Sedition Act were intended to vindicate the reputations of Congress and the President.

The development of a FEDERAL COMMON LAW OF CRIMES, expanding the jurisdiction of the national courts, fit the nationalist pattern. Whether the courts could try nonstatutory offenses was a question that first arose in Henfield's case (1793). Wilson maintained that an American citizen serving on a French privateer commissioned in an American port and attacking ships of England, with whom the United States was at peace, had committed an indictable offense under the Proclamation of Neutrality, the law of nations, and the treaty with England, even though Congress had not made his act a crime.

The same nationalist pattern unified several of the Court's opinions in cases dealing with various issues. In CHISHOLM v. GEORGIA (1793) the Court's holding, that its jurisdiction extended to suits against a state by citizens of another state, was founded on nationalist principles as well as on the text of Article III. Wilson, for example, began with the principles that the people of the United States form a nation, making ridiculous the "haughty notions of state independence, state SOVEREIGNTY, and state supremacy." "As to the purposes of the Union," he said, "therefore, Georgia is not a sovereign state." Jay's opinion also stressed "the national character" of the United States and the "inexpediency" of allowing state courts to decide questions that involved the performance of national treaties. The denunciation of the Court for its "consolidation of the Union" and its "annihilation of the sovereignty of the States" led to the ELEVENTH AMENDMENT, which was intended to nullify *Chisholm.*

In *Glass v. Sloop Betsy* (1794) the Court supported

the government's neutrality policy by ruling that France, after capturing a neutral ship, could not hold or award her as a prize in an American port. Only the United States courts could determine the lawfulness of prizes brought into its ports, and no foreign nation controlled its admiralty law or could subvert American rights under international law. In *Penhallow v. Doane* (1795) the Court resolved an old dispute over the ownership of a prize. One party's claims relied on decisions of a New Hampshire court, the other's on a decision of a prize court established by the old Congress of the Confederation. Paterson, in the Supreme Court's principal opinion, upheld the lower federal courts, which had decided against the state court and claimed jurisdiction. No nation, he said, had recognized the states as sovereign for the purpose of awarding prizes. The old Congress had been the supreme council of the nation and center of the Union, he claimed, whose sovereignty was approved by the people of America and recognized by foreign nations. The federal courts succeeded to that sovereignty in prize matters. New Hampshire angrily remonstrated against the "destruction" of its sovereignty but the Court's ruling prevailed.

Its decision in *Hylton v. United States* gave life to the government's revenue powers. When the Court upheld federal treaties as paramount to state laws, in *Ware v. Hylton* (1796), Chase, in the principal opinion for the Court, indulged in fanciful nationalism when declaring, "There can be no limitation on the power of the people of the United States. By their authority the State Constitutions were made."

Other notable cases of the first decade were VAN HORNE'S LESSEE V. DORRANCE (1794) and CALDER V. BULL (1798), in which the Court laid the foundation for the judicial doctrine of VESTED RIGHTS, which it developed further in contract clause and HIGHER LAW decisions during Marshall's chief justiceship. Although the Court was left out of the planning for the new national capital, it had been enunciating doctrines—of judicial review, national supremacy, and vested rights—that helped shape the United States and would in time make the judicial branch of government impossible to ignore.

LEONARD W. LEVY

Bibliography

CURRIE, DAVID P. 1981 The Constitution in the Supreme Court: 1789–1801. *University of Chicago Law Review* 48:819–885.

GOEBEL, JULIUS 1971 *Antecedents and Beginnings.* Vol. I of the *Oliver Wendell Holmes Devise History of the Supreme Court,* ed. Paul Freund. New York: Macmillan.

HAINES, CHARLES GROVE 1944 *The Role of the Supreme Court in American Government and Politics, 1789–1835.* Berkeley: University of California Press.

HENDERSON, DWIGHT F. 1971 *Courts for a New Nation.* Washington, D.C.: Public Affairs Press.

WARREN, CHARLES 1923 *The Supreme Court in United States History.* Vol. I. Boston: Little, Brown.

SUPREME COURT PRACTICE

The SUPREME COURT is the only judicial body created by the Constitution. Article III, Section 1, specifies that "The JUDICIAL POWER OF THE UNITED STATES, shall be vested in one supreme Court, and in such inferior Courts as the Congress may from time to time ordain and establish." The judges of that "one supreme Court," like the judges of the inferior courts created by Congress, are to hold their offices "during GOOD BEHAVIOUR" and to suffer no diminution of compensation during their continuance in office. Supreme Court Justices can be impeached, however. And it is not constitutionally clear that their "good Behaviour" term of office is the equivalent of a life term, as generally thought.

In practice, this "one supreme Court" has always acted as a unitary body. That means that the Court never divides into panels or groups of Justices for purposes of resolving matters submitted to the Court. All petitions and briefs are circulated to, and considered by, all participating Justices; and all Court decisions are rendered on behalf of the Court as a unit of nine Justices.

Article III of the Constitution, in establishing the judicial institution known as the Supreme Court, vests in the Court two basic kinds of jurisdiction: ORIGINAL JURISDICTION and APPELLATE JURISDICTION. The Court's original jurisdiction is its power to decide certain cases and controversies in the first instance. Its appellate jurisdiction is its power to review certain cases and controversies decided in the first instance by lower courts.

In COHENS V. VIRGINIA (1821), Chief Justice JOHN MARSHALL stated that the Court "must decide" a case before it that is properly within one of these two areas of jurisdiction, and that the Court has "no more right to decline the exercise of jurisdiction which is given, than to usurp that which is not given . . . [either of which] would be treason to the Constitution." But in the Court's judicial world, Marshall's proposition is no longer universally true, if it ever was. The modern need to control and limit the voluminous number of cases clamoring for review has forced the Court to resist demands that every facet of the Court's vested jurisdiction be exercised. Limitations of time and human energy simply do not permit the luxury of resolving every dispute that comes before the Court. Notions of judicial prudence and sound discretion, given these limitations, have thus become dominant in the Court's selection of those relatively few cases it feels it can afford to review in a plenary fashion and to resolve the merits. Such factors are evident in the Court's control of both its original docket and its appellate docket.

Section 2 of Article III specifies that the Supreme Court "shall have original jurisdiction" in all cases "affecting Ambassadors, other public Ministers and Consuls, and those in which a State shall be Party." Compared with cases on the appellate docket, cases on the original docket are quite few in number. Indeed, cases involving ambassadors, ministers, and consuls have never been common and have virtually disappeared from the original docket. The typical original case has thus become that in which a state is the plaintiff or defendant; most frequent are suits between two or more states over boundaries and water rights, suits that cannot appropriately be handled by any other tribunal. States have also sued each other over state financial obligations, use of natural resources, multistate domiciliary and escheat problems, breaches of contracts between states, and various kinds of injuries to the public health and welfare of the complaining state.

States can also invoke the Court's original jurisdiction to sue private nonresident citizens, or ALIENS, for alleged injuries to the sovereign interests of the complaining state. And a state may bring such suits on behalf of all its citizens to protect the economy and natural resources of the state, as well as the health and welfare of the citizens. The ELEVENTH AMENDMENT bars an original action against a defendant state brought by a private plaintiff who is a citizen of another state; and the sovereign immunity principle recognized by that Amendment also bars such an action by a citizen of the defendant state. Because that amendment does not apply to the federal sovereign as plaintiff, the United States can bring an original action in the Supreme Court against a defendant state. All cases brought by a state against a private party defendant, however, fall within the nonexclusive category of the Court's original jurisdiction; such suits can alternatively be brought in some other federal or state court. The Court in recent years has sought to reduce its original docket workload by rejecting some nonexclusive causes of action and requiring the parties to proceed in an available alternative forum.

Original cases often involve factual disputes. In processing such cases, the Court considers itself the equivalent of a federal trial court, though with significant differences. The Court's rules and procedures in this respect are not very specific, and practices may vary from case to case. The case starts with a motion for leave to file a complaint, a requirement that permits the Court to consider and resolve jurisdictional and prudential objections. If the Court denies the motion for leave to file, the case terminates. If the motion is granted, the complaint is ordered filed, the defendant files an answer, and in most instances a trial ensues.

The Justices themselves do not conduct trials in original cases. Instead, they appoint a member of the bar or a retired lower court judge to serve as a special master. The special master then takes evidence, hears witnesses, makes fact-findings, and recommends legal conclusions. But all rulings, findings, and conclusions of the special master are subject to review by the Court. That review occurs after parties aggrieved by the special master's actions have filed exceptions thereto; all parties then brief and orally argue the exceptions before the entire Court, which decides the case by written opinion. A complicated case may require more than one hearing before the special master and more than one opinion by the Court, prolonging the case for years.

The Court itself has admitted that it is "ill-equipped for the task of factfinding and so forced, in original cases, awkwardly to play the role of factfinder without actually presiding over the introduction of evidence." Original cases take away valuable time and attention from the Court's main mission, the exercise of its appellate jurisdiction, where the Court serves as the prime overseer of important matters of federal constitutional and statutory law. The Court is thus increasingly disposed to construe its original jurisdiction narrowly, exercising that jurisdiction only where the parties cannot secure an initial resolution of their controversy in another tribunal. If there is such an alternative proceeding, the Court prefers to REMAND the parties to the lower court and to deal with any important issues in the case on review of the lower court's determination.

The Court's appellate jurisdiction is also defined and vested by Article III, Section 2. That jurisdiction extends to all categories of CASES AND CONTROVERSIES, decided in the first instance by lower federal courts or state courts, that fall within the JUDICIAL POWER OF THE UNITED STATES. Those categories include: cases arising under the Constitution, laws, and treaties of the United States; cases affecting ambassadors, ministers, and consuls; cases of ADMIRALTY AND MARITIME JURISDICTION; controversies to which the United States is a party; controversies between two or more states; and controversies between a state and citizens of another state, between citizens of different states, between citizens of the same state claiming lands under grants of different states, or between a state or its citizens and foreign states or citizens. The Court's appellate jurisdiction extends "both as to Law and Fact, with such Exceptions, and under such Regulations as the Congress shall make."

The exceptions clause in Section 2 contains within it a constitutional enigma, as yet unsolved. The problem is the extent of Congress's power to control and limit the Supreme Court's appellate jurisdiction. The Court has never held that its appellate jurisdiction is coterminous with the Section 2 categories of judicial power. Consistently since *Wiscart v. Dauchy* (1796) the Court has said, albeit often by way of OBITER DICTUM, that it can exercise appellate jurisdiction only to the extent permitted by acts of Congress, and that a legislative denial of jurisdiction may be implied from a failure by Congress to make an affirmative grant of jurisdiction. The Court, in other words, assumes that its appellate jurisdiction comes from statutes, not directly from Section 2 of Article III. The assumption is that Congress cannot add to the constitutional definitions of appellate jurisdiction, but that Congress can subtract from or make exceptions to those definitions.

It is clear that Congress has made broad statutory grants of jurisdiction to the Court, though not to the full extent permitted by Section 2. These affirmative grants have always been sufficient to permit the Court to fulfill its essential function of interpreting and applying the Constitution and of insuring the supremacy of federal law. So far, the statutory omissions and limitations have not hobbled the performance of that function.

At the same time, periodic proposals have been made in Congress to use the exceptions clause to legislate certain exclusions from the appellate jurisdiction previously granted by Congress. Such proposals usually spring from displeasure with Court decisions dealing with specific constitutional matters. The proponents would simply excise those areas of appellate jurisdiction that permit the Court to render the objectionable decisions. Many commentators contend that the exceptions clause was not designed to authorize Congress to strip the Court of power to perform its essential function of overseeing the development of constitutional doctrines and guarantees. Objections are also raised that such legislative excisions are mere subterfuges for overruling constitutional rights established by the Court, a most serious infringement of the separation of powers doctrine. Because no jurisdictional excisions of this broad nature have been enacted, the Court has yet to speak to this constitutional conundrum. (See JUDICIAL SYSTEM.)

Whatever the outer limits of the exceptions clause, Congress since 1789 has vested in the Court broad appellate power to review lower court decisions that fall within the constitutional "case or controversy" categories. Statutes permit the Court to review virtually all decisions of lower federal appellate courts, as well as a limited number of decisions of federal trial courts. And Congress has from the start given the Court jurisdiction to review decisions of the highest state courts that deal with federal constitutional, treaty, or statutory matters.

An ingredient of most jurisdictional statutes are legislative directions as to the mode by which the Court's appellate powers are to be invoked. In modern times, most lower court decisions are made reviewable by way of WRIT OF CERTIORARI or, in a declining number of specialized instances, by way of APPEAL. Congress permits the Court to issue its own extraordinary writs, such as HABEAS CORPUS or MANDAMUS, and to review certain matters not otherwise reviewable on certiorari or appeal; and there is a rarely used authorization for lower federal appellate court CERTIFICATION of difficult questions to be answered by the Supreme Court.

At COMMON LAW, the term "certiorari" means an original writ commanding lower court judges or officers to certify and transfer the record of the lower court proceedings in a case under review by a higher court. In the Supreme Court lexicon, the common law meaning of the term has been modified and expanded. Certiorari refers generally to the entire process of discretionary review by the Supreme Court of a lower court decision. Such review is sought by filing a petition for writ of certiorari. That document sets forth in short order the reasons why the questions presented by the decision below are so nationally important that the Court should review the case and resolve those questions on the merits. In most cases, the record in the court below is not routinely filed in the Court along with the petition.

Each Justice, after reviewing the petition for certiorari, the brief in opposition, and the opinion below, makes his or her own subjective assessment as to the appropriateness of plenary review by the entire Court. Such review is granted only if at least four Justices vote to grant the petition, a practice known as the RULE OF FOUR. If the petition is granted, a formal order to that effect is entered; copies of the order are sent to the parties and to the court below, which is then requested to transmit a certified copy of the record. But at no time does any writ of certiorari issue from the Court. The parties proceed thereafter to brief and argue orally the questions presented in the petition.

An appeal, on the other hand, refers to a theoretically obligatory type of review by the Supreme Court. That means that once the appeal is properly filed and docketed, the Court must somehow consider and dispose of the case on its merits. There is said to be no discretion to refuse to make such a decision on the merits of the appeal, which serves to distinguish an appeal from a certiorari case.

To invoke the Court's review powers by way of appeal, the aggrieved party first files a short notice of appeal in the lower court and then dockets the appeal in the Supreme Court by filing a document entitled "jurisdictional statement." Apart from the different title, a jurisdictional statement is remarkably like a petition for writ of certiorari. Like a petition, the jurisdictional statement sets forth briefly the reasons why the issues are so substantial, or important, "as to require plenary consideration, with briefs on the merits and oral argument, for their resolution." The Rule of Four is followed in considering whether to grant plenary consideration of an appeal. Such a grant takes the form of an order to the effect that "probable jurisdiction is noted," although if there remains any question as to whether the case complies with the technical jurisdictional requirements of an appeal, the order is changed to read: "further consideration of the question of jurisdiction is postponed to the hearing of the case on the merits." The appeal then follows the pattern of a certiorari case with respect to obtaining the record from the lower court(s), briefing the questions presented, and arguing orally before the Court.

As if to underscore the similarity between a jurisdictional statement and a petition for writ of certiorari, Congress has directed the Court, in situations where a party has "improvidently" taken an appeal "where the proper mode of review is by petition for certiorari," to consider and act on the jurisdictional statement as if it were a petition for writ of certiorari, and then either granting or denying certiorari. Thus a party cannot be prejudiced by seeking the wrong mode of Supreme Court review.

There is, however, one historical and confusing difference in the Court's summary disposition of certiorari cases and appeals, a difference springing from the notion that the Court is obliged to dispose of all appeals on their merits. When a petition for writ of certiorari is denied, the order denying the petition has no precedential value. It means only that fewer than four Justices, or perhaps none at all, want to hear and decide the merits of the questions presented. That is the end of the case.

But when fewer than four Justices wish to hear an appeal in a plenary manner, the long-held theory is that the Court is still compelled to dispose of the appeal on the merits of the questions presented. To comply with this theory, which is judge-made and not dictated by Congress, the Court has constructed a number of one-line orders, any one of which can be used to dismiss or dispose of the appeal without further briefing or oral argument. A typical order of this nature, used particularly in appeals from state court decisions, reads: "the appeal is dismissed for want of a substantial FEDERAL QUESTION." Such summary orders, which are devoid of explanation of the insubstantiality of the question involved, consistently have been held to be precedents. The Court has said that they must be understood and followed by state and lower federal courts.

In 1978, all nine Justices publicly conceded to the Congress that, while these summary dispositions of appeals are decisions on the merits, experience has shown that they "often are uncertain guides to the courts bound to follow them and not infrequently create more confusion than clarity." The Justices accordingly asked Congress to eliminate virtually all appeals, thereby recognizing formally that the Court's appellate jurisdiction is almost wholly discretionary. Congress has yet to respond.

At the start in 1789 and for a century thereafter, the Court was authorized to exercise only mandatory jurisdiction, either by way of appeal or a closely related process known as WRIT OF ERROR. But as the nation expanded and matured, litigation proliferated. It became evident toward the end of the nineteenth century that the Court could not keep up with its growing docket if it had to continue resolving the merits of every case that was filed. Gradually, Congress began to withdraw some of this mandatory jurisdiction from the Court, replacing it with discretionary jurisdiction by way of certiorari. But it was not until 1925 that Congress decreed a major shift toward discretionary review powers. At that time the dockets of the Court were so clogged with mandatory appeals and writs of error that litigants had to wait two and three years to have their cases decided. In the JUDICIARY ACT OF 1925, written largely at the suggestion of the Court, Congress transferred large segments of appellate jurisdiction from the obligatory to the discretionary category. Fully eighty percent of the

Court's docket thereafter was of the certiorari variety.

But the 1925 transfer proved insufficient. During the 1970s, Congress eliminated many of the remaining appeals that could be taken from lower federal courts, leaving only a handful within the federal sector of Supreme Court jurisdiction. The largest pocket of mandatory appeals left untouched consists of appeals from state court decisions validating state statutes in the face of federal constitutional challenges. The caseload explosions in the 1970s and 1980s, which saw the Court's annual case filings rising near the 5,000 mark, created pressure to eliminate all significant remnants of mandatory appeal jurisdiction.

Nearly one-half of these filed cases are petitions and applications filed by prisoners, petitions that are often frivolous and thus quickly disposed of. But from the overall pool of some 5,000 cases the Justices select about 150 cases each term for plenary review and resolution. The Justices feel that time limitations do not permit them to dispose of many more than 150 important and complex controversies, although they do manage to dispose of another 200 or so cases in a summary fashion, without briefs or oral arguments. In any event, the number of cases granted full review has hovered around the 150 mark for many of the last fifty years. This constancy is largely the product of the discretion and the docket control inherent in the certiorari jurisdiction. Without discretion to deny review to more than ninety-five percent of the certiorari petitions filed each year, the Court's ability to function efficiently would soon cease.

The procedures by which the Court achieves this docket control and makes this vital selection of cases for plenary review are simple but not well understood by the public. And some of the processes change as workloads increase and issues tend to become more difficult of resolution. As of the 1980s, the procedures may be summarized as follows:

By law, the Supreme Court begins its annual TERM, or working session, on the first Monday in October. Known as the October Term, this session officially runs for a full year, eliminating the prior practice of convening special sessions during the summer to hear urgent matters. But for most administrative purposes, each term continues for about nine months, October through June, or until all cases considered ready for disposition have been resolved. At that point, the Court normally recesses without formally adjourning until the following October.

The Court usually disposes of requests for review, hears oral arguments, and issues written opinions only during the nine-month working portion of the term. But the Court never closes for purposes of accepting new cases, as well as briefs and motions in pending cases. That means that filing time requirements are never waived during the summer recess; parties must respect those requirements in all seasons. In most civil cases, certiorari petitions and jurisdictional statements must be filed within ninety days from the entry of judgment, or from the denial of rehearing, in the court below. This filing period is only sixty days in criminal cases, federal or state.

As soon as opposing parties have filed briefs or motions in response to a certiorari petition or jurisdictional statement, these documents are circulated to all nine Justices. These circulations occur on a weekly basis all year round. The circulated cases are then scheduled by the Court's clerk for disposition by the Justices at the next appropriate CONFERENCE. Cases circulated during the summer recess accumulate for consideration at a lengthy conference held just before the opening of the new October term. Cases circulated during term time are considered at a conference held about two weeks after a given weekly circulation.

The massive numbers of case filings make it impossible for every Justice personally to examine these thousands of documents, although some may try. Most are aided in this task by law CLERKS, each Justice being entitled to employ four. The clerks often have the task of reading these documents and reducing them to short memoranda for the convenience of their respective Justices. In recent years, a number of Justices have used a "cert pool" system, whereby law clerk resources in several chambers are pooled to produce memoranda for the joint use of all the participating Justices. But whether a Justice reads all these matters or is assisted by law clerk memoranda, the ultimate discretionary judgments made respecting the grant or denial of review are necessarily those of each Justice. Law clerks simply do not make critical judgments or cast votes.

Law clerks are selected personally by each Justice, a practice dating back to 1882 when Justice HORACE GRAY first employed a top Harvard Law School graduate. In modern times, clerks are invariably selected from among recent law school graduates with superior academic records. And many Justices require that their clerks also have clerked for lower court judges. The clerks normally stay with their Justices for one term only, though some have served longer. Many law clerks have gone on to distinguished legal careers of their own. Three of them have become Supreme Court Justices: Justices BYRON R. WHITE, WILLIAM H. REHNQUIST, and JOHN PAUL STEVENS.

An important element of each Justice's workload is to act in the capacity of Circuit Justice, a vestigial remnant of the earlier circuit-riding tasks. For this purpose, each Justice is assigned one or more federal judicial circuits, which divide the nation into twelve geographical areas. The Justice assigned to a particular circuit handles a variety of preliminary motions and applications in cases originating in the area covered by the circuit. Included are such matters as applications for stays of lower court judgments pending action on a petition for certiorari, applications in criminal cases for bail or release pending such action, and applications to extend the time for filing certiorari or appeal cases. Law clerks frequently assist in processing these applications, and on occasion an application may be disposed of by a written "in chambers" opinion of the Circuit Justice.

The Court no longer discusses every certiorari petition at conference. The excessive number of petitions makes it necessary and appropriate to curtail collegial discussion of petitions at the formal conferences of the Justices. At present, the Chief Justice circulates a "discuss list," a list of cases in a given weekly circulation deemed worthy of discussion and formal voting at conference. All appeals are discussed at conference, but rarely more than thirty percent of the certiorari cases are listed for discussion. Any Justice may add an omitted case to the list, however. Review is then automatically denied to any unlisted case, without conference consideration.

Decisions whether to grant or deny review of cases on the "discuss list" are reached at one of the periodic secret conferences. During term time, conferences are normally held each Friday during the weeks when oral arguments are heard, and on the Friday just before the commencement of each two-week oral argument period. Conferences can be held on other days as well. Only the Justices are present at these conferences; no law clerks or secretaries are permitted to attend.

Conferences are held in a well-appointed room adjacent to the Chief Justice's chambers, which are to the rear of the courtroom. The conference begins with exchanges of handshakes among the Justices, a custom originating in 1888. Coffee is available from a silver urn. The typical conference begins with discussion and disposition of the "discuss list" cases, appeals being considered first. The Chief Justice leads the discussion of each case, followed by each associate Justice in order of seniority. Any formal voting takes place in reverse order of seniority. Then, if there are argued cases to be decided, a similar order of discussion and voting is followed. Argued cases, however, may be discussed at other conferences scheduled immediately after a day or two of oral arguments, thus making the Friday conferences less lengthy.

Using the Rule of Four at these conferences, the Court selects from the pool of "discuss list" cases those that it will review and resolve on the merits, following full briefs and oral argument. A few cases, however, may be granted review and then resolved immediately in a summary manner without briefs or oral argument, by way of a PER CURIAM written opinion. Such summary disposition has been much criticized by those who lose their cases without being fully heard, but the practice has been codified in the Court's rules. The important point is that it is the cases that are selected at these conferences for plenary review that account for the 150 or so cases at the core of the Court's workload each term.

The cases thus selected for full review reflect issues that, in the Justices' view, are of national significance. It is not enough that the issues are important to the parties to the case; they must be generally important. But the Court rarely if ever explains why review is denied, or why the issues were not deemed important enough to warrant plenary attention. There are occasional written explanatory dissents from the denial of review, but these can only express the views of a minority. Review is granted only when four or more Justices are subjectively convinced that there are special and important reasons for reviewing the questions presented, which may or may not involve a conflict among lower courts as to how to resolve such questions. It bears emphasis that the exercise of this kind of discretionary judgment enables the Court to control its docket and to limit the extent of its plenary workload.

When a "discuss list" case is granted review, the petitioning party has forty-five days in which to file a brief on the merits, together with a printed record appendix. The opposing party then has thirty days to file a brief on the merits. Briefs of intervening parties and AMICI CURIAE, if there are any in a given case, are filed during these periods. When all briefs are in, the case is ready to be scheduled for oral argument.

Oral argument before the Justices occurs only on Monday, Tuesday, and Wednesday of a scheduled week of argument, leaving the other weekdays available for work and conferences. Usually, fourteen weeks of oral argument are scheduled, in two-week segments from October through April. One hour of argument is allowed in most cases, one-half hour for each side. Arguments start promptly at 10 A.M. and end at 3 P.M., with a lunch adjournment from noon to 1

P.M. The Justices are well prepared, having read the briefs. Some may also be aided by "bench memos" prepared by their law clerks, memoranda that outline the critical facts and the opposing arguments. Counsel arguing a case may thus expect sharp and penetrating questions from the bench; and counsel are warned by the Court's rules not to read arguments from a prepared text.

Sometime during the week in which a particular case has been argued, the Court meets in secret conference to decide the merits of that case. With the Chief Justice presiding and leading the discussion, the normal pattern of collegial discussion and voting takes place. But the vote reached at conference is necessarily tentative and subject to change as work begins on opinion writing. Shortly after the vote is taken, the case is assigned to one of the Justices to draft an opinion for the Court. The assignment is made by the senior Justice in the majority, if the vote is split. Normally, the assignment is made by the Chief Justice, unless he is in dissent.

The Justice assigned to write an opinion for the Court then begins work on a draft. This is essentially a lonely task. Following the conference discussion, there is little time for further collegial consultation among the Justices in the preparation of an opinion. Depending upon the work patterns of a particular Justice, the law clerks may engage in much of the research and analysis that underlie scholarly opinions; some clerks may be assigned the task of producing drafts of an opinion, while some Justices may do all the drafting themselves. Since 1981, drafting of opinions has been mechanically made easier by the installation of word processors in each Justice's chambers.

Once the draft of the majority opinion has been completed, it is circulated to all other members of the Court. The other Justices may suggest various changes or additions to the draft. To become an opinion of the Court, the draft opinion must attract the adherence and agreement of a majority of five Justices, which sometimes requires the author of the draft to accept modifications suggested by another Justice as the price of the latter's adherence. One or more of the Justices who cannot accept the reasoning or the result of the draft opinion then may produce their own drafts of CONCURRING or DISSENTING OPINIONS. The circulation of these separate opinion drafts may in turn cause the author of the majority draft to make further changes by way of answer to arguments made in a draft concurrence or dissent. Thus nothing is truly final until the collegial exchange of opinions is complete, the votes are set in concrete, and the result is considered ready for public announcement. Even then, there are cases in which the Court cannot reach a majority censensus, resulting in simply an announcement of the judgment of the Court accompanied by a number of PLURALITY, concurring, and dissenting opinions. The difficulty sometimes encountered in reaching a clear-cut majority result, while distressing to the bar and the lower courts, is generally reflective of the difficulty and complexity of some of the momentous issues that reach the Court.

The opinions and judgments of the Court in argued cases are announced publicly in the courtroom. At one time, opinions were uniformly announced on what became known as Opinion Monday. But the Court found that too many opinions announced on a Monday, particularly toward the end of a term, made it difficult for the press to give adequate media coverage to important Court rulings. The Court now announces opinions on any day it sits, thereby spreading out opinion announcements. In weeks in which oral arguments are scheduled for three days, the practice is to announce opinions only on a Tuesday or Wednesday, leaving Monday for the announcement of summary orders. Opinions may still be announced on a Monday, particularly if no oral arguments are scheduled for that day. After all oral arguments have been heard, usually by the end of April, opinions can be announced on any given Monday, when the Court sits to announce summary orders, or on any other day of the week that the Court wishes to sit solely to announce opinions.

The practices regarding the announcement of opinions in open court change from time to time. At one time, many opinions were read by the authors in full or in substantial part. More recently the Justices have tended merely to give short summaries save in the most important cases; in some less important cases only the result is announced. All opinions and orders are made available to the public and the news media a few moments after the courtroom announcements. Eventually, opinions and orders appear in bound volumes known as the United States Reports.

When the Court first convened in February of 1790, one of its first actions was to prescribe qualifications for lawyers wishing to practice before the Court. The original rule, in language very like that of the present rule, established two requirements: the attorney must have been admitted to practice in a state supreme court "for three years past," and the attorney's "private and professional character" must appear to be good.

Nearly 200,000 attorneys have been admitted to

the Supreme Court bar since the Court was established. In recent times, as many as 6,000 have been admitted in a year. Prior to 1970, an attorney could be admitted only on motion of a sponsor in open court, before all the Justices. But the Court found that so much time was taken in listening to these routine motions and admissions and that it was often so expensive for a lawyer to travel to Washington from afar just to engage in this briefest of ceremonies, that an alternative "mail-order" procedure should be made available. Most attorneys today are admitted by mail, although some prefer to follow the earlier practice of being admitted in open court.

The modern Supreme Court bar has no formal structure or leadership. It is largely a heterogeneous collection of individual lawyers located in all parts of the nation. Many members of the bar never practice before the Court, and even fewer ever have the opportunity to argue orally. Most private practitioners who do have occasion to argue orally do so on a "once-in-a-lifetime" basis. Those who appear with some regularity before the Court are usually connected with an organization or governmental group specializing in Supreme Court litigation, such as the office of the SOLICITOR GENERAL of the United States. Gone are the days when private legal giants, such as DANIEL WEBSTER, were repeatedly employed specially by litigants to present oral arguments before the Court.

While a lay litigant may prepare and file petitions and briefs on the litigant's own behalf, without the aid of a member of the bar, the complexities and subtleties of modern practice make such self-help increasingly inadvisable. Only in the rarest of circumstances will the Court permit a lay litigant to present oral argument. Those imprisoned have frequently filed their own petitions for certiorari, seeking some sort of review of their criminal convictions. Indeed, about half of the nearly 5,000 case filings per year can be ascribed to prisoner petitions. The Court catalogues these petitions on its IN FORMA PAUPERIS docket but gives them the same careful treatment it gives petitions filed on behalf of clients who can afford to pay filing and printing costs.

The Court will, on application by an impecunious litigant or prisoner, appoint a member of the Court's bar to prepare briefs on the merits and to present oral arguments, once review has been granted in the case. But the Court will not appoint a lawyer to aid in preparing and filing a petition for certiorari or jurisdictional statement. Legal aid programs operating in most lower courts usually insure that a lawyer appointed or volunteering to represent a prisoner in the lower courts will be available to file such documents in the Supreme Court.

Such are the basic processes and procedures that enable the Court to perform its historic missions. As the Court approaches its third century, the Justices are deeply concerned with the Court's growing workload and the resulting effect upon the quality of its decision making. The Court's internal and external procedures have been streamlined and perfected about as much as possible. Some restructuring of its jurisdiction and functions seems necessary. Yet despite these perceived shortcomings, the Court has managed to maintain its prime role in the evolving history of the American legal system. The Court's effective performance of that role is due in no small part to the procedures and rules established for those who practice before it.

EUGENE GRESSMAN

Bibliography

STERN, ROBERT L.; GRESSMAN, EUGENE; and SHAPIRO, STEPHEN M. 1986 *Supreme Court Practice,* 6th ed. Washington, D.C.: Bureau of National Affairs.

SUSPECT CLASSIFICATION

Long before the term "suspect classification" gained currency, Justice HARLAN FISKE STONE captured the idea in his opinion for the Supreme Court in UNITED STATES V. CAROLENE PRODUCTS CO. (1938). While insisting on RATIONAL BASIS as the appropriate STANDARD OF REVIEW for cases involving ECONOMIC REGULATION, Stone suggested that "prejudice against DISCRETE AND INSULAR MINORITIES [that is, religious, or national, or racial minorities] may be a special condition, which tends seriously to curtail the operation of those political processes ordinarily to be relied upon to protect minorities, and which may call for a correspondingly more searching judicial inquiry." In modern idiom, to call a legislative classification "suspect" is to suggest the possibility that it resulted from prejudice against the group it burdens, a possibility that justifies strict judicial scrutiny to assure that it is necessary to achieve a COMPELLING STATE INTEREST. In practice, most laws subject to this exacting standard are held invalid.

Irony attends the origins of the expression. Justice HUGO L. BLACK, writing for a majority in *Korematsu v. United States* (1944), one of the JAPANESE AMERICAN CASES, found no denial of EQUAL PROTECTION in an EXECUTIVE ORDER excluding American citizens of Japanese ancestry from the West Coast. Along the way to this extraordinary conclusion, however, he said: "all legal restrictions which curtail the civil rights of a single racial group are immediately suspect. That is not to say that all such restrictions are unconstitutional. It is to say that courts must subject them to the most rigid scrutiny." In *Korematsu* itself, the Court did no such thing; it paid the greatest deference to a "military" judgment that was chiefly political and steeped in racial prejudice. Yet *Korematsu*'s main doctrinal legacy was that racial classifications were suspect.

In one view, this two-stage analysis, first identifying a classification as suspect and then subjecting it to STRICT SCRUTINY, is a roundabout way of addressing the issue of illicit legislative motives. (See LEGISLATION; WASHINGTON v. DAVIS, 1976.) Strict scrutiny is required in order to allay the suspicion that a law was designed to disadvantage a minority that lacked effective power in the legislature. That suspicion is laid to rest only by a showing that the law is well designed to achieve a legitimate purpose that has real importance. In another view, a classification based on race should be subjected to strict scrutiny because the immutable characteristic of race lends itself so well to a system thought dominated by stereotype, which automatically consigns a person to a general category, often implying inferiority. This concern for stigmatic harm is part of the substantive core of the equal protection clause, the principle of equal citizenship; the concern retains vitality even in an era when members of racial minorities have become electoral majorities in many of our major cities.

A number of egalitarian decisions in the later years of the WARREN COURT suggested a wide range of classifications that were candidates for inclusion by the Supreme Court in the "suspect" category: alienage, sex, ILLEGITIMACY, age, indigency. In the event, none of these candidates was accepted fully. Some classifications disadvantaging ALIENS were held "suspect," but many were not. The Court did significantly heighten the standard of review for most cases involving claimed denials of SEX DISCRIMINATION and gave some "bite" to the rational basis standard in cases involving illegitimacy. On the whole, however, the Court's behavior since the late 1970s suggests a determination to limit expansion of the list of suspect classifications, and thus to limit the occasions for active judicial supervision of legislation.

Some racial classifications are adopted as remedies for past societal discrimination based on race. Such an AFFIRMATIVE ACTION program presents neither of the principal dangers that have been said to require strict judicial scrutiny of racial classifications. There is less reason to suspect an illicit motive when a majoritarian body such as a legislature discriminates in favor of a historically disadvantaged minority, and the risk of stigmatic harm to a racial group is much reduced. Thus, varying majorities of the Supreme Court have consistently agreed that the appropriate standard of review for such remedial legislation, including RACIAL QUOTAS, is considerably less exacting than the strictest form of strict scrutiny.

The whole "suspect classifications" idea would seem to have outlived its usefulness. Surely the Supreme Court no longer needs the doctrine to justify its highest levels of intensity of judicial review. In race cases, for example, the Court needs no such locution in order to continue imposing on government a "heavy burden of justification" of laws imposing invidious racial discrimination. Abandonment of the rhetoric of suspect classifications would promote candor, by easing the way for open recognition of the sliding scale of standards of review now serving to cloak the Court's interest balancing. It would also remove a barrier, built into the very language of suspect "classifications," to doctrinal growth in the direction of affirmative governmental responsibility to alleviate those inequalities that prevent the realization of the principle of equal citizenship.

KENNETH L. KARST

Bibliography

BREST, PAUL A. 1976 The Supreme Court, 1975 Term—Foreword: In Defense of the Antidiscrimination Principle. *Harvard Law Review* 90:1–54.

ELY, JOHN HART 1980 Democracy and Distrust: A Theory of Judicial Review. Cambridge, Mass.: Harvard University Press.

SUTHERLAND, GEORGE
(1862–1942)

George Sutherland, Supreme Court Justice from 1922 to 1938, was born in England in 1862. A year thereafter, he was brought by his parents to Brigham Young's Utah. Although he himself was never a Mormon, Sutherland attended a Mormon academy; in 1882–1883, he studied at the law school at the University of Michigan. On leaving the university, Sutherland was admitted to the Utah bar. He attained immediate prominence, both professionally and politically. He was elected to the House of Representatives as a Republican in 1900 and to the Senate in 1905, where he remained until 1917.

Sutherland's tenure in Congress forced him to confront issues in a political context that he would later deal with as a Supreme Court Justice. Generally he supported a conservative position. Yet his most enduring legislative achievements centered on improving conditions for seamen; advancing a federal WORKER'S COMPENSATION program; and promoting woman suffrage. Sutherland's congressional tenure enabled him as early as 1910 to establish his credentials for appointment to the Supreme Court. The 1920 election of Warren Harding, attributed in considerable part to Sutherland in his role of principal confidential adviser to the candidate, virtually assured him the nomination. The nomination was sent to an approving Senate on September 5, 1922.

Anyone interested in the new Justice's approach to legal and political problems had not far to look. In the five years since his retirement from the Senate, Sutherland had delivered major addresses setting forth his conservative philosophy. In his presidential address to the American Bar Association in 1917, he chose to speak on "Private Rights and Government Control." The message was clear. "Prying Commissions" and "governmental intermeddling" were unnecessary and at war with the "fundamental principle upon which our form of government depends, namely, that it is an empire of laws and not of men." Four years later Sutherland was telling the New York State Bar Association "that government should confine its activities, as a general rule, to preserving a free market and preventing fraud." He further explained that "fundamental social and economic laws" were beyond the "power of official control."

Once on the Court, Sutherland readily joined his conservative colleagues invoking SUBSTANTIVE DUE PROCESS to strike down exertions of governmental power. His first major opinion, in ADKINS V. CHILDREN'S HOSPITAL (1923), was directed at the minimum wage. Here, in the area of FREEDOM OF CONTRACT, no presumptive validity could be accorded to the exercise of legislative power. Rather, its legitimacy could be established only by "exceptional circumstances" and certainly not by considerations of a worker's needs or bargaining power. In short order, state attempts to regulate prices of gasoline, theater tickets, and employment agency services were similarly condemned. Other forms of state regulation fared no better. Nor was substantive due process the sole doctrinal reliance. In the Court's continuing battle with state legislatures, Sutherland led his colleagues in discovering hitherto unrealized prohibitions in the EQUAL PROTECTION, COMMERCE, and CONTRACT CLAUSES. And, under his hand, the PRIVILEGES AND IMMUNITIES clause of the FOURTEENTH AMENDMENT, neglected and forgotten for decades, sprang to life as a restraint on state power in COLGATE V. HARVEY (1935).

Eventually, of course, the Court repudiated the Sutherland approach to state legislative power and little of it remains. Yet, in at least two respects, his contribution in this area is of continuing significance. The first has to do with his seminal opinion in *Frost and Frost Trucking v. Railroad Commission* (1926) where he elaborated the theory of unconstitutional conditions. This theory destroyed the notion that a state's power to withhold a privilege somehow gives it authority to discriminate without check in granting the privilege. The second is his opinion for a divided court in EUCLID V. AMBLER REALTY (1926) which furnishes the constitutional foundation for the modern law of ZONING.

When Sutherland came to deal with the actions of Congress and the President, he exhibited the same jealousy of authority that characterized his response to state legislatures. Accordingly, he remained to the end unconvinced of the constitutionality of many of the New Deal enactments and in time was overwhelmed by the arrival of our modern-day Constitution of "powers." Even so, Sutherland's lasting impact will be found on close examination to have been highly significant. Particularly, he made highly personalized contributions to our *structural* Constitution; he had a distinctive role in shaping the Constitution as a guarantor of CIVIL RIGHTS; and he, more than anyone else, supplied the intellectual underpinnings for the FOREIGN AFFAIRS power.

As for the structural Constitution, Sutherland's opinion in *Massachusetts v. Mellon* (1923), and its companion case of FROTHINGHAM V. MELLON (1923), is still, despite scores of intervening qualifying decisions, the basic starting point in determining when a federal "taxpayer" has STANDING to raise a constitutional question in actions in the federal courts. Here plainly is one of the most telling limitations on federal judicial power. In a number of cases, Sutherland wrote opinions enforcing restraint on Supreme Court review of state decisions that were found to rest on independent and ADEQUATE STATE GROUNDS. In still others, he resisted effectively the pleas of reformers to whittle down guarantees of the right to TRIAL BY JURY, in civil as well as criminal cases. And in the highly technical matter of the relationship between state and federal courts, Sutherland's influence continues. Finally, Sutherland's views have been decisive in regard to the President's power to remove federal office holders. Early in his judicial career he concurred in Chief

Justice WILLIAM HOWARD TAFT's unnecessarily wide-ranging opinion in MYERS V. UNITED STATES (1926), sanctioning a presidential power to remove without restraint. In HUMPHREY'S EXECUTOR V. UNITED STATES (1935) he started the Court on the way to new DOCTRINE. The removal power must take account of the nature of the office involved.

Sutherland's tenure on the Court spanned the years in which the Court began to take the BILL OF RIGHTS seriously as a check on STATE ACTION. His role in this development was not all of one piece. But he did write a leading opinion, in GROSJEAN V. AMERICAN PRESS COMPANY (1936), condemning a state tax on the press because of the levy's impermissible *motive* to make costly the criticism of public officials. And in POWELL V. ALABAMA (1932), he charted for the Court the first steps a state must take to assure counsel in legal proceedings. His problem there was counsel in a capital case. But Sutherland's opinion was not so confined in its implications and has proved influential even beyond the bounds of the criminal law.

Long before he went on the Court, Sutherland was given to speculation about the foreign relations powers, producing in 1919 a book on the subject, *Constitutional Power and World Affairs.* In his book and elsewhere, Sutherland developed the theory that the powers of the United States in respect to foreign affairs were largely unrelated to any grant from the states and existed as an incident of SOVEREIGNTY devolved directly on the United States from Great Britain. Their employment and their distribution were to be governed by rules not applicable to the specific delegations of the Constitution. In 1936, in CURTISS-WRIGHT EXPORT CORP. V. UNITED STATES, Sutherland was able to incorporate these views in an opinion for a unanimous Court.

Sutherland retired from the Court in 1938. He died in 1942.

FRANCIS PASCHAL

Bibliography

PASCHAL, JOEL FRANCIS 1951 *Mr. Justice Sutherland: A Man against the State.* Princeton, N.J.: Princeton University Press.

SWAIN v. ALABAMA
380 U.S. 202 (1965)

A 6–3 Court, speaking through Justice BYRON R. WHITE, rejected the claim of a black defendant to proportional representation of his race on grand and petit juries. Although blacks were substantially underrepresented on the jury panel, and although the prosecutor had used his peremptory challenges to exclude blacks in this case (there had been eight blacks on the venire), the Court found no evidence on the record of purposeful discrimination. The Court hinted that systematic use of peremptory challenges to exclude blacks from all juries would be unconstitutional, but it said that the record in *Swain* failed to show such systematic discrimination. In *Batson v. Kentucky* (1986) the Court partially overruled *Swain,* holding that a prosecutor cannot constitutionally use peremptory challenges to exclude potential jurors solely on account of their race.

DENNIS J. MAHONEY

(SEE ALSO: *Jury Discrimination.*)

SWANN v. CHARLOTTE-MECKLENBURG BOARD OF EDUCATION
402 U.S. 1 (1971)

Three years before *Swann* was decided, the Supreme Court had established a school board's affirmative duty to dismantle a school system that had been racially segregated by the command of law or by the board's deliberate actions. (See GREEN V. COUNTY SCHOOL BOARD, 1968.) In *Swann,* the Court was asked to apply this standard to a large metropolitan school district including the city of Charlotte, North Carolina, and its surrounding county. President RICHARD M. NIXON had made two appointments to the Court in the intervening years, and some observers expected the Justices' previous unanimity in school DESEGREGATION cases to be shattered in this case. In the event, no such thing happened; a unanimous Court affirmed a sweeping order by the federal district judge, James B. McMillan, calling for districtwide busing of children for the purpose of improving the schools' RACIAL BALANCE. (After issuing this order, Judge McMillan received death threats and was given police protection.) The *Swann* opinion was signed by Chief Justice WARREN E. BURGER. However, internal evidence strongly suggests that the opinion was a negotiated patchwork of drafts, and investigative journalists have asserted plausibly that Justice POTTER STEWART contributed its main substantive points.

Once a constitutional violation was found, the Court said, the school board had an obligation to take steps to remedy both present de jure segregation (see DE FACTO/DE JURE) and the present effects of past de jure segregation. These steps must achieve "the greatest possible degree of actual desegregation, taking into account the practicalities of the situation." The Court thus approved Judge McMillan's use of districtwide racial percentages as "a starting point" in shaping a remedy and placed on the school board the very difficult burden of showing that the continued existence of one-race schools was not the result of present or past de jure segregation. Finally, the Court approved the busing of children to schools not in their own neighborhoods as one permissible remedy within a court's discretion. The matter of busing, however, was not left to lower court discretion. In a COMPANION CASE from Mobile, Alabama, *Davis v. Board of School Commissioners,* the Court *required* busing the lower courts had not ordered.

Swann set the pattern for school desegregation litigation not only in southern cities but in the North and West as well. Once a court finds deliberate acts of segregation, *Swann's* affirmative duties arise.

KENNETH L. KARST

(SEE ALSO: *Keyes v. School District No. 1, 1973; Columbus Board of Education v. Penick, 1979; School Busing.*)

Bibliography

FISS, OWEN M. 1974 School Desegregation: The Uncertain Path of the Law. *Philosophy & Public Affairs* 4:3–39.

WOODWARD, BOB and ARMSTRONG, SCOTT 1979 *The Brethren: Inside the Supreme Court.* Pages 96–112. New York: Simon & Schuster.

SWAYNE, NOAH H. (1804–1884)

Noah Haynes Swayne was the first of President ABRAHAM LINCOLN's five Supreme Court appointees. Geography, antislavery credentials, and support for the Union constituted Lincoln's chief criteria when he made his first appointments to the Court. Swayne fulfilled these qualifications.

Because of his hostility to slavery, Swayne left his native Virginia and in 1823 moved to Ohio, where he served in the state legislature. In 1830 President ANDREW JACKSON named him United States Attorney. During the next several decades, he continued his active political career, and he appeared as counsel in a number of FUGITIVE SLAVERY cases. In 1855, he joined the fledgling Republican party and became a leading figure in the Ohio group. His close friend, Justice JOHN MCLEAN, had suggested Swayne as his successor. When McLean died early in 1861, Swayne quickly marshaled support from leading Ohio Republicans; Lincoln appointed him in January 1862.

On the Supreme Court, Swayne enthusiastically supported the administration, approving of Lincoln's blockade of southern ports in the PRIZE CASES (1862), upholding the Legal Tender Act of 1862 in *Roosevelt v. Meyer* (1863), and sustaining military trials in EX PARTE VALLANDIGHAM (1864). After the war, in EX PARTE MILLIGAN (1866), he joined the Court's minority faction which declined to discuss the question of congressionally authorized military tribunals.

During Reconstruction, Swayne again demonstrated consistent support for the congressional Republican program. For example, he dissented in the TEST OATH CASES (1867), and he voted to decline JURISDICTION in the unreported case of *Mississippi v. Stanton* (1868), when the Court divided evenly on whether to take another case that might have decided the fate of the Reconstruction program. Perhaps Swayne's clearest deference to congressional determination of Reconstruction was expressed in his dissent in TEXAS V. WHITE (1869). He rejected the majority fiction that Texas was not out of the Union and insisted that Texas's relationship to the Union must be determined by Congress. Swayne recognized that the FOURTEENTH AMENDMENT had been designed in part to benefit the freedmen, as evidenced by his vote in STRAUDER V. WEST VIRGINIA (1880), striking down RACIAL DISCRIMINATION in jury selection. Yet he repeatedly supported the Court's narrow construction of the FIFTEENTH AMENDMENT, thus limiting black VOTING RIGHTS.

After the Civil War, Swayne continued to back Republican programs. He dissented when the majority struck down the legal tender laws in 1870, but the next year he joined the new majority that reversed that decision. (See LEGAL TENDER CASES.) A decade later, just before his retirement, Swayne delivered the Court's opinion in SPRINGER V. UNITED STATES (1881) upholding the Civil War income tax. He impressively rejected arguments that the tax confiscated property without DUE PROCESS OF LAW and that it was a DIRECT TAX, and therefore need not be apportioned among the states according to population. That decision subsequently was temporarily overruled in POLLOCK V. FARMER'S LOAN AND TRUST (1895), but Swayne's opinion generally is regarded as the more historically valid.

In its time, Swayne's opinion in GELPCKE V. CITY OF DUBUQUE (1864) had enormous influence. Speaking for the Court, Swayne held that a state court could invalidate a lawfully controlled municipal bonding arrangement. The decision left countless municipalities responsible for maintaining railroad financing, despite popular protests against the practice as well as deceitful activities on the part of the railroads. Later, Swayne joined JOSEPH P. BRADLEY, STEPHEN J. FIELD, and SALMON P. CHASE in dissent in the SLAUGHTERHOUSE CASES (1873). Swayne's dissent lacked the elaborate rhetoric and logic of the Bradley and Field dissents, but he invoked the same mystical faith in the sanctity of property.

Swayne ranks as an ordinary Justice, not greatly appreciated even in his own time. His colleagues disapproved of his aggressive campaigning for the Chief Justiceship in 1864 and 1873, and he remained on the bench long after his physical and mental capacities had noticeably declined. He wrote few major opinions in his two decades on the bench.

STANLEY I. KUTLER

Bibliography

FAIRMAN, CHARLES 1939 *Mr. Justice Miller and the Supreme Court, 1862–1890.* Cambridge, Mass.: Harvard University Press.

GILLETTE, WILLIAM 1969 Noah H. Swayne. In Leon Friedman and Fred L. Israel, eds., *The Justices of the Supreme Court,* Vol. 2:789–1010. New York: Chelsea House.

SWEATT v. PAINTER
339 U.S. 629 (1950)
MCLAURIN v. OKLAHOMA STATE REGENTS
339 U.S. 637 (1950)

Texas had established a separate law school for blacks; the state university law school thus rejected Sweatt, a black applicant. In *McLaurin,* the state university admitted a black to graduate study in education but made him sit in segregated classroom alcoves and at separate tables in the library and cafeteria. In both cases, state courts upheld the challenged SEGREGATION. In *Sweatt* the NAACP recruited some law professors to file a brief AMICUS CURIAE urging the Supreme Court to abandon the SEPARATE BUT EQUAL DOCTRINE and hold that state-sponsored segregation was unconstitutional. Eleven states supported the Texas position.

The Court unanimously held the practices of segregation in these cases unconstitutional, but it did not reach the broader issue. Chief Justice FRED M. VINSON wrote both opinions. In *Sweatt* he emphasized the intangibles of legal education: faculty reputation, influential alumni, traditions, prestige, and—most significant for the doctrinal future—a student body including members of a race that would produce an overwhelming majority of the judges, lawyers, witnesses, and jury members Sweatt might face. Assuming the continued vitality of "separate but equal," the new law school for blacks was not equal to the state university law school, and Sweatt must be admitted to the latter.

The *McLaurin* opinion, too, avoided direct attack on the separate-but-equal principle, but it sapped that principle's foundations: segregation impaired McLaurin's ability to study and learn, to discuss questions with other students and be accepted by them on his merits; thus the state must lift its restrictions on him.

In neither case did the Court discuss segregation's stigmatizing effects. In neither did the Court consider any asserted justifications for segregation. The only question was whether segregation produced significant inequality; affirmative answers to that question ended the Court's inquiries. Taken seriously, these decisions must lead—as they did, four years later—to the conclusion that racial segregation in public education is unconstitutional. (See BROWN V. BOARD OF EDUCATION, 1954.)

KENNETH L. KARST

SWEEZY v. NEW HAMPSHIRE

See: *Watkins v. United States*

SWIFT v. TYSON
41 U.S. (16 Peters) 1 (1842)

In *Swift v. Tyson* the Supreme Court gave to the Rules of Decision Act (JUDICIARY ACT OF 1789, section 34) a construction that was to stand until ERIE RAILROAD CO. V. TOMPKINS (1938), almost a century later. As a result of this construction, the federal courts came to exercise COMMON LAW authority over a wide variety of disputes, some of which involved matters outside the limits of federal legislative power. Because these federal court decisions did not purport to bind state courts, the result was often the parallel existence of two different rules of law applicable to the same controversy.

Proceeding on the basis of diversity of citizenship (see DIVERSITY JURISDICTION), Swift sued Tyson in a New York federal court on a bill of exchange. A critical question in the case was whether, in light of the particular facts, Swift was a "purchaser for value" of that bill. The Supreme Court, in an opinion by Justice JOSEPH STORY, held that he was, resolving the question on the basis of "general principles and doctrines of commercial jurisprudence," not on the basis of the decisional law of New York.

Tyson had argued that although there was no relevant state statute, the decisions of the New York state courts were controlling because the Rules of Decision Act provided that the "laws of the several states . . . shall be regarded as rules of decision . . . in cases where they apply." This provision, the Court replied, was limited in application to "the positive statutes of the state, and the construction thereof by the local tribunals, and to rights and titles to things having a permanent locality." It did not require adherence to state judicial decisions on such matters as "questions of general commercial law, where the state tribunals are called upon to perform the like functions as ourselves, that is, to ascertain, upon general reasoning and legal analogies . . . what is the just rule furnished by the principles of commercial law to govern the case."

Historians disagree on the justification and soundness of the *Swift* decision. But there is general agreement that in the years that followed, *Swift* was expanded well beyond its originally intended scope, and that its OVERRULING, in *Erie,* reflected a very different perception of the proper role of the federal courts.

DAVID L. SHAPIRO

(SEE ALSO: *Federal Common Law, Civil.*)

SWIFT & COMPANY v. UNITED STATES
196 U.S. 375 (1905)

Justice OLIVER WENDELL HOLMES's opinion for a unanimous Supreme Court in *Swift* announced the STREAM OF COMMERCE doctrine, fundamental to constitutional COMMERCE CLAUSE adjudication ever since.

In 1902 Attorney General PHILANDER C. KNOX ordered that an EQUITY complaint be filed against the Beef Trust, the five largest meat-packing concerns in the country. The complaint alleged conspiracy and combination in restraint of interstate trade, suppression of competition, and price-fixing, all in violation of the SHERMAN ANTITRUST ACT. In 1903 federal district court judge PETER S. GROSSCUP issued a perpetual INJUNCTION against the packers. On appeal to the Supreme Court, the packers, though admitting the truth of the government allegations, contended that they were not involved in INTERSTATE COMMERCE. The entire transaction between the packers and those who purchased meat from them had occurred completely within the state where the packers slaughtered and prepared their meat. The sale had been consumated in-state and thus only INTRASTATE COMMERCE was involved. Knox's successor, WILLIAM H. MOODY, asserted that the restraint of trade directly affected interstate commerce even if no interstate acts were involved. Armed with the packers' admissions, Moody stressed the unity of the transactions, arguing that the operation had to be viewed as a whole.

The Court accepted Moody's view. The trust's "EFFECT UPON COMMERCE is not accidental, secondary, remote, or merely probable," Holmes declared, as he revised the Court's view of interstate commerce, affecting decisions for decades to come: "Commerce among the states is not a technical legal conception, but a practical one, drawn from the course of the business." Livestock moving from the range to the retailer, "with the only interruption necessary to find a purchaser at the stock yards," created "a current of commerce among the states, and the purchase of cattle is a part and incident of such commerce." Thus a local activity might be seen as part of interstate commerce. This stream of commerce doctrine fundamentally redirected the Court's examination of commerce clause questions and brought the Court face-to-face with economic reality, modifying the doctrinal effect of UNITED STATES v. E. C. KNIGHT COMPANY (1895).

DAVID GORDON

Bibliography

GORDON, DAVID 1983 The Beef Trust: Antitrust Law and the Meat Packing Industry, 1902–1922. Ph.D. diss., Claremont Graduate School.

SWISHER, CARL BRENT
(1897–1968)

Carl Brent Swisher taught constitutional history for many years at Johns Hopkins University. A pioneer in the field of judicial biography, Swisher published *Stephen J. Field: Craftsman of the Law* (1930), still highly regarded. His *Roger B. Taney* (1935), the leading biography, and his posthumously published *The Taney Period, 1836–1864* (1974; Vol. 5, Holmes Devise History of the Supreme Court) describe Taney's accomplishments as Chief Justice as well as his failures of judgment and proslavery bias, thereby rescuing Taney from the limbo to which most historians had consigned him in the wake of DRED SCOTT V. SANDFORD (1857). Swisher also published several general studies of constitutional law and the Supreme Court, including *American Constitutional Development* (1943; rev. ed. with E. M. Sait, 1954) and *The Supreme Court in Modern Role* (1958; rev. ed., 1965). In the most influential of these works, *The Growth of Constitutional Power in the United States* (1946; rev. ed., 1963), Swisher questioned the continuing usefulness of the doctrine of SEPARATION OF POWERS, fearing that it prevented government from achieving the ends which society increasingly expected government to achieve; he also urged government supervision of large corporations to check their political and economic power.

RICHARD B. BERNSTEIN

SYMBOLIC SPEECH

Does communication by conduct rather than by words constitute "speech" within the FIRST AMENDMENT's guarantee of FREEDOM OF SPEECH? The status of communicative conduct, as with most free speech questions, is usually presented in an emotion-laden context: does the burning of a flag, or of a draft card, constitute a First-Amendment-protected activity? Is the act of marching in a public DEMONSTRATION (as distinguished from the placards which the marchers carry) a form of protected "speech?" Are school or other governmental regulations of hair styles an abridgment of freedom of speech? Does nude dancing constitute a form of First Amendment "speech?" Although the lower federal and state courts frequently have wrestled with all of these questions, the United States Supreme Court has yet to articulate a theoretical base that explains the status of symbolic speech under the First Amendment.

At least since STROMBERG V. CALIFORNIA (1931), the Supreme Court has assumed that "speech" within the meaning of the First Amendment's guarantee of "freedom of speech" includes more than merely verbal communications. In *Stromberg* the Court declared invalid a California statute that prohibited the public display of "any flag, badge, banner or device . . . as a sign, symbol or emblem of opposition to organized government." Among other decisions applying the First Amendment to nonverbal conduct, perhaps the most striking was TINKER V. DES MOINES INDEPENDENT COMMUNITY SCHOOL DISTRICT (1969). The Court there upheld the right of high school students to wear black armbands as a protest against American participation in the VIETNAM WAR, calling their conduct "the type of symbolic act that is within the Free Speech Clause of the First Amendment."

But if conduct sometimes constitutes protected "speech," sometimes it does not. UNITED STATES V. O'BRIEN (1968) affirmed a conviction for draft card burning. Chief Justice EARL WARREN, speaking for the Court, answered the defendant's symbolic speech defense by opining, "We cannot accept the view that an apparently limitless variety of conduct can be labeled 'speech' whenever the person engaging in the conduct intends thereby to express an idea."

Any attempt to disentangle "speech" from conduct that is itself communicative will not withstand analysis. The speech element in symbolic speech is entitled to no lesser (and also no greater) degree of protection than that accorded to so-called pure speech. Indeed, in one sense all speech is symbolic. At this moment the reader is observing black markings on paper which curl and point in various directions. We call such markings letters, and in groups they are referred to as words. What is being said in this sentence is meaningful only because the reader recognizes these markings as symbols for particular ideas. The same is true of oral speech which is simply the use of symbolic sounds. Outside the science fiction realm of mind-to-mind telepathic communication, all communications necessarily involve the use of symbols.

But because all expression necessarily requires the use of symbols, it does not necessarily follow as a matter of logic that First Amendment protection is or should be available for all symbolic expressions. The "speech" protected by the First Amendment might be limited to expressions in which the symbols employed consist of conventional words. The Supreme Court has found so restrictive a reading of the First Amendment to be unacceptable. Significantly, in First Amendment cases, the Court often refers to "freedom of expression" as the equivalent of freedom of speech. Justice OLIVER WENDELL HOLMES's "free trade in ideas" may not be reduced to mere trade in words. It is the freedom to express ideas and feelings, not merely the freedom to engage in verbal locutions, that must be protected if the First Amendment's central values are to be realized.

In COHEN V. CALIFORNIA (1971) the Supreme Court held that the emotive form of speech is as entitled to First Amendment protection as is its cognitive content. Emotive expression can be fully as important as intellectual, or cognitive, content in the competition of ideas for acceptance in the marketplace. Of course, most communications encompass both cognitive and emotive content. But even if a communication is substantially devoid of all cognitive content, its emotive content surely lies within the First Amendment scope. Symphonic compositions or nonrepresentational art are protected against governmental censorship, notwithstanding their lack of verbal or cognitive content.

Of course, not all conduct should be regarded as "speech" within the meaning of the First Amendment. Not even the most ardent free speech advocate would contend that all legislation regulating human conduct is subject to First Amendment restrictions. If, as the Court stated in the *O'Brien* opinion, the First Amendment is not to apply to a "limitless variety of conduct," what standards should be applied in determining whether given restrictions on conduct constitute First Amendment abridgment of symbolic speech?

If government's purpose in restricting is to suppress the message conveyed by the conduct, then the state should not be heard to deny the actor's claim that the conduct in question was intended to communicate a message. Such a message-restricting motivation by the state should also establish that the conduct in question constitutes symbolic speech. But such a conclusion does not necessarily imply that the speech is entitled to First Amendment protection. Even speech in words may in some circumstances be subordinated to a counter-speech interest. Likewise, no First Amendment ABSOLUTISM will protect communicative conduct. In some contexts symbolic speech may be overbalanced by counter-speech interests. If, however, the asserted or actual counter-speech interest is simply commitment to a particular view of the world—political, ethical, aesthetic, or otherwise—this interest will not justify abridgment of the right to express a contrary view, either by words or by conduct.

Just as First Amendment principles apply equally to expression in the symbols of the English or French languages, for example, the same principles govern when the symbols are of neither of these languages, nor of any conventional language. The crucial question under the First Amendment is whether meaningful symbols are being employed by one who wishes to communicate to others.

The courts have resisted equating symbolic speech with verbal speech because of a fear of immunizing all manner of conduct from the controls of the law. This fear is unjustifiable; it stems from a false premise as to the First Amendment protection accorded to verbal speech. In fact, speech in words is not immune from regulation. For example, an interest in excluding trespassers will justify abridging the verbal speech of those who wish to speak on property from which they may properly be excluded. Similarly, words that presage an imminent and likely BREACH OF THE PEACE will justify regulation just as much as if the idea be conveyed by nonverbal symbols. These are but two of many instances when verbal speech is subordinated to counter-speech interests.

According full and equal status to symbolic speech under the First Amendment will not open the floodgates to abuses, immunizing *O'Brien's* "apparently limitless variety of conduct" from legal regulation. Recognition of such equality of forms of expression would mean that no one will be penalized because he chooses to communicate—or is able to communicate—only in a language other than conventional words. We shall all be the richer for such recognition.

MELVILLE B. NIMMER

Bibliography

NIMMER, MELVILLE B. 1973 The Meaning of Symbolic Speech to the First Amendment. *UCLA Law Review* 21:29–62.

T

TAFT, ROBERT A. (1889–1953)

Senator Robert Alphonso Taft, the son of President and Chief Justice WILLIAM HOWARD TAFT, was a leader of Republican opposition to the New Deal policies of FRANKLIN D. ROOSEVELT. A graduate of Yale University and Harvard Law School, Taft served in the Ohio legislature from 1921 to 1933. His public crusade against the Roosevelt revolution began in 1935; in 1938 he was elected to the United States Senate, sworn to do battle against "the mistaken belief that government can remove all poverty, redistribute all wealth, and bestow happiness on every citizen."

An advocate of STRICT CONSTRUCTION of constitutional provisions that confer power on government, Taft severely criticized Roosevelt's appointees to the Supreme Court for acting as if "constitutional principles are weak as water" by abdicating their duty to keep the government within the limits set by the Constitution. He strongly urged that Congress become the locus of responsible CONSTITUTIONALISM, and he opposed, both in peacetime and wartime, DELEGATIONS OF POWER to the executive branch.

Taft continued to oppose expansion of the executive power after HARRY S. TRUMAN became President. During the STEEL SEIZURE CONTROVERSY Taft argued that if the President could increase his own powers by simply declaring a national emergency the Constitution would become a dead letter. Taft used his position as chairman of the Senate Labor Committee to sponsor a comprehensive reform of federal labor law, now known as the TAFT-HARTLEY ACT.

After a decade and a half of being "Mr. Republican," Taft felt entitled to his party's presidential nomination in 1952. However, the nomination, and election to the presidency, went to General DWIGHT D. EISENHOWER, hero of World War II. Nevertheless, Taft had a major share in formulating the domestic policy of the new administration during its first year in office.

DENNIS J. MAHONEY

Bibliography

KIRK, RUSSEL and MCCLELLAN, JAMES 1967 *The Political Principles of Robert A. Taft.* New York: Fleet Press Corporation.

TAFT, WILLIAM HOWARD (1857–1930)

William Howard Taft's life was amazing both for length of public service (1881–1930) and for the variety of his activities: prosecuting attorney in his native state of Ohio, superior court judge in Cincinnati, SOLICITOR GENERAL of the United States, federal circuit court judge, governor general of the Philippine Islands, cabinet member, President of the United States (1908–1912), professor of law at Yale, and Chief Justice of the United States (1921–1930).

Taft appeared to be almost the prototype of a Chief Justice. Large of frame and good-natured, weighing well over 350 pounds, he filled out the popular image. His gallantry was famous. "I heard recently," Justice DAVID J. BREWER reported, "that he arose in a street car and gave his seat to three women."

Taft idolized Chief Justice JOHN MARSHALL. One day, passing by the west entrance to the Capitol, he paused in front of the bronze statue of Marshall. "Would you rather have been Marshall than President?" a friend asked. "Of course," Taft answered, "I would rather have been Marshall than any other American unless it had been Washington, and I am inclined to think I would rather have been Marshall than Washington. He made this country." Taft himself became the only man in history to occupy both the White House and the Supreme Court's center chair.

During Roosevelt's administration Taft rejected two opportunities to join the Supreme Court as associate justice. As successor to Roosevelt in the White House, Taft thought longingly about the future and pined to succeed aging Chief Justice MELVILLE W. FULLER. "If the Chief Justice would only retire," Taft lamented, "how simple everything would become!"

As President Taft signed Associate Justice EDWARD D. WHITE's commission as Chief Justice, he grieved: "There is nothing I would have liked more than being Chief Justice of the United States. I can't help seeing the irony in the fact that I, who desired that office so much, should now be signing the commission of another man." Rating Supreme Court appointments as among his most important presidential functions, Taft had the opportunity to appoint five associate Justices as well as the Chief—WILLIS VAN DEVANTER, HORACE H. LURTON, JOSEPH R. LAMAR, CHARLES EVANS HUGHES, and MAHLON PITNEY. Each appointment was a continuing source of pride to Taft, who at every opportunity underscored the importance of the judiciary.

Taft's cordial relations with Roosevelt did not last. Differences developed during Taft's presidency over questions of policy and administration. Finally the clash led to a split in the Republican Party. As a result, when Taft ran for reelection in 1912 Roosevelt ran as a Progressive. The upshot was a Democratic victory and the election of WOODROW WILSON as President.

After Justice Lamar died, rumor began to spread that the new President might, rising above party politics, follow the example of his predecessor's high-mindedness when in 1910 Taft had selected as Chief Justice a southern Democrat and Roman Catholic, Associate Justice Edward D. White. But Wilson appointed LOUIS D. BRANDEIS instead, and Taft, outraged by that appointment, declared that Brandeis was "not a fit person to be a member of the Court."

In 1919, Taft was off the public payroll for the first time. Soon he took a position at Yale, teaching constitutional law. Meanwhile, the chief justiceship seemed a remote possibility. Prospects brightened in 1920 with the smashing Republican victory of WARREN G. HARDING. Shortly after Harding's election the unblushing aspirant made the pilgrimage to Marion, Ohio. Taft was "nearly struck dumb" when the President-elect broached a Supreme Court appointment. Of course, the former President was available, but he made it clear that, having appointed three of the present bench and three others and, having vigorously opposed Brandeis's appointment in 1916, he would accept only the chief justiceship.

Taft's opportunity to achieve his ambition was not altogether accidental. During his presidency, when Chief Justice Fuller died, two choices loomed as possibilities—CHARLES EVANS HUGHES and Edward D. White. The latter, seventeen years Hughes's senior, received the nod. Had Taft chosen Hughes, instead of White, his lifelong ambition would not have been realized.

The office of Chief Justice carries scant inherent power. He manages the docket, presents the cases in conference, and guides discussion. When in the majority, he assigns the writing of opinions. In 1921 Taft remarked: "The Chief Justice goes into a monastery." Yet it is difficult to think of a Chief Justice who more frequently violated the American Bar Association's canons of judicial propriety on so many fronts. During the presidency of CALVIN COOLIDGE he was often a White House visitor. His political activities ranged widely over legislation and judicial appointments at all levels. In his choice of judges his alleged purpose was competence. But Taft even opposed selection of the eminent New York Judge BENJAMIN N. CARDOZO, fearful lest he "herd with [OLIVER WENDELL] HOLMES and Brandeis." At the outset, he had kind words for HARLAN F. STONE, indeed claimed credit for his appointment to the Court. But when Stone began to join Holmes and Brandeis, the Chief Justice became increasingly critical.

As institutional architect, Taft ranks second only to OLIVER ELLSWORTH, the third Chief Justice, who originally devised the judicial system. Taft's best known extrajudicial achievement, "The Judges' Bill" of 1925, giving the Supreme Court control over its docket, passed with only token opposition. Soon Congress authorized other procedural changes Taft had long advocated. To achieve these reforms Taft lobbied Presidents and members of Congress and sought press support. The most striking example of his effectiveness as a lobbyist was his campaign for the marble palace in which the Court now sits. At the cornerstone ceremony, in October 1932, Chief Justice Hughes declared: "For this enterprise progressing to completion we are indebted to the late Chief Justice William Howard Taft more than anyone else. The building is the result of his intelligent persistence."

Taft's goals as Chief Justice were efficiency, prompt dispatch of the Court's business, and harmonious relations among his colleagues. His overwhelming desire was to "mass" the Court. For the ex-President, Brandeis's appointment had been "one of the deepest wounds that I have had as an American and a lover of the constitution and a believer in progressive conservatism." Naturally Taft anticipated strained relations with his new colleague. To smooth this possible difficulty he wrote Brandeis long letters on the desirability of taking prompt steps to make the Court more efficient. Such friendly appeals moved his brother Horace to predict: "I expect to see you and Brandeis hobnobbing together with the utmost good will." Taft's strategy worked. Soon he was able to write: "I've come to like Brandeis very much." The feeling was mutual. Brandeis thought of Taft as "a cultivated man" and enjoyed talking with him. The Chief Justice's brother thought Brandeis "had been taken into camp." Justice JOHN H. CLARKE resigned because he believed that Brandeis could no longer be counted on to uphold the liberal stance.

"Things go happily in the CONFERENCE room with Taft," Brandeis commented. "The judges go home less tired emotionally and less weary physically than in White's day. When we differ, we agree to differ without any ill feelings." It seems likely that certain of Brandeis's unpublished opinions reflect his high regard for the Chief Justice. In one decision in particular, the second child labor case, BAILEY V. DREXEL FURNITURE CO. (1922), Taft writing for the Court invoked the authority of HAMMER V. DAGENHART (1918), a singularly conservative ruling. Yet, Brandeis went along with the majority, explaining: "I can't always dissent. I sometimes endorse an opinion with which I do not agree. I acquiesce." Brandeis's silence may have been the measure of Taft's gift for leadership.

In ALEXANDER BICKEL's volume, *The Unpublished Opinions of Mr. Justice Brandeis* (1957), eight out of eleven were prepared during less than ten years of Taft's chief justiceship. Taft went to great pains to create esprit de corps. Seemingly trivial personal considerations—the sending of a salmon to Justice WILLIS VAN DEVANTER, the customary ride he gave Holmes and Brandeis after the Saturday conference, the Christmas card that always went out to Justice JOSEPH MCKENNA—all such thoughtful attention to highly dissimilar human beings contributed immeasurably to judicial teamwork.

Justice Van Devanter posed a unique problem. He was indispensable in conference where Taft was not always acquainted with judicial technicalities or even facts of the cases. But Van Devanter was "opinion shy." This, however, evoked no complaint from the Chief Justice, even if he wrote no opinions at all. Taft regarded him as "the mainstay of the Court" and dubbed him "my Lord Chancellor."

Taft was determined to make the Court's promptness "a model for the courts of the country." His colleagues, as Holmes said, approved the Chief's "way of conducting business . . . especially his disinclination to put cases over." To accelerate the Court's work, Taft urged cutting vacations from seventeen to twelve weeks and using various time-saving devices.

Taft's first major opinion, TRUAX V. CORRIGAN (1921), involved the constitutionality of an Arizona statute barring state courts from issuing injunctions in LABOR cases, except under special conditions. Owners of a restaurant sought an injunction against a BOYCOTT and PICKETING of their place of business. A majority of five Justices, concluding that the bar against injunctions denied DUE PROCESS OF LAW and EQUAL PROTECTION OF THE LAW, declared the act unconstitutional. "A law which operates to make lawful such a wrong as described in the plaintiff's complaint," the Chief Justice observed, "deprives the owner of the business and the premises of his property without due process of law and cannot be held valid under the FOURTEENTH AMENDMENT. . . . The Constitution was intended, its very purpose was to prevent experimentation with the fundamental rights of the individual."

Taft's next major opinion, STAFFORD V. WALLACE (1922), upheld broad federal power under the COMMERCE CLAUSE, announcing that Congress had a "wide area of discretion, free from judicial second guessing." At issue was the PACKERS AND STOCKYARD ACT of 1929, regulating the business of packers done in INTERSTATE COMMERCE. The "chief evil" Congress aimed at was the monopoly of packers, "enabling them unduly and arbitrarily to lower prices to the shipper who sells, and unduly and arbitrarily to increase the price to the consumer who buys." In deciding *Stafford* Taft relied mainly on Holmes's majority opinion in SWIFT V. UNITED STATES (1905). "That case," wrote the Chief Justice, "was a milestone in the interpretation of the Commerce Clause of the Constitution. It recognized the great changes and development in the business of this vast country and drew again the dividing line between interstate and intrastate commerce where the Constitution intended it to be. It refused to permit local incidents of great interstate movements which, taken alone, were intrastate, to characterize the movement as such. The *Swift* case merely fitted the Commerce Clause to the real and practical essence of modern business growth."

Another example of Taft's effort to keep the Court "consistent with itself" was ADKINS V. CHILDREN'S HOSPITAL (1923) involving an act of Congress fixing the minimum wage for women and minors. Speaking for the Court, Justice Sutherland invalidated the act, relying primarily on Justice RUFUS PECKHAM'S reactionary decision in LOCHNER V. NEW YORK (1905). Refusing to endorse *Lochner*, Taft and Holmes dissented: "It is impossible," the Chief Justice explained, "for me to reconcile the *Bunting* [*v. Oregon*] case of 1917 and the *Lochner* case and I have always supposed that the *Lochner* case was thus overruled *sub silentio.*" Although Sutherland and Taft disagreed in *Adkins*, Taft could not bring himself to endorse Holmes's dissent because of its irreverent treatment of the FREEDOM OF CONTRACT doctrine. And in *Wolff Packing Co. v. Court of Industrial Relations* (1923) Taft for the Court approvingly cited Sutherland's *Adkins* opinion on that doctrine.

The year 1926 witnessed a significant decision in American constitutional history: the 6–3 ruling in MYERS V. UNITED STATES upholding the President's power to remove a postmaster without the consent of the Senate. Said Taft: "I never wrote an opinion that I felt to be so important in its effect." The Chief Justice's unqualified appraisal reflects his White House experience. There were three dissenters—Holmes, JAMES C. MCREYNOLDS, and Brandeis. Brandeis wrote: "The separation of powers of government did not make each branch completely autonomous. It left each in some measure dependent on the other. . . . The doctrine of SEPARATION OF POWERS was adopted by the [CONSTITUTIONAL] CONVENTION OF 1787, not to promote efficiency but to preclude the exercise of arbitrary power. The purpose was not to avoid friction, but by means of the inevitable friction incident to the distribution of governmental powers among the departments, to save the people from autocracy."

Taft did not live to see the Court's later qualification of the President's power to remove executive officers. In HUMPHREY'S EXECUTOR V. UNITED STATES (1935) the President was denied executive power to remove a federal trade commissioner, appointed for seven years with the ADVICE AND CONSENT of the Senate, on the score of inefficiency or neglect of duty. Speaking for the Court in that later case, Justice Sutherland, who had enjoyed most cordial relations with Taft, went out of his way to say that the authority of the *Myers* case remained intact. The Court did not adopt the views of the *Myers* dissenters, but shifted emphasis from the "simple logic" of Article II of the Constitution—that the removal power is inherently "executive"—to the theory that a postmaster "is merely one of the units in the executive department and hence inherently subject to the exclusive and illimitable power of removal by the Chief Executive whose subordinate and aide he is."

As Taft's tenure drew to a close, dissents came more frequently and vehemently. Holmes and Brandeis, who had dissented from Taft's first major opinion in *Truax*, dissented from his last major opinion in OLMSTEAD V. UNITED STATES (1928). Justice Stone and even Justice PIERCE BUTLER joined the dissenters. Taft, a crusader for stricter enforcement of the criminal law, narrowly construed the FOURTH AMENDMENT'S ban on unreasonable searches and seizures by ruling that evidence obtained by wiretapping could be introduced at a criminal trial. In the face of hostile criticism of his *Olmstead* opinion, Taft declared privately, "If they think we are going to be frightened in our effort to stand by the law and give the public a chance to punish criminals, they are mistaken, even though we are condemned for lack of high ideals." Taft thought that Holmes's dissent was sentimental in declaring that "it is a lesser evil that some criminals should escape than that the Government should play an ignoble part."

Near the end, Taft winced nervously whenever he contemplated his probable successor. Knowing that President HERBERT C. HOOVER's attachment to Stone was "very great," Taft feared the worst: "I have no doubt that if I were to retire or die, the President would appoint Stone head of the Court." Once in the Chief Justice's good graces, Stone had fallen into profound disfavor. "He definitely has ranged himself with Brandeis and with Holmes in a good many of our constitutional differences." Nor was Stone's "herding" with the Court's "kickers" his only shortcoming. He was "not a great leader and would have a great deal of trouble in massing the Court." The Chief was not entirely without hope: "With Van and Mac and Sutherland and you and Sanford," he wrote to Justice Butler in 1929, "there will be five to steady the boat. So there would be a great deal of difficulty in working through reversals of present positions, even if I either had to retire or were gathered to my fathers, so that we must not give up at once."

Taft's triumphant march continued to the end, but

the future was clouded with uncertainty. By 1929 the world he had known and the people on whom he relied were in eclipse. As the economy slid rapidly toward the abyss, government intervention was openly advocated. To combat these forces, Taft's determination stiffened. "As long as things continue as they are and I am able to answer in my place," he resolved to "stay on the Court in order to prevent the Bolsheviki from getting control." President Hoover, Taft thought, "would put in some rather extreme destroyers of the Constitution. . . ."

None of Taft's predecessors, with the possible exception of Marshall, entertained so expansive a view of the chief justiceship, or used it so effectively on so many fronts. Taft was a great administrator, a great judicial architect, a skillful harmonizer of human relations. Yet he is not commonly considered a great Chief Justice.

ALPHEUS THOMAS MASON

Bibliography

MASON, ALPHEUS THOMAS 1930 The Labor Decisions of Chief Justice Taft. *University of Pennsylvania Law Review* 78:585–625.

——— 1979 *The Supreme Court from Taft to Burger.* Baton Rouge: Louisiana State University Press.

——— 1964 *William Howard Taft: Chief Justice.* New York: Simon & Schuster.

MCHALE, FRANCIS 1931 *President and Chief Justice: The Life and Public Services of William Howard Taft.* Philadelphia: Dorrance.

MURPHY, W. F. 1962 Chief Justice Taft and the Lower Court Bureaucracy. *Journal of Politics* 24:453–476.

——— 1961 In His Own Image: Mr. Justice Taft and Supreme Court Appointments. *Supreme Court Review* 1961:159–193.

PRINGLE, H. F. 1939 *The Life and Times of William Howard Taft.* New York: Farrar & Rinehart.

TAFT COURT (1921–1930)

WILLIAM HOWARD TAFT became Chief Justice of the United States on June 30, 1921. Never before or since has any person brought such a range of distinguished experience in public affairs and professional qualifications to the bench. Taft presided over a court that included Justices of highly varied abilities and achievements. In 1921, OLIVER WENDELL HOLMES, already a great figure of the law, had served nineteen years on the Supreme Court. He remained on the Court throughout Taft's tenure and beyond. Holmes's only equal on the Court was LOUIS D. BRANDEIS, who had been on the Court barely five years at Taft's accession. Taft, a private citizen in 1916, had vigorously opposed the appointment of Brandeis to the High Court. Although they remained ideological opponents and although some mistrust persisted on both sides, they maintained cordial relations, carrying on their opposition in a highly civil manner.

The rest of the Court that Taft inherited lacked the stature or ability of Holmes and Brandeis. Three Justices, JOHN J. CLARKE, MAHLON PITNEY, and WILLIAM R. DAY would retire within the first two years of Taft's tenure. Their retirements gave President WARREN C. HARDING a chance to reconstitute the Court. The President appointed his former Senate colleague GEORGE H. SUTHERLAND to one of the vacancies. The other two spots were filled by men strongly recommended by Taft: PIERCE BUTLER and EDWARD T. SANFORD.

The other Justices on the Court in 1921 were WILLIS VAN DEVANTER, JAMES C. MCREYNOLDS, and JOSEPH MCKENNA. Van Devanter had been appointed to the bench by Taft when he was President. He, like Butler and Sanford, continued to be strongly influenced by the Chief Justice. During the Taft years, he served the Chief Justice in the performance of many important institutional tasks outside the realm of decision making and opinion writing. For example, Van Devanter led the drive to revamp the JURISDICTION of the Supreme Court in the "Judges' Bill," the JUDICIARY ACT OF 1925. McReynolds, a Wilson appointee, was an iconoclastic conservative of well-defined prejudices.

Finally, Taft inherited Joseph McKenna, whose failing health impaired his judicial performance. In 1925, Taft, after consulting the other justices, urged McKenna to retire. McKenna was succeeded by HARLAN F. STONE. Though deferential to Taft at the outset, by the end of the decade Stone became increasingly identified with the dissenting positions of Holmes and Brandeis. From early 1923 through Taft's resignation only that one change took place.

Because of the substantial continuity of personnel the Taft Court can be thought of as an institution with a personality and with well-defined positions on most critical issues that came before it. Outcomes were as predictable as they ever can be, and the reasoning, persuasive or not, was consistent.

Taft was a strong Chief Justice. He lobbied powerfully for more federal judges, for a streamlined federal procedure, for reorganization of the federal judiciary, and for greater control by the Supreme Court over the cases it would decide. The most concrete of Taft's reforms was a new building for the Court itself, though the building was not completed until after his death.

A second major institutional change was completed during Taft's term. In 1925 Congress passed the "Judges' Bill." The Supreme Court's agenda is one of the most important factors in determining the evolution of constitutional law. Until 1891 that agenda had been determined largely at the initiative of litigants. In 1891 the Court received authority to review certain classes of cases by the discretionary WRIT OF CERTIORARI. However, many lower court decisions had continued to be reviewable as of right in the Supreme Court even after 1891. The 1925 act altered the balance by establishing the largely discretionary certiorari jurisdiction of the Supreme Court as it has remained for six decades. The act was one of Taft's major projects. It relieved the docket pressure occasioned by the press of obligatory jurisdiction, and placed agenda control at the very center of constitutional politics.

The successful initiatives of the Court in seizing control of its own constitutional agenda and constructing a new home should not obscure the fact that the Court's institutional position was, as always, under attack during the 1920s. A spate of what were perceived as antilabor decisions in 1921–1922 led to calls from the labor movement and congressional progressives to circumscribe the Court's powers. In the 1924 election Robert LaFollette, running as a third-party candidate on the Progressive ticket, called for a constitutional amendment to limit JUDICIAL REVIEW. Both the Republican incumbent, CALVIN COOLIDGE, and the 1924 Democratic candidate, JOHN W. DAVIS, defended the Court against LaFollette. The upshot of the unsuccessful LaFollette campaign was a heightened sensitivity to judicial review as an issue and a firm demonstration of the consensus as to its legitimacy and centrality in the American constitutional system.

Much of the labor movement had supported LaFollette's initiatives against judicial review, but labor specifically sought limitations on federal court labor INJUNCTIONS. Labor's campaign against injunctions peaked in 1927 after the Supreme Court simultaneously declined to review a series of controversial injunctions in the West Virginia coal fields and approved an injunction in BEDFORD CUT STONE COMPANY V. JOURNEYMAN STONECUTTERS, holding that a union's nationwide refusal to handle nonunion stone should be enjoined as an agreement in RESTRAINT OF TRADE. Between 1928 and 1930 the shape of what was to become the NORRIS-LAGUARDIA ACT OF 1932 emerged in Congress. The impetus behind that law, the politics of it, indeed, the language and theory of the statute itself are rooted in the Taft years.

A description of the Court's institutional role must consider the relations between CONGRESS AND THE COURT in shaping constitutional law and constitutional politics. During the Taft years a dialogue between Court and Congress persisted on a variety of crucial constitutional issues. The decision of the Court striking down the first Child Labor Act in HAMMER V. DAGENHART (1918) led to congressional interest in using the taxing power to circumvent apparent limitations on the direct regulatory authority of Congress under the COMMERCE CLAUSE. The second Child Labor Act imposed an excise tax on the profits of firms employing child labor. That act was struck down as unconstitutional in 1922.

From 1922 on Congress had before it various versions of antilynching legislation—most notably the Dyer Bill, which had actually passed the House. Opponents of the antilynching legislation argued that it was an unconstitutional federal usurpation of state functions. In *Moore v. Dempsey* (1923), decided shortly after the Dyer Bill had nearly succeeded in passage, the Court held that a state criminal trial dominated by a mob constituted a denial of DUE PROCESS OF LAW, appropriately redressed in a federal HABEAS CORPUS proceeding. *Moore v. Dempsey* did not establish that an antilynching law would be constitutional. Yet a conclusion that mob domination of a criminal trial did *not* deny due process surely would have been a constitutional nail in the coffin of antilynching laws. And, prior to *Moore v. Dempsey* the relatively recent PRECEDENT of FRANK V. MANGUM (1915) had pointed toward just such a conclusion. Considerations concerning the response of Congress regularly influenced the constitutional decision making of the Taft Court. When Taft was appointed, three important labor cases were pending that had been argued but not decided by the WHITE COURT. The Court had reached an impasse. Two of the cases presented questions about the use of injunctions to restrain labor picketing. Section 20 of the Clayton Act appeared to deny the federal courts the power to issue such injunctions subject to certain exceptions, most notably the power to use the injunction to protect property from damage. *American Steel Foundries v. Tri-City Labor Council* presented questions of construction of this section, and TRUAX V. CORRIGAN, involving a state law, presented a constitutional variant of the Clayton Act problem.

In *American Steel Foundries,* Taft's first significant opinion as Chief Justice, the Court read section 20 to encompass protection of the property interest in an ongoing business from unreasonable or intimidating picketing or from illegal BOYCOTTS or strikes. Statutory construction thus preserved the injunction as a restraint on labor.

But not all state courts saw the issue as the Taft Court did. The Arizona Supreme Court read its statute to bar injunctions in labor disputes, at least where actual destruction of physical property was not threatened. In *Truax v. Corrigan,* decided a week after *American Steel Foundries,* Taft wrote for a majority of five, holding that Arizona had unconstitutionally denied employers the injunction in labor disputes. *Truax* in effect created a constitutional *right* to a labor injunction. It did so on two grounds. First, it held that employers were denied the EQUAL PROTECTION OF THE LAWS insofar as their particular type of property interest was denied the same protection afforded other property interests. Second, it held that the failure to protect the interest in the continued operation of a business deprived the business owner of property without due process of law. *Truax v. Corrigan* was the cornerstone of the Taft Court edifice of industrial relations. Not only did the decision suggest that Congress could not constitutionally prevent the federal courts from granting labor injunctions, but it also ushered in a decade of the most intensive use of the labor injunction the country had ever seen. A desperate battle was fought to save the unionized sector of coal from competition from the newer, largely nonunion, southern mines. That union campaign was broken by dozens of labor injunctions upheld by the Fourth Circuit in a consolidated appeal. The Supreme Court's refusal to review those decisions in 1927 attracted larger headlines than all but the most significant of Supreme Court opinions ever get. The Fourth Circuit opinion later cost Circuit Judge John J. H. Parker a seat on the Supreme Court. In fact, however, his conclusion was an all but inevitable consequence of the Supreme Court's position in *Truax v. Corrigan.*

The industrial order that the Taft Court sought to protect from labor insurgency was itself built upon uncertain constitutional foundations. The Taft Court was not committed, unambiguously, to a laissez-faire market. The Court distinguished sharply between legislation regulating the price (wage or rent) terms of a contract and laws regulating other terms. Thus, in the best known of its apparent inconsistencies, the Taft Court held void a District of Columbia law prescribing a minimum wage for women, although only a year later it upheld a New York law establishing maximum hours for women. The Court also struck down a state statute regulating fees or commissions for employment brokers while intimating that other reasonable regulatory measures directed at employment brokerage would be upheld.

Sutherland, in his peculiar majority opinion in the minimum wage case—ADKINS V. CHILDREN'S HOSPITAL (1923)—seemed preoccupied with the redistributive aspects of the minimum wage law. There was nothing wrong with a legislative preference for a living (minimum) wage; the problem lay in imposing an obligation on the employer to pay it. One person's need, he argued, could not, in itself, justify another's obligation to satisfy it. The regulation of nonprice terms need not be redistributive in effect, for the costs of any such regulation could be recaptured by negotiated changes in price. If the Court was seeking to protect bargains against regulation with redistribution effect, then shielding price terms from governmental interference was the most visible and easily understood way to accomplish its purpose.

In general the Taft Court sought to maintain principled distinctions among three forms of economic activity. Government enterprise was subject to the usual constitutional constraints upon government. This form of economic activity was relatively unimportant in the 1920s, although in cases involving municipal utilities the Court had some opportunity to address such issues as contractual rate structure. The Court spoke more frequently to the problem of transition from private to public or from public to private enterprise. World War I had seen government control of the railroads, shipping, coal, and, to a lesser degree, labor relations generally. The Court had to develop principles of compensation to govern the takeover and return of such large-scale enterprises.

More important than the dichotomy between governmental and private economic activity was the distinction drawn between private activity AFFECTED WITH A PUBLIC INTEREST and the more general run of private economic endeavor. Upon this distinction turned the constitutionality of public regulation—including price regulation in some circumstances—of various forms of economic activity. Although the category of business affected with a public interest had been part of the Court's rhetorical stock in trade for almost half a century when Taft took his seat, it assumed particular significance through the decade beginning with a case from Kansas. In 1920, having survived the effects of a bitter coal strike, Kansas passed its Industrial Court Act, declaring all production and distribution of food, clothing, shelter, and fuel for human consumption or use to be business affected with a public interest. Public transportation and public utilities were also so labeled. The act forbade strikes, lockouts, and plant closings in all such industries except by order of the Kansas Court of Industrial Relations. Moreover, that court upon its own motion or upon the petition of virtually any person could adjudicate the fitness or adequacy of wages and prices in any such business. The act contemplated a form of compulsory arbitration to replace labor bargaining against a background of strikes and lockouts.

In a series of unanimous opinions the Supreme Court struck down one after another of these innovative aspects of the Kansas act. Taft, in the leading opinion, WOLFF PACKING CORPORATION V. COURT OF INDUSTRIAL RELATIONS (1923) held that the state could not, by legislative fiat, declare businesses to be affected with a public interest for purposes so comprehensive as to include supervision of their wage and price structures. Taft's opinion wholly failed to state a principled distinction between those businesses traditionally subject to price regulation (such as grain elevators), on the one hand, and meat packing, on the other. In OBITER DICTUM he suggested that the competitive structure of the industry was not determinative of the legislature's power to regulate. But the opinion did acknowledge that long-established law permitted regulation of publicly conferred monopolies and of common carriers or inns even if not monopolies.

The Taft Court thus rejected a generalization, based on the war experience, that all basic economic activity could be defined as affected with a public interest. But the Court was not unmindful of the war's lessons. Unanimously it upheld the recapture provisions of the [Railroad] Transportation Act of 1920 despite the overt redistributive effect of the law. The act required the payment into a federal trust fund of half the profits earned by strong railroads, for redistribution to failing ones. The Chief Justice, at least, understood the recapture provisions as justified in part because the alternative to such a scheme might have to be nationalization. Furthermore, the Court had already gone to great lengths to uphold other, seemingly inevitable, characteristics of rate regulation in an integrated transportation system. The Interstate Commerce Commission (ICC), if it were to be effective at all, needed power to regulate joint rates over hauls using more than one line for a single journey. It was apparent that the apportionment of joint rates could be used to redistributive effect. In the *New England Divisions Case* (1923) the Court had already upheld the ICC's explicit consideration of the need to strengthen the weaker New England lines when it apportioned revenues from joint rates. It was a short step from such use of joint rates to the recapture provisions.

The Court's willingness to accept some qualifications of vested property rights in the interest of planning was not confined to such traditional areas of regulation as transportation and public utilities. The Court decided its first cases challenging general ZONING ordinances in the 1920s and, on the whole, upheld the power, though not without significant dissent and important qualifications.

Despite the Court's upholding of zoning and of regulatory initiatives such as the recapture provisions, the Taft Court has long been considered to have been ardent in imposing constitutional limits upon legislation that restricted vested property interests. That reputation is soundly based, although the extent to which the Taft Court differed from predecessor and successor Courts has been substantially exaggerated by FELIX FRANKFURTER and his followers.

Perhaps the best known of the Taft Court pronouncements on the constitutional protection of property is Justice Holmes's opinion for the Court in *Pennsylvania Coal Company v. Mahon* (1923). Pennsylvania's Kohler Act required anthracite coal mining to be done so as to avoid subsidence of surface areas at or near buildings, streets, and other structures used by human beings. The Court held unconstitutional the application of the law to mining in an area where the mining company had conveyed surface rights, expressly reserving to itself and to its successors the subsurface mining rights.

Despite Brandeis's dissenting opinion, Holmes's opinion was moderate in tone and antithetical to the sort of dogmatics that characterized Sutherland's opinions in the wage and price regulation area. Indeed, Holmes's methodology was explicitly one that reduced the takings/regulation distinction to a matter of degree—as Holmes himself once recognized in a flippant reference to "the petty larceny of the police power." Moreover, the Court that decided *Pennsylvania Coal* decided the case of *Miller v. Schoene* (1928) five years later, upholding a Virginia law providing for the uncompensated (or less than fully compensated) destruction of cedar trees infected with cedar rust, a condition harmful only to neighboring apple trees.

The Court also had to face the implications of the constitutional protection of property in considering the methodology of public utility rate regulation. In a series of cases beginning in 1923 and proceeding throughout the Taft period, Justice Brandeis posed a major challenge to the "fair value" methodology of SMYTH V. AMES (1895). Industry during the 1920s argued that the rate base—the "property" upon which the Constitution guaranteed a reasonable rate of permissible return—should be valued according to the replacement cost of capital items—despite a general inflationary trend, accelerated by World War I. Brandeis formulated a comprehensive critique both of this particular windfall calculation and of the rule that produced it. Brandeis first reformulated the problem in a characteristically daring way. The issue was not so much a vested right to a return on capital as it was the necessity for a level of profit that could attract the new capital required for effective operation of the public utility. Brandeis lost the battle for a new approach to rate-making. Yet here, no less than in other arenas for disputes over the constitutional protection of property, doctrinal lines had been drawn that anticipated the issues of the New Deal.

Traditional, genteel conservativism is neither overtly ideological in content nor strident in manner. In most respects the Taft Court was traditionally conservative. The Court was hostile to labor and to any insurgency from the left, but the hostility usually took the form of a neutral defense of civil order. That neutrality, though it almost always worked against the left, was not explicitly one-sided and was, in fact, applied occasionally against rightist militant politics and street activity as well.

The constitutional defense of civil order entailed a strong commitment to ratify the acts of local government and of the national political branches so long as their power and authority were used to put down militant politics and especially politics of the street. Thus, the Court consistently upheld CRIMINAL SYNDICALISM LAWS, even while recognizing, in GITLOW V. NEW YORK (1925), that the FIRST AMENDMENT limited state as well as federal legislative power. Moreover, in a theoretically interesting, though practically less significant case, the Court upheld a New York law requiring the registration and disclosure of names of members of certain secret societies—a measure directed against the Ku Klux Klan. Brandeis and Holmes repeatedly dissented in the criminal syndicalism cases, sketching an alternative version of the political process far more hospitable to insurgent initiatives for change.

A second pillar of the defense of civic order was the reliance upon independent courts as guarantors of vested property rights against street politics. To this end the injunction was elevated to a constitutional pedestal. *Truax v. Corrigan,* which constitutionalized capital's right to a labor injunction, must be seen not only as a part of a larger antilabor *corpus* but also as the link between that work and the principle of civic order.

For traditional conservatives the injunction had much to commend it. It was in the hands of politically independent judges, who were less susceptible than other officials to mass pressure. It was governed—or supposed to be governed—by neutral principles rather than special interests; it permitted the adaptation of principle to local needs and adjusted the level of intervention to that necessary to shore up appropriately sound local elites. No wonder, then, that the issue of the injunction pervaded the constitutional politics of the 1920s.

If Taft was committed to the courts' playing a dominant role in labor discipline and the guarantee of civic order, he was at the same time committed to an efficient, unintimidated, and uncorrupted judiciary to do the job. In *Tumey v. Ohio* (1927) he wrote for a unanimous Court striking down as a denial of due process an Ohio scheme through which a public official judging traffic violations was paid a percentage of the fines collected. Of greater significance was MOORE V. DEMPSEY (1923), in which a divided Court upheld the power of a federal district court in federal HABEAS CORPUS proceedings to go behind the record of a state court murder conviction to determine whether the trial had been dominated by a mob.

Racist justice was a deeply rooted problem, not high on the conservative agenda for reform. Taft was, however, very concerned with the potential for corruption of the courts inherent in the great national experiment of the decade, prohibition. The Chief Justice realized that there were many opportunities for organized crime in the liquor business to buy friendly judges and other officials, especially in states where prohibition was unpopular. The Court refused to extend the protection of the DOUBLE JEOPARDY principle to cases of successive prosecutions under state and federal law for substantially the same conduct. Part of the reason for this limit upon the double jeopardy principle was the potential under any contrary rule of insulating conduct from federal prosecution by securing a state conviction and paying a small fine. The Court's interpretation of FEDERALISM to tolerate structural redundancy was thus a major prophylactic against the dangers of local corruption of courts.

Like all its predecessors, however conservative, the Taft Court paid lip service to the idea that the people are sovereign and, consequently, that popular government is a pervasive and overriding principle in constitutional interpretation. Even though dissenters within the court (Holmes and Brandeis) and critical commentators without (Frankfurter, EDWARD S. CORWIN, and

THOMAS REED POWELL) claimed that the Justices ignored the presumption of constitutionality that ought to attach to the work of the popular branches, the simple fact is that no Justice denied, as an abstract principle, either the presumption of constitutionality or the deference that ought to be paid to legislative judgments. It was the application of the principle that divided the Court.

Most of the Justices were skeptical of the capacity of the masses intelligently to exercise the rights and discharge the obligations of participatory, popular government. Taft himself welcomed a leading role for elites in suppressing, or at least damping, the demands of the rabble and in representing the "better class" of citizens. But Taft's views in these matters were not very different from those of Holmes. Holmes doubted the capacity of the masses and considered a dominant role for elites in politics to be almost a natural law. Brandeis, the only real contrast, was considerably more committed to reform and to its promise. But he, in his own way, also distrusted the masses. He saw hope for change in a shift from a propertied oligarchy to a technically trained meritocracy. At the same time Brandeis understood the limits of this vision. His support of STATES' RIGHTS and localism in politics and his hostility to concentration in industry had common roots: the recognition of limits to techniques of effective organization; the affirmation of political principles limiting concentrations of power; and the affirmation of the principles of maximum participation in public affairs. Chiefly in this last respect, Brandeis stood committed to a principle that the other Justices ignored or rejected.

In what ways did the general attitudes of the Justices to popular government affect the work of the Court? Perhaps the most direct effect was visible in the great, perennial debate over the power of judicial review. The Justices appear to have been unanimous in their private opposition to schemes such as that of LaFollette to limit the power of judicial review by statute or constitutional amendment. Even Brandeis, who was personally close to LaFollette and who supported the Wisconsin senator's positions on many substantive issues, opposed initiatives to curb the Court.

In at least one important area the Taft Court initiated a significant reform in the mechanics of popular government itself. The Court struck down the first version of the Texas system of white primaries which, through official state action, denied blacks the right to vote in statewide PRIMARY ELECTIONS. NIXON V. HERNDON (1927) was the first in a line of cases that ultimately destroyed the white primary device.

The Court upheld the power of Congress to conduct LEGISLATIVE INVESTIGATIONS and to use COMPULSORY PROCESS to that end. The Court also appeared to uphold an enlarged vision of an exclusive PRESIDENTIAL POWER to remove executive officers. A special constitutional status for government of TERRITORIES was approved. Finally, the Court struggled mightily but produced no satisfactory or consistent principles in the area of STATE TAXATION OF COMMERCE and STATE REGULATION OF COMMERCE.

The 1920s saw a determined attack upon the ethnic pluralism, the cultural and ethical relativism, and the absence of traditional controls that characterized a newly emergent urban America. The prohibition movement, resurgent religious fundamentalism, virulent nativism, and racism gave rise to a reactionary program for legal reform. In the area of prohibition the Court did more than give full effect to a constitutional amendment and its implementing legislation. The Justices also decided a host of criminal procedure issues in such a way as to arm the enforcers against what was perceived as a concerted attack on law and order themselves.

But the Court was actively hostile to groups like the "new" Ku Klux Klan. It not only upheld a Klan registration statute but also, in PIERCE V. SOCIETY OF SISTERS (1925), held invalid an Oregon statute that had effectively outlawed private schools. The law was the product of a popular initiative organized and vigorously supported by the Klan as part of its nativist and anti-Catholic crusade. The decision in MEYER V. NEBRASKA (1923) striking down laws forbidding the teaching of German in the schools also reflected the Justices' unwillingness to permit nativist sentiment to cut too deeply into the social fabric.

But the Court did uphold state ALIEN land ownership laws directed principally against Asian immigrants and upheld the disgraceful national discrimination against Asian immigration in the face of constitutional attack. The Court also permitted the continuation of restrictive covenants in housing (CORRIGAN V. BUCKLEY, 1926) and segregation in public schools (GONG LUM V. RICE, 1927), though in each instance it avoided an explicit articulation of constitutional approval for these practices.

The constitutional work of the Taft Court extended over the customary broad area of national life, but it was dominated by the motif of conflict between property and labor. Civil strife, policies toward insurgency, free or regulated markets, confiscation—all were issues that arose principally from the overarching conflict. It is a measure of the Taft Court's achievement that, through Brandeis on the one hand and

Taft on the other, a measure of clarity was achieved in articulating the implications of this conflict for constitutional structure and doctrine over a wide range of subjects. It was Taft's vision alone, however, that dominated the Court's action—consistently hostile to labor and its interests. The traditional conservative structure of property and order was one legacy of Taft's Court to the era of the Great Depression; Brandeis's vision—as yet wholly unrealized—was the other.

ROBERT M. COVER

Bibliography

BERNSTEIN, IRVING 1960 *The Lean Years: A History of the American Worker, 1920–1933.* Boston: Houghton Mifflin.

BICKEL, ALEXANDER M. 1957 *The Unpublished Opinions of Mr. Justice Brandeis: The Supreme Court at Work.* Cambridge, Mass.: Belknap Press of Harvard University Press.

DANELSKI, DAVID J. 1964 *A Supreme Court Justice Is Appointed.* New York: Random House.

FRANKFURTER, FELIX AND GREENE, NATHAN 1930 *The Labor Injunction.* New York: Macmillan.

MASON, ALPHEUS THOMAS 1946 *Brandeis: A Free Man's Life.* New York: Viking.

——— 1956 *Harlan Fiske Stone: Pillar of the Law.* New York: Viking.

——— 1964 *William Howard Taft: Chief Justice.* New York: Simon & Schuster.

MURPHY, WALTER F. 1964 *Elements of Judicial Strategy.* Chicago: University of Chicago Press.

PRINGLE, HENRY F. 1939 *The Life and Times of William Howard Taft.* New York: Farrar & Rinehart.

RABBAN, DAVID M. 1983 The Emergence of Modern First Amendment Doctrine. *University of Chicago Law Review* 50:1205–1355.

TAFT-HARTLEY LABOR RELATIONS ACT

61 Stat. 136 (1947)

Passed over President HARRY S. TRUMAN's veto, the Taft-Hartley Act represented Republican hostility to the power of labor unions and the National Labor Relations Board (NLRB); its provisions limit the authority and conduct of unions and their officials and curtail the Board's authority.

In amending the WAGNER (NATIONAL LABOR RELATIONS) ACT, the measure banned the CLOSED SHOP; permitted employers to sue unions for strike-incurred damages; forbade union contributions to political campaigns; required public disclosure of union finances; required unions to give sixty days notice before inaugurating strikes; and allowed the President to halt a major strike by seeking a court INJUNCTION for an eighty-day "cooling off" period. Although the right to COLLECTIVE BARGAINING was further guaranteed, section 14b permitted states to adopt RIGHT-TO-WORK LAWS, forbidding any requirement that workers join unions to hold jobs. Most constitutionally suspect were provisions requiring labor union officials, in order to use the facilities of the NLRB, to sign affidavits denying communist party membership or belief. These noncommunist oath provisions were unsuccessfully challenged in the courts in AMERICAN COMMUNICATIONS ASSOCIATION v. DOUDS (1950).

PAUL L. MURPHY

Bibliography

SUTHERLAND, ARTHUR E. 1948 The Constitutionality of the Taft-Hartley Law. *Industrial and Labor Relations Review* 1:177–205.

TAKAHASHI v. FISH AND GAME COMMISSION

334 U.S. 410 (1948)

Under California law, ALIENS ineligible for CITIZENSHIP (mainly Asians) could not hold commercial fishing licenses. Citing the broad power of Congress to regulate aliens, the Supreme Court held, 7–2, that the PREEMPTION DOCTRINE barred the law. The CIVIL RIGHTS ACT OF 1866 was taken to protect the rights of aliens to pursue their livelihoods under nondiscriminatory state laws. The opinion also conveyed overtones of FOURTEENTH AMENDMENT reasoning.

KENNETH L. KARST

TAKING OF PROPERTY

The authority of government to acquire private property from an involuntary owner (usually called the power of EMINENT DOMAIN) is recognized in the Fifth Amendment to the Constitution, which provides: "nor shall private property be taken for public use, without JUST COMPENSATION." The public use and compensation requirements of the Constitution apply not only to acquisitions by the federal government but—by INCORPORATION in the FOURTEENTH AMENDMENT—to acquisitions by the states as well. Similar provisions appear in the state constitutions, and the state and federal requirements are usually identically interpreted. It is, however, possible that a taking would pass muster under the federal Constitution and still be held to violate the state constitutional provision (or vice versa).

The requirement of PUBLIC USE has been liberally interpreted by the courts, which rarely find that a taking is not for a public use. For example, property may be taken for resale to private developers in an urban renewal project, or for the development of an industrial park. Indeed, the courts have permitted authority to take private property to be vested by LEGISLATION in privately owned public utilities, such as water companies. The test is not ultimate public ownership, or even direct public benefit, but rather the general benefit to the public from projects that are publicly sponsored or encouraged to promote the economy or the public welfare. The only clear limits on the broad interpretation of "public use" would be (1) the grant of the taking authority to a private company simply to improve its private economic position; or (2) the use of the taking power by the government if government itself were simply seeking to make money by engaging in strictly entrepreneurial activities.

The requirement of "just compensation" has been interpreted to mean the amount a willing seller would get from a willing buyer in the absence of the government's desire to acquire the property. The owner is not entitled to receive more for the property simply because the government has an urgent need for it—as for a military base. Neither may the owner receive less compensation because the government's plan for the area—to install a garbage dump, for example, has depressed neighborhood values. Nor is the owner entitled to increased compensation merely because the property has special value to him, such as sentimental or family value, or because he would not sell the property at any price. Compensation must be given in cash immediately upon the taking; government cannot oblige the owner to accept future promises of payment which may be unmarketable, or marketable only at a discount from the just compensation value.

Ordinarily there is no ambiguity about whether a property has been taken. Nor is there any ambiguity about the principle of takings law, stated at the most general level: if the public wants something, it should pay for it and not coerce private owners into contributing their property to the public. If government wants a site for a post office, for example, it is obliged to institute condemnation proceedings in court, leading to an involuntary transfer of title and possession, at which time it will pay the owner just compensation. But in many instances government legislates or behaves in a way that reduces or destroys the value of private property without formally taking title or possession and without instituting condemnation proceedings. If the owner complains, seeking just compensation for a taking, government may reply that it has simply regulated under the POLICE POWER, but has not "taken" the property and thus need not compensate. The great bulk of all legal controversies over the taking of property turn on the question whether there has been a "taking" at all.

Plainly government sometimes gets the benefits of a taking without any of the formal incidents of ownership. A celebrated case, *Causby v. United States* (1946), involved the flight of military planes just above the surface of privately owned farmland adjacent to a military airport. As a result of noise from the overflights the farm was made virtually worthless for agricultural purposes. The farmer claimed that his farm had in practical effect been taken, that government was using it as a sort of extension of the runway, and that government should have to pay for it as it had for the rest of the airport. The Supreme Court agreed that this use of the farmland was a taking in effect, if not in form, and that the farmer was entitled to just compensation for what is called INVERSE CONDEMNATION.

This ruling does not mean that the neighbors of a public airport or highway subjected to noise that reduces their property values will always be compensated. In general such disadvantaged neighbors are not viewed by the courts as having had their property taken in the constitutional sense. The reason is that although a nearly total loss (such as the farmer sustained) is judicially viewed as a taking, some modest diminution of value resulting from neighboring public activities is viewed as one of the disadvantages of modern life that must be accepted by property owners.

The judicial focus on the quantum of loss as a test of a taking is called the diminution of value theory and was put forward many years ago by Justice OLIVER WENDELL HOLMES in *Pennsylvania Coal Co. v. Mahon* (1922). There is no clear line, Holmes believed, between the formal taking of property by government (in which title and possession are acquired) and the various forms of government regulation (such as zoning and pollution control), which do not transfer ownership formally, but restrict private owners' uses and values for the benefit of the general public. In both cases, according to Holmes, the traditional rights of private owners are being restricted for the benefit of the public. If there were no legal limits on such restrictions, he said, private property would be worthless and wholly at the mercy of government. On the other hand, Holmes said, if every value-diminishing regulation were viewed as a compensable taking of property, government would be unable to function, for essentially all of its regulatory activities (speed limits, liquor control, safety standards, rent control) disadvantage property owners to some degree.

He thus devised a practical test. We must all accept some impairment of property values so that society can function in a civilized way, and government must be permitted to make regulations requiring such impairments. If, however, the losses from such regulations become extreme—nearing total destruction of the property's value for any owner—then the society should compensate the owner and bear the losses of the regulation commonly. Thus, under the Holmesian theory, the amount of the loss and the ability of the owner to continue to earn some return from his property after the regulation has been imposed become the critical determinants of the constitutional question: has there been a taking for which compensation must be paid?

Although Holmes's test continues to dominate taking cases, there are a number of other theories that are widely found in the literature and in judicial opinions. One theory holds that prohibitions of certain socially undesirable uses do not qualify as compensable takings despite considerable loss to the owners, because one cannot be viewed as having a property right to engage in "noxious" conduct, and losses flowing from prohibition of such conduct is not a taking away of property. The illegalization of manufacture and sale of a dangerous drug, or of polluting activity, has been so categorized.

Another theory sometimes advanced is that certain government restrictions imposed on property owners are not a taking of property from the owners by the government, but are the merely regulation by the government of activities by which it mediates between various private uses in conflict with each other. Under this theory compensation is required only when the government as an enterprise itself benefits directly from the regulation (it gets additional space for its military airport, for example). The enterprise/regulation theory has sometimes been used to justify ZONING and other LAND USE controls that restrict the amount or type of building permitted to a landowner on his land. Modern historic preservation ordinances as well as safety and environmental controls are sometimes justified on this theory.

Still another view suggests that government may, without compensation, impose much greater restrictions to prevent future additional exploitation of property, while leaving existing uses, than it may cut back on existing uses. Thus, in PENN CENTRAL TRANSPORTATION CO. V. NEW YORK (1978), an important case, the Supreme Court upheld a historic preservation ordinance prohibiting the owners of Grand Central Station in New York from building a high rise office tower above the railroad station, noting that the existing station did produce some economic return to the owners. The claimed "taking" of a property right to build a bigger building was rejected.

Although no single theory wholly dominates taking law, two guidelines permit safe prediction about the great majority of cases. Courts will find a taking and require just compensation if (1) the government acquires physical possession of the property; or if (2) regulation so reduces the owner's values that virtually no net economic return is left to the proprietor.

JOSEPH L. SAX

(SEE ALSO: *Dames & Moore v. Regan, 1981; Hawaii Housing Authority v. Midkiff, 1984.*)

Bibliography

ACKERMAN, BRUCE A. 1977 *Private Property and the Constitution.* New Haven, Conn.: Yale University Press.

BOSSELMAN, FRED; CALLIES, DAVID; and BANTA, JOHN 1973 *The Taking Issue.* Washington, D.C.: Council on Environmental Quality.

MICHELMAN, FRANK I. 1967 Property, Utility and Fairness: Comments on the Ethical Foundations of "Just Compensation" Law. *Harvard Law Review* 80:1165–1258.

SAX, JOSEPH L. 1971 Taking and the Police Power. *Yale Law Journal* 74:36–76.

——— 1971 Takings, Private Property and Public Rights. *Yale Law Journal* 81:149–186.

TANEY, ROGER BROOKE (1777–1864)

Roger B. Taney, Chief Justice of the United States from 1836 until his death in 1864, profoundly shaped American constitutional development in cases dealing with states' regulatory powers, corporations, slavery, and the JURISDICTION OF FEDERAL COURTS. His reputation long suffered from invidious and inappropriate comparisons with his predecessor Chief Justice JOHN MARSHALL and because of his disastrous opinion in DRED SCOTT V. SANDFORD (1857). But his influence has been enduring and, on balance, beneficial.

Taney was born in 1777 in Calvert County, Maryland. His father, a well-to-do planter, destined him for a career in law. After graduation from Dickinson College (Pennsylvania), he was admitted to the bar in 1799 and began a thirty-six-year career of politics and law practice in Maryland. He served intermittently in both houses of the state legislature until 1821, at first as a Federalist. But finding that affiliation intolerable because of the conduct of New England Federalists during the War of 1812, he assumed leadership of a local faction known as Coodies and then after 1825 supported ANDREW JACKSON. Practicing first in Frederick, where he maintained his lifelong residence, and then in Baltimore, he became a preeminent member of the Maryland bar, state attorney general from 1827 to 1831, and then attorney general of the United States, a position he held until 1833, when he served for a year as secretary of the treasury.

Taney urged President Jackson to veto the bill to recharter the Bank of the United States and contributed that part of JACKSON'S VETO OF THE BANK BILL in which the President denied that the Supreme Court's opinion on constitutional matters bound the President. As treasury secretary, Taney ordered removal of the federal deposits from the Bank and their distribution to certain "pet banks." In these bank matters, Taney was not the mere pliant tool of Jackson; rather, he acted in accord with his own deep suspicions of centralized and monopolistic economic power.

As attorney general, Taney also had occasion to explore issues involving slavery and free blacks. Upholding South Carolina's Negro Seamen's Act, which prohibited black seamen from disembarking from their vessels while in Carolina waters, Taney insisted that the state's sovereign right to control slaves and free blacks overrode any inconsistent exercise of federal treaty and commerce powers. Presaging his *Dred Scott* opinion, he maintained that blacks were "a separate and degraded people," incapable of being citizens. He also expressed doubt that a Supreme Court decision holding the statute unconstitutional would bind the states.

As Chief Justice of the United States after 1836, Taney left an enduring imprint on the American Constitution. Most of the landmark cases coming before the Court in the first decade of his tenure involved questions of the power of the states to regulate the economic behavior of persons or corporations within their jurisdictions. In CHARLES RIVER BRIDGE V. WARREN BRIDGE (1837) Taney employed a paradigmatic balance between investors' demands for autonomy and the states' insistence on public control of that new legal creature, the private corporation. Refusing to read into a bridge company's charter an implicit grant of a transportation monopoly, Taney held that "in charters, . . . no rights are taken from the public, or given to the corporation, beyond those which the words of the charter, by their natural and proper construction, purport to convey." (See RESERVED POLICE POWERS.)

Subsequent decisions of the Taney Court confirmed the *Charles River Bridge* DOCTRINE: where the state had explicitly conveyed monopoly rights or otherwise conferred valuable privileges, a majority of the Court honored the grant and held the state to it under CONTRACT CLAUSE doctrines deriving from FLETCHER V. PECK (1810). On the other hand, the Court refused to infer monopoly grants or other restrictions on state regulatory power if they were not explicitly conferred in a corporate charter. Thus in BANK OF AUGUSTA V. EARLE (1839) Taney held that states could regulate the activities of foreign corporations within their jurisdictions, or exclude them altogether, but that such regulations would have to be explicit. Absent express declarations of state policy, the TANEY COURT refused to hold that banking corporations could not enter into contracts outside the state that chartered them.

Yet Taney entertained an instinctive sympathy for states' efforts to control economic activity within their jurisdictions. In another case from his maiden term, BRISCOE V. BANK OF KENTUCKY (1837), Taney supported the majority's holding that a state was not precluded from creating a bank wholly owned by it and exercising note-issuing powers, so long as the state did not pledge its credit to back the notes. Such notes would have been a subterfuge form of the state BILLS OF CREDIT that had been struck down in CRAIG V. MISSOURI (1830). In BRONSON V. KINZIE (1843), however, Taney invalidated state statutes that restricted foreclosure sales and granted mortgagors rights to redeem foreclosed property. Even here, however, he emphasized that states could modify contractual remedies so long as they did not tamper with the substance of existing contracts.

Taney's opinions dealing with the jurisdiction of federal courts proved to be among his most significant. Some of these restricted the autonomy of the states in the interests of protecting the national market. Thus in SWIFT V. TYSON (1842) the Court unanimously supported an opinion by Justice JOSEPH STORY holding that in commercial law matters, federal courts need not look to the forum state's COMMON LAW for rules of decision, but instead might formulate commercial law doctrines out of "the general principles and doctrines of commercial jurisprudence," a principle that survived until *Swift* was overruled in ERIE RAILROAD V. TOMPKINS (1938). (See FEDERAL COMMON LAW.) In PROPELLER GENESEE CHIEF V. FITZHUGH (1851), Taney discarded the English tidewater rule of ADMIRALTY JURISDICTION that Story had imported into American law, and held instead that the inland jurisdiction of federal courts in admiralty matters extended to all navigable waters, tidal or not, thus expanding the reach of federal admiralty jurisdiction to the Great Lakes and the interior rivers. But in LUTHER V. BORDEN (1849), he reasserted the POLITICAL QUESTION doctrine, holding that a challenge to the legitimacy of Rhode Island's government after the Dorr Rebellion of 1842 was to be resolved only by the legislative and executive branches of the national government, not the judicial.

It might be expected that Taney would have been warmly sympathetic to the emerging doctrine of the POLICE POWER, first fully articulated by Massachusetts Chief Justice LEMUEL SHAW in *Commonwealth v. Alger* (1851). But Taney held unspoken reservations about the police power doctrine, fearing that if the states' regulatory powers were defined too explicitly or couched under a rubric, they might somehow be restricted by the federal Constitution. He thus preferred to avoid an explicit definition of the police power, and instead emphasized the states' inherent powers of SOVEREIGNTY over persons and things within their jurisdiction, believing that if the issue were framed in terms of sovereignty rather than regulatory power, the states' autonomy from external interference might be more secure.

This issue of state regulatory power remained sensitive throughout Taney's tenure and was prominent in cases arising out of the attempt of Democratic majorities in the Ohio legislature to levy taxes on banks that had been exempted from certain forms of taxation by their charters. In *Ohio Life Insurance & Trust Co. v. Debolt* (1854) Taney held, in accordance with the *Charles River Bridge* paradigm, that the Court would not read into bank charters an implicit exemption from taxes. But in DODGE V. WOOLSEY (1856), Taney joined a majority in defending an explicit charter exemption against a state constitutional amendment empowering the state to tax exempted banks. Taney was not hostile to banks and corporations as such; he had an alert appreciation of the role that they would play in developing the national market.

Another issue—indeed, the critical one—that kept Taney and his colleagues sensitized to issues of state regulatory power was the protean matter of slavery and black people. This issue, deep in the background, skewed all but one of the Taney Court's COMMERCE CLAUSE decisions. In his first term, the Court skirted slavery complications in a case, MAYOR OF NEW YORK V. MILN (1837), challenging the right of a state to impose some measure of control over the ingress of foreign passengers, by holding that the challenged authority was not a regulation of commerce but rather an exercise of the police power. But this evasion would not dispose of subsequent cases challenging the power of the state to control the importation of liquor or the immigration of persons. In the LICENSE CASES (1847), the Court rendered six opinions, including one by Taney who was with the majority for the result, sustaining the efforts of three New England states to prohibit the importation and sale of liquor. But in the PASSENGER CASES (1849), raising issues similar to *Miln,* the court produced eight opinions, this time with Taney in the minority, striking down state laws regulating or taxing the influx of ALIENS. Taney was consistent throughout, insisting that no federal constitutional restraints existed on the power of the states to control persons or objects coming into their borders. His brush with the controversy over the Negro Seamen's Act as United States attorney general had left him hostile to any constitutional restraints that might inhibit the power of the slave states to control the ingress of free blacks, slaves, abolitionists, or antislavery propaganda.

The Taney Court did manage to filter slavery complications out of one major commerce clause case, thereby producing another paradigm of state regulatory power. In COOLEY V. BOARD OF WARDENS OF PHILADELPHIA (1851) the Court, with Taney in the majority, held that the commerce clause did not restrain the states from regulating matters essentially local in nature (such as, in this case, pilotage fees or harbor regulations) even if they had some impact on interstate or foreign commerce.

Curiously, the Court was more successful, in the short run, in disposing of cases where the question of slavery was overt rather than implicit. Taney, deeply dedicated to the welfare of his state and region, and anxious above all to protect the slave states from external meddling that would threaten their control of the black population, free or slave, or that would promote widespread emancipation, adopted passionate and extremist postures in slavery cases. In GROVES V. SLAUGHTER (1841), which involved the validity of a contract for sale of a slave under a state constitution that prohibited the commercial importation of slaves, Taney was provoked to a sharp reiteration of his attorney general's opinion, insisting that the power of a state to control blacks within its borders was exclusive of all federal power, including that under the commerce clause.

In PRIGG V. PENNSYLVANIA (1842) Taney was again prodded into another concurrence. Though he agreed with most of Justice Joseph Story's opinion for the majority holding unconstitutional a Pennsylvania PERSONAL LIBERTY LAW, he firmly disavowed Story's dictum that states need not participate in the recapture and rendition of fugitive slaves. Taney rejected Story's assertion that states could not enact legislation supplemental to the federal Fugitive Slave Act, and maintained that states must do so; his colleagues PETER V. DANIEL and SMITH THOMPSON merely asserted that a state could adopt such laws.

In STRADER v. GRAHAM (1851) Taney spoke for the Court in a case raising American variants of issues earlier canvassed in SOMERSET'S CASE (1772), a doctrinally seminal English decision that had passed into the mainstream of American constitutional thought. Appellant sought to have the Court overturn a Kentucky Court of Appeals decision that slaves permitted by their master to sojourn in a free state who then returned to their slave domicile did not become liberated because of their free-state sojourn. Taney held that the state court determination of the slaves' status was conclusive on federal courts (a point consistent with his emphasis on state control of blacks and a doctrinal opportunity for evading the issues of *Dred Scott* later). But Taney uttered OBITER DICTA disturbing to the free states. He suggested that the power of states over persons in their jurisdictions was unfettered "except in so far as the powers of the states in this respect are restrained . . . by the Constitution of the United States," thus hinting that there might be some federal constitutional impediment to the abolition statutes of the free states. He further insisted, needlessly, that the antislavery provisions of the NORTHWEST ORDINANCE were defunct, no longer an effective prohibition of the introduction of slavery in the states that had been carved out of the Northwest Territory.

Dred Scott (1857) was Taney's definitive utterance on the slavery question. His opinion, though one of nine, was taken by contemporaries to be for the Court, and Taney himself so considered it. Taney first excluded blacks descended from slaves from the status of "Citizens" as that term was used both in the Article III diversity clause and the Article IV PRIVILEGES AND IMMUNITIES clause. In order to support this conclusion, Taney asserted, incorrectly, that blacks in 1787 had been "considered as a subordinate and inferior class of beings, who . . . had no rights which the white man was bound to respect." Taney further insisted that the meaning of the Constitution does not change over time, so that the connotations of its words in 1787 remained rigid and static, unalterable except by formal amendment.

In the second half of his long opinion, Taney held that the federal government lacked power to exclude slavery from the territories, thus holding the MISSOURI COMPROMISE unconstitutional (even though it had already been declared void by the KANSAS-NEBRASKA ACT of 1854). He grounded this lack of federal power not in the territories clause of Article IV, but in its textual sibling, the new states clause, insisting that Congress could not impose conditions on the admission of new states that would put them in a position inferior to those already admitted. Taney also suggested in passing that the DUE PROCESS clause of the Fifth Amendment prohibited Congress from interfering with the property rights of slaveholders. But the significance of this utterance as a source of the later doctrine of SUBSTANTIVE DUE PROCESS has been overrated. Taney was not a devotee of HIGHER LAW doctrines, such as those enunciated by Justice SAMUEL CHASE in CALDER v. BULL (1798), by Justice Story in cases like TERRETT v. TAYLOR (1815) and *Wilkinson v. Leland* (1829), and by numerous state court judges, most recently in the landmark case of WYNEHAMER v. NEW YORK (1856).

In his *Dred Scott* opinion Taney also adopted three points of proslavery constitutional thought previously voiced in Southern legislatures and doctrinal writings: the federal government had no power over slavery except to protect the rights of slaveholders; the federal government was the "trustee" of the states for the territories, and as such must protect the interests of all of them there; and the territorial legislature could not exclude slavery during the territorial period. His performance in the *Dred Scott* case was widely condemned. Justice BENJAMIN R. CURTIS effectively controverted it in his scholarly dissent in *Dred Scott;* northern legislators, political leaders, attorneys, and polemicists poured forth innumerable rebuttals; and the Vermont legislature and the Maine Supreme Judicial Court flatly rejected its doctrines. ABRAHAM LINCOLN insisted that *Dred Scott*'s doctrine must be overruled.

Taney remained unmoved by such criticism, insisting in private correspondence that his position would be validated in time. Though aged and in intermittent ill health, he continued his judicial labors unabated. In ABLEMAN v. BOOTH (1859), a magisterial treatise on the role of the federal judiciary in the American federal system, Taney held that state courts could not interfere with the judgment of a federal court through use of the writ of HABEAS CORPUS. He adumbrated the doctrine of dual sovereignty: the federal and state governments "are yet separate and distinct sovereignties, acting separately and independently of each other." (See DUAL FEDERALISM.) But he insisted on the unfettered independence of federal courts in their execution of federal laws. In *dictum,* he asserted that the Fugitive Slave Act of 1850 was constitutional.

Taney produced significant published and unpublished opinions during the Civil War. In private communications, he supported SECESSION and condemned Lincoln's resort to force to save the Union. In keeping with such views, he drafted opinions, probably to be incorporated into conventional judicial opinions when the opportunity arose, condemning the EMANCIPATION PROCLAMATION, CONSCRIPTION, and the Legal Tender Acts. He also extended the first half of his *Dred Scott* opinion to exclude all blacks, not just those descended from slaves, from CITIZENSHIP; and he reasserted the obligation of the free states to return fugitive slaves. In an official opinion on circuit he condemned Lincoln's suspension of the writ of *habeas corpus* in EX PARTE MERRYMAN (1861), an opinion Lincoln refused to honor. He also joined the dissenters in the PRIZE CASES (1863), who insisted that because only Congress can declare war, Lincoln's military response to secession and southern military actions was "private" and of no legal effect. His death in 1864 relieved him from the painful necessity of seeing his vision of the constitutional and social order destroyed by the victory of Union arms.

Taney's lasting contributions consisted of his reinforcement of the political question doctrine, his strong defense of the states' regulatory powers, and his vigorous aggrandizement of the jurisdiction of the federal courts. More than his colleagues, he keenly appreciated the role of technological change in American law, a sensitivity apparent in *Charles River Bridge* and *Genesee Chief.* His defense of regional autonomy and his hostility to the power of concentrated capital retain a perennial relevance. His instinct for dynamic balance in the formulation of enduring rules of law, as in the *Charles River Bridge* paradigm, evinced judicial statesmanship of the first rank.

Constitutional problems related to slavery combined with Taney's personal failings to blight his reputation and eclipse his real achievements. *Dred Scott* remains a monument to judicial hubris, and all the slavery cases that came before the Taney Court bear the impress of Taney's determination to bend the Constitution to the service of sectional interest. Though he manumitted nearly all his own slaves and was in his personal relations a kind and loving man, Taney as Chief Justice was immoderate and willful when the times called for judicial caution. His tolerance of multiple opinions permitted dissents and concurrences to proliferate, blurring the clarity of doctrine in commerce clause cases. In any case touched directly or indirectly by slavery, Taney's sure instincts for viable doctrine, as well as his nobler personal qualities, deserted him and gave way to a blind and vindictive sectionalism unworthy of the Chief Justice of the United States.

It is the tragic irony of Taney's career that his virtues were so closely linked to his faults, especially in their results. He fully merited FELIX FRANKFURTER's warm appreciation of his role in shaping the American federal system: "the intellectual power of his opinions and their enduring contribution to a workable adjustment of the theoretical distribution of authority between two governments for a single people, place Taney second only to Marshall in the constitutional history of our country." Yet no other Justices have so gravely damaged the federal system because of sectional bias, and the real merits of Taney's defense of localist values have been obscured by his racial antipathies and sectional dogmatism.

WILLIAM M. WIECEK

Bibliography

FEHRENBACHER, DON E. 1979 *The Dred Scott Case: Its Significance in American Law and Politics.* New York: Oxford University Press.

HARRIS, ROBERT J. 1957(1966) Chief Justice Taney: Prophet of Reform and Reaction. Pages 93–118 in Leonard W. Levy, ed., *American Constitutional Law: Historical Essays.* New York: Harper & Row.

LEWIS, WALKER 1965 *Without Fear or Favor: A Biography of Chief Justice Roger Brooke Taney.* Boston: Houghton Mifflin.

SWISHER, CARL B. 1935 *Roger B. Taney.* New York: Macmillan.

——— 1974 *The Taney Period, 1835–64.* Volume 5 of *The Oliver Wendell Holmes Devise History of The Supreme Court of the United States.* New York: Macmillan.

TANEY COURT
(1836–1864)

The Supreme Court under Chief Justice ROGER B. TANEY (1836–1864) has not been a favorite among historians, perhaps because it defies easy generalization. There were few great constitutional moments and no dramatic lawmaking decisions comparable to those handed down by the MARSHALL COURT. The fifteen Justices who served with Taney (not counting ABRAHAM LINCOLN's Civil War appointees) varied immensely in ability—from JOSEPH STORY of Massachusetts who was the leading scholar on the bench until his death in 1845 to JOHN MCKINLEY of Alabama whose twenty-five years on the Court left barely a trace. Institutional unity and efficiency were often disrupted by abrasive personalities like HENRY BALDWIN (who became mentally unstable shortly after his appointment in 1830) and PETER V. DANIEL (whose passion for STATES' RIGHTS drove him into chronic dissent). Division was constant and bitter as the Justices disagreed openly over corporation, banking, and slavery questions—all of which tended to be seen from a sectional point of view. Fortunately for the ongoing work of the Court, most of its members shared a respect for the Constitution and had a common commitment to economic progress and property rights that cut across ideological and sectional differences. All were Democrats, too, except Story, JOHN MCLEAN, and BENJAMIN R. CURTIS. Most of the Court respected the Chief Justice—whose legal mind was of a high order—and responded well to his patient, democratic style of leadership. Still the Court under Taney did not quite cohere. There was no "leading mind," as DANIEL WEBSTER complained, and no clear-cut doctrinal unity.

Clearly the Taney Court was not the Marshall Court—but then again it was not the age of Marshall. The society that conditioned the Taney Court and defined the perimeters within which it made law was democratic in its politics, pluralistic in social composition, divided in ideology, and shaped by capitalist forces which increasingly sought freedom from traditional governmental restraints. Most threatening to judicial unity, because it was directly reflected in the opinions of the Court, was the intensification of sectional rivalry. As northern states committed themselves to commerce and manufacturing, they came to see themselves—taking their cultural cues from the abolitionists—as a section united in defense of liberty and freedom. The South found ideological conservatism an ideal umbrella for an expansive social-economic system based on cotton and organized around plantation slavery. As the sections competed for political power and control of the new West, each came to think of itself as the last best hope of mankind. And each insisted that the Constitution accommodate its policy preferences—a demand that the Supreme Court could satisfy only by compromising doctrinal purity and finally could not satisfy at all.

In short, the political and economic problems of the new age became constitutional problems just as ALEXIS DE TOCQUEVILLE had said they would. Whether the Supreme Court would be the primary agency to resolve those problems was, of course, a matter of debate. ANDREW JACKSON, armed with a mandate from the people, did not believe that the Court had a monopoly of constitutional wisdom. Newly organized POLITICAL PARTIES stood ready to dispute judicial decisions that offended their constituencies. States armed with JOHN C. CALHOUN's theory of NULLIFICATION insisted that they, not the Court, had the final word on the Constitution. Accordingly, the margin of judicial error was drastically reduced. The Court was obliged to make the Constitution of 1787 work for a new age; the high nationalism of the Marshall Court, along with its Augustan style of judging, would have to be toned down. Changes would have to come. The question—and it was as yet a new one in American constitutional law—was whether they could be made without disrupting the continuity upon which the authority of the law and the prestige of the Court rested.

The moment of testing came quickly. Facing the Court in its 1837 term were three great constitutional questions dealing with state banking, the COMMERCE CLAUSE, and corporate contracts. Each had been argued before the Marshall Court and each involved a question of FEDERALISM which pitted new historical circumstances against a precedent from the Marshall period. The Court's decisions in these cases would set the constitutional tone for the new age.

In BRISCOE V. BANK OF KENTUCKY the challenge was simple and straightforward. The issue was whether notes issued by the state-owned Commonwealth Bank were prohibited by Article I, section 10, of the Constitution, which prevented states from issuing BILLS OF CREDIT. The Marshall Court had ruled broadly against state bills of credit in CRAIG V. MISSOURI (1830), but the new Jacksonian majority ruled for the state bank. Justice McLean's opinion paid deference to legal continuity by distinguishing *Briscoe* from *Craig*, but political and economic expediency controlled the decision as Story's bitter dissent made clear. The fact was that, after the demise of the second Bank of the United States, state bank notes were the main currency of the country. To rule against the bank would put such notes in jeopardy, a risk the new Court refused to take.

Policy considerations of a states' rights nature also overwhelmed doctrinal consistency in commerce clause litigation, the Court's primary means of drawing the line between national and state power. Marshall's opinion in GIBBONS V. OGDEN (1824) had conceded vast power over INTERSTATE COMMERCE to Congress, although the Court had not gone so far as to rule that national power automatically excluded states from passing laws touching FOREIGN and INTERSTATE COMMERCE. The new age needed a flexible interpretation of the commerce clause that would please states' rights forces in both the North and the South and at the same time encourage the growth of a national market.

In MAYOR OF NEW YORK V. MILN, the second of the trio of great cases in 1837, the Court struggled toward such a reinterpretation. A New York law required masters of all vessels arriving at the port of New York to make bond that none of their passengers should become wards of the city. The practical need for such a law seemed clear enough; the question was whether it encroached unconstitutionally on federal power over interstate commerce as laid out in the *Gibbons* decision. The Chief Justice assigned the opinion to Justice SMITH THOMPSON who was prepared to justify the New York law as a police regulation and as a legitimate exercise of concurrent commerce power. His narrow definition of STATE POLICE POWER displeased some of his brethren, however, and even more so his position on CONCURRENT POWER. When he refused to compromise, the opinion was reassigned to PHILIP P. BARBOUR, who upheld the state regulation as a valid exercise of state police power. Barbour's contention that police power was "unqualified and exclusive" far exceeded anything that precedent could justify, however, as Story pointed out in his dissent. Indeed, Barbour's opinion, so far as it ruled that states could regulate interstate passengers, went beyond the position agreed upon in CONFERENCE and lacked the full concurrence of a majority.

The *Miln* case settled little except that the New York regulation was constitutional. The Court remained sharply divided over the basic questions: whether congressional power over foreign and interstate commerce was exclusive of the states or concurrent with them and, if it was concurrent, how much congressional action would be necessary to sustain national predominance. The doctrine of state police power had taken a tentative step toward maturity, but its relation to the commerce clause remained unsettled. That the states reserved some power to legislate for the health and welfare of their citizens seemed clear enough, but to establish an enclave of state power prior to, outside the scope of, and superior to powers delegated explicitly to Congress was to beg, not settle the crucial constitutional question.

The uncertainty regarding the questions generated by *Miln* continued throughout the 1840s in such cases as GROVES V. SLAUGHTER (1841) where the Court refused to rule on whether the provision of the Mississippi Constitution of 1832 touching the interstate slave trade was a violation of national commerce power. Confusion increased in the LICENSE CASES (1847) and the PASSENGER CASES (1849), which dealt with state regulation of alcohol and immigration respectively. The Justices upheld state authority in the first and denied it in the second, but in neither did they clarify the relation of state police power to federal authority over interstate commerce.

Not until COOLEY V. BOARD OF WARDENS (1852), which considered the constitutionality of a Pennsylvania law regulating pilotage in the port of Philadelphia, did the Court supply guidelines for commerce clause litigation. Congress had twice legislated on pilotage, but in neither case was there any conflict with the Pennsylvania law. The issue came, therefore, precisely and unavoidably to focus on EXCLUSIVE POWER versus concurrent power: whether the constitutional grant of commerce power to Congress automatically prohibited STATE REGULATION OF COMMERCE or whether the states could regulate commerce as long as such regulations did not actually conflict with congressional legislation.

Justice Curtis's majority opinion upheld the state law and in the process salvaged some doctrinal regularity. Starting from the undeniable premise that the commerce power granted to Congress did not expressly exclude the states from exercising authority over interstate commerce, he ruled that exclusive congressional JURISDICTION obtained only when the subject matter itself required it. The SUBJECTS OF COMMERCE, however, were vast and varied and did not require blanket exclusiveness. Some matters, he said, needed a "single uniform rule, operating equally on the commerce of the United States in every port." Some just as certainly admitted of local regulation. Power, in other words, followed function: if the subject matter required uniform regulation, the power belonged to Congress; if it did not, the states might regulate it. State police power remained to be settled, but the pressure to do so was lessened because the concurrent commerce power of the states was now clearly recognized.

SELECTIVE EXCLUSIVENESS, as the Court's approach in *Cooley* came to be called, was not a certain and final answer to the problem of allocating commerce power between the national government and the states, however. The rule was clear enough but how to apply it was not, which is to say that Curtis gave no guidelines for determining which aspects of commerce required uniform regulation or which permitted diversity. What was clear was that the Court had retreated from the constitutional formalism of the Marshall period. The opinion was short, only ten pages long; it made no reference to precedent, not even *Gibbons*. The Justices now willed to do what they had previously done unwillingly: they decided cases without a definitive pronouncement of DOCTRINE. The important difference in *Cooley* was that the Court devised a rule of thumb recognizing the judicial interest-balancing that previously had been carried on covertly in the name of formal distinctions. Ordered process, not logical categories, would be the new order of the day.

The Court's flexibility also signaled a shift of power in the direction of the states. The constitutional legacy of the Marshall Court had been altered to fit Jacksonian priorities. Still, national authority had not been destroyed. The Taney Court had refused to extend the nationalist principles of MCCULLOCH V. MARYLAND (1819) and *Gibbons,* to be sure, but the principles stood. The Court's new federalism did not rest on new states' rights constitutional doctrine. Neither did the new federalism threaten economic growth, as conservatives had predicted. Agrarian capitalism, for example, fared as well under the Taney Court as it had under its predecessor. The Justices did sometimes resist the most exorbitant demands of land speculators, and occasionally a dissenting Justice spoke for the little man as did Daniel in *Arguello v. United States* (1855). But the majority took their cue from FLETCHER V. PECK (1810), which is to say that plungers in the land market mostly got free rein, as for example in *Cervantes v. United States* (1854) and *Fremont v. United States* (1855). That slaveholding agrarian capitalists were to benefit from this judicial largess was clear from the decision in DRED SCOTT V. SANDFORD (1857).

The Court's promotion of commercial-industrial-corporate capitalism proved more difficult because of the sectional disagreements among the Justices. But there is no doubt that the Taney Court served as a catalyst for the release of American entrepreneurial energies. Its plan for a democratic, nonmonopolistic capitalism, Jacksonian style, was unveiled in CHARLES RIVER BRIDGE V. WARREN BRIDGE, the last of the three landmark decisions of the 1837 term. Here the question was whether the toll-free Warren Bridge, chartered and built in 1828 a few hundred feet from the Charles River Bridge, destroyed the property rights of the old bridge, in violation of its charter as protected by DARTMOUTH COLLEGE V. WOODWARD (1819). The difficulty was that the charter of 1785, although granting the Charles River Bridge the right to collect tolls, had not explicitly granted a monopoly. The fate of the old bridge depended, therefore, on the willingness of the Taney Court to extend the principle of *Dartmouth College* by implication.

Taney, who spoke for the new Jacksonian majority on the Court, refused to do so. The Chief Justice agreed that "the rights of private property are sacredly guarded," but he insisted "that the community also have rights, and that the happiness and well-being of every citizen depends on their faithful preservation." The Court should not venture into the no-man's land of inference and construction when the public interest rested in the balance, Taney argued. He cleverly supported this position by citing Marshall's opinion in PROVIDENCE BANK V. BILLINGS (1830). And the public interest, as Taney saw it, lay in extending equality of economic opportunity. "Modern science," he said with an eye on new railroad corporations, would be throttled and transportation set back to the last century if turnpike and canal companies could turn charter rights into monopoly grants.

The *Bridge* decision, like the Court's decisions in banking and commerce, revealed a distinct instrumentalist tone as well as a new tolerance for state legislative discretion. The Court also showed its preference for dynamic over static capital. Still, property rights were not generally threatened. To be sure, in WEST RIVER BRIDGE COMPANY V. DIX (1848) the Court recognized the power of state legislatures to take property for public purposes with JUST COMPENSATION, but conservatives themselves were willing to recognize that power. The Court also took a liberal view of state DEBTORS' RELIEF LEGISLATION, especially laws applying to mortgages for land, but even here the Court could claim the Marshall Court's decision in OGDEN V. SAUNDERS (1827) as its guide. There was no doubt, on the other hand, as BRONSON V. KINZIE (1843) showed, that state relief laws that impaired substantial contractual rights would not be tolerated.

Corporate property also remained secure under the *Bridge* ruling. Indeed, corporate expansion was strongly encouraged by the Taney Court despite the resistance of some of the southern agrarian Justices. After 1837 the Court consistently refused to extend charter rights by implication, but it also upheld corporate charters that explicitly granted monopoly rights even though in some cases such rights appeared hostile to community interest. Corporations also greatly profited from BANK OF AUGUSTA V. EARLE (1839), which raised the question whether corporations chartered in one state could do business in another. Taney conceded that the legislature could prohibit foreign corporations from doing business in the state and some such laws were subsequently passed. But such prohibitions, he went on to say, had to be explicit; practically speaking, this limitation assured corporations the right to operate across state lines. Hardly less important to corporate expansion was *Louisville Railroad v. Letson* (1844) which held that corporations could be considered citizens of the states in which they were chartered for purposes of DIVERSITY JURISDICTION—thus removing the increasingly unworkable fiction created in *Bank of United States v. Deveaux* (1809) and assuring corporate access to federal courts where the bias in favor of local interests would be minimized.

The Court's promotion of capitalism showed the basic continuity between the Marshall and Taney periods and the fact that antebellum law followed the contours of economic development. Acknowledgment of this continuity, however, should not obscure the real changes in constitutional federalism as the Taney Court deferred more to state power and legislative discretion. Overall the Court spoke more modestly, too, readily acknowledging former errors and generally toning down its rhetoric. In LUTHER V. BORDEN (1849), it went so far as to promise judicial self-restraint regarding POLITICAL QUESTIONS, though that promise ought not to be confused with a hard-and-fast doctrine, which it clearly was not. Although the Court avoided stridency, it did not claim less power. The constitutional nationalism which the Taney Court reduced was not the same as the judicial nationalism which it actually extended. In short, the Court did things differently, but it did not surrender its power to do them. Although the *Bridge* case conceded new power to state legislatures and promised judicial restraint, the Court still monitored the federal system in corporate contract questions. The Court's commerce clause decisions worked to make the federal system more flexible. But in every case from *Miln* through *Cooley,* the Court retained the right to judge—and often, as in *Cooley,* by vague constitutional standards. This judicial authority, moreover, was used throughout the Taney period to expand the jurisdiction of the Court, often at the expense of state judiciaries which the Court claimed to respect.

Never was federal judicial expansion more striking than in SWIFT V. TYSON (1842), a commercial law case which arose under federal diversity jurisdiction. For a unanimous Court, Story held that, in matters of general commercial law, state "laws," which section 34 of the JUDICIARY ACT OF 1789 obliged the federal courts to follow in diversity cases, did not include state court decisions. In the absence of controlling state statutes, then, federal courts were free to apply general principles of commercial law, which they proceeded to do until *Swift* was overruled in 1938. Almost as expansive was Taney's opinion in PROPELLER GENESEE CHIEF V. FITZHUGH (1851), which bluntly overturned the tidewater limitation imposed by the Marshall Court and extended the admiralty jurisdiction of the federal courts over the vast network of inland lakes and rivers.

Both these decisions were part of the Court's consistent effort to establish a system of uniform commercial principles conducive to the interstate operation of business. Both paved the way for federal judicial intrusion into state judicial authority. When state courts objected to this judicial nationalism, as the Wisconsin Supreme Court did in the slave rendition case of ABLEMAN V. BOOTH (1859), Jacksonian Roger Taney put them in their place with a ringing defense of federal judicial authority that was every bit as unyielding as was Federalist John Marshall's in COHENS V. VIRGINIA (1821). *Ableman* was an assertion of power that would have astonished conservative critics in 1837 who predicted the imminent decline and fall of the Court. Instead, by 1850 the Taney Court was even more popular than the Marshall Court had been and the Chief Justice was praised by men of all political persuasions. All this would change when the Court confronted the issue of slavery.

Adjudicating the constitutional position of slavery fell mainly to the Taney Court; there was no escape. Slavery was the foundation of the southern economy, a source of property worth billions, a social institution that shaped the cultural values of an entire section and the politics of the whole nation. Moreover, it was an integral part of the Constitution, which the Court had to interpret. At the same time, it was, of all the issues facing the antebellum Court, least amenable to a rational legal solution—and in this respect, it foreshadowed social issues like abortion and AFFIRMATIVE ACTION which have troubled the contemporary Court. No other single factor so much accounts for the divisions on the Taney Court or its inability to clearly demarcate power in the federal system.

Given the slavery question's explosive nature, the Justices not surprisingly tried to avoid confronting it directly. Thus the obfuscation in *Groves v. Slaughter* (1841), where the issue was whether a provision in the Mississippi Constitution prohibiting the importation of slaves for sale after 1833 illegally encroached upon federal power over interstate commerce. The Court circumvented this issue by ruling that the state constitutional clause in question was not self-activating—a position that, while avoiding trouble for the Court, also guaranteed the collection of millions of dollars of outstanding debts owed slave traders and in effect put the judicial seal of approval on the interstate slave trade. The Court also dodged the substantive issue in STRADER V. GRAHAM (1851), which raised the question whether slaves who resided in Kentucky had become free by virtue of their temporary residence in the free state of Ohio. The Court refused jurisdiction on the ground that Kentucky law reasserted itself over the slaves on their return, so that no federal question was involved.

Where the substantive question could not be sidestepped, the Court aimed to decide cases on narrow grounds and in such a way as to please both North and South. Thus in *The Amistad* (1841), Justice Story ruled that Africans on their way to enslavement who escaped their Spanish captors were free by virtue of principles of international law and a close reading of the Treaty of 1794 with Spain. Extremists in neither section were pleased. Even less were they content with Story's efforts to juggle sectional differences, morality, and objective adjudication in PRIGG V. PENNSYLVANIA (1842). There the question was whether and to what extent states were allowed to pass PERSONAL LIBERTY LAWS protecting the rights of free Negroes in rendition cases. The South was pleased when Story declared the Pennsylvania liberty law of 1826 to be a violation of the constitutional and statutory obligation to return fugitive slaves. He went on to say, with his eye on northern opinion (and with doubtful support from a majority on the Court), that the power over fugitives belonged exclusively to the federal government and that states were not obliged to cooperate in their return. The decision encouraged northern states to pass personal liberty laws but also necessitated the more stringent federal fugitive slave law of 1850. Both developments fueled sectional conflict. (See FUGITIVE SLAVERY.)

The Court's strategy of avoidance aimed to keep slavery on the state level where the Constitution had put it, but the slavery question would not stay put. What brought it forth politically and legally as a national question was SLAVERY IN THE TERRITORIES, a problem which confronted the Court and the nation in *Dred Scott.* The nominal issue in that famous case was whether a Negro slave named Scott, who had resided in the free state of Illinois and the free territory of Minnesota (made free by the MISSOURI COMPROMISE of 1820) and who returned to the slave state of Missouri, could sue in the federal courts. Behind this jurisdictional issue lay the explosive political question of whether Congress could prohibit slavery in the territories, or to put it another way, whether the Constitution guaranteed it there. The future of slavery itself was on the line.

The first inclination of the Justices when they confronted the case early in 1856 was to continue the strategy of avoidance by applying *Strader v. Graham* (1851); by that precedent Scott would have become a slave on his return to Missouri with no right to sue in the federal courts. This compromise was abandoned: in part because of pressure from President JAMES BUCHANAN and Congress; in part because northern Justices McLean and Curtis planned to confront the whole issue in dissent; in part because the proslave, pro-South wing of the Court (led by Taney and Wayne) wanted to silence the abolitionists by putting the Constitution itself behind slavery in the territories; in part because the Justices pridefully believed they could put the troublesome question to rest and save the Union.

Taney's was the majority opinion so far as one could be gleaned from the cacophony of separate opinions and dissents. It was totally prosouthern and brutally racist: Scott could not sue in the federal courts because he was not a citizen of the United States. He was not a citizen because national CITIZENSHIP followed state citizenship, and in 1787 the states had looked upon blacks as racially inferior (which the states in fact did) and unqualified for citizenship (which several states did not). Scott's argument that he was free by virtue of residence in a free state was wrong, said Taney, because of *Strader* (which had been relied upon by the Supreme Court of Missouri); Scott's argument that residence in a free territory made him free carried no weight because Congress had no authority to prohibit slavery in the territories—an assertion that ignored seventy years of constitutional practice and permitted Taney to set forth the SUBSTANTIVE DUE PROCESS theory of the Fifth Amendment against the TAKING OF PROPERTY. Scott was still a slave. Congress could not prohibit slavery in the territories, because the Constitution guaranteed it there; neither, as the creatures of Congress, could territorial legislatures prohibit slavery as claimed by proponents of the doctrine of POPULAR SOVEREIGNTY. Taney's Constitution was for whites only.

Instead of saving the Union the decision brought it closer to civil war and put the Court itself in jeopardy. In effect, the decision outlawed the basic principle of the Republican party (opposition to the extension of slavery in the territories), forcing that party to denounce the Court. The Democratic party, the best hope for political compromise, was now split between a southern wing (which in 1860 chose the certainty of *Dred Scott* over the vagueness of popular sovereignty) and northern antislavery forces who, if they did not defect to the Republicans, went down to defeat with STEPHEN DOUGLAS and popular sovereignty. Sectional hatred intensified and the machinery of political compromise was seriously undercut—along with the prestige of the Court. From its peak of popularity in 1850 the Taney Court descended to an all-time low. After SECESSION it served only the section of the Union that ignored *Dred Scott* entirely, condemned the Court as a tool of southern expansionism, and looked upon the Chief Justice as an arch-traitor to liberty and national union.

Fortunately, these disabilities were not permanent. Northern hatred focused less on the Court as an institution and more on the particular decision of *Dred Scott,* which was obliterated by the THIRTEENTH and FOURTEENTH AMENDMENTS. *Dred Scott* seemed less important, too, after President Lincoln "Republicanized" the Court with new appointments (five, including a new Chief Justice who had been an abolitionist). More important, the Court brought itself into harmony with the northern war effort by doing what the Supreme Court has always done in wartime: deferring to the political branches of government and bending law to military necessity. Sometimes the Court deferred by acting (as in the PRIZE CASES of 1863 where it permitted the President to exercise WAR POWERS and still not recognize the belligerent status of the Confederacy) and sometimes it deferred by not acting (as when it refused to interfere with the broad use of martial law during the war).

The Taney Court not only survived but it also salvaged its essential powers—and with time even a grudging respect from historians. The memory of *Dred Scott* could not be totally exorcised, of course, but it diminished along with the idealism of the war years and with the recognition that the racism of the opinion was shared by a majority of white Americans. In any case, the reform accomplishments of the Taney Court helped to balance the reactionary ones. Its modest style of judging fit the new democratic age. Through its decisions ran a new appreciation of the democratic nature and reform potential of state action and a tacit recognition as well of the growing maturity of legislative government. The Court's pragmatic federalism, while it could support the evil of slavery, also embodied a tradition of cultural pluralism, local responsibility, and suspicion of power. This it did without destroying the foundations of constitutional nationalism established by the Marshall Court. Change is the essence of American experience. The Taney Court accepted this irresistible premise and accommodated the Constitution to it. The adjustment was often untidy, but the Court's preference for process over substance looked to the modern age and prefigured the main direction of American constitutional law.

R. KENT NEWMYER

Bibliography

COVER, ROBERT M. 1975 *Justice Accused: Antislavery and the Judicial Process.* New Haven: Yale University Press.

FEHRENBACHER, DON E. 1978 *The Dred Scott Case: Its Significance in American Law and Politics.* New York: Oxford University Press.

FRANKFURTER, FELIX 1937 *The Commerce Clause under Marshall, Taney and Waite.* Chapel Hill: University of North Carolina Press.

HARRIS, ROBERT J. 1957 Chief Justice Taney: Prophet of Reform and Reaction. *Vanderbilt Law Review* 10:227–257.

KUTLER, STANLEY 1971 *Privilege and Creative Destruction: The Charles River Bridge Case.* Philadelphia: J. B. Lippincott.

SWISHER, CARL B. 1974 *The Taney Period, 1836–1864.* Volume V of *The Oliver Wendell Holmes Devise History of the Supreme Court of the United States.* New York: Macmillan.

WARREN, CHARLES 1926 *The Supreme Court in United States History,* Vol. 2. New and revised ed. Boston: Little, Brown.

TARIFF ACT
4 Stat. 270 (1828)

Known as the "Tariff of Abominations," this act was designed to embarrass JOHN QUINCY ADAMS and help ANDREW JACKSON win the Presidency. Jacksonians controlling the House Committee on Manufactures wrote a tariff with excessively high duties for iron, hemp, flax, and numerous other raw materials. The bill's authors believed Adams's New England supporters would have to oppose the bill, and that the failure to pass a tariff would cost Adams the Middle States and the election. When New Englanders tried to amend the bill they were voted down by a coalition of southern and Middle State representatives organized by MARTIN VAN BUREN. The plan ultimately failed when representatives from everywhere but the South voted for the bill. Legislatures in South Carolina, Georgia, Mississippi, and Virginia denounced the act. JOHN C. CALHOUN anonymously wrote the South Carolina EXPOSITION AND PROTEST which laid out a theory of state NULLIFICATION of federal laws. While not adopting the Exposition, the South Carolina legislature printed 5,000 copies for distribution and declared the tariff unconstitutional. Although nullification was defeated at this juncture, and the tariff was amended in 1832, the 1828 act set the stage for the nullification crisis of 1832–1833.

PAUL FINKELMAN

Bibliography

FREEHLING, WILLIAM W. 1965 *Prelude to Civil War: The Nullification Controversy in South Carolina, 1816–1836.* New York: Harper & Row.

TAXATION OF INTERSTATE COMMERCE

See: State Taxation of Commerce

TAXATION WITHOUT REPRESENTATION

Taxation without representation was the primary underlying cause of the American Revolution. Taxation by consent, through representatives chosen by local electors, is a fundamental principle of American CONSTITUTIONALISM. From the colonial period, REPRESENTATION had been actual: a legislator was the deputy of his local electors. He represented a particular geographic constituency, and like his electors he had to meet local residence requirements. Thus, representation of the body politic and government by consent of the governed were structurally connected in American thought.

Taxation without representation deprived one of his property contrary to the first principles of the SOCIAL COMPACT and of the British constitution. No Englishmen endorsed the constitutionality of taxation without representation; that it violated FUNDAMENTAL LAW was the teaching of the CONFIRMATIO CARTARUM, the PETITION OF RIGHT, and the BILL OF RIGHTS. Englishmen claimed, however, that Parliament "virtually" represented the colonies—every member of Parliament represented the English nation, not a locality—and therefore could raise a revenue in America. Rejecting the concept of virtual representation, Americans insisted that they were not and could not be represented in Parliament. The argument of virtual representation implicitly conceded the American contention that taxation was the function of a representative body, not merely a legislative or sovereign body. American legislatures, facing parliamentary taxation for the first times in 1764 and 1765, resolved that Parliament had no constitutional authority to raise a revenue in America. Pennsylvania's assembly, for example, resolved "that the taxation of the people of this province, by any other . . . than . . . their representatives in assembly is unconstitutional." Similarly, the STAMP ACT CONGRESS resolved that the colonies could not be constitutionally taxed except by their own assemblies. The resolutions of the colonies, individually and collectively, claimed an exemption from all parliamentary taxation including customs duties and trade regulations whose purpose was to raise revenue.

The American claims were not simply concocted to meet the unprecedented taxation levied by Parliament in 1764 and after. The experience of Virginia, the first colony, was typical. Its charter guaranteed the rights of Englishmen, which Virginia assumed included the exclusive right of its own representative assembly to tax its inhabitants; the assembly so declared in a statute of 1624. In 1652 planters in a county not represented in the assembly protested the imposition of a tax. In 1674, when Virginia sought confirmation from the crown of its exclusive right to tax its inhabitants, the crown's attorney in England endorsed "the right of Virginians, as well as other Englishmen, not to be taxed but by their consent, expressed by their representatives." The Committee for Foreign Plantations and the Privy Council approved, too, but the king withheld approval because of Bacon's Rebellion. Virginia nevertheless persisted in its position. In 1717 the imposition of a royal postal fee produced, in the words of the colony's royal governor, "a great clamor. . . . The people were made to believe that Parliament could not levy any tax (for so they called the rates of postage) here without consent of the General Assembly." In 1753, when Virginia's governor imposed a trivial fee for the use of his seal on each land patent, the assembly lectured him on the theme that subjects cannot be "deprived of the least part of their property but by their own consent: Upon this excellent principle is our constitution funded." The history of any colony would yield similar incidents, showing how entrenched were the claims that Americans advanced when Parliament first sought to tax the colonies.

When the Declaratory Act of 1766 claimed for Parliament a power to "legislate" for America "in all cases whatsoever," some members of Parliament argued the American position that Parliament could tax only in its representative capacity and therefore could not tax America. WILLIAM PITT and Lord Camden (CHARLES PRATT) endorsed that position. Pitt denounced virtual representation as a contemptible idea and declared that taxation "is no part of the governing or legislative power"; he also distinguished taxes levied for revenue from trade regulations that incidentally but not deliberately produced some revenue. The dominant British position, however, assumed that because taxation was inseparable from SOVEREIGNTY, Parliament as the sovereign legislature in the empire had the power to tax in matters of imperial concern, even though the tax fell on unrepresented members of the empire. That position provoked Americans to distinguish the powers belonging to local governments (the idea of FEDERALISM); to develop the concepts of LIMITED GOVERNMENT, fundamental law, and a CONSTITUTION as supreme law over all government; and to frame written constitutions that enumerated the powers of government.

LEONARD W. LEVY

Bibliography

BAILYN, BERNARD 1967 *The Ideological Origins of the American Revolution.* Cambridge, Mass.: Harvard University Press.

MORGAN, EDMUND S. 1976 *The Challenge of the American Revolution.* Chap. 1. New York: W. W. Norton.

MORTON, RICHARD L. 1960 *Colonial Virginia,* 2 vols. Chapel Hill: University of North Carolina Press.

TAX COURT OF THE UNITED STATES

When the Internal Revenue Service determines a deficiency, a taxpayer who disagrees can either pay the additional tax and sue for a refund in a federal district court or withhold payment and petition the Tax Court to set aside the deficiency. Tax Court decisions are reviewed in the UNITED STATES COURTS OF APPEALS.

The Tax Court, until 1942 called the Board of Tax Appeals, was declared by Congress in 1970 to be a "court." It is not, however, a CONSTITUTIONAL COURT created under Article III, but a LEGISLATIVE COURT. Its members do not have life tenure but serve for fifteen-year terms.

KENNETH L. KARST

TAX CREDITS AND RELIGIOUS SCHOOLS

See: Government Aid to Religious Institutions

TAXING AND SPENDING POWER

A principal weakness of the ARTICLES OF CONFEDERATION was that Congress had no power of taxation. It could request the states to contribute their fair shares to the national treasury but it had no power to collect when, as often happened, the states did not pay. Hence, the first grant of power to Congress in the Constitution was to "have Power to Lay and collect Taxes, Duties, Imposts and Excises, to pay the Debts and provide for the common Defense and general Welfare of the United States; but all Duties, Imposts and Excises shall be uniform throughout the United States." The Constitution also imposed two other limitations. Congress could not tax exports nor lay a "Capitation, or other direct, Tax" unless "in Proportion to the Census or Enumeration herein before directed to be taken."

The direct limitations on taxing power pose few problems. Congress does not impose capitation or property taxes, which would be direct taxes and require apportionment among the states in accordance with population. Other taxes must be uniform—which means that the same subject or activity must be taxed at the same rate wherever it is found. Congress, like the states, cannot tax exports to foreign countries.

More difficult problems have risen because taxes not only raise revenue but also regulate. A tax on liquor may be designed to raise money but also to discourage consumption. A deduction for interest in computing income tax encourages home ownership. A tax may be high enough to virtually stop the production and sale of a particular product. Before the Civil War the federal government derived most of its revenue from the customs and in many years had no internal revenue beyond that. But beginning with the Civil War, Congress expanded the scope of federal taxation at a time when the Supreme Court had fairly restrictive views as to congressional powers to regulate local activities. The question became how far Congress could use taxation to achieve policies that were forbidden to it through direct regulation.

When Congress imposed a ten percent tax on local banknotes for the purpose of achieving a federal government monopoly in the issuing of currency, the Court in VEAZIE BANK V. FENNO (1869) indicated that the tax was constitutional but said that in any event no regulatory problem was presented; Congress did have an independent MONETARY POWER, and the tax was merely a means of implementing it. Thirty-five years later the Court faced the problem more directly. Congress had imposed a ten cents per pound tax on oleomargarine that was colored and only one-quarter cent per pound if it was white. The Court in MCCRAY V. UNITED STATES (1904) said that even though Congress did not have the power to pass a statute forbidding the sale of colored oleomargarine, it could still tax it and the courts would not interfere merely on the grounds that the tax was too high. And the Court also held that Congress could impose a tax on distributing narcotic drugs and include in the same statute regulations as to how such drugs were to be distributed. The Court in UNITED STATES v. DOREMUS (1919) said that a tax was not invalid just because it had regulatory as well as taxation purposes and that the regulations attached to the tax were constitutional as facilitating the collection of the tax.

But in the Child Labor Tax Case (1922) the Court concluded that a tax might really be a regulation and thus invalid. A federal statute prohibiting interstate transportation of goods made by child labor had been held to exceed Congress's power under the COMMERCE CLAUSE in HAMMER v. DAGENHART (1918). So Congress imposed a tax of ten percent of the net profits for the year for any manufacturing business that employed children within certain age limits. Here, the court said, the challenge was not merely that the tax was too high. Rather, Congress had imposed a regulation and used the tax as a penalty for violation. "[A] court must be blind not to see that the so-called tax is imposed to stop the employment of children within the age limits prescribed. Its prohibitory and regulatory effect and purpose are palpable." In *United States v. Constantine* (1935) the Court similarly held invalid a special tax of $1,000 upon anyone dealing in liquor in a state or locality where such dealing was illegal. The Court said that the law clearly was not a tax but rather a penalty for violating state law.

In a series of later cases, however, the Court upheld the taxes. A heavy tax on sale of special weapons such as sawed-off shotguns was upheld in SONZINSKY v. UNITED STATES (1937). In *United States v. Sanchez* (1950) and *United States v. Kahriger* (1953) the Court upheld taxes on narcotics and gambling in which taxpayers were required to register with the federal government, even though that registration would make it easier for the states to enforce their gambling and narcotics laws. In *Sanchez* the Court said: "It is beyond serious question that a tax does not cease to be valid merely because it regulates, discourages, or even definitely deters the activities taxed. . . . The principle applies even though the revenue obtained is obviously negligible, . . . or the revenue purpose of the tax may be secondary. . . . Nor does a statute necessarily fall because it touches on activities which Congress might not otherwise regulate. . . . These principles are controlling here. The tax in question is a legitimate exercise of the taxing power despite its collateral regulatory purpose and effect." Later, in MARCHETTI v. UNITED STATES (1968), the Court eliminated the use of the taxing power to compel violators of state laws to register with the federal government on the grounds that it violates the RIGHT AGAINST SELF-INCRIMINATION. And since the power of the federal government to regulate has received such major expansion in modern times, there is little need to use the taxing power to expand federal powers. Even though the Child Labor Tax Case may still be good law in defining when a tax ceases to be a tax and becomes a regulation, it is of minor importance. Congress will almost always have power to regulate and can cast its regulation in the form of a tax.

The spending power has also raised constitutional questions. Before the early 1900s, Congress spent money chiefly to defray its routine powers of government. It made a few grants to the states to encourage the construction of roads and universities, granting the money outright with no matching requirements or federal supervision. In 1902 the grants amounted to only seven million dollars per year. Soon, however, Congress began to see that grants could be used to encourage states to take action meeting federal standards even with respect to parts of the economy then thought to be outside congressional power.

The SHEPPARD-TOWNER MATERNITY ACT of 1921 provided for federal grants to states that would agree to spend the money for reducing maternal and infant mortality. Massachusetts, which had refused the grants, and Frothingham, a citizen and taxpayer, brought suits. The Supreme Court in *Massachusetts v. Mellon* and FROTHINGHAM v. MELLON (1923) held that neither had STANDING to litigate the issue. Massachusetts had no real interest at stake, for it had refused the grant. Frothingham had no standing as a taxpayer because her interest in the funds spent was miniscule and shared with all other federal taxpayers. The result of this suit was to make most government spending programs impossible to challenge in court.

As a result, it was not until 1936 that a major question as to the scope of the spending power was settled. Congress has power to levy taxes "to pay the Debts and provide for the common Defence and general Welfare of the United States." What does the GENERAL WELFARE CLAUSE mean? JAMES MADISON had argued that money could be spent only to carry out the other powers given to Congress—that there was not, in essence, any additional power granted by the general welfare language. ALEXANDER HAMILTON had said that the clause granted a substantive power to tax and spend so long as it was for the general welfare of the United States.

The Court finally had an opportunity to decide the issue in 1936 in UNITED STATES v. BUTLER. The AGRI-

CULTURE ADJUSTMENT ACT of 1933 had provided for agreements between the secretary of agriculture and farmers to reduce acreage in exchange for benefit payments. The money for the payments came from a tax levied on the processors of the commodity concerned with all of the tax proceeds directed to that purpose. The Court held first that the processors upon whom the tax was levied did have standing to challenge the expenditure, because they paid a substantial tax earmarked for that expenditure. Next, the Court adopted the Hamilton position that the power to spend might be exercised for the general welfare and was not limited to the other direct grants of legislative power. Finally, the Court said it did not have to decide whether the expenditure in this case was for the general welfare, because this law was a regulation, not an expenditure, and invalid as going beyond congressional regulatory power.

The *Butler* interpretation of the spending power, however, soon became the basis to uphold expenditures. In HELVERING V. DAVIS (1937) the Court upheld the SOCIAL SECURITY ACT, concluding that expenditures for old age pensions were expenditures for the general welfare. And in BUCKLEY V. VALEO (1976) the Court held that expenditures of funds to finance campaigns of presidential candidates was valid as an expenditure for the general welfare. (See CAMPAIGN FINANCING.) The Court said: "Congress was legislating for the 'general welfare'—to reduce the deleterious influence of large contributions on our political process, to facilitate communication by candidates with the electorate, and to free candidates from the rigors of fundraising. . . . Congress has concluded that the means are 'necessary and proper' to promote the general welfare, and we thus decline to find this legislation without the grant of power in Art. I, § 8."

The use of grants to states as a means of federal regulation has proceeded apace, almost totally free of challenge by the courts. Only where the challenge is based on the ESTABLISHMENT OF RELIGION has the Court recognized standing to challenge by taxpayers. And that holding, in FLAST V. COHEN (1968), is not absolute, as was shown by VALLEY FORGE CHRISTIAN COLLEGE V. AMERICANS UNITED FOR SEPARATION OF CHURCH AND STATE (1982). The seven million dollars of such grants in 1902 had risen to seven billion in 1960 and to over one hundred billion in the early 1980s—about one-third percent of state and local receipts from their own sources. Again, however, the constitutional issues have lost their former importance. If the expenditure can be said to be for the general welfare, the intrusion of the federal government into a local area does not matter. Because congressional powers to spend for the general welfare and to regulate under the commerce clause are so broad, there is little prospect of a successful constitutional challenge to federal spending.

Both as to taxation and as to expenditure, no major constitutional problems remain. Congress has such broad regulatory powers that it no longer needs to attempt to get around power limitations by using taxation and expenditure. These methods of regulation are used today as convenient devices for accomplishing goals within congressional power. The major limitations on them are political. If the increase in federal grants to states appears to be slowing and if some recent Presidents have talked about a New Federalism policy to decrease such federal spending, the reasons lie not in constitutional limitations but in governmental policy.

EDWARD L. BARRETT

(SEE ALSO: *Direct and Indirect Taxes; Economic Regulation; Import-Export Clause; Impoundment of Funds; National Police Power.)*

Bibliography

GRANT, J. A. C. 1936 Commerce, Production, and the Fiscal Powers of Congress. *Yale Law Journal* 45:751–778.

POWELL, THOMAS R. 1922 Child Labor, Congress and the Constitution. *North Carolina Law Review* 1:61–81.

TRIBE, LAURENCE H. 1978 *American Constitutional Law.* Pages 225–227, 244–250. Mineola, N.Y.: Foundation Press.

TAXPAYERS' AND CITIZENS' SUITS

Federal courts will rule on the merits of a legal claim only at the request of one with a "personal stake in the outcome of the controversy." As a corollary of this central, entrenched STANDING doctrine, the federal judiciary turns away attacks on the legality of government behavior by citizens suing only as such. The rule stems from a SEPARATION OF POWERS premise: that federal judges should not review conduct of Congress or the Executive absent the need to protect a plaintiff from distinct personal injury. The rule has been applied mostly to reject challenges by United States citizens to acts of the political branches of the federal government, although it also appears to bar federal court suits by state or local citizens against acts of their governments. In essence, the citizen interest in lawful governance is viewed as an ideological, not a personal, interest, an interest best left to political rather than judicial resolution. Nonetheless, if a plaintiff can show concrete individual injury, as in SIERRA CLUB V. MORTON (1972), the public interest may then be argued in behalf of the personal claim, even if the primary motive for suing is not the personal but the citizen interest.

The law of taxpayer standing is more elaborate, because taxpayers' suits are sometimes deemed sufficiently personal to permit standing and sometimes rejected as disguised citizens' suits. Taxpayers contesting their own tax liability have a "personal stake," of course, but such an individualized interest is less clear for taxpayers disputing how tax revenues are spent. In FROTHINGHAM V. MELLON (1923) the Supreme Court found the pecuniary interest of a federal taxpayer in federal spending too remote to justify JUDICIAL REVIEW of congressional appropriations, but it reaffirmed its previous approval of federal court suits by local taxpayers attacking local spending programs. In FLAST V. COHEN (1968) the Court created an exception, allowing federal taxpayers to challenge congressional spending as an ESTABLISHMENT OF RELIGION because the establishment clause gives taxpayers a special interest in challenging the use of tax dollars to support religion. The dissent objected that the Court was recognizing standing to bring a "public action" having no effect on the suing taxpayer's financial interest.

Since *Flast,* the Court has denied standing to federal taxpayers who raised other constitutional objections in *United States v. Richardson* (1974) and *Schlesinger v. Reservists Committee* (1974). And in VALLEY FORGE CHRISTIAN COLLEGE V. AMERICANS UNITED (1982), a decision that substantially undermines the premise of *Flast,* the Court denied standing to taxpayers who raised establishment clause objections, but challenged federal distribution of surplus property rather than congressional appropriations of money. Even at the state taxpayer level, invoking the establishment clause will not suffice if the claim is not of government financial support of religion but of regulatory support, as in DOREMUS V. BOARD OF EDUCATION (1952). In short, a federal court will recognize taxpayer standing only when there is a tangible financial connection between a local or state taxpayer's interest and government spending, or when a local, state, or federal taxpayer challenges legislative appropriations on establishment clause grounds.

The federal judiciary's rejection of citizen suits and most taxpayer attacks on spending reflects a view that the power of judicial review is only a by-product of the need to apply law, including constitutional law, to decide the rights of those claiming injury. To entertain public actions would be to expand judicial scrutiny of acts of the elected branches of government—usurpation that might bring retaliation, in the eyes of those who take this view. For those who think judicial review is founded on a broader obligation to assure government adherence to the Constitution, such an expanded scrutiny would be desirable. If Congress were to authorize the federal courts to take jurisdiction over public actions, the Supreme Court probably would not find Article III's "case" or "controversy" requirement an insurmountable barrier. But the Court has always been reluctant to entertain public actions on its own authority.

JONATHAN D. VARAT

Bibliography

WRIGHT, CHARLES A.; MILLER, ARTHUR R.; and COOPER, EDWARD H. 1984 *Federal Practice and Procedure.* Vol. 13:634–663. St. Paul, Minn.: West Publishing Co.

TAYLOR, JOHN
(1753–1824)

John Taylor of Caroline read law in the office of his uncle, EDMUND PENDLETON. He became involved early in Virginia revolutionary politics and was a delegate to the FIRST CONTINENTAL CONGRESS. He served as an Army officer and almost continuously as a member of the House of Delegates (1779–1785). In the legislature he supported a measure to end ESTABLISHMENT OF RELIGION in Virginia.

As a delegate to the state convention in 1788 Taylor opposed RATIFICATION OF THE CONSTITUTION, which lacked a BILL OF RIGHTS, gave too much power to the general government, and was insufficiently republican. Even so, he involved himself immediately in the politics of the new government, becoming the foremost publicist of Jeffersonian democracy. Both in the Senate (1792–1794) and in the public press he was a leading opponent of the economic policies of ALEXANDER HAMILTON. In the controversy over the ALIEN AND SEDITION ACTS, Taylor introduced the Virginia Resolutions (written by JAMES MADISON) in the state legislature. (See VIRGINIA AND KENTUCKY RESOLUTIONS.)

An ardent supporter of THOMAS JEFFERSON, Taylor returned briefly to the Senate in 1803. He supported the TWELFTH AMENDMENT and defended the constitutionality of the LOUISIANA PURCHASE when even the President doubted it. Taylor broke with the Republican party over the War of 1812 and the renomination of President Madison, but he did not deviate from its principles. In his final term in the Senate

(1822–1824) and in his last books Taylor denounced the growing power of the federal judiciary, JOHN MARSHALL'S decision in MCCULLOCH V. MARYLAND (1819), and HENRY CLAY'S AMERICAN SYSTEM, with its INTERNAL IMPROVEMENTS and protective tariff. He advocated STRICT CONSTRUCTION of constitutional grants of power to the federal government.

Taylor saw himself as the defender of a liberty in constant danger and a republic in perpetual crisis. He thought that, in every generation, the American people were presented with a choice between the political principles and practice of Thomas Jefferson and those of JOHN ADAMS—the former conducive to, and the latter destructive of, self-government and public happiness. He believed that the civic virtue of farmers, tradesmen, and professional persons was the indispensable basis of free institutions; and for him banks and corporations raised the specter of economic oligarchy, undermining both that virtue and those institutions. Big government was the creature and ally of big business; and bigness was the enemy of liberty and equality. Incongruously, for all his concern with liberty and equality he unqualifiedly supported black slavery. Taylor is probably best known as a theorist of STATES' RIGHTS: his ideas bridged the gap between the Virginia and Kentucky Resolutions and JOHN C. CALHOUN'S doctrine of NULLIFICATION.

Taylor's most important books are *An Enquiry into the Principles and Policies of the Government of the United States* (1814), a comprehensive statement of the political theory of agrarian democracy, and *Construction Construed and Constitutions Vindicated* (1820), an attack on the expansion of federal court JURISDICTION and the use of JUDICIAL REVIEW to reduce the independence of the states.

DENNIS J. MAHONEY

Bibliography

HILL, CHARLES W. 1977 *The Political Theory of John Taylor of Caroline.* Rutherford, N.J.: Fairleigh Dickinson University Press.

LLOYD, THOMAS GORDON 1973 *The Danger Not Yet Over: The Political Thought and Practice of John Taylor of Caroline.* Ph.D. dissertation, Claremont Graduate School.

TAYLOR, ZACHARY
(1784–1850)

A professional soldier and hero of the Mexican War, Zachary Taylor was elected President as a Whig in 1848. A moderate on most issues, Taylor was a Louisiana slaveholder who was politically close to New Yorkers Thurlow Weed and WILLIAM SEWARD. Taylor opposed any interference with slavery in the South but also opposed opening the Mexican Cession to slavery. Similarly, he opposed the WILMOT PROVISO but advocated immediate admission of California and New Mexico as free states. He opposed the COMPROMISE OF 1850 and would probably have vetoed most of its provisions, had he not died in July 1850.

PAUL FINKELMAN

Bibliography

HAMILTON, HOLMAN 1941 *Zachary Taylor: Soldier of the Republic.* Indianapolis: Bobbs-Merrill.

TAYLOR v. LOUISIANA
419 U.S. 522 (1975)

Under Louisiana law women were selected for jury service only when they explicitly volunteered for duty; men were selected irrespective of their desires. In *Hoyt v. Florida* (1961), the Supreme Court had employed a RATIONAL BASIS standard of review to uphold a similar law against DUE PROCESS and EQUAL PROTECTION attacks. In *Taylor,* however, the Court invalidated this jury selection system as a denial of the Sixth Amendment right of the accused to "a jury drawn from a fair cross section of the community." That the accused was male was irrelevant to this claim. The vote was 8–1; Justice WILLIAM H. REHNQUIST dissented, and Chief Justice WARREN E. BURGER concurred only in the result.

Writing for the other seven Justices, Justice BYRON R. WHITE declined to follow *Hoyt;* if the fair cross section requirement ever "permitted the almost total exclusion of women, this is not the case today." Women had entered the work force in large numbers, undermining their exemption "solely on their sex and the presumed role in the home." *Taylor* is not only an important JURY DISCRIMINATION precedent but also a strong judicial rejection of laws resting on stereotypical assumptions about "woman's role."

KENNETH L. KARST

TEN BROEK, JACOBUS
(1911–1968)

The major contribution of Jacobus ten Broek to American constitutional scholarship was *The Antislavery Origins of the Fourteenth Amendment* (1951; rev. ed.,

Equal under Law, 1965), in which he described the influence of the abolitionist movement on the drafting and ratification of the FOURTEENTH AMENDMENT. Ten Broek argued that the abolitionists identified the NATURAL RIGHTS of human beings as constitutional rights requiring a national constitutional power of enforcement. He maintained that the PRIVILEGES AND IMMUNITIES clause of the amendment protected these natural rights and the auxiliary rights necessary to their enjoyment; that the EQUAL PROTECTION clause required the states to supply full legal protection to natural rights and authorized Congress to protect these rights if the states failed to do so; and that the amendment applied to the states those provisions of the federal BILL OF RIGHTS guaranteeing natural rights, as well as those natural rights not mentioned in the Bill of Rights. Ten Broek, a lawyer, was a political scientist at the University of California, Berkeley.

RICHARD B. BERNSTEIN

TENNESSEE v. GARNER
105 S.Ct. 1694 (1985)

At the time of this case a majority of police departments in the nation prohibited the use of deadly force against nonviolent suspects, and the Supreme Court sought by its decision to stimulate a uniformity of that practice. Justice BYRON R. WHITE for a 6–3 majority held unconstitutional on FOURTH AMENDMENT grounds a state act authorizing an officer to shoot to kill in order to prevent an escape after he gave notice of an intent to arrest. The DOCTRINE of the case is that to kill a fleeing, unarmed felon as a last resort in order to prevent his getaway constitutes an unreasonable seizure unless the officer believes that failure to use deadly force will result in serious harm to himself or others. Justice SANDRA DAY O'CONNOR, for the dissenters, would have permitted deadly force at least against residential burglars who resist arrest by attempting to flee the scene of the crime.

LEONARD W. LEVY

(SEE ALSO: *Unreasonable Search.*)

TENNESSEE v. SCOPES

See: *State of Tennessee v. Scopes*

TENNESSEE VALLEY AUTHORITY ACT
48 Stat. 58 (1933)

A debate over the best use for an uncompleted defense plant site at Muscle Shoals—in the heart of a chronically depressed region—emerged after World War I, ending with passage of the Tennessee Valley Authority Act. In 1933, President FRANKLIN D. ROOSEVELT urged creation of "a corporation clothed with the power of government but possessed of the flexibility and initiative of a private enterprise" to rehabilitate and develop the resources of the Tennessee River valley.

The resultant act, largely written by Senator GEORGE W. NORRIS, encompassed a variety of objectives including national defense; flood control and the improvement of navigation; the development of agriculture, industry, and electric power; and even reforestation. To accomplish these goals, Congress created the Tennessee Valley Authority (TVA), granting it the power to construct dams and power works in the valley and to increase production of badly needed fertilizers. The act also authorized the TVA to sell any energy produced in excess of its needs, giving preference to publicly owned organizations; the TVA further received authority to build power lines to facilitate sales and transmission of power. A series of amendments in 1935 and 1939 sought to liquidate the system's costs by providing for sales of electric power, producing "gross revenues in excess of the costs of production," to acquire major utility properties, and even to issue credit to assist the distribution of its power.

Supporters of the act relied on arguments including the GENERAL WELFARE CLAUSE, the commerce power, and the WAR POWERS. The Supreme Court sustained a TVA contract for the sale of surplus power in ASHWANDER V. TENNESSEE VALLEY AUTHORITY (1936), thus effectively sustaining the act's constitutionality.

DAVID GORDON

TENNEY v. BRANDHOVE
341 U.S. 367 (1951)

This decision established the absolute immunity of state legislative officials from damages actions, brought under SECTION 1983, TITLE 42, UNITED STATES CODE, alleging violations of constitutional rights. William Brandhove claimed that Senator Jack

B. Tenney and other members of a California state legislative committee had violated his constitutional rights by conducting hearings to intimidate and silence him. In an opinion by Justice FELIX FRANKFURTER, the Supreme Court noted the history of parliamentary immunity in England, and cited the SPEECH OR DEBATE CLAUSE as a recognition of the need for a fearless and independent legislature. It held that, despite the unequivocal language of section 1983, Congress had not meant to "impinge on a tradition so well grounded in history and reason." (See LEGISLATIVE IMMUNITY.)

THEODORE EISENBERG

TEN POUND ACT CASES
N.H. (1786–1787)

These cases, about which little is known (not even the names of the litigants are known), are notable as the first instances in our history of a state court's holding unconstitutional an act of a state legislature. The Inferior Court of Common Pleas of Rockingham County, sitting in Portsmouth, New Hampshire, in 1786 and 1787, voided the "Ten Pound Act," which had been passed in 1785 for the speedy recovery of small debts. Our scanty knowledge of the cases derives from newspaper reports and legislative records. The act of 1785 allowed justices of the peace to try certain civil cases, involving sums less than ten pounds, without juries. The state constitutional guarantee of TRIAL BY JURY extended to all civil cases except those which juries customarily did not try. New Hampshire practice had previously allowed a justice of the peace to try a case without a jury if the sum amounted to less than two pounds. After the court ruled that the act conflicted with the right to trial by jury, petitions to the state House of Representatives demanded IMPEACHMENT of the judges. The house, by a 3–1 majority, voted that the act was constitutional, but the judges stood by their initial decision or reaffirmed it in another case. Following the failure of a motion to impeach the judges, the house capitulated and repealed the Ten Pound Act.

LEONARD W. LEVY

TENTH AMENDMENT

Adopted in 1791 as part of the BILL OF RIGHTS, the Tenth Amendment declares that "powers not delegated to the United States by the Constitution . . . are reserved to the States respectively, or to the people." This language was an attempt to satisfy the public that the new constitution would not make a reality of that most repeated of Anti-Federalist fears: a completely centralized or "consolidated" government. But while the Tenth Amendment reminded Congress that its concerns were limited, the Constitution envisioned the effective exercise of national power, as the NECESSARY AND PROPER CLAUSE and the SUPREMACY CLAUSE indicated. The inevitable question was to be: what happens when Congress's responsibilities require measures the states say are beyond Congress's powers? JOHN MARSHALL attempted the Supreme Court's first answer to this question in MCCULLOCH V. MARYLAND (1819). *McCulloch* is best interpreted as advancing the following propositions: by granting and enumerating powers, the Constitution envisions the pursuit of a limited number of ends (see ENUMERATED POWERS); the framers did not and could not have enumerated all the legislative means appropriate to achieving constitutional ends in changing historical circumstances; Congress can select appropriate means to authorized national ends without regard for state prerogatives; the states, by contrast, cannot enact measures conflicting with lawful congressional policies.

To reach these conclusions Marshall observed that in drafting the Tenth Amendment the First Congress had refused to limit national powers to those "expressly granted," as the ARTICLES OF CONFEDERATION had done, and that a STRICT CONSTRUCTION of national powers would defeat the vital purposes for which the Constitution had been established. By rejecting a rigid line between state and national powers *McCulloch* opened the way to the future assumption of state responsibilities by the national government as needed to achieve national ends. Critics charged that Marshall would consolidate all power in the national government by permitting unlimited means to an ostensibly limited number of national ends. Marshall defended his theory by insisting that judges should invalidate pretextual congressional acts, that is, congressional acts cloaked in the commerce power and other national powers but actually aimed at state concerns, not at the free flow of commerce or other authorized national ends. The Court did not always conform to this view of *McCulloch* in upholding the expansions of national power in the twentieth century. The SOCIAL SECURITY ACT, the FAIR LABOR STANDARDS ACT, and the CIVIL RIGHTS ACT of 1964 were good faith exercises of national power because they were plausible as means to the nation's economic health or the ends of the Civil War amendments. The same cannot be said for the MANN ACT, the Little Lindbergh Act, and other uses of national power for POLICE POWER purposes. (See GENERAL WELFARE CLAUSE.)

From the late 1840s to the late 1930s judges unfriendly either to national power or to government generally lapsed into a static conception of state–federal powers that exempted "state instrumentalities" from federal taxation (see INTERGOVERNMENTAL IMMUNITIES) and removed aspects of the nation's economic life (such as labor relations and other incidents of manufacturing) from Congress's reach. (See COMMERCE CLAUSE.) Scholars have imputed a theory of DUAL FEDERALISM to many of the decisions of this period because the Court seemed to say that the RESERVED POWERS of the states constituted a line Congress could not cross in exercising its admitted powers. The most infamous of dual federalist decisions, HAMMER V. DAGENHART (1918), prevented Congress from using its power over INTERSTATE COMMERCE to combat child labor, a practice then considered reserved to state control. After the Depression changed attitudes toward federal power, the Court all but eliminated the tax immunity doctrine, leaving only hypothetical protection from federal taxes that might interfere with "essential state functions," as might a federal tax on a statehouse. And in the landmark case of UNITED STATES V. DARBY (1941) the Court overruled *Hammer,* holding that Congress, regardless of its underlying purposes, could stop any goods from moving in interstate commerce, even though they were produced in conformity to state policies toward child labor and other conditions of manufacturing. For the *Darby* majority Justice HARLAN FISKE STONE said that the Tenth Amendment declared the "truism" that Congress could only exercise granted powers but that it had no effect on the question of what powers had actually been granted. Stone thus returned the Court to Marshall's view that Congress could disregard state prerogatives in the pursuit of what it saw as the nation's economic health in changing circumstances. But by disavowing judicial inquiries into underlying legislative purposes, Stone rejected the view that judges should invalidate pretextual uses of power—the essence of Marshall's defense of *McCulloch* as a decision compatible with the concept of a national government with limited concerns. Time had run out on this concept by the mid-1940s as Congress had advanced far in the use of its commerce, taxing, and spending powers for purposes of admitted state concern. (See NATIONAL POLICE POWER.)

Such was the general picture in the postwar constitutional law of state–federal power until a surprise decision in 1976 invalidated federal wage and hour standards for state employees. A plurality opinion in NATIONAL LEAGUE OF CITIES V. USERY (1976) likened STATES' RIGHTS "regarding the conduct of integral governmental functions" to the rights of individuals protected by the Bill of Rights. Here was an even clearer statement of dual federalism than *Hammer,* and critics charged that this radical departure from *McCulloch* threatened federal standards in areas such as CIVIL RIGHTS and environmental protection. But after evading extension of *Usery* for a decade the Court overruled *Usery* in GARCIA V. SAN ANTONIO METROPOLITAN TRANSIT AUTHORITY (1985), on the theory that representation of state governmental interests in Congress, as opposed to judicial vindication of states' rights, is the constitutionally preferred way to protect state prerogatives. *Garcia* thus abandoned *Usery* without returning to the theory of *McCulloch.*

Beyond fluctuations in judicial doctrine one can attribute the decline of the Tenth Amendment to the social and economic interdependencies of an industrial society and an enhanced public commitment to minority and other fundamental rights with which states' rights historically clashed.

SOTIRIOS A. BARBER

Bibliography

CORWIN, EDWARD S. 1950 The Passing of Dual Federalism. *Virginia Law Review* 36:1–24.

FLAX, KAREN H. 1983 In the Wake of National League of Cities v. Usery: A "Derelict" Makes Waves. *South Carolina Law Review* 34:649–686.

WECHSLER, HERBERT 1954 The Political Safeguards of Federalism: The Role of the States in the Composition and Selection of the National Government. *Columbia Law Review* 54:543–560.

TENURE OF OFFICE ACT
14 Stat. 430 (1867)

After a complete political rupture between President ANDREW JOHNSON and congressional Republicans over Reconstruction policy, Congress enacted the Tenure of Office Act in March 1867, providing that all officials of the executive branch, except cabinet officers whose appointment had required Senate confirmation, would hold office until their successors had likewise been confirmed. Cabinet officers were to hold office only during the term of the president appointing them plus one month. The act also provided for interim appointments while the Senate was not in session.

In February 1868, President Johnson removed Secretary of War EDWIN M. STANTON, who was hostile to his Reconstruction policies, and appointed General Lorenzo Thomas in his place. The House promptly voted to impeach Johnson. Though Republicans sought to remove him from office because of his stubborn obstruction of their Reconstruction program, debates in his Senate trial turned on the constitutionality of the statute. The President's counsel maintained that it was unconstitutional as an interference with the president's removal power, a prerogative distinct from the APPOINTIVE POWER. The Senate could not muster the two-thirds vote necessary for conviction. Congress repealed the act in 1887.

WILLIAM M. WIECEK

Bibliography

BENEDICT, MICHAEL LES 1973 *The Impeachment and Trial of Andrew Johnson.* New York: Norton.

TERM
(Supreme Court)

As prescribed by congressional statute, the Supreme Court holds a regular annual term of court, beginning on the first Monday in October. The term usually concludes in late June or early July of the following year. The Court is also authorized to hold special terms outside the normal October terms but does so only infrequently, in urgent circumstances (EX PARTE QUIRIN, 1942, German saboteurs convicted by military commission; O'BRIEN V. BROWN, 1972, seating of delegates to Democratic National Convention).

Although Congress manipulated the Court's terms to postpone decision of MARBURY V. MADISON (1803) for nearly a year, modern times have seen no similar stratagems.

KENNETH L. KARST

TERMINIELLO v. CHICAGO
337 U.S. 1 (1949)

Terminiello was convicted of disorderly conduct after a meeting in a private hall outside of which a thousand persons violently protested his anti-Semitic, antiblack, and anticommunist harangue. The Court reversed because the jury had been instructed that it might convict on a finding that Terminiello's speech "invite[d] dispute." This instruction failed to require a finding of CLEAR AND PRESENT DANGER of violence. *Terminiello* frequently is coupled with FEINER V. NEW YORK (1951) as illustrations of the HOSTILE AUDIENCE problem.

MARTIN SHAPIRO

TERRETT v. TAYLOR
9 Cranch 43 (1815)

This was the first case and one of the very few in which the Supreme Court relied exclusively upon the concept of a HIGHER LAW as the sole basis for holding a state act unconstitutional. After adopting THOMAS JEFFERSON'S statute of religious liberty, which separated church and state in Virginia, the legislature confiscated certain Episcopal glebe lands and sold them, using the proceeds for charity. The lands in question having been donated to the church by private persons, no contract and therefore no CONTRACT CLAUSE issue existed. Justice JOSEPH STORY for the Court held the confiscation act void, offering as grounds: "we think ourselves standing upon the principles of natural justice, upon the fundamental laws of every free government, upon the spirit and letter of the constitution. . . ." Story did not mention *which* letter. Usually the Court applied the DOCTRINE of VESTED RIGHTS in a way that absorbed the higher law within express provisions of the Constitution.

LEONARD W. LEVY

TERRITORIAL COURT

From the beginning the United States has held TERRITORIES outside the existing states. Some territories have been destined for statehood, others for independence, and still others for "permanent" territorial status. (See COMMONWEALTH STATUS.) Early in our history Congress established courts to serve the territories, but it did not give their judges the life tenure and salary guarantees demanded by Article III for judges of CONSTITUTIONAL COURTS. The constitutional status of these territorial courts was thus uncertain.

Chief Justice John Marshall sought to resolve the uncertainty in AMERICAN INSURANCE CO. V. CANTER (1828) by inventing a new category called LEGISLATIVE COURTS. Such a court, Marshall said, is not created under Article III, which provides for the establishment of constitutional courts to exercise the JUDICIAL POWER OF THE UNITED STATES. Rather it is created by Congress in carrying out its general legislative powers under Article I, including the power to provide for the government of the territories. Although the case at hand was one of ADMIRALTY AND MARITIME JURISDICTION, plainly within the federal judicial power, the fact that it arose in a territory made it appropriate for disposition by such a "legislative" territorial court. The result made good sense in a territory (Florida) that was to become a state; upon statehood, most of the work of the territorial courts would be taken over by the state courts, and there would be no place for a large body of life-tenured judges in the new federal courts. Furthermore, independence from the President and Congress receded in importance in a territorial government that had essentially the same power as a state to discard the principle of SEPARATION OF POWERS.

Today legislative courts continue to serve in territories such as Guam and the Virgin Islands. In the Commonwealth of PUERTO RICO, Congress has created a dual court system matching that of the DISTRICT OF COLUMBIA: one set of constitutional courts, operating wholly within the terms of Article III, and one set of commonwealth courts roughly equivalent to state courts.

KENNETH L. KARST

Bibliography

WRIGHT, CHARLES ALAN 1983 *The Law of Federal Courts*, 4th ed. Pages 14–15, 40–42, 49, 139–140. St. Paul, Minn.: West Publishing Co.

TERRITORY

At the time of independence several states had extensive claims to territory on the western frontier. A dispute over whether such territories were to be administered by the claimant states or by and for the United States long delayed ratification of the ARTICLES OF CONFEDERATION. In 1780 Congress passed a resolution urging the states to cede their claims to the United States. The resolution contained three promises which became the basic principles of American CONSTITUTIONALISM as extended to the territories: that the territories would be "disposed of for the common benefit of the United States"; that they would be "settled and formed into distinct republican states"; and that they would eventually "become members of the federal union and have the same rights of SOVEREIGNTY, freedom, and independence as the other states." After the cession was complete and the western boundary was settled by the Treaty of Paris (1783), Congress embodied these three principles in measures for the temporary government of the territories: the ORDINANCE OF 1784 and the NORTHWEST ORDINANCE OF 1787. The same principles were reaffirmed by the CONSTITUTIONAL CONVENTION OF 1787. Although some delegates advocated maintaining the western lands as a federal colony to be exploited and governed permanently by the existing states, the Constitution provided for the admission of new states on an equal basis with the original states.

The first acquisition of territory beyond the original borders of the nation was the LOUISIANA PURCHASE. After brief debate about the constitutional propriety of such territorial expansion, Congress proceeded to organize the Louisiana Territory following the model of the Northwest Ordinance. Exploration, purchase, and cession, as well as the conquests of the Mexican War, resulted in further territorial expansion.

Congress's power to make rules and regulations for the territories derives from the second clause of Article IV, section 3. In the first important case on territories to be decided by the Supreme Court, AMERICAN INSURANCE COMPANY V. CANTER (1828), Chief Justice JOHN MARSHALL suggested that the power to govern the territories was also implied in the power to acquire them through the use of the TREATY POWER or the WAR POWERS. He added that, whatever its source, Congress's power over the territories was plenary, whether exercised directly or through a local legislature, and extended even to creation of TERRITORIAL COURTS with JURISDICTION beyond the JUDICIAL POWER OF THE UNITED STATES.

In the early nineteenth century the question of SLAVERY IN THE TERRITORIES divided the country and sparked new controversy over the constitutional status of territories. Southerners maintained that the federal government held the territories in trust for the states and that Congress could not properly prohibit slavery in them, while northern Whigs such as ABRAHAM LINCOLN maintained that the territories were national possessions and failure to prohibit slavery in them would constitute a national endorsement of the institution. STEPHEN A. DOUGLAS proposed to avoid the issue by leaving it to a vote of the settlers in each territory. Congress sought to allay sectional contention in the MISSOURI COMPROMISE by permitting slavery in one part of the Louisiana Purchase while prohibiting it in the rest. In the COMPROMISE OF 1850, Douglas's formula (which he called POPULAR SOVEREIGNTY) was adopted for the territory acquired in the Mexican War (except California). In DRED SCOTT V. SANDFORD (1857) the Supreme Court held that Congress did not have the power to exclude slavery from the territories. The Civil War, by eliminating the slavery issue, ended the sectional dispute over the status of territories.

By 1869 American territorial acquisition on the mainland of North America was complete. A new debate about the status of territories began when, at the end of the nineteenth century, the United States started to acquire overseas possessions, not a part of the continent and apparently not destined for statehood. The place of this "colonial empire" in the constitutional system was a subject of political dispute in the 1900 elections; but it was not resolved until the Supreme Court decided the INSULAR CASES. In these cases the Court formulated the doctrine of INCORPORATION OF TERRITORIES, according to which territorial possessions do not become part of the United States until Congress, by some positive action, makes them so.

Territories may be either incorporated or unincorporated, and either organized or unorganized. The former refers to the degree of constitutional protection enjoyed by inhabitants and to Congress's ultimate intention to confer statehood or not; the latter refers to the provision Congress has made for government of the territory. There are now no incorporated territories, but there are both organized and unorganized unincorporated territories. In 1934 the special status of "commonwealth" was created for the Philippines, which became independent after World War II; PUERTO RICO and the Northern Marianas currently have COMMONWEALTH STATUS and enjoy virtually complete internal self-government. After World War II the United States accepted a mandate over the Trust Territory of the Pacific Islands. Authority over that territory was exercised by virtue of the UNITED NATIONS CHARTER until the trusteeship ended in 1981.

DENNIS J. MAHONEY

Bibliography

BLOOM, JOHN PORTER, ed. 1973 *The American Territorial System.* Athens: Ohio University Press.

LIEBOWITZ, A. H. 1979 United States Federalism: States and Territories. *American University Law Review* 28:449–482.

PERKINS, WHITNEY T. 1962 *Denial of Empire.* Leyden, Netherlands: A. W. Sythoff.

TERRY v. ADAMS
345 U.S. 461 (1953)

With confidence, we can call *Terry* the last of the series of "Texas primary cases" beginning with NIXON V. HERNDON (1927). The decision is also a clear modern example of the "public function" strand of STATE ACTION doctrine. In a Texas county, a group called the Jaybird Democratic Association conducted pre-PRIMARY ELECTIONS, from which black voters were excluded. The winners of these elections consistently won both the Democratic primaries and the general elections. The Supreme Court held that black plaintiffs were entitled to a DECLARATORY JUDGMENT that their exclusion from the Jaybird election amounted to state action in violation of the FIFTEENTH AMENDMENT. There was no MAJORITY OPINION. Three Justices said that the state could not constitutionally permit a racial exclusion from the only election that mattered in the county. The electoral process was inescapably public, subject to the Fifteenth Amendment's commands. Four other Justices said the Jaybirds were an auxiliary of the local Democratic party organization, and thus included within the doctrine of SMITH V. ALLWRIGHT (1944). Justice FELIX FRANKFURTER found state action in the participation of state election officials as voters in the Jaybird election. Justice SHERMAN MINTON dissented, calling the Jaybirds nothing but a "pressure group."

KENNETH L. KARST

TERRY v. OHIO
392 U.S. 1 (1968)
SIBRON v. NEW YORK
392 U.S. 40 (1968)

Terry v. Ohio marked the first attempt by the Supreme Court to deal with a pervasive type of police conduct known as STOP AND FRISK. Where an individual's suspicious conduct gives rise to an apprehension of danger, but PROBABLE CAUSE for an arrest does not exist, it is common police practice to stop the suspect for questioning and to pat down (frisk) his outer clothing in a search for concealed weapons. While this may be an effective way to deter crime it is susceptible to abuse. Though far less intrusive on privacy and security than formal arrest and thorough search, a stop and, especially, a frisk can be a frightening and humiliating experience.

It was this consideration that led the Court in *Terry* to hold that stop and frisk is subject to limitations established by the FOURTH AMENDMENT. Chief Justice EARL WARREN declared that the forcible restraint of an individual, however temporary, is a "seizure," and a frisk, though limited in scope, is a "search," within the meaning of the Fourth Amendment. However, the imperative of sound law enforcement, as well as the need of the police to assure their own safety and that of the citizenry, requires that the amendment's reasonableness clause—rather than the probable cause standard of the warrant clause—should govern this type of police conduct. Balancing individual freedom against community needs, Warren concluded that if "a reasonably prudent [officer] in the circumstances [is] warranted in the belief that his safety or that of others [is] in danger," he is, under the reasonableness clause, entitled to stop and frisk the suspect in order to avoid the threatened harm. Any weapon thus seized is admissible at trial. However, in *Terry*'s companion case, *Sibron v. New York* the Court held that where the motivation for the frisk is the discovery of EVIDENCE rather than the confiscation of weapons, the evidence seized is inadmissible.

The officer's apprehension of danger must be based on articulable facts rather than mere hunch; the difference between probable cause and the less strict standard authorized in *Terry* is a difference between reasonable belief and reasonable suspicion. Paradoxically, the case both significantly limited and momentously expanded the police search power: it placed "on the street" police–citizen encounters under the protection of the Fourth Amendment even as it allowed, for the first time, a standard less exacting than probable cause to meet the requirement of reasonableness for searches made in EXIGENT CIRCUMSTANCES.

JACOB W. LANDYNSKI

TEST CASE

Whenever a unit of government, or an interest in the private sector, wants a favorable constitutional decision on a point in question, a test case is often organized to gain a ruling from the Supreme Court. The Court has not defined the term, and need not, as there is no judicial criterion for "test case" under the CASES AND CONTROVERSIES clause of Article III. Scholarship on the judicial process provides the best understanding of the term as a strategy employed by different interests, for differing ends. FLETCHER V. PECK (1810) showed that systematically plotting a test case, so framing it as to elicit particular answers based on prediction concerning how the Justices are likely to respond, and then using the judicial decision for political advantage is not a strategy unique to recent CIVIL RIGHTS cases but a durable aspect of constitutional litigation since the early years of the Republic.

Organizers of test cases sometimes look upon victory in the Supreme Court as a secondary goal. For example, the arguments of the National Woman Suffrage Association that women, as citizens, were already enfranchised by terms of the FOURTEENTH AMENDMENT breathed new life into the organization through publicity of test cases. MINOR V. HAPPERSETT (1875) and two other cases failed but they produced national news.

The Department of Justice took little initiative in enforcing new legislation in the nineteenth century, largely because Congress intended enforcement to come through complaints of individuals entitled to sue violators. An example of this is the CIVIL RIGHTS CASES (1883). Individuals challenged about a hundred violations of the CIVIL RIGHTS ACT OF 1875. Eventually, five came to the Supreme Court as test cases, where they were unsuccessfully argued by the SOLICITOR GENERAL. These test cases were not managed; they simply happened as individual blacks complained.

Business interests may bring test cases to prevent enforcement of new regulatory legislation, as in 1917 when David Clark for the Southern Cotton Manufacturers sought to invalidate the KEATING-OWEN ACT which prohibited shipment in INTERSTATE COMMERCE of designated products manufactured in plants employing children. Stephen Wood reports the advice of a Philadelphia lawyer to the manufacturers:

> No legal proceeding will lie until the [Keating-Owen] bill is in operation. Some action must be taken under some provision of the bill so that a real and not a moot question is raised. A court, in order to pass upon any phase of it, must have before it an actual case, and if the measure is to be contested, the case should not only be carefully selected in order that the constitutional principle desired to be raised may be clearly presented, but I believe then that when the issue is raised, if possible, a judicial district should be selected in which the judge is a man of known courage. This is no case to try before a weak character [1968: 87–88].

Clark proceeded to raise money, select suitable counsel, identify Judge James Edmund Boyd as courageous, and locate cotton companies in the western district of North Carolina ready to cooperate. After searching for the "perfect combination of factors," Clark worked up four possible test cases to submit to the attorneys in New York. There the *Dagenhart* case was selected as the best. The Dagenharts, a father and two minor sons, and the company "were mere figureheads" whom Clark persuaded to set up the case. First, the company posted notices that under-age employees would be dismissed when the Keating-Owen law went into effect. The attorneys employed by Clark then prepared a complaint for Dagenhart asserting that this threat would deprive him of his VESTED RIGHTS, because he was entitled to the services of his minor sons and the compensation arising from their labors. By moving before the law became effective, the cotton manufacturers put the Department of Justice on the defensive, trapped within the confines of their test case. Judge Boyd, who ruled the Keating-Owen Act invalid under the Fifth and TENTH AMENDMENTS, was upheld by the Supreme Court in 1918 in HAMMER V. DAGENHART.

Success in managing constitutional litigation requires understanding of both substantive law and litigation practice. Following enactment of the WAGNER ACT in 1935, lawyers for the National Labor Relations Board combined these talents in impressive fashion, gaining a stunning triumph from the Supreme Court in *NLRB v. Jones & Laughlin* in March 1937. (See WAGNER ACT CASES.) Against hostile attacks by the National Lawyers' Committee of the American Liberty League, NLRB lawyers carefully developed cases running the gamut of size and type to make the first tests establishing wide congressional power to regulate labor practices in businesses affecting interstate commerce.

NLRB lawyers, even before the Wagner Act was signed, had designed a "master plan" envisioning test cases built around COMMERCE CLAUSE issues stressing the type of industry, characteristics of individual businesses, the degree of actual or threatened obstruction of commerce, and the type of unfair labor practices charged. In Peter Irons's words, this "master plan" gave clear directions for "sifting through their massive case loads in search of ideal test cases, charting a clear path from the picket line to the Supreme Court." The NLRB staff functioned as legal craftsmen, "as much meticulous technicians as partisan advocates," who "winnowed and selected cases with care; scrutinized records with a fine-tooth comb; chose courts with a shopper's discriminating eye; wrote briefs to draw the issues narrowly and precisely."

Although numerous voluntary associations with litigation programs, such as the Anti-Saloon League of America, the National Consumers' League, and the AMERICAN JEWISH CONGRESS, have sponsored test cases as a way of influencing public policy, the organizations most noted for this practice have been the National Association for the Advancement of Colored People (NAACP), formed in 1909, and the NAACP LEGAL DEFENSE FUND, INC., organized in 1939.

Modern test cases by associations, public interest law firms, or lawyers working *pro bono publico* are often cast as CLASS ACTIONS under the FEDERAL RULES OF CIVIL PROCEDURE. Although they may attack conditions that are widespread, these cases rest on particularized explorations of fact, often through discovery and expert testimony. In attacking school segregation in the five cases styled as BROWN V. BOARD OF EDUCATION, the NAACP sought to develop full factual records, building upon the experience of THURGOOD MARSHALL and others as counsel in the earlier white primary cases and racial RESTRICTIVE COVENANT cases. Widespread test cases will continue because both government and private counsel can approach the Supreme Court only by representing particular parties with particular concrete claims.

CLEMENT E. VOSE

Bibliography

CORTNER, RICHARD C. 1964 *The Wagner Act Cases.* Pages 106–141. Knoxville: University of Tennessee Press.

FREUND, PAUL A. 1951 *On Understanding the Supreme Court.* Pages 77–116. Boston: Little, Brown.

IRONS, PETER 1982 *The New Deal Lawyers.* Pages 234–289. Princeton, N.J.: Princeton University Press.

KLUGER, RICHARD 1975 *Simple Justice: The History of Brown v. Board of Education and Black America's Struggle for Equality.* Pages 256–540. New York: Vintage Books.

VOSE, CLEMENT E. 1959 *Caucasians Only: The Supreme Court, the NAACP, and the Restrictive Covenant Cases.* Pages 50–73, 151–176. Berkeley: University of California Press.

WOOD, STEPHEN B. 1968 *Constitutional Politics in the Progressive Era.* Pages 81–110. Chicago: University of Chicago Press.

TESTIMONIAL AND NONTESTIMONIAL COMPULSION

In the 1960s the Supreme Court ruled that the RIGHT AGAINST SELF-INCRIMINATION was not infringed when police compelled the driver of an accident vehicle to give a blood sample for analysis of its alcoholic content, compelled a suspect in a LINEUP to utter before witnesses the words used by a bank robber, and compelled another suspected bank robber to submit a sample of his handwriting for comparison with a note given to a bankteller. In the 1970s the Court held that the right against self-incrimination did not protect a person from the compulsory production of business and tax records in the possession of his or her accountant or lawyer, and did not protect a person from a court order to make a voice recording for a federal GRAND JURY seeking to identify a criminal by the sound of a voice on a legally intercepted telephone conversation. All these decisions shared a thorny problem: if a person is compelled to provide the state with evidence to incriminate him, is he necessarily a witness against himself in the Fifth Amendment sense?

The Court prefers a different formulation: does nontestimonial compulsion force a person to be a witness against himself criminally? The consistent answer has been "no," even if there was a testimonial dimension to the forced admissions. If that testimonial dimension loomed too large, the Court loosened its distinction between testimonial and nontestimonial compulsion and relied on some other distinction. Thus, when the driver of a vehicle involved in an accident was required by state law to stop and identify himself, though doing so subjected him to criminal penalties, the Court saw no Fifth Amendment issue, only a regulation promoting the satisfaction of civil liabilities. Similarly, when a lawyer or accountant was forced to turn over a client's incriminating records, the client had not been compelled at all, though he paid the criminal penalty and lost the chance to make a Fifth Amendment plea. And when the police during the course of a lawful search found incriminating business records, the records were introduced in evidence, although they could not have been subpoenaed directly from the businessman. In these cases, where the compulsion was communicative or testimonial in character, the Court inconsistently discoursed on the need to decide as it did in order to avoid a decision against the introduction of nontestimonial evidence that had been compelled.

More often the Court relied on a supposed distinction between forcing a person to furnish evidence against himself of a testimonial nature and forcing him to be the source of nontestimonial or physical evidence against himself, usually derived from his body. The word "witness" implies giving testimony based on one's knowledge, not displaying one's person. Compulsion to reveal information other than one's physical characteristics is generally unconstitutional, especially if the information is derived directly from the party himself, though not if the police lawfully find his records. The Court's distinction between testimonial and nontestimonial compulsion is obviously a bit porous. That distinction derived from the realistic need to prevent the Fifth Amendment from disabling police identifications based on fingerprints, handwriting, photographs, blood samples, voice exemplars, and lineups. The distinction had its origin in a passing remark by Justice OLIVER WENDELL HOLMES in 1910, when he dismissed as "an extravagant extension of the Fifth Amendment" the claim that requiring a defendant to model a shirt for identification purposes breached the right against self-incrimination.

The trouble with the distinction, apart from the Court's own inconsistency, is that physical or identifying evidence can be communicative in character, as when a laboratory report, the result of a drunken driver's blood sample, is introduced against him, or when a grand jury indicts one whose voice identifies him as the culprit. Whether by writing, speaking, or giving blood involuntarily, an individual has been compelled to furnish evidence against himself. That he has not been forced to "testify" is a distinction less persuasive than semantically catchy. However, some such distinction seems necessary. The fundamental meaning of the Fifth Amendment is that a person need not be the unwilling instrument of his own undoing and that the state must find its own evidence against him without his involuntary cooperation, and a literal reading of the amendment would prevent the police from fingerprinting a suspect or making him stand in a lineup for identification purposes. Thus the Court must find ways around the amendment.

A minority of Justices have sought a compromise by permitting as nontestimonial that evidence which does not require volition or affirmative cooperation; thus, the lineup and taking blood, photographs, and fingerprints require merely passive conduct. If, however, incriminating evidence can be secured only by the active volition of one asked to repeat certain words, model clothing, or give a handwriting sample, these minority Justices would sustain a Fifth Amendment plea. But their distinction between volitional and passive acts is as hairsplitting as the majority's between testimonial and nontestimonial compulsion. Anyone overpowered to give a sample of his blood would scarcely think he affirmatively cooperated.

The Justices in the majority also make unreal distinctions, as between the physical properties of one's voice and the testimonial content of what he says: "This is a stickup" communicates more than pitch and resonance. If the right against self-incrimination protects a defendant at his trial from having to speak up for the benefit of witnesses, why does it not protect him in the grand jury room, the interrogation room, or the lineup?

The distinction between testimonial and nontestimonial compulsion derives from the needs of law enforcement and seems to be a permanent addition to constitutional law. The Court, which can reach whatever results it desires, probably will add to the roster of nontestimonial evidence that can be compelled and will narrow the meaning of testimonial compulsion or find exceptions to it.

LEONARD W. LEVY

Bibliography

BAUER, W. J. 1977 Formalism, Legal Realism, & Constitutionally Protected Privacy under the Fourth & Fifth Amendments. *Harvard Law Review* 90:945–991.

KOONTZ, HAL and STODEL, JEFFREY 1973 The Scope of Testimonial Immunity under the Fifth: *Kastigar v. United States. Loyola* (Los Angeles) *Law Review* 6:350–383.

TESTIMONIAL IMMUNITY

See: Use Immunity

TEST OATH CASES

Cummings v. Missouri
4 Wallace 277 (1867)
Ex Parte Garland
4 Wallace 333 (1867)

Historically test oaths were weapons to inflict penalties and punishments on obnoxious minorities and were enemies of freedom of political and religious thought. A test or LOYALTY OATH should not be confused with an oath of allegiance, which is a promissory oath by which one swears to support the government and, if assuming office, to discharge its duties faithfully. An oath of allegiance concerns future conduct. A test oath is retroactive and purgative, because it is a disclaimer of specific beliefs, associations, and behavior deemed criminal or disloyal.

Missouri by its constitution prescribed a series of disavowals of belief and past conduct in the form of oaths to be taken by all voters, jurors, state officers, clergymen, lawyers, teachers, and corporation officers. All must swear as a condition of voting, holding office, teaching, and the like, that they had never been in armed hostility to the United States, had never by word or deed manifested adherence to the enemies of the country or desired their victory, had never been connected with any organization inimical to the United States, and had never been a Southern sympathizer. Anyone teaching, preaching, voting, or engaging in any of the specified activities without first taking the oaths was subject to fine and imprisonment. Cummings, a Roman Catholic priest, carried on his religious duties without taking the oath and was convicted.

The test oath prescribed by Congress was a disclaimer of having served the Confederacy and applied only to federal officials until extended in 1865 to members of the federal bar. It could be construed as a wartime qualification for office until it was extended to peacetime and to members of the federal bar. Until then it was not passed to inflict punishment for past offenses. The oath disqualified AUGUSTUS H. GARLAND, who had spent the war as a member of the Confederate Congress, from resuming his prewar practice before the Supreme Court, although he had been given a presidential pardon.

The Supreme Court, Justice STEPHEN J. FIELD writing for a bare majority, held unconstitutional both the Missouri requirement of a test oath and the federal requirement of 1865. Field reasoned that each violated the bans against EX POST FACTO laws and BILLS OF ATTAINDER. To conclude that they constituted ex post facto laws, Field had to demonstrate that they retroactively imposed punishment for acts not criminal when committed. Missouri's dragnet covered not only hostile acts against the government but "words, desires, and sympathies also," and some of the acts were not even blameworthy. The federal statute reached acts that under certain circumstances might not have been offenses, such as assisting persons in armed hostility to the United States, serving in innocuous positions in the South, or reluctantly obeying the existing order. Persons who were incapable of truthfully taking the oaths suffered disabilities that constituted punishment, such as the deprivation of civil and political rights, disqualifications from office and from the pursuit of lawful professions, and, in the case of Garland, disbarment. Justice SAMUEL F. MILLER for the dissenters replied that an ex post facto law punished only in a criminal sense by imposing fines and imprisonment, not civil disabilities.

Field described a bill of attainder as a legislative act that inflicts punishment without a judicial trial. Attainders, he insisted, could be directed against whole classes, not just named individuals, and might inflict punishments conditionally, as in these cases. Cummings the priest and Garland the lawyer were presumed guilty until they removed that presumption by their expurgatory oaths; if it was not removed, they faced the punishment of being deprived of their professions without trial and conviction. Miller could see no attainder because the required oaths designated no criminal by name or description, declared no guilt, and inflicted neither sentence nor punishment. He saw merely a qualification for office, a position that Field savaged. Miller accurately argued, however, that Field stretched the conventional meanings of ex post facto laws and bills of attainder to cover the cases before the Court. For that reason, these decisions are today considered triumphs for CIVIL LIBERTIES; in their time, however, they exposed the Court to accusations of sympathizing with the Confederate cause, opposing Reconstruction, and assisting enemies of the Union.

LEONARD W. LEVY

Bibliography

FAIRMAN, CHARLES 1939 *Mr. Justice Miller and the Supreme Court.* Pages 129–136. Cambridge, Mass.: Harvard University Press.

SWISHER, CARL BRENT (1930)1963 *Stephen J. Field: Craftsman of the Law.* Pages 138–154. Hamden, Conn.: Archon Books.

TEXAS v. BROWN
460 U.S. 730 (1983)

This case is significant for Justice WILLIAM H. REHNQUIST'S exposition of the scope and applicability of the PLAIN VIEW DOCTRINE, which had emerged in COOLIDGE V. NEW HAMPSHIRE (1971) as an exception to the warrant requirement for a SEARCH AND SEIZURE. According to Rehnquist, the answer to the question whether property in plain view may be seized depends on the lawfulness of the intrusion that allows the police to see that property. Plain view therefore provides the basis for seizure if an officer's access to the object has a prior FOURTH AMENDMENT justification. The police may seize a suspicious object if they are engaged in a lawful activity; they do not have to know at once that the object inadvertently exposed to their sight is EVIDENCE of a crime. Reasonable suspicion on PROBABLE CAUSE is sufficient even if the property seized was not immediately apparent as evidence of crime. No Justice dissented in this case, but Rehnquist spoke for a mere plurality, and a mere plurality had announced the plain view doctrine in *Coolidge.* Accordingly, judicial controversy about the doctrine will continue, as will controversy about its application to particular facts.

LEONARD W. LEVY

TEXAS v. WHITE
7 Wallace 700 (1869)

In 1867 the Court accepted ORIGINAL JURISDICTION of *Texas v. White* because one party was a state (Article III, section 2). So doing, the Court raised again, as in EX PARTE MILLIGAN (1866) and the TEST OATH cases, a possibility of judicial intervention into military reconstruction. Some decision on the state-status question was needed. Democrats insisted that the nation was not empowered to answer the state-status question and that the South's states, like bottom-weighted dolls, had sprung up, fully restored, with prevailing race hierarchies intact, in the wake of Union Army advances. Almost all Republicans assumed that the South's states, by attempting to secede, had twisted themselves out of their proper federal relations; that the Constitution (Article IV, section 4) imposed a duty on the nation to guarantee every state a REPUBLICAN FORM OF GOVERNMENT; and that the nation also possessed temporary "grasp of war" dominion over the defeated states.

Post-Appomattox Texas wished to recover possession of state bonds that secessionist Texas had sold. Counsel for bond buyers argued in 1869, when the Supreme Court heard *Texas v. White,* that Texas was always a state and the sales were valid. Special counsel for Texas, Unionist George Washington Paschal, author of a recent treatise on the Constitution, insisted that though Texas remained a state, its acts adverse to federal responsibilities invalidated the bond sales; the state should recover the bonds.

Chief Justice SALMON P. CHASE, for the majority of the Court, accepted and restated Paschal's position. The Constitution "looks to an indestructible Union composed of indestructible States." SECESSION was void. Texas's acts supportive of rebellion, performed while seceded, were unsupportable.

Justices ROBERT C. GRIER, SAMUEL F. MILLER, and NOAH SWAYNE insisted that Texas was as much out of the Union in 1869 as in 1861. Therefore the original jurisdiction clause of the Constitution did not apply.

Both the majority and the minority stressed Congress's primacy in defining a state's status. Chase, though insisting that he was not pronouncing upon military reconstruction, by implication approved its constitutional bases and reinforced Court pretensions to at least an equal share, if not more, in implementation of policy, through its review authority.

HAROLD M. HYMAN

TEXAS ANNEXATION

See: Annexation of Texas

THAYER, JAMES BRADLEY
(1831–1902)

American jurist, Harvard law professor, and author of a masterful treatise on EVIDENCE, Thayer is important in constitutional studies for his powerful advocacy of judicial self-restraint, or deference to legislation challenged as unconstitutional. He influenced Justices LOUIS D. BRANDEIS, FELIX FRANKFURTER, and OLIVER WENDELL HOLMES, and Judge LEARNED HAND.

Thayer invoked a supposedly established judicial rule which, recognizing that the Constitution admitted of different interpretations and allowed legislatures a vast range of permissible choice, required that all rational legislative choices be adjudged constitutional. Properly holding legislation unconstitutional only in cases clear beyond REASONABLE DOUBT, courts should not consider their own views on unconstitutionality, but should consider instead whether the legislature could reasonably have thought its actions constitutional. (See RATIONAL BASIS.)

Thayer regarded JUDICIAL REVIEW as a legitimate outgrowth of American experience and as a valuable conservative admixture in popular government. But he warned that this "outside" corrective threatened to curtail the people's political education. His strictures against JUDICIAL ACTIVISM were published just as the Supreme Court was embarking on a course of active defense of FREEDOM OF CONTRACT against ECONOMIC REGULATION. In a later era, when the Court's activism turned to personal liberties of another kind, Thayer's rule came under criticism: it was not an "established rule," but a policy preference; its reasonable doubt standard either would enfeeble judicial review or would be too flexible to restrain courts effectively; its applicability in Supreme Court review of state legislation was unclear; it was particularly inappropriate for legislation affecting specific BILL OF RIGHTS guarantees. Regrettably, Thayer himself had not adequately explored either the strengths and weaknesses of his rule or the broader underlying problem—how to square JUDICIAL REVIEW AND DEMOCRACY.

HOWARD E. DEAN

Bibliography

THAYER, JAMES BRADLEY 1893 The Origin and Scope of the American Doctrine of Constitutional Law. *Harvard Law Review* 7:129–156.

THEORIES OF THE UNION

Political unions are organizations of states possessing specific powers for carrying out purposes of mutual interest to constituent polities. Unions are formed by means of confederation or federation, and by definition are combinative or compound in nature rather than unitary or homogeneous. In American history the Union refers to the general structure of political authority created during the Revolution by the American people, acting through their colonial and state governments, for the pursuit of common purposes as an expression of their incipient nationality. Theories of the Union are explanations of the American state system, descriptive and normative in purpose, which have been formulated to guide political action and resolve controversies among the member states. Especially important in the period from 1789 to 1868, theories of the Union have been concerned with four principal issues: the origin and nature of statehood; the nature and extent of state powers; the origin, nature, and extent of the powers of the central government; and the manner of resolving conflicts between the states and the central authority.

Although intercolonial cooperation occurred intermittently before the Revolution, in an effective political sense the formation by the colonies in 1774 of an assembly to deal with imperial matters of common concern marked the beginning of the American Union. In 1776 this assembly, the CONTINENTAL CONGRESS, issued the DECLARATION OF INDEPENDENCE, proclaiming that the colonies "are, and of right ought to be, free and independent states." Yet the Declaration also referred to the people in the colonies as "one people," and to the colonies as "the United States of America." The practical effect was to announce the existence of a national Union comprising thirteen state governments and a central body, Congress, which, although not constituted as a government and incapable of legislating for individuals in the states, was more than merely the agent of the states. Although theory and principle to explain this new compound political organization were yet to be formulated, the fact of a division of SOVEREIGNTY characterized the American Union from the outset.

The Union thus existed as political reality before it was rationalized in a formal instrument of government, the ARTICLES OF CONFEDERATION (1781). Asserting that "[e]ach State retains its sovereignty, freedom and independence, and every Power, JURISDICTION, and right which is not by this confederation expressly delegated to the United States," the Articles conformed to the model of a league of autonomous states. However, the language of state sovereignty notwithstanding, the states were not perfect states. And Congress, although empowered only to make resolutions and recommendations rather than to make law, in matters submitted to its consideration acted as a real government. In practical effect the Union resembled the operation of the British empire, in which sovereignty had been divided between the colonial governments managing local affairs and the authority of Parliament regulating matters of general interest in the empire.

Theory of the Union was relevant to territorial problems of the 1780s, which raised the question of the origin and nature of statehood. The original colonies based their claim to statehood on their COLONIAL CHARTERS and the fact of succession to previously existing political establishments. This theory of the creation of states implied a fixed or determinate Union, and was useless to those people—either in existing states or outside them—who desired to form new states and join the Union. An alternative approach was to claim a revolutionary right of self-government; Vermont may be said to have employed this principle in its struggle to separate from New York and achieve statehood. A third method of state making was to form a political community and secure recognition from the other states. This technique was developed in the 1780s when Virginia and other states with extensive land claims, desiring to confirm their sovereignty, ceded some of their lands to Congress and secured in return approval of their claims and state boundaries. Implicit in these transactions was an expansive rather than static conception of the Union: although states might proclaim their sovereignty, the determination of statehood—the very existence of the states—depended on the sanction of the other states acting through Congress.

The CONSTITUTIONAL CONVENTION OF 1787 altered the nature and structure of the Union by creating a central government, capable of making law and regulating individuals, in place of the noncoercive authority of the Confederation. Precisely how much and in what ways the restructured Union differed from the Confederation was debated during the process of RATIFICATION OF THE CONSTITUTION. These debates gave rise to the classic theories of the Union expounded by statesmen of the early national period.

In providing for a government based on the SEPARATION OF POWERS and comprising a legislature elected in part by the people, the Framers of the Constitution applied republican principles to the problem of organizing the American Union. They did not, however, completely reject the essential principle of the Confederation, the idea that the states were the constituent power. This principle was retained in the provisions for equal state representation in the Senate and for the contingency plan for electing the President in the House of Representatives, where each state was to have had one vote. The result, as JAMES MADISON wrote in THE FEDERALIST #39, was a government partly national and partly federal in respect of the source, operation, and extent of its powers; the constituent basis on which it was established; and the nature of the amending authority. Some of these functions embodied the idea that the American people as a single national community were the constituent power; others, the idea that the states as separate political communities were constituting the central government.

In contemporary usage the term "federal" referred to a confederation of sovereign states, and the word "national" to a unitary government operating directly on individuals. Accordingly, the Articles of Confederation were described as a federal government. But the supporters of the new government, combining elements of both a confederation and a unitary national government, called *it* a federal government. In doing so they gave a new definition to FEDERALISM as the division of sovereignty among a central government and separate state governments operating on the same population in the same area.

In the ratification controversy Federalists and Anti-Federalists combined arguments from history, the constitutional text, and political theory to fashion competing theories of the Union in pursuit of their divergent political goals. Denying that sovereignty could be divided, Anti-Federalists warned that the proposed central government would transform the Union into a consolidated state. The Federalists, in order to allay STATES' RIGHTS apprehensions, stressed the division of authority between the states and the central government and the ultimate sovereignty of the people. Although the Federalists glossed over conflicts that were bound to arise in a governmental system based on a division of sovereign authority, their constitutional theory confirmed the main tendencies in the operation of the American Union from its inception.

Perhaps the single most important formulation of Unionist theory was contained in the VIRGINIA AND KENTUCKY RESOLUTIONS of 1798–1799, written by JAMES MADISON and THOMAS JEFFERSON. Seeking a constitutionally legitimate way to prevent the enforcement of the ALIEN AND SEDITION ACTS, the Republican party leaders advanced the compact theory of the Union. On this theory were based all subsequent assertions of states' rights and state sovereignty, including those supporting SECESSION in 1861.

Jefferson and Madison argued that the Union was a compact made by the states, which as the constituent parties retained the right to judge whether the central government had violated the compact. Exercising this right by the accepted practices for implementing compacts, the states, according to Madison, could "interpose" their authority to stop unconstitutional acts of the central government. In the Kentucky Resolutions of 1799 Jefferson declared that a NULLIFICATION by the sovereign states of all unauthorized acts of the federal government was "the rightful remedy." The theory thus propounded held that the states created the Union; the federal government could exercise only delegated powers, not including regulation of speech and press, which were reserved to the states; and the states had authority to question the exercise of central authority and by implication to settle constitutional disputes over federal–state relations.

Whether Madison and Jefferson contemplated peaceful concerted action by the states, or single-state defiance of federal authority (possibly by force, as was later proposed in South Carolina), their action served as precedent and model for one of the basic strategies of constitutional politics throughout the antebellum period. From the standpoint of constitutional law the most significant feature of the compact theory was the proposition that the states had created the Constitution and the Union. The argument could mean any number of things depending on how a state was defined. A state could be considered to be the territory occupied by a political community, the governing institutions and officers of the community, or the people forming the community. In his report to the Virginia legislature in 1800, Madison used the third of these definitions to explain how the states, through the ratification process, had made the Constitution. On this theory, the TENTH AMENDMENT expressed the equivalence of state and people, reserving powers not delegated to the federal government "to the States respectively or to the people." A fixed feature of later states' rights and state sovereignty teaching, this popular conception of statehood enabled compact theorists to define the nation as self-governing political communities founded on common republican principles.

An alternative theory of the Union was propounded by the Federalist party. Federalists held that the Constitution and the Union had been made by the people of the United States, who as the constituent power had divided sovereignty between the states and the central government. The government of the United States possessed limited powers, but within its sphere of action it was supreme. Federalists, and their Whig political descendants in the 1830s, further reasoned that according to the original constitutional design conflicts in federal–state relations were to be resolved by the federal judiciary. In his debate with Robert Y. Hayne of South Carolina in 1830 on the nature of the Union, DANIEL WEBSTER said the judicial article and the SUPREMACY CLAUSE were the "key-stone of the arch" of Union. "With these," he declared, "it is a constitution; without them, it is a confederacy."

Distrusting localism, Federalists identified the nation with the central government, and theirs is often referred to as the nationalist theory of the Union. This reference is misleading, however, insofar as it implies that the compact theory was not a valid expression of American nationality. Properly regarded, the Federalist-Whig doctrine is the central supremacy theory of the Union. Acknowledging divided sovereignty and the limited nature of federal authority, Federalists and Whigs recognized states' rights as essential to the Union. But, believing the nation could act only through the central government, they insisted on the supremacy of federal power when it conflicted with an otherwise legitimate state power. The supremacy clause of the Constitution was the positive expression of the principle of federal paramountcy that its proponents believed was intended to guide national development.

In refuting the compact theory, central supremacy theorists made the popular origins of the Union their most distinctive tenet. They insisted that the Constitution was not a compact made by the states but an instrument of government made by "the people of the United States." The meaning of this term is not self-evident. It might be taken to mean that the American people constituted and could act as a single political community. Webster seemed to have this conception in mind when in the debate with Hayne he argued that the Constitution "pronounces that it is established by the people of the United States in the aggregate," not by the states or even by the people of the several states. JOHN MARSHALL stated the popular-origins thesis more carefully in MCCULLOCH V. MARYLAND (1819). Marshall observed that the Constitution was "submitted to the people" for ratification, and they acted on it "by assembling in Convention." In a sense Marshall conceded the compact theorists' main point—that the Constitution had been ratified by the people acting as separate political communities. "It is true," he wrote, "they assembled in their several States." But he discounted the significance of this fact, adding: "and where else should they have assembled? No political dreamer was ever wild enough to think of breaking down the lines which separate the States, and of compounding the American people into one common mass. Of consequence, when they act they act in their States." Thus the same facts on which the compact theorists based their conclusion that the Union was made by the states supported the central supremacy contention that the Union was made by the people of the United States.

From 1830 to 1860 theories of the Union continued to have political significance as Americans expanded territorially and struggled with the slavery question. Two variations of the compact theory were developed to protect slavery within the state system: DUAL FEDERALISM and the nullification theory of JOHN C. CALHOUN of South Carolina. Within the central supremacy theory, meanwhile, the idea of the Union as perpetual and indissoluble was elaborated.

Although formally accepting divided sovereignty, dual federalists in a practical sense sought to remove actual or potential central government restraints on state power, including the power to protect slavery. Insisting that the reserved powers of the states constituted a limitation on the federal government, they regarded the Tenth Amendment as a kind of supremacy clause for the states. Accordingly, in cases such as NEW YORK V. MILN (1837) the Supreme Court under Chief Justice ROGER B. TANEY, reversing the effect of Marshall's central supremacy unionism, held that state powers over matters of "police" had not been surrendered to federal authority.

Calhoun's doctrine of nullification, employed in South Carolina's fight against the tariff in 1832, was a more radical extension of the compact theory of the Union. Calhoun held that federal powers were granted in trust by the states, which he defined as the people exercising indivisible sovereignty in separate political communities. He thus rejected the principle of divided sovereignty. Picking up where Madison and Jefferson had left off, Calhoun sought to devise a constitutional means of obstructing unconstitutional acts of the central government. His ingenious, if ultimately perverse, solution was to transform the creative constituent power of the states, identified in the Article V amending power, into an instrument of negation. Calhoun reasoned that a state, acting in popular convention, might interpose its authority to nullify a federal measure. The states would then be consulted, and if three-fourths of them did not approve the objectionable measure it would be withdrawn. If, however, the states upheld the central government, the nullifying state could secede from the Union.

Placed on the defensive by the nullificationists, central supremacy advocates were moved to insist on the perpetuity of the Union. This idea was implicit in the very creation of the Constitution. The fact that the Articles of Confederation referred to the Union as "perpetual" did not prevent men from believing that a state might withdraw its membership; by the same token the omission from the Constitution of the language of perpetuity did not mean that the Framers considered the Union to be anything less than a permanent government. It is nevertheless significant that while the terms disunion and secession were employed in the early nineteenth century, not until the nullification crisis did central supremacy theorists like Webster and JOHN QUINCY ADAMS explicate the perpetuity idea. Their argument may be described as declaratory in nature. But it was not only Whig keepers of the central supremacy tradition but also Democrats who met the South Carolina challenge by asserting perpetual Unionism. In his Proclamation to South Carolina (1832) President ANDREW JACKSON condemned secession as unconstitutional and affirmed the Constitution as a binding obligation on the states.

Changing little as constitutional doctrine, the central supremacy theory of the Union formed part of a nationalist ideology that emerged in the North in the pre-Civil War period. In contrast to the universalistic, democratic, and decentralized nationalism associated with the compact school, northern nationalism, based on New England Federalist sources and developed by Whig and Republican politicians, was historical, ethnic, cultural, and religious in nature. Whereas President GEORGE WASHINGTON in his Farewell Address had said it was the "unity of government which constitutes you one people," central supremacy theorists such as FRANCIS LIEBER turned the equation around by regarding the American people as forming a sovereign national community, from which emanated the Constitution and the Union. In this sectionally sponsored nationalism, the Union, without ceasing to be a means of securing liberty, became as well an end in itself: an organically rooted thing of absolute and intrinsic value.

Theories of the Union had a configurative as well as causative effect on the Civil War and Reconstruction. The existence of the compact theory—and the reiteration of this theory from 1798 to 1860 as the basis for states' rights, nullification, and disunionist demands—provided an arguably constitutional course of action for Southerners to follow in seceding from the Union in response to the antislavery threat. In the North the tradition of central supremacy constitutionalism was available to rationalize and sustain the Republican party's decision to resist secession. Pronouncing secession "the essence of anarchy," President ABRAHAM LINCOLN in 1861 affirmed the perpetuity of the Union, declared its primacy over the states, and asserted that "the States have their *status* in the Union, and they have no other *legal status.*" The war would be fought, Congress resolved in 1861, "to defend and maintain the supremacy of the Constitution and to preserve the Union, with all the dignity, equality, and rights of the several States unimpaired."

Applying central supremacy tenets, the United States government between 1861 and 1868 regarded the Union as unbroken in a constitutional sense. It denied any legal effect to secession, treated the rebellious states as disorganized communities, and adopted measures to form loyal state governments capable of resuming their place in the Union. Acknowledging at most that the seceded states were out of their proper practical relation with the Union, federal authorities were forced to consider the fundamental question in Unionist theory: the origin, nature, and meaning of statehood.

Was a state to be defined as territory, population, governmental institutions and officers, or political community? Federal reconstruction policy held that a state was a body of people constituting a political community whose existence was dependent on and qualified by the Union. Implicit in the history of the state system, this relationship was explicitly rationalized in Article IV, section 4, of the Constitution, which states: "The United States shall guarantee to every State in this Union a Republican Form of Government." In choosing the guarantee clause as a reconstruction basis, Congress rejected the idea that a state was mere territory, or population, or governmental institutions and officers whose acts of disloyalty could destroy the state and cause it to revert to a territorial condition, subject to the plenary power of Congress. The progression to statehood out of the territorial condition, if not a constitutional right enjoyed by the people as a political community, was at least irreversible.

Although compact theorists had long feared the transformation of the Union into a consolidated government, when political conditions in the 1860s were most favorable for this development, reconstruction policymakers evinced a concern for states' rights and divided sovereignty as essential to Unionism. The Supreme Court expressed this outlook in TEXAS V. WHITE (1869), confirming the congressional view of statehood as an irreversible condition. The Court declared that a "State, in the ordinary sense of the Constitution, is a political community of free citizens, occupying a territory of defined boundaries." Without the states in the Union, the Court reasoned, there could be no such political body as the United States. The conclusion therefore followed that "the preservation of the States, and the maintenance of their governments, are as much within the design and care of the Constitution as the preservation of the Union and the maintenance of the National government. The Constitution, in all its provisions, looks to an indestructible Union, composed of indestructible States."

The triumph of the central government in the Civil War signified the rejection of the compact theory of the Union as a framework for national development. Although aspects of the theory continued to be used in political and constitutional debate, it was repudiated in relation to the practical question that made it a vital element in antebellum politics: the mounting of single or concerted state resistance to central authority, including the possibility of secession. After the war secession was no longer a constitutionally conceivable or politically practical course of action. The central supremacy theory prevailed as the framework for constitutional development.

Although it is doubtful whether the American people, to use John Marshall's formulation, could in a constitutional sense be described as having been compounded into a single common mass as a result of the war, nevertheless in a political and ideological sense the idea of the people as a single national community, rather than as similar yet separate political communities, gained wider acceptance. Moreover, within the central supremacy theory the adoption of the THIRTEENTH, FOURTEENTH, and FIFTEENTH AMENDMENTS greatly altered federal–state relations. The nature and extent of federal and state powers of course continued to be a major issue in constitutional law and politics. But the nature of statehood, the nature of the Union, and the propriety of federal resolution of conflicts in the operation of the state system were now settled issues. Theories of the Union, associated with fundamentally different conceptions of nationalism, ceased to be relevant to basic political choices as Americans entered the period of industrialization.

HERMAN BELZ

Bibliography

ARIELI, YEHOSHUA 1966 *Individualism and Nationalism in American Ideology.* Baltimore: Penguin Books.

BENNETT, WALTER HARTWELL 1964 *American Theories of Federalism.* University: University of Alabama Press.

CARPENTER, JESSE T. 1930 *The South as a Conscious Minority 1789–1861: A Study in Political Thought.* New York: New York University Press.

DAVIS, S. RUFUS 1978 *The Federal Principle: A Journey through Time in Quest of Meaning.* Berkeley: University of California Press.

DIAMOND, MARTIN 1974 What the Framers Meant by Federalism. In R. A. Goldwin, ed., *A Nation of States: Essays on the American Federal System.* Chicago: Rand McNally.

ONUF, PETER S. *The Origins of the Federal Republic: Jurisdictional Controversies in the United States, 1775–1787.* Philadelphia: University of Pennsylvania Press.

STAMPP, KENNETH M. 1978 The Concept of a Perpetual Union. *Journal of American History* 65:5–33.

THIRD AMENDMENT

Quartering of troops in private houses, except in cases of military necessity, has long been regarded as contrary to British political traditions. Illegal quartering figured in important controversies between the king and the people, and it was condemned in the PETITION OF RIGHT (1628) and the English BILL OF RIGHTS (1689).

The British government sent regular troops to America in 1765 to discourage resistance to parliamentary taxation. Parliament, in the Quartering Act, required that the soldiers be housed at the expense of the province to which they were sent, and provided that, if existing barracks were insufficient, private buildings would be commandeered for the purpose. This measure was one of the specific grievances cited in the DECLARATION OF INDEPENDENCE.

During the debates over RATIFICATION OF THE CONSTITUTION several state conventions suggested a prohibition against quartering of troops. It was among JAMES MADISON's original proposals for the BILL OF RIGHTS, and the First Congress approved it unanimously and virtually without change. The amendment affirms the sanctity of private property in our constitutional system: the refusal of an individual property owner is an absolute bar to quartering in peacetime. The amendment represents a principle so fundamental that no act of Congress has ever been seriously challenged under it.

DENNIS J. MAHONEY

THIRD-PARTY BUGGING

See: Electronic Eavesdropping

THIRTEENTH AMENDMENT
(Framing)

Scholars and jurists have virtually ignored the Thirteenth Amendment, the Constitution's first formal addition in sixty-one years. Reasons for this indifference seem, initially, to be both obvious and adequate. The Thirteenth Amendment, ratified in December 1865, appears to be a simple, brief statement of the noble, limited effect of the Civil War.

Its succinct text, written by Illinois Senator LYMAN TRUMBULL, echoed clauses of the NORTHWEST ORDINANCE. In the Civil War's last weeks, during the closing session of the 38th Congress, Senator CHARLES SUMNER tried to substitute for the proposed Amendment's second section one specifying that every person was equal before both national and state laws. Trumbull, a constitutional specialist, favored section 2 in its present form. Sumner and many other congressmen assumed that all parts of the Constitution, including amendments, implicitly authorized enforcement; Trumbull wished to have the amendment empower enforcement explicitly. There was almost no other discussion on the amendment. In a sense, abolition had been before the congressmen and the nation since 1861.

Persons who celebrated abolition's arrival in 1865 did not foresee that race problems and derivative strains in federal relations were to require a FOURTEENTH and a FIFTEENTH AMENDMENT plus enforcement legislation, and would lead to the first IMPEACHMENT of a President. Celebrants of 1865 stressed the "war-gulf" that separated the ratified Thirteenth Amendment from one in early 1861 that Congress had proposed and three states had ratified in a desperate effort to seduce the South from seceding. The aborted Thirteenth Amendment would have forbidden the nation perpetually from curtailing slavery in states where it existed. Thereafter the nation steadily raised both its sense of self-interest and its moral sights. Union troops in the South reported that the only trustworthy residents were black. Though few Negroes lived outside the South, most Northern states had long been racist in laws and customs, if never so fiercely as in the slave states. During the war Northern racism softened, partially as a result of pro-Negro reports from Union soldiers and partly from the diffusion of ABOLITIONIST CONSTITUTIONAL THEORY. Before the war, abolitionists, long hard-pressed even in the North, had come to scorn the Constitution, for it did not protect them against unpunished harassments. But once the war started, Union and abolition became identified. Gradually, Congress and ABRAHAM LINCOLN caught up to Union soldiers' needs, constituents' altering race sentiments, and abolitionists' aspirations and perceptions.

In 1861 and 1862, CONFISCATION ACTS threatened disloyal individuals with the loss of their title to property, including slaves, after individual prosecutions in federal courts. In September 1862, Lincoln's EMAN-

CIPATION PROCLAMATION, an executive, war-power order, offered slaveowners ninety days in which to give up the rebellion or lose their slaves. That grace period having expired, Lincoln in January 1863 ordered also the recruitment of Negroes, most of whom lived in the South, into the Union's armies. In December 1863 and July 1864 respectively, Reconstruction policies issued by the President and the Congress provided for emancipation as a prerequisite for state restorations. The fall 1864 election proved the growth of a Northern consensus in favor of irreversible emancipation as a war result, though, save for abolitionists, it had not been an original war aim. Therefore the 38th Congress, with Lincoln's warm support, prepared the present Thirteenth Amendment, and when the war ended it sent it to the states for ratification.

Despite its simplicity, the Thirteenth Amendment was a momentous, perhaps revolutionary change in constitutional relationships. It prohibited not only the national or state governments or officials but every American institution and person from allowing slavery or involuntary servitude to exist, and it specifically authorized Congress to enforce the prohibition. If states, the traditional parents of slavery, did not comply with the prohibition and allowed individuals to hold other people in a slave status, the nation now had authority to punish directly either the oppressing persons or the states.

Democrats strongly opposed ratification. Even before the Civil War, most Democrats rejected a view of the Constitution as an adaptable, organic instrument. The amendment's enforcement clause allowed Congress to initiate changes in race relationships beyond abolition. Some Democrats insisted that abolition was illicit even by means of an amendment; that slave property remained totally a state's right to define; and that the unrepresented Southern states could not properly be asked to ratify the amendment.

Republicans argued for the amendment's ratification, in part because Lincoln's Emancipation Proclamation might have left slavery alive in the unseceded border states and in some Confederate areas earlier reconquered. It was clear also that individual confiscation trials could never reach the millions of slaveholders and slaves. Republicans also worried because the amendment voided the Constitution's THREE-FIFTHS CLAUSE. The South's Negroes were now to count as whole persons in determining the size of a state's congressional representation. Ironically, the South, after initiating and carrying on a civil war for four years, would substantially increase its strength in the House of Representatives. "Radical" Republicans looked at the Thirteenth Amendment as the culmination of abolitionist constitutional theory. Radicals asserted that the amendment, freeing slaves, also equalized all Americans in the protections due to them in their states for the exercise of both public and private rights. The DECLARATION OF INDEPENDENCE and the BILL OF RIGHTS defined the duties all states owed to every resident; the nation's duty was to see to state performance. State justice, down to the remotest hamlet, must protect every resident equally against hurtful positive acts or discriminatory nonacts by public officers and private persons, in both civil and criminal relationships.

No Republicans advocated centralization; all Republicans were STATES' RIGHTS nationalists. State sovereignty was dead but state rights flourished. State wrongs that diminished individuals' rights as defined by state laws, were, however, unacceptable; they again threatened the nation's stability. Republicans assumed that the ex-rebel states would emulate, in their formal law at least, the lessened racism of the rest of the nation, and afford Negroes the same protections that whites enjoyed. But it became apparent from evidence such as the BLACK CODES that the South would not behave as expected.

All through 1865, Democrats criticized the fact that President ANDREW JOHNSON required the reconstructing states to ratify the Thirteenth Amendment, and they insisted that those states were entitled to be represented in Congress. The Johnson provisional states, excepting Florida and Texas where reconstruction proceeded slowly, did ratify the Thirteenth Amendment, though reluctantly, with spokesmen expressing special distaste for the enforcement clause. Johnson pressured recalcitrant states with threats of indefinite military rule if ratification failed; Secretary of State WILLIAM SEWARD calmed Southerners by asserting that the amendment restricted Congress to enforcing only a prohibition of formal slavery, a dubious interpretation. On December 15, 1865, Seward proclaimed the amendment to be in effect. Were the southern states truly states for the purposes of ratification? The question asked in 1865 and again in 1868 and 1870 when the Fourteenth and Fifteenth Amendments were ratified, and repeated endlessly since, has a metaphysical quality. Ratification was a mandate to the nation by a clear majority of the American people, not an act of the national government. Lincoln's insight that the South's states were still states, although out of their proper relationship to the Union of states, neither supported immediate restorations of those states nor diminished their capacities to perform certain state functions including ratification of amendments. In 1865 the southern states ratified in number beyond the Constitution's requirement (Article V) that three-fourths of the states approve an amendment. Additional states ratified subsequently to end all doubts as to the amendment's validity. But in 1865, those doubts existed and enhanced the doubts that Democrats spread, and Republicans also felt, about President Johnson's unlimited authority over the South.

The 39th Congress assembled in December 1865 for its first postwar session. Its Republican members, upon examination of the Black Codes and other evidence from the South of lingering vestiges of servitude, resorted immediately to the just-ratified Thirteenth Amendment's enforcement clause. Sharing a mobile, organic view of the Constitution, Republicans were ready to confirm that the nation had an interest in and a duty to personal equality in states, as defined by state law and customs; their readiness is evident in the quick formulation of the CIVIL RIGHTS BILL (the world's first), the second FREEDMAN'S BUREAU BILL, and the Fourteenth Amendment. Republicans created these measures in light of the Thirteenth Amendment, a far more complex and inclusive statement than most accounts suggest.

HAROLD M. HYMAN

Bibliography

BUCHANAN, SIDNEY G. 1976 *The Quest for Freedom: A Legal History of the Thirteenth Amendment.* Houston: Reprint from *Houston Law Review.*

HOWE, MARK A. DEWOLFE 1965 Federalism and Civil Rights. [Massachusetts Historical Society] *Proceedings* 77:15–67.

HYMAN, HAROLD M. and WIECEK, WILLIAM M. 1982 *Equal Justice under Law: Constitutional Development 1835–1875.* Chaps. 10–11. New York. Harper & Row.

TEN BROEK, JACOBUS 1951 *The Antislavery Origins of the Fourteenth Amendment.* Chap. 13. Berkeley: University of California Press.

THIRTEENTH AMENDMENT
(Judicial Interpretation)

Ratification of the Thirteenth Amendment in 1865 not only diminished the urgency of the debate over the constitutionality of the EMANCIPATION PROCLAMATION but also wrote a new substantive value into the Constitution. The amendent's first section abolished slavery and involuntary servitude throughout the nation, and its second section empowered Congress to enforce abolition. If any of the amendment's framers expected it to end the system of racial dominance and dependence, they were soon divested of that illusion. The persistence of a plantation economy and the adoption in southern states of the BLACK CODES kept blacks in a position of subordination that was not only economic but political and social as well.

The question thus arose whether section 2 of the Thirteenth Amendment gave Congress the power to do more than provide sanctions against slavery or involuntary servitude, narrowly defined. Over a presidential veto, Congress adopted the CIVIL RIGHTS ACT OF 1866, which not only declared the CITIZENSHIP of the freed slaves but also protected them against the sort of RACIAL DISCRIMINATION that had been embodied in the Black Codes, such as disqualification to own property, to make contracts, or to serve on juries. President ANDREW JOHNSON had explained his veto of the bill partly on the ground that the Thirteenth Amendment had not empowered Congress to adopt legislation aimed at such purposes. Reacting to this argument, Congress proposed the FOURTEENTH AMENDMENT as a means of assuring the validity of the 1866 Act and placing beyond doubt the power of Congress to enforce the CIVIL RIGHTS of the freed slaves.

From the beginning it was arguable that the abolition of slavery implied that the persons so freed would take on the status of free citizens—that the amendment should be read broadly as a response to the whole social system of racial subordination associated with slavery. But in the early years, this view did not prosper in the Supreme Court; it was found mainly in OBITER DICTA and in dissenting opinions. All agreed that section 1 of the amendment was self-executing: slavery and involuntary servitude were abolished, whether or not Congress enacted civil or criminal sanctions to enforce the abolition. Because the amendment contained no STATE ACTION limitation, it operated directly, of its own force, against either public or private conduct that imposed slavery. But the Court limited the notion of "involuntary servitude" to personal servitude, refusing to extend it (by analogy to feudal servitudes) to cover the granting of monopolies or other similar privileges. (See SLAUGHTERHOUSE CASES, 1873). By the end of the nineteenth century, the Court was saying that slavery implied no more than "a state of bondage," and the lack of "a legal right to the disposal of [one's] own person, property, and services"; thus the Thirteenth Amendent standing alone did not even forbid a state to impose racial segregation on seating in railroad cars. (See PLESSY V. FERGUSON, 1896.)

This narrow view of the Thirteenth Amendment's self-executing reach was reflected in the Supreme

Court's treatment of the power granted to Congress by section 2. In the CIVIL RIGHTS CASES (1883) the Court, in the face of a powerful dissenting opinion by Justice JOHN MARSHALL HARLAN, held invalid the CIVIL RIGHTS ACT OF 1875, a congressional statute forbidding racial discrimination in such PUBLIC ACCOMMODATIONS as hotels, theaters, and railroads. Both the majority and the dissent agreed that the Thirteenth Amendment was designed to put an end to the "incidents" of slavery as well as slavery itself. The question was whether racially based refusals of access to public accommodations amounted to "badges of slavery and servitude," and the majority held that they did not. This severely restrictive interpretation of the power of Congress to enforce the Thirteenth Amendment culminated in 1906, when the Court decided HODGES V. UNITED STATES. Congress could prohibit no more than the "entire subjection" of one person to another, as in laws forbidding PEONAGE; Congress was not empowered by section 2 to go further in erasing "badges" or "incidents" of slavery.

So matters stood for six decades. The Thirteenth Amendment, like the Fourteenth Amendment's guarantee of the EQUAL PROTECTION OF THE LAWS, lay dormant, offering no effective protection against racial discrimination. The judicial interpretation of the Thirteenth Amendment mirrored the nation's political history; Congress adopted no civil rights legislation from the time of Reconstruction to the late 1950s. The first modern civil rights law of major importance was the CIVIL RIGHTS ACT OF 1964; its public accommodations provisions were upheld by the Supreme Court, but on the basis of the COMMERCE CLAUSE, not the Thirteenth or Fourteenth Amendments. (See HEART OF ATLANTA MOTEL V. UNITED STATES, 1964; *Katzenbach v. McClung,* 1964.) The Court seemed determined to uphold congressional legislation aimed at establishing racial equality, and in UNITED STATES V. GUEST (1966) six Justices agreed in two separate opinions that Congress could reach even private conduct that interfered with the exercise of Fourteenth Amendment rights. The state action limitation, in other words, would not bar congressional enforcement of the equal protection clause of the Fourteenth Amendment's prohibition on private discrimination.

The reach of the equal protection clause, of course, is not limited to racial inequalities. Perhaps some of the Justices were reluctant to pursue the line of doctrinal development suggested by the separate opinions in *Guest,* for fear of giving Congress an invitation without apparent limitation. The solution to this puzzle—if it was a puzzle—came only two years after the *Guest* decision, in the form of a complete turnabout in the interpretation of the power of Congress to enforce the Thirteenth Amendment.

The turnabout came in JONES V. ALFRED H. MAYER CO. (1968), when the Court interpreted the 1866 Civil Rights Act to prohibit all racial discrimination in the sale of property and upheld the act as so construed. The Court overruled the *Hodges* decision and essentially adopted the dissenting views of Justice Harlan in the *Civil Rights Cases.* The Thirteenth Amendment was held to empower Congress not only to eliminate slavery but also to eliminate slavery's "badges and incidents." Furthermore, said the Court, it is for Congress itself "rationally to determine what are the badges and incidents of slavery," and to enact laws to eradicate any such "relic of slavery" it might find.

This broad language is not limited to racial discrimination. Commentators have asked whether the Court, in seeking to avoid an open-ended interpretation of congressional power under the Fourteenth Amendment, has offered Congress a different set of constitutional bootstraps. In the quoted passage from the *Jones* opinion, the Court appears to authorize Congress to define a given right—any right—as one that is essential to freedom, to define its impairment as an incident of slavery, and to enact a law protecting the right against both public and private interference.

When the right in question is a right to be free from racial discrimination, this line of reasoning accords not only with the language of the *Jones* opinion but also with the decision's place in the historical process of constitutional validation of modern civil rights legislation. Outside the racial context, however, the reasoning is unlikely to be adopted by the Supreme Court. Of course the Thirteenth Amendment prohibits the enslavement of anyone, of any race. And the Court has upheld an application of the 1866 act to a case of racial discrimination against whites, evidently (but without discussion) on the basis of Congress's power to enforce the Thirteenth Amendment, in *McDonald v. Santa Fe Trail Transportation Co.* (1976). The decision is defensible, despite the lack of historic links between slavery and discrimination against whites. There is a basis in experience for a congressional conclusion that discrimination against one racial group affects attitudes toward race generally and promotes discrimination against other races. It would be much harder to justify a similar conclusion about the effects of discrimination on the basis of gender, or sexual preference, or physical handicap. Even if the analogy were stronger, the doctrinal context of the *Jones* decision cautions against a prediction that its "badges and incidents" reasoning will be extended beyond cases of racial discrimination. The Thirteenth Amendment seems to have had its main appeal as a basis for congressional power precisely because that power could be contained within the confines of remedies for racial discrimination. The "badges and incidents of slavery" which justify congressional intervention are to be found in racial discrimination if they are to be found at all.

The power of Congress to enforce the Thirteenth Amendment, like any other congressional power, is subject to the limitations of the BILL OF RIGHTS. Without question, the amendment empowers Congress to prohibit racial discrimination in all the public areas of life, including commercial dealings. In RUNYON V. MCCRARY (1976), for example, the Supreme Court relied on the Thirteenth Amendment to uphold application of the 1866 act to a private school that accepted applicants from children in the public at large but excluded blacks. The potential limitations of the Bill of Rights found expression in that case. Justice LEWIS F. POWELL, concurring, cautioned that some hypothetical congressional enforcements of the Thirteenth Amendment might violate constitutional rights of PRIVACY or associational freedom, as when a litigant might seek application of the 1866 act to a case of racial discrimination in the selection of a home tutor or babysitter.

The expansion of the power of Congress to enforce the Thirteenth Amendment has not been accompanied by a corresponding expansion of the amendment's reach as a self-executing provision. The *Jones* opinion left open the question whether the amendment "by its own terms did anything more than abolish slavery," and although MEMPHIS V. GREENE (1981) raised the issue, the Court did not reach it. Thus, even though a great many forms of private racial discrimination may constitute "badges and incidents of slavery" justifying congressional action to secure their elimination, if Congress has not acted, these same "badges and incidents" are insufficient to trigger the operation of the amendment's section 1. The practical significance of this difference, however, is slight. The Supreme Court has construed existing civil rights legislation broadly enough to prohibit a wide range of private acts of racial discrimination.

Even assuming that the Thirteenth Amendment's self-executing force is limited to cases of bondage to personal service, there is room for debate about the kinds of compulsion that constitute involuntary servitude. Debt bondage—the requirement that a person work in discharge of a debt—is a classic case of peonage and is plainly forbidden by the amendment. However, compulsory military service (or alternative service for CONSCIENTIOUS OBJECTORS), hard labor for persons imprisoned for crime, and restrictions on the right to strike all have been sustained against Thirteenth Amendment attacks.

KENNETH L. KARST

Bibliography

CASPER, GERHARD 1968 Jones v. Mayer: Clio, Bemused and Confused Muse. *Supreme Court Review* 1968:89–132.

FAIRMAN, CHARLES 1971 *Reconstruction and Reunion: 1864–1888, Part One.* Chapter XIX. New York: Macmillan Company.

NOTE 1969 The "New" Thirteenth Amendment: A Preliminary Analysis. *Harvard Law Review* 82:1294–1321.

THOMAS v. REVIEW BOARD
450 U.S. 707 (1981)

Reaffirming its decision in SHERBERT V. VERNER (1963), the Supreme Court, 8–1, invalidated Indiana's refusal of unemployment compensation to a Jehovah's Witness who, for religious reasons, had quit his job rather than work on weapons production. The state had not shown that denying benefits was the LEAST RESTRICTIVE MEANS of achieving a COMPELLING STATE INTEREST.

KENNETH L. KARST

THOMAS v. UNION CARBIDE AGRICULTURAL PRODUCTS CO.
473 U.S. (1985)

The Supreme Court's decision in NORTHERN PIPELINE CONSTRUCTION CO. V. MARATHON PIPE LINE CO. (1982) left considerable confusion about the power of Congress to confer JURISDICTION on administrators or LEGISLATIVE COURTS over cases falling within the JUDICIAL POWER OF THE UNITED STATES. *Thomas* provided some useful clarification.

The Federal Insecticide, Fungicide, and Rodenticide Act (FIFRA) requires a manufacturer, as a condition on registering a pesticide, to supply research data on the pesticide's health, safety, and environmental effects to the Environmental Protection Agency (EPA). These data may be used in evaluating a second manufacturer's registration of a similar product, provided that the second manufacturer offers to compensate the first. If the two manufacturers cannot agree on the compensation, FIFRA requires binding arbitration of the dispute. An arbitrator's decision is reviewable by a court only for "fraud, misrepresentation or other misconduct."

Various pesticide manufacturers sued the EPA administrator challenging the constitutionality of the scheme of binding arbitration with limited court review. The federal district court held that the scheme violated Article III of the Constitution; on direct APPEAL, the Supreme Court unanimously reversed, upholding the law.

Justice SANDRA DAY O'CONNOR, writing for the Court, recognized a broad policy in Article III "that federal judicial power shall be vested in courts whose judges enjoy life tenure and fixed compensation." *Marathon* effectuated a part of that policy but was distinguishable here. Considering the origin of the claims to compensation in federal law, along with the reasons of public policy that persuaded Congress to impose binding arbitration, the manufacturers' claimed rights were properly considered "public rights," the adjudication of which Congress could place in administrative hands. Cases involving "public rights" were not limited to those in which the government itself was a party. Nor, said the Court in an important OBITER DICTUM, is Article III's requirement of independent judges irrelevant merely because the government is a party. Here the assignment of decision to nonjudicial arbitrators was softened somewhat by FIFRA's provision of some minimal review by CONSTITUTIONAL COURTS of arbitrators' decisions. (In some cases, the Court noted, DUE PROCESS considerations might independently require further court review.)

Thomas thus adopted a flexible approach to Article III's limitations on Congress's employment of nonjudicial tribunals—the very approach urged by the *Marathon* dissenters. Justice WILLIAM J. BRENNAN, for three Justices, concurred separately on the basis of his PLURALITY OPINION in *Marathon.* Justice JOHN PAUL STEVENS concurred, saying the manufacturers lacked STANDING to challenge the law's validity.

KENNETH L. KARST

THOMPSON, SMITH
(1763–1843)

Smith Thompson was among the most experienced judges ever appointed to the Supreme Court, and his tenure on the bench (1823–1843) linked the constitutional doctrines of the MARSHALL COURT and the TANEY COURT. After sixteen years on the New York Supreme Court (1802–1818), four years as chief justice, Thompson had been secretary of the navy (1818–1823). His experience in JAMES MONROE's cabinet made Monroe feel so comfortable with Thompson, presumably including his constitutional views, that the President insisted that the New Yorker fill the seat vacated by the death of a fellow New Yorker, H. BROCKHOLST LIVINGSTON.

Thompson did not change his jurisprudence significantly during his twenty years on the Court. He remained a black-letter lawyer, whose most interesting contributions to constitutional jurisprudence can be traced to his New York judicial and cabinet experiences. Besides adhering to precedent, Thompson concerned himself with maintaining judicial independence while showing a willingness to let the legislature have free rein. Having served in an era when Congress was relatively inactive, Thompson appears today as a STATES' RIGHTS advocate, or more precisely an adherent to states' responsibilities. Yet his values did not differ greatly from those of his nationalistic brethren on the Marshall Court. He was, for example, aware of the business community's needs. Unlike Livingston, his predecessor on the Marshall Court, Thompson was more willing to express his differences with the rest of the Court.

He was absent when GIBBONS V. OGDEN (1824) was argued, but in *Livingston v. Van Ingen* (1812), decided by the New York court, he had resolved some of the questions involved in *Gibbons* in favor of the steamboat monopoly. Although Thompson's *Van Ingen* opinion did not consider the commerce clause question, that of his colleague, JAMES KENT, did and commerce clause cases subsequent to *Gibbons* show that Thompson subscribed to Kent's doctrine of concurrent powers to regulate commerce. JOHN MARSHALL's language in *Gibbons* was, moreover, sufficiently broad to allow Thompson to render lip service to *Gibbons* while taking a contrary position. In BROWN V. MARYLAND (1827), Thompson dissented from Marshall's majority opinion holding that Maryland's law imposing license taxes on wholesalers of imported goods violated both the import and export and the COMMERCE CLAUSE. Like Kent, Thompson did not examine the nature of the power underlying state regulations. Whether the state regulated commerce or not was immaterial so long as the statute did not conflict with a congressional act. In rejecting Marshall's ORIGINAL PACKAGE DOCTRINE in *Brown,* Thompson set forth the position that goods became subject to a state's jurisdiction upon crossing its borders. Thompson continued his adherence to the doctrine of concurrent commerce powers in MAYOR OF

NEW YORK v. MILN (1837), to the extent that he wrote separately rather than subscribe to the majority's reasoning that regulation of immigrant passengers was simply a valid exercise of the STATE POLICE POWER. Subsequently, the concurrent powers doctrine became an integral part of ROGER B. TANEY's constitutional thought. Taney had not advanced that doctrine while arguing for the state in *Brown,* and it is reasonable to assume that he borrowed it from Thompson.

On the slavery question, Thompson assumed the doughface position later followed by his replacement on the Court, SAMUEL NELSON, of providing support for the peculiar institution, while striving to confine the question at hand and giving the appearance of sticking rigidly to precedent. Typical, in this respect, was GROVES v. SLAUGHTER (1841), where Thompson, speaking for the Court's majority, was able to avoid the question whether Mississippi's constitutional ban on uncontrolled slave shipments from other states violated the commerce clause. In PRIGG v. PENNSYLVANIA (1842), Thompson differed from JOSEPH STORY's opinion that the fugitive slave clause did not prohibit state laws designed "faithfully" to enforce the clause. In contrast with Thompson's adherence to legal formalism in slavery cases was his activism in *Cherokee Nation v. Georgia* (1831). Dissenting, in the most elaborate opinion of his career, he asserted that regardless of their relative weakness to their white neighbors, the Cherokees constituted an independent, foreign, sovereign, nation. The following year, Thompson's dissent became the majority position in WORCESTER v. GEORGIA. (See CHEROKEE INDIAN CASES.)

Thompson's conservative attitude toward government and business sometimes put him at odds with both Marshall and Taney. Perhaps none of his contemporaries had more concern for protecting VESTED RIGHTS than did Thompson. He joined Story's CHARLES RIVER BRIDGE dissent (1837), and in his own WHEATON v. PETERS (1834) dissent he said that as a matter of "sound reason and abstract morality" the COMMON LAW provided COPYRIGHT protection. It was his concern for vested rights alone with his administrative experience that caused Thompson to distinguish between cabinet officers' political and ministerial duties. Only the latter functions were "subject to the control of the law, and the direction of the president," he said in *United States ex rel. Stokes et al. v. Kendall* (1838). Thompson's conservatism meshed with his adherence to states' responsibilities in interpreting the CONTRACT CLAUSE. In his view contracts were subject to the existing law of a place, including insolvency laws. Such laws, like the long-standing New York system, were also good for business. These beliefs explain Thompson's opposition to Marshall in OGDEN v. SAUNDERS (1837), and partially explains his CRAIG v. MISSOURI dissent (1830). Thompson's impact on constitutional law was slight, and only a few Whig politicians lamented his death.

DONALD ROPER

Bibliography

DUNNE, GERALD T. 1969 Smith Thompson. In Leon Friedman and Fred L. Israel, eds., *The Justices of the United States Supreme Court.* Pages 475–492. New York: Chelsea House.

THORNHILL v. ALABAMA 310 U.S. 88 (1940)

This case involved a FIRST AMENDMENT challenge to convictions under an Alabama antipicketing statute. Normally one has STANDING only to plead one's own constitutional rights. In *Thornhill,* however, the Supreme Court did not ask whether the particular activity in which the pickets had engaged was constitutionally protected. Instead it asked whether the statute itself, rather than its application to these particular persons, violated the First Amendment. Because the statute was INVALID ON ITS FACE, it could be challenged, even by a union that itself might have engaged in violent picketing not protected by the First Amendment. The theory was that the statute's general ban on all labor dispute picketing would threaten peaceful picketers as well, even though no peaceful picketers had even been prosecuted.

Justice FRANK MURPHY acknowledged that the state legislature legitimately might have written a narrowly drawn statute that condemned only violent or mass picketing. Instead it wrote a general ban on all picketing in labor–management disputes. "The existence of such a statute . . . which does not aim specifically at evils within the allowable area of state control but, on the contrary, sweeps within its ambit other activities that in ordinary circumstances constitute an exercise of freedom of speech . . . readily lends itself to . . . discriminatory enforcement by local prosecuting officials [and] results in a continuous and pervasive unconstitutional restraint on all freedom of discussion." Subsequently the Court was to speak of the unconstitutional CHILLING EFFECT of such "facially overbroad" statutes.

MARTIN SHAPIRO

THORNTON v. CALDOR, INC.
105 S. Ct. 2914 (1985)

The Supreme Court held unconstitutional, on establishment clause grounds, a state act authorizing employees to designate a sabbath day and not work that day. Applying the three-part test of LEMON v. KURTZMAN (1971), Chief Justice WARREN E. BURGER found that by vesting in employees an "absolute and unqualified" right not to work on the sabbath of one's choice, and by forcing employers to adjust work schedules to the religious practices of employees, the act constituted a law respecting an ESTABLISHMENT OF RELIGION. In purpose and effect it advanced religion, preferring those who believe in not working on the sabbath to those who hold no such belief. By implication, a statute giving employers some leeway would be constitutional. Only Justice WILLIAM H. REHNQUIST dissented, without opinion. No member of the Court defended the statute as a state effort to prevent discrimination against sabbath believers by preventing the imposition of employment penalties on those acting in obedience to conscience by refusing to work. (See SHERBERT v. VERNER, 1963.)

LEONARD W. LEVY

THORPE, FRANCIS N.
(1857–1926)

Francis Newton Thorpe, professor of history at the University of Pennsylvania, edited seven volumes of *American Charters and Constitutions.* He also wrote several books on political and constitutional history from a post-Civil War nationalist viewpoint. He emphasized the UNWRITTEN CONSTITUTION by which the written Constitution is continually extended and adapted.

DENNIS J. MAHONEY

THREE-FIFTHS CLAUSE

Article I, section 2, clause 3, of the United States Constitution originally provided that members of the House of Representatives would be apportioned among the states on a formula that added to "free Persons" (including indentured servants but excluding untaxed Indians) "three fifths of all other Persons." The 1840 publication of JAMES MADISON's notes of debates in the CONSTITUTIONAL CONVENTION OF 1787 revealed that the euphemism "all other Persons" referred to slaves.

The clause originated in an unsuccessful 1783 proposal in the Confederation Congress to amend the ARTICLES OF CONFEDERATION by changing the method of apportioning taxes among the states to a per capita basis that would include all free persons and "three-fifths of all other persons." At the Philadelphia convention, JAMES WILSON, a Pennsylvania delegate, resurrected the three-fifths formula as an amendment to the VIRGINIA PLAN and thereby touched off heated debates on counting slaves for apportionment purposes. The underlying conflict of interests between slave and free states provoked a great crisis of the convention. The deadlock was resolved by a complex formula that was part of the GREAT COMPROMISE basing both representation and DIRECT TAXES on the three-fifths formula and, for good measure, making the direct-tax provisions of Article I, section 9, unamendable (Article V).

Madison in THE FEDERALIST #54 defended the clause as an arbitrary but reasonable compromise that roughly reflected the anomalous legal status of a slave, a human for certain purposes and a chattel for others. The slave was "debased by servitude below the equal level of free inhabitants, which regards the slave as divested of two-fifths of the man." NATHANIEL GORHAM of Massachusetts had earlier agreed, accepting the clause as "pretty near the just proportion."

The three-fifths formula gave the slave states an additional political weight in Congress quite close to what they would have enjoyed if they had counted all slaves for purposes of apportionment. In 1811 this produced eighteen slave-state representatives more than the southern states would have had if slaves had been excluded altogether from apportionment. The clause therefore rankled New England and middle-state Federalists, who used the clause as a vehicle to voice their resentment at the Virginia Dynasty and the rising political power of the west. Reviving arguments of 1787 that if Virginia counted its slaves Massachusetts should be able to count its cattle, New Englanders complained with JOHN QUINCY ADAMS that "slave representation has governed the union." The HARTFORD CONVENTION demanded in 1814 that the clause be abrogated.

Later debates during the abolition controversy renewed this dispute. Abolitionists either disingenuously tried to construe the clause as referring to persons other than slaves (indentured servants or ALIENS) or demanded that the clause be expunged. Defenders of slavery and Garrisonian abolitionists both cited the clause as an explicit assurance of the privileged constitutional status of that unique form of property, human chattels.

Though the abolitionist debates proved inconclusive, the clause bedeviled Republicans during Reconstruction. After the abolition of slavery, all blacks became "free Persons" and thus the congressional representation of the former Confederate states would be augmented by perhaps a dozen congressmen, endangering the Republicans' objectives for the war and Reconstruction. To forestall this, Republicans first temporarily excluded ten of the former seceded states from representation in Congress, then forced ratification of the FOURTEENTH AMENDMENT, whose section 2 provides that representatives shall be apportioned simply on "the whole number of persons in each State," and that a state's representation should be reduced in proportion to its denial of the vote to male citizens over twenty-one years old, except for participation in rebellion or crime.

WILLIAM M. WIECEK

Bibliography

OHLINE, HOWARD A. 1971 Republicanism and Slavery: Origins of the Three-Fifths Clause in the United States Constitution. *William and Mary Quarterly* 28:563–594.

SIMPSON, ALBERT F. 1941 The Political Significance of Slave Representation, 1787–1821. *Journal of Southern History* 7:315–342.

THREE-JUDGE COURT

The Supreme Court's decision in EX PARTE YOUNG (1908) made it possible for one federal judge to tie up an entire state legislative program by granting preliminary injunctive relief. In 1910 Congress required certain applications for federal-court INTERLOCUTORY injunctions against state officers to be heard by three judges. Such a court's order was made directly appealable to the Supreme Court. A similar statutory scheme had been devised earlier for certain ANTITRUST and railroad regulation cases. The 1948 revision of the JUDICIAL CODE made clear that the three-judge requirement applied to all hearings on applications for interlocutory or permanent INJUNCTIONS against state officers.

A considerable body of law developed out of this statute. Applications for DECLARATORY JUDGMENTS were not subject to the requirement, although injunctive relief is authorized to enforce a declaratory judgment. Three-judge courts were required only for actions seeking to enjoin state officers in carrying out statutes of general and statewide application, not local ordinances. While three judges were ordinarily necessary to deny injunctive relief as well as grant it, a single judge could dismiss such an action when it was "insubstantial."

The system of three-judge courts was enormously burdensome, both on the lower federal courts and on the Supreme Court. In 1976, Congress drastically limited the three-judge requirement, retaining it only in certain cases involving legislative REAPPORTIONMENT or VOTING RIGHTS and some cases under the CIVIL RIGHTS ACT OF 1964.

KENNETH L. KARST

Bibliography

WRIGHT, CHARLES ALAN 1983 *The Law of Federal Courts,* 4th ed. Pages 295–299, 728–729. St. Paul, Minn.: West Publishing Co.

TIEDEMAN, CHRISTOPHER G. (1857–1903)

Christopher G. Tiedeman, a professor of law, published *A Treatise on the Limitations of Police Power in the United States* (1886). Second only to THOMAS COOLEY'S *Constitutional Limitations* in its influence on American constitutional law, Tiedeman's book spurred the conversion of the FOURTEENTH AMENDMENT into a bulwark of VESTED RIGHTS. He believed that liberty found its highest expression in laissez-faire economics and that the POLICE POWER, which he sought to reduce to the role of policeman, was making "socialism, communism, and anarchism . . . rampant in America." He found evidence for that claim in the advocacy of prolabor legislation and state protection of the weak against the strong. Conservatism, he wrote, feared "the advent of an absolutism more tyrannical and more unreasoning than any before experienced by man, the absolutism of a democratic majority." JUDICIAL REVIEW in support of written constitutions that limited government provided the only hope, and Tiedeman's exposition of cases was calculated to assist courts in their task of thwarting invasions of private rights. In 1900, in the preface to a revised second edition, Tiedeman expressed gratification that "the first edition of this book has been quoted by the courts in hundreds of cases."

LEONARD W. LEVY

TILTON v. RICHARDSON

See: *Lemon v. Kurtzman*

TIMBER CULTURE ACT

See: Environmental Regulation

TIMES-MIRROR CO. v. CALIFORNIA

See: *Bridges v. California*

TINKER v. DES MOINES INDEPENDENT COMMUNITY SCHOOL DISTRICT
393 U.S. 503 (1969)

Tinker is a leading modern decision on the subjects of SYMBOLIC SPEECH and CHILDREN'S RIGHTS. A group of adults and students in Des Moines planned to protest the VIETNAM WAR by wearing black armbands during the 1965 holiday season. On learning of this plan, the public school principals adopted a policy to forbid the wearing of armbands. Two high school students and one junior high school student wore armbands to school, refused to remove them, and were suspended until they might return without armbands. They sued in federal court to enjoin enforcement of the principals' policy and for nominal damages. The district court dismissed the complaint, and the court of appeals affirmed by an equally divided court. The Supreme Court reversed, 7–2, in an opinion by Justice ABE FORTAS.

The wearing of these armbands was "closely akin to 'pure speech' " and protected by the FIRST AMENDMENT. The school environment did imply limitations on the freedom of expression, but here the principals lacked justification for imposing any such limitations. The authorities' "undifferentiated fear" of disturbance was insufficient. While student expression could be forbidden when it materially disrupted school work or school discipline, these students had undertaken "a silent, passive expression of opinion, unaccompanied by any disorder or disturbance." Furthermore, only this "particular symbol . . . was singled out for prohibition"; political campaign buttons had been allowed, and even "the Iron Cross, traditionally a symbol of Nazism." (Justice Fortas may have been unaware of the vogue among surfers and their inland imitators.)

Justice HUGO L. BLACK dissented, accusing the majority of encouraging students to defy their teachers and arguing that the wearing of the armbands had, in fact, diverted other students' minds from their schoolwork. He did not ask how much the principals' reaction to the planned protest might have contributed to that diversion.

KENNETH L. KARST

TITLES OF NOBILITY

In the twentieth century, the idea of a hereditary ruling elite using titles of nobility as a device for maintaining its authority seems a bit frivolous. To the founding generation, however, the threat was only too real. Moreover, the threat that a foreign potentate might suborn an American citizen or official by proffering such a title was also perceived as significant. The ARTICLES OF CONFEDERATION forbade the acceptance of foreign titles by any person holding federal or state office and forbade the granting of titles by the United States or by any state. The prohibitions were carried over into the Constitution, except that there is no longer a ban on state officers accepting foreign titles, and Congress may authorize acceptance of titles by federal officers. In both documents, titles of nobility are treated, along with gifts and offices, as items of value that foreign governments might offer in exchange for favors, and Governor EDMUND RANDOLPH, at the CONSTITUTIONAL CONVENTION, asserted that the provision was designed to guard against corruption.

As it appears in the Constitution, the prohibition against accepting foreign titles applies only to those holding a federal office of trust or profit. On the eve of the War of 1812, Congress proposed to the states a constitutional amendment extending the prohibition to every citizen of the United States. Under the proposed amendment, acceptance of a title of nobility would have caused automatic forfeiture of United States CITIZENSHIP and permanent disqualification from holding federal or state office. The titles-of-nobility amendment was one of only six constitutional amendments ever proposed by Congress to fall short of ratification by the states.

DENNIS J. MAHONEY

TOCQUEVILLE, ALEXIS DE
(1805–1859)

The French magistrate and political theorist Alexis Clerel de Tocqueville spent nine months of 1831 and 1832 in the United States. He believed that democracy was the inescapable destiny of all nations and that America, as the first avowedly democratic nation in the modern world, offered an opportunity for the student of politics to observe democracy in action. One product of Tocqueville's sojourn on our shores was *Democracy in America.*

Tocqueville thought that the main problem of democracy was a tendency toward radical equality of condition which was destructive of the liberty necessary for excellence in human endeavors. He perceived in America two undesirable developments: a pervasive tyranny of the majority and a centrifugal individualism. He proposed, as a solution to democracy's problems, a "new science of politics" based on enlightened self-interest. He emphasized the utility, rather than the beauty or nobility, of virtue and public-spiritedness.

A shrewd observer of political affairs, Tocqueville was one of the first to discern the American tendency toward JUDICIAL SUPREMACY. American judges, he noted, although confined to deciding particular cases, and only those presenting justiciable controversies, possess immense political power. This is possible because "scarcely any political question arises in the United States which is not resolved, sooner or later, into a judicial question," and because of the simple fact that the Americans have acknowledged the right of judges to found their decisions on the Constitution rather than on the laws, or, in other words, they have permitted them not to apply such laws as may appear to them to be unconstitutional. The political power of the judges, arising out of the exercise of JUDICIAL REVIEW, appeared to Tocqueville a salutary check on potential legislative excess. Tocqueville's observation, made when the Supreme Court had voided only a single federal law as unconstitutional, seems all the more perceptive today.

Tocqueville also recognized the unique status of the Constitution in American political life. The English constitution was alterable by ordinary legislation and the constitutions of continental monarchies were immutable save by violent revolution; only in America was the Constitution regarded as an expression of the SOVEREIGNTY of the people, not subject to change at the whim of legislators, but amendable by the common consent of the citizens in accordance with established rules.

Not all of Tocqueville's observations remain valid. For example, he wrote that the states were more powerful than the national government and that Congress was more powerful than the President. In each case, however, he identified the factors that have caused those relationships to be reversed in our own day.

Tocqueville's purpose in writing *Democracy in America* was not merely to describe American institutions. He addressed himself to the universal problems of modern politics—economic and social, as well as governmental. America provided illustrations and examples, and from the American experience he made generalizations applicable to all modern nations. In America Tocqueville learned how to make democracy safe for the world.

DENNIS J. MAHONEY

Bibliography

PIERSON, G. W. 1959 *Tocqueville in America.* New York: Basic Books.

ZETTERBAUM, MARVIN 1965 *Tocqueville and the Problem of Democracy.* New York: Basic Books.

TODD, THOMAS
(1765–1826)

Thomas Todd served as a Justice of the United States Supreme Court for nearly nineteen years, but he had only a small impact on the Court's decisions. Born into a fairly prominent Virginia family, he was orphaned at an early age. Because the bulk of his father's estate went to his eldest brother, he was forced to fend for himself. Following a short enlistment in the army during the Revolutionary War he went to Liberty Hall in Lexington, Virginia (later Washington and Lee University), where he studied the classics and mathematics. Todd then entered the household of his cousin Harry Innes, an accomplished lawyer and respected member of the Virginia legislature, where he served as a tutor in return for room and board. In 1784 Innes and his family removed to Kentucky where he became a judge, and Todd accompanied them. Through his cousin's political connections Todd quickly became involved in the movement to make Kentucky a separate state, serving as secretary and clerk for the various conventions that were called, and helped to write Kentucky's first CONSTITUTION in 1792.

Admitted to the bar in 1788, Todd developed a lucrative law practice, with a specialty in land titles. During the 1790s he served as secretary to the Kentucky legislature and as clerk to the federal district court. In 1799 he was appointed judge of that court, and five years later he became chief judge. In 1807 Congress increased the number of United States Supreme Court Justices from five to six in order to accommodate the newly created western circuit (Ohio, Kentucky, and Tennessee) and to resolve the special problems in land law arising there. As this was Todd's area of expertise and because Todd was popular with the congressmen from the western states, President THOMAS JEFFERSON appointed him to the newly created post.

Although a Republican, Todd invariably supported the strongly nationalist and probusiness decisions of the MARSHALL COURT. Reportedly he was opposed to the Supreme Court's ruling in DARTMOUTH COLLEGE V. WOODWARD (1819), but he was absent when it was handed down. In fact, bad health combined with the difficulties of riding the western circuit forced him to miss many of the Supreme Court sessions. He wrote only fourteen decisions, eleven for the majority, two concurring, and one dissenting in the relatively unimportant case of *Finley v. Lynn* (1810). With the exception of his last opinion, *Riggs v. Taylor* (1824), which dealt with an evidentiary problem, all his opinions dealt with problems involving land titles. He remained active in various local and state civic affairs until his death.

RICHARD E. ELLIS

Bibliography

ISRAEL, FRED L. 1969 Thomas Todd. Pages 407–412 in Leon Friedman and Fred L. Israel, eds., *Justices of the Supreme Court, 1789–1969. New York: Chelsea House.*

TOLERATION ACT
1 William & Mary ch. 18 (1689)

The principle of RELIGIOUS LIBERTY denies that the state has any legitimate authority over the individual's religion or irreligion; the principle of toleration insists that a state which maintains an ESTABLISHMENT OF RELIGION indulge the existence of nonconformist religious groups. Toleration is a step between persecution and liberty. The Toleration Act, which accompanied the Glorious Revolution of 1688–1689, was a political necessity that restored peace to a religiously pluralistic England and ended a period of persecution during which thousands of nonconformist Protestant ministers had died in jail.

The act, entitled "A Bill of Indulgence," exempted most nonconformists from the penalties of the persecutory laws of the Restoration, leaving those laws in force but inapplicable to persons qualifying for indulgence. Subjects who took the requisite oaths to support the new king and reject the authority of the pope might have the privilege of worshipping as they pleased, because they were exempted from the penalties that had suppressed them. Baptists and Quakers received special indulgences. Thus the act had the effect of permitting the existence of lawful nonconformity, though nonconformists still had to pay tithes to the established church and endure many civil disabilities. One section of the act excluded from its benefits Roman Catholic recusants and Protestant antitrinitarians. England still regarded the former as political subversives, the latter as virtual atheists. For all its faults the statute of 1689 ushered in an era of toleration under the established church and ultimately benefited dissenters in those American colonies that maintained establishments of religion.

LEONARD W. LEVY

Bibliography

SEATON, A. (1911)1972 *The Theory of Toleration under the Later Stuarts.* Pages 92–236. New York: Octagon Books.

TONKIN GULF RESOLUTION

See: Gulf of Tonkin Resolution

TOOMBS, ROBERT A.
(1810–1885)

A Georgia attorney educated at Schenectady's Union College, Robert Augustus Toombs was a congressman (1843–1853) and senator (1853–1861) before becoming a SECESSION leader. Initially a conservative Whig and an ally of ALEXANDER STEPHENS, Toombs became a Democrat, but not a fire-eater, after the COMPROMISE OF 1850. In 1856 he supported the admission of Kansas without slavery, if the settlers there voted for statehood on that basis. In 1860 Toombs worked for a united Democratic Party, but despite this goal and his previous support for STEPHEN A. DOUGLAS in the Senate, Toombs opposed Douglas's presidential aspirations. After ABRAHAM LINCOLN's election Toombs supported the Crittenden Compromise, and he also offered his own. When compromise failed, he returned to Georgia as a secession leader, writing a report for the Georgia Secession Convention explaining why disunion was necessary. Appointed Confederate secretary of state, Toombs resigned after five months to accept a rebel army commission. When he was denied a promotion after Antietam, Toombs left the army and became a critic of JEFFERSON DAVIS's economic inefficiency, confederate violations of CIVIL LIBERTIES, and CONSCRIPTION. In 1865 he escaped to England; he returned in 1867 to lead Georgia's anti-Reconstruction forces. He dominated Georgia's 1877 CONSTITUTIONAL CONVENTION, which paved the way for black disfranchisement, and, at Toombs's insistence, severely limited corporate charters and railroad development. Toombs never petitioned for CITIZENSHIP, and although a successful attorney, never again held public office.

PAUL FINKELMAN

Bibliography

THOMPSON, ROBERT Y. 1966 *Robert Toombs of Georgia.* Baton Rouge: Louisiana State University Press.

TOOMER v. WITSELL
334 U.S. 385 (1948)

South Carolina required state residents to pay a $25-per-boat license fee to gather shrimp in state waters; for nonresidents, the fee was $2,500. The Supreme Court, speaking through Chief Justice FRED M. VINSON, held that this discrimination violated both the PRIVILEGES AND IMMUNITIES clause of Article IV and the COMMERCE CLAUSE. (See STATE REGULATION OF COMMERCE.) The commerce ground was easy and unanimously supported by the Justices. The decision's main importance lay in its approach to the privileges and immunities clause; on this issue the Court divided, 6–3. Earlier decisions had suggested that the clause protected only "fundamental rights." *Toomer* redirected the inquiry: discrimination against nonresidents was permissible only if it bore a substantial relation to solving a problem distinctively presented by nonresidents. South Carolina's discriminatory tax failed this test.

KENNETH L. KARST

TORCASO v. WATKINS
367 U.S. 488 (1961)

The Maryland Constitution provided: "No RELIGIOUS TEST ought ever to be required as a qualification to any office . . . other than a declaration of belief in the existence of God. . . ." For Justice HUGO L. BLACK, speaking for the Supreme Court, the Maryland requirement contravened the ESTABLISHMENT OF RELIGION clause of the FIRST AMENDMENT. Black, quoting his own opinion for the Court in EVERSON V. BOARD OF EDUCATION (1947), repeated that government may not "force a person to profess a belief . . . in any religion."

RICHARD E. MORGAN

TORT CLAIMS ACT

See: Federal Tort Claims Act

TOTH, UNITED STATES ex rel., v. QUARLES
350 U.S. 11 (1955)

Five months after his honorable discharge from the Air Force, Toth was charged with committing murder while on active duty in Korea. Taken to Korea for trial by court martial, Toth sought HABEAS CORPUS in a DISTRICT OF COLUMBIA court. On APPEAL, the Supreme Court held, 6–3, that a civilian was entitled to TRIAL BY JURY in a civilian court established under Article III; court-martial JURISDICTION was constitutionally limited to actual members of the armed forces.

KENNETH L. KARST

(SEE ALSO: *Judicial Power of the United States; Military Justice and the Constitution.*)

TOWNSEND v. SAIN
372 U.S. 29 (1963)

When a state prisoner seeks federal HABEAS CORPUS review of a constitutional error in his or her case, the federal court must decide what weight to give the state court fact findings that are relevant to the prisoner's claim. The fairness and accuracy of such findings are crucial to the proper adjudication of federal constitutional rights, because most habeas corpus petitions raise mixed questions of law and fact, such as the VOLUNTARINESS of a WAIVER OF CONSTITUTIONAL RIGHTS, or the suggestiveness of a LINE-UP identification. In *Townsend,* a unanimous Supreme Court held that a federal court in a habeas corpus proceeding always has the power to try the facts anew, and that it must do so if the defendant did not receive a full and fair evidentiary hearing in any state court proceeding. The Court split 5–4 over the need for more specific directives concerning mandatory hearings, with Chief Justice EARL WARREN setting forth the majority's view that a hearing is required in six particular circumstances.

In 1966, Congress enacted a modified form of the *Townsend* criteria in an amendment to the JUDICIAL CODE, specifying eight circumstances when the validity of state court findings may not be presumed. In other circumstances, the habeas corpus petitioner bears the burden of proving that the state fact findings were erroneous.

CATHERINE HANCOCK

TOWNSHEND ACTS (1767)

The Townshend Acts imposed duties upon American imports of glass, lead, paint, paper, and tea and authorized WRITS OF ASSISTANCE as one means of enforcing payment. Although "external" in form, the duties were not levied to regulate trade but to raise revenue to help pay for maintaining British soldiers and officials in America. The colonists protested that the levies constituted TAXATION WITHOUT REPRESENTATION. The Townshend Act duties (except that on tea) were repealed in 1770.

DENNIS J. MAHONEY

TRADE UNIONS

See: Labor and the Constitution

TRANSACTIONAL IMMUNITY

See: Immunity Grant

TRANS-MISSOURI FREIGHT ASSOCIATION v. UNITED STATES 166 U.S. 290 (1897)

A 5–4 Supreme Court, holding that the SHERMAN ANTITRUST ACT extended to railroads, rejected the RULE OF REASON advanced by Justice EDWARD D. WHITE in dissent. In 1889, eighteen railroads had combined to form the Trans-Missouri Freight Association "for the purpose of mutual protection, by establishing and maintaining reasonable rates, rules and regulations [over their mutual] freight traffic." Any member's proposed rate reduction for a route shared with another member needed Association approval.

Justice RUFUS PECKHAM, the Court's spokesman, found two questions: Did the Sherman Act apply to railroads and, if so, was the Freight Association agreement a violation of that act? He dismissed the railroads' claim of exemption on two grounds. Their business was commerce, and the lower courts and the dissenters had relied on a mistaken belief that the Sherman Act could not apply to railroads because the INTERSTATE COMMERCE ACT already regulated carriers. He refused "to read into the act by way of judicial legislation an exception that is not placed there [by Congress]." Policy matters were not questions for judicial determination; any alteration of the law was for Congress to undertake. Peckham concluded that the Sherman Act prohibited all restraints of INTERSTATE COMMERCE; adopting the rule of reason would "substantially . . . leave the question of reasonableness to the companies themselves." Endorsing free competition, the Court declared that intent need not be proved: the Association agreement clearly restrained commerce.

DAVID GORDON

TRAVEL

See: Right to Travel

TREASON

Treason is the only crime defined in the United States Constitution. Article III, section 3, declares that

> Treason against the United States shall consist only in levying war against them, or in adhering to their enemies, giving them aid and comfort. No person shall be convicted of treason unless on the testimony of two witnesses to the same overt act, or on confession in open court. The Congress shall have power to declare the punishment of treason, but no ATTAINDER OF TREASON shall work corruption of blood, or forfeiture except during the life of the person attainted.

State constitutions contain similar limiting definitions of treason against a state. However, since national independence there has been little action or development of doctrine under the state provisions. The notable exceptions are the trials of Thomas Wilson Dorr (1844) and of John Brown (1859) which ended in convictions of treason by levying war against the states of Rhode Island and Virginia, respectively. State histories include a few abortive attempts to employ treason INDICTMENTS against people who incurred the wrath of powerful elements in the community. Thus indictments were brought against Mormon leaders in Missouri in 1838 and in Illinois in 1844; for political reasons the Missouri charge was not pressed and the defendants escaped jail; a mob murdered Joseph Smith shortly after his arrest on the Illinois indictment. Such isolated instances aside, the law of treason in the United States has been almost wholly the product of debates over making the national Constitution and decisions of federal courts under Article III, section 3.

As it has developed under the Constitution, the law regarding treason has strikingly mingled concern for the security of government and the legal order and concern for the freedom of private individuals and groups. The crime deals with the most serious threats to the existence of the state. In adopting the Constitution everyone took for granted that, since the people were creating a new SOVEREIGNTY, it must have authority to protect itself. Congress has reflected this judgment of the gravity of the matter by prescribing penalties that may extend to life imprisonment, or perhaps even to execution. Where charges have fallen fairly within the constitutional definition of the offense, judges have not hesitated to make firm application of the law. However, on its face the Constitution takes a limiting approach to the crime. Treason, says Article III, section 3, shall consist "only" in two named types of conduct; Congress is thus barred from adding new categories of treason, as it is also explicitly limited in fixing penalties. Moreover, the treason clause puts a stringent limit on the executive in prosecuting the crime; absent a confession in open court, by constitutional mandate the prosecution must muster testimony of two witnesses to the same overt act that the accused committed in seeking to carry out the treason. Federal judges in cases arising under the treason clause have followed a restrictive approach in marking the outer boundaries of the crime. Thus in one aspect the treason clause guards the security of the government. But in another dimension it sets limitations that make it functionally analogous to provisions of the BILL OF RIGHTS, protecting CIVIL LIBERTIES of private individuals and groups.

The constitutional emphasis on restricting the scope of the crime of treason is a marked departure from the main directions the law had taken in England and in this country before 1789. Before the eighteenth century, in practice, official policy had given clear primacy to the security of government, often more obviously to serve the interests of particular powerholders than to serve the common good.

From the fourteenth to the eighteenth century, English political history included aggressive use of charges of treason as weapons of partisan conflict; prosecution was usually vindictive and pressed with scant regard to fair procedure or careful insistence on clear proof or reliable evidence. The only counterweight to this abusive trend was the continuance of the statute of 25 Edward III (1350), stating seven categories of high treason—notably those of levying war, adhering to enemies, or seeking "to compass or imagine the death of our lord the King"—and asserting that only Parliament might enlarge the definitions of treason, thus forbidding judges to extend the offense by interpretation. The restrictive emphasis of the statute of Edward III was stressed by the English treatise writers from whom lawmakers in the new United States got most of their knowledge of the course of English policy regarding treason. In particular, EDWARD COKE, Matthew Hale, and WILLIAM BLACKSTONE spoke of abuse of vague, extended definitions of the crime as instruments of partisan combat, imperiling the general liberty. Thus Hale warned, "How dangerous it is by construction and analogy to make treasons, where the letter of the law has not done it; for such a method admits of no limits or bounds, but runs as far as the wit and invention of accusers, and the odiousness and detestation of persons accused will carry men." Offsetting such warnings, however, the English treatises also brought to the knowledge of lawmakers in North America a considerable range of decisions in which English judges had, despite the limit declared in Edward III's statute, greatly enlarged the offense of treason by construction.

Security in the most elemental sense was at stake for the English colonies in North America under the threat of French and Indian wars and in the new states torn through the American Revolution by bitter divisions between those loyal to the Crown and those asserting independence. Thus in the colonies and in the new states during the years of the Revolutionary War, statute books included many broadly and sometimes vaguely defined offenses of subversion, in dramatic contrast to the limited definition of treason later written into the national Constitution and thereafter typically included in constitutions of the states. Though colonial and early state legislation sometimes borrowed the language of the act of Edward III, we must realize that at least by the late eighteenth century lawyers here would be familiar, through the standard English treatises, with the expansive readings which English courts had given the old statute.

With adoption of the national Constitution we encounter introduction of a restrictive emphasis to balance the security concerns previously dominant in the law of treason. There is not a great deal about the treason clause in the records of the framing and RATIFICATION OF THE CONSTITUTION. But what there is shows sensitivity to lessons that policymakers here felt they should draw from English experience of the dangers to individual and political liberty of loose resort to treason prosecutions. JAMES WILSON was probably the ablest lawyer on the CONSTITUTIONAL CONVENTION's Committee of Detail, which took the responsibility of adopting a restrictive rather than an extensive approach to defining treason. In the Pennsylvania ratifying convention, Wilson twice—on his own initiative and without any criticisms of the provision voiced by an alert and suspicious opposition—praised the treason clause as including protection of civil liberty along with protection of government. In his law lectures delivered at the College of Philadelphia in 1790 and 1791, Wilson emphasized the constitutional provision by devoting an entire lecture to it. He made the centerpoint of his analysis the importance of carefully bounding the crime: "It is the observation of the celebrated MONTESQUIEU, that if the crime of treason be indeterminate, this alone is sufficient to make any government degenerate into arbitrary power." Two fears were prominent in the limited attention given the treason clause in adopting the Constitution: that holders of official power would use the treason charge to suppress legitimate, peaceful political opposition and to destroy those who were out of official favor, and that popular fear and emotion might be stirred under the dread charge to produce convictions without additional evidence. Subsequent federal court opinions recognized this restrictive background, in decisions limiting extension of the offense. Speaking for the Supreme Court in EX PARTE BOLLMAN AND SWARTWOUT (1807) in a matter indirectly involving a treason charge, Chief Justice JOHN MARSHALL declared that "to prevent the possibility of those calamities which result from the extension of treason to offences of minor importance, that great fundamental law which defines and limits the various departments of our government, has given a rule on the subject both to the legislature and the courts of America, which neither can be permitted to transcend." In the first treason case to reach the Supreme Court, CRAMER V. UNITED STATES (1945), the Court reaffirmed the propriety of this approach, quoting with approval Marshall's further admonition that "It is, therefore, more safe, as well as more consonant to the principles of our constitution, that the crime of treason should not be extended by construction to doubtful cases; and that crimes not clearly within the constitutional definition, should receive such punishment as the legislature in its wisdom may provide."

Three key elements enter into the crime of treason: an obligation of allegiance to the legal order, and intent and action to violate that obligation. First, treason is a breach of allegiance. A citizen owes loyal support to the sovereignty within which he lives or from which he derives his citizen's status. There are circumstances under which by the law of a foreign state an individual may owe it allegiance at the same time that he owes fealty to the United States; thus an individual may be a citizen of the United States because he was born here, and also be a citizen of another nation because he was born to nationals of that country. But dual nationality does not relieve an individual of obligation to refrain from volunteering aid or comfort to the foreign nation when it is at war with the United States. The restrictive tone attending treatment of treason charges had an analogy in World War II decisions which put on the government the burden of proving by clear and convincing evidence that citizens of the United States who had been lawfully present in an enemy country at the outbreak of war and were conscripted into enemy military service on the basis of their dual nationality had not complied under duress. However, in 1961 Congress amended the governing legislation to put the burden of proving duress on the individual claiming to hold United States CITIZENSHIP. The change from the court decisions to Congress's amendment revealed the persistence of tension between values placed on governmental security and on individual security, familiar in the treatment of the treason offense. One other facet of the allegiance element deserves note. Though the matter has not been presented to a court in this country, a resident alien enjoying the nation's protection owes it obedience to its laws while he is a resident. Such an individual is probably guilty of treason if he commits acts that would constitute the offense if done by a citizen.

To convict one of treason, the government must prove that the accused had a treasonable intent to levy war or to adhere to an enemy and to give aid and comfort to that enemy. Since betrayal of allegiance is at the heart of the offense, the requisite wrongful intent must be specific—a focused purpose to bring about a betrayal. In many crimes requiring proof of a guilty mind, the law holds an individual responsible as intending the reasonably foreseeable consequences of his conduct, even though he pleads that he did not intend to bring about the particular outcome for which he is charged. In *Cramer v. United States* the Supreme Court opinion included some incautious language which appeared to adopt that position. But the weight of authority in earlier federal court decisions and in rulings after *Cramer* indicates that the prosecution must prove that the defendant did intend to challenge the full authority of government at home (levy war) or to deliver aid to an enemy, as a substantial, independent element in his purpose, whatever other ends he may have had in mind. To this extent it appears that the prosecution must prove that the accused had a specific intent to levy war or to aid enemies. However, this requirement does not necessitate proof of guilty purpose by explicit statement or direct admission; the prosecution may prove the guilty intent by strong inference from the context of the accused's behavior.

The calculated limitations of the treason clause of the Constitution offer persuasive evidence that proof of the crime should require showing a specific intent. The Constitution obviously narrows the prior scope of treason by omitting any analogue to the offense of "compassing" or "imagining" the death of the king. Under that head, old English doctrine erected "constructive" treasons by inferring the wrongful intent from speech or writings that complaisant judges ruled might have the "natural consequences" of stirring popular discontent out of which violence might erupt to endanger the state. The weight of authority in federal court decisions has recognized that the policy of Article III, section 3, is to prevent expansion of the offense by building upon loose inferences of intention.

The character of the requisite wrongful intent varies according to which of the two heads of the offense is in issue. To be guilty of levying war against the United States, the individual must intend to use organized force to overthrow the government. Under the older English law treason existed if there was intent by collective force to prevent enforcement of a particular statute or other lawful order, or to obtain some particular benefit for a group, contrary to law. This English doctrine was followed in two early instances involving violent group resistance to enforcing particular federal laws—collection of a federal excise on whiskey (the WHISKEY REBELLION in western Pennsylvania in 1794) and collection of a federal property tax (the FRIES REBELLION, also in Pennsylvania, 1799). However, the later weight of authority is that nothing short of intention to overthrow the government suffices to make out the offense. Significant of this trend was the disposition of a late nineteenth-century effort to revive the old English doctrine. Following the Homestead Riot of 1892, several strike leaders were indicted for levying war against the state of Pennsylvania. But the indictments were later quietly dropped, while use of the treason charge met with prompt criticism even from conservative legal commentators. Violent group actions short of challenge to the existence of the government are now treated under heads of INCITEMENT, riot, or unlawful assembly.

Adhering to an enemy requires intent to render the enemy tangible support ("aid and comfort"). Established doctrine has defined "enemies" as only those against whom a legally declared STATE OF WAR exists. However, in the twentieth century, experience of such undeclared shooting hostilities as the Korean POLICE ACTION has raised the question of the continued vitality of the older limitation. The accused does not rebut the existence of the requisite intent for treason by pleading that he acted for mixed purposes, as to make money by selling goods to an enemy, if one of his purposes was in fact to render performance useful to the enemy. However, the accused may seek to persuade the court that he acted solely for a nontreasonable purpose, as when out of parental affection a father gave shelter to his son who was present in the country in wartime as an enemy agent. So, too, one whom the outbreak of war finds in a hostile country probably will not be found to have had treasonable intent merely because he took a job there to meet the necessities of earning a living, though the employment may have made some contributions to the enemy's strength.

In addition to proving wrongful intent, the government must prove that the accused committed some overt act to carry out his treasonable purpose. The calculated omission from the constitutional definition of treason of any counterpart of the English charge of compassing the death of the king underlines the requirement of proving overt action. The function of the overt act element, said the Supreme Court in *Cramer v. United States,* is to ensure "that mere mental attitudes or expression should not be treason." However, the Court's opinion in *Cramer* clouded definition of the requirement thus put on the prosecution; the Court seemed to say that the act must be of such character as itself to be evidence of the treasonable intent—a position apparently contrary to the emphasis common in other court rulings that the intent and the act elements are distinct. But in HAUPT V. UNITED STATES (1947) the Court somewhat clarified the matter: the behavior of the accused proved by the required testimony of two witnesses need not on its face evidence treasonable intent; an act apparently innocent, such as a transfer of money, might suffice if, in the light of other evidence of the context of the action, what the accused did could fairly be understood to aid an enemy. However, *Haupt* indicated that evidence of the context illuminating the significance of the overt act must also be supplied by two witnesses to the same circumstances. On the other hand, by the weight of authority, to prove the offense the prosecution need not establish that the accused succeeded in delivering aid to the enemy; it is enough that he took overt action to attempt delivery, though the *Cramer* opinion also contains language suggesting that effective delivery of aid should be shown. Mindful of abuses of charges of treason to suppress peaceful political opposition, English doctrine, adopted by judges in the United States, declares that a meeting to plan against the government is not a sufficient overt act to establish treason; conspiracy to levy war is not the levy of war, said Coke. But there is no comparable line of authority that a meeting to plan giving aid to an enemy is insufficient as an overt act of adherence to the enemy.

About the constitutional requirement of "testimony of two witnesses to the same overt act" hangs the uncertainty earlier noted, created by the Supreme Court opinion in *Cramer,* whether the act so proved must itself evidence treasonable intent or constitute actual delivery of aid to the enemy. Otherwise, rulings under the two-witness requirement have been straightforward. Courts have shown care to enforce the substance of the requirement, but not with doctrinaire rigidity. Two witnesses must testify directly to the act charged in the indictment; it will not suffice that there is two-witness evidence of a separate act from which it might be inferred that the charged act occurred. Two-witness testimony to the accused's admissions of an act does not meet the requirement of two-witness evidence to the act itself. However, the testimony of the two witnesses need not be identical or precise as to all aspects of the behavior cited as the overt act, nor need the testimony minutely cover every element into which an episode of behavior might be analyzed; the evidence is sufficient if it joins in identifying what reasonable jurors can regard as a connected transaction. Thus in *Haupt* the Supreme Court held that it was not fatal to the government's case that two-witness testimony did not show the enemy agent entering the accused's apartment, where it did show that he entered the building in which the accused had an apartment, and entered only as the accused's licensee, since the prosecution showed by other two-witness testimony that no other tenant in the building sheltered the agent.

This record suggests regard for the restrictive policy embodied in the constitutional history of treason. However, probably in large measure it also indicates that through most of its history the country has enjoyed substantial political stability. In any event the record shows little vindictive resort to the charge and few cases carrying politically controversial tones. Most actions taken against Loyalists in the American Revolution were to confiscate property. Because of the scale of the Civil War and the de facto belligerent status which events assigned the Confederacy, there was no material resort to treason prosecutions in that contest, though clearly those who took arms in behalf of the seceded states levied war against the United States. JEFFERSON DAVIS, President of the Confederacy, was indicted for treason. But the government faced strong arguments that it improperly charged treason against those conducting a rebel government which had achieved the status of a recognized belligerent. Though the government did not formally concede the point, neither did it bring Davis to trial on the indictment. Treason cases arising out of the Whiskey Rebellion (1795), the Fries disturbance (1799–1800), the Burr conspiracy (1807), THOMAS JEFFERSON's embargo (1808), and resistance to enforcement of the Fugitive Slave Law (1850), grew out of difficult domestic political issues but were of limited practical impact. Treason prosecutions by state authorities incident to the Dorr Rebellion in Rhode Island (1844) and John Brown's raid in Virginia (1859) were exceptional for their broad political bearing. Some cases carried tones of domestic ideological disputes over the country's entry into World War I. But this cast was notably absent from treason prosecutions incident to World War II.

By its terms the constitutional definition of treason puts some limits on governmental agencies in dealing with subversion. Congress may not increase the categories of conduct which the government may prosecute under the name of treason, nor may it extend the reach of the offense by including under the heads of adherence to enemies or levying war conduct lacking the historic elements of those crimes, or by mandating an extensive view of the evidence deemed relevant to establishing the elements of such treasons. The treason clause pointedly restricts Congress's authority to fixing penalties for the crime, and the position of the clause in Article III (establishing the JUDICIAL POWER OF THE UNITED STATES) underlines the implication that problems of applying the law of treason are ultimately for the courts. In their turn, federal judges have generally found in the language and history of Article III, section 3, a mandate against extending the range of the offense in doubtful cases. The two-witness requirement implies a further limitation on Congress. In light of that strict limitation on the prosecution's case, Congress should not have authority to avoid the two-witness requirement simply by changing labels and legislating under other names against offenses that involve all the elements of treason within the constitutional definition. However, the Supreme Court's decision in EX PARTE QUIRIN (1942) cast doubt on the validity of this analysis. One of several Nazi agents landed secretly on the east coast of the United States to sabotage war production plants was an American citizen. The Court rejected the argument that he must be prosecuted for treason by adhering to the enemy, and not for an offense against the laws of war incorporated in an act of Congress. Clearly the accused had committed treason. But the Court focused on the fact that the offense under the laws of war included another element—that the accused, having the status of an enemy belligerent, had passed the country's defenses in civilian dress with a hostile purpose.

Though it approaches the borderline of propriety, the Court's decision in *Quirin* might find support in analogues that date from the First Congress. There is no evidence that those who adopted the limiting constitutional definition of "treason" meant thereby to bar legislators from creating other crimes of subversion, the elements of which did not turn on the distinctive character of levying war or adhering to enemies. Congress in fact has defined and provided for punishment of other offenses of subversive or hostile activity against the security of the government, and federal courts have sustained such statutes. *United States v. Rosenberg* (1953) presented charges of conspiracy to violate the Federal ESPIONAGE ACT, which provides penalties for "whoever, with intent or reason to believe that it is to be used to the injury of the United States or to the advantage of a foreign nation," communicates or delivers to any foreign government or its agents information relating to the national defense. The federal court of appeals held that the treason clause did not bar creation of this offense, because "in the Rosenbergs' case, an essential element of treason, giving aid to an 'enemy' is irrelevant to the espionage offense." In *United States v. Drummond* (1965) the same appeals court dealt with a charge of conspiracy to violate the same statute by a serviceman in the United States Navy who between 1957 and 1962 delivered classified military materials to Soviet agents. Reaffirming that the treason clause did not bar creation of the espionage offense, the court found it "unnecessary" to invoke the difference relied on in *Rosenberg,* because it found differences in the required mental element in the crimes of treason and espionage. It pointed out that the espionage act required a showing only (1) that the defendant transmitted information with intent "or reason to believe" that it would be used for a forbidden result; and (2) with intent or reason to believe that it would be used either "to the injury of the United States or to the advantage of a foreign nation." In contrast, the court implied, treason requires proof of a specific intent, and a specific intent both to aid an enemy and to injure the United States.

Though the constitutional definition of treason may do no more formally than limit the kinds of conduct that may be prosecuted under the name of treason, there are respects in which it may have broader practical effect in restricting action of official agencies. The Constitution abolished the barbarous or oppressive penalties that were once a distinguishing mark of the crime. But legislation still allows heavy penalties for the offense; in light of Supreme Court limitations put on resort to the death penalty in other crimes there may be doubt whether a court may order execution of a convicted traitor, but the law still permits imposing a life sentence. Thus it may be of consequence whether the prosecutor can make out a case of "treason" or is limited to another charge which may carry a lesser penalty. Political history teaches that the mere accusation of treason, rather than of another crime, carries peculiar intimidation and stigma. Federalist treason prosecutions arising out of the Whiskey Rebellion (1794) were designed to stain supporters of Jefferson and JAMES MADISON with the imputation of subversive intent. The Jefferson administration sought to use the charge of treason (1808) to make examples against widespread opposition to the Embargo imposed to press England to respect rights of neutral use of the high seas. Democratic accusations of treason against the HARTFORD CONVENTION protesting the conduct of war with England (1814–1815) helped that venture to weaken a tottering Federalist party structure. A prosecution for treason undertook to discredit opposition to enforcement of the Fugitive Slave Law (1850). To break rank-and-file morale, Pennsylvania authorities brought treason indictments against leaders of the Homestead Strike (1892). In the cold war emotions of the 1950s, epithets of "treason" were employed in reckless attacks on the record of Democratic administrations in conducting relations with communist Russia and China. Such episodes validate the cautions expressed among those who adopted the national Constitution, that the definition of treason be limited so that this country would not repeat the old English experience of using the charge to destroy legitimate, peaceful political competition. Adoption of the FIRST AMENDMENT guarantees of free speech, press, assembly, and petition provided more direct and comprehensive declarations of the values of free political processes, and eventually these guarantees found substantial enforcement in decisions of the Supreme Court. That the First Amendment tended to preempt the field was early indicated when it became the prime reliance of those who attacked the constitutionality of the Sedition Act of 1798. (See ALIEN AND SEDITION ACTS.) However, given the extent to which concern for safeguarding peaceful public policy debate and activity figured in adopting a restrictive definition of treason, constitutional history here offers as yet unrealized possibilities for safeguarding First Amendment values.

JAMES WILLARD HURST

Bibliography

ABRAMS, STUART E. 1976 Threats to the President and the Constitutionality of Constructive Treason. *Columbia Journal of Law and Social Problems* 12:351–392.

CHAPIN, BRADLEY 1964 *The American Law of Treason: Revolutionary and Early National Origins.* Seattle: University of Washington Press.

HILL, L. M. 1968 The Two-Witness Rule in English Treason Trials. *American Journal of Legal History* 12:95–111.

HURST, JAMES WILLARD 1971 *The Law of Treason in the United States.* Westport, Conn.: Greenwood Press.

SIMON, WALTER G. 1961 The Evolution of Treason. *Tulane Law Review* 35:667–704.

STILLMAN, ARTHUR M. AND ARNER, FREDERICK R. 1954 *Federal Case Law Concerning the Security of the United States.* 83rd Congress, 2d session. Printed for the use of the Senate Committee on Foreign Relations. Washington, D.C.: Government Printing Office.

WIENER, FREDERICK BERNAYS 1962 Uses and Abuses of Legal History. *The Law Society's Gazette* 59:311–315.

TREATY OF GUADALUPE HIDALGO
9 Stat. 922 (1850)

In 1821 Mexico, having declared its independence from Spain, took control of the territory that now includes all of California, Arizona, New Mexico, and Texas, and parts of Nevada, Utah, and Colorado. But within twenty-five years, present-day Texas had been annexed by the United States, and at the end of the Mexican War the remaining areas were ceded to the United States under the Treaty of Guadalupe Hidalgo.

The treaty, signed in 1848, was not ratified by the Senate until 1850; the delay was caused by the unsuccessful efforts of Republicans to attach to the treaty the WILMOT PROVISO, banning slavery in the newly acquired territory. For more than a decade an important constitutional issue was debated but not resolved: the question whether the treaty's provisions preserving Spanish or Mexican local law in the territory were themselves sufficient to abolish slavery.

The Treaty of Guadalupe Hidalgo gave all inhabitants of the affected territory the option of becoming United States citizens or of relocating within the new Mexican borders. Although some moved to Mexico, the overwhelming majority remained at home in what had become United States territory. As a result, for the first time in the nation's history United States CITIZENSHIP was conferred on people who were not citizens of any state. This action added fuel to a constitutional debate about the relation of national citizenship to state citizenship, a debate that continued until the FOURTEENTH AMENDMENT was ratified in 1868.

The international border remained unmarked and for most purposes unreal. Until 1894 there was no formal control over the border; United States IMMIGRATION statistics recorded the arrival of Mexicans only at seaports. Many border areas remained integrated economic regions, with workers traveling in both directions to fill fluctuating labor demands. Many Mexicans, especially those in direct conflict with Americans in the border region, continued to think of the southwest as "lost" territory that was rightfully Mexico's. These views, long expressed by the Mexican government, are echoed among today's Chicanos in support of diffuse if underdeveloped positions concerning the legal (including constitutional) effects of the Treaty of Guadalupe Hidalgo: for example, that the territory rightfully belongs to Mexicans or Chicanos, or that United States violations of the treaty have voided its effects. Whatever one may think of such claims, one should appreciate the collective sense of group identification reflected in their public assertion.

GERALD P. LÓPEZ
KENNETH L. KARST

(SEE ALSO: *Compromise of 1850; Slavery in the Territories.*)

TREATY ON THE EXECUTION OF PENAL SENTENCES
24 U.S.T. 7399 (1977)

The Mexican-American Treaty on the Execution of Penal Sentences was signed on November 25, 1976. Legislation implementing the treaty became law on October 28, 1977. Since that time, thousands of prisoners have been exchanged under its provisions.

The treaty, a model for later agreements with countries such as Canada, responded to concerns about the treatment of Americans imprisoned in Mexican jails, concerns that became increasingly acute as the two countries in the 1970s began a crackdown on drug traffic from Mexico to the United States. Preexisting procedures for monitoring and improving the conditions of Americans incarcerated in Mexico, mainly action taken by United States consular offices, had proven unsatisfactory.

Under the treaty, any American imprisoned in Mexico can, with his consent and the consent of Mexico and the United States, be sent to serve his sentence in the American prison system. Mexican prisoners can similarly be transferred from the United States to Mexico. Once transferred, the prisoner's sentence can be reduced by any procedures such as parole or conditional release applicable in the receiving country. The treaty covers only acts criminal in both countries, and does not extend to political crimes or to infractions of IMMIGRATION laws or "purely military" laws.

The attorney general administers the obligations of the United States under the treaty. The implementing legislation requires the attorney general to verify the prisoner's consent to transfer, and also provides a right to appointed counsel during the verification proceedings should the prisoner be unable to pay.

Lower federal courts have held that the treaty does not violate the Constitution despite the fact that under it the United States incarcerates United States citizens whose trials may not have complied with the BILL OF RIGHTS.

GERALD P. LÓPEZ

(SEE ALSO: *Prisoners' Rights.*)

TREATY POWER

To enhance the pledged word of the United States in foreign relations, the Framers of the Constitution granted to the President, in cooperation with the Senate, the power to make and enter into treaties. They also provided that this power should vest exclusively in the federal government. The Framers neglected to define the term "treaty," however, leaving its meaning to subsequent clarification. Today, under international law, the term is used for all manner of formal instruments of agreement between or among nations that, regardless of the titles used, create relationships of reciprocal rights and obligations. Under United States law, the term "treaty" usually denotes only those international agreements that are concluded by the federal government and ratified by the President upon receiving the ADVICE AND CONSENT of the Senate. All other international agreements—EXECUTIVE AGREEMENTS, for example—are brought into force for the United States upon a constitutional basis other than senatorial advice and consent.

The process of treaty making involves negotiation, signature, ratification, exchange of instruments of ratification, publication, and proclamation; but, other than prescribing that two-thirds of the senators present must give their advice and consent to the ratification of a treaty, the Constitution is silent on the subject. In the early days of the Republic, it was thought that the Senate would participate with the President by giving its advice and consent at every negotiating juncture. Today, it is the accepted practice for the President to solicit the advice and consent of the Senate only after a treaty has been negotiated and signed, although in many—especially important—instances, Senate and even House committees play active roles in advance of the conclusion of a treaty, sometimes on their own initiative, sometimes at the behest of the executive branch.

Once the negotiation of a treaty is complete, the President decides whether to sign the treaty and, if so, whether to submit it to the Senate for advice and consent to ratification. If the Senate is perceived as hostile, the President may choose to let the treaty die rather than suffer defeat. If the Senate receives the treaty, it refers the treaty to the Committee on Foreign Relations, which may or may not report the treaty to the full Senate for its advice and consent. Committee inaction is the usual method for withholding consent to controversial treaties. Sometimes the executive branch will request that the committee withhold or suspend action. Few treaties are defeated by direct vote of the full Senate.

After the Senate gives its advice and consent to ratification, often subject to "reservations," "understandings," and "declarations" initiated by the Senate or the executive branch itself (to clarify, alter, or amend the treaty), the treaty is returned to the President for ratification. The President may choose to ratify the treaty or to return it to the Senate for further consideration. The President also may choose not to ratify the treaty at that time.

After a treaty is ratified, which is a national act, some international act—typically the exchange or deposit of instruments of ratification—usually is required to bring the treaty into force. Also upon ratification, the President issues a proclamation making the treaty officially public. There is disagreement over whether proclamation of a treaty is constitutionally required before the treaty takes effect domestically, but it is the norm to issue such a proclamation which, in any event, is useful in determining the date on which the treaty enters into force.

The Constitution does not limit the treaty power explicitly. Moreover, no treaty or treaty provision has ever been held unconstitutional. Nevertheless, it is generally agreed that such limitations exist. For example, the Supreme Court held, in REID V. COVERT (1957), that treaties may not contravene any constitutional prohibition, such as those in the BILL OF RIGHTS or in the THIRTEENTH, FOURTEENTH, and FIFTEENTH AMENDMENTS. Further, although MISSOURI V. HOLLAND (1920) largely disposed of the argument that the subject matter of treaties is limited by the TENTH AMENDMENT, it remains possible, as the Court hinted in *DeGeofroy v. Riggs* (1890), that the treaty power may be limited by "restraints . . . arising from the nature . . . of the states."

Beyond these limitations, however, the treaty power is perceived as a broad power, extending to all matters of "international concern," a phrase that some claim limits the treaty power, but that the courts have used to illustrate the power's broad scope. Ordinarily it is difficult to show that a treaty matter is not of international concern even in the presence of domestic effects.

In addition to granting the power to make and enter into treaties, the Framers of the Constitution provided that resulting treaties, together with the duly enacted laws of the United States, should constitute part of the "supreme law of the land." Thus, as well as giving rise to international legal obligations, treaties have force as domestic law, to be applied as federal statutes and consequently to prevail at all times over inconsistent state laws (assuming no conflict with the Constitution).

Still, not all treaties are automatically binding on American courts. Aside from the general constitutionality requirement, two additional conditions must obtain for treaties to have domestic effect. First, a treaty must not conflict with a subsequent act of Congress. This is in keeping with the judiciary's interpretation of the SUPREMACY CLAUSE, ranking treaties and acts of Congress equally and therefore ruling that the law later in time prevails. With the sole exception of *Cook v. United States* (1933), cases in this area have involved conflicts between an earlier treaty and a later statute, with the latter prevailing. The courts presume, however, that Congress does not intend to supersede treaties, and consequently the courts are disposed toward interpretations that will achieve compatibility between treaties and federal statutes on the same subject.

Second, for a treaty to bind courts it must be "self-executing" or, alternatively, "non–self-executing" but supported by enabling legislation. Such was the holding in *Foster v. Neilson* (1829). Judicial decisions vary widely in their application of this requirement, however. The distinction between "self-executing" and "non–self-executing" treaties is more easily stated than applied. A determination that a treaty fits one category or the other often may be shown to depend on subjective, at times political, considerations.

Although the Constitution is silent on the question of who has the power to suspend or terminate treaties and under what circumstances, it is generally accepted that the President has such power, *without* the advice and consent of the Senate, based on the President's established constitutional authority to conduct the foreign affairs of the United States. A challenge to the President's authority in this connection has thus far arisen only in the one case of GOLDWATER V. CARTER (1979), and that case was decided, on purely jurisdictional grounds, against the challenge. Were the Senate to consent to a treaty on the condition that its advice and consent would be required for the treaty's suspension or termination, however, such a condition might be binding on the President. Also, based on the power of Congress to declare war, it is arguable that the entire Congress (not just the Senate) might legitimately claim a voice in the termination of a treaty where such termination might threaten war.

BURNS H. WESTON

Bibliography

AMERICAN LAW INSTITUTE 1965 *Restatement of the Law, Second—Foreign Relations Law of the United States.* Pages 361–448. St. Paul, Minn.: American Law Institute.

_____ 1980 *Restatement of the Law—Foreign Relations Law of the United States (Revised), Tentative Draft No. 1.* Pages 71–144. Philadelphia: American Law Institute.

FOSTER, J. 1901 The Treaty-Making Power under the Constitution. *Yale Law Journal* 11:69–79.

HENKIN, LOUIS 1972 *Foreign Affairs and the Constitution.* Mineola, N.Y.: Foundation Press.

MCLAUGHLIN, C. H. 1958 The Scope of the Treaty Power in the United States. *Minnesota Law Review* 42:709–771; 43:651–725.

WRIGHT, QUINCY 1919 The Constitutionality of Treaties. *American Journal of International Law* 13:242–266.

TRENCHARD, JOHN

See: Cato's Letters

TRESPASS

A person commits trespass when he or she enters or remains on the property of another without the permission of the property owner. Violation of trespass laws may result in civil action by the property owner or criminal prosecution. Constitutional issues arise in civil or criminal trespass actions when a defendant claims that the basis for his or her exclusion from the property violates the Constitution. A defendant may assert that she was excluded from the property because she engaged in an activity protected by the Constitution (such as the FREEDOM OF SPEECH protected by the FIRST AMENDMENT) or because she is a member of a constitutionally protected class (such as a racial group) disfavored by the property owner.

If a property owner uses the property to perform a public function or if the property owner has become associated with the government in the operation of a business located on the property, the owner may not exclude persons on a basis that is incompatible with constitutional values. A public function is an activity that traditionally has been within the exclusive province of government, such as the operation of a municipality. When a state allowed a private company to own and operate a company town, which included residential and business districts, the First Amendment protection for freedom of speech prohibited exclusion of a woman who wished to distribute religious literature within the town. Operation of a store or SHOPPING CENTER on privately owned property is not held to be a public function. Thus, the First Amendment is not violated when a shopping center owner relies on trespass laws to exclude persons from the shopping mall who wish to engage in speech, PICKETING, or distribution of leaflets.

The Supreme Court will not allow trespass laws to be used to exclude persons from private property because of their race or political activity if the property owner has been directed or encouraged by the government to use the trespass laws in such a discriminatory manner. The Court has held that statutes requiring or specifically allowing a restaurant owner to provide separate areas for customers of different races encouraged racial segregation so that the owner could not use the trespass laws to exclude persons seeking service on a race neutral, integrated basis. Similarly, the owner of a restaurant operated in a government building could not exclude persons from the premises because of their race.

Federal statutes or state law may also limit the use of trespass laws. The National Labor Relations Board, for example, may order store or shopping center owners to allow labor picketers to walk on privately owned sidewalks or parking lots adjacent to businesses involved in a labor dispute. A state supreme court may interpret its state constitution to prohibit shopping center owners from excluding persons who wish to engage in political speech. These state and federal limitations on property owners' use of the trespass laws to exclude persons from their property do not violate any right guaranteed the property owners by the United States Constitution.

JOHN E. NOWAK

Bibliography

NOWAK, JOHN E.; ROTUNDA, RONALD D.; and YOUNG, J. NELSON 1983 *Constitutional Law.* Pages 497–525. St. Paul, Minn.: West Publishing Co.

VAN ALSTYNE, WILLIAM W. and KARST, KENNETH L. 1961 State Action. *Stanford Law Review* 14:3–58.

TREVETT v. WEEDEN (Rhode Island, 1786)

A Rhode Island case of 1786, this is the best known of the alleged state precedents for JUDICIAL REVIEW. The Superior Court of Judicature, the state's highest tribunal, did not hold a state act unconstitutional but it did construe it in a manner that left it inoperative. The case arose under a force act passed by the legislature to compel observance of the state paper-money laws; anyone refusing to accept paper money at par with specie was triable without a jury or right of appeal "according to the laws of the land" and on conviction was subject to a 100 pound fine and costs or be committed "till sentence be performed." Trevett filed an INFORMATION before the state chief justice charging that Weeden refused tender of paper money at face value. James Varnum, representing Weeden, argued that the force act violated the right to TRIAL BY JURY, guaranteed by the unwritten state constitution, which was FUNDAMENTAL LAW that limited legislative powers; the legislature could make law "not repugnant to the constitution" and the judiciary had "the sole power of judging those laws . . . but cannot admit any act of the legislative as law, which is against the constitution."

The court refused to decide the issue, ruling that it lacked JURISDICTION. Its JUDGMENT was simply that Trevett's complaint "does not come under the cognizance of the Justices . . . and it is hereby dismissed." Orally, however, some of the judges, according to the newspaper accounts, declared the force act "to be repugnant and unconstitutional," and one of them pointed out that its phrase, "without trial by jury, according to the laws of the land," was self-contradictory and thus unenforceable.

The governor called the legislature into special session, and the legislature summoned the high court judges to explain their reasons, the legislature said, for holding an act "unconstitutional, and so absolutely void," an "unprecedented" judgment that tended "to abolish the legislative authority." Judge David Howell, the court's main spokesman, defended judicial review and judicial independence. Although he summarized Varnum's argument that the act was unconstitutional, Howell insisted that the legislature had confused the argument, for the judgment was just that the complaint was "cognizable."

The legislature, unconvinced by the court's technical distinction, recognized that the judgment made the paper money laws unenforceable; in effect the court had exercised judicial review, which the legislature deemed subversive of its supremacy. Howell, by contrast, had claimed that if the legislature could pass on the court's judgment, "the Legislature would become the supreme judiciary—a perversion of power totally subversive of civil liberty." Anticipating a motion to unseat them, the judges presented a memorial demanding DUE PROCESS OF LAW. Varnum and the attorney general supported them, arguing that they could not be removed except on a criminal charge. The motion to remove the judges failed, and the legislature even repealed the force act, but it revenged itself on the judges by failing to reelect four of the five members when their annual terms expired, and by ousting Congressman Varnum and the state attorney general. Varnum published a one-sided pamphlet on the case, giving it publicity even in Philadelphia while the CONSTITUTION CONVENTION OF 1787 met. Although the pamphlet popularized the doctrine of judicial review, in Rhode Island no judge endorsed it for seventy years after.

LEONARD W. LEVY

TRIAL BY JURY

The right to jury trial is provided in three clauses of the Constitution of the United States. Jury trial in federal criminal cases is required by Article III, which is otherwise given to defining the role of the federal judiciary: "The Trial of all Crimes, except in Cases of IMPEACHMENT, shall be by Jury." This provision is repeated in the Sixth Amendment, which is otherwise given to the rights of the accused: "In all criminal prosecutions, the accused shall enjoy the right to a speedy and PUBLIC TRIAL, by an impartial jury . . ." The BILL OF RIGHTS also included a provision for jury trial in civil matters; this right is embodied in the SEVENTH AMENDMENT: "In Suits at common law, where the value in controversy shall exceed twenty dollars, the right of trial by jury shall be preserved. . . ."

The federal Constitution makes no explicit provision regarding the right to trial by jury in proceedings in state courts. State constitutions contain many similar provisions, although the interpretations of the right in state courts have varied significantly from the standards applied in federal courts. Substantial variation survived the enactment of the FOURTEENTH AMENDMENT, which for the first time subjected the state courts to the strictures of the DUE PROCESS clause. It was early held, and appears still to be the law, that the Fourteenth Amendment does not incorporate the Seventh, that there is no federal constitutional requirement of a right to jury trial in *civil* cases in state court. (See WALKER V. SAUVINET, 1875.) More recently, the Supreme Court has held that due process does require some form of access to a jury in major criminal prosecutions in state courts. (See DUNCAN V. LOUISIANA, 1968.)

Although the institution of jury trial has been known to American and English courts for a millennium, there have been significant changes in its form and nature over that period. Indeed, the origins of the institution are shrouded in the uncertainties of prehistory. Germanic tribes, like most stable societies, made early use of laymen in official resolution of disputes. Such practices were well known to Saxons and their neighbors at the time of the Norman Conquest in 1066. Nevertheless, at that time and place, more common resort was made to various ordeals, which were essentially religious services purporting to reveal the will of the deity. One variation on trial by ordeal was trial by battle, in which the Saxon disputants, or their champions, waged a ritual struggle to determine the side of the diety. Yet another variation was trial by wager of law, which engaged the services of the neighbors as oath helpers. By their willingness in numbers to risk salvation to stand up for a disputant, the oath helpers were perceived to express a divine will. In some sense witnesses and in some sense decision makers, these laymen can be viewed as early jurors. The nature, origin, and extent of the use of such institutions in the several shires of Saxon England doubtless varied and are the subject of some uncertainty.

The royal judges appointed by Norman kings embraced Saxon traditions, including trial by ordeal, oath helping, wager of law, and the use of laymen to share responsibility for official decisions. A papal decree in 1215, which withdrew the clergy from participation in trials by ordeal, had the effect of withdrawing the imprimatur of the deity from the decisions of the royal courts. This apparently stimulated interest in alternative methods of trial that might deflect some of the odium of decision from the royal surrogate. Thus, the PETIT JURY (to be distinguished from the GRAND JURY) emerged in more nearly contemporary form in the thirteenth century as a feature of the Norman royal courts.

Thirteenth-century jury trial emerged chiefly in proceedings of TRESPASS, a form of action in which the lash of royal power was applied to maintain the peace of the realm. As trespass and its derivative forms of action came to dominate the COMMON LAW, so trial by jury became the dominant method of trial in civil matters coming before the royal law courts. Thus, jury trial was associated with the various forms of trespass on the case (from which the modern law of torts emerged), of assumpsit (from which the modern law of contracts emerged), and of replevin, an action important to the development of personal property rights. Indeed, one reason for the demise of some of the earlier royal writs, such as the writ of right, or even the writ of debt, was dissatisfaction with the mode of trial that accompanied the use of such writs.

A concurrent evolution led to the emergence of the jury as an important element of criminal justice in the royal courts. The royal inquest was a feature of early Norman royal governance; it was an important device for centralizing power in the royal government and was a proceeding for calling local institutions and affairs to account. The grand jury was a group of local subjects of the crown who were called upon to investigate, or answer from their own knowledge, regarding the observance by their neighbors of the obligations imposed upon them by royal command. By stages, the inquest came to be followed by a further proceeding to impose royal punishment on apparent wrongdoers. In the latter half of the twelfth century, the royal government was initiating such enforcement proceedings, thus supplementing the trespass proceedings which had earlier provided protection for the peace of the realm, but only on the initiative of a victim of wrongdoing. By 1164, there was a clear beginning of the use of petit juries in crown proceedings. By 1275, it was established that the petit jury of twelve neighbors would try the guilt of an accused, provided the accused consented to such a means of trial, which he was coerced to do.

One major theme in the evolution of the right to jury trial in royal courts was the development of a system of accountability to constrain lawlessness by juries. For some time, the only method available to royal courts to deal with such behavior was to prosecute (or, more precisely, to attaint) the jurors for rendering a false verdict. If a second jury so decided, a jury could be punished for this offense. The harshness of this remedy led to its demise, for the attaint jurors were reluctant to expose an earlier jury to disgrace and punishment. In the seventeenth century the writ of attaint was gradually replaced by the practice of granting a new trial when the first verdict was against the weight of the evidence. This practice came to be equally applicable to criminal as well as civil proceedings, except insofar as an accused could not twice be placed in jeopardy of conviction. (See DOUBLE JEOPARDY.)

A second major theme in the evolution of the right to jury trial in civil cases was its confinement to the common law courts when the Chancery emerged as an alternative system of adjudicating the use of the royal power. English chancellors were exercising a form of judicial power as early as the fifteenth century. An important feature of the Chancery (or proceedings in EQUITY as they came to be known) was the absence of the jury. Another important feature was the use by the chancellor of a broader range of judicial remedies, most prominently including the INJUNCTION, which were personal commands of the judge under threat of punishment for contumacy.

Nineteenth-century English law reform ultimately brought about the demise not only of equity as a separate judicial system, but also of the right to jury trial in civil cases. In a search for greater efficiency and dispatch, the jury system in the law courts was modified and limited, so that the jury trial is now seldom used in the United Kingdom, or in other parts of the Commonwealth, except in criminal cases.

The right to jury trial took quite a different turn in the United States. At the time of the Revolution, that right came to be celebrated as a means of nullifying the power of a mistrusted sovereign; hence the several constitutional provisions guaranteeing the continued exercise of the right. Moreover, there was a special mistrust of equity (where the English recognized no right to jury trial) in eighteenth-century America, based in large part on its close connection to the royal power. Accordingly, some of the states abolished it, others conferred its powers on their legislatures, while only some retained its colonial forms or created state chanceries to continue the English tradition.

In many parts of the early United States, there was a widely shared mistrust of professional lawyers and of judges drawn from that profession. Mistrust of officials in general and professional judges in particular was a feature of the Jacksonian politics of the first half of the nineteenth century, which was reflected in provisions for the election of judges and the reaffirmation of the importance of jury trial as a means of deprofessionalizing the exercise of judicial power. These political impulses were magnified in the populism of the late nineteenth century.

Indeed, the American legal profession came to be shaped in important degree around the institution of the jury; jury advocacy became in the popular mind the central activity of the American lawyer. During much of the nineteenth century, the most powerful intellectual force in American law was the work of WILLIAM BLACKSTONE, an English scholar of the previous century. Blackstone's *Commentaries* (1776) was the one book read by almost all American lawyers, and perhaps the only law book read by some. By no coincidence Blackstone was a staunch advocate of the right to jury trial in civil cases, an institution already in decline in his own country; his belief in the institution of the lay jury was one of his strongest links to the frontier society which he so significantly influenced.

Beginning as early as 1848 in New York, most American states adopted "merged" systems of procedure in civil cases. Merger united law and equity in a single judicial system; reformers were careful to retain the right to jury trial in actions "at law" and in some states even extended it to some matters properly described under the former system as "suits in equity." Through most of the nineteenth century, the federal courts played a secondary role in the American legal system, and Congress required their procedures to conform "as near as may be" to the procedural legislation of the states in which they sat. For the most part, this conformity seemed to apply to the forms of jury practice as well as to other details of procedure. It was not until 1938 that the FEDERAL RULES OF CIVIL PROCEDURE were promulgated for the federal courts, for the first time formally merging law and equity in federal courts in accordance with national standards. The FEDERAL RULES OF CRIMINAL PROCEDURE soon followed. A national system or method of conducting jury trials in federal courts for defining the scope of the jury's power and the judge's responsibility and for prescribing the limits of the right to jury trial at last emerged.

For a period of several decades following the reform era of the 1930s, the Supreme Court made the protection of the right to jury trial in civil cases a major item on its agenda. A number of its decisions enlarged on previous expectations about the scope of the right and increased the authority of the jury, for example, BEACON THEATERS, INC. V. WESTOVER (1959) and ROGERS V. MISSOURI PACIFIC RAILROAD CO. (Justice FELIX FRANKFURTER's dissent, 1957). Interest in the right to jury trial became very intense in the mid-1960s as a result of widespread CIVIL RIGHTS litigation, preoccupation with EQUAL PROTECTION, and the possible NULLIFICATION or impairment of federal law by locally selected juries.

In the last decade, there may have been some growth in consciousness of the disadvantages of jury trial in civil cases. Increasing attention has focused on trial efficiency, the effectiveness of the law, and alternative methods of dispute resolution. But it is too early to say that we have entered a period in which the distinctly American institution of jury trial will be seriously reexamined.

As much as for any procedural right, the beauty of the right to jury trial is in the eye of the beholder. For as long as there have been lay decision makers, there have been strong-minded critics and devoted defenders who have disputed the wisdom of the system with equal vehemence. The practice rests on values so basic and so unsuitable to proof or disproof that the debate seems unlikely to terminate. It is at least in part for this reason that so many reforms, from the Seventh Amendment to the Rules Enabling Act, sought to evade debate on the fundamental issues by ostensibly preserving the status quo in regard to the right to jury trial, leaving the issues of the scope of jury trial to other times and other forums. Rarely has Congress or any state legislature been able to address the merit of the right to jury trial without having its deliberative processes impaled on the sharp point of the debate. For the same reason, decisions to expand or contract, preserve or alter, existing practices have been and will continue to be greatly influenced by the predominance of one view or the other of the merits of the institution.

Supporters of the right to jury trial regard it as a keystone of democratic government. It is, indeed, a method of sharing power with those who are governed. It deflects the hostility toward public institutions otherwise engendered by the lash of public power. It is a remedy for judicial megalomania, the occupational hazard of judging. Particularly in regard to criminal legislation, the right to jury trial provides a limit on the power of legislatures who eventually must countenance the nonenforceability of laws which citizens are unwilling to enforce. It is also a means of education: jurors learn about the law and share their learning with families and neighbors. In all these respects, it engenders trust. In general, supporters and critics alike agree that those benefits are more substantial in criminal than in civil litigation.

Critics observe, however, that juries are inefficient

and may well be quite inaccurate in their perceptions and decisions. Involving many people in the making of a decision is inherently inefficient. It is necessary to invest time and expense in the selection of jurors. Trials proceed much more slowly because of the shorter attention span of lay persons in courtroom contexts and because additional participants entail additional interruptions and delays for personal reasons. Because of the inexperience of jurors, there has developed a substantial body of rules governing the admission of EVIDENCE which have as their purpose the protection of the jury from confusion and inflammation of prejudice. These strictures operate at times to increase the complexity of trials and to enlarge the possibility of mistrial or new trial, which is the result of error in the application of such rules of evidence. For these reasons, jury trials take substantially longer than nonjury trials and are substantially more expensive for the participants.

Moreover, as other critics emphasize, the deliberations of juries are undisciplined. Although jurors tend to be conscientious in the application of the governing law, the controlling rules are often dimly understood and not infrequently sacrificed in order to secure the requisite consensus. Whatever guidance or control the trial judge may supply, the chance of erratic decision is greater in jury than in nonjury trials.

Other adverse factors are less frequently mentioned. Jury service is in many cases a substantial burden to jurors; although they receive token payment, they are coerced to perform a duty that can sometimes be onerous. Particularly in communities characterized by disorder and social disintegration, jurors may even be frequent objects of intimidation and bribery; they are, in general, more difficult to protect from these vices than are judges, and they are perhaps also more vulnerable to such pernicious influences.

To a substantial degree, the perceived merits or demerits of the system will depend on particular features of the system which are designed to respond to the problems the system presents. Unfortunately, techniques for diminishing the demerits of jury trial often tend also to diminish its merits: the more control exercised over juries, the less advantage there is in assembling them. In the final analysis, almost every issue regarding the right to jury trial turns on the degree to which power is to be confided in professional officers of the law. Consensus on that basic issue being so distant a prospect, the contours of the institution as described below must be regarded as an unstable compromise, quite subject to change.

Instability is nowhere more clearly exemplified than in regard to JURY SIZE. Perhaps as early as the thirteenth century, Englishmen understood that a jury is a group composed of twelve persons. The method of selecting the jury might have varied, the duties assigned to the group may have been altered, but the one element of stability was their number, twelve. Some states experimented with the use of smaller juries, particularly in the trial of lesser crimes, and the Supreme Court in WILLIAMS V. FLORIDA (1970) held that the use of such groups as six is not itself a deprivation of due process of law. It was, however, long presumed that a common law jury is twelve and that such a number was required in federal courts by the Sixth and Seventh Amendments, unless a smaller number be agreed to by the parties. This presumption is reflected in the language of Federal Rule of Civil Procedure 48, which authorizes parties to agree to smaller juries.

Nevertheless, most federal district courts have in the last decade adopted local rules of court designating civil juries to consist of six persons. The validity of these local rules was sustained by the Supreme Court in *Colegrove v. Battin* (1973). The Court rested its decision on the absence of any straightforward legislative prohibition on juries of less than twelve and on the dubious assumption that there were no solid data demonstrating that twelve-person juries reach substantially different verdicts from six-person juries. The Court also manifested a conviction that six-person juries are more efficient than those composed of larger numbers, a conviction which is itself not amenable to solid empirical proof. However, in BALLEW V. GEORGIA (1978) the Court held that a five-member group was too small to be properly deliberative, representative, and free from intimidation and therefore did not afford due process. The Court's decisions have stimulated increased interest in the scientific examination of judicial institutions; the decisions have also called into question other traditional presumptions about juries, none of which carries more historical weight than did the tradition of twelve.

A second traditional feature of the common law jury has been the requirement of JURY UNANIMITY in reaching a verdict. Some states have experimented with the acceptance of verdicts supported by juries that are less than unanimous. In general, such provisions have called for super-majorities, such as a vote of ten or twelve jurors. The Supreme Court held in *Minneapolis and St. Louis Railway Co. v. Bombolis* (1916) that such provisions were not denials of due process for state court proceedings involving issues of federal law, but later, in BURCH V. LOUISIANA (1979), it invalidated a Louisiana law that authorized verdicts of conviction on the basis of a five-to-one vote of a six-person jury. Despite these variations at the state level, however, the unanimity requirement remains a standard feature of federal jury practice, unless, as the Federal Rules authorize in civil cases, the parties agree on a lesser majority.

One effect of the unanimity requirement is to assure that the jury will deliberate on its decision rather than settle for a mere nose count. A secondary effect is to increase the likelihood that no decision will be reached, with the result that a new trial before a new jury will be required, unless the controversy is privately resolved without further litigation. A third effect is to enhance the role and responsibility of each individual juror, making each an important actor with power to control the ultimate outcome of the process. To the extent that the jury is intended to be a representative body, the unanimity requirement tends to protect litigants and interests that are associated with minority groups.

A third important feature of traditional common law jury practice was the mode of selecting the jury. Using the Norman nomenclature, the court administrative arm assembles a VENIRE of citizens from whom the jury will be selected. Veniremen may be excused or disqualified by the judge and those remaining are then subject to a further process of selection by the parties. The latter process, known as VOIR DIRE examination, proceeds from a questioning of the jurors to their challenge by the parties on grounds of cause, or peremptorily if the parties would simply prefer other members of the venire. Peremptory challenges have perhaps always been limited in number, a somewhat larger number being allowed in criminal than in civil cases.

In recent decades, this traditional process has been subject to substantial criticism and pressure. Criticism proceeds from the premise that the jury should be in some degree representative of the community it helps to govern. Most of the criticism has been directed at the process of selecting veniremen, the usual earlier practice in this country having been to authorize a court administrator to select prospective jurors by methods that were usually elitist in premise and effect. In many communities, the usual method was the "key man" system, which invoked the assistance of community leaders to identify citizens of stature who would be deserving of the trust reposed in jurors. Such systems were common in federal courts. Indeed, it was not uncommon for a federal court to maintain a BLUE RIBBON list of veniremen of more than ordinary intelligence and experience who might be summoned to decide cases requiring more than ordinary skill on the part of the decision maker. Such methods produced juries that were anything but representative, in the proportional sense, of the communities from which they were selected.

In a legal environment favoring egalitarianism, such practices were doomed. As early as 1945, in *Thiel v. Southern Pacific Co.*, the Supreme Court upheld a challenge by a federal litigant to a venire selection method that seemed likely to result in underrepresentation of the working class in local jurors. In *Carter v. Jury Commission of Greene County* (1970), the Supreme Court refused to declare a state key-man system invalid on its face absent a showing that the scheme was purposefully adopted as a means of preventing some group (usually blacks) from being represented. Nevertheless, when such a scheme underrepresents a group consistently, a prima facie case of JURY DISCRIMINATION is established and the scheme may then be found unconstitutional as applied, as in *Turner v. Fouche* (1970). Congress anticipated these holdings by enacting federal jury selection legislation in 1968. Current legislation does repose some authority in local federal courts to administer jury selection, on condition that their methods produce juries that bear proximate resemblances to randomness. Of course, individual litigants are not entitled under the statute or the Constitution to have a jury that actually reflects the demography of the community; all that is assured is that the method of selection be one that is reasonably likely to produce such a panel.

In recent years, mounting attention has been given to the process of peremptory challenge and the practice of some local prosecutors to use these challenges to prevent minority representation on particular juries, especially those called to try minority members on serious criminal charges. The Supreme Court has held that a prosecutor's use of peremptory challenges in any single case is immune from attack; the Court held in SWAIN V. ALABAMA (1965) that the very concept of peremptory challenges entailed the right to act without explanation. Still, the Court did leave open the possibility that systematic use of peremptories to exclude members of some group might be found to violate the equal protection guarantee of the Fourteenth Amendment. In subsequent cases, however, proving to the Court's satisfaction that systematic discrimination did exist has been virtually impossible. Some state courts have gone beyond the federal standards and ruled that peremptory challenge of veniremen on the basis of membership in any group violates provisions of their state constitutions, for example, California in *People v. Wheeler* (1978).

Partly as a result of the practice of making juries

more representative, a new issue has arisen regarding the competence of juries to deal with intricate technical disputes beyond the ken of ordinary citizens. The Third Circuit Court of Appeals held in *Matsushita Electric Industrial Company v. Zenith Radio Corporation* (1980) that the Seventh Amendment is subject to the Fifth Amendment, that the use of juries in very complex civil cases may be a denial of due process of law. This question, also, has not reached the Supreme Court.

Litigants having a right to jury trial are entitled to a jury decision only on questions of fact, not on matters of law. The distinction between questions of fact and law can be stated clearly enough: the former pertain to the specific events in dispute; the latter to the legal principles to be applied. But the application of the distinction is often problematic. For this reason, juries often have to deal with issues containing substantial elements of legal interpretation. The classic example, which arises in both civil and criminal contexts, is a decision applying a general standard of negligence to the conduct of the accused or the defendant; the general standard takes more specific shape in the minds of jurors as they apply it to the events at hand.

Since the seventeenth century, it has been the responsibility of the trial judge to assure that the controlling law is obeyed by the jury; the trial judge is accountable to the appellate court for the effective performance of this duty. There are several steps in the usual common law jury trial at which the trial judge is obliged to perform this function.

A major function of the judge at a jury trial is to instruct the jury on the controlling law. This instruction is usually the last event before the jury retires to deliberate. If either party makes a timely objection to the judge's statement of law in his charge to the jury, any error in the instructions will be a solid ground for reversal.

In a civil trial, the judge should not instruct the jury at all unless there is a dispute in the evidence presented which might raise some doubt in a reasonable mind or about which jurors might reasonably differ. If the judge finds that there is no such dispute, he should direct the jury to find a verdict for the part entitled under the law to JUDGMENT. In cases of doubt about the application of this standard, the judge may prefer to reserve his ruling on a motion for directed verdict until after the jury has rendered a verdict. If the verdict is rendered contrary to the law, the judge may then enter a judgment notwithstanding the verdict in favor of the verdict loser. The Supreme Court has held in *Baltimore and Carolina Line v. Redman* (1935) that the judge may not take this latter step unless the motion for directed verdict was timely and the question properly reserved; otherwise, there is a violation of the Seventh Amendment because the judgment notwithstanding the verdict was unknown to English practice at the time of adoption of the Amendment.

In a criminal case the judge should direct a verdict for the accused when the prosecution has failed to offer proof of one or more elements of the offense charged. But the trial judge may not direct a verdict of guilty in a criminal case; to this extent, the Sixth Amendment assures the role of the jury as a bulwark against punishment deemed oppressive by the community, even if the punishment is required by the positive law. An element of natural justice is thereby introduced to the legal system.

In addition to his role as law officer, the trial judge also has some responsibility for the quality of fact-finding done by the jury. In either civil or criminal cases, he may set aside a verdict as contrary to the weight of the evidence. When exercising this prerogative, the trial judge is obliged to order a new trial before a second jury. In a criminal case, the power to order the new trial is confined by the constitutional constraint against double jeopardy. In a civil case, the power to grant a new trial may be exercised conditionally, but this power is subject to constitutional limitations. A conditional order of new trial is likely to occur where the trial judge regards a jury verdict as correct on the matter of liability but excessive in regard to the award of damages.

Some factual issues arising in jury-tried cases may be reserved for the judge. For example, in civil cases, issues of fact arising in a determination of the jurisdiction of the court must be decided by the judge. In criminal cases, sentencing is a function of the judge, not the jury, although the wisdom and propriety of the sentence often require factual determination.

With the exceptions noted, the division of function between judge and jury in federal courts has not been deemed a matter for constitutional adjudication. *A fortiori,* state practice in respect to these issues has not generally been regarded as presenting any constitutional problems of due process of law. The Supreme Court, however, has on occasion intervened to reverse state court judgments in actions arising under federal law on the ground that the federal law posed an issue for a jury which under the state practice was incorrectly left to the decision of a judge. Particularly in cases arising under the federal EMPLOYERS LIABILITY ACT, the Court was strict in limiting the role of the trial judge. Its decisions, based upon statutory grounds, may indicate that state jury practice must meet federal standards when state courts are called upon to enforce federal law. It is even possible that the Seventh Amendment will be found to be applicable to litigation of federal claims in state courts, not by reason of the Fourteenth Amendment, but by an inference of congressional intent.

The Sixth Amendment applies only to criminal proceedings that could have been tried by a jury at the time of its adoption in 1791. Even at that time, it was well understood that "petty" offenses might be tried without a jury. Federal legislation gives specific meaning to such offenses as those involving a punishment of imprisonment for six months or less and fines of $500 or less. In BALDWIN V. NEW YORK (1970) the Supreme Court held that due process requires jury trial in state court prosecutions for offenses involving imprisonment for more than six months. In *Bloom v. Illinois* (1968) the Court applied a similar standard to punishments imposed for contempt of court, although it conceded that there was some historical basis for treating contempt as a matter between litigant and judge, particularly where the contumacious act is committed in the presence of the court. In MCKEIVER V. PENNSYLVANIA (1971), however, the Court held that the right to jury trial is not applicable to a proceeding to determine the delinquency of a juvenile, even though a decision adverse to the juvenile might result in imprisonment for a period significantly in excess of six months; such proceedings, the Court said, are not strictly criminal because they involve less moral judgment about the conduct of the juvenile.

The Seventh Amendment has proved much more complex and troublesome. One major question has been the applicability of the amendment to claims brought under federal legislation enacted after the adoption of the amendment. A narrowly historical view would preclude the application of the right to such legislation-based claims, since they are not strictly actions "at common law." The Court has, however, generally extended the right to jury trial to statutory actions where the remedy pursued in the judicial proceeding was one that resembled a common law remedy. Thus, in *Pernell v. Southall Realty Co.* (1974) the Court held that there was a right to jury trial in a statutory action of eviction that was closely analogous to a common law action for ejectment. And in *Curtis v. Loether* (1974) the Court held that there was a right to jury trial in an action brought under the fair housing provisions of the CIVIL RIGHTS ACT OF 1964 because the remedy sought was compensatory damages of the sort that might have been recoverable in a common law action of trespass on the case.

In other cases, however, the Court has approved legislation creating administrative procedures and remedies that displace common law rights and thus eliminate jury-triable actions. In *National Labor Relations Board v. Jones & Laughlin Steel Corp.* (1937), the Court upheld the award of back pay in proceedings before the board, despite the close analogy to common law contract actions. This decision was extended in *Atlas Roofing Co. v. Occupational Safety and Health Administration* (1977), in which the Court upheld legislation providing for the recovery by a government agency of a civil penalty in a court proceeding where there was no right to jury trial. The Court emphasized that the case involved a "public right," to be distinguished from common law rights of private parties. In *Lorillard v. Pons* (1978) the Court interpreted the legislature to intend a statutory right to jury trial in proceedings brought under the AGE DISCRIMINATION ACT. In that case, as in *Curtis*, the Court avoided any indication of the applicability of the Seventh Amendment to the employment discrimination provisions of the Civil Rights Act, which, like the Age Discrimination Act, provides for back pay awards to be made by courts, not administrative agencies.

The most complex issues of the scope of the right to jury trial arise in complex litigation where matters that are within the compass of the Seventh Amendment coincide with other matters outside that compass. In general, the Supreme Court has tended to insist upon protection of the right to jury trial in such situations, even at the risk of submitting to a jury matters that would not be jury-triable if litigated alone. Illustrative is DAIRY QUEEN, INC. V. WOOD (1962) in which the plaintiff sought both an injunction and compensatory damages. Injunctive relief, unlike compensatory damages, is an equitable rather than a legal remedy and so is not subject to the right of trial by jury. The trial court deemed the injunction to be the primary relief sought and undertook to try the case without a jury, albeit with the intention of seating a jury to decide the measure of damages should it appear that a wrong had been committed. The Supreme Court reversed, holding that the jury-triable claim for damages must be tried first in order to protect the constitutional right to jury trial, leaving it for the judge later to decide on the availability of injunctive relief if the jury should determine that a wrong had been committed. Similarly, in BEACON THEATERS, INC. V. WESTOVER (1959) the Court held that a jury-triable counterclaim would have to be tried first, before a determination could be made on a related claim by the plaintiff that was not jury-triable.

These cases illustrate that the constitutional right to jury trial now tends to depend on the specific substantive right and remedy involved in the litigation, not on the general (common law or equity) context in which that right is disputed. This approach was illustrated in *Ross v. Bernhard* (1970), in which the Court held that a claim brought by a shareholder on behalf of the CORPORATION was jury-triable when the claim would have been triable by a jury had it been brought by the corporation itself; this decision would seem to be applicable as well to claims for damages brought by class representatives. This is so even though the procedures of STOCKHOLDER SUITS and CLASS ACTIONS are derived from the equity tradition, not from the practices of law courts. Thus, the increasingly widespread use of complex procedural devices that unite equitable and legal matters may in fact operate to enlarge the practical scope of the right to jury trial. This seems true despite the disclaimers set forth in such law reforms as the Federal Declaratory Judgment Act and the Federal Rules Enabling Act, which express the intent not to alter the existing scope of the right. That intent was not practicably attainable consistent with achieving the other aims of the procedural reforms, which include efficiency and dispatch.

On the other hand, a rule that the Seventh Amendment right to jury trial depends on the substantive right and remedy involved in the litigation is not always applied. Illustrative is *Katchen v. Landy* (1966), which upholds the power of the court to determine without a jury claims brought against a bankrupt estate, whether or not the claims might have been jury-triable if asserted directly against the bankrupt. The Court emphasized the practical needs of the bankruptcy system for dispatch in making such decisions; it was said that these considerations justified Congress in directing that they be made without juries. Thus, the scope of the constitutional right to jury trial in civil cases is a complex question, drawing heavily on historical analogues but also influenced by considerations of contemporary practicality. It is not a static right, but it is likely to take on new dimensions in the hands of future courts.

It may be concluded that the right of accused persons to a trial by jury has become a deeply entrenched feature of criminal litigation in the United States, broadly protected by the Sixth and Fourteenth Amendments, with the selection and role of the jury being aspects of the right that are themselves subject to constitutional control. The right to jury trial in civil cases, on the other hand, rests upon a different constitutional provision, which is inapplicable in state courts and may be somewhat less rigidly maintained even in federal courts, for the reason that it is less assuredly beneficial to the citizens to be protected.

PAUL D. CARRINGTON

Bibliography

DAWSON, JOHN P. 1962 *A History of Lay Judges.* Cambridge, Mass.: Harvard University Press.

HELLER, FRANCIS H. 1951 *The Sixth Amendment to the Constitution of the United States.* Lawrence: University of Kansas Press.

JAMES, FLEMING 1963 Right to Jury Trial in Civil Cases. *Yale Law Journal* 72:655–693.

KALVEN, HARRY and ZEISEL, HANS 1966 *The American Jury.* Boston: Little, Brown.

MCCART, SAMUEL N. 1964 *Trial by Jury.* Philadelphia: Chilton Books.

SCHULTZ, MARJORIE S., ED. 1980 The American Jury. *Law and Contemporary Problems.* Durham, N.C.: Duke University.

SPOONER, LYSANDER 1852 *An Essay on the Trial by Jury.* Boston: John P. Jewett Co.

VAN DYKE, JON M. 1977 *Jury Selection Procedures.* Cambridge, Mass.: Ballinger.

WOLFRAM, CHARLES 1973 The Constitutional History of the Seventh Amendment. *Minnesota Law Review* 57:639–747.

TRIMBLE, ROBERT
(1776–1828)

Robert Trimble, appointed to the Supreme Court by JOHN QUINCY ADAMS on April 11, 1826, was born in Virginia and raised in Kentucky. He studied law, began practice in Paris, Kentucky, and became one of the leading lawyers of the state with a specialty in land litigation. To the Supreme Court he brought an independence of character, a respect for legality, and considerable judicial experience. From 1807 to 1808 he served on the Kentucky Court of Appeals and from 1817 to 1826 on the federal district court. His years on the district bench corresponded to a period of political-economic upheaval during which Kentucky openly resisted federal ADMIRALTY JURISDICTION and federal judicial interference with state relief measures. Both as district judge and as circuit partner with his friend Justice THOMAS TODD, Trimble held the line for federal judicial authority and objective legality as he saw it—so firmly in fact that he was threatened with IMPEACHMENT.

His integrity, ability, and nationalism won him an appointment to the Court on Todd's death. He served only twenty-seven months before his own death but long enough to have won the respect of JOHN MARSHALL and JOSEPH STORY; Story eulogized him as belonging "to that school, of which Mr. Chief Justice Marshall (himself a host) is the acknowledged head and expositor." Trimble spoke for the Court only fifteen times; ironically his lone constitutional opinion in OGDEN V. SAUNDERS (1827) called forth Marshall's only dissent in a constitutional case. The question was whether a state bankruptcy law applying to contracts made after the passage of the law was a violation of the CONTRACT CLAUSE. Trimble's clear-headed, practical opinion upholding state power remained controlling for most of the nineteenth century despite the dissents of Marshall and Story.

R. KENT NEWMYER

Bibliography

STORY, JOSEPH 1829 Memoir of Judge Trimble. *American Jurist and Law Magazine* 1:149–157.

TRIMBLE v. GORDON
430 U.S. 762 (1977)

A year before this decision, the Supreme Court had refused, in *Mathews v. Lucas* (1976), to hold that ILLEGITIMACY was a SUSPECT CLASSIFICATION requiring strict judicial scrutiny. In *Trimble,* a 5–4 majority invalidated an Illinois law that prevented illegitimate children from inheriting from their fathers who had not made wills. Discriminations based on illegitimacy, said Justice LEWIS F. POWELL for the majority, must be "carefully attuned to alternative considerations." Although paternity might be hard to prove in some cases, wholesale disinheritance of illegitimate children was unjustified. In this case a judicial paternity proceeding had determined the decedent to be the father.

Justice WILLIAM H. REHNQUIST dissented at length, criticizing the development of modern EQUAL PROTECTION doctrine. Except for classifications based on race or national origin, he would abandon all forms of STRICT SCRUTINY, requiring no more than a RATIONAL BASIS for legislative discrimination. Laws classifying according to legitimacy of parentage deserved no more heightened judicial scrutiny than did "other laws regulating economic and social conditions."

Only a year later, in LALLI V. LALLI (1978), a fragmented Court made *Trimble*'s precedential status uncertain.

KENNETH L. KARST

TROP v. DULLES
356 U.S. 86 (1958)
PEREZ v. BROWNELL
356 U.S. 44 (1958)

In two cases decided the same day the Supreme Court ruled on the constitutionality of the EXPATRIATION provisions of the Nationality Act of 1940. In *Perez* the Court held (5–4) that revocation of CITIZENSHIP for voting in a foreign election was a valid exercise of governmental control over FOREIGN AFFAIRS.

In *Trop,* however, the Court held unconstitutional (5–4) the involuntary expatriation of a wartime deserter. Chief Justice EARL WARREN, for a plurality, contended that expatriation is CRUEL AND UNUSUAL PUNISHMENT; but WILLIAM J. BRENNAN, the one justice who changed sides, argued only that Congress's power over citizenship is less extensive when foreign affairs are not involved.

DENNIS J. MAHONEY

TRUAX v. CORRIGAN
257 U.S. 312 (1921)

A 1913 Arizona law, similar to the labor provisions of the CLAYTON ANTITRUST ACT, prohibited state court INJUNCTIONS against peaceful PICKETING. Following a dispute with restaurant proprietor William Truax, a local union peacefully picketed and distributed handbills calling for a BOYCOTT. Truax's business receipts dropped dramatically, and after the Arizona courts denied him relief, he appealed to the Supreme Court, contending that the state law deprived him of his property without DUE PROCESS OF LAW and violated the EQUAL PROTECTION clause of the FOURTEENTH AMENDMENT.

Chief Justice WILLIAM HOWARD TAFT, speaking for a 5–4 majority, held the state statute unconstitutional. He reasoned that Truax held a property right in his business; free access to it by employees and customers was incidental to that right. Concerted action that intentionally injured that right was a conspiracy and a tort. In this case, the union's activities constituted an "unlawful annoyance and hurtful nuisance." Such wrongs, Taft concluded, could not be remediless, and he declared that the anti-injunction law deprived Truax of due process. He also ruled that the law violated equal protection by limiting the application of an injunction to a particular class.

JUSTICE LOUIS D. BRANDEIS, dissenting, maintained that even if the employer had a constitutional right to be free from boycotting and picketing, the state was not compelled to protect that right with an injunction, as states were free to expand or control their EQUITY jurisdiction. In a separate dissent, Justice OLIVER WENDELL HOLMES argued that the state law was a valid "social experiment," however "futile or even noxious." Beyond that, he challenged the assumption equating "business" with a property right. Business, he asserted, was "a course of conduct," and like any other was subject to modification regarding what would justify doing it a harm.

STANLEY I. KUTLER

TRUMAN, HARRY S. (1884–1972)

The thirty-third President began his career in local Democratic politics in Missouri. Truman served in various capacities, including county judge and planning official, and helped coordinate employment and relief programs during the early 1930s. After his election to the United States Senate in 1934, he supported the New Deal programs and specialized in transportation policy. Declining President FRANKLIN D. ROOSEVELT's offer of an appointment to the Interstate Commerce Commission, he was reelected to the Senate in 1940. During the war years he attracted notice as the effective chairman of a Senate investigating committee established to oversee the efficiency and fairness of defense contracting. Elected vice-president in 1944, he succeeded to the presidency the next year when Roosevelt died. He returned to the White House in 1949 for a second term, following an unexpected election victory.

Truman believed in a strong and active presidency, operating within a Constitution sufficiently flexible to accommodate executive initiatives for the public good. The Framers of the Constitution, Truman said, had deliberately left vague the details of presidential power, allowing the "experience of the nation to fill in the outlines." He disagreed with scholars who claimed that history makes the man: "I think that it is the man who makes history." His roster of favorite Presidents included GEORGE WASHINGTON, THOMAS JEFFERSON, ANDREW JACKSON, ABRAHAM LINCOLN, GROVER CLEVELAND, THEODORE ROOSEVELT, WOODROW WILSON, and Franklin Roosevelt.

Although criticized at times by liberals for providing inadequate leadership and action on CIVIL RIGHTS, Truman's record is impressive. In 1946 he created the President's Committee on Civil Rights. A year later it issued an important document, *To Secure These Rights,* that took a firm stand against various forms of RACIAL DISCRIMINATION. In 1948 Truman issued EXECUTIVE ORDER 9981, ending discrimination in the armed services, and in that same year delivered a powerful civil rights message to Congress and supported the inclusion of a civil rights plank in the Democrats' platform.

Truman's commitment to the BILL OF RIGHTS was tested by the issue of subversion that overshadowed his administration. As a student of history he was keenly aware of the hysteria that had fanned repressive episodes, from the Salem witch trials to the Red Scare of 1919. He felt prepared to handle the new cycle that took the form of anticommunism and indiscriminate labeling of "subversives." (See SUBVERSIVE ACTIVITIES AND THE CONSTITUTION.)

EXECUTIVE ORDER 9835, issued by Truman in 1947, established procedures to control subversive infiltration of the federal government. The effect was to deprive agency employees of fundamental elements of DUE PROCESS, including the right to receive specific charges against them and to confront their accusers. Even when an accused received clearance from a loyalty board, the data remained in the files, forcing the employee to answer the same charges with each move to a new job. Truman later admitted that the program, which thrived on secret evidence and secret informers, was filled with defects and injustices.

Truman began to give closer attention to CIVIL LIBERTIES. In a message to Congress on August 8, 1950, he warned that pending legislation on internal security would forbid dissent. When the internal security bill reached his desk in the fall of 1950, he delivered a ringing denunciation, protesting in his veto message that the bill would put government in the "thought control business." Especially objectionable to him was a provision requiring "Communist-front" and "Communist-action" groups to register with the attorney general. This placed on the government the responsibility for probing the "attitudes and states of mind" of organization leaders. Groups could be linked to the Communist party whenever their positions failed to "deviate" from those of the Communist movement. Thus, any organization dedicated to low-cost housing or other humanitarian goals espoused by the party could be branded a communist front. Truman called this feature "the greatest danger to FREEDOM OF SPEECH, press and assembly, since the ALIEN AND SEDITION LAWS of 1798." The veto message, delivered in the midst of an election campaign that featured charges from some Republicans about Democrats being soft on communism, was courageous and principled. Within a day both Houses of Congress easily overrode the veto. (See INTERNAL SECURITY ACT.)

Following North Korea's invasion of the south in June 1950, Truman dispatched American soldiers to Korea without seeking congressional support or approval. A month later the State Department issued a belated memorandum defending the President's legal authority to repel the attack. The memo claimed that Truman's action was justified by international law, the UNITED NATIONS CHARTER, "and the resolution pursuant thereto." However, the United Nations issued *two* resolutions on Korea, one of June 25 calling for the cessation of hostilities and the withdrawal of North Korean forces to the 38th parallel, and a second resolution (adopted two days later) recommending armed force to repel the attack. Truman intervened militarily before passage of the second resolution. (See KOREAN WAR.)

Truman placed General Douglas MacArthur in command of American forces in Korea. MacArthur wanted to widen the military front, probing deeply into North Korea. He objected repeatedly, in public, to the limited war policy adopted by the administration. Eventually he alienated Truman, top cabinet officials, the Joint Chiefs of Staff, and the National Security Council. Over the course of almost a year, Truman became convinced that MacArthur was untrustworthy and insubordinate, but his abrupt dismissal of the general on April 11, 1951, triggered a storm of protest across the nation. In explaining his decision, Truman said it was fundamental that "military commanders must be governed by the policies and directives issued to them in the manner provided by our laws and Constitution."

Only a few members of Congress questioned Truman's authority to send troops to Korea, but as part of a "Great Debate" in 1951, legislators challenged his constitutional power to send ground forces to Europe. Resolutions were introduced in each house to require congressional authorization before military forces could be sent abroad. Although these measures were not enacted, uneasiness about the scope of presidential war-making power persisted. After President LYNDON B. JOHNSON's commitment of American troops to Southeast Asia and subsequent military actions there by President RICHARD M. NIXON, Congress passed the WAR POWERS RESOLUTION of 1973 to restrict the President's military powers. (See EMERGENCY POWER.)

Truman's attitude about presidential power and constitutional constraints is illuminated by his 1952 seizure of steel mills. He believed that a pending strike would prevent production of materials needed for the war in Korea. (See EXECUTIVE ORDER 10340; STEEL SEIZURE CONTROVERSY.) At a news conference on April 17 he was asked whether his INHERENT POWERS permitted seizure of newspapers and radio stations. To the consternation of the press he replied that the President could act "for whatever is for the best of the country." A week later, complaining that speculation about him seizing the press and the radio was "hooey," he stated that he had "difficulty imagining the Government taking over and running those industries." Continuing to respond to concerns about his views of emergency power, on April 27 he wrote in a letter that presidential powers are "derived from the Constitution, and they are limited, of course, by the provisions of the Constitution, particularly those that protect the rights of individuals."

Meanwhile, the Justice Department was developing a different scenario for District Judge David Pine. Assistant Attorney General Homer Baldridge told Pine on April 24 that "there is not power in the Courts to restrain the President. . . ." After Pine had declared the seizure invalid, Truman claimed at a news conference on May 22 that "nobody" (including Congress and the Court) could take from the President his power to seize private property and to protect the welfare of the people. However, he said that he would abide by the Supreme Court's verdict, and when the decision fell on June 2 (see YOUNGSTOWN SHEET & TUBE CO. V. SAWYER, 1952), declaring the seizure invalid, he immediately ordered the government to relinquish possession of the mills.

Often careless with his remarks at press conference, for which he paid dearly, Truman came to the White House with a solid understanding of history and governmental institutions and processes. He maintained a deep respect for individual rights and civilian government. Through his personal integrity and honesty he helped moderate many of the repressive forces that operated during his years in office.

LOUIS FISHER

Bibliography

HAMBY, ALONZO L. 1973 *Beyond the New Deal: Harry S. Truman and American Liberalism.* New York: Columbia University Press.

TRUMAN, HARRY S. 1960 *Mr. Citizen.* New York: Bernard Geis.

_____ 1955 *Year of Decisions.* Garden City, N.Y.: Doubleday.

_____ 1956 *Years of Trial and Hope.* Garden City, N.Y.: Doubleday.

TRUMBULL, LYMAN
(1813–1896)

An Illinois state supreme court judge (1848–1853) and United States senator (1855–1873), Lyman Trumbull opposed all slavery expansion before 1861, and during the SECESSION crisis he argued that the Constitution already adequately protected slavery and no amendments, concessions, or compromises were necessary. A strong supporter of the Union war effort, Trumbull nevertheless believed that the war should be fought within the framework of the Constitution. Thus, he opposed President ABRAHAM LINCOLN's unilateral suspension of HABEAS CORPUS, arbitrary arrests, and the closing of northern newspapers. Nonetheless, he supported legislation authorizing such actions. Trumbull gave mild support to the EMANCIPATION PROCLAMATION but doubted its constitutionality, and thus he introduced the resolution which led to the THIRTEENTH AMENDMENT. As chairman of the Senate Judiciary Committee during the war and Reconstruction, Trumbull initiated the first and second CONFISCATION ACTS, the CIVIL RIGHTS ACT OF 1866, the FREEDMEN'S BUREAU Extension Act (1866), and the first civil service reform legislation (1870). Despite his opposition to slavery and support of CIVIL RIGHTS, Trumbull was at heart a white supremacist and only reluctantly voted for the FIFTEENTH AMENDMENT. He opposed both punitive legislation for southern states that discriminated against blacks and the 1871 Ku Klux Klan Act, because of his lack of sympathy for blacks and his refusal to accept the fact that the Civil War had radically altered the nature of STATES' RIGHTS. He gave unenthusiastic support for ANDREW JOHNSON in 1865–1866, and, although disgusted with Johnson's vetos of his Civil Rights and Freedman's Bureau Bills, Trumbull voted against conviction of Johnson in the trial following IMPEACHMENT because he doubted Johnson had committed an impeachable act under the Constitution. A successful corporate lawyer, Trumbull argued EX PARTE MCCARDLE (1867) at the express request of General ULYSSES S. GRANT and was paid $10,000 for his services, even though he was a senator at the time. In 1876 Trumbull unsuccessfully argued the cause of Samuel Tilden before the Election Commission that considered the disputes over the Tilden-Hayes presidential election. (See COMPROMISE OF 1877.) Late in life he supported populism and the rights of workers, and in his last Supreme Court case he defended the labor organizer Eugene V. Debs in IN RE DEBS (1895).

PAUL FINKELMAN

Bibliography

KRUG, MARK M. 1965 *Lyman Trumbull: Conservative Radical.* New York: A. S. Barnes & Co.

TRUPIANO v. UNITED STATES

See: Search and Seizure; Search Incident to Arrest

TUCKER, HENRY ST. GEORGE
(1780–1848)

A political leader, scholar, and jurist, Henry St. George Tucker studied law under his father, ST. GEORGE TUCKER. He was a congressman (1815–1819), state judge (1824–1841), and professor of law at the University of Virginia (1841–1848). In his classroom lectures and in his textbook entitled *Lectures on Constitutional Law* (1843), he took a moderate STATES' RIGHTS position, steering, as he said, "a middle course between [the] dangerous extremes" of NULLIFICATION and centralization. His book is intended as a refutation of the nationalist position of JOSEPH STORY, but, although he regarded the Constitution as a compact among the states, he rejected nullification and SECESSION as remedies for violations by the federal government.

DENNIS J. MAHONEY

Bibliography

BAUER, ELIZABETH KELLEY 1952 *Commentaries on the Constitution, 1790–1860.* New York: Columbia University Press.

TUCKER, JOHN RANDOLPH
(1823–1897)

A political leader, scholar, and attorney, John Randolph Tucker was the son of HENRY ST. GEORGE TUCKER and the grandson of ST. GEORGE TUCKER. He was attorney general of Virginia (1857–1865), congressman (1875–1887), professor of law at Washington and Lee University (1870–1875, 1888–1897), and president of the American Bar Association (1894). From his retirement from Congress until his death he worked on his two-volume commentary, *The Constitution of the United States,* which was published posthumously in 1899. Tucker continued the family's tradition of STATES' RIGHTS constitutionalism, proposing that the TENTH AMENDMENT was the key to understanding the Constitution. He was strikingly influenced by European political theorists, including J. K. Bluntschli, and rejected the ideas of NATURAL RIGHTS, human equality, and SOCIAL COMPACT in favor of the concept of an organic state.

DENNIS J. MAHONEY

TUCKER, N. BEVERLEY (1784–1851)

Jurist, scholar, and novelist Nathaniel Beverley Tucker developed his political views under the influence of his half-brother, JOHN RANDOLPH. As a judge and politician in Missouri (1815–1830) he fiercely resisted the MISSOURI COMPROMISE. Later, as a professor of law at William and Mary College (1834–1851) he was one of the most extreme advocates of a STATES' RIGHTS interpretation of the Constitution. He argued that SOVEREIGNTY resided in the several states and that the people of Virginia were obliged to obey federal law only because Virginia commanded them to do so. He defended slavery and supported NULLIFICATION. His novel, *The Partisan Leader* (1836), advocated SECESSION and predicted a civil war.

DENNIS J. MAHONEY

Bibliography

BAUER, ELIZABETH KELLEY 1952 *Commentaries on the Constitution, 1790–1860.* New York: Columbia University Press.

TUCKER, ST. GEORGE (1751–1827)

St. George Tucker, who became known as the "American Blackstone," wrote the first commentary on the Constitution since THE FEDERALIST, a book that he recommended as a "masterly discussion." After a dozen years as a judge in Virginia, Tucker succeeded GEORGE WYTHE, with whom he had studied law, as professor of law at the College of William and Mary. Using WILLIAM BLACKSTONE's *Commentaries on the Laws of England* as his text, Tucker updated and domesticated Blackstone in his lectures, showing how the English law had changed in the United States and in Virginia. His lectures led in 1803 to the publication in five volumes of an annotated edition of Blackstone. Notwithstanding Tucker's 1,400 notes, the most creative parts of his work are to be found in his appendices, which run to 425 pages in the first volume, mostly an analysis of the United States Constitution. Although Tucker preferred a "federal" to a "consolidated" Union, he was a moderate who defended the American constitutional system, championed democracy, opposed SLAVERY, and made constructive criticisms. The appendix argued against a FEDERAL COMMON LAW OF CRIMES. Volume two's appendices included an extended proposal for the gradual abolition of slavery and a libertarian essay on FIRST AMENDMENT freedoms, in which Tucker discoursed on the reasons that religion, speech, and press should be "absolute" and "unrestricted," except for laws against personal defamation. Tucker's edition of Blackstone led to his appointment to the highest court of Virginia, where he served with distinction, followed in 1813 by an appointment as a United States district judge. Tucker held that position until shortly before his death. He ranks with the best of Jeffersonian jurists and theorists.

LEONARD W. LEVY

TUCKER ACT 24 Stat. 505 (1887)

Thirty-two years after establishing the Court of Claims, Congress enacted the Tucker Act, expanding that court's JURISDICTION to decide claims against the United States. Henceforth, the court might decide not only contract claims but also claims against the government founded on the Constitution and other damage claims not based on tort. Today the act confers jurisdiction over such cases on the United States CLAIMS COURT, along with jurisdiction over claims founded on various federal statutes and regulations. If the amount in controversy in such a case is less than $10,000, the UNITED STATES DISTRICT COURT exercises CONCURRENT JURISDICTION—thus allowing persons with small claims to bring suit in their home districts rather than in Washington, D.C. The act creates no substantive rights but merely provides jurisdiction in cases in which the government's liability is founded on other principles of law. In effect, however, the act amounts to a waiver of the federal government's SOVEREIGN IMMUNITY, in recognition of the vital principle that government should not be above the law.

KENNETH L. KARST

(SEE ALSO: *Federal Tort Claims Act.*)

Bibliography

WRIGHT, CHARLES A.; MILLER, ARTHUR R.; and COOPER, EDWARD H. 1985 *Federal Practice and Procedure,* 2nd ed. Vol. 14:270–294. St. Paul, Minn.: West Publishing Co.

TUGWELL, REXFORD G. (1891–1979)

Economist Rexford Guy Tugwell was a member of President FRANKLIN D. ROOSEVELT's "brain trust" and an advocate of centralized economic planning by the federal government. After serving as undersecretary of agriculture and governor of Puerto Rico, he began a second career as a historian and constitutional theorist. His books on the Roosevelt years include *The Democratic Roosevelt* (1957, 1969) and *The Brains Trust* (1968). Tugwell's years as a government official convinced him that only a rewriting of the Constitution, emphasizing provisions for centralization, economic planning, and emergency powers, would produce an effective form of government. He denounced as undemocratic the accepted principles of JUDICIAL REVIEW, FEDERALISM, and SEPARATION OF POWERS, and he stressed the need for total revision of the Constitution rather than gradual evolution through judicial interpretation. Tugwell frequently published his own proposals for a rewritten constitution. In *The Emerging Constitution* (1975) his proposals included: reduction of the states to administrative districts of a unitary national government; expansion of executive power, including EXECUTIVE PRIVILEGE; curtailment of the judiciary's power to pass judgment on actions of the national government to supervise the economy; and periodic revision of the Constitution through a simplified AMENDING PROCESS.

RICHARD B. BERNSTEIN

TUITION GRANTS

While parents have a constitutional right to send their children to private rather than public schools (see PIERCE V. SOCIETY OF SISTERS, 1925), the exercise of that right costs money. Such parents not only bear their share of the taxes that support public schools but also pay tuition to their children's schools. Not surprisingly, a regular item of business in Congress and the state legislatures is a proposal to relieve this "double burden" through some form of governmental relief. Two types of constitutional problems beset such proposals. Governmental aid to private schools may be attacked as STATE ACTION that promotes racial SEGREGATION or as an unconstitutional ESTABLISHMENT OF RELIGION.

Soon after the decision in BROWN V. BOARD OF EDUCATION (1954–1955), a number of southern states adopted a series of devices aimed at evading DESEGREGATION. One such device was the payment of state grants to private schools or to parents of private school children. The assumption was that when public schools were ordered to desegregate, white children would be withdrawn and placed in private schools. Some states went so far as to give local school boards the option of closing public schools and even selling those schools' physical plants to the operators of private schools which would be supported by tuition subsidized by the state. These private schools, it was expected, would be limited to white students. (More recently, federal CIVIL RIGHTS legislation has been applied to forbid that type of "segregation academy" to refuse black applicants. See RUNYON V. MCCRARY, (1976.) The Supreme Court held these tuition grant programs unconstitutional as evasions of *Brown* in cases such as GRIFFIN V. COUNTY SCHOOL BOARD (1964) and *Poindexter v. Louisiana Financial Assistance Commission* (PER CURIAM, 1968).

More recently, private schools in the North and West have acquired new white students following orders desegregating urban school systems. "White flight" means not only the departure of white families for the suburbs but also the transfer of white students from public to private schools. Estimates in the late 1970s suggested that as many as one-fifth of all enrollments in the nation's private schools were the result of "white flight." Proposals for governmental aid to private school children and their parents must therefore face a challenge based on the likely racially discriminatory impacts of various proposed forms of aid. Such impacts would not, of themselves, establish a constitutional violation; they would, however, be some evidence of an improper governmental purpose. (See LEGISLATION.)

Tuition grants limited to low-income parents of children enrolled in religious schools were held to violate the establishment clause in COMMITTEE FOR PUBLIC EDUCATION V. NYQUIST (1973). That decision did not settle the question of the constitutionality of a hypothetical program in which the state gave *all* parents education vouchers, to be used to support schools of their choosing, public or private, religious or secular. (See GOVERNMENT AID TO RELIGIOUS INSTITUTIONS; MUELLER V. ALLEN, 1983.)

Proponents of voucher plans designed to aid private schools and their clienteles have gone to some lengths in an effort to tailor their proposals to meet these two types of constitutional objection. One proposal provides elaborate incentives for racial integration, such as bonuses for integrated schools. In the absence of strong incentives of some kind, it seems obvious that significant aid to private elementary and secondary education will have the effect of increasing racial segregation by increasing the educational mobility of middle class whites.

KENNETH L. KARST

Bibliography

SUGARMAN, STEPHEN D. 1974 Family Choice: The Next Step in the Quest for Equal Educational Opportunity? *Law and Contemporary Problems* 38:513–565.

TWELFTH AMENDMENT

The ELECTORAL COLLEGE, as contemplated in Article II of the Constitution, was to be a kind of "search committee," nominating outstanding men of various regions from among whom Congress would elect the President and vice-president. The Framers expected each elector to cast his first vote for a candidate from his home state and his second for a national figure from another state. The delegates to the CONSTITUTIONAL CONVENTION assumed that the primary electoral divisions in the country were, and would remain, sectional.

The rise of POLITICAL PARTIES, which began almost immediately after the Constitution went into effect, belied that assumption. The parties nominated candidates, and the Electoral College had only to choose between the party slates; sectional loyalties were subordinated to ideological ones. In 1796, when party discipline was still developing, the Electoral College chose a Federalist President and a Republican vice-president. In 1800 straight party voting produced a tie between THOMAS JEFFERSON and AARON BURR, the Republican nominees for President and vice-president, respectively. The disgraceful performance of the House of Representatives, which required thirty-five ballots to ratify the voters' choice, led directly to adoption of the Twelfth Amendment.

The amendment provided that the electors would vote for President and vice-president in separate ballots; if no candidate obtained a majority of electoral votes, the House of Representatives (voting by states) would elect the President and the Senate the vice-president. Introduced by Senator DeWitt Clinton of New York, the amendment faced congressional opposition from Federalists and representatives of small states, each group fearing that its influence on presidential selection would be diminished. Once Congress proposed the Twelfth Amendment in 1804, the necessary thirteen states ratified it in less than six months—only the TWENTY-SIXTH AMENDMENT (1971) was ratified more quickly.

DENNIS J. MAHONEY

TWENTIETH AMENDMENT

Congress proposed the Twentieth Amendment, sponsored by Senator GEORGE W. NORRIS of Nebraska, on March 2, 1932; ratification was completed on January 23, 1933. The amendment provided that the President, vice-president, and Congress begin their terms in the January following their election. Under the old scheme of Article I, section 4, congressmen had not taken their seats until thirteen months after their election, and a short "lame duck" session in election years included members who had already been defeated. The amendment also made provisions for PRESIDENTIAL SUCCESSION and authorized Congress to provide for a situation in which a President-elect or vice-president-elect does not qualify by inauguration day.

DENNIS J. MAHONEY

TWENTY-FIFTH AMENDMENT

Congress proposed the Twenty-Fifth Amendment in July 1965, and ratification by the state legislatures was completed in February 1967. The amendment revised the constitutional provisions dealing with PRESIDENTIAL SUCCESSION, specifically providing that when a vacancy occurs in the office of President the VICE-PRESIDENT becomes (rather than "acts as") President. The amendment also provides for the orderly transfer of executive power in the event of a temporary presidential disability and for filling a vacancy in the office of vice-president.

DENNIS J. MAHONEY

Bibliography

FEERICK, JOHN D. 1976 *The Twenty-Fifth Amendment.* New York: Fordham University Press.

TWENTY-FIRST AMENDMENT

The Twenty-First Amendment repealed the EIGHTEENTH AMENDMENT and rescinded the constitutional mandate for national PROHIBITION of alcoholic beverages. Congress proposed the amendment in February 1933; RATIFICATION was complete in December 1933. To the extent that the VOLSTEAD ACT depended upon the constitutional authority of the Eighteenth Amendment, that statute became inoperative upon the passage of the Twenty-First Amendment.

The second clause of the Twenty-First Amendment prohibits transportation or importation of intoxicating liquors into states or territories in contravention of local law. The clause apparently gives the states power to regulate interstate commerce in alcoholic beverages, including the authority to discriminate against out-of-state producers and distributors, thus freeing the states, as far as liquor is concerned, from COMMERCE CLAUSE restrictions. The Supreme Court has upheld that interpretation in several cases, notably *State Board v. Young's Market* (1936). The Court suggested an even broader scope for state regulatory power under the amendment in *California v. LaRue* (1972), when it upheld a regulation banning sexually explicit entertainment in licensed taverns, and in *Elks' Lodge v. Ingraham* (1973), when it upheld a statute denying liquor licenses to private clubs that practiced RACIAL DISCRIMINATION.

The Twenty-First Amendment is the only constitutional amendment to have been ratified by state conventions rather than by the state legislatures. Congress chose this variant of the AMENDING PROCESS because proponents of repeal feared that antiliquor sentiment was dominant in many state legislatures, because of the overrepresentation of rural areas.

DENNIS J. MAHONEY

TWENTY-FOURTH AMENDMENT

The Twenty-Fourth Amendment, written by Senator Spessard Holland of Florida, was proposed by Congress on August 27, 1962, and became part of the Constitution on February 4, 1964. The amendment provides that the right of United States citizens to vote for federal officers shall not be denied or abridged for nonpayment of a POLL TAX or other tax.

A poll tax is simply a per capita tax and has no necessary relationship to election polling. However, several southern states made payment of the poll tax an electoral qualification in order to diminish the VOTING RIGHTS of black citizens. Bills to abolish the practice were introduced every year from 1939 on, and Holland, who believed statutory abolition to be beyond Congress's power, introduced his amendment every year from 1949 on.

By 1964, only five states retained payment of the poll tax as a qualification for voting. Because the Twenty-Fourth Amendment governed only federal elections, four states divided their elections, continuing to require poll tax payment for voting in state elections; but the Supreme Court held, in HARPER V. VIRGINIA BOARD OF ELECTIONS (1966), that this practice violated the Constitution by denying EQUAL PROTECTION OF THE LAWS.

DENNIS J. MAHONEY

TWENTY-SECOND AMENDMENT

Although, as ALEXANDER HAMILTON explained in THE FEDERALIST #69, the President was "to be re-eligible as often as the people of the United States shall think him worthy of their confidence," a constitutional custom dating back to the administration of GEORGE WASHINGTON limited the President of the United States to two terms in office. In 1940, however, with the Great Depression finally coming to an end and with most of the world already engaged in World War II, FRANKLIN D. ROOSEVELT sought and won election to a third term. He was subsequently elected to a fourth term, although he died sixty days after that term began.

The Twenty-Second Amendment makes the two-term limit a part of the formal Constitution. Congress proposed the amendment in March 1947 and RATIFICATION was complete four years later.

The effect of the amendment on the balance of power between the executive and the legislature is not clear. Hamilton, who personally had advocated a life term for the President, speculated in *The Federalist* #71 that Presidents would become more submissive to Congress as elections approached; and DWIGHT D. EISENHOWER argued during his second term that his ineligibility for reelection was a guarantee that he was more disinterestedly public-spirited than congressmen who opposed him. In the 1980s, on the other hand, journalists and political scientists who had come to see elections as retroactively legitimating, rather than prospectively legitimating, began referring to President RONALD REAGAN as a "lame duck" even before his second inauguration.

The two-term limit is no longer controversial. Ever since the CONSTITUTIONAL CONVENTION OF 1789 there have been proposals for limiting the President to a single term, generally longer than four years, but none of these has ever been seriously considered as a constitutional amendment.

DENNIS J. MAHONEY

TWENTY-SIXTH AMENDMENT

Congress proposed the Twenty-Sixth Amendment on March 23, 1971. Ratification was completed in 107 days, the shortest time ever required to complete the

AMENDING PROCESS. The amendment standardized the voting age in all federal, state, and local elections at eighteen.

Under the Constitution the power to establish qualifications for voting in all elections was left to the states, except that the qualifications to vote for representatives in Congress (and, after the SEVENTEENTH AMENDMENT, for senators) had to be the same as those to vote for members of the most numerous branch of the state legislature. Under various amendments, VOTING RIGHTS could not constitutionally be denied or abridged on account of race, color, previous servitude, sex, or failure to pay taxes; the FOURTEENTH AMENDMENT set twenty-one as the highest minimum age a state could require for voters. Before 1970 only four states had enacted a minimum voting age lower than twenty-one.

In the VOTING RIGHTS AMENDMENTS of 1970, Congress purported to lower the voting age to eighteen for all elections. The Supreme Court, in OREGON V. MITCHELL (1970), upheld the statute, insofar as it pertained to federal elections, under Article I, section 4, which authorizes Congress to regulate the time and manner of elections of its members; but the Court held the act unconstitutional insofar as it pertained to state elections. The decision threatened to throw the 1972 elections into chaos, because in most states the voting age for balloting for federal officials would have been different from the voting age for state races. The rapidity with which the amendment was ratified is attributable to a general desire to avoid such chaos.

Although Congress, in proposing the amendment, expressed confidence in the "idealism and concern and energy" the new voters would bring to the political system, the actual effect of the amendment has been less than revolutionary. Empirical studies have shown that eighteen-to-twenty-one-year-olds have the lowest voter turnout rate of any age group; and those who do vote do not differ markedly from the rest of the population concerning political parties or issues.

DENNIS J. MAHONEY

TWENTY-THIRD AMENDMENT

Proposed by Congress on June 17, 1960, the Twenty-Third Amendment became effective on March 29, 1961. The amendment includes residents of the DISTRICT OF COLUMBIA in the process of electing the President and vice-president by allowing them to choose members of the ELECTORAL COLLEGE. The influence of the district is limited by the proviso permitting it no more electoral votes than the least populous state—in practice fixing the district's electoral votes at three.

As the amendment was introduced by Senator Kenneth Keating, of New York, it would have allocated the District of Columbia as many electoral votes as a state with the same population and would have permitted the district to elect representatives to Congress on the same basis. Representative Emmanuel Celler, of New York, chairman of the House Judiciary Committee, reduced it to its final form in order to insure passage. Celler's committee also separated the District of Columbia suffrage amendment from two other amendments (on Congressional vacancies and POLL TAXES) to which the Senate had linked it.

There was some opposition from Republicans, who predicted the district would inevitably support Democratic candidates, and Southerners, who feared the amendment would increase the political power of blacks.

DENNIS J. MAHONEY

TWINING v. NEW JERSEY
211 U.S. 78 (1908)

Twining formed part of the line of decisions, from HURTADO V. CALIFORNIA (1884) and MAXWELL V. DOW (1900) to PALKO V. CONNECTICUT (1937), in which the Supreme Court denied that the traditional Fifth and SIXTH AMENDMENT rights of accused persons were FUNDAMENTAL RIGHTS protected against state infringement by the FOURTEENTH AMENDMENT. In *Twining*, an eight-man majority, speaking through Justice WILLIAM H. MOODY, held that neither the PRIVILEGES AND IMMUNITIES clause nor the DUE PROCESS clause incorporated the RIGHT AGAINST SELF-INCRIMINATION. The Court also considered whether some of the personal rights safeguarded by the BILL OF RIGHTS might be safeguarded against the states because to deny those rights would be to deny due process of law. That is, apart from the question whether the Fourteenth Amendment's protection of immunities and liberty had the effect of incorporating the Fifth Amendment right, the Court also decided the question whether the concept of due process itself was of such a nature as to include the right against self-incrimination. Was a denial of that right a denial of due process?

Although Moody admitted that the Court would

not allow history to "strait-jacket" constitutional law, he resorted to "every historical test" to determine how history "rated" the right in question. Moody was a pathetically poor historian; his mangling of the little evidence he knew led him wrongly to conclude that the right against self-incrimination was neither a fundamental right nor part of due process of law. On that reading of history he decided that the state had not violated the Constitution by permitting a trial court to instruct the jury that they might draw adverse inferences against a defendant because of his reliance on the right against self-incrimination or his failure to testify.

Justice JOHN MARSHALL HARLAN delivered another lone dissenting opinion, arguing that immunity against self-incrimination, like the right to INDICTMENT by GRAND JURY and the right to TRIAL BY JURY, should be deemed fundamental and applicable to the states. Whether he believed that the privileges and immunities clause or the due process clause, or both, incorporated the right is not clear; but he certainly believed it to be essential to due process.

At the time the Court held a narrower view of PROCEDURAL DUE PROCESS, it used an expanded SUBSTANTIVE DUE PROCESS to protect CORPORATIONS and prevent Congress from protecting trade unions (see ADAIR V. UNITED STATES, 1908). ADAMSON V. CALIFORNIA (1947) reaffirmed *Twining,* but the Court overruled both cases in MALLOY V. HOGAN (1964).

LEONARD W. LEVY

(SEE ALSO: *Incorporation Doctrine.*)

TWO GUYS FROM HARRISON-ALLENTOWN v. MCGINLEY

See: Sunday Closing Laws

TWO-LEVEL THEORY

In an important 1960 article, Harry Kalven, Jr., coined the phrase "two-level theory." As he described it, FIRST AMENDMENT methodology classified speech at two levels. Some speech was so unworthy as to be beneath First Amendment protection: no First Amendment review was necessary. Thus the Court in CHAPLINSKY V. NEW HAMPSHIRE (1942) had referred to "certain well-defined and narrowly limited classes of speech, the prevention and punishment of which has never been thought to raise any constitutional problem. These include the lewd and obscene, the profane, the libelous, and the insulting or fighting words." At the second level, speech of constitutional value was protected unless it presented a CLEAR AND PRESENT DANGER of a substantive evil.

In a subsequent article Kalven observed that in NEW YORK TIMES V. SULLIVAN (1964) neither the two-level approach nor the clear and present danger test was an organizing strategy or guiding methodology. He expressed the hope that the *Sullivan* Court's unwillingness to employ the two-level theory presaged the theory's demise along with the clear and present danger test. Kalven's hopes have been only partially realized. Perhaps partly as a result of his persuasive efforts, the Court has been willing to scrutinize state justifications for regulating some types of speech previously thought to raise no constitutional problem. *Chaplinsky*'s off-hand assumption that each class of speech in its litany raises no constitutional problem is no longer credible. Nonetheless, the Court continues to be impressed by *Chaplinsky*'s famous OBITER DICTUM that speech beneath the protection of the First Amendment occupies that status because its slight contribution to truth is outweighed by the state interests in order and morality.

Kalven's hope for the complete repudiation of the clear and present danger doctrine also remains unfulfilled. A variation of the doctrine occupies a secure doctrinal place in the context of INCITEMENT TO UNLAWFUL CONDUCT, and the DENNIS V. UNITED STATES (1951) version of the test has been employed by the Court in other contexts, as in *Landmark Communications, Inc. v. Virginia* (1978) and NEBRASKA PRESS ASSOCIATION V. STUART (1976).

If doctrine were described today in terms of levels, many levels would be necessary. At one level, there is the question whether a First Amendment problem is presented: an effort to communicate a message by assassination presumably raises no First Amendment problem. If cognizable First Amendment values are present, there remains the question whether any legal protection is appropriate: advocacy of illegal action often is unprotected despite the existence of cognizable First Amendment interests. If some protection is appropriate, further questions remain: what protection in what contexts, at what times, in what places, and concerning what modes of expression? A multitude of doctrinal tests now govern a multitude of contexts. Harry Kalven would appreciate the Court's sensitivity to the vicissitudes of human conduct, but likely would regret the absence of an overall vision.

STEVEN SHIFFRIN

Bibliography

KALVEN, HARRY, JR. 1960 The Metaphysics of the Law of Obscenity. *Supreme Court Review* 1960:1–45.

——— 1964 The New York Times Case: A Note on "The Central Meaning of the First Amendment." *Supreme Court Review* 1964:191–221.

TWO SOVEREIGNTIES RULE

This rule, which the Supreme Court repudiated in *Murphy v. Waterfront Commission* (1964), was a limitation on the RIGHT AGAINST SELF-INCRIMINATION. Based on the federal principle that one sovereignty has no interest in the law enforcement activities of another, the rule was that a person could not refuse to testify on the grounds that his disclosure would subject him to prosecution by another sovereignty or JURISDICTION. Thus he could be convicted of a federal crime on the basis of testimony compelled in a state proceeding or of a state crime on the basis of testimony compelled in a federal proceeding. In matters involving national supremacy, Congress can grant immunity against state prosecutions, but a state cannot immunize against a federal prosecution and one state cannot immunize against prosecution in another.

The rule entered American constitutional law in 1906 in *Hale v. Henkel* as a result of the Court's factual mistakes. In that case the appellant, who had received a grant of immunity against federal prosecution, sought reversal of his conviction for contempt by a federal court for refusing to answer questions that exposed him to state prosecution. The Court needlessly declared that English COMMON LAW had settled the question by a rule that "the only danger to be considered is one arising within the same jurisdiction and under that same sovereignty." The Court cited two English cases, one not in point and the other soon discredited by a decision unknown to the Court. In *United States v. Murdock* (1933), a unanimous Court "definitely settled that one under examination in a federal tribunal could not refuse to answer on account of probable incrimination under state law," a proposition resting on *Hale* and the two English precedents. By 1944 the Court made the two sovereignties rule reciprocal, so that a suspect could be whipsawed into incriminating himself in one jurisdiction by receiving a grant of immunity from another. State and federal authorities sometimes assisted each other, one compelling disclosure, the other prosecuting. So matters stood until the *Murphy* case.

Although granted immunity by New York and New Jersey, Murphy remained silent because his answers might incriminate him under federal law. He won a reversal of his conviction when the Supreme Court, in an opinion by Justice ARTHUR J. GOLDBERG, exposed the erroneous basis of the precedents and concluded that the two sovereignties rule had no support in history or in the policies underlying the Fifth Amendment right. On the same day, in MALLOY V. HOGAN (1964), the Court extended that right to the states. Given that extension and a broad view of the right, the Court held that a state witness is protected against incrimination under both federal and state law and a federal witness is similarly protected. Justices BYRON R. WHITE and POTTER STEWART concurred separately. *Murphy* also stands for the proposition that use immunity rather than TRANSACTIONAL IMMUNITY satisfies the demand of the Fifth Amendment at least in a two sovereignties case.

A two sovereignties rule still operates with respect to DOUBLE JEOPARDY: a person may be prosecuted for both state and federal crimes committed by the same act.

LEONARD W. LEVY

TYLER, JOHN
(1790–1862)

A Virginia lawyer, governor, and United States senator, John Tyler, a Democrat elected vice-president as a Whig in 1840 became America's first accidential President upon the death of WILLIAM HENRY HARRISON in 1841. This peaceful transition of leaders underscored the strength of the Constitution even though it frustrated the Whig politicians who had nominated Harrison. As President, Tyler was usually a constitutional strict constructionist, and many of his policies resembled those of ANDREW JACKSON. Tyler refused to interfere with the SOVEREIGNTY of Rhode Island during Dorr's Rebellion, but he was an early advocate of Texas annexation which was accomplished in the last months of his administration. In 1861 Tyler chaired the Washington Peace Conference, but after its failure he advocated SECESSION. The only former President to serve the Confederacy, Tyler was elected to the provisional Congress and the Confederate House of Representatives.

PAUL FINKELMAN

Bibliography

MORGAN, ROBERT J. 1954 *A Whig Embattled: The Presidency of John Tyler.* Lincoln: University of Nebraska Press.

TYSON & BROTHER v. BANTON
273 U.S. 418 (1927)

Citing Chief Justice WILLIAM HOWARD TAFT's opinion in WOLFF PACKING COMPANY V. COURT OF INDUSTRIAL RELATIONS (1923), Justice GEORGE SUTHERLAND found unconstitutional a New York statute regulating ticket "scalpers." The state based the law on a declaration that theater prices were AFFECTED WITH A PUBLIC INTEREST, but because the theater business did not fit Taft's categories, the law fell as a violation of FREEDOM OF CONTRACT and a denial of DUE PROCESS OF LAW.

Justice OLIVER WENDELL HOLMES dissented: "a state legislature may do whatever it sees fit to do unless it is restrained by some express prohibition in the [federal or state] constitution." Justice LOUIS D. BRANDEIS joined him and Justice HARLAN FISKE STONE wrote a separate dissent. All three urged rejection of the public interest concept—"a fiction intended to beautify what is disagreeable to the sufferers"—in favor of state regulation wherever the public welfare demanded it.

DAVID GORDON

(SEE ALSO: *Ribnik v. McBride, 1928; New State Ice Company v. Liebmann, 1932.*)

ULLMANN v. UNITED STATES
350 U.S. 422 (1956)

Ullmann, relying on his right not to be a witness against himself, refused to testify before a federal GRAND JURY concerning his alleged communist activities. Though he received immunity against prosecution for any criminal transaction concerning which he was compelled to testify, he continued pertinacious. Ullmann argued against the constitutionality of the congressional Immunity Act of 1954 on the grounds that it did not immunize him from such disabilities as loss of job, expulsion from labor unions, compulsory registration as a subversive, passport ineligibility, and general public opprobrium. Thus he distinguished his case from BROWN V. WALKER (1896) on the theory that he had not received full transactional immunity. The Court rejected Ullmann's argument, 7–2. Justice FELIX FRANKFURTER for the majority reasoned that the Fifth Amendment's right to silence operated only to prevent the compulsion of testimony that might expose one to a criminal charge. The disabilities to which Ullmann claimed exposure were not criminal penalties. Justices WILLIAM O. DOUGLAS and HUGO L. BLACK, dissenting, would have held the immunity act unconstitutional on the ground that the right of silence created by the Fifth Amendment is beyond the reach of Congress. Douglas contended that the amendment was designed to protect against INFAMY, as well as prosecution, and against forfeitures—those disabilities of which Ullmann spoke—as well as criminal fines and imprisonment.

LEONARD W. LEVY

(SEE ALSO: *Right against Self-Incrimination.*)

ULTRA VIRES

(Latin: "Beyond powers.") This term applies either to acts taken by a CORPORATION beyond the limits of its chartered (legally authorized) powers or to acts of a public official beyond his or her delegated authority.

DAVID GORDON

"ULYSSES," ONE BOOK ENTITLED, UNITED STATES v.
5F. Supp. 182 (1933); 72 F.2d 705 (1934)

Although it was not a decision of the Supreme Court, *Ulysses* was not merely a case involving a famous book and prominent judges but also a harbinger of modern decisions on OBSCENITY. Its standards for construing the COMMON LAW terms embodied in federal customs regulations were transmuted in UNITED STATES V. ROTH (1957) into constitutional principles for testing both federal and state legislation on the subject.

The handful of early obscenity cases that reached the Supreme Court mainly presented claims of technical error in the trials below. *Ulysses* presented clear questions of substantive standards for adjudging obscenity and lewdness. The established reputation of the book insured careful attention; Judge John M. Woolsey's lower court opinion was unmistakably written for the anthologies it ultimately graced. Judge AUGUSTUS N. HAND's appellate majority opinion was straightforward, but Judge Martin T. Manton's dissent was somewhat verbose.

Woolsey declared that the book successfully showed "how the screen [sic] of consciousness with its ever-shifting kaleidoscopic impression carries, as it were on a plastic palimpsest, . . . a penumbral zone residual of past impressions . . . not unlike the result of a double or, if that is possible, a multiple exposure on a cinema film. . . ."

The relevant statute on importation of books prohibited not pandering but obscenity. Woolsey announced without discussion that the test for obscenity required examination of the whole work. The standard was the effect on "what the French would call *l'homme moyen sensuel*—who plays, in this branch of legal inquiry . . . the same role . . . as does the "reasonable man in the law of torts. . . ." With this standard he found the book "somewhat emetic, nowhere . . . an aphrodisiac." He also found Joyce to have been sincere and lacking pornographic intent or the "leer of the sensualist."

At the appellate level Augustus Hand for himself and LEARNED HAND managed to come to grips with the central legal issue—whether isolated passages could render a work of art obscene. This was the test derived from *Regina v. Hicklin* (1868), the classic British case, and, they conceded, followed in *United States v. Bennett* (1879), a CIRCUIT COURT decision by Justice SAMUEL BLATCHFORD. They discounted other alleged precedents and argued that the isolated passages concept was not followed for works of science or medicine and should not be followed for literature either. They cited state decisions embracing the "dominant effect" notion, and read that test (together with their definition of the relevant audience) into the statute, concluding that other readings would be impractical and overrestrictive.

Manton, dissenting, insisted that federal decisions in the past had accepted the "isolated passages" test. As literature was for amusement only, the community could reasonably demand that it meet moral standards—those of average, not exceptional, individuals.

SAMUEL KRISLOV

Bibliography

LOCKHART, WILLIAM B. and MCCLURE, ROBERT C. 1954 Literature, the Law of Obscenity, and the Constitution. *Minnesota Law Review* 38:295–395.

UNCONSTITUTIONAL CONDITIONS

Although government may not be obligated to provide its citizens with a certain benefit or privilege, it is not free to condition granting the benefit or privilege on the recipient's relinquishing a constitutional right. Likewise, the government may not withhold or cancel the benefit by way of penalizing the assertion of a constitutional right. For example, in SHERBERT V. VERNER (1963) the Supreme Court held South Carolina's unemployment compensation act unconstitutional as applied to exclude a Seventh Day Adventist from benefits when she would not find a job releasing her from work on Saturdays. Withholding the benefits effectively penalized exercise of the claimant's RELIGIOUS LIBERTY.

It has sometimes been argued that a legislature's greater power of withholding a benefit must necessarily include the lesser power of granting the benefit with restrictions. On this theory, the recipient of the benefit is deprived of no right, for the right can be retained simply by rejecting the proffered benefit. This logic leads to drastic consequences as government becomes increasingly involved in supplying such vital needs as jobs, housing, welfare, and EDUCATION.

As early as *Frost & Frost Trucking Company v. Railroad Commission* (1926) the Court recognized the potential for excess conditions on the exercise of constitutional rights: "If the state may compel the surrender of one constitutional right as a condition of its favor, it may, in like manner, compel a surrender of all. It is inconceivable that guarantees embedded in the Constitution of the United States may thus be manipulated out of existence."

Subsequent courts have rarely been persuaded by arguments claiming an absolute power of government to condition and limit the grant of general benefits. Rather, they have generally recognized that the revocation of benefits amounts to regulatory activity by government, for which sufficient justification must be established if constitutional rights are restricted. This doctrine of unconstitutional conditions has been successfully applied to restrain assertions of unlimited governmental power in four major substantial areas: the privilege of out-of-state corporations to engage in local business; the use of public property and facilities; the receipt of entitlements and social service benefits; and government employment.

As early as 1839, the Supreme Court announced that a state might exclude out-of-state corporations from conducting business within its borders. In early cases, this power to exclude was held sufficient to justify highly unreasonable conditions on entry and even the arbitrary revocation of a corporation's license. Subsequent Court decisions, however, have subjected such regulations to DUE PROCESS standards. Given the Court's increasing sensitivity to national interests in economic growth and the smooth functioning of the federal system, it is not surprising that the Court invoked the doctrine of unconstitutional conditions to check a power previously thought to be virtually absolute.

In 1897 the Court upheld an ordinance that prohibited public speaking in a municipal park without a permit from the mayor. The Court reasoned that ownership of the land gave the city the right to withhold access completely; the city therefore could grant access on any conditions, including those restricting FIRST AMENDMENT freedoms. This logic has been invalidated by later decisions which have viewed the manipulation of access to streets and parks as regulatory activity subject to constitutional attack. (See PUBLIC FORUM.)

Given the large number of benefits now provided by government, the imposition of conditions on the recipients of such benefits raises a significant possibility of undermining individual liberties. The Supreme Court has used unconstitutional condition analysis to prevent such a result in cases involving unemployment compensation, WELFARE BENEFITS, public housing, tax exemptions, public education, and the mail services. One leading doctrinal basis for these decisions has been the guarantee of PROCEDURAL DUE PROCESS.

In *McAuliffe v. Mayor of New England* (1892) the Massachusetts Supreme Judicial Court denied the petition of a policeman who had been fined for violating a regulation restricting his political activity. Justice OLIVER WENDELL HOLMES, speaking for the state court, stated: "The petitioner may have a constitutional right to talk politics, but he has no constitutional right to be a policeman. . . . There are few employments for hire in which the servant does not agree to suspend his constitutional right of free speech, as well as of idleness, by the implied terms of his contract. The servant cannot complain, as he takes his employment on the terms which are offered him." More recently, however, courts have found conditions on employees unconstitutional irrespective of any abstract right to public employment. The courts have asked whether the condition restricts employment in a "patently arbitrary and discriminatory manner" in violation of due process, as set forth in WIEMAN V. UPDEGRAFF (1952), and whether, in withholding or revoking employment under conditions capable of improper application, the state is penalizing specific constitutional freedoms.

Although claims of unconstitutional conditions in these four areas have become less common in recent years, the doctrine has recently emerged in the sphere of CRIMINAL PROCEDURE, particularly in cases involving the guilty plea. PLEA BARGAINING effectively penalizes the exercise of the right to trial by rewarding those who plead guilty. In addition, it denies the individual the RIGHT AGAINST SELF-INCRIMINATION and the right to confront and cross-examine witnesses against him. The Court, however, has endorsed the use of plea bargaining. Rather than address the challenges raised by the unconstitutional conditions doctrine, the Court has insisted only that guilty pleas be "voluntary and intelligent" and that the plea bargaining process conform to certain standards of fairness. The tension between the principle of unconstitutional conditions and the Court's endorsement of plea bargaining seems likely to produce future controversy.

ARTHUR ROSETT

Bibliography

VAN ALSTYNE, WILLIAM W. 1968 The Demise of the Right–Privilege Distinction in Constitutional Law. *Harvard Law Review* 81:1439–1464.

UNCONSTITUTIONALITY

The American concept of unconstitutionality was born before the Constitution was adopted. The STAMP ACT CONGRESS of 1765, for example, declared that acts of Parliament imposing TAXATION WITHOUT REPRESENTATION were unconstitutional and need not be obeyed. Then as now, of course, the British constitution was an unwritten collection of customs and usages, only partly reflected in statutes and COMMON LAW principles. Since the adoption of the earliest state constitutions, however, the statement that a governmental action is unconstitutional has been taken as an assertion that the action violates a written constitution. In common speech, "unconstitutional" normally refers to an action's invalidity under the United States Constitution, but in law the term also refers to invalidity under a state constitution. Legislation is not the only form of governmental action that may be unconstitutional. When police officers conduct unreasonable SEARCHES AND SEIZURES, for example, they act unconstitutionally. Similarly, a state court acts unconstitutionally when it enforces a racially RESTRICTIVE COVENANT.

An assertion of unconstitutionality can be made by anyone: a citizen making a complaint, a newspaper editorial writer, a lawyer arguing a case. The assertion may take on a more authoritative character when it is made by a public officer acting in a governmental capacity. Thus, the President might veto a bill passed by Congress on the ground that it is unconstitutional. (See CIVIL RIGHTS ACT OF 1866; JACKSON'S VETO OF THE BANK BILL.) Or, the President might refuse to enforce an act of Congress on similar grounds. Such a presidential refusal led the House of Representatives to adopt ARTICLES OF IMPEACHMENT against ANDREW JOHNSON, thus registering its view that Johnson's conduct was itself unconstitutional. An executive officer may decline to enforce a law for the purpose of allowing others to frame a TEST CASE, thus allowing the courts to rule on the law's validity. BOARD OF EDUCATION V. ALLEN (1968) resulted from one such refusal.

The official in *Allen* thought it important to get a judicial ruling on the constitutionality of the law in question. In fact, Americans have become accustomed to identifying the idea of unconstitutionality with a judicial declaration of unconstitutionality—and, in particular, with such a declaration by the Supreme Court. A lawyer, asked by a client whether a law is or is not constitutional, ordinarily will respond with a prediction of what the courts will hold.

From MARBURY V. MADISON (1803) forward, American courts have assumed that they have the power to disregard a statute that violates a constitutional norm. When a court holds a statute unconstitutional it refuses to give effect to the law in the case before it. Indeed, the *Marbury* opinion grounded the principle of JUDICIAL REVIEW in the need for a court to decide the case before it according to law, including the Constitution as the supreme law. Federal courts are not permitted to give ADVISORY OPINIONS on the law but make their constitutional rulings only in the context of concrete CASES AND CONTROVERSIES. Yet there is a sense in which any opinion is, in part, advisory. The statement of a reason for decision requires a court to move from the particulars of the case before it to the more abstract level of a rule or principle which can be applied later as a PRECEDENT in deciding another appropriate case. Occasionally, particularly in the area of the FREEDOMS OF SPEECH and of the PRESS, a court may hold a law INVALID ON ITS FACE. But even if the court merely says it is holding the law "invalid as applied," the ruling becomes a precedent for other applications to similar facts.

In a statement now famous for its inaccuracy, the Supreme Court said in *Norton v. Shelby County* (1886) that an unconstitutional law "is not a law; it confers no rights; it imposes no duties; it affords no protection; it creates no office; it is, in legal contemplation, as inoperative as though it had never been passed." The statement is misleading in two respects. First, courts are no better than anyone else at undoing the past. A great many actions may be taken on the basis of a statute in the time between its enactment and its judicial invalidation. Justice often requires that those actions be given effect: a corporation organized under an invalid statute will be bound under its contracts; an official who enforces a law in good faith before the law is held invalid will not be liable in damages for the action. In *Lemon v. Kurtzman II* (1973), the Supreme Court allowed Pennsylvania to reimburse church schools for educational services performed under a statute before the Court had held the law invalid in LEMON V. KURTZMAN I (1971).

Second, the *Norton* statement is misleading in the context of an OVERRULING of a previous decision that has held a statute invalid. In ADKINS V. CHILDREN'S HOSPITAL (1923) the Supreme Court had held the DISTRICT OF COLUMBIA MINIMUM WAGE LAW unconstitutional, but in WEST COAST HOTEL CO. V. PARRISH (1937), the Court overruled *Adkins.* Was it then necessary for Congress to reenact the law for it to be effective? The attorney general issued an opinion answering this question negatively, and no one now challenges that opinion's soundness.

Determining whether a court has actually held a law unconstitutional may prove more difficult than identifying the court's HOLDING on the underlying constitutional law. In dealing with a federal statute, for example, the Supreme Court may make clear its view of the Constitution's command, but it may not make clear whether it has held the statute invalid or construed the statute narrowly to avoid holding it unconstitutional. Such an ambiguity still bemuses collectors of antique trivia when they contemplate HODGSON V. BOWERBANK (1809).

Ultimately, the notion of unconstitutionality refers not so much to a fact—or even an opinion, judicial or otherwise—as to a decisional process. In that process courts play the most prominent role, but now and then they yield the center of the stage to other actors. (See ABRAHAM LINCOLN; THOMAS JEFFERSON; WATERGATE AND THE CONSTITUTION.)

KENNETH L. KARST

Bibliography

BICKEL, ALEXANDER M. 1962 *The Least Dangerous Branch: The Supreme Court at the Bar of Politics.* Indianapolis: Bobbs-Merrill.

FIELD, OLIVER P. 1935 *The Effect of an Unconstitutional Statute.* Minneapolis: University of Minnesota Press.

UNIFORM CODE OF MILITARY JUSTICE ACT

See: Military Justice

UNION PACIFIC RAILROAD COMPANY v. UNITED STATES

See: Sinking Fund Cases

UNITED BUILDING & CONSTRUCTION TRADES COUNCIL v. MAYOR AND COUNCIL OF CAMDEN

See: Privileges and Immunities

UNITED JEWISH ORGANIZATIONS v. CAREY

430 U.S. 144 (1977)

Under the VOTING RIGHTS ACT OF 1965 New York sought approval of the United States attorney general for its REAPPORTIONMENT of voters in state legislative districts in Greater New York City. To increase the nonwhite majorities in certain districts, and thus secure approval, the legislature divided a Hasidic Jewish community into two districts, each with a nonwhite majority. Petitioners claimed that assignment of voters solely on the basis of race violated the FOURTEENTH and FIFTEENTH AMENDMENTS.

By a 7–1 vote, the Supreme Court upheld the race-conscious reapportionment. There was no majority opinion but a series of overlapping alignments. Four Justices, noting that the percentage of nonwhite-majority districts was less than the percentage of nonwhites in the county in question, said that the use of racial criteria to comply with the act was not limited to compensating for past discrimination. Other Justices emphasized the lack of stigma or legislative purpose to disadvantage the Hasidim. Justice WILLIAM J. BRENNAN, in a comprehensive opinion on race-conscious remedies, appeared to look ahead to REGENTS OF UNIVERSITY OF CALIFORNIA V. BAKKE (1978). Chief Justice WARREN E. BURGER dissented.

KENNETH L. KARST

UNITED MINE WORKERS v. CORONADO COAL COMPANY

259 U.S. 344 (1922)

CORONADO COAL COMPANY v. UNITED MINE WORKERS

268 U.S. 295 (1925)

In two nearly identical cases, the Supreme Court provided opposite answers to the same question: does the SHERMAN ANTITRUST ACT apply to local strikes that indirectly restrain commerce? The United Mine Workers (UMW) struck to prevent an employer from closing its mines despite valid union contracts; violence and property damage resulted. The company sued the union claiming a Sherman Act conspiracy to restrain INTERSTATE COMMERCE. In its defense, the UMW claimed that it was exempt from suit because it was unincorporated and, because mining was local, that there had been no Sherman Act violation. On APPEAL to the Supreme Court, Chief Justice WILLIAM HOWARD TAFT declared for a unanimous bench that, although unions (even though unincorporated) could clearly be sued, the union had not violated the Sherman Act here. Mining was merely local; any interference concerned the PRODUCTION rather than the distribution of goods. Taft said no restraint of trade existed, absent an explicit showing of intent to restrain trade, unless the obstruction had "such a direct, material and substantial effect to restrain [commerce] that intent reasonably may be inferred." Taft thus introduced new tests of reasonableness (see RULE OF REASON) and intent.

The company soon appealed with new EVIDENCE. Again unanimous, the Supreme Court now said that when intent to restrain trade attended a decrease in production, a previously "indirect and remote obstruction" became a direct interference in violation of the law. The Court asserted that the evidence at the second trial demonstrated such intent. The Court's near reversal, a finding of intent where none had previously existed, probably resulted from a fear of the implications of the first decision. The effect of the later opinion was to hamper union organizing efforts and cast doubt on the legality of strikes generally; certainly intent could be found by Justices who were looking for it.

DAVID GORDON

(SEE ALSO: *Labor and the Antitrust Laws.*)

UNITED MINE WORKERS v. UNITED STATES
330 U.S. 258 (1947)

When John L. Lewis and the United Mine Workers went on strike in the spring of 1946 against coal operators throughout the country, President HARRY S TRUMAN, acting as COMMANDER-IN-CHIEF, seized the mines by EXECUTIVE ORDER to protect the national interest during the emergency. The failure of subsequent negotiations prompted a call that autumn for a second strike, which the government forestalled by obtaining an INJUNCTION in federal district court. Lewis defied the injunction, incurring contempt citations, a personal fine of $10,000, and a fine against his union of $3,500,000.

Lewis appealed to the Supreme Court. Chief Justice FRED M. VINSON, for a 7–2 majority, held that neither the NORRIS-LAGUARDIA nor the CLAYTON ACT deprived the district court of JURISDICTION to issue the injunction pending judicial interpretation of the contract between the government and the miners. The majority denied the assertion that the "employer" referred to in the acts included the government; neither legislative history nor subsequent policy demonstrated any intent to make those acts applicable to government–employee disputes. Moreover, even if the Norris-LaGuardia Act applied, the Court could legitimately issue an injunction to maintain existing conditions pending the court's decision on its jurisdiction. The Court upheld the contempt findings—asserting that the same conduct might constitute both civil and criminal contempt for which both coercive and punitive measures might be imposed—and the fine against Lewis, but remanded the case for redetermination of the union fine.

DAVID GORDON

UNITED NATIONS CHARTER
59 Stat. 1031 (1945)

The United Nations Charter, a multilateral treaty which serves as the "constitution" of the United Nations Organization, was drafted in San Francisco at the United Nations Conference on International Organization in 1945 and ratified by fifty-one original member states. Like the Constitution of the United States, the charter has proved to be a flexible instrument subject to broad interpretation.

The charter was ratified by the United States Senate, 89–2, and it became law, binding both internally and externally, when it entered into force on October 24, 1945. Treaties, properly executed and ratified, are international law, at least formally, and in the United States they also are domestic law by virtue of the SUPREMACY CLAUSE of Article IV of the Constitution.

Despite the charter's nearly unanimous endorsement by the Senate, it was eagerly suggested that, in removing the right of the United States to go to war at will and in authorizing the Security Council to commit the member states to war in certain circumstances, the charter improperly delegated to the United Nations powers and functions belonging to the federal government, including the power to declare war, vested in Congress, and the power to conduct war, vested primarily in the President as commander-in-chief.

Congress and the President are not, however, deprived by the charter of the powers to declare and conduct war, only of the right to exercise these powers in contravention of international law (including the charter). All treaties, the charter included, limit only the international legal right—not the constitutional authority—of states to do freely that which is within their power to do freely in the absence of a treaty. Moreover, as a sovereign nation, the United States has the final authority to decide how it will comply with the particular terms and requirements of a treaty; and as a permanent member of the Security Council, the United States retains, in any event, an absolute veto over any action that would commit the United States to unwelcome policy. When Congress and the President act to comply with their charter obligations, in accordance with the United Nations Participation Act of 1945, they do so pursuant to the TREATY POWER and to their more general FOREIGN AFFAIRS powers.

Another, more recent, matter of constitutional concern is the question of whether United States courts, state and federal, are bound by the human rights clauses of the charter and related instruments, such as the Universal Declaration of Human Rights. The United States Supreme Court has never addressed the question of whether the charter's human rights provisions are self-executing in the United States; lower courts have answered that question in the negative.

BURNS H. WESTON

Bibliography

CAHILL, J. 1952 "The United Nations Charter as Law of the Land." *Albany Law Review* 15–16:51–57.

Charter of the United Nations and Statute of the International Court of Justice. Office of Public Information, United Nations, New York.

GOODRICH, M. and HAMBRO, E. 1949 *Charter of the United Nations: Commentary and Documents.* Boston: World Peace Foundation.

HENKIN, LOUIS 1972 *Foreign Affairs and the Constitution.* Mineola, N.Y.: Foundation Press.

UNITED RAILWAYS & ELECTRIC CO. OF BALTIMORE v. WEST
280 U.S. 234 (1930)

This obscure case has no significance except to illustrate how the Supreme Court manipulated the FAIR RETURN rule of SMYTH V. AMES (1898) to prevent rate regulation, which the Court disapproved. A public service commission fixed rates that permitted the company to earn a profit of 6.26 percent. The company sought rates returning 7.44 percent. The Court used SUBSTANTIVE DUE PROCESS to void the commission's rates and decided that rates returning "7½ percent, or even 8 percent, on the value of the property" might be "necessary to avoid confiscation." Justices LOUIS D. BRANDEIS, OLIVER W. HOLMES, and HARLAN FISKE STONE dissented.

LEONARD W. LEVY

UNITED STATES v. . . .

See entry under name of other party

UNITED STATES COIN & CURRENCY, UNITED STATES v.

See: *United States v. Marchetti*

UNITED STATES COURT OF APPEALS FOR THE FEDERAL CIRCUIT

This court was created by the FEDERAL COURTS IMPROVEMENT ACT (1982), to take over the JURISDICTION of the COURT OF CUSTOMS AND PATENT APPEALS and the COURT OF CLAIMS. Its first judges were the judges of the superseded courts. It is a CONSTITUTIONAL COURT, whose twelve judges serve for life during good behavior.

The Federal Circuit, like the other UNITED STATES COURTS OF APPEALS, is an intermediate appellate court; its jurisdiction, however, is defined not by region but by subject matter. It has nationwide jurisdiction to hear APPEALS in cases chiefly of the types previously heard by the superseded courts: customs and patent matters, and claims against the United States. In the future, however, other types of cases may be added to the Federal Circuit's jurisdiction—tax appeals, for example. Such developments might relieve some of the pressure on the Supreme Court's docket, effectively removing certain technical and specialized areas from the Court's workload. Many proponents of the 1982 act regard the creation of this opportunity as the act's most important achievement.

KENNETH L. KARST

UNITED STATES COURTS OF APPEALS

The United States Courts of Appeals form the intermediate component of the three-tiered federal judiciary, lying between the UNITED STATES DISTRICT COURTS and the SUPREME COURT of the United States. As such, they normally serve as the first courts of review in the federal JUDICIAL SYSTEM. But because of the natural limitations upon the Supreme Court's capacity, the Courts of Appeals are often also the final courts of review.

Article III, section 1, of the Constitution provides: "The JUDICIAL POWER OF THE UNITED STATES, shall be vested in one supreme Court, and in such inferior Courts as the Congress may from time to time ordain and establish." Thus, in contrast to the Supreme Court, inferior federal courts were not required by the Constitution; rather, their creation was left to the discretion of Congress. Such treatment reflected a compromise between two views, one favoring the mandatory creation of inferior courts, and the other completely opposed to the existence of any such courts.

The Courts of Appeals are relative newcomers to the federal judicial system, having been born with the CIRCUIT COURTS OF APPEALS ACT (Evarts Act) of 1891. The Courts of Appeals were created to solve an acute crisis in the federal judiciary stemming from the limited capacity of the existing system, which had remained largely unchanged since the JUDICIARY ACT

OF 1789. That act had established a bilevel system of inferior federal courts. There were, first of all, single-judge "district courts," generally one per state. The Union was also divided into several "circuits." CIRCUIT COURT was to be held twice a year in each of the districts encompassed by a given circuit. At these sittings, cases would be heard by a three-judge panel consisting of two Supreme Court Justices and the district judge for the district in which the circuit court was being held.

Having determined to avail itself of its constitutional prerogative to establish inferior federal courts, Congress faced the further issue of those courts' appropriate function and JURISDICTION. In the debates over Article III, there had been substantial support for giving Congress the power to create only admiralty courts, rather than inferior courts of general jurisdiction. No such limitation was adopted, however. It has therefore been generally assumed that Congress is constitutionally free to define the role of the inferior federal courts however it chooses.

The manner that Congress selected in the 1789 act is of some interest. The district courts were, and remain today, trial courts or courts of first instance. The circuit courts, in distinct contrast to today's middle-tier courts, also functioned primarily as trial courts. In the area of private civil law, the circuit courts' jurisdiction was largely concurrent with that of the district courts: it encompassed cases within the DIVERSITY JURISDICTION, but not FEDERAL QUESTION cases. (Original federal jurisdiction was not extended to federal question cases until 1875.) Similarly, with respect to civil suits by the United States, both circuit and district courts were given ORIGINAL JURISDICTION, the only difference being that the requisite amount in controversy was higher for circuit court jurisdiction.

The circuit courts even had certain original jurisdiction that the district courts lacked. The first removal jurisdiction was vested in the circuit courts alone. And the circuit courts had exclusive jurisdiction over most federal crimes.

Nonetheless, the seeds of the modern federal courts of appeals were planted by the first Judiciary Act. The early circuit courts had appellate jurisdiction in civil cases involving disputes over amounts exceeding $50, and in admiralty cases exceeding $300. (A district judge sitting as a circuit judge was not, however, permitted to vote on appeals from his own decisions.) Unlike the modern courts of appeals, however, the circuit courts were the final federal forum for many of these cases. In civil suits, circuit court judgments were reviewable only when the amount in dispute exceeded $2,000. Judgments in criminal cases were categorically unreviewable.

The early circuit courts proved problematic, in the main because of the burden that circuit riding placed on the Supreme Court Justices. Congress attempted to alleviate that hardship by reducing from two to one the number of Justices required to sit on a circuit court, but the benefit of the reduction was more than outweighed by several important augmentations of the High Court's jurisdiction that were enacted by Congress during the century following the 1789 Judiciary Act. Most notable of such legislation was the JUDICIARY ACT OF 1875, which granted the lower courts, as well as the Supreme Court, nearly the full scope of Article III jurisdiction, including original federal question jurisdiction in the district and circuit courts. The federal courts, already vastly overloaded with cases, were virtually submerged after this act. Reform was inevitable.

Indeed, attempts to improve the judicial system had more than once been made. In 1801 Congress had enacted the JUDICIARY ACT OF 1801 (the "Law of the Midnight Judges"), which among other things had established permanent circuit judgeships, three to a circuit. When political tides shifted the following year, however, the act was repealed, and the system reverted essentially to its original condition, except that Congress permitted circuit court to be held by a single judge, rather than three. Much later, in 1869, Congress partially restored the plan of 1801 by creating a single permanent circuit judgeship for each of the nine circuits then in existence. And in 1887 and 1888 Congress passed a series of measures aimed at pruning the expanded jurisdiction of the lower federal courts.

But it was not until the Evarts Act that Congress provided structural reforms adequate to the crisis of judicial overload. The act established three-judge courts of appeals for each of the nine circuits, and increased the number of permanent circuit judgeships to two per circuit. The third appeals judge would in most instances be a district judge (though Supreme Court Justices remained eligible), but the act, following the rule set down by the Act of 1789, barred district judges from reviewing their own decisions.

Curiously, the Evarts Act left the old circuit courts standing, although it did remove their APPELLATE JURISDICTION. Until these courts were abolished in 1911, there thus functioned two sets of federal trial courts.

The Evarts Act provided for direct review by the Supreme Court of the decisions of the district courts and the old circuit courts, in some important cases.

The new circuit courts of appeals would review the remainder. Under the act, a circuit court's decision in an admiralty or diversity case would be final, unless that court certified a question to the Supreme Court or the Supreme Court granted a WRIT OF CERTIORARI in order to review the circuit court's decision. In most other cases, circuit court decisions were appealable as of right.

Since the Evarts Act, only a few significant alterations have been made to the federal judicial system in general, and the courts of appeals in particular. The rules governing Supreme Court review are perhaps the most important arena of change. In 1925, Congress replaced appeal as of right with discretionary review for all circuit court judgments except those holding a state statute unconstitutional. In 1937, Congress passed a law permitting appeal to the Supreme Court from any judgment by a federal court holding an act of Congress unconstitutional in any civil case to which the United States is a party.

In 1948 the circuit courts established by the Evarts Act were renamed; each court is now known as the United States Court of Appeals for the______Circuit. The number of circuits has also been increased; and there is now a "Federal Circuit" court to hear appeals from the CLAIMS COURT and from district courts in patent cases or in cases arising under the TUCKER ACT. Finally, procedures in the various courts of appeals were standardized in 1968 in the Federal Rules of Appellate Procedure. Each circuit, however, retains its own rule-making power for matters not covered by the Federal Rules.

The chief work of the courts of appeals is the review of final judgments of the United States district courts. The courts, however, are also empowered to review certain orders that are not strictly final, essentially when the benefit of such review clearly outweighs any attendant disruption and delay of district court proceedings. In addition, Congress has enabled the appeals courts to issue the extraordinary WRIT OF MANDAMUS and WRIT OF PROHIBITION in cases in which district courts may abuse their constitutional powers. Finally, the statutes governing many of the various federal administrative agencies provide for direct review of agency adjudication and rule-making in the court of appeals for the circuit in which the party seeking review resides, or in the Court of Appeals for the District of Columbia Circuit. The latter circuit court has been a frequent forum for challenges, constitutional and otherwise, to federal agency action.

To understand the role of the courts of appeals in the development of constitutional law, it is necessary to understand the relationship between the appeals courts and the Supreme Court. As was noted above, since the JUDICIARY ACT OF 1925, the "Judges Bill," the Supreme Court has had a discretionary power of review of most circuit court decisions. Again, however, appeal as of right lies in cases in which the appeals court has held a state statute to be repugnant to the Constitution, laws, or treaties of the United States, and in civil cases in which either a court of appeals or a district court has held an act of Congress unconstitutional and the United States is a party. Nonetheless, neither type of case in which appeal is of right bulks very large in the overall volume of appeals from circuit courts, and of those, many are denied Supreme Court review for want of a substantial federal question.

Accordingly, the Supreme Court has the discretion to review or not to review the vast majority of decisions by the courts of appeals. Not surprisingly, because of the limited capacity of the High Court, its discretion is much more often exercised to deny review than to grant it. As a general rule, in fact, the Supreme Court tends not to review appeals court decisions unless the issues involved either have an urgent importance or have received conflicting treatment by different circuits, or both.

One might conclude that, because the Supreme Court does review important cases, the appeals courts have no significant role in the development of constitutional law. Constitutional law, however, is not the product solely of the Supreme Court.

To begin, the Supreme Court can only review a decision that a party seeks to have reviewed; not every losing party in the court of appeals may do so. For example, in *Kennedy v. Sampson* (1974) the District of Columbia Circuit construed the POCKET VETO clause of the Constitution (Article 1, section 7, clause 2) to bar the President from exercising the pocket veto power during brief, intrasession adjournments of Congress. The President then declined to seek review in the Supreme Court; he chose instead to acquiesce in the rule laid down by the appeals court. The court's decision thus became a cornerstone of the law respecting the presentation of laws for presidential approval.

Of course, as a glance at any constitutional law textbook or casebook reveals, the vast majority of important constitutional PRECEDENTS are produced not by the courts of appeals but by the Supreme Court. Decisions like *Kennedy* are thus the exception, not the rule. Nonetheless, in several ways the appeals courts contribute significantly to the development of constitutional law.

Before a constitutional issue is decided by the Supreme Court, it will often have received a thorough ventilation by one or more circuit courts. The Supreme Court thus has the benefit of the circuit judges' consideration of difficult constitutional matters, and may sometimes explicitly adopt the reasoning of the court of appeals. For example, in *United States v. Dennis* (1950) the Second Circuit faced the difficult issue of whether, and if so, how, the CLEAR AND PRESENT DANGER test applied to a conspiracy to advocate the overthrow of the government by force and violence and to organize a political party for the purpose of such advocacy. The Court of Appeals, in an opinion by Judge LEARNED HAND, held that such advocacy was unprotected by the FIRST AMENDMENT even though the actual forceful overthrow of the government was not imminent. The Supreme Court affirmed the decision in DENNIS V. UNITED STATES (1951), and its opinion adopted much of Judge Hand's analysis, including Judge Hand's "clear and present danger" formula, namely, "whether the gravity of the 'evil,' discounted by its improbability, justifies such invasion of free speech as is necessary to avoid the danger."

The role of the courts of appeals in resolving novel issues of constitutional law, however, is only half of the picture. Equally important is the appeals courts' adjudication of cases raising issues on which the Supreme Court has already spoken. Because the High Court can only sketch the broad outlines of constitutional DOCTRINE, it remains for the lower courts to apply precedent, elaborate or clarify it, and extrapolate from it. Because appeal from the district courts to the appeals court is of right, and because most litigation never reaches the Supreme Court, it is in the courts of appeals that the Supreme Court's sketch is worked into a fully drawn landscape.

When the Supreme Court decides not to give plenary review to a case arising from an appeals court, what implication should be drawn concerning the value of the appeals court's opinion as a precedent? By denying a petition for certiorari or dismissing an appeal as of right for want of jurisdiction, the Court formally indicates no view of the merits or demerits of the appeals court's decision. Nonetheless, it is commonly thought that the Supreme Court generally does not decline to review an appeals court decision that it finds clearly incorrect. Similarly, when the Supreme Court summarily affirms an appeals court's decision, it is formally signaling its agreement with the result only, and not necessarily the reasoning of the lower court. Yet, such affirmances are popularly thought to indicate at least the Court's tentative agreement with the substance of the lower court's opinion.

Since the early 1960s, the federal courts at all three levels have experienced a dramatic and continuing increase in their workload. At the district and circuit levels, Congress has responded by adding judges to existing courts. When the number of judges in a circuit has become sufficiently great, Congress has divided the circuit into two. That course is not entirely satisfactory, however, because it tends to push the appeals courts in the direction of being regional, rather than national courts, and increases the likelihood of intercircuit conflict.

At the Supreme Court level, Congress has made no significant changes. Various proposals for reducing the Court's workload would also affect adjudication at the appeals court level. A frequent suggestion has been to establish a national court of appeals. In one version, the national court would sit only to resolve conflicts among the circuits, thereby eliminating a significant share of the Supreme Court's annual docket. In another version, the national court would screen cases to determine those worthy of Supreme Court review. Another proposal would reduce the Supreme Court's workload by eliminating appeal as of right. One effect of such a measure, of course, would be to increase the number of appeals court decisions that are effectively final.

CARL MCGOWAN

Bibliography

BATOR, PAUL M.; MISHKIN, PAUL J.; SHAPIRO, DAVID L.; and WECHSLER, HERBERT 1973 *Hart and Wechsler's The Federal Courts and the Federal System,* 2nd ed. Mineola, N.Y.: Foundation Press.

WRIGHT, CHARLES A. 1983 *Handbook of the Law of Federal Courts.* St. Paul, Minn.: West Publishing Co.

UNITED STATES DISTRICT COURT FOR THE EASTERN DISTRICT OF MICHIGAN, UNITED STATES v.
407 U.S. 297 (1972)

Most Presidents have claimed inherent executive authority to use electronic surveillance for national security purposes without complying with conventional FOURTH AMENDMENT requirements such as prior court approval. In several earlier decisions, such as KATZ V. UNITED STATES (1967), and in the 1968 statute authorizing federal and state officials to use ELECTRONIC EAVESDROPPING, the issue had been left open.

During the VIETNAM WAR, Attorney General John N. Mitchell approved a wiretap "to gather intelligence information deemed necessary to protect the nation from attempts of domestic organizations to attack and subvert the existing structure of the government." The Supreme Court unanimously ruled that where threats by *domestic* organizations were concerned, neither section 2511(3) of the 1968 act nor the Constitution gave the President authority to use electronic surveillance without first obtaining a warrant from a magistrate. The Court thus rejected the President's claim of INHERENT POWER. The Court did not decide whether the Fourth Amendment's warrant requirement applied to activities of foreign powers or their agents; a 1978 statute now governs this. The Court also suggested that Congress could authorize standards for intelligence gathering for domestic security purposes that are less stringent than for law enforcement; Congress has not done so.

HERMAN SCHWARTZ

UNITED STATES DISTRICT COURTS

In enacting Article III, the Framers of the Constitution authorized the establishment of a federal judicial system consisting of a SUPREME COURT and such inferior courts as Congress might decide to establish. In the JUDICIARY ACT OF 1789 Congress created a Supreme Court, divided the country into three circuits, authorized a CIRCUIT COURT to sit in each circuit, and established a federal district court in each of the states. The Supreme Court was the only truly appellate court in the system. Unlike the modern courts of appeal, the old circuit courts, while exercising some appellate jurisdiction, were intended to be the chief federal trial courts. A Supreme Court Justice riding the circuit and judges of the district courts in the circuit manned each of these circuit courts.

The federal district courts were empowered to sit at various times in specified locations within the states where they were located. They were tribunals of very limited JURISDICTION and originally had as their main function the adjudication of admiralty and maritime matters. It was anticipated that the state trial courts or federal circuit courts would handle, as trial courts, the most important legal issues facing the new nation. The federal district courts were empowered to try minor criminal cases. In addition, they had CONCURRENT JURISDICTION with the circuit courts over suits by ALIENS for tort violations of a treaty or the law of nations, suits against consuls, and disputes in which the federal government initiated the proceeding and the matter in controversy was $100 or less. However, district court jurisdiction was exclusive in admiralty, over seizures of land for violation of federal statutes, and over seizures under import, navigation, and trade statutes.

This limited and specialized jurisdiction has steadily expanded. Today the district court is the only federal nonspecialized court, handling both criminal and civil matters. Among the latter are admiralty cases, federal question cases, and cases within the DIVERSITY JURISDICTION (cases between different states). In a diversity case the matter in controversy must exceed $10,000. No jurisdictional amount is normally required for the other exercises of the district court's civil jurisdiction. Appeals from a district court go to the UNITED STATES COURT OF APPEALS.

The first district court to be organized was the district court of New York. That court began functioning on November 3, 1789, and was the predecessor to the current district court for the Southern District of New York. Even today judges of the Southern District refer to theirs as the "Mother Court."

As the system was originally conceived, each state was to contain at least one federal district and one federal court. There has been no deviation from this pattern as the country has expanded from thirteen to fifty states. In addition, the DISTRICT OF COLUMBIA and the federal TERRITORIES (the Virgin Islands, PUERTO RICO, and Guam) are each organized as a federal district with a district court. In over half the states, although there may be a number of federal district judges who sit in separate locations throughout the state, there is only one federal district. Twelve states are divided into two federal districts; some states have three federal districts; and California, New York, and Texas are subdivided into four federal districts.

As the country has expanded, the number of federal district judges has increased. Since 1954 the roster of federal judges has grown through enactment of legislation authorizing additional judgeships for federal district courts nationwide. The Omnibus Judgeship Act of 1978 raised the number of authorized district judges from 399 to 516. The Southern District of New York has twenty-seven authorized judgeships, the largest number of any district in the country.

Federal district judges are nominated by the President and appointed with the ADVICE AND CONSENT of the Senate. The prevailing practice is for the selection of the nominee to come to the President from the Department of Justice. If one or both of the senators from the state in question belong to the President's party, the candidate for nomination is proposed by one or both senators and submitted to the Department of Justice for approval and recommendation to the President for nomination. Today few candidates are nominated and sent to the Senate for confirmation without first being found qualified by the American Bar Association. When the President decides to nominate a candidate, the Federal Bureau of Investigation undertakes a security check. If the candidate is cleared, the President announces the nomination and sends the name to the Senate. The Senate Judiciary Committee holds hearings, which are usually one-day affairs for candidates for federal district courts. If the Senate Judiciary Committee approves, the nomination is voted on by the full Senate.

An Article III judge has life tenure during GOOD BEHAVIOR, and his salary cannot be diminished while he is in office. The only way to remove a federal district judge from office is by IMPEACHMENT. Of course, a federal judge, like any other person, may be prosecuted for criminal law violations. Bribery has been the most frequent charge, but criminal prosecutions of federal judges are rare and attempts to remove them by impeachment have been infrequent.

When the first change of political power occurred in the United States at the national level, from the Federalist party to the Republican party of THOMAS JEFFERSON, the Jeffersonians commenced impeachment proceedings against two judges appointed by the Federalists and disliked by the Republicans: JOHN PICKERING, a judge of the district court in New Hampshire, and SAMUEL CHASE, an Associate Justice of the Supreme Court. Pickering was convicted by the Senate in 1803, but the requisite two-thirds Senate majority could not be mustered to convict Chase. Since that time impeachment to unseat a federal judge has not been a successful political weapon. Partisan politics has from time to time generated unsuccessful calls for impeachment of various judges.

A federal district court judgeship carries considerable prestige. It is a presidential appointment; it is a national rather than a local office; and federal district court judgeships are limited in number. District judges in the main have had prior careers as prominent or distinguished lawyers before going on the bench. They are drawn for the most part from the middle and upper strata of our society. They are generally alumni of the best known law schools of the nation or of the state in which they will serve. They have generally had successful careers in private practice, often with backgrounds as federal, state, or local prosecutors. A few are former academics, and some come to court from public service careers outside government.

Until the twentieth century, all federal district judges were white males. The first woman to be confirmed as a federal judge was Florence Allen, who was appointed to the Court of Appeals for the Sixth Circuit in 1934. The first woman appointed to the district court was Burneta Matthews, who was given an interim appointment to the District of Columbia bench in 1949. She was confirmed by the Senate in 1950 for a permanent appointment. Constance Baker Motley was the first black woman to be appointed to the federal bench. She was appointed to the District Court for the Southern District of New York in 1966, and in 1982 became chief judge of that court.

WILLIAM HASTIE was the first black to be made a federal judge. He was appointed to the District Court of the Virgin Islands in 1937 and in 1949 was named to the Court of Appeals for the Third Circuit. James Parsons, appointed judge of the Northern District of Illinois in 1961, was the first black named a district judge in the continental United States. Since these initial appointments the number of blacks, women, and members of other ethnic minorities has grown steadily.

The first Judiciary Act authorized each court to make rules for conducting its own business, and in 1842 the Supreme Court was empowered to regulate process, pleading, proof and DISCOVERY in EQUITY, admiralty, and law cases in the district and circuit courts. In 1938 uniform rules for conducting civil cases, entitled the FEDERAL RULES OF CIVIL PROCEDURE, were adopted for the federal system. In 1946 the FEDERAL RULES OF CRIMINAL PROCEDURE were enacted. These rules have achieved uniformity of procedure and practice in the federal district courts throughout the nation.

The typical calendar of civil cases in a federal district court contains a plethora of complex cases involving PATENT, trademark, and COPYRIGHT infringement claims; federal securities law violations; CIVIL RIGHTS infractions; private antitrust claims; shareholders' derivative suits; IMMIGRATION and NATURALIZATION cases; employment, age, and housing discrimination claims; and claims under a variety of other federal statutes, such as the FREEDOM OF INFORMATION ACT, Investment Advisers Act, Commodities Exchange Act, FAIR LABOR STANDARDS ACT, and Federal Employers' Liability Act. In addition, there are seamen's injury and cargo damage claims, HABEAS CORPUS petitions by both state and federal prisoners, and litigation based on diversity jurisdiction. The criminal case load involves a variety of infractions defined in the United States criminal code.

Among the primary functions of the federal district courts are the vindication of federal rights secured by the Constitution and laws of the United States.

The federal district court is often called upon to hold a state law or act unconstitutional because it violates federal constitutional guarantees or has been preempted by federal legislation. Obviously, the exercise of this power by federal district courts has the potential for creating friction and disharmony between state and federal courts. A lower federal court's power to strike down a state law on federal constitutional grounds, in the face of a contrary ruling by the highest court of the state, is not an easy pill for state judges to swallow. Federal courts have devised doctrines of COMITY and ABSTENTION to ease the friction. A growing number of federal judges, recognizing that state judges, too, have a duty to protect and enforce federal rights, have been inclined to give increasing deference to state court determinations of federal constitutional questions.

A burgeoning federal caseload undoubtedly promotes this inclination toward accommodation and also promotes a tightening of limitations on federal habeas corpus review of state court criminal convictions. A habeas corpus petition enables a state prisoner, after unsuccessfully appealing his conviction through the state court system, to have the matter reviewed by the federal district court to determine whether the trial and conviction violated the defendant's federal constitutional rights. Not surprisingly, habeas corpus petitions have inundated the federal courts. While most are without merit, the few petitions of substance that succeed are another cause of federal–state court friction. Rules of limitations have been imposed requiring exhaustion of state remedies and forbidding review if the state court's denial of the appeal of the criminal conviction rests on the defendant's failure to conform to state governing procedure absent a showing of cause and prejudice. (See WAINWRIGHT V. SYKES, 1977.)

Diversity jurisdiction brings to the federal courts issues of state law that would ordinarily be tried in the state courts. The initial justification for giving federal courts jurisdiction over such cases was concern that parochialism would put the out-of-state complainant at a disadvantage in seeking redress in state court against a resident of the forum state.

Exercise of federal diversity jurisdiction was at one time a cause of federal–state confusion if not friction. The district courts in diversity cases have been required to follow applicable state statutes, but until 1938 they were free to disregard state decisional law and decide on the basis of their own notions of what the COMMON LAW was or should be. With the Supreme Court's decision in ERIE RAILROAD V. TOMPKINS (1938) federal courts were no longer free to disregard state court decisions. Federal courts may apply their own rules as to pleading and practice but on substantive issues must function as adjuncts of the state judiciary.

ERIE V. TOMPKINS has made clear that the diversity jurisdiction is a wasteful use of federal judicial resources. State court parochialism is no longer a justifiable basis for federal diversity jurisdiction. Because the federal court must apply state law, apart from federal procedural rules, the litigant is seldom better off in federal court than he would be if relegated to state courts, where increasing numbers of federal judges feel such cases belong. Congress, however, has shown little interest in divesting federal district courts of the diversity jurisdiction.

The federal district court is the place where litigation usually commences to test the constitutional validity of state or federal governmental action with national implication. These TEST CASES usually seek injunctive relief or DECLARATORY JUDGMENTS. These are suits in EQUITY; thus no jury is empaneled, and the district judge must determine both the facts and the law. The judge will articulate his or her findings of the facts and legal conclusions as to the constitutional validity of the governmental action being tested. The trial record and the district court's analysis are thus extremely important for appellate courts, particularly in cases of first impression.

It is the district court that decides in the first instance whether the government is violating a newspaper's FIRST AMENDMENT rights, an accused's RIGHT AGAINST SELF-INCRIMINATION, or a minority citizen's right to the equal protection of the laws. Organizations such as the AMERICAN CIVIL LIBERTIES UNION, the National Association for the Advancement of Colored People, Jehovah's Witnesses, environmental groups, corporations, and individuals initiate litigation in the district court to test the constitutionality of some federal, state, or local legislation or practice. (See TEST CASES.)

Such a case was *McLean v. Arkansas Board of Education* (D. Ark., 1982). The American Civil Liberties Union sought to challenge an Arkansas law requiring that creationism—a biblical story of man's and the world's creation, as opposed to Darwin's evolutionary theory for explaining the genesis of mankind—be taught in the public schools. The issue was tried first in the federal district court, which framed the issue in these terms: is creationism a religious doctrine or a valid scientific theory? The court heard and weighed testimony, chiefly from experts on both sides, and held that the Arkansas statute was an unconstitutional ESTABLISHMENT OF RELIGION.

Sometimes prior DOCTRINE has forecast the outcome. For instance, although the SEPARATE BUT EQUAL DOCTRINE on which school SEGREGATION had been founded was not overruled until BROWN V. BOARD OF EDUCATION (1954), earlier decisions such as SWEATT V. PAINTER (1950) and *McLaurin v. Oklahoma State Regents* (1950) pointed to that overruling. Nonetheless, the record amassed by several district courts, showing the psychological and education deprivation inflicted by segregation on black children, was crucial in enabling the Supreme Court to take the final step of overruling PLESSY V. FERGUSON (1896) and holding that segregated schools violated the right of minority school children to equal protection of the law.

Similarly, a federal district court facing a constitutional challenge to the HYDE AMENDMENT, a congressional provision largely denying Medicaid funds for the cost of abortions, held hearings for about a year. The trial record contained some 400 exhibits and 5,000 pages of testimony. The judge was required to digest this mountain of testimonial and documentary evidence and prepare cohesive findings of facts and conclusions of law. (See HARRIS V. MCRAE, 1980.)

The need for so long a trial and the condensation of so voluminous a record into a coherent decision is not commonplace. However, it is not unusual for a district judge to be required to master the facts in a complex trial lasting many months, and to set forth the facts found and legal conclusions in a comprehensive fashion.

In some cases the district court, as a supplement to its own adjudicative fact-finding, must make findings as to LEGISLATIVE FACTS as well. For instance, in FULLILOVE V. KLUTZNICK (1980) Congress had required at least ten percent of federal funds granted for local public works projects to be set aside for minority businesses. This legislation was attacked as unconstitutional racial discrimination. The district court framed the issue as the power of Congress to remedy past discrimination. The district judge relied on congressional findings that minorities had been denied access to entrepreneurial opportunities provided in building construction works financed by public funds. Based on this legislative finding and Congress's purpose to take remedial action, the district court found the set-aside to be a legitimate remedial act. The Supreme Court adopted this rationale, and upheld the quota.

At times, in a constitutional controversy, the district court, although adhering to judicial precedent requiring it to dismiss the constitutional challenge, may help to bring about a reversal of precedent by recognizing that a wrong exists which should be remedied. BAKER V. CARR (1962) was a challenge to Tennessee's malapportioned legislature. The district court, in its opinion, carefully and sympathetically tracked the contentions of the plaintiffs that the legislators had condoned gross inequality in legislative REPRESENTATION and debased the VOTING RIGHTS of a large number of citizens. The court, however, relied on COLEGROVE V. GREEN (1946) and dismissed the action. On review of this order, the Supreme Court ruled that the plaintiffs' allegations had stated a case within the district court's jurisdiction. Subsequently, REYNOLDS V. SIMS (1964) embodied the Supreme Court's famous ONE PERSON, ONE VOTE principle, requiring legislative districts to be constructed as nearly as possible of an equal number of voters. (See REAPPORTIONMENT.)

Issues of such magnitude are highly charged; it is not unusual, in these controversial circumstances, for the judge who decides a case contrary to the majority's view to face public criticism and in some cases even social ostracism.

Judge Waties Waring's unpopular decision in favor of blacks in voting and school cases led to his social ostracism in Charleston, South Carolina; Judge Skelly Wright became anathema to many whites in New Orleans for the same reason, and escaped that environment through appointment to the Court of Appeals of the District of Columbia Circuit. Similarly, Judge William Ray Overton, who decided the creationism case adversely to local sentiments, and Judge James B. MacMillan, who ordered a complex program of SCHOOL BUSING in Charlotte, North Carolina, were subjected to severe community criticism.

Although not so dramatic as the examples given, public criticism meets almost every district judge at one time or another for rendering an unpopular decision. Because most public controversies have a way of ending up in the federal courts, district judges must decide whether seniority systems must be modified to prevent the employment gains of minorities and women from being wiped out; whether regulations requiring physicians to report to parents abortions performed on teenagers are valid; whether the overcrowding and the rundown conditions of a prison require it to be closed; or whether permitting school authorities to provide for prayer or meditation violates the SEPARATION OF CHURCH AND STATE. The district judge normally sits alone, and does not share decision with others, as do federal appellate judges—and therefore is singularly exposed to abuse and pressure.

Life tenure helps secure the independence of the district judge in facing such issues. This independence is crucial, not only for the judge but also for a constitutional system that seeks to secure the rights of the unpopular and despised.

ROBERT L. CARTER

Bibliography

ADMINISTRATIVE OFFICE OF THE UNITED STATES COURT. *Annual Report of the Director.* Washington, D.C.: Government Printing Office.

CLARK, D. S. 1981 Adjudication to Administration: A Statistical Analysis of Federal District Courts in the 20th Century. *Southern California Law Review* 55:65–152.

HALL, KERMIT 1976 The Antebellum Lower Federal Judiciary, 1829–1861. *Vanderbilt Law Review* 29:1089–1129.

——— 1981 California's Lower Federal First Judicial Appointments. *Hastings Law Journal* 32:819–837.

HENDERSON, DWIGHT F. 1971 *Courts for a New Nation.* Washington, D.C.: Public Affairs Press.

HOUGH, CHARLES M. 1934 *The U.S. District Court for the Southern District of New York.* New York: Maritime Law Association.

Management Statistic for United States Courts. 1981.

STECKLER, WILLIAM E. 1978 Future of the Federal District Courts. *Indiana Law Review* 11:601–620.

SURRENCY, ERWIN C. 1963 History of Federal Courts. *Missouri Law Review* 28:214–244.

THOMPSON, FRANK, JR. 1970 Impeachment of Federal Judges: A Historical Overview. *North Carolina Law Review* 49:87–121.

UNITED STATES RAILROAD RETIREMENT BOARD v. FRITZ

See: Rational Basis; Substantive Due Process

UNITED STATES TRUST CO. v. NEW JERSEY
431 U.S. 1 (1977)

This decision marked the beginning of the modern revitalization of the CONTRACT CLAUSE as a limitation on state legislative power. New York and New Jersey had promised, on issuing bonds to support their Port Authority, to limit severely their use of Authority revenues to subsidize rail passenger transportation. Twelve years later the states sought to divert commuters from automobiles to railroads; they raised bridge and tunnel tolls and, repealing their earlier promise, authorized use of the increased revenues to subsidize commuter railroads. The Supreme Court, 4–3, held the repeal unconstitutional as an impairment of the OBLIGATION OF CONTRACT.

The dissenters, led by Justice WILLIAM J. BRENNAN, accurately described the decision as the first in nearly forty years to invalidate economic legislation under the contract clause and argued vigorously for maintaining judicial deference to legislative power. For the majority, Justice HARRY A. BLACKMUN commented that the outright repeal had deprived bondholders of an important security interest and could be justified only if it were both "reasonable and necessary to serve an important public purpose." The repeal failed this heightened STANDARD OF REVIEW, because alternative means of diverting commuters to railroads were available: taxing parking or gasoline, for example.

KENNETH L. KARST

(SEE ALSO: *Allied Structural Steel Co. v. Spannaus, 1978.*)

UNITED STEELWORKERS OF AMERICA v. WEBER
443 U.S. 193 (1979)

This was one of an important series of decisions upholding the legality of AFFIRMATIVE ACTION. In *Weber,* the Court held, 5–2, in an opinion by Justice WILLIAM J. BRENNAN, that a private affirmative action plan reserving for blacks fifty percent of the openings in a training program leading to plant employment did not violate Title VII of the CIVIL RIGHTS ACT OF 1964. *Weber* left open important questions about the permissible scope of affirmative action, including whether governments might resort to affirmative action without violating the Fifth or FOURTEENTH AMENDMENT, and the extent to which private affirmative action programs may "trammel the interests" of white employees.

THEODORE EISENBERG

UNREASONABLE SEARCH

"Unreasonable" is the controlling word in the FOURTH AMENDMENT. In its first clause the amendment guarantees the right of the people to be free from unreasonable SEARCHES AND SEIZURES; its second clause stipulates the terms for issuance of a judicial warrant: probable cause, oath or affirmation, particularity of description. What is an unreasonable and therefore forbidden search? Conversely, what is a reasonable and permitted one? The amendment does not say. The answer, in large measure, depends on one's understanding of the relationship of the two clauses.

Two polar positions have dominated debate in the Supreme Court on this matter. The view that was in the ascendancy before 1946 and that has generally prevailed again since CHIMEL V. CALIFORNIA (1969), treats the two clauses in conjunction so that the unreasonable searches forbidden by the first clause are defined by the warrant requirements in the second clause: a reasonable search is one conducted subject to a proper warrant, an unreasonable search is one that is not. A second view, generally dominant between HARRIS V. UNITED STATES (1946) and 1969, holds that reasonableness is an autonomous principle, to be measured by all the circumstances rather than by the securing of a warrant (although this is one factor to be considered).

The conflict between the two readings of "unreasonable" essentially has centered on SEARCH INCIDENT TO ARREST, a recognized "emergency" exception to the warrant requirement since WEEKS V. UNITED STATES (1914). According to the second interpretation, once the privacy of the dwelling has legitimately been invaded to make a lawful arrest, it is reasonable to allow the search (for the purpose of disarming the arrestee and seizing EVIDENCE which he may seek to destroy) to blanket the entire premises in which the arrest was made. This is a matter of the greatest consequence, for the vast majority of searches are carried out incident to arrest. If, however, the warrant requirement is considered to be the core of the amendment, the search must be circumscribed to the extent required by the emergency and therefore confined to the person arrested and the area within his immediate reach.

To treat reasonableness as an independent standard is contrary to both history and logic. On logical grounds there seems little value to stringent warrant requirements that can be readily negated by "reasonable" WARRANTLESS SEARCHES. History, too, sets its face against the notion. The Fourth Amendment's proscription of unreasonable searches, alone among the provisions of the BILL OF RIGHTS to set fair standards for the apprehension and trial of accused persons, has a rich historical background in American, as well as English, experience. The amendment is rooted in the restrictions which seventeenth- and eighteenth-century COMMON LAW judges in England placed on the search power (for example, WILKES CASES, 1763–1770). This power had been abused through the government's relentless hunt for political and religious dissidents during a phase of English history well understood in the colonies. The amendment stems more directly from the public outcry against indiscriminate searches for smuggled goods (authorized by GENERAL WARRANTS known as WRITS OF ASSISTANCE) during the last years of the colonial period in America, notably in Massachusetts. The main object of the Fourth Amendment, to prevent the recurrence of the detested general warrant, was to be accomplished by placing strict limits on the issuance of a warrant. The reasonableness clause, as seems clear from the historical record of the amendment's drafting in the first Congress, was meant to reemphasize, and perhaps strengthen, the warrant requirements in the second clause. To detach the reasonableness clause from the warrant clause by infusing it with independent potency serves to dilute the amendment's protection, exactly the opposite of the result its framers intended. It is insufficient to leave the initial determination of reasonableness to the police, with JUDICIAL REVIEW taking place retrospectively when the prosecutor seeks to introduce the fruits of the search in evidence. Many searches will produce no evidence, and even when evidence is found, the pressure on judges to rule against obviously guilty defendants will be great despite the illegality of the searches.

Consonant with the amendment's history, the Court at one time assigned an even broader meaning to "unreasonable" than is taken by the first view. In BOYD V. UNITED STATES (1886) the Court held that private papers are immune to seizure even under warrant—on the theory that one test of the reasonableness of a search is whether or not its purpose is to seize evidence that will force the person to incriminate himself. In contrast, contraband goods and fruits and instrumentalities of crime are deemed seizable because their possessor has no legal property right in them. In *Gouled v. United States* (1921) the Court logically extended the immunity granted private papers to all kinds of evidentiary materials (for example; clothing). However, this MERE EVIDENCE RULE, as it came to be known, was overturned as "wholly irrational" in WARDEN V. HAYDEN (1967), and probably little remains of the immunity granted to private papers (*Fisher v. United States,* 1976).

Other EXIGENT CIRCUMSTANCES, in addition to search incidental to arrest, which, in either view, permit the police to bypass the warrant requirement, include the rule of CARROLL V. UNITED STATES, (1925), which permits the search of a moving vehicle on PROBABLE CAUSE to believe that it is transporting contraband; the ruling in *Schmerber v. California* (1966), which permits the compulsory taking of a blood sample from a driver to measure its alcoholic content where there is probable cause to believe he was intoxicated while driving; and the rule of *Warden v. Hayden* (1967), which permits the "hot pursuit" of a felon into a dwelling. Even in the absence of evidence that a crime has been committed, where the suspicious conduct of an individual leads an officer to believe that he or others are in danger and imminent action is imperative, he may stop the suspect and "frisk" the individual's outer clothing in order to disarm him of weapons he may be carrying. (See TERRY V. OHIO, 1968.)

In the case of search incidental to arrest, hot pursuit, or STOP AND FRISK, the emergency is self-evident, but it is no less genuine in the case of a moving vehicle or a blood test, for the delay involved in the obtaining of a warrant will usually defeat the object of the search. The automobile might by that time be far away, perhaps in another jurisdiction, and the percentage of alcohol in the blood gradually diminishes once intake ceases. These are only examples. Clearly any real emergency, as the sound of a shot or a cry for help coming from behind closed doors, would justify a warrantless search by the police.

The only kinds of searches known to the framers, and to which the Fourth Amendment was originally addressed, contained two elements: (1) entry into the dwelling (2) for the purpose of seizing evidence of crime. At first the Court considered the definition of search to be governed by this experience and maintained that warrants were not required for more modern types of searches that lacked one or the other of these elements. Thus searches for oral utterances conducted by WIRETAPPING which do not involve entry onto premises, as in OLMSTEAD V. UNITED STATES (1928), or inspection of dwellings to uncover nuisances to public health or safety, as in *Frank v. Maryland* (1959), were held not to be covered by the amendment. Subsequently, however, ELECTRONIC EAVESDROPPING (including wiretapping) and ADMINISTRATIVE SEARCHES were both brought under the amendment's protective umbrella in KATZ V. UNITED STATES (1967) and CAMARA V. MUNICIPAL COURT (1967), respectively. But a visit to the home by a caseworker for the purpose of determining whether a public assistance grant is being properly used does not amount to an unreasonable search and requires no warrant, as the Court held in WYMAN V. JAMES (1971).

A court order for the surgical removal of a bullet from the body of a suspect was ruled unreasonable in *Winston v. Lee* (1985)—at least when the need for the evidence is not "compelling"—because of the serious intrusion on privacy and the medical risks entailed.

In order to prevent the Fourth Amendment from being reduced to a mere parchment guarantee, evidence obtained through unreasonable search has since 1914 been excluded from trials in the federal courts (*Weeks v. United States*), and in the state courts as well since MAPP V. OHIO (1961). (See EXCLUSIONARY RULE.) Although the amendment contains no express command of exclusion, it has been construed to authorize the judiciary to apply such sanctions as are necessary to ensure compliance with the standard of reasonableness.

Like the rest of the Bill of Rights, the ban on unreasonable searches was originally intended to place restrictions only on the federal government. That ban became applicable to the states, as an element of FOURTEENTH AMENDMENT due process, in 1961 (*Mapp v. Ohio*), and the same standard of reasonableness now governs searches made by federal and state authorities (KER V. CALIFORNIA, 1963). (See INCORPORATION DOCTRINE.)

JACOB W. LANDYNSKI

Bibliography

FELLMAN, DAVID 1976 *The Defendant's Rights Today.* Pages 277–284. Madison: University of Wisconsin Press.

LAFAVE, WAYNE R. 1978 *Search and Seizure: A Treatise on the Fourth Amendment.* Vol. 2:406–476, 498–609; vol. 3:2–140. St. Paul, Minn.: West Publishing Co.

LANDYNSKI, JACOB W. 1966 *Search and Seizure and the Supreme Court.* Pp. 30–44, 387–417. Baltimore: Johns Hopkins University Press.

______ 1971 "The Supreme Court's Search for Fourth Amendment Standards: The Warrantless Search." *Connecticut Bar Journal* 45:2–39.

LEVY, LEONARD W. 1974 *Against the Law: The Nixon Court and American Justice.* Pages 75–117. New York: Harper & Row.

UNWRITTEN CONSTITUTION

When the American colonists charged that some British colonial policies and practices were unconstitutional, they appealed to what was generally conceived as an unwritten constitutional tradition that combined the practical good sense of English experience with standards of conduct that were simply, or naturally, equitable and right. Though the principles of this constitutional tradition were scattered among state documents, reported cases of the COMMON LAW, treatises, and other writings, their status derived not from having been written or enacted but from their perceived origin in sources like custom, divine will, reason, and nature. These principles were thought superior to acts of Parliament, whose status did depend on their enactment.

While invoking unwritten HIGHER LAW, however, the colonists were implicitly challenging its efficacy. To the charge of TAXATION WITHOUT REPRESENTATION, Parliament responded with the theory of virtual representation. The colonists rejected this DOCTRINE and insisted that as a practical matter responsible government depended on the ballot, not on government's respect for natural justice. Belief in a higher law thus coexisted with a pessimistic view of human nature and a corresponding distrust of government.

Unlike Britain's constitution, the American Constitution was established through RATIFICATION, a form of enactment. As the supreme law of the land this enacted Constitution consigns appeals from its authority to the category of extralegal considerations. But foreclosing the constitutionality of appeals from the highest written law did not depreciate unwritten law as such, for the written or enacted law could still reflect unwritten standards of natural justice and reason whose status did not depend on enactment. This was the claim of those who campaigned for ratification, as was to be expected from the rhetoric typical of public attempts to persuade.

This is not to say that anyone saw the proposed constitution as entirely consistent with the dictates of reason and justice. Slavery and the equal REPRESENTATION in the Senate of small and large states are examples of acknowledged compromises with contingencies that would not bend to principle. Nevertheless, the argument for ratification was full of references to higher norms as standards for evaluating constitutions, as principles behind its rules and institutions, and as objectives of the system as a whole. In THE FEDERALIST #9 and #10, ALEXANDER HAMILTON and JAMES MADISON not only presented the Constitution as an attempt to reconcile democracy with minority rights and the common good, but they also stated that the fate of democracy justly depended on that reconciliation. In *The Federalist* #78 Hamilton defended JUDICIAL REVIEW and recognized the role of judges in "mitigating the severity and confining the operations" of "unjust and partial" enactments. In *The Federalist* #51 Madison said, "Justice is the end of government" and that it "ever will be pursued until it is obtained, or until liberty be lost in the pursuit." And in the same number he described CHECKS AND BALANCES as a "policy of supplying, by opposite and rival interests, the defects of better motives." Taking this statement at face value would require as a prerequisite to a full understanding of the Constitution knowledge of the "better motives" that constituted part of the model for what the Framers wrote.

It is a matter of central importance that appeals to ideas like justice were not expressed as appeals to this or that particular version but to the general idea itself. Aware of the difference, Hamilton urged readers of *The Federalist* #1 to rise above "local prejudices little favorable to the discovery of truth." He recalled the frequent claim that Americans would decide the possibility of rational government for the whole of mankind, a claim that might redouble efforts to rise above parochialism by adding "the inducements of philanthropy to those of patriotism." Equally important, however, was his acknowledgment of the great number and power of "causes which . . . give a false bias to . . . judgement." And he urged "moderation" on those "ever so thoroughly persuaded of their being in the right." This appeal suggests the value of self-critical striving for truth, an attitude more of confidence in progress toward truth than in claims to possess it.

Further indication of the Constitution's dependence on commitments that some theorists believe written constitutions can displace is the fact that properties of the Constitution as a whole influence the interpretation of its parts. In addition to the rhetoric of its PREAMBLE and of its draftsmen, the document reflects a concern for simple justice by virtue of its written character. As written communication to an audience of indefinite composition, size, and duration, the document presupposes that virtually anyone can come to understand what it means. Presupposing a large and lasting community of meaning, it anticipates a community of interests embracing all to whom it would potentially apply or who would accept it as a model.

Because of their content, provisions like the TENTH AMENDMENT and the old fugitive slave clause are at odds with the community of interests presupposed by the Constitution as a whole. They are at odds with themselves by virtue of their enunciation as parts of the whole. This tension justified JOHN MARSHALL's nationalist construction of the Tenth Amendment, ABRAHAM LINCOLN's view that the Constitution had put slavery on the path of ultimate extinction, and the Supreme Court's application of the BILL OF RIGHTS to the states through the INCORPORATION DOCTRINE. Observers have interpreted the acceptance of this kind of construction as a sign that the nation has an unwritten constitution. But therapeutic constructions might as easily indicate the power of a written constitution to undermine the parochial and particularistic aspects of its content, separable as the written word is from the physical presence of its authors and their particular needs and conceptions.

The implications of the Constitution's written character bear on a protracted debate among constitutional theorists over the possibility of limiting the discretion of judges in difficult constitutional cases involving human rights, especially rights to SUBSTANTIVE DUE PROCESS and EQUAL PROTECTION. Many participants in the debate share an academic moral skepticism that finds no meaning in general normative concepts beyond the particular conceptions of historical individuals or communities. They diminish simple justice with quotation marks, and they hold particular conceptions of justice interesting primarily as facts that influence other facts, not as beliefs that can be morally better or worse than other beliefs. Rejecting the object of its quest, they also reject traditional moral philosophy as a method of acquiring knowledge. They treat the beliefs of persons and communities as matters essentially of historical fact, to be established by empirical methods, with some room for conceptual analysis, but not for judgments of right and wrong.

To these commentators, talk of reason and justice is essentially rationalization of personal preference, class interest, community morality, and the like. And because they tend to believe that elected officials have a stronger claim to represent the community, they argue that judicial review often involves the imposition of minority preferences on the majority. In an effort to reconcile judicial review with majoritarianism these theorists have tried to link the meaning of general constitutional norms with the intentions of the Framers, tradition, existing and projected community morality, the institutional prerequisites of democratic decision, and other sources whose content they perceive essentially as matters of fact or uncontroversial inference. The effort has failed largely because each source yields conflicting options, not simple, consistent answers. And when the skeptics make their selections, they inevitably (if covertly and therefore irresponsibly) make normative judgments whose rationality their position would force them to deny.

The failure of these skeptical theorists to extirpate normative judgments from decisions about the meaning of constitutional provisions has strengthened the case for moral philosophy in constitutional inquiry, which, in turn, has exacerbated apprehension of unrestrained judicial power. But renewed concern for natural justice need not threaten hopes for limiting judicial discretion. Those who take seriously the idea of justice as something higher than their particular conceptions will value the self-critical striving for moral and political truth recommended in *The Federalist* #1. This attitude is itself a limitation on discretion of the most objectionable variety because it is the antithesis of willful assertiveness.

Arguments for taking natural justice seriously might begin by reflecting on the apparent power of ordinary political debate to change minds about justice and related ideas. This familiar fact shows that, as ordinary citizens understand it, political life presupposes simple justice. Moral skeptics err in supposing that continuing disagreement about justice proves that debate is pointless or that there is nothing to debate about. If there are moral truths to be known, as is ordinarily presupposed, agreement is not the test of what is right. Holding that agreement is the test may signal that one abandons ordinary presuppositions, but it is not an argument for doing so. Academic inquiry begins with ordinary presuppositions. And though constitutional theorists have not reached agreement (a good thing, for universal consensus would remove the impetus for reflection and improvement), they have been unable to avoid ordinary presuppositions about justice and the value of reasoning in deciding what the Constitution means. Perhaps this is a reason to value self-critical striving for the best constructions to which constitutional language, tradition, and opinion are open.

SOTIRIOS A. BARBER

(SEE ALSO: *Higher Law; Limited Government; Natural Rights and the Constitution.*)

Bibliography

BREST, PAUL 1981 The Fundamental Rights Controversy: The Essential Contradictions of Normative Constitutional Scholarship. *Yale Law Journal* 90:1063–1109.

GREY, THOMAS C. 1978 Origins of the Unwritten Constitution: Fundamental Law in American Revolutionary Thought. *Stanford Law Review* 30:843–893.

HARRIS, WILLIAM F., II 1982 Bonding Word and Polity: The Logic of American Constitutionalism. *American Political Science Review* 76:34–45.

MOORE, MICHAEL S. 1985 A Natural Law Theory of Interpretation. *Southern California Law Review* 58:277–398.

——— 1982 Moral Reality. *Wisconsin Law Review* 1982:1061–1156.

UPHAUS v. WYMAN
360 U.S. 72 (1959)

In PENNSYLVANIA V. NELSON (1956) the Court appeared to hold that the Smith Act preempted state antisubversion laws. Here the Court held that state JURISDICTION over sedition against the state, as opposed to sedition against the federal government, was not preempted. In *Sweezy v. New Hampshire* (1956) the Court had invalidated a subversion investigation by the New Hampshire attorney general. Here, using the interest-balancing techniques of BARENBLATT V. UNITED STATES (1959), decided the same day, the Court upheld a similar investigation by him in his capacity as a one-man legislative investigating committee.

MARTIN SHAPIRO

USE IMMUNITY

See: Immunity Grant

UTILITY REGULATION

See: Economic Regulation

VACCINATION

Vaccination is the introduction into the body of a vaccine to prevent disease. In the late nineteenth and early twentieth centuries a number of states made smallpox vaccination compulsory. The Supreme Court upheld the constitutionality of such a law in JACOBSON V. MASSACHUSETTS (1905), and *Jacobson*'s continuing vitality as a PRECEDENT is routinely assumed.

The *Jacobson* opinion was written by Justice OLIVER WENDELL HOLMES, who regarded the case as he regarded LOCHNER V. NEW YORK (1905), decided later the same year over his dissent. For Holmes, the question in both cases was whether the legislative judgment had passed the bounds of reason. For the majority who found a violation of SUBSTANTIVE DUE PROCESS in *Lochner's* sixty-hour limit on bakers' weekly work but validated compulsory vaccination, the difference surely was that they saw vaccination as a soundly based health requirement. Yet the subsequent collapse of substantive due process as a constitutional limit on ECONOMIC REGULATION should not be taken as a return to the Holmes view equating invasions of the body with the general run of restrictions on liberty. Undoubtedly the standard of judicial review in such cases today is far more demanding than it was for Holmes in *Jacobson.*

A patient who refuses medical treatment, for example, surely has a constitutional right to do so, founded on the liberty protected by the due process clauses, absent the most compelling justification for state-ordered intrusion into his or her body. The right may come to be described in the PRIVACY language used to explain the abortion decisions, which really rest not so much on privacy in its ordinary sense as on a woman's control over her own body and her own life. Similarly, the decisions involving invasion of the body to extract blood or other EVIDENCE for use in detecting crime make clear that such invasions must pass the test of strict judicial scrutiny of their justifications. Claims of RELIGIOUS LIBERTY may be added to the constitutional mix, as when a Jehovah's Witness refuses a blood transfusion, but with or without that ingredient the constitutional claim to autonomy over the body is strong.

The strength of the countervailing governmental interest in compelling vaccination would, of course, depend on the degree of danger to the public posed by unvaccinated persons. Now that smallpox is approaching worldwide eradication, the constitutional claim of a latter-day Jacobson would be far more substantial. Many doctors now recommend against smallpox vaccination, because—as Jacobson himself argued—the procedure involves a risk of contracting the disease. Given the vastly reduced public health justification for the inoculation, it is by no means clear that a compulsory smallpox vaccination law would survive constitutional challenge today. Undoubtedly, however, a state could constitutionally require vaccination for other diseases that significantly endanger public health.

KENNETH L. KARST

Bibliography

TRIBE, LAURENCE H. 1978 *American Constitutional Law.* Pages 913–921. Mineola, N.Y.: Foundation Press.

VAGRANCY LAWS

Historically, society has used vagrancy laws to punish undesirable or immoral persons considered to be dangerous because of their potential for engaging in criminal conduct. Such laws differed significantly from traditional criminal statutes in that they made it a crime to be a person of a specified status or condition. In the United States, the types of persons punished as "vagrants" have included rogues, vagabonds, habitual loafers, and others considered to be of immoral character.

The first vagrancy laws, which originated in England, required workers to live in specified locations and proscribed giving assistance to able-bodied beggars who refused to work. Late-fifteenth-century vagrancy laws provided that beggars and idle persons, after punishment, were to be banished.

Vagrancy legislation in the United States began in colonial times and closely followed the English model. In the nineteenth century, the Supreme Court in MAYOR OF NEW YORK V. MILN (1837) implicitly recognized both the objectives and necessity of such laws, stating in OBITER DICTUM: "We think it as competent and as necessary for a state to provide precautionary measures against this moral pestilence of paupers, vagabonds, and possible convicts; as it is to guard against the physical pestilence. . . ." More recently, the Court in EDWARDS V. CALIFORNIA (1941) expressly rejected this notion, observing that "[w]hatever may have been the notion then prevailing, we do not think that it will now be seriously contended that because a person is without employment and without funds he constitutes a 'moral pestilence.' Poverty and immorality are not synonymous."

Edwards, however, was a narrow decision, which struck down under the COMMERCE CLAUSE a California statute making it a misdemeanor to bring an indigent, nonresident alien into the state. Thus, notwithstanding *Edwards,* vagrancy laws continued broadly to proscribe various types of status crimes until the Supreme Court's decision in *Papachristou v. City of Jacksonville* (1972).

In *Papachristou* the Court held under the VAGUENESS DOCTRINE that a vagrancy statute was unconstitutional on its face. The ordinance, a typical example of a traditional vagrancy law, subjected the following persons to criminal penalty because the city deemed them to be "vagrants":

> Rogues and vagabonds . . . dissolute persons who go about begging, common gamblers, persons who use juggling or unlawful games or plays, common drunkards, common night walkers, thieves, pilferers or pickpockets, traders in stolen property, lewd, wanton and lascivious persons, keepers of gambling places, common railers and brawlers, persons wandering or strolling around from place to place without any lawful purpose or object, habitual loafers, disorderly persons, persons neglecting all lawful business and habitually spending their time by frequenting houses of ill fame, gaming houses, or places where alcoholic beverages are sold or served, [and] persons able to work but habitually living upon the earnings of their wives or minor children.

Two fundamental constitutional defects arise from the vagueness inherent in traditional vagrancy laws. Initially, the definition of "vagrant" fails to give adequate notice of what criminal conduct is proscribed. As recognized in *Connally v. General Construction Co.* (1926), when a criminal statute "either forbids or requires the doing of an act in terms so vague that men of common intelligence must necessarily guess at its meaning and differ as to its application," the DUE PROCESS CLAUSE requires its invalidation under the vagueness doctrine. This doctrine was first applied to a vagrancy-type statute in *Lanzetta v. New Jersey* (1939), which held unconstitutional for vagueness a New Jersey "gangster" statute punishing any "person not engaged in any lawful occupation, known to be a member of a gang consisting of two or more persons, who has been convicted [of a crime or at least three disorderly person offenses]." *Papachristou* applied this doctrine to traditional vagrancy laws, in which the generalized and all-inclusive definitions may encompass many types of innocent behavior.

The second aspect of the vagueness doctrine, even more important than the requirement of fair notice, is that a criminal statute must set forth minimal guidelines to govern law enforcement. Absent such guidelines, a criminal statute is subject to substantial abuse by police officers, prosecutors, and jurors on the basis of their own personal predilections. Imprecise definitions, like those contained in traditional vagrancy statutes, give law enforcement officers virtually unbridled discretion to make arrests on mere suspicion rather than on PROBABLE CAUSE, and to use such arrests as a law enforcement tool to gather information and to interview persons about unrelated crimes. Moreover, as suggested in Justice HUGO L. BLACK'S dissenting opinion in *Edelman v. California* (1953), they are also easily susceptible of being used against persons expressing unpopular views, as well as against the poor and minorities.

Traditional vagrancy statutes may also suffer from other constitutional defects. For example, *Robinson v. California* (1962) struck down a provision of a California vagrancy statute that made it a crime to be a "narcotics addict," on the ground that the statute violated the CRUEL AND UNUSUAL PUNISHMENT clause of the Eighth Amendment. In *Powell v. Texas* (1968), by contrast, the Court upheld a state statute that proscribed public drunkenness, even though the person so charged might suffer from chronic alcoholism. The Court noted in *Powell* that such a proscription differs from convicting someone for being an addict, a chronic alcoholic, mentally ill, or a leper. Rather than punishing mere status, the proscription focuses on the specific act of appearing drunk in public on a particular occasion—conduct that the state has an interest in prohibiting.

To the extent that vagrancy laws have been used to exclude undesirables from a state or otherwise to confine them geographically, *Edwards* recognizes that they may unreasonably burden INTERSTATE COMMERCE. Moreover, such restrictions also may unconstitutionally impair the RIGHT TO TRAVEL. And provisions of vagrancy laws that prohibit association with known thieves and other undesirables not only suffer from vagueness but also may violate an individual's right of association.

In view of the Supreme Court's decisions in the area of vagrancy laws, most of the antiquated provisions of such laws—which focus on controlling undesirables by proscribing various types of status or condition—no longer can withstand constitutional scrutiny.

JAMES R. ASPERGER

(SEE ALSO: *Kolender v. Lawson, 1983.*)

Bibliography

AMSTERDAM, ANTHONY G. 1967 Federal Constitutional Restrictions on the Punishment of Crimes of Status, Crimes of General Obnoxiousness, Crimes of Displeasing Police Officers, and the Like. *Criminal Law Bulletin* 3:205–241.

FOOTE, CALEB 1956 Vagrancy-Type Law and Its Administration. *University of Pennsylvania Law Review* 104:603–650.

LACEY, FORREST W. 1953 Vagrancy and Other Crimes of Personal Condition. *Harvard Law Review* 66:1203–1226.

VAGUENESS

The Fifth Amendment and FOURTEENTH AMENDMENT respectively prohibit the federal and state governments from taking life, liberty, or property without DUE PROCESS OF LAW. These provisions forbid the enforcement of any law that, in the classic words of *Connally v. General Construction Co.* (1926), "either forbids or requires the doing of an act in terms so vague that men of common intelligence must necessarily guess at its meaning and differ as to its application." Vagueness imperils the fair administration of legal sanctions in several ways. First, it threatens punishment of people who had no fair warning of what conduct to avoid. Second, by creating interpretive latitude for those who apply the law—police, prosecutors, judges, juries, and others—vagueness permits punishment to be inflicted selectively for arbitrary or improper reasons. Third, a law's vagueness hinders the efforts of reviewing courts to control such abuses in the law's enforcement; the less clear the law is, the less visible—and correspondingly more difficult to detect and correct—are irregular instances of its administration.

To minimize these dangers, the due process requirement of reasonable clarity forbids enforcement even if the legislature constitutionally could have prohibited, through a clearer law than it did enact, all the behavior its vague law might have been intended to reach. When the uncertain coverage of a vague law might extend into areas of behavior that are constitutionally protected from regulation, however, the ordinary dangers of arbitrary enforcement are heightened, and two additional concerns emerge: the risk that a vague law, which inevitably poses an uncertain risk of prosecution, will inhibit people from exercising precious liberties that the government has no right to outlaw, and the possibility that the legislature did not explicitly focus on the liberty interest and thus did not actually decide that there was compelling reason to regulate it.

The deterrence of constitutionally guaranteed activity that vagueness may produce is akin to the deterrence produced by overbroad laws that encompass both behavior that legitimately may be regulated and behavior that is constitutionally protected. Vagueness differs from overbreadth in that the source of potential inhibition is the law's lack of clarity, not its excessive reach. Yet in both cases the ultimate threat is that those who wish to exercise constitutional rights will refrain from doing so for fear of being penalized. That vagueness may have the practical effect of overbroad regulation explains the common doctrinal confusion between the two concepts. Vagueness also differs from OVERBREADTH in another way: an uncertain law that addresses, even in its most expansive interpretation, only behavior that constitutionally may be regulated may still be void for vagueness, but, by definition, cannot be void for overbreadth.

Two questions dominate the law of vagueness: how much vagueness is tolerable before the law violates due process, and who may raise the vagueness objection. The Supreme Court appears to give different answers to each question, depending on whether or not the vagueness implicates constitutionally protected activity. Still, the constitutional issue of vagueness is always a question of degree, of how much interpretive uncertainty is tolerable before the legitimate regulatory interests of government must yield to the perils of vagueness. If the constitutional definition of vagueness is itself uncertain, the reason is that language is inherently imprecise. The public interest in regulating antisocial behavior would be sacrificed if due process mandated impossible standards of clarity before laws validly could be enforced.

The starting point for vagueness analysis is to ascertain the nature of the standard that the law sets. This inquiry requires judges to consider not only the statutory language but also all interpretive aids that may add to the law's precision, such as accepted meanings in the relevant community (or in other areas of law) for terms contained in the statute, implementing regulations, past judicial interpretations that have clarified uncertain terms, and even judicial clarification in the very case raising the vagueness objection—if this after-the-fact clarification does not disregard the legislature's intent and if the challenger reasonably could have anticipated that the law could be construed to cover his conduct. The interpretive option often allows the Supreme Court and lower federal courts to avoid invalidating vague federal laws. When federal courts confront state laws, however, they are limited to determining whether state court clarification has cured any constitutional problems of vagueness. This difference largely explains why state laws are stricken for vagueness more often than are federal laws.

Once a law has received the benefit of all available clarification, a wide range of factors affects a court's judgment whether the law's remaining vagueness renders it unconstitutional. In a case in which the vagueness does not bear on constitutionally shielded behavior, only two vagueness objections are permitted: that the law is vague as applied to the particular behavior of the individual challenger, or that the law is INVALID ON ITS FACE for being unduly vague as applied to anyone, including the challenger, because no one who consulted it could derive fair warning of what conduct was prohibited or could determine whether the legislature meant one thing rather than another. In *Hoffman Estates v. Flipside* (1982) the Supreme Court confirmed that in deciding cases in which the latter objection is raised, greater uncertainty is constitutionally permissible when the law regulates a relatively narrow subject matter; when the law regulates economic behavior (because businesses more reasonably can be expected to consult laws in advance of acting than can individuals); when the law imposes civil rather than criminal penalties (because the consequences of noncompliance are less severe); and when the law applies only to those who intentionally or knowingly violate it (because there is less risk of unfair surprise). Historically, once the Supreme Court determined that ECONOMIC REGULATION posed no significant threat to constitutional freedoms, it became more tolerant of the imprecision in laws banning "unreasonable," "unjust," or "unfair" prices or business practices, as *United States v. National Dairy Products Corp.* (1963) illustrates. Moreover, the Court permits more uncertainty when it perceives the government's regulatory objective to be especially important—as SCREWS V. UNITED STATES (1945) demonstrated in upholding a rather vague CIVIL RIGHTS law protecting individuals—and also when it would be difficult for the legislature to delineate more precisely the penalized behavior.

The Court is especially receptive to a challenge based on vagueness when a law's uncertain coverage risks inhibiting constitutionally safeguarded freedoms. In the last half-century this receptivity has been manifested primarily in FIRST AMENDMENT cases. One indicator of the Court's increased sensitivity is the wide range of people who may now raise the vagueness objection. In cases implicating constitutionally protected activity, the Court not only entertains complaints that a law is vague as applied to the individual litigant or vague in all applications, but it sometimes permits those to whom a law clearly applies to object that it is facially invalid because it is unduly vague as to others. Despite Supreme Court rulings to the contrary both in earlier periods and in cases as recent as PARKER V. LEVY (1974) and BROADRICK V. OKLAHOMA (1973), and despite continuing voices of dissent that this practice allows one as to whom enforcement is fair to assert the hypothetical rights of others and confuses vagueness and overbreadth, the Court currently maintains, in such cases as YOUNG V. AMERICAN MINI THEATRES (1976) and KOLENDER V. LAWSON (1983), that such a person may have the whole law invalidated if the deterrent effect of its vagueness on others is real and substantial.

All of the factors that bear on the acceptable degree of vagueness in laws encompassing only unprotected conduct still apply, some more heavily, to laws that potentially reach constitutionally protected conduct. In addition, the Supreme Court seems to be concerned with other factors: how much protected freedom the vagueness might deter; how important the asserted freedom is; the judges' capacity to preserve the freedom through case-by-case application; the legislature's ability to reformulate the law in less inhibiting fashion; and the extent and importance of legitimate regulation that must be foregone if the law is voided for vagueness.

Although the Court does not always articulate these considerations, they appear to underlie many decisions. In *Baggett v. Bullitt* (1964) and *Cramp v. Board of Public Instruction* (1961), for example, the invalidation of LOYALTY OATH requirements for undue vagueness arrayed important freedoms of association against dubious government needs for assurance. More generally, when the enactment's vagueness risks suppression of unpopular expression or criticism of government, the Court's tolerance level is low. Thus in *Coates v. Cincinnati* (1971) an ordinance barring assembly of three or more persons "annoying" passers-by was held void, as was a law prohibiting "contemptuous treatment" of the American flag in *Smith v. Goguen* (1974).

On the other hand, even vagueness that inhibits valued expression is sometimes indulged if regulatory interests are perceived as powerful. Good examples are the extreme vagueness *Parker v. Levy* permitted the military in punishing "conduct unbecoming an officer and a gentleman" and the lesser, yet undoubted, uncertainty of laws prohibiting partisan political activity by PUBLIC EMPLOYEES that the Court upheld in *Broadrick v. Oklahoma*.

Similarly divergent assessments of the acceptable level of indefiniteness in statutes defining and proscribing OBSCENITY reflect conflict within the Court over the value of sexually explicit, but constitutionally protected, materials. The judgment that deterrence of some sexually explicit adult movies was no cause for alarm led a plurality in *Young v. American Mini Theatres* to uphold a ZONING ordinance restricting the concentration of adult theaters and bookstores in downtown Detroit. A similar judgment underlies the Court's willingness to permit inevitably vague definitions of obscenity to serve as the basis for criminal punishment. By contrast, Justice WILLIAM J. BRENNAN, who is more concerned about the potentially protected sexual expression that might be lost, declared in his important dissent in *Paris Adult Theatre I v. Slaton* (1973) his firm, if belated, conviction that vagueness in defining obscenity is virtually an insuperable problem. Even he, however, did not conclude that the distribution of obscene materials must consequently remain unregulated; rather, he suggested that the protection of juveniles and the privacy of unconsenting adults might render vagueness tolerable, though protection of consenting adults and community mores and aesthetics would not.

The complexity of the vagueness doctrine stems, then, from the dual nature of the constitutional protection that it offers. Individuals are protected in any case from arbitrary enforcement without a fair opportunity to conform their conduct to legitimate law, and the social interest in maximizing constitutional freedoms is central to judgments about vagueness when the law's indefiniteness threatens to inhibit those freedoms.

JONATHAN D. VARAT

Bibliography

AMSTERDAM, ANTHONY B. 1960 The Void-for-Vagueness Doctrine in the Supreme Court. *University of Pennsylvania Law Review* 109:67–116.

BOGEN, DAVID S. 1978 First Amendment Ancillary Doctrines. *Maryland Law Review* 37:679, 714–726.

SCHAUER, FREDERICK 1978 Fear, Risk and the First Amendment: Unravelling the "Chilling Effect." *Boston University Law Review* 58:685.

VALENTINE v. CHRESTENSEN

See: Commercial Speech

VALLANDIGHAM, EX PARTE
1 Wallace 243 (1864)

In 1863, soldiers arrested, tried, and found guilty Negrophobic Democratic congressman Clement L. Vallandigham (Ohio) for violating Army orders against public expressions of Confederate sympathies. After returning to this country from banishment in rebel lines, which ABRAHAM LINCOLN had ordered, Vallandigham applied to the Supreme Court for a WRIT OF CERTIORARI to annul the military proceedings. The Court, accepting JURISDICTION, decided, without dissent, that it had no jurisdiction over appeals from military courts. The likelihood of direct clashes between the Court and the COMMANDER-IN-CHIEF thus receded to revive in EX PARTE MILLIGAN (1867).

HAROLD M. HYMAN

VALLEY FORGE CHRISTIAN COLLEGE v. AMERICANS UNITED FOR SEPARATION OF CHURCH AND STATE

454 U.S. 464 (1982)

Severely limiting the precedent of FLAST V. COHEN (1968), the Supreme Court here tightened the requirements for STANDING in a TAXPAYER'S SUIT against the federal government.

Under a general power from Congress to dispose of surplus federal property, the Department of Health, Education and Welfare (HEW) transferred land and buildings worth over $500,000 to a religious college that trained students for the ministry. Because HEW calculated that the government benefited from the transfer at a rate of 100 percent, the college paid nothing.

Federal taxpayers sued to set aside the transfer, contending that it amounted to an ESTABLISHMENT OF RELIGION. The Supreme Court held, 5–4, that the taxpayers lacked standing. The majority distinguished *Flast,* which had upheld taxpayer standing to challenge federal subsidies to church schools: *Flast* challenged an act of Congress; here plaintiffs challenged a decision by HEW. Furthermore, *Flast* involved injury to the plaintiffs as taxpayers: tax money was to be spent unconstitutionally. Here the Court dealt not with Congress's spending power but with the power to dispose of property.

The dissenters emphasized what everyone knew: absent taxpayer standing, no one has standing to challenge government donations of property to churches. In such cases the establishment clause is enforceable in the consciences of government officials, but not in court.

KENNETH L. KARST

VAN BUREN, MARTIN

(1782–1862)

Martin Van Buren of Kinderhook, New York, was admitted to the bar in 1803 and quickly established himself as a successful lawyer and politician. While serving in the New York legislature, Van Buren and a group of close associates known as the Albany Regency constituted the first political machine with a modern cast in the nation. As such the Regency gave a new direction to American politics.

But Van Buren did not consider the political process an end in itself; he saw in it a mode for achieving his notion of a Jeffersonian republic, in which a judicious division of power and responsibility between the central government and the states turned on a STRICT CONSTRUCTION of the Constitution. Opposition was expressed in BROAD CONSTRUCTION, along Hamiltonian lines. Between these two positions, the one emphasizing state power, the other national, the very essence of SOVEREIGNTY would be in constant conflict over public questions, a conflict he thought essential to the democratic governance of the states and the nation. He carried his ideas of an adversarial party system to Washington when elected a United States senator in 1821, and over the two terms he served, developed, and promoted them. Van Buren bound together into a cohesive program the personal factions that constituted his party. As he had planned, his partisan coalition gave impetus to a specific political opposition. Thus, he played a significant role in the formation of the current two-party system.

Van Buren articulated a historical view of strict construction. He was a frequent critic of the centralizing doctrines of the MARSHALL COURT and supported measures to curb JUDICIAL REVIEW. He drafted ANDREW JACKSON's veto of the MAYSVILLE ROAD BILL, the first comprehensive treatment of the responsibility of the central government to fund INTERNAL IMPROVEMENTS in the various states. Van Buren distinguished projects that were clearly intrastate from those that were interstate in character. In withholding the support of the national government for the economic development of the individual states, he relied partly on JAMES MONROE's veto of the Cumberland Road Bill, but he took care to assert that many projects purely local in character and initiated by a state might deserve support under constitutional provisions that provided for the common defense and the GENERAL WELFARE. His distinction depended upon many variables which could change with time and with circumstance.

Van Buren's second expression of what might be properly called the New Jeffersonianism was in the financial policy he pursued as President (1837–1841): the subtreasury system, which looked to the separation of the federal government from the state deposit banks. The federal government held most of the nation's specie currency, the basis of the paper money supply; thus it would act as a restraint on state banks, curbing their tendencies to speculation and ensuring a more equitable distribution of credit. His means may have been orthodox and deflationary, but they acted as a restriction upon state power, contrary to THOMAS JEFFERSON's ideas on government.

Van Buren's stand on the powers of Congress over

the TERRITORIES, however, was a restatement of Jeffersonian views expressed in the NORTHWEST ORDINANCE of 1787. Van Buren added his own interpretation of Article IV, section 3, of the Constitution, which delegates to the Congress the power "to make needful rules and regulations respecting the territory or other property of the United States." In doing so he went further than JOHN MARSHALL and agreed with JOSEPH STORY who asserted that the power was exclusive and that "rules and regulations" covered all possible contingencies. Van Buren had supported the MISSOURI COMPROMISE as a proper exercise of congressional power even though, as a matter of precedent, he thought the Ordinance of 1787 excluded slavery from all territories. In the United States Senate he voted against the bill organizing a territorial government for Florida because it sustained slavery. The most complete exposition of his stand on the territorial question of the late 1840s and 1850s is expressed in an address he prepared for the New York Democratic legislative caucus. It was the basis for the platform of the Free Soil party in the campaign of 1848 and the spirit and the substance of the Republican party platform in the campaigns of 1856 and 1860.

W. JOHN NIVEN

Bibliography

NIVEN, W. JOHN 1983 *Martin Van Buren and the Romantic Age of American Politics.* New York: Oxford University Press.

VAN DEVANTER, WILLIS
(1859–1941)

Colleagues and contemporary observers agreed that Willis Van Devanter was enormously influential during his twenty-six years on the Supreme Court. Chief Justice WILLIAM HOWARD TAFT, who as President appointed him in 1911, described his Wyoming associate as "my mainstay," "the most valuable man in our court," and the Justice who had "more influence" than any other. Justice LOUIS D. BRANDEIS, Van Devanter's ideological antipode, praised him as a "master of formulas that decided cases without creating precedents." Harvard's Professor FELIX FRANKFURTER aptly dubbed him Taft's "Lord Chancellor."

Van Devanter's backstage prominence contrasted vividly with his well-known "pen paralysis." He rarely spoke for the Court in major constitutional cases. During his tenure, Van Devanter averaged only fourteen written opinions each year; during the 1930s he averaged only three a year.

Van Devanter came to the Court after a career in Wyoming law and politics, followed by five years in the Interior Department. President THEODORE ROOSEVELT appointed him to the Eighth Circuit Court of Appeals in 1903; eight years later, President Taft elevated him to the Supreme Court. Taft, himself a former circuit judge, prized judicial experience as a criterion for appointment to the Supreme Court.

Although Van Devanter was one of the conservative "Four Horsemen" of the New Deal era, two of his earlier opinions aligned him with the "liberal nationalistic" wing of the Court. In the second of the EMPLOYERS' LIABILITY CASES (1913) he upheld a federal statute holding railroads liable for injuries suffered by workers engaged in INTERSTATE COMMERCE. He boldly generalized about the sweep of the COMMERCE CLAUSE, describing the commerce power as "complete in itself," but he added that it did not extend to matters that had no "real or substantial relation to some part of such commerce." The previous year, in *Southern Railway Co. v. United States* (1911), he had written for the Court to sustain federal railroad safety legislation in a case involving an intrastate railroad which carried goods that had passed through interstate commerce. Again, Van Devanter found the commerce power plenary and operative if an intrastate matter affected interstate commerce. The decision anticipated Justice CHARLES EVANS HUGHES's consideration of intrastate effects on the commerce power in the *Shreveport Case* (HOUSTON, EAST AND WEST TEXAS RAILROAD COMPANY V. UNITED STATES, 1914), an opinion Van Devanter supported; yet, in the 1930s he consistently rejected similar arguments to expand the scope of federal ECONOMIC REGULATION.

Van Devanter's most important and enduring contribution to constitutional law came with his opinion broadly approving Congress's investigative powers. In MCGRAIN V. DAUGHERTY (1927) the plaintiffs had challenged a Senate committee's investigation of Harding administration scandals. Van Devanter recognized that historically "the power of inquiry—with process to enforce it—is an essential and appropriate auxiliary to the legislative function"; that the power might be abused, he added, was no argument against its existence.

Van Devanter usually supported governmental repression of political dissent in the World War I era. In the early 1930s, however, he deviated from his ideological allies as he joined the majority in invalidating a section of California's criminal anarchy law in STROMBERG V. CALIFORNIA (1931). He also supported

Justice GEORGE H. SUTHERLAND's pathbreaking opinion on Sixth Amendment rights in POWELL v. ALABAMA (1932). But a few years later, when the Court reverted to the CLEAR AND PRESENT DANGER doctrine for FIRST AMENDMENT cases, Van Devanter led the "Four Horsemen" in dissent. In HERNDON v. LOWRY (1937), which involved a black communist who had been convicted under Georgia state law, Van Devanter thought that Herndon's appeal to blacks was especially dangerous; Van Devanter's dissent reflected the suppressive BAD TENDENCY TEST and racist rhetoric, as well.

During the constitutional struggles over the New Deal, Van Devanter opposed the administration in every case except ASHWANDER v. TENNESSEE VALLEY AUTHORITY (1936). Even when his conservative colleagues resurrected the restrictive doctrines of UNITED STATES v. E. C. KNIGHT COMPANY (1895), a decision which he had circumvented in some of his early opinions, Van Devanter steadfastly opposed the expansion of national regulatory power. But he never spoke for that viewpoint, either in the majority or in dissent. Fittingly, however, he played a key role in what may have been FRANKLIN D. ROOSEVELT's most significant political defeat. During the consideration of Roosevelt's court-packing proposal in April 1937, Van Devanter announced his intention to take advantage of a new law allowing Justices to retire at full pay. The impending vacancy offered promise of a shift in the Court's ideological stance, and made the President's plan unnecessary for many administrative supporters. After his retirement from the Supreme Court, Van Devanter apparently was the first retired Justice who served regularly as a reserve judge.

STANLEY I. KUTLER

Bibliography

PASCHAL, JOEL F. 1951 *Mr. Justice Sutherland: A Man Against the State.* Princeton, N.J.: Princeton University Press.

PRINGLE, HENRY F. 1939 *The Life and Times of William Howard Taft.* New York: Farrar & Rinehart.

VAN HORNE'S LESSEE v. DORRANCE

2 Dallas 304 (1795)

Van Horne's Lessee, a circuit court case in the District of Pennsylvania, is memorable because of Justice WILLIAM PATERSON'S charge to the jury, instructing them that a state act unconstitutionally violated property rights. His opinion can be read as a roadmap of the direction that constitutional law would take as a law of judicially implied limitations on legislation adversely affecting property rights. In lucid nonlegal language, Paterson spelled out judicial presuppositions and constitutional principles that were to become orthodox for well over a century. In discussing "What is a Constitution?" and analyzing the legislature's authority to pass its act divesting land titles, Paterson joined together the doctrines of JUDICIAL REVIEW and VESTED RIGHTS. Prefiguring FLETCHER v. PECK (1810) as well as the basic principle of MARBURY v. MADISON (1803), Paterson invoked the HIGHER LAW concept and the CONTRACT CLAUSE against the statute.

Having declared that "it will be the duty of the Court to adhere to the constitution, and to declare the act null and void" if it exceeds the legislature's authority, Paterson discoursed on the relationship between FUNDAMENTAL LAW and the rights of property. He found such rights inalienable, their preservation a primary object of "the social compact." Property, when vested, must be secure. For the government to take property without providing a recompense in value would be "an outrage," a "dangerous" display of unlimited authority, "a monster in legislation" that would "shock all mankind." To divest a citizen of his freehold even with compensation was a necessary "despotic" power to be exercised only in "cases of the first necessity." The reason was that the Constitution "encircles, and renders [a vested right] an holy thing. . . . It is a right not *ex gratia* from the legislature, but *ex debito* from the constitution. It is sacred. . . ."

Paterson informed the jury that courts must hold unconstitutional legislative encroachments on sacred property rights even in the absence of a written constitutional limitation on legislative powers. He relied on "reason, justice, and moral recitude," "the principles of social alliance in every free government," and the "letter and spirit of the constitution." The letter, in this instance, turned out to be the clause in Article I, section 10, of the Constitution, prohibiting a state law impairing the OBLIGATION OF A CONTRACT. Paterson assumed that the contract clause extended to contracts to which the state was a party; that a previous state act recognizing a property interest of the original claimant was a contract within the protection of the contract clause; and that the divestiture of the titles, even with compensation, violated the clause. Paterson's charge was a textbook exposition of SOCIAL COMPACT THEORY, CONSTITUTIONALISM, higher law limitations, judicial review, courts as bulwarks of property rights, and the contract clause.

LEONARD W. LEVY

VATTEL, EMERICH DE (1714–1767)

Emerich de Vattel, the Swiss-born statesman and theorist of LIMITED GOVERNMENT, wrote his *Law of Nations* (1758) as an attempt to explain international law on the basis of NATURAL RIGHTS. He argued that men compacted to form sovereign states, and the state ordained a CONSTITUTION superior to any prince or legislature. Vattel reasoned that because the "legislature derives its power from the constitution, it cannot overleap the bounds of it without destroying its own foundation"—and this maxim was frequently cited by American revolutionary leaders including JAMES OTIS and SAMUEL ADAMS. Even more important for American constitutional thought was his assertion, often quoted by JAMES MADISON, that states joining a federal union retained their SOVEREIGNTY but were nevertheless bound by the terms of the union.

DENNIS J. MAHONEY

VEAZIE BANK v. FENNO 8 Wallace 533 (1869)

During the Civil War, Congress introduced national bank notes, secured by United States bonds, as one form of currency. Congress then decided to make its money supreme by driving out of circulation bank notes issued by state banks, and to that end it imposed a prohibitory ten percent tax on those notes. Veazie Bank objected on the grounds that the tax was not levied for revenue purposes but to drive state notes out of existence by the device of a DIRECT TAX, which must be apportioned among the states on the basis of population. Chief Justice SALMON P. CHASE, for a seven-member majority, upheld the constitutionality of the congressional tax statute. Chase declared that only taxes on land and CAPITATION TAXES were direct taxes. He found the constitutional authority for the statute in Congress's power to control the currency of the nation and for that purpose to restrain "the circulation as money of any notes not issued under its own authority." Without such a restraining power the attempt by Congress to secure a "sound and uniform currency for the country must be futile."

LEONARD W. LEVY

VENUE

"Venue" refers to the location of a trial. Article III of the Constitution specifies that federal crimes be tried "in the State where the said Crimes shall have been committed." This provision is reinforced by the SIXTH AMENDMENT's guarantee of TRIAL BY JURY "of the State and district wherein the crime shall have been committed." Although the INCORPORATION DOCTRINE has made the Sixth Amendment's jury trial guarantee applicable to the states, the Supreme Court has not yet had occasion to decide whether that amendment's venue provision also limits the states. However, state law itself usually provides for trial in the locality where the crime is alleged to have been committed.

Both the FEDERAL RULES OF CRIMINAL PROCEDURE and a number of state laws contemplate a change of venue when trial in the district otherwise appropriate risks prejudicing the fairness of a criminal trial. The availability of a change of venue has been offered by the Supreme Court as one argument against GAG ORDERS forbidding the press to publish information about pending prosecutions. (See FREE PRESS/FAIR TRIAL.)

Some crimes are committed in more than one place: interstate transportation of a stolen automobile, for example, or certain criminal conspiracies. The Supreme Court has upheld congressional legislation allowing prosecution in any of the districts in which such a crime is committed.

Venue in civil actions is not limited by the Constitution. By statute, Congress has established an elaborate set of rules governing venue in federal civil cases. Because these rules are designed for the parties' convenience, the right to assert them can be waived. Thus a defendant in a federal court civil action must raise the objection of improper venue before trial, at the pleadings stage of the case.

KENNETH L. KARST

Bibliography

WRIGHT, CHARLES ALAN 1983 *The Law of Federal Courts,* 4th ed. Chap. 7. St. Paul, Minn.: West Publishing Co.

VERMONT CONSTITUTION OF 1777 (July 8, 1777)

In significant respects Vermont's early constitutional history was unique. It was never a colony, had no charter, and was not recognized as a separate government or state by the original thirteen, although it fully supported the American cause during the Revolution. Vermonters declared their independence not only from Great Britain but also from New York. A "convention" adopted a CONSTITUTION, prefaced by a declaration of rights, that was modeled after the extremely democratic PENNSYLVANIA CONSTITUTION OF 1776, but Vermont added three notable provisions. Its constitution was the first to outlaw slavery, the first to allow all male residents over twenty-one to vote even if they owned no property and paid no taxes, and the first to include a provision for JUST COMPENSATION in cases of EMINENT DOMAIN. Vermont joined the union as the fourteenth state in 1791.

LEONARD W. LEVY

VESTED RIGHTS

"Vested rights" are claims enforceable under law. Early in the history of the Republic, an assertive concept of vested rights became the core of a highly refined legal and constitutional doctrine that was invoked as a shield for private property against regulation by government. In EDWARD S. CORWIN's phrase, this became "the basic doctrine of American constitutional law."

An early expression of the doctrine was Justice WILLIAM PATERSON's opinion in VAN HORNE'S LESSEE V. DORRANCE (1795), stating that preservation of private property is "a primary object of the SOCIAL COMPACT," so that any law taking one person's freehold and vesting it in another without compensation must be seen as "inconsistent with the principles of reason, justice and moral rectitude . . . [and] contrary to the principle of social alliance in every free government." In expounding this doctrine, judges and treatise writers cited general principles of justice from natural law, civil law, and COMMON LAW. In pre-1860 contract and property law, the doctrine served in tandem with the CONTRACT CLAUSE and was regularly invoked by those opposing the expansion of state interventions under the taxation, EMINENT DOMAIN, and POLICE POWERS.

There is a difference between "vested interests" and "vested rights." The former are claims and expectations based on private contractual relationships and upon a property owner's understanding of the privileges, immunities, and responsibilities associated by law with the property in question. Interests become "rights" when courts agree to enforce such contractual relationships and understandings concerning property. This difference was recognized by Justice ROBERT H. JACKSON, in his opinion in *United States v. Willow Run Power Company* (1945), declaring: "Not all economic interests are 'property rights'; only those economic advantages are 'rights' which have the law back of them. . . ." A claim to a right (or "advantage"), Jackson stated, "is really a question to be answered" in judicial proceedings and decisions; it is not something to be taken a priori, even when ancient maxims and rules can be adduced in favor of the claim.

Justice Jackson's robust LEGAL REALISM was not the view that prevailed in legal and constitutional discourse during the nineteenth century. On occasion, individual judges or courts did defend legislative prerogatives against claims of vested rights in terms that foreshadowed Jackson's formulation. For example, a New York judge in 1835 denounced vested rights as an "indefinite" term that was "resorted to when no better argument exists." Any governmental action, he contended, imposed "burthens and duties" that redefined rights. Much more commonly found, however, were views founded on the notion that it was "manifest injustice by positive law" when legislation took away what Justice SAMUEL CHASE described in CALDER V. BULL (1798) as "that security for personal liberty, or private property, for the protection whereof the government was established."

State judges regularly invoked the vested rights doctrine, often explicitly merged with DUE PROCESS declarations, to review and sometimes invalidate legislation. Many judges applied natural-law principles associated with the Fifth Amendment, contending that they were a check upon the abuse of legislative power no less important than explicit state constitutional provisions or than the contract clause. Much relied upon, in such decisions, was Justice JOSEPH STORY's opinion in *Wilkinson v. Leland* (1829), contending that "the fundamental maxims of a free government seem to require that the rights of personal liberty and private property should be held sacred."

During JOHN MARSHALL's tenure as Chief Justice, the court introduced "vested rights" doctrine into contract clause rulings, as in Marshall's opinions in FLETCHER V. PECK (1810) and DARTMOUTH COLLEGE V. WOODWARD (1819). When conservative, property-minded state and federal judges applied Marshall's doctrines in broad terms in the 1830s and 1840s, the debate over vested rights began to center on whether or not corporate privileges, broadly construed, should be given the same protection as property held by individuals and quasi-public institutions. To conservatives such as DANIEL WEBSTER and Justice Story, a corporation's privileges and property rights under a franchise were merely a variant of an individual's rights in fee simple to a house or a tract of farmland. Webster, for example, viewed the action of Massachusetts in CHARLES RIVER BRIDGE COMPANY V. WARREN BRIDGE COMPANY (1837) as part of a "revolution against the foundations on which property rests." He raised the alarm again in his argument in WEST RIVER BRIDGE V. DIX (1848), denouncing broad use of the power of eminent domain as a dangerous kind of agrarian radicalism. There was a pragmatic side, as well, to the arguments of conservatives; both Story and Webster warned on many occasions that to allow legislatures unrestrained use of the police power or eminent domain, in derogation of vested property rights whether personal or corporate, would risk bringing all new investment (and material progress) to a halt.

Beginning with the decision in the *Charles River Bridge* case, the antebellum Supreme Court softened its stand on vested rights; state judges, however, kept the doctrine before the bar and the public. The high-sounding rhetoric of vested rights doctrine can easily obscure one of the important facts of the pre-Civil War period—the irony that in practice the antebellum state courts, as James Willard Hurst has shown, "tended to uphold vested rights only so long as they were felt to yield substantial or present returns in social function." Seldom did the courts support claims of vested rights that were invoked to protect "static" economic interests, attempting to block technological innovation or new forms of investment. Judges favored instead claims of "dynamic" rights that could be seen as forces for change and growth.

The adoption of the FOURTEENTH AMENDMENT opened the way to revival of vested rights doctrine in federal constitutional law. If anything, "vested rights" were now championed in enlarged forms. Leading conservative lawyers such as WILLIAM M. EVARTS, former Justice JOHN A. CAMPBELL, and John N. Jewett seized on the Fourteenth Amendment to forge the new, broader doctrine. Citing the concept of property as an "established expectation," they denied that government could deprive property owners of any expectation unless it paid compensation. They expanded the notion of property to include the right to engage in occupations; and they contended broadly that the rights of ownership included the right to compete freely in the quest for profits. Taking up arguments presented earlier by Campbell, Justice STEPHEN J. FIELD even attempted in his dissenting opinion in the SLAUGHTERHOUSE CASES (1873) to fuse the Fourteenth Amendment with the DECLARATION OF INDEPENDENCE—and thereby to throw the mantle of vested rights over economic interests and activities that he viewed as embraced by the phrase "pursuit of happiness." As he believed, such rights were beyond the legitimate reach of state regulation. Some conservative jurists and lawyers also found in the amendment's PRIVILEGES AND IMMUNITIES clause another prop for vested rights doctrine.

The newly expanded version of vested rights soon found its way into constitutional law, as Justice Field's views came to prevail with those of his colleagues. The traditional rhetoric of vested rights was harnessed to the FREEDOM OF CONTRACT doctrine, which became standard fare in the Court's decisions concerning the validity of laws regulating labor and business practices. In giving content to the doctrine of SUBSTANTIVE DUE PROCESS in the field of economic and social regulation, the Supreme Court marked out a meandering, uncertain, often absurd boundary between what it found to be legitimate police power and the "sacred" rights of property. The view, as Laurence Tribe has phrased it, "that certain settled expectations of a focused and crystallized sort should be secure against governmental disruption, at least without appropriate compensation" became a powerful weapon in the hands of the new industrial corporate interests—and at the same time became the center of political storms in the Populist and Progressive eras. Only with abandonment of economic due process in the late 1930s, together with the ascendancy of views such as Justice Jackson's harshly realist version of vested rights, did the concept recede in importance in constitutional law and in political strife.

In HOME BUILDING & LOAN ASSOCIATION V. BLAISDELL (1934), the Court gave notice that it was ready to uphold even so dramatic a state abridgment of private rights as a mortgage moratorium law. The Court would not, the majority declared, "throttle the capacity of the States to protect their fundamental interests." The common good, or the public interest, must also be honored in any system allocating constitutional powers and immunities. Thus the career of vested rights in the Webster-Story-Field tradition clearly had run its course. Nor for more than thirty years did debates in legislatures and courts return to the concerns of the conservative era; and even then the notion of "settled expectations" and related vested rights ideas were exhumed for application only in a fairly narrow context, relating to land use regulation and INVERSE CONDEMNATION. To that degree, at least, echoes of a doctrine rooted in natural law do continue to be heard in our own day.

HARRY N. SCHEIBER

Bibliography

CORWIN, EDWARD S. 1914 The Basic Doctrine of American Constitutional Law. *Michigan Law Review* 12:247–276.

HURST, JAMES WILLARD 1956 *Law and the Conditions of Freedom in the Nineteenth Century United States.* Madison: University of Wisconsin Press.

MCCLELLAN, JAMES 1971 *Joseph Story and the American Constitution.* Norman: University of Oklahoma Press.

MCCURDY, CHARLES W. 1975 Justice Field and the Jurisprudence of Government–Business Relations. *Journal of American History* 61:970–1005.

TWISS, BENJAMIN R. 1942 *Lawyers and the Constitution: How Laissez Faire Came to the Supreme Court.* Princeton, N.J.: Princeton University Press.

VETO POWER

After rejecting an absolute veto for the President, the delegates at the CONSTITUTIONAL CONVENTION OF 1787 granted the President a qualified power to veto congressional legislation, subject to an override by a two-thirds majority of each house of Congress. Some anti-Federalists objected to the veto as an encroachment upon the legislative power in violation of the SEPARATION OF POWERS doctrine, but ALEXANDER HAMILTON answered in THE FEDERALIST #73 that the President needed a veto to protect the executive branch from "depredations" by the legislature. The veto was also designed to be used against bills that were constitutionally defective, poorly drafted, or injurious to the community.

The Constitution provides that any bill not returned by the President "within ten Days (Sundays excepted)" shall become law "unless the Congress by their Adjournment prevent its Return, in which Case it shall not be a Law." The latter procedure, known as the POCKET VETO, was first used by President JAMES MADISON in 1812. In the POCKET VETO CASE of 1929, the Supreme Court decided that "adjournment" did not refer merely to final adjournment at the end of a Congress. The pocket veto could be used during any adjournment, final or interim, that "prevented" a bill's return to Congress. However, in *Wright v. United States* (1938) the Court considered a three-day recess by the Senate too short a period to constitute adjournment.

Further clarification of the pocket veto resulted from an action by President RICHARD M. NIXON. In 1970, during an adjournment of Congress for less than a week, he pocket-vetoed the Family Practice of Medicine Bill. An appellate court, in *Kennedy v. Sampson* (1974), held that an *intra*session adjournment of Congress does not prevent the President from returning a bill so long as Congress makes appropriate arrangements to receive presidential messages. The GERALD R. FORD and JIMMY CARTER administrations renounced pocket vetoes during *inter*session adjournments as well. This political accommodation restricted the pocket veto to the final adjournment at the end of the second session. President RONALD W. REAGAN, however, has used the pocket veto between the first and second sessions, provoking renewed litigation.

Other court decisions have clarified the boundaries of the veto power. In 1919, in *Missouri Pacific Railway Co. v. Kansas,* the Supreme Court announced that the Constitution required only two-thirds of a quorum in each House to override a veto, not two-thirds of the total membership. In 1899 the Court decided, in *La Abra Silver Mining Co. v. United States,* that the President could sign a bill after Congress recessed, and in *Edwards v. United States* (1932) the Court ruled that he could sign a bill after a final adjournment of Congress.

Statistics underscore the effectiveness of the President's veto. Of the 1,380 regular (return) vetoes from GEORGE WASHINGTON through Jimmy Carter, Congress overrode only ninety-four. There have also been 1,011 pocket vetoes, more than half of them directed by GROVER CLEVELAND and FRANKLIN D. ROOSEVELT against private relief bills.

Most of the governors of the states have been granted authority to veto individual items of a bill (the "item veto"). Congress has thus far resisted giving this power to the President, despite popular belief that such a power would increase "economy and efficiency" by combating "logrolling" and "pork-barrel" politics in Congress. Prominent among the arguments against the item veto is the danger that Presidents could use the authority to control the votes of individual members of Congress. A project in a member's district or state could be held hostage until he or she agreed to support a nominee or legislative proposal backed by the White House.

An informal type of item veto has evolved because Presidents selectively enforce the law. In signing a bill, Presidents have announced that they would refuse to carry out certain provisions which they considered unconstitutional or undesirable. The IMPOUNDMENT of funds has been a common example, but Presidents have also severed from authorization bills a number of sections they considered a "nullity," without binding force or effect.

LOUIS FISHER

Bibliography

FISHER, LOUIS 1985 *Constitutional Conflicts between Congress and the President.* Princeton, N.J.: Princeton University Press.

JACKSON, CARLTON 1967 *Presidential Vetoes, 1792–1945.* Athens: University of Georgia Press.

MASON, EDWARD CAMPBELL 1890 *The Veto Power.* New York: Russell & Russell.

VICE-PRESIDENCY

The American vice-presidency has historically occupied an ambiguous position. Although protocol ranks it the nation's second office, the duties assigned it have not been commensurate with that status. Pundits have frequently ridiculed the office and reformers have generously proposed modifying it. Yet for an institution that has engendered so much criticism the vice-presidency has undergone remarkably little constitutional change.

The office was conceived in the final days of the CONSTITUTIONAL CONVENTION OF 1787 for reasons that remain obscure. Some delegates suggested the need for an officer to preside over the Senate and resolve tie votes. Others viewed the vice-presidency as a way to handle unexpected presidential vacancies. Finally, some saw the office as an expedient to ensure the election of a national President. They feared that presidential electors would invariably support their own state's favorite son, thereby frustrating efforts to select a chief executive. By creating a second office and by giving electors a second vote subject to the proviso that one of the votes must go to a person from a state other than the elector's these constitutional architects believed they would overcome provincial tendencies and provide the new nation with a consensus leader. The candidate with the most votes (provided that they constituted a majority) would be President, the runner-up vice-president.

The system provided not only a national President but also vice-presidents of rare ability—JOHN ADAMS, THOMAS JEFFERSON, and AARON BURR. In 1800, however, the electoral votes for Jefferson and Burr deadlocked, although the Republican party had clearly intended Jefferson to be President. The constitutional crisis required thirty-six ballots of the House of Representatives before Jefferson prevailed. The initial system accordingly fell into disfavor, and in 1804 the states ratified the TWELFTH AMENDMENT which provided for separate election of President and vice-president. Many legislators feared that the vice-presidency would attract only inferior candidates and accordingly proposed its abolition.

Although the office survived, the high caliber of its occupants did not. Most vice-presidents during the remainder of the nineteenth century were nonentities who brought few credentials to the office, did little while in it, and disappeared from public attention once their term ended. Presidents had little influence on the selection of their running mates. Party leaders typically chose the second candidate from a different wing of the party in order to balance the ticket. Presidents and vice-presidents frequently feuded over policy and personal differences. The vice-president presided over the Senate, but did little else. As WOODROW WILSON wrote, "The chief embarrassment in discussing his office is, that in explaining how little there is to be said about it one has evidently said all there is to say."

The nineteenth century did, however, provide four occasions for vice-presidents to succeed to the presidency on the death of the incumbent. JOHN TYLER, MILLARD FILLMORE, ANDREW JOHNSON, and CHESTER A. ARTHUR all became President when their predecessors died in office. None, however, won a term of his own.

The ambiguous constitutional status of the office was one source of its problem. The office was a hybrid between the legislative and executive branches; its occupant was selected with the President, and yet his only constitutional duty resided in the legislative branch. Neither the Senate not the President was disposed to give great power to an officer which neither had selected and neither could remove. Some Presidents have viewed the vice-presidency as a legislative office and argued that the principle of SEPARATION OF POWERS precludes delegation of duties. Some vice-presidents have advanced this reasoning (or rationalization) to resist executive assignments. Moreover, since the presidency itself was relatively inactive for much of the nineteenth century, the President typically had little need to delegate duties to a vice-president, especially one not politically or personally compatible.

During the twentieth century, the vice-presidency achieved greater importance. The rise in status of the office occurred primarily because of political change rather than constitutional reform. The presidency became the main beneficiary of increased activity of the federal government, especially from the New Deal onward. The President became the distributor of increased patronage, and therefore other political actors responded more willingly to his influence. Accordingly, presidential candidates, rather than party leaders, began to assume a larger role in selecting the running mate. Presidents thus had a chance to select compatible vice-presidents and an incentive to provide them with some assignments. Moreover, increased demands on the presidency provided opportunities for vice-presidential activity. Presidents have tended to use their vice-presidents as foreign envoys, commission chairmen, party leaders, public spokesmen, legislative liaison, and advisers. Ratification in 1967 of the TWENTY-FIFTH AMENDMENT, which in part provided a means for filling unexpected vice-presidential vacancies, recognized the new significance of the office. With a few notable exceptions, twentieth-century vice-presidents have been men of some accomplishment. Many have been presidential candidates prior to accepting the second position: virtually all subsequently were considered for their party's presidential nomination or received it. Since 1900, five vice-presidents—THEODORE ROOSEVELT, CALVIN COOLIDGE, HARRY S. TRUMAN, LYNDON B. JOHNSON, and GERALD FORD—have succeeded to the presidency upon death or resignation of the incumbent. Each one except Ford subsequently won his own term—and Ford lost but narrowly. Presidents JIMMY CARTER and RONALD REAGAN have done much to enhance the office by granting Vice-Presidents Walter F. Mondale and George Bush, respectively, broad access to, and influence in, decision making.

The vice-presidency's enlarged significance this century has not silenced its critics. Some prominent students of American government recommend abolishing the office: they would generally handle an unexpected presidential vacancy by designating an interim President and holding special elections. Others would retain the vice-presidency but would attempt to augment its powers either by requiring that the vice-president hold a leading cabinet position or have a vote or significant powers in the Senate. Finally, a third group of reformers seeks to change the process of nominating or electing vice-presidents. Proposals range from having presidential and vice-presidential candidates run together during primaries to holding separate elections for President and vice-president. Although these proposals stimulate interesting debates, the prospects of significant formal changes in the vice-presidency are slim. Constitutional change rarely, if ever, comes easily. Proposed reforms of the vice-presidency would tend to create as many problems as they would solve. Growth in the office will probably depend largely on further changes in American politics and on the relation between future Presidents and vice-presidents.

JOEL K. GOLDSTEIN

Bibliography

FEERICK, JOHN 1965 *From Failing Hands.* New York: Fordham University Press.

GOLDSTEIN, JOEL K. 1982 *The Modern American Vice Presidency: Transformation of a Political Institution.* Princeton, N.J.: Princeton University Press.

WILLIAMS, IRVING G. 1956 *The Rise of the Vice Presidency.* Washington, D.C.: Public Affairs Press.

VICINAGE

Of all the features constituting a citizen's right to a TRIAL BY JURY, none is so outdated or less of service than the Sixth Amendment provision guaranteeing "an impartial jury of the State and district wherein the crime [charged] shall have been committed." This specification of the geographic area from which jurors must be drawn should not be confused, however, with VENUE, which fixes the location of the trial itself.

The clause providing for a jury of the vicinage or neighborhood enjoys a time-worn heritage. In the thirteenth century jurors were usually witnesses or had personal knowledge of the event at issue. Although jurors eventually lost their character as witnesses, both EDWARD COKE and WILLIAM BLACKSTONE discussed the precise number of jurors who must come from the immediate locality. Vicinage became an issue in the colonial debate with England, and the Virginia Assembly, in 1769, asserted the colonists' right to "the inestimable Privilege of being tried by a Jury from the vicinage," a position echoed by the Continental Congress and listed as a grievance against the king in the DECLARATION OF INDEPENDENCE. The Sixth Amendment, framed shortly after the JUDICIARY ACT OF 1789, probably refers to the judicial districts established by that act.

Nevertheless, a federal defendant today "does not have a right under the Sixth Amendment to have jurors drawn from the entire district" (*Zicarelli v. Dietz,* 1980), and the Supreme Court has denied that trial juries "must mirror the community and reflect the various distinctive groups in the population" (*Taylor v. Louisiana,* 1975). State courts have generally been willing to narrow the vicinage requirement to a unit as small as an individual county, although federal courts have asserted that the Sixth Amendment clause applies "only to federal criminal trials, not to state criminal trials" (*Zicarelli*).

DAVID GORDON

VIETNAM WAR

Throughout American history, Presidents have dispatched armed forces abroad to protect the lives and property of United States citizens as well as American security interests. However, these military operations usually were limited in scope and duration, were conducted against relatively defenseless nations, and did not involve major powers. Thus, there was little opportunity to test the President's constitutional authority to send armed forces abroad without prior congressional authorization or a DECLARATION OF WAR. For various reasons, the KOREAN WAR did not furnish the occasion to test President HARRY S. TRUMAN's constitutional powers. The Vietnam War (1965–1973) was the first modern undeclared war that provided the opportunity to test the President's authority as COMMANDER-IN-CHIEF.

During the Vietnam War numerous litigants challenged the President's authority to initiate and conduct military hostilities without a congressional declaration of war or other explicit prior authorization. Such litigants denied that the GULF OF TONKIN resolution constituted authorization. Despite these challenges, the federal courts exhibited extreme caution in entering this twilight zone of concurrent power. The federal judiciary's reluctance to decide WAR POWERS controversies reveals a respect for the constitutional SEPARATION OF POWERS, an appreciation for the respective constitutional functions of Congress and the President in FOREIGN AFFAIRS, and a sense of judicial self-restraint. Nevertheless, toward the end of the Vietnam War, several lower federal courts entered the political thicket to restore the constitutional balance between Congress and the President.

Despite factual variations, the Vietnam War cases can be classified into four broad categories. One federal district court asserted categorically that the complaint raised a POLITICAL QUESTION beyond the court's JURISDICTION. A second agreed that the President's authority to conduct military activities without a declaration of war posed a nonjusticiable political question, but proceeded to determine whether the President had acted on his own authority, pursuant to, or in conflict with either the expressed or implied will of Congress. Courts in the third category concluded that the political question doctrine did not foreclose them from inquiring into the existence and constitutional sufficiency of joint congressional-presidential participation in prosecuting the war. Finally, some district courts decided cases on the substantive merits. Yet the Vietnam War ended without an authoritative Supreme Court decision.

At the war's end Congress enacted the War Powers Resolution (1973), which attempted to resolve the constitutional ambiguities posed by the separation of the congressional war powers from the President's office of commander-in-chief. Under the resolution, Congress can alternatively authorize continuation of military hostilities that the President has initiated or require him to disengage armed forces from foreign combat within sixty to ninety days. Practical problems aside, the resolution seems constitutionally flawed. The Supreme Court's decision in IMMIGRATION AND NATURALIZATION SERVICE V. CHADHA (1983) cast doubt on the constitutionality of the resolution's LEGISLATIVE VETO provision, which states that Congress can direct the disengagement of troops by CONCURRENT RESOLUTION. Moreover, if the Constitution vests the authority to initiate military hostilities exclusively in the Congress, can Congress constitutionally delegate this authority to the President, even for a limited period? Is the War Powers Resolution an undated declaration of war that allows the President to choose the time, the place, and the enemy?

The Framers of the Constitution conferred only a limited set of defensive war powers on the President. As commander-in-chief he superintends the armed forces in war and peace, defending the nation, its armed forces, and its citizens and their property against attack, and directing military operations in wartime. The Framers did not authorize the President to initiate military hostilities, to transform defensive actions into aggressive wars, or to defend allies against attack.

In the Framers' view, only Congress could change the nation's condition from peace to war. Yet neither the constitutional text nor the records of the CONSTITUTIONAL CONVENTION conclusively draw the boundary between congressional power to initiate war and presidential power to defend against attack. In the twentieth century, international terrorism, the Vietnam War, guerrilla and insurgency warfare, wars of "national liberation," and the global conflict between the United States and the Soviet Union have virtually erased the Framers' distinction between defensive and offensive war.

A long history of undeclared war and military hostilities demonstrates that the constitutional questions raised during the Vietnam War are inherent in the American constitutional system. Presidents will be confronted with demands and opportunities to intervene militarily to protect American national security interests and the security interests of the nation's allies. Before yielding to this temptation, future Presidents should recall one of the Vietnam War's most important lessons: the nation should not wage a protracted undeclared war without a continuing agreement between Congress and the President that reflects broad, sustained public support.

EDWARD KEYNES

Bibliography

KEYNES, EDWARD 1982 *Undeclared War: Twilight Zone of Constitutional Power.* University Park: Pennsylvania State University Press.

REVELEY, W. TAYLOR, III 1981 *War Powers of the President and Congress: Who Holds the Arrows and Olive Branch?* Charlottesville: University Press of Virginia.

SOFAER, ABRAHAM D. 1976 *War, Foreign Affairs, and Constitutional Power.* Cambridge, Mass.: Ballinger Publishing Co.

VILLAGE OF . . .

See entry under name of village

VINSON, FRED M. (1890–1953)

Fred M. Vinson was appointed thirteenth CHIEF JUSTICE of the United States by President HARRY S. TRUMAN in 1946 and served in that office until his death. His appointment followed a distinguished career in all three branches of the federal government. That career profoundly influenced his performance as Chief Justice.

Born and raised in the jail of Louisa, Kentucky—his father was the town jailer—he devoted almost his entire professional career to the public sector. Shortly after his admission to the bar, he served as city attorney and as Commonwealth attorney. Elected to Congress in 1928, he was an influential member of that legislative body during the New Deal years. His judicial experience commenced with appointment as judge of the United States Court of Appeals for the District of Columbia in 1937, and was broadened in 1942 when Chief Justice HARLAN FISKE STONE named him Chief Judge of the EMERGENCY COURT OF APPEALS. His executive branch experience began with his 1943 appointment as director of Economic Stabilization, followed in 1945 by three posts in rapid succession: Federal Loan administrator, director of War Mobilization and Reconversion, and secretary of the Treasury.

He was appointed Chief Justice in 1946 to a Court widely regarded as ridden not only with the usual ideological disagreements but also with severe personal animosities. One successful aspect of his tenure as Chief Justice was the substantial reduction of public exposure of these conflicts.

In 1949, the deaths of Justices FRANK MURPHY and WILEY B. RUTLEDGE were followed by the appointments of TOM C. CLARK and SHERMAN MINTON. These changes, which occurred just short of the midpoint of his tenure, shifted the balance of the Court to a more conservative position, one more consonant with his own judicial and political philosophy.

That philosophy must be ascertained more by inference than through direct revelation. During his seven years as Chief Justice, the number of cases heard by the Court declined; as Chief Justice he assigned comparatively few opinions to himself. The evidence makes clear, however, that his philosophy reflected his public and political experience, acquired during the New Deal and World War II years, when a strong national government was deemed a *sine qua non* and loyalty to one's party and political confreres was a necessary condition of the success of the political process.

For him, the governmental institutions were democratically based, sound, and trustworthy; they were entitled to the loyalty of those whom they served and to protection from those who would destroy them. The judgments of the President and Congress that communism threatened both from without and from within were entitled to respect. The nation and its people fared better with a stable regime than with one of disruption; government was entitled at least to have time to respond to conflicts. The lowest person could rise to the highest office. Concomitantly—although the enactments of legislatures were normally to be respected—legal restrictions based upon race, disabling handicaps to the realization of the American dream, were disfavored. Even as his extensive federal governmental experience made him sympathetic to a strong central government, so his executive branch experience rendered him unafraid of strong executive power.

His tenure as Chief Justice spanned the Cold War era in which pro-Soviet attitudes that had developed during World War II became suspect. The rise of McCarthyism, the trial of Alger Hiss, the KOREAN

WAR, the theft of atomic secrets, and like events dominated public discussion and government reaction.

These events pervaded the atmosphere in which major constitutional issues were presented. Thus, his views about loyalty are perhaps best represented in those cases that sustained noncriminal deprivations addressed to communists and those considered disloyal, for example, his opinion for the Court in AMERICAN COMMUNICATIONS ASSOCIATION v. DOUDS (1950); denial of TAFT-HARTLEY COLLECTIVE BARGAINING benefits); and his votes in *Bailey v. Richardson* (1951; denial of federal employment) and JOINT ANTI-FASCIST REFUGEE COMMITTEE v. MCGRATH (1951; blacklisting of suspected organizations).

His lack of sympathy for those whose purpose he viewed as destructive of the governmental institutions is evidenced in his plurality opinion in DENNIS v. UNITED STATES (1951), which sustained against a FIRST AMENDMENT claim the criminal convictions of communist leaders under the Smith Act, and his majority opinion in FEINER v. NEW YORK (1951), affirming the conviction of an antigovernment speaker who refused to stop speaking when ordered to do so by a police officer after members of the audience threatened to assault him.

His concern for institutional stability is reflected in his opinion in UNITED STATES v. UNITED MINE WORKERS (1947), sustaining the judiciary's use of the CONTEMPT POWER to halt a disruptive strike, and his dissenting opinion in YOUNGSTOWN SHEET & TUBE CO. v. SAWYER (1951), where he would have sustained the power of the President to seize steel mills to maintain steel production interrupted by a strike.

Overtaken by later cases, several of Vinson's most significant opinions advanced the elimination of RACIAL DISCRIMINATION and in theoretical terms expanded the interpretation of the EQUAL PROTECTION clause. Although the unanimous opinions he authored in SWEATT v. PAINTER (1950) and MCLAURIN v. BOARD OF REGENTS (1950) did not in terms overrule the SEPARATE BUT EQUAL DOCTRINE of PLESSY v. FERGUSON (1896), the rejection of the separate Texas law school in *Sweatt* and of the special treatment of *McLaurin* made the demise of that doctrine inevitable. His most interesting and venturesome equal protection opinion was SHELLEY v. KRAEMER (1948), the RESTRICTIVE COVENANT case, whose doctrinal implications have yet to be satisfactorily delineated.

Vinson accorded the federal government expansive legislative power under the COMMERCE CLAUSE. Perceived conflicts between the federal government and the states were resolved in favor of a strong central government. Where the federal government had not spoken, his concern focused on discrimination against INTERSTATE COMMERCE and the out-of-stater, a position most clearly seen in the STATE TAXATION OF COMMERCE cases and TOOMER v. WITSELL (1948), the path-breaking interpretation of the PRIVILEGES AND IMMUNITIES clause of Article IV, which in effect extended his commerce clause philosophy to areas he thought the clause did not reach.

His general judicial approach inclined Vinson to focus on the particular facts of the case and to eschew promulgation of sweeping legal principles. He was slow to overrule earlier opinions and DOCTRINES. The power of the Court to invalidate federal executive and legislative actions on constitutional grounds was to be used sparingly; he never voted to invalidate an act of Congress or a presidential action. He was as apt as any member of his Court, save perhaps Justice FELIX FRANKFURTER, to avoid constitutional questions and, when those issues were faced, to take an intermediate rather than ultimate constitutional position. Clearly, Fred M. Vinson belonged to the "judicial restraint" school of Supreme Court Justices.

MURRAY L. SCHWARTZ

Bibliography

KIRKENDALL, K. 1969 Fred M. Vinson. In Leon Friedman and Fred L. Israel, *The Justices of the United States Supreme Court.* Vol. 4:2639–2649. New York: Chelsea House.

PRITCHETT, C. HERMAN 1954 *Civil Liberties and the Vinson Court.* Chicago: University of Chicago Press.

SYMPOSIUM 1954 *Northwestern University Law Review* 49:1–76.

VINSON COURT
(1946–1953)

FRED M. VINSON was Chief Justice of the United States from June 24, 1946, until his death on September 8, 1953. During his seven-year period of service the Supreme Court was considerably less interesting, colorful, or originative of significant constitutional DOCTRINE than its predecessor, the STONE COURT, or its successor, the WARREN COURT. However, the Vinson Court did deal with serious and important issues, particularly Cold War challenges to CIVIL LIBERTIES and awakening concerns about RACIAL DISCRIMINATION.

Vinson was a close friend of President HARRY S. TRUMAN and an active Democrat who had had the unique experience of serving in all three branches of the federal government. Immediately preceding his appointment to the Court he had been secretary of the treasury. President Truman had made one previous appointment, naming HAROLD BURTON, a Republican and former Senate colleague of Truman, to replace OWEN ROBERTS in 1945. The other seven justices were of course all holdovers from the Stone Court, which guaranteed a continuation of the judicial dialogue that had pitted the liberal activism of HUGO L. BLACK, WILLIAM O. DOUGLAS, FRANK MURPHY, and WILEY B. RUTLEDGE against the brilliant critiques of FELIX FRANKFURTER and ROBERT H. JACKSON, with the moderate STANLEY F. REED somewhere in the center.

The four-judge liberal bloc had within itself the votes required to grant CERTIORARI petitions, which ensured that civil liberties issues would continue to appear on the Court's agenda. When the liberals agreed, they needed only one additional vote to constitute a majority. But in the summer of 1949 Justices Murphy and Rutledge died, cutting the liberal bloc in half. President Truman filled these two vacancies by the appointment of TOM C. CLARK, his attorney general, and SHERMAN MINTON, who had been a New Deal senator from Indiana. The two new justices joined with Vinson, Reed, and Burton in a moderately conservative bloc which dominated the remaining four terms of the Vinson Court. An indication of the balance of power on the Court is provided by the number of dissents registered by each of the Justices during this four-year period: Clark 15, Vinson 40, Burton 44, Minton 47, Reed 59, Jackson 80, Frankfurter 101, Douglas 130, Black 148.

The most famous decision of the Vinson Court in terms of public reaction, and probably the most noteworthy as a contribution to constitutional theory, was YOUNGSTOWN SHEET & TUBE CO. V. SAWYER (1952), generally known as the Steel Seizure Case. Here the Court by a vote of 6–3 held unconstitutional President Truman's seizure of the nation's steel mills in 1952, an action he justified as necessary to avert a nationwide strike that might have affected the flow of munitions to American troops in Korea. The President had no statutory authority for the seizure, which consequently had to be justified on a theory of inherent presidential power to meet emergencies.

Justice Black, supported by Douglas, flatly denied the existence of any inherent presidential powers. Justices Jackson and Frankfurter were less dogmatic, and the doctrine of the case is generally drawn from their opinions. As they saw it, the controlling factor was that Congress had considered granting the President seizure power to deal with nationwide strikes when adopting the TAFT-HARTLEY ACT in 1947 but had decided against it. In addition, Jackson contributed a situational scale for ruling on claims of executive emergency power. Vinson, in his most famous dissent, upheld the President as having moved in an emergency to maintain the status quo until Congress could act, and he rejected the majority's "messenger boy" concept of the presidential office.

The fact that the Court could have avoided the constitutional issue in the Steel Seizure Case by various alternatives suggested that most of the justices believed it important to announce a check on presidential power. The decision was enormously popular with the press and public and has subsequently been accepted as an authoritative statement on the SEPARATION OF POWERS, establishing that actions of the president are subject to JUDICIAL REVIEW. There had been some doubt on this point since the failure of the post-Civil War suit against the president in MISSISSIPPI V. JOHNSON (1867). It established also that executive claims of power for which statutory authority is lacking, and which must consequently rely on the President's general Article II authority, are subject to strict judicial scrutiny.

Less significant in its doctrine than the Steel Seizure Case but almost as controversial was the Court's contempt ruling against John L. Lewis, leader of the coal miners, in 1947 (UNITED STATES V. UNITED MINE WORKERS). The government had seized the nation's bituminous coal mines in 1946 to end a crippling strike and had entered into a contract with Lewis on wages and working conditions. When Lewis subsequently terminated the contract unilaterally and resumed the strike, the government secured a contempt JUDGMENT and heavy fine against Lewis and the union. In his first major opinion Vinson upheld the conviction for contempt, ruling that the NORRIS-LAGUARDIA ACT limiting the issuance of labor INJUNCTIONS was not binding on the government as an employer.

A significant difference between the Stone and Vinson Courts was that World War II had ended and the Cold War against communism had begun. The hunt for subversives in which the nation was caught up soon after the shooting war was over tainted the entire period of the Vinson Court and created difficult civil liberties issues. The government's principal weapon against suspected subversion was the Smith Act of 1940, which made it unlawful to teach and advocate the overthrow of the United States government by force and violence, or to organize a group for such a purpose.

Convictions of eleven leaders of the American Communist party under the Smith Act were upheld by the Supreme Court in DENNIS V. UNITED STATES

(1951). In the most memorable event of his judicial career, Chief Justice Vinson wrote the Court's majority opinion defending the Smith Act against contentions that it violated the FIRST AMENDMENT. The defendants admittedly had taken no action with the immediate intention of initiating a revolution. But Vinson held that the CLEAR AND PRESENT DANGER TEST, developed by Justice OLIVER WENDELL HOLMES and LOUIS D. BRANDEIS, did not require the government to wait until a "putsch" was about to be executed before acting against a conspiracy. Vinson accepted the reformulation of the test developed by Judge LEARNED HAND: "Whether the gravity of the 'evil,' discounted by its improbability, justifies such invasion of free speech as is necessary to avoid the danger." He considered the communist "evil" to be that grave. Justices Black and Douglas dissented; Douglas pointed out that the prosecution had introduced no evidence of Communist party action aimed at overthrow of the government.

Vinson also wrote the Court's opinion in AMERICAN COMMUNICATIONS ASSOCIATION V. DOUDS (1950), upholding the Taft-Hartley Act noncommunist oath. This statute denied the protections and services of the WAGNER (NATIONAL LABOR RELATIONS) ACT to any labor organization whose officers failed to file affidavits that they were not members of the Communist party. The Chief Justice held that Congress in adopting this statute was acting to prevent the obstruction of commerce by "political strikes." The law was not aimed at speech but rather at harmful conduct carried on by persons who could be identified by their political affiliations and beliefs.

The Vinson Court was caught up in the final moments of the Cold War's most spectacular event, the execution of Julius and Ethel Rosenberg, who were charged with passing atomic "secrets" to the Russians. Review of the lower court conviction and subsequent APPEALS was routinely denied by the Supreme Court in 1952 and early 1953, as were also the initial petitions for STAY OF EXECUTION. But Justice Douglas thought that one final petition filed the day before execution was scheduled raised a new legal issue deserving consideration. He consequently granted a stay which the full Court set aside the next day, and the executions were then carried out. Douglas's action caused a brief furor and a congressman demanded his IMPEACHMENT. In the last opinion before his death Vinson defended Douglas's action as a proper response to protect the Court's JURISDICTION over the case pending a consideration of the legal issue raised. Black and Frankfurter joined Douglas in asserting that the stay should have been granted.

During the era of the Vinson Court, congressional committee investigations of communism developed into major political and media events. Senator Joseph McCarthy's pursuit of "Fifth Amendment Communists" got under way in 1950, too late to create issues for the Vinson Court. But the HOUSE COMMITTEE ON UN-AMERICAN ACTIVITIES had begun operations in 1938, and by 1947 petitions for review of contempt citations against witnesses who had refused to reply to committee interrogation began to reach the Supreme Court. However, it declined review of all the cases that would have required a ruling on the constitutionality of the use of investigatory power, and it dealt only with certain less controversial issues of committee procedure and use of the Fifth Amendment privilege by witnesses.

A prominent feature of the Cold War period was concern about the loyalty of government employees. A LOYALTY OATH fad developed in nearly every state, which the Vinson Court legitimated in GERENDE V. BOARD OF SUPERVISORS OF ELECTIONS (1951) by upholding a Maryland law that required candidates for public office to file affidavits that they were not "subversive persons."

A loyalty program covering federal employees was set up by President Truman in 1947 and was continued by President DWIGHT D. EISENHOWER. It required checking the loyalty of all incumbent employees and all applicants for federal employment. A complex administrative organization of loyalty review boards was created, and to assist the boards the attorney general issued a list of organizations he found to be "totalitarian, fascist, communist, or subversive." Consideration of the constitutionality of this program split the Court 4–4 in *Bailey v. Richardson* (1951). But in JOINT ANTI-FASCIST REFUGEE COMMITTEE V. MCGRATH (1951), decided the same day, the Court by a vote of 5–3 challenged the attorney general's list as having been drawn up without appropriate investigation or DUE PROCESS. The dissenters were Reed, Vinson, and Minton. In spite of this opinion the list continued to be used for a number of years in government hiring and investigation.

At the state level a New York law providing for the removal of public school teachers on grounds of membership in listed subversive organizations was upheld in ADLER V. BOARD OF EDUCATION OF CITY OF NEW YORK (1952), Justice Minton reasoning that the purpose was constitutional and that procedural protections provided by the statute were adequate. Justices Black and Douglas dissented, and Frankfurter would have denied the appeal on technical grounds of STANDING and RIPENESS.

Apart from Cold War cases, FREEDOM OF SPEECH and FREEDOM OF THE PRESS did not suffer seriously at the hands of the Vinson Court. BURSTYN V. WILSON (1952) was in fact an advance in its holding that a motion picture could not be censored on the ground that it was "sacrilegious." A law censoring magazines featuring bloodshed and lust was struck down in *Winters v. New York* (1948) as void for vagueness. *Poulos v. New Hampshire* (1953) upheld licensing of meetings in public parks and streets, but only if the licenses were granted without discrimination, and the use of licensing ordinances to prevent unpopular religious groups or preachers from holding meetings in public parks was rebuffed in NIEMOTKO V. MARYLAND (1951) and KUNZ V. NEW YORK (1951).

In TERMINIELLO V. CHICAGO (1949) a divided Court reversed on rather technical grounds the conviction of a rabble-rouser for BREACH OF THE PEACE resulting from an incendiary speech. But FEINER V. NEW YORK (1951) upheld the conviction of a soapbox orator even though the situation was much less inflammatory than in *Terminiello.* Moreover, BEAUHARNAIS V. ILLINOIS (1952) approved a state law treating critical comments about racial groups as criminal and subjecting their authors to prosecution for GROUP LIBEL.

The Vinson Court dealt with a number of conflicts between freedom of expression and privacy but without producing any theories justifying or limiting privacy claims such as those subsequently developed in GRISWOLD V. CONNECTICUT (1965) by the Warren Court. Use of sound trucks in streets and parks was initially upheld in *Saia v. New York* (1948) against contentions of infringement on privacy, but in the following year the Court conceded that "loud and raucous" sound trucks could be forbidden (KOVACS V. COOPER). Radio broadcasts including commercial messages in DISTRICT OF COLUMBIA streetcars were permitted to continue by *Public Utilities Commission v. Pollak* (1952), even though CAPTIVE AUDIENCES might suffer, but *Breard v. City of Alexandria* (1951) protected householders by approving an ordinance forbidding door-to-door selling of magazine subscriptions. Justice Black charged that the latter decision violated the "preferred position" for First Amendment freedoms originated by the Roosevelt Court. The severest blow to that philosophy was *United Public Workers v. Mitchell* (1947) which upheld by a vote of 4–3 the HATCH ACT limits on political activity by public employees.

In a 1940 case, THORNHILL V. ALABAMA, the Court had strongly asserted that PICKETING in labor disputes was protected by the First Amendment. Almost immediately, however, the Court found it necessary to announce limits on this holding, a process the Vinson Court continued. The most significant case was GIBONEY V. EMPIRE STORAGE & ICE CO. (1949), where the Court ruled unanimously against a union that was picketing to force an employer to enter into an illegal restrictive contract.

The issue of public financial aid to religious schools required the Vinson Court to make the first significant effort to interpret and apply the First Amendment ban on ESTABLISHMENT OF RELIGION. EVERSON V. BOARD OF EDUCATION (1947) involved a state arrangement under which parents could be reimbursed from public moneys for their children's bus fare to parochial schools. An unusual five-judge majority composed of three liberals (Black, Douglas, and Murphy) and two conservatives (Vinson and Reed) held that the subsidy was simply a social welfare measure and that the First Amendment did not require exclusion of persons of any faith from the benefits of "public welfare legislation." Rutledge's vigorous dissent regarded payment for transportation to church schools as a direct aid to religious education and so unconstitutional.

The following year MCCOLLUM V. BOARD OF EDUCATION presented another church–state issue. The case involved a RELEASED TIME program of religious education under which public school children attended classes in Protestant, Roman Catholic, or Jewish religious instruction during school hours and in the school building. The Court's almost unanimous verdict of UNCONSTITUTIONALITY aroused a storm of criticism in church circles, and within four years the Court substantially reversed this ruling, upholding a New York City released time program that differed from *McCollum* only in that the classes were held off the school grounds (ZORACH V. CLAUSEN, 1952.) A similar reluctance to disturb the religious community was seen as the Court avoided on technical grounds of standing a ruling on the constitutionality of Bible-reading in the public schools (DOREMUS V. BOARD OF EDUCATION).

The Vinson Court's civil liberties record was distinctly better than that of its predecessors in one area, protection of minorities from discrimination. The prevailing constitutional rule was that established by PLESSY V. FERGUSON in 1896—that SEGREGATION of the races was constitutional provided treatment or facilities were equal. In practice, they were never equal, but over the years the Court had consistently avoided the difficult task of enforcing the *Plessy* rule. In the field of education, none of the few efforts to challenge unequal facilities had been successful. But in 1938 the HUGHES COURT made a small beginning, ruling in MISSOURI EX REL. GAINES V. CANADA that Missouri, which denied blacks admission to state law schools, must do so or set up a separate law school for blacks. MORGAN V. VIRGINIA (1946) invalidated a state Jim Crow law requiring racial segregation of passengers on public motor carriers, but the constitutional ground given was burden on INTERSTATE COMMERCE rather than denial of EQUAL PROTECTION.

The Vinson Court undertook cautiously to build on these beginnings. The COMMERCE CLAUSE justification used in the Virginia bus case was likewise employed in BOB-LO EXCURSION CO. V. MICHIGAN (1948). But the Vinson Court's boldest action against segregation came shortly thereafter in SHELLEY V. KRAEMER (1948). With Vinson writing the opinion, the Court declared that RESTRICTIVE COVENANTS binding property owners not to sell to minorities, although within the legal rights of property owners, were unenforceable. For a court to give effect to such a discriminatory contract, Vinson held, would amount to STATE ACTION in violation of the FOURTEENTH AMENDMENT.

The separate law school for blacks that Texas had established was declared unequal in SWEATT V. PAINTER (1950). The University of Oklahoma, forced to admit a black graduate student, required him to sit in a separate row in class, at a separate desk in the library, and at a separate table in the cafeteria. MCLAURIN V. OKLAHOMA STATE REGENTS (1950), with Vinson again writing the opinion, held these practices to be an unconstitutional impairment of the student's ability to learn his profession.

Vinson's opinion, however, rejected the opportunity to consider the broader issue of the *Plessy* SEPARATE BUT EQUAL rule. So attacks on the segregation principle continued, and the TEST CASES moved from the universities and graduate schools to the primary and secondary schools. In December 1952 BROWN V. BOARD OF EDUCATION OF TOPEKA and four other school segregation cases were argued for three days before the Court. But instead of a decision in June, the Court set the cases for reargument in October. The Chief Justice died in September, and so the Vinson Court's most momentous issue was passed on to the Warren Court.

Although the Stone Court had broken some new ground in CRIMINAL PROCEDURE, its record was mixed, particularly in guaranteeing the RIGHT TO COUNSEL and protection against UNREASONABLE SEARCHES and seizures. This latter issue surfaced in the Vinson Court's first term. One of the oldest problems in American constitutional law is whether the due process clause of the Fourteenth Amendment "incorporated" and made effective in state criminal proceedings the protections of the Fourth through the Eighth Amendments. As recently as 1937 in PALKO V. CONNECTICUT the Court had reiterated the principle that all state procedures consistent with ORDERED LIBERTY are acceptable.

In ADAMSON V. CALIFORNIA (1947) the *Palko* doctrine survived on the Vinson Court, but by only a 5–4 vote. Justice Black led the minority. He relied on legislative history to establish his version of the intention of the framers of the Fourteenth Amendment and attacked the ORDERED LIBERTY test as substituting natural law and the notions of individual Justices for the precise and protective language of the BILL OF RIGHTS.

Although Black lost in *Adamson,* "ordered liberty" was a standard powerful enough to bring state criminal processes within the ambit of the FOURTH AMENDMENT in WOLF V. COLORADO (1949). However, Justice Frankfurter for the six-judge majority held only that SEARCHES AND SEIZURES by state law officers are bound by the standard of reasonableness; he declined to go further and impose on state prosecutions the EXCLUSIONARY RULE which prevents EVIDENCE secured by unconstitutional means from being offered in federal prosecutions. Justices Murphy, Douglas, and Rutledge, dissenting, contended that the exclusionary rule provided the only effective protection against police violation of the Fourth Amendment, and their view was finally adopted on the Warren Court in MAPP V. OHIO (1961).

With respect to right to counsel, the Vinson Court accepted the rule announced by the Stone Court in BETTS V. BRADY (1942) that the necessity for counsel depended upon the circumstances, such as the seriousness of the crime, the age and mental capacity of the defendant, and the ability of the judge. Applying the "special circumstances" rule in twelve cases, the Vinson Court concluded that in six the absence of counsel had resulted in denial of a FAIR TRIAL. In only one of the twelve was the Court unanimous. This experience was a factor in the Warren Court's decision in GIDEON V. WAINWRIGHT (1963) to abolish the confusing special circumstances rule and make counsel mandatory in all state felony prosecutions.

What was potentially one of the Vinson Court's most significant decisions for the federal system was nullified by Congress. In 1947 the Court ruled that subsurface land and mineral rights in California's three-mile coastal area belonged to the federal government (*United States v. California*), and in 1950 the Court applied the same rule to Texas. Congress retaliated in 1953 by ceding to the states ownership of land and resources under adjoining seas up to a distance of three miles from shore or to the states' historic boundaries.

In summary, the tendency of the Vinson Court was to follow a policy of judicial restraint, rejecting innovation or activism. The number of cases decided by full opinion fell below one hundred during three of the last four years, far less than the number typically decided by earlier Courts. The five justices who dominated the Court in its latter period were capable but lacking in style or originality. The four Justices of intellectual distinction—Black, Douglas, Frankfurter, and Jackson—generally paired off and pulled in opposite directions.

The pall of the Cold War hung over the Court. Confronted with the scandal of McCarthyism, it was quiescent. Facing Smith Act prosecutions, the loyalty inquisition of federal employees, lists of subversive organizations, scrutiny of school teachers' associates, loyalty oaths, and deportation of ex-communists, the Court's response was usually to legitimate the government's action.

But in one field, significantly, there was a different kind of response. The Vinson Court did not evade the issue of racial discrimination. Although moving cautiously, as was appropriate considering the enormity of the problem, the Court nevertheless proceeded to bring denial of equal protection out of the limbo of neglect and unconcern into the focus of national consciousness and thereby prepared the way for its successor's historic decision on May 17, 1954.

C. HERMAN PRITCHETT

Bibliography

FRANK, JOHN P. 1954 Fred Vinson and the Chief Justiceship. *University of Chicago Law Review* 21:212–246.

MURPHY, PAUL L. 1972 *The Constitution in Crisis Times, 1919–1969.* New York: Harper & Row.

PRITCHETT, C. HERMAN (1954)1966 *Civil Liberties and the Vinson Court.* Chicago: University of Chicago Press.

SWINDLER, WILLIAM F. 1970 *Court and Constitution in the Twentieth Century: The New Legality, 1932–1968.* Indianapolis: Bobbs-Merrill.

VIRGINIA, EX PARTE

See: *Strauder v. West Virginia*

VIRGINIA v. RIVES

See: *Strauder v. West Virginia*

VIRGINIA v. TENNESSEE

See: Interstate Compacts

VIRGINIA AND KENTUCKY RESOLUTIONS (1798–1799)

These resolutions declared the ALIEN AND SEDITION ACTS unconstitutional and sought to arouse political opposition by appealing to the legislatures of the several states. The strategy was devised by THOMAS JEFFERSON, the vice-president, who secretly drafted the resolutions that were adopted by the Kentucky legislature. A similar but milder series was drafted by JAMES MADISON for the Virginia assembly. Both set forth the compact theory of the Constitution, holding that the general government was one of strictly delegated powers; that acts beyond its powers were void; and that, there being no ultimate arbiter of the Constitution, each state had "an equal right to judge for itself, as well of infractions as of the mode and measure of redress." (See THEORIES OF THE UNION.) Jefferson baptized the theory "NULLIFICATION," though the name was omitted by Kentucky; and Virginia spoke instead of the right of each state to "interpose" to arrest the evil.

Five of the nine Kentucky Resolutions were devoted to proving the unconstitutionality of the Alien and Sedition Laws. The Alien Law was attacked for want of power, for violation of a specific constitutional provision (Article I, section 9), and for denial of TRIAL BY JURY and other fair procedures. The Sedition Act was asserted to be outside the scope of the Constitution as well as a direct violation of the FIRST AMENDMENT. The resolutions offered no broadly philosophical plea for FREEDOM OF SPEECH and PRESS but met the threat of the Sedition Law at its most vulnerable point, as an invasion of rights reserved to the states. It belonged to each state, not the general government, to determine "how far the licentiousness of speech and of the press may be abridged without lessening their useful freedom." Kentucky urged the other state legislatures to concur in declaring the acts unconstitutional and void.

Replies to the resolutions, mostly from Northern legislatures under Federalist control, were uniformly unfavorable. Prodded by Jefferson, Kentucky adopted a second set of resolutions in November 1799, reaffirming the principles of the first and, incidentally, introducing the word "nullification." In January 1800 the Virginia assembly adopted Madison's Report, a masterly exposition of the dual sovereignty theory of the federal union and a powerful defense of CIVIL LIBERTIES.

The principal object of the resolutions was to secure the freedom of opposition, of debate, and of change through the political process. This object was secured by the Republican victory in the election of 1800. But in pursuing "a political resistance for political effect," in Jefferson's words, he and his associates were somewhat careless on points of constitutional theory. Whether the resolutions were meant as a declaration of opinion or as a "nullification" of federal law, whether the right claimed for the state was limited to "usurpations" of the compact or extended to "abuses" as well, whether the ultimate recourse was the natural right of revolution or a constitutional right of SECESSION, these points were left unclear. It mattered little in 1800, after the resolutions had done their work and then were forgotten; but it mattered a great deal a generation later when the "Resolutions of '98" were revived and tortured by JOHN C. CALHOUN into a defense, not of liberty, but of slavery.

MERRILL D. PETERSON

Bibliography

KOCH, ADRIENNE and AMMON, HARRY 1948 The Virginia and Kentucky Resolutions: An Episode in Jefferson's and Madison's Defense of Civil Liberties. *William and Mary Quarterly* (3rd. ser.) 5:145–176.

MALONE, DUMAS 1962 *Jefferson and the Ordeal of Liberty.* Boston: Little, Brown.

VIRGINIA CHARTER OF 1606
(April 10, 1606)

This was the first royal charter issued for the planting of a colony in America. Charters were usually issued to private trading companies, as in this case, or to proprietary lords. The charter laid out boundaries, defined the relationship of the colony to the crown, and provided for a government. In this first charter, the government consisted only of a council. Subsequent charters for Virginia in 1609 and 1612 established the office of the governor; by 1619, in accord with a document called the "Great Charter" of 1618, elections were held and the first representative legislature in American history met at Jamestown. The enduring significance of Virginia's first charter lies in its provision that the colonists and their descendants "shall have and enjoy all Liberties, Franchises, and Immunities . . . as if they had been abiding and born, within this our Realm of England. . . ." Later charters for Virginia contained similar clauses. Their meaning was doubtless restricted at the time to legal rights of land tenure and inheritance, trial by jury, and little else; but the vague language (repeated in numerous other charters for colonies from New England to the South) allowed American colonists to believe that they were entitled to all the rights of Englishmen—their constitutional system and common law. Charters could be revoked and some were, but the American experience eventually led to written constitutions of fundamental law that contained bills of rights.

LEONARD W. LEVY

VIRGINIA DECLARATION OF RIGHTS AND CONSTITUTION OF 1776
(June 12 and 29, 1776)

Virginia, the oldest, largest, and most prestigious of the original states, adopted a Declaration of Rights on June 12, 1776, and two weeks later its "Constitution or Form of Government." Each document was the first of its kind and considerably influenced constitution-making in the other states. The primary draftsman of both documents was GEORGE MASON, although the self-styled "convention" that adopted them included many luminaries, among them JAMES MADISON. The convention was actually an extralegal or provisional legislature similar in membership to the last House of Burgesses under the royal charter before the Revolution. The same convention enacted ordinary legislation and elected a governor under the new CONSTITUTION.

THOMAS JEFFERSON in his *Notes on Virginia,* written in 1781, observed that "capital defects" marred the work of the constitution-makers of 1776 who were acting without precedent. Property qualifications on the right to vote disfranchised about half the men of the state who served in the militia or paid taxes, and gross malapportionment, which benefited the old tidewater counties, diminished the representative character of the new government. The governor was little more than a ceremonial figurehead. The assembly elected him and his councillors as well as the state judges, and the governor had no veto power. Jefferson believed that concentrating the powers of government in the legislature, notwithstanding recognition of the principle of separation of powers, "is precisely the definition of despotic government. . . . An elective despotism was not the government we fought for." In fact, however, legislative supremacy characterized all the new state governments, excepting those of Massachusetts and New York.

The gravest deficiency of the Virginia system, according to Jefferson, was that the legislature, having framed the constitution and declaration of rights without having provided that they be perpetual and unalterable, could change them by ordinary legislation. That was true in theory, although the constitution lasted over half a century and rarely did the legislature enact measures inconsistent with it. In practice it was regarded a FUNDAMENTAL LAW, especially the declaration of rights.

That declaration was the most significant achievement of the convention. As the first such American document, it contained many constitutional "firsts," such as the statements that "all men" are equally free and have inherent rights which cannot be divested even by compact; that among these rights are the enjoyment of life, liberty, property, and the pursuit of happiness; and that all power derives from the people who retain a right to change the government if it fails to secure the people's objectives. The declaration recognized "the free exercise of religion" and FREEDOM OF THE PRESS, and included clauses that were precursors, sometimes in rudimentary form, of the FOURTH through the Eighth AMENDMENTS of the Constitution of the United States. Inexplicably the convention voted down a ban on BILLS OF ATTAINDER and on EX POST FACTO LAWS and omitted the FREEDOMS OF SPEECH, assembly, and petition, the right to the writ of HABEAS CORPUS, GRAND JURY proceedings, the right to compulsory process to secure EVIDENCE in one's own behalf, the right to counsel, and freedom from DOUBLE JEOPARDY. Although RELIGIOUS LIBERTY was guaranteed, the ban on an ESTABLISHMENT OF RELIGION awaited enactment of the VIRGINIA STATUTE OF RELIGIOUS FREEDOM in 1786. Madison's familiarity with his own state's bill of rights strongly influenced his draft of the amendments that became the BILL OF RIGHTS of the Constitution.

LEONARD W. LEVY

Bibliography

LINGLEY, CHARLES R. 1910 *The Transition of Virginia from Colony to Commonwealth.* New York: Columbia University Press.

VIRGINIA PLAN

At the CONSTITUTIONAL CONVENTION OF 1787, EDMUND RANDOLPH, arguing that the government of the union under the ARTICLES OF CONFEDERATION could not defend itself against state encroachments, introduced the alternative of a "national plan," probably the work of JAMES MADISON. In effect Virginia proposed to supersede the Articles by providing for a strong, central government of three branches, each with broad, undefined powers. The plan included a congress of two houses, the first elected by the people and the second by the first, both to be apportioned on the basis of a state's population of free inhabitants or its contributions to the national treasury. The most significant provision empowered congress to legislate in all cases of state incompetency or whenever state legislation might disrupt national harmony. Congress was also empowered to veto state laws. The sole check on congress was a qualified veto power vested in a council consisting of the executive and some judges. One provision required state officers to swear support of the new constitution, and another authorized the use of force against recalcitrant states. The Virginia Plan structured the deliberations of the Constitutional Convention and became the nucleus of the Constitution of the United States.

LEONARD W. LEVY

Bibliography

BRANT, IRVING 1950 *James Madison: Father of the Constitution, 1787–1800.* Pages 23–54. Indianapolis: Bobbs-Merrill.

VIRGINIA PRIVATE SCHOOL CASES

See: *Runyon v. McCrary*

VIRGINIA STATE BOARD OF PHARMACY v. VIRGINIA CITIZENS CONSUMER COUNCIL

425 U.S. 748 (1976)

Traditionally COMMERCIAL SPEECH was assumed to lie outside the FIRST AMENDMENT's protection. This decision made clear that this assumption was obsolete. Virginia's rules governing professional pharmacists forbade the advertising of prices of prescription drugs. The Supreme Court, 7–1, held this rule invalid at the behest of a consumers' group, thus promoting the notion of a "right to receive" in the FREEDOM OF SPEECH. (See LISTENERS' RIGHTS.) The Court's opinion indicated that false or misleading commercial advertising might be regulated—a rule the Court would never apply to political speech. For a few years, this decision stood as the Court's principal commercial speech precedent, only to be assimilated in the comprehensive opinion in CENTRAL HUDSON GAS V. PUBLIC SERVICE COMMISSION (1980).

MARTIN SHAPIRO

VIRGINIA STATUTE OF RELIGIOUS FREEDOM (1786)

This historic statute, one of the preeminent documents in the history of RELIGIOUS LIBERTY, climaxed a ten-year struggle for the SEPARATION OF CHURCH AND STATE in Virginia. On the eve of the Revolution Baptists were jailed for unlicensed preaching, and JAMES MADISON exclaimed that the "diabolical Hell conceived principle of persecution rages." The Church of England (Episcopal) was the established church of Virginia, supported by public taxes imposed on all. The state CONSTITUTION of 1776 guaranteed that everyone was "equally entitled to the free exercise of religion," but the convention defeated a proposal by Madison that would have ended any form of an ESTABLISHMENT OF RELIGION. By the close of 1776 the legislature, responding to dissenter petitions, repealed all laws punishing any religious opinions or modes of worship, exempted dissenters from compulsory support of the established church, and suspended state taxation on its behalf. But the legislature reserved for future decision the question whether religion ought to be supported by voluntary contributions or by a new establishment of all Christian churches.

In 1779 an indecisive legislature confronted two diametrically opposed bills. One was a general assessment bill, providing that the Christian religion should be "the established religion" supported by public taxation and allowing every taxpayer to designate the church that would receive his money. The other was THOMAS JEFFERSON's Bill for Religious Freedom, which later provided the philosophical basis for the religion clauses of the FIRST AMENDMENT. The preamble, a classic expression of the American creed on intellectual as well as religious liberty, stressed that everyone had a "natural right" to his opinions and that religion was a private, voluntary matter of individual conscience beyond the scope of the civil power to support or restrain. Jefferson rejected the BAD TENDENCY TEST for suppressing opinions and proposed "that it is time enough for the rightful purposes of the civil government for its officers to interfere when principles break out into overt acts against peace and good order. . . ." The bill, which protected even freedom of irreligion, provided that no one should be compelled to frequent or support any worship. Neither Jefferson's bill nor the other could muster a majority, and for several years the legislature deadlocked.

Each year, however, support for an establishment grew. When a liberalized general assessment bill was introduced in 1784, omitting subscription to articles of faith and giving secular reasons for the support of religion, the Presbyterian clergy backed it. Madison angrily declared that they were "as ready to set up an establishment which is to take them in as they were to pull down that which shut them out." Only Madison's shrewd politicking delayed passage of the general assessment bill until the legislature had time to evaluate the state of public opinion. MADISON'S MEMORIAL AND REMONSTRANCE turned public opinion against the assessment; even the Presbyterian clergy now endorsed Jefferson's bill. Madison reintroduced it in late 1785, and it became law in early 1786, completing the separation of church and state in Virginia and providing a model for a nation.

LEONARD W. LEVY

Bibliography

STOKES, ANSON PHELPS 1950 *Church and State in the United States.* Vol. 1:366–394. New York: Harper & Row.

VIRTUAL REPRESENTATION

See: Representation; Taxation without Representation

VLANDIS v. KLINE 412 U.S. 441 (1973)

A Connecticut statute gave resident students at a state university certain tuition preferences. A student who had entered the university as a nonresident was relegated to that status for his or her full student career. The Supreme Court, 6–3, held the latter provision unconstitutional. A majority of five Justices, speaking through Justice POTTER STEWART, held that the provision created "a permanent and IRREBUTTABLE PRESUMPTION of non-residence." Because this presumption was "not necessarily or universally true in fact," it denied a student PROCEDURAL DUE PROCESS by denying a hearing on the issue of residence. Justice BYRON R. WHITE concurred on EQUAL PROTECTION GROUNDS. The dissenters suggested that the Court had, in fact, drifted into an area of SUBSTANTIVE DUE

PROCESS that the Court had abandoned in the 1930s. The irrebuttable presumptions DOCTRINE had a brief vogue, but *Weinberger v. Salfi* (1975) placed it in mothballs.

KENNETH L. KARST

VOICE SAMPLES

See: Testimonial Compulsion

VOID FOR VAGUENESS

See: Vagueness

VOIR DIRE

Voir dire (Old French: "to speak the truth") refers to the questioning by the court or counsel of prospective jurors to determine their qualification for jury service.

Two types of objections may be raised to disqualify prospective jurors: peremptory challenges and challenges for cause. A peremptory challenge allows dismissal of a juror without cause. Most states provide each side with twenty such challenges for a capital offense, and a lesser number for other felonies and misdemeanors.

A challenge for cause requires the challenging party to prove potential prejudice to the case if the challenged juror should be accepted. There is generally no limit to such challenges. The typical statute permits such an objection if the juror is of unsound mind, lacks the qualifications required by law, is related to a party in the litigation, has served in a related case or GRAND JURY investigation, or has a "state of mind" that will prevent him from acting with impartiality.

In *Wainwright v. Witt* (1985) the Supreme Court stated that the standard to determine when a prospective juror should be excluded for cause is whether the juror's views would prevent or substantially impair the juror's duties in accordance with his/her instructions and oath.

Commonly, a prosecutor calls and examines twelve veniremen, exercises his challenges for cause and peremptory challenges, replaces those excused with others, and then tenders a group of twelve to the defense. The defendant follows a similar procedure. This process continues until the parties have exhausted their challenges or expressed their satisfaction with the jury.

Voir dire proceedings are usually open to the public. In *Press-Enterprise v. Superior Court* (1984) the trial judge had ordered that all but three days of a six-week voir dire for a rape-murder trial of a teenage girl be closed to the public and press and had refused to grant the defendant's pretrial motion for release of the voir dire transcript. The Supreme Court unanimously reversed, holding that voir dire proceedings in criminal trials should be presumptively open to the public, unless fair trial interests would be better served by closure.

Voir dire vests broad authority in the trial judge. A judge may refuse to allow questions deemed irrelevant or inappropriate. The Constitution, however, requires certain inquiries. In *Ham v. South Carolina* (1973) the Supreme Court held that where racial issues permeate or are inextricably bound up in a trial, the defendant is entitled to questioning specifically directed at racial prejudice. In *Ristano v. Ross* (1976), however, the Court held that this right does not extend to all cases in which the victim and the defendant are of different races. Questioning about general bias or prejudice will normally suffice. The Court held in *Rosales-Lopez v. United States* (1981) that judges may decide on a case-by-case basis whether racial overtones justify such questioning.

Finally, voir dire violates DUE PROCESS if its exclusion of a particular group seriously detracts from the jury's impartiality and ability to reflect dominant community values. In *Witherspoon v. Illinois* (1968) the Supreme Court invalidated a statute that had the effect of screening out jurors not enthusiastic about CAPITAL PUNISHMENT, but accepting those who were. Jurors may constitutionally be disqualified, however, by expressing an absolute refusal to impose the death penalty.

CHARLES H. WHITEBREAD

Bibliography

KALVEN, HARRY and ZEISEL, HANS 1966 *The American Jury.* Boston: Little, Brown.

VOLSTEAD ACT
41 Stat. 305 (1919)

Congress passed the Volstead National Prohibition Act, sponsored by Representative Andrew J. Volstead (Republican, Minnesota), on October 28, 1919. The act provided both for the continuation of wartime PROHIBITION and for enforcement of the EIGH-

TEENTH AMENDMENT. It was enacted over the veto of President WOODROW WILSON, who objected to the linking of those "two distinct phases of prohibition legislation."

To enforce the Eighteenth Amendment against private conduct the Volstead Act defined "intoxicating beverages" as any beverages containing at least 0.5% alcohol by volume, and provided stringent penalties for their manufacture, importation, transportation, sale, possession, or use. The constitutionality of the act was upheld in the National Prohibition Cases (*Rhode Island v. Palmer,* 1920), in which the Supreme Court, speaking through Justice WILLIS VAN DEVANTER, held that Congress's power under the amendment was complete and extended to intrastate as well as interstate transactions.

The Beer-Wine Revenue Act of March 1933 amended the Volstead Act by permitting the manufacture and sale of beer and wine with an alcohol content of up to 3.2%. Passage of the TWENTY-FIRST AMENDMENT later the same year rendered the Volstead Act void.

DENNIS J. MAHONEY

VOLUNTARINESS

See: Police Interrogation and Confessions

VON HOLST, HERMANN EDUARD (1841–1904)

A German immigrant who became chairman of the department of history at the University of Chicago, Hermann E. von Holst published a seven-volume *Constitutional and Political History of the United States* (1876–1892). The work is malproportioned; the last four volumes cover 1850–1861. Intent on condemning the "slavocracy," the author blamed the ANNEXATION OF TEXAS, the Mexican War, the KANSAS-NEBRASKA ACT, and the Civil War on a slaveholders' conspiracy. The decision in DRED SCOTT V. SANDFORD (1857), wrote von Holst, was "an unparalleled prostitution of the judicial ermine." Von Holst believed that centralized sovereignty and a free society stood for morality and national salvation. Despite his valuable use of newspapers and public documents, his style is so turgid and his judgments are so biased that he is no longer read.

LEONARD W. LEVY

VOTING RIGHTS

"The right to vote freely for the candidate of one's choice is of the essence of a democratic society, and any restrictions on that right strike at the heart of representative government." So spoke Chief Justice EARL WARREN, on behalf of the Supreme Court, in REYNOLDS V. SIMS (1964).

The Chief Justice's words were in direct philosophic succession to principles of the primacy of representative political institutions announced by the FIRST CONTINENTAL CONGRESS 190 years before, in the Declaration and Resolves of October 14, 1774:

> [T]he foundation of English liberty, and of all free government, is a right in the people to participate in their legislative council: and as the English colonists are not represented, and from their local and other circumstances, cannot properly be represented in the British parliament, they are entitled to a free and exclusive power of legislation in their several provincial legislatures, where their right of representation can alone be preserved, in all cases of taxation and internal policy, subject only to the negative of their sovereign, in such manner as has been heretofore used and accustomed.

The failure of King George III, through his ministers, to recognize the urgency of the colonists' demand for true representative institutions was one of the chief causes of revolution set forth in the DECLARATION OF INDEPENDENCE: "He has dissolved Representative Houses repeatedly, for opposing with manly firmness his invasions in the rights of the people. He has refused for a long time, after such dissolutions, to cause others to be elected; whereby the Legislative Powers, incapable of Annihilation, have returned to the People at large for their exercise."

The severing of the ties with Britain required the establishment, at the state level and at the national level, of new and more representative institutions of government. American constitutional history is characterized in part by the continuing enlargement of the right to vote, the mechanism which, in the American political tradition, has become the *sine qua non* of a valid system of REPRESENTATION. An anomaly presents itself: The Constitution, as amended, addresses aspects of the right to vote with far greater frequency than any other topic. Nonetheless, it has never been the function of the Constitution affirmatively to define the universe of voters. The Constitution's function has been narrower—progressively to limit the permissible grounds of disenfranchisement.

Prior to the American Revolution, eligibility to vote was not uniform among the colonies, but the variations were relatively minor. Broadly speaking, voting for colonial (as distinct from township or borough) officials was reserved to adult (generally meaning twenty-one or older) "freeholders." In equating property ownership and suffrage, the colonies were following a familiar English model. But landowning was far more widely dispersed in the colonies than in the mother country, so the proportion of colonists eligible to vote was larger.

There were not more than a few black or women freeholders in any of the colonies, and pursuant either to convention or to formal legal specification those few did not vote. Religious restrictions were also commonplace but varied somewhat among the colonies and at different times. In general, the franchise was the prerogative of the propertied, Protestant, white male.

With the coming of independence, all of the newly sovereign states except Connecticut and Rhode Island adopted new charters of government—"constitutions." Impelled by the rhetoric of revolution and the eagerness of thousands of militiamen to participate in the processes of governance, the drafters of the new state constitutions relaxed but did not abandon the property and religious qualifications for voting for state officials (and the correlative, and generally more stringent, qualifications for holding state office). As Max Farrand observed, Americans

> might declare that "all men are created equal," and bills of rights might assert that government rested upon the consent of the governed; but these constitutions carefully provided that such consent should come from property owners, and, in many of the States, from religious believers and even followers of the Christian faith. "The man of small means might vote, but none save well-to-do Christians could legislate, and in many states none but a rich Christian could be a governor." In South Carolina, for example, a freehold of 10,000 currency was required of the Governor, Lieutenant Governor, and members of the council; 2,000 of the members of the Senate; and, while every elector was eligible to the House of Representatives, he had to acknowledge the being of a God and to believe in a future state of rewards and punishments, as well as to hold "a freehold at least of fifty acres of land, or a town lot."

Under the ARTICLES OF CONFEDERATION, the state delegates in Congress constituted the nation's government. The Articles limited the numbers of delegates (no fewer than two and no more than seven per state) but left each state legislature free to determine the qualifications of those selected and the mode of their annual selection. The Articles did not preclude popular election of delegates, but the word "appointed," in the phrase "appointed in such manner as the legislature of each State shall direct," suggests that it was not anticipated that legislatures would remit to their constituents the power to choose those who would speak and vote for the states in Congress.

At the CONSTITUTIONAL CONVENTION OF 1787, the Framers divided on how the lower house was to be selected. JAMES MADISON told his fellow delegates that he "considered an election of one branch at least of the legislature by the people immediately, as a clear principle of true government." Madison's view carried the day. But then the Convention faced the question whether the Constitution should set the qualifications of those who were to elect representatives. GOUVERNEUR MORRIS of Pennsylvania proposed that only freeholders should vote. Colonel GEORGE MASON of Virginia found this proposal regressive: "Eight of nine States have extended the right of suffrage beyond the freeholders. What will the people there say, if they should be disfranchised." OLIVER ELLSWORTH of Connecticut also challenged Morris's proposal: "How shall the freehold be defined? Ought not every man who pays a tax to vote for the representative who is to levy and dispose of his money?" Morris was unpersuaded: "He had long learned not to be the dupe of words. . . . Give the votes to people who have no property, and they will sell them to the rich who will be able to buy them." But BENJAMIN FRANKLIN took decisive issue with his fellow Pennsylvanian: "It is of great consequence that we should not depress the virtue and public spirit of our common people; of which they displayed a great deal during the war, and which contributed principally to the favorable issue of it." Morris's proposal was decisively defeated. The Convention instead approved the provision that has endured ever since, under which eligibility to vote for representatives is keyed, in each state, to that state's rules of eligibility to vote for members of the most numerous house of the state legislature.

When it came to designing the method of selecting the President and vice-president, the Convention devised the indirect election system of the ELECTORAL COLLEGE. The expectation was that the electors—themselves chosen from among the leading citizens of their respective states—would, through disinterested deliberation, select as the nation's chief executive officials the two persons of highest civic virtue, wholly without regard for the vulgar demands of "politics." According to ALEXANDER HAMILTON in THE FEDERALIST #68, "[t]he mode of appointment of the Chief Magistrate of the United States is almost the only part of the system, of any consequence, which has escaped without severe censure, or which has received the slightest mark of approbation from its opponents." But, measured against its intended purpose, no other structural aspect of the Constitution has wound up wider of the mark. The Framers of the Constitution wholly failed to anticipate the development of national political parties whose chief political goal would be the election of the party leader as President. That development has meant that since the fourth presidential election—that of 1800, in which THOMAS JEFFERSON defeated JOHN ADAMS—the electors in each state have themselves been selected as adherents of the political party prevailing in that state and thus have, with the rarest of exceptions, cast their electoral votes for the party's presidential and vice-presidential candidates. The system of electors remains to this day, but it has been entirely drained of its intended function.

Those who drafted the Constitution in 1787, and who saw it through ratification to the launching of the new ship of state in 1789, were America's aristocracy. The transformation of American politics from 1789 to the Civil War can be measured in the marked shift in class status of those who occupied the Presidency. The Presidents from GEORGE WASHINGTON to JOHN QUINCY ADAMS were all patricians. Most of the Presidents from ANDREW JACKSON to ABRAHAM LINCOLN were not. The growth of national parties, beginning with Jefferson and accelerating with Jackson, democratized politics by putting politicians in the business of seeking to enlarge their voting constituencies. Property qualifications gave way, for the most part, to taxpayer qualifications. And, in many states, these in turn were soon largely abandoned.

The erosion of property tests for voting did not mean that anything approximating universal suffrage was at hand. As one political scientist has summarized the situation:

> Apart from a few midwestern states, hungry for settlers, no one was very warm to the prospect of aliens and immigrants at the polls; all the states but Maine, Massachusetts, Vermont, New Hampshire, Rhode Island, and New York explicitly barred free blacks from voting, and New York imposed special property requirements on blacks which, while repeatedly challenged, were repeatedly upheld in popular referenda. Even in the tiny handful of northern states that did not exclude blacks by law, social pressures tended to accomplish the same end. New Hampshire and Vermont in 1857 and 1858 had to pass special laws against excluding blacks from voting. Chancellor James Kent concluded that only in Maine could the black man participate equally with the white man in civil and political rights. Women were universally denied the vote [Elliott 1974, p. 40].

In 1848, a year of revolution in Europe, 300 people gathered in a church in the little upstate New York town of Seneca Falls to consider the status of women. The most revolutionary item on the agenda was voting. Half a century before there had been a small outcropping of female voting in New Jersey, whose 1776 constitution had, perhaps inadvertently, used the word "inhabitants" to describe those who, if they met the property qualifications, could vote. It appears that by 1807, respectable New Jersey opinion had reached the consensus that laxity was slipping into license (at a local election in Trenton even slaves and Philadelphians were said to have cast ballots). At this point, "reform" was clearly called for: the legislature promptly altered the electoral code to bring New Jersey's voting qualifications back into conformity with the white maleness that characterized the electorate in the rest of the country and remained the accepted order of things until Seneca Falls.

The chief driving energies behind the Seneca Falls Convention were Elizabeth Cady Stanton and Lucretia Mott. Stanton drafted the "Declaration of Principles" and the several resolutions which the convention was asked to adopt. The only resolution to receive less-than-unanimous endorsement was the ninth: "Resolved, that it is the duty of the women of this country to secure to themselves their sacred right to the elective franchise." That the franchise was a far more chimerical goal than other concerns (for example, property rights for married women) was recognized by Mott. She had asked Stanton not to submit the ninth resolution for the reason that "Thou will make us ridiculous." The factor that may have tipped the balance in Stanton's decision not to subordinate her principle to Mott's pragmatism was the strong encouragement of Frederick Douglass. The great black leader supported the ninth resolution. He joined the cause of equal rights for women to the cause of abolition.

The women's movement maintained its close association with abolitionism through the Civil War. After the freeing of the slaves, the country's attention focused on the terms on which American blacks were to be brought into the mainstream of American life. The leaders of the women's movement hoped that the drive for women's suffrage would complement and be reinforced by the drive for black suffrage. But that was not to be. As the war neared its end, a number of Republican leaders began to recognize a strong partisan interest in creating black voters to counter the feared resurgence of the Democratic party; there were no comparable reasons for creating women voters. Many of the women leaders, recognizing the political realities, accepted—albeit with no enthusiasm—the priority given to the rights of blacks. But not Elizabeth Cady Stanton and Susan B. Anthony. Said Anthony: "I will cut off this right arm before I will ever work for or demand the ballot for the Negro and not the woman." (Anthony and Stanton then formed the National Woman Suffrage Association, while the other leaders worked through the American Woman Suffrage Association; the split was not to be healed for twenty-five years.)

In 1864 Abraham Lincoln appointed SALMON P. CHASE—Lincoln's former secretary of the treasure and one of his chief rivals for the Republican presidential nomination in 1860—to succeed ROGER B. TANEY as CHIEF JUSTICE of the United States. Chase's elevation to the Court did not abate his presidential ambitions and his attendant interest in promoting a favorable political environment. The new Chief Justice wrote to Lincoln, as he subsequently wrote to President ANDREW JOHNSON, urging that black suffrage be made a condition of the reconstruction of the rebel states. And by 1867 Chase had taken the position that Congress had constitutional authority to enfranchise blacks as a mode of enforcing the THIRTEENTH AMENDMENT: "Can anything be clearer than that the National Legislature charged with the duty of 'enforcing by appropriate legislation' the condition of universal freedom, is authorized and bound to provide for universal suffrage? Is not *suffrage* the best security against *slavery* and *involuntary servitude*? Is not the legislation which provides the *best* security the most *appropriate*?" Chase lost interest in active promotion of black voting when it became apparent that his modest chances of being nominated for the presidency were more likely to be realized in the Democratic party than in the Republican party. In any event, the question whether the Thirteenth Amendment could have been a platform for enlarging the franchise became moot upon the adoption of the two other post-Civil War Amendments, both of which expressly addressed the franchise—for blacks, not for women.

The FOURTEENTH AMENDMENT, ratified in 1868, dealt with black voting by indirection. By declaring that "[a]ll persons born or naturalized in the United States, and subject to the jurisdiction thereof, are citizens of the United States and of the State wherein they reside," the first sentence of the first section of the amendment overruled Roger B. Taney's pronouncement in DRED SCOTT V. SANDFORD (1857), that blacks, whether slave or free, could not be citizens within the contemplation of the Constitution. The second sentence of the first section sought to protect the CIVIL RIGHTS of blacks: First, it guaranteed "the privileges and immunities of citizens of the United States" against state abridgment and, second, it prohibited state denial to any person, whether citizen or not, of "life, liberty or property without DUE PROCESS OF LAW," or deprivation of the "EQUAL PROTECTION OF THE LAWS." The second section of the amendment spoke to the political rights of blacks. It provided that any state that denied participation in federal or state elections to "any of the male inhabitants of such State, being twenty-one years of age, and citizens of the United States . . . except for participation in rebellion, or other crime," should have its allocation of representatives and of presidential electors proportionately reduced. The framers of the amendment thus preserved the states' entitlement to discriminate but proposed a substantial penalty as the price of discrimination.

By 1869, after General ULYSSES S. GRANT's narrow victory in the 1868 presidential election, the Republican party recognized that black votes were essential to its survival. So the Republican leadership in Congress fashioned the FIFTEENTH AMENDMENT. That amendment, ratified in 1870, addressed the question of black voting directly. A citizen's entitlement to vote could not be "abridged by the United States or by any State on account of race, color, or previous condition of servitude."

Notwithstanding that the express language of the Fourteenth Amendment addressed male voting, and that the express language of the Fifteenth Amendment addressed discriminations rooted in "race, color or previous condition of servitude," some leaders of the women's movement contended that women were constitutionally entitled to vote. Arguing that the right to vote in a federal election was a privilege of national citizenship protected by section 1 of the Fourteenth Amendment, Susan B. Anthony actually persuaded election officials in Rochester, New York, to let her vote in 1872 notwithstanding that the New York constitution limited the franchise to men. Anthony was promptly charged with the crime of casting a ballot in a federal election in which she was not an eligible voter. The presiding judge was Justice WARD HUNT of the Supreme Court. Justice Hunt rejected Anthony's constitutional claim in the following words:

> The right of voting, or the privilege of voting, is a right or privilege arising under the constitution of the state, and not under the Constitution of the United States. The qualifications are different in the different states. Citizenship, age, sex, residence, are variously required in the different states, or may be so. If the right belongs to any particular person, it is because such person is entitled to it by the laws of the state where he offers to exercise it, and not because of citizenship of the United States. If the state of New York

should provide that no person should vote until he had reached the age of thirty years, or after he had reached the age of thirty years, or after he had reached the age of fifty, or that no person having grey hair, or who had not the use of all his limbs, should be entitled to vote, I do not see how it could be held to be a violation of any right derived or held under the Constitution of the United States. We might say that such regulations were unjust, tyrannical, unfit for the regulation of an intelligent state; but, if rights of a citizen are thereby violated they are of that fundamental class, derived from his position as a citizen of the state, and not those limited rights belonging to him as a citizen of the United States.

Read through the prism of a century of doctrinal hindsight, Justice Hunt's words seem—at least at first blush—somewhat surprising. The surprise is not occasioned by the fact that the Justice gave such short shrift to arguments based on the Fourteenth Amendment's PRIVILEGES AND IMMUNITIES CLAUSE, for we are accustomed to the fact that, ever since the SLAUGHTERHOUSE CASES (1873), the Supreme Court has read the grant of privileges and immunities flowing from national citizenship very restrictively. The surprise stems from Hunt's failure—which may also have been counsel's failure—to approach sex-based denial of the franchise (not to mention the assertedly analogous hypothetical denials based on age, physical handicap, or color of hair) in equal protection terms. The likely explanation is that in *Slaughterhouse* the Court doubted that "any action of a State not directed by way of discrimination against the negroes as a class, or on account of their race, will ever be held to come within the" equal protection clause.

Justice Hunt directed the jury to return a verdict of guilty and imposed a fine of $100.

Justice Hunt's rejection of Anthony's privileges and immunities claim was vindicated two years later by Chief Justice MORRISON R. WAITE'S opinion for the unanimous Court in MINOR V. HAPPERSETT (1875). This was a civil suit brought in a Missouri state court by Virginia L. Minor, and her lawyer husband Francis Minor, to challenge the refusal of a Missouri election official to register her as a voter. The Minors contended that the provision of the Missouri constitution limiting the electorate to male citizens transgressed the privileges and immunities clause. In rejecting the Minors' contention, Chief Justice Waite demonstrated that limitation of the franchise to males had been the norm, despite the fact that women were citizens. Voting had not been a privilege of national citizenship prior to the Fourteenth Amendment. As the amendment "did not add to the privileges and immunities of a citizen," but merely "furnished an additional guaranty for the protection of such as he already had," Missouri's refusal to let Minor vote was not unconstitutional. *Minor v. Happersett* ended attempts to win the campaign for woman's suffrage by litigation. The road to the ballot box was to be political—persuading male legislators to pass laws giving women the vote.

It was to be a long road. In 1870 Wyoming's territorial legislature enacted a law entitling women to vote. Utah followed suit, but the victory there was temporary. An 1887 congressional statute forbidding Utah's Mormons from practicing polygamy also overrode the territorial legislature's grant of the franchise to women. Three years later Wyoming's first state constitution called for women's suffrage. Thereafter progress was slow. Many state campaigns were fought and most were lost. In the South, votes for women were seen as a harbinger of votes for blacks, and the states resisted accordingly; in the East, many industrialists mistrusted the links between some women's suffragists and trade union and other reform groups; in the Midwest, the women's suffrage movement was seen by the brewing interests as the advance guard of prohibition. By 1913 women could vote in only nine states; in that year Illinois admitted women to participation in presidential elections.

In 1912, THEODORE ROOSEVELT'S Progressive party endorsed women's suffrage. This endorsement served as a reminder that Susan B. Anthony and her associates had sought to achieve women's suffrage not state-by-state but by amending the Constitution. Pressure for a women's suffrage amendment mounted during World War I when women entered the work force in record numbers. In 1918 WOODROW WILSON announced support for the proposed amendment, notwithstanding that women's suffrage was anathema to the white Democratic South. In 1919, with Democrats divided and Republicans strongly in favor, Congress submitted to the states a proposed amendment barring denial or abridgment of the right to vote in any election on grounds of sex. In 1920, the NINETEENTH AMENDMENT was ratified. In the 1920 elections one of the voters was Charlotte Woodward Pierce who, as a nineteen-year-old farm girl, had attended the Seneca Falls Convention in 1848.

Following the Civil War, the military occupation of the South ushered in a period in which blacks not only voted but were elected to office. With the adoption of the Fifteenth Amendment, there appeared to be some ground for supposing that black voting had achieved a legal infrastructure which might suffice even after the army departed. However, although the amendment bars race, color, and previous condition of servitude as criteria of eligibility to vote, it does not proscribe other criteria—such as literacy or taxpayer status—susceptible of adaptation as surrogates for racism. The lesson was that most blacks might be prevented from voting by educational or property qualifications.

Following the COMPROMISE OF 1877, which led to the withdrawal from the South of the last military units, the twilight of black participation in the southern political process began. Through the 1880s, some black voting continued—frequently in Populist alliance with poor whites. But in the 1890s, as a corollary of the spreading gospel of Jim Crow, the southern white political leadership forged a consensus to exclude blacks from the ballot box. Some of this was achieved by force, and some by skulduggery, but in large measure the forms of law were utilized. LITERACY TESTS and POLL TAXES were common exclusionary devices, as was closing Democratic primaries—the only real elections in most of the South—to blacks. The underlying rationale was that offered by Senator James Vardaman of Mississippi: "I am just as much opposed to Booker Washington as a voter, with all his Anglo-Saxon reinforcements, as I am to the cocoanut-headed, chocolate-covered, typical little coon, Andy Dottson, who blacks my shoes every morning. Neither is fit to perform the supreme function of citizenship."

By and large, the legal stratagems employed by the southern states to disenfranchise blacks succeeded. Poll taxes and literacy tests which did not on their face show a discriminatory purpose easily passed constitutional muster from BREEDLOVE V. SUTTLES (1937) to *Lassiter v. Northampton Election Board* (1959). To be sure, the Supreme Court did intervene in those rare instances in which the purpose to discriminate was evident on the face of the challenged restraint. A flagrant example was the so-called GRANDFATHER CLAUSE in Oklahoma's 1910 constitution, which exempted from the literacy requirement any would-be voter "who was, on January 1, 1866, or at any time prior thereto, entitled to vote under any form of government, or who at that time resided in some foreign nation, and [any] lineal descendant thereof." In GUINN V. UNITED STATES (1915) the Supreme Court held this literacy test invalid.

Because during the first half of the twentieth century the decisive voting in the South took place in Democratic primaries, not in the general elections, the cases of greatest practical as well as doctrinal consequence were those that challenged devices to maintain the whiteness of the "white primary."

In NIXON V. HERNDON (1927) a unanimous Court, speaking through Justice OLIVER WENDELL HOLMES, sustained the complaint of L. A. Nixon, who contended that he had been unconstitutionally barred from voting in a Texas Democratic primary through enforcement of a Texas statute that recited that "in no event shall a negro be eligible to participate in a Democratic party primary election held in the state of Texas." The Court held that this statutory racial exclusion contravened the Fourteenth Amendment.

The consequence of this ruling was described by Justice BENJAMIN N. CARDOZO in his opinion in NIXON V. CONDON (1932): "Promptly after the announcement of [the Herndon] decision, the legislature of Texas enacted a new statute . . . repealing the article condemned by this court; declaring that the effect of the decision was to create an emergency with a need for immediate action; and substituting for the article so repealed another bearing the same number. By the article thus substituted, 'every political party in this State through its State Executive Committee shall have the power to prescribe the qualifications of its own members and shall in its own way determine who shall be qualified to vote or otherwise participate in such political party. . . .' " Thereupon the executive committee of the Texas Democratic party voted to limit party membership and participation to whites, and L. A. Nixon was once again barred from voting in the Democratic primary. Once again Nixon brought a lawsuit, and once again he prevailed in the Supreme Court. Justice Cardozo, speaking for a majority of five, concluded that the new Texas statute delegated exercise of the state's power over primaries to party executive committees, with the result that the racial exclusion decided on by the executive committee was in effect the racially discriminatory act of the State of Texas and hence prohibited by the Fourteenth Amendment. Justice JAMES C. MCREYNOLDS, joined by three other Justices, dissented.

Three years later, in GROVEY V. TOWNSEND (1935), the Court considered the next refinement in the Texas Democratic primary—exclusion of blacks by vote of the party convention. Speaking through Justice OWEN J. ROBERTS, the Court this time unanimously concluded that the action taken by the Texas Democratic party was an entirely private decision for which the State of Texas was not accountable; accordingly, neither the Fourteenth nor the Fifteenth Amendment was transgressed.

Nine years later, toward the end of World War II, the Court, in SMITH V. ALLWRIGHT (1944), again considered the *Grovey v. Townsend* question. In the interval, seven of the Justices who had participated in *Grovey v. Townsend* had died or retired. Approaching the matter in a common sense way, the Court, with

Justice Roberts dissenting, concluded that the role of the primary as a formal and vital predicate of the election made it an integral part of the state's voting processes and hence subject to the requirement of the Fifteenth Amendment. Accordingly, the Court in *Smith v. Allwright* overruled *Grovey v. Townsend.*

The resumption, after three-quarters of a century, of significant black participation in the southern political process dates from the decision in *Smith v. Allwright.* But the elimination of the most egregious legal barriers did not mean that all blacks were automatically free to vote. Hundreds of thousands of would-be black voters were still kept from the polls by fraud or force or both. In 1957, three years after the Court, in BROWN V. BOARD OF EDUCATION (1954), held that legally mandated racial SEGREGATION contravened the Fourteenth Amendment, Congress passed the first federal civil rights law enacted since the 1870s: a voting rights law which authorized modest federal supervision of the southern voting process. And the year 1964 witnessed ratification of the TWENTY-FOURTH AMENDMENT, barring exclusion of American citizens from voting in any federal election on grounds of failure to pay any poll tax or other tax. But as black demands for equal treatment multiplied, responsive abuses escalated.

In the spring of 1965, a Boston minister, one of scores of clergymen who had gone to Selma, Alabama, to help MARTIN LUTHER KING, JR., launch a voter registration drive, was murdered. A few days later, on March 15, 1965, President LYNDON B. JOHNSON addressed Congress:

> Many of the issues of civil rights are very complex and most difficult. But about this there can and should be no argument. Every American citizen must have an equal right to vote. There is no reason which can excuse the denial of that right. There is no duty which weighs more heavily on us than the duty we have to ensure that right.
>
> Yet the harsh fact is that in many places in this country men and women are kept from voting simply because they are Negroes.
>
> Every device of which human ingenuity is capable has been used to deny this right. The Negro citizen may go to register only to be told that the day is wrong, or the hour is late, or the official in charge is absent. And if he persists and if he manages to present himself to the registrar, he may be disqualified because he did not spell out his middle name or because he abbreviated a word on the application. And if he manages to fill out an application, he is given a test. The registrar is the sole judge of whether he passes this test. He may be asked to recite the entire constitution, or explain the most complex provisions of state laws. And even a college degree cannot be used to prove that he can read and write.
>
> For the fact is that the only way to pass these barriers is to show a white skin.
>
> Experience has clearly shown that the existing process of law cannot overcome systematic and ingenious discrimination. No law that we now have on the books—and I have helped to put three of them there—can ensure the right to vote when local officials are determined to deny it. . . .
>
> This time, on this issue, there must be no delay, or no hesitation or no compromise with our purpose.
>
> We cannot, we must not refuse to protect the right of every American to vote in every election that he may desire to participate in. And we ought not, we must not wait another eight months before we get a bill. We have already waited a hundred years and more and the time for waiting is gone. . . .
>
> But even if we pass this bill, the battle will not be over. What happened in Selma is part of a far larger movement which reaches into every section and state of America. It is the effort of American Negroes to secure for themselves the full blessings of American life.
>
> Their cause must be our cause too. Because it is not just Negroes, but really it is all of us, who must overcome the crippling legacy of bigotry and injustice. And we shall overcome.
>
> As a man whose roots go deeply into Southern soil I know how agonizing racial feelings are. I know how difficult it is to reshape the attitudes and the structure of our society.
>
> But a century has passed, more than a hundred years, since the Negro was freed. And he is not fully free tonight.
>
> It was more than a hundred years ago that Abraham Lincoln, the great President of the Northern party, signed the Emancipation Proclamation, but emancipation is a proclamation and not a fact.
>
> A century has passed, more than a hundred years since equality was promised. And yet the Negro is not equal.
>
> A century has passed since the day of promise. And the promise is unkept.
>
> The time of justice has now come. I tell you that I believe sincerely that no force can hold it back. It is right in the eyes of man and God that it should come. And when it does, I think that day will brighten the lives of every American.

Congress enacted the VOTING RIGHTS ACT OF 1965. The act provided, among other things, for the suspension of literacy tests for five years in states or political subdivisions thereof in which fewer than "50 per cent of its voting-age residents were registered on November 1, 1964, or voted in the presidential election of November, 1964." This and other major provisions of the 1965 act were thereafter sustained in SOUTH CAROLINA V. KATZENBACH (1966), *Rome v. United States* (1980), and KATZENBACH V. MORGAN (1966), as appropriate ways of enforcing the Fifteenth and Fourteenth Amendments. Subsequent amendments to the 1965 act have broadened its coverage.

The 1944 decision in *Smith v. Allwright* was more than a new and hospitable judicial approach to the right of blacks to participate in the American political process. It was a major advance (as, four years later, was SHELLEY V. KRAEMER, 1948) toward the day—May 17, 1954—when a unanimous Court, speaking through Chief Justice Warren, was to hold, in *Brown v. Board of Education,* that the equal protection clause barred the legally mandated racial segregation of school children. Subsequent decisions, building on *Brown v. Board of Education,* soon made it plain that the equal protection clause barred all the legal trappings of Jim Crow. *Brown v. Board of Education* worked a fundamental change in the Court's and the nation's perception of the scope of judicial responsibility to vindicate those values.

In 1962, eight years after *Brown v. Board of Education,* the Court, in *Baker v. Carr,* held that allegations that a state legislature suffered from systematic malapportionment, under which districts of widely different populations were each represented by one legislator, stated a claim cognizable under the equal protection clause. The importance of *Baker v. Carr* cannot be overestimated. Chief Justice Warren thought it the most significant decision handed down by the Court during his sixteen years in the center chair. Even those who rank *Brown v. Board of Education* ahead of *Baker v. Carr* must nonetheless acknowledge that the latter decision set in motion a process that resulted in the redesign of numerous state legislatures and a myriad of local governing bodies, and, indeed, of the House of Representatives. That redesign has been required to meet the Court's pronouncement, in GRAY V. SANDERS (1963), that "[t]he conception of political equality from the Declaration of Independence, to Lincoln's Gettysburg Address, to the Fifteenth, Seventeenth, and Nineteenth Amendments can mean only one thing—one person, one vote." Long-standing patterns of malapportionment in which rural districts with relatively few inhabitants were represented on equal terms with heavily populated urban districts have become a thing of the past. (See REAPPORTIONMENT.)

Guaranteeing the voting rights of women and blacks and overcoming rampant malapportionment have cured the major inexcusable deficiencies of the American political process. In recent decades, certain lesser inequalities have also begun to be addressed.

From the beginning of the republic, Americans residing in the continental United States but not within any state—for example, those who lived in federal territories—had no way of voting in national elections. In the most egregious of anomalies, residents of the nation's capital were voiceless in the selection of the President who dwelt and governed in their own home town. So matters stood until 1964, when the TWENTY-THIRD AMENDMENT was added to the Constitution, giving the DISTRICT OF COLUMBIA a minimum of three electoral votes in presidential elections.

In the late 1960s, profound divisions in American opinion about America's military involvement in the VIETNAM WAR forced recognition of another anomaly—that tens of thousands of young men were being drafted to fight in an unpopular foreign war although they were not old enough to vote in national elections choosing the officials responsible for making decisions for war or for peace. In 1970, Congress, in amending the Voting Rights Act, included a provision forbidding abridgment of the right of any citizen to vote "on account of age if such citizen is eighteen years or older." The statute was promptly challenged in OREGON V. MITCHELL (1970). Four Justices concluded that Congress had the power to lower the voting age to eighteen. Four Justices concluded that Congress had no such power. The casting vote was that of Justice Hugo L. Black, who held that Congress could regulate the voting age in national elections but not in state elections. Because Americans vote every two years for state and national officials at the same time, *Oregon v. Mitchell* was an invitation to chaos. Within six months, Congress proposed and the requisite three-fourths of the states ratified, the TWENTY-SIXTH Amendment which accomplished by constitutional mandate what Congress had been unable to achieve by statute.

In the course of two centuries law and conscience have combined to make the American suffrage almost truly universal. One massive obstacle remains: apathy. In recent national elections in the European democracies, seventy-two percent of the eligible electorate voted in Great Britain, seventy-nine percent in Spain, eighty-five percent in France, and eighty-nine percent in Italy and West Germany. By contrast, in the American presidential election of 1980, only fifty-three percent of those eligible voted. In America's 1984 presidential election, after both major parties had made massive efforts to register new voters, not more than fifty-five percent of those who could have voted made their way to the ballot box. A fateful question confronting American democracy is whether tens of millions of self-disenfranchised Americans will in the years to come find the energy and good sense to exercise the precious right won at such great labor at the Constitutional Convention, in Congress and state legislatures and the Supreme Court, and at Selma and Seneca Falls.

LOUIS H. POLLAK

(SEE ALSO: *Rogers v. Lodge, 1982.*)

Bibliography

CHUTE, MARCHETTE G. 1969 *First Liberty: A History of the Right to Vote in America, 1619–1850.* New York: Dutton.

DUBOIS, ELLEN CAROL, ed. 1981 *Elizabeth Cady Stanton, Susan B. Anthony: Correspondence, Writings, Speeches.* New York: Shocken.

ELLIOTT, WARD E. Y. 1974 *The Rise of Guardian Democracy: The Supreme Court's Role in Voting Rights Disputes, 1845–1969.* Cambridge, Mass.: Harvard University Press.

FAIRMAN, CHARLES 1971 *Reconstruction and Reunion, 1864–1888.* New York: Macmillan.

FARRAND, MAX, ed 1921 *The Fathers of the Constitution.* New Haven, Conn.: Yale University Press.

———, ed. 1911 *The Records of the Federal Convention of 1787.* New Haven, Conn.: Yale University Press.

FLEXNER, ELEANOR 1975 *Century of Struggle: The Woman's Right to Vote Movement in the United States.* Rev. ed. Cambridge, Mass.: Harvard University Press.

HIGGINBOTHAM, A. L., JR. 1984 "States' 'Rights' and States' 'Wrongs' ": Apartheid, Virginia and South African Style." Dubois Lecture, Harvard University.

MCKAY, ROBERT B. 1965 *Reapportionment: The Law and Politics of Equal Representation.* New York: Twentieth Century Fund.

WILLIAMSON, CHILTON 1960 *American Suffrage from Property to Democracy, 1760–1860.* Princeton, N.J.: Princeton University Press.

WOODWARD, C. VANN 1951 *Origins of the New South, 1877–1913.* Baton Rouge: Louisiana State University Press.

——— 1957 *The Strange Career of Jim Crow.* New York: Oxford University Press.

VOTING RIGHTS ACT OF 1965 AND ITS AMENDMENTS

79 Stat. 437 (1965)

Despite Congress's efforts in the CIVIL RIGHTS ACTS of 1957, 1960, and 1964 to protect the right to vote, the case-by-case approach of these laws proved ineffective in dealing with denials of VOTING RIGHTS to millions of blacks. By 1965, only seventy-one voting rights cases had been filed by the Department of Justice. And in 1964 only 19.4, 6.4, and 31.8 percent of eligible blacks were registered to vote in Alabama, Mississippi, and Louisiana, respectively. In Louisiana, comparable white registration stood at 80.2 percent.

The Voting Rights Act of 1965, amended in 1970, 1975, and 1982, provided additional protection of the right to vote. The 1965 act's most extraordinary features, its preclearance requirements, applied only to states or political subdivisions with low voter registration or participation. In such jurisdictions, most of which were in the South, the act suspended literacy, educational, and character tests of voter qualifications used to deny the right to vote in any elections. In addition, with a view to New York's Puerto Rican population, the act prohibited conditioning the right to vote on any English comprehension requirement for anyone who had completed sixth grade in a school in which the predominant classroom language was other than English. States and political subdivisions subject to the suspension of voting tests were barred from implementing other voting practices that had the effect of denying or abridging the right to vote without obtaining preclearance from a federal court or the ATTORNEY GENERAL.

The Voting Rights Act Amendments of 1970 and 1975 enhanced the preclearance provisions. The 1965 act's coverage had been triggered by low electoral participation in the 1964 election. The 1970 amendments extended the preclearance requirement through 1975 and suspended voting qualification tests or devices until 1975 in all jurisdictions, not just in jurisdictions covered by other provisions of the original 1965 act. The 1975 amendments extended the preclearance requirement through 1982 and suspended tests or devices indefinitely. The 1970 and 1975 amendments also added 1968 and 1972 to 1964 as years in which low electoral participation would trigger the act's coverage. The 1982 amendments imposed new preclearance standards to be effective until 2007.

The Supreme Court has taken an expansive view of the procedures covered by the act's preclearance requirement. In *Allen v. State Board of Elections* (1969), *Dougherty County Board of Education v. White* (1978), and other cases, the Court applied the act to voting practices that might affect minority voter effectiveness, as well as to practices directly limiting voter registration. Under these rulings, the act's preclearance requirements would govern changes in voting districts, or a county board of education's requirement that employees seeking elective office take an unpaid leave of absence.

A change in voting procedure raises the question

whether the change triggers the act's preclearance requirement by having the effect of denying or abridging the right to vote. In deciding whether the requisite effect exists, the Supreme Court has held that the act covers effects even if they are not discriminatorily motivated. This standard, which is more stringent than the purposeful discrimination requirement the Court applies under the FOURTEENTH AMENDMENT and FIFTEENTH AMENDMENT, was upheld against constitutional attack in *Rome v. United States* (1980).

In addition to the preclearance requirements, the 1965 act included a nationwide prohibition upon voting qualifications or standards that deny or abridge voting rights on account of race. This prohibition applies whether the governmental unit is subject to the act's preclearance requirements or not. And, unlike the preclearance requirements, which apply only to changes in voting procedures, it applies to procedures that have long been in effect. A plurality opinion in MOBILE V. BOLDEN (1980) suggested that this provision only proscribed purposeful discrimination prohibited by the Constitution. In the 1982 amendments, however, Congress rejected a purposeful discrimination requirement and set forth standards governing findings of discriminatory effect.

In one of its remedies, the 1965 act continued and expanded a method of guaranteeing voting rights initiated in the FORCE ACT OF 1871. On a showing of widespread denials of voting rights, the act authorized a federal court to appoint federal voting examiners who themselves would examine and register voters for all elections, thereby superseding state election officials.

Addressing problems not covered by the 1965 act, the 1970 amendments lowered from twenty-one to eighteen the minimum voting age for all elections, prohibited states from imposing RESIDENCY REQUIREMENTS in presidential elections, and provided for uniform national rules for absentee voting in presidential elections. The 1975 amendments also sought to overcome linguistic barriers to political participation by requiring bilingual elections in certain political subdivisions. These language provisions brought Texas and Florida under the act's coverage. The 1982 amendments changed the expiration date of these provisions from 1985 to 1992, and added voter assistance provisions for the handicapped.

In general, the 1965 act and amendments have fared well in the Supreme Court. In SOUTH CAROLINA V. KATZENBACH (1966) and KATZENBACH V. MORGAN (1966) the Court upheld the constitutionality of the act. Following the Court's decision in NATIONAL LEAGUE OF CITIES V. USERY (1976) that certain integral state operations are beyond Congress's power to regulate under the COMMERCE CLAUSE, the constitutional attack was renewed. In *Rome v. United States* (1980) the Court held this argument inapplicable to cases involving Congress's power to enforce the Civil War amendments. In UNITED JEWISH ORGANIZATIONS OF WILLIAMSBURGH, INC. V. CAREY (1977) the Court held that use of racial criteria to favor minority voters in an effort to comply with the Voting Rights Act did not violate the Fourteenth or Fifteenth Amendments. In OREGON V. MITCHELL (1970) the Supreme Court sustained most of the 1970 amendments but invalidated lowering the voting age in state and local elections. The latter ruling in *Mitchell*, however, soon was overturned by the TWENTY-SIXTH Amendment.

The Voting Rights Act has been the most measurably successful CIVIL RIGHTS statute. In most southern states the gap between black and white voter registration shrank dramatically, and the number of elected black officials tripled between 1970 and 1975. Overt racial appeals no longer are a routinely successful part of southern political campaigns. The 1975 amendments confirmed a shift in attitude on civil rights matters. For the first time in the twentieth century, a majority of southern congressmen voted in favor of a federal civil rights statute.

THEODORE EISENBERG

Bibliography

BELL, DERRICK A., JR. 1980 *Race, Racism and American Law,* 2nd ed. Boston: Little, Brown.

DORSEN, NORMAN; BENDER, PAUL; NEUBORNE, BURT; and LAW, SYLVIA 1979 Emerson, Haber, and Dorsen's *Political and Civil Rights in the United States,* 4th ed. Vol. 2:609–685. Boston: Little, Brown.

UNITED STATES SENATE, COMMITTEE ON THE JUDICIARY 1982 Senate Report No. 97–417, 97th Congress, 2d Session.

W

WABASH, ST. LOUIS & PACIFIC RAILWAY v. ILLINOIS
118 U.S. 557 (1886)

Tremendous growth in a national railroad network after the Civil War led to increasingly scandalous and harmful abuses. State efforts to control the problems were generally ineffective until *Munn v. Illinois* (1877). In that case, Chief Justice MORRISON R. WAITE allowed state regulation of railroads where Congress had not yet acted, "even though it may indirectly affect" those outside the state. Illinois had attempted to curb one area of abuse by forbidding LONG HAUL–SHORT HAUL DISCRIMINATION. So pervasive was this evil that it would be outlawed later in the INTERSTATE COMMERCE and MANN-ELKINS ACTS. The state sued the Wabash company to prevent it from charging more for shorter hauls; because significant portions of most long hauls lay outside Illinois, the issue lay in the constitutionality of a state regulation of INTERSTATE COMMERCE.

A 6–3 Supreme Court struck down the Illinois statute, undercutting the decisions in the GRANGER CASES (1877) without impairing the DOCTRINE of AFFECTATION WITH A PUBLIC INTEREST. Justice SAMUEL F. MILLER looked to the COMMERCE CLAUSE as securing a "freedom of commerce" across the country. The imposition, by individual states, of varying patterns of rates and regulations on interstate commerce was "oppressive" and rendered the commerce clause a "very feeble and almost useless provision." Miller then relied on the decision in COOLEY V. BOARD OF WARDENS OF PHILADELPHIA (1851) to declare that such regulation was clearly national, not local, in character even though Congress had not yet acted. In so doing, he altered the thrust of the *Cooley* test by examining the impact of state regulation on the nation instead of on the subjects involved. Miller concluded that "it is not, and never has been, the deliberate opinion of a majority of this court that a statute of a state which attempts to regulate the fare and charges by railroad companies [affecting interstate commerce] is a valid law."

Justices HORACE GRAY, JOSEPH P. BRADLEY, and Chief Justice Waite dissented, contending that the *Granger Cases* should have ruled the decision here. Citing WILLSON V. BLACK BIRD CREEK MARSH COMPANY (1829), Gray and his colleagues argued that "in the absence of congressional legislation to the contrary, [the railroads] are not only susceptible of state regulation, but properly amenable to it." They recited the litany of rights and powers granted the railroads by the state: "its being, its franchises, its powers, its road, its right to charge" all confirmed the state's right to regulate the road. The dissenters asserted that the Illinois statute affected interstate commerce only "incidentally" and not adversely. Subject to future congressional action, they would have affirmed the state action.

This decision effectively created a vacuum—Congress had not acted and the states were forbidden to act or even to control intrastate abuses. Together with an increasingly powerful reform movement, *Wabash* helped contribute to the passage of the Interstate Commerce Act in 1887, creating the first national regulatory body.

DAVID GORDON

WADE, UNITED STATES v.
388 U.S. 218 (1967)

Wade's conviction of bank robbery depended heavily on the identification of him as the robber by two bank employees. After he was indicted and counsel appointed for him, the Federal Bureau of Investigation arranged a LINEUP, which included Wade and five or six other people. Wade's counsel was not notified of the procedure; neither he nor anyone else representing Wade's interests was present.

The Supreme Court held that the lineup was a "critical stage" of the proceedings; thus, the Sixth Amendment guarantees a right to the presence of counsel at the pretrial identification if evidence of the lineup were to be used at the trial. The Court reasoned that counsel was necessary at this early stage in order to assure the fairness of the trial itself. The two premises were that eyewitness identification is treacherously subject to mistake, and that police methods in obtaining identifications are often and easily unduly suggestive. If a lawyer has been present at the lineup, later, at the trial, by his questioning of the eyewitnesses he will be able to show how any irregularities have tainted the in-court identification of the defendant.

Wade established a per se rule: if counsel is absent at the pretrial confrontation, the government may not use EVIDENCE that such an event happened. Whether the witness can nevertheless make an in-court identification depends on whether the unfair procedure tainted his present ability to identify: if he had not seen the uncounseled lineup, would he still be able to pick out the defendant?

Finally, the Court suggested that the pretrial confrontation might not be a "critical stage" if other methods were developed to assure against the risk of irreparable mistaken identification. In KIRBY V. ILLINOIS (1972) the Court restricted the holding in *Wade* to lineups held after defendants have been formally charged with crime.

BARBARA ALLEN BABCOCK

WADE-DAVIS BILL
(July 2, 1864)

Republicans worried that under LINCOLN'S PLAN OF RECONSTRUCTION (December 8, 1863), the old state leadership might reverse emancipation. On July 2, 1864, Ohio's Senator Benjamin Wade and Maryland's Representative Henry Winter Davis passed a state-restoration bill that emphasized emancipation's permanence and equalized freedmen's CIVIL RIGHTS.

Their bill, implementing the Constitution's guarantee to each state of a REPUBLICAN FORM OF GOVERNMENT (Article IV, section 4), authorized the President to appoint a provisional governor for each conquered state. When a majority of white male citizens swore future loyalty to the Union, the governor was to initiate a CONSTITUTIONAL CONVENTION. Each new CONSTITUTION must incorporate emancipation, disfranchise high Confederates, and repudiate Confederate debts; then a majority of state voters, the President, and Congress must approve each constitution, and elections could proceed. State laws were to prevail excepting those on slavery. Criminal laws were to apply equally to whites and blacks.

ABRAHAM LINCOLN, unwilling to upset Arkansas's and Louisiana's progress under his 1863 policy, pocket-vetoed the bill. Advocating an abolition constitutional amendment to insure the legitimacy of emancipation, Lincoln suggested that Wade-Davis procedures, though vetoed, were satisfactory.

An election impended. If reelected, LINCOLN would serve until 1869. His educability on race was outstanding. Almost all Republicans, including Wade and Davis, supported him. Had Lincoln signed their bill, it would have committed his successor to equal state justice for all residents.

HAROLD M. HYMAN

Bibliography

HYMAN, HAROLD M. 1963 *A More Perfect Union: The Impact of the Civil War and Reconstruction on the Constitution.* Chap. 16. New York: Knopf.

WAGNER ACT CASES
NLRB v. Jones & Laughlin Steel Corp.
301 U.S. 1 (1937)
NLRB v. Fruehauf Trailer Co.
301 U.S. 49 (1937)
NLRB v. Friedman-Harry Marks Clothing Co.
301 U.S. 58 (1937)
Associated Press Co. v. NLRB
301 U.S. 103 (1937)

The reinvigoration of the COMMERCE CLAUSE as a source of congressional power began with the first cases to reach the Supreme Court under the WAGNER (NATIONAL LABOR RELATIONS) ACT. That statute had been passed in 1935 in an effort to preserve the rights of employees in interstate industries to choose their own representatives and to bargain collectively with their employers. In 1930 the Supreme Court had held that the Railway Labor Act gave such rights to railroad employees. The NATIONAL INDUSTRIAL RECOVERY ACT (NIRA) of 1933 sought to extend such rights to other employees by requiring all codes of fair competition for other industries to contain similar provisions. The code system collapsed when the NIRA was invalidated in SCHECHTER POULTRY CORP. V. UNITED STATES in May 1935. The President and Congress believed that the denial of COLLECTIVE BARGAINING rights would lead to industrial unrest and strikes, which would necessarily obstruct INTERSTATE COMMERCE, and would also aggravate the Great Depression by depressing wage rates and the purchasing power of wage earners. As a result the National Labor Relations Act became law less than six weeks after the *Schechter* decision.

The act authorized the newly created National Labor Relations Board (NLRB), which succeeded similar boards created under the NIRA, to prevent employers from engaging in unfair labor practices "affecting [interstate] commerce," which was defined to mean "in commerce, or burdening or obstructing commerce," or which had led or might lead to a labor dispute burdening or obstructing commerce. These definitions were designed to embody the decisional law upholding the authority of Congress to regulate acts that "directly" obstructed interstate commerce. Congress assumed, correctly as it turned out, that the courts would construe the statute as "contemplating the exercise of control within constitutional bounds."

The NLRB's first cases were brought against employers engaged in interstate transportation and communication (bus lines and the Associated Press) and manufacturers who purchased their supplies and sold their products across state lines. Before these cases were decided, the Supreme Court, in CARTER V. CARTER COAL CO. (1936), held that the substantially identical provisions of the Guffey-Snyder (Bituminous Coal Conservation) Act, enacted shortly after the Labor Relations Act, did not fall within the commerce power of Congress. In the *Carter* case the government had proved that coal strikes would burden not merely the interstate commerce of the immediate employers but also the interstate rail system and many other industries dependent upon coal. No stronger showing could be made under the Wagner Act for employers engaged in mining or manufacturing. As was to be expected, the courts of appeals, though sustaining the act as to companies engaged in interstate transportation and communication, deemed themselves bound by *Carter,* as well as *Schechter* and UNITED STATES V. BUTLER (1936) to hold that the act did not extend to manufacturers.

The first five NLRB cases to reach the Supreme Court involved a bus line, the Associated Press, and three manufacturers. The cases were argued together, beginning on February 8, 1937. Three days before, President FRANKLIN D. ROOSEVELT had announced his plan to appoint up to six new Supreme Court Justices, one for each justice over 70 years of age. On April 12, the Court affirmed the NLRB's rulings in all five cases. The opinions on the commerce clause issue in the bus and press cases were unanimous, although in the press case, four Justices dissented on FIRST AMENDMENT grounds. The cases against manufacturers—the Jones & Laughlin Steel Corporation, the Fruehauf Trailer Co., and a medium-size men's clothing manufacturer—were decided by a 5–4 vote. The membership of the Court had not changed since *Schechter* and *Carter.* But Chief Justice CHARLES EVANS HUGHES and Justice OWEN ROBERTS, who had been part of the majority of six who had rejected the labor relations provisions of the Guffey Act in *Carter,* now joined with Justices LOUIS D. BRANDEIS, HARLAN FISKE STONE, and BENJAMIN N. CARDOZO. The Chief Justice wrote the opinions in the manufacturers' cases.

In the *Carter* case, the majority opinion of Justice GEORGE SUTHERLAND had not denied the magnitude of the effect of coal strikes upon interstate commerce. The question, he held, was whether the effect was "direct," and that did not turn upon the "extent of the effect" or its "magnitude," but "entirely upon the manner in which the effect has been brought about"; "it connotes the absence of an efficient intervening agency or condition." The effect must "operate proximately—not mediately, remotely, or collaterally." Why "direct" should be so defined was not otherwise explained, except by the need for preserving the power of the states over PRODUCTION, even in interstate industries in which interstate competition would preclude state regulation. (See EFFECTS ON COMMERCE.)

The opinion of Chief Justice Hughes in the *Jones & Laughlin* case flatly rejected the *Butler* approach.

Giving full weight to respondent's contention with respect to a break in the complete continuity of the "STREAM OF COMMERCE" by reason of respondent's manufacturing operations, the fact remains that the stoppage of those operations by industrial strife would have a most serious effect upon interstate commerce. In view of respondent's far-flung activities, it is idle to say that the effect would be indirect or remote. It is obvious that it would be immediate and might be catastrophic. We are asked to shut our eyes to the plainest facts of our national life and to deal with the question of direct and indirect effects in an intellectual vacuum. . . . When industries organize themselves on a national scale, making their relation to interstate commerce the dominant factor in their activities, how can it be maintained that their industrial labor relations constitute a forbidden field into which Congress may not enter when it is necessary to protect interstate commerce from the paralyzing consequences of industrial war? We have often said that interstate commerce itself is a practical conception. It is equally true that interferences with that commerce must be appraised by a judgment that does not ignore actual experience.

The Chief Justice also met head on the argument that the federal power did not extend to activities in the course of production or manufacturing. Citing many antitrust cases, he declared: "The close and intimate effect which brings the subject within the reach of Federal power may be due to activities in relation to productive industry although the industry when separately viewed is local. . . . It is thus apparent that the fact that the employees here concerned were engaged in production is not determinative."

"The fundamental principle," Hughes stated, "is that the power to regulate commerce is the power to enact 'all appropriate legislation' for 'its protection and advancement'; to adopt measures 'to promote its growth and insure its safety'; 'to foster, protect, control and restrain.' That power is plenary and may be exerted to protect interstate commerce 'no matter what the source of the dangers which threatened it.' " Hughes also invoked the SHREVEPORT DOCTRINE he had announced in HOUSTON EAST AND WEST TEXAS RAILWAY V. UNITED STATES (1914): "Although activities may be intrastate in character when separately considered, if they have such a close and substantial relation to interstate commerce that their control is essential or appropriate to protect that commerce from burdens and obstructions, Congress cannot be denied the power to exercise that control."

In deference to his own opinion in *Schechter,* the Chief Justice declared that "undoubtedly the scope of this power must be considered in the light of our dual system of government" so as not to "obliterate the distinction between what is national and what is local." In *Schechter* the effect upon commerce had been too "remote"; "to find 'immediacy or directness' there was to find it 'almost everywhere', a result inconsistent with the maintenance of our Federal system." With little explanation Hughes added that *Carter* was "not controlling."

Within a few weeks the Court sustained the constitutionality of the SOCIAL SECURITY ACT. Soon after Justices WILLIS VAN DEVANTER and Sutherland retired. And President Roosevelt's court-packing plan, not very surprisingly, got nowhere.

Subsequent Labor Board cases extended the application of the Labor Act far beyond the three manufacturers in the center of the interstate movement; it was sufficient that a strike would interfere with interstate movement of products (for example, *Santa Cruz Fruit Packing Co. v. NLRB,* 1938; *NLRB v. Fainblatt,* 1939; *Consolidated Edison Co. v. NLRB,* 1938). The unanimous opinion of the Court speaking through Justice Stone, with Hughes and Roberts still on the bench, in UNITED STATES V. DARBY (1941) explicitly rejected the concept that the TENTH AMENDMENT limited the powers granted Congress by the Constitution. And other cases by now have extended the commerce power "almost everywhere." Nevertheless, the opinion in *Jones & Laughlin* remains a landmark in the interpretation of the commerce clause, as the definitive acceptance of the modern theories which recognize the power of Congress to control all aspects of the nation's integrated economic system.

ROBERT L. STERN

Bibliography

CORTNER, RICHARD C. 1970 *The Jones & Laughlin Case.* New York: Knopf.

——— 1964 *The Wagner Act Cases.* Knoxville: University of Tennessee Press.

DODD, E. MERRICK 1945 The Supreme Court and Organized Labor, 1941–1945. *Harvard Law Review* 58:1018–1071.

GROSS, JAMES A. 1974 *The Making of the National Labor Relations Board: A Study in Economics, Politics, and the Law,* Vol. 1 (1933–1937). Albany: State University of New York Press.

STERN, ROBERT L. 1946 The Commerce Clause and the National Economy, 1933–1946. *Harvard Law Review* 59:645–693, 888–947.

WAGNER (NATIONAL LABOR RELATIONS) ACT
49 Stat. 449 (1935)

Named after the New York senator who introduced and fought for it, the National Labor Relations Act (NLRA) extended the protection of the United States to organized labor. Robert Wagner framed the act to provide a constitutional basis for the protections given to labor by section 7(a) of the NATIONAL INDUSTRIAL RECOVERY ACT (NIRA) and by a National Labor Relations Board, which had been established and was operating under the sole authority of Public Resolution 44 and an EXECUTIVE ORDER. The Supreme Court confirmed the need for new legislation when, eleven days after the NLRA's enactment, it voided the NIRA in SCHECHTER POULTRY CORP. V. UNITED STATES (1935).

Congress based the Wagner Act on the COMMERCE CLAUSE: the denial by employers of employees' rights to organize and bargain collectively caused "strikes and other forms of industrial strife or unrest, which have the intent or necessary effect of burdening or obstructing [interstate] commerce." Congress added that unequal bargaining positions had exacerbated national economic instability. One section of the act guaranteed employees the right to organize, "to bargain collectively through representatives of their own choosing," and to act together to further these ends. Another section reinforced these rights by delineating employers' obligations; it defined and prohibited "unfair labor practices," including interference with the exercise of the above-mentioned rights, or discrimination to encourage or discourage union formation, administration, or membership. This section also outlawed discrimination against an employee for filing a complaint against his employer under the act and made it illegal to refuse to bargain collectively with a union's legal representative.

The act also provided for a National Labor Relations Board with broad supervisory powers to administer its provisions. The Board could issue complaints, hear and determine charges, and issue CEASE-AND-DESIST ORDERS which were enforceable upon application to federal circuit courts. Congress further empowered the board to hold representation elections and to certify the winner.

Wagner drafted the act carefully so that it would withstand scrutiny by the Supreme Court. Section 1—outlining the NLRA's policy—was rewritten after the decision in *Schechter* to specify the burdens placed upon INTERSTATE COMMERCE by labor unrest. The act's policy statement attributed that discord to the denial of workers' rights which this act would secure. Wagner's diligence paid off. A 5–4 majority of the Court upheld the NLRA in *N.L.R.B. v. Jones & Laughlin Steel Corporation* (1937). (See WAGNER ACT CASES.) The Wagner Act provided for strong independent unions in an effort to promote COLLECTIVE BARGAINING. By thus indirectly stimulating higher wages and increased consumer demand, the act helped guarantee a stable national economy and social justice for American labor. The TAFT-HARTLEY LABOR MANAGEMENT RELATIONS ACT, passed in 1947 partly to plug loopholes in the NLRA, governed union conduct much as employers' actions had earlier been regulated.

DAVID GORDON

Bibliography

MILLIS, HARRY A. and BROWN, EMILY C. 1950 *From the Wagner Act to Taft-Hartley: A Study of National Labor Policy.* Chicago: University of Chicago Press.

TAYLOR, BENJAMIN J. and WITNEY, FRED (1970)1975 *Labor Relations Law,* 2nd ed. Pages 134–199. Englewood Cliffs, N.J.: Prentice-Hall.

WAINWRIGHT v. SYKES
433 U.S. 72 (1977)

In *Sykes* the ADEQUATE STATE GROUND bar to federal HABEAS CORPUS, buried in FAY V. NOIA (1963), was unearthed and returned to service with little more than a coat of paint for disguise. *Noia* had held that a state prisoner was not barred from seeking federal habeas corpus relief merely because the applicant had failed to raise his or her federal constitutional claim in the earlier state proceeding as required by state law. *Noia* was attacked within the Supreme Court and by some scholars for sacrificing finality of decision. State judges trumpeted their resentment at giving federal district courts the last word in the state criminal process.

Sykes was the culmination of the attack on *Noia* from within the Court. A state prisoner sought federal habeas corpus, arguing that his rights to a warning under MIRANDA V. ARIZONA (1966) had been violated when his statement was admitted into EVIDENCE at his state trial. He had not objected when the evidence was offered, as state law required. The Supreme Court held, 7–2, that federal habeas corpus was barred.

Justice WILLIAM H. REHNQUIST, for the majority, announced that failure to raise a federal constitutional claim in the manner required by state law bars resort to federal habeas corpus unless the applicant shows "cause" for the procedural default and "prejudice" from the forfeiture of the federal claim. Defendant had asserted no cause for the absence of timely objection, and prejudice was negated by other evidence of his guilt, independent of his statement.

KENNETH L. KARST

WAITE, MORRISON R.
(1816–1888)

Morrison Remick Waite, sixth Chief Justice of the United States, successfully led the Supreme Court in dealing with major constitutional problems concerning Reconstruction and business–government relations between 1874 and 1888.

Son of Henry Matson Waite, Chief Justice of the Connecticut Supreme Court of Errors, Morrison Waite read law after graduating from Yale College in 1837. In 1838 he removed to Ohio, where he built a flourishing legal practice specializing in commercial law, acquired substantial property interests, and joined the Whig party. Although prominent in the legal profession, Waite was virtually unknown in national affairs prior to his appointment as Chief Justice. He served one term in the Ohio legislature and a term on the Toledo city council, was appointed counsel to the Geneva Tribunal to negotiate the *Alabama* claims in 1872, and was elected president of the Ohio CONSTITUTIONAL CONVENTION of 1873.

The circumstances of Waite's appointment to the Court were remarkable, not so much because he lacked national political recognition as because he was the fifth person whom President ULYSSES S. GRANT nominated or asked to serve as Chief Justice. Yet Waite had early been touted for the position by leading Ohio politicians, and Grant had considered him a possibility from the beginning. His effective service at the Geneva Arbitration, professional reputation, and unwavering Republican party loyalty recommended him, and in January 1874 the Senate confirmed him by a 63–0 vote.

Waite's significance in American constitutional history is threefold. He wrote the first Supreme Court opinions interpreting the FOURTEENTH and FIFTEENTH AMENDMENTS in cases involving Negroes' CIVIL RIGHTS. Second, his 1877 opinions in *Munn v. Illinois* and the other GRANGER CASES established the basic principles of constitutional law governing state governments as they attempted to deal with economic changes caused by the industrial revolution. Third, Waite expressed a conception of JUDICIAL REVIEW that summarized dominant nineteenth-century ideas about constitutional adjudication and provided a model for twentieth-century theorists of judicial restraint.

The northern retreat from Reconstruction was well underway when Waite became Chief Justice, and the WAITE COURT did not attempt to reverse this political development. Under the circumstances, and given the circumscribed role of the judiciary in nineteenth-century constitutional politics, it had little choice but to acquiesce. In determining the meaning of the Fourteenth and Fifteenth Amendments and in applying federal civil rights laws, however, the Court could choose among several possible conceptions of national legislative power and federal–state relations. Waite guided the Court toward a moderate position of STATES' RIGHTS nationalism which upheld national power to protect civil rights within the framework of traditional FEDERALISM.

To understand this development it is necessary to advert to the SLAUGHTERHOUSE CASES (1873) and to Justice JOSEPH P. BRADLEY's circuit court opinion in UNITED STATES V. CRUIKSHANK (1874). In the former, the Supreme Court confirmed the theory of dual American CITIZENSHIP, stated that the Fourteenth Amendment did not add to the rights of national citizenship, and concluded that ordinary civil rights were attributes of state citizenship, regulation of which was beyond the authority of the United States. In the *Cruikshank* case, involving prosecution of whites in Colfax, Louisiana, for violating the civil rights of Negro citizens, Justice Bradley held that although the Fourteenth Amendment prohibited state rather than private denial of civil rights, under certain conditions the federal government was authorized to guarantee civil rights against interference by private individuals. The relevant circumstance, according to Bradley, was state failure to fulfill its affirmative duty to protect citizens' rights.

Chief Justice Waite wrote the majority opinion when *United States v. Cruikshank* (1876) was decided in the Supreme Court. Defendants were indicted under a section of the Force Act of 1870 that declared it a federal crime for two or more persons to deprive any citizen of rights secured by the Constitution or laws of the United States. Like Bradley in the CIRCUIT COURT, Waite found numerous flaws in the INDICTMENTS and on that ground ordered the defendants to be discharged, thus frustrating the federal civil rights enforcement effort. Nevertheless, Waite asserted national authority to enforce civil rights.

The Chief Justice followed the *Slaughterhouse* opinion in positing separate federal and state citizenships and in stating that the federal government could protect only those rights placed within its JURISDICTION. He held further that the FREEDOM OF ASSEMBLY, which the defendants were charged with violating, was a right of state rather than federal citizenship. The indictment, however, had incorrectly stated that denial of freedom of assembly by private persons was a federal crime within the meaning of the Force Act; therefore the indictment was invalid. Yet federal authority was not nugatory in civil rights matters. Waite pointed out that if the indictment had charged a violation of the right to assemble in order to petition the national government, it would have been proper under the act. Thus in protecting a federal right national authority was putatively effective against private individuals as well as states. Waite furthermore asserted an indirect federal power to protect rights of state citizenship against both state and private interference. The ordinary right of assembly was a state right, said Waite, over which "no direct power" was granted to Congress. This appeared to mean that if states failed to uphold civil rights within their jurisdiction, the federal government could provide the needed protection. Finally Waite noted that the indictments did not allege that the full and equal benefit of laws for the protection of whites was denied to blacks on account of race; accordingly the CIVIL RIGHTS ACT OF 1866 was not in point. The implication was that if a racially discriminatory purpose had been alleged, federal authority under the 1866 law could have been employed against private as well as against state denial of rights.

Waite also gave the opinion in UNITED STATES V. REESE (1876), the first Supreme Court case involving Fifteenth Amendment VOTING RIGHTS. State officials in Kentucky were indicted for refusing to accept the vote of a Negro citizen. Again the Court ruled against the federal government. Waite declared two provisions of the Force Act of 1870 unconstitutional because they did not in express terms limit the offense of state officials to denial of the right to vote on account of color. Insisting on the need for STRICT CONSTRUCTION of criminal statutes, he interpreted the act in a strained and technical manner as preventing any wrongful interference with voting rights, rather than simply interferences that were racially motivated. The Fifteenth Amendment authorized the federal government to deal only with the latter. It did not, said Waite, secure the right to vote, but only the right not to be discriminated against in voting on racial grounds. Observing that "Congress has not as yet provided by 'appropriate legislation' for the punishment of the offense charged in the indictment," Waite in effect invited Republican lawmakers to enact a more tightly drawn enforcement act.

Waite's personal sympathies were enlisted in efforts to assist Negroes. As a trustee of the Peabody Fund in 1874 he signed a report endorsing a constitutional argument for federal aid to education, thus breaking the rule against extra-Court political involvement to which he scrupulously adhered throughout his judicial career. Although Waite accepted the abandonment of Reconstruction and held that Congress had no power "to do mere police duty in the States," his opinions nevertheless authorized federal interference against state and in some circumstances private denial of rights when racially motivated. In subsequent cases, most notably UNITED STATES V. HARRIS (1883), the CIVIL RIGHTS CASES (1883), and EX PARTE YARBROUGH (1884), the Waite Court amplified the principles set forth in the *Cruikshank* and *Reese* cases.

In the sphere of government–business relations, Waite was sympathetic to regulatory legislation within a political and legal framework that encouraged industrial expansion and a national free trade area. In the early 1870s, in response to farmers' and merchants' demands for relief from high shipping costs, several midwestern states adopted legislation setting maximum railroad rates. These laws appeared to discourage further railroad construction, and within a few years most of them were repealed or modified. Nevertheless, in the landmark *Granger Cases* the Supreme Court ruled on the constitutionality of these regulatory measures.

Munn v. Illinois (1877), Waite's most famous opinion, sustained an 1871 Illinois law that established maximum rates for grain elevators. Waite based his approval of the legislation on a broad conception of the STATE POLICE POWER, which he said authorized states to regulate the use of private property "when such regulation becomes necessary for the public good." He rejected the contention that state regulation of the rates charged by ferries, common carriers, or bakers was a deprivation of property without DUE PROCESS OF LAW in violation of the Fourteenth Amendment. Support for Waite's conclusion lay in numerous state COMMON LAW precedents asserting a public interest in certain kinds of property, such as lands bordering on watercourses, which were subject to government regulation. Like other judges in similar cases, and influenced by a memorandum prepared by Justice Bradley dealing with the instant case, Waite relied on a treatise of the seventeenth-century English judge Lord Chief Justice Sir Matthew Hale in asserting: "When property is 'AFFECTED WITH A PUBLIC INTEREST, it ceases to be juris privati only.' " The grain elevator companies, Waite explained, exercised a virtual monopoly in the regional market structure; thus, they were affected with a public interest and subject to regulation by the state legislature. In the other *Granger Cases* Waite employed this principle to uphold state regulation of railroad rates.

Waite also approved state regulation of CORPORATIONS in a series of decisions that carried to a logical conclusion the principle by which the CONTRACT CLAUSE of the Constitution did not prevent state legislatures from reserving the power to alter charter grants. These cases included STONE V. MISSISSIPPI (1880), *Ruggles v. Illinois* (1883), and *Spring Valley Water Works v. Schotteler* (1883). This trend culminated in STONE V. FARMERS LOAN AND TRUST CO.

(1886), known as the *Railroad Commission Cases*, in which Waite held that a state charter authorizing railroads to set reasonable rates did not divest a state of the power ultimately to determine what was a reasonable rate.

While generally approving regulatory legislation, Waite placed limitations on the POLICE POWER with a view toward protecting private property. In the *Railroad Commission Cases* he admonished: "This power to regulate is not a power to destroy; and limitation is not the equivalent of confiscation. Under pretence of regulating fares and freights the state cannot require a railroad corporation to carry persons or property without reward; neither can it do that which in law amounts to a TAKING of private property without due process of law." Rather than suggesting an irresistible tendency to accept the argument for SUBSTANTIVE DUE PROCESS that was later adopted by the Supreme Court, these and similar dicta indicate that Waite, like Justice STEPHEN J. FIELD who dissented in *Munn* and the other *Granger* cases, believed the essential constitutional problem in cases involving government–business relations was to determine the extent of the police power. Shortly after the *Munn* decision Waite wrote: "The great difficulty in the future will be to establish the boundary between that which is private, and that in which the public has an interest."

Waite epitomized nineteenth-century thinking about the nature of the judicial function and the power of judicial review. He believed the judiciary should play a subordinate role in public-policy making, and should especially defer to the political branches in questions concerning the reasonableness of legislation. His clearest and most forceful expression of this view appeared in *Munn v. Illinois* when he stated: "For us the question is one of power, not of expediency. If no state of circumstances could justify such a statute, then we may declare this one void, because in excess of the legislative power of the States. But if it could we must presume it did. Of the propriety of legislative interference within the scope of legislative power, the legislature is the exclusive judge." Waite acknowledged that legislative power might be abused. But "[f]or protection against abuses by legislatures," he observed, "the people must resort to the polls, not to the courts."

Waite effectively balanced the competing demands of state and federal authority as constitutional equilibrium was restored after the end of Reconstruction. In addition to the decisions already noted, he wrote the opinions in *Louisiana v. Jumel* (1882) and *New Hampshire v. Louisiana* (1882), both of which held that the ELEVENTH AMENDMENT prevented suits by bondholders attempting to force a state government to redeem its bonds. These decisions expressed the political logic of the COMPROMISE OF 1877 and marked a significant broadening of states' SOVEREIGN IMMUNITY under the Eleventh Amendment. In another notable case involving state power and women's rights, MINOR V. HAPPERSETT (1875), Waite adhered to a narrow interpretation of the Fourteenth Amendment in deciding that the right to vote was not an attribute of federal citizenship and that states could regulate the suffrage as they saw fit.

On the other hand, Waite upheld federal authority in the controversial SINKING FUND CASES (1879) and in PENSACOLA TELEGRAPH CO. V. WESTERN UNION TELEGRAPH CO. (1878). In the former, the Court confirmed the constitutionality of an act of Congress requiring the Union Pacific and Central Pacific railroads to set aside money from current income for the subsequent payment of its mortgage debts. In the latter case the Court upheld the rights of an interstate telegraph company operating under authority of an act of Congress against the rights of a company acting under a state charter. Waite also voted to strike down state tax legislation when it interfered with INTERSTATE COMMERCE, although he was less inclined than his colleagues to regard STATE TAXATION OF COMMERCE in this light.

Overcoming the resentment of several Justices who had aspired to the Chief Justiceship, Waite performed the administrative and other tasks of his position with great skill. In a larger political sense he was also a successful judicial statesman. During his tenure, as at few times in American constitutional history, the Supreme Court was remarkably free of congressional criticism. Waite achieved this success by confining JUDICIAL POLICYMAKING within limits approved by the nation's representative political institutions and public opinion.

HERMAN BELZ

Bibliography

BENEDICT, MICHAEL LES 1979 Preserving Federalism: Reconstruction and the Waite Court. *Supreme Court Review* 1978:39–79.

FRANTZ, LAUREN B. 1964 Congressional Power to Enforce the Fourteenth Amendment Against Private Acts. *Yale Law Journal* 73:1352–1384.

MAGRATH, PETER C. 1963 *Morrison R. Waite: The Triumph of Character.* New York: Macmillan.

SCHEIBER, HARRY N. 1971 The Road to *Munn:* Eminent Domain and the Concept of Public Purpose in the State Courts. *Perspectives in American History* 5:329–402.

TRIMBLE, BRUCE R. 1938 *Chief Justice Waite: Defender*

of the Public Interest. Princeton, N.J.: Princeton University Press.

WAITE COURT
(1874–1888)

A new age of American constitutional law was at hand when MORRISON R. WAITE became CHIEF JUSTICE of the United States in 1874. Not only had the Civil War discredited many antebellum glosses on the "old" Constitution, consisting of the venerable document framed in 1787 and the twelve amendments adopted during the early republic, but it had also generated a "new" Constitution consisting of the THIRTEENTH AMENDMENT, the FOURTEENTH AMENDMENT, and the FIFTEENTH AMENDMENT. The range of choices at the Court's disposal was virtually unlimited as it reconstituted the old organic law and integrated the new. CHARLES SUMNER said it best just four years before Waite took the Court's helm. The tumultuous events of 1861–1869, he exclaimed, had transformed the Constitution into "molten wax" ready for new impression. An extraordinarily homogeneous group of men made this impression. Of the fourteen associate Justices who sat with Waite between 1874 and his death in 1888, only NATHAN CLIFFORD had been appointed by a Democrat and all but two—SAMUEL F. MILLER and JOHN MARSHALL HARLAN, both of Kentucky—had been born in the free states. All of them were Protestants. Thus the Republican party, which had subdued the South and created the "new" Constitution, had also reconstructed the federal judiciary. As the Waite Court proceeded to refashion the structure of American constitutional law, its work ineluctably reflected the values, aspirations, and fears that had animated the Republican party's northern Protestant constituency since the 1850s.

Fierce opposition to state SOVEREIGNTY concepts was a core element of Republican belief from the party's very inception. Republicans asociated state sovereignty with proslavery constitutionalism in the 1850s, with SECESSION in 1861, and ultimately with the tragic war both engendered. Waite and his colleagues shared this aversion to state sovereignty dogma and repeatedly expressed it in controversies involving the IMPLIED POWERS of Congress under the "old" Constitution. In case after case the Court resisted limitations on federal power derived from state sovereignty premises and held, in effect, that Congress's authority to enact statutes deemed NECESSARY AND PROPER for the ENUMERATED POWERS had the same scope under the Constitution as it would if the states did not exist. On several occasions the Court even revived the idea that Congress might exercise any power inherent in national sovereignty as long as it was not specifically prohibited by the Constitution. This doctrine, first expounded by Federalist congressmen during debate on the SEDITION ACT of 1798, had been regarded as "exploded" by most antebellum statesmen. But its revival after the Civil War did have a certain logic. If there was one impulse that every member of the Waite Court had in common, it was the urge to extirpate every corollary of "southern rights" theory from American constitutional law and to confirm the national government's authority to exercise every power necessary to maintain its existence.

The revival of the implied powers doctrine began in the often overlooked case of *Kohl v. United States* (1876). There counsel challenged Congress's authority to take private property in Cincinnati as a site for public buildings on the ground that the Constitution sanctioned federal exercise of the EMINENT DOMAIN power only in the DISTRICT OF COLUMBIA. Article I, section 8, vested Congress with authority to acquire land elsewhere "for the erection of forts . . . and other needful buildings" only "by the consent of the legislature of the State in which the same shall be." This was by no means a novel argument. JAMES MADISON and JAMES MONROE had pointed to the national government's lack of a general eminent domain power when vetoing INTERNAL IMPROVEMENT bills, and proslavery theorists had invoked the same principle as a bar to compensated emancipation and colonization schemes. In *Pollard's Lessee v. Hagan* (1845), moreover, the TANEY COURT had said that "the United States have no constitutional capacity to exercise municipal jurisdiction, sovereignty, or eminent domain within the limits of a State or elsewhere, except in the cases in which it is expressly granted." But WILLIAM STRONG, speaking for the Court in *Kohl*, refused to take this doctrine "seriously." Congress's war, commerce, and postal powers necessarily included the right to acquire property for forts, lighthouses, and the like. "If the right to acquire property for such uses be made a barren right by the unwillingness of property holders to sell, or by the action of a State prohibiting a sale to the Federal Government," Strong explained, "the constitutional grants of power may be rendered nugatory. . . . This cannot be." Congress's eminent domain power must be implied, Strong concluded, for commentators on the law of nations had always regarded it as "the offspring of political necessity, and . . . inseparable from sovereignty."

HORACE GRAY sounded the same theme in the Legal Tender Cases (*Juilliard v. Greenman,* 1884), where the Court sustained Congress's authority to emit legal tender notes even in peacetime. With only STEPHEN J. FIELD dissenting, Gray asserted that because the power to make government paper a legal tender was "one of the powers belonging to sovereignty in other civilized nations, and not expressly withheld from Congress by the Constitution," it was unquestionably "an appropriate means, conducive and plainly adapted" to the execution of Congress's power to borrow money. In EX PARTE YARBROUGH (1884), decided the same day, the Court spoke the language of national sovereignty in an especially significant case. At issue there was the criminal liability of a Georgia man who had savagely beaten a black voter en route to cast his ballot in a federal election. The Court unanimously sustained the petitioner's conviction under the 1870 CIVIL RIGHTS ACT, which made it a federal crime to "injure, oppress, threaten, or intimidate any citizen in the free exercise or enjoyment of any right or privilege secured to him by the Constitution or laws of the United States." It did so on the ground that Congress's duty "to provide in an ELECTION held under its authority, for security of life and limb to the voter" arose not from its interest in the victim's rights so much as "from the necessity of the government itself." Samuel F. Miller explained that Congress's power to regulate the time, place, and manner of holding federal elections, conferred in Article I, section 4, implied a "power to pass laws for the free, pure, and safe exercise" of the suffrage. "But it is a waste of time," he added, "to seek for specific sources to pass these laws. . . . If this government is anything more than a mere aggregation of delegated agents of other States and governments, each of which is superior to the general government, it must have the power to protect the elections on which its existence depends from violence and corruption."

The Court's decisions in *Kohl, Juilliard,* and *Yarbrough* merely jettisoned antebellum canons of STRICT CONSTRUCTION. They did not impair the autonomy of state governments. The eminent domain power of the several states was not threatened by *Kohl,* the Constitution expressly prohibited the states from making anything but gold and silver a legal tender, and *Yarbrough* did not jeopardize Georgia's power to prosecute political assassins for assault or murder. Yet the Waite Court was as quick to defend exercises of Congress's powers in situations where counsel claimed that the states' autonomy was in jeopardy as in cases where their reserved powers remained unimpaired. *Ex parte Siebold* (1880) was the leading case in point. There the Court sustained a conviction for ballot stuffing under the 1871 ENFORCEMENT ACT, which made it a federal crime for any state official at a congressional election to neglect duties required of him by either state or federal law. Counsel for the petitioner argued that in PRIGG V. PENNSYLVANIA (1842) and KENTUCKY V. DENNISON (1861) the Taney Court had held that the principle of divided sovereignty precluded acts of Congress compelling the cooperation of state officials in the execution of national law. "We cannot yield to such a transcendental view of State sovereignty," JOSEPH BRADLEY proclaimed for the Court in *Siebold.* "As a general rule," he said, "it is no doubt expedient and wise that the operations of the State and National Governments should, as far as practicable, be conducted separately, in order to avoid undue jealousies and jars." But the Constitution neither mandated an immutable boundary between spheres of federal and state power nor restricted Congress's choice of means in implementing its enumerated authority to regulate federal elections.

The Court's constitutional nationalism did have limits. Like most Republicans of the age, Waite and his colleagues resisted the idea of centralization with as much ardor as the concept of state sovereignty. They regarded the national government's competence as deriving from the powers specified in the Constitution or fairly implied from it; the residual powers of government, usually called "internal police," belonged exclusively to the several states. Thus decisions like *Kohl* and *Siebold,* as Waite and his associates understood them, did not contract the ambit of state JURISDICTION. Rather the court simply refused to recognize implied limitations on the powers of Congress derived from state sovereignty premises. The *Trade-Mark Cases* (1879) underscored the Waite Court's allegiance to this view of the federal system. There a unanimous Court, speaking through Miller, held that Congress had no authority to enact a "universal system of trade-mark registration." Miller's method of analysis was more revealing than the result. His first impulse was to determine which sphere of government ordinarily had responsibility for such matters in the constitutional scheme. "As the property in trade-marks and the right to their exclusive use rest on the laws of the States, and like the great body of the rights of persons and of property, depend on them for security and protection," he explained, "the power of Congress to legislate on the subject . . . must be found in the Constitution of the United States, which is the source of all the powers the Congress can lawfully exercise." This two-tier method not only reified DUAL FEDERALISM but also put the burden of demonstrating Congress's authority to act on the government. In the *Trade-Mark Cases* it could not do so. Trade-marks lacked "the essential characteristics" of creative work in the arts and sciences, consequently the statute could not be sustained under the COPYRIGHT or PATENT powers. And the commerce power, though admittedly "broad," could not be construed as to permit federal regulation of commercial relations between persons residing in the same state.

When the Waite Court turned to cases involving the "new" Constitution, the instinct to conceptualize rights and powers in terms of dual federalism had fateful consequences. Beginning in UNITED STATES V. CRUIKSHANK (1876), the Court emasculated Congress's power "to enforce, by appropriate legislation," the rights guaranteed by the Fourteenth and Fifteenth Amendments. At issue was the validity of conspiracy convictions under the 1870 Civil Rights Act against a band of whites who had attacked a conclave of blacks in Grants Parish, Louisiana, killing from sixty to one hundred of them. The government claimed that the defendants had deprived the black citizens of their constitutional rights to hold a peaceful assembly, to bear arms, to vote, and to EQUAL PROTECTION OF THE LAWS safeguarding persons and property. The Court unanimously overturned the convictions. The CONSPIRACY law was not voided; indeed, the Court sustained a conviction under that very statute in *Yarbrough.* But Waite and his associates were determined to confine Congress's power to enact "appropriate legislation" in such a way to preserve what Miller called "the main features of the federal system." The Court had no choice in the matter, Joseph Bradley remarked on circuit in 1874, unless it was prepared "to clothe Congress with power to pass laws for the general preservation of social order in every State," or, in short, with a plenary power of "internal police."

Waite's opinion for the Court in *Cruikshank* contained two separate lines of argument. He began the first foray by pointing out that every American citizen "owes allegiance to two sovereigns, and claims protection from both." Because the two levels of government could protect the rights of citizens only "within their respective spheres," federal authorities could assert jurisdiction over perpetrators of violence only if the rights denied to victims were derived from the Constitution and laws of the United States. But in the SLAUGHTERHOUSE CASES (1873), decided ten months before Waite came to the Court, a majority of five had concluded that there were very few PRIVILEGES OR IMMUNITIES of national CITIZENSHIP and that the Fourteenth Amendment had not created any new ones. Fundamental rights of life, liberty, and property still rested upon the laws of the states, and citizens had to rely upon the states for the protection of those rights. Among the privileges of state citizenship, Waite explained in *Cruikshank,* were the rights to assemble, to bear arms, and to vote. Although guaranteed against infringement by Congress in the BILL OF RIGHTS, the rights to assemble and bear arms were not "granted by the Constitution" or "in any manner dependent upon that instrument for existence." The right to vote in state and local elections stood on the same footing because "the right to vote in the States comes from the States." The Fifteenth Amendment did give citizens a new right under the Constitution—exemption from RACIAL DISCRIMINATION when attempting to vote. Because the Grants Parish indictments did not aver that the defendants had prevented their victims "from exercising the right to vote on account of race," however, that count was as defective as the rest.

Waite's second line of argument in *Cruikshank* was designed to hold the votes of Joseph Bradley, Stephen J. Field, and NOAH SWAYNE. They had dissented in the *Slaughterhouse Cases,* claiming that the Fourteenth Amendment had been designed to reconstruct the federal system by creating a third sphere in the constitutional scheme—that of the individual whose FUNDAMENTAL RIGHTS were now protected against unequal and discriminatory state laws. Waite satisfied them by stating what came to be known as the STATE ACTION doctrine. He not only conceded that "[t]he equality of the rights of citizens is a principle of republicanism" but strongly implied that the Fourteenth Amendment had nationalized this principle under the equal protection clause, if not the privileges or immunities clause. But the amendment, he added, "does not . . . add any thing to the rights which one citizen had under the Constitution against another." The very language of the amendment's first section—"No state shall . . ."—suggested that it must be read not as a grant of power to Congress but as a limitation on the states. It followed that the exercise of fundamental rights did not come under the Constitution's protection until jeopardized by the enactment or enforcement of a state law. "This the amendment guarantees, but no more," Waite declared. "The power of the national government is limited to the enforcement of this guaranty."

The principles announced in *Cruikshank* doomed the rest of Congress's CIVIL RIGHTS program, all of which had been based on the assumption that the "new" Constitution might be employed as a sword to protect any interference with fundamental rights.

A voting rights statute went down in UNITED STATES v. REESE (1876) because Congress had failed to limit federal jurisdiction over state elections to the prevention of racially motivated fraud or dereliction; the antilynching provisions of the 1871 Civil Rights Act were invalidated for want of state action in UNITED STATES v. HARRIS (1883). One latent function of *Cruikshank*, however, was to draw renewed attention to the equal protection clause as a shield for blacks and other racial minorities whose civil rights were imperiled by discriminatory state laws. Soon the docket was crowded with such cases, and the Court was compelled to wrestle with longstanding ambiguities in the Republican party's commitment to racial equality.

Republicans had always been quick to defend equal rights in the market, for it was the rights to make contracts and own property that distinguished free people from slaves. But many Republicans regarded the idea of equality before the law as wholly compatible with legalized race prejudice in the social realm. Words like "nation" and "race" were not merely descriptive terms in the nineteenth century; they were widely understood as objective manifestations of natural communities, the integrity of which government had a duty to maintain. Thus most Republicans never accepted the proposition that blacks ought to be free to marry whites and many denied the right of blacks to associate with whites even in public places. The framers of the "new" Constitution had neither abjured this qualified view of equality not incorporated it into the Fourteenth Amendment. The discretion of Waite and his colleagues was virtually unfettered. They could weave prevailing prejudices into equal protection jurisprudence or they could interpret the equality concept broadly, declare that the "new" Constitution was colorblind, and put the Court's enormous prestige squarely behind the struggle for racial justice.

Exponents of racial equality were greatly encouraged by STRAUDER v. WEST VIRGINIA (1880), the case of first impression. There a divided Court reversed the murder conviction of a black defendant who had been tried under a statute that limited jury service to "white male persons." The Fourteenth Amendment, William Strong explained for the majority, "was designed to secure the colored race the enjoyment of all the civil rights that under the law are enjoyed by white persons." This formulation was acceptable even to the two dissenters. According to Stephen J. Field and Nathan Clifford, however, jury service was not a "civil right." It was a "political right." The only rights Congress intended to protect with the Fourteenth Amendment, they contended, were those enumerated in the Civil Rights Act of 1866—to own property, to make and enforce contracts, to sue and give evidence. The equal protection clause, Field said, "secures to all persons their civil rights upon the same terms; but it leaves political rights . . . and social rights . . . as they stood previous to its adoption." But the *Strauder* majority was unimpressed by Field's version of the "original understanding" and it set a face of flint against his typology of rights. "The Fourteenth Amendment makes no attempt to enumerate the rights it designed to protect," Strong declared. "It speaks in general terms, and those are as comprehensive as possible." The very term equal protection, he added, implied "that no discrimination shall be made against [blacks] by the law because of their color."

Strauder seemed to open the door for judicial proscription of all racial classifications in state laws. John R. Tompkins, counsel for an interracial couple that had been sentenced to two years in prison for violating Alabama's antimiscegenation law, certainly read the case that way. But the idea of distinct spheres of rights—"civil" and "social" if no longer "political"—furtively reentered the Waite Court's jurisprudence in PACE v. ALABAMA (1883). Field, speaking for a unanimous Court, held that antimiscegenation laws were not barred by the Fourteenth Amendment as long as both parties received the same punishment for the crime. Equal protection mandated equal treatment, not freedom of choice; antimiscegenation laws restricted the liberty of blacks and whites alike. Underlying this disingenuous view was an unarticulated premise of enormous importance. In settings involving the exercise of "social rights" the equal protection clause did not prohibit state legislatures from enacting statutes that used race as a basis for regulating the rights of persons. The legal category "Negro" was not suspect per se. (See SUSPECT CLASSIFICATION.)

The concept of "social rights" also figured prominently in the CIVIL RIGHTS CASES (1883), decided ten months after *Pace.* There the Court struck down the CIVIL RIGHTS ACT OF 1875, which forbade the owners of theaters, inns, and public conveyances to deny any citizen "the full and equal benefit" of their facilities. Joseph Bradley, speaking for the majority, rejected the claim that the businesses covered by the act were quasi-public agencies; consequently the state action doctrine barred federal intervention under the Fourteenth Amendment. But Bradley conceded that the state action doctrine was not applicable in Thirteenth Amendment contexts. It not only "nullif[ies] all state laws which establish or uphold slavery," he said, but also "clothes Congress with power to pass all laws necessary and proper for abolishing all badges and incidents of slavery in the United States." With the exception of John Marshall Harlan, however, every member of the Waite Court equated the "badges and incidents of slavery" with the denial of "civil rights" and concluded that Congress had nearly exhausted its authority to enact appropriate legislation under the Thirteenth Amendment with the CIVIL RIGHTS ACT OF 1866. "[A]t that time," Bradley explained, "Congress did not assume, under the authority given by the Thirteenth Amendment, to adjust what may be called the social rights of man and races in the community; but only to declare and vindicate those fundamental rights which appertain to the essence of citizenship, and the enjoyment or deprivation of which constitutes the essential distinction between freedom and slavery." Bradley's opinion was circumspect in only one respect. Whether denial of equal accommodation "might be a denial of a right which, if sanctioned by the state law, would be obnoxious to the [equal protection] prohibitions of the Fourteenth Amendment," he said, "is another question." But that was true only in the most formal sense. Once the Court had identified two distinct spheres of rights under the Thirteenth Amendment, one "civil" and another "social," it was difficult to resist the impulse to link that standard with the doctrine expounded in *Pace* when deciding equal protection cases. Stephen J. Field and Horace Gray, the only members of the *Civil Rights Cases* majority still alive when PLESSY V. FERGUSON (1896) was decided, had no qualms about state laws that required SEPARATE BUT EQUAL accommodations for blacks on public conveyances. Harlan was the sole dissenter on both occasions.

Equal opportunity in the market was one civil right that every member of the Waite Court assumed was guaranteed by the equal protection clause. Thus in YICK WO V. HOPKINS (1886) the Court invalidated the racially discriminatory application of a San Francisco ordinance that required all laundries, except those specifically exempted by the board of supervisors, to be built of brick or stone with walls one foot thick and metal roofs. No existing San Francisco laundry could meet such stringent building regulations, but the ordinance had the desired effect. The authorities promptly exempted the city's white operators and denied the petitions of their 240 Chinese competitors. "[T]he conclusion cannot be resisted," STANLEY MATTHEWS asserted for a unanimous Court, "that no reason for [this discrimination] exists except hostility to the race and nationality to which the petitioners belong, and which in the eye of the law is not justified." Yet the type of right divested was at least as important in *Yick Wo* as the fact of discrimination. The Court described laws that arbitrarily impaired entrepreneurial freedom as "the essence of slavery" while laws that denied racial minorities free choice in the selection of marriage partners and theater seats were not. But that was not all. The court invoked the absence of standards for administering the laundry ordinance as an independent ground for its unconstitutionality. The boundless discretion, or, as Matthews put it, "the naked and arbitrary power" delegated to the authorities was as decisive for the Court as the fact that the ordinance had been applied with "an evil eye and an unequal hand." In the Waite Court's view, however, the same kind of concern about official discretion was neither possible nor desirable in jury-service cases. In *Strauder* Strong conceded that jury selection officials might constitutionally employ facially neutral yet impossibly vague tests of good character, sound judgment, and the like. The Court had no choice but to presume that the jury commissioners had acted properly, Harlan explained in *Bush v. Kentucky* (1883), in the absence of state laws expressly restricting participation to whites. As blacks began to disappear from jury boxes throughout the South, it became clear that although *Strauder* put jury service in the "civil rights" category, in practical application it stood on a far lower plane than the rights enumerated in the Civil Rights Act of 1866. When Booker T. Washington counseled blacks to place economic opportunities ahead of all others in 1895, he expressed priorities that the Waite Court had long since embroidered into equal protection jurisprudence.

The path of DUE PROCESS was at once more tortuous and less decisive than the development of equal protection doctrine. In *Dent v. West Virginia* (1888), decided at the close of the Waite era, the Court conceded, as it had in the beginning, that "it may be difficult, if not impossible, to give to the terms 'due process of law' a definition which will embrace every permissible exertion of power affecting private rights and exclude such as are forbidden." Yet two generalizations about the Waite Court's understanding of due process can be advanced with confidence. First, the modern distinction between PROCEDURAL and SUBSTANTIVE DUE PROCESS had no meaning for Waite and his colleagues. In their view, the Fifth and Fourteenth Amendments furnished protection for fundamental rights against arbitrary action, regardless of the legal form in which the arbitrary act had been clothed. In HURTADO V. CALIFORNIA (1884), where the majority rejected counsel's claim that the Fourteenth Amendment INCORPORATED the Bill of Rights, Stanley Matthews explained that because the due process concept embraced "broad and general maxims of liberty and justice," it "must be held to guaranty not particular forms of procedure, but the very substance of individual rights to life, liberty, and property." Even Miller, the most circumspect member of the Court, agreed in 1878 that a law declaring the property of A to be vested in B, "without more," would "deprive A of his property without due process of law." It is equally clear that the Court assumed that CORPORATIONS were PERSONS within the meaning of the Fifth and Fourteenth Amendments long before Waite acknowledged as much during oral argument in *Santa Clara County v. Southern Pacific Railroad Co.* (1886). As early as the GRANGER CASES (1877) the Court decided controversies in which railroad corporations challenged state regulation on due process grounds, and neither the defendant states nor the Justices breathed a doubt about the Court's jurisdiction. In the SINKING FUND CASES (1879), moreover, Waite stated emphatically in obiter dictum that the Fifth Amendment had always barred Congress "from depriving persons or corporations of property without due process of law."

Although every member of the Court accepted the essential premises of substantive due process, no statute was voided on due process grounds during the Waite era. Conventional assumptions about the boundary between the legislative and judicial spheres were largely responsible for the Court's reticence. In due process cases, at least, most of the period's Justices meant it when they stated, as Waite did in the *Sinking Fund Cases,* that "[e]very possible presumption is in favor of the validity of a statute, and this continues until the contrary is shown beyond a reasonable doubt." The most disarming demonstration of that Court's adherence to this principle came in *Powell v. Pennsylvania* (1888). At issue was an act that prohibited the manufacture and sale of oleomargarine. The legislature had labeled the statute as a public health measure, but it was no secret that the law really had been designed to protect the dairy industry against a new competitor. Harlan, speaking for everyone but Field, conceded that counsel for the oleomargarine manufacturer had stated "a sound principle of constitutional law" when he argued that the Fourteenth Amendment guaranteed every person's right to pursue "an ordinary calling or trade" and to acquire and possess property. Indeed, the Court had furnished protection for those very rights in *Yick Wo.* "But we cannot adjudge that the defendant's rights of liberty and property, as thus defined, have been infringed," Harlan added, "without holding that, although it may have been enacted in good faith for the objects expressed in its title . . . it has, in fact, no real or substantial relation to those objects." And this the Court was not prepared to do. Defendant's offer of proof as to the wholesomeness of his product was insufficient, for it was the legislature's duty, not the judiciary's, "to conduct investigations of facts entering into questions of public policy." Nor could the Court consider the reasonableness of the means selected by the legislature: "Whether the manufacture of oleomargarine . . . is, or may be, conducted in such a way . . . as to baffle ordinary inspection, or whether it involves such danger to the public health as to require . . . the entire suppression of the business, rather than its regulation . . . are questions of fact and of public policy which belong to the legislative department to determine." Field, dissenting, claimed that the majority had not simply deferred to the legislature but had recognized it as "practically omnipotent."

Field overstated the predisposition of his colleagues, and he knew it. The Court seldom spoke with a luminous, confident voice in due process cases; majority opinions almost invariably revealed lingering second thoughts. Each time the Court said yes to legislatures, it reminded them that someday the Court might use the due process clause to say no. In *Powell,* for example, Harlan warned lawmakers that the Court was ready to intercede "if the state legislatures, under the pretence of guarding the public health, the public morals, or the public safety, should invade the rights of life, liberty, and property." Harlan did not explain how the Court might identify an act that had been passed "under the pretence" of exercising the police power, but he seemed to be confident that the Justices would be able to identify a tainted statute once they saw one. Waite's opinion in *Munn v. Illinois* (1877) was equally ambiguous. In one series of paragraphs he stated that the power to regulate prices was inherent in the police power; in another he suggested that price fixing was legitimate only if the regulated concern was a "business AFFECTED WITH A PUBLIC INTEREST." It followed from the latter proposition, though not from the former, that "under some circumstances" the Court might disallow regulation of prices charged by firms that were "purely and exclusively private." In *Munn* Waite was more certain about the reasonableness of rates lawfully fixed. "We know that it is a power which may be abused," he said; "but . . . [f]or protection against abuses by the legislatures the people must resort to the polls, not the courts." By 1886, however, Waite and some of his colleagues were not so sure. "[U]nder the pretense of regulating fares and freights," Waite declared in the *Railroad*

Commission Cases (1886), "the State cannot require a railroad corporation to carry persons or property without reward; neither can it do that which in law amounts to a taking of private property for public use without JUST COMPENSATION, or without due process of law." This statement, like Harlan's similar remark in *Powell,* warranted many conflicting inferences. At the close of the Waite era, then, the scope of the JUDICIAL POWER under the due process clause was as unsettled as the clause's meaning.

When Waite died in 1888, a St. Louis law journal observed that he had been "modest, conscientious, careful, conservative, and safe." It was a shrewd appraisal not only of the man but of his Court's work in constitutional law. The Court's unwillingness to use judicial power as an instrument of moral leadership evoked scattered protests from racial egalitarians, who accused Waite and his colleagues of energizing bigotry, and from exponents of laissez-faire who complained that the Court had failed to curb overweening regulatory impulses in the state legislatures. But no criticism was heard from the Republican party's moderate center, where the Court had looked for bearings as it reconstructed the "old" Constitution and integrated the "new." In retrospect, it was THOMAS M. COOLEY, not Charles Sumner, who supplied the Waite Court with an agenda and suggested an appropriate style for its jurisprudence. The Republican party had resorted to "desperate remedies" and had treated the Constitution as if it were "wax" during the Civil War, he said in 1867. Now it was time for the bench and bar to ensure that postwar institutions were "not mere heaps of materials from which to build something new, but the same good old ship of state, with some progress toward justice and freedom."

CHARLES W. MCCURDY

Bibliography

BENEDICT, MICHAEL LES 1979 Preserving Federalism: Reconstruction and the Waite Court. *Supreme Court Review* 1978:39–79.

CORWIN, EDWARD S. 1913 *National Supremacy: Treaty Power versus State Power.* New York: Henry Holt.

——— 1948 *Liberty against Government.* Baton Rouge: Louisiana State University Press.

MAGRATH, C. PETER 1963 *Morrison R. Waite: The Triumph of Character.* New York: Macmillan.

MCCURDY, CHARLES W. 1975 Justice Field and the Jurisprudence of Government–Business Relations. *Journal of American History* 61:970–1005.

SCHMIDT, BENNO C. 1983 Juries, Jurisdiction, and Race Discrimination: The Lost Promise of Strauder v. West Virginia. *Texas Law Review* 61:1401–1499.

WAIVER OF CONSTITUTIONAL RIGHTS

A potential beneficiary may waive almost any constitutional claim. Rights not of constitutional dimension also may be waived. The Supreme Court has struggled with the questions whether any special DOCTRINE governs waivers of constitutional rights and, if so, whether the special doctrine applies to all constitutional rights. These waiver issues, like much of the rest of constitutional law, took on massive new proportions with the rapid expansion of constitutional rights in the 1960s and 1970s. Prior to that era, there were relatively few rights eligible for waiver.

Distinctions between waivers of constitutional rights and waivers of other rights do not appear in very early cases. The most frequent waiver issue probably was whether a civil litigant had waived the SEVENTH AMENDMENT right to TRIAL BY JURY. *Hodges v. Easton* (1882), a case raising this issue, was the setting for one of the Supreme Court's important statements concerning waiver. In *Hodges* the Court acknowledged that litigants may waive the right but cautioned, in an oft-quoted statement that seemed to contemplate special treatment for waivers of constitutional rights, that "every reasonable presumption should be indulged against . . . waiver."

Then, as later would be true, there seemed to be a gap between the Court's statement of the waiver standard and its application of the standard in deciding cases. The Court's casual attitude toward waiver emerged in *Pierce v. Somerset Railway* (1898) and *Eustis v. Bolles* (1893), in which the Court found waivers of claims that state laws unconstitutionally impaired the OBLIGATION OF CONTRACT. In each case not only was "every reasonable presumption" against waiver not indulged; the Court went so far as to indicate that a state court's finding of waiver of constitutional rights did not even raise a federal issue reviewable by the Supreme Court. It may be, however, that the Court was insufficiently attentive to differences between the waiver issue and the existence of an independent and ADEQUATE STATE GROUND for decision, which would preclude Supreme Court review of the state court's judgment.

Although the Court had not become deeply involved in waiver issues, the legal community knew that waiver doctrine might have to be attuned to differences among constitutional rights. Through eight editions from 1868 to 1927, THOMAS M. COOLEY's treatise on constitutional law acknowledged that litigants may waive constitutional rights but it stated that in criminal cases this "must be true to a very limited extent only." Subsequent Supreme Court waiver doctrine at first would adhere to, and later partially undermine, Cooley's suggested distinction. But in his time, Cooley, himself a state supreme court justice, was on safe ground. As long as there were few constitutional rights regulating CRIMINAL PROCEDURE, one easily could limit their waivability.

The Court became more involved with waivers of constitutional rights in the 1930s. In *Aetna Insurance Co. v. Kennedy* (1937) and JOHNSON V. ZERBST (1938), cases raising civil and criminal procedure waiver issues, the Court seemed to indulge presumptions against waiver. And *Johnson v. Zerbst* supplied a new guiding rhetoric. Waiver required "an intentional relinquishment or abandonment of a known right or privilege." Again, though, the Court's articulated waiver standard sometimes was difficult to reconcile with the standard it applied. In *Rogers v. United States* (1951) a GRAND JURY witness who answered many questions was held to have waived her Fifth Amendment RIGHT AGAINST SELF-INCRIMINATION with respect to additional information.

The 1930s doctrinal seeds restricting waiver flowered in the 1960s. The most significant waiver developments concerned the question of a state criminal defendant's waiver of the right to assert a federal constitutional claim in a federal HABEAS CORPUS proceeding. A habeas corpus case, FAY V. NOIA (1963), became the touchstone for analysis of waiver of constitutional rights. *Fay* reaffirmed *Johnson v. Zerbst*'s waiver standard and required a conscious decision to forgo the privilege of seeking to vindicate federal rights. On the language of *Fay,* accidental waivers seemed impossible. The Court's reluctance to allow waivers of constitutional rights reached a high point in MIRANDA V. ARIZONA (1966), when the Court required that police inform suspects of their constitutional rights to assure that any waiver would be knowing.

The late WARREN COURT's reluctance to allow waivers of constitutional rights contrasts with the BURGER COURT's attitude. In one respect, a retreat from the 1960s standard seemed inevitable. For *Fay* and *Johnson* soon collided with the realities of the American criminal justice system. Through the PLEA BARGAINING process, the entire system depends upon widespread waivers of constitutional rights. In the trilogy of *McMann v. Richardson* (1970), *Parker v. North Carolina* (1970), and *Brady v. United States* (1970), holdings difficult to reconcile with the *Fay-Johnson* standard, this reality took hold. The trilogy effectively made a plea of guilty a waiver of nearly all constitutional procedure rights, known or unknown.

Another waiver issue, one with perhaps less of a foregone conclusion, further signaled the Court's shift in attitude. The FOURTH AMENDMENT guarantees the right to be free of UNREASONABLE SEARCHES and seizures and often requires police to obtain a warrant before conducting a search. For many years there was doubt about the relationship between searches conducted with consent, which need not comply with the Fourth Amendment's warrant requirement, and the concept of waiver. If consent were equated with a waiver of Fourth Amendment rights, then the *Johnson* standard seemed applicable. But since few who consent to searches are informed of their Fourth Amendment rights, it was difficult to characterize any waiver as knowing. The widespread practice of CONSENT SEARCHES seemed to hang in the balance.

A Court reluctant to allow waivers of constitutional rights might have adopted the *Miranda*-like solution of generally requiring the police to inform suspects of their Fourth Amendment rights before obtaining consent to a search. In SCHNECKLOTH V. BUSTAMONTE (1973) the Court, opting for a different extreme, preempted most Fourth Amendment waiver problems. It found that the *Johnson* standard had, almost without exception, "been applied only to those rights which the Constitution guarantees to a criminal defendant in order to preserve a FAIR TRIAL." Fourth Amendment claims were held not to be subject to the knowing and intelligent waiver requirement.

Schneckloth's reasoning may have implications for other constitutional rights. It suggests that rights other than those relating to a fair trial are subject to a waiver standard more lenient than the *Johnson* test. But it did not signal a wholesale retreat from *Johnson.* After *Schneckloth,* in cases such as EDWARDS V. ARIZONA (1981), the Court reaffirmed that the *Johnson* standard governs waivers of the RIGHT TO COUNSEL.

In WAINWRIGHT V. SYKES (1977), where the Court squarely confronted *Fay,* it further limited 1960s waiver doctrine. Under *Wainwright,* failure to comply with state procedural rules effectively waives the right to raise a constitutional claim on federal habeas corpus. A habeas applicant must both explain his failure to comply with state procedures and show that his case was prejudiced by the constitutional flaw. The Court rejected *Fay*'s requirement of a knowing and deliberate waiver. In effect, the burden of proving nonwaiver had been placed on the defendant.

The waiver question also continued to arise in contexts not involving criminal procedure. In *D. H. Over-*

myer Co. v. Frick Company (1972) and *Swarb v. Lennox* (1972) the Court reconfirmed earlier holdings that at least some civil litigants may contractually waive due process rights to NOTICE and hearing prior to a JUDGMENT and thereby effectively waive the opportunity to contest the validity of a debt. In *Parden v. Terminal Railway* (1964) states may have been surprised to learn that certain activities effectively waived their constitutional immunity from suit in federal court. For many years prior to *Parden,* it appeared that only an express waiver by states would be effective. But the Court found that by operating a railroad in INTERSTATE COMMERCE, a state effectively waived its immunity from employees' suits in federal court under the federal EMPLOYERS LIABILITY ACT. *Parden*'s reach was limited by *Employees v. Department of Public Health and Welfare* (1973), which refused to rely on the FAIR LABOR STANDARDS ACT to subject states to federal damage suits by employees. More important, EDELMAN V. JORDAN (1974) held that state participation in a federal program did not amount to consent to suit in federal court on claims relating to the program.

THEODORE EISENBERG

Bibliography

COVER, ROBERT M. and ALEINIKOFF, T. ALEXANDER 1977 Dialectical Federalism: Habeas Corpus and the Court. *Yale Law Journal* 86:1035–1102.

LAFAVE, WAYNE R. 1978 *Search and Seizure: A Treatise on the Fourth Amendment* §§ 8.1, 8.2, 11.1, 11.7 (f). St. Paul, Minn.: West Publishing Co.

TIGAR, MICHAEL E. 1970 Foreword: Waiver of Constitutional Rights: A Disquiet in the Citadel. *Harvard Law Review* 84:1–28.

TRIBE, LAURENCE H. 1978 *American Constitutional Law.* Pages 133–138. Mineola, N.Y.: Foundation Press.

WALKER, TIMOTHY
(1802–1856)

Born in Massachusetts, Timothy Walker attended Harvard College and Harvard Law School where he studied with Justice JOSEPH STORY. He settled in Cincinnati in 1830 and opened a private law school, which eventually became part of the University of Cincinnati. He wrote on various legal subjects, but his primary contribution was his compilation of his lectures, *An Introduction to American Law* (1837), which he dedicated to Story, whose teachings and viewpoint he spread. A third of the work is on constitutional law, strongly nationalist in its orientation. By 1905 the book had gone through eleven editions.

LEONARD W. LEVY

WALKER v. BIRMINGHAM
388 U.S. 307 (1967)

The Supreme Court, 5–4, upheld criminal contempt convictions of eight black ministers, including MARTIN LUTHER KING, JR., for holding a CIVIL RIGHTS protest parade in violation of an INJUNCTION issued by an Alabama state court. The injunction, which forbade them from engaging in street parades without a permit, was issued EX PARTE, two days before the intended march. The order was based on a city ordinance that the Court later held unconstitutional for VAGUENESS in *Shuttlesworth v. Birmingham* (1969), a case arising out of the same events.

For the majority, Justice POTTER STEWART concluded that the ministers, once enjoined by a court order, were not entitled to disregard the injunction even if it had been granted unconstitutionally. Rather, they were obliged to ask the court to modify the order, or to seek relief from the injunction in another court.

Justice WILLIAM J. BRENNAN, for the four dissenters, pointed out that, in the absence of a court order, the FIRST AMENDMENT would have entitled the marchers to disregard the ordinance, which was INVALID ON ITS FACE. It was incongruous, he argued, to let the state alter this result simply by obtaining "the ex parte stamp of a judicial officer on a copy of the invalid ordinance." These views were echoed in separate dissents by Chief Justice EARL WARREN and Justice WILLIAM O. DOUGLAS. The *Walker* principle, though much criticized, remains the DOCTRINE of the Court.

KENNETH L. KARST

(SEE ALSO: *Demonstration.*)

WALKER v. SAUVINET
92 U.S. 90 (1876)

Walker lost a civil judgment in a trial decided by a judge, in conformance with state law, after the jury deadlocked and after Walker had demanded TRIAL BY JURY. The Court held, 7–2, that the SEVENTH AMENDMENT to the Constitution, guaranteeing trial by jury in civil actions at law, applied only in federal courts, and that the right to a jury trial in similar state cases was not a privilege of United States citizenship guaranteed by the PRIVILEGES AND IMMUNITIES clause of the FOURTEENTH AMENDMENT. This was the earliest rejection of the INCORPORATION DOCTRINE. Its result is still good law, long after the latter doctrine's triumph.

LEONARD W. LEVY

WALLACE v. JAFFREE
472 U.S. (1985)

A 6–3 Supreme Court, in an opinion by Justice JOHN PAUL STEVENS, held unconstitutional an Alabama statute that required public school children to observe a period of silence "for meditation or voluntary prayer." No member of the Court contested the constitutionality of the period of silence for meditation. As Justice SANDRA DAY O'CONNOR said in her CONCURRING OPINION, no threat to RELIGIOUS LIBERTY could be discerned from a room of "silent, thoughtful school children." Chief Justice WARREN E. BURGER added that there was no threat "even if they chose to pray." Burger willfully misunderstood or missed the point. Any student in any public school may pray voluntarily and silently at almost any time of the school day, if so moved. The state, in this case, sought to orchestrate group prayer by capitalizing on the impressionability of youngsters. Compulsory attendance laws and the coercive setting of the school provided a CAPTIVE AUDIENCE for the state to promote religion. Justice JOHN PAUL STEVENS emphasized the fact that the state act was "entirely motivated by a purpose to advance religion" and had "*no* secular purpose." The evidence irrefutably showed that. Accordingly, the Alabama act failed to pass the test of LEMON V. KURTZMAN (1971) used by the Court to determine whether a state violated the FIRST AMENDMENT's prohibition against an ESTABLISHMENT OF RELIGION.

Justice O'Connor, observing that Alabama already had a moment of silence law on its books, noted that during the silence, no one need be religious, no one's religious beliefs could be compromised, and no state encouragement of religion existed. "The crucial question," she wrote, "is whether the State has conveyed or attempted to convey the message that children should use the moment of silence for prayer." The only possible answer was that the state, by endorsing the decision to pray during the moment of silence, sponsored a religious exercise, thereby breaching the First Amendment's principle of SEPARATION OF CHURCH AND STATE.

LEONARD W. LEVY

WALZ v. TAX COMMISSION
397 U.S. 664 (1970)

In this 8–1 decision, the Supreme Court added a new element to the test for the constitutionality of financial aid to religious institutions. Chief Justice WARREN E. BURGER rejected Walz's claim that a state's grant of tax exemption to property used only for religious purposes violated the ESTABLISHMENT OF RELIGION clause of the FIRST AMENDMENT. Adding to tests already elaborated in ABINGTON SCHOOL DISTRICT V. SCHEMPP (1963), Burger required assurance that "the end result—the effect—[of a grant of tax exemption] is not an excessive government entanglement with religion. The test is inescapably one of degree." Commenting that "the course of constitutional neutrality in this area cannot be an absolutely straight line," he said that taxing a church would have involved even more "entanglement" than exempting them. Justice WILLIAM O. DOUGLAS, dissenting, believed that TORCASO V. WATKINS (1961) governed. He concluded that "a tax exemption is a subsidy."

DAVID GORDON

(SEE ALSO: *Government Aid to Sectarian Institutions.*)

WAR, DECLARATION OF

See: Declaration of War

WAR, STATE OF

See: State of War

WARD v. ILLINOIS
431 U.S. 767 (1977)

The Supreme Court upheld, 5–4, a conviction for selling "sado-masochistic" materials. (See MISHKIN V. NEW YORK, 1966). Justice BYRON R. WHITE, for the majority, said that a state law could pass the "patent offensiveness" part of the test of MILLER V. CALIFORNIA (1973) although it did not specifically define the proscribed materials; state court interpretations had followed *Miller*'s guidelines. The dissenters, led by Justice JOHN PAUL STEVENS, argued that the absence of the statutory definition specified by *Miller* left the law unconstitutionally vague.

KENNETH L. KARST

WARDEN v. HAYDEN
387 U.S. 294 (1976)

In *Gouled v. United States* (1921) the Court announced a rule that rings strange to the modern ear; when conducting an otherwise lawful search, police are authorized to search for contraband, fruits of crime, means and instrumentalities of crime, or weapons of escape, but they are not authorized to search for "mere evidence." The rationale for the MERE EVIDENCE RULE was never clear, but its main theme was that police could not take objects from an accused without asserting a superior property interest in the object seized. This requirement spurred judicial creativity in recognizing property interests and in broadly defining their scope.

In *Warden v. Hayden* the Supreme Court rejected this property-centered conception of FOURTH AMENDMENT jurisprudence. Police could seize evidence after all. Questions remained concerning the scope of searches for items previously regarded as mere evidence (such as diaries) and concerning the applicable standards for SEARCHES AND SEIZURES of "mere evidence" belonging to innocent parties.

STEVEN SHIFFRIN

WARE v. HYLTON
3 Dallas 199 (1796)

Ware established the fundamental principle of constitutional law that a state act may not violate a national treaty. An act of Virginia during the Revolution sequestered sterling debts owed by Virginians to British subjects and provided that such debts be discharged on payment (in depreciated currency) to the state. The Treaty of Paris of 1783 provided that creditors should meet with no lawful impediments to the recovery of full value in sterling, and Article VI of the Constitution made treaties of the United States the supreme law of the land. Ware, a British subject, brought an action in a federal court seeking such a recovery from Hylton, a Virginian. The prewar debts of Virginians to British creditors exceeded $2,000,000. Justice JAMES IREDELL, on circuit, ruled that the treaty did not revive any debt that had been discharged, and on the WRIT OF ERROR from the circuit court, JOHN MARSHALL, for Hylton, argued that a United States treaty could not annul a statute passed when the state was sovereign. He also denied the authority of the Supreme Court to question the validity of a state law, arguing that the Constitution had not expressly granted such an authority.

Iredell persisted in his opinion expressed below, but Justice SAMUEL CHASE, supported by the concurring opinions of the remainder of the Justices, declared that the SUPREMACY CLAUSE (Article VI), operating retroactively, nullified the state act, thereby reviving the sterling debt. Chase cloaked his opinion in sweeping nationalist doctrine that twisted history: "There can be no limitations on the power of the people to change or abolish the state constitutions, or to make them yield to the general government, and to treaties made by their authority." A treaty, he ruled, could not be supreme law if any state act could stand in its way; state laws contrary to the treaty were prostrated before it and the Constitution, which was the "creator" of the states. The *Ware* decision intensified Jeffersonian hostility to the consolidating and procreditor opinions of the federal courts. The decision's imperishable principle of the supremacy of national treaties survived its origins—no doubt in part because JAY'S TREATY of 1794 had provided that the United States should assume the payment of the controversial debts.

LEONARD W. LEVY

WAR, FOREIGN AFFAIRS, AND THE CONSTITUTION

The United States became a nation among nations on July 4, 1776, fully endowed with SOVEREIGNTY, that is, the capacity to do whatever nations do in world politics. International law acknowledges that nations have the power to breach their international legal obligations and take the consequences so far as other nations are concerned. Constitutionally, breaches of international law by Congress or the President are binding on courts and citizens alike as official acts within the discretion of the political branches of the government. Thus the FOREIGN AFFAIRS powers, including the WAR POWERS, draw their substance from the matrix of public international law. In the language of PEREZ V. BROWNELL (1958), the Constitution recognizes in the national government "the powers indispensable to its functioning effectively in the company of sovereign nations."

In the CONSTITUTIONAL CONVENTION, a majority led by JAMES WILSON insisted that an "energetic" and independent President was needed to maintain the unity of a country that was already large and destined to become larger, and above all to help assure its safety in a turbulent and dangerous world. As EDWARD S. CORWIN wrote:

> [T]he fact is that what the Framers had in mind was not the cabinet system, as yet nonexistent even in Great

Britain, but the "balanced constitution" of [JOHN] LOCKE, MONTESQUIEU, and [WILLIAM] BLACKSTONE, which carried with it the idea of a *divided initiative in the matter of legislation and a broad range of autonomous executive power or "prerogative."* Sir Henry Maine's dictum that "the American constitution is the British constitution with the monarchy left out," is, from the point of view of 1789, almost the exact reverse of the truth, for the presidency was designed in great measure to reproduce the monarchy of George III with the corruption left out, and also of course the hereditary feature [1957, pp. 14–15].

Actually, all comparisons of the British and American constitutions break down. The President is effectively both king and prime minister, but Congress is not Parliament, and its relation to the President is necessarily at arm's length.

The entire authority of the United States to act as a sovereign nation in world politics is confined by the Constitution to the national government and denied to the states. It is divided by the Constitution between the President and Congress.

The President is head of state as well as head of government, and therefore the ultimate embodiment of the nation's sovereignty, especially in times of crisis. ABRAHAM LINCOLN turned to his prerogative and residual powers as the source of much of his authority during the Civil War. In addition, the Constitution endows the President with "the" executive power of the United States, including without limitation the power to conduct diplomacy; to make treaties, with the ADVICE AND CONSENT of the Senate; and to serve as COMMANDER-IN-CHIEF of the armed forces; moreover, he is enjoined to see to it that the laws are faithfully executed.

The constitutional definition of the role of Congress in foreign affairs is comparably broad. Article I provides that "all LEGISLATIVE POWERS herein granted shall be vested in a Congress of the United States." Among the powers expressly granted to Congress are the powers to lay and collect taxes and provide for the common defense; regulate foreign commerce; establish an uniform rule of NATURALIZATION; define and punish piracies and FELONIES committed on the high seas and offenses against the law of nations; declare war, grant LETTERS OF MARQUE AND REPRISAL, and make rules concerning captures on land and water; and raise and support the armed forces, make rules for their government and regulation, and provide for organizing, arming, and disciplining the militia and calling forth the armed forces and the militia to execute the laws of the Union, suppress insurrections, and repel invasions. The problems of CITIZENSHIP and of foreign affairs in their more general aspects are not mentioned, but Congress's authority to legislate on such issues has been readily inferred by the Supreme Court as inherent in national sovereignty.

In short, the Constitution prescribes that the foreign affairs powers of the nation—including the war power—be shared between Congress and the President in accordance with the overriding principle of functional necessity. All the powers the nation requires in the international environment exist. Those which are executive in character are to be exercised by the President. Those which are legislative in nature are reserved for Congress. When in recess, however, Congress can meet only at the President's call, and can act in all cases only subject to the President's VETO POWER. As Corwin concluded, the Constitution invites the President and Congress "to struggle for the privilege of directing American foreign policy."

Sooner or later, most aspects of the conduct of foreign affairs involve both legislative and executive decisions; they are therefore the proper business of both Congress and the President, in a pattern that reflects subtle political judgments about how their cooperation can best be organized under the circumstances. A few functions are unique to each branch. Only the President can command the armed forces, call a special session of Congress, or conduct the diplomacy of the nation; and only Congress can declare war, appropriate money, or make certain conduct criminal. On the other hand, the President sometimes asks members of Congress to serve on diplomatic delegations. And Congress sometimes attempts to restrict the President's power to deploy or use the armed forces, although many constitutional authorities have regarded such restrictions as invasions of the President's executive power.

The flexibility of the constitutional arrangements for making and carrying out foreign policy is not peculiar to the field of foreign affairs. As JAMES MADISON saw from the beginning, the principle of the SEPARATION OF POWERS does not mean that the three branches of the government are really separate. Most of their powers are commingled. The branches are not independent but interdependent, and the preservation of the functional boundaries between the legislative and the executive depends as much on the reflexes of the political system as on rulings of the Supreme Court.

It was realized from the beginning that rigid rules about how Congress and the President should work together in the field of foreign affairs would be undesirable and indeed dangerous. As ALEXANDER HAMILTON wrote in THE FEDERALIST #23, "the authorities essential to the common defense . . . ought to exist without limitation, *because it is impossible to foresee or define the extent and variety of national exigencies or the correspondent extent and variety of the means which may be necessary to satisfy them.* The circumstances that endanger the safety of nations are infinite, and for this reason no constitutional shackles can wisely be imposed on the power to which the care of it is committed."

Diplomacy without force behind it has been and will remain a nullity. The use or the threat of armed force has been a normal instrument of American diplomacy, from secret warnings, "showing the flag," and conducting maneuvers, at one end of the spectrum, to programs of rearmament, partial mobilization, and the actual use of armed force—in times of "war" and of "peace," as international law defines those words—at the other. In the early days of the Republic, raids across the borders were commonplace. The problems of piracy and the slave trade required the frequent use of force, pursuant to treaty, statute, or the decisions of the President acting alone. Then and now, international law recognized the right of all states to use limited force in peacetime to cure forceful breaches of international law when no peaceful remedy was available. The United States has taken advantage of its rights in this regard to protect its borders, its ships, its citizens in peril abroad, and indeed, the rights of citizens whose monetary claims had not been paid by foreign governments. Moreover, the United States and other Western nations have sometimes intervened abroad on humanitarian grounds where organized government has broken down. Such exercises by the United States of its "inherent" right of self-defense have been carried out mainly, but not exclusively, on the authority of the President.

The threat to use force and even the use of force have been familiar features of diplomacy from the opening of Japan to President RICHARD M. NIXON's secret nuclear warnings that induced the Soviet Union not to attack Chinese nuclear installations. At the end of the Civil War, we deployed 50,000 troops along the Mexican border. France heeded our suggestion, withdrew its troops from Mexico, and left Maximilian to his fate. Similarly, in 1962, President JOHN F. KENNEDY assembled some 250,000 troops in Florida, and halted a Soviet vessel carrying military supplies to Cuba; the Soviet Union withdrew its nuclear missiles from Cuba. A few years earlier, at a moment of severe Soviet pressure against Turkey, President HARRY S. TRUMAN ordered the battleship *Missouri* to carry the body of a deceased Turkish ambassador to Istanbul for burial—manifestly a journey intended to be more than a courteous gesture to the people of Turkey. Such threats of force have been almost entirely within the province of the President.

The list of such incidents is long enough to demonstrate that throughout its history the United States government has called upon its armed forces to perform a wide variety of functions in support of its foreign policy. There have been five DECLARATIONS OF WAR in our national experience, and more than 200 episodes in which the President ordered the armed forces into combat, sometimes with the support of a treaty or of legislation passed before or after the event, more often on his own authority. The number of occasions on which the President secretly threatened to use force in aid of his diplomacy cannot be counted accurately, but is surely considerable.

The pattern of cooperation between the President and Congress with respect to war and foreign affairs has been the same since the first administration of President GEORGE WASHINGTON. This continuity of practice arises from the nature of things. Congress could and did admonish the President to protect frontier settlements from Indian raids but could not meet and vote every time the risk arose. In any event, it was the President's duty to protect the settlements with or without the support of a statute. The circumstances which may require the use of or the threat to use armed force are too protean, and pervade the conduct of foreign affairs too completely, to be compressed within a single procedure.

From the beginning of our government under the Constitution, a great deal of energy has been absorbed by attempts to define the respective roles of the President and of Congress in carrying out these functions. The participants in the debate are divided into two camps.

Hamilton's view of the Presidency dominates the judicial opinions, the pattern of practice, the writings of scholars, and the pronouncements of senators and representatives. To Hamiltonians, all national powers not granted to Congress or the courts are "executive" and therefore presidential, especially if they concern relations with foreign powers or the duties of the nation under international law.

But a dissenting opinion has persisted, based on the fear of executive power as dictatorship in disguise. Corwin calls it the "ultra-Whig" view. It opposes almost all claims to presidential independence, and regards the executive as no more than an obstreperous but indispensable servant of a "sovereign" Congress. This conception of the Presidency has been a mainstay of political attacks on Presidents for unpopular wars.

The Hamiltonian position crystallized during the neutrality controversy of 1793, an episode of immense importance to the formation of the Constitution. France had declared war against Great Britain. The United States was bound to France by the 1778 treaties of perpetual alliance which seemed to require the infant Republic, in the event of war between France and Britain, to give various forms of belligerent aid to France. Any such assistance would have been an act of war against Great Britain, which could easily have snuffed out the new nation. Washington and his cabinet were determined to preserve neutrality despite the treaties with France and the strongly pro-French bias of public opinion. After the Supreme Court refused Washington's request for an ADVISORY OPINION determining whether the President could issue a proclamation of neutrality on his own authority, Washington did so, and took special precautions to assure Great Britain of America's pacific intentions.

The concurrent nature of the foreign relations power was soon demonstrated. Juries would not convict American seamen for violating the President's neutrality proclamation. Congress then grudgingly passed a Neutrality Act, supporting the President's interpretation of the treaties with France. In due course, the Neutrality Act was enforced. Congress had the last word, but acted under circumstances carefully arranged by the President, acting independently.

Hamilton's *Pacificus* papers, defending the President's right to issue the Proclamation of neutrality, are among the most cogent of all our state papers on the conduct of foreign affairs. The President, said Hamilton, has the foreign affairs and war powers of the British monarch minus the limitations on those powers mentioned in the Constitution. Those limitations, being exceptions to the President's executive powers, should be strictly construed.

The President is the sole officer of the government empowered to communicate with foreign nations. This is an executive power. It was therefore the President's role to inform the nations about the position of the United States with respect to the European war. Next, Hamilton argued, it is the President's duty to preserve peace until Congress declares war. In this case, the President's duty required him faithfully to execute the international law of neutrality, and thus avoid giving offense to foreign powers. To carry out that duty, the President had to determine for himself whether a status of neutrality conformed to our national interests and was compatible with our obligations under the French treaties, and then to announce his position diplomatically. Hamilton said that the President has the authority and the duty to determine the operation of treaties in the first instance, an important example of his right as President to decide upon the obligations of the country to foreign nations until Congress does so within its own sphere.

Hamilton's analysis would lead to the conclusion that while only Congress can move the nation into a state of general war, the President can authorize more limited uses of force in peacetime for purposes of self-defense, the protection of citizens abroad, the fulfillment of treaty obligations, and the support of diplomacy.

The Ultra-Whig dissenting view draws an altogether different boundary between the respective war powers of the President and Congress. For the dissenters, Congress's power to "declare" war gives Congress entire control over every aspect of the war power, including neutrality. It means, they contend, that the President can never employ the armed forces, save to repel a sudden attack, unless Congress has first passed a "declaration of war." Some dissenters agree that Congress may authorize limited war in the international law sense, but insist that the declaration of war clause requires congressional action before the President uses force at all, except in cases of sudden attack. A few concede that circumstances may justify congressional approval after the event—after Pearl Harbor, for example, or the firing on Fort Sumter. And some even accept the decision of the Supreme Court in THE PRIZE CASES (1863), which upheld acts of Congress ratifying President Lincoln's blockade of the Confederacy, enacted some months after the President had instituted the blockade. But all the dissenters are dubious about statutes, treaties, or joint resolutions—and many have been put on the books since 1792—that may be invoked to support presidential uses of force years later. The Ultra-Whigs admit that the United States may, like other nations, sign treaties that have military provisions, but they are uneasy about the propriety of such commitments unless they are reiterated by Congress when they become the basis for military action.

There is no reason for such confusion to persist. The "declaration of war" authorized in the Constitution is bracketed in Article I, section 8, with "letters of marque and reprisal" and "captures on land and sea." All are terms of specific meaning in international law. A declaration of war has far-reaching consequences, including: the authorization of unlimited hostilities, the possible internment of enemy ALIENS, the sequestration of enemy property, and the imposition of regulations, such as censorship, that would be unthinkable in peacetime. But many kinds of hostilities recognized as legitimate under international law do not constitute "general war," and can therefore be initiated by official action less sweeping than a declaration of war. Most familiar are exercises of the right of self-defense against certain breaches of international law. Many are short, quick responses to a sudden threat; others become more prolonged conflicts. International law limits all such defensive campaigns to the use of as much force as is reasonably necessary to eliminate the original breach.

Hamilton's theory of presidential power is clearly the operative model of American constitutional law with respect to the international use of force. But the practice has not been nearly so symmetrical as Hamilton's logic. Every American President who has felt obliged to use the armed forces has vividly remembered the political attacks on "JOHN ADAMS' Undeclared War," and therefore sought to obtain congressional support for his policies as soon as it was politically feasible to do so. But such prudence has never helped a President saddled with an unpopular war. John Adams was supported by four successive statutes; they had no effect on the political outcry against him, or the fate of the Federalist party. Presidents Truman and LYNDON B. JOHNSON endured similar trials. As Johnson commented: "I said early in my Presidency that if I wanted Congress with me on the landing of Vietnam, I'd have to have them on the take off. And I did just that. . . . But I failed to reckon with one thing: the parachute. I got them on the take off, but a lot of them bailed out before the end of the flight."

Between the Congress of Vienna and the turn of the twentieth century, the United States was not a major actor in world politics; the central features of American foreign policy were Manifest Destiny and the MONROE DOCTRINE. Nonetheless, there were periods of tension between Congress and the President with respect to the conduct of foreign relations. The most acute of these episodes concerned the expansion of the nation to the Pacific and controversies about problems in Latin America and Canada. Some of the controversies reflected deep divisions between the parties and among the people, others no more than normal rivalry between the political branches of the government.

But the collapse of the old state system in 1914 imposed new burdens on the United States, which in turn gave rise to profound disquiet in American opinion, exacerbating the traditional tension between Congress and the President with respect to the war power, and reaching a climax during the early 1970s. The VIETNAM WAR dragged on, accompanied by antiwar rioting of a kind the nation had not experienced since the Civil War. At the same time, the controversy over President Nixon's behavior with respect to Watergate poisoned the political atmosphere, and produced so strong a movement for the President's impeachment that he resigned.

In this atmosphere of extreme political excitement, Congress passed the War Powers Resolution of 1973. Its political purpose was to assure the people that Congress could and would protect the nation against future Vietnams. For the first time in nearly two hundred years, the Hamiltonian view of the Presidency and the war power suffered at least a nominal defeat.

The Resolution asserts congressional supremacy with regard to the war power, but it does not adopt an extreme form of the Ultra-Whig view. It does not say, for example, that the President can use force only if Congress has first declared war. Not does it seek to confine the President's use of force without prior congressional approval to cases of "sudden attack."

The Resolution purports to fulfill the intent of the Framers of the Constitution, as summarized in three propositions. First, the armed forces should not be involved in hostilities without the collective judgment of Congress and the President. Second, Congress has the power to pass all laws NECESSARY AND PROPER for carrying into execution the powers of the President. Third, the constitutional powers of the President as Commander-in-Chief can be exercised by him to introduce the forces into hostile situations only pursuant to a declaration of war or a "specific" statute, or in a national emergency created by an attack upon the United States. Clearly, this attempt at restatement omits the nation's obligations under treaties.

The Resolution requires the President to consult with Congress "in every possible instance" before introducing the armed forces into situations where hostilities are an imminent risk, and also to "consult" regularly with Congress after hostilities have begun until they are terminated. The resolution makes no attempt to define the term "consult," which is a word of political but not of constitutional meaning.

The War Powers Resolution requires the President to report to Congress within forty-eight hours and regularly thereafter whenever he has introduced armed forces into situations risking hostilities without a declaration of war. It further requires the President to terminate such a use of the armed forces within sixty days unless Congress has declared war, authorized hostilities in another "specific" form, or extended the sixty-day period to not more than ninety days. Where hostilities are being conducted abroad without a declaration of war or "specific" authorization in another form, the resolution authorizes Congress, by CONCURRENT RESOLUTION, to require the President to terminate hostilities and remove the armed forces.

If the War Powers Resolution were carried out literally, it would constitute the most revolutionary change in the Constitution ever accomplished—far more drastic in its effects than the shift of authority from the states to the national government which began after Civil War. It would subject the President to the orders of an omnipotent Congress. No future President could do what Lincoln did during the Civil War, or rely on the behavior of every strong President between Washington and Lyndon Johnson as precedents. The deterrent influence of American military power and of American treaties, already weakened after Vietnam, would decline even further. The United States would be the only country in the world that lacked the capacity to enter into treaties or conduct secret negotiations contemplating the use of force, and it would be hampered in many other ways in the conduct of its foreign relations. Enforcing the resolution would produce paradoxes. Although no future President could do what President Kennedy did during the Cuban Missile Crisis in 1962, the highly "specific" legal arrangements for the Vietnam War would have satisfied the Resolution's requirements. That war was authorized not only by the United Nations Charter and the Southeast Asia Collective Defense Treaty of 1954, but by the GULF OF TONKIN RESOLUTION of 1963 and other explicit acts of Congress as well. On the other hand, the sponsors of the Resolution have said that it does not affect the President's unique responsibilities with regard to the nuclear weapon. Above all, as has been evident in the decade since it was passed, the Resolution would convert almost every serious foreign policy problem into a debate between Congress and the President about constitutional power, making the conduct of foreign relations even more cumbersome and contentious than is the case already.

The War Powers Resolution is in profound conflict with the necessities of governance in a turbulent world and with the concept of the Presidency that has evolved from the experience of the nation under the Constitution. We can therefore predict that the Hamiltonian conception of the war powers will prevail as the constitutional norm, and that the War Powers Resolution will become a footnote to history, either through repudiation or desuetude.

Institutional pride may keep Congress from repealing the resolution, although repeal disguised as revision is not unthinkable. The courts will almost surely declare the Resolution unconstitutional if an appropriate case should arise. The ruling of the Supreme Court in IMMIGRATION AND NATURALIZATION SERVICE V. CHADHA (1983) is applicable to the chief operative parts of the War Powers Resolution. *Chadha* ruled that congressional action can have legislative effect only through acts or joint resolutions fully subject to the President's veto. If Congress cannot constitutionally terminate a war by passing a concurrent resolution, it can hardly do so by failing to pass such a resolution within sixty or ninety days.

In holding the War Powers Resolution unconstitutional, the Supreme Court may well go beyond *Chadha* to deal with more fundamental aspects of the separation of powers principle: the resolution's effect, for example, on the President's hitherto unquestioned power to conduct secret negotiations, receive surrenders, or negotiate cease-fire agreements; and its attempt, recalling the proposed BRICKER AMENDMENT, to require legislation before treaties can become the supreme law of the land.

Even if the resolution is neither repealed nor declared unconstitutional by the courts, it is unlikely to be an important influence on Presidents. The resolution does not correspond to the nature of the problems of foreign policy and national security with which the government has to deal, and therefore cannot function as effective law. At least eleven episodes involving the use of force or the imminent risk of using force occurred during the first decade after the War Powers Resolution was passed. In each case the President, while protesting that the resolution was unconstitutional, consulted with congressional leaders and kept Congress informed about events. In no case did the procedure mandated by the resolution prove convenient or appropriate, and in no case was it followed. In each case there were some congressional protests that the War Powers Resolution was being violated, and even suggestions that the President be impeached.

The President and Congress, separately and together, have been entrusted by history with sovereign prerogatives in exercising the foreign affairs and war powers of the nation. Those prerogatives have been in uneasy balance for two hundred years, an instance of the friction between the branches of government on which the Founding Fathers relied to preserve the liberties of the people. Over a wide range, the President and Congress can exercise their joint and several political discretion in dealing quickly with complex and swiftly moving events, often on the basis of fragmentary information. Within that zone, the only constitutional restraints on which the people can rely to secure them from the abuse of such political discretion is the electoral process itself, as Chief Justice Marshall remarked in GIBBONS V. OGDEN (1824).

But the choices committed by the Constitution to the care of Congress and the President are not unlimited, even when one gives full weight to the view that the war power is the power to wage war successfully. The foreign affairs and war powers are aspects of a government organized under a written Constitution dominated by the principle of democratic responsibility. Although the Supreme Court has hesitated to pass on many conflicts between the President and Congress, it has intervened where exercises of the war power impinged upon CIVIL RIGHTS, or attempted radically to alter the equilibrium of the constitutional order.

Thus, certain constitutional limits on the President's war power emerged in its first major test—the neutrality crisis of 1793. President Washington could have used the armed forces or called up the militia to keep French privateers at the docks of Philadelphia or Charleston; in the event, he prudently refrained from such action. But he could not get American juries to convict American citizens indicted for violating a presidential proclamation. Similarly, YOUNGSTOWN SHEET & TUBE CO. V. SAWYER (1952) decided that the President had no INHERENT POWERS to seize steel mills as a step toward settling a strike during the Korean War when Congress had rejected such a procedure.

There are comparable constitutional limits on what Congress and the President acting together can do in the name of the war power. Congress can make it an offense to recruit soldiers within the United States for wars in which the United States is neutral, but it is doubtful whether it would be constitutional for Congress to forbid American citizens from going abroad to fight. In *Ex parte Merryman* (1861) and *Ex parte Milligan* (1867) the courts held that even in the midst of the Civil War, courts-martial could not try civilians while the ordinary courts were available. And in REID V. COVERT (1957) and *Kinsella v. United States* (1960) the Supreme Court struck down convictions imposed by courts-martial on the wives of military personnel living on American bases abroad.

The only exceptions to this line of cases are the JAPANESE AMERICAN CASES, decided during World War II. These cases upheld the constitutionality of a statute authorizing the President to exclude citizens of Japanese descent from California, Oregon, and Washington, and requiring their internment in camps until they could be resettled in other parts of the country. These decisions have been severely criticized, and the Court's opinion in DUNCAN V. KAHANAMOKU (1946) can be interpreted as overruling them *sub silentio.* Until they are more decisively repudiated, however, they remain, as Justice Jackson said in KOREMATSU V. UNITED STATES (1944), "a loaded weapon ready for the hand of any authority that can bring forward a plausible claim of an urgent need."

EUGENE V. ROSTOW

Bibliography

CORWIN, EDWARD S. (1940)1957 *The President: Office and Powers, 1787–1957.* New York: New York University Press.

HENKIN, LOUIS 1972 *Foreign Affairs and the Constitution.* Mineola, N.Y.: Foundation Press.

RANDALL, JAMES G. (1926)1951 *Constitutional Problems under Lincoln.* Urbana: University of Illinois Press.

REVELY, W. TAYLOR, III 1981 *The War Powers of the President and Congress.* Charlottesville: University Press of Virginia.

ROSTOW, EUGENE V. 1945 The Japanese-American Cases: A Disaster. *Yale Law Journal* 54:489–533, reprinted in *The Sovereign Prerogative* (1962). New Haven: Yale University Press.

——— 1973 Statement, in Appendix to *War Powers,* Hearings before Subcommittee on National Security Policy and Scientific Developments, Committee on Foreign Affairs, House of Representatives, 93rd Congress, 1st Session, March 7–20, 1973, pp. 395–502; also in Rostow, Eugene V. 1972 Great Cases Make Bad Law: The War Powers Act. *Texas Law Review* 50:833–900.

SOFAER, ABRAHAM D. 1976 *War, Foreign Affairs, and Constitutional Power: The Origins.* Cambridge, Mass.: Ballinger Publishing Co.

TURNER, ROBERT F. 1983 *The War Powers Resolution: Its Implementation in Theory and Practice.* Philadelphia: Foreign Policy Research Institute.

WAR POWERS

Not appearing in the Constitution, the phrase "war powers" nonetheless describes a cluster of powers exercised by the President or Congress, together or separately, to combat both domestic insurgency and foreign military enemies. They comprise those activities necessary "to wage war successfully," including the raising of troops, the provision of equipment and supplies, the mobilization of opinion, and the maintenance of security in loyal areas (during civil war or insurgency) or on the home front (during foreign war).

As with all governmental activity, the legitimacy of the war powers depends ultimately on explicit or implicit sources in the Constitution. Among these are the grants to Congress of authority "to declare War," to raise, maintain, and make rules for federal military forces, and "to provide for calling forth the Militia to execute the Laws of the Union, suppress Insurrections and repel Invasions." Other sources include the Article I authorization to suspend the privilege of the writ of HABEAS CORPUS "when in Cases of Rebellion or Invasion the public Safety may require it," the Article II clauses making the President COMMANDER-IN-CHIEF, giving him power to make treaties subject to Senate consent, and charging him to "take Care that the Laws be faithfully executed," and the Article IV commitments guaranteeing "to every State . . . a REPUBLICAN FORM OF GOVERNMENT" and pledging protection against invasion and domestic violence. Magnifying all these grants is the NECESSARY AND PROPER CLAUSE.

Contrariwise, only in exceptional circumstances have officials instituted TREASON prosecutions, for in Article III the Framers laid out strict evidentiary requirements, owing to the crime's draconian connotations. But such seemingly plausible restrictions as the FIRST AMENDMENT and Fifth Amendment, the principle of SEPARATION OF POWERS, and the rule against delegation of power have seldom proved real barriers to effective wartime government; and generally JUDICIAL REVIEW has had little impact on the power to make war.

As early as 1792, Congress empowered the President to call forth state militias when "combinations too powerful to be suppressed by the ordinary course of judicial proceedings" prevented the execution of federal law. Used during the WHISKEY REBELLION (1794), and subsequently modified to include regular military forces and to clarify the President's authority to determine the existence of emergency, this provision later helped undergird President ABRAHAM LINCOLN's response to the siege of Fort Sumter. The ALIEN AND SEDITION ACTS of 1798 provide another early illustration of legislative-executive collaboration; adopted during the Quasi-War with France, they posed the enduring issue of reconciling CIVIL LIBERTIES with the perceived requirements of internal security.

Although Presidents THOMAS JEFFERSON and ANDREW JACKSON confronted serious opposition to enforcement of federal law during the Embargo and NULLIFICATION crises, the Civil War produced the first comprehensive test of the war powers' true potential. With only a slender statutory base—or none at all—for much of his action, Lincoln called out the militia, requested federal volunteer troops, increased the size of the regular army and navy, spent money from the treasury, established a naval blockade of the Confederacy, and suspended the privilege of the writ of habeas corpus. When Congress finally met at Lincoln's call, on July 4, 1861, it confronted not only a program already in place but also the President's explanation that his actions, "whether strictly legal or not, were ventured upon under what appeared to be a popular demand and a public necessity, trusting . . . that Congress would readily ratify them."

Besides retroactively endorsing much of the Lincoln program, Congress voted appropriations and passed confiscation, legal tender, and draft legislation to support the defeat of the rebellion. It also authorized Lincoln's seizure of the Union's telegraphs and railways in January 1862. The general rule of the Civil War, however, was executive initiative under the theory that the Constitution had been intended to provide government adequate to all contingencies. This view built on THE FEDERALIST #23 and LUTHER V. BORDEN (1849) and gained important wartime endorsement in the PRIZE CASES (1863). Its fullest elaboration appeared in *War Powers under the Constitution of the United States,* a massive exposition and compilation by William Whiting, the War Department's solicitor.

Even Lincoln's internal security program, which emphasized military arrest without warrant, detention without trial, and release once danger had passed, escaped serious censure during the war itself, despite the short-term imprisonment of some 13,000 to 25,000 northern civilians. Typical of Court review of war powers disputes, Chief Justice ROGER B. TANEY's attack on the suspension of habeas corpus, in *Ex parte Merryman* (1861), was feeble and futile, while the more serious blow in EX PARTE MILLIGAN came in 1866, after the war had ended.

In World War I, WOODROW WILSON by no means ignored the Lincoln model; such key agencies as the War Industries Board and the Committee on Public Information rested solely on executive authority. But the bulk of the internal effort during 1917–1918 relied on congressional delegation of power. Wilson in turn delegated authority to a host of administrative agencies that exercised direct control of the sinews of war.

The resulting intervention contrasted markedly with the Civil War experience. Bolstering prewar statutes that had given the President power to place mandatory defense contracts with private firms, the Lever Act (1917) constituted the war's largest delegation of power. It allowed sweeping regulation of priorities, production, and prices throughout the economy; yet in only a minor detail did the Supreme Court eventually rule the act unconstitutional, in UNITED STATES v. COHEN GROCERY COMPANY (1921). The Trading with the Enemy Act (1917) permitted control of foreign commodity and currency transactions, encountered no significant judicial challenge, and later provided a statutory base for President FRANKLIN D. ROOSEVELT's "Bank Holiday" during the economic emergency of the Great Depression. (Not until 1977 did Congress limit the law's availability to periods of declared war—and then provided a slightly narrower set of financial powers for use in other crises.) The SELECTIVE SERVICE ACT (1917) gave free rein to Wilson in establishing draft machinery and received strong endorsement in the SELECTIVE DRAFT LAW CASES (1918), a decision supplying precedent for upholding selective service legislation in World War II and the Cold War. The ESPIONAGE ACT (1917) and SEDITION ACT (1918) enlisted the judicial system and were upheld in SCHENCK V. UNITED STATES (1919), ABRAMS V. UNITED STATES (1919), and PIERCE V. UNITED STATES (1920). Over 1,900 prosecutions took place under these two measures, with 930 convictions.

In World War II, President Roosevelt effectively combined the Lincoln and Wilson approaches. He based many actions and agencies on his INHERENT POWERS as commander-in-chief, even when tackling problems of domestic mobilization. The National War Labor Board is an example. Created in January 1942 to insure against labor strife and work stoppages in war industries, its orders were in theory only "informatory," "at most advisory"; yet companies violating the orders were denied federal contracts and needed materials. Recalcitrant workers risked revocation of their draft exemptions and denial of other jobs within the jurisdiction of the United States Employment Service. Although avowedly established under authority vested in Roosevelt "by the Constitution and the statutes of the United States" (a commonly used formula for World War II agencies), until June 1943 the Board actually had no statutory base but rather fell under the Office of Emergency Management, itself a creation within the Executive Office of the President.

Other action rested on legislation. In September 1939, well before American entry into the war, Roosevelt's declaration of a national emergency activated laws, some dating to before World War I, that empowered him to increase the size of the army and navy, regulate banking and currency dealing, take over factories and power plants, reallocate appropriations among executive departments and agencies, and censor wire and radio communications. The Lend-Lease Act (1941) delegated the broadest procurement powers ever given to a President, yet it was never challenged judicially. The Office of Price Administration, established under the Emergency Price Control Act (1942), provided the major wartime inflation fighting program; like the nonstatutory agencies, it often employed indirect sanction that proved impossible to challenge judicially. Decisions validating the act included YAKUS V. UNITED STATES (1944), *Bowles v. Willingham* (1944), and *Steuart and Brothers v. Bowles* (1944). Not surprisingly, the war's proliferation of alphabetical agencies dwarfed the New Deal's.

In addition, the government had a sedition law available (the Smith Act of 1940), but widespread support for the war meant relatively few prosecutions. The Japanese American relocation program—the single most blatant obstruction of CIVIL LIBERTIES in the nation's history—instead had its own flimsy legislative base and for practical purposes received judicial sanction in the JAPANESE AMERICAN CASES—*Hirabayashi v. United States* (1943) and *Korematsu v. United States* (1944).

The lesson of the two world wars, as Clinton Rossiter accurately summarized, is "that in time of war Congress can pass just about any law it wants as a 'necessary and proper' accessory to the delegated war powers; that the President can make just about any use of such law he sees fit; and that the people with their overt or silent resistance, not the Court with its power of judicial review, will set the only practical limits to arrogance of abuse." Indeed, even popular resistance, real or imagined, generally has proved more of a challenge to be subdued than a restrictive hurdle.

Punctuated by limited wars in Korea and Vietnam, the period of Cold War since 1945 conveys a similar lesson: if Congress and the President act together, little likelihood exists of judicial challenge. In this respect President HARRY S. TRUMAN erred during the KOREAN WAR, when a plant seizure triggered YOUNGSTOWN SHEET AND TUBE CO. V. SAWYER (1952). As for the VIETNAM WAR, Presidents LYNDON B. JOHNSON and RICHARD M. NIXON found that despite flagging public support, Congress kept voting supplies until the main fighting was over. For its part, the judiciary moved only gingerly when limiting use of war-related powers, as in NEW YORK TIMES V. UNITED STATES (1971) (government secrecy), and

UNITED STATES V. UNITED STATES DISTRICT COURT (1972) (national security electronic surveillance). Moreover, the Supreme Court in LAIRD V. TATUM (1972) held that the courts lacked jurisdiction over a challenge to the use of military personnel to gather domestic intelligence pertaining to potential public disorder; and other courts managed to discover executive-legislative *agreement* in Congress's decision finally to cut appropriations for operations in or over Cambodia.

Future Presidents may not benefit so readily from legislative acquiescence. Soon after enacting the War Powers Resolution (1973) to control external warmaking by the President, Congress passed the NATIONAL EMERGENCIES ACT (1976). Recent studies had disclosed that four declarations of national emergency were still in effect, one dating to 1933 and another to 1950; these proclamations activated 470 provisions of federal law, many of which lingered from the two world wars and Korea. The 1976 law ended these existing emergencies two years after its passage, mandated periodic six-month review of any future emergency declarations, and made them terminable by CONCURRENT RESOLUTION—a procedure of doubtful constitutionality under IMMIGRATION AND NATURALIZATION SERVICE V. CHADHA (1983). The act also required Presidents to inform Congress fully of the legislative basis for emergency actions. But subsequent response to President JIMMY CARTER's declaration of national emergency over the Iranian hostage crisis (1979) indicated little congressional desire to adhere rigorously to the new requirements.

Whenever a crisis plausibly justifies their exercise, the war powers seem likely to continue to generate government centered in the executive branch, emphasizing energetic administration that transcends normal restrictions, and on occasion sufficiently vigorous to warrant the label "constitutional dictatorship."

CHARLES A. LOFGREN

Bibliography

CORWIN, EDWARD S. (1957)1984 *The President: Office and Powers, 1787–1984,* 5th ed., revised by Randall W. Bland, Theodore T. Hindson, and Jack W. Peltason. New York: New York University Press.

FISHER, LOUIS 1985 *Constitutional Conflicts between Congress and the President.* Princeton, N.J.: Princeton University Press.

ROSSITER, CLINTON (1948)1963 *Constitutional Dictatorship: Crisis Government in the Modern Democracies.* New York: Harcourt, Brace.

——— (1951)1976 *The Supreme Court and the Commander in Chief.* Expanded edition by Richard P. Longaker. Ithaca, N.Y.: Cornell University Press.

WAR POWERS ACTS

First War Powers Act 55 Stat. 838 (1941)

Second War Powers Act 56 Stat. 176 (1942)

Enacted less than two weeks after the bombing of Pearl Harbor, the First War Powers Act was similar to the World War I Overman Act (1917). It delegated to the President virtually complete authority to reorganize the executive branch, the independent government agencies, and government corporations in any manner he deemed appropriate to expedite prosecution of the war. That power, and reorganizations accomplished under it, were to remain in force until six months after the end of the war. The act also authorized the President to censor mail and other forms of communication between the United States and foreign countries.

The Second War Powers Act, passed three months after the first, further strengthened the executive branch for conduct of the war. It authorized acquisition of land for military or naval purposes, by condemnation if necessary. It also suspended some provisions of the HATCH ACT (1939), relaxed NATURALIZATION standards for ALIENS serving in the armed forces, established procedures for war production contracting, and authorized several other adjustments of governmental affairs.

The War Powers Acts, like their predecessors, represented an attempt to accommodate the concentration of power necessary for the prosecution of the war to the accustomed forms of constitutional government.

DENNIS J. MAHONEY

WARRANT

See: Arrest Warrant; General Warrant; Search Warrant

WARRANTLESS SEARCH

The FOURTH AMENDMENT makes no explicit provision for warrantless searches. The first clause of the amendment provides simply that "the right of the people to be secure in their persons, houses, papers, and effects, against unreasonable SEARCHES AND SEIZURES, shall not be violated." This general prohibition is followed by another clause that provides more particularly for the issuance of SEARCH WARRANTS. The amendment itself does not indicate what connection there is between the two clauses (which are separated only by a comma and the word "and"). Accordingly, its application to various kinds of warrantless searches has depended heavily on which clause the Supreme Court favors. On the one hand, the first clause might be regarded as the main provision, searches pursuant to a warrant being only one type of reasonable search that is authorized. Or, if the second clause be emphasized, the absence of a search warrant might be regarded ordinarily as itself making a search unreasonable, the requirement of a warrant being disregarded only in exceptional circumstances including particularly lack of an opportunity to obtain one.

Some kinds of warrantless search are obviously necessary to the performance of other official duties. A police officer who unexpectedly makes an ARREST of someone committing a violent crime may necessarily search him for weapons. If the Fourth Amendment were deemed to prohibit every search without a warrant, one would be driven to the conclusion that the arresting officer's conduct was not a search at all within its contemplation. Current interpretation of the Fourth Amendment has avoided such an all-or-nothing approach. The amendment is applicable to a very wide range of official conduct interfering with expectations of privacy; within that context, the prevailing rules have established a number of situations in which a warrant to search is unnecessary.

The first such situation is the SEARCH INCIDENT TO AN ARREST. The need for an arresting officer to ensure that the person whom he arrests does not have in his possession a weapon or means of escape is the basis for the most frequently applied exception to the requirement of a warrant. Because police actively engaged in crime prevention often come on circumstances calling for an arrest without advance notice, a search incident to the arrest must be made without a warrant. Although not strictly necessary to effectuate the arrest, another reason for allowing a search is to prevent the arrestee from destroying EVIDENCE in his possession. The Supreme Court said in CHIMEL V. CALIFORNIA (1969) that all three justifications are sufficient to authorize a search of the arrestee's person and the area "within his immediate control" from which he might grab something. That general rule defines an area that may be searched without a warrant following an arrest, whether or not there is particular reason to believe that anything subject to seizure is there to be grabbed and, indeed, whether or not there is reason to believe that the arrestee is likely to grab anything. In effect, the rule authorizes a not-too-intensive search of the arrestee, including small containers on his person like a wallet or purse, and a small area around the place of the arrest. If a person were arrested in his home, the rule would authorize a limited search of the table or desk at which he sat, but not all the contents of the room or the contents of other rooms.

The scope of this rule illustrates a general feature of the exceptions to the warrant requirement. Although from time to time the Court has intimated that such exceptions depend on an emergency that demands a search before a warrant could practicably be obtained, the rule does not depend on a particularized finding of that kind. In some cases, the rule has been applied to uphold a search even though the arresting officers could easily have (or even had) removed the person from the area searched or immobilized him. (One might note also that the rule applies fully to arrests that are not unanticipated, even though in that case a warrant could presumably have been obtained.) The evident rationale is that a warrantless search incident to an arrest is so often necessary that it is impractical to require particular justification in each case.

Warrants are not required for AUTOMOBILE SEARCHES in various circumstances. Although automobiles (and other motor vehicles) as private places enjoy the protection of the Fourth Amendment, two distinct lines of analysis have markedly limited the application to them of the requirement of a search warrant. Automobiles, the Supreme Court has said, are subject to much greater regulation and inspection than dwellings; the expectation of privacy in them is much less. Having reached that judgment, the Court has not modified it to differentiate between areas like the back seat that are generally open to view and closed or concealed areas like the trunk or glove compartment that are not.

If police officers obtain lawful custody of an automobile which they have PROBABLE CAUSE to search for evidence of a crime, a warrantless search is allowed for some period, a few hours at least, after custody is obtained. This rule is based not only on the lesser expectation of privacy attached to an automobile but also on its mobility and the unpredictability with which custody often is obtained. The Supreme Court has not been persuaded that the immobilization of the car while it is in custody ordinarily makes it unnecessary to allow a search until a warrant has been obtained. Second, if officers have lawful custody of an automobile and routinely follow a regular custodial procedure, like an inventory of its contents, a search performed as part of the procedure is permitted. The routine nature of such practices, which are followed by many police departments, has persuaded the Supreme Court that they are reasonable. (Also, the arrest-incident exception authorizes a thorough search of the passenger compartment of an automobile, including all containers within it, as an incident of the arrest of an occupant.)

A search at the time and place of an arrest is likely to be limited by the circumstances to weapons or means of escape and only the most obvious evidentiary items. Later, when the person is about to be placed in detention or while he is in detention, there is opportunity for a more thorough search; sometimes, the evidentiary significance of an item is not plain at the time of the arrest and is revealed as the investigation proceeds. The police have authority to make a very thorough search without a warrant of items removed from the arrested person and held by them while he is lawfully detained temporarily in a jail or similar facility. The arrest, it has been said, being the more significant interference with liberty, includes the lesser intrusion on privacy occasioned by the search. Furthermore, a search is authorized at the time and place of the arrest and it is routine administrative procedure to impound and perhaps inventory a person's effects before he is placed in a cell; therefore, it is reasoned, the fact that some time elapses between the arrest and the search has no constitutional significance.

The most general exception to the requirement of a search warrant allows the police and other public officials to search without a warrant in EXIGENT CIRCUMSTANCES: an emergency furnishing adequate grounds for a search that has to be carried out before a warrant can be obtained. A search incident to the unanticipated arrest of a potentially dangerous person is an example of this more general category, although justified by a special rule. Another example is an entry and search of private premises while in "hot pursuit" of someone who has just committed a crime; police officers are not required to interrupt the chase until they have obtained a warrant. Similarly, officers responding to a cry for help or acting to avert a danger inside private premises need not wait to obtain a warrant. It has usually been held also that if officers have particular, reliable information that specific evidence of crime is about to be destroyed and there is not time to obtain a warrant, they can enter to prevent its destruction.

In such cases, authority to search without a warrant is tailored to the emergency. The officers claiming the authority must not themselves be responsible for the existence of the emergency; if, for example, they unreasonably delayed applying for a warrant until it was too late, they could not then assert their inability to obtain a warrant. Also, the authority extends only as far as the emergency requires. Entering in hot pursuit, officers could also search for weapons that the person whom they are pursuing might use against them; but once having him in custody, they could not continue to search solely for evidence.

The regulation of persons and goods entering or leaving the country has always been understood to provide a special basis for warrantless searches. Public officials who supervise traffic across the border are authorized to inspect goods and to require a person crossing the border to submit to a thorough search. (See BORDER SEARCHES.) Some comprehensive statutory programs for the regulation of industry and commerce have authorized warrantless entries and inspections. Such procedures have been upheld if a requirement of a warrant might be expected to frustrate the regulatory program and the business in question is generally subject to close governmental supervision: for example, gun and liquor dealerships, and mines. Similarly, the Supreme Court has held that inspection visits to the home by a welfare official can be made a condition of receipt of public welfare. In other cases, the Court has concluded that the regulatory purpose of a statute did not require that warrantless (unannounced) searches be allowed.

In some circumstances, a brief invasion of personal privacy less intrusive than a full search is allowed without a warrant. Most common is the protective "frisk" or pat-down of a person whose conduct a police officer has reason to investigate and who he reasonably suspects may be armed. There being no opportunity to obtain a warrant, the safe performance of the officer's investigative duty justifies a limited search for weapons. Likewise, traffic officers are allowed to make routine checks for driver's licenses and automobile registrations, so long as the checks follow an established pattern or there are specific grounds for a departure from the pattern. Routine inspection of passengers and carry-on luggage has been upheld as a regulatory measure to prevent airplane hijacking. In these cases, not only is the procedure in question thought to be less objectionable than a full search; there is no way to accomplish the legitimate objective of the procedure consistently with a requirement of a warrant.

The Fourth Amendment does not insist that persons protect a privacy that they are willing to forego. Accordingly, a warrant to search is not required if a person having authority to do so voluntarily admits public officials and permits them to search. A consensual search that is successful often is challenged later on the grounds that consent was not given fully voluntarily or did not extend to the actual search; or, if the premises are shared by others, it may be claimed that the person who consented did not have the independent authority to do so. While a resolution of such issues may depend on difficult matters of fact, the basic principle that a search with consent does not require a warrant is unquestioned.

Those who believe that the requirement of a search warrant is a significant protection against UNREASONABLE SEARCHES may conclude that the Supreme Court has drawn the categories of lawful warrantless searches too broadly. Categories like the search incident to arrest, automobile search, and jail search appear to depend only on the premises that such searches often are fruitful and sometimes have to be made before a warrant can be obtained. But the categories are general and require neither premise to be fulfilled in the particular case; each of them encourages the police to make a large number of searches routinely, without particular justification. This approach, it can be argued, is inconsistent with the plain purpose of the Fourth Amendment to prohibit *general* searches: unfocused, unlimited rummaging in the privacy of individuals.

Critics of the Court have observed also that its analysis of warrantless searches is to a considerable degree incoherent. Why, for example, should an arrest justify the search of any area surrounding the arrestee, if he can be and often is removed from that place before the search is made? Why should automobiles, which often are used for the same private purposes as dwellings, be treated categorically as less private? Why should an arrest automatically defeat the person's separate interest in the privacy of items in his possession? The Court's failure to provide convincing answers to such questions has rendered this part of Fourth Amendment DOCTRINE only a set of rules without supporting rationale.

A defense of the rules for warrantless searches begins with the premise that warrants are peculiarly appropriate for planned investigative searches and have much less utility in the ordinary unplanned encounters between police or other public officials and private persons. If legitimate police duties justify an encounter, then a search related in purpose is also legitimate. This approach places a great deal of emphasis on the requirement that a search be "reasonable" and construes that term with attention to common police practices as well as the individual interest in privacy. To limit warrantless searches to cases of manifest necessity would blink the natural—and therefore reasonable—impulse of police officers to search whatever is legitimately in their custody and may furnish evidence of crime. Some explanation for the breadth of the exceptions to the requirement of a warrant may lie also in the fact that the issue is almost always tested in the context of a criminal prosecution, when the defendant seeks the protection of the EXCLUSIONARY RULE to avoid the admission of incriminating evidence that a search has uncovered.

LLOYD L. WEINREB

Bibliography

AMERICAN LAW INSTITUTE 1975 *A Model Code of Pre-Arraignment Procedure.* Philadelphia: American Law Institute.

AMSTERDAM, ANTHONY G. 1974 Perspectives on the Fourth Amendment. *Minnesota Law Review* 58:349–477.

LAFAVE, WAYNE R. 1978 *Search and Seizure.* St. Paul, Minn.: West Publishing Co.

LANDYNSKI, JACOB W. 1966 *Search and Seizure and the Supreme Court.* Baltimore: Johns Hopkins University Press.

WEINREB, LLOYD L. 1974 Generalities of the Fourth Amendment. *University of Chicago Law Review* 42:47–85.

WARREN, CHARLES
(1868–1954)

Charles Warren was a Boston lawyer who, as assistant attorney general of the United States, drafted the ESPIONAGE ACT and argued many cases before the Supreme Court. He became an expert on constitutional and legal history. He wrote excellent books in the tradition of the old school of high-minded conservative nationalists who rejected CHARLES BEARD's economic interpretation. Among his leading books are *A History of the American Bar, A History of Harvard Law School, The Supreme Court in United States History,* which won the Pulitzer Prize, *Congress, the Constitution, and the Supreme Court,* and *The Making of the Constitution.* His works still merit reading and remain influential. His article on the JUDICIARY ACT OF 1789 helped lead the Supreme Court in ERIE RAILROAD V. TOMKINS (1938) to overrule almost a century of decisions based on SWIFT V. TYSON (1842).

LEONARD W. LEVY

WARREN, EARL
(1891–1974)

The fourteenth Chief Justice of the United States, Earl Warren presided over the most sweeping judicial reinterpretation of the Constitution in generations. He served from October 1953 to June 1969. In that time the SUPREME COURT, overruling the doctrine that SEPARATE BUT EQUAL facilities for black persons satisfied the requirement of EQUAL PROTECTION, outlawed official racial SEGREGATION in every area of life. The Court ended the long-established rural bias of legislative representation by opening the question to judicial scrutiny and then ruling that citizens must be represented equally in state legislatures and the national House of Representatives. It imposed constitutional restraints for the first time on the law of LIBEL, hitherto a matter entirely of state concern. It applied to the states the standards set by the BILL OF RIGHTS for federal CRIMINAL PROCEDURE: the right of all poor defendants to free counsel, for example, and the prohibition of unreasonable SEARCHES AND SEIZURES, enforced by the EXCLUSIONARY RULE. It limited government power to punish unorthodox beliefs and enlarged the individual's freedom to express herself or himself in unconventional, even shocking ways.

The WARREN COURT, as it was generally called, had as profound an impact on American life as any Supreme Court since the time of JOHN MARSHALL. It was extraordinary not only in the scale but in the direction of its exercise of power. From Marshall's day to the Court's clash with President FRANKLIN D. ROOSEVELT in the 1930s judges had exercised a conservative influence in the American system. Shortly before his appointment to the Court in 1941 ROBERT H. JACKSON wrote that "never in its entire history can the Supreme Court be said to have for a single hour been representative of anything except the relatively conservative forces of its day." But the Warren Court in its time was perhaps *the* principal engine of American liberal reform.

Earl Warren seemed an unlikely figure to lead such a judicial revolution. He was a Republican politician, the elected attorney general of California and for three terms its phenomenally popular governor. In 1948 he was the Republican candidate for vice-president, on the ticket headed by Thomas E. Dewey. On naming him Chief Justice, President DWIGHT D. Eisenhower emphasized his "middle-of-the-road philosophy." Yet within a few years billboards in the South demanded Warren's IMPEACHMENT, and the paranoid right charged that he was doing the work of communism. Putting aside the rantings of extremists, there was no doubt that as Chief Justice Warren consistently favored liberal values and unembarrassedly translated them into constitutional doctrine. Where did that commitment come from in a man whose appearance was that of a bland, hearty political figure?

There were in fact clues in his life and earlier career. He was born in Los Angeles in 1891, the son of a Norwegian immigrant who worked for the Southern Pacific Railroad. He knew poverty and personal tragedy. As a young man he was a railroad callboy, waking up the gangs, and he saw men with their legs cut off in accidents carried in on planks. His father was murdered, the murderer never found: a traumatic event that must have helped to point Warren in the direction of justice, legal and social. He put himself through college and law school at the University of California. After a brief try at private practice he spent all his life in public office, as a local prosecutor and crusading district attorney before winning statewide office.

In California politics he at first had the support of conservatives. As attorney general he blocked the nomination of Max Radin, a law professor known as a legal realist, to the state supreme court because Radin was a "radical." As attorney general and governor Warren was a leading proponent of the World War II federal order removing all persons of Japanese ancestry from the West Coast and putting them in desolate camps; opposing their return in 1943, he said, "If the Japs are released, no one will be able to tell a saboteur from any other Jap." (In a memoir published after his death, Warren wrote: "I have since deeply regretted the removal order and my own testimony advocating it, because it was not in keeping with our American concept of freedom and the rights of citizens. . . .")

But in 1945 Warren astounded political California by proposing a state program of prepaid medical insurance. Characteristically, he did so not for ideological but for human, practical reasons: he had fallen ill and realized how catastrophic serious illness would be for a person without resources. Then, in his last two terms as governor, he became an apostle of liberal Republicanism. A later Democratic governor, Edmund G. Brown, said Warren "was the best governor California ever had. . . . He felt the people of California were in his care, and he cared for them."

Many Americans and other people around the world saw that same paternal image in Earl Warren the Chief Justice, for he became an international symbol. He represented the hope of authority bringing justice to the downtrodden, an American vision of change by law rather than by rebellion. A single case gave Warren that status: BROWN V. BOARD OF EDUCATION, the 1954 school segregation decision. In recent years the Supreme Court had chipped away at PLESSY V. FERGUSON, the 1896 decision allowing what were termed "separate but equal" facilities but what were almost always in fact grossly inferior schools and other public institutions for blacks. Yet in 1953 seventeen southern and border states, with forty percent of the national enrollment, still confined black children to separate public schools; moreover, there was involved here, unlike higher education, the compulsory daily association of children. The emotional content of the legal question was high. The Court had given the most gingerly handling to the question, restoring the issue to the calendar for reargument.

Warren became Chief Justice before the second argument. The following May he delivered the opinion for a unanimous Court holding public school segregation unconstitutional. The unanimity was itself a striking feature of the result, and a surprising one. Expected southern resistance made unanimity politically essential, but the known attitudes of some members of the Court had suggested the likelihood of dissents. Richard Kluger's exhaustive study has demonstrated that the new Chief Justice played a crucial part in his management of the process inside the Court. After argument he delayed formal discussion of the cases in conference to avoid the development of rigid positions among the nine Justices. Then he stated as his view that the separate-but-equal doctrine could not be maintained unless one thought blacks inherently inferior: an approach likely to induce shame in any judge prepared to argue for that outcome. He persuaded his colleagues even then to avoid a formal vote but to continue discussing the cases, in tight secrecy, among themselves. He wrote an opinion in simple terms. Finally, he persuaded reluctant members of the Court to join for the sake of unanimity. A law clerk present at a late meeting between the Chief Justice and the most reluctant, STANLEY F. REED, remembers him saying, "Stan, you're all by yourself in this now. You've got to decide whether it's really the best thing for the country."

What is known about the process of decision in the school cases throws lights on one question asked during his lifetime: did Chief Justice Warren exercise leadership or have influence in the Court beyond his own vote in conference? He shared that bench with men of strong personality and conviction: in particular HUGO L. BLACK, who said the judicial duty was to follow the literal language of the Constitution and found in it absolutes, and FELIX FRANKFURTER, who scorned absolutes and said the Court should defer to the political branches of government in applying the uncertain commands of the Constitution. Warren came to the Court utterly inexperienced in its work; how could he have effective influence? The school cases show that he did.

No Chief Justice can command his associates' beliefs. If Warren had served with different, more conservative colleagues, many of the views that made history might have been expressed by him in dissent. Changes while he was on the Court greatly affected the trend of doctrine, in particular the retirement of Justice Frankfurter in 1962 and his replacement by ARTHUR J. GOLDBERG, who was much readier to join Warren in intervening on behalf of liberal values. But the identification of that Court with its Chief Justice, for all its logical imperfection, has substantial basis in reality.

Warren wrote the opinions of the Court not only in *Brown* but in later cases that dramatically overturned expectations. The most important of these—Warren himself thought them the weightiest decisions of his years on the Court—were the REAPPORTIONMENT cases. A divided Supreme Court in COLEGROVE V. GREEN (1946) had refused to entertain an attack on numerical inequality in political districts, an opinion by Justice Frankfurter saying that courts must stay out of the "political thicket." In 1962 the Warren Court, in an opinion by Justice WILLIAM J. BRENNAN, overthrew that doctrine of reluctance and said that federal courts could consider issues of fairness in districting. The decision in BAKER V. CARR left open the substantive questions: must the population be the test of equality, or may states weigh geography or other factors in districting? Does the same standard apply to both houses of legislatures? The answers were given by Chief Justice Warren in 1964, in terms so firm that some who listened in the courtroom felt as if they were at a second American constitutional convention. In REYNOLDS V. SIMS Warren said for a 6–3 majority that every house of every state legislature must be apportioned on the basis of population alone, with the districts as nearly equal as practicable. Few cases in any court ever had so direct and immediate an impact on a nation's politics; reapportionment was required in most of the fifty states, ancient legislative expectations were upset, new suburban power vindicated. Justice JOHN MARSHALL HARLAN predicted in dissent, as had Justice Frankfurter in *Baker v. Carr*, that the courts would not be able to manage the apportionment litigation—or to enforce their decisions against political resistance. But the gloomy prediction was wrong. Resistance from political incumbents quickly collapsed; nothing like the emotional public opposition to the school segregation cases developed in any region.

Emotions were aroused by Warren's opinion in MIRANDA V. ARIZONA (1966), holding that before questioning an arrested person the police must warn him that he has a right to remain silent and a right to see a lawyer first—one provided by the state if he cannot afford one—and that a confession obtained in violation of that rule is inadmissible at trial. The decision touched a nerve among police, prosecutors, and others convinced that judges were impeding the fight against crime. *Miranda* climaxed a series of cases holding local police to the standards of the Bill of Rights: for example, MAPP V. OHIO (1961), exclusion of illegally obtained evidence; GIDEON V. WAINWRIGHT (1963), RIGHT TO COUNSEL; GRIFFIN V. CALIFORNIA (1965), RIGHT AGAINST SELF-INCRIMINATION; each overruling an earlier decision. In *Spano v. New York* (1959) Warren commented: "The abhorrence of society to the use of involuntary confessions does not turn alone on their inherent untrustworthiness. It also turns on the deep-rooted feeling that the police must obey the law while enforcing the law; that in the end life and liberty can be as much endangered from illegal methods used to convict those thought to be criminals as from the actual criminals themselves." Impatient with reviewing the facts in case after case of claimed coercion, the Court under Warren sought a general prophylactic rule—and wrote it in *Miranda.*

Objection to the *Miranda* decision came not only from the law enforcement community. More dispassionate critics saw it as an example of overreaching by the Warren Court. The opinion seemed more legislative in character than judicial, laying out what amounted to a code of police procedure with little basis in precedent. Moreover, the Court did not confront a situation in which reform by other means was blocked, as it had with school segregation and malapportioned legislatures; various reformers were working on the confession problem.

Freedom of expression was another subject of fundamental constitutional development during the Warren years. The most important single decision was probably NEW YORK TIMES V. SULLIVAN (1964), holding that a public official may not recover libel damages unless the statement was published with knowledge of its falsity or in reckless disregard of truth or falsity. That opinion was by Justice Brennan. Justice WILLIAM O. DOUGLAS wrote for the Court in LAMONT V. POSTMASTER GENERAL (1965), holding that a statute requiring the post office to detain "Communist political propaganda" from abroad unless the addressee requested its delivery violated the FIRST AMENDMENT—the first federal statute that the Supreme Court ever held invalid under that amendment. Warren joined in these and other expansive decisions. He wrote for a 5–4 majority in UNITED STATES V. ROBEL (1967), striking down a law that forbade the employment in defense plants of any member of an organization required to register under the Subversive Activities Control Act. Warren's opinion for a unanimous Court in *Bond v. Floyd* (1966) held that the Georgia legislature could not exclude a duly elected member because he had expressed admiration for draft resisters.

The one area of expression in which Warren departed from the majority of his colleagues was OBSCENITY. He thought that local and national authorities should have a relatively free hand to combat what he evidently regarded as a social evil. Thus, while in *Miranda* imposing a national standard for fair pretrial procedures in criminal cases, he argued in dissent in JACOBELLIS V. OHIO (1964) that each local community should be allowed to fix its own standard of obscenity, a view that became the law under Chief Justice WARREN E. BURGER in MILLER V. CALIFORNIA (1973). Another example of a departure from Warren's usual approach came when gambling was involved. He generally favored broad application of the right against self-incrimination; but when the rule was applied for the benefit of a gambler in MARCHETTI V. UNITED STATES (1968), he alone dissented. Once again he saw a social evil.

Scholarly critics of Chief Justice Warren saw the obscenity and gambling cases as illustrating a fundamental shortcoming in a judge: a concern to reach particular results rather than to work out principles applicable whoever the parties in a case might be. In Warren's view, it seemed, justice consisted not in providing a philosophically satisfactory process and basis of decision but in seeing that the right side, the good side, won in each case. Many of the commentators regretted the lack of a consistent doctrinal thread in his opinions. There was nothing like Justice Black's exaltation of the constitutional text, or Justice Frankfurter's institutional concern for self-restraint.

G. Edward White, in a full-length study of Warren's work, rejected the general scholarly view that Warren had no rudder as a judge and lacked craftsmanship. He was an ethicist, White concluded, who saw his craft as "discovering ethical imperatives in a maze of confusion"—and in the Constitution. Thus the prosecutor so hard on corruption that he was called a boy scout, the Californian politician who stood aloof from party machines lest he be sullied, became a judicial enforcer of ethical imperatives. In general his sympathy lay with the little person, with victims, with people excluded from the benefits of our democracy.

But he also was in the tradition of the American Progressives, who thought that government could be made to work for the people. Those two themes came together in the reapportionment cases, decisions designed to make democracy work better by making the electoral process fairer. John Hart Ely, in an analysis of judicial review as practiced in the Warren years, suggested that many of the pathbreaking decisions had a democratic structural purpose: to assure access for the powerless and thus make the system work.

There was a directness, a simplicity in Warren's opinions on the largest issues. "Legislators represent people," he wrote in the reapportionment cases, "not acres or trees. Legislators are elected by voters, not farms or cities or economic interests. . . . The weight of a citizen's vote cannot be made to depend on where he lives." When the Court held unconstitutional a statute depriving a native-born American of his citizenship for deserting the armed forces in time of war, TROP V. DULLES (1958), Warren for a plurality argued that EXPATRIATION was a CRUEL AND UNUSUAL PUNISHMENT in violation of the Eighth Amendment. The death penalty would not have been "cruel," he conceded, but the deprivation of citizenship was, for it caused "the total destruction of the individual's status in organized society" and cost him "the right to have rights."

Warren's whole career suggests that he was a person born not to muse but to act—and to govern. That view provides a connecting thread through all the offices he held. In each he exerted his powerful abilities in the ways open to him. As a prosecutor he fought crime. As wartime attorney general and governor he was a patriot, worrying about spies. In the postwar years, he turned to the social problems of an expanding California. As Chief Justice, too, he was committed to action, to using the opportunities available to make an impression on American life: to break the pattern of malapportionment, to attack local police abuses, to condemn racial discrimination. The instinct to govern did not leave Earl Warren when he put on a robe.

Many regarded him as a heroic figure because he put aside philosophical concerns and technical legal issues and dealt squarely with what he considered outrageous situations. And there were outrages in American life: official racism, political discrimination, abuse of police authority, suppression of free expression. Warren as Chief Justice had the conviction, the humanity, and the capacity for growth to deal effectively with those issues inside that prickly institution, the Supreme Court. But there were those who shared Justice LEARNED HAND's doubts about rule by judges, however beneficent. "For myself," Hand wrote in 1958, with the contemporary Supreme Court in mind, "it would be most irksome to be ruled by a bevy of Platonic Guardians, even if I knew how to choose them, which I assuredly do not." Earl Warren may have been the closest thing the United States has had to a constitutional Platonic Guardian, dispensing law without any sensed limit of authority except what he saw as the good of society. He was a decent, kindly law-giver. But the exercise of such power by other judges—before and after Warren—has not always had kindly or rational results. The questions about judicial power remain after its extraordinary uses in the Warren years.

ANTHONY LEWIS

Bibliography

ELY, JOHN HART 1980 *Democracy and Distrust: A Theory of Judicial Review.* Cambridge, Mass.: Harvard University Press.

KLUGER, RICHARD 1975 *Simple Justice: The History of Brown v. Board of Education and Black America's Struggle for Equality.* New York: Knopf.

SCHWARTZ, BERNARD 1983 *Superchief.* Garden City, N.Y.: Doubleday.

WHITE, G. EDWARD 1982 *Earl Warren: A Public Life.* New York: Oxford University Press.

WARREN COURT

It was surely the best known Supreme Court in history, and probably the most controversial. Its grand themes—racial equality, REAPPORTIONMENT, the separation of religion and education, DUE PROCESS—became matters of public consciousness. Its leading judges—HUGO L. BLACK, WILLIAM O. DOUGLAS, FELIX FRANKFURTER, JOHN MARSHALL HARLAN, and EARL WARREN—became personages in whom the general public took an interest. When the Warren Court came into being in October 1953, the Supreme Court was the least known and least active of the major branches of government; by the retirement of Chief Justice Warren in June 1969, nearly everyone in American life had been affected by a Warren Court decision, and a great many Americans had firm opinions about the Supreme Court. When Warren was appointed Chief Justice, few commentators took note of the fact that he had had no previous judicial experience and had spent the last twelve years as a state politician. By the time WARREN E. BURGER succeeded Warren as Chief Justice the process of nominating a Justice to the Supreme Court had become an elaborate search for the "experienced," uncontroversial, and predictable nominee, and the Court was to lower its profile again.

The Warren Court years, then, were years in which the Supreme Court of the United States made itself a vital force in American culture. A striking pattern of interchange between the Court and the general public emerged in these years. As public issues, such as CIVIL RIGHTS or legislative malapportionment surfaced, these issues became translated into constitutional law cases. The Court, expanding the conventional ambit of its JURISDICTION, reached out to decide those cases, thereby making an authoritative contribution to the public debate. As the Court continued to reach out, the public came to rely on its presence, and the American JUDICIAL SYSTEM came to be perceived as a forum for the resolution of contemporary social problems. The use of the Supreme Court as an institution for redressing grievances ignored by Congress or state legislatures became common with the Warren Court.

The origins of the Warren Court can officially be traced to September 8, 1953, when Chief Justice FRED M. VINSON died of a heart attack. By September 30, President DWIGHT D. EISENHOWER had named Warren, the governor of California who had been a rival candidate for the Republican presidential nomination in 1952, as Vinson's successor. This nominal creation of the Warren Court did not, however, hint at its character. Indeed that character was not immediately apparent. Even the Court's first momentous decision, BROWN V. BOARD OF EDUCATION (1954), announced in May of its first term, was in some respects a holdover from the VINSON COURT. *Brown* had been argued before the Vinson Court, was based in part on Vinson Court precedents chipping away at RACIAL DISCRIMINATION in education, and was decided by a Court whose only new member was its Chief Justice. It was a cautious decision, apparently assuming that DESEGREGATION would be a long and slow process.

But *Brown* was also the Warren Court's baptism of fire. All the elements that were to mark subsequent major Warren Court decisions were present in *Brown*. *Brown* involved a major social problem, racial discrimination, translated into a legal question, the constitutionality of SEPARATE BUT EQUAL public schools. It posed an issue that no other branch of government was anxious to address. It raised questions that had distinctively moral implications: in invalidating racial SEGREGATION the Court was condemning the idea of racial supremacy. And it affected the lives of ordinary citizens, not merely in the South, not merely in public education, for the Court's series of PER CURIAM decisions after *Brown* revealed that it did not consider racial segregation any more valid in other public facilities than it had in schools. The Warren Court had significantly altered race relations in America.

The context of the Warren Court's first momentous decision was decisive in shaping the Court's character as a branch of government that was not disinclined to resolve difficult social issues, not hesitant to foster social change, not reluctant to involve itself in controversy. By contrast, the legislative and executive branches appeared as equivocators and fainthearts. The Warren Court was deluged with criticism for its decision in *Brown,* both from persons who resisted having to change habits of prejudice and from scholars who faulted the reasoning of the Court's opinion. This response only seemed to make the Court more resolute.

The deliberations of *Brown* also served to identify some of the Justices whose presence was to help shape the character of the Warren Court. Earl Warren transformed a closely divided Court, which had postponed a decision on *Brown* because it was uncertain and fragmented on the case's resolution, into a unanimous voice. That transformation was a testament to Warren's remarkable ability to relate to other people and to convince them of the rightness of his views. In *Brown* he had argued that those who would support the separate but equal doctrine should recognize that it was based on claims of racial superiority. That argument struck home to at least two Justices, TOM C. CLARK and STANLEY F. REED, who had grown up in the South. When Warren had finished his round of office visits and discussions, he had secured nine votes for his majority opinion and had suppressed the writing of separate concurrences. ROBERT H. JACKSON, a long holdout in *Brown* who was dubious about the possibility of finding a doctrinal rationale to invalidate the separate but equal principle, joined Warren's opinion and left a hospital bed to appear in court the day the decision was announced.

A silent partner in the *Brown* decision had been Felix Frankfurter. By the late 1950s Frankfurter's jurisprudence, which stressed a limited role for judges in reviewing the constitutionality of legislative decisions, had rigidified, isolating Frankfurter from many other justices and identifying him as one of the guardians of a theory of judicial self-restraint. Judicial self-restraint in *Brown* would have supported the separate but equal doctrine, since that doctrine itself signified a judicial reluctance to disturb legislative enactments forcibly separating persons on the basis of race. Frankfurter, however, could not abide the consequences of continued deference to the separate but equal doctrine, but he did not want to expose the lack of "restraint" that his position assumed. He accordingly confided his views on *Brown* only to Warren and worked toward fashioning a decree—containing the controversial phrase ALL DELIBERATE SPEED as a guideline for implementing desegregation—that would temper the shock of the *Brown* mandate. At the appropriate moment he joined Warren's opinion.

The partnership of Warren and Frankfurter in the segregation cases contrasted with the usual posture of both Justices on the Warren Court. Warren's approach to judging, with its relative indifference to doctrinal reasoning and to institutional considerations, its emphasis on the morally or ethically appropriate result, and its expansive interpretation of the Court's review powers, was the antithesis of Frankfurter's. For the most part the two men sharply disagreed over the results or the reasoning of major Warren Court decisions, with Frankfurter enlisting a stable of academic supporters in his behalf and Warren seeking to bypass doctrinal or institutional objections to make broad ethical appeals to the public at large.

The presence of two other significant Warren Court Justices, Hugo Black and William O. Douglas, was also felt in *Brown.* Black, a native of Clay County, Alabama, and fleetingly a member of the Ku Klux Klan, had been an opponent of racial discrimination since being elected to the Senate in 1926. He had supported the Vinson Court precedents crippling "separate but equal," for which he had received outspoken criticism in his home state. His position in *Brown* was well known early on: an uncompromising opposition to discriminatory practices. Such positions were characteristic of Black on the Warren Court. He staked out positions decisively, held them with tenacity, and constantly sought to convert others to his views. His theory of constitutional adjucation, which placed great emphasis on a "literal" but "liberal" construction of BILL OF RIGHTS protections, was a major contribution to Warren Court jurisprudence.

Equally outspoken and tenacious, and even more activist than Black, was William O. Douglas, whose academic experience, which paralleled Frankfurter's, had generated a strikingly different conception of judicial behavior. Douglas did not agonize over issues of institutional deference and doctrinal principle; he took his power to make law as a given and sought to use it to promote values in which he believed. The values were principally those associated with twentieth-century libertarianism and egalitarianism. Douglas spoke out for small business, organized labor, disadvantaged minorities, consumers, the poor, dissidents, and those who valued their privacy and their freedom from governmental restraint. Douglas's role on the Warren Court was that of an ideologue, anxious to secure results and confident that he could find doctrinal justifications. Together, Black and Douglas prodded the Court to vindicate even the most unpopular forms of free expression and minority rights.

While the Warren Court was generally regarded as an activist Court and a liberal Court, it was not exclusively so, and not all its members could be characterized as either activists or liberals. Until his retirement in 1962, at the midway point of Warren's tenure, Frankfurter had vociferously protested against an excessively broad interpretation of the Court's review powers, a position that resulted in his supporting the constitutionality of a number of "conservative" legislative policies. Other Justices on the Warren Court were either disinclined to exercise sweeping review powers or less enthusiastic than Warren, Black, or Douglas about the policies of twentieth-century liberalism. Most influential among those Justices was John Harlan, an Eisenhower appointee who joined the Court in 1955 and remained until 1971.

Harlan frequently and adroitly rejected the assumptions of Warren Court majorities that "every major social ill in this country can find its cure in some constitutional 'principle' " and that the Court could be "a general haven for reform movements." Moreover, in a group of Justices who were often impatient to reach results and not inclined to linger over the niceties of doctrinal analysis, Harlan distinguished himself by producing painstakingly crafted opinions. Often Harlan's quarrels with a majority would be over the method by which results were reached; his concurrences and dissents regularly demonstrated the complexities of constitutional adjudication.

The Warren Court will be best known for its identification with three themes: egalitarianism, liberalism, and activism. From *Brown* through POWELL V. MCCORMACK (1969), Earl Warren's last major opinion, the Court demonstrated a dedication to the principle of equality, a principle that, in Archibald Cox's felicitous phrase, "once loosed . . . is not easily cabined." Race relations were the initial context in which the Court attempted to refine the meaning of equal justice in America. Once the ordeal of *Brown* was concluded, that meaning seemed comparatively straightforward. In a series of *per curiam* opinions, the Court extended *Brown* to public beaches, parks, recreational facilities, housing developments, public buildings, eating facilities, and hospitals. The conception of equality embodied by these decisions was that of equality of opportunity: blacks could not be denied the opportunity of access to public places.

Brown had been rationalized by the Court on similar grounds: the gravamen of the injustice in a segregated school system was a denial of equal educational opportunities to blacks. But equality of opportunity became difficult to distinguish, in the race cases, from the conception of equality of condition. The Court presumed that classifications based on race were constitutionally suspect and seemed to suggest that equal justice in the race relations area required something like color-blindness. Classifications based on race or skin color not only denied black Americans equal opportunities, they also were not based on any rational judgment, since the human condition transcended superficial differences of race. After the *per curiams,* the massive resistance to *Brown,* and the civil rights movement of the 1960s, the Court gradually perceived that equality in race relations necessitated the eradication of stigmas based on skin color. This momentum of egalitarianism culminated in *Loving v. Virginia* (1967), in which the Court invalidated state prohibitions of miscegenous marriages, thereby affirming the absence of fundamental differences between blacks and whites.

Between the *per curiams* and *Loving* had come skirmishes between the Court and groups resisting its mandates for change in race relations. COOPER V. AARON (1963) involved a challenge by the governor of Arkansas to compulsory integration in the Little Rock school system. The Court, in an unprecedented opinion signed individually by all nine Justices, reaffirmed the obligations of Southern schools to integrate. *Goss v. Board of Education* (1963) invalidated minority-to-majority transfer plans whose purpose was to allow students to attend schools outside their districts in which their race was in the majority. HEART OF ATLANTA MOTEL V. UNITED STATES (1964) and *Katzenbach v. McClung* (1964) used the Constitution's COMMERCE CLAUSE and the CIVIL RIGHTS ACT OF 1964 to prevent hotels and restaurants from refusing service to blacks. BURTON V. WILMINGTON PARKING AUTHORITY (1961) and *Evans v. Newton* (1966) showed the Court's willingness to use the DOCTRINE of "STATE ACTION" to compel ostensibly private establishments (restaurants and parks) to admit blacks.

After *Loving* the Court grew impatient with resistance to the implementation of its decrees in *Brown.* In GREEN V. NEW KENT COUNTY SCHOOL BOARD (1968) the Court scrutinized the actual effect of "freedom of choice" plans, where students attended schools of their own choice. The Court found that the system perpetuated segregation when eighty-five percent of the black children in a school district had remained in a previously all-black school and no white child had chosen to attend that school, and advised that "delays are no longer tolerable." Finally, in ALEXANDER V. HOLMES COUNTY BOARD OF EDUCATION (1969) the Court declared that the time for racial integration of previously segregated school systems was "at once." *Green* and *Alexander* compelled integration of schools and other public facilities. Equality of condition had become the dominant means to achieve the goal of equality.

One can see a similar trend in the area of reapportionment. For the first half of the twentieth century, including the early years of the Warren Court, state legislatures were not apportioned solely on the basis of population. Upper houses of legislatures had a variety of means for electing their members, some deliberately unresponsive to demographic concerns, and few states apportioned legislative seats on the basis of ONE PERSON, ONE VOTE. In *Baker v. Carr* (1962), however, the Court announced that it would scrutinize Tennessee's system of electing state legislators to see if it conformed to the population of districts in the state. Justice WILLIAM J. BRENNAN, a former student of Frankfurter's, rejected the POLITICAL QUESTION doctrine Frankfurter had consistently imposed as a barrier to Court determination of reapportionment cases. Frankfurter wrote an impassioned dissent in *Baker,* but the way was clear for constitutional challenges to malapportioned legislatures. By 1964 suits challenging legislative apportionment schemes had been filed in more than thirty states.

Chief Justice Warren's opinion for the Court in REYNOLDS V. SIMS (1964), a case testing Alabama's reapportionment system, demonstrated how the idea of equality had infused the reapportionment cases. "We are cautioned," he wrote, "about the dangers of entering into political thickets and mathematical quagmires. Our answer to this: a denial of constitutionally protected rights demands judicial protection; our oath and our office require no less of us. . . . To the extent that a citizen's right to vote is debased, he is that much less a citizen." Equality did not mean merely an equal opportunity to have representatives from one's district in a state legislature, but that all votes of all citizens were to be treated equally: voting, like race relations, was to be an area in which equality of condition was to prevail.

The Court provided for such equality even where the state's citizens had indicated a preference for another scheme. In LUCAS V. FORTY-FOURTH GENERAL ASSEMBLY (1964), the Court invalidated Colorado's districting plan apportioning only one house of the legislature on a population basis. This plan had been adopted after a statewide referendum in which a majority rejected population-based apportionment for both houses. Warren found that the scheme did not satisfy the equal protection clause because it was not harmonious with the principle of one person, one vote. Voting was a condition of CITIZENSHIP, not just an opportunity to participate in government.

In free speech cases, the Warren Court struggled to move beyond a "marketplace" approach, in which majorities could perhaps suppress speech with distasteful content, to an approach where all speakers were presumed to have an equal right to express their thoughts. The approach was first developed in "communist sympathizer" cases, where a minority of the Court objected to laws making it a crime to be a member of the Communist party or to advocate Communist party doctrine. Eventually, in BRANDENBURG V. OHIO (1969), a unanimous Court distinguished between "mere advocacy" of views and "incitement to imminent lawless action." That case involved statements made by a member of the Ku Klux Klan at a rally that were derogatory of blacks and Jews. The fact that the speaker was known to belong to an organization historically linked to racism and violence was not enough to hinder expression of his views.

Brandenburg united, without entirely clarifying, a number of strands of Warren Court FIRST AMENDMENT doctrine. In the OVERBREADTH cases, such as *NAACP v. Alabama ex rel. Flowers* (1964), APTHEKER V. SECRETARY OF STATE (1964), KEYISHIAN V. BOARD OF REGENTS (1967), and UNITED STATES V. ROBEL (1967), the Court found that legitimate governmental prohibitions on speech that employed "means which sweep unnecessarily broadly" violated the First Amendment, because they might deter the behavior of others who could not legitimately be prohibited from speaking. In the SYMBOLIC SPEECH cases, the Court considered the permissibility of wearing black arm bands (TINKER V. DES MOINES COMMUNITY SCHOOL DISTRICT, 1969) or burning draft cards (UNITED STATES V. O'BRIEN, 1968) or mutilating flags (STREET V. NEW YORK, 1969) as a means of protesting the Vietnam War. Finally, in the "sit-in" and "picketing" cases, such as COX V. LOUISIANA (1964), BROWN V. LOUISIANA (1966), and ADDERLEY V. FLORIDA (1966), the Court sought to distinguish protected "expression" from unprotected but related "conduct." In none of these areas was the Court's doctrinal position clear—draft card burners and picketers were denied constitutional protection, although flag mutilators and "sit-in" demonstrators were granted it—but the decisions revealed the Warren Court's interest in carving out an area of First Amendment protection that was not dependent on public support for the speaker or his actions.

The Warren Court also attempted to extend the First Amendment's reach into other doctrinal areas, notably defamation and OBSCENITY. In NEW YORK TIMES V. SULLIVAN (1964) the Court concluded that common law libel actions could raise First Amendment issues. The Court's opinion, which found that the First Amendment gave rise to a constitutional privilege to make false and defamatory statements about public officials if the statements were not made with recklessness or malice, expressed concern that libel law could be used as a means of punishing "unpopular" speech. Justice Brennan's majority opinion referred to "a profound national commitment to the principle that debate on public issues should be uninhibited, robust, and wide-open," and spoke of the "inhibiting" effects of civil damages on "those who would give voice to public criticism."

Once the First Amendment was seen as relevant to defamation cases, the future of common law principles in the area of libel and slander seemed precarious. *New York Times v. Sullivan* had established a constitutional privilege to publish information about "public officials." *Rosenblatt v. Baer* (1966) widened the meaning of "public official" to include a supervisor of a county-owned ski resort; *Curtis Publishing Co. v. Butts* (1967) and *Associated Press v. Walker* (1967) included "public figures" as well as public officials in the category of those in whose affairs the general public had a special interest; *Time, Inc. v. Hill* (1967) found a privilege to disclose "private" but newsworthy information.

The defamation cases showed the tendency of the equality principle to expand once set in motion: it seemed hard to distinguish different rules for public officials, public figures, and matters of public interest. Such was also true in the area of obscenity. Once the Court recognized, as it did in ROTH V. UNITED STATES (1957), that First Amendment concerns were relevant in obscenity cases, and yet a core of unprotected expression remained, it was forced to define obscenity. Thirteen obscenity cases between 1957 and 1968 produced fifty-five separate opinions from the Justices, but the meaning of "obscene" for constitutional purposes was not made much clearer. Some Justices, such as Black and Douglas, decided that obscene speech was entitled to as much constitutional protection as any other speech, but a shifting majority of the Court continued to deny protection for expressions that, by one standard or another, could be deemed "obscene." Among the criteria announced by Court majorities for labeling a work "obscene" was that it appeal to a "prurient interest," and that it be "patently offensive" and "utterly without redeeming social value." Justice Stewart, in JACOBELLIS V. OHIO (1964), announced a different criterion: "I know [obscenity] when I see it." Eventually, after *Redrup v. New York* (1967), the Court began to reverse summarily all obscenity convictions whenever five Justices, for whatever reason, adjudged a work not to be obscene.

A final area of unprotected expression involved the FIGHTING WORDS doctrine of CHAPLINSKY V. NEW HAMPSHIRE (1942). A series of Warren Court cases, including *Edwards v. South Carolina* (1963), *Gregory v. Chicago* (1969) and even *New York Times v. Sullivan,* with its language about "vehement, caustic, and sometimes unpleasantly sharp attacks on government and public officials," may have reduced *Chaplinsky* to insignificance.

The pattern of First Amendment decisions, taken with its opinions on race relations and reapportionment, not only demonstrated the Warren Court's shifting conceptions of equality but stamped it in the popular mind as a "liberal" Court. Liberalism has been identified, in the years after World War II, with support for affirmative government and protection of civil rights; the Warren Court was notable for its efforts to insure that interventionist government and civil libertarianism could coexist. But in so doing the Warren Court redefined the locus of interventionist government in America. *Brown v. Board of Education* was a classic example. Congress and the state legislatures were not taking sufficient action to preserve the rights of blacks, so the Court intervened to scrutinize their conduct and, where necessary, to compel them to act. This role for the Court was a major change from that performed by its predecessors. "Liberal" judging in the early twentieth century, according to such defenders of interventionist government as Felix Frankfurter and LOUIS D. BRANDEIS, meant judicial self-restraint: the Supreme Court was to *avoid* scrutiny of state and federal legislation whose purpose was to aid disadvantaged persons. The Warren Court eschewed that role to become the principal interventionist branch of government in the 1950s and 1960s.

In addition to its decisions in race relations and reapportionment, two other areas of Warren Court activity helped augment its public reputation as a "liberal" Court. The first area was CRIMINAL PROCEDURE: here the Court virtually rewrote the laws of the states to conform them to its understanding of the Constitution's requirements. The most important series of its criminal procedure decisions, from a doctrinal perspective, were the INCORPORATION DOCTRINE cases, where the Court struggled with the question of whether, and to what extent, the due process clause of the FOURTEENTH AMENDMENT incorporates procedural protections in the Bill of Rights, making those protections applicable against the states. The Warren Court began a process of "selective incorporation" of Bill of Rights safeguards, applying particular protections in given cases but refusing to endorse the incorporation doctrine in its entirety. This process produced some landmark decisions, notably MAPP V. OHIO (1961), which applied FOURTH AMENDMENT protections against illegal SEARCHES AND SEIZURES to state trials, and BENTON V. MARYLAND (1969), which held that the Fifth Amendment's DOUBLE JEOPARDY guarantee applied to the states. Other important "incorporation" cases were GRIFFIN V. CALIFORNIA (1965), maintaining a RIGHT AGAINST SELF-INCRIMINATION; MALLOY V. HOGAN (1964), applying the Fifth Amendment's self-incrimination privilege to state proceedings; and DUNCAN V. LOUISIANA (1968), incorporating the Sixth Amendment's right to TRIAL BY JURY in criminal cases.

A major consequence of selective incorporation was that fewer criminal convictions were obtained in state trials. Particularly damaging to state prosecutors were the decisions in *Mapp* and *Mallory,* which eliminated from state court trials illegally secured evidence and coerced statements of incrimination. The Court also tightened the requirements for police conduct during the incarceration of criminal suspects. *Malloy v. United States* (1957) insisted that criminal defendants be brought before a magistrate prior to being interrogated. MIRANDA V. ARIZONA (1966) announced a series of constitutional "warnings" that the police were required to give persons whom they had taken into custody. *Miranda* had been preceded by another significant case, ESCOBEDO V. ILLINOIS (1964), which had required that a lawyer be present during police investigations if a suspect requested one. Further, the landmark case of GIDEON V. WAINWRIGHT (1963) had insured that all persons suspected of crimes could secure the services of a lawyer if they desired such, whether they could afford them or not.

The result of this activity by the Warren Court in the area of criminal procedure was that nearly every stage of a POLICE INTERROGATION was fraught with constitutional complexities. The decisions, taken as a whole, seemed to be an effort to buttress the position of persons suspected of crimes by checking the power of the police: some opinions, such as *Miranda,* were explicit in stating that goal. By intervening in law enforcement proceedings to protect the rights of allegedly disadvantaged persons—a high percentage of criminals in the 1960s were poor and black—the Warren Court Justices were acting as liberal policymakers.

Church and state cases were another area in which the Court demonstrated its liberal sensibility, to the concern of many observers. Affirmative state action to promote religious values in the public schools—heretofore an aspect of America's educational heritage—was likely to be struck down as a violation of the establishment clause. In ENGEL V. VITALE (1962) the Court struck down nondenominational prayer readings in New York public schools. A year after *Engel* the Court also invalidated a Pennsylvania law that required reading from the Bible in ABINGTON TOWNSHIP SCHOOL DISTRICT V. SCHEMPP (1963) and a Maryland law that required recitation of the Lord's Prayer in *Murrary v. Curlett* (1963). (See RELIGION IN PUBLIC SCHOOLS.) In *McGowan v. Maryland* (1961), however, the Court permitted the state to impose SUNDAY CLOSING LAWS. Chief Justice Warren, for the Court, distinguished between laws with a religious purpose and laws "whose present purpose and effect" was secular, even though they were originally "motivated by religious forces." The Court invoked *McGowan* in a subsequent case, BOARD OF EDUCATION V. ALLEN (1968), which sustained a New York law providing for the loaning of textbooks from public to parochial schools.

Liberalism, as practiced by the Warren Court, produced a different institutional posture from earlier "reformist" judicial perspectives. As noted, liberalism required that the Court be both an activist governmental institution and a defender of minority rights. This meant that unlike previously "activist" Courts, such as the Courts of the late nineteenth and early twentieth century, its beneficiaries would be nonelites, and unlike previously "reformist" Courts, such as the Court of the late 1930s and 1940s, it would assume a scrutinizing rather than a passive stance toward the actions of other branches of government. Had the Warren Court retained either of these former roles, *Brown, Baker v. Carr,* and *Miranda* would likely not have been decided as they were. These decisions all offended entrenched elites and required modifications of existing governmental practices. In so deciding these cases the Warren Court was assuming that activism by the judiciary was required in order to produce liberal results. With this assumption came a mid-twentieth-century fusion of affirmative governmental action and protection for CIVIL LIBERTIES.

Maintaining a commitment to liberal theory while at the same time modifying its precepts required some analytical refinements in order to reconcile the protection of civil liberties with claims based on affirmative governmental action. In *Brown* the desires of some whites and some blacks to have a racially integrated educational experience conflicted with the desires of some whites and some blacks to limit their educational experiences to persons of their own race. The Court chose to prefer the former desire, basing its judgment on a theory of the educational process that minimized the relevance of race. That theory then became a guiding assumption for the Court's subsequent decisions in the race relations area.

Similar sets of intermediate distinctions between goals of liberal theory were made in other major cases. In the REAPPORTIONMENT cases the distinction was between REPRESENTATION based on population, a claim put forth by a disadvantaged minority, and other forms of proportional representation that had been endorsed by legislative majorities. The Court decided to prefer the former claim as more democratic and then made the one-person, one-vote principle the basis of its subsequent decisions. In the school prayer cases the distinction was between the choice of a majority to ritualize the recognition of a public deity in the public school and the choice of a minority to deny that recognition as out of place. The Court decided to prefer the latter choice as more libertarian. In the criminal procedure cases the distinction was between a majoritarian decision to protect the public against crime by advantaging law enforcement personnel in their encounters with persons suspected of committing crimes, and the claims of such persons that they were being unfairly disadvantaged. The Court chose to prefer the latter claims as being more consistent with principles of equal justice.

When the Warren Court reached the end of its tenure, liberalism clearly did not merely mean deference toward the decisions of democratic and representative bodies of government. It meant deference toward these decisions only if they promoted the goals of liberal policy: equality, fairness, protection of civil rights, support for disadvantaged persons. Under this model of liberal policymaking, the Supreme Court was more concerned with achieving enlightened results than it was with the constitutional process by which these results were reached. Liberalism and judicial activism went hand in hand.

As it became clear that the Court's activism was designed to promote a modified version of liberalism, the Court became vulnerable to public dissatisfaction with liberal policies. Such dissatisfaction emerged in the 1970s. The internal contradictions of liberalism became exposed in such areas as AFFIRMATIVE ACTION in higher education and forced busing in primary education, and the saving distinctions made by the Court in earlier cases appeared as naked policy choices whose legitimacy was debatable. If affirmative preference, based on race, for one class of applicants to an institution of higher learning results in disadvantage to other classes, equality of condition has not been achieved and equality of educational opportunity has been undermined. If some families are compelled to send their children to schools where they are racial minorities in order to achieve "racial balance" throughout the school system, the resulting "balance" may well disadvantage more people than it advantages. Equality and social justice have turned out to be more complicated concepts than mid-twentieth-century liberalism assumed.

The egalitarianism and the liberalism of the Warren Court paled in significance when compared to its activism. If contemporary America has become a "litigious society," as it is commonly portrayed, the Warren Court helped set in motion such trends. Social issues have habitually been transformed into legal questions in America, but the Warren Court seemed to welcome such a transformation, finding constitutional issues raised in contexts as diverse as reapportionment and prayers in the public schools. As the Court created new sources of constitutional protection, numerous persons sought to make themselves the beneficiaries. Sometimes the Court went out of its way to help the organizations litigating a case, as in the civil rights area. The result was that the lower courts and the Supreme Court became "activist" institutions—repositories of grievances, scrutinizers of the conduct of other branches of government, havens for the disadvantaged.

In the academic community, Warren Court activism was from the first regarded as more controversial than Warren Court egalitarianism. The reason was the prominence in academic circles of a two-pronged theory of JUDICIAL REVIEW, one prong of which stressed the necessity of grounding judicial decisions, in the area of constitutional law, in textually supportable principles of general applicability, and the other prong of which resurrected Frankfurter's conception of a limited, deferential role for the Court as a lawmaking institution. The Warren Court, according to academic critics, repeatedly violated the theory's dual standards. Decisions like *Brown v. Board, Baker v. Carr,* GRISWOLD V. CONNECTICUT (1965), a case discovering a RIGHT OF PRIVACY in the Constitution that was violated by statutes forbidding the use of BIRTH CONTROL pills, and HARPER V. VIRGINIA BOARD OF Elections (1966), a case invalidating POLL TAX requirements on voting as violating the EQUAL PROTECTION clause because such requirements conditioned VOTING RIGHTS on wealth, had not been sufficiently grounded in constitutional doctrine. There was no evidence that the Fourteenth Amendment was intended to reach segregated schools and there were no judicial decisions supporting that position. The Constitution did not single out for protection a right to vote, let alone a right to have one's vote weighed equally with the votes of others. "Privacy" was nowhere mentioned in the constitutional text. The framers of the Constitution had assumed a variety of suffrage restrictions, including ones based on wealth. In short, leading Warren Court decisions were not based on "neutral principles" of constitutional law.

Nor had the Court been mindful, critics felt, of its proper lawmaking posture in a democratic society where it was a conspicuously nondemocratic institution. In *Brown* it had ostensibly substituted its wisdom for that of Congress and several Southern states. In *Baker* it had forced legislatures to reapportion themselves even when a majority of a state's voters had signified their intention to staff one house of the legislature on grounds other than one person, one vote. In *Engel v. Vitale* it had told the public schools that they could not have government-formulated compulsory prayers, even though the vast majority of school officials and parents desired them. It had fashioned codes of criminal procedure for the police, ignoring Congress's abortive efforts in that direction. It had decided, after more than 200 years of defamation law, that the entire area needed to be reconsidered in light of the First Amendment.

A role for the Court as a deferential, principled decision maker was, however, not sacrosanct. Few Supreme Courts had assumed such a role in the past. All of the "great cases" in American constitutional history could be said to have produced activist decisions: MARBURY V. MADISON (1803), establishing the power of judicial review; MCCULLOCH V. MARYLAND (1819) and GIBBONS V. OGDEN (1824), delineating the scope of the federal commerce power; DRED SCOTT V. SANDFORD (1857), legitimizing SLAVERY IN THE TERRITORIES; the LEGAL TENDER CASES, deciding the constitutionality of legal tender notes; POLLOCK V. FARMERS LOAN AND TRUST (1895), declaring an income tax unconstitutional; LOCHNER V. NEW YORK (1905), scuttling state hours and wages legislation; UNITED STATES V. BUTLER (1936), invalidating a major portion of the New Deal's administrative structure. Activism was an ancient judicial art.

The Warren Court's activism differed from other

Courts' versions principally not because its reasoning was more specious or its grasp of power more presumptuous but because its beneficiaries were different. Previous activist decisions had largely benefited entrenched elites, whether slaveowners, entrepreneurs, "combinations of capital," or businesses that sought to avoid government regulation. The activist decisions of the Warren Court benefited blacks, disadvantaged suburban voters, atheists, criminals, pornographers, and the poor. The Warren Court's activism facilitated social change rather than preserving the status quo. The critics of the Court had forgotten that the role they espoused for the judiciary had been created in order to facilitate change and promote the interests of the disadvantaged. In the 1950s and 1960s the "democratic" institutions charged with that responsibility had become unresponsive, so the Warren Court had acted in their stead. It was ironic that the same critics who were shocked at the Court of the 1930s' resistance to the New Deal should protest against a Court that was reaching the results they had then sought.

Activism was the principal basis of the Court's controversiality; egalitarianism its dominant instinctual reaction; liberalism its guiding political philosophy. The combination of these ingredients, plus the presence of some judicial giants, gave the Warren Court a prominence and a visibility that are not likely to be surpassed for some time. But even though countless persons in the American legal profession today were shaped by Warren Court decisions, one can see the Warren Court receding into history. That Court seemed to have been led, in the final analysis, by a conception of American life that appeared vindicated by the first fifty years of twentieth-century experience. That conception held that American society was continually progressing toward a nobler and brighter and more enlightened future. As Earl Warren wrote in a passage that appears on his tombstone:

> Where there is injustice, we should correct it;
> where there is poverty, we should eliminate it;
> where there is corruption, we should stamp it out;
> where there is violence, we should punish it;
> where there is neglect, we should provide care;
> where there is war, we should restore peace;
> and wherever corrections are achieved we should add them permanently to our storehouse of treasures.

In that passage appears the Warren Court sensibility: a sensibility dedicated to the active pursuit of ideals that have seemed less tangible and achievable with the years.

G. EDWARD WHITE

Bibliography

BICKEL, ALEXANDER 1970 *The Supreme Court and the Idea of Progress.* New York: Harper & Row.

BLACK, CHARLES 1970 The Unfinished Business of the Warren Court. *University of Washington Law Review* 46:3–45.

COX, ARCHIBALD 1968 *The Warren Court.* Cambridge, Mass.: Harvard University Press.

KURLAND, PHILIP 1970 *Politics, the Constitution, and the Warren Court.* Chicago: University of Chicago Press.

LEVY, LEONARD W.,ed. 1972 *The Supreme Court under Earl Warren.* New York: Quadrangle Books.

MCCLOSKEY, ROBERT 1960 *The American Supreme Court.* Chicago: University of Chicago Press.

WECHSLER, HERBERT 1959 Toward Neutral Principles of Constitutional Law. *Harvard Law Review* 73:1–23.

WHITE, G. EDWARD 1976 *The American Judicial Tradition.* New York: Oxford University Press.

——— 1982 *Earl Warren: A Public Life.* New York: Oxford University Press.

WARTH v. SELDIN

See: *Simon v. Eastern Kentucky Welfare Rights Organization*

WASHINGTON, BUSHROD
(1762–1829)

Bushrod Washington served on the United States Supreme Court for thirty-one years, but he did not hand down many important decisions. Lacking the analytical sweep of JOHN MARSHALL and the erudition and energy of JOSEPH STORY, he invariably supported their opinions which strengthened the power of the central government and encouraged the development of the economy. In fact, he was so closely allied with Chief Justice Marshall that another Justice on that Court, WILLIAM JOHNSON of South Carolina, observed that the two "are commonly estimated as a single judge."

Washington was well connected by birth. His mother came from a prominent Virginia family and his father, John, was a particularly close brother of GEORGE WASHINGTON. He graduated from the College of William and Mary in 1778 and served in the Continental Army. After the war he studied law in Philadelphia under JAMES WILSON. Returning to Virginia in 1787, he was admitted to the bar and elected to the Virginia state ratifying convention, where he supported the adoption of the United States Constitution. Following this he practiced law in Richmond, where he developed a reputation for being diligent and extremely knowledgeable. Many young men, including HENRY CLAY, came to read law under his direction. During the 1790s he joined the Federalist Party, and in 1798 JOHN ADAMS appointed him to the Supreme Court. A short time later, as the "favorite nephew" of the former President, he became executor of Washington's will and inherited Mount Vernon and his uncle's public and private papers, which he made available to Marshall for his *Life of George Washington.*

Bushrod Washington was particularly effective and conscientious in the performance of his circuit-riding duties, especially when he presided over jury trials. His tact and sense of fair play allowed him to enforce the Sedition Act of 1798 in a number of cases without engaging in the partisan politics that made SAMUEL CHASE and WILLIAM PATERSON so controversial. His most famous circuit court decision came in the case *United States v. Bright* (1809). This was the TREASON trial of a general of the Pennsylvania state militia who had been formally authorized to resist the United States Supreme Court's decision in *United States v. Peters* (1809). Following a confrontation with a federal marshal, and after President JAMES MADISON threatened to use force, the state eventually backed down, whereupon Bright and several other officers were arrested, tried, and convicted. (Madison eventually pardoned them on humanitarian grounds.) Bushrod Washington handled the trial, which took place in Philadelphia amid a highly charged atmosphere, with great skill, maintaining both decorum and the authority of the federal government. Sentencing Bright, he declared, "A State has no constitutional power . . . to employ force to resist the execution of a decree of a federal court, though such decree is deemed to have been beyond the JURISDICTION of the Court to make. . . ."

Several other decisions rendered by Bushrod Washington are of interest. In a concurring opinion in DARTMOUTH COLLEGE V. WOODWARD (1819) he tried to reign in some of the implications of Marshall's more sweeping decision. In GREEN V. BIDDLE (1823) he handed down what proved to be an unenforceable decision invalidating various Kentucky statutes adopted to protect settlers from absentee landlords. Finally, in OGDEN V. SAUNDERS (1827), he openly broke with Marshall, abandoned his own earlier circuit court decision in *Golden v. Prince* (1814), and declared that a state BANKRUPTCY ACT that had a prospective application did not violate the CONTRACT CLAUSE.

Bushrod Washington died in Philadelphia on November 26, 1829.

RICHARD E. ELLIS

Bibliography

BLAUSTEIN, ALBERT P. and MERSKY, ROY M. 1969 Bushrod Washington. Pages 243–257 in Leon Friedman and Fred L. Israel, eds., *Justices of the Supreme Court, 1789–1969.* New York: Chelsea House.

WASHINGTON, GEORGE (1732–1799)

The people of the United States are indebted to no man so much as they are to George Washington. And the debt extends to his role in the creation of the American Constitution. As the general who led the revolutionary armies to victory and so vindicated American independence, as one of the few men who had traveled in virtually every part of the United States, including the vast Western wilderness, and as a leading citizen of northern Virginia, Washington was actively involved in the movement of affairs that culminated in the CONSTITUTIONAL CONVENTION OF 1787. When the Convention met, he became its presiding officer. During the controversy over the RATIFICATION OF THE CONSTITUTION, the opposition to a strong executive was overcome by the universal assumption that Washington would be the first man to hold the office. When the Constitution was ratified and Washington did become President, he self-consciously seized the opportunity to set precedents for the conduct of governmental affairs. And when, after two terms in that office he handed over the reins of executive authority, he did so in perfect constitutional order and retired to his country seat.

The third son of a prosperous planter, Washington learned the surveying trade in his teens, and as a surveyor he traveled widely in the area west of the Appalachian Mountains. At twenty-one he was appointed to major in the Virginia militia, and when the French and Indian War broke out in 1754 he was promoted to lieutenant colonel and placed second in command of a regiment dispatched to the Ohio Valley. On his colonel's death, Washington took command and managed, without supplies, funds, competent subordinates, or trained noncommissioned officers and troops, to achieve initial military success. He was subsequently made an aide to the British commanding general, and in 1755, at the age of twenty-three, was promoted to colonel and made commander-in-chief of all Virginia forces, the highest ranking American military officer.

In 1759, Washington married Martha Custis, the wealthiest widow in Virginia, and, adding her holdings to his own, achieved a financial independence that would subsequently permit him to engage in a career of uncompensated public service. For a decade and a half he lived the life of a gentleman planter, with the attendant civic duties of serving as a justice of the peace and as a member of the House of Burgesses.

In 1769 Washington introduced in the House of Burgesses a series of resolutions (drafted by his friend and neighbor GEORGE MASON) denying the right of the British Parliament to tax the colonies and initiating the first ASSOCIATION. After passage of the Intolerable Acts in 1774, Washington introduced in the house the Fairfax County Resolves closing Virginia's trade with Britain. He was also elected a delegate to the FIRST CONTINENTAL CONGRESS, which he attended in military uniform.

The Revolutionary War began in Spring 1775 when the Massachusetts militia forcibly resisted the attempt of British troops to seize its weapons and supplies. In June, on the motion of JOHN ADAMS, the CONTINENTAL CONGRESS adopted the Massachusetts militia as the Continental Army and appointed Washington commander-in-chief. The war lasted eight and one-half years, and Washington was the American commander for the whole period. The war was not an unrelieved military success on the American side, but the commander did learn to deal with Congress and with foreign allies, and he became, in his own person, the symbol of American national unity. Just before resigning his commission in 1783, he resisted the suggestion that the army, which had been shamefully left unpaid, should overthrow the Congress and establish its own government.

After his return to private life in 1784, Washington devoted his time to management of his property in Virginia and in the Ohio Valley. He became president of the Potomac Company, which had as its object the development of the Potomac River as a navigable waterway. And he engaged in a wide correspondence, always urging, in letters dealing with politics, the strengthening of the Union and an increase in the powers of Congress under the ARTICLES OF CONFEDERATION. In March 1785 he was host to a conference of commissioners from Maryland and Virginia that was supposed to discuss the navigation of the Potomac River but that, in the event, called for a broader conference—the Annapolis Convention—that ultimately led to the Constitutional Convention of 1787.

Pleading pressures of financial reverses and ill health, Washington was reluctant to accept election as a delegate to the Convention, but he did so at the repeated urging of JAMES MADISON and EDMUND RANDOLPH. At Philadelphia he was unanimously elected president of the Convention, although, as most of the debates were conducted in a committee of the whole house, he did not actually have to preside on most occasions. Although Washington did not take an active part in the recorded debates of the Convention, his attendance and his signature on the document as president of the Convention were offered as a guarantee of the result.

The first ELECTORAL COLLEGE under the new Constitution was elected in January 1789, and every member cast one of his two votes for George Washington. Washington learned of the result on April 14. His journey from Virginia to New York took a week, and involved parades and ceremonies in every town he passed through along the way; the affection and gratitude of the population were genuine, and Washington's task was to retain them while directing the executive affairs of the government.

Following his inauguration on April 30, Washington immediately began the business of running the executive branch of government. Everything he did set a precedent, not only for America but for the world, because his position as a republican chief executive was unique. Attention had to be given to such matters as the form of address and the conduct of social events so as to insure both the dignity of the federal executive and the republicanism of the country.

Every act in the process of governing had to be done a first time: the performance of each executive task, however routine, set the pattern for the permanent conduct of the presidency. The first bill to pass the new Congress was presented for Washington's signature on June 1: he affixed his signature, and the first statute under the Constitution became law. The first occasion for negotiating a treaty arose in August; in strict compliance with Article II, section 2, Washington appeared in person before the Senate to ask for ADVICE AND CONSENT and, when the Senate referred the matter to committee he stalked out. Since that day, Presidents have submitted treaties to the Senate after they are negotiated, but no President has asked for the Senate's advice before negotiations begin.

Statutes creating the three executive departments of state, war, and treasury were enacted during the summer of 1789. Washington appointed his fellow Virginian THOMAS JEFFERSON to be the first secretary of state, his wartime chief of artillery, General Henry Knox, to be secretary of war, and his former aide, Colonel ALEXANDER HAMILTON, to be secretary of the treasury. Although the Constitution provides only that the President may require written opinions from the principal executive officers, and that only as to their peculiar duties, Washington began the practice of meeting regularly with the three secretaries and the attorney general, Edmund Randolph, to discuss affairs of state generally. From this practice has come the notion of the American CABINET, as well as the accepted opinion that the heads of the executive departments are responsible primarily to the President, and not to Congress, for their official conduct.

But Washington had to appoint not only his cabinet officers but also every official in the executive branch down to customs inspectors and lighthouse keepers. Although the Constitution permitted Congress to vest inferior appointments in the chiefs of the departments, Congress did not immediately do so. Washington was besieged with applications from would-be federal bureaucrats. Indeed, had Congress desired to hamstring the President it might have been enough just to leave all federal appointments in his hands.

Besides the cabinet officers, the most important appointees were the Justices of the Supreme Court. The JUDICIARY ACT OF 1789 provided for six Justices. Washington nominated his friend JOHN JAY, who had been secretary of foreign affairs in the old government, to be Chief Justice. The other five nominees were drawn from different states, both to facilitate their performance of circuit duty and to make the Court representative of the whole country. Among them were three men who had been Washington's fellow delegates to the Constitutional Convention, JAMES WILSON, JOHN RUTLEDGE, and JOHN BLAIR. (See SUPREME COURT, 1789–1801.)

Once the machinery was in place, the issue became what policy the new government would follow. Washington, who had relied on Congressman James Madison for the machinery, turned to Secretary of the Treasury Hamilton for the policy. Hamilton's program was set forth in a series of reports submitted over the next two years. The program called for an alliance between the federal government and the wealthier citizens to promote the unity and prosperity of the nation. The Hamiltonian program provoked a controversy over the proper interpretation of constitutional provisions conferring power on the national government. Hamilton argued for BROAD CONSTRUCTION; Jefferson, for STRICT CONSTRUCTION. The arguments were reduced to writing at Washington's request to help him to decide whether to sign or to veto the BANK OF THE UNITED STATES ACT (1790). Washington, convinced by Hamilton's doctrine of IMPLIED POWERS, signed the act.

The French Revolution of 1789 provoked a further division between Washington's chief advisers. Most Americans initially sympathized with the French overthrow of the monarchy and the attempt to establish a republican form of government. But as the French Revolution became more extreme and expansionary, and as the conservative states of Europe mobilized to resist it, opinion became divided. Jefferson and his supporters continued to sympathize with the revolution, while Hamilton and his allies were inclined to side with the embattled British.

By 1793, the Wars of the French Revolution had become global, and American interests, particularly American shipping, were suffering the effects. Washington, with the assent of his whole cabinet, issued a PROCLAMATION OF NEUTRALITY in April 1793, warning American citizens to refrain from becoming involved on either side. Hamilton published a series of newspaper articles asserting, among other things, that the proclamation had been necessary because of the active support of France on the part of the Jeffersonians. Madison, replying in his own newspaper essays, claimed that Washington, by his unilateral issuance of the proclamation, had usurped the power of Congress to declare war and of the Senate to share in treaty making.

The first party lines in American politics under the Constitution had been drawn, and drawn on constitutional grounds. Jefferson resigned from the cabinet at the end of 1793. Thereafter, Washington's was a "Federalist" administration, with Jefferson, Madison, and the "Republicans" in opposition.

The WHISKEY REBELLION of 1794 presented the first organized resistance to the national government. Western Pennsylvania farmers, upset by an excise on whiskey that seemed unduly to burden their section of the country, threatened to use force to impede collection of the tax. Washington called 15,000 militiamen into federal service and himself set out to command the expedition. The rebellion was ultimately put down without bloodshed, and when two rebel leaders were subsequently convicted of TREASON, Washington pardoned them.

The administration's foreign policy also led to controversy at about the same time. Chief Justice Jay had been sent to Britain to negotiate a settlement of certain continuing difficulties in relations between the two countries. JAY'S TREATY contained many provisions favorable to British interests, and apparently detrimental to the economic interests of some regions of the United States, especially the South and West. The treaty also provoked constitutional controversy about the operation of the TREATY POWER. For example, would the Senate be required to advise and consent to the treaty as it was presented, or could the Senate amend a treaty? And could the President and the Senate enter into treaty commitments that would involve the expenditure of funds without the concurrence of the House of Representatives whose agreement was required for the appropriation of the funds? The treaty was approved in a partisan vote, but with a reservation suspending operation of certain objectionable provisions.

Washington chose not to seek a third term as President in the election of 1796. He was dismayed and distressed by the bitterness of the partisan rivalries that had grown up among men who had once been close colleagues, and he himself attempted always to remain above the partisan fray. WASHINGTON'S FAREWELL ADDRESS to his countrymen contained his strictures against the spirit of party, as well as his advice on foreign affairs and on public morality.

Even after his retirement to his estate at Mount Vernon, Washington could not escape either public service or partisan intrigue. When war with France seemed inevitable in 1798, President JOHN ADAMS nominated and the Senate unanimously confirmed Washington as COMMANDER-IN-CHIEF. There immediately followed a scramble among Federalist military men for the subordinate general officer positions. Washington supported Hamilton, who ultimately became second in command. Under the circumstances it is not surprising that Washington thought of the Republicans, who had been pro-French, as dangerous men and that he supported the ALIEN AND SEDITION ACTS.

Nevertheless, when Washington died in 1799 he was eulogized by Federalists and Republicans alike. More than any other individual, Washington was responsible for America's being independent, adopting the Constitution, and having a functioning republican government.

DENNIS J. MAHONEY

Bibliography

COOKE, JACOB E. 1987 Organizing the National Government. In Levy, Leonard W., and Mahoney, Dennis J., eds., *The Constitution: A History of Its Framing and Ratification.* New York: Macmillan.

FLEXNER, JAMES THOMAS 1965–1972 *George Washington.* 4 Vols. Boston: Little, Brown.

FREEMAN, DOUGLAS SOUTHALL 1948–1957 *George Washington.* 7 Vols. New York: Scribner's.

MARSHALL, JOHN (1804–1807)1925 *The Life of George Washington.* 5 Vols. New York: Wm. H. Wise & Co.

MATTESON, DAVID M. 1970 *The Organization of the Government under the Constitution.* New York: Da Capo Press.

WASHINGTON v. DAVIS
426 U.S. 229 (1976)

This landmark decision concerns the relevance of a decision maker's motives in EQUAL PROTECTION cases. Black candidates for the Washington, D.C., police force alleged that the District's selection criteria had an adverse discriminatory effect upon the employment prospects of minorities and that the effect violated the FOURTEENTH AMENDMENT's equal protection clause and ANTIDISCRIMINATION LEGISLATION. In an opinion by Justice BYRON R. WHITE, the Supreme Court held that discriminatory effects, standing alone, are insufficient to establish an equal protection violation. Proof of purposeful discrimination is necessary. The Court also rejected the candidates' statutory claim. In an opinion that did not address the constitutional question, Justice WILLIAM J. BRENNAN, joined by Justice THURGOOD MARSHALL, dissented from the Court's disposition of the statutory issue. In a concurring opinion, Justice JOHN PAUL STEVENS discussed the relationship between discriminatory effects and proof of discriminatory intent and articulated his reasons for rejecting the statutory claim.

In settling a long-standing controversy over whether a decision maker's motives may constitute the basis for an equal protection claim, the Court climbed two interesting doctrinal hills. Prior to *Davis,* cases such as *Whitcomb v. Chavis* (1971) and *White v. Regester* (1973) expressly had suggested that unintentional disproportionate effects on a minority may constitute the basis for an equal protection claim. Justice White's opinion ignores these precedents but warns against the broad consequences of such a HOLDING. Such a rule "would raise serious questions about, and perhaps invalidate, a whole range of tax, welfare, public service, regulatory, and licensing statutes that may be more burdensome to the poor and to the average black than to the more affluent white."

In addition, contrary to *Davis*'s holding, a line of opinions dating back to FLETCHER V. PECK (1810) and reaffirmed in UNITED STATES V. O'BRIEN (1968) and PALMER V. THOMPSON (1971), clearly had stated that legislators' motives may not form the basis of constitutional attacks on statutes. Without alluding to all of the relevant precedents, the Court reinterpreted *Palmer* and suggested that some of its language had constituted mere OBITER DICTA.

As a practical matter, *Davis*, when combined with subsequent similar cases such as ARLINGTON HEIGHTS V. METROPOLITAN HOUSING DEVELOPMENT CORP. (1977) and MOBILE V. BOLDEN (1980), curtailed litigants' ability to bring successful equal protection claims. Proof of intentional discrimination is difficult to obtain and judges are reluctant to deem officials intentional wrongdoers. Indeed, it was six years after *Davis* before the Court, in *Rogers v. Lodge* (1982), sustained a finding of intentional discrimination in a racial equal protection case.

THEODORE EISENBERG

WASHINGTON v. TEXAS

See: Compulsory Process; Evidence

WASHINGTON'S FAREWELL ADDRESS
(September 17, 1796)

When President GEORGE WASHINGTON decided, in the summer of 1796, not to seek a third term, he published an address to the American people embodying his advice on how to insure the survival of the new constitutional order. The first draft was prepared by Washington himself; the final version was drafted under Washington's direction by ALEXANDER HAMILTON, incorporating suggestions from JAMES MADISON and JOHN JAY.

The first, and longest, section of the address comprises an encomium of the federal union and a warning against the dangers of factionalism, and especially of sectionalism. Washington urged that Americans regard the Union as "the support of your tranquility at home, your peace abroad, of your safety, of your prosperity, of that very liberty which you so highly prize." The central section of the address commends religion as a support for free government. Anything that weakened religious belief, he argued, would corrupt public morals, undermine the efficacy of oaths, and threaten the national capacity for self-government. The final section of the address contains Washington's advice on FOREIGN AFFAIRS and defense. Washington opposed permanent alliances and standing armies as incompatible with constitutional democracy.

Advice in the address concerning specific constitutional questions includes Washington's deprecation of the "spirit of encroachment" that would subvert the SEPARATION OF POWERS and his admonition against hasty adoption of constitutional amendments.

DENNIS J. MAHONEY

Bibliography

EIDELBERG, PAUL 1974 *A Discourse on Statesmanship: The Design and Transformation of the American Polity.* Chicago: University of Illinois Press.

WATERGATE AND THE CONSTITUTION

The Watergate scandal, starting with an illegal break-in at Democratic National Committee headquarters in June 1972 and ending with President GERALD R. FORD pardoning RICHARD M. NIXON in September 1974, produced one of the most significant constitutional crises in modern times. It raised a number of unsettling issues central to the constitutional structure of SEPARATION OF POWERS.

The two major constitutional issues Watergate brought into focus were EXECUTIVE PRIVILEGE and the scope of the IMPEACHMENT power. In September 1972 a GRAND JURY indicted the Watergate burglars but the Justice Department closed the investigation despite evidence of a wider conspiracy. Following the November election, the Watergate burglary trial began. In it defendants claimed they had been pressured to remain silent and plead guilty; that perjury was committed; and that "others" were involved. Such allegations led to the creation of a Senate Watergate Committee, headed by SAM ERVIN, which began taking testimony, revealing a White House program of political espionage that included Watergate. Witnesses suggested that the President was participating in a coverup and that the President had made tape recordings of conversations in his office. The Ervin Committee attempted to subpoena such tapes, but the President refused to surrender them, claiming executive privilege. The committee then went to the courts, which in two cases (*Nixon v. Sirica,* 1973, and *Senate Select Committee on Presidential Campaign Activities v. Nixon,* 1974, attempted to define the line between a committee's power to compel testimony in order to perform its functions and the need for privacy in presidential communications. A third case, UNITED STATES V. NIXON (1974), arose out of a criminal prosecution of the President's aides. Both the prosecutor and the defense sought to subpoena the tapes, and the President again resisted. Chief Justice WARREN E. BURGER, for a unanimous Supreme Court, conceded a "presumptive privilege" for executive communications, but ruled that respect of the integrity of the judicial process required the courts to weigh any such claim against the importance of assuring the production in court of relevant evidence and ultimately of protecting the system of criminal justice. The Court thus ordered certain tapes produced. Their disclosures, which came at the height of the House of Representatives' impeachment process, demonstrated the President's active complicity in the coverup conspiracy from the first moment. This led Nixon to resign to avoid impeachment for "high crimes and misdemeanors."

The impeachment process was fraught with constitutional difficulties. Nixon's firing of a Senate-approved special prosecutor, given sweeping powers to investigate the Watergate scandal, had produced the initial demands for his impeachment. In October the House Judiciary Committee launched an impeachment inquiry. Questions promptly arose as to what constituted an impeachable offense, and what "other high crimes and misdemeanors" might include. Must these be criminal in nature and intent, or might they be quasi-political, involving gross breach of public trust? Was maladministration impeachable, or must a statutory offense or a serious crime be demonstrated? The President's attorneys argued the latter. The committee staff indicated a President might be removed for "substantial misconduct," not necessarily of specific criminal nature. This controversy was mooted by the revelations of the disputed tapes and by the resignation, but not before the House committee recommended three ARTICLES OF IMPEACHMENT to the House at large. Rejecting two articles dealing with income tax violations and the secret bombing of Cambodia, which raised the question of the extent of presidential emergency power in FOREIGN AFFAIRS, the Committee contended that "Richard M. Nixon warrants impeachment and trial and removal from office" for other charges. These were: that he prevented, obstructed, and impeded the administration of justice; that he repeatedly engaged in conduct violating the constitutional rights of citizens, impairing the due and proper administration of justice and the conduct of lawful inquiries, or contravening the laws governing agencies of the executive branch and the purposes of these agencies; and that he failed without lawful cause or excuse to produce papers and things as directed by duly authorized subpoenas issued by the Committee on the Judiciary of the House of Representatives. Included as substantiating detail were fourteen examples of interfering or endeavoring to interfere with conduct of investigations by the Department of Justice of the United States, the Federal Bureau of Investigation, the Watergate special prosecutor, and congressional committees; endeavoring to misuse the Central Intelligence Agency; the electronic surveillance of private citizens; the break-in of a psychiatrist's office; and the unlawful campaign financing practices of the Committee to Re-elect the President.

An unresolved constitutional issue arose in September 1974: whether a subsequent President can issue a pardon in the absence of either a conviction or an INDICTMENT. A final question will trouble historians for years: did the Constitution work in Watergate, or did the crisis demonstrate fundamental failures in the governmental system?

PAUL L. MURPHY

Bibliography

KURLAND, PHILIP 1978 *Watergate and the Constitution.* Chicago: University of Chicago Press.

MILLER, ARTHUR S. 1979 *Social Change and Fundamental Law.* Westport, Conn.: Greenwood Press.

MURPHY, PAUL L. 1979 Misgovernment by Judiciary? Watergate and the Constitution. *Harvard Civil Rights/Civil Liberties Law Review* 14:783–799.

WATER POLLUTION CONTROL ACT

See: Environmental Regulation

WATER POWER ACT
41 Stat. 1063 (1920)

The failure to capitalize on the vast water power resources of the country led increasingly, in the early twentieth century, to efforts to develop and regulate unused power on public lands and navigable rivers. After a number of failed attempts at national legislation, Congress finally passed the Water Power Act in 1920.

The act established a Federal Power Commission

(FPC), to be composed of the secretaries of war, agriculture, and interior, with authority to approve water power projects "for the development and improvement of navigation, and for the development, transmission, and utilization of power" on any navigable river or public lands. The act empowered the FPC to license projects for up to fifty years; it also directed preferential treatment for state or municipal projects. The rates charged for the use of water were to include only FPC expenses; moreover, the act required licensees to charge "reasonable, nondiscriminatory and just" rates and prohibited combinations or other agreements to limit output or fix prices. The act stipulated that rate-fixing and regulation be administered according to the procedures outlined in the INTERSTATE COMMERCE ACT.

The Supreme Court approved extensive federal controls in UNITED STATES V. APPALACHIAN ELECTRIC POWER COMPANY (1940).

DAVID GORDON

WATER QUALITY IMPROVEMENT ACT

See: Environmental Regulation

WATKINS v. UNITED STATES 354 U.S. 178 (1957) *SWEEZY v. NEW HAMPSHIRE* 354 U.S. 234 (1957)

Watkins, a labor leader called to testify before the House Committee on Un-American Activities, had been told by the union president that he would lose his position if he claimed his RIGHT AGAINST SELF-INCRIMINATION. He thus claimed a FIRST AMENDMENT privilege when he declined to answer the committee's questions about the membership of other people in the Communist party. He also objected that these questions were beyond the scope of the committee's activities. For his refusal to answer, Watkins was convicted of contempt of Congress. The Supreme Court reversed his conviction, 8–1.

Writing for the Court, Chief Justice EARL WARREN rested decision on a narrow point: Watkins had been denied PROCEDURAL DUE PROCESS, for he had not been given a sufficient explanation of the subject of inquiry, and thus could not know whether the committee's questions were "pertinent to the questions under inquiry," as the contempt statute specified. Warren's opinion, however, strongly suggested that the Court would be prepared to confront the whole issue of LEGISLATIVE INVESTIGATIONS into political association. He remarked on the use of such investigations to subject people to public stigma, and the absence in such proceedings of effective protection of procedural fairness. "We have no doubt that there is no congressional power to expose for the sake of exposure," Warren wrote. "Who can define the meaning of 'un-American'?" Justice TOM C. CLARK, the sole dissenter, appeared to object as much to these broad OBITER DICTA as to the actual decision. He complained of the Court's "mischievous curbing of the informing function of Congress."

In *Sweezy,* a COMPANION CASE to *Watkins,* the Court held, 6–2, that a state legislative investigation could not constitutionally compel Sweezy to answer questions about the Progressive party and about a lecture he had given at the University of New Hampshire. Chief Justice Warren wrote a PLURALITY OPINION for four Justices, concluding that Sweezy's contempt conviction violated procedural due process because the state legislature had not clearly authorized the attorney general, who conducted the investigation, to inquire into those subjects. Justice FELIX FRANKFURTER, joined by Justice JOHN MARSHALL HARLAN, concurred, arguing that the state had unconstitutionally invaded Sweezy's FOURTEENTH AMENDMENT liberty—here, his "political autonomy," a plain reference to the First Amendment. Justice Frankfurter used a (for him) familiar BALANCING TEST, but articulated a COMPELLING STATE INTEREST standard for cases of invasions of political privacy. The Frankfurter opinion is notable for its early articulation of the constitutional dimension of ACADEMIC FREEDOM. It also led, the following year, to the Court's explicit recognition of the FREEDOM OF ASSOCIATION in NAACP V. ALABAMA (1958). Justice Clark again dissented, now joined by Justice HAROLD H. BURTON.

A number of members of Congress reacted angrily to these opinions and others decided the same year, such as YATES V. UNITED STATES (1957) and *Jencks v. United States* (1957). (See JENCKS ACT.) Bills were proposed in Congress to limit the Supreme Court's jurisdiction over cases involving controls of subversive activities. In the event, not much "curbing" was done, and in retrospect *Watkins* and *Sweezy* appeared to be no more than trial balloons. Two years later, in BARENBLATT V. UNITED STATES (1959), a majority of the Court backed away from the expected confrontation with Congress.

KENNETH L. KARST

WAYNE, JAMES M.
(1790?–1867)

After service as an elected official and judge in Georgia and as a Jacksonian Democrat in Congress, James Moore Wayne served thirty-two years as an Associate Justice of the United States Supreme Court. Despite this lengthy tenure he produced no significant opinions, though he consistently strove to protect national authority, corporations, and slavery. During the Civil War, his nationalist outlook induced him to remain on the Court as a Unionist.

Wayne, son of a well-to-do Savannah factor and rice planter, was educated at the College of New Jersey (Princeton), read law in New Haven and in his native Savannah, and was admitted to the Georgia bar in 1811. He was a member of the Georgia House of Representatives from 1815 to 1817, mayor of Savannah from 1817 to 1819, and successively judge of a court of common pleas and of the Superior Court. He later served in two state CONSTITUTIONAL CONVENTIONS, the second time as president. In 1829, Wayne was elected to the United States House of Representatives, where he prominently supported ANDREW JACKSON. He promoted Indian removal from his native state, backed Jackson's Bank policies, and stood by the President during the NULLIFICATION Crisis in South Carolina. He was the only member of the Georgia delegation to support the FORCE BILL. In his last term, he became chairman of the Foreign Relations Committee.

Jackson nominated Wayne to take the seat of Justice WILLIAM JOHNSON of South Carolina, and he was confirmed in 1835. Justice BENJAMIN R. CURTIS later called Wayne one of the "most high-toned Federalists on the bench," referring to Wayne's tenacious nationalism. This outlook was most apparent in COMMERCE CLAUSE cases. In the PASSENGER CASES (1849), Wayne was one of a majority that held unconstitutional state statutes regulating the ingress of ship passengers on the ground that insofar as such laws "practically operated as regulations of commerce, or as restraints upon navigation," they were unconstitutional. The power to regulate foreign and INTERSTATE COMMERCE was "exclusively vested in congress." Unlike his fellow Southerner, Chief Justice ROGER B. TANEY, he was not troubled by the implications of this position for the states' control of slavery. Wayne joined in Justice JOHN MCLEAN's nationalist dissent in COOLEY V. BOARD OF WARDENS (1851), arguing that Congress's control of interstate and FOREIGN COMMERCE was exclusive of state power.

The same nationalist spirit produced other opinions upholding federal authority. In *Dobbins v. Erie County* (1842) Wayne struck down a local tax on a federal officer. He was an enthusiastic proponent of federal admiralty jurisdiction, and in *Waring v. Clarke* (1847) he extended that jurisdiction to tidal waters of the Mississippi River well above New Orleans. In *Louisville, Cincinnati, and Charleston Railroad Co. v. Letson* (1844) Wayne rejected a rule, originally fashioned by Chief Justice JOHN MARSHALL, that restricted the access of corporations to federal courts by requiring that for purposes of DIVERSITY JURISDICTION, all their shareholders be citizens of a state different from all parties on the other side. Wayne instead adopted the rule that a corporation's CITIZENSHIP for diversity purposes is derived from the state where it was chartered and where its officers conducted business.

Wayne was sympathetic to corporate investors, as his CONTRACT CLAUSE opinions reveal. He dissented without opinion in WEST RIVER BRIDGE V. DIX (1848), in which the Court permitted a state to use its EMINENT DOMAIN powers to destroy a corporate charter. In the Ohio Bank Tax cases, Wayne consistently voted to strike down state attempts to modify tax exemptions claimed by banks. One of these cases, DODGE V. WOOLSEY (1856), produced what was probably Wayne's most memorable opinion. Condemning the effort of Ohio Democrats to destroy a tax exemption by an amendment to the state constitution, Wayne sermonized: "moral obligations never die. If broken by states and nations, though the terms of reproach are not the same with which we are accustomed to designate the faithlessness of individuals, the violation of justice is not the less."

Wayne was himself a slaveholder and no less dedicated to his section than other southern jurists such as Taney and PETER DANIEL. He considered slavery a vital component of southern society, beyond control of the federal government except for purposes of protection. But, unlike Taney, Wayne remained coolly assured about the constitutional security of slavery, and he was not blinded by the state-sovereignty dogmatism that warped his Chief's opinions in slavery cases. The Constitution itself, Wayne believed, incorporated express protections for slavery's security. In his concurrence in PRIGG V. PENNSYLVANIA (1842) Wayne went along with JOSEPH STORY's assertion that states need not support enforcement of the federal Fugitive Slave Act, but only on the ground that to admit any state role at all would be to invite Northern states to interfere with the capture and rendition of fugitives.

Wayne played a mischievous role in DRED SCOTT v. SANDFORD (1857) though his brief concurring opinion merely endorsed entirely Taney's opinion. Wayne first urged that the Chief Justice write the opinion for the Court's majority rather than Justice SAMUEL NELSON, whose opinion would evade the larger issues in the case by a narrow jurisdictional ruling, and he formally moved that the Court address itself to all issues, not just the jurisdictional ones. Scholars have suggested that Taney's opinion incorporated portions of a draft opinion that Wayne did not submit. Yet Wayne was no fanatic on the subject of slavery. On circuit, he delivered a vigorous jury charge in the trial of officers of the notorious slave ship *Wanderer*, upholding the power of the federal government to hang slavers.

The Civil War forced a severe test of Wayne's conflicting loyalties. After SECESSION, he supported his son's decision to resign his commission in the United States Army and accept appointment as Georgia's adjutant general, but Wayne elected to remain on the federal bench. Georgia retaliated by confiscating his property and declaring him an enemy alien. In 1861, Wayne denied a HABEAS CORPUS petition from a soldier who claimed that ABRAHAM LINCOLN's call for troops was illegal. In conformity with that position, Wayne joined the five-member majority in the PRIZE CASES (1863), upholding the legality of Lincoln's action in imposing a blockade around the seceding states. He wrote for the Court in EX PARTE VALLANDIGHAM (1864), refusing to review the conviction of an Ohio Copperhead congressman by a military commission. In EX PARTE MILLIGAN (1866), where the majority held that Congress could not authorize military commissions for areas outside the theater of war, Wayne joined the four-man minority who argued for congressional discretion in using military commissions. But there are indications that Wayne's Unionist views would not be extrapolated to accept all aspects of Republican Reconstruction. He joined the majority in the TEST OATH CASES (1867), holding state and federal proscriptive oaths unconstitutional. He refused to hold CIRCUIT COURTS in his circuit in areas under military occupation. His death on July 5, 1867, ended his grief at the devastation that secession, war, and Reconstruction had brought to his beloved state.

WILLIAM M. WIECEK

Bibliography

GATELL, FRANK O. 1969 James M. Wayne. In Leon Friedman and Fred L. Israel eds., *The Justices of the United States Supreme Court 1789–1969: Their Lives and Major Opinions.* New York: Chelsea House Publishers.

LAWRENCE, ALEXANDER A. 1943 *James Moore Wayne: Southern Unionist.* Chapel Hill: University of North Carolina Press.

WAYTE v. UNITED STATES
471 U.S. (1985)

After a presidential proclamation directing young men to register for a possible draft, David Wayte did not register, but wrote letters to government officials stating that he did not intend to do so. These letters went into a Selective Service file of men who had given similar notices or who had been reported by others for failing to register. The government adopted a policy of "passive enforcement" of registration: it would prosecute only men named in this file. Government officials wrote letters warning the men to register or face prosecution, and Federal Bureau of Investigation agents urged Wayte in person to register during a grace period. He refused and was indicted for failure to register. The federal district court dismissed Wayte's indictment, holding that the government had not rebutted his preliminary showing of selective prosecution. The court of appeals reversed, holding that Wayte had not shown that the government had prosecuted him because of his protest. The Supreme Court affirmed, 7–2.

Justice LEWIS F. POWELL wrote the OPINION OF THE COURT. Claims of selective prosecution, he said, must be judged under ordinary EQUAL PROTECTION standards, which, as the Court held in WASHINGTON v. DAVIS (1976), require a showing of intentional discrimination. Here, the government's awareness that "passive enforcement" would fall disproportionately on protesters was an insufficient showing of intent to punish protest. Given the government's policy of urging compliance after receiving notice of failure to register, Wayte was not prosecuted for protesting, but for persisting in refusing registration.

Wayte's FIRST AMENDMENT challenge also focused on the enforcement system's disparate impact on protesters. Applying the formula of UNITED STATES v. O'BRIEN (1968), Justice Powell concluded that "passive enforcement" passed the test. The government interest in national security was important, and unrelated to the suppression of expression; and the enforcement system burdened speech no more than was necessary to secure registration.

Justice THURGOOD MARSHALL dissented, joined by Justice WILLIAM J. BRENNAN, arguing that Wayte had been denied effective opportunity for DISCOVERY of information concerning the motivations of high government officials for prosecuting him. Thus, he could not fully support his claim that the prosecution was designed to punish his protest. The majority dismissed this argument, saying—contrary to the dissenters' view—that Wayte had not presented the issue to the Supreme Court.

KENNETH L. KARST

WEALTH DISCRIMINATION

Wealth discrimination—the state's allocation of resources on the basis of ability to pay—has received the attention of the courts only recently. Sensitivity to the plight of the poor was an outgrowth of the CIVIL RIGHTS movement of the 1960s. Thus, the first constitutional issue raised by EQUAL PROTECTION claims of the poor was whether poverty-based discrimination is analogous to RACIAL DISCRIMINATION for purposes of the applicable STANDARD OF REVIEW.

Advocates of this analogy stress the poor's lack of political power and the public's antipathy to the poor and to programs, such as welfare, enacted to ameliorate poverty. They argue that the Supreme Court should give less deference to legislative judgments when reviewing poverty discrimination claims than it does when reviewing ECONOMIC REGULATIONS challenged by those able to pursue nonjudicial means of redress. However, at no time during the more than quarter of a century since the Court's first decision in this area, GRIFFIN V. ILLINOIS (1956), has a majority of the Court ever embraced the analogy to race for purposes of equal protection review.

The *Griffin* decision held unconstitutional a state's refusal to provide an INDIGENT convicted criminal defendant with a free transcript necessary to obtain meaningful appellate review. In so holding, *Griffin* enunciated a potentially expansive principle of "equal justice": "[A] state can no more discriminate on account of poverty than on account of religion, race, or color. . . . There can be no equal justice when the kind of trial [or APPEAL] a man gets depends on the amount of money he has."

Since *Griffin,* the Supreme Court has struck down poverty-based discrimination in only a few other cases, most notably DOUGLAS V. CALIFORNIA (1963) and BODDIE V. CONNECTICUT (1971). *Douglas* held unconstitutional a state's refusal to appoint counsel for an indigent seeking appellate review of a criminal conviction; and *Boddie* held unconstitutional a state's refusal to waive court access fees which deprived an indigent plaintiff of access to the only available forum for obtaining a divorce.

In the vast majority of poverty-based discrimination cases, however, the Supreme Court has treated the poor's claims, whether they involve access to the judicial process itself, equal educational opportunity, or the very means of survival, the same as any other challenged "social and economic" regulation. Thus, the Court has applied the RATIONAL BASIS standard of review to uphold a $50 bankruptcy filing fee against a debtor too poor to pay it; a state financing system that allocated educational resources according to the tax bases of school districts; and an allocation of WELFARE BENEFITS that discriminated on the basis of family size. (See *United States v. Kras,* 1973; SAN ANTONIO INDEPENDENT SCHOOL DISTRICT V. RODRIGUEZ, 1973; DANDRIDGE V. WILLIAMS, 1971.)

Several reasons may underlie the Court's refusal actively to scrutinize legislation adversely affecting the poor. If the Court holds a payment requirement unconstitutional as applied to the poor, someone must decide who is poor enough to qualify for this affirmative relief. Moreover, such a holding may require the legislative branch to reallocate its budget to provide the funds necessary to pay for what the poor cannot afford, something which the courts are always reluctant to do, especially in times of economic recession.

Another reason for judicial restraint lies in the need for line-drawing. If not all poverty-based inequalities or deprivations are unconstitutional—as surely they are not in a market economy—then the Court must delineate those interests that are sufficiently "vital" or "fundamental" to justify stricter judicial scrutiny when the state allocates such interests through a pricing system that deprives poor people from access to them. Obvious candidates include basic necessities such as food, housing, and other means of subsistence. Beginning with its 1971 decision in *Dandridge,* however, the Supreme Court consistently has refused to treat any such interests as entitled to a heightened equal protection standard of review. Moreover, in MAHER V. ROE (1977) the Court carried this refusal to apply a meaningful equal protection standard to any discriminatory "social and economic" legislation to the extreme of validating a provision prohibiting Medicaid funding of abortion although other, including pregnancy-related medical care costs, were funded and the choice to seek an abortion rather than bear a child had been held to be constitutionally protected. Moreover, *Maher* upheld this discrimination even though, unlike the discrimination upheld in all similar prior cases, it cost rather than saved taxpayer dollars. (See HARRIS V. MCRAE, 1980.)

The Court's refusal since 1971 to treat "vital interests" of the poor as comparable to constitutionally guaranteed rights is one matter. In *Maher,* however, the Court validated discrimination only among the poor and solely on the basis of the poor's attempt to exercise a constitutionally guaranteed right of choice otherwise available to everyone. The recent jurisprudence of wealth discrimination legitimates and reinforces a dual system of constitutional rights, leaving the poor—who disproportionately are composed of women, children, the aged, and racial minorities—with paper rights beyond their financial reach.

BARBARA BRUDNO

Bibliography

BINION, GAYLE 1982 The Disadvantaged Before the Burger Court: The Newest Unequal Protection. *Law & Policy Quarterly* 4:37–69.

BRUDNO, BARBARA 1976 *Poverty, Inequality, and the Law.* St. Paul, Minn.: West Publishing Co.

——— 1980 Wealth Discrimination in the Supreme Court: Equal Protection for the Poor from *Griffin* to *Maher.* Pages 229–246 in Ron Collins, ed., *Constitutional Government in America.* Durham, N.C.: Carolina Academic Press.

WEBB-KENYON ACT
37 Stat. 699 (1913)

Although the Supreme Court had generally refused to uphold laws that it characterized as STATE REGULATION OF COMMERCE, a series of decisions in the late nineteenth and early twentieth centuries deferred to such action. Reacting to a clear invitation in the Court's opinion in LEISY V. HARDIN (1890), holding that absent congressional authorization a state could not prevent the importation and first sale of liquor in the original package, Congress passed the Wilson Act. The law subjected intoxicating liquor "to the operation and effect of the laws of [a] State or territory enacted in the exercise of its [STATE] POLICE POWERS" despite the liquor's journey in INTERSTATE COMMERCE and the ORIGINAL PACKAGE DOCTRINE. The Court sustained that act in *In re Rahrer* (1891).

The Webb-Kenyon Act, passed over the veto of President WILLIAM HOWARD TAFT, divested liquor of its interstate character when introduced in violation of state law. Congress thus effectively allowed state prohibition laws to regulate national commerce in liquor. The Court upheld this act in CLARK DISTILLING COMPANY V. WESTERN MARYLAND RAILWAY CO. (1917).

DAVID GORDON

Bibliography

SEMONCHE, JOHN E. 1978 *Charting the Future: The Supreme Court Responds to a Changing Society, 1890–1920.* Westport, Conn.: Greenwood Press.

WEBSTER, DANIEL
(1782–1852)

As a leading lawyer and politician for forty years, Daniel Webster influenced constitutional development as few others have. When the young New Hampshire representative arrived in Washington in 1813, he immediately became a spokesman for New England interests and remained so until the mid-1820s despite an interruption of congressional service (1817–1823) upon moving to Boston. For most of the time from 1827 to his death in 1852, he was an eloquent nationalist in the Senate. Except for two periods as secretary of state under Tyler and Fillmore, he spent the last quarter-century of his life in that body, expounding the principles of a perpetual Union and a flexible Constitution. In either role, sectionalist or nationalist, he applied constitutional ideas to political issues with uncommon ability.

During the early years his Federalist partisanship and loyalty to a commercial constitutency led him to oppose Republican policies of embargo and war. Using economic coercion to maintain maritime rights, he believed, intolerably stretched the power to regulate commerce, indeed, it destroyed commerce. And prosecuting an offensive war against Britain caused other constitutional errors: misuse of militia, proposals for federal conscription, encroachment on STATES' RIGHTS. Though not a delegate to the HARTFORD CONVENTION, Webster approved its resolutions. Later he sought, unconvincingly, to dissociate himself from it. His sectionalism persisted when he opposed the postwar trend toward a protective tariff (1816–1824). Again he voiced a strict constructionist interpretation of the COMMERCE CLAUSE to promote low rates desired by merchants and a system of laissez-faire in the first phase of industrialization.

In the late 1820s, he shifted to a nationalist position concurrently with JOHN C. CALHOUN's shift in the opposite direction. In behalf of rising manufacturers, he joined HENRY CLAY in advocating governmental policies to achieve economic growth and American self-sufficiency. No longer did he oppose use of the commerce power for broad goals. When South Carolina nullified the tariff of 1832, his oratorical duel with

Calhoun provided an opportunity to reiterate more comprehensively his constitutional thought, dramatically set forth in his earlier debate with ROBERT HAYNE. Beyond the tariff question, he countered the doctrines of state sovereignty and NULLIFICATION with the concept of a perpetual Union, created by the people, not the states, and composed of two spheres of authority, national and state, both responsible to the people. In event of conflict, Article VI of the Constitution required national supremacy; and the Supreme Court had long performed its proper duty of upholding that rule.

Soon slavery became the focus of politics. Ever since writing a memorial on the Missouri question in 1820, Webster had advocated a national power to prevent western extension of slavery; but he conceded Congress could not touch it in existing states and he soft-pedaled the moral question. Subsequently he opposed ANNEXATION OF TEXAS and further territorial acquisitions from Mexico, fearing they would disrupt the Union. When, in the great congressional debate of 1850, controversy reached a climax, he preferred compromise to save the Union instead of legislation against extension of slavery, constitutionally possible though it was. Antislavery forces attacked him furiously—the more so when the fugitive slave law, a part of the compromise, appeared to violate CIVIL LIBERTIES. As senator, he had inclined toward TRIAL BY JURY for suspected runaways; as secretary of state he insisted upon strict observance of the statute prescribing summary process.

He was very active in the Supreme Court as well as in Congress. Altogether, he argued 168 cases, of which twenty-five involved constitutional questions. He won about half and influenced doctrinal development even in some he lost. Regularly, he set forth nationalistic arguments to limit state power in a day when most congressional powers were dormant. More successful when JOHN MARSHALL was Chief Justice (to 1835) than when ROGER B. TANEY presided, he made a deep impression on the governmental structure. Of the cases strengthening nationalism, MCCULLOCH V. MARYLAND (1819) stands out. Here, though overshadowed by WILLIAM PINKNEY, Webster contributed to a definition of the Union identical to that in his Senate speeches against nullification. And he introduced the aphorism that the power to tax involves the power to destroy. OSBORN V. BANK OF THE UNITED STATES (1824) provided opportunities to advocate expansion of federal court JURISDICTION in the whole field of corporate rights.

The first commerce case the Court heard involved the New York steamboat monopoly (GIBBONS V. OGDEN, 1824). Contending for an exclusive congressional power over INTERSTATE COMMERCE, Webster would have been satisfied with a rule of partially concurrent power. Marshall sympathized with the first option but did not rest his decision on either formula, therefore postponing a judicial guideline. Over the next twenty-five years, Webster participated in several other cases, such as the LICENSE CASES (1847) and the PASSENGER CASES (1849), in an unavailing effort to obtain an exclusive-power decision. At last, in COOLEY V. BOARD OF WARDENS (1851), his protégé, Justice BENJAMIN CURTIS, spoke for a majority in laying down a partially concurrent-power standard which preserved about as much exclusive national authority as Webster wished. *Cooley* remains good constitutional law.

Webster's nationalism was not an abstract idea. He connected it with the sanctity of property rights as the very foundation of a dynamic economy. Best illustrating this belief are the CONTRACT CLAUSE cases in which he appeared. DARTMOUTH COLLEGE V. WOODWARD (1819) is a classic in the long history of VESTED RIGHTS shielded from state interference. He relied upon the contract clause of the Constitution as if it were an early version of SUBSTANTIVE DUE PROCESS of law. Though the contract clause, even the concept of vested rights of property, has declined, the notion of active judicial defense of individual constitutional rights flourishes in the area of civil liberties. The *Dartmouth* case was only Webster's first of several dealing with the contract clause.

Webster's career reflected the junction of personal capacity with a favorable setting to establish nationhood and to invigorate a capitalist economy. Still, he may have been flawed by moral oversights and may have encouraged an inequitable distribution of wealth and privilege. Perhaps his contemporaries sensed weaknesses such as these as they passed over him in electing their presidents.

MAURICE G. BAXTER

(SEE ALSO: *Constitutional History, 1801–1829; 1829–1848.*)

Bibliography

BARTLETT, IRVING H. 1978 *Daniel Webster.* New York: W. W. Norton.

BAXTER, MAURICE G. 1966 *Daniel Webster and the Supreme Court.* Amherst: University of Massachusetts Press.

______ 1984 *One and Inseparable: Daniel Webster and the Union.* Cambridge, Mass.: Harvard University Press.

FUESS, CLAUDE M. 1930 *Daniel Webster,* 2 vols. Boston: Little, Brown.

WEEKS v. UNITED STATES
232 U.S. 383 (1914)

Weeks v. United States was the Court's single most creative decision under the FOURTH AMENDMENT. To save the amendment as a living constitutional guarantee, the Court endowed it with an enforcement feature, ordering the exclusion from federal trials of EVIDENCE obtained through unlawful seizure. Without this EXCLUSIONARY RULE, seized evidence, regardless of its origin, would always be admissible. The rule thus has provided the occasion for judicial articulation of Fourth Amendment reasonableness in later cases.

Under COMMON LAW, and for the first century of the Constitution's existence, evidence unlawfully seized by government officers was nonetheless admissible in evidence. In BOYD V. UNITED STATES (1886) the Court implicitly discarded this common law principle, but the exclusionary rule, as it has come to be called, was not explicitly enthroned until the *Weeks* decision. The reason for admitting unlawfully seized evidence, a standard still followed in nearly all other countries, is readily understood. Unlike coerced confessions, which are excluded from trial in all civilized countries because of their untrustworthiness, the fruit of an illegal search is just as reliable when taken without a shadow of authority as when taken under warrant. To exclude the evidence allows a criminal to go free. Absent the exclusionary rule, however, the Fourth Amendment might become a mere paper guarantee of freedom from UNREASONABLE SEARCHES without an effective enforcement process. Unlike other guarantees in the BILL OF RIGHTS (for example, RIGHT TO COUNSEL), the Fourth Amendment affects the pretrial stage of the case and is—apart from the exclusionary rule—not within the power of the trial court to enforce. The secrecy in which searches are planned and executed makes it impossible to seek the advance protection of an INJUNCTION, a regular practice when FIRST AMENDMENT freedoms are threatened.

The unanimous *Weeks* opinion said that if unconstitutionally seized evidence were admitted, the Fourth Amendment "might as well be stricken from the Constitution." Furthermore, if the evidence were admitted, courts become parties to the misdeeds of the police, thus compromising the integrity of the judicial process.

The opinion did not, however, make clear whether the exclusionary rule was required by the Constitution or merely was the product of the Court's supervisory power over the lower federal courts and thus subject to negation by Congress. Even if the rule is rooted in the Fourth Amendment, the question remains whether it is a personal right of the defendant or just a deterrent against unlawful searches, discardable if other deterrents can be found. The *Weeks* opinion appeared to endorse the first position; use of the evidence, said the Court, would constitute "a denial of the constitutional rights of the accused." More recent decisions, however, favor the deterrent theory. Nonetheless, one who is not himself the victim of an unlawful search but is implicated in crime by the seizure does not have STANDING to challenge admission of the evidence.

JACOB W. LANDYNSKI

WEEMS v. UNITED STATES
217 U.S. 349 (1910)

In *Weems,* the Court held that punishment is cruel and unusual if it is grossly excessive for the crime. Paul Weems, a government official in the Philippines, was convicted of falsifying pay records. Under a territorial law inherited from the Spanish penal code, Weems was sentenced to *cadeña temporal,* a punishment involving fifteen years of hard labor in chains, permanent deprivation of political rights, and surveillance by the authorities for life. Since the Philippine Bill of Rights was Congress's extension to the Philippines of rights guaranteed by the Constitution, the meaning of CRUEL AND UNUSUAL PUNISHMENT was the same in both documents.

DENNIS J. MAHONEY

WELFARE BENEFITS

Nothing in the Constitution requires the United States or any state to provide public relief to those unable to earn adequate subsistence. Throughout most of history that relief has been the responsibility of private charity or local government. But several provisions of the Constitution impose an obligation on government officials, where such relief is provided, to refrain from imposing arbitrary standards or procedures. That obligation is generally recognized by legislative bodies and, since the late 1960s, has become a special concern of the federal courts.

The courts have treated questions concerning the extension or withdrawal of public welfare benefits under the PRIVILEGES AND IMMUNITIES, EQUAL PROTEC-

TION, and DUE PROCESS clauses of the Constitution. In SHAPIRO V. THOMPSON (1969) the Supreme Court held that a one-year RESIDENCE REQUIREMENT for welfare eligibility infringed the right of interstate migration, a privilege protected by Article IV and the FOURTEENTH AMENDMENT, and also denied equal protection of the laws to indigent interstate travelers. In GRAHAM V. RICHARDSON (1971) the Court held that denial of benefits to resident ALIENS was a denial of equal protection. However, in DANDRIDGE V. WILLIAMS (1970) the Court decisively rejected argument that WEALTH DISCRIMINATION was a SUSPECT CLASSIFICATION or that welfare subsistence was a FUNDAMENTAL INTEREST. And in *Jefferson v. Hackney* (1972), the Court declined to hold that the equal protection clause required a state to compute the need for public assistance according to the same standard for each of the various welfare programs. Nonetheless in GOLDBERG V. KELLY (1970) the Court held that once benefits were granted they could not be discontinued without PROCEDURAL DUE PROCESS, including NOTICE and FAIR HEARING.

DENNIS J. MAHONEY

WELSH v. WISCONSIN
466 U.S. 740 (1984)

In *Welsh* the Supreme Court considered and rejected an exception to its rule of PAYTON V. NEW YORK (1984) that the FOURTH AMENDMENT prohibits a warrantless arrest in one's home in the absence of EXIGENT CIRCUMSTANCES. Police made a warrantless night entry of a private home to arrest a man for committing the nonjailable offense of driving while drunk. Justice WILLIAM J. BRENNAN for a 6–2 Court rejected the state's reliance on the hot pursuit doctrine because the police had not in fact engaged in a pursuit. In view of the state's classification of a first-offense drunk-driving offense as a minor crime meriting merely a fine, the Court also rejected the argument that the need to get a blood-alcohol test without delay provided an exigent circumstance.

LEONARD W. LEVY

WENGLER v. DRUGGISTS MUTUAL INSURANCE COMPANY
446 U.S. 142 (1980)

Missouri's workers' compensation law provided death benefits to all widows but only to widowers who proved actual dependence on their wives or incapacity to earn a living. The Supreme Court, 8–1, held this SEX DISCRIMINATION invalid, following CRAIG V. BOREN (1976) and CALIFANO V. GOLDFARB (1977).

KENNETH L. KARST

WESBERRY v. SANDERS
376 U.S. 1 (1964)

After BAKER V. CARR (1962) held that legislative districting presented a justiciable controversy, the Supreme Court held in *Wesberry*, 8–1, that a state's congressional districts are required by Article I, section 2, of the Constitution to be as equal in population as is practicable. That section provides that representatives are to be chosen "by the People of the several States." Justice JOHN MARSHALL HARLAN dissented on both textual and historical grounds.

Later decisions make clear that no justifications can excuse substantial deviation from population equality in congressional districting.

KENNETH L. KARST

(SEE ALSO: *Reapportionment.*)

WEST COAST HOTEL COMPANY v. PARRISH
300 U.S. 379 (1937)

This decision sustaining a Washington state minimum wage statute in March 1937 signaled a seismic shift in judicial philosophy toward acceptance of the validity of social and economic legislation. Together with the WAGNER ACT CASES, the decision reflected a new, favorable judicial attitude toward the New Deal, thus defusing FRANKLIN D. ROOSEVELT's court-packing proposal.

The constitutionality of minimum wage legislation had a peculiar history. In MULLER V. OREGON (1908) and BUNTING V. OREGON (1917) the Justices had approved state laws regulating maximum working hours, including provisions for overtime wages. In 1917, the Court divided evenly on an Oregon minimum wage law. WILLIAM HOWARD TAFT, among others, confidently presumed that LOCHNER V. NEW YORK's (1905) rigorous FREEDOM OF CONTRACT doctrines no longer applied. Yet in 1923, a 5–3 majority of the Court reaffirmed the *Lochner* ruling, and in ADKINS V. CHILDREN'S HOSPITAL (1923) the Court invalidated a DISTRICT OF COLUMBIA minimum wage statute. New Chief Justice Taft sharply attacked the majority's reasoning. He found no distinction between MAXIMUM HOUR AND MINIMUM WAGE LAWS: one was the "multiplier and the other the multiplicand." Although Taft reiterated his belief that *Lochner* had been tacitly overruled, *Lochner* nevertheless persisted until the *Parrish* decision in 1937.

After *Adkins,* the Court invalidated other state minimum wage laws. The Great Depression, however, stimulated new state laws, perhaps encouraged by Justice GEORGE SUTHERLAND'S OBITER DICTUM that "exceptional circumstances" might justify such legislation. But in MOREHEAD V. NEW YORK EX REL. TIPALDO (1936), a 5–4 majority held to the *Adkins* precedent and invalidated a recent New York law. The Court's opinion masked Justice OWEN J. ROBERTS'S uneasiness. Roberts had supported PIERCE BUTLER, JAMES C. MCREYNOLDS, George Sutherland, and WILLIS VAN DEVANTER in *Tipaldo,* but he later revealed that the state counsel's argument that *Adkins* merely be distinguished, and not overthrown, had obliged him to follow the precedent. Six months later, Roberts provided the key vote to consider the Washington law. On the surface, the procedure was justified on the ground that the state court had upheld the statute, but the combination of the *Tipaldo* dissenters' strongly held views on constitutionality and Roberts's skepticism toward *Adkins* dictated a full-scale review of the issue.

Roberts later stated that he had decided in favor of the statutes after arguments in December 1936 and that he had successfully urged delaying the decision pending HARLAN FISKE STONE'S recovery from illness in order to mass a majority. Stone returned shortly after Roosevelt submitted his court-packing proposal in early February. Chief Justice CHARLES EVANS HUGHES then withheld the announcement until March 29, perhaps to avoid appearances of political submission.

Hughes's majority opinion decisively repudiated *Lochner* and *Adkins.* He argued that the Constitution nowhere enshrined freedom of contract and that "regulation which is reasonable in relation to its subject and is adopted in the interests of the community is DUE PROCESS." Seeking to deflect the outraged protests of his more conservative brethren, Hughes invoked Taft's *Adkins* dissent: "That challenge persists and is without any satisfactory answer."

Invoking the public interest doctrine of NEBBIA V. NEW YORK (1934), Hughes asked what could be "closer to the public interest than the health of women and their protection from unscrupulous and overreaching employers?" Accordingly, Hughes held that the minimum wage statute was reasonable and not "arbitrary or capricious." That, he concluded, "is all we have to decide."

Sutherland, speaking for the dissenters, passionately reiterated his *Adkins* doctrine. More broadly, Sutherland also implicitly addressed Stone's scathing dissent in UNITED STATES V. BUTLER (1936), which had pleaded for judicial self-restraint and an end to judges' imposition of their own social and economic predilections. The notion of self-restraint, Sutherland retorted, was "ill considered and mischievous"; it belonged "in the domain of will and not of judgment." Judges were bound to enforce the Constitution, he said, according to their own "conscientious and informed convictions." Sutherland concluded that freedom of contract remained the rule. The intervening economic conditions altered nothing, for "the meaning of the Constitution," he said, "does not change with the ebb and flow of economic events." Sutherland's dissent was both an apologia and an obituary for a judicial philosophy eclipsed by new realities.

STANLEY I. KUTLER

Bibliography

MASON, ALPHEUS T. 1956 *Harlan Fiske Stone.* New York: Viking Press.

WESTON v. CITY COUNCIL OF CHARLESTON

2 Peters 449 (1829)

The Supreme Court, in an opinion by Chief Justice JOHN MARSHALL, held unconstitutional a city ordinance taxing interest-bearing stock of the United States, on the grounds that the tax burdened the ENUMERATED POWER of the United States to borrow money on its credit. The principle of the opinion, that an instrumentality of the United States is immune from taxation by state and local governments, derived from MCCULLOCH V. MARYLAND (1819).

LEONARD W. LEVY

(SEE ALSO: *Intergovernmental Immunities.*)

WEST RIVER BRIDGE COMPANY v. DIX

6 Howard 529 (1848)

The *West River Bridge* case challenged a Vermont law of 1839 authorizing county officials to expropriate the rights of way, real estate, or entire franchises of chartered companies in order to provide their communities with free public roads. County officials condemned the entire franchise and property of the West River Bridge Company, which had been given a hundred-year franchise under a charter of 1795 for a bridge near Brattleboro, an important market town. The stockholders were awarded $4,000 in damages. The company's appeal was rejected by the Vermont Supreme Court, and the case was then carried to the United States Supreme Court.

DANIEL WEBSTER, as counsel for the company, sought in his arguments to reopen virtually all the issues of CHARLES RIVER BRIDGE V. WARREN BRIDGE COMPANY (1837). He contended that rising popular disregard for franchised rights of corporations would legitimate the worst "levelling ultraisms or Antirentism or Agrarianism or Abolitionism." Eminent domain was a power inappropriate to republican government, he contended, and the bridge taking was in blatant violation of the CONTRACT CLAUSE. Nonetheless, the Court, with Justice JAMES M. WAYNE dissenting, upheld Vermont's action. Each of the three opinions filed declared that eminent domain was a power fundamental to the states, had long been exercised by them, was not restrained by the contract clause, and extended as much to franchises as to any other type of property. As the first Supreme Court ruling that dealt directly with the states' power of eminent domain and related procedural matters, *West River Bridge* complemented the *Charles River Bridge* decision; both supported the states' authority to accommodate technological change and social and entrepreneurial needs.

HARRY N. SCHEIBER

WEST VIRGINIA STATE BOARD OF EDUCATION v. BARNETTE

See: Flag Salute Cases

WHALEN v. ROE
429 U.S. 589 (1977)

Rejecting a claim based on the constitutional RIGHT OF PRIVACY, a unanimous Supreme Court upheld a New York law requiring storage in a computer file of the names and addresses of persons who obtain, by doctors' prescriptions, such drugs as opium, methadone, cocaine, and amphetamines. Justice JOHN PAUL STEVENS, writing for the Court, noted that previous decisions recognizing a right of privacy had involved two different kinds of interests: (1) "avoiding disclosure of personal matters"; and (2) "independence in making certain kinds of important decisions." Both interests were arguably implicated here; there was some risk of disclosure of a drug user's name, and that risk could have deterred the prescription or use of such drugs even when they were medically advisable. Nonetheless, and despite a district court finding that the state had not proved the necessity of storing this personal information, the Court concluded that the law was valid. The state's interest in DRUG REGULATION was vital; the legislature was entitled to experiment with reasonable means for achieving that end. Balanced against this objective, the invasions of privacy were too slight to constitute invasions of either patients' or doctors' constitutional liberties.

KENNETH L. KARST

WHEATON, HENRY
(1785–1848)

Henry Wheaton read law in his native Providence, Rhode Island, and studied civil law in France in 1805–1806. While in France he translated the new *Code Napoléon* into English. He became the first official reporter for the United States Supreme Court under an 1816 statute creating that position. From 1816 to 1827 Wheaton edited twelve volumes of United States Reports. While official reporter he argued a number of cases, including GIBBONS V. OGDEN (1824). In *Wheaton v. Peters* (1834) he unsuccessfully sued his successor, Richard Peters. The Supreme Court ruled that no individual could hold a COPYRIGHT on Supreme Court opinions. From 1827 to 1846 Wheaton held various diplomatic positions and wrote extensively on international law. His works included *Elements of International Law, History of the Law of Nations* (1842) and an essay on the African slave trade (1842). He was the foremost American expert on international law during his lifetime.

PAUL FINKELMAN

Bibliography

BAKER, ELIZABETH F. 1937 *Henry Wheaton, 1785–1848.* Philadelphia: University of Pennsylvania Press.

WHEELER, BURTON K.
(1882–1975)

A Montana Democrat, Burton K. Wheeler ranked with GEORGE NORRIS of Nebraska and William Borah of Idaho as one of the major liberal leaders of the

United States Senate, where Wheeler served from 1923 to 1946. In the 1924 presidential campaign, ROBERT M. LA FOLLETTE of Wisconsin headed the Progressive party ticket, with Wheeler as his running mate. They attracted more votes than any previous third party, and their platform provided an agenda for the New Deal. One plank urged an amendment to the Constitution providing that a two-thirds majority in both houses of Congress might override any judicial decision holding a congressional enactment unconstitutional. Although Wheeler was a critic of the Supreme Court and of JUDICIAL REVIEW, he insisted that a constitutional amendment was the only proper means of reform; accordingly, he broke with FRANKLIN D. ROOSEVELT in 1937 by opposing his Court-packing plan. It was Wheeler, an ally of Justice LOUIS D. BRANDEIS, who produced the letter by Chief Justice CHARLES EVANS HUGHES that contributed to the 10–8 vote against the bill by the Senate Judiciary Committee. Wheeler remained a liberal, though he was an isolationist in foreign affairs.

LEONARD W. LEVY

Bibliography

WHEELER, BURTON K., with PAUL F. HEALY 1962 *Yankee from the West.* New York: Doubleday.

WHISKEY REBELLION (1794)

The "rebellion" in western Pennsylvania provided the first test of the power of the federal government to suppress insurrections and enforce obedience to its laws. Frontier farmers, who were also small distillers, resisted the whiskey excise from its passage in 1791. When the resistance erupted in violence in July 1794, President GEORGE WASHINGTON issued a proclamation ordering the rebels to submit to the law or face military coercion under an act authorizing employment of the militia in such cases. After a peace mission failed, he called up 15,000 militia from Pennsylvania and neighboring states. The army marched, and the rebellion quickly collapsed without bloodshed; two ringleaders, tried and convicted of TREASON, were subsequently pardoned by the President. Federalist leaders exulted in this crushing of rebellion, which they viewed as part of a plot against the government, while their Republican counterparts denounced the force as excessive and intended to overawe opposition to the administration.

MERRILL D. PETERSON

Bibliography

BALDWIN, LELAND D. 1939 *Whiskey Rebels: The Story of a Frontier Uprising.* Pittsburgh: University of Pittsburgh Press.

WHITE, BYRON R. (1917–)

In 1962 President JOHN F. KENNEDY appointed Byron R. White to replace CHARLES E. WHITTAKER and become the ninety-third Justice to serve on the Supreme Court. White was forty-four years old and had no previous judicial experience. He had been a CLERK for Chief Justice FRED N. VINSON in 1946–1947, however, and was the first former law clerk subsequently appointed to that tribunal. His only other significant government experience had come during the preceding year, after President Kennedy had appointed him deputy attorney general. White had managed the Justice Department, recruited lawyers, and evaluated candidates for federal judgeships. His CIVIL RIGHTS enforcement experience included a stint in Montgomery, Alabama, where local authorities had failed to prevent mob violence against the freedom riders, an interracial group protesting racial SEGREGATION in public transportation. White restored order with the help of 400 federal marshals, providing Kennedy with a significant national victory over recalcitrant state officials.

Whatever White lacked in government experience, he made up in personal capacities. Born in rural Colorado, White came of age there during the Depression. He worked in the beet fields as a boy and later won a scholarship to the University of Colorado, where he was first in his class and an all-American football player. He played professional football, and for several months, until the European outbreak of World War II, he studied as a Rhodes scholar in England, where he first met John Kennedy. He began studying law at Yale in 1939 and again topped his class. The war interrupted his studies, and he served as a naval intelligence officer in the South Pacific, where he again encountered Kennedy. He was graduated in 1946, and after his clerkship, returned to Colorado to practice law. In 1959 he organized support for Kennedy as the Democratic nominee for President. Following Kennedy's nomination, he chaired Citizens for Kennedy, a nationwide volunteer group. His public service followed.

When White joined the WARREN COURT, its most vigorous efforts to nationalize CIVIL LIBERTIES and limit government power in favor of individual rights and egalitarian values lay just ahead. White voted regularly with the majority to invalidate discrimination against racial minorities and the politically powerless in areas such as school DESEGREGATION and REAPPORTIONMENT, and to sustain the constitutionality of federal civil rights legislation. Nonetheless, he acquired a reputation as a moderate-to-conservative Justice for his frequent dissents in major decisions, such as MIRANDA V. ARIZONA (1966), which imposed new constitutional limits on police discretion; for his willingness to uphold laws excluding communists from government positions; and for his general inclination toward judicial self-restraint.

With President RICHARD M. NIXON's four Court appointments from 1969–1971, the deferential positions White previously had articulated in dissent increasingly became majority views in the BURGER COURT. But White also dissented from decisions undermining egalitarian opinions he had joined in the Warren era. The Court had changed around him—not an uncommon occurrence for Justices serving for long periods.

The Court's shift, together with White's failure to articulate a comprehensive personal vision of an ideal balance of individual liberty and government power, has led some observers to conclude that White lacks a coherent judicial philosophy. The votes and written opinions of this independent, tough-minded jurist, however, do reveal a distinctive vision of the Supreme Court's role in constitutional law, a vision compatible with White's personal history.

One pervasive attitude in White's approach is skepticism and humility about the authority and capacity of the Court to second-guess the efforts of other government officials in dealing with difficult societal problems. White's opinions reflect deference to the good faith assessments and pragmatic judgments of police, administrative officials, and state and federal judges—particularly when he is convinced that they have readier access to relevant information than the Court does, or that government flexibility is needed. He reserves the highest deference for legislative judgments, out of respect for LEGISLATIVE POWER, especially that of the national Congress, as the most legitimate source of law in a democratic society. This second tenet emphasizes the primacy of legislative decisions in allocating the benefits and burdens of government programs, balancing individual rights and community needs, and structuring government operations.

The corollary is that White's deference disappears if good faith and pragmatism are absent. When prejudice infects government decision making, when the interests of the disadvantaged systematically are excluded from consideration in government processes, or when individual liberty is sacrificed for minimal public gain, White readily and consistently supports constitutional prohibitions. He embraces a strongly individualistic ideology that demands fair government treatment of citizens as individuals and holds ordinary citizens and government officials accountable for their individual conduct.

White's individualism produces a powerful egalitarian ethic that takes two different forms. One is constitutional invalidation of government action that treats people stereotypically, with insufficient regard for their individual worth, merits, and capacities. The other is constitutional approval of government efforts to equalize opportunities for the disadvantaged.

These general themes explain much of Justice White's participation in the Court's work. His opposition to stringent constitutional limits on law enforcement practices, absent significant abuse of a particular defendant's liberty, reflects deference to the difficulties of enforcement and the flexibility it requires, as well as to the judgment that guilty individuals have no great claim to benefit from police misconduct that has not harmed them. Deference, pragmatism, and rugged individualism underlie White's position in *Miranda* and his majority opinion in *United States v. Leon* (1984), establishing a GOOD FAITH EXCEPTION to the EXCLUSIONARY RULE. His Court opinions holding that the states must provide TRIAL BY JURY if substantial imprisonment is possible, but that the states may convict with less than unanimous verdicts and with juries of only six members, illustrate a compromise between a belief in the importance of the jury in protecting individual liberty and tolerance for pragmatic modifications of its traditional features when the modifications do not seriously undermine its basic value. The heavy weight he has placed behind sanctioning guilty individuals gives way, however, when government interferes with a fair presentation of the defendant's side, as by denying the RIGHT TO COUNSEL. In civil cases, too, in contexts as diverse as PROCEDURAL DUE PROCESS and the CONTRACT CLAUSE, he has tolerated pragmatic (and unbiased) responses to perceived governmental needs.

White's deference to national LEGISLATIVE POWER has led him to reject both FEDERALISM objections that Congress has usurped reserved state power, as in OREGON V. MITCHELL (1970) and NATIONAL LEAGUE OF CITIES V. USERY (1976), and SEPARATION OF POWERS objections that Congress has invaded the Court's or the President's power, as in his provocative dissents in NORTHERN PIPELINE CONSTRUCTION CO. V.

MARATHON PIPE LINE CO. (1982), dealing with the powers of LEGISLATIVE COURTS in BANKRUPTCY cases, and IMMIGRATION AND NATURALIZATION SERVICE V. CHADHA (1983), in which the majority struck down the LEGISLATIVE VETO. He also opposed individual rights challenges to legislative efforts that promote equality, such as the affirmative action program upheld in FULLILOVE V. KLUTZNICK (1980), and Congress's attempt to equalize campaign spending, partially invalidated over White's dissent in BUCKLEY V. VALEO (1976). In these cases, deference and attachment to egalitarian values worked together; when they are in conflict, however, White tends to put aside deference and vote to strike down federal laws that discriminate on such invidious bases as race or sex.

White is as vigorous in opposing biased or arbitrary government judgments as he is in supporting justifiable, pragmatic ones. He will not invoke the Constitution to impose affirmative obligations on government, but will do so to prevent the government from imposing unfair burdens. He is reluctant to recognize constitutional immunities for even the highest level officials, preferring to hold that no one is above the law. That frequent theme appears most prominently in his dissent in NIXON V. FITZGERALD (1982), arguing that the President is legally accountable for abuse of government power, and in his opinions interpreting the SPEECH AND DEBATE CLAUSE as fully immunizing members of Congress from inquiry into legislative conduct, but providing no immunity for nonlegislative acts.

More broadly, White has voted to invalidate government policies founded on prejudice or bad motive without more, but usually would not invalidate laws adopted with proper motives, whatever their impact. Thus, in WASHINGTON V. DAVIS (1976) White led the Court in making proof of intentional discrimination a necessary condition for finding a violation of the equal protection clause. He also would have made intent a sufficient condition, however, as he articulated in dissent in PALMER V. THOMPSON (1971). He has been both generous in finding proof of illicit intent and forceful in insisting that, once wrongdoing is shown, the harm be remedied fully, especially in cases of RACIAL DISCRIMINATION. And when the impact of governmental action significantly impairs the democratic process, as in reapportionment cases, White also has supported judicial intervention.

In FIRST AMENDMENT cases, too, White is strict about disallowing government discrimination against disfavored viewpoints, but tolerant of significant limitations on individual expression that are inevitable byproducts of legitimate government aims, a theme illustrated by his opinion in BROADRICK V. OKLAHOMA (1973). That opinion also represents White's consistent belief that the OVERBREADTH and VAGUENESS doctrines should be used only sparingly to strike statutes with a neutral and uncertain inhibiting effect on the general populace—a position readily held by a believer in hardy individualism. He is likewise unreceptive to arguments that the press needs wide immunity from libel and other actions lest fear of liability deter them from vigorous and important expression. Thus, although this Justice with considerable personal experience as the object of media attention strongly supported First Amendment limits on press liability for reporting about public officials, he vigorously dissented in GERTZ V. ROBERT WELCH, INC. (1974) from the Court's granting the powerful media constitutional immunity from liability to helpless individuals who seek redress for the ravaging of their reputations. Indeed, he generally opposes affording the press any special privileges, except in cases of prior restraint or when the press serves as the public's monitor of government. Finally, White has been relatively deferential to regulations of OBSCENITY and SUBVERSIVE ADVOCACY, the former an example of deference to strong community views which invade little important freedom and the latter an example of deference to the community's right to protect its democratic character.

White's concern for the constitutional obligation to purge arbitrariness from government decision making extends naturally to questions of procedural fairness. Although White would allow government considerable flexibility in defining procedures, he has insisted that appropriate procedures be provided if government deprives a person of a government-created liberty or property entitlement, even if the government was under no initial obligation to create it. So conceived, procedural due process promotes individualized application of law on the basis of personal responsibility and guards against arbitrary decisions.

White's emphasis on equality and fair, if flexible, process generally stops short of imposing substantive limits on government policy. His normal disinclination to go beyond constitutional text or history and recognize new fundamental liberties tends to yield, however, when a state restricts personal autonomy by a law that deviates from most other states' laws or is of minimal efficacy in achieving proper objectives. Thus, White dissented in ROE V. WADE (1973), where the Court used SUBSTANTIVE DUE PROCESS analysis to invalidate laws regulating abortion, but he concurred in GRISWOLD V. CONNECTICUT (1965), arguing that the state's atypical law against marital use of contraceptives violated substantive due process because of its "marginal utility to the declared objective" of deterring illicit sexual relationships. Similarly, he initially voted against the death penalty in *Furman v. Georgia* (1972), not because it constituted CRUEL AND UNUSUAL PUNISHMENT but because it was administered arbitrarily and too infrequently to achieve its deterrent aims. Later, he voted to uphold mandatory death penalty laws applied broadly and consistently. Still, he wrote the major opinion in COKER V. GEORGIA (1977), holding the death penalty for rape cruel and unusual, largely because most states had refrained from imposing it for crimes not producing death.

Normally, White's limited belief in NATURAL RIGHTS jurisprudence surfaces as increased scrutiny of legislative means when government policy implicates broadly accepted liberties and the threat of inequality or arbitrariness is high. Perhaps not surprisingly, given his personal experience, he not only finds family choice fundamental, but educational opportunity, too. Thus, he has been especially adamant to invalidate school SEGREGATION, inequality of expenditures among a state's school districts, and school discipline that involves corporal punishment or lacks procedural safeguards. He is equally adamant that public aid to the secular functions of parochial schools, a policy that supports educational choice and quality, does not constitute a prohibited ESTABLISHMENT OF RELIGION—a distinct minority view on the Court.

JONATHAN D. VARAT

Bibliography

ISRAEL, FRED 1969 Byron R. White. In Leon Friedman and Fred Israel, eds., *The Justices of the Supreme Court: Their Lives and Major Opinions.* Vol. 4:2951–2961. New York: Chelsea House.

LIEBMAN, LANCE 1972 Swing Man on the Supreme Court. *New York Times Magazine,* October 8, 1972.

SCHWARTZ, BERNARD 1983 *Super Chief: Earl Warren and His Supreme Court: A Judicial Biography.* New York: New York University Press.

WOODWARD, BOB and ARMSTRONG, SCOTT 1979 *The Brethren: Inside the Supreme Court.* New York: Simon & Schuster.

WHITE, EDWARD D. (1845–1921)

Born and raised in Louisiana, the son of a slaveholding sugar planter and a Confederate veteran, Edward Douglass White was an archetype of the "New South" political leader. The masters of the region's economic and social development from the 1880s until World War I combined the interests of antebellum planters with those of northern and local capitalists eager to build railroads and tap the area's coal, iron, and timber. The South's new ruling class "redeemed" Dixie from the egalitarian schemes of Radical Republicans and carpetbaggers by supporting RUTHERFORD B. HAYES for President and accepting the national hegemony of the GOP's conservative wing. In return, these leaders of the "New South" received from the Republicans a promise to remove federal troops from the region, a free hand with respect to the Negro, and a junior partnership in the management of the nation's economic affairs. (See COMPROMISE OF 1877.)

While tending his family's plantation and building a prosperous legal practice in New Orleans, White became a chief political confidant and ally of Governor Francis Nicholls, the leader of the state's conservative Democrats, who rewarded him with an appointment to the Louisiana Supreme Court and then a seat in the United States Senate in 1891. While in Washington, the portly, florid, long-haired junior senator from Louisiana adopted a rigid STATES' RIGHTS and laissez-faire posture on most issues. However, he fervently supported high duties on foreign sugar and lavish federal bounties to the planters in his home state. White led the Senate's successful revolt against President GROVER CLEVELAND's efforts to lower the protective tariff in 1893. Nevertheless, the beleaguered head of the Democratic party nominated him to the Supreme Court a year later, following the death of SAMUEL BLATCHFORD and the Senate's rejection of two earlier nominees.

White took his seat as the junior member of the FULLER COURT at one of the important turning points in the history of the federal judiciary. The country seethed with unrest generated by the worst depression of the nineteenth century. Violent confrontations between workers and employers erupted on the nation's major railroads as well as in coal mines, steel mills, and other factories. Debt-ridden farmers formed the radical Populist Party, which demanded government control of the money supply and banking system and nationalization of the major trunk rail lines. Insurgent Democrats nominated the youthful William Jennings Bryan, who ran on a platform promising inflation of the money supply, higher taxes on the wealthy, and a curb on trusts and other monopolies. In this atmosphere of class strife and regional polarization, men of property and standing looked to the Supreme Court to defend the constitutional ark against dangerous innovations. Fuller and most of his colleagues were equal to the task of repelling the radical hordes.

Even before the economic collapse, a majority of the Justices had served warning that they would not tolerate legislative attacks on corporate property and profits. Legislative power to fix railroad rates, they warned, was not without limits; corporations were PERSONS, entitled to the judicial protection of the FOURTEENTH AMENDMENT'S DUE PROCESS clause; and no rate imposed by legislative fiat could be deemed "reasonable" without final judicial review. Then, in a series of cases that reached the Court together during the depths of the depression in 1895, the Justices quashed federal efforts to prosecute the sugar trust under the SHERMAN ANTITRUST ACT in UNITED STATES V. E. C. KNIGHT CO. (1895); upheld the contempt conviction of the labor leader Eugene V. Debs for his role in the Pullman boycott in IN RE DEBS (1895); and declared unconstitutional the first federal income tax levied since the Civil War in POLLACK V. FARMER'S LOAN AND TRUST CO. (1895). These three decisions displayed the FULLER COURT'S conservative colors and represented a major victory for big business, the wealthy, and the enemies of organized labor.

Like the majority of his brethren, Justice White showed no sympathy for Debs and the militant working class movement he represented. White also endorsed Fuller's reasoning in the sugar trust case, which limited the scope of the Sherman Act to monopolies of interstate trade or commerce and left to the individual states all authority to curb monopolies over production. But he joined Justice JOHN MARSHALL HARLAN, the outspoken champion of nationalism and federal power, in denouncing the majority's assault on the income tax statute. White had been a member of the Senate that passed the income tax measure as part of the tariff package in 1892, and, although he did not endorse the levy, neither did he doubt the constitutional power of Congress to adopt it. In order to invalidate the law, the majority had to ignore two weighty precedents, one dating from 1796. This was too much for White, who argued eloquently that "the conservation and orderly development of our institutions rests on our acceptance of the results of the past, and their use as lights to guide our steps in the future. Teach the lesson that settled principles may be overthrown at any time, and confusion and turmoil must ultimately result."

The income tax dissent revealed an important aspect of White's jurisprudence which remained constant during his years as an associate Justice and later as Chief Justice after 1911. Although deeply conservative and devoted to the judicial protection of private property, White was also a pragmatist capable of endorsing moderate reforms that had clear constitutional sanction and that served to cap the pressures for more radical change. Though not adverse to overturning a few precedents himself, White usually did so in the pursuit of policies that strengthened rather than weakened the dominant economic forces of corporate capitalism.

In this spirit, he endorsed the judicial imperialism inherent in Justice Harlan's opinion in SMYTH V. AMES (1898), which made the federal judiciary the final arbiter of utility rates, but he also enforced the progressive reforms of the THEODORE ROOSEVELT-WILLIAM HOWARD TAFT era which revitalized the regulatory authority of the Interstate Commerce Commission (ICC) over the nation's major railroads. In a series of decisions, culminating in White's opinion in INTERSTATE COMMERCE COMMISSION V. ILLINOIS CENTRAL RAILROAD CO. (1910), the majority sustained the ICC's fact-finding and rate-fixing powers as mandated by Congress. White's views were compatible with the interests of the railroads, which looked to the ICC to prevent financially ruinous rate wars, and with those of reformers like Roosevelt, who believed that such regulation would curb the appetite for government ownership of the carriers.

White rendered his greatest service to the conservative cause in the area of antitrust law by promoting the view that the Sherman Act prohibited only "unreasonable" restraints of trade, a perspective pregnant with possibilities for enlarged judicial control over the country's economic structure, yet wholly compatible with the desires of big business. But it took White over a decade to defeat the contrary views of other Justices, who remained more wedded to the old Jacksonian belief in competition and the dangers of monopoly.

In the wake of the *E. C. Knight* decision restricting federal antitrust efforts to INTERSTATE COMMERCE, the Department of Justice began a campaign to stamp out railroad cartels and pools designed to divide up traffic and fix rates. A majority of the Justices, led by Harlan and RUFUS W. PECKHAM, a passionate spokesman for laissez-faire economics, sustained the government's efforts in this area on the theory that the Sherman Act outlawed *all* restraints of trade, even those that might be deemed "reasonable" in view of particular business conditions such as rate wars and destructive competition. In the first of these cases, UNITED STATES V. TRANS-MISSOURI FREIGHT ASSOCIATION (1897), White wrote a long, rambling dissent which accused the majority of misreading the antitrust law, defying the traditions of the COMMON LAW with respect to restraints of trade, and jeopardizing the economic progress brought to the nation by business combinations and consolidations.

White continued to dissent in the *Joint Traffic Association Case* (1898) and in NORTHERN SECURITIES CO. V. UNITED STATES (1904), where a five-Justice majority upheld the government's suit against the Morgan-Harriman rail monopoly between Chicago and the Pacific Northwest. In each case, White argued that the antitrust law, incorporating the ancient doctrines of the common law, prohibiting only "unreasonable" restraints of trade. Technically, White was correct, but all of the methods condemned in *Trans-Missouri, Joint Traffic Association,* and *Northern Securities* would have been indictable at common law as well, because their fundamental objective had been to fix prices contrary to the public interest. This fact seems to have eluded White, who believed that the Harlan-Peckham approach threatened the demise of valuable business enterprises by virtue of judicial abdication to the prosecutorial zeal of misguided reformers in the executive branch. In this perception, he enjoyed the support of three other justices, including OLIVER WENDELL HOLMES, who also looked upon the Rockefellers, Morgans, and Harrimans as agents of social and economic progress.

Four changes in the personnel of the Court between 1909 and 1911 gave White a new majority for his doctrine a year later when the government's suits against Standard Oil and American Tobacco finally reached the Justices after years of litigation. Speaking now as Chief Justice of the United States, having been appointed to the center chair by President Taft, White sustained the government's case against the monopolists but cast aside the Harlan-Peckham interpretation of the Sherman Act. Henceforth, the majority decreed, only "unreasonable" trade restraints would be indictable under the Sherman Act and the Justices on the Supreme Court would determine where the line should be drawn between legal and illegal competitive behavior. Harlan wrote a melancholy dissent against this sharp reversal of doctrine, which seemed to teach that "settled principles may be overthrown at any time, and confusion and turmoil must ultimately result."

White's RULE OF REASON doctrine provoked a storm of protest from progressives in the Congress, who denounced the Justices for mutilating the antitrust law, arrogating to themselves too much power over the economic system, and giving big business a hunting license to continue its predatory ways. Although Congress added the CLAYTON ACT amendments to the antitrust law in 1914, specifically outlawing a substantial list of business practices, White's rule of reason carried the day. The Court quashed the government's efforts to break up the shoe machinery monopoly in 1913 and also threw out the case against United States Steel in 1920, a year before White died. There was extraordinary historical irony in the fact that it was a Southerner and a veteran of the Rebel army who advanced antitrust doctrines that sealed the triumph of industrial capitalism and big business in American life.

For a Southerner, a Democrat, and a spokesman for states' rights in the Senate, White displayed considerable toleration for the expansion of federal economic controls by means of the COMMERCE CLAUSE and the TAXING AND SPENDING POWER. In the Senate he had taken an active role in fighting a federal law to regulate the trade in agricultural "futures," noting that it would invade the JURISDICTION of the states and create "the most unlimited and arbitrary government on the face of God's earth." As a Justice, however, he joined Harlan's path-breaking opinion in the Lottery Case, CHAMPION V. AMES (1903), which greatly expanded the NATIONAL POLICE POWER via the interstate commerce clause. A year later he wrote the Court's opinion in MCCRAY V. UNITED STATES (1904), which affirmed the power of Congress to impose a prohibitive levy upon oleomargarine and thus employ its tax powers for regulatory purposes.

White drew back, however, from the logical implications of the national police power when Congress sought to apply it to other areas of social and economic life. He was willing to permit the extension of the commerce power to federal regulation of adulterated foods and interstate traffic in prostitution, but he joined Justice WILLIAM R. DAY's opinion in HAMMER V. DAGENHART (1918), which declared unconstitutional Congress's attempt to eradicate child labor. He also rejected federal efforts to tax and regulate narcotics traffic in UNITED STATES V. DOREMUS (1919), although the majority found this use of the federal taxing power compatible with White's own views in *McCray.* He sanctioned Congress's adoption of an eight-hour day for interstate train crews which brought an end to the disastrous nationwide rail strike, but he joined three other dissenters in *Block v. Hirsh* (1921) when Holmes and the majority upheld the national legislature's power to impose rent controls upon property in the DISTRICT OF COLUMBIA during the emergency of World War I.

White displayed equal inconsistency in cases where state ECONOMIC REGULATIONS came under DUE PROCESS challenge. The one thread of coherence seemed to be his growing conservatism and abiding dislike for organized labor. He dissented in LOCHNER V. NEW YORK (1905) along with Harlan and Day, noting that "no evils arising from such legislation could be more far-reaching than those that might come to our system of government if the judiciary . . . should enter the domain of legislation, and upon grounds merely of justice or reason or wisdom, annul statutes that had received the sanction of the people's representatives." He also voted to sustain the Oregon and California maximum hours laws for women in MULLER V. OREGON (1908) and *Miller v. Wilson* (1915). But he balked at the overtime pay provisions and general maximum hours limitation in BUNTING V. OREGON (1917) and sided with the majority in the three leading cases of the period which protected employers' use of YELLOW DOG CONTRACTS against both state and federal efforts to eliminate this notorious antiunion device: ADAIR V. UNITED STATES (1908), COPPAGE V. KANSAS (1915), and HITCHMAN V. HITCHMAN COAL & COKE CO. (1917).

In 1919, White joined JOSEPH MCKENNA, WILLIS VAN DEVANTER, and JAMES C. MCREYNOLDS in dissent against the Court's opinion in the *Arizona Employers' Liability Cases* (1919), which upheld that state's law shifting the cost of industrial accidents to employers. And during his final term on the Court, he joined the majority in scuttling the anti-INJUNCTION provisions of the Clayton Antitrust Act and affirming the illegality of secondary boycotts. If not the most reactionary member of the Supreme Court with respect to organized labor, White certainly ran a close race for that honor with Justices Day, MAHLON PITNEY, and McReynolds.

White had been elevated to the chief justiceship by William Howard Taft, who coveted the position for himself and feared that a younger nominee might forever prevent that happy development. Taft realized his lifelong ambition in 1921, when White died. Predictably, White's eulogizers compared his career to that of John Marshall and other immortals of the bench, but a more accurate assessment is that constitutional law showed his imprint until 1937.

MICHAEL E. PARRISH

Bibliography

DISHMAN, ROBERT 1951 Mr. Justice White and the Rule of Reason. *The Review of Politics* 13:229–248.

HIGHSAW, ROBERT B. 1981 *Edward Douglass White: Defender of the Conservative Faith.* Baton Rouge: Louisiana State University Press.

KLINKHAMER, MARIE CAROLYN 1943 *Edward Douglass White, Chief Justice of the United States.* Washington, D.C.: Catholic University Press.

SEMONCHE, JOHN E. 1978 *Charting the Future: The Supreme Court Responds to a Changing Society, 1890–1920.* Westport, Conn.: Greenwood Press.

WHITE, UNITED STATES *v.*
401 U.S. 745 (1971)

During the reign of OLMSTEAD V. UNITED STATES (1927) the Supreme Court consistently ruled, in cases including ON LEE V. UNITED STATES (1952) and LOPEZ V. UNITED STATES (1963), that government informers who deceptively interrogated criminal suspects and either secretly transmitted the conversations to eavesdropping government agents with concealed recorders or secretly recorded the conversations, had committed no TRESPASS, and therefore the FOURTH AMENDMENT was inapplicable. The use of spies without complying with Fourth Amendment controls was reaffirmed in HOFFA V. UNITED STATES (1966). KATZ V. UNITED STATES (1967), however, abolished the trespass requirement for Fourth Amendment protection and focused on the personal PRIVACY interests that were entitled to protection. Some therefore thought *On Lee* was no longer good law. In *United States v. White,* however, the Court held otherwise. Though there was no clear majority for either approving or disapproving *On Lee,* four Justices voted to reaffirm that decision, and Justice HUGO L. BLACK concurred to make a majority on the ground that *Olmstead*'s trespass requirement should be retained. The *On Lee* doctrine was thus reaffirmed.

Justice BYRON R. WHITE, for the plurality, ruled that a person is not protected by the Fourth Amendment against a faithless friend, regardless of whether a trespass is involved. An expectation of such protection is not "justifiable" under the *Katz* standard. Police have always been allowed to use the evidence of faithless associates who turn to the police or are informers: "one contemplating illegal activities must realize and risk that his companions may be reporting to the police." The fact that the faithless friend was wired, transmitting the conversation to others or recording it for later replaying, makes no constitutional difference.

The dissents focused on the latter point. Justice JOHN MARSHALL HARLAN rejected the "assumption of risk" rationale of the majority, stressing that the real question was which risks the law *should* force people to assume. Whereas the use of unwired spies or contemporaneous recording to ensure reliability are both justifiable, simultaneous overhearing by third parties is different; free discourse would be seriously jeopardized if people were forced to assume the risk that their words were being simultaneously transmitted to third parties and transcribed. "Were third-party bugging a prevalent practice, it might well smother that spontaneity—reflected in frivolous, impetuous, sacrilegious, and defiant discourse—that liberates daily life." Justice Harlan emphasized that the dissenters' views would not prohibit the use of wired informers but would only bring the practice under Fourth Amendment warrant and other procedures.

Even though the principal *White* opinion did not command a majority, it kept *On Lee* in effect and freed the government from Fourth Amendment restrictions on the use of spies and informers, wired or otherwise.

HERMAN SCHWARTZ

(SEE ALSO: *Electronic Eavesdropping.*)

WHITE COURT
(1910–1921)

"The condition of the Supreme Court is pitiable, and yet those old fools hold on with a tenacity that is most discouraging," President WILLIAM HOWARD TAFT wrote in May 1909 to his old friend HORACE H. LURTON. Taft would have his day. One year later, Chief Justice MELVILLE W. FULLER spoke at the Court's memorial service for Justice DAVID J. BREWER: "As our brother Brewer joins the great procession, there pass before me the forms of Mathews and Miller, of Field and Bradley and Lamar and Blatchford, of Jackson and Gray and of Peckham, whose works follow them now that they rest from their labors." These were virtually Fuller's last words from the bench, for he died on Independence Day, 1910, in his native Maine. RUFUS W. PECKHAM had died less than a year earlier. WILLIAM H. MOODY, tragically and prematurely ill, would within a few months have to cut short by retirement one of the few notable short tenures on the Court. JOHN MARSHALL HARLAN had but one year left in his remarkable thirty-four-year tenure. By 1912, five new Justices had come to the Court who were not there in 1909: a new majority under a new Chief Justice.

The year 1910 was a significant divide in the history of the country as well. The population was nearly half urban, and immigration was large and growing. The country stood on the verge of enacting humane and extensive labor regulation. A year of Republican unrest in Congress and THEODORE ROOSEVELT's decisive turn to progressive agitation, 1910 was the first time in eight elections that the Democrats took control of the House. In the same year, the National Association for the Advancement of Colored People was founded. It was a year of progressive tremors that would eventually shake the Supreme Court to its foundations with the appointment of LOUIS D. BRANDEIS in 1916. But the five appointments with which President Taft rehabilitated his beloved Court between 1909 and 1912 had no such dramatic impact. There was a significant strengthening of a mild progressive tendency earlier evident within the Court, but the new appointments brought neither a hardening nor a decisive break with the DOCTRINES of laissez-faire constitutionalism and luxuriant individualism embodied in such decisions as LOCHNER V. NEW YORK (1905) and ADAIR V. UNITED STATES (1908). Taft's aim was to strengthen the Court with active men of sound, if somewhat progressive, conservative principles. Neither Taft nor the nation saw the Court, as both increasingly would a decade later, as the storm center of pressures for fundamental constitutional change.

Taft's first choice when Peckham died in 1909 was his friend Lurton, then on the Sixth Circuit, and a former member of the Tennessee Supreme Court. Lurton, a Democrat, had been a fiery secessionist in his youth, and in his short and uneventful four-year tenure he combined conservationism on economic regulation, race, and labor relations. Taft's second choice was not so modest. When Taft went to Governor CHARLES EVANS HUGHES of New York to replace Brewer, he brought to the Court for the first of his two tenures a Justice who would emerge as one of the greatest figures in the history of American law, and a principal architect of modern CIVIL LIBERTIES and CIVIL RIGHTS jurisprudence. As governor of New York, Hughes was already one of the formidable reform figures of the Progressive era, and his later career as a presidential candidate who came within a whisper of success in 1916, secretary of state during the 1920s, and Chief Justice during the tumultuous years of the New Deal, mark him as one of the most versatile and important public figures to sit on the Court since JOHN MARSHALL.

Taft's choice of the Chief Justice to fill the center seat left vacant by Fuller was something of a surprise, although reasons are obvious in retrospect. EDWARD D. WHITE was a Confederate veteran from Louisiana, who had played a central role in the Democratic reaction against Reconstruction in that state and had emerged as a Democratic senator in 1891. He had been appointed Associate Justice in 1894 by President GROVER CLEVELAND and had compiled a respectable but unobtrusive record in sixteen years in the side seat. He had dissented with able force from the self-inflicted wound of POLLOCK V. FARMERS' LOAN & TRUST CO. (1895), holding unconstitutional the federal income tax, and his antitrust dissents in TRANS-MISSOURI FREIGHT ASSOCIATION (1897) and UNITED STATES V. NORTHERN SECURITIES COMPANY (1904) embodied sound good sense. He had done "pioneer work," as Taft later called it, in ADMINISTRATIVE LAW. White had a genius for friendship and, despite a habit of constant worrying, extraordinary personal warmth. OLIVER WENDELL HOLMES summed him up in these words in 1910: "His writing leaves much to be desired, but his thinking is profound, especially in the legislative direction which we don't recognize as a judicial requirement but which is so, especially in our Court, nevertheless." White was sixty-five, a Democrat, a Confederate veteran, and a Roman Catholic, and his selection by Taft was seen as adventurous. But given Taft's desire to bind up sectional wounds, to spread his political advantage, to put someone in the center seat who might not occupy Taft's own ultimate ambition for too long, to exemplify bipartisanship in the choice of Chief Justice, and on its own sturdy merits, the selection of White seems easy to understand.

Along with White's nomination, Taft sent to the Senate nominations of WILLIS VAN DEVANTER of Wyoming and JOSEPH R. LAMAR of Georgia. Van Devanter would sit for twenty-seven years, and would become one of the Court's most able, if increasingly conservative, legal craftsmen. Lamar would last only five years, and his death in 1915, along with Lurton's death in 1914 and Hughes's resignation to run for President, opened up the second important cycle of appointments to the White Court.

The Taft appointees joined two of the most remarkable characters ever to sit on the Supreme Court. John Marshall Harlan, then seventy-eight, had been on the Court since his appointment by President RUTHERFORD B. HAYES in 1877. He was a Justice of passionate strength and certitude, a man who, in the fond words of Justice Brewer, "goes to bed every night with one hand on the Constitution and the other on the Bible, and so sleeps the sleep of justice and righteousness." He had issued an apocalyptic dissent in *Pollock*, the income tax case, and his dissent in PLESSY V. FERGUSON (1986), the notorious decision upholding racial SEGREGATION on railroads, was an appeal to the conscience of the Constitution without equal in our history. The other, even more awesome, giant on the Court in 1910 was Holmes, then seventy, but still not quite recognized as the jurist whom BENJAMIN N. CARDOZO would later call "probably the greatest legal intellect in the history of the English-speaking judiciary." The other two members of the Court were JOSEPH MCKENNA, appointed by President WILLIAM MCKINLEY in 1898, and WILLIAM R. DAY, appointed by President Theodore Roosevelt in 1903.

The Supreme Court in 1910 remained in "truly republican simplicity," as Dean Acheson would recall, in the old Senate chamber, where the Justices operated in the midst of popular government, and in the sight of visitors to the Capitol. No office space was available, and the Justices worked in their homes. Their staff allowance provided for a messenger and one clerk, and their salaries were raised in 1911 to $14,500 for the Associate Justices and $15,000 for the Chief Justice. The Court was badly overworked and the docket was falling further and further behind, not to be rescued until the JUDICIARY ACT OF 1925 gave the Court discretion to choose the cases it would review.

In the public's contemporaneous view, if not in retrospect, the most important cases before the White Court between 1910 and 1921 did not involve the Constitution at all, but rather the impact of the SHERMAN ANTITRUST ACT on the great trusts. UNITED STATES V. STANDARD OIL COMPANY (1911) and *American Tobacco Company v. United States* (1911) had been initiated by the Roosevelt administration to seek dissolution of the huge combinations, and when the cases were argued together before the Supreme Court in 1911, the *Harvard Law Review* thought public attention was concentrated on the Supreme Court "to a greater extent than ever before in its history."

The problem for the Court was to determine the meaning of restraint of trade amounting to monopoly. The answer offered by Chief Justice White for the Court was the famous RULE OF REASON, under which not all restraints of trade restrictive of competition were deemed to violate the Sherman Act, but rather only those "undue restraints" which suggested an "intent to do wrong to the general public . . . thus restraining the free flow of commerce and tending to bring about the evils, such as enhancement of riches, which were considered to be against public policy." Under this test, the Court deemed Standard Oil to have engaged in practices designed to dominate the oil industry, exclude others from trade, and create a monopoly. It was ordered to divest itself of its subsidiaries, and to make no agreements with them that would unreasonably restrain trade. The court ruled that the American Tobacco Company was also an illegal combination and forced it into dissolution.

Antitrust was perhaps the dominant political issue of the 1912 presidential campaign, and the rule of reason helped to fuel a heated political debate that produced the great CLAYTON ACT and FEDERAL TRADE COMMISSION ACT of 1914. Further great antitrust cases came to the White Court, notably *United States v. United States Steel Company,* begun in 1911, postponed during the crisis of World War I, and eventually decided in 1920. A divided Court held that United States Steel had not violated the Sherman Act, mere size alone not constituting an offense.

The tremendous public interest generated by the antitrust cases before the White Court was a sign of the temper of the political times, in which the regulation of business and labor relations was the chief focus of progressive attention. In this arena of constitutional litigation, the White Court's record was mixed, with perhaps a slight progressive tinge. On the great questions of legislative power to regulate business practices and working arrangements, the White Court maintained two parallel but opposing lines of doctrines, the one protective of laissez-faire constitutionalism and freedom from national regulation, the other receptive to the progressive reforms of the day.

In the first four years after its reconstitution by Taft, the Supreme Court handed down a number of important decisions upholding national power to regulate commerce for a variety of ends. The most expansive involved federal power to regulate railroads—and to override competing state regulation when necessary. *Atlantic Coast Line Railroad v. Riverside Mills* (1911) upheld Congress's amendment of the HEPBURN ACT imposing on the initial carrier of goods liability for any loss occasioned by a connecting carrier, notwithstanding anything to the contrary in the bill of lading. FREEDOM OF CONTRACT gave way to the needs of shippers for easy and prompt recovery. More significantly, in the second of the EMPLOYERS' LIABILITY CASES (1912), the Court upheld congressional legislation imposing liability for any injury negligently caused to any employee of a carrier engaged in INTERSTATE COMMERCE. This legislation did away with the fellow-servant rule and the defense of contributory negligence, again notwithstanding contracts to the contrary. In 1914, in the famous *Shreveport Case* (HOUSTON, EAST & WEST TEXAS RAILWAY COMPANY V. UNITED STATES) the Court upheld the power of the Interstate Commerce Commission to set the rates of railroad hauls entirely within Texas, because those rates competed against traffic between Texas and Louisiana. The Court overrode the rates set by the Texas Railroad Commission in the process. And in the most important COMMERCE CLAUSE decision of the early years of the White Court, the MINNESOTA RATE CASES (1913), the Court upheld the power of the states to regulate railroad rates for intrastate hauls, even when that regulation would force down interstate rates, so long as there had been no federal regulation of those rates. Thus, state power over rates was not invalidated because of the possibility of prospective federal regulation, and a large loophole between state and federal power was closed.

Outside the area of carrier regulation, the White Court was also friendly to national regulation by expanding the NATIONAL POLICE POWER doctrine. HIPOLITE EGG CO. V. UNITED STATES (1911) upheld the PURE FOOD AND DRUG ACT of 1906 in regulating adulterated food and drugs shipped in interstate commerce, whether or not the material had come to rest in the states. "Illicit articles" that traveled in interstate commerce were subject to federal control, the Court said, although with a doctrinal vagueness and confusion that would come back to haunt the Court in HAMMER V. DAGENHART (1918). In HOKE V. UNITED STATES (1913) the Court upheld the MANN ACT, which punished the transportation in interstate commerce of women "for the purpose of prostitution or debauchery, or for any other immoral purpose."

Taft got his opportunity for a sixth appointment—more appointments in one term than any President in our history since GEORGE WASHINGTON—when Harlan died in 1911. He filled the vacancy with MAHLON PITNEY, chancellor of New Jersey. The reasons for this appointment are obscure, but like other Taft appointments Pitney was a sound, middle-of-the-road, good lawyer with little flair or imagination. As if to prepare for the coming flap over Brandeis, the Pitney appointment ran into trouble because of the nominee's alleged antilabor positions. But Pitney prevailed, and he would serve on the Court until 1922.

If ever in the history of the Supreme Court successive appointments by one President have seemed to embrace dialectical opposites, WOODROW WILSON's appointments of JAMES C. MCREYNOLDS in 1914 and Louis D. Brandeis in 1916 are the ones. McReynolds would become an embittered and crude anti-Semite; Brandeis was the first Jew to sit on the Supreme Court. McReynolds would become the most rigid and doctrinaire apostle of laissez-faire conservatism in constitutional history, the most recalcitrant of the "Four Horsemen of Reaction" who helped to scuttle New Deal legislation in the early 1930s. Brandeis was the greatest progressive of his day, on or off the Court. McReynolds was an almost invariable foe of CIVIL LIB-

ERTIES and CIVIL RIGHTS for black people; Brandeis was perhaps the driving force of his time for the development of civil liberties, especially freedom of expression and rights of personal privacy. What brought these opposites together in Wilson's esteem, although he came to regret the McReynolds appointment, was antitrust fervor. McReynolds's aggressive individualism and Brandeis's progressive concern for personal dignity and industrial democracy coalesced around antitrust law, and this was the litmus test of the day for Wilson. Thus, possibly the most difficult and divisive person ever to sit on the Supreme Court and possibly the most intellectually gifted and broadly influential Justice in the Court's history took their seats in spurious, rather Wilsonian, juxtaposition.

Wilson's third appointment was handed him by the resignation of his rival in the presidential election of 1916. As it became plain that Hughes was the only person who could unite the Republican party, he came under increasing pressure from Taft and others to make himself available. He did. Wilson nominated JOHN J. CLARK of Ohio to replace Hughes. One of the most pregnant speculations about the history of the Supreme Court is what might have happened had Hughes remained on the bench. He might well have become a Chief Justice in 1921 instead of Taft, and under his statesmanlike influence, the hardening of doctrine that led to the confrontation over the New Deal and the Court-packing plan might not have happened.

Although two of Wilson's three appointments were staunch progressives, the Supreme Court seemed to adopt a somewhat conservative stance as it moved toward the decade of erratic resistance to reform that would follow in the 1920s. Federal reform legislation generally continued to pass muster, but there was the staggering exception of the *Child Labor Case* in 1918. And the Court seemed to strike out at labor unions, in both constitutional and antitrust decisions.

In *Hammer v. Dagenhart* (1918) the Supreme Court stunned Congress and most of the country when it invalidated the first federal CHILD LABOR ACT. The extent of child labor in the United States during the Progressive era was an affront to humanitarian sensibilities. One child out of six between the ages of ten and fifteen was a wage earner. Prohibition and regulation of child labor became the central reform initiatives of the progressive impulse. In 1916, overcoming constitutional doubts, Wilson signed the KEATING-OWEN ACT, which forbade the shipment in interstate or foreign commerce of the products of mines where children sixteen and under had been employed, or of factories where children younger than fourteen worked, or where children fourteen to sixteen had worked more than eight hours a day, six days a week. Child labor was not directly forbidden, but was severely discouraged by closing the channels of interstate commerce.

A narrow majority of the Court, in an opinion by Justice Day, held that this law exceeded the federal commerce power. Day reasoned that the goods produced by child labor were in themselves harmless, and that the interstate transportation did not in itself accomplish any harm. This reasoning was entirely question-begging, because it was the possibility of interstate commerce that imposed a competitive disadvantage in states that outlawed child labor in comparison with less humanitarian states. Moreover, the reasoning was flatly inconsistent with the opinion in *Hipolite Egg* and *Hoke.* But the majority plainly regarded the federal child labor legislation as an invasion of the domestic preserves of the states. Holmes, joined by McKenna, Brandeis, and Clarke, issued a classic dissent.

With the preparations for an advent of American involvement in World War I, the Supreme Court recognized broad federal power to put the economy on a wartime footing. The burden of constitutional resistance to reform legislation shifted to cases involving state laws. Here the main hardening in doctrinal terms came in cases involving labor unions. Otherwise, a reasonable progressivism prevailed. Thus, in BUNTING V. OREGON (1917) the Court upheld the maximum ten-hour day for all workers in mills and factories, whether men or women. However, two minimum wage cases from Oregon were upheld only by the fortuity of an equally divided Supreme Court, Brandeis having recused himself.

The most chilling warning to progressives that laissez-faire constitutionalism was not dead came in COPPAGE V. KANSAS (1915). The issue was the power of a state to prohibit by legislation the so-called YELLOW DOG CONTRACT, under which workers had to promise their employers not to join a union. The Court in *Coppage* held such laws unconstitutional: to limit an employer's freedom to offer employment on its own terms was a violation of freedom of contract.

The Supreme Court's race relations decisions between 1910 and 1921 constitute one of the Progressive era's most notable, and in some ways surprising, constitutional developments. Each of the Civil War amendments was given unprecedented application. For the first time, in the *Grandfather Clause Cases* (1915), the Supreme Court applied the FIFTEENTH AMENDMENT and what was left of the federal civil rights statutes to strike down state laws calculated to deny blacks the right to vote. For the first time, in BAILEY V. ALABAMA (1911) and UNITED STATES V. REYNOLDS (1914), the Court used the THIRTEENTH AMENDMENT to strike down state laws that supported PEONAGE by treating breach of labor contracts as criminal fraud and by encouraging indigent defendants to avoid the chain gang by having employers pay their fines in return for commitments to involuntary servitude. For the first time, in BUCHANAN V. WARLEY (1917), it found in the FOURTEENTH AMENDMENT constitutional limits on the spread of laws requiring racial separation in residential areas of cities and towns, and also for the first time, in *McCabe v. Atchison, Topeka & Santa Fe Railway* (1914), it put some teeth in the equality side of the SEPARATE BUT EQUAL DOCTRINE by striking down an Oklahoma law that said that railroads need not provide luxury car accommodations for blacks on account of low demand.

To be sure, only with respect to peonage could the White Court be said to have dismantled the legal structure of racism in any fundamental way. After the White Court passed into history in 1921, blacks in the South remained segregated and stigmatized by Jim Crow laws, disfranchised by invidiously administered LITERACY TESTS, white PRIMARY ELECTIONS, and POLL TAXES; and victimized by a criminal process from whose juries and other positions of power they were wholly excluded. But if the White Court did not stem the newly aggressive and self-confident ideology of racism inundating America in the Progressive era, neither did it put its power and prestige behind the flood, as had the WAITE COURT and FULLER COURT that preceded it—and, at critical points, it resisted. The White Court's principled countercurrents were more symbols of hope than effective bulwarks against the racial prejudice that permeated American law. But the decisions taken together mark the first time in American history that the Supreme Court opened itself in more than a passing way to the promises of the Civil War amendments.

World War I generated the first set of cases that provoked the Supreme Court for the first time since the FIRST AMENDMENT was ratified in 1791 to consider the meaning of freedom of expression. The cases, not surprisingly, involved dissent and agitation against the war policies of the United States. The war set off a major period of political repression against critics of American policy.

In the first three cases, SCHENCK V. UNITED STATES, FROHWERK V. UNITED STATES, and IN RE DEBS (1919), following the lead of Justice Holmes, the Supreme Court looked not to the law of SEDITIOUS LIBEL for justification in punishing speech but rather to traditional principles of legal responsibility for attempted crimes. In English and American COMMON LAW, an unsuccessful attempt to commit a crime could be punished if the attempt came dangerously close to success, while preparations for crime—in themselves harmless—could not be punished. With his gift of great utterance, Holmes distilled these doctrinal nuances into the rule that expression could be punished only if it created a CLEAR AND PRESENT DANGER of bringing about illegal action, such as draft resistance or curtailment of weapons production. Given his corrosive skepticism and his Darwinian sense of flux, the clear and present danger rule later became in Holmes's hands a fair protection for expression. But in the hands of judges and juries more passionate or anxious, measuring protection for expression by the likelihood of illegal action proved evanescent and unpredictable.

There were other problems with the clear and present danger rule. It took no account of the value of a particular expression, but considered only its tendency to cause harmful acts. Because the test was circumstantial, legislative declarations that certain types of speech were dangerous put the courts in the awkward position of having to second-guess the legislature's factual assessments of risk in order to protect the expression. This problem became clear to Holmes in ABRAMS V. UNITED STATES (1919), in which a statute punishing speech that urged curtailment of war production was used to impose draconian sanctions on a group of radical Russian immigrants who had inveighed against manufacture of war material that was to be used in Russia. In this case, Holmes and Brandeis joined in one of the greatest statements of political tolerance ever uttered.

In 1921, the year Edward Douglass White died and Taft became Chief Justice, Benjamin Cardozo delivered his immortal lectures, "The Nature of the Judicial Process." Cardozo pleaded for judges to "search for light among the social elements of every kind that are the living forces behind the facts they deal with." The judge must be "the interpreter for the community of its sense of law and order . . . and harmonize results with justice through a method of free decision." Turning to the Supreme Court, Cardozo stated: "Above all in the field of constitutional law, the method of free decision has become, I think, the dominant one today."

In this view, we can see that Cardozo was too hopeful, although his statement may have been offered more as an admonition than a description. The method of "free decision," exemplified for Cardozo by the opinions of Holmes and Brandeis, remained in doubt notwithstanding the inconsistent progressivism of the White Court, and would become increasingly embattled in the decades to come.

BENNO C. SCHMIDT, JR.

Bibliography

BICKEL, ALEXANDER M. and SCHMIDT, BENNO C., JR. 1984 *The Judiciary and Responsible Government 1910–1921.* Vol. IX of the Holmes Devise History of the Supreme Court. New York: Macmillan.

CARDOZO, BENJAMIN N. 1921 *The Nature of the Judicial Process.* New Haven, Conn.: Yale University Press.

CHAFEE, ZECHARIAH 1949 *Free Speech in the United States.* Cambridge, Mass.: Harvard University Press.

HIGHSAW, ROBERT B. 1981 *Edward Douglass White.* Baton Rouge: Louisiana State University Press.

SEMONCHE, JOHN E. 1978 *Charting the Future: The Supreme Court Responds to a Changing Society 1890–1920.* Westport, Conn.: Greenwood Press.

SWINDLER, WILLIAM F. 1969 *Court and Constitution in the 20th Century: The Old Legality 1889–1932.* Indianapolis: Bobbs-Merrill.

WHITE PRIMARIES

See: *Grovey v. Townsend; Nixon v. Condon; Nixon v. Herndon;* Primary Elections; *Smith v. Allwright; Terry v. Adams*

WHITING, WILLIAM

See: Commentators on the Constitution

WHITNEY v. CALIFORNIA
274 U.S. 357 (1927)

SCHENCK V. UNITED STATES (1919), ABRAMS V. UNITED STATES (1919), GITLOW V. NEW YORK (1925), and *Whitney* are the four leading FREEDOM OF SPEECH cases of the 1920s in which the CLEAR AND PRESENT DANGER rule was announced but then rejected by the majority in favor of the BAD TENDENCY test announced in *Gitlow.* In *Whitney,* Justice EDWARD SANFORD repeated his *Gitlow* argument that a state law does not violate FIRST AMENDMENT rights by employing the "bad tendency" test as the standard of reasonableness in speech cases. The state may reasonably proscribe "utterances . . . tending to . . . endanger the foundations of organized government." Here Justice Sanford added that "united and joint action involves even greater danger to the public peace and security than the isolated utterances . . . of individuals." Miss Whitney had been convicted of organizing and becoming a member of an organization that advocated and taught CRIMINAL SYNDICALISM in violation of the California Criminal Syndicalism Act of 1919. The Court upheld the act's constitutionality.

After *Schenck,* the clear and present danger position had been reiterated in dissenting opinions by OLIVER WENDELL HOLMES and LOUIS D. BRANDEIS in *Abrams* and *Gitlow.* Brandeis, joined by Holmes, concurred in *Whitney.* Brandeis's reason for concurring rather than dissenting was that Whitney had not properly argued to the California courts that their failure to invoke the danger test was error, and that the Supreme Court might not correct errors by state courts unless those errors were properly raised below.

Brandeis's concurrence was a forceful reiteration of the value to a democracy of freedom of speech for even the most dissident speakers. The framers knew that "fear breeds repression; that repression breeds hate; that hate menaces stable government; that the path of safety lies in the opportunity to discuss freely supposed grievances . . . and that the fitting remedy for evil counsels is good ones." Brandeis reemphasized the imminence requirement of the danger rule. "To courageous, self-reliant men, with confidence in the power of free and fearless reasoning applied through the processes of popular government, no danger flowing from speech can be deemed clear and present, unless the incidence of the evil apprehended is so imminent that it may befall before there is opportunity for full discussion. If there be time . . . to avert the evil by the process of education, the remedy to be applied is more speech, not enforced silence."

Whitney is often cited for an addition by Brandeis to the original clear and present danger formula. The evil anticipated must be not only substantive but also serious. "The fact that speech is likely to result in some violence or in destruction of property is not enough to justify its suppression. There must be the probability of serious injury to the state. . . ."

The Court overruled *Whitney* in BRANDENBURG V. OHIO (1969).

MARTIN SHAPIRO

WHITTAKER, CHARLES
(1901–1973)

A considerable number of Justices who served on the United States Supreme Court resembled T. S. Eliot's famous Mr. Prufrock: "an attendant lord, one that will do [to swell a progress, start a scene or two, . . .] Deferential, glad to be of use, [Politic, cautious, and meticulous;] Full of high sentence, but a bit obtuse. . . ." Charles Whittaker, a self-made man from Kansas, appointed to the Court by President DWIGHT D. EISENHOWER, was one of these.

Whittaker joined the WARREN COURT in 1957, after earlier service on the Eighth Circuit Court of Appeals. His tenure was distinguished only by its brevity and by his own inability to develop a coherent judicial philosophy apart from the orthodox political and social conservatism of the Republican Middle West. His retirement and that of Justice FELIX FRANKFURTER in 1962 marked the beginning of the Warren Court's most liberal and activist phase.

Several DEPORTATION and coerced confession cases best exemplified Whittaker's ad hoc approach to constitutional issues and the confusion that often plagued his opinions. Writing for a majority of six Justices in *Bonetti v. Roger* (1958), he overturned the federal government's attempt to deport an ALIEN who had entered the country in 1923, joined the Communist party for a brief period during the 1930s, left the country to fight in the Spanish Civil War, and finally returned to the United States without rejoining the party. Earlier, Whittaker had voted to sustain the deportation of another alien who had resided continuously in the United States for forty years and whose only offense did not constitute a crime when he committed it (*Lehmann v. Carson*). Two years after *Bonetti,* he voted to uphold the termination of Social Security benefits to aliens deported for their membership in the Communist party during the Great Depression in *Fleming v. Nestor* (1960).

Whittaker displayed little more consistency in the coerced confession cases. In *Moore v. Michigan* (1957), he voted to reverse the murder conviction of a black teenager with a seventh-grade education and a history of head injuries, who had confessed to the crime without the benefit of a lawyer. During the next term, however, he voted, in *Thomas v. Arizona* (1958), to sustain the murder conviction of a black man in Arizona, who had confessed after a twenty-hour interrogation which included the placing of a rope around his neck by a member of the sheriff's posse.

Sometimes, Whittaker joined the Warren Court's liberal bloc, as in TROP V. DULLES (1958), where five Justices declared unconstitutional a provision of the Nationality Act of 1940 depriving wartime deserters of their CITIZENSHIP. He also joined the liberals in *Perez v. Brownell* (1958) when they dissented against the EXPATRIATION of American citizens who voted in foreign elections. (See TROP V. DULLES, 1958.) Whittaker also wrote the opinion in *Staub v. Baxley* (1958), invalidating a city ordinance that required union organizers to secure a permit before soliciting new members.

More frequently, however, Whittaker cast his vote with the Court's conservative bloc led by Justices JOHN MARSHALL HARLAN, TOM C. CLARK, and FELIX FRANKFURTER. In *Beilan v. Board of Education* (1958) he helped to sanction the firing of public school teachers who refused to answer questions about their possible affiliation with the Communist party. He approved the contempt conviction of a college professor who refused to cooperate with a state legislative committee investigating subversive groups in UPHAUS V. WYMAN (1959). He likewise voted to compel the registration of the Communist party under the Subversive Activities Control Act and to allow bar examiners in California to deny admission to a candidate who refused to answer their inquiries about his past membership in the party. (See COMMUNIST PARTY V. SUBVERSIVE ACTIVITIES CONTROL BOARD, 1961; KONIGSBERG V. STATE BAR OF CALIFORNIA, 1961.)

During his final term on the Court, Whittaker continued to affirm his conservative leanings by dissenting in MAPP V. OHIO (1961). He also joined in the Court's dismissal on jurisdictional grounds of an attack on Connecticut's anti-birth control statute in *Poe v. Ullman* (1961). After retiring from the bench, he became a legal adviser to the General Motors Corporation as well as a shrill critic of the CIVIL RIGHTS and anti-Vietnam War protest movements.

MICHAEL E. PARRISH

Bibliography

BERMAN, D. M. 1959 Mr. Justice Whittaker: A Preliminary Appraisal. *Missouri Law Review* 24:1–28.

FRIEDMAN, LEON 1969 Charles Whittaker. Pages 2893–2904 in Leon Friedman and Fred L. Israel, eds., *The Justices of the United States Supreme Court, 1789–1969: Their Lives and Major Opinions.* New York: Chelsea House.

WICKARD v. FILBURN
317 U.S. 111 (1942)

In 1941, by an amendment to the AGRICULTURAL ADJUSTMENT ACT of 1938, Congress brought the national power to regulate the economy to a new extreme, yet the Supreme Court unanimously sustained the regulation in a far-reaching expansion of the commerce power. The price of wheat, despite marketing controls, had fallen. A bushel on the world market in 1941 sold for only forty cents as a result of a worldwide glut, and the wheat in American storage bins had reached record levels. To enable American growers to benefit from government fixed prices of $1.16 per bushel, Congress authorized the secretary of agriculture to fix production quotas for all wheat, even that consumed by individual growers. Filburn sowed twenty-three acres of wheat, despite his quota of only eleven, and produced an excess of 239 bushels for which the government imposed a penalty of forty-nine cents a bushel. Filburn challenged the constitutionality of the statute, arguing that it regulated production and consumption, both local in character; their effects upon INTERSTATE COMMERCE, he maintained, were "indirect."

Justice ROBERT H. JACKSON for the Court wrote that the question would scarcely merit consideration, given UNITED STATES v. DARBY (1941), "except for the fact that this Act extends federal regulation to production not intended in any part for commerce but wholly for consumption on the farm." The Court had never before decided whether such activities could be regulated "where no part of the product is intended for interstate commerce intermingled with the subjects thereof." Taking its law on the scope of the commerce power from GIBBONS v. OGDEN (1824) and the SHREVEPORT DOCTRINE, the Court repudiated the use of mechanical legal formulas that ignored the reality of a national economic market; no longer would the reach of the COMMERCE CLAUSE be limited by a finding that the regulated activity was "production" or its economic effects were "indirect." The rule laid down by Jackson, which still controls, is that even if an activity is local and not regarded as commerce, "it may still, whatever its nature, be reached by Congress if it exerts a substantial economic effect on interstate commerce, and this irrespective of whether such effect is what might at some earlier time have been defined as 'direct' or 'indirect.'" (See EFFECTS ON COMMERCE.)

How could the wheat grown by Filburn, which he fed to his own animals, used for his own food, and kept for next year's seed, be regarded as having a "substantial economic effect" on interstate commerce? Wheat consumed on the farm by its growers, the government had proved, amounted to over twenty percent of national production. Filburn consumed a "trivial" amount, but if he had not produced what he needed for his own use in excess of his allotted quota, he would have had to buy it. By not buying wheat, such producer-consumers depressed the price by cutting the demand. His own contribution to the demand for wheat was trivial, but "when taken with that of others similarly situated," it was significant. Congress had authorized quotas to increase the price of the commodity; wheat consumed on the farm where grown could burden a legitimate congressional purpose to stimulate demand and force up the price. Thus, even if a single bushel of Filburn's infinitesimal production never left his farm, Congress could reach and regulate his activity, because all the Filburns, taken collectively, substantially affected commerce.

LEONARD W. LEVY

Bibliography

STERN, ROBERT L. 1946 The Commerce Clause and the National Economy, 1933–1946. *Harvard Law Review* 59:901–909.

WICKERSHAM, GEORGE
(1858–1936)

Appointed attorney general in 1909 by WILLIAM HOWARD TAFT, George Wickersham argued and won STANDARD OIL COMPANY v. UNITED STATES (1911) and *American Tobacco Company v. United States* (1911). He initiated more prosecutions under the SHERMAN ANTITRUST ACT in four years than his predecessor had in seven, prompting business leaders to call for his resignation. As chairman of the Wickersham Committee from 1929 to 1931, he directed an investigation of the entire system of federal jurisprudence. The commission reported on problems raised by political penetrations of courts, lax criminal law enforcement, abuses of constitutional rights, and various sociological influences contributing to crime.

DAVID GORDON

WIDMAR v. VINCENT
454 U.S. 263 (1981)

In order to avoid activity that might constitute an ESTABLISHMENT OF RELIGION, the University of Missouri at Kansas City barred a student religious group from meeting on the campus for religious teaching or worship. The Supreme Court, 8–1, held that the University, having "created a forum generally open for use by student groups," was forbidden by the FIRST AMENDMENT'S guarantee of the FREEDOM OF SPEECH to exclude the religious group. Because the exclusion was based on the content of the group's speech, it was unconstitutional unless necessary to serve a COMPELLING STATE INTEREST. The exclusion was not necessary to avoid establishment clause problems, for no state sponsorship of religion was implied when the university provided a forum generally open to all student groups.

Justice JOHN PAUL STEVENS, concurring, said that any university necessarily makes many distinctions based on speech content. Here, however, the university discriminated on the basis of the viewpoint of particular speakers, and that was forbidden by the First Amendment.

Justice BYRON R. WHITE dissented, arguing that the state could constitutionally "attempt to disentangle itself from religious worship."

KENNETH L. KARST

(SEE ALSO: *Public Forum.*)

WIEMAN v. UPDEGRAFF
344 U.S. 183 (1952)

In an opinion written by Justice TOM C. CLARK, the Supreme Court struck down an Oklahoma LOYALTY OATH for state employees that required signers to affirm that they were not and had not been for five years members of organizations designated by the attorney general of the United States as "communist front" or "subversive." Clark, who as attorney general had initiated the federal list in 1947, held that the statute violated the DUE PROCESS clause because it did not distinguish innocent membership from knowing membership in the proscribed organizations.

MICHAEL E. PARRISH

WIGMORE, JOHN HENRY
(1863–1943)

John Henry Wigmore was perhaps the foremost American legal scholar and educator of the twentieth century. A professor of law at Northwestern University Law School for fifty years (1893–1943), nearly thirty of them as its dean (1901–1929), Wigmore played the leading role in developing it into one of the nation's leading law schools. Wigmore also helped to found numerous professional and academic organizations, among them the American Institute of Law and Criminology (1909) and the American Bar Association's Sections on Criminal Law (1920) and on International and Comparative Law (1934).

Wigmore wrote an extraordinary number of books and articles on almost every field of the law, but his most significant works focused on evidence, criminal law and criminology, and international and comparative law. His great *Treatise on Evidence* (1904; third ed., 1940; subsequently revised by others) established itself as the dominant work in its field and was acclaimed as the greatest treatise on any single subject of the law. Although some critics objected to the *Treatise*'s introduction of new terms, its length and elaborate organization, and its occasional divergence from the current state of the law, most scholars welcomed it as the most systematic overview of its subject, and it had great influence on many states' revisions of their rules of EVIDENCE and on the Federal Rules of Evidence (1969–1975). Wigmore's other major works on evidence were his *Pocket Code of Evidence* (1910; third ed., 1942) and his *Principles of Judicial Proof* (1913, third ed., 1937). His other books include *A Panorama of the World's Legal Systems* (1928; second ed., 1936), *A Kaleidoscope of Justice* (1941), *Problems of Law: Its Past, Present and Future* (1920), and casebooks on evidence (1906; third ed., 1932) and on torts (1910–1912).

RICHARD B. BERNSTEIN

Bibliography

ROALFE, WILLIAM R. 1977 *John Henry Wigmore: Scholar and Reformer.* Evanston, Ill.: Northwestern University Press.

WILKES CASES
19 Howell's State Trials (1763–1768)

Counting derivative trials, the Wilkes Cases embraced at least forty cases from 1763 to 1769; all emanated ultimately from a single GENERAL WARRANT issued by the British secretaries of state on April 26, 1763, against *The North Briton,* No. 45, a periodical trenchantly critical of the Grenville administration. Numerous categories of the general warrant, which allowed its bearer to arrest, search, and seize at his discretion, had operated in England for centuries. The warrant of April 26, however, was of an atypical variety, based on custom rather than statute, which the government used against dissident publications; it resulted in the search of at least five houses, the arrest of forty-nine persons, and the seizure of thousands of manuscripts and books.

Although hundreds of such warrants had issued since the Restoration, the latest crop of victims included John Wilkes, a powerful member of Parliament and principal author of *The North Briton.* When Wilkes sued every official connected with the warrant, many of the others arrested promptly did the same.

The trials unfolded in distinct series. In *Huckle v. Money,* the first trial on July 6, 1763, CHARLES PRATT, the Chief Justice of the Court of Common Pleas, criticized the *North Briton* warrant because it specified no person, had been issued without a formal complaint under oath, and thus lacked PROBABLE CAUSE. When this case reached the full Common Pleas, Pratt extended his attack to the general search feature of the warrant, holding that it, as well as its companion power of general arrest, violated MAGNA CARTA.

The outcome of the *North Briton* trials incited suits by earlier victims of secretarial warrants. In the most famous of these trials, *Entick v. Carrington* (1765), which accrued from a general warrant against *The Monitor,* the emphasis shifted to the powers of general, confiscatory seizure in such warrants. Pratt, now ennobled as Lord Camden, condemned the use of seized personal papers against their owner as self-incriminatory. Moreover, Camden continued, because private property was inherently sacred, any invasion of it without express legal authority was a trespass even if it merely involved touching the soil or grass. He conceded that the inspection of private papers was not itself a legal trespass, but he insisted that the disclosure of the personal secrets they contained greatly magnified the harm from the physical trespass of their seizure.

Although Pratt in *Wilkes v. Wood* (1763) had condemned even general warrants authorized by statute, WILLIAM MURRAY (Lord Mansfield), in a final appeal of *Huckle v. Money,* upheld statutory warrants and denounced only those not based on parliamentary enactment. When Pratt shifted to the same grounds in *Entick,* the effect was to confine the assault on general warrants to the variant based on custom, and to preserve a greater number that derived from statute. In 1766 a resolution against general warrants did emerge from the House of Commons, but an effort to transform it into binding, comprehensive legislation failed.

WILLIAM CUDDIHY

Bibliography

HOLDSWORTH, SIR WILLIAM 1938 *A History of English Law.* 7th ed. 15 vols. Vol. 10:99–100, 658–672. London: Methuen.

NOBBE, GEORGE 1939 *The North Briton.* New York: Columbia University Press.

WILLIAMS, ROGER
(1603–1683)

Arriving in New England in 1631, Roger Williams preached in Plymouth and Salem, but almost immediately clashed with the Massachusetts authorities over issues involving both church and state. He attacked Massachusetts's right to its land on the grounds that the land had not been purchased from the Indians—only granted by the king. He claimed that the colonial churches had not broken sharply enough with the Church of England, and he denied that magistrates had power to punish in religious matters. Under sentence of banishment from Massachusetts, Williams fled to Providence in 1636 and formed a settlement there. By 1644 he had secured a patent from the English government combining his own and neighboring towns into the colony of Rhode Island and Providence Plantations.

Although always a Calvinist, Williams adhered to no church after his departure from Massachusetts except for a brief period as a Baptist; rather, he lived as a Seeker. RELIGIOUS LIBERTY was his abiding passion, and he defended it primarily for its benefits to religion. Drawing the analogy of church as garden and world as wilderness, he insisted that only a wall between the two could preserve the integrity of the church.

Williams believed that allowing the state any power in church affairs made the state the arbiter of religious truth, an area in which its lack of competence only perverted religion. To demonstrate the absurdity of state attempts to proclaim the true church, he cited history, especially the recent multiple changes in religious allegiance on the part of the English government, and he expressed the psychological insights that rulers tended to advance their own religious preferences as truth and that persecutors always justified their actions in religion's name.

Williams's political views flowed from his religious theories. For him the Israel of the Old Testament was a figurative entity and not, as Massachusetts Puritans claimed, a model for government. He saw government as a SOCIAL COMPACT drawn up between citizens for secular purposes only. Just as civil interference ruined religion, so religious interference disrupted government—by accusations of heresy against civil leaders and demands for their removal from office. He believed that governing was an art, for which Christianity did not necessarily constitute a gift.

Carrying his arguments in favor of religious liberty

to their logical and remarkably radical conclusions, Williams contended that liberty should be extended to all law-abiding citizens, including Roman Catholics (whom he abhorred), non-Christians, and even those he considered blasphemers. By opposing monopolization of Rhode Island's land by its original settlers, he strove to keep the colony open to newcomers of all religions and to enable them to settle there on an equal social and economic basis with already-established inhabitants.

Beyond Rhode Island's fidelity to his ideals of religious freedom, Williams exerted hardly any influence. His views shocked his contemporaries, and throughout his life he bore the stigma of radicalism. During the colonial years, his writings almost disappeared. Succeeding centuries, however, have restored his reputation by correctly perceiving him as a prophet and forerunner of modern religious liberty.

THOMAS CURRY

Bibliography

MILLER, PERRY 1953 *Roger Williams: His Contribution to the American Tradition.* Indianapolis: Bobbs-Merrill.

MORGAN, EDMUND S. 1967 *Roger Williams: The Church and the State.* New York: Harcourt, Brace & World.

WILLIAMS v. FLORIDA
399 U.S. 78 (1970)

The rule of *Williams* is that trial by a jury of six in a noncapital FELONY case does not violate the constitutional right to TRIAL BY JURY in a state prosecution. Trial by jury had historically meant trial by a jury of twelve, neither more nor less. Justice BYRON R. WHITE for the Supreme Court found no rationale for the figure of twelve, which he called "accidental" and "superstitious." If Congress enacted a statute providing for juries of less than twelve in federal prosecutions, the Sixth Amendment would be no bar, according to this case. A jury of six is practical: it can be selected in half the time, costs only half as much, and may reach its verdict more quickly. According to White, "there is no discernible difference between the results reached by the two different-sized juries," but in fact a jury of six hangs less frequently, significantly changes the probability of conviction, and convicts different persons. White claimed that the size of the jury should be large enough to promote group deliberation and allow for a representative cross-section of the community, and he claimed that a jury of six serves those functions as well as a jury of twelve. In fact the Court was wrong. Only Justice THURGOOD MARSHALL dissented on the question of jury size, in an opinion that rested strictly on precedent. Williams also contended that Florida violated his RIGHT AGAINST SELF-INCRIMINATION by its notice-of-alibi rule, but he convinced only Justices HUGO L. BLACK and WILLIAM O. DOUGLAS.

LEONARD W. LEVY

(SEE ALSO: *Jury Size.*)

WILLIAMS v. MISSISSIPPI
170 U.S. 213 (1898)

Williams is a realistic snapshot of our constitutional law on race at the turn of the century. A black man was tried in Mississippi for the murder of a white, convicted by an all-white jury, and sentenced to death. He alleged that he had been denied the EQUAL PROTECTION OF THE LAWS guaranteed by the FOURTEENTH AMENDMENT, because the laws of the state were rigged in such a way as to exclude members of his race from jury service. In Mississippi, to be eligible for jury service one must be qualified to vote. To be a voter one must have paid his POLL TAX and have satisfied registration officials that he could not only pass a LITERACY TEST but also could understand or reasonably interpret any clause of the state constitution; registration officials had sole discretion to decide whether an applicant had the requisite understanding. In Mississippi at that time, a black graduate of Harvard Law School could not satisfy white officials. The state convention of 1890 clearly adopted new qualifications on the right to vote in order to insure white supremacy by disfranchising black voters. Under prior laws there were 190,000 black voters; by 1892 only 8,600 remained, and these were soon eliminated. Blacks disappeared from jury lists after 1892.

A unanimous Supreme Court, speaking through Justice JOSEPH MCKENNA, held that the state constitution and laws passed under it, prescribing the qualifications of voters and jurors, did not on their face discriminate racially. McKenna also declared that the discretion vested in state and local officials who managed elections and selected juries, while affording the opportunity for unconstitutional RACIAL DISCRIMINATION, was not constitutionally excessive. Yet McKenna said, "We gather . . . that this discretion can be and has been exercised against the colored race, and from these lists jurors are selected." The Court recognized that a law on its face might be impartial and be administered "with an evil eye and an unequal hand," but it held that "it has not been shown that their actual administration was evil; only that evil was possible under them."

LEONARD W. LEVY

WILLIAMS v. VERMONT
472 U.S. (1985)

Vermont levied a use tax on automobiles, collected upon each car's registration. No tax was imposed if the car was bought in Vermont, and a Vermont sales tax was paid. If the car was purchased outside Vermont, the use tax was reduced by the amount of any sales tax paid to the other state—but only if the registrant was then a Vermont resident. Persons who had bought cars outside Vermont before becoming Vermont residents sued in state court, challenging the constitutionality of this scheme. The Vermont courts denied relief, but the Supreme Court, 6–3, held that the discrimination against newcomers violated the EQUAL PROTECTION clause. Justice BYRON R. WHITE wrote the OPINION OF THE COURT.

As it had done for half a century, the Court avoided the much-discussed question whether a state must give a credit for payment of another state's sales tax in such circumstances. Instead, the Court followed ZOBEL V. WILLIAMS (1982) and held that the discrimination against newcomers to Vermont served no legitimate statutory purpose. As in *Zobel,* Justice WILLIAM J. BRENNAN, concurring, wrote that the discrimination threatened the "federal interest in free interstate migration." (See RIGHT TO TRAVEL.) Justice HARRY A. BLACKMUN, for the dissenters, favored a REMAND to the state courts for clarification whether the law in fact so discriminated. Even if it did, he argued, Vermont could legitimately tax in rough proportion to automobiles' use on Vermont roads.

KENNETH L. KARST

WILLIAMSON, HUGH
(1735–1819)

Hugh Williamson, mathemetician, physician, and Presbyterian minister, signed the Constitution as a North Carolina delegate to the CONSTITUTIONAL CONVENTION OF 1787. A frequent but not very influential speaker, he was the first to propose the six-year term for senators. He supported RATIFICATION in the North Carolina convention and served in the first two Congresses.

DENNIS J. MAHONEY

WILLIAMSON v. LEE OPTICAL CO.
348 U.S. 483 (1955)

Justice WILLIAM O. DOUGLAS, for an 8–0 Supreme Court, announced that "the day is gone when this Court uses the DUE PROCESS CLAUSE" to strike down state business regulation. Without any inquiry into actual legislative history, Douglas upheld an Oklahoma law regulating eyeglass sales, suggesting various hypothetical reasons why the legislature might have thought it necessary.

DENNIS J. MAHONEY

WILLOUGHBY, WESTEL W.
(1867–1945)

Westel Woodbury Willoughby taught political science at Johns Hopkins University (1894–1933) and was a founder of the American Political Science Association. He wrote nearly two dozen books, including *The Supreme Court of the United States* (1890), *The Nature of the State* (1896), *The American Constitutional System* (1904), and *The Constitutional Law of the United States* (1910; second edition, 1922).

Willoughby rejected the notion that FEDERALISM implied division of SOVEREIGNTY between the central government and the states. He described the Constitution in terms of LIMITED GOVERNMENT, but regarded the central government as possessing the ultimate authority in the country and believed that in crisis situations (such as civil war) the rights of both states and citizens must yield to the INHERENT POWER of national self-preservation. Because he thought the government must at other times be limited to constitutionally DELEGATED POWERS he was especially critical of the decisions in the INSULAR CASES.

DENNIS J. MAHONEY

WILLSON v. BLACK BIRD CREEK MARSH CO.
2 Peters 245 (1829)

Chief Justice JOHN MARSHALL's opinion for a unanimous Supreme Court cannot be reconciled with his opinions in GIBBONS V. OGDEN (1824) and BROWN V. MARYLAND (1827), neither of which he mentioned in Willson. Delaware had authorized the company to dam a navigable tidewater creek, obstructing the navigation of Willson's sloop, licensed under the same Federal Coastal Licensing Act that had proved decisive in *Gibbons.* The Court sustained the constitutionality of the state statute as a measure calculated to improve marshland property and the health of its inhabitants. The Coastal Licensing Act notwithstanding, the Court found that Congress had chosen not to govern the many small navigable creeks of the eastern coast. In effect, the Court sustained the POLICE POWER in a case involving local circumstances affecting the COMMERCE CLAUSE "in its dormant state," that is, unexercised by Congress.

Marshall's *Willson* opinion is so laconic, almost unreasoned, and uncharacteristic of the great Chief Justice that it has never been satisfactorily explained. FELIX FRANKFURTER, in his book *The Commerce Clause,* surmised that Marshall understood that a completely exclusive commerce power might overdiminish STATES' RIGHTS and that Marshall realized the need for effective state regulation of local problems. Taking into consideration "the circumstances of the case," Marshall acknowledged the state interest in enhancing property values and improving the public health. Accordingly he opened the door to the police power because the state's objectives, unlike the situations in *Gibbons* and *Brown,* were not the regulation of commerce per se. *Willson,* however, left a confused legacy for the TANEY COURT, which divided in MAYOR OF NEW YORK v. MILN (1837) and produced doctrinal chaos in the LICENSE CASES (1847) and the PASSENGER CASES (1849). Not until COOLEY v. BOARD OF WARDENS (1851) did the Taney Court find a formula that purported to reconcile Marshall's doctrines in *Gibbons* and *Willson.*

LEONARD W. LEVY

WILMOT PROVISO
(1846)

The proviso was introduced by Congressman David Wilmot (Democrat, Pennsylvania) as an amendment to a $2,000,000 appropriations bill requested by President JAMES K. POLK to finance the Mexican War. The proviso prohibited slavery in any territory acquired from Mexico, thus enabling northern Democrats, like Wilmot, to support the war without supporting slave expansion and more slave states. The proviso passed the House, but the Senate adjourned without acting on the appropriations bill. In 1847 the proviso was added to a new $3,000,000 war appropriations bill. The Senate refused to accept the proviso, and in a bitterly debated compromise, the House agreed to the appropriation without the proviso. Despite its failure in Congress, the proviso raised serious constitutional and political issues. Southerners argued that they had contributed to the war effort and ought to be allowed to settle in the conquered territories without any special disabilities. Northerners condemned the war, especially after the defeat of the proviso, as aggression by an expansionist "slave power." The proviso led to the formation of the Free Soil Party, which was committed to prohibiting SLAVERY IN THE TERRITORIES. Free Soilers ran particularly well in some northern Democratic districts.

PAUL FINKELMAN

Bibliography

MORRISON, CHAPLAIN W. 1967 *Democratic Politics and Sectionalism: The Wilmot Proviso Controversy.* Chapel Hill: University of North Carolina Press.

WILSON, JAMES
(1742–1798)

James Wilson was one of the most influential members of the founding generation. He was born in Scotland and educated as a classical scholar at the University of St. Andrews. He immigrated to America in 1765, whereupon he served as a tutor at the College of Philadelphia while he studied law with the celebrated JOHN DICKINSON. His keen and perceptive mind, superb classical education, and excellent legal training prepared him to play a major role in the creation of the new American republic. He was a frequent delegate from Pennsylvania to the Second CONTINENTAL CONGRESS, one of six men who signed both the DECLARATION OF INDEPENDENCE and the Constitution, and second only to JAMES MADISON in his contribution to the deliberations of the CONSTITUTIONAL CONVENTION. He produced what was probably the most widely distributed and discussed defense of the new Constitution in his Statehouse Speech of October 6, 1787. He was the principal figure in the efforts to secure RATIFICATION OF THE CONSTITUTION by Pennsylvania, whose approval was indispensable to the success of the whole constitutional movement. He was a major architect of the significant Pennsylvania Constitution of 1790. He was one of the six original Justices of the United States Supreme Court. He was the first professor of law appointed after the founding of the new republic, and he was the only Framer to formulate a general theory of government and law—this in his lectures on law, delivered in 1791–1792 at what would later become the University of Pennsylvania.

Wilson was and remains influential, however, not so much because of the roles he played as for the ideas he articulated, the arguments he made, and the institutional arrangements he favored. Among the principal Framers, Wilson was the most committed to, and trusting of, unmitigated majoritarian democracy. He favored the simplicity of immediate consent and self-restraint to the complexity of procedural protections and constitutional contrivances. Relying heavily on the Scottish moralists (especially Thomas Reid), Wilson argued that men are naturally social; imbued with a sense of goodness, veracity, and benevolence; and possessed of a progressive intuitive sense that can be improved with practice so as to carry society "above any limits which we can now assign." As a consequence, he trusted them to elect leaders who would govern soberly and well, especially over a large and "comprehensive Federal Republic" such as the United States. He saw no need to protect the people from themselves. Madison's "republican remed[ies] for the diseases most incident to republican government" were, he believed, unnecessary. The government would be good to the extent that its branches were prompted, through their competition with one another, to serve the people and to reflect faithfully their wishes. Wilson brought this view of government and his commitment to majoritarianism to the Federal Convention, where his influence was clearly felt. He contributed significantly to the Convention's understanding of SEPARATION OF POWERS, figured prominently in determining the institutional arrangements and powers of the legislative, executive, and judicial branches, and helped to make FEDERALISM possible with his arguments concerning the dual SOVEREIGNTY of the people.

Wilson contributed to the Convention's understanding of separation of powers by arguing that it properly consists not of functionally separated branches but of coordinate and equal branches that perform a blend of functions in order to balance, not separate, powers. As he declared, "The separation of the departments does not require that they should have separate objects but that they should act separately tho' on the same objects." Wilson was aware that the various governmental branches, even though popularly elected, would occasionally be activated by "an official sentiment opposed to that of the General Government and perhaps to that of the people themselves." On those occasions, separation of powers would be necessary to insure the fidelity of these popular agents. Wilson also contributed to the Convention's understanding by stressing that separation of powers not only prevents governmental tyranny but also contributes to governmental efficiency. Aware that the democratic process of mutual deliberation and consent can paralyze government when swift and decisive action is necessary, he argued that government would be more efficient if its different functions were performed by separate and distinct agencies.

Wilson's influence on the legislative branch was felt primarily in the House of Representatives and in his promotion of reflective, as opposed to refining, representation. He argued in the Convention that "the Government ought to possess not only first, the force but secondly, the mind or sense of the people at large. The Legislature ought to be the most exact transcript of the whole Society." Wilson regarded representation as a "chain of communication" between the people and those to whom they have delegated the powers of government. Its purpose is not to "refine" the people's sentiments; rather, it is to communicate through links "sound and strong" the exact feelings of the people. Strong as this chain might be, however, Wilson was unwilling to trust it completely. So long as the legislature was perfectly reflective of the people, no problem was presented; however, there was no way to ensure this. On occasion, the legislature might come to possess and perceive an interest distinct from, and perhaps contrary to, the public at large. On that occasion, a single legislature would be dangerous, and thus Wilson argued for a divided legislature with a numerous House of Representatives, so close in political style and feelings to those it represented that it would constitute their "exact transcript," and a popularly elected Senate organized around the principle of proportional representation, thereby providing a "double representation" for the people. Wilson was one of the first to argue that it is possible for the people, simply through the electoral process, to have two different agents or representatives speaking for them at the same time. He did not fear that this common election would erode the material distinctions, and consequently the benefits that resulted from these material distinctions, between the two branches of the legislature. He trusted in the development of a "point of honor" between the two branches: they would "be rivals in duty, rivals in fame, rivals for the good graces of their common constituents." His views on the Senate, though unsuccessful at the Convention, were largely vindicated with the passage of the SEVENTEENTH AMENDMENT.

Wilson's contributions to the shape and powers of the executive branch were perhaps most significant of all. He was the first delegate to propose "that the Executive consist of a single person." He argued that the executive, no less than the legislature, needed to be restrained and controlled. But, "in order to control the legislative authority, you must divide it. In order to control the Executive, you must unite it." The advantage of clear-cut responsibility would reinforce and assure those other "very important advantages" that are also obtained from a single executive, including energy, vigor, dispatch, firmness, consistency, and stability. Wilson was also the first delegate at the Convention to suggest that the President should be elected directly by the people. When this proposal failed to gain general support, he was then the first to propose an ELECTORAL COLLEGE scheme, a modification of which ultimately found its way into the Constitution. He also favored a relatively brief presidential tenure of three years and reeligibility. These features would insure that the President would become and remain "the Man of the People."

Wilson's "Man of the People" was to be more than simply derived from their midst; he was also to be capable of acting vigorously on their behalf. As Wilson stressed in the Pennsylvania ratifying convention, the President was to be captain of the ship of state, holding firmly to the helm and allowing the vessel to "proceed neither in one direction or another without his concurrence." He was to be powerful and independent enough to protect the people from the excesses, instabilities, and injustices of legislative dominance. Wilson's captain was to take his bearings from the people and set his course according to their dictates. Because the people would not be easily misled, Wilson, unlike THE FEDERALIST, would not have the President provide the people with direction or resist them when they were wrong.

Wilson also labored at the Convention for the establishment of a powerful judiciary. Because the judges would be appointed by the President and confirmed by the Senate, he understood the judiciary to be "drawn from the same source, animated by the same principles, and directed to the same ends" and therefore "as much the friend of the people" as the other branches. As a consequence, it could be entrusted with the power of JUDICIAL REVIEW. So entrusted, it could serve as a "noble guard" defending the fundamental principles and will of the people as expressed in the Constitution from governmental sentiments—especially legislative sentiments—which from time to time might come to oppose them.

Wilson also helped to make federalism possible by arguing in the Convention that the people could create and assign power to more than "one set of immediate representatives." The delegates could preserve the states and at the same time establish a new national government because of the dual sovereignty of the people. He argued that both the states and the national government receive their authority directly from the people and owe their responsibility directly to them. The people are the sovereign foundation of all governments. As such, they can construct two levels of government and assign different powers to them. They can take powers from the state governments and place them in the national government. Wilson employed this same argument in the Pennsylvania ratifying convention to taunt those Anti-Federalists who contended that the people could not give to the national government whatever powers and for whatever purposes they pleased. He also operated from these premises in CHISHOLM V. GEORGIA (1793), his only truly important Supreme Court decision, in which he declared that the people of the United States had formed themselves into "a nation for national purposes" and that, consequently, states as well as individual persons were subject to the JUDICIAL POWER OF THE UNITED STATES.

Wilson embraced and defended the "comprehensive Federal Republic" created by the Constitution not only because the people had chosen to construct such a level of government over them but also because he believed that a reciprocating relationship existed between the structure of government and the character of the people. A petty state would produce, he believed, petty men. The only lessons they would learn would be those of "low Vice" and "illiberal Cunning." Only a large republic would sustain and nourish the good qualities of the people. Only a large republic would produce noble citizens, worthy of the great political trust Wilson would place in them.

Central to Wilson's constitutional thought was his confidence in the good qualities of the people. In this regard, he differed from his fellow Framers, in that he relied upon what The Federalist considered "the weaker springs of human character." This difference was critical then and remains so now: Wilson's commitment to unrestrained majoritarian democracy stands in sharp contrast to the Constitution's more complex mitigated democracy that relies not so much on men as on institutions for our political salvation.

RALPH A. ROSSUM

Bibliography

ADAMS, RANDOLPH GREENFIELD, ED. 1930 *Selected Political Essays of James Wilson.* New York: Knopf.

MCCLOSKEY, ROBERT GREEN, ED. 1967 *The Works of James Wilson.* 2 Vols. Cambridge, Mass.: Harvard University Press.

ROSSUM, RALPH A. 1976 James Wilson and the "Pyramid of Government": The Federal Republic. *Political Science Reviewer* 6:113–142.

SMITH, CHARLES PAGE 1956 *James Wilson: Founding Father.* Chapel Hill: University of North Carolina Press.

WILSON, WOODROW
(1856–1924)

Dr. Thomas Woodrow Wilson was both a scholar and an active participant in American constitutional development. Trained in history and law, Wilson became one of the first practitioners of the new academic political science that was born in America toward the close of the nineteenth century. He taught at Bryn Mawr College and Wesleyan University, and became a professor at, and later president of, Princeton University.

As a political scientist, Wilson urged fundamental reforms in the American system of government. In his first book, *Congressional Government* (1885), he argued that instead of the balance of powers envisaged by the Founders, American government was dominated by the legislative branch and, in particular, by a few powerful congressional committees. Wilson advocated cabinet government as he supposed it to exist in Great Britain, dominated by a strong executive. In *Constitutional Government in the United States* (1908), Wilson argued that under the Constitution the President had authority to exercise vigorous leadership of the whole American political system. In other works, Wilson advocated the scientific study of techniques of public administration and the training of a new class of civil servants who would be independent of political influence or control. Professional administrators, Wilson believed, should be left free to devise the most efficient means of carrying into effect the general policy decisions of the political branches of the government. (See PROGRESSIVE CONSTITUTIONAL THOUGHT.)

A progressive Democrat, Wilson was elected governor of New Jersey in 1910, and President of the United States two years later, when THEODORE ROOSEVELT broke with President WILLIAM HOWARD TAFT and split the Republican party. Wilson's platform called for a "New Freedom," characterized by a vigorous ANTITRUST policy, reduced tariffs, legislation to benefit organized labor, and creation of the federal reserve banking system.

During Wilson's terms of office, the SEVENTEENTH, EIGHTEENTH, and NINETEENTH AMENDMENTS were added to the Constitution. But ordinary legislation did as much to change the distribution and use of governmental power as did formal constitutional amendments. The FEDERAL RESERVE ACT (1913) placed control of the nation's money and credit in the hands of an independent, semi-private banking system. The FEDERAL TRADE COMMISSION ACT (1914), brainchild of Boston attorney LOUIS D. BRANDEIS, created an independent REGULATORY AGENCY with specific authority to make regulations having the force of law.

Among the least creditable achievements of the Wilson administration was the introduction of official racial SEGREGATION in executive departments of the federal government for the first time since the Civil War. Wilson himself approved the change of policy, arguing that segregation was in the best interests of black federal employees, but he did not regard it as a matter of major concern.

Wilson asserted a broad conception of executive power in military and FOREIGN AFFAIRS. In 1913 the United States assumed control of the foreign policy of Nicaragua and American marines put down an insurgent movement in that country. Wilson also deployed marines twice, in 1914 and 1916, to suppress insurrections in the Dominican Republic. Between 1913 and 1917 the United States intervened continuously, and ultimately unsuccessfully, in the internal politics of Mexico. For none of these military adventures did Wilson have specific congressional authorization; he relied instead on his power as COMMANDER-IN-CHIEF of the armed forces.

Although Wilson campaigned for reelection in 1916 on the slogan, "He kept us out of war," the United States entered World War I just one month after his second inauguration. The war emergency provided the rationale for a vast expansion of federal power. The Overman Act (1917) created a virtual presidential dictatorship over the machinery of the government; the RAILROAD CONTROL ACT commandeered the private rail network and consolidated it under government auspices; the SELECTIVE SERVICE ACT authorized the drafting of millions of young men into the military; and the ESPIONAGE ACT and the SEDITION ACT provided a basis for controlling civilian dissent. In a sense, the war provided the essential basis—a strongly held vision of the public good—for many of the reforms the Progressives had long advocated. For at least two decades afterward, political activists and reformers would hark back to the sense of unity that World War I provided.

American intervention enabled Britain and France to defeat the Germans and their allies, and so the American government was entitled to a leading voice in dictating the peace terms. Wilson was unable, however, to secure ratification of the Treaty of Versailles and the League of Nations Covenant by the United

States Senate. Republicans, led by Senator HENRY CABOT LODGE, opposed these measures, which seemingly would have subordinated American SOVEREIGNTY to an international body and permanently involved the United States in European quarrels.

In 1919, exhausted by a national campaign to win support for the Versailles Treaty, Wilson suffered a debilitating stroke. For the last year of his presidency the erstwhile advocate of strong presidential leadership tried, and failed, to govern the country from his sickbed. The constitutional problem of presidential disability would not be resolved until passage of the TWENTY-FIFTH AMENDMENT.

DENNIS J. MAHONEY

Bibliography

BETH, LOREN P. 1971 *The Development of the American Constitution: 1877–1917.* New York: Harper & Row.

BRAGDON, HENRY W. 1967 *Woodrow Wilson: The Academic Years.* Cambridge, Mass.: Belknap Press.

LINK, ARTHUR S. 1947–1974 *Woodrow Wilson,* 6 vols. Princeton, N.J.: Princeton University Press.

WILSON v. NEW
243 U.S. 332 (1917)

Congress passed the ADAMSON EIGHT-HOUR ACT in 1916 to avert a threatened nationwide railroad strike and to prevent disruption of INTERSTATE COMMERCE. The act prescribed an eight-hour day for railway workers and prohibited any reduction in pay for the shorter hours. Congress thereby regulated wages (pending the report of a commission established by the act) as well as hours. A United States District Court enjoined enforcement of the act, and that decision was appealed to the Supreme Court.

Chief Justice EDWARD D. WHITE, for a 5–4 Supreme Court, sustained the act as a legitimate exercise of congressional power. Asserting that Congress's power to establish working hours was "so clearly sustained as to render the subject not disputable," White faced the issue: did the COMMERCE CLAUSE give Congress the power to set wages? Despite reservations about government interference with FREEDOM OF CONTRACT, the majority held that the Adamson Act only supplemented contracting parties' rights. Moreover, Congress might set a temporary wage standard to protect interstate commerce when private parties failed to exercise their contract rights. Although the strike threatened an emergency, the emergency created no new powers, but it might provide an occasion for exercise of the commerce power.

The dissenters contended either that the act violated the Fifth Amendment as a TAKING OF PROPERTY or that the act lay outside the scope of Congress's commerce power because wages and hours were only remotely connected with interstate commerce.

DAVID GORDON

WINSHIP, IN RE
397 U.S. 358 (1970)

A 6–3 Supreme Court, speaking through Justice WILLIAM J. BRENNAN, held here that among the constitutional rights available in juvenile proceedings is the STANDARD OF PROOF beyond a REASONABLE DOUBT. A twelve-year-old was charged with a crime which, if done by an adult, would be larceny. The applicable New York statute required only a preponderance of evidence for conviction, and three successive New York courts rejected the contention that the FOURTEENTH AMENDMENT required a higher standard of proof. Tracing the requirement back to early United States history, Brennan found "virtually unanimous adherence" to the reasonable doubt standard in COMMON LAW jurisdictions. He extolled its protective value and spoke of the "vital role" of this "indispensable" standard. "We explicitly hold that the DUE PROCESS Clause protects the accused against conviction except upon proof beyond a reasonable doubt of every fact necessary to constitute the crime with which he is charged." Moreover, Brennan could find no obstacle to extending this right to juveniles. Justice HUGO L. BLACK, dissenting, charged the majority with amending the BILL OF RIGHTS. "Nowhere in that document is there any statement that conviction of crime requires proof of guilt beyond a reasonable doubt."

DAVID GORDON

(SEE ALSO: *Jackson v. Virginia, 1979.*)

WIRETAPPING

Telephone tapping is probably the best known form of electronic surveillance. The Supreme Court originally ruled in OLMSTEAD V. UNITED STATES (1928) that neither the Fifth nor the FOURTH AMENDMENT could be used to control wiretapping. In KATZ V. UNITED STATES (1967), however, the Supreme Court declared that what people reasonably expect to keep private is entitled to constitutional protection under the Fourth Amendment.

Both before and after the *Katz* decision, wiretapping was regulated by statute. Between 1934 and 1968, Section 605 of the COMMUNICATIONS ACT prohibited virtually all wiretapping except for NATIONAL SECURITY purposes. The Justice Department construed the statute so narrowly, however, that it had little effect: federal and state officials tapped extensively, as did private parties, and there were few prosecutions.

In 1968, Congress enacted Title III of the OMNIBUS CRIME CONTROL AND SAFE STREETS ACT, which prohibits telephone tapping except by federal and state officials who obtain prior judicial approval. Before issuing such approval, the court must have PROBABLE CAUSE to believe that EVIDENCE of a specific crime listed in the statute, and relating to a particular person, will be found by tapping a specific phone. Interceptions must be minimized, and notice of the interception must ultimately be given to the target of the surveillance.

Critics claim that the minimization and judicial supervision requirements are ineffective, that wiretapping is inherently indiscriminate, and that it is of little value for major crimes. Proponents assert that the technique is useful, and that the procedural protections are effective.

Wiretapping within the United States to obtain foreign national security intelligence is governed by the Foreign Intelligence Surveillance Act (1978), which creates a special warrant procedure for judicial issuance of permission to wiretap. Both wiretap statutes have been held constitutional.

HERMAN SCHWARTZ

(SEE ALSO: *Electronic Eavesdropping.*)

Bibliography

SCHWARTZ, HERMAN 1977 *Taps, Bugs, and Fooling the People.* New York: Field Foundation.

WIRT, WILLIAM
(1772–1834)

A Virginian lawyer, William Wirt helped defend James Callender in his SEDITION trial (1800) and helped prosecute AARON BURR for TREASON (1806). As United States attorney general under JAMES MONROE and JOHN QUINCY ADAMS (1817–1829), Wirt initiated the system of preserving the "opinions of the Attorneys General" for future use. While attorney general, Wirt followed the common practice of arguing private cases. In association with DANIEL WEBSTER he helped successfully to argue DARTMOUTH COLLEGE V. WOODWARD (1819), MCCULLOCH V. MARYLAND (1819), and GIBBONS V. OGDEN (1824). Wirt's national perspective in these cases was similar to his official policy as attorney general.

PAUL FINKELMAN

Bibliography

KENNEDY, JOHN P. 1850 *Memoirs of the Life of William Wirt.* Philadelphia: Lea & Blanchard.

WISCONSIN v. YODER
406 U.S. 205 (1972)

Wisconsin's school-leaving age was sixteen. Members of the Old Order Amish religion declined, on religious grounds, to send their children to school beyond the eighth grade. Wisconsin chose to force the issue, and counsel for the Amish defendants replied that while the requirement might be valid as to others, the free exercise clause of the FIRST AMENDMENT required exemption in the case of the Amish.

Chief Justice WARREN E. BURGER, speaking for the Supreme Court, was much impressed by the Amish way of life. He rejected Wisconsin's argument that belief but not action was protected by the free exercise clause, and cited SHERBERT V. VERNER (1963). Nor was the Chief Justice convinced by the state's assertion of a COMPELLING STATE INTEREST. Nothing indicated that Amish children would suffer from the lack of high school education. Burger stressed that the Amish would have lost had they based their claim on "subjective evaluations and rejections of the contemporary social values accepted by the majority."

Justice BYRON R. WHITE filed a concurring opinion in which Justices WILLIAM J. BRENNAN and POTTER STEWART joined. White found the issue in *Yoder* much closer than Burger. White pointed out that many Amish children left the religious fold upon attaining their majority and had to make their way in the larger world like everyone else.

Justice WILLIAM O. DOUGLAS dissented in part. He saw the issue as one of CHILDREN'S RIGHTS in which Frieda Yoder's personal feelings and desires should be determinative. Justice Stewart, joined by Justice Brennan, filed a brief concurrence which took issue with Douglas on this point, and noted that there was nothing in the record which indicated that the religious beliefs of the children in the case differed in any way from those of the parents.

RICHARD E. MORGAN

WOLF v. COLORADO
338 U.S. 25 (1949)

In *Wolf* the Supreme Court held that "the core" of the FOURTH AMENDMENT's freedom from UNREASONABLE SEARCHES was "basic" and thus incorporated in the FOURTEENTH AMENDMENT as a restriction on searches by state officers, but that its enforcement feature, the EXCLUSIONARY RULE (in effect for federal trials since 1914), was not. The refusal to require the exclusionary rule for state trials was largely based on considerations of FEDERALISM. The Court reasoned, first, that the exclusionary rule could scarcely be considered "basic" when the COMMON LAW rule of admissibility was still followed both in the English-speaking world outside the United States and in most of the American states, and second, that suits in tort against offending officers could be "equally effective" in deterring unlawful searches. The experience of the following twelve years proved the suit in tort to be a paper remedy rather than an effective sanction, leading the Court to overrule *Wolf* and impose the exclusionary rule on the states in MAPP V. OHIO (1961).

JACOB W. LANDYNSKI

WOLFF PACKING COMPANY v. COURT OF INDUSTRIAL RELATIONS
262 U.S. 522 (1923)

Reversing a trend of broad definitions of public utilities, the Supreme Court voided a Kansas law declaring certain businesses to be AFFECTED WITH A PUBLIC INTEREST, and thus subject to regulation. A unanimous Court could find no justification for the statute and held that affectation derived from the nature of a business, not from the declaration of a state legislature. The Court thus returned to a concept implicit in *Munn v. Illinois* (1877): that a public interest inhered in monopolistic enterprises. (see GRANGER CASES.) Chief Justice WILLIAM HOWARD TAFT defined three categories of businesses clothed with a public interest: public utilities, occupations traditionally regulated (such as innkeepers), and those "businesses which, though not public at their inception, may be fairly said to have risen to be such, and have become subject in consequence to some government regulation."

DAVID GORDON

(SEE ALSO: *Public Use; Economic Regulation and the Constitution.*)

WOLMAN v. WALTER
433 U.S. 229 (1977)

Ohio's aid plan for independent schools had six components: (1) the loan of textbooks; (2) the supply of standardized testing and scoring material; (3) the provision of diagnostic services aimed at identifying speech, hearing, and psychological problems; (4) the provision, off non-public school premises, of therapeutic, guidance, and remedial services; (5) the loan to pupils of instructional materials such as slide projectors, tape recorders, maps, and scientific gear; and (6) the provision of transportation for field trips similar to the transportation provided public school students.

Justice HARRY BLACKMUN delivered what was in part an opinion of the Supreme Court and in part a PLURALITY OPINION in which only Chief Justice WARREN E. BURGER, Justice POTTER STEWART, and Justice LEWIS F. POWELL joined.

The Court upheld the loan of textbooks, the supply of testing materials, the therapeutic services, and the provision of diagnostic services on non-public school premises. The Court found unconstitutional the provisions for lending secular instructional materials and for field trip transportation.

This case indicated the extent to which the "wall between church and state" was in fact a blurred, indistinct, and variable barrier.

RICHARD E. MORGAN

WOMEN

See: Sex Discrimination

WONG KIM ARK, UNITED STATES v.
169 U.S. 649 (1898)

This case, decided at a time when prejudice against people of Chinese ancestry was widespread, maintained the integrity of the CITIZENSHIP clause of section one of the FOURTEENTH AMENDMENT. Congressional legislation, known as the CHINESE EXCLUSION ACTS, denied citizenship to Chinese immigrants, and a treaty with China provided that no subject of China in the United States could be naturalized. Neither the exclusion acts nor the treaty applied in this case, however, because Wong Kim Ark had been born in San Francisco. When he was about twenty-one he visited his parents who had returned to China after living in the United States approximately twenty years. On his return to San Francisco, he was denied entry to the United States on the grounds that he was not a citizen. The Supreme Court held, 6–2, that the government's policy in refusing NATURALIZATION to persons of Chinese ancestry could not constitutionally be applied to anyone born in the United States whose parents, regardless of ancestry, were domiciled in this country and did not have diplomatic status.

LEONARD W. LEVY

WONG SUN v. UNITED STATES
371 U.S. 471 (1963)

In *Wong Sun* the Supreme Court held that an incriminating oral statement made by a suspect that derives immediately from his unlawful arrest is inadmissible in evidence as a FRUIT OF THE POISONOUS TREE, no less than the derivative EVIDENCE obtained from an unlawful search, as in SILVERTHORNE V. UNITED STATES (1920), or from unlawful wiretapping, as in NARDONE V. UNITED STATES (1939). However, when the taint of the earlier illegality is dissipated (as it was in this case, by a suspect voluntarily returning to make a statement several days after his arraignment and release on his own recognizance), the evidence is admissible.

In addition, *Wong Sun* contributed to the elaboration of PROBABLE CAUSE standards by holding that flight from an officer is not in itself such a strong inference of guilt as to establish probable cause for an arrest.

JACOB W. LANDYNSKI

WOOD v. STRICKLAND
420 U.S. 308 (1975)

This was an early case in the development of EXECUTIVE IMMUNITY from DAMAGES in CIVIL RIGHTS actions alleging constitutional violations. The case involved the liability of school board members for alleged violations of students' DUE PROCESS rights. The Supreme Court, in an opinion by Justice BYRON R. WHITE, clarified its holding in SCHEUER V. RHODES (1974) by expressly stating that the good faith defense of executive officials contained both subjective and objective elements. An official must subjectively believe he is doing right and must not act in "ignorance or disregard of settled, indisputable law." *Harlow v. Fitzgerald* (1982) later undermined the subjective component of *Wood*'s test. (See NIXON V. FITZGERALD, 1982.)

THEODORE EISENBERG

WOODBURY, LEVI
(1789–1851)

Levi Woodbury was a New Hampshire lawyer, state supreme court justice (1817–1823), governor (1823–1824), United States senator (1825–1831; 1841–1842), secretary of the navy (1831–1834), secretary of the treasury (1834–1841), and United States Supreme Court Justice (1845–1851). A staunch Jacksonian Democrat, Woodbury supported territorial expansion, STRICT CONSTRUCTION, and STATES' RIGHTS, while opposing the BANK OF THE UNITED STATES, abolitionists, and high tariffs. Although a conservative, Woodbury advocated public schools, female education, and prison reform. He personally disliked slavery but believed it was constitutionally protected and that all agitation over it should cease.

On the New Hampshire bench Woodbury supported the state in DARTMOUTH COLLEGE V. WOODWARD (1819). As treasury secretary, Woodbury continued President ANDREW JACKSON's Bank War and advocated an independent treasury. He believed that Congress lacked constitutional power to recharter the Bank, and as late as 1841 he asserted that MCCULLOCH V. MARYLAND (1819) neither set a valid precedent nor determined the constitutionality of any future bank charter.

In 1830, as a senator, Woodbury criticized the Supreme Court for its "manifest and sleepless opposition . . . to the strict construction of the Constitution" which had created "a diseased enlargement of the powers of the General Government and throwing chains over States-Rights. . . ." Woodbury attempted to stop these tendencies in his brief tenure on the Supreme Court. In the LICENSE CASES (1847), Woodbury joined the majority in upholding state PROHIBITION statues. In the PASSENGER CASES (1849), he asserted, in dissent, that states could constitutionally regulate immigrants without violating the Constitution's COMMERCE CLAUSE. In LUTHER V. BORDEN (1848), he agreed with the majority that the case involved a POLITICAL QUESTION beyond the court's JURISDICTION, but he nevertheless modified his states' rights position to condemn the use of martial law in Rhode Island. In *Warning v. Clarke* (1847), he again dissented, this time to assert state jurisdiction over navigable rivers. In a rare deviation from his states' rights philosophy, Woodbury wrote the majority opinion in *Planters' Bank v. Sharpe* (1848), overturning a Mississippi statute and court decision because both impaired the OBLIGATION OF CONTRACTS in violation of the Constitution.

Woodbury's most important majority opinion was written in *Jones v. Van Zandt* (1847), where he upheld a particularly harsh interpretation of the Fugitive Slave Law of 1793. Van Zandt, an Ohio Quaker, had given a ride to a group of blacks walking on a road in Ohio. Woodbury held Van Zandt financially liable for the escape of these fugitive slaves, even though at the time Van Zandt had no notice they were fugitives. Woodbury asserted that the Constitution had "flung its shield" over slavery, giving masters a COMMON LAW right to recapture their property. Woodbury held that the Fugitive Slave Law was a constitutionally proper enforcement of this right. Somewhat inconsistently, he then asserted that slavery itself was "a political question, settled by each State for itself." In 1848 Woodbury sought the presidential nomination. He was considered a likely candidate in 1852, because his *Van Zandt* opinion gave him southern support, while as a Northerner he might get grudging support from Free Soil Democrats. He campaigned for the nomination from the bench until his death in 1851.

PAUL FINKELMAN

Bibliography

GATELL, FRANK O. 1968 Levi Woodbury. Pages 843–872 in Leon Friedman and Fred L. Israel, eds., *The Justices of the United States Supreme Court, 1789–1969: Their Lives and Major Opinions.* New York: Chelsea House.

WOODRUFF v. PARHAM
8 Wallace 123 (1869)

Woodruff produced a retreat from the broad enunciation of the ORIGINAL PACKAGE DOCTRINE in BROWN v. MARYLAND (1827). In that case Chief Justice JOHN MARSHALL had said in an OBITER DICTUM that the DOCTRINE applied "equally to importations from a sister State. . . ." In this case the city of Mobile, Alabama, had taxed various commodities and transactions including goods imported from other states and sold in their original and unbroken packages. Woodruff alleged that this tax violated the constitutional clause forbidding state IMPOSTS or duties on imports. The Court ruled unanimously that the clause applied only to goods imported from foreign countries. Because the tax did not discriminate against the products of other states, it did not burden INTERSTATE COMMERCE. In effect, the Court limited the original package doctrine to FOREIGN COMMERCE.

LEONARD W. LEVY

WOODS, WILLIAM B.
(1824–1887)

William Burnham Woods of Ohio was appointed to the Supreme Court in 1880 after eleven years of service as United States circuit judge for the Fifth Circuit. His tenure on the Supreme Court was brief (1881–1887); virtually all of his opinions for the Court dealt with private law questions that came up under DIVERSITY JURISDICTION. He is remembered primarily for his collaboration with Justice JOSEPH P. BRADLEY, first on circuit, then on the Supreme Court, in the formulation of a jurisprudence for the FOURTEENTH AMENDMENT. Although initially disposed to give the amendment a BROAD CONSTRUCTION, Woods ultimately retreated in the face of a more circumspect majority on the Supreme Court.

Woods's first meeting with Bradley, who had been assigned to the circuit upon his appointment to the Supreme Court, occurred at New Orleans in 1870. There they advanced a broad interpretation of the Fourteenth Amendment's PRIVILEGES AND IMMUNITIES clause in *Live Stock Dealers & Butchers Assn. v. Crescent City Co. & Board of Metropolitan Police* (1870), the first case, Woods noted in the report, in which the amendment was fully considered by a federal tribunal. The privileges and immunities of United States citizens, they contended, embraced all "fundamental rights," including that of pursuing any lawful employment in a lawful manner. "It is possible," Bradley admitted, "that those who framed the article were not themselves aware of the far reaching character of its terms," but its language clearly applied "as well to white as colored persons" and protected the rights of both against arbitrary state laws. Working from memoranda prepared by Bradley, Woods indicated in *United States v. Hall* (1871) that FREEDOM OF SPEECH and FREEDOM OF ASSEMBLY were among the FUNDAMENTAL RIGHTS guaranteed by the Fourteenth Amendment, opening the door for INCORPORATION of the BILL OF RIGHTS through the privileges and immunities clause. Over the dissents of Bradley and three others, however, the Supreme Court rejected each of these pioneering doctrinal formulations in the landmark SLAUGHTERHOUSE CASES (1873). Eleven years later, in BUTCHERS UNION SLAUGHTERHOUSE

CO. V. CRESCENT CITY LIVE STOCK CO. (1884), Woods joined with Bradley and Justices STEPHEN J. FIELD and JOHN MARSHALL HARLAN in one last trenchant protest against the majority's emasculation of the privileges and immunities clause. Woods surrendered altogether in *Presser v. Illinois* (1886), where he spoke for a unanimous Court in holding that the Bill of Rights was a limitation only on the power of the federal government and in no way restricted the states.

Woods's initial construction of Congress's affirmative powers under the Fourteenth Amendment was especially spacious. In *Hall,* the case of first impression, Woods overruled defendants' demurrer to a conspiracy INDICTMENT under the Civil Rights Act of 1870. A federal statute punishing private action such as assault, he asserted, was certainly an "appropriate" exercise of national power, for "denying the EQUAL PROTECTION OF THE LAWS included the omission to protect, as well as the omission to pass laws for protection." (See STATE ACTION.) In UNITED STATES V. CRUIKSHANK (1874), however, Bradley led a retreat from this position. There counsel for the defendants again attacked the constitutionality of the conspiracy measure, insisting that it usurped the state's exclusive JURISDICTION over crimes such as murder. Woods disagreed and stood on the doctrine advanced in his *Hall* opinion. But Bradley conceded that protection of rights against private action was primarily the duty of the states, and his views prevailed in the Supreme Court. Woods then abandoned the *Hall* formulation. Seven years later in UNITED STATES V. HARRIS (1883), his most important Supreme Court opinion, Woods prominently displayed his penchant for following the lead of others. The results were tragic. In *Harris* he not only embraced Bradley's *Cruikshank* position but also invalidated the Klu Klux Klan Act (FORCE ACT OF 1871) on the grounds that it failed to restrict criminal liability to persons who conspired to divest rights because of the victim's race. As drafted, Woods explained for the Court, the statute covered instances even where whites assaulted whites; consequently it was "broader than is warranted" by the Thirteenth Amendment.

CHARLES W. MCCURDY

Bibliography

FILLER, LOUIS 1969 William B. Woods. In Leon Friedman and Fred L. Israel (eds.), *The Justices of the United States Supreme Court 1789–1969: Their Lives and Major Opinions.* Pp. 1327–1336. New York: Chelsea House.

FRANTZ, LAURENT B. 1964 Congressional Power to Enforce the Fourteenth Amendment against Private Acts. *Yale Law Journal* 73:1353–1384.

WOODS v. CLOYD W. MILLER COMPANY

333 U.S. 138 (1948)

A unanimous Supreme Court here upheld the Housing and Rent Act of 1947 which had extended wartime price controls into peacetime. Writing for the Court, Justice WILLIAM O. DOUGLAS declared that legislation adopted under the WAR POWERS could constitutionally be continued in effect in economically essential areas of public policy even after the cessation of hostilities.

DAVID GORDON

WOODSON v. NORTH CAROLINA

See: Capital Punishment Cases, 1976

WORCESTER v. GEORGIA

See: Cherokee Indian Cases

WORKERS' COMPENSATION LEGISLATION

Workers' compensation legislation provides workers compensation for losses resulting from injury, disablement, or death when the losses result from work-related accidents, casualties, or disease. The legislation replaces tort liability with a schedule of benefits based upon the loss or impairment of the wage-earning capacity of the worker. All fifty states in the Union have workers' compensation statutes.

Under the COMMON LAW, employers often were able to defeat employees' tort actions by invoking the doctrines of contributory negligence, negligence of fellow servants, or assumption of risk. Frequently the employer did not even need these defenses, for the employee first had to prove the employer's negligence in order to recover. Accordingly, many victims of work-related injuries went uncompensated.

In order to extend the protection afforded workers and to contain costly and time-consuming litigation of industrial accidents, states enacted workers' compensation legislation with no requirement of negligence or fault as a prerequisite to liability. Employers were simultaneously protected against what were perceived to be excessively large JUDGMENTS through a limited and determinant payout. The statutes essentially substitute a system of insurance for liability based on fault.

In *Ives v. South Buffalo Railway Company* (1911) New York's highest court struck down the state's first compulsory compensation requirements as unconstitutional, on the ground that they violated the state and federal DUE PROCESS clauses. However, the Supreme Court held in NEW YORK CENTRAL RAILROAD COMPANY V. WHITE (1917) that a compulsory compensation system does not violate the United States Constitution, at least for "hazardous employment." In the case of the New York statute, New York promptly amended its constitution to authorize compulsory plans.

The general rule in this area of law is that if an injury is fully or partly covered by the statute, the statutory remedy is exclusive. Many jurisdictions do not allow compensation for injuries caused by a worker's willful misconduct or unreasonable failure to observe safety rules or use safety devices.

WILLIAM B. GOULD

Bibliography

MALONE, WEX S; PLANT, MARCUS L; and LITTLE, JOSEPH W. 1980 *Cases and Materials on Workers' Compensation and Employment Rights,* 2nd ed. St. Paul, Minn: West Publishing Co.

WORTMAN, TUNIS
(?–1822)

A New York lawyer prominent in Tammany politics, Tunis Wortman contributed significantly to the emergence of a libertarian theory of the FIRST AMENDMENT following the Sedition Act of 1798. His philosophic book, *An Enquiry, Concerning the Liberty, and Licentiousness of the Press* (1800), whose publication ALBERT GALLATIN and other Jeffersonian congressmen helped underwrite, was the era's most systematic presentation of the case for an absolutist interpretion of freedom of publication (excluding personal libels). Wortman regarded prosecutions for SEDITIOUS LIBEL as incompatible with republican government.

LEONARD W. LEVY

WRIGHT v. VINTON BRANCH OF MOUNTAIN TRUST BANK OF ROANOKE
300 U.S. 440 (1937)

Despite the decision in LOUISVILLE JOINT STOCK LAND BANK V. RADFORD (1935), Congress had to act on behalf of farmers losing their farms through foreclosures. A revised FRAZIER-LEMKE ACT fixed a three-year stay of proceedings with the proviso that a federal bankruptcy court might shorten that period if the economic emergency ended. The new act also provided that the mortgagee retained a lien on the property. But except for a few other minor changes the act remained the same, allowing the bankrupt mortgagor to retain possession of the property and to purchase it at its newly appraised value. Justice LOUIS D. BRANDEIS, for a unanimous Supreme Court, found that the new act was free of the objectionable features of the original and did not violate the Fifth Amendment's DUE PROCESS clause. President FRANKLIN D. ROOSEVELT's court-packing plan may have influenced the Court to temper its views.

LEONARD W. LEVY

WRIGHTWOOD DAIRY CO., UNITED STATES v.
315 U.S. 110 (1942)
ROCK ROYAL CO-OP, INC., UNITED STATES v.
307 U.S. 533 (1939)

These decisions are among the more significant results of the post-1936 interpretation of the COMMERCE CLAUSE as a source of federal power extending to virtually the entire national economy. The AGRICULTURAL MARKETING AGREEMENT ACT of 1937 authorized the secretary of agriculture to fix minimum prices for all milk in INTERSTATE COMMERCE, or burdening or affecting commerce. In *Rock Royal* the price-fixing provisions governed sales by local dairy farmers to dealers who processed the milk and transported it. Those opposing federal authority contended that the regulated transactions included INTRASTATE COMMERCE whose sales were fully completed *before* any interstate commerce began. Holding the statute constitutional, the Court declared that the national power to fix production quotas and prices applied to local milk because its marketing was "inextricably intermingled with and directly affected the marketing of milk which moved across state lines." In *Wrightwood,* the milk subject to regulation under the same statute was entirely intrastate and none of it was intermingled with milk that crossed state lines. Nevertheless the Court unanimously held that it was the EFFECT ON INTERSTATE COMMERCE, not the source of the injury to it, that was "the sole criterion of Congressional power." Accordingly, the commerce power extended to intrastate transactions whose regulation made the regulation of interstate commerce effective, including intrastate transactions whose competitive price affected interstate ones. Both cases were decided on a thoroughgoing application of the SHREVEPORT DOCTRINE.

LEONARD W. LEVY

WRIT OF ASSISTANCE

See: Assistance, Writ of

WRIT OF CERTIORARI

See: Certiorari, Writ of

WRIT OF ERROR

See: Error, Writ of

WRIT OF HABEAS CORPUS

See: Habeas Corpus

WRIT OF MANDAMUS

See: Mandamus, Writ of

WRIT OF PROHIBITION

See: Prohibition, Writ of

WRITS OF ASSISTANCE CASE

See: Paxton's Case

WYMAN v. JAMES
400 U.S. 309 (1971)

In *Wyman* the Supreme Court held that a recipient of Aid to Families with Dependent Children must permit a home visit by a caseworker, when the law requires it, or forfeit her right to public assistance. The Supreme Court did not consider it to be a search in FOURTH AMENDMENT terms. Even if the visit were a search, the Court said it was reasonable: it was made for the benefit of the child; it was "a gentle means" of assuring that tax funds are properly spent; the caseworker was not a "uniformed authority"; and the recipient had the choice of invoking her right to refuse or forfeiting the benefits. Three dissenting Justices (WILLIAM O. DOUGLAS, WILLIAM J. BRENNAN, THURGOOD MARSHALL) protested that the Court had granted more protection to a commercial warehouse than to a "poor woman's home."

JACOB W. LANDYNSKI

WYNEHAMER v. PEOPLE OF NEW YORK
13 N.Y. 378 (1856)

Although out of joint with its times, *Wynehamer* became a classic case of pre-1937 American constitutional history, exemplifying our constitutional law as a law of judicially implied limitations on legislative powers, drawn from the DUE PROCESS clause for the benefit of VESTED RIGHTS. The case involved the constitutionality of a state prohibition act. More than a dozen states had such legislation before the Civil War. The New York law involved in *Wynehamer* prohibited the sale of intoxicating liquor and the possession of liquors for sale, and it ordered the forfeiture and destruction of existing supplies as public nuisances. The fundamental issue raised by such legislation was whether property which had not been taken for a public use could be destroyed in the name of the public health and morals, without any compensation to the owner. Everywhere, except in New York, the state courts held that a mere license to sell liquor was not a contract in the meaning of the CONTRACT CLAUSE, and that a charter to make and sell liquor was subject to the RESERVED POLICE POWER to alter, amend, or repeal it. Moreover, liquor, like explosives or narcotics, was a peculiar kind of property, dangerous to the public safety, morals, and health. Legislatures could never relinquish their control over such matters, not even by a contract in the form of a charter. As Chief Justice ROGER B. TANEY had said in the 1847 LICENSE CASES, nothing in the United States Constitution prevented a state from regulating the liquor traffic "or from prohibiting it altogether."

The New York Court of Appeals, however, held the state prohibition statute unconstitutional on the grounds that it violated the due process clause of the state constitution. The various opinions of the state judges used the novel concept of SUBSTANTIVE DUE

PROCESS about half a century before the Supreme Court of the United States accepted that concept. The conventional and previously sole understanding of due process had been that it referred to regularized and settled procedures insuring mainly a fair accusation, hearing, and conviction. And, the doctrine of vested rights notwithstanding, the orthodox view of the POLICE POWER authorized the legislature, as Chief Justice LEMUEL SHAW of Massachusetts had said, "to declare the possession of certain articles of property . . . unlawful because they would be injurious, dangerous, and noxious; and by due process of law, by proceeding IN REM, to provide both for the abatement of the nuisance and for the punishment of the offender, by the seizure and confiscation of the property, by the removal, sale or destruction of the noxious article" (*Fisher v. McGirr,* 1854). Accordingly the opinion of the New York court was startling when it said, "All property is alike in the characteristic of inviolability. If the legislature has no power to confiscate and destroy property in general, it has no such power over any particular species." The court showed that the prohibition statute simply annihilated existing property right in liquors. The crucial lines of the opinion declared that the right not to be deprived of life, liberty, or property without due process of law "necessarily imports that the legislature cannot make the mere existence of the rights secured the occasion of depriving a person of any of them, even by the forms which belong to 'due process of law.' For if it does not necessarily import this, then the legislative power is absolute."

Thus even if the legislature provided all the forms of due process by laying down proper procedures for prosecuting violators of the statute, as in this case, due process had still been denied. The court, in effect, looked at the substance of the statute, found it denied persons of their property, and then held it unconstitutional for denying "due process," even if it did not deny due process. One can make sense out of this by realizing that the court had rewritten the due process clause to mean that property cannot be deprived with or without due process. The Court in effect redpenciled the due process clause out of the constitution, or as EDWARD S. CORWIN said, *Wynehamer* stands for "nothing less than the elimination of the very phrase under construction from the constitutional clause in which it occurs." The difficulty, however, is that the court had to its own mind kept and relied on the due process clause. It added a new meaning to supplement the old one. It constitutionally changed process into substance by holding that the statute's infirmity lay in what it did, not how it did it. Due process as a substantive limitation on legislative powers was then an absurd concept. Substantive process was oxymoronic, like thunderous silence.

Another way of understanding *Wynehamer*'s substantive due process is to realize that the court believed that due process had substance. The court in effect accused the legislature of retaining the forms of due process without its substance, that is, of providing mere empty formalities and labeling them due process, because the effective deprivation of property was not by judicial process but by legislative fiat.

Wynehamer, an aberration at the time, was everywhere repudiated yet destined for ultimate acceptance by the highest court of the land and destined, too, to become the source of a major doctrine in American constitutional history.

LEONARD W. LEVY

Bibliography

CORWIN, EDWARD S. 1948 *Liberty against Government.* Chap. 3. Baton Rouge: Louisiana State University Press.

MOTT, RODNEY L. 1926 *Due Process of Law.* Pages 311–326. Indianapolis: Bobbs-Merrill.

WYTHE, GEORGE
(1726–1806)

George Wythe served almost uninterruptedly in Virginia's House of Burgesses from 1754 to 1775 and was a delegate to the First Continental Congress in 1774, later signing the DECLARATION OF INDEPENDENCE. With his pupil THOMAS JEFFERSON (JOHN MARSHALL and HENRY CLAY were also his students) and EDMUND PENDLETON, Wythe revised Virginia's laws. He was appointed to the Virginia Court of Chancery in 1778; one year later he became the first professor of law in the United States, enabling him to influence the course of American jurisprudence. His opinion in COMMONWEALTH V. CATON (1782) approved, in theory, a court's right to restrain a legislative act violative of the constitution. Wythe was a delegate to the CONSTITUTIONAL CONVENTION OF 1787 and chairman of its rules committee, but judicial duties obliged him to leave the convention early. At the Virginia convention he worked for RATIFICATION OF THE CONSTITUTION. Wythe opposed slavery and freed the slaves he inherited.

DAVID GORDON

Bibliography

CLARKIN, WILLIAM 1970 *Serene Patriot: A Life of George Wythe.* Albany, N.Y.: Alan Publications.

Y

YAKUS v. UNITED STATES
321 U.S. 414 (1944)

The EMERGENCY PRICE CONTROL ACT of 1942 delegated power to fix prices and rents to the Office of Price Administration (OPA). Under the act, challenges to the legality of OPA regulations could not be made in federal district court enforcement proceedings, even those aimed at imposing criminal penalties, but must be made in separate proceedings in the EMERGENCY COURT OF APPEALS. The Supreme Court sustained this limitation on the district courts in civil enforcement proceedings in *Lockerty v. Phillips* (1944). In *Yakus,* the Court upheld the limitation in the context of a criminal prosecution. The Court also rejected attacks on the act as an unconstitutional DELEGATION OF POWER for failing to provide sufficient guidelines. Chief Justice HARLAN FISKE STONE, for the Court, said that the act contained specific objectives: "to stabilize prices and to prevent speculative, unwarranted and abnormal increases in prices and rents." It also mentioned standards for price-setting: administrators should consult industry and consider current prices. Because the act accorded with earlier decisions and because its standards were "sufficiently definite and precise," Stone could find no unauthorized delegation of power. Justice OWEN ROBERTS, dissenting, believed that the case presented substantially the same issue as SCHECHTER POULTRY CORPORATION V. UNITED STATES (1935) which the majority, he said, had clearly overruled. Justice WILEY RUTLEDGE also dissented, joined by Justice FRANK MURPHY. Rutledge argued that Congress could not constitutionally command the federal courts to enforce administrative orders, disregarding their possible unconstitutionality. The Rutledge view seems likely to prevail in the absence of a wartime emergency.

DAVID GORDON

YAMASHITA, IN RE
327 U.S. 1 (1947)

A 6–2 Supreme Court here refused to consider the claim of an enemy officer, charged with war crimes before an American military tribunal in the Philippines, that he had been denied the DUE PROCESS OF LAW guaranteed by the Fifth Amendment. The Court held that it had JURISDICTION only to consider whether the military tribunal had authority to try the accused.

When General Tomoyuki Yamashita surrendered in 1945, an American military commission tried him on charges that he permitted atrocities against both civilians and prisoners of war, in violation of the law of war. Yamashita's military counsel applied to the Supreme Court for leave to file petitions for writs of HABEAS CORPUS and prohibition, challenging the jurisdiction and legal authority of the commission. Chief Justice HARLAN FISKE STONE, for the majority, denied leave to file but wrote an opinion on the jurisdictional issues. He found that Congress had legally authorized the commission's establishment under the WAR POWERS, and that the charge was adequate to state a violation of the law of war. Stone also denied that the American Articles of War (which incorporated the law of war) forbade the admission of hearsay and opinion EVIDENCE.

Justices FRANK MURPHY and WILEY RUTLEDGE, dissenting, argued eloquently for the extension of the due process clause.

DAVID GORDON

YARBROUGH, EX PARTE
110 U.S. 651 (1884)

This is the only nineteenth-century case in which the Supreme Court sustained the power of the United States to punish private persons for interfering with VOTING RIGHTS. Yarbrough and other members of the Ku Klux Klan assaulted a black citizen who voted in a congressional election. The United States convicted the Klansmen under a federal statute making it a crime to conspire to injure or intimidate any citizen in the free exercise of any right secured to him by the laws of the United States. The Court, in a unanimous opinion by Justice SAMUEL F. MILLER, held that the United States "must have the power to protect the elections on which its existence depends, from violence and corruption." Miller's reasoning is confused. Congress had passed the statute in contemplation of its power to enforce the FOURTEENTH AMENDMENT. In UNITED STATES V. CRUIKSHANK (1876) the Court had ruled that the same statute could not reach private, rather than state, actions. Miller thought the situation different when Congress sought to protect rights constitutionally conferred, and he stressed Article I, section 4, which empowered Congress to alter state regulations for the election of members of Congress. But that provision did not apply here. In UNITED STATES V. REESE (1876) the Court had ruled that the FIFTEENTH AMENDMENT did not confer the right to vote on anyone, but only a right to be free from RACIAL DISCRIMINATION in voting. Here, however, Miller ruled that "under some circumstances," the Fifteenth Amendment, which was not the basis of the statute, may operate as the source of a right to vote. In the end Miller declared, "But it is a waste of time to seek for specific sources of the power to pass these laws." In JAMES V. BOWMAN (1903), involving the right to vote in a federal election, the Court held unconstitutional an act of Congress without reference to *Yarbrough.*

LEONARD W. LEVY

YATES, ROBERT
(1738–1801)

Judge Robert Yates, who in 1777 had served on the committee that drafted the state constitution, was a delegate from New York to the CONSTITUTIONAL CONVENTION OF 1787. A trusted, if undistinguished, follower of Governor George Clinton, Yates represented the antinationalist viewpoint then dominant in New York politics. He and JOHN LANSING consistently outvoted ALEXANDER HAMILTON and kept New York in the STATES' RIGHTS camp. But on July 10 Yates and Lansing walked out, charging that the Convention was exceeding its authority.

In the contest over RATIFICATION OF THE CONSTITUTION Yates was an active anti-Federalist. His "Brutus" letters were an able and articulate presentation of the dangers opponents feared would result from adoption of the Constitution, including annihilation of the states and usurpation by the federal courts. Yates was a delegate to the New York ratifying convention where he voted against ratification.

Yates kept notes of the debates of the federal convention from its first meeting through July 5. He did not publish the notes himself, but they were published in 1821 and are, after JAMES MADISON's, the best record of the early proceedings.

DENNIS J. MAHONEY

Bibliography

ROSSITER, CLINTON 1966 *1787: The Grand Convention.* New York: Macmillan.

YATES v. UNITED STATES
354 U.S. 298 (1957)

Following DENNIS V. UNITED STATES (1951), Smith Act conspiracy prosecutions were brought against all second-rank United States Communist party officials, and convictions were secured in every case brought to trial between 1951 and 1956. In June 1957, however, the Supreme Court, in *Yates,* reversed the convictions of fourteen West Coast party leaders charged with Smith Act violations. The Court, speaking through Justice JOHN MARSHALL HARLAN, declared that the *Dennis* decision had been misunderstood. The Smith Act did not outlaw advocacy of the abstract doctrine of violent overthrow, because such advocacy was too remote from concrete action to be regarded as the kind of indoctrination preparatory to action condemned in *Dennis.* The essential distinction, Harlan argued, was that those to whom the advocacy was addressed had to be urged to *do* something, now or in the future, rather than merely *believe* in something. Without formally repudiating the "sliding scale" reformulation of CLEAR AND PRESENT DANGER set forth in the *Dennis* opinion, the Court erected a stern new standard for evaluating convictions under the Smith Act, making conviction under the measure difficult. As to INDICTMENTS for involvement in organizing the Communist party in the United States, the Court also took a narrow view. Organizing, Harlan maintained, was only the original act of creating such a group, not any continuing process of proselytizing and recruiting. Since the indictments had been made some years following the postwar organizing of their party, the federal three-year statute of limitations had run out. The Court cleared five of the defendants, remanding the case of nine others for retrial. The ruling brought an abrupt end to the main body of Smith Act prosecutions then under way.

PAUL L. MURPHY

YBARRA v. ILLINOIS
444 U.S. 85 (1979)

Although three dissenting Justices complained that the Supreme Court majority had narrowed the STOP-AND-FRISK RULE of TERRY V. OHIO (1968), Justice POTTER STEWART for the Court did not doubt that an officer may pat down a suspect for a concealed weapon. Stewart regarded *Terry* as an exception to the requirement of PROBABLE CAUSE. Here no such cause existed to search a person suspected neither of criminal activity nor of having a weapon. A police officer, having a warrant to search a tavern and its bartender, patted down a bystander, felt no weapon, but removed from his pocket a cigarette pack containing heroin. The Court reversed the man's conviction, because the warrant did not include him, and probable cause to search him was absent.

LEONARD W. LEVY

YELLOW DOG CONTRACT

The yellow dog contract was a device used by employers prior to the New Deal era to prevent collective bargaining by employees. By a yellow dog contract a worker agreed not to join or remain a member of a labor organization and to quit his job if he joined one. At a time in our history when the courts shaped the law so that its major beneficiary was industrial capitalism, yellow dog contracts were enforceable, even though workers had little choice in accepting their terms. Workers either signed such contracts or forfeited the opportunity of working. In effect, a yellow dog contract blackmailed an employee into promising not to join a union; his supposed free choice to accept a job or look elsewhere for work turned out to be a choice between being blackmailed or blacklisted. In one perspective, yellow dog contracts robbed workers of their FREEDOM OF CONTRACT. The courts thought otherwise, however.

In the 1890s fifteen states enacted laws that promoted COLLECTIVE BARGAINING by outlawing yellow dog contracts, and in 1898 section 10 of the ERDMAN ACT, passed by Congress, also outlawed their use by interstate railroads. In ADAIR V. UNITED STATES (1908) the Supreme Court held the Erdman Act unconstitutional. SUBSTANTIVE DUE PROCESS of law provided one ground of decision. The Court reasoned that section 10 abridged freedom of contract, a liberty the Court found in the Fifth Amendment's DUE PROCESS CLAUSE, because Congress had violated the right of workers to make contracts for the sale of their labor. In COPPAGE V. KANSAS (1915) the Court applied this reasoning to state statutes that had banned yellow dog contracts.

Having disabled both the national commerce power and the STATE POLICE POWER from forbidding yellow dog contracts, the Court then sustained the legality of such contracts. In HITCHMAN COAL AND COKE CO. V. MITCHELL (1917) the Court reversed a federal circuit court's determination that a yellow dog contract was not an enforceable contract. Justice MAHLON PITNEY for a six-member majority declared, "The employer is as free to make non-membership a condition of employment as the worker is free to join the union." The Court added that the right to make such a contract was "part of the constitutional rights of personal liberty and private property, not to be taken away even by legislation," which the Court had already voided. The extent to which these decisions thwarted unionization cannot be gauged.

Congress revived the Erdman Act's provision when it passed the Railway Labor Act of 1926, and in the NORRIS-LAGUARDIA ACT of 1932 declared yellow dog contracts to be contrary to American public policy and unenforceable "in any court of the United States." The major industrial states passed "little Norris-LaGuardia acts." By the time these statutes came before the Supreme Court, it found ways to sustain them.

LEONARD W. LEVY

YICK WO v. HOPKINS
118 U.S. 356 (1886)

This is one of the basic decisions interpreting the EQUAL PROTECTION OF THE LAWS clause of the FOURTEENTH AMENDMENT. A San Francisco ordinance made criminal the conduct of a laundry business in any building not made of stone or brick, with such exceptions for wooden structures as administrative officials might make. Officials used their discretion in a grossly discriminatory manner, licensing about eighty wooden laundries run by Caucasians and denying licenses to about two hundred applicants of Chinese extraction. The Supreme Court unanimously held, in an opinion by Justice STANLEY MATTHEWS, that the ordinance, though racially neutral on its face, was applied so unequally and oppressively by public authorities as to deny equal protection. Thus the Court looked beyond the law's terms to its racially discriminatory administration and applied the benefits of the Fourteenth Amendment to Oriental ALIENS, that is, "to all persons . . . without regard to any difference of race, of color, or of nationality."

LEONARD W. LEVY

YOUNG, EX PARTE
209 U.S. 123 (1908)

The question in this case—one of the most important of the present century—was whether a citizen might resort to a federal court to vindicate a constitutional right against state infringement and, pending a final JUDGMENT, obtain freedom from civil or criminal suits by a temporary INJUNCTION directed to an officer of the state. The Supreme Court held that, the ELEVENTH AMENDMENT notwithstanding, a federal court might issue such an injunction.

A Minnesota statute fixed railroad rates and (to deter institution of a TEST CASE) made the officers and employees of the railroads personally liable to heavy fines and imprisonment if those rates were exceeded. A STOCKHOLDER'S SUIT in EQUITY was filed in federal Circuit Court to prevent enforcement of or compliance with the statute, on the ground that it violated the FOURTEENTH AMENDMENT by depriving the railroads of property without DUE PROCESS OF LAW. The federal court issued a temporary injunction restraining the state attorney general, Edward T. Young, from taking steps to enforce the statute. When Young defied the injunction the court found him in contempt and committed him to the custody of the United States marshal.

Young petitioned the Supreme Court for a writ of HABEAS CORPUS, contending that the suit for injunction was really against the state and that, under the Eleventh Amendment, the state could not be sued in federal court without its consent. The Court denied Young's petition, Justice JOHN MARSHALL HARLAN alone dissenting.

Justice RUFUS PECKHAM, for the Court, argued that if the Minnesota law was unconstitutional, then Young, attempting to enforce it, was stripped of his official character and became merely a private individual using the state's name to further his own illegitimate end. Incongruously, the end Young was furthering was unconstitutional only because it involved STATE ACTION. The "private wrong" was a fiction adopted by the Court to circumvent the Eleventh Amendment.

Congress reacted to the *Young* decision by passing a law (substantially repealed in 1976) requiring that federal court injunctions against enforcement of state laws alleged to be unconstitutional issue only from special THREE-JUDGE COURTS and providing, in such cases, for direct APPEAL to the Supreme Court.

The doctrine of *Young* remains valid law today. Although it originally arose in connection with due process protection of economic liberty, the doctrine provides a remedy for state action infringing CIVIL RIGHTS or CIVIL LIBERTIES. But the doctrine of *Young* applies only to equitable relief, and the Eleventh Amendment remains bar to actions for monetary damages that will be paid out of the state treasury.

DENNIS J. MAHONEY

(SEE ALSO: *Osborn v. Bank of the United States, 1824; Edelman v. Jordan, 1974.*)

YOUNG v. AMERICAN MINI THEATRES, INC.
427 U.S. 50 (1976)

In *Young v. American Mini Theatres, Inc.* the Supreme Court upheld a Detroit ZONING ordinance requiring adult theaters to be located certain distances from residential areas and specified businesses. Four Justices led by Justice JOHN PAUL STEVENS argued that adult movies ranked low in the hierarchy of FIRST AMENDMENT values. Four dissenting Justices led by Justice POTTER STEWART argued that the First Amendment recognized no hierarchy for types of protected speech. Justice LEWIS F. POWELL agreed with the dissent, but voted to uphold the ordinance, arguing that the theater owners had asserted no First

Amendment interest of their own and that the First Amendment interests of others, including moviemakers and potential audiences, were not endangered.

STEVEN SHIFFRIN

YOUNGER v. HARRIS
401 U.S. 37 (1971)

Harris, indicted under California's CRIMINAL SYNDICALISM LAW, sought a federal court INJUNCTION to compel the district attorney to cease prosecution in the state court. The district court held the law unconstitutional and issued the injunction. The Supreme Court reversed, 8–1, severely limiting DOMBROWSKI v. PFISTER (1965).

Justice HUGO L. BLACK, for the Court, rested decision on two interlocking grounds. First, a state prosecution was pending; because any claim that the underlying state law was unconstitutional could be made in the state proceeding, there was no "irreparable injury" to justify an injunction. Second, the national government should avoid intruding into "the legitimate activities of the state." Although a federal court might enjoin a state prosecution commenced in bad faith to harass the exercise of FIRST AMENDMENT rights, the claim that the law was unconstitutional on its face did not satisfy this bad-faith harassment requirement. (See ABSTENTION DOCTRINES.)

After *Younger,* the California courts held the syndicalism law invalid.

KENNETH L. KARST

YOUNGSTOWN SHEET & TUBE CO. v. SAWYER
343 U.S. 579 (1952)

In a landmark restriction on presidential power, the Supreme Court in 1952 held invalid President HARRY S. TRUMAN's seizure of the steel mills. Justice HUGO L. BLACK, joined by five other Justices, delivered the opinion of the Court. Chief Justice FRED M. VINSON, dissenting with Justices STANLEY F. REED and SHERMAN MINTON, believed that military and economic emergencies justified Truman's action.

Each of the five concurring Justices wrote separate opinions, advancing different views of the President's emergency power. Only Justices Black and WILLIAM O. DOUGLAS insisted on specific constitutional or statutory authority to support presidential seizure of private property. Assigning the lawmaking function exclusively to Congress, they allowed the President a role only in recommending or vetoing laws. On existing precedent, this concept of the SEPARATION OF POWERS doctrine was far too rigid. Previous Presidents had engaged directly in the lawmaking function without express constitutional or statutory authority, often with the acquiescence and even blessing of Congress and the courts.

The other four concurring Justices (FELIX FRANKFURTER, ROBERT H. JACKSON, HAROLD BURTON, and TOM C. CLARK) did not draw such a strict line between the executive and legislative branches, nor did they try to delimit the President's authority to act in future emergencies. Frankfurter thought it inadvisable to attempt a comprehensive definition of presidential power, based on abstract principles, without admitting powers that had evolved by custom: a "systematic, unbroken, executive practice, long pursued to the knowledge of the Congress and never before questioned . . . may be treated as a gloss on 'executive Power.' " Burton withheld opinion on the President's constitutional power when facing an "imminent invasion or threatened attack," while Clark agreed that the Constitution gave the President extensive authority in time of grave and imperative national emergency.

Jackson identified three categories of presidential power, ranging from actions based on express or implied congressional authorization (putting executive authority at its maximum) to executive measures that were incompatible with congressional policy (reducing presidential power to its lowest ebb). In between lay a "zone of twilight" in which President and Congress shared authority. Jackson said that congressional inertia, indifference, or acquiescence might enable, if not invite, independent presidential action. He further argued that the ENUMERATED POWERS of the President required "scope and elasticity" and said he would "indulge the widest latitude of interpretation" when presidential powers were turned against the outside world for the security of the United States.

Considering the four concurrences and three dissents, the Steel Seizure Case was far from a repudiation of the inherent power doctrine. Nevertheless, a majority of the Court did reach agreement on important principles: presidential actions, including those of an "emergency" nature, are subject to JUDICIAL REVIEW; the courts may enjoin executive officers from carrying out presidential orders that conflict with statutory policy or the Constitution; and independent presidential powers in domestic affairs are especially vulnerable to judicial scrutiny when Congress has adopted a contrary statutory policy. The Steel Seizure Case has supplied the Supreme Court with an important precedent for curbing subsequent exercises of presidential power in areas such as the Pentagon Papers case (NEW YORK TIMES V. UNITED STATES, 1971), electronic surveillance, IMPOUNDMENT, and EXECUTIVE PRIVILEGE.

LOUIS FISHER

(SEE ALSO: *Steel Seizure Controversy; Executive Order 10340; Harry S. Truman.)*

Bibliography

MARCUS, MAEVA 1977 *Truman and the Steel Seizure Case: The Limits of Presidential Power.* New York: Columbia University Press.

WESTIN, ALAN F. 1958 *The Anatomy of a Constitutional Law Case.* New York: Macmillan.

ZABLOCKI v. REDHAIL
434 U.S. 374 (1978)

In LOVING V. VIRGINIA (1967) the Supreme Court had struck down a MISCEGENATION statute flatly forbidding interracial marriage, resting decision on both EQUAL PROTECTION and SUBSTANTIVE DUE PROCESS grounds. In *Zablocki* the Court protected the "right to marry" in a setting where race was irrelevant. Wisconsin required a court's permission for the marriage of a resident parent who had been ordered to support a child not in his or her custody. Permission would be granted only when the candidate proved compliance with the support obligation and showed that the children were not likely to become public charges. Because he could not comply with the law, Redhail was denied a marriage license. The Supreme Court held, 8–1, that this denial was unconstitutional.

The case produced six opinions. Justice THURGOOD MARSHALL, for the majority, rested on equal protection grounds. Marriage was a FUNDAMENTAL INTEREST, protected by the constitutional RIGHT OF PRIVACY. The Wisconsin law interfered "directly and substantially" with the right to marry and was not necessary to effectuate important state interests. Justice POTTER STEWART concurred on due process grounds. Justice LEWIS F. POWELL, also concurring, objected to the Court's STRICT SCRUTINY test; such an inquiry would cast doubt on such limits on marriage as "bans on incest, bigamy, and homosexuality, as well as various preconditions to marriage, such as blood tests." Using a more relaxed STANDARD OF REVIEW, he nonetheless found the statute wanting on both due process and equal protection grounds. Justice JOHN PAUL STEVENS concurred, calling the law a "clumsy and deliberate legislative discrimination between the rich and poor" whose irrationality violated equal protection. Justice WILLIAM H. REHNQUIST, in lone dissent, rejected the notion that marriage was a "fundamental" right and argued for the strict judicial nonscrutiny that had become his trademark.

For all the diversity of the Justices' views, little turns on the choice between equal protection and due process grounds, or on conclusory assertions about the proper standard of review. *Zablocki* makes clear that significant state interference with the freedom to marry demands correspondingly weighty justification.

KENNETH L. KARST

(SEE ALSO: *Freedom of Intimate Association; Marriage and the Constitution.*)

ZEMEL v. RUSK
381 U.S. 1 (1965)

In *Zemel* the Supreme Court sustained (6–3) the constitutionality of the secretary of state's refusal to validate passports for travel to Cuba. Chief Justice EARL WARREN, for the majority, rejected two arguments for the petitioner: that he had a RIGHT TO TRAVEL under the DUE PROCESS clause of the Fifth Amendment; and that he had a FIRST AMENDMENT right to travel to Cuba to gather information.

DENNIS J. MAHONEY

(SEE ALSO: *Richmond Newspapers, Inc. v. Virginia, 1980.*)

ZENGER'S CASE
(1735)

Had John Peter Zenger, the printer of the *New-York Weekly Journal,* attacked the provincial assembly of New York instead of its hated royal governor, he would have been summarily convicted at the bar of the house, jailed, and forgotten by posterity. But he was tried by a jury, brilliantly defended by a great lawyer, and saved for posterity by James Alexander's report of *A brief Narrative of the Case and Tryal of John Peter Zenger* (1736). Alexander, the editor of the paper which Zenger printed, probably wrote the articles that led to the prosecution and, as a lawyer, prepared the case for Andrew Hamilton.

Scalded by the paper's weekly articles against his administration, Governor William Cosby ordered an information against its printer for SEDITIOUS LIBEL; a GRAND JURY had refused to indict, the assembly had refused to cooperate, and the local government, defending "liberty of the press," protested. Zenger, in other words, symbolized the popular party against a detested administration. Not surprisingly the jury acquitted him after brief deliberation, against the instructions of Chief Justice James DeLancey, who presided at the trial before the Supreme Court of Judicature.

The law was against Zenger. Both the prosecutor and the judge accurately informed the jury that seditious libel consisted of scandalizing the government by adversely reflecting on those entrusted with its administration, by publishing material tending to breed popular contempt for the administration, or by alienating the affections of the people for government in any way. Moreover, the truth of a libel magnified its criminality. But Hamilton's reply had greater appeal. If the people could not remonstrate against the oppressions and villainies of their governors, confining themselves always to truthful accusations, they would in no time lose their liberty and property. Hamilton did not repudiate the law of seditious libel; he argued, rather, that Zenger's statements being true were not libels. When the court rejected the proposition that truth should be a defense to a charge of seditious libel, Hamilton appealed to the jury over the court. He argued that the jury, like the press, was a bastion of popular liberty. It should ignore the court's instruction to return a special verdict on the question whether Zenger had, in fact, published the statements charged; a special verdict would leave to the court a ruling on the question of law whether those statements were criminal. Hamilton urged the jury, instead, to return a general verdict of "not guilty," thus deciding the law as well as the fact. The jury returned a general verdict of "not guilty."

The jury's general verdict was a safe way of striking at the unpopular governor and endorsing the right of the people, through the press, to criticize their government. The jury's verdict did not, however, alter the settled law. Not until the Sedition Act of 1798 (see ALIEN AND SEDITION ACTS) did truth as a defense and the power of the jury to render a general verdict in cases of seditious libel become part of American law; and, as the enforcement of that infamous statute showed, embattled libertarians came to discover that they should have repudiated the doctrine of seditious libel rather than grasp at Zengerian principles.

LEONARD W. LEVY

(SEE ALSO: *People v. Croswell*, 1804; *New York Times v. Sullivan*, 1964.)

Bibliography

KATZ, STANLEY NIDER 1972 *A Brief Narrative of the Case and Trial of John Peter Zenger. . . by James Alexander.* Cambridge, Mass.: Harvard University Press.

LEVY, LEONARD W. 1960 Did the Zenger Case Really Matter? Freedom of the Press in Colonial New York. *William and Mary Quarterly,* 3d ser., 17:35–50.

ZOBEL v. WILLIAMS

See: Privileges and Immunities; Right to Travel

ZONING

When a local government decides how to allocate land uses it acts under the POLICE POWER exercised by the states and their governmental subdivisions to regulate for the public health, safety, and welfare. The first zoning ordinances appeared early in the twentieth century as a result of urbanization and the encroachment of factories and noxious uses in residential neighborhoods. In EUCLID V. AMBLER REALTY (1926) the Supreme Court upheld a comprehensive local zoning ordinance, rejecting a SUBSTANTIVE DUE PROCESS attack. Although today's zoning ordinances are more sophisticated than the simple division of land uses upheld in *Euclid,* the basic constitutional issues raised by zoning decisions remain an unusually stable area of constitutional law.

Because a zoning ordinance is adopted by a legislative body, and because zoning amendments are legislative decisions in most states, the constitutional scrutiny applied to zoning is no different from that applied to LEGISLATION at any governmental level. The courts use the due process analysis of *Euclid* to uphold zoning if they find a reasonable relationship between the zoning and the city's police power objectives. Like other social and economic legislation, zoning comes to court clothed with a presumption of validity. A court will not question the wisdom or the motives of legislators. If a court finds any RATIONAL BASIS to support zoning as an implementation of the public health, safety, and welfare, the ordinance will be held valid. A court considers factors such as increased traffic and congestion, compatibility with adjacent uses, and impact on land values of neighboring properties. Courts often apply a fairly debatable rule: if reasonable minds can differ on the reasonableness of an ordinance, the municipal decision must be upheld. Some state courts are more willing than the federal courts to use theories of STATE CONSTITUTIONAL LAW to strike down zoning regulations.

Although a court may be reluctant to question the police power objectives of zoning, it may be more inclined to examine the effects of a zoning restriction on the value of property. Even when a zoning ordinance achieves public objectives, it may be held to be a TAKING OF PROPERTY if it denies a property owner all economic use of his land. The leading case is *Pennsylvania Coal Co. v. Mahon* (1972).

Other guarantees may also serve as bases for constitutional challenges to zoning ordinances. The FIRST AMENDMENT repeatedly forms the basis of attacks on local sign ordinances and ordinances regulating adult businesses. In the 1960s and 1970s, a series of "exclusionary zoning" cases challenged a municipal refusal to rezone to allow mobile homes, apartments, or anything other than single family homes on large lots. Arguing that such practices violated the EQUAL PROTECTION clause, landowners and hopeful future residents had varying success. The Supreme Court was originally not interested in fashioning a federal constitutional remedy. In ARLINGTON HEIGHTS V. METROPOLITAN HOUSING DEVELOPMENT CORP. (1977) it severely restricted the authority of the federal courts to find RACIAL DISCRIMINATION in exclusionary zoning. Some state courts have been more aggressive. In *Southern Burlington County NAACP v. Mount Laurel* (1975), for example, the New Jersey Supreme Court held, on both substantive due process and equal protection grounds, that a municipality cannot close its doors to the housing needs of the region, including low-cost housing. Then, in CLEBURNE V. CLEBURNE LIVING CENTER, INC. (1985) the Supreme Court gave some indication that it would examine more rigorously the exclusionary classifications in zoning ordinances.

Zoning ordinances also require landowners to obtain development permission under a host of administrative procedures that vary from one JURISDICTION to another. Whether it be subdivision or site plan approval, variances, special or conditional uses, or environmental permits, the process is rife with constitutional pitfalls for local administrative bodies. The standards for approving or denying permits must be made specific in the ordinance; otherwise, a state court may hold that the ordinance unconstitutionally delegates legislative authority to an administrative body. Applicants must be given PROCEDURAL DUE PROCESS, including NOTICE and an opportunity to be heard, and, in some states, even quasi-judicial procedures. The agency's decision must be based on evidence sufficient to support it.

Perhaps the most serious danger to the constitutional status of zoning is the threat of a radical departure in the judicial relief afforded a victorious landowner. Under the SEPARATION OF POWERS doctrine, the traditional judicial relief for invalid zoning has been to grant an INJUNCTION prohibiting its enforcement and allow the municipality to rezone. A few courts in the 1970s held that confiscatory zoning amounted to taking of property for public purposes and required cities to compensate landowners. The Supreme Court has not yet decided the availability of this remedy under the federal Constitution.

Damages for a taking may be available under SECTION 1983, TITLE 42, UNITED STATES CODE. In MONELL V. DEPARTMENT OF SOCIAL SERVICES (1978) the Supreme Court held that municipalities can be sued under Section 1983, and the specter of money damages for any denial of constitutional rights in the zoning process became a reality. The damage to a landowner whose economic return is restricted by zoning and who must proceed through a time-consuming local zoning process perhaps including litigation can be substantial. The traditional constitutional deference afforded local government under its police power remains, but the possible consequences of stepping outside constitutional bounds have become severe.

Zoning ordinances now include sophisticated techniques, such as computer-based point systems for approving new development, incentive and bonus programs, and the transfer of development rights. These new techniques have not yet been extensively tested in the courts, but they raise constitutional problems similar to those raised by conventional zoning. Judicial attention in the years to come will focus on the constitutionality of these techniques and on the suitability of a damage remedy in zoning cases.

DANIEL R. MANDELKER
BARBARA ROSS

Bibliography

MANDELKER, DANIEL R. 1982 *Land Use Law.* Charlottesville, Va.: Michie Co.

WILLIAMS, NORMAN, JR. 1974 *American Land Planning Law.* Chicago: Callaghan & Co.

ZORACH v. CLAUSEN
343 U.S. 306 (1952)

This was the Supreme Court's second encounter with a RELEASED TIME program. In MCCOLLUM V. BOARD OF EDUCATION (1948), the Court had invalidated an arrangement by which teachers entered public schools to provide religious instruction. *Zorach* involved New York City's released time program in which instruction was offered off school premises. According to the requests of their parents, public school children were allowed to leave school for specific periods of time to go to church facilities. Nonparticipating students remained in their regular classrooms.

Justice WILLIAM O. DOUGLAS delivered the OPINION OF THE COURT sustaining the constitutionality of New York's program. Douglas emphasized that, as opposed to *McCollum,* no public facilities were used. The schools, Douglas said, were merely rearranging their schedules to accommodate the needs of religious people.

Justices HUGO L. BLACK, ROBERT H. JACKSON, and FELIX FRANKFURTER dissented. Black and Jackson argued that children were compelled by law to attend public schools and that to release them for religious instruction used governmental compulsion to promote religion. In a slap at Douglas's presumed presidential ambitions, Jackson said, "Today's judgment will be more interesting to students of psychology and of the judicial process than to students of constitutional law."

RICHARD E. MORGAN

ZURCHER v. STANFORD DAILY
436 U.S. 547 (1978)

In *Zurcher v. Stanford Daily* the police chief of Palo Alto, California, appealed from a federal district court decision declaring that a search of a college newspaper's office conducted pursuant to a duly authorized search warrant had infringed upon FOURTH AMENDMENT and FIRST AMENDMENT rights. There was no contention that the newspaper or any of its staff was reasonably suspected of the commission of a crime, nor was it contended that weapons, contraband, or fruits of a crime were likely to be found on the premises. Rather, the police secured a warrant on a showing of PROBABLE CAUSE for the conclusion that photographic evidence of a crime was to be found somewhere on the premises. The Supreme Court thus addressed the general question of the standards that should govern the issuance of warrants to search the premises of persons not themselves suspected of criminal activity and the specific question whether any different standards should apply to press searches.

The Court ruled that the innocence of the party to be searched was of no constitutional importance. So long as there was probable cause to believe that evidence of a crime was to be found on premises particularly described, no further showing was needed. Specifically, the Court declined to "reconstrue the Fourth Amendment" to require a showing that it would be impracticable to secure a subpoena *duces tecum* before a warrant could be issued.

That the party to be searched was a newspaper the Court regarded as of some moment but not enough to prefer subpoenas over warrants. Instead, the Court observed that warrant requirements should be applied with "particular exactitude when First Amendment interests would be endangered by the search."

The Court expressed confidence that magistrates would safeguard the interests of the press. Magistrates could guard against the type of intrusions that might interfere with the timely publication of a newspaper or otherwise deter normal editorial and publication decisions. Nor, said the Court, "will there be any occasion or opportunity for officers to rummage at large in newspaper files." The Court asserted that "the warrant in this case authorized nothing of this sort." Yet, as the *Zurcher* opinion discloses, the police searched "the Daily's photographic laboratories, filing cabinets, desks, and wastepaper baskets." The Court's application of the particular exactitude standard seems neither particular nor exact.

Zurcher is the first case squarely to authorize the search and seizure of mere evidence from an innocent party; it has raised difficult questions of Fourth Amendment reasonableness as applied to searches of other innocent third parties such as lawyers and judges. By suggesting that press values be considered in an assessment of reasonableness, it opens the door for further distinctions between searches of media and nonmedia persons. By suggesting that the reasonableness of a search is a requirement that may go beyond probable cause and specificity, it reopens discussion about the relationship between the two clauses of the Fourth Amendment.

STEVEN SHIFFRIN

Appendix 1

The Call for the Federal Constitutional Convention

RESOLUTION OF CONGRESS

1787, February 21

WHEREAS there is provision in the Articles of Confederation & perpetual Union for making alterations therein by the Assent of a Congress of the United States and of the legislatures of the several States; And whereas experience hath evinced that there are defects in the present Confederation, as a means to remedy which several of the States and particularly the State of New York by express instruction to their delegates in Congress have suggested a convention for the purposes expressed in the following resolution and such Convention appearing to be the most probable means of establishing in these states a firm national government

Resolved that in the opinion of Congress it is expedient that on the second Monday in May next a Convention of delegates who shall have been appointed by the several states be held at Philadelphia for the sole and express purpose of revising the Articles of Confederation and reporting to Congress and the several legislatures such alterations and provisions therein as shall when agreed to in Congress and confirmed by the states render the federal constitution adequate to the exigencies of Government & the preservation of the Union.

Appendix 2

Articles of Confederation

Articles of Confederation and perpetual Union between the States of New Hampshire, Massachusetts Bay, Rhode Island and Providence Plantations, Connecticut, New York, New Jersey, Pennsylvania, Delaware, Maryland, Virginia, North Carolina, South Carolina, and Georgia.

ARTICLE I. The style of this Confederacy shall be "The United States of America."

ART. II. Each State retains its sovereignty, freedom, and independence, and every power, jurisdiction, and right, which is not by this Confederation expressly delegated to the United States in Congress assembled.

ART. III. The said States hereby severally enter into a firm league of friendship with each other, for their common defence, the security of their liberties, and their mutual and general welfare, binding themselves to assist each other against all force offered to, or attacks made upon them, or any of them, on account of religion, sovereignty, trade, or any other pretence whatever.

ART. IV. The better to secure and perpetuate mutual friendship and intercourse among the people of the different States in this Union, the free inhabitants of each of these States, paupers, vagabonds, and fugitives from justice excepted, shall be entitled to all the privileges and immunities of free citizens in the several States, and the people of each State shall have free ingress and regress to and from any other State, and shall enjoy therein all the privileges of trade and commerce, subject to the same duties, impositions, and restrictions as the inhabitants thereof respectively, provided that such restrictions shall not extend so far as to prevent the removal of property imported into any State, to any other State of which the owner is an inhabitant; provided also, that no imposition, duties, or restriction shall be laid by any State, on the property of the United States, or either of them.

If any person guilty of or charged with treason, felony, or other high misdemeanor in any State, shall flee from justice, and be found in any of the United States, he shall, upon demand of the governor or executive power of the State from which he fled, be delivered up and removed to the State having jurisdiction of his offence.

Full faith and credit shall be given in each of these States to the records, acts, and judicial proceedings of the courts and magistrates of every other State.

ART. V. For the more convenient management of the general interests of the United States, delegates shall be annually appointed in such manner as the legislature of each State shall direct, to meet in Congress on the first Monday in November, in every year, with a power reserved to each State to recall its delegates, or any of them, at any time within the year, and to send others in their stead, for the remainder of the year.

No State shall be represented in Congress by less than two, nor by more than seven members; and no person shall be capable of being a delegate for more than three years in any term of six years, nor shall any person, being a delegate, be capable of holding any office under the United States for which he or another for his benefit receives any salary, fees, or emolument of any kind.

Each State shall maintain its own delegates in a meeting of the States, and while they act as members of the committee of the States.

In determining questions in the United States, in Congress assembled, each State shall have one vote.

Freedom of speech and debate in Congress shall not be impeached or questioned in any court or place out of Congress, and the members of Congress shall be protected in their persons from arrests and imprisonments, during the time of their going to or from, and attendance on, Congress, except for treason, felony, or breach of the peace.

ART VI. No State, without the consent of the United States in Congress assembled, shall send any embassy to, or receive any embassy from, or enter into any conference, agreement, alliance, or treaty with, any king, prince, or state; nor shall any person holding any office of profit or trust under the United States, or any of them accept of any present, emolument, office, or title of any kind whatever from any king, prince, or foreign state; nor shall the United States in Congress assembled, or any of them, grant any title of nobility.

No two or more States shall enter into any treaty, confederation, or alliance whatever between them, without the consent of the United States in Congress assembled, specifying accurately the purposes for which the same is to be entered into, and how long it shall continue.

No State shall lay any imposts or duties, which may interfere with any stipulations in treaties entered into by the United States in Congress assembled, with any king, prince, or state, in pursuance of any treaties already proposed by Congress, to the courts of France and Spain.

No vessels of war shall be kept up in time of peace by any State, except such number only as shall be deemed necessary by the United States in Congress assembled, for the defence of such State or its trade; nor shall any body of forces be kept up by any State, in time of peace, except such number only as in the judgment of the United States in Congress assembled shall be deemed requisite to garrison the forts necessary for the defence of such State; but every State shall always keep up a well regulated and disciplined militia, sufficiently armed and accoutred, and shall provide and constantly have ready for use, in public stores, a due number of field-pieces and tents, and a proper quantity of arms, ammunition, and camp equipage.

No State shall engage in any war without the consent of the United States in Congress assembled, unless such State be actually invaded by enemies, or shall have received certain advice of a resolution being formed by some nation of Indians to invade such State, and the danger is so imminent as not to admit of a delay till the United States in Congress assembled can be consulted; nor shall any State grant commissions to any ships or vessels of war, nor letters of marque or reprisal, except it be after a declaration of war by the United States in Congress assembled, and then only against the kingdom or state, and the subjects thereof, against which war has been so declared, and under such regulations as shall be established by the United States in Congress assembled, unless such State be infested by pirates, in which case vessels of war may be fitted out for that occasion, and kept so long as the danger shall continue, or until the United States in Congress assembled shall determine otherwise.

ART. VII. When land forces are raised by any State for the common defence, all officers of or under the rank of colonel shall be appointed by the legislature of each State respectively, by whom such forces shall be raised, or in such manner as such State shall direct; and all vacancies shall be filled up by the State which first made the appointment.

ART. VIII. All charges of war and all other expenses that shall be incurred for the common defence or general welfare, and allowed by the United States in Congress assembled, shall be defrayed out of a common treasury, which shall be supplied by the several States, in proportion to the value of all land within each State, granted to or surveyed for any person, and such land and the buildings and improvements thereon shall be estimated according to such mode as the United States in Congress assembled shall from time to time direct and appoint.

The taxes for paying that proportion shall be laid and levied by the authority and direction of the legislatures of the several States within the time agreed upon by the United States in Congress assembled.

ART. IX. The United States in Congress assembled shall have the sole and exclusive right and power of determining on peace and war, except in the cases mentioned in the sixth article—of sending and receiving ambassadors—entering into treaties and alliances, provided that no treaty of commerce shall be made whereby the legislative power of the respective States shall be restrained from imposing such imposts and duties on foreigners as their own people are subjected to, or from prohibiting the exportation or importation of any species of goods or commodities whatsoever—of establishing rules for deciding, in all cases, what captures on land or water shall be legal, and in what manner prizes taken by land or naval forces in the service of the United States shall be divided or appropriated—of granting letters of marque and reprisal in times of peace—appointing courts for the trial of piracies and felonies committed on the high seas, and establishing courts for receiving and determining finally appeals in all cases of captures, provided that no member of Congress shall be appointed a judge of any of the said courts.

The United States in Congress assembled shall also be the last resort on appeal in all disputes and differences now subsisting or that hereafter may arise between two or more States concerning boundary, jurisdiction, or any other cause whatever; which authority shall always be exercised in the manner following:—Whenever the legislative or executive authority or lawful agent of any State in controversy with another shall present a petition to Congress stating the matter in question and praying for a hearing, notice thereof shall be given by order of Congress to the legislative or executive authority of the other State in controversy, and a day assigned for the appearance of the parties by their lawful agents, who shall then be directed to appoint, by joint consent, commissioners or judges to constitute a court for hearing and determining the matter in question; but if they cannot agree, Congress shall name three persons out of each of the United States, and from the list of such persons each party shall alternately strike out one, the petitioners beginning, until the number shall be reduced to thirteen; and from that number not less than seven nor more than nine names, as Congress shall direct, shall, in the presence of Congress, be drawn out by lot, and the persons whose names shall be so drawn, or any five of them, shall be commissioners or judges, to hear and finally determine the controversy, so always as a major part of the judges who shall hear the cause shall agree in the determination; and if either party shall neglect to attend at the day appointed, without showing reasons, which Congress shall judge sufficient, or, being present, shall refuse to strike, the Congress shall proceed to nominate three persons out of each State, and the Secretary of Congress shall strike in behalf of such party absent or refusing; and the judgment and sentence of the court to be appointed, in the manner before prescribed, shall be final and conclusive; and if any of the parties shall refuse to submit to the authority of such court, or to appear or defend their claim or cause, the court shall nevertheless proceed to pronounce sentence or judgment, which shall in like manner be final and decisive, the judgment or sentence and other proceedings being in either case transmitted to Congress, and lodged among the acts of Congress for the security of the parties concerned: provided that every commissioner, before he sits in judgment, shall take an oath, to be administered by one of the judges of the Supreme or Superior Court of the State where the cause shall be tried, *"well and truly to hear and determine the matter in question according to the best of his judgment, without favor, affection, or hope of reward,"* provided also that no State shall be deprived of territory for the benefit of the United States.

All controversies concerning the private right of soil, claimed under different grants of two or more States, whose jurisdictions as they may respect such lands and the States which passed such grants are adjusted, the said grants or either of them being at the same time claimed to have originated antecedent to such settlement of jurisdiction, shall, on the petition of either party to the Congress of the United States, be finally determined as near as may be in the same manner as is before prescribed for deciding disputes respecting territorial jurisdiction between different States.

The United States in Congress assembled shall also have the sole and exclusive right and power of regulating the alloy and value of coin struck by their own authority, or by that of the respective States—fixing the standard of weights and measures throughout the United States—regulating the trade and managing all affairs with the Indians, not members of any of the States, provided that the legislative right of any State within its own limits be not infringed or violated—establishing and regulating post-offices from one State to another, throughout all the United States, and exacting such postage on the papers passing through the same as may be requisite to defray the expenses of the said office—appointing all officers of the land forces in the service of the United States, excepting regimental officers—appointing all the officers of the naval forces, and commissioning all officers whatever in the service of the United States—making rules for the government and regulation of the said land and naval forces, and directing their operations.

The United States in Congress assembled shall have authority to appoint a committee, to sit in the recess of Congress, to be denominated "A Committee of the States," and to consist of one delegate from each State; to appoint such other committees and civil officers as may be necessary for managing the general affairs of the United States under their direction; and to appoint one of their number to preside, provided that no person be allowed to serve in the office of president more than one year in any term of three years—to ascertain the necessary sums of money to be raised for the service of the United States, and to appropriate and apply the same for defraying the public expenses—to borrow money, or emit bills on the credit of the United States, transmitting every half-year to the respective States an account of the sums of money so borrowed or emitted—to build and equip a navy—to agree upon the number of land forces, and to make requisitions from each State for its quota, in proportion to the number of white inhabitants in such State; which requisition shall be binding, and thereupon the legislature of each State shall appoint the regimental officers, raise the men, and clothe, arm, and equip them in a soldier-like manner, at the expense of the United States, and the officers and men so clothed, armed, and equipped shall march to the place appointed, and within the time agreed on by the United States in Congress assembled; but if the United States in Congress assembled shall, on consideration of circumstances, judge proper that any State should not raise men, or should raise a smaller number than its quota, and that any other State should raise a greater number of men than the quota thereof, such extra number shall be raised, officered, clothed, armed, and equipped in the same manner as the quota of such State, unless the legislature of such State shall judge that such extra number cannot be safely spared out of the same, in which case they shall raise, officer, clothe, arm, and equip as many of such extra number as they judge can be safely spared: and the officers and men, so clothed, armed, and equipped shall march to the place appointed, and within the time agreed on, by the United States in Congress assembled.

The United States in Congress assembled shall never engage in a war, nor grant letters of marque and reprisal in time of peace, nor enter into any treaties or alliances, nor coin money, nor regulate the value thereof, nor ascertain the sums and expenses necessary for the defence and welfare of the United States, or any of them, nor emit bills, nor borrow money on the credit of the United States, nor appropriate money, nor agree upon the number of vessels of war to be built or purchased, or the number of land or sea forces to be raised, nor appoint a commander-in-chief of the army or navy, unless nine States assent to the same; nor shall a question on any other point, except for adjourning from day to day, be determined, unless by the votes of a majority of the United States in Congress assembled.

The Congress of the United States shall have power to adjourn to any time within the year, and to any place within the United States, so that no period of adjournment be for a longer duration than the space of six months, and shall publish the journal of their proceedings monthly, except such parts thereof relating to treaties, alliances, or military operations, as in their judgment require secrecy, and the yeas and nays of the delegates of each State on any question shall be entered on the journal, when it is desired by any delegate; and the delegates of a State, or any of them, at his or their request, shall be furnished with a transcript of the said journal, except such parts as are above excepted, to lay before the legislatures of the several States.

ART. X. The Committee of the States, or any nine of them, shall be authorized to execute, in the recess of Congress, such of the powers of Congress as the United States in Congress assembled, by the consent of nine States, shall from time to time think expedient to vest them with: provided that no power be delegated to the said Committee, for the exercise of which, by the Articles of Confederation, the voice of nine States in the Congress of the United States assembled is requisite.

ART. XI. Canada, acceding to this Confederation, and joining in the measures of the United States, shall be admitted into and entitled to all the advantages of this Union; but no other colony shall be admitted into the same, unless such admission be agreed to by nine States.

ART. XII. All bills of credit emitted, moneys borrowed, and debts contracted by or under the authority of Congress, before the assembling of the United States in pursuance of the present Confederation, shall be deemed and considered as a charge against the United States, for payment and satisfaction whereof the said United States and the public faith are hereby solemnly pledged.

ART. XIII. Every State shall abide by the determinations of the United States in Congress assembled, on all questions which by this Confederation are submitted to them. And the Articles of this Confederation shall be inviolably observed by every State, and the Union shall be perpetual; nor shall any alteration at any time hereafter be made in any of them, unless such alteration be agreed to in a Congress of the United States, and be afterwards confirmed by the legislatures of every State.

AND WHEREAS it hath pleased the Great Governor of the world to incline the hearts of the legislatures we respectfully represent in Congress to approve of and to authorize us to ratify the said Articles of Confederation and perpetual Union, KNOW YE, That we, the undersigned delegates, by virtue of the power and authority to us given for that purpose, do by these presents, in the name and in behalf of our respective constituents, fully and entirely ratify and confirm each and every of the said Articles of Confederation and perpetual Union, and all and singular the matters and things therein contained: and we do further solemnly plight and engage the faith of our respective constituents that they shall abide by the determinations of the United States in Congress assembled, on all questions which by the said Confederation are submitted to them. And that the Articles thereof shall be inviolably observed by the States we respectively represent, and the Union shall be perpetual.

Appendix 3

The Constitution of the United States

In the following printed copy of the Constitution, spelling, capitalization, and punctuation conform to the text of the engrossed parchment.

We the People of the United States, in Order to form a more perfect Union, establish Justice, insure domestic Tranquility, provide for the common defence, promote the general Welfare, and secure the Blessings of Liberty to ourselves and our Posterity, do ordain and establish this Constitution for the United States of America.

ARTICLE. I.

SECTION. 1. All legislative Powers herein granted shall be vested in a Congress of the United States, which shall consist of a Senate and House of Representatives.

SECTION. 2. The House of Representatives shall be composed of Members chosen every second Year by the People of the several States, and the Electors in each State shall have the Qualifications requisite for Electors of the most numerous Branch of the State Legislature.

No Person shall be a Representative who shall not have attained to the Age of twenty five Years, and been seven Years a Citizen of the United States, and who shall not, when elected, be an Inhabitant of that State in which he shall be chosen.

Representatives and direct Taxes shall be apportioned among the several States which may be included within this Union, according to their respective Numbers, which shall be determined by adding to the whole Number of free Persons, including those bound to Service for a Term of Years, and excluding Indians not taxed, three fifths of all other Persons. The actual Enumeration shall be made within three Years after the first Meeting of the Congress of the United States, and within every subsequent Term of ten Years, in such Manner as they shall by Law direct. The Number of Representatives shall not exceed one for every thirty Thousand, but each State shall have at Least one Representative; and until such enumeration shall be made, the State of New Hampshire shall be entitled to chuse three, Massachusetts eight, Rhode-Island and Providence Plantations one, Connecticut five, New-York six, New Jersey four, Pennsylvania eight, Delaware one, Maryland six, Virginia ten, North Carolina five, South Carolina five, and Georgia three.

When vacancies happen in the Representation from any State, the Executive Authority thereof shall issue Writs of Election to fill such Vacancies.

The House of Representatives shall chuse their Speaker and other Officers; and shall have the sole Power of Impeachment.

SECTION. 3. The Senate of the United States shall be composed of two Senators from each State, chosen by the Legislature thereof, for six Years; and each Senator shall have one Vote.

Immediately after they shall be assembled in Consequence of the first Election, they shall be divided as equally as may be into three Classes. The Seats of the Senators of the first Class shall be vacated at the Expiration of the second Year, of the second Class at the Expiration of the fourth Year, and of the third Class at the Expiration of the sixth Year, so that one third may be chosen every second Year; and if Vacancies happen by Resignation, or otherwise, during the Recess of the Legislature of any State, the Executive thereof may make temporary Appointments until the next Meeting of the Legislature, which shall then fill such Vacancies.

No Person shall be a Senator who shall not have attained to the Age of thirty Years, and been nine Years a Citizen of the United States, and who shall not, when elected, be an Inhabitant of that State for which he shall be chosen.

The Vice President of the United States shall be President of the Senate, but shall have no Vote, unless they be equally divided.

The Senate shall chuse their other Officers, and also a President pro tempore, in the Absence of the Vice President, or when he shall exercise the Office of President of the United States.

The Senate shall have the sole Power to try all Impeachments. When sitting for that Purpose, they shall be on Oath or Affirmation. When the President of the United States is tried, the Chief Justice shall preside: And no Person shall be convicted without the Concurrence of two thirds of the Members present.

Judgment in Cases of Impeachment shall not extend further than to removal from Office, and disqualification to hold and enjoy any Office of honor, Trust or Profit under the United States: but the Party convicted shall nevertheless be liable and subject to Indictment, Trial, Judgment and Punishment, according to Law.

SECTION. 4. The Times, Places and Manner of holding Elections for Senators and Representatives, shall be prescribed in each State by the Legislature thereof; but the Congress may at any time by Law make or alter such Regulations, except as to the Places of chusing Senators.

The Congress shall assemble at least once in every Year, and such Meeting shall be on the first Monday in December, unless they shall by Law appoint a different Day.

SECTION. 5. Each House shall be the Judge of the Elections, Returns and Qualifications of its own Members, and a Majority of each shall constitute a Quorum to do Business; but a smaller Number may adjourn from day to day, and may be authorized to compel the Attendance of absent Members, in such Manner, and under such Penalties as each House may provide.

Each House may determine the Rules of its Proceedings, punish its Members for disorderly Behaviour, and, with the Concurrence of two thirds, expel a Member.

Each House shall keep a Journal of its Proceedings, and from time to time publish the same, excepting such Parts as may in their Judgment require Secrecy; and the Yeas and Nays of the Members of either House on any question shall, at the Desire of one fifth of those Present, be entered on the Journal.

Neither House, during the Session of Congress, shall, without the Consent of the other, adjourn for more than three days, nor to any other Place than that in which the two Houses shall be sitting.

SECTION. 6. The Senators and Representatives shall receive a Compensation for their Services, to be ascertained by Law, and paid out of the Treasury of the United States. They shall in all Cases, except Treason, Felony and Breach of the Peace, be privileged from Arrest during their Attendance at the Session of their respective Houses, and in going to and returning from the same; and for any Speech or Debate in either House, they shall not be questioned in any other Place.

No Senator or Representative shall, during the Time for which he was elected, be appointed to any civil Office under the Authority of the United States, which shall have been created, or the Emoluments whereof shall have been encreased during such time; and no Person holding any Office under the United States, shall be a Member of either House during his Continuance in Office.

SECTION. 7. All Bills for raising Revenue shall originate in the House of Representatives; but the Senate may propose or concur with Amendments as on other Bills.

Every Bill which shall have passed the House of Representatives and the Senate, shall, before it become a Law, be presented to the President of the United States; If he approve he shall sign it, but if not he shall return it, with his Objections to that House in which it shall have originated, who shall enter the Objections at large on their Journal, and proceed to reconsider it. If after such Reconsideration two thirds of that House shall agree to pass the Bill, it shall be sent, together with the Objections, to the other House, by which it shall likewise be reconsidered, and if approved by two thirds of that House, it shall become a Law. But in all such Cases the Votes of both Houses shall be determined by yeas and Nays, and the Names of the Persons voting for and against the Bill shall be entered on the Journal of each House respectively. If any Bill shall not be returned by the President within ten Days (Sundays excepted) after it shall have been presented to him, the Same shall be a Law, in like Manner as if he had signed it, unless the Congress by their Adjournment prevent its Return, in which Case it shall not be a Law.

Every Order, Resolution, or Vote to which the Concurrence of the Senate and House of Representatives may be necessary (except on a question of Adjournment) shall be presented to the President of the United States; and before the Same shall take Effect, shall be approved by him, or being disapproved by him, shall be repassed by two thirds of the Senate and House of Representatives, according to the Rules and Limitations prescribed in the Case of a Bill.

SECTION. 8. The Congress shall have Power To lay and collect Taxes, Duties, Imposts and Excises, to pay the Debts and provide for the common Defence and general Welfare of the United States; but all Duties, Imposts and Excises shall be uniform throughout the United States;

To borrow Money on the credit of the United States;

To regulate Commerce with foreign Nations, and among the several States, and with the Indian tribes;

To establish an uniform Rule of Naturalization, and uniform Laws on the subject of Bankruptcies throughout the United States;

To coin Money, regulate the Value thereof, and of foreign Coin, and fix the Standard of Weights and Measures;

To provide for the Punishment of counterfeiting the Securities and current Coin of the United States;

To establish Post Offices and post Roads;

To promote the Progress of Science and useful Arts, by securing for limited Times to Authors and Inventors the exclusive Right to their respective Writings and Discoveries;

To constitute Tribunals inferior to the supreme Court;

To define and punish Piracies and Felonies committed on the high Seas, and Offences against the Law of Nations;

To declare War, grant Letters of Marque and Reprisal, and make Rules concerning Captures on Land and Water;

To raise and support Armies, but no Appropriation of Money to that Use shall be for a longer Term than two Years;

To provide and maintain a Navy;

To make Rules for the Government and Regulation of the land and naval Forces;

To provide for calling forth the Militia to execute the Laws of the Union, suppress Insurrections and repel Invasions;

To provide for organizing, arming, and disciplining, the Militia, and for governing such Part of them as may be employed in the Service of the United States, reserving to the States respectively, the Appointment of the Officers, and the Authority of training the Militia according to the discipline prescribed by Congress;

To exercise exclusive Legislation in all Cases whatsoever, over such District (not exceeding ten Miles square) as may, by Cession of particular States, and the Acceptance of Congress, become the Seat of the Government of the United States, and to exercise like Authority over all Places purchased by the Consent of the Legislature of the State in which the Same shall be, for the Erection of Forts, Magazines, Arsenals, dock- Yards, and other needful Buildings;—And

To make all Laws which shall be necessary and proper for carrying into Execution the foregoing Powers, and all other Powers vested by this Constitution in the Government of the United States, or in any Department or Officer thereof.

SECTION. 9. The Migration or Importation of such Persons as any of the States now existing shall think proper to admit, shall not be prohibited by the Congress prior to the Year one thousand eight hundred and eight, but a Tax or duty may be imposed on such Importation, not exceeding ten dollars for each Person.

The Privilege of the Writ of Habeas Corpus shall not be suspended, unless when in Cases of Rebellion or Invasion the public Safety may require it.

No Bill of Attainder or ex post facto Law shall be passed.

No Capitation, or other direct, Tax shall be laid, unless in Proportion to the Census or Enumeration herein before directed to be taken.

No Tax or Duty shall be laid on Articles exported from any State.

No Preference shall be given by any Regulation of Commerce or Revenue to the Ports of one State over those of another: nor shall Vessels bound to, or from, one State, be obliged to enter, clear, or pay Duties in another.

No Money shall be drawn from the Treasury, but in Consequence of Appropriations made by Law; and a regular Statement and Account of the Receipts and Expenditures of all public Money shall be published from time to time.

No Title of Nobility shall be granted by the United States: And no Person holding any Office of Profit or Trust under them, shall, without the Consent of the Congress, accept of any present, Emolument, Office, or Title, of any kind whatever, from any King, Prince, or foreign State.

SECTION. 10. No State shall enter into any Treaty, Alliance, or Confederation; grant Letters of Marque and Reprisal; coin Money; emit Bills of Credit; make any Thing but gold and silver Coin a Tender in Payment of Debts; pass any Bill of Attainder, ex post facto Law, or Law impairing the Obligation of Contracts, or grant any Title of Nobility.

No State shall, without the Consent of the Congress, lay any Imposts or Duties on Imports or Exports, except what may be absolutely necessary for executing it's inspection Laws: and the net Produce of all Duties and Imposts, laid by any State on Imports or Exports, shall be for the Use of the Treasury of the United States; and all such Laws shall be subject to the Revision and Controul of the Congress.

No State shall, without the Consent of Congress, lay any Duty of Tonnage, keep Troops, or Ships of War in time of Peace, enter into any Agreement or Compact with another State, or with a foreign Power, or engage in War, unless actually invaded, or in such imminent Danger as will not admit of delay.

ARTICLE II.

SECTION. 1. The executive Power shall be vested in a President of the United States of America. He shall hold his Office during the Term of four Years, and, together with the Vice President, chosen for the same Term, be elected, as follows

Each State shall appoint, in such Manner as the Legislature thereof may direct, a Number of Electors, equal to the whole Number of Senators and Representatives to which the State may be entitled in the Congress: but no Senator or Representative, or Person holding an Office of Trust or Profit under the United States, shall be appointed an Elector.

The Electors shall meet in their respective States, and vote by Ballot for two Persons, of whom one at least shall not be an inhabitant of the same State with themselves. And they shall make a List of all the Persons voted for, and of the Number of Votes for each; which List they shall sign and certify, and transmit sealed to the Seat of the Government of the United States, directed to the President of the Senate. The President of the Senate shall, in the Presence of the Senate and House of Representatives, open all the Certificates, and the Votes shall then be counted. The Person having the greatest Number of Votes shall be the President, if such Number be a Majority of the whole Number of Electors appointed; and if there be more than one who have such Majority, and have an equal Number of Votes, then the House of Representatives shall immediately chuse by Ballot one of them for President; and if no Person have a Majority, then from the five highest on the List the said House shall in like Manner chuse the President. But in chusing the President, the Votes shall be taken by States, the Representation from each State having one Vote; A quorum for this purpose shall consist of a Member or Members from two thirds of the States, and a Majority of all the States shall be necessary to a Choice. In every Case, after the Choice of the President, the Person having the greatest Number of Votes of the Electors shall be the Vice President. But if there should remain two or more who have equal Votes, the Senate shall chuse from them by Ballot the Vice President.

The Congress may determine the Time of chusing the Electors, and the Day on which they shall give their Votes; which Day shall be the same throughout the United States.

No Person except a natural born Citizen, or a Citizen of the United States, at the time of the Adoption of this Constitution, shall be eligible to the Office of President; neither shall any Person be eligible to that Office who shall not have attained to the Age of thirty five Years, and been fourteen Years a Resident within the United States.

In Case of the Removal of the President from Office, or of his Death, Resignation, or Inability to discharge the Powers and Duties of the said Office, the Same shall devolve on the Vice President, and the Congress may by Law provide for the Case of Removal, Death, Resignation or Inability, both of the President and Vice President, declaring what Officer shall then act as President, and such Officer shall act accordingly, until the Disability be removed, or a President shall be elected.

The President shall, at stated Times, receive for his Services, a Compensation, which shall neither be encreased nor diminished during the Period for which he shall have been elected, and he shall not receive within that Period any other Emolument from the United States, or any of them.

Before he enter on the Execution of his Office, he shall take the following Oath or Affirmation:—"I do solemnly swear (or affirm) that I will faithfully execute the Office of President of the United States, and will to the best of my Ability, preserve, protect and defend the Constitution of the United States."

SECTION. 2. The President shall be Commander in Chief of the Army and Navy of the United States, and of the Militia of the several States, when called into the actual Service of the United States; he may require the Opinion, in writing, of the principal Officer in each of the executive Departments, upon any Subject relating to the Duties of their respective Offices, and he shall have Power to grant Reprieves and Pardons for Offences against the United States, except in Cases of Impeachment.

He shall have Power, by and with the Advice and Consent of the Senate, to make Treaties, provided two thirds of the Senators present concur; and he shall nominate, and by and with the Advice and Consent of the Senate, shall appoint Ambassadors, other public Ministers and Consuls, Judges of the supreme Court, and all other Officers of the United States, whose Appointments are not herein otherwise provided for, and which shall be established by Law: but the Congress may by Law vest the Appointment of such inferior Officers, as they think proper, in the President alone, in the Courts of Law, or in the Heads of Departments.

The President shall have Power to fill up all Vacancies that may happen during the Recess of the Senate, by granting Commissions which shall expire at the End of their next Session.

SECTION. 3. He shall from time to time give to the Congress Information of the State of the Union, and recommend to their Consideration such Measures as he shall judge necessary and expedient; he may, on extraordinary Occasions, convene both Houses, or either of them, and in Case of Disagreement between them, with Respect to the Time of Adjournment, he may adjourn them to such Time as he shall think proper; he shall receive Ambassadors and other public Ministers; he shall take Care that the Laws be faithfully executed, and shall Commission all the Officers of the United States.

SECTION. 4. The President, Vice President and all civil Officers of the United States, shall be removed from Office on Impeachment for, and Conviction of, Treason, Bribery, or other high Crimes and Misdemeanors.

ARTICLE III.

SECTION. 1. The judicial Power of the United States, shall be vested in one supreme Court, and in such inferior Courts as the Congress may from time to time ordain and establish. The Judges, both of the supreme and inferior Courts, shall hold their Offices during good Behaviour, and shall, at stated Times, receive for their Services, a Compensation, which shall not be diminished during their Continuance in Office.

SECTION. 2. The judicial Power shall extend to all Cases, in Law and Equity, arising under this Constitution, the Laws of the United States, and Treaties made, or which shall be made, under their Authority;—to all Cases affecting Ambassadors, other public Ministers and Consuls;—to all Cases of admiralty and maritime Jurisdiction;—to Controversies to which the United States shall be a Party;—to Controversies between two or more States;—between a State and Citizens of another State;—between Citizens of different States,—between Citizens of the same State claiming Lands under Grants of different States, and between a State, or the Citizens thereof, and foreign States, Citizens or Subjects.

In all Cases affecting Ambassadors, other public Ministers and Consuls, and those in which a State shall be Party, the supreme Court shall have original Jurisdiction. In all the other Cases before mentioned, the supreme Court shall have appellate Jurisdiction, both as to Law and Fact, with such Exceptions, and under such Regulations as the Congress shall make.

The Trial of all Crimes, except in Cases of Impeachment, shall be by Jury; and such Trial shall be held in the State where the said Crimes shall have been committed; but when not committed within any State, the Trial shall be at such Place or Places as the Congress may by Law have directed.

SECTION. 3. Treason against the United States, shall consist only in levying War against them, or in adhering to their Enemies, giving them Aid and Comfort. No Person shall be convicted of Treason unless on the Testimony of two Witnesses to the same overt Act, or on Confession in open Court.

The Congress shall have Power to declare the Punishment of Treason, but no Attainder of Treason shall work Corruption of Blood, or Forfeiture except during the Life of the Person attainted.

ARTICLE IV.

SECTION. 1. Full Faith and Credit shall be given in each State to the public Acts, Records, and judicial Proceedings of every other State. And the Congress may by general Laws prescribe the Manner in which such Acts, Records and Proceedings shall be proved, and the Effect thereof.

SECTION. 2. The Citizens of each State shall be entitled to all Privileges and Immunities of Citizens in the several States.

A Person charged in any State with Treason, Felony, or other Crime, who shall flee from Justice, and be found in another State, shall on Demand of the executive Authority of the State from which he fled, be delivered up, to be removed to the State having Jurisdiction of the Crime.

No Person held to Service or Labour in one State, under the Laws thereof, escaping into another, shall, in Consequence of any Law or Regulation therein, be discharged from such Service or Labour, but shall be delivered up on Claim of the Party to whom such Service or Labour may be due.

SECTION. 3. New States may be admitted by the Congress into this Union; but no new State shall be formed or erected within the Jurisdiction of any other State; nor any State be formed by the Junction of two or more States, or Parts of States, without the Consent of the Legislatures of the States concerned as well as of the Congress.

The Congress shall have Power to dispose of and make all needful Rules and Regulations respecting the Territory or other Property belonging to the United States; and nothing in this Constitution shall be so construed as to Prejudice any Claims of the United States, or of any particular State.

SECTION. 4. The United States shall guarantee to every State in this Union a Republican Form of Government, and shall protect each of them against Invasion; and on Application of the Legislature, or of the Executive (when the Legislature cannot be convened) against domestic Violence.

ARTICLE V.

The Congress, whenever two thirds of both Houses shall deem it necessary, shall propose Amendments to this Constitution, or, on the Application of the Legislatures of two thirds of the several States, shall call a Convention for proposing Amendments, which, in either Case, shall be valid to all Intents and Purposes, as Part of this Constitution, when ratified by the legislatures of three fourths of the several States, or by Conventions in three fourths thereof, as the one or the other Mode of Ratification may be proposed by the Congress; Provided that no Amendment which may be made prior to the Year One thousand eight hundred and eight shall in any Manner affect the first and fourth Clauses in the Ninth Section of the first Article; and that no State, without its Consent, shall be deprived of it's equal Suffrage in the Senate.

ARTICLE VI.

All Debts contracted and Engagements entered into, before the Adoption of this Constitution, shall be as valid against the United States under this Constitution, as under the Confederation.

This Constitution, and the Laws of the United States which shall be made in Pursuance thereof; and all Treaties made, or which shall be made, under the Authority of the United States, shall be the supreme Law of the Land; and the Judges in every State shall be bound thereby, any Thing in the Constitution or Laws of any State to the Contrary notwithstanding.

The Senators and Representatives before mentioned, and the Members of the several State Legislatures, and all executive and judicial Officers, both of the United States and of the several States, shall be bound by Oath or Affirmation, to support this Constitution; but no religious Test shall ever be required as a Qualification to any Office or public Trust under the United States.

ARTICLE VII.

The Ratification of the Conventions of nine States, shall be sufficient for the Establishment of this Constitution between the States so ratifying the Same.

The Word "the", being interlined between the seventh and eighth Lines of the first Page, the Word "Thirty" being partly written on an Erazure in the fifteenth Line of the first Page, The Words "is tried" being interlined between the thirty second and thirty third Lines of the first Page and the Word "the" being interlined between the forty third and forty fourth Lines of the second Page.

Attest William Jackson
Secretary

DONE in Convention by the Unanimous Consent of the States present the Seventeenth Day of September in the Year of our Lord one thousand seven hundred and Eighty seven and of the Independance of the United States of America the Twelfth. IN WITNESS whereof We have hereunto subscribed our Names.

G° WASHINGTON

Presid[t] and deputy from Virginia

DELAWARE: GEO: READ, GUNNING BEDFORD jun, JOHN DICKINSON, RICHARD BASSETT, JACO: BROOM

MARYLAND: JAMES MCHENRY, DAN OF ST. THOS. JENIFER, DANL. CARROLL

VIRGINIA: JOHN BLAIR—, JAMES MADISON JR.

NORTH CAROLINA: WM. BLOUNT, RICHD. DOBBS SPAIGHT, HU WILLIAMSON

SOUTH CAROLINA: J. RUTLEDGE, CHARLES COTESWORTH PINCKNEY, CHARLES PINCKNEY, PIERCE BUTLER

GEORGIA: WILLIAM FEW, ABR BALDWIN

NEW HAMPSHIRE: JOHN LANGDON, NICHOLAS GILMAN

MASSACHUSETTS: NATHANIEL GORHAM, RUFUS KING

CONNECTICUT: WM. SAML. JOHNSON, ROGER SHERMAN

NEW YORK: ALEXANDER HAMILTON

NEW JERSEY: WIL: LIVINGSTON, DAVID BREARLEY, WM. PATERSON, JONA: DAYTON

PENNSYLVANIA: B. FRANKLIN, THOMAS MIFFLIN, ROBT. MORRIS, GEO. CLYMER, THOS. FITZSIMONS, JARED INGERSOLL, JAMES WILSON, GOUV MORRIS

AMENDMENT I

Congress shall make no law respecting an establishment of religion, or prohibiting the free exercise thereof; or abridging the freedom of speech, or of the press; or the right of the people peaceably to assemble, and to petition the Government for a redress of grievances.

AMENDMENT II

A well regulated Militia, being necessary to the security of a free State, the right of the people to keep and bear Arms, shall not be infringed.

AMENDMENT III

No Soldier shall, in time of peace be quartered in any house, without the consent of the Owner, nor in time of war, but in a manner to be prescribed by law.

AMENDMENT IV

The right of the people to be secure in their persons, houses, papers, and effects, against unreasonable searches and seizures, shall not be violated, and no Warrants shall issue, but upon probable cause, supported by Oath or affirmation, and particularly describing the place to be searched, and the persons or things to be seized.

AMENDMENT V

No person shall be held to answer for a capital, or otherwise infamous crime, unless on a presentment or indictment of a Grand Jury, except in cases arising in the land or naval forces, or in the Militia, when in actual service in time of War or public danger; nor shall any person be subject for the same offence to be twice put in jeopardy of life or limb; nor shall be compelled in any criminal case to be a witness against himself, nor be deprived of life, liberty, or property, without due process of law; nor shall private property be taken for public use, without just compensation.

AMENDMENT VI

In all criminal prosecutions, the accused shall enjoy the right to a speedy and public trial, by an impartial jury of the State and district wherein the crime shall have been committed, which district shall have been previously ascertained by law, and to be informed of the nature and cause of the accusation; to be confronted with the witnesses against him; to have compulsory process for obtaining Witnesses in his favor, and to have the assistance of counsel for his defence.

AMENDMENT VII

In Suits at common law, where the value in controversy shall exceed twenty dollars, the right of trial by jury shall be preserved, and no fact tried by a jury, shall be otherwise re-examined in any Court of the United States, than according to the rules of the common law.

AMENDMENT VIII

Excessive bail shall not be required, nor excessive fines imposed, nor cruel and unusual punishments inflicted.

AMENDMENT IX

The enumeration in the Constitution, of certain rights, shall not be construed to deny or disparage others retained by the people.

AMENDMENT X

The powers not delegated to the United States by the Constitution, nor prohibited by it to the States, are reserved to the States respectively, or to the people.

AMENDMENT XI

The Judicial power of the United States shall not be construed to extend to any suit in law or equity, commenced or prosecuted against one of the United States by Citizens of another State, or by Citizens or Subjects of any Foreign State.

AMENDMENT XII

The Electors shall meet in their respective states, and vote by ballot for President and Vice-President, one of whom, at least, shall not be an inhabitant of the same state with themselves; they shall name in their ballots the person voted for as President, and in distinct ballots the person voted for as Vice-President, and they shall make distinct lists of all persons voted for as President, and of all persons voted for as Vice-President, and of the number of votes for each, which lists they shall sign and certify, and transmit sealed to the seat of the government of the United States, directed to the President of the Senate;—The President of the Senate shall, in the presence of the Senate and House of Representatives, open all the certificates and the votes shall then be counted;—The person having the greatest number of votes for President, shall be the President, if such number be a majority of the whole number of Electors appointed; and if no person have such majority, then from the persons having the highest numbers not exceeding three on the list of those voted for as President, the House of Representatives shall choose immediately, by ballot, the President. But in choosing the President, the votes shall be taken by states, the representation from each state having one vote; a quorum for this purpose shall consist of a member or members from two-thirds of the states, and a majority of all the states shall be necessary to a choice. And if the House of Representatives shall not choose a President whenever the right of choice shall devolve upon them, before the fourth day of March next following, then the Vice-President shall act as President, as in the case of the death or other constitutional disability of the President.—The person having the greatest number of votes as Vice-President, shall be the Vice-President, if such number be a majority of the whole number of Electors appointed, and if no person have a majority, then from the two highest numbers on the list, the Senate shall choose the Vice-President; a quorum for the purpose shall consist of two-thirds of the whole number of Senators, and a majority of the whole number shall be necessary to a choice. But no person constitutionally ineligible to the office of President shall be eligible to that of Vice-President of the United States.

AMENDMENT XIII

SECTION 1. Neither slavery nor involuntary servitude, except as a punishment for crime whereof the party shall have been duly convicted, shall exist within the United States, or any place subject to their jurisdiction.

SECTION 2. Congress shall have power to enforce this article by appropriate legislation.

AMENDMENT XIV

SECTION 1. All persons born or naturalized in the United States, and subject to the jurisdiction thereof, are citizens of the United States and of the State wherein they reside. No State shall make or enforce any law which shall abridge the privileges or immunities of citizens of the United States; nor shall any State deprive any person of life, liberty, or property, without due process of law; nor deny to any person within its jurisdiction the equal protection of the laws.

SECTION 2. Representatives shall be apportioned among the several States according to their respective numbers, counting the whole number of persons in each State, excluding Indians not taxed. But when the right to vote at any election for the choice of electors for President and Vice President of the United States, Representatives in Congress, the Executive and Judicial officers of a State, or the members of the Legislature thereof, is denied to any of the male inhabitants of such State, being twenty-one years of age, and citizens of the United States, or in any way abridged, except for participation in rebellion, or other crime, the basis of representation therein shall be reduced in the proportion which the number of such male citizens shall bear to the whole number of male citizens twenty-one years of age in such State.

SECTION 3. No person shall be a Senator or Representative in Congress, or elector of President and Vice President, or hold any office, civil or military, under the United States, or under any State, who, having previously taken an oath, as a member of Congress, or as an officer of the United States, or as a member of any State legislature, or as an executive or judicial officer of any State, to support the Constitution of the United States, shall have engaged in insurrection or rebellion against the same, or given aid or comfort to the enemies thereof. But Congress may by a vote of two-thirds of each House, remove such disability.

SECTION 4. The validity of the public debt of the United States, authorized by law, including debts incurred for payment of pensions and bounties for services in suppressing insurrection or rebellion, shall not be questioned. But neither the United States nor any State shall assume or pay any debt or obligation incurred in aid of insurrection or rebellion against the United States, or any claim for the loss or emancipation of any slave; but all such debts, obligations and claims shall be held illegal and void.

SECTION 5. The Congress shall have power to enforce, by appropriate legislation, the provisions of this article.

AMENDMENT XV

SECTION 1. The right of citizens of the United States to vote shall not be denied or abridged by the United States or by any State on account of race, color, or previous condition of servitude.

SECTION 2. The Congress shall have power to enforce this article by appropriate legislation.

AMENDMENT XVI

The Congress shall have power to lay and collect taxes on incomes, from whatever source derived, without apportionment among the several States, and without regard to any census or enumeration.

AMENDMENT XVII

The Senate of the United States shall be composed of two Senators from each State, elected by the people thereof, for six years; and each Senator shall have one vote. The electors in each State shall have the qualifications requisite for electors of the most numerous branch of the State legislatures.

When vacancies happen in the representation of any State in the Senate, the executive authority of such State shall issue writs of election to fill such vacancies: *Provided,* That the legislature of any State may empower the executive thereof to make temporary appointments until the people fill the vacancies by election as the legislature may direct.

This amendment shall not be so construed as to affect the election or term of any Senator chosen before it becomes valid as part of the Constitution.

AMENDMENT XVIII

SECTION 1. After one year from the ratification of this article the manufacture, sale, or transportation of intoxicating liquors within, the importation thereof into, or the exportation thereof from the United States and all territory subject to the jurisdiction thereof for beverage purposes is hereby prohibited.

SECTION 2. The Congress and the several States shall have concurrent power to enforce this article by appropriate legislation.

SECTION 3. This article shall be inoperative unless it shall have been ratified as an amendment to the Constitution by the legislatures of the several States, as provided in the Constitution, within seven years from the date of the submission hereof to the States by the Congress.

AMENDMENT XIX

The right of citizens of the United States to vote shall not be denied or abridged by the United States or by any State on account of sex.

Congress shall have power to enforce this article by appropriate legislation.

AMENDMENT XX

SECTION 1. The terms of the President and Vice President shall end at noon on the 20th day of January, and the terms of Senators and Representatives at noon on the 3d day of January, of the years in which such terms would have ended if this article had not been ratified; and the terms of their successors shall then begin.

SECTION 2. The Congress shall assemble at least once in every year, and such meeting shall begin at noon on the 3d day of January, unless they shall by law appoint a different day.

SECTION 3. If, at the time fixed for the beginning of the term of the President, the President elect shall have died, the Vice President elect shall become President. If a President shall not have been chosen before the time fixed for the beginning of his term, or if the President elect shall have failed to qualify, then the Vice President elect shall act as President until a President shall have qualified; and the Congress may by law provide for the case wherein neither a President elect nor a Vice President elect shall have qualified, declaring who shall then act as President, or the manner in which one who is to act shall be selected, and such person shall act accordingly until a President or Vice President shall have qualified.

SECTION 4. The Congress may by law provide for the case of the death of any of the persons from whom the House of Representatives may choose a President whenever the right of choice shall have devolved upon them, and for the case of the death of any of the persons from whom the Senate may choose a Vice President whenever the right of choice shall have devolved upon them.

SECTION 5. Sections 1 and 2 shall take effect on the 15th day of October following the ratification of this article.

SECTION 6. This article shall be inoperative unless it shall have been ratified as an amendment to the Constitution by the legislatures of three-fourths of the several States within seven years from the date of its submission.

AMENDMENT XXI

SECTION 1. The eighteenth article of amendment to the Constitution of the United States is hereby repealed.

SECTION 2. The transportation or importation into any State, Territory, or possession of the United States for delivery or use therein of intoxicating liquors, in violation of the laws thereof, is hereby prohibited.

SECTION 3. This article shall be inoperative unless it shall have been ratified as an amendment to the Constitution by conventions in the several States, as provided in the Constitution, within seven years from the date of the submission hereof to the States by the Congress.

AMENDMENT XXII

SECTION 1. No person shall be elected to the office of the President more than twice, and no person who has held the office of President, or acted as President, for more than two years of a term to which some other person was elected President shall be elected to the office of the President more than once. But this Article shall not apply to any person holding the office of President when this Article was proposed by the Congress, and shall not prevent any person who may be holding the office of

President, or acting as President, during the term within which this Article becomes operative from holding the office of President or acting as President during the remainder of such term.

SECTION 2. This article shall be inoperative unless it shall have been ratified as an amendment to the Constitution by the legislatures of three-fourths of the several States within seven years from the date of its submission to the States by the Congress.

AMENDMENT XXIII

SECTION 1. The District constituting the seat of Government of the United States shall appoint in such manner as the Congress may direct:

A number of electors of President and Vice President equal to the whole number of Senators and Representatives in Congress to which the District would be entitled if it were a State, but in no event more than the least populous State; they shall be in addition to those appointed by the States, but they shall be considered, for the purposes of the election of President and Vice President, to be electors appointed by a State; and they shall meet in the District and perform such duties as provided by the twelfth article of amendment.

SECTION 2. The Congress shall have power to enforce this article by appropriate legislation.

AMENDMENT XXIV

SECTION 1. The right of citizens of the United States to vote in any primary or other election for President or Vice President, for electors for President or Vice President, or for Senator or Representatives in Congress, shall not be denied or abridged by the United States or any State by reason of failure to pay any poll tax or other tax.

SECTION 2. The Congress shall have power to enforce this article by appropriate legislation.

AMENDMENT XXV

SECTION 1. In case of the removal of the President from office or of his death or resignation, the Vice President shall become President.

SECTION 2. Whenever there is a vacancy in the office of the Vice President, the President shall nominate a Vice President who shall take office upon confirmation by a majority vote of both Houses of Congress.

SECTION 3. Whenever the President transmits to the President pro tempore of the Senate and the Speaker of the House of Representatives his written declaration that he is unable to discharge the powers and duties of his office, and until he transmits to them a written declaration to the contrary, such powers and duties shall be discharged by the Vice President as Acting President.

SECTION 4. Whenever the Vice President and a majority of either the principal officers of the executive departments or of such other body as Congress may by law provide, transmit to the President pro tempore of the Senate and the Speaker of the House of Representatives their written declaration that the President is unable to discharge the powers and duties of his office, the Vice President shall immediately assume the powers and duties of the office as Acting President.

Thereafter, when the President transmits to the President pro tempore of the Senate and the Speaker of the House of Representatives his written declaration that no inability exists, he shall resume the powers and duties of his office unless the Vice President and a majority of either the principal officers of the executive department or of such other body as Congress may by law provide, transmit within four days to the President pro tempore of the Senate and the Speaker of the House of Representatives their written declaration that the President is unable to discharge the powers and duties of his office. Thereupon Congress shall decide the issue, assembling within forty-eight hours for that purpose if not in session. If the Congress, within twenty-one days after receipt of the latter written declaration, or, if Congress is not in session, within twenty-one days after Congress is required to assemble, determines by two-thirds vote of both Houses that the President is unable to discharge the powers and duties of his office, the Vice President shall continue to discharge the same as Acting President; otherwise, the President shall resume the powers and duties of his office.

AMENDMENT XXVI

SECTION 1. The right of citizens of the United States, who are eighteen years of age or older, to vote shall not be denied or abridged by the United States or by any State on account of age.

SECTION 2. The Congress shall have power to enforce this article by appropriate legislation.

Appendix 4

Resolution Transmitting the Constitution to Congress

IN CONVENTION

Monday, September 17, 1787

PRESENT, *The States of New-Hampshire, Massachusetts, Connecticut, Mr. Hamilton from New-York, New Jersey, Pennsylvania, Delaware, Maryland, Virginia, North Carolina, South Carolina, and Georgia.*

Resolved, That the [following] Constitution be laid before the United States in Congress assembled, and that it is the opinion of this convention, that it should afterwards be submitted to a convention of delegates, chosen in each State by the people thereof, under the recommendation of its legislature, for their assent and ratification; and that each convention assenting to, and ratifying the same should give notice thereof to the United States in Congress assembled.

Resolved, That it is the opinion of this convention, that as soon as the conventions of nine States shall have ratified this Constitution, the United States in Congress assembled should fix a day on which electors should be appointed by the States which shall have ratified the same, and a day on which the electors should assemble to vote for the President, and the time and place for commencing proceedings under this Constitution; that after such publication the electors should be appointed, and the senators and representatives elected; that the electors should meet on the day fixed for the election of the President, and should transmit their votes certified, signed, sealed, and directed, as the Constitution requires, to the secretary of the United States in Congress assembled; that the senators and representatives should convene at the time and place assigned; that the senators should appoint a president of the Senate, for the sole purpose of receiving, opening, and counting the votes for President; and that after he shall be chosen, the Congress, together with the President, should without delay proceed to execute this Constitution.

By the unanimous order of the convention.

GEORGE WASHINGTON, *President.*

WILLIAM JACKSON, *Secretary.*

Appendix 5

Washington's Letter of Transmittal

IN CONVENTION

September 17, 1787

SIR,
WE HAVE now the honor to submit to the consideration of the United States in Congress assembled, that Constitution which has appeared to us the most advisable.

The friends of our country have long seen and desired, that the power of making war, peace, and treaties, of levying money and regulating commerce, and the correspondent executive and judicial authorities should be fully and effectually vested in the general government of the Union: but the impropriety of delegating such extensive trust to one body of men is evident—Hence results the necessity of a different organization.

It is obviously impracticable in the federal government of these States, to secure all rights of independent sovereignty to each, and yet provide for the interest and safety of all—Individuals entering into society, must give up a share of liberty to preserve the rest. The magnitude of the sacrifice must depend as well on situation and circumstances as on the object to be obtained. It is at all times difficult to draw with precision the line between those rights which must be surrendered, and those which may be reserved; and on the present occasion this difficulty was increased by a difference among the several States as to their situation, extent, habits, and particular interests.

In all our deliberations on this subject we kept steadily in our view, that which appears to us the greatest interest of every true American, the consolidation of our Union, in which is involved our prosperity, felicity, safety, perhaps our national existence. This important consideration, seriously and deeply impressed on our minds, led each State in the Convention to be less rigid on points of inferior magnitude, than might have been otherwise expected; and thus the Constitution, which we now present, is the result of a spirit of amity, and of that mutual deference and concession which the peculiarity of our political situation rendered indispensable.

That it will meet the full and entire approbation of every State is not perhaps to be expected; but each will doubtless consider, that had her interest alone been consulted, the consequences might have been particularly disagreeable or injurious to others; that it is liable to as few exceptions as could reasonably have been expected, we hope and believe; that it may promote the lasting welfare of that country so dear to us all, and secure her freedom and happiness, is our most ardent wish.

With great respect,
We have the honor to be
SIR,
Your Excellency's most
Obedient and Humble Servants,
GEORGE WASHINGTON, President

By Unanimous Order of the Convention
HIS EXCELLENCY
THE PRESIDENT OF CONGRESS

Appendix 6

The Birth of the Constitution: A Chronology

1786

September 11–14	Annapolis Convention.
September 20	Report of Annapolis Convention, calling for a Constitutional Convention, submitted to Congress.
October 11	Congress sends Annapolis Convention report to committee.
November 23	New Jersey elects delegates.
December 4	Virginia elects delegates.
December 30	Pennsylvania elects delegates.

1787

January 6	North Carolina elects delegates.
January 17	New Hampshire elects delegates.
February 3	Delaware elects delegates.
February 10	Georgia elects delegates.
February 21	Congress calls Constitutional Convention.
March 3	Massachusetts elects delegates.
March 6	New York elects delegates.
March 8	South Carolina elects delegates.
March 14	Rhode Island refuses to elect delegates.
April 23–May 6	Maryland elects delegates.
May 14	Day appointed for beginning of Convention; quorum not present.
May 14–17	Connecticut elects delegates.
May 25	Quorum is present (seven states represented); Convention begins.
May 29	Governor Edmund Randolph introduces the Virginia Plan.
June 15	William Paterson introduces the New Jersey Plan.
July 16	Great Compromise approved: voting power in first house of Congress to be apportioned by population; states to have equal voting power in the second house.
August 6	Committee on Detail submits draft to Convention.
September 12	Committee on Style submits draft to Convention.
September 15	Draft Constitution approved by unanimous vote of the states represented in the Convention.
September 17	Constitution is signed; Convention adjourns.

September 26–28	Proposed Constitution debated in Congress.
September 28	Congress transmits Constitution to the states for ratification action.
September 29	Pennsylvania calls state convention.
October 17	Connecticut calls state convention.
October 25	Massachusetts calls state convention.
October 26	Georgia calls state convention.
October 31	Virginia calls state convention.
November 1	New Jersey calls state convention.
November 6	Delegates to Pennsylvania convention elected.
November 10	Delaware calls state convention.
November 12	Delegates to Connecticut convention elected.
November 19–January 7, 1788	Delegates to Massachusetts convention elected.
November 20	Pennsylvania convention begins.
November 26	Delegates to Delaware convention elected.
November 27–December 1	Delegates to New Jersey convention elected.
December 1	Maryland calls state convention.
December 3	Delaware convention begins.
December 4–5	Delegates to Georgia convention elected.
December 6	North Carolina calls state convention.
December 7	Delaware convention ratifies Constitution (30–0).
December 11	New Jersey convention begins.
December 12	Pennsylvania convention ratifies Constitution (46–23).
December 14	New Hampshire calls state convention.
December 18	New Jersey convention ratifies constitution (38–0).
December 25	Georgia convention begins.
31 December–February 12, 1788	Delegates to New Hampshire convention elected.

1788

January 3	Connecticut convention begins.
January 9	Connecticut convention ratifies Constitution (128–40).
January 9	Massachusetts convention begins.
January 19	South Carolina calls state convention.
February 1	New York calls state convention.
February 6	Massachusetts convention ratifies Constitution (187–168) and proposes amendments.
February 13–22	New Hampshire convention holds first session.
March 1	Rhode Island calls state referendum on Constitution.
March 3–31	Delegates to Virginia convention elected.
March 24	Rhode Island voters reject Constitution in referendum (2711–239).
March 28–29	Delegates to North Carolina convention elected.
April 7	Delegates to Maryland convention elected.
April 11–12	Delegates to South Carolina convention elected.
April 21	Maryland convention begins.
April 26	Maryland convention ratifies Constitution (63–11).
April 29–May 3	Delegates to New York convention elected.
May 12	South Carolina convention begins.
May 23	South Carolina convention ratifies Constitution (149–73) and proposes amendments.
June 2	Virginia convention begins.
June 17	New York convention begins.
June 18	New Hampshire convention begins second session.
June 21	New Hampshire convention ratifies Constitution (57–47) and proposes amendments.
June 25	Virginia convention ratifies Constitution (89–79) and proposes amendments.

July 2	New Hampshire's ratification received by Congress; as this is the ninth state ratification, a committee is appointed to effect the transition from government under the Articles of Confederation to government under the Constitution.
July 21	North Carolina convention begins.
July 26	New York convention ratifies Constitution (30–27) and proposes amendments.
August 2	North Carolina convention proposes amendments, but does not ratify the Constitution.
September 13	Congress sets dates for presidential election and for first meeting of Congress under the Constitution.
November 20	Virginia legislature requests Congress to call a second constitutional convention.
November 30	North Carolina calls second state convention.

1789

May 4	Representative James Madison announces, during congressional debate, his intention to introduce constitutional amendments.
May 5–6	Petitions to Congress from legislatures of Virginia and New York, asking Congress to call a second constitutional convention, are reported and filed.
June 8	Madison, in a speech in the House of Representatives, introduces amendments that will become the Bill of Rights.
July 21	Madison's proposed amendments referred to select committee of the House of Representatives.
July 28	Select committee reports back the proposed amendments; its report is tabled.
August 14–18	Congress debates proposed amendments in Committee of the Whole.
August 21–22	Delegates to second North Carolina convention elected.
August 24	House of Representatives approves and sends to the Senate seventeen proposed amendments, including the provisions of the Bill of Rights.
September 2	Senate begins debate on the Bill of Rights.
September 9	Senate approves a version of the Bill of Rights.
September 21	The Senate and House versions of the Bill of Rights are referred to a conference committee.
September 24	House of Representatives approves (37–14) conference committee version of the Bill of Rights.
September 25	Senate approves conference committee version of the Bill of Rights. Twelve amendments to the Constitution, including the ten now known as the Bill of Rights, are proposed by Congress to the states.
November 16	Second North Carolina convention begins.
November 20	New Jersey legislature ratifies the Bill of Rights.
November 21	North Carolina convention ratifies Constitution (194–77) and proposes amendments.
December 19	Maryland legislature ratifies the Bill of Rights.
December 22	North Carolina legislature ratifies Bill of Rights.

1790

January 17	Rhode Island calls state convention.
January 18	South Carolina legislature ratifies the Bill of Rights.
January 25	New Hampshire legislature ratifies the Bill of Rights.
January 28	Delaware legislature ratifies the Bill of Rights.
February 8	Delegates to Rhode Island convention elected.
February 24	New York legislature ratifies the Bill of Rights.
March 1	Rhode Island convention begins.
March 10	Pennsylvania legislature ratifies the Bill of Rights.

May 29	Rhode Island convention ratifies Constitution (34–32) and proposes amendments.
June	Rhode Island legislature ratifies the Bill of Rights. (N.B.: exact date in June of Rhode Island's ratification is unknown.)

1791

March 4	Vermont admitted to the Union.
November 3	Vermont legislature ratifies Bill of Rights.
December 15	Virginia legislature ratifies the Bill of Rights.

Appendix 7

Important Events in the Development of American Constitutional Law

1215	Magna Carta.
1225	Magna Carta reissued in the modified form that became the English statute.
1295	Parliament of three estates established, the model for all future English parliaments.
1297	Confirmatio Cartarum.
1322	That no statute could be made except by consent of both lords and commons was established and declared.
1354	The phrase "due process of law" was first used in a statute.
1387	By statute the king was forbidden to levy imposts, duties, or surcharges without consent of Parliament; the king could no longer legally raise revenue by his own authority alone.
1407	The king agreed that all revenue measures must originate in the House of Commons; this practice was followed in Article I, Section 7, of the Constitution.
1606	Edward Coke was appointed Chief Justice of Common Pleas. He was made Chief Justice of the King's Bench ("Lord Chief Justice of England") in 1613.
	First Virginia Charter.
1608	*Calvin's Case.*
1610	*Bonham's Case.*
1619	The General Assembly of Virginia met, the first representative assembly in the New World.
1620	Mayflower Compact.
1628	Petition of Right.
1629	Charter of Massachusetts Bay Company.
1635	Massachusetts General Court established a committee to write fundamental laws to limit magistrate, "in resemblance to a Magna Carta."
	Roger Williams banished by the General Court of Massachusetts. He founded Providence Plantation in 1636.
	In instructions to Governor Wyatt, the Virginia Assembly was officially recognized as a permanent institution, to meet at least annually.
1639	Fundamental Orders of Connecticut.
1641	Courts of High Commission and Star Chamber abolished; oath *ex officio* abolished.
	Massachusetts Body of Liberties.
	The Grand Remonstrance charged King Charles I with various unlawful acts and demanded that executive power be exercised by ministers in whom Parliament had confidence.
1643	Roger Williams's *The Bloudy Tenent of Persecution.*
1644	John Milton's *Areopagitica,* a plea against prior restraint and censorship, published.

1644	Massachusetts General Court became bicameral, as Assistants met separately from Assembly.
1647	Massachusetts General Laws and Liberties.
1649	Maryland Toleration Act.
1652	Roger Williams's pamphlet *The Bloudy Tenent Yet More Bloudy* published.
1653	The Instrument of Government, the short-lived written constitution of the English commonwealth, promulgated by Oliver Cromwell.
1660–1696	Navigation Acts.
1662	Royal Charter for Connecticut (constitution until 1818).
1663	Royal Charter of Rhode Island (constitution until 1842).
1664	New York granted to Duke of York as proprietary colony; the proprietor to have complete power to make laws.
1670	*Bushell's Case.*
1679	Habeas Corpus Act.
1682	Pennsylvania Frame of Government.
1687	William Penn's *The Excellent Priviledge of Liberty and Property* published; it included the first text of and commentary on Magna Carta published in America.
1689	Act of Toleration.
	English Bill of Rights.
	John Locke's *Letter Concerning Toleration.*
1690	John Locke's *Two Treatises of Government.*
1695	The last English licensing act, restricting freedom of the press, expired.
1698	Algernon Sidney's *Discourses Concerning Government.*
1701	Pennsylvania Charter of Liberties.
1720–1721	Trenchard and Gordon's essays, *Cato's Letters* and *The Independent Whig,* first published.
1733	Molasses Act.
1735	*Zenger's Case.*
1748	Montesquieu's *Spirit of the Laws.*
1754	Albany Plan of Union proposed by the Albany Congress.
1758	Emerich de Vattel's *Law of Nations and of Nature.*
1762	Massachusetts General Court voted a ban on general warrants; it was disallowed by the Governor.
1763	*Paxton's Case* (Writs of Assistance Case).
1764	James Otis, in *The Rights of the British Colonies Asserted and Proved,* denied the right of Parliament to tax the Americans and maintained that a court could judge an act of Parliament void if it was contrary to natural justice.
	The Sugar Act (American Revenue Act) was the first attempt by the British Parliament to tax the colonists for revenue purposes.
1765	*Entick v. Carrington.*
	Stamp Act.
	Stamp Act Congress.
1765–1769	William Blackstone's *Commentaries on the Laws of England* published.
1766	A county court in Northhampton County, Virginia, in an advisory opinion, declared the Stamp Act unconstitutional and therefore void.
	Declaratory Act.
1767–1768	John Dickinson's *Letters from a Farmer in Pennsylvania* published.
1768	Massachusetts Circular Letter.
1772	*Somerset's Case.*
1773	Constitutional debate in Massachusetts; Governor James Hutchinson, in a message to the General Court, asserted that supreme power must rest somewhere; the alternatives were parliamentary rule or independence. The General Court replied that sovereignty could be, and, in fact, already was, divided.
1774	Coercive Acts (Intolerable Acts), including Administration of Justice Act.
	First Continental Congress.
	The Association.
	Joseph Galloway proposes his Plan of Union.
	Thomas Jefferson's *Summary View of the Rights of British America.*
1775	Second Continental Congress convened.
	Declaration of the Causes and Necessity of Taking Up Arms.

1776	Thomas Paine's *Common Sense.*
	Declaration of Independence.
	Dickinson's draft of Articles of Confederation submitted to Congress.
1776–1780	First state constitutions written.
1777	Articles of Confederation approved by Congress and submitted to states.
1779	Congressional resolution asked states to cede their western lands to the United States.
1780	*Holmes v. Walton* (New Jersey).
1781	Articles of Confederation ratified and in force.
1783	*Quock Walker's Case* (Massachusetts).
1784	*Rutgers v. Waddington* (New York).
	James Madison's "Memorial and Remonstrance" against religious assessments.
1786	Virginia Statute for Religious Freedom.
	Ten Pound Act Cases (New Hampshire).
	Trevett v. Weeden (Rhode Island).
	Annapolis Convention.
1787	*Bayard v. Singleton.*
	Congress adopted resolution calling federal Constitutional Convention.
	John Adams's *Defense of the Constitutions of Government of the United States.*
	Constitutional Convention met in Philadelphia and drafted Constitution of the United States.
	Northwest Ordinance.
	Congress transmitted Constitution to the states for ratification.
1787–1788	*The Federalist.*
1788	Constitution ratified by required nine states.
	Congress adopted ordinance to put Constitution into effect.
1789	George Washington chosen President.
	Departments of State, War, and Treasury created.
	Jucidiary Act of 1789.
	Habeas Corpus Act.
	Bill of Rights proposed.
	President Washington appeared in person to ask the Senate's advice and consent relative to an Indian treaty; failure to act cost the Senate a role as the President's council of advice.
1790	Alexander Hamilton's Report on the Public Credit.
	Treason Act.
1791	*Champion and Dickason v. Casey.*
	Bank of the United States Act.
	Bill of Rights ratified and in effect.
	Hamilton's Report on Manufactures.
1792	*Hayburn's Case.*
	President Washington used the presidential veto power for the first time, vetoing a reapportionment bill he thought unconstitutional.
1793	*Chisholm v. Georgia.*
	First Fugitive Slave Act.
	The Supreme Court, presented with a list of questions from the president and the cabinet concerning relations with France, refused to give an advisory opinion.
	Washington's Proclamation of Neutrality in the Wars of the French Revolution.
1794	Jay's Treaty.
	Whiskey Rebellion in Pennsylvania against federal alcohol tax. Suppressed by militia of four states under federal control.
1795	*Van Horne's Lessee v. Dorrance.*
	Post Office Department created.
	Ware v. Hylton.
1796	*Hylton v. United States.*
	Washington's Farewell Address.
	XYZ Affair began three-year undeclared war with France.
1798	Alien and Sedition Acts.
	Calder v. Bull.
	Department of the Navy created.

	Eleventh Amendment ratified and in effect.
	Virginia and Kentucky Resolutions.
1799	Second set of Kentucky Resolutions claimed states could nullify unconstitutional acts of Congress.
1801	Electoral College tie between Thomas Jefferson and Aaron Burr resolved in House of Representatives; this led to the Twelfth Amendment.
	John Marshall became Chief Justice.
	Judiciary Act of 1801.
1802	Judiciary Act of 1801 repealed; Judiciary Act of 1802 enacted.
1803	*Marbury v. Madison.*
	Stuart v. Laird.
	Louisiana Purchase Treaty.
1804	John Pickering, United States District Court judge for New Hampshire, having been impeached by the House of Representatives of malfeasance and intemperance, was convicted by the Senate and removed from office.
	Twelfth Amendment ratified and in effect.
1805	Samuel Chase, Associate Justice of the Supreme Court, having been impeached by the House of Representatives of oppressive and partisan conduct, was acquitted by the Senate.
1807	*Ex Parte Bollman and Swartwout.*
	Abolition of the Slave Trade Act.
	Embargo Act.
	Trial of Aaron Burr (*United States v. Burr*).
1809	Massachusetts Resolutions declared the Embargo unconstitutional and not legally binding.
	United States v. Judge Peters (Olmstead Case).
1810	*Fletcher v. Peck.*
1812	*New Jersey v. Wilson.*
	United States v. Hudson and Goodwin.
1814	Hartford Convention.
1815	*Terrett v. Taylor.*
	Second Bank of the United States Act.
1816	*Martin v. Hunter's Lessee.*
1817	Madison's veto of Bonus Bill (on constitutional grounds).
1819	Secretary of War Calhoun recommended a program of internal improvements as a defense measure.
	Dartmouth College v. Woodward.
	McCulloch v. Maryland.
	Sturges v. Crowninshield.
1820	John Taylor of Caroline's *Construction Construed* published, arguing that the Supreme Court was destroying the independence of the states and of the other branches of the federal government.
	Missouri Compromise.
1821	*Cohens v. Virginia.*
1822	Cumberland Road Bill vetoed by President James Monroe, who also recommended a constitutional amendment authorizing the United States to build and operate internal improvements.
1823	Monroe Doctrine.
	Corfield v. Coryell.
1824	*Gibbons v. Ogden.*
	Osborn v. Bank of the United States.
1825	John Quincy Adams (who had finished second in the Electoral College vote) elected president by the House of Representatives.
	Eakin v. Raub.
1826–1830	James Kent's *Commentaries on American Law.*
1827	*Brown v. Maryland.*
	Martin v. Mott.
	Ogden v. Saunders.

1828	South Carolina Exposition and Protest.
	American Insurance Company v. Canter.
1829	*Willson v. Black Bird Creek Marsh Company.*
1830	Maysville Road Bill vetoed by President Andrew Jackson.
	Daniel Webster and Robert Young Hayne participated in a great debate in the Senate on the nature of the Constitution.
	Craig v. Missouri.
	Providence Bank v. Billings.
1831	William Lloyd Garrison founded *The Liberator.*
	Cherokee Nation v. Georgia (first of the Cherokee Indian Cases).
1832	Jackson's Veto of the Bank Bill.
	Vice-President John C. Calhoun, in his Fort Hill Address, explained his theory of nullification.
	South Carolina Ordinance of Nullification of the Tariff Act of 1828.
	Jackson's Proclamation to the People of South Carolina.
	Worcester v. Georgia.
1833	Force Act of 1833.
	Joseph Story's *Commentaries on the Constitution.*
	Barron v. Baltimore.
1836	First congressional "gag rule" on antislavery petitions imposed.
	Roger B. Taney became Chief Justice.
1837	Membership of Supreme Court increased from seven to nine.
	New York v. Miln.
	Briscoe v. Bank of Kentucky.
	Charles River Bridge v. Warren Bridge Company.
1839	*Bank of Augusta v. Earle.*
1841	*Groves v. Slaughter.*
1842	Reapportionment Act required representatives to be elected by district.
	Dobbins v. Erie Company.
	Swift v. Tyson.
	Prigg v. Pennsylvania.
1843	*Bronson v. Kinzie.*
1844	Texas Annexation Treaty signed; rejected by Senate.
1845	Congress, by joint resolution, approved the annexation of Texas and provided for admission of Texas as a state.
	Congress provided for uniform presidential election day.
1847	License Cases.
1848	Oregon Act.
	Treaty of Guadalupe Hidalgo.
	West River Bridge Company v. Dix.
1849	Passenger Cases.
	Luther v. Borden.
1850	Compromise of 1850.
	Nashville Convention Resolutions asserted right of secession.
	Strader v. Graham.
1850–1858	Personal Liberty Laws adopted by states: Vermont in 1850; Connecticut and Rhode Island in 1854; Maine, Massachusetts, and Michigan in 1855; Kansas in 1857; Wisconsin in 1858.
1851	*Cooley v. Board of Wardens.*
1852	*Pennsylvania v. Wheeling Bridge Company.*
	The Genesee Chief v. Fitzhugh.
1854	Kansas-Nebraska Act.
	Ohio Life Insurance & Trust Company v. DeBolt.
	In re Booth (Wisconsin Supreme Court held Fugitive Slave Act of 1850 unconstitutional).
1855	Connecticut adopted law requiring literacy test for voting.
	Court of Claims created.
1856	*Murray's Lessee v. Hoboken Land Improvement Company.*

	Wynehamer v. New York.
	Dodge v. Woolsey.
1857	*Dred Scott v. Sandford.*
1858	Lincoln-Douglas debates.
1859	*Ableman v. Booth.*
1860	Crittenden Compromise proposed.
	Senator Jefferson Davis introduced a proposal for a federal slave code.
	South Carolina Ordinance of Secession.
1861	First federal income tax imposed as a war measure.
	President Abraham Lincoln proclaimed insurrection, called for troops, suspended habeas corpus.
	Secession of ten other states; Confederate Constitution adopted.
	Kentucky v. Dennison.
1862	Abolition of slavery in the territories.
	Emancipation Proclamation.
	Homestead Act.
1863	Gettysburg Address.
	Lincoln's Proclamation of Amnesty and Reconstruction.
1864	Lincoln's pocket veto of the Wade-Davis Bill.
	Salmon P. Chase became Chief Justice.
1865	Freedmen's Bureau founded.
	Joint Committee on Reconstruction established.
	Thirteenth Amendment ratified and in effect.
	Writ of habeas corpus restored by presidential proclamation.
1866	Civil Rights Act of 1866.
	Ex Parte Milligan.
1867	First Reconstruction Act.
	Habeas Corpus Act.
	Tenure of Office Act.
1868	*Ex parte McCardle.*
	Fourteenth Amendment ratified and in effect.
	Impeachment of Andrew Johnson.
	Johnson's proclamation of general amnesty.
	Texas v. White.
1869	Wyoming adopts women's suffrage.
1870	Department of Justice established.
	Fifteenth Amendment ratified and in effect.
	Hepburn v. Griswold.
1871	Force Act of 1871.
	Knox v. Lee.
	Ku Klux Klan Act.
1872	Congress established uniform date for congressional elections.
1873	Slaughterhouse Cases.
1874	Morrison R. Waite became Chief Justice.
1875	Civil Rights Act of 1875.
1876	Disputed election: Tilden-Hayes.
	Munn v. Illinois.
	United States v. Cruikshank.
	United States v. Reese.
1877	Compromise of 1877 settled disputed election and ended Reconstruction.
1880	Chinese Exclusion Treaty.
	Strauder v. West Virginia.
1881	Kansas adopted prohibition of alcohol (first state prohibition statute).
	Springer v. United States.
	Kilbourn v. Thompson.
1882	Chinese Exclusion Act (enacted over presidential veto).
1883	Civil Rights Cases.

1884	*Juilliard v. Greenman.*
	Ex parte Yarbrough.
	Hurtado v. California.
1886	*Wabash, St. Louis & Pacific Railway v. Illinois.*
	Boyd v. United States.
	Yick Wo v. Hopkins.
1887	Interstate Commerce Act.
1888	Melville W. Fuller became Chief Justice.
1890	*Chicago, Milwaukee & St. Paul Railroad v. Minnesota.*
	Leisy v. Hardin.
	Sherman Antitrust Act.
1892	*Counselman v. Hitchcock.*
1894	Force Act of 1871 repealed.
	Reagan v. Farmers' Loan and Trust Company.
1895	*United States v. E. C. Knight Company.*
	Pollock v. Farmers' Loan and Trust Company.
	In re Debs.
1896	*Plessy v. Ferguson.*
	Allgeyer v. Louisiana.
1897	Trans-Missouri Freight Case.
	Chicago, Burlington & Quincy Railroad v. Chicago.
1898	*Holden v. Hardy.*
	Smyth v. Ames.
	Williams v. Mississippi.
1899	*United States v. Wong Kim Ark.*
1901	New Alabama constitution: literacy and property tests, plus grandfather clause, required for voting (effect was to disenfranchise blacks).
1903	*Champion v. Ames.*
	First direct primary elections (in Wisconsin).
	Panama Canal Treaty (Hay-Bunau Treaty).
1904	*Northern Securities Company v. United States.*
1905	*Swift & Company v. United States.*
	Lochner v. New York.
1906	Hepburn Act.
1908	*Muller v. Oregon.*
	Adair v. United States.
	Loewe v. Lawlor.
	Ex parte Young.
	Twining v. New Jersey.
1910	Edward D. White became Chief Justice.
	Mann-Elkins Act.
1911	*United States v. Grimaud.*
	Standard Oil Company v. United States.
1913	Federal Reserve Act (Owen-Glass Act).
	Sixteenth Amendment ratified and in effect.
1914	Federal Trade Commission Act.
	Weeks v. United States.
	Shreveport Rate Case.
1916	Child Labor Act (Keating-Owen Act).
1917	Selective Service Act.
1918	Selective Draft Law Cases.
	Hammer v. Dagenhart.
1919	Eighteenth Amendment ratified and in effect.
	Schenck v. United States.
	Senate rejects Treaty of Versailles.
	Volstead Act.
	Abrams v. United States.

1920	Esch-Cummings Transportation Act.
	Missouri v. Holland.
	United States v. United States Steel Corporation.
	Nineteenth Amendment ratified and in effect.
	Palmer Raids.
1921	*Bailey v. Drexel Furniture Company.*
	Budget and Accounting Act.
	William Howard Taft became Chief Justice.
1923	*Adkins v. Children's Hospital.*
	Moore v. Dempsey.
	Massachusetts v. Mellon.
1924	Child Labor Amendment proposed by Congress.
1925	*State v. Scopes* (Tennessee).
	Pierce v. Society of Sisters.
	Gitlow v. New York.
1926	*Meyers v. United States.*
1927	*Nixon v. Herndon.*
1928	*Olmstead v. United States.*
1930	Charles Evans Hughes became Chief Justice.
1931	*Near v. Minnesota.*
1932	Norris-La Guardia Act.
	Powell v. Alabama.
1933	National Industrial Recovery Act.
	Securities Act of 1933.
	Tennessee Valley Authority Act.
	Twentieth Amendment ratified and in effect.
	Twenty-First Amendment ratified and in effect.
1934	Communications Act.
	Nebbia v. New York.
	Home Building and Loan Company v. Blaisdell.
	Securities Exchange Act of 1934.
1935	National Labor Relations Act (Wagner Act).
	Social Security Act.
	Schechter Poultry Corporation v. United States.
	Norris v. Alabama.
	Humphrey's Executor v. United States.
1936	*Brown v. Mississippi.*
	United States v. Butler.
	Ashwander v. Tennessee.
	Carter v. Carter Coal Company.
1937	Franklin D. Roosevelt announced Court-packing scheme.
	West Coast Hotel Company v. Parrish.
	Wagner Act Cases.
	Social Security Act Cases.
	United States v. Curtiss-Wright Export Corporation.
	Palko v. Connecticut.
1938	Fair Labor Standards Act.
	Food, Drug and Cosmetics Act.
	House of Representatives establishes committee to investigate un-American activities.
	Johnson v. Zerbst.
	Missouri ex rel. Gaines v. Canada.
1939	*Graves, New York ex rel., v. O'Keefe.*
	Hatch Act.
1940	Alien Registration Act (Smith Act).
	Cantwell v. Connecticut.
1941	Fair Employment Practices Commission established by executive order.
	Harlan F. Stone became Chief Justice.

	United States v. Darby Lumber Company.
1942	*Wickard v. Filburn.*
	Betts v. Brady.
	President Roosevelt approved program of relocation of Japanese Americans.
	Skinner v. Oklahoma.
1943	*McNabb v. United States.*
	Hirabayashi v. United States.
	West Virginia Board of Education v. Barnette (Second Flag Salute Case).
1944	*Korematsu v. United States.*
	Smith v. Allwright.
1946	Frederick M. Vinson became Chief Justice.
1947	*Everson v. Board of Education.*
	First Hoover Commission established.
	National Labor-Management Relations Act (Taft-Hartley Act) passed over President Harry S. Truman's veto.
	National Security Act.
1948	Executive orders banned racial segregation in the armed forces and in civilian federal employment.
	Illinois ex rel. McCollum v. Board of Education.
	Shelley v. Kraemer.
	Selective Service Act.
	Sipuel v. Board of Regents.
1949	*Wolf v. Colorado.*
1950	*American Communications Association v. Douds.*
	Internal Security Act (McCarran Act).
	Sweatt v. Painter.
	McLaurin v. Oklahoma State Regents for Higher Education.
1951	*Dennis v. United States.*
	Twenty-Second Amendment ratified and in effect.
1952	Immigration and Nationality Act (McCarran-Walter Act) became law over Truman's veto.
	President Truman ordered seizure of steel mills.
	Youngstown Sheet & Tube Company v. Sawyer (Steel Seizure Case).
1953	Earl Warren became Chief Justice.
1954	*Brown v. Board of Education of Topeka.*
	Censure of Joseph McCarthy by the United States Senate.
	Communist Control Act.
1955	*Brown v. Board of Education II* ("all deliberate speed").
1956	*Ullmann v. United States.*
1957	Civil Rights Act of 1957.
	President Dwight D. Eisenhower ordered federal troops to enforce desegregation order in Little Rock, Arkansas.
	Watkins v. United States.
	Yates v. United States.
	Mallory v. United States.
	Roth v. United States, Alberts v. California.
1958	*Cooper v. Aaron.*
1959	*Barenblatt v. United States.*
1960	Civil Rights Act of 1960.
1961	*Communist Party v. Subversive Activities Control Board.*
	Mapp v. Ohio.
	Twenty-Third Amendment ratified and in effect.
1962	*Baker v. Carr.*
	Engel v. Vitale.
1963	*Edwards v. South Carolina.*
	Gray v. Sanders.
	Gideon v. Wainwright.

1964	Civil Rights Act of 1964.
	Gulf of Tonkin Resolution.
	Wesberry v. Sanders.
	Reynolds v. Sims.
	New York Times Co. v. Sullivan.
	Heart of Atlanta Motel v. United States.
	Malloy v. Hogan.
	Escobedo v. Illinois.
1965	*Pointer v. Texas.*
	Albertson v. Subversive Activities Control Board.
	Griswold v. Connecticut.
	Voting Rights Act of 1965.
1966	*Miranda v. Arizona.*
	South Carolina v. Katzenbach.
	Harper v. Virginia State Board of Elections.
	Miranda v. Arizona.
1967	*Klopfer v. North Carolina.*
	In re Gault.
	Warden v. Hayden.
	Katz v. United States.
1968	*Duncan v. Louisiana.*
	Jones v. Alfred H. Mayer Co.
	Terry v. Ohio.
1969	*Benton v. Maryland.*
	Chimel v. California.
	Warren E. Burger became Chief Justice.
1970	*In re Winship.*
	Williams v. Florida.
1971	*New York Times Company v. United States* (Pentagon Papers Case).
	Swann v. Charlotte-Mecklenburg County Board of Education.
	McKeiver v. Pennsylvania, In re Burrus.
	Lemon v. Kurtzman.
	New York Times Co. v. United States, United States v. The Washington Post.
1972	Equal Rights Amendment proposed by Congress.
	Furman v. Georgia (Capital Punishment Cases of 1972).
	Kastigar v. United States.
	Johnson v. Louisiana.
	Apodaca v. Oregon.
	Jackson v. Georgia.
	Branch v. Texas.
	Argersinger v. Hamlin.
	Branzburg v. Hayes.
1973	*Miller v. California.*
	Roe v. Wade.
1974	Resignation of President Richard M. Nixon.
	United States v. Nixon.
1976	*Buckley v. Valeo.*
	National League of Cities v. Usery.
	Gregg v. Georgia, Proffitt v. Florida, Jurek v. Texas (Capital Punishment Cases of 1976).
1977	Panama Canal Treaties.
1978	*Ballew v. Georgia.*
	First National Bank of Boston v. Bellotti.
	Regents of University of California v. Bakke.
	District of Columbia Representation Amendment proposed by Congress.
	Simple majority of Congress voted to extend ratification deadline for Equal Rights Amendment (original proposal had required a two-thirds vote).

1979	*United Steelworkers of America v. Weber.*
1982	Extended deadline for ratification of Equal Rights Amendment expired.
	Plyler v. Doe.
1983	*Immigration and Naturalization Service v. Chadha.*
1985	Deadline for ratification of District of Columbia Representation Amendment expired.
	Gramm-Rudman-Hollings Balanced Budget Act.

Glossary

abstention Any of several doctrines by which federal courts delay or avoid decision, allowing issues of state law or entire cases to be decided by state courts.*

action A court case. Before the unification of law and equity, an "action" at law was distinguished from a proceeding in equity.

advisory opinion A judicial opinion on a question of law, rendered without deciding the rights of parties to an adversary proceeding. In the federal courts, advisory opinions are barred by the "case or controversy" requirement.*

amicus curiae [Latin: friend of the court] One who, although not a party to the case, submits a brief suggesting how the case, or certain issues in the case, should be decided.*

appeal Review of a court decision by a higher court to determine whether errors of law were made. Appeal is a particular type of review, but the word is sometimes used more generally, to refer to any review of a lower court decision.*

appellate jurisdiction The legitimate authority of a higher court to hear and decide appeals from lower courts.*

bail Money deposited with a court to guarantee the appearance of a defendant for trial, permitting his release from jail until trial.*

bill of attainder A legislative finding of guilt and imposition of punishment without a court trial.*

brief A document filed on behalf of a litigant, at trial or on appeal, stating the facts of the case and arguing the legal basis for a decision in the litigant's favor.*

case law The body of law established in court decisions, as distinct from customary and statutory law. Case law is the most important component of the common law.

certification A procedure by which a lower court requests from a higher court (or a federal court requests from a state court) guidance on questions of law relative to a case pending in the lower court.*

certiorari [Latin: to be made more certain] A form of writ directing a lower court to forward the record of a case to a higher court for review; it is the primary form of discretionary appellate review by the U.S. Supreme Court.*

civil law (1) the body of law dealing with the private rights and duties of individuals, distinguished from criminal law; (2) a body of law derived from the Roman legal codes that is in force in continental Europe and elsewhere, distinguished from common law. Civil law, in the latter sense, is the basis of much of the private law of Louisiana, and it is the original source of some aspects of property law in Texas and in states formed from the Mexican Cession.

* Entries marked with an asterisk have a separate article in the *Encyclopedia*.

class action A legal action brought by one or more litigants in the name of a numerous class of whom the particular litigants claim to be representative, or an action against a numerous class of defendants.*

comity The respect owed by one court or governmental agency to the official acts of a court or agency in another jurisdiction.*

common law The body of legal custom and accumulated precedent inherited from England, sometimes inaccurately described as "judge-made law."*

concurrent powers Governmental powers that may be exercised either by the national or by the state government.*

concurring opinion A separate opinion filed by a judge of a multimember court indicating agreement with the decision of a case but setting forth alternative or additional reasons for reaching the result.*

consent decree A court order that makes legally binding an agreement between the parties to a case to settle it without further litigation.*

declaratory judgment A judicial order determining the legal rights of the parties in a particular case, anticipating future controversy rather than remedying past injury. Equitable in form, declaratory relief is available in federal court by virtue of an act of Congress.*

de facto [Latin: in fact] Existing in fact, whether or not existing in law or by right.*

defendant The party against whom an action is brought. At the appellate level the party moved against is called the appellee or respondent.

de jure [Latin: in law] Existing in law or by virtue of official acts; distinguished from de facto (q.v.).

dictum (pl. dicta) [Latin: something said] Formerly, an authoritative pronouncement. Now, commonly used as an abbreviation of "obiter dictum" (q.v.).

dissenting opinion An opinion by a judge of a multimember court who disagrees with the court's decision in a case.*

diversity jurisdiction The legitimate authority of federal courts to hear cases in which the parties have "diversity of citizenship," that is, when they are citizens of different states or of a state and a foreign country.*

dual federalism A doctrine of constitutional interpretation according to which the reserved powers of the states operate as limitations on the power of the national government.*

due process of law The fair and regular procedures established by law. Under the Fifth and Fourteenth Amendments, the government may deprive a person of life, liberty, or property only after due process. The due process clauses of the Constitution protect both procedural and substantive rights.*

equity A system of jurisprudence parallel to and corrective of the common law, based on principles of fairness rather than on the letter of the law. In most American jurisdictions, law and equity have been merged.*

error A form of writ issued by a higher court directing a lower court to submit a case for appellate review. The writ of error is no longer used in the federal courts, having been superseded by appeal (q.v.).*

exclusionary rule A rule excluding evidence obtained in violation of a defendant's rights from admission at the defendant's trial as proof of guilt.*

ex parte [Latin: from one party; from the part (of)] (1) A hearing or other legal act at which only one side of a case is represented; (2) in the heading of a case, an identification of the party who is applying for judicial relief.*

ex post facto [Latin: from after the fact] A law that makes criminal, or that increases the criminal penalty for, an act committed before the law was passed.*

ex relatione [Latin: from what has been related (by)] Legal actions brought by the state upon information supplied by or at the instigation of a private party are said to be "ex relatione." In reports, it is abbreviated *"ex rel."*

federal question jurisdiction The legitimate authority of a federal court to hear and decide cases "arising under" the Constitution, laws, or treaties of the United States.*

grand jury An investigatory body that is usually empowered to issue indictments or presentments charging persons with crimes.*

habeas corpus [Latin: you shall have the body] A form of writ directing a custodial official to appear before a judge with the person of a prisoner and to give a satisfactory legal justification for having the person in custody. The writ of habeas corpus is frequently used by state prisoners to obtain federal court review of their convictions.*

immunity In criminal cases, a grant of exemption from prosecution made in return for testimony; in intergovernmental relations, the exemption of government instrumentalities from taxation by other levels of government. In general, an exemption from a legally imposed duty or liability; along with privileges, immunities are protected by Article IV and by the Fourteenth Amendment.

incorporation (1) A doctrine according to which certain specific provisions of the Bill of Rights are made applicable against state authority by virtue of the "due process" clause of the Fourteenth Amendment; (2) a doctrine according to which certain territories are made so intimately a part of the United States that certain constitutional protections become applicable to the inhabitants.*

indictment A formal statement by a grand jury charging a person with a criminal offense.*

in forma pauperis [Latin: in the manner of a poor person] A proceeding in which the court waives requirements that a litigant pay certain fees and comply with certain formal requirments, granted because the litigant cannot afford to comply but ought not to be barred from access to the court.*

injunction A form of writ prohibiting or requiring the performance of a specific act by a particular person. An injunction is a form of remedy available under a court's equity power.*

in personam [Latin: against the person] A manner of proceeding in a case so that the decision and remedy are directed against a particular person.*

in re [Latin: in the matter (of)] A way of titling the report of a case in which there are no adversary parties.*

in rem [Latin: against the thing] A manner of proceeding in a case so that the decision and remedy affect the status of property with reference to the whole world rather than to particular individuals.*

judgment The official decision by a court of a case or controversy, including the remedy ordered, excluding the reasons for the ruling.*

judicial review The power of a court to review legislation or other governmental acts, including the acts of administrative agencies. The term is used especially for court review to determine whether an act is in conformance with the Constitution.*

jurisdiction Legitimate authority. The term is sometimes limited to the legitimate authority of courts to hear and decide cases.*

jury A body of lay citizens exercising responsibility for hearing and deciding facts in the judicial system; a jury is either a grand jury (q.v.) or a petit jury (q.v.).

justiciability The status of a case or controversy indicating that it may appropriately be heard and decided by a court.*

litigant A party to a legal action.

magistrate At the time the Constitution was written and in general, a government official, especially of the executive or judicial branch. In contemporary technical usage, a judicial officer authorized to conduct certain kinds of hearings, to issue certain kinds of orders, or to try minor offenses.

mandamus [Latin: we command] A form of writ directed to a government official or a lower court directing the performance of an act appropriate to that offical's or court's duties.*

mootness The status of a case or controversy indicating that it no longer involves a legal question appropriate to be heard and decided by a court.*

nolo contendere [Latin: I do not wish to contest (it).] A plea entered by a criminal defendant equivalent in effect to a plea of guilty in the criminal case but not amounting to an admission of guilt that might be used in another case, either civil or criminal.*

obiter dictum [Latin: said by the way] Any words in a court's opinion that are not required for the decision of the case, and that are therefore, in theory, not binding as precedent. The term is often misleadingly abbreviated to "dictum" or to its plural, "dicta."*

original jurisdiction The legitimate authority of a court to hear and decide cases in the first instance. Original jurisdiction is distinguished from appellate jurisdiction (q.v.).*

ordinance Any statute. In recent times, most commonly used for enactments by cities, counties, or other local governments.

per curiam [Latin: by the court] An unsigned opinion, attributable to the whole court and not to an individual judge as author.*

petit jury The ordinary trial jury; a body of lay persons who hear evidence and decide questions of fact in a civil or criminal case.*

plaintiff The party who brings an action. At the appellate level, the moving party is called the appellant or the petitioner.

police power The general authority of government to regulate the health, safety, morals, and welfare of the public.*

political question An issue reserved for decision by the legislative and executive branches of government, and so not appropriately decided by a court.*

precedent A past decision, resolving issues of law, which is relied on in the decision of later cases.*

preemption A doctrine according to which legislation by the national government explicitly displaces or conflicts with state legislation or has so pervaded a particular area or topic of regulation as to preclude state legislation on the same subject.*

presentment A formal report of a grand jury charging a person with a criminal offense; a presentment differs from an indictment in that the former is prepared on the grand jury's own initiative while the latter is initiated by the public prosecutor. Reports of the results of grand jury investigations are often referred to as "presentments" even when they do not contain criminal charges.*

ratio decidendi [Latin: reason for being decided] The reasoning supporting the decision of a court in a particular case, establishing a precedent.*

remand The action of a higher court in returning a case to a lower court for decision or for further proceedings.*

ripeness The status of a case when circumstances have advanced to the point of sufficient specificity and concreteness to justify decision or review.*

seriatim [Latin: serially] One at a time, in sequence; used to describe the opinions of judges on multimember tribunals where custom does not permit a single "opinion of the court."*

special master A person appointed by a court to perform certain functions in a case, especially to hear evidence and to make findings of fact.*

standing The legal status of a litigant indicating that he is a proper party to litigate an issue or a case or controversy.*

stare decisis [Latin: to stand by what has been decided] A doctrine requiring that courts, in deciding cases, should adhere to the principles of law established in prior cases, called precedents (q.v.).*

state action Official action by a state or under color of state law, an essential element of a claim of right raised under the "due process" or "equal protection" clause of the Fourteenth Amendment.*

statute A law enacted by a legislature; a part of the formal, written law. Also called an "act" of Congress or of the legislature, a statute is to be distinguished from a constitution and also from customary or common law and case law.

subpoena [Latin: under penalty] An order to appear and testify at a proceeding (*subpoena ad testificandum*) or to produce physical evidence at a proceeding (*subpoena duces tecum*).*

transactional immunity Immunity from prosecution for any offense mentioned in testimony given in exchange for the grant of immunity, regardless of other evidence that may be acquired independently.

ultra vires [Latin: beyond (its) power] An action by a person, corporation, or public agency that is beyond the actor's legitimate authority.

use immunity Immunity from prosecution based upon or using evidence of an offense given by a witness in exchange for the grant of immunity. Prosecution may occur only if it is based on independently acquired evidence.

venue The place where a case is to be heard.*

vested rights Legally recognized rights, especially property rights, of which a person may not be deprived without due process of law.*

writ A court order.

Case Index

HOW TO READ A CASE CITATION

A case citation tells the reader where the decision and opinion in a case have been reported. It gives, in shorthand form, all the information necessary to find a copy of the report.

The elements of a typical citation are: the volume number, the name of the reporter or of the compilation, (the series number,) the page number of the first page of the report, (the court or jurisdiction,) and the year in which the case was decided. Any information that is unnecessary or inapplicable is omitted. Thus,

384 U.S. 346 (1966)

is the citation to the case reported in volume 384 of the United States Reports, beginning on page 346; the case (*Miranda v. Arizona*) was decided in 1966 by the Supreme Court of the United States. So far, there is only one series of volumes in the United States Reports, and all cases in the United States Reports are Supreme Court cases or matters disposed of by Supreme Court Justices. And

13 N.Y. 378 (1858)

is the citation to the case reported in volume 13 of the New York Reports beginning on page 378; the case (*Wynehamer v. People*) was decided in 1858 by the New York Court of Appeals (the highest court of New York).

Many volumes of reports, especially reports of older cases, bear the name of the reporter rather than of the jurisdiction. Some volumes of reports, especially specialized volumes, have names indicating neither the reporter nor the jurisdiction. The table that follows lists the reports in which cases cited in this *Encyclopedia* are to be found:

U.S.	United States Reports
Dall.	Dallas (= United States Reports, vols. 1–4)
Cranch	Cranch (= U.S. Reports vols. 5–13)
Wheat.	Wheaton (= U.S. Reports vols. 14–25)
Pet.	Peters (= U.S. Reports vols. 26–41)
How.	Howard (= U.S. Reports vols. 42–65)
Black	Black (= U.S. Reports vols. 66–67)
Wall.	Wallace (= U.S. Reports vols. 68–90)
S.Ct.	West's Supreme Court Reporter (cited only when the citation to U.S. Reports was unavailable at the time of compilation)

F.	Federal Reporter (F. 2d = Federal Reporter, 2d series)
F.Supp.	Federal Supplement
F.Cas.	Federal Cases
Ct.Cl.	U.S. Court of Claims Reports
Dane Abr.	Dane's Abridgment of American Law
Gill & J.	Gill & Johnson (Maryland)
Pick.	Pickering (= Massachusetts Reports vols. 18–41)
Metc.	Metcalf (= Massachusetts Reports vols. 42–54)
Cush.	Cushing (= Massachusetts Reports vols. 55–66)
Gray	Gray (= Massachusetts Reports vols. 67–82)
Quincy	Quincy's Reports (Massachusetts)
Hals.	Halsted's New Jersey Reports
N.J. Super.	New Jersey Superior Court Reports
Abb. Prac.	Abbott's New York Practice Reports
Hill	Hill's New York Reports
Johns.	Johnson's New York Reports
Johns. Cas.	Johnson's New York Cases
N.Y.S.	New York Supplement (N.Y.S. 2d = N.Y. Supplement, 2d series)
Martin	Martin's North Carolina Reports
Serg. & R.	Sergeant & Rawles's Pennsylvania Reports
Whart.	Wharton's Pennsylvania Reports
Bay	Bay's South Carolina Reports
P.	West's Pacific Reporter (P. 2d = Pacific Reporter, 2d series)
State Abbreviations	Reports of the state's highest court
A.C.	Appeal Cases (English)
E.R.	East's King's Bench Reports (English)
Eng. Rep.	English Reports
How. St. Tr.	Howell's State Trials (English)
Mod.	Modern English Cases

Numbers in **boldface** refer to the main entry on the subject.

A

B

C

D

E

F

G

H

I

J

K

L

M

N

O

P

Q

R

T

U

V

W

Y

Z

Name Index

Numbers in **boldface** *refer to the main entry on the subject.*

C

D

E

F

G

H

I

J

K

L

M

S

T

U

V

W

Y

Z

Subject Index

*Numbers in **boldface** refer to the main entry on the subject.*

A

B

D

F

G

H

I

J

K

L

M

N

O

P

Q

R

S

U

V

Y

Z